Statistical yearbook | Annuaire statistique | Anuario estadístico | 1986

statistical yearbook
annuaire statistique
anuario estadístico

1986

Reference tables
Education
Educational expenditure
Science and technology
Libraries
Book production
Newspapers and other periodicals
Cultural paper
Archives
Museums and related institutions
Film and cinema
Radio and television broadcasting

Tableaux de référence
Education
Dépenses de l'enseignement
Science et technologie
Bibliothèques
Édition de livres
Journaux et autres périodiques
Papier culturel
Archives
Musées et institutions similaires
Film et cinéma
Radiodiffusion sonore et télévision

Cuadros de referencia
Educación
Gastos de la educación
Ciencia y tecnología
Bibliotecas
Edición de libros
Periódicos y otras publicaciones periódicas
Papel cultural
Archivos
Museos e instituciones similares
Películas y cines
Radiodifusión sonora y televisión

unesco

Published in 1986 by the United Nations Educational, Scientific and Cultural Organization
7, place de Fontenoy, 75700 Paris
Photocomposition by Computaprint Ltd. London.
Printed by Imprimerie Duculot Gembloux (Belgium)

Publié en 1986 par l'Organisation des Nations Unies pour l'Éducation, la Science et la Culture,
7, place de Fontenoy, 75700 Paris
Photocomposition effectuée par Computaprint Ltd. London.
Imprimé par Imprimerie Duculot, Gembloux (Belgique)

Publicado en 1986 por la Organización de las Naciones Unidas para la Educación, la Ciencia y la Cultura,
7, place de Fontenoy, 75700 Paris
Fotocomposición efectuada por Computaprint Ltd. London.
Impreso por Imprimerie Duculot Gembloux (Bélgica)

ISBN 92-3-002445-7

Printed in Belgium

Table of contents

New table introduced in this issue.

Table de matières

\# Nouveau tableau introduit dans le présent Annuaire

Indice

Nuevo cuadro introducido en el presente Anuario

Introduction

This issue of the *Unesco Statistical Yearbook* has been prepared by the Office of Statistics with the co-operation of the National Commissions for Unesco and national statistical services, and with the help of the Statistical Office and the Population Division of the United Nations.

Each Member State is requested to report periodically to the Organization on its laws, regulations and statistics relating to its educational, scientific and cultural life and activities in accordance with Article VIII of the Constitution of Unesco. Data are gathered mainly from official replies to Unesco questionnaires and special surveys but also from official reports and publications, supplemented by information available to the Secretariat from other national and international sources. Where available data differ from the recommendations adopted or other concepts and definitions employed by Unesco, the statistical practice used in the country is followed, with a footnote where possible.

Some 200 countries and territories reply within the limits of their capabilities to Unesco questionnaires directly and the data they have kindly provided are incorporated in this *Yearbook*. The improvements in the tables and the additional information provided are referred to in the introduction to each subject chapter. As in the past, the aim of the 1986 edition of the *Yearbook* has been to present figures for the latest years for which data are available ; however by using the present *Yearbook* in combination with the earlier editions, a meaningful time series can be developed for most areas.

As in the previous edition the introductory texts to the tables are included with the relative chapters at the beginning of each subject and are presented in English, French and Spanish.

A number of other Unesco publications present statistical data. A list of these publications will be found at the end of this volume. All questions and comments, as well as any suggestions for further improvements in subsequent editions of the *Yearbook*, will be received gratefully by the Office of Statistics, Unesco, 75700 Paris (France).

Explanatory note

The data presented in this publication relate in general to territorial units within de facto boundaries as at October 1985 depending in part on the availability of official statistics relating to such territories.

Table 1.1 on population is the most comprehensive in terms of geographic description ; it constitutes the reference table of the *Yearbook* in respect of country nomenclature of geographic and administrative units. Changes in name, administration and status which occured during 1984 and 1985 are given in the footnotes to Table 1.1.

The designations employed and the presentation of the material in this publication do not imply the expression of any opinion whatsoever on the part of the Unesco Secretariat concerning the legal status of any country or territory, or of its authorities, or concerning the delimitations of the frontiers of any country or territory.

Data presented for *Jordan*, unless otherwise indicated, refer to the East Bank only.

The data which relate to the *Federal Republic of Germany* and the *German Democratic Republic* include the relevant data relating to Berlin for which separate data have not been supplied. This is without prejudice to any question of status which may be involved.

Data presented for the *Holy See* refer to the State of the Vatican City.

The figures presented for the *Byelorussian S.S.R.* and the *Ukrainian S.S.R.* are already included with those of the *U.S.S.R.*

In some tables, the designation "developed" and "developing" countries is intended for statistical convenience and does not, necessarily, express a judgement about the stage reached by a particular country or area in the development process.

Data presented in this edition of the *Yearbook* which differ from the corresponding data for the same year given in earlier editions should be taken to reflect revisions made as a result of the receipt of further information.

Owing to the rounding of figures, the totals and sub-totals shown in the tables do not always correspond exactly to the sums of their component items.

Explanatory notes concerning selected figures are indicated by footnote indicators shown against the name of the relevant continents, regions, countries or territories, and indicated by the symbol ‡ . The corresponding texts will be found at the end of each table ; each note is composed of the name of the continent, region, country or territory (in English), followed by the required explanation, for which the English text is preceded by the symbol E—> , the French text by FR=> , and the Spanish text by ESP >. For a certain number of tables, there is also a general note which precedes the notes for individual countries ; the reader's attention is drawn to these general notes for the explanatory material which they contain.

The following symbols are used :

–	Magnitude nil
0 or 0.0	Magnitude less than half of unit employed
...	Data not available
.	Category not applicable
*	Provisional or estimated data
./.	Data included elsewhere with another category
———>	The figure immediately to the left of the arrow includes data relative to the columns where this symbol is indicated.
<———	The figure immediately to the right of the arrow includes data relative to the columns where this symbol is indicated.

A break in the continuity of a time series is indicated by a vertical or horizontal line.

Introduction

Cette édition de l'*Annuaire statistique de l'Unesco* a été établie par l'Office des statistiques, avec la coopération des commissions nationales pour l'Unesco et des services nationaux de statistique, et avec le concours du Bureau de statistique et de la Division de la Population de l'Organisation des Nations Unies.

En vertu de l'article VIII de l'Acte constitutif de l'Unesco, chaque État membre est tenu d'adresser à l'Organisation un rapport périodique sur les lois, règlements et statistiques relatifs à ses institutions et à son activité dans les domaines de l'éducation, de la science et de la culture. Les données sont recueillies par le Secrétariat, principalement au moyen de questionnaires et d'enquêtes spéciales, mais aussi dans les publications et rapports officiels, le tout étant complété par des renseignements provenant d'autres sources nationales et internationales. Lorsque les données disponibles ne sont pas conformes aux recommandations adoptées ou aux autres concepts et définitions utilisés par l'Unesco, on a suivi la pratique adoptée par les pays, si possible avec une note explicative.

Quelque 200 pays et territoires répondent dans la mesure de leurs possibilités aux questionnaires de l'Unesco, et les données qu'ils ont bien voulu fournir sont incorporées dans cet *Annuaire*. Les améliorations apportées à la présentation des tableaux, ainsi que les données supplémentaires qui y sont contenues, sont précisées dans l'introduction de chaque chapitre. Comme par le passé, le but de l'édition de 1986 a été de présenter des chiffres concernant les dernières années pour lesquelles on dispose de statistiques. Toutefois, l'ensemble constitué par le présent *Annuaire* et les éditions précédentes offre aux utilisateurs une série chronologique valable pour la plupart des domaines.

Comme dans la précédente édition de l'*Annuaire*, les textes d'introduction aux différents chapitres et aux tableaux correspondants sont groupés au début de chaque chapitre et présentés successivement en anglais, en français et en espagnol.

Un certain nombre d'autres publications de l'Unesco contiennent également des renseignements statistiques ; on en trouvera la liste à la fin de ce volume. Prière d'adresser toutes questions ou observations concernant le présent *Annuaire*, ainsi que toutes suggestions en vue d'améliorer les éditions ultérieures, à l'Office des statistiques de l'Unesco, 75700 Paris (France).

Notice explicative

Les données présentées dans cette publication se rapportent, en général, aux territoires tels qu'ils étaient délimités en octobre 1985 par les frontières de faits ; elles proviennent en partie des statistiques officielles relatives à ces territoires.

Le tableau 1.1 (population) est le plus complet du point de vue géographique ; il constitue le tableau de référence de l'*Annuaire* pour ce qui est de la nomenclature des pays, ainsi que des unités géographiques et administratives. Les changements survenus entre 1984 et 1985 en matière de noms, d'administration et de statut juridique sont indiqués en note dans le tableau 1.1.

Les désignations employées et la présentation adoptée dans cette publication ne sauraient être interprétées comme exprimant une prise de position du Secrétariat de l'Unesco sur le statut juridique ou le régime d'un pays ou d'un territoire quelconque, non plus que sur le tracé de ses frontières.

Les données relatives à la *Jordanie* se réfèrent, sauf indication contraire, à la rive orientale seulement.

Les données relatives à la *République fédérale d'Allemagne* et à la *République démocratique allemande* incluent les données pertinentes relatives à Berlin, pour lequel des données séparées n'ont pas été fournies. Cela sans préjudice des questions de statut qui peuvent se poser à cet égard.

Les données relatives au *Saint Siège* se réfèrent à l'Etat de la Cité du Vatican.

Les chiffres séparés présentés pour la *R.S.S. de Biélorussie* et la *R.S.S. d'Ukraine* sont déjà inclus dans l'*U.R.S.S.*

Dans quelques tableaux, la désignation pays "développés" et "en développement" est donnée pour des convenances statistiques et n'implique pas nécessairement un jugement sur le niveau atteint par tel pays ou région, en particulier dans leur processus de développement.

Lorsque les données présentées dans cette édition de l'*Annuaire* diffèrent des données correspondant à la même année qui figuraient dans les éditions précédentes, on doit considérer qu'il s'agit de chiffres révisés à la suite de nouveaux renseignements reçus.

Les chiffres et pourcentages ayant été arrondis, les totaux et les sous-totaux figurant dans les tableaux ne correspondent pas toujours exactement à la somme des éléments qui les composent.

Les notes explicatives concernant certains chiffres sont signalées par des appels de notes suivant immédiatement le nom des continents, des régions, des pays ou territoires auxquels ils s'appliquent et sont indiqués par le symbole ‡. On trouvera les textes correspondants à la fin de chaque tableau ; chaque note est composée du nom du continent, de la région, du pays ou du territoire (en anglais), suivi de l'explication nécessaire. Le texte anglais est précédé du symbole E —> , le texte français de FR -> et le texte espagnol de ESP > . Il y a aussi, pour un certain nombre de tableaux, une note générale précédant les notes spécifiques aux pays. Ces notes générales doivent particulièrement retenir l'attention du lecteur par les explications essentielles qu'elles contiennent.

Les symboles utilisés sont les suivants :

–	Chiffre nul
0 ou 0.0	Chiffre inférieur à la moitié de l'unité employée
...	Données non disponibles
.	Catégorie sans objet
*	Chiffre provisoire ou estimé
./.	Données comprises dans une autre rubrique
——>	Le chiffre immédiatement à gauche de la flèche comprend les données relatives aux colonnes où figure ce symbole.
<——	Le chiffre immédiatement à droite de la flèche comprend les données relatives aux colonnes où figure ce symbole.

Une discontinuité dans l'homogénéité des séries est indiquée par un trait vertical ou horizontal.

Introducción

La presente edición del *Anuario estadístico de la Unesco* ha sido preparada por la Oficina de Estadística, con la cooperación de la comisiones nacionales para la Unesco y de los servicios nacionales de estadística y con la ayuda de la Oficina de Estadística y de la División de Población de las Naciones Unidas.

En virtud del artículo VIII de la Constitución de la Unesco cada Estado miembro debe someter a la Organización un informe periódico sobre las leyes, reglamentos y estadísticas relativos a sus instituciones y actividades educativas, científicas y culturales. Esos datos los reúne la Secretaría principalmente por medio de cuestionarios y de encuestas especiales, pero también utilizando las publicaciones e informes oficiales, completándose el todo mediante información procedente de otras fuentes nacionales e internacionales. Cuando los datos disponibles difieren de las recomendaciones aprobadas o de los demás conceptos y definiciones utilizados por la Unesco, se ha seguido el procedimiento adoptado en el país considerado, dando la explicación correspondiente, cuando ello es posible, en una nota.

Unos 200 países y territorios han respondido en la medida de sus posibilidades a los cuestionarios de la Unesco y los datos que han tenido a bien facilitar se incorporan en este *Anuario*. Las mejoras introducidas en la presentación de los cuadros, así como los datos suplementarios contenidos en los mismos, se indican en la introducción de cada capítulo. Como en el pasado, la finalidad de la edición de 1986 es la de presentar cifras relativas a los últimos años sobre los cuales se dispone de estadísticas.

No obstante, el conjunto que constituye el presente *Anuario* y las ediciones precedentes ofrece a los usuarios una serie cronológica válida para la mayor parte de los campos de actividades de que se trata.

Como en la precedente edición del *Anuario*, los textos de introducción a los diferentes capítulos y a los cuadros correspondientes se agrupan al comienzo de cada capítulo y se presentan sucesivamente en inglés, francés y español.

Un cierto número de otras publicaciones de la Unesco contienen también información estadística. La lista de las mismas figura al final de este volumen. Se ruega que toda cuestión u observación relativa al presente *Anuario*, así como todas las sugerencias destinadas a mejorar las ediciones ulteriores, se dirijan a la Oficina de Estadística de la Unesco, 75700 Paris (Francia).

Nota explicativa

Los datos que figuran en la presente publicación se referien, en general, a los territorios tal como estaban delimitados en octubre 1985 por sus fronteras de hecho, y proceden en parte de las estadísticas oficiales relativas a esos mismos territorios.

El cuadro 1.1 (Población) es el más completo desde el punto de vista geográfico. Constituye el cuadro de referencia del *Anuario* por lo que se refiere a la nomenclatura de los países, así como de las unidades geográficas y administrativas. Los cambios habidos entre 1984 y 1985 en materia de nombres, de administración y de estatuto jurídico se indican mediante nota en el cuadro 1.1.

Las designaciones empleadas y la presentación utilizada en esta publicación no deben interpretarse en el sentido de que expresen una opinión de la Secretaría de la Unesco sobre el estatuto jurídico o el régimen de un país o de un territorio cualquiera, como tampoco sobre el trazado de sus fronteras.

Los datos presentados para *Jordania*, salvo indicación contraria, se refieren a la orilla oriental solamente.

Los datos de la *República Federal de Alemania* y de la *República Democrática Alemana* comprenden los datos pertinentes relativos a Berlín, que no nos han sido procurados separadamente, lo que no prejuzga las cuestiones de estatuto que pueden plantearse al respecto.

Los datos relativos a la *Santa Sede* se refieren al Estado de la Ciudad del Vaticano.

Los datos separados que se presentan para la *R.S.S. de Bielorrusia* y la *R.S.S. de Ucrania* ya están incluidos en los de la *U.R.S.S.*

En algunos cuadros, la denominación países "desarrollados" y "en desarrollo" se da por conveniencias estadísticas, y no supone en ningún caso una toma de posición sobre el nivel alcanzado por tal o cual país o región en particular, en su proceso de desarrollo.

Cuando los datos presentados en esta edición del *Anuario* difieren de los datos correspondientes al mismo año que figuran en las ediciones anteriores, debe considerarse que se trata de cifras revisadas de acuerdo con las nuevas informaciones recibidas.

Como las cifras y porcentajes se han redondeado, los totales y los sub-totales que figuran en los cuadros no siempre corresponden exactamente a la suma de los elementos que los componen.

Las notas explicativas relativas a ciertas cifras se señalan por medio de llamadas de nota que figuran inmediatamente después del nombre de los continentes, regiones, países o territorios a que se refieren y se indican con el símbolo ‡ . Los textos correspondientes aparecen al final de cada cuadro, las notas se componen del nombre del continente, región, país o territorio (en inglés), seguido de la debida explicación. Los textos en inglés, francés y español están precedidos respectivamente de los símbolos E—> , FR=> y ESP> . En un determinado número de cuadros figura igualmente una nota general, que precede las notas correspondientes a los países. Estas notas generales deben retener particularmente la atención del lector, dadas las explicaciones esenciales que contienen.

Los signos convencionales utilizados son los siguientes :

—	Cifra nula
0 ó 0.0	Cifra inferior a la mitad de la unidad empleada
...	Datos no disponibles
.	Categoría sin objeto
*	Cifra provisional o estimada
./.	Datos comprendidos en otra rúbrica
———>	La cifra situada immediatemente a la izquierda de la flecha comprende los datos relativos a las columnas donde figura dicho símbolo.
<———	La cifra situada immediatemente a la derecha de la flecha comprende los datos relativos a las columnas donde figura dicho símbolo.

Una interrupción en la homogeneidad de las series se indica mediante un trazo vertical u horizontal.

List of countries and territories

Liste des pays et territoires

Lista de paŝes y territorios

To facilitate the presentation of the tables in the body of this publication, the names of countries and territories and the different groupings of countries have been given in English only. For purposes of cross-reference, lists of the names of countries and territories, grouped according to continent and arranged in alphabetical order in English, French and Spanish are given in the following pages. The names of countries in French and Spanish are preceded by a numerical reference (in parentheses). The equivalent name in English can thus be read off opposite the number indicated.

En vue de faciliter la présentation des tableaux, les noms des pays, des territoires et des différents groupes de pays ont été donnés en anglais seulement. Il sera néanmoins aisé de trouver l'équivalent anglais des noms en français et en espagnol en se servant de la liste ci-après, où les pays ont été classés séparément en anglais, français et espagnol et groupés, par continents, dans l'ordre alphabétique de chaque langue. Les noms des pays en espagnol et en français sont précédés d'un numéro entre parenthèses qui les renvoie à leur équivalent en anglais.

Con vistas a facilitar la presentación de los cuadros, los nombres de los países y territorios sólo se indican en inglés. Sin embargo, se podrá encontrar fácilmente el equivalente inglés de los nombres en español y en francés sirviéndose de la lista que figura a continuación, en la que los países se han clasificado separadamente en inglés, español y francés, agrupados por continentes, de acuerdo con el orden alfabético propio a cada lengua. Al lado de los nombres de los países en español y en francés figura un número entre paréntesis que corresponde al equivalente del orden alfabético inglés.

Africa	Afrique	Africa
1 Algeria	(44) Afrique du Sud	(2) Angola
2 Angola	(1) Algérie	(1) Argelia
3 Benin	(2) Angola	(3) Benín
4 Botswana	(3) Bénin	(4) Botswana
5 Burkina Faso	(4) Botswana	(5) Burkina Faso
6 Burundi	(5) Burkina Faso	(6) Burundi
7 Cameroon	(6) Burundi	(8) Cabo Verde
8 Cape Verde	(7) Cameroun	(7) Camerún
9 Central African Republic	(8) Cap-Vert	(11) Comores
10 Chad	(11) Comores	(12) Congo
11 Comoros	(12) Congo	(13) Côte d'Ivoire
12 Congo	(13) Côte-d'Ivoire	(10) Chad
13 Côte d'Ivoire	(14) Djibouti	(15) Egipto
14 Djibouti	(15) Egypte	(17) Etiopià
15 Egypt	(17) Ethiopie	(18) Gabón
16 Equatorial Guinea	(18) Gabon	(19) Gambia
17 Ethiopia	(19) Gambie	(20) Ghana
18 Gabon	(20) Ghana	(21) Guinea
19 Gambia	(21) Guiné	(22) Guinea-Bissau
20 Ghana	(22) Guiné-Bissau	(16) Guinea Ecuatorial
21 Guinea	(16) Guiné équatoriale	(26) Jamahiriya Arabe Libia
22 Guinea-Bissau	(26) Jamahiriya arabe libyenne	(23) Kenia
23 Kenya	(23) Kenya	(24) Lesotho
24 Lesotho	(24) Lesotho	(25) Liberia
25 Liberia	(25) Libéria	(27) Madagascar
26 Libyan Arab Jamahiriya	(27) Madagascar	(28) Malawi
27 Madagascar	(28) Malawi	(29) Malí
28 Malawi	(29) Mali	(32) Marruecos
29 Mali	(32) Maroc	(31) Mauricio
30 Mauritania	(31) Maurice	(30) Mauritania
31 Mauritius	(30) Mauritanie	(33) Mozambique
32 Morocco	(33) Mozambique	(34) Namibia
33 Mozambique	(34) Namibie	(35) Níger
34 Namibia	(35) Niger	(36) Nigeria
35 Niger	(36) Nigéria	(37) Reunión
36 Nigeria	(50) Ouganda	(9) República Centroafricana
37 Reunion	(9) République centrafricaine	(51) República Unida de Tanzania
38 Rwanda	(51) République-Unie de Tanzanie	(38) Rwanda
39 St Helena	(37) Réunion	(52) Sahara Occidental

40 Sao Tome and Principe	(38) Rwanda	(39) Santa Elena
41 Senegal	(52) Sahara occidental	(40) Santo Tomé y Príncipe
42 Seychelles	(39) Sainte-Hélène	(41) Senegal
43 Sierra Leone	(40) Sao Tome et Principe	(42) Seychelles
44 Somalia	(41) Sénégal	(43) Sierra Leona
45 South Africa	(42) Seychelles	(44) Somalia
46 Sudan	(43) Sierra Leone	(45) Sudáfrica
47 Swaziland	(44) Somalie	(46) Sudán
48 Togo	(46) Soudan	(47) Swazilandia
49 Tunisia	(47) Swaziland	(48) Togo
50 Uganda	(10) Tchad	(49) Túnez
51 United Republic of Tanzania	(48) Togo	(50) Uganda
52 Western Sahara	(49) Tunisie	(14) Yibuti
53 Zaire	(53) Zaïre	(53) Zaire
54 Zambia	(54) Zambie	(54) Zambia
55 Zimbabwe	(55) Zimbabwe	(55) Zimbabwe
North America	Amérique du Nord	América del Norte
56 Antigua and Barbuda	(56) Antigua et Barbuda	(56) Antigua y Barbuda
57 Bahamas	(79) Antilles néerlandaises	(79) Antillas Neerlandesas
58 Barbados	(57) Bahamas	(57) Bahamas
59 Belize	(58) Barbade	(58) Barbados
60 Bermuda	(59) Belize	(59) Belize
61 British Virgin Islands	(60) Bermudes	(60) Bermudas
62 Canada	(63) Iles Caïmanes	(62) Canadá
63 Cayman Islands	(62) Canada	(63) Islas Caimán
64 Costa Rica	(64) Costa Rica	(64) Costa Rica
65 Cuba	(65) Cuba	(65) Cuba
66 Dominica	(66) Dominique	(66) Dominica
67 Dominican Republic	(68) El Salvador	(68) El Salvador
68 El Salvador	(90) Etats-Unis	(90) Estados Unidos
69 Greenland	(70) Grenade	(70) Granada
70 Grenada	(69) Groënland	(69) Groenlandia
71 Guadeloupe	(71) Guadeloupe	(71) Guadalupe
72 Guatemala	(72) Guatemala	(72) Guatemala
73 Haiti	(73) Haïti	(73) Haiti
74 Honduras	(74) Honduras	(74) Honduras
75 Jamaica	(75) Jamaïque	(75) Jamaica
76 Martinique	(76) Martinique	(76) Martinica
77 Mexico	(77) Mexique	(77) México
78 Montserrat	(78) Montserrat	(78) Montserrat
79 Netherlands Antilles	(80) Nicaragua	(80) Nicaragua
80 Nicaragua	(81) Panama	(81) Panamá
81 Panama	(82) Ancienne Zone du Canal	(82) Antigua Zona del Canal
82 Former Canal Zone	(83) Porto Rico	(83) Puerto Rico
83 Puerto Rico	(67) République dominicaine	(67) República Dominicana
84 St Christopher and Nevis and Anguilla	(84) Saint-Christophe et Nevis et Anguilla	(84) San Cristóbal y Nevis y Anguilla
85 St Lucia	(85) Sainte-Lucie	(85) Santa Lucía
86 St Pierre and Miquelon	(86) Saint-Pierre-et-Miquelon	(86) San Pedro y Miquelón
87 St Vincent and the Grenadines	(87) Saint-Vincent-et-Grenadines	(87) San Vicente y Granadinas
88 Trinidad and Tobago	(88) Trinité-et-Tobago	(88) Trinidad y Tabago
89 Turks and Caicos Islands	(89) Iles Turques et Caïques	(89) Islas Turcas y Caicos
90 United States	(91) Iles Vierges américaines	(91) Islas Vírgenes Americanas
91 United States Virgin Islands	(61) Iles Vierges britanniques	(61) Islas Vírgenes Británicas
South America	Amérique du Sud	América del Sur
92 Argentina	(92) Argentine	(92) Argentina
93 Bolivia	(93) Bolivie	(93) Bolivia
94 Brazil	(94) Brésil	(94) Brasil
95 Chile	(95) Chili	(96) Colombia
96 Colombia	(96) Colombie	(95) Chile
97 Ecuador	(97) Equateur	(97) Ecuador
98 Falkland Islands (Malvinas)	(98) Iles Falkland (Malvinas)	(98) Islas Falkland (Malvinas)
99 French Guiana	(100) Guyana	(100) Guyana
100 Guyana	(99) Guyane française	(99) Guyana Francesa
101 Paraguay	(101) Paraguay	(101) Paraguay
102 Peru	(102) Pérou	(102) Perú
103 Suriname	(103) Suriname	(103) Suriname
104 Uruguay	(104) Uruguay	(104) Uruguay
105 Venezuela	(105) Venezuela	(105) Venezuela
Asia	Asie	Asia
106 Afghanistan	(106) Afghanistan	(106) Afganistán
107 Bahrain	(142) Arabie saoudite	(142) Arabia Saudita
108 Bangladesh	(107) Bahrein	(107) Bahrein
109 Bhutan	(108) Bangladesh	(108) Bangladesh
110 Brunei Darussalam	(109) Bhoutan	(111) Birmania
111 Burma	(111) Birmanie	(110) Brunei Darussalam
112 China	(110) Brunéi Darussalam	(109) Bután
113 Cyprus	(112) Chine	(112) China
114 Democratic Kampuchea	(113) Chypre	(113) Chipre
115 Democratic Yemen	(148) Emirats arabes unis	(148) Emiratos Arabes Unidos
116 East Timor	(117) Hong-kong	(140) Filipinas
117 Hong Kong	(118) Inde	(117) Hong-Kong
118 India	(119) Indonésie	(118) India
119 Indonesia	(120) Iran, République Islamique d'	(119) Indonesia
120 Iran, Islamic Republic of	(121) Iraq	(120) Irán, República Islámica de
121 Iraq	(122) Israël	(121) Iraq
122 Israel	(123) Japon	(122) Israel

123 Japan	(124) Jordanie	(123) Japón
124 Jordan	(114) Kampuchéa démocratique	(124) Jordania
125 Korea, Democratic People's Republic of	(127) Koweït	(114) Kampuchea Democrática
126 Korea, Republic of	(129) Liban	(127) Kuweit
127 Kuwait	(130) Macao	(129) Líbano
128 Lao People's Democratic Republic	(131) Malaisie	(130) Macao
129 Lebanon	(132) Malaisie péninsulaire	(131) Malasia
130 Macau	(133) Sabah	(132) Malasia peninsular
131 Malaysia	(134) Sarawak	(133) Sabah
132 Peninsular Malaysia	(135) Maldives	(134) Sarawak
133 Sabah	(136) Mongolie	(135) Maldivas
134 Sarawak	(137) Népal	(136) Mongolia
135 Maldives	(138) Oman	(137) Nepal
136 Mongolia	(139) Pakistan	(138) Omán
137 Nepal	(140) Philippines	(139) Paquistán
138 Oman	(141) Qatar	(145) República Arabe Siria
139 Pakistan	(145) République arabe syrienne	(126) República de Corea
140 Philippines	(126) République de Corée	(128) República Democrática Popular Lao
141 Qatar	(128) République démocratique populaire lao	(125) República Popular Democrática de Corea
142 Saudi Arabia	(125) République populaire démocratique de Corée	(141) Qatar
143 Singapore	(143) Singapour	(143) Singapur
144 Sri Lanka	(144) Sri Lanka	(144) Sri Lanka
145 Syrian Arab Republic	(146) Thaïlande	(146) Tailandia
146 Thailand	(116) Timor oriental	(116) Timor Oriental
147 Turkey	(147) Turquie	(147) Turquía
148 United Arab Emirates	(149) Viet-nam	(149) Viet Nam
149 Viet Nam	(150) Yémen	(150) Yemen
150 Yemen	(115) Yémen démocratique	(115) Yemen Democrático
Europe	Europe	Europa
151 Albania	(151) Albanie	(151) Albania
152 Andorra	(162) Allemagne, République fédérale d'	(162) Alemania, República Federal de
153 Austria	(152) Andorre	(152) Andorra
154 Belgium	(153) Autriche	(153) Austria
155 Bulgaria	(154) Belgique	(154) Bélgica
156 Czechoslovakia	(155) Bulgarie	(155) Bulgaria
157 Denmark	(157) Danemark	(156) Checoslovaquia
158 Faeroe Islands	(180) Espagne	(157) Dinamarca
159 Finland	(158) Iles Féroé	(180) España
160 France	(159) Finlande	(158) Islas Feroé
161 German Democratic Republic	(160) France	(159) Finlandia
162 Germany, Federal Republic of	(163) Gibraltar	(160) Francia
163 Gibraltar	(164) Grèce	(163) Gibraltar
164 Greece	(166) Hongrie	(164) Grecia
165 Holy See	(168) Irlande	(166) Hungría
166 Hungary	(167) Islande	(168) Irlanda
167 Iceland	(169) Italie	(167) Islandia
168 Ireland	(170) Liechtenstein	(169) Italia
169 Italy	(171) Luxembourg	(170) Liechtenstein
170 Liechtenstein	(172) Malte	(171) Luxemburgo
171 Luxembourg	(173) Monaco	(172) Malta
172 Malta	(175) Norvège	(173) Mónaco
173 Monaco	(174) Pays-Bas	(175) Noruega
174 Netherlands	(176) Pologne	(174) Países Bajos
175 Norway	(177) Portugal	(176) Polonia
176 Poland	(161) République démocratique allemande	(177) Portugal
177 Portugal	(178) Roumanie	(183) Reino Unido
178 Romania	(183) Royaume-Uni	(161) República Democrática Alemana
179 San Marino	(179) Saint-Marin	(178) Rumania
180 Spain	(165) Saint-Siège	(179) San Marino
181 Sweden	(181) Suède	(165) Santa Sede
182 Switzerland	(182) Suisse	(181) Suecia
183 United Kingdom	(156) Tchécoslovaquie	(182) Suiza
184 Yugoslavia	(184) Yougoslavie	(184) Yugoslavia
Oceania	Océanie	Oceanía
185 American Samoa	(186) Australie	(186) Australia
186 Australia	(187) Iles Cook	(187) Islas Cook
187 Cook Islands	(188) Fidji	(190) Guam
188 Fiji	(190) Guam	(191) Kiribati
189 French Polynesia	(191) Kiribati	(192) Nauru
190 Guam	(192) Nauru	(195) Niue
191 Kiribati	(195) Nioué	(196) Isla Norfolk
192 Nauru	(196) Ile Norfolk	(193) Nueva Caledonia
193 New Caledonia	(193) Nouvelle-Calédonie	(194) Nueva Zelandia
194 New Zealand	(194) Nouvelle-Zélande	(197) Islas del Pacífico
195 Niue	(197) Iles du Pacifique	(198) Papúa Nueva Guinea
196 Norfolk Island	(198) Papouasie - Nouvelle-Guinée	(189) Polinesia Francesa
197 Pacific Islands	(189) Polynésie française	(200) Islas Salomón
198 Papua New Guinea	(200) Iles Salomon	(199) Samoa
199 Samoa	(199) Samoa	(185) Samoa Americanas
200 Solomon Islands	(185) Samoa américaines	(201) Tokelau
201 Tokelau	(201) Tokelaou	(202) Tonga
202 Tonga	(202) Tonga	(203) Tuvalu
203 Tuvalu	(203) Tuvalu	(204) Vanuatú
204 Vanuatu	(204) Vanuatu	(188) Viti

English	Français	Español
U.S.S.R.	U.R.S.S.	U.R.S.S.
205 U.S.S.R.	(205) U.R.S.S.	(205) U.R.S.S.
206 Byelorussian S.S.R.	(206) R.S.S. de Biélorussie	(206) R.S.S. de Bielorrusia
207 Ukrainian S.S.R.	(207) R.S.S. d'Ukraine	(207) R.S.S. de Ucrania
Continents, major areas and groups of countries	Continents, grandes régions et groupes de pays	Continentes, grandes regiones y grupos de paises
World	Monde	Mundo
Africa	Afrique	Africa
America	Amérique	América
Asia	Asie	Asia
Europe (inc. U.S.S.R.)	Europe (y compris U.R.S.S.)	Europa (incl. U.R.S.S.)
Oceania	Océanie	Oceania
Developed countries	Pays développés	Paises desarrollados
Developing countries	Pays en développement	Paises en desarrollo
Africa (excluding Arab States)	Afrique (sans les Etats arabes)	Africa (sin los Estados árabes)
Asia (excluding Arab States)	Asie (sans les Etats arabes)	Asia (sin los Estados árabes)
Arab States	Etats arabes	Estados árabes
Northern America	Amérique septentrionale	América septentrional
Latin America and the Caribbean	Amérique latine et les caraïbes	América latina y el Caribe

1 Reference tables

Tableaux de référence

Cuadros de referencia

The first part of the *Yearbook* consists of two tables on population, one on illiteracy and one on educational attainment. They provide reference material for all the other tables presented in the *Yearbook* which are concerned with education, science, culture and mass media.

The size and density of a country's population directly affect the development of its educational institutions and facilities. Estimates of the population aged 0-24 in suitably combined age-groups are presented in order to show major fluctuations by region of the younger cohorts, those which can be expected to affect most directly the demand for education.

Estimates of illiteracy and data on educational attainment provide an educational profile of the adult population which can serve as a complement to statistics on school and university enrolments.

Table 1.1

Table 1.1 contains data on total population, area and density for the world, for each continent, and for 204 countries and territories. It is the most comprehensive table in the *Yearbook* in the sense that practically all countries and territories of the world are included. The population data given are official mid-year estimates for the years 1970, 1975, 1980, 1983 and 1984, prepared by the Population Division of the United Nations (medium variant, as assessed in 1984). Area figures, unless otherwise noted, include inland waters. Population density figures (inhabitants per square kilometre) are not given for areas of less than 1,000 square kilometres. Readers interested in more detailed information on area, population and age structure are referred to the various editions of the *Demographic Yearbook* and the *Statistical Yearbook* of the United Nations.

Table 1.2

Table 1.2 presents estimates and projections of the total population and the population below age 25, for the world, by continents, major areas and groups of countries, for the years 1970, 1975, 1980, 1985, 1990 and 2000. Separate estimates are given for age-groups 0-4, 5-9, 10-14, 15-19 and 20-24 years, covering the ages of most relevance for education. The figures presented in table 1.2 correspond to the medium variant of the projections which were prepared by the United Nations Population Division in 1984.

The table is broken down into the five major areas of the world, and then into various other groupings which are described, where necessary, in general footnote 1 at the head of the table.

Figure 1 shows the differences of population growth for each continent. Over the thirty years from 1970 to 2000, Europe's population (including U.S.S.R.) will rise by only 18.0% and that of Northern America by 31.2%, whereas that of Latin America and the Caribbean will rise by 92.8%, the population of Africa by 141.7% and that of Asia by 68.8%. The population of Asia will continue to constitute over half the world's total during these thirty years.

Figure 2 shows graphically world population for ages 0 to 24 and for the period 1970-2000. When the world total is anaylsed by major areas, the developing countries, and the Arab States in particular show the highest rates of increase.

Table 1.3

Table 1.3 presents data relating to the illiterate population and percentage illiterate by age and sex from the latest census or survey held since 1970 for which figures are available. Data for 122 countries are shown: the figures were provided by the United Nations Statistical Office or were derived from regional or national publications. Readers interested in obtaining comparable data for earlier years are referred to the 1977 Unesco publication *Statistics of Educational Attainment and Illiteracy, 1945-1974*, and to the 1983 document *Statistics of Educational Attainment and Illiteracy, 1970-1980*, CSR-E-44.

Table 1.4

Table 1.4 shows the percentage distribution of the highest level of educational attainment of the adult population by sex, and wherever possible, by urban and rural areas. The data are derived from national censuses or sample surveys and were provided by the United Nations Statistical Office or were derived from regional or national publications. The purpose of this table is to present the most recent data on educational attainment received by the Unesco Office of Statistics for each country and territory. Readers interested in data for earlier years or in breakdowns by age are referred to the 1977 Unesco publication *Statistics of Educational Attainment and Illiteracy, 1945-1974*, and to the 1983 document *Statistics of Educational Attainment and Illiteracy, 1970-1980*, CSR-E-44.

The six levels of educational attainment, ranging from no schooling to third level, are conceptually based on a selection of the level categories of the International Standard Classification of Education (ISCED) and may be defined as follows:

No schooling. This term applies to those who have completed less than one year of schooling.

Incompleted first level. The duration of education at the first level may vary depending on the country: this category includes all those who completed at least one year of education at the first level but who did not complete the final year at this level. The current structure of all countries' first and second level education can be found in Table 3.1.

Completed first level. Those who completed the final year of education at the first level (ISCED level category '1') but did not go on to second level studies are included in this group. In some cases (as indicated by a footnote) the data for the two final years of the first level were combined, so that some individuals who reached only the penultimate year of study were counted in this group.

Entered second level, first stage. This group comprises those whose level of educational attainment was limited to the lower stage of education at the second level as defined in Table 3.1 and corresponds to ISCED level category '2'.

Entered second level, second stage (ISCED level category '3'). This group consists of those who moved to the higher stage of second level education from the lower stage, but did not proceed to studies at the third level.

Third level. Anyone who undertook third level studies (ISCED level categories '5', '6' or '7'), whether or not they completed the full course, would be counted in this group.

The number of people whose level of education was not stated has been subtracted from the total population.

The proportion of the 15-24 age group with some third level education is frequently smaller than that of the 25-34 age group, since a sizeable proportion of the 15-24 age group is too young to have reached the entrance age to the third level of education. For this reason the total adult age range is taken as 25+ and not 15+ for the purposes of this table.

La première partie de l'*Annuaire statistique* se compose de deux tableaux sur la population, d'un sur l'analphabétisme et d'un autre sur le niveau d'instruction. Ces tableaux fournissent des données de référence pour tous les autres tableaux qui portent sur l'enseignement, la science, la culture et les moyens d'information.

Le nombre et la densité des habitants d'un pays influent directement sur le développement de ses établissements et de ses moyens d'enseignement. Les estimations de la population âgée de 0 à 24 ans, classée par groupes d'âge de façon appropriée, sont présentées pour faire connaître les principales fluctuations par région des cohortes qui concernent les jeunes, qui sont certainement celles qui jouent le plus grand rôle dans les demandes formulées relatives à l'enseignement.

Les estimations concernant l'analphabétisme et les données sur le niveau d'instruction présentent un profil éducatif de la population adulte et peuvent servir comme un complément aux statistiques sur les effectifs scolaires et universitaires.

Tableau 1.1

Le tableau 1.1 contient des données sur la population totale, la supercifie et la densité de peuplement de l'ensemble du monde, de chaque continent et de 204 pays et territoires. C'est le tableau le plus complet de l'*Annuaire*, en ce sens que presque tous les pays et territoires du monde y figurent. Les chiffres relatifs à la population sont fondés sur les estimations faites au milieu de l'année indiquée pour les années 1970, 1975, 1980, 1983 et 1984, et préparées par la Division de la Population de l'Organisation des Nations Unies (variante moyenne évaluée en 1984). Sauf indication contraire, les chiffres relatifs à la superficie comprennent les eaux intérieures. La densité de la population (nombre d'habitants au kilomètre carré) n'est pas indiquée lorsque la superficie est inférieure à 1.000 km2. Les lecteurs désireux d'avoir des renseignements plus détaillés sur la superficie, la population et la structure par âge sont priés de se reporter aux diverses éditions de l'*Annuaire statistique* et de l'*Annuaire démographique* de l'Organisation des Nations Unies.

Tableau 1.2

Dans le tableau 1.2 figurent les estimations et les projections pour les années 1970, 1975, 1980, 1985, 1990 et 2000 de la population totale et de la population de moins de 25 ans pour le monde entier, par continents, par grandes régions et par groupes de pays. Des estimations sont données séparément pour les groupes d'âge 0-4, 5-9, 10-14, 15-19 et 20-24 ans, qui sont ceux qui présentent le plus d'intérêt du point de vue de l'éducation. Les données présentées dans le tableau 1.2 correspondent à la variante moyenne des projections préparées par la Division de la population de l'Organisation des Nations Unies en 1984.

Le tableau présente les cinq grandes régions du monde, divisées elles-mêmes en divers autres groupes dont la composition, si nécessaire, est indiquée dans la note générale qui figure en-tête de ce tableau.

Le graphique 1 montre les différences d'accroissement de la population entre les continents. Au cours des trente années qui s'étendent de 1970 à 2000, la population européenne (y compris l'U.R.S.S.) n'augmentera que de 18.0% et celle de l'Amérique septentrionale de 31.2% alors que celle de l'Amérique latine et des Caraïbes augmentera de 92.8%, celle de l'Afrique de 141.7% et celle de l'Asie de 68.8%. Pendant ces trente années la population de l'Asie continuera de représenter plus de la moitié de la population mondiale.

Le graphique 2 représente la population mondiale âgée de 0 à 24 ans pour la période 1970-2000. Quand le total mondial est analysé par grandes régions, on constate que ce sont les pays en développement, et en particulier les Etats arabes, qui ont le taux d'accroissement le plus élevé.

Tableau 1.3

Le tableau 1.3 présente des données sur la population analphabète et le pourcentage d'analphabètes, par âge et par sexe. Ces données sont tirées des derniers recensements ou enquêtes faits depuis 1970 pour lesquels les chiffres sont disponibles. Ce tableau contient des données pour 122 pays: les chiffres ont été fournis par l'Office des Statistiques de l'Organisation des Nations Unies ou extraits de publications nationales ou régionales. Les lecteurs intéressés par des données comparables pour les années antérieures sont priés de consulter la publication de l'Unesco *Statistiques sur le niveau d'instruction et l'analphabétisme, 1945-1974*, parue en 1977, et le document *Statistiques sur le niveau d'instruction et l'analphabétisme, 1970-1980*, CSR-E-44, paru en 1983.

Tableau 1.4

Le tableau 1.4 présente la répartition en pourcentage de la population adulte d'après le plus haut degré d'instruction atteint, par sexe et, dans la mesure du possible, par zones urbaine et rurale. Les données sont tirées des recensements nationaux et des enquêtes par sondage, dont les résultats nous on été communiqués par l'Office des statistiques de l'Organisation des Nations Unies, ainsi que des publications régionales ou nationales.

Le but de ce tableau est de présenter les données les plus récentes sur le niveau d'instruction, reçues à l'Office des Statistiques de l'Unesco pour chaque pays ou territoire. Les lecteurs qui voudraient prendre connaissance de la répartition par âge ou des données relatives aux années précédentes doivent consulter la publication de l'Unesco *Statistiques sur le niveau d'instruction et l'analphabétisme, 1945-1974*, parue en 1977, et le document *Statistiques sur le niveau d'instruction et l'analphabétisme, 1970-1980*, CSR-E-44, paru en 1983.

Les six niveaux d'instruction retenus, qui s'étendent du groupe de personnes n'ayant reçu aucune éducation scolaire à celui des personnes ayant atteint le troisième degré d'enseignement, sont conçus à partir d'une sélection de catégories par degré de la Classification Internationale Type de l'Education (CITE), et peuvent être définis comme suit:

Sans scolarité. Il s'agit des personnes qui ont fait moins d'une année de scolarité.

Premier degré non complété. La durée de l'enseignement du premier degré est différente selon les pays: cette catégorie comprend toutes les personnes qui ont fait au moins une année d'enseignement du premier degré mais qui n'ont pas terminé la dernière année de ce degré. La structure en vigueur de l'enseignement du premier et du second degré figure pour tous les pays dans le tableau 3.1.

Premier degré complété. Comprend les personnes qui ont terminé la dernière année de l'enseignement du premier degré (catégorie par degré '1' de la CITE), mais qui n'ont pas accédé aux études du second degré. Dans quelques cas (indiqués par une note), les données correspondant aux deux dernières années de l'enseignement de premier degré ont été réunies, de sorte que les personnes n'ayant terminé que l'avant-dernière année sont comptées aussi dans ce groupe.

Accédé au second degré, premier cycle. Ce groupe, qui correspond à la catégorie par degré '2' de la CITE, comprend toutes les personnes dont les études n'ont pas été au-delà du premier cycle de l'enseignement du second degré, tel qu'il est défini dans le tableau 3.1.

Accédé au second degré, deuxième cycle (catégorie par degré '3' de la CITE). Ce groupe comprend les personnes qui sont passées du premier au deuxième cycle de l'enseignement du second degré, mais qui n'ont pas fait d'études du troisième degré.

Troisième degré (catégories par degré '5', '6' ou '7' de la CITE). Toutes les personnes qui ont entrepris des études du troisième degré, qu'elles les aient ou non terminées, sont comptées dans ce groupe.

Le nombre des personnes dont le niveau d'instruction n'est pas connu a été soustrait du total de la population.

En ce qui concerne l'enseignement du troisième degré, la proportion du groupe d'âge 15-24 ans est souvent inférieure à celle du groupe d'âge 25-34 ans, par le fait qu'une proportion notable du groupe d'âge 15-24 ans est encore trop jeune pour accéder à l'enseignement du troisième degré. Pour cette raison, on a choisi comme total de la population adulte dans ce tableau le groupe d'âge 25 ans et plus et non 15 ans et plus.

El cuadro 1.1 contiene datos sobre la población total, la superficie y la densidad demográfica de todo el mundo, de cada continente y de 204 países y territorios. Se trata del cuadro más completo del *Anuario*, en el sentido de que prácticamente figuran en él todo los países y territorios del globo. Las cifras relativas a la población se basan en las estimaciones efectuadas a mediados del año indicado (1970, 1975, 1980, 1983 y 1984), preparados por la División de la Población de la Organización de las Naciones Unidas (variante media evaluada en 1984). Cuando no se dice otra cosa, las cifras de superficie comprenden las aguas continentales. No se indica la densidad demográfica (número de habitantes por kilómetro cuadrado) cuando la superficie es inferior a 1 000 km2. Los lectores que deseen datos más detallados sobre la superficie, la población y la estructura por edades pueden consultar las diversas ediciones del *Statistical Yearbook - Annuaire Statistique* y *Demographic Yearbook - Annuaire Démografique* de las Naciones Unidas.

Cuadro 1.2

En el cuadro 1.2 figuran las estimaciones y las proyecciones de la población total y de la población de menos de 25 años en todo el mundo, en los distintos continentes, grandes regiones y grupos de países, para los años 1970, 1975, 1980, 1985, 1990 y 2000. Se presentan por separado unas estimaciones relativas a los grupos de 0-4, 5-9, 10-14, 15-19, y 20-24 años de edad, que son los que ofrecen más interés desde el punto de vista de la educación. Los datos presentados en el cuadro 1.2 corresponden a la variante media de las proyecciones preparados, en 1984, por la División de Población de las Naciones Unidas.

Se indican en el cuadro las cinco regiones principales del mundo, subdivididas en otros varios grupos cuya composición, cuando procede, se señala en la nota general que figura en el encabezamiento del cuadro.

En el gráfico 1 se indican las diferencias de crecimiento entre cada continente. En los 30 años que van de 1970 a 2000 la población europea (incluída la U.R.S.S.) sólo aumentará en un 18.0% y, en cambio, la de América septentrional en un 31.2%, la de América Latina y el Caribe en un 92.8%, la de Africa en un 141.7% y la de Asia en un 68.8%. Durante esos 30 años, la población de Asia seguirá representando más de la mitad de la población mundial.

El gráfico 2 representa la población mundial de 0 a 24 años de edad para el período 1970-2000. Cuando se analiza el total mundial por grandes regiones, se observa que los que tienen una tasa de crecimiento más alta son los países en desarrollo, y en particular los Estados Arabes.

Cuadro 1.3

El cuadro 1.3 presenta datos sobre la población analfabeta y el porcentaje de analfabetos por edad y sexo. Estos datos han sido obtenidos de los últimos censos o encuestas llevados a cabo desde 1970 donde las cifras son disponibles. Este cuadro presenta datos para 122 países: las cifras han sido proporcionados por la Oficina de Estadística de la Organización de Naciones Unidas u obtenidas a partir de publicaciones nacionales o regionales. Los lectores interesados en datos comparables para años anteriores, se las suplica consultar la publicación de la Unesco *Estadísticas sobre el nivel de instrucción y el analfabetismo, 1945-1974*, aparecida en 1977, y al documento *Estadísticas sobre el nivel de instrucción y el analfabetismo, 1970-1980*, CSR-E-44, aparecido en 1983.

Cuadro 1.4

El cuadro 1.4 presenta la distribución en porcentaje de la población adulta según el mas alto nivel de instrucción alcanzado, por sexo y, cuando es posible, según las zonas urbana y rural. Los datos están tomados de censos nacionales y de encuestas por sondeo cuyos resultados nos han sido comunicados por la Oficina de Estadística de las Naciones Unidas y de publicaciones regionales o nacionales. La finalidad de este cuadro es la de presentar los datos más recientes sobre nivel de instrucción recibidos en la Oficina de Estadística de la Unesco para cada país y territorio. Los lectores que se interesen en los datos relativos a los años anteriores o a la distribución por edad deben consultar la publicación de la Unesco *Estadísticas sobre el nivel de instrucción y el analfabetismo, 1945-1974*, aparecida en 1977, y al documento *Estadísticas sobre el nivel de instrucción y el analfabetismo, 1970-1980*, CSR-E-44, aparecido en 1983.

Los seis niveles de instrucción presentados, que van del grupo de personas sin escolaridad al de las personas que alcanzaron el tercer grado de enseñanza, están basados conceptualmente en una selección de las categorías generales de la Clasificación Internacional Normalizada de la Educación (CINE) y que pueden ser definidos de la maniera siguiente:

Sin escolaridad: Se trata de las personas que no llegaron a completar un año de estudios.

Primer grado incompleto. La duración de la enseñanza de primer grado puede variar según los países: esta categoría comprende todas las personas que terminaron como mínimo un año de enseñanza de primer grado, pero que no finalizaron el último año de este nivel. La estructura en vigor de las enseñanzas de primero y de segundo grado figura, para todos los países, en el cuadro 3.1.

Primer grado completo. Comprende las personas que terminaron el último año de enseñanza de primer grado (categoría general '1' de la CINE), pero que no accedieron a la enseñanza de segundo grado. En algunos casos (indicados en una nota) se han reunido los datos correspondientes a los dos últimos años de enseñanza de primer grado, y las personas que sólo terminaron el penúltimo año se cuentan también en este grupo.

Accedieron al segundo grado, primer ciclo. Este grupo comprende todas las personas cuyos estudios no sobrepasaron el primer ciclo de la enseñanza de segundo grado, tal y como se define en el cuadro 3.1 y corresponde a la categoría general '2' de la CINE.

Accedieron al segundo grado, segundo ciclo (categoría general '3' de la CINE). Este grupo comprende las personas que pasaron del primero al segundo ciclo de la enseñanza de segundo grado, pero que no hicieron estudios de tercer grado.

Tercer grado. Todas las personas que empezaron estudios de tercer grado, (categorías generales '5', '6' o '7' de la CINE) que los hayan o no terminado, figuran en este grupo.

El número de personas sobre las cuales se desconoce el nivel de instrucción ha sido sustraído del total de la población.

En lo que concierne a la enseñanza de tercer grado, la proporción del grupo de edad de 15 a 24 años es a menudo inferior a la del grupo de 25 a 34 años de edad, ya que una proporción notable de aquél es todavía demasiado joven para poder ingresar en ese grado de enseñanza. Por este motivo, se ha escogido como total de la población adulta en el cuadro el grupo de edad de 25 años y más, y no el de 15 años y más.

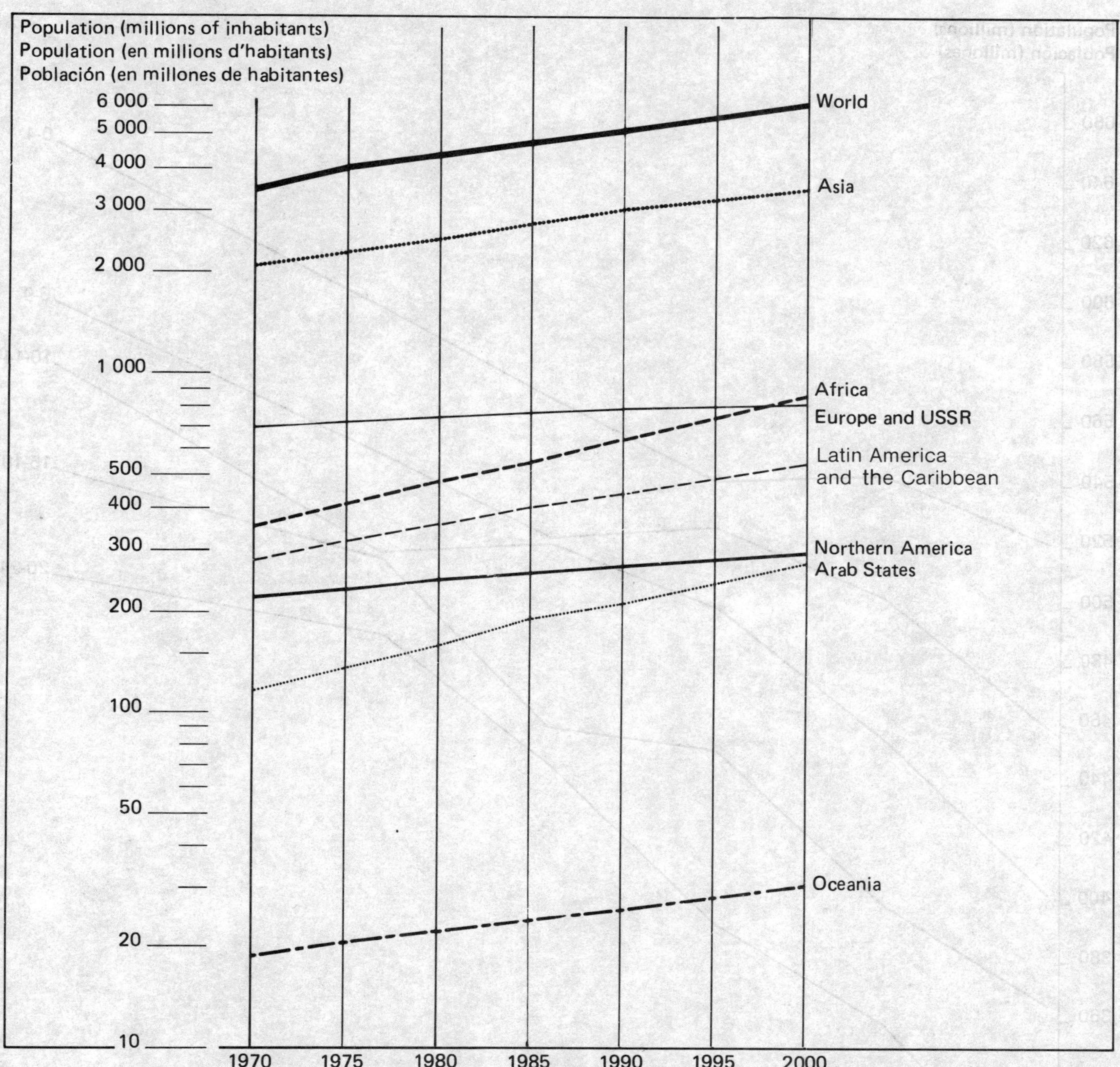

Figure 1: **Growth in the population of the world and of major areas, 1970-2000.**
Source: Table 1.2.

Graphique 1 : **Evolution de la population mondiale par grandes régions, 1970-2000.**
Source : Tableau 1.2.

Gráfico 1: **Evolución de la población mundial por grandes regiones, 1970-2000.**
Fuente: Cuadro 1.2.

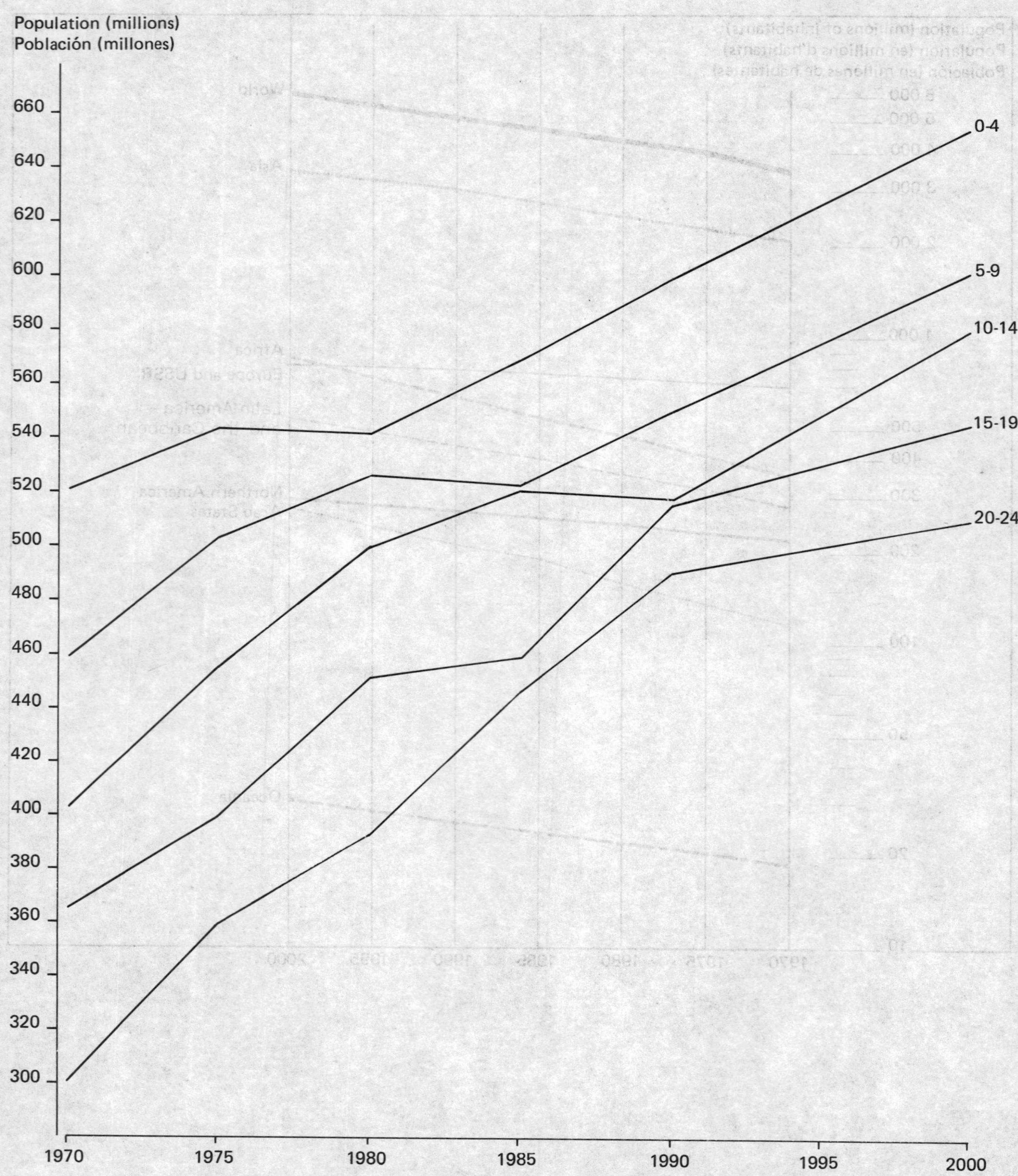

Figure 2: **World population aged 0-24, by 5-year age-groups, 1970-2000.**
Source: Table 1.2.

Graphique 2 : **Population mondiale âgée de 0 à 24 ans, par groupe d'âge quinquennal, 1970-2000.**
Source: Tableau 1.2.

Gráfico 2: **Población mundial de 0 à 24 años de edad, por grupos quinquenales, 1970-2000.**
Fuente: Cuadro 1.2.

1.1 Population, area and density, 1970, 1975, 1980, 1983 and 1984

Population, superficie et densité, 1970, 1975, 1980, 1983 et 1984

Población, superficie y densidad, 1970, 1975, 1980, 1983 y 1984

NUMBER OF COUNTRIES AND TERRITORIES PRESENTED IN THIS TABLE: 204

NOMBRE DE PAYS ET DE TERRITOIRES PRESENTES DANS CE TABLEAU: 204

NUMERO DE PAISES Y DE TERRITORIOS PRESENTADOS EN ESTE CUADRO: 204

CONTINENTS, MAJOR AREAS, GROUPS OF COUNTRIES AND COUNTRIES / CONTINENTS, GRANDES REGIONS, GROUPES DE PAYS ET PAYS / CONTINENTES, GRANDES REGIONES, GRUPOS DE PAISES Y PAISES	ESTIMATES OF MID-YEAR POPULATION (THOUSANDS) / ESTIMATIONS DE LA POPULATION AU MILIEU DE L'ANNEE (MILLIERS) / ESTIMACIONES DE LA POBLACION A MEDIADOS DE AÑO (EN MILES)					AREA (SQ. KM) / SUPERFICIE (KM CARRES) / SUPERFICIE (KM CUADRADOS)	INHABITANTS PER SQ. KM / NOMBRE D'HABITANTS AU KM CARRE / HABITANTES POR KM CUADRADO
	1970	1975	1980	1983	1984		1984
	(1)	(2)	(3)	(4)	(5)	(6)	(7)
WORLD TOTAL	3 693	4 076	4 450	4 679	4 757	135 743	35
AFRICA	361	413	479	523	539	30 313	18
AMERICA	510	560	613	646	657	42 073	16
ASIA‡	2 102	2 354	2 584	2 725	2 771	27 572	101
EUROPE (INCLUDING U.S.S.R.)	701	728	750	761	765	27 276	28
OCEANIA‡	19	21	23	24	24	8 509	3
DEVELOPED COUNTRIES	1 053	1 102	1 147	1 169	1 178	55 944	22
DEVELOPING COUNTRIES	2 641	2 974	3 303	3 510	3 579	79 799	46
AFRICA (EXCLUDING ARAB STATES)	274	315	366	400	412	20 363	19
ASIA (EXCLUDING ARAB STATES)	2 067	2 313	2 535	2 671	2 715	23 841	114
ARAB STATES	122	140	163	177	182	13 680	14
NORTHERN AMERICA‡	227	239	252	259	261	21 525	12
LATIN AMERICAN AND THE CARIBBEAN	283	321	361	387	396	20 548	19
AFRICA							
ALGERIA	13 747	16 018	18 666	20 449	21 073	2 381 741	9
ANGOLA	5 589	6 520	7 723	8 322	8 535	1 246 700	7
BENIN	2 707	3 041	3 494	3 812	3 929	112 622	35
BOTSWANA	624	754	915	1 025	1 065	581 730	2
BURKINA FASO	5 077	5 569	6 159	6 615	6 776	274 200	25
BURUNDI	3 457	3 747	4 100	4 453	4 584	27 834	165
CAMEROON	6 744	7 581	8 623	9 346	9 604	475 442	20
CAPE VERDE	270	283	296	313	320	4 033	79
CENTRAL AFRICAN REPUBLIC	1 875	2 058	2 299	2 458	2 516	622 984	4
CHAD	3 652	4 030	4 477	4 791	4 902	1 284 000	4
COMOROS	272	321	381	418	431	2 171	198
CONGO	1 201	1 351	1 529	1 651	1 695	342 000	5
COTE D'IVOIRE‡	5 552	6 768	8 172	9 107	9 452	322 463	29
DJIBOUTI	160	214	310	341	352	22 000	16
EGYPT	33 053	36 291	41 520	44 647	45 758	1 001 449	46
EQUATORIAL GUINEA	291	319	352	375	383	28 051	14
ETHIOPIA	30 622	34 311	38 521	41 417	42 464	1 221 900	35
GABON	950	1 002	1 064	1 114	1 132	267 667	4
GAMBIA	469	525	584	618	630	11 295	56
GHANA	8 614	9 801	11 561	12 734	13 153	238 537	55
GUINEA	4 387	4 852	5 407	5 791	5 930	245 857	24
GUINEA-BISSAU	527	628	809	856	873	36 125	24
KENYA	11 291	13 702	16 766	18 965	19 765	582 646	34
LESOTHO	1 065	1 188	1 339	1 444	1 481	30 355	49
LIBERIA	1 365	1 581	1 871	2 054	2 121	111 369	19

CONTINENTS, MAJOR AREAS, GROUPS OF COUNTRIES AND COUNTRIES CONTINENTS, GRANDES REGIONS, GROUPES DE PAYS ET PAYS CONTINENTES, GRANDES REGIONES, GRUPOS DE PAISES Y PAISES	ESTIMATES OF MID-YEAR POPULATION (THOUSANDS) ESTIMATIONS DE LA POPULATION AU MILIEU DE L'ANNEE (MILLIERS) ESTIMACIONES DE LA POBLACION A MEDIADOS DE AÑO (EN MILES)					AREA (SQ. KM) SUPERFICIE (KM CARRES) SUPERFICIE (KM CUADRADOS)	INHABITANTS PER SQ. KM NOMBRE D'HABITANTS AU KM CARRE HABITANTES POR KM CUADRADO
	1970	1975	1980	1983	1984		1984
	(1)	(2)	(3)	(4)	(5)	(6)	(7)
LIBYAN ARAB JAMAHIRIYA	1 987	2 429	2 973	3 334	3 467	1 759 540	2
MADAGASCAR	6 717	7 603	8 704	9 459	9 731	587 041	17
MALAWI	4 520	5 166	5 951	6 522	6 729	118 484	57
MALI	5 685	6 292	7 023	7 632	7 853	1 240 000	6
MAURITANIA	1 245	1 422	1 631	1 779	1 833	1 030 700	2
MAURITIUS	848	868	955	1 011	1 031	2 045	504
MOROCCO	15 310	17 305	19 382	20 930	21 433	446 550	48
MOZAMBIQUE	8 142	9 720	12 123	13 196	13 574	801 590	17
NAMIBIA	1 041	1 181	1 349	1 465	1 507	824 292	2
NIGER	4 145	4 665	5 311	5 771	5 939	1 267 000	5
NIGERIA	57 220	67 671	80 556	89 010	92 048	923 768	100
REUNION	442	483	510	523	527	2 510	210
RWANDA	3 718	4 359	5 144	5 680	5 872	26 338	223
ST. HELENA	5	5	5	5	5	314	.
SAO TOME AND PRINCIPE	74	80	85	92	95	964	.
SENEGAL	4 008	4 772	5 672	6 121	6 280	196 192	32
SEYCHELLES	52	58	65	71	73	280	.
SIERRA LEONE	2 834	3 045	3 296	3 471	3 535	71 740	49
SOMALIA	2 634	3 251	4 019	4 383	4 516	637 657	7
SOUTH AFRICA	22 761	25 502	28 612	30 821	31 593	1 221 037	26
SUDAN	13 859	16 013	18 681	20 340	20 935	2 505 813	8
SWAZILAND	425	483	559	611	630	17 363	36
TOGO	2 020	2 252	2 554	2 788	2 872	56 785	51
TUNISIA	5 129	5 612	6 392	6 808	6 944	163 610	42
UGANDA	9 805	11 171	13 106	14 470	14 963	236 036	63
UNITED REPUBLIC OF TANZANIA	13 513	15 901	18 868	20 956	21 714	945 087	23
WESTERN SAHARA	76	117	135	147	151	266 000	1
ZAIRE	19 481	22 398	25 847	28 219	29 064	2 345 409	12
ZAMBIA	4 191	4 841	5 648	6 236	6 447	752 614	9
ZIMBABWE	5 308	6 219	7 368	8 181	8 474	390 580	22
AMERICA, NORTH							
ANGUILLA	6	6	7	7	7	...	...
ANTIGUA AND BARBUDA	66	71	75	78	79	440	.
BAHAMAS	171	204	210	222	226	13 935	16
BARBADOS	239	245	249	253	253	431	.
BELIZE	120	131	145	154	158	22 965	7
BERMUDA	55	63	71	76	78	53	.
BRITISH VIRGIN ISLANDS	10	10	12	12	12	153	.
CANADA	21 407	22 727	24 090	24 880	25 153	9 976 139	3
CAYMAN ISLANDS	10	14	17	18	19	259	.
COSTA RICA	1 732	1 966	2 279	2 467	2 532	50 700	50
CUBA	8 572	9 331	9 732	9 950	9 995	110 861	92
DOMINICA	71	72	73	75	75	751	.
DOMINICAN REPUBLIC	4 289	4 945	5 558	5 977	6 110	48 734	125
EL SALVADOR	3 583	4 142	4 797	5 241	5 395	21 041	256
GREENLAND	47	50	52	53	54	2 175 600	
GRENADA	94	100	107	110	111	344	.
GUADELOUPE	320	330	327	333	334	1 779	188
GUATEMALA	5 246	6 023	6 917	7 535	7 746	108 889	71
HAITI‡	4 605	5 158	5 809	6 268	6 425	27 750	232
HONDURAS	2 640	3 093	3 691	4 089	4 229	112 088	38
JAMAICA	1 869	2 043	2 173	2 278	2 309	10 991	210
MARTINIQUE	327	331	326	330	329	1 102	299
MEXICO	51 176	60 152	69 393	75 192	77 094	1 972 547	39
MONTSERRAT	11	12	12	12	12	98	.
NETHERLANDS ANTILLES	222	239	252	258	260	961	.
NICARAGUA	2 054	2 408	2 771	3 063	3 166	130 000	24
PANAMA	1 531	1 748	1 957	2 092	2 137	77 082	28
PUERTO RICO	2 719	2 995	3 199	3 351	3 401	8 897	382
ST. CHRISTOPHER AND NEVIS	46	45	45	46	46	...	...
ST. LUCIA	101	111	120	126	128	616	.
ST. PIERRE AND MIQUELON	5	6	6	6	6	242	.
ST. VINCENT AND THE GRENADINES	88	93	99	102	103	388	.
TRINIDAD AND TOBAGO	956	1 008	1 095	1 150	1 168	5 130	228
TURKS AND CAICOS ISLANDS	6	6	7	7	7	430	.
UNITED STATES	205 051	215 972	227 704	234 191	236 104	9 372 614	25
U.S. VIRGIN ISLANDS	64	95	98	102	104	342	.

CONTINENTS, MAJOR AREAS, GROUPS OF COUNTRIES AND COUNTRIES CONTINENTS, GRANDES REGIONS, GROUPES DE PAYS ET PAYS CONTINENTES, GRANDES REGIONES, GRUPOS DE PAISES Y PAISES	ESTIMATES OF MID-YEAR POPULATION (THOUSANDS) ESTIMATIONS DE LA POPULATION AU MILIEU DE L'ANNEE (MILLIERS) ESTIMACIONES DE LA POBLACION A MEDIADOS DE AÑO (EN MILES)					AREA (SQ. KM) SUPERFICIE (KM CARRES) SUPERFICIE (KM CUADRADOS)	INHABITANTS PER SQ. KM NOMBRE D'HABITANTS AU KM CARRE HABITANTES POR KM CUADRADO
	1970	1975	1980	1983	1984		1984
	(1)	(2)	(3)	(4)	(5)	(6)	(7)
AMERICA, SOUTH							
ARGENTINA	23 962	26 050	28 237	29 592	30 070	2 766 889	11
BOLIVIA	4 324	4 892	5 570	6 038	6 202	1 098 581	6
BRAZIL	95 847	108 030	121 286	129 754	132 633	8 511 965	16
CHILE	9 455	10 338	11 127	11 687	11 865	756 945	16
COLOMBIA	20 803	23 177	25 794	27 537	28 119	1 138 914	25
ECUADOR	6 052	7 036	8 123	8 861	9 116	283 561	32
FALKLAND ISLANDS (MALVINAS)	2	2	2	2	2	12 173	.
FRENCH GUIANA	48	56	69	76	79	91 000	1
GUYANA	710	781	865	918	936	214 969	4
PARAGUAY	2 291	2 689	3 168	3 469	3 573	406 752	9
PERU	13 194	15 162	17 295	18 715	19 201	1 285 216	15
SURINAME	374	364	355	369	372	163 265	2
URUGUAY	2 808	2 829	2 908	2 974	2 994	176 215	17
VENEZUELA	10 603	12 666	15 024	16 361	16 831	912 050	18
ASIA							
AFGHANISTAN	13 622	15 378	16 063	16 328	16 420	647 497	25
BAHRAIN	219	272	347	391	411	622	.
BANGLADESH	66 671	76 582	88 219	95 913	98 531	143 998	684
BHUTAN	1 045	1 158	1 281	1 362	1 389	47 000	30
BRUNEI DARUSSALAM	130	156	185	211	220	5 765	38
BURMA	27 101	30 442	33 714	35 799	36 481	676 552	54
CHINA	830 674	927 271	996 134	1 035 795	1 047 315	9 596 961	109
CYPRUS	615	610	629	652	660	9 251	71
DEMOCRATIC KAMPUCHEA	6 938	7 099	6 400	6 817	7 012	181 035	39
DEMOCRATIC YEMEN	1 498	1 656	1 861	2 024	2 079	332 968	6
EAST TIMOR	603	671	581	619	636	14 874	43
HONG KONG	3 942	4 396	5 039	5 350	5 449	1 045	5 214
INDIA	554 910	620 701	688 856	731 086	745 026	3 287 590	227
INDONESIA	120 281	135 666	150 958	160 427	163 461	1 904 569	86
IRAN, ISLAMIC REPUBLIC OF	28 398	33 344	38 635	42 142	43 368	1 648 000	26
IRAQ	9 357	11 020	13 291	14 798	15 338	434 924	35
ISRAEL	2 975	3 455	3 878	4 098	4 173	20 770	201
JAPAN	104 331	111 524	116 807	118 964	119 830	377 708	317
JORDAN	2 299	2 600	2 923	3 267	3 389	97 740	35
KOREA, DEMOCRATIC PEOPLE'S REPUBLIC OF	13 892	15 853	18 025	19 451	19 923	120 538	165
KOREA, REPUBLIC OF	31 924	35 281	38 124	40 114	40 713	98 484	413
KUWAIT	745	1 008	1 375	1 605	1 703	17 818	96
LAO PEOPLE'S DEMOCRATIC REPUBLIC	3 019	3 427	3 683	3 938	4 026	236 800	17
LEBANON	2 469	2 767	2 669	2 684	2 677	10 400	257
MACAU	245	260	323	363	378	16	.
MALAYSIA	10 865	12 308	13 763	14 833	15 191	329 749	46
MALDIVES	114	133	155	171	176	298	.
MONGOLIA	1 248	1 445	1 663	1 807	1 857	1 565 000	1
NEPAL	11 488	13 000	14 667	15 746	16 113	140 797	114
OMAN	654	766	984	1 126	1 183	212 457	6
PAKISTAN	65 707	74 733	86 143	94 427	97 336	796 095	122
PHILIPPINES	37 542	42 566	48 317	51 992	53 238	300 000	177
QATAR	111	171	225	270	291	11 000	26
SAUDI ARABIA	5 745	7 254	9 372	10 577	11 049	2 149 690	5
SINGAPORE	2 075	2 263	2 415	2 503	2 531	581	.
SRI LANKA	12 514	13 603	14 819	15 657	15 933	65 610	243
SYRIAN ARAB REPUBLIC	6 258	7 438	8 800	9 792	10 143	185 180	55
THAILAND	36 370	41 387	46 516	49 483	50 445	514 000	98
TURKEY	35 322	40 026	44 468	47 427	48 366	780 576	62
UNITED ARAB EMIRATES	224	504	980	1 147	1 231	83 600	15
VIET-NAM	42 730	48 031	54 175	57 574	58 663	329 556	178
YEMEN	4 833	5 282	5 981	6 488	6 665	195 000	34
EUROPE							
ALBANIA	2 138	2 424	2 731	2 923	2 986	28 748	104
ANDORRA	20	27	35	38	39	453	.
AUSTRIA	7 448	7 521	7 505	7 498	7 499	83 849	89
BELGIUM	9 639	9 796	9 852	9 873	9 886	30 513	324
BULGARIA	8 514	8 722	8 862	8 964	9 013	110 912	81

CONTINENTS, MAJOR AREAS, GROUPS OF COUNTRIES AND COUNTRIES / CONTINENTS, GRANDES REGIONS, GROUPES DE PAYS ET PAYS / CONTINENTES, GRANDES REGIONES, GRUPOS DE PAISES Y PAISES	ESTIMATES OF MID-YEAR POPULATION (THOUSANDS) / ESTIMATIONS DE LA POPULATION AU MILIEU DE L'ANNEE (MILLIERS) / ESTIMACIONES DE LA POBLACION A MEDIADOS DE AÑO (EN MILES)					AREA (SQ. KM) / SUPERFICIE (KM CARRES) / SUPERFICIE (KM CUADRADOS)	INHABITANTS PER SQ. KM / NOMBRE D'HABITANTS AU KM CARRE / HABITANTES POR KM CUADRADO
	1970	1975	1980	1983	1984		1984
	(1)	(2)	(3)	(4)	(5)	(6)	(7)
CZECHOSLOVAKIA	14 362	14 802	15 311	15 421	15 491	127 869	121
DENMARK	4 929	5 060	5 123	5 122	5 122	43 069	119
FAEROE ISLANDS	39	40	41	41	42	1 399	30
FINLAND	4 606	4 712	4 780	4 834	4 861	337 032	14
FRANCE	50 670	52 706	53 714	54 129	54 351	547 026	99
GERMAN DEMOCRATIC REPUBLIC‡	17 066	16 850	16 737	16 708	16 720	108 178	155
GERMANY, FEDERAL REPUBLIC OF‡	60 700	61 832	61 566	61 107	60 966	248 577	245
GIBRALTAR	26	27	29	30	31	6	.
GREECE	8 792	9 046	9 643	9 781	9 829	131 944	74
HOLY SEE‡	1	1	1	1	1	...	...
HUNGARY	10 353	10 541	10 711	10 679	10 682	93 030	115
ICELAND	204	218	228	237	240	103 000	2
IRELAND	2 954	3 206	3 401	3 530	3 570	70 283	51
ITALY	53 564	55 830	57 070	57 172	57 238	301 225	190
LIECHTENSTEIN	21	24	26	28	28	157	.
LUXEMBOURG	339	363	364	363	363	2 586	140
MALTA	326	345	369	376	379	316	.
MONACO	24	25	26	27	27	1	.
NETHERLANDS	13 033	13 795	14 150	14 359	14 430	40 844	353
NORWAY	3 878	4 007	4 086	4 119	4 131	324 219	13
POLAND	32 657	34 023	35 574	36 448	36 798	312 677	118
PORTUGAL	8 628	9 425	9 884	10 085	10 148	92 082	110
ROMANIA	20 360	21 245	22 201	22 635	22 814	237 500	96
SAN MARINO	19	20	21	22	22	61	.
SPAIN	33 779	35 596	37 430	38 110	38 335	504 782	76
SWEDEN	8 042	8 193	8 311	8 325	8 337	449 964	19
SWITZERLAND	6 266	6 406	6 327	6 353	6 364	41 288	154
UNITED KINGDOM	55 480	56 035	55 945	56 052	56 088	244 046	230
YUGOSLAVIA	20 372	21 351	22 299	22 746	22 934	255 804	90
OCEANIA							
AMERICAN SAMOA	27	30	32	35	35	197	.
AUSTRALIA	12 551	13 628	14 695	15 297	15 498	7 686 848	2
COOK ISLANDS	21	18	18	19	20	236	.
FIJI	520	577	629	667	679	18 274	37
FRENCH POLYNESIA	109	133	148	157	160	4 000	40
GUAM	86	96	106	110	112	549	.
KIRIBATI	49	54	59	62	63	728	.
NAURU	7	7	8	8	8	21	.
NEW CALEDONIA	110	133	139	148	151	19 058	8
NEW ZEALAND	2 819	3 088	3 169	3 261	3 291	268 676	12
NIUE	5	4	3	3	3	259	.
NORFOLK ISLAND	1	2	2	2	2	36	.
PACIFIC ISLANDS	103	121	136	147	150	1 779	84
PAPUA NEW GUINEA	2 423	2 696	3 086	3 337	3 422	461 691	7
SAMOA	143	150	155	160	161	2 842	57
SOLOMON ISLANDS	164	194	225	250	259	28 446	9
TOKELAU	2	2	2	2	2	10	.
TONGA	85	88	97	103	105	699	.
TUVALU	6	6	8	8	8	...	...
VANUATU	83	96	117	132	137	14 763	...
U.S.S.R.							
U.S.S.R.	241 700	253 393	265 493	272 428	275 339	22 402 200	12
BYELORUSSIAN S.S.R.‡	9 038	9 351	9 643	9 806	...	207 600	47
UKRAINIAN S.S.R.‡	47 307	49 020	50 040	50 546	...	603 700	84

General note/Note générale/Nota general:

E--> Area shown includes land area and inland waters, but excludes uninhabited polar regions and some uninhabited islands. Population density is not shown for territories less than 1,000 square kilometres in area.

FR-> La superficie indiquée est celle des terres et des eaux intérieures, non compris les zones polaires ni quelques îles inhabitées. La densité n'est pas indiquée lorsque la superficie est inférieure à 1 000 kilomètres carrés.

ESP> La superficie incluye las tierras y las aguas continentales, pero no las regiones polares y ciertas islas inhabitadas. No se indica la densidad demografica en el caso de territorios de menos de 1 000 kilometros cuadrados de superficie.

Asia:

E--> Excluding the U.S.S.R., but including both the Asian and the European portions of Turkey.

FR-> Non compris l'U.R.S.S., mais y compris la partie asiatique et la partie européenne de la Turquie.

ESP> Excluida la U.R.S.S., pero incluida la Turquía europea y la asiática.

Oceania:

E--> Hawaii, a State of the United States, is included in Northern America, rather than in Oceania.

FR-> Hawaii, Etat des Etats-Unis, est compris dans l'Amérique Septentrionale plutôt que dans l'Océanie.

Oceania: (Cont):

ESP> Hawai, estado de los Estados Unidos, figura en América Septentrional, y no en Oceania.

Northern America:

E--> Hawaii, a State of the United States, is included in Northern America, rather than Oceania.

FR-> Hawaii, Etat des Etats-Unis, est compris dans l'Amérique septentrionale plutôt que dans l'Océanie.

ESP> Hawai, estado de los Estados Unidos, figura en America septentrional y no en Oceania.

AFRICA:

Côte d'Ivoire:

E--> Formerly listed as Ivory Coast.

FR-> Antérieurement montré sous le nom de Ivory Coast (en anglais) et de Costa de Marfil (en espagnol).

ESP> Anteriormente clasificado con el nombre de Costa de Marfil.

EUROPE:

German Democratic Republic:

Germany, Federal Republic of:

E--> The data which relate to the Federal Republic of Germany and the German Democratic Republic include the relevant data relating to Berlin for which separate data have not been supplied. This is without prejudice to any question of status which may be involved.

FR-> Les données se rapportant à la République fédérale d'Allemagne et à la République démocratique allemande incluent les données pertinentes relatives à Berlin pour laquelle des données séparées n'ont pas été fournies. Cela sans préjudice des questions de statut qui peuvent se

Germany, Federal Republic of: (Cont):

poser à cet égard.

ESP> Los datos relativos a la Republica federal de Alemania y de la Republica democratica alemana comprenden los datos pertinentes correspondientes a Berlin, que no nos han sido procurados separadamente, lo que no prejuzga las cuestiones de estatuto que puenden plantearse al respecto.

Holy See:

E--> Data refer to the State of the Vatican City, of which the area is 0.44 square kilometres.

FR-> Les données se réfèrent à l'Etat de la Cité du Vatican, dont la superficie est de 0,44 kilomètres carrés.

ESP> Los datos se refieren al Estado de la Ciudad del Vaticano, cuya superficie es de 0,44 kilometros cuadrados.

U.S.S.R.:

Byelorussian S.S.R.:

E--> The number of inhabitants per square kilometre refers to 1983.

FR-> Le nombre d'habitants au kilomètre carré se réfère à 1983.

ESP> El número de habitantes por kilometro cuadrado se refiere a 1983.

Ukrainian S.S.R.:

E--> The number of inhabitants per square kilometre refers to 1983.

FR-> Le nombre d'habitants au kilomètre carré se réfère à 1983.

ESP> El número de habitantes por kilometro cuadrado se refiere a 1983.

1.2 Estimated total population and population 0-24 years old, by continents, major areas and groups of countries, 1970-2000

Estimation de la population totale et de la population de 0 à 24 ans, par continents, grandes régions et groupes de pays, 1970-2000

Estimación de la población total y de la poblacíon de 0 a 24 años, por continentes, grandes regiones y grupos de países, 1970-2000

DEVELOPED COUNTRIES:
ALL EUROPEAN COUNTRIES (EXCEPT FOR YUGOSLAVIA), U.S.S.R., UNITED STATES, CANADA, JAPAN, ISRAEL, AUSTRALIA, NEW ZEALAND AND SOUTH AFRICA.

DEVELOPING COUNTRIES:
REST OF THE WORLD.

NORTHERN AMERICA:
BERMUDA, CANADA, GREENLAND, ST. PIERRE AND MIQUELON, AND UNITED STATES.

LATIN AMERICA AND THE CARIBBEAN:
REST OF AMERICA.

ARAB STATES:
ALGERIA, DJIBOUTI, EGYPT, LIBYAN ARAB JAMAHIRIYA, MAURITANIA, MOROCCO, SOMALIA, SUDAN, TUNISIA, BAHRAIN, DEMOCRATIC YEMEN, IRAQ, JORDAN, KUWAIT, LEBANON, OMAN, QATAR, SAUDI ARABIA, SYRIAN ARAB REPUBLIC, UNITED ARAB EMIRATES AND YEMEN.

A = ALL AGES

PAYS DEVELOPPES:
TOUS LES PAYS D'EUROPE (SAUF LA YOUGOSLAVIE), U.R.S.S., ETATS-UNIS, CANADA, JAPON, ISRAEL, AUSTRALIE, NOUVELLE-ZELANDE ET AFRIQUE DU SUD.

PAYS EN DEVELOPPEMENT:
LE RESTE DU MONDE.

AMERIQUE SEPTENTRIONALE:
BERMUDES, CANADA, GROENLAND, SAINT-PIERRE-ET-MIQUELON, ET ETATS-UNIS.

AMERIQUE LATINE ET LES CARAIBES:
LE RESTE DE L'AMERIQUE.

ETATS ARABES:
ALGERIE, DJIBOUTI, EGYPTE, JAMAHIRIYA ARABE LIBYENNE, MAURITANIE, MAROC, SOMALIE, SOUDAN, TUNISIE, BAHREIN, YEMEN DEMOCRATIQUE, IRAK, JORDANIE, KOWEIT, LIBAN, OMAN, QATAR, ARABIE SAOUDITE, REPUBLIQUE ARABE SYRIENNE, EMIRATS ARABES UNIS ET YEMEN.

A = TOUS LES AGES

PAISES DESAROLLADOS:
TODOS LOS PAISES DE EUROPA (A LA EXCEPCION DE YUGOSLAVIA), LA U.R.S.S., LOS ESTADOS UNIDOS, CANADA, JAPON, ISRAEL, AUSTRALIA, NUEVA ZELANDIA Y SUDAFRICA.

PAISES EN DESAROLLO:
LOS DEMAS PAISES DEL MONDO.

AMERICA SEPTENTRIONAL:
BERMUDES, CANADA, GROENLANDIA, SAN PEDRO Y MIQUELON, Y LOS ESTADOS UNIDOS.

AMERICA LATINA Y EL CARIBE:
LOS DEMAS PAISES DE AMERICA.

ESTADOS ARABES:
ARGELIA, YIBUTI, EGIPTO, JAMAHIRIYA ARABE LIBYA, MAURITANIA, MARRUECOS, SOMALIA, SUDAN, TUNEZ, BAHREIN, YEMEN DEMOCRATICO, IRAK, JORDANIA, KUWEIT, LIBANO, OMAN, QATAR, ARABIA SAUDITA, REPUBLICA ARABE SIRIA, EMIRATOS ARABES UNIDOS Y YEMEN.

A = TODAS LAS EDADES

CONTINENTS MAJOR AREAS AND GROUPS OF COUNTRIES CONTINENTS GRANDES REGIONS ET GROUPES DE PAYS CONTINENTES GRANDES REGIONES Y GRUPOS DE PAISES	AGE GROUP GROUPE D'AGE GRUPO DE EDAD	ESTIMATED POPULATION (THOUSANDS) ESTIMATION DE LA POPULATION (EN MILLIERS) POBLACION ESTIMADA (EN MILES)						ANNUAL AVERAGE INCREASE ACCROISSEMENT MOYEN ANNUEL CRECIMIENTO MEDIO ANNUAL		
		1970	1975	1980	1985	1990	2000	1970–80 (%)	1980–90 (%)	1990–2000 (%)
		(1)	(2)	(3)	(4)	(5)	(6)	(7)	(8)	(9)
WORLD TOTAL										
	A	3 693 220	4 076 167	4 449 533	4 836 645	5 246 209	6 121 813	1.9	1.7	1.6
	0–4	521 548	543 689	540 759	569 278	599 752	654 162	0.4	1.0	0.9
	5–9	458 637	503 263	526 267	523 016	552 889	617 439	1.4	0.5	1.1
	10–14	403 082	455 307	499 458	521 107	518 361	580 520	2.2	0.4	1.1
	15–19	365 017	399 628	451 322	495 268	517 244	545 015	2.1	1.4	0.5
	20–24	301 333	359 652	393 938	446 325	490 453	510 520	2.7	2.2	0.4
	0–24	2 049 618	2 261 539	2 411 743	2 554 993	2 678 698	2 907 656	1.6	1.1	0.8
AFRICA										
	A	360 752	413 340	479 456	554 928	645 282	871 817	2.9	3.0	3.1
	0–4	65 586	75 227	87 466	101 328	117 572	152 528	2.9	3.0	2.6
	5–9	52 122	60 216	69 624	81 371	95 116	128 177	2.9	3.2	3.0
	10–14	43 746	50 354	58 889	67 786	79 504	109 125	3.0	3.0	3.2
	15–19	36 521	42 567	49 314	57 695	66 581	91 760	3.0	3.0	3.3
	20–24	30 379	35 374	41 640	48 084	56 416	76 732	3.2	3.1	3.1
	0–24	228 354	263 738	306 933	356 264	415 189	558 322	3.0	3.1	3.0

CONTINENTS MAJOR AREAS AND GROUPS OF COUNTRIES / CONTINENTS GRANDES REGIONS ET GROUPES DE PAYS / CONTINENTES GRANDES REGIONES Y GRUPOS DE PAISES	AGE GROUP / GROUPE D'AGE / GRUPO DE EDAD	ESTIMATED POPULATION (THOUSANDS) / ESTIMATION DE LA POPULATION (EN MILLIERS) / POBLACION ESTIMADA (EN MILES)						ANNUAL AVERAGE INCREASE / ACCROISSEMENT MOYEN ANNUEL / CRECIMIENTO MEDIO ANNUAL		
		1970	1975	1980	1985	1990	2000	1970–80 (%)	1980–90 (%)	1990–2000 (%)
		(1)	(2)	(3)	(4)	(5)	(6)	(7)	(8)	(9)
AMERICA										
	A	509 971	560 011	613 295	668 391	726 397	843 730	1.9	1.7	1.5
	0–4	63 947	66 250	69 969	76 592	80 628	83 958	0.9	1.4	0.4
	5–9	62 853	63 150	65 550	69 037	75 745	82 247	0.4	1.5	0.8
	10–14	57 888	63 220	63 345	65 355	68 886	79 788	0.9	0.8	1.5
	15–19	50 925	57 934	63 209	63 113	65 180	75 516	2.2	0.3	1.5
	20–24	43 101	50 611	57 641	62 857	62 845	68 594	2.9	0.9	0.9
	0–24	278 714	301 165	319 714	336 954	353 284	390 103	1.4	1.0	1.0
ASIA										
	A	2 102 044	2 353 885	2 583 891	2 818 214	3 057 649	3 548 994	2.1	1.7	1.5
	0–4	331 314	342 491	323 893	330 626	340 549	357 998	–0.2	0.5	0.5
	5–9	279 025	318 880	331 798	313 376	321 462	346 809	1.7	–0.3	0.8
	10–14	236 883	276 396	316 263	328 753	310 811	330 780	2.9	–0.2	0.6
	15–19	216 957	234 499	273 432	313 588	326 349	317 282	2.3	1.8	–0.3
	20–24	173 242	213 230	230 293	270 213	310 482	306 205	2.9	3.0	–0.1
	0–24	1 237 421	1 385 496	1 475 679	1 556 556	1 609 653	1 659 075	1.8	0.9	0.3
EUROPE (INC. USSR)										
	A	701 125	727 796	750 040	770 468	790 414	827 210	0.7	0.5	0.5
	0–4	58 561	57 458	57 258	58 361	58 522	57 077	–0.2	0.2	–0.2
	5–9	62 531	58 857	57 028	57 051	58 186	57 639	–0.9	0.2	–0.1
	10–14	62 594	63 200	58 712	56 924	56 957	58 312	–0.6	–0.3	0.2
	15–19	58 836	62 633	63 247	58 607	56 827	58 037	0.7	–1.1	0.2
	20–24	52 964	58 647	62 372	63 023	58 419	56 739	1.6	–0.7	–0.3
	0–24	295 486	300 795	298 617	293 965	288 911	287 806	0.1	–0.3	–0.0
OCEANIA										
	A	19 329	21 131	22 850	24 644	26 467	30 062	1.7	1.5	1.3
	0–4	2 140	2 264	2 173	2 372	2 481	2 601	0.2	1.3	0.5
	5–9	2 106	2 159	2 267	2 181	2 379	2 567	0.7	0.5	0.8
	10–14	1 972	2 135	2 248	2 289	2 203	2 513	1.3	–0.2	1.3
	15–19	1 778	1 994	2 120	2 265	2 306	2 419	1.8	0.8	0.5
	20–24	1 648	1 790	1 992	2 147	2 291	2 250	1.9	1.4	–0.2
	0–24	9 644	10 342	10 800	11 254	11 660	12 350	1.1	0.8	0.6
DEVELOPED COUNTRIES										
	A	1 052 648	1 102 341	1 146 696	1 187 162	1 227 103	1 303 490	0.9	0.7	0.6
	0–4	90 257	89 559	88 498	92 040	93 330	93 920	–0.2	0.5	0.1
	5–9	96 081	90 881	89 423	88 279	91 854	93 672	–0.7	0.3	0.2
	10–14	96 222	97 511	91 396	89 476	88 345	93 281	–0.5	–0.3	0.5
	15–19	91 350	96 751	97 959	91 478	89 573	92 062	0.7	–0.9	0.3
	20–24	84 516	91 378	96 689	97 967	91 534	88 594	1.4	–0.5	–0.3
	0–24	458 426	466 080	463 964	459 242	454 637	461 529	0.1	–0.2	0.1
DEVELOPING COUNTRIES										
	A	2 640 572	2 973 826	3 302 837	3 649 483	4 019 106	4 818 323	2.3	2.0	1.8
	0–4	431 291	454 130	452 261	477 238	506 422	560 243	0.5	1.1	1.0
	5–9	362 556	412 382	436 843	434 737	461 034	523 768	1.9	0.5	1.3
	10–14	306 860	357 796	408 062	431 630	430 015	487 238	2.9	0.5	1.3
	15–19	273 667	302 877	353 363	403 789	427 670	452 952	2.6	1.9	0.6
	20–24	216 817	268 274	297 248	348 357	398 918	421 926	3.2	3.0	0.6
	0–24	1 591 192	1 795 459	1 947 778	2 095 750	2 224 060	2 446 126	2.1	1.3	1.0
AFRICA (EXCLUDING ARAB STATES)										
	A	273 715	314 885	366 057	425 428	497 967	686 584	2.9	3.1	3.3
	0–4	50 620	58 507	68 427	80 256	94 736	128 073	3.1	3.3	3.1
	5–9	39 390	46 130	53 932	63 237	74 869	104 957	3.2	3.3	3.4
	10–14	32 708	38 073	44 934	52 337	61 604	87 222	3.2	3.2	3.5
	15–19	27 406	31 907	37 400	43 927	51 305	71 897	3.2	3.2	3.4
	20–24	23 393	26 584	31 161	36 366	42 838	59 184	2.9	3.2	3.3
	0–24	173 517	201 201	235 855	276 124	325 352	451 334	3.1	3.3	3.3
ASIA (EXCLUDING ARAB STATES)										
	A	2 067 284	2 312 762	2 534 645	2 759 483	2 987 855	3 452 820	2.1	1.7	1.5
	0–4	324 907	334 963	314 831	319 922	328 170	342 358	–0.3	0.4	0.4
	5–9	273 770	312 774	324 514	304 568	310 989	332 910	1.7	–0.4	0.7
	10–14	232 683	271 187	310 212	321 537	302 060	318 672	2.9	–0.3	0.5
	15–19	213 516	230 362	268 279	307 583	319 162	306 916	2.3	1.8	–0.4
	20–24	170 343	209 787	226 065	265 021	304 440	297 520	2.9	3.0	–0.2
	0–24	1 215 218	1 359 073	1 443 900	1 518 631	1 564 821	1 598 376	1.7	0.8	0.2
ARAB STATES										
	A	121 797	139 578	162 644	188 231	217 108	281 406	2.9	2.9	2.6
	0–4	21 373	24 247	28 100	31 775	35 215	40 095	2.8	2.3	1.3
	5–9	17 987	20 192	22 976	26 942	30 721	37 118	2.5	2.9	1.9
	10–14	15 238	17 490	20 006	22 664	26 650	34 012	2.8	2.9	2.5
	15–19	12 556	14 797	17 067	19 773	22 463	30 229	3.1	2.8	3.0
	20–24	9 885	12 233	14 707	16 910	19 620	26 233	4.1	2.9	2.9
	0–24	77 039	88 959	102 857	118 064	134 669	167 686	2.9	2.7	2.2

CONTINENTS MAJOR AREAS AND GROUPS OF COUNTRIES / CONTINENTS GRANDES REGIONS ET GROUPES DE PAYS / CONTINENTES GRANDES REGIONES Y GRUPOS DE PAISES	AGE GROUP / GROUPE D'AGE / GRUPO DE EDAD	ESTIMATED POPULATION (THOUSANDS) / ESTIMATION DE LA POPULATION (EN MILLIERS) / POBLACION ESTIMADA (EN MILES)						ANNUAL AVERAGE INCREASE / ACCROISSEMENT MOYEN ANNUEL / CRECIMIENTO MEDIO ANNUAL		
		1970	1975	1980	1985	1990	2000	1970–80 (%)	1980–90 (%)	1990–2000 (%)
		(1)	(2)	(3)	(4)	(5)	(6)	(7)	(8)	(9)
NORTHERN AMERICA										
	A	226 566	238 818	251 923	263 585	275 325	297 335	1.1	0.9	0.8
	0–4	19 040	17 884	18 233	20 573	21 169	21 026	-0.4	1.5	-0.1
	5–9	22 229	19 522	18 364	18 431	20 772	21 575	-1.9	1.2	0.4
	10–14	23 163	22 998	20 137	18 578	18 644	21 588	-1.4	-0.8	1.5
	15–19	21 417	23 597	23 424	20 352	18 799	21 211	0.9	-2.2	1.2
	20–24	19 068	21 619	23 937	23 684	20 626	19 168	2.3	-1.5	-0.7
	0–24	104 917	105 620	104 094	101 618	100 010	104 567	-0.1	-0.4	0.4
LATIN AMERICAN AND THE CARIBBEAN										
	A	283 408	321 194	361 373	404 806	451 072	546 395	2.5	2.2	1.9
	0–4	44 907	48 365	51 736	56 019	59 459	62 932	1.4	1.4	0.6
	5–9	40 623	43 628	47 186	50 606	54 974	60 672	1.5	1.5	1.0
	10–14	34 726	40 222	43 208	46 777	50 242	58 201	2.2	1.5	1.5
	15–19	29 510	34 337	39 785	42 761	46 381	54 305	3.0	1.5	1.6
	20–24	24 034	28 993	33 705	39 173	42 218	49 426	3.4	2.3	1.6
	0–24	173 800	195 545	215 619	235 336	253 274	285 537	2.2	1.6	1.2

1.3 Illiterate population 15 years of age and over and percentage illiteracy, by age group and by sex

Population analphabète de 15 ans et plus et pourcentage d'analphabètes, par groupe d'âge et par sexe

Población analfabeta de 15 años y más y porcentaje de analfabetos, por grupo de edad y por sexo

NUMBER OF COUNTRIES AND TERRITORIES PRESENTED IN THIS TABLE: 122

NOMBRE DE PAYS ET DE TERRITOIRES PRESENTES DANS CE TABLEAU: 122

NUMERO DE PAISES Y DE TERRITORIOS PRESENTADOS EN ESTE CUADRO: 122

COUNTRY AND YEAR OF CENSUS OR SURVEY / PAYS ET ANNEE DU RECENSEMENT OU DE L'ENQUETE / PAIS Y AÑO DEL CENSO O DE LA ENCUESTA		AGE GROUP / GROUPE D'AGE / GRUPO DE EDAD	ILLITERATE POPULATION / POPULATION ANALPHABETE / POLACION ANALFABETA			PERCENTAGE OF ILLITERATES / POURCENTAGE D'ANALPHABETES / PORCENTAJE DE ANALFABETOS		
			TOTAL TOTALE	MALE MASCULINE MASCULINA	FEMALE FEMININE FEMENINA	TOTAL TOTALE	MALE MASCULIN MASCULINO	FEMALE FEMININ FEMININO
			(1)	(2)	(3)	(4)	(5)	(6)
AFRICA								
ALGERIA	1982	15+	5 880 350	2 297 347	3 583 003	55.3	42.7	68.3
		15–19	571 397	146 489	424 908	22.8	11.5	34.5
		20–24	588 031	192 407	395 624	34.4	21.0	49.9
		25–29	587 513	177 264	410 249	47.7	29.0	66.2
		30–59	3 234 237	1 277 426	1 956 811	77.1	63.9	89.0
		60+	899 172	503 761	395 411	90.8	86.1	97.4
BENIN	1979	15+	1 418 051	563 351	854 700	83.5	74.8	90.5
		10–14	170 516	73 035	97 481	52.5	41.1	66.1
		15–19	159 265	57 505	101 760	64.5	49.9	77.2
		20–24	190 852	56 197	134 655	75.8	59.6	85.5
		25–29	203 083	67 543	135 540	81.3	68.6	89.6
		30+	864 851	382 106	482 745	91.1	85.9	95.7
BOTSWANA‡	1971	15+	182 944	83 011	99 933	59.0	63.1	56.0
		10–14	34 465	19 027	14 918	46.0	51.7	39.2
		15–19	21 886	11 334	10 552	39.6	46.3	34.2
		20–24	15 357	6 022	9 335	40.7	45.2	38.2
		25–34	31 223	12 771	18 452	53.4	55.9	51.9
		35–44	27 128	13 002	14 126	58.3	65.7	52.8
		45–54	27 210	12 792	14 418	71.8	72.8	71.0
		55–64	20 490	9 503	10 987	80.4	81.3	79.6
		65+	39 650	17 587	22 063	81.7	80.4	82.7
BURKINA FASO	1975	15+	2 803 440	1 272 593	1 530 847	91.2	85.3	96.7
		10–14	543 329	277 378	265 951	83.6	79.2	88.8
		15–19	459 118	217 592	241 526	84.4	77.3	92.0
		20–24	357 104	145 652	211 452	86.9	77.8	94.6
		25–34	693 730	282 038	411 692	91.7	84.9	97.3
		35–44	497 851	222 574	275 277	93.7	88.4	98.4
		45–54	360 700	175 243	185 457	95.0	91.2	98.9
		55–59	114 883	61 438	53 445	94.8	91.4	99.1
		60+	320 054	168 056	151 998	96.6	94.4	99.2
BURUNDI‡	1982	10+	...	...	...	66.2	57.2	74.3
CAMEROON‡	1976	15+	2 360 088	863 884	1 496 204	58.8	45.4	70.9
		10–14	171 609	74 925	96 684	21.5	17.8	25.6
		15–24	384 887	119 686	265 201	31.2	20.4	40.9
		25–34	519 516	155 797	363 719	56.9	38.0	72.3
		35–44	528 584	185 763	342 821	70.0	52.6	85.4
		45–54	414 896	168 927	245 969	78.6	64.6	92.3
		55–64	278 841	125 418	153 423	85.4	75.9	95.1
		65+	233 364	108 293	125 071	90.5	84.9	95.9
CAPE VERDE	1970	14+	134 633	...	...	63.1	...	...
CENTRAL AFRICAN REPUBLIC	1975	15+	...	...	...	73.0	67.0	85.0
COMOROS	1980	15+	88 780	36 429	52 351	52.1	44.0	60.0
		10–14	4 741	2 194	2 547	24.4	21.2	28.1
		15–19	10 079	3 835	6 244	33.4	26.2	40.0
		20–24	10 792	4 037	6 755	44.4	36.5	51.1
		25–34	20 405	7 826	12 579	52.5	43.9	59.7
		35–44	17 428	7 265	10 163	57.8	48.7	66.6
		45–54	12 007	5 346	6 661	60.5	52.0	70.0
		55–64	8 281	3 715	4 566	63.1	54.0	73.1
		65+	9 788	4 405	5 383	70.4	61.6	79.6

COUNTRY AND YEAR OF CENSUS OR SURVEY PAYS ET ANNEE DU RECENSEMENT OU DE L'ENQUETE PAIS Y AÑO DEL CENSO O DE LA ENCUESTA		AGE GROUP GROUPE D'AGE GRUPO DE EDAD	ILLITERATE POPULATION POPULATION ANALPHABETE POLACION ANALFABETA			PERCENTAGE OF ILLITERATES POURCENTAGE D'ANALPHABETES PORCENTAJE DE ANALFABETOS		
			TOTAL TOTALE	MALE MASCULINE MASCULINA	FEMALE FEMININE FEMENINA	TOTAL TOTALE	MALE MASCULIN MASCULINO	FEMALE FEMININ FEMININO
			(1)	(2)	(3)	(4)	(5)	(6)
EGYPT	1976	15+	13 317 501	5 051 502	8 265 999	61.8	46.4	77.6
		15–19	1 817 203	757 342	1 059 861	46.6	36.1	58.7
		20–24	1 564 243	564 773	999 470	52.1	38.2	65.6
		25–34	2 825 314	984 057	1 841 257	59.8	42.5	76.5
		35–44	2 602 651	957 244	1 645 407	67.1	49.5	84.7
		45–54	2 090 345	797 933	1 292 412	71.0	53.5	89.0
		55–64	1 375 302	563 614	811 688	75.2	59.4	92.2
		65+	1 042 443	426 539	615 904	82.0	68.4	95.2
EQUATORIAL GUINEA‡	1980	15+	105 100	...	...	63.0	...	...
ETHIOPIA	1983	10+	8 500 000	...	...	37.6	...	...
GHANA	1970	15+	3 293 320	1 285 320	2 008 000	69.8	56.9	81.6
		15–19	311 840	115 740	196 100	38.5	27.9	49.6
		20–24	379 980	110 620	269 360	55.7	36.1	71.8
		25–34	862 520	291 440	571 080	71.2	53.4	85.7
		35–44	679 880	274 100	405 780	81.4	68.5	93.2
		45–54	488 580	224 140	264 440	87.9	80.2	95.7
		55–64	274 860	130 420	144 440	89.8	83.5	96.4
		65+	295 660	138 860	156 800	92.8	87.9	97.7
GUINEA-BISSAU	1979	15+	342 393	130 922	211 471	80.0	66.7	91.4
		10–14	37 342	14 717	22 625	46.0	33.1	61.4
		15–19	40 904	11 824	29 080	56.8	34.7	76.6
		20–24	42 807	11 729	31 078	71.8	48.2	88.2
		25–34	87 539	27 744	59 795	81.8	63.8	94.1
		35–44	64 244	25 068	39 176	87.9	77.5	96.2
		45–54	44 366	20 080	24 286	91.6	86.0	96.8
		55–64	29 199	15 564	13 635	92.0	87.8	97.2
		65+	33 334	18 913	14 421	93.0	89.8	97.7
LIBERIA	1974	15+	714 502	313 658	400 844	80.4	71.0	89.7
		10–14	116 498	58 879	57 619	71.3	68.8	76.0
		15–19	98 922	35 827	63 095	62.2	47.4	75.6
		20–24	85 238	26 942	58 296	70.1	49.5	86.9
		25–34	185 810	69 885	115 925	82.4	69.3	93.1
		35–44	139 183	66 629	72 554	86.8	79.8	94.5
		45–54	93 454	49 980	43 474	90.5	86.5	95.6
		55–64	59 126	33 639	25 487	93.3	91.2	96.3
		65+	52 769	30 756	22 013	95.0	93.9	96.5
LIBYAN ARAB JAMAHIRIYA	1973	15+	608 050	200 813	407 237	61.0	38.7	85.2
		10–14	33 792	2 410	31 382	12.8	1.8	25.0
		15–19	47 261	4 548	42 713	27.9	5.1	53.0
		20–24	58 092	9 551	48 541	42.8	13.6	74.2
		25–34	127 442	31 345	96 097	58.0	28.0	89.2
		35–44	132 384	45 974	86 410	71.5	48.0	96.8
		45–54	99 370	40 998	58 372	78.5	61.0	98.4
		55–64	63 510	29 143	34 367	86.5	75.2	99.1
		65+	79 991	39 254	40 737	92.2	85.7	99.6
MALI	1976	15+	3 236 240	1 469 632	1 766 608	90.6	86.5	94.3
		15–19	503 492	222 156	281 336	78.7	72.3	84.7
		20–24	399 048	163 222	235 826	82.5	74.8	88.8
		25–34	816 223	341 797	474 426	93.0	88.7	96.3
		35–44	586 119	278 219	307 900	95.4	92.5	98.2
		45–54	402 437	202 363	200 074	96.3	93.8	99.1
		55–64	135 939	73 475	62 464	96.8	94.7	99.4
		65+	392 982	188 400	204 582	98.3	97.0	99.5
MAURITANIA	1976	6+	895 877	...	...	82.6	...	...
MOROCCO‡	1971	15+	6 407 137	2 654 041	3 753 096	78.6	66.4	90.2
		10–14	1 256 130	541 413	714 717	60.2	49.1	72.6
		15–19	853 185	333 836	519 349	58.8	44.9	73.6
		20–24	696 330	247 734	448 596	66.6	49.7	82.1
		25–34	1 440 365	514 548	925 817	80.8	65.3	93.0
		35–44	1 332 603	549 728	782 875	86.2	74.5	97.0
		45–54	882 203	421 173	461 030	88.0	79.8	97.0
		55–64	555 852	269 005	286 847	89.2	82.3	96.9
		65+	646 599	318 017	328 582	91.4	85.9	97.5
MOZAMBIQUE	1980	15+	4 557 751	1 650 952	2 906 799	72.8	56.0	87.8
		10–14	860 050	411 037	449 013	58.5	52.3	65.7
		15–19	545 900	185 130	360 770	49.2	32.6	66.7
		20–24	588 553	161 056	427 497	64.9	40.9	83.2
		25–39	1 521 170	489 844	1 031 326	74.4	53.8	91.0
		40–59	1 303 358	548 431	754 927	84.1	72.0	95.9
		60+	598 770	266 491	332 279	92.2	85.4	98.4

COUNTRY AND YEAR OF CENSUS OR SURVEY PAYS ET ANNEE DU RECENSEMENT OU DE L'ENQUETE PAIS Y AÑO DEL CENSO O DE LA ENCUESTA		AGE GROUP GROUPE D'AGE GRUPO DE EDAD	ILLITERATE POPULATION POPULATION ANALPHABETE POLACION ANALFABETA			PERCENTAGE OF ILLITERATES POURCENTAGE D'ANALPHABETES PORCENTAJE DE ANALFABETOS		
			TOTAL TOTALE	MALE MASCULINE MASCULINA	FEMALE FEMININE FEMENINA	TOTAL TOTALE	MALE MASCULIN MASCULINO	FEMALE FEMININ FEMININO
			(1)	(2)	(3)	(4)	(5)	(6)
REUNION	1982	15+	73 220	38 861	34 359	21.4	23.5	19.5
		10–14	2 204	1 393	811	3.4	4.3	2.5
		15–19	2 310	1 673	637	3.3	4.7	1.8
		20–24	2 876	2 025	851	5.9	8.5	3.4
		25–34	7 755	4 980	2 775	10.6	14.1	7.4
		35–44	13 137	7 493	5 644	24.5	28.1	20.9
		45–54	18 181	9 654	8 527	44.0	47.7	40.4
		55–64	14 364	7 140	7 224	49.4	52.0	47.0
		65+	14 597	5 896	8 701	57.6	59.6	56.3
RWANDA	1978	15+	1 619 117	620 852	998 265	61.8	49.2	73.4
		10–14	246 501	114 253	132 248	42.2	39.1	45.2
		15–19	272 181	122 614	149 567	47.2	42.1	52.3
		20–24	227 808	91 144	136 664	48.4	38.2	59.0
		25–34	304 974	100 633	204 341	55.4	38.0	71.4
		35–44	253 344	74 981	178 363	66.6	44.9	83.6
		45–54	237 377	87 907	149 470	81.4	66.0	94.2
		55–64	188 652	77 954	110 698	90.7	82.2	97.8
		65+	134 781	65 619	69 162	94.6	91.0	98.3
ST. HELENA	1976	16+	92	50	42	2.9	3.2	2.5
SAO TOME AND PRINCIPE	1981	15+	22 080	6 755	15 325	42.6	26.8	57.6
		10–14	1 641	751	890	13.9	12.4	15.4
		15–19	1 464	440	1 024	14.0	8.4	19.5
		20–24	1 780	402	1 378	22.3	10.2	34.2
		25–34	3 435	806	2 629	35.9	17.6	52.6
		35–44	3 948	1 227	2 721	54.3	34.3	73.5
		45–54	4 468	1 603	2 865	64.9	46.7	82.9
		55–64	3 447	1 206	2 241	69.8	50.3	88.3
		65+	3 538	1 071	2 467	75.5	53.1	92.4
SEYCHELLES	1971	15+	12 494	6 465	6 029	42.3	44.4	40.2
		10–14	1 592	1 007	585	22.4	27.6	17.0
		15–19	945	644	301	19.8	25.7	13.3
		20–24	965	583	382	27.7	31.0	23.8
		25–34	2 063	1 123	940	38.0	41.5	34.5
		35–44	2 359	1 205	1 154	45.4	47.0	43.8
		45–54	2 070	1 051	1 019	50.1	52.0	48.4
		55–64	1 934	912	1 022	61.3	61.1	61.5
		65+	2 158	947	1 211	63.7	67.5	61.0
SUDAN	1973	10–49	5 221 323	2 090 554	3 130 769	68.6	55.2	82.1
SWAZILAND	1976	15+	115 836	49 281	66 555	44.8	42.7	46.5
		10–14	17 412	9 271	8 141	26.1	28.1	24.2
		15–19	11 573	5 275	6 298	22.3	22.4	22.1
		20–24	10 604	3 983	6 621	27.6	26.2	28.6
		25–34	22 418	8 508	13 910	38.4	34.3	41.5
		35–44	22 613	9 855	12 758	52.2	48.0	56.1
		45–54	19 245	8 996	10 249	65.2	62.6	67.6
		55–64	13 475	6 222	7 253	73.9	70.3	77.3
		65+	15 908	6 442	9 466	84.7	79.5	88.7
TOGO	1981	15+	927 712	328 497	599 215	68.6	53.3	81.5
		12–14	50 403	18 605	31 798	28.0	18.8	39.2
		15–19	104 790	30 963	73 827	39.1	22.7	56.3
		20–29	113 598	28 145	85 453	56.5	33.6	72.7
		30–39	138 591	38 674	99 917	68.8	48.1	82.7
		40–49	203 651	66 589	137 062	76.9	59.9	89.2
		50–59	146 581	59 880	86 701	83.8	72.4	93.9
		60–69	86 016	38 790	47 226	87.7	79.7	95.5
		70+	134 485	65 456	69 029	93.3	88.8	98.0
TUNISIA	1980	15+	1 973 777	710 150	1 263 627	53.5	38.9	67.7
		10–14	158 824	35 939	122 885	19.0	8.3	30.5
		15–19	150 584	33 690	116 894	20.7	9.2	32.3
		20–24	154 769	29 307	125 462	26.8	10.4	42.4
		25–34	340 411	87 422	252 989	46.4	25.7	64.1
		35–44	373 455	128 089	245 366	69.2	48.3	89.3
		45–54	419 909	169 330	250 579	83.5	69.5	96.6
		55–64	288 276	132 627	155 649	86.6	76.4	97.8
		65+	246 373	129 685	116 688	88.9	83.0	96.5
UNITED REPUBLIC OF TANZANIA‡	1978	15+	5 058 986	1 728 025	3 330 961	53.7	37.8	68.6
		10–14	535 899	251 722	284 177	25.5	23.6	27.5
		15–19	491 733	139 994	351 739	28.6	16.6	40.1
		20–24	527 095	136 065	391 030	39.7	23.2	52.7
		25–34	1 087 683	291 564	796 119	47.8	27.3	65.9
		35–44	952 958	305 711	647 247	61.2	40.2	81.4
		45–54	793 648	303 600	490 048	72.0	54.8	89.3
		55–64	580 021	249 442	330 579	79.7	66.0	94.3
		65+	625 848	301 649	324 199	87.3	78.8	97.0

COUNTRY AND YEAR OF CENSUS OR SURVEY / PAYS ET ANNEE DU RECENSEMENT OU DE L'ENQUETE / PAIS Y AÑO DEL CENSO O DE LA ENCUESTA		AGE GROUP / GROUPE D'AGE / GRUPO DE EDAD	ILLITERATE POPULATION / POPULATION ANALPHABETE / POLACION ANALFABETA			PERCENTAGE OF ILLITERATES / POURCENTAGE D'ANALPHABETES / PORCENTAJE DE ANALFABETOS		
			TOTAL TOTALE	MALE MASCULINE MASCULINA	FEMALE FEMININE FEMENINA	TOTAL TOTALE	MALE MASCULIN MASCULINO	FEMALE FEMININ FEMENINO
			(1)	(2)	(3)	(4)	(5)	(6)
AMERICA, NORTH								
BARBADOS‡	1970	15+	1 093	493	600	0.7	0.7	0.7
		15–19	50	31	19	0.2	0.2	0.2
		20–24	62	41	21	0.3	0.4	0.2
		25–34	84	53	31	0.4	0.5	0.3
		35–44	65	35	30	0.3	0.4	0.2
		45–54	133	60	73	0.6	0.7	0.6
		55–64	291	131	160	1.5	1.5	1.6
		65+	408	142	266	2.1	2.1	2.1
BELIZE‡	1970	15+	5 353	2 656	2 699	8.8	8.8	8.8
		15–19	331	162	169	2.6	2.6	2.7
		20–24	324	164	160	3.9	4.0	3.8
		25–34	764	388	376	6.5	6.6	6.4
		35–44	1 034	513	521	10.3	10.3	10.4
		45–54	979	487	402	13.6	13.3	11.2
		55–64	925	450	475	15.9	15.6	16.3
		65+	998	492	506	19.4	20.1	18.8
BERMUDA‡	1970	15+	586	391	195	1.6	2.1	1.1
		15–19	17	9	8	0.4	0.4	0.4
		20–24	13	9	4	0.3	0.4	0.2
		25–34	68	40	28	0.8	0.9	0.7
		35–44	133	99	34	1.9	2.8	1.0
		45–54	166	119	47	3.1	4.5	1.8
		55–64	93	64	29	2.4	3.4	1.4
		65+	96	51	45	2.9	3.6	2.3
BRITISH VIRGIN ISLANDS‡	1970	15+	100	61	39	1.7	1.9	1.5
		15–19	5	2	3	0.5	0.4	0.7
		20–24	6	4	2	0.6	0.6	0.5
		25–34	7	5	2	0.5	0.7	0.3
		35–44	11	8	3	1.3	1.7	0.8
		45–54	17	6	11	2.4	1.7	3.2
		55–64	13	8	5	2.9	3.3	2.5
		65+	41	28	13	8.3	10.9	5.5
CAYMAN ISLANDS‡	1970	15+	152	70	82	2.5	2.5	2.4
		15–19	12	5	7	1.3	1.1	1.4
		20–24	14	8	6	2.1	2.6	1.7
		25–34	25	13	12	2.0	2.2	1.8
		35–44	22	8	14	2.1	1.7	2.4
		45–54	20	8	12	2.5	2.3	2.7
		55–64	21	12	9	3.1	4.2	2.3
		65+	38	16	22	5.0	5.6	4.7
COSTA RICA‡	1973	15+	121 312	59 084	62 228	11.6	11.4	11.8
		10–14	14 083	8 035	6 048	5.1	5.7	4.5
		15–19	9 379	5 105	4 274	4.2	4.6	3.8
		20–24	9 749	4 966	4 783	5.8	6.0	5.6
		25–34	21 899	10 760	11 139	9.8	9.7	9.8
		35–44	26 238	12 409	13 829	15.4	14.7	16.1
		45–54	20 125	9 630	10 495	17.0	16.3	17.8
		55–64	17 046	8 236	8 810	21.7	20.9	22.5
		65+	16 876	7 978	8 898	25.6	24.4	26.7
CUBA‡	1981	15–49	105 901	...	...	2.2	...	...
		10–14	9 473	...	...	0.8	...	...
		15–19	3 589	...	...	0.3	...	...
		20–24	4 820	...	...	0.6	...	...
		25–34	19 199	...	...	1.4	...	...
		35–44	47 859	...	...	4.2	...	...
		45–49	30 434	...	...	7.1	...	...
		10–49	...	...	...	1.9	1.7	2.1
		10+	...	...	...	3.8	3.8	3.8
DOMINICA‡	1970	15+	2 083	944	1 139	5.9	6.0	5.8
		15–19	42	21	21	0.6	0.7	0.6
		20–24	55	26	29	1.1	1.2	1.1
		25–34	161	89	72	2.8	3.5	2.2
		35–44	251	127	124	4.9	5.8	4.3
		45–54	334	152	182	6.8	7.0	6.7
		55–64	486	230	256	12.5	13.1	11.9
		65+	754	299	455	18.4	19.3	17.8
DOMINICAN REPUBLIC	1981	5+	1 519 198	770 758	748 440	31.4	31.8	30.9
EL SALVADOR	1980	15+	818 100	...	...	32.7	...	...
		10–14	126 900	...	...	20.1	...	...
		15–19	83 900	...	...	16.6	...	...
		20–24	69 100	...	...	19.8	...	...
		25–34	129 300	...	...	26.2	...	...
		35–44	144 000	...	...	35.6	...	...
		45–54	149 900	...	...	47.9	...	...
		55–64	118 100	...	...	52.8	...	...
		65+	124 800	...	...	58.7	...	...

COUNTRY AND YEAR OF CENSUS OR SURVEY PAYS ET ANNEE DU RECENSEMENT OU DE L'ENQUETE PAIS Y AÑO DEL CENSO O DE LA ENCUESTA		AGE GROUP GROUPE D'AGE GRUPO DE EDAD	ILLITERATE POPULATION POPULATION ANALPHABETE POLACION ANALFABETA			PERCENTAGE OF ILLITERATES POURCENTAGE D'ANALPHABETES PORCENTAJE DE ANALFABETOS		
			TOTAL TOTALE	MALE MASCULINE MASCULINA	FEMALE FEMININE FEMENINA	TOTAL TOTALE	MALE MASCULIN MASCULINO	FEMALE FEMININ FEMININO
			(1)	(2)	(3)	(4)	(5)	(6)
GRENADA‡	1970	15+	1 070	424	646	2.2	2.0	2.4
		15–19	91	51	40	0.9	1.0	0.8
		20–24	83	45	38	1.2	1.4	1.1
		25–34	96	38	58	1.2	1.1	1.4
		35–44	144	54	90	2.0	1.7	2.2
		45–54	180	71	109	2.9	2.7	3.1
		55–64	193	77	116	3.6	3.4	3.8
		65+	283	88	195	5.2	4.7	5.5
GUADELOUPE	1982	15+	22 359	11 231	11 128	10.0	10.4	9.6
		10–14	716	432	284	1.7	2.1	1.4
		15–19	490	302	188	1.2	1.4	0.9
		20–24	609	408	201	2.0	2.5	1.4
		25–34	1 582	960	622	3.6	4.6	2.7
		35–44	2 122	1 242	880	6.4	7.8	5.1
		45–54	4 117	2 295	1 822	15.2	17.9	12.7
		55–64	4 403	2 325	2 078	19.6	21.7	17.7
		65+	9 036	3 699	5 337	35.9	34.4	37.1
GUATEMALA‡	1973	15+	1 528 732	651 915	876 817	54.0	46.4	61.5
		10–14	298 559	139 943	158 616	44.1	40.2	48.2
		15–19	243 253	101 424	141 829	43.5	37.0	49.7
		20–24	223 809	91 023	132 786	47.6	39.4	55.6
		25–34	334 850	138 435	196 415	53.2	44.7	61.5
		35–44	291 765	122 960	168 805	58.6	49.7	67.4
		45–54	206 807	92 492	114 315	62.5	54.9	70.3
		55–64	125 924	58 244	67 680	64.8	58.2	71.7
		65+	102 324	47 337	54 987	68.6	63.9	73.2
HAITI	1982	15+	2 004 791	926 751	1 078 040	65.2	62.7	67.5
		10–14	298 692	160 908	137 784	51.6	55.6	47.6
		15–19	229 764	116 949	112 815	44.9	46.5	43.5
		20–24	243 385	109 656	133 729	53.2	51.4	54.8
		25–34	437 083	188 767	248 316	64.4	60.9	67.4
		35–44	368 294	164 944	203 350	73.6	69.4	77.4
		45–54	293 847	143 543	150 304	75.8	71.9	80.0
		55–64	187 646	91 275	96 371	78.7	75.7	81.9
		65+	244 772	111 617	133 155	82.0	79.1	84.7
HONDURAS‡	1974	15+	594 194	274 815	319 379	43.1	41.1	44.9
		10–14	112 465	61 357	51 108	30.6	32.8	28.4
		15–19	77 741	40 400	37 341	26.9	28.9	25.1
		20–24	70 009	32 750	37 259	30.6	30.2	31.1
		25–34	123 264	56 581	66 683	40.3	38.4	42.1
		35–44	123 752	54 705	69 047	53.4	48.5	57.9
		45–54	95 382	43 051	52 331	60.7	55.6	65.8
		55–64	58 670	27 096	31 574	62.2	57.4	67.0
		65+	45 376	20 232	25 144	61.8	56.7	66.6
JAMAICA‡	1970	15+	38 063	20 374	17 689	3.9	4.4	3.5
		15–19	1 897	1 151	746	1.2	1.5	0.9
		20–24	1 918	1 087	831	1.5	1.9	1.3
		25–34	4 369	2 489	1 880	2.4	2.9	2.0
		35–44	5 913	3 244	2 669	3.8	4.4	3.2
		45–54	6 927	3 725	3 202	5.1	5.7	4.6
		55–64	7 959	4 230	3 729	7.2	7.8	6.6
		65+	9 080	4 448	4 632	9.2	10.2	8.4
MARTINIQUE	1982	15+	16 814	8 824	7 990	7.2	8.0	6.6
		10–14	548	313	235	1.4	1.5	1.2
		15–19	393	269	124	0.9	1.2	0.6
		20–24	477	307	170	1.4	1.7	1.1
		25–34	864	544	320	2.1	2.8	1.4
		35–44	1 099	658	441	3.4	4.4	2.5
		45–54	2 703	1 652	1 051	9.0	11.8	6.6
		55–64	3 281	1 871	1 410	13.7	16.7	11.0
		65+	7 997	3 523	4 474	29.2	30.7	28.1
MEXICO	1980	15+	6 451 740	2 545 171	3 906 569	17.0	13.8	20.1
		15–19	541 947	239 380	302 567	7.1	6.4	7.8
		20–24	570 231	226 465	343 766	9.3	7.6	10.8
		25–34	1 148 797	449 183	699 614	13.3	10.7	15.8
		35–44	1 245 638	477 782	767 856	20.2	15.8	24.5
		45–54	1 076 731	407 398	669 333	25.8	19.9	31.4
		55–64	798 883	314 674	484 209	31.0	24.7	37.1
		65+	1 069 513	430 289	639 224	41.8	35.7	47.1
MONTSERRAT‡	1970	15+	231	100	131	3.4	3.2	3.4
		15–19	13	7	6	1.2	1.3	1.1
		20–24	11	5	6	1.2	1.1	1.4
		25–34	11	4	7	1.2	0.9	1.6
		35–44	28	15	13	3.6	4.4	2.9
		45–54	32	19	13	3.4	4.9	2.3
		55–64	54	24	30	5.1	5.2	5.1
		65+	82	26	56	6.6	6.1	6.9

1.3 Illiterate population
Population analphabète
Población analfabeta

COUNTRY AND YEAR OF CENSUS OR SURVEY / PAYS ET ANNEE DU RECENSEMENT OU DE L'ENQUETE / PAIS Y AÑO DEL CENSO O DE LA ENCUESTA		AGE GROUP / GROUPE D'AGE / GRUPO DE EDAD	ILLITERATE POPULATION / POPULATION ANALPHABETE / POLACION ANALFABETA			PERCENTAGE OF ILLITERATES / POURCENTAGE D'ANALPHABETES / PORCENTAJE DE ANALFABETOS		
			TOTAL TOTALE	MALE MASCULINE MASCULINA	FEMALE FEMININE FEMENINA	TOTAL TOTALE	MALE MASCULIN MASCULINO	FEMALE FEMININ FEMENINO
			(1)	(2)	(3)	(4)	(5)	(6)
NETHERLANDS ANTILLES‡	1971	15+	8 699	4 083	4 616	7.5	7.4	7.6
		10–14	266	163	103	11.4	13.9	8.8
		15–19	592	358	234	4.4	5.3	3.5
		20–24	624	362	262	3.6	4.2	2.9
		25–34	1 089	545	544	3.8	4.1	3.6
		35–44	1 123	509	614	5.1	4.9	5.3
		45–54	1 173	576	597	7.9	8.0	7.8
		55–64	1 856	823	1 033	16.8	15.8	17.8
		65+	2 242	910	1 332	27.7	26.5	28.6
NICARAGUA‡	1971	15+	410 755	193 475	217 277	42.5	42.0	42.9
		10–14	108 317	58 483	49 834	41.0	43.5	38.4
		15–19	69 205	35 966	33 239	34.1	36.9	31.6
		20–24	56 669	27 268	29 401	36.9	37.7	36.2
		25–34	90 176	41 542	48 631	42.1	41.1	42.9
		35–44	80 391	36 962	43 429	47.4	45.3	49.3
		45–54	53 347	24 613	28 734	50.3	48.0	52.5
		55–64	32 932	14 971	17 961	51.0	48.5	53.3
		65+	28 035	12 153	15 882	49.8	47.6	51.6
PANAMA	1980	15+	156 531	74 737	81 794	14.4	13.7	15.1
		10–14	17 594	9 778	7 816	7.7	8.4	7.0
		15–19	10 036	4 467	5 569	5.0	4.5	5.5
		20–24	11 263	4 743	6 520	6.9	5.9	7.9
		25–34	28 336	12 803	15 533	10.9	9.9	11.9
		35–44	29 247	14 039	15 208	16.6	15.7	17.5
		45–54	27 645	13 705	13 940	22.5	21.7	23.4
		55–59	11 212	5 597	5 615	23.9	22.9	24.8
		60+	38 792	19 383	19 409	32.4	31.7	33.3
PUERTO RICO‡	1980	15+	239 095	107 372	131 723	10.9	10.3	11.5
		15–19	19 946	10 856	9 090	5.9	6.4	5.4
		20–24	16 607	8 804	7 803	6.1	6.8	5.5
		25–34	31 711	16 460	15 251	6.8	7.5	6.2
		35–44	31 778	14 854	16 924	8.8	8.8	8.9
		45–54	29 275	12 069	17 206	10.7	9.4	11.9
		55–64	34 869	13 752	21 117	15.4	12.6	17.9
		65+	74 909	30 577	44 332	29.6	25.4	33.5
ST. CHRISTOPHER AND NEVIS AND ANGUILLA‡	1970	15+	546	247	299	2.4	2.4	2.3
		15–19	74	39	35	1.5	1.6	1.5
		20–24	29	15	14	1.3	1.4	1.2
		25–34	47	23	24	1.7	2.1	1.6
		35–44	56	22	34	1.8	1.7	1.9
		45–54	89	41	48	2.5	2.6	2.5
		55–64	107	51	56	2.9	3.1	2.8
		65+	144	56	88	4.6	5.0	4.3
ST. LUCIA‡	1970	15+	9 195	4 251	4 944	18.3	19.2	17.6
		15–19	370	229	141	3.9	4.9	2.8
		20–24	481	264	217	7.1	9.0	5.7
		25–34	1 314	638	676	15.1	16.8	13.7
		35–44	1 812	817	995	23.4	25.1	22.2
		45–54	1 809	880	929	25.9	27.2	24.8
		55–64	1 521	692	829	29.4	29.6	29.2
		65+	1 888	731	1 157	35.8	37.5	34.8
ST. VINCENT AND THE GRENADINES‡	1970	15+	1 839	779	1 060	4.4	4.2	4.5
		15–19	173	89	84	1.9	2.0	1.8
		20–24	132	59	73	2.2	2.2	2.3
		25–34	221	91	130	3.2	3.0	3.3
		35–44	272	125	144	4.4	4.8	4.0
		45–54	312	131	181	5.9	5.8	5.9
		55–64	353	160	193	8.1	8.3	8.1
		65+	376	124	252	9.0	8.4	9.3
TRINIDAD AND TOBAGO	1980	15+	34 800	11 890	22 910	5.1	3.5	6.6
		10–14	700	390	310	0.6	0.7	0.5
		15–19	970	530	440	0.7	0.8	0.7
		20–24	900	430	470	0.8	0.8	0.9
		25–34	1 800	890	910	1.1	1.1	1.2
		35–44	3 420	1 110	2 310	3.4	2.2	4.5
		45–54	7 200	1 910	5 290	10.0	5.5	14.1
		55–64	8 220	2 550	5 670	14.6	8.9	20.6
		65+	12 290	4 470	7 820	20.0	16.2	23.1
TURKS AND CAICOS ISLANDS‡	1970	15+	56	18	38	1.9	1.4	2.3
		15–19	6	2	4	1.0	0.7	1.4
		20–24	2	–	2	0.7	–	1.2
		25–34	6	2	4	1.3	0.9	1.7
		35–44	6	2	4	1.3	1.2	1.3
		45–54	6	3	3	1.3	1.5	1.2
		55–64	6	2	4	1.7	1.3	2.1
		65+	24	7	17	7.0		8.1

COUNTRY AND YEAR OF CENSUS OR SURVEY / PAYS ET ANNEE DU RECENSEMENT OU DE L'ENQUETE / PAIS Y AÑO DEL CENSO O DE LA ENCUESTA		AGE GROUP / GROUPE D'AGE / GRUPO DE EDAD	ILLITERATE POPULATION / POPULATION ANALPHABETE / POLACION ANALFABETA			PERCENTAGE OF ILLITERATES / POURCENTAGE D'ANALPHABETES / PORCENTAJE DE ANALFABETOS		
			TOTAL TOTALE	MALE MASCULINE MASCULINA	FEMALE FEMININE FEMENINA	TOTAL TOTALE	MALE MASCULIN MASCULINO	FEMALE FEMININ FEMENINO
			(1)	(2)	(3)	(4)	(5)	(6)
UNITED STATES	1979	14+	...	...	...	0.5	...	...
		14–24	...	...	...	0.2	...	...
		25–44	...	...	...	0.3	...	...
		45–64	...	...	...	0.7	...	...
		65+	...	...	...	1.4	...	...
AMERICA, SOUTH								
ARGENTINA	1980	15+	1 184 964	543 174	641 790	6.1	5.7	6.4
		10–14	79 686	45 682	34 004	3.2	3.7	2.8
		15–19	70 135	41 832	28 303	3.0	3.6	2.4
		20–24	72 197	38 673	33 524	3.2	3.5	3.0
		25–29	83 473	43 882	39 591	3.9	4.2	3.7
		30–34	93 199	48 050	45 149	4.7	4.9	4.5
		35–39	90 098	44 030	46 068	5.2	5.1	5.3
		40–44	87 116	41 902	45 214	5.6	5.4	5.8
		45–49	88 451	41 585	46 866	5.9	5.6	6.3
		50–54	96 896	42 871	54 025	6.6	6.0	7.2
		55–59	98 384	43 258	55 126	7.7	7.0	8.4
		60–64	93 436	39 558	53 878	9.3	8.4	10.1
		65+	311 579	117 533	194 046	13.6	11.9	14.9
BOLIVIA	1976	15+	993 437	315 460	677 977	36.8	24.2	48.6
		10–14	57 885	19 004	38 881	10.6	6.8	14.7
		15–19	69 145	18 150	50 995	13.9	7.3	20.5
		20–24	79 628	19 931	59 697	19.5	10.0	28.5
		25–34	183 943	49 036	134 907	29.9	16.3	42.8
		35–44	196 862	58 833	138 029	45.0	28.1	60.6
		45–54	183 575	61 631	121 944	54.2	37.8	69.5
		55–64	136 014	50 802	85 212	64.6	51.1	76.5
		65+	144 270	57 077	87 193	74.5	65.3	82.0
BRAZIL	1980	15+	18 716 847	8 560 176	10 156 671	25.5	23.7	27.2
		10–14	3 676 448	2 029 877	1 646 571	25.8	28.4	23.2
		15–19	2 235 370	1 258 297	977 073	16.5	18.8	14.2
		20–24	1 799 071	900 410	898 661	15.6	15.9	15.4
		25–34	3 382 290	1 565 180	1 817 110	19.8	18.5	20.9
		35–44	3 380 639	1 490 425	1 890 214	28.0	24.9	31.0
		45–54	2 951 392	1 264 454	1 686 938	33.7	29.2	38.1
		55–64	2 335 250	993 481	1 341 769	41.8	36.2	47.3
		65+	2 632 835	1 087 929	1 544 906	53.8	47.5	59.3
CHILE‡	1983	15+	...	...	...	5.6	...	...
COLOMBIA	1981	15+	2 407 458	1 091 407	1 316 051	14.8	13.6	16.1
		10–14	474 631	254 416	221 215	13.9	14.6	13.1
ECUADOR‡	1982	15+	758 272	298 018	460 254	19.8	15.8	23.8
		10–14	71 092	36 289	34 803	6.9	7.0	6.8
		15–19	46 139	20 187	25 952	5.2	4.6	5.9
		20–24	57 821	22 695	35 126	7.4	5.9	8.9
		25–34	123 618	45 638	77 980	11.0	8.3	13.7
		35–44	143 034	53 126	89 908	19.3	14.4	24.1
		45–54	138 518	55 253	83 265	26.8	21.6	31.9
		55–64	115 613	47 577	68 036	33.9	28.0	39.8
		65+	133 529	53 542	79 987	41.5	34.5	48.0
FRENCH GUIANA	1982	15+	8 372	...	...	17.2	...	...
		10–14	457	...	...	5.8	...	...
		15–19	454	...	...	6.5	...	...
		20–24	792	...	...	10.9	...	...
		25–34	2 242	...	...	16.7	...	...
		35–44	1 719	...	...	19.8	...	...
		45–54	1 203	...	...	22.4	...	...
		55–64	907	...	...	25.2	...	...
		65+	1 055	...	...	30.7	...	...
GUYANA‡	1970	15+	31 042	10 454	20 588	8.4	5.7	11.0
		15–19	1 237	589	648	1.6	1.5	1.6
		20–24	1 318	569	749	2.3	2.1	2.6
		25–34	3 395	1 355	2 040	4.6	3.8	5.4
		35–44	6 061	1 800	4 261	10.1	6.1	14.0
		45–54	7 463	2 161	5 302	16.7	9.5	24.1
		55–64	6 328	2 119	4 209	20.4	13.2	27.9
		65+	5 240	1 861	3 379	20.9	16.7	24.2
PARAGUAY	1982	15+	219 120	84 340	134 780	12.5	9.7	15.2
		10–14	28 410	15 140	13 270	7.6	7.9	7.2
		15–19	17 790	8 500	9 290	5.5	5.3	5.6
		20–24	17 920	7 440	10 480	6.3	5.3	7.3
		25–34	35 100	14 850	20 250	8.6	7.2	10.1
		35–44	36 590	14 220	22 370	13.1	10.1	16.0
		45–54	37 940	14 380	23 560	19.1	14.7	23.3
		55–64	32 170	11 760	20 410	24.4	18.2	30.3
		65+	41 610	13 190	28 420	33.2	23.5	41.1

COUNTRY AND YEAR OF CENSUS OR SURVEY / PAYS ET ANNEE DU RECENSEMENT OU DE L'ENQUETE / PAIS Y AÑO DEL CENSO O DE LA ENCUESTA		AGE GROUP / GROUPE D'AGE / GRUPO DE EDAD	ILLITERATE POPULATION / POPULATION ANALPHABETE / POLACION ANALFABETA			PERCENTAGE OF ILLITERATES / POURCENTAGE D'ANALPHABETES / PORCENTAJE DE ANALFABETOS		
			TOTAL TOTALE	MALE MASCULINE MASCULINA	FEMALE FEMININE FEMENINA	TOTAL TOTALE	MALE MASCULIN MASCULINO	FEMALE FEMININ FEMININO
			(1)	(2)	(3)	(4)	(5)	(6)
PERU‡	1981	15+	1 799 458	485 486	1 313 972	18.1	9.9	26.1
		10–14	169 446	68 447	100 999	7.8	6.2	9.5
		15–19	115 013	32 448	82 565	6.2	3.5	8.9
		20–24	122 706	27 452	95 254	7.7	3.5	11.8
		25–34	277 203	60 311	216 892	12.1	5.3	18.7
		35–39	186 199	41 776	144 423	21.1	9.7	32.0
		40+	1 098 337	323 499	774 838	33.0	19.6	46.2
SURINAME	1978	15–59	60 305	20 677	39 628	35.0	31.6	37.1
URUGUAY‡	1975	15+	124 664	65 007	59 657	6.1	6.6	5.7
		10–14	5 925	3 667	2 258	2.3	2.8	1.8
		15–19	3 213	1 988	1 225	1.4	1.7	1.0
		20–24	4 269	2 911	1 358	2.1	2.9	1.3
		25–34	8 685	5 240	3 445	2.4	2.9	1.9
		35–44	14 701	8 539	6 162	4.1	4.9	3.4
		45–54	20 448	11 084	9 364	6.0	6.6	5.5
		55–64	26 532	14 317	12 215	10.2	11.4	9.2
		65+	46 816	20 928	25 888	17.2	17.5	16.9
VENEZUELA	1981	15+	1 319 265	579 180	740 085	15.3	13.5	17.0
		10–14	143 167	84 651	58 516	7.9	9.3	6.5
		15–19	112 289	64 807	47 482	6.8	7.8	5.7
		20–24	106 145	55 040	51 105	7.3	7.7	7.0
		25–34	198 884	92 072	106 812	9.0	8.4	9.6
		35–44	216 561	90 593	125 968	16.4	13.7	19.1
		45–54	240 800	97 065	143 735	25.7	20.5	30.9
		55–64	209 666	83 783	125 883	35.6	28.6	42.5
		65+	234 920	95 820	139 100	48.6	44.0	52.3
ASIA								
AFGHANISTAN‡	1979	15+	5 832 988	2 583 581	3 249 407	81.8	69.7	95.0
		10–14	948 950	353 850	595 100	61.5	42.6	83.5
		15–19	805 581	348 739	456 842	67.2	51.8	87.1
		20–24	757 878	313 006	444 872	73.0	57.2	90.8
		25–34	1 265 547	466 411	799 136	81.9	65.8	95.4
		35–44	1 113 414	476 943	636 471	88.3	77.8	98.3
		45–54	855 869	415 319	440 550	89.2	80.8	98.9
		55–64	564 422	300 228	264 194	91.1	84.9	99.3
		65+	470 277	262 935	207 342	93.1	88.6	99.4
BAHRAIN	1981	15+	71 160	34 398	36 762	30.2	23.5	41.4
		10–14	2 157	469	1 688	6.3	2.7	9.9
		15–19	3 590	971	2 619	10.1	5.5	14.8
		20–24	6 955	3 421	3 534	16.7	13.8	21.2
		25–34	15 819	8 888	6 931	21.0	16.9	30.5
		35–44	14 893	6 657	8 236	38.1	26.1	60.7
		45–54	14 085	6 651	7 434	58.7	45.6	78.9
		55–64	9 049	4 569	4 480	74.6	64.2	89.5
		65+	6 769	3 241	3 528	87.2	79.8	95.4
BANGLADESH	1981	15+	32 923 083	14 501 583	18 421 500	70.8	60.3	82.0
		10–14	8 715 441	4 545 096	4 170 345	74.8	73.0	76.9
		15–19	5 232 801	2 375 362	2 857 439	64.2	57.2	71.1
		20–24	4 371 789	1 727 112	2 644 677	64.5	53.2	74.8
		25–34	7 796 087	3 245 033	4 551 054	68.5	56.6	80.5
		35–44	6 020 420	2 670 465	3 349 955	74.0	62.4	86.9
		45–54	4 276 890	1 958 337	2 318 553	77.0	65.2	90.9
		55–64	2 832 959	1 331 169	1 501 790	79.4	67.6	93.9
		65+	2 392 137	1 194 105	1 198 032	81.0	70.0	95.9
BRUNEI DARUSSALAM	1981	15+	26 224	9 574	16 650	22.2	14.8	31.0
		10–14	1 224	612	612	5.7	5.6	5.8
		15–19	933	463	470	4.6	4.3	4.9
		20–24	1 786	905	881	7.9	7.3	8.5
		25–34	4 140	1 365	2 775	12.1	7.3	17.9
		35–44	5 318	1 452	3 866	30.5	14.6	51.3
		45–54	5 836	1 894	3 942	50.4	30.2	74.2
		55+	8 211	3 495	4 716	68.6	52.7	88.4
BURMA	1973	15+	4 761 785	1 286 314	3 475 471	29.0	15.9	41.7
		10–14	781 005	321 817	459 188	22.4	18.3	26.7
		15–19	547 314	182 507	364 807	18.7	12.6	24.5
		20–24	465 463	135 544	329 919	20.2	11.9	28.1
		25–34	904 163	247 517	656 646	26.1	14.6	37.3
		35–44	1 013 343	260 285	753 058	33.1	17.1	48.9
		45–54	787 560	209 697	577 863	35.8	19.1	52.3
		55–64	583 818	144 320	439 498	40.4	20.3	60.0
		65+	460 124	106 444	353 680	44.7	21.9	65.0

COUNTRY AND YEAR OF CENSUS OR SURVEY PAYS ET ANNEE DU RECENSEMENT OU DE L'ENQUETE PAIS Y AÑO DEL CENSO O DE LA ENCUESTA		AGE GROUP GROUPE D'AGE GRUPO DE EDAD	ILLITERATE POPULATION POPULATION ANALPHABETE POLACION ANALFABETA			PERCENTAGE OF ILLITERATES POURCENTAGE D'ANALPHABETES PORCENTAJE DE ANALFABETOS		
			TOTAL TOTALE	MALE MASCULINE MASCULINA	FEMALE FEMININE FEMENINA	TOTAL TOTALE	MALE MASCULIN MASCULINO	FEMALE FEMININ FEMININO
			(1)	(2)	(3)	(4)	(5)	(6)
CHINA‡	1982	15+	230 146 750	71 110 590	159 036 130	34.5	20.8	48.9
		15–19	11 783 220	2 710 540	9 072 680	9.4	4.3	14.7
		20–24	10 642 090	2 159 880	8 482 210	14.3	5.7	23.3
		25–34	39 953 810	9 587 710	30 366 100	24.1	11.2	38.0
		35–44	33 968 230	9 837 370	24 130 860	33.1	18.1	50.0
		45–54	49 905 630	16 850 740	33 054 890	56.6	36.2	79.4
		55–59	23 020 990	8 293 690	14 727 300	67.9	47.4	89.8
		60+	60 872 780	21 670 660	39 202 120	79.4	60.9	95.5
CYPRUS	1976	10+	...	...	...	9.5	15.2	3.5
		15+	...	...	...	*11.0	*4.0	*17.0
		15–39	...	...	...	*1.0	...	...
		40+	...	...	...	*23.0	...	...
DEMOCRATIC YEMEN	1973	10+	736 224	254 177	482 047	72.9	52.3	92.1
HONG KONG‡	1971	15+	571 840	126 152	445 688	22.7	9.9	35.9
		10–14	10 011	3 996	6 015	1.9	1.5	2.4
		15–19	13 039	5 026	8 013	3.0	2.3	3.8
		20–24	16 124	6 035	10 089	4.8	3.5	6.2
		25–34	48 755	15 554	33 201	12.0	6.9	18.2
		35–44	131 072	32 184	98 888	26.2	12.2	41.6
		45–54	136 995	30 782	106 213	33.7	14.4	55.2
		55–64	116 419	22 426	93 993	43.7	17.6	67.6
		65+	110 436	14 145	96 291	62.2	23.9	81.3
INDIA	1981	15+	238 097 747	93 899 834	144 197 913	59.2	45.2	74.3
		10–14	37 290 123	14 957 724	22 332 399	43.5	33.1	55.2
		15–19	28 582 428	11 480 784	17 101 644	44.6	33.9	56.7
		20–24	27 497 781	9 690 257	17 807 524	48.0	33.5	62.8
		25–34	51 160 336	18 596 823	32 563 513	54.9	39.3	71.0
		35–59	96 946 774	39 730 709	57 216 065	67.2	52.5	83.5
		60+	33 910 428	14 401 261	19 509 167	78.5	65.4	92.2
INDONESIA	1980	15+	28 325 026	9 490 915	18 834 111	32.7	22.5	42.3
		10–14	1 759 845	849 169	910 676	10.0	9.3	10.7
		15–19	1 993 655	739 759	1 253 896	13.1	9.9	16.1
		20–24	2 123 457	663 893	1 459 564	16.3	11.1	20.8
		25–34	4 332 996	1 406 854	2 926 142	22.2	14.6	29.6
		35–44	6 064 249	1 821 514	4 242 735	38.0	23.3	52.2
		45–49	3 110 924	1 032 886	2 078 038	50.6	34.3	66.3
		50+	10 699 745	3 826 009	6 873 736	63.8	46.8	79.9
IRAN, ISLAMIC REPUBLIC OF	1976	15+	11 733 299	4 875 377	6 857 922	63.5	51.8	75.6
		10–14	1 109 749	318 190	791 559	25.8	14.1	38.8
		15–19	1 387 733	463 505	924 228	38.7	25.6	52.2
		20–24	1 380 444	451 049	929 395	49.8	33.9	64.5
		25–34	2 300 095	832 343	1 467 752	60.9	45.5	75.3
		35–44	2 418 114	1 064 927	1 353 187	74.4	63.0	86.9
		45–54	2 145 278	1 038 017	1 107 261	80.2	71.4	90.7
		55–64	1 058 566	515 728	542 838	83.8	75.6	93.5
		65+	1 043 069	509 808	533 261	89.7	83.5	96.5
ISRAEL‡	1983	15+	224 080	67 020	157 140	8.2	5.0	11.3
		15–17	2 175	635	1 540	0.1	0.1	0.1
		18–24	7 495	2 625	4 870	1.6	1.1	2.2
		25–34	15 515	4 635	10 880	2.5	1.5	3.5
		35–44	26 540	6 810	19 730	6.3	3.3	9.2
		45–54	49 580	13 645	35 935	14.7	8.4	20.6
		55–64	49 385	13 980	35 405	16.2	10.0	21.7
		65+	73 390	24 610	48 780	20.2	14.5	25.3
		15–29	15 768	4 237	11 531	12.0	6.2	18.5
		30–44	17 357	4 575	12 782	27.9	14.6	41.6
		45+	23 996	9 137	14 859	32.6	24.5	40.9
JORDAN	1979	15+	...	...	...	34.6	19.9	49.5
		15–19	...	...	...	7.5	2.4	13.2
		20–24	...	...	...	14.6	5.2	23.5
		25–29	...	...	...	23.3	7.7	37.0
		30–34	...	...	...	32.0	11.2	53.0
		35–44	...	...	...	49.1	25.7	72.1
		45–54	...	...	...	59.9	38.5	84.0
		55–64	...	...	...	69.7	52.6	87.4
		65+	...	...	...	84.3	73.7	94.5
KOREA, REPUBLIC OF‡	1970	15+	2 263 783	500 196	1 763 587	12.4	5.6	19.0
		10–14	35 540	13 818	21 722	0.8	0.6	1.0
		15–19	24 424	10 228	14 196	0.8	0.7	0.9
		20–24	28 744	10 396	18 348	1.1	0.8	1.5
		25–34	145 068	29 375	115 693	3.3	1.3	5.3
		35–44	327 419	48 954	278 465	9.9	3.0	16.3
		45–54	510 976	108 078	402 898	22.1	9.5	34.3
		55+	1 227 152	293 165	933 987	47.9	26.5	64.4

COUNTRY AND YEAR OF CENSUS OR SURVEY PAYS ET ANNEE DU RECENSEMENT OU DE L'ENQUETE PAIS Y AÑO DEL CENSO O DE LA ENCUESTA		AGE GROUP GROUPE D'AGE GRUPO DE EDAD	ILLITERATE POPULATION POPULATION ANALPHABETE POLACION ANALFABETA			PERCENTAGE OF ILLITERATES POURCENTAGE D'ANALPHABETES PORCENTAJE DE ANALFABETOS		
			TOTAL TOTALE	MALE MASCULINE MASCULINA	FEMALE FEMININE FEMENINA	TOTAL TOTALE	MALE MASCULIN MASCULINO	FEMALE FEMININ FEMENINO
			(1)	(2)	(3)	(4)	(5)	(6)
KUWAIT	1980	15+	263 840	135 869	127 971	32.5	27.2	40.9
		15–19	20 125	8 822	11 303	16.8	13.7	20.3
		20–24	31 208	16 770	14 438	25.1	23.1	27.8
		25–34	71 917	39 233	32 684	27.7	24.3	33.6
		35–44	63 876	32 836	31 040	36.7	28.5	52.8
		45–54	41 487	22 021	19 466	48.7	38.4	70.1
		55–59	11 340	5 551	5 789	59.4	46.4	81.1
		60+	23 887	10 636	13 251	77.7	65.6	91.1
LEBANON	1970	10+	...	...	...	...	21.5	42.1
		10–14	...	...	...	...	6.1	15.3
		15–19	...	...	...	...	8.5	20.7
		20–24	...	...	...	...	11.0	28.6
		25–29	...	...	...	...	15.2	37.8
		30–39	...	...	...	...	25.0	51.3
		40–49	...	...	...	...	31.2	59.8
		50–59	...	...	...	...	35.4	66.8
		60+	...	...	...	...	53.9	79.4
MACAU	1970	15+	31 917	11 894	20 023	20.6	15.2	26.1
		10–14	6 480	3 969	2 511	15.9	18.3	13.2
		15–19	5 400	2 570	2 830	13.7	12.5	14.9
		20–24	1 390	282	1 108	6.2	2.3	11.0
		25–34	3 380	1 336	2 044	16.1	12.9	19.3
		35–44	5 678	1 814	3 864	21.5	14.0	28.8
		45–54	7 102	3 093	4 009	34.5	29.5	39.7
		55–64	4 043	1 335	2 708	28.9	18.7	39.5
		65+	4 924	1 464	3 460	42.3	30.7	50.4
MALAYSIA	1980	15+	2 399 790	791 000	1 608 790	30.4	20.4	40.3
		10–14	236 460	113 100	123 360	15.0	14.0	15.0
		15–19	156 100	62 300	93 800	11.0	9.0	12.0
		20–29	351 100	116 300	234 800	15.0	11.0	20.0
		30–39	415 900	123 100	292 800	27.0	16.0	38.0
		40–49	503 070	150 300	352 770	46.0	28.0	65.0
		50–59	426 820	135 900	290 920	58.0	38.0	79.0
		60+	546 800	203 100	343 700	74.0	56.0	91.0
PENINSULAR MALAYSIA	1980	15+	1 801 365	559 948	1 246 417	27.0	16.7	36.9
		10–14	166 946	85 655	81 291	12.3	12.4	12.2
		15–19	99 738	44 120	55 618	8.0	7.2	8.8
		20–24	111 806	40 316	71 490	10.8	8.2	13.1
		25–34	252 660	68 762	188 898	15.1	8.7	23.0
		35–44	351 226	92 133	259 093	32.5	16.9	48.4
		45–54	369 440	102 353	267 087	50.0	28.0	71.1
		55–64	306 290	95 076	211 214	62.0	39.6	83.2
		65+	310 205	117 188	193 017	74.5	38.9	92.1
SABAH	1980	10+	276 400	118 400	158 000	42.0	34.0	51.0
SARAWAK	1980	15+	351 847	135 801	216 046	48.9	38.4	59.2
		10–14	45 780	22 157	23 623	28.6	27.0	30.2
		15–19	32 142	11 854	20 288	23.6	17.9	28.9
		20–24	31 417	10 538	20 879	28.6	20.3	36.1
		25–34	67 116	21 620	45 496	38.8	25.3	52.1
		35–44	69 851	26 652	43 199	61.0	46.1	76.2
		45–54	64 124	25 615	38 509	76.5	62.9	89.4
		55–64	49 256	21 595	27 661	83.7	73.3	94.0
		65+	37 941	17 927	20 014	87.8	79.4	96.9
MALDIVES	1977	15+	13 814	7 378	6 436	17.6	17.5	17.7
		15–19	2 531	1 458	1 073	15.6	17.8	13.4
		20–24	1 471	772	699	12.6	13.0	12.2
		25–34	1 827	905	922	12.4	11.9	12.9
		35–44	3 190	1 579	1 611	19.8	18.4	21.4
		45–54	2 595	1 446	1 149	24.3	23.1	26.0
		55–64	1 339	692	647	23.7	20.6	28.4
		65+	861	526	335	26.5	24.2	31.2
NEPAL	1981	15+	6 998 148	3 053 083	3 945 065	79.4	68.3	90.8
		10–14	1 045 467	452 238	593 229	61.2	49.2	75.3
		15–19	882 010	360 317	521 693	66.4	51.8	82.5
		20–24	981 835	371 373	610 462	73.5	58.3	87.4
		25–34	1 681 560	682 519	999 041	78.7	65.7	90.9
		35–44	1 379 493	621 745	757 748	83.8	74.1	93.8
		45–54	1 005 383	490 314	515 069	86.6	79.1	95.2
		55–64	629 830	309 991	319 839	88.3	81.6	95.9
		65+	438 037	216 824	221 213	89.5	83.6	96.1

COUNTRY AND YEAR OF CENSUS OR SURVEY PAYS ET ANNEE DU RECENSEMENT OU DE L'ENQUETE PAIS Y AÑO DEL CENSO O DE LA ENCUESTA		AGE GROUP GROUPE D'AGE GRUPO DE EDAD	ILLITERATE POPULATION POPULATION ANALPHABETE POLACION ANALFABETA			PERCENTAGE OF ILLITERATES POURCENTAGE D'ANALPHABETES PORCENTAJE DE ANALFABETOS		
			TOTAL TOTALE	MALE MASCULINE MASCULINA	FEMALE FEMININE FEMENINA	TOTAL TOTALE	MALE MASCULIN MASCULINO	FEMALE FEMININ FEMENINO
			(1)	(2)	(3)	(4)	(5)	(6)
PAKISTAN	1981	15+	33 597 018	15 511 984	18 085 034	73.8	64.0	84.8
		10–14	7 996 604	4 021 378	3 975 226	74.0	68.7	80.4
		15–19	4 925 199	2 303 788	2 621 411	63.4	55.0	73.4
		20–24	4 049 781	1 766 736	2 283 045	65.0	54.0	77.2
		25–34	7 195 519	3 145 008	4 050 511	71.3	59.6	84.1
		35–44	6 190 519	2 631 646	3 558 873	76.8	64.9	88.9
		45–54	4 892 509	2 335 328	2 557 181	81.0	71.9	91.5
		55–59	1 332 384	626 449	705 935	82.7	72.9	94.0
		60+	5 011 107	2 703 029	2 308 078	87.4	81.6	95.4
PHILIPPINES‡	1980	15+	4 626 922	2 200 485	2 426 437	16.7	16.1	17.2
		10–14	1 193 311	669 133	524 178	20.1	22.1	18.0
		15–19	411 567	222 412	189 155	7.9	8.7	7.1
		20–24	391 090	200 206	190 884	8.6	9.2	8.1
		25–34	749 296	381 964	367 332	11.0	11.2	10.8
		35–44	753 538	371 678	381 860	16.8	16.4	17.2
		45–54	772 292	350 816	421 476	25.4	23.3	27.4
		55–64	743 571	324 292	419 279	37.2	33.5	40.7
		65+	805 568	349 117	456 451	49.3	44.0	54.3
QATAR	1981	10+	92 375	62 057	30 318	48.9	48.8	49.1
SINGAPORE	1980	15+	300 994	75 422	225 572	17.1	8.4	26.0
		15–19	9 640	5 276	4 364	3.4	3.6	3.1
		20–24	12 023	5 536	6 487	4.1	3.6	4.5
		25–34	32 370	8 956	23 414	7.0	3.8	10.3
		35–44	50 773	9 804	40 969	19.0	7.2	31.1
		45–54	68 124	14 584	53 540	34.0	14.1	55.0
		55–64	57 249	13 271	43 978	43.7	19.9	68.4
		65+	70 815	17 995	52 820	62.2	35.1	84.2
SRI LANKA‡	1981	15+	1 335 882	451 587	884 295	13.9	9.2	18.8
		10–14	190 007	97 135	92 872	11.2	11.2	11.2
		15–19	165 727	82 088	83 639	10.3	10.1	10.6
		20–24	131 123	56 315	74 808	8.7	7.5	9.9
		25–34	205 779	74 626	131 153	8.6	6.2	11.0
		35–44	207 856	58 700	149 156	13.5	7.5	19.8
		45–54	236 123	63 612	172 511	20.5	10.7	30.8
		55–64	183 342	52 201	131 141	24.0	12.9	36.6
		65+	205 932	64 045	141 887	32.0	18.9	46.5
SYRIAN ARAB REPUBLIC‡	1970	15+	1 851 949	629 904	1 222 045	60.0	40.4	80.0
		10–14	260 719	65 537	195 182	32.1	15.3	50.8
		15–19	237 396	60 893	176 503	40.8	20.5	61.9
		20–24	200 406	54 782	145 624	45.2	23.8	68.1
		25–34	358 338	95 123	263 215	55.4	30.7	78.1
		35–44	376 735	134 583	242 152	67.1	46.9	88.1
		45–54	250 430	98 223	152 207	72.5	54.6	91.9
		55–64	195 114	82 746	112 368	81.6	68.3	95.2
		65+	233 530	103 554	129 976	87.1	76.9	97.5
THAILAND‡	1980	15+	3 296 606	1 049 664	2 246 942	12.0	7.7	16.0
		10–14	184 177	87 979	96 198	3.2	3.0	3.4
		15–19	155 746	63 602	92 144	2.9	2.4	3.4
		20–24	154 209	55 859	98 350	3.4	2.5	4.3
		25–34	308 632	105 643	202 989	4.9	3.4	6.4
		35–44	451 448	148 534	302 914	10.1	6.7	13.4
		45–54	528 166	178 305	389 481	15.7	10.8	22.7
		55–64	715 645	209 740	505 905	37.2	22.3	51.5
		65+	943 140	287 981	655 159	61.9	42.2	77.9
TURKEY	1980	15+	9 384 000	2 559 295	6 824 705	34.4	18.7	50.2
		10–14	790 505	263 414	527 091	14.4	9.2	20.0
		15–19	685 959	168 553	517 406	13.8	6.6	21.5
		20–24	694 073	127 088	566 985	17.1	6.1	28.7
		25–34	1 515 354	253 160	1 262 994	25.0	8.2	42.4
		35–44	1 712 752	387 993	1 324 759	40.3	18.8	60.6
		45–54	1 910 635	597 141	1 313 494	51.1	31.3	71.7
		55–64	1 168 180	403 809	764 371	60.1	41.8	78.4
		65+	1 697 047	621 551	1 075 496	74.5	59.8	86.9
	1984	15+	...	...	...	25.8	14.1	37.5
UNITED ARAB EMIRATES	1975	15+	186 058	126 586	59 472	46.5	41.6	61.9
		10–14	5 095	2 154	2 941	13.8	10.5	17.8
		15–19	13 948	7 804	6 144	34.3	30.1	41.6
		20–24	28 092	20 963	7 129	38.4	36.4	45.7
		25–34	59 806	44 823	14 983	40.5	37.6	52.7
		35–44	39 016	26 543	12 473	50.7	44.1	74.6
		45–54	22 619	13 934	8 685	64.6	55.6	87.0
		55–64	12 040	6 786	5 254	80.2	72.6	92.7
		65+	10 537	5 733	4 804	89.9	85.4	95.9

COUNTRY AND YEAR OF CENSUS OR SURVEY PAYS ET ANNEE DU RECENSEMENT OU DE L'ENQUETE PAIS Y AÑO DEL CENSO O DE LA ENCUESTA		AGE GROUP GROUPE D'AGE GRUPO DE EDAD	ILLITERATE POPULATION POPULATION ANALPHABETE POLACION ANALFABETA			PERCENTAGE OF ILLITERATES POURCENTAGE D'ANALPHABETES PORCENTAJE DE ANALFABETOS		
			TOTAL TOTALE	MALE MASCULINE MASCULINA	FEMALE FEMININE FEMENINA	TOTAL TOTALE	MALE MASCULIN MASCULINO	FEMALE FEMININ FEMENINO
			(1)	(2)	(3)	(4)	(5)	(6)
VIET-NAM	1979	15+	4 846 849	1 340 445	3 506 404	16.0	9.5	21.7
		10-14	532 964	262 345	270 619	7.6	7.2	7.9
		15-19	298 845	124 120	174 725	5.0	4.2	5.7
		20-24	245 802	79 032	166 770	5.0	3.5	6.4
		25-34	414 989	129 467	285 522	6.7	4.4	8.7
		35-45	525 882	141 731	384 151	11.7	6.8	15.9
		46-50	365 314	92 783	272 531	17.4	9.3	24.9
		51+	2 996 017	773 312	2 222 705	45.7	27.3	59.7
EUROPE								
GREECE	1981	15+	701 056	140 544	560 512	9.5	3.9	14.7
		10-14	5 665	2 722	2 943	0.7	0.7	0.8
		15-19	7 281	3 507	3 774	1.0	1.0	1.1
		20-24	7 390	3 319	4 071	1.0	0.9	1.2
		25-34	18 426	7 629	10 797	1.4	1.2	1.6
		35-44	52 544	12 425	40 119	4.4	2.1	6.4
		45-54	121 528	29 147	92 381	9.2	4.5	13.7
		55-64	108 678	19 001	89 677	12.2	4.5	18.9
		65+	385 209	65 516	319 693	31.2	12.0	46.6
HUNGARY	1980	15+	95 542	27 756	67 786	1.1	0.7	1.5
		15-19	4 510	2 204	2 306	0.7	0.7	0.7
		20-24	4 699	2 133	2 566	0.6	0.5	0.6
		25-34	9 162	3 603	5 559	0.6	0.4	0.7
		35-44	12 387	4 206	8 181	0.9	0.6	1.2
		45-54	14 163	4 446	9 717	1.0	0.7	1.4
		55-64	9 976	2 791	7 185	0.9	0.6	1.2
		65+	40 645	8 373	32 272	2.8	1.4	3.7
ITALY	1971	15+	2 487 142	928 403	1 558 739	6.1	4.7	7.4
		15-19	35 680	19 994	15 686	0.9	1.1	0.8
		20-24	49 723	25 491	24 232	1.2	1.2	1.2
		25-34	152 122	66 271	85 851	2.1	1.8	2.3
		35-44	334 172	134 527	199 645	4.5	3.7	5.4
		45-54	335 569	126 420	209 149	5.4	4.2	6.5
		55-64	549 530	204 580	344 950	9.3	7.3	11.1
		65+	1 030 346	351 120	679 226	16.9	13.8	19.1
LIECHTENSTEIN	1981	10+	68	33	35	*.3	*.3	*.3
POLAND	1978	15+	334 586	92 609	241 977	1.2	0.7	1.7
		15-19	5 557	3 176	2 381	0.2	0.2	0.2
		20-24	7 273	3 978	3 295	0.2	0.2	0.2
		25-34	11 781	6 145	5 636	0.2	0.2	0.2
		35-44	11 148	5 498	5 650	0.3	0.3	0.3
		45-54	21 832	9 115	12 717	0.5	0.5	0.6
		55-64	27 562	8 985	18 577	1.0	0.7	1.2
		65+	249 433	55 712	193 721	7.0	4.0	8.9
PORTUGAL	1981	15+	1 506 206	524 461	981 745	20.6	15.2	25.4
		10-14	14 268	8 243	6 025	1.7	1.9	1.4
		15-19	16 704	9 895	6 809	1.9	2.3	1.6
		20-24	16 812	9 245	7 567	2.2	2.4	2.0
		25-34	39 323	17 479	21 844	3.0	2.7	3.3
		35-44	144 913	48 854	96 059	12.7	9.0	16.1
		45-54	318 764	111 132	207 632	27.5	20.3	34.0
		55-64	366 996	128 626	238 370	38.1	28.7	46.2
		65+	602 694	199 230	403 464	53.6	43.6	60.3
SAN MARINO	1976	10+	640	260	380	3.9	3.2	4.7
SPAIN	1981	15+	1 971 695	541 480	1 430 215	7.1	4.0	9.9
		10-14	19 886	10 337	9 549	0.6	0.6	0.6
		15-19	27 377	14 280	13 097	0.8	0.9	0.8
		20-24	32 069	14 652	17 417	1.1	1.0	1.2
		25-34	86 653	32 884	53 769	1.7	1.3	2.2
		35-44	187 373	54 891	132 482	4.4	2.6	6.2
		45-54	363 885	110 240	253 645	7.9	4.9	10.8
		55-64	368 460	104 050	264 410	10.2	6.1	13.7
		65+	905 878	210 483	695 395	21.4	12.2	27.7
YUGOSLAVIA	1981	15+	1 764 042	370 558	1 393 484	10.4	4.5	16.1
		10-14	16 860	6 515	10 345	0.9	0.7	1.2
		15-19	22 836	7 443	15 393	1.2	0.8	1.7
		20-24	28 758	8 367	20 391	1.5	0.9	2.2
		25-34	72 165	16 864	55 301	2.0	0.9	3.2
		35-44	156 651	24 179	132 472	5.7	1.8	9.6
		45-54	389 603	60 674	328 929	13.1	4.1	21.7
		55-64	356 605	58 091	298 514	20.1	7.5	29.8
		65+	737 424	194 940	542 484	34.6	21.5	44.2

COUNTRY AND YEAR OF CENSUS OR SURVEY PAYS ET ANNEE DU RECENSEMENT OU DE L'ENQUETE PAIS Y AÑO DEL CENSO O DE LA ENCUESTA		AGE GROUP GROUPE D'AGE GRUPO DE EDAD	ILLITERATE POPULATION POPULATION ANALPHABETE POLACION ANALFABETA TOTAL TOTALE			PERCENTAGE OF ILLITERATES POURCENTAGE D'ANALPHABETES PORCENTAJE DE ANALFABETOS TOTAL TOTALE		
				MALE MASCULINE MASCULINA	FEMALE FEMININE FEMENINA		MALE MASCULIN MASCULINO	FEMALE FEMININ FEMENINO
			(1)	(2)	(3)	(4)	(5)	(6)
OCEANIA								
FIJI	1976	15+	65 957	24 305	41 652	21.0	16.0	26.0
		15–19	2 501	909	1 592	6.0	4.0	7.0
		20–24	5 066	1 920	3 146	9.0	7.0	11.0
		25–29	5 635	2 016	3 619	13.0	9.0	16.0
		30–39	12 808	4 158	8 650	19.0	12.0	25.0
		40–49	14 461	5 278	9 183	31.0	22.0	40.0
		50+	25 486	10 024	15 462	47.0	36.0	59.0
GUAM	1980	15+	2 470	1 317	1 153	3.6	3.6	3.5
		15–19	514	272	242	4.7	4.7	4.7
		20–24	456	279	177	4.1	4.6	3.5
		25–34	504	286	218	2.6	2.8	2.3
		35–44	284	170	114	2.5	2.8	2.2
		45–54	240	135	105	2.9	3.1	2.8
		55–64	196	88	108	4.0	3.3	4.9
		65+	276	87	189	9.2	6.2	12.0
NEW CALEDONIA	1976	15+	7 133	3 370	3 763	8.7	7.8	9.7
		15–19	300	180	120	2.2	2.6	1.8
		20–24	328	205	123	3.0	3.5	2.4
		25–34	759	341	418	3.8	3.2	4.5
		35–39	577	254	323	6.9	5.7	8.1
		40–49	1 285	562	723	10.0	8.1	12.2
		50–59	1 434	636	798	17.9	14.7	21.6
		60+	2 450	1 192	1 258	30.2	29.0	31.3
PAPUA NEW GUINEA	1971	10+	1 106 880	512 713	594 167	67.9	60.7	75.6
SAMOA	1971	15+	1 581	819	762	2.2	2.2	2.1
		10–14	–	–	–	–	–	–
		15–19	–	–	–	–	–	–
		20–24	–	–	–	–	–	–
		25–34	15	8	7	0.1	0.1	0.1
		35–44	56	29	27	0.5	0.5	0.4
		45–54	147	77	70	1.7	1.7	1.6
		55–64	297	155	142	6.0	6.1	5.9
		65+	1 066	550	516	26.4	29.6	23.7
TONGA‡	1976	15+	193	81	112	0.4	0.3	0.5
		10–14	48	30	18	0.4	0.5	0.3
		15–19	22	10	12	0.2	0.2	0.2
		20–24	9	4	5	0.1	0.1	0.1
		25–34	22	9	13	0.2	0.2	0.3
		35–44	24	9	15	0.3	0.2	0.4
		45–54	24	12	12	0.4	0.4	0.4
		55–64	20	11	9	0.6	0.6	0.5
		65+	72	26	46	2.6	2.0	3.2
VANUATU	1979	15+	28 647	13 823	14 824	47.1	42.7	52.2
		10–14	5 004	2 538	2 466	34.7	33.1	36.4
		15–19	3 125	1 431	1 694	25.7	22.6	29.0
		20–24	3 157	1 364	1 793	31.1	26.2	36.3
		25–34	6 243	2 700	3 543	42.3	35.9	49.0
		35–44	6 018	2 793	3 225	59.0	50.8	68.6
		45–54	4 327	2 264	2 063	69.3	63.8	76.5
		55–64	3 059	1 679	1 380	75.8	71.6	81.8
		65+	2 718	1 592	1 126	83.9	81.8	87.0
U.S.S.R.								
U.S.S.R.	1979	9–49	...	...	...	0.2	0.2	0.2
BYELORUSSIAN S.S.R.	1979	9–49	...	...	...	0.1	0.1	0.1
UKRAINIAN S.S.R.	1979	9–49	...	...	...	0.1	0.1	0.1

AFRICA:

Botswana:

E--> *De jure* population excluding 24,012 residents absent for less than one year and nomad population estimated at 10,550 at 1971 census.

FR-> Population de droit. Non compris 24 012 résidents hors du pays pour moins d'une année et les nomades estimés à 10 550 au recensement de 1971.

ESP> Población de jure, excluídas 24 012 personas residentes fuera del país por un período inferior a un año y los nómadas que se estimaron a 10 550 en el censo de 1971.

Burundi:

E--> Estimates made by National authorities.

FR-> Estimations effectuées par les autorités nationales.

Burundi: (Cont):

ESP> Estimaciones establecidos por las autoridades nacionales.

Cameroun:

E--> *De jure* population.

FR-> Population de droit.

ESP> Población de jure.

Equatorial Guinea:

E--> Estimate made by national authorities.

FR-> Estimations effectuées par les autorités nationales.

ESP> Estimaciones establecidos por las autoridades nacionales.

Morocco:

E--> Estimates for *de jure* population, based on results of a sample survey.

FR-> Estimation de la population de droit, fondée sur les résultats

Morocco: (Cont):
d'une enquête par sondage.
ESP> Estimación de la población de jure fundada en los resultados de una encueta por sondeo.
United Republic of Tanzania:
E--> Illiterates in Kiswahili.
FR-> Analphabètes en Kiswahili.
ESP> Analfabetos en Kiswahili.
AMERICA, NORTH:
Barbados:
E--> Persons with no schooling are defined as illiterates.
FR-> Les personnes sans scolarité ont été considérées comme étant analphabètes.
ESP> Las personas sin escolaridad han sido consideradas como analfabetos.
Belize:
E--> Persons with no schooling are defined as illiterates.
FR-> Les personnes sans scolarité ont été considérées comme étant analphabètes.
ESP> Las personas sin escolaridad han sido consideradas como analfabetos.
Bermuda:
E--> Persons with no schooling are defined as illiterates.
FR-> Les personnes sans scolarité ont été considérées comme étant analphabètes.
ESP> Las personas sin escolaridad han sido consideradas como analfabetos.
British Virgin Islands:
E--> Persons with no schooling are defined as illiterates.
FR-> Les personnes sans scolarité ont été considérées comme étant analphabètes.
ESP> Las personas sin escolaridad han sido consideradas como analfabetos.
Cayman Islands:
E--> Persons with no schooling are defined as illiterates.
FR-> Les personnes sans scolarité ont été considérées comme étant analphabètes.
ESP> Las personas sin escolaridad han sido consideradas como analfabetos.
Costa Rica:
E--> *De jure* population.
FR-> Population de droit.
ESP> Población de jure.
Cuba:
E--> Not including functionally and physically handicapped.
FR-> Non compris les handicapés physiques et fonctionnels.
ESP> Excluídos los incapacitados funcionales y físicos.
Dominica:
E--> Persons with no schooling are defined as illiterates.
FR-> Les personnes sans scolarité ont été considérées comme étant analphabètes.
ESP> Las personas sin escolaridad han sido consideradas como analfabetos.
Grenada:
E--> Persons with no schooling are defined as illiterates.
FR-> Les personnes sans scolarité ont été considérées comme étant analphabètes.
ESP> Las personas sin escolaridad han sido consideradas como analfabetos.
Guatemala:
E--> *De jure* population, based on a 5% sample.
FR-> Population de droit, d'après un échantillonage portant sur 5%.
ESP> Población de jure, según un muestreo referente al 5%.
Honduras:
E--> *De jure* population.
FR-> Population de droit.
ESP> Población de jure.
Jamaica:
E--> Persons with no schooling are defined as illiterates.
FR-> Les personnes sans scolarité ont été considérées comme étant analphabètes.
ESP> Las personas sin escolaridad han sido consideradas como analfabetos.
Montserrat:
E--> Persons with no schooling are defined as illiterates.
FR-> Les personnes sans scolarité ont été considérées comme étant analphabètes.
ESP> Las personas sin escolaridad han sido consideradas como analfabetos.
Netherlands Antilles:
E--> *De jure* population.
FR-> Population de droit.
ESP> Población de jure.
Nicaragua:
E--> *De jure* population. In 1980, after the National Literacy Campaign, the Ministry of Education estimated that of the 722,431 illiterates identified in the census of October 1979, 130,372 were *analfabetos inaptos*, and 406,056 were made literate, leaving only

Nicaragua: (Cont):
186,003 *analfabetos aptos* (or 12.96% of the population of 10 years and over).
FR-> Population de droit. En 1980, à la fin de la campagne nationale d'alphabétisation, le Ministère de l'Education a estimé que parmi les 722 431 analphabètes recensés en octobre 1979, 130 372 étaient *analfabetos inaptos*, que 406 056 étaient devenus alphabètes, laissant seulement 186 003 *analfabetos aptos* (ou 12.96% de la population âgée de 10 ans et plus).
ESP> Población de jure. En 1980, después de la Cruzadda Nacional de Alfabetización, el Ministerio de Education estimó que de los 722 431 analfabetos, según el Censo de octubre de 1979, 130 372 eran *analfabetos inaptos*, 406 056 fueron alfabetizados quedando solamente *186 003 analfabetos aptos*, (o sea 12.96% de la población de 10 años y más).
Puerto Rico:
E--> *De jure* population but not including armed forces stationed in this area.
FR-> Population de droit mais non compris les militaires en garnison sur le territoire.
ESP> Pobliación de jure, pero excluyendo los militares destacados en la zona.
St. Christopher and Nevis and Anguilla:
E--> Persons with no schooling are defined as illiterates.
FR-> Les personnes sans scolarité ont été considérées comme étant analphabètes.
ESP> Las personas sin escolaridad han sido consideradas como analfabetos.
St. Lucia:
E--> Persons with no schooling are defined as illiterates.
FR-> Les personnes sans scolarité ont été considérées comme étant analphabètes.
ESP> Las personas sin escolaridad han sido consideradas como analfabetos.
St. Vincent and the Grendadines:
E--> Persons with no schooling are defined as illiterates.
FR-> Les personnes sans scolarité ont été considérées comme étant analphabètes.
ESP> Las personas sin escolaridad han sido consideradas como analfabetos.
Turks and Caicos Islands:
E--> Persons with no schooling are defined as illiterates.
FR-> Les personnes sans scolarité ont été considérées comme étant analphabètes.
ESP> Las personas sin escolaridad han sido consideradas como analfabetos.
AMERICA, SOUTH:
Chile:
E--> Estimates made by National authorities.
FR-> Estimations effectuées par les autorités nationales.
ESP> Estimaciones establecidos por las autoridades nacionales.
Ecuador:
E--> Excluding nomadic Indian tribes.
FR-> Non compris les tribus indiennes nomades.
ESP> Excluídas las tribus indias nómadas.
Guyana:
E--> Persons with no schooling are defined as illiterates.
FR-> Les personnes sans scolarité ont été considérées comme étant analphabètes.
ESP> Las personas sin escolaridad han sido consideradas como analfabetos.
Peru:
E--> Excluding Indian jungle population.
FR-> Non compris les indiens de la jungle.
ESP> Excluidos los indios de la selva.
Uruguay:
E--> Based on a sample tabulation of census returns.
FR-> D'après un échantillonage des bulletins de recensement.
ESP> Según un muestro de los boletines de censo.
ASIA:
Afghanistan:
E--> Excluding nomad populations.
FR-> Non compris les populations nomades.
ESP> Excluídas las poblaciones nómades.
China:
E--> Data are based on a 10% sample of census returns.
FR-> Les données ont été établies d'après un échantillonage portant sur 10% des bulletins de recensement.
ESP> Los datos se han establecidos según un muestreo referente al 10% de los boletines de censo.
Hong Kong:
E--> Persons with no schooling are defined as illiterates.
FR-> Les personnes sans scolarité ont été considérées comme étant analphabètes.
ESP> Las personas sin escolaridad han sido consideradas como analfabetos.
Israel:
E--> Persons with no schooling are defined as illiterates.

Israel: (Cont):
FR-> Les personnes sans scolarité ont été considérées comme étant analphabètes.
ESP> Las personas sin escolaridad han sido consideradas como analfabetos.
Korea, Republic of:
E--> Based on a sample survey. Excluding alien armed forces, civilian aliens employed by armed forces and foreign diplomatic personnel and their dependents.
FR-> D'après une enquête par sondage. Non compris les militaires étrangers, les civils étrangers employés par les forces armées, ni le personnel diplomatique étranger et les membres de leur famille les accompagnant.
ESP> Según una encuestra por sondeo. Excluídos los militares extranjeros, los civiles extranjeros empleados por las fuerzas armadas y los diplomáticos extranjeros y los miembros de sus familias que les acompañan.
Philippines:
E--> Based on a 20% sample of census returns.
FR-> D'après un échantillonage portant sur 20% des bulletins de recensement.
ESP> Según un muestreo referente al 20% de los boletines de censo.
Sri Lanka:
E--> Data are based on a 10% sample of census returns.
FR-> Les données ont été établies d'après un échantillonage portant sur 10% des bulletins de recensement.
ESP> Los datos se han establecidos según un muestreo referente al 10% de los boletines de censo.
Syrian Arab Republic:
E--> National population only.
FR-> Population nationale seulement.
ESP> Población nacional solamente.
Thailand:
E--> Based on a 20% sample.
FR-> D'après un échantillonage à 20%.
ESP> Según un muestreo a 20%.
OCEANIA:
Tonga:
E--> *De jure* population.
FR-> Population de droit.
ESP> Población de jure.

1.4 Percentage distribution of population 25 years of age and over, by educational attainment and by sex

Répartition en pourcentage de la population de 25 ans et plus selon le niveau d'instruction, par sexe

Distribución en porcentaje de la población de 25 años y más según el nivel de instrucción, por sexo

S1 = FIRST STAGE
S2 = SECOND STAGE

A = ALL AGES

NUMBER OF COUNTRIES AND TERRITORIES PRESENTED IN THIS TABLE: 135

S1 = PREMIER CYCLE
S2 = DEUXIEME CYCLE

A = TOUS LES AGES

NOMBRE DE PAYS ET DE TERRITOIRES PRESENTES DANS CE TABLEAU: 135

S1 = PRIMER CICLO
S2 = SEGUNDO CICLO

A = TODAS LAS EDADES

NUMERO DE PAISES Y DE TERRITORIOS PRESENTADOS EN ESTE CUADRO: 135

COUNTRY / PAYS / PAIS	YEAR SEX / ANNEE SEXE / AÑO SEXO		AGE GROUP / GROUPE D'AGE / GRUPO DE EDAD	TOTAL POPULATION / POPULATION TOTALE / POBLACION TOTAL	HIGHEST LEVEL ATTAINED / NIVEAU D'INSTRUCTION ATTEINT / NIVEL DE INSTRUCCION ALCANZADO					
					NO SCHOOLING / SANS SCOLARITE / SIN ESCOLARIDAD	FIRST LEVEL / PREMIER DEGRE / PRIMER GRADO		ENTERED SECOND LEVEL / ACCEDE AU SECOND DEGRE / ACCEDIERON AL SEGUNDO GRADO		POST-SECONDARY / POST-SECONDAIRE / POST-SECUNDARIA
						INCOMPLETED / NON COMPLETE / INCOMPLETO	COMPLETED / COMPLETE / COMPLETO	S-1	S-2	
				(1)	(2)	(3)	(4)	(5)	(6)	(7)
AFRICA										
ALGERIA										
TOTAL POPULATION	1971	MF	25+	4 173 435	84.4	13.0	——>	2.2	——>	0.3
		F	25+	2 256 695	95.9	3.3	——>	0.7	——>	0.1
URBAN POPULATION		MF	25+	1 410 185	73.5	20.5	——>	5.2	——>	0.8
		F	25+	741 965	89.5	8.3	——>	2.0	——>	0.2
RURAL POPULATION		MF	25+	2 763 250	89.9	9.2	——>	0.6	——>	0.1
		F	25+	1 514 730	99.0	0.9	——>	0.1	——>	0.0
BENIN										
	1979	MF	25+	1 191 179	89.2	8.3	——>	1.4	0.8	0.3
		F	25+	651 159	94.3	4.4	——>	0.9	0.4	0.1
BOTSWANA										
BOTSWANA CITIZENS	1981	MF	25+	310 303	54.7	31.1	9.4	3.1	1.3	0.5
		F	25+	172 274	51.4	36.3	8.7	2.5	0.8	0.2
TOTAL POPULATION		MF	12+	569 765	43.2	35.1	14.6	4.4	1.8	0.9
		F	12+	311 706	39.8	38.4	15.6	4.3	1.4	0.5
URBAN POPULATION		MF	12+	114 274	23.3	32.0	25.5	10.1	6.1	3.0
		F	12+	54 253	19.4	35.3	27.3	10.6	5.5	2.0
RURAL POPULATION		MF	12+	455 491	48.1	35.9	11.9	3.0	0.7	0.4
		F	12+	257 453	44.1	39.1	13.1	3.0	0.5	0.2
CAMEROON										
TOTAL POPULATION	1976	MF	25+	2 780 576	71.3	24.0	——>	4.4	——>	0.3
		F	25+	1 462 952	84.3	13.9	——>	1.6	——>	0.1
URBAN POPULATION		MF	25+	685 943	57.0	29.0	——>	12.9	——>	1.0
		F	25+	325 300	67.4	26.5	——>	5.7	——>	0.4
RURAL POPULATION		MF	25+	2 094 633	78.4	19.9	——>	1.7	——>	0.0
		F	25+	1 137 652	89.2	10.3	——>	0.5	——>	0.0
EGYPT‡										
	1976	MF	25+	14 641 740	86.3	4.7	——>	5.7	——>	3.4
		F	25+	7 326 340	92.9	2.6	——>	3.1	——>	1.3
GAMBIA										
	1973	MF	25+	203 986	94.9	0.8	0.5	2.6	1.0	0.2
		F	25+	97 345	97.1	0.5	0.2	1.5	0.5	0.1
GHANA										
	1970	MF	25+	3 227 660	77.7	5.8	——>	12.8	3.3	0.4
		F	25+	1 689 000	88.0	4.8	——>	6.0	1.1	0.1

COUNTRY / PAYS / PAIS	YEAR / ANNEE / AÑO	SEX / SEXE / SEXO	AGE GROUP / GROUPE D'AGE / GRUPO DE EDAD	TOTAL POPULATION / POPULATION TOTALE / POBLACION TOTAL	HIGHEST LEVEL ATTAINED / NIVEAU D'INSTRUCTION ATTEINT / NIVEL DE INSTRUCCION ALCANZADO: NO SCHOOLING / SANS SCOLARITE / SIN ESCOLARIDAD	FIRST LEVEL / PREMIER DEGRE / PRIMER GRADO: INCOMPLETED / NON COMPLETE / INCOMPLETO	FIRST LEVEL / PREMIER DEGRE / PRIMER GRADO: COMPLETED / COMPLETE / COMPLETO	ENTERED SECOND LEVEL / ACCEDE AU SECOND DEGRE / ACCEDIERON AL SEGUNDO GRADO: S-1	ENTERED SECOND LEVEL / ACCEDE AU SECOND DEGRE / ACCEDIERON AL SEGUNDO GRADO: S-2	POST-SECONDARY / POST-SECONDAIRE / POST-SECUNDARIA
				(1)	(2)	(3)	(4)	(5)	(6)	(7)
GUINEA-BISSAU‡										
	1979	MF	7+	483 336	91.1	7.5	0.5	0.6	0.2	0.1
KENYA‡										
	1979	MF	25+	4 818 310	58.6	32.2	——>	7.9	1.3	——>
		F	25+	2 442 417	73.0	23.0	——>	3.4	0.6	——>
LESOTHO										
	1976	MF	25+	483 002	34.3	52.0	9.1	4.6	——>	0.1
		F	25+	255 898	24.8	61.3	10.2	3.6	——>	0.1
LIBERIA										
TOTAL POPULATION	1974	MF	25+	607 806	87.1	2.6	1.2	3.6	3.9	1.5
		F	25+	296 114	94.3	1.1	0.5	1.4	1.8	0.8
URBAN POPULATION		MF	25+	157 100	67.3	4.6	2.5	8.7	11.9	5.1
		F	25+	66 589	81.0	2.6	1.5	4.7	7.0	3.2
RURAL POPULATION		MF	25+	450 706	94.1	1.9	0.8	1.8	1.2	0.3
		F	25+	229 525	98.2	0.6	0.2	0.5	0.3	0.1
LIBYAN ARAB JAMAHIRIYA‡										
	1973	MF	25+	691 054	72.7	18.8	3.5	4.0	——>	1.0
		F	25+	331 711	95.3	3.1	0.9	0.7	——>	0.1
MALAWI										
	1977	MF	25+	2 064 965	55.4	37.3	4.7	1.5	1.0	0.2
		F	25+	1 086 793	68.8	28.7	1.6	0.5	0.4	0.1
MALI‡										
TOTAL POPULATION	1976	MF	25+	2 445 774	95.4	3.0	0.8	0.6	——>	0.2
		F	25+	1 273 821	98.1	1.3	0.4	0.2	——>	0.1
URBAN POPULATION		MF	25+	372 189	83.5	8.8	3.7	2.7	——>	1.4
		F	25+	190 796	91.5	5.0	1.9	1.2	——>	0.4
RURAL POPULATION		MF	25+	2 073 585	97.5	2.0	0.3	0.2	——>	0.0
		F	25+	1 083 052	99.2	0.7	0.1	0.0	——>	0.0
MAURITIUS										
	1983	MF	25+	440 134	23.9	52.0	——>	20.6	——>	3.6
		F	25+	230 126	32.4	48.1	——>	17.5	——>	1.9
MOROCCO										
TOTAL POPULATION	1971	MF	25+	5 750 690	92.5	1.9	1.2	4.4	——>	——>
		F	25+	2 953 936	96.3	0.9	0.7	2.1	——>	——>
URBAN POPULATION		MF	25+	1 992 086	82.6	3.6	3.0	10.7	——>	——>
		F	25+	1 028 861	90.1	2.2	2.0	5.7	——>	——>
RURAL POPULATION		MF	25+	3 758 604	97.8	0.9	0.3	1.0	——>	——>
		F	25+	1 925 075	99.6	0.1	0.1	0.2	——>	——>
MOZAMBIQUE‡										
	1980	MF	5+	11 928 785	61.5	35.9	2.0	0.5	0.1	0.1
		F	5+	5 926 697	72.8	25.9	1.0	0.2	0.0	0.0
NIGER										
	1977	MF	10+	3 341 708	88.5	10.3	——>	1.0	——>	0.1
		F	10+	1 715 803	95.4	3.9	——>	0.6	——>	0.0
RWANDA‡										
	1978	MF	25+	1 568 661	77.0	16.8	4.0	2.0	——>	0.3
		F	25+	779 613	88.2	8.9	1.5	1.3	——>	0.1
SAO TOME AND PRINCIPE‡										
	1981	MF	25+	33 308	56.6	18.0	19.3	4.6	1.3	0.3
		F	25+	17 330	74.6	11.8	9.7	3.0	0.7	0.1
SENEGAL										
	1970	MF	6+	2 857 310	95.3	——>	1.8	2.1	0.7	0.1
		F	6+	1 508 619	97.2	——>	1.1	1.2	0.4	0.0
SEYCHELLES										
	1971	MF	25+	21 193	28.3	34.5	21.5	7.3	5.9	2.6
		F	25+	11 089	25.6	36.8	22.7	8.1	5.1	1.7
SOUTH AFRICA‡										
TOTAL POPULATION	1970	MF	25+	8 685 224	42.1	21.4	5.3	20.7	6.7	3.7
		F	25+	4 448 424	43.7	20.8	5.6	20.9	6.0	3.1
URBAN POPULATION		MF	25+	4 749 910	23.6	21.9	7.1	31.2	10.6	5.6
		F	25+	2 159 486	19.9	21.2	8.0	35.1	10.7	5.1
RURAL POPULATION		MF	25+	3 935 314	64.6	20.8	3.3	8.1	1.9	1.3
		F	25+	2 288 938	66.1	20.3	3.4	7.5	1.5	1.2

COUNTRY / PAYS / PAIS	YEAR / ANNEE / AÑO	SEX / SEXE / SEXO	AGE GROUP / GROUPE D'AGE / GRUPO DE EDAD	TOTAL POPULATION / POPULATION TOTALE / POBLACION TOTAL	HIGHEST LEVEL ATTAINED / NIVEAU D'INSTRUCTION ATTEINT / NIVEL DE INSTRUCCION ALCANZADO					
					NO SCHOOLING / SANS SCOLARITE / SIN ESCOLARIDAD	FIRST LEVEL / PREMIER DEGRE / PRIMER GRADO		ENTERED SECOND LEVEL / ACCEDE AU SECOND DEGRE / ACCEDIERON AL SEGUNDO GRADO		POST-SECONDARY / POST-SECONDAIRE / POST-SECUNDARIA
						INCOMPLETED / NON COMPLETE / INCOMPLETO	COMPLETED / COMPLETE / COMPLETO	S-1	S-2	
				(1)	(2)	(3)	(4)	(5)	(6)	(7)
SWAZILAND‡										
	1976	MF	25+	168 168	53.6	25.4	9.2	7.9	3.9	——>
		F	25+	91 516	56.3	26.3	8.3	6.3	2.7	——>
TOGO										
	1981	MF	25+	1 084 488	76.5	13.5	——>	8.7	——>	1.3
		F	25+	604 296	87.3	7.9	——>	4.2	——>	0.5
TUNISIA										
TOTAL POPULATION	1984	MF	25+	2 714 100	66.3	18.9	——>	12.0	——>	2.8
		F	25+	1 347 700	79.0	12.7	——>	6.9	——>	1.3
URBAN POPULATION		MF	25+	1 504 300	53.4	23.7	——>	18.2	——>	4.7
		F	25+	746 600	67.9	18.2	——>	11.6	——>	2.3
RURAL POPULATION		MF	25+	1 209 800	82.3	12.8	——>	4.4	——>	0.6
		F	25+	601 100	92.7	5.9	——>	1.2	——>	0.2
UNITED REPUBLIC OF TANZANIA										
	1978	MF	10+	5 637 889	48.6	40.7	8.7	1.6	0.1	0.2
AMERICA, NORTH										
ANTIGUA AND BARBUDA‡										
	1970	MF	A	64 316	15.0	79.2	——>	4.5	——>	1.3
		F	A	34 004	14.4	80.6	——>	4.1	——>	0.9
BARBADOS										
	1980	MF	25+	116 874	0.8	63.5	——>	32.3	——>	3.3
		MF	25+	68 807	0.9	65.2	——>	32.0	——>	1.9
BELIZE										
	1980	MF	25+	45 596	10.7	75.3	——>	11.7	——>	2.3
		F	25+	22 632	10.5	76.6	——>	11.7	——>	1.2
BERMUDA										
	1970	MF	25+	28 015	2.0	43.8	——>	46.8	——>	7.4
		F	25+	14 050	1.3	41.5	——>	51.0	——>	6.2
BRITISH VIRGIN ISLANDS										
	1980	MF	25+	5 136	2.4	65.8	——>	23.3	——>	8.5
		F	25+	2 437	2.4	64.7	——>	25.4	——>	7.4
CANADA										
TOTAL POPULATION	1981	MF	25+	13 971 280	2.0	14.2	9.5	36.8	——>	37.4
		F	25+	7 161 655	2.2	14.2	9.4	39.6	——>	34.7
URBAN POPULATION		MF	25+	10 743 370	1.9	13.1	8.5	39.4	——>	37.1
		F	25+	5 597 975	2.2	13.6	8.7	39.1	——>	36.3
RURAL POPULATION		MF	25+	3 227 895	2.3	18.1	12.7	37.6	——>	29.3
		F	25+	1 563 690	2.0	16.2	11.9	41.0	——>	28.8
CAYMAN ISLANDS										
	1970	MF	25+	4 533	2.8	79.1	——>	15.2	——>	2.9
		F	25+	2 571	2.7	82.0	——>	14.0	——>	1.3
COSTA RICA‡										
TOTAL POPULATION	1973	MF	25+	657 543	16.1	49.1	17.8	6.3	4.9	5.8
		F	25+	331 240	16.0	49.8	17.7	6.5	4.5	5.4
URBAN POPULATION		MF	25+	297 887	7.2	37.4	24.8	10.9	9.0	10.6
		F	25+	161 996	8.1	39.3	24.4	10.9	8.1	9.3
RURAL POPULATION		MF	25+	359 656	23.6	58.8	12.1	2.4	1.4	1.8
		F	25+	169 244	23.6	59.9	11.4	2.3	1.1	1.7
CUBA										
TOTAL POPULATION	1981	MF	25–49	3 013 315	3.7	22.6	27.6	40.2	——>	5.9
		F	25–49	1 511 380	4.1	27.0	28.4	35.9	——>	4.5
URBAN POPULATION		MF	25–49	2 165 853	2.0	16.8	26.0	47.4	——>	7.8
RURAL POPULATION		MF	25–49	847 462	8.1	37.5	31.6	21.9	——>	1.0
DOMINICA										
	1981	MF	25+	27 508	6.6	80.5	——>	11.1	——>	1.7
		F	25+	14 581	6.8	81.6	——>	10.6	——>	1.0
DOMINICAN REPUBLIC										
TOTAL POPULATION	1970	MF	25+	1 145 090	40.1	41.6	4.3	9.6	2.5	1.9
		F	25+	563 150	42.8	40.9	3.9	8.7	2.4	1.3
URBAN POPULATION		MF	25+	487 675	22.9	42.1	7.4	18.3	5.2	4.1
RURAL POPULATION		MF	25+	657 415	52.8	41.2	2.0	3.2	0.5	0.3

COUNTRY / PAYS / PAIS	YEAR SEX / ANNEE SEXE / AÑO SEXO		AGE GROUP / GROUPE D'AGE / GRUPO DE EDAD	TOTAL POPULATION / POPULATION TOTALE / POBLACION TOTAL	HIGHEST LEVEL ATTAINED / NIVEAU D'INSTRUCTION ATTEINT / NIVEL DE INSTRUCCION ALCANZADO					
					NO SCHOOLING / SANS SCOLARITE / SIN ESCOLARIDAD	FIRST LEVEL / PREMIER DEGRE / PRIMER GRADO		ENTERED SECOND LEVEL / ACCEDE AU SECOND DEGRE / ACCEDIERON AL SEGUNDO GRADO		POST-SECONDARY / POST-SECONDAIRE / POST-SECUNDARIA
						INCOMPLETED / NON COMPLETE / INCOMPLETO	COMPLETED / COMPLETE / COMPLETO	S-1	S-2	
				(1)	(2)	(3)	(4)	(5)	(6)	(7)
EL SALVADOR‡										
TOTAL POPULATION	1980	MF	10+	3 132 400	30.2	60.7	—>	6.9	—>	2.3
		F	10+	1 635 100	33.1	58.3	—>	6.6	—>	1.9
URBAN POPULATION		MF	10+	1 405 000	15.5	66.2	—>	13.5	—>	4.8
		F	10+	776 200	19.6	64.0	—>	12.5	—>	3.9
RURAL POPULATION		MF	10+	1 727 400	42.2	56.2	—>	1.4	—>	0.2
		F	10+	858 900	45.4	53.1	—>	1.3	—>	0.2
GRENADA	1981	MF	25+	33 401	2.2	87.8	—>	8.5	—>	1.5
		F	25+	18 362	2.3	88.3	—>	8.5	—>	0.8
GUADELOUPE	1982	MF	25+	150 253	10.7	54.6	—>	29.5	—>	5.2
		F	25+	79 984	10.3	53.6	—>	31.8	—>	4.2
GUATEMALA‡										
TOTAL POPULATION	1973	MF	25+	1 785 720	93.9	—>	—>	4.9	—>	1.2
		F	25+	897 960	94.7	—>	—>	4.8	—>	0.5
URBAN POPULATION		MF	25+	639 780	85.2	—>	—>	11.8	—>	2.9
RURAL POPULATION		MF	25+	1 145 940	98.7	—>	—>	1.1	—>	0.2
HAITI	1982	MF	25+	2 103 124	77.0	15.2	—>	7.2	—>	0.7
		F	25+	1 093 992	81.3	12.3	—>	5.9	—>	0.4
HONDURAS‡	1983	MF	25+	...	33.5	51.3	—>	4.3	7.6	3.3
		F	25+	...	34.1	51.1	—>	4.4	8.3	2.2
		MF	25+	...	17.3	51.8	—>	8.2	15.4	7.4
		F	25+	...	19.4	51.8	—>	8.4	15.8	4.6
		MF	25+	...	46.1	51.0	—>	1.2	1.6	0.1
		F	25+	...	46.9	50.3	—>	1.0	1.7	0.1
JAMAICA	1981	MF	14+	1 377 400	2.0	69.7	—>	28.4	—>	—>
MEXICO‡	1980	MF	25+	24 116 344	38.1	31.7	17.3	6.4	1.7	4.9
MONTSERRAT	1980	MF	25+	5 544	1.7	84.6	—>	7.9	—>	5.8
		F	25+	3 023	1.7	84.4	—>	9.9	—>	4.0
NETHERLANDS ANTILLES‡	1971	MF	25+	90 564	52.2	25.0	—>	18.4	—>	4.4
		F	25+	48 988	74.9	13.8	—>	8.9	—>	2.4
NICARAGUA	1971	MF	25+	593 100	53.9	41.8	—>	—>	4.4	—>
PANAMA	1980	MF	25+	718 509	17.4	27.3	23.4	11.7	11.8	8.4
		F	25+	355 390	18.3	26.5	23.3	11.7	12.3	7.8
FORMER CANAL ZONE‡										
TOTAL POPULATION	1970	MF	25+	19 855	1.0	2.6	17.9	8.9	38.9	30.7
		F	25+	9 279	0.8	2.8	19.9	11.2	38.2	27.1
URBAN POPULATION		MF	25+	1 441	0.3	1.9	7.8	9.3	35.5	45.1
		F	25+	741	0.4	3.1	11.2	8.9	34.1	42.2
RURAL POPULATION		MF	25+	18 414	1.1	2.6	18.7	8.8	39.2	29.5
		F	25+	8 538	0.8	2.8	20.6	11.4	38.6	25.8
PUERTO RICO‡	1980	MF	25+	1 577 686	8.0	17.8	11.4	16.4	27.9	18.4
		F	25+	839 399	9.1	17.8	11.9	15.7	27.2	18.3
ST. CHRISTOPHER-NEVIS AND ANGUILLA	1980	MF	25+	16 695	1.1	29.6	—>	67.2	—>	2.1
		F	25+	9 233	1.0	30.3	—>	67.5	—>	1.2
ST. LUCIA	1980	MF	25+	39 599	17.5	74.5	—>	6.8	—>	1.3
		F	25+	21 756	16.8	75.6	—>	6.8	—>	0.7
ST. VINCENT AND THE GRENADINES	1980	MF	25+	32 444	2.4	88.0	—>	8.2	—>	1.4
		MF	25+	17 893	2.5	88.6	—>	8.0	—>	0.9

COUNTRY PAYS PAIS	YEAR ANNEE AÑO	SEX SEXE SEXO	AGE GROUP GROUPE D'AGE GRUPO DE EDAD	TOTAL POPULATION POPULATION TOTALE POBLACION TOTAL	HIGHEST LEVEL ATTAINED / NIVEAU D'INSTRUCTION ATTEINT / NIVEL DE INSTRUCCION ALCANZADO: NO SCHOOLING SANS SCOLARITE SIN ESCOLARIDAD	FIRST LEVEL / PREMIER DEGRE / PRIMER GRADO: INCOMPLETED NON COMPLETE INCOMPLETO	FIRST LEVEL / PREMIER DEGRE / PRIMER GRADO: COMPLETED COMPLETE COMPLETO	ENTERED SECOND LEVEL / ACCEDE AU SECOND DEGRE / ACCEDIERON AL SEGUNDO GRADO: S–1	ENTERED SECOND LEVEL / ACCEDE AU SECOND DEGRE / ACCEDIERON AL SEGUNDO GRADO: S–2	POST-SECONDARY POST-SECONDAIRE POST-SECUNDARIA
				(1)	(2)	(3)	(4)	(5)	(6)	(7)
TRINIDAD AND TOBAGO										
	1980	MF	25+	408 215	1.3	29.4	42.6	19.7	4.0	2.9
		F	25+	201 148	1.3	29.9	42.4	20.4	4.1	1.9
TURKS AND CAICOS ISLANDS										
	1980	MF	25+	2 859	0.9	74.6	——>	16.9	——>	7.7
		F	25+	1 545	1.0	77.5	——>	16.4	——>	5.1
UNITED STATES										
	1981	MF	25+	132 899 000	3.3	——>	64.6	——>	——>	32.2
		F	25+	70 390 000	3.1	——>	68.8	——>	——>	28.0
U.S. VIRGIN ISLANDS‡										
TOTAL POPULATION	1970	MF	25+	28 891	1.6	7.0	73.8	——>	——>	17.6
		F	25+	14 449	1.6	6.6	75.8	——>	——>	16.0
URBAN POPULATION		MF	25+	7 308	1.3	6.1	82.5	——>	——>	10.2
		F	25+	3 834	1.4	5.7	82.9	——>	——>	10.0
RURAL POPULATION		MF	25+	21 583	1.7	7.3	70.9	——>	——>	20.1
		F	25+	10 615	1.7	6.9	73.2	——>	——>	18.1
AMERICA, SOUTH										
ARGENTINA										
	1980	MF	25+	14 913 575	7.1	33.4	33.0	20.4	——>	6.1
		F	25+	7 711 356	6.7	32.1	35.2	20.1	——>	5.8
BOLIVIA										
TOTAL POPULATION	1976	MF	25+	1 759 432	48.6	28.5	——>	10.8	7.1	5.0
		F	25+	918 709	62.2	20.7	——>	8.2	5.6	3.3
URBAN POPULATION		MF	25+	690 374	23.2	30.6	——>	19.7	15.6	10.9
		F	25+	368 977	34.3	28.6	——>	17.0	13.0	7.2
RURAL POPULATION		MF	25+	1 069 058	65.0	27.2	——>	5.1	1.5	1.3
		F	25+	549 732	80.8	15.4	——>	2.3	0.7	0.7
BRAZIL‡										
TOTAL POPULATION	1980	MF	25+	48 310 722	32.9	50.4	4.9	6.9	——>	5.0
		F	25+	24 576 023	35.2	48.8	4.6	7.2	——>	4.1
URBAN POPULATION		MF	25+	34 355 258	22.8	54.7	6.5	9.2	——>	6.8
		F	25+	17 928 564	25.9	53.1	6.0	9.4	——>	5.6
RURAL POPULATION		MF	25+	13 955 463	57.7	40.0	0.9	1.0	——>	0.4
		F	25+	6 647 459	60.5	37.3	0.9	1.1	——>	0.3
CHILE										
TOTAL POPULATION	1970	‡‡	25+	3 721 125	12.4	57.2	——>	26.6	——>	3.8
		F	25+	1 945 921	13.3	57.7	——>	26.5	——>	2.5
URBAN POPULATION		MF	25+	2 712 020	8.3	34.1	26.0	27.0	——>	4.8
RURAL POPULATION		MF	25+	792 400	29.8	54.2	10.0	5.4	——>	0.6
COLOMBIA										
	1973	MF	20+	8 478 100	22.4	55.9	——>	18.4	——>	3.3
		F	20+	4 483 086	23.7	56.0	——>	18.5	——>	1.8
		MF	20+	5 593 002	14.2	54.8	——>	26.1	——>	4.9
		F	20+	3 108 408	16.1	56.2	——>	25.1	——>	2.6
		MF	20+	2 885 098	38.4	58.0	——>	3.5	——>	0.2
		F	20+	1 374 677	40.8	55.6	——>	3.5	——>	0.1
ECUADOR										
	1982	MF	25+	2 887 330	25.4	17.0	34.1	8.1	7.9	7.6
		F	25+	1 457 435	29.6	16.8	31.1	8.3	8.7	5.6
FRENCH GUIANA										
	1982	MF	25+	34 145	20.8	40.5	——>	32.4	——>	6.4
GUYANA										
	1980	MF	25+	270 849	8.1	72.9	——>	17.3	——>	1.8
		F	25+	138 083	10.6	73.0	——>	15.5	——>	0.9
PARAGUAY‡										
TOTAL POPULATION	1972	MF	25+	842 223	19.6	57.7	10.3	5.9	4.6	2.0
		F	25+	438 419	25.4	53.8	10.6	5.1	4.0	1.2
URBAN POPULATION		MF	25+	346 870	11.3	46.8	16.5	11.0	9.8	4.6
		F	25+	192 086	15.4	47.0	17.5	9.5	8.0	2.5
RURAL POPULATION		MF	25+	495 353	25.5	65.3	5.9	2.2	0.9	0.2
		F	25+	246 333	33.2	59.1	5.1	1.6	0.8	0.1
PERU‡										
	1981	MF	25+	6 526 328	24.0	27.3	17.2	10.7	10.7	10.1
		F	25+	3 308 370	34.2	24.4	15.5	8.6	9.7	7.7

COUNTRY / PAYS / PAIS	YEAR SEX / ANNEE SEXE / AÑO SEXO		AGE GROUP / GROUPE D'AGE / GRUPO DE EDAD	TOTAL POPULATION / POPULATION TOTALE / POBLACION TOTAL	HIGHEST LEVEL ATTAINED / NIVEAU D'INSTRUCTION ATTEINT / NIVEL DE INSTRUCCION ALCANZADO					
					NO SCHOOLING / SANS SCOLARITE / SIN ESCOLARIDAD	FIRST LEVEL / PREMIER DEGRE / PRIMER GRADO		ENTERED SECOND LEVEL / ACCEDE AU SECOND DEGRE / ACCEDIERON AL SEGUNDO GRADO		POST-SECONDARY / POST-SECONDAIRE / POST-SECUNDARIA
						INCOMPLETED / NON COMPLETE / INCOMPLETO	COMPLETED / COMPLETE / COMPLETO	S-1	S-2	
				(1)	(2)	(3)	(4)	(5)	(6)	(7)
URUGUAY										
	1975	MF	25+	1 590 200	9.9	36.7	29.6	17.4	—>	6.3
		F	25+	824 700	10.4	34.9	31.2	16.6	—>	6.8
VENEZUELA										
	1981	MF	25+	5 542 852	23.5	47.2	—>	22.3	—>	7.0
		F	25+	2 802 602	26.4	46.2	—>	21.9	—>	5.5
ASIA										
AFGHANISTAN										
TOTAL POPULATION	1979	MF	25+	4 891 473	89.0	6.5	0.3	1.1	—>	3.0
		F	25+	2 405 187	97.6	1.4	0.1	0.3	—>	0.6
URBAN POPULATION		MF	25+	717 983	72.1	12.0	1.1	3.5	—>	11.4
		F	25+	335 968	88.2	5.7	0.8	1.6	—>	3.7
RURAL POPULATION		MF	25+	4 173 490	92.0	5.5	0.2	0.7	—>	1.6
		F	25+	2 069 219	99.2	0.7	0.0	0.0	—>	0.0
BAHRAIN										
	1971	MF	25+	81 520	77.4	5.5	4.2	9.2	—>	3.8
		F	25+	34 633	86.2	3.6	2.4	5.6	—>	2.2
BANGLADESH										
	1974	MF	25+	24 896 064	82.3	10.0	—>	6.9	—>	0.9
		F	25+	12 053 928	93.0	5.4	—>	1.4	—>	0.1
BRUNEI DARUSSALAM										
	1981	MF	25+	75 283	32.1	28.3	—>	30.1	—>	9.4
		F	25+	33 701	45.8	21.7	—>	25.6	—>	6.9
BURMA										
	1973	MF	25+	11 118 272	78.3	12.4	—>	7.0	2.1	0.2
		F	25+	5 559 102	82.0	12.9	—>	4.0	1.1	0.0
CHINA‡										
	1982	MF	25+	466 915 380	44.5	—>	32.7	16.1	5.6	1.0
		F	25+	227 191 450	62.3	—>	23.6	9.9	3.7	0.5
CYPRUS										
	1976	MF	10+	...	0.7	54.9	—>	36.7	—>	7.7
		F	10+	...	0.7	59.0	—>	34.0	—>	6.3
HONG KONG‡										
	1981	MF	25+	2 601 296	22.5	16.7	23.1	13.2	17.3	7.1
		F	25+	1 239 697	35.9	15.3	19.5	9.9	14.4	5.0
INDIA										
	1981	MF	25+	280 599 720	72.5	11.3	—>	13.7	—>	2.5
		F	25+	135 517 843	85.2	7.2	—>	6.6	—>	1.1
INDONESIA										
TOTAL POPULATION	1980	MF	25+	58 441 240	41.1	31.6	16.8	4.7	4.9	0.8
		F	25+	29 764 530	53.9	26.6	12.9	3.3	3.0	0.4
URBAN POPULATION		MF	25+	12 518 959	21.9	26.0	23.1	12.1	14.1	2.9
		F	25+	6 288 212	34.8	24.2	20.3	9.8	9.5	1.4
RURAL POPULATION		MF	25+	45 922 281	45.9	33.6	15.1	2.7	2.5	0.2
		F	25+	23 476 318	59.0	27.3	10.8	1.5	1.3	0.1
ISRAEL										
TOTAL POPULATION	1982	MF	25+	2 003 500	9.7	30.6	—>	36.6	—>	23.1
		F	25+	1 030 200	14.1	30.2	—>	34.8	—>	20.9
JEWISH POPULATION		MF	25+	1 785 400	7.4	28.3	—>	39.2	—>	25.1
		F	25+	918 500	10.5	28.8	—>	37.7	—>	23.0
NON JEWISH POP.		MF	25+	218 100	28.1	49.0	—>	15.6	—>	7.2
		F	25+	111 700	43.5	41.1	—>	11.2	—>	4.2
JAPAN										
TOTAL POPULATION	1980	MF	25+	73 368 684	0.4	—>	45.3	—>	39.7	14.3
		F	25+	38 110 839	0.6	—>	47.6	—>	42.1	9.5
URBAN POPULATION		MF	25+	55 235 050	0.3	—>	40.3	—>	42.5	16.5
		F	25+	28 596 309	0.4	—>	42.5	—>	45.8	11.0
RURAL POPULATION		MF	25+	18 133 634	0.7	—>	60.6	—>	31.0	7.6
		F	25+	9 514 530	0.9	—>	62.9	—>	30.9	5.1
KOREA, REPUBLIC OF										
	1980	MF	25+	16 457 362	19.7	34.5	—>	18.2	18.7	8.9
		F	25+	8 503 065	26.9	39.4	—>	16.7	12.9	4.0

COUNTRY / PAYS / PAIS	YEAR / ANNEE / AÑO	SEX / SEXE / SEXO	AGE GROUP / GROUPE D'AGE / GRUPO DE EDAD	TOTAL POPULATION / POPULATION TOTALE / POBLACION TOTAL	HIGHEST LEVEL ATTAINED / NIVEAU D'INSTRUCTION ATTEINT / NIVEL DE INSTRUCCION ALCANZADO: NO SCHOOLING / SANS SCOLARITE / SIN ESCOLARIDAD	FIRST LEVEL / PREMIER DEGRE / PRIMER GRADO: INCOMPLETED / NON COMPLETE / INCOMPLETO	FIRST LEVEL / PREMIER DEGRE / PRIMER GRADO: COMPLETED / COMPLETE / COMPLETO	ENTERED SECOND LEVEL / ACCEDE AU SECOND DEGRE / ACCEDIERON AL SEGUNDO GRADO: S-1	ENTERED SECOND LEVEL / ACCEDE AU SECOND DEGRE / ACCEDIERON AL SEGUNDO GRADO: S-2	POST-SECONDARY / POST-SECONDAIRE / POST-SECUNDARIA
				(1)	(2)	(3)	(4)	(5)	(6)	(7)
KUWAIT										
TOTAL POPULATION	1980	MF	25+	568 086	58.0	7.6	——>	9.6	14.8	10.1
		F	25+	205 573	62.7	6.4	——>	8.7	14.7	7.4
KUWAITI POPULATION		MF	25+	176 011	69.5	7.8	——>	9.5	9.0	4.2
		F	25+	89 718	80.0	4.5	——>	6.1	6.6	2.8
NON KUWAITI POP.		MF	25+	392 075	52.8	7.5	——>	9.6	17.4	12.7
		F	25+	115 855	49.3	7.9	——>	10.7	21.0	11.0
LEBANON										
TOTAL POPULATION	1970	MF	25+	836 060	45.6	28.5	10.8	7.1	4.9	3.1
		F	25+	412 010	59.5	18.8	9.9	6.9	3.8	1.1
URBAN POPULATION		MF	25+	504 485	38.5	26.6	13.9	9.6	6.9	4.6
		F	25+	245 450	50.6	19.0	13.0	9.9	5.7	1.8
RURAL POPULATION		MF	25+	331 575	56.5	31.4	6.1	3.2	2.0	0.8
		F	25+	166 650	72.7	18.4	5.4	2.4	0.8	0.2
MACAU‡										
	1970	MF	25+	93 557	26.9	58.0	——>	13.7	——>	1.4
		F	25+	47 800	33.7	55.3	——>	10.2	——>	0.9
MALAYSIA										
TOTAL POPULATION	1970	MF	A	10 319 324	43.4	30.0	12.6	8.8	5.1	——>
		F	A	5 120 906	51.0	27.6	10.6	7.1	3.7	——>
URBAN POPULATION		MF	A	2 780 254	32.5	29.7	12.8	14.1	10.9	——>
		F	A	1 378 254	39.5	28.5	11.6	12.0	8.3	——>
RURAL POPULATION		MF	A	7 539 070	47.5	30.1	12.5	6.9	3.0	——>
		F	A	3 742 652	55.3	27.2	10.3	5.2	2.0	——>
NEPAL										
TOTAL POPULATION	1981	MF	25+	1 012 465	41.2	29.4	——>	22.7	——>	6.8
		F	25+	197 209	36.8	42.1	——>	16.4	——>	4.7
URBAN POPULATION		MF	25+	156 646	26.9	19.0	——>	33.0	——>	21.2
		F	25+	43 738	28.5	25.0	——>	31.5	——>	14.9
RURAL POPULATION		MF	25+	855 819	43.8	31.3	——>	20.8	——>	4.1
		F	25+	153 471	39.2	46.9	——>	12.1	——>	1.8
PAKISTAN‡										
TOTAL POPULATION	1981	MF	25+	30 707 279	78.9	8.7	——>	10.5	——>	1.9
		F	25+	14 400 805	90.4	4.7	——>	4.2	——>	0.7
URBAN POPULATION		MF	25+	8 709 327	59.5	12.9	——>	22.1	——>	5.4
		F	25+	3 901 096	73.9	10.8	——>	12.8	——>	2.6
RURAL POPULATION		MF	25+	21 997 952	86.8	6.9	——>	5.9	——>	0.5
		F	25+	10 499 709	96.5	2.4	——>	1.0	——>	0.1
PHILIPPINES										
	1980	MF	25+	17 865 290	11.7	31.3	22.8	18.9	——>	15.2
		F	25+	8 980 215	13.3	31.4	23.7	16.6	——>	15.1
QATAR‡										
	1981	MF	10+	188 940	48.9	15.0	——>	11.7	12.8	11.6
		F	10+	61 732	49.1	15.9	——>	11.7	13.6	9.7
SINGAPORE										
	1980	MF	25+	1 176 282	43.7	38.3	——>	9.6	5.0	3.4
		F	25+	583 726	54.3	31.2	——>	8.7	3.8	2.0
SRI LANKA										
		MF	30+	5 146 092	17.8	50.5	——>	14.9	14.5	2.3
		F	30+	2 477 507	26.0	45.9	——>	13.0	13.3	1.9
SYRIAN ARAB REPUBLIC										
	1970	MF	25+	2 061 729	68.6	25.9	——>	4.3	——>	1.3
		F	25+	1 028 918	87.5	10.2	——>	2.0	——>	0.4
THAILAND										
	1980	MF	25+	17 491 470	20.5	67.3	2.4	4.5	2.3	2.9
		F	25+	9 000 623	26.3	65.4	1.6	2.6	1.7	2.4
TURKEY										
	1980	MF	25+	18 277 340	52.4	35.3	——>	8.7	——>	3.6
		F	25+	9 207 179	68.3	24.5	——>	5.7	——>	1.5
UNITED ARAB EMIRATES‡										
	1975	MF	25+	285 947	72.2	5.2	——>	16.7	——>	6.0
		F	25+	65 743	79.3	2.5	——>	14.1	——>	4.1

COUNTRY / PAYS / PAIS	YEAR / ANNEE / AÑO	SEX / SEXE / SEXO	AGE GROUP / GROUPE D'AGE / GRUPO DE EDAD	TOTAL POPULATION / POPULATION TOTALE / POBLACION TOTAL	NO SCHOOLING / SANS SCOLARITE / SIN ESCOLARIDAD	FIRST LEVEL / PREMIER DEGRE / PRIMER GRADO: INCOMPLETED / NON COMPLETE / INCOMPLETO	FIRST LEVEL / PREMIER DEGRE / PRIMER GRADO: COMPLETED / COMPLETE / COMPLETO	ENTERED SECOND LEVEL / ACCEDE AU SECOND DEGRE / ACCEDIERON AL SEGUNDO GRADO: S-1	ENTERED SECOND LEVEL / ACCEDE AU SECOND DEGRE / ACCEDIERON AL SEGUNDO GRADO: S-2	POST-SECONDARY / POST-SECONDAIRE / POST-SECUNDARIA
				(1)	(2)	(3)	(4)	(5)	(6)	(7)
					HIGHEST LEVEL ATTAINED / NIVEAU D'INSTRUCTION ATTEINT / NIVEL DE INSTRUCCION ALCANZADO					
EUROPE										
AUSTRIA										
	1981	MF	25+	4 558 681	.	49.3	→	→	47.5	3.3
		F	25+	2 508 936	.	61.9	→	→	36.6	1.6
BELGIUM										
	1977	MF	14+	6 995 797	79.1	→	→	→	13.4	7.5
		F	14+	3 630 767	82.9	→	→	→	11.9	5.3
CZECHOSLOVAKIA										
	1980	MF	25+	9 274 694	0.4	47.6	→	45.9	→	6.0
		F	25+	4 899 960	0.5	58.3	→	37.2	→	4.0
FINLAND‡										
	1980	MF	20+	3 442 000	*1.2	50.0	→	7.7	29.2	11.9
		F	20+	1 815 000	*1.0	51.2	→	8.9	28.5	10.4
GERMAN DEMOCRATIC REPUBLIC										
	1981	MF	25+	10 714 841	–	30.1	→	52.6	→	17.3
		F	25+	5 935 267	–	42.0	→	43.9	→	14.1
GREECE										
	1981	MF	25+	5 966 511	11.5	16.9	44.3	6.1	13.6	7.6
		F	25+	3 113 632	17.7	18.4	41.7	4.2	13.1	4.9
HUNGARY										
	1980	MF	25+	6 903 881	1.3	8.0	3.2	57.0	23.6	7.0
		F	25+	3 670 474	1.7	8.7	3.4	61.5	19.6	5.0
IRELAND										
	1971	MF	25+	1 562 091	67.9	→	→	27.4	→	4.6
		F	25+	790 413	65.8	→	→	30.6	→	3.6
ITALY‡										
	1971	MF	25+	32 965 274	7.3	23.7	48.9	17.5	→	2.6
		F	25+	17 310 402	8.8	27.3	47.5	14.9	→	1.5
LIECHTENSTEIN										
	1970	MF	25+	11 483	0.3	80.2	→	14.1	→	5.4
		F	25+	5 814	0.4	82.6	→	16.2	→	0.8
NETHERLANDS‡										
	1971	MF	25+	5 679 695	–	47.0	→	36.7	9.1	7.2
		F	25+	2 851 945	–	52.5	→	34.0	8.7	4.8
NORWAY‡										
	1980	MF	25+	2 574 641	1.8	0.0	→	60.0	26.2	11.9
		F	25+	1 324 409	1.6	0.0	→	65.7	23.8	8.8
POLAND										
TOTAL POPULATION	1978	MF	25+	20 271 991	2.8	12.7	44.9	33.9	→	5.7
		F	25+	10 752 794	3.7	14.8	47.5	29.6	→	4.4
URBAN POPULATION		MF	25+	11 922 514	1.5	5.8	39.2	44.7	→	8.8
		F	25+	6 419 326	2.2	7.3	43.8	40.0	→	6.7
RURAL POPULATION		MF	25+	8 349 477	4.5	22.6	53.1	18.6	→	1.2
		F	25+	4 333 468	6.1	25.8	52.9	14.3	→	0.9
PORTUGAL										
	1970	MF	25+	4 800 335	44.2	17.3	30.0	6.8	→	1.6
		F	25+	2 710 085	52.4	18.4	23.2	5.1	→	0.9
ROMANIA										
	1977	MF	25+	12 622 808	55.6	→	→	39.8	→	4.6
SAN MARINO										
	1976	MF	15+	14 473	4.6	64.3	→	28.7	→	2.4
		F	15+	7 263	5.4	66.0	→	26.8	→	1.9
SPAIN‡										
TOTAL POPULATION	1981	MF	25+	21 758 499	35.1	11.8	32.7	7.6	5.7	7.1
		F	25+	11 411 664	38.9	11.8	32.5	7.2	4.1	5.5
URBAN POPULATION		MF	25+	17 054 758	33.7	11.1	31.4	8.9	6.7	8.2
		F	25+	9 023 931	37.6	11.2	31.7	8.5	4.8	6.2
RURAL POPULATION		MF	25+	4 703 741	40.6	14.3	37.3	2.7	2.0	3.1
		F	25+	2 387 733	44.1	14.0	35.7	2.4	1.4	2.5
SWEDEN										
	1979	MF	25–74	4 998 000	41.6	→	→	7.3	35.7	15.4
		F	25–74	2 540 000	43.6	→	→	8.1	34.2	14.1

COUNTRY / PAYS / PAIS	YEAR / ANNEE / AÑO	SEX / SEXE / SEXO	AGE GROUP / GROUPE D'AGE / GRUPO DE EDAD	TOTAL POPULATION / POPULATION TOTALE / POBLACION TOTAL	HIGHEST LEVEL ATTAINED / NIVEAU D'INSTRUCTION ATTEINT / NIVEL DE INSTRUCCION ALCANZADO					
					NO SCHOOLING / SANS SCOLARITE / SIN ESCOLARIDAD	FIRST LEVEL / PREMIER DEGRE / PRIMER GRADO		ENTERED SECOND LEVEL / ACCEDE AU SECOND DEGRE / ACCEDIERON AL SEGUNDO GRADO		POST-SECONDARY / POST-SECONDAIRE / POST-SECUNDARIA
						INCOMPLETED / NON COMPLETE / INCOMPLETO	COMPLETED / COMPLETE / COMPLETO	S-1	S-2	
				(1)	(2)	(3)	(4)	(5)	(6)	(7)
SWITZERLAND‡										
	1970	MF	25+	3 196 376	5.1	73.8	→	→	21.2	→
		F	25+	1 730 620	5.6	75.2	→	→	19.3	→
UNITED KINGDOM‡										
	1976	MF	25-69	...	89.0	→	→	→	→	11.0
		F	20-69	...	92.0	→	→	→	→	8.0
YUGOSLAVIA										
	1981	MF	25+	13 083 762	15.8	53.9	→	23.4	→	6.8
		F	25+	6 786 385	23.3	56.1	→	15.8	→	4.8
OCEANIA										
AMERICAN SAMOA										
	1974	MF	25+	10 157	..	16.0	15.6	32.3	23.5	12.6
		F	25+	4 943	..	17.3	17.7	34.0	21.8	9.3
AUSTRALIA										
	1971	MF	25+	6 878 445	0.9	29.3	→	48.3	→	21.5
		F	25+	3 472 417	0.9	30.1	→	59.0	→	10.0
COOK ISLANDS										
	1971	MF	25+	7 702	3.9	28.4	54.4	11.2	→	2.1
		F	25+	3 627	4.3	27.6	58.4	9.0	→	0.7
FIJI										
	1976	MF	25+	213 707	19.7	45.8	20.5	6.7	3.9	3.3
		F	25+	105 689	27.0	45.4	17.1	5.6	2.4	2.5
GUAM										
	1980	MF	25+	46 906	1.5	16.5	3.3	44.4	→	34.4
		F	25+	22 366	2.1	19.4	3.5	44.2	→	30.8
NEW CALEDONIA‡										
	1976	MF	14+	76 774	9.4	75.6	→	13.1	→	2.0
		F	14+	36 291	10.5	75.9	→	12.2	→	1.4
NEW ZEALAND										
TOTAL POPULATION	1981	MF	25+	1 720 383	1.2	41.5	→	→	26.6	30.6
		F	25+	884 310	1.2	42.3	→	→	28.9	27.6
URBAN POPULATION		MF	25+	1 450 758	1.2	41.3	→	→	26.0	31.5
		F	25+	757 791	1.3	42.8	→	→	28.3	27.6
RURAL POPULATION		MF	25+	269 625	1.0	42.8	→	→	30.1	26.1
		F	25+	126 519	0.9	39.1	→	→	32.3	27.7
NIUE										
	1976	MF	25+	1 337	–	53.5	5.8	23.6	15.2	1.9
		F	25+	734	–	57.5	5.4	24.0	12.5	0.5
PACIFIC ISLANDS‡										
	1970	MF	25+	32 155	34.1	20.7	25.3	6.8	6.6	6.4
		F	25+	15 374	38.5	25.2	24.4	4.5	4.2	3.2
PAPUA NEW GUINEA										
	1980	MF	25+	1 135 783	82.6	8.2	5.0	3.9	0.3	→
		F	25+	551 886	87.3	7.2	3.6	1.8	0.0	→
SAMOA										
	1976	MF	25+	47 031	60.0	→	→	31.5	6.3	2.2
		F	25+	23 665	62.1	→	→	31.1	5.5	1.3
SOLOMON ISLANDS										
	1976	MF	25+	68 102	55.5	39.5	→	3.3	→	1.6
		F	25+	31 714	64.8	32.6	→	1.7	→	1.0
VANUATU										
	1979	MF	25+	38 488	37.2	34.3	6.5	14.7	7.3	→
		F	25+	17 612	43.5	33.7	5.8	11.8	5.2	→
U.S.S.R.										
U.S.S.R.										
TOTAL POPULATION	1979	MF	10+	...	36.2	→	→	44.8	10.7	8.3
		F	10+	...	40.3	→	→	40.6	11.5	7.6
URBAN POPULATION		MF	10+	...	27.6	→	→	47.6	13.3	11.4
		F	10+	...	30.7	→	→	44.3	14.5	10.5
RURAL POPULATION		MF	10+	...	50.8	→	→	39.9	6.3	3.0
		F	10+	...	56.4	→	→	34.4	6.6	2.6

COUNTRY / PAYS / PAIS	YEAR SEX / ANNEE SEXE / AÑO SEXO	AGE GROUP / GROUPE D'AGE / GRUPO DE EDAD	TOTAL POPULATION / POPULATION TOTALE / POBLACION TOTAL	HIGHEST LEVEL ATTAINED / NIVEAU D'INSTRUCTION ATTEINT / NIVEL DE INSTRUCCION ALCANZADO					
				NO SCHOOLING / SANS SCOLARITE / SIN ESCOLARIDAD	FIRST LEVEL / PREMIER DEGRE / PRIMER GRADO		ENTERED SECOND LEVEL / ACCEDE AU SECOND DEGRE / ACCEDIERON AL SEGUNDO GRADO		POST-SECONDARY / POST-SECONDAIRE / POST-SECUNDARIA
					INCOMPLETED / NON COMPLETE / INCOMPLETO	COMPLETED / COMPLETE / COMPLETO	S-1	S-2	
			(1)	(2)	(3)	(4)	(5)	(6)	(7)
BYELORUSSIAN S.S.R.									
TOTAL POPULATION	1979 MF	10+	...	40.6	--->	--->	41.5	10.2	7.7
	F	10+	...	45.1	--->	--->	36.8	11.1	7.0
URBAN POPULATION	MF	10+	...	24.0	--->	--->	49.9	14.2	12.0
	F	10+	...	26.4	--->	--->	46.9	15.6	11.1
RURAL POPULATION	MF	10+	...	60.2	--->	--->	31.7	5.5	2.6
	F	10+	...	66.6	--->	--->	25.1	5.8	2.5
UKRAINIAN S.S.R.									
	1970 MF	20+	31 482 631	48.8	--->	--->	44.7	--->	6.5
	F	20+	18 157 359	54.5	--->	--->	40.2		5.3

AFRICA:

Egypt:

E--> Second level also includes third level education not leading to a university degree.

FR-> Le second degré inclut aussi l'enseignement du troisième degré ne conduisant pas à un grade universitaire.

ESP> El segundo grado incluye también la enseñanza de tercer grado no conducente a un título universitario.

Guinea-Bissau:

E--> The category *completed first level* comprises the last two years of education at the first level.

FR-> La catégorie *premier degré complété* comprend les deux dernières années de l'enseignement du premier degré.

ESP> La categoría *primer grado completo* comprende los dos últimos años de la enseñanza de primer grado.

Kenya:

E--> Those persons who did not state their level of education have been included in the category *no schooling.*

FR-> La catégorie *sans scolarité* comprend les personnes dont le niveau d'instruction est inconnu.

ESP> Las personas cuyo nivel de instrucción se desconoce figuran en la categoría *sin escolaridad.*

Libyan Arab Jamahiriya:

E--> Illiteracy data have been used for the category *no schooling.*

FR-> Les données relatives à l'analphabétisme ont été utilisées pour les personnes *sans scolarité.*

ESP> Se han utilizado los datos relativos al analfabetismo con respecto a las personas *sin escolaridad.*

Mali:

E--> The category *completed first level* comprises the last two years of education at the first level.

FR-> La catégorie *premier degré complété* comprend les deux dernières années de l'enseignement du premier degré.

ESP> La categoría *primer grado completo* comprende los dos últimos años de la enseñanza de primer grado.

Mozambique:

E--> Illiteracy data have been used for the category *no schooling.* The category *completed first level* comprises the last two years of education at the first level.

FR-> Les données relatives à l'analphabétisme ont été utilisées pour les personnes *sans scolarité.* La catégorie *premier degré complété* comprend les deux dernières années de l'enseignement du premier degré.

ESP> Se han utilizado los datos relativos al analfabetismo con respecto a las personas *sin escolaridad.* La categoría *primer grado completo* comprende los dos últimos años de la enseñanza de primer grado.

Rwanda:

E--> Those persons who did not state their level of education have been included in the category *no schooling.*

FR-> La catégorie *sans scolarité* comprend les personnes dont le niveau d'instruction est inconnu.

ESP> Las personas cuyo nivel de instrucción se desconoce figuran en la categoría *sin escolaridad.*

Sao Tome and Principe:

E--> Illiteracy data have been used for the category *no schooling.*

FR-> Les données relatives à l'analphabétisme ont été utilisées pour les personnes *sans scolarité.*

ESP> Se han utilizado los datos relativos al analfabetismo con respecto a las personas *sin escolaridad.*

South Africa:

E--> Those persons who did not state their level of education have been included in the category *no schooling.*

South Africa: (Cont):

FR-> La catégorie *sans scolarité* comprend les personnes dont le niveau d'instruction est inconnu.

ESP> Las personas cuyo nivel de instrucción se desconoce figuran en la categoría *sin escolaridad.*

Swaziland:

E--> The category *completed first level* comprises the last two years of education at the first level.

FR-> La catégorie *premier degré complété* comprend les deux dernières années de l'enseignement du premier degré.

ESP> La categoría *primer grado completo* comprende los dos últimos años de la enseñanza de primer grado.

AMERICA, NORTH:

Antigua and Barbuda:

E--> *De jure* population.
FR-> Population de droit.
ESP> Población *de jure.*

Costa Rica:

E--> *De jure* population.
FR-> Population de droit.
ESP> Población *de jure.*

El Salvador:

E--> Illiteracy data have been used for the category *no schooling.*

FR-> Les données relatives à l'analphabétisme ont été utilisées pour les personnes *sans scolarité.*

ESP> Se han utilizado los datos relativos al analfabetismo con respecto a las personas *sin escolaridad.*

Guatemala:

E--> *De jure* population.
FR-> Population de droit.
ESP> Población *de jure.*

Honduras:

E--> Based on a sample survey referring to 51,372 persons.

FR-> D'après une enquête par sondage portant sur 51 372 personnes.

ESP> Según un encuestra por muestro representa a 51 372 personas.

Mexico:

E--> Illiteracy data have been used for the category *no schooling.*

FR-> Les données relatives à l'analphabétisme ont été utilisées pour les personnes *sans scolarité.*

ESP> Se han utilizado los datos relativos al analfabetismo con respecto a las personas *sin escolaridad.*

Netherlands Antilles:

E--> *De jure* population. Those persons who did not state their level of education, have been included in the category *no schooling.*

FR-> Population de droit. Les personnes dont le niveau d'instruction est inconnu sont incluses dans la catégorie *sans scolarité.*

ESP> Población *de jure.* Las personas cuyo nivel de instrucción se desconoce figuran en la categoría *sin escolaridad.*

Panama (Former Canal Zone):

E--> *De jure* population, including armed forces stationed in the area.

FR-> Population de droit, y compris les militaires en garnison sur le territoire.

ESP> Población *de jure,* incluidos los militares destacados en la zona.

Puerto Rico:

E--> *De jure* population, including armed forces stationed in the

Puerto Rico: (Cont):
area.
FR-> Population de droit, y compris les militaires en garnison sur le territoire.
ESP> Población *de jure*, incluidos los militares destacados en la zona.
U. S. Virgin Islands:
E--> *De jure* population, including armed forces stationed in the area.
FR-> Population de droit, y compris les militaires en garnison sur le territoire.
ESP> Población *de jure*, incluidos los militares destacados en la zona.
AMERICA, SOUTH:
Brazil:
E--> *De jure* population.
FR-> Population de droit.
ESP> Población *de jure*. Paraguay:
E--> Those persons who did not state their level of education have been included in the category *no schooling*.
FR-> Les personnes dont la niveau d'instruction est inconnu sont incluses dans la catégorie *sans scolarité*.
ESP> Las personas cuyo nivel de instrucción se desconoce figuran en la categoría *sin escolaridad*.
Peru:
E--> Those persons who did not state their level of education have been included in the category *no schooling*.
FR-> Les personnes dont le niveau d'instruction est inconnu sont incluses dans la catégorie *sans scolarité*.
ESP> Las personas cuyo nivel de instrucción se desconoce figuran en la categoría *sin escolaridad*.
ASIA:
China:
E--> Data are based on a 10% sample of census returns.
FR-> Les données ont été établies d'après un échantillonnage portant sur 10% des bulletins de recensement.
ESP> Los datos se han establecidos según un muestreo referente al 10% de los boletinos de censo.
Hong Kong:
E--> The category *completed first level* comprises the last two years of education at the first level.
FR-> La catégorie *premier degré complété* comprend les deux dernières années de l'enseignement du premier degré.
ESP> La categoría *primer grado completo* comprende los dos últimos años de la enseñanza de primer grado.
Macau:
E--> Illiteracy data have been used for the category *no schooling*.
FR-> Les données relatives à l'analphabétisme ont été utilisées pour les personnes *sans scolarité*.
ESP> Se han utilizado los datos relativos al analfabetismo con respecto a las personas *sin escolaridad*.
Pakistan:
E--> The category *no schooling* comprises illiterates and those persons who did not state their level of education.
FR-> La catégorie *sans scolarité* comprend les analphabètes et les personnes dont le niveau d'instruction est inconnu.
ESP> La categoría *sin escolaridad* comprende los analfabetos y las personas cuyo nivel de instrucción se desconoce.
Qatar:
E--> Illiteracy data have been used for the category *no schooling*.
FR-> Les données relatives à l'analphabétisme ont été utilisées pour les personnes *sans scolarité*.
ESP> Se han utilizado los datos relativos al analfabetismo con respecto a las personas *sin escolaridad*.
United Arab Emirates:
E--> The category *no schooling* comprises illiterates and those

United Arab Emirates: (Cont):
persons who did not state their level of education.
FR-> La catégorie *sans scolarité* comprend les analphabètes et les personnes dont le niveau d'instruction est inconnu.
ESP> La categoría *sin escolaridad* comprende los analfabetos y las personas cuyo nivel de instrucción se desconoce.
EUROPE:
Finland:
E--> Data on education at the second and third levels refer to highest level completed.
FR-> Les données relatives aux enseignements du second et du troisième degré se réfèrent au niveau d'instruction complété.
ESP> Los datos relativos a las enseñanzas del segundo grado y tercer grado se refieren al nivel de instrucción completo.
Italy:
E--> *De jure* population. Illiteracy data have been used for the category *no schooling*.
FR-> Population de droit. Les données relatives à l'analphabétisme ont été utilisées pour les personnes *sans scolarité*.
ESP> Población *de jure*. Se han utilizado los datos relativos al analfabetismo con respecto a las personas *sin escolaridad*.
Netherlands:
E--> Not including persons for which the level of education is unknown.
FR-> Non compris les personnes dont le niveau d'instruction est inconnu.
ESP> Excluidas las personas cuyo nivel de instrucción se desconoce.
Norway:
E--> Those persons who did not state their level of education have been included in the category *no schooling*.
FR-> La catégorie *sans scolarité* comprend les personnes dont le niveau d'instruction est inconnu.
ESP> Las personas cuyo nivel de instrucción se desconoce figuran en la categoría *sin escolaridad*.
Spain:
E--> The category *no schooling* comprises illiterates and those persons who did not state their level of education.
FR-> La catégorie *sans scolarité* comprend les analphabètes et les personnes dont le niveau d'instruction est inconnu.
ESP> La categoría *sin escolaridad* comprende los analfabetos y las personas cuyo nivel de instrucción se desconoce.
Switzerland:
E--> Excluding population still in schools.
FR-> Non compris la population fréquentant les établissements scolaires.
ESP> Excluída la población en curso de escolarización. United Kingdom:
E--> Figures do not include data for Northern Ireland.
FR-> Les chiffres n'incluent pas les données relatives à l'Irlande du Nord.
ESP> Las cifras excluyen los datos relativos a Irlanda del Norte.
OCEANIA:
New Caledonia:
E--> Those persons who did not state their level of education have been included in the category *no schooling*.
FR-> La catégorie *sans scolarité* comprend les personnes dont le niveau d'instruction est inconnu.
ESP> Las personas cuyo nivel de instrucción se desconoce figuran en la categoría *sin escolaridad*.
Pacific Islands:
E--> *De jure* population, including armed forces stationed in the area.
FR-> Population de droit, y compris les militaires en garnison sur le territoire.
ESP> Población *de jure*, incluidos los militares destacados en la zona.

Education

Education

Educación

The following three chapters of the *Yearbook* assemble most of the basic statistical information collected and compiled by Unesco regarding public and private educational institutions at all levels. This collection of tables provides world-wide statistical data on such subjects as the number of schools; teachers and pupils by sex and by level and type of education; students and graduates in higher education by sex, field of study and level of programme; foreign students in higher education by country of origin and by host country; and public expenditure on education by purpose and by level of education. As far as possible, data refer to the school years beginning in 1975 and 1980, as well as the four most recent years.

For the purpose of these tables, the definitions and classifications set out in the revised Recommendation concerning the International Standardization of Educational Statistics, adopted by the General Conference of Unesco at its twentieth session (Paris, 1978), and those presented in the International Standard Classification of Education (ISCED) have been applied as far as possible. In accordance therewith education is classified by level as follows:

Education preceding the first level (ISCED level 0), which provides education for children who are not old enough to enter a school at the first level (e.g. at nursery school, kindergarten, infant school).

Education at the first level (ISCED level 1), of which the main function is to provide the basic elements of education (e.g. at elementary school, primary school).

Education at the second level (ISCED levels 2 and 3), based upon at least four years' previous instruction at first level, and providing general or specialized instruction, or both (e.g. at middle school, secondary school, high school, teacher-training school at this level, schools of a vocational or technical nature).

Education at the third level (ISCED levels 5, 6 and 7), which requires, as a minimum condition of admission, the successful completion of education at the second level, or evidence of the attainment of an equivalent level of knowledge (e.g. at university, teachers' college, higher professional school).

Special education, covering all types of education given to children who suffer from physical, mental, visual, social, hearing or speech handicaps, or from reading and writing difficulties.

The following definitions are reproduced from the Recommendation:

A pupil (student) is a person enrolled in a school for systematic instruction at any level of education.

A teacher is a person directly engaged in instructing a group of pupils (students). Heads of educational institutions, supervisory and other personnel should be counted as teachers only when they have regular teaching functions.

A school (educational institution) is a group of pupils (students) of one or more grades organized to receive instruction of a given type and level under one teacher, or under more than one teacher and with an immediate head.

(a) *A public school* is a school operated by a public authority (national, federal, state or provincial, or local), whatever the origin of its financial resources.

(b) *A private school* is a school not operated by a public authority, whether or not it receives financial support from such authorities. Private schools may be defined as aided or non-aided, respectively, according as they derive or do not derive financial support from public authorities.

The enrolment data throughout these tables refer, in general, to the beginning of the school or academic year. In this connection, it should be pointed out that enrolment data may vary substantially according to the date at which the count is taken, i.e. at the beginning, in the middle, at the end of the school year, an average count, etc. The years stated indicate the calendar year in which the school or academic year begins. It is important to keep in mind that only in some forty countries does the school year begin in January, i.e. actually coincides with calendar year. In the majority of countries and territories, the school year begins in one fiscal year and ends in the following year. Appendix B gives information on the dates of commencement and end of the school and fiscal year in each country and territory.

Les trois chapitres de l'*Annuaire* qui suivent contiennent la plupart des données statistiques de base recueillies et élaborées par l'Unesco au sujet des établissements d'enseignement, publics et privés, de tous les degrés. La série de tableaux qui suit présente, pour l'ensemble du monde, des données statistiques sur: le nombre d'écoles; le nombre de maîtres et d'élèves par sexe et par degré et type d'enseignement; le nombre d'étudiants et de diplômés de l'enseignement supérieur, par sexe, par domaine d'études et par niveau des programmes; le nombre d'étudiants étrangers, par pays d'origine et par pays d'accueil; enfin, les dépenses publiques afférentes à l'enseignement, selon leur destination et par degré d'enseignement. Dans la mesure du possible, les chiffres présentés se rapportent aux années scolaires commençant en 1975 et en 1980 et aux quatre années les plus récentes.

Les définitions et classifications qui figurent dans la Recommandation révisée concernant la normalisation internationale des statistiques de l'éducation, adoptée par la Conférence générale de l'Unesco à sa vingtième session (Paris, 1978), ainsi que celles qui apparaissent dans la Classification

Internationale Type de l'Education (CITE), ont été utilisées, autant qu'il a été possible, dans ces tableaux. Aux termes de ces définitions, l'enseignement est classé par degré, de la façon suivante:

Enseignement précèdant le premier degré (Niveau 0 de la CITE), dispensé, par exemple, dans les écoles maternelles, les écoles gardiennes ou les jardins d'enfants, qui assure l'éducation des enfants trop jeunes pour être admis à l'enseignement du premier degré.

Enseignement du premier degré (Niveau 1 de la CITE), dispensé, par exemple, dans les écoles élémentaires ou les écoles primaires, qui a pour fonction principale de fournir les premiers éléments de l'instruction.

Enseignement du second degré (Niveaux 2 et 3 de la CITE), dispensé, par exemple dans les écoles moyennes, les lycées, les collèges, les gymnases, les athénées, les écoles complémentaires, ainsi que dans les écoles de ce degré destinées à la formation des maîtres et les écoles de caractère technique ou professionnel), qui implique quatre années au moins d'études préalables dans le premier degré et qui donne une formation générale ou spécialisée (ou les deux).

Enseignement du troisième degré (Niveaux 5, 6 et 7 de la CITE), dispensé, par exemple, dans les universités, les diverses grandes écoles et instituts supérieurs, y compris les ecoles normales supérieures, qui exige comme condition minimale d'admission d'avoir suivi avec succès un enseignement complet du second degré ou de faire preuve de connaissances équivalentes.

Education spéciale, englobant tous les types d'enseignement destinés aux enfants déficients physiques, mentaux, visuels, auditifs, souffrant de difficultés de la parole ou de troubles de lecture et d'écriture et aux inadaptés sociaux.

Les définitions ci-après sont tirées de la Recommandation:

Elève (étudiant): personne inscrite dans un établissement d'enseignement pour recevoir un enseignement systématique de n'importe quel degré.

Maître: personne assurant directement l'instruction d'un groupe d'élèves (étudiants); les chefs d'établissement, ainsi que les membres du personnel d'inspection, de surveillance et autres, ne devraient être rangés parmi les maîtres que s'ils exercent régulièrement des fonctions d'enseignement.

Etablissement d'enseignement (école, institut, etc.): institution groupant des élèves (étudiants) d'une ou plusieurs années en vue de leur faire donner un enseignement d'un certain type et d'un certain degré par un ou plusieurs maîtres placés sous l'autorité directe d'un chef d'établissement.

(a) *Etablissement d'enseignement public*: établissement dont le fonctionnement est assuré par les pouvoirs publics (nationaux, fédéraux, d'état ou provinciaux, ou locaux) quelle que soit l'origine de ses ressources financières.

(b) *Etablissement d'enseignement privé*: le fonctionnement n'est pas assuré par les pouvoirs publics qu'il reçoive ou non une aide financière de ceux-ci. Les établissements d'enseignement privé peuvent être classés en établissements subventionnés et établissements non subventionnés, selon qu'ils reçoivent ou non une aide financière des pouvoirs publics. Dans tous les tableaux, les données concernant les effectifs se rapportent d'ordinaire au début de l'année scolaire ou universitaire. A ce propos, il y a lieu de rappeler que les effectifs peuvent varier sensiblement, selon qu'il s'agit de chiffres relevés au début, au milieu ou à la fin de l'année scolaire ou encore de moyennes, etc...

Les années indiquées sont les années civiles pendant lesquelles commencent les années scolaires ou universitaires. Il ne faut pas oublier que l'année scolaire ne commence en janvier (c'est-à-dire coïncide avec l'année civile) que dans une quarantaine de pays du monde. Dans la plupart des pays et territoires, l'année scolaire commence dans une année civile et termine dans l'année suivante. L'annexe B fournit des renseignements sur le commencement et la fin des années scolaires et budgétaires dans chaque pays et territoire.

Los tres capítulos siguientes del *Anuario* contienen la mayor parte de los datos estadísticos básicos solicitados por la Unesco en relación con los establecimientos docentes, públicos y privados, de todos los grados (niveles) de la enseñanza. En los cuadros que figuran a continuación se presentan datos estadísticos mundiales sobre el número de establecimientos docentes; el número de maestros y profesores y de alumnos por sexo, grado (nivel) y tipo de enseñanza; el número de estudiantes y diplomados de la enseñanza de tercer grado (superior), por sexo, sector de estudios y por nivel de los programas; el número de estudiantes extranjeros, por país de origen y por país huésped; por último, los gastos públicos de educación desglosados según su destino y por grado de enseñanza. En la medida de lo posible los datos se refieren los años escolares que empezaron en 1975 y en 1980 y a los cuatro años más recientes.

En esos cuadros se han utilizado en lo posible las definiciones y clasificaciones que figuran en la Recomendación revisada sobre la normalización internacional de las estadísticas relativas a la educación aprobada por la Conferencia General de la Unesco en su 20a reunión (París, 1978) y las deficiones que se encuentran en la Classificación Internacional Normalizada de la Educación (CINE). Con arreglo a esas definiciones, la enseñanza queda clasificada por grados como sigue:

Enseñanza anterior al primer grado (Nivel 0 de la CINE), por ejemplo, la que se da en guarderías infantiles, escuelas de párvulos o jardines de infancia : para los niños que no están aún en edad de ser admitidos en la enseñanza de primer grado.

Enseñanza de primer grado (Nivel 1 de la CINE), por ejemplo, la que se da en escuelas elementales o en escuelas primarias, cuya función principal consiste en proporcionar los primeros elementos de la instrucción.

Enseñanza de segundo grado (Niveles 2 y 3 de la CINE), por ejemplo, la que se da en escuelas de enseñanza media, secundarias, institutos, liceos, colegios, escuelas técnicas, escuelas normales de este grado, que implica cuatro años como mínimo de estudios previos en el primer grado y que da una formación general o especializada, o de ambas clases.

Enseñanza de tercer grado (Niveles 5, 6 y 7 de la CINE), por ejemplo, la que se da en las universidades, las escuelas técnicas superiores, las grandes escuelas especiales y las escuelas normales superiores, para la admisión a la cual se exige como condición mínima haber completado con éxito la enseñanza de segundo grado o demostrar la posesión de conocimientos equivalentes.

Educación especial: comprende toda la enseñanza general o profesional destinada a los deficientes físicos o mentales, visuales, auditivos, que sufren de dificultades de la palabra o de trastornos para la lectura y a los inadaptados sociales.

Las siguientes definiciones están tomadas de la recomendación:

Alumno (estudiante) : la persona matriculada en un establecimiento docente para recibir una enseñanza sistemática de cualquier grado.

Maestro o profesor. La persona que se ocupa directamente de la instrucción de un grupo de alumnos (estudiantes). No debería incluirse entre los maestros o profesores a los directores de los establecimientos docentes, ni al personal de inspección, vigilancia, etc, más que cuando ejerzan regularmente funciones de enseñanza.

Establecimiento docente (escuela, instituto, etc.): grupo de alumnos (estudiantes) de uno o de varios años de estudios organizado para recibir una enseñanza de determinado tipo y determinado grado dada por uno o varios maestros o profesores, bajo la autoridad de un director de establecimiento.

(a) *Establecimiento docente público*: Establecimiento cuyo funcionamiento depende del poder público (nacional, federal, provincial o local), cualquiera que sea el origen de sus recursos económicos.

(b) *Establecimiento docente privado*: establecimiento cuyo funcionamiento no depende del poder público, tanto si recibe una ayuda económica de éste como en caso contrario. Los establecimientos docentes privados pueden clasificarse en establecimientos subvencionados y establecimientos no subvencionados, según reciban o no una ayuda económica de los poderes públicos.

En todos los cuadros, los datos relativos a la matrícula se

refieren habitualmente al principio del año escolar o universitario. Procede recordar a este respecto que la matrícula puede variar sensiblemente según se trate de cifras calculadas al principio, a mediados o al final del año escolar, de promedios, etc.

Los años indicados son los años civiles durante los cuales empiezan los años escolares o universitarios. No hay que olvidar que el año escolar empieza en enero (es decir, coincide con el año civil) en sólo unos 40 países. En la mayoría de los países y territorios, el año escolar empieza en un año civil y termina en el año subsiguiente. En el apéndice B se presentan datos sobre el comienzo y el final de los años escolares y de los ejercicios económicos en cada país y territorio.

---

2 Summary tables for all levels of education, by continents, major areas and groups of countries

Tableaux récapitulatifs pour tous les degrés d'enseignement, par continents, grandes régions et groupes de pays

Cuadros recapitulativos para todos los grados de enseñanza, por continentes, grandes regiones y grupos de países

This chapter, comprising 12 tables, provides a summary presentation of data for all levels of education. Together these tables convey a general picture of the quantitative development since 1970 and also of the present situation of education and expenditure on education in the whole world and in each major area and group of countries.

Table 2.1

The data in this table provide for the latest year available a regional summary of the information given in Table 3.1 of this *Yearbook*. The variations in the duration of compulsory education, the entrance ages to first level education and the duration of first level and second level general education are shown by continents, major areas and groups of countries.

Tables 2.2 - 2.6

The definitions for each level of education are given in the introductory text to the *Education* section. Data in the present edition are based mainly on the enrolment and the teachers figures shown for each individual country and territory in Tables 3.4, 3.7 and 3.11 of the *Yearbook*. It should be noted that the breakdown and percentage distribution by level of education are influenced by the length of schooling at each level, which, in turn depends on the criteria applied in the national definitions of levels (see Table 3.1). Since these criteria, particularly as concerns primary and secondary education, vary from country to country, caution should be exercised in making comparisons between areas and also in interpreting changes observed within a given area during the period under review.

Table 2.7

This table provides a frequency distribution of pupil-teacher ratios at the first level of education, based on the figures shown in Table 3.4.

Table 2.8

The data in this table are based mainly on the enrolment and teachers' figures shown for each individual country and territory in Table 3.3 of the *Yearbook*.

Table 2.9

The data in this table are based mainly on the enrolment and teachers' figures shown for each individual country and territory in Table 3.7 of the *Yearbook*. Care should be exercised when making comparisons between areas and also in interpreting changes observed within a given area during the period under review because of the differences in the curricula and classifications used by countries and territories to define the role and function of teacher training and technical and vocational education at the second level.

Table 2.10

This table presents adjusted gross enrolment ratios by level of education, by sex, by continents, major areas and groups of countries for 1960, 1965, 1970, 1975, 1980 and 1985. It must be noted that the data presented in this table are based on estimates and projections as assessed by the Unesco Office of Statistics in 1985, and use the medium variant of the population as assessed by the United Nations in 1982. A gross enrolment ratio for a given level of education is derived by dividing the total enrolment for this level of education, regardless of age, by the population of the age group which according to national regulations, should be enrolled at this level. The term ***adjusted*** indicates that the population groups used in deriving these ratios for a particular region have been obtained by taking into account the structure of education of each country in a region. However, for third level education, a standard duration of 5 years following the end of second level general education was used for all countries.

All ratios are expressed as percentages and may be greater than 100 because of late entry, repetition, etc.

Table 2.11

This table presents age-specific enrolment ratios for 1960, 1965, 1970, 1975, 1980 and 1985, and for the age-groups 6-11, 12-17, 18-23, and 6-23 years. It must be noted that the data presented in this table are based on estimates and projections as assessed by the Unesco Office of Statistics in 1985, and use the medium variant of the population as assessed by the United Nations in 1982.

These ratios, which are expressed as percentages, show the proportion of the population in the above age-groups enrolled at any level of education. They are thus purely demographic measures and must not be interpreted as referring to the coverage of first, second or third level education. It should be noted that these figures do not take into account education preceding the first level and that the ratios for the age-group 6-11 may be underestimated because for certain countries the entrance age at first level education is 7 years.

Table 2.12

The purpose of this table is to show the general trends in public expenditure on education, expressed in United States dollars at current market prices, between 1970 and 1984.

For most countries statistics for Gross National Product (GNP) and exchange rates have been obtained from the World Bank and the International Monetary Fund respectively. For certain countries with centrally planned economies, the Material Product and educational expenditure are converted using the non-commercial rates of exchange published by the United Nations.

The data shown in this table should be considered as general approximate indications of the public resources allocated to education. The comparative analysis of data expressed in U.S. dollars should be treated with great caution, due to the fact that the official exchange rates used for the conversions produce unrealistic U.S. dollar values for a number of countries. In particular, figures for recent years are greatly influenced by the appreciation of the U.S. dollar. Moreover, these values are expressed at current prices and are therefore affected by inflation.

Ce chapitre, qui comprend 12 tableaux, présente des données récapitulatives pour tous les degrés d'enseignement. Ces tableaux donnent également une idée générale sur le développement quantitatif à partir de 1970, ainsi que sur la situation actuelle de l'enseignement et des dépenses afférentes à l'enseignement dans l'ensemble du monde et dans chaque grande région et groupe de pays.

Tableau 2.1

Les données de ce tableau présentent pour la dernière année disponible, un résumé régional de l'information qui figure dans le tableau 3.1 de cet *Annuaire*. Les variations dans les durées de la scolarité obligatoire, les âges d'admission dans l'enseignement du premier degré et la durée des enseignements du premier degré et général du second degré sont présentées par continents, grandes régions et groupes de pays.

Tableaux 2.2 - 2.6

Pour la définition de chaque degré d'enseignement se reporter au texte introductif de la partie *Education*. Les données de ce tableau sont basées, pour la plupart, sur les effectifs scolaires et le personnel enseignant indiqués pour chaque pays et territoire dans les tableaux 3.4, 3.7 et 3.11 de l'*Annuaire*. Il y a lieu de noter que la répartition, en chiffres absolus ou en pourcentage, entre les différents degrés d'enseignement dépend du nombre d'années d'études correspondant à chaque degré et, par suite, des critères appliqués dans chaque pays pour définir les degrés d'enseignement (voir tableau 3.1). Comme ces critères varient d'un pays à un autre, notamment en ce qui concerne le premier et le second degré, il convient de faire preuve de prudence lorsqu'on veut procéder à des comparaisons entre les régions ou interpréter les modifications constatées dans une région donnée pendant la période considérée.

Tableau 2.7

Ce tableau présente en distribution de fréquence le nombre d'élèves par maître, dans l'enseignement du premier degré d'après les données qui figurent dans le tableau 3.4.

Tableau 2.8

Les données présentées dans ce tableau sont basées, pour la plupart, sur les effectifs scolaires et le personnel enseignant indiqués pour chaque pays et territoire dans le tableau 3.3 de l'*Annuaire*.

Tableau 2.9

Les données présentées dans ce tableau sont basées, pour la plupart, sur les effectifs scolaires et le personnel enseignant indiqués pour chaque pays et territoire dans le tableau 3.7 de l'*Annuaire*. Il convient de faire preuve de prudence lorsqu'on veut procéder à des comparaisons entre les régions ou interpréter les modifications constatées dans une région donnée pendant la période considérée, compte tenu des différences existant dans les programmes d'études et les classifications utilisées par les pays et territoires pour définir le rôle et la fonction de l'enseignement normal et de l'enseignement technique et professionel.

Tableau 2.10

Ce tableau présente les taux d'inscription scolaire bruts ajustés par degré d'enseignement, par sexe, par continents, grandes régions et groupes de pays pour 1960, 1965, 1970, 1975, 1980 et 1985. Signalons que les données présentées dans ce tableau correspondent à des estimations et projections établies par l'Office des Statistiques de l'Unesco en 1985 en utilisant la variante moyenne de la population évaluée par les Nations Unies en 1982.

Un taux d'inscription scolaire brut pour un niveau d'éducation donné est obtenu en divisant le total des effectifs scolaires de ce niveau d'éducation, sans tenir compte de l'âge, par la population scolarisable du groupe d'âge, suivant les systèmes nationaux. Le terme *ajusté* indique que les groupes de population utilisés pour le calcul de ces taux pour une région donnée ont été obtenus en tenant compte des systèmes d'éducation pour chaque pays de la région. Cependant, pour l'enseignement du troisième degré, une durée normalisée de 5 ans, à partir de la fin de l'enseignement du second degré, a été utilisée pour tous les pays.

Tous les taux sont exprimés en pourcentages et peuvent être supérieurs à 100, en raison des admissions tardives, redoublements, etc.

Tableau 2.11

Ce tableau présente les taux d'inscription par âge pour 1960, 1965, 1970, 1975, 1980 et 1985 pour les groupes d'âge 6-11, 12-17, 18-23 et 6-23. Signalons que les données présentées dans ce tableau correspondent à des estimations et projections établies par l'Office des Statistiques de l'Unesco en 1985 en utilisant la variante moyenne de la population évaluée par les Nations Unies en 1982.

Ces taux d'inscription, qui sont exprimés en pourcentages, montrent la proportion de la population des groupes d'âge ci-dessus, inscrite dans n'importe quel degré d'enseignement. Ils ne représentent donc qu'un rapport purement démographique, qui ne doit pas être interprété comme se référant aux enseignements du premier, du second et du troisième degré.

Il faut souligner que ces données ne tiennent pas compte de l'enseignement précédant le premier degré et que les taux pour le groupe d'âge 6-11 peuvent être sous-estimés parce que dans certains pays l'âge d'admission dans l'enseignement du premier degré est de 7 ans.

Tableau 2.12

Ce tableau a pour objet de montrer l'évolution des dépenses publiques d'enseignement exprimées en dollars des Etats-Unis aux prix courants du marché entre les années 1970 et 1984.

Pour la majeure partie des pays, les données sur le produit national brut (PNB) et les taux de change sont fournis par la Banque Mondiale et le Fonds Monétaire International respectivement. Pour certains pays dont l'économie est soumise à une planification centralisée, le produit matériel et les dépenses d'enseignement sont convertis d'après les taux de change non-commerciaux publiés par les Nations Unies.

Toutes les données doivent être considérées comme des indications générales et approximatives de l'ordre de grandeur des ressources publiques consacrées à l'enseignement. L'analyse comparative des données exprimées en dollars des Etats-Unis, doit être faite avec beaucoup de prudence, car les taux de change officiels utilisés pour les conversions fournissent des valeurs en dollars irréalistes pour un certain nombre de pays. Au cours des dernières années, les chiffres sont particulièrement influencés par la révaluation du dollar des Etats-Unis. Il faut aussi prendre en compte que ces valeurs sont exprimées en prix courants et sont donc affectées par l'inflation.

Este capítulo, que comprende 12 cuadros, presenta datos recapitulativos para todos los grados de enseñanza. Estos cuadros dan igualmente una idea general del desarrollo cuantitativo a partir de 1970, así como de la situación actual de la enseñanza y de los gastos destinados a la educación en el conjunto del mundo y en cada una de las grandes regiones y grupos de países.

Cuadro 2.1

Los datos de este cuadro presentan para el último año disponible, un resumen regional de la información que figura en el cuadro 3.1 de este *Anuario*. Las variaciones en la duración de la escolaridad obligatoria, las edades de admisión en la enseñanza de primer grado y la duración de las enseñanza de primer grado y general de segundo grado, se presentan por continentes, grandes regiones y grupos de países.

Cuadros 2.2-2.6

Puede verse la definición de los distintos grados de enseñanza en la introducción del capítulo *Educación*. La mayoría de los datos de este cuadro, se basan en las cifras de la matrícula escolar y del personal docente indicadas en los cuadros 3.4, 3.7 y 3.11 del *Anuario* con respecto a cada país o territorio. Procede señalar que la distribución, en valor absoluto y en porcentajes, entre los distintos grados de enseñanza depende del número de años de estudios correspondiente a cada grado y, por ende, de los criterios aplicados en cada país para definir dichos grados (véase el cuadro 3.1). Como estos criterios varían según los países, en particular en el caso del primero y del segundo grado, habrá que tener presente estas circunstancias al hacer comparaciones entre las regiones o al interpretar las modificaciones observadas en una región dada durante el período considerado.

Cuadro 2.7

Este cuadro presenta en distribución de frecuencia el número de alumnos por maestro, para la enseñanza de primer grado con base en los datos que figuran en el cuadro 3.4.

Cuadro 2.8

Los datos de este cuadro se basan principalmente en las cifras de matrícula escolar y de personal docente que figuran para cada país y territorio en el cuadro 3.3 del *Anuario*.

Cuadro 2.9

Los datos presentados en este cuadro se basan principalmente en las cifras de matrícula escolar y de personal docente que figuran para cada país y territorio en el cuadro 3.7 del *Anuario*. Las comparaciones entre regiones deben efectuarse con mucha prudencia, al igual que la interpretacion de los cambios que se observen en el interior de una misma región durante el período considerado, debido a las diferencias existentes en los programas de estudio y las clasificaciones utilizadas por los países y territorios para definir el papel y las funciones de la enseñanza normal y de la enseñanza técnica y profesional.

Cuadro 2.10

Este cuadro presenta las tasas brutas de escolarización por nivel de educación, por sexo, por continentes, grandes regiones y grupos de países para 1960, 1965, 1970, 1975, 1980 y 1985. Señalamos que los datos presentados en este cuadro se refieren a las estimaciones y proyecciones establecidas por la Oficina de Estadística de la Unesco en 1985 utilizando la variante media de la población evaluada por las Nationes Unidas en 1982.

Una tasa bruta para un nivel de educación dado, se obtiene dividiendo el total de escolarización para el nivel de educación en cuestión, independientemente de la edad, por la población del grupo de edad, que de acuerdo con las normas nacionales, deben de estar inscritos en ese nivel. El término *ajustado* indica que los grupos de población utilizados para obtener estas tasas para una región en particular, han sido obtenidos tomando en consideración la estructura educacional para cada país en la región. Alternativamente, para la educación de tercer grado, una duración fija de 5 años al final de la educación secundaria general, fue utilizada para todos los países.

Todas las tasas están expresadas como porcentajes y pueden ser superiores a 100 como consecuencia de inscripciones retrasadas, repetidores, etc.

Cuadro 2.11

Este cuadro presenta las tasas específicas de escolarización por edad para 1960, 1965, 1970, 1975, 1980 y 1985 y para los grupos de edad 6-11, 12-17, 18-23 y 6-23. Señalamos que los datos presentados en este cuadro se refieren a las estimaciones y proyecciones establecidas por la Oficina de Estadística de la Unesco en 1985 utilizando la variante media de la población evaluada por las Naciones Unidas en 1982.

Las tasas de escolarización, expresadas en porcentaje, muestran la proporción de la población de los grupos de edad arriba mencionados, inscrita en no importa que grado de enseñanza. Dichas tasas sólo representan una relación puramente demográfica, que no debe ser interpretada como expresión de las enseñanzas de primer, segundo y tercer grado.

Se debe notar que estos datos no toman en cuenta la enseñanza anterior al primer grado y que las tasas para el grupo de edad 6-11 pueden estar subestimadas, ya que en ciertos países la edad de admisión en la enseñanza del primer grado es de 7 años.

Cuadro 2.12

La finalidad de este cuadro consiste en exponer la evolución de los gastos públicos de educación, expresados a precios corrientes del mercado y en dólares de los Estados Unidos, entre los años 1970 y 1984.

Para la mayoría de los países, los datos relativos al producto nacional bruto (PNB) y los tipos de cambio nos han sido proporcionados por el Banco Mundial y el Fondo Monetario Internacional respectivamente. Para los países cuya economía está sometida a una planificación centralizada, el producto material y los gastos de enseñanza han sido convertidos de acuerdo con los tipos de cambio no comerciales publicados por las Naciones Unidas.

Los datos del presente cuadro han de considerarse como una indicación general y aproximada del orden de magnitud de los recursos públicos dedicados al sector de la educación. El análisis comparativo de los datos expresados en dólares de los Estados Unidos debe ser llevado a cabo con mucha prudencia ya que los tipos de cambio oficiales utilizados, proporcionan valores en dólares completamente irrealistas para un cierto número de países. En los últimos años, las cifras han estado particularmente influenciadas por la continua reevaluación del dólar de los Estados Unidos. Hay que tomar también en cuenta que éstos valores están expresados en precios corrientes y por ende modificados por la inflación.

2.1 Education systems

Systèmes d'enseignement

Sistemas de enseñanza

FOR COMPOSITION OF THE MAJOR AREAS AND GROUPS OF COUNTRIES, SEE THE HEAD NOTE TO TABLE 1.2.

POUR LA COMPOSITION DES GRANDES REGIONS ET DES GROUPES DE PAYS, VOIR LA NOTE EN-TETE DU TABLEAU 1.2.

PUEDE VERSE LA COMPOSICION DE LAS GRANDES REGIONES Y GRUPOS DE PAISES EN LA NOTA ENCABEZANDO EL CUADRO 1.2.

	WORLD / MONDE / MUNDO	AFRICA / AFRIQUE / AFRICA	AMERICA / AMERIQUE / AMERICA	ASIA / ASIE / ASIA	EUROPE (INCLUDING U.S.S.R.) / EUROPE (Y COMPRIS L'U.R.S.S.) / EUROPA (INCLUIDA LA U.R.S.S.)	OCEANIA / OCEANIE / OCEANIA
DURATION (IN YEARS) OF COMPULSORY EDUCATION DUREE DE LA SCOLARITE OBLIGATOIRE (ANNEES) DURACION DE LA ENSEÑANZA OBLIGATORIA (ANOS)						
5	12	2	1	8	–	1
6	35	13	11	9	1	1
7	9	5	3	1	–	–
8	31	11	5	5	8	2
9	35	5	8	8	12	2
10	35	6	10	2	11	6
11	9	–	5	–	2	2
12	5	–	3	–	1	1
13	–	–	–	–	–	–
NO COMPULSORY EDUCATION PAS DE SCOLARITE OBLIGATOIRE ENSEÑANZA NO OBLIGATORIA	28	12	3	8	–	5
NOT SPECIFIED NON SPECIFIE SIN ESPECIFICAR	1	–	–	1	–	–
TOTAL COUNTRIES NOMBRE TOTAL DE PAYS NUMERO TOTAL DE PAISES	200	54	49	42	35	20
ENTRANCE AGE, FIRST LEVEL OF EDUCATION AGE D'ENTREE DANS L'EN-SEIGNEMENT DU 1ER DEGRE EDAD DE INGRESO EN LA ENSEÑANZA DE PRIMER GRADO						
4	1	–	–	–	1	–
5	34	5	16	5	2	6
6	116	30	25	28	21	12
7	47	18	8	8	11	2
8	2	1	–	1	–	–
NOT SPECIFIED NON SPECIFIE SIN ESPECIFICAR	–	–	–	–	–	–
TOTAL COUNTRIES NOMBRE TOTAL DE PAYS NUMERO TOTAL DE PAISES	200	54	49	42	35	20

DEVELOPED COUNTRIES PAYS DEVELOPPES PAISES DESARROLLADOS	DEVELOPING COUNTRIES PAYS EN DEVELOPPEMENT PAISES EN DESARROLLO	AFRICA (EXCLUDING ARAB STATES) AFRIQUE (NON COMPRIS LES ETATS ARABES) AFRICA (EXCLUIDOS LOS ESTADOS ARABES)	ASIA (EXCLUDING ARAB STATES) ASIE (NON COMPRIS LES ETATS ARABES) ASIA (EXCLUIDOS LOS ESTADOS ARABES)	ARAB STATES ETATS ARABES ESTADOS ARABES	NORTHERN AMERICA AMERIQUE SEPTENTRIONALE AMERICA SEPTENTRIONAL	LATIN AMERICA AND THE CARIBBEAN AMERIQUE LATINE ET LES CARAIBES AMERICA LATINA Y EL CARIBE
–	12	2	8	–	–	1
1	34	12	5	5	–	11
–	9	4	1	1	–	3
7	24	8	3	5	–	5
16	19	3	6	4	1	7
12	23	6	2	–	1	9
3	6	–	–	–	1	4
1	4	–	–	–	1	2
–	–	–	–	–	–	–
–	28	10	4	6	–	3
–	1	–	1	–	–	–
40	160	45	30	21	4	45
1	–	–	–	–	–	–
3	31	5	5	–	1	15
26	90	24	18	16	3	22
10	37	15	6	5	–	8
–	2	1	1	–	–	–
–	–	–	–	–	–	–
40	160	45	30	21	4	45

	WORLD MONDE MUNDO	AFRICA AFRIQUE AFRICA	AMERICA AMERIQUE AMERICA	ASIA ASIE ASIA	EUROPE (INCLUDING U.S.S.R.) EUROPE (Y COMPRIS L'U.R.S.S.) EUROPA (INCLUIDA LA U.R.S.S.)	OCEANIA OCEANIE OCEANIA
DURATION (IN YEARS) OF 1ST LEVEL EDUCATION DUREE DE L'ENSEIGNEMENT DU 1ER DEGRE (ANNEES) DURACION DE LA ENSEÑANZA DE PRIMER GRADO (ANOS)						
3	1	–	–	1	–	–
4	8	3	–	2	3	–
5	35	4	5	15	10	1
6	102	33	25	21	14	9
7	26	10	11	–	–	5
8	23	3	7	3	6	4
9	4	1	1	–	1	1
10	1	–	–	–	1	–
NOT SPECIFIED NON SPECIFIE SIN ESPECIFICAR	–	–	–	–	–	–
TOTAL COUNTRIES NOMBRE TOTAL DE PAYS NUMERO TOTAL DE PAISES	200	54	49	42	35	20
DURATION (IN YEARS) OF GENERAL EDUCATION AT THE SECOND LEVEL DUREE DE L'ENSEIGNEMENT GENERAL DU 2ND DEGRE (ANNEES) DURACION DE LA ENSEÑANZA GENERAL DE 2NDO GRADO (ANOS)						
2	3	1	–	–	1	1
3	3	–	2	–	1	–
4	23	2	6	4	5	6
5	32	8	14	4	4	2
6	72	20	18	19	10	5
7	61	23	9	14	9	6
8	5	–	–	1	4	–
9	1	–	–	–	1	–
NOT SPECIFIED NON SPECIFIE SIN ESPECIFICAR	–	–	–	–	–	–
TOTAL COUNTRIES NOMBRE TOTAL DE PAYS NUMERO TOTAL DE PAISES	200	54	49	42	35	20

DEVELOPED COUNTRIES PAYS DEVELOPPES PAISES DESARROLLADOS	DEVELOPING COUNTRIES PAYS EN DEVELOPPEMENT PAISES EN DESARROLLO	AFRICA (EXCLUDING ARAB STATES) AFRIQUE (NON COMPRIS LES ETATS ARABES) AFRICA (EXCLUIDOS LOS ESTADOS ARABES)	ASIA (EXCLUDING ARAB STATES) ASIE (NON COMPRIS LES ETATS ARABES) ASIA (EXCLUIDOS LOS ESTADOS ARABES)	ARAB STATES ETATS ARABES ESTADOS ARABES	NORTHERN AMERICA AMERIQUE SEPTEN-TRIONALE AMERICA SEPTEN-TRIONAL	LATIN AMERICA AND THE CARIBBEAN AMERIQUE LATINE ET LES CARAIBES AMERICA LATINA Y EL CARIBE
–	1	–	1	–	–	–
2	6	3	1	1	–	–
10	25	3	14	2	1	4
18	84	26	12	16	1	24
0	26	10	–	–	1	10
8	15	2	2	2	1	6
1	3	1	–	–	–	1
1	–	–	–	–	–	–
–	–	–	–	–	–	–
40	160	45	30	21	4	45
1	2	1	–	–	–	–
1	2	–	–	–	–	2
7	16	1	3	2	1	5
5	27	7	4	1	1	13
12	60	16	10	13	1	17
10	51	20	13	4	1	8
3	2	–	–	1	–	–
1	–	–	–	–	–	–
–	–	–	–	–	–	–
40	160	45	30	21	4	45

2.2 Estimated total enrolment and teaching staff by level of education

Estimation des effectifs et du personnel enseignant, par degré d'enseignement

Estimación de la matrícula escolar y del personal docente, por grado de enseñanza

(SEE INTRODUCTORY TEXT CONCERNING TABLES 2.2 – 2.6)

% 1970–80 AND 1980–84 = ANNUAL AVERAGE INCREASE IN ENROLMENT AND TEACHING STAFF FROM 1970 TO 1980 AND FROM 1980 TO 1984, AS PERCENTAGE.

(VOIR LE TEXTE D'INTRODUCTION RELATIF AUX TABLEAUX 2.2 – 2.6)

% 1970–80 ET 1980–84 = ACCROISSEMENT MOYEN ANNUEL DES EFFECTIFS SCOLAIRES ET DU PERSONNEL ENSEIGNANT DE 1970 A 1980 ET DE 1980 A 1984, EN POURCENTAGE.

(VEASE EL TEXTO DE INTRODUCCION RELATIVO A LOS CUADROS 2.2 – 2.6)

% 1970–80 Y 1980–84 = CRECIMIENTO MEDIO ANUAL DE LA MATRICULA ESCOLAR Y DEL PERSONAL DOCENTE DE 1970 A 1980 Y DE 1980 A 1984, EN PORCENTAJE.

CONTINENTS, MAJOR AREAS AND GROUPS OF COUNTRIES / CONTINENTS, GRANDES REGIONS ET GROUPES DE PAYS / CONTINENTES, GRANDES REGIONES Y GRUPOS DE PAISES	YEAR / ANNEE / AÑO	ENROLMENT (THOUSANDS) / EFFECTIFS SCOLAIRES (MILLIERS) / MATRICULA ESCOLAR (MILES)				TEACHING STAFF (THOUSANDS) / PERSONNEL ENSEIGNANT (MILLIERS) / PERSONAL DOCENTE (MILES)			
		TOTAL / TOTAL / TOTAL	1ST LEVEL / 1ER DEGRE / 1ER GRADO	2ND LEVEL / 2ND DEGRE / 2DO GRADO	3RD LEVEL / 3EME DEGRE / 3ER GRADO	TOTAL / TOTAL / TOTAL	1ST LEVEL / 1ER DEGRE / 1ER GRADO	2ND LEVEL / 2ND DEGRE / 2DO GRADO	3RD LEVEL / 3EME DEGRE / 3ER GRADO
		(1)	(2)	(3)	(4)	(5)	(6)	(7)	(8)
WORLD TOTAL‡	1970	615 944	430 147	157 700	28 097	25 924	14 837	8 957	2 130
	1975	758 074	511 876	206 663	39 534	32 341	17 859	11 602	2 880
	1980	843 221	554 594	241 412	47 216	37 392	19 700	14 065	3 626
	1983	870 807	568 191	250 934	51 682	39 587	20 857	14 779	3 952
	1984	886 497	574 314	258 990	53 194	40 233	21 136	15 046	4 051
	% 1970–80	3.2	2.6	4.4	5.3	3.7	2.9	4.6	5.5
	% 1980–84	1.3	0.9	1.8	3.0	1.8	1.8	1.7	2.8
AFRICA‡	1970	34 226	29 371	4 454	401	967	735	202	29
	1975	48 796	40 066	7 917	814	1 383	1 021	315	47
	1980	74 312	59 238	13 701	1 374	2 155	1 523	545	87
	1983	85 345	65 345	18 246	1 755	2 534	1 721	697	116
	1984	87 628	66 393	19 390	1 846	2 639	1 771	746	121
	% 1970–80	8.1	7.3	11.9	13.1	8.3	7.6	10.4	11.6
	% 1980–84	4.2	2.9	9.1	7.7	5.2	3.8	8.2	8.6
AMERICA	1970	118 123	79 021	28 321	10 781	5 453	2 928	1 750	775
	1975	136 889	87 852	33 386	15 651	6 584	3 497	2 060	1 028
	1980	146 673	94 443	34 388	17 842	7 381	3 745	2 328	1 309
	1983	153 114	98 109	35 988	19 018	7 779	3 962	2 402	1 414
	1984	154 275	98 246	36 533	19 496	7 984	4 038	2 490	1 456
	% 1970–80	2.2	1.8	2.0	5.2	3.1	2.5	2.9	5.4
	% 1980–84	1.3	1.0	1.5	2.2	2.0	1.9	1.7	2.7
ASIA‡	1970	324 012	242 939	74 186	6 886	11 472	7 420	3 483	569
	1975	427 049	310 977	105 794	10 278	15 583	9 703	5 094	785
	1980	478 485	330 718	133 939	13 827	18 753	10 732	6 983	1 038
	1983	489 253	335 690	137 412	16 151	20 073	11 453	7 445	1 175
	1984	501 568	341 171	143 487	16 910	20 376	11 626	7 543	1 207
	% 1970–80	4.0	3.1	6.1	7.2	5.0	3.8	7.2	6.2
	% 1980–84	1.2	0.8	1.7	5.2	2.1	2.0	1.9	3.8
EUROPE (INCL. USSR)	1970	135 396	76 226	49 364	9 806	7 849	3 658	3 449	742
	1975	140 786	70 408	57 939	12 439	8 553	3 525	4 035	992
	1980	138 976	67 490	57 730	13 756	8 834	3 576	4 096	1 162
	1983	138 228	66 419	57 502	14 306	8 927	3 600	4 111	1 216
	1984	138 141	65 925	57 739	14 477	8 949	3 582	4 132	1 234
	% 1970–80	0.3	–1.2	1.6	3.4	1.2	–0.2	1.7	4.6
	% 1980–84	–0.2	–0.6	0.0	1.3	0.3	0.0	0.2	1.5
OCEANIA	1970	4 188	2 590	1 374	224	182	96	72	15
	1975	4 553	2 573	1 627	353	238	112	98	28
	1980	4 776	2 704	1 655	417	269	126	112	30
	1983	4 867	2 629	1 786	452	275	122	123	31
	1984	4 885	2 579	1 842	465	285	120	133	32
	% 1970–80	1.3	0.4	1.9	6.4	4.0	2.8	4.5	7.2
	% 1980–84	0.6	–1.2	2.7	2.8	1.5	–1.2	4.4	1.6

CONTINENTS, MAJOR AREAS AND GROUPS OF COUNTRIES / CONTINENTS, GRANDES REGIONS ET GROUPES DE PAYS / CONTINENTES, GRANDES REGIONES Y GRUPOS DE PAISES	YEAR / ANNEE / AÑO	ENROLMENT (THOUSANDS) EFFECTIFS SCOLAIRES (MILLIERS) MATRICULA ESCOLAR (MILES)				TEACHING STAFF (THOUSANDS) PERSONNEL ENSEIGNANT (MILLIERS) PERSONAL DOCENTE (MILES)			
		TOTAL / TOTAL / TOTAL	1ST LEVEL / 1ER DEGRE / 1ER GRADO	2ND LEVEL / 2ND DEGRE / 2DO GRADO	3RD LEVEL / 3EME DEGRE / 3ER GRADO	TOTAL / TOTAL / TOTAL	1ST LEVEL / 1ER DEGRE / 1ER GRADO	2ND LEVEL / 2ND DEGRE / 2DO GRADO	3RD LEVEL / 3EME DEGRE / 3ER GRADO
		(1)	(2)	(3)	(4)	(5)	(6)	(7)	(8)
DEVELOPED COUNTRIES‡	1970	217 682	119 212	77 691	20 779	12 021	5 472	5 033	1 516
	1975	226 951	113 303	86 933	26 714	13 189	5 467	5 799	1 924
	1980	222 724	110 134	83 352	29 239	13 801	5 635	5 858	2 308
	1983	222 547	108 723	83 497	30 327	13 980	5 689	5 878	2 414
	1984	222 076	107 532	83 912	30 632	14 031	5 656	5 921	2 454
	% 1970–80	0.2	–0.8	0.7	3.5	1.4	0.3	1.5	4.3
	% 1980–84	–0.1	–0.6	0.2	1.2	0.4	0.1	0.3	1.5
DEVELOPING COUNTRIES‡	1970	398 262	310 935	80 009	7 318	13 903	9 365	3 924	614
	1975	531 123	398 573	119 730	12 820	19 152	12 392	5 803	956
	1980	620 497	444 460	158 060	17 977	23 591	14 065	8 207	1 318
	1983	648 260	459 468	167 437	21 355	25 607	15 168	8 901	1 538
	1984	664 421	466 782	175 078	22 562	26 202	15 480	9 125	1 597
	% 1970–80	4.5	3.6	7.0	9.4	5.4	4.2	7.7	7.9
	% 1980–84	1.7	1.2	2.6	5.8	2.7	2.4	2.7	4.9
AFRICA (EXCLUDING ARAB STATES)‡	1970	22 451	20 331	2 019	101	609	502	96	11
	1975	32 998	28 757	4 051	189	882	711	155	17
	1980	53 993	45 720	7 892	382	1 421	1 113	277	31
	1983	61 703	50 157	11 018	528	1 636	1 239	351	46
	1984	63 116	50 879	11 698	540	1 681	1 260	373	48
	% 1970–80	9.2	8.4	14.6	14.2	8.8	8.3	11.2	10.9
	% 1980–84	4.0	2.7	10.3	9.0	4.3	3.1	7.7	11.6
ASIA (EXCLUDING ARAB STATES)‡	1970	319 216	239 399	73 075	6 742	11 277	7 288	3 426	562
	1975	419 648	305 679	103 963	10 006	15 263	9 496	4 995	772
	1980	468 062	323 629	131 053	13 380	18 286	10 451	6 825	1 010
	1983	477 189	327 589	133 990	15 609	19 499	11 116	7 242	1 141
	1984	488 927	332 696	139 898	16 333	19 771	11 273	7 327	1 171
	% 1970–80	3.9	3.1	6.0	7.1	5.0	3.7	7.1	6.0
	% 1980–84	1.1	0.7	1.6	5.1	2.0	1.9	1.8	3.8
ARAB STATES	1970	16 571	12 581	3 547	444	553	365	163	25
	1975	23 200	16 607	5 697	896	820	517	260	44
	1980	30 742	20 607	8 695	1 440	1 201	691	426	84
	1983	35 706	23 288	10 649	1 768	1 472	819	550	104
	1984	37 153	23 989	11 281	1 883	1 563	864	590	110
	% 1970–80	6.4	5.1	9.4	12.5	8.1	6.6	10.1	12.9
	% 1980–84	4.8	3.9	6.7	6.9	6.8	5.7	8.5	7.0
NORTHERN AMERICA	1970	61 837	32 445	20 252	9 140	3 139	1 403	1 121	615
	1975	64 438	31 587	20 848	12 003	3 449	1 474	1 254	722
	1980	59 510	29 640	16 885	12 986	3 647	1 510	1 225	912
	1983	59 228	29 453	16 336	13 440	3 664	1 539	1 178	946
	1984	58 753	29 077	16 110	13 566	3 672	1 538	1 175	959
	% 1970–80	–0.4	–0.9	–1.8	3.6	1.5	0.7	0.9	4.0
	% 1980–84	–0.3	–0.5	–1.2	1.1	0.2	0.5	–1.0	1.3
LATIN AMERICAN AND THE CARIBBEAN	1970	56 286	46 576	8 070	1 640	2 314	1 525	629	160
	1975	72 451	56 265	12 538	3 648	3 135	2 023	806	306
	1980	87 163	64 803	17 503	4 856	3 734	2 235	1 103	396
	1983	93 886	68 656	19 652	5 578	4 115	2 423	1 224	468
	1984	95 522	69 169	20 423	5 931	4 312	2 499	1 315	497
	% 1970–80	4.5	3.4	8.0	11.5	4.9	3.9	5.8	9.5
	% 1980–84	2.3	1.6	3.9	5.1	3.7	2.8	4.5	5.8

General note / Note générale / Nota general:

E--> For composition of major areas and groups of countries, see head note to table 1.2. The school year begins in the calendar year indicated. More information on this point is given in the general introduction to the 'Education' section. The figures in this table do not include data relating to pre-primary, special and adult education. Second level education includes general, teacher training and vocational education. Third level education includes universities and other institutions of higher education. Owing to the rounding of figures, the totals and sub-totals shown in this table do not always correspond exactly to the sums of their component items.

FR-> Pour la composition des grandes régions et des groupes de pays, voir la note en-tête du tableau 1.2. L'année scolaire commence pendant l'année civile indiquée. Pour plus de détails, se reporter à l'introduction générale de la partie 'Education'. Les chiffres de ce tableau ne comprennent pas l'enseignement préprimaire, l'éducation spéciale et l'éducation des adultes. L'enseignement du second degré comprend les enseignements

General note / Note générale / Nota general: (Cont):

général, normal et technique. L'enseignement du troisième degré comprend les universités et autres établissements d'enseignement supérieur. Les chiffres ayant été arrondis, les totaux et les sous-totaux figurant dans ce tableau ne correspondent pas toujours exactement à la somme des éléments qui les composent.

ESP> Puede verse la composición de las grandes regiones y grupos de paises en la nota encabezando el cuadro 1.2. El año escolar empieza durante el año civil indicado. Pueden verse mas detalles a este respecto en la introducción general de la sección 'Educación'. Las cifras de este cuadro no comprenden la enseñanza preprimaria, la educación especial y la educación de adultos. La enseñanza de segundo grado incluye las enseñanzas general, normal y técnica. La enseñanza de tercer grado incluye las universidades y otros establecimientos de enseñanza superior. Como las cifras se han redondeado, los totales y los sub-totales que figuran en este cuadro no siempre corresponden exactamente a la suma de los elementos que los componen.

World total, Africa, Developed countries, Africa (excluding Arab States):

E--> Not including South Africa.
FR-> Non compris l'Afrique du Sud.
ESP> Excluída Sudáfrica.

World total, Asia, Developing countries, Asia (excl. Arab States):

E--> Not including the Democratic People's Republic of Korea.
FR-> Non compris la République populaire démocratique de Corée.
ESP> Excluída la República popular democrática de Corea.

2.3 Total enrolment and teaching staff: percentage distribution by level of education

Répartition en pourcentage des effectifs scolaires et du personnel enseignant, par degré d'enseignement

Distribución en porcentaje de la matrícula escolar y del personal docente, por grado de enseñanza

(SEE INTRODUCTORY TEXT CONCERNING TABLES 2.2 – 2.6)

(VOIR LE TEXTE D'INTRODUCTION RELATIF AUX TABLEAUX 2.2 – 2.6)

(VEASE EL TEXTO DE INTRODUCCION RELATIVO A LOS CUADROS 2.2 – 2.6)

CONTINENTS, MAJOR AREAS AND GROUPS OF COUNTRIES / CONTINENTS, GRANDES REGIONS ET GROUPES DE PAYS / CONTINENTES, GRANDES REGIONES Y GRUPOS DE PAISES	YEAR / ANNEE / AÑO	PERCENTAGE DISTRIBUTION / REPARTITION EN POURCENTAGE / DISTRIBUCION PORCENTUAL							
		ENROLMENT / EFFECTIFS SCOLAIRES / MATRICULA ESCOLAR				TEACHING STAFF / PERSONNEL ENSEIGNANT / PERSONAL DOCENTE			
		TOTAL / TOTAL / TOTAL	1ST LEVEL / 1EE DEGRE / 1ER GRADO	2ND LEVEL / 2ND DEGRE / 2DO GRADO	3RD LEVEL / 3EME DEGRE / 3ER GRADO	TOTAL / TOTAL / TOTAL	1ST LEVEL / 1ER DEGRE / 1ER GRADO	2ND LEVEL / 2ND DEGRE / 1DO GRADO	3RD LEVEL / 3EME DEGRE / 3ER GRADO
		(1)	(2)	(3)	(4)	(5)	(6)	(7)	(8)
WORLD TOTAL‡	1970	100.0	69.8	25.6	4.6	100.0	57.2	34.6	8.2
	1975	100.0	67.5	27.3	5.2	100.0	55.2	35.9	8.9
	1980	100.0	65.8	28.6	5.6	100.0	52.7	37.6	9.7
	1983	100.0	65.2	28.8	5.9	100.0	52.7	37.3	10.0
	1984	100.0	64.8	29.2	6.0	100.0	52.5	37.4	10.1
AFRICA‡	1970	100.0	85.8	13.0	1.2	100.0	76.0	20.9	3.0
	1975	100.0	82.1	16.2	1.7	100.0	73.8	22.8	3.4
	1980	100.0	79.7	18.4	1.8	100.0	70.7	25.3	4.0
	1983	100.0	76.6	21.4	2.1	100.0	67.9	27.5	4.6
	1984	100.0	75.8	22.1	2.1	100.0	67.1	28.3	4.6
AMERICA	1970	100.0	66.9	24.0	9.1	100.0	53.7	32.1	14.2
	1975	100.0	64.2	24.4	11.4	100.0	53.1	31.3	15.6
	1980	100.0	64.4	23.4	12.2	100.0	50.7	31.5	17.7
	1983	100.0	64.1	23.5	12.4	100.0	50.9	30.9	18.2
	1984	100.0	63.7	23.7	12.6	100.0	50.6	31.2	18.2
ASIA‡	1970	100.0	75.0	22.9	2.1	100.0	64.7	30.4	5.0
	1975	100.0	72.8	24.8	2.4	100.0	62.3	32.7	5.0
	1980	100.0	69.1	28.0	2.9	100.0	57.2	37.2	5.5
	1983	100.0	68.6	28.1	3.3	100.0	57.1	37.1	5.9
	1984	100.0	68.0	28.6	3.4	100.0	57.1	37.0	5.9
EUROPE (INCL. USSR)	1970	100.0	56.3	36.5	7.2	100.0	46.6	43.9	9.5
	1975	100.0	50.0	41.2	8.8	100.0	41.2	47.2	11.6
	1980	100.0	48.6	41.5	9.9	100.0	40.5	46.4	13.2
	1983	100.0	48.1	41.6	10.3	100.0	40.3	46.1	13.6
	1984	100.0	47.7	41.8	10.5	100.0	40.0	46.2	13.8
OCEANIA	1970	100.0	61.8	32.8	5.3	100.0	52.7	39.6	8.2
	1975	100.0	56.5	35.7	7.8	100.0	47.1	41.2	11.8
	1980	100.0	56.6	34.7	8.7	100.0	46.8	41.6	11.2
	1983	100.0	54.0	36.7	9.3	100.0	44.4	44.7	11.3
	1984	100.0	52.8	37.7	9.5	100.0	42.1	46.7	11.2
DEVELOPED COUNTRIES‡	1970	100.0	54.8	35.7	9.5	100.0	45.5	41.9	12.6
	1975	100.0	49.9	38.3	11.8	100.0	41.5	44.0	14.6
	1980	100.0	49.4	37.4	13.1	100.0	40.8	42.4	16.7
	1983	100.0	48.9	37.5	13.6	100.0	40.7	42.0	17.3
	1984	100.0	48.4	37.8	13.8	100.0	40.3	42.2	17.5
DEVELOPING COUNTRIES‡	1970	100.0	78.1	20.1	1.8	100.0	67.4	28.2	4.4
	1975	100.0	75.0	22.5	2.4	100.0	64.7	30.3	5.0
	1980	100.0	71.6	25.5	2.9	100.0	59.6	34.8	5.6
	1983	100.0	70.9	25.8	3.3	100.0	59.2	34.8	6.0
	1984	100.0	70.3	26.4	3.4	100.0	59.1	34.8	6.1

2.3 Total enrolment and teaching staff: percentage distribution
Effectifs scolaires et personnel enseignant: répartition en pourcentage
Matrícula escolar y personal docente: distribución en porcentaje

CONTINENTS, MAJOR AREAS AND GROUPS OF COUNTRIES / CONTINENTS, GRANDES REGIONES ET GROUPES DE PAYS / CONTINENTES, GRANDES REGIONES Y GRUPOS DE PAISES	YEAR / ANNEE / AÑO	PERCENTAGE DISTRIBUTION / REPARTITION EN POURCENTAGE / DISTRIBUCION PORCENTUAL							
		ENROLMENT / EFFECTIFS SCOLAIRES / MATRICULA ESCOLAR				TEACHING STAFF / PERSONNEL ENSEIGNANT / PERSONAL DOCENTE			
		TOTAL / TOTAL / TOTAL	1ST LEVEL / 1EE DEGRE / 1ER GRADO	2ND LEVEL / 2ND DEGRE / 2DO GRADO	3RD LEVEL / 3EME DEGRE / 3ER GRADO	TOTAL / TOTAL / TOTAL	1ST LEVEL / 1ER DEGRE / 1ER GRADO	2ND LEVEL / 2ND DEGRE / 1DO GRADO	3RD LEVEL / 3EME DEGRE / 3ER GRADO
		(1)	(2)	(3)	(4)	(5)	(6)	(7)	(8)
AFRICA (EXCLUDING ARAB STATES)‡	1970	100.0	90.6	9.0	0.4	100.0	82.4	15.8	1.8
	1975	100.0	87.1	12.3	0.6	100.0	80.6	17.6	1.9
	1980	100.0	84.7	14.6	0.7	100.0	78.3	19.5	2.2
	1983	100.0	81.3	17.9	0.9	100.0	75.7	21.5	2.8
	1984	100.0	80.6	18.5	0.9	100.0	75.0	22.2	2.9
ASIA (EXCLUDING ARAB STATES)‡	1970	100.0	75.0	22.9	2.1	100.0	64.6	30.4	5.0
	1975	100.0	72.8	24.8	2.4	100.0	62.2	32.7	5.1
	1980	100.0	69.1	28.0	2.9	100.0	57.2	37.3	5.5
	1983	100.0	68.6	28.1	3.3	100.0	57.0	37.1	5.9
	1984	100.0	68.0	28.6	3.3	100.0	57.0	37.1	5.9
ARAB STATES	1970	100.0	75.9	21.4	2.7	100.0	66.0	29.5	4.5
	1975	100.0	71.6	24.6	3.9	100.0	63.0	31.7	5.4
	1980	100.0	67.0	28.3	4.7	100.0	57.5	35.5	7.0
	1983	100.0	65.2	29.8	5.0	100.0	55.6	37.4	7.1
	1984	100.0	64.6	30.4	5.1	100.0	55.3	37.7	7.0
NORTHERN AMERICA	1970	100.0	52.5	32.8	14.8	100.0	44.7	35.7	19.6
	1975	100.0	49.0	32.4	18.6	100.0	42.7	36.4	20.9
	1980	100.0	49.8	28.4	21.8	100.0	41.4	33.6	25.0
	1983	100.0	49.7	27.6	22.7	100.0	42.0	32.2	25.8
	1984	100.0	49.5	27.4	23.1	100.0	41.9	32.0	26.1
LATIN AMERICAN AND THE CARIBBEAN	1970	100.0	82.7	14.3	2.9	100.0	65.9	27.2	6.9
	1975	100.0	77.7	17.3	5.0	100.0	64.5	25.7	9.8
	1980	100.0	74.3	20.1	5.6	100.0	59.9	29.5	10.6
	1983	100.0	73.1	20.9	5.9	100.0	58.9	29.7	11.4
	1984	100.0	72.4	21.4	6.2	100.0	58.0	30.5	11.5

General note / Note générale / Nota general:

E--> For composition of major areas and groups of countries, see head note to table 1.2. The school year begins in the calendar year indicated. More information on this point is given in the general introduction to the 'Education' section. The figures in this table do not include data relating to pre-primary, special and adult education. Second level education includes general, teacher training and vocational education. Third level education includes universities and other institutions of higher education. Owing to the rounding of figures, the totals and sub-totals shown in this table do not always correspond exactly to the sums of their component items.

FR-> Pour la composition des grandes régions et des groupes de pays, voir la note en-tête du tableau 1.2. L'année scolaire commence pendant l'année civile indiquée. Pour plus de détails, se reporter à l'introduction générale de la partie 'Education'. Les chiffres de ce tableau ne comprennent pas l'enseignement préprimaire, l'éducation spéciale et l'éducation des adultes. L'enseignement du second degré comprend les enseignements général, normal et technique. L'enseignement du troisième degré comprend les universités et autres établissements d'enseignement supérieur. Les chiffres ayant été arrondis, les totaux et les sous-totaux figurant dans ce tableau ne correspondent pas toujours exactement à la

General note / Note générale / Nota general: (Cont):
somme des éléments qui les composent.

ESP> Puede verse la composición de las grandes regiones y grupos de paises en la nota encabezando el cuadro 1.2. El año escolar empieza durante el año civil indicado. Pueden verse mas detalles a este respecto en la introducción general de la sección 'Educación'. Las cifras de este cuadro no comprenden la enseñanza preprimaria, la educación especial y la educación de adultos. La enseñanza de segundo grado incluye las enseñanzas general, normal y técnica. La enseñanza de tercer grado incluye las universidades y otros establecimientos de enseñanza superior. Como las cifras se han redondeado, los totales y los sub-totales que figuran en este cuadro no siempre corresponden exactamente a la suma de los elementos que los componen.

World total, Africa, Developped countries, Africa (excl. Arab States):

E--> Excluding South Africa.

FR-> Non compris l'Afrique du Sud.

ESP> Excluída Sudáfrica.

World total, Asia, Developing countries, Asia (excl. Arab States):

E--> Not including the Democratic People's Republic of Korea.

FR-> Non compris la République populaire démocratique de Corée.

ESP> Excluída la República popular democrática de Corea.

2.4 Estimated female enrolment by level of education

Estimation des effectifs scolaires féminins par degré d'enseignement

Estimación de la matrícula escolar femenina por grado de enseñanza

(SEE INTRODUCTORY TEXT CONCERNING TABLES 2.2 – 2.6)

(VOIR LE TEXTE D'INTRODUCTION RELATIF AUX TABLEAUX 2.2 – 2.6)

(VEASE EL TEXTO DE INTRODUCCION RELATIVO A LOS CUADROS 2.2 – 2.6)

% 1970–80 AND 1980–84 = ANNUAL AVERAGE INCREASE IN ENROLMENT FROM 1970 TO 1980 AND FROM 1980 TO 1984, AS PERCENTAGE.

% 1970–80 ET 1980–84 = ACCROISSEMENT MOYEN ANNUEL DES EFFECTIFS SCOLAIRES DE 1970 A 1980 ET DE 1980 A 1984, EN POURCENTAGE.

% 1970–80 Y 1980–84 = CRECIMIENTO MEDIO ANUAL DE LA MATRICULA ESCOLAR DE 1970 A 1980 Y DE 1980 A 1984, EN PORCENTAJE.

CONTINENTS, MAJOR AREAS AND GROUPS OF COUNTRIES / CONTINENTS, GRANDES REGIONS ET GROUPES DE PAYS / CONTINENTES, GRANDES REGIONES Y GRUPOS DE DE PAISES	YEAR / ANNEE / AÑO	FEMALE ENROLMENT (THOUSANDS) / EFFECTIFS SCOLAIRES FEMININS (MILLIERS) / MATRICULA ESCOLAR FEMENINA (MILES)				% OF FEMALES IN TOTAL ENROLMENT / % DES EFFECTIFS FEMININS PAR RAPPORT AU TOTAL DES EFFECTIFS / % DE LA MATRICULAR ESCOLAR FEMENINA CON RESPECTO A LA MATRICULA TOTAL			
		TOTAL / TOTAL / TOTAL	1ST LEVEL / 1ER DEGRE / 1ER GRADO	2ND LEVEL / 2ND DEGRE / 2DO GRADO	3RD LEVEL / 3EME DEGRE / 3ER GRADO	TOTAL / TOTAL / TOTAL	1ST LEVEL / 1ER DEGRE / 1ER GRADO	2ND LEVEL / 2ND DEGRE / 2DO GRADO	3RD LEVEL / 3EME DEGRE / 3ER GRADO
		(1)	(2)	(3)	(4)	(5)	(6)	(7)	(8)
WORLD TOTAL (INCLUDING CHINA)‡	1970	...	...	...	...	...	...	...	...
	1975	334 789	229 161	89 735	15 895	44	45	43	40
	1980	373 492	248 645	104 837	20 010	44	45	43	42
	1983	385 093	254 447	108 486	22 160	44	45	43	43
	1984	392 669	257 831	112 032	22 806	44	45	43	43
	% 1970–80	.	.	.	.				
	% 1980–84	1.3	0.9	1.7	3.3				
WORLD TOTAL (EXCLUDING CHINA)‡	1970	212 738	144 540	57 639	10 559	44	44	44	38
	1975	248 602	160 918	71 954	15 732	44	45	45	40
	1980	285 707	183 471	82 496	19 740	45	45	45	43
	1983	307 152	195 075	90 247	21 831	45	45	44	54
	1984	313 444	198 454	92 591	22 398	45	45	44	43
	% 1970–80	3.0	2.4	3.7	6.5				
	% 1980–84	2.3	2.0	2.9	3.2				
AFRICA‡	1970	12 746	11 332	1 323	90	37	39	30	22
	1975	19 240	16 375	2 657	208	39	41	34	26
	1980	30 629	25 405	4 860	365	41	43	35	27
	1983	35 235	28 475	6 275	485	41	44	34	28
	1984	36 192	28 974	6 698	520	41	44	35	28
	% 1970–80	9.2	8.4	13.9	15.0				
	% 1980–84	4.3	3.3	8.3	9.3				
AMERICA	1970	56 779	38 551	13 881	4 346	48	49	49	40
	1975	66 073	42 765	16 378	6 929	48	49	49	44
	1980	71 905	46 003	17 127	8 775	49	49	50	49
	1983	74 794	47 427	17 959	9 408	49	48	50	49
	1984	75 346	47 576	18 121	9 649	49	48	50	49
	% 1970–80	2.4	1.8	2.1	7.3				
	% 1980–84	1.2	0.8	1.4	2.4				
ASIA‡	1970	74 807	56 315	16 624	1 867	39	41	35	27
	1975	91 404	66 347	22 255	2 802	40	41	37	29
	1980	111 736	78 028	29 719	3 988	41	42	39	31
	1983	125 852	85 703	35 225	4 923	41	43	39	33
	1984	130 676	88 705	36 841	5 130	41	43	39	33
	% 1970–80	4.1	3.3	6.0	7.9				
	% 1980–84	4.0	3.3	5.5	6.5				

2.4 School enrolment (female)
Effectifs scolaires (féminins)
Matrícula escolar (femenina)

CONTINENTS, MAJOR AREAS AND GROUPS OF COUNTRIES / CONTINENTS, GRANDES REGIONS ET GROUPES DE PAYS / CONTINENTES, GRANDES REGIONES Y GRUPOS DE DE PAISES	YEAR / ANNEE / AÑO	FEMALE ENROLMENT (THOUSANDS) / EFFECTIFS SCOLAIRES FEMININS (MILLIERS) / MATRICULA ESCOLAR FEMENINA (MILES)				% OF FEMALES IN TOTAL ENROLMENT / % DES EFFECTIFS FEMININS PAR RAPPORT AU TOTAL DES EFFECTIFS / % DE LA MATRICULAR ESCOLAR FEMENINA CON RESPECTO A LA MATRICULA TOTAL			
		TOTAL / TOTAL / TOTAL	1ST LEVEL / 1ER DEGRE / 1ER GRADO	2ND LEVEL / 2ND DEGRE / 2DO GRADO	3RD LEVEL / 3EME DEGRE / 3ER GRADO	TOTAL / TOTAL / TOTAL	1ST LEVEL / 1ER DEGRE / 1ER GRADO	2ND LEVEL / 2ND DEGRE / 2DO GRADO	3RD LEVEL / 3EME DEGRE / 3ER GRADO
		(1)	(2)	(3)	(4)	(5)	(6)	(7)	(8)
EUROPE (INCL. USSR)	1970	66 445	37 109	25 158	4 179	49	49	51	43
	1975	69 737	34 208	29 877	5 652	50	49	52	45
	1980	69 149	32 743	29 978	6 429	50	49	52	47
	1983	68 936	32 214	29 911	6 812	50	49	52	48
	1984	68 885	31 970	30 027	6 888	50	48	52	48
	% 1970–80	0.4	–1.2	1.8	4.4				
	% 1980–84	–0.1	–0.6	0.0	1.7				
OCEANIA	1970	1 961	1 232	653	76	47	48	48	34
	1975	2 149	1 223	787	140	47	48	48	40
	1980	2 288	1 292	812	183	48	48	49	44
	1983	2 335	1 256	876	203	48	48	49	45
	1984	2 344	1 230	904	210	48	48	49	45
	% 1970–80	1.6	0.5	2.2	9.2				
	% 1980–84	0.6	–1.2	2.7	3.5				
DEVELOPED COUNTRIES‡	1970	105 736	58 054	39 229	8 453	49	49	50	41
	1975	111 201	55 100	44 305	11 797	49	49	51	44
	1980	110 174	53 515	42 731	13 928	49	49	51	48
	1983	110 143	52 755	42 772	14 616	52	49	51	72
	1984	109 905	52 226	42 900	14 779	49	49	51	48
	% 1970–80	0.4	–0.8	0.9	5.1				
	% 1980–84	–0.1	–0.6	0.1	1.5				
DEVELOPING COUNTRIES‡	1970	107 002	86 486	18 410	2 106	40	42	34	29
	1975	137 401	105 818	27 649	3 935	41	43	37	32
	1980	175 533	129 956	39 765	5 812	42	44	39	35
	1983	197 009	142 320	47 475	7 215	42	44	39	36
	1984	203 539	146 228	49 691	7 619	43	44	39	36
	% 1970–80	5.1	4.2	8.0	10.7				
	% 1980–84	3.8	3.0	5.7	7.0				
AFRICA (EXCLUDING ARAB STATES)‡	1970	8 583	7 968	598	17	38	39	30	17
	1975	13 413	12 025	1 353	34	41	42	33	18
	1980	22 695	19 935	2 690	70	42	44	34	18
	1983	25 702	22 151	3 453	98	42	44	31	19
	1984	26 267	22 481	3 685	101	42	44	32	19
	% 1970–80	10.2	9.6	16.2	15.2				
	% 1980–84	3.7	3.1	8.2	9.6				
ASIA (EXCLUDING ARAB STATES)‡	1970	73 236	55 110	16 290	1 836	39	41	35	27
	1975	88 754	64 409	21 625	2 720	40	42	37	29
	1980	107 546	75 067	28 641	3 838	41	42	39	31
	1983	120 940	82 313	33 898	4 729	41	43	39	33
	1984	125 516	85 153	35 440	4 922	41	43	39	33
	% 1970–80	3.9	3.1	5.8	7.7				
	% 1980–84	3.9	3.2	5.5	6.4				
ARAB STATES	1970	5 734	4 570	1 059	105	35	36	30	24
	1975	8 477	6 288	1 934	256	37	38	34	29
	1980	12 124	8 431	3 248	445	39	41	37	31
	1983	14 444	9 714	4 149	582	40	42	39	33
	1984	15 086	10 045	4 413	628	41	42	39	33
	% 1970–80	7.8	6.3	11.9	15.5				
	% 1980–84	5.6	4.5	8.0	9.0				
NORTHERN AMERICA	1970	29 599	15 792	10 043	3 765	48	49	50	41
	1975	31 124	15 378	10 343	5 403	48	49	50	45
	1980	29 474	14 429	8 377	6 668	50	49	50	51
	1983	29 223	14 266	8 046	6 911	49	48	49	51
	1984	28 984	14 135	7 873	6 975	49	49	49	51
	% 1970–80	–0.0	–0.9	–1.8	5.9				
	% 1980–84	–0.4	–0.5	–1.5	1.1				
LATIN AMERICAN AND THE CARIBBEAN	1970	27 179	22 760	3 838	582	48	49	48	35
	1975	34 948	27 387	6 035	1 526	48	49	48	42
	1980	42 431	31 575	8 750	2 107	49	49	50	43
	1983	45 571	33 161	9 913	2 497	49	48	50	45
	1984	46 363	33 441	10 248	2 673	49	48	50	45
	% 1970–80	4.6	3.3	8.6	13.7				
	% 1980–84	2.2	1.4	4.0	6.1				

General note / Note générale / Nota general:

E--> For composition of major areas and groups of countries, see head note to table 1.2. The school year begins in the calendar year indicated. More information on this point is given in the general introduction to the 'Education' section. The figures in this table do not include data relating to pre-primary, special and adult education. Second level education includes general, teacher training and vocational education. Third level education includes universities and other institutions of higher education. Owing to the rounding of figures, the totals and sub-totals shown in this table do not always correspond exactly to the sums of their component items.

FR-> Pour la composition des grandes régions et des groupes de pays, voir la note en-tête du tableau 1.2. L'année scolaire commence pendant l'année civile indiquée. Pour plus de détails, se reporter à l'introduction générale de la partie 'Education'. Les chiffres de ce tableau ne comprennent pas l'enseignement préprimaire, l'éducation spéciale et l'éducation des adultes. L'enseignement du second degré comprend les enseignements général, normal et technique. L'enseignement du troisième degré comprend les universités et autres établissements d'enseignement supérieur. Les chiffres ayant été arrondis, les totaux et les sous-totaux figurant dans ce tableau ne correspondent pas toujours exactement à la somme des éléments qui les composent.

ESP> Puede verse la composición de las grandes regiones y grupos de paises en la nota encabezando el cuadro 1.2. El año escolar empieza durante el año civil indicado. Pueden verse mas detalles a este respecto en la introducción general de la sección 'Educación'. Las cifras de este cuadro no comprenden la enseñanza preprimaria, la educación especial y la educación de adultos. La enseñanza de segundo grado incluye las enseñanzas general, normal y técnica. La enseñanza de tercer grado incluye las universidades y otros establecimientos de enseñanza superior. Como las cifras se han redondeado, los totales y los sub-totales que figuran en este cuadro no siempre corresponden exactamente a la suma de los elementos que los componen.

World Total (incl. China), World Total (excl. China):

E--> Since for China it was not possible to estimate 1970 data, two world totals are shown; the available data for China are included in the first total only. Both totals exclude the Democratic People's Republic of Korea.

FR-> Pour la Chine, il n'était pas possible d'estimer les données pour 1970. C'est pourquoi ce tableau présente deux totaux; les données disponibles pour la Chine sont incluses dans le premier total seulement. Les deux totaux ne comprennent pas la République populaire démocratique de Corée.

ESP> Para China no fue posible estimar los datos relativos al año 1970. Por ello este cuadro presenta dos totales; los datos disponibles para China se incluyen en el primer total solamente. Los dos totales no incluyen la República popular democrática de Corea.

World Total, Africa, Developed countries, Africa (excl. Arab States):

E--> Not including South Africa.

FR-> Non compris l'Afrique du Sud.

ESP> Excluída Sudáfrica.

Asia, Developing countries, Asia (excl. Arab States):

E--> Not including China and the Democratic People's Republic of Korea.

FR-> Non compris la Chine et la République populaire démocratique de Corée.

ESP> Excluídas China y la República popular democrática de Corea.

2.5 Estimated female teaching staff by level of education (first and second levels only)

Estimation du personnel enseignant féminin, par degré d'enseignement (premier et second degrés seulement)

Estimación del personal docente femenino, por grado de enseñanza (primer y segundo grado solamente)

(SEE INTRODUCTORY TEXT CONCERNING TABLES 2.2 – 2.6)

(VOIR LE TEXTE D'INTRODUCTION RELATIF AUX TABLEAUX 2.2 – 2.6)

(VEASE EL TEXTO DE INTRODUCCION RELATIVO A LOS CUADROS 2.2 – 2.6)

CONTINENTS, MAJOR AREAS AND GROUPS OF COUNTRIES / CONTINENTS, GRANDES REGIONS ET GROUPES DE PAYS / CONTINENTES, GRANDES REGIONES Y GRUPOS DE PAISES	YEAR / ANNEE / AÑO	FIRST LEVEL/PREMIER DEGRE/PRIMER GRADO		SECOND LEVEL/SECOND DEGRE/SEGUNDO GRADO	
		TOTAL FEMALE TEACHING STAFF / TOTAL DU PERSONNEL ENSEIGNANT FEMININ / TOTAL DEL PERSONAL DOCENTE FEMENINO (000)	AS % OF TOTAL TEACHING STAFF / EN % DU TOTAL DU PERSONNEL ENSEIGNANT / EN % DEL TOTAL DEL PERSONAL DOCENTE %	TOTAL FEMALE TEACHING STAFF / TOTAL DU PERSONNEL ENSEIGNANT FEMININ / TOTAL DEL PERSONAL DOCENTE FEMENINO (000)	AS % OF TOTAL TEACHING STAFF / EN % DU TOTAL DU PERSONNEL ENSEIGNANT / EN % DEL TOTAL DEL PERSONAL DOCENTE %
		(1)	(2)	(3)	(4)
WORLD TOTAL (INCLUDING CHINA)‡	1970	...	...	...	...
	1975	9 239	52	...	...
	1980	10 224	52	5 552	39
	1983	10 782	52	5 871	40
	1984	11 043	28	6 077	40
WORLD TOTAL (EXCLUDING CHINA)‡	1970	6 529	58	3 427	44
	1975	7 350	58	4 241	45
	1980	8 185	58	4 764	44
	1983	8 774	57	5 133	43
	1984	8 950	26	5 294	43
AFRICA‡	1970	208	28	55	27
	1975	306	30	85	27
	1980	510	33	152	28
	1983	605	35	199	29
	1984	625	35	215	29
AMERICA	1970	2 354	80	796	45
	1975	2 796	80	959	47
	1980	2 940	79	1 082	46
	1983	3 121	79	1 118	47
	1984	3 182	79	1 163	47
ASIA‡	1970	1 361	36	608	27
	1975	1 673	37	870	30
	1980	2 095	40	1 169	31
	1983	2 369	39	1 437	31
	1984	2 473	10	1 516	31
EUROPE (INCL. USSR)	1970	2 546	70	1 935	56
	1975	2 502	71	2 282	57
	1980	2 558	72	2 311	56
	1983	2 600	72	2 326	57
	1984	2 593	72	2 340	57
OCEANIA	1970	60	63	33	46
	1975	73	65	45	46
	1980	81	64	51	46
	1983	79	65	54	44
	1984	77	64	62	47
DEVELOPED COUNTRIES‡	1970	3 922	72	2 560	51
	1975	3 979	73	2 975	51
	1980	4 111	73	3 008	51
	1983	4 177	73	3 024	51
	1984	4 161	74	3 050	52

CONTINENTS, MAJOR AREAS AND GROUPS OF COUNTRIES / CONTINENTS, GRANDES REGIONS ET GROUPES DE PAYS / CONTINENTES, GRANDES REGIONES Y GRUPOS DE PAISES	YEAR / ANNEE / AÑO	FIRST LEVEL/PREMIER DEGRE/PRIMER GRADO: TOTAL FEMALE TEACHING STAFF / TOTAL DU PERSONNEL ENSEIGNANT FEMININ / TOTAL DEL PERSONAL DOCENTE FEMENINO (000)	FIRST LEVEL: AS % OF TOTAL TEACHING STAFF / EN % DU TOTAL DU PERSONNEL ENSEIGNANT / EN % DEL TOTAL DEL PERSONAL DOCENTE %	SECOND LEVEL/SECOND DEGRE/SEGUNDO GRADO: TOTAL FEMALE TEACHING STAFF / TOTAL DU PERSONNEL ENSEIGNANT FEMININ / TOTAL DEL PERSONAL DOCENTE FEMENINO (000)	SECOND LEVEL: AS % OF TOTAL TEACHING STAFF / EN % DU TOTAL DU PERSONNEL ENSEIGNANT / EN % DEL TOTAL DEL PERSONAL DOCENTE %
		(1)	(2)	(3)	(4)
DEVELOPING COUNTRIES‡	1970	2 607	45	867	32
	1975	3 371	47	1 266	35
	1980	4 074	48	1 756	35
	1983	4 597	47	2 109	35
	1984	4 789	17	2 244	35
AFRICA (EXCLUDING ARAB STATES)‡	1970	123	25	28	29
	1975	198	28	41	26
	1980	351	32	70	25
	1983	404	33	86	25
	1984	411	33	92	25
ASIA (EXCLUDING ARAB STATES)‡	1970	1 312	36	591	27
	1975	1 592	37	836	30
	1980	1 966	40	1 114	30
	1983	2 192	39	1 360	31
	1984	2 287	9	1 433	31
ARAB STATES	1970	134	37	44	27
	1975	189	37	78	30
	1980	289	42	137	32
	1983	379	46	190	35
	1984	400	46	205	35
NORTHERN AMERICA	1970	1 157	82	508	45
	1975	1 210	82	571	46
	1980	1 227	81	561	46
	1983	1 251	81	541	46
	1984	1 250	81	541	46
LATIN AMERICAN AND THE CARIBBEAN	1970	1 197	78	289	46
	1975	1 587	78	388	48
	1980	1 713	77	521	47
	1983	1 870	77	576	47
	1984	1 931	77	622	47

General note / Note générale / Nota general:

E--> For composition of major areas and groups of countries, see head note to table 1.2. The school year begins in the calendar year indicated. More information on this point is given in the general introduction to the 'Education' section. Second level education includes general, teacher training and vocational education. Owing to the rounding of figures, the totals and sub-totals shown in this table do not always correspond exactly to the sums of their component items.

FR-> Pour la composition des grandes régions et des groupes de pays, voir la note en-tête du tableau 1.2. L'année scolaire commence pendant l'année civile indiquée. Pour plus de détails, se reporter à l'introduction générale de la partie 'Education'. L'enseignement du second degré comprend les enseignements général, normal et technique. Les chiffres ayant été arrondis, les totaux et les sous-totaux figurant dans ce tableau ne correspondent pas toujours exactement à la somme des éléments qui les composent.

ESP> Puede verse la composición de las grandes regiones y grupos de paises en la nota encabezando el cuadro 1.2. El año escolar empieza durante el año civil indicado. Pueden verse mas detalles a este respecto en la introducción general de la sección 'Educación'. La enseñanza de segundo grado incluye las enseñanzas general, normal y técnica. Como las cifras se han redondeado, los totales y los sub-totales que figuran en este cuadro no siempre corresponden exactamente a la suma de los elementos que los componen.

World Total (incl. China), World Total (excl. China):

E--> Since for China it was not possible to estimate data for 1970 and 1975, two world totals are shown; the available data for China are included in the first total only. Both totals exclude the Democratic People's Republic of Korea.

FR-> Pour la Chine, il n'était pas possible d'estimer les données pour 1970 et 1975. C'est pourquoi ce tableau présente deux totaux; les données disponibles pour la Chine sont incluses dans le premier total seulement. Les deux totaux ne comprennent pas la République populaire démocratique de Corée.

ESP> Para China no fue posible estimar los datos para 1970 y 1975. Por ello este cuadro presenta dos totales; los datos disponibles para China se incluyen en el primer total solamente. Los dos totales no incluyen la República popular democrática de Corea.

World Total, Africa, Developed countries, Africa (excl. Arab States):

E--> Not including South Africa.

FR-> Non compris l'Afrique du Sud.

ESP> Excluída Sudáfrica.

Asia, Developing countries, Asia (excl. Arab States):

E--> Not including China and the Democratic People's Republic of Korea.

FR-> Non compris la Chine et la République populaire démocratique de Corée.

ESP> Excluídas China y la República popular democrática de Corea.

2.6 Index numbers of total and female enrolment and teaching staff by level of education (1970 = 100)

Indices: total des effectifs scolaires, effectifs féminins et personnel enseignant, par degré d'enseignement (1970 = 100)

Indices: total de la matrícula escolar, matrícula escolar femenina y personal docente, por grado de enseñanza (1970 = 100)

(SEE INTRODUCTORY TEXT CONCERNING TABLES 2.2 – 2.6)

(VOIR LE TEXTE D'INTRODUCTION RELATIF AUX TABLEAUX 2.2 – 2.6)

(VEASE EL TEXTO DE INTRODUCCION RELATIVO A LOS CUADROS 2.2 – 2.6)

CONTINENTS, MAJOR AREAS AND GROUPS OF COUNTRIES / CONTINENTS, GRANDES REGIONS ET GROUPES DE PAYS / CONTINENTES, GRANDES REGIONES Y GRUPOS DE PAISES	YEAR / ANNEE / AÑO	TOTAL ENROLMENT / TOTAL DES EFFECTIFS SCOLAIRES / TOTAL DE LA MATRICULA ESCOLAR				FEMALE ENROLMENT / EFFECTIFS FEMININS / MATRICULA FEMENINA				TEACHING STAFF / PERSONNEL ENSEIGNANT / PERSONAL DOCENTE			
		TOTAL / TOTAL / TOTAL	1ST LEVEL / 1ER DEGRE / 1ER GRADO	2ND LEVEL / 2ND DEGRE / 2DO GRADO	3RD LEVEL / 3EME DEGRE / 3ER GRADO	TOTAL / TOTAL / TOTAL	1ST LEVEL / 1ER DEGRE / 1ER GRADO	2ND LEVEL / 2ND DEGRE / 2DO GRADO	3RD LEVEL / 3EME DEGRE / 3ER GRADO	TOTAL / TOTAL / TOTAL	1ST LEVEL / 1ER DEGRE / 1ER GRADO	2ND LEVEL / 2ND DEGRE / 2DO GRADO	3RD LEVEL / 3EME DEGRE / 3ER GRADO
		(1)	(2)	(3)	(4)	(5)	(6)	(7)	(8)	(9)	(10)	(11)	(12)
WORLD TOTAL (INCLUDING CHINA)‡	1970	100	100	100	100	...	...	...	...	100	100	100	100
	1975	123	119	131	140	.	.	.	.	124	120	129	135
	1980	136	128	153	168	.	.	.	.	144	132	157	170
	1983	141	132	159	183	.	.	.	.	152	140	164	185
	1984	143	133	164	189	.	.	.	.	155	142	167	190
WORLD TOTAL (EXCLUDING CHINA)‡	1970	100	100	100	100	100	100	100	100	100	100	100	100
	1975	115	111	122	139	116	111	124	148	118	112	121	136
	1980	131	125	140	164	134	126	143	186	135	126	140	168
	1983	141	133	155	179	144	134	156	206	147	137	154	182
	1984	144	135	160	184	147	137	160	212	151	140	159	186
AFRICA‡	1970	100	100	100	100	100	100	100	100	100	100	100	100
	1975	142	136	177	202	150	144	200	231	143	138	155	162
	1980	217	201	307	342	240	224	367	405	222	207	269	300
	1983	249	222	409	437	276	251	474	538	262	234	345	400
	1984	256	226	435	460	283	255	506	580	272	240	369	417
AMERICA	1970	100	100	100	100	100	100	100	100	100	100	100	100
	1975	115	111	117	145	116	110	117	159	120	119	117	132
	1980	124	119	121	165	126	119	123	201	135	127	133	168
	1983	129	124	127	176	131	123	129	216	142	135	137	182
	1984	130	124	128	180	132	123	130	222	146	137	142	187
ASIA‡	1970	100	100	100	100	100	100	100	100	100	100	100	100
	1975	119	116	126	142	122	117	133	150	123	118	129	142
	1980	142	133	161	185	149	138	178	213	150	137	167	179
	1983	159	145	190	218	168	152	211	263	176	158	203	198
	1984	164	149	198	226	174	157	221	274	183	164	212	202
EUROPE (INCL. USSR)	1970	100	100	100	100	100	100	100	100	100	100	100	100
	1975	103	92	117	126	104	92	118	135	108	96	116	133
	1980	102	88	116	140	104	88	119	153	112	97	118	156
	1983	102	87	116	145	103	86	118	163	113	98	119	163
	1984	102	86	116	147	103	86	119	164	114	97	119	166
OCEANIA	1970	100	100	100	100	100	100	100	100	100	100	100	100
	1975	108	99	118	157	109	99	120	184	130	116	136	186
	1980	114	104	120	186	116	104	124	240	147	131	155	200
	1983	116	101	129	201	119	101	134	267	151	127	170	206
	1984	116	99	134	207	119	99	138	276	156	125	184	213
DEVELOPED COUNTRIES‡	1970	100	100	100	100	100	100	100	100	100	100	100	100
	1975	104	95	111	128	105	94	112	139	109	99	115	126
	1980	102	92	107	140	104	92	108	164	114	102	116	152
	1983	102	91	107	145	104	90	109	172	116	103	116	159
	1984	102	90	108	147	103	89	109	174	116	103	117	161

CONTINENTS, MAJOR AREAS AND GROUPS OF COUNTRIES / CONTINENTS, GRANDES REGIONS ET GROUPES DE PAYS / CONTINENTES, GRANDES REGIONES Y GRUPOS DE PAISES	YEAR / ANNEE / AÑO	TOTAL ENROLMENT / TOTAL DES EFFECTIFS SCOLAIRES / TOTAL DE LA MATRICULA ESCOLAR				FEMALE ENROLMENT / EFFECTIFS FEMININS / MATRICULA FEMENINA				TEACHING STAFF / PERSONNEL ENSEIGNANT / PERSONAL DOCENTE			
		TOTAL / TOTAL / TOTAL	1ST LEVEL / 1ER DEGRE / 1ER GRADO	2ND LEVEL / 2ND DEGRE / 2DO GRADO	3RD LEVEL / 3EME DEGRE / 3ER GRADO	TOTAL / TOTAL / TOTAL	1ST LEVEL / 1ER DEGRE / 1ER GRADO	2ND LEVEL / 2ND DEGRE / 2DO GRADO	3RD LEVEL / 3EME DEGRE / 3ER GRADO	TOTAL / TOTAL / TOTAL	1ST LEVEL / 1ER DEGRE / 1ER GRADO	2ND LEVEL / 2ND DEGRE / 2DO GRADO	3RD LEVEL / 3EME DEGRE / 3ER GRADO
		(1)	(2)	(3)	(4)	(5)	(6)	(7)	(8)	(9)	(10)	(11)	(12)
DEVELOPING COUNTRIES‡	1970	100	100	100	100	100	100	100	100	100	100	100	100
	1975	125	120	138	169	128	122	150	186	129	124	134	165
	1980	156	144	189	231	164	150	215	275	163	148	185	221
	1983	174	157	226	276	184	164	257	342	190	169	224	254
	1984	179	161	236	290	190	169	269	361	198	175	236	264
AFRICA (EXCLUDING ARAB STATES)‡	1970	100	100	100	100	100	100	100	100	100	100	100	100
	1975	146	141	200	187	156	150	226	200	144	141	161	154
	1980	240	224	390	378	264	250	449	411	233	221	288	281
	1983	274	246	545	522	299	277	577	576	268	246	365	418
	1984	281	250	579	534	306	282	616	594	276	250	388	436
ASIA (EXCLUDING ARAB STATES)‡	1970	100	100	100	100	100	100	100	100	100	100	100	100
	1975	118	115	125	141	121	116	132	148	122	116	127	142
	1980	140	132	159	182	146	136	175	209	148	134	165	176
	1983	156	143	188	214	165	149	208	257	173	154	199	193
	1984	161	146	195	222	171	154	217	268	179	160	208	197
ARAB STATES	1970	100	100	100	100	100	100	100	100	100	100	100	100
	1975	140	132	160	201	147	137	182	243	148	141	159	176
	1980	185	163	245	324	211	184	306	423	217	189	261	336
	1983	215	185	300	398	251	212	391	554	266	224	337	416
	1984	224	190	318	424	263	219	416	600	282	236	361	440
NORTHERN AMERICA	1970	100	100	100	100	100	100	100	100	100	100	100	100
	1975	104	97	102	131	105	97	102	143	109	105	111	117
	1980	96	91	83	142	99	91	83	177	116	107	109	148
	1983	95	90	80	147	98	90	80	183	116	109	105	153
	1984	95	89	79	148	97	89	78	185	116	109	104	155
LATIN AMERICAN AND THE CARIBBEAN	1970	100	100	100	100	100	100	100	100	100	100	100	100
	1975	128	120	155	222	128	120	157	262	135	132	128	191
	1980	154	139	216	296	156	138	227	362	161	146	175	247
	1983	166	147	243	340	167	145	258	429	177	158	194	292
	1984	169	148	253	361	170	146	267	459	186	163	209	310

General note / Note générale / Nota general:

E--> For composition of major areas and groups of countries, see head note to table 1.2. The school year begins in the calendar year indicated. More information on this point is given in the general introduction to the 'Education' section. The figures in this table do not include data relating to pre-primary, special and adult education. Second level education includes general, teacher training and vocational education. Third level education includes universities and other institutions of higher education. Owing to the rounding of figures, the totals and sub-totals shown in this table do not always correspond exactly to the sums of their component items.

FR-> Pour la composition des grandes régions et des groupes de pays, voir la note en-tête du tableau 1.2. L'année scolaire commence pendant l'année civile indiquée. Pour plus de détails, se reporter à l'introduction générale de la partie 'Education'. Les chiffres de ce tableau ne comprennent pas l'enseignement préprimaire, l'éducation spéciale et l'éducation des adultes. L'enseignement du second degré comprend les enseignements général, normal et technique. L'enseignement du troisième degré comprend les universités et autres établissements d'enseignement supérieur. Les chiffres ayant été arrondis, les totaux et les sous-totaux figurant dans ce tableau ne correspondent pas toujours exactement à la somme des éléments qui les composent.

ESP> Puede verse la composición de las grandes regiones y grupos de paises en la nota encabezando el cuadro 1.2. El año escolar empieza durante el año civil indicado. Pueden verse mas detalles a este respecto en la introducción general de la sección 'Educación'. Las cifras de este cuadro no comprenden la enseñanza preprimaria, la educación especial y la educación de adultos. La enseñanza de segundo grado incluye las enseñanzas general, normal y técnica. La enseñanza de tercer grado incluye las universidades y otros establecimientos de enseñanza superior. Como las cifras se han redondeado, los totales y los sub-totales que figuran en este cuadro no siempre corresponden exactamente a la suma de los elementos que los componen.

World Total (incl. China), World Total (excl. China):

E--> Since for China it was not possible to estimate data on female enrolment for 1970, two world totals are shown; the available data for China are included in the first total only. Both totals exclude the Democratic People's Republic of Korea.

FR-> Pour la Chine, il n'était pas possible d'estimer les données relatives aux effectifs féminins pour 1970. C'est pourquoi ce tableau présente deux totaux; les données disponibles pour la Chine sont incluses dans le premier total seulement. Les deux totaux ne comprennent pas la République populaire démocratique de Corée.

ESP> Para China no fue posible estimar los datos relativos a la matrícula feminina en 1970. Por ello este cuadro presenta dos totales; los datos disponibles para China se incluyen en el primer total solamente. Los dos totales no incluyen la República popular democrática de Corea.

World Total, Africa, Developed countries, Africa (excl. Arab States):

E--> Not including South Africa.

FR-> Non compris l'Afrique du Sud.

ESP> Excluída Sudáfrica.

Asia, Developing countries, Asia (excl. Arab States):

E--> Not including China and the Democratic People's Republic of Korea.

FR-> Non compris la Chine et la République populaire démocratique de Corée.

ESP> Excluídas China y la República popular democrática de Corea.

2.7 Pupil-teacher ratios at the first level of education

Nombre d'élèves par maître pour le premier degré d'enseignement

Número de alumnos por maestro por el primer grado de enseñanza

CONTINENTS, MAJOR AREAS AND GROUPS OF COUNTRIES / CONTINENTS, GRANDES REGIONS ET GROUPES DE PAYS / CONTINENTES, GRANDES REGIONES Y GRUPOS DE PAISES	YEAR / ANNEE / AÑO	FREQUENCY DISTRIBUTION ACCORDING TO THE PUPIL-TEACHER RATIO IN FIRST LEVEL EDUCATION / DISTRIBUTION DE FREQUENCE SELON LE NOMBRE D'ELEVES PAR MAITRE DANS L'ENSEIGNEMENT DU PREMIER DEGRE / DISTRIBUCION DE FRECUENCIA SEGUN EL NUMERO DE ALUMNOS POR MAESTRO EN LA ENSEÑANZA DE PRIMER GRADO					
		– 21	21–30	31–40	41–50	51–60	+ 60
WORLD TOTAL‡	1970	23	80	51	28	8	5
	1975	37	71	48	21	13	4
	1980	50	67	43	20	9	5
	1983	52	70	40	19	9	4
	1984	51	72	43	14	10	4
AFRICA‡	1970	1	6	20	18	3	5
	1975	1	6	19	14	9	4
	1980	3	7	18	14	6	5
	1983	2	9	21	11	6	4
	1984	2	10	21	8	8	4
AMERICA	1970	4	22	17	4	2	–
	1975	6	24	14	3	1	–
	1980	13	22	11	3	–	–
	1983	14	22	10	3	–	–
	1984	14	22	10	3	–	–
ASIA‡	1970	4	19	10	6	3	–
	1975	7	17	11	3	3	–
	1980	7	16	12	3	3	–
	1983	8	17	8	5	3	–
	1984	8	17	11	3	2	–
EUROPE (INCL. USSR)	1970	11	19	3	–	–	–
	1975	19	12	2	–	–	–
	1980	19	13	1	–	–	–
	1983	21	11	1	–	–	–
	1984	21	11	1	–	–	–
OCEANIA	1970	3	14	2	–	–	–
	1975	4	12	2	–	–	–
	1980	8	9	1	–	–	–
	1983	7	11	1	–	–	–
	1984	6	12	–	–	–	–
DEVELOPED COUNTRIES‡	1970	12	23	3	–	–	–
	1975	21	15	2	–	–	–
	1980	23	14	1	–	–	–
	1983	25	12	1	–	–	–
	1984	25	12	1	–	–	–
DEVELOPING COUNTRIES‡	1970	11	57	48	28	8	5
	1975	16	56	46	21	13	4
	1980	27	53	42	20	9	5
	1983	27	58	39	19	9	4
	1984	26	60	42	14	10	4
AFRICA (EXCLUDING ARAB STATES)‡	1970	1	4	15	16	3	5
	1975	1	5	13	13	8	4
	1980	2	7	11	13	6	5
	1983	1	8	16	9	6	4
	1984	1	7	18	6	8	4
ASIA (EXCLUDING ARAB STATES)‡	1970	2	13	7	6	2	–
	1975	2	14	7	3	3	–
	1980	2	11	10	3	3	–
	1983	3	12	7	5	2	–
	1984	3	12	10	3	1	–

CONTINENTS, MAJOR AREAS AND GROUPS OF COUNTRIES CONTINENTS, GRANDES REGIONS ET GROUPES DE PAYS CONTINENTES, GRANDES REGIONES Y GRUPOS DE PAISES	YEAR ANNEE AÑO	FREQUENCY DISTRIBUTION ACCORDING TO THE PUPIL-TEACHER RATIO IN FIRST LEVEL EDUCATION DISTRIBUTION DE FREQUENCE SELON LE NOMBRE D'ELEVES PAR MAITRE DANS L'ENSEIGNEMENT DU PREMIER DEGRE DISTRIBUCION DE FRECUENCIA SEGUN EL NUMERO DE ALUMNOS POR MAESTRO EN LA ENSEÑANZA DE PRIMER GRADO					
		− 21	21–30	31–40	41–50	51–60	+ 60
ARAB STATES	1970	2	8	8	2	1	–
	1975	5	4	10	1	1	–
	1980	6	5	9	1	–	–
	1983	6	6	6	2	1	–
	1984	6	8	4	2	1	–
NORTHERN AMERICA	1970	–	4	–	–	–	–
	1975	1	3	–	–	–	–
	1980	3	1	–	–	–	–
	1983	4	–	–	–	–	–
	1984	4	–	–	–	–	–
LATIN AMERICAN AND THE CARIBBEAN	1970	4	18	17	4	2	–
	1975	5	21	14	4	1	–
	1980	10	21	11	3	–	–
	1983	10	22	10	3	–	–
	1984	10	22	10	3	–	–

General note / Note générale / Nota general:
E--> For composition of major areas and groups of countries, see the head note to table 1.2.
FR-> Pour la composition des grandes régions et des groupes de pays, voir la note en-tête du tableau 1.2.
ESP> Puede verse la composición de las grandes regiones y grupos de países en la nota encabezando del cuadro 1.2.

World Total, Africa, Developed countries, Africa (excl. Arab States):
E--> Not including South Africa.

World Total, Africa, Developed countries, Africa (excl. Arab (Cont):
FR-> Non compris l'Afrique du Sud.
ESP> Excluída Sudáfrica.

World Total, Asia, Developing countries, Asia (excluding Arab States):
E--> All data exclude the Democratic People's Republic of Korea.
FR-> Toutes les données excluent la République populaire démocratique de Corée.
ESP> Todos los datos excluyen la Républica popular democrática de Corea.

2.8 Estimated teaching staff and enrolment by sex for education preceding the first level

Estimation du personnel enseignant et des effectifs scolaires, par sexe, pour l'enseignement précédant le premier degré

Estimación del personal docente y de la matrícula escolar, por sexo, para la enseñanza anterior al primer grado

% 1970–80 AND 1980–84 = ANNUAL AVERAGE INCREASE IN TEACHING STAFF AND ENROLMENT FROM 1970 TO 1980 AND 1980 TO 1984, AS PERCENTAGE.

% 1970–80 ET 1980–84 = ACCROISSEMENT MOYEN ANNUEL DU PERSONNEL ENSEIGNANT ET DES EFFECTIFS SCOLAIRES DE 1970 A 1980 ET DE 1980 A 1984, EN POURCENTAGE.

% 1970–80 Y 1980–84 = CRECIMIENTO MEDIO ANUAL DEL PERSONAL DOCENTE Y DE LA MATRICULA ESCOLAR DE 1970 A 1980 Y DE 1980 A 1984, EN PORCENTAJE.

CONTINENTS, MAJOR AREAS AND GROUPS OF COUNTRIES / CONTINENTS, GRANDES REGIONS ET GROUPES DE PAYS / CONTINENTES, GRANDES REGIONES Y GRUPOS DE PAISES	YEAR / ANNEE / AÑO	TEACHING STAFF / PERSONNEL ENSEIGNANT / PERSONAL DOCENTE			ENROLMENT / EFFECTIFS SCOLAIRES / MATRICULA ESCOLAR			
		TOTAL (000)	FEMALE / FEMMES / FEMENINO (000)	% F	TOTAL (000)	FEMALE / FILLES / FEMENINA (000)	% F	PRIVATE / PRIVE / PRIVADA %
		(1)	(2)	(3)	(4)	(5)	(6)	(7)
WORLD TOTAL (INCLUDING CHINA)‡	1970	...	...	...	...	...	...	...
	1975	2 148	...	...	43 422	...	...	23
	1980	3 029	...	...	57 062	...	...	21
	1983	3 419	3 267	96	61 157	29 101	48	19
	1984	3 582	3 451	96	64 250	30 408	47	19
	% 1970–80	.	.		.	.		
	% 1980–84	4.3	.		3.0	.		
WORLD TOTAL (EXCLUDING CHINA)‡	1970	1 432	1 403	98	28 558	13 926	49	26
	1975	1 912	1 850	97	37 222	18 020	48	27
	1980	2 618	2 537	97	45 555	21 634	47	26
	1983	2 986	2 888	97	49 755	23 676	48	24
	1984	3 091	2 988	97	51 302	24 390	48	24
	% 1970–80	6.2	6.1		4.8	4.5		
	% 1980–84	4.2	4.2		3.0	3.0		
AFRICA‡	1970	7	7	100	274	123	45	72
	1975	33	13	39	874	327	37	77
	1980	67	35	52	2 132	846	40	58
	1983	74	40	54	2 329	997	43	64
	1984	77	43	56	2 429	1 030	42	66
	% 1970–80	25.3	17.5		22.8	21.3		
	% 1980–84	3.5	5.3		3.3	5.0		
AMERICA	1970	264	259	98	6 380	3 118	49	28
	1975	331	321	97	8 306	4 062	49	31
	1980	413	400	97	10 310	5 009	49	32
	1983	499	486	97	12 672	6 269	49	30
	1984	541	523	97	13 543	6 698	49	29
	% 1970–80	4.6	4.4		4.9	4.9		
	% 1980–84	7.0	6.9		7.1	7.5		
ASIA‡	1970	143	122	85	4 092	1 909	47	54
	1975	202	177	88	6 045	2 857	47	49
	1980	307	277	90	8 479	4 116	49	45
	1983	347	307	88	9 139	4 334	47	46
	1984	367	326	89	9 540	4 504	47	45
	% 1970–80	7.9	8.5		7.6	8.0		
	% 1980–84	4.6	4.2		3.0	2.3		
EUROPE (INCL. USSR)	1970	1 011	1 008	100	17 579	8 662	49	18
	1975	1 338	1 332	100	21 749	10 656	49	17
	1980	1 823	1 815	100	24 377	11 540	47	14
	1983	2 058	2 047	99	25 370	11 957	47	9
	1984	2 098	2 089	100	25 546	12 037	47	9
	% 1970–80	6.1	6.1		3.3	2.9		
	% 1980–84	3.6	3.6		1.2	1.1		

CONTINENTS, MAJOR AREAS AND GROUPS OF COUNTRIES / CONTINENTS, GRANDES REGIONS ET GROUPES DE PAYS / CONTINENTES, GRANDES REGIONES Y GRUPOS DE PAISES	YEAR / ANNEE / AÑO	TEACHING STAFF / PERSONNEL ENSEIGNANT / PERSONAL DOCENTE TOTAL (000)	FEMALE / FEMMES / FEMENINO (000)	% F	ENROLMENT / EFFECTIFS SCOLAIRES / MATRICULA ESCOLAR TOTAL (000)	FEMALE / FILLES / FEMENINA (000)	% F	PRIVATE / PRIVE / PRIVADA %
		(1)	(2)	(3)	(4)	(5)	(6)	(7)
OCEANIA	1970	8	6	75	233	113	48	60
	1975	8	8	100	247	119	48	33
	1980	9	9	100	256	125	49	36
	1983	8	8	100	245	120	49	40
	1984	8	8	100	245	120	49	41
	% 1970–80	1.2	4.1		0.9	1.0		
	% 1980–84	−2.9	−2.9		−1.1	−1.0		
DEVELOPED COUNTRIES‡	1970	1 286	1 270	99	24 145	11 846	49	24
	1975	1 661	1 635	98	29 813	14 566	49	24
	1980	2 154	2 126	99	32 543	15 455	47	22
	1983	2 397	2 365	99	33 581	15 981	48	18
	1984	2 436	2 405	99	33 703	16 036	48	18
	% 1970–80	5.3	5.3		3.0	2.7		
	% 1980–84	3.1	3.1		0.9	0.9		
DEVELOPING COUNTRIES‡	1970	146	133	91	4 413	2 080	47	37
	1975	251	215	86	7 409	3 454	47	37
	1980	464	411	89	13 012	6 179	47	36
	1983	589	523	89	16 174	7 695	48	36
	1984	655	583	89	17 599	8 354	47	35
	% 1970–80	12.3	11.9		11.4	11.5		
	% 1980–84	9.0	9.1		7.8	7.8		
AFRICA (EXCLUDING ARAB STATES)‡	1970	5	5	100	203	88	43	65
	1975	9	9	100	390	177	45	56
	1980	30	28	93	1 284	574	45	35
	1983	33	31	94	1 333	653	49	44
	1984	34	32	94	1 376	669	49	46
	% 1970–80	19.6	18.8		20.3	20.6		
	% 1980–84	3.2	3.4		1.7	3.9		
ASIA (EXCLUDING ARAB STATES)‡	1970	138	117	85	3 874	1 809	47	53
	1975	195	169	87	5 776	2 733	47	49
	1980	291	261	90	8 137	3 957	49	45
	1983	326	287	88	8 730	4 141	47	45
	1984	346	305	88	9 109	4 302	47	44
	% 1970–80	7.7	8.4		7.7	8.1		
	% 1980–84	4.4	4.0		2.9	2.1		
ARAB STATES‡	1970	7	7	100	290	135	47	81
	1975	30	11	37	753	274	36	83
	1980	53	23	43	1 190	430	36	84
	1983	61	28	46	1 404	537	38	83
	1984	64	31	48	1 484	563	38	83
	% 1970–80	22.4	12.6		15.2	12.3		
	% 1980–84	4.8	7.7		5.7	7.0		
NORTHERN AMERICA	1970	200	196	98	4 652	2 248	48	28
	1975	234	225	96	5 541	2 678	48	31
	1980	235	225	96	5 562	2 644	48	33
	1983	248	238	96	5 876	2 879	49	34
	1984	249	239	96	5 898	2 890	49	34
	% 1970–80	1.6	1.4		1.8	1.6		
	% 1980–84	1.5	1.5		1.5	2.2		
LATIN AMERICAN AND THE CARIBBEAN	1970	64	63	98	1 728	870	50	28
	1975	97	96	99	2 764	1 384	50	31
	1980	178	175	98	4 749	2 365	50	30
	1983	251	247	98	6 796	3 390	50	26
	1984	292	284	97	7 645	3 808	50	25
	% 1970–80	10.8	10.8		10.6	10.5		
	% 1980–84	13.2	12.9		12.6	12.6		

General note / Note générale / Nota general:

E--> For composition of major areas and groups of countries, see head note to table 1.2. The school year begins in the calendar year indicated. More information on this point is given in the general introduction to the 'Education' section. Owing to the rounding of figures, the totals and sub-totals shown in this table do not always correspond exactly to the sums of their component items.

FR-> Pour la composition des grandes régions et des groupes de pays, voir la note en-tête du tableau 1.2. L'année scolaire commence pendant l'année civile indiquée. Pour plus de détails, se reporter à l'introduction générale de la partie 'Education'. Les chiffres ayant été arrondis, les totaux et les sous-totaux figurant dans ce tableau ne correspondent pas toujours exactement à la somme des éléments qui les composent.

General note / Note générale / Nota general: (Cont):

ESP> Puede verse la composición de las grandes regiones y grupos de países en la nota encabezando el cuadro 1.2. El año escolar empieza durante el año civil indicado. Pueden verse mas detalles a este respecto en la introducción general de la sección 'Educación'. Como las cifras se han redondeado, los totales y los sub-totales que figuran en este cuadro no siempre corresponden exactamente a la suma de los elementos que los componen.

World Total (incl. China), World Total (excl. China):

E--> Since for China it was not possible to estimate the complete series of data, two world totals are shown; the available data for China are included in the first total only. Both totals exclude the Democratic People's Republic of Korea.

FR-> Pour la Chine, il n'était pas possible d'estimer la série complète de données. C'est pourquoi ce tableau présente deux totaux; les données disponibles pour la Chine sont incluses dans le premier total seulement. Les deux totaux ne comprennent pas la République populaire démocratique de Corée.

ESP> Para China no fue posible estimar la serie completa de datos. Por ello este cuadro presenta dos totales; los datos disponibles para China se incluyen en el primer total solamente. Los dos totales no incluyen la República popular democrática de Corea.

World Total, Africa, Developed countries, Africa (excl. Arab States):

E--> Not including South Africa.

World Total, Africa, Developed countries, Africa (excl. Arab (Cont):

FR-> Non compris l'Afrique du Sud.

ESP> Excluída Sudáfrica.

Asia, Developing countries, Asia (excluding Arab States):

E--> Not including China and the Democratic People's Republic of Korea.

FR-> Non compris la Chine et la République populaire démocratique de Corée.

ESP> Excluídas China y la República popular democrática de Corea.

Arab States:

E--> The inclusion of Koranic schools from 1975 affects the comparability of this series.

FR-> L'inclusion des écoles coraniques à partir de 1975 affecte la comparabilité de cette série.

ESP> La inclusión de las escuelas coránicas a partir de 1975, affecta la comparabilidad de esta serie.

2.9 Percentage distribution of education at the second level by type: enrolment and teaching staff

Répartition en pourcentage de l'enseignement du second degré par type: effectifs scolaires et personnel enseignant

Repartición en porcentaje de la enseñanza de segundo grado, por tipo: matrícula escolar y personal docente

CONTINENTS, MAJOR AREAS AND GROUPS OF COUNTRIES / CONTINENTS, GRANDES REGIONS ET GROUPES DE PAYS / CONTINENTES, GRANDES REGIONES Y GRUPOS DE PAISES	YEAR / ANNEE / AÑO	ENROLMENT / EFFECTIFS SCOLAIRES / MATRICULA ESCOLAR				TEACHING STAFF / PERSONNEL ENSEIGNANT / PERSONAL DOCENTE			
		TOTAL / TOTAL / TOTAL (%)	GENERAL EDUCATION / ENSEIGNEMENT GENERAL / ENSEÑANZA GENERAL (%)	TEACHER TRAINING / ENSEIGNEMENT NORMAL / ENSEÑANZA NORMAL (%)	VOCATIONAL / ENSEIGNEMENT TECHNIQUE / ENSEÑANZA TECNICA (%)	TOTAL / TOTAL / TOTAL (%)	GENERAL EDUCATION / ENSEIGNEMENT GENERAL / ENSEÑANZA GENERAL (%)	TEACHER TRAINING / ENSEIGNEMENT NORMAL / ENSEÑANZA NORMAL (%)	VOCATIONAL / ENSEIGNEMENT TECHNIQUE / ENSEÑANZA TECNICA (%)
		(1)	(2)	(3)	(4)	(5)	(6)	(7)	(8)
WORLD TOTAL (INCLUDING CHINA)‡	1970	100.0	87.1	...	...	100.0	...	...	...
	1975	100.0	88.0	...	...	100.0	...	...	...
	1980	100.0	87.5	1.3	11.2	100.0	85.0	1.6	13.4
	1983	100.0	86.9	1.2	11.9	100.0	84.0	1.6	14.4
	1984	100.0	86.7	1.3	12.1	100.0	83.5	1.6	14.9
WORLD TOTAL (EXCLUDING CHINA)‡	1970	100.0	84.1	1.4	14.5	100.0	79.9	2.1	18.0
	1975	100.0	84.6	1.3	14.1	100.0	81.4	1.7	16.9
	1980	100.0	84.2	1.4	14.4	100.0	81.6	1.7	16.7
	1983	100.0	84.9	1.3	13.8	100.0	81.9	1.6	16.4
	1984	100.0	84.9	1.3	13.8	100.0	81.9	1.6	16.6
AFRICA‡	1970	100.0	83.5	4.2	12.3	100.0	77.7	6.4	16.3
	1975	100.0	86.3	4.5	9.2	100.0	79.4	6.3	14.3
	1980	100.0	85.9	5.0	9.1	100.0	80.9	5.5	13.6
	1983	100.0	86.8	5.0	8.2	100.0	82.6	5.2	12.1
	1984	100.0	86.9	5.0	8.1	100.0	82.8	5.2	11.9
AMERICA‡	1970	100.0	62.7	6.8	30.5	100.0	56.2	9.0	34.7
	1975	100.0	71.6	4.5	23.9	100.0	67.3	5.7	27.1
	1980	100.0	72.5	4.0	23.6	100.0	69.6	4.9	25.5
	1983	100.0	74.0	3.2	22.8	100.0	70.2	4.5	25.3
	1984	100.0	74.0	2.9	23.1	100.0	69.9	4.1	26.0
ASIA‡	1970	100.0	91.4	0.7	7.9	100.0	89.4	1.0	9.6
	1975	100.0	91.5	0.6	7.9	100.0	89.0	0.9	10.1
	1980	100.0	92.0	0.6	7.4	100.0	90.4	0.9	8.7
	1983	100.0	92.7	0.4	6.8	100.0	91.1	0.7	8.2
	1984	100.0	92.7	0.5	6.8	100.0	91.0	0.7	8.3
EUROPE (INCL. USSR)	1970	100.0	80.4	1.1	18.5	100.0	78.0	1.4	20.6
	1975	100.0	80.0	0.8	19.2	100.0	78.8	1.2	20.0
	1980	100.0	77.0	0.8	22.1	100.0	76.7	1.2	22.2
	1983	100.0	75.5	0.8	23.7	100.0	75.0	1.2	23.8
	1984	100.0	75.2	0.8	23.9	100.0	74.7	1.2	24.1
OCEANIA	1970	100.0	...	...	...	100.0	...	...	...
	1975	100.0	...	...	...	100.0	...	...	...
	1980	100.0	...	...	...	100.0	...	...	...
	1983	100.0	...	...	...	100.0	...	...	...
	1984	100.0	...	...	...	100.0	...	...	...
DEVELOPED COUNTRIES‡	1970	100.0	80.7	1.0	18.3	100.0	78.3	1.2	20.4
	1975	100.0	80.5	0.7	18.8	100.0	79.0	1.1	19.9
	1980	100.0	78.2	0.7	21.1	100.0	77.2	1.0	21.7
	1983	100.0	77.2	0.7	22.1	100.0	75.8	1.0	23.1
	1984	100.0	77.1	0.7	22.2	100.0	75.7	1.0	23.3

2.9 Enrolment and teachers at the second level: % distribution
Effectifs et personnel enseignant du second degré: répartition en %
Matrícula escolar y personal docente de segundo grado: repartición en %

CONTINENTS, MAJOR AREAS AND GROUPS OF COUNTRIES / CONTINENTS, GRANDES REGIONS ET GROUPES DE PAYS / CONTINENTES, GRANDES REGIONES Y GRUPOS DE PAISES	YEAR / ANNEE / AÑO	ENROLMENT / EFFECTIFS SCOLAIRES / MATRICULA ESCOLAR: TOTAL / TOTAL / TOTAL (%)	GENERAL EDUCATION / ENSEIGNEMENT GENERAL / ENSEÑANZA GENERAL (%)	TEACHER TRAINING / ENSEIGNEMENT NORMAL / ENSEÑANZA NORMAL (%)	VOCATIONAL / ENSEIGNEMENT TECHNIQUE / ENSEÑANZA TECNICA (%)	TEACHING STAFF / PERSONNEL ENSEIGNANT / PERSONAL DOCENTE: TOTAL / TOTAL / TOTAL (%)	GENERAL EDUCATION / ENSEIGNEMENT GENERAL / ENSEÑANZA GENERAL (%)	TEACHER TRAINING / ENSEIGNEMENT NORMAL / ENSEÑANZA NORMAL (%)	VOCATIONAL / ENSEIGNEMENT TECHNIQUE / ENSEÑANZA TECNICA (%)
		(1)	(2)	(3)	(4)	(5)	(6)	(7)	(8)
DEVELOPING COUNTRIES‡	1970	100.0	87.6	2.0	10.4	100.0	82.0	3.4	14.5
	1975	100.0	88.3	1.7	10.0	100.0	84.3	2.5	13.1
	1980	100.0	88.1	1.8	10.0	100.0	85.5	2.3	12.1
	1983	100.0	89.1	1.6	9.3	100.0	86.5	2.0	11.4
	1984	100.0	89.0	1.6	9.4	100.0	86.4	2.0	11.6
AFRICA (EXCLUDING ARAB STATES)‡	1970	100.0	84.2	6.5	9.3	100.0	78.1	9.4	12.5
	1975	100.0	86.9	6.9	6.2	100.0	82.6	8.4	9.0
	1980	100.0	86.9	7.4	5.8	100.0	81.6	7.2	10.8
	1983	100.0	87.5	7.0	5.5	100.0	84.6	7.1	8.0
	1984	100.0	87.4	7.1	5.5	100.0	84.7	7.2	8.0
ASIA (EXCLUDING ARAB STATES)‡	1970	100.0	91.3	0.6	8.0	100.0	89.4	0.9	9.7
	1975	100.0	91.4	0.6	8.0	100.0	88.9	0.8	10.2
	1980	100.0	91.9	0.6	7.5	100.0	90.4	0.8	8.7
	1983	100.0	92.8	0.4	6.8	100.0	91.2	0.6	8.1
	1984	100.0	92.7	0.4	6.8	100.0	91.1	0.7	8.3
ARAB STATES	1970	100.0	86.8	2.1	11.1	100.0	81.0	3.7	14.7
	1975	100.0	88.6	1.9	9.5	100.0	82.3	3.5	14.2
	1980	100.0	87.5	1.8	10.7	100.0	83.8	2.8	13.4
	1983	100.0	87.7	1.7	10.5	100.0	83.5	2.7	13.8
	1984	100.0	88.0	1.8	10.3	100.0	83.7	2.7	13.6
NORTHERN AMERICA	1970	100.0	...	...	...	100.0	...	...	...
	1975	100.0	...	...	...	100.0	...	...	...
	1980	100.0	...	...	...	100.0	...	...	...
	1983	100.0	...	...	...	100.0	...	...	...
	1984	100.0	...	...	...	100.0	...	...	...
LATIN AMERICAN AND THE CARIBBEAN	1970	100.0	62.6	6.8	30.6	100.0	56.1	9.1	34.8
	1975	100.0	71.6	4.5	23.9	100.0	67.2	5.7	27.1
	1980	100.0	72.5	4.0	23.6	100.0	69.6	4.9	25.5
	1983	100.0	74.0	3.2	22.8	100.0	70.2	4.5	25.3
	1984	100.0	74.0	2.9	23.1	100.0	69.9	4.1	26.1

General note / Note générale / Nota general:

E--> For composition of major areas and groups of countries, see head note to table 1.2. The school year begins in the calendar year indicated. More information on this point is given in the general introduction to the 'Education' section.

FR-> Pour la composition des grandes régions et des groupes de pays, voir la note en-tête du tableau 1.2. L'année scolaire commence pendant l'année civile indiquée. Pour plus de détails, se reporter à l'introduction générale de la partie 'Education'.

ESP> Puede verse la composición de las grandes regiones y grupos de países en la nota encabezando el cuadro 1.2. El año escolar empieza durante el año civil indicado. Pueden verse mas detalles a este respecto en la introducción general de la sección 'Educación'.

World Total (incl. China), World Total (excl. China):

E--> Since for China it was not possible to estimate data for 1970 and 1975, two world totals are shown; the available data for China are included in the first total only. Both totals exclude Northern America, Democratic People's Republic of Korea, Australia, New Zealand and South Africa.

FR-> Pour la Chine, il n'était pas possible d'estimer les données pour 1970 et 1975. C'est pourquoi ce tableau présente deux totaux; les données disponibles pour la Chine sont incluses dans le premier total seulement. Les deux totaux ne comprennent pas l'Amérique septentrionale, la République populaire démocratique de Corée, l'Australie, la Nouvelle-Zélande et l'Afrique du Sud.

ESP> Para China no fue posible estimar los datos para 1970 y 1975. Por ello este cuadro presenta dos totales; los datos disponibles para China se incluyen en el primer total solamente. Los dos totales no incluyen America septentrional, la República popular democrática de Corea, Australia, Nueva Zelandia y Sudáfrica..

World total, Africa, Developed countries, Africa (excluding Arab States):

E--> Not including South Africa.

FR-> Non compris l'Afrique du Sud.

ESP> Excluída Sudáfrica.

America:

E--> Not including Northern America.

FR-> Non compris l'Amérique septentrionale.

ESP> Excluída America septentrional.

Asia, Developing countries, Asia (excl. Arab States):

E--> Not including China and the Democratic People's Republic of Korea.

FR-> Non compris la Chine et la République populaire démocratique de Corée.

ESP> Excluídas China y la República popular democrática de Corea.

Developed countries:

E--> Not including Northern America, Australia, New Zealand and South Africa.

FR-> Non compris l'Amérique septentrionale, l'Australie, la Nouvelle-Zélande et l'Afrique du Sud.

ESP> Excluídas America septentrional, Australia Nueva Zelandia y Sudáfrica.

2.10 Gross enrolment ratios by level of education

Taux d'inscription bruts par degré d'enseignement

Tasas de escolarización brutas por grado de enseñanza

CONTINENTS, MAJOR AREAS AND GROUPS OF COUNTRIES / CONTINENTS, GRANDES REGIONS ET GROUPES DE PAYS / CONTINENTES, GRANDES REGIONES Y GRUPOS DE PAISES	YEAR / ANNEE / AÑO	LEVEL OF EDUCATION / DEGRE D'ENSEIGNEMENT / GRADO DE ENSEÑANZA											
		FIRST LEVEL / PREMIER DEGRE / PRIMER GRADO			SECOND LEVEL / SECOND DEGRE / SEGUNDO GRADO			THIRD LEVEL / TROISIEME DEGRE / TERCER GRADO			ALL LEVELS / TOUS LES DEGRES / TODOS LOS GRADOS		
		MF	M	F	MF	M	F	MF	M	F	MF	M	F
		(1)	(2)	(3)	(4)	(5)	(6)	(7)	(8)	(9)	(10)	(11)	(12)
WORLD TOTAL‡	1960	80.7	91.1	69.9	27.5	31.2	23.6	5.2	6.9	3.4	43.8	49.8	37.6
	1965	85.0	95.3	74.3	32.1	36.9	27.1	7.4	9.5	5.3	48.3	54.8	41.6
	1970	83.8	90.9	76.3	35.2	39.6	30.7	8.8	10.8	6.7	48.1	53.0	43.0
	1975	94.7	102.7	86.4	43.1	48.3	37.7	10.3	12.0	8.5	54.1	59.3	48.6
	1980	94.4	102.3	86.2	45.1	50.6	39.5	11.2	12.6	9.7	54.7	60.0	49.3
	1985	98.8	106.3	90.9	46.3	51.5	40.9	11.8	13.4	10.2	55.5	60.5	50.2
AFRICA	1960	43.5	55.4	31.5	5.2	7.4	3.0	0.7	1.2	0.3	20.2	26.1	14.3
	1965	51.6	63.2	39.9	8.0	11.3	4.7	1.1	1.8	0.4	24.9	31.3	18.6
	1970	56.0	67.1	44.8	11.2	15.3	7.2	1.5	2.4	0.7	28.3	34.7	21.9
	1975	65.0	75.2	54.7	15.6	20.2	10.9	2.5	3.7	1.3	33.8	40.1	27.4
	1980	79.7	90.4	68.8	23.1	28.9	17.3	3.2	4.7	1.7	42.5	49.5	35.6
	1985	84.3	92.8	75.7	33.0	40.1	25.8	4.3	6.2	2.4	48.3	54.9	41.8
AMERICA‡	1960	81.4	82.9	79.9	50.6	50.7	50.4	13.4	17.0	9.8	57.3	59.0	55.6
	1965	86.4	87.7	85.1	57.0	57.3	56.7	17.5	21.4	13.4	61.9	63.6	60.1
	1970	90.5	91.5	89.6	58.6	58.9	58.3	23.1	27.3	18.8	64.7	66.4	63.0
	1975	98.0	99.2	96.8	60.5	60.8	60.2	29.0	32.0	25.9	68.8	70.3	67.3
	1980	104.0	105.2	102.7	59.1	58.5	59.7	29.6	29.7	29.4	70.0	70.5	69.6
	1985	106.4	108.0	104.8	65.2	64.2	66.3	31.6	31.9	31.3	73.5	74.0	73.0
ASIA‡	1960	80.3	95.7	64.0	20.5	25.7	15.0	2.5	3.7	1.2	39.7	47.9	31.0
	1965	85.7	100.6	69.8	22.5	29.3	15.4	3.4	4.9	1.8	43.9	52.9	34.5
	1970	82.0	91.7	71.8	26.2	32.1	20.0	3.8	5.3	2.1	42.4	48.7	35.7
	1975	98.7	109.7	87.2	35.9	43.4	27.9	4.4	6.1	2.7	50.8	57.8	43.3
	1980	93.5	103.8	82.8	39.2	46.9	31.1	5.5	7.4	3.5	50.5	57.6	43.1
	1985	99.5	109.8	88.7	38.8	45.7	31.6	6.3	8.3	4.3	49.8	56.5	42.8
EUROPE (INCL. USSR)	1960	106.3	107.1	105.6	51.3	53.0	49.5	10.2	12.9	7.6	61.0	62.8	59.2
	1965	104.7	105.3	104.0	64.8	66.5	63.1	16.0	19.2	12.7	67.4	69.1	65.6
	1970	105.1	105.6	104.6	70.8	72.0	69.6	17.4	19.6	15.1	68.1	69.3	66.7
	1975	101.9	102.4	101.3	79.1	78.5	79.7	20.3	21.7	18.8	69.1	69.6	68.7
	1980	103.7	104.1	103.3	82.1	80.9	83.4	21.8	22.6	20.9	70.0	69.9	70.0
	1985	103.8	104.1	103.5	85.9	84.7	87.2	23.8	24.4	23.2	72.2	72.1	72.3
OCEANIA	1960	101.6	102.1	101.1	53.1	54.4	51.8	9.9	14.0	5.6	62.9	64.5	61.3
	1965	102.4	104.2	100.4	61.6	63.1	59.9	11.4	15.4	7.2	64.6	66.8	62.2
	1970	103.5	105.5	101.3	68.1	69.8	66.4	13.9	17.8	9.7	67.1	69.5	64.5
	1975	98.0	100.2	95.7	72.3	72.7	71.9	19.7	23.2	15.9	67.2	69.3	65.1
	1980	99.4	101.1	97.6	70.3	69.8	70.9	20.6	22.5	18.7	66.5	67.4	65.4
	1985	97.2	99.0	95.3	74.5	74.0	75.0	22.9	24.2	21.5	67.4	68.3	66.5
DEVELOPED COUNTRIES‡	1960	101.5	102.4	100.6	62.1	63.3	60.9	13.3	17.1	9.4	65.6	67.5	63.7
	1965	100.3	101.0	99.6	74.7	75.8	73.5	19.2	23.6	14.6	70.5	72.4	68.5
	1970	100.1	100.6	99.5	78.6	79.4	77.9	23.2	27.2	19.1	71.1	72.7	69.4
	1975	100.7	101.1	100.2	83.5	82.8	84.2	28.1	31.0	25.2	73.2	74.1	72.3
	1980	101.8	102.1	101.4	83.9	82.7	85.1	29.9	30.7	29.0	73.3	73.4	73.3
	1985	102.3	102.7	101.9	87.9	86.8	89.1	33.1	33.9	32.2	76.1	76.1	76.0
DEVELOPING COUNTRIES‡	1960	72.8	86.8	58.1	15.1	19.8	10.3	2.0	2.9	1.0	35.5	43.1	27.6
	1965	79.8	93.3	65.7	17.5	23.6	11.1	2.7	3.9	1.5	40.5	48.6	31.9
	1970	78.6	87.8	69.0	22.4	27.9	16.7	3.1	4.3	1.8	40.6	46.5	34.3
	1975	93.1	103.2	82.7	31.4	38.3	24.3	4.3	5.7	2.8	48.4	55.0	41.6
	1980	92.7	102.3	82.7	35.8	42.8	28.6	5.4	7.1	3.7	49.9	56.5	43.1
	1985	97.8	107.2	88.4	37.7	44.2	31.0	6.4	8.1	4.6	50.8	56.9	44.4

CONTINENTS, MAJOR AREAS AND GROUPS OF COUNTRIES / CONTINENTS, GRANDES REGIONS ET GROUPES DE PAYS / CONTINENTES, GRANDES REGIONES Y GRUPOS DE PAISES	YEAR / ANNEE / AÑO	FIRST LEVEL / PREMIER DEGRE / PRIMER GRADO			SECOND LEVEL / SECOND DEGRE / SEGUNDO GRADO			THIRD LEVEL / TROISIEME DEGRE / TERCER GRADO			ALL LEVELS / TOUS LES DEGRES / TODOS LOS GRADOS		
		MF	M	F	MF	M	F	MF	M	F	MF	M	F
		(1)	(2)	(3)	(4)	(5)	(6)	(7)	(8)	(9)	(10)	(11)	(12)
AFRICA (EXCLUDING ARAB STATES)	1960	41.3	52.7	30.1	3.6	5.1	2.2	0.3	0.5	0.1	18.8	24.2	13.6
	1965	48.3	58.8	37.9	5.5	7.6	3.4	0.5	0.8	0.2	22.7	28.0	17.5
	1970	53.4	63.3	43.5	8.2	11.0	5.5	0.8	1.2	0.3	26.1	31.5	20.8
	1975	63.1	72.0	54.2	11.6	15.0	8.2	1.1	1.8	0.5	31.7	37.0	26.5
	1980	80.0	90.2	69.9	19.1	24.1	14.1	1.6	2.6	0.7	41.8	48.2	35.4
	1985	84.6	92.6	76.7	29.1	35.9	22.3	2.7	4.3	1.1	47.4	53.6	41.3
ASIA (EXCLUDING ARAB STATES)‡	1960	80.8	96.2	64.6	20.7	25.8	15.2	2.5	3.7	1.2	39.9	48.1	31.3
	1965	86.2	101.1	70.4	22.6	29.4	15.5	3.4	4.9	1.8	44.1	53.1	34.7
	1970	82.4	91.9	72.3	26.3	32.1	20.1	3.7	5.3	2.1	42.5	48.7	35.9
	1975	99.1	110.0	87.8	36.0	43.5	28.0	4.4	6.0	2.6	50.9	57.8	43.5
	1980	93.6	103.9	82.9	39.1	46.8	31.0	5.4	7.3	3.4	50.4	57.4	43.1
	1985	99.6	109.9	88.9	38.5	45.4	31.3	6.2	8.2	4.2	49.6	56.2	42.6
ARAB STATES	1960	50.0	65.0	34.4	10.3	15.2	5.3	2.0	3.2	0.7	24.6	32.9	16.1
	1965	60.9	76.8	44.1	16.1	23.1	8.7	3.3	5.2	1.3	31.9	41.8	21.7
	1970	63.7	79.2	47.4	21.1	28.8	12.9	4.3	6.5	2.0	35.3	45.2	24.9
	1975	73.6	89.4	57.0	28.3	36.3	19.8	6.9	9.6	4.0	42.0	51.9	31.5
	1980	81.9	94.7	68.5	37.0	45.2	28.3	8.4	11.2	5.4	47.8	56.4	38.7
	1985	86.4	97.2	75.2	47.4	55.0	39.5	9.8	12.5	6.9	53.9	61.4	45.9
NORTHERN AMERICA‡	1960	91.3	92.2	90.4	105.1	104.3	106.0	27.9	34.8	20.8	80.1	82.0	78.1
	1965	92.7	93.5	91.8	113.5	112.7	114.4	34.0	41.2	26.8	83.0	85.1	80.9
	1970	89.3	89.9	88.7	112.1	111.2	113.1	44.5	51.7	37.1	82.8	84.8	80.6
	1975	98.0	98.6	97.5	104.6	103.4	105.8	52.3	56.8	47.7	85.8	87.2	84.4
	1980	100.1	100.5	99.7	93.2	92.0	94.4	53.7	51.3	56.0	82.7	81.9	83.6
	1985	102.9	103.6	102.2	99.7	98.5	101.0	62.6	60.6	64.6	88.9	88.3	89.5
LATIN AMERICAN AND THE CARIBBEAN	1960	73.0	74.9	71.1	14.2	14.9	13.6	3.0	4.2	1.8	40.0	41.4	38.5
	1965	81.5	83.1	79.9	19.4	20.2	18.7	4.2	5.6	2.8	45.9	47.2	44.5
	1970	91.4	92.6	90.2	24.9	25.7	24.0	6.3	8.0	4.5	52.1	53.4	50.8
	1975	98.0	99.6	96.5	35.4	36.2	34.4	11.7	13.6	9.9	58.5	60.0	57.0
	1980	105.8	107.5	104.2	43.5	43.0	44.1	13.4	15.1	11.7	63.3	64.4	62.3
	1985	107.9	109.9	105.9	52.2	51.2	53.3	15.0	16.3	13.6	66.6	67.6	65.7

General note / Note générale / Nota general:

E--> For composition of major areas and groups of countries, see head note to table 1.2. It should, however, be noted, that in this table, Yugoslavia is included with the developed countries.

FR-> Pour la composition des grandes régions et groupes de pays, voir la note en-tête du tableau 1.2. On doit cependant noter, que dans ce tableau, la Yougoslavie est incluse avec les pays développés.

ESP> Veáse la nota encabezando el cuadro 1.2 para la composición de las grandes regiones y grupos de países. Debe tomarse nota, sin embargo, que en este cuadro, Yugoslavia esta incluída con los países desarrollados.

2.11 Enrolment ratios by age-group and sex

Taux d'inscription par groupe d'âge et par sexe

Tasas de escolarización por grupo de edad y por sexo

CONTINENTS, MAJOR AREAS AND GROUPS OF COUNTRIES / CONTINENTS, GRANDES REGIONS ET GROUPES DE PAYS / CONTINENTES, GRANDES REGIONES Y GRUPOS DE PAISES	YEAR / ANNEE / AÑO	AGE GROUPS / GROUPES D'AGE / GRUPOS DE EDAD											
		6 – 11			12 – 17			18 – 23			6 – 23		
		MF	M	F	MF	M	F	MF	M	F	MF	M	F
		(1)	(2)	(3)	(4)	(5)	(6)	(7)	(8)	(9)	(10)	(11)	(12)
WORLD TOTAL (EXCLUDING CHINA)‡	1960	62.3	68.7	55.8	37.9	42.9	32.8	8.0	10.4	5.6	38.8	43.6	33.9
	1965	66.3	72.5	59.8	44.3	49.7	38.7	12.2	15.1	9.2	44.2	49.3	38.9
	1970	67.7	73.6	61.6	46.1	51.5	40.5	14.3	17.1	11.3	45.6	50.6	40.6
	1975	70.3	76.4	64.1	48.6	53.2	43.9	16.8	19.7	13.8	47.7	52.3	42.8
	1980	74.3	80.0	68.2	51.3	55.8	46.6	17.7	20.0	15.3	49.7	54.0	45.2
	1985	76.8	82.0	71.3	55.6	60.1	50.8	19.4	21.9	16.8	52.4	56.6	48.0
AFRICA	1960	32.7	41.0	24.5	17.3	23.4	11.3	1.9	3.1	0.8	19.2	24.9	13.6
	1965	38.9	46.9	30.9	22.1	29.2	15.0	2.8	4.4	1.3	23.7	29.8	17.7
	1970	41.9	49.4	34.4	26.7	34.2	19.2	4.3	6.4	2.2	27.0	33.2	20.8
	1975	49.0	55.9	42.1	32.6	40.2	25.0	6.3	9.0	3.5	32.3	38.4	26.2
	1980	60.6	68.0	53.2	42.5	50.9	34.1	8.6	12.0	5.3	40.8	47.4	34.1
	1985	65.9	71.6	60.2	50.7	59.6	41.8	11.5	15.5	7.5	46.4	52.7	40.1
AMERICA	1960	75.2	75.5	74.9	60.2	62.4	57.9	15.4	18.2	12.5	54.5	56.2	52.8
	1965	78.5	78.5	78.4	64.4	66.6	62.2	22.1	25.2	18.8	58.7	60.3	57.0
	1970	81.1	81.0	81.2	66.3	68.4	64.2	26.5	29.7	23.2	60.7	62.4	59.1
	1975	83.4	83.6	83.2	72.0	73.4	70.6	32.1	34.9	29.2	64.2	65.6	62.7
	1980	87.2	87.5	86.9	71.2	71.7	70.6	33.7	34.1	33.4	64.8	65.2	64.3
	1985	87.9	88.4	87.4	78.0	78.6	77.4	35.7	36.1	35.4	67.8	68.3	67.3
ASIA‡	1960	54.2	65.3	42.7	24.8	31.7	17.7	4.4	6.7	2.0	30.4	37.7	22.9
	1965	60.0	70.9	48.8	31.3	39.2	23.1	6.3	9.2	3.3	36.0	43.7	28.0
	1970	61.8	71.7	51.5	32.3	40.1	24.2	7.7	10.9	4.3	37.6	45.0	29.9
	1975	65.7	75.4	55.5	33.8	40.6	26.7	9.4	13.2	5.4	39.7	46.8	32.2
	1980	69.8	78.5	60.5	37.6	44.1	30.8	10.4	14.0	6.7	42.2	48.8	35.2
	1985	73.6	81.5	65.1	42.1	48.2	35.6	12.5	16.4	8.5	45.1	51.3	38.6
EUROPE (INCL. USSR)	1960	86.5	86.4	86.6	60.2	62.4	57.9	12.8	15.5	10.2	54.6	56.3	52.9
	1965	87.8	87.7	87.9	66.8	68.8	64.8	22.3	25.6	18.9	62.2	63.9	60.5
	1970	89.5	89.3	89.6	70.5	72.1	68.9	22.9	25.2	20.6	62.5	63.7	61.2
	1975	90.0	90.2	89.8	74.1	74.0	74.2	25.4	26.5	24.2	63.4	63.8	62.9
	1980	90.2	90.0	90.4	77.3	76.9	77.7	25.6	26.0	25.1	63.4	63.4	63.4
	1985	89.8	89.7	89.9	80.7	80.4	81.1	27.9	28.0	27.8	65.1	65.0	65.2
OCEANIA	1960	85.5	85.3	85.7	58.8	60.8	56.7	8.4	11.9	4.7	55.8	57.3	54.3
	1965	87.9	88.6	87.1	63.0	65.6	60.3	10.2	13.9	6.3	57.4	59.5	55.1
	1970	89.9	91.1	88.7	68.4	70.7	66.0	12.1	15.7	8.3	59.2	61.4	56.8
	1975	88.0	89.4	86.6	70.7	71.6	69.8	17.1	20.6	13.4	60.4	62.3	58.4
	1980	90.2	91.4	88.9	68.3	68.1	68.6	18.0	19.8	16.0	59.6	60.5	58.6
	1985	88.5	89.5	87.4	70.3	70.4	70.2	20.5	21.8	19.1	60.0	60.9	59.2
DEVELOPED COUNTRIES	1960	90.5	90.5	90.5	68.9	70.9	66.8	14.9	18.2	11.6	60.6	62.4	58.7
	1965	91.0	90.9	91.0	74.5	76.3	72.8	24.2	28.2	20.1	66.2	68.0	64.3
	1970	91.7	91.6	91.8	76.3	77.8	74.8	26.7	30.0	23.2	66.0	67.6	64.4
	1975	91.7	91.8	91.7	80.4	80.3	80.5	30.5	32.9	28.0	67.7	68.5	66.8
	1980	92.1	92.0	92.3	80.9	80.4	81.3	30.9	31.5	30.2	67.2	67.2	67.1
	1985	91.6	91.5	91.6	85.5	85.2	85.8	33.8	34.3	33.2	69.4	69.4	69.3
DEVELOPING COUNTRIES‡													
	1960	47.5	57.1	37.7	21.1	27.6	14.5	3.8	5.6	2.0	26.8	33.2	20.2
	1965	54.8	63.9	45.4	27.6	35.0	20.0	5.5	7.8	3.2	32.8	39.6	25.9
	1970	57.9	66.2	49.4	31.3	38.6	23.8	7.1	9.7	4.4	35.9	42.4	29.2
	1975	62.8	70.9	54.4	34.9	41.4	28.2	9.7	12.8	6.4	39.2	45.4	32.7
	1980	68.8	76.3	60.8	40.3	46.6	33.8	11.6	14.6	8.5	43.2	49.1	37.1
	1985	72.7	79.4	65.7	46.0	52.1	39.6	13.7	17.0	10.3	46.9	52.4	41.1

2.11 Enrolment ratios by age-group and sex
Taux d'inscription par groupe d'âge et par sexe
Tasas de escolarización por grupo de edad y por sexo

CONTINENTS, MAJOR AREAS AND GROUPS OF COUNTRIES / CONTINENTS, GRANDES REGIONS ET GROUPES DE PAYS / CONTINENTES, GRANDES REGIONES Y GRUPOS DE PAISES	YEAR / ANNEE / AÑO	AGE GROUPS / GROUPES D'AGE / GRUPOS DE EDAD											
		6 - 11			12 - 17			18 - 23			6 - 23		
		MF	M	F	MF	M	F	MF	M	F	MF	M	F
		(1)	(2)	(3)	(4)	(5)	(6)	(7)	(8)	(9)	(10)	(11)	(12)
AFRICA (EXCLUDING ARAB STATES)	1960	30.0	37.6	22.6	17.3	23.1	11.7	1.4	2.3	0.6	18.0	23.1	13.0
	1965	35.0	41.8	28.3	21.6	27.9	15.4	2.0	3.1	1.0	21.7	26.7	16.6
	1970	38.6	44.8	32.3	26.1	32.8	19.5	3.0	4.6	1.5	25.0	30.2	19.9
	1975	45.7	51.1	40.3	32.4	39.3	25.5	4.2	6.2	2.2	30.4	35.4	25.4
	1980	59.0	65.6	52.5	43.6	51.9	35.4	6.4	9.2	3.7	40.1	46.3	34.0
	1985	64.3	69.3	59.3	51.5	60.4	42.7	9.3	13.1	5.6	45.7	51.7	39.7
ASIA (EXCLUDING ARAB STATES)‡	1960	54.7	65.7	43.2	24.9	31.7	17.9	4.3	6.7	2.0	30.6	37.9	23.2
	1965	60.5	71.2	49.3	31.4	39.2	23.3	6.2	9.0	3.3	36.2	43.8	28.2
	1970	62.1	71.9	52.0	32.3	40.0	24.3	7.6	10.8	4.3	37.7	45.0	30.1
	1975	65.7	75.3	55.7	33.6	40.3	26.7	9.2	12.9	5.3	39.5	46.5	32.2
	1980	69.6	78.3	60.4	37.3	43.6	30.5	10.2	13.8	6.5	41.9	48.4	35.0
	1985	73.3	81.2	64.9	41.5	47.6	35.1	12.3	16.1	8.3	44.7	50.8	38.2
ARAB STATES	1960	40.0	51.1	28.5	18.3	26.4	10.1	4.0	6.6	1.4	23.3	31.2	15.2
	1965	49.0	60.7	36.6	24.8	35.0	14.3	6.5	10.4	2.7	30.2	39.5	20.4
	1970	51.5	63.0	39.4	29.5	40.0	18.4	8.9	13.4	4.5	33.5	43.1	23.6
	1975	61.1	73.3	48.3	35.2	44.9	25.0	13.5	18.6	8.1	40.1	49.6	30.1
	1980	68.9	78.9	58.6	42.2	51.3	32.5	15.9	20.6	10.8	45.5	53.6	36.9
	1985	73.7	82.0	65.1	51.2	59.6	42.4	18.8	23.3	14.1	51.2	58.4	43.7
NORTHERN AMERICA	1960	100.0	100.0	100.0	92.1	94.0	90.2	29.3	34.3	24.3	79.1	81.2	77.0
	1965	100.0	100.0	100.0	93.3	95.0	91.6	40.3	45.6	35.0	81.2	83.4	79.1
	1970	100.0	100.0	100.0	89.8	91.3	88.1	45.7	50.5	40.8	79.2	81.3	77.0
	1975	100.0	100.0	100.0	94.4	94.5	94.2	50.4	54.2	46.5	80.6	81.9	79.1
	1980	100.0	100.0	100.0	86.5	86.0	87.0	49.0	47.5	50.5	76.3	75.7	77.0
	1985	100.0	100.0	100.0	95.7	95.6	95.7	55.4	54.1	56.7	81.7	81.2	82.2
LATIN AMERICAN AND THE CARIBBEAN	1960	57.7	58.1	57.3	36.4	38.8	33.9	5.7	7.1	4.4	36.9	38.3	35.6
	1965	64.0	63.9	64.0	43.0	45.5	40.6	8.1	9.7	6.4	42.5	43.7	41.3
	1970	71.2	70.9	71.5	49.9	52.1	47.5	11.6	13.5	9.6	48.3	49.5	47.1
	1975	76.6	76.9	76.4	57.9	59.9	55.8	18.7	20.8	16.6	54.3	55.7	52.9
	1980	82.0	82.5	81.6	63.2	64.3	62.1	23.3	24.8	21.8	58.7	59.7	57.7
	1985	83.5	84.2	82.8	70.5	71.2	69.6	24.6	25.8	23.4	61.5	62.4	60.6

General note / Note générale / Nota general:

E--> For composition of major areas and groups of countries, see head note to table 1.2. It should, however, be noted, that in this table, Yugoslavia is included with the developed countries.

FR-> Pour la composition des grandes régions et groupes de pays, voir la note en-tête du tableau 1.2. On doit cependant noter, que dans ce tableau, la Yougoslavie est incluse avec les pays développés.

ESP> Veáse la nota encabezando el cuadro 1.2 para la composición de las grandes regiones y grupos de países. Debe tomarse nota, sin embargo, que en este cuadro, Yugoslavia esta incluída con los países desarrollados.

World Total, Asia, Developing countries, Asia (excl. Arab States):

E--> Not including China and the Democratic People's Republic of Korea.

FR-> Non compris la Chine et la République populaire démocratique de Corée.

ESP> Excluídas China y la República popular democrática de Corea.

2.12 Estimated public expenditure on education, in United States dollars

Estimation des dépenses publiques afférentes à l'enseignement, en dollars des Etats-Unis

Estimación de los gastos destinados a la educación, en dólares de los Estados Unidos

CONTINENTS, MAJOR AREAS AND GROUPS OF COUNTRIES CONTINENTS, GRANDES REGIONS ET GROUPES DE PAYS CONTINENTES, GRANDES REGIONES Y GRUPOS DE PAISES	PUBLIC EXPENDITURE ON EDUCATION (IN MILLIONS OF DOLLARS) DEPENSES PUBLIQUES AFFERENTES A L'ENSEIGNEMENT (EN MILLIONS DE DOLLARS) GASTOS PUBLICOS DESTINADOS A LA EDUCACION (EN MILLIONES DE DOLARES)				PUBLIC EXPENDITURE ON EDUCATION AS % OF GNP DEPENSES PUBLIQUES AFFERENTES A L'ENSEI-GNEMENT EN % DU PNB GASTOS PUBLICOS DESTINADOS A LA EDUCACION EN % DEL PNB				PUBLIC EXPENDITURE ON EDUCATION PER INHABITANT ($) DEPENSES PUBLIQUES AFFERENTES A L'ENSEI-GNEMENT, PAR HABITANT ($) GASTOS PUBLICOS DESTINADOS A LA EDUCACION POR HABITANTE ($)			
	1970	1975	1980	1984	1970	1975	1980	1984	1970	1975	1980	1984
WORLD TOTAL	159 900	330 713	612 098	651 171	5.2	5.6	5.6	5.7	45	84	142	141
AFRICA	2 406	6 955	16 677	16 969	4.2	4.8	4.8	5.4	7	18	38	34
AMERICA	77 479	127 583	233 132	300 055	6.2	6.0	6.3	6.4	152	228	380	457
ASIA	13 933	46 128	101 589	117 772	3.1	4.3	4.5	4.6	7	20	41	44
EUROPE (INCL. USSR)	64 098	143 079	250 275	204 006	5.1	5.8	5.6	5.5	92	197	335	268
OCEANIA	1 984	6 968	10 425	12 369	4.4	6.2	5.9	5.9	103	332	460	514
DEVELOPED COUNTRIES	145 444	289 684	520 052	556 277	5.7	6.1	6.1	6.1	142	270	466	487
DEVELOPING COUNTRIES	14 456	41 029	92 046	94 894	3.0	3.6	3.8	4.0	6	14	29	27
AFRICA (EXCLUDING ARAB STATES)	1 151	3 553	9 305	7 688	3.3	4.2	4.3	4.9	5	13	29	21
ASIA (EXCLUDING ARAB STATES)	13 389	41 091	91 543	104 906	3.0	4.2	4.6	4.5	7	18	37	40
ARAB STATES	1 799	8 439	17 418	22 147	5.1	5.9	4.6	5.5	15	62	109	123
NORTHERN AMERICA	71 830	113 288	200 231	270 053	6.7	6.6	7.0	6.8	317	474	795	1 033
LATIN AMERICA AND THE CARIBBEAN	5 649	14 295	32 901	30 002	3.4	3.6	4.0	4.4	20	45	91	76

General note / Note générale / Nota general:

E--> For composition of major areas and groups of countries, see head note to table 1.2. Data for the following countries are not included in the world total nor in the totals by region: Democratic Kampuchea, Democratic People's Republic of Korea, Lao People's Democratic Republic, Lebanon, Mongolia, Mozambique, South Africa and Viet-nam.

FR-> Pour la composition des grandes régions et groupes de pays, voir la note en-tête du tableau 1.2. Pour les pays suivants les données ne sont incluses ni dans le total mondial ni dans les totaux par régions: Afrique du

General note / Note générale / Nota general: (Cont):
Sud, Kampuchea démocratique, Liban, Mongolie, Mozambique, République démocratique populaire Lao, République populaire démocratique de Corée, et Viet-nam.

ESP> Veáse la nota encabezando el cuadro 1.2 para la composición de las grandes regiones y grupos de países. Los datos relativos a los países siguientes no éstan incluídos ni en el total mondial ni en los totales por regiones: Kampuchea democrática, Líbano, Mongolia, Mozambique, República democrática popular Lao, República popular democrática popular de Corea, Sudáfrica y Viet-nam.

3 Education

Education

Educación

This chapter provides statistics on education preceding the first level, as well as on that at the first, second, and third levels of education. Data are also provided on educational systems and on enrolment ratios for the different levels. Data on the number of students and teachers are provided for all levels of education; data on number of institutions are provided for education preceding the first level and for education at the first level; data on enrolment and graduates at the third level are provided according to different types of disaggregation.

The text which follows is subdivided into three sections according to the type of data included in the tables of this chapter.

Section A.

This section, which refers to tables 3.1 to 3.2, provides information by country on the entrance ages and duration of compulsory education for first and second level general education and enrolment ratios by level of education.

Section B.

This section consists of seven tables, 3.3 to 3.9 concerned with education preceding the first level, and first and second level education. In consulting the tables in this chapter, reference should be made to the information on duration of schooling, etc., contained in Tables 3.1, 3.1a and 3.1b.

In general, the data shown in these tables are for the years 1975, 1980, 1981, 1982, 1983 and 1984.

Section C.

This section consists of seven tables on the development of third level education in the world.

According to the definition adopted by Unesco, education at the third level requires, as a minimum condition of entry, the successful completion of education at the second level or proof of equivalent knowledge or experience. It can be given in different types of institutions, such as universities, teacher-training institutes, technical institutes, etc.

The categories of data contained in this chapter are as follows:

Students: Number of students enrolled per 100,000 inhabitants (Table 3.10), students by type of institution (Table 3.11), by field of study (Table 3.12) and by level of programmes and field of study (Table 3.13). The two last tables are compiled according to the International Standard Classification of Education (ISCED).

Teachers: Total and by type of institution (Table 3.11).

Graduates: Breakdown by ISCED level of programmes and field of study (Table 3.14).

Foreign students: Total and by country of study and by country of origin (Tables 3.15 and 3.16).

Figure 3 below shows the increase or decrease in the number of students per 100,000 inhabitants in the different continents, regions and groups of countries. In 1984, the ratio was more than four times higher in developed countries than in the developing countries. However, considerable differences persist within these major groups of countries; in the developed countries, the ratio for *Northern America* in 1984 was about three times that of *Oceania* and *Europe and the U.S.S.R.*; in the developing countries the ratio for *Latin America and the Caribbean* in 1984 was more than four times that of *Africa*.

Definitions of fields of study according to ISCED (International Standard Classification of Education)

ISCED Codes

LEVELS	FIELDS OF STUDY		
5, 6, 7	14	EDUCATION SCIENCE AND TEACHER TRAINING	General teacher training, teacher training programmes with specialization in vocational subjects, education science.
5, 6, 7	22, 26	HUMANITIES, RELIGION AND THEOLOGY	Languages and literature, linguistics, comparative literature, programmes for interpreters and translators, history, archaeology, philosophy. Religion and theology.
5, 6, 7	18	FINE AND APPLIED ARTS	Art studies, drawing and painting, sculpturing, handicrafts, music, drama, photography and cinematography, interior design, history and philosophy of art.
5, 6, 7	38	LAW	Law, programmes for "notaires", local magistrates, jurisprudence.
5, 6, 7	30	SOCIAL AND BEHAVIOURAL SCIENCE	Social and behavioural science, economics, demography, political science, sociology, anthropology, psychology, geography, studies of regional cultures.
5, 6, 7	34	COMMERCIAL AND BUSINESS ADMINISTRATION	Business administration and commercial programmes, accountancy, secretarial programmes, business machine operation and electronic data processing, financial management, public administration, institutional administration.
5, 6, 7	84	MASS COMMUNICATION AND DOCUMENTATION	Journalism, programmes in radio and television broadcasting, public relations, communications arts, library science, programmes for technicians in museums and similar repositories, documentation techniques.
5, 6, 7	66	HOME ECONOMICS (domestic science)	Household arts, consumer food research and nutrition.
5	78	SERVICE TRADES	Cooking (restaurant and hotel-type), retailing, tourist trades, other service trades programmes.
5, 6, 7	42	NATURAL SCIENCE	Biological science, chemistry, geological science, physics, astronomy, meteorology, oceanography.
5, 6, 7	46	MATHEMATICS AND COMPUTER SCIENCE	General programmes in mathematics, statistics, actuarial science, computer science.
5, 6, 7	50	MEDICAL SCIENCE AND HEALTH-RELATED	Medicine, surgery and medical specialities, hygiene and public health, physiotherapy and occupational therapy; nursing, midwifery, medical X-ray techniques and other programmes in medical diagnostic and treatment techniques; medical technology, dentistry, stomatology and odontology, dental techniques, pharmacy, optometry.
5, 6, 7	54	ENGINEERING	Chemical engineering and materials techniques, civil engineering, electrical and electronics engineering, surveying, industrial engineering, metallurgical engineering, mining engineering, mechanical engineering, agricultural and forestry engineering techniques, fishery engineering techniques.
5, 6, 7	58	ARCHITECTURE AND TOWN PLANNING	Architecture, town planning, landscape architecture.
5	52	TRADE, CRAFT AND INDUSTRIAL PROGRAMMES	Food processing; electrical and electronics trades, metal trades, mechanical trades, air-conditioning trades; textile techniques, graphic arts, laboratory technicians, optical lens making.
5	70	TRANSPORT AND COMMUNICATIONS	Air crew and ships' officer programmes, railway operating trades, road motor vehicle operation programmes, postal service programmes.
5, 6, 7	62	AGRICULTURE, FORESTRY AND FISHERY	General programmes in agriculture, animal husbandry, horticulture, crop husbandry, agricultural economics, food sciences and technology, soil and water sciences, veterinary medicine, forestry, forest products technology, fishery science and technology.
6	01		General programmes.
5, 6, 7	89	OTHER PROGRAMMES	Criminology, civil security and military programme, social welfare, vocational counselling, physical education, environmental studies, nautical science. Other programmes.

Ce chapitre présente des statistiques relatives à l'enseignement précédant le premier degré, ainsi qu'aux enseignements du premier, du second et du troisième degré. Des données sont présentées sur les systèmes nationaux d'enseignement et les taux d'inscription scolaire ainsi que sur le personnel enseignant et les effectifs scolaires pour tous les niveaux d'enseignement; le nombre d'écoles est également indiqué pour les enseignements précédant le premier degré et le premier degré; les chiffres sur les effectifs et les diplômés du troisième degré sont présentés selon différentes répartitions.

Le texte qui suit est subdivisé en trois sections, en accord avec le type de données qui figurent dans les tableaux de ce chapitre.

Section A.

Cette section, relative aux tableaux 3.1 à 3.2, procure des informations par pays sur l'âge d'admission et la durée de l'enseignement obligatoire dans les enseignements du premier degré et du second degré général, ainsi que les taux d'inscription par degré d'enseignement.

Section B.

Cette section comprend sept tableaux, 3.3 à 3.9, qui se réfèrent à l'enseignement précédant le premier degré et aux enseignements du premier et du second degré. En consultant les tableaux de ce chapitre, il faut se référer aux renseignements sur la durée de la scolarité, etc. contenus dans les tableaux 3.1, 3.1a et 3.1b.

En général, les données présentées dans ces tableaux correspondent aux années 1975, 1980, 1981, 1982, 1983 et 1984.

Section C.

La présente section comprend sept tableaux statistiques sur le développement de l'enseignement du troisième degré dans le monde.

L'enseignement du troisième degré, d'après la définition adoptée par l'Unesco, est celui qui exige comme condition minimale d'admission d'avoir suivi avec succès un enseignement complet du second degré ou de faire preuve de connaissances ou expériences équivalentes. Il peut être dispensé dans différents types d'établissements tels que les universités, les écoles normales supérieures, les écoles techniques supérieures, etc.

Les catégories de données présentées dans ce chapitre sont les suivantes:

Etudiants: Nombre d'étudiants inscrits par 100 000 habitants (tableau 3.10), étudiants par type d'établissement (tableau 3.11, par domaine d'études (tableau 3.12) et par niveau de programme et domaine d'études (tableau 3.13). Ces deux derniers tableaux sont présentés selon les critères de la Classification Internationale Type de l'Education (CITE).

Personnel enseignant: Nombre total et par type d'établissement (tableau 3.11).

Diplômés: Répartition par niveau de programmes et domaine d'études de la CITE (tableau 3.14).

Etudiants étrangers: Nombre total, par pays d'études, et par pays d'origine (tableaux 3.15 et 3.16).

Le graphique 3 ci-après montre l'accroissement ou la diminution du nombre d'étudiants par 100 000 habitants dans les différents continents, régions ou groupes de pays. En 1984, ce rapport était plus de quatre fois plus élevé dans les pays développés que dans les pays en développement. Néanmoins, des écarts considérables persistent entre les groupes de pays; dans les pays développés, le taux de l'*Amérique septentrionale* en 1984 était environ trois fois celui de l'*Océanie* et de l'*Europe et l'U.R.R.S.*; dans les pays en développement, le taux de l'*Amérique latine et les caraïbes* en 1984 était plus de quatre fois celui de l'*Afrique*.

Définitions des domaines d'études d'après la CITE (Classification internationale type de l'éducation)

Codes CITE			
Niveaux	Domaines d'études		
5, 6, 7	14	SCIENCES DE L'EDUCATION ET FORMATION D'ENSEIGNANTS	Formation de personnel enseignant, préparation générale à l'enseignement, préparation à l'enseignement avec spécialisation dans des disciplines à caractère professionnel, sciences de l'éducation.
5, 6, 7	22, 26	LETTRES, RELIGION ET THEOLOGIE	Langues et littératures, linguistique, littérature comparée, formation d'interprètes et de traducteurs, histoire, archéologie, philosophie. Religion et théologie.
5, 6, 7	18	BEAUX-ARTS ET ARTS APPLIQUES	Etudes artistiques, dessin et peinture, sculpture, arts artisanaux, musique, arts du spectacle, photographie et cinématographie, décoration, histoire et philosophie de l'art.
5, 6, 7	38	DROIT	Droit, notariat, formation de magistrats locaux, jurisprudence.
5, 6, 7	30	SCIENCES SOCIALES ET SCIENCES DU COMPORTEMENT	Sciences sociales et sciences du comportement, sciences économiques, science politique, démographie, sociologie, anthropologie, psychologie, géographie, études des cultures régionales.
5, 6, 7	34	FORMATION AU COMMERCE ET A L'ADMINISTRATION DES ENTREPRISES	Administration des entreprises et enseignement commercial, comptabilité, secrétariat, mécanographie et traitement électronique de l'information, gestion financière, administration publique, administration d'établissements et de collectivités.
5, 6, 7	84	INFORMATION ET DOCUMENTATION	Journalisme, formations pour la radio et la télévision, relations avec le public, techniques de l'information, bibliothéconomie, formation des techniciens pour les musées et établissements analogues, techniques de la documentation.
5, 6, 7	66	ENSEIGNEMENT MENAGER	Arts ménagers, alimentation familiale, diététique et nutrition.
5	78	FORMATION POUR LE SECTEUR TERTIAIRE	Hôtellerie et restauration, commerce de détail, services de tourisme, autres formations pour le secteur tertiaire.
5, 6, 7	42	SCIENCES EXACTES ET NATURELLES	Sciences biologiques, chimie, sciences géologiques, physique, astronomie, meteorologie, océanographie.
5, 6, 7	46	MATHEMATIQUES ET INFORMATIQUE	Mathématiques générales, statistique, science actuarielle, informatique.
5, 6, 7	50	SCIENCES MEDICALES, SANTE ET HYGIENE	Médecine, chirurgie et spécialisations médicales, hygiène et santé publique, physiothérapie et ergothérapie; formation d'infirmiers, de sages-femmes, de radiologues et autres formations aux techniques du diagnostic et du traitement des maladies, technologie médicale, art dentaire, stomatologie et odontologie, technologie dentaire, pharmacie, optométrie.
5, 6, 7	54	SCIENCES DE L'INGENIEUR	Génie chimique et technologie des matériaux, génie civil, électrotechnique et éloctronique, topographie, organisation industrielle, métallurgie, techniques minières, mécanique, technologie agricole et forestière, techniques de la pêche.
5, 6, 7	58	ARCHITECTURE ET URBANISME	Architecture, urbanisme, formation d'architectes paysagistes.
5	52	METIERS DE LA PRODUCTION INDUSTRIELLE	Traitement des denrées alimentaires; formation en électricité, en électronique, au travail des métaux, à la mécanique, aux techniques du conditionnement d'air; technologie des textiles, arts graphiques, techniciens de laboratoire, fabrication de verres optiques.
5	70	TRANSPORTS ET TELECOMMUNICATIONS	Formation de personnel des transports aériens, maritimes, ferroviaires, routiers et des services postaux.
5, 6, 7	62	AGRICULTURE, SYLVICULTURE ET HALIEUTIQUE	Enseignement agricole, zootechnie, horticulture, culture de plein champ, économie agricole, science et technologie de l'alimentation, pédologie et hydrologie, médecine vétérinaire, sylviculture, technologie des produits forestiers, halieutique (science et technologie de la pêche).
6	01		Programmes d'enseignement général.
5, 6, 7	89	AUTRES PROGRAMMES	Criminologie, formation militaire et pour la sécurité civile, formation de personnel des services sociaux, formation des conseillers d'orientation professionnelle, éducation physique, programmes relatifs à l'environnement, sciences nautiques. Autres programmes.

Este capítulo facilita datos estadísticos sobre la enseñanza anterior al primer grado, asi como sobre las enseñanzas de primero, segundo y tercer grado. También se presentan datos relativos a los sistemas de enseñanza y las tasas de escolarización, para todos los grados de enseñanza. Se indican asimismo el número de escuelas en las enseñanzas anterior al primer grado y de primer grado, y las cifras relativas a los efectivos y los diplomados de la enseñanza de tercer grado se presentan bajo distintas formas.

El texto que sigue se subdivide en tres secciones, de acuerdo con los tipos de datos que figuran en este capítulo.

Sección A.

Esta sección, que comprende los cuadros 3.1 a 3.2, facilita la información, por países, sobre la edad de admisión, la duración de la enseñanza obligatoria en las enseñanzas de primero y de segundo grado, y las tasas de escolarización para los diferentes grados de enseñanza.

Sección B.

Esta sección comprende siete cuadros, 3.3 a 3.9, que se refieren a la enseñanza anterior al primer grado y a las enseñanzas de primero y de segundo grado. Al consultar los cuadros de este capítulo, hay que referirse a las informaciones sobre la duración de la escolaridad, etc. que figuran en los cuadros 3.1, 3.1a y 3.1b.

En general, los datos presentados en estos cuadros corresponden a los años 1975, 1980, 1981, 1982, 1983 y 1984.

Sección C.

Esta sección comprende siete cuadros estadísticos sobre el desarrollo de la enseñanza de tercer grado en los distintos países del mundo.

Según la definición adoptada por la Unesco, la enseñanza de tercer grado es aquella en la que se exige, como condición mínima de admisión, haber terminado con éxito la enseñanza de segundo grado o demostrar la posesión de conocimientos equivalentes. Puede dispensarse en distintos tipos de establecimientos docentes tales como las universidades, las escuelas normales superiores, las escuelas técnicas superiores, etc.

Los datos presentados en este capítulo corresponden a las siguientes categorías:

Estudiantes: número de estudiantes inscritos por 100 000 habitantes (cuadro 3.10), estudiantes por tipo de establecimiento por sectores de estudios (cuadro 3.12) y por nivel de programas y sector de estudios (cuadro 3.13). Estos dos últimos cuadros se presentan según los criterios de la Clasificación Internacional Normalizada de la Educación (CINE).

Personal docente: número total y por tipo de establecimiento (cuadro 3.11).

Diplomados: distribución por nivel de programas y sector de estudios de la CINE (cuadro 3.14).

Estudiantes extranjeros: número total y por países de orígen (cuadros 3.15 y 3.16).

En el gráfico 3 que aparece al final del texto puede verse el aumento o la disminución del número de estudiantes por 100 000 habitantes en los diferentes continentes, regiones o grupos de países. En 1984 esta relación era más de cuatro veces más elevada en los países desarrollados que en los países en desarrollo. Sin embargo, persisten considerables diferencias entre los grupos de países; en los países desarrollados, la tasa de *América septentrional* en 1984 era aproximadamente tres veces la de *Oceanía* y de *Europa y U.R.S.S.*; en los países en desarrollo, la tasa de *América Latina y el Caribe* en 1984 era más de cuatro veces la de Africa.

Definiciones de los sectores de estudio según la CINE (Clasificación Internacional Normalizada de la Educación)

Cifra de la CINE			
Grados	Sectores de estudios		
5, 6, 7	14	CIENCIAS DE LA EDUCACION Y FORMACION DE PERSONAL DOCENTE	Programas generales de formación de personal docente, formación de personal docente con especialización en materias profesionales o técnicas, ciencias de la educación.
5, 6, 7	22, 26	HUMANIDADES, RELIGION Y TEOLOGIA	Lenguas y literatura, lingüística, literatura comparada, formación de traductores e intérpretes, historia, arqueología, filosofía. Religión y teología.
5, 6, 7	18	BELLAS ARTES Y ARTES APLICADAS	Estudios artísticos, dibujo y pintura, escultura, artesanía, música, arte dramático, fotografía y cinematografía, decoración, historia y filosofía del arte.
5, 6, 7	38	DERECHO	Derecho, formación de notarios, formación de magistrados locales, jurisprudencia.
5, 6, 7	30	CIENCIAS SOCIALES Y DEL COMPORTAMIENTO	Ciencias sociales y del comportamiento, economía, ciencias políticas, demografía, sociología, antropología, psicología, geografía, estudio de las culturas regionales.
5, 6, 7	34	ENSEÑANZA COMERCIAL Y DE ADMINISTRACION DE EMPRESAS	Administración de empresas y enseñanza comercial, contabilidad, programas de secretaría, manejo de máquinas de oficina y tratamiento electrónico de datos, gestión financiera, administración pública, administración de instituciones.
5, 6, 7	84	DOCUMENTACION Y COMUNICACION SOCIAL	Periodismo, formación de personal de radio y televisión, relaciones públicas, comunicación, bibliotecología, formación de personal técnico de museos y establecimientos análogos, técnicas de la documentación.
5, 6, 7	66	ECONOMIA DOMESTICA (ENSEÑANZA DEL HOGAR)	Artes del hogar, nutrición e investigación sobre el consumo de alimentos y la alimentación familiar.
5	78	FORMACION PARA EL SECTOR DE LOS SERVICIOS	Arte culinario (hotelería y restaurantes), venta al detalle, turismo, otros programas relativos al sector de los servicios.
5, 6, 7	42	CIENCIAS NATURALES	Ciencias biológicas, química, ciencias geológicas, física, astronomía, meteorología, oceanografía.
5, 6, 7	46	MATEMATICAS E INFORMATICA	Programas generales de matemáticas, estadística, ciencia actuarial, informática.
5, 6, 7	50	CIENCIAS MEDICAS, SANIDAD E HIGIENE	Medicina, cirugía y especialidades médicas, higiene y sanidad pública, fisioterapía y ergoterapía; formación de enfermeros y de comadronas, tecnología médica de los rayos X y otras tecnologías del diagnóstico y tratamiento médicos, tecnología médica; odontología y estomatología, tecnología dentaria, farmacia, optometría.
5, 6, 7	54	INGENIERIA Y TECNOLOGIA	Ingeniería química y tecnología de materiales, ingeniería civil, ingeniería eléctrica y electrónica, topografía, organización industrial, ingeniería metalúrgica, ingeniería de minas, ingeniería mecánica, ingeniería agronómica, ingeniería forestal (de montes).
5, 6, 7	58	ARQUITECTURA Y URBANISMO	Arquitectura, urbanismo, arquitectura paisajística.
5	52	ARTES Y OFICIOS INDUSTRIALES	Tratamiento y elaboración de alimentos; oficios de la electricidad, de la electrónica, del metal, oficios relativos a la mecánica, al acondicionamiento de aire; técnicas textiles, artes gráficas, técnicos de laboratorio, fabricación de cristales y lentes ópticos.
5	70	TRANSPORTES Y COMUNICACIONES	Formación de personal para los transportes aéreos, marítimos, por ferrocarril y por carretera;. programas relativos a los servicios postales.
5, 6, 7	62	ENSEÑANZA AGRONOMICA, DASONOMICA Y PESQUERA	Agronomía, zootecnía, horticultura, agricultura, economía agraria, tecnología y ciencias de la alimentación, hidrología y edafología, veterinaria, dasonomía, tecnología de los produtos forestales, ciencia y tecnología pesquera (haliéutica).
6	01		Enseñanza general.
5, 6, 7	89	OTROS PROGRAMAS	Criminología, enseñanza militar y programas relativos a la seguridad civil, asistencia social, orientación profesional, educación física, estudios mesológicos, ciencia náutica. Otros programas.

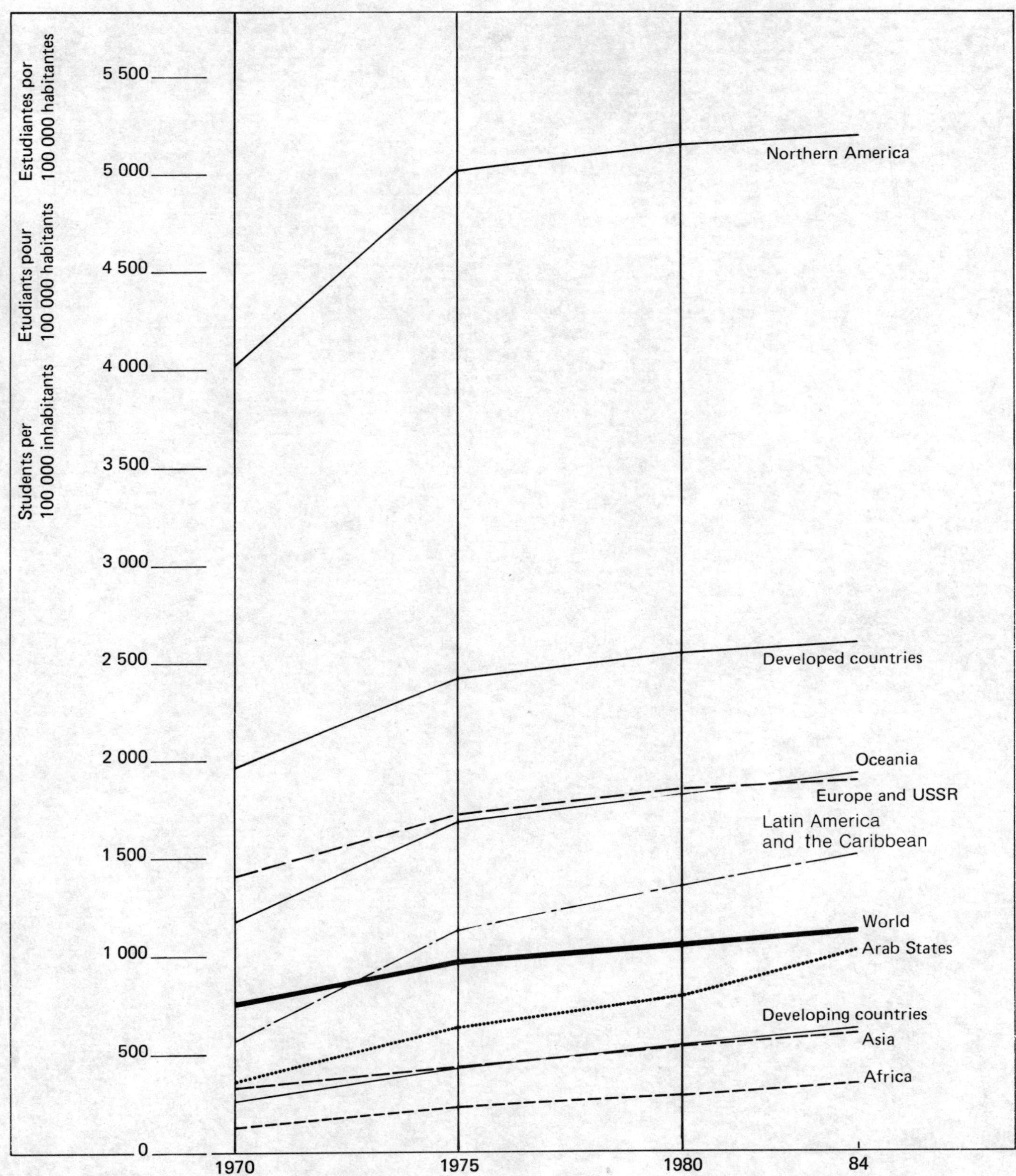

Figure 3: **Number of students at the third level per 100 000 inhabitants**
Not including the D.P.R. of Korea.

Graphique 3 : **Nombre d'étudiants du troisième degré pour 100 000 habitants**
Non compris la R.D.P. de Corée.

Gráfico 3: **Número de estudiantes de tercer grado por 100 000 habitantes**
Excluida la R.D.P. de Corea.

3.1 National education systems
Systèmes nationaux d'enseignement
Sistemas nacionales de enseñanza

P—P = FIRST LEVEL
S—S = SECOND LEVEL
S1–S1 = SECOND LEVEL, FIRST STAGE
S2–S2 = SECOND LEVEL, SECOND STAGE

FOR COUNTRIES MARKED WITH THE SYMBOL #, THE EDUCATIONAL SYSTEM ALLOWS FOR OTHER ALTERNATIVES (SEE TABLE 3.1A)

PLEASE REFER TO EXPLANATORY TEXT AT END OF TABLE

NUMBER OF COUNTRIES AND TERRITORIES PRESENTED IN THIS TABLE: 200

P—P = PREMIER DEGRE
S—S = SECOND DEGRE
S1–S1 = SECOND DEGRE, PREMIER CYCLE
S2–S2 = SECOND DEGRE, DEUXIEME CYCLE

POUR LES PAYS SIGNALES PAR LE SYMBOLE #, LE SYSTEME D'ENSEIGNEMENT PERMET D'AUTRES STRUCTURES (VOIR LE TABLEAU 3.1A)

PRIERE DE SE REFERER AU TEXTE EXPLICATIF A LA FIN DU TABLEAU

NOMBRE DE PAYS ET DE TERRITOIRES PRESENTES DANS CE TABLEAU: 200

P—P = PRIMER GRADO
S—S = SEGUNDO GRADO
S1–S1 = SEGUNDO GRADO, PRIMER CICLO
S2–S2 = SEGUNDO GRADO, SEGUNDO CICLO

PARA LOS PAISES SENALADOS CON EL SIMBOLO #, EL SISTEMA DE LA ENSEÑANZA PERMITE OTRAS ESTRUCTURAS (VEASE EL CUADRO 3.1A)

REFERIRSE AL TEXTO EXPLICATIVO AL FINAL DEL CUADRO

NUMERO DE PAISES Y DE TERRITORIOS PRESENTADOS EN ESTE CUADRO: 200

COUNTRY / PAYS / PAIS	COMPULSORY EDUCATION / SCOLARITE OBLIGATOIRE / ESCOLARIDAD OBLIGATORIA: AGE LIMITS / LIMITES D'AGE / LIMITES DE EDAD	DURATION (YEARS) / DUREE (ANNEES) / DURACION (ANOS)	ENTRANCE AGE TO EDUCATION PRECEDING THE FIRST LEVEL / AGE D'ADMISSION DANS L'ENSEIGNEMENT PRECEDANT LE PREMIER DEGRE / EDAD DE ADMISION EN LA ENSEÑANZA ANTERIOR AL PRIMER GRADO	ENTRANCE AGE AND DURATION OF FIRST AND SECOND LEVEL (GENERAL) EDUCATION / AGE D'ADMISSION ET DUREE DES ENSEIGNEMENTS DU PREMIER ET DU SECOND DEGRE (GENERAL) / EDAD DE ADMISION Y DURACION DE LAS ENSEÑANZAS DE PRIMER Y DE SEGUNDO GRADO (GENERAL) — AGE / AGE / EDAD: 4	5	6	7	8	9	10	11	12	13	14	15	16	17	18	19	20
AFRICA																				
ALGERIA	6–15	9	–			P	P	P	P	P	P	S1	S1	S1	S1	S2	S2	S2		
ANGOLA	7–15	8	3				P	P	P	P	S1	S1	S1	S1	S2	S2				
BENIN	5–11	5	3		P	P	P	P	P	P	S1	S1	S1	S1	S2	S2	S2			
BOTSWANA	–	–	–			P	P	P	P	P	P	P	S1	S1	S2	S2	S2			
BURKINA FASO	7–13	6	3				P	P	P	P	P	P	S1	S1	S1	S1	S2	S2	S2	
BURUNDI	7–13	6	5				P	P	P	P	P	P	S1	S1	S1	S1	S2	S2	S2	
CAMEROON																				
EASTERN	6–12	6	4			P	P	P	P	P	P	S1	S1	S1	S1	S2	S2	S2		
WESTERN	–	–	3			P	P	P	P	P	P	P	S1	S1	S1	S1	S1	S2	S2	
CAPE VERDE	7–13	6	–				P	P	P	P	P	P	S1	S1	S1	S2	S2			
CENTRAL AFRICAN REPUBLIC	6–14	8	4			P	P	P	P	P	P	S1	S1	S1	S1	S2	S2	S2		
CHAD	8–14	6	4			P	P	P	P	P	P	S1	S1	S1	S1	S2	S2	S2		
COMOROS	7–15	8	4			P	P	P	P	P	P	S1	S1	S1	S1	S2	S2	S2		
CONGO	6–16	10	3			P	P	P	P	P	P	S1	S1	S1	S1	S2	S2	S2		
COTE D'IVOIRE	–	–	4				P	P	P	P	P	P	S1	S1	S1	S1	S2	S2	S2	
DJIBOUTI	6–14	8	...			P	P	P	P	P	P	S1	S1	S1	S1	S2	S2	S2		

COUNTRY / PAYS / PAIS	COMPULSORY EDUCATION / SCOLARITE OBLIGATOIRE / ESCOLARIDAD OBLIGATORIA: AGE LIMITS / LIMITES D'AGE / LIMITES DE EDAD	COMPULSORY EDUCATION / SCOLARITE OBLIGATOIRE / ESCOLARIDAD OBLIGATORIA: DURATION (YEARS) / DUREE (ANNEES) / DURACION (AÑOS)	ENTRANCE AGE TO EDUCATION PRECEDING THE FIRST LEVEL / AGE D'ADMISSION DANS L'ENSEIGNEMENT PRECEDANT LE PREMIER DEGRE / EDAD DE ADMISION EN LA ENSEÑANZA ANTERIOR AL PRIMER GRADO	ENTRANCE AGE AND DURATION OF FIRST AND SECOND LEVEL (GENERAL) EDUCATION / AGE D'ADMISSION ET DUREE DES ENSEIGNEMENTS DU PREMIER ET DU SECOND DEGRE (GENERAL) / EDAD DE ADMISION Y DURACION DE LAS ENSEÑANZAS DE PRIMER Y DE SEGUNDO GRADO (GENERAL) — AGE / AGE / EDAD: 4	5	6	7	8	9	10	11	12	13	14	15	16	17	18	19	20
EGYPT #	6–12	6	–			P	P	P	P	P	P	S1	S1	S1	S2	S2	S2			
EQUATORIAL GUINEA #	6–14	8	2			P	P	P	P	P	P	S1	S1	S1	S1	S2	S2			
ETHIOPIA	–	–	4				P	P	P	P	P	P	S1	S1	S2	S2	S2	S2		
GABON	6–16	10	3			P	P	P	P	P	P	S1	S1	S1	S1	S2	S2	S2		
GAMBIA	–	–	2					P	P	P	P	P	P	S1	S1	S1	S1	S2	S2	
GHANA	6–16	10	4			P	P	P	P	P	P	S1	S1	S1	S1	S2	S2	S2		
GUINEA	7–13	6	–				P	P	P	P	P	P	S1	S1	S1	S2	S2	S2		
GUINEA-BISSAU	7–13	6	3				P	P	P	P	P	P	S1	S1	S1	S2	S2			
KENYA	–	–	3			P	P	P	P	P	P	P	S1	S1	S1	S2	S2	S2		
LESOTHO	6–13	7	...			P	P	P	P	P	P	P	S1	S1	S1	S2	S2			
LIBERIA	6–16	10	4			P	P	P	P	P	P	S1	S1	S1	S2	S2	S2			
LIBYAN ARAB JAMAHIRIYA	6–15	9	4			P	P	P	P	P	P	S1	S1	S1	S2	S2	S2			
MADAGASCAR	6–13	6	3			P	P	P	P	P	S1	S1	S1	S1	S2	S2	S2			
MALAWI	–	–	–			P	P	P	P	P	P	P	P	S1	S1	S2	S2			
MALI	6–15	9	3			P	P	P	P	P	P	S1	S1	S1	S2	S2	S2			
MAURITANIA	6–14	8	3			P	P	P	P	P	P	S1	S1	S1	S2	S2	S2			
MAURITIUS	5–12	7	3		P	P	P	P	P	P	S1	S1	S1	S2	S2	S2	S2			
MOROCCO	7–14	7	3				P	P	P	P	P	S1	S1	S1	S1	S2	S2	S2		
MOZAMBIQUE	–	–	6				P	P	P	P	S1	S1	S1	S2	S2					
NAMIBIA	7–16	9	...				P	P	P	P	P	P	P	S	S	S	S	S		
NIGER	7–15	8	4				P	P	P	P	P	P	S1	S1	S1	S1	S2	S2	S2	
NIGERIA	6–12	6	3			P	P	P	P	P	P	S1	S1	S1	S2	S2	S2			
REUNION	6–16	10	2			P	P	P	P	P	S1	S1	S1	S1	S2	S2	S2			
RWANDA	7–15	8	–				P	P	P	P	P	P	P	P	S1	S1	S1	S2	S2	S2
ST. HELENA	5–15	10	3		P	P	P	P	P	P	S1	S1	S1	S1	S2	S2				
SAO TOME AND PRINCIPE #	6–12	6	5				P	P	P	P	S1	S1	S2	S2	S2	S2	S2			
SENEGAL	6–12	5	...			P	P	P	P	P	P	S1	S1	S1	S1	S2	S2	S2		
SEYCHELLES	6–15	9	4			P	P	P	P	P	P	P	P	P	S	S				
SIERRA LEONE	–	–	3		P	P	P	P	P	P	P	S1	S1	S1	S1	S1	S2	S2		
SOMALIA	6–14	8	4			P	P	P	P	P	P	P	P	S	S	S	S			
SUDAN	–	–	5				P	P	P	P	P	P	S1	S1	S1	S2	S2	S2		
SWAZILAND	6–13	7	–			P	P	P	P	P	P	P	S1	S1	S1	S2	S2			
TOGO	6–12	6	3			P	P	P	P	P	P	S1	S1	S1	S1	S2	S2	S2		
TUNISIA #	–	–	3			P	P	P	P	P	P	S1	S1	S1	S2	S2	S2	S2		
UGANDA	–	–	...			P	P	P	P	P	P	P	S1	S1	S1	S1	S2	S2		
UNITED REPUBLIC OF TANZANIA	7–14	7	3				P	P	P	P	P	P	P	S1	S1	S1	S1	S2	S2	
WESTERN SAHARA	6–16	8	4			P	P	P	P	P	S1	S1	S1	S2	S2	S2				
ZAIRE	6–12	6	3			P	P	P	P	P	P	S1	S1	S2	S2	S2	S2			
ZAMBIA	–	–	3				P	P	P	P	P	P	P	S1	S1	S1	S2	S2		

COUNTRY / PAYS / PAIS	COMPULSORY EDUCATION / SCOLARITE OBLIGATOIRE / ESCOLARIDAD OBLIGATORIA: AGE LIMITS / LIMITES D'AGE / LIMITES DE EDAD	DURATION (YEARS) / DUREE (ANNEES) / DURACION (AÑOS)	ENTRANCE AGE TO EDUCATION PRECEDING THE FIRST LEVEL / AGE D'ADMISSION DANS L'ENSEIGNEMENT PRECEDANT LE PREMIER DEGRE / EDAD DE ADMISION EN LA ENSEÑANZA ANTERIOR AL PRIMER GRADO	ENTRANCE AGE AND DURATION OF FIRST AND SECOND LEVEL (GENERAL) EDUCATION / AGE D'ADMISSION ET DUREE DES ENSEIGNEMENTS DU PREMIER ET DU SECOND DEGRE (GENERAL) / EDAD DE ADMISION Y DURACION DE LAS ENSEÑANZAS DE PRIMER Y DE SEGUNDO GRADO (GENERAL) — AGE / AGE / EDAD																
				4	5	6	7	8	9	10	11	12	13	14	15	16	17	18	19	20
ZIMBABWE	7–15	8	5				P	P	P	P	P	P	P	S	S	S	S	S	S	
AMERICA, NORTH																				
ANTIGUA #	5–16	11	–		P	P	P	P	P	P	S1	S1	S1	S2	S2					
BAHAMAS	5–14	10	...		P	P	P	P	P	P	S1	S1	S1	S2	S2	S2				
BARBADOS	5–16	11	3		P	P	P	P	P	P	S1	S1	S1	S2	S2	S2				
BELIZE #	6–14	8	3			P	P	P	P	P	P	P	P	S	S	S	S			
BERMUDA	5–16	11,12	4		P	P	P	P	P	P	P	S	S	S	S	S				
BRITISH VIRGIN ISLANDS #	5–15	10	3		P	P	P	P	P	P	P	S1	S1	S1	S2	S2				
CANADA #	6–16	8–10	5			P	P	P	P	P	P	S1	S1	S1	S2	S2	S2			
CAYMAN ISLANDS	5–15	10	–		P	P	P	P	P	P	S	S	S	S	S	S	S			
COSTA RICA #	6–15	9	5			P	P	P	P	P	P	S1	S1	S1	S2	S2				
CUBA	6–11	6	5			P	P	P	P	P	P	S1	S1	S1	S2	S2	S2			
DOMINICA	5–15	10	3		P	P	P	P	P	P	P	S1	S1	S1	S1	S1	S2	S2		
DOMINICAN REPUBLIC	7–14	6	3				P	P	P	P	P	P	S1	S1	S2	S2	S2	S2		
EL SALVADOR	7–15	9	4				P	P	P	P	P	P	P	P	P	S	S	S		
GRENADA	5–16	11	3		P	P	P	P	P	P	P	S	S	S	S	S				
GUADELOUPE	6–16	10	2			P	P	P	P	P	S1	S1	S1	S1	S2	S2	S2			
GUATEMALA	7–14	6	4				P	P	P	P	P	P	S1	S1	S1	S2	S2	S2		
HAITI #	6–12	6	4			P	P	P	P	P	P	S1	S1	S1	S2	S2	S2			
HONDURAS	7–13	6	4				P	P	P	P	P	P	S1	S1	S1	S2	S2			
JAMAICA	6–15	10	4		P	P	P	P	P	P	P	S1	S1	S1	S2	S2	S2	S2		
MARTINIQUE	6–16	10	2			P	P	P	P	P	S1	S1	S1	S1	S2	S2	S2			
MEXICO	6–12	6	4			P	P	P	P	P	P	S1	S1	S1	S2	S2	S2			
MONTSERRAT	5–14	9	3		P	P	P	P	P	P	P	S1	S1	S1	S1	S1	S2	S2		
NETHERLANDS ANTILLES	–	–	3			P	P	P	P	P	P	S	S	S	S	S				
NICARAGUA	7–12	6	3				P	P	P	P	P	P	S1	S1	S1	S2	S2			
PANAMA	6–15	9	5			P	P	P	P	P	P	S1	S1	S1	S2	S2	S2			
FORMER CANAL ZONE	6–14	–	5			P	P	P	P	P	P	S	S	S	S	S	S			
PUERTO RICO‡ #	8–14	7	...		P	P	P	P	P	P	P	P	S	S	S	S				
ST. CHRISTOPHER AND NEVIS #	5–17	12	3		P	P	P	P	P	P	P	S1	S1	S1	S1	S2	S2			
ST. LUCIA	5–15	11	–		P	P	P	P	P	P	P	S1	S1	S1	S2	S2				
ST. PIERRE AND MIQUELON	6–16	10	2			P	P	P	P	P	S1	S1	S1	S1	S2	S2	S2			
ST. VINCENT AND THE GRENADINES	–	–	3		P	P	P	P	P	P	P	S1	S1	S1	S1	S1	S2	S2		
TRINIDAD AND TOBAGO	6–12	7	–		P	P	P	P	P	P	P	S1	S1	S1	S2	S2				
TURKS AND CAICOS ISLANDS	4 1/2–14	9 1/2	4 1/2	P	P	P	P	P	P	P	P	S	S	S	S	S				
UNITED STATES‡ #	6–16	11	3			P	P	P	P	P	P	P	P	S	S	S	S			
U.S. VIRGIN ISLANDS‡ #	5–16	12	4			P	P	P	P	P	P	P	P	S	S	S	S			

COUNTRY / PAYS / PAIS	COMPULSORY EDUCATION / SCOLARITE OBLIGATOIRE / ESCOLARIDAD OBLIGATORIA: AGE LIMITS / LIMITES D'AGE / LIMITES DE EDAD	DURATION (YEARS) / DUREE (ANNEES) / DURACION (AÑOS)	ENTRANCE AGE TO EDUCATION PRECEDING THE FIRST LEVEL / AGE D'ADMISSION DANS L'ENSEIGNEMENT PRECEDANT LE PREMIER DEGRE / EDAD DE ADMISION EN LA ENSEÑANZA ANTERIOR AL PRIMER GRADO	ENTRANCE AGE AND DURATION OF FIRST AND SECOND LEVEL (GENERAL) EDUCATION / AGE D'ADMISSION ET DUREE DES ENSEIGNEMENTS DU PREMIER ET DU SECOND DEGRE (GENERAL) / EDAD DE ADMISION Y DURACION DE LAS ENSEÑANZAS DE PRIMER Y DE SEGUNDO GRADO (GENERAL) — AGE / AGE / EDAD: 4	5	6	7	8	9	10	11	12	13	14	15	16	17	18	19	20
AMERICA, SOUTH																				
ARGENTINA #	6–14	7	3			P	P	P	P	P	P	P	S1	S1	S1	S2	S2			
BOLIVIA	6–13	8	4			P	P	P	P	P	P	P	P	S	S	S	S			
BRAZIL	7–14	8	4				P	P	P	P	P	P	P	P	S	S	S			
CHILE	6–13	8	4			P	P	P	P	P	P	P	P	S	S	S	S			
COLOMBIA	6–14	5	5			P	P	P	P	P	S1	S1	S1	S1	S2	S2				
ECUADOR	6–14	6	4			P	P	P	P	P	P	S1	S1	S1	S2	S2	S2			
FALKLAND ISLANDS (MALVINAS)	5–15	10	–		P	P	P	P	P	P	S	S	S	S	S					
FRENCH GUIANA	6–16	10	2			P	P	P	P	P	S1	S1	S1	S1	S2	S2	S2			
GUYANA #	6–14	8	4			P	P	P	P	P	P	S1	S1	S1	S1	S2	S2			
PARAGUAY	7–14	6	5				P	P	P	P	P	P	S1	S1	S1	S2	S2	S2		
PERU	6–12	6	3			P	P	P	P	P	P	S1	S1	S2	S2	S2				
SURINAME #	6–12	6	4			P	P	P	P	P	P	S1	S1	S1	S2	S2	S2			
URUGUAY	6–15	9	3			P	P	P	P	P	P	S1	S1	S1	S2	S2	S2			
VENEZUELA	7–15	9	3				P	P	P	P	P	P	S1	S1	S1	S2	S2	S2		
ASIA																				
AFGHANISTAN	7–15	8	2				P	P	P	P	P	P	P	P	S	S	S	S		
BAHRAIN	6–15	9	3			P	P	P	P	P	P	S1	S1	S1	S2	S2	S2			
BANGLADESH	6–11	5	4			P	P	P	P	P	S1	S1	S1	S1	S1	S2	S2			
BHUTAN	–	–	5				P	P	P	P	P	S1	S1	S1	S2	S2				
BRUNEI DARUSSALAM	5–16	9	5			P	P	P	P	P	P	S1	S1	S1	S1	S1	S2	S2		
BURMA	5–10	5	4		P	P	P	P	P	S1	S1	S1	S1	S2	S2					
CHINA #	7–16	9	3				P	P	P	P	P	S1	S1	S1	S2	S2				
CYPRUS‡ #	6–12	6	3		P	P	P	P	P	P	S1	S1	S1	S2	S2	S2				
DEMOCRATIC KAMPUCHEA	6–12	6	5			P	P	P	P	P	P	S1	S1	S1	S1	S2	S2	S2		
DEMOCRATIC YEMEN	7–14	8	3				P	P	P	P	P	P	P	P	S	S	S	S		
EAST TIMOR	...	...	...			P	P	P	P	S1	S1	S1	S1	S1	S2	S2				
HONG KONG #	6–15	9	4			P	P	P	P	P	P	S1	S1	S1	S1	S1	S2	S2		
INDIA‡	6–11	5	3			P	P	P	P	P	S1	S1	S1	S2	S2	S2	S2			
INDONESIA	7–13	6	5				P	P	P	P	P	P	S1	S1	S1	S2	S2	S2		
IRAN, ISLAMIC REP. OF	6–14	8	5			P	P	P	P	P	S1	S1	S1	S2	S2	S2	S2			
IRAQ	6–12	6	4			P	P	P	P	P	P	S1	S1	S1	S2	S2	S2			
ISRAEL #	5–15	9	3			P	P	P	P	P	P	P	P	S	S	S	S			
JAPAN #	6–15	9	3			P	P	P	P	P	P	S1	S1	S1	S2	S2	S2			
JORDAN	6–15	9	3			P	P	P	P	P	P	S1	S1	S1	S2	S2	S2			
KOREA, DEMOCRATIC PEOPLE'S REP. OF	5–15	10	4			P	P	P	P	S	S	S	S	S	S					
KOREA, REPUBLIC OF	6–12	6	5			P	P	P	P	P	P	S1	S1	S1	S2	S2	S2			
KUWAIT	6–14	8	4			P	P	P	P	S1	S1	S1	S1	S2	S2	S2	S2			
LAO PEOPLE'S DEMOCRATIC REPUBLIC	7–12	5	3			P	P	P	P	P	S1	S1	S1	S2	S2	S2				

COUNTRY / PAYS / PAIS	COMPULSORY EDUCATION / SCOLARITE OBLIGATOIRE / ESCOLARIDAD OBLIGATORIA: AGE LIMITS / LIMITES D'AGE / LIMITES DE EDAD	DURATION (YEARS) / DUREE (ANNEES) / DURACION (AÑOS)	ENTRANCE AGE TO EDUCATION PRECEDING THE FIRST LEVEL / AGE D'ADMISSION DANS L'ENSEIGNEMENT PRECEDANT LE PREMIER DEGRE / EDAD DE ADMISION EN LA ENSEÑANZA ANTERIOR AL PRIMER GRADO	ENTRANCE AGE AND DURATION OF FIRST AND SECOND LEVEL (GENERAL) EDUCATION / AGE D'ADMISSION ET DUREE DES ENSEIGNEMENTS DU PREMIER ET DU SECOND DEGRE (GENERAL) / EDAD DE ADMISION Y DURACION DE LAS ENSEÑANZAS DE PRIMER Y DE SEGUNDO GRADO (GENERAL) — AGE / AGE / EDAD: 4	5	6	7	8	9	10	11	12	13	14	15	16	17	18	19	20
LEBANON	–	–	4			P	P	P	P	P	S1	S1	S1	S1	S2	S2	S2			
MACAU	6–12	5	4			P	P	P	P	P	S1	S1	S2	S2	S2					
MALAYSIA	6–15	9	4			P	P	P	P	P	P	S1	S1	S1	S2	S2	S2	S2		
MALDIVES	–	–	4			P	P	P	P	P	S1	S1	S1	S1	S1	S2	S2			
MONGOLIA	8–16	8	3					P	P	P	S1	S1	S1	S1	S1	S2	S2			
NEPAL	6–11	5	3			P	P	P	P	P	S1	S1	S2	S2	S2					
OMAN	–	–	4			P	P	P	P	P	P	S1	S1	S1	S2	S2	S2			
PAKISTAN	–	–	3		P	P	P	P	P	S1	S1	S1	S2	S2	S2	S2				
PHILIPPINES	7–13	6	3				P	P	P	P	P	P	S	S	S	S				
QATAR	–	–	2			P	P	P	P	P	P	S1	S1	S1	S2	S2	S2			
SAUDI ARABIA	–	–	4			P	P	P	P	P	P	S1	S1	S1	S2	S2	S2			
SINGAPORE #	–	–	4			P	P	P	P	P	P	S1	S1	S1	S1	S2	S2			
SRI LANKA	5–15	10	4		P	P	P	P	P	P	S1	S1	S1	S1	S1	S2	S2			
SYRIAN ARAB REPUBLIC	6–11	6	3			P	P	P	P	P	P	S1	S1	S1	S2	S2	S2			
THAILAND	7–15	7	4				P	P	P	P	P	P	S1	S1	S1	S2	S2	S2		
TURKEY	6–14	5	3			P	P	P	P	P	S1	S1	S1	S2	S2	S2				
UNITED ARAB EMIRATES	6–12	6	4			P	P	P	P	P	P	S1	S1	S1	S2	S2	S2			
VIET-NAM	6–11	5	3			P	P	P	P	P	S1	S1	S1	S1	S2	S2	S2			
YEMEN	6–12	6	3				P	P	P	P	P	P	S1	S1	S1	S2	S2	S2		
EUROPE																				
ALBANIA	6–13	8	3			P	P	P	P	P	P	P	P	S	S	S	S			
ANDORRA # FRENCH SCHOOLS	6–16	10	3			P	P	P	P	P	S1	S1	S1	S1	S2	S2	S2			
SPANISH SCHOOLS	6–15	10	2			P	P	P	P	P	S1	S1	S1	S2	S2	S2	S2			
AUSTRIA #	6–15	9	3			P	P	P	P	S1	S1	S1	S1	S2	S2	S2	S2			
BELGIUM	6–14,15	9	3			P	P	P	P	P	P	S1	S1	S1	S2	S2	S2			
BULGARIA #	7–14	8	3				P	P	P	P	P	P	P	P	S	S	S			
CZECHOSLOVAKIA	6–15	9	3			P	P	P	P	P	P	P	P	S	S	S	S			
DENMARK	7–15	9	5			P	P	P	P	P	P	S1	S1	S1	S2	S2	S2			
FINLAND	7–16	9	3				P	P	P	P	P	P	S1	S1	S1	S2	S2	S2		
FRANCE	6–16	10	3			P	P	P	P	P	S1	S1	S1	S1	S2	S2	S2			
GERMAN DEMOCRATIC REPUBLIC	6–16	10	3			P	P	P	P	P	P	P	P	P	P	S	S			
GERMANY, FEDERAL REPUBLIC OF‡ #	6–15	9	3			P	P	P	P	S1	S1	S1	S1	S1	S1	S2	S2	S2		
GIBRALTAR	4–15	11	3	P	P	P	P	P	P	P	P	S1	S1	S1	S1	S2	S2			
GREECE #	6–15	9	4			P	P	P	P	P	P	S1	S1	S1	S2	S2	S2			
HUNGARY	6–16	10	3			P	P	P	P	P	P	P	P	S	S	S	S			
ICELAND	7–15	8	6				P	P	P	P	P	P	S1	S1	S1	S2	S2	S2	S2	
IRELAND #	6–15	9	4			P	P	P	P	P	P	S1	S1	S1	S2	S2				
ITALY	6–13	8	3			P	P	P	P	P	S1	S1	S1	S2	S2	S2	S2	S2		

COUNTRY / PAYS / PAIS	COMPULSORY EDUCATION / SCOLARITE OBLIGATOIRE / ESCOLARIDAD OBLIGATORIA: AGE LIMITS / LIMITES D'AGE / LIMITES DE EDAD	DURATION (YEARS) / DUREE (ANNEES) / DURACION (AÑOS)	ENTRANCE AGE TO EDUCATION PRECEDING THE FIRST LEVEL / AGE D'ADMISSION DANS L'ENSEIGNEMENT PRECEDANT LE PREMIER DEGRE / EDAD DE ADMISION EN LA ENSEÑANZA ANTERIOR AL PRIMER GRADO	ENTRANCE AGE AND DURATION OF FIRST AND SECOND LEVEL (GENERAL) EDUCATION / AGE D'ADMISSION ET DUREE DES ENSEIGNEMENTS DU PREMIER ET DU SECOND DEGRE (GENERAL) / EDAD DE ADMISION Y DURACION DE LAS ENSEÑANZAS DE PRIMER Y DE SEGUNDO GRADO (GENERAL) — AGE / AGE / EDAD																
				4	5	6	7	8	9	10	11	12	13	14	15	16	17	18	19	20
LIECHTENSTEIN #	6–14	8	4			P	P	P	P	P	S1	S1	S1	S2	S2	S2				
LUXEMBOURG	6–15	9	4			P	P	P	P	P	P	S1	S1	S1	S2	S2	S2	S2		
MALTA	5–16	12	4		P	P	P	P	P	P	S1	S1	S1	S1	S1	S2	S2			
MONACO	6–16	10	3			P	P	P	P	P	S1	S1	S1	S1	S2	S2	S2			
NETHERLANDS #	6–16	10	4			P	P	P	P	P	P	S1	S1	S1	S2	S2	S2			
NORWAY	7–16	9	5				P	P	P	P	P	P	S1	S1	S1	S2	S2	S2		
POLAND	7–14	8	3				P	P	P	P	P	P	P	P	S	S	S	S		
PORTUGAL	6–14	6	3			P	P	P	P	P	P	S1	S1	S1	S2	S2	S2			
ROMANIA #	6–16	10	3			P	P	P	P	P	P	P	P	S	S	S	S			
SAN MARINO	6–13	8	3			P	P	P	P	P	S1	S1	S1	S2	S2	S2	S2	S2		
SPAIN	6–15	10	2			P	P	P	P	P	S1	S1	S1	S2	S2	S2	S2			
SWEDEN #	7–16	9	3				P	P	P	P	P	P	S1	S1	S1	S2	S2	S2		
SWITZERLAND #	7–16	8,9	4				P	P	P	P	P	P	S1	S1	S1	S2	S2	S2	S2	
UNITED KINGDOM	5–16	11	3		P	P	P	P	P	P	S1	S1	S1	S2	S2	S2	S2			
YUGOSLAVIA	7–15	8	3				P	P	P	P	S1	S1	S1	S1	S2	S2	S2	S2		
OCEANIA																				
AMERICAN SAMOA	6–18	12	3			P	P	P	P	P	P	P	P	S1	S1	S2	S2			
AUSTRALIA #	6–16	9,10	4			P	P	P	P	P	P	S1	S1	S1	S2	S2				
COOK ISLANDS	6–16	10	3			P	P	P	P	P	P	P	P	S1	S1	S2	S2			
FIJI #	–	–	3			P	P	P	P	P	P	S	S	S	S	S	S			
FRENCH POLYNESIA	6–14	8	3			P	P	P	P	P	S1	S1	S1	S1	S2	S2	S2			
GUAM	5–16	11	5			P	P	P	P	P	P	S1	S1	S1	S2	S2	S2			
KIRIBATI #	6–10	5	4			P	P	P	P	P	P	S1	S1	S1	S2	S2	S2			
NAURU	6–16	10	4			P	P	P	P	P	P	P	S	S	S	S				
NEW CALEDONIA	6–16	10	3			P	P	P	P	P	S1	S1	S1	S1	S2	S2	S2			
NEW ZEALAND #	5–15	10	3		P	P	P	P	P	P	S1	S1	S1	S1	S2	S2	S2			
NIUE	5–15	10	2		P	P	P	P	P	P	P	S	S	S	S	S	S			
NORFOLK ISLAND	5–16	11	–		P	P	P	P	P	P	P	S	S	S	S					
PACIFIC ISLANDS	6–14	8	4			P	P	P	P	P	P	P	P	S1	S1	S2	S2			
PAPUA NEW GUINEA	–	–	5				P	P	P	P	P	P	S1	S1	S1	S1	S2	S2		
SAMOA	–	–	3		P	P	P	P	P	P	P	S1	S1	S1	S1	S2	S2	S2		
SOLOMON ISLANDS #	–	–	3			P	P	P	P	P	P	S1	S1	S1	S2	S2				
TOKELAU ISLANDS	5–15	10	3		P	P	P	P	P	P	P	P	P	S	S					
TONGA	6–14	6	3			P	P	P	P	P	P	S	S	S	S	S	S	S		
TUVALU	7–15	9	–		P	P	P	P	P	P	P	S	S	S	S	S	S			
VANUATU	–	–	3			P	P	P	P	P	P	S1	S1	S1	S1	S2	S2	S2		
U.S.S.R.																				
U.S.S.R.‡ #	7–17	10	3				P	P	P	P	P	S1	S1	S1	S2	S2				
BYELORUSSIAN S.S.R‡ #	7–17	10	3				P	P	P	P	P	S1	S1	S1	S2	S2				
UKRAINIAN S.S.R.‡ #	7–17	10	3				P	P	P	P	P	S1	S	S1	S2	S2				

This table provides a summary presentation of selected elements of the educational systems. The information given here facilitates the correct interpretation of the figures shown in the educational tables in the *Yearbook*.

The first and the second columns provide data on compulsory education regulations. The first column shows lower and upper age limits. Thus 6-14, for example, means that children are subject to compulsory education laws, unless otherwise exempted, from their sixth birthday to their fourteenth birthday. The second column shows the number of years of compulsory school attendance. For example, regulations may stipulate that the duration of compulsory education shall be six years between the ages of 6 and 14. This means that a child would cease to be subject to the regulations either on his fourteenth birthday or on completion of six years' schooling (though he might then be only 12 or 13 years old).

However, in many countries and territories where the urgent problem is to provide sufficient schools for all children, the existence of compulsory school laws may be only of academic interest since almost all such regulations exempt a child from attending if there is no suitable school within reasonable distance of his home.

The third column gives the age at which children are accepted for education preceding the first level. For most countries education preceding the first level is still provided on a limited basis, often restricted to urban areas where only a small proportion of children within the ages shown is actually receiving pre-school education. The diagrams for all countries and territories which follow these three columns provide a pictorial representation of the duration and age of admission into first level and second level general education according to the education system presently in force. Information on teacher training and technical and vocational education are not presented. The symbol *P* shows the duration of first level education, the symbol *S1* that for the first stage of second level general education and the symbol *S2* the duration of the second stage of second level general education. It should be noted that for some countries and territories no distinction is made between the two stages of second level general education. In these cases the duration of this level of education is shown simply by the symbol *S*. Further, for a certain number of countries, the entrance age and duration of education at these two levels may vary depending on the area or type of school. For these countries the most common system is shown in the diagram. Table 3.1a indicates the other existing possibilities.

Finally Table 3.1b shows changes in the educational system which have occurred in certain countries since 1975. This table should be consulted when referring to the enrolment data given in tables 3.3 to 3.9.

Ce tableau présente des données sommaires sélectionnées sur les systèmes d'enseignement. L'information ainsi présentée doit aider à interpréter correctement les chiffres qui figurent dans les tableaux de l'*Annuaire* consacrés à l'éducation.

Les première et deuxième colonnes présentent les données relatives à l'obligation scolaire. Dans la première colonne sont précisées les limites d'âge inférieure et supérieure. C'est ainsi que les deux chiffres 6-14 signifient que les lois instituant la scolarité obligatoire s'appliquent, sauf exception, aux enfants de 6 à 14 ans. La deuxième colonne indique le nombre d'années pendant lesquelles les enfants sont tenus de fréquenter l'école. Les réglements peuvent stipuler, par exemple, que la durée de l'enseignement obligatoire est de six années (entre 6 et 14 ans). En d'autres termes, l'enfant cesse d'être soumis à l'obligation scolaire soit lorsqu'il a atteint l'âge de 14 ans, soit lorsqu'il a terminé sa sixième année d'études (même s'il n'a alors que 12 ou 13 ans).

Néanmoins, dans beaucoup de pays et territoires, le problème le plus urgent consiste à disposer d'un nombre suffisant d'écoles pour tous les enfants, l'existence d'une loi sur la scolarité obligatoire n'ayant qu'un intérêt théorique, puisque la plupart de ces règlementations dispensent un enfant de fréquentation scolaire s'il n'existe pas une école à une distance raisonnable de son domicile.

La troisième colonne indique l'âge d'admission des enfants dans l'enseignement précédant le premier degré. Pour la plupart des pays, l'enseignement précédant le premier degré n'est encore dispensé que d'une façon limitée généralement aux zones urbaines, où une faible proportion seulement des enfants compris dans l'âge indiqué peuvent en bénéficier. Le diagramme qui suit et qui comprend les trois colonnes présente pour tous les pays et territoires une représentation graphique de la durée et de l'âge d'admission dans l'enseignement du premier degré et l'enseignement général du second degré, en accord avec les systèmes d'enseignement actuellement en vigueur. Les renseignements concernant l'enseignement normal et l'enseignement technique et profesionnel du second degré ne sont pas présentés. Le symbole *P* montre la durée de l'enseignement du premier degré, le symbole *S1* celle du premier cycle de l'enseignement général du second degré et le symbole *S2* la durée du deuxième cycle de l'enseignement général du second degré. Il faut noter que pour quelques pays et territoires il n'est pas fait de distinction entre les deux cycles de l'enseignement général du second degré. Dans ces cas, la durée de l'enseignement est montrée par le symbole S . De plus, pour un certain nombre de pays, l'âge d'admission et la durée de l'enseignement dans ces deux degrés peuvent varier selon la zone ou le type d'école. Pour ces pays, le système le plus courant a été porté sur le diagramme. Le tableau 3.1a indique les autres possibilités existantes.

Finalement, le tableau 3.1b précise les changements qui se sont produits dans le système d'enseignement d'un certain nombre de pays depuis 1975. Ce tableau doit être consulté lorsque l'on se réfère aux effectifs scolaires qui figurent dans les tableaux 3.3 à 3.9.

Este cuadro presenta un resumen de datos seleccionados sobre los sistemas de enseñanza. La información así procurada debe facilitar una interpretación correcta de las cifras que figuran en los cuadros del *Anuario* correspondientes a la educación.

En las columnas primera y segunda figuran datos relativos a la escolaridad obligatoria. En la primera se precisan los límites de edad inferior y superior. Así, por ejemplo, las cifras 6-14 significan que la ley que instituye la escolaridad obligatoria se aplica sin excepción a los niños de 6 a 14 años de edad. En la segunda columna puede verse el número de años durante los cuales los niños han de asistir a la escuela. Se puede estipular, por ejemplo, que la duración de la enseñanza obligatoria es de 6 años, entre los 6 y los 14 años de edad. En otras palabras, el niño deja de estar sometido a la obligación escolar o bien al cumplir los 14 años o bien cuando termina su sexto año de estudios (aunque sólo tenga entonces 12 o 13 años).

Ahora bien, en muchos países y territorios el problema más urgente consiste en disponer de un número suficiente de escuelas para todos los niños; la existencia de una ley sobre la escolaridad obligatoria no tiene sino un interés teórico, dado que la mayoría de esas disposiciones eximen a los niños de la asistencia escolar si no existe una escuela a distancia razonable de su domicilio.

La tercera columna indica la edad de admisión de los niños en la enseñanza anterior al primer grado. Para la mayoría de los países, la enseñanza anterior al primer grado sigue dispensándose todavía de un modo limitado generalmente a las zonas urbanas, donde sólo puede beneficiarse de ella una pequeña proporción de los niños de la edad indicada. El diagrama siguiente que comprende las tres columnas muestra para todos los países y territorios una representación gráfica sobre la duración y la edad de admisión en la enseñanza de primer grado y en la enseñanza general de segundo grado, de acuerdo con los sistemas de educación actualmente en vigor. Las informaciones relativas a la enseñanza normal y a la enseñanza técnica y profesional no se presentan. Los símbolos *P* indican la duración del primer grado de enseñanza, los símbolos *S1* la duración del primer ciclo de la enseñanza general de segundo grado y los símbolos *S2* la duración del segundo ciclo de la enseñanza general de segundo grado. Es de notar que para algunos países y territorios no existe ninguna distinción entre los dos ciclos de enseñanza general de segundo grado. En tales casos, la duración de este grado de enseñanza se muestra en los símbolos *S*. Además, para un cierto número de países, la edad de admisión y la duración de la enseñanza en estos dos grados pueden variar según la zona o el tipo de escuela. Para estos países, en el diagrama se ha indicado el sistema más corriente. El cuadro 3.1a señala las otras posibilidades existentes.

Finalmente, en el cuadro 3.1b se precisan los cambios que

se han producido en el sistema de enseñanza de un determinado número de países desde 1975. Este cuadro debe consultarse al referirse a los efectivos escolares que figuran en los cuadros 3.3 a 3.9.

General Note/Note générale/Nota general:

E--> For countries marked with the symbol #
, the educational system allows for other alternatives (see Table 3.1a).

FR-> Pour les pays signalés par le symbole #
, le système d'enseignement permet d'autres structures (voir le tableau 3.1a).

ESP> Para los países señalados con el símbolo #
el sistema de la enseñanza permite otras estructuras (véase el cuadro 3.1a).

AMERICA, NORTH:

Puerto Rico:

E--> From 1979, for technical reasons, the first level of education is considered to have a duration of 8 years and the second level of education 4 years, instead of 6 years for each level.

FR-> A partir de 1979, pour des raisons d'ordre technique, on considère une durée de 8 années dans l'enseignement du premier degré et de 4 années dans l'enseignement du second degré au lieu de 6 années dans chaque degré.

ESP> A partir de 1979, por razones técnicas, se considera que la educación de primer grado tiene una duración de 8 años, y la educación de segundo grado de 4 años en vez de 6 años para cada uno de los dos grados.

United States:

E--> From 1979, for technical reasons, the duration of first level education is taken as 8 years for the entire country (4 years at the second level); previously the actual duration of education at the two levels for each state was taken into account (6 or 8 years for first level, 6 or 4 years for second level).

FR-> A partir de 1979, pour des raisons d'ordre technique, on a considéré une durée de l'enseignement du premier degré de 8 années dans tout le pays (4 années pour le second degré); précédemment on tenait compte de la durée effective dans chaque état (6 ou 8 années pour l'enseignement du premier degré, 6 ou 4 années pour le second degré).

ESP> A partir de 1979, por razones técnicas, se considera que la enseñanza de primer grado tiene una duración de 8 años en todo el país (4 años para le enseñanza de segundo grado); anteriormente se tomaba en cuenta la duración efectiva de cada estado (6 u 8 años para la enseñanza de primer grado, 6 ó 4 años para la enseñanza de segundo grado).

U. S. Virgin Islands:

E--> From 1979, for technical reasons, the first level of education is considered to have a duration of 8 years and the second level of education 4 years, instead of 6 years for each level.

FR-> A partir de 1979, pour des raisons d'ordre technique, on considère une durée de 8 années dans l'enseignement du premier degré et de 4 années dans l'enseignement du second degré au lieu de 6 années dans chaque degré.

U. S. Virgin Islands: (Cont):

ESP> A partir de 1979, por razones técnicas, se considera que la educación de primer grado tiene una duración de 8 años, y la educación de segundo grado de 4 años en vez de 6 años para cada uno de los dos grados.

ASIA:

Cyprus:

E--> Greek education only.

FR-> Enseignement grec seulement.

ESP> Enseñanza griego solamente.

India:

E--> This information pertains to the majority of states.

FR-> Ces informations concernent la majorité des états.

ESP> Estos datos se refieren a la majoría de los estados.

EUROPE:

Germany, Federal Republic of:

E--> In addition to alternative education structures (see table 3.1a) there are also three years of compulsory part-time vocational education.

FR-> En plus des autres structures du système d'enseignement (voir le tableau 3.1a), il existe aussi une scolarité obligatoire de trois ans à temps partiel dans l'enseignement technique.

ESP> Además de las otras estructuras sobre el sistema de enseñanza (véase el cuadro 3.1a), también existe una escolaridad obligatoria de tres años de jornada parcial en la enseñanza técnica.

U.S.S.R.:

U.S.S.R.:

E--> For consistency with ISCED, the educational structure, according to which the data are classified in this chapter, is taken to comprise 5 years of primary education and 5 years of secondary education (whereas the institutional system comprises 8 and 2 years respectively).

FR-> Pour s'uniformiser avec la CITE, la structure de l'enseignement, selon laquelle on présente les données de ce chapitre, comporte 5 années d'enseignement du premier degré et 5 années d'enseignement du second degré (alors que le système institutionnel comporte 8 et 2 années respectivement).

ESP> Para conformarse con la CINE, la estructura de enseñanza, según la cual se presentan los datos de este capítulo, consiste de 5 años de enseñanza de primer grado y 5 años de segundo grado (mientras que el sistema institucional consiste de 8 y 2 años respectivamente).

Byelorussian S.S.R.:

E--> See note for the U.S.S.R.

FR-> Voir la note de l'U.R.S.S.

ESP> Véase la nota de la U.R.S.S.

Ukrainian S.S.R.:

E--> See note for the U.S.S.R.

FR-> Voir la note de l'U.R.S.S.

ESP> Véase la nota de la U.R.S.S.

TABLE 3.1A: NATIONAL EDUCATIONAL SYSTEMS: OTHER STRUCTURES

TABLEAU 3.1A: SYSTEMES NATIONAUX D'ENSEIGNEMENT: AUTRES STRUCTURES EN VIGUEUR

CUADRO 3.1A: SISTEMAS NACIONALES DE ENSEÑANZA: OTRAS ESTRUCTURAS EN VIGOR

COUNTRY / PAYS / PAIS	ENTRANCE AGE / AGE D'ADMISSION / EDAD DE ADMISION		DURATION (YEARS) / DUREE (ANNEE) / DURACION (AÑOS)	
	1ST LEVEL / 1ER DEGRE / 1ER GRADO	2ND LEVEL (GENERAL) / 2EME DEGRE (GENERAL) / 2NDO GRADO (GENERAL)	1ST LEVEL / 1ER DEGRE / 1ER GRADO	2ND LEVEL (GENERAL) / 2EME DEGRE (GENERAL) / 2NDO GRADO (GENERAL)
AFRICA				
EGYPT	5	11		
EQUATORIAL GUINEA			8	
SAO TOME AND PRINCIPE		12		
TUNISIA			8	
AMERICA, NORTH				
ANTIGUA			7	
BELIZE				5
BRITISH VIRGIN ISLANDS			8	
CANADA		14	8	3+4,5
COSTA RICA				3+3
HAITI			7	3+4
PUERTO RICO		13	6	3+3
ST. CHRISTOPHER AND NEVIS				5+2
UNITED STATES	5	12	6	6
U.S. VIRGIN ISLANDS		14	6	3+3
AMERICA, SOUTH				
ARGENTINA				3+3 3+4
GUYANA				5+2
SURINAME				2+3
ASIA				
CHINA			6	3+3
CYPRUS			7	3+4
HONG KONG				3+2

COUNTRY / PAYS / PAIS	ENTRANCE AGE / AGE D'ADMISSION / EDAD DE ADMISION		DURATION (YEARS) / DUREE (ANNEE) / DURACION (AÑOS)	
	1ST LEVEL / 1ER DEGRE / 1ER GRADO	2ND LEVEL (GENERAL) / 2EME DEGRE (GENERAL) / 2NDO GRADO (GENERAL)	1ST LEVEL / 1ER DEGRE / 1ER GRADO	2ND LEVEL (GENERAL) / 2EME DEGRE (GENERAL) / 2NDO GRADO (GENERAL)
ISRAEL				5
JAPAN				3+4
SINGAPORE			8	4+3
EUROPE				
ANDORRA (SPANISH SCHOOLS) (ECOLES ESPAG.) (ESCUELAS ESP.)				4+4
AUSTRIA				4+5
BULGARIA				4
GERMANY, FEDERAL REPUBLIC OF			4–9	4–6+3
GREECE				3+4
IRELAND				4+2
LIECHTENSTEIN				5+3
NETHERLANDS				4+2
ROMANIA			10	
SWEDEN				3+2
SWITZERLAND	6		4–6	4+4 3+5 5+2
OCEANIA				
AUSTRALIA	5		7	
FIJI			8	4
KIRIBATI			6–9	
NEW ZEALAND			7	
SOLOMON ISLANDS	7,8,9	12,13,14		3+3
U.S.S.R.				
U.S.S.R.				3+3
BYELORUSSIAN S.S.R.				3+3
UKRAINIAN S.S.R.				

TABLE 3.1B : STRUCTURAL CHANGES IN EDUCATIONAL SYSTEMS SINCE 1975
TABLEAU 3.1B: CHANGEMENTS DE STRUCTURE DANS LES SYSTEMES D'ENSEIGNEMENT DEPUIS 1975
CUADRO 3.1B : CAMBIOS DE ESTRUCTURA EN LOS SISTEMAS DE ENSEÑANZA DESDE 1975

COUNTRY PAYS PAIS	YEAR OF CHANGE ANNEE DU CHANGEMENT AÑO DEL CAMBIO	FIRST LEVEL OF EDUCATION / ENSEIGNEMENT DU PREMIER DEGRE / ENSEÑANZA DE PRIMER GRADO DURATION (YEARS) / DUREE (ANNEES) / DURACION (AÑOS) FROM / DE	 TO / A	GENERAL EDUCATION AT THE SECOND LEVEL / ENSEIGNEMENT GENERAL DU SECOND DEGRE / ENSEÑANZA GENERAL DE SEGUNDO GRADO DURATION (YEARS) / DUREE (ANNEES) / DURACION (AÑOS) FROM / DE	 TO / A
AFRICA					
MADAGASCAR	1976	6	5		
MAURITANIA	1977			4+3	3+3
	1979	7	6		
MOZAMBIQUE	1982			3+4	3+2
NIGERIA	1982			5+2	3+3
RWANDA	1979	6	8		
SEYCHELLES	1980	6	9	3+4	4
	1984			4	2
SOMALIA	1976	4	6	4+4	4
	1980	6	8		
AMERICA, NORTH					
CAYMAN ISLANDS	1979			6	7
CUBA	1977			4+3	3+3
HAITI	1976	7	6	3+4	3+3
NICARAGUA	1980			3+3	3+2
ASIA					
BAHRAIN	1977			2+3	3+3
DEMOCRATIC YEMEN	1978	6	7	3+3	2+3
	1979	7	8	2+3	4
IRAN, ISLAMIC REP. OF	1977			3+3	3+4
LAO PEOPLE'S DEMOCRATIC REP.	1976	6	5	4+3	3+3
NEPAL	1981	3	5	4+3	2+3
SINGAPORE	1979	6	6,8		
SRI LANKA	1978	5	6		
THAILAND	1978	7	6	3+2	3+3
VIET NAM	1976			3+3	4+3
EUROPE					
PORTUGAL	1980			3+2	3+3
OCEANIA					
SOLOMON ISLANDS	1976	7	6		

3.2 Enrolment ratios for the first, second and third levels of education

Taux d'inscription dans les enseignements du premier, du second et du troisième degré

Tasas de escolarización para las enseñanzas de primero, segundo y tercer grado

PLEASE REFER TO EXPLANATORY TEXT AT END OF TABLE

NUMBER OF COUNTRIES AND TERRITORIES PRESENTED IN THIS TABLE: 146

PRIERE DE SE REFERER AU TEXTE EXPLICATIF A LA FIN DU TABLEAU

NOMBRE DE PAYS ET DE TERRITOIRES PRESENTES DANS CE TABLEAU: 146

REFERIRSE AL TEXTO EXPLICATIVO AL FINAL DEL CUADRO

NUMERO DE PAISES Y DE TERRITORIOS PRESENTADOS EN ESTE CUADRO: 146

COUNTRY / PAYS / PAIS	YEAR / ANNEE / AÑO	SEX / SEXE / SEXO	ENROLMENT RATIOS / TAUX D'INSCRIPTION / TASAS DE ESCOLARIZACION					
			FIRST LEVEL / PREMIER DEGRE / PRIMER GRADO		SECOND LEVEL / SECOND DEGRE / SEGUNDO GRADO		1ST + 2ND LEVELS / 1ER + 2ND DEGRE / 1ER + 2DO GRADO	3RD LEVEL / 3EME DEGRE / 3ER GRADO
			GROSS / BRUT / BRUTA	NET / NET / NETA	GROSS / BRUT / BRUTA	NET / NET / NETA	GROSS / BRUT / BRUTA	GROSS / BRUT / BRUTA
AFRICA								
ALGERIA	1975			(6–11)		(12–18)	(6–18)	(20–24)
		MF	93	77	20	...	59	3.2
		M	109	89	26	...	70	...
		F	75	64	14	...	46	...
	1980							
		MF	95	81	33	...	65	4.9
		M	108	91	40	...	75	7.1
		F	81	71	26	...	54	2.7
	1981							
		MF	94	81	36	...	66	4.7
		M	107	91	43	...	76	6.4
		F	81	71	29	...	56	2.9
	1982							
		MF	94	81	...	...	...	5.5
		M	106	91	...	...	...	7.2
		F	81	72	...	...	...	3.7
	1983							
		MF	94	83	43	...	69	...
		M	106	92	51	...	79	...
		F	82	74	36	...	59	...
	1984							
		MF	94	84	47	...	71	5.8
		M	106	93	54	...	80	7.5
		F	83	75	39	...	61	4.0
ANGOLA	1980			(7–10)		(11–16)	(7–16)	(20–24)
		MF	158	...	19	...	80	0.3
	1981							
		MF	148	70	13	...	73	0.4
		M	158	74	...	...	...	0.7
		F	137	67	...	...	...	0.1
	1982							
		MF	134	66	12	...	66	0.4
		M	146	71	...	...	...	...
		F	121	61	...	...	...	...

COUNTRY / PAYS / PAIS	YEAR / ANNEE / AÑO	SEX / SEXE / SEXO	ENROLMENT RATIOS / TAUX D'INSCRIPTION / TASAS DE ESCOLARIZACION					
			FIRST LEVEL / PREMIER DEGRE / PRIMER GRADO		SECOND LEVEL / SECOND DEGRE / SEGUNDO GRADO		1ST + 2ND LEVELS / 1ER + 2ND DEGRE / 1ER + 2DO GRADO	3RD LEVEL / 3EME DEGRE / 3ER GRADO
			GROSS / BRUT / BRUTA	NET / NET / NETA	GROSS / BRUT / BRUTA	NET / NET / NETA	GROSS / BRUT / BRUTA	GROSS / BRUT / BRUTA
BENIN	1975			(5–10)		(11–17)	(5–17)	(20–24)
		MF	50	...	9	...	31	0.8
		M	70	...	13	...	43	1.4
		F	31	...	5	...	19	0.2
	1980							
		MF	64	...	16	...	41	1.4
		M	88	...	24	...	58	...
		F	40	...	9	...	25	...
	1981							
		MF	65	...	19	...	43	1.9
		M	89	...		...	...	3.1
		F	42	...	...	...	...	0.7
	1982							
		MF	67	...	22	...	45	2.0
		M	91	...	32	...	63	3.5
		F	43	...	12	...	28	0.7
	1983							
		MF	64	45	21	...	44	2.1
		M	86	60	30	...	60	3.6
		F	42	30	11	...	28	0.8
	1984							
		MF	64	46	19	...	43	...
		M	86	61	28	...	59	...
		F	42	31	11	...	28	...
BOTSWANA	1975			(6–12)		(13–17)	(6–17)	(20–24)
		MF	72	58	16	11	52	0.7
		M	65	52	16	10	47	1.1
		F	79	63	16	12	56	0.4
	1980							
		MF	91	75	19	15	65	1.1
		M	82	68	18	12	59	1.4
		F	100	82	21	17	71	0.9
	1982							
		MF	93	...	20	...	66	1.5
		M	86	...	18	...	61	...
		F	100	...	22	...	71	...
	1983							
		MF	95	75	21	...	68	1.6
		M	88	70	19	...	63	1.8
		F	102	81	22	...	73	1.3
	1984							
		MF	97	76	25	18	70	1.9
		M	91	71	23	15	66	...
		F	103	81	27	20	75	...
	1985							
		MF	99	...	28	...	73	...
		M	94	...	26	...	69	...
		F	104	...	30	...	77	...
BURKINA FASO	1975			(7–12)		(13–19)	(7–19)	(20–24)
		MF	16	...	2	...	9	0.2
		M	21	...	3	...	12	0.4
		F	12	...	1	...	7	0.1
	1980							
		MF	21	17	3	...	12	0.3
		M	26	22	4	...	15	0.5
		F	15	13	2	...	9	0.1
	1981							
		MF	22	19	3	...	13	...
		M	28	24	4	...	17	...
		F	17	14	2	...	10	...
	1982							
		MF	24	20	3	3	14	0.6
		M	31	25	5	4	18	0.9
		F	18	15	2	2	10	0.2

COUNTRY / PAYS / PAIS	YEAR / ANNEE / AÑO	SEX / SEXE / SEXO	ENROLMENT RATIOS / TAUX D'INSCRIPTION / TASAS DE ESCOLARIZACION					
			FIRST LEVEL / PREMIER DEGRE / PRIMER GRADO		SECOND LEVEL / SECOND DEGRE / SEGUNDO GRADO		1ST + 2ND LEVELS / 1ER + 2ND DEGRE / 1ER + 2DO GRADO	3RD LEVEL / 3EME DEGRE / 3ER GRADO
			GROSS / BRUT / BRUTA	NET / NET / NETA	GROSS / BRUT / BRUTA	NET / NET / NETA	GROSS / BRUT / BRUTA	GROSS / BRUT / BRUTA
BURKINA FASO (CONT)	1983							
		MF	26	22	4	...	15	0.6
		M	33	28	5	...	20	0.9
		F	19	16	3	...	11	0.3
	1984							
		MF	29	25	4	3	17	0.7
		M	37	31	6	...	22	1.0
		F	22	18	3	...	13	0.3
BURUNDI	1975			(6–11)		(12–18)	(6–18)	(20–24)
		MF	22	...	3	2	13	0.3
		M	28	...	4	3	16	0.6
		F	17	...	2	1	9	0.1
	1980			(7–12)		(13–19)	(7–19)	(20–24)
		MF	29	21	3	...	16	0.6
		M	35	26	5	...	20	0.9
		F	22	17	2	...	12	0.3
	1981							
		MF	33	24	3	2	18	0.6
		M	41	30	4	3	23	...
		F	25	19	2	2	14	...
	1982							
		MF	39	...	...	...	...	...
	1983							
		MF	44	35	4	...	25	0.7
		M	54	41	5	...	30	1.0
		F	35	28	3	...	20	0.3
	1984							
		MF	49	39	...	...	...	...
		M	58	45	...	...	...	...
		F	40	32	...	...	...	...
CAMEROON	1975			(6–11)		(12–18)	(6–18)	(20–24)
		MF	97	69	13	11	56	1.3
		M	108	76	17	14	63	2.2
		F	87	63	8	7	48	0.4
	1980							
		MF	104	...	19	15	62	1.6
		M	113	...	24	20	70	...
		F	94	...	13	11	55	...
	1981							
		MF	105	...	19	...	63	1.6
		M	114	...	25	...	71	...
		F	95	...	14	...	56	...
	1982							
		MF	107	...	21	...	66	1.7
		M	117	...	26	...	74	...
		F	98	...	15	...	58	...
	1983							
		MF	106	...	22	...	66	2.0
		M	115	...	28	...	73	...
		F	96	...	16	...	58	...
	1984							
		MF	107	...	23	...	67	2.2
		M	116	...	29	...	75	...
		F	97	...	18	...	59	...
CAPE VERDE	1975			(7–12)		(13–17)	(7–17)	(20–24)
		MF	125	...	7	...	75	–
		M	130	...	8	...	78	–
		F	120	...	7	...	71	–
	1980							
		MF	112	89	8	...	65	–
		M	117	91	9	...	68	–
		F	108	86	7	...	62	–
	1983							
		MF	110	89	11	...	64	–
		M	113	90	13	...	66	–
		F	107	88	10	...	62	–

COUNTRY / PAYS / PAIS	YEAR / ANNEE / AÑO	SEX / SEXE / SEXO	FIRST LEVEL / PREMIER DEGRE / PRIMER GRADO: GROSS / BRUT / BRUTA	FIRST LEVEL / PREMIER DEGRE / PRIMER GRADO: NET / NET / NETA	SECOND LEVEL / SECOND DEGRE / SEGUNDO GRADO: GROSS / BRUT / BRUTA	SECOND LEVEL / SECOND DEGRE / SEGUNDO GRADO: NET / NET / NETA	1ST + 2ND LEVELS / 1ER + 2ND DEGRE / 1ER + 2DO GRADO: GROSS / BRUT / BRUTA	3RD LEVEL / 3EME DEGRE / 3ER GRADO: GROSS / BRUT / BRUTA
CENTRAL AFRICAN REPUBLIC	1975			(6–11)		(12–18)	(6–18)	(20–24)
		MF	73	...	8	...	40	0.4
		M	96	...	13	...	55	0.7
		F	51	...	3	...	27	0.1
	1980							
		MF	71	57	14	...	43	0.9
		M	93	73	21	...	57	1.7
		F	51	42	7	...	30	0.1
	1981							
		MF	73	59	15	...	45	1.3
		M	95	75	23	...	60	2.4
		F	52	42	8	...	30	0.3
	1982							
		MF	74	60	16	...	46	1.1
		M	98	79	24	...	62	2.1
		F	51	42	8	...	30	0.1
	1983							
		MF	77	...	...	...	...	1.2
		M	...	...	...	...	...	2.2
		F	...	...	...	...	...	0.2
CHAD	1975			(6–11)		(12–18)	(6–18)	(20–24)
		MF	35	...	3	...	19	0.2
		M	51	...	...	...	...	0.3
		F	18	...	...	...	...	0.02
	1984							
		MF	38	...	6	...	22	0.4
		M	55	...	11	...	33	0.7
		F	21	...	2	...	12	0.1
COMOROS	1980			(6–11)		(12–18)	(6–18)	(20–24)
		MF	93	...	24	...	60	–
		M	109	...	31	...	72	–
		F	78	...	16	...	48	–
CONGO‡	1975			(6–11)		(12–18)	(6–18)	(20–24)
		MF	...	...	...	...	...	2.9
		M	...	...	...	...	...	5.2
		F	...	...	...	...	...	0.6
	1980							
		MF	...	...	...	...	...	5.6
		M	...	...	...	...	...	9.6
		F	...	...	...	...	...	1.6
	1981							
		MF	...	...	...	...	...	6.7
		M	...	...	...	...	...	11.8
		F	...	...	...	...	...	1.8
COTE D'IVOIRE	1975			(6–11)		(12–18)	(6–18)	(20–24)
		MF	62	...	13	...	38	1.3
		M	77	...	18	...	48	2.0
		F	47	...	7	...	28	0.5
	1980							
		MF	77	...	20	...	50	2.9
		M	93	...	27	...	61	4.6
		F	62	...	12	...	38	1.1
	1981							
		MF	...	...	...	...	...	2.7
	1982							
		MF	79	...	20	...	51	...
		M	93	...	28	...	62	...
		F	64	...	11	...	39	...
	1983							
		MF	77	...	20	...	50	2.4
		M	91	...	28	...	61	3.8
		F	63	...	12	...	39	0.9

COUNTRY / PAYS / PAIS	YEAR / ANNEE / AÑO	SEX / SEXE / SEXO	ENROLMENT RATIOS / TAUX D'INSCRIPTION / TASAS DE ESCOLARIZACION — FIRST LEVEL / PREMIER DEGRE / PRIMER GRADO: GROSS / BRUT / BRUTA	FIRST LEVEL: NET / NET / NETA	SECOND LEVEL / SECOND DEGRE / SEGUNDO GRADO: GROSS / BRUT / BRUTA	SECOND LEVEL: NET / NET / NETA	1ST + 2ND LEVELS / 1ER + 2ND DEGRE / 1ER + 2DO GRADO: GROSS / BRUT / BRUTA	3RD LEVEL / 3EME DEGRE / 3ER GRADO: GROSS / BRUT / BRUTA
EGYPT	1975			(6–11)		(12–17)	(6–17)	(20–24)
		MF	75	...	43	...	60	13.5
		M	89	...	55	...	73	18.5
		F	60	...	31	...	46	8.3
	1980							
		MF	78	...	54	...	66	17.6
		M	90	...	65	...	78	23.4
		F	65	...	41	...	53	11.4
	1981							
		MF	80	...	55	...	68	18.9
		M	92	...	67	...	80	25.0
		F	67	...	43	...	56	12.4
	1982							
		MF	82	...	58	...	70	19.9
		M	93	...	69	...	82	25.9
		F	70	...	45	...	58	13.4
	1983							
		MF	84	...	58	...	72	21.0
		M	94	...	70	...	83	27.4
		F	72	...	46	...	60	14.1
EQUATORIAL GUINEA	1975			(6–11)		(12–17)	(6–17)	(20–24)
		MF	83	...	11	...	50	–
		M	...	...	20	...	...	–
		F	...	...	4	...	...	–
	1980							
		MF	84	...	...	...	...	–
	1981							
		MF	84	...	...	...	...	3.8
		M	...	...	...	...	...	6.9
		F	...	...	...	...	...	0.7
	1982							
		MF	93	...	10	...	56	...
	1983							
		MF	108	...	...	...	...	...
ETHIOPIA	1975			(7–12)		(13–18)	(7–18)	(20–24)
		MF	20	...	5	...	13	...
		M	27	...	8	...	18	...
		F	13	...	3	...	9	...
	1980							
		MF	35	...	9	...	23	0.4
		M	46	...	11	...	30	...
		F	25	...	6	...	16	...
	1981							
		MF	38	...	10	...	25	0.4
		M	49	...	13	...	33	0.8
		F	28	...	7	...	18	0.1
	1982							
		MF	40	...	10	...	26	0.5
		M	50	...	13	...	33	0.8
		F	29	...	7	...	19	0.1
	1983							
		MF	39	...	11	...	26	0.4
		M	48	...	14	...	33	0.8
		F	29	...	8	...	19	0.1
GABON	1975			(6–11)		(12–18)	(6–18)	(20–24)
		MF	102	...	17	...	59	1.3
		M	105	...	22	...	63	2.0
		F	100	...	12	...	55	0.5
	1980							
		MF	115	...	21	...	67	...
		M	117	...	25	...	71	...
		F	113	...	17	...	64	...

3.2 **School enrolment ratios**
Taux d'inscription scolaire
Tasas de escolarización

COUNTRY / PAYS / PAIS	YEAR / ANNEE / AÑO	SEX / SEXE / SEXO	ENROLMENT RATIOS / TAUX D'INSCRIPTION / TASAS DE ESCOLARIZACION — FIRST LEVEL / PREMIER DEGRE / PRIMER GRADO: GROSS / BRUT / BRUTA	FIRST LEVEL: NET / NET / NETA	SECOND LEVEL / SECOND DEGRE / SEGUNDO GRADO: GROSS / BRUT / BRUTA	SECOND LEVEL: NET / NET / NETA	1ST + 2ND LEVELS / 1ER + 2ND DEGRE / 1ER + 2DO GRADO: GROSS / BRUT / BRUTA	3RD LEVEL / 3EME DEGRE / 3ER GRADO: GROSS / BRUT / BRUTA
GABON (CONT)	1981							
		MF	117	...	21	...	69	...
		M	119	...	26	...	72	...
		F	115	...	17	...	65	...
	1982							
		MF	119	...	23	...	70	3.3
		M	121	...	28	...	73	5.0
		F	118	...	18	...	67	1.7
	1983							
		MF	123	...	25	...	73	3.6
		M	124	...	30	...	76	5.2
		F	121	...	20	...	70	1.9
GAMBIA	1975			(8–13)		(14–19)	(8–19)	(20–24)
		MF	33	21	10	7	22	–
		M	44	29	15	10	31	–
		F	21	13	5	3	14	–
	1980							
		MF	52	50	13	...	34	–
		M	68	65	19	...	46	–
		F	36	35	8	...	23	–
	1981							
		MF	58	54	15	...	38	–
		M	74	70	21	...	49	–
		F	41	39	9	...	26	–
	1982							
		MF	62	58	17	13	41	–
		M	79	75	23	19	54	–
		F	45	42	10	8	29	–
	1983							
		MF	68	62	19	15	46	–
		M	85	77	27	21	58	–
		F	51	47	12	9	33	–
	1984							
		MF	73	63	21	19	49	–
		M	91	78	29	26	63	–
		F	55	49	13	11	36	–
GHANA	1975			(6–11)		(12–18)	(6–18)	(20–24)
		MF	71	...	37	...	55	1.1
		M	80	...	45	...	64	1.8
		F	62	...	28	...	45	0.3
	1980							
		MF	72	...	37	...	55	...
		M	80	...	46	...	64	...
		F	64	...	28	...	47	...
	1981							
		MF	76	...	37	...	57	1.6
		M	85	...	46	...	66	2.6
		F	66	...	28	...	48	0.7
	1982							
		MF	77	...	38	...	58	...
		M	86	...	47	...	67	...
		F	67	...	28	...	49	...
	1983							
		MF	78	...	38	...	59	...
		M	87	...	47	...	68	...
		F	68	...	28	...	49	...
	1984							
		MF	67	...	36	...	52	1.5
		M	75	...	45	...	61	2.3
		F	59	...	27	...	44	0.6
GUINEA	1975			(7–12)		(13–18)	(7–18)	(20–24)
		MF	27	...	12	...	20	3.0
		M	36	...	18	...	28	4.9
		F	18	...	6	...	13	1.1

COUNTRY / PAYS / PAIS	YEAR / ANNEE / AÑO	SEX / SEXE / SEXO	ENROLMENT RATIOS / TAUX D'INSCRIPTION / TASAS DE ESCOLARIZACION					
			FIRST LEVEL / PREMIER DEGRE / PRIMER GRADO		SECOND LEVEL / SECOND DEGRE / SEGUNDO GRADO		1ST + 2ND LEVELS / 1ER + 2ND DEGRE / 1ER + 2DO GRADO	3RD LEVEL / 3EME DEGRE / 3ER GRADO
			GROSS / BRUT / BRUTA	NET / NET / NETA	GROSS / BRUT / BRUTA	NET / NET / NETA	GROSS / BRUT / BRUTA	GROSS / BRUT / BRUTA
GUINEA (CONT)	1980							
		MF	31	...	14	...	24	3.9
		M	42	...	21	...	32	6.4
		F	21	...	8	...	15	1.5
	1981							
		MF	30	...	13	...	22	2.8
		M	...	...	19	...	...	4.4
		F	...	...	7	...	...	1.2
	1982							
		MF	29	...	13	...	22	2.7
		M	39	...	19	...	30	4.3
		F	19	...	7	...	13	1.2
	1983							
		MF	28	23	13	...	21	2.5
		M	38	31	19	...	29	...
		F	18	15	7	...	13	...
	1984							
		MF	32	26	13	...	24	2.1
		M	44	35	20	...	33	3.2
		F	20	16	7	...	14	1.1
GUINEA–BISSAU	1975			(7–12)		(13–17)	(7–17)	(20–24)
		MF	64	59	3	3	38	–
		M	90	83	5	5	54	–
		F	39	37	2	2	23	–
	1980							
		MF	67	59	6	3	41	–
		M	95	83	10	4	59	–
		F	41	36	2	1	25	–
	1981							
		MF	66	56	8	3	41	–
		M	93	79	13	6	60	–
		F	40	35	3	1	24	–
	1982							
		MF	63	55	10	...	41	–
		M	88	76	17	...	58	–
		F	40	35	4	...	25	–
	1983							
		MF	62	53	11	3	41	–
		M	84	73	19	6	58	–
		F	40	35	4	1	25	–
KENYA	1975			(5–11)		(12–17)	(5–17)	(20–24)
		MF	95	72	13	8	63	0.8
		M	103	76	16	9	69	...
		F	87	68	9	7	57	...
	1980							
		MF	104	71	18	...	71	0.9
		M	109	73	21	...	75	1.5
		F	99	70	15	...	66	0.4
	1981							
		MF	101	69	17	...	69	0.9
		M	105	70	20	...	72	1.5
		F	97	68	14	...	65	0.4
	1982							
		MF	101	...	17	...	69	...
		M	105	...	21	...	73	...
		F	98	...	14	...	66	...
	1983							
		MF	100	...	19	...	69	0.9
		M	104	...	23	...	73	1.5
		F	97	...	16	...	65	0.3
	1984							
		MF	97	...	19	...	67	...
		M	101	...	22	...	70	...
		F	94	...	16	...	64	...

COUNTRY / PAYS / PAIS	YEAR / ANNEE / AÑO	SEX / SEXE / SEXO	ENROLMENT RATIOS / TAUX D'INSCRIPTION / TASAS DE ESCOLARIZACION					
			FIRST LEVEL / PREMIER DEGRE / PRIMER GRADO		SECOND LEVEL / SECOND DEGRE / SEGUNDO GRADO		1ST + 2ND LEVELS / 1ER + 2ND DEGRE / 1ER + 2DO GRADO	3RD LEVEL / 3EME DEGRE / 3ER GRADO
			GROSS / BRUT / BRUTA	NET / NET / NETA	GROSS / BRUT / BRUTA	NET / NET / NETA	GROSS / BRUT / BRUTA	GROSS / BRUT / BRUTA
LESOTHO	1975			(6–12)		(13–17)	(6–17)	(20–24)
		MF	105	...	13	...	71	0.5
		M	87	...	12	...	59	0.7
		F	123	...	14	...	82	0.4
	1980							
		MF	102	66	17	13	71	1.6
		M	85	54	14	9	59	...
		F	120	78	20	16	82	...
	1981							
		MF	105	66	19	13	73	1.8
		M	89	55	15	9	62	1.3
		F	122	77	22	17	85	2.2
	1982							
		MF	110	71	19	14	76	1.9
		M	94	60	16	10	65	1.4
		F	126	82	23	18	87	2.3
	1983							
		MF	111	71	21	12	78	1.9
		M	97	60	17	8	67	1.4
		F	126	81	26	17	89	2.3
	1984							
		MF	...	...	...	...	...	1.8
		M	...	...	...	...	...	1.4
		F	...	...	...	...	...	2.2
LIBERIA	1975			(6–11)		(12–17)	(6–17)	(20–24)
		MF	62	...	17	...	42	1.8
		M	80	...	25	...	56	2.8
		F	45	...	8	...	28	0.8
	1980							
		MF	76	...	23	...	52	...
		M	95	...	33	...	67	...
		F	57	...	13	...	37	...
LIBYAN ARAB JAMAHIRIYA‡	1975			(6–11)		(12–17)	(6–17)	(20–24)
		MF	...	...	...	...	...	6.3
		M	...	...	...	...	...	9.8
		F	...	...	...	...	...	2.3
	1980							
		MF	...	...	...	...	...	8.2
		M	...	...	...	...	...	11.9
		F	...	...	...	...	...	4.3
	1981							
		MF	...	...	...	...	...	9.5
		M	...	...	...	...	...	13.8
		F	...	...	...	...	...	5.0
	1982							
		MF	...	...	...	...	...	10.8
		M	...	...	...	...	...	15.7
		F	...	...	...	...	...	5.7
MADAGASCAR	1975			(6–11)		(12–18)	(6–18)	(20–24)
		MF	102	...	15	...	60	1.3
		M	117	...	17	...	69	1.3
		F	87	...	12	...	51	1.3
	1980			(6–10)		(11–17)	(6–17)	(20–24)
		MF	148	...	...	...	...	3.1
		M	152	...	...	...	...	...
		F	144	...	...	...	...	...
	1981							
		MF	144	...	...	...	...	4.0
		M	147	...	...	...	...	...
		F	140	...	...	...	...	...
	1982							
		MF	136	...	...	...	...	4.2
		M	145	...	...	...	...	...
		F	127	...	...	...	...	...

COUNTRY / PAYS / PAIS	YEAR / ANNEE / AÑO	SEX / SEXE / SEXO	ENROLMENT RATIOS / TAUX D'INSCRIPTION / TASAS DE ESCOLARIZACION					
			FIRST LEVEL / PREMIER DEGRE / PRIMER GRADO		SECOND LEVEL / SECOND DEGRE / SEGUNDO GRADO		1ST + 2ND LEVELS / 1ER + 2ND DEGRE / 1ER + 2DO GRADO	3RD LEVEL / 3EME DEGRE / 3ER GRADO
			GROSS / BRUT / BRUTA	NET / NET / NETA	GROSS / BRUT / BRUTA	NET / NET / NETA	GROSS / BRUT / BRUTA	GROSS / BRUT / BRUTA
MADAGASCAR (CONT)	1983							
		MF	128	...	37	...	79	4.3
		M	133	...	...	...	...	...
		F	122	...	...	...	...	...
	1984							
		MF	121	...	36	...	76	4.6
		M	125	...	43	...	82	...
		F	118	...	30	...	71	...
MALAWI	1975			(6–13)		(14–17)	(6–17)	(20–24)
		MF	57	...	3	...	42	0.5
		M	71	...	5	...	52	0.9
		F	44	...	2	...	32	0.1
	1980							
		MF	61	44	4	...	45	0.7
		M	74	49	5	...	54	1.0
		F	49	39	2	...	36	0.4
	1981							
		MF	65	...	4	...	47	0.7
		M	...	...	5	...	...	1.0
		F	...	...	2	...	...	0.4
	1982							
		MF	62	44	4	...	45	0.7
		M	73	48	5	...	54	1.0
		F	52	40	2	...	37	0.4
	1983							
		MF	60	42	4	...	43	0.7
		M	69	45	6	...	51	1.0
		F	50	39	2	...	36	0.4
	1984							
		MF	62	44	4	...	45	0.7
		M	71	47	6	...	52	1.0
		F	53	41	2	...	38	0.4
MALI	1975			(6–11)		(12–17)	(6–17)	(20–24)
		MF	24	...	7	...	17	0.6
		M	32	...	11	...	23	1.1
		F	17	...	3	...	11	0.1
	1980							
		MF	25	17	8	...	17	0.3
		M	32	...	12	...	23	0.5
		F	18	...	5	...	12	0.1
	1981							
		MF	24	16	8	...	17	0.8
		M	30	...	11	...	22	1.5
		F	18	...	4	...	12	0.2
	1982							
		MF	24	16	7	...	16	0.9
		M	30	...	10	...	21	1.8
		F	17	...	4	...	11	0.2
MAURITANIA	1975			(6–12)		(13–19)	(6–19)	(20–24)
		MF	19	...	4	...	12	...
		M	24	...	...	...	...	...
		F	13	...	...	...	...	...
	1980			(6–11)		(12–17)	(6–17)	(20–24)
		MF	34	...	10	...	23	...
		M	44	...	16	...	31	...
		F	24	...	4	...	15	...
	1982							
		MF	37	...	12	...	26	...
		M	45	...	19	...	33	...
		F	29	...	6	...	19	...
MAURITIUS	1975			(5–10)		(11–17)	(5–17)	(20–24)
		MF	107	82	39	34	70	1.4
		M	108	83	42	37	72	2.4
		F	106	81	35	32	68	0.4

COUNTRY / PAYS / PAIS	YEAR / ANNEE / AÑO	SEX / SEXE / SEXO	ENROLMENT RATIOS / TAUX D'INSCRIPTION / TASAS DE ESCOLARIZACION — FIRST LEVEL / PREMIER DEGRE / PRIMER GRADO		SECOND LEVEL / SECOND DEGRE / SEGUNDO GRADO		1ST + 2ND LEVELS / 1ER + 2ND DEGRE / 1ER + 2DO GRADO	3RD LEVEL / 3EME DEGRE / 3ER GRADO
			GROSS BRUT BRUTA	NET NET NETA	GROSS BRUT BRUTA	NET NET NETA	GROSS BRUT BRUTA	GROSS BRUT BRUTA
MAURITIUS (CONT)	1980	MF	108	93	48	...	73	1.1
		M	109	92	49	...	74	1.4
		F	108	93	47	...	72	0.7
	1981	MF	114	95	48	...	76	0.9
		M	114	95	50	...	77	1.2
		F	114	96	47	...	75	0.5
	1982	MF	114	99	49	...	77	0.8
		M	114	99	51	...	78	1.2
		F	114	100	47	...	76	0.4
	1983	MF	112	98	51	...	78	0.6
		M	112	98	53	...	80	0.8
		F	112	99	49	...	77	0.4
	1984	MF	106	97	51	...	76	0.6
		M	105	96	54	...	78	0.9
		F	106	98	48	...	75	0.3
MOROCCO				(7–11)		(12–18)	(7–18)	(20–24)
	1975	MF	62	47	16	14	37	3.2
		M	78	58	21	17	47	5.2
		F	45	35	12	10	27	1.2
	1980	MF	78	58	25	20	50	6.0
		M	96	71	32	24	62	9.3
		F	59	45	19	15	38	2.8
	1981	MF	81	58	27	...	52	6.6
		M	100	70	33	...	64	10.1
		F	62	45	21	...	40	3.2
	1982	MF	85	...	28	...	54	5.9
		M	104	...	34	...	66	8.8
		F	66	...	22	...	42	3.0
	1983	MF	86	63	29	...	55	6.7
		M	105	75	35	...	66	9.9
		F	66	50	24	...	43	3.7
	1984	MF	80	63	31	...	52	7.8
		M	97	76	37	...	63	11.4
		F	62	50	25	...	41	4.2
MOZAMBIQUE				(6– 9)		(10–16)	(6–16)	(20–24)
	1976	MF	111	...	3	...	47	0.1
		M	133	...	4	...	57	0.1
		F	90	...	2	...	38	0.1
	1980	MF	99	36	5	...	43	0.1
		M	114	39	8	...	51	0.1
		F	84	34	3	...	36	0.1
	1981	MF	94	36	5	4	41	0.1
		M	107	38	8	5	48	0.2
		F	81	34	3	2	35	0.1
				(7–10)		(11–17)	(7–17)	(20–24)
	1982	MF	92	49	5	...	40	0.1
		M	104	54	8	...	47	...
		F	79	45	3	...	34	...
	1983	MF	83	48	6	...	37	...
		M	94	53	8	...	43	...
		F	71	43	4	...	31	...

COUNTRY / PAYS / PAIS	YEAR / ANNEE / AÑO	SEX / SEXE / SEXO	FIRST LEVEL / PREMIER DEGRE / PRIMER GRADO: GROSS / BRUT / BRUTA	FIRST LEVEL: NET / NET / NETA	SECOND LEVEL / SECOND DEGRE / SEGUNDO GRADO: GROSS / BRUT / BRUTA	SECOND LEVEL: NET / NET / NETA	1ST + 2ND LEVELS / 1ER + 2ND DEGRE / 1ER + 2DO GRADO: GROSS / BRUT / BRUTA	3RD LEVEL / 3EME DEGRE / 3ER GRADO: GROSS / BRUT / BRUTA
			ENROLMENT RATIOS / TAUX D'INSCRIPTION / TASAS DE ESCOLARIZACION					
MOZAMBIQUE (CONT)	1985							
		MF	...	...	...	...	...	0.1
		M	...	...	...	...	...	0.2
		F	...	...	...	...	...	0.1
NIGER	1975			(7–12)		(13–19)	(7–19)	(20–24)
		MF	20	...	2	2	11	0.1
		M	25	...	3	3	15	0.2
		F	14	...	1	1	8	0.03
	1980							
		MF	27	21	5	4	17	0.3
		M	35	...	7	5	22	0.5
		F	19	...	3	2	11	0.1
	1981							
		MF	27	...	6	...	17	0.4
		M	34	...	...	...	...	0.7
		F	19	...	...	...	...	0.1
	1982							
		MF	27	...	6	...	17	0.5
		M	...	...	...	...	...	0.8
		F	...	...	...	...	...	0.1
	1983							
		MF	28	...	7	...	18	0.5
		M	...	...	...	...	...	0.8
		F	...	...	...	...	...	0.2
	1984							
		MF	...	...	...	...	...	0.6
		M	...	...	...	...	...	0.9
		F	...	...	...	...	...	0.2
NIGERIA	1975			(6–11)		(12–18)	(6–18)	(20–24)
		MF	51	...	8	...	31	0.8
		M	...	...	...	...	...	1.4
		F	...	...	...	...	...	0.2
	1980							
		MF	97	...	19	...	60	2.2
		M	110	...	24	...	70	...
		F	84	...	13	...	51	...
	1981							
		MF	98	...	22	...	62	2.5
		M	112	...	31	...	74	...
		F	84	...	13	...	50	...
	1982			(6–11)		(12–17)	(6–17)	(20–24)
		MF	97	...	28	...	67	...
		M	110	...	42	...	80	...
		F	84	...	14	...	53	...
	1983							
		MF	92	...	29	...	64	3.3
		M	103	...	...	...	...	...
		F	81	...	...	...	...	...
REUNION‡				(6–10)		(11–17)	(6–17)	(20–24)
RWANDA	1975			(7–12)		(13–18)	(7–18)	(20–24)
		MF	56	...	2	...	32	0.3
		M	61	...	3	...	35	...
		F	51	...	1	...	29	...
	1980			(7–14)		(15–20)	(7–20)	(20–24)
		MF	63	60	2	2	41	0.3
		M	66	62	2	2	43	0.5
		F	60	57	1	1	39	0.1
	1981							
		MF	64	61	2	2	42	0.3
		M	67	63	2	2	44	0.6
		F	62	59	1	1	40	0.1
	1982							
		MF	63	59	2	2	41	0.3
		M	65	61	3	3	42	0.6
		F	60	57	2	1	39	0.1

COUNTRY / PAYS / PAIS	YEAR / ANNEE / AÑO	SEX / SEXE / SEXO	ENROLMENT RATIOS / TAUX D'INSCRIPTION / TASAS DE ESCOLARIZACION					
			FIRST LEVEL / PREMIER DEGRE / PRIMER GRADO		SECOND LEVEL / SECOND DEGRE / SEGUNDO GRADO		1ST + 2ND LEVELS / 1ER + 2ND DEGRE / 1ER + 2DO GRADO	3RD LEVEL / 3EME DEGRE / 3ER GRADO
			GROSS / BRUT / BRUTA	NET / NET / NETA	GROSS / BRUT / BRUTA	NET / NET / NETA	GROSS / BRUT / BRUTA	GROSS / BRUT / BRUTA
RWANDA (CONT)	1983	MF	62	59	2	2	40	0.3
		M	64	60	3	3	42	0.6
		F	60	57	1	1	39	0.1
SENEGAL	1975			(6–11)		(12–18)	(6–18)	(20–24)
		MF	41	...	10	...	26	2.0
		M	48	...	...	...	...	3.3
		F	34	...	...	...	...	0.7
	1980	MF	46	37	11	...	29	2.8
		M	55	44	15	...	36	4.5
		F	36	30	7	...	22	1.0
	1981	MF	48	39	12	...	31	2.5
		M	58	47	16	...	38	4.1
		F	38	31	8	...	23	0.9
	1982	MF	51	41	12	...	32	...
		M	61	49	16	...	40	...
		F	41	33	8	...	25	...
	1983	MF	53	43	12	...	34	2.2
		M	64	51	17	...	41	3.6
		F	43	35	8	...	26	0.9
	1984	MF	55	44	13	...	35	...
		M	66	52	17	...	42	...
		F	44	36	8	...	27	...
SIERRA LEONE	1975			(5–11)		(12–18)	(5–18)	(20–24)
		MF	39	...	11	...	26	0.6
		M	47	...	16	...	33	1.1
		F	30	...	7	...	20	0.2
	1980	MF	54	...	14	...	36	0.6
		M	64	...	20	...	44	...
		F	45	...	8	...	28	...
	1981	MF	59	...	15	...	39	...
		M	69	...	21	...	48	...
		F	48	...	9	...	30	...
	1982	MF	58	...	17	...	39	...
		M	68	...	23	...	48	...
		F	48	...	11	...	31	...
SOMALIA	1975			(6– 9)		(10–17)	(6–17)	(20–24)
		MF	56	21	6	...	25	0.7
		M	73	25	8	...	33	1.3
		F	40	17	3	...	17	0.2
	1980			(6–13)		(14–17)	(6–17)	(20–24)
		MF	34	25	13	7	28	...
		M	43	32	19	10	36	...
		F	24	18	7	4	19	...
	1981	MF	29	21	17	7	25	...
		M	37	27	23	10	33	...
		F	21	15	10	5	17	...
	1982	MF	25	18	18	...	23	...
		M	33	23	24	...	30	...
		F	18	13	12	...	16	...
	1983	MF	25	...	17	...	22	...
		M	32	...	23	...	29	...
		F	18	...	12	...	16	...

COUNTRY / PAYS / PAIS	YEAR / ANNEE / AÑO	SEX / SEXE / SEXO	ENROLMENT RATIOS / TAUX D'INSCRIPTION / TASAS DE ESCOLARIZACION: FIRST LEVEL / PREMIER DEGRE / PRIMER GRADO — GROSS / BRUT / BRUTA	FIRST LEVEL — NET / NET / NETA	SECOND LEVEL / SECOND DEGRE / SEGUNDO GRADO — GROSS / BRUT / BRUTA	SECOND LEVEL — NET / NET / NETA	1ST + 2ND LEVELS / 1ER + 2ND DEGRE / 1ER + 2DO GRADO — GROSS / BRUT / BRUTA	3RD LEVEL / 3EME DEGRE / 3ER GRADO — GROSS / BRUT / BRUTA
SUDAN	1975			(7–12)		(13–18)	(7–18)	(20–24)
		MF	47	...	14	...	32	1.5
		M	59	...	19	...	41	2.5
		F	34	...	8	...	22	0.5
	1980	MF	50	...	16	...	35	1.8
		M	59	...	20	...	41	2.6
		F	41	...	12	...	28	1.0
	1981	MF	50	...	17	...	35	2.0
		M	60	...	20	...	42	2.8
		F	41	...	14	...	29	1.2
	1982	MF	50	...	18	...	36	2.1
		M	59	...	21	...	42	2.7
		F	42	...	15	...	30	1.4
	1983	MF	49	...	19	...	36	2.0
		M	57	...	23	...	42	2.6
		F	41	...	16	...	30	1.5
SWAZILAND	1975			(6–12)		(13–17)	(6–17)	(20–24)
		MF	99	74	32	21	74	2.5
		M	100	72	35	20	77	...
		F	97	75	29	22	72	...
	1980	MF	106	83	39	...	81	3.9
		M	106	...	40	...	82	4.8
		F	106	...	38	...	81	3.1
	1981	MF	110	86	40	...	84	3.5
		M	110	84	41	...	85	4.1
		F	109	88	40	...	84	2.8
	1982	MF	111	85	42	...	86	3.4
		M	111	84	43	...	86	4.1
		F	110	87	42	...	85	2.7
	1983	MF	111	84	44	...	86	3.3
		M	111	81	44	...	87	3.9
		F	110	87	43	...	86	2.6
	1984	MF	111	85	44	...	87	...
		M	112	82	44	...	87	...
		F	110	87	43	...	86	...
TOGO	1975			(6–11)		(12–18)	(6–18)	(20–24)
		MF	99	...	19	...	60	1.2
		M	130	...	29	...	81	2.1
		F	68	...	9	...	40	0.3
	1980	MF	122	...	34	...	79	2.2
		M	150	...	...	...	...	3.8
		F	93	...	...	...	...	0.6
	1981	MF	116	78	32	...	76	1.9
		M	141	93	48	...	96	3.3
		F	92	62	16	...	55	0.6
	1982	MF	111	76	29	...	71	1.8
		M	134	89	43	...	90	3.0
		F	88	63	14	...	52	0.5
	1983	MF	100	69	24	...	63	1.8
		M	122	82	36	...	81	3.0
		F	79	55	12	...	46	0.5

COUNTRY / PAYS / PAIS	YEAR / ANNEE / AÑO	SEX / SEXE / SEXO	ENROLMENT RATIOS / TAUX D'INSCRIPTION / TASAS DE ESCOLARIZACION					
			FIRST LEVEL / PREMIER DEGRE / PRIMER GRADO		SECOND LEVEL / SECOND DEGRE / SEGUNDO GRADO		1ST + 2ND LEVELS / 1ER + 2ND DEGRE / 1ER + 2DO GRADO	3RD LEVEL / 3EME DEGRE / 3ER GRADO
			GROSS BRUT BRUTA	NET NET NETA	GROSS BRUT BRUTA	NET NET NETA	GROSS BRUT BRUTA	GROSS BRUT BRUTA
TOGO (CONT)	1984	MF	97	67	21	...	60	1.8
		M	118	80	32	...	77	3.1
		F	75	54	10	...	43	0.6
TUNISIA	1975			(6–11)		(12–18)	(6–18)	(20–24)
		MF	97	...	21	17	60	4.2
		M	116	...	28	21	72	6.3
		F	78	...	15	12	46	2.1
	1980	MF	103	83	27	23	64	5.5
		M	117	92	33	28	74	7.9
		F	88	73	20	17	53	3.2
	1981	MF	106	86	30	27	66	5.4
		M	120	95	36	33	76	7.6
		F	93	77	23	20	56	3.3
	1982	MF	111	90	31	28	69	5.3
		M	124	98	38	34	78	7.3
		F	98	81	24	22	60	3.5
	1983	MF	114	93	34	30	72	5.3
		M	125	100	40	35	81	7.0
		F	102	85	27	24	63	3.6
	1984	MF	116	94	36	32	75	5.6
		M	127	100	42	37	83	7.2
		F	105	87	30	26	66	4.0
UGANDA‡	1975			(6–12)		(13–18)	(6–18)	(20–24)
		MF	44	...	4	...	28	0.6
		M	53	...	6	...	34	0.9
		F	35	...	2	...	22	0.2
	1980	MF	50	...	5	...	32	0.5
		M	56	...	7	...	37	0.8
		F	43	...	3	...	27	0.2
	1981	MF	52	39	5	...	33	0.6
		M	60	43	7	...	39	0.9
		F	45	35	3	...	28	0.3
	1982	MF	58	40	8	...	38	0.6
		M	66	43	11	...	44	0.9
		F	50	38	5	...	32	0.3
UNITED REPUBLIC OF TANZANIA	1975			(7–13)		(14–19)	(7–19)	(20–24)
		MF	53	...	3	...	33	0.2
		M	62	...	4	...	39	0.4
		F	44	...	2	...	27	0.1
	1980	MF	93	...	3	...	57	...
		M	100	...	4	...	62	...
		F	86	...	2	...	53	...
	1981	MF	94	66	3	...	58	0.4
		M	100	68	4	...	62	0.6
		F	88	65	2	...	54	0.1
	1982	MF	90	61	3	...	55	0.4
		M	94	62	4	...	58	0.6
		F	85	61	2	...	52	0.1
	1983	MF	87	...	3	...	54	0.4
		M	91	...	4	...	57	0.6
		F	84	...	2	...	51	0.1

COUNTRY / PAYS / PAIS	YEAR / ANNEE / AÑO	SEX / SEXE / SEXO	ENROLMENT RATIOS / TAUX D'INSCRIPTION / TASAS DE ESCOLARIZACION — FIRST LEVEL / PREMIER DEGRE / PRIMER GRADO: GROSS / BRUT / BRUTA	FIRST LEVEL: NET / NET / NETA	SECOND LEVEL / SECOND DEGRE / SEGUNDO GRADO: GROSS / BRUT / BRUTA	SECOND LEVEL: NET / NET / NETA	1ST + 2ND LEVELS / 1ER + 2ND DEGRE / 1ER + 2DO GRADO: GROSS / BRUT / BRUTA	3RD LEVEL / 3EME DEGRE / 3ER GRADO: GROSS / BRUT / BRUTA
UNITED REPUBLIC OF TANZANIA (CONT)	1984							
		MF	...	...	...	...	...	0.4
		M	...	...	...	...	...	0.6
		F	...	...	...	...	...	0.1
ZAIRE	1975		(6–11)		(12–17)		(6–17)	(20–24)
		MF	98	...	17	...	61	1.3
		M	117	...	25	...	75	...
		F	78	...	9	...	47	...
	1980							
		MF	98	...	35	...	70	1.3
		M	114	...	51	...	86	...
		F	82	...	19	...	54	...
	1981							
		MF	98	...	41	...	73	1.3
		M	114	...	59	...	90	...
		F	82	...	23	...	56	...
	1982							
		MF	98	75	49	42	76	1.3
		M	113	86	70	60	94	...
		F	83	64	27	24	59	...
	1983							
		MF	98	75	57	49	80	...
		M	112	86	81	70	99	...
		F	84	65	33	28	61	...
ZAMBIA	1975		(7–13)		(14–18)		(7–18)	(20–24)
		MF	97	...	15	...	67	2.1
		M	105	...	20	...	74	3.6
		F	88	...	10	...	60	0.6
	1980							
		MF	98	84	17	...	69	1.6
		M	103	86	22	...	74	...
		F	92	81	12	...	63	...
	1981							
		MF	97	...	17	...	68	1.5
		M	102	...	21	...	73	2.4
		F	92	...	12	...	63	0.6
	1982							
		MF	98	...	17	...	69	1.6
		M	103	...	22	...	74	2.5
		F	93	...	12	...	64	0.7
	1983							
		MF	100	...	17	...	71	1.6
		M	105	...	22	...	76	2.6
		F	95	...	12	...	65	0.7
ZIMBABWE	1975		(7–13)		(14–19)		(7–19)	(20–24)
		MF	73	...	9	...	47	1.6
		M	79	...	10	...	52	...
		F	67	...	7	...	43	...
	1980							
		MF	88	...	8	...	56	1.3
	1981							
		MF	118	...	15	...	77	1.9
		M	122	...	18	...	81	...
		F	113	...	13	...	73	...
	1982							
		MF	126	100	23	...	85	2.2
		M	131	100	27	...	89	2.6
		F	121	100	19	...	80	1.8
	1983							
		MF	130	...	30	...	91	2.6
		M	135	...	36	...	96	3.0
		F	126	...	25	...	86	2.1
	1984							
		MF	131	100	39	...	94	2.6
		M	135	100	46	...	100	3.1
		F	127	100	31	...	89	2.2

COUNTRY / PAYS / PAIS	YEAR / ANNEE / AÑO	SEX / SEXE / SEXO	ENROLMENT RATIOS / TAUX D'INSCRIPTION / TASAS DE ESCOLARIZACION: FIRST LEVEL / PREMIER DEGRE / PRIMER GRADO		SECOND LEVEL / SECOND DEGRE / SEGUNDO GRADO		1ST + 2ND LEVELS / 1ER + 2ND DEGRE / 1ER + 2DO GRADO	3RD LEVEL / 3EME DEGRE / 3ER GRADO
			GROSS BRUT BRUTA	NET NET NETA	GROSS BRUT BRUTA	NET NET NETA	GROSS BRUT BRUTA	GROSS BRUT BRUTA
AMERICA, NORTH								
BARBADOS	1975			(5–10)		(11–16)	(5–16)	(20–24)
		MF	110	100	78	73	93	10.0
		M	109	100	76	70	91	...
		F	111	100	81	76	95	...
	1980							
		MF	99	96	89	86	94	15.6
		M	98	94	90	86	94	14.9
		F	100	97	89	85	94	16.3
	1981							
		MF	101	97	88	84	94	18.7
		M	102	98	85	82	94	...
		F	99	96	91	87	95	...
	1982							
		MF	102	99	89	85	96	18.7
		M	106	100	87	83	96	...
		F	99	95	91	86	95	...
	1983							
		MF	108	...	89	85	99	18.9
		M	108	...	88	84	97	20.0
		F	109	...	91	86	100	17.8
	1984							
		MF	110	...	93	89	101	19.4
		M	113	...	93	89	102	19.9
		F	108	...	94	90	101	19.0
CANADA	1975			(6–11)		(12–17)	(6–17)	(20–24)
		MF	99	...	91	...	95	39.3
		M	99	...	90	...	94	43.3
		F	99	...	92	...	95	35.3
	1980							
		MF	102	...	92	...	97	38.3
		M	102	...	91	...	96	38.1
		F	102	...	93	...	97	38.5
	1981							
		MF	108	99	96	88	102	39.4
		M	109	99	96	87	102	38.7
		F	107	99	97	89	102	40.1
	1982							
		MF	107	98	99	...	103	41.8
		M	108	98	99	...	103	40.7
		F	106	98	99	...	102	42.9
	1983							
		MF	106	97	102	...	104	44.0
		M	107	97	102	...	105	42.6
		F	105	97	102	...	103	45.5
COSTA RICA	1975			(6–11)		(12–16)	(6–16)	(20–24)
		MF	107	92	42	35	79	17.5
		M	108	92	40	33	78	...
		F	106	92	45	37	79	...
	1980							
		MF	106	90	47	39	79	23.0
		M	107	89	44	36	77	...
		F	105	91	51	43	80	...
	1981							
		MF	106	91	47	39	78	23.5
		M	107	90	43	36	78	...
		F	105	91	50	42	80	...
	1982							
		MF	103	89	46	37	77	22.7
		M	104	88	43	35	76	...
		F	102	89	49	40	78	...
	1983							
		MF	102	...	44	...	75	22.1
		M	103	...	41	...	75	...
		F	100	...	46	...	76	...

COUNTRY / PAYS / PAIS	YEAR / ANNEE / AÑO	SEX / SEXE / SEXO	ENROLMENT RATIOS / TAUX D'INSCRIPTION / TASAS DE ESCOLARIZACION: FIRST LEVEL / PREMIER DEGRE / PRIMER GRADO: GROSS / BRUT / BRUTA	FIRST LEVEL: NET / NET / NETA	SECOND LEVEL / SECOND DEGRE / SEGUNDO GRADO: GROSS / BRUT / BRUTA	SECOND LEVEL: NET / NET / NETA	1ST + 2ND LEVELS / 1ER + 2ND DEGRE / 1ER + 2DO GRADO: GROSS / BRUT / BRUTA	3RD LEVEL / 3EME DEGRE / 3ER GRADO: GROSS / BRUT / BRUTA
COSTA RICA (CONT)	1984	MF	101	...	42	...	75	22.1
		M	102	...	40	...	75	...
		F	100	...	45	...	75	...
CUBA	1975			(6–11)		(12–18)	(6–18)	(20–24)
		MF	124	...	42	...	85	11.0
		M	126	...	42	...	86	...
		F	122	...	42	...	84	...
	1980			(6–11)		(12–17)	(6–17)	(20–24)
		MF	108	98	73	...	91	19.5
		M	111	98	71	...	91	19.8
		F	105	97	76	...	90	19.3
	1981	MF	107	97	75	...	90	19.9
		M	110	97	72	...	90	18.8
		F	104	97	77	...	90	21.0
	1982	MF	109	98	72	...	90	19.1
		M	112	99	70	...	90	17.8
		F	105	98	75	...	90	20.6
	1983	MF	108	97	74	...	90	19.6
		M	111	97	71	...	89	18.0
		F	105	97	77	...	90	21.2
	1984	MF	106	95	75	...	89	20.1
		M	110	95	71	...	88	18.1
		F	102	94	79	...	89	22.2
DOMINICAN REPUBLIC	1975			(7–12)		(13–18)	(7–18)	(20–24)
		MF	104	...	36	...	74	10.1
		M	...	...	...	...	...	11.3
		F	...	...	...	...	...	8.9
	1980	MF	114	...	43	...	81	...
	1981	MF	116	70	45	...	83	...
		M	115	70	...	...	...	...
		F	117	70	...	...	...	...
	1982	MF	109	71	44	...	79	...
		M	104	72	...	...	...	...
		F	115	70	...	...	...	...
	1983	MF	112	73	45	...	81	...
		M	107	74	...	...	...	...
		F	117	72	...	...	...	...
EL SALVADOR	1975			(7–15)		(16–18)	(7–18)	(20–24)
		MF	75	...	19	...	63	7.9
		M	76	...	21	...	64	10.4
		F	74	...	17	...	62	5.4
	1980	MF	74	...	23	...	63	3.9
		M	74	...	24	...	63	5.3
		F	74	...	23	...	63	2.4
	1981	MF	61	56	20	...	52	5.7
		M	61	56	19	...	52	7.9
		F	61	57	21	...	53	3.5
	1982	MF	68	...	23	...	58	10.1
		M	68	...	22	...	58	12.3
		F	68	...	23	...	58	7.8
	1983	MF	69	64	24	...	60	11.9
		M	69	64	23	...	59	13.5
		F	69	63	25	...	60	10.3

COUNTRY / PAYS / PAIS	YEAR / ANNEE / AÑO	SEX / SEXE / SEXO	FIRST LEVEL / PREMIER DEGRE / PRIMER GRADO: GROSS / BRUT / BRUTA	FIRST LEVEL / PREMIER DEGRE / PRIMER GRADO: NET / NET / NETA	SECOND LEVEL / SECOND DEGRE / SEGUNDO GRADO: GROSS / BRUT / BRUTA	SECOND LEVEL / SECOND DEGRE / SEGUNDO GRADO: NET / NET / NETA	1ST + 2ND LEVELS / 1ER + 2ND DEGRE / 1ER + 2DO GRADO: GROSS / BRUT / BRUTA	3RD LEVEL / 3EME DEGRE / 3ER GRADO: GROSS / BRUT / BRUTA
EL SALVADOR (CONT)	1984							
		MF	70	62	24	14	60	...
		M	69	61	23	12	59	...
		F	70	62	26	16	61	...
GUADELOUPE‡				(6–10)		(11–17)	(6–17)	(20–24)
GUATEMALA	1975			(7–12)		(13–18)	(7–18)	(20–24)
		MF	63	53	12	10	40	4.3
		M	69	57	13	10	43	6.5
		F	57	49	11	9	37	2.0
	1980							
		MF	71	58	17	13	46	8.4
		M	77	...	18	...	50	...
		F	65	...	15	...	43	...
	1981							
		MF	75	61	17	...	49	...
		M	81	65	18	...	53	...
		F	69	57	16	...	45	...
	1982							
		MF	70	58	17	14	46	7.4
		M	75	61	17	...	49	...
		F	65	55	16	...	43	...
	1983							
		MF	75	62	17	...	49	...
		M	80	65	17	...	52	...
		F	69	58	16	...	45	...
	1984							
		MF	76	...	17	...	50	...
HAITI	1975			(7–12)		(13–19)	(7–19)	(20–24)
		MF	60	...	8	...	34	0.7
		M	...	...	8	...	...	1.0
		F	...	...	7	...	...	0.3
	1980			(6–11)		(12–17)	(6–17)	(20–24)
		MF	67	33	12	...	42	0.9
		M	72	34	13	...	45	1.3
		F	62	33	12	...	39	0.5
	1981							
		MF	67	38	12	...	42	...
		M	72	39	13	...	45	...
		F	63	37	12	...	39	...
	1982							
		MF	72	42	14	...	46	1.0
		M	77	42	14	...	48	...
		F	68	41	14	...	43	...
	1983							
		MF	76	39	16	...	49	1.1
		M	81	40	16	...	51	1.5
		F	72	38	16	...	46	0.8
HONDURAS	1975			(7–12)		(13–17)	(7–17)	(20–24)
		MF	88	...	16	...	59	4.6
		M	89	...	16	...	60	6.0
		F	86	...	17	...	59	3.2
	1980							
		MF	95	76	30	...	69	8.2
		M	96	76	29	...	69	10.2
		F	95	75	30	...	69	6.2
	1982							
		MF	99	85	32	...	72	9.7
		M	100	85	30	...	72	11.1
		F	98	84	34	...	72	8.3
	1983							
		MF	101	86	33	24	73	9.7
		M	101	86	31	23	73	11.1
		F	100	86	34	26	73	8.3

COUNTRY / PAYS / PAIS	YEAR / ANNEE / AÑO	SEX / SEXE / SEXO	ENROLMENT RATIOS / TAUX D'INSCRIPTION / TASAS DE ESCOLARIZACION					
			FIRST LEVEL / PREMIER DEGRE / PRIMER GRADO		SECOND LEVEL / SECOND DEGRE / SEGUNDO GRADO		1ST + 2ND LEVELS / 1ER + 2ND DEGRE / 1ER + 2DO GRADO	3RD LEVEL / 3EME DEGRE / 3ER GRADO
			GROSS / BRUT / BRUTA	NET / NET / NETA	GROSS / BRUT / BRUTA	NET / NET / NETA	GROSS / BRUT / BRUTA	GROSS / BRUT / BRUTA
HONDURAS (CONT)	1984							
		MF	102	87	33	20	74	9.1
		M	102	86	31	18	73	...
		F	101	87	36	22	75	...
	1985							
		MF	102	...	...	...	...	...
		M	103	...	...	...	...	...
		F	102	...	...	...	...	...
JAMAICA	1975			(6–11)		(12–18)	(6–18)	(20–24)
		MF	97	90	58	56	78	6.7
		M	97	89	53	52	75	...
		F	98	90	63	61	81	...
	1980							
		MF	101	94	59	57	78	6.2
		M	100	93	55	54	76	...
		F	101	95	63	60	81	...
	1981							
		MF	104	...	60	...	80	6.0
	1982							
		MF	106	99	60	...	81	5.9
		M	105	97	...	...	...	...
		F	107	100	...	...	...	...
	1983							
		MF	106	94	58	...	80	...
		M	106	93	56	...	78	...
		F	107	96	60	...	81	...
MARTINIQUE‡				(6–10)		(11–17)	(6–17)	(20–24)
MEXICO	1975			(6–11)		(12–17)	(6–17)	(20–24)
		MF	109	...	34	...	76	10.6
		M	112	...	41	...	80	...
		F	106	...	28	...	71	...
	1980							
		MF	120	...	47	...	87	14.1
		M	121	...	50	...	89	18.8
		F	119	...	45	...	85	9.4
	1981							
		MF	119	...	51	...	89	14.7
		M	120	...	54	...	90	19.1
		F	118	...	49	...	87	10.2
	1982							
		MF	119	...	53	...	89	14.9
		M	121	...	56	...	91	19.0
		F	117	...	51	...	87	10.7
	1983							
		MF	119	...	55	...	89	15.2
		M	120	...	56	...	91	19.3
		F	117	...	53	...	87	11.1
	1984							
		MF	116	97	55	...	88	...
		M	118	...	...	...	...	...
		F	115	...	...	...	...	...
NICARAGUA	1975			(7–12)		(13–18)	(7–18)	(20–24)
		MF	82	65	24	...	56	8.3
		M	80	...	23	...	54	11.0
		F	85	...	24	...	58	5.7
	1980			(7–12)		(13–17)	(7–17)	(20–24)
		MF	99	74	43	23	76	14.1
		M	96	73	40	21	73	...
		F	102	75	45	25	79	...
	1982							
		MF	100	73	39	...	75	12.2
		M	97	72	36	...	73	13.1
		F	103	74	42	...	78	11.4

COUNTRY / PAYS / PAIS	YEAR / ANNEE / AÑO	SEX / SEXE / SEXO	ENROLMENT RATIOS / TAUX D'INSCRIPTION / TASAS DE ESCOLARIZACION					
			FIRST LEVEL / PREMIER DEGRE / PRIMER GRADO		SECOND LEVEL / SECOND DEGRE / SEGUNDO GRADO		1ST + 2ND LEVELS / 1ER + 2ND DEGRE / 1ER + 2DO GRADO	3RD LEVEL / 3EME DEGRE / 3ER GRADO
			GROSS / BRUT / BRUTA	NET / NET / NETA	GROSS / BRUT / BRUTA	NET / NET / NETA	GROSS / BRUT / BRUTA	GROSS / BRUT / BRUTA
NICARAGUA (CONT)	1983							
		MF	103	73	44	21	79	12.8
		M	100	72	39	16	75	14.1
		F	106	75	48	27	82	11.5
	1984							
		MF	99	73	43	...	76	11.0
		M	...	...	...	...	...	11.6
		F	...	...	...	...	...	10.5
	1985							
		MF	...	...	...	...	...	9.8
		M	...	...	...	...	...	8.5
		F	...	...	...	...	...	11.0
PANAMA	1975			(6–11)		(12–17)	(6–17)	(20–24)
		MF	114	87	55	39	87	17.3
		M	116	87	52	37	87	17.1
		F	111	88	57	41	87	17.5
	1980							
		MF	106	88	61	46	85	22.0
		M	108	88	57	43	84	19.3
		F	104	89	65	49	86	24.8
	1981							
		MF	104	88	60	46	84	22.3
		M	106	87	57	43	83	19.9
		F	102	88	64	49	84	24.8
	1982							
		MF	104	87	59	46	83	22.9
		M	106	87	56	43	82	20.2
		F	102	88	63	49	83	25.8
	1983							
		MF	104	87	59	46	82	22.0
		M	106	87	55	43	82	17.9
		F	101	87	62	49	82	26.3
	1984							
		MF	105	87	59	47	83	25.1
		M	107	87	56	44	82	21.8
		F	102	87	63	50	83	28.5
PUERTO RICO	1975			(5–10)		(11–16)	(5–16)	(20–24)
		MF	107	...	78	...	92	32.8
		M	...	...	...	...	...	31.3
		F	...	...	...	...	...	34.3
	1979			(5–12)		(13–16)	(5–16)	(20–24)
		MF	...	...	...	...	...	45.4
		M	...	...	...	...	...	39.6
		F	...	...	...	...	...	50.9
	1981							
		MF	94	...	74	...	87	...
TRINIDAD AND TOBAGO	1975			(5–11)		(12–16)	(5–16)	(20–24)
		MF	105	87	51	...	83	5.1
		M	104	86	49	...	81	6.0
		F	106	89	54	...	85	4.2
	1980							
		MF	98	88	68	...	85	4.9
		M	95	85	...	...	...	5.7
		F	101	91	...	...	...	4.2
	1981							
		MF	98	90	72	63	87	4.8
		M	95	88	71	62	85	5.8
		F	100	93	72	63	88	3.8
	1982							
		MF	99	...	73	63	88	4.4
		M	95	...	72	63	86	5.0
		F	102	...	74	64	90	3.7
	1984							
		MF	96	91	76	63	88	...
		M	94	90	75	61	86	...
		F	98	93	78	65	90	...

COUNTRY / PAYS / PAIS	YEAR / ANNEE / AÑO	SEX / SEXE / SEXO	ENROLMENT RATIOS / TAUX D'INSCRIPTION / TASAS DE ESCOLARIZACION — FIRST LEVEL / PREMIER DEGRE / PRIMER GRADO: GROSS / BRUT / BRUTA	FIRST LEVEL: NET / NET / NETA	SECOND LEVEL / SECOND DEGRE / SEGUNDO GRADO: GROSS / BRUT / BRUTA	SECOND LEVEL: NET / NET / NETA	1ST + 2ND LEVELS / 1ER + 2ND DEGRE / 1ER + 2DO GRADO: GROSS / BRUT / BRUTA	3RD LEVEL / 3EME DEGRE / 3ER GRADO: GROSS / BRUT / BRUTA
UNITED STATES	1975						(6–17)	(20–24)
		MF	...	...	...	...	99	57.3
		M	...	...	...	...	...	62.5
		F	...	...	...	...	...	52.0
	1980			(6–13)		(14–17)	(6–17)	(20–24)
		MF	98	94	90	81	95	56.0
		M	99	93	89	80	95	53.9
		F	98	94	91	83	96	58.1
	1981							
		MF	101	97	94	84	99	56.3
		M	101	96	93	83	99	53.6
		F	101	97	94	85	99	59.1
	1982							
		MF	101	97	94	84	98	56.4
		M	102	97	94	83	99	53.8
		F	100	97	93	85	98	59.2
	1983							
		MF	102	97	95	85	99	56.4
		M	103	97	94	83	100	...
		F	101	96	96	86	99	...
	1984							
		MF	101	96	95	85	99	57.3
		M	102	96	95	84	99	...
		F	100	96	95	87	98	...
AMERICA, SOUTH								
ARGENTINA	1975			(6–12)		(13–17)	(6–17)	(20–24)
		MF	106	96	54	42	85	27.2
		M	106	96	51	39	84	28.1
		F	106	97	57	45	86	26.2
	1980							
		MF	106	...	...	...	...	21.6
		M	106	...	...	...	...	21.2
		F	106	...	...	...	...	22.1
	1982							
		MF	108	...	...	...	...	24.0
		M	108	...	...	...	...	22.2
		F	107	...	...	...	...	25.8
	1983							
		MF	107	...	60	...	89	25.2
		M	107	...	57	...	89	23.1
		F	107	...	62	...	90	27.4
	1984							
		MF	107	...	65	...	91	29.3
		M	107	...	62	...	90	27.1
		F	107	...	69	...	93	31.6
	1985							
		MF	108	...	70	...	94	36.4
		M	107	...	66	...	92	34.2
		F	108	...	75	...	96	38.8
BOLIVIA	1975			(6–13)		(14–17)	(6–17)	(20–24)
		MF	85	73	31	21	69	11.7
		M	94	...	...	...	...	...
		F	76	...	...	...	...	...
	1980							
		MF	84	77	36	16	70	16.5
		M	90	82	41	18	76	...
		F	78	72	31	14	64	...
	1981							
		MF	86	...	34	...	70	16.5
		M	93	...	37	...	77	...
		F	78	...	31	...	64	...
	1982							
		MF	85	...	35	...	71	16.4

COUNTRY / PAYS / PAIS	YEAR / ANNEE / AÑO	SEX / SEXE / SEXO	ENROLMENT RATIOS / TAUX D'INSCRIPTION / TASAS DE ESCOLARIZACION					
			FIRST LEVEL / PREMIER DEGRE / PRIMER GRADO		SECOND LEVEL / SECOND DEGRE / SEGUNDO GRADO		1ST + 2ND LEVELS / 1ER + 2ND DEGRE / 1ER + 2DO GRADO	3RD LEVEL / 3EME DEGRE / 3ER GRADO
			GROSS / BRUT / BRUTA	NET / NET / NETA	GROSS / BRUT / BRUTA	NET / NET / NETA	GROSS / BRUT / BRUTA	GROSS / BRUT / BRUTA
BOLIVIA (CONT)	1983							
		MF	87	...	35	...	72	...
		M	94	...	38	...	78	...
		F	81	...	32	...	67	...
	1984							
		MF	91	81	37	25	75	...
		M	96	86	40	27	80	...
		F	85	77	34	23	70	...
BRAZIL	1975			(7–14)		(15–17)	(7–17)	(20–24)
		MF	88	71	26	9	72	10.7
		M	89	...	24	8	73	...
		F	87	...	28	10	72	...
	1980							
		MF	99	81	34	14	81	11.9
		M	101	...	31	13	82	12.2
		F	97	...	36	16	80	11.7
	1981							
		MF	97	79	34	14	80	11.6
		M	99	...	...	...	...	...
		F	95	...	...	...	...	...
	1982							
		MF	101	82	34	14	83	11.4
		M	101	...	...	...	...	...
		F	100	...	...	...	...	...
	1983							
		MF	103	83	35	14	86	11.3
		M	108	...	...	...	...	11.3
		F	99	...	...	...	...	11.4
	1984							
		MF	103	83	...	...	...	...
	1985							
		MF	104	...	...	...	...	...
CHILE	1975			(6–13)		(14–17)	(6–17)	(20–24)
		MF	115	96	47	33	93	16.2
		M	115	95	44	31	92	17.6
		F	115	97	51	36	94	14.7
	1980							
		MF	112	...	53	...	92	13.0
		M	113	...	50	...	91	14.7
		F	111	...	57	...	93	11.3
	1981							
		MF	110	...	56	...	91	13.0
		M	110	...	51	...	90	14.8
		F	109	...	60	...	93	11.2
	1982							
		MF	108	98	58	42	91	13.3
		M	109	98	55	40	91	15.4
		F	106	99	61	44	91	11.1
	1983							
		MF	108	92	63	46	93	14.7
		M	109	92	60	44	93	16.8
		F	107	93	66	48	93	12.5
	1984							
		MF	107	92	66	...	93	15.3
		M	108	...	63	...	93	17.3
		F	106	...	69	...	94	13.2
	1985							
		MF	...	...	...	...	...	15.8
COLOMBIA	1975			(7–11)		(12–17)	(7–17)	(20–24)
		MF	118	...	39	...	77	8.0
		M	116	...	39	...	76	10.1
		F	120	...	39	...	79	5.8

COUNTRY / PAYS / PAIS	YEAR / ANNEE / AÑO	SEX / SEXE / SEXO	ENROLMENT RATIOS / TAUX D'INSCRIPTION / TASAS DE ESCOLARIZACION — FIRST LEVEL / PREMIER DEGRE / PRIMER GRADO — GROSS / BRUT / BRUTA	FIRST LEVEL — NET / NET / NETA	SECOND LEVEL / SECOND DEGRE / SEGUNDO GRADO — GROSS / BRUT / BRUTA	SECOND LEVEL — NET / NET / NETA	1ST + 2ND LEVELS / 1ER + 2ND DEGRE / 1ER + 2DO GRADO — GROSS / BRUT / BRUTA	3RD LEVEL / 3EME DEGRE / 3ER GRADO — GROSS / BRUT / BRUTA
COLOMBIA (CONT)	1980			(6–10)		(11–16)	(6–16)	(20–24)
		MF	128	...	44	...	82	10.6
		M	127	...	43	...	81	11.7
		F	130	...	45	...	83	9.5
	1982							
		MF	121	78	46	...	80	12.1
		M	120	...	45	...	79	13.1
		F	122	...	47	...	81	11.2
	1983							
		MF	121	...	46	...	80	12.4
		M	120	...	43	...	78	...
		F	122	...	50	...	83	...
	1984							
		MF	119	76	49	...	81	12.8
		M	119	...	48	...	81	13.3
		F	119	...	49	...	82	12.4
	1985							
		MF	117	75	50	...	82	12.9
		M	116	...	50	...	81	...
		F	119	...	51	...	83	...
ECUADOR	1975			(6–11)		(12–17)	(6–17)	(20–24)
		MF	101	78	39	28	73	26.9
		M	103	78	41	28	75	...
		F	99	78	38	27	72	...
	1980							
		MF	113	...	51	...	85	36.5
		M	115	...	51	...	85	45.2
		F	112	...	51	...	84	27.5
	1981							
		MF	115	...	53	...	86	34.1
		M	...	...	53	...	...	42.2
		F	...	...	53	...	...	25.9
	1982							
		MF	116	...	55	...	87	32.1
		M	...	...	54	...	...	...
		F	...	...	56	...	...	...
	1983							
		MF	117	...	52	...	86	32.5
		M	117	...	51	...	86	39.4
		F	117	...	53	...	87	25.5
	1984							
		MF	114	...	55	...	86	33.1
GUYANA	1975			(6–11)		(12–17)	(6–17)	(20–24)
		MF	95	84	54	...	75	3.8
		M	96	84	53	...	75	5.0
		F	95	84	55	...	75	2.7
	1980							
		MF	100	...	60	...	80	2.6
		M	101	...	58	...	80	2.9
		F	99	...	62	...	81	2.3
	1981							
		MF	99	90	60	...	80	2.8
		M	99	89	58	...	79	3.1
		F	99	91	62	...	80	2.5
	1982							
		MF	95	...	57	...	76	2.0
		M	...	...	...	...	...	2.3
		F	...	...	...	...	...	1.7
	1983							
		MF	90	...	55	...	73	2.0
		M	...	...	...	...	...	2.1
		F	...	...	...	...	...	1.9
PARAGUAY	1975			(7–12)		(13–18)	(7–18)	(20–24)
		MF	102	85	20	16	64	7.0
		M	106	87	20	16	66	...
		F	97	83	20	16	61	...

COUNTRY / PAYS / PAIS	YEAR / ANNEE / AÑO	SEX / SEXE / SEXO	ENROLMENT RATIOS / TAUX D'INSCRIPTION / TASAS DE ESCOLARIZACION: FIRST LEVEL / PREMIER DEGRE / PRIMER GRADO — GROSS / BRUT / BRUTA	FIRST LEVEL — NET / NET / NETA	SECOND LEVEL / SECOND DEGRE / SEGUNDO GRADO — GROSS / BRUT / BRUTA	SECOND LEVEL — NET / NET / NETA	1ST + 2ND LEVELS / 1ER + 2ND DEGRE / 1ER + 2DO GRADO — GROSS / BRUT / BRUTA	3RD LEVEL / 3EME DEGRE / 3ER GRADO — GROSS / BRUT / BRUTA
PARAGUAY (CONT)	1980	MF	103	...	27	...	68	8.8
	1981	MF	103	...	28	...	68	9.1
	1982	MF	103	90	30	...	69	9.3
		M	107	92	30	...	71	...
		F	99	89	29	...	66	...
	1983	MF	102	...	30	...	69	10.3
	1984	MF	101	...	31	...	69	9.7
PERU	1975			(6–11)		(12–16)	(6–16)	(20–24)
		MF	113	...	46	...	85	14.6
		M	...	...	50	...	...	19.6
		F	...	...	41	...	...	9.5
	1980	MF	114	86	59	...	91	19.4
		M	117	...	63	...	94	24.8
		F	111	...	54	...	87	13.9
	1981	MF	115	93	61	...	92	20.6
		M	117	95	65	...	95	26.1
		F	112	91	57	...	89	14.8
	1982	MF	118	92	61	...	94	21.5
		M	122	...	64	...	98	27.4
		F	115	...	57	...	90	15.6
	1985	MF	122	97	65	...	98	...
		M	125	...	68	...	101	...
		F	120	...	61	...	95	...
SURINAME	1975			(6–11)		(12–17)	(6–17)	(20–24)
		MF	110	...	52	...	84	5.8
		M	115	...	47	...	84	8.1
		F	106	...	57	...	84	3.5
	1980	MF	...	...	...	...	...	7.0
	1981	MF	...	...	...	...	...	7.3
	1982	MF	...	...	...	...	...	7.6
	1983	MF	...	...	...	...	...	7.3
	1984	MF	133	98	66	...	98	6.9
		M	136	98	...	...	...	6.7
		F	130	97	...	...	...	7.1
URUGUAY	1975			(6–11)		(12–17)	(6–17)	(20–24)
		MF	107	...	60	...	84	16.0
		M	107	...	...	...	...	17.8
		F	106	...	...	...	...	14.2
	1980	MF	106	...	60	...	84	16.1
		M	107	...	59	...	84	15.0
		F	106	...	61	...	84	17.2
	1981	MF	122	...	64	...	94	15.9
		M	124	...	...	...	...	...
		F	120	...	...	...	...	...

COUNTRY / PAYS / PAIS	YEAR / ANNEE / AÑO	SEX / SEXE / SEXO	ENROLMENT RATIOS / TAUX D'INSCRIPTION / TASAS DE ESCOLARIZACION — FIRST LEVEL / PREMIER DEGRE / PRIMER GRADO: GROSS / BRUT / BRUTA	FIRST LEVEL / PREMIER DEGRE / PRIMER GRADO: NET / NET / NETA	SECOND LEVEL / SECOND DEGRE / SEGUNDO GRADO: GROSS / BRUT / BRUTA	SECOND LEVEL / SECOND DEGRE / SEGUNDO GRADO: NET / NET / NETA	1ST + 2ND LEVELS / 1ER + 2ND DEGRE / 1ER + 2DO GRADO: GROSS / BRUT / BRUTA	3RD LEVEL / 3EME DEGRE / 3ER GRADO: GROSS / BRUT / BRUTA
URUGUAY (CONT)	1982							
		MF	113	...	65	...	90	20.4
		M	...	...	...	...	...	17.9
		F	...	...	...	...	...	22.8
	1983							
		MF	109	88	67	...	89	20.8
		M	110	...	...	...	...	17.8
		F	107	...	...	...	...	23.8
	1984							
		MF	...	...	...	...	...	26.1
	1985							
		MF	...	...	...	...	...	31.7
VENEZUELA	1975			(7–12)		(13–17)	(7–17)	(20–24)
		MF	100	81	45	35	77	18.1
		M	99	...	42	33	75	...
		F	100	...	48	37	79	...
	1980			(7–12)		(13–18)	(7–18)	(20–24)
		MF	109	86	41	34	76	21.4
		M	...	...	36	...	...	...
		F	...	...	45	...	...	...
	1981							
		MF	110	87	41	35	77	22.3
		M	110	...	37	31	75	...
		F	110	...	46	38	80	...
	1982							
		MF	111	88	43	36	79	22.8
		M	111	...	38	32	76	...
		F	111	...	48	40	81	...
	1983							
		MF	108	86	43	36	77	24.3
		M	108	...	39	33	75	...
		F	108	...	48	40	79	...
	1984							
		MF	109	86	45	38	78	23.4
		M	109	...	40	34	76	...
		F	108	...	49	41	80	...
ASIA								
AFGHANISTAN	1975			(6–13)		(14–17)	(6–17)	(20–24)
		MF	25	...	7	...	20	1.0
		M	41	...	13	...	33	1.7
		F	8	...	2	...	6	0.3
	1980			(7–14)		(15–18)	(7–18)	(20–24)
		MF	34	29	10	...	27	...
		M	54	46	16	...	43	...
		F	12	11	4	...	10	...
	1981							
		MF	36	31	12	...	29	...
		M	57	48	18	...	46	...
		F	14	12	5	...	11	...
	1982							
		MF	13	12	7	...	12	1.4
		M	18	15	10	...	16	...
		F	9	8	5	...	7	...
	1984							
		MF	16	14	8	...	14	...
		M	22	19	10	...	19	...
		F	10	9	5	...	9	...
BAHRAIN	1975			(6–11)		(12–16)	(6–16)	(20–24)
		MF	96	70	52	36	77	2.3
		M	107	76	51	34	82	1.9
		F	85	64	55	39	72	3.1

COUNTRY / PAYS / PAIS	YEAR / ANNEE / AÑO	SEX / SEXE / SEXO	FIRST LEVEL / PREMIER DEGRE / PRIMER GRADO: GROSS / BRUT / BRUTA	FIRST LEVEL / PREMIER DEGRE / PRIMER GRADO: NET / NET / NETA	SECOND LEVEL / SECOND DEGRE / SEGUNDO GRADO: GROSS / BRUT / BRUTA	SECOND LEVEL / SECOND DEGRE / SEGUNDO GRADO: NET / NET / NETA	1ST + 2ND LEVELS / 1ER + 2ND DEGRE / 1ER + 2DO GRADO: GROSS / BRUT / BRUTA	3RD LEVEL / 3EME DEGRE / 3ER GRADO: GROSS / BRUT / BRUTA
BAHRAIN (CONT)	1980			(6–11)		(12–17)	(6–17)	(20–24)
		MF	104	80	64	55	85	4.7
		M	111	84	70	58	92	4.6
		F	97	76	58	52	79	4.9
	1981							
		MF	104	79	68	57	87	5.9
		M	112	84	73	59	94	5.4
		F	95	74	62	54	80	6.7
	1982							
		MF	104	82	78	65	92	8.9
		M	109	86	84	68	97	7.0
		F	99	78	72	62	86	11.3
	1983							
		MF	108	86	77	61	94	10.1
		M	112	88	81	61	97	8.1
		F	104	83	74	61	90	12.6
	1984							
		MF	110	90	82	...	97	10.4
		M	112	91	85	...	99	8.1
		F	109	90	79	...	95	13.4
BANGLADESH	1975			(5– 9)		(10–16)	(5–16)	(20–24)
		MF	73	...	19	...	44	...
		M	95	...	29	...	60	...
		F	51	...	8	...	28	...
	1980							
		MF	62	60	18	...	38	3.0
		M	76	75	26	...	50	5.1
		F	46	45	9	...	26	0.9
	1982			(6–10)		(11–17)	(6–17)	(20–24)
		MF	61	...	...	...	...	3.5
		M	71	...	...	...	...	5.4
		F	51	...	...	...	...	1.5
	1983							
		MF	62	56	18	...	39	4.5
		M	77	69	26	...	50	7.2
		F	47	43	10	...	28	1.7
	1984							
		MF	62	55	19	18	39	4.9
		M	67	60	26	25	45	7.9
		F	55	50	11	11	32	1.8
	1985							
		MF	60	54	18	17	38	...
		M	70	63	26	...	46	...
		F	50	45	10	...	29	...
BHUTAN	1976			(6–11)		(12–16)	(6–16)	(20–24)
		MF	9	...	1	...	6	–
		M	13	...	2	...	8	–
		F	5	...	0.3	...	3	–
	1980							
		MF	15	...	...	...	...	0.3
		M	...	...	...	...	...	0.4
		F	...	...	...	...	...	0.1
	1981							
		MF	17	...	...	...	...	...
	1982			(7–11)		(12–16)	(7–16)	(20–24)
		MF	22	...	3	...	13	...
		M	29	...	...	...	...	...
		F	15	...	...	...	...	...
	1983							
		MF	24	...	4	...	14	0.05
		M	31	...	6	...	19	0.1
		F	16	...	1	...	9	0.01
	1984							
		MF	25	...	4	...	15	...
		M	32	...	6	...	20	...
		F	17	...	1	...	10	...

COUNTRY / PAYS / PAIS	YEAR / ANNEE / AÑO	SEX / SEXE / SEXO	FIRST LEVEL / PREMIER DEGRE / PRIMER GRADO: GROSS / BRUT / BRUTA	FIRST LEVEL: NET / NET / NETA	SECOND LEVEL / SECOND DEGRE / SEGUNDO GRADO: GROSS / BRUT / BRUTA	SECOND LEVEL: NET / NET / NETA	1ST + 2ND LEVELS / 1ER + 2ND DEGRE / 1ER + 2DO GRADO: GROSS / BRUT / BRUTA	3RD LEVEL / 3EME DEGRE / 3ER GRADO: GROSS / BRUT / BRUTA
BURMA	1975			(5– 9)		(10–15)	(5–15)	(20–24)
		MF	85	...	22	...	53	2.1
		M	88	...	24	...	55	...
		F	82	...	20	...	50	...
	1980	MF	91	...	22	...	56	...
	1981	MF	96	...	24	...	58	5.1
	1982	MF	99	...	24	...	59	...
	1983	MF	102	...	24	...	61	...
CHINA	1975			(7–11)		(12–16)	(7–16)	(20–24)
		MF	122	...	46	...	88	0.6
		M	130	...	54	...	96	0.7
		F	114	...	38	...	80	0.4
	1980	MF	112	...	46	...	80	1.3
		M	121	...	54	...	88	2.0
		F	103	...	37	...	71	0.6
	1981	MF	112	...	39	...	76	1.5
		M	122	...	47	...	84	2.1
		F	102	...	32	...	67	0.7
	1982	MF	112	...	36	...	73	1.3
		M	122	...	43	...	82	1.8
		F	101	...	29	...	64	0.7
	1983	MF	113	...	35	...	73	1.3
		M	124	...	42	...	81	1.8
		F	102	...	29	...	64	0.7
	1984	MF	118	...	37	...	75	1.4
		M	129	...	43	...	83	1.9
		F	107	...	31	...	66	0.8
CYPRUS‡				(5–10)		(11–16)	(5–16)	(20–24)
DEMOCRATIC YEMEN	1975			(7–12)		(13–18)	(7–18)	(20–24)
		MF	81	...	23	...	56	1.0
		M	109	...	36	...	79	1.7
		F	51	...	10	...	34	0.4
	1980			(7–14)		(15–18)	(7–18)	(20–24)
		MF	65	...	18	...	51	2.3
		M	93	...	25	...	73	2.3
		F	36	...	11	...	29	2.3
	1981	MF	64	...	18	...	50	2.3
		M	93	...	24	...	73	2.3
		F	34	...	11	...	27	2.4
	1982	MF	64	...	19	...	51	...
		M	94	...	26	...	74	...
		F	34	...	11	...	27	...
	1983	MF	66	...	19	...	52	...
		M	96	...	26	...	76	...
		F	35	...	11	...	28	...
HONG KONG	1975			(6–11)		(12–18)	(6–18)	(20–24)
		MF	119	92	49	46	78	10.1
		M	122	93	51	48	80	14.7
		F	117	91	47	44	76	5.3

COUNTRY / PAYS / PAIS	YEAR / ANNEE / AÑO	SEX / SEXE / SEXO	ENROLMENT RATIOS / TAUX D'INSCRIPTION / TASAS DE ESCOLARIZACION — FIRST LEVEL / PREMIER DEGRE / PRIMER GRADO: GROSS / BRUT / BRUTA	FIRST LEVEL / PREMIER DEGRE / PRIMER GRADO: NET / NET / NETA	SECOND LEVEL / SECOND DEGRE / SEGUNDO GRADO: GROSS / BRUT / BRUTA	SECOND LEVEL / SECOND DEGRE / SEGUNDO GRADO: NET / NET / NETA	1ST + 2ND LEVELS / 1ER + 2ND DEGRE / 1ER + 2DO GRADO: GROSS / BRUT / BRUTA	3RD LEVEL / 3EME DEGRE / 3ER GRADO: GROSS / BRUT / BRUTA
HONG KONG (CONT)	1980							
		MF	107	95	64	61	81	10.5
		M	107	95	63	59	81	14.2
		F	106	96	65	62	82	6.4
	1981							
		MF	106	96	66	62	82	10.8
		M	107	95	64	60	82	14.2
		F	105	96	68	64	83	7.2
	1982							
		MF	106	96	67	63	84	11.9
		M	107	96	64	60	82	15.2
		F	105	96	70	66	85	8.3
	1983							
		MF	106	96	68	64	84	12.4
		M	107	96	65	61	83	15.5
		F	105	96	71	67	86	9.0
	1984							
		MF	105	95	69	64	85	12.8
		M	106	95	66	61	83	16.0
		F	104	95	72	68	86	9.3
INDIA	1975			(5– 9)		(10–15)	(5–15)	(20–24)
		MF	81	...	28	...	54	8.6
		M	96	...	37	...	66	12.7
		F	64	...	18	...	40	4.2
	1980							
		MF	83	...	32	...	57	...
		M	98	...	42	...	69	...
		F	67	...	22	...	44	...
	1981							
		MF	82	...	34	...	57	...
		M	96	...	44	...	69	...
		F	66	...	23	...	44	...
	1982							
		MF	85	...	35	...	59	...
		M	100	...	45	...	71	...
		F	69	...	24	...	45	...
	1983			(6–10)		(11–17)	(6–17)	(20–24)
		MF	90	...	34	...	59	...
		M	105	...	44	...	71	...
		F	73	...	23	...	45	...
INDONESIA	1975			(7–12)		(13–18)	(7–18)	(20–24)
		MF	86	72	20	17	55	2.4
		M	94	78	25	21	62	...
		F	78	67	15	13	49	...
	1980							
		MF	107	88	29	...	72	...
		M	115	93	35	...	79	...
		F	100	83	23	...	65	...
	1981							
		MF	111	94	31	...	75	3.9
		M	117	98	37	...	81	5.5
		F	105	90	25	...	69	2.4
	1982							
		MF	113	98	35	...	77	4.2
		M	116	100	40	...	82	5.8
		F	109	95	29	...	72	2.7
	1983							
		MF	116	96	37	...	79	5.6
		M	119	98	42	...	84	7.8
		F	113	94	31	...	75	3.5
	1984							
		MF	118	98	39	...	82	6.5
		M	121	100	45	...	86	8.9
		F	116	96	34	...	77	4.2

COUNTRY / PAYS / PAIS	YEAR / ANNEE / AÑO	SEX / SEXE / SEXO	ENROLMENT RATIOS / TAUX D'INSCRIPTION / TASAS DE ESCOLARIZACION — FIRST LEVEL / PREMIER DEGRE / PRIMER GRADO: GROSS / BRUT / BRUTA	FIRST LEVEL: NET / NET / NETA	SECOND LEVEL / SECOND DEGRE / SEGUNDO GRADO: GROSS / BRUT / BRUTA	SECOND LEVEL: NET / NET / NETA	1ST + 2ND LEVELS / 1ER + 2ND DEGRE / 1ER + 2DO GRADO: GROSS / BRUT / BRUTA	3RD LEVEL / 3EME DEGRE / 3ER GRADO: GROSS / BRUT / BRUTA
IRAN, ISLAMIC REPUBLIC OF	1975			(6–10)		(11–16)	(6–16)	(20–24)
		MF	93	...	45	...	69	4.9
		M	114	...	57	...	86	7.0
		F	71	...	33	...	52	2.8
	1980			(6–10)		(11–17)	(6–17)	(20–24)
		MF	88	...	...	...	...	...
	1981	MF	94	...	43	...	66	...
		M	110	...	52	...	78	...
		F	77	...	33	...	53	...
	1982	MF	97	...	39	...	66	3.6
		M	112	...	47	...	77	5.0
		F	82	...	32	...	55	2.2
	1983	MF	102	84	40	...	68	3.9
		M	115	92	48	...	78	5.4
		F	89	76	33	...	58	2.3
	1984	MF	107	88	43	...	72	4.4
		M	117	95	51	...	81	6.1
		F	95	81	35	...	62	2.6
IRAQ	1975			(6–11)		(12–17)	(6–17)	(20–24)
		MF	94	79	35	25	67	9.0
		M	122	100	48	34	89	11.8
		F	64	55	21	16	45	6.0
	1980	MF	115	100	57	47	89	9.4
		M	120	100	75	62	100	12.5
		F	109	95	38	31	77	6.1
	1981	MF	111	...	59	49	88	9.8
		M	115	...	77	64	98	13.3
		F	107	...	40	33	77	6.2
	1982	MF	106	92	55	...	83	10.0
		M	111	96	70	...	93	13.4
		F	101	88	39	...	73	6.5
	1983	MF	104	...	53	...	82	10.0
		M	111	...	67	...	92	13.2
		F	98	...	37	...	71	6.6
ISRAEL	1975			(6–13)		(14–17)	(6–17)	(20–24)
		MF	97	...	66	...	87	...
		M	96	...	60	...	85	...
		F	97	...	71	...	89	...
	1980	MF	93	...	70	...	87	31.1
		M	...	...	...	...	...	29.6
		F	...	...	...	...	...	32.6
	1981	MF	94	...	72	...	87	33.9
		M	...	...	...	...	...	35.6
		F	...	...	...	...	...	32.1
	1982	MF	97	...	73	...	89	34.2
		M	96	...	69	...	88	35.5
		F	97	...	78	...	91	32.7
	1983	MF	98	92	74	...	91	34.3
		M	97	91	70	...	89	35.1
		F	99	93	78	...	93	33.4

COUNTRY / PAYS / PAIS	YEAR / ANNEE / AÑO	SEX / SEXE / SEXO	ENROLMENT RATIOS / TAUX D'INSCRIPTION / TASAS DE ESCOLARIZACION — FIRST LEVEL / PREMIER DEGRE / PRIMER GRADO: GROSS / BRUT / BRUTA	FIRST LEVEL: NET / NET / NETA	SECOND LEVEL / SECOND DEGRE / SEGUNDO GRADO: GROSS / BRUT / BRUTA	SECOND LEVEL: NET / NET / NETA	1ST + 2ND LEVELS / 1ER + 2ND DEGRE / 1ER + 2DO GRADO: GROSS / BRUT / BRUTA	3RD LEVEL / 3EME DEGRE / 3ER GRADO: GROSS / BRUT / BRUTA
ISRAEL (CONT)	1984	MF	...	...	...	...	...	34.2
		M	...	...	...	...	...	35.0
		F	...	...	...	...	...	33.4
JAPAN	1975			(6–11)		(12–17)	(6–17)	(20–24)
		MF	99	...	91	...	95	24.6
		M	99	...	91	...	95	33.0
		F	99	...	92	...	95	16.0
	1980	MF	100	100	93	93	97	30.5
		M	100	100	92	92	96	40.6
		F	100	100	94	94	97	20.2
	1981	MF	100	100	94	94	97	30.6
		M	100	100	94	93	97	40.6
		F	100	100	95	94	97	20.4
	1982	MF	100	100	94	94	97	30.3
		M	100	100	93	93	97	39.9
		F	100	100	96	95	98	20.5
	1983	MF	100	100	94	...	97	30.2
		M	100	100	93	...	97	39.4
		F	100	100	95	...	98	20.7
	1984	MF	100	100	95	95	97	29.6
		M	100	100	94	...	97	38.2
		F	101	100	95	...	98	20.7
JORDAN‡	1980			(6–11)		(12–17)	(6–17)	(20–24)
		MF	104	93	76	68	91	26.6
		M	105	94	79	70	93	28.9
		F	102	91	73	60	90	24.2
	1981	MF	103	92	77	69	91	31.6
		M	105	95	79	71	93	37.0
		F	100	90	76	68	90	25.3
	1982	MF	100	89	78	71	90	33.3
		M	101	91	79	71	91	38.9
		F	98	88	77	70	89	27.8
	1983	MF	99	88	79	...	90	37.4
		M	98	88	80	...	90	41.5
		F	99	88	78	...	90	33.2
KOREA, REPUBLIC OF	1975			(6–11)		(12–17)	(6–17)	(20–24)
		MF	107	99	56	52	81	9.6
		M	107	99	64	58	85	13.7
		F	107	100	48	45	77	5.4
	1980	MF	110	100	76	69	93	15.0
		M	109	100	81	72	95	22.0
		F	111	100	71	65	90	7.5
	1982	MF	107	100	84	76	95	21.7
		M	107	100	87	79	97	31.1
		F	107	100	80	73	93	11.6
	1983	MF	103	99	87	...	95	23.9
		M	103	99	91	...	97	33.4
		F	104	99	84	...	93	13.7
	1984	MF	99	96	91	...	95	26.1
		M	99	96	94	...	97	35.9
		F	99	96	88	...	94	15.5

COUNTRY / PAYS / PAIS	YEAR / ANNEE / AÑO	SEX / SEXE / SEXO	ENROLMENT RATIOS / TAUX D'INSCRIPTION / TASAS DE ESCOLARIZACION — FIRST LEVEL / PREMIER DEGRE / PRIMER GRADO: GROSS / BRUT / BRUTA	FIRST LEVEL: NET / NET / NETA	SECOND LEVEL / SECOND DEGRE / SEGUNDO GRADO: GROSS / BRUT / BRUTA	SECOND LEVEL: NET / NET / NETA	1ST + 2ND LEVELS / 1ER + 2ND DEGRE / 1ER + 2DO GRADO: GROSS / BRUT / BRUTA	3RD LEVEL / 3EME DEGRE / 3ER GRADO: GROSS / BRUT / BRUTA
KOREA, REPUBLIC OF (CONT)	1985	MF	96	93	94	...	95	...
		M	96	93	97	...	96	...
		F	96	93	91	...	94	...
KUWAIT	1975			(6- 9)		(10–17)	(6–17)	(20–24)
		MF	92	68	66	57	77	9.0
		M	99	72	71	61	83	7.1
		F	85	64	61	53	72	11.2
	1980	MF	102	85	80	...	89	10.9
		M	105	89	84	...	92	8.0
		F	100	80	76	...	85	14.9
	1981	MF	102	84	81	...	89	12.6
		M	103	89	85	...	92	10.0
		F	101	80	77	...	86	16.3
	1982	MF	103	86	82	74	90	14.2
		M	104	90	85	77	92	10.7
		F	101	82	78	71	87	18.9
	1983	MF	104	86	82	...	90	14.6
		M	105	88	85	...	93	11.5
		F	102	83	79	...	88	18.9
	1984	MF	103	86	82	...	90	15.6
		M	105	88	85	...	92	12.4
		F	102	83	79	...	88	20.3
LAO PEOPLE'S DEMOCRATIC REPUBLIC	1975			(6–11)		(12–18)	(6–18)	(20–24)
		MF	58	...	7	...	34	...
	1980			(6–10)		(11–16)	(6–16)	(20–24)
		MF	94	...	18	...	56	0.5
		M	102	...	21	...	61	0.6
		F	86	...	14	...	50	0.3
	1981	MF	92	...	18	...	55	0.9
		M	100	...	21	...	60	1.2
		F	85	...	14	...	49	0.6
	1982	MF	91	...	18	...	54	1.2
		M	...	...	23	...	...	1.6
		F	...	...	13	...	...	0.8
	1983	MF	90	...	19	...	54	1.4
		M	103	...	22	...	62	...
		F	77	...	15	...	45	...
LEBANON	1980			(6–10)		(11–17)	(6–17)	(20–24)
		MF	111	...	59	...	82	33.7
		M	...	...	...	...	...	47.6
		F	...	...	...	...	...	22.2
	1981	MF	112	...	60	...	82	28.7
		M	116	...	59	...	83	39.3
		F	108	...	61	...	81	19.8
	1982	MF	111	...	62	...	82	28.9
		M	115	...	61	...	84	39.2
		F	105	...	63	...	81	20.1
MALAYSIA	1975			(6–11)		(12–18)	(6–18)	(20–24)
		MF	91	...	44	...	67	2.8
		M	92	...	40	...	66	4.0
		F	89	...	47	...	68	1.6

COUNTRY / PAYS / PAIS	YEAR / ANNEE / AÑO	SEX / SEXE / SEXO	ENROLMENT RATIOS / TAUX D'INSCRIPTION / TASAS DE ESCOLARIZACION — FIRST LEVEL / PREMIER DEGRE / PRIMER GRADO — GROSS / BRUT / BRUTA	NET / NET / NETA	SECOND LEVEL / SECOND DEGRE / SEGUNDO GRADO — GROSS / BRUT / BRUTA	NET / NET / NETA	1ST + 2ND LEVELS / 1ER + 2ND DEGRE / 1ER + 2DO GRADO — GROSS / BRUT / BRUTA	3RD LEVEL / 3EME DEGRE / 3ER GRADO — GROSS / BRUT / BRUTA
MALAYSIA (CONT)	1980							
		MF	93	...	48	...	70	4.3
		M	...	...	...	...	...	5.4
		F	...	...	...	...	...	3.2
	1982							
		MF	94	...	49	...	71	4.7
		M	95	...	...	...	...	5.4
		F	93	...	...	...	...	4.2
	1983							
		MF	96	...	50	...	72	5.2
		M	96	...	51	...	73	6.1
		F	95	...	50	...	72	4.4
	1984							
		MF	97	...	53	...	74	6.1
		M	98	...	53	...	74	6.8
		F	97	...	53	...	74	5.4
	1985							
		MF	99	...	53	...	75	...
		M	100	...	53	...	75	...
		F	99	...	53	...	75	...
MONGOLIA	1975			(8–10)		(11–17)	(8–17)	(20–24)
		MF	108	...	81	...	90	8.4
		M	111	...	77	...	89	8.2
		F	104	...	84	...	91	8.6
	1980							
		MF	106	...	88	...	94	...
		M	108	...	84	...	92	...
		F	105	...	92	...	96	...
	1981							
		MF	106	...	88	...	93	25.5
		M	106	...	84	...	91	18.8
		F	106	...	92	...	96	32.3
	1982							
		MF	107	99	87	...	93	...
		M	105	...	82	...	90	...
		F	108	...	91	...	96	...
	1983							
		MF	107	...	87	...	94	...
		M	106	...	82	...	90	...
		F	107	...	92	...	97	...
	1984							
		MF	105	...	88	...	94	...
		M	104	...	84	...	91	...
		F	106	...	92	...	96	...
NEPAL	1975			(6– 8)		(9–15)	(6–15)	(20–24)
		MF	51	...	13	...	26	2.3
		M	86	...	23	...	44	...
		F	16	...	4	...	8	...
	1980							
		MF	83	...	21	...	43	3.2
		M	115	...	33	...	62	4.7
		F	48	...	9	...	22	1.3
	1981			(6–10)		(11–15)	(6–15)	(20–24)
		MF	65	...	18	...	44	4.8
		M	92	...	29	...	64	7.1
		F	36	...	7	...	23	2.0
	1982							
		MF	67	...	21	...	46	4.8
		M	93	...	32	...	66	...
		F	39	...	9	...	25	...
	1983							
		MF	73	54	22	17	50	4.8
		M	100	75	34	26	70	7.4
		F	43	32	10	8	28	1.9

COUNTRY / PAYS / PAIS	YEAR / ANNEE / AÑO	SEX / SEXE / SEXO	FIRST LEVEL / PREMIER DEGRE / PRIMER GRADO: GROSS / BRUT / BRUTA	FIRST LEVEL: NET / NET / NETA	SECOND LEVEL / SECOND DEGRE / SEGUNDO GRADO: GROSS / BRUT / BRUTA	SECOND LEVEL: NET / NET / NETA	1ST + 2ND LEVELS / 1ER + 2ND DEGRE / 1ER + 2DO GRADO: GROSS / BRUT / BRUTA	3RD LEVEL / 3EME DEGRE / 3ER GRADO: GROSS / BRUT / BRUTA
			ENROLMENT RATIOS / TAUX D'INSCRIPTION / TASAS DE ESCOLARIZACION					
NEPAL (CONT)	1984							
		MF	77	56	23	18	52	...
		M	104	76	35	27	72	...
		F	47	35	11	9	30	...
OMAN	1975			(6–11)		(12–17)	(6–17)	(20–24)
		MF	44	32	1	1	25	–
		M	63	44	2	2	36	–
		F	24	20	0.5	0.4	14	–
	1980							
		MF	60	50	14	12	40	–
		M	77	62	21	17	52	–
		F	42	37	7	6	26	–
	1981							
		MF	63	53	17	14	43	–
		M	80	65	24	20	56	–
		F	46	41	9	8	30	–
	1982							
		MF	69	57	22	...	48	–
		M	84	66	31	...	61	–
		F	53	47	12	...	35	–
	1983							
		MF	75	65	25	...	54	–
		M	88	74	35	...	66	–
		F	62	56	15	...	42	–
	1984							
		MF	83	69	30	...	60	–
		M	93	75	40	...	71	–
		F	72	62	19	...	49	–
PAKISTAN	1975			(5– 9)		(10–16)	(5–16)	(20–24)
		MF	41	...	15	...	27	1.9
		M	56	...	22	...	38	2.7
		F	25	...	7	...	15	0.9
	1979							
		MF	42	...	14	...	27	2.0
		M	...	...	...	...	...	2.8
		F	...	...	...	...	...	1.1
	1980							
		MF	39	...	14	...	25	...
		M	51	...	20	...	34	...
		F	26	...	8	...	16	...
	1981							
		MF	40	...	14	...	26	...
		M	51	...	20	...	34	...
		F	27	...	8	...	16	...
	1982							
		MF	42	...	15	...	27	...
		M	54	...	21	...	36	...
		F	28	...	8	...	17	...
	1983							
		MF	42	...	15	...	27	...
		M	54	...	...	...	...	...
		F	29	...	...	...	...	...
PHILIPPINES	1975			(7–12)		(13–16)	(7–16)	(20–24)
		MF	107	95	54	...	87	18.4
	1980							
		MF	113	94	65	46	95	27.7
		M	113	94	61	43	94	26.8
		F	113	94	69	49	96	28.5
	1981							
		MF	111	94	64	45	93	28.2
		M	110	93	62	43	92	27.4
		F	111	96	66	47	94	29.0
	1982							
		MF	109	93	66	46	93	29.1
		M	109	91	63	44	92	...
		F	110	94	68	49	94	...

COUNTRY / PAYS / PAIS	YEAR / ANNEE / AÑO	SEX / SEXE / SEXO	ENROLMENT RATIOS / TAUX D'INSCRIPTION / TASAS DE ESCOLARIZACION					
			FIRST LEVEL / PREMIER DEGRE / PRIMER GRADO		SECOND LEVEL / SECOND DEGRE / SEGUNDO GRADO		1ST + 2ND LEVELS / 1ER + 2ND DEGRE / 1ER + 2DO GRADO	3RD LEVEL / 3EME DEGRE / 3ER GRADO
			GROSS / BRUT / BRUTA	NET / NET / NETA	GROSS / BRUT / BRUTA	NET / NET / NETA	GROSS / BRUT / BRUTA	GROSS / BRUT / BRUTA
PHILIPPINES (CONT)	1983							
		MF	109	92	67	50	93	...
		M	108	94	64	46	92	...
		F	109	90	69	53	94	...
	1984							
		MF	107	88	68	51	92	...
		M	106	87	65	47	91	...
		F	107	89	71	55	94	...
QATAR	1975			(6–11)		(12–17)	(6–17)	(20–24)
		MF	111	81	52	34	83	4.3
		M	116	81	48	30	82	2.4
		F	107	81	56	39	84	11.2
	1980							
		MF	107	87	68	52	89	9.4
		M	111	90	66	51	90	5.4
		F	104	84	70	54	89	17.5
	1981							
		MF	111	90	66	52	90	12.8
		M	115	94	62	49	90	8.4
		F	107	86	71	55	91	21.0
	1982							
		MF	116	91	67	54	92	17.4
		M	118	92	62	49	90	11.9
		F	113	90	74	60	95	27.2
	1983							
		MF	117	97	66	53	92	19.5
		M	122	100	60	47	90	15.0
		F	113	94	74	60	95	27.2
	1984							
		MF	121	100	68	54	94	18.3
		M	123	100	61	49	91	11.3
		F	118	99	76	61	98	30.7
SAUDI ARABIA	1975			(6–11)		(12–17)	(6–17)	(20–24)
		MF	58	42	22	13	42	4.1
		M	72	54	28	17	52	6.0
		F	43	29	15	9	30	1.8
	1980							
		MF	63	50	30	22	48	7.3
		M	75	62	36	27	58	8.8
		F	50	37	23	16	38	5.0
	1981							
		MF	64	51	31	22	50	8.2
		M	76	62	37	27	59	9.9
		F	52	39	25	17	40	5.9
	1982							
		MF	65	51	33	24	51	9.4
		M	76	62	39	29	60	11.2
		F	54	40	27	18	42	7.0
	1983							
		MF	68	53	38	26	55	9.8
		M	77	...	47	31	64	11.2
		F	58	...	29	20	46	7.9
SINGAPORE	1975			(6–11)		(12–17)	(6–17)	(20–24)
		MF	110	100	52	...	78	9.0
		M	113	100	51	...	80	10.7
		F	107	100	52	...	77	7.3
	1980							
		MF	108	99	58	...	81	7.8
		M	109	100	56	...	81	9.3
		F	106	99	59	...	81	6.3
	1981							
		MF	106	97	62	...	83	8.6
		M	107	98	61	...	83	10.0
		F	104	97	63	...	83	7.0

COUNTRY / PAYS / PAIS	YEAR / ANNEE / AÑO	SEX / SEXE / SEXO	FIRST LEVEL / PREMIER DEGRE / PRIMER GRADO: GROSS / BRUT / BRUTA	FIRST LEVEL: NET / NET / NETA	SECOND LEVEL / SECOND DEGRE / SEGUNDO GRADO: GROSS / BRUT / BRUTA	SECOND LEVEL: NET / NET / NETA	1ST + 2ND LEVELS / 1ER + 2ND DEGRE / 1ER + 2DO GRADO: GROSS / BRUT / BRUTA	3RD LEVEL / 3EME DEGRE / 3ER GRADO: GROSS / BRUT / BRUTA
SINGAPORE (CONT)	1982	MF	109	98	65	...	86	10.3
		M	111	98	64	...	87	11.9
		F	107	98	65	...	85	8.6
	1983	MF	113	100	69	...	90	11.8
		M	115	100	68	...	91	13.3
		F	110	100	69	...	89	10.2
	1984	MF	115	100	71	...	92	...
		M	118	100	70	...	93	...
		F	113	100	73	...	92	...
SRI LANKA	1975			(6–10)		(11–17)	(6–17)	(20–24)
		MF	77	...	48	...	61	1.3
		M	81	...	47	...	62	1.7
		F	74	...	49	...	60	1.0
	1980			(5–10)		(11–17)	(5–17)	(20–24)
		MF	103	...	55	...	77	2.8
		M	105	...	53	...	77	3.2
		F	100	...	57	...	77	2.5
	1981	MF	105	...	56	...	79	2.9
		M	107	...	53	...	78	3.3
		F	103	...	59	...	79	2.5
	1982	MF	105	...	57	...	79	3.7
		M	107	...	54	...	78	...
		F	102	...	60	...	80	...
	1983	MF	104	...	59	...	80	4.1
		M	106	...	56	...	79	4.6
		F	101	...	62	...	81	3.6
	1984	MF	103	...	61	...	81	...
		M	105	...	58	...	80	...
		F	101	...	64	...	82	...
SYRIAN ARAB REPUBLIC	1975			(6–11)		(12–17)	(6–17)	(20–24)
		MF	96	87	43	37	71	12.1
		M	112	100	57	48	86	17.5
		F	78	72	28	25	55	6.3
	1980	MF	102	91	47	40	77	16.9
		M	114	100	58	49	88	22.6
		F	89	81	36	31	65	10.7
	1981	MF	103	91	49	45	79	16.5
		M	114	100	60	54	90	21.5
		F	91	82	38	35	67	11.0
	1982	MF	103	92	52	47	81	15.9
		M	113	100	63	57	91	20.6
		F	92	83	41	37	70	10.7
	1983	MF	105	94	56	...	84	16.4
		M	114	100	68	...	94	21.2
		F	96	86	44	...	73	11.1
	1984	MF	107	95	59	52	86	...
		M	115	100	70	62	95	...
		F	98	89	47	42	76	...
THAILAND	1975			(7–13)		(14–18)	(7–18)	(20–24)
		MF	83	...	26	...	62	3.4
		M	87	...	28	...	65	4.0
		F	80	...	23	...	59	2.7

COUNTRY / PAYS / PAIS	YEAR / ANNEE / AÑO	SEX / SEXE / SEXO	FIRST LEVEL / PREMIER DEGRE / PRIMER GRADO: GROSS / BRUT / BRUTA	NET / NET / NETA	SECOND LEVEL / SECOND DEGRE / SEGUNDO GRADO: GROSS / BRUT / BRUTA	NET / NET / NETA	1ST + 2ND LEVELS / 1ER + 2ND DEGRE / 1ER + 2DO GRADO: GROSS / BRUT / BRUTA	3RD LEVEL / 3EME DEGRE / 3ER GRADO: GROSS / BRUT / BRUTA
THAILAND (CONT)	1980			(7–12)		(13–18)	(7–18)	(20–24)
		MF	98	...	29	...	66	13.1
		M	99	...	30	...	67	...
		F	96	...	28	...	64	...
	1981							
		MF	98	...	29	...	65	19.3
	1982							
		MF	...	...	...	...	...	21.8
	1983							
		MF	97	...	30	...	64	22.5
TURKEY	1975			(6–10)		(11–16)	(6–16)	(20–24)
		MF	108	...	29	...	66	9.3
		M	...	...	40	...	...	14.8
		F	...	...	19	...	...	3.1
	1980							
		MF	97	...	...	...	...	6.0
		M	103	...	...	...	...	8.4
		F	92	...	...	...	...	3.2
	1981							
		MF	100	...	36	...	66	6.0
		M	105	...	45	...	73	8.3
		F	95	...	26	...	59	3.3
	1982							
		MF	...	...	36	...	...	6.4
		M	...	...	46	...	...	8.5
		F	...	...	26	...	...	4.1
	1983							
		MF	111	...	38	...	72	7.4
		M	116	...	47	...	79	9.4
		F	107	...	28	...	65	5.2
	1984							
		MF	113	82	...	...	...	8.9
		M	116	...	...	...	...	11.8
		F	109	...	...	...	...	5.8
UNITED ARAB EMIRATES	1975			(6–11)		(12–17)	(6–17)	(20–24)
		MF	101	...	33	...	72	–
		M	104	...	36	...	73	–
		F	97	...	29	...	70	–
	1980							
		MF	92	76	54	...	77	2.3
		M	93	75	57	...	79	1.7
		F	92	78	50	...	76	4.0
	1981							
		MF	96	82	58	...	81	3.2
		M	96	81	57	...	80	2.2
		F	96	83	59	...	82	5.6
	1982							
		MF	97	77	58	...	81	4.6
		M	97	76	55	...	79	3.2
		F	97	77	62	...	84	7.6
	1983							
		MF	97	76	58	...	81	6.6
		M	98	76	54	...	79	4.8
		F	97	77	64	...	85	10.3
	1984							
		MF	97	76	58	...	81	7.8
		M	97	75	52	...	78	4.8
		F	97	77	65	...	85	13.9
VIET-NAM	1975			(6–10)		(11–16)	(6–16)	(20–24)
		MF	107	...	39	...	72	2.1
		M	106	...	38	...	71	2.6
		F	108	...	41	...	73	1.6

COUNTRY / PAYS / PAIS	YEAR / ANNEE / AÑO	SEX / SEXE / SEXO	ENROLMENT RATIOS / TAUX D'INSCRIPTION / TASAS DE ESCOLARIZACION					
			FIRST LEVEL / PREMIER DEGRE / PRIMER GRADO		SECOND LEVEL / SECOND DEGRE / SEGUNDO GRADO		1ST + 2ND LEVELS / 1ER + 2ND DEGRE / 1ER + 2DO GRADO	3RD LEVEL / 3EME DEGRE / 3ER GRADO
			GROSS / BRUT / BRUTA	NET / NET / NETA	GROSS / BRUT / BRUTA	NET / NET / NETA	GROSS / BRUT / BRUTA	GROSS / BRUT / BRUTA
VIET-NAM (CONT)	1980			(6–10)		(11–17)	(6–17)	(20–24)
		MF	111	96	40	...	70	2.2
		M	114	...	42	...	72	3.4
		F	107	...	38	...	67	1.0
YEMEN	1975			(7–12)		(13–18)	(7–18)	(20–24)
		MF	29	22	4	3	19	0.7
		M	50	38	8	6	34	1.6
		F	7	5	1	1	4	0.1
	1980							
		MF	46	...	5	...	27	1.2
		M	80	...	8	...	47	2.5
		F	12	...	1	...	7	0.2
	1981							
		MF	53	...	6	...	32	...
		M	90	...	10	...	54	...
		F	15	...	2	...	9	...
	1982							
		MF	62	...	7	...	37	...
		M	105	...	13	...	64	...
		F	18	...	2	...	11	...
	1983							
		MF	67	...	10	...	42	...
		M	112	...	17	...	69	...
		F	22	...	3	...	13	...
EUROPE								
ALBANIA	1980			(6–13)		(14–17)	(6–17)	(20–24)
		MF	106	...	65	...	93	5.4
		M	109	...	71	...	97	5.3
		F	103	...	60	...	89	5.4
	1981							
		MF	104	...	60	...	90	...
		M	106	...	65	...	93	...
		F	101	...	55	...	86	...
	1982							
		MF	100	...	59	...	87	6.0
		M	100	...	63	...	89	6.2
		F	99	...	55	...	85	5.9
	1983							
		MF	98	...	62	...	87	6.6
		M	99	...	66	...	89	7.0
		F	97	...	58	...	84	6.3
	1984							
		MF	98	...	63	...	87	7.0
		M	100	...	67	...	90	7.6
		F	96	...	58	...	84	6.5
AUSTRIA	1975			(6– 9)		(10–17)	(6–17)	(20–24)
		MF	102	89	74	71	83	18.9
		M	102	...	73	...	82	23.2
		F	101	...	76	...	84	14.4
	1980							
		MF	98	87	74	...	81	23.6
		M	99	86	73	...	80	26.9
		F	98	88	75	...	82	20.3
	1981							
		MF	99	...	73	...	80	23.6
		M	99	...	71	...	79	26.4
		F	98	...	75	...	82	20.7
	1982							
		MF	98	...	74	...	81	23.8
		M	99	...	73	...	80	26.2
		F	98	...	76	...	82	21.4
	1983							
		MF	98	...	74	...	81	24.5
		M	98	...	73	...	80	26.7
		F	97	...	76	...	82	22.2

COUNTRY / PAYS / PAIS	YEAR / ANNEE / AÑO	SEX / SEXE / SEXO	ENROLMENT RATIOS / TAUX D'INSCRIPTION / TASAS DE ESCOLARIZACION					
			FIRST LEVEL / PREMIER DEGRE / PRIMER GRADO		SECOND LEVEL / SECOND DEGRE / SEGUNDO GRADO		1ST + 2ND LEVELS / 1ER + 2ND DEGRE / 1ER + 2DO GRADO	3RD LEVEL / 3EME DEGRE / 3ER GRADO
			GROSS / BRUT / BRUTA	NET / NET / NETA	GROSS / BRUT / BRUTA	NET / NET / NETA	GROSS / BRUT / BRUTA	GROSS / BRUT / BRUTA
AUSTRIA (CONT)	1984							
		MF	97	86	76	...	82	25.9
		M	97	86	73	...	80	28.0
		F	97	86	79	...	84	23.6
BELGIUM	1975			(6–11)		(12–17)	(6–17)	(20–24)
		MF	102	...	84	...	92	22.7
		M	102	...	84	...	92	26.0
		F	102	...	83	...	92	19.2
	1980							
		MF	101	97	86	...	93	26.3
		M	102	97	83	...	92	29.2
		F	101	98	88	...	94	23.2
	1981							
		MF	101	98	87	83	93	26.8
		M	101	97	84	82	92	29.1
		F	100	98	89	85	94	24.3
	1982							
		MF	98	94	87	...	92	27.4
		M	97	94	84	...	91	29.3
		F	98	95	90	...	94	25.3
	1983							
		MF	97	94	89	84	92	28.0
		M	96	93	86	83	91	29.7
		F	97	94	91	86	94	26.3
	1984							
		MF	98	93	91	86	94	30.6
		M	98	92	88	84	93	32.8
		F	99	94	94	88	96	28.3
BULGARIA	1975			(7–14)		(15–17)	(7–17)	(20–24)
		MF	99	96	89	68	96	19.2
		M	99	96	...	...	...	16.2
		F	99	97	...	...	...	22.2
	1980							
		MF	98	96	84	...	94	16.1
		M	98	96	85	...	95	13.8
		F	98	96	84	...	94	18.5
	1981							
		MF	100	98	82	69	96	15.6
		M	100	98	83	69	96	14.0
		F	100	98	82	69	95	17.2
	1982							
		MF	102	99	82	69	97	15.3
		M	102	99	83	70	97	14.0
		F	102	99	82	69	96	16.7
	1983							
		MF	102	98	86	74	98	15.8
		M	102	98	85	73	98	14.3
		F	101	98	86	74	97	17.4
	1984							
		MF	102	97	90	78	99	16.8
		M	102	98	90	78	99	15.1
		F	101	97	91	78	98	18.5
CZECHOSLOVAKIA	1975			(6–14)		(15–18)	(6–18)	(20–24)
		MF	96	...	35	...	77	12.1
		M	96	...	27	...	74	14.1
		F	97	...	44	...	80	9.9
	1980							
		MF	92	...	44	...	78	17.1
		M	91	...	33	...	74	19.5
		F	92	...	56	...	82	14.5
	1981							
		MF	90	...	46	...	77	17.6
		M	89	...	34	...	74	20.0
		F	91	...	58	...	81	15.1

COUNTRY / PAYS / PAIS	YEAR / ANNEE / AÑO	SEX / SEXE / SEXO	ENROLMENT RATIOS / TAUX D'INSCRIPTION / TASAS DE ESCOLARIZACION — FIRST LEVEL / PREMIER DEGRE / PRIMER GRADO: GROSS / BRUT / BRUTA	FIRST LEVEL: NET / NET / NETA	SECOND LEVEL / SECOND DEGRE / SEGUNDO GRADO: GROSS / BRUT / BRUTA	SECOND LEVEL: NET / NET / NETA	1ST + 2ND LEVELS / 1ER + 2ND DEGRE / 1ER + 2DO GRADO: GROSS / BRUT / BRUTA	3RD LEVEL / 3EME DEGRE / 3ER GRADO: GROSS / BRUT / BRUTA
CZECHOSLOVAKIA (CONT)	1982	MF	89	...	46	...	77	17.3
		M	88	...	34	...	73	19.4
		F	89	...	58	...	81	15.0
	1983	MF	88	...	44	...	76	16.4
		M	87	...	33	...	72	18.4
		F	88	...	57	...	80	14.4
	1984	MF	87	...	42	...	75	15.9
		M	87	...	31	...	72	17.9
		F	88	...	54	...	79	13.8
DENMARK	1975			(6–11)		(12–17)	(6–17)	(20–24)
		MF	104	...	80	...	92	29.4
		M	...	...	...	...	...	32.0
		F	...	...	...	...	...	26.7
	1980	MF	97	...	105	...	101	28.6
		M	97	...	105	...	101	28.6
		F	97	...	104	...	101	28.6
	1981	MF	98	...	105	...	102	28.4
		M	98	...	106	...	102	28.0
		F	98	...	105	...	102	28.8
	1982	MF	100	...	105	77	103	29.0
		M	100	...	106	76	103	29.0
		F	100	...	105	79	103	29.0
	1983	MF	101	...	104	75	103	29.2
		M	101	...	105	74	103	29.0
		F	101	...	104	76	103	29.3
	1984	MF	101	...	...	...	...	...
FINLAND‡	1975			(7–12)		(13–18)	(7–18)	(20–24)
		MF	102	...	89	...	95	27.2
		M	103	...	83	...	93	28.0
		F	101	...	94	...	97	26.3
	1980	MF	96	...	98	...	97	32.1
		M	97	...	93	...	95	32.4
		F	96	...	104	...	100	31.7
	1981	MF	97	...	99	...	98	32.5
		M	97	...	93	...	95	32.5
		F	97	...	104	...	101	32.5
	1982	MF	100	...	98	...	99	33.1
		M	100	...	93	...	96	32.9
		F	99	...	104	...	102	33.4
	1983	MF	102	...	101	...	101	30.9
		M	102	...	93	...	97	31.7
		F	102	...	108	...	105	30.2
	1984	MF	103	...	101	...	102	30.6
		M	104	...	94	...	98	...
		F	103	...	109	...	106	...
FRANCE	1975			(6–10)		(11–17)	(6–17)	(20–24)
		MF	109	98	82	76	93	24.5
		M	...	...	...	...	...	25.1
		F	...	...	...	...	...	23.8
	1980	MF	111	100	85	79	96	25.5
		M	112	...	77	...	92	...
		F	111	...	93	...	100	...

COUNTRY / PAYS / PAIS	YEAR / ANNEE / AÑO	SEX / SEXE / SEXO	FIRST LEVEL / PREMIER DEGRE / PRIMER GRADO: GROSS / BRUT / BRUTA	FIRST LEVEL / PREMIER DEGRE / PRIMER GRADO: NET / NET / NETA	SECOND LEVEL / SECOND DEGRE / SEGUNDO GRADO: GROSS / BRUT / BRUTA	SECOND LEVEL / SECOND DEGRE / SEGUNDO GRADO: NET / NET / NETA	1ST + 2ND LEVELS / 1ER + 2ND DEGRE / 1ER + 2DO GRADO: GROSS / BRUT / BRUTA	3RD LEVEL / 3EME DEGRE / 3ER GRADO: GROSS / BRUT / BRUTA
FRANCE (CONT)	1981							
		MF	110	99	86	79	96	27.2
		M	111	99	81	76	94	27.6
		F	109	99	90	83	98	26.8
	1982							
		MF	109	97	88	81	96	27.8
		M	110	97	83	77	94	27.7
		F	108	97	92	85	98	27.8
	1983							
		MF	108	...	90	...	97	26.8
		M	109	...	84	...	94	...
		F	107	...	96	...	100	...
GERMAN DEMOCRATIC REPUBLIC	1975			(7–16)		(17–18)	(7–18)	(20–24)
		MF	94	...	89	...	93	29.5
		M	...	...	...	...	...	25.1
		F	...	...	...	...	...	34.0
	1980			(6–15)		(16–17)	(6–17)	(20–24)
		MF	96	...	88	...	94	30.3
		M	95	...	90	...	94	24.8
		F	97	...	85	...	95	36.1
	1981							
		MF	96	...	88	...	94	30.1
		M	94	...	90	...	93	24.4
		F	97	...	85	...	95	36.2
	1982							
		MF	95	...	88	...	93	29.4
		M	94	...	90	...	93	23.7
		F	96	...	85	...	94	35.4
	1983							
		MF	97	...	87	...	95	30.9
		M	97	...	...	...	...	26.8
		F	98	...	...	...	...	35.2
	1984							
		MF	98	...	87	...	95	30.3
		M	97	...	...	...	...	26.6
		F	98	...	...	...	...	34.3
GERMANY, FEDERAL REPUBLIC OF‡	1975			(6– 9)		(10–18)	(6–18)	(20–24)
		MF	...	...	...	...	80	24.5
		M	...	...	...	...	79	29.8
		F	...	...	...	...	81	19.0
	1980							
		MF	...	...	...	...	79	26.2
		M	...	...	...	...	77	29.9
		F	...	...	...	...	80	22.3
	1981							
		MF	...	...	...	...	80	27.6
		M	...	...	...	...	79	31.0
		F	...	...	...	...	81	24.0
	1982							
		MF	...	...	...	...	80	28.4
		M	...	...	...	...	79	31.8
		F	...	...	...	...	81	24.9
	1983							
		MF	99	...	74	...	80	29.0
		M	100	...	72	...	78	32.6
		F	99	...	76	...	81	25.2
	1984							
		MF	...	...	...	...	...	29.1
		M	...	...	...	...	...	32.8
		F	...	...	...	...	...	25.2
GREECE	1975			(6–11)		(12–17)	(6–17)	(20–24)
		MF	104	97	78	64	92	18.3
		M	105	97	87	68	96	22.2
		F	104	97	69	59	87	14.2

COUNTRY / PAYS / PAIS	YEAR / ANNEE / AÑO	SEX / SEXE / SEXO	ENROLMENT RATIOS / TAUX D'INSCRIPTION / TASAS DE ESCOLARIZACION — FIRST LEVEL / PREMIER DEGRE / PRIMER GRADO: GROSS / BRUT / BRUTA	FIRST LEVEL: NET / NET / NETA	SECOND LEVEL / SECOND DEGRE / SEGUNDO GRADO: GROSS / BRUT / BRUTA	SECOND LEVEL: NET / NET / NETA	1ST + 2ND LEVELS / 1ER + 2ND DEGRE / 1ER + 2DO GRADO: GROSS / BRUT / BRUTA	3RD LEVEL / 3EME DEGRE / 3ER GRADO: GROSS / BRUT / BRUTA
GREECE (CONT)	1980							
		MF	103	96	81	...	92	17.4
		M	103	96	85	...	94	20.0
		F	103	97	77	...	89	14.6
	1981							
		MF	104	89	84	76	94	17.7
		M	105	89	88	77	96	19.8
		F	104	90	81	75	92	15.4
	1982							
		MF	106	91	85	...	95	...
		M	106	91	89	...	97	...
		F	106	91	82	...	93	...
HUNGARY	1975			(6–13)		(14–17)	(6–17)	(20–24)
		MF	99	...	63	...	86	11.7
		M	99	...	67	...	87	11.8
		F	99	...	58	...	84	11.5
	1980							
		MF	96	95	69	...	88	12.9
		M	96	94	72	...	89	12.7
		F	97	95	67	...	88	13.1
	1981							
		MF	99	97	71	...	90	13.7
		M	98	96	72	...	90	13.1
		F	99	97	70	...	90	14.2
	1982							
		MF	99	97	73	...	91	14.1
		M	99	96	73	...	91	13.4
		F	99	98	72	...	91	14.8
	1983							
		MF	99	97	73	71	91	14.7
		M	99	97	73	71	91	13.6
		F	99	98	72	71	91	15.8
	1984							
		MF	99	97	73	71	91	15.2
		M	98	96	73	70	91	14.0
		F	99	98	73	71	91	16.6
ICELAND	1975			(7–12)		(13–19)	(7–19)	(20–24)
		MF	100	...	80	...	89	15.7
		M	98	...	85	...	91	19.1
		F	102	...	75	...	87	12.0
	1980							
		MF	99	...	86	...	92	24.3
		M	...	...	89	...	...	28.4
		F	...	...	82	...	...	19.9
	1981							
		MF	99	...	87	...	92	20.0
		M	...	...	...	...	...	19.5
		F	...	...	...	...	...	20.6
	1982							
		MF	99	...	88	...	93	22.8
		M	97	...	91	...	94	21.8
		F	101	...	85	...	92	23.7
	1983							
		MF	101	...	90	...	95	23.2
		M	99	...	94	...	97	21.7
		F	102	...	86	...	93	24.8
	1984							
		MF	100	...	93	...	96	22.8
IRELAND	1975			(6–11)		(12–16)	(6–16)	(20–24)
		MF	103	91	86	75	96	18.8
		M	103	91	82	72	94	24.1
		F	103	92	91	77	98	13.2
	1980							
		MF	100	90	90	78	95	20.4
		M	100	89	85	75	93	23.8
		F	100	91	95	80	98	16.9

COUNTRY / PAYS / PAIS	YEAR / ANNEE / AÑO	SEX / SEXE / SEXO	ENROLMENT RATIOS / TAUX D'INSCRIPTION / TASAS DE ESCOLARIZACION — FIRST LEVEL / PREMIER DEGRE / PRIMER GRADO: GROSS / BRUT / BRUTA	FIRST LEVEL / PREMIER DEGRE / PRIMER GRADO: NET / NET / NETA	SECOND LEVEL / SECOND DEGRE / SEGUNDO GRADO: GROSS / BRUT / BRUTA	SECOND LEVEL / SECOND DEGRE / SEGUNDO GRADO: NET / NET / NETA	1ST + 2ND LEVELS / 1ER + 2ND DEGRE / 1ER + 2DO GRADO: GROSS / BRUT / BRUTA	3RD LEVEL / 3EME DEGRE / 3ER GRADO: GROSS / BRUT / BRUTA
IRELAND (CONT)	1981							
		MF	99	89	92	78	96	21.5
		M	99	89	87	76	94	25.2
		F	100	90	97	81	99	17.6
	1982							
		MF	100	89	93	79	97	22.1
		M	100	89	88	77	95	25.6
		F	100	90	98	81	99	18.6
ITALY	1975			(6–10)		(11–18)	(6–18)	(20–24)
		MF	106	98	70	66	84	25.1
		M	107	98	74	68	87	30.1
		F	106	99	66	64	82	19.9
	1980							
		MF	101	...	72	...	83	27.2
		M	101	...	73	...	83	30.7
		F	100	...	71	...	82	23.6
	1981							
		MF	100	...	72	...	83	25.7
		M	100	...	73	...	83	28.9
		F	100	...	71	...	82	22.4
	1982							
		MF	100	...	73	...	83	25.4
		M	100	...	73	...	83	27.8
		F	100	...	72	...	82	22.8
	1983							
		MF	99	...	73	...	83	25.4
		M	99	...	74	...	83	27.7
		F	99	...	73	...	82	23.1
	1984							
		MF	99	...	74	...	83	26.3
		M	...	...	...	...	...	28.2
		F	...	...	...	...	...	24.2
LUXEMBOURG‡	1975			(6–11)		(12–18)	(6–18)	(20–24)
		MF	...	...	59	56	...	1.9
		M	...	...	59	55	...	2.1
		F	...	...	59	56	...	1.6
	1980							
		MF	...	...	62	56	...	2.6
		M	...	...	61	53	...	3.3
		F	...	...	63	59	...	1.8
	1981							
		MF	...	...	63	...	...	2.4
		M	...	...	62	...	...	3.1
		F	...	...	65	...	...	1.7
	1982							
		MF	...	...	64	59	...	3.2
		M	...	...	63	58	...	4.4
		F	...	...	66	61	...	2.1
	1983							
		MF	...	...	68	...	...	3.4
		M	...	...	69	...	...	4.3
		F	...	...	67	...	...	2.5
MALTA	1975			(5–10)		(11–17)	(5–17)	(20–24)
		MF	94	84	75	71	83	4.6
		M	96	85	81	76	88	6.8
		F	92	82	69	67	79	2.5
	1980							
		MF	100	87	66	62	81	2.7
		M	104	90	71	65	86	4.1
		F	96	83	60	59	77	1.3
	1981							
		MF	98	87	71	67	84	2.7
		M	100	89	77	70	88	4.3
		F	95	86	65	64	79	1.2

COUNTRY / PAYS / PAIS	YEAR / ANNEE / AÑO	SEX / SEXE / SEXO	ENROLMENT RATIOS / TAUX D'INSCRIPTION / TASAS DE ESCOLARIZACION — FIRST LEVEL / PREMIER DEGRE / PRIMER GRADO: GROSS / BRUT / BRUTA	FIRST LEVEL: NET / NET / NETA	SECOND LEVEL / SECOND DEGRE / SEGUNDO GRADO: GROSS / BRUT / BRUTA	SECOND LEVEL: NET / NET / NETA	1ST + 2ND LEVELS / 1ER + 2ND DEGRE / 1ER + 2DO GRADO: GROSS / BRUT / BRUTA	3RD LEVEL / 3EME DEGRE / 3ER GRADO: GROSS / BRUT / BRUTA
MALTA (CONT)	1982							
		MF	95	86	74	69	84	3.0
		M	98	88	80	72	89	4.6
		F	92	83	68	66	80	1.3
	1983							
		MF	95	87	76	71	86	4.1
		M	97	89	83	75	90	5.9
		F	94	85	69	68	81	2.1
	1984							
		MF	...	...	...	...	...	4.4
		M	...	...	...	...	...	5.9
		F	...	...	...	...	...	2.7
NETHERLANDS	1975			(6–11)		(12–17)	(6–17)	(20–24)
		MF	98	91	88	79	93	25.2
		M	98	90	92	80	95	33.3
		F	99	92	84	79	91	16.8
	1980							
		MF	100	93	92	81	96	30.0
		M	99	91	95	80	97	35.5
		F	101	94	90	82	95	24.3
	1981							
		MF	99	91	94	...	96	30.5
		M	98	89	96	...	97	35.1
		F	100	92	93	...	96	25.7
	1982							
		MF	97	89	97	83	97	30.7
		M	96	87	99	82	98	34.8
		F	98	90	96	85	97	26.4
	1983							
		MF	95	87	101	85	98	30.8
		M	94	86	103	84	99	34.8
		F	96	89	99	86	98	26.6
	1984							
		MF	95	87	102	...	98	31.4
		M	94	85	103	...	99	35.5
		F	96	88	100	...	98	27.1
NORWAY	1975			(7–12)		(13–18)	(7–18)	(20–24)
		MF	101	100	88	79	95	22.1
		M	101	100	88	79	95	26.8
		F	101	100	88	79	95	17.1
	1980							
		MF	100	98	94	84	97	25.6
		M	100	98	92	82	96	26.1
		F	100	99	96	86	98	25.0
	1981							
		MF	99	98	95	84	97	26.5
		M	99	98	92	82	95	26.6
		F	99	99	98	86	99	26.4
	1982							
		MF	98	...	97	...	98	28.4
		M	98	...	95	...	96	28.3
		F	99	...	99	...	99	28.4
	1983							
		MF	98	...	...	...	...	29.3
		M	...	...	...	...	...	28.9
		F	...	...	...	...	...	29.7
	1984							
		MF	97	...	...	...	...	...
POLAND	1975			(7–14)		(15–18)	(7–18)	(20–24)
		MF	100	...	72	...	89	16.8
		M	102	...	70	...	89	15.2
		F	99	...	74	...	89	18.5
	1980							
		MF	100	98	77	70	92	17.6
		M	100	98	75	68	91	15.3
		F	99	98	80	74	92	20.1

COUNTRY / PAYS / PAIS	YEAR / ANNEE / AÑO	SEX / SEXE / SEXO	FIRST LEVEL / PREMIER DEGRE / PRIMER GRADO: GROSS / BRUT / BRUTA	FIRST LEVEL: NET / NET / NETA	SECOND LEVEL / SECOND DEGRE / SEGUNDO GRADO: GROSS / BRUT / BRUTA	SECOND LEVEL: NET / NET / NETA	1ST + 2ND LEVELS / 1ER + 2ND DEGRE / 1ER + 2DO GRADO: GROSS / BRUT / BRUTA	3RD LEVEL / 3EME DEGRE / 3ER GRADO: GROSS / BRUT / BRUTA
POLAND (CONT)	1981	MF	100	98	76	70	92	16.8
		M	100	98	74	67	92	14.5
		F	99	98	79	73	92	19.2
	1982	MF	100	99	75	69	92	15.8
		M	101	99	73	66	92	13.9
		F	99	98	78	72	92	17.9
	1983	MF	101	99	75	69	93	15.9
		M	101	99	73	66	92	13.9
		F	100	99	79	73	93	18.0
	1984	MF	101	99	77	72	94	15.9
		M	102	99	75	68	93	13.8
		F	100	99	80	75	94	18.1
PORTUGAL	1975			(6–11)		(12–16)	(6–16)	(20–24)
		MF	113	87	53	28	86	10.5
		M	114	87	53	27	87	11.7
		F	111	88	52	29	85	9.3
	1980			(6–11)		(12–17)	(6–17)	(20–24)
		MF	122	97	37	...	78	11.1
		M	125	98	35	...	78	11.4
		F	119	97	39	...	78	10.8
	1981	MF	121	...	37	...	78	11.2
		M	121	...	35	...	77	11.2
		F	121	...	40	...	79	11.3
	1982	MF	121	81	43	...	81	11.5
		M	122	82	40	...	80	11.3
		F	121	80	46	...	83	11.6
	1983	MF	120	97	47	...	83	...
		M	120	98	43	...	81	...
		F	119	96	51	...	85	...
ROMANIA	1975			(6–13)		(14–17)	(6–17)	(20–24)
		MF	107	...	65	...	93	9.2
		M	108	...	64	...	93	9.9
		F	107	...	66	...	93	8.4
	1980	MF	102	...	71	...	93	11.0
		M	102	...	73	...	94	12.4
		F	101	...	69	...	92	9.5
	1981	MF	104	...	67	...	93	11.3
		M	104	...	67	...	93	12.7
		F	104	...	67	...	93	9.9
	1982	MF	100	...	71	...	91	11.4
		M	101	...	69	...	91	12.8
		F	100	...	73	...	91	9.9
	1983	MF	99	...	72	...	90	11.7
		M	99	...	71	...	90	13.0
		F	99	...	74	...	90	10.3
	1984	MF	98	...	73	...	89	11.7
		M	99	...	72	...	89	12.9
		F	98	...	74	...	90	10.4
SPAIN	1975			(6–10)		(11–17)	(6–17)	(20–24)
		MF	111	100	73	63	89	20.4
		M	111	100	74	65	90	26.2
		F	111	100	71	61	89	14.6

COUNTRY / PAYS / PAIS	YEAR / ANNEE / AÑO	SEX / SEXE / SEXO	ENROLMENT RATIOS / TAUX D'INSCRIPTION / TASAS DE ESCOLARIZACION					
			FIRST LEVEL / PREMIER DEGRE / PRIMER GRADO		SECOND LEVEL / SECOND DEGRE / SEGUNDO GRADO		1ST + 2ND LEVELS / 1ER + 2ND DEGRE / 1ER + 2DO GRADO	3RD LEVEL / 3EME DEGRE / 3ER GRADO
			GROSS BRUT BRUTA	NET NET NETA	GROSS BRUT BRUTA	NET NET NETA	GROSS BRUT BRUTA	GROSS BRUT BRUTA
SPAIN (CONT)	1980	MF	109	100	87	74	96	23.7
		M	110	100	86	74	96	26.3
		F	109	100	89	75	97	21.1
	1981	MF	110	...	92	...	100	24.0
		M	111	...	91	...	99	26.0
		F	109	...	94	...	100	22.0
	1982	MF	109	100	91	75	99	24.4
		M	110	100	88	75	97	25.7
		F	109	100	94	75	100	23.1
	1983	MF	108	100	89	...	97	25.8
		M	108	100	88	...	96	26.4
		F	107	100	91	...	98	25.2
SWEDEN	1975		(7–12)		(13–18)		(7–18)	(20–24)
		MF	101	100	78	...	90	28.8
		M	101	100	75	...	88	33.7
		F	102	100	82	...	92	23.7
	1980	MF	97	...	88	...	92	36.6
		M	96	...	83	...	90	...
		F	97	...	93	...	95	...
	1981	MF	97	96	87	81	92	36.8
		M	97	96	81	78	89	38.9
		F	97	96	92	84	94	34.7
	1982	MF	98	...	86	...	91	38.5
		M	97	...	81	...	89	...
		F	98	...	91	...	94	...
	1983	MF	98	...	85	...	91	39.2
		M	98	...	80	...	89	41.0
		F	98	...	90	...	94	37.4
	1984	MF	98	...	83	...	90	38.2
		M	...	...	79	...	...	...
		F	...	...	88	...	...	...
SWITZERLAND‡	1975							(20–24)
		MF	...	...	...	...	...	13.6
		M	...	...	...	...	...	19.5
		F	...	...	...	...	...	7.9
	1980	MF	...	...	...	...	...	18.2
		M	...	...	...	...	...	25.5
		F	...	...	...	...	...	11.0
	1981	MF	...	...	...	...	...	18.6
		M	...	...	...	...	...	25.5
		F	...	...	...	...	...	11.7
	1982	MF	...	...	...	...	...	18.7
		M	...	...	...	...	...	25.1
		F	...	...	...	...	...	12.2
	1983	MF	...	...	...	...	...	19.4
		M	...	...	...	...	...	25.7
		F	...	...	...	...	...	12.9
	1984	MF	...	...	...	...	...	21.2
		M	...	...	...	...	...	28.3
		F	...	...	...	...	...	13.8

COUNTRY / PAYS / PAIS	YEAR / ANNEE / AÑO	SEX / SEXE / SEXO	ENROLMENT RATIOS / TAUX D'INSCRIPTION / TASAS DE ESCOLARIZACION — FIRST LEVEL / PREMIER DEGRE / PRIMER GRADO		SECOND LEVEL / SECOND DEGRE / SEGUNDO GRADO		1ST + 2ND LEVELS / 1ER + 2ND DEGRE / 1ER + 2DO GRADO	3RD LEVEL / 3EME DEGRE / 3ER GRADO
			GROSS / BRUT / BRUTA	NET / NET / NETA	GROSS / BRUT / BRUTA	NET / NET / NETA	GROSS / BRUT / BRUTA	GROSS / BRUT / BRUTA
UNITED KINGDOM	1975			(5–10)		(11–17)	(5–17)	(20–24)
		MF	105	98	83	78	93	18.9
		M	105	98	82	77	93	23.6
		F	106	98	83	78	94	13.9
	1980	MF	104	96	84	80	92	20.2
		M	103	96	83	78	92	25.1
		F	104	97	85	81	93	15.1
	1981	MF	102	95	85	80	92	20.4
		M	102	95	84	79	91	25.0
		F	103	95	86	82	93	15.6
	1982	MF	101	93	86	81	92	20.3
		M	101	94	84	80	91	24.4
		F	101	93	87	83	93	16.0
	1983	MF	...	...	...	...	...	20.3
		M	...	...	...	...	...	24.2
		F	...	...	...	...	...	16.2
YUGOSLAVIA	1975			(7–10)		(11–18)	(7–18)	(20–24)
		MF	103	79	76	71	84	20.0
		M	104	...	79	...	87	23.5
		F	101	...	72	...	82	16.3
	1980	MF	100	80	83	76	89	21.8
		M	100	...	86	...	91	23.3
		F	99	...	80	...	86	20.2
	1981	MF	101	...	82	...	88	21.5
		M	101	...	85	...	90	22.9
		F	100	...	79	...	86	20.0
	1982	MF	101	...	83	...	89	20.8
		M	101	...	85	...	90	22.3
		F	101	...	80	...	87	19.3
	1983	MF	100	...	82	...	88	20.2
		M	100	...	84	...	90	21.8
		F	100	...	80	...	87	18.6
	1984	MF	98	...	82	...	88	...
		M	98	...	84	...	89	...
		F	98	...	80	...	86	...
OCEANIA								
AUSTRALIA	1975			(6–11)		(12–16)	(6–16)	(20–24)
		MF	107	96	87	79	98	24.0
		M	107	96	87	79	98	28.0
		F	107	97	87	80	98	19.8
	1980	MF	109	100	84	76	98	25.4
		M	109	100	83	75	97	27.3
		F	109	100	86	78	98	23.4
	1981	MF	109	100	84	77	98	25.9
		M	109	100	83	76	97	27.9
		F	109	100	86	78	98	23.8
	1982	MF	109	100	86	79	98	25.9
		M	109	100	85	78	98	27.6
		F	109	100	88	80	99	24.2
	1983	MF	108	99	90	82	100	26.6
		M	108	99	89	81	99	28.0
		F	108	99	92	83	100	25.2

COUNTRY / PAYS / PAIS	YEAR / ANNEE / AÑO	SEX / SEXE / SEXO	ENROLMENT RATIOS / TAUX D'INSCRIPTION / TASAS DE ESCOLARIZACION — FIRST LEVEL / PREMIER DEGRE / PRIMER GRADO: GROSS / BRUT / BRUTA	FIRST LEVEL: NET / NET / NETA	SECOND LEVEL / SECOND DEGRE / SEGUNDO GRADO: GROSS / BRUT / BRUTA	SECOND LEVEL: NET / NET / NETA	1ST + 2ND LEVELS / 1ER + 2ND DEGRE / 1ER + 2DO GRADO: GROSS / BRUT / BRUTA	3RD LEVEL / 3EME DEGRE / 3ER GRADO: GROSS / BRUT / BRUTA
AUSTRALIA (CONT)	1984							
		MF	107	97	94	84	100	27.1
		M	107	97	92	83	100	28.3
		F	106	97	95	85	101	25.8
FIJI	1975			(6–11)		(12–17)	(6–17)	(20–24)
		MF	115	...	66	...	90	2.9
		M	115	...	65	...	90	4.2
		F	115	...	66	...	90	1.6
	1980							
		MF	112	100	76	...	94	2.7
		M	113	100	74	...	94	...
		F	111	100	78	...	95	...
	1981							
		MF	112	100	75	...	94	2.9
		M	113	100	73	...	93	3.7
		F	111	100	78	...	95	2.0
	1982							
		MF	111	...	77	...	94	3.3
	1983							
		MF	110	100	77	...	95	...
		M	111	100	75	...	94	...
		F	109	100	80	...	95	...
	1984							
		MF	110	100	78	...	95	...
		M	111	100	77	...	95	...
		F	109	100	79	...	95	...
NEW ZEALAND	1975			(5–10)		(11–17)	(5–17)	(20–24)
		MF	106	100	81	79	92	25.7
		M	107	100	80	79	92	31.8
		F	106	100	81	80	92	19.3
	1980							
		MF	109	100	82	...	94	28.1
		M	109	100	81	...	94	32.8
		F	109	100	83	...	94	23.3
	1981							
		MF	107	100	82	...	93	28.7
		M	108	100	81	...	93	32.8
		F	107	100	83	...	93	24.4
	1982							
		MF	107	100	82	...	93	28.5
		M	108	100	81	...	93	32.8
		F	106	100	84	...	94	24.0
	1983							
		MF	106	100	85	...	94	28.5
		M	107	100	84	...	94	32.5
		F	105	100	86	...	94	24.3
PAPUA NEW GUINEA	1975			(7–12)		(13–18)	(7–18)	(20–24)
		MF	57	...	12	...	37	2.5
		M	69	...	16	...	45	3.5
		F	44	...	7	...	27	1.4
	1980							
		MF	59	...	12	...	38	1.9
		M	66	...	15	...	43	2.8
		F	51	...	8	...	32	0.9
	1981							
		MF	58	...	12	...	37	...
		M	65	...	15	...	42	...
		F	51	...	8	...	32	...
	1982							
		MF	60	...	11	...	38	1.6
		M	66	...	14	...	42	2.3
		F	53	...	8	...	33	0.8
	1983							
		MF	...	...	...	...	...	1.7
		M	...	...	...	...	...	2.4
		F	...	...	...	...	...	0.9

COUNTRY / PAYS / PAIS	YEAR / ANNEE / AÑO	SEX / SEXE / SEXO	FIRST LEVEL / PREMIER DEGRE / PRIMER GRADO: GROSS / BRUT / BRUTA	FIRST LEVEL: NET / NET / NETA	SECOND LEVEL / SECOND DEGRE / SEGUNDO GRADO: GROSS / BRUT / BRUTA	SECOND LEVEL: NET / NET / NETA	1ST + 2ND LEVELS / 1ER + 2ND DEGRE / 1ER + 2DO GRADO: GROSS / BRUT / BRUTA	3RD LEVEL / 3EME DEGRE / 3ER GRADO: GROSS / BRUT / BRUTA
PAPUA NEW GUINEA (CONT)	1984	MF	...	...	...	...	...	2.1
		M	...	...	...	...	...	2.9
		F	...	...	...	...	...	1.0
U.S.S.R.								
U.S.S.R.	1975			(7-11)		(12-16)	(7-16)	(20-24)
		MF	97	...	92	...	95	22.2
		M	...	...	...	...	...	21.6
		F	...	...	...	...	...	22.9
	1980	MF	106	...	93	...	100	21.2
	1981	MF	107	...	96	...	101	21.2
	1982	MF	107	...	97	...	102	21.3
	1983	MF	106	...	99	...	103	21.2
	1984	MF	106	...	100	...	103	21.4

This table presents enrolment ratios which are shown for countries and territories whose population exceed 250,000. For countries whose population is less than 250,000, population data by single years of age are not available. Demographic data have been obtained from the Population Division of the United Nations and the enrolment data used to calculate the gross enrolment ratios appear in tables 3.4, 3.7 and 3.11 of this *Yearbook*. Where enrolment data by age for the primary and secondary levels are also available, a net enrolment ratio has been calculated.

All ratios are expressed as percentages. The gross enrolment ratio is the total enrolment of all ages divided by the population of the specific age groups which correspond to the age groups of primary and secondary schooling. The net enrolment ratio has been calculated by using only that part of the enrolment which corresponds to the age groups of primary and secondary schooling.

These ratios have been calculated taking into account the differing national systems of education and the duration of schooling at the first and second levels. At the third level the figures for the population aged 20-24 have been used throughout.

The age groups used to calculate enrolment ratios for the primary and secondary levels shown in the table, have been determined according to the following rules:

1. For countries which have a single school system at eac[h] level, the age group is defined in conformity with the norma[l] entrance age and normal duration of general schooling at th[e] first and second levels as given in table 3.1.
2. In the case of countries with several systems of differing durations, the system followed by the majority of the pupils has been used.
3. The durations used are those which were operative in that year.

The age group for the combined ratio for the first and secon[d] levels is defined by taking a whole range covered by two ag[e] groups defined for the first and second levels.

Enrolment ratios for the second level are based on the tota[l] enrolment including general education, teacher-training an[d] technical and vocational education. Table 3.7 should be consulte[d] for more details on enrolment data. It should be emphasized tha[t] the gross enrolment ratio at the first and second levels include[s] pupils of all possible ages, whereas the population is limited to th[e] range of official school ages defined according to the above mentioned rules. Therefore, for countries with almost universa[l] education among the school-age population at the first level, th[e] gross enrolment ratio will exceed 100 if the actual age distributio[n] of pupils spreads over outside the official school ages.

Ce tableau présente des taux d'inscription pour les pays et territoires dont la population est supérieure à 250 000 habitants. Pour les pays dont la population est inférieure à 250 000 habitants, les données de population par années d'âge simple ne sont pas disponibles. Les données démographiques nous ont été fournies par la Division de la Population de l'Organisation des Nations Unies et les effectifs qui ont servi pour calculer les taux d'inscription bruts sont ceux qui figurent dans les tableaux 3.4, 3.7 et 3.11 de cet *Annuaire*. Lorsqu'on disposait des effectifs par âge des enseignements du premier et du second degré, on a calculé un taux d'inscription net. Tous les taux d'inscription sont exprimés en pourcentages. Le taux d'inscription brut pour les enseignements du premier et du second degré est le rapport entre les effectifs scolaires, quel que soit l'âge des élèves, et la population d'un groupe d'âge déterminé d'après la durée de la scolarité à chacun de ces niveaux. Le calcul du taux d'inscription net est basé seulement sur la partie des effectifs dont les groupes d'âge correspondent à la durée de la scolarité du premier et d[u] second degré. Les taux ont été calculés en tenant compte de l[a] diversité des systèmes nationaux d'enseignement et de la duré[e] des études du premier et du second degré. Pou[r] l'enseignement du troisième degré, on a pris en considération l[e] groupe d'âge 20-24. Les groupes d'âge utilisés pour calculer le[s] taux d'inscription relatifs aux enseignements du premier et d[u] second degré, qui figurent dans le tableau ont été déterminés e[n] accord avec les normes suivantes:

1. Pour les pays qui ont un type d'enseignement unique à tous les degrés, le groupe d'âge est déterminé conformément à l'âge normal d'admission et à la durée normale des études générales primaires et secondaires qui figurent dans le tableau 3.1.
2. Dans le cas des pays qui ont plusieurs types d'enseignement de durée différente, on a choisi le système qui s'applique à la majorité des élèves.

3. Les durées d'enseignement sont celles qui étaient en vigueur pour chaque année considérée.

Le groupe d'âge considéré pour le calcul du taux concernant la totalité du premier et du second degré est déterminé par les limites extrêmes de l'ensemble des deux groupes d'âge définis pour le premier et le second degré.

Les taux d'inscription pour le second degré sont fondés sur les effectifs globaux des trois types d'enseignement du second degré (général, normal, technique et professionnel). On trouvera des renseignements plus détaillés sur ces effectifs dans le tableau 3.7. Il convient de noter que le taux d'inscription brut dans le premier et le second degré comprend les élèves de tous les âges possibles alors que la population considérée est limitée aux groupes d'âge officiels déterminés selon les règles susmentionnées. Par conséquent, dans les pays où, pour le premier degré, la population d'âge scolaire est presque entièrement scolarisée, le taux d'inscription brut dépassera 100 si la répartition réelle des élèves par âge déborde les limites d'âge officielles.

Este cuadro presenta las tasas de escolarización para los países y territorios de una población superior a 250 000 habitantes. Para los países cuya población es inferior a 250 000 habitantes, no se dispone de los datos de población por años de edad simple. Los datos demográficos nos han sido procurados por la División de la Población de la Organización de las Naciones Unidas y la matrícula escolar que ha permitido el cálculo de las tasas de escolarización es la que figura en los cuadros 3.4, 3.7 y 3.11 del presente *Anuario.* Cuando se disponía de la matrícula por edad relativa a las enseñanzas de primer y de segundo grado, se ha calculado una tasa de escolarización neta. Todas las tasas de escolarización se expresan en porcentaje. La tasa de escolarización bruta para las enseñanzas de primer y de segundo grado es la relación entre la matrícula escolar, cualesquiera que sea la edad de los alumnos, y la población de un grupo de edad determinado según la duración de los estudios en cada uno de dichos niveles. El cálculo de la tasa de escolarización neta se basa únicamente en los efectivos cuyos grupos de edad corresponden a la duración de los estudios de primer y de segundo grado. Las tasas se han calculado teniendo en cuenta la diversidad de los sistemas de enseñanza y de la duración de los estudios de primer y de segundo grado. Para la enseñanza de tercer grado, se tomó en consideración el grupo de edad 20-24. Los grupos de edad utilizados para calcular las tasas de escolarización relativas a las enseñanzas de primer y de segundo grado que figuran en el cuadro han sido determinados como sigue:

1. Para los países que tienen un solo sistema de enseñanza para cada grado, el grupo de edad ha sido determinado de acuerdo con la edad normal de admisión y la duración normal de los estudios generales primario y secundario, tal como figuran en el cuadro 3.1.
2. En el caso de los países que tienen varios sistemas de enseñanza de diferente duración, se ha escogido el sistema que se aplica a la mayoría de los alumnos.
3. Las duraciones de escolaridad consideradas son las que estaban en vigor en los años correspondientes.

El grupo de edad considerado para el cálculo de la tasa combinada relativa al total de las enseñanzas de primer y de segundo grado queda determinado por los límites extremos del conjunto de los dos grupos de edad, definidos para ambos grados.

Las tasas de escolarización para el segundo grado se fundan en la matrícula global de los tres tipos de enseñanza (general, normal y técnica y profesional). Si se desean más detalles relativos a tales efectivos, puede consultarse el cuadro 3.7. Conviene señalar que la tasa de escolarización bruta comprende los alumnos de todas las edades para las enseñanzas de primer y de segundo grado, mientras que la población considerada se limita a los grupos de edad oficiales, determinados según las normas antes mencionadas. Por consiguiente, los países donde, para el primer grado, la población de edad escolar está casi completamente escolarizada, la tasa de escolarización bruta sobrepasará 100 si la distribución de los alumnos por edad desborda los límites de edad oficiales.

General note/Note générale/Nota general:

E--> The existence of inconsistencies either in the enrolment and/or population data have led to the suppression of the enrolment ratios for first and second level education.

FR-> L'existence d'inconsistances dans les données des effectifs scolaires et/ou de la population a entrainé la suppression des taux d'inscription des enseignements du premier et du second degré.

ESP> La existencia de inconsistencias en los efectivos y/o en los datos de población, ha provocado la supresión de las tasas de escolarización para las enseñanzas de primero y segundo grado.

AFRICA:

Congo:

E--> See general note.
FR-> Voir la note générale.
ESP> Véase la nota general.

Libyan Arab Jamahiriya:

E--> See general note.
FR-> Voir la note générale.
ESP> Véase la nota general.

Reunion:

E--> See general note.
FR-> Voir la note générale.
ESP> Véase la nota general.

Uganda:

E--> Government maintained and aided schools only.
FR-> Ecoles publiques et subventionnées seulement.
ESP> Escuelas públicas y subvencionadas solamente.

AMERICA, NORTH:

Guadeloupe:

E--> See general note.
FR-> Voir la note générale.
ESP> Véase la nota general.

Martinique:

E--> See general note.
FR-> Voir la note générale.
ESP> Véase la nota general.

ASIA:

Cyprus:

E--> Ratios are not shown since available data refer to only a subset of the population.

FR-> Les taux ne sont pas publiés car les effectifs scolaires ne correspondent qu'à une partie de la population.

ESP> No se publican las tasas porque la matrícula escolar sólo corresponde a una parte de la población.

Jordan:

E--> Ratios refer to the enrolment and corresponding population of the East Bank only.

FR-> Les taux ont été calculés en utilisant les effectifs scolaires et la population de la rive orientale seulement.

ESP> Las tasas se han calculado utilizando la matrícula escolar y la población de la orilla oriental solamente.

EUROPE:

Finland:

E--> The ratios include integrated special education.
FR-> Les taux d'inscription incluent l'éducation spéciale intégrée.
ESP> Las tasas incluyen la educación especial integrada.

Germany, Federal Republic of:

E--> For the years 1975 to 1982 the individual enrolment ratios for the first and second levels have been suppressed since they are distorted because of an overlap of durations for these two levels of education between states. The combined enrolment ratio, however, for these two levels of education does not suffer from this defect.

FR-> Pour les années 1975 à 1982 les taux d'inscription scolaire séparés pour les enseignements du premier et du second degré ont été supprimés, car ils se trouvaient faussés. En effet, il peut y avoir, d'une part un chevauchement entre les enseignements du premier et du second degré et d'autre part, la durée de l'enseignement de chacun de ces degrés peut varier d'un état à l'autre. Néanmoins, le taux combiné d'inscription du premier et du second degré n'est pas affecté pas ces différences.

ESP> Para los años 1975 a 1982 las tasas separadas de escolarización para las enseñanzas de primer y de segundo grado han sido suprimadas, ya que son deformadas. En efecto, puede haber imbricación entre las enseñanzas de primer y de segundo grado y existir diferencias de un Estado a otro en lo que se refiere a la duración de los estudios de estos dos grados de enseñanza. Sin embargo, la tasa combinada de enseñanza de

Germany, Federal Republic of: (Cont):
escolarización para las enseñanzas de primer y segundo grado no se va afectada por estas diferencias.

Luxembourg:

E--> The existence of inconsistencies either in the enrolment and/or population data have led to the suppression of the enrolment ratios for first level education.

FR-> L'existence d'inconsistances dans les données des effectifs scolaires et/ou de la population a entrainé la suppression des taux d'inscription de l'enseignement du premier degré.

ESP> La existencia de inconsistencias en los efectivos y/o en los datos de población, ha provocado la supresión de las tasas de escolarización para la enseñanza de primero grado.

Switzerland:

E--> No ratios are shown for either first or second level education because of the lack of a uniform education structure.

FR-> Aucun taux d'inscription n'est publié pour les enseignements du premier et du second degré en l'absence d'une structure uniforme d'enseignement.

ESP> No se ha publicado ninguna tasa de escolarización para las enseñanzas de primero y segundo grado debido a que no existe una estructura uniforme de la enseñanza.

3.3 Education preceding the first level: institutions, teachers and pupils

Enseignement précédant le premier degré: établissements, personnel enseignant et élèves

Enseñanza anterior al primer grado: establecimientos, personal docente y alumnos

PLEASE REFER TO EXPLANATORY TEXT AT END OF TABLE

PRIERE DE SE REFERER AU TEXTE EXPLICATIF A LA FIN DU TABLEAU

REFERIRSE AL TEXTO EXPLICATIVO AL FINAL DEL CUADRO

NUMBER OF COUNTRIES AND TERRITORIES PRESENTED IN THIS TABLE: 158

NOMBRE DE PAYS ET DE TERRITOIRES PRESENTES DANS CE TABLEAU: 158

NUMERO DE PAISES Y DE TERRITORIOS PRESENTADOS EN ESTE CUADRO: 158

COUNTRY PAYS PAIS	YEAR ANNEE AÑO	SCHOOLS ECOLES ESCUELAS	TEACHING STAFF PERSONNEL ENSEIGNANT PERSONAL DOCENTE			PUPILS ENROLLED ELEVES INSCRITS ALUMNOS MATRICULADOS			
			TOTAL	FEMALE FEMININ FEMENINO	% F	TOTAL	FEMALE FEMININ FEMENINO	% F	% PRIVATE PRIVE PRIVADA
		(1)	(2)	(3)	(4)	(5)	(6)	(7)	(8)
AFRICA									
ANGOLA‡	1980	...	...	...	...	390 512	157 803	40	...
	1981	...	...	...	...	342 316	163 478	48	...
	1982	...	...	...	...	292 457	...	...	...
BENIN	1980	92	174	...	...	3 779	...	...	–
	1981	128	246	129	52	4 925	2 160	44	–
	1982	140	267	147	55	5 667	2 538	45	–
	1983	174	344	181	53	7 655	3 386	44	–
	1984	209	438	234	53	9 895	4 348	44	–
BURKINA FASO	1975	...	19	19	100	497	239	48	87
	1980	...	...	...	...	732	319	44	90
	1981	14	...	...	...	727	308	42	90
	1982	...	...	...	...	641	278	43	88
	1984	...	...	...	...	1 805	865	48	80
BURUNDI‡	1975	...	10	...	...	594	292	49	...
	1980	...	15	15	100	1 004	498	50	...
	1981	...	23	23	100	1 049	539	51	31
	1983	15	29	29	100	1 333	624	47	39
	1984	15	25	25	100	1 446	691	48	31
CAMEROON	1975	...	...	...	...	21 752	10 558	49	42
	1980	436	1 512	1 494	99	40 574	19 920	49	49
	1981	...	...	...	...	39 861	...	...	48
	1982	431	1 715	1 710	100	41 038	19 467	47	46
	1983	500	2 037	2 037	100	55 490	27 415	49	45
	1984	567	2 357	2 348	100	67 688	34 253	51	46
CENTRAL AFRICAN REPUBLIC‡	1975	...	213	213	100	10 673	4 932	50	8
	1980	1	14	14	100	598	268	45	–
	1981	1	14	14	100	631	331	52	–
COMOROS	1980	600	600	200	33	17 778	8 598	48	–
CONGO	1980	36	334	334	100	3 498	1 736	50	–
	1981	35	405	405	100	3 607	1 782	49	–
	1982	42	482	482	100	4 567	2 295	50	–
	1984	44	543	543	100	5 369	2 593	48	–
COTE D'IVOIRE	1975	...	108	108	100	4 656	2 260	49	60
	1980	...	179	179	100	6 291	2 953	47	76
	1982	81	233	233	100	7 200	3 574	50	66
	1983	...	230	230	100	7 493	3 745	50	63
DJIBOUTI	1975	1	2	2	100	159	91	57	100
	1978	1	8	8	100	273	...	...	100
EGYPT	1975	...	...	...	...	41 948	20 719	49	100
	1980	433	...	...	...	74 921	36 809	49	94
	1981	465	1 731	1 701	98	76 732	37 677	49	93
	1982	503	...	...	...	84 539	41 226	49	91

3.3 Education preceding the first level
Enseignement précédant le premier degré
Enseñanza anterior al primer grado

COUNTRY / PAYS / PAIS	YEAR / ANNEE / AÑO	SCHOOLS / ECOLES / ESCUELAS	TEACHING STAFF / PERSONNEL ENSEIGNANT / PERSONAL DOCENTE			PUPILS ENROLLED / ELEVES INSCRITS / ALUMNOS MATRICULADOS			
			TOTAL	FEMALE / FEMININ / FEMENINO	% F	TOTAL	FEMALE / FEMININ / FEMENINO	% F	% PRIVATE / PRIVE / PRIVADA
		(1)	(2)	(3)	(4)	(5)	(6)	(7)	(8)
ETHIOPIA	1982	573	1 125	...	...	52 749	...	...	–
	1983	610	1 325	...	...	52 255	...	...	–
	1984	676	1 345	...	...	60 298	...	...	–
GHANA‡	1980	1 160	...	...	...	158 395	72 682	46	11
	1981	1 052	...	...	...	142 755	65 210	46	...
	1982	1 052	...	...	...	143 820	...	...	...
	1983	...	...	...	...	151 011	69 239	46	...
	1984	2 093	...	...	...	158 597	...	...	...
GUINEA-BISSAU	1976	...	...	...	...	29	...	...	...
	1980	6	46	45	98	459	225	49	...
	1981	8	46	43	93	479	224	47	...
	1982	19	70	70	100	1 645	640	39	...
	1983	8	39	36	92	708	377	53	...
KENYA	1982	*9 141	*11 594	...	...	*485 194	*237 148	*49	...
	1983	10 610	12 807	12 658	99	537 878	269 687	50	81
LIBYAN ARAB JAMAHIRIYA	1975	62	364	364	100	7 727	3 346	43	38
	1980	45	515	515	100	9 008	4 146	46	–
	1982	56	701	701	100	12 493	5 938	48	–
MAURITIUS	1975	283	358	356	99	9 233	4 498	49	100
	1980	349	453	451	100	11 704	5 712	49	100
	1981	365	524	521	99	11 105	5 423	49	100
	1982	340	543	532	98	10 617	5 210	49	100
MOROCCO‡	1975	...	...	...	...	375 567	...	...	...
	1980	27 245	29 611	1 532	5	579 547	143 127	25	100
	1981	27 488	30 034	2 351	8	603 604	163 140	27	100
	1982	28 517	31 327	2 942	9	635 283	175 095	28	100
	1983	29 267	31 833	1 986	6	683 510	195 770	29	100
	1984	29 957	33 585	3 056	9	730 933	207 537	28	100
MOZAMBIQUE‡	1981	...	...	...	...	90 151	41 987	47	...
	1982	...	...	...	...	85 955	39 349	46	...
	1983	...	...	...	...	57 522	26 504	46	...
NIGER	1975	6	19	19	100	874	424	49	100
	1980	21	85	25	29	2 561	1 268	50	54
	1981	20	82	...	...	2 713	1 357	50	50
REUNION‡	1975	...	514	...	...	26 700	...	...	10
	1980	...	...	...	...	33 816	...	...	8
	1981	136	1 020	916	98	35 886	...	...	8
	1982	143	1 128	*1 114	*99	37 466	...	...	8
	1983	147	1 193	1 164	98	36 845	...	...	8
ST. HELENA	1976	3	10	10	100	85	46	54	–
	1980	3	9	9	100	60	36	60	–
	1981	3	...	...	...	68	34	50	–
	1982	3	8	8	100	65	31	48	–
	1983	3	7	7	100	62	37	60	–
SAO TOME AND PRINCIPE	1976	...	...	...	...	1 627	760	47	–
	1980	...	...	...	...	2 430	...	...	...
	1981	...	...	...	...	2 664	...	...	...
	1982	...	...	...	...	2 842	1 392	49	...
	1983	...	...	...	...	2 998	1 531	51	...
	1984	...	...	...	...	3 023	...	...	...
SENEGAL‡	1980	98	85	85	100	8 445	4 315	51	80
	1981	90	156	108	69	8 515	4 377	51	74
	1982	99	156	108	69	9 164	4 605	50	68
	1983	...	...	...	...	3 631	1 763	49	...
SEYCHELLES	1976	41	...	...	...	1 787	909	51	96
	1980	34	91	91	100	2 568	...	...	–
	1982	37	121	121	100	3 526	...	...	–
	1983	38	94	94	100	2 917	...	...	–
	1984	38	110	110	100	3 110	...	...	–
	1985	38	109	109	100	3 180	...	...	–
SOMALIA	1975	9	68	61	90	1 080	499	46	–
	1980	17	143	134	94	2 089	1 087	52	–
	1981	24	148	142	96	1 752	823	47	–
	1982	20	151	146	97	1 938	1 018	53	–
	1983	16	135	128	95	1 201	651	54	–
SUDAN‡	1980	3 135	3 183	...	...	148 879	...	...	69
	1982	3 973	3 588	...	...	164 131	...	...	61
	1983	4 105	3 828	...	...	167 872	...	...	61

COUNTRY / PAYS / PAIS	YEAR / ANNEE / AÑO	SCHOOLS / ECOLES / ESCUELAS	TEACHING STAFF / PERSONNEL ENSEIGNANT / PERSONAL DOCENTE			PUPILS ENROLLED / ELEVES INSCRITS / ALUMNOS MATRICULADOS			
			TOTAL	FEMALE / FEMININ / FEMENINO	% F	TOTAL	FEMALE / FEMININ / FEMENINO	% F	% PRIVATE / PRIVE / PRIVADA
		(1)	(2)	(3)	(4)	(5)	(6)	(7)	(8)
SWAZILAND	1976	39	67	67	100	1 605	850	53	30
	1978	50	32	32	100	1 880	...	...	–
TOGO	1975	94	133	119	89	6 723	3 270	49	64
	1980	148	237	237	100	8 424	4 121	49	54
	1981	171	265	264	100	9 000	4 381	49	46
	1982	190	329	326	99	9 393	4 603	49	50
	1983	195	343	337	98	9 248	4 580	50	49
	1984	202	346	346	100	9 279	4 640	50	47
ZAMBIA	1979	...	...	...	...	6 022	...	...	100
AMERICA, NORTH									
ANTIGUA AND BARBUDA	1975	26	43	43	100	985	502	51	100
	1978	...	...	...	...	912	504	55	100
	1983	...	...	...	...	677	365	54	100
BARBADOS‡	1975	*114	86	...	...	*2 661	*1 400	*53	*7
	1980	132	*151	...	...	3 936	1 962	50	*20
	1981	128	*154	...	...	3 610	1 879	52	*17
	1982	126	132	...	...	3 052	1 482	49	*19
BELIZE	1975	25	...	...	...	1 084	...	...	100
	1980	55	*130	...	...	*2 000	...	...	...
BERMUDA‡	1975	10	...	...	...	396	192	48	...
	1980	31	...	...	...	1 067	545	51	60
	1981	30	37	36	97	1 085	538	50	61
	1982	30	37	37	100	1 006	517	51	57
	1983	32	37	37	100	1 284	621	48	66
	1984	32	37	37	100	1 287	637	49	66
BRITISH VIRGIN ISLANDS	1975	6	10	10	100	155	67	43	100
	1980	8	15	12	80	299	134	45	100
	1982	6	21	20	95	184	88	48	100
	1983	6	15	14	93	190	98	52	100
	1984	...	...	...	...	226	110	49	100
CANADA	1975	...	*16 600	*16 600	*100	398 476	193 620	49	2
	1980	...	...	...	...	397 266	193 807	49	3
	1981	...	...	...	...	391 969	190 804	49	3
	1982	...	...	...	...	400 219	194 522	49	4
	1983	...	...	...	...	402 264	195 590	49	3
CAYMAN ISLANDS	1979	5	5	5	100	158	79	50	100
COSTA RICA	1975	318	500	500	100	15 608	7 789	50	11
	1980	370	673	...	...	21 857	10 792	49	13
	1981	424	739	727	98	23 969	11 857	49	9
	1982	450	752	...	...	27 584	13 539	49	11
	1983	483	841	...	...	31 008	15 324	49	11
	1984	492	...	...	...	29 220	14 393	49	11
CUBA	1975	...	4 358	...	...	126 565	61 951	49	–
	1980	...	5 047	4 998	99	123 741	60 386	49	–
	1981	...	5 248	5 094	97	123 302	60 156	49	–
	1982	...	5 258	5 255	100	118 072	57 346	49	–
	1983	...	4 898	4 881	100	107 660	52 201	48	–
	1984	...	4 931	4 924	100	109 061	52 925	49	–
DOMINICA	1975	52	60	58	97	2 300	1 269	55	100
	1976	52	65	53	82	2 400	1 373	57	100
	1978	58	65	65	100	2 280	1 176	52	100
DOMINICAN REPUBLIC	1975	...	...	...	...	24 015	...	...	...
	1980	286	...	...	...	27 278	...	...	87
	1981	292	...	...	...	27 983	...	...	87
	1982	...	...	...	...	39 907	...	...	61
	1983	...	...	...	...	43 365	...	...	60
EL SALVADOR‡	1975	320	592	592	100	42 227	22 101	52	13
	1980	459	1 036	1 036	100	48 684	25 350	52	20
	1981	347	1 055	927	88	44 834	23 414	52	16
	1982	*347	961	927	96	55 763	29 196	52	23
	1983	550	1 100	1 068	97	60 805	31 417	52	25
	1984	770	1 144	1 112	97	61 223	31 672	52	26
GRENADA‡	1976	71	94	94	100	2 487	1 293	52	100
	1980	67	115	113	98	2 500	...	...	...
	1981	70	117	115	98	2 616	...	...	4
	1982	70	131	130	99	2 823	...	...	5
	1983	76	150	148	99	2 790	1 481	53	7

3.3 Education preceding the first level
Enseignement précédant le premier degré
Enseñanza anterior al primer grado

COUNTRY / PAYS / PAIS	YEAR / ANNEE / AÑO	SCHOOLS / ECOLES / ESCUELAS	TEACHING STAFF / PERSONNEL ENSEIGNANT / PERSONAL DOCENTE			PUPILS ENROLLED / ELEVES INSCRITS / ALUMNOS MATRICULADOS			
			TOTAL	FEMALE / FEMININ / FEMENINO	% F	TOTAL	FEMALE / FEMININ / FEMENINO	% F	% PRIVATE / PRIVE / PRIVADA
		(1)	(2)	(3)	(4)	(5)	(6)	(7)	(8)
GUADELOUPE‡	1975	...	...	...	...	11 313	...	...	15
	1980	...	...	...	...	16 875	...	...	11
	1981	65	537	471	*97	16 391	...	...	11
	1982	70	553	487	*98	16 256	...	...	11
	1983	73	565	561	99	16 733	...	...	10
GUATEMALA	1975	342	999	927	93	30 254	14 877	49	36
	1980	564	1 700	...	...	48 869	24 464	50	38
	1981	657	1 738	1 597	92	51 744	25 766	50	42
	1982	738	1 891	...	...	53 085	...	...	42
	1983	839	2 036	1 869	92	59 885	29 730	50	42
	1984	889	2 278	...	...	61 897	...	...	43
HAITI‡	1983	497	181	181	100	24 850	...	...	64
HONDURAS	1975	234	406	406	100	16 136	8 073	50	16
	1980	441	833	...	...	33 034	*13 874	*42	16
	1981	445	884	...	...	36 016	*16 567	*46	...
	1982	460	820	820	100	37 957	18 357	48	18
	1983	615	1 224	1 224	100	46 228	23 599	51	15
	1984	650	1 267	1 267	100	44 793	22 782	51	15
JAMAICA	1975	1 705	3 163	...	...	126 217	67 771	54	83
	1980	...	...	...	...	119 508	61 592	52	*85
	1981	...	...	...	...	123 374	...	...	...
	1982	1 549	...	...	...	116 718	...	...	*83
	1983	1 594	...	...	...	122 164	62 523	51	*83
MARTINIQUE‡	1980	...	...	...	...	17 678	...	...	4
	1981	70	586	564	*99	16 915	...	...	4
	1982	70	642	601	*97	16 900	...	...	4
	1983	73	653	641	98	17 355	...	...	4
MEXICO	1975	4 156	14 073	*14 073	*100	537 090	265 705	49	8
	1980	13 021	32 368	32 368	100	1 071 619	531 704	50	11
	1981	17 798	43 531	43 531	100	1 411 316	703 561	50	12
	1982	23 305	53 265	53 265	100	1 690 964	842 879	50	8
	1983	28 245	60 937	60 937	100	1 893 643	947 049	50	7
	1984	31 022	72 325	72 325	100	2 147 495	1 073 250	50	7
MONTSERRAT‡	1976	10	23	23	100	444	...	...	...
	1981	9	20	19	95	278	124	45	...
NETHERLANDS ANTILLES	1981	94	348	...	...	8 694	4 220	49	80
	1982	93	349	...	...	8 707	4 310	50	81
NICARAGUA	1975	...	...	...	...	8 986	...	...	67
	1980	463	924	915	99	30 524	15 649	51	43
	1982	646	1 212	1 203	99	38 534	20 219	52	30
	1983	953	1 420	1 392	98	50 163	26 004	52	29
	1984	...	1 701	...	...	60 557	...	...	...
PANAMA	1975	224	457	457	100	12 398	6 297	51	40
	1980	365	645	644	100	18 136	9 063	50	34
	1981	498	851	848	100	22 616	11 373	50	32
	1982	537	966	961	99	24 656	12 364	50	30
	1983	608	1 016	1 011	100	25 843	12 637	49	30
	1984	...	...	...	...	*27 090	...	...	...
PUERTO RICO	1975	...	...	...	...	19 756	...	...	...
ST. CHRISTOPHER AND NEVIS	1983	4	23	23	100	322	153	48	–
ST. PIERRE AND MIQUELON	1980	4	18	18	100	356	169	47	78
	1981	4	18	18	100	350	172	49	78
	1982	4	18	18	100	350	168	48	77
	1983	4	18	18	100	357	178	50	81
	1984	4	18	18	100	364	183	50	80
ST. VINCENT AND THE GRENADINES	1981	30	...	...	...	967	468	48	100
	1983	40	...	...	...	*1 415	...	...	*100
TRINIDAD AND TOBAGO‡	1980	39	117	...	...	1 739	...	...	...
	1981	39	117	...	...	1 733	...	...	...
	1982	43	129	...	...	1 928	...	...	...
	1984	44	132	132	100	1 805	...	...	...
TURKS AND CAICOS ISL.	1975	2	6	5	83	95	...	...	100
UNITED STATES	1975	...	...	...	...	5 141 000	...	...	33
	1980	...	...	...	...	5 163 000	2 449 000	47	36
	1981	...	...	...	...	5 219 000	2 469 000	47	37
	1982	...	...	...	...	5 452 000	2 673 000	49	*36
	1983	...	...	...	...	*5 472 000	...	...	*36

COUNTRY PAYS PAIS	YEAR ANNEE AÑO	SCHOOLS ECOLES ESCUELAS	TEACHING STAFF PERSONNEL ENSEIGNANT PERSONAL DOCENTE TOTAL	FEMALE FEMININ FEMENINO	% F	PUPILS ENROLLED ELEVES INSCRITS ALUMNOS MATRICULADOS TOTAL	FEMALE FEMININ FEMENINO	% F	% PRIVATE PRIVE PRIVADA
		(1)	(2)	(3)	(4)	(5)	(6)	(7)	(8)
U.S. VIRGIN ISLANDS	1980	...	...	...	...	2 561	...	...	31
	1981	...	...	...	...	2 631	...	...	29
AMERICA, SOUTH									
ARGENTINA	1975	5 694	18 991	18 928	100	369 082	185 743	50	30
	1981	6 953	25 409	25 306	100	526 964	265 871	50	32
	1982	7 345	27 454	27 377	100	570 353	287 100	50	31
	1983	*7 280	*29 597	*29 531	*100	*602 226	*302 809	*50	*32
	1984	7 659	32 785	32 632	100	654 645	327 586	50	32
	1985	8 015	36 287	36 117	100	693 259	348 639	50	31
BOLIVIA‡	1975	373	1 472	...	...	40 242	22 148	55	11
	1980	...	...	...	...	90 031	44 503	49	...
	1981	...	...	...	...	105 399	36 262	49	8
	1982	...	...	...	...	111 043	...	...	...
	1983	...	...	...	...	116 614	...	...	...
	1984	1 065	3 814	...	...	132 837	66 029	50	11
BRAZIL	1975	9 158	26 393	26 086	99	566 008	281 283	50	49
	1980	15 320	58 788	57 458	98	1 335 317	660 412	49	46
	1981	18 028	66 824	65 261	98	1 543 822	766 237	50	45
	1982	23 098	81 049	...	...	1 866 868	...	...	41
	1983	27 436	88 149	...	...	2 084 109	...	...	37
CHILE‡	1975	1 761	2 512	2 504	100	124 697	...	...	21
	1980	...	...	...	...	174 909	64 381	51	20
	1981	...	...	...	...	175 450	64 151	50	21
	1982	...	...	...	...	184 526	67 675	49	27
	1983	...	...	...	...	146 369	72 284	49	39
	1984	...	...	...	...	176 183	87 066	49	41
COLOMBIA	1975	2 013	3 887	...	...	95 908	...	...	70
	1980	3 736	9 126	8 480	93	215 085	110 796	52	*65
	1982	3 723	7 701	...	...	194 005	...	...	63
	1983	4 396	9 140	8 821	97	221 262	112 963	51	62
	1984	4 681	9 506	5 694	60	259 845	129 663	50	62
	1985	5 127	10 891	...	...	285 286	142 380	50	61
ECUADOR	1975	254	778	741	95	23 864	12 067	51	35
	1980	736	1 858	1 768	95	50 819	25 760	51	42
	1981	811	2 034	1 925	95	57 830	29 479	51	41
	1982	975	2 331	2 234	96	65 959	33 055	50	39
	1983	1 235	2 777	2 645	95	80 079	40 280	50	44
FRENCH GUIANA‡	1975	8	56	...	...	3 359	...	...	...
	1980	...	...	...	...	3 879	...	...	12
	1981	18	144	122	97	4 045	...	...	12
	1982	18	141	123	98	4 063	...	...	11
	1983	18	152	149	98	4 117	...	...	12
GUYANA	1976	356	1 662	1 643	99	25 784	12 910	50	–
	1980	374	2 018	1 975	98	27 955	14 020	50	–
	1981	368	1 783	1 761	99	29 958	14 974	50	–
	1982	...	...	...	...	30 460	15 291	50	–
PARAGUAY	1982	32	...	...	...	13 590	6 994	51	63
PERU	1975	2 098	4 459	4 390	98	172 051	85 062	49	27
	1980	3 271	6 778	6 689	99	228 168	114 940	50	27
	1981	3 514	7 741	7 504	97	250 212	125 210	50	28
	1982	3 886	8 076	7 973	99	279 504	140 099	50	29
SURINAME	1975	309	589	589	100	17 581	8 722	50	59
	1979	279	653	...	...	18 191	...	...	...
	1984	281	...	...	...	16 935	8 405	50	54
URUGUAY‡	1975	...	921	...	...	40 239	...	...	32
	1980	...	1 001	...	...	42 444	...	...	25
	1981	772	...	...	...	44 415	...	...	24
	1982	872	1 026	...	...	49 539	...	...	28
	1983	928	...	...	...	53 999	...	...	23
VENEZUELA	1975	327	6 246	6 230	100	224 600	112 272	50	21
	1980	...	16 487	...	...	421 183	...	...	17
	1981	...	16 683	16 393	98	461 017	230 274	50	17
	1982	1 164	18 181	...	...	499 093	...	...	16
	1983	1 266	19 448	19 128	98	523 318	260 428	50	15
	1984	...	...	...	...	*591 524	...	...	...
ASIA									
AFGHANISTAN‡	1975	8	95	95	100	1 891	919	49	–
	1980	36	369	369	100	4 470	2 010	45	–
	1981	37	430	430	100	4 970	2 196	44	–
	1982	37	319	319	100	4 735	2 116	45	–

3.3 Education preceding the first level
Enseignement précédant le premier degré
Enseñanza anterior al primer grado

COUNTRY / PAYS / PAIS	YEAR / ANNEE / AÑO	SCHOOLS / ECOLES / ESCUELAS	TEACHING STAFF / PERSONNEL ENSEIGNANT / PERSONAL DOCENTE			PUPILS ENROLLED / ELEVES INSCRITS / ALUMNOS MATRICULADOS			
			TOTAL	FEMALE / FEMININ / FEMENINO	% F	TOTAL	FEMALE / FEMININ / FEMENINO	% F	% PRIVATE / PRIVE / PRIVADA
		(1)	(2)	(3)	(4)	(5)	(6)	(7)	(8)
BAHRAIN	1975	...	...	...	...	1 983	964	49	100
	1980	...	...	...	...	3 730	1 768	47	100
	1981	...	104	104	100	4 383	2 079	47	100
	1982	30	160	159	99	5 053	2 417	48	100
	1983	33	189	189	100	5 217	2 518	48	100
BRUNEI DARUSSALAM	1975	14	39	39	100	1 496	688	46	100
	1980	143	324	248	77	6 760	3 251	48	51
	1981	146	352	289	82	6 879	3 360	49	54
	1982	150	348	306	88	7 224	3 482	48	53
	1983	140	336	293	87	7 345	3 595	49	50
	1984	145	363	323	89	7 655	3 737	49	48
CHINA	1975	171 749	236 500	...	...	6 200 000	...	...	–
	1980	170 419	410 700	335 100	82	11 507 700	...	...	–
	1981	130 360	401 100	328 400	82	10 562 200	...	...	–
	1982	122 107	415 200	349 600	84	11 130 900	...	...	–
	1983	136 300	433 000	378 200	87	11 402 500	5 424 800	48	–
	1984	166 500	491 100	463 000	94	12 947 400	6 018 600	46	–
CYPRUS‡	1975	96	222	218	98	4 229	2 067	49	74
	1980	259	418	416	100	10 397	5 007	48	49
	1981	281	451	449	100	11 541	5 481	47	48
	1982	308	481	479	100	12 466	5 928	48	47
	1983	333	547	540	99	13 960	6 753	48	52
DEMOCRATIC YEMEN	1975	11	157	145	92	2 820	1 262	45	–
	1980	26	311	307	99	5 541	2 562	46	–
	1981	28	367	365	99	6 076	2 801	46	–
	1982	28	384	379	99	6 737	3 179	47	–
	1983	28	423	420	99	9 657	4 841	50	–
HONG KONG	1975	839	4 168	4 025	97	160 184	76 755	48	100
	1980	761	5 177	5 064	98	197 410	94 788	48	100
	1981	729	5 361	5 227	98	200 426	96 200	48	100
	1982	709	5 472	5 349	98	205 200	99 330	48	100
	1983	724	5 946	5 844	98	209 869	101 698	48	100
	1984	775	6 602	6 489	98	226 450	109 637	48	100
INDIA	1975	5 658	...	...	...	569 296	256 187	45	...
	1980	10 802	...	...	...	918 238	416 848	45	...
	1981	10 920	...	...	...	836 484	381 404	46	...
	1982	12 716	...	...	...	1 021 093	458 291	45	...
INDONESIA	1976	12 935	24 503	24 400	100	579 876	320 889	55	95
	1980	19 868	37 100	...	...	1 005 226	...	...	99
	1981	20 289	37 845	...	...	1 245 825	...	...	99
	1982	22 062	42 688	...	...	1 141 215	...	...	99
	1983	23 836	46 228	...	...	1 220 686	...	...	100
	1984	25 380	56 489	...	...	1 233 793	...	...	100
IRAN, ISLAMIC REPUBLIC OF	1975	1 804	6 985	6 952	100	175 424	79 978	46	26
	1980	2 791	9 356	...	...	172 000	...	...	–
	1981	2 738	7 946	7 938	100	195 639	92 554	47	–
	1982	2 410	8 394	*8 338	*99	177 525	85 329	48	–
	1983	2 735	9 229	9 220	100	202 899	100 960	50	–
IRAQ	1975	245	1 913	1 913	100	44 413	20 578	46	–
	1980	387	3 235	3 235	100	76 507	36 671	48	–
	1981	437	3 696	3 696	100	81 449	39 315	48	–
	1982	507	4 170	4 170	100	79 457	38 137	48	–
	1983	523	4 244	4 244	100	76 663	36 855	48	–
ISRAEL‡	1975	5 289	6 122	5 518	100	200 710	79 233	49	19
	1980	...	...	...	...	269 506	*127 832	*47	17
	1981	...	...	...	...	278 800	...	...	...
	1982	...	...	...	...	284 480	...	...	...
	1983	...	...	...	...	285 040	138 190	48	...
JAPAN	1975	13 108	93 853	82 255	88	2 292 591	1 121 244	49	75
	1980	14 893	110 037	97 083	88	2 407 093	1 177 453	49	73
	1981	15 059	109 317	96 390	88	2 292 810	1 122 006	49	74
	1982	15 152	108 834	95 762	88	2 227 615	1 089 873	49	75
	1983	15 189	109 090	95 997	88	2 192 808	1 074 052	49	75
	1984	15 211	108 267	95 380	88	2 132 942	1 044 724	49	75
JORDAN	1975	158	453	451	100	14 952	6 343	42	99
	1980	207	737	731	99	19 598	8 372	43	99
	1981	221	747	744	100	21 198	9 346	44	100
	1982	239	854	850	100	22 930	10 128	44	99
	1983	273	936	936	100	24 579	10 863	44	99
	1984	304	1 055	1 055	100	27 236	12 463	46	99

COUNTRY / PAYS / PAIS	YEAR / ANNEE / AÑO	SCHOOLS / ECOLES / ESCUELAS	TEACHING STAFF / PERSONNEL ENSEIGNANT / PERSONAL DOCENTE: TOTAL	FEMALE / FEMININ / FEMENINO	% F	PUPILS ENROLLED / ELEVES INSCRITS / ALUMNOS MATRICULADOS: TOTAL	FEMALE / FEMININ / FEMENINO	% F	% PRIVATE / PRIVE / PRIVADA
		(1)	(2)	(3)	(4)	(5)	(6)	(7)	(8)
KOREA, REPUBLIC OF‡	1975	611	2 153	1 689	78	32 032	14 150	44	100
	1980	901	3 339	2 846	85	66 433	30 041	45	97
	1981	2 958	3 961	3 409	86	153 823	70 189	46	50
	1982	3 463	4 349	3 905	90	168 653	77 035	46	49
	1983	4 276	6 421	5 703	89	206 404	94 897	46	55
	1984	5 183	7 513	6 718	89	254 438	118 324	47	54
KUWAIT	1975	101	1 299	1 299	100	24 097	11 223	47	40
	1980	109	1 696	1 696	100	29 965	14 262	48	41
	1981	124	1 913	1 913	100	33 038	15 901	48	40
	1982	131	2 055	2 055	100	35 096	16 811	48	39
	1983	138	2 158	2 157	100	37 028	18 780	51	40
	1984	143	2 232	2 231	100	39 185	18 674	48	38
LAO PEOPLE'S DEMOCRATIC REPUBLIC	1980	153	252	252	100	5 296	2 719	51	–
	1981	224	544	544	100	9 736	4 774	49	–
	1982	...	723	723	100	10 399	...	...	–
	1983	298	793	793	100	13 269	...	...	–
LEBANON	1980	943	6 604	...	...	123 530	...	...	81
	1981	914	6 744	...	...	120 431	57 509	48	82
	1982	...	...	...	...	120 873	57 892	48	84
MACAU	1975	41	130	...	...	5 072	...	...	98
	1978	55	241	...	...	8 960	...	...	99
MALAYSIA	1984	...	8 745	8 674	99	269 477	...	...	...
	1985	5 757	9 056	8 889	98	293 801	...	...	...
MALDIVES	1981	1	...	...	...	1 651	...	...	...
	1982	1	...	...	...	1 909	...	...	...
MONGOLIA	1975	542	1 699	...	...	36 974	19 497	53	–
	1980	617	1 813	1 813	100	49 800	...	...	–
	1981	624	...	...	...	52 300	...	...	–
	1982	630	1 900	1 900	100	53 800	29 600	55	–
	1983	641	...	...	...	55 700	...	...	–
	1984	957	...	...	...	59 100	...	...	–
NEPAL	1983	153	706	430	61	14 952	5 642	38	100
	1984	176	733	450	61	16 864	6 854	41	100
OMAN	1975	1	4	4	100	160	68	43	100
	1980	3	11	10	91	472	251	53	100
	1981	5	28	28	100	674	280	42	100
	1982	3	32	32	100	865	390	45	100
	1983	2	37	37	100	872	381	44	100
	1984	2	81	81	100	1 643	764	47	100
PHILIPPINES	1975	...	...	...	...	86 443	...	...	...
	1980	...	...	...	...	*123 571	...	...	...
	1981	2 280	3 522	...	...	152 262	77 719	51	66
	1982	2 155	3 774	1 846	49	159 633	77 841	49	58
	1983	2 364	4 543	...	...	181 726	89 832	49	62
QATAR	1975	12	38	38	100	1 434	635	44	100
	1980	19	...	...	...	2 587	1 203	47	100
	1981	21	152	152	100	3 301	1 482	45	100
	1982	28	131	131	100	3 178	1 440	45	100
	1983	29	154	154	100	3 559	1 587	45	100
	1984	33	155	145	94	3 461	1 586	46	100
SAUDI ARABIA	1975	92	439	425	97	15 485	6 528	42	91
	1980	195	1 127	1 098	97	28 045	12 375	44	87
	1981	244	1 506	1 470	98	35 326	15 651	44	87
	1982	324	1 610	1 573	98	41 202	18 551	45	84
	1983	315	2 298	2 266	99	47 197	20 985	44	83
SINGAPORE‡	1975	52	278	276	99	4 883	2 320	48	...
	1980	251	832	832	100	22 256	10 630	48	31
	1981	239	818	818	100	22 227	10 684	48	35
	1982	235	815	815	100	23 389	11 148	48	37
	1983	226	820	820	100	23 469	11 045	47	38
	1984	222	864	864	100	24 775	11 733	47	41
SYRIAN ARAB REPUBLIC	1975	323	1 012	980	97	33 477	14 940	45	100
	1980	351	1 082	1 052	97	33 611	14 985	45	100
	1981	371	1 176	1 146	97	37 703	16 543	44	100
	1982	460	1 405	1 385	99	45 197	19 939	44	93
	1983	493	1 574	1 555	99	52 228	23 424	45	93
	1984	515	1 723	1 710	99	59 929	27 201	45	...
THAILAND	1975	2 864	...	...	...	214 620	103 582	48	58
	1980	...	...	...	...	367 313	178 662	49	55
	1981	...	...	...	...	379 400	...	...	59
	1983	...	...	...	...	471 597	...	...	53

COUNTRY / PAYS / PAIS	YEAR / ANNEE / AÑO	SCHOOLS / ECOLES / ESCUELAS	TEACHING STAFF / PERSONNEL ENSEIGNANT / PERSONAL DOCENTE			PUPILS ENROLLED / ELEVES INSCRITS / ALUMNOS MATRICULADOS			
			TOTAL	FEMALE / FEMININ / FEMENINO	% F	TOTAL	FEMALE / FEMININ / FEMENINO	% F	% PRIVATE / PRIVE / PRIVADA
		(1)	(2)	(3)	(4)	(5)	(6)	(7)	(8)
TURKEY‡	1980	117	262	255	97	4 691	2 090	45	80
	1981	122	279	273	98	5 582	2 549	46	73
	1982	120	290	283	98	5 725	2 554	45	72
	1983	125	308	290	94	6 103	2 806	46	74
UNITED ARAB EMIRATES‡	1975	11	186	186	100	7 603	3 895	51	51
	1980	20	359	359	100	17 263	7 930	46	69
	1981	34	494	494	100	24 490	11 762	48	62
	1982	34	564	564	100	30 128	14 248	47	65
	1983	34	505	505	100	29 744	14 021	47	64
	1984	33	559	559	100	32 012	14 804	46	63
VIET-NAM	1975	...	*22 300	...	...	*764 400	...	...	...
	1980	6 121	57 605	57 605	100	1 595 724	823 806	52	–
	1981	...	62 900	62 900	100	1 527 000	...	...	–
	1982	...	63 000	63 000	100	1 468 000	...	...	–
YEMEN	1975	2	4	4	100	322	157	49	100
EUROPE									
ALBANIA	1980	2 667	4 162	4 162	100	92 490	...	...	–
	1981	2 753	4 430	4 430	100	96 790	...	...	–
	1982	2 836	4 480	4 480	100	99 120	...	...	–
	1983	2 931	4 600	4 600	100	103 000	...	...	–
	1984	2 990	4 753	4 753	100	107 450	...	...	–
ANDORRA	1974	...	...	...	...	1 594	754	47	...
	1982	13	151	129	85	1 925	944	49	17
AUSTRIA‡	1975	2 882	5 578	5 522	99	154 318	75 551	49	33
	1980	3 423	7 069	7 030	99	165 611	81 262	49	28
	1981	3 478	7 212	7 158	99	163 373	79 677	49	28
	1982	3 497	7 299	7 242	99	163 735	79 850	49	27
	1983	3 580	7 689	7 644	99	166 542	81 029	49	27
	1984	3 541	7 941	7 904	100	171 881	83 626	49	27
BELGIUM‡	1975	5 226	17 460	17 460	100	435 896	213 355	49	58
	1980	4 325	17 116	17 075	100	383 955	188 248	49	58
	1981	4 232	17 174	...	...	386 100	189 718	49	58
	1982	4 231	...	...	...	388 602	190 470	49	58
	1983	4 106	16 802	16 756	100	391 204	191 176	49	58
	1984	4 091	19 062	18 957	99	395 232	192 687	49	58
BULGARIA	1975	7 550	24 137	24 137	100	392 625	191 806	49	–
	1980	6 185	28 996	28 996	100	420 804	204 002	48	–
	1981	5 918	29 092	29 092	100	407 297	197 711	49	–
	1982	5 733	29 257	29 257	100	403 518	195 164	48	–
	1983	5 551	29 317	29 317	100	391 902	190 115	49	–
	1984	5 285	29 089	29 089	100	380 430	184 125	48	–
CZECHOSLOVAKIA	1975	9 226	34 755	34 755	100	475 004	...	...	–
	1980	11 119	47 290	47 290	100	694 720	...	...	–
	1981	11 283	48 408	48 408	100	707 184	...	...	–
	1982	11 397	49 437	49 437	100	714 921	...	...	–
	1983	11 523	50 622	50 622	100	713 135	...	...	–
	1984	11 601	51 181	51 181	100	700 478	...	...	–
DENMARK	1975	...	...	...	...	44 859	21 776	49	7
	1980	...	...	...	...	62 936	30 864	49	8
	1981	...	...	...	...	65 942	32 457	49	6
	1982	...	...	...	...	61 478	29 878	49	6
	1983	...	...	...	...	59 335	29 015	49	6
	1984	...	...	...	...	58 788	...	...	...
FINLAND‡	1975	...	1 639	1 639	100	59 526	...	...	20
	1980	1 683	...	...	...	78 628	...	...	...
	1981	1 756	5 245	...	...	82 639	...	...	10
	1982	1 851	5 472	...	...	86 756	...	...	9
	1983	1 930	...	...	...	89 858	...	...	...
	1984	...	...	...	...	93 450	...	...	...
FRANCE‡	1975	13 051	57 658	57 514	100	2 591 142	...	...	14
	1980	16 080	66 948	...	...	2 383 465	1 163 500	49	13
	1981	16 362	79 646	67 912	98	2 373 940	1 157 388	49	13
	1982	16 688	81 977	69 687	98	2 406 418	1 171 107	49	13
	1983	17 012	73 002	*71 177	*98	2 461 362	*1 197 509	*49	13
GERMAN DEMOCRATIC REPUBLIC	1975	11 648	51 998	*51 998	*100	693 163	...	...	–
	1980	12 145	56 448	56 448	100	663 491	...	...	–
	1981	12 340	59 284	59 284	100	709 117	...	...	–
	1982	12 563	61 815	61 815	100	750 718	...	...	–
	1983	12 821	65 298	65 298	100	785 159	...	...	–
	1984	13 025	67 429	67 429	100	788 730	...	...	–

COUNTRY PAYS PAIS	YEAR ANNEE AÑO	SCHOOLS ECOLES ESCUELAS	TEACHING STAFF / PERSONNEL ENSEIGNANT / PERSONAL DOCENTE TOTAL	 FEMALE FEMININ FEMENINO	 % F	PUPILS ENROLLED / ELEVES INSCRITS / ALUMNOS MATRICULADOS TOTAL	 FEMALE FEMININ FEMENINO	 % F	 % PRIVATE PRIVE PRIVADA
		(1)	(2)	(3)	(4)	(5)	(6)	(7)	(8)
GERMANY, FEDERAL REPUBLIC OF	1975	26 305	...	...	...	1 655 825	801 640	48	...
	1980	26 793	...	...	...	*1 535 959	*751 010	*49	...
	1981	26 920	...	...	...	*1 544 519	*744 041	*48	...
	1982	27 103	...	...	...	*1 582 035	*755 264	*48	...
	1983	*26 836	...	...	...	*1 581 069	*754 805	*48	...
GIBRALTAR‡	1975	1	1	1	100	13	6	46	–
	1980	1	2	2	100	28	11	39	–
	1981	2	5	5	100	72	29	40	–
	1982	2	5	5	100	75	36	48	–
	1983	2	5	5	100	75	38	51	–
GREECE	1975	3 279	4 137	4 137	100	108 357	52 459	48	15
	1980	4 576	6 514	6 514	100	145 924	71 173	49	9
	1981	4 743	6 901	6 901	100	151 666	73 975	49	8
	1982	4 922	6 913	6 913	100	153 587	75 020	49	7
HUNGARY	1975	4 077	20 512	20 512	100	329 408	159 052	48	–
	1980	4 690	29 437	29 437	100	478 100	230 493	48	–
	1981	4 800	31 018	31 018	100	477 038	230 452	48	–
	1982	4 826	31 972	31 972	100	466 402	225 949	48	–
	1983	4 842	32 715	32 715	100	455 205	221 537	49	–
	1984	4 824	33 245	33 245	100	440 773	214 742	49	–
ICELAND	1975	...	...	...	...	3 502	...	...	8
	1980	...	...	...	...	4 041	...	...	...
	1981	...	...	...	...	4 195	...	...	...
	1982	...	...	...	...	4 235	2 045	48	...
	1983	...	...	...	...	3 989	1 955	49	...
	1984	...	...	...	...	4 208	...	...	...
IRELAND	1975	...	4 408	3 218	73	135 783	66 179	49	100
	1980	...	4 782	3 523	74	137 533	66 568	48	100
	1981	...	4 896	3 642	74	139 846	67 579	48	100
	1982	...	5 071	3 799	75	142 501	69 198	49	100
ITALY	1975	27 485	63 523	63 523	100	1 822 527	892 143	49	*39
	1980	30 295	108 261	...	...	1 870 477	917 854	49	38
	1981	30 027	107 799	...	...	1 804 708	885 801	49	37
	1982	29 898	107 924	...	...	1 757 411	860 131	49	35
	1983	29 473	108 207	...	...	1 695 911	829 887	49	35
	1984	28 823	...	...	...	1 639 377	...	...	...
LUXEMBOURG	1975	...	394	394	100	8 625	4 230	49	
	1980	...	415	411	99	7 621	3 703	49	1
	1981	...	426	421	99	7 551	3 652	48	1
	1982	...	413	408	99	7 579	3 670	48	
MALTA	1975	43	406	347	85	6 237	2 940	47	60
	1980	42	428	372	87	7 691	3 630	47	51
	1981	36	403	355	88	7 603	3 490	46	52
	1982	42	363	309	85	7 645	3 485	46	53
	1983	45	414	352	85	7 744	3 648	47	53
MONACO‡	1976	...	...	...	...	352	...	...	...
	1980	5	...	...	...	330	151	46	...
	1981	5	...	...	...	357	162	45	...
	1982	9	...	...	...	658	...	...	37
NETHERLANDS	1975	7 568	20 565	20 565	100	518 890	252 806	49	71
	1980	8 050	22 361	22 361	100	409 576	198 795	49	70
	1981	8 108	22 533	22 490	100	399 769	194 069	49	69
	1982	8 170	22 645	22 567	100	398 804	193 832	49	69
	1983	8 059	22 286	22 160	99	396 946	193 136	49	69
	1984	7 951	...	...	...	399 453	194 654	49	69
NORWAY	1975	...	5 516	...	...	30 479	...	...	...
	1980	2 554	16 866	...	...	78 189	...	...	41
	1981	2 756	18 115	...	...	82 933	...	...	40
	1982	...	...	...	...	86 315	...	...	...
	1983	...	...	...	...	89 898	...	...	...
POLAND	1975	31 176	44 542	43 957	99	1 107 648	...	...	–
	1980	31 014	57 730	57 137	99	1 349 528	...	...	0.0
	1981	27 016	63 230	62 341	99	1 295 629	...	...	0.0
	1982	26 184	68 428	67 479	99	1 276 653	...	...	0.0
	1983	26 460	71 692	69 490	97	1 236 659	...	...	0.0
	1984	26 337	74 368	73 089	98	1 290 903	...	...	0.0
PORTUGAL‡	1975	679	1 903	1 842	97	44 832	21 354	48	91
	1980	1 916	5 047	4 974	99	100 178	48 389	48	31
	1981	2 325	5 528	5 414	98	112 412	54 083	48	28
	1982	2 429	2 883	...	...	114 640	...	...	23
	1983	2 551	6 039	5 992	99	117 859	56 960	48	27

3.3 Education preceding the first level
Enseignement précédant le premier degré
Enseñanza anterior al primer grado

COUNTRY / PAYS / PAIS	YEAR / ANNEE / AÑO	SCHOOLS / ECOLES / ESCUELAS	TEACHING STAFF / PERSONNEL ENSEIGNANT / PERSONAL DOCENTE			PUPILS ENROLLED / ELEVES INSCRITS / ALUMNOS MATRICULADOS			
			TOTAL	FEMALE / FEMININ / FEMENINO	% F	TOTAL	FEMALE / FEMININ / FEMENINO	% F	% PRIVATE / PRIVE / PRIVADA
		(1)	(2)	(3)	(4)	(5)	(6)	(7)	(8)
ROMANIA	1975	13 537	33 789	33 789	100	812 420	404 766	50	–
	1980	13 467	38 512	38 512	100	935 711	461 084	49	–
	1981	13 387	38 977	38 977	100	931 217	458 662	49	–
	1982	13 255	34 955	34 955	100	902 608	445 106	49	–
	1983	13 068	34 365	34 365	100	893 101	440 790	49	–
	1984	12 938	33 955	33 955	100	886 199	437 152	49	–
SAN MARINO	1975	16	68	68	100	735	356	48	31
	1980	17	91	91	100	877	430	49	...
	1981	17	92	92	100	864	420	49	...
	1982	16	98	98	100	866	433	50	...
	1983	16	99	99	100	848	423	50	...
SPAIN	1975	...	24 621	24 287	99	920 336	471 437	51	62
	1980	...	35 588	34 386	97	1 182 425	593 030	50	45
	1981	...	36 846	35 352	96	1 197 897	597 480	50	44
	1982	...	37 343	35 666	96	1 187 617	589 861	50	42
	1983	3 176	38 084	36 351	95	1 171 062	581 976	50	40
SWEDEN	1975	5 913	...	...	...	206 726	...	...	...
	1980	8 504	...	...	...	226 571	...	...	...
	1981	...	...	...	...	235 424	...	...	...
	1982	9 238	...	...	...	232 878	...	...	...
	1983	9 425	...	...	...	237 385	...	...	...
	1984	...	...	...	...	251 122	...	...	...
SWITZERLAND	1976	...	...	...	...	130 116	60 417	46	12
	1980	...	...	...	...	120 315	58 402	49	7
	1981	...	...	...	...	118 764	57 993	49	4
	1982	...	...	...	...	120 076	58 463	49	4
	1983	...	...	...	...	119 261	57 861	49	3
	1984	...	...	...	...	120 727	58 632	49	4
UNITED KINGDOM	1975	1 040	...	...	...	388 309	189 836	49	5
	1980	1 251	...	...	...	336 972	164 986	49	8
	1981	1 254	...	...	...	315 335	153 871	49	6
	1982	1 259	...	...	...	319 000	156 000	49	6
	1983	1 260	...	...	...	349 700	170 500	49	5
YUGOSLAVIA	1975	2 308	17 794	16 889	95	188 526	90 792	48	–
	1980	3 177	29 436	27 632	94	290 870	139 284	48	–
	1981	3 427	31 351	29 672	95	317 507	152 232	48	–
	1982	3 621	32 993	31 095	94	336 364	162 139	48	–
	1983	3 740	34 231	32 175	94	347 235	166 783	48	–
OCEANIA									
AMERICAN SAMOA‡	1980	...	...	...	...	1 922	891	46	7
	1981	...	...	...	...	1 578	...	...	...
	1983	...	94	92	98	1 715	859	50	...
	1984	...	95	95	100	1 816	906	50	...
AUSTRALIA‡	1975	...	...	...	...	186 652	90 903	49	19
	1980	...	...	...	...	165 742	80 485	49	22
	1981	...	...	...	...	160 580	78 044	49	23
	1982	...	...	...	...	158 188	76 859	49	24
	1983	...	...	...	...	158 468	76 968	49	25
	1984	...	...	...	...	156 641	76 234	49	26
COOK ISLANDS	1982	...	...	...	...	446	...	...	...
FIJI	1975	117	256	256	100	3 339	1 603	48	100
	1980	163	196	196	100	4 493	2 201	49	100
	1981	168	217	217	100	4 536	2 270	50	100
	1982	184	...	...	...	4 815	...	...	100
	1983	199	253	253	100	5 393	2 675	50	100
	1984	219	255	255	100	5 340	...	...	100
FRENCH POLYNESIA	1975	9	265	265	100	8 117	3 949	49	26
	1981	47	350	350	100	9 354	4 566	49	22
	1982	59	406	*406	*100	10 485	5 113	49	20
	1983	63	...	...	...	11 256	5 512	49	19
	1984	67	462	*462	*100	11 937	5 854	49	19
GUAM	1983	...	99	93	94	2 892	1 249	43	13
NEW CALEDONIA‡	1975	...	...	...	...	6 195	...	...	...
	1980	...	...	...	...	10 313	5 121	50	25
	1982	46	147	144	98	8 062	4 026	50	32
	1983	...	344	...	...	8 675	4 298	50	34
	1984	54	364	...	...	9 028	4 490	50	35
	1985	52	355	...	...	8 647	4 280	49	33

COUNTRY PAYS PAIS	YEAR ANNEE AÑO	SCHOOLS ECOLES ESCUELAS	TEACHING STAFF / PERSONNEL ENSEIGNANT / PERSONAL DOCENTE TOTAL	 FEMALE FEMININ FEMENINO	 % F	PUPILS ENROLLED / ELEVES INSCRITS / ALUMNOS MATRICULADOS TOTAL	 FEMALE FEMININ FEMENINO	 % F	 % PRIVATE PRIVE PRIVADA
		(1)	(2)	(3)	(4)	(5)	(6)	(7)	(8)
NEW ZEALAND	1975	401	836	835	100	32 357	15 957	49	100
	1980	...	...	...	...	40 410	19 720	49	97
	1981	521	...	...	...	39 794	19 502	49	97
	1982	535	1 140	...	...	41 092	20 400	50	97
	1983	539	1 145	...	...	41 594	20 623	50	97
NIUE	1975	13	45	45	100	352	171	49	–
PACIFIC ISLANDS	1975	...	...	...	...	691	367	53	52
PAPUA NEW GUINEA	1975	...	...	...	...	51	21	41	...
	1981	...	...	...	...	333	142	43	...
	1982	...	...	...	...	370	161	44	...
SAMOA	1975	21	80	68	85	1 926	982	51	100
	1976	26	96	83	86	2 113	1 085	51	100
	1977	40	123	...	...	2 200	...	...	100
TOKELAU	1981	3	3	3	100	56	27	48	–
	1982	3	3	3	100	48	21	44	–
	1983	3	5	3	60	71	25	35	–
TONGA	1975	11	25	25	100	568	337	59	100
VANUATU	1976	26	41	41	100	1 076	522	49	53
	1980	34	49	49	100	1 187	557	47	66
	1981	...	...	...	...	1 092	527	48	...
U.S.S.R.									
U.S.S.R.	1975	99 392	730 723	730 723	100	8 403 162	...	...	–
	1980	116 000	1 081 000	...	...	10 212 000	...	...	–
	1981	119 000	1 115 000	...	...	10 626 000	...	...	–
	1982	122 000	1 170 000	...	...	10 891 000	...	...	–
	1983	125 000	1 264 000	...	...	11 195 000	...	...	–
	1984	128 000	1 293 000	...	...	11 339 000	...	...	–
BYELORUSSIAN S.S.R.	1976			...	...	371 601	...	...	–
	1980	3 488	36 400	...	...	345 300	...	...	–
	1981	3 653	38 700	...	...	362 300	...	...	–
	1982	3 849	40 700	...	...	376 200	...	...	–
	1983	4 090	43 500	...	...	387 600	...	...	–
UKRAINIAN S.S.R.	1975	17 707	...	...	...	1 886 000	...	...	–
	1980	21 200	...	...	...	1 779 300	...	...	–
	1981	21 500	...	...	...	1 819 100	...	...	–
	1982	21 700	...	...	...	1 845 800	...	...	–
	1983	22 000	...	...	...	1 881 000	...	...	–
	1984	22 300	...	...	...	1 888 900	...	...	–

The data refer to education preceding the first level, e.g. kindergartens, nursery schools as well as infant classes attached to schools at higher levels. Nursery play centres, etc. have been excluded whenever possible. Figures on teachers refer, in general, to both full-time and part-time teachers. Unless otherwise stated, data cover both public and private schools. The enrolment in private institutions (aided and unaided) as a percentage of the total number of children enrolled in education preceding the first level has also been shown. However, data in this table should be considered as a minimum indication of the amount of pre-primary education since complete data are not available in all cases. Table 3.1 should be consulted for complementary information.

Les données se rapportent à l'enseignement qui précède le premier degré (jardins d'enfants, écoles maternelles et classes enfantines ouvertes dans des écoles de niveau plus élevé). Les garderies, crèches, etc. ont été, dans la mesure du possible, exclues. Les chiffres relatifs au personnel enseignant englobent, en général, le personnel à plein temps et le personnel à temps partiel. Sauf indication contraire, les données se rapportent à la fois aux établissements publics et aux établissements privés. Le pourcentage des effectifs inscrits dans les établissements privés (subventionnés et non subventionnés) par rapport au total des effectifs de l'enseignement précédant le premier degré a été indiqué. Il convient cependant de considérer les données de ce tableau comme une indication minimale de l'importance de l'enseignement précédant le premier degré, car on ne dispose pas de données complètes dans tous les cas. Pour des renseignements complémentaires, veuillez consulter le tableau 3.1.

Los datos se refieren a la enseñanza anterior al primer grado (jardines de la infancia, escuelas maternales y clases de párvulos adscritas a establecimientos docentes de grado superior). En la medida de lo posible, se han excluído las guarderías, centros de juego, etc. Las cifras relativas al personal docente abarcan, en general, el personal que trabaja en régimen de jornada completa y el de jornada parcial. Cuando no se indica otra cosa, los datos comprenden a la vez los establecimientos públicos y los privados. Se indica el porcentaje de la matrícula correspondiente a los establecimientos privados (subvencionados y no subvencionados) con respecto a la matrícula total de la enseñanza anterior al primer grado. Procede, sin embargo, considerar los datos de este cuadro como una indicación mínima de la importancia de la enseñanza anterior al primer grado, ya que no se dispone de datos completos en todos los casos. Para toda información complementaria debe consultarse el cuadro 3.1.

AFRICA:

Angola:

E--> Data refer to initiation classes where pupils learn portuguese.

FR-> Les données se réfèrent aux classes d'initiation où les élèves apprennent le portugais.

ESP> Los datos se refieren a las clases de iniciación donde los alumnos aprenden el portugués.

Burundi:

E--> Data for 1975 and 1980, refer to public education only.

FR-> Pour 1975 et 1980, les données se réfèrent à l'enseignement public seulement.

ESP> Para 1975 y 1980, los datos se refieren a la enseñanza pública solamente.

Central African Republic:

E--> For 1975, the figures shown in columns 6 and 7 refer to public education only. For 1980 and 1981, data exclude kindergartens attached to the Ministry of Social Affairs.

FR-> En 1975 les données des colonnes 6 et 7 se réfèrent à l'enseignement public seulement. En 1980 et 1981, les données n'incluent pas les jardins d'enfants qui dépendent du Ministère des Affaires Sociales.

ESP> En 1975 los datos de las columnas 6 y 7 se refieren a la enseñanza pública solamente. En 1980 y 1981, los datos excluyen los jardines infantiles dependientes del Ministerio de los Asuntos Sociales.

Ghana:

E--> For 1981 and 1982, data refer to public education only.

FR-> En 1981 et 1982, les données se réfèrent à l'enseignement public seulement.

ESP> En 1981 y 1982, los datos se refieren a la enseñanza pública solamente.

Morocco:

E--> 1975 data and columns 2 to 4 for 1980, 1983 and 1984 refer to Koranic schools only.

FR-> Les données de 1975 et celles des colonnes 2 à 4 pour 1980, 1983 et 1984 se réfèrent aux écoles coraniques seulement.

ESP> Los datos para 1975 y los de las columnas 2 a 4 para 1980, 1983 y 1984 se refieren a las escuelas coránicas solamente.

Mozambique:

E--> Data refer to initiation classes where pupils learn portuguese.

FR-> Les données se réfèrent aux classes d'initiation où les élèves apprennent le portugais.

ESP> Los datos se refieren a las clases de iniciacio×

Reunion:

E--> The figures shown in columns 2 for 1975, and 3 and 4 for 1981 refer to public education only.

FR-> Les chiffres de la colonne 2 pour 1975, et ceux des colonnes 3 et 4 pour 1981 se réfèrent à l'enseignement public seulement.

ESP> Las cifras de la columna 2 en 1975 y las de las columnas 3 y 4 en 1981 se refieren a la enseñanza pública solamente.

Senegal:

E--> All data on teachers and data on pupils for 1983 refer to public education only.

FR-> Toutes les données relatives au personnel enseignant et celles relatives aux élèves pour 1983, se réfèrent à l'enseignement public seulement.

ESP> Todos los datos relativos al personal docente y los relativos a los alumnos para 1983 se refieren a la enseñanza pública solamente.

Sudan:

E--> Data include Koranic schools 'khalwas' which accept pupils of all ages (100,900 pupils in 1983).

FR-> Les données incluent les écoles coraniques 'khalwas' qui acceptent des élèves de tous âges (100 900 élèves en 1983).

ESP> Los datos incluyen las escuelas coránicas 'khalwas' que admiten a los alumnos de todas las edades (100 900 alumnos en 1983).

AMERICA, NORTH:

Barbados:

E--> Data on teachers refer to public education only.

FR-> Les données relatives au personnel enseignant se réfèrent à l'enseignement public seulement.

ESP> Los datos relativos al personal docente se refieren a la enseñanza pública solamente.

Bermuda:

E--> Data on teachers and all data for 1975 refer to public education only.

FR-> Les données relatives au personnel enseignant et toutes les données de l'année 1975 se réfèrent à l'enseignement public seulement.

ESP> Los datos sobre el personal docente y todos los datos relativos a 1975 se refieren a la enseñanza pública solamente.

El Salvador:

E--> For 1975, data on teachers refer to public education only.

FR-> Pour 1975, les données relatives au personnel enseignant se réfèrent à l'enseignement public seulement.

ESP> En 1975, los datos sobre el personal docente se refieren a la enseñanza pública solamente.

Grenada:

E--> For 1980, data on pupils refer to public education only.

FR-> Pour 1980, les chiffres relatifs aux élèves se réfèrent à l'enseignement public seulement.

ESP> En 1980, las cifras relativas a los alumnos se refieren a la enseñanza pública solamente.

Guadeloupe:

E--> Data on female teachers for 1981 and 1982 refer to public education only.

FR-> Les données sur le personnel enseignant féminin en 1981 et 1982 se réfèrent à l'enseignement public seulement.

ESP> Las cifras sobre el personal docente femenino en 1981 y 1982 se refieren a la enseñanza pública solamente.

Haiti:

E--> Data on teachers refer to public education only.

FR-> Les données sur le personnel enseignant se réfèrent à l'enseignement public seulement.

ESP> Las cifras sobre el personal docente se refieren a la enseñanza pública solamente.

Martinique:

E--> Data on female teachers for 1981 and 1982 refer to public education only.

FR-> Les données relatives au personnel enseignant féminin en 1981 et 1982 se réfèrent à l'enseignement public seulement.

ESP> Los datos sobre el personal docente femenino en 1981 y 1982 se refieren a la enseñanza pública solamente.

Montserrat:

E--> Data refer to public education only.

FR-> Les données se réfèrent à l'enseignement public seulement.

ESP> Los datos se refieren a la enseñanza pública solamente.

Trinidad and Tobago:

E--> Data refer to public education only.

FR-> Les données se réfèrent à l'enseignement public seulement.

ESP> Los datos se refieren a la enseñanza pública solamente.

AMERICA, SOUTH:

Bolivia:

E--> The figures shown in columns 5, 6 and 7 for 1975 and 6 and 7 for 1981 do not include data on public rural schools.

FR-> Les chiffres des colonnes 5, 6 et 7 en 1975 et 6 et 7 en 1981 n'incluent pas les écoles publiques rurales.

ESP> Las cifras de las columnas 5, 6 y 7 en 1975 y 6 y 7 en 1981 no incluyen las escuelas públicas rurales.

Chile:

E--> For 1980, 1981 and 1982 data on female pupils (columns 6 and 7) and all data for 1983 do not include kindergartens de la junta nacional.

FR-> Pour 1980, 1981 et 1982 les données relatives aux élèves de sexe féminin (colonnes 6 et 7) et toutes les données pour 1983 n'incluent pas les écoles maternelles de la junte nationale.

ESP> En 1980, 1981 y 1982 los datos relativos a la matrícula femenina (columnas 6 y 7) y todos los datos para 1983 no incluyen las escuelas de párvulos de la junta nacional.

French Guiana:

E--> Data on teachers for 1975 and those on female teachers (columns 3 and 4) for 1981 and 1982 refer to public education only.

FR-> Les chiffres relatifs au personnel enseignant pour 1975 ainsi que ceux relatifs au personnel enseignant féminin (colonnes 3 et 4) pour 1981 et 1982 se réfèrent à l'enseignement public seulement.

ESP> Las cifras sobre el personal docente en 1975 y las sobre el personal docente femenino (columnas 3 y 4) en 1981 y 1982 se refieren a la enseñanza pública solamente.

Uruguay:

E--> Data on teachers refer to public education only.

FR-> Les données relatives au personnel enseignant se réfèrent à l'enseignement public seulement.

ESP> Los datos sobre el personal docente se refieren a la enseñanza pública solamente.

ASIA:

Afghanistan:

E--> The figures for 1975 refer to Kabul only.

FR-> Les données pour 1975 se réfèrent à Kaboul seulement.

ESP> Los datos para 1975 se refieren a Kabul solamente.

Cyprus:

E--> Not including Turkish schools.

FR-> Non compris les écoles turques.

ESP> Excluídas las escuelas turcas.

Israel:

E--> For 1975 the figures on female teachers (columns 3 and 4) and those on female students (columns 6 and 7) refer to public education only.

FR-> Pour 1975 les chiffres relatifs au personnel enseignant féminin (colonnes 3 et 4) et ceux relatifs aux élèves de sexe féminin (colonnes 6 et 7) se réfèrent à l'enseignement public seulement.

ESP> En 1975 las cifras sobre el personal docente femenino (columnas 3 y 4) y las sobre la matrícula femenina (columnas 6 y 7) se refieren a la enseñanza pública solamente.

Korea, Republic of:

E--> From 1981, due to a change of school system, the data are not comparable with the previous years.

FR-> A partir de 1981, à la suite d'un changement dans le système

Korea, Republic of: (Cont):
scolaire, les données ne sont pas comparables à celles des années précédentes.

ESP> A partir de 1981, de acuerdo con un cambio del sistema escolar, los datos no son comparables a los de los años anteriores.

Singapore:

E--> Data for 1975 refer to private education only.

FR-> Les données pour 1975 se réfèrent à l'enseignement privé seulement.

ESP> Los datos para 1975 se refieren a la enseñanza privada solamente.

Turkey:

E--> Data refer to kindergartens only.

FR-> Les données se réfèrent aux jardins d'enfants seulement.

ESP> Los datos se refieren a los jardines infantiles solamente.

United Arab Emirates:

E--> The figures in columns 1, 2, 3 and 4 refer to public education only.

FR-> Les chiffres des colonnes 1,2, 3 et 4 se réfèrent à l'enseignement public seulement.

ESP> Las cifras de las columnas 1, 2, 3 y 4 se refieren a la enseñanza pública solamente.

EUROPE:

Austria:

E--> For 1975 data on pupils include special education and exclude 'Vorschulklassen'.

FR-> Pour 1975 les chiffres relatifs aux élèves incluent l'éducation spéciale et excluent les 'Vorschulklassen'.

ESP> Para 1975 los datos sobre los alumnos incluyen la educación especial y excluyen las 'Vorschulklassen'.

Belgium:

E--> Data on teachers for 1984 and all data on pupils include special education.

FR-> Les données sur le personnel enseignant pour 1984 et toutes les données relatives aux élèves incluent l'éducation spéciale.

ESP> Los datos sobre el personal docente para 1984 y todos los datos relativos a los alumnos incluyen la educación especial.

Finland:

E--> Figures shown in columns 2, 3 and 4 for 1975 refer to public education only; all other data include special education.

FR-> Les chiffres des colonnes 2, 3 et 4 en 1975 se réfèrent à l'enseignement public seulement; toutes les autres données incluent l'education spéciale.

ESP> Los datos de las columnas 2, 3 y 4 en 1975 se refieren a la enseñanza pública solamente; todos los otros datos incluyen la educación especial.

France:

E--> The figures shown in columns 2, 3 and 4 for 1975, 1980, 1983 and data shown in columns 3 and 4 for 1981 and 1982 refer to public education only.

FR-> Les chiffres des colonnes 2, 3 et 4 en 1975, 1980 et 1983 ainsi que ceux des colonnes 3 et 4 en 1981 et 1982 se réfèrent à l'enseignement public seulement.

ESP> Las cifras de las columnas 2, 3 y 4 en 1975, 1980, 1983 y los datos de las columnas 3 y 4 para 1981 y 1982 se refieren a la enseñanza pública solamente.

Gibraltar:

E--> Data refer to public education only.

FR-> Les données se réfèrent à l'enseignement public seulement.

ESP> Los datos se refieren a la enseñanza pública solamente.

Monaco:

E--> Data for 1976, 1980 and 1981 refer to public education only.

FR-> Les données de 1976, 1980 et 1981 se réfèrent à l'enseignement public seulement.

ESP> Los datos para 1976, 1980 y 1981 se refieren a la enseñanza pública solamente.

Portugal:

E--> For 1982, data on teachers refer to public education only.

FR-> Pour 1982, les données relatives au personnel enseignant se réfèrent à l'enseignement public seulement.

ESP> Para 1982, los datos sobre el personal docente se refieren a la enseñanza pública solamente.

OCEANIA:

American Samoa:

E--> Except for 1980, data refer to public education only.

FR-> A l'exception de 1980, les données se réfèrent à l'enseignement public seulement.

ESP> A la excepción de 1980, los datos se refieren a la enseñanza pública solamente.

Australia:

E--> Data refer only to preprimary classes in primary schools (pre-year 1).

FR-> Les données se réfèrent seulement aux classes maternelles rattachées aux écoles primaires ('pre-year 1').

ESP> Los datos se refieren solamente a las clases maternales adscritas a las escuelas primarias ('pre-year 1').

New Caledonia:

E--> For 1982, data on teachers refer to public education only.

FR-> En 1982, les données sur le personnel enseignant se réfèrent à l'enseignement public seulement.

ESP> En 1982, los datos sobre el personal docente se refieren a la enseñanza pública solamente.

3.4 Education at the first level: institutions, teachers and pupils

Enseignement du premier degré: établissements, personnel enseignant et élèves

Enseñanza de primer grado: establecimientos, personal docente y alumnos

PLEASE REFER TO EXPLANATORY TEXT AT END OF TABLE

PRIERE DE SE REFERER AU TEXTE EXPLICATIF A LA FIN DU TABLEAU

REFERIRSE AL TEXTO EXPLICATIVO AL FINAL DEL CUADRO

NUMBER OF COUNTRIES AND TERRITORIES PRESENTED IN THIS TABLE: 193

NOMBRE DE PAYS ET DE TERRITOIRES PRESENTES DANS CE TABLEAU: 193

NUMERO DE PAISES Y DE TERRITORIOS PRESENTADOS EN ESTE CUADRO: 193

COUNTRY / PAYS / PAIS	YEAR / ANNEE / AÑO	SCHOOLS / ECOLES / ESCUELAS	TEACHING STAFF / PERSONNEL ENSEIGNANT / PERSONAL DOCENTE			PUPILS ENROLLED / ELEVES INSCRITS / ALUMNOS MATRICULADOS			PUPIL/ TEACHER RATIO / NOMBRE D'ELEVES PAR MAITRE / NUMERO DE ALUMNOS POR MAESTRO
			TOTAL	FEMALE / FEMININ / FEMENINO	% F	TOTAL	FEMALE / FEMININ / FEMENINO	% F	
		(1)	(2)	(3)	(4)	(5)	(6)	(7)	(8)
AFRICA									
ALGERIA‡	1975	7 798	65 043	...	...	2 663 248	1 064 576	40	41
	1980	9 263	88 481	32 506	37	3 122 566	1 309 246	42	35
	1981	9 399	94 216	34 475	37	3 178 912	1 338 761	42	34
	1982	9 864	100 288	37 244	37	3 241 924	1 375 135	42	32
	1983	10 453	109 173	40 847	37	3 336 536	1 422 855	43	31
	1984	10 842	115 242	43 904	38	3 414 705	1 469 043	43	30
ANGOLA‡	1980	6 090	...	...	...	1 300 673	...	...	...
	1981	7 026	40 027	...	...	1 258 858	588 532	47	40
	1982	6 308	32 004	...	...	1 178 430	536 105	45	46
BENIN	1975	1 325	4 864	...	...	259 880	81 623	31	53
	1980	2 275	7 994	1 848	23	379 926	121 745	32	48
	1981	2 480	10 381	2 473	24	404 297	130 547	32	39
	1982	2 723	11 339	2 803	25	428 185	139 406	33	38
	1983	2 560	12 163	3 024	25	429 190	142 416	33	35
	1984	2 667	13 269	3 200	24	444 232	147 808	33	33
BOTSWANA	1975	323	3 509	2 333	66	116 293	63 949	55	33
	1980	415	5 316	3 827	72	171 914	93 793	55	32
	1982	484	5 767	4 402	76	187 065	99 802	53	32
	1983	502	6 360	4 855	76	198 328	105 735	53	31
	1984	512	6 794	5 169	76	209 772	110 767	53	31
	1985	528	6 980	5 435	78	223 608	117 185	52	32
BURKINA FASO‡	1975	712	2 997	544	18	141 177	52 275	37	47
	1980	936	3 700	747	20	201 595	74 367	37	54
	1981	1 037	3 744	780	21	223 843	82 473	37	60
	1982	1 176	4 153	875	21	250 628	92 389	37	60
	1983	...	4 103	880	21	276 732	101 764	37	62
	1984	1 537	5 550	1 287	23	313 520	115 340	37	56
BURUNDI‡	1975	580	4 209	1 814	43	129 597	50 045	39	31
	1980	686	4 805	2 258	47	175 856	69 352	39	35
	1981	792	5 252	2 487	47	206 408	79 400	38	39
	1982	...	...	...	...	252 973	...	...	...
	1983	875	6 135	2 784	45	301 278	120 648	40	49
	1984	943	6 689	3 045	46	343 027	140 521	41	51
CAMEROON	1975	4 506	22 209	3 055	14	1 122 900	500 049	45	51
	1980	4 971	26 763	5 248	20	1 379 205	626 966	45	52
	1981	5 148	28 585	5 973	21	1 443 728	657 638	46	51
	1982	5 460	31 588	7 045	22	1 535 582	699 231	46	49
	1983	5 582	31 030	7 349	24	1 563 852	712 773	46	50
	1984	5 742	32 082	8 016	25	1 634 428	743 750	46	51
CAPE VERDE‡	1975	477	1 243	...	...	64 794	*31 000	*48	48
	1980	...	1 436	...	...	57 587	27 985	49	36
	1983	...	1 445	...	...	55 751	27 396	49	33
CENTRAL AFRICAN REPUBLIC	1975	732	3 329	592	18	221 432	79 554	36	67
	1980	825	4 130	1 016	25	246 174	90 468	37	60
	1981	853	4 284	1 009	24	259 525	94 884	37	61
	1982	894	4 364	1 129	26	271 117	95 118	35	62
	1983	931	4 225	...	...	291 444	...	...	69

COUNTRY / PAYS / PAIS	YEAR / ANNEE / AÑO	SCHOOLS / ECOLES / ESCUELAS	TEACHING STAFF / PERSONNEL ENSEIGNANT / PERSONAL DOCENTE			PUPILS ENROLLED / ELEVES INSCRITS / ALUMNOS MATRICULADOS			PUPIL/TEACHER RATIO / NOMBRE D'ELEVES PAR MAITRE / NUMERO DE ALUMNOS POR MAESTRO
			TOTAL	FEMALE FEMININ FEMENINO	% F	TOTAL	FEMALE FEMININ FEMENINO	% F	
		(1)	(2)	(3)	(4)	(5)	(6)	(7)	(8)
CHAD‡	1975	...	*2 512	*133	*5	*212 983	*55 963	*26	77
	1984	1 231	4 494	...	...	288 478	78 974	27	64
COMOROS	1980	236	1 292	95	7	59 709	24 777	41	46
CONGO	1975	1 033	5 434	945	17	319 101	148 445	47	59
	1980	1 335	7 186	1 794	25	390 676	188 431	48	54
	1981	1 377	6 997	1 801	26	406 835	196 690	48	58
	1982	1 428	7 329	1 983	27	422 874	205 508	49	58
	1983	...	...	...	...	443 143	214 237	48	...
	1984	1 522	7 549	2 217	29	458 237	222 625	49	61
COTE D'IVOIRE	1975	2 904	15 358	1 906	12	672 707	253 582	38	44
	1980	4 807	26 460	4 070	15	1 024 585	409 859	40	39
	1982	5 501	31 297	5 420	17	1 134 915	461 945	41	36
	1983	5 795	32 414	5 838	18	1 159 824	476 170	41	36
DJIBOUTI	1975	...	268	95	35	9 764	3 464	35	36
	1980	45	419	...	...	16 841	...	...	40
	1981	47	382	...	...	18 896	7 866	42	49
	1982	48	423	...	...	20 433	8 583	42	48
	1983	52	496	...	...	21 847	9 244	42	44
EGYPT‡	1975	10 346	118 251	56 323	48	4 181 198	1 601 608	38	35
	1980	12 120	...	...	...	4 662 816	1 875 949	40	...
	1981	12 306	141 375	66 808	47	4 876 462	1 983 954	41	34
	1982	12 013	165 308	77 071	47	5 036 608	2 087 822	41	30
	1983	...	170 904	80 223	47	5 349 579	2 255 782	42	31
EQUATORIAL GUINEA	1975	...	...	...	...	*39 000	...	...	...
	1980	...	647	...	...	44 499	...	...	69
	1981	...	664	...	...	45 428	...	...	68
	1982	...	...	...	...	52 021	...	...	...
	1983	...	...	...	...	61 532	...	...	...
ETHIOPIA	1975	3 706	24 469	3 779	15	1 084 307	349 003	32	44
	1980	5 822	33 322	7 296	22	2 130 716	744 068	35	64
	1981	6 209	37 854	8 609	23	2 374 362	847 152	36	63
	1982	6 582	42 347	10 012	24	2 511 050	923 915	37	59
	1983	7 096	46 674	11 443	25	2 497 114	936 602	38	54
GABON	1975	746	2 664	535	20	128 552	62 736	49	48
	1980	864	3 441	939	27	155 081	76 209	49	45
	1981	886	3 526	1 000	28	160 349	78 966	49	45
	1982	901	3 781	1 118	30	165 559	81 589	49	44
	1983	929	3 802	1 139	30	172 201	84 961	49	45
GAMBIA	1975	103	948	...	...	24 617	8 169	33	26
	1980	148	1 808	610	34	43 432	15 147	35	24
	1981	161	2 119	713	34	48 903	17 480	36	23
	1982	164	2 347	770	33	53 774	19 481	36	23
	1983	179	2 439	814	33	60 529	22 696	37	25
	1984	189	2 640	890	34	66 257	25 083	38	25
GHANA‡	1975	6 966	38 381	12 674	33	1 156 758	502 479	43	30
	1980	7 848	47 921	20 123	42	1 416 893	629 080	44	30
	1981	8 029	50 685	22 200	44	1 499 732	655 383	44	30
	1982	8 214	51 109	23 255	46	1 574 719	688 152	44	31
	1983	8 403	58 434	26 588	46	1 653 455	722 560	44	28
	1984	8 965	56 100	25 526	46	1 464 624	640 041	44	26
GUINEA	1975	2 115	4 977	482	10	198 849	66 909	34	40
	1980	2 555	7 165	985	14	257 547	85 842	33	36
	1981	...	7 723	...	...	249 905	...	...	32
	1982	2 635	7 902	1 243	16	247 702	80 793	33	31
	1983	...	7 867	1 357	17	246 129	79 842	32	31
	1984	2 385	7 947	1 677	21	287 804	90 664	32	36
GUINEA-BISSAU‡	1975	*550	2 163	...	...	81 890	28 819	35	*34
	1980	...	3 257	782	24	74 539	23 549	32	23
	1981	732	3 315	774	23	74 803	23 733	32	23
	1982	719	3 363	802	24	74 359	24 370	33	22
	1983	730	3 303	755	23	74 979	25 158	34	23
KENYA	1975	8 161	86 107	24 594	29	2 881 155	1 319 654	46	33
	1980	10 268	102 489	...	...	3 926 629	1 864 014	47	38
	1981	10 950	110 911	...	...	3 981 162	1 902 586	48	36
	1982	11 497	115 094	36 181	31	4 184 602	2 006 433	48	36
	1983	11 966	117 705	...	...	4 323 822	2 074 580	48	37
	1984	12 535	122 738	39 680	32	4 380 232	2 110 992	48	36

COUNTRY / PAYS / PAIS	YEAR / ANNEE / AÑO	SCHOOLS / ECOLES / ESCUELAS	TEACHING STAFF / PERSONNEL ENSEIGNANT / PERSONAL DOCENTE: TOTAL	FEMALE / FEMININ / FEMENINO	% F	PUPILS ENROLLED / ELEVES INSCRITS / ALUMNOS MATRICULADOS: TOTAL	FEMALE / FEMININ / FEMENINO	% F	PUPIL/TEACHER RATIO / NOMBRE D'ELEVES PAR MAITRE / NUMERO DE ALUMNOS POR MAESTRO
		(1)	(2)	(3)	(4)	(5)	(6)	(7)	(8)
LESOTHO	1975	1 079	4 226	2 939	70	221 922	131 014	59	53
	1980	1 074	5 097	3 818	75	244 838	143 472	59	48
	1981	1 085	5 350	4 011	75	259 046	149 938	58	48
	1982	1 103	5 295	4 002	76	277 945	158 567	57	52
	1983	1 152	5 670	...	...	289 590	163 690	57	51
LIBERIA‡	1975	...	*3 832	*1 140	*30	157 821	56 750	36	*41
	1980	1 651	9 099	2 069	23	227 431	85 874	38	*41
LIBYAN ARAB JAMAHIRIYA	1975	2 042	24 331	7 086	29	556 169	256 065	46	23
	1980	2 607	36 591	17 160	47	662 843	314 570	47	18
	1982	2 729	42 696	22 627	53	721 710	341 979	47	17
MADAGASCAR‡	1975	7 960	20 134	...	...	1 210 841	526 201	43	60
	1980	13 594	39 474	...	...	1 723 779	844 822	49	44
	1981	14 769	42 197	...	...	1 731 383	849 038	49	41
	1982	14 390	43 898	...	...	1 701 601	796 816	47	39
	1983	14 050	43 157	...	...	1 651 012	*789 175	*48	38
	1984	13 973	42 462	...	...	1 625 216	783 716	48	38
MALAWI‡	1975	2 140	10 588	...	...	641 709	253 563	40	61
	1980	2 340	12 540	...	...	809 862	333 495	41	65
	1981	2 402	13 143	...	...	882 903	...	...	67
	1982	...	13 476	...	...	868 849	367 262	42	60
	1983	...	14 499	4 562	31	847 157	359 103	42	58
	1984	2 468	14 932	4 940	33	899 459	383 776	43	60
MALI	1975	1 063	6 213	1 148	18	252 393	90 033	36	41
	1980	1 248	6 862	1 368	20	291 159	105 115	36	42
	1981	...	7 278	1 400	19	291 546	106 757	37	40
	1982	1 301	7 932	1 598	20	296 301	108 514	37	37
MAURITANIA‡	1975	...	1 439	...	...	50 465	18 106	36	35
	1980	599	2 183	198	9	90 530	32 057	35	41
	1982	637	2 401	292	12	107 390	42 041	39	45
MAURITIUS‡	1975	...	5 791	...	...	150 573	73 711	49	26
	1980	267	6 379	2 729	44	128 758	63 033	49	20
	1981	268	6 638	2 858	44	135 462	66 764	49	20
	1982	272	6 623	2 806	44	137 004	67 504	49	21
	1983	278	6 572	2 785	44	138 790	68 498	49	21
	1984	281	6 465	2 745	44	135 391	67 020	50	21
MOROCCO‡	1975	1 928	37 226	7 725	21	1 547 647	555 589	36	40
	1980	2 332	56 908	16 990	30	2 172 289	804 056	37	37
	1981	2 767	63 675	20 280	32	2 309 696	863 450	37	36
	1982	2 990	67 682	22 343	33	2 442 726	921 526	38	36
	1983	3 164	71 731	24 214	34	2 467 611	931 370	38	34
	1984	3 443	82 874	27 111	33	2 278 734	863 884	38	27
MOZAMBIQUE‡	1976	5 853	15 000	...	...	1 276 500	518 966	41	85
	1980	5 730	17 030	3 714	22	1 387 192	590 101	43	81
	1981	5 709	18 751	3 937	21	1 286 714	552 406	43	73
	1982	5 430	20 368	4 373	21	1 247 095	534 783	43	65
	1983	5 886	20 769	4 242	20	1 162 617	495 569	43	59
NIGER	1975	1 249	3 617	1 124	31	142 182	50 029	35	39
	1980	1 686	5 518	1 673	30	228 855	80 784	35	41
	1981	1 708	5 475	1 741	32	233 441	83 913	36	43
	1982	1 715	...	...	...	244 758	...	...	...
	1983	1 728	6 940	2 286	33	261 531	...	...	38
NIGERIA	1975	...	...	...	...	5 950 296	...	...	...
	1980	...	369 636	121 497	33	13 760 030	5 970 244	43	37
	1981	...	386 826	...	...	14 285 437	6 137 088	43	37
	1982	...	383 989	...	...	14 654 798	6 306 728	43	38
	1983	...	359 701	...	...	14 383 487	6 331 658	44	40
REUNION‡	1975	371	3 661	...	...	95 810	...	...	26
	1980	...	...	...	...	79 143	...	...	...
	1981	355	3 290	2 118	69	81 329	...	...	25
	1982	357	3 398	2 160	68	78 004	...	...	23
	1983	358	3 355	2 257	67	76 448	...	...	23
RWANDA‡	1975	1 668	8 022	2 355	29	401 521	184 814	46	50
	1980	1 567	11 912	4 577	38	704 924	337 625	48	59
	1981	1 558	13 043	5 179	40	743 067	357 144	48	57
	1982	1 556	13 590	5 701	42	747 172	360 795	48	55
	1983	1 572	14 105	5 993	42	761 955	369 034	48	54

COUNTRY / PAYS / PAIS	YEAR / ANNEE / AÑO	SCHOOLS / ECOLES / ESCUELAS	TEACHING STAFF / PERSONNEL ENSEIGNANT / PERSONAL DOCENTE			PUPILS ENROLLED / ELEVES INSCRITS / ALUMNOS MATRICULADOS			PUPIL/TEACHER RATIO / NOMBRE D'ELEVES PAR MAITRE / NUMERO DE ALUMNOS POR MAESTRO
			TOTAL	FEMALE / FEMININ / FEMENINO	% F	TOTAL	FEMALE / FEMININ / FEMENINO	% F	
		(1)	(2)	(3)	(4)	(5)	(6)	(7)	(8)
ST. HELENA	1975	8	...	...	...	755	365	48	...
	1980	8	39	37	95	717	369	51	18
	1981	8	...	...	...	647	334	52	...
	1982	8	37	36	97	583	318	55	16
	1983	8	32	31	97	589	299	51	18
SAO TOME AND PRINCIPE	1975	...	422	...	...	14 290	...	...	34
	1980	...	588	...	...	16 376	...	...	28
	1981	...	617	...	...	16 382	...	...	27
	1982	64	628	...	...	16 102	7 873	49	26
	1983	...	538	325	60	15 874	7 756	49	30
	1984	...	517	...	...	16 013	...	...	31
SENEGAL	1975	...	7 577	...	...	311 913	131 315	42	41
	1980	1 672	9 175	2 202	24	419 748	166 913	40	46
	1981	1 795	10 586	2 787	26	452 679	179 594	40	43
	1982	1 969	11 378	2 928	26	496 066	197 728	40	44
	1983	2 150	12 934	3 580	28	533 394	213 205	40	41
SEYCHELLES‡	1975	36	428	406	95	10 232	5 268	51	24
	1980	27	658	529	80	14 468	7 356	51	22
	1982	25	683	619	91	14 470	7 143	49	21
	1983	25	656	618	94	14 361	7 076	49	22
	1984	25	679	*640	*94	14 256	7 006	49	21
	1985	25	652	555	85	14 368	7 073	49	22
SIERRA LEONE	1975	1 074	6 373	1 530	24	205 910	81 470	40	32
	1980	1 199	9 528	...	...	315 145	131 661	42	33
	1981	1 223	10 025	...	...	346 703	141 488	41	35
	1982	1 219	10 451	2 290	22	350 160	143 397	41	34
SOMALIA‡	1975	730	3 481	565	16	197 706	70 122	35	57
	1980	1 408	8 122	2 365	29	271 704	98 053	36	33
	1981	1 357	8 391	2 524	30	239 916	85 856	36	29
	1982	1 337	10 065	2 956	29	218 726	76 711	35	22
	1983	1 308	9 460	3 015	32	220 680	78 997	36	23
SUDAN	1975	4 719	31 695	9 990	32	1 169 279	416 156	36	37
	1980	6 027	43 451	13 497	31	1 464 227	591 173	40	34
	1981	6 176	46 437	*16 301	*35	1 524 381	608 501	40	33
	1982	6 758	47 084	18 913	40	1 579 286	643 448	41	34
	1983	6 544	47 754	18 946	40	1 599 181	655 367	41	33
SWAZILAND	1975	412	2 363	1 805	76	89 528	43 984	49	38
	1980	450	3 278	2 590	79	112 019	55 937	50	34
	1981	470	3 586	2 833	79	119 913	59 664	50	33
	1982	468	3 769	3 001	80	125 303	62 325	50	33
	1983	468	3 922	3 058	78	129 767	64 275	50	33
	1984	467	4 039	3 240	80	134 528	66 732	50	33
TOGO	1975	1 362	6 080	1 224	20	362 895	126 041	35	60
	1980	2 205	9 193	...	...	506 356	194 064	38	55
	1981	2 251	9 619	2 044	21	498 639	196 384	39	52
	1982	2 291	10 214	2 132	21	492 329	194 608	40	48
	1983	2 317	10 145	2 143	21	457 376	178 837	39	45
	1984	2 329	10 225	2 074	20	454 209	175 276	39	44
TUNISIA	1975	2 319	23 320	*5 597	*24	932 787	364 370	39	40
	1980	2 661	27 375	8 003	29	1 054 027	438 252	42	39
	1981	2 829	28 764	8 781	31	1 088 822	461 901	42	38
	1982	2 960	30 411	9 726	32	1 150 580	495 150	43	38
	1983	3 087	33 347	11 410	34	1 198 447	524 147	44	36
	1984	3 230	36 610	13 350	36	1 245 262	549 314	44	34
UGANDA‡	1975	3 472	28 681	8 216	29	973 604	390 461	40	34
	1980	4 276	38 422	*11 410	*30	1 292 377	*558 300	*43	34
	1981	4 585	40 489	11 913	29	1 407 158	600 119	43	35
	1982	4 945	44 426	12 802	30	1 616 791	688 636	43	36
UNITED REPUBLIC OF TANZANIA‡	1975	5 804	29 735	9 709	33	1 592 396	668 112	42	54
	1980	9 794	81 153	29 927	37	3 367 644	1 585 140	47	41
	1981	9 980	81 659	30 352	37	3 538 183	1 687 235	48	43
	1982	10 035	88 370	34 248	39	3 512 799	1 697 401	48	40
	1983	...	85 308	...	...	3 552 923	1 724 976	49	42
ZAIRE	1975	...	...	...	...	3 544 498	1 405 657	40	...
	1980	...	...	...	...	4 195 699	1 745 385	42	...
	1981	...	...	...	...	4 342 470	1 818 918	42	...
	1982	...	...	...	...	4 495 346	1 902 442	42	...
	1983	10 065	112 077	...	...	4 654 613	1 990 710	43	42

COUNTRY / PAYS / PAIS	YEAR / ANNEE / AÑO	SCHOOLS / ECOLES / ESCUELAS	TEACHING STAFF / PERSONNEL ENSEIGNANT / PERSONAL DOCENTE			PUPILS ENROLLED / ELEVES INSCRITS / ALUMNOS MATRICULADOS			PUPIL/TEACHER RATIO / NOMBRE D'ELEVES PAR MAITRE / NUMERO DE ALUMNOS POR MAESTRO
			TOTAL	FEMALE / FEMININ / FEMENINO	% F	TOTAL	FEMALE / FEMININ / FEMENINO	% F	
		(1)	(2)	(3)	(4)	(5)	(6)	(7)	(8)
ZAMBIA	1975	2 710	18 096	6 735	37	872 392	396 384	45	48
	1980	2 819	21 455	8 584	40	1 041 938	487 435	47	49
	1981	...	22 258	8 861	40	1 073 203	505 227	47	48
	1982	...	...	...	...	1 121 769	528 095	47	...
	1983	...	...	...	...	*1 194 070	*562 097	*47	...
ZIMBABWE‡	1975	3 623	21 202	7 214	34	862 736	395 114	46	40
	1980	3 157	28 118	...	...	1 235 036	...	...	44
	1981	3 563	37 773	14 290	38	1 714 266	822 164	48	45
	1982	3 880	45 467	18 074	40	1 905 437	915 373	48	42
	1983	3 960	52 502	21 127	40	2 044 029	984 175	48	39
	1984	4 161	54 086	22 634	42	2 130 487	1 029 687	48	39
AMERICA, NORTH									
ANTIGUA AND BARBUDA‡	1975	59	524	443	85	11 340	5 507	49	*26
	1978	53	390	334	86	9 557	4 706	49	*25
	1983	...	...	...	...	11 394	5 276	46	...
BAHAMAS‡	1975	...	1 294	...	...	31 707	15 915	50	*26
	1980	...	1 261	...	...	32 854	...	...	*24
	1981	228	1 151	...	...	32 687	16 358	50	*24
	1982	226	1 555	1 072	92	32 664	16 127	49	21
	1983	225	2 899	...	...	30 570	...	...	*21
BARBADOS‡	1975	...	...	...	...	*32 884	*16 426	*50	...
	1980	134	*1 172	...	...	31 147	15 497	50	28
	1981	135	*1 473	...	...	30 728	15 070	49	22
	1982	137	1 492	...	...	30 337	14 645	48	18
	1983	128	1 317	...	...	30 907	15 327	50	21
	1984	125	1 421	975	*74	30 161	14 605	48	21
BELIZE‡	1975	194	1 207	871	72	33 444	...	...	*27
	1980	197	1 421	...	...	34 615	...	...	24
	1981	198	1 463	...	...	35 113	...	...	24
	1982	208	...	...	...	37 158	18 121	49	...
BERMUDA‡	1975	22	...	...	...	6 808	3 288	48	...
	1980	22	312	227	88	5 934	2 885	49	19
	1981	22	326	226	86	5 881	2 872	49	18
	1982	22	322	284	88	5 750	2 826	49	18
	1983	22	316	280	89	5 530	2 769	50	18
	1984	22	309	278	90	5 398	2 692	50	17
BRITISH VIRGIN ISLANDS	1975	22	113	102	90	2 096	1 042	50	19
	1980	18	109	92	84	1 974	982	50	18
	1982	19	121	93	77	2 009	988	49	17
	1983	19	117	97	83	2 054	966	47	18
	1984	19	...	...	...	2 069	987	48	...
CANADA‡	1975	...	*119 300	*85 500	*72	2 440 016	1 190 489	49	*20
	1980	...	...	...	...	2 184 919	1 064 543	49	...
	1981	...	...	...	...	2 296 996	1 109 685	48	...
	1982	12 990	142 533	94 460	66	2 271 784	1 092 978	48	*18
	1983	12 913	142 283	94 737	67	2 251 535	1 082 843	48	*18
CAYMAN ISLANDS‡	1975	16	55	46	84	1 933	948	49	*23
	1980	15	65	55	85	2 123	1 045	49	*19
COSTA RICA‡	1975	2 770	12 429	...	...	361 303	176 792	49	29
	1980	2 936	12 596	...	...	348 674	169 403	49	28
	1981	2 944	10 556	8 316	79	348 616	169 052	48	33
	1982	2 971	10 312	...	...	342 373	166 194	49	*33
	1983	2 993	10 316	...	...	343 800	166 507	48	*33
	1984	3 035	...	...	...	350 658	169 567	48	...
CUBA	1975	14 886	77 472	55 543	72	1 795 752	862 687	48	23
	1980	12 196	84 041	63 339	75	1 468 538	698 138	48	17
	1981	11 771	83 113	63 761	77	1 409 765	670 946	48	17
	1982	11 213	83 358	63 710	76	1 363 078	647 619	48	16
	1983	10 866	83 424	64 105	77	1 282 989	610 778	48	15
	1984	10 477	79 610	61 646	77	1 174 453	554 614	47	15
DOMINICA‡	1975	57	674	477	71	17 166	8 276	48	*27
	1980	...	...	...	...	14 815	7 472	50	...
	1981	...	...	...	...	14 803	7 025	47	...
	1983	66	665	...	...	13 283	6 287	47	20
DOMINICAN REPUBLIC‡	1975	5 487	17 932	...	...	911 142	...	...	51
	1980	4 606	...	...	...	1 105 730	...	...	...
	1981	...	...	...	...	1 149 805	460 302	*50	...
	1982	6 009	23 578	...	...	1 092 838	565 266	52	46
	1983	4 846	20 607	...	...	1 121 851	478 698	*52	*46

COUNTRY / PAYS / PAIS	YEAR / ANNEE / AÑO	SCHOOLS / ECOLES / ESCUELAS	TEACHING STAFF / PERSONNEL ENSEIGNANT / PERSONAL DOCENTE			PUPILS ENROLLED / ELEVES INSCRITS / ALUMNOS MATRICULADOS			PUPIL/TEACHER RATIO / NOMBRE D'ELEVES PAR MAITRE / NUMERO DE ALUMNOS POR MAESTRO
			TOTAL	FEMALE / FEMININ / FEMENINO	% F	TOTAL	FEMALE / FEMININ / FEMENINO	% F	
		(1)	(2)	(3)	(4)	(5)	(6)	(7)	(8)
EL SALVADOR‡	1975	3 103	14 256	9 677	68	759 460	366 612	48	44
	1980	3 196	17 364	11 315	65	834 101	412 743	49	48
	1981	2 311	17 441	11 732	67	709 567	352 291	50	41
	1982	2 390	17 853	11 886	67	810 827	400 582	49	45
	1983	2 464	17 633	11 902	67	851 895	420 212	49	48
	1984	2 631	21 145	14 018	66	883 329	438 883	50	42
GRENADA	1975	63	...	...	...	21 195	10 125	48	...
	1980	57	776	506	65	18 076	8 647	48	23
	1981	59	760	500	66	17 331	8 237	48	23
	1982	64	764	521	68	17 704	8 469	48	23
	1983	64	775	536	69	20 460	9 725	48	26
GUADELOUPE‡	1975	257	2 018	...	...	62 813	...	...	31
	1980	...	...	...	...	53 581	...	...	...
	1981	238	2 186	1 404	64	52 947	...	...	24
	1982	232	2 408	1 445	60	50 576	...	...	21
	1983	230	2 173	1 487	68	47 733	...	...	22
GUATEMALA	1975	6 122	18 129	11 162	62	627 126	280 719	45	35
	1980	6 959	23 770	...	...	803 404	362 083	45	34
	1981	7 015	23 900	14 897	62	874 697	395 155	45	37
	1982	6 791	24 456	...	...	848 116	388 111	46	35
	1983	7 490	25 862	16 052	62	930 130	421 460	45	36
	1984	7 820	26 963	...	...	979 888	...	...	36
HAITI‡	1975	2 788	11 816	...	...	487 135	...	...	41
	1980	3 271	14 581	7 124	49	642 391	294 712	46	44
	1981	3 321	14 927	...	...	658 102	304 103	46	44
	1982	3 241	16 986	8 902	52	723 041	336 567	47	43
	1983	3 406	18 483	9 197	50	783 070	365 188	47	42
HONDURAS	1975	4 602	13 045	...	...	460 744	225 965	49	35
	1980	5 524	16 385	12 187	74	601 337	298 163	50	37
	1982	5 857	17 930	13 355	74	671 786	331 566	49	37
	1983	6 205	18 966	14 046	74	703 608	349 021	50	37
	1984	6 304	19 155	14 194	74	736 902	366 008	50	38
	1985	...	...	...	...	765 809	380 074	50	...
JAMAICA‡	1975	923	11 531	...	...	371 876	185 568	50	*39
	1980	894	8 676	7 506	87	359 488	178 053	50	40
	1981	...	...	...	...	363 593	...	...	...
	1982	883	...	...	...	363 368	180 505	50	...
	1983	881	10 374	9 047	87	341 748	168 688	49	33
MARTINIQUE‡	1975	238	2 273	...	...	58 747	...	...	26
	1980	...	...	...	...	47 382	...	...	...
	1981	230	2 056	1 401	68	45 245	...	...	22
	1982	226	1 927	1 316	68	41 928	...	...	22
	1983	224	2 004	1 505	75	39 050	...	...	19
MEXICO	1975	55 618	255 939	*159 055	*62	11 461 415	5 450 446	48	45
	1980	76 179	375 220	...	...	14 666 257	7 151 826	49	39
	1981	76 286	400 417	...	...	14 981 028	7 301 482	49	37
	1982	77 900	415 425	...	...	15 222 916	7 356 458	48	37
	1983	78 903	428 029	...	...	15 376 153	7 439 855	48	36
	1984	76 183	437 408	...	...	15 219 245	7 405 543	49	35
MONTSERRAT	1975	16	106	91	86	2 635	1 261	48	25
	1980	16	...	...	...	1 846	892	48	...
	1981	15	86	75	87	1 725	865	50	20
NETHERLANDS ANTILLES	1980	...	...	...	...	32 856	16 243	49	...
	1981	125	1 543	...	...	32 832	16 140	49	21
	1982	122	...	...	...	32 380	15 902	49	...
NICARAGUA‡	1975	2 297	8 817	...	...	341 533	*174 182	*51	*40
	1980	4 421	13 318	10 391	78	472 167	239 968	51	35
	1982	4 056	14 105	11 153	79	509 240	258 245	51	36
	1983	5 221	15 329	12 014	78	536 656	272 392	51	35
	1984	...	17 969	...	...	534 317	...	...	*35
PANAMA	1975	2 171	12 459	10 053	81	334 607	160 588	48	27
	1980	2 306	12 361	9 909	80	337 522	162 510	48	27
	1981	2 316	12 598	10 112	80	335 239	161 272	48	27
	1982	2 347	12 853	10 234	80	336 740	161 991	48	26
	1983	2 378	12 912	10 264	79	335 651	160 805	48	26
	1984	2 438	13 255	10 483	79	339 101	161 796	48	26
PUERTO RICO‡	1975	...	17 270	...	...	385 903	...	...	22
	1981	...	...	...	...	492 908	...	...	...

COUNTRY / PAYS / PAIS	YEAR / ANNEE / AÑO	SCHOOLS / ECOLES / ESCUELAS	TEACHING STAFF / PERSONNEL ENSEIGNANT / PERSONAL DOCENTE: TOTAL	FEMALE / FEMININ / FEMENINO	% F	PUPILS ENROLLED / ELEVES INSCRITS / ALUMNOS MATRICULADOS: TOTAL	FEMALE / FEMININ / FEMENINO	% F	PUPIL/TEACHER RATIO / NOMBRE D'ELEVES PAR MAITRE / NUMERO DE ALUMNOS POR MAESTRO
		(1)	(2)	(3)	(4)	(5)	(6)	(7)	(8)
ST. CHRISTOPHER AND NEVIS	1975	...	...	...	...	8 804	4 246	48	...
	1980	...	...	...	...	7 149	3 488	49	...
	1981	...	...	...	...	7 074	3 007	43	...
	1983	33	357	282	79	8 070	3 976	49	23
	1984	32	339	277	82	7 655	3 525	46	23
ST. LUCIA	1975	76	953	...	...	29 859	14 576	49	31
	1980	77	957	768	80	29 605	15 079	51	31
	1981	78	1 012	809	80	31 199	15 469	50	31
	1982	79	985	766	78	31 795	15 711	49	32
	1983	80	1 084	841	78	32 107	15 788	49	30
ST. PIERRE AND MIQUELON	1980	5	36	26	72	747	364	49	21
	1981	5	39	28	72	703	353	50	18
	1982	5	41	28	68	673	337	50	16
	1983	5	38	29	76	656	324	49	17
	1984	5	39	28	72	612	300	49	16
ST. VINCENT AND THE GRENADINES	1975	61	1 210	518	43	21 854	10 605	49	18
	1981	62	1 184	736	62	21 497	10 436	49	18
	1983	64	...	...	...	22 454	10 793	48	...
TRINIDAD AND TOBAGO‡	1975	473	6 471	4 022	62	199 033	98 990	50	31
	1980	464	7 002	4 623	66	167 039	83 524	50	24
	1981	466	7 298	4 950	68	167 950	83 182	50	23
	1982	467	7 522	5 460	73	169 853	84 927	50	23
	1984	468	7 627	5 357	70	168 308	83 708	50	22
TURKS AND CAICOS ISLANDS‡	1975	17	83	75	90	1 764	...	...	21
	1980	17	80	74	93	1 483	712	48	19
	1984	17	68	67	99	1 429	697	49	21
UNITED STATES‡	1975	*77 619	*1 354 000	...	...	*26 846 000	...	...	*20
	1980	...	*1 390 000	...	...	27 448 000	13 361 000	49	*20
	1981	...	*1 370 000	...	...	27 794 000	13 558 000	49	*20
	1982	...	1 352 000	...	...	27 411 000	13 310 000	49	20
	1983	...	1 415 000	...	...	27 195 000	13 180 000	48	19
	1984	...	1 414 000	...	...	26 839 000	13 059 000	49	19
U.S. VIRGIN ISLANDS‡	1975	*42	*1 111	...	...	*17 997	...	...	*16
	1980	...	819	...	...	21 738	...	...	*15
	1981	...	786	...	...	21 597	...	...	*15
AMERICA, SOUTH									
ARGENTINA	1975	20 646	195 997	181 141	92	3 571 180	1 758 729	49	18
	1980	...	...	...	...	3 917 449	1 927 389	49	...
	1982	20 201	206 535	189 438	92	4 197 372	2 061 532	49	20
	1983	*20 339	*212 932	*197 029	*93	*4 315 752	*2 123 487	*49	*20
	1984	20 619	218 520	202 074	92	4 430 513	2 183 532	49	20
	1985	20 700	229 715	212 033	92	4 589 291	2 268 227	49	20
BOLIVIA	1975	9 519	38 737	...	...	859 413	383 882	45	22
	1980	...	48 894	23 293	48	978 250	456 411	47	20
	1981	...	45 024	...	...	1 022 624	468 604	46	23
	1982	...	...	...	...	1 049 921	...	...	...
	1983	...	...	...	...	1 105 922	512 116	46	...
	1984	8 038	47 224	...	...	1 181 246	554 224	47	25
BRAZIL	1975	188 260	896 652	764 527	85	19 549 249	9 636 448	49	22
	1980	201 926	884 257	748 927	85	22 598 254	10 993 176	49	26
	1981	192 629	942 955	...	...	22 472 979	10 965 652	49	24
	1982	198 030	960 905	837 010	87	23 563 884	11 685 538	50	25
	1983	190 917	967 975	...	...	24 555 789	*11 724 670	*48	25
CHILE	1975	8 461	65 817	48 615	74	2 298 998	1 130 358	49	35
	1980	...	...	...	...	2 185 459	1 069 048	49	...
	1981	8 658	...	...	...	2 139 319	1 046 326	49	...
	1982	8 311	62 746	...	...	2 092 597	1 016 101	49	33
	1983	8 479	...	...	...	2 085 128	1 015 518	49	...
	1984	8 862	...	...	...	2 045 893	995 317	49	...
COLOMBIA	1975	33 202	121 957	...	...	3 911 244	1 974 005	50	32
	1980	33 557	136 381	107 744	79	4 168 200	2 083 500	50	31
	1982	34 725	131 741	...	...	3 930 303	1 958 720	50	30
	1983	35 470	133 957	...	...	3 983 141	1 984 142	50	30
	1984	35 984	135 417	...	...	4 009 423	1 987 204	50	30
	1985	34 004	132 940	105 014	79	4 039 533	2 019 305	50	30

COUNTRY / PAYS / PAIS	YEAR / ANNEE / AÑO	SCHOOLS / ECOLES / ESCUELAS	TEACHING STAFF / PERSONNEL ENSEIGNANT / PERSONAL DOCENTE: TOTAL	FEMALE / FEMININ / FEMENINO	% F	PUPILS ENROLLED / ELEVES INSCRITS / ALUMNOS MATRICULADOS: TOTAL	FEMALE / FEMININ / FEMENINO	% F	PUPIL/TEACHER RATIO / NOMBRE D'ELEVES PAR MAITRE / NUMERO DE ALUMNOS POR MAESTRO
		(1)	(2)	(3)	(4)	(5)	(6)	(7)	(8)
ECUADOR	1975	9 479	32 279	20 960	65	1 216 233	591 241	49	38
	1980	11 451	42 415	27 696	65	1 534 258	746 014	49	36
	1981	12 012	45 459	29 509	65	1 589 997	...	...	35
	1982	12 316	45 225	29 571	65	1 633 516	...	...	36
	1983	13 011	50 347	32 526	65	1 677 364	823 800	49	33
	1984	...	51 300	...	...	1 672 608	...	...	33
FALKLAND ISLANDS (MALVINAS)	1975	18	23	11	48	206	99	48	9
	1980	...	15	5	33	223	130	58	15
FRENCH GUIANA‡	1975	46	259	...	...	7 594	...	...	29
	1980	...	...	...	...	9 276	...	...	...
	1981	47	409	256	70	9 424	...	...	23
	1982	50	409	250	69	9 787	...	...	24
	1983	51	423	305	72	9 780	...	...	23
GUYANA	1975	...	4 052	2 791	69	130 240	64 015	49	32
	1980	425	3 909	2 721	70	130 832	64 242	49	33
	1981	423	3 493	2 433	70	130 003	63 966	49	37
PARAGUAY	1975	...	...	...	...	452 249	214 459	47	...
	1980	...	18 948	...	...	518 968	...	...	27
	1981	...	19 748	...	...	530 083	...	...	27
	1982	3 613	20 746	...	...	539 889	256 952	48	26
	1983	...	21 524	...	...	549 637	...	...	26
	1984	...	22 090	...	...	559 080	...	...	25
PERU	1975	19 701	72 641	...	...	2 840 625	...	...	39
	1980	20 776	84 360	50 676	60	3 161 375	1 514 621	48	37
	1981	20 981	86 893	52 534	60	3 251 807	1 564 967	48	37
	1982	21 335	89 370	...	...	3 412 769	1 624 197	48	38
	1985	24 327	106 600	64 036	60	3 711 592	1 787 244	48	35
SURINAME	1975	309	2 552	1 659	65	80 171	38 248	48	31
	1984	...	...	...	...	71 454	34 488	48	...
URUGUAY	1975	2 308	13 572	...	...	322 602	156 947	49	24
	1980	2 294	14 768	...	...	331 247	161 293	49	22
	1981	2 543	18 017	...	...	387 150	187 510	48	21
	1982	2 292	16 821	...	...	363 179	...	...	22
	1983	2 295	17 036	...	...	350 178	170 094	49	21
VENEZUELA	1975	11 859	69 466	...	...	2 108 413	1 041 196	49	30
	1980	...	92 551	...	...	2 530 263	...	...	27
	1981	12 788	97 045	80 241	83	2 591 051	1 274 791	49	27
	1982	12 990	100 681	83 611	83	2 660 440	1 305 833	49	26
	1983	12 691	100 078	83 292	83	2 641 380	1 294 767	49	26
ASIA									
AFGHANISTAN‡	1975	3 371	18 558	3 353	18	784 568	115 795	15	42
	1980	3 824	35 364	7 413	21	1 115 993	198 580	18	32
	1981	4 018	37 537	7 742	21	1 198 286	223 235	19	32
	1982	635	15 008	7 009	47	449 948	141 948	32	30
	1984	754	14 865	8 349	56	545 959	166 013	30	37
BAHRAIN‡	1975	...	2 044	946	46	44 857	19 569	44	21
	1980	...	2 577	1 242	48	48 451	22 439	46	17
	1981	...	2 543	1 245	49	49 298	22 491	46	17
	1982	...	2 736	1 341	49	50 217	23 813	47	17
	1983	...	2 910	1 454	50	53 575	25 614	48	16
	1984	...	2 892	1 486	51	55 496	27 392	49	17
BANGLADESH	1975	39 914	164 717	8 397	5	8 349 834	2 839 021	34	51
	1980	43 936	153 859	12 128	8	8 240 169	3 044 989	37	54
	1982	44 028	...	...	...	*8 400 000	*3 400 000	*40	...
	1983	43 472	171 349	13 702	8	8 808 028	3 254 459	37	51
	1984	44 119	189 884	14 879	8	8 915 442	3 891 969	44	47
	1985	44 180	189 900	15 192	8	8 920 293	3 568 116	40	47
BHUTAN	1976	...	...	...	...	16 671	4 481	27	...
	1980	...	...	...	...	29 899	...	...	...
	1981	...	...	...	...	33 610	...	...	...
	1982	127	1 050	...	...	37 404	11 813	32	36
	1983	136	1 167	...	...	41 372	13 401	32	35
	1984	141	1 149	...	...	44 275	14 658	33	39
BRUNEI DARUSSALAM	1975	139	1 582	684	43	30 109	14 324	48	19
	1980	137	1 671	760	45	30 513	14 547	48	18
	1981	142	1 800	864	48	31 677	15 119	48	18
	1982	183	1 923	944	49	31 682	15 170	48	16
	1983	176	2 048	1 038	51	32 771	15 645	48	16
	1984	144	2 331	1 274	55	34 373	16 391	48	15

COUNTRY PAYS PAIS	YEAR ANNEE AÑO	SCHOOLS ECOLES ESCUELAS	TEACHING STAFF / PERSONNEL ENSEIGNANT / PERSONAL DOCENTE TOTAL	 FEMALE FEMININ FEMENINO	 % F	PUPILS ENROLLED / ELEVES INSCRITS / ALUMNOS MATRICULADOS TOTAL	 FEMALE FEMININ FEMENINO	 % F	PUPIL/TEACHER RATIO NOMBRE D'ELEVES PAR MAITRE NUMERO DE ALUMNOS POR MAESTRO
		(1)	(2)	(3)	(4)	(5)	(6)	(7)	(8)
BURMA	1975	18 670	66 251	...	...	3 475 749	1 658 078	48	52
	1980	21 999	80 343	...	...	4 148 300	...	...	52
	1981	23 499	86 354	...	...	4 392 500	...	...	51
	1982	25 499	95 435	...	...	4 541 900	...	...	48
	1983	27 499	104 754	...	...	4 696 300	...	...	45
CHINA	1975	1 093 317	5 203 000	1 888 500	36	150 941 000	68 243 000	45	29
	1980	917 316	5 499 400	2 039 100	37	146 270 000	65 174 000	45	27
	1981	894 074	5 580 100	2 027 000	36	143 328 000	63 012 000	44	26
	1982	880 516	5 504 600	1 997 200	36	139 720 400	60 998 800	44	25
	1983	862 165	5 424 600	2 007 400	37	135 780 400	59 372 200	44	25
	1984	853 700	5 369 600	2 093 600	39	135 571 200	59 377 200	44	25
CYPRUS‡	1975	402	2 101	916	44	56 602	27 388	48	27
	1980	443	2 193	993	45	48 701	23 789	49	22
	1981	438	2 203	1 020	46	46 095	22 552	49	21
	1982	435	2 221	1 038	47	46 198	22 459	49	21
	1983	413	2 221	1 054	47	46 653	22 584	48	21
DEMOCRATIC YEMEN‡	1975	962	6 659	1 743	26	228 544	71 004	31	34
	1980	897	10 072	3 439	34	267 456	73 696	28	27
	1981	861	10 832	3 399	31	270 167	70 307	26	25
	1982	911	11 152	3 579	32	279 096	72 472	26	25
	1983	924	11 281	3 921	35	294 028	77 390	26	26
HONG KONG	1975	1 126	20 666	14 172	69	642 611	308 075	48	31
	1980	803	17 937	13 015	73	540 260	258 685	48	30
	1981	781	17 864	13 066	73	537 123	256 962	48	30
	1982	765	19 388	14 185	73	538 458	256 898	48	28
	1983	760	19 431	14 242	73	539 856	257 175	48	28
	1984	753	19 621	14 451	74	536 220	255 531	48	27
INDIA‡	1975	453 530	1 559 137	387 122	25	65 660 022	25 010 985	38	42
	1980	485 538	1 345 376	343 399	26	72 687 840	28 111 612	39	*43
	1981	495 007	1 365 431	352 771	26	73 563 270	28 586 643	39	*43
	1982	503 741	1 389 356	354 362	26	77 038 922	29 763 280	39	*43
INDONESIA	1975	72 760	603 327	...	...	17 776 617	8 088 266	45	29
	1980	128 875	787 400	...	...	25 537 053	11 786 487	46	32
	1981	134 021	855 876	...	...	27 026 488	12 652 293	47	32
	1982	144 133	971 893	318 610	33	27 990 275	13 431 482	48	29
	1983	153 359	1 056 447	...	...	29 108 580	13 997 881	48	28
	1984	158 590	1 131 271	...	...	29 909 188	14 405 718	48	26
IRAN, ISLAMIC REPUBLIC OF‡	1975	36 738	152 106	79 492	52	4 468 299	1 685 364	38	29
	1980	39 213	...	...	...	4 799 000	...	...	...
	1981	42 805	192 719	109 917	57	5 283 377	2 113 369	40	27
	1982	45 490	280 649	131 768	47	5 592 808	2 284 600	41	20
	1983	47 567	297 298	156 065	52	5 994 403	2 525 480	42	20
	1984	48 982	307 718	161 645	53	6 343 300	2 723 424	43	21
IRAQ	1975	7 595	69 812	25 557	37	1 776 095	591 613	33	25
	1980	11 284	94 000	45 516	48	2 615 910	1 212 828	46	28
	1981	10 816	98 422	47 489	48	2 637 023	1 239 448	47	27
	1982	10 243	107 479	62 151	58	2 620 883	1 217 335	46	24
	1983	10 138	112 428	68 040	61	2 698 542	1 233 059	46	24
ISRAEL‡	1975	1 503	32 657	...	...	535 320	261 338	49	15
	1980	1 576	41 468	...	...	621 912	...	...	14
	1981	1 591	42 068	...	...	641 668	...	...	14
	1982	1 592	42 395	...	...	667 207	326 899	49	14
	1983	1 607	42 536	...	...	685 714	338 083	49	14
JAPAN‡	1975	24 650	402 553	228 728	57	10 280 642	5 056 696	49	26
	1980	24 945	470 991	266 971	57	11 750 543	5 764 765	49	25
	1981	25 005	477 101	269 898	57	11 848 653	5 814 092	49	25
	1982	25 043	478 349	269 337	56	11 827 000	5 804 311	49	25
	1983	25 045	476 991	267 464	56	11 665 452	5 725 900	49	24
	1984	25 064	471 724	264 383	56	11 464 221	5 592 698	49	24
JORDAN‡	1975	1 165	11 136	5 719	51	386 012	179 394	46	35
	1980	1 115	14 303	8 416	59	454 391	216 578	48	32
	1981	1 149	14 891	9 114	61	467 696	222 225	48	31
	1982	1 129	14 873	9 687	65	473 027	226 308	48	32
	1983	1 148	15 179	10 110	67	487 890	233 663	48	32
	1984	1 173	15 799	10 275	65	504 226	245 412	49	32
KOREA, DEMOCRATIC PEOPLE'S REP. OF	1976	4 700	...	...	...	2 561 674	1 242 980	49	...

COUNTRY / PAYS / PAIS	YEAR / ANNEE / AÑO	SCHOOLS / ECOLES / ESCUELAS	TEACHING STAFF / PERSONNEL ENSEIGNANT / PERSONAL DOCENTE			PUPILS ENROLLED / ELEVES INSCRITS / ALUMNOS MATRICULADOS			PUPIL/TEACHER RATIO / NOMBRE D'ELEVES PAR MAITRE / NUMERO DE ALUMNOS POR MAESTRO
			TOTAL	FEMALE / FEMININ / FEMENINO	% F	TOTAL	FEMALE / FEMININ / FEMENINO	% F	
		(1)	(2)	(3)	(4)	(5)	(6)	(7)	(8)
KOREA, REPUBLIC OF	1975	6 367	108 126	36 440	34	5 599 074	2 709 133	48	52
	1980	6 487	119 064	43 792	37	5 658 002	2 745 382	49	48
	1981	6 517	122 727	47 230	38	5 586 494	2 712 067	49	46
	1982	6 501	124 572	49 720	40	5 465 248	2 652 240	49	44
	1983	6 500	126 163	52 124	41	5 257 164	2 550 371	49	42
	1984	6 528	126 233	53 158	42	5 040 958	2 446 787	49	40
KUWAIT	1975	177	6 360	3 471	55	111 820	51 099	46	18
	1980	238	8 035	4 466	56	148 983	71 249	48	19
	1981	242	8 385	4 648	55	154 772	74 749	48	18
	1982	238	8 346	4 677	56	160 188	77 862	49	19
	1983	252	8 968	5 303	59	165 696	80 680	49	18
	1984	263	9 448	6 371	67	170 616	82 900	49	18
LAO PEOPLE'S DEMOCRATIC REP.‡	1975	...	11 848	...	...	317 126	...	...	27
	1980	6 339	16 109	4 849	30	479 291	217 297	45	30
	1981	6 349	16 130	...	...	480 535	218 643	46	30
	1982	...	16 454	5 201	32	480 871	...	...	29
	1983	6 544	17 789	5 229	29	485 741	204 799	42	27
LEBANON‡	1980	1 168	22 646	...	...	405 402	...	...	18
	1981	1 108	22 810	...	...	398 977	189 876	48	17
	1982	...	...	...	...	382 500	179 761	47	...
MACAU	1975	59	753	...	...	20 758	...	...	28
	1976	66	1 196	...	...	24 700	...	...	21
	1978	66	801	...	...	24 145	...	...	30
MALAYSIA	1975	6 387	59 343	...	...	1 893 323	908 717	48	32
	1980	6 457	73 304	...	...	2 008 587	...	...	27
	1982	6 464	79 275	...	...	2 079 438	*1 007 939	*48	26
	1983	6 490	81 664	38 108	47	2 120 050	1 029 111	49	26
	1984	6 557	83 760	40 174	48	2 148 748	1 044 999	49	26
	1985	6 629	91 099	45 493	50	2 191 676	1 064 590	49	24
MALDIVES	1980	...	...	...	...	30 621	...	...	...
	1982	...	...	...	...	34 090	...	...	...
MONGOLIA	1975	...	...	...	...	129 802	63 420	49	...
	1980	...	...	...	...	145 200	71 200	49	...
	1981	...	...	...	...	146 500	72 500	49	...
	1982	103	4 700	...	...	150 100	74 700	50	32
	1983	...	...	...	...	152 700	75 300	49	...
	1984	...	...	...	...	153 700	76 000	49	...
NEPAL‡	1975	8 314	18 874	...	...	542 524	84 008	15	29
	1980	10 130	27 805	2 681	10	1 067 912	299 512	28	38
	1981	10 628	29 134	...	...	1 388 001	373 736	27	48
	1982	10 912	32 259	...	...	1 474 698	406 962	28	46
	1983	11 299	38 131	3 503	9	1 626 437	455 430	28	43
	1984	11 660	46 484	*4 596	*10	1 747 857	510 571	29	38
OMAN	1975	181	2 055	550	27	54 611	14 901	27	27
	1980	178	3 959	1 362	34	91 895	31 455	34	23
	1981	183	4 130	1 393	34	102 011	36 370	36	25
	1982	213	4 649	1 614	35	117 295	44 456	38	25
	1983	311	5 101	1 906	37	135 815	54 573	40	27
	1984	328	5 494	2 242	41	156 947	66 555	42	29
PAKISTAN‡	1975	52 800	130 295	44 149	34	5 236 203	1 546 406	30	40
	1980	59 165	150 004	48 652	32	5 473 578	1 782 378	33	36
	1981	61 117	159 062	49 557	31	5 741 490	1 895 852	33	36
	1982	71 358	176 700	50 462	29	6 179 400	2 010 000	33	35
	1983	72 053	206 000	57 400	28	6 412 000	2 092 000	33	31
PHILIPPINES‡	1975	30 839	261 817	...	...	7 597 279	...	...	29
	1980	30 595	264 241	211 271	80	8 033 642	3 905 036	49	30
	1981	31 729	273 492	...	...	8 518 283	4 155 165	49	31
	1982	32 304	272 134	232 454	85	8 591 267	4 186 389	49	32
	1983	32 809	281 456	238 478	85	8 717 469	4 254 207	49	31
	1984	...	286 246	272 129	95	8 793 763	4 299 487	49	31
QATAR	1975	100	1 252	678	54	23 615	11 246	48	19
	1980	101	2 029	1 159	57	30 078	14 472	48	15
	1981	100	2 303	1 373	60	32 618	15 432	47	14
	1982	106	2 508	1 586	63	34 805	16 527	47	14
	1983	108	2 798	1 718	61	35 920	17 025	47	13
	1984	103	2 871	1 837	64	37 967	18 127	48	13
SAUDI ARABIA	1975	3 460	34 481	10 568	31	677 803	246 559	36	20
	1980	5 719	50 511	19 645	39	926 531	360 030	39	18
	1981	6 270	55 836	23 040	41	994 901	397 416	40	18
	1982	6 776	60 539	26 320	43	1 070 291	436 411	41	18
	1983	7 259	67 854	28 736	42	1 171 654	495 373	42	17

COUNTRY / PAYS / PAIS	YEAR / ANNEE / AÑO	SCHOOLS / ECOLES / ESCUELAS	TEACHING STAFF / PERSONNEL ENSEIGNANT / PERSONAL DOCENTE: TOTAL	FEMALE / FEMININ / FEMENINO	% F	PUPILS ENROLLED / ELEVES INSCRITS / ALUMNOS MATRICULADOS: TOTAL	FEMALE / FEMININ / FEMENINO	% F	PUPIL/TEACHER RATIO / NOMBRE D'ELEVES PAR MAITRE / NUMERO DE ALUMNOS POR MAESTRO
		(1)	(2)	(3)	(4)	(5)	(6)	(7)	(8)
SINGAPORE	1975	391	10 777	7 223	67	328 401	154 995	47	30
	1980	335	9 463	6 289	66	291 649	139 276	48	31
	1981	328	9 505	6 290	66	285 179	136 000	48	30
	1982	321	10 286	7 063	69	289 092	136 597	47	28
	1983	305	9 921	6 778	68	290 800	137 317	47	29
	1984	275	10 657	7 385	69	288 623	135 556	47	27
SRI LANKA‡	1975	...	99 067	51 526	52	1 367 860	646 171	47	*30
	1980	8 772	...	...	...	2 081 391	999 173	48	...
	1981	9 176	131 656	...	...	2 132 596	1 026 432	48	*32
	1982	9 209	129 210	...	...	2 142 377	1 033 247	48	*32
	1983	...	133 658	...	...	2 153 595	1 037 997	48	*32
	1984	9 240	135 514	...	...	2 156 522	1 040 304	48	*32
SYRIAN ARAB REPUBLIC‡	1975	7 018	37 621	17 035	45	1 273 944	504 939	40	34
	1980	7 846	55 346	29 616	54	1 555 921	667 780	43	28
	1981	8 098	59 110	32 440	55	1 642 888	718 168	44	28
	1982	8 288	62 959	36 240	58	1 716 795	759 161	44	27
	1983	8 489	67 057	39 776	59	1 823 684	817 698	45	27
	1984	8 747	71 122	43 013	60	1 924 242	872 975	45	27
THAILAND‡	1975	42 179	239 128	...	...	6 686 477	3 161 807	47	28
	1980	...	299 473	145 950	49	7 392 563	3 562 975	48	*23
	1981	...	333 351	...	...	7 449 219	...	...	*22
	1983	...	355 984	...	...	7 272 153	...	...	*22
TURKEY	1975	41 981	171 032	...	...	5 463 684	...	...	32
	1980	45 549	212 456	86 205	41	5 656 494	2 568 623	45	27
	1981	45 842	212 795	88 375	42	5 859 711	2 697 369	46	28
	1983	47 326	208 891	86 111	41	6 497 308	3 034 145	47	31
	1984	47 161	209 395	86 198	41	6 514 189	3 064 561	47	31
UNITED ARAB EMIRATES‡	1975	...	3 191	1 563	49	52 207	23 694	45	15
	1980	200	5 424	2 949	54	88 617	42 343	48	14
	1981	...	4 838	2 602	54	103 937	49 489	48	17
	1982	...	5 290	2 939	56	115 211	54 989	48	17
	1983	...	5 278	2 846	54	126 726	60 792	48	18
	1984	...	5 691	3 056	54	137 700	66 135	48	18
VIET-NAM	1975	...	204 998	114 331	56	7 403 715	3 650 762	49	36
	1980	...	204 104	133 652	65	7 887 439	3 732 913	47	39
YEMEN‡	1975	2 139	6 604	562	9	254 651	28 201	11	38
	1980	3 094	10 576	...	...	455 913	56 990	13	44
	1981	3 711	11 700	...	...	541 602	76 445	14	44
	1982	4 169	13 165	1 696	13	652 050	94 940	15	46
	1983	4 645	13 305	1 321	10	731 989	117 866	16	51
EUROPE									
ALBANIA	1980	1 559	25 980	13 060	50	552 651	260 895	47	21
	1981	1 577	26 100	13 100	50	545 900	259 300	48	21
	1982	1 617	26 440	13 520	51	532 300	256 600	48	20
	1983	1 621	27 100	13 748	51	531 520	254 667	48	20
	1984	1 631	27 387	14 017	51	540 332	256 767	48	20
ANDORRA‡	1975	...	...	...	...	3 802	1 802	47	...
	1982	13	355	204	57	3 453	1 639	47	10
AUSTRIA‡	1975	3 590	26 374	18 608	71	501 843	244 462	49	19
	1980	3 450	27 525	20 776	75	400 397	195 074	49	15
	1981	3 451	27 561	21 110	77	384 986	187 401	49	14
	1982	3 434	27 731	21 377	77	367 691	179 108	49	13
	1983	3 421	27 942	21 589	77	354 479	172 607	49	13
	1984	3 414	28 175	22 175	79	342 779	166 861	49	12
BELGIUM‡	1975	7 773	48 625	27 777	57	917 557	449 474	49	19
	1980	4 968	46 430	27 278	59	842 117	409 890	49	*18
	1981	4 850	45 130	...	...	821 059	399 899	49	*18
	1982	4 600	...	...	...	780 408	381 600	49	...
	1983	4 497	40 894	24 835	61	758 663	371 547	49	*18
	1984	4 383	43 958	25 799	59	755 576	368 400	49	17
BULGARIA	1975	3 419	48 445	34 159	71	980 318	475 402	48	20
	1980	3 247	51 581	36 953	72	994 018	482 258	49	19
	1981	3 119	57 682	43 032	75	1 029 747	499 935	49	18
	1982	3 091	60 168	44 554	74	1 052 925	511 350	49	18
	1983	3 033	61 819	46 093	75	1 063 329	515 783	49	17
	1984	2 992	61 358	45 955	75	1 072 048	519 709	48	17

COUNTRY / PAYS / PAIS	YEAR / ANNEE / AÑO	SCHOOLS / ECOLES / ESCUELAS	TEACHING STAFF / PERSONNEL ENSEIGNANT / PERSONAL DOCENTE: TOTAL	FEMALE / FEMININ / FEMENINO	% F	PUPILS ENROLLED / ELEVES INSCRITS / ALUMNOS MATRICULADOS: TOTAL	FEMALE / FEMININ / FEMENINO	% F	PUPIL/TEACHER RATIO / NOMBRE D'ELEVES PAR MAITRE / NUMERO DE ALUMNOS POR MAESTRO
		(1)	(2)	(3)	(4)	(5)	(6)	(7)	(8)
CZECHOSLOVAKIA	1975	9 285	95 634	73 210	77	1 881 414	921 541	49	20
	1980	6 753	90 380	71 460	79	1 904 476	937 307	49	21
	1981	6 612	90 282	72 015	80	1 930 634	950 517	49	21
	1982	6 516	90 702	72 920	80	1 956 634	964 317	49	22
	1983	6 445	92 435	75 043	81	1 992 400	979 435	49	22
	1984	6 398	94 404	77 103	82	2 037 126	1 001 171	49	22
DENMARK‡	1975	...	58 012	...	...	490 891	...	...	*16
	1980	2 346	...	...	...	434 635	211 959	49	...
	1981	2 346	...	...	...	432 127	211 131	49	...
	1982	2 352	...	...	...	431 946	211 502	49	...
	1983	2 361	66 008	37 175	56	426 766	208 738	49	*17
	1984	...	...	...	...	412 699	...	...	...
FINLAND‡	1975	...	24 494	14 990	61	453 737	219 795	48	19
	1980	4 245	25 949	...	...	373 347	181 879	49	14
	1981	4 234	26 664	...	...	365 418	179 014	49	14
	1982	4 238	24 752	...	...	365 965	178 173	49	15
	1983	4 230	25 139	...	...	369 047	179 762	49	15
	1984	...	...	...	...	374 413	182 242	49	...
FRANCE‡	1975	55 886	204 311	139 877	68	4 601 550	...	...	*20
	1980	51 448	208 847	138 538	66	4 610 361	2 235 963	48	*20
	1981	50 792	203 978	118 595	*65	4 535 613	2 192 922	48	22
	1982	50 187	206 198	119 648	*65	4 387 003	2 124 144	48	21
	1983	49 356	173 757	*116 590	*67	4 259 598	*2 065 905	*49	*21
GERMAN DEMOCRATIC REPUBLIC‡	1975	5 067	158 543	...	...	2 578 782	...	...	16
	1980	5 106	168 849	...	...	2 203 991	1 089 366	49	13
	1981	5 127	170 115	115 848	68	2 106 463	1 041 725	49	12
	1982	5 156	171 381	117 823	69	2 024 220	1 000 665	49	12
	1983	5 183	167 143	113 076	68	2 031 824	995 874	49	12
	1984	...	168 580	116 052	69	2 008 332	984 786	49	12
GERMANY, FEDERAL REPUBLIC OF‡	1975	18 107	273 041	164 202	60	6 425 217	3 106 972	48	24
	1980	18 411	273 556	170 742	62	5 044 424	2 405 520	48	18
	1981	18 541	270 922	169 553	63	4 775 189	2 267 481	47	18
	1982	18 468	267 417	167 500	63	4 500 991	2 134 493	47	17
	1983	18 653	140 365	110 529	79	2 366 211	1 156 265	49	17
GIBRALTAR	1975	14	158	139	88	2 808	1 390	50	18
	1980	13	157	131	83	2 750	1 374	50	18
	1981	13	168	134	80	2 844	1 418	50	17
	1982	...	...	...	...	2 852	1 397	49	...
	1983	13	177	136	77	2 934	1 433	49	17
GREECE	1975	9 633	30 953	14 565	47	935 730	450 506	48	30
	1980	9 461	37 315	17 845	48	900 641	435 000	48	24
	1981	9 400	37 947	18 236	48	891 488	430 386	48	23
	1982	9 282	37 310	18 033	48	890 171	430 813	48	24
HUNGARY	1975	4 468	66 861	...	...	1 051 095	510 180	49	16
	1980	3 633	75 422	60 673	80	1 162 203	565 243	49	15
	1981	3 604	78 053	63 119	81	1 213 465	590 060	49	16
	1982	3 567	80 798	65 686	81	1 244 094	605 171	49	15
	1983	3 546	83 496	68 226	82	1 269 899	617 933	49	15
	1984	3 539	86 367	70 806	82	1 286 648	626 674	49	15
ICELAND‡	1975	183	1 380	751	54	26 418	12 912	49	*21
	1980	...	...	...	...	24 736	...	...	...
	1981	...	...	...	...	24 809	...	...	...
	1982	...	...	...	...	25 018	12 167	49	...
	1983	...	...	...	...	25 280	12 293	49	...
	1984	...	...	...	...	25 058	...	...	...
IRELAND	1975	3 558	13 060	8 472	65	404 818	197 491	49	31
	1980	3 385	14 636	10 795	74	419 998	205 447	49	29
	1981	3 361	14 829	11 046	74	420 871	205 739	49	28
	1982	3 356	15 117	11 357	75	421 539	205 815	49	28
ITALY	1975	33 233	255 267	211 337	83	4 833 415	2 348 516	49	19
	1980	30 305	273 744	238 299	87	4 422 888	2 150 146	49	16
	1981	29 712	279 082	242 151	87	4 332 584	2 108 638	49	16
	1982	29 214	276 716	242 589	88	4 204 272	2 044 540	49	15
	1983	28 727	281 311	249 103	89	4 062 756	1 976 551	49	14
	1984	28 328	...	...	...	3 909 365	...	...	...
LUXEMBOURG	1975	...	1 521	810	53	29 430	14 468	49	19
	1980	...	1 765	882	50	24 628	11 954	49	14
	1981	...	1 734	886	51	23 841	11 625	49	14
	1982	...	1 685	859	51	22 826	11 072	49	14

COUNTRY / PAYS / PAIS	YEAR / ANNEE / AÑO	SCHOOLS / ECOLES / ESCUELAS	TEACHING STAFF / PERSONNEL ENSEIGNANT / PERSONAL DOCENTE			PUPILS ENROLLED / ELEVES INSCRITS / ALUMNOS MATRICULADOS			PUPIL/TEACHER RATIO / NOMBRE D'ELEVES PAR MAITRE / NUMERO DE ALUMNOS POR MAESTRO
			TOTAL	FEMALE / FEMININ / FEMENINO	% F	TOTAL	FEMALE / FEMININ / FEMENINO	% F	
		(1)	(2)	(3)	(4)	(5)	(6)	(7)	(8)
MALTA	1975	104	*1 421	*974	*69	29 834	14 465	48	*21
	1980	89	1 557	993	64	33 063	15 944	48	21
	1981	86	1 617	1 052	65	33 187	16 124	49	21
	1982	88	1 656	1 062	64	33 208	15 893	48	20
	1983	87	1 648	1 059	64	33 987	16 422	48	21
MONACO‡	1976	...	...	...	...	1 145	...	...	...
	1980	3	...	...	...	1 017	471	46	...
	1981	3	...	...	...	961	443	46	...
	1982	6	...	...	...	1 354	...	...	...
NETHERLANDS‡	1975	8 568	52 700	24 216	46	1 453 467	714 053	49	28
	1980	8 727	57 536	26 421	46	1 333 342	658 509	49	23
	1981	8 727	55 874	25 311	45	1 269 868	627 180	49	23
	1982	8 745	60 434	29 527	49	1 201 512	593 650	49	20
	1983	8 607	57 293	27 371	48	1 139 955	563 897	49	20
	1984	8 454	...	...	...	1 094 980	541 837	49	...
NORWAY‡	1975	3 424	46 901	23 818	51	390 129	190 060	49	*17
	1980	3 518	47 739	26 709	56	390 186	190 252	49	*17
	1981	3 526	47 802	26 789	56	383 599	187 349	49	*17
	1982	3 539	...	...	...	372 705	182 172	49	...
	1983	3 543	...	...	...	362 146	...	...	...
	1984	3 539	...	...	...	347 768	...	...	...
POLAND‡	1975	14 738	208 173	167 976	81	4 309 823	2 081 313	48	*20
	1980	12 593	212 050	176 113	83	4 167 313	2 025 824	49	*21
	1981	13 156	233 004	194 064	83	4 255 678	2 066 598	49	*22
	1982	13 601	253 037	206 757	82	4 377 472	2 126 668	49	*22
	1983	15 233	279 013	225 450	81	4 535 041	2 201 558	49	*22
	1984	15 683	294 516	242 662	82	4 676 779	2 267 604	48	*21
PORTUGAL	1975	13 111	59 485	48 074	81	1 204 567	581 147	48	20
	1980	12 460	68 746	...	...	1 240 307	594 090	48	18
	1981	11 665	67 452	...	...	1 223 127	600 277	49	18
	1982	12 295	68 188	...	...	1 221 539	...	...	18
	1983	12 373	69 048	...	...	1 203 119	...	...	17
ROMANIA	1975	14 695	144 978	97 201	67	2 889 208	1 404 360	49	20
	1980	14 381	156 817	109 017	70	3 236 808	1 578 403	49	21
	1981	14 299	157 709	109 627	70	3 285 073	1 600 283	49	21
	1982	14 244	152 228	105 980	70	3 140 101	1 526 264	49	21
	1983	14 213	150 539	105 530	70	3 067 446	1 492 930	49	20
	1984	14 134	148 407	104 463	70	3 035 209	1 478 124	49	20
SAN MARINO	1975	15	116	100	86	1 692	789	47	15
	1980	14	145	128	88	1 509	733	49	10
	1981	13	160	141	88	1 488	723	49	9
	1982	13	164	147	90	1 493	736	49	9
	1983	13	165	144	87	1 456	711	49	9
SPAIN‡	1975	...	172 122	100 477	58	3 653 320	1 786 175	49	*29
	1980	...	112 879	...	...	3 609 623	1 753 535	49	32
	1981	...	113 583	...	...	3 633 713	1 758 234	48	32
	1982	...	117 382	82 268	70	3 633 906	1 756 190	48	31
	1983	6 410	117 873	83 760	71	3 607 755	1 740 980	48	31
SWEDEN	1975	...	34 185	27 575	81	698 677	341 764	49	20
	1980	4 928	...	...	...	666 679	325 121	49	...
	1981	4 922	40 709	33 212	82	662 581	323 159	49	16
	1982	4 879	40 800	33 278	82	658 127	321 525	49	16
	1983	4 826	40 488	33 102	82	647 557	315 995	49	16
	1984	4 770	...	...	...	630 505	...	...	...
SWITZERLAND‡	1975	...	...	...	...	556 885	274 382	49	...
	1980	...	...	...	...	450 942	220 942	49	...
	1981	...	...	...	...	434 288	212 366	49	...
	1982	...	...	...	...	415 478	203 437	49	...
	1983	...	...	...	...	398 931	195 580	49	...
	1984	...	...	...	...	385 474	188 860	49	...
UNITED KINGDOM‡	1975	26 981	285 786	230 659	81	5 725 167	2 793 625	49	...
	1980	26 504	260 283	203 643	78	4 910 724	2 393 020	49	...
	1981	26 072	250 510	195 584	78	4 688 572	2 285 248	49	...
	1982	25 755	245 000	192 000	78	4 474 000	2 180 000	49	...
YUGOSLAVIA	1975	13 442	60 904	40 766	67	1 494 825	725 255	49	25
	1980	12 671	59 391	41 449	70	1 431 582	692 074	48	24
	1981	12 537	60 264	42 203	70	1 446 228	699 901	48	24
	1982	12 402	61 432	42 867	70	1 456 916	705 796	48	24
	1983	12 314	61 441	43 012	70	1 460 214	708 648	49	24
	1984	12 189	62 219	43 010	69	1 455 439	704 734	48	23

COUNTRY / PAYS / PAIS	YEAR / ANNEE / AÑO	SCHOOLS / ECOLES / ESCUELAS	TEACHING STAFF / PERSONNEL ENSEIGNANT / PERSONAL DOCENTE: TOTAL	FEMALE / FEMININ / FEMENINO	% F	PUPILS ENROLLED / ELEVES INSCRITS / ALUMNOS MATRICULADOS: TOTAL	FEMALE / FEMININ / FEMENINO	% F	PUPIL/TEACHER RATIO / NOMBRE D'ELEVES PAR MAITRE / NUMERO DE ALUMNOS POR MAESTRO
		(1)	(2)	(3)	(4)	(5)	(6)	(7)	(8)
OCEANIA									
AMERICAN SAMOA‡	1975	...	*270	...	...	6 052	...	...	*22
	1981	24	330	...	...	6 744	3 229	48	17
	1983	32	346	183	53	7 227	3 427	47	21
	1984	33	359	224	62	7 650	3 620	47	21
AUSTRALIA‡	1975	8 009	78 390	56 185	72	1 603 408	780 896	49	20
	1980	...	91 280	64 311	70	1 688 121	823 857	49	21
	1981	...	91 386	63 964	70	1 679 987	819 115	49	20
	1982	...	...	...	...	1 659 734	809 238	49	...
	1983	...	...	...	...	1 619 609	788 387	49	...
	1984	...	102 853	73 880	72	1 571 238	763 808	49	17
COOK ISLANDS	1975	...	...	...	...	5 339	...	...	...
	1982	...	...	...	...	4 181	...	...	...
	1983	...	231	...	...	3 998	...	...	17
FIJI‡	1975	641	4 274	2 281	53	134 971	66 131	49	32
	1980	652	4 097	2 349	57	116 139	56 646	49	28
	1981	656	4 150	2 316	56	116 318	56 716	49	28
	1982	661	...	...	...	117 522	...	...	...
	1983	660	4 304	2 446	57	120 174	58 501	49	28
	1984	665	4 384	2 470	56	123 340	59 991	49	28
FRENCH POLYNESIA	1975	167	1 213	950	78	28 533	13 853	49	24
	1981	...	1 544	1 069	69	29 012	13 893	48	19
	1982	240	1 361	...	...	29 384	13 955	47	22
	1983	178	...	...	...	27 944	13 385	48	...
	1984	198	1 337	...	...	27 401	13 173	48	20
GUAM	1975	39	*919	...	...	*20 215	...	...	*22
	1983	39	672	609	91	15 676	7 519	48	23
KIRIBATI	1975	106	449	...	...	14 862	...	...	33
	1980	100	435	210	48	13 235	6 457	49	30
	1982	104	450	220	49	13 836	6 822	49	31
	1983	106	453	225	50	13 612	6 709	49	30
	1984	108	471	229	49	13 194	6 507	49	28
	1985	112	460	236	51	13 440	6 625	49	29
NAURU	1974	...	...	...	...	1 392	648	47	...
	1985	7	71	43	61	1 451	679	47	20
NEW CALEDONIA‡	1975	235	1 431	...	...	24 943	12 207	49	21
	1981	...	1 518	...	...	26 779	12 976	48	23
	1982	268	*1 305	...	...	26 513	12 825	48	*20
	1983	273	1 226	...	...	22 934	11 201	49	19
	1984	224	*1 175	...	...	24 410	11 811	48	*21
	1985	211	1 131	...	...	22 517	10 838	48	20
NEW ZEALAND‡	1975	2 471	21 187	13 517	64	391 399	190 087	49	*23
	1980	2 345	22 893	15 178	66	381 262	185 824	49	22
	1981	2 342	22 277	14 707	66	367 986	179 132	49	22
	1982	2 323	17 306	12 013	69	359 011	174 460	49	21
	1983	...	...	...	...	346 797	168 418	49	...
NIUE‡	1975	8	65	27	42	1 122	543	48	17
	1980	...	45	...	...	666	...	...	15
	1981	...	42	...	...	592	...	...	14
	1982	...	65	37	57	591	273	46	*15
	1983	7	35	23	66	490	231	47	14
	1984	7	29	18	62	496	216	44	17
PACIFIC ISLANDS	1975	248	1 526	499	33	30 285	14 544	48	20
	1980	249	...	...	...	30 159	...	...	...
	1981	245	*1 374	*374	*27	31 099	...	...	*23
PAPUA NEW GUINEA	1975	1 762	7 544	1 721	23	238 267	88 994	37	32
	1980	*2 130	*9 549	*2 559	*27	299 823	*123 805	*41	*31
	1981	2 150	9 935	2 917	29	300 536	125 991	42	30
	1982	2 197	10 163	3 010	30	313 790	134 174	43	31
SAMOA	1975	152	1 216	773	64	32 642	16 713	51	27
	1980	152	1 438	1 026	71	33 012	15 694	48	*23
	1981	...	1 288	...	...	32 206	15 377	48	25
	1982	162	1 460	1 050	72	31 567	15 202	48	22
	1983	164	1 502	1 078	72	31 457	15 104	48	21
SOLOMON ISLANDS‡	1975	344	1 071	312	29	28 219	10 743	38	26
	1980	370	1 148	303	26	28 870	11 980	41	25
	1981	369	1 171	313	27	29 253	12 163	42	25
	1982	376	1 199	335	28	30 616	12 917	42	26
	1983	409	1 390	391	28	34 953	14 928	43	25
	1984	423	1 536	...	...	37 522	...	...	24

3.4 Education at the first level
Enseignement du premier degré
Enseñanza de primer grado

COUNTRY / PAYS / PAIS	YEAR / ANNEE / AÑO	SCHOOLS / ECOLES / ESCUELAS	TEACHING STAFF / PERSONNEL ENSEIGNANT / PERSONAL DOCENTE			PUPILS ENROLLED / ELEVES INSCRITS / ALUMNOS MATRICULADOS			PUPIL/ TEACHER RATIO / NOMBRE D'ELEVES PAR MAITRE / NUMERO DE ALUMNOS POR MAESTRO
			TOTAL	FEMALE FEMININ FEMENINO	% F	TOTAL	FEMALE FEMININ FEMENINO	% F	
		(1)	(2)	(3)	(4)	(5)	(6)	(7)	(8)
TOKELAU‡	1976	...	...	...	...	386	201	52	...
	1981	...	21	16	76	434	213	49	21
	1982	...	27	19	70	426	203	48	16
	1983	...	48	28	58	411	196	48	12
TONGA	1975	126	688	368	53	19 260	9 176	48	28
	1980	110	781	...	...	19 012	...	...	24
	1981	110	695	412	59	17 364	8 245	47	25
	1982	110	793	485	61	16 701	7 889	47	21
	1983	111	832	501	60	16 329	7 721	47	20
TUVALU	1976	...	...	...	...	1 540	...	...	...
	1980	...	...	...	...	1 327	...	...	...
	1981	...	...	...	...	1 269	...	...	...
	1984	11	61	43	70	1 349	583	43	22
VANUATU‡	1975	...	...	...	...	20 095	9 029	45	...
	1980	278	986	...	...	23 264	10 593	46	24
	1981	289	1 076	422	39	22 969	10 474	46	21
	1983	244	934	...	...	22 244	...	...	24
U.S.S.R.									
U.S.S.R.‡	1975	147 083	2 399 299	1 692 153	71	21 366 200	...	...	*17
	1980	130 000	2 321 000	*1 653 000	*71	21 713 900	...	...	*17
	1981	129 000	2 332 000	...	...	22 231 900	...	...	*17
	1982	128 000	2 338 000	...	...	22 660 000	...	...	*17
	1983	127 000	2 361 000	...	...	22 976 000	...	...	*17
	1984	127 000	2 430 000	...	...	23 245 000	...	...	*17
BYELORUSSIAN S.S.R.‡	1975	8 408	106 893	...	...	770 500	...	...	*15
	1980	6 600	90 800	...	...	750 300	...	...	*15
	1981	6 400	90 600	...	...	765 300	...	...	*15
	1982	6 300	90 300	...	...	774 700	...	...	*15
	1983	6 100	90 600	...	...	782 900	...	...	*15
UKRAINIAN S.S.R.‡	1975	23 435	445 400	...	...	5 970 000	...	...	*16
	1980	21 000	389 900	...	...	3 595 200	...	...	*15
	1981	20 800	387 500	...	...	3 650 800	...	...	*15
	1982	20 700	387 700	...	...	3 678 300	...	...	*15
	1983	20 500	387 600	...	...	3 703 000	...	...	*16
	1984	20 400	395 200	...	...	3 709 100	...	...	*15

In general, data in this table cover both public and private schools at the first level of education, including primary classes attached to secondary schools but excluding schools and classes organized for adults or for handicapped children. In consulting this table, reference should be made to the information given on duration of schooling in Table 3.1, 3.1a and 3.1b. Figures on teaching staff refer, in principle, to both full- and part-time teachers. Data comparability may thus be affected, particularly as regards the pupil/teacher ratios presented in column 8, as the proportion of part-time teachers varies greatly from one country to another. Data exclude other instructional personnel without teaching function (e.g. certain principals, librarians, guidance personnel, etc.). However, it has not been possible to ascertain whether for certain countries such other instructional personnel are included.

En général, les données de ce tableau se rapportent aux établissements d'enseignement du premier degré, publics et privés, y compris les classes primaires rattachées aux établissements du second degré, mais non compris les écoles et les classes destinées aux adultes et aux enfants déficients. Il convient, en consultant ce tableau, de se reporter aux renseignements donnés sur la durée de la scolarité aux tableaux 3.1, 3.1a et 3.1b. Les chiffres relatifs au personnel enseignant représentent, en général, le nombre total de maîtres à plein temps et à temps partiel. Ceci peut affecter la comparabilité des données, surtout en ce qui concerne le nombre d'élèves par maître, présenté à la colonne 8, car la proportion des enseignants à temps partiel peut varier considérablement d'un pays à l'autre. Les données excluent le personnel qui n'est pas chargé d'enseignement (proviseurs, bibliothécaires, conseillers d'orientation professionnelle, etc.). Il n'a pas été possible de vérifier si cette règle a été suivie par tous les pays.

En general, los datos de este cuadro se refieren a los establecimientos de enseñanza de primer grado, públicos y privados, incluídos los adscritos a establecimientos de segundo grado; quedan excluídas, en cambio, las escuelas y las clases destinadas a los adultos y a los niños deficientes. Al consultar este cuadro, habrá que tener presentes los datos sobre la duración de la escolaridad que figuran en los cuadros 3.1, 3.1a y 3.1b. Las cifras relativas al personal docente, representan, en general, el número total de maestros de jornada completa y de jornada parcial. Esto puede afectar la comparabilidad de los datos, sobre todo en lo que concierne al número de alumnos por maestro, tal como se presenta en la columna 8, ya que la proporción de maestros a tiempo parcial puede variar considerablemente de un país a otro. Las cifras excluyen el personal que no se dedica a la enseñanza (por ejemplo, ciertos directores, los bibliotecarios, los consejeros de orientación profesional, etc.). Todavia, no ha sido posible comprobar si esta regla se aplica en todos los países.

AFRICA:

Algeria:

E--> For 1975 and 1980, the figures in columns 1, 2, 3, 4 and 8 and all the data from 1981 exclude *OUCFA schools* for which enrolment was 3,739 (F 1,696) in 1980.

FR-> Pour 1975 et 1980 les chiffres des colonnes 1, 2, 3, 4 et 8 et toutes les données à partir de 1981 excluent les écoles de l'OUCFA qui comptaient 3 739 élèves (dont 1 696 filles) en 1980.

ESP> Para 1975 y 1980, las cifras de las columnas 1, 2, 3, 4 y 8 y todos los datos a partir de 1981 excluyen las escuelas de la *OUCFA* que tenían 3 739 alumnos (F 1 696) en 1980.

Angola:

E--> For 1981 and 1982 data in columns 2 and 8 include initiation classes (education preceding the first level).

FR-> Pour 1981 et 1982 les données des colonnes 2 et 8 incluent les classes d'initiation (enseignement précédant le premier degré).

ESP> En 1981 y 1982 los datos de las columnas 2 y 8 incluyen las clases de iniciación (enseñanza anterior al primer grado).

Burkina Faso:

E--> For 1983, the data on teachers (columns 2, 3, 4 and 8) refer to public education only.

FR-> Pour 1983, les données sur le personnel enseignant (colonnes 2, 3, 4 et 8) se réfèrent à l'enseignement public seulement.

ESP> Para 1983, los datos sobre el personal docente (columnas 2, 3, 4 y 8) se refieren a la enseñanza pública solamente.

Burundi:

E--> The figures on teachers (columns 2, 3, 4 and 8) for 1980 and those in column 5 for 1982 refer to public education only.

FR-> Les données sur le personnel enseignant (colonnes 2, 3, 4 et 8) pour 1980, et celles de la colonne 5 pour 1982 se réfèrent à l'enseignement public seulement.

ESP> Los datos sobre el personal docente (columnas 2, 3, 4 y 8) en 1980 y los de la columna 5 en 1982 se refieren a la enseñanza pública solamente.

Cape Verde:

E--> Data in columns 2 and 8 refer to *ensino básico elementar* (grades 1-4) only.

FR-> Les données des colonnes 2 et 8 se réfèrent à l'*ensino básico elementar* (années d'études 1 à 4) seulement.

ESP> Los datos de las columnas 2 y 8 se refieren al *ensino básico elementar* (años de estudios 1-4) solamente.

Chad:

E--> For 1975, the figures on teachers (columns 2, 3, 4 and 8) refer to public education only.

FR-> En 1975 les chiffres sur le personnel enseignant (colonnes 2, 3, 4 et 8) se réfèrent à l'enseignement public seulement.

ESP> En 1975 las cifras sobre el personal docente (columnas 2, 3, 4 y 8) se refieren a la enseñanza pública solamente.

Egypt:

E--> Data on teachers (columns 2, 3 4 and 8) for 1975 and 1981, and all data for 1982 and 1983 do not include Al Azhar.

FR-> Les données relatives au personnel enseignant (colonnes 2, 3, 4 et 8) pour 1975 et 1981 et toutes les données pour 1982 et 1983 ne comprennent pas Al Azhar.

ESP> Los datos relativos al personal docente (columnas 2, 3, 4 y 8) para 1975 y 1981 y todos los datos para 1982 y 1983 no incluyen Al Azhar.

Ghana:

E--> Data refer to public education only.

FR-> Les données se réfèrent à l'enseignement public seulement.

ESP> Los datos se refieren a la enseñanza publica solamente.

Guinea-Bissau:

E--> For 1975, data on teaching staff do not include the *Instituto Amizade* and those on pupils include initiation classes (education preceding the first level).

FR-> Pour 1975 les données relatives au personnel enseignant ne comprennent pas l'*Instituto Amizade* et les données relatives aux élèves incluent les classes d'initiation (enseignement précédant le premier degré).

ESP> En 1975, los datos relativos al personal docente no incluyen el Instituto Amizade; los datos relativos a los alumnos incluyen las clases de iniciación (enseñanza anterior al primer grado).

Liberia:

E--> Data include education preceding the first level. For 1980, the figures in columns 1, 2, 3 and 4 include the first stage of general education at the second level.

FR-> Les données incluent l'enseignement précédant le premier degré. En 1980, les données des colonnes 1, 2, 3 et 4 incluent le premier cycle de l'enseignement général du second degré.

ESP> Los datos incluyen la enseñanza anterior al primer grado. En 1980, los datos de las columnas 1, 2, 3 y 4 incluyen el primer ciclo de la enseñanza general de segundo grado.

Madagascar:

E--> See Table 3.1b.

FR-> Voir le tableau 3.1b.

ESP> Véase el cuadro 3.1b.

Malawi:

E--> Figures on teachers (columns 2 and 8) for 1982 refer to public education only.

FR-> Les données relatives au personnel enseignant (colonnes 2 et 8) pour 1982 se réfèrent à l'enseignement public seulment.

ESP> Los datos sobre el personal docente (columnas 2 y 8) para 1982 se refieren a la enseñanza pública solamente.

Mauritania:

E--> See Table 3.1b.

FR-> Voir le tableau 3.1b.

ESP> Véase el cuadro 3.1b.

Mauritius:

E--> From 1980, data on female teachers (columns 3 and 4) do not include Rodriguez.

FR-> A partir de 1980, les données relatives au personnel enseignant féminin (colonnes 3 et 4) n'incluent pas Rodriguez.

ESP> A partir de 1980, los datos relativos al personal docente femenino (columnas 3 y 4) no incluyen Rodriguez.

Morocco:

E--> The figures in columns 2, 3, 4 and 8 for 1975 and 1980 as well as those in column 1 for 1980 refer to public education only. For 1982, enrolment does not include MUCF (7,100 pupils, F 3,407 in 1981).

FR-> Les données des colonnes 2, 3, 4 et 8 pour 1975 et 1980 ainsi que celles de la colonne 1 pour 1980 se réfèrent à l'enseignement public seulement. Pour 1982, les données sur les effectifs n'incluent pas la MUCF (7 100 élèves, F 3 407 en 1981)

ESP> Los datos de las columnas 2, 3, 4 y 8 en 1975 y 1980 y los de la columna 1 en 1980 se refieren a la enseñanza pública solamente. En 1982, los datos sobre los alumnos la matrícula no incluye la MUCF (7 100 alumnos, F 3 407 en 1981).

Mozambique:

E--> All data for 1976 and 1980 and those in columns 1, 2, 3, 4 and 8 for 1981, 1982 and 1983 include initiation classes (education preceding the first level).

FR-> Toutes les données pour 1976 et 1980 et celles des colonnes 1, 2, 3, 4 et 8 pour 1981, 1982 et 1983 incluent les classes d'initiation (enseignement précédant le premier degré).

ESP> Todos los datos para 1976 y 1980 y los de las columnas 1, 2, 3, 4 y 8 para 1981, 1982 y 1983 incluyen las clases de iniciación (enseñanza anterior al primer grado).

Reunion:

E--> Data on female teachers (columns 3 and 4) for 1981 and 1982 refer to public education only.

FR-> Les données sur le personnel enseignant féminin (colonnes 3 et 4) pour 1981 et 1982 se réfèrent à l'enseignement public seulement.

ESP> Los datos sobre el personal docente femenino (columnas 3 y 4) para 1981 y 1982 se refieren a la enseñanza pública solamente.

Rwanda:

E--> See Table 3.1b.

FR-> Voir le tableau 3.1b.

ESP> Véase el cuadro 3.1b.

Seychelles:

E--> See Table 3.1b.

FR-> Voir le tableau 3.1b.

ESP> Véase el cuadro 3.1b.

Somalia:

E--> See Table 3.1b.

FR-> Voir le tableau 3.1b.

ESP> Véase el cuadro 3.1b.

Uganda:

E--> All data from 1975 to 1981 and data on female teachers (columns 3 and 4) for 1982 refer to government-maintained and aided schools only.

FR-> Toutes les données de 1975 à 1981 et celles relatives au personnel enseignant féminin (colonnes 3 et 4) pour 1982 se réfèrent aux écoles publiques et subventionnées seulement.

ESP> Todos los datos de 1975 a 1981 y los sobre el personal docente femenino para 1982 se refieren a las escuelas públicas y subvencionadas solamente.

United Republic of Tanzania:

E--> All data refer to Tanzania mainland only. For 1980, data in columns 1, 2, 3 and 4 refer to government-maintained and aided schools only.

FR-> Toutes les données se réfèrent à la Tanzanie continentale seulement. Pour 1980 les données des colonnes 1, 2, 3 et 4 se réfèrent aux écoles publiques et subventionnées seulement.

ESP> Todos los datos se refieren a Tanzania continental solamente. En 1980 los datos de las columnas 1, 2, 3 y 4 se refieren a las escuelas publicas y subvencionadas solamente.

Zimbabwe:

E--> For 1975, data on teaching staff (columns 2, 3, 4 and 8) refer to government-maintained and aided schools only.

FR-> Pour 1975, les données sur le personnel enseignant (colonnes 2, 3, 4 et 8) se réfèrent aux écoles publiques et subventionnées seulement.

ESP> Para 1975 los datos sobre el personal docente (columnas 2, 3, 4 y 8) se refieren a las escuelas públicas y subvencionadas solamente.

AMERICA, NORTH:

Antigua and Barbuda:

E--> All data on teaching staff and figures on pupils for 1983

Antigua and Barbuda: (Cont):
include secondary classes attached to primary schools.

FR-> Toutes les données sur le personnel enseignant ainsi que celles sur les élèves pour 1983 incluent les classes secondaires rattachées aux écoles primaires.

ESP> Todos los datos sobre el personal docente y los sobre los alumnos en 1983 incluyen las clases secundarias adscritas a las escuelas primarias.

Bahamas:

E--> The figures shown in column 2 for 1975, 1980 and 1981, and those in columns 3 and 4 for 1982 refer to public education only. For 1983, the figure in column 2 refers to education at both first and second level.

FR-> Le chiffre de la colonne 2 en 1975, 1980, 1981 et ceux des colonnes 3 et 4 pour 1982 se réfèrent à l'enseignement public seulement. Pour 1983 le chiffre de la colonne 2 se réfère à l'enseignement du premier et du second degré.

ESP> La cifra de la columna 2 en 1975, 1980, y 1981 y las de las columnas 3 y 4 para 1982 se refieren a la enseñanza pública solamente. Para 1983 la cifra de la columna 2 se refiere a la enseñanza de primer grado y de segundo grado.

Barbados:

E--> From 1980 to 1983 data on teachers (columns 2 and 8) and those on female teachers for 1984 refer to public education only.

FR-> De 1980 à 1983, les données relatives au personnel enseignant (colonnes 2 et 8) et celles sur le personnel enseignant féminin pour 1984 se réfèrent à l'enseignement public seulement.

ESP> De 1980 a 1983 los datos relativos al personal docente (columnas 2 y 8) y las sobre el personal docente femenino para 1984 se refieren a la enseñanza pública solamente.

Belize:

E--> For 1975, data on teachers (columns 2, 3, 4 and 8) and all data from 1980 refer to government-maintained and aided shools only.

FR-> En 1975, les données sur le personnel enseignant (colonnes 2, 3, 4 et 8) et tous les chiffres à partir de 1980 se réfèrent aux écoles publiques et subventionnées seulement.

ESP> En 1975, los datos sobre el personal docente (columnas 2, 3, 4 y 8) y todos los datos a partir de 1980, se refieren a las escuelas públicas y subvencionadas solamente.

Bermuda:

E--> Data on female teachers (columns 3 and 4) for 1980 and 1981 refer to public education only.

FR-> Les données sur le personnel enseignant féminin (colonnes 3 et 4) pour 1980 et 1981 se réfèrent à l'enseignement public seulement.

ESP> Los datos sobre el personal docente femenino (columnas 3 y 4) por 1980 y 1981 se refieren a la enseñanza pública solamente.

Canada:

E--> For 1982 and 1983 the figures shown in columns 1 to 4 include education preceding the first level.

FR-> Pour 1982 et 1983 les chiffres des colonnes 1 à 4 incluent l'enseignement précédant le premier degré.

ESP> Para 1982 y 1983 las cifras de las columnas 1 a 4 incluyen la enseñanza anterior al primer grado.

Cayman Islands:

E--> The figures shown in columns 2, 3 and 4 refer to public education only.

FR-> Les chiffres des colonnes 2, 3 et 4 se réfèrent à l'enseignement public seulement.

ESP> Las cifras de las columnas 2, 3 y 4 se refieren a la enseñanza pública solamente.

Costa Rica:

E--> For 1982 and 1983 data on teaching staff refer to public education only.

FR-> En 1982 et 1983 les données relatives au personnel enseignant se réfèrent à l'enseignement public seulement.

ESP> En 1982 y 1983 los datos relativos al personal docente se refieren a la enseñanza pública solamente.

Dominica:

E--> For 1975 data on teaching staff (columns 2, 3 and 4) include general education at the second level.

FR-> Pour 1975, les données relatives au personnel enseignant (colonnes 2, 3, et 4) incluent l'enseignement général du second degré.

ESP> Para 1975 los datos relativos al personal docente (columnas 2, 3 y 4) incluyen la enseñanza general de segundo grado.

Dominican Republic:

E--> For 1981, figure shown in column 6 and for 1983 those in columns 1, 2 and 6 refer to public education only.

FR-> Pour 1981 le chiffre de la colonne 6 et pour 1983 ceux des colonnes 1, 2 et 6 se réfèrent à l'enseignement public seulement.

ESP> En 1981, la cifra de la columna 6 y para 1983 las de las columnas 1, 2 y 6 se refieren a la enseñanza pública solamente.

El Salvador:

E--> For 1975, all data include evening schools and the figures on teachers (columns 2, 3, 4 and 8) refer to public education only.

FR-> Pour 1975, toutes les données comprennent les écoles du soir et les chiffres relatifs au personnel enseignant (colonnes 2, 3, 4 et 8) se réfèrent à l'enseignement public seulement.

ESP> Para 1975 todos los datos incluyen las escuelas nocturnas y las

El Salvador: (Cont):
cifras sobre el personal docente (columnas 2, 3, 4 y 8) se refieren a la enseñanza pública solamente.

Guadeloupe:

E--> For 1981 and 1982 data on female teachers (columns 3 and 4) refer to public education only.

FR-> Pour 1981 et 1982, les données relatives au personnel enseignant féminin (colonnes 3 et 4) se réfèrent à l'enseignement public seulement.

ESP> Para 1981 y 1982, los datos sobre el personal docente femenino (columnas 3 y 4) se refieren a la enseñanza pública solamente.

Haiti:

E--> See Table 3.1b.

FR-> Voir le tableau 3.1b.

ESP> Véase el cuadro 3.1b.

Jamaica:

E--> Data on teachers for 1975 include senior departments of all-age schools (second level). The figures shown in columns 2, 3, 4 and 8 for 1980 and all data for 1983 refer to public education only.

FR-> Les données relatives au personnel enseignant pour 1975 incluent les classes supérieures des écoles complètes (second degré). Les données des colonnes 2, 3, 4 et 8 en 1980 et toutes les données pour 1983 se réfèrent à l'enseignement public seulement.

ESP> Los datos sobre el personal docente por 1975 incluyen las clases superiores de *las escuelas completas* (segundo grado). Las cifras de las columnas 2, 3, 4 y 8 en 1980 y todos los datos para 1983 se refieren a la enseñanza pública solamente.

Martinique:

E--> For 1981 and 1982 data on female teachers (columns 3 and 4) refer to public education only.

FR-> Pour 1981 et 1982, les données relatives au personnel enseignant féminin (colonnes 3 et 4) se réfèrent à l'enseignement public seulement.

ESP> Para 1981 y 1982, los datos sobre el personal docente femenino (columnas 3 y 4) se refieren a la enseñanza pública solamente.

Nicaragua:

E--> For 1975, data shown in columns 1 and 2 include education preceding the first level and for 1984 data on teachers include the 'primaria acelerada'.

FR-> Pour 1975, les données des colonnes 1 et 2 incluent l'enseignement précédant le premier degré et pour 1984 les données sur le personnel enseignant comprennent l'école 'primaria acelerada'.

ESP> Para 1975, los datos de las columnas 1 y 2 incluyen la enseñanza anterior al primer grado y para 1984 los datos sobre el personal docente incluyen la enseñanza primaria acelerada.

Puerto Rico:

E--> For 1975 and 1981, data refer to public education only. For 1981, data refer to grades 1 to 8, previously to grades 1 to 6.

FR-> En 1975 et 1981, les données se réfèrent à l'enseignement public seulement. En 1981, les données se réfèrent aux classes allant de la première à la huitième année d'études; antérieurement aux classes de I à VI.

ESP> En 1975 y 1981 los datos se refieren a la enseñanza pública solamente. En 1981, los datos se refieren a las clases comprendidas entre el primer y el octavo año de estudios; anteriormente comprendían las clases de I a VI.

Trinidad and Tobago:

E--> The data refer to government-maintained and aided schools only and include intermediate departments of secondary schools.

FR-> Les données se réfèrent aux écoles publiques et subventionnées seulement et incluent les sections intermédiaires des écoles secondaires.

ESP> Los datos se refieren a las escuelas públicas y subvencionadas solamente y incluyen las secciones intermedias de las escuelas secundarias.

Turks and Caicos Islands:

E--> For 1980 and 1984 data refer to public education only.

FR-> En 1980 et 1984 les données se réfèrent à l'enseignement public seulement.

ESP> En 1980 y 1984 los datos se refieren a la enseñanza pública solamente.

United States:

E--> All data include special education. Beginning 1980, all data refer to grades 1 to 8; previously to grades 1 to 6 or 1 to 8 according to States.

FR-> Toutes les données incluent l'éducation spéciale. A partir de 1980, toutes les données se réfèrent aux classes allant de la première à la huitième année d'études; antérieurement les données étaient présentées suivant la structure de l'enseignement de chaque Etat (6 ou 8 années).

ESP> Todos los datos incluyen la enseñanza especial. A partir de 1980, todos los datos se refieren a las clases comprendidas entre el primer y el octavo año de estudios; anteriormente los datos se presentaban de acuerdo con la estructura de enseñanza de cada estado (6 u 8 años).

U.S. Virgin Islands:

E--> From 1980, data on teaching staff include education preceding the first level and refer to public education only; data on pupils refer to grades 1 to 8; previously to grades 1 to 6.

FR-> A partir de 1980, les données du personnel enseignant incluent l'enseignement précédant le premier degré et se réfèrent à

U.S. Virgin Islands: (Cont):
l'enseignement public seulement; les données relatives aux élèves se réfèrent aux classes allant de la première à la huitième année d'études; antérieurement aux classes de I à VI.

ESP> A partir de 1980, los datos relativos al personal docente incluyen la enseñanza anterior al primer grado y se refieren a la enseñanza pública solamente; los datos relativos a los alumnos se refieren a las clases comprendidas entre el primer y el octavo año de estudios; anteriormente a las clases de I a VI.

AMERICA, SOUTH:

French Guiana:

E--> For 1981 and 1982 data on female teachers (columns 3 and 4) refer to public education only.

FR-> Pour 1981 et 1982 les données sur le personnel enseignant féminin (colonnes 3 et 4) se réfèrent à l'enseignement public seulement.

ESP> Para 1981 y 1982 los datos sobre el personal docente femenino (columnas 3 y 4) se refieren a la enseñanza pública solamente.

ASIA:

Afghanistan:

E--> For 1975 the figures shown in columns 2, 3, 4 and 8 do not include primary classes attached to middle and secondary schools.

FR-> En 1975 les chiffres des colonnes 2, 3, 4 and 8 ne comprennent pas les classes primaires rattachées aux écoles moyennes et secondaires.

ESP> En 1975 las cifras de las columnas 2, 3, 4 y 8 no incluyen las clases primarias adscritas a las escuelas medias y secundarias.

Bahrain:

E--> Data on teaching staff (columns 2, 3, 4 and 8) include part of intermediate education and, apart from 1975, refer to public education only.

FR-> Les données relatives au personnel enseignant (colonnes 2, 3, 4 et 8) comprennent une partie de l'enseignement intermédiaire et, à l'exception de 1975, se réfèrent à l'enseignement public seulement.

ESP> Los datos sobre el personal docente (columnas 2, 3, 4 y 8) comprenden una parte de la enseñanza intermedia y, a la excepción de 1975, se refieren a la enseñanza pública solamente.

Cyprus:

E--> Not including Turkish schools.

FR-> Non compris les écoles turques.

ESP> Excluídas las escuelas turcas.

Democratic Yemen:

E--> See Table 3.1b. For 1975, 1980 and 1981 data on teachers (columns 2, 3, 4 and 8) do not include schools for nomads.

FR-> Voir le tableau 3.1b. Pour 1975, 1980 et 1981 les données sur le personnel enseignant (colonnes 2, 3, 4 et 8) n'incluent pas les écoles de nomades.

ESP> Vease el cuadro 3.1b. Para 1975, 1980 y 1981 los datos sobre el personal docente (columnas 2, 3, 4 y 8) no incluyen las escuelas para nómadas.

India:

E--> From 1980, the figures on teaching staff do not include primary classes attached to secondary schools.

FR-> A partir de 1980, les données relatives au personnel enseignant ne comprennent pas les classes primaires rattachées aux écoles secondaires.

ESP> A partir de 1980, los datos relativos al personal docente no incluyen las clases primarias adscritas a las escuelas secundarias.

Iran, Islamic Rep. of:

E--> For 1982 data on female teachers refer to full-time only.

FR-> Pour 1982 le chiffre sur le personnel enseignant féminin se réfère au personnel à plein temps seulement.

ESP> Para 1982 la cifra sobre el personal docente femenino se refiere al personal de jornada completa solamente.

Israel:

E--> Data on teaching staff (columns 2 and 8) do not include intermediate classes attached to primary schools.

FR-> Les données relatives au personnel enseignant (colonnes 2 et 8) n'incluent pas les classes intermédiaires rattachées aux écoles primaires.

ESP> Los datos relativos al personal docente (columnas 2 y 8) no incluyen las clases intermedias adscritas a las escuelas primarias.

Japan:

E--> For 1975, the figures shown in columns 3, 4, 6 and 7, from 1980 to 1983 those in columns 2, 3, 4, 6, 7 and 8 and all data for 1984 include special education.

FR-> Pour 1975, les chiffres des colonnes 3, 4, 6 et 7, et de 1980 à 1983 ceux des colonnes 2, 3, 4, 6, 7 et 8, et toutes les données pour 1984 incluent l'éducation spéciale.

ESP> Para 1975 las cifras de las columnas 3, 4, 6 y 7, de 1980 a 1983 las de las columnas 2, 3, 4, 6, 7 y 8 y todos los datos para 1984 incluyen la educación especial.

Jordan:

E--> Including UNRWA schools with 2,349 teachers (f: 1,200) and 91,590 pupils (f: 44,727) in 1984.

FR-> Y compris les écoles de l'*UNRWA* qui comptaient 2 349 maîtres (dont f: 1 200) et 91 590 élèves (dont f 44 727) en 1984.

ESP> Incluídas las escuelas del O.O.P.S.R.P. (Organización de Obras Publicas y Socorro para los Refugiados de Palestina) que tenían 2 349 maestros (f: 1 200) y 91 590 alumnos (f: 44 727) en 1984.

Lao People's Democratic Republic:

E--> See Table 3.1b.

FR-> Voir le tableau 3.1b.

ESP> Véase el cuadro 3.1b.

Lebanon:

E--> Including UNRWA schools with 770 teachers and 23,221 pupils (F: 11,637) in 1982.

FR-> Y compris les écoles de l'*UNRWA* qui comptaient 770 maîtres et 23 221 élèves (F: 11 637) en 1982.

ESP> Incluídas las escuelas del O.O.P.S.R.P. que tenían 770 maestros y 23 221 alumnos (F: 11 637) en 1982.

Nepal:

E--> See Table 3.1b.

FR-> Voir le tableau 3.1b.

ESP> Véase el cuadro 3.1b.

Pakistan:

E--> Data include education preceding the first level.

FR-> Les données incluent l'enseignement précédant le premier degré.

ESP> Los datos incluyen la enseñanza anterior al primer grado.

Philippines:

E--> For 1980, data refer to public education only.

FR-> Pour 1980 les données se réfèrent à l'enseignement public seulement.

ESP> Para 1980 los datos se refieren a la enseñanza pública solamente.

Sri Lanka:

E--> See Table 3.1b. The figures on teaching staff include general education at the second level For 1975 and 1984, data on pupils refer to public education only.

FR-> Voir le tableau 3.1b. Les chiffres relatifs au personnel enseignant incluent l'enseignement général du second degré. En 1975 et 1984 les chiffres relatifs aux élèves se réfèrent à l'enseignement public seulement.

ESP> Véase el cuadro 3.1b. Las cifras relativas al personal docente incluyen la enseñanza general de segundo grado. En 1975 y 1984 las cifras relativas a los alumnos se refieren a la enseñanza pública solamente.

Syrian Arab Republic:

E--> Including UNRWA schools with 978 teachers and 34,533 pupils in 1984.

FR-> Y compris les écoles de l'*UNRWA* qui comptaient 978 maîtres et 34 533 élèves en 1984.

ESP> Incluídas las escuelas del O.O.P.S.R.P. que tenian 978 maestros y 34 533 alumnos en 1984.

Thailand:

E--> See Table 3.1b. From 1980, data on teaching staff refer to public education only and include education preceding the first level.

FR-> Voir le tableau 3.1b. A partir de 1980, les données relatives au personnel enseignant se réfèrent à l'enseignement public seulement et incluent l'enseignement précédant le premier degré.

ESP> Véase el cuadro 3.1b. A partir de 1980 los datos relativos al personal docente se refieren a la enseñanza pública solamente y incluyen la enseñanza anterior al primer grado.

United Arab Emirates:

E--> Data on teaching staff (columns 2, 3, 4 and 8) refer to public education only.

FR-> Les chiffres sur le personnel enseignant (colonnes 2, 3, 4 et 8) se réfèrent à l'enseignement public seulement.

ESP> Las cifras sobre el personal docente (columnas 2, 3, 4 y 8) se refieren a la enseñanza pública solamente.

Yemen:

E--> The figures on teaching staff (columns 2, 3, 4 and 8) refer to public education only.

FR-> Les chiffres sur le personnel enseignant (colonnes 2, 3, 4 et 8) se réfèrent à l'enseignement public seulement.

ESP> Las cifras sobre el personal docente (columnas 2, 3, 4 y 8) se refieren a la enseñanza pública solamente.

EUROPE:

Andorra:

E--> For 1975, data include education preceding the first level.

FR-> Pour 1975, les données incluent l'enseignement précédant le premier degré.

ESP> Para 1975, los datos incluyen la enseñanza anterior al primer grado.

Austria:

E--> For 1975, data on teaching staff include grades V-VIII of the 'Volksschulen' classified under education at the second level.

FR-> En 1975, les données relatives au personnel enseignant comprennent les classes allant de la cinquième à la huitième année des 'Volksschulen' qui font partie de l'enseignement du second degré.

ESP> En 1975, los datos relativos al personal docente comprenden las clases que van del quinto al octavo año de las 'Volksschulen' que se clasifican en la enseñanza de segundo grado.

Belgium:

E--> Data on pupils include special education.

FR-> Les données relatives aux élèves incluent l'éducation spéciale.

ESP> Los datos relativos a los alumnos incluyen la educación especial.

Denmark:

E--> Data on teaching staff include general education at the second level.

FR-> Les données relatives au personnel enseignant incluent l'enseignement général du second degré.

ESP> Los datos relativos al personal docente incluyen la enseñanza general de segundo grado.

Finland:

E--> Data include integrated special education.

FR-> Les données incluent l'education spéciale intégrée.

ESP> Los datos incluyen la educación especial integrada.

France:

E--> The figures shown in columns 2, 3, and 4 for 1975, 1980 and 1983 and those in column 3 for 1981 and 1982 refer to public education only.

FR-> Les chiffres des colonnes 2, 3, et 4 en 1975, 1980 et 1983 et ceux de la colonne 3 en 1981 et 1982 se réfèrent à l'enseignement public seulement.

ESP> Las cifras de las columnas 2, 3, y 4 en 1975, 1980 y 1983 y las de la columna 3 en 1981 y 1982 se refieren a la enseñanza pública solamente.

German Democratic Republic:

E--> Data on teaching staff include general education at the second level and special education.

FR-> Les données relatives au personnel enseignant incluent l'enseignement général du second degré et l'éducation spéciale.

ESP> Los datos relativos al personal docente incluyen la enseñanza general de segundo grado y la educación especial.

Germany, Federal Republic of:

E--> For 1983, due to a new method of estimation, data are not comparable with those of previous years.

FR-> Pour 1983, suite à une nouvelle méthode d'estimation, les données ne sont pas comparables avec celles des années précédentes.

ESP> Para 1983, de acuerdo con un nuevo método de estimación, los datos no son comparables a los de los años anteriores.

Iceland:

E--> For 1975, data on teaching staff include education preceding the first level.

FR-> En 1975, les données sur le personnel enseignant incluent l'enseignement précédant le premier degré.

ESP> En 1975, los datos sobre el personal docente incluyen la enseñanza anterior al primer grado.

Monaco:

E--> Except for 1982, data refer to public education only.

FR-> A l'exception de l'année 1982, les données se réfèrent à l'enseignement public seulement.

ESP> Excepto para 1982, los datos se refieren a la enseñanza pública solamente.

Netherlands:

E--> For 1975 data on teaching staff refer to full-time teachers only.

FR-> Pour 1975, les données relatives au personnel enseignant se réfèrent au personnel enseignant à plein temps seulement.

ESP> Para 1975 los datos relativos al personal docente se refieren al personal docente de jornada completa solamente.

Norway:

E--> Data on teachers include general education at the second level.

FR-> Les données relatives au personnel enseignant incluent l'enseignement général du second degré.

ESP> Los datos relativos al personal docente incluyen la enseñanza general de segundo grado.

Poland:

E--> Data on teaching staff (columns 2, 3 and 4) include evening and correspondence courses.

FR-> Les données relatives au personnel enseignant (colonnes 2, 3 et 4) incluent les cours du soir et par correspondance.

ESP> Los datos relativos al personal docente (columnas 2, 3 y 4) incluyen los cursos nocturnos y por correspondencia.

Spain:

E--> For 1975, data on teaching staff include part of general education at the second level.

FR-> Pour 1975 les données sur le personnel enseignant incluent une partie de l'enseignement général du second degré.

ESP> Para 1975 los datos sobre el personal docente incluyen una parte de la enseñanza general de segundo grado.

Switzerland:

E--> Data for 1975 refer to public education only and include special education.

FR-> En 1975, les données se réfèrent à l'enseignement public seulement et incluent l'éducation spéciale.

ESP> En 1975, los datos se refieren a la enseñanza pública solamente e incluyen la educación especial.

United Kingdom:

E--> Data on teaching staff include education preceding the first level.

FR-> Les données sur le personnel enseignant incluent l'enseignement précédant le premier degré.

United Kingdom: (Cont):

ESP> Los datos sobre el personal docente incluyen la enseñanz anterior al primer grado.

OCEANIA:

American Samoa:

E--> Data for 1975, and the figures in columns 1, 2 and 8 for 198 refer to public education only.

FR-> Les données pour 1975, et celles des colonnes 1, 2 et 8 pou 1981 se réfèrent à l'enseignement public seulement.

ESP> Los datos en 1975, y los de las columnas 1, 2 y 8 en 1981 s refieren a la enseñanza pública solamente.

Australia:

E--> The figures on teachers (columns 2, 3, 4 and 8) include pr primary classes, special education, upgraded and correspondenc courses.

FR-> Les données sur le personnel enseignant (colonnes 2, 3, 4 e 8) comprennent les classes préprimaires, l'éducation spéciale, le 'upgraded courses' et les cours par correspondance.

ESP> Los datos sobre el personal docente (columnas 2, 3, 4 y 8 comprenden las clases preprimarias, la educación especial, las 'upgrade courses' y los cursos por correspondencia.

Fiji:

E--> For 1975, data on enrolment include Forms I and II (educatio at the second level).

FR-> Pour 1975, les données relatives aux élèves incluent les 'Form I et II (enseignement du second degré).

ESP> Para 1975 los datos sobre los alumnos incluyen las 'Forms' I II (enseñanza de segundo grado).

New Caledonia:

E--> For 1975 and 1981, the figures on teaching staff (columns 2 an 8) include education preceding the first level. In 1983, data do not includ 'fin d'études' classes.

FR-> Pour 1975 et 1981, les chiffres relatifs au personne enseignant (colonnes 2 et 8) incluent l'enseignement précédant l premier degré. En 1983, les données n'incluent pas les classes de fi d'études.

ESP> Para 1975 y 1981, las cifras relativas al personal docent (columnas 2 y 8) incluyen la enseñanza anterior al primer grado. En 1983 los datos no incluyen las clases de 'fin d'études'.

New Zealand:

E--> Except for 1982, data on teaching staff include Forms I and (education at the second level). For 1975, these figures also include specia education.

FR-> A l'exception de 1982, les données sur le personnel enseignan incluent les 'Forms' I et II (enseignement du second degré). Pour 1975, ce chiffres comprennent également l'éducation spéciale.

ESP> A la excepción de 1982, los datos sobre el personal docent comprenden las 'Forms' I y II (enseñanza de segundo grado). Para 1975 estas cifras incluyen también la educación especial.

Niue:

E--> For 1975, data refer to grades I-VIII; for the other years to grade I-VII. For 1982, data on teaching staff include general education at th second level.

FR-> En 1975, les données se rapportent aux classes allant de l première à la huitième année d'études; pour les autres années aux classe allant de la première à la septième année. Pour 1982, les données relative au personnel enseignant incluent l'enseignement général du secon degré.

ESP> En 1975, los datos se refieren a las clases I-VIII; para los otro años a las clases I-VII. En 1982, los datos relativos al personal docent incluyen la enseñanza general de segundo grado.

Solomon Islands:

E--> See Table 3.1b.

FR-> Voir le tableau 3.1b.

ESP> Véase el cuadro 3.1b.

Tokelau:

E--> For 1983 data on taeching staff (columns 2, 3, 4 and 8) includ general education the second level.

FR-> Pour 1983, les données relatives au personnel enseignan (colonnes 2, 3, 4 et 8) incluent l'enseignement général du second degré

ESP> En 1983, los datos relativos al personal docente (columns 2, 3 4 y 8) incluyen la enseñanza general de segundo grado.

Vanuatu:

E--> For 1983, data refer to public education only.

FR-> Pour 1983, les données se réfèrent à l'enseignement publi seulement.

ESP> En 1983, los datos se refieren a la enseñanza públic solamente.

U.S.S.R.:

U.S.S.R.:

E--> Figures in columns 1, 2, 3 and 4 include general education at the second level.

FR-> Les données des colonnes 1, 2, 3 et 4 incluent l'enseignemen général du second degré.

ESP> Los datos de las columnas 1, 2, 3 y 4 incluyen la enseñanz general de segundo grado.

Byelorussian S.S.R.:

E--> Figures in columns 1 and 2 include general education at the

Byelorussian S.S.R.: (Cont):
second level.

FR-> Les données des colonnes 1 et 2 incluent l'enseignement général du second degré.

ESP> Los datos de las columnas 1 y 2 incluyen la enseñanza general de segundo grado.

Ukrainian S.S.R.:

E--> Figures in columns 1 and 2 include general education at the second level. From 1980, data on pupils refer to the first 5 years of primary school instead of 8 years.

FR-> Les données des colonnes 1 et 2 incluent l'enseignement général du second degré. A partir de 1980, les données relatives aux élèves se réfèrent aux 5 premières années de l'enseignement du premier degré au lieu de 8 années.

ESP> Los datos de las columnas 1 y 2 incluyen la enseñanza general de segundo grado. A partir de 1980, los datos relativos a los alumnos se refieren a los 5 primeros años de la enseñanza de primer grado, en vez de 8 años.

3.5 Education at the first level: Percentage distribution of enrolment by grade

Enseignement du premier degré: répartition en pourcentage des effectifs par année d'études

Enseñanza de primer grado: distribución en porcentaje de la matrícula escolar por año de estudios

PLEASE REFER TO EXPLANATORY TEXT AT END OF TABLE

NUMBER OF COUNTRIES AND TERRITORIES PRESENTED IN THIS TABLE: 182

PRIERE DE SE REFERER AU TEXTE EXPLICATIF A LA FIN DU TABLEAU

NOMBRE DE PAYS ET DE TERRITOIRES PRESENTES DANS CE TABLEAU: 182

REFERIRSE AL TEXTO EXPLICATIVO AL FINAL DEL CUADRO

NUMERO DE PAISES Y DE TERRITORIOS PRESENTADOS EN ESTE CUADRO: 182

COUNTRY PAYS PAIS	YEAR ANNEE AÑO	SEX SEXE SEXO	GRADES / ANNEES / AÑOS DE ESTUDIOS									
			I	II	III	IV	V	VI	VII	VIII	IX	X
AFRICA												
ALGERIA‡	1975	MF	19	17	17	16	14	12	5			
		F	20	17	17	16	14	12	4			
	1980	MF	18	17	17	16	15	13	4			
		F	18	18	17	16	15	13	3			
	1983	MF	19	17	16	15	17	15	2			
		F	19	17	16	15	17	14	1			
	1984	MF	18	18	16	15	14	17	1			
		F	19	18	17	16	14	16	1			
ANGOLA	1980	MF	41	30	18	11						
	1981	MF	39	31	19	12						
		F	40	32	18	10						
	1982	MF	38	30	19	13						
BENIN	1975	MF	26	21	16	13	12	12				
		F	27	20	16	13	12	12				
	1980	MF	28	18	19	13	10	11				
		F	28	19	19	13	10	11				
	1983	MF	24	18	17	14	13	13				
		F	25	19	18	14	13	12				
	1984	MF	25	19	17	14	13	13				
		F	25	19	17	14	12	12				
BOTSWANA	1975	MF	22	18	17	12	9	9	12			
		F	21	17	18	12	9	9	13			
	1980	MF	19	16	14	14	13	12	12			
		F	18	15	13	14	13	13	13			
	1984	MF	17	15	14	16	13	12	13			
		F	17	14	14	16	13	12	14			
	1985	MF	17	15	14	15	13	12	14			
		F	16	15	13	14	13	13	15			
BURKINA FASO	1975	MF	24	20	18	14	12	13				
		F	24	20	18	14	12	12				
	1980	MF	25	20	17	14	11	14				
		F	25	20	17	14	11	13				
	1983	MF	24	21	17	14	11	13				
		F	24	21	17	14	11	13				
	1984	MF	26	19	18	14	11	13				
		F	26	20	17	14	11	12				

COUNTRY PAYS PAIS	YEAR ANNEE AÑO	SEX SEXE SEXO	GRADES / ANNEES / AÑOS DE ESTUDIOS									
			I	II	III	IV	V	VI	VII	VIII	IX	X
BURUNDI	1975	MF	22	17	17	15	15	13				
		F	23	18	17	16	14	12				
	1980	MF	24	18	16	14	14	13				
		F	25	18	16	14	14	13				
	1983	MF	27	24	13	12	12	12				
		F	28	24	13	12	11	11				
	1984	MF	25	21	19	11	12	11				
		F	27	22	19	11	11	11				
CAMEROON	1975	MF	27	18	17	13	12	12	1			
		F	27	18	17	13	12	11	1			
	1980	MF	26	17	17	13	12	13	2			
		F	26	17	17	13	12	12	2			
	1983	MF	25	17	18	13	12	12	2			
		F	25	17	18	14	13	12	2			
	1984	MF	25	17	18	14	13	12	2			
		F	25	17	18	14	13	12	2			
CAPE VERDE	1975	MF	44	21	15	12	4	3				
		F	*45	*22	*15	*10	*4	*3				
	1980	MF	25	23	21	19	7	5				
	1983	MF	26	21	20	17	9	6				
		F	26	21	20	18	8	6				
CENTRAL AFRICAN REPUBLIC	1975	MF	27	21	17	12	10	12				
		F	29	23	17	12	9	10				
	1980	MF	27	20	17	13	11	12				
		F	29	21	18	12	10	10				
	1981	MF	27	21	18	12	10	12				
		F	29	22	18	12	10	9				
	1982	MF	26	22	18	13	10	11				
		F	29	22	18	13	10	9				
CHAD‡	1975	MF	35	19	15	10	9	12				
		F	39	21	16	9	8	8				
	1984	MF	40	21	15	10	7	7				
		F	45	21	14	9	7	5				
COMOROS	1980	MF	26	22	19	11	12	11				
		F	27	22	20	10	11	10				
CONGO	1975	MF	23	19	19	15	13	12				
		F	24	19	19	15	12	11				
	1980	MF	21	16	20	17	14	12				
		F	21	16	20	17	14	12				
	1982	MF	22	16	21	16	14	11				
		F	22	16	21	17	14	11				
	1984	MF	21	16	21	16	14	11				
		F	21	16	21	16	14	11				
COTE D'IVOIRE	1975	MF	20	17	16	14	14	18				
		F	22	18	17	14	14	15				
	1980	MF	20	18	16	14	12	19				
		F	21	19	17	14	12	17				
	1982	MF	19	17	16	14	13	20				
		F	20	18	16	15	13	17				
	1983	MF	19	16	16	14	14	20				
		F	20	17	17	14	14	18				
DJIBOUTI	1975	MF	20	21	15	14	13	16				
		F	18	20	20	15	15	13				
	1980	MF	21	16	13	21	15	14				
	1982	MF	21	20	16	12	11	20				
		F	22	20	16	11	11	20				
	1983	MF	19	19	18	14	11	18				
		F	19	20	18	14	10	18				

3.5 **Percentage distribution (first level) by grade**
Répartition en pourcentage (premier degré) par année d'études
Distribución en porcentaje (primer grado) por año de estudios

COUNTRY / PAYS / PAIS	YEAR / ANNEE / AÑO	SEX / SEXE / SEXO	I	II	III	IV	V	VI	VII	VIII	IX	X
			GRADES / ANNEES / AÑOS DE ESTUDIOS									
EGYPT	1975	MF	18	20	14	17	15	16				
		F	19	20	14	17	14	15				
	1980	MF	19	19	17	17	15	13				
		F	20	20	17	17	14	13				
	1982	MF	19	19	17	16	15	14				
		F	*20	*20	*17	*16	*14	*13				
	1983	MF	19	19	17	16	14	14				
		F	20	19	17	16	14	13				
ETHIOPIA	1975	MF	34	18	15	13	10	10				
		F	34	18	14	13	11	10				
	1980	MF	39	21	14	10	8	7				
		F	42	21	13	10	7	7				
	1982	MF	32	20	18	14	10	8				
		F	34	20	17	13	9	7				
	1983	MF	30	18	17	15	12	9				
		F	32	18	17	14	11	8				
GABON	1975	MF	34	18	15	11	10	11				
		F	35	18	15	11	10	10				
	1980	MF	33	18	16	12	10	11				
		F	34	18	16	12	10	10				
	1982	MF	33	18	16	11	10	11				
		F	33	18	16	11	10	11				
	1983	MF	33	18	16	12	10	12				
		F	33	18	16	12	10	11				
GAMBIA	1975	MF	21	17	17	15	13	18				
		F	21	19	17	15	12	16				
	1980	MF	23	19	17	13	12	15				
		F	28	20	16	12	11	13				
	1983	MF	22	18	17	15	14	15				
		F	24	20	18	14	13	12				
	1984	MF	21	17	16	15	14	17				
		F	23	18	17	15	13	13				
GHANA	1975	MF	23	18	17	16	14	13				
		F	23	18	17	15	14	12				
	1980	MF	22	18	17	16	15	13				
		F	22	19	17	15	14	13				
	1984	MF	19	18	17	16	15	14				
		F	20	18	17	16	15	14				
GUINEA	1975	MF	26	21	14	14	11	13				
		F	31	21	14	13	10	11				
	1980	MF	21	20	19	16	13	12				
		F	23	21	19	15	12	10				
	1983	MF	24	18	17	15	13	13				
		F	25	18	17	15	12	12				
	1984	MF	35	15	14	13	11	12				
		F	34	16	14	13	11	11				
GUINEA-BISSAU‡	1975	MF	66	15	9	6	2	2				
		F	76	12	6	4	2	1				
	1980	MF	36	22	16	15	7	4				
		F	42	23	15	10	6	3				
	1982	MF	36	23	16	14	8	4				
		F	40	23	15	11	8	4				
	1983	MF	35	23	16	14	8	4				
		F	39	23	15	12	8	4				
KENYA	1975	MF	23	25	15	12	9	8	8			
		F	24	26	15	12	9	8	7			
	1980	MF	23	18	14	13	12	11	9			
		F	24	19	14	13	12	11	8			
	1983	MF	21	16	15	14	12	12	9			
		F	21	17	16	15	13	12	8			

COUNTRY PAYS PAIS	YEAR ANNEE AÑO	SEX SEXE SEXO	GRADES / ANNEES / AÑOS DE ESTUDIOS									
			I	II	III	IV	V	VI	VII	VIII	IX	X
KENYA (CONT)	1984	MF	20	16	15	14	13	12	10			
		F	20	16	15	15	13	12	10			
LESOTHO	1975	MF	23	20	17	13	11	9	8			
		F	20	19	16	14	12	10	9			
	1980	MF	26	18	16	13	11	9	8			
		F	24	17	15	13	12	10	9			
	1982	MF	28	18	15	12	10	9	8			
		F	25	17	15	12	11	10	9			
	1983	MF	28	18	15	12	10	8	8			
		F	25	17	15	13	11	10	9			
LIBERIA‡	1975	MF	34	——>	18	13	11	9	8	7		
		F	38	——>	18	13	10	8	7	5		
	1980	MF	35	——>	17	13	11	9	8	7		
		F	39	——>	17	12	10	8	7	6		
LIBYAN ARAB JAMAHIRIYA	1975	MF	19	16	16	18	17	15				
		F	20	16	17	18	17	12				
	1980	MF	19	18	17	18	16	13				
		F	19	18	17	18	15	13				
	1982	MF	18	17	16	18	16	14				
		F	19	17	17	18	16	13				
MADAGASCAR	1980	MF	38	22	17	12	10					
		F	39	21	16	12	11					
	1982	MF	34	22	18	14	12					
		F	35	22	18	14	12					
	1983	MF	33	21	18	15	13					
MALAWI	1975	MF	29	20	15	11	8	6	4	6		
		F	33	21	16	11	7	5	4	4		
	1980	MF	29	18	14	10	8	8	6	9		
		F	33	19	14	10	7	7	5	6		
	1983	MF	24	18	15	11	8	8	6	10		
		F	26	19	16	11	8	7	6	7		
	1984	MF	27	17	14	10	8	8	6	10		
		F	29	18	15	11	8	7	6	7		
MALI	1975	MF	26	20	18	14	13	9				
		F	27	20	19	14	12	9				
	1980	MF	22	21	18	16	13	10				
		F	23	21	18	16	12	9				
	1981	MF	23	19	19	15	13	11				
		F	24	20	19	15	12	9				
	1982	MF	24	19	18	15	13	11				
		F	25	20	18	15	12	10				
MAURITANIA	1975	MF	26	12	15	17	11	10	10			
		F	26	16	15	17	11	9	8			
	1980	MF	20	17	17	15	15	15				
		F	21	19	18	15	14	14				
	1982	MF	22	18	16	14	14	16				
		F	23	18	17	14	13	15				
MAURITIUS	1975	MF	14	15	14	16	15	26				
		F	14	15	14	16	15	26				
	1980	MF	17	15	15	15	16	23				
		F	17	15	15	15	16	22				
	1983	MF	17	16	20	15	13	19				
		F	16	16	21	15	13	18				
	1984	MF	11	17	16	21	16	20				
		F	11	17	16	21	16	20				
MOROCCO	1975	MF	25	20	19	17	19					
		F	25	20	19	17	18					
	1980	MF	24	20	18	17	20					
		F	25	20	18	17	20					

3.5 Percentage distribution (first level) by grade
Répartition en pourcentage (premier degré) par année d'études
Distribución en porcentaje (primer grado) por año de estudios

COUNTRY PAYS PAIS	YEAR ANNEE AÑO	SEX SEXE SEXO	GRADES / ANNEES / AÑOS DE ESTUDIOS									
			I	II	III	IV	V	VI	VII	VIII	IX	X
MOROCCO (CONT)	1983	MF	22	21	19	17	21					
		F	22	21	19	17	20					
	1984	MF	19	21	21	19	20					
		F	19	21	21	18	20					
MOZAMBIQUE	1982	MF	42	30	17	11						
		F	45	30	16	8						
	1983	MF	41	30	19	11						
		F	44	30	18	8						
NIGER	1975	MF	29	22	16	13	10	11				
		F	28	22	16	13	10	10				
	1980	MF	21	19	17	15	13	15				
		F	21	20	17	15	13	14				
	1981	MF	18	20	17	15	14	15				
		F	19	20	18	16	14	15				
	1983	MF	16	18	18	17	15	17				
NIGERIA	1982	MF	21	18	17	16	15	14				
REUNION	1975	MF	22	20	20	20	18					
	1982	MF	21	19	19	20	22					
	1983	MF	21	19	19	20	21					
RWANDA	1975	MF	28	18	16	14	12	11				
		F	29	18	17	14	12	10				
	1980	MF	21	18	16	13	11	9	6	7		
		F	21	18	16	13	11	8	6	6		
	1982	MF	21	17	15	13	11	9	7	6		
		F	22	17	15	14	11	9	7	6		
	1983	MF	22	17	15	13	11	9	8	6		
		F	22	17	15	13	11	9	7	5		
ST. HELENA	1982	MF	19	14	15	19	17	16				
		F	19	13	16	20	15	16				
	1983	MF	17	16	15	14	22	15				
		F	16	15	16	16	21	14				
SAO TOME AND PRINCIPE	1980	MF	30	27	25	18						
	1983	MF	31	26	23	21						
		F	30	26	23	21						
	1984	MF	32	25	23	21						
SENEGAL	1980	MF	20	19	17	15	13	16				
		F	21	19	17	15	13	15				
	1982	MF	22	19	16	14	13	16				
		F	23	19	16	14	13	15				
	1983	MF	21	20	17	14	13	15				
		F	22	20	17	14	13	14				
SEYCHELLES	1975	MF	17	17	17	16	17	16				
		F	16	17	17	16	16	17				
	1980	MF	11	11	12	11	11	11	11	11	11	
		F	11	11	11	10	11	11	11	12	13	
	1984	MF	11	11	12	13	11	11	12	11	10	
		F	11	11	12	12	11	11	11	10	10	
	1985	MF	12	11	10	12	12	11	11	11	10	
		F	12	11	11	12	12	11	11	11	10	
SIERRA LEONE	1975	MF	26	18	15	13	11	9	8			
		F	27	18	15	13	11	8	7			
SOMALIA	1975	MF	68	19	8	5						
		F	73	17	6	4						
	1980	MF	22	15	15	11	7	8	9	13		
		F	20	15	15	12	8	8	11	12		
	1982	MF	17	15	14	13	14	10	6	10		
		F	16	14	13	13	14	11	7	10		
	1983	MF	19	14	13	12	12	12	9	8		
		F	20	14	12	12	12	12	9	9		

COUNTRY PAYS PAIS	YEAR ANNEE AÑO	SEX SEXE SEXO	GRADES / ANNEES / AÑOS DE ESTUDIOS									
			I	II	III	IV	V	VI	VII	VIII	IX	X
SUDAN	1975	MF	22	19	16	15	14	14				
		F	22	19	16	15	14	14				
	1980	MF	22	19	17	15	14	13				
		F	21	19	17	15	14	14				
	1982	MF	21	19	17	16	14	13				
		F	21	19	17	16	14	14				
	1983	MF	22	19	17	15	14	13				
		F	22	19	17	15	14	13				
SWAZILAND	1975	MF	20	16	16	14	13	11	10			
		F	19	16	16	14	13	11	11			
	1980	MF	21	18	16	14	12	10	9			
		F	20	17	16	14	12	11	10			
	1983	MF	19	17	16	14	12	10	10			
		F	19	17	16	14	13	11	10			
	1984	MF	19	17	16	14	13	11	10			
		F	19	16	16	14	13	11	10			
TOGO	1975	MF	29	19	17	12	11	11				
		F	33	20	17	12	10	8				
	1980	MF	*25	*19	*18	*13	*12	*13				
		F	*26	*20	*18	*13	*11	*11				
	1983	MF	25	19	18	13	12	12				
		F	27	20	19	13	11	10				
	1984	MF	27	19	18	13	12	11				
		F	29	20	19	13	11	9				
TUNISIA	1975	MF	17	16	16	16	16	19				
		F	18	17	16	16	16	17				
	1980	MF	19	17	16	15	14	18	–	–		
		F	21	18	17	15	14	16	–	–		
	1983	MF	20	18	17	15	15	14	2	0		
		F	21	19	17	15	14	13	2	0		
	1984	MF	19	18	17	16	15	13	1	0		
		F	20	19	17	15	14	13	1	0		
UGANDA‡	1975	MF	20	17	15	13	12	12	11			
		F	22	18	16	13	12	11	9			
	1981	MF	23	18	15	13	11	10	10			
		F	25	18	15	13	11	10	8			
	1982	MF	24	18	15	12	10	10	9			
		F	26	19	16	12	10	9	7			
UNITED REPUBLIC OF TANZANIA‡	1975	MF	29	16	14	12	10	10	9			
		F	31	17	14	12	10	9	8			
	1980	MF	14	16	24	15	14	11	6			
		F	15	16	24	15	13	11	6			
	1981	MF	14	13	15	21	14	13	10			
		F	15	14	15	21	14	12	9			
	1982	MF	14	13	13	14	20	14	12			
		F	15	14	13	14	20	13	11			
ZAIRE	1975	MF	*26	*20	*18	*14	*12	*10				
		F	*28	*20	*19	*14	*11	*8				
	1980	MF	26	18	17	15	13	11				
		F	27	19	17	14	12	10				
	1982	MF	26	17	17	15	13	12				
		F	27	19	16	14	13	11				
	1983	MF	26	17	17	15	14	12				
		F	26	19	16	15	13	11				
ZAMBIA	1975	MF	17	16	16	16	12	11	11			
		F	18	17	17	16	12	10	10			
	1980	MF	16	16	16	15	13	12	12			
		F	17	17	16	15	12	12	11			
	1981	MF	16	16	15	15	13	12	12			
		F	17	17	16	15	13	12	11			

3.5 Percentage distribution (first level) by grade
Répartition en pourcentage (premier degré) par année d'études
Distribución en porcentaje (primer grado) por año de estudios

COUNTRY PAYS PAIS	YEAR ANNEE AÑO	SEX SEXE SEXO	GRADES / ANNEES / AÑOS DE ESTUDIOS									
			I	II	III	IV	V	VI	VII	VIII	IX	X
ZIMBABWE	1975	MF	20	18	16	15	13	10	9			
		F	21	19	17	15	13	10	8			
	1980	MF	30	17	14	12	10	9	8			
	1983	MF	18	18	19	16	11	9	8			
		F	19	19	20	16	10	9	8			
	1984	MF	17	16	17	17	15	10	8			
		F	17	16	17	18	14	9	8			
AMERICA, NORTH												
ANTIGUA AND BARBUDA	1975	MF	18	13	13	15	14	14	13			
		F	17	13	14	15	15	13	13			
BAHAMAS	1981	MF	17	17	17	16	16	17				
		F	17	17	17	16	16	17				
	1982	MF	18	17	16	17	16	16				
		F	17	17	17	17	16	17				
BARBADOS‡	1975	MF	18	16	17	17	17	16				
		F	17	16	17	17	16	17				
	1980	MF	16	16	17	18	17	17				
		F	16	16	17	18	17	16				
	1983	MF	17	16	16	16	17	18				
		F	17	16	16	16	17	18				
	1984	MF	24	14	15	15	16	16				
		F	22	15	15	16	16	16				
BELIZE‡	1975	MF	19	14	13	13	11	11	10	9		
		F	19	13	13	12	13	11	9	10		
	1979	MF	19	14	13	12	12	11	10	10		
	1980	MF	19	13	13	13	11	11	10	10		
BERMUDA‡	1975	MF	13	14	14	14	15	16	15			
		F	13	13	13	14	14	17	16			
	1980	MF	14	14	14	15	15	15	14			
		F	14	14	13	15	15	15	15			
	1983	MF	14	15	15	14	14	14	15			
		F	14	14	16	13	14	14	16			
	1984	MF	15	14	15	15	14	14	14			
		F	14	14	15	15	13	14	14			
BRITISH VIRGIN ISLANDS	1975	MF	15	13	14	13	14	12	15	4		
		F	11	13	15	13	14	13	17	4		
	1980	MF	12	12	15	15	15	14	14	3		
		F	12	10	15	13	17	14	15	3		
	1983	MF	17	11	14	13	15	14	15	0		
		F	16	10	13	13	16	15	17	0		
	1984	MF	16	14	14	15	14	13	13	0		
		F	15	13	14	14	14	15	14	0		
CANADA	1975	MF	16	15	15	16	18	19				
		F	16	15	16	16	18	19				
	1980	MF	17	16	16	17	17	17				
		F	16	16	16	17	17	17				
	1982	MF	17	17	16	16	16	17				
		F	17	17	16	16	16	17				
	1983	MF	17	17	17	16	16	17				
		F	17	17	17	16	16	17				
CAYMAN ISLANDS	1975	MF	18	18	14	15	18	18				
		F	17	18	14	15	18	17				
	1980	MF	16	15	16	16	18	19				
		F	16	15	17	17	18	16				
COSTA RICA	1975	MF	18	17	19	16	15	14				
		F	18	17	19	17	15	15				
	1980	MF	18	18	18	16	16	14				
		F	18	18	17	16	17	14				

COUNTRY PAYS PAIS	YEAR ANNEE AÑO	SEX SEXE SEXO	GRADES / ANNEES / AÑOS DE ESTUDIOS									
			I	II	III	IV	V	VI	VII	VIII	IX	X
COSTA RICA (CONT)	1983	MF	21	18	18	16	14	13				
		F	21	18	18	16	14	14				
	1984	MF	22	19	17	16	14	12				
		F	21	19	17	16	14	12				
CUBA	1975	MF	17	17	17	18	16	13				
		F	17	17	17	18	17	14				
	1980	MF	14	19	17	18	15	16				
		F	14	18	18	18	16	16				
	1983	MF	13	18	16	17	18	19				
		F	13	17	16	17	18	19				
	1984	MF	12	17	17	18	18	19				
		F	13	16	17	17	18	19				
DOMINICA	1975	MF	16	13	15	14	15	14	12			
		F	15	14	15	14	15	14	12			
	1980	MF	13	13	15	17	15	13	14			
		F	12	12	16	16	15	14	14			
	1981	MF	13	13	14	14	17	16	14			
		F	13	13	13	13	16	16	16			
	1983	MF	12	13	13	13	14	16	19			
		F	12	12	13	13	13	15	21			
DOMINICAN REPUBLIC	1980	MF	34	18	16	13	10	8				
	1982	MF	33	19	16	13	11	9				
		F	31	18	16	14	11	9				
	1983	MF	32	19	16	14	11	9				
EL SALVADOR‡	1975	MF	28	18	13	10	8	7	6	5	4	
		F	28	18	13	10	8	7	6	5	4	
	1980	MF	24	16	14	11	10	8	6	5	5	
		F	24	16	14	12	10	8	6	5	5	
	1983	MF	27	17	13	10	8	7	7	6	5	
		F	27	17	13	10	8	8	7	6	5	
	1984	MF	26	17	14	11	8	7	7	6	5	
		F	26	17	14	11	8	7	7	6	5	
GRENADA	1975	MF	16	13	13	14	15	15	14			
		F	16	13	13	14	15	15	14			
	1980	MF	16	14	14	14	14	13	14			
		F	15	14	14	14	14	13	15			
	1982	MF	15	14	15	15	14	14	14			
		F	14	14	15	15	14	14	14			
	1983	MF	24	12	13	13	12	11	16			
		F	24	12	13	13	12	12	15			
GUADELOUPE	1975	MF	23	20	20	20	17					
	1982	MF	19	19	20	21	20					
	1983	MF	19	19	20	22	21					
GUATEMALA	1975	MF	37	20	16	11	9	7				
		F	37	20	15	11	9	7				
	1980	MF	36	20	15	11	9	8				
		F	37	20	15	11	9	8				
	1983	MF	36	20	16	12	9	7				
		F	36	21	16	11	9	7				
	1984	MF	35	21	16	12	9	8				
HAITI	1980	MF	32	20	16	13	10	8	2			
		F	32	20	15	13	10	8	2			
	1982	MF	42	18	14	11	9	7				
		F	42	17	14	11	9	6				
	1983	MF	38	19	16	12	9	6				
		F	38	19	16	12	9	6				
HONDURAS	1975	MF	36	21	16	12	9	7				
		F	35	21	16	12	9	7				

3.5 Percentage distribution (first level) by grade
Répartition en pourcentage (premier degré) par année d'études
Distribución en porcentaje (primer grado) por año de estudios

COUNTRY PAYS PAIS	YEAR ANNEE AÑO	SEX SEXE SEXO	GRADES / ANNEES / AÑOS DE ESTUDIOS									
			I	II	III	IV	V	VI	VII	VIII	IX	X
HONDURAS (CONT)	1980	MF	35	21	16	12	9	7				
		F	34	21	16	12	10	8				
	1984	MF	33	21	16	12	10	8				
		F	32	20	16	13	10	8				
	1985	MF	32	21	16	13	10	8				
		F	31	20	17	13	10	9				
JAMAICA	1975	MF	17	17	18	17	16	14				
		F	17	17	18	17	16	15				
	1980	MF	17	17	18	17	16	15				
		F	16	17	18	17	16	16				
	1982	MF	17	17	17	17	16	16				
		F	17	17	16	17	16	17				
	1983	MF	17	17	17	16	16	16				
		F	17	17	17	16	16	17				
MARTINIQUE	1975	MF	21	21	20	20	18					
	1982	MF	18	19	19	21	23					
	1983	MF	18	18	20	22	22					
MEXICO	1975	MF	27	20	17	14	12	10				
		F	27	20	17	14	12	10				
	1980	MF	25	19	17	15	13	11				
		F	25	19	17	15	13	11				
	1983	MF	22	18	17	16	14	12				
		F	22	18	17	16	14	12				
	1984	MF	22	18	17	16	15	13				
		F	21	18	17	16	15	13				
MONTSERRAT‡	1975	MF	14	9	13	11	14	12	12	6	8	
		F	13	9	12	10	14	13	14	5	9	
	1981	MF	15	8	14	16	17	14	15	2	–	
		F	15	8	12	15	18	14	17	2	–	
NETHERLANDS ANTILLES	1980	MF	17	18	17	17	16	16				
		F	16	16	17	17	16	17				
NICARAGUA	1975	MF	38	20	15	12	9	7				
	1980	MF	43	20	13	10	8	6				
		F	41	20	13	11	8	7				
	1983	MF	38	21	17	11	8	5				
		F	36	21	17	11	9	6				
	1984	MF	32	24	17	13	9	5				
PANAMA	1975	MF	21	19	17	16	15	12				
		F	21	18	17	16	16	12				
	1980	MF	21	18	17	16	15	13				
		F	21	17	17	16	15	14				
	1983	MF	21	18	17	16	14	14				
		F	21	18	17	16	14	14				
	1984	MF	21	18	17	16	15	13				
		F	21	18	17	16	15	14				
PUERTO RICO‡	1975	MF	17	16	17	17	17	16				
	1981	MF	13	12	12	13	13	12	13	12		
ST. CHRISTOPHER AND NEVIS‡	1984	MF	12	14	14	14	13	14	18			
		F	12	14	14	14	13	15	18			
ST. LUCIA‡	1975	MF	11	12	12	13	12	13	12	8	8	
		F	11	12	12	13	12	13	12	8	8	
	1980	MF	12	12	13	12	10	11	12	8	10	
		F	11	11	13	13	10	11	13	7	11	
	1982	MF	12	12	12	11	11	11	13	7	10	
		F	12	12	11	11	11	11	14	7	10	
	1983	MF	12	12	12	11	11	11	13	8	10	
		F	12	12	12	11	11	11	13	8	10	

COUNTRY PAYS PAIS	YEAR ANNEE AÑO	SEX SEXE SEXO	GRADES / ANNEES / AÑOS DE ESTUDIOS									
			I	II	III	IV	V	VI	VII	VIII	IX	X
ST. PIERRE AND MIQUELON	1980	MF	18	19	20	22	21					
		F	17	19	19	24	21					
	1983	MF	20	17	18	21	24					
		F	20	18	17	21	23					
	1984	MF	20	19	19	19	24					
		F	16	21	19	19	25					
ST. VINCENT AND THE GRENADINES	1975	MF	20	14	13	14	14	13	12			
		F	19	14	12	14	14	14	13			
	1981	MF	20	16	15	14	14	11	10			
		F	19	16	15	14	13	12	11			
	1983	MF	18	15	14	15	15	12	12			
		F	17	14	14	15	14	13	13			
TRINIDAD AND TOBAGO	1975	MF	12	11	12	12	12	11	18	8	5	
		F	12	11	12	12	12	11	19	8	5	
	1980	MF	14	13	13	13	13	11	17	5	2	
		F	13	13	13	12	13	12	17	5	2	
	1982	MF	13	13	13	12	12	12	18	5	1	
		F	13	13	13	12	12	12	18	5	1	
	1984	MF	14	14	14	13	13	11	17	3	1	
		F	14	14	14	13	13	12	17	3	1	
UNITED STATES‡	1975	MF	15	14	14	14	15	16	6	6		
	1980	MF	12	12	12	13	14	13	13	13		
		F	12	11	12	13	14	13	12	13		
	1983	MF	13	12	12	12	12	12	14	13		
		F	13	12	12	12	12	12	14	13		
	1984	MF	13	12	12	12	12	12	13	13		
		F	13	12	12	12	13	13	12	13		
U.S. VIRGIN ISLANDS‡	1975	MF	18	16	17	17	16	15				
	1980	MF	12	12	13	13	13	12	15	11		
	1981	MF	12	12	12	13	13	12	15	11		
AMERICA, SOUTH												
ARGENTINA	1975	MF	20	17	15	14	13	12	10			
		F	19	16	15	14	13	12	11			
	1980	MF	19	17	15	14	13	11	10			
		F	19	17	15	14	13	12	10			
	1981	MF	20	16	15	14	13	12	10			
		F	19	16	15	14	13	12	10			
BOLIVIA	1975	MF	28	18	15	12	9	7	6	5		
		F	30	19	15	11	9	7	6	5		
	1980	MF	27	18	14	11	9	8	7	6		
		F	28	18	15	12	9	8	6	5		
	1983	MF	22	17	15	12	10	9	8	6		
		F	24	18	15	12	10	8	7	6		
	1984	MF	23	17	15	12	11	9	7	6		
		F	24	18	15	12	10	8	6	6		
BRAZIL‡	1975	MF	31	16	13	11	10	8	6	5		
	1980	MF	31	16	13	10	10	8	6	5		
	1982	MF	31	16	13	11	11	8	6	5		
	1983	MF	28	17	13	11	11	8	6	5		
CHILE	1975	MF	16	15	14	13	13	11	10	8		
		F	16	15	14	13	13	11	10	8		
	1980	MF	16	14	14	13	12	12	11	9		
		F	15	14	13	13	12	12	11	9		
	1983	MF	12	13	14	14	14	12	11	10		
		F	12	13	14	14	14	13	11	10		
	1984	MF	12	12	13	14	14	13	12	10		
		F	12	12	13	14	14	13	12	11		

3.5 **Percentage distribution (first level) by grade**
Répartition en pourcentage (premier degré) par année d'études
Distribución en porcentaje (primer grado) por año de estudios

COUNTRY PAYS PAIS	YEAR ANNEE AÑO	SEX SEXE SEXO	GRADES / ANNEES / AÑOS DE ESTUDIOS I	II	III	IV	V	VI	VII	VIII	IX	X
COLOMBIA	1975	MF	35	23	18	13	11					
		F	34	23	18	13	11					
	1980	MF	32	22	18	15	13					
		F	31	22	18	15	13					
	1984	MF	30	22	19	16	14					
		F	29	22	19	16	14					
	1985	MF	31	22	18	16	13					
		F	30	21	19	17	14					
ECUADOR	1975	MF	27	19	17	14	12	11				
		F	27	19	17	15	12	11				
	1980	MF	25	19	17	15	13	11				
		F	25	19	17	15	13	11				
	1983	MF	24	19	17	15	13	12				
		F	23	18	17	15	13	12				
	1984	MF	24	18	17	15	14	12				
FALKLAND ISLANDS (MALVINAS)	1975	MF	17	22	10	18	16	18				
		F	13	19	13	18	16	20				
	1980	MF	17	15	16	18	16	17				
		F	18	14	15	18	16	18				
FRENCH GUIANA	1975	MF	27	22	20	17	14					
	1982	MF	23	21	20	18	18					
	1983	MF	23	21	21	17	18					
GUYANA	1975	MF	18	17	17	17	15	16				
		F	17	17	17	18	15	16				
	1980	MF	17	17	18	17	16	15				
		F	17	17	17	17	16	15				
	1981	MF	17	17	17	17	16	15				
		F	17	17	17	17	17	16				
PARAGUAY	1975	MF	27	22	18	14	11	8				
		F	27	22	18	14	11	8				
	1980	MF	26	22	18	14	11	9				
	1983	MF	24	21	18	15	12	10				
	1984	MF	24	21	18	15	12	10				
PERU	1975	MF	24	20	17	15	12	10				
	1980	MF	25	17	16	15	14	12				
		F	26	18	16	15	14	12				
	1982	MF	26	19	16	15	14	12				
		F	26	19	16	14	13	11				
	1985	MF	26	19	16	15	13	12				
		F	26	19	16	14	13	11				
SURINAME	1975	MF	21	18	17	17	15	13				
		F	20	17	17	17	16	14				
	1984	MF	19	17	17	17	16	14				
		F	18	17	17	17	17	15				
URUGUAY‡	1975	MF	19	17	17	16	16	14				
	1980	MF	20	18	17	17	15	13				
		F	19	17	17	17	16	14				
	1981	MF	20	18	17	17	15	14				
	1983	MF	20	18	17	16	15	14				
VENEZUELA	1975	MF	23	19	17	16	14	11				
		F	22	19	17	16	14	12				
	1980	MF	22	19	17	16	14	12				
	1982	MF	22	19	17	16	14	12				
		F	21	18	17	16	14	13				
	1983	MF	22	19	17	16	14	12				
		F	21	18	17	16	14	13				

COUNTRY PAYS PAIS	YEAR ANNEE AÑO	SEX SEXE SEXO	GRADES / ANNEES / AÑOS DE ESTUDIOS									
			I	II	III	IV	V	VI	VII	VIII	IX	X
ASIA												
AFGHANISTAN	1975	MF	22	18	17	13	11	8	7	5		
		F	23	19	17	13	10	8	6	4		
	1980	MF	21	16	14	14	11	9	8	6		
		F	22	17	15	14	11	8	7	6		
	1982	MF	16	16	13	13	12	11	10	9		
		F	17	17	14	13	12	10	9	8		
	1984	MF	18	16	14	12	12	11	10	8		
		F	19	16	14	12	11	10	9	7		
BAHRAIN	1975	MF	18	18	18	18	15	13				
		F	18	18	18	18	15	13				
	1980	MF	17	18	17	17	16	15				
		F	19	18	17	17	15	14				
	1983	MF	19	18	18	16	15	14				
		F	21	18	18	16	14	13				
	1984	MF	18	18	17	17	16	15				
		F	18	19	17	17	15	14				
BANGLADESH	1980	MF	41	21	16	12	9					
		F	41	22	16	12	9					
	1984	MF	46	19	15	11	9					
		F	48	19	14	11	8					
	1985	MF	45	20	15	12	8					
		F	47	20	14	11	8					
BHUTAN‡	1983	MF	46	17	13	10	8	6				
		F	50	16	12	10	7	5				
	1984	MF	45	17	13	11	8	6				
		F	48	17	12	10	7	6				
BRUNEI DARUSSALAM	1975	MF	15	15	14	22	16	17				
		F	15	15	15	22	16	17				
	1980	MF	18	8	16	15	17	26				
		F	17	8	17	15	16	27				
	1983	MF	19	17	16	14	11	23				
		F	18	17	16	14	10	24				
	1984	MF	19	17	16	14	14	20				
		F	18	16	16	15	14	21				
BURMA‡	1975	MF	37	21	17	14	10					
		F	38	22	17	14	9					
CHINA	1980	MF	25	21	20	18	16					
	1983	MF	23	20	19	19	17	2				
	1984	MF	22	20	19	18	17	3				
		F	23	20	19	18	16	3				
CYPRUS‡	1975	MF	19	15	17	16	15	17	0	0		
		F	19	15	17	16	15	17	0	0		
	1980	MF	14	13	17	18	18	21	0			
		F	14	13	17	17	18	21	0			
	1982	MF	19	16	15	14	18	19	0			
		F	19	16	15	14	18	19	0			
	1983	MF	19	19	16	14	14	18	0			
		F	19	18	16	15	14	18	0			
DEMOCRATIC YEMEN‡	1975	MF	23	21	19	14	12	11				
		F	26	23	20	13	10	8				
	1980	MF	16	15	14	13	13	12	10	9		
		F	15	15	15	14	12	12	10	8		
	1982	MF	18	16	14	13	12	11	9	8		
		F	19	16	14	13	12	10	8	8		
	1983	MF	19	17	14	12	12	10	9	8		
		F	21	17	14	12	11	10	8	7		
HONG KONG	1975	MF	15	15	17	18	18	17				
		F	15	15	17	18	18	17				

3.5 **Percentage distribution (first level) by grade**
Répartition en pourcentage (premier degré) par année d'études
Distribución en porcentaje (primer grado) por año de estudios

COUNTRY PAYS PAIS	YEAR ANNEE AÑO	SEX SEXE SEXO	GRADES / ANNEES / AÑOS DE ESTUDIOS									
			I	II	III	IV	V	VI	VII	VIII	IX	X
HONG KONG (CONT)	1980	MF	17	17	17	17	16	16				
		F	17	17	17	17	16	16				
	1983	MF	16	16	17	18	17	16				
		F	16	16	17	18	17	16				
	1984	MF	16	16	17	17	17	17				
		F	16	16	17	17	18	17				
INDIA	1975	MF	33	22	18	14	12					
		F	35	22	18	14	11					
	1979	MF	30	23	19	15	12					
		F	32	23	19	15	12					
INDONESIA	1975	MF	27	21	17	14	11	9				
		F	28	21	17	14	11	8				
	1980	MF	23	23	18	14	12	10				
		F	24	23	16	15	12	10				
	1983	MF	22	19	17	16	14	11				
		F	22	19	18	16	14	11				
	1984	MF	21	19	17	16	14	13				
		F	21	19	17	16	14	13				
IRAN, ISLAMIC REPUBLIC OF	1975	MF	27	23	18	16	16					
		F	30	23	17	15	14					
	1983	MF	27	21	19	17	16					
		F	28	21	18	17	15					
	1984	MF	26	21	19	17	16					
		F	27	22	19	17	15					
IRAQ	1975	MF	25	19	15	15	15	10				
		F	29	20	15	14	14	8				
	1980	MF	15	18	24	15	16	12				
		F	15	19	27	14	14	10				
	1982	MF	18	15	16	18	21	12				
		F	18	16	16	19	22	10				
	1983	MF	19	16	15	16	19	16				
		F	19	17	15	16	19	15				
ISRAEL	1975	MF	14	13	13	13	13	12	11	11		
		F	14	13	13	13	13	12	11	11		
	1980	MF	14	13	13	13	13	12	11	10		
	1982	MF	14	13	13	13	12	12	12	11		
		F	14	13	13	13	12	12	12	11		
	1983	MF	13	14	13	13	12	12	12	11		
		F	13	14	13	13	12	12	12	11		
JAPAN‡	1975	MF	18	18	15	16	17	16				
		F	18	18	15	16	17	16				
	1980	MF	17	17	17	16	16	16				
		F	17	17	17	16	16	16				
	1983	MF	15	16	17	17	17	17				
		F	15	16	17	18	17	17				
	1984	MF	15	16	16	17	18	18				
		F	15	15	16	17	18	18				
JORDAN‡	1975	MF	18	17	18	17	16	14				
		F	19	17	18	17	16	13				
	1980	MF	17	18	17	17	17	15				
		F	17	18	17	17	17	15				
	1983	MF	17	16	16	17	18	16				
		F	17	16	16	17	18	16				
	1984	MF	18	17	16	16	17	17				
		F	18	17	16	16	17	16				
KOREA, REPUBLIC OF	1975	MF	18	16	17	16	16	17				
		F	17	16	17	16	16	17				
	1980	MF	16	17	18	16	16	16				
		F	16	17	18	16	16	16				

COUNTRY PAYS PAIS	YEAR ANNEE AÑO	SEX SEXE SEXO	GRADES / ANNEES / AÑOS DE ESTUDIOS									
			I	II	III	IV	V	VI	VII	VIII	IX	X
KOREA, REP. OF (CONT)	1983	MF	14	15	17	17	18	19				
		F	14	15	17	17	18	19				
	1984	MF	15	15	16	17	18	19				
		F	15	15	16	17	18	19				
KUWAIT	1975	MF	29	26	23	21						
		F	29	26	23	21						
	1980	MF	27	26	24	23						
		F	28	26	24	22						
	1983	MF	28	25	24	22						
		F	28	25	24	23						
	1984	MF	27	26	24	22						
		F	27	26	24	22						
LAO PEOPLE'S DEMOCRATIC REPUBLIC	1980	MF	41	21	16	12	9					
		F	40	21	16	13	9					
	1983	MF	44	22	15	11	9					
		F	43	22	15	11	8					
MALAYSIA	1984	MF	18	17	17	17	16	16				
		F	18	17	17	17	16	16				
	1985	MF	17	17	17	17	16	15				
		F	18	17	17	17	16	15				
MONGOLIA	1975	MF	35	34	31							
		F	35	34	32							
	1980	MF	35	33	32							
	1983	MF	34	34	32							
	1984	MF	34	33	33							
NEPAL	1975	MF	57	24	19							
		F	58	24	18							
	1980	MF	55	25	20							
		F	57	25	17							
	1983	MF	43	19	16	13	10					
		F	45	19	15	12	9					
	1984	MF	42	19	15	13	10					
		F	44	19	15	12	10					
OMAN	1975	MF	23	29	20	15	9	3				
		F	30	31	21	11	5	2				
	1980	MF	23	19	18	17	13	10				
		F	27	20	19	15	11	8				
	1983	MF	25	20	16	16	12	11				
		F	29	22	16	14	10	9				
	1984	MF	25	21	17	15	12	10				
		F	28	23	18	13	11	8				
PAKISTAN‡	1975	MF	31	22	18	16	13					
		F	35	21	17	15	12					
	1980	MF	34	21	17	15	13					
		F	38	20	16	13	12					
	1982	MF	35	21	17	15	12					
		F	38	21	16	13	12					
	1983	MF	35	21	17	15	12					
		F	34	20	18	15	13					
PHILIPPINES	1975	MF	21	19	17	16	14	13				
	1980	MF	21	18	17	18	14	12				
		F	21	18	17	18	14	13				
	1983	MF	22	18	17	16	15	13				
		F	21	18	17	16	15	14				
	1984	MF	22	18	17	15	14	13				
		F	21	18	17	16	15	14				
QATAR‡	1975	MF	20	19	17	17	15	12				
		F	21	19	18	17	15	11				

3.5 Percentage distribution (first level) by grade
Répartition en pourcentage (premier degré) par année d'études
Distribución en porcentaje (primer grado) por año de estudios

COUNTRY PAYS PAIS	YEAR ANNEE AÑO	SEX SEXE SEXO	GRADES / ANNEES / AÑOS DE ESTUDIOS									
			I	II	III	IV	V	VI	VII	VIII	IX	X
QATAR (CONT)‡	1980	MF	19	18	17	17	16	13				
		F	19	18	17	17	16	13				
	1983	MF	18	17	16	17	17	14				
		F	18	17	16	17	16	14				
	1984	MF	18	17	17	16	17	15				
		F	18	18	17	16	16	15				
SAUDI ARABIA	1975	MF	24	19	17	17	13	10				
		F	24	20	17	16	13	9				
	1980	MF	23	19	18	16	13	11				
		F	25	19	17	15	13	11				
	1982	MF	23	20	17	16	14	11				
		F	24	20	17	15	13	10				
	1983	MF	23	19	17	16	14	11				
		F	25	19	17	15	13	10				
SINGAPORE	1975	MF	14	14	16	16	17	22				
		F	14	15	16	17	18	21				
	1980	MF	16	17	16	18	16	17				
		F	16	17	16	17	16	17				
	1983	MF	15	14	15	16	17	17	5	2		
		F	15	14	15	17	17	17	4	2		
	1984	MF	13	15	14	15	17	17	4	5		
		F	14	15	14	15	17	18	3	4		
SRI LANKA	1975	MF	25	23	19	14	19					
		F	25	23	20	13	20					
	1980	MF	17	17	17	19	16	14				
		F	18	17	17	19	16	14				
	1983	MF	18	18	17	17	16	14				
		F	18	18	17	17	15	15				
	1984	MF	18	18	17	17	16	14				
		F	18	18	17	17	16	14				
SYRIAN ARAB REPUBLIC‡	1975	MF	20	18	17	17	15	13				
		F	21	19	18	17	14	11				
	1980	MF	21	19	17	16	14	13				
		F	22	20	17	15	14	11				
	1983	MF	21	18	17	16	15	13				
		F	22	18	17	16	14	12				
	1984	MF	21	19	17	15	15	14				
		F	21	20	17	15	14	13				
THAILAND	1975	MF	23	19	19	17	9	7	6			
		F	24	19	19	17	9	7	6			
	1980	MF	20	18	19	17	15	12				
		F	19	17	19	17	16	12				
	1981	MF	19	17	17	18	16	13				
	1983	MF	18	16	16	16	16	16				
TURKEY	1980	MF	23	21	20	19	18					
		F	23	21	20	19	17					
	1983	MF	26	20	20	18	16					
		F	27	20	20	17	16					
	1984	MF	22	23	20	19	17					
		F	22	23	20	19	16					
UNITED ARAB EMIRATES‡	1975	MF	22	21	18	16	13	9				
		F	24	22	18	15	13	8				
	1980	MF	20	18	17	17	15	13				
		F	21	18	17	17	15	13				
	1983	MF	22	19	18	16	14	12				
		F	22	19	18	16	13	12				
	1984	MF	22	19	17	16	14	11				
		F	22	19	17	16	14	11				
VIET-NAM	1980	MF	27	21	19	17	16					
		F	26	21	19	17	16					

COUNTRY PAYS PAIS	YEAR ANNEE AÑO	SEX SEXE SEXO	GRADES / ANNEES / AÑOS DE ESTUDIOS I	II	III	IV	V	VI	VII	VIII	IX	X
YEMEN‡	1975	MF	42	23	16	9	6	4				
		F	41	19	16	11	7	5				
	1980	MF	39	23	16	11	7	5				
		F	43	20	14	10	7	6				
	1982	MF	30	24	19	13	8	6				
		F	36	25	17	10	6	5				
	1983	MF	29	21	19	15	10	7				
		F	35	23	18	12	7	5				
EUROPE												
ALBANIA	1980	MF	12	12	12	12	13	13	13	12		
		F	13	12	12	12	13	13	12	12		
	1983	MF	13	13	13	12	13	12	12	12		
		F	13	13	13	12	12	12	12	12		
	1984	MF	12	13	13	12	13	12	12	12		
		F	12	13	13	12	13	12	12	12		
AUSTRIA	1975	MF	25	25	25	25						
		F	25	25	25	25						
	1980	MF	24	24	25	27						
		F	24	24	25	27						
	1983	MF	24	24	26	26						
		F	24	24	26	26						
	1984	MF	25	24	25	26						
		F	24	24	25	26						
BELGIUM‡	1975	MF	17	16	16	17	17	17				
		F	18	16	16	17	17	17				
	1980	MF	17	16	17	17	17	16				
		F	17	16	17	17	17	16				
	1983	MF	17	16	16	16	17	17				
		F	17	16	16	16	17	17				
	1984	MF	18	17	16	16	17	17				
		F	18	17	16	16	17	17				
BULGARIA	1975	MF	14	12	12	12	12	13	12	12		
		F	14	12	12	12	12	13	12	12		
	1980	MF	14	13	13	13	13	13	11	10		
		F	14	13	13	13	13	13	11	10		
	1983	MF	14	13	14	13	12	12	12	11		
		F	14	13	14	13	12	12	12	11		
	1984	MF	14	13	13	14	12	11	11	11		
		F	14	13	13	14	12	11	11	11		
CZECHOSLOVAKIA	1975	MF	11	11	11	11	12	12	11	10	9	
		F	11	11	11	11	12	12	11	11	9	
	1980	MF	15	13	12	12	11	11	10	10	5	
		F	15	13	12	12	11	11	10	10	6	
	1983	MF	14	14	14	14	12	11	11	10	0	
		F	14	14	14	14	12	11	11	10	0	
	1984	MF	13	13	13	13	13	12	11	10	–	
		F	13	13	13	13	13	12	11	10	–	
DENMARK	1975	MF	15	16	18	18	17	16				
	1980	MF	16	17	17	16	16	17				
		F	16	17	17	16	16	17				
	1982	MF	17	16	16	17	17	16				
		F	17	16	16	17	17	16				
	1983	MF	15	17	16	17	17	17				
		F	15	17	16	17	18	17				
FINLAND‡	1975	MF	16	16	16	16	18	18				
	1980	MF	15	16	16	17	17	19				
		F	15	16	16	17	17	19				
	1983	MF	18	18	17	15	16	16				
		F	18	17	17	15	16	17				

3.5 Percentage distribution (first level) by grade
Répartition en pourcentage (premier degré) par année d'études
Distribución en porcentaje (primer grado) por año de estudios

COUNTRY PAYS PAIS	YEAR ANNEE AÑO	SEX SEXE SEXO	GRADES / ANNEES / AÑOS DE ESTUDIOS									
			I	II	III	IV	V	VI	VII	VIII	IX	X
FINLAND (CONT)‡	1984	MF	18	18	17	16	15	16				
		F	18	18	17	17	15	16				
FRANCE	1975	MF	22	19	19	20	20					
	1980	MF	20	20	20	20	20					
		F	20	20	20	20	20					
	1981	MF	19	19	20	21	21					
		F	19	19	20	21	21					
	1982	MF	19	19	20	21	21					
		F	19	19	20	21	21					
GERMAN DEMOCRATIC REPUBLIC	1983	MF	10	9	9	9	9	11	11	11	10	10
		F	10	9	9	9	9	11	11	11	11	11
	1984	MF	11	10	9	9	8	9	11	11	10	10
		F	11	10	9	9	8	9	11	11	11	11
GERMANY, FEDERAL REPUBLIC OF‡	1975	MF	24	25	25	25						
		F	24	25	25	25						
	1980	MF	23	24	26	28						
		F	22	24	26	28						
	1982	MF	25	25	25	26						
		F	24	25	25	26						
	1983	MF	25	25	25	25						
		F	25	25	25	25						
GIBRALTAR	1975	MF	11	12	12	12	13	13	14	14		
		F	11	11	13	12	12	13	14	14		
	1980	MF	13	13	13	11	12	13	13	12		
		F	13	12	13	12	12	13	14	11		
	1982	MF	13	13	13	12	13	11	12	13		
		F	12	12	14	12	14	12	13	13		
	1983	MF	12	13	12	13	13	13	11	13		
		F	12	12	12	14	12	14	12	13		
GREECE‡	1975	MF	17	17	17	17	16	15				
		F	17	17	17	17	16	15				
	1980	MF	17	16	16	16	16	17				
		F	17	16	16	16	16	17				
	1981	MF	16	18	17	17	16	17				
		F	17	17	17	17	17	17				
	1982	MF	17	16	17	17	17	16				
		F	17	16	17	17	16	16				
HUNGARY	1975	MF	15	14	13	12	12	12	11	11		
		F	15	14	13	12	12	12	11	11		
	1980	MF	15	13	12	12	13	12	12	11		
		F	15	13	12	12	13	12	12	11		
	1983	MF	14	14	15	13	12	11	11	11		
		F	14	14	15	13	12	11	11	11		
	1984	MF	13	13	14	14	13	11	11	10		
		F	13	14	14	14	13	11	11	10		
ICELAND	1975	MF	15	16	17	17	17	18				
		F	15	16	17	17	18	17				
IRELAND	1975	MF	17	17	17	17	17	16				
		F	17	17	17	17	17	16				
	1980	MF	17	17	17	17	16	16				
		F	16	17	17	17	16	16				
	1981	MF	17	16	17	17	17	17				
		F	16	16	17	17	17	17				
	1982	MF	17	16	16	17	17	17				
		F	16	16	16	17	17	17				
ITALY	1975	MF	19	20	20	21	21					
		F	19	20	20	21	21					
	1980	MF	19	20	20	21	21					
		F	19	20	20	21	21					

COUNTRY PAYS PAIS	YEAR ANNEE AÑO	SEX SEXE SEXO	GRADES / ANNEES / AÑOS DE ESTUDIOS									
			I	II	III	IV	V	VI	VII	VIII	IX	X
ITALY (CONT)	1982	MF	18	20	21	21	21					
		F	18	20	21	21	21					
	1983	MF	17	19	20	21	22					
		F	17	19	20	21	22					
LUXEMBOURG	1975	MF	18	16	17	17	17	15				
		F	17	16	17	17	17	16				
	1980	MF	16	13	18	18	18	17				
		F	16	13	17	18	18	18				
	1981	MF	18	15	14	17	18	18				
		F	18	15	14	17	18	18				
	1982	MF	18	17	16	14	17	17				
		F	18	17	16	14	17	18				
MALTA‡	1975	MF	20	16	17	15	17	14	0	0		
		F	20	16	17	16	17	14	0	0		
	1980	MF	17	17	16	16	16	18				
		F	17	17	16	16	16	18				
	1982	MF	17	17	17	16	17	16				
		F	17	17	17	16	17	16				
	1983	MF	17	17	17	17	17	15				
		F	17	17	17	17	16	16				
NETHERLANDS	1975	MF	18	17	16	16	17	16				
		F	17	17	16	16	17	17				
	1980	MF	15	16	17	17	18	18				
		F	15	16	17	17	18	18				
	1983	MF	16	16	16	16	17	19				
		F	16	16	16	16	18	19				
	1984	MF	17	16	16	16	17	18				
		F	17	16	16	16	17	18				
NORWAY	1975	MF	17	17	17	17	16	16				
		F	17	17	17	17	16	16				
	1980	MF	16	16	17	17	17	17				
		F	16	16	17	17	17	17				
	1981	MF	16	16	17	17	17	18				
		F	16	16	17	17	17	18				
POLAND	1975	MF	12	11	12	12	13	13	13	13		
	1980	MF	14	13	13	13	12	12	12	12		
	1983	MF	14	14	13	13	12	12	11	10		
	1984	MF	14	14	13	13	13	12	11	10		
PORTUGAL	1975	MF	16	25	18	17	13	11				
		F	16	24	18	17	13	11				
	1980	MF	40	——>	34	——>	14	12				
		F	39	——>	35	——>	14	12				
	1982	MF	38	——>	33	——>	15	13				
		F	*37	——>	*33	——>	*16	*14				
	1983	MF	38	——>	34	——>	15	13				
		F	*36	——>	*34	——>	*16	*14				
SAN MARINO	1975	MF	19	21	19	20	20					
		F	18	21	21	20	21					
	1980	MF	20	19	20	20	20					
		F	21	20	22	18	20					
	1982	MF	19	19	20	20	22					
		F	18	19	20	20	23					
	1983	MF	19	20	20	21	21					
		F	20	19	19	21	21					
SPAIN	1975	MF	21	20	20	20	20					
		F	21	20	20	20	20					
	1980	MF	21	20	20	20	20					
		F	21	20	20	20	20					

3.5 Percentage distribution (first level) by grade
Répartition en pourcentage (premier degré) par année d'études
Distribución en porcentaje (primer grado) por año de estudios

COUNTRY PAYS PAIS	YEAR ANNEE AÑO	SEX SEXE SEXO	GRADES / ANNEES / AÑOS DE ESTUDIOS									
			I	II	III	IV	V	VI	VII	VIII	IX	X
SPAIN (CONT)	1982	MF	20	21	20	20	20					
		F	20	21	20	20	20					
	1983	MF	19	21	20	20	21					
		F	19	21	20	20	21					
SWEDEN	1975	MF	16	17	17	17	17	16				
		F	16	17	17	17	17	16				
	1980	MF	17	17	17	16	16	17				
		F	17	17	17	16	16	17				
	1982	MF	16	17	17	17	17	16				
		F	16	17	17	17	17	17				
	1983	MF	15	16	17	17	17	17				
		F	15	16	17	17	17	17				
SWITZERLAND‡	1975	MF	17	17	18	18	16	13				
		F	17	17	18	18	16	13				
	1980	MF	17	18	19	20	15	12				
		F	17	18	19	20	15	12				
	1983	MF	17	18	19	19	15	12				
		F	18	18	19	19	15	12				
	1984	MF	18	18	18	19	15	12				
		F	18	19	18	19	15	12				
YUGOSLAVIA‡	1975	MF	25	25	25	25						
		F	25	25	25	25						
	1980	MF	26	25	25	24						
		F	26	25	25	24						
	1982	MF	26	25	25	24						
		F	26	25	25	24						
	1983	MF	25	25	25	25						
		F	25	25	25	25						
OCEANIA												
AMERICAN SAMOA‡	1975	MF	13	14	12	12	12	13	12	12		
	1983	MF	14	14	13	12	11	12	12	12		
		F	13	13	12	13	11	12	13	12		
	1984	MF	13	13	14	13	12	11	12	12		
AUSTRALIA	1975	MF	17	16	15	15	15	16	5			
		F	17	16	15	15	15	16	5			
	1980	MF	15	16	16	16	16	15	5			
		F	15	16	16	17	16	15	5			
	1983	MF	15	15	15	16	16	17	6			
		F	15	15	15	16	16	17	6			
	1984	MF	15	15	15	16	16	17	6			
		F	15	15	15	16	16	17	6			
COOK ISLANDS	1982	MF	13	11	12	11	12	13	14	14		
	1983	MF	12	12	13	11	12	13	13	14		
FIJI‡	1975	MF	13	13	14	13	13	13	11	11		
		F	13	13	14	13	13	13	11	11		
	1980	MF	16	14	14	14	14	14	8	7		
		F	15	14	14	14	14	14	8	7		
	1983	MF	16	15	14	14	13	13	8	7		
		F	16	15	14	14	13	13	8	7		
	1984	MF	16	15	14	14	14	12	8	7		
		F	16	15	14	14	13	12	8	7		
FRENCH POLYNESIA‡	1975	MF	21	20	19	17	13	10				
		F	20	20	19	17	14	10				
	1983	MF	20	18	19	19	16	8				
		F	19	18	19	20	18	6				
	1984	MF	20	19	19	19	17	7				
		F	19	18	18	20	18	6				

COUNTRY PAYS PAIS	YEAR ANNEE AÑO	SEX SEXE SEXO	GRADES / ANNEES / AÑOS DE ESTUDIOS									
			I	II	III	IV	V	VI	VII	VIII	IX	X
GUAM‡	1975	MF	51	--->	--->	16	17	16				
	1983	MF	18	17	16	17	17	17				
		F	18	17	16	16	16	17				
KIRIBATI	1980	MF	12	12	11	13	13	17	10	7	6	
		F	12	12	11	13	12	16	10	7	5	
	1984	MF	12	11	12	10	11	11	13	10	10	
		F	12	11	12	10	11	12	13	10	10	
	1985	MF	14	11	11	12	10	11	13	8	9	
		F	14	11	12	12	10	11	12	9	10	
NAURU	1985	MF	17	16	18	16	15	15	4			
		F	18	16	18	18	14	13	3			
NEW CALEDONIA‡	1975	MF	21	17	17	18	15	11				
		F	21	17	17	18	16	11				
	1984	MF	19	17	18	19	20	8	--->	--->		
		F	18	17	18	19	20	8	--->	--->		
	1985	MF	19	18	17	19	19	8	--->	--->		
		F	20	18	17	19	20	6	--->	--->		
NEW ZEALAND	1975	MF	36	--->	16	16	16	16				
		F	36	--->	16	16	16	16				
	1980	MF	15	16	4	16	17	17	16			
		F	15	16	3	16	17	17	16			
	1982	MF	15	15	3	16	16	17	18			
		F	15	15	3	16	17	17	18			
	1983	MF	15	15	3	15	16	17	18			
		F	15	15	3	15	16	17	18			
NIUE	1975	MF	13	9	11	10	18	13	15	12		
		F	12	8	10	11	16	14	16	12		
	1980	MF	12	14	15	13	15	17	14			
	1983	MF	14	11	14	16	14	16	14			
	1984	MF	16	15	13	13	14	13	17			
		F	13	13	18	13	17	14	13			
PACIFIC ISLANDS	1975	MF	15	13	13	13	12	12	11	12		
		F	14	13	13	13	12	12	12	11		
PAPUA NEW GUINEA	1975	MF	22	17	18	15	15	14				
		F	22	18	18	14	15	13				
	1981	MF	23	19	18	14	14	12				
		F	24	19	18	14	14	11				
	1982	MF	22	20	17	16	13	13				
		F	23	20	17	16	12	12				
SAMOA	1975	MF	14	18	13	14	14	13	13			
		F	14	15	13	20	13	13	13			
	1980	MF	14	15	14	15	14	14	14			
		F	14	15	15	15	14	14	14			
	1982	MF	13	14	14	15	15	15	15			
		F	13	13	14	15	15	15	15			
	1983	MF	14	14	13	14	15	15	14			
		F	14	13	13	14	16	15	14			
SOLOMON ISLANDS	1975	MF	21	16	17	15	14	9	8			
		F	23	17	18	14	13	8	7			
	1980	MF	23	16	16	15	15	14				
		F	25	17	17	15	14	13				
	1983	MF	26	19	17	16	12	11				
		F	27	20	16	15	11	11				
	1984	MF	23	20	17	15	14	10				
TOKELAU	1982	MF	9	11	11	9	12	12	12	12	12	
		F	9	9	9	7	16	12	11	12	13	
	1983	MF	14	9	10	9	11	10	9	15	12	
		F	14	10	9	9	12	9	8	18	12	

3.5 Percentage distribution (first level) by grade
Répartition en pourcentage (premier degré) par année d'études
Distribución en porcentaje (primer grado) por año de estudios

COUNTRY PAYS PAIS	YEAR ANNEE AÑO	SEX SEXE SEXO	GRADES / ANNEES / AÑOS DE ESTUDIOS									
			I	II	III	IV	V	VI	VII	VIII	IX	X
TONGA	1975	MF	18	22	16	14	11	19				
		F	18	23	16	14	11	18				
	1982	MF	15	14	14	16	15	26				
		F	15	15	14	16	16	24				
	1983	MF	15	15	14	15	16	25				
		F	16	15	15	14	16	24				
VANUATU	1975	MF	20	20	17	16	13	12	3			
		F	20	20	17	16	12	12	3			
	1980	MF	19	18	16	15	14	13	5			
		F	20	18	16	14	13	13	5			
	1981	MF	20	18	16	14	14	14	4			
		F	21	18	16	14	14	13	4			
U.S.S.R.												
U.S.S.R.	1975	MF	19	19	20	20	21					
	1980	MF	21	21	20	19	19					
	1982	MF	21	20	20	20	19					
	1983	MF	24	19	19	19	19					
BYELORUSSIAN S.S.R.‡	1975	MF	11	11	12	12	13	13	14	15		
	1980	MF	24	19	19	19	19					
	1981	MF	25	19	19	19	19					
	1982	MF	25	19	19	19	19					
UKRAINIAN S.S.R.‡	1975	MF	12	12	12	12	13	13	13	14		
	1980	MF	22	20	20	19	19					
	1982	MF	22	20	19	20	19					
	1983	MF	22	19	19	19	20					

The percentage distribution by grade appearing in this table is presented for the first level only and refers to total enrolment (MF) and female enrolment. These percentages are presented for 1975, 1980 and the two latest years available.

In most cases the data appearing in this table have bee calculated on the basis of the duration of education at the fir level as shown for each country in Table 3.1.

La répartition en pourcentage par année d'études qui figure dans ce tableau est présentée pour l'enseignement du premier degré seulement et se réfère au total des effectifs (MF) et aux effectifs féminins. Ces pourcentages sont présentés pour l'année 1975, 1980 et les deux dernières années disponibles.

En général, les données présentées dans ce tableau ont ét calculées en fonction de la durée de l'enseignement du premi degré, telle qu'elle figure pour chaque pays et territoire dans tableau 3.1.

La repartición en porcentaje por año de estudios que figura en este cuadro se presenta para la enseñanza de primer grado solamente y se refiere a la matrícula escolar total (MF) y femenina. Los porcentajes se refieren a los años 1975, 1980 y los dos últimos años disponibles.

En general, los datos de este cuadro se han calculado e función de la duración de la enseñanza de primer grado tal com figura, en relación con cada país y territorio, en el cuadro 3.1.

AFRICA:

Algeria:

E--> Enrolment in grade VII refers to terminal classes.

FR-> Les données sur les effectifs de la septième année d'études se réfèrent aux classes de fin d'études.

ESP> Los datos sobre los efectivos del séptimo año de estudios se refieren a las clases de *fin d'études*.

Chad:

E--> For 1975, data do not include Moslem private education (9,453 pupils).

FR-> Pour 1975, les données n'incluent pas l'enseignement privé musulman (9 453 élèves).

ESP> Para 1975, los datos no incluyen la enseñanza privada musulmana (9 453 alumnos).

Guinea-Bissau:

E--> For 1975, data include initiation classes (education precedir the first level).

FR-> Pour 1975, les données incluent les classes d'initiatio (enseignement précédant le premier degré).

ESP> En 1975, los datos incluyen las clases de iniciación (enseñanz anterior al primer grado).

Liberia:

E--> Data include education preceding the first level.

FR-> Les données incluent l'éducation précédant le premier degré.

ESP> Los datos incluyen la enseñanza anterior al primer grado.

Uganda:

E--> Data refer to government-maintained and aided schools only.

FR-> Les données se réfèrent aux écoles publiques et subventionnée seulement.

Uganda: (Cont):
ESP> Los datos se refieren a las escuelas públicas y subvencionadas solamente.
United Republic of Tanzania:
E--> Tanzania mainland only.
FR-> Tanzanie continentale seulement.
ESP> Tanzania continental solamente.
AMERICA, NORTH:
Barbados:
E--> For 1984, enrolment in grade 1 refers to infant classes.
FR-> En 1984, les données sur les effectifs de la première année d'études se rapportent aux 'Infant classes'.
ESP> En 1984, los datos sobre los alumnos del primer año de estudios se refieren a las 'Infant classes'.
Belize:
E--> Data refer to government-maintained and aided schools only.
FR-> Les données se réfèrent aux écoles publiques et subventionnées seulement.
ESP> Los datos se refieren a las escuelas públicas y subvencionadas solamente.
Bermuda:
E--> For 1975, data refer to public education only.
FR-> Pour 1975, les données se réfèrent à l'enseignement public seulement.
ESP> Para 1975, los datos se refieren a la enseñanza pública solamente.
El Salvador:
E--> Data include evening schools.
FR-> Les données incluent les écoles du soir.
ESP> Los datos incluyen las escuelas nocturnas.
Montserrat:
E--> Enrolment in grades VIII and IX refers to terminal classes and data for 1981 refer to public education only.
FR-> Les données sur les effectifs des huitième et neuvième années d'études se réfèrent aux classes de fin d'études et les données pour 1981 se réfèrent à l'enseignement public seulement.
ESP> Los datos sobre la matrícula para el octavo y noveno año de estudios se refieren a las clases de *fin d'études* y los datos para 1981 se refieren a la enseñanza pública solamente.
Puerto Rico:
E--> All data refer to public education only. For 1981, data refer to enrolment in grades I to VIII instead of I to VI.
FR-> Toutes les données se réfèrent à l'enseignement public seulement. En 1981, les données se réfèrent aux effectifs des classes allant de la première à la huitième année d'études, antérieurement aux classes allant de la première à la sixième année.
ESP> Todos los datos se refieren a la enseñanza pública solamente. En 1981, los datos se refieren a la matrícula del primero al octavo año de estudios, anteriormente a la matrícula del primero al sexto año.
St. Christopher and Nevis:
E--> Data refer to public education only.
FR-> Les données se réfèrent à l'enseignement public seulement.
ESP> Los datos se refieren a la enseñanza pública solamente.
St. Lucia:
E--> Enrolment in grades VIII and IX refers to terminal classes.
FR-> Les données sur les effectifs des huitième et neuvième années d'études se réfèrent aux classes de fin d'études.
ESP> Los datos sobre la matrícula del octavo y noveno año de estudios se refieren a las clases de *fin d'études*.
United States:
E--> For 1980, 1983 and 1984 data refer to the first eight grades. For 1975 figures for grades VII and VIII only include enrolment in public schools organized as elementary schools.
FR-> Pour 1980, 1983 et 1984 les données se réfèrent aux huit premières années d'études. Pour 1975 les chiffres pour les septième et huitième années d'études se réfèrent seulement aux effectifs des écoles publiques qui ne dispensent que l'enseignement du premier degré.
ESP> En 1980, 1983 y 1984 los datos se refieren a los ocho primeros años de estudios. En 1975 las cifras para el séptimo y octavo año de estudios se refieren únicamente a las escuelas públicas que sólo otorgan la enseñanza de primer grado.
U.S. Virgin Islands:
E--> All data refer to public education only. In 1975 data refer to enrolment in the first six grades; for 1980 and 1981 data refer to enrolment in the first eight grades.
FR-> Toutes les données se réfèrent à l'enseignement public seulement. En 1975 les données ne représentent que les effectifs des six premières années d'études; pour 1980 et 1981 les données se réfèrent aux effectifs allant de la première à la huitième année d'études.
ESP> Todos los datos se refieren a la enseñanza pública solamente. En 1975 los datos se refieren a los efectivos de los seis primeros años de estudios; para 1980 y 1981 los datos se refieren a los ocho primeros años de estudios.
AMERICA, SOUTH:
Brazil:
E--> In 1983, data do not include literacy classes (1,032,621 pupils).
FR-> En 1983, les données ne comprennent pas les classes d'alphabétisation (1 032 621 élèves).
ESP> En 1983, los datos excluyen las clases de alfabetización (1 032 621 alumnos).
Uruguay:
E--> For 1975 and 1980, data refer to public education only.
FR-> Pour 1975 et 1980, les données se réfèrent à l'enseignement public seulement.
ESP> Para 1975 y 1980, los datos se refieren a la enseñanza pública solamente.
ASIA:
Bhutan:
E--> Data for grade 1 refer to kindergarten.
FR-> Les données relatives à la première année d'études se réfèrent aux jardins d'enfants.
ESP> Los datos del primer año de estudios se refieren a los jardines infantiles.
Burma:
E--> Data for grade I refer to kindergarten.
FR-> Les données relatives à la première année d'études se réfèrent aux jardins d'enfants.
ESP> Los datos relativos al primer año de estudios se refieren a los jardines infantiles.
Cyprus:
E--> Not including Turkish schools. Enrolment in grades VII and VIII exists only in private schools.
FR-> Non compris les écoles turques. Les effectifs des septième et huitième années d'études se réfèrent seulement aux écoles privées.
ESP> Excluídas las escuelas turcas. Los efectivos para el séptimo y el octavo año de estudios se refieren solamente a las escuelas privadas.
Democratic Yemen:
E--> For 1975, data include schools for nomads.
FR-> Pour 1975, les données incluent les écoles de nomades.
ESP> En 1975, los datos incluyen las escuelas para nómadas.
Japan:
E--> Data include special education.
FR-> Les données incluent l'éducation spéciale.
ESP> Los datos incluyen la educación especial.
Jordan:
E--> Including UNRWA schools.
FR-> Y compris les écoles de l'UNRWA.
ESP> Incluídas las escuelas del O.O.P.S.R.P. (Organización de Obras Públicas y Socorro para los Refugiados de Palestina).
Pakistan:
E--> Data for grade 1 include preprimary classes.
FR-> Les données relatives à la première année d'études incluent les classes préprimaires.
ESP> Los datos relativos al primero año de estudios incluyen las clases preprimarias.
Qatar:
E--> Data refer to public education only.
FR-> Les données se réfèrent à l'enseignement public seulement.
ESP> Los datos se refieren a la enseñanza pública solamente.
Syrian Arab Republic:
E--> Including UNRWA schools.
FR-> Y compris les écoles de l'UNRWA.
ESP> Incluídas las escuelas del O.O.P.S.R.P.
United Arab Emirates:
E--> Data refer to public education only.
FR-> Les données se réfèrent à l'enseignement public seulement.
ESP> Los datos se refieren a la enseñanza pública solamente.
Yemen:
E--> Data refer to public education only.
FR-> Les données se réfèrent à l'enseignement public seulement.
ESP> Los datos se refieren a la enseñanza pública solamente.
EUROPE:
Belgium:
E--> Except for 1984, data include special education.
FR-> A l'exception de l'année 1984, les données incluent l'éducation spéciale.
ESP> Excepto para 1984, los datos incluyen la educación especial.
Finland:
E--> Data include integrated special education.
FR-> Les données comprennent l'éducation spéciale intégrée.
ESP> Los datos incluyen la educación especial integrada.
Germany, Federal Republic of:
E--> Data refer to the first 4 grades of first level education only.
FR-> Les données se réfèrent aux quatre premières années de l'enseignement du premier degré seulement.
ESP> Los datos se refieren a los cuatro primeros años de la enseñanza de primer grado solamente.
Greece:
E--> Data include evening schools.
FR-> Les données incluent les écoles du soir.
ESP> Los datos incluyen las escuelas nocturnas.
Malta:
E--> Enrolment in grades VII and VIII refers to private schools only.
FR-> Les données sur les effectifs des septième et huitième années

Malta: (Cont):
d'études se réfèrent seulement aux écoles privées.
ESP> Los datos sobre la matrícula del séptimo y octavo año de estudios se refieren solamente a las escuelas privadas.
Switzerland:
E--> In 1975, data include special education.
FR-> En 1975, les données incluent l'éducation spéciale.
ESP> En 1975, los datos incluyen la educación especial.
Yugoslavia:
E--> In 1975, data include special education.
FR-> En 1975, les données incluent l'éducation spéciale.
ESP> En 1975, los datos incluyen la educación especial.
OCEANIA:
American Samoa:
E--> For 1975 and 1984, data refer to public education only.
FR-> Pour 1975 et 1984, les données se réfèrent à l'enseignement public seulement.
ESP> Para 1975 y 1984, los datos se refieren a la enseñanza pública solamente.
Fiji:
E--> For 1975, data on grades VII and VIII include forms I and II (education at the second level).
FR-> Pour 1975, les données relatives aux septième et huitième années d'études incluent les 'forms' I et II (enseignement du second degré).
ESP> En 1975, los datos relativos a los séptimo y octavo años de estudios incluyen las 'forms' I y II (enseñanza de segundo grado).
French Polynesia:
E--> Enrolment in grade VI refers to terminal classes.
FR-> Les données sur les effectifs de la sixième année d'études se réfèrent aux classes de 'fin d'études'.

French Polynesia: (Cont):
ESP> Los datos sobre los efectivos del sexto año de estudios se refieren a las clases de 'fin d'études'.
Guam:
E--> For 1975, data refer to public education only.
FR-> Pour 1975, les données se réfèrent à l'enseignement public seulement.
ESP> Para 1975, los datos se refieren a la enseñanza pública solamente.
New Caledonia:
E--> Grades VI, VII and VIII refer to terminal classes.
FR-> Les sixième, septième et huitième années d'études se réfèrent aux classes de fin d'études.
ESP> Los sexto, séptimo y octavo años de estudios se refieren a las clases de *fin d'études*.
U.S.S.R.:
Byelorussian S.S.R:
E--> For 1980, 1981 and 1982, enrolment in grades VI to VIII is included with general education at the second level.
FR-> Pour 1980, 1981 et 1982, les effectifs des classes allant de la sixième à la huitième année d'études sont inclus dans l'enseignement général du second degré.
ESP> En 1980, 1981 y 1982, la matrícula del sexto al octavo año de estudios está incluída en la enseñanza general de segundo grado.
Ukrainian S.S.R.:
E--> For 1980, 1982 and 1983, enrolment in grades VI to VIII is included with the second level of general education.
FR-> Pour 1980, 1982 et 1983, les effectifs des classes allant de la sixième à la huitième année d'études sont inclus dans l'enseignement général du second degré.
ESP> En 1980, 1982 y 1983, la matrícula del sexto al octavo año de estudios está incluída en la enseñanza general de segundo grado.

3.6 Education at the first level: percentage repeaters by grade

Enseignement du premier degré: pourcentage de redoublants par année d'études

Enseñanza de primer grado: porcentaje de repetidores por año de estudios

PLEASE REFER TO EXPLANATORY TEXT AT END OF TABLE

PRIERE DE SE REFERER AU TEXTE EXPLICATIF A LA FIN DU TABLEAU

REFERIRSE AL TEXTO EXPLICATIVO AL FINAL DEL CUADRO

NUMBER OF COUNTRIES AND TERRITORIES PRESENTED IN THIS TABLE: 130

NOMBRE DE PAYS ET DE TERRITOIRES PRESENTES DANS CE TABLEAU: 130

NUMERO DE PAISES Y DE TERRITORIOS PRESENTADOS EN ESTE CUADRO: 130

COUNTRY / PAYS / PAIS	YEAR / ANNEE / AÑO	SEX / SEXE / SEXO	TOTAL / TOTAL / TOTAL	PERCENTAGE REPEATERS BY GRADE / POURCENTAGE DE REDOUBLANTS PAR ANNEE D'ETUDES / PORCENTAJE DE REPETIDORES POR AÑO DE ESTUDIOS									
				TOTAL	I	II	III	IV	V	VI	VII	V III	IX
AFRICA													
ALGERIA‡	1975	MF	333 877	13	7	9	13	12	13	21	22		
		F	128 261	12	7	9	13	12	13	21	20		
	1980	MF	364 710	12	8	9	11	10	11	19	25		
		F	139 610	11	8	8	11	10	10	18	20		
	1983	MF	229 588	7	5	5	5	4	7	14	21		
		F	84 268	6	5	5	5	3	6	12	17		
	1984	MF	233 498	7	6	6	6	6	4	12	18		
		F	84 410	6	5	5	5	5	3	10	17		
ANGOLA	1980	MF	379 254	29	31	31	25	26					
	1981	MF	453 069	36	30	51	26	34					
BENIN	1975	MF	55 172	21	17	16	20	19	27	36			
		F	19 013	23	18	19	21	23	30	40			
	1980	MF	74 378	20	16	18	18	20	22	31			
		F	26 290	22	18	20	21	22	25	33			
	1983	MF	122 384	29	21	25	30	28	30	46			
		F	42 695	30	22	26	32	31	33	46			
	1984	MF	115 143	26	21	21	28	25	30	37			
		F	40 369	27	21	23	29	28	34	38			
BOTSWANA	1975	MF	3 361	3	0	0	0	0	0	0	21		
	1980	MF	5 040	3	0	0	1	0	1	1	20		
	1984	MF	12 337	6	1	1	1	14	1	1	24		
		F	6 573	6	1	1	1	12	1	1	26		
	1985	MF	12 713	6	1	1	1	12	1	1	23		
		F	6 638	6	1	1	1	11	1	1	24		
BURKINA FASO	1975	MF	24 638	17	15	14	14	14	14	37			
		F	9 754	19	17	15	16	16	16	38			
	1980	MF	34 453	17	14	13	15	13	16	37			
		F	13 424	18	15	14	15	15	18	37			
	1983	MF	45 692	17	12	12	14	13	15	40			
		F	15 862	16	12	11	13	13	15	36			
	1984	MF	44 151	14	10	10	12	12	13	35			
		F	16 993	15	10	11	12	13	15	35			

3.6 Percentage repeaters by grade (first level)
Pourcentage de redoublants par année d'études (premier degré)
Porcentaje de repetidores por año de estudios (primer grado)

COUNTRY PAYS PAIS	YEAR ANNEE AÑO	SEX SEXE SEXO	TOTAL TOTAL TOTAL	PERCENTAGE REPEATERS BY GRADE / POURCENTAGE DE REDOUBLANTS PAR ANNEE D'ETUDES / PORCENTAJE DE REPETIDORES POR AÑO DE ESTUDIOS									
				TOTAL	I	II	III	IV	V	VI	VII	VIII	IX
BURUNDI	1975	MF	33 171	26	19	18	25	27	32	40			
		F	12 083	24	18	17	24	26	29	38			
	1980	MF	53 107	30	26	22	23	29	40	49			
		F	21 106	30	27	21	23	29	40	50			
	1983	MF	41 262	14	12	8	13	14	19	24			
		F	16 726	14	12	7	13	14	20	26			
	1984	MF	53 086	15	12	13	10	16	22	27			
		F	21 886	16	12	13	10	17	24	30			
CAMEROON	1975	MF	281 517	25	30	22	23	18	21	33	4		
		F	122 450	24	30	22	23	18	21	32	4		
	1980	MF	413 356	30	35	25	30	24	27	38	12		
		F	184 772	29	34	25	30	23	27	38	12		
	1983	MF	461 928	30	36	25	30	23	27	34	7		
		F	206 382	29	35	24	30	23	27	34	7		
	1984	MF	471 822	29	35	25	31	23	26	32	8		
		F	208 862	28	34	24	30	23	26	31	8		
CAPE VERDE	1980	MF	16 123	28	39	26	24	21	27	23			
	1983	MF	16 421	29	35	31	24	24	32	30			
		F	7 795	28	33	30	23	23	33	29			
CENTRAL AFRICAN REPUBLIC	1975	MF	78 173	35	41	31	32	29	29	46			
		F	27 310	34	40	30	32	29	30	43			
	1980	MF	86 402	35	33	33	36	32	34	46			
		F	33 139	37	34	36	38	35	36	46			
	1981	MF	90 231	35	34	33	35	33	32	45			
		F	33 637	35	35	35	34	35	33	44			
	1982	MF	95 611	35	35	32	35	31	33	49			
		F	35 090	37	37	33	39	36	34	47			
CHAD‡	1975	MF	74 299	37	40	33	31	27	30	54			
		F	18 784	35	39	34	32	27	26	44			
	1976	MF	79 342	38	40	32	34	26	31	58			
		F	20 233	36	37	34	35	27	31	50			
COMOROS	1980	MF	14 666	25	31	21	17	27	23	28			
CONGO	1975	MF	83 438	26	31	23	29	22	21	28			
		F	37 940	26	30	22	28	23	21	27			
	1980	MF	100 439	26	27	19	32	27	24	23			
		F	47 529	25	26	18	32	27	24	22			
	1982	MF	130 084	31	30	22	39	36	31	24			
		F	61 151	30	29	21	38	35	30	22			
	1984	MF	152 140	33	33	23	43	37	32	27			
		F	71 280	32	31	22	42	35	31	26			
COTE D'IVOIRE	1975	MF	140 548	21	17	15	16	15	21	41			
		F	52 207	21	18	16	17	16	21	38			
	1980	MF	201 279	20	15	13	14	13	15	43			
		F	80 118	20	16	14	15	14	16	41			
	1982	MF	278 241	25	20	17	19	18	20	47			
		F	112 950	24	21	17	21	19	22	46			
	1983	MF	299 428	26	20	18	20	19	23	48			
		F	122 017	26	21	19	20	20	25	47			
DJIBOUTI	1975	MF	1 843	19	3	20	23	19	21	32			
		F	549	16	4	18	17	17	16	25			
EGYPT	1975	MF	279 831	7	–	12	–	16	–	11			
		F	109 907	7	–	13	–	16	–	10			
	1980	MF	*366 482	*8	–	19	–	21	–	4			
		F	165 382	9	–	35	–	9	–	4			
	1981	MF	*129 659	*3	–	7	–	8	–	–			
		F	*48 669	*2	–	*7	–	7	–	–			
	1982	MF	*106 229	*2	–	6	–	6	–	–			
		F	*36 300	*2	–	5	–	5	–	–			

COUNTRY / PAYS / PAIS	YEAR / ANNEE / AÑO	SEX / SEXE / SEXO	TOTAL / TOTAL / TOTAL	PERCENTAGE REPEATERS BY GRADE / POURCENTAGE DE REDOUBLANTS PAR ANNEE D'ETUDES / PORCENTAJE DE REPETIDORES POR AÑO DE ESTUDIOS									
				TOTAL	I	II	III	IV	V	VI	VII	V III	IX
ETHIOPIA‡	1981	MF	289 062	12	17	11	9	8	8	9			
		F	118 528	14	19	13	10	10	10	12			
GABON	1975	MF	43 752	34	49	33	30	21	22	20			
		F	21 576	34	49	32	31	22	22	20			
	1980	MF	54 017	35	50	33	32	22	21	21			
		F	26 192	34	49	32	32	21	22	22			
	1982	MF	53 798	32	48	30	29	20	20	22			
		F	26 637	33	48	30	29	20	20	21			
	1983	MF	56 972	33	45	31	30	20	19	33			
		F	27 747	33	44	30	30	20	20	33			
GAMBIA	1975	MF	2 568	10	7	4	4	5	6	35			
		F	798	10	6	4	3	3	6	37			
	1980	MF	5 817	13	9	7	7	8	12	41			
		F	1 952	13	9	7	7	7	13	41			
	1983	MF	8 040	13	10	14	8	8	10	31			
		F	2 412	11	10	8	8	7	9	27			
	1984	MF	8 087	12	10	7	7	7	8	32			
		F	2 599	10	10	8	7	6	7	27			
GHANA	1975	MF	26 854	2	5	2	2	2	1	1			
		F	12 353	2	5	2	2	2	1	1			
	1980	MF	28 994	2	4	2	2	1	1	1			
		F	13 580	2	4	2	2	1	1	1			
GUINEA	1976	MF	19 944	9	9	9	9	9	8	10			
	1980	MF	56 384	22	22	21	19	19	21	33			
	1983	MF	46 577	19	17	20	17	17	18	27			
		F	17 396	22	16	20	22	23	23	33			
	1984	MF	69 617	24	15	28	26	24	27	42			
		F	23 816	26	17	27	30	27	33	43			
GUINEA-BISSAU	1975	MF	11 490	14	11	25	18	18	16	13			
	1980	MF	21 529	29	38	28	22	23	24	11			
		F	7 108	30	38	29	20	20	32	15			
	1982	MF	23 163	31	35	30	28	31	29	19			
		F	7 975	33	35	34	29	27	34	26			
	1983	MF	22 520	30	34	30	27	29	29	20			
		F	7 879	31	33	31	29	29	33	24			
KENYA	1975	MF	150 919	5	5	3	4	5	4	7	16		
	1981	MF	523 450	13	15	13	11	12	13	15	13		
		F	247 339	13	14	12	11	13	13	16	12		
LESOTHO	1975	MF	13 385	6	9	4	4	3	3	3	18		
		F	8 030	6	9	4	4	3	3	3	19		
	1980	MF	50 581	21	25	22	21	17	16	14	22		
		F	28 294	20	25	21	20	16	16	14	23		
	1982	MF	64 981	23	30	26	23	18	17	15	22		
		F	35 503	22	29	24	22	17	17	15	23		
	1983	MF	70 948	24	33	26	24	19	17	14	20		
		F	37 729	23	33	24	22	18	17	14	22		
LIBERIA	1978	MF	22 033	11	12	——>	13	12	11	10	9	8	
		F	8 985	12	13	——>	14	13	13	12	10	10	
LIBYAN ARAB JAMAHIRIYA	1975	MF	91 358	16	10	11	13	28	15	21			
		F	40 591	16	10	11	13	28	16	19			
	1980	MF	60 926	9	7	4	5	13	15	12			
		F	25 094	8	7	4	5	11	13	9			
	1982	MF	69 173	10	7	5	6	14	15	10			
		F	28 279	8	6	5	5	13	13	8			

3.6 Percentage repeaters by grade (first level)
Pourcentage de redoublants par année d'études (premier degré)
Porcentaje de repetidores por año de estudios (primer grado)

COUNTRY PAYS PAIS	YEAR ANNEE AÑO	SEX SEXE SEXO	TOTAL TOTAL TOTAL	PERCENTAGE REPEATERS BY GRADE POURCENTAGE DE REDOUBLANTS PAR ANNEE D'ETUDES PORCENTAJE DE REPETIDORES POR AÑO DE ESTUDIOS									
				TOTAL	I	II	III	IV	V	VI	VII	V III	IX
MALAWI	1975	MF	105 732	16	19	16	15	11	8	10	13	37	
		F	42 846	17	19	16	16	13	9	11	15	37	
	1980	MF	141 132	17	19	17	15	12	3	12	15	43	
		F	56 925	17	19	17	15	12	3	13	17	42	
	1983	MF	133 588	16	18	15	12	9	5	12	14	39	
		F	55 090	15	18	16	13	9	5	13	15	38	
	1984	MF	140 393	16	17	16	13	9	4	11	13	38	
		F	58 613	15	17	16	13	10	4	12	15	37	
MALI	1975	MF	57 843	23	22	23	23	21	23	28			
	1980	MF	86 153	30	28	26	32	29	33	34			
		F	31 934	30	30	29	33	24	35	35			
	1982	MF	91 942	31	28	29	33	31	33	37			
MAURITANIA	1975	MF	7 460	15	8	16	14	14	16	19	29		
		F	3 175	18	10	14	17	20	20	26	34		
	1980	MF	12 683	14	12	11	12	13	10	27			
		F	5 363	17	15	14	16	16	13	28			
	1982	MF	18 459	17	13	14	15	15	17	30			
MOROCCO	1975	MF	434 392	28	23	20	26	30	44				
	1980	MF	639 807	29	26	21	25	28	47				
		F	223 525	28	25	20	24	26	45				
	1983	MF	768 176	31	32	22	25	28	47				
		F	270 521	29	31	20	23	25	45				
	1984	MF	495 072	22	24	20	18	16	31				
		F	173 249	20	22	18	16	14	29				
MOZAMBIQUE	1982	MF	379 163	30	31	31	31	26					
		F	173 858	33	32	33	34	29					
	1983	MF	332 855	29	28	31	27	26					
		F	150 887	30	29	33	30	28					
NIGER	1975	MF	18 580	13	6	10	14	12	18	33			
		F	6 638	13	7	10	14	13	19	33			
	1980	MF	32 825	14	2	11	15	15	17	34			
REUNION	1975	MF	20 949	22	31	21	18	19	19				
	1976	MF	20 987	22	32	19	18	21	22				
	1977	MF	17 488	19	24	17	15	19	19				
RWANDA	1976	MF	73 336	17	21	13	14	14	13	24			
		F	33 191	16	20	12	14	14	13	23			
	1980	MF	40 459	6	15	10	4	0	0	0			
		F	19 219	6	15	10	4	0	0	0			
	1982	MF	105 752	14	22	14	13	12	10	9	8	18	
		F	49 878	14	21	14	13	12	10	8	8	18	
	1983	MF	90 488	12	20	13	11	10	9	7	7	4	
		F	42 894	12	20	13	10	10	8	7	7	4	
SAO TOME AND PRINCIPE	1976	MF	5 900	47	51	42	44	46					
		F	2 403	40	40	40	40	40					
	1980	MF	4 831	30	35	28	27	26					
	1983	MF	3 025	19	26	18	16	13					
		F	1 405	18	24	17	15	14					
	1984	MF	3 339	21	27	21	17	15					
SENEGAL	1980	MF	65 349	16	11	11	12	12	15	33			
		F	26 552	16	11	12	13	13	16	34			
	1982	MF	78 013	16	11	11	12	13	15	35			
		F	31 419	16	12	11	13	13	16	34			
	1983	MF	81 272	15	11	10	11	12	15	34			
		F	32 737	15	12	11	12	13	16	33			

COUNTRY PAYS PAIS	YEAR ANNEE AÑO	SEX SEXE SEXO	TOTAL TOTAL TOTAL	PERCENTAGE REPEATERS BY GRADE / POURCENTAGE DE REDOUBLANTS PAR ANNEE D'ETUDES / PORCENTAJE DE REPETIDORES POR AÑO DE ESTUDIOS									
				TOTAL	I	II	III	IV	V	VI	VII	VIII	IX
SEYCHELLES	1975	MF	117	1	0	0	0	1	1	4			
		F	70	1	0	0	0	2	1	4			
	1980	MF	–	–	–	–	–	–	–	–	–	–	–
		F	–	–	–	–	–	–	–	–	–	–	–
	1984	MF	–	–	–	–	–	–	–	–	–	–	–
		F	–	–	–	–	–	–	–	–	–	–	–
	1985	MF	–	–	–	–	–	–	–	–	–	–	–
		F	–	–	–	–	–	–	–	–	–	–	–
SUDAN			–	–	–	–	–	–	–	–			
SWAZILAND	1975	MF	9 084	10	9	6	8	11	11	11	18		
		F	4 001	9	8	5	7	8	10	11	18		
	1980	MF	12 185	11	10	9	11	10	12	11	16		
		F	5 245	9	9	7	8	8	11	11	15		
	1983	MF	16 745	13	14	12	13	11	13	12	16		
		F	7 217	11	13	9	11	9	11	11	15		
	1984	MF	16 924	13	13	12	13	11	12	11	16		
		F	7 187	11	11	9	11	9	11	11	15		
TOGO	1975	MF	104 553	29	37	24	26	20	25	34			
		F	37 759	30	36	25	28	22	27	34			
	1981	MF	183 391	37	41	35	36	30	33	44			
		F	74 698	38	41	35	38	33	36	46			
	1983	MF	163 852	36	40	34	37	28	31	41			
		F	66 349	37	40	35	39	30	33	43			
	1984	MF	166 074	37	38	34	37	30	35	46			
		F	66 864	38	38	35	39	34	38	48			
TUNISIA	1975	MF	180 346	19	11	13	14	14	19	41			
		F	65 990	18	11	12	13	13	18	41			
	1980	MF	217 164	21	18	16	18	20	25	28	–	–	
		F	83 464	19	18	15	16	18	23	26	–	–	
	1983	MF	238 058	20	19	16	17	19	24	30	–	–	
		F	96 821	18	18	15	15	17	21	29	–	–	
	1984	MF	260 523	21	20	17	18	19	25	31	–	–	
		F	106 213	19	19	16	16	17	23	29	–	–	
UGANDA‡	1975	MF	99 358	10	12	11	11	11	11	12	2		
	1979	MF	117 531	10	12	10	10	9	9	12	2		
	1982	MF	163 106	10	11	10	11	10	11	14	4		
		F	70 950	11	11	10	11	11	11	14	4		
UNITED REPUBLIC OF TANZANIA‡	1975	MF	7 763	0	0	0	0	0	0	0	3		
		F	2 862	0	0	0	0	0	0	0	2		
	1981	MF	43 218	1	3	3	3	0	0	0	0		
		F	20 835	1	3	3	2	0	0	0	0		
	1982	MF	42 928	1	3	3	3	0	0	0	0		
		F	20 193	1	3	3	2	0	0	0	0		
ZAIRE	1975	MF	748 274	*21	24	23	22	19	17	15			
		F	305 160	*22	25	23	23	20	18	15			
	1980	MF	789 640	19	21	20	21	18	16	13			
		F	334 252	19	21	19	22	19	17	13			
	1982	MF	846 034	19	21	21	21	18	15	13			
		F	358 123	19	21	19	22	18	16	12			
	1983	MF	876 009	19	21	22	21	18	15	12			
		F	370 811	19	21	19	22	18	15	11			
ZAMBIA	1975	MF	17 922	2	0	1	1	3	1	1	8		
		F	6 955	2	0	1	1	3	1	1	7		
	1980	MF	19 278	2	0	0	0	2	1	1	9		
		F	7 798	2	0	0	0	2	1	1	8		
	1981	MF	15 704	1	0	0	0	2	0	1	7		
		F	6 436	1	0	0	0	2	0	1	7		

3.6 Percentage repeaters by grade (first level)
Pourcentage de redoublants par année d'études (premier degré)
Porcentaje de repetidores por año de estudios (primer grado)

COUNTRY / PAYS / PAIS	YEAR / ANNEE / AÑO	SEX / SEXE / SEXO	TOTAL / TOTAL / TOTAL	PERCENTAGE REPEATERS BY GRADE / POURCENTAGE DE REDOUBLANTS PAR ANNEE D'ETUDES / PORCENTAJE DE REPETIDORES POR AÑO DE ESTUDIOS									
				TOTAL	I	II	III	IV	V	VI	VII	VIII	IX
ZIMBABWE	1983	MF	–	–	–	–	–	–	–	–	–		
		F	–	–	–	–	–	–	–	–	–		
	1984	MF	17 423	1	1	1	1	1	0	0	1		
		F	8 059	1	1	1	1	0	0	0	1		
AMERICA, NORTH													
ANTIGUA AND BARBUDA	1975	MF	216	2	4	1	1	1	2	1	4		
		F	97	2	4	1	1	0	1	0	5		
BRITISH VIRGIN ISLANDS	1984	MF	199	10	12	8	7	5	10	10	15	43	
		F	81	8	11	8	4	4	7	9	14	–	
COSTA RICA	1975	MF	23 394	6	–	13	14	–	8	3			
		F	9 428	5	–	11	12	–	6	2			
	1980	MF	27 459	8	–	20	14	–	9	2			
		F	12 022	7	–	19	13	–	8	2			
	1983	MF	39 821	12	15	18	12	8	10	2			
	1984	MF	38 436	11	17	13	12	9	6	2			
CUBA	1975	MF	145 897	8	20	10	6	6	3	2			
	1980	MF	83 747	6	–	14	2	8	5	3			
	1983	MF	62 767	5	0	15	3	6	3	2			
	1984	MF	48 031	4	0	14	3	4	2	1			
DOMINICAN REPUBLIC	1980	MF	199 142	18	27	16	13	12	11	14			
	1982	MF	151 861	14	23	10	9	6	13	13			
EL SALVADOR‡	1975	MF	55 428	7	15	8	6	4	3	2	1	0	
	1982	MF	64 787	8	16	8	7	6	4	3	2	2	1
		F	30 258	8	15	7	7	6	4	3	2	1	1
	1983	MF	66 310	8	16	8	6	5	4	3	2	1	1
		F	31 370	7	16	8	6	5	4	3	2	1	1
	1984	MF	74 114	8	18	9	6	5	4	3	2	1	1
		F	35 581	8	18	9	6	5	4	3	2	1	1
GRENADA‡	1975	MF	1 288	6	9	5	4	5	7	5	7		
	1982	MF	979	6	10	4	5	3	5	4	7		
		F	380	4	9	3	4	3	4	2	7		
GUADELOUPE	1975	MF	12 508	20	27	17	17	19	19				
	1977	MF	9 667	17	21	14	17	18	14				
GUATEMALA	1975	MF	93 022	15	26	12	11	7	5	2			
	1980	MF	120 278	15	26	13	11	7	5	2			
	1982	MF	155 509	18	26	13	33	7	4	2			
	1983	MF	143 533	15	26	14	11	7	5	2			
HAITI	1979	MF	121 345	21	27	21	19	18	15	7	6		
		F	55 134	21	27	21	19	19	15	7	8		
	1982	MF	95 129	13	13	14	14	14	13	8			
		F	43 651	13	12	14	15	15	13	8			
HONDURAS	1980	MF	97 244	16	26	15	12	10	6	3			
		F	45 856	15	25	15	12	10	6	3			
	1982	MF	107 669	16	26	16	13	9	7	2			
		F	49 973	15	25	15	12	9	6	2			
	1984	MF	113 932	15	26	15	11	8	6	2			
		F	53 199	15	26	14	11	8	5	2			

COUNTRY PAYS PAIS	YEAR ANNEE AÑO	SEX SEXE SEXO	TOTAL TOTAL TOTAL	PERCENTAGE REPEATERS BY GRADE / POURCENTAGE DE REDOUBLANTS PAR ANNEE D'ETUDES / PORCENTAJE DE REPETIDORES POR AÑO DE ESTUDIOS									
				TOTAL	I	II	III	IV	V	VI	VII	V III	IX
JAMAICA	1975	MF	13 431	4	7	3	2	2	2	6			
		F	5 909	3	6	2	1	2	2	7			
	1980	MF	13 984	4	7	3	2	2	2	8			
		F	6 348	4	6	2	2	1	2	9			
	1983	MF	16 311	5	8	3	2	2	3	9			
		F	7 477	4	7	2	2	2	2	11			
MARTINIQUE	1975	MF	10 364	18	22	15	14	16	21				
	1977	MF	9 196	17	21	14	15	16	17				
MEXICO	1975	MF	1 266 286	11	17	12	10	9	7	2			
		F	569 828	10	16	11	10	9	7	2			
	1980	MF	1 432 143	10	19	10	8	7	5	1			
	1983	MF	1 566 703	10	20	12	9	7	5	1			
		F											
	1984	MF	1 528 012	10	20	11	9	7	5	1			
NICARAGUA	1980	MF	79 926	17	26	13	11	9	6	4			
		F	38 450	16	26	12	11	9	5	3			
	1982	MF	78 033	15	24	11	9	9	6	4			
		F	37 115	14	23	11	9	8	6	3			
	1983	MF	95 125	18	32	13	8	8	6	4			
		F	45 571	17	31	13	8	7	5	4			
PANAMA	1975	MF	42 183	13	21	17	14	10	6	2			
		F	17 289	11	19	14	12	8	5	2			
	1980	MF	42 943	13	20	16	13	11	9	3			
		F	17 220	11	17	13	11	9	7	3			
	1983	MF	39 365	12	19	14	12	9	7	3			
		F	16 014	10	18	12	10	8	6	2			
	1984	MF	41 896	12	20	16	13	10	7	3			
		F	16 770	10	18	13	11	8	6	3			
ST. LUCIA‡	1982	MF	1 022	3	3	1	1	2	2	1	9	5	5
		F	506	3	2	1	0	3	2	1	10	4	5
	1983	MF	2 205	7	5	4	3	3	5	2	14	6	21
		F	999	6	3	3	2	3	4	1	15	7	18
ST. PIERRE AND MIQUELON	1980	MF	110	15	20	9	11	18	16				
	1983	MF	93	14	10	9	18	15	18				
	1984	MF	37	6	13	5	5	2	5				
TRINIDAD AND TOBAGO	1981	MF	6 504	4	2	1	1	0	1	2	13	6	23
		F	3 211	4	3	1	1	0	1	1	14	5	23
	1984	MF	8 161	5	2	1	1	0	0	1	21	12	25
		F	4 611	6	2	1	0	0	0	1	26	11	24
AMERICA, SOUTH													
ARGENTINA	1975	MF	309 003	9	18	10	9	7	5	3	1		
		F	134 608	8	16	9	8	6	4	3	1		
	1976	MF	292 138	8	15	10	9	7	5	3	1		
		F	126 025	7	14	9	8	6	4	3	1		
BRAZIL	1975	MF	2 980 865	15	23	17	10	10	12	12	10	7	
	1980	MF	4 570 951	20	29	19	15	12	19	18	16	11	
	1981	MF	4 574 768	20	29	19	16	12	20	18	15	11	
	1982	MF	4 861 964	21	28	20	16	13	21	19	16	12	
CHILE	1975	MF	287 170	12	20	15	13	11	10	8	10	6	
		F	124 968	11	19	13	11	10	9	7	8	5	
	1977	MF	281 700	13	18	15	13	12	13	11	9	5	
		F	137 778	13	18	15	13	12	13	11	9	5	
	1983	MF	151 731	7	12	9	7	7	8	5	5	3	
		F	61 985	6	11	7	6	6	6	5	4	3	

3.6 Percentage repeaters by grade (first level)
Pourcentage de redoublants par année d'études (premier degré)
Porcentaje de repetidores por año de estudios (primer grado)

COUNTRY / PAYS / PAIS	YEAR / ANNEE / AÑO	SEX / SEXE / SEXO	TOTAL / TOTAL / TOTAL	PERCENTAGE REPEATERS BY GRADE / POURCENTAGE DE REDOUBLANTS PAR ANNEE D'ETUDES / PORCENTAJE DE REPETIDORES POR AÑO DE ESTUDIOS									
				TOTAL	I	II	III	IV	V	VI	VII	V III	IX
COLOMBIA	1984	MF	494 551	12	19	13	10	8	5				
		F	230 287	12	18	12	10	8	5				
	1985	MF	684 832	17	25	18	14	11	7				
		F	338 253	17	24	18	15	11	7				
ECUADOR	1975	MF	138 613	11	16	13	10	9	7	6			
		F	65 044	11	16	12	10	9	7	5			
	1980	MF	148 134	10	14	12	9	8	5	4			
	1983	MF	144 714	9	13	11	8	7	5	3			
	1984	MF	143 929	9	13	11	8	7	5	3			
FRENCH GUIANA	1975	MF	1 274	17	23	15	15	14	15				
	1976	MF	1 316	17	24	15	15	14	12				
	1977	MF	1 212	15	21	13	15	14	10				
GUYANA	1975	MF	10 880	8	16	5	6	5	5	14			
		F	4 969	8	15	4	5	4	4	15			
	1979	MF	10 643	8	15	5	6	4	4	14			
		F	5 005	8	13	5	5	3	4	16			
	1981	MF	4 711	4	6	2	3	2	3	6			
		F	2 196	3	5	2	3	2	3	6			
PARAGUAY	1975	MF	69 378	15	24	19	15	10	6	3			
		F	29 582	14	22	17	13	8	4	2			
	1980	MF	70 578	14	20	17	14	9	6	3			
	1983	MF	56 231	10	15	13	11	8	5	2			
	1984	MF	62 479	11	15	15	12	9	5	2			
PERU‡	1975	MF	289 700	10	16	12	9	8	7	4			
	1980	MF	594 817	19	28	20	18	15	14	8			
		F	276 711	18	28	19	18	15	12	7			
	1981	MF	602 791	19	28	18	19	16	14	8			
		F	291 854	19	28	18	19	16	14	8			
	1985	MF	524 270	14	21	13	12	13	11	8			
SURINAME	1975	MF	19 157	24	27	25	21	26	23	20			
		F	8 178	21	25	21	16	23	21	21			
	1978	MF	21 938	26	30	26	23	26	26	22			
		F	9 496	23	27	21	19	24	25	24			
	1984	MF	15 500	22	25	21	22	21	21	19			
		F	6 726	20	21	17	18	19	21	21			
URUGUAY‡	1976	MF	44 521	17	29	18	15	14	12	8			
		F	19 612	15	26	14	12	12	13	11			
	1979	MF	42 447	15	27	17	14	13	11	7			
		F	*18 053	*14	24	14	11	11	10	8			
	1980	MF	41 151	15	27	16	13	13	10	7			
		F	17 135	13	24	14	11	11	8	7			
VENEZUELA	1975	MF	57 389	3	–	–	–	10	8	–			
	1980	MF	248 987	10	14	11	10	10	7	3			
	1982	MF	265 328	10	14	11	11	10	7	2			
	1983	MF	261 075	10	14	11	10	9	7	3			
ASIA													
AFGHANISTAN	1980	MF	165 621	15	19	13	13	18	14	12	15	11	
		F	31 442	16	18	15	14	20	14	12	18	9	
	1982	MF	48 545	11	5	5	11	11	14	14	16	16	
		F	15 227	11	5	5	10	10	15	15	18	18	
	1984	MF	31 758	6	5	5	5	5	5	6	8	10	
		F	9 538	6	5	5	5	5	5	6	8	10	

COUNTRY PAYS PAIS	YEAR ANNEE AÑO	SEX SEXE SEXO	TOTAL TOTAL TOTAL	PERCENTAGE REPEATERS BY GRADE POURCENTAGE DE REDOUBLANTS PAR ANNEE D'ETUDES PORCENTAJE DE REPETIDORES POR AÑO DE ESTUDIOS									
				TOTAL	I	II	III	IV	V	VI	VII	V III	IX
BAHRAIN	1981	MF	5 572	11	12	11	11	14	12	7			
		F	2 330	10	14	11	11	11	8	5			
	1983	MF	5 905	11	11	9	11	14	13	8			
		F	2 615	10	12	10	11	12	10	5			
	1984	MF	4 118	7	8	7	8	8	8	5			
		F	1 888	7	8	8	8	7	6	4			
BANGLADESH	1976	MF	1 608 984	19	24	16	15	15	13				
		F	556 721	19	24	16	15	15	13				
	1981	MF	1 472 899	18	25	12	17	9	9				
		F	601 198	18	25	12	17	9	9				
BHUTAN‡	1976	MF	1 826	11	–	26	15	16	17	33			
	1978	MF	683	3	1	4	3	9	9	8			
		F	249	5	–	9	9	13	11	6			
	1979	MF	2 924	13	14	14	12	12	7	12			
		F	789	12	12	13	13	11	6	15			
BRUNEI DARUSSALAM	1975	MF	2 492	8	5	3	4	5	3	28			
		F	1 068	7	4	3	3	5	3	27			
	1980	MF	3 831	13	6	23	12	10	10	18			
		F	1 458	10	4	17	9	7	7	16			
	1983	MF	2 951	9	10	9	6	6	13	10			
		F	1 050	7	7	5	4	4	10	9			
	1984	MF	3 514	10	10	10	8	4	9	18			
		F	1 407	9	7	7	5	7	6	17			
CYPRUS‡	1975	MF	552	1	4	1	0	0	0	0	–	–	
		F	225	1	3	1	0	0	0	0	–	–	
	1980	MF	280	1	3	1	0	–	–	0	–		
		F	110	0	3	1	0	–	–	0	–		
	1982	MF	200	0	2	0	0	0	0	0	–		
		F	72	0	2	0	–	–	0	–	–		
	1983	MF	281	1	3	0	0	0	0	0	–		
		F	112	0	2	0	–	–	0	0	–		
HONG KONG	1980	MF	19 192	4	5	4	5	5	3	0			
		F	7 069	3	4	3	3	4	2	0			
	1983	MF	12 733	2	2	3	3	4	2	0			
		F	4 852	2	2	2	3	3	2	0			
	1984	MF	10 988	2	2	2	3	3	2	0			
		F	4 201	2	2	2	2	3	2	0			
INDONESIA	1975	MF	1 906 099	11	15	12	11	9	7	2			
	1980	MF	2 119 921	8	17	9	7	5	3	1			
	1983	MF	2 672 205	9	15	12	10	7	5	1			
	1984	MF	2 783 919	9	16	11	10	8	6	1			
IRAN, ISLAMIC REPUBLIC OF	1983	MF	708 944	12	17	10	8	10	13				
	1984	MF	684 669	11	17	9	6	9	11				
IRAQ	1975	MF	278 693	16	14	13	11	14	26	18			
		F	89 863	15	14	14	12	15	26	11			
	1979	MF	265 899	10	2	9	10	12	21	7			
		F	106 064	9	2	9	9	11	20	6			
	1982	MF	609 042	23	13	19	23	28	28	30			
		F	258 898	21	12	19	22	27	23	24			
JAPAN‡			–	–	–	–	–	–	–	–			
JORDAN‡	1975	MF	15 892	4	0	0	6	8	6	5			
		F	7 713	4	0	0	6	9	6	5			
	1980	MF	14 680	3	0	0	0	4	8	7			
		F	7 053	3	0	0	0	4	8	7			
	1983	MF	22 629	5	0	0	0	9	10	8			
		F	10 559	5	0	0	0	9	9	8			

3.6 **Percentage repeaters by grade (first level)**
Pourcentage de redoublants par année d'études (premier degré)
Porcentaje de repetidores por año de estudios (primer grado)

COUNTRY PAYS PAIS	YEAR ANNEE AÑO	SEX SEXE SEXO	TOTAL TOTAL TOTAL	PERCENTAGE REPEATERS BY GRADE / POURCENTAGE DE REDOUBLANTS PAR ANNEE D'ETUDES / PORCENTAJE DE REPETIDORES POR AÑO DE ESTUDIOS									
				TOTAL	I	II	III	IV	V	VI	VII	V III	IX
JORDAN (CONT)‡	1984	MF	23 760	5	0	0	0	9	10	8			
		F	11 087	5	0	0	0	10	10	8			
KOREA, REPUBLIC OF‡			–	–	–	–	–	–	–	–			
KUWAIT‡	1975	MF	12 105	13	13	13	16	11					
		F	5 632	13	14	15	16	10					
	1980	MF	9 177	7	7	9	9	4					
		F	4 483	7	8	9	9	4					
	1983	MF	9 984	6	6	7	7	4					
		F	4 957	6	6	8	7	4					
	1984	MF	9 626	6	6	6	7	4					
		F	4 777	6	6	6	7	4					
MALAYSIA‡			–	–	–	–	–	–	–	–			
MONGOLIA	1978	MF	3 808	3	2	3	3						
	1979	MF	2 528	2	2	2	2						
OMAN	1975	MF	5 097	9	11	7	12	11	4	8			
		F	1 352	9	9	8	9	16	5	5			
	1983	MF	14 363	11	9	9	9	16	11	11			
		F	4 619	8	9	8	8	10	8	8			
	1984	MF	17 594	11	10	9	8	18	14	12			
		F	5 917	9	9	8	7	12	10	8			
PHILIPPINES	1980	MF	202 934	2	3	3	3	2	2	1			
		F	82 628	2	3	2	2	2	2	1			
	1983	MF	187 047	2	3	3	2	2	1	1			
		F	71 572	2	3	2	2	1	1	1			
	1984	MF	122 856	1	2	1	1	1	1	1			
		F	59 959	1	2	1	1	1	1	1			
QATAR‡	1975	MF	4 692	22	23	22	21	24	25	14			
		F	2 165	21	22	20	20	22	28	11			
	1980	MF	3 181	13	16	12	10	17	13	5			
		F	1 567	13	17	10	10	18	14	6			
	1983	MF	3 038	10	11	7	7	15	14	7			
		F	1 210	9	10	6	5	12	13	4			
	1984	MF	3 479	11	10	9	10	15	15	9			
		F	1 372	9	10	8	9	12	11	6			
SAUDI ARABIA	1975	MF	103 091	15	17	14	14	21	14	9			
		F	28 922	12	13	11	11	16	11	6			
	1980	MF	145 168	16	16	17	16	19	15	10			
		F	35 749	10	10	10	10	13	10	4			
	1982	MF	145 335	14	16	14	13	16	13	7			
		F	39 839	9	11	9	9	11	9	4			
	1983	MF	154 386	13	15	13	13	16	13	7			
		F	44 851	9	11	9	8	11	9	4			
SINGAPORE	1975	MF	25 758	8	0	0	2	3	4	28			
		F	8 633	6	0	0	2	2	3	21			
	1980	MF	19 309	7	1	1	1	8	11	18			
		F	7 772	6	0	1	0	7	9	16			
	1983	MF	3 668	1	0	0	0	0	0	7	0	–	
		F	1 794	1	0	0	0	0	0	7	–	–	
	1984	MF	3 257	1	0	0	0	0	0	5	–	4	
		F	1 716	1	0	0	0	0	–	6	–	6	
SRI LANKA	1975	MF	221 337	15	15	12	15	25	13				
	1980	MF	217 122	10	6	12	14	11	10	8			
	1983	MF	220 180	10	8	10	11	12	11	9			
	1984	MF	204 463	9	8	10	10	11	9	8			

COUNTRY / PAYS / PAIS	YEAR / ANNEE / AÑO	SEX / SEXE / SEXO	TOTAL / TOTAL / TOTAL	PERCENTAGE REPEATERS BY GRADE / POURCENTAGE DE REDOUBLANTS PAR ANNEE D'ETUDES / PORCENTAJE DE REPETIDORES POR AÑO DE ESTUDIOS									
				TOTAL	I	II	III	IV	V	VI	VII	V III	IX
SYRIAN ARAB REPUBLIC‡	1975	MF	129 136	10	12	11	11	9	7	9			
		F	49 965	10	12	11	11	9	7	5			
	1980	MF	126 628	8	11	9	8	6	6	8			
		F	47 871	7	11	8	7	6	4	4			
	1983	MF	141 072	8	11	9	7	6	5	7			
		F	57 789	7	11	9	7	5	4	4			
	1984	MF	149 816	8	12	8	7	6	5	7			
		F	61 461	7	12	8	7	5	4	4			
THAILAND	1975	MF	688 053	10	19	12	11	4	7	4	2		
		F	295 924	9	18	10	10	3	7	3	1		
	1980	MF	610 229	8	16	9	7	4	8	2			
		F	260 913	7	14	7	6	4	8	3			
TURKEY	1983	MF	573 106	9	13	9	10	6	3				
		F	261 124	9	13	9	9	6	3				
	1984	MF	596 777	9	20	7	9	5	2				
		F	274 014	9	20	7	9	5	2				
UNITED ARAB EMIRATES‡	1975	MF	7 072	15	12	16	16	20	18	8			
		F	3 177	15	13	16	15	20	17	7			
	1980	MF	6 629	9	6	6	12	13	11	7			
		F	3 081	9	6	7	12	12	11	5			
	1983	MF	7 118	6	4	5	4	8	8	7			
		F	3 160	5	4	5	4	7	7	5			
	1984	MF	8 789	6	4	5	5	9	9	8			
		F	3 845	6	4	5	5	7	8	6			
YEMEN‡	1980	MF	104 265	25	16	29	28	24	42	48			
		F	1 336	3	2	2	1	1	6	13			
	1981	MF	118 394	23	6	18	35	52	52	19			
		F	8 328	12	2	1	20	43	48	14			
	1982	MF	122 113	20	4	11	27	47	48	19			
		F	12 042	14	1	8	17	35	62	15			
EUROPE													
AUSTRIA‡	1976	MF	17 834	4	3	5	3	3					
	1978	MF	13 768	3	2	4	3	3					
BELGIUM‡	1975	MF	225 439	24	14	20	25	26	31	28			
		F	104 927	23	14	20	24	25	28	27			
	1980	MF	163 040	19	13	17	20	21	23	22			
		F	72 924	18	12	16	18	20	21	21			
	1983	MF	137 710	18	10	15	19	21	23	22			
		F	61 391	17	9	14	17	19	21	20			
	1984	MF	130 891	18	10	14	16	19	21	20			
		F	58 814	16	10	13	16	19	21	20			
BULGARIA‡	1975	MF	20 173	2	3	2	1	2	4	2	2	1	
	1980	MF	17 170	2	3	2	1	2	2	2	1	1	
		F	4 679	1	...	...	...	...	...	...	...	...	
	1983	MF	19 493	2	2	1	1	2	2	2	2	1	
		F	4 770	1	...	...	...	...	...	...	...	...	
	1984	MF	19 786	2	3	1	1	2	2	2	2	1	
		F	4 373	1	...	...	...	...	...	...	...	...	
CZECHOSLOVAKIA	1975	MF	15 664	1	0	2	1	1	1	1	1	0	
		F	5 940	1	0	2	1	1	1	1	0	0	
	1980	MF	16 329	1	1	1	1	1	0	1	1	0	
		F	6 265	1	1	1	1	1	0	1	1	0	
	1983	MF	18 974	1	2	1	1	1	1	1	1	0	
		F	7 112	1	2	1	1	1	1	1	0	0	
	1984	MF	17 724	1	2	1	1	1	1	1	1	0	–
		F	6 547	1	1	1	1	1	1	0	0	0	–

3.6 **Percentage repeaters by grade (first level)**
Pourcentage de redoublants par année d'études (premier degré)
Porcentaje de repetidores por año de estudios (primer grado)

COUNTRY / PAYS / PAIS	YEAR / ANNEE / AÑO	SEX / SEXE / SEXO	TOTAL / TOTAL / TOTAL	PERCENTAGE REPEATERS BY GRADE / POURCENTAGE DE REDOUBLANTS PAR ANNEE D'ETUDES / PORCENTAJE DE REPETIDORES POR AÑO DE ESTUDIOS									
				TOTAL	I	II	III	IV	V	VI	VII	V III	IX
FRANCE	1975	MF	424 459	9	14	7	6	7	11				
	1979	MF	427 541	9	13	8	7	8	11				
GERMANY, FEDERAL REPUBLIC OF‡	1975	MF	126 768	3	5	4	2	2					
		F	52 931	3	4	3	2	2					
	1980	MF	60 390	2	2	3	2	2					
		F	25 092	2	2	3	2	1					
	1982	MF	47 061	2	1	3	2	2					
		F	20 306	2	1	3	2	2					
	1983	MF	42 112	2	1	2	2	2					
		F	17 948	2	1	2	1	1					
GREECE‡	1975	MF	26 860	3	7	3	3	1	1	0			
		F	10 592	2	6	3	2	1	1	0			
	1980	MF	9 685	1	3	1	1	0	0	0			
		F	3 796	1	3	1	1	0	0	0			
	1981	MF	1 215	0	0	0	0	0	0	0			
		F	418	0	0	0	0	0	0	0			
	1982	MF	1 762	0	0	0	0	0	0	0			
		F	698	0	0	0	0	0	0	0			
HUNGARY	1975	MF	28 457	3	5	3	2	2	4	3	2	0	
		F	10 700	2	5	2	2	1	3	2	1	0	
	1980	MF	24 225	2	4	2	2	1	3	2	1	0	
		F	9 078	2	3	2	1	1	2	1	1	0	
	1983	MF	34 742	3	5	3	2	2	4	3	2	0	
		F	12 598	2	4	2	2	2	3	2	1	0	
	1984	MF	37 846	3	5	3	2	2	4	3	3	0	
		F	13 527	2	4	2	2	2	3	2	2	0	
ITALY	1975	MF	143 873	3	5	4	3	2	2				
		F	56 497	2	4	3	2	2	1				
	1980	MF	54 036	1	2	1	1	1	1				
		F	20 464	1	1	1	1	1	1				
	1982	MF	52 437	1	2	1	1	1	1				
		F	19 749	1	1	1	1	1	1				
	1983	MF	48 257	1	2	1	1	1	1				
		F	17 920	1	1	1	1	1	1				
LUXEMBOURG	1975	MF	1 809	6	12	7	7	5	3	3			
		F	792	5	11	5	7	4	2	3			
	1978	MF	1 688	6	12	7	8	5	3	2			
		F	700	5	11	6	6	3	3	2			
	1982	MF	1 363	6	11	6	7	7	3	2			
		F	549	5	11	4	5	5	3	1			
MALTA‡	1975	MF	310	1	0	1	1	2	1	1	2	–	
		F	169	1	0	1	1	3	1	1	3	–	
	1980	MF	649	2	1	1	3	3	2	2			
		F	242	2	1	1	2	2	2	2			
	1982	MF	525	2	1	2	2	2	1	1			
		F	211	1	1	1	2	1	2	1			
	1983	MF	447	1	1	1	2	1	1	1			
		F	199	1	1	1	2	1	1	1			
NETHERLANDS	1975	MF	35 673	2	5	3	2	2	1	1			
		F	14 546	2	4	3	2	2	1	1			
	1980	MF	33 789	3	6	4	2	2	1	1			
		F	12 859	2	4	3	2	1	1	1			
	1983	MF	24 725	2	4	4	2	1	1	1			
		F	9 792	2	3	3	2	1	1	1			
	1984	MF	23 856	2	4	4	2	1	1	1			
		F	9 603	2	3	3	2	1	1	1			

COUNTRY PAYS PAIS	YEAR ANNEE AÑO	SEX SEXE SEXO	TOTAL TOTAL TOTAL	PERCENTAGE REPEATERS BY GRADE POURCENTAGE DE REDOUBLANTS PAR ANNEE D'ETUDES PORCENTAJE DE REPETIDORES POR AÑO DE ESTUDIOS									
				TOTAL	I	II	III	IV	V	VI	VII	V III	IX
POLAND	1975	MF	107 828	3	2	1	1	1	5	4	4	1	
	1980	MF	92 315	2	2	1	1	2	4	3	3	1	
	1983	MF	166 996	4	3	2	3	5	6	5	5	1	
	1984	MF	144 897	3	3	2	2	4	5	4	4	1	
PORTUGAL‡	1975	MF	136 656	11	3	16	10	14	10	15			
		F	56 808	10	2	14	8	13	8	12			
	1982	MF	*238 591	*20	25	——>	15	——>	*20	*16			
	1983	MF	*234 993	*20	25	——>	14	——>	*21	*18			
		F	*98 923	*17	22	——>	13	——>	*16	*14			
SAN MARINO	1982	MF	17	1	0	3	0	1	1				
	1983	MF	6	0	.	0	.	1	1				
SPAIN	1980	MF	231 424	6	6	6	6	7	8				
		F	96 882	6	5	5	5	6	7				
	1982	MF	221 975	6	3	7	6	7	9				
		F	94 239	5	2	6	5	6	8				
	1983	MF	184 549	5	3	7	3	4	8				
		F	75 834	4	2	6	3	3	7				
SWITZERLAND‡	1976	MF	12 362	2	2	2	3	2	2	2			
		F	5 318	2	2	2	2	2	2	2			
	1980	MF	8 799	2	2	2	2	2	2	2			
		F	3 794	2	1	2	2	2	2	1			
	1983	MF	8 784	2	2	3	2	2	2	2			
		F	3 726	2	1	2	2	2	2	2			
	1984	MF	7 967	2	2	2	2	2	2	2			
		F	3 374	2	1	2	2	2	2	2			
YUGOSLAVIA	1975	MF	55 334	4	6	4	3	2					
	1980	MF	23 712	2	3	1	1	1					
	1982	MF	22 912	2	3	1	1	1					
	1983	MF	23 041	2	3	1	1	1					
OCEANIA													
FIJI‡	1976	MF	5 761	4	6	2	4	3	4	5	4	7	
	1980	MF	5 601	5	6	4	4	4	5	5	6	6	
		F	2 331	4	5	3	4	3	4	5	5	7	
	1983	MF	4 547	4	5	3	3	3	4	4	4	4	
		F	1 846	3	5	2	3	2	3	4	4	3	
	1984	MF	3 934	3	5	3	3	3	3	3	4	3	
		F	1 541	3	4	2	2	2	2	3	3	2	
FRENCH POLYNESIA‡	1982	MF	2 936	10	10	10	10	10	10	10			
		F	1 392	10	10	10	10	10	10	10			
KIRIBATI	1980	MF	609	5	4	1	3	4	3	13	2	2	5
		F	286	4	3	1	3	3	3	13	2	2	5
	1984	MF	377	3	6	3	2	2	3	1	2	1	5
		F	186	3	6	2	3	2	2	2	3	1	4
	1985	MF	374	3	5	2	1	1	1	1	3	2	10
		F	187	3	5	2	1	1	1	1	3	1	9
NEW CALEDONIA‡	1984	MF	4 058	17	20	15	13	16	22	9	——>	–	
		F	1 810	15	17	14	13	15	21	6	——>	–	
	1985	MF	3 848	17	20	15	14	19	22	6	——>	–	
		F	1 632	15	17	13	12	17	19	6	——>	–	
SOLOMON ISLANDS	1975	MF	1 541	5	8	5	6	5	3	2	9		
		F	603	6	7	5	6	7	4	2	8		
	1980	MF	1 409	5	4	6	4	3	4	10			
		F	556	5	4	5	4	3	3	9			
	1982	MF	1 297	4	4	3	3	4	4	9			
		F	528	4	4	3	3	4	4	10			

3.6 **Percentage repeaters by grade (first level)**
Pourcentage de redoublants par année d'études (premier degré)
Porcentaje de repetidores por año de estudios (primer grado)

COUNTRY PAYS PAIS	YEAR ANNEE AÑO	SEX SEXE SEXO	TOTAL TOTAL TOTAL	PERCENTAGE REPEATERS BY GRADE POURCENTAGE DE REDOUBLANTS PAR ANNEE D'ETUDES PORCENTAJE DE REPETIDORES POR AÑO DE ESTUDIOS									
				TOTAL	I	II	III	IV	V	VI	VII	V III	IX
SOLOMON ISLANDS (CONT)	1983	MF	1 402	4	4	2	4	2	4	10			
		F	553	4	4	2	4	2	3	10			
TONGA	1979	MF	1 013	5	–	–	–	–	–	24			
		F	483	5	–	–	–	–	–	24			
	1982	MF	1 320	8	–	–	–	–	–	31			
		F	610	8	–	–	–	–	–	32			
	1983	MF	1 238	8	–	–	–	–	–	31			
		F	500	6	–	–	–	–	–	27			
U.S.S.R.													
U.S.S.R.	1975	MF	173 533	1	1	1	1	1	1				
	1980	MF	102 919	0	1	0	0	1	1				
	1982	MF	117 828	1	1	0	0	0	1				
	1983	MF	106 000	0	1	0	0	0	0				
BYELORUSSIAN S.S.R.‡	1975	MF	5 689	0	1	0	0	0	0	0	0	0	
	1980	MF	2 600	0	1	0	0	0	0				
	1981	MF	2 900	0	1	0	0	0	0				
	1982	MF	2 600	0	1	0	0	0	0				
UKRAINIAN S.S.R.‡	1975	MF	11 100	0	0	0	0	0	0	0	0	0	
	1980	MF	7 800	0	1	0	0	0	0				
	1982	MF	10 900	0	1	0	0	0	0				
	1983	MF	13 100	0	1	0	0	0	0				

These data refer to total and female repeaters at the first level of education in 1975, 1980 and the two latest years available.

The total number of repeaters together with its percentage of total enrolment as well as the percentage repeaters in each grade appearing in this table have been calculated from figures taken from questionnaire replies and national publications.

The percentages presented in this table have been calculated by dividing the number of repeaters by the enrolment for the same year.

To maintain a consistent and coherent series on repetition as well as to facilitate the comparison of these data with those for enrolment by grade presented in Table 3.5, estimates have been made when the number of repeaters in private institutions was not available. In no case did the missing data constitute more than 5% of the total enrolment. The identification of these estimates is facilitated by the introduction of an asterisk which precedes the total number of repeaters.

The method of estimation used takes into account all available information. For example, the proportion of repeaters in private schools for previous years was used if available; when no other information was available, the data on repeaters were adjusted to reflect the incidence of private enrolment.

Ces données se réfèrent aux redoublants (total et filles) dans l'enseignement du premier degré en 1975, 1980 et les deux dernières années disponibles.

Le nombre total de redoublants avec le pourcentage par rapport au total des effectifs d'élèves ainsi que le pourcentage de redoublants dans chaque année d'études qui figurent dans ce tableau ont été calculés avec les données provenant des réponses aux questionnaires et des publications nationales.

Les pourcentages présentés dans ce tableau ont été calculés en divisant le nombre de redoublants par les effectifs de la même année.

Afin d'assurer une série cohérente et consistante sur les redoublants et de faciliter la comparabilité de ces données avec celles des effectifs par année d'études présentés dans le tableau 3.5, des estimations ont été faites sur le nombre de redoublants dans les écoles privées, lorsque ces chiffres n'étaient pas disponibles. Les données manquantes ne représentent en aucun cas plus de 5% du total des effectifs. L'identification de ces estimations est facilitée par l'introduction d'un astérisque qui précède le nombre de redoublants.

La méthode d'estimation utilisée prend en considération toutes les informations disponibles; par exemple, la proportion des redoublants dans les écoles privées au cours des années antérieures est utilisée, lorsque ces chiffres sont connus. Si l'on ne dispose pas d'autres informations, les données sur les redoublants sont ajustées en accord avec l'importance des effectifs de l'enseignement privé.

Estos datos se refieren a los repetidores (total y de sexo femenino) en la enseñanza de primer grado en 1975, 1980 y los dos ultimos años disponibles.

El número total de repetidores con el porcentaje en relación con la matrícula total así como los porcentajes de repetidores en cada año de estudios que figuran en este cuadro se han calculado con los datos provenientes de las respuestas a los cuestionarios y de las publicaciones nacionales.

El cálculo de los porcentajes se ha efectuado dividiendo el número de repetidores por la matrícula escolar relativa al mismo año.

Con el fin de asegurar una serie coherente y consistente sobre los repetidores y de facilitar la comparabilidad de estos datos con los de los efectivos por año de estudios presentados en el cuadro 3.5, se han efectuado estimaciones relativas al número de repetidores en las escuelas privadas cuando no se disponía de tales datos. En estos casos, la cantidad que faltaba nunca era superior al 5% del efectivo total. La identificación de estas estimaciones se ve facilitada con la introducción de un asterisco que figura delante del número de repetidores.

El método de estimación utilizado toma en consideración todas las informaciones disponibles. Por ejemplo, la proporción de los repetidores en las escuelas privadas para los años anteriores se ha utilizado, cuando se dispone de tales datos. Si no se dispone de otra información, los datos relativos a los repetidores se ajustan de acuerdo con la importancia de los efectivos de la enseñanza privada.

AFRICA:

Algeria:

E--> Enrolment in grade VII refers to terminal classes.

FR-> Les données sur les effectifs de la septième année d'études se réfèrent aux classes de fin d'études.

ESP> Los datos sobre los efectivos del séptimo año de estudios se refieren a las clases de *fin d'études*.

Chad:

E--> Data do not include Moslem private education.

FR-> Les données ne tiennent pas compte de l'enseignement privé musulman.

ESP> Los datos no incluyen la enseñanza privada musulmana.

Ethiopia:

E--> Data refer to public education only.

FR-> Les données se réfèrent à l'enseignement public seulement.

ESP> Los datos se refieren a la enseñanza pública solamente.

Uganda:

E--> Government-maintained and aided schools only.

FR-> Ecoles publiques et subventionnées seulement.

ESP> Escuelas públicas y subvencionadas solamente.

United Republic of Tanzania:

E--> Tanzania mainland only.

FR-> Tanzanie continentale seulement.

ESP> Tanzania continental solamente.

AMERICA, NORTH:

El Salvador:

E--> Data include evening schools.

FR-> Les données incluent les écoles du soir.

ESP> Los datos incluyen las escuelas nocturnas.

Grenada:

E--> For 1982, data refer to public education only.

FR-> Pour 1982, les données se réfèrent à l'enseignement public seulement.

ESP> Para 1982, los datos se refieren a la enseñanza pública solamente.

St. Lucia:

E--> Enrolment in grades VIII and IX refer to terminal classes.

FR-> Les données sur les effectifs des huitième et neuvième années d'études se réfèrent aux classes de fin d'études.

ESP> Los datos sobre los efectivos del octavo y noveno año de estudios se refieren a las clases de 'fin d'études'.

AMERICA, SOUTH:

Peru:

E--> In 1975, data include evening schools.

FR-> Pour 1975, les données incluent les écoles du soir.

ESP> En 1975, los datos incluyen las escuelas nocturnas.

Uruguay:

E--> Data refer to public education only.

FR-> Les données se réfèrent à l'enseignement public seulement.

ESP> Los datos se refieren a la enseñanza pública solamente.

ASIA:

Bhutan:

E--> Data for grade 1 refer to kindergartens.

FR-> Les données relatives à la première année d'études se réfèrent aux jardins d'enfants.

ESP> Los datos relativos al primer año de estudios se refieren a los jardines infantiles.

Cyprus:

E--> Not including Turkish schools. Enrolment in grades VII and VIII exists only in private schools.

FR-> Non compris les écoles turques. Les données sur les effectifs des septième et huitième années d'études se réfèrent seulement aux écoles privées.

ESP> Excluídas las escuelas turcas. Los datos sobre los efectivos para el séptimo y octavo año de estudios se refieren a las escuelas privadas solamente.

Japan:

E--> A policy of automatic promotion is practiced in first level education.

FR-> Une politique de promotion automatique est appliquée pour l'enseignement du premier degré.

ESP> Se aplica una política de promoción automática para la enseñanza de primer grado.

Jordan:

E--> Including UNRWA schools.

FR-> Y compris les écoles de l'UNRWA.

ESP> Incluídas las escuelas del O.O.P.S.R.P. (Organización de Obras Públicas y Socorro para Los Refugiados de Palestina).

Korea, Republic of:

E--> A policy of automatic promotion is practiced in first level education.

FR-> Une politique de promotion automatique est appliquée pour l'enseignement du premier degré.

ESP> Se aplica una política de promoción automática para la enseñanza de primer grado.

Kuwait:

E--> For 1975 and 1980, data refer to public education only.

FR-> Pour 1975 et 1980, les données se réfèrent à l'enseignement public seulement.

ESP> Para 1975 y 1980, los datos se refieren a la enseñanza pública solamente.

Malaysia:

E--> A policy of automatic promotion is practiced in first level education.

FR-> Une politique de promotion automatique est appliquée pour l'enseignement du premier degré.

ESP> Se aplica una política de promoción automática para la enseñanza de primer grado.

Qatar:

E--> Data refer to public education only.

FR-> Les données se réfèrent à l'enseignement public seulement.

ESP> Los datos se refieren a la enseñanza pública solamente.

Syrian Arab Republic:

E--> Including UNRWA schools.

FR-> Y compris les écoles de l'UNRWA.

ESP> Incluídas las escuelas del O.O.P.S.R.P.

United Arab Emirates:

E--> Data refer to public education only.

FR-> Les données se réfèrent à l'enseignement public seulement.

ESP> Los datos se refieren a la enseñanza pública solamente.

Yemen:

E--> Data refer to public education only.

FR-> Les données se réfèrent à l'enseignement public seulement.

ESP> Los datos se refieren a la enseñanza pública solamente.

EUROPE:

Austria:

E--> For 1976 and 1978, data include special education.

FR-> Pour 1976 et 1978, les données incluent l'éducation spéciale.

ESP> Para 1976 y 1978, los datos incluyen la educación especial.

Belgium:

E--> Except for 1984, data include special education.

FR-> A l'exception de l'année 1984, les données incluent l'éducation spéciale.

ESP> Salvo para 1984, los datos incluyen la educación especial.

Bulgaria:

E--> For 1975, data include evening schools.

FR-> Pour 1975, les données incluent les écoles du soir.

ESP> Para 1975, los datos incluyen las escuelas nocturnas.

Germany, Federal Republic of:

E--> Data refer to the first four grades of first level education.

FR-> Les données se réfèrent aux quatre premières années de l'enseignement du premier degré.

ESP> Los datos se refieren a los cuatros primeros años de la enseñanza de primer grado.

Greece:

E--> For 1975, data include evening schools.

FR-> Pour 1975, les données incluent les écoles du soir.

ESP> Para 1975, los datos incluyen las escuelas nocturnas.

Malta:

E--> For 1975, enrolment in grades VII and VIII exists only in private schools.

FR-> En 1975, les données sur les effectifs des septième et huitième années d'études se réfèrent seulement aux écoles privées.

ESP> En 1975, los datos sobre los efectivos para el séptimo y octavo año de estudios se refieren a las escuelas privadas solamente.

Portugal:

E--> Beginning 1975, data on preparatory education previously classified at the second level are shown at the first level.

FR-> A partir de 1975, les données relatives aux cours préparatoires antérieurement classées dans l'enseignement du second degré ont été incluses dans l'enseignement du premier degré.

ESP> A partir de 1975, los datos relativos a los cursos preparatorios, anteriormente clasificados en la enseñanza de segundo grado, han sido incluídos en la enseñanza de primer grado.

Switzerland:

E--> For 1976, data include special education.

FR-> Pour 1976, les données incluent l'éducation spéciale.

ESP> Para 1976, los datos incluyen la educación especial.

OCEANIA:

Fiji:

E--> For 1975, data on grades VII and VIII include Forms I and II (education at the second level.

FR-> Pour 1975, les données relatives aux septième et huitième années d'études incluent les forms I et II (enseignement de second degré).

ESP> En 1975, los datos relativos a los septimo y octavo años de estudios incluyen las forms I y II (enseñanza de segundo grado).

French Polynesia:

E--> Enrolment in grade VI refers to terminal classes.

French Polynesia: (Cont):
FR–> Les données sur les effectifs de la sixième année d'études se réfèrent aux classes de fin d'études.
ESP> Los datos sobre los efectivos del sexto año de estudios se refieren a las clases de 'fin d'études'.
New Caledonia:
E––> Enrolment in grade VI and VII refers to terminal classes.
FR–> Les données sur les effectifs de la sixième et septième année d'études se réfèrent aux classes de fin d'études.
ESP> Los datos sobre los efectivos del sexto y séptimo año de estudios se refieren a las clases de *fin d'études*.
U.S.S.R.:
Byelorussian S.S.R.:
E––> From 1980, enrolment in grades VI to VIII is included in general education at the second level.

Byelorussian S.S.R.: (Cont):
FR–> A partir de 1980, les effectifs des classes allant de la sixième à la huitième année d'études sont inclus dans l'enseignement général du second degré.
ESP> A partir de 1980, los efectivos del sexto al octavo año de estudios están incluídos en la enseñanza general de segundo grado.
Ukrainian S.S.R.:
E––> From 1980, enrolment in grades VI to VIII is included in general education at the second level.
FR–> A partir de 1980, les effectifs des classes allant de la sixième à la huitième année d'études sont inclus dans l'enseignement général du second degré.
ESP> A partir de 1980, los efectivos del sexto al octavo año de estudios están incluídos en la enseñanza general de segundo grado.

3.7 Education at the second level (general, teacher-training and vocational): teachers and pupils

Enseignement du second degré (général, normal et technique): personnel enseignant et élèves

Enseñanza de segundo grado (general, normal y técnica): personal docente y alumnos

TOTAL SECOND LEVEL = TOTAL DU SECOND DEGRE = TOTAL DEL SEGUNDO GRADO
GENERAL EDUCATION = ENSEIGNEMENT GENERAL = ENSEÑANZA GENERAL
TEACHER TRAINING = ENSEIGNEMENT NORMAL = ENSEÑANZA NORMAL
VOCATIONAL EDUCATION = ENSEIGNEMENT TECHNIQUE = ENSEÑANZA TECNICA

NUMBER OF COUNTRIES AND TERRITORIES PRESENTED IN THIS TABLE: 192

NOMBRE DE PAYS ET DE TERRITOIRES PRESENTES DANS CE TABLEAU: 192

NUMERO DE PAISES Y DE TERRITORIOS PRESENTADOS EN ESTE CUADRO: 192

COUNTRY / PAYS / PAIS	TYPE OF EDUCATION / TYPE D'ENSEIGNEMENT / TIPO DE ENSEÑANZA	YEAR / ANNEE / AÑO	TEACHING STAFF / PERSONNEL ENSEIGNANT / PERSONAL DOCENTE: TOTAL	FEMALE / FEMININ / FEMENINO	% F	PUPILS ENROLLED / ELEVES INSCRITS / ALUMNOS MATRICULADOS: TOTAL	FEMALE / FEMININ / FEMENINO	% F
			(1)	(2)	(3)	(4)	(5)	(6)
AFRICA								
ALGERIA‡	TOTAL SECOND LEVEL	1975	19 764	...	...	512 428	172 769	34
		1980	41 137	...	...	1 031 791	397 959	39
		1981	47 771	...	...	1 154 709	455 498	39
		1982	...	...	...	...	...	...
		1983	...	...	...	1 473 053	...	...
		1984	...	...	...	...	...	...
	GENERAL	1975	18 205	...	...	490 818	167 200	34
		1980	...	...	...	1 003 983	389 982	39
		1981	...	...	...	1 124 100	446 713	40
		1983	61 961	...	...	1 420 303	581 266	41
		1984	69 466	23 479	34	1 569 167	648 950	41
	TEACHER TRAINING	1975	792	...	...	8 809	2 891	33
		1980	...	...	...	13 315	4 911	37
		1981	1 311	...	...	14 261	4 930	35
		1982	...	...	...	16 771	...	...
		1983	...	...	...	20 664	...	...
	VOCATIONAL	1975	767	...	...	12 801	2 678	21
		1980	...	...	...	14 493	3 066	21
		1981	...	...	...	16 348	3 855	24
		1983	...	...	...	32 086	8 617	27
		1984	...	...	...	42 577	12 078	28
ANGOLA	TOTAL SECOND LEVEL	1980	...	...	...	190 702	...	...
		1981	...	...	...	139 784	...	...
		1982	...	...	...	131 918	...	...
	GENERAL	1980	...	...	...	185 904	...	...
		1981	...	...	...	134 578	...	...
		1982	...	...	...	124 858	...	...
	TEACHER TRAINING	1980	...	...	...	2 086	...	...
		1981	...	...	...	2 564	793	31
		1982	...	...	...	3 141	787	25
	VOCATIONAL	1980	...	...	...	2 712	...	...
		1981	...	...	...	2 642	...	...
		1982	...	...	...	3 919	753	19

COUNTRY / PAYS / PAIS	TYPE OF EDUCATION / TYPE D'ENSEIGNEMENT / TIPO DE ENSEÑANZA	YEAR / ANNEE / AÑO	TEACHING STAFF / PERSONNEL ENSEIGNANT / PERSONAL DOCENTE			PUPILS ENROLLED / ELEVES INSCRITS / ALUMNOS MATRICULADOS		
			TOTAL	FEMALE / FEMININ / FEMENINO	% F	TOTAL	FEMALE / FEMININ / FEMENINO	% F
			(1)	(2)	(3)	(4)	(5)	(6)
BENIN	TOTAL SECOND LEVEL	1975	...	...	...	43 123	...	...
		1980	...	...	...	89 969	...	...
		1981	...	...	...	106 908	...	...
		1982	...	...	...	126 485	...	...
		1983	...	...	...	123 884	...	...
		1984	...	...	...	120 582	35 266	29
	GENERAL	1975	1 092	...	...	41 802	12 261	29
		1980	1 854	...	...	83 207	21 765	26
		1981	...	...	...	99 295	...	...
		1982	...	...	...	117 724	32 688	28
		1983	2 481	...	...	115 362	32 324	28
		1984	2 409	...	...	112 267	32 206	29
	TEACHER TRAINING	1975	10	5	50	170	29	17
		1980	...	...	...	788	...	...
		1981	...	...	...	989	...	...
		1982	...	...	...	1 146	...	...
		1983	...	...	...	1 386	...	...
		1984	...	...	...	*1 441	*435	*30
	VOCATIONAL	1975	...	...	...	1 151	...	...
		1980	...	...	...	5 974	...	...
		1981	...	...	...	6 624	...	...
		1982	...	...	...	7 615	...	...
		1983	609	...	...	7 136	...	...
		1984	...	...	...	6 874	2 625	38
BOTSWANA	TOTAL SECOND LEVEL	1975	860	256	30	14 286	7 418	52
		1980	1 137	417	37	20 969	11 434	55
		1982	...	...	...	...	...	...
		1983	...	...	...	25 010	13 569	54
		1984	1 565	614	39	30 902	16 506	53
		1985	...	...	...	...	...	...
	GENERAL	1975	570	167	29	12 098	6 392	53
		1980	851	300	35	18 325	10 283	56
		1982	984	395	40	20 965	11 522	55
		1983	1 046	422	40	22 252	12 125	54
		1984	1 216	506	42	27 364	14 812	54
		1985	1 283	545	42	32 172	17 175	53
	TEACHER TRAINING	1975	48	20	42	489	373	76
		1980	59	15	25	844	700	83
		1982	59	17	29	984	847	86
		1983	59	20	34	948	822	87
		1984	67	26	39	999	840	84
		1985	73	27	37	1 188	996	84
	VOCATIONAL	1975	242	69	29	1 699	653	38
		1980	227	102	45	1 800	451	25
		1983	...	...	...	1 810	622	34
		1984	282	82	29	2 539	854	34
BURKINA FASO	TOTAL SECOND LEVEL	1975	818	...	...	16 227	5 123	32
		1980	...	...	...	27 539	9 224	33
		1981	...	...	...	31 398	11 043	35
		1982	1 451	...	...	32 605	10 970	34
		1983	...	...	...	35 904	12 337	34
		1984	...	...	...	43 843	15 345	35
	GENERAL	1975	580	...	...	13 167	4 037	31
		1980	903	...	...	23 420	7 632	33
		1981	1 112	...	...	25 273	8 112	32
		1982	...	...	...	27 618	8 918	32
		1983	1 433	...	...	31 474	10 255	33
		1984	1 715	...	...	39 369	13 006	33
	TEACHER TRAINING	1975	28	14	50	391	117	30
		1980	...	...	...	248	57	23
		1981	...	...	...	255	58	23
		1982	...	...	...	204	58	28
		1983	...	...	...	197	62	31
		1984	...	...	...	261	62	24
	VOCATIONAL	1975	210	40	19	2 669	969	36
		1980	194	...	...	3 871	1 535	40
		1981	272	...	...	5 870	2 873	49
		1982	...	...	...	4 783	1 994	42
		1983	444	...	...	4 233	2 020	48
		1984	325	...	...	4 213	2 277	54
BURUNDI	TOTAL SECOND LEVEL	1975	731	156	21	13 623	4 204	31
		1980	...	...	...	19 013	*6 079	*32
		1981	...	...	...	20 398	7 456	37
		1983	1 543	331	21	26 415	9 653	37

COUNTRY / PAYS / PAIS	TYPE OF EDUCATION / TYPE D'ENSEIGNEMENT / TIPO DE ENSEÑANZA	YEAR / ANNEE / AÑO	TEACHING STAFF / PERSONNEL ENSEIGNANT / PERSONAL DOCENTE			PUPILS ENROLLED / ELEVES INSCRITS / ALUMNOS MATRICULADOS		
			TOTAL	FEMALE / FEMININ / FEMENINO	% F	TOTAL	FEMALE / FEMININ / FEMENINO	% F
			(1)	(2)	(3)	(4)	(5)	(6)
BURUNDI (CONT)	GENERAL	1975	326	71	22	7 143	1 934	27
		1980	...	...	...	8 899	2 265	25
		1981	521	92	18	10 509	3 342	32
		1983	552	144	26	14 955	5 085	34
	TEACHER TRAINING	1975	302	85	28	5 381	2 245	42
		1980	*412	*84	*20	6 849	*3 213	*47
		1981	420	99	24	6 983	3 346	48
		1983	453	118	26	7 905	3 598	46
	VOCATIONAL	1975	103	–	–	1 099	25	2
		1980	*239	*25	*10	3 265	*601	*18
		1981	...	...	...	2 906	768	26
		1983	538	69	13	3 555	970	27
CAMEROON	TOTAL SECOND LEVEL	1975	4 805	970	20	143 812	46 813	33
		1980	8 926	...	...	234 090	82 720	35
		1981	9 335	1 896	20	248 786	89 553	36
		1982	9 680	1 954	20	273 660	99 080	36
		1983	10 439	2 167	21	296 538	109 895	37
		1984	12 807	...	...	328 423	124 569	38
	GENERAL	1975	3 309	628	19	106 266	33 398	31
		1980	5 944	1 044	18	169 298	57 438	34
		1981	6 227	1 134	18	180 248	62 427	35
		1982	6 482	1 120	17	200 412	70 123	35
		1983	6 795	1 188	17	218 057	78 579	36
		1984	8 381	...	...	238 075	88 303	37
	TEACHER TRAINING	1975	132	22	17	1 284	327	25
		1980	218	47	22	2 118	768	36
		1981	215	55	26	2 282	792	35
		1982	275	58	21	2 953	1 084	37
		1983	388	98	25	3 596	1 493	42
		1984	482	122	25	3 880	1 586	41
	VOCATIONAL	1975	1 364	320	23	36 262	13 088	36
		1980	2 764	...	...	62 674	24 514	39
		1981	2 893	707	24	66 256	26 334	40
		1982	2 923	776	27	70 295	27 873	40
		1983	3 256	881	27	74 885	29 823	40
		1984	3 944	...	...	86 468	34 680	40
CAPE VERDE	TOTAL SECOND LEVEL	1975	...	...	...	...	...	...
		1980	...	...	...	...	...	...
		1981	...	...	...	...	...	...
		1983	...	...	...	...	...	...
	GENERAL	1975	...	...	...	2 025	957	47
		1980	121	...	...	2 733	1 167	43
		1981	144	...	...	3 073	1 250	41
		1983	...	...	...	3 885	1 683	43
	VOCATIONAL	1975	33	...	...	680	...	...
		1980	40	...	...	504	...	...
		1981	43	...	...	504	...	...
		1983	...	...	...	711	272	38
CENTRAL AFRICAN REPUBLIC‡	TOTAL SECOND LEVEL	1975	...	...	...	23 011	4 150	18
		1980	724	114	16	45 211	11 936	26
		1981	...	...	...	50 345	13 123	26
		1982	998	...	...	55 368	...	...
	GENERAL	1975	515	134	26	20 635	3 495	17
		1980	510	62	12	41 811	10 396	25
		1981	547	69	13	44 973	11 355	25
		1982	773	...	...	52 155	13 043	25
	TEACHER TRAINING	1975	47	12	26	404	194	48
		1980	88	21	24	677	195	29
		1981	65	12	18	678	162	24
		1982	74	...	...	695	...	...
	VOCATIONAL	1975	...	...	...	1 972	461	23
		1980	126	31	25	2 723	1 345	49
		1981	...	...	...	4 694	1 606	34
		1982	151	...	...	2 518	1 262	50
CHAD	TOTAL SECOND LEVEL	1975	...	...	...	16 391	...	...
		1984	...	...	...	45 612	6 945	15
	GENERAL	1975	...	...	...	15 128	...	...
		1984	...	...	...	43 053	6 529	15
	TEACHER TRAINING	1975	...	...	...	549	...	...
		1984	59	5	8	200	3	2

COUNTRY / PAYS / PAIS	TYPE OF EDUCATION / TYPE D'ENSEIGNEMENT / TIPO DE ENSEÑANZA	YEAR / ANNEE / AÑO	TEACHING STAFF / PERSONNEL ENSEIGNANT / PERSONAL DOCENTE			PUPILS ENROLLED / ELEVES INSCRITS / ALUMNOS MATRICULADOS		
			TOTAL	FEMALE / FEMININ / FEMENINO	% F	TOTAL	FEMALE / FEMININ / FEMENINO	% F
			(1)	(2)	(3)	(4)	(5)	(6)
CHAD (CONT)	VOCATIONAL	1975	...	...	...	714	...	...
		1984	...	...	...	2 359	413	18
COMOROS	TOTAL SECOND LEVEL	1980	449	91	20	13 798	4 665	34
	GENERAL	1980	432	88	20	13 528	4 597	34
	TEACHER TRAINING	1980	8	2	25	119	29	24
	VOCATIONAL	1980	9	1	11	151	39	26
CONGO	TOTAL SECOND LEVEL	1975	2 413	266	11	102 110	36 782	36
		1980	*5 117	...	...	187 585	77 222	41
		1981	4 899	...	...	190 668	81 327	43
		1982	...	...	...	...	...	...
		1984	5 437	...	...	202 908	86 473	43
	GENERAL	1975	2 042	182	9	94 276	33 720	36
		1980	3 649	...	...	168 718	67 583	40
		1981	3 451	278	8	169 924	70 235	41
		1982	3 996	287	7	189 831	77 333	41
		1984	4 120	...	...	182 294	75 976	42
	TEACHER TRAINING	1975	34	8	24	705	185	26
		1980	229	...	...	1 934	488	25
		1981	187	...	...	1 938	573	30
		1984	193	27	14	1 655	506	31
	VOCATIONAL	1975	337	76	23	7 129	2 877	40
		1980	*1 239	...	...	16 933	9 151	54
		1981	1 261	...	...	18 806	*10 519	*56
		1984	1 124	...	...	18 959	9 991	53
COTE D'IVOIRE‡	TOTAL SECOND LEVEL	1975	...	...	...	126 800	33 427	26
		1980	...	...	...	238 508	71 044	30
		1981	...	...	...	...	...	...
		1982	...	...	...	...	...	...
		1983	...	...	...	...	...	...
	GENERAL	1975	3 247	...	...	102 387	25 207	25
		1980	5 192	...	...	198 190	55 826	28
		1982	...	...	...	217 824	61 342	28
		1983	...	...	...	229 872	65 507	28
	TEACHER TRAINING	1975	...	...	...	1 337	368	28
		1980	...	...	...	2 454	423	17
		1982	...	...	...	1 525	922	60
		1983	...	...	...	1 081	316	29
	VOCATIONAL	1975	...	...	...	23 076	7 852	34
		1980	...	...	...	37 864	14 795	39
		1981	1 947	...	...	38 587	12 591	33
DJIBOUTI	TOTAL SECOND LEVEL	1975	148	57	39	1 994	531	27
		1980	278	...	...	5 156	...	...
		1981	301	...	...	5 542	...	...
		1982	314	...	...	5 929	2 185	37
		1983	334	...	...	6 331	2 282	36
	GENERAL	1975	85	41	48	1 398	443	32
		1980	179	...	...	3 812	...	...
		1981	191	...	...	4 076	...	...
		1982	200	...	...	4 429	1 397	32
		1983	211	...	...	4 791	1 507	31
	TEACHER TRAINING	1975	4	1	25	36	7	19
		1980	11	...	...	65	...	...
		1981	13	...	...	90	*45	*50
		1982	15	...	...	89	34	38
		1983	15	...	...	80	29	36
	VOCATIONAL	1975	59	15	25	560	81	14
		1980	88	...	...	1 279	...	...
		1981	97	...	...	1 376	...	...
		1982	99	...	...	1 411	754	53
		1983	108	...	...	1 460	746	51
EGYPT‡	TOTAL SECOND LEVEL	1975	78 789	20 962	27	2 176 362	744 997	34
		1980	121 999	37 851	31	2 929 168	1 081 504	37
		1981	120 958	38 755	32	3 085 465	1 157 262	38
		1982	142 916	47 510	33	3 089 002	1 199 197	39
		1983	149 712	51 121	34	3 201 703	...	...
	GENERAL	1975	51 740	16 105	31	1 765 853	603 618	34
		1980	83 364	28 858	35	2 238 882	813 072	36
		1981	79 317	28 246	36	2 326 209	858 845	37
		1982	97 182	35 276	36	2 287 796	880 115	38
		1983	101 107	37 609	37	2 436 646	947 459	39

COUNTRY PAYS PAIS	TYPE OF EDUCATION TYPE D'ENSEIGNEMENT TIPO DE ENSEÑANZA	YEAR ANNEE AÑO	TEACHING STAFF / PERSONNEL ENSEIGNANT / PERSONAL DOCENTE TOTAL	 FEMALE FEMININ FEMENINO	 % F	PUPILS ENROLLED / ELEVES INSCRITS / ALUMNOS MATRICULADOS TOTAL	 FEMALE FEMININ FEMENINO	 % F
			(1)	(2)	(3)	(4)	(5)	(6)
EGYPT (CONT)‡	TEACHER TRAINING	1975	2 755	1 048	38	33 014	14 509	44
		1980	4 148	1 766	43	56 377	25 458	45
		1981	4 509	1 989	44	57 355	29 657	52
		1982	5 107	2 254	44	63 429	33 831	53
		1983	5 778	2 538	44	71 545	39 414	55
	VOCATIONAL	1975	24 294	3 809	16	377 495	126 870	34
		1980	34 487	7 227	21	633 909	242 974	38
		1981	37 132	8 520	23	701 901	268 760	38
		1982	40 627	9 980	25	737 777	285 251	39
		1983	42 827	10 974	26	693 512	...	...
EQUATORIAL GUINEA	TOTAL SECOND LEVEL	1975	165	18	11	4 523	751	17
		1979	158	...	...	2 729	...	...
		1982	...	...	...	4 368	...	...
	GENERAL	1975	115	14	12	3 984	709	18
	TEACHER TRAINING	1975	21	4	19	169	42	25
	VOCATIONAL	1975	29	–	–	370	–	–
ETHIOPIA	TOTAL SECOND LEVEL	1975	...	...	...	...	...	...
		1980	...	...	...	...	...	...
		1981	...	...	...	...	...	...
		1982	...	...	...	...	...	...
		1983	...	...	...	...	...	...
	GENERAL	1975	6 791	714	11	230 908	68 904	30
		1980	9 962	1 003	10	426 277	151 542	36
		1981	11 184	1 139	10	487 179	171 607	35
		1982	12 570	1 363	11	535 152	190 478	36
		1983	13 192	1 455	11	579 834	207 542	36
	VOCATIONAL	1983	233	20	9	3 949	1 313	33
GABON	TOTAL SECOND LEVEL	1975	1 016	...	...	22 542	7 870	35
		1980	1 587	387	24	29 406	11 776	40
		1981	1 583	402	25	30 222	11 907	39
		1982	1 743	411	24	32 692	13 035	40
		1983	2 135	523	24	36 160	14 704	41
	GENERAL	1975	812	248	31	19 721	7 174	36
		1980	1 034	285	28	19 998	8 402	42
		1981	1 045	289	28	20 697	8 704	42
		1982	1 161	312	27	22 350	9 492	42
		1983	1 457	395	27	24 651	10 615	43
	TEACHER TRAINING	1975	36	...	...	371	124	33
		1980	181	40	22	3 878	1 810	47
		1981	170	44	26	3 683	1 661	45
		1982	200	36	18	4 263	1 894	44
		1983	232	49	21	4 703	2 088	44
	VOCATIONAL	1975	168	38	23	2 450	572	23
		1980	372	62	17	5 530	1 564	28
		1981	368	69	19	5 842	1 542	26
		1982	382	63	16	6 079	1 649	27
		1983	446	79	18	6 806	2 001	29
GAMBIA	TOTAL SECOND LEVEL	1975	347	89	26	6 618	*1 785	*27
		1980	620	158	25	9 657	2 853	30
		1981	...	...	...	*10 569	...	...
		1982	774	202	26	12 424	3 785	30
		1983	829	208	25	14 430	4 402	31
		1984	959	227	24	15 939	4 813	30
	GENERAL	1975	304	78	26	6 178	1 690	27
		1980	536	144	27	9 081	2 740	30
		1981	587	148	25	10 029	3 046	30
		1982	626	159	25	11 366	3 379	30
		1983	705	171	24	13 390	4 022	30
		1984	780	177	23	14 599	4 325	30
	TEACHER TRAINING	1975	13	5	38	111	45	41
		1980	30	3	10	262	53	20
		1981	–	–	–	–	–	–
		1982	19	4	21	95	20	21
		1983	24	7	29	124	21	17
		1984	30	7	23	323	74	23
	VOCATIONAL	1975	30	6	20	329	*50	*15
		1980	54	11	20	314	60	19
		1981	...	...	...	*540	...	...
		1982	129	39	30	963	386	40
		1983	100	30	30	916	359	39
		1984	149	43	29	1 017	414	41

3.7 Education at the second level: teachers and pupils
Enseignement du second degré: personnel enseignant et élèves
Enseñanza de segundo grado: personal docente y alumnos

COUNTRY / PAYS / PAIS	TYPE OF EDUCATION / TYPE D'ENSEIGNEMENT / TIPO DE ENSEÑANZA	YEAR / ANNEE / AÑO	TEACHING STAFF / PERSONNEL ENSEIGNANT / PERSONAL DOCENTE			PUPILS ENROLLED / ELEVES INSCRITS / ALUMNOS MATRICULADOS		
			TOTAL	FEMALE / FEMININ / FEMENINO	% F	TOTAL	FEMALE / FEMININ / FEMENINO	% F
			(1)	(2)	(3)	(4)	(5)	(6)
GHANA‡	TOTAL SECOND LEVEL	1975	25 142	5 443	22	555 980	212 667	38
		1980	30 694	6 458	21	668 387	254 191	38
		1981	34 195	7 347	21	693 505	263 741	38
		1982	35 045	7 497	21	729 565	273 855	38
		1983	35 907	...	...	753 665	281 719	37
		1984	34 871	...	...	751 192	282 641	38
	GENERAL	1975	23 181	5 139	22	532 520	207 214	39
		1980	29 156	6 213	21	644 305	248 569	39
		1981	*32 668	*7 104	*22	*667 942	*257 814	*39
		1982	*33 369	*7 240	*22	702 764	267 726	38
		1983	34 168	...	...	725 831	275 391	38
		1984	33 017	...	...	723 260	275 714	38
	TEACHER TRAINING	1975	939	201	21	4 541	1 932	43
		1980	881	194	22	11 600	4 698	41
		1981	907	200	22	12 189	4 937	41
		1982	935	206	22	12 523	5 072	41
		1983	952	210	22	12 893	5 222	41
		1984	822	...	...	14 880	6 026	40
	VOCATIONAL	1975	1 022	103	10	18 919	3 521	19
		1980	657	51	8	12 482	924	7
		1981	620	43	7	13 374	990	7
		1982	741	51	7	14 278	1 057	7
		1983	787	54	7	14 941	1 106	7
		1984	1 032	...	...	13 052	901	7
GUINEA‡	TOTAL SECOND LEVEL	1975	...	...	...	...	...	...
		1980	...	...	...	98 305	27 599	28
		1981	...	...	...	93 660	26 282	28
		1982	5 109	492	10	94 848	25 968	27
		1983	...	...	...	97 719	27 286	28
		1984	...	...	...	101 121	27 157	27
	GENERAL	1975	2 738	133	5	69 908	18 064	26
		1980	3 520	...	...	89 900	24 942	28
		1981	3 833	...	...	86 285	23 897	28
		1982	4 365	444	10	87 055	23 296	27
		1983	5 091	465	9	89 756	24 404	27
		1984	...	...	...	93 815	24 433	26
	TEACHER TRAINING	1981	...	...	...	1 325	...	...
		1982	103	22	21	1 222	469	38
		1983	...	...	...	997	462	46
		1984	115	10	9	890	407	46
	VOCATIONAL	1975	...	...	...	1 260	150	12
		1981	...	...	...	6 050	...	...
		1982	641	26	4	6 571	2 203	34
		1983	...	...	...	6 966	2 420	35
		1984	714	39	5	6 416	2 317	36
GUINEA-BISSAU	TOTAL SECOND LEVEL	1975	213	...	...	2 153	660	31
		1980	462	99	21	4 757	939	20
		1981	465	104	22	6 294	1 107	18
		1982	...	...	...	8 432	1 678	20
		1983	795	118	15	9 634	1 818	19
	GENERAL	1975	161	...	...	1 720	540	31
		1980	387	78	20	4 068	876	22
		1981	388	84	22	5 631	1 064	19
		1982	543	80	15	7 667	1 628	21
		1983	678	88	13	8 804	1 755	20
	TEACHER TRAINING	1975	12	...	...	90	43	48
		1980	46	20	43	412	25	6
		1981	45	18	40	480	32	7
		1982	59	21	36	546	43	8
		1983	54	23	43	578	56	10
	VOCATIONAL	1975	40	5	13	343	77	22
		1980	29	1	3	277	38	14
		1981	32	2	6	183	11	6
		1982	...	...	...	219	7	3
		1983	63	7	11	252	7	3
KENYA‡	TOTAL SECOND LEVEL	1975	9 730	...	...	240 969	84 782	35
		1980	17 081	...	...	428 023	174 281	41
		1981	17 809	...	...	422 446	172 786	41
		1982	18 103	...	...	449 829	182 394	41
		1983	20 381	...	...	517 033	208 925	40
		1984	...	...	...	...	...	...

COUNTRY / PAYS / PAIS	TYPE OF EDUCATION / TYPE D'ENSEIGNEMENT / TIPO DE ENSEÑANZA	YEAR / ANNEE / AÑO	TEACHING STAFF / PERSONNEL ENSEIGNANT / PERSONAL DOCENTE			PUPILS ENROLLED / ELEVES INSCRITS / ALUMNOS MATRICULADOS		
			TOTAL	FEMALE / FEMININ / FEMENINO	% F	TOTAL	FEMALE / FEMININ / FEMENINO	% F
			(1)	(2)	(3)	(4)	(5)	(6)
KENYA (CONT)‡	GENERAL	1975	...	...	...	226 835	81 529	36
		1980	15 916	...	...	407 322	...	...
		1981	16 706	...	...	400 727	...	...
		1982	16 848	...	...	429 225	...	...
		1983	18 960	...	...	493 710	199 550	40
		1984	19 368	...	...	510 943	214 596	42
	TEACHER TRAINING	1975	541	170	31	8 666	3 253	38
		1980	732	...	...	12 126	4 880	40
		1981	694	...	...	12 596	5 269	42
		1982	720	...	...	11 405	4 709	41
		1983	919	...	...	13 792	5 386	39
		1984	1 027	...	...	15 413	6 112	40
	VOCATIONAL	1975	...	...	...	5 468	–	–
		1980	433	...	...	8 575	...	...
		1981	409	...	...	9 123	...	...
		1982	535	...	...	9 199	...	...
		1983	502	...	...	9 531	3 989	42
LESOTHO	TOTAL SECOND LEVEL	1975	740	387	52	16 462	9 154	56
		1980	1 244	591	48	24 591	14 615	59
		1981	1 372	708	52	27 331	16 393	60
		1982	1 495	754	50	28 730	17 103	60
		1983	1 699	850	50	32 619	19 707	60
	GENERAL	1975	605	302	50	15 611	8 552	55
		1980	1 122	534	48	23 355	13 922	60
		1981	1 248	662	53	25 997	15 608	60
		1982	1 368	703	51	27 799	16 637	60
		1983	1 552	789	51	31 422	19 095	61
	TEACHER TRAINING	1975	69	46	67	304	221	73
		1980	–	–	–	–	–	–
		1981	–	–	–	–	–	–
		1982	–	–	–	–	–	–
		1983	–	–	–	–	–	–
	VOCATIONAL	1975	66	39	59	547	381	70
		1980	122	57	47	1 236	693	56
		1981	124	46	37	1 334	785	59
		1982	127	51	40	931	466	50
		1983	147	61	41	1 197	612	51
LIBERIA‡	TOTAL SECOND LEVEL	1975	...	...	...	34 151	8 498	25
		1980	...	...	...	54 623	15 343	28
	GENERAL	1975	...	...	...	32 978	8 331	25
		1980	1 129	...	...	51 666	14 632	28
	TEACHER TRAINING	1975	53	12	23	322	55	17
		1980	...	...	...	635	84	13
	VOCATIONAL	1975	...	...	...	851	112	13
		1980	...	...	...	2 322	627	27
LIBYAN ARAB JAMAHIRIYA	TOTAL SECOND LEVEL	1975	11 819	...	...	166 122	55 722	34
		1980	24 323	5 750	24	296 197	118 953	40
		1982	30 673	8 483	28	340 703	141 077	41
	GENERAL	1975	9 464	1 287	14	140 486	43 464	31
		1980	20 327	4 942	24	253 201	98 134	39
		1982	25 056	7 637	30	280 208	113 522	41
	TEACHER TRAINING	1975	1 832	437	24	20 748	12 258	59
		1980	2 488	631	25	26 988	16 838	62
		1982	2 730	604	22	32 132	21 303	66
	VOCATIONAL	1975	523	...	...	4 888	–	–
		1980	1 508	177	12	16 008	3 981	25
		1982	2 887	242	8	28 363	6 252	22
MADAGASCAR‡	TOTAL SECOND LEVEL	1975	...	...	...	...	...	...
		1980	...	...	...	...	...	...
		1981	...	...	...	...	...	...
		1982	...	...	...	...	...	...
		1983	...	...	...	530 021	...	...
		1984	...	...	...	...	...	...
	GENERAL	1975	...	...	...	78 954	32 146	41
		1983	...	...	...	518 538	...	...
		1984	10 383	...	...	288 543	122 529	42
	TEACHER TRAINING	1980	157	...	...	1 619	...	...
		1981	168	...	...	1 753	...	...
		1982	166	...	...	1 738	...	...
		1983	...	...	...	1 837	...	...

COUNTRY / PAYS / PAIS	TYPE OF EDUCATION / TYPE D'ENSEIGNEMENT / TIPO DE ENSEÑANZA	YEAR / ANNEE / AÑO	TEACHING STAFF / PERSONNEL ENSEIGNANT / PERSONAL DOCENTE			PUPILS ENROLLED / ELEVES INSCRITS / ALUMNOS MATRICULADOS		
			TOTAL	FEMALE FEMININ FEMENINO	% F	TOTAL	FEMALE FEMININ FEMENINO	% F
			(1)	(2)	(3)	(4)	(5)	(6)
MADAGASCAR (CONT)‡	VOCATIONAL	1975	858	...	...	7 504	...	...
		1980	1 121	...	...	9 393	1 067	11
		1981	1 153	...	...	8 291	...	...
		1982	1 125	...	...	8 987	...	...
		1983	1 023	...	...	9 646	...	...
		1984	1 136	...	...	9 204	2 274	25
MALAWI	TOTAL SECOND LEVEL	1975	794	...	...	15 018	4 117	27
		1980	868	...	...	18 653	5 248	28
		1981	1 000	...	...	19 948	5 654	28
		1982	1 027	...	...	20 346	5 720	28
		1983	1 115	...	...	22 767	6 451	28
		1984	1 202	...	...	24 843	7 426	30
	GENERAL	1975	748	...	...	14 489	4 117	28
		1980	834	...	...	18 006	5 248	29
		1981	952	...	...	19 329	5 654	29
		1982	980	...	...	19 832	5 720	29
		1983	1 072	...	...	22 245	6 451	29
		1984	1 150	...	...	24 343	7 426	31
	TEACHER TRAINING		–	–	–	–	–	–
	VOCATIONAL	1975	46	–	–	529	–	–
		1980	34	–	–	647	–	–
		1981	48	–	–	619	–	–
		1982	47	–	–	514	–	–
		1983	43	–	–	522	–	–
		1984	52	–	–	500	–	–
MALI	TOTAL SECOND LEVEL	1975	...	...	...	55 444	14 287	26
		1979	...	...	...	78 707	...	...
		1981	...	...	...	75 819	21 172	28
		1982	...	...	...	68 732	18 945	28
	GENERAL	1975	2 567	452	18	48 488	12 358	25
		1979	...	...	...	70 514	...	...
		1981	...	...	...	66 669	18 308	27
		1982	3 870	...	...	64 148	18 412	29
	TEACHER TRAINING	1975	...	...	...	1 948	359	18
		1979	...	...	...	2 711	508	19
		1981	...	...	...	4 313	737	17
		1982	...	...	...	2 444	211	9
	VOCATIONAL	1975	...	...	...	*5 008	*1 570	*31
		1979	...	...	...	5 482	1 895	35
		1981	...	...	...	4 837	2 127	44
		1982	...	...	...	2 140	322	15
MAURITANIA‡	TOTAL SECOND LEVEL	1975	...	...	...	...	...	...
		1980	...	...	...	22 102	4 528	20
		1982	...	...	...	...	...	...
	GENERAL	1975	...	...	...	6 571	...	...
		1980	646	54	8	20 248	4 291	21
		1982	864	...	...	25 700	6 238	24
	TEACHER TRAINING	1975	...	...	...	160	...	...
		1980	51	6	12	850	164	19
		1982	57	...	...	1 027	253	25
	VOCATIONAL	1980	...	...	...	1 004	73	7
MAURITIUS	TOTAL SECOND LEVEL	1975	2 177	...	...	65 113	28 869	44
		1980	...	...	...	81 926	39 602	48
		1981	...	...	...	79 534	37 880	48
		1982	...	...	...	77 779	36 795	47
		1983	...	...	...	77 838	36 605	47
		1984	...	...	...	74 795	34 690	46
	GENERAL	1975	2 065	...	...	63 492	28 195	44
		1980	3 101	*1 220	*39	81 656	39 542	48
		1981	3 121	*1 226	*39	79 314	37 820	48
		1982	3 175	*1 247	*39	77 442	36 723	47
		1983	3 010	*1 193	*40	77 188	36 464	47
		1984	3 563	*1 413	*40	73 961	34 405	47
	TEACHER TRAINING	1975	19	8	42	589	245	42
		1980	–	–	–	–	–	–
		1981	–	–	–	–	–	–
		1982	–	–	–	–	–	–
		1983	–	–	–	–	–	–
		1984	–	–	–	–	–	–

COUNTRY / PAYS / PAIS	TYPE OF EDUCATION / TYPE D'ENSEIGNEMENT / TIPO DE ENSEÑANZA	YEAR / ANNEE / AÑO	TEACHING STAFF / PERSONNEL ENSEIGNANT / PERSONAL DOCENTE			PUPILS ENROLLED / ELEVES INSCRITS / ALUMNOS MATRICULADOS		
			TOTAL	FEMALE / FEMININ / FEMENINO	% F	TOTAL	FEMALE / FEMININ / FEMENINO	% F
			(1)	(2)	(3)	(4)	(5)	(6)
MAURITIUS (CONT)	VOCATIONAL	1975	93	26	28	1 032	429	42
		1980	...	...	...	270	60	22
		1981	...	...	...	220	60	27
		1982	...	...	...	337	72	21
		1983	...	...	...	650	141	22
		1984	...	...	...	834	285	34
MOROCCO‡	TOTAL SECOND LEVEL	1975	*20 099	...	...	486 173	...	...
		1980	36 526	...	...	797 110	300 665	38
		1981	42 517	11 174	26	888 123	341 623	38
		1982	46 619	12 775	27	968 327	379 728	39
		1983	53 457	14 814	28	1 046 136	414 152	40
		1984	...	...	...	1 130 185	446 186	39
	GENERAL	1975	19 613	5 381	27	468 870	160 119	34
		1980	...	...	...	787 004	298 344	38
		1981	...	...	...	872 021	341 623	39
		1982	...	...	...	948 232	370 373	39
		1983	...	...	...	1 022 107	401 776	39
		1984	52 920	15 365	29	1 103 663	432 066	39
	TEACHER TRAINING	1975	*486	...	...	3 953	1 716	43
		1980	–	–	–	–	–	–
		1981	–	–	–	–	–	–
		1982	–	–	–	–	–	–
		1983	–	–	–	–	–	–
		1984	–	–	–	–	–	–
	VOCATIONAL	1975	...	...	...	13 350	...	...
		1980	...	...	...	10 106	2 321	23
		1981	...	...	...	*16 102	...	...
		1982	...	...	...	20 095	9 355	47
		1983	...	...	...	24 029	12 376	52
		1984	...	...	...	26 522	14 120	53
MOZAMBIQUE‡	TOTAL SECOND LEVEL	1976	...	...	...	46 656	14 905	32
		1980	...	...	...	...	...	...
		1981	3 388	752	22	107 849	30 606	28
		1982	3 363	709	21	108 916	32 075	29
		1983	3 519	666	19	121 033	36 659	30
	GENERAL	1976	...	...	...	37 255	...	...
		1980	2 151	590	27	90 041	25 979	29
		1981	2 211	576	26	89 835	27 693	31
		1982	2 361	572	24	93 224	29 255	31
		1983	2 523	552	22	105 395	33 915	32
	TEACHER TRAINING	1976	–	–	–	–	–	–
		1981	270	44	16	4 236	602	14
		1982	199	13	7	3 659	599	16
		1983	223	12	5	3 594	542	15
	VOCATIONAL	1976	...	...	...	9 401	...	...
		1980	680	102	15	12 704	2 127	17
		1981	907	132	15	13 778	2 311	17
		1982	803	124	15	12 033	2 221	18
		1983	773	102	13	12 044	2 202	18
NIGER‡	TOTAL SECOND LEVEL	1975	637	146	23	14 462	3 983	28
		1980	1 284	267	21	38 861	11 334	29
		1981	...	...	...	44 788	...	...
		1982	...	...	...	45 094	...	...
		1983	...	...	...	47 188	...	...
	GENERAL	1975	571	137	24	13 621	3 785	28
		1980	1 164	255	22	36 510	10 765	29
		1981	...	...	...	42 967	...	...
		1982	...	...	...	42 164	...	...
		1983	...	...	...	44 650	...	...
	TEACHER TRAINING	1975	41	4	10	608	184	30
		1980	80	6	8	1 830	525	29
		1981	...	...	...	1 062	373	35
		1982	...	...	...	2 355	...	...
		1983	...	...	...	1 593	...	...
	VOCATIONAL	1975	25	5	20	233	14	6
		1980	40	6	15	521	44	8
		1981	...	...	...	759	...	...
		1982	...	...	...	575	...	...
		1983	...	...	...	945	...	...
NIGERIA	TOTAL SECOND LEVEL	1975	...	...	...	854 785	...	...
		1980	81 492	16 326	20	2 345 604	821 784	35
		1981	89 076	...	...	2 880 280	832 752	29
		1982	108 664	...	...	3 393 186	867 142	26
		1983	98 487	...	...	3 561 207	...	...

COUNTRY / PAYS / PAIS	TYPE OF EDUCATION / TYPE D'ENSEIGNEMENT / TIPO DE ENSEÑANZA	YEAR / ANNEE / AÑO	TEACHING STAFF / PERSONNEL ENSEIGNANT / PERSONAL DOCENTE: TOTAL	FEMALE / FEMININ / FEMENINO	% F	PUPILS ENROLLED / ELEVES INSCRITS / ALUMNOS MATRICULADOS: TOTAL	FEMALE / FEMININ / FEMENINO	% F
			(1)	(2)	(3)	(4)	(5)	(6)
NIGERIA (CONT)	GENERAL	1975	...	...	...	704 917	...	...
		1980	61 755	4 928	8	1 995 417	708 832	36
		1981	77 822	...	...	2 503 952	732 466	29
		1982	93 054	...	...	3 009 751	798 447	27
		1983	82 749	...	...	3 169 624	...	...
	TEACHER TRAINING	1975	...	...	...	123 627	...	...
		1980	8 952	7 289	81	282 244	101 390	36
		1981	8 080	...	...	292 429	91 604	31
		1982	9 946	...	...	296 439	60 973	21
		1983	9 932	...	...	303 737	...	...
	VOCATIONAL	1975	...	...	...	26 241	...	...
		1980	10 785	4 109	38	67 943	11 562	17
		1981	3 174	...	...	83 899	8 682	10
		1982	5 664	...	...	86 996	7 722	9
		1983	5 806	...	...	87 846	...	...
REUNION‡	TOTAL SECOND LEVEL	1975	2 363	...	...	50 467	27 954	55
		1980	...	...	...	62 613	...	...
		1981	3 618	1 601	44	65 425	35 853	55
		1982	3 685	1 604	44	67 353	36 618	54
		1983	3 713	1 641	44	68 391	36 879	54
	GENERAL	1975	...	...	...	44 524	25 134	56
		1981	2 889	1 345	47	45 131	26 309	58
		1982	2 939	1 347	46	45 036	26 358	59
		1983	...	...	...	45 602	26 445	58
	TEACHER TRAINING		–	–	–	–	–	–
	VOCATIONAL	1975	...	...	...	5 943	2 820	47
		1981	729	256	35	20 294	9 544	47
		1982	746	257	34	22 317	10 260	46
		1983	...	...	...	22 789	10 434	46
RWANDA	TOTAL SECOND LEVEL	1975	752	194	26	12 046	3 978	33
		1980	887	234	26	10 667	3 718	35
		1981	984	261	27	12 505	4 478	36
		1982	1 037	248	24	14 230	5 148	36
		1983	1 082	254	23	14 761	4 997	34
	GENERAL	1975	...	...	...	8 704	2 680	31
		1980	...	...	...	5 022	1 388	28
		1981	...	...	...	4 156	807	19
		1982	...	...	...	5 330	1 065	20
		1983	...	...	...	5 488	1 030	19
	TEACHER TRAINING	1975	...	...	...	1 552	665	43
		1980	...	...	...	3 580	1 606	45
		1981	...	...	...	5 124	2 465	48
		1982	...	...	...	5 362	2 622	49
		1983	...	...	...	5 433	2 438	45
	VOCATIONAL	1975	...	...	...	1 790	633	35
		1980	...	...	...	2 065	724	35
		1981	...	...	...	3 225	1 206	37
		1982	...	...	...	3 538	1 461	41
		1983	...	...	...	3 840	1 529	40
ST. HELENA	TOTAL SECOND LEVEL	1975	...	...	...	524	281	54
		1980	47	35	74	638	304	48
		1981	68	60	88	652	309	47
		1982	48	35	73	602	282	47
		1983	43	30	70	555	282	51
	GENERAL	1975	...	...	...	509	276	54
		1980	40	32	80	601	295	49
		1981	...	...	...	604	299	50
		1982	39	31	79	561	277	49
		1983	33	26	79	507	274	54
	TEACHER TRAINING	1975	...	...	...	5	5	100
		1980	4	3	75	5	5	100
		1981	6	4	67	10	10	100
		1982	7	4	57	10	4	40
		1983	7	4	57	17	8	47
	VOCATIONAL	1975	...	...	...	10	–	–
		1980	3	–	–	32	4	13
		1981	...	–	–	38	–	–
		1982	2	–	–	31	1	3
		1983	3	–	–	31	–	–

COUNTRY / PAYS / PAIS	TYPE OF EDUCATION / TYPE D'ENSEIGNEMENT / TIPO DE ENSEÑANZA	YEAR / ANNEE / AÑO	TEACHING STAFF / PERSONNEL ENSEIGNANT / PERSONAL DOCENTE: TOTAL	FEMALE / FEMININ / FEMENINO	% F	PUPILS ENROLLED / ELEVES INSCRITS / ALUMNOS MATRICULADOS: TOTAL	FEMALE / FEMININ / FEMENINO	% F
			(1)	(2)	(3)	(4)	(5)	(6)
SAO TOME AND PRINCIPE	TOTAL SECOND LEVEL	1975	...	...	...	4 010	...	...
		1980	...	...	...	3 815	...	...
		1981	...	...	...	4 878	...	...
		1982	...	...	...	6 303	...	...
		1983	325	...	...	6 436	...	...
	GENERAL	1975	...	...	...	3 776	...	...
		1980	...	...	...	3 685	...	...
		1981	273	...	...	4 698	2 119	45
		1982	268	...	...	6 160	2 777	45
		1983	300	...	...	6 195	...	...
	TEACHER TRAINING		–	–	–	–	–	–
	VOCATIONAL	1975	...	...	...	234	...	...
		1980	...	...	...	130	...	...
		1981	...	...	...	180	...	...
		1982	...	...	...	143	...	...
		1983	25	...	...	241	...	...
SENEGAL‡	TOTAL SECOND LEVEL	1975	...	...	...	...	...	...
		1980	4 302	...	...	95 604	31 307	33
		1981	4 834	...	...	103 821	34 976	34
		1982	...	...	...	109 937	36 356	33
		1983	4 980	767	15	113 561	37 204	33
	GENERAL	1975	...	...	...	69 590	...	...
		1980	...	...	...	83 431	28 133	34
		1981	...	...	...	91 081	31 153	34
		1982	3 053	447	15	99 542	33 779	34
		1983	4 380	680	16	103 510	34 646	33
	TEACHER TRAINING	1980	...	...	...	2 241	724	32
		1981	...	...	...	1 920	610	32
		1982	83	4	5	735	114	16
		1983	97	13	13	612	97	16
	VOCATIONAL	1975	...	...	...	8 182	...	...
		1980	...	...	...	9 932	2 450	25
		1981	...	...	...	10 820	3 213	30
		1982	...	...	...	9 660	2 463	25
		1983	*503	*74	*15	9 439	2 461	26
SEYCHELLES‡	TOTAL SECOND LEVEL	1975	177	102	58	3 778	2 125	56
		1980	127	47	37	924	*438	*47
		1982	213	90	42	3 168	1 793	57
		1983	...	...	...	3 567	1 896	53
		1984	290	...	...	3 889	1 948	50
		1985	364	107	29	3 975	1 997	50
	GENERAL	1975	145	90	62	3 465	1 901	55
		1980	67	30	45	478	226	47
		1982	109	37	34	2 362	1 189	50
		1983	91	...	...	2 603	1 308	50
		1984	147	...	...	2 605	1 278	49
		1985	193	54	28	2 435	1 233	51
	TEACHER TRAINING	1975	–	–	–	–	–	–
		1980	–	–	–	–	–	–
		1982	20	12	60	172	158	92
		1983	23	...	...	210	189	90
		1984	25	...	...	226	...	...
		1985	22	14	64	170	148	87
	VOCATIONAL	1975	32	12	38	313	224	72
		1980	60	17	28	446	*212	*48
		1982	84	41	49	634	446	70
		1983	...	...	...	754	399	53
		1984	118	...	...	1 058	...	...
		1985	149	39	26	1 370	616	45
SIERRA LEONE	TOTAL SECOND LEVEL	1975	2 596	901	35	50 478	15 991	32
		1980	...	...	...	...	...	...
		1981	...	...	...	...	...	...
		1982	...	...	...	...	...	...
	GENERAL	1975	2 378	854	36	48 534	15 589	32
		1980	2 985	...	...	64 808	19 374	30
		1981	3 282	...	...	72 367	22 232	31
		1982	3 828	789	21	81 759	26 048	32
	TEACHER TRAINING	1975	120	34	28	1 145	355	31
		1980	...	...	...	1 500	523	35
		1981	...	...	...	1 788	676	38
		1982	...	...	...	2 130	840	39
	VOCATIONAL	1975	98	13	13	799	47	6

COUNTRY / PAYS / PAIS	TYPE OF EDUCATION / TYPE D'ENSEIGNEMENT / TIPO DE ENSEÑANZA	YEAR / ANNEE / AÑO	TEACHING STAFF / PERSONNEL ENSEIGNANT / PERSONAL DOCENTE			PUPILS ENROLLED / ELEVES INSCRITS / ALUMNOS MATRICULADOS		
			TOTAL	FEMALE / FEMININ / FEMENINO	% F	TOTAL	FEMALE / FEMININ / FEMENINO	% F
			(1)	(2)	(3)	(4)	(5)	(6)
SOMALIA‡	TOTAL SECOND LEVEL	1975	1 529	130	9	31 857	7 566	24
		1980	2 089	153	7	43 841	11 689	27
		1981	2 850	247	9	56 693	16 921	30
		1982	3 671	326	9	63 942	20 934	33
		1983	3 018	226	7	63 255	21 434	34
	GENERAL	1975	1 161	102	9	26 611	6 119	23
		1980	1 345	138	10	33 132	9 294	28
		1981	2 008	166	8	43 823	13 741	31
		1982	2 832	238	8	51 927	17 433	34
		1983	2 201	151	7	53 591	18 685	35
	TEACHER TRAINING	1975	181	–	–	3 422	1 128	33
		1980	119	14	12	3 005	853	28
		1981	164	25	15	3 376	1 263	37
		1982	173	27	16	2 960	1 482	50
		1983	133	16	12	1 836	1 005	55
	VOCATIONAL	1975	187	28	15	1 824	319	17
		1980	625	1		7 704	1 542	20
		1981	678	56	8	9 494	1 917	20
		1982	666	61	9	9 055	2 019	22
		1983	684	59	9	7 828	1 744	22
SUDAN	TOTAL SECOND LEVEL	1975	13 166	...	...	281 839	86 806	31
		1980	18 831	...	...	384 194	141 736	37
		1981	18 689	...	...	426 932	174 778	41
		1982	20 600	...	...	455 969	182 155	40
		1983	20 176	5 675	28	507 206	209 225	41
	GENERAL	1975	12 097	2 528	21	268 120	*84 196	*31
		1980	17 452	4 487	26	362 992	136 016	37
		1981	17 105	4 497	26	403 236	167 988	42
		1982	18 812	5 159	27	427 954	173 167	40
		1983	18 644	5 331	29	474 927	200 043	42
	TEACHER TRAINING	1975	420	...	...	4 723	1 993	42
		1980	695	180	26	5 657	2 429	43
		1981	738	207	28	6 566	2 616	40
		1982	730	...	...	6 722	2 858	43
		1983	545	200	37	6 067	2 752	45
	VOCATIONAL	1975	649	–	–	8 996	617	7
		1980	684	...	...	15 545	3 291	21
		1981	846	...	...	17 130	4 174	24
		1982	1 058	...	...	21 293	6 130	29
		1983	987	144	15	26 212	6 430	25
SWAZILAND	TOTAL SECOND LEVEL	1975	...	...	...	16 876	...	...
		1980	...	...	...	23 665	...	...
		1981	...	...	...	...	...	...
		1982	...	...	...	...	...	...
		1983	...	...	...	...	...	...
		1984	...	...	...	...	...	...
	GENERAL	1975	739	291	39	16 227	7 378	45
		1980	1 292	624	48	23 198	11 370	49
		1981	1 433	657	46	24 826	12 234	49
		1982	1 501	694	46	26 469	13 041	49
		1983	1 518	705	46	27 801	13 787	50
		1984	1 569	743	47	28 833	14 163	49
	TEACHER TRAINING	1975	...	...	...	205	168	82
		1980	...	...	...	283	218	77
		1981	...	...	...	286	...	...
		1982	...	...	...	307	...	...
		1983	...	...	...	723	...	...
		1984	...	...	...	719	...	...
	VOCATIONAL	1975	...	...	...	444	...	...
		1980	...	...	...	184	...	...
TOGO‡	TOTAL SECOND LEVEL	1975	1 634	*268	*16	64 404	15 330	24
		1980	...	...	...	...	...	...
		1981	...	...	...	130 231	33 053	25
		1982	...	...	...	119 106	29 804	25
		1983	...	...	...	101 989	25 084	25
		1984	...	...	...	90 990	21 884	24
	GENERAL	1975	1 358	204	15	59 162	13 760	23
		1980	...	...	...	125 122	...	...
		1981	3 982	508	13	122 925	30 779	25
		1982	4 146	558	13	112 861	28 108	25
		1983	4 200	530	13	95 941	23 664	25
		1984	3 985	519	13	85 745	20 557	24

COUNTRY / PAYS / PAIS	TYPE OF EDUCATION / TYPE D'ENSEIGNEMENT / TIPO DE ENSEÑANZA	YEAR / ANNEE / AÑO	TEACHING STAFF / PERSONNEL ENSEIGNANT / PERSONAL DOCENTE — TOTAL	FEMALE / FEMININ / FEMENINO	% F	PUPILS ENROLLED / ELEVES INSCRITS / ALUMNOS MATRICULADOS — TOTAL	FEMALE / FEMININ / FEMENINO	% F
			(1)	(2)	(3)	(4)	(5)	(6)
TOGO (CONT)‡	TEACHER TRAINING	1975	25	*5	*20	124	26	21
		1981	38	3	8	374	120	32
		1982	44	3	7	308	112	36
		1983	30	4	13	421	86	20
		1984	...	...	...	58	58	100
	VOCATIONAL	1975	251	59	24	5 118	1 544	30
		1981	...	...	...	6 932	2 154	31
		1982	...	...	...	5 937	1 584	27
		1983	...	...	...	5 627	1 334	24
		1984	303	43	14	5 187	1 269	24
TUNISIA‡	TOTAL SECOND LEVEL	1975	8 769	2 475	28	201 845	67 971	34
		1980	14 328	4 091	29	293 351	107 074	37
		1981	16 186	4 789	30	331 606	122 853	37
		1982	18 521	5 645	30	355 161	*133 611	*38
		1983	20 493	6 332	31	387 445	148 733	38
		1984	22 781	7 053	31	419 337	166 293	40
	GENERAL	1975	...	...	...	144 812	49 889	34
		1980	...	...	...	209 060	80 493	39
		1981	...	...	...	243 879	94 646	39
		1982	...	...	...	267 477	*104 561	*39
		1983	...	...	...	299 514	118 340	40
		1984	...	...	...	332 683	134 205	40
	TEACHER TRAINING	1975	...	...	...	1 059	554	52
		1980	148	36	24	4 101	2 557	62
		1981	164	43	26	4 062	2 624	65
		1982	202	54	27	3 969	2 558	64
		1983	219	60	27	3 962	2 635	67
		1984	226	62	27	4 013	2 789	69
	VOCATIONAL	1975	...	...	...	55 974	17 528	31
		1980	...	...	...	80 190	24 024	30
		1981	...	...	...	83 665	25 583	31
		1982	...	...	...	83 715	26 492	32
		1983	...	...	...	83 969	27 758	33
		1984	...	...	...	82 641	29 299	35
UGANDA‡	TOTAL SECOND LEVEL	1975	2 599	...	...	55 263	14 357	26
		1980	...	...	...	...	...	...
		1981	4 382	837	19	94 614	28 995	31
		1982	7 022	958	14	145 389	47 977	33
	GENERAL	1975	1 994	392	20	45 871	12 112	26
		1980	3 202	...	...	73 092	*21 123	*29
		1981	3 732	744	20	83 000	25 261	30
		1982	6 287	*878	*14	132 051	43 799	33
	TEACHER TRAINING	1975	330	...	...	6 096	2 160	35
		1981	408	92	23	8 157	3 476	43
		1982	496	79	16	9 157	3 881	42
	VOCATIONAL	1975	275	*1		3 296	85	3
		1981	242	1		3 457	258	7
		1982	239	1		4 181	297	7
UNITED REPUBLIC OF TANZANIA‡	TOTAL SECOND LEVEL	1975	3 218	...	...	62 031	19 439	31
		1980	...	...	...	78 715	...	...
		1981	4 006	1 074	27	76 411	26 312	34
		1982	4 162	...	...	78 655	26 960	34
		1983	...	...	...	81 787	28 614	35
	GENERAL	1975	2 606	740	28	52 290	15 208	29
		1980	...	...	...	67 292	22 388	33
		1981	3 262	924	28	67 602	23 015	34
		1982	3 362	...	...	69 145	23 835	34
		1983	2 213	...	...	71 219	24 947	35
	TEACHER TRAINING	1975	612	...	...	9 741	4 231	43
		1980	...	...	...	11 423	...	...
		1981	581	139	24	7 449	3 161	42
		1982	627	...	...	8 101	2 972	37
		1983	786	...	...	9 404	3 516	37
	VOCATIONAL	1981	163	11	7	1 360	136	10
		1982	173	...	...	1 409	153	11
		1983	181	...	...	1 164	151	13
ZAIRE	TOTAL SECOND LEVEL	1975	...	...	...	511 481	135 341	26
		1980	...	...	...	1 207 112	327 587	27
		1981	...	...	...	1 461 101	401 679	27
		1982	...	...	...	1 771 177	494 292	28
		1983	43 459	...	...	2 151 900	610 374	28

3.7 Education at the second level: teachers and pupils
Enseignement du second degré: personnel enseignant et élèves
Enseñanza de segundo grado: personal docente y alumnos

COUNTRY / PAYS / PAIS	TYPE OF EDUCATION / TYPE D'ENSEIGNEMENT / TIPO DE ENSEÑANZA	YEAR / ANNEE / AÑO	TEACHING STAFF / PERSONNEL ENSEIGNANT / PERSONAL DOCENTE: TOTAL	TEACHING STAFF: FEMALE / FEMININ / FEMENINO	TEACHING STAFF: % F	PUPILS ENROLLED / ELEVES INSCRITS / ALUMNOS MATRICULADOS: TOTAL	PUPILS ENROLLED: FEMALE / FEMININ / FEMENINO	PUPILS ENROLLED: % F
			(1)	(2)	(3)	(4)	(5)	(6)
ZAIRE (CONT)	GENERAL	1975	...	...	...	360 888	89 484	25
		1980	...	...	...	881 192	239 138	27
		1981	...	...	...	1 066 604	293 226	27
		1982	...	...	...	1 292 959	360 833	28
		1983	...	...	...	1 570 887	445 573	28
	TEACHER TRAINING	1975	...	...	...	95 688	27 607	29
		1980	...	...	...	205 209	58 966	29
		1981	...	...	...	248 387	72 302	29
		1982	...	...	...	301 100	88 973	30
		1983	...	...	...	365 823	109 867	30
	VOCATIONAL	1975	...	...	...	54 905	18 250	33
		1980	...	...	...	120 711	29 483	24
		1981	...	...	...	146 110	36 151	25
		1982	...	...	...	177 118	44 486	25
		1983	...	...	...	215 190	54 934	26
ZAMBIA	TOTAL SECOND LEVEL	1975	...	...	...	77 672	...	...
		1980	4 882	...	...	102 019	35 718	35
		1981	...	...	...	104 652	37 230	36
		1982	...	...	...	110 416	39 085	35
		1983	...	...	...	...	...	...
		1984	...	...	...	...	...	...
	GENERAL	1975	3 202	1 042	33	73 049	25 066	34
		1980	4 334	...	...	95 771	33 309	35
		1981	...	...	...	98 862	34 866	35
		1982	4 602	...	...	104 859	37 237	36
		1983	...	...	...	*115 088	*41 324	*36
	TEACHER TRAINING	1975	220	49	22	2 246	1 022	46
		1980	313	60	19	3 742	1 750	47
		1981	341	62	18	3 598	1 677	47
		1982	...	...	...	3 241	1 256	39
		1983	...	...	...	3 555	1 390	39
		1984	...	...	...	3 770	1 517	40
	VOCATIONAL	1975	...	...	...	2 377	...	...
		1980	235	7	3	2 506	659	26
		1981	...	...	...	2 192	687	31
		1982	...	...	...	2 316	592	26
ZIMBABWE‡	TOTAL SECOND LEVEL	1975	3 788	1 526	40	70 005	29 052	42
		1980	3 782	...	...	74 746	...	...
		1981	6 148	...	...	149 018	62 661	42
		1982	8 549	...	...	227 613	93 761	41
		1983	10 440	...	...	316 435	129 038	41
		1984	...	...	...	...	...	...
	GENERAL	1975	3 737	1 477	40	68 693	27 984	41
		1980	3 736	...	...	74 012	...	...
		1981	6 112	...	...	148 378	62 021	42
		1982	8 529	...	...	227 294	93 442	41
		1983	10 420	3 399	33	316 104	128 707	41
		1984	14 718	4 426	30	416 136	168 154	40
	TEACHER TRAINING		–	–				–
	VOCATIONAL	1975	51	49	96	1 312	1 068	81
		1980	46	...	...	734	734	100
		1981	36	...	...	640	640	100
		1982	20	...	...	319	319	100
		1983	20	...	...	331	331	100
AMERICA, NORTH								
ANTIGUA AND BARBUDA‡	TOTAL SECOND LEVEL	1975	313	197	63	6 827	...	...
		1983	...	...	...	...	...	...
	GENERAL	1975	280	181	65	6 629	3 465	52
		1983	...	...	...	4 104	2 328	57
	TEACHER TRAINING	1975	13	11	85	96	77	80
	VOCATIONAL	1975	20	5	25	102	...	...
BAHAMAS‡	TOTAL SECOND LEVEL	1975	...	...	...	...	...	...
		1980	1 018	...	...	...	...	...
		1981	940	...	...	...	...	...
		1982	1 316	...	...	...	...	...
		1983	...	...	...	...	...	...

COUNTRY / PAYS / PAIS	TYPE OF EDUCATION / TYPE D'ENSEIGNEMENT / TIPO DE ENSEÑANZA	YEAR / ANNEE / AÑO	TEACHING STAFF / PERSONNEL ENSEIGNANT / PERSONAL DOCENTE			PUPILS ENROLLED / ELEVES INSCRITS / ALUMNOS MATRICULADOS		
			TOTAL	FEMALE / FEMININ / FEMENINO	% F	TOTAL	FEMALE / FEMININ / FEMENINO	% F
			(1)	(2)	(3)	(4)	(5)	(6)
BAHAMAS (CONT)‡	GENERAL	1975	...	...	...	28 056	14 468	52
		1980	...	...	...	28 136	...	...
		1981	...	...	...	23 346	12 101	52
		1982	...	...	...	27 649	14 476	52
		1983	...	...	...	29 496	...	...
	TEACHER TRAINING	1975	21	...	...	731	...	...
	VOCATIONAL	1975	92	...	...	1 823	...	...
BARBADOS‡	TOTAL SECOND LEVEL	1975	1 421	...	...	29 025	14 963	52
		1980	1 231	...	...	28 818	14 363	50
		1981	1 231	...	...	27 787	14 324	52
		1982	1 209	...	...	27 640	13 979	51
		1983	1 368	...	...	27 715	14 053	51
		1984	1 449	...	...	28 695	14 445	50
	GENERAL	1980	1 231	...	...	28 818	14 363	50
		1981	1 231	...	...	27 787	14 324	52
		1982	1 209	...	...	27 640	13 979	51
		1983	1 368	...	...	27 715	14 053	51
		1984	1 449	...	...	28 695	14 445	50
	TEACHER TRAINING		–	–	–	–	–	–
	VOCATIONAL		–	–	–	–	–	–
BELIZE	TOTAL SECOND LEVEL	1975	...	...	...	...	...	...
		1980	...	...	...	...	...	...
		1981	...	...	...	5 694	...	...
		1982	...	...	...	6 308	*3 280	*52
	GENERAL	1975	...	...	...	5 008	2 759	55
		1980	338	159	47	5 435	*2 989	*55
		1981	345	150	43	5 562	*3 004	*54
		1982	...	...	...	*6 118	...	...
	TEACHER TRAINING		–	–	–	–	–	–
	VOCATIONAL	1981	...	...	...	132	...	...
		1982	...	...	...	190	...	...
BERMUDA‡	TOTAL SECOND LEVEL	1975	...	...	...	...	...	...
		1980	...	...	...	...	...	...
		1981	...	...	...	...	...	...
		1982	...	...	...	...	...	...
		1983	...	...	...	...	...	...
		1984	...	...	...	...	...	...
	GENERAL	1975	...	...	...	4 824	2 517	52
		1980	367	151	*51	4 347	2 165	50
		1981	369	165	*51	4 213	2 085	49
		1982	360	210	58	4 178	2 063	49
		1983	357	207	58	4 227	2 093	50
		1984	418	218	52	4 741	2 391	50
	TEACHER TRAINING		–	–	–	–	–	–
BRITISH VIRGIN ISLANDS	TOTAL SECOND LEVEL	1975	48	25	52	821	456	56
		1980	55	33	60	791	448	57
		1982	70	40	57	897	516	58
		1983	100	60	60	1 323	762	58
		1984	...	...	...	...	...	...
	GENERAL	1980	...	...	...	510	279	55
		1983	...	...	...	1 014	559	55
		1984	...	...	...	1 078	593	55
	TEACHER TRAINING		–	–	–	–	–	–
	VOCATIONAL	1980	...	...	...	281	169	60
		1983	26	16	62	309	203	66
CANADA	TOTAL SECOND LEVEL	1975	*144 300	*60 300	*42	2 589 862	*1 276 542	*49
		1980	...	...	...	2 323 228	1 146 714	49
		1981	...	...	...	2 340 255	1 149 336	49
		1982	129 256	57 189	44	2 321 381	1 132 164	49
		1983	130 551	59 456	46	2 323 105	1 132 044	49
	TEACHER TRAINING		–	–	–	–	–	–
CAYMAN ISLANDS‡	TOTAL SECOND LEVEL	1975	106	55	52	1 495	794	53
		1980	207	114	55	2 075	1 001	48
	GENERAL	1975	106	55	52	1 495	794	53
		1980	207	114	55	2 075	1 001	48

3.7 **Education at the second level: teachers and pupils**
Enseignement du second degré: personnel enseignant et élèves
Enseñanza de segundo grado: personal docente y alumnos

COUNTRY / PAYS / PAIS	TYPE OF EDUCATION / TYPE D'ENSEIGNEMENT / TIPO DE ENSEÑANZA	YEAR / ANNEE / AÑO	TEACHING STAFF / PERSONNEL ENSEIGNANT / PERSONAL DOCENTE: TOTAL	FEMALE / FEMININ / FEMENINO	% F	PUPILS ENROLLED / ELEVES INSCRITS / ALUMNOS MATRICULADOS: TOTAL	FEMALE / FEMININ / FEMENINO	% F
			(1)	(2)	(3)	(4)	(5)	(6)
CAYMAN ISLANDS (CONT)‡	TEACHER TRAINING		–	–	–	–	–	–
	VOCATIONAL		–	–	–	–	–	–
COSTA RICA‡	TOTAL SECOND LEVEL	1975	4 929	...	...	111 538	57 763	52
		1980	7 157	...	...	135 830	72 014	53
		1981	6 955	3 784	54	133 909	70 405	53
		1982	7 307	...	...	130 337	68 360	52
		1983	7 107	...	...	122 836	64 308	52
		1984	...	...	...	117 412	60 691	52
	GENERAL	1975	3 866	1 995	52	91 227	48 736	53
		1980	4 903	...	...	105 220	56 586	54
		1981	4 747	2 690	57	103 196	55 194	53
		1982	5 295	...	...	100 043	53 213	53
		1983	5 177	...	...	95 152	50 124	53
		1984	...	...	...	91 086	47 501	52
	TEACHER TRAINING		–	–	–	–	–	–
	VOCATIONAL	1975	1 063	...	...	20 311	9 027	44
		1980	2 254	...	...	30 610	15 428	50
		1981	2 208	1 094	50	30 713	15 211	50
		1982	2 012	...	...	30 294	15 147	50
		1983	1 930	...	...	27 684	14 184	51
		1984	...	...	...	26 326	13 190	50
CUBA‡	TOTAL SECOND LEVEL	1975	42 306	20 032	47	554 365	273 106	49
		1980	80 665	38 422	48	1 046 884	527 018	50
		1981	86 578	40 898	47	1 056 763	531 667	50
		1982	88 199	41 945	48	1 017 556	516 467	51
		1983	89 826	42 285	47	1 024 113	522 487	51
		1984	93 704	42 452	45	1 031 365	530 632	51
	GENERAL	1975	32 755	16 317	50	420 315	224 804	53
		1980	63 685	31 976	50	837 261	423 084	51
		1981	65 088	33 021	51	826 477	417 514	51
		1982	65 101	33 027	51	774 410	396 925	51
		1983	64 683	33 364	52	773 781	399 184	52
		1984	64 495	32 383	50	793 516	410 297	52
	TEACHER TRAINING	1975	2 640	1 512	57	34 076	23 494	69
		1980	3 888	2 119	55	38 496	24 999	65
		1981	3 492	2 010	58	35 223	22 897	65
		1982	3 563	2 034	57	35 071	22 736	65
		1983	3 535	2 018	57	35 886	23 948	67
		1984	3 905	1 866	48	33 471	23 215	69
	VOCATIONAL	1975	6 911	2 203	32	99 974	24 808	25
		1980	13 092	4 327	33	171 127	78 935	46
		1981	17 998	5 867	33	195 063	91 256	47
		1982	19 535	6 884	35	208 075	96 806	47
		1983	21 608	6 903	32	214 446	99 355	46
		1984	25 304	8 203	32	204 378	97 120	48
DOMINICA‡	TOTAL SECOND LEVEL	1975	...	...	...	6 487	3 826	59
		1983	...	...	...	7 622	...	...
	GENERAL	1975	...	...	...	5 896	3 282	56
		1983	...	...	...	7 186	3 994	56
	TEACHER TRAINING	1975	13	8	62	43	32	74
		1983	10	6	60	60	...	...
	VOCATIONAL	1975	...	...	...	548	512	93
		1983	25	...	...	376	...	...
DOMINICAN REPUBLIC‡	TOTAL SECOND LEVEL	1975	...	...	...	260 133	...	...
		1980	...	...	...	356 091	...	...
		1981	...	...	...	379 377	...	...
		1982	...	...	...	343 322	...	...
		1983	...	...	...	379 998	...	...
	GENERAL	1975	...	...	...	239 424	...	...
		1980	...	...	...	331 471	...	...
		1981	...	...	...	353 729	...	...
		1982	...	...	...	316 801	...	...
		1983	...	...	...	352 328	...	...
	TEACHER TRAINING	1975	...	...	...	1 389	...	...
		1980	...	...	...	1 722	...	...
		1981	...	...	...	1 956	...	...
		1982	...	...	...	2 008	1 446	72
		1983	144	103	72	2 338	1 645	70

COUNTRY / PAYS / PAIS	TYPE OF EDUCATION / TYPE D'ENSEIGNEMENT / TIPO DE ENSEÑANZA	YEAR / ANNEE / AÑO	TEACHING STAFF / PERSONNEL ENSEIGNANT / PERSONAL DOCENTE TOTAL	FEMALE / FEMININ / FEMENINO	% F	PUPILS ENROLLED / ELEVES INSCRITS / ALUMNOS MATRICULADOS TOTAL	FEMALE / FEMININ / FEMENINO	% F
			(1)	(2)	(3)	(4)	(5)	(6)
DOMINICAN REP. (CONT)‡	VOCATIONAL	1975	...	...	...	19 320	...	...
		1980	...	...	...	22 898	...	...
		1981	...	...	...	23 692	...	...
		1982	...	...	...	24 513	18 302	75
		1983	491	...	...	25 332	...	...
EL SALVADOR	TOTAL SECOND LEVEL	1975	2 869	...	...	51 731	22 987	44
		1980	3 080	844	27	73 030	34 929	48
		1981	...	...	...	64 702	33 320	51
		1982	2 792	756	27	74 941	38 246	51
		1983	3 390	1 001	30	81 318	42 049	52
		1984	3 590	1 097	31	85 081	44 968	53
	GENERAL	1975	...	...	...	29 559	13 037	44
		1980	1 805	437	24	24 280	10 436	43
		1981	1 675	408	24	20 861	9 976	48
		1982	...	...	...	22 310	10 327	46
		1983	...	...	...	24 220	11 616	48
		1984	...	...	...	26 784	12 993	49
	TEACHER TRAINING	1975	25	13	52	620	374	60
		1980	65	24	37	3 451	2 560	74
		1981	...	...	...	3 012	2 310	77
		1982	...	...	...	2 458	1 954	79
		1983	...	...	...	905	857	95
		1984	...	...	...	849	849	100
	VOCATIONAL	1975	...	...	...	21 552	9 576	44
		1980	1 210	383	32	45 299	21 933	48
		1981	1 102	342	31	40 829	21 034	52
		1982	...	...	...	50 173	25 965	52
		1983	...	...	...	56 193	29 576	53
		1984	...	...	...	57 448	31 126	54
GRENADA	TOTAL SECOND LEVEL	1975	...	...	...	...	...	...
		1980	...	...	...	...	...	...
		1981	...	...	...	...	...	...
		1982	...	...	...	...	...	...
		1983	...	...	...	...	...	...
	GENERAL	1975	...	...	...	10 197	...	...
		1980	...	...	...	8 626	5 056	59
		1981	...	...	...	8 645	5 138	59
		1982	264	137	52	8 578	4 912	57
		1983	321	162	50	6 799	3 890	57
GUADELOUPE‡	TOTAL SECOND LEVEL	1975	2 147	...	...	43 805	23 291	53
		1980	...	...	...	49 398	...	...
		1981	2 765	1 346	49	48 457	26 244	54
		1982	2 964	1 435	48	49 062	26 608	54
		1983	2 987	1 503	50	49 897	27 029	54
	GENERAL	1975	...	...	...	37 009	19 947	54
		1981	2 180	1 082	50	32 966	18 727	57
		1982	2 394	1 194	50	33 218	18 918	57
		1983	...	...	...	33 605	19 033	57
	TEACHER TRAINING		–	–	–	–	–	–
	VOCATIONAL	1975	...	...	...	6 796	3 344	49
		1981	585	264	45	15 491	7 517	49
		1982	570	241	42	15 844	7 690	49
		1983	...	...	...	16 292	7 996	49
GUATEMALA	TOTAL SECOND LEVEL	1975	5 994	2 252	38	99 233	45 749	46
		1980	...	...	...	156 612	70 809	45
		1981	11 173	4 063	36	165 492	76 559	46
		1982	12 941	...	...	161 801	75 044	46
		1983	11 828	4 269	36	167 724	79 062	47
		1984	12 023	...	...	174 653	...	...
	GENERAL	1975	...	...	...	73 947	32 387	44
		1980	...	...	...	104 588	45 190	43
		1981	...	...	...	109 810	48 410	44
		1982	...	...	...	106 221	47 218	44
		1983	...	...	...	113 048	50 200	44
	TEACHER TRAINING	1975	...	...	...	13 631	7 464	55
		1980	...	...	...	22 256	13 880	62
		1981	...	...	...	20 233	12 593	62
		1982	...	...	...	17 734	11 268	64
		1983	...	...	...	17 407	10 890	63
	VOCATIONAL	1975	...	...	...	11 655	5 898	51
		1980	...	...	...	29 768	11 739	39
		1981	...	...	...	35 449	15 556	44
		1982	...	...	...	37 846	16 558	44
		1983	...	...	...	37 269	17 972	48

3.7 Education at the second level: teachers and pupils
Enseignement du second degré: personnel enseignant et élèves
Enseñanza de segundo grado: personal docente y alumnos

COUNTRY / PAYS / PAIS	TYPE OF EDUCATION / TYPE D'ENSEIGNEMENT / TIPO DE ENSEÑANZA	YEAR / ANNEE / AÑO	TEACHING STAFF / PERSONNEL ENSEIGNANT / PERSONAL DOCENTE: TOTAL	TEACHING STAFF: FEMALE / FEMININ / FEMENINO	TEACHING STAFF: % F	PUPILS ENROLLED / ELEVES INSCRITS / ALUMNOS MATRICULADOS: TOTAL	PUPILS ENROLLED: FEMALE / FEMININ / FEMENINO	PUPILS ENROLLED: % F
			(1)	(2)	(3)	(4)	(5)	(6)
HAITI‡	TOTAL SECOND LEVEL	1975	...	...	...	...	...	...
		1980	4 392	...	...	99 894	...	...
		1981	...	...	...	101 519	...	...
		1982	5 693	...	...	120 316	...	...
		1983	...	...	...	137 513	...	...
	GENERAL	1975	3 388	311	9	55 213	25 630	46
		1980	4 034	...	...	96 596	45 867	47
		1981	4 239	...	...	98 562	47 052	48
		1982	5 367	579	11	117 081	57 809	49
		1983	5 257	...	...	134 278	64 662	48
	TEACHER TRAINING	1980	123	...	...	723	519	72
		1981	...	...	...	833	590	71
		1982	128	...	...	861	...	...
		1983	108	...	...	859	581	68
	VOCATIONAL	1980	235	...	...	2 575	...	...
		1981	...	...	...	2 124	...	...
		1982	198	...	...	2 374	...	...
		1983	...	...	...	2 376	...	...
HONDURAS	TOTAL SECOND LEVEL	1975	*3 132	...	...	56 705	...	...
		1980	4 489	2 152	48	127 293	64 182	50
		1982	5 227	2 532	48	147 990	78 545	53
		1983	5 342	2 553	48	156 665	81 308	52
		1984	6 313	3 043	48	164 453	88 374	54
	GENERAL	1975	...	...	...	36 956	18 925	51
		1980	...	...	...	93 806	46 534	50
		1982	...	...	...	106 398	53 451	50
		1983	...	...	...	110 661	56 054	51
		1984	...	...	...	112 956	57 065	51
	TEACHER TRAINING	1975	...	...	...	2 004	1 415	71
		1980	...	...	...	5 156	3 802	74
		1982	...	...	...	6 829	4 860	71
		1983	...	...	...	8 110	5 056	62
		1984	...	...	...	10 032	6 882	69
	VOCATIONAL	1975	...	...	...	17 745	...	...
		1980	...	...	...	28 331	13 846	49
		1982	...	...	...	34 763	20 234	58
		1983	...	...	...	37 894	20 198	53
		1984	...	...	...	41 465	24 427	59
JAMAICA‡	TOTAL SECOND LEVEL	1975	6 473	...	...	216 248	115 784	54
		1980	7 525	4 991	66	248 001	131 745	53
		1981	...	...	...	...	...	...
		1982	...	...	...	249 648	...	...
		1983	8 193	5 419	66	233 354	119 724	51
	GENERAL	1975	6 181	...	...	211 309	113 379	54
		1980	7 110	4 760	67	233 723	122 450	52
		1981	...	...	...	241 735	...	...
		1982	...	...	...	241 195	...	...
		1983	7 685	5 158	67	224 846	115 496	51
	TEACHER TRAINING		–	–	–	–	–	–
	VOCATIONAL	1975	292	...	...	4 939	2 405	49
		1980	415	231	56	14 278	9 295	65
		1982	...	...	...	8 453	...	...
		1983	508	261	51	8 508	4 228	50
MARTINIQUE‡	TOTAL SECOND LEVEL	1975	2 357	...	...	45 260	24 576	54
		1980	...	...	...	47 745	...	...
		1981	3 077	1 609	52	45 531	24 664	54
		1982	3 142	1 628	52	47 087	25 778	55
		1983	3 065	1 638	53	46 709	25 460	55
	GENERAL	1975	...	...	...	39 234	21 077	54
		1981	2 459	1 314	53	30 695	17 263	56
		1982	2 489	1 333	54	31 677	18 073	57
		1983	2 416	1 331	55	31 912	18 001	56
	TEACHER TRAINING		–	–	–	–	–	–
	VOCATIONAL	1975	...	...	...	6 026	3 499	58
		1981	618	295	48	14 836	7 401	50
		1982	653	295	45	15 410	7 705	50
		1983	...	...	...	14 797	7 459	50

COUNTRY PAYS PAIS	TYPE OF EDUCATION TYPE D'ENSEIGNEMENT TIPO DE ENSEÑANZA	YEAR ANNEE AÑO	TEACHING STAFF / PERSONNEL ENSEIGNANT / PERSONAL DOCENTE TOTAL	 FEMALE FEMININ FEMENINO	 % F	PUPILS ENROLLED / ELEVES INSCRITS / ALUMNOS MATRICULADOS TOTAL	 FEMALE FEMININ FEMENINO	 % F
			(1)	(2)	(3)	(4)	(5)	(6)
MEXICO	TOTAL SECOND LEVEL	1975	169 781	55 218	33	2 938 972	1 159 319	39
		1980	268 178	...	...	4 741 850	2 214 442	47
		1981	301 939	...	...	5 332 131	2 508 918	47
		1982	316 987	...	...	5 716 238	2 690 268	47
		1983	337 914	...	...	6 064 264	2 887 320	48
		1984	...	...	...	...	...	...
	GENERAL	1975	141 730	42 016	30	2 506 014	853 580	34
		1980	226 532	...	...	4 042 188	1 750 873	43
		1981	252 487	...	...	4 512 582	1 993 707	44
		1982	263 353	...	...	4 817 198	2 131 696	44
		1983	279 391	...	...	5 152 572	2 332 113	45
		1984	...	...	...	5 396 936	...	...
	TEACHER TRAINING	1975	8 396	3 089	37	111 502	74 706	67
		1980	12 988	...	...	207 997	138 669	67
		1981	13 127	...	...	203 557	141 630	70
		1982	13 266	...	...	190 167	136 554	72
		1983	14 085	...	...	159 140	115 765	73
		1984	...	...	...	113 313	...	...
	VOCATIONAL	1975	19 655	10 113	51	321 456	231 033	72
		1980	28 658	...	...	491 665	324 900	66
		1981	36 325	...	...	615 992	373 581	61
		1982	40 368	...	...	708 873	422 018	60
		1983	44 438	...	...	752 552	439 442	58
MONTSERRAT	TOTAL SECOND LEVEL	1975	...	...	...	535	...	...
		1980	37	...	...	887	...	...
		1981	...	...	...	...	...	...
	GENERAL	1975	35	...	...	482	...	...
		1980	32	...	...	828	...	...
		1981	...	...	...	871	453	52
	TEACHER TRAINING		–	–	–	–	–	–
	VOCATIONAL	1975	8	3	38	53	24	45
		1980	5	...	...	59	...	...
NETHERLANDS ANTILLES	TOTAL SECOND LEVEL	1980	...	...	...	...	...	...
		1981	1 403	...	...	21 249	11 197	53
		1982	...	...	...	...	...	...
	GENERAL	1980	...	...	...	11 427	6 929	61
		1981	669	...	...	10 931	6 808	62
		1982	684	...	...	11 032	6 881	62
	TEACHER TRAINING	1981	...		...	34	34	100
	VOCATIONAL	1980	...	...	...	10 532	4 472	42
		1981	734	...	...	10 284	4 355	42
		1982	747	...	...	10 088	4 249	42
NICARAGUA‡	TOTAL SECOND LEVEL	1975	2 308	...	...	80 202	40 434	50
		1980	4 221	...	...	139 743	74 328	53
		1982	4 103	...	...	136 629	73 494	54
		1983	5 027	...	...	157 076	85 682	55
		1984	6 014	...	...	161 745	...	...
	GENERAL	1975	1 628	...	...	66 958	32 875	49
		1980	...	...	...	120 522	63 000	52
		1982	...	...	...	114 868	60 262	52
		1983	...	...	...	126 738	66 976	53
		1984	...	...	...	115 996	...	...
	TEACHER TRAINING	1975	55	...	...	822	601	73
		1980	...	...	...	2 560	2 027	79
		1982	...	...	...	3 779	3 033	80
		1983	...	...	...	6 172	5 075	82
		1984	...	...	...	9 740	...	...
	VOCATIONAL	1975	625	...	...	12 422	6 958	56
		1980	...	...	...	16 661	9 301	56
		1982	...	...	...	17 982	10 199	57
		1983	...	...	...	24 166	13 631	56
		1984	...	...	...	36 009	...	...
PANAMA	TOTAL SECOND LEVEL	1975	5 666	3 101	55	133 181	68 848	52
		1980	8 138	4 319	53	171 273	89 328	52
		1981	8 610	4 594	53	174 078	90 775	52
		1982	8 924	4 937	55	174 791	91 050	52
		1983	9 184	4 871	53	176 441	92 077	52
		1984	9 491	4 667	49	181 774	94 696	52

3.7 Education at the second level: teachers and pupils
Enseignement du second degré: personnel enseignant et élèves
Enseñanza de segundo grado: personal docente y alumnos

COUNTRY / PAYS / PAIS	TYPE OF EDUCATION / TYPE D'ENSEIGNEMENT / TIPO DE ENSEÑANZA	YEAR / ANNEE / AÑO	TEACHING STAFF / PERSONNEL ENSEIGNANT / PERSONAL DOCENTE			PUPILS ENROLLED / ELEVES INSCRITS / ALUMNOS MATRICULADOS		
			TOTAL	FEMALE / FEMININ / FEMENINO	% F	TOTAL	FEMALE / FEMININ / FEMENINO	% F
			(1)	(2)	(3)	(4)	(5)	(6)
PANAMA (CONT)	GENERAL	1975	3 472	1 939	56	89 364	45 242	51
		1980	6 005	3 316	55	130 496	67 037	51
		1981	6 328	3 519	56	129 787	66 986	52
		1982	6 502	3 613	56	129 203	66 501	51
		1983	6 652	3 690	55	129 913	66 738	51
		1984	6 835	3 408	50	133 123	68 208	51
	TEACHER TRAINING	1975	244	141	58	5 850	4 300	74
		1980	48	26	54	984	663	67
		1981	47	30	64	1 094	688	63
		1982	43	24	56	1 224	731	60
		1983	46	21	46	1 071	635	59
		1984	42	18	43	942	585	62
	VOCATIONAL	1975	1 950	1 021	52	37 967	19 306	51
		1980	2 085	977	47	39 793	21 628	54
		1981	2 235	1 045	47	43 197	23 101	53
		1982	2 379	1 300	55	44 364	23 818	54
		1983	2 486	1 160	47	45 457	24 704	54
		1984	2 614	1 241	47	47 709	25 903	54
PUERTO RICO‡	TOTAL SECOND LEVEL	1975	*8 526	...	...	292 847	...	...
		1981	...	...	...	191 015	...	...
	TEACHER TRAINING		–	–	–	–	–	–
ST. CHRISTOPHER AND NEVIS	TOTAL SECOND LEVEL	1975	...	...	...	...	...	...
		1980	...	...	...	...	...	...
		1981	...	...	...	...	...	...
		1983	289	139	48	4 060	1 965	48
		1984	235	159	68	4 197	2 028	48
	GENERAL	1975	...	...	...	4 740	2 430	51
		1980	...	...	...	4 214	2 053	49
		1981	...	...	...	4 334	2 187	50
		1983	271	135	50	3 881	1 921	49
		1984	218	155	71	4 038	1 985	49
	TEACHER TRAINING		–	–	–	–	–	–
	VOCATIONAL	1983	18	4	22	179	44	25
		1984	17	4	24	159	43	27
ST. LUCIA	TOTAL SECOND LEVEL	1975	297	115	39	4 522	...	...
		1980	...	...	...	4 607	2 551	55
		1981	336	...	...	5 148	2 905	56
		1982	319	162	51	5 313	2 960	56
		1983	350	184	53	5 314	3 028	57
	GENERAL	1975	231	*97	*42	4 136	2 325	56
		1980	229	120	52	4 306	2 400	56
		1981	288	162	56	4 827	2 732	57
		1982	272	146	54	4 982	2 766	56
		1983	298	164	55	4 989	2 854	57
	TEACHER TRAINING	1975	25	13	52	156	...	...
		1980	...	...	...	122	*90	*74
		1981	14	11	79	128	100	78
		1982	13	9	69	131	117	89
		1983	17	13	76	109	88	81
	VOCATIONAL	1975	41	5	12	230	59	26
		1980	...	...	...	179	61	34
		1981	34	...	...	193	73	38
		1982	34	7	21	200	77	39
		1983	35	7	20	216	86	40
ST. PIERRE AND MIQUELON	TOTAL SECOND LEVEL	1980	62	31	50	748	392	52
		1981	63	32	51	761	389	51
		1982	65	32	49	748	394	53
		1983	71	34	48	751	408	54
		1984	...	...	...	777	415	53
	GENERAL	1980	49	28	57	527	278	53
		1981	50	29	58	530	281	53
		1982	52	29	56	531	290	55
		1983	56	30	54	535	293	55
		1984	...	...	...	526	294	56
	TEACHER TRAINING		–	–	–	–	–	–
	VOCATIONAL	1980	13	3	23	221	114	52
		1981	13	3	23	231	108	47
		1982	13	3	23	217	104	48
		1983	15	4	27	216	115	53
		1984	...	...	...	251	121	48

COUNTRY / PAYS / PAIS	TYPE OF EDUCATION / TYPE D'ENSEIGNEMENT / TIPO DE ENSEÑANZA	YEAR / ANNEE / AÑO	TEACHING STAFF / PERSONNEL ENSEIGNANT / PERSONAL DOCENTE			PUPILS ENROLLED / ELEVES INSCRITS / ALUMNOS MATRICULADOS		
			TOTAL	FEMALE / FEMININ / FEMENINO	% F	TOTAL	FEMALE / FEMININ / FEMENINO	% F
			(1)	(2)	(3)	(4)	(5)	(6)
ST. VINCENT AND THE GRENADINES	TOTAL SECOND LEVEL	1975	243	104	43	5 084	2 974	58
		1981	...	...	...	8 058	4 739	59
		1983	...	...	...	7 473	4 357	58
	GENERAL	1975	217	94	43	4 685	2 771	59
		1981	327	171	52	7 771	4 580	59
		1983	...	...	...	7 267	4 271	59
	TEACHER TRAINING	1975	14	8	57	291	172	59
		1981	...	...	...	183	126	69
		1983	...	...	...	105	49	47
	VOCATIONAL	1975	12	2	17	108	31	29
		1981	...	...	...	104	33	32
		1983	...	...	...	101	37	37
TRINIDAD AND TOBAGO	TOTAL SECOND LEVEL	1975	...	...	...	67 872	...	...
		1980	4 377	...	...	89 355	...	...
		1981	4 511	2 334	52	90 724	45 766	50
		1982	4 653	...	...	90 815	45 912	51
		1984	4 750	2 478	52	92 017	46 249	50
	GENERAL	1975	1 631	850	52	64 039	...	...
		1980	...	...	...	*82 434	...	...
		1981	...	...	...	*84 203	*42 526	*51
	TEACHER TRAINING		–	–	–	–	–	–
	VOCATIONAL	1975	...	...	...	3 833	1 110	29
		1980	...	...	...	6 921	3 389	49
		1981	...	...	...	6 521	3 240	50
TURKS AND CAICOS ISLANDS	TOTAL SECOND LEVEL	1975	35	*13	*37	671	...	...
		1980	47	28	60	691	...	...
		1984	51	34	67	707	...	...
	GENERAL	1975	35	*13	*37	671	...	...
		1980	47	28	60	691	...	...
		1984	51	34	67	707	...	...
	TEACHER TRAINING		–	–	–	–	–	–
	VOCATIONAL		–	–	–	–	–	–
UNITED STATES‡	TOTAL SECOND LEVEL	1975	*1 109 000	...	...	*20 546 000	...	...
		1980	*1 095 000	...	...	14 556 000	7 228 000	50
		1981	*1 051 000	...	...	14 643 000	7 211 000	49
		1982	1 033 000	...	...	14 122 000	6 917 000	49
		1983	1 047 000	...	...	14 007 000	6 911 000	49
		1984	1 043 000	...	...	13 779 000	6 737 000	49
	TEACHER TRAINING		–	–	–	–	–	–
U.S. VIRGIN ISLANDS‡	TOTAL SECOND LEVEL	1975	*592	...	...	*10 590	...	...
		1980	617	...	...	6 737	...	...
		1981	666	...	...	7 135	...	...
	TEACHER TRAINING		–	–	–	–	–	–
AMERICA, SOUTH								
ARGENTINA	TOTAL SECOND LEVEL	1975	161 859	101 216	63	1 243 058	650 902	52
		1981	...	...	...	1 366 444	725 620	53
		1983	*193 551	*126 474	*65	*1 466 424	*752 516	*51
		1984	213 961	140 120	65	1 635 654	850 667	52
		1985	230 093	151 168	66	1 800 049	942 768	52
	GENERAL	1975	62 334	45 526	73	454 194	275 784	61
		1981	77 956	58 415	75	528 140	335 653	64
		1983	*79 728	*60 223	*76	*614 615	*382 721	*62
		1984	86 874	64 677	74	656 521	406 645	62
		1985	93 675	69 472	74	715 518	442 107	62
	TEACHER TRAINING		–	–	–	–	–	–
	VOCATIONAL	1975	99 525	55 690	56	788 864	375 118	48
		1981	...	...	...	838 304	389 967	47
		1983	*113 823	*66 251	*58	*851 809	*369 795	*43
		1984	127 087	75 443	59	979 133	444 022	45
		1985	136 418	81 696	60	1 084 531	500 661	46

3.7 Education at the second level: teachers and pupils
Enseignement du second degré: personnel enseignant et élèves
Enseñanza de segundo grado: personal docente y alumnos

COUNTRY / PAYS / PAIS	TYPE OF EDUCATION / TYPE D'ENSEIGNEMENT / TIPO DE ENSEÑANZA	YEAR / ANNEE / AÑO	TEACHING STAFF / PERSONNEL ENSEIGNANT / PERSONAL DOCENTE: TOTAL (1)	FEMALE / FEMININ / FEMENINO (2)	% F (3)	PUPILS ENROLLED / ELEVES INSCRITS / ALUMNOS MATRICULADOS: TOTAL (4)	FEMALE / FEMININ / FEMENINO (5)	% F (6)
BOLIVIA	TOTAL SECOND LEVEL	1975	7 143	...	...	130 029	...	...
		1980	...	...	...	170 710	73 991	43
		1981	...	...	...	166 325	75 961	46
		1982	...	...	...	176 216	...	...
		1983	...	...	...	182 760	83 506	46
		1984	...	...	...	199 944	92 369	46
BRAZIL	TOTAL SECOND LEVEL	1975	*133 070	...	...	1 935 903	1 033 096	53
		1980	198 087	105 945	53	2 819 182	1 515 859	54
		1981	205 610	...	...	2 820 998	...	...
		1982	203 676	...	...	2 874 505	...	...
		1983	180 354	...	...	2 944 097	...	...
	GENERAL	1975	...	...	...	882 059	563 427	64
	TEACHER TRAINING	1975	...	...	...	271 337	246 838	91
	VOCATIONAL	1975	...	...	...	782 507	222 831	28
CHILE	TOTAL SECOND LEVEL	1975	29 567	14 730	50	448 911	238 533	53
		1980	...	...	...	538 309	284 784	53
		1981	...	...	...	554 749	296 324	53
		1982	...	...	...	565 745	293 910	52
		1983	...	...	...	613 546	317 818	52
		1984	...	...	...	637 092	327 960	51
	GENERAL	1975	17 799	9 802	55	285 806	166 363	58
		1980	...	...	...	369 180	204 802	55
		1981	...	...	...	392 940	218 068	55
		1982	...	...	...	418 649	226 976	54
		1983	...	...	...	488 346	257 224	53
		1984	...	...	...	524 906	272 628	52
	TEACHER TRAINING		–	–	–	–	–	–
	VOCATIONAL	1975	11 768	4 928	42	163 105	72 170	44
		1980	...	...	...	169 129	79 982	47
		1981	...	...	...	161 809	78 256	48
		1982	...	...	...	147 096	66 934	46
		1983	...	...	...	125 200	60 594	48
		1984	...	...	...	112 186	55 332	49
COLOMBIA	TOTAL SECOND LEVEL	1975	70 451	29 237	42	1 370 567	683 639	50
		1980	85 135	35 756	42	1 733 192	870 276	50
		1982	90 171	38 593	43	1 816 628	914 851	50
		1983	90 006	39 500	44	1 816 599	963 779	53
		1984	93 121	...	...	1 889 023	942 622	50
		1985	95 981	...	...	1 934 032	965 082	50
	GENERAL	1975	50 480	20 292	40	1 031 237	512 381	50
		1980	61 836	25 290	41	1 313 004	660 502	50
		1982	65 426	27 413	42	1 374 692	687 693	50
		1983	67 827	29 254	43	1 424 419	722 074	51
		1984	67 770	...	...	1 432 234	714 684	50
		1985	69 871	...	...	1 468 709	731 399	50
	TEACHER TRAINING	1975	4 897	2 962	60	82 843	61 323	74
		1980	4 096	2 433	59	67 583	50 958	75
		1982	3 922	2 266	58	63 846	49 788	78
		1983	4 026	2 330	58	64 243	46 711	73
		1984	3 987	...	...	65 472	32 671	50
		1985	3 817	...	...	60 721	33 631	55
	VOCATIONAL	1975	15 074	5 983	40	256 487	109 935	43
		1980	19 203	8 033	42	352 605	158 816	45
		1982	20 823	8 914	43	378 090	177 370	47
		1983	18 153	7 916	44	327 937	194 994	59
		1984	21 364	...	...	391 317	195 267	50
		1985	22 293	...	...	404 602	200 052	49
ECUADOR	TOTAL SECOND LEVEL	1975	23 446	8 315	35	383 624	182 678	48
		1980	34 868	...	...	591 969	...	...
		1981	37 318	14 147	38	634 933	313 507	49
		1982	40 770	15 941	39	672 575	338 186	50
		1983	40 840	15 758	39	655 219	328 667	50
		1984	...	...	...	...	...	...
	GENERAL	1975	18 335	6 514	36	339 771	156 333	46
		1980	27 048	*10 278	*38	516 548	246 141	48
		1981	28 565	10 928	38	552 847	*263 150	*48
		1982	30 082	11 779	39	581 403	283 140	49
		1983	29 319	11 402	39	560 473	270 876	48
		1984	32 572	...	...	608 765	...	...

COUNTRY / PAYS / PAIS	TYPE OF EDUCATION / TYPE D'ENSEIGNEMENT / TIPO DE ENSEÑANZA	YEAR / ANNEE / AÑO	TEACHING STAFF / PERSONNEL ENSEIGNANT / PERSONAL DOCENTE: TOTAL	FEMALE / FEMININ / FEMENINO	% F	PUPILS ENROLLED / ELEVES INSCRITS / ALUMNOS MATRICULADOS: TOTAL	FEMALE / FEMININ / FEMENINO	% F
			(1)	(2)	(3)	(4)	(5)	(6)
ECUADOR (CONT)	TEACHER TRAINING	1975	130	31	24	913	488	53
		1980	258	65	25	4 945	3 452	70
		1981	266	68	26	6 299	4 551	72
		1982	1 032	447	43	8 471	5 779	68
		1983	931	289	31	4 941	3 354	68
	VOCATIONAL	1975	4 981	1 770	36	42 940	25 857	60
		1980	7 562	...	...	70 476	...	...
		1981	8 487	3 151	37	75 787	45 806	60
		1982	9 656	3 715	38	81 357	49 267	61
		1983	10 590	4 067	38	89 805	...	...
		1984	12 016	...	...	97 011	...	...
FALKLAND ISLANDS (MALVINAS)	TOTAL SECOND LEVEL	1975	...	...	...	126	55	44
		1980	11	4	36	90	50	56
	GENERAL	1975	...	...	...	126	55	44
		1980	11	4	36	90	50	56
	TEACHER TRAINING		–	–	–	–	–	–
	VOCATIONAL		–	–	–	–	–	–
FRENCH GUIANA‡	TOTAL SECOND LEVEL	1975	338	...	...	5 534	2 867	52
		1980	...	...	...	7 421	...	...
		1981	545	269	49	7 728	4 110	53
		1982	537	273	51	8 014	4 188	52
		1983	578	302	52	8 485	4 435	52
	GENERAL	1975	...	...	...	3 998	2 166	54
		1981	402	214	53	5 364	2 952	55
		1982	389	218	56	5 537	2 969	54
		1983	...	...	...	5 862	3 164	54
	TEACHER TRAINING		–	–	–	–	–	–
	VOCATIONAL	1975	...	...	...	1 536	701	46
		1981	143	55	38	2 364	1 158	49
		1982	148	55	37	2 477	1 219	49
		1983	...	...	...	2 623	1 271	48
GUYANA	TOTAL SECOND LEVEL	1975	...	...	...	71 327	36 021	51
		1980	...	...	...	...	...	...
		1981	...	...	...	...	...	...
	GENERAL	1975	3 202	1 144	36	66 326	33 530	51
		1980	4 236	1 897	45	75 335	38 504	51
		1981	4 797	2 697	56	73 762	37 664	51
	TEACHER TRAINING		–	–	–	–	–	–
	VOCATIONAL	1975	...	...	...	5 001	2 491	50
PARAGUAY	TOTAL SECOND LEVEL	1975	...	...	...	75 424	37 363	50
		1980	...	...	...	118 828	...	...
		1981	...	...	...	126 498	...	...
		1982	...	...	...	137 146	...	...
		1983	...	...	...	143 786	...	...
		1984	...	...	...	150 566	...	...
	GENERAL	1975	...	...	...	70 048	36 107	52
		1980	...	...	...	111 905	...	...
		1981	...	...	...	119 199	...	...
		1982	...	...	...	128 363	63 212	49
		1983	...	...	...	134 995	...	...
		1984	...	...	...	140 872	...	...
	TEACHER TRAINING		–	–	–	–	–	–
	VOCATIONAL	1975	...	...	...	5 376	1 256	23
		1980	...	...	...	6 923	...	...
		1981	...	...	...	7 299	...	...
		1982	...	...	...	8 783	...	...
		1983	...	...	...	8 791	...	...
		1984	...	...	...	9 694	...	...
PERU	TOTAL SECOND LEVEL	1975	34 136	...	...	813 489	...	...
		1980	...	...	...	1 203 116	547 393	45
		1981	...	...	...	...	...	...
		1982	...	...	...	...	...	...
		1985	...	...	...	...	...	...
	GENERAL	1975	26 033	...	...	627 059	...	...
		1980	...	...	...	1 151 748	526 780	46
		1981	49 569	22 970	46	1 226 130	565 643	46
		1982	50 075	...	...	1 249 293	578 047	46
		1985	68 541	...	...	1 427 261	667 399	47

3.7 Education at the second level: teachers and pupils
Enseignement du second degré: personnel enseignant et élèves
Enseñanza de segundo grado: personal docente y alumnos

COUNTRY / PAYS / PAIS	TYPE OF EDUCATION / TYPE D'ENSEIGNEMENT / TIPO DE ENSEÑANZA	YEAR / ANNEE / AÑO	TEACHING STAFF / PERSONNEL ENSEIGNANT / PERSONAL DOCENTE			PUPILS ENROLLED / ELEVES INSCRITS / ALUMNOS MATRICULADOS		
			TOTAL	FEMALE / FEMININ / FEMENINO	% F	TOTAL	FEMALE / FEMININ / FEMENINO	% F
			(1)	(2)	(3)	(4)	(5)	(6)
PERU (CONT)	TEACHER TRAINING		–	–	–	–	–	–
	VOCATIONAL	1975	8 103	...	...	186 430	...	...
		1980	...	...	...	51 368	20 613	40
SURINAME	TOTAL SECOND LEVEL	1975	1 793	901	50	30 603	16 726	55
		1979	2 326	...	...	35 742	...	...
		1984	...	...	...	...	...	...
	GENERAL	1975	1 127	733	65	26 442	14 850	56
		1979	1 899	...	...	30 152	...	...
		1984	...	...	...	30 246	...	...
	TEACHER TRAINING	1975	399	124	31	1 894	1 454	77
		1979	158	...	...	949	...	...
		1984	160	...	...	2 028	1 770	87
	VOCATIONAL	1975	267	44	16	2 267	422	19
		1979	269	...	...	4 641	...	...
URUGUAY‡	TOTAL SECOND LEVEL	1975	...	...	...	182 195	...	...
		1980	...	...	...	148 294	78 487	53
		1981	...	...	...	188 123	...	...
		1982	...	...	...	190 053	...	...
		1983	...	...	...	197 890	...	...
	GENERAL	1975	...	...	...	144 497	...	...
		1980	...	...	...	125 438	72 390	58
		1981	...	...	...	162 106	...	...
		1982	...	...	...	164 036	...	...
		1983	...	...	...	171 137	...	...
	TEACHER TRAINING		–	–	–	–	–	–
	VOCATIONAL	1975	...	...	...	37 698	14 439	38
		1980	...	...	...	22 856	6 097	27
		1981	...	...	...	26 017	12 362	48
		1982	...	...	...	26 017	12 362	48
		1983	...	...	...	26 753	11 987	45
VENEZUELA	TOTAL SECOND LEVEL	1975	37 232	...	...	669 138	351 890	53
		1980	48 910	...	...	850 470	464 486	55
		1981	50 048	...	...	884 233	483 087	55
		1982	51 261	...	...	939 678	*512 613	*55
		1983	55 314	29 212	53	963 363	525 026	54
	GENERAL	1975	...	...	...	622 428	...	...
		1980	...	...	...	782 829	...	...
		1981	...	...	...	822 527	...	...
		1983	...	...	...	912 185	496 462	54
	TEACHER TRAINING	1975	...	...	...	16 445	14 708	89
		1980	...	...	...	24 414	...	...
		1981	...	...	...	15 805	...	...
		1982	...	...	...	6 090	...	...
		1983	–	–	–	–	–	–
	VOCATIONAL	1975	...	...	...	30 265	...	...
		1980	...	...	...	43 227	...	...
		1981	...	...	...	45 901	...	...
		1982	...	...	...	49 376	...	...
		1983	...	...	...	51 178	28 564	56
ASIA								
AFGHANISTAN‡	TOTAL SECOND LEVEL	1975	8 089	1 090	13	93 497	10 505	11
		1980	7 532	...	...	136 898	...	...
		1981	...	...	...	159 390	32 068	20
		1982	...	...	...	...	...	...
		1984	...	...	...	...	...	...
	GENERAL	1975	7 425	1 049	14	87 537	9 854	11
		1980	6 270	1 331	21	124 488	26 143	21
		1981	6 409	1 393	22	144 858	30 016	21
		1982	4 303	1 448	34	93 933	29 593	32
		1984	6 943	2 191	32	99 729	32 615	33
	TEACHER TRAINING		–	–	–	–	–	–
	VOCATIONAL	1975	664	*41	*6	5 960	651	11
		1980	1 262	...	...	12 410	...	...
		1981	...	...	...	14 532	2 052	14

COUNTRY / PAYS / PAIS	TYPE OF EDUCATION / TYPE D'ENSEIGNEMENT / TIPO DE ENSEÑANZA	YEAR / ANNEE / AÑO	TEACHING STAFF / PERSONNEL ENSEIGNANT / PERSONAL DOCENTE			PUPILS ENROLLED / ELEVES INSCRITS / ALUMNOS MATRICULADOS		
			TOTAL	FEMALE FEMININ FEMENINO	% F	TOTAL	FEMALE FEMININ FEMENINO	% F
			(1)	(2)	(3)	(4)	(5)	(6)
BAHRAIN‡	TOTAL SECOND LEVEL	1975	...	...	...	18 617	8 847	48
		1980	1 184	603	51	26 528	12 092	46
		1981	1 430	716	50	28 710	13 160	46
		1982	1 656	817	49	33 629	15 394	46
		1983	1 812	923	51	33 476	15 762	47
		1984	...	...	...	35 901	17 040	47
	GENERAL	1975	704	346	49	16 962	8 389	49
		1980	...	...	...	23 718	11 104	47
		1981	1 101	662	60	24 647	11 600	47
		1982	1 176	685	58	27 785	13 077	47
		1983	1 282	779	61	26 409	12 998	49
		1984	...	...	...	28 253	14 242	50
	TEACHER TRAINING		–	–		–	–	–
	VOCATIONAL	1975	...	...	...	1 655	458	28
		1980	...	...	...	2 810	988	35
		1981	329	54	16	4 063	1 560	38
		1982	480	132	28	5 844	2 317	40
		1983	530	144	27	7 067	2 764	39
		1984	544	137	25	7 648	2 798	37
BANGLADESH‡	TOTAL SECOND LEVEL	1976	...	...	...	2 183 413	...	...
		1980	111 927	7 489	7	2 659 208	636 584	24
		1981	...	...	...	2 407 888	448 745	19
		1983	114 612	...	...	2 959 437	...	...
		1984	118 602	10 979	9	3 111 267	885 444	28
		1985	...	...	...	3 125 219	...	...
	GENERAL	1976	98 965	6 365	6	2 164 328	531 745	25
		1980	110 096	7 314	7	2 632 904	634 372	24
		1981	85 067	6 540	8	2 381 346	446 905	19
		1983	112 077	8 108	7	2 930 757	806 198	28
		1984	115 751	10 636	9	3 083 643	882 656	29
		1985	110 757	9 426	9	3 097 871	868 411	28
	TEACHER TRAINING	1976	...	...	...	7 610	1 368	18
		1980	772	127	16	6 704	1 782	27
		1981	734	115	16	6 825	1 493	22
		1983	1 362	214	16	7 699	1 685	22
		1984	1 497	303	20	8 109	1 879	23
		1985	...	...	...	8 303	...	...
	VOCATIONAL	1976	...	...	...	11 475	...	...
		1980	1 059	48	5	19 600	430	2
		1981	...	...	...	19 717	347	2
		1983	1 173	...	...	20 981	...	...
		1984	1 354	40	3	19 515	909	5
		1985	1 427	48	3	19 045	995	5
BHUTAN‡	TOTAL SECOND LEVEL	1976	...	...	...	...	...	...
		1979	...	...	...	...	...	...
		1982	...	...	...	...	...	...
		1983	394	...	...	5 298	903	17
		1984	581	...	...	5 872	1 026	17
	GENERAL	1976	...	...	...	817	164	20
		1979	...	...	...	1 488	339	23
		1982	...	...	...	2 660	...	...
		1983	251	...	...	3 109	802	26
		1984	431	...	...	3 608	874	24
	TEACHER TRAINING	1976	...	...	...	30	10	33
		1979	...	...	...	117	...	...
		1983	20	...	...	99	26	26
		1984	20	...	...	94	47	50
	VOCATIONAL	1983	123	...	...	2 090	75	4
		1984	130	...	...	2 170	105	5
BRUNEI DARUSSALAM	TOTAL SECOND LEVEL	1975	782	287	37	14 614	6 946	48
		1980	1 413	479	34	17 441	8 716	50
		1981	1 538	537	35	17 869	9 027	51
		1982	...	...	...	18 734	9 475	51
		1983	...	...	...	19 940	10 195	51
		1984	1 801	554	31	19 904	10 196	51
	GENERAL	1975	684	276	40	13 687	6 666	49
		1980	1 214	453	37	16 532	8 349	51
		1981	1 326	501	38	16 805	8 665	52
		1982	1 396	536	38	17 698	9 115	52
		1983	...	...	...	18 854	9 782	52
		1984	1 526	521	34	18 565	9 670	52

3.7 Education at the second level: teachers and pupils
Enseignement du second degré: personnel enseignant et élèves
Enseñanza de segundo grado: personal docente y alumnos

COUNTRY / PAYS / PAIS	TYPE OF EDUCATION / TYPE D'ENSEIGNEMENT / TIPO DE ENSEÑANZA	YEAR / ANNEE / AÑO	TEACHING STAFF / PERSONNEL ENSEIGNANT / PERSONAL DOCENTE: TOTAL (1)	FEMALE / FEMININ / FEMENINO (2)	% F (3)	PUPILS ENROLLED / ELEVES INSCRITS / ALUMNOS MATRICULADOS: TOTAL (4)	FEMALE / FEMININ / FEMENINO (5)	% F (6)
BRUNEI DARUSSALAM (CONT)	TEACHER TRAINING	1975	37	11	30	613	273	45
		1980	81	23	28	450	296	66
		1981	85	28	33	494	268	54
		1982	...	...	...	389	247	63
		1983	91	26	29	382	270	71
		1984	87	24	28	591	379	64
	VOCATIONAL	1975	61	–	–	314	7	2
		1980	118	3	3	459	71	15
		1981	127	8	6	570	94	16
		1982	...	...	...	647	113	17
		1983	160	9	6	704	143	20
		1984	188	9	5	748	147	20
BURMA	TOTAL SECOND LEVEL	1975	24 911	...	...	933 486	...	...
		1980	31 248	...	...	1 066 300	...	...
		1981	36 981	...	...	1 164 000	...	...
		1982	40 194	...	...	1 195 400	...	...
		1983	43 368	...	...	1 234 000	...	...
	GENERAL	1975	23 812	...	...	917 896	406 237	44
		1980	30 048	...	...	1 046 100	...	...
		1981	35 725	...	...	1 142 800	...	...
		1982	38 681	...	...	1 170 500	...	...
		1983	41 668	...	...	1 210 300	...	...
	TEACHER TRAINING	1975	289	...	...	4 890	2 827	58
		1980	394	...	...	5 700	...	...
		1981	394	...	...	5 600	...	...
		1982	422	...	...	5 900	...	...
		1983	592	...	...	5 900	...	...
	VOCATIONAL	1975	810	...	...	10 700	...	...
		1980	806	...	...	*14 500	...	...
		1981	862	...	...	*15 600	...	...
		1982	1 091	...	...	16 300	...	...
		1983	1 108	...	...	17 800	...	...
CHINA	TOTAL SECOND LEVEL	1975	2 164 601	...	...	45 368 000	17 781 000	39
		1980	3 171 564	787 700	25	56 778 000	22 341 000	39
		1981	3 008 789	761 600	25	50 146 000	19 501 000	39
		1982	2 870 455	750 800	26	47 027 900	18 406 800	39
		1983	2 826 764	737 600	26	46 340 661	18 239 600	39
		1984	2 721 400	782 900	29	48 608 800	19 440 200	40
	GENERAL	1975	2 092 155	505 200	24	44 661 000	17 537 000	39
		1980	3 019 700	750 300	25	55 081 000	21 801 000	40
		1981	2 844 000	719 300	25	48 596 000	18 954 000	39
		1982	2 680 500	700 600	26	45 284 900	17 774 400	39
		1983	2 596 900	678 200	26	43 977 300	17 351 200	39
		1984	2 456 600	708 800	29	45 541 500	18 218 700	40
	TEACHER TRAINING	1975	24 618	...	...	302 288	...	...
		1980	37 664	8 300	22	482 108	125 214	26
		1981	37 489	8 200	22	436 904	125 880	29
		1982	39 255	9 000	23	411 381	139 411	34
		1983	40 464	10 000	25	454 861	169 387	37
		1984	42 600	10 700	25	511 400	208 800	41
	VOCATIONAL	1975	47 828	...	...	405 030	...	...
		1980	114 200	29 100	25	1 214 900	414 800	34
		1981	127 300	34 100	27	1 113 000	421 200	38
		1982	150 700	41 200	27	1 331 600	493 000	37
		1983	189 400	49 400	26	1 908 500	719 000	38
		1984	222 200	63 400	29	2 555 900	1 012 700	40
CYPRUS‡	TOTAL SECOND LEVEL	1975	2 451	985	40	49 373	23 435	47
		1980	2 953	1 237	42	47 599	23 286	49
		1981	3 047	1 291	42	48 881	24 038	49
		1982	3 093	1 301	42	48 527	24 033	50
		1983	3 137	1 342	43	49 274	24 401	50
	GENERAL	1975	2 066	913	44	43 261	23 049	53
		1980	2 449	1 140	47	41 794	22 463	54
		1981	2 550	1 199	47	43 338	23 172	53
		1982	2 581	1 199	46	43 000	23 066	54
		1983	...	...	...	45 599	24 104	53
	TEACHER TRAINING		–	–	–	–	–	–
	VOCATIONAL	1975	385	72	19	6 112	386	6
		1980	504	97	19	5 805	823	14
		1981	497	92	19	5 543	866	16
		1982	512	102	20	5 527	967	17
		1983	...	...	...	3 675	297	8

COUNTRY / PAYS / PAIS	TYPE OF EDUCATION / TYPE D'ENSEIGNEMENT / TIPO DE ENSEÑANZA	YEAR / ANNEE / AÑO	TEACHING STAFF / PERSONNEL ENSEIGNANT / PERSONAL DOCENTE: TOTAL	FEMALE / FEMININ / FEMENINO	% F	PUPILS ENROLLED / ELEVES INSCRITS / ALUMNOS MATRICULADOS: TOTAL	FEMALE / FEMININ / FEMENINO	% F
			(1)	(2)	(3)	(4)	(5)	(6)
DEMOCRATIC YEMEN‡	TOTAL SECOND LEVEL	1975	2 332	...	...	47 463	...	...
		1980	1 649	329	20	31 490	9 183	29
		1981	2 016	516	26	31 705	9 795	31
		1982	1 720	372	22	33 816	9 883	29
		1983	1 946	521	27	34 807	10 327	30
	GENERAL	1975	2 071	431	21	44 829	9 924	22
		1980	1 199	276	23	26 160	8 557	33
		1981	1 497	490	33	27 301	9 078	33
		1982	1 210	316	26	28 290	9 198	33
		1983	1 493	462	31	29 205	9 592	33
	TEACHER TRAINING	1975	62	8	13	794	231	29
		1980	81	8	10	1 229	266	22
		1981	93	7	8	1 173	284	24
		1982	82	10	12	1 279	227	18
		1983	74	9	12	1 261	229	18
	VOCATIONAL	1975	199	...	...	1 840	...	...
		1980	369	45	12	4 101	360	9
		1981	426	19	4	3 231	433	13
		1982	428	46	11	4 247	458	11
		1983	379	50	13	4 341	506	12
HONG KONG	TOTAL SECOND LEVEL	1975	15 149	6 198	41	368 655	172 405	47
		1980	15 986	7 784	49	468 975	231 238	49
		1981	16 039	7 806	49	464 923	231 433	50
		1982	16 871	8 164	48	459 611	230 674	50
		1983	17 480	8 509	49	453 369	226 980	50
		1984	17 840	8 785	49	447 813	223 782	50
	GENERAL	1975	...	...	...	347 146	166 083	48
		1980	...	...	...	437 956	221 280	51
		1981	...	...	...	432 431	220 435	51
		1982	...	...	...	428 117	220 387	51
		1983	...	...	...	422 405	216 710	51
		1984	...	...	...	416 125	213 090	51
	TEACHER TRAINING		–	–	–	–	–	–
	VOCATIONAL	1975	...	...	...	21 509	6 322	29
		1980	...	...	...	31 019	9 958	32
		1981	...	...	...	32 492	10 998	34
		1982	...	...	...	31 494	10 287	33
		1983	...	...	...	30 964	10 270	33
		1984	...	...	...	31 688	10 692	34
INDIA‡	TOTAL SECOND LEVEL	1975	...	...	...	23 638 666	7 195 555	30
		1980	...	...	...	...	...	...
		1981	...	...	...	...	...	...
		1982	...	...	...	...	...	...
	GENERAL	1975	1 180 233	303 644	26	23 447 697	7 116 654	30
		1980	1 731 978	511 841	30	29 337 454	9 409 745	32
		1981	1 788 596	535 998	30	32 600 864	10 585 358	32
		1982	1 849 504	556 929	30	34 032 130	11 199 558	33
	TEACHER TRAINING	1975	...	...	...	19 379	8 704	45
	VOCATIONAL	1975	...	...	...	171 590	70 197	41
INDONESIA‡	TOTAL SECOND LEVEL	1975	...	...	...	3 570 080	1 366 151	38
		1980	385 186	...	...	5 721 815	...	...
		1981	403 422	...	...	6 320 013	2 558 911	40
		1982	*469 631	...	...	7 222 213	3 026 351	42
		1983	...	...	...	*7 445 917	*3 118 711	*42
		1984	...	...	...	...	...	...
	GENERAL	1975	...	...	...	2 709 953	1 088 838	40
		1980	261 864	...	...	4 879 361	...	...
		1981	289 979	...	...	5 475 099	2 234 126	41
		1982	336 336	...	...	6 328 508	2 672 099	42
		1983	384 219	...	...	6 511 390	2 731 456	42
		1984	433 750	...	...	7 042 001	2 974 369	42
	TEACHER TRAINING	1975	8 311	1 830	22	102 847	59 865	58
		1980	16 648	...	...	232 024	139 271	60
		1981	17 397	...	...	233 633	140 206	60
		1982	18 246	...	...	233 668	139 047	60
		1983	17 588	...	...	253 695	153 546	61
		1984	18 424	...	...	280 313	167 214	60
	VOCATIONAL	1975	...	...	...	757 280	217 448	29
		1980	...	...	...	610 430	*166 872	*27
		1981	...	...	...	611 281	184 579	30
		1982	...	...	...	660 037	215 205	33
		1983	...	...	...	*680 832	*233 709	*34

3.7 Education at the second level: teachers and pupils
Enseignement du second degré: personnel enseignant et élèves
Enseñanza de segundo grado: personal docente y alumnos

COUNTRY / PAYS / PAIS	TYPE OF EDUCATION / TYPE D'ENSEIGNEMENT / TIPO DE ENSEÑANZA	YEAR / ANNEE / AÑO	TEACHING STAFF / PERSONNEL ENSEIGNANT / PERSONAL DOCENTE: TOTAL	FEMALE / FEMININ / FEMENINO	% F	PUPILS ENROLLED / ELEVES INSCRITS / ALUMNOS MATRICULADOS: TOTAL	FEMALE / FEMININ / FEMENINO	% F
			(1)	(2)	(3)	(4)	(5)	(6)
IRAN, ISLAMIC REPUBLIC OF‡	TOTAL SECOND LEVEL	1975	81 855	32 306	39	2 183 137	778 875	36
		1981	...	...	...	2 836 144	1 085 616	38
		1982	188 064	...	...	2 693 540	1 061 293	39
		1983	196 541	69 879	36	2 832 841	1 127 685	40
		1984	206 244	74 366	36	3 107 548	1 235 035	40
	GENERAL	1975	73 056	30 560	42	1 988 670	727 458	37
		1981	...	...	...	2 677 634	1 063 625	40
		1982	171 418	...	...	2 566 151	1 043 622	41
		1983	178 869	68 093	38	2 685 076	1 101 456	41
		1984	...	...	...	2 922 576	1 193 801	41
	TEACHER TRAINING	1975	1 733	485	28	43 958	22 352	51
		1981	–	–	–	–	–	–
		1982	–	–	–	–	–	–
		1983	–	–	–	–	–	–
		1984	...	...	...	5 769	469	8
	VOCATIONAL	1975	7 066	1 261	18	150 509	29 065	19
		1981	12 836	1 267	10	158 510	21 991	14
		1982	16 646	...	...	127 389	17 671	14
		1983	17 672	1 786	10	147 765	26 229	18
		1984	19 663	2 510	13	179 203	40 765	23
IRAQ	TOTAL SECOND LEVEL	1975	21 454	8 542	40	525 255	152 487	29
		1980	33 514	13 400	40	1 033 418	333 771	32
		1981	35 825	15 214	42	1 110 655	366 856	33
		1982	38 678	17 372	45	1 065 588	368 657	35
		1983	42 374	20 818	49	1 068 224	371 422	35
	GENERAL	1975	19 397	8 008	41	493 384	141 497	29
		1980	28 552	11 890	42	954 536	303 154	32
		1981	30 580	13 467	44	1 028 348	335 929	33
		1982	32 735	15 139	46	974 250	333 629	34
		1983	36 144	18 229	50	962 003	331 480	34
	TEACHER TRAINING	1975	403	262	65	8 096	5 485	68
		1980	814	517	64	21 958	13 939	63
		1981	919	557	61	25 468	14 785	58
		1982	1 070	619	58	27 695	16 179	58
		1983	1 115	638	57	28 788	17 193	60
	VOCATIONAL	1975	1 654	272	16	23 775	5 505	23
		1980	4 148	993	24	56 924	16 678	29
		1981	4 326	1 190	28	56 839	16 142	28
		1982	4 873	1 614	33	63 643	18 849	30
		1983	5 115	1 951	38	77 433	22 749	29
ISRAEL‡	TOTAL SECOND LEVEL	1975	...	...	...	170 168	89 229	52
		1980	31 650	18 150	57	199 859	...	...
		1981	31 570	...	...	210 047	...	...
		1982	33 361	19 073	57	219 670	113 469	52
		1983	35 508	...	...	229 146	118 313	52
	GENERAL	1975	...	...	...	96 625	55 509	57
		1980	...	...	...	117 527	...	...
		1981	...	...	...	124 588	...	...
		1982	...	...	...	133 417	74 231	56
		1983	...	...	...	139 500	77 628	56
	TEACHER TRAINING		–	–	–	–	–	–
	VOCATIONAL	1975	...	...	...	73 543	33 720	46
		1980	...	...	...	82 332	38 236	46
		1981	...	...	...	85 459	...	...
		1982	...	...	...	86 253	39 238	45
		1983	...	...	...	89 646	40 685	45
JAPAN‡	TOTAL SECOND LEVEL	1975	502 946	124 792	25	8 795 780	4 362 848	50
		1980	554 078	145 943	26	9 520 948	4 718 610	50
		1981	553 684	145 330	26	9 798 282	4 855 000	50
		1982	578 694	156 690	27	10 036 175	4 974 914	50
		1983	589 577	160 860	27	10 244 607	5 075 830	50
		1984	603 098	165 952	28	10 613 444	5 225 838	49
	GENERAL	1975	...	...	...	7 290 748	3 655 221	50
		1980	...	...	...	8 110 230	4 057 997	50
		1982	...	...	...	8 699 975	4 348 414	50
		1983	...	...	...	8 911 407	4 449 530	50
		1984	...	...	...	9 232 444	4 589 397	50
	TEACHER TRAINING		–	–	–	–	–	–

COUNTRY PAYS PAIS	TYPE OF EDUCATION TYPE D'ENSEIGNEMENT TIPO DE ENSEÑANZA	YEAR ANNEE AÑO	TEACHING STAFF PERSONNEL ENSEIGNANT PERSONAL DOCENTE TOTAL (1)	FEMALE FEMININ FEMENINO (2)	% F (3)	PUPILS ENROLLED ELEVES INSCRITS ALUMNOS MATRICULADOS TOTAL (4)	FEMALE FEMININ FEMENINO (5)	% F (6)
JAPAN (CONT)‡	VOCATIONAL	1975	...	...	...	1 505 032	707 627	47
		1980	...	...	...	1 410 718	660 613	47
		1982	...	...	...	1 336 200	626 500	47
		1983	...	...	...	1 333 200	626 300	47
		1984	...	...	...	1 381 000	636 441	46
JORDAN‡	TOTAL SECOND LEVEL	1975	7 768	3 027	39	164 186	66 856	41
		1980	12 848	5 486	43	266 430	119 022	45
		1981	13 610	5 914	43	281 192	128 824	46
		1982	14 126	6 330	45	295 989	136 454	46
		1983	14 443	6 767	47	311 402	144 759	46
		1984	17 325	8 520	49	332 430	155 495	47
	GENERAL	1975	7 410	2 945	40	157 745	64 963	41
		1980	11 999	5 248	44	252 367	114 833	46
		1981	12 668	5 639	45	263 950	123 381	47
		1982	13 118	6 045	46	275 440	129 999	47
		1983	13 153	6 365	48	286 092	135 995	48
		1984	15 503	7 897	51	303 404	145 148	48
	TEACHER TRAINING		–	–	–	–	–	–
	VOCATIONAL	1975	358	82	23	6 441	1 893	29
		1980	849	238	28	14 063	4 189	30
		1981	942	275	29	17 242	5 443	32
		1982	1 008	285	28	20 549	6 455	31
		1983	1 290	402	31	25 310	8 764	35
		1984	1 822	623	34	29 026	10 347	36
KOREA, REPUBLIC OF‡	TOTAL SECOND LEVEL	1975	83 811	16 596	20	3 111 510	1 268 430	41
		1980	109 546	28 127	26	4 285 889	1 948 972	45
		1981	116 559	30 539	26	4 335 025	1 981 261	46
		1982	121 704	33 049	27	4 435 000	2 035 842	46
		1983	128 967	36 142	28	4 571 459	2 109 709	46
		1984	134 509	38 729	29	4 718 225	2 198 150	47
	GENERAL	1975	67 332	14 659	22	2 674 972	1 126 247	42
		1980	82 338	22 744	28	3 404 602	1 561 667	46
		1981	87 612	24 749	28	3 521 608	1 628 409	46
		1982	91 804	26 910	29	3 610 623	1 673 391	46
		1983	97 782	29 479	30	3 746 005	1 741 809	46
		1984	102 954	31 854	31	3 880 856	1 812 923	47
	TEACHER TRAINING		–	–	–	–	–	–
	VOCATIONAL	1975	16 479	1 937	12	436 538	142 183	33
		1980	27 208	5 383	20	881 287	387 305	44
		1981	28 947	5 790	20	813 417	352 852	43
		1982	29 900	6 139	21	824 377	362 451	44
		1983	31 185	6 663	21	825 454	367 900	45
		1984	31 555	6 875	22	837 369	385 227	46
KUWAIT	TOTAL SECOND LEVEL	1975	9 371	4 564	49	108 219	49 127	45
		1980	15 342	7 607	50	181 882	83 227	46
		1981	16 329	8 215	50	196 413	89 948	46
		1982	17 155	8 536	50	209 592	96 418	46
		1983	16 965	8 664	51	220 981	102 482	46
		1984	...	...	...	230 678	108 046	47
	GENERAL	1975	9 008	4 498	50	106 891	48 928	46
		1980	15 257	7 607	50	181 461	83 227	46
		1981	16 237	8 215	51	195 741	89 948	46
		1982	17 040	8 536	50	208 589	96 418	46
		1983	16 821	8 652	51	219 758	102 412	47
		1984	*17 958	*9 233	*51	229 738	107 966	47
	TEACHER TRAINING		–	–	–	–	–	–
	VOCATIONAL	1975	363	66	18	1 328	199	15
		1980	85	–	–	421	–	–
		1981	92	–	–	672	–	–
		1982	115	–	–	1 003	–	–
		1983	144	12	8	1 223	70	6
		1984	...	...	...	940	80	9
LAO PEOPLE'S DEMOCRATIC REPUBLIC‡	TOTAL SECOND LEVEL	1976	...	...	...	48 669	15 930	33
		1980	4 703	...	...	90 435	34 913	39
		1981	...	...	...	...	...	...
		1982	...	...	...	...	...	...
		1983	8 419	...	...	105 012	...	...
	GENERAL	1976	...	...	...	42 049	12 928	31
		1980	3 764	967	26	78 925	30 306	38
		1981	4 098	...	...	80 177	31 099	39
		1982	4 779	1 599	33	82 335	29 082	35
		1983	6 219	...	...	88 775	35 282	40

3.7 Education at the second level: teachers and pupils
Enseignement du second degré: personnel enseignant et élèves
Enseñanza de segundo grado: personal docente y alumnos

COUNTRY > PAYS / PAIS	TYPE OF EDUCATION / TYPE D'ENSEIGNEMENT / TIPO DE ENSEÑANZA	YEAR / ANNEE / AÑO	TEACHING STAFF / PERSONNEL ENSEIGNANT / PERSONAL DOCENTE			PUPILS ENROLLED / ELEVES INSCRITS / ALUMNOS MATRICULADOS		
			TOTAL	FEMALE FEMININ FEMENINO	% F	TOTAL	FEMALE FEMININ FEMENINO	% F
			(1)	(2)	(3)	(4)	(5)	(6)
LAO PEOPLE'S DEM. REPUBLIC (CONT)‡	TEACHER TRAINING	1976	...	...	...	5 726	2 767	48
		1980	650	223	34	9 508	4 048	43
		1983	1 093	267	24	9 481	...	...
	VOCATIONAL	1976	...	...	...	894	235	26
		1980	289	...	...	2 002	559	28
		1983	1 107	...	...	6 756	...	...
LEBANON‡	TOTAL SECOND LEVEL	1980	...	...	...	287 310	...	...
		1981	...	...	...	...	...	...
		1982	...	...	...	...	...	...
	GENERAL	1980	21 344	...	...	254 444	...	...
		1981	...	...	...	250 028	128 308	51
		1982	...	...	...	258 353	134 001	52
	TEACHER TRAINING	1980	392	123	31	1 663	1 316	79
	VOCATIONAL	1980	...	...	...	31 203	...	...
		1981	...	...	...	39 045	15 775	40
		1982	3 866	301	8	39 933	15 834	40
MACAU	TOTAL SECOND LEVEL	1975	564	...	...	11 758	...	...
		1976	737	...	...	14 305	...	...
	GENERAL	1975	382	...	...	7 867	...	...
		1976	527	...	...	9 701	...	...
	TEACHER TRAINING	1975	6	...	...	61	...	...
		1976	6	...	...	42	...	...
	VOCATIONAL	1975	176	...	...	3 830	...	...
		1976	204	...	...	4 562	...	...
MALAYSIA‡	TOTAL SECOND LEVEL	1975	34 133	...	...	933 411	...	...
		1980	48 284	...	...	1 094 715	...	...
		1982	54 695	...	...	1 155 779	...	...
		1983	54 787	25 121	46	1 173 202	568 452	48
		1984	...	...	...	1 272 930	623 129	49
		1985	58 630	27 728	47	1 299 114	638 617	49
	GENERAL	1975	32 394	...	...	899 669	396 473	44
		1980	46 801	...	...	1 076 137	...	...
		1982	53 141	...	...	1 137 701	...	...
		1983	53 176	24 762	47	1 156 466	563 383	49
		1984	...	...	...	1 252 746	617 331	49
		1985	56 931	27 320	48	*1 278 394	*632 605	*49
	TEACHER TRAINING		–	–	–	–	–	–
	VOCATIONAL	1975	1 739	...	...	33 742	...	...
		1980	1 483	...	...	18 578	...	...
		1982	1 554	...	...	18 078	...	...
		1983	1 611	359	22	16 736	5 069	30
		1984	...	...	...	20 184	5 798	29
		1985	1 699	408	24	20 720	6 012	29
MALDIVES	TOTAL SECOND LEVEL	1980	...	...	...	998	...	...
		1981	...	...	...	1 217	...	...
		1982	...	...	...	1 870	...	...
		1983	...	...	...	2 756	...	...
	GENERAL	1975	...	...	...	459	255	56
		1980	...	...	...	875	...	...
		1981	...	...	...	1 116	...	...
		1982	...	...	...	1 466	...	...
		1983	...	...	...	2 344	...	...
	TEACHER TRAINING		–	–	–	–	–	–
	VOCATIONAL	1980	...	...	...	123	...	...
		1981	...	...	...	101	...	...
		1982	...	...	...	404	...	...
		1983	...	...	...	412	...	...
MONGOLIA	TOTAL SECOND LEVEL	1975	...	...	...	184 688	95 719	52
		1980	...	...	...	245 600	...	...
		1981	...	...	...	252 200	...	...
		1982	11 500	...	...	256 700	135 100	53
		1983	...	...	...	266 100	...	...
		1984	...	...	...	273 900	...	...
	GENERAL	1975	...	...	...	172 134	87 715	51
		1980	...	...	...	226 900	117 000	52
		1981	...	...	...	232 400	119 700	52
		1982	10 400	...	...	236 000	121 600	52
		1983	...	...	...	244 700	127 000	52
		1984	...	...	...	252 100	128 600	51

COUNTRY PAYS PAIS	TYPE OF EDUCATION TYPE D'ENSEIGNEMENT TIPO DE ENSEÑANZA	YEAR ANNEE AÑO	TEACHING STAFF / PERSONNEL ENSEIGNANT / PERSONAL DOCENTE TOTAL	FEMALE FEMININ FEMENINO	% F	PUPILS ENROLLED / ELEVES INSCRITS / ALUMNOS MATRICULADOS TOTAL	FEMALE FEMININ FEMENINO	% F
			(1)	(2)	(3)	(4)	(5)	(6)
MONGOLIA (CONT)	TEACHER TRAINING	1975	137	63	46	1 618	1 343	83
		1982	200	100	50	2 300	1 900	83
	VOCATIONAL	1975	...	...	...	10 936	6 661	61
		1982	900	400	44	18 400	11 600	63
NEPAL‡	TOTAL SECOND LEVEL	1976	11 295	*1 055	*9	262 748	45 932	17
		1980	16 376	1 498	9	512 434	102 502	20
		1981	17 154	...	...	313 895	61 627	20
		1982	16 454	...	...	370 082	76 003	21
		1983	15 910	*1 462	*9	418 085	91 041	22
		1984	17 069	*1 490	*9	455 401	104 509	23
	GENERAL	1976	10 609	...	...	243 231	...	...
	TEACHER TRAINING	1976	173	...	...	2 702	...	...
	VOCATIONAL	1976	513	...	...	16 815	...	...
OMAN	TOTAL SECOND LEVEL	1975	208	33	16	1 379	227	16
		1980	...	...	...	16 785	...	...
		1981	1 915	576	30	21 226	...	...
		1982	2 530	674	27	28 221	7 523	27
		1983	3 148	895	28	33 913	9 717	29
		1984	...	...	...	41 749	12 933	31
	GENERAL	1975	188	33	18	1 295	227	18
		1980	1 733	461	27	15 280	3 828	25
		1981	1 794	540	30	19 591	5 420	28
		1982	2 171	621	29	25 796	7 054	27
		1983	2 667	824	31	31 193	9 199	29
		1984	2 858	921	32	38 844	12 428	32
	TEACHER TRAINING	1975	–	–	–	–	–	–
		1980	65	28	43	483	230	48
		1981	78	36	46	634	296	47
		1982	87	38	44	813	358	44
		1983	119	50	42	799	348	44
		1984	92	40	43	658	304	46
	VOCATIONAL	1975	20	–	–	84	–	–
		1980	...	...	...	1 022	...	...
		1981	...	...	...	1 001	...	...
		1982	272	15	6	1 612	111	7
		1983	362	21	6	1 921	170	9
		1984	...	...	...	2 247	201	9
PAKISTAN	TOTAL SECOND LEVEL	1975	106 960	31 492	29	1 935 849	451 729	23
		1980	123 817	...	...	2 165 832	558 029	26
		1981	128 467	38 270	30	2 253 298	582 680	26
		1982	141 613	42 419	30	2 341 143	606 688	26
		1983	154 759	46 585	30	2 402 121	...	...
	GENERAL	1975	104 086	30 687	29	1 901 344	442 284	23
		1980	120 646	...	...	2 125 418	551 305	26
		1981	*125 059	*37 527	*30	2 208 216	575 008	26
		1982	137 997	41 644	30	2 291 856	599 011	26
		1983	150 935	45 761	30	2 347 789	...	...
	TEACHER TRAINING	1975	987	422	43	8 790	3 853	44
		1980	1 177	316	27	6 922	916	13
		1981	1 305	332	25	7 419	1 086	15
		1982	1 498	381	25	8 841	1 552	18
		1983	1 691	430	25	10 263	2 018	20
	VOCATIONAL	1975	1 887	383	20	25 715	5 592	22
		1980	1 994	395	20	33 492	5 808	17
		1981	2 103	411	20	37 663	6 586	17
		1982	2 118	394	19	40 446	6 125	15
		1983	2 133	394	18	44 069	6 506	15
PHILIPPINES	TOTAL SECOND LEVEL	1975	72 778	...	...	2 291 707	...	...
		1980	85 779	...	...	2 928 525	1 559 313	53
		1981	85 465	...	...	2 935 732	1 503 287	51
		1982	90 266	...	...	3 092 128	1 583 409	51
		1983	91 602	...	...	3 204 551	1 622 767	51
		1984	103 493	*98 387	*95	3 323 512	1 683 026	51
	TEACHER TRAINING		–	–	–	–	–	–
QATAR	TOTAL SECOND LEVEL	1975	829	372	45	10 109	4 829	48
		1980	1 624	817	50	15 901	7 680	48
		1981	1 755	903	51	17 158	8 291	48
		1982	2 139	1 086	51	18 864	9 187	49
		1983	2 210	1 173	53	19 607	9 689	49
		1984	2 316	1 274	55	20 979	10 475	50

3.7 Education at the second level: teachers and pupils
Enseignement du second degré: personnel enseignant et élèves
Enseñanza de segundo grado: personal docente y alumnos

COUNTRY / PAYS / PAIS	TYPE OF EDUCATION / TYPE D'ENSEIGNEMENT / TIPO DE ENSEÑANZA	YEAR / ANNEE / AÑO	TEACHING STAFF / PERSONNEL ENSEIGNANT / PERSONAL DOCENTE: TOTAL	FEMALE / FEMININ / FEMENINO	% F	PUPILS ENROLLED / ELEVES INSCRITS / ALUMNOS MATRICULADOS: TOTAL	FEMALE / FEMININ / FEMENINO	% F
			(1)	(2)	(3)	(4)	(5)	(6)
QATAR (CONT)	GENERAL	1975	698	335	48	9 416	4 560	48
		1980	1 538	817	53	15 461	7 680	50
		1981	1 668	903	54	16 696	8 291	50
		1982	2 053	1 086	53	18 346	9 187	50
		1983	2 119	1 173	55	19 037	9 689	51
		1984	2 228	1 274	57	20 398	10 475	51
	TEACHER TRAINING	1975	56	37	66	324	269	83
		1980	–	–	–	–	–	–
		1981	–	–	–	–	–	–
		1982	–	–	–	–	–	–
		1983	–	–	–	–	–	–
		1984	–	–	–	–	–	–
	VOCATIONAL	1975	75	–	–	369	–	–
		1980	86	–	–	440	–	–
		1981	87	–	–	462	–	–
		1982	86	–	–	518	–	–
		1983	91	–	–	570	–	–
		1984	88	–	–	581	–	–
SAUDI ARABIA	TOTAL SECOND LEVEL	1975	13 956	3 360	24	202 741	65 996	33
		1980	26 634	8 980	34	348 996	132 368	38
		1981	29 573	10 584	36	379 575	146 818	39
		1982	32 482	12 289	38	419 031	163 433	39
		1983	35 478	12 953	37	503 074	185 902	37
	GENERAL	1975	12 154	3 038	25	184 404	61 673	33
		1980	24 254	8 058	33	328 328	122 307	37
		1981	27 232	9 836	36	360 174	139 181	39
		1982	30 168	11 673	39	400 564	157 939	39
		1983	33 264	12 533	38	483 683	182 089	38
	TEACHER TRAINING	1975	1 156	288	25	14 015	4 064	29
		1980	1 619	922	57	15 562	10 061	65
		1981	1 492	748	50	13 467	7 637	57
		1982	1 436	616	43	11 817	5 494	46
		1983	981	420	43	9 069	3 813	42
	VOCATIONAL	1975	646	34	5	4 322	259	6
		1980	761	–	–	5 106	–	–
		1981	849	–	–	5 934	–	–
		1982	878	–	–	6 650	–	–
		1983	1 233	–	–	10 322	–	–
SINGAPORE	TOTAL SECOND LEVEL	1975	7 951	...	...	183 364	89 980	49
		1980	9 298	4 863	52	180 817	90 306	50
		1981	9 162	4 816	53	186 212	...	...
		1982	10 231	5 511	54	187 148	92 156	49
		1983	9 704	5 194	54	193 007	95 036	49
		1984	9 644	5 092	53	197 183	97 799	50
	GENERAL	1975	7 211	*3 406	*47	176 224	89 471	51
		1980	8 275	4 613	56	171 426	88 182	51
		1981	8 273	4 611	56	177 238	90 716	51
		1982	9 032	5 282	58	176 845	90 026	51
		1983	8 644	4 956	57	182 343	92 283	51
		1984	8 236	4 743	58	187 764	94 968	51
	TEACHER TRAINING		–	–	–	–	–	–
	VOCATIONAL	1975	740	...	...	7 140	509	7
		1980	1 023	250	24	9 391	2 124	23
		1981	889	205	23	8 974	...	...
		1982	1 199	229	19	10 303	2 130	21
		1983	1 060	238	22	10 664	2 753	26
		1984	1 408	349	25	9 419	2 831	30
SRI LANKA‡	TOTAL SECOND LEVEL	1976	...	...	...	1 088 089	554 442	51
		1980	...	...	...	...	...	...
		1981	...	...	...	...	...	...
		1982	...	...	...	...	...	...
		1983	...	...	...	...	...	...
		1984	...	...	...	...	...	...
	GENERAL	1976	57 854	...	...	1 076 502	548 898	51
		1980	...	...	...	1 258 002	641 045	51
		1981	...	...	...	1 293 213	669 512	52
		1982	...	...	...	1 315 062	683 628	52
		1983	...	...	...	1 367 754	708 793	52
		1984	...	...	...	1 382 574	718 238	52
	TEACHER TRAINING	1976	...	...	...	6 809	3 946	58
		1980	689	...	...	9 321	...	...
		1981	–	–	–	–	–	–
		1982	–	–	–	–	–	–
		1983	–	–	–	–	–	–
		1984	–	–	–	–	–	–

COUNTRY / PAYS / PAIS	TYPE OF EDUCATION / TYPE D'ENSEIGNEMENT / TIPO DE ENSEÑANZA	YEAR / ANNEE / AÑO	TEACHING STAFF / PERSONNEL ENSEIGNANT / PERSONAL DOCENTE: TOTAL	FEMALE / FEMININ / FEMENINO	% F	PUPILS ENROLLED / ELEVES INSCRITS / ALUMNOS MATRICULADOS: TOTAL	FEMALE / FEMININ / FEMENINO	% F
			(1)	(2)	(3)	(4)	(5)	(6)
SRI LANKA (CONT)‡	VOCATIONAL	1976	1 239	72	6	4 778	1 598	33
SYRIAN ARAB REPUBLIC‡	TOTAL SECOND LEVEL	1975	24 895	7 506	30	488 409	152 060	31
		1980	...	...	...	604 327	220 939	37
		1981	35 357	7 826	22	635 355	235 010	37
		1982	40 119	9 073	23	687 435	258 503	38
		1983	45 035	10 248	23	755 095	288 386	38
		1984	48 599	11 085	23	815 071	318 840	39
	GENERAL	1975	22 704	7 062	31	463 348	146 925	32
		1980	29 573	6 536	22	577 990	213 345	37
		1981	31 573	7 269	23	600 716	226 288	38
		1982	35 185	8 430	24	643 847	247 989	39
		1983	38 480	9 384	24	701 330	276 255	39
		1984	41 503	10 052	24	757 228	304 718	40
	TEACHER TRAINING	1975	514	253	49	3 015	1 371	45
		1980	...	...	...	147	88	60
		1981	–	–	–	–	–	–
		1982	–	–	–	–	–	–
		1983	–	–	–	–	–	–
		1984	–	–	–	–	–	–
	VOCATIONAL	1975	1 677	191	11	22 046	3 764	17
		1980	3 280	...	...	26 190	7 506	29
		1981	3 784	557	15	34 639	8 722	25
		1982	4 934	643	13	43 588	10 514	24
		1983	6 555	864	13	53 765	12 131	23
		1984	*7 096	1 033	*15	57 843	14 122	24
THAILAND‡	TOTAL SECOND LEVEL	1975	43 830	...	...	1 193 741	523 203	44
		1980	...	...	...	1 919 967	...	...
		1981	...	...	...	1 990 866	...	...
		1983	...	...	...	2 191 713	...	...
	GENERAL	1975	29 527	...	...	956 427	414 461	43
		1980	70 201	39 818	57	1 617 465	740 077	46
		1981	76 339	...	...	1 572 587	...	...
		1983	85 081	...	...	1 754 925	...	...
	TEACHER TRAINING	1975	4 588	2 343	51	46 248	22 944	50
		1980	...	...	...	5 388	2 746	51
		1981	...	...	...	1 632	...	...
		1983	80	...	...	963	...	...
	VOCATIONAL	1975	*9 715	*3 991	*41	191 066	85 798	45
		1980	...	...	...	297 114	...	...
		1981	...	...	...	416 647	...	...
		1983	19 715	...	...	435 825	...	...
TURKEY	TOTAL SECOND LEVEL	1975	...	...	...	1 746 160	549 551	31
		1981	117 644	41 414	35	2 310 113	792 901	34
		1982	129 268	45 082	35	2 393 477	833 477	35
		1983	132 217	46 578	35	2 540 636	891 879	35
		1984	...	...	...	...	...	...
	GENERAL	1975	...	...	...	1 371 444	433 492	32
		1981	81 155	29 144	36	1 779 618	637 919	36
		1982	88 600	31 335	35	1 852 530	677 372	37
		1983	90 759	32 547	36	1 980 523	733 976	37
	TEACHER TRAINING	1975	...	...	...	53 445	25 181	47
		1980	1 012	...	...	15 785	...	...
		1981	968	232	24	15 776	5 083	32
		1982	986	281	28	16 819	5 532	33
		1983	983	282	29	17 815	5 744	32
	VOCATIONAL	1975	...	...	...	*321 271	*90 878	*28
		1981	35 521	12 038	34	514 719	149 899	29
		1982	39 682	13 466	34	524 128	150 573	29
		1983	40 475	13 749	34	542 298	152 159	28
		1984	41 020	16 473	40	576 067	160 568	28
UNITED ARAB EMIRATES‡	TOTAL SECOND LEVEL	1975	...	...	...	12 562	4 661	37
		1980	...	...	...	32 362	14 451	45
		1981	...	...	...	39 868	18 253	46
		1982	...	...	...	45 957	21 126	46
		1983	...	...	...	51 892	24 134	47
		1984	...	...	...	56 733	27 006	48
	GENERAL	1975	1 389	564	41	12 148	4 569	38
		1980	2 829	1 344	48	31 940	14 451	45
		1981	2 788	1 386	50	39 266	18 253	46
		1982	3 311	1 651	50	45 235	21 126	47
		1983	3 462	1 759	51	51 277	24 134	47
		1984	3 660	1 898	52	56 126	27 006	48

COUNTRY / PAYS / PAIS	TYPE OF EDUCATION / TYPE D'ENSEIGNEMENT / TIPO DE ENSEÑANZA	YEAR / ANNEE / AÑO	TEACHING STAFF / PERSONNEL ENSEIGNANT / PERSONAL DOCENTE: TOTAL	FEMALE / FEMININ / FEMENINO	% F	PUPILS ENROLLED / ELEVES INSCRITS / ALUMNOS MATRICULADOS: TOTAL	FEMALE / FEMININ / FEMENINO	% F
			(1)	(2)	(3)	(4)	(5)	(6)
UNITED ARAB EMIRATES (CONT)‡	TEACHER TRAINING	1975	...	...	...	118	92	78
		1980	–	–	–	–	–	–
		1981	–	–	–	–	–	–
		1982	–	–	–	–	–	–
		1983	–	–	–	–	–	–
		1984	–	–	–	–	–	–
	VOCATIONAL	1975	90	1	1	296	–	–
		1980	...	...	...	422	–	–
		1981	...	...	...	602	–	–
		1982	...	...	...	722	–	–
		1983	...	...	...	615	–	–
		1984	...	...	...	607	–	–
VIET-NAM‡	TOTAL SECOND LEVEL	1976	127 635	73 389	57	3 200 912	1 563 012	49
		1980	...	...	...	...	...	...
	GENERAL	1976	119 388	71 230	60	3 108 629	1 522 217	49
		1980	148 973	86 182	58	3 846 737	1 808 028	47
	TEACHER TRAINING	1976	2 336	607	26	25 730	17 803	69
		1980	...	...	...	20 397	4 601	23
	VOCATIONAL	1976	5 911	1 552	26	66 553	22 992	35
YEMEN‡	TOTAL SECOND LEVEL	1975	...	...	...	24 606	3 200	13
		1980	...	...	...	40 733	*5 402	*13
		1981	...	...	...	50 178	6 930	14
		1982	...	...	...	63 933	*8 083	*13
		1983	...	...	...	84 835	11 132	13
	GENERAL	1975	1 042	...	...	22 581	2 557	11
		1980	2 023	...	...	38 293	*4 637	*12
		1981	2 446	...	...	47 699	*6 240	*13
		1982	3 432	293	9	60 032	*6 891	*11
		1983	3 679	308	8	78 665	9 616	12
	TEACHER TRAINING	1975	113	38	34	1 459	643	44
		1980	...	...	...	1 548	673	43
		1981	...	...	...	1 547	594	38
		1982	297	72	24	2 763	1 069	39
		1983	...	...	...	4 489	1 372	31
	VOCATIONAL	1975	...	...	...	566	–	–
		1980	...	...	...	892	92	10
		1981	...	...	...	932	96	10
		1982	...	...	...	1 138	123	11
		1983	273	...	...	1 681	144	9
EUROPE								
ALBANIA‡	TOTAL SECOND LEVEL	1980	5 392	1 903	35	163 866	73 288	45
		1981	5 630	2 100	37	150 700	67 540	45
		1982	5 000	1 850	37	148 285	...	...
		1983	5 500	2 050	37	156 248	...	...
		1984	6 957	2 652	38	159 440	72 264	45
	GENERAL	1980	1 008	468	46	30 780	18 070	59
		1981	1 100	410	37	29 460	17 500	59
		1982	1 250	450	36	29 992	...	...
		1983	1 370	510	37	32 500	...	...
		1984	1 552	592	38	35 643	20 566	58
	TEACHER TRAINING	1980	21	19	90	604	532	88
		1981	30	10	33	900	800	89
		1982	80	30	38	1 400	1 100	79
		1983	110	40	36	1 713	1 221	71
		1984	118	45	38	2 387	1 580	66
	VOCATIONAL	1980	4 363	1 416	32	132 482	54 686	41
		1981	4 500	1 680	37	120 340	49 240	41
		1982	3 670	1 370	37	63 400	29 300	46
		1983	4 020	1 500	37	69 354	32 264	47
		1984	5 287	2 015	38	121 410	50 118	41
ANDORRA	TOTAL SECOND LEVEL	1975	...	...	...	1 753	1 092	62
		1982	...	...	...	2 516	1 271	51
	GENERAL	1975	...	...	...	1 753	1 092	62
		1982	...	...	...	2 516	1 271	51
	TEACHER TRAINING		–	–	–	–	–	–
	VOCATIONAL		–	–	–	–	–	–

COUNTRY / PAYS / PAIS	TYPE OF EDUCATION / TYPE D'ENSEIGNEMENT / TIPO DE ENSEÑANZA	YEAR / ANNEE / AÑO	TEACHING STAFF / PERSONNEL ENSEIGNANT / PERSONAL DOCENTE: TOTAL	FEMALE / FEMININ / FEMENINO	% F	PUPILS ENROLLED / ELEVES INSCRITS / ALUMNOS MATRICULADOS: TOTAL	FEMALE / FEMININ / FEMENINO	% F
			(1)	(2)	(3)	(4)	(5)	(6)
AUSTRIA‡	TOTAL SECOND LEVEL	1975	...	...	...	755 670	374 266	50
		1980	63 678	32 594	51	739 702	368 154	50
		1981	65 747	34 055	52	713 106	358 996	50
		1982	66 756	35 257	53	705 441	353 493	50
		1983	68 755	36 585	53	682 983	342 643	50
		1984	67 975	36 839	54	671 925	340 663	51
	GENERAL	1975	...	...	...	629 852	307 616	49
		1980	47 841	25 861	54	583 382	284 271	49
		1981	49 285	26 909	55	565 276	275 466	49
		1982	49 734	27 592	55	548 838	266 965	49
		1983	50 694	28 349	56	524 067	255 039	49
		1984	50 613	28 626	57	500 702	243 556	49
	TEACHER TRAINING	1975	...	...	...	6 283	6 247	99
		1980	708	574	81	5 339	5 289	99
		1981	803	618	77	5 277	5 214	99
		1982	864	701	81	5 218	5 146	99
		1983	841	685	81	5 011	4 934	98
		1984	863	697	81	4 863	4 766	98
	VOCATIONAL	1975	...	...	...	119 535	60 403	51
		1980	15 129	6 159	41	150 981	78 594	52
		1981	15 659	6 528	42	142 553	78 316	55
		1982	16 158	6 964	43	151 385	81 382	54
		1983	17 220	7 551	44	153 905	82 670	54
		1984	16 499	7 516	46	166 360	92 341	56
BELGIUM‡	TOTAL SECOND LEVEL	1975	...	...	...	795 203	387 798	49
		1980	...	...	...	835 524	415 108	50
		1981	...	...	...	835 177	413 756	50
		1982	...	...	...	818 611	407 571	50
		1983	...	...	...	825 108	407 730	49
		1984	...	...	...	827 839	409 333	49
	GENERAL	1975	...	...	...	494 684	232 727	47
	TEACHER TRAINING		–	–	–	–	–	–
	VOCATIONAL	1975	...	...	...	300 519	155 071	52
		1980	...	...	...	264 911	...	...
		1981	...	...	...	227 720	114 685	50
		1982	...	...	...	237 469	117 338	49
		1983	...	...	...	376 227	181 186	48
		1984	...	...	...	374 519	178 704	48
BULGARIA	TOTAL SECOND LEVEL	1975	27 045	14 079	52	344 015	...	...
		1980	25 666	13 656	53	314 753	151 529	48
		1981	25 684	13 906	54	306 240	148 240	48
		1982	25 102	14 100	56	305 577	147 901	48
		1983	25 201	14 270	57	318 201	155 236	49
		1984	25 692	14 712	57	336 044	164 047	49
	GENERAL	1975	7 637	4 822	63	101 206	...	...
		1980	7 159	4 604	64	91 863	62 673	68
		1981	7 986	5 083	64	99 229	66 824	67
		1982	8 459	5 632	67	112 436	73 443	65
		1983	8 577	5 716	67	134 233	86 707	65
		1984	8 992	6 079	68	152 838	96 871	63
	TEACHER TRAINING		–	–	–	–	–	–
	VOCATIONAL	1975	19 408	9 257	48	242 809	101 406	42
		1980	18 507	9 052	49	222 890	88 856	40
		1981	17 698	8 823	50	207 011	81 416	39
		1982	16 643	8 468	51	193 141	74 458	39
		1983	16 624	8 554	51	183 968	68 529	37
		1984	16 700	8 633	52	183 206	67 176	37
CZECHOSLOVAKIA	TOTAL SECOND LEVEL	1975	32 739	14 132	43	320 531	196 646	61
		1980	33 227	15 280	46	388 561	240 160	62
		1981	33 364	15 590	47	393 343	243 767	62
		1982	32 852	15 686	48	390 051	241 787	62
		1983	32 386	15 784	49	372 503	232 327	62
		1984	32 460	15 981	49	355 069	222 763	63
	GENERAL	1975	9 213	5 113	55	121 283	77 136	64
		1980	9 850	5 512	56	145 395	89 785	62
		1981	10 143	5 662	56	149 210	92 745	62
		1982	10 152	5 761	57	149 055	93 522	63
		1983	10 329	5 891	57	143 512	90 460	63
		1984	10 581	6 011	57	137 125	86 117	63

3.7 Education at the second level: teachers and pupils
Enseignement du second degré: personnel enseignant et élèves
Enseñanza de segundo grado: personal docente y alumnos

COUNTRY / PAYS / PAIS	TYPE OF EDUCATION / TYPE D'ENSEIGNEMENT / TIPO DE ENSEÑANZA	YEAR / ANNEE / AÑO	TEACHING STAFF / PERSONNEL ENSEIGNANT / PERSONAL DOCENTE			PUPILS ENROLLED / ELEVES INSCRITS / ALUMNOS MATRICULADOS		
			TOTAL	FEMALE / FEMININ / FEMENINO	% F	TOTAL	FEMALE / FEMININ / FEMENINO	% F
			(1)	(2)	(3)	(4)	(5)	(6)
CZECHOSLOVAKIA (CONT)	TEACHER TRAINING	1975	699	404	58	8 786	8 615	98
		1980	986	606	61	14 457	14 293	99
		1981	1 026	644	63	14 590	14 457	99
		1982	973	631	65	13 141	12 975	99
		1983	888	605	68	11 487	11 360	99
		1984	820	555	68	10 110	9 939	98
	VOCATIONAL	1975	22 827	8 615	38	190 462	110 895	58
		1980	22 391	9 162	41	228 709	136 082	60
		1981	22 195	9 284	42	229 543	136 565	59
		1982	21 727	9 294	43	227 855	135 290	59
		1983	21 169	9 288	44	217 504	130 507	60
		1984	21 059	9 415	45	207 834	126 707	61
DENMARK‡	TOTAL SECOND LEVEL	1975	...	...	...	365 561	...	...
		1980	...	...	...	498 944	242 206	49
		1981	...	...	...	498 462	242 307	49
		1982	...	...	...	495 950	239 760	48
		1983	...	...	...	486 541	235 522	48
	GENERAL	1975	...	...	...	327 588	...	...
		1980	...	...	...	372 948	190 742	51
		1981	...	...	...	368 564	188 420	51
		1982	...	...	...	357 654	182 960	51
		1983	...	...	...	345 682	177 179	51
	TEACHER TRAINING		–	–	–	–	–	–
	VOCATIONAL	1975	...	...	...	37 973	...	...
		1980	...	...	...	125 996	51 464	41
		1981	...	...	...	129 898	53 887	41
		1982	...	...	...	138 296	56 800	41
		1983	...	...	...	140 859	58 343	41
FINLAND‡	TOTAL SECOND LEVEL	1975	...	...	...	419 808	218 933	52
		1980	33 958	...	...	444 165	229 820	52
		1981	34 248	...	...	441 232	228 991	52
		1982	37 098	...	...	432 761	225 314	52
		1983	37 356	...	...	433 646	229 446	53
		1984	...	...	...	...	...	...
	GENERAL	1975	23 139	...	...	337 575	180 566	53
		1980	19 822	...	...	341 054	181 292	53
		1981	19 863	...	...	336 605	179 608	53
		1982	22 279	...	...	325 763	174 143	53
		1983	22 356	...	...	316 740	169 990	54
		1984	...	...	...	310 639	166 746	54
	TEACHER TRAINING	1975	...	...	...	703	470	67
		1980	188	43	23	872	574	66
		1981	82	40	49	891	568	64
		1982	84	43	51	860	558	65
		1983	86	...	...	917	622	68
	VOCATIONAL	1975	...	...	...	81 530	37 897	46
		1980	13 948	5 834	42	102 239	47 954	47
		1981	14 303	6 070	42	103 736	48 815	47
		1982	14 735	6 307	43	106 138	50 613	48
		1983	14 914	...	...	115 989	58 834	51
		1984	14 800	...	...	114 457	58 645	51
FRANCE‡	TOTAL SECOND LEVEL	1975	316 341	...	...	4 890 152	...	...
		1980	256 369	...	...	5 013 666	2 677 574	53
		1981	288 714	159 097	55	5 050 028	2 603 341	52
		1982	318 452	174 315	55	5 124 403	2 637 123	51
		1983	310 698	172 437	56	5 225 994	*2 735 287	*52
	GENERAL	1975	...	...	...	3 864 720	...	...
		1980	...	...	...	3 911 054	1 929 406	49
		1981	238 852	138 194	58	3 791 497	2 007 429	53
		1982	260 480	150 192	58	3 803 119	2 027 170	53
		1983	...	...	...	3 926 016	*2 036 860	*52
	TEACHER TRAINING	1975	...	...	...	16 000	...	...
		1980	–	–	–	–	–	–
		1981	–	–	–	–	–	–
		1982	–	–	–	–	–	–
		1983	–	–	–	–	–	–
	VOCATIONAL	1975	58 546	...	...	1 009 432	...	...
		1980	...	...	...	1 102 612	748 168	68
		1981	49 862	20 903	42	1 258 531	595 912	47
		1982	57 972	24 123	42	1 321 284	609 953	46
		1983	...	...	...	1 299 978	*698 427	*54

COUNTRY PAYS PAIS	TYPE OF EDUCATION TYPE D'ENSEIGNEMENT TIPO DE ENSEÑANZA	YEAR ANNEE AÑO	TEACHING STAFF / PERSONNEL ENSEIGNANT / PERSONAL DOCENTE TOTAL	 FEMALE FEMININ FEMENINO	 % F	PUPILS ENROLLED / ELEVES INSCRITS / ALUMNOS MATRICULADOS TOTAL	 FEMALE FEMININ FEMENINO	 % F
			(1)	(2)	(3)	(4)	(5)	(6)
GERMAN DEMOCRATIC REPUBLIC‡	TOTAL SECOND LEVEL	1975	...	...	...	460 639	...	...
		1980	...	...	...	506 412	...	...
		1981	...	...	...	494 451	...	...
		1982	...	...	...	476 334	...	...
		1983	...	...	...	456 151	...	...
		1984	...	...	...	435 892	...	...
	GENERAL	1975	...	...	...	47 854	...	...
		1980	...	...	...	46 927	25 085	53
		1981	...	...	...	46 051	24 451	53
		1982	...	...	...	45 334	24 079	53
		1983	...	...	...	44 985	...	...
		1984	...	...	...	44 266	...	...
	TEACHER TRAINING		–	–	–	–	–	–
	VOCATIONAL	1975	14 379	...	...	412 785	...	...
		1980	16 355	...	...	459 485	...	...
		1981	16 553	...	...	448 400	...	...
		1982	16 640	...	...	431 000	...	...
		1983	...	...	...	411 166	...	...
		1984	...	...	...	391 626	...	...
GERMANY, FEDERAL REPUBLIC OF‡	TOTAL SECOND LEVEL	1975	...	...	...	3 638 200	1 842 645	51
		1980	298 277	121 823	41	4 300 740	2 220 663	52
		1981	306 966	...	...	4 318 013	2 229 613	52
		1982	307 179	...	...	4 254 046	2 200 834	52
		1983	*437 559	...	...	5 967 864	2 981 859	50
	GENERAL	1975	210 891	81 694	39	3 176 508	1 593 215	50
		1980	237 656	100 482	42	3 690 340	1 892 766	51
		1981	243 490	103 621	43	3 655 459	1 879 474	51
		1982	241 449	102 316	42	3 554 861	1 829 161	51
		1983	*371 072	*168 836	*46	5 280 370	2 609 167	49
	TEACHER TRAINING		–	–	–	–	–	–
	VOCATIONAL	1975	...	...	...	461 692	249 430	54
		1980	60 621	21 341	35	610 400	327 897	54
		1981	63 476	...	...	662 554	350 139	53
		1982	65 730	...	...	699 185	371 673	53
		1983	66 487	...	...	687 494	372 692	54
GIBRALTAR	TOTAL SECOND LEVEL	1975	132	53	40	1 629	824	51
		1980	...	...	...	1 811	899	50
		1981	143	55	38	1 842	917	50
		1982	145	51	35	1 832	915	50
		1983	145	53	37	1 825	912	50
	GENERAL	1975	114	53	46	1 587	823	52
		1980	123	52	42	1 770	899	51
		1981	125	54	43	1 794	916	51
		1982	126	50	40	1 764	914	52
		1983	126	52	41	1 749	908	52
	TEACHER TRAINING		–	–	–	–	–	–
	VOCATIONAL	1975	18	–	–	42	1	2
		1980	...	...	...	41	–	–
		1981	18	1	6	48	1	2
		1982	19	1	5	68	1	1
		1983	19	1	5	76	4	5
GREECE	TOTAL SECOND LEVEL	1975	...	...	...	661 796	283 855	43
		1980	39 571	19 429	49	740 058	337 816	46
		1981	41 023	20 328	50	778 024	360 169	46
		1982	...	...	...	...	...	...
	GENERAL	1975	18 719	9 952	53	529 205	266 493	50
		1980	31 737	17 547	55	639 633	317 863	50
		1981	33 613	18 746	56	669 812	333 537	50
		1982	35 996	20 162	56	677 712	338 276	50
	TEACHER TRAINING		–	–	–	–	–	–
	VOCATIONAL	1980	7 834	1 882	24	100 425	19 953	20
		1981	7 410	1 582	21	108 212	26 632	25
HUNGARY‡	TOTAL SECOND LEVEL	1975	22 781	...	...	371 898	168 126	45
		1980	...	...	...	357 334	165 679	46
		1981	...	...	...	375 588	179 612	48
		1982	...	...	...	395 976	189 994	48
		1983	...	...	...	409 585	196 934	48
		1984	...	...	...	420 104	202 916	48

3.7 **Education at the second level: teachers and pupils**
Enseignement du second degré: personnel enseignant et élèves
Enseñanza de segundo grado: personal docente y alumnos

COUNTRY / PAYS / PAIS	TYPE OF EDUCATION / TYPE D'ENSEIGNEMENT / TIPO DE ENSEÑANZA	YEAR / ANNEE / AÑO	TEACHING STAFF / PERSONNEL ENSEIGNANT / PERSONAL DOCENTE: TOTAL	FEMALE / FEMININ / FEMENINO	% F	PUPILS ENROLLED / ELEVES INSCRITS / ALUMNOS MATRICULADOS: TOTAL	FEMALE / FEMININ / FEMENINO	% F
			(1)	(2)	(3)	(4)	(5)	(6)
HUNGARY (CONT)‡	GENERAL	1975	6 663	...	...	99 656	64 905	65
		1980	6 639	4 027	61	89 400	58 286	65
		1981	6 888	4 197	61	93 104	60 676	65
		1982	7 155	4 405	62	97 588	63 871	65
		1983	7 409	4 630	62	101 230	66 028	65
		1984	7 709	4 867	63	104 534	68 012	65
	TEACHER TRAINING	1975	...	...	...	4 913	4 913	100
		1980	...	...	...	5 897	5 894	100
		1981	...	...	...	5 332	5 329	100
		1982	...	...	...	4 938	4 934	100
		1983	...	...	...	4 950	4 947	100
		1984	...	...	...	5 025	5 021	100
	VOCATIONAL	1975	...	...	...	267 329	98 308	37
		1980	...	...	...	262 037	101 499	39
		1981	...	...	...	277 152	113 607	41
		1982	...	...	...	293 450	121 189	41
		1983	...	...	...	303 405	125 959	42
		1984	...	...	...	310 545	129 883	42
ICELAND	TOTAL SECOND LEVEL	1975	2 387	699	29	*25 853	11 566	*45
		1980	...	...	...	26 643	12 447	47
		1981	...	...	...	26 769	...	...
		1982	...	...	...	26 627	12 537	47
		1983	...	...	...	26 803	12 559	47
		1984	...	...	...	27 237	...	...
	GENERAL	1975	1 538	506	33	20 292	10 089	50
		1980	...	...	...	19 091	...	...
		1982	...	...	...	19 221	9 702	50
	TEACHER TRAINING	1975	30	17	57	210	172	82
		1980	...	...	...	168	...	...
		1982	...	...	...	171	117	68
	VOCATIONAL	1975	819	176	21	*5 351	*1 305	*24
		1980	...	...	...	7 384	...	...
		1982	...	...	...	7 235	2 718	38
IRELAND‡	TOTAL SECOND LEVEL	1975	18 913	9 537	50	270 956	138 851	51
		1980	19 878	...	...	300 601	155 304	52
		1981	20 663	...	...	309 600	159 792	52
		1982	21 060	10 532	50	316 878	162 821	51
	GENERAL	1975	...	...	...	260 999	130 601	50
		1980	19 878	...	...	286 619	145 295	51
		1981	20 402	...	...	294 973	149 274	51
		1982	20 850	10 458	50	301 956	152 380	50
	TEACHER TRAINING		–	–	–	–	–	–
	VOCATIONAL	1975	...	...	...	9 957	8 250	83
		1980	...	...	...	13 982	10 009	72
		1981	261	...	...	14 627	10 518	72
		1982	210	...	...	14 922	10 441	70
ITALY	TOTAL SECOND LEVEL	1975	432 867	...	...	4 875 179	2 251 250	46
		1980	519 128	302 040	58	5 307 989	2 550 177	48
		1981	527 302	312 314	59	5 300 387	2 562 611	48
		1982	532 264	316 596	59	5 319 934	2 578 676	48
		1983	533 977	320 164	60	5 324 122	2 584 598	49
		1984	...	...	...	5 344 538	...	...
	GENERAL	1975	294 322	...	...	3 343 085	1 587 955	48
		1980	325 718	209 981	64	3 484 339	1 680 440	48
		1981	330 808	217 758	66	3 452 509	1 670 701	48
		1982	332 996	219 624	66	3 446 449	1 669 435	48
		1983	333 271	221 786	67	3 413 087	1 657 007	49
		1984	...	...	...	3 404 524	...	...
	TEACHER TRAINING	1975	18 899	...	...	198 426	183 161	92
		1980	22 308	15 447	69	237 471	223 310	94
		1981	22 580	15 893	70	241 063	226 787	94
		1982	22 756	16 171	71	238 140	223 790	94
		1983	21 932	15 533	71	222 376	208 517	94
		1984	...	...	...	210 600	...	...
	VOCATIONAL	1975	119 646	...	...	1 333 668	480 134	36
		1980	171 102	76 612	45	1 586 179	646 427	41
		1981	173 914	78 663	45	1 606 815	665 123	41
		1982	176 512	80 801	46	1 635 345	685 451	42
		1983	178 774	82 845	46	1 688 659	719 074	43
		1984	...	...	...	1 729 414	...	...

COUNTRY / PAYS / PAIS	TYPE OF EDUCATION / TYPE D'ENSEIGNEMENT / TIPO DE ENSEÑANZA	YEAR / ANNEE / AÑO	TEACHING STAFF / PERSONNEL ENSEIGNANT / PERSONAL DOCENTE: TOTAL	FEMALE / FEMININ / FEMENINO	% F	PUPILS ENROLLED / ELEVES INSCRITS / ALUMNOS MATRICULADOS: TOTAL	FEMALE / FEMININ / FEMENINO	% F
			(1)	(2)	(3)	(4)	(5)	(6)
LUXEMBOURG	TOTAL SECOND LEVEL	1975	...	...	...	22 652	11 038	49
		1980	1 927	...	...	24 171	12 059	50
		1981	1 958	...	...	24 375	12 149	50
		1982	2 020	...	...	24 341	12 112	50
		1983	...	...	...	25 221	12 064	48
	GENERAL	1975	959	...	...	15 191	7 573	50
		1980	...	...	...	16 974	8 668	51
		1981	...	...	...	17 339	8 728	50
		1982	...	...	...	18 973	9 485	50
		1983	...	...	...	18 975	8 897	47
	TEACHER TRAINING	1975	–	–	–	–	–	–
		1980	...	...	...	53	50	94
		1981	...	...	...	46	44	96
		1982	...	...	...	83	76	92
	VOCATIONAL	1975	...	...	...	7 461	3 465	46
		1980	...	...	...	7 144	3 341	47
		1981	...	...	...	6 990	3 377	48
		1982	...	...	...	5 285	2 551	48
MALTA	TOTAL SECOND LEVEL	1975	2 498	934	37	32 409	14 927	46
		1980	*2 141	*783	*37	25 501	11 458	45
		1981	2 180	787	36	26 700	12 050	45
		1982	2 253	795	35	27 257	12 459	46
		1983	2 032	730	36	27 901	12 711	46
	GENERAL	1975	*2 089	*897	*43	28 022	14 196	51
		1980	*1 691	*695	*41	21 377	10 562	49
		1981	*1 769	...	...	22 077	11 058	50
		1982	*1 828	*717	*39	21 986	11 434	52
		1983	*1 589	*652	*41	22 664	11 754	52
	TEACHER TRAINING		–	–	–	–	–	–
	VOCATIONAL	1975	409	37	9	4 387	731	17
		1980	450	88	20	4 124	896	22
		1981	411	...	...	4 623	992	21
		1982	425	78	18	5 271	1 025	19
		1983	443	78	18	5 237	957	18
MONACO‡	TOTAL SECOND LEVEL	1976	...	...	...	1 993	...	...
		1980	...	...	...	2 065	...	...
		1981	...	...	...	2 071	...	...
		1982	...	...	...	3 132	...	...
	GENERAL	1976	...	...	...	1 395	...	...
		1980	...	...	...	1 314	...	...
		1981	...	...	...	1 318	...	...
		1982	...	...	...	1 914	...	...
	TEACHER TRAINING		–	–	–	–	–	–
	VOCATIONAL	1976	...	...	...	598	...	...
		1980	...	...	...	751	383	51
		1981	...	...	...	753	380	50
		1982	...	...	...	1 218	...	...
NETHERLANDS	TOTAL SECOND LEVEL	1975	...	...	...	1 283 585	600 323	47
		1980	...	...	...	1 391 485	663 695	48
		1981	...	...	...	1 412 714	676 503	48
		1982	...	...	...	1 440 242	691 345	48
		1983	...	...	...	1 466 956	703 972	48
		1984	...	...	...	1 445 991	697 526	48
	GENERAL	1975	48 193	11 859	25	766 391	380 114	50
		1980	54 369	13 997	26	823 730	428 252	52
		1981	54 901	14 360	26	828 731	434 883	52
		1982	55 919	14 936	27	836 220	440 673	53
		1983	53 770	14 342	27	832 990	439 841	53
		1984	53 375	14 242	27	822 615	434 962	53
	TEACHER TRAINING	1975	...	...	...	10 830	10 789	100
		1980	1 124	583	52	7 190	7 119	99
		1981	1 165	609	52	7 490	7 394	99
		1982	1 210	615	51	8 069	7 961	99
		1983	1 182	591	50	7 818	7 674	98
		1984	...	...	...	4 785	4 700	98
	VOCATIONAL	1975	...	...	...	506 364	209 420	41
		1980	...	...	...	560 565	228 324	41
		1981	...	...	...	576 493	234 226	41
		1982	...	...	...	595 953	242 711	41
		1983	...	...	...	626 148	256 457	41
		1984	...	...	...	618 591	257 864	42

3.7 Education at the second level: teachers and pupils
Enseignement du second degré: personnel enseignant et élèves
Enseñanza de segundo grado: personal docente y alumnos

COUNTRY / PAYS / PAIS	TYPE OF EDUCATION / TYPE D'ENSEIGNEMENT / TIPO DE ENSEÑANZA	YEAR / ANNEE / AÑO	TEACHING STAFF / PERSONNEL ENSEIGNANT / PERSONAL DOCENTE: TOTAL	FEMALE / FEMININ / FEMENINO	% F	PUPILS ENROLLED / ELEVES INSCRITS / ALUMNOS MATRICULADOS: TOTAL	FEMALE / FEMININ / FEMENINO	% F
			(1)	(2)	(3)	(4)	(5)	(6)
NORWAY	TOTAL SECOND LEVEL	1975	...	...	...	326 640	159 629	49
		1980	...	...	...	360 776	180 226	50
		1981	...	...	...	368 624	185 117	50
		1982	...	...	...	381 603	189 992	50
	GENERAL	1975	...	...	...	263 941	131 998	50
		1980	...	...	...	279 266	141 888	51
		1981	...	...	...	282 231	144 177	51
		1982	...	...	...	284 508	145 748	51
	TEACHER TRAINING	1975	–	–	–	–	–	–
		1980	...	...	...	345	288	83
		1981	...	...	...	368	307	83
		1982	...	...	...	451	364	81
	VOCATIONAL	1975	10 332	3 387	33	62 699	27 631	44
		1980	...	...	...	81 165	38 050	47
		1981	...	...	...	86 025	40 633	47
		1982	...	...	...	96 644	43 880	45
POLAND‡	TOTAL SECOND LEVEL	1975	169 635	78 403	46	1 946 366	980 709	50
		1980	139 412	72 938	52	1 673 869	840 888	50
		1981	138 888	72 034	52	1 608 017	810 515	50
		1982	140 046	72 770	52	1 542 344	778 418	50
		1983	142 696	74 624	52	1 520 819	772 864	51
		1984	141 661	75 009	53	1 548 297	785 258	51
	GENERAL	1975	34 114	21 899	64	471 594	334 944	71
		1980	26 380	18 157	69	345 214	244 242	71
		1981	26 542	18 418	69	336 511	239 264	71
		1982	26 899	18 446	69	329 015	235 623	72
		1983	28 184	19 125	68	326 085	235 865	72
		1984	28 013	19 512	70	329 916	239 934	73
	TEACHER TRAINING	1975	...	...	...	17 588	14 230	81
		1980	...	...	...	18 703	16 277	87
		1981	...	...	...	18 606	16 528	89
		1982	...	...	...	18 879	17 091	91
		1983	...	...	...	19 299	17 690	92
		1984	...	...	...	20 942	19 156	91
	VOCATIONAL	1975	135 521	56 504	42	1 457 184	631 535	43
		1980	113 032	54 781	48	1 309 952	580 369	44
		1981	112 346	53 616	48	1 252 900	554 723	44
		1982	113 147	54 324	48	1 194 450	525 704	44
		1983	114 512	55 499	48	1 175 435	519 309	44
		1984	113 648	55 497	49	1 197 439	526 168	44
PORTUGAL‡	TOTAL SECOND LEVEL	1975	29 714	16 586	56	466 491	226 858	49
		1980	32 028	18 963	59	398 320	190 612	*52
		1981	34 619	...	...	399 043	193 674	*52
		1982	36 219	...	...	451 426	218 971	*52
		1983	36 327	...	...	489 696	261 224	53
	GENERAL	1975	14 903	8 816	59	330 008	171 949	52
		1980	...	...	...	398 320	190 612	*52
		1981	34 619	...	...	399 043	193 674	*52
		1982	36 219	...	...	451 426	218 971	*52
		1983	36 327	...	...	489 696	261 224	53
	TEACHER TRAINING	1975	826	501	61	9 166	7 841	86
		1980	–	–	–	–	–	–
		1981	–	–	–	–	–	–
		1982	–	–	–	–	–	–
		1983	–	–	–	–	–	–
	VOCATIONAL	1975	13 985	7 269	52	127 317	47 068	37
		1980	–	–	–	–	–	–
		1981	–	–	–	–	–	–
		1982	–	–	–	–	–	–
		1983	–	–	–	–	–	–
ROMANIA‡	TOTAL SECOND LEVEL	1975	46 907	20 720	44	870 161	434 205	50
		1980	48 082	20 829	43	871 257	412 381	47
		1981	49 394	22 150	45	1 168 829	535 727	46
		1982	49 159	22 560	46	1 347 169	635 012	47
		1983	51 431	23 749	46	1 453 769	682 916	47
		1984	49 547	23 487	47	1 500 323	698 649	47
	GENERAL	1975	14 713	8 120	55	256 135	177 639	69
		1980	8 254	4 353	53	80 879	52 330	65
		1981	8 909	4 798	54	135 376	85 016	63
		1982	6 770	3 594	53	121 213	79 813	66
		1983	6 648	3 547	53	112 716	76 193	68
		1984	7 292	3 899	53	106 375	73 450	69

COUNTRY / PAYS / PAIS	TYPE OF EDUCATION / TYPE D'ENSEIGNEMENT / TIPO DE ENSEÑANZA	YEAR / ANNEE / AÑO	TEACHING STAFF / PERSONNEL ENSEIGNANT / PERSONAL DOCENTE: TOTAL	FEMALE / FEMININ / FEMENINO	% F	PUPILS ENROLLED / ELEVES INSCRITS / ALUMNOS MATRICULADOS: TOTAL	FEMALE / FEMININ / FEMENINO	% F
			(1)	(2)	(3)	(4)	(5)	(6)
ROMANIA (CONT)‡	TEACHER TRAINING	1975	1 248	728	58	18 898	16 958	90
		1980	1 134	689	61	6 317	6 019	95
		1981	1 103	644	58	6 080	5 830	96
		1982	779	464	60	5 444	5 222	96
		1983	686	431	63	4 644	4 458	96
		1984	697	412	59	4 314	4 124	96
	VOCATIONAL	1975	30 946	11 872	38	595 128	239 608	40
		1980	38 694	15 787	41	784 061	354 032	45
		1981	39 382	16 708	42	1 027 373	444 881	43
		1982	41 610	18 502	44	1 220 512	549 977	45
		1983	44 097	19 771	45	1 336 409	602 265	45
		1984	41 558	19 176	46	1 389 634	621 075	45
SAN MARINO	TOTAL SECOND LEVEL	1975	108	62	57	1 211	575	47
		1980	112	69	62	1 219	593	49
		1981	147	79	54	1 354	617	46
		1982	170	104	61	1 317	589	45
		1983	155	88	57	1 266	582	46
	GENERAL	1975	108	62	57	1 211	575	47
		1980	112	69	62	1 219	593	49
		1981	147	79	54	1 354	617	46
		1982	170	104	61	1 317	589	45
		1983	155	88	57	1 266	582	46
	TEACHER TRAINING		–	–	–	–	–	–
	VOCATIONAL		–	–	–	–	–	–
SPAIN	TOTAL SECOND LEVEL	1975	...	...	...	3 188 619	1 530 843	48
		1980	...	...	...	3 976 747	1 979 208	50
		1981	...	...	...	4 228 827	...	...
		1982	190 859	81 528	43	4 169 047	2 101 847	50
		1983	192 574	82 889	43	4 112 760	2 048 465	50
	GENERAL	1975	...	...	...	2 638 551	1 295 197	49
		1980	...	...	...	3 088 026	1 569 844	51
		1981	...	...	...	3 120 490	1 587 036	51
		1982	143 312	66 201	46	3 117 212	1 582 383	51
		1983	144 528	67 544	47	3 167 562	1 606 810	51
	TEACHER TRAINING		–	–	–	–	–	–
	VOCATIONAL	1975	37 744	10 283	27	550 068	235 646	43
		1980	40 696	12 661	31	888 721	409 364	46
		1981	...	...	...	1 108 337	...	...
		1982	47 547	15 327	32	1 051 835	519 464	49
		1983	48 046	15 345	32	945 198	441 655	47
SWEDEN	TOTAL SECOND LEVEL	1975	54 200	24 303	45	507 642	258 556	51
		1980	...	...	...	606 833	311 945	51
		1981	...	...	...	606 152	314 843	52
		1982	51 397	23 914	47	607 199	314 684	52
		1983	51 466	24 019	47	604 067	313 312	52
		1984	...	...	...	596 104	308 255	52
	GENERAL	1975	...	...	...	369 012	189 047	51
		1980	...	...	...	443 355	226 649	51
		1981	...	...	...	437 515	224 652	51
		1982	...	...	...	420 973	216 684	51
		1983	...	...	...	405 342	209 472	52
	TEACHER TRAINING	1975	...	...	...	1 078	759	70
		1980	...	...	...	73	43	59
		1981	...	...	...	74	29	39
		1983	...	...	...	104	77	74
	VOCATIONAL	1975	...	...	...	137 552	68 750	50
		1980	...	...	...	163 405	85 253	52
		1981	...	...	...	168 563	90 162	53
		1982	...	...	...	186 226	98 000	53
		1983	...	...	...	198 621	103 763	52
SWITZERLAND‡	TOTAL SECOND LEVEL	1975	...	...	...	371 978	184 124	49
		1980	...	...	...	459 590	233 312	51
		1981	...	...	...	455 975	232 558	51
		1982	...	...	...	450 372	230 180	51
		1983	...	...	...	443 427	226 963	51
		1984	...	...	...	430 615	220 581	51
	GENERAL	1975	...	...	...	334 629	163 961	49
		1980	...	...	...	425 203	210 161	49
		1981	...	...	...	420 273	208 403	50
		1982	...	...	...	413 778	205 283	50
		1983	...	...	...	406 093	201 637	50
		1984	...	...	...	393 874	195 997	50

COUNTRY / PAYS / PAIS	TYPE OF EDUCATION / TYPE D'ENSEIGNEMENT / TIPO DE ENSEÑANZA	YEAR / ANNEE / AÑO	TEACHING STAFF / PERSONNEL ENSEIGNANT / PERSONAL DOCENTE: TOTAL	FEMALE / FEMININ / FEMENINO	% F	PUPILS ENROLLED / ELEVES INSCRITS / ALUMNOS MATRICULADOS: TOTAL	FEMALE / FEMININ / FEMENINO	% F
			(1)	(2)	(3)	(4)	(5)	(6)
SWITZERLAND (CONT)‡	TEACHER TRAINING	1975	...	...	...	11 070	7 564	68
		1980	...	...	...	10 128	7 819	77
		1981	...	...	...	9 736	7 649	79
		1982	...	...	...	10 573	8 252	78
		1983	...	...	...	10 634	8 407	79
		1984	...	...	...	9 950	8 035	81
	VOCATIONAL	1975	...	...	...	26 279	12 599	48
		1980	...	...	...	24 259	15 332	63
		1981	...	...	...	25 966	16 506	64
		1982	...	...	...	26 021	16 645	64
		1983	...	...	...	26 700	16 919	63
		1984	...	...	...	26 791	16 549	62
UNITED KINGDOM	TOTAL SECOND LEVEL	1975	...	...	...	5 154 371	2 525 945	49
		1980	...	...	...	5 341 849	2 644 645	50
		1981	...	...	...	5 329 275	2 640 435	50
		1982	...	...	...	5 296 000	2 624 000	50
	GENERAL	1975	308 827	147 810	48	4 945 770	2 413 008	49
		1980	332 585	162 490	49	5 087 036	2 498 999	49
		1981	329 720	160 805	49	5 040 235	2 478 696	49
		1982	...	...	...	4 977 000	2 450 000	49
	TEACHER TRAINING		–	–	–	–	–	–
	VOCATIONAL	1980	...	...	...	254 813	145 646	57
		1981	...	...	...	289 040	161 739	56
		1982	...	...	...	319 000	174 000	55
YUGOSLAVIA‡	TOTAL SECOND LEVEL	1975	...	...	...	2 264 101	1 061 877	*47
		1980	131 348	64 735	49	2 426 077	1 140 228	47
		1981	134 360	66 390	49	2 381 378	1 122 138	47
		1982	...	...	...	2 389 620	1 132 155	47
		1983	...	...	...	2 370 102	1 125 593	47
		1984	131 570	66 231	50	2 362 746	1 121 018	47
	GENERAL	1975	...	...	...	1 693 749	814 509	*48
		1980	...	...	...	1 835 636	873 550	48
		1981	...	...	...	1 798 375	858 589	48
		1982	...	...	...	1 864 713	898 843	48
		1983	...	...	...	1 832 033	879 485	48
		1984	...	...	...	1 779 332	853 189	48
	TEACHER TRAINING	1975	849	325	38	9 133	6 762	74
		1980	...	...	...	2 633	2 195	83
		1981	...	...	...	1 982	1 621	82
		1982	...	...	...	15 934	12 971	81
		1983	...	...	...	16 146	13 347	83
		1984	...	...	...	18 877	15 774	84
	VOCATIONAL	1975	18 867	9 674	51	561 219	240 606	43
		1980	...	...	...	587 808	264 483	45
		1981	...	...	...	581 021	261 928	45
		1982	...	...	...	508 973	220 341	43
		1983	...	...	...	521 923	232 761	45
		1984	...	...	...	564 537	252 055	45
OCEANIA								
AMERICAN SAMOA‡	TOTAL SECOND LEVEL	1975	*70	...	...	*2 097	...	...
		1981	132	...	...	2 960	1 405	47
		1983	145	40	28	3 051	1 442	47
		1984	*149	*28	*19	3 287	1 564	48
	TEACHER TRAINING		–	–	–	–	–	–
AUSTRALIA	TOTAL SECOND LEVEL	1975	74 041	34 463	47	1 095 691	534 215	49
		1980	85 340	38 604	45	1 095 610	544 028	50
		1981	86 364	38 988	45	1 110 319	552 687	50
		1982	...	...	...	1 139 820	566 819	50
		1983	...	...	...	1 200 318	594 474	50
		1984	103 064	49 700	48	1 247 468	618 012	50
	GENERAL	1975	74 041	34 463	47	1 095 691	534 215	49
		1980	85 340	38 604	45	1 095 610	544 028	50
		1981	86 364	38 988	45	1 110 319	552 687	50
		1982	...	...	...	1 139 820	566 819	50
		1983	...	...	...	1 200 318	594 474	50
		1984	103 064	49 700	48	1 247 468	618 012	50
	TEACHER TRAINING		–	–	–	–	–	–
	VOCATIONAL		–	–	–	–	–	–

COUNTRY / PAYS / PAIS	TYPE OF EDUCATION / TYPE D'ENSEIGNEMENT / TIPO DE ENSEÑANZA	YEAR / ANNEE / AÑO	TEACHING STAFF / PERSONNEL ENSEIGNANT / PERSONAL DOCENTE			PUPILS ENROLLED / ELEVES INSCRITS / ALUMNOS MATRICULADOS		
			TOTAL	FEMALE / FEMININ / FEMENINO	% F	TOTAL	FEMALE / FEMININ / FEMENINO	% F
			(1)	(2)	(3)	(4)	(5)	(6)
COOK ISLANDS	TOTAL SECOND LEVEL	1975	...	...	...	...	...	...
		1982	...	...	...	...	...	...
		1983	...	...	...	...	...	...
	GENERAL	1975	...	...	...	1 276	...	...
		1982	...	...	...	1 592	...	...
		1983	...	...	...	1 542	...	...
FIJI‡	TOTAL SECOND LEVEL	1975	...	...	...	30 545	15 056	49
		1980	2 564	1 043	41	49 963	25 380	51
		1981	2 749	1 164	42	48 608	24 728	51
		1982	...	...	...	47 687	...	...
		1983	2 868	1 139	40	47 231	24 107	51
		1984	2 909	1 219	42	47 073	23 537	50
	GENERAL	1975	1 184	430	36	28 072	13 826	49
		1980	2 254	962	43	47 119	23 747	50
		1981	2 442	1 077	44	45 843	23 150	50
		1983	2 572	1 067	41	44 357	22 461	51
		1984	2 656	1 152	43	43 277	21 756	50
	TEACHER TRAINING	1975	...	...	...	535	297	56
		1980	75	20	27	514	247	48
		1981	72	19	26	369	203	55
		1983	44	11	25	256	119	46
		1984	14	5	36	88	55	63
	VOCATIONAL	1975	...	...	...	1 938	933	48
		1980	235	61	26	2 330	1 386	59
		1981	235	68	29	2 396	1 375	57
		1983	252	61	24	2 618	1 527	58
		1984	239	62	26	3 708	1 726	47
FRENCH POLYNESIA	TOTAL SECOND LEVEL	1975	569	253	44	9 035	5 074	56
		1981	870	...	...	13 306	7 314	55
		1982	986	...	...	15 492	7 691	50
		1983	...	...	...	15 747	8 564	54
		1984	1 166	448	38	17 052	9 273	54
	GENERAL	1975	434	190	44	7 280	4 164	57
		1981	...	...	...	10 451	6 028	58
		1982	789	...	...	12 049	6 385	53
		1983	...	...	...	12 356	7 056	57
		1984	804	333	41	13 611	7 620	56
	TEACHER TRAINING	1975	6	3	50	111	85	77
		1981	–	–	–	–	–	–
		1982	–	–	–	–	–	–
		1983	–	–	–	–	–	–
		1984	–	–	–	–	–	–
	VOCATIONAL	1975	129	60	47	1 644	825	50
		1981	...	...	...	2 855	1 286	45
		1982	197	...	...	3 443	1 306	38
		1983	...	...	...	3 391	1 508	44
		1984	362	115	32	3 441	1 653	48
GUAM‡	TOTAL SECOND LEVEL	1975	*595	...	...	*13 242	...	...
		1979	...	...	...	7 389	...	...
		1983	720	451	63	13 375	6 457	48
	GENERAL	1983	654	420	64	12 507	6 063	48
	TEACHER TRAINING		–	–	–	–	–	–
	VOCATIONAL	1983	66	31	47	868	394	45
KIRIBATI	TOTAL SECOND LEVEL	1975	...	...	...	...	...	...
		1980	154	60	39	2 440	1 112	46
		1982	131	41	31	1 896	933	49
		1983	130	45	35	1 901	935	49
		1984	146	...	...	2 074	988	48
		1985	160	60	38	2 196	1 099	50
	GENERAL	1975	...	...	...	795	378	48
		1980	70	30	43	957	490	51
		1982	65	26	40	950	492	52
		1983	64	28	44	1 022	527	52
		1984	67	29	43	1 104	550	50
		1985	88	44	50	1 437	734	51
	TEACHER TRAINING	1975	13	...	...	55	...	...
		1980	13	4	31	107	56	52
		1982	17	3	18	113	64	57
		1983	13	2	15	80	53	66
		1984	10	3	30	87	58	67
		1985	12	4	33	97	68	70

3.7 **Education at the second level: teachers and pupils**
Enseignement du second degré: personnel enseignant et élèves
Enseñanza de segundo grado: personal docente y alumnos

COUNTRY / PAYS / PAIS	TYPE OF EDUCATION / TYPE D'ENSEIGNEMENT / TIPO DE ENSEÑANZA	YEAR / ANNEE / AÑO	TEACHING STAFF / PERSONNEL ENSEIGNANT / PERSONAL DOCENTE: TOTAL	FEMALE / FEMININ / FEMENINO	% F	PUPILS ENROLLED / ELEVES INSCRITS / ALUMNOS MATRICULADOS: TOTAL	FEMALE / FEMININ / FEMENINO	% F
			(1)	(2)	(3)	(4)	(5)	(6)
KIRIBATI (CONT)	VOCATIONAL	1980	71	26	37	1 376	566	41
		1982	49	12	24	833	377	45
		1983	53	15	28	799	355	44
		1984	69	...	...	883	380	43
		1985	60	12	20	662	297	45
NAURU	TOTAL SECOND LEVEL	1985	40	18	45	482	242	50
	GENERAL	1985	36	18	50	465	234	50
	TEACHER TRAINING	1985	–	–	–	–	–	–
	VOCATIONAL	1985	4	–	–	17	8	47
NEW CALEDONIA‡	TOTAL SECOND LEVEL	1975	...	...	...	7 960	3 995	50
		1980	839	...	...	11 945	6 449	54
		1982	1 188	...	...	15 477	7 790	50
		1983	1 289	...	...	16 854	8 661	51
		1984	1 224	...	...	17 745	9 278	52
		1985	1 265	...	...	18 351	9 530	52
	GENERAL	1975	379	217	57	5 604	3 016	54
		1980	545	...	...	9 139	4 988	55
		1982	780	376	48	11 095	6 160	56
		1983	...	...	...	11 920	6 482	54
		1984	...	...	...	12 481	6 815	55
		1985	...	...	...	12 922	7 017	54
	TEACHER TRAINING	1975	30	6	*35	135	85	63
		1980	–	–	–	–	–	–
		1982	–	–	–	–	–	–
		1983	–	–	–	–	–	–
		1984	–	–	–	–	–	–
		1985	–	–	–	–	–	–
	VOCATIONAL	1975	...	...	...	2 221	894	40
		1980	294	94	32	2 806	1 461	52
		1982	408	...	...	4 382	1 630	37
		1983	...	...	...	4 934	2 179	44
		1984	...	...	...	5 264	2 463	47
		1985	...	...	...	5 429	2 513	46
NEW ZEALAND‡	TOTAL SECOND LEVEL	1975	...	...	...	354 107	174 178	49
		1980	...	...	...	352 427	174 175	49
		1981	...	...	...	350 895	173 842	50
		1982	...	...	...	351 034	174 946	50
		1983	...	...	...	360 411	179 091	50
	GENERAL	1975	12 107	4 784	40	351 720	172 313	49
		1980	13 278	*5 485	*41	349 356	171 668	49
		1981	13 883	5 885	42	348 423	171 829	49
		1982	17 412	7 608	44	348 504	172 771	50
		1983	...	...	...	357 820	176 936	49
	TEACHER TRAINING		–	–	–	–	–	–
	VOCATIONAL	1975	...	...	...	2 387	1 865	78
		1980	...	...	...	3 071	2 507	82
		1981	...	...	...	2 472	2 013	81
		1982	...	...	...	2 530	2 175	86
		1983	...	...	...	2 591	2 155	83
NIUE	TOTAL SECOND LEVEL	1975	22	9	41	271	133	49
		1980	25	...	...	397	...	...
		1981	27	...	...	406	...	...
		1982	...	...	...	386	188	49
		1983	17	11	65	357	170	48
		1984	27	8	30	360	171	48
	GENERAL	1975	22	9	41	271	133	49
		1980	25	...	...	397	...	...
		1981	27	...	...	406	...	...
		1982	...	...	...	386	188	49
		1983	17	11	65	357	170	48
		1984	...	...	...	353	168	48
	TEACHER TRAINING		–	–	–	–	–	–
	VOCATIONAL	1975	–	–	–	–	–	–
		1980	–	–	–	–	–	–
		1981	–	–	–	–	–	–
		1982	–	–	–	–	–	–
		1983	–	–	–	–	–	–
		1984	...	...	...	7	3	43
PACIFIC ISLANDS	TOTAL SECOND LEVEL	1975	528	156	30	7 951	3 500	44
		1980	...	...	...	6 885	...	...
		1981	*445	*143	*32	6 872	...	...

COUNTRY / PAYS / PAIS	TYPE OF EDUCATION / TYPE D'ENSEIGNEMENT / TIPO DE ENSEÑANZA	YEAR / ANNEE / AÑO	TEACHING STAFF / PERSONNEL ENSEIGNANT / PERSONAL DOCENTE			PUPILS ENROLLED / ELEVES INSCRITS / ALUMNOS MATRICULADOS		
			TOTAL	FEMALE / FEMININ / FEMENINO	% F	TOTAL	FEMALE / FEMININ / FEMENINO	% F
			(1)	(2)	(3)	(4)	(5)	(6)
PACIFIC ISLANDS (CONT)	GENERAL	1975	528	156	30	7 951	3 500	44
		1980	...	...	...	6 885	...	...
		1981	*445	*143	*32	6 872	...	...
	TEACHER TRAINING		–	–	–	–	–	–
	VOCATIONAL		–	–	–	–	–	–
PAPUA NEW GUINEA	TOTAL SECOND LEVEL	1975	2 034	700	34	41 391	*11 731	*28
		1980	...	...	...	...	...	...
		1981	2 289	738	32	49 334	...	...
		1982	2 348	768	33	50 353	...	...
	GENERAL	1975	1 282	482	38	29 762	9 379	32
		1980	*1 586	533	*34	38 690	12 523	32
		1981	1 625	513	32	39 701	13 065	33
		1982	1 715	583	34	41 471	14 710	35
	TEACHER TRAINING	1975	166	76	46	1 990	715	36
		1980	*154	64	*42	1 704	637	37
		1981	165	68	41	1 649	619	38
		1982	120	43	36	1 660	645	39
	VOCATIONAL	1975	586	142	24	9 639	*1 637	*17
		1981	499	157	31	7 984	...	...
		1982	513	142	28	7 222	...	...
SAMOA	TOTAL SECOND LEVEL	1975	...	...	...	15 943	*8 062	*51
		1980	...	...	...	19 785	9 691	49
		1981	...	...	...	19 876	...	...
		1982	...	...	...	21 643	...	...
		1983	...	...	...	...	...	...
	GENERAL	1975	...	...	...	15 098	7 712	51
		1980	...	...	...	19 299	9 459	49
		1981	...	...	...	19 438	9 491	49
		1982	...	...	...	20 747	10 449	50
		1983	...	...	...	20 494	10 273	50
	TEACHER TRAINING	1975	30	15	50	490	263	54
		1980	15	7	47	222	124	56
		1981	17	...	...	228	...	...
		1982	29	16	55	304	184	61
		1983	12	7	58	314	186	59
	VOCATIONAL	1975	*48	*3	*6	355	*87	*25
		1980	35	16	46	264	108	41
		1981	31	...	...	210	...	...
		1982	44	...	...	592	...	...
SOLOMON ISLANDS	TOTAL SECOND LEVEL	1975	131	37	28	2 014	503	25
		1980	257	67	26	4 030	...	...
		1981	306	...	...	5 004	...	...
		1982	313	...	...	5 542	...	...
		1983	325	...	...	5 837	...	...
		1984	...	...	...	...	...	...
	GENERAL	1975	87	28	32	1 555	412	26
		1980	196	61	31	3 547	1 063	30
		1981	239	...	...	4 265	1 338	31
		1982	249	...	...	4 594	1 491	32
		1983	265	...	...	4 807	1 594	33
		1984	267	...	...	5 118	1 738	34
	TEACHER TRAINING	1975	18	5	28	146	46	32
		1980	24	3	13	116	...	...
		1981	31	...	...	177	42	24
		1982	28	...	...	227	70	31
		1983	25	...	...	260	123	47
		1984	28	...	...	372	156	42
	VOCATIONAL	1975	26	4	15	313	45	14
		1980	37	3	8	367	18	5
		1981	36	...	...	562	...	...
		1982	36	...	...	721	...	...
		1983	35	...	...	770	...	...
TOKELAU	TOTAL SECOND LEVEL	1979	18	9	50	277	129	47
		1983	...	...	...	488	245	50
	GENERAL	1979	6	3	50	80	43	54
		1983	...	...	...	108	56	52
	TEACHER TRAINING		–	–	–	–	–	–
	VOCATIONAL	1979	12	6	50	197	86	44
		1983	...	...	...	380	189	50

3.7 Education at the second level: teachers and pupils
Enseignement du second degré: personnel enseignant et élèves
Enseñanza de segundo grado: personal docente y alumnos

COUNTRY PAYS PAIS	TYPE OF EDUCATION TYPE D'ENSEIGNEMENT TIPO DE ENSEÑANZA	YEAR ANNEE AÑO	TEACHING STAFF / PERSONNEL ENSEIGNANT / PERSONAL DOCENTE TOTAL	 FEMALE FEMININ FEMENINO	 % F	PUPILS ENROLLED / ELEVES INSCRITS / ALUMNOS MATRICULADOS TOTAL	 FEMALE FEMININ FEMENINO	 % F
			(1)	(2)	(3)	(4)	(5)	(6)
TONGA‡	TOTAL SECOND LEVEL	1975	...	...	...	11 351	5 482	48
		1981	...	...	...	16 566	7 812	47
		1982	...	...	...	17 085	8 166	48
		1983	...	...	...	...	...	...
	GENERAL	1975	...	...	...	10 685	5 229	49
		1981	686	337	49	15 760	7 447	47
		1982	761	360	47	16 348	7 827	48
		1983	...	...	...	16 268	7 686	47
	TEACHER TRAINING	1975	11	7	64	117	71	61
		1981	14	8	57	182	113	62
		1982	18	7	39	125	79	63
		1983	...	...	...	145	87	60
	VOCATIONAL	1975	23	4	17	549	182	33
		1981	...	...	...	624	252	40
		1982	...	...	...	612	260	42
TUVALU	TOTAL SECOND LEVEL	1976	...	...	...	248	...	...
		1980	...	...	...	248	...	...
		1981	...	...	...	265	...	...
		1984	...	...	...	...	...	...
	GENERAL	1984	...	...	...	243	136	56
	TEACHER TRAINING		–	–	–	–	–	–
VANUATU	TOTAL SECOND LEVEL	1975	...	...	...	1 505	636	42
		1980	...	...	...	2 426	1 018	42
		1981	*188	*59	*31	2 480	1 003	40
		1983	...	...	...	2 904	1 093	38
	GENERAL	1975	...	...	...	1 263	555	44
		1980	...	...	...	1 970	866	44
		1981	126	49	39	1 883	818	43
		1983	...	...	...	2 186	920	42
	TEACHER TRAINING	1975	...	...	...	103	50	49
		1980	...	...	...	106	59	56
		1981	12	2	17	83	47	57
		1983	13	3	23	85	35	41
	VOCATIONAL	1975	...	...	...	139	31	22
		1980	45	...	...	350	93	27
		1981	*50	*8	*16	514	138	27
		1983	...	...	...	633	138	22
U.S.S.R.								
U.S.S.R.‡	TOTAL SECOND LEVEL	1975	...	...	...	23 171 700	...	...
		1980	...	...	...	20 274 500	...	...
		1981	...	...	...	19 899 900	...	...
		1982	...	...	...	19 669 000	...	...
		1983	...	...	...	19 743 000	...	...
		1984	...	...	...	20 008 000	...	...
	GENERAL	1975	...	...	...	20 808 100	...	...
		1980	...	...	...	17 355 900	...	...
		1981	...	...	...	16 937 700	...	...
		1982	...	...	...	16 815 000	...	...
		1983	...	...	...	16 868 000	...	...
		1984	...	...	...	17 051 000	...	...
	TEACHER TRAINING	1975	...	...	...	156 800	...	...
		1980	...	...	...	160 200	...	...
		1981	...	...	...	163 700	...	...
		1982	...	...	...	169 800	...	...
		1983	...	...	...	174 800	...	...
		1984	...	...	...	194 100	...	...
	VOCATIONAL	1975	218 428	109 214	50	2 206 800	...	...
		1980	...	...	...	2 758 400	...	...
		1981	...	...	...	2 798 500	...	...
		1982	...	...	...	2 684 200	...	...
		1983	...	...	...	2 700 200	...	...
		1984	...	...	...	2 762 900	...	...
BYELORUSSIAN S.S.R.‡	TOTAL SECOND LEVEL	1975	...	...	...	882 600	...	...
		1980	...	...	...	759 700	...	...
		1981	...	...	...	736 400	...	...
		1982	...	...	...	722 100	...	...
		1983	...	...	...	714 700	...	...

COUNTRY PAYS PAIS	TYPE OF EDUCATION TYPE D'ENSEIGNEMENT TIPO DE ENSEÑANZA	YEAR ANNEE AÑO	TEACHING STAFF / PERSONNEL ENSEIGNANT / PERSONAL DOCENTE TOTAL	 FEMALE FEMININ FEMENINO	 % F	PUPILS ENROLLED / ELEVES INSCRITS / ALUMNOS MATRICULADOS TOTAL	 FEMALE FEMININ FEMENINO	 % F
			(1)	(2)	(3)	(4)	(5)	(6)
BYELORUSSIAN S.S.R. (CONT)‡	GENERAL	1975	...	...	...	800 000	...	...
		1980	...	...	...	645 200	...	...
		1981	...	...	...	617 800	...	...
		1982	...	...	...	600 000	...	...
		1983	...	...	...	591 500	...	...
	TEACHER TRAINING	1975	...	...	...	3 300	...	...
		1980	...	...	...	3 700	...	...
		1981	...	...	...	4 300	...	...
		1982	...	...	...	5 500	...	...
		1983	...	...	...	6 800	...	...
	VOCATIONAL	1975	...	...	...	79 300	...	...
		1980	...	...	...	110 800	...	...
		1981	...	...	...	114 300	...	...
		1982	...	...	...	116 600	...	...
		1983	...	...	...	116 400	...	...
UKRAINIAN S.S.R.‡	TOTAL SECOND LEVEL	1975	...	...	...	821 900	...	...
		1980	...	...	...	3 406 400	...	...
		1981	...	...	...	3 340 100	...	...
		1982	...	...	...	3 316 200	...	...
		1983	...	...	...	3 316 700	...	...
		1984	...	...	...	3 352 800	...	...
	GENERAL	1975	...	...	...	1 038 100	...	...
		1980	...	...	...	2 904 000	...	...
		1981	...	...	...	2 824 800	...	...
		1982	...	...	...	2 801 800	...	...
		1983	...	...	...	2 796 200	...	...
		1984	...	...	...	2 814 200	...	...
	TEACHER TRAINING	1980	...	...	...	22 500	...	...
		1981	...	...	...	23 500	...	...
		1982	...	...	...	19 200	...	...
		1983	...	...	...	17 100	...	...
		1984	...	...	...	19 700	...	...
	VOCATIONAL	1975	40 400	...	...	783 800	...	...
		1980	...	...	...	479 900	...	...
		1981	...	...	...	491 800	...	...
		1982	...	...	...	495 200	...	...
		1983	...	...	...	503 400	...	...
		1984	...	...	...	518 900	...	...

This table gives the number of teachers and pupils by sex enrolled in each of the three types of education at the second level, i.e. general, teacher-training, and technical and vocational. Unless otherwise stated, data cover public and private schools.

In most cases, data include part-time teachers and their proportion is particularly substantial in technical and vocational education. Generally, it can be stated that, whenever the number of teachers seems disproportionately high in relation to the number of pupils enrolled, this is due to the fact that the figures include various categories of part-time teachers. Instructional personnel without teaching functions (e.g. librarians, guidance personnel, certain principals, etc.) have been excluded whenever possible.

Second level, General: The term *second level, general* refers to education in *secondary schools* that provide general or specialized instruction based upon at least four years previous instruction at the first level, and which do not aim at preparing the pupils directly for a given trade or occupation. Such schools may be called high schools, middle schools, lyceums, gymnasiums, etc., and offer courses of study whose completion is a minimum condition for admission to university. In many countries, because of the desire to provide other types of training for students not proceeding to university, there has been a development of schools with the aim of providing both academic and vocational training. These *composite* secondary schools are considered as equivalent to the academic type of secondary school and are classified as *second level, general.*

Second level, Teacher-training: The term *second level, teacher-training* refers to education in secondary schools whose purpose is the training of students for the teaching profession.

Second level, Technical and vocational: The term *second level, technical and vocational* is here used to cover education provided in those *secondary schools* which aim at preparing the pupils directly for a trade or occupation other than teaching. Such schools have many different names and vary greatly as to type and duration of training. Part-time courses and short courses abound and are excluded in as much as they refer to adult education. The abreviation vocational education has been used in the table headings.

For international comparisons, this table should be consulted in conjunction with Tables 3.1, 3.1a and 3.1b. Please note that for all the countries where education at the second level consists of two stages the data refer to both stages.

Ce tableau indique le nombre et la répartition par sexe du personnel enseignant et des élèves inscrits dans chacun des trois types d'enseignement du second degré: général, normal et technique et professionel. Sauf indication contraire, les données se réfèrent aux écoles publiques et privées.

Dans la plupart des cas, les chiffres comprennent les enseignants temps partiel, qui sont particulièrement nombreux dans l'enseignement technique et professionnel. D'une manière générale, on peut affirmer que, lorsque l'effectif des enseignants paraît anormalement élevé par rapport à celui des élèves, ceci est dû au fait que les chiffres comprennent diverses catégories de personnel à temps partiel. Dans toute la mesure du possible, est exclu le personnel qui n'exerce pas de fonctions d'enseignement (par exemple les bibliothécaires, les orientateurs, certains chefs d'établissements, etc.).

Second degré, enseignement général: La formule *second degré, enseignement général* désigne l'enseignement, général ou spécialisé, dispensé dans les *écoles secondaires* à des enfants ayant déjà fait au moins quatre années d'études dans le premier degré, et qui ne vise pas à préparer directement les élèves à une profession ou à un emploi. Les écoles de ce type s'appellent collèges, lycées, gymnases, etc., et elles dispensent un enseignement qu'il faut obligatoirement avoir terminé pour pouvoir être admis à l'université. Dans de nombreux pays, où l'on souhaite dispenser d'autres types de formation aux élèves qui ne se destinent pas aux études supérieures, on assiste au développement d'écoles qui offrent une formation tant générale que professionnelle. On considère que ces écoles secondaires *composites* sont d'un niveau équivalent à celui des écoles secondaires traditionnelles: elles sont de ce fait classées dans la catégorie *second degré, enseignement général*.

Second degré, enseignement normal: La formule *second degré, enseignement normal* désigne l'enseignement dispensé dans les écoles secondaires dont le but est de préparer à la profession enseignante.

Enseignement technique et professionnel: La formule *enseignement technique et professionel* désigne ici l'enseignement dispensé dans des *écoles secondaires* qui visent à préparer directement leurs élè à un emploi ou une profession autre que l'enseignement. C écoles peuvent porter divers noms et la formation qu'e dispensent varie largement quant à sa nature et à sa durée. type d'enseignement comporte fréquemment des cours à temps ou des cours de brève durée, qui ont été exclus dans mesure où ils se réfèrent à l'éducation des adultes. La form abrégée 'enseignement technique' est utilisée dans les entê des tableaux.

Pour effectuer des comparaisons internationales, ce table doit être consulté conjointement avec les tableaux 3.1, 3.1a 3.1b. Il convient de noter que, pour tous les pays l'enseignement du second degré se compose de deux cycles, chiffres se réfèrent à l'ensemble des deux cycles.

En este cuadro se indican el número y la distribución por sexo del personal docente y de los alumnos matriculados en cada uno de los tres tipos de enseñanza de segundo grado (general, normal, y técnica y profesional). Salvo indicación contraria, los datos se refieren a las escuelas públicas y privadas.

En la mayoría de los casos, las cifras engloban a los profesores de jornada parcial, cuyo número es particularmente importante en la enseñanza técnica y profesional. Cabe decir que, en general, cuando el número de profesores parece desproporcionadamente alto comparado con el de los alumnos matriculados, se debe a que las cifras comprenden diversas categorías de personal de jornada parcial. En la medida de lo posible, ha quedado excluido el personal que no ejerce funciones docentes (por ejemplo, bibliotecarios, el personal de orientación, ciertos directores de establecimientos de enseñanza, etc.).

Segundo grado, enseñanza general: En la categoría *enseñanza general de segundo grado* se han incluído las *escuelas de segundo grado* (es decir, las que dan una enseñanza general o especializada que implica cuatro años como mínimo de estudios previos en el primer grado) cuya finalidad no consiste en preparar directamente a los alumnos para un oficio o una profesión determinada. Esas escuelas, que pueden llamarse escuelas secundarias, escuelas medias, liceos, gimnasios, etc., tienen un plan de estudios que conduce a la obtención de un diploma que es condición indispensable para el ingreso en la enseñanza superior. Bastantes países, para ofrecer otros tipos de formación a los alumnos que no aspiran a cursar estudios superiores, han creado escue donde se da una instrucción a la vez general y técnica. E escuelas secundarias de carácter mixto se consideran c siempre como equivalentes a las escuelas secundarias de t general y deben ser agrupadas bajo la rúbrica *enseñanza genera segundo grado.*

Segundo grado, enseñanza normal (formación de perso docente): La expresión *segundo grado, enseñanza normal*, se refi a la enseñanza en escuelas secundarias destinadas a preparar p la profesión docente.

Segundo grado, enseñanza técnica y profesional: La expres *enseñanza técnica y profesional* se utiliza para designar las *escuela segundo grado* que tienen como finalidad preparar directament los alumnos para un oficio o una profesión determinada que sea la docente. El nombre y el tipo de esas escuelas, var considerablemente. Son frecuentes los ciclos de estudios horario parcial y los de breve duración, que han sido excluidos la medida en que se refieren a la educacón de adultos. Por razo prácticas se ha utilizado el término enseñanza técnica en títulos de los cuadros.

Para efectuar comparaciones internacionales, este cua debe consultarse conjuntamente con los cuadros 3.1, 3.1 3.1b. Nótese que, par todos los países donde la enseñanza segundo grado comprende dos ciclos, los datos se refieren al t de los dos ciclos.

AFRICA:

Algeria:

E--> *General education:* For 1975 data on teachers and all data for 1981, 1983 and 1984 exclude *OUCFA* schools (pupils: 3,497, f: 1,714, in 1980). For 1984, data on teachers include vocational education.

FR-> *Enseignement général*: Pour 1975 les données relatives au personnel enseignant et toutes les données pour 1981, 1983 et 1984 ne comprennent pas les écoles de l'OUCFA (3 497 élèves dont 1 714 filles en 1980). Pour 1984, les données relatives au personnel enseignant comprennent l'enseignement technique.

ESP> *Enseñanza general:* En 1975 los datos relativos al personal docente y todos los datos para 1981, 1983 y 1984 excluyen las escuelas del *OUCFA* (3 497 alumnos, f: 1 714 en 1980). En 1984, los datos sobre el personal docente incluyen la enseñanza técnica.

Central African Republic:

E--> *Teacher training:* For 1975, data on teachers include teacher training at the third level of education.

FR-> *Enseignement normal:* Pour 1975, les données relatives au personnel enseignant incluent l'enseignement normal du troisième degré.

ESP> *Enseñanza normal:* En 1975, los datos relativos al personal docente incluyen la enseñanza normal de tercer grado.

Côte d'Ivoire:

E--> *General education:* For 1975 and 1980, data on teachers refer to public education only.

FR-> *Enseignement général:* Pour 1975 et 1980 les données relatives au personnel enseignant se réfèrent à l'enseignement public seulement.

ESP> *Enseñanza general:* Para 1975 y 1980 los datos relativos al personal docente se refieren a la enseñanza pública solamente.

Egypt:

E--> *General education:* All data on teachers and data on pupils for 1982 and 1983 do not include secondary classes at Al Azhar (pupils: 166,201, f: 36,789 in 1981). *Teacher training:* Except for 1975 and pupils in 1980, data exclude Al Azhar.

FR-> *Enseignement général:* Toutes les données relatives au personnel enseignant et celles relatives aux élèves pour 1982 et 198 comprennent pas les classes secondaires rattachées à Al Azhar (166 élèves dont 36 789 filles en 1981). *Enseignement normal:* A l'excep de 1975 et des élèves en 1980, les données n'incluent pas Al Azhar

ESP> *Enseñanza general:* Todos los datos relativos al pers docente y los sobre los alumnos para 1982 y 1983 excluyen las cla secundarias adscritas a Al Azhar (166 201 alumnos, f: 36 789 1981). *Enseñanza normal:* A la excepción de 1975 y de los alumnos 1980, los datos excluyen Al Azhar.

Ghana:

E--> *General and vocational education:* From 1980, comme schools are included in general education. *Teacher training:* For 19 data on teachers include teacher training at the third level of educa Beginning 1980, due to a reorganization of the teacher training educa data are not comparable with the previous years. *Vocational educa* Beginning 1980, certain vocational courses are classified at the third l of education.

FR-> *Enseignement général et enseignement technique:* A parti 1980, les écoles commerciales sont incluses dans l'enseignem général. *Enseignement normal:* Pour 1975 les données relatives personnel enseignant incluent l'enseignement normal du troisi degré. A partir de 1980, suite à la réorganisation de l'enseignement nor les données ne sont pas comparables à celles des années précéden *Enseignement technique:* A partir de 1980, certains cours techniques s classés dans l'enseignement du troisième degré.

ESP> *Enseñanza general y técnica:* A partir de 1980, las escu comerciales han sido incluídas en la enseñanza general. *Enseña normal:* En 1975, los datos relativos al personal docente incluye enseñanza normal de tercer grado. A partir de 1980, de acuerdo co reorganización de la enseñanza normal, los datos no son comparables a de los años anteriores. *Enseñanza técnica:* A partir de 1980, ciertos cu técnicos figuran en la enseñanza de tercer grado.

Guinea:

E--> *General education:* For 1975, data on teachers inc vocational education.

Guinea: (Cont):
FR-> *Enseignement général:* Pour 1975, les données relatives au personnel enseignant incluent l'enseignement technique.
ESP> *Enseñanza general:* Para 1975, los datos relativos al personal docente incluyen la enseñanza técnica.
Kenya:
E--> *Teacher training:* For 1980, 1981 and 1982 data on teachers include teacher training at the third level of education.
FR-> *Enseignement normal:* Pour 1980, 1981 et 1982 les données relatives au personnel enseignant comprennent l'enseignement normal du troisième degré.
ESP> *Enseñanza normal:* En 1980, 1981 y 1982 los datos relativos al personal docente incluyen la enseñanza normal de tercer grado.
Liberia:
E--> *General education:* For 1980, data on teachers exclude the first stage of general education, included at the first level of education.
FR-> *Enseignement général:* Pour 1980, les données relatives au personnel enseignant ne comprennent pas le premier cycle de l'enseignement général, inclus dans le premier degré.
ESP> *Enseñanza general:* En 1980, los datos relativos al personal docente excluyen el primer ciclo de la enseñanza general, incluído en el primer grado.
Madagascar:
E--> *General education:* Data for 1975 and 1984 refer to public education only.
FR-> *Enseignement général:* Les données pour 1975 et 1984 se réfèrent à l'enseignement public seulement.
ESP> *Enseñanza general:* Los datos para 1975 y 1984 se refieren a la enseñanza pública solamente.
Mauritania:
E--> See Table 3.1b.
FR-> Voir le tableau 3.1b.
ESP> Véase el cuadro 3.1b.
Morocco:
E--> *General education:* For 1975, data on teachers, include vocational education and refer to public education only. *Vocational education:* For 1980, data exclude professional schools.
FR-> *Enseignement général:* Pour 1975, les données relatives au personnel enseignant comprennent l'enseignement technique et se réfèrent à l'enseignement public seulement. *Enseignement technique:* Pour 1980 les données ne comprennent pas les écoles professionnelles.
ESP> *Enseñanza general:* Para 1975, los datos relativos al personal docente incluyen la enseñanza técnica y se refieren a la enseñanza pública solamente. *Enseñanza técnica:* En 1980, los datos excluyen las escuelas profesionales.
Mozambique:
E--> See Table 3.1b.
FR-> Voir le tableau 3.1b.
ESP> Véase el cuadro 3.1b.
Niger:
E--> *General education:* Data for 1982 and 1983 refer to public education only.
FR-> *Enseignement général:* Pour 1982 et 1983, les données se réfèrent à l'enseignement public seulement.
ESP> Para 1982 y 1983, los datos se refieren a la enseñanza pública solamente.
Reunion:
E--> For 1981 and 1982, data on teachers refer to public education only. *General education:* For 1975, data include teacher training.
FR-> Pour 1981 et 1982, les données relatives au personnel enseignant se réfèrent à l'enseignement public seulement. *Enseignement général:* Pour 1975 les données incluent l'enseignement normal.
ESP> Para 1981 y 1982, los datos sobre el personal docente se refieren a la enseñanza pública solamente. *Enseñanza general:* En 1975 los datos incluyen la enseñanza normal.
Senegal:
E--> *General education:* For 1982, data on teachers refer to public education only.
FR-> *Enseignement général:* En 1982, les données sur le personnel enseignant se réfèrent à l'enseignement public seulement.
ESP> *Enseñanza general:* En 1982, los datos sobre el personal docente se refieren a la enseñanza pública solamente.
Seychelles:
E--> See Table 3.1b.
FR-> Voir le tableau 3.1b.
ESP> Véase el cuadro 3.1b.
Somalia:
E--> See Table 3.1b.
FR-> Voir le tableau 3.1b.
ESP> Véase el cuadro 3.1b.
Togo:
E--> *Teacher training:* Data on teachers include teacher training at the third level of education.
FR-> *Enseignement normal:* Les données relatives au personnel enseignant incluent l'enseignement normal du troisième degré.
ESP> *Enseñanza normal:* Los datos relativos al personal docente incluyen la enseñanza normal de tercer grado.
Tunisia:
E--> For 1975 data on teachers refer to public education only.
FR-> Pour 1975, les données relatives au personnel enseignant se réfèrent à l'enseignement public seulement.
ESP> En 1975, los datos relativos al personal docente se refieren a la enseñanza pública solamente.
Uganda:
E--> *General education:* Except for 1982, data refer to government-maintained and aided schools only.
FR-> *Enseignement général:* A l'exception de 1982, les données se rapportent aux écoles publiques et subventionnées seulement.
ESP> *Enseñanza general:* A la excepción de 1982, los datos se refieren a las escuelas públicas y subvencionadas solamente.
United Republic of Tanzania:
E--> *General and vocational education:* For 1975, data on general education include vocational education. For other years, data on pupils include only a part of vocational education.
FR-> *Enseignement général et technique:* Pour 1975 les données relatives à l'enseignement général incluent l'enseignement technique. Pour les autres années, les chiffres relatifs aux effectifs ne comprennent qu'une partie de l'enseignement technique.
ESP> *Enseñanza general y técnica:* En 1975 los datos relativos a la enseñanza general incluyen la enseñanza técnica. Para los otros años, los datos relativos a los alumnos comprenden solamente una parte de la enseñanza técnica.
Zimbabwe:
E--> *General education:* Data on teachers for 1975 refer to government-maintained and aided schools only.
FR-> *Enseignement général:* Les données relatives au personnel enseignant en 1975 se rapportent aux écoles publiques et subventionnées seulement.
ESP> *Enseñanza general:* Los datos relativos al personal docente en 1975 se refieren a las escuelas públicas y subvencionadas solamente.
AMERICA, NORTH:
Antigua and Barbuda:
E--> *General education:* In 1975, data on teachers and for 1983 data on pupils do not include post-primary classes.
FR-> *Enseignement général:* Pour 1975, les données relatives au personnel enseignant et pour 1983 celles relatives aux élèves ne comprennent pas les classes secondaires rattachées aux écoles primaires.
ESP> *Enseñanza general:* En 1975 los datos relativos al personal docente y en 1983 los datos sobre los alumnos no incluyen las clases secundarias adscritas a las escuelas primarias.
Bahamas:
E--> *Teacher training:* Data on pupils for 1975 include teacher training at the third level. *Vocational education:* 1975 data on pupils include part-time education.
FR-> *Enseignement normal:* Les données relatives aux élèves pour 1975 incluent l'enseignement normal du troisième degré. *Enseignement technique:* Pour 1975 les données relatives aux élèves comprennent les élèves à temps partiel.
ESP> *Enseñanza normal:* Los datos relativos a los alumnos para 1975 incluyen la enseñanza normal de tercer grado. *Enseñanza técnica:* Para 1975 los datos relativos a la matrícula comprenden los alumnos de jornada parcial.
Barbados:
E--> *Total:* For 1980, 1981 and 1982, data on teachers refer to public education only.
FR-> *Total:* Pour 1980, 1981 et 1982, les données relatives au personnel enseignant se réfèrent à l'enseignement public seulement.
ESP> *Total:* En 1980, 1981 y 1982, los datos relativos al personal docente se refieren a la enseñanza pública solamente.
Bermuda:
E--> *General education:* For 1980 and 1981 data on female teachers, refer to public education only.
FR-> *Enseignement général:* Pour 1980 et 1981 les données relatives au personnel enseignant féminin, se réfèrent à l'enseignement public seulement.
ESP> *Enseñanza general:* En 1980 y 1981 los datos relativos al personal docente femenino, se refieren a la enseñanza pública solamente.
Cayman Islands:
E--> See Table 3.1b. For 1975, data on teachers refer to public education only.
FR-> Voir le tableau 3.1b. Pour 1975 les données relatives au personnel enseignant se réfèrent à l'enseignement public seulement.
ESP> Véase el cuadro 3.1b. En 1975 los datos relativos al personal docente se refieren a la enseñanza pública solamente.
Costa Rica:
E--> For 1982 and 1983, data on teachers refer to public education only.
FR-> Pour 1982 et 1983, les données relatives au personnel enseignant se réfèrent à l'enseignement public seulement.
ESP> En 1982 y 1983, los datos relativos al personal docente se refieren a la enseñanza pública solamente.
Cuba:
E--> See Table 3.1b.

Cuba: (Cont):
FR-> Voir le tableau 3.1b.
ESP> Véase el cuadro 3.1b.
Dominica:
E--> *General education:* Data on teachers are included with education at the first level.
FR-> *Enseignement général:* Les données relatives au personnel enseignant sont incluses dans l'enseignement du premier degré.
ESP> *Enseñanza general:* Los datos sobre el personal docente están incluídos en la enseñanza de primer grado.
Dominican Republic:
E--> *General education:* For 1982 and 1983 data on pupils refer to public education only. *Vocational education:* For 1983 data on teachers refer to public education only.
FR-> *Enseignement général:* Pour 1982 et 1983 les données relatives aux élèves se réfèrent à l'enseignement public seulement. *Enseignement technique:* Pour 1983 les données relatives au personnel enseignant se réfèrent à l'enseignement public seulement.
ESP> *Enseñanza general:* Para 1982 y 1983 los datos sobre los alumnos se refieren a la enseñanza pública solamente. *Enseñanza técnica:* Para 1983 los datos relativos al personal docente se refieren a la enseñanza pública solamente.
Guadeloupe:
E--> For 1981 and 1982 data on teaching staff refer to public education only. *General education:* For 1975 data include teacher training.
FR-> Pour 1981 et 1982 les données relatives au personnel enseignant se réfèrent à l'enseignement public seulement. *Enseignement général:* Pour 1975 les données incluent l'enseignement normal.
ESP> En 1981 y 1982 los datos relativos al personal docente se refieren a la enseñanza pública solamente. *Enseñanza general:* Para 1975 los datos incluyen la enseñanza normal.
Haiti:
E--> See Table 3.1b.
FR-> Voir le tableau 3.1b.
ESP> Véase el cuadro 3.1b.
Jamaica:
E--> *General education:* Data on teachers for 1975 and 1980 do not include senior departments of all-age schools and those for 1983 refer to public education only. *Vocational education:* All data for 1975, 1982, 1983, and data on teachers for 1980 refer to public education only.
FR-> *Enseignement général:* Les données relatives au personnel enseignant pour 1975 et 1980, ne comprennent pas les sections supérieures des 'all-age schools' et celles pour 1983 se réfèrent à l'enseignement public seulement. *Enseignement technique:* Toutes les données pour 1975, 1982 et 1983, ainsi que celles relatives au personnel enseignant pour 1980 se réfèrent à l'enseignement public seulement.
ESP> *Enseñanza general:* Los datos relativos personal docente para 1975 y 1980 no comprenden las secciones superiores de las 'all-age schools' y los para 1983 se refieren a la enseñanza pública solamente. *Enseñanza técnica:* Todos los datos para 1975, 1982, 1983 y los datos relativos al personal docente en 1980 se refieren a la enseñanza pública solamente.
Martinique:
E--> *General education:* For 1975 data on pupils include teacher training.
FR-> *Enseignement général:* Pour 1975 les données se rapportant aux élèves incluent l'enseignement normal.
ESP> *Enseñanza general:* Para 1975 los datos relativos a los alumnos incluyen la enseñanza normal.
Nicaragua:
E--> See Table 3.1b.
FR-> Voir le tableau 3.1b.
ESP> Véase el cuadro 3.1b.
Puerto Rico:
E--> Data refer to public education only. For 1981 data refer to grades IX to XII; previous figures refer to grades VII to XII.
FR-> Les données se réfèrent à l'enseignement public seulement. Les données pour 1981 se réfèrent aux classes allant de la neuvième à la douzième année d'études. Pour les années précédentes les chiffres se référaient aux classes allant de la septième à la douzième année d'études.
ESP> Los datos se refieren a la enseñanza pública solamente. Los datos de 1981 se refieren a los años de estudios IX a XII. Anteriormente, las cifras se referían a los años de estudios VII a XII.
United States:
E--> All data include special education. From 1980 data on pupils refer to grades IX to XII. For previous years data referred to grades VII to XII or IX to XII according to States.
FR-> Toutes les données incluent l'éducation spéciale. A partir de 1980 les données relatives aux élèves se réfèrent aux classes allant de la neuvième à la douzième année d'études. Les années précédentes, les chiffres correspondaient aux années d'études VII-XII ou IX-XII, selon les Etats.
ESP> Todos los datos incluyen la educación especial. A partir de 1980 los datos relativos a los alumnos se refieren a los años de estudios IX a XII. Anteriormente, los datos incluían los años de estudios VII a XII o IX a XII según los Estados.
U.S. Virgin Islands:
E--> From 1980 data on pupils refer to public education only to grades IX to XII; previously they referred to grades VII to XII.
FR-> A partir de 1980 les données relatives aux élèves se réfère l'enseignement public seulement et aux classes allant de la neuvième douzième année d'études; les chiffres des années précédentes se référa aux classes allant de la septième à la douzième année d'études.
ESP> A partir de 1980 los datos relativos a los alumnos se refiere la enseñanza pública solamente y a los años de estudios IX a anteriormente, las cifras se referían a los años de estudios VII a XII.
AMERICA, SOUTH:
French Guiana:
E--> For 1981 and 1982 data on teaching staff refer to pu education only. *General education:* For 1975, data include teac training.
FR-> Pour 1981 et 1982 les données sur le personnel enseign se réfèrent à l'enseignement public seulement. *Enseignement général:* P 1975 les données incluent l'enseignement normal.
ESP> Para 1981 y 1982 los datos sobre el personal docente refieren a la enseñanza pública solamente. *Enseñanza general:* Para 19 los datos incluyen la enseñanza normal.
Uruguay:
E--> *General education:* For 1980, data do not include course U.T.U. (Universidad del Trabajo del Uruguay). *Vocational education:* F 1980, data refer to public education only.
FR-> *Enseignement général:* Pour 1980, les données comprennent pas les cours de la U.T.U. (Universidad del Trabajo Uruguay). *Enseignement technique:* A partir de 1980, les données réfèrent à l'enseignement public seulement.
ESP> *Enseñanza general:* En 1980, los datos no incluyen los cursos la U.T.U. (Universidad del Trabajo del Uruguay). *Enseñanza técnica:* A p de 1980, los datos se refieren a la enseñanza pública solamente.
ASIA:
Afghanistan:
E--> See Table 3.1b. *General education:* For 1975, data on teach include primary classes attached to middle and secondary schools.
FR-> Voir le tableau 3.1b. *Enseignement général:* Pour 1975 données relatives au personnel enseignant comprennent les clas primaires rattachées aux écoles moyennes et secondaires.
ESP> Véase el cuadro 3.1b. *Enseñanza general:* En 1975 los da relativos al personal docente incluyen las clases primarias adscritas a escuelas medias y secundarias.
Bahrain:
E--> See Table 3.1b. *General education:* For 1975, data on teach exclude a part of intermediate education and from 1981 they refe public education only.
FR-> Voir le tableau 3.1b. *Enseignement général:* Pour 1975, données relatives au personnel enseignant excluent une partie l'enseignement intermédiaire et à partir de 1981, elles se réfèren l'enseignement public seulement.
ESP> Véase el cuadro 3.1b. *Enseñanza general:* Para 1975, los da relativos al personal docente excluyen una parte de la enseñanza interme y a partir de 1981, ellos se refieren a la enseñanza pública solamente
Bangladesh:
E--> *General education:* For 1981, data on teachers do include religious schools.
FR-> *Enseignement général:* Pour 1981, les données relatives personnel enseignant ne comprennent pas les écoles religieuses.
ESP> *Enseñanza general:* Para 1981, los datos relativos al perso docente no incluyen las escuelas religiosas.
Bhutan:
E--> *General education:* From 1976 to 1982, data on teachers included with education at the first level.
FR-> *Enseignement général:* De 1976 à 1982, les données relati au personnel enseignant sont incluses dans l'enseignement du prem degré.
ESP> *Enseñanza general:* De 1976 a 1982, los datos relativos personal docente quedan incluídos en la enseñanza de primer grado.
Cyprus:
E--> Not including Turkish schools. *General and vocational:* 1983, data on commercial schools are included with general educati
FR-> Compte non tenu des écoles turques. *Enseignement généra technique:* Pour 1983, les données relatives aux écoles commerciales s comprises avec l'enseignement général.
ESP> Excluídas las escuelas turcas. *Enseñanza general y técnica:* P 1983, los datos relativos a las escuelas comerciales estan incluídos e enseñanza general.
Democratic Yemen:
E--> See table 3.1b. *General education:* For 1975, 1982 and 19 data on pupils include schools for nomads.
FR-> Voir le tableau 3.1b. *Enseignement général:* Pour 1975, 19 et 1983, les données relatives aux élèves incluent les écoles nomades.
ESP> Véase el cuadro 3.1b. *Enseñanza general:* En 1975, 198 1983, los datos relativos a los alumnos incluyen las escuelas p nómadas.
India:
E--> *General education:* From 1980, data on teachers incl

India: (Cont):
primary classes attached to secondary schools.

FR-> *Enseignement général:* A partir de 1980, les données relatives au personnel enseignant comprennent les classes primaires rattachées aux écoles secondaires.

ESP> *Enseñanza general:* A partir de 1980, los datos relativos al personal docente incluyen las clases primarias adscritas a las escuelas secundarias.

Indonesia:

E--> *General education:* All data on teachers and data on pupils for 1983 and 1984 do not include religious schools.

FR-> *Enseignement général:* Toutes les données relatives au personnel enseignant et celles relatives aux élèves pour 1983 et 1984 ne comprennent pas les écoles religieuses.

ESP> *Enseñanza general:* Todos los datos sobre el personal docente y los relativos a los alumnos para 1983 y 1984 no incluyen las escuelas religiosas.

Iran, Islamic Republic, of:

E--> See Table 3.1b.

FR-> Voir le tableau 3.1b.

ESP> Véase el cuadro 3.1b.

Israel:

E--> Data on teaching staff include intermediate classes attached to primary schools.

FR-> Les données relatives au personnel enseignant incluent les classes intermédiaires rattachées aux écoles primaires.

ESP> Los datos relativos al personal docente incluyen las clases intermedias adscritas a las escuelas primarias.

Japan:

E--> For 1975, data on female teachers and from 1980 all data on teachers include special education. *General education:* Until 1983, data on female pupils and for 1984 all data on pupils include special education.

FR-> Pour 1975, les données relatives au personnel enseignant féminin et à partir de 1980, toutes les données sur le personnel enseignant incluent l'éducation spéciale. *Enseignement général:* Jusqu'à 1983 les données relatives aux effectifs féminins et pour 1984 toutes les données sur les effectifs incluent l'éducation spéciale.

ESP> Para 1975, los datos relativos al personal docente femenino y a partir de 1980 todos los datos relativos al personal docente incluyen la educación especial. *Enseñanza general:* Hasta 1983, los datos relativos a la matrícula femenina y para 1984 todos los datos sobre los alumnos incluyen la educación especial.

Jordan:

E--> Including UNRWA schools with 1,358 teachers (f: 617) and 44,592 pupils (f: 21,355) in general education in 1984.

FR-> Y compris les écoles de l'UNRWA qui comptaient 1 358 maîtres (f: 617) et 44 592 élèves (f: 21 355) dans l'enseignement général en 1984.

ESP> Incluídas las escuelas del O.O.P.S.R.P. que tenían 1 358 profesores (f: 617) y 44 592 alumnos (f: 21 355) en la enseñanza general en 1984.

Korea, Republic of:

E--> *Vocational education:* For 1980 data on pupils include part-time education.

FR-> *Enseignement technique:* Pour 1980 les données relatives aux élèves incluent l'enseignement à temps partiel.

ESP> *Enseñanza técnica:* En 1980 los datos sobre la matrícula incluyen la enseñanza de jornada parcial.

Lao People's Democratic Republic:

E--> See Table 3.1b.

FR-> Voir le tableau 3.1b.

ESP> Véase el cuadro 3.1b.

Lebanon:

E--> Including UNRWA schools with 9,425 pupils (f: 4,911) enrolled in general education in 1982.

FR-> Y compris les écoles de l'UNRWA qui comptaient 9 425 élèves (f: 4 911) dans l'enseignement général en 1982.

ESP> Incluídas las escuelas del O.O.P.S.R.P. que en 1982 tenían 9 425 alumnos (f: 4 911) en la enseñanza general.

Malaysia:

E--> *General education:* For 1983 data do not include form VI (25,804 pupils (f: 13,712) in 1981).

FR-> *Enseignement général:* Pour 1983, les données n'incluent pas la 'form' VI (25 804 élèves, dont 13 712 filles, en 1981).

ESP> *Enseñanza general:* Para 1983, los datos no incluyen la 'form' VI (25 804 alumnos, f: 13 712 en 1981).

Nepal:

E--> See Table 3.1b.

FR-> Voir le tableau 3.1b.

ESP> Véase el cuadro 3.1b.

Sri Lanka:

E--> See table 3.1b. *General education:* For 1976 and 1984, data refer to public education only. *Vocational education:* Data refer to technical institutes attached to the Ministry of Education only.

FR-> Voir le tableau 3.1b. *Enseignement général:* Pour 1976 et 1984, les données se réfèrent à l'enseignement public seulement. *Enseignement technique:* Les données se réfèrent aux instituts techniques rattachés au Ministère de l'Education seulement.

Sri Lanka: (Cont):

ESP> Véase el cuadro 3.1b. *Enseñanza general:* En 1976 y 1984, los datos se refieren a la enseñanza pública solamente. *Enseñanza técnica:* Los datos se refieren a los institutos técnicos dependientes del Ministerio de Educación solamente.

Syrian Arab Republic:

E--> Including UNRWA schools with 620 teachers and 16,330 pupils in general education in 1984. *Teacher training:* Data on teachers for 1975 include teacher training at the third level of education.

FR-> Y compris les écoles de l'UNRWA qui comptaient 620 maîtres et 16 330 élèves dans l'enseignement général en 1984. *Enseignement normal:* Les données relatives au personnel enseignant pour 1975 incluent l'enseignement normal du troisième degré.

ESP> Incluídas las escuelas del O.O.P.S.R.P. que en 1984 tenían 620 maestros y 16 330 alumnos en la enseñanza general. *Enseñanza normal:* Para 1975, los datos relativos al personal docente incluyen la enseñanza normal de tercer grado.

Thailand:

E--> See Table 3.1b. *General education:* Data on teachers refer to public education only. *Teacher training:* For 1975, data on teachers include teacher training at the third level of education.

FR-> Voir le tableau 3.1b. *Enseignement général:* Les données relatives au personnel enseignant se réfèrent à l'enseignement public seulement. *Enseignement normal:* Pour 1975, les données relatives au personnel enseignant comprennent l'enseignement normal du troisième degré.

ESP> Véase el cuadro 3.1b. *Enseñanza general:* Los datos relativos al personal docente se refieren a la enseñanza pública solamente. *Enseñanza normal:* Para 1975, los datos relativos al personal docente comprenden la enseñanza normal de tercer grado.

United Arab Emirates:

E--> *General education:* Data on teachers refer to public education only.

FR-> *Enseignement général:* Les données relatives au personnel enseignant se réfèrent à l'enseignement public seulement.

ESP> *Enseñanza general:* Los datos relativos al personal docente se refieren a la enseñanza pública solamente.

Viet-nam:

E--> See Table 3.1b.

FR-> Voir le tableau 3.1b.

ESP> Véase el cuadro 3.1b.

Yemen:

E--> *General education:* Data on teaching staff refer to public education only.

FR-> *Enseignement général:* Les données relatives au personnel enseignant se réfèrent à l'enseignement public seulement.

ESP> *Enseñanza general:* Los datos relativos al personal docente se refieren a la enseñanza pública solamente.

EUROPE:

Albania:

E--> *Vocational education:* For 1982 and 1983, data on pupils do not include evening courses.

FR-> *Enseignement technique:* Pour 1982 et 1983, les données relatives aux élèves n'incluent pas les cours du soir.

ESP> *Enseñanza técnica:* En 1982 y 1983, los datos relativos a los alumnos no incluyen los cursos nocturnos.

Austria:

E--> *General education:* Data for 1975 include special education.

FR-> *Enseignement général:* Pour 1975 les données comprennent l'éducation spéciale.

ESP> *Enseñanza general:* En 1975 los datos incluyen la educación especial.

Belgium:

E--> Data include special education. *Vocational education:* For 1981 and 1982, data refer to the dutch-speaking sector only.

FR-> Les données comprennent l'éducation spéciale. *Enseignement technique:* Pour 1981 et 1982, les données se réfèrent au régime linguistique néerlandais seulement.

ESP> Los datos incluyen la educación especial. *Enseñanza técnica:* En 1981 y 1982, los datos se refieren solamente a la enseñanza de lengua holandesa.

Denmark:

E--> *General education:* Data on teachers are included with education at the first level. *Vocational education:* Except for 1975, data include apprenticeship training.

FR-> *Enseignement général:* Les données relatives au personnel enseignant sont incluses avec l'enseignement du premier degré. *Enseignement technique:* A l'exception de 1975, les données comprennent la formation pratique.

ESP> *Enseñanza general:* Los datos relativos al personal docente quedan incluídos en la enseñanza de primer grado. *Enseñanza técnica:* Excepto 1975, los datos incluyen la formación práctica.

Finland:

E--> *General education:* For 1975, data on teaching staff include primary classes attached to secondary schools. From 1980, data on pupils include integrated special education. *Teacher training:* For 1980, data on teaching staff include teacher training at the third level.

FR-> *Enseignement général:* Pour 1975 les données relatives au

Finland: (Cont):
personnel enseignant comprennent les classes primaires rattachées aux écoles secondaires. A partir de 1980, les données relatives aux élèves incluent l'éducation spéciale intégrée. *Enseignement normal:* Pour 1980 les données relatives au personnel enseignant incluent l'enseignement normal du troisième degré.

ESP> *Enseñanza general:* Pour 1975 los datos relativos al personal docente comprenden las clases primarias adscritas a las escuelas secundarias; a partir de 1980, los datos relativos a los alumnos incluyen la educación especial integrada. *Enseñanza normal:* Para 1980 los datos relativos al personal docente incluyen la enseñanza normal de tercer grado.

France:

E--> For 1975, data on teachers refer to full-time only; from 1980, they refer to public education only.

FR-> Pour 1975, les données relatives au personnel enseignant se réfèrent au personnel à plein temps seulement; à partir de 1980, elles se réfèrent à l'enseignement public seulement.

ESP> Para 1975, los datos relativos al personal docente se refieren al personal de jornada completa solamente; a partir de 1980, ellos se refieren a la enseñanza pública solamente.

German Democratic Republic:

E--> *General education:* Data on teachers are included with education at the first level.

FR-> *Enseignement général:* Les données relatives au personnel enseignant sont incluses avec l'enseignement du premier degré.

ESP> *Enseñanza general:* Los datos relativos al personal docente están incluídos en la enseñanza de primer grado.

Germany, Federal Republic of:

E--> Beginning 1983, due to a new method of estimation, data are not comparable with those of previous years.

FR-> A partir de 1983, suite à une nouvelle méthode d'estimation, les données ne sont pas comparables avec celles des années antérieures.

ESP> A partir de 1983, debido a un nuevo método de estimación, los datos no son comparables a los de los años anteriores.

Hungary:

E--> *Vocational education:* Data include full-time apprenticeship training.

FR-> *Enseignement technique:* Les données comprennent l'apprentissage à plein temps.

ESP> *Enseñanza ténica:* Los datos incluyen las escuelas de aprendizaje de jornada completa.

Ireland:

E--> The number of teachers is expressed in full-time equivalent. *General education:* Data on teachers include a part of teaching staff of vocational education.

FR-> Le nombre de professeurs est compté en équivalent plein temps. *Enseignement général:* Les données sur le personnel enseignant incluent une partie du personnel enseignant de l'enseignement technique.

ESP> El número de profesores se presenta en equivalencia de jornada completa. *Enseñanza general:* Los datos sobre el personal docente incluyen una parte del personal docente de la enseñanza técnica.

Monaco:

E--> Except for 1982, data refer to public education only.

FR-> A l'exception de l'ann
ee 1982 les données se réfèrent à l'enseignement public seulement.

ESP> Salvo para el año 1982, los datos se refieren a la enseñanza pública solamente.

Poland:

E--> *Vocational education:* Data on teachers include teacher training.

FR-> *Enseignement technique:* Les données relatives au personnel enseignant incluent l'enseignement normal.

ESP> *Enseñanza técnica:* Los datos relativos al personal docente incluyen la enseñanza normal.

Portugal:

E--> See Table 3.1b. *General education:* For 1980,1981 and 1982 data on female pupils refer to public education only.

FR-> Voir le tableau 3.1b. *Enseignement général:* Pour 1980, 1981 et 1982 les données relatives aux effectifs féminins se réfèrent à l'enseignement public seulement.

ESP> Véase el cuadro 3.1b. *Enseñanza general:* En 1980, 1981 y 1982 los datos relativos a la matrícula femenina se refieren a la enseñanza pública solamente.

Romania:

E--> *General and vocational education:* From 1981, data include evening and correspondence courses.

FR-> *Enseignement général et technique:* A partir de 1981, les données incluent les cours du soir et par correspondance.

ESP> *Enseñanza general y técnica:* A partir de 1981, los datos incluyen los cursos nocturnos y por correspondencia.

Switzerland:

E--> For 1975, data refer to public education only.

FR-> Pour 1975 les données se réfèrent à l'enseignement public seulement.

ESP> En 1975 los datos se refieren a la enseñanza pública

Switzerland: (Cont):
solamente.

Yugoslavia:

E--> *General education:* For 1975, data on female pupils include special education. *Vocational education:* For 1980 and 1981, data on pupils include a part of enrolment of teacher training.

FR-> *Enseignement général:* Pour 1975 les données relatives aux effectifs féminins incluent l'éducation spéciale. *Enseignement technique:* Pour 1980 et 1981, les données sur les élèves incluent une partie des effectifs de l'enseignement normal.

ESP> *Enseñanza general:* En 1975 los datos relativos a la matrícula femenina incluyen la educación especial. *Enseñanza técnica:* Para 1980 y 1981, los datos sobre los alumnos incluyen una parte de la matrícula de la enseñanza normal.

OCEANIA:

American Samoa:

E--> For 1975, data refer to public education only.

FR-> Pour 1975, les données se réfèrent à l'enseignement public seulement.

ESP> Para 1975, los datos se refieren a la enseñanza pública solamente.

Fiji:

E--> *General education:* For 1975, enrolment in forms I and II are included in first level education. *Teacher training:* In 1984, a part of teacher training has been reclassified as third level education.

FR-> *Enseignement général:* Pour 1975, les effectifs des 'forms' I et II sont inclus dans l'enseignement du premier degré. *Enseignement normal:* En 1984, une partie de l'enseignement normal a été reclassée dans l'enseignement du troisième degré.

ESP> *Enseñanza general:* En 1975, la matrícula de las 'forms' I y II está incluída en la enseñanza de primer grado. *Enseñanza normal:* En 1984 una parte de la enseñanza normal ha sido reclasificada en la enseñanza de tercer grado.

Guam:

E--> For 1979 data refer to public education only.

FR-> Pour 1979 les chiffres se réfèrent à l'enseignement public seulement.

ESP> En 1979 las cifras se refieren a la enseñanza pública solamente.

New Caledonia:

E--> *Teacher training:* For 1975 data on female teachers refer to public education only.

FR-> *Enseignement normal:* Pour 1975 les données relatives au personnel enseignant féminin se réfèrent à l'enseignement public seulement.

ESP> *Enseñanza normal:* En 1975 los datos relativos al personal docente femenino se refieren a la enseñanza pública solamente.

New Zealand:

E--> *General education:* Until 1981, data on teachers in forms I and II are included with first level education. For 1975 data on pupils include special education.

FR-> *Enseignement général:* Jusqu'à 1981, les données relatives au personnel enseignant des 'forms' I et II sont incluses dans l'enseignement du premier degré. Pour 1975 les données relatives aux élèves incluent l'éducation spéciale.

ESP> *Enseñanza general:* Hasta 1981, los datos relativos al personal docente de las 'forms' I y II están incluídos en la enseñanza de primer grado. En 1975 los datos relativos a los alumnos incluyen la educación especial.

Tonga:

E--> *General education:* For 1982, data on teachers refer to public education only.

FR-> *Enseignement général:* Pour 1982, les données relatives au personnel enseignant se réfèrent à l'enseignement public seulement.

ESP> *Enseñanza general:* Para 1982, los datos relativos al personal docente se refieren a la enseñanza pública solamente.

U.S.S.R.:

U.S.S.R.:

E--> *General education:* Data on teachers are included with education at the first level. *Vocational education:* Data on teachers include teacher training as well as evening and correspondence courses.

FR-> *Enseignement général:* Les données relatives au personnel enseignant sont incluses avec l'enseignement du premier degré. *Enseignement technique:* Les données relatives au personnel enseignant comprennent l'enseignement normal ainsi que les cours du soir et par correspondance.

ESP> *Enseñanza general:* Los datos relativos al personal docente están incluídos en la enseñanza de primer grado. *Enseñanza técnica:* Los datos relativos al personal docente comprenden la enseñanza normal y los cursos nocturnos y por correspondencia.

Byelorussian S.S.R.:

E--> *General education:* Data on teachers are included with education at the first level. *Vocational education:* Data on teachers include teacher training as well as evening and correspondence courses.

FR-> *Enseignement général:* Les données relatives au personnel enseignant sont incluses dans l'enseignement du premier degré. *Enseignement technique:* Les données relatives au personnel enseignant comprennent l'enseignement normal ainsi que les cours du soir et par

Byelorussian S.S.R.: (Cont):
correspondance.

ESP> *Enseñanza general:* Los datos relativos al personal docente quedan incluídos en la enseñanza de primer grado. *Enseñanza técnica:* Los datos relativos al personal docente comprenden la enseñanza normal y los cursos nocturnos y por correspondencia.

Ukrainian S.S.R.:

E--> *General education:* Data on teachers are included with education at the first level. From 1980 data refer to 6 years instead of 3 years in order to be consistent with ISCED. *Vocational education:* For 1975, all data include teacher training as well as evening and correspondence courses.

Ukrainian S.S.R.: (Cont):

FR-> *Enseignement général:* Les données relatives au personnel enseignant sont incluses avec l'enseignement du premier degré. A partir de 1980 les données se réfèrent à 6 années d'études au lieu de 3 années afin d'être en accord avec la C.I.T.E. *Enseignement technique:* Pour 1975, toutes les données incluent l'enseignement normal ainsi que les cours du soir et par correspondance.

ESP> *Enseñanza general:* Los datos relativos al personal docente quedan incluídos en la enseñanza de primer grado. A partir de 1980, los datos se refieren a 6 años de estudios en vez de 3 años para conformarse con la C.I.N.E. *Enseñanza técnica:* En 1975, todos los datos incluyen la enseñanza normal y los cursos nocturnos y por correspondencia.

3.8 Education at the second level (general): percentage distribution of enrolment by grade

Enseignement du second degré (général): répartition en pourcentage des effectifs par année d'études

Enseñanza de segundo grado (general): distribución en porcentaje de la matrícula escolar por año de estudios

PLEASE REFER TO EXPLANATORY TEXT AT END OF TABLE

PRIERE DE SE REFERER AU TEXTE EXPLICATIF A LA FIN DU TABLEAU

REFERIRSE AL TEXTO EXPLICATIVO AL FINAL DEL CUADRO

NUMBER OF COUNTRIES AND TERRITORIES PRESENTED IN THIS TABLE: 176

NOMBRE DE PAYS ET DE TERRITOIRES PRESENTES DANS CE TABLEAU: 176

NUMERO DE PAISES Y DE TERRITORIOS PRESENTADOS EN ESTE CUADRO: 176

COUNTRY / PAYS / PAIS	YEAR / ANNEE / AÑO	SEX / SEXE / SEXO	GRADE / ANNEES / AÑOS DE ESTUDIOS									
			I	II	III	IV	V	VI	VII	VIII	IX	X
AFRICA												
ALGERIA	1975	MF	25	23	19	16	8	6	5			
		F	26	24	19	16	7	5	4			
	1980	MF	23	21	19	17	9	6	5			
		F	23	21	19	17	8	6	5			
	1983	MF	24	21	17	18	7	6	7			
		F	24	21	17	17	8	6	7			
	1984	MF	24	21	18	17	8	6	6			
		F	24	21	18	17	8	7	7			
ANGOLA	1981	MF	58	24	11	5	2	——>				
	1982	MF	59	26	9	4	3	——>				
BENIN	1975	MF	22	23	20	18	7	7	4			
		F	23	23	20	17	7	7	4			
	1980	MF	33	19	16	15	7	5	6			
		F	34	20	15	15	6	5	6			
	1982	MF	18	25	23	15	4	6	8			
		F	21	27	22	15	3	6	7			
	1983	MF	17	20	25	20	5	4	9			
		F	19	23	25	19	4	4	7			
BOTSWANA	1975	MF	36	30	21	8	6					
		F	38	33	20	5	4					
	1980	MF	33	28	23	9	7					
		F	36	29	24	7	5					
	1984	MF	40	26	20	8	6					
		F	42	27	20	7	4					
	1985	MF	33	32	21	7	6					
		F	33	34	22	5	5					
BURKINA FASO	1975	MF	23	19	18	18	8	7	7			
		F	27	20	19	18	6	5	5			
	1980	MF	25	21	18	15	8	6	7			
		F	28	22	18	15	7	5	6			
	1983	MF	26	19	17	15	10	6	7			
		F	23	22	19	17	8	5	6			
	1984	MF	30	20	16	16	7	5	6			
		F	32	21	16	16	6	4	4			

COUNTRY PAYS PAIS	YEAR ANNEE AÑO	SEX SEXE SEXO	GRADE / ANNEES / AÑOS DE ESTUDIOS									
			I	II	III	IV	V	VI	VII	VIII	IX	X
BURUNDI	1975	MF	19	20	21	15	11	8	7			
		F	22	21	22	18	8	6	3			
	1980	MF	17	18	19	16	10	10	9			
		F	14	17	18	20	12	11	9			
	1981	MF	19	18	19	18	12	8	6			
		F	21	19	20	17	12	6	5			
CAMEROON	1975	MF	28	21	17	16	7	7	4			
		F	31	23	18	16	6	4	2			
	1980	MF	24	21	19	18	7	7	4			
		F	27	23	20	17	6	5	3			
	1983	MF	25	20	18	18	8	7	5			
		F	28	22	18	18	6	5	3			
	1984	MF	25	20	18	17	7	7	5			
		F	28	22	18	17	6	5	3			
CAPE VERDE	1975	MF	42	27	12	10	8					
	1980	MF	36	26	22	9	7					
		F	38	27	20	8	7					
	1981	MF	34	26	20	12	8					
		F	37	27	20	9	8					
	1983	MF	36	25	18	11	10					
		F	36	28	15	11	10					
CENTRAL AFRICAN REPUBLIC	1975	MF	28	23	19	17	8	4	2			
		F	38	26	18	10	4	2	2			
	1980	MF	30	21	17	13	8	6	5			
		F	39	23	16	11	5	3	2			
	1981	MF	29	21	16	15	8	5	5			
		F	34	22	17	14	7	3	3			
	1982	MF	28	21	17	14	9	6	6			
		F	37	23	17	12	6	3	2			
CHAD	1975	MF	28	22	18	18	6	4	4			
	1984	MF	20	20	20	19	8	5	7			
		F	23	21	18	17	9	5	6			
COMOROS	1980	MF	26	23	17	20	9	3	2			
		F	28	26	17	18	8	2	1			
CONGO	1975	MF	31	23	18	13	7	4	3			
		F	36	25	19	13	4	2	1			
	1980	MF	30	20	17	20	5	3	5			
		F	34	22	17	19	3	2	2			
	1982	MF	30	20	17	17	8	4	5			
		F	34	22	17	16	6	3	2			
COTE D'IVOIRE	1975	MF	29	23	20	16	5	4	4			
		F	33	25	18	14	4	3	3			
	1980	MF	29	25	19	15	5	5	2			
		F	33	26	18	13	4	3	2			
	1982	MF	26	23	20	16	6	6	2			
		F	31	26	20	15	4	4	1			
	1983	MF	25	23	20	17	6	6	2			
		F	30	24	20	16	4	4	1			
DJIBOUTI	1975	MF	24	26	17	12	10	6	5			
		F	22	20	14	13	15	10	7			
	1980	MF	31	24	19	14	5	4	3			
	1982	MF	28	27	19	17	5	3	2			
		F	29	28	18	16	3	3	3			
	1983	MF	27	26	18	17	6	4	2			
		F	28	28	17	16	5	3	3			
EGYPT	1975	MF	29	23	27	7	7	7				
		F	30	23	26	7	6	7				

3.8 Percentage distribution (second level general) by grade
Répartition en % (second degré général) par année d'études
Distribución en % (segundo grado general) por año de estudios

COUNTRY PAYS PAIS	YEAR ANNEE AÑO	SEX SEXE SEXO	GRADE / ANNEES / AÑOS DE ESTUDIOS									
			I	II	III	IV	V	VI	VII	VIII	IX	X
EGYPT (CONT)	1980	MF	26	22	28	8	7	9				
		F	27	22	28	7	7	9				
	1981	MF	27	24	25	8	7	9				
		F	28	25	24	7	7	9				
	1982	MF	26	25	27	7	7	9				
		F	26	25	27	7	7	8				
ETHIOPIA	1975	MF	33	28	18	13	8	0				
		F	35	31	17	12	6	0				
	1980	MF	27	22	18	14	11	8				
		F	26	23	19	13	10	8				
	1982	MF	29	23	18	13	10	7				
		F	27	25	19	13	10	7				
	1983	MF	29	24	17	13	10	7				
		F	27	25	18	13	10	6				
GABON	1975	MF	29	24	18	13	7	5	5			
		F	33	25	17	12	7	4	3			
	1980	MF	27	20	19	14	9	6	6			
		F	31	20	19	13	7	5	4			
	1982	MF	28	21	17	13	9	7	6			
		F	30	22	17	13	7	6	5			
	1983	MF	29	21	17	13	8	6	6			
		F	32	21	17	12	7	5	5			
GAMBIA	1975	MF	27	23	23	21	6	1				
		F	29	23	23	19	5	1				
	1980	MF	26	24	21	20	7	1				
		F	27	24	21	20	6	1				
	1983	MF	26	25	23	19	5	1				
		F	27	25	23	19	5	1				
	1984	MF	27	25	23	20	4	1				
		F	28	27	22	18	5	2				
GHANA	1975	MF	28	25	23	20	2	1	1			
		F	29	26	23	19	2	0	0			
	1979	MF	28	26	23	19	3	1	1			
		F	30	26	23	18	2	0	0			
	1984	MF	27	25	24	21	3	1	1			
		F	29	25	23	20	2	0	0			
GUINEA	1975	MF	30	21	15	13	12	9				
		F	31	22	16	13	10	7				
	1980	MF	22	21	22	11	17	7				
		F	22	22	24	11	16	6				
	1983	MF	24	20	21	11	17	7				
		F	24	21	23	11	16	5				
	1984	MF	21	19	19	15	13	13				
		F	21	20	21	15	12	11				
GUINEA–BISSAU	1975	MF	43	27	16	8	6					
		F	46	28	14	6	6					
	1980	MF	45	27	12	10	6					
		F	46	34	9	6	4					
	1982	MF	41	27	14	10	9					
		F	46	27	14	7	6					
	1983	MF	34	27	16	13	10					
		F	37	29	15	10	8					
KENYA‡	1975	MF	32	28	20	16	2	2				
		F	35	29	19	13	2	1				
	1980	MF	28	25	21	21	3	2				
		F	29	26	21	20	2	2				
	1983	MF	28	26	21	21	2	2				
		F	28	26	21	21	2	2				
	1984	MF	29	23	22	21	3	2				
		F	29	23	22	21	3	2				

COUNTRY PAYS PAIS	YEAR ANNEE AÑO	SEX SEXE SEXO	GRADE / ANNEES / AÑOS DE ESTUDIOS									
			I	II	III	IV	V	VI	VII	VIII	IX	X
LESOTHO	1975	MF	32	29	23	7	8					
		F	34	29	22	7	7					
	1980	MF	35	30	18	11	6					
		F	36	30	17	10	6					
	1982	MF	36	27	19	11	7					
		F	37	28	19	9	6					
	1983	MF	35	29	19	10	7					
		F	36	29	19	10	6					
LIBERIA	1975	MF	27	22	20	14	10	8				
		F	30	24	19	12	9	7				
	1978	MF	22	19	19	16	12	10				
		F	23	20	19	16	12	9				
	1979	MF	23	21	18	16	11	11				
		F	24	20	18	15	12	11				
LIBYAN ARAB JAMAHIRIYA	1975	MF	44	25	18	6	4	3				
		F	49	25	17	4	3	2				
	1980	MF	33	27	22	9	6	4				
		F	36	28	23	7	4	2				
	1982	MF	31	26	22	8	6	6				
		F	33	27	23	7	5	4				
MADAGASCAR‡	1975	MF	22	21	20	17	7	7	6			
		F	22	21	20	18	7	7	5			
	1979	MF	32	23	17	12	7	6	4			
	1983	MF	22	20	20	23	7	5	3			
	1984	MF	20	20	19	23	7	6	5			
		F	21	18	20	24	7	6	5			
MALAWI	1975	MF	30	30	20	19						
		F	34	34	17	15						
	1980	MF	30	30	21	19						
		F	32	32	19	17						
	1983	MF	30	28	22	20						
		F	31	31	20	18						
	1984	MF	28	28	21	22						
		F	30	30	21	19						
MALI	1975	MF	32	26	24	8	7	4				
		F	36	27	23	6	5	3				
	1981	MF	28	24	29	4	12	4				
		F	31	27	30	3	7	2				
	1982	MF	28	23	30	3	8	8				
		F	31	25	29	2	6	6				
MAURITANIA	1975	MF	30	21	17	13	9	6	4			
	1980	MF	26	29	16	12	9	8				
		F	33	31	16	9	7	5				
	1982	MF	27	22	18	16	9	9				
		F	33	23	19	14	6	5				
MAURITIUS	1975	MF	23	20	17	18	18	2	2			
		F	24	21	17	18	16	2	2			
	1980	MF	17	18	20	20	19	3	3			
		F	18	19	20	20	18	3	2			
	1983	MF	19	17	17	20	19	4	5			
		F	19	18	16	20	19	3	4			
	1984	MF	17	18	17	20	20	4	5			
		F	18	18	17	20	19	3	4			
MOROCCO	1975	MF	24	19	17	17	9	7	7			
		F	26	20	18	16	9	6	6			
	1980	MF	20	18	16	17	12	8	8			
		F	21	19	17	17	11	8	8			
	1982	MF	20	18	16	16	11	9	10			
		F	20	18	16	17	11	8	10			

3.8 Percentage distribution (second level general) by grade
Répartition en % (second degré général) par année d'études
Distribución en % (segundo grado general) por año de estudios

COUNTRY PAYS PAIS	YEAR ANNEE AÑO	SEX SEXE SEXO	GRADE / ANNEES / AÑOS DE ESTUDIOS									
			I	II	III	IV	V	VI	VII	VIII	IX	X
MOROCCO (CONT)	1984	MF	21	17	16	17	10	9	10			
		F	21	17	16	17	10	9	10			
MOZAMBIQUE	1982	MF	50	36	6	4	3					
		F	53	34	6	4	3					
	1983	MF	49	37	6	4	3					
		F	51	37	6	4	3					
NIGER	1975	MF	31	24	21	14	4	3	3			
		F	33	22	21	14	4	3	3			
	1980	MF	28	24	20	17	5	3	2			
		F	29	24	19	18	5	3	2			
	1981	MF	34	22	20	15	3	3	2			
REUNION‡	1975	MF	30	25	26	11	4	2	2			
		F	29	24	26	12	4	2	2			
	1979	MF	24	22	32	12	5	2	2			
		F	23	22	29	13	6	3	3			
	1982	MF	32	24	17	15	6	3	4			
		F	29	23	17	16	7	3	4			
	1983	MF	31	26	16	16	6	3	4			
		F	28	25	17	17	7	3	4			
RWANDA	1975	MF	39	24	22	6	5	5				
		F	39	29	25	3	3	2				
	1980	MF	3	10	57	10	10	9				
		F	–	7	81	5	4	3				
	1981	MF	41	3	14	15	13	13				
		F	45	–	16	14	15	10				
	1983	MF	33	29	20	2	5	10				
		F	44	29	15	–	–	11				
ST. HELENA	1982	MF	21	21	27	27	3	1				
		F	20	22	28	23	4	3				
	1983	MF	17	24	23	32	3	1				
		F	19	20	23	31	4	2				
SAO TOME AND PRINCIPE	1976	MF	45	24	15	8	5	2	1			
		F	41	28	15	10	3	3	0			
	1982	MF	54	17	13	6	5	3	2			
		F	56	17	13	6	4	3	1			
SENEGAL	1976	MF	26	21	18	17	7	6	5			
		F	27	22	19	17	6	5	4			
	1980	MF	24	22	19	18	8	7	3			
		F	25	23	20	18	6	5	2			
	1982	MF	25	21	18	18	7	7	4			
		F	26	21	19	19	7	5	3			
	1983	MF	24	21	18	18	8	7	3			
		F	25	22	18	18	7	6	3			
SEYCHELLES	1975	MF	40	37	14	4	3	1	1			
		F	40	36	16	4	3	0	0			
	1980	MF	32	51	10	7						
		F	31	56	7	5						
	1984	MF	52	48								
		F	51	49								
	1985	MF	51	49								
		F	54	46								
SIERRA LEONE	1976	MF	30	24	19	16	11	1	0			
SOMALIA‡	1975	MF	–	28	26	28	5	7	6			
		F	–	31	28	29	3	5	3			
	1980	MF	60	20	13	7						
		F	66	17	11	6						
	1982	MF	27	33	29	11						
		F	30	33	28	8						
	1983	MF	19	26	28	28						
		F	18	28	27	27						

COUNTRY PAYS PAIS	YEAR ANNEE AÑO	SEX SEXE SEXO	GRADE / ANNEES / AÑOS DE ESTUDIOS									
			I	II	III	IV	V	VI	VII	VIII	IX	X
SUDAN	1975	MF	29	24	25	*9	*7	*6				
		F	*32	*24	*25	*8	*6	*5				
	1980	MF	28	22	24	8	8	9				
		F	29	22	24	8	8	8				
	1982	MF	26	25	24	9	9	7				
		F	26	26	25	8	8	7				
	1983	MF	24	23	24	9	9	11				
		F	25	23	25	9	8	11				
SWAZILAND	1975	MF	35	27	20	10	7					
		F	38	28	19	9	7					
	1980	MF	31	27	22	11	9					
		F	32	28	22	10	8					
	1983	MF	31	27	21	12	9					
		F	32	28	21	12	8					
	1984	MF	31	27	21	12	9					
		F	32	28	20	11	8					
TOGO	1975	MF	37	24	16	13	5	4	2			
		F	42	24	15	11	4	3	1			
	1979	MF	28	23	19	18	5	3	3			
		F	34	24	18	16	3	2	2			
	1983	MF	27	21	20	20	4	5	4			
		F	32	23	21	17	2	3	2			
	1984	MF	25	21	21	20	4	5	4			
		F	29	24	22	17	3	3	2			
TUNISIA‡	1975	MF	23	20	17	11	10	9	10			
		F	24	21	17	11	10	9	8			
	1980	MF	26	18	19	12	9	8	8			
		F	26	18	18	12	9	8	8			
	1983	MF	24	20	19	12	9	7	8			
		F	24	20	19	12	9	7	8			
	1984	MF	23	20	18	14	10	7	8			
		F	24	20	18	14	10	7	8			
UGANDA‡	1975	MF	25	23	22	21	5	5				
		F	28	24	22	19	4	3				
	1979	MF	25	23	22	21	4	4				
		F	27	24	23	20	3	3				
	1981	MF	28	23	21	19	5	4				
		F	31	25	21	17	4	3				
UNITED REPUBLIC OF TANZANIA‡	1975	MF	26	25	21	20	4	4				
		F	28	27	22	19	2	2				
	1980	MF	23	25	23	23	3	3				
		F	24	26	24	22	2	2				
	1981	MF	24	23	25	23	3	3				
		F	25	24	24	23	2	2				
ZAIRE	1975	MF	*49	*33	*7	*5	*3	*2				
		F	*58	*33	*5	*2	*1	*1				
	1980	MF	48	37	6	4	3	2				
		F	53	37	4	3	2	1				
	1982	MF	48	37	6	4	3	2				
		F	53	37	4	3	2	1				
	1983	MF	48	37	6	4	3	2				
		F	53	37	4	3	2	1				
ZAMBIA	1975	MF	29	26	23	11	10					
		F	32	27	24	10	7					
	1980	MF	27	25	25	12	11					
		F	28	27	25	11	9					
ZIMBABWE	1975	MF	29	27	20	15	7	2				
		F	30	27	20	15	7	1				
	1980	MF	30	23	21	17	6	2				

3.8 Percentage distribution (second level general) by grade
Répartition en % (second degré général) par année d'études
Distribución en % (segundo grado general) por año de estudios

COUNTRY PAYS PAIS	YEAR ANNEE AÑO	SEX SEXE SEXO	GRADE / ANNEES / AÑOS DE ESTUDIOS									
			I	II	III	IV	V	VI	VII	VIII	IX	X
ZIMBABWE (CONT)	1983	MF	35	30	24	8	2	1				
		F	36	30	24	8	2	1				
	1984	MF	33	25	22	18	1	1				
		F	35	25	21	17	1	0				
AMERICA, NORTH												
ANTIGUA AND BARBUDA	1975	MF	25	21	24	15	13	2				
		F	24	22	23	16	13	3				
	1977	MF	31	22	22	13	11	0				
		F	25	22	24	15	13	0				
BAHAMAS	1982	MF	19	18	18	17	16	12				
		F	19	17	18	17	17	13				
BARBADOS‡	1975	MF	24	22	23	14	16	1				
		F	22	21	22	15	19	1				
	1983	MF	21	20	18	18	22	1				
		F	20	19	17	18	24	1				
	1984	MF	20	20	19	18	22	1				
		F	19	20	18	17	25	1				
BELIZE	1980	MF	34	27	22	16	1					
		F	*35	*26	*22	*15	*1					
	1981	MF	34	27	22	15	1					
		F	*34	*28	*21	*16	*1					
BERMUDA	1980	MF	20	20	20	20	18	2				
		F	19	20	19	20	20	2				
	1983	MF	21	22	20	19	17	2				
		F	21	22	19	17	18	2				
	1984	MF	21	22	21	19	16	2				
		F	21	21	21	19	16	2				
BRITISH VIRGIN ISLANDS	1983	MF	21	19	25	17	19					
		F	21	20	25	16	18					
	1984	MF	24	19	17	23	17					
		F	23	21	19	21	17					
CANADA	1975	MF	18	18	19	18	16	11	——>			
		F	*18	*18	*19	*18	*16	*11	——>			
	1980	MF	16	16	18	18	17	14	——>			
		F	16	16	18	18	18	14	——>			
	1982	MF	17	16	17	17	16	11	5			
		F	17	17	17	17	16	12	5			
	1983	MF	17	16	17	17	16	12	5			
		F	17	17	17	17	16	12	5			
COSTA RICA	1975	MF	29	24	25	14	9					
		F	28	24	25	14	8					
	1980	MF	27	28	19	14	12	0				
		F	26	27	19	16	12	0				
	1983	MF	31	21	19	16	13	0				
		F	30	21	19	16	14	0				
	1984	MF	32	22	18	15	12	0				
		F	30	22	19	16	13	0				
CUBA	1975	MF	37	29	16	10	4	3	2			
		F	37	29	16	10	4	3	2			
	1980	MF	30	28	23	9	6	4				
		F	29	27	24	9	6	5				
	1983	MF	30	25	24	9	7	6				
		F	29	24	23	10	7	6				
	1984	MF	30	27	23	9	7	6				
		F	28	26	22	10	8	6				
DOMINICA	1983	MF	29	26	27	10	7	1				
		F	28	26	25	11	8	1				
DOMINICAN REPUBLIC	1983	MF	24	20	18	15	12	10				

COUNTRY PAYS PAIS	YEAR ANNEE AÑO	SEX SEXE SEXO	GRADE / ANNEES / AÑOS DE ESTUDIOS									
			I	II	III	IV	V	VI	VII	VIII	IX	X
EL SALVADOR	1975	MF	43	33	24							
		F	43	33	24							
	1980	MF	35	33	32							
		F	36	33	31							
	1983	MF	45	31	25							
		F	45	30	25							
	1984	MF	39	34	27							
		F	39	34	28							
GRENADA	1976	MF	35	31	15	9	8	1	1			
		F	34	31	15	9	9	1	1			
	1981	MF	35	27	18	10	10	0				
		F	34	26	18	12	10	0				
	1982	MF	34	27	18	11	10					
		F	31	27	18	12	12					
	1983	MF	22	25	19	17	16					
		F	21	25	20	18	16					
GUADELOUPE‡	1976	MF	26	24	22	18	4	2	2			
		F	26	25	21	19	4	3	3			
	1981	MF	26	25	17	18	7	3	3			
		F	25	24	18	19	8	4	3			
	1982	MF	27	25	18	17	6	4	3			
		F	25	24	18	18	7	4	4			
	1983	MF	29	25	17	17	6	3	4			
		F	26	24	18	18	7	3	4			
GUATEMALA‡	1975	MF	31	22	17	14	11	6				
		F	30	22	16	14	11	7				
	1980	MF	39	29	25	3	3	0				
		F	39	31	26	2	2	0				
	1981	MF	40	30	24	4	3	0				
		F	40	30	26	2	1	0				
	1982	MF	38	29	26	3	3	0				
	1983	MF	41	30	24	3	2	0				
HAITI	1976	MF	25	20	17	14	12	9	3			
		F	26	21	18	15	11	8	2			
	1980	MF	27	20	17	14	10	10	3			
		F	28	21	18	14	10	8	2			
	1982	MF	27	20	17	14	10	9	3			
		F	27	20	18	14	10	8	2			
	1983	MF	25	18	17	15	12	10	3			
		F	26	19	17	15	12	9	2			
HONDURAS‡	1975	MF	42	27	21	6	4					
	1980	MF	42	27	21	*6	*4					
		F	42	28	23	*5	*2					
	1982	MF	41	27	21	6	4	0				
		F	41	29	23	4	3	0				
	1984	MF	39	28	22	6	4	0				
JAMAICA‡	1975	MF	28	25	23	13	11	1	1			
		F	27	24	23	13	11	1	1			
	1980	MF	25	24	23	14	12	1	1			
		F	24	24	24	14	12	1	1			
	1983	MF	24	24	22	16	13	1	0			
		F	23	23	23	16	13	1	1			
MARTINIQUE‡	1976	MF	25	22	28	15	5	2	3			
		F	25	22	25	16	6	3	3			
	1981	MF	27	26	18	17	6	3	3			
		F	25	25	19	18	6	3	3			
	1982	MF	27	26	18	18	5	3	3			
		F	25	24	19	19	6	3	4			
	1983	MF	26	27	18	18	5	3	3			
		F	24	26	18	20	7	3	3			

3.8 Percentage distribution (second level general) by grade
Répartition en % (second degré général) par année d'études
Distribución en % (segundo grado general) por año de estudios

COUNTRY PAYS PAIS	YEAR ANNEE AÑO	SEX SEXE SEXO	GRADE / ANNEES / AÑOS DE ESTUDIOS									
			I	II	III	IV	V	VI	VII	VIII	IX	X
MEXICO	1975	MF	31	24	20	12	8	4	0			
		F	36	28	23	7	5	3	0			
	1980	MF	30	25	21	12	8	5				
		F	32	27	22	9	6	3				
	1982	MF	30	25	20	12	8	5				
		F	31	27	22	9	7	4				
	1983	MF	28	24	21	13	8	5				
NETHERLANDS ANTILLES	1980	MF	24	22	21	23	7	3				
		F	24	22	22	23	6	2				
NICARAGUA	1975	MF	33	25	21	12	9	–				
	1980	MF	35	26	18	12	9					
		F	35	26	18	11	9					
	1982	MF	34	24	21	11	10					
		F	34	25	22	10	9					
	1983	MF	35	24	20	13	8					
		F	35	24	20	13	8					
PANAMA‡	1975	MF	31	26	23	9	6	4				
		F	31	27	24	8	5	4				
	1980	MF	29	24	22	10	8	8				
		F	28	24	23	10	8	7				
	1983	MF	25	21	17	14	12	10				
		F	24	20	18	15	13	10				
	1984	MF	25	21	17	14	12	10				
		F	24	21	18	15	13	10				
PUERTO RICO‡	1975	MF	21	20	18	17	13	11				
	1981	MF	29	28	24	20						
ST. LUCIA	1980	MF	26	26	22	14	10	2	1			
		F	26	26	22	14	9	2	1			
	1982	MF	23	23	27	14	11	3				
		F	23	23	27	15	10	2				
	1983	MF	25	22	26	14	11	1	1			
		F	26	22	26	13	11	1	1			
ST. PIERRE AND MIQUELON	1980	MF	27	23	18	16	9	4	3			
		F	29	21	17	16	8	5	4			
	1983	MF	26	26	15	17	7	5	4			
		F	27	23	16	17	7	4	5			
	1984	MF	27	23	16	14	10	6	4			
		F	24	22	16	16	12	5	4			
ST. VINCENT AND THE GRENADINES‡	1981	MF	31	23	22	13	10	1	0			
		F	29	24	22	14	10	1	0			
	1983	MF	31	24	20	13	11	1	–			
		F	29	24	20	15	12	1	–			
TRINIDAD AND TOBAGO‡	1975	MF	16	17	16	26	17	8				
		F	16	16	16	26	17	8				
	1981	MF	20	20	20	19	18	3				
		F	20	20	19	19	18	3				
	1982	MF	20	20	19	19	19	4				
		F	20	19	20	19	19	4				
	1984	MF	22	21	19	16	18	4				
		F	21	21	19	16	18	5				
UNITED STATES‡	1975	MF	13	13	21	20	18	16				
	1980	MF	26	25	25	24						
	1983	MF	27	25	24	24						
		F	27	24	24	24						
	1984	MF	27	26	24	24						
		F	27	25	24	24						

COUNTRY PAYS PAIS	YEAR ANNEE AÑO	SEX SEXE SEXO	GRADE / ANNEES / AÑOS DE ESTUDIOS I	II	III	IV	V	VI	VII	VIII	IX	X
U.S. VIRGIN ISLANDS‡	1980	MF	36	27	22	16						
	1981	MF	35	26	21	19						
AMERICA, SOUTH												
ARGENTINA	1975	MF	25	22	19	18	15	1	0			
		F	25	22	20	18	15	1	0			
	1979	MF	25	21	19	18	15	1	0			
		F	25	22	20	18	15	1	0			
BOLIVIA‡	1975	MF	36	28	20	16						
	1980	MF	36	27	21	16						
		F	38	27	20	15						
	1983	MF	36	27	22	16						
		F	36	26	23	15						
	1984	MF	36	27	21	17						
		F	35	28	21	16						
BRAZIL‡	1975	MF	46	30	23	2						
		F	44	30	24	2						
	1980	MF	43	31	24	2						
		F	43	31	24	2						
	1981	MF	43	31	24	2						
	1982	MF	43	31	24	2						
CHILE	1975	MF	34	27	23	16						
		F	33	27	24	16						
	1980	MF	33	27	23	17						
		F	33	27	23	17						
	1983	MF	35	27	21	16						
		F	34	27	22	17						
	1984	MF	34	30	20	16						
		F	33	29	21	17						
COLOMBIA‡	1975	MF	24	27	17	14	10	8				
		F	24	26	18	15	11	7				
	1980	MF	29	20	16	13	12	9				
		F	29	20	17	14	12	9				
	1984	MF	25	20	17	15	13	11				
		F	25	20	17	15	13	11				
	1985	MF	25	20	17	15	13	11				
		F	25	20	17	15	13	11				
ECUADOR‡	1975	MF	33	23	19	11	8	6				
		F	34	25	19	9	7	6				
	1980	MF	27	20	17	16	12	9				
	1983	MF	25	20	17	16	12	10				
		F	24	20	18	16	12	10				
	1984	MF	25	20	17	16	12	10				
FALKLAND ISLANDS (MALVINAS)	1975	MF	20	22	14	28	16					
		F	16	20	18	27	18					
	1979	MF	24	20	20	19	17					
		F	15	23	18	22	22					
	1980	MF	20	22	22	20	16					
		F	18	20	22	26	14					
FRENCH GUIANA‡	1976	MF	26	24	20	15	7	4	4			
		F	26	22	19	16	8	4	4			
	1979	MF	25	24	20	17	7	3	4			
		F	22	24	20	17	8	4	5			
	1982	MF	28	25	17	16	7	4	4			
		F	25	25	17	16	8	4	5			
	1983	MF	28	27	16	15	7	3	4			
		F	27	25	17	15	8	3	5			

3.8 Percentage distribution (second level general) by grade
Répartition en % (second degré général) par année d'études
Distribución en % (segundo grado general) por año de estudios

COUNTRY PAYS PAIS	YEAR ANNEE AÑO	SEX SEXE SEXO	GRADE / ANNEES / AÑOS DE ESTUDIOS									
			I	II	III	IV	V	VI	VII	VIII	IX	X
GUYANA	1975	MF	30	26	25	9	9	1				
		F	30	26	25	9	9	1				
	1980	MF	27	25	22	16	9	1				
		F	27	25	22	16	10	0				
PARAGUAY‡	1975	MF	27	21	17	14	11	9				
		F	25	21	17	15	12	10				
	1980	MF	27	21	17	15	12	9				
	1983	MF	26	21	17	14	11	9				
	1984	MF	25	21	18	15	12	10				
PERU	1975	MF	30	24	18	15	13					
	1980	MF	29	22	19	16	13					
		F	29	22	19	17	13					
	1981	MF	29	22	18	16	14					
		F	29	22	19	17	14					
	1985	MF	29	22	18	16	14					
		F	30	22	18	16	14					
SURINAME	1975	MF	39	31	18	11	2	1				
		F	37	32	19	10	1	1				
	1977	MF	32	29	22	13	3	1				
		F	32	30	22	13	2	1				
URUGUAY‡	1976	MF	28	19	17	14	13	9				
		F	24	19	18	15	14	10				
	1980	MF	23	21	18	15	13	9				
		F	22	21	18	15	14	10				
	1983	MF	26	22	18	15	12	8				
VENEZUELA‡	1975	MF	33	23	19	14	9	1				
		F	32	23	19	14	10	1				
	1980	MF	33	23	18	14	10	2				
		F	31	23	19	14	11	2				
	1982	MF	33	24	19	13	10	1				
		F	32	24	19	14	10	2				
	1983	MF	33	24	19	14	10	1				
		F	31	24	20	14	10	1				
ASIA												
AFGHANISTAN	1975	MF	33	28	22	17						
		F	36	27	21	16						
	1980	MF	37	23	21	20						
		F	41	24	19	16						
	1982	MF	36	26	21	18						
		F	38	25	21	17						
	1984	MF	37	26	21	16						
		F	39	24	21	16						
BAHRAIN‡	1975	MF	29	25	18	14	13					
		F	26	24	20	15	15					
	1980	MF	30	25	19	8	4	13				
		F	28	25	19	11	5	13				
	1982	MF	29	26	24	7	7	7				
		F	26	24	24	9	8	9				
	1983	MF	28	24	24	10	7	7				
		F	25	23	22	13	8	8				
BANGLADESH‡	1976	MF	28	22	19	14	12	3	2			
		F	28	26	21	11	9	3	2			
	1984	MF	27	21	19	13	11	5	4			
	1985	MF	27	21	19	13	11	5	4			
BHUTAN	1976	MF	34	29	19	8	10					
		F	45	29	16	9	2					
	1979	MF	32	30	21	9	8					
		F	35	36	15	8	6					

COUNTRY PAYS PAIS	YEAR ANNEE AÑO	SEX SEXE SEXO	GRADE / ANNEES / AÑOS DE ESTUDIOS									
			I	II	III	IV	V	VI	VII	VIII	IX	X
BHUTAN (CONT)	1983	MF	34	28	23	8	7					
		F	35	30	21	8	6					
	1984	MF	35	28	22	9	6					
		F	34	31	21	8	6					
BRUNEI DARUSSALAM	1975	MF	30	21	23	12	10	2	2			
		F	30	21	24	13	9	2	1			
	1980	MF	27	23	20	12	14	2	3			
		F	26	22	20	12	14	2	3			
	1983	MF	24	20	19	16	16	3	3			
		F	22	20	19	16	18	2	2			
	1984	MF	20	21	20	15	18	3	3			
		F	19	20	20	15	20	3	3			
BURMA	1975	MF	26	20	18	15	12	10				
		F	25	20	17	15	12	11				
	1976	MF	27	20	17	18	7	11				
		F	25	19	17	19	7	13				
CHINA	1980	MF	30	29	23	7	10	0				
	1983	MF	32	29	24	6	6	2				
	1984	MF	31	29	25	6	6	4				
		F	31	30	25	6	6	3				
CYPRUS‡	1975	MF	20	18	17	16	15	14	1			
		F	19	18	17	16	15	14	1			
	1980	MF	19	20	18	14	15	14	1			
		F	17	19	17	15	16	15	0			
	1981	MF	21	18	19	15	13	14	1			
		F	20	17	18	16	14	15	0			
	1982	MF	19	21	17	16	14	12	1			
		F	17	20	16	17	15	13	0			
DEMOCRATIC YEMEN‡	1975	MF	33	27	18	9	6	6				
		F	33	28	17	10	6	6				
	1978	MF	40	30	13	10	8					
		F	38	31	12	11	7					
	1983	MF	33	26	24	17						
		F	29	26	25	19						
HONG KONG	1975	MF	26	23	19	15	12	3	1			
		F	26	23	20	16	12	3	1			
	1980	MF	20	20	20	17	16	5	2			
		F	20	20	21	18	16	4	2			
	1983	MF	19	19	17	17	19	6	3			
		F	19	19	17	18	20	6	2			
	1984	MF	20	19	17	16	18	6	3			
		F	20	19	17	17	19	5	3			
INDIA	1975	MF	27	23	19	15	12	4	0			
		F	28	24	19	14	11	4	0			
	1979	MF	26	24	19	15	12	2	1			
		F	27	28	18	14	11	2	1			
INDONESIA‡	1975	MF	34	26	21	7	6	5				
		F	36	26	21	7	5	5				
	1980	MF	30	25	21	10	8	6				
		F	31	26	22	10	7	5				
	1983	MF	27	24	21	11	9	8				
		F	28	24	21	10	9	7				
	1984	MF	28	24	21	10	9	8				
		F	28	24	22	9	9	7				
IRAN, ISLAMIC REPUBLIC OF	1975	MF	38	27	17	2	9	8				
		F	38	27	17	2	9	7				
	1981	MF	25	21	19	9	10	8	8			
		F	24	20	19	10	10	9	8			

3.8 Percentage distribution (second level general) by grade
Répartition en % (second degré général) par année d'études
Distribución en % (segundo grado general) por año de estudios

COUNTRY PAYS PAIS	YEAR ANNEE AÑO	SEX SEXE SEXO	GRADE / ANNEES / AÑOS DE ESTUDIOS									
			I	II	III	IV	V	VI	VII	VIII	IX	X
IRAN, ISLAMIC REPUBLIC OF (CONT)	1983	MF	29	22	17	10	8	7	7			
		F	26	21	17	11	9	8	8			
	1984	MF	30	22	18	10	8	7	6			
		F	28	21	17	11	9	8	7			
IRAQ	1975	MF	31	24	20	9	8	8				
		F	31	25	18	9	9	9				
	1980	MF	32	25	19	8	7	8				
		F	34	25	18	8	7	7				
	1982	MF	29	26	21	7	8	9				
		F	33	26	19	8	7	7				
	1983	MF	26	27	22	9	7	10				
		F	28	28	20	9	7	8				
ISRAEL	1975	MF	39	23	20	18	0					
		F	36	24	21	19	0					
	1980	MF	37	23	21	19	0					
	1982	MF	38	22	21	20	0					
		F	35	23	22	21	–					
	1983	MF	38	22	21	20						
		F	35	23	21	21						
JAPAN‡	1975	MF	22	21	21	13	12	11	0			
	1980	MF	22	19	20	14	12	12	0			
		F	22	19	20	14	13	12	0			
	1983	MF	21	21	21	14	11	12	0			
		F	21	20	21	14	12	12	0			
	1984	MF	22	21	20	14	13	11	0			
JORDAN‡	1975	MF	32	23	19	10	9	8				
		F	32	23	19	10	8	7				
	1980	MF	25	22	19	13	11	11				
		F	25	22	19	14	11	10				
	1983	MF	*25	*22	*19	12	11	10				
		F	*25	*22	*19	13	12	10				
	1984	MF	68	→	→	13	10	10				
		F	66	→	→	13	11	10				
KOREA, REPUBLIC OF	1975	MF	27	25	24	10	8	6				
		F	27	26	23	9	8	6				
	1980	MF	25	25	23	10	9	8				
		F	26	25	23	9	9	8				
	1983	MF	24	23	24	10	10	9				
		F	25	24	24	10	9	8				
	1984	MF	25	23	22	11	10	9				
		F	26	24	23	10	9	8				
KUWAIT	1975	MF	24	17	15	12	11	8	6	5		
		F	23	17	15	12	12	9	7	6		
	1980	MF	21	17	15	12	12	9	7	6		
		F	21	17	15	12	12	10	8	6		
	1983	MF	18	16	15	14	14	10	7	7		
		F	18	16	15	14	13	10	7	7		
	1984	MF	17	16	14	13	15	10	8	6		
		F	17	16	14	13	14	10	8	6		
LAO PEOPLE'S DEMOCRATIC REPUBLIC	1976	MF	49	29	15	4	2	2				
		F	50	29	15	3	2	1				
	1980	MF	34	26	22	8	6	4				
		F	35	26	21	8	6	4				
	1982	MF	33	25	20	8	7	7				
		F	35	25	18	9	7	7				
	1983	MF	34	25	20	9	6	6				
		F	35	25	20	9	6	5				

COUNTRY PAYS PAIS	YEAR ANNEE AÑO	SEX SEXE SEXO	GRADE / ANNEES / AÑOS DE ESTUDIOS I	II	III	IV	V	VI	VII	VIII	IX	X
MALAYSIA	1984	MF	30	21	20	13	12	2	2			
		F	30	21	20	13	12	2	2			
	1985	MF	*30	*21	*21	*12	*12	*2	*2			
		F	*30	*21	*20	*12	*12	*2	*2			
MONGOLIA	1975	MF	24	22	19	15	13	4	3			
		F	22	21	19	16	14	4	4			
	1980	MF	19	19	17	17	15	6	7			
	1983	MF	19	18	18	16	16	7	6			
	1984	MF	19	18	17	17	16	7	6			
NEPAL‡	1976	MF	29	20	16	13	9	7	7			
	1980	MF	27	21	16	12	10	8	6			
		F	29	22	16	12	9	7	5			
	1983	MF	29	23	19	15	13					
		F	31	24	18	15	12					
	1984	MF	29	24	19	16	12					
		F	31	24	18	15	11					
OMAN	1975	MF	52	19	13	8	5	2				
		F	32	27	15	17	8	—				
	1980	MF	46	27	17	5	3	2				
		F	46	28	16	5	3	1				
	1983	MF	35	24	19	11	7	4				
		F	36	24	19	11	7	3				
	1984	MF	34	23	18	11	8	5				
		F	36	24	17	11	7	5				
PAKISTAN	1975	MF	25	22	18	14	12	5	4			
		F	26	22	19	13	11	5	4			
	1980	MF	27	22	18	13	11	6	4			
		F	27	21	17	13	11	6	5			
	1982	MF	26	22	17	14	12	5	4			
		F	27	22	16	13	10	6	5			
	1983	MF	26	22	17	14	12	5	4			
PHILIPPINES‡	1975	MF	31	27	22	20						
	1980	MF	29	27	24	21						
		F	29	26	24	21						
	1983	MF	30	26	23	20						
		F	30	26	23	21						
	1984	MF	30	26	23	20						
		F	30	26	23	21						
QATAR‡	1975	MF	25	22	19	14	11	9				
		F	26	23	21	14	9	8				
	1980	MF	29	18	17	15	11	11				
		F	28	18	17	14	12	11				
	1983	MF	25	20	16	17	11	11				
		F	24	20	16	18	11	11				
	1984	MF	24	20	18	15	13	10				
		F	22	20	18	16	14	10				
SAUDI ARABIA	1975	MF	33	25	19	10	8	6				
		F	33	26	19	10	8	5				
	1980	MF	28	23	21	12	8	8				
		F	29	24	20	13	8	7				
	1982	MF	27	22	20	13	10	8				
		F	27	22	20	13	11	8				
	1983	MF	27	22	20	13	9	9				
		F	26	22	19	13	10	9				
SINGAPORE	1975	MF	24	24	24	20	4	4				
		F	24	23	24	21	4	4				
	1980	MF	28	24	20	19	4	5				
		F	27	24	20	19	5	5				

3.8 Percentage distribution (second level general) by grade
Répartition en % (second degré général) par année d'études
Distribución en % (segundo grado general) por año de estudios

COUNTRY PAYS PAIS	YEAR ANNEE AÑO	SEX SEXE SEXO	GRADE / ANNEES / AÑOS DE ESTUDIOS I	II	III	IV	V	VI	VII	VIII	IX	X
SINGAPORE (CONT)	1983	MF	21	21	25	22	5	4	1			
		F	20	21	25	22	6	5	2			
	1984	MF	20	20	21	26	6	5	1			
		F	20	20	21	26	6	6	1			
SRI LANKA‡	1975	MF	20	18	16	12	26	3	4			
		F	20	18	16	12	27	3	4			
	1980	MF	20	17	13	9	25	6	10			
		F	19	16	13	8	25	7	11			
	1983	MF	22	18	16	14	20	3	7			
		F	21	18	16	14	21	3	9			
	1984	MF	20	19	16	14	21	4	5			
		F	19	19	16	14	22	4	6			
SYRIAN ARAB REPUBLIC‡	1975	MF	29	21	22	9	8	11				
		F	30	22	22	10	8	9				
	1980	MF	28	21	23	10	7	10				
		F	28	21	23	10	8	10				
	1983	MF	30	22	22	9	7	11				
		F	29	22	21	10	8	10				
	1984	MF	30	22	21	10	8	10				
		F	29	22	20	11	8	10				
THAILAND	1975	MF	34	29	25	7	4	0				
		F	33	29	25	8	5	0				
	1980	MF	24	21	20	19	9	8				
		F	23	20	20	19	9	9				
	1981	MF	26	23	21	11	10	8				
	1983	MF	25	23	22	12	10	9				
TURKEY	1975	MF	27	24	20	12	9	7	0			
		F	26	24	20	13	10	7	0			
	1982	MF	32	22	17	12	8	7	0			
		F	29	23	17	13	9	8	0			
	1983	MF	33	23	17	11	8	7	0			
		F	29	23	18	13	9	8	0			
UNITED ARAB EMIRATES‡	1975	MF	33	25	17	12	8	6				
		F	35	25	16	12	7	5				
	1981	MF	30	23	19	13	9	8				
		F	29	23	18	13	9	8				
	1983	MF	28	22	19	14	10	8				
		F	27	22	18	14	10	8				
	1984	MF	27	21	18	15	10	8				
		F	26	22	18	15	11	8				
VIET-NAM	1976	MF	32	26	22	4	7	5	4			
		F	31	26	22	4	6	6	5			
	1980	MF	30	25	22	5	7	6	5			
		F	29	25	23	5	7	6	5			
YEMEN‡	1975	MF	31	22	19	12	9	7				
		F	36	20	25	10	5	4				
	1980	MF	31	21	20	11	7	10				
		F	32	20	20	10	8	10				
	1982	MF	37	24	17	9	6	6				
		F	35	27	17	8	6	6				
	1983	MF	37	24	18	10	6	6				
		F	33	24	18	10	7	8				
EUROPE												
ALBANIA	1980	MF	34	25	22	18						
		F	32	26	23	19						
	1983	MF	38	26	20	16						
		F	37	27	21	16						
	1984	MF	36	27	22	16						
		F	34	27	22	17						

COUNTRY PAYS PAIS	YEAR ANNEE AÑO	SEX SEXE SEXO	GRADE / ANNEES / AÑOS DE ESTUDIOS									
			I	II	III	IV	V	VI	VII	VIII	IX	X
AUSTRIA	1975	MF	22	21	21	19	9	3	3	2	0	
		F	22	21	21	20	8	3	3	3	0	
	1980	MF	19	20	21	20	10	3	3	3	0	
		F	19	20	21	21	8	4	3	3	0	
	1983	MF	18	19	20	21	10	4	4	3	0	
		F	18	19	20	21	9	4	4	4	0	
	1984	MF	19	19	20	21	10	4	4	4	0	
		F	19	19	20	21	9	4	4	4	0	
BELGIUM‡	1975	MF	25	21	19	14	11	9	0			
		F	25	22	20	13	11	9	0			
	1979	MF	25	22	16	14	12	11	0			
		F	24	22	17	14	13	11	0			
	1984	MF	18	18	18	18	15	12	1			
		F	17	17	18	17	15	13	2			
BULGARIA‡	1975	MF	37	31	31							
		F	38	31	31							
	1980	MF	39	30	31							
		F	38	30	31							
	1983	MF	45	30	25	0						
		F	45	30	25	0						
	1984	MF	41	32	26	1						
		F	41	32	26	1						
CZECHOSLOVAKIA	1975	MF	27	25	24	24						
		F	27	25	25	24						
	1980	MF	26	27	24	22						
		F	27	27	24	22						
	1983	MF	24	25	25	26						
		F	24	25	25	25						
	1984	MF	24	25	26	26						
		F	23	25	26	26						
DENMARK	1975	MF	23	22	22	20	7	6				
	1977	MF	23	22	20	23	6	6				
		F	22	21	20	23	7	6				
FINLAND‡	1975	MF	25	26	22	10	10	8				
	1980	MF	22	23	23	12	11	9				
		F	20	21	22	13	13	10				
	1983	MF	21	22	23	12	12	10				
		F	20	20	22	14	13	12				
	1984	MF	20	21	23	13	12	11				
		F	19	19	21	14	14	12				
FRANCE	1976	MF	23	23	19	17	8	5	6			
		F	22	21	19	17	9	6	6			
	1980	MF	23	21	19	17	9	8	4			
	1981	MF	24	22	16	16	10	6	6			
		F	22	21	16	16	10	7	7			
	1982	MF	24	23	16	16	8	6	6			
		F	22	22	16	16	10	6	7			
GERMANY, FEDERAL REPUBLIC OF	1975	MF	18	18	18	17	14	6	3	3	2	
		F	18	18	18	17	14	7	3	3	2	
	1980	MF	14	15	17	17	16	10	4	4	3	
		F	14	15	17	17	16	10	4	4	3	
	1982	MF	13	14	16	17	17	11	4	4	4	
		F	13	14	15	17	17	12	4	4	4	
	1983	MF	12	14	15	16	17	12	5	4	4	
		F	12	13	15	16	17	13	5	4	4	
GIBRALTAR	1975	MF	25	26	23	16	5	5				
		F	24	27	20	17	6	6				
	1980	MF	23	23	25	18	7	4				
		F	22	23	23	20	8	3				

3.8 Percentage distribution (second level general) by grade
Répartition en % (second degré général) par année d'études
Distribución en % (segundo grado general) por año de estudios

COUNTRY PAYS PAIS	YEAR ANNEE AÑO	SEX SEXE SEXO	GRADE / ANNEES / AÑOS DE ESTUDIOS									
			I	II	III	IV	V	VI	VII	VIII	IX	X
GIBRALTAR (CONT)	1982	MF	22	22	22	17	10	7				
		F	23	20	20	19	11	6				
	1983	MF	24	23	21	16	11	5				
		F	22	23	20	16	14	5				
GREECE‡	1975	MF	21	19	17	16	14	13	0			
		F	21	19	17	16	14	13	0			
	1980	MF	26	22	19	12	11	10	0			
		F	24	21	19	13	12	10	0			
	1981	MF	25	22	19	14	10	9	0			
		F	24	21	19	15	11	10	0			
	1982	MF	25	22	19	14	11	9	0			
		F	23	21	19	15	12	10	0			
HUNGARY	1975	MF	25	25	25	24						
		F	26	25	25	24						
	1980	MF	28	26	24	22						
		F	28	26	24	22						
	1983	MF	28	27	24	22						
		F	28	27	24	21						
	1984	MF	27	26	25	22						
		F	27	26	25	22						
ICELAND	1975	MF	22	21	21	17	8	6	4			
		F	22	21	21	17	9	6	4			
	1976	MF	22	22	20	19	6	5	6			
		F	22	22	20	21	6	5	5			
IRELAND	1975	MF	25	24	21	2	15	13				
		F	24	23	21	2	16	14				
	1980	MF	23	23	21	3	16	14				
		F	22	22	21	3	17	16				
	1981	MF	23	22	21	2	17	15				
		F	22	21	20	2	18	16				
	1982	MF	23	22	21	3	17	15				
		F	22	21	20	2	18	17				
ITALY	1975	MF	32	27	24	4	3	3	3	3		
		F	31	27	24	4	3	3	3	3		
	1980	MF	30	27	25	4	4	4	3	3		
		F	29	27	26	4	4	4	3	3		
	1982	MF	30	27	26	4	3	3	3	3		
		F	29	27	26	4	4	4	3	4		
	1983	MF	30	28	25	4	3	3	3	3		
		F	28	27	26	5	4	4	4	3		
LUXEMBOURG	1975	MF	34	20	16	12	6	5	6			
		F	34	21	17	12	6	5	6			
	1980	MF	30	26	19	7	7	5	6			
		F	29	26	19	7	7	6	6			
	1981	MF	28	27	20	7	6	6	6			
		F	26	27	20	8	7	6	7			
	1982	MF	25	24	27	6	6	6	6			
		F	25	23	26	7	7	5	7			
MALTA	1975	MF	22	27	22	15	10	2	1			
		F	21	25	22	18	12	2	1			
	1980	MF	24	24	22	14	10	3	3			
		F	23	23	27	14	9	2	2			
	1982	MF	24	26	17	14	11	4	3			
		F	23	25	19	16	12	3	3			
	1983	MF	25	23	21	13	11	7	——>			
		F	24	22	22	15	12	6	——>			
NETHERLANDS	1975	MF	23	22	20	21	10	4				
		F	23	22	21	21	9	3				
	1980	MF	21	21	20	23	11	4				
		F	21	21	21	23	11	4				

COUNTRY PAYS PAIS	YEAR ANNEE AÑO	SEX SEXE SEXO	GRADE / ANNEES / AÑOS DE ESTUDIOS									
			I	II	III	IV	V	VI	VII	VIII	IX	X
NETHERLANDS (CONT)	1983	MF	21	21	20	22	12	4				
		F	21	21	21	23	11	4				
	1984	MF	20	21	20	23	12	5				
		F	20	21	21	23	11	4				
NORWAY‡	1975	MF	23	23	23	15	9	8				
		F	23	22	23	16	9	8				
	1980	MF	24	24	23	13	9	8				
		F	23	23	22	15	9	9				
	1981	MF	24	23	23	13	9	8				
		F	23	22	22	15	9	9				
POLAND	1975	MF	25	26	25	23						
		F	26	26	25	23						
	1980	MF	26	25	25	24						
	1983	MF	26	26	25	23						
		F	27	51	--->	22						
	1984	MF	28	25	24	23						
		F	28	49	--->	23						
PORTUGAL‡	1975	MF	33	17	26	9	16					
		F	31	18	27	9	15					
	1980	MF	27	21	18	12	12	10				
		F	25	20	18	13	13	11				
	1982	MF	27	21	17	12	14	10				
		F	25	20	17	12	15	10				
	1983	MF	28	21	16	13	12	11				
		F	26	21	16	13	13	11				
SAN MARINO	1975	MF	31	29	27	3	3	3	2	2		
		F	30	31	26	3	2	4	2	2		
	1980	MF	30	31	29	4	3	2	2	1		
		F	29	32	28	4	2	2	2	2		
	1982	MF	25	24	27	11	7	3	2	1		
		F	23	27	28	11	7	2	2	1		
	1983	MF	26	25	24	9	8	2	2	2		
		F	29	23	27	6	9	2	2	2		
SPAIN	1975	MF	29	22	21	11	11	0	7			
		F	28	22	21	11	10	0	7			
	1980	MF	24	22	19	10	9	8	7			
		F	23	21	19	11	10	9	8			
	1982	MF	24	21	19	11	9	8	8			
		F	23	21	19	11	10	9	8			
	1983	MF	24	21	19	11	9	8	8			
		F	22	21	19	11	10	9	8			
SWEDEN	1975	MF	28	27	27	7	6	4				
		F	27	26	26	8	8	4				
	1980	MF	27	28	28	8	7	3				
		F	26	26	26	10	8	4				
	1982	MF	26	27	29	7	7	4				
		F	24	26	27	9	9	5				
	1983	MF	27	26	28	7	7	4				
		F	25	25	26	9	9	6				
SWITZERLAND	1980	MF	6	10	24	23	21	7	4	3	2	
		F	6	10	23	23	21	8	4	3	2	
	1983	MF	6	10	23	23	21	7	4	4	2	
		F	5	10	23	23	22	8	4	3	2	
	1984	MF	5	9	23	23	22	7	4	4	3	
		F	5	9	22	22	22	9	5	4	2	
YUGOSLAVIA‡	1975	MF	22	21	20	19	8	4	3	3		
		F	23	20	19	18	9	4	4	3		
	1980	MF	20	19	19	19	11	10	1	1		
	1982	MF	19	18	18	17	14	11	1	1		
		F	19	18	18	17	14	11	1	2		

3.8 Percentage distribution (second level general) by grade
Répartition en % (second degré général) par année d'études
Distribución en % (segundo grado general) por año de estudios

COUNTRY PAYS PAIS	YEAR ANNEE AÑO	SEX SEXE SEXO	GRADE / ANNEES / AÑOS DE ESTUDIOS									
			I	II	III	IV	V	VI	VII	VIII	IX	X
YUGOSLAVIA (CONT)‡	1983	MF	20	19	18	18	13	11	0	1		
		F	20	19	18	18	13	11	0	1		
OCEANIA												
AMERICAN SAMOA‡	1983	MF	27	27	23	23						
		F	29	26	21	24						
	1984	MF	31	25	23	21						
		F	33	25	23	19						
AUSTRALIA	1975	MF	15	24	23	19	11	7				
		F	15	24	23	20	11	7				
	1980	MF	15	22	22	20	12	8				
		F	15	22	22	20	13	9				
	1983	MF	15	22	22	20	13	8				
		F	15	22	22	20	13	9				
	1984	MF	14	22	21	20	13	9				
		F	14	22	21	20	13	9				
FIJI‡	1975	MF	./.	./.	35	36	24	5				
		F	./.	./.	36	37	24	4				
	1980	MF	12	13	24	25	17	8	0			
		F	12	13	24	26	17	7	0			
	1983	MF	11	11	24	25	18	10	1			
		F	11	11	25	25	18	9	1			
	1984	MF	10	10	25	25	18	10	1			
		F	10	11	25	26	18	10	1			
FRENCH POLYNESIA	1979	MF	31	27	17	14	4	3	3			
	1983	MF	29	25	16	17	7	3	3			
		F	28	24	17	18	7	3	3			
	1984	MF	30	23	14	16	7	5	5			
		F	29	23	15	17	7	5	5			
GUAM‡	1979	MF	27	29	23	21						
	1983	MF	18	17	20	16	16	14				
		F	18	17	19	17	16	14				
KIRIBATI	1975	MF	29	25	20	11	10	5				
		F	31	26	18	12	9	4				
	1980	MF	24	29	25	12	8	2				
		F	24	31	25	13	7	0				
	1984	MF	31	24	22	10	8	4				
		F	30	25	24	10	8	3				
	1985	MF	29	26	23	13	6	3				
		F	27	28	25	13	6	3				
NAURU‡	1985	MF	28	25	24	16	4	4				
		F	23	23	28	17	7	3				
NEW CALEDONIA	1980	MF	30	25	18	16	5	4	3			
		F	30	25	18	16	5	4	3			
	1984	MF	31	27	16	14	5	3	3			
		F	29	27	16	15	6	3	3			
	1985	MF	30	28	16	14	6	3	3			
		F	29	26	17	15	7	4	3			
NEW ZEALAND‡	1975	MF	19	19	19	18	16	8	2			
		F	18	19	19	18	16	8	2			
	1980	MF	18	17	18	17	18	10	3			
		F	18	17	17	17	18	10	3			
	1982	MF	18	18	18	17	17	9	3			
		F	18	17	17	17	18	10	3			
	1983	MF	18	18	17	17	17	10	3			
		F	18	18	17	17	18	10	3			
NIUE	1980	MF	22	29	23	14	11	1				
	1983	MF	25	25	23	13	14	——>				
		F	22	24	25	12	16	——>				
	1984	MF	20	25	25	23	7	——>				
		F	21	24	24	24	8	——>				

COUNTRY PAYS PAIS	YEAR ANNEE AÑO	SEX SEXE SEXO	GRADE / ANNEES / AÑOS DE ESTUDIOS									
			I	II	III	IV	V	VI	VII	VIII	IX	X
PAPUA NEW GUINEA	1980	MF	32	29	18	16	2	2				
		F	33	30	18	15	2	2				
	1981	MF	32	28	19	17	2	2				
		F	34	29	18	16	2	2				
	1982	MF	32	28	19	17	2	2				
		F	34	28	19	16	1	2				
SAMOA	1975	MF	26	22	20	19	10	3	1			
		F	24	22	21	19	12	2	0			
	1980	MF	23	21	18	16	16	5	1			
		F	22	21	18	17	16	5	1			
	1982	MF	22	21	18	17	15	6	1			
		F	21	21	18	17	16	6	1			
	1983	MF	22	21	19	17	15	6	1			
		F	21	20	19	18	16	6	1			
SOLOMON ISLANDS	1975	MF	28	31	17	13	11					
	1980	MF	36	34	11	10	8	2				
		F	39	33	12	9	7	1				
	1983	MF	29	29	25	8	8	2				
		F	32	31	24	6	6	1				
	1984	MF	30	26	26	9	7	2				
		F	33	28	27	7	5	1				
TOKELAU	1983	MF	47	53								
		F	43	57								
TONGA	1975	MF	34	20	18	14	10	4	0			
		F	34	20	18	12	10	5	0			
	1979	MF	22	17	17	17	15	11	2			
		F	21	17	17	17	16	11	2			
	1982	MF	21	21	19	15	14	8	2			
		F	21	23	19	15	15	7	1			
	1983	MF	*21	*24	*21	*14	*12	*7	*1			
		F	20	24	*23	*14	*12	*7	*1			
TUVALU	1984	MF	19	17	21	23	10	11				
		F	21	17	20	24	7	11				
VANUATU	1980	MF	36	28	20	7	5	2	1			
		F	36	29	20	7	5	2	2			
	1981	MF	34	31	19	7	3	4	1			
		F	37	32	17	6	3	4	2			
	1983	MF	26	26	19	17	8	4	——>			
		F	25	27	20	19	6	3	——>			
U.S.S.R.												
U.S.S.R.	1975	MF	23	23	24	15	14	0				
	1980	MF	23	23	24	15	15	0				
	1982	MF	24	24	23	14	14	0				
	1983	MF	25	24	23	14	14	0				
BYELORUSSIAN S.S.R.‡	1975	MF	51	49	0							
	1980	MF	22	23	24	15	16	0				
	1981	MF	23	23	24	15	15	0				
	1982	MF	24	23	24	14	15	0				
UKRAINIAN S.S.R.‡	1975	MF	52	48	0							
	1980	MF	23	24	24	14	15	0				
	1982	MF	25	24	24	13	14	0				
	1983	MF	25	25	24	13	13	0				

The percentage distribution by grade appearing in this table is presented for second level general education only and refers to total enrolment (MF) and female enrolment. These percentages are presented for 1975, 1980 and the two latest years available.

In most cases the data appearing in this table have been calculated on the basis of the duration of general education at the second level as shown for each country in Table 3.1.

La répartition en pourcentage par année d'études qui figure dans ce tableau concerne l'enseignement général du second degré seulement et se réfère au total des effectifs (MF) et aux effectifs féminins. Ces pourcentages sont présentés pour les années 1975, 1980 et les deux dernières années disponibles.

Dans la plupart des cas, les données présentées dans ce tableau ont été calculées en fonction de la durée de l'enseignement général du second degré, telle qu'elle figure pour chaque pays territoire dans le tableau 3.1.

La repartición en porcentaje por año de estudios que figura en este cuadro se presenta para la enseñanza general de segundo grado solamente y se refiere a la matrícula escolar total (MF) y femenina. Los porcentajes se refieren a los años 1975, 1980 y los dos últimos años disponibles.

En la mayoría de los casos, los datos de este cuadro se han calculado en función de la duración de la enseñanza general de segundo grado tal como figura, en relación con cada país territorio, en el cuadro 3.1.

AFRICA:

Kenya:

E--> For 1975, data include vocational education.

FR-> Pour 1975, les données comprennent l'enseignement technique.

ESP> Para 1975, los datos comprenden la enseñanza técnica.

Madagascar:

E--> Data refer to public education only.

FR-> Les données se réfèrent à l'enseignement public seulement.

ESP> Los datos se refieren a la enseñanza pública solamente.

Reunion:

E--> For 1975, figures include teacher training.

FR-> Pour 1975, les chiffres incluent l'enseignement normal.

ESP> En 1975, las cifras incluyen la enseñanza normal.

Somalia:

E--> In 1975, due to the reform of the educational system, progressively applied, no pupils were reported in grade I.

FR-> En 1975, suite à la réforme du système scolaire, appliquée progressivement, aucun élève n'a été inscrit en première année d'études.

ESP> En 1975, de acuerdo con el cambio del sistema escolar aplicado progresivamente, ningún alumno estuvo inscrito en el primer año de estudios.

Tunisia:

E--> For 1975 and 1980, data refer to public education only.

FR-> Pour 1975 et 1980, les données se réfèrent à l'enseignement public seulement.

ESP> Para 1975 y 1980, los datos se refieren a la enseñanza pública solamente.

Uganda:

E--> Data refer to government-maintained and aided schools only.

FR-> Les données se réfèrent aux écoles publiques et subventionnées seulement.

ESP> Los datos se refieren a las escuelas públicas y subvencionadas solamente.

United Republic of Tanzania:

E--> Data include vocational education.

FR-> Les chiffres comprennent l'enseignement technique.

ESP> Los datos comprenden la enseñanza técnica.

AMERICA, NORTH:

Barbados:

E--> For 1975 data include vocational education.

FR-> Pour 1975, les données comprennent l'enseignement technique.

ESP> En 1975, los datos incluyen la enseñanza técnica.

Guadeloupe:

E--> For 1976, figures include teacher training.

FR-> Pour 1976, les chiffres incluent l'ensei- gnement normal.

ESP> En 1976, los datos comprenden la enseñanza normal.

Guatemala:

E--> Data for 1975 refer to all second level education and all other figures include data 'por cooperativa' which refer mainly to evening classes.

FR-> Les données relatives à 1975 se réfèrent à l'ensemble de l'enseignement du second degré et tous les autres chiffres incluent les données de l'enseignement 'por cooperativa' qui se réfèrent surtout aux cours du soir.

ESP> Los datos en 1975 se refieren al total de la enseñanza de segundo grado y las otras cifras incluyen los datos de la enseñanza 'por cooperativa' que se refieren principalmente a los cursos nocturnos.

Honduras:

E--> For 1975, data include part-time students.

FR-> Pour 1975, les données comprennent les élèves à temps partiel.

ESP> Para 1975, los datos comprenden los alumnos de jornada parcial.

Jamaica:

E--> Data refer to public education only.

FR-> Les données se réfèrent à l'enseignement public seulement.

Jamaica: (Cont):

ESP> Los datos se refieren a la enseñanza pública solamente.

Martinique:

E--> For 1976, data include teacher training.

FR-> Pour 1976, les données incluent l'enseignement normal.

ESP> En 1976, los datos comprenden la enseñanza normal.

Panama:

E--> For 1975, data refer to public education only and for 1983 and 1984 they refer to all second level.

FR-> Pour 1975, les données se réfèrent à l'enseignement public seulement et pour 1983 et 1984 elles se réfèrent à l'ensemble de l'enseignement du second degré.

ESP> En 1975, los datos se refieren a la enseñanza pública solamente y en 1983 y 1984 se refieren al total de la enseñanza de segundo grado.

Puerto Rico:

E--> For 1975, data refer to public education only. For 1981, figures refer to grades IX to XII; data for previous years refer to grades VII to XII.

FR-> Pour 1975, les données se réfèrent à l'enseignement public seulement. Pour 1981, les chiffres se réfèrent aux classes allant de la neuvième à la douzième année d'études. Pour les années précédentes, les chiffres incluent les classes allant de la septième à la douzième année d'études.

ESP> Para 1975, los datos se refieren a la enseñanza pública solamente. En 1981, las cifras se refieren a los años de estudios IX a XII. Para los años anteriores las cifras se refieren a los años de estudios VII a XII.

St. Vincent and the Grenadines:

E--> For 1983, data refer to all second level.

FR-> Pour 1983, les données se réfèrent à l'ensemble de l'enseignement du second degré.

ESP> En 1983, los datos se refieren al total de la enseñanza de segundo grado.

Trinidad and Tobago:

E--> For 1975, data refer to government-maintained and aided schools only and for 1981, 1982 and 1984 they refer to all second level.

FR-> Pour 1975, les données se réfèrent aux écoles publiques et subventionnées seulement et pour 1981, 1982 et 1984 elles se réfèrent à l'ensemble de l'enseignement du second degré.

ESP> En 1975, los datos se refieren a las escuelas públicas y subvencionadas solamente y en 1981, 1982 y 1984 ellos se refieren al total de la enseñanza de segundo grado.

United States:

E--> Data refer public education only. From 1980, data refer to grades IX to XII; in previous years for certain States data also included grades VII and VIII.

FR-> Les données se réfèrent à l'enseignement public seulement. À partir de 1980, les données se réfèrent aux classes allant de la neuvième à la douzième année d'études. Les années précédentes pour certains Etats les chiffres incluaient également les classes correspondant à la septième et à la huitième année d'études.

ESP> Los datos se refieren a la enseñanza pública solamente. A partir de 1980, las cifras se refieren a los años de estudios IX a XII; anteriormente para ciertos Estados las cifras incluían también los años de estudios VII y VIII.

U.S. Virgin Islands:

E--> Data relate to public education only and refer to grades IX to XII.

FR-> Les données se rapportent à l'enseignement public seulement et se réfèrent aux classes allant de la neuvième à la douzième année d'études.

ESP> Los datos se refieren a la enseñanza pública solamente y se refieren a los años de estudios IX a XII.

AMERICA, SOUTH:

Bolivia:

E--> Data refer to all second level education.

FR-> Les données se réfèrent à l'ensemble de l'enseignement du

Bolivia: (Cont):
second degré.
ESP> Los datos se refieren al total de la enseñanza de segundo grado.
Brazil:
E--> Data refer to all second level education.
FR-> Les données se réfèrent à l'ensemble de l'enseignement du second degré.
ESP> Los datos se refieren al total de la enseñanza de segundo grado.
Colombia:
E--> Data refer to all second level education.
FR-> Les données se réfèrent à l'ensemble de l'enseignement du second degré.
ESP> Los datos se refieren al total de la enseñanza de segundo grado.
Ecuador:
E--> From 1980, data include vocational education.
FR-> A partir de 1980, les données incluent l'enseignement technique.
ESP> A partir de 1980, los datos incluyen la enseñanza técnica.
French Guiana:
E--> For 1976, data include teacher training.
FR-> Pour 1976, les données incluent l'enseignement normal.
ESP> En 1976, los datos incluyen la enseñanza normal.
Paraguay:
E--> From 1980, data include commercial education.
FR-> A partir de 1980, les données incluent l'enseignement commercial.
ESP> A partir de 1980, los datos incluyen la enseñanza comercial.
Uruguay:
E--> For 1976, data include the first stage of vocational education and for 1980, they do not include courses of the U.T.U. (Universidad del Trabajo de Uruguay).
FR-> Pour 1976, les données comprennent le premier cycle de l'enseignement technique et pour 1980, elles n'incluent pas les cours de la U.T.U. (Universidad del Trabajo del Uruguay).
ESP> En 1976, los datos incluyen el primer ciclo de la enseñanza técnica y en 1980 no incluyen los cursos de la U.T.U. (Universidad del Trabajo del Uruguay).
Venezuela:
E--> Data refer to all second level education.
FR-> Les données se réfèrent à l'ensemble de l'enseignement du second degré.
ESP> Los datos se refieren al total de la enseñanza de segundo grado.
ASIA:
Bahrain:
E--> Data refer to public education and do not include religious schools.
FR-> Les données se réfèrent à l'enseignement public et ne comprennent pas les écoles religieuses.
ESP> Los datos se refieren a la enseñanza pública y no comprenden las escuelas religiosas.
Bangladesh:
E--> For 1984 and 1985, data refer to all second level.
FR-> Pour 1984 et 1985, les données se réfèrent à l'ensemble de l'enseignement du second degré.
ESP> Para 1984 y 1985, los datos se refieren al total de la enseñanza de segundo grado.
Cyprus:
E--> Not including Turkish schools.
FR-> Non compris les écoles turques.
ESP> Excluídas las escuelas turcas.
Democratic Yemen:
E--> Data include schools for nomads.
FR-> Les données incluent les écoles de nomades.
ESP> Los datos incluyen las escuelas para nómadas.
Indonesia:
E--> Data do not include religious schools.
FR-> Les données ne comprennent pas les écoles religieuses.
ESP> Los datos no comprenden las escuelas religiosas.
Japan:
E--> Data include special education and part-time pupils.
FR-> Les données comprennent l'éducation spéciale et les élèves à temps partiel.
ESP> Los datos comprenden la educación especial y los alumnos de jornada parcial.
Jordan:
E--> Including UNRWA schools.
FR-> Y compris les écoles de l'UNRWA.
ESP> Incluídas la escuelas del O.O.P.S.R.P.
Nepal:
E--> Except for 1976, data refer to all second level education.
FR-> A l'exception de l'année 1976, les données se réfèrent à l'ensemble de l'enseignement du second degré.
ESP> A la excepción del año 1976, los datos se refieren al total de la enseñanza de segundo grado.
Philippines:
E--> Data refer to all second level education.
FR-> Les données se réfèrent à l'ensemble de l'enseignement du second degré.
ESP> Los datos se refieren al total de la enseñanza de segundo grado.
Qatar:
E--> Data refer to public education only.
FR-> Les données se réfèrent à l'enseignement public seulement.
ESP> Los datos se refieren a la enseñanza pública solamente.
Sri Lanka:
E--> Data refer to public education only.
FR-> Les données se réfèrent à l'enseignement public seulement.
ESP> Los datos se refieren a la enseñanza pública solamente.
Syrian Arab Republic:
E--> Data include UNRWA schools.
FR-> Les données comprennnent les écoles de l'UNRWA.
ESP> Los datos incluyen las escuelas del O.O.P.S.R.P.
United Arab Emirates:
E--> For 1975, data refer to public education and do not include religious schools.
FR-> Pour 1975, les données se réfèrent à l'enseignement public et ne comprennent pas les écoles religieuses.
ESP> Para 1975, los datos se refieren a la enseñanza pública y no incluyen las escuelas religiosas.
Yemen:
E--> Data refer to public education only.
FR-> Les données se réfèrent à l'enseignement public seulement.
ESP> Los datos se refieren a la enseñanza pública solamente.
EUROPE:
Belgium:
E--> Data include special education.
FR-> Les données comprennent l'éducation spéciale.
ESP> Los datos incluyen la educación especial.
Bulgaria:
E--> For 1975, data include evening and correspondence courses.
FR-> Pour 1975, les données comprennent les cours du soir et par correspondance.
ESP> En 1975, los datos incluyen los cursos nocturnos y por correspondencia.
Finland:
E--> Data include integrated special education.
FR-> Les données incluent l'éducation spéciale intégrée.
ESP> Los datos incluyen la educación especial integrada.
Greece:
E--> For 1975 and 1980, data include evening schools whose duration is 7 years.
FR-> En 1975 et 1980, les données comprennent les écoles du soir qui ont une durée de 7 ans.
ESP> En 1975 y 1980, los datos comprenden las escuelas nocturnas que tienen una duración de 7 años.
Norway:
E--> For 1975, data include part-time education.
FR-> Pour 1975, les données comprennent l'enseignement à temps partiel.
ESP> En 1975, los datos incluyen la enseñanza de jornada parcial.
Portugal:
E--> For 1980 and 1982, data on female enrolment refer to public education only.
FR-> Pour 1980 et 1982, les données relatives aux effectifs féminins se réfèrent à l'enseignement public seulement.
ESP> En 1980 y 1982, los datos relativos a la matrícula femenina se refieren a la enseñanza pública solamente.
Yugoslavia:
E--> For 1975, data on female enrolment include special education.
FR-> Pour 1975, les données relatives aux effectifs féminins incluent l'éducation spéciale.
ESP> En 1975, los datos relativos a la matrícula femenina incluyen la educación especial.
OCEANIA:
American Samoa:
E--> Data refer to the total of second level education.
FR-> Les données se réfèrent au total de l'enseignement du second degré.
ESP> Los datos se refieren al total de la enseñanza de segundo grado.
Fiji:
E--> For 1975 the 'forms' I and II are included in the first level of education.
FR-> Pour 1975 les 'forms' I et II sont incluses dans l'enseignement du premier degré.
ESP> Para 1975 las 'forms' I y II quedan incluídas en la enseñanza de primer grado.
Guam:
E--> For 1979, data refer to the total of public second level education and for 1983 to the total of second level education.
FR-> Pour 1979, les données se réfèrent au total de l'enseignement

Guam: (Cont):
public du second degré et pour 1983 à l'ensemble de l'enseignement du second degré.

ESP> Para 1979, los datos se refieren al total de la enseñanza pública de segundo grado y para 1983 al total de la enseñanza de segundo grado.

Nauru:

E--> Data include vocational education.

FR-> Les données incluent l'enseignement technique.

ESP> Los datos incluyen la enseñanza técnica.

New Zealand:

E--> For 1975 data include special education.

FR-> Pour 1975 les données incluent l'éducation spéciale.

ESP> En 1975 los datos incluyen la educación especial.

U.S.S.R.:

Byelorussian S.S.R.:

E--> For 1975, data refer to grades IX to XI. For other years, figures refer to grades VI to XI.

FR-> Pour 1975, les chiffres se réfèrent aux classes allant de la neuvième à la onzième année d'études. Pour les autres années, les chiffres se réfèrent aux classes allant de la sixième à la onzième année d'études.

ESP> Las cifras para 1975 se refieren a los años de estudios IX a XI. Para los otros años, las cifras se refieren a los años de estudios VI a XI.

Ukrainian S.S.R.:

E--> For 1975, data refer to grades IX to XI. For other years, figures refer to grades VI to XI.

FR-> Pour 1975, les chiffres se réfèrent aux classes allant de la neuvième à la onzième année d'études. Pour les autres années, les chiffres se réfèrent aux classes allant de la sixième à la onzième année d'études.

ESP> Las cifras para 1975 se refieren a los años de estudios IX a XI. Para los otros años, las cifras se refieren a los años de estudios VI a XI.

3.9 Education at the second level (general): percentage repeaters by grade

Enseignement du second degré (général): pourcentage de redoublants par année d'études

Enseñanza de segundo grado (general): porcentaje de repetidores por año de estudios

PLEASE REFER TO EXPLANATORY TEXT AT END OF TABLE

PRIERE DE SE REFERER AU TEXTE EXPLICATIF A LA FIN DU TABLEAU

REFERIRSE AL TEXTO EXPLICATIVO AL FINAL DEL CUADRO

NUMBER OF COUNTRIES AND TERRITORIES PRESENTED IN THIS TABLE: 115

NOMBRE DE PAYS ET DE TERRITOIRES PRESENTES DANS CE TABLEAU: 115

NUMERO DE PAISES Y DE TERRITORIOS PRESENTADOS EN ESTE CUADRO: 115

COUNTRY PAYS PAIS	YEAR ANNEE AÑO	SEX SEXE SEXO	TOTAL TOTAL TOTAL	PERCENTAGE REPEATERS BY GRADE POURCENTAGE DE REDOUBLANTS PAR ANNEE D'ETUDES PORCENTAJE DE REPETIDORES POR AÑO DE ESTUDIOS									
				TOTAL	I	II	III	IV	V	VI	VII	V III	IX
AFRICA													
ALGERIA	1975	MF	26 431	5	4	5	4	10	4	3	13		
		F	8 615	5	3	4	4	10	4	2	18		
	1979	MF	66 514	7	5	5	7	13	5	5	15		
		F	21 296	6	4	4	6	12	5	5	16		
	1983	MF	119 357	8	4	3	4	19	7	4	28		
		F	40 521	7	2	2	2	18	6	4	28		
	1984	MF	*120 162	*8	4	4	5	17	5	4	21		
		F	*38 854	*6	3	2	3	15	4	3	21		
BENIN	1975	MF	5 861	14	10	9	17	18	4	24	32		
		F	1 965	16	14	11	19	25	5	18	23		
	1980	MF	7 891	9	5	7	12	16	3	5	32		
		F	2 572	12	7	9	16	22	5	6	25		
	1982	MF	24 211	21	27	14	19	16	13	33	33		
		F	7 472	23	29	15	22	21	15	32	38		
	1983	MF	39 809	35	25	36	34	38	15	37	54		
		F	11 971	37	27	37	37	43	17	47	52		
BURKINA FASO	1975	MF	1 913	15	9	14	10	21	11	17	33		
		F	*524	*13	*9	*9	*11	*23	*14	*16	*24		
	1980	MF	3 207	14	10	12	13	20	9	8	30		
	1982	MF	4 663	17	13	12	20	20	12	18	33		
	1983	MF	4 694	15	11	13	14	23	10	11	30		
BURUNDI	1976	MF	585	9	9	9	9	9	9	9	8		
		F	214	12	11	12	13	13	11	14	5		
	1980	MF	*896	*10	7	6	9	9	15	18	13		
		F	*275	*12	6	5	14	13	14	22	14		
	1981	MF	880	8	5	7	8	8	9	17	14		
		F	326	10	6	8	10	12	13	14	12		
CAMEROON	1975	MF	11 385	11	8	7	9	18	8	17	21		
		F	3 918	12	9	8	11	20	10	19	24		
	1980	MF	32 154	19	13	14	18	29	12	34	32		
		F	11 490	20	14	15	20	31	14	37	35		
	1983	MF	36 052	17	12	11	16	26	13	24	25		
		F	13 788	18	12	12	18	28	15	27	29		

3.9 Percentage repeaters by grade (second level general)
% de redoublants par année d'études (second degré général)
% de repetidores por año de estudios (segundo grado general)

COUNTRY / PAYS / PAIS	YEAR / ANNEE / ANO	SEX / SEXE / SEXO	TOTAL / TOTAL / TOTAL	PERCENTAGE REPEATERS BY GRADE / POURCENTAGE DE REDOUBLANTS PAR ANNEE D'ETUDES / PORCENTAJE DE REPETIDORES POR AÑO DE ESTUDIOS									
				TOTAL	I	II	III	IV	V	VI	VII	V III	IX
CAMEROON (CONT)	1984	MF	45 850	19	13	14	18	29	15	29	37		
		F	17 122	19	12	15	20	31	16	29	39		
CAPE VERDE	1980	MF	615	23	22	27	24	11	16				
		F	293	25	25	29	29	10	14				
	1981	MF	513	17	19	16	21	5	16				
		F	221	18	22	18	18	3	14				
	1983	MF	862	22	24	26	28	12	6				
		F	386	23	25	28	29	12	6				
CENTRAL AFRICAN REPUBLIC	1980	MF	10 466	25	25	24	27	27	22	15	32		
		F	3 000	29	27	27	33	34	26	20	43		
	1981	MF	10 416	23	23	21	24	23	24	22	29		
		F	2 978	26	29	27	25	23	20	25	31		
	1982	MF	12 112	23	24	21	22	27	20	21	28		
		F	3 449	26	25	22	24	29	35	43	48		
COMOROS	1980	MF	1 507	11	9	5	5	26	11	18	7		
		F	482	10	8	3	5	30	10	11	8		
CONGO	1975	MF	16 429	17	19	18	17	20	9	16	14		
		F	7 107	21	22	20	20	26	10	22	10		
	1980	MF	54 846	33	27	29	35	43	19	20	45		
		F	22 499	33	28	30	35	45	27	20	58		
	1982	MF	70 409	37	38	37	35	49	22	24	33		
		F	30 333	39	38	39	37	49	22	33	46		
COTE D'IVOIRE	1975	MF	13 009	13	9	11	16	17	11	14	26		
		F	3 860	15	13	13	19	20	10	13	25		
	1980	MF	23 628	12	8	9	12	16	13	26	43		
		F	8 486	15	13	12	17	20	15	27	45		
	1982	MF	34 377	16	12	14	17	17	15	31	26		
		F	12 630	21	17	19	23	25	18	32	21		
	1983	MF	37 330	16	11	13	16	22	14	37	22		
		F	13 160	20	15	18	21	29	14	39	21		
DJIBOUTI	1975	MF	92	7	5	4	7	10	7	11	12		
		F	31	7	6	3	10	9	6	12	7		
EGYPT	1975	MF	247 941	14	5	6	32	5	4	28			
	1979	MF	*376 185	*17	7	8	29	4	21	34			
		F	108 244	14	7	4	28	5	2	31			
	1982	MF	304 896	12	4	3	24	5	5	39			
GABON	1980	MF	4 448	22	21	24	29	22	16	14	23		
	1982	MF	*4 480	*20	*19	*21	*20	*24	18	18	17		
	1983	MF	5 458	22	22	23	28	20	19	17	21		
GAMBIA	1975	MF	85	1	0	0	1	2	9	3			
		F	24	1	0	1	1	2	14	–			
	1980	MF	180	2	1	1	2	4	2	1			
		F	59	2	1	1	3	4	6	–			
	1983	MF	360	3	0	1	2	7	9	1			
		F	96	2	1	1	3	5	10	–			
	1984	MF	419	3	2	2	3	5	5	1			
		F	136	3	3	2	3	4	7	–			
GHANA	1975	MF	*7 796	*1	*2	*2	*2	*0	*1	–	*0		
		F	*3 741	*2	*2	*2	*3	*0	*0	–	*0		
	1976	MF	*7 796	*1	*1	*2	*2	*0	*0	–	*0		
		F	*3 741	*2	*2	*2	*3	*0	*0	–	*0		
GUINEA	1980	MF	41 043	46	32	38	54	36	64	55			
	1984	MF	36 751	39	39	37	42	31	52	36			
		F	9 780	40	43	38	47	30	49	28			
GUINEA-BISSAU	1975	MF	251	15	12	17	21	12	8				
	1982	MF	1 790	23	20	21	60	5	10				
		F	505	31	27	26	77	4	6				

COUNTRY PAYS PAIS	YEAR ANNEE AÑO	SEX SEXE SEXO	TOTAL TOTAL TOTAL	PERCENTAGE REPEATERS BY GRADE / POURCENTAGE DE REDOUBLANTS PAR ANNEE D'ETUDES / PORCENTAJE DE REPETIDORES POR AÑO DE ESTUDIOS									
				TOTAL	I	II	III	IV	V	VI	VII	VIII	IX
GUINEA-BISSAU (CONT)	1983	MF	1 368	16	21	17	11	15	3				
		F	317	18	25	15	19	11	4				
LIBYAN ARAB JAMAHIRIYA‡	1975	MF	12 004	9	6	11	13	7	7	12			
		F	4 553	10	13	7	11	6	2	10			
	1980	MF	37 704	15	20	15	15	6	3	9			
		F	12 688	13	17	12	12	6	2	6			
	1982	MF	32 256	12	15	11	11	9	7	5			
		F	12 039	11	13	9	11	11	4	3			
MADAGASCAR‡	1984	MF	57 856	20	13	11	17	34	21	22	27		
		F	25 073	20	13	13	18	35	19	19	22		
MALI	1975	MF	10 701	22	20	21	28	3	33	20			
	1982	MF	22 429	35	28	29	48	8	31	43			
MAURITANIA	1980	MF	1 544	8	10	4	8	7	8	14			
		F	415	10	14	5	11	9	5	15			
	1982	MF	2 795	11	11	9	14	6	8	24			
MAURITIUS	1975	MF	4 238	7	4	5	5	9	11	2	12		
		F	2 302	8	4	7	7	10	13	2	13		
	1979	MF	7 441	9	6	5	6	12	18	2	17		
		F	3 497	9	4	5	6	13	19	2	14		
	1982	MF	9 600	12	6	6	6	17	23	16	——>		
		F	4 461	12	7	5	5	18	21	17	——>		
	1984	MF	12 506	17	7	6	8	25	33	7	34		
MOROCCO‡	1975	MF	72 937	16	9	11	14	28	12	10	33		
		F	23 569	15	8	11	14	28	11	9	32		
	1980	MF	119 352	15	9	10	11	26	16	9	33		
		F	43 376	15	9	9	11	27	14	9	31		
	1982	MF	148 967	16	9	10	12	25	17	10	33		
		F	58 097	16	8	9	13	25	16	10	35		
	1984	MF	231 151	21	16	16	16	31	23	14	34		
		F	89 834	21	15	15	16	32	23	14	34		
MOZAMBIQUE	1982	MF	19 702	21	20	26	14	13	13				
		F	7 265	25	24	29	20	15	15				
	1983	MF	25 735	24	24	28	18	14	22				
		F	9 572	28	28	30	24	19	26				
NIGER	1975	MF	1 582	12	9	12	15	12	15	12	10		
		F	432	11	9	13	16	11	6	7	8		
	1980	MF	2 581	7	5	5	5	15	9	6	14		
		F	870	8	4	5	5	21	10	1	26		
REUNION‡	1975	MF	5 327	12	13	11	12	12	7	9	20		
	1979	MF	6 067	12	15	16	6	10	15	11	20		
	1982	MF	7 035	16	19	19	8	12	12	8	27		
	1983	MF	6 632	15	19	16	7	10	12	8	30		
RWANDA	1975	MF	499	6	6	8	4	3	6	2			
		F	222	8	8	12	6	4	3	2			
	1979	MF	524	7	15	10	3	7	7	3			
	1981	MF	214	5	–	7	22	4	5	3			
	1983	MF	263	5	7	6	1	9	6	3			
		F	38	4	4	6	–	–	–	1			
SAO TOME AND PRINCIPE	1976	MF	950	26	21	38	39	15	2	–	–		
		F	504	30	23	42	47	17	–	–	–		
	1977	MF	976	31	36	37	37	7	5	–	–		
		F	478	33	33	42	42	4	3	–	–		

3.9 Percentage repeaters by grade (second level general)
% de redoublants par année d'études (second degré général)
% de repetidores por año de estudios (segundo grado general)

COUNTRY PAYS PAIS	YEAR ANNEE AÑO	SEX SEXE SEXO	TOTAL TOTAL TOTAL	PERCENTAGE REPEATERS BY GRADE / POURCENTAGE DE REDOUBLANTS PAR ANNEE D'ETUDES / PORCENTAJE DE REPETIDORES POR AÑO DE ESTUDIOS									
				TOTAL	I	II	III	IV	V	VI	VII	V III	IX
SENEGAL	1976	MF	9 538	13	10	12	13	19	16	12	16		
	1980	MF	11 430	14	11	11	13	18	14	21	15		
	1982	MF	18 008	18	11	16	17	28	15	28	23		
	1983	MF	16 617	16	11	11	13	24	15	29	29		
SEYCHELLES‡			–	–	–	–	–	–					
SIERRA LEONE	1977	MF	8 675	16	17	16	17	18	11	2	2		
		F	3 066	18	19	16	18	20	14	4	4		
	1978	MF	9 566	17	18	18	16	18	12	4	–		
		F	3 606	19	21	22	18	18	9	4	–		
SWAZILAND	1975	MF	712	4	4	6	4	4	2				
		F	329	4	4	6	4	5	2				
	1980	MF	988	4	4	5	5	3	1				
		F	554	5	4	6	6	4	1				
	1983	MF	1 650	6	5	9	6	6	1				
		F	851	6	5	10	6	6	0				
	1984	MF	1 734	6	5	9	6	6	0				
		F	864	6	5	9	7	5	0				
TOGO	1975	MF	9 067	15	14	10	16	27	12	25	15		
		F	2 542	18	17	14	19	32	12	28	19		
	1979	MF	30 081	25	23	20	26	36	14	18	34		
		F	7 849	28	26	23	29	40	14	18	39		
	1983	MF	32 653	34	25	25	35	52	17	52	42		
		F	8 541	36	28	30	39	54	15	54	48		
	1984	MF	29 010	34	28	24	34	49	27	40	44		
		F	7 071	34	31	26	36	49	20	42	43		
TUNISIA‡	1975	MF	17 052	13	13	12	12	10	12	10	23		
		F	5 450	12	12	10	9	10	14	11	24		
	1980	MF	21 723	11	8	10	13	8	10	9	29		
		F	7 803	10	6	9	13	8	9	9	29		
	1983	MF	44 793	15	14	15	15	10	13	10	32		
		F	16 718	14	12	14	14	10	13	10	33		
	1984	MF	55 383	17	19	14	19	11	12	12	32		
		F	20 270	15	15	13	18	10	11	12	31		
UGANDA‡	1976	MF	1 367	2	1	2	3	4	4	4			
	1977	MF	1 134	2	1	2	2	4	1	4			
ZAIRE	1980	MF	69 721	8	8	7	7	7	11	18			
		F	23 764	10	10	8	9	11	20	32			
	1982	MF	102 301	8	8	7	7	7	11	18			
		F	34 872	10	10	8	9	11	20	32			
	1983	MF	124 292	8	8	7	7	7	11	18			
		F	42 367	10	10	8	8	11	19	31			
ZAMBIA	1976	MF	617	1	0	0	3	0	0				
		F	329	1	0	0	5	0	0				
	1980	MF	1 062	1	0	0	4	0	0				
ZIMBABWE	1984	MF	473	0	0	0	0	0	0	0			
		F	242	0	0	0	0	1	–	1			
AMERICA, NORTH													
COSTA RICA	1981	MF	8 468	8	–	15	9	13	3	–			
		F	4 224	8	–	14	9	12	2	–			
	1983	MF	11 272	12	12	20	10	10	3	13			
	1984	MF	9 950	11	14	11	9	11	3	13			
CUBA	1975	MF	9 627	2	3	2	1	3	2	2	2		
	1980	MF	36 944	4	7	4	3	3	2	1			
	1983	MF	20 218	3	4	3	2	2	1	0			
	1984	MF	17 200	2	3	2	2	3	1	0			

COUNTRY PAYS PAIS	YEAR ANNEE AÑO	SEX SEXE SEXO	TOTAL TOTAL TOTAL	PERCENTAGE REPEATERS BY GRADE POURCENTAGE DE REDOUBLANTS PAR ANNEE D'ETUDES PORCENTAJE DE REPETIDORES POR AÑO DE ESTUDIOS									
				TOTAL	I	II	III	IV	V	VI	VII	VIII	IX
EL SALVADOR	1975	MF	171	1	1	1	0						
		F	57	0	1	1	0						
	1983	MF	152	1	1	1	0						
		F	82	1	1	1	0						
	1984	MF	161	1	1	1	0						
		F	79	1	1	1	0						
GRENADA	1982	MF	1 525	18	13	20	22	14	27				
		F	846	17	14	17	19	16	25				
GUADELOUPE	1976	MF	4 538	12	9	12	12	13	18	17	23		
	1979	MF	4 967	13	10	14	14	11	16	12	22		
	1982	MF	4 714	14	11	17	11	18	18	16	18		
	1983	MF	4 741	14	11	15	13	17	19	15	23		
GUATEMALA‡	1975	MF	4 143	4	6	5	5	2	2	2			
		F	1 744	4	5	4	4	2	1	2			
	1979	MF	3 813	3	4	3	3	2	1	1			
	1980	MF	3 985	3	4	3	3	3	2	7			
HAITI	1976	MF	3 553	6	5	5	5	7	9	11	2		
		F	1 491	6	5	6	5	7	8	11	3		
	1980	MF	5 578	6	6	5	4	4	5	11	13		
		F	2 483	5	5	4	4	4	6	10	16		
	1981	MF	6 837	7	7	6	6	6	7	13	8		
		F	3 361	7	7	6	6	7	8	13	6		
	1982	MF	10 914	9	8	8	8	9	11	19	3		
		F	5 395	9	8	8	8	9	11	17	3		
JAMAICA‡	1975	MF	6 198	3	3	2	6	2	3	1	2		
		F	2 979	3	2	2	6	2	3	0	2		
	1980	MF	5 243	2	2	1	4	1	3	0	2		
		F	2 676	2	2	1	5	1	3	0	2		
	1983	MF	5 192	2	2	2	4	1	3	0	1		
		F	2 444	2	1	2	4	1	3	0	0		
MARTINIQUE‡	1976	MF	5 639	14	12	12	15	16	19	13	29		
	1979	MF	6 487	17	11	18	19	14	25	15	26		
	1982	MF	5 408	17	14	19	12	21	21	19	26		
	1983	MF	5 578	17	14	19	13	21	27	19	27		
MEXICO	1976	MF	51 700	2	1	1	1	6	5	3			
	1980	MF	98 517	2	2	3	2	2	5	4			
	1981	MF	102 911	2	1	1	1	5	7	8			
	1982	MF	110 209	2	1	1	1	5	6	8			
NICARAGUA	1979	MF	22 383	20	20	22	20	21	19	7			
PANAMA‡	1975	MF	4 386	6	7	6	4	5	7	2			
	1979	MF	10 651	9	11	10	8	9	8	8			
	1983	MF	18 234	10	15	11	7	9	8	6			
	1984	MF	17 160	9	13	11	8	9	7	4			
ST. LUCIA	1982	MF	146	3	1	0	3	13	–	2			
		F	95	3	1	1	2	15	–	2			
	1983	MF	285	6	2	1	8	19	3	–			
ST. PIERRE AND MIQUELON	1980	MF	83	16	14	21	12	25	7	–	11		
	1983	MF	70	13	10	18	8	16	14	4	17		
	1984	MF	50	10	5	11	5	12	14	20	18		
TRINIDAD AND TOBAGO‡	1984	MF	2 293	2	–	0	0	0	12	8			
		F	1 291	3	–	–	–	0	14	7			

3.9 Percentage repeaters by grade (second level general)
% de redoublants par année d'études (second degré général)
% de repetidores por año de estudios (segundo grado general)

COUNTRY / PAYS / PAIS	YEAR / ANNEE / AÑO	SEX / SEXE / SEXO	TOTAL / TOTAL / TOTAL	PERCENTAGE REPEATERS BY GRADE / POURCENTAGE DE REDOUBLANTS PAR ANNEE D'ETUDES / PORCENTAJE DE REPETIDORES POR AÑO DE ESTUDIOS									
				TOTAL	I	II	III	IV	V	VI	VII	VIII	IX
AMERICA, SOUTH													
ARGENTINA	1975	MF	27 895	6	9	7	6	5	1	0	2		
BRAZIL‡	1975	MF	90 137	5	6	5	3	1					
		F	42 391	4	5	4	2	0					
	1980	MF	204 845	7	10	6	3	1					
		F	100 413	7	10	6	3	1					
	1981	MF	262 450	9	13	9	4	2					
	1982	MF	289 617	10	14	9	4	3					
CHILE	1975	MF	35 131	12	15	13	14	4					
		F	22 032	13	15	14	15	5					
	1977	MF	24 725	8	10	8	9	2					
		F	13 981	8	10	8	9	2					
	1983	MF	39 310	8	9	7	11	3					
		F	20 455	8	9	7	11	3					
COLOMBIA‡	1984	MF	378 851	20	41	23	15	10	9	3			
		F	188 264	20	39	24	16	9	10	3			
	1985	MF	380 778	20	40	22	14	10	9	3			
		F	189 222	20	38	23	16	9	9	3			
ECUADOR‡	1975	MF	26 867	8	9	8	7	11	7	2			
		F	10 776	7	8	7	6	8	6	1			
	1980	MF	58 219	10	11	11	10	12	8	3			
	1983	MF	74 324	11	13	12	12	14	11	4			
	1984	MF	79 144	11	12	12	12	13	11	4			
FRENCH GUIANA	1978	MF	264	6	2	6	3	7	14	12	18		
	1982	MF	654	12	9	14	7	14	15	9	22		
	1983	MF	821	14	11	17	12	14	12	5	28		
GUYANA	1975	MF	13 335	20	10	12	44	7	29	4			
		F	6 569	20	9	11	44	6	29	4			
	1978	MF	6 599	9	4	4	8	26	18	6			
		F	3 359	9	3	4	8	27	17	5			
	1979	MF	7 531	10	5	5	8	24	24	7			
		F	3 789	10	4	4	8	24	22	10			
PERU	1975	MF	57 528	9	11	11	10	9	3				
	1980	MF	102 961	9	13	11	7	6	3				
		F	40 460	8	11	10	7	5	2				
	1981	MF	123 299	10	15	12	8	7	3				
		F	56 526	10	15	12	8	7	3				
	1985	MF	141 964	10	15	12	8	7	4				
SURINAME	1975	MF	3 806	14	19	14	9	9	–	–			
		F	1 983	13	18	14	7	8	–	–			
	1977	MF	3 573	13	14	14	12	13	–	–			
		F	1 901	12	13	14	11	15	–	–			
VENEZUELA‡	1975	MF	72 000	11	12	11	13	9	4	2			
		F	36 389	10	11	10	14	8	4	1			
	1980	MF	102 992	12	14	13	16	9	4	2			
	1982	MF	109 901	12	13	13	14	9	4	2			
		F	57 918	11	12	13	15	9	4	2			
	1983	MF	109 066	11	12	13	14	9	5	4			
		F	56 603	11	11	12	14	8	4	4			
ASIA													
AFGHANISTAN	1977	MF	16 934	20	22	28	17	9					
		F	1 885	15	19	17	10	13					
	1980	MF	14 847	12	13	18	10	5					
		F	4 239	16	22	17	11	6					

COUNTRY / PAYS / PAIS	YEAR / ANNEE / AÑO	SEX / SEXE / SEXO	TOTAL / TOTAL / TOTAL	PERCENTAGE REPEATERS BY GRADE / POURCENTAGE DE REDOUBLANTS PAR ANNEE D'ETUDES / PORCENTAJE DE REPETIDORES POR AÑO DE ESTUDIOS									
				TOTAL	I	II	III	IV	V	VI	VII	VIII	IX
AFGHANISTAN (CONT)	1982	MF	4 372	5	8	4	2	2					
		F	1 589	5	10	3	3	2					
	1984	MF	3 843	4	6	3	3	1					
		F	1 285	4	6	3	3	1					
BAHRAIN‡	1975	MF	3 525	22	22	25	26	13	24				
		F	1 655	21	17	25	25	12	27				
	1980	MF	1 732	8	8	7	5	6	12	14			
		F	631	6	7	7	4	4	5	7			
	1982	MF	2 472	11	14	11	10	4	6	10			
		F	875	8	9	9	9	2	6	7			
	1983	MF	1 737	7	12	6	6	3	2	7			
		F	463	4	6	3	5	2	1	6			
BHUTAN	1976	MF	174	21	16	23	27	42	10				
	1979	MF	53	4	3	4	6	1	1				
		F	10	3	2	2	8	–	5				
BRUNEI DARUSSALAM	1975	MF	860	6	0	0	14	1	24	–	25		
		F	424	6	0	0	17	1	20	–	23		
	1980	MF	2 253	14	10	7	15	6	36	0	19		
		F	1 113	13	8	7	16	5	37	–	19		
	1983	MF	1 785	9	6	5	7	5	25	0	31		
		F	918	9	4	3	9	4	27	–	29		
	1984	MF	2 022	11	8	4	10	6	26	1	24		
		F	975	10	5	3	10	5	25	–	27		
CYPRUS‡	1975	MF	586	1	2	2	1	1	1	0	–		
		F	162	1	1	1	1	1	0	0	–		
	1979	MF	810	2	3	2	2	3	1	0	–		
		F	338	1	2	2	1	3	1	0	–		
HONG KONG	1980	MF	30 497	7	8	7	6	6	11	–	–		
		F	12 888	6	6	5	6	6	8	–	–		
	1983	MF	33 125	8	7	6	1	8	20	–	–		
		F	14 521	7	5	5	1	7	17	–	–		
	1984	MF	31 846	8	6	5	1	9	21	–	–		
		F	14 245	7	4	4	1	8	19	–	–		
INDONESIA‡	1975	MF	53 875	3	3	2	2	4	3	3			
	1980	MF	84 177	2	2	2	2	2	2	2			
	1983	MF	106 294	2	2	2	2	1	1	2			
	1984	MF	117 270	2	1	2	2	1	1	2			
IRAN, ISLAMIC REPUBLIC OF	1983	MF	312 781	12	17	12	13	6	5	4	8		
	1984	MF	372 471	13	16	15	13	9	6	4	11		
IRAQ‡	1975	MF	98 833	20	18	21	25	8	11	33			
		F	24 600	17	20	19	16	9	10	22			
	1979	MF	271 930	30	31	32	36	12	14	42			
		F	70 022	26	29	29	26	11	11	33			
	1982	MF	347 505	36	43	35	38	25	10	41			
		F	98 244	29	37	32	25	21	7	27			
JAPAN‡			–	–	–	–	–	–	–	–	–		
JORDAN‡	1975	MF	12 901	8	10	8	12	4	1	6			
		F	5 266	8	10	8	12	4	2	4			
	1980	MF	11 813	5	7	5	2	4	2	8			
		F	4 392	4	7	4	2	4	1	3			
	1981	MF	15 721	6	8	6	3	5	3	9			
		F	6 155	5	8	6	3	5	3	3			
	1982	MF	17 713	6	9	7	4	6	3	7			
		F	7 566	6	9	7	3	5	3	3			
KOREA, REPUBLIC OF	1983	MF	440	0	0	0	0	0	0	0			
		F	174	0	0	0	0	0	0	0			

3.9 Percentage repeaters by grade (second level general)
% de redoublants par année d'études (second degré général)
% de repetidores por año de estudios (segundo grado general)

COUNTRY / PAYS / PAIS	YEAR / ANNEE / AÑO	SEX / SEXE / SEXO	TOTAL / TOTAL / TOTAL	PERCENTAGE REPEATERS BY GRADE / POURCENTAGE DE REDOUBLANTS PAR ANNEE D'ETUDES / PORCENTAJE DE REPETIDORES POR AÑO DE ESTUDIOS									
				TOTAL	I	II	III	IV	V	VI	VII	VIII	IX
KOREA, REP. OF (CONT)	1984	MF	212	0	0	0	0	0	0	0			
		F	42	0	0	0	0	0	0	0			
KUWAIT‡	1975	MF	17 130	19	28	22	20	12	15	17	10	10	
		F	6 003	15	24	18	16	7	9	13	8	7	
	1980	MF	18 642	19	28	22	20	12	15	17	10	10	
		F	6 971	15	24	18	16	7	9	13	8	7	
	1983	MF	20 223	9	11	9	6	2	17	14	9	5	
		F	8 266	8	8	7	5	2	17	14	9	4	
	1984	MF	19 608	9	10	8	6	3	15	11	8	5	
		F	7 354	7	7	6	5	2	13	10	7	3	
MONGOLIA	1975	MF	5 834	3	7	5	3	1	0	1	0		
	1979	MF	1 325	1	1	1	1	0	0	0	0		
OMAN	1975	MF	16	1	1	2	2	1	–	–			
		F	8	4	3	2	11	3	–	–			
	1983	MF	*3 081	*10	13	7	14	4	3	0			
		F	670	7	11	5	8	4	2	–			
	1984	MF	*3 993	*10	14	9	14	4	3	3			
		F	*843	*7	9	7	8	3	2	1			
QATAR‡	1975	MF	763	10	12	11	7	9	6	9			
		F	194	5	5	7	4	6	2	8			
	1980	MF	2 199	15	27	17	12	7	6	8			
		F	806	11	22	9	7	6	6	8			
	1983	MF	2 298	13	21	15	9	12	9	4			
		F	1 004	11	15	11	6	15	10	6			
	1984	MF	2 313	13	19	11	11	16	6	6			
		F	895	9	12	8	7	15	6	6			
SAUDI ARABIA	1975	MF	16 546	9	13	8	8	7	3	3			
		F	3 186	5	7	5	4	6	1	2			
	1980	MF	51 557	16	16	16	20	13	7	17			
		F	11 112	9	9	10	11	9	5	6			
	1982	MF	48 891	12	14	11	16	13	4	11			
		F	13 617	9	8	8	12	10	3	8			
	1983	MF	69 591	14	14	14	20	13	6	12			
		F	17 694	10	9	10	15	9	3	7			
SINGAPORE	1975	MF	6 618	4	0	4	4	7	1	6			
		F	2 870	3	0	3	4	6	0	4			
	1980	MF	21 199	12	17	11	10	12	3	11			
		F	9 425	11	16	10	8	9	3	8			
	1983	MF	9 020	5	0	0	4	15	2	6	9		
		F	3 780	4	0	0	3	13	2	5	6		
	1984	MF	9 016	5	0	0	3	13	3	6	8		
		F	3 984	4	0	0	3	12	3	5	4		
SRI LANKA‡	1975	MF	160 806	15	9	8	6	1	36	6	30		
	1980	MF	109 820	9	7	5	5	5	15	2	18		
	1983	MF	94 404	7	7	6	4	2	10	2	20		
	1984	MF	90 353	7	7	5	4	2	8	1	28		
SYRIAN ARAB REPUBLIC‡	1975	MF	*75 951	*16	*15	*11	*29	*4	*3	*25			
		F	*19 177	*13	*13	*9	*23	*4	*1	*22			
	1980	MF	83 829	15	14	9	24	3	3	24			
		F	25 530	12	13	8	20	2	1	20			
	1983	MF	107 553	15	14	8	24	3	2	35			
		F	35 815	13	12	7	21	3	1	29			
	1984	MF	106 079	14	14	9	20	3	2	31			
		F	36 121	12	12	8	17	2	1	27			
THAILAND	1975	MF	44 165	5	4	4	3	11	10	–			
		F	15 669	4	3	3	2	10	11	–			
	1977	MF	35 257	3	4	4	2	1	⟶				
		F	11 576	2	3	3	2	1	⟶				

COUNTRY / PAYS / PAIS	YEAR / ANNEE / ANO	SEX / SEXE / SEXO	TOTAL / TOTAL / TOTAL	PERCENTAGE REPEATERS BY GRADE / POURCENTAGE DE REDOUBLANTS PAR ANNEE D'ETUDES / PORCENTAJE DE REPETIDORES POR AÑO DE ESTUDIOS									
				TOTAL	I	II	III	IV	V	VI	VII	V III	IX
TURKEY	1975	MF	222 004	16	18	17	8	27	15	12	4		
		F	58 032	13	14	14	7	24	13	10	3		
	1981	MF	497 381	28	24	30	23	38	32	29	8		
		F	135 733	21	17	23	17	30	24	22	4		
	1982	MF	577 181	31	30	29	26	45	33	31	16		
		F	171 118	25	23	24	21	38	27	25	12		
	1983	MF	487 215	25	27	24	18	32	23	21	9		
		F	149 533	20	21	21	15	28	20	17	8		
UNITED ARAB EMIRATES‡	1975	MF	868	9	11	10	7	10	4	4			
		F	291	7	7	9	7	8	2	0			
	1979	MF	2 359	10	13	12	14	5	4	2			
		F	918	9	10	11	12	5	4	3			
	1983	MF	4 723	11	16	12	13	7	4	4			
		F	1 574	8	12	10	6	6	2	2			
	1984	MF	4 952	9	14	9	7	8	4	4			
		F	1 630	6	10	6	3	6	2	3			
VIET–NAM	1978	MF	155 574	5	5	4	4	4	5	4	4		
EUROPE													
AUSTRIA‡	1976	MF	29 127	5	4	4	4	5	7	9	9	3	3
	1978	MF	27 031	5	3	3	4	4	8	15	14	4	1
BELGIUM‡	1975	MF	103 775	21	17	20	24	26	20	21	23		
		F	49 267	21	18	21	24	27	20	19	15		
	1979	MF	109 589	26	26	28	26	26	23	23	15		
		F	51 029	24	24	26	25	27	19	20	5		
BULGARIA‡	1975	MF	1 687	1	1	2	1						
	1980	MF	294	0	0	0	0						
	1983	MF	564	0	1	0	0	–					
	1984	MF	684	0	1	0	0	–					
CZECHOSLOVAKIA	1975	MF	417	0	0	1	0	0					
		F	216	0	0	0	0	0					
	1980	MF	521	0	0	0	0	0					
		F	301	0	0	0	0	0					
	1983	MF	760	1	1	1	1	0					
		F	457	1	1	1	0	0					
	1984	MF	644	0	0	1	1	0					
		F	417	0	0	1	1	0					
FRANCE	1976	MF	358 626	9	10	7	9	8	11	7	18		
	1979	MF	405 129	10	9	10	7	8	15	13	25		
	1981	MF	470 031	12	12	13	9	13	14	9	20		
	1982	MF	474 008	12	11	14	9	12	16	9	20		
GERMANY, FEDERAL REPUBLIC OF	1975	MF	263 841	5	2	4	6	5	5	7	7	5	3
		F	100 128	4	1	3	4	4	4	6	5	4	2
	1980	MF	199 336	3	1	2	4	5	4	4	4	2	1
		F	77 666	3	1	2	3	4	4	3	3	1	1
	1982	MF	229 598	4	1	3	5	6	5	4	6	2	2
		F	96 114	3	1	2	4	5	5	4	5	2	2
	1983	MF	217 860	4	1	3	5	6	5	4	5	2	1
		F	94 204	4	1	2	4	6	5	4	5	2	1
GREECE‡	1975	MF	27 574	5	7	6	5	5	3	1	6		
		F	10 272	4	6	5	4	4	3	0	7		
	1979	MF	30 887	5	10	6	1	3	4	1	5		
		F	10 630	3	7	4	1	2	3	1	3		
	1981	MF	30 595	5	9	5	1	3	3	1	12		
		F	10 304	3	7	4	1	2	2	0	11		
	1982	MF	37 689	6	11	7	1	5	3	1	7		
		F	12 976	4	8	5	1	4	2	0	7		

3.9 Percentage repeaters by grade (second level general)
% de redoublants par année d'études (second degré général)
% de repetidores por año de estudios (segundo grado general)

COUNTRY / PAYS / PAIS	YEAR / ANNEE / AÑO	SEX / SEXE / SEXO	TOTAL / TOTAL / TOTAL	PERCENTAGE REPEATERS BY GRADE / POURCENTAGE DE REDOUBLANTS PAR ANNEE D'ETUDES / PORCENTAJE DE REPETIDORES POR AÑO DE ESTUDIOS									
				TOTAL	I	II	III	IV	V	VI	VII	VIII	IX
HUNGARY	1980	MF	596	1	1	1	1	0					
		F	359	1	1	1	0	0					
	1983	MF	916	1	1	1	1	0					
		F	579	1	1	1	0	0					
	1984	MF	816	1	1	1	1	0					
		F	535	1	1	1	0	0					
ITALY	1975	MF	174 341	5	8	6	3	4	4	4	2	2	
		F	61 445	4	6	4	2	3	3	3	2	2	
	1980	MF	282 812	8	11	9	5	6	5	5	4	4	
		F	97 693	6	8	7	4	5	4	3	3	2	
	1982	MF	295 735	9	13	10	5	6	4	6	4	3	
		F	100 500	6	9	7	4	4	3	4	3	2	
	1983	MF	243 548	7	13	5	5	5	4	5	3	3	
		F	91 172	6	9	6	3	4	3	4	2	2	
LUXEMBOURG‡	1975	MF	1 172	8	7	10	8	4	7	7	10		
		F	479	6	6	8	7	5	7	5	7		
	1980	MF	2 234	13	15	15	10	11	8	7	22		
		F	1 026	12	13	13	9	9	7	5	21		
	1981	MF	2 189	13	14	12	9	14	12	9	23		
		F	1 060	12	13	11	9	13	12	10	24		
	1982	MF	3 045	16	18	17	15	13	12	10	23		
		F	1 412	15	16	14	15	13	11	8	28		
MALTA	1975	MF	145	1	1	0	1	1	0	0	0		
		F	53	0	1	0	0	0	0	–	–		
	1980	MF	438	2	2	2	3	1	2	0	–		
		F	216	2	2	2	2	1	3	0	–		
	1982	MF	547	2	2	2	4	3	2	1	–		
		F	290	3	3	2	3	2	2	1	–		
	1983	MF	455	2	2	2	2	2	2	1	——>		
		F	219	2	2	2	2	3	2	0	——>		
NETHERLANDS	1975	MF	87 071	11	10	13	12	11	11	10			
		F	37 986	10	8	12	11	9	10	10			
	1980	MF	92 530	11	7	12	12	14	12	8			
		F	44 767	10	6	11	12	13	12	8			
	1983	MF	87 161	10	7	10	11	13	14	10			
		F	43 888	10	6	10	10	12	14	10			
	1984	MF	86 651	11	7	10	11	12	13	9			
		F	43 297	10	6	10	11	11	13	8			
POLAND	1975	MF	12 413	3	3	4	3	0					
	1980	MF	5 991	2	2	3	2	0					
	1983	MF	8 196	3	2	4	3	1					
	1984	MF	7 073	2	2	3	3	0					
PORTUGAL	1975	MF	41 488	13	0	15	25	4	20				
		F	21 646	13	0	14	25	3	20				
	1977	MF	81 915	20	15	21	24	6	30				
		F	42 002	20	14	20	24	5	29				
SAN MARINO	1975	MF	69	6	5	7	6	6	–	5	–	–	
SPAIN	1980	MF	351 616	11	13	11	9	10	13	11	12		
		F	161 716	10	12	10	8	10	12	10	12		
	1982	MF	389 438	12	14	12	10	12	14	13	16		
		F	181 744	11	12	10	9	12	14	12	16		
	1983	MF	385 006	12	13	11	9	12	14	13	16		
		F	176 654	11	11	10	9	11	14	12	15		
SWITZERLAND	1980	MF	18 853	4	9	6	6	2	4	4	4	3	1
		F	8 140	4	8	5	5	2	3	4	3	3	1
	1983	MF	13 375	3	2	4	3	3	4	4	5	5	3
		F	5 720	3	2	3	3	2	3	3	4	4	2

COUNTRY / PAYS / PAIS	YEAR / ANNEE / AÑO	SEX / SEXE / SEXO	TOTAL / TOTAL / TOTAL	PERCENTAGE REPEATERS BY GRADE / POURCENTAGE DE REDOUBLANTS PAR ANNEE D'ETUDES / PORCENTAJE DE REPETIDORES POR AÑO DE ESTUDIOS: TOTAL	I	II	III	IV	V	VI	VII	VIII	IX
SWITZERLAND (CONT)	1984	MF	19 523	5	9	6	6	3	4	5	6	6	3
		F	8 990	5	8	5	6	3	4	4	5	6	2
YUGOSLAVIA	1975	MF	77 515	5	7	5	5	1	7	5	3	1	
	1982	MF	68 645	4	4	3	3	1	8	5	2	1	
	1983	MF	71 956	4	4	3	3	1	9	5	3	1	
OCEANIA													
FIJI‡	1977	MF	4 959	15	./.	./.	1	14	34	25			
	1980	MF	4 381	9	1	1	1	14	22	18	4		
		F	2 214	9	0	1	1	15	23	17	8		
	1983	MF	4 533	10	0	1	1	14	22	22	3		
		F	2 320	10	1	1	1	14	21	29	4		
	1984	MF	4 033	9	1	1	0	12	21	21	4		
		F	1 990	9	1	1	0	13	22	18	1		
FRENCH POLYNESIA	1981	MF	1 605	15	15	15	14	17	18	25	15		
	1982	MF	1 208	10	10	10	10	10	11	11	11		
	1983	MF	2 108	17	14	19	12	23	21	11	24		
KIRIBATI	1980	MF	10	1	–	–	4	–	1	–			
		F	6	1	–	–	4	–	3	–			
	1983	MF	19	2	3	1	1	3	1	–			
		F	12	2	5	1	–	6	–	–			
	1984	MF	16	1	2	0	3	2	–	–			
		F	6	1	1	1	3	–	–	–			
NEW CALEDONIA	1982	MF	1 633	15	17	15	13	17	12	8	13		
		F	880	14	16	14	12	17	13	8	10		
	1984	MF	2 508	20	22	19	20	21	18	12	17		
		F	1 381	20	19	21	22	23	19	8	17		
	1985	MF	2 606	20	21	21	18	20	17	16	18		
		F	1 433	20	21	22	18	22	18	17	18		
NEW ZEALAND	1980	MF	9 516	3	–	–	–	–	15				
		F	4 695	3	–	–	–	–	15				
	1981	MF	9 570	3	–	–	–	–	16				
		F	4 885	3	–	–	–	–	16				
SOLOMON ISLANDS	1980	MF	10	0	0	0	1	1	0	–			
		F	4	0	–	0	2	–	–	–			
TONGA	1982	MF	1 681	10	8	6	9	11	19	15	13		
		F	830	11	8	7	9	11	19	17	5		
	1983	MF	1 436	9	*7	*5	*7	*7	*22	*14	*10		
		F	626	8	4	5	*6	*7	*22	*14	*8		
U.S.S.R.													
U.S.S.R.	1975	MF	106 100	1	1	1	0	1	0	0			
	1980	MF	50 100	0	0	0	0	1	0	0			
	1982	MF	46 100	0	0	0	0	1	0	0			
	1983	MF	56 040	0	0	0	0	1	0	0			
BYELORUSSIAN S.S.R.‡	1975	MF	1 313	1	1	0	–						
	1980	MF	2 000	0	0	0	0	1	0	–			
	1981	MF	2 200	0	0	0	0	1	0	–			
	1982	MF	2 200	0	0	0	0	1	0	–			
UKRAINIAN S.S.R.‡	1975	MF	2 100	0	0	0	–						
	1980	MF	4 000	0	0	0	0	0	0	–			
	1982	MF	4 700	0	0	0	0	0	0	–			
	1983	MF	5 600	0	0	0	0	0	0	–			

These data refer to total and female repeaters in second level general education only in 1975, 1980 and the latest two years available.

The total number of repeaters together with its percentage of total enrolment as well as the percentage repeaters in each grade appearing in this table have been calculated from figures taken from questionnaire replies and national publications.

The percentages presented in this table have been calculated by dividing the number of repeaters by the enrolment for the same year.

To maintain a consistent and coherent series on repetition as well as to facilitate the comparison of these data with those for enrolment by grade presented in Table 3.8, estimates have been made when the number of repeaters in private institutions was not available. In no case did the missing data constitute more than 5% of the total enrolment. The identification of these estimates is facilitated by the introduction of an asterisk which precedes the total number of repeaters.

The method of estimation used takes into account all available information. For example, the proportion of repeaters in private schools for previous years was used if available; when no other information was available, the data on repeaters were adjusted to reflect the incidence of private enrolment.

Ces données se réfèrent aux redoublants (total et filles) dans l'enseignement général du second degré seulement en 1975, 1980 et les deux dernières années disponibles.

Le nombre total de redoublants avec le pourcentage par rapport au total des effectifs d'élèves ainsi que le pourcentage de redoublants dans chaque année d'études qui figurent dans ce tableau ont été calculés avec les données provenant des réponses aux questionnaires et des publications nationales.

Les pourcentages présentés dans ce tableau ont été calculés en divisant le nombre de redoublants par les effectifs de la même année.

Afin d'assurer une série cohérente et consistante sur les redoublants et de faciliter la comparabilité de ces données avec celles des effectifs par année d'études présentés dans le tableau 3.8, des estimations ont été faites sur le nombre de redoublants dans les écoles privées, lorsque ces chiffres n'étaient pas disponibles. Les données manquantes ne représentent en aucun cas plus de 5% du total des effectifs. L'identification de ces estimations est facilitée par l'introduction d'un astérisque qui précède le nombre de redoublants.

La méthode d'estimation utilisée prend en considération toutes les informations disponibles; par exemple, la proportion des redoublants dans les écoles privées au cours des années antérieures est utilisée, lorsque ces chiffres sont connus. Si l'on ne dispose pas d'autres informations, les données sur les redoublants sont ajustées en accord avec l'importance des effectifs de l'enseignement privé.

Estos datos se refieren a los repetidores (total y de sexo femenino) en la enseñanza general de segundo grado solamente en 1975, 1980 y los dos ultimos años disponibles.

El número total de repetidores con el porcentaje en relación con la matrícula total así como los porcentajes de repetidores en cada año de estudios que figuran en este cuadro se han calculado con los datos provenientes de las respuestas a los cuestionarios y de las publicaciones nacionales.

El cálculo de los porcentajes se ha efectuado dividiendo el número de repetidores por la matrícula escolar relativa al mismo año.

Con el fin de asegurar una serie coherente y consistente sobre los repetidores y de facilitar la comparabilidad de estos datos con los de los efectivos por año de estudios presentados en el cuadro 3.8, se han efectuado estimaciones relativas al número de repetidores en las escuelas privadas cuando no se disponía de tales datos. En estos casos, la cantidad que faltaba nunca era superior al 5% del efectivo total. La identificación de estas estimaciones se ve facilitada con la introducción de un asterisco que figura delante del número de repetidores.

El método de estimación utilizado toma en consideración todas las informaciones disponibles. Por ejemplo, la proporción de los repetidores en las escuelas privadas para los años anteriores se ha utilizado, cuando se dispone de tales datos. Si no se dispone de otra información, los datos relativos a los repetidores se ajustan de acuerdo con la importancia de los efectivos de la enseñanza privada.

AFRICA:

Libyan Arab Jamahiriya:

E--> For 1975, data refer to public education only.

FR-> Pour 1975, les données se réfèrent à l'enseignement public seulement.

ESP> En 1975, los datos se refieren a la enseñanza pública solamente.

Madagascar:

E--> Data refer to public education only.

FR-> Les données se réfèrent à l'enseignement public seulement.

ESP> Los datos se refieren a la enseñanza pública solamente.

Morocco:

E--> For 1980, data include vocational education.

FR-> Pour 1980, les données incluent l'enseignement technique.

ESP> Para 1980, los datos incluyen la enseñanza técnica.

Reunion:

E--> For 1975, data include teacher training.

FR-> Pour 1975, les données incluent l'enseignement normal.

ESP> En 1975, los datos incluyen la enseñanza normal.

Seychelles:

E--> A policy of automatic promotion is practised in second level education.

FR-> Une politique de promotion automatique est appliquée pour l'enseignement du second degré.

ESP> Se aplica una política de promoción automática para la enseñanza de segundo grado.

Tunisia:

E--> For 1975 and 1980, data refer to public education only.

FR-> Pour 1975 et 1980, les données se réfèrent à l'enseignement public seulement.

ESP> Para 1975 y 1980, los datos se refieren a la enseñanza pública solamente.

Uganda:

E--> Data refer to public and aided schools only.

FR-> Les données se réfèrent aux écoles publiques et subventionnées seulement.

ESP> Datos relativos a las escuelas públicas y subvencionadas

Uganda: (Cont):
solamente.

AMERICA, NORTH:

Guatemala:

E--> For 1975, data refer to all second level education. For 1979 and 1980, figures include data *por cooperativa* which refer mainly to evening classes.

FR-> Pour 1975, les données se réfèrent à l'ensemble de l'enseignement du second degré. Pour 1979 et 1980, les chiffres incluent les données de l'enseignement 'por cooperativa' qui se réfèrent surtout aux cours du soir.

ESP> En 1975, los datos se refieren al total de la enseñanza de segundo grado. En 1979 y 1980 las cifras incluyen los datos de la educación 'por cooperativa' que se refieren principalmente a los cursos nocturnos.

Jamaica:

E--> Data refer to public education only.

FR-> Les données se réfèrent à l'enseignement public seulement.

ESP> Los datos se refieren a la enseñanza pública solamente.

Martinique:

E--> For 1976, data include teacher training.

FR-> Pour 1976, les données incluent l'ensei- gnement normal.

ESP> En 1976, los datos incluyen la enseñanza normal.

Panama:

E--> For 1975 and 1979, data refer to public education only and for 1983 and 1984, they refer to all second level.

FR-> Pour 1975 et 1979, les données se réfèrent à l'enseignement public seulement et pour 1983 et 1984, elles se réfèrent à l'ensemble de l'enseignement du second degré.

ESP> En 1975 y 1979, los datos se refieren a la enseñanza pública solamente y en 1983 y 1984, ellos se refieren al total de la enseñanza de segundo grado.

Trinidad and Tobago:

E--> Data refer to all second level education.

FR-> Les données se réfèrent à l'ensemble de l'enseignement du second degré.

ESP> Los datos se refieren al total de la enseñanza de segundo

Trinidad and Tobago: (Cont):
grado.
AMERICA, SOUTH:
Brazil:
E--> Data refer to all second level education.
FR-> Les données se réfèrent à l'ensemble de l'enseignement du second degré.
ESP> Los datos se refieren al total de la enseñanza de segundo grado.
Colombia:
E--> Data refer to all second level.
FR-> Les données se réfèrent à l'ensemble de l'enseignement du second degré.
ESP> Los datos se refieren al total de la enseñanza de segundo grado.
Ecuador:
E--> From 1980, data include vocational education.
FR-> A partir de 1980, les données incluent l'enseignement technique.
ESP> A partir de 1980, los datos incluyen la enseñanza técnica.
Venezuela:
E--> From 1980, data refer to all second level education.
FR-> A partir de 1980, les données se réfèrent à l'ensemble de l'enseignement du second degré.
ESP> A partir de 1980, los datos se refieren al total de la enseñanza de segundo grado.
ASIA:
Bahrain:
E--> Data refer to public education and do not include religious schools.
FR-> Les données se réfèrent à l'enseignement public et ne comprennent pas les écoles religieuses.
ESP> Los datos se refieren a la enseñanza pública y no comprenden las escuelas religiosas.
Cyprus:
E--> Not including Turkish schools.
FR-> Non compris les écoles turques.
ESP> Excluídas las escuelas turcas.
Indonesia:
E--> Data do not include religious schools.
FR-> Les données ne comprennent pas les écoles religieuses.
ESP> Los datos no incluyen las escuelas religiosas.
Iraq:
E--> For 1975 and 1979, data refer to failing pupils at the end of the school year.
FR-> Pour 1975 et 1979, les données se réfèrent aux élèves ayant échoué en fin d'année scolaire.
ESP> Para 1975 y 1979, los datos se refieren a los alumnos que no terminaron con éxito el fin del año escolar.
Japan:
E--> A policy of automatic promotion is practised in second level education.
FR-> Une politique de promotion automatique est appliquée pour l'enseignement du second degré.
ESP> Se aplica una política de promoción automática para la enseñanza de segundo grado.
Jordan:
E--> Including UNRWA schools.
FR-> Y compris les écoles de l'UNRWA.
ESP> Incluídas las escuelas del O.O.P.S.R.P.
Kuwait:
E--> Data for 1975 and 1980 refer to public education only.
FR-> Pour 1975 et 1980, les données se réfèrent à l'enseignement public seulement.
ESP> Para 1975 y 1980 los datos se refieren a la enseñanza pública solamente.
Qatar:
E--> Data refer to public education only.
FR-> Les données se réfèrent à l'enseignement public seulement.
Qatar: (Cont):
ESP> Los datos se refieren a la enseñanza pública solamente.
Sri Lanka:
E--> Data refer to public education only.
FR-> Les données se réfèrent à l'enseignement public seulement.
ESP> Los datos se refieren a la enseñanza pública solamente.
Syrian Arab Republic:
E--> Including UNRWA schools.
FR-> Y compris les écoles de l'UNRWA.
ESP> Incluídas las escuelas del O.O.P.S.R.P.
United Arab Emirates:
E--> Data refer to public education and do not include religious schools.
FR-> Les données se réfèrent à l'enseignement public et ne comprennent pas les écoles religieuses.
ESP> Los datos se refieren a la enseñanza pública y no incluyen las escuelas religiosas.
EUROPE:
Austria:
E--> Data include special education.
FR-> Y compris l'éducation spéciale.
ESP> Incluída la educación especial.
Belgium:
E--> Data include special education.
FR-> Les données comprennent l'éducation spéciale.
ESP> Los datos incluyen la educación especial.
Bulgaria:
E--> For 1975, data include evening and correspondence courses.
FR-> Pour 1975, les données comprennent les cours du soir et par correspondance.
ESP> Para 1975, los datos incluyen los cursos nocturnos y por correspondencia.
Greece:
E--> Data include evening schools which have a duration of 7 years.
FR-> Y compris les écoles du soir qui ont une durée de 7 ans.
ESP> Incluídas las escuelas nocturnas que tienen una duración de 7 años.
Luxembourg:
E--> Data for 1980 and 1981 do not include repeaters in the 'enseignement complémentaire'.
FR-> Les données pour 1980 et 1981 ne comprennent pas les redoublants de l'enseignement complémentaire.
ESP> Los datos para 1980 y 1981 no incluyen los repetidores de la 'enseignement complémentaire'.
OCEANIA:
Fiji:
E--> For 1977, the forms I and II are included in the first level of education.
FR-> Pour 1977, les 'forms' I et II sont incluses dans l'enseignement du premier degré.
ESP> Pour 1977, las 'forms' I y II quedan incluidas en la enseñanza de primer grado.
U.S.S.R.
Byelorussian S.S.R.:
E--> For 1975, figures refer to grades IX to XI. From 1980, figures refer to grades VI to XI.
FR-> Pour 1975, les chiffres incluent les classes de la neuvième à la onzième année d'études. A partir de 1980, les chiffres se réfèrent aux classes allant de la sixième à la onzième année d'études.
ESP> Para 1975, las cifras incluyen los años de estudios IX a XI. A partir de 1980, las cifras se refieren a los años de estudios VI a XI.
Ukrainian S.S.R.:
E--> For 1975, figures refer to grades IX to XI. From 1980, figures refer to grades VI to XI.
FR-> Pour 1975, les chiffres incluent les classes de la neuvième à la onzième année d'études. A partir de 1980, les chiffres se réfèrent aux classes allant de la sixième à la onzième année d'études.
ESP> Para 1975, las cifras incluyen los años de estudios IX a XI. A partir de 1980, las cifras se refieren a los años de estudios VI a XI.

3.10 Education at the third level: number of students per 100,000 inhabitants

Enseignement du troisième degré: nombre d'étudiants par 100 000 habitants

Enseñanza de tercer grado: número de estudiantes por 100 000 habitantes

Ø DATA FOR 1982 FOR COUNTRIES SHOWN WITH THIS SYMBOL ARE FOR 1981.

Ø LES DONNEES DE 1982 RELATIVES AUX PAYS ACCOMPAGNES DE CE SYMBOLE SE REFERENT A 1981.

Ø LOS DATOS DE 1982 RELATIVOS A LOS PAISES EN LOS QUE APARECE ESTO SIMBOLO SE REFIEREN A 1981.

NUMBER OF COUNTRIES AND TERRITORIES PRESENTED IN THIS TABLE: 139

NOMBRE DE PAYS ET DE TERRITOIRES PRESENTES DANS CE TABLEAU: 139

NUMERO DE PAISES Y DE TERRITORIOS PRESENTADOS EN ESTE CUADRO: 139

COUNTRY / PAYS / PAIS	SEX / SEXE / SEXO	NUMBER OF STUDENTS PER 100,000 INHABITANTS / NOMBRE D'ETUDIANTS PAR 100 000 HABITANTS / NUMERO DE ESTUDIANTES POR 100 000 HABITANTES				
		1975	1980	1982	1983	1984
AFRICA						
ALGERIA	MF	261	425	483	...	529
	M	...	630	653	...	700
	F	...	224	316	...	359
ANGOLA	MF	...	28	33	...	...
	M	...	...	...	...	...
	F	...	...	...	...	...
BENIN	MF	70	138	170	179	...
	M	121	...	290	298	...
	F	20	...	55	64	...
BOTSWANA	MF	62	101	134	140	166
	M	90	128	...	163	...
	F	38	78	...	119	...
BURKINA FASO	MF	19	27	48	51	57
	M	31	42	75	81	88
	F	8	11	21	23	26
BURUNDI	MF	27	46	...	54	...
	M	49	71	...	83	...
	F	6	22	...	26	...
CAMEROON‡	MF	113	136	148	167	185
	M	197	...	...	...	...
	F	33	...	...	...	...
CENTRAL AFRICAN REPUBLIC	MF	33	75	90	98	...
	M	61	142	175	183	...
	F	6	12	10	19	...
CHAD	MF	14	...	...	...	34
	M	26	...	...	...	62
	F	1	...	...	...	6
CONGO Ø	MF	241	475	552	...	...
	M	441	821	972	...	...
	F	47	139	145	...	...
COTE D'IVOIRE‡ Ø	MF	106	240	213	207	...
	M	170	385	...	...	...
	F	37	87	...	...	...
EGYPT‡	MF	1 323	1 724	1 895	1 957	...
	M	1 821	2 327	2 515	2 606	...
	F	808	1 103	1 256	1 287	...
EQUATORIAL GUINEA Ø	MF	–	324	...	...	...
	M	–	597	...	...	...
	F	–	62	...	...	...
ETHIOPIA	MF	...	37	40	39	...
	M	...	...	70	69	...
	F	...	...	10	8	...

COUNTRY PAYS PAIS	SEX SEXE SEXO	NUMBER OF STUDENTS PER 100,000 INHABITANTS NOMBRE D'ETUDIANTS PAR 100 000 HABITANTS NUMERO DE ESTUDIANTES POR 100 000 HABITANTES				
		1975	1980	1982	1983	1984
GABON	MF	101	...	273	290	...
	M	164	...	414	430	...
	F	41	...	137	154	...
GHANA Ø	MF	93	...	133	...	152
	M	158	...	212	...	240
	F	29	...	55	...	66
GUINEA	MF	256	338	233	212	180
	M	423	553	369	...	271
	F	91	128	101	...	91
KENYA‡ Ø	MF	66	77	74	75	...
	M	...	126	120	122	...
	F	...	30	28	29	...
LESOTHO	MF	46	141	162	160	155
	M	55	...	120	122	118
	F	37	...	200	195	191
LIBERIA‡	MF	152	203	...	...	...
	M	238	295	...	...	...
	F	67	111	...	...	...
LIBYAN ARAB JAMAHIRIYA	MF	553	678	859	...	...
	M	860	958	1 213	...	...
	F	207	364	463	...	...
MADAGASCAR	MF	110	260	354	361	388
	M	108	...	...	...	...
	F	113	...	...	...	...
MALAWI	MF	43	58	58	59	58
	M	76	83	86	87	86
	F	12	35	31	32	31
MALI‡	MF	47	23	78	...	...
	M	87	43	142	...	...
	F	9	5	18	...	...
MAURITIUS	MF	126	109	93	69	77
	M	221	153	141	99	113
	F	34	65	47	41	41
MOROCCO	MF	262	580	558	631	723
	M	426	892	827	910	1 044
	F	97	268	288	350	402
MOZAMBIQUE‡	MF	...	8	9	...	11
	M	...	12	...	...	17
	F	...	5	...	...	5
NIGER	MF	12	27	38	42	48
	M	21	44	64	67	79
	F	2	11	12	18	18
NIGERIA Ø	MF	66	186	206	204	...
	M	114	...	...	...	...
	F	20	...	...	...	...
RWANDA	MF	25	24	29	30	...
	M	...	44	52	53	...
	F	...	5	7	8	...
SENEGAL Ø	MF	172	239	210	193	...
	M	287	394	345	309	...
	F	59	88	78	79	...
SIERRA LEONE	MF	54	55	...	...	...
	M	92	...	...	...	...
	F	17	...	...	...	...
SOMALIA‡	MF	63	72	...	...	...
	M	114	130	...	...	...
	F	13	16	...	...	...
SUDAN	MF	133	154	177	175	...
	M	224	224	233	224	...
	F	43	84	121	126	...
SWAZILAND‡	MF	210	336	287	278	...
	M	288	412	346	335	...
	F	134	261	229	223	...
TOGO	MF	104	186	149	152	156
	M	183	322	260	260	267
	F	28	54	42	47	48
TUNISIA	MF	365	498	511	520	559
	M	536	696	681	677	711
	F	191	297	338	361	405

3.10 Third level: number of students per 100,000 inhabitants
Troisième degré: nombre d'étudiants par 100 000 habitants
Tercer grado: número de estudiantes por 100 000 habitantes

COUNTRY / PAYS / PAIS	SEX / SEXE / SEXO	NUMBER OF STUDENTS PER 100,000 INHABITANTS / NOMBRE D'ETUDIANTS PAR 100 000 HABITANTS / NUMERO DE ESTUDIANTES POR 100 000 HABITANTES 1975	1980	1982	1983	1984
UGANDA	MF	49	45	52	...	...
	M	81	70	77	...	...
	F	18	20	28	...	...
UNITED REPUBLIC OF TANZANIA‡	MF	19	...	31	31	29
	M	34	...	52	51	49
	F	5	...	11	11	10
ZAIRE	MF	111	110	115	...	...
	M	...	...	...	...	...
	F	...	...	...	...	...
ZAMBIA	MF	174	133	134	141	...
	M	301	...	210	...	...
	F	48	...	58	...	...
ZIMBABWE	MF	136	113	189	219	224
	M	...	...	222	257	264
	F	...	...	156	181	185
AMERICA, NORTH						
BARBADOS Ø	MF	938	1 620	1 955	2 028	2 065
	M	...	1 579	...	2 262	2 213
	F	...	1 656	...	1 815	1 931
CANADA‡	MF	3 600	3 688	4 016	4 203	...
	M	3 980	3 708	3 978	4 156	...
	F	3 222	3 668	4 054	4 249	...
COSTA RICA‡	MF	1 691	2 440	2 454	2 389	2 381
	M	...	...	...	...	...
	F	...	...	...	...	...
CUBA	MF	886	1 559	1 751	1 939	2 123
	M	...	1 578	1 638	1 800	1 929
	F	...	1 539	1 870	2 084	2 324
DOMINICAN REPUBLIC	MF	900	...	...	...	...
	M	999	...	...	...	...
	F	798	...	...	...	...
EL SALVADOR‡	MF	683	351	923	1 095	...
	M	903	483	1 133	1 244	...
	F	460	218	711	944	...
GUATEMALA‡	MF	380	736	647	...	...
	M	577	...	...	...	...
	F	178	...	...	...	...
HAITI	MF	56	80	87	100	...
	M	86	114	...	135	...
	F	26	48	...	67	...
HONDURAS	MF	385	700	842	843	798
	M	506	869	963	964	...
	F	263	529	720	721	...
JAMAICA	MF	470	644	668	...	...
	M	...	...	...	...	...
	F	...	...	...	...	...
MEXICO	MF	934	1 294	1 382	1 425	...
	M	...	1 729	1 778	1 822	...
	F	...	857	985	1 028	...
NICARAGUA‡	MF	759	1 273	1 201	1 036	916
	M	1 002	...	1 316	1 086	799
	F	517	...	1 085	986	1 033
PANAMA	MF	1 504	2 063	2 201	2 130	2 444
	M	1 482	1 821	1 943	1 728	2 109
	F	1 528	2 316	2 469	2 549	2 793
PUERTO RICO	MF	3 256	...	...	...	...
	M	3 096	...	...	...	...
	F	3 410	...	...	...	...
TRINIDAD AND TOBAGO‡	MF	490	516	483	...	...
	M	593	597	553	...	...
	F	383	435	413	...	...
UNITED STATES	MF	5 179	5 313	5 350	5 292	5 281
	M	5 836	5 299	5 315	...	...
	F	4 553	5 325	5 384	...	...
AMERICA, SOUTH						
ARGENTINA	MF	2 291	1 741	1 890	1 962	2 253
	M	2 406	1 736	1 783	1 829	2 121
	F	2 175	1 745	1 995	2 093	2 383

COUNTRY / PAYS / PAIS	SEX / SEXE / SEXO	NUMBER OF STUDENTS PER 100,000 INHABITANTS / NOMBRE D'ETUDIANTS PAR 100 000 HABITANTS / NUMERO DE ESTUDIANTES POR 100 000 HABITANTES				
		1975	1980	1982	1983	1984
BOLIVIA‡	MF	1 019	1 436	1 429	...	...
	M	...	...	...	...	...
	F	...	...	...	...	...
BRAZIL	MF	1 009	1 162	1 132	1 140	...
	M	...	1 202	...	1 141	...
	F	...	1 121	...	1 140	...
CHILE‡	MF	1 448	1 308	1 550	1 614	1 660
	M	1 605	1 501	1 804	1 866	...
	F	1 292	1 118	1 300	1 367	...
COLOMBIA‡	MF	760	1 053	1 320	1 375	1 384
	M	967	1 165	...	1 432	...
	F	553	941	...	1 318	...
ECUADOR‡	MF	2 419	3 321	3 019	3 047	3 072
	M	...	4 137	...	3 815	...
	F	...	2 496	...	2 270	...
GUYANA	MF	365	285	227	230	...
	M	473	321	267	239	...
	F	258	249	188	221	...
PARAGUAY	MF	681	850	897	986	929
	M	...	...	...	...	...
	F	...	...	...	...	...
PERU	MF	1 290	1 771	2 001	...	...
	M	1 738	2 276	2 556	...	...
	F	836	1 258	1 439	...	...
SURINAME	MF	413	669	817	813	783
	M	578	...	...	...	769
	F	248	...	...	...	796
URUGUAY‡	MF	1 153	1 248	1 698	2 143	2 588
	M	1 307	1 189	1 494	...	...
	F	1 003	1 306	1 896	...	...
VENEZUELA	MF	1 686	2 044	2 199	2 351	2 267
	M	...	...	...	...	...
	F	...	...	...	...	...
ASIA						
AFGHANISTAN	MF	80	...	121	...	...
	M	134	...	...	...	...
	F	22	...	...	...	...
BAHRAIN	MF	259	550	939	1 023	1 031
	M	223	555	740	789	772
	F	301	542	1 216	1 349	1 397
BANGLADESH‡	MF	207	272	319	403	443
	M	351	455	488	638	706
	F	54	78	140	153	164
BHUTAN	MF	–	25	...	...	...
	M	–	38	...	...	...
	F	–	11	...	...	...
BURMA Ø	MF	184	...	470	...	...
	M	...	...	...	...	...
	F	...	...	...	...	...
CHINA‡	MF	54	117	115	119	138
	M	71	174	164	170	192
	F	36	56	62	66	80
CYPRUS	MF	99	308	280	338	391
	M	119	361	316	372	435
	F	79	256	244	303	347
DEMOCRATIC YEMEN Ø	MF	76	177	185	...	...
	M	121	173	179	...	...
	F	33	181	191	...	...
EAST TIMOR	MF	...	...	...	...	...
	M	...	...	...	...	...
	F	...	...	...	...	...
HONG KONG‡	MF	1 012	1 201	1 360	1 394	1 410
	M	1 480	1 636	1 735	1 746	1 759
	F	521	727	947	1 005	1 025
INDIA‡	MF	744	776	...	...	...
	M	1 103	1 107	...	...	...
	F	358	420	...	...	...

3.10 **Third level: number of students per 100,000 inhabitants**
Troisième degré: nombre d'étudiants par 100 000 habitants
Tercer grado: número de estudiantes por 100 000 habitantes

COUNTRY PAYS PAIS	SEX SEXE SEXO	NUMBER OF STUDENTS PER 100,000 INHABITANTS NOMBRE D'ETUDIANTS PAR 100 000 HABITANTS NUMERO DE ESTUDIANTES POR 100 000 HABITANTES				
		1975	1980	1982	1983	1984
INDONESIA	MF	205	...	392	518	600
	M	...	...	535	717	816
	F	...	...	250	321	385
IRAN, ISLAMIC REPUBLIC OF‡	MF	456	–	331	359	409
	M	647	–	458	494	566
	F	260	–	201	219	245
IRAQ	MF	781	803	860	856	...
	M	1 033	1 077	1 153	1 139	...
	F	522	519	556	563	...
ISRAEL‡	MF	2 462	2 504	2 741	2 755	2 769
	M	2 641	2 445	2 950	2 928	2 943
	F	2 283	2 562	2 534	2 584	2 596
JAPAN‡	MF	2 017	2 065	2 024	2 026	2 006
	M	2 773	2 820	2 743	2 728	2 675
	F	1 284	1 333	1 329	1 345	1 357
JORDAN	MF	457	1 250	1 569	1 722	...
	M	594	1 313	1 763	1 906	...
	F	313	1 183	1 362	1 526	...
KOREA, REPUBLIC OF	MF	842	1 614	2 417	2 682	2 930
	M	1 215	2 427	3 552	3 848	4 147
	F	464	785	1 258	1 493	1 691
KUWAIT	MF	804	991	1 183	1 196	1 287
	M	635	739	908	958	1 045
	F	1 009	1 330	1 552	1 518	1 619
LAO PEOPLE'S DEMOCRATIC REP.‡	MF	...	38	102	122	...
	M	...	52	139	...	...
	F	...	24	64	...	...
LEBANON	MF	...	2 962	2 715	...	...
	M	...	3 854	3 483	...	...
	F	...	2 101	1 981	...	...
MALAYSIA	MF	266	419	474	524	614
	M	375	512	521	594	677
	F	154	325	427	453	550
MONGOLIA Ø	MF	683	...	2 173	...	...
	M	666	...	1 612	...	...
	F	699	...	2 735	...	...
NEPAL‡	MF	181	262	403	406	...
	M	...	415	...	639	...
	F	...	103	...	162	...
OMAN	MF	...	...	...	...	...
	M	...	...	...	...	...
	F	...	...	...	...	...
PAKISTAN‡	MF	171	182	...	...	...
	M	253	256	...	...	...
	F	84	101	...	...	...
PHILIPPINES	MF	1 808	2 641	2 781	...	...
	M	...	2 455	...	...	...
	F	...	2 828	...	...	...
QATAR	MF	455	1 011	1 596	1 712	1 588
	M	290	606	1 103	1 317	973
	F	787	1 717	2 443	2 396	2 662
SAUDI ARABIA	MF	364	662	811	830	...
	M	555	882	1 022	992	...
	F	154	403	563	639	...
SINGAPORE	MF	999	963	1 252	1 406	...
	M	1 183	1 150	1 464	1 601	...
	F	807	768	1 031	1 203	...
SRI LANKA‡	MF	113	288	373	405	...
	M	141	320	...	447	...
	F	84	255	...	363	...
SYRIAN ARAB REPUBLIC	MF	990	1 535	1 496	1 568	...
	M	1 449	2 113	1 994	2 077	...
	F	512	932	979	1 041	...
THAILAND‡	MF	316	1 290	2 178	2 264	...
	M	379	...	...	...	...
	F	253	...	...	...	...
TURKEY‡	MF	817	554	607	707	863
	M	1 348	805	822	909	1 149
	F	269	286	378	491	560

COUNTRY / PAYS / PAIS	SEX / SEXE / SEXO	NUMBER OF STUDENTS PER 100,000 INHABITANTS / NOMBRE D'ETUDIANTS PAR 100 000 HABITANTS / NUMERO DE ESTUDIANTES POR 100 000 HABITANTES				
		1975	1980	1982	1983	1984
UNITED ARAB EMIRATES	MF	–	279	411	511	557
	M	–	211	289	367	343
	F	–	431	671	821	1 016
VIET-NAM‡	MF	167	212	...	...	...
	M	208	333	...	...	...
	F	129	97	...	...	...
YEMEN	MF	46	76	...	...	...
	M	86	142	...	...	...
	F	9	16	...	...	...
EUROPE						
ALBANIA‡	MF	...	533	612	673	713
	M	...	531	632	712	774
	F	...	536	592	633	650
AUSTRIA	MF	1 286	1 822	1 951	2 056	2 205
	M	1 699	2 233	2 308	2 412	2 557
	F	919	1 454	1 628	1 733	1 885
BELGIUM‡	MF	1 735	2 111	2 226	2 283	2 486
	M	2 085	2 451	2 491	2 524	2 780
	F	1 400	1 787	1 973	2 052	2 205
BULGARIA‡	MF	1 474	1 144	1 073	1 100	1 158
	M	1 258	1 006	1 012	1 027	1 076
	F	1 690	1 281	1 133	1 172	1 238
CZECHOSLOVAKIA	MF	1 048	1 287	1 252	1 177	1 129
	M	1 283	1 542	1 472	1 376	1 327
	F	824	1 044	1 043	988	939
DENMARK‡	MF	2 179	2 074	2 162	2 209	...
	M	2 452	2 148	2 239	2 273	...
	F	1 912	2 001	2 088	2 148	...
FINLAND	MF	2 425	2 577	2 653	2 482	2 459
	M	2 646	2 761	2 785	2 683	...
	F	2 218	2 404	2 530	2 293	...
FRANCE	MF	1 971	2 005	2 186	2 114	...
	M	2 101	2 207	2 266	...	...
	F	1 845	1 810	2 108	...	...
GERMAN DEMOCRATIC REPUBLIC‡	MF	2 291	2 395	2 412	2 599	2 582
	M	2 160	2 147	2 122	2 454	2 454
	F	2 404	2 613	2 672	2 730	2 698
GERMANY, FEDERAL REPUBLIC OF	MF	1 684	1 987	2 293	2 409	2 465
	M	2 168	2 447	2 777	2 929	2 993
	F	1 241	1 566	1 848	1 930	1 979
GREECE Ø	MF	1 296	1 256	1 281	...	...
	M	1 667	1 498	1 491	...	...
	F	940	1 023	1 078	...	...
HUNGARY‡	MF	1 020	944	941	935	936
	M	1 087	980	942	913	910
	F	957	911	941	956	961
ICELAND	MF	1 363	2 287	2 158	2 199	2 136
	M	1 690	2 735	2 110	2 105	...
	F	1 023	1 831	2 208	2 295	...
IRELAND	MF	1 440	1 610	1 838	...	...
	M	1 889	1 901	2 149	...	...
	F	990	1 316	1 524	...	...
ITALY	MF	1 749	1 959	1 910	1 960	2 065
	M	2 184	2 302	2 187	2 225	2 314
	F	1 333	1 630	1 646	1 706	1 827
LUXEMBOURG‡	MF	133	205	259	270	...
	M	155	271	360	355	...
	F	112	142	162	190	...
MALTA	MF	413	257	271	356	372
	M	626	406	444	556	544
	F	221	120	112	172	214
NETHERLANDS‡	MF	2 088	2 544	2 653	2 675	2 737
	M	2 831	3 090	3 103	3 122	3 195
	F	1 355	2 007	2 209	2 234	2 285
NORWAY	MF	1 663	1 936	2 155	2 217	...
	M	2 087	2 039	2 228	2 265	...
	F	1 244	1 836	2 084	2 170	...

3.10 Third level: number of students per 100,000 inhabitants
Troisième degré: nombre d'étudiants par 100 000 habitants
Tercer grado: número de estudiantes por 100 000 habitantes

COUNTRY / PAYS / PAIS	SEX / SEXE / SEXO	NUMBER OF STUDENTS PER 100,000 INHABITANTS / NOMBRE D'ETUDIANTS PAR 100 000 HABITANTS / NUMERO DE ESTUDIANTES POR 100 000 HABITANTES				
		1975	1980	1982	1983	1984
POLAND‡	MF	1 692	1 656	1 372	1 305	1 241
	M	1 593	1 504	1 263	1 197	1 133
	F	1 785	1 800	1 477	1 408	1 344
PORTUGAL	MF	846	932	989	...	...
	M	984	1 016	1 038	...	...
	F	722	857	946	...	...
ROMANIA‡	MF	775	868	806	769	729
	M	869	1 010	939	884	832
	F	683	730	675	656	628
SPAIN‡	MF	1 518	1 819	1 930	2 067	...
	M	1 985	2 079	2 092	2 180	...
	F	1 073	1 569	1 774	1 958	...
SWEDEN	MF	1 985	2 451	2 602	2 682	2 651
	M	2 381	...	...	2 902	...
	F	1 594	...	...	2 467	...
SWITZERLAND	MF	1 010	1 346	1 428	1 506	1 664
	M	1 457	1 928	1 985	2 078	2 326
	F	585	793	899	962	1 035
UNITED KINGDOM‡	MF	1 308	1 478	1 562	1 600	...
	M	1 716	1 924	1 972	2 000	...
	F	920	1 056	1 171	1 219	...
YUGOSLAVIA	MF	1 850	1 848	1 715	1 650	...
	M	2 260	2 045	1 897	1 841	...
	F	1 453	1 655	1 538	1 464	...
OCEANIA						
AUSTRALIA	MF	2 016	2 203	2 239	2 283	2 313
	M	2 386	2 413	2 438	2 458	2 477
	F	1 644	1 993	2 041	2 108	2 150
FIJI‡	MF	287	288	351	...	...
	M	403	...	...	...	...
	F	168	...	...	...	...
NEW ZEALAND	MF	2 143	2 419	2 559	2 599	...
	M	2 718	2 889	3 031	3 053	...
	F	1 566	1 953	2 091	2 150	...
PAPUA NEW GUINEA	MF	217	163	138	145	177
	M	302	243	206	215	262
	F	124	76	64	69	84
U.S.S.R.						
U.S.S.R.‡	MF	1 916	1 972	1 970	1 946	1 918
	M	2 045	...	...	...	...
	F	1 803	...	...	...	...

This table shows the number of students enrolled at the third level of education per 100,000 inhabitants. The ratios are provided for the years 1975, 1980, 1982, 1983, and 1984 and have been calculated using the enrolment data shown in Table 3.11 and the population figures provided by the Populat Division of the United Nations. When data in Table 3.11 incomplete, estimates have been used in order to maintain comparability of the ratios presented for different years.

Ce tableau présente le nombre d'étudiants inscrits dans l'enseignement du troisième degré par 100,000 habitants. Les taux se réfèrent aux années 1975, 1980, 1982, 1983, et 1984 et ont été calculés en utilisant les effectifs indiqués dans le tableau 3.11 et les chiffres de population fournis par la Division de la Population des Nations Unies. Lorsque les données tableau 3.11 sont imcomplètes, des estimations ont été utilis afin de maintenir la comparabilité des taux présentés pour différentes années.

Este cuadro presenta el número de estudiantes inscritos en la enseñanza de tercer grado por 100 000 habitantes. Las tasas se facilitan para los años 1975, 1980, 1982, 1983 y 1984 y han sido calculadas utilizando los efectivos que figuran en el cuadro 3.11 y las cifras de población que nos han sido comunicadas por la División de la Población de las Nacio Unidas. Cuando los datos en el cuadro 3.11 son incompletos han utilizado estimaciones a fin de mantener la comparabilidac las tasas presentadas para los diferentes años.

General note/Note générale/Nota general:

E--> Please see the notes to Table 3.11 for countries marked with a footnote indicator.

FR-> Voir les notes du tableau 3.11 pour les pays signalés avec un appel de note.

ESP> Véase las notas del cuadro 3.11 para los países en los que figura una indicación de nota. AFRICA:

Liberia:

E--> Data for 1980 refer to 1979.

FR-> Les données de 1980 se réfèrent à 1979.

ESP> Los datos de 1980 se refieren a 1979.

Mozambique:

E--> Data for 1984 refer to 1985.

FR-> Les données de 1984 se réfèrent à 1985.

ESP> Los datos de 1984 se refieren a 1985.

Somalia:

E--> Data for 1980 refer to 1979.

FR-> Les données de 1980 se réfèrent à 1979.

ESP> Los datos de 1980 se refieren a 1979.

AMERICA, NORTH:

Nicaragua:

E--> Data for 1982, 1983 and 1984 refer respectively to 1983, 1984 and 1985.

FR-> Les données de 1982, 1983, et 1984 se réfèrent respectivement à 1983, 1984 et 1985.

ESP> Los datos de 1982, 1983 y 1984 se refieren respectivamente a 1983, 1984 y 1985.

AMERICA, SOUTH:

Chile:

E--> Data for 1982, 1983 and 1984 refer respectively to 1983, 1984 and 1985.

Chile: (Cont):

FR-> Les données de 1982, 1983 et 1984 se réfèrent respectivement à 1983, 1984 et 1985.

ESP> Los datos de 1982, 1983 y 1984 se refieren respectivamente a 1983, 1984 y 1985.

Colombia:

E--> Data for 1982, 1983 and 1984 refer respectively to 1983, 1984 and 1985.

FR-> Les données de 1982, 1983 et 1984 se réfèrent respectivement à 1983, 1984 et 1985.

ESP> Los datos de 1982, 1983 y 1984 se refieren respectivamente a 1983, 1984 y 1985.

Uruguay:

E--> Data for 1982, 1983 and 1984 refer respectively to 1983, 1984 and 1985.

FR-> Les données de 1982, 1983 et 1984 se réfèrent respectivement à 1983, 1984 et 1985.

ESP> Los datos de 1982, 1983 y 1984 se refieren respectivamente a 1983, 1984 y 1985.

ASIA:

Bangladesh:

E--> Data for 1975 refer to 1976.

FR-> Les données de 1975 se réfèrent à 1976.

ESP> Los datos de 1975 se refieren a 1976.

India:

E--> Data for 1980 refer to 1979.

FR-> Les données de 1980 se réfèrent à 1979.

ESP> Los datos de 1980 se refieren a 1979.

Israel:

E--> Data for 1975 refer to 1976.

FR-> Les données de 1975 se réfèrent à 1976.

ESP> Los datos de 1975 se refieren a 1976.

3.11 Education at the third level: teachers and students by type of institution

Enseignement du troisième degré: personnel enseignant et étudiants par type d'établissement

Enseñanza de tercer grado: personal docente y estudiantes por tipo de establecimiento

ALL INSTITUTIONS = TOTAL DES ETABLISSEMENTS = TODOS LOS ESTABLECIMIENTOS
UNIVERSITIES AND EQ. INSTS. = UNIVERSITES ET ETAB. EQUIV. = UNIVERSIDADES Y ESTAB. EQUIV.
OTHER THIRD LEVEL INSTS. = AUTRES ETAB. DU TROISIEME DEGRE = OTROS ESTAB. DE TERCER GRADO

PLEASE REFER TO EXPLANATORY TEXT AT END OF TABLE

PRIERE DE SE REFERER AU TEXTE EXPLICATIF A LA FIN DU TABLEAU

REFERIRSE AL TEXTO EXPLICATIVO AL FINAL DEL CUADRO

NUMBER OF COUNTRIES AND TERRITORIES PRESENTED IN THIS TABLE: 160

NOMBRE DE PAYS ET DE TERRITOIRES PRESENTES DANS CE TABLEAU: 160

NUMERO DE PAISES Y DE TERRITORIOS PRESENTADOS EN ESTE CUADRO: 160

COUNTRY / PAYS / PAIS	TYPE OF INSTITUTION / TYPE D'ETABLISSEMENT / TIPO DE ESTABLECIMIENTO	YEAR / ANNEE / AÑO	TEACHING STAFF / PERSONNEL ENSEIGNANT / PERSONAL DOCENTE			STUDENTS ENROLLED / ETUDIANTS INSCRITS / ESTUDIANTES MATRICULADOS		
			TOTAL	FEMALE FEMININ FEMENINO	% F	TOTAL	FEMALE FEMININ FEMENINO	% F
			(1)	(2)	(3)	(4)	(5)	(6)
AFRICA								
ALGERIA‡	ALL INSTITUTIONS	1975	...	...	...	41 847	...	...
		1980	8 962	...	...	79 351	21 014	26
		1981	9 778	...	...	78 027	23 561	30
		1982	11 601	...	...	95 867	31 489	33
		1984	...	...	...	111 507	35 627	32
	UNIVERSITIES & EQ. INSTS.	1975	...	...	...	41 847	...	...
		1980	8 962	...	...	79 351	21 014	26
		1981	9 778	...	...	78 027	23 561	30
		1982	11 601	...	...	95 867	31 489	33
		1984	...	...	...	111 507	35 627	32
ANGOLA	ALL INSTITUTIONS	1980	225	...	...	2 183	...	...
		1981	374	...	...	2 666	*430	*16
		1982	316	...	...	2 674	...	...
	UNIVERSITIES & EQ. INSTS.	1980	225	...	...	2 183	...	...
		1981	374	...	...	2 666	*430	*16
		1982	316	...	...	2 674	...	...
BENIN	ALL INSTITUTIONS	1975	153	...	...	2 118	315	15
		1980	...	...	...	4 822	...	...
		1981	803	...	...	5 680	1 063	19
		1982	...	...	...	6 302	1 035	16
		1983	...	...	...	6 818	1 249	18
	UNIVERSITIES & EQ. INSTS.	1975	148	...	...	2 102	314	15
		1981	607	...	...	4 931	906	18
		1982	...	...	...	5 445	883	16
		1983	...	...	...	6 013	1 106	18
	OTHER THIRD LEVEL INSTS.	1975	5	...	...	16	1	6
		1981	196	...	...	749	157	21
		1982	...	...	...	857	152	18
		1983	...	...	...	805	143	18
BOTSWANA	ALL INSTITUTIONS	1975	56	12	21	469	152	32
		1980	94	...	...	928	372	40
		1981	144	...	...	1 022	387	38
		1982	...	...	...	1 317	...	...
		1983	137	...	...	1 435	632	44
		1984	142	...	...	1 773	...	...
	UNIVERSITIES & EQ. INSTS.	1975	56	12	21	469	152	32
		1980	94	...	...	928	372	40
		1981	144	...	...	1 022	387	38
		1982	...	...	...	1 317	...	...
		1983	137	...	...	1 435	632	44
		1984	142	...	...	1 773	...	...

COUNTRY / PAYS / PAIS	TYPE OF INSTITUTION / TYPE D'ETABLISSEMENT / TIPO DE ESTABLECIMIENTO	YEAR / ANNEE / AÑO	TEACHING STAFF / PERSONNEL ENSEIGNANT / PERSONAL DOCENTE			STUDENTS ENROLLED / ETUDIANTS INSCRITS / ESTUDIANTES MATRICULADOS		
			TOTAL	FEMALE / FEMININ / FEMENINO	% F	TOTAL	FEMALE / FEMININ / FEMENINO	% F
			(1)	(2)	(3)	(4)	(5)	(6)
BURKINA FASO	ALL INSTITUTIONS	1975	166	22	13	1 067	212	20
		1980	140	...	...	1 643	354	22
		1982	289	40	14	3 086	688	22
		1983	333	...	...	3 406	757	22
		1984	...	...	...	3 845	882	23
	UNIVERSITIES & EQ. INSTS.	1975	166	22	13	1 067	212	20
		1980	140	...	...	1 643	354	22
		1982	289	40	14	3 086	688	22
		1983	333	...	...	3 406	757	22
		1984	...	...	...	3 845	882	23
BURUNDI	ALL INSTITUTIONS	1975	223	...	...	1 002	112	11
		1980	...	...	...	1 879	464	25
		1981	...	...	...	2 068	...	...
		1983	...	...	...	2 411	601	25
	UNIVERSITIES & EQ. INSTS.	1975	123	...	...	652	72	11
		1980	...	...	...	1 793	438	24
		1981	...	...	...	1 900	...	...
		1983	...	...	...	2 009	482	24
	OTHER THIRD LEVEL INSTS.	1975	100	...	...	350	40	11
		1980	...	...	...	86	26	30
		1981	...	...	...	168	57	34
		1983	...	...	...	402	119	30
CAMEROON‡	ALL INSTITUTIONS	1975	...	...	...	...	...	...
		1980	...	...	...	11 686	...	...
		1981	...	...	...	12 510	...	...
		1982	...	...	...	13 493	...	...
		1983	...	...	...	15 563	...	...
		1984	...	...	...	17 741	...	...
	UNIVERSITIES & EQ. INSTS.	1975	...	...	...	7 191	1 081	15
		1980	...	...	...	10 631	...	...
		1981	447	65	15	11 435	...	...
		1982	...	...	...	12 184	...	...
		1983	...	...	...	13 687	...	...
		1984	...	...	...	15 761	...	...
	OTHER THIRD LEVEL INSTS.	1980	...	...	...	1 055	...	...
		1981	...	...	...	1 075	...	...
		1982	...	...	...	1 309	...	...
		1983	...	...	...	1 876	...	...
		1984	...	...	...	1 980	...	...
CENTRAL AFRICAN REPUBLIC	ALL INSTITUTIONS	1975	...	...	...	669	...	...
		1980	444	68	15	1 719	143	8
		1981	412	50	12	2 549	269	11
		1982	380	51	13	2 162	128	6
		1983	376	60	16	2 413	240	10
	UNIVERSITIES & EQ. INSTS.	1975	85	20	24	555	31	6
		1980	379	63	17	1 394	119	9
		1981	239	37	15	1 904	230	12
		1982	272	44	16	1 704	99	6
		1983	322	55	17	1 889	167	9
	OTHER THIRD LEVEL INSTS.	1975	...	...	...	114	...	...
		1980	65	5	8	325	24	7
		1981	173	13	8	645	39	6
		1982	108	7	6	458	29	6
		1983	54	5	9	524	73	14
CHAD	ALL INSTITUTIONS	1975	...	...	...	547	29	5
		1976	62	7	11	758	40	5
		1984	141	11	8	1 643	142	9
	UNIVERSITIES & EQ. INSTS.	1975	...	...	...	547	29	5
		1976	62	7	11	758	40	5
		1984	104	5	5	1 470	139	9
	OTHER THIRD LEVEL INSTS.	1984	37	6	16	173	3	2
CONGO	ALL INSTITUTIONS	1975	165	25	15	3 249	321	10
		1980	292	27	9	7 255	1 079	15
		1981	354	37	10	8 886	1 182	13
	UNIVERSITIES & EQ. INSTS.	1975	165	25	15	3 249	321	10
		1980	292	27	9	7 255	1 079	15
		1981	354	37	10	8 886	1 182	13

3.11 Third level: teachers and students by type of institution
Troisième degré: professeurs et étudiants par type d'établissement
Tercer grado: profesores y estudiantes por tipo de establecimiento

COUNTRY / PAYS / PAIS	TYPE OF INSTITUTION / TYPE D'ETABLISSEMENT / TIPO DE ESTABLECIMIENTO	YEAR / ANNEE / AÑO	TEACHING STAFF / PERSONNEL ENSEIGNANT / PERSONAL DOCENTE			STUDENTS ENROLLED / ETUDIANTS INSCRITS / ESTUDIANTES MATRICULADOS		
			TOTAL	FEMALE / FEMININ / FEMENINO	% F	TOTAL	FEMALE / FEMININ / FEMENINO	% F
			(1)	(2)	(3)	(4)	(5)	(6)
COTE D'IVOIRE‡	ALL INSTITUTIONS	1975	...	...	...	7 174	1 218	17
		1980	...	...	...	19 633	...	...
		1981	1 204	...	...	18 732	...	...
		1983	...	...	...	18 872	...	...
	UNIVERSITIES & EQ. INSTS.	1975	...	...	...	6 274	1 123	18
		1980	625	...	...	12 742	2 376	19
		1981	666	...	...	12 541	...	...
		1983	...	...	...	12 859	2 519	20
	OTHER THIRD LEVEL INSTS.	1975	...	...	...	900	*95	*11
		1980	...	...	...	6 891	...	...
		1981	538	...	...	6 191	...	...
		1983	...	...	...	6 013	...	...
EGYPT‡	ALL INSTITUTIONS	1975	...	...	...	480 016	144 096	30
		1980	...	...	...	715 701	225 562	32
		1981	...	...	...	778 216	247 245	32
		1982	34 261	...	...	825 800	269 589	33
		1983	33 200	...	...	873 565	283 114	32
	UNIVERSITIES & EQ. INSTS.	1975	...	...	...	451 187	136 422	30
		1980	...	...	...	663 418	210 072	32
		1981	25 503	6 641	26	722 434	230 178	32
		1982	32 190	7 001	22	766 377	251 495	33
		1983	31 234	6 885	22	808 309	263 308	33
	OTHER THIRD LEVEL INSTS.	1975	...	...	...	28 829	7 674	27
		1980	...	...	...	52 283	15 490	30
		1981	...	...	...	55 782	17 067	31
		1982	2 071	...	...	59 423	18 094	30
		1983	1 966	...	...	65 256	19 806	30
EQUATORIAL GUINEA‡	ALL INSTITUTIONS	1981	68	...	...	1 140	112	10
ETHIOPIA	ALL INSTITUTIONS	1976	...	...	...	6 966	...	...
		1980	1 051	...	...	14 368	...	...
		1981	1 137	...	...	14 985	2 007	13
		1982	1 269	102	8	16 117	2 018	13
		1983	1 446	134	9	16 030	1 761	11
	UNIVERSITIES & EQ. INSTS.	1976	...	...	...	4 971	...	...
		1980	787	...	...	9 291	...	...
		1981	884	...	...	9 670	1 030	11
		1982	1 001	82	8	10 512	1 084	10
		1983	920	85	9	10 526	917	9
	OTHER THIRD LEVEL INSTS.	1976	...	...	...	1 995	...	...
		1980	264	...	...	5 077	...	...
		1981	253	...	...	5 315	957	18
		1982	268	20	7	5 605	934	17
		1983	526	49	9	5 504	844	15
GABON	ALL INSTITUTIONS	1975	...	...	...	1 014	207	20
		1979	...	...	...	1 663	371	22
		1982	594	80	13	2 992	766	26
		1983	616	83	13	3 228	873	27
	UNIVERSITIES & EQ. INSTS.	1975	...	...	...	651	148	23
		1979	...	...	...	1 663	371	22
		1982	345	46	13	2 118	600	28
		1983	359	47	13	2 059	604	29
	OTHER THIRD LEVEL INSTS.	1975	...	...	...	363	59	16
		1979	...	...	...	605	109	18
		1982	249	34	14	874	166	19
		1983	257	36	14	1 169	269	23
GHANA	ALL INSTITUTIONS	1975	1 103	...	...	9 079	1 439	16
		1979	...	...	...	...	...	...
		1981	...	...	...	16 350	3 398	21
		1984	...	...	...	...	...	...
	UNIVERSITIES & EQ. INSTS.	1975	963	...	...	7 179	919	13
		1979	...	...	...	9 745	1 232	13
		1981	1 091	105	10	7 981	1 389	17
		1984	...	...	...	7 649	1 309	17
	OTHER THIRD LEVEL INSTS.	1975	*140	...	...	*1 900	*520	*27
		1981	...	...	...	*8 369	*2 009	*24

COUNTRY / PAYS / PAIS	TYPE OF INSTITUTION / TYPE D'ETABLISSEMENT / TIPO DE ESTABLECIMIENTO	YEAR / ANNEE / AÑO	TEACHING STAFF / PERSONNEL ENSEIGNANT / PERSONAL DOCENTE: TOTAL	FEMALE / FEMININ / FEMENINO	% F	STUDENTS ENROLLED / ETUDIANTS INSCRITS / ESTUDIANTES MATRICULADOS: TOTAL	FEMALE / FEMININ / FEMENINO	% F
			(1)	(2)	(3)	(4)	(5)	(6)
GUINEA	ALL INSTITUTIONS	1975	...	...	...	12 411	2 237	18
		1980	1 289	40	3	18 270	3 497	19
		1981	...	...	...	13 161	2 839	22
		1982	1 373	52	4	13 182	2 883	22
		1983	...	...	...	12 304	...	...
		1984	1 925	65	3	10 664	2 737	26
	UNIVERSITIES & EQ. INSTS.	1980	577	31	5	5 319	726	14
		1981	556	19	3	3 573	571	16
		1982	614	23	4	3 750	833	22
		1984	636	20	3	4 379	816	19
	OTHER THIRD LEVEL INSTS.	1980	712	9	1	12 951	2 771	21
		1981	...	...	...	9 588	2 268	24
		1982	759	29	4	9 432	2 050	22
		1984	1 289	45	3	6 285	1 921	31
KENYA‡	ALL INSTITUTIONS	1975	...	...	...	...	...	...
		1980	...	...	...	12 986	...	...
		1981	...	...	...	13 398	...	...
		1983	...	...	...	22 157	...	...
	UNIVERSITIES & EQ. INSTS.	1975	...	...	...	6 327	...	...
		1980	...	...	...	9 155	2 302	25
		1981	...	...	...	9 312	2 243	24
		1983	1 183	...	...	9 223	2 653	29
	OTHER THIRD LEVEL INSTS.	1980	...	...	...	3 831	...	...
		1981	...	...	...	4 086	...	...
		1983	...	...	...	12 934	...	...
LESOTHO	ALL INSTITUTIONS	1975	83	...	...	543	229	42
		1980	192			1 889	...	...
		1981	221	...	...	2 095	1 340	64
		1982	217	...	...	2 275	1 460	64
		1983	282	...	...	2 308	1 458	63
		1984	247	...	...	2 303	1 461	63
	UNIVERSITIES & EQ. INSTS.	1975	73	...	...	502	212	42
		1980	137	...	...	995	...	...
		1981	149	...	...	1 091	502	46
		1982	160	...	...	1 139	535	47
		1983	212	...	...	1 350	711	53
		1984	170	...	...	1 170	539	46
	OTHER THIRD LEVEL INSTS.	1975	10	8	80	41	17	41
		1980	55	...	...	894	761	85
		1981	72	...	...	1 004	838	83
		1982	57	...	...	1 136	925	81
		1983	70	...	...	958	747	78
		1984	77	...	...	1 133	922	81
LIBERIA	ALL INSTITUTIONS	1975	...	...	...	2 404	536	22
		1979	...	...	...	3 789	1 050	28
	UNIVERSITIES & EQ. INSTS.	1975	...	...	...	2 404	536	22
		1979	...	...	...	3 702	1 050	28
	OTHER THIRD LEVEL INSTS.	1979	...	...	...	87	–	–
LIBYAN ARAB JAMAHIRIYA	ALL INSTITUTIONS	1975	951	...	...	13 427	2 358	18
		1980	...	...	...	20 166	5 096	25
		1981	...	...	...	23 767	6 076	26
		1982	...	...	...	27 535	7 010	25
	UNIVERSITIES & EQ. INSTS.	1975	951	...	...	13 427	2 358	18
		1980	...	...	...	20 166	5 096	25
		1981	...	...	...	23 767	6 076	26
		1982	...	...	...	27 535	7 010	25
MADAGASCAR	ALL INSTITUTIONS	1975	...	...	...	8 385	4 350	52
		1980	451	...	...	22 632	...	...
		1981	590	...	...	30 000	...	...
		1982	706	...	...	32 599	...	...
		1983	960	...	...	34 162	...	...
		1984	1 059	...	...	37 746	...	...
	UNIVERSITIES & EQ. INSTS.	1975	...	...	...	8 385	4 350	52
		1980	451	...	...	22 632	...	...
		1981	590	...	...	30 000	...	...
		1982	706	...	...	32 599	...	...
		1983	960	...	...	34 162	...	...
		1984	1 059	...	...	37 746	...	...

3.11 Third level: teachers and students by type of institution
Troisième degré: professeurs et étudiants par type d'établissement
Tercer grado: profesores y estudiantes por tipo de establecimiento

COUNTRY / PAYS / PAIS	TYPE OF INSTITUTION / TYPE D'ETABLISSEMENT / TIPO DE ESTABLECIMIENTO	YEAR / ANNEE / AÑO	TEACHING STAFF / PERSONNEL ENSEIGNANT / PERSONAL DOCENTE			STUDENTS ENROLLED / ETUDIANTS INSCRITS / ESTUDIANTES MATRICULADOS		
			TOTAL	FEMALE / FEMININ / FEMENINO	% F	TOTAL	FEMALE / FEMININ / FEMENINO	% F
			(1)	(2)	(3)	(4)	(5)	(6)
MALAWI	ALL INSTITUTIONS	1975	244	...	...	2 198	314	14
		1980	281	...	...	3 476	1 078	31
		1981	415	...	...	3 586	1 033	29
		1982	413	...	...	3 657	1 000	27
		1983	352	...	...	3 851	1 082	28
		1984	391	...	...	3 884	1 068	27
	UNIVERSITIES & EQ. INSTS.	1975	150	14	9	1 148	138	12
		1980	173	34	20	1 722	427	25
		1981	301	...	...	1 829	374	20
		1982	305	...	...	1 849	373	20
		1983	229	...	...	1 961	354	18
		1984	270	...	...	1 964	359	18
	OTHER THIRD LEVEL INSTS.	1975	94	...	...	1 050	176	17
		1980	108	...	...	1 754	651	37
		1981	114	...	...	1 757	659	38
		1982	108	...	...	1 808	653	36
		1983	123	...	...	1 890	728	39
		1984	121	...	...	1 920	709	37
MALI‡	ALL INSTITUTIONS	1975	...	...	...	2 936	302	10
		1980	321	...	...	1 631	184	11
		1981	475	...	...	4 498	495	11
		1982	499	...	...	5 792	708	12
	OTHER THIRD LEVEL INSTS.	1975	101	...	...	2 936	302	10
		1980	321	...	...	1 631	184	11
		1981	...	...	...	4 498	495	11
		1982	499	...	...	5 792	708	12
MAURITIUS	ALL INSTITUTIONS	1975	155	9	6	1 096	150	14
		1980	210	32	15	1 038	317	31
		1981	192	27	14	901	263	29
		1982	175	28	16	926	234	25
		1983	201	26	13	702	208	30
		1984	189	32	17	794	216	27
	UNIVERSITIES & EQ. INSTS.	1975	155	9	6	1 096	150	14
		1980	125	8	6	470	88	19
		1981	105	9	9	388	61	16
		1982	96	9	9	490	74	15
		1983	122	7	6	430	111	26
		1984	110	13	12	344	66	19
	OTHER THIRD LEVEL INSTS.	1980	85	24	28	568	229	40
		1981	87	18	21	513	202	39
		1982	79	19	24	436	160	37
		1983	79	19	24	272	97	36
		1984	79	19	24	450	150	33
MOROCCO‡	ALL INSTITUTIONS	1975	1 642	...	...	45 322	8 440	19
		1980	...	...	...	112 405	...	...
		1981	...	...	...	125 804	...	...
		1982	...	...	...	114 005	...	...
		1983	...	...	...	126 897	...	...
		1984	...	...	...	...	...	...
	UNIVERSITIES & EQ. INSTS.	1975	937	160	17	35 081	6 726	19
		1980	2 757	486	18	86 731	21 663	25
		1981	3 284	596	18	96 953	25 304	26
		1982	3 901	725	19	82 944	23 930	29
		1983	3 736	...	...	99 637	31 649	32
		1984	4 375	856	20	126 481	41 073	32
	OTHER THIRD LEVEL INSTS.	1975	705	...	...	10 241	1 714	17
		1980	...	...	...	25 674	...	...
		1981	...	...	...	28 851	...	...
		1982	...	...	...	31 061	...	...
		1983	...	...	...	27 260	...	...
MOZAMBIQUE‡	ALL INSTITUTIONS	1976	164	39	24	906	304	34
		1980	300	...	...	1 000	*212	*21
		1981	323	...	...	1 266	254	20
		1982	327	...	...	1 110	...	...
		1985	331	70	21	1 442	332	23
	UNIVERSITIES & EQ. INSTS.	1976	164	39	24	906	304	34
		1980	300	...	...	1 000	*212	*21
		1981	323	...	...	1 266	254	20
		1982	327	...	...	1 110	...	...
		1985	331	70	21	1 442	332	23

COUNTRY / PAYS / PAIS	TYPE OF INSTITUTION / TYPE D'ETABLISSEMENT / TIPO DE ESTABLECIMIENTO	YEAR / ANNEE / AÑO	TEACHING STAFF / PERSONNEL ENSEIGNANT / PERSONAL DOCENTE			STUDENTS ENROLLED / ETUDIANTS INSCRITS / ESTUDIANTES MATRICULADOS		
			TOTAL	FEMALE / FEMININ / FEMENINO	% F	TOTAL	FEMALE / FEMININ / FEMENINO	% F
			(1)	(2)	(3)	(4)	(5)	(6)
NIGER	ALL INSTITUTIONS	1975	74	11	15	541	56	10
		1980	224	29	13	1 435	285	20
		1981	289	35	12	1 853	325	18
		1982	267	33	12	2 118	339	16
		1983	322	46	14	2 450	526	21
		1984	314	33	11	2 863	526	18
	UNIVERSITIES & EQ. INSTS.	1975	74	11	15	541	56	10
		1980	224	29	13	1 435	285	20
		1981	289	35	12	1 853	325	18
		1982	267	33	12	2 118	339	16
		1983	322	46	14	2 450	526	21
		1984	314	33	11	2 863	526	18
NIGERIA	ALL INSTITUTIONS	1975	...	...	...	44 964	...	...
		1980	10 742	...	...	150 072	...	...
		1981	14 417	...	...	176 904	...	...
		1983	...	...	...	181 945	...	...
	UNIVERSITIES & EQ. INSTS.	1975	5 019	...	...	32 971	5 114	16
		1980	5 475	...	...	70 395	...	...
		1981	7 759	...	...	83 357	...	...
		1983	8 470	...	...	93 740	...	...
	OTHER THIRD LEVEL INSTS.	1975	...	...	...	11 993	...	...
		1980	5 267	...	...	79 677	...	...
		1981	6 658	...	...	93 547	...	...
		1983	...	...	...	88 205	...	...
RWANDA	ALL INSTITUTIONS	1975	175	...	...	1 108	...	...
		1980	240	21	9	1 243	122	10
		1981	...	...	...	...	...	...
		1982	...	...	...	...	...	...
		1983	305	16	5	1 705	229	13
	UNIVERSITIES & EQ. INSTS.	1975	89	...	...	672	...	...
		1980	126	11	9	920	101	11
		1981	290	23	8	1 212	141	12
		1982	...	...	...	1 317	191	15
		1983	229	15	7	1 367	221	16
	OTHER THIRD LEVEL INSTS.	1975	86	...	...	436	...	...
		1980	114	10	9	323	21	7
		1983	76	1	1	338	8	2
ST. HELENA	ALL INSTITUTIONS	1979	11	4	36	38	7	18
		1980	9	4	44	36	9	25
		1981	9	5	56	37	5	14
	OTHER THIRD LEVEL INSTS.	1979	11	4	36	38	7	18
		1980	9	4	44	36	9	25
		1981	9	5	56	37	5	14
SENEGAL	ALL INSTITUTIONS	1975	...	...	...	...	...	...
		1980	1 024	...	...	13 560	2 507	18
		1981	925	...	...	12 522	2 348	19
		1983	...	...	...	11 809	2 434	21
	UNIVERSITIES & EQ. INSTS.	1975	412	...	...	8 213	1 428	17
		1980	591	...	...	12 673	2 412	19
		1981	580	...	...	11 754	2 250	19
		1983	640	83	13	11 293	2 359	21
	OTHER THIRD LEVEL INSTS.	1980	433	...	...	887	95	11
		1981	345	...	...	768	98	13
		1983	...	...	...	516	75	15
SEYCHELLES‡	ALL INSTITUTIONS	1979	14	6	43	104	73	70
		1980	28	16	57	144	128	89
		1981	–	–	–	–	–	–
	OTHER THIRD LEVEL INSTS.	1979	14	6	43	104	73	70
		1980	28	16	57	144	128	89
		1981	–	–	–	–	–	–
SIERRA LEONE	ALL INSTITUTIONS	1975	289	38	13	1 642	266	16
		1980	270	...	...	1 809	...	...
	UNIVERSITIES & EQ. INSTS.	1975	289	38	13	1 642	266	16
		1980	270	...	...	1 809	...	...
SOMALIA	ALL INSTITUTIONS	1975	324	...	...	2 040	218	11
		1979	...	...	...	...	...	...

3.11 Third level: teachers and students by type of institution
Troisième degré: professeurs et étudiants par type d'établissement
Tercer grado: profesores y estudiantes por tipo de establecimiento

COUNTRY / PAYS / PAIS	TYPE OF INSTITUTION / TYPE D'ETABLISSEMENT / TIPO DE ESTABLECIMIENTO	YEAR / ANNEE / AÑO	TEACHING STAFF / PERSONNEL ENSEIGNANT / PERSONAL DOCENTE			STUDENTS ENROLLED / ETUDIANTS INSCRITS / ESTUDIANTES MATRICULADOS		
			TOTAL	FEMALE / FEMININ / FEMENINO	% F	TOTAL	FEMALE / FEMININ / FEMENINO	% F
			(1)	(2)	(3)	(4)	(5)	(6)
SOMALIA (CONT)	UNIVERSITIES & EQ. INSTS.	1975	286	...	...	1 936	192	10
		1979	...	...	...	2 899	...	...
	OTHER THIRD LEVEL INSTS.	1975	38	...	...	104	26	25
SUDAN	ALL INSTITUTIONS	1975	1 420	97	7	21 342	3 408	16
		1980	1 276	98	8	28 788	7 791	27
		1981	1 139	74	6	33 527	10 240	31
		1982	1 184	77	7	35 063	11 970	34
		1983	1 464	95	6	35 648	12 764	36
	UNIVERSITIES & EQ. INSTS.	1975	1 178	51	4	19 208	2 973	15
		1980	1 027	41	4	25 699	7 026	27
		1981	877	37	4	30 346	9 443	31
		1982	941	39	4	31 819	10 991	35
		1983	1 161	57	5	31 852	11 618	36
	OTHER THIRD LEVEL INSTS.	1975	242	46	19	2 134	435	20
		1980	249	57	23	3 089	765	25
		1981	262	37	14	3 465	797	23
		1982	243	38	16	3 244	979	30
		1983	303	38	13	3 796	1 146	30
SWAZILAND‡	ALL INSTITUTIONS	1975	136	25	18	1 012	...	...
		1980	183	64	35	1 875	741	40
		1981	247	98	40	1 699	701	41
		1982	...	...	...	1 201	459	38
		1983	...	...	...	...	...	...
	UNIVERSITIES & EQ. INSTS.	1975	86	12	14	336	...	...
		1980	108	37	34	1 009	370	37
		1981	111	37	33	1 069	413	39
		1982	113	28	25	1 064	395	37
		1983	...	...	...	1 063	395	37
	OTHER THIRD LEVEL INSTS.	1975	50	13	26	676	235	35
		1980	75	27	36	866	371	43
		1981	136	61	45	630	288	46
		1982	...	...	...	137	64	47
TOGO‡	ALL INSTITUTIONS	1975	...	...	...	2 353	323	14
		1980	...	...	...	4 750	703	15
		1981	...	...	...	4 307	630	15
		1982	...	...	...	4 034	570	14
		1983	...	...	...	4 234	661	16
		1984	...	...	...	...	...	...
	UNIVERSITIES & EQ. INSTS.	1975	236	39	17	2 167	308	14
		1980	272	35	13	4 345	664	15
		1981	269	28	10	4 008	601	15
		1982	260	27	10	3 833	550	14
		1983	266	29	11	3 954	629	16
		1984	283	36	13	4 192	628	15
	OTHER THIRD LEVEL INSTS.	1975	...	...	...	186	15	8
		1980	...	...	...	405	39	10
		1981	...	...	...	299	29	10
		1982	...	...	...	201	20	10
		1983	...	...	...	280	32	11
TUNISIA	ALL INSTITUTIONS	1975	1 427	217	15	20 505	5 273	26
		1980	4 031	357	9	31 827	9 437	30
		1981	...	...	...	32 832	10 266	31
		1982	4 105	568	14	34 077	11 209	33
		1983	4 397	...	...	35 426	12 223	35
		1984	4 672	...	...	38 829	13 974	36
	UNIVERSITIES & EQ. INSTS.	1975	1 427	217	15	20 505	5 273	26
		1980	4 031	357	9	31 827	9 437	30
		1981	...	...	...	32 832	10 266	31
		1982	4 105	568	14	34 077	11 209	33
		1983	4 397	...	...	35 426	12 223	35
		1984	4 672	...	...	38 829	13 974	36
UGANDA	ALL INSTITUTIONS	1975	617	58	9	5 474	988	18
		1980	...	...	...	5 856	1 323	23
		1981	569	...	...	6 563	1 501	23
		1982	640	45	7	7 312	1 964	27
	UNIVERSITIES & EQ. INSTS.	1975	444	33	7	3 914	619	16
		1980	...	...	...	4 035	795	20
		1981	362	...	...	4 623	942	20
		1982	369	27	7	4 854	1 055	22

COUNTRY / PAYS / PAIS	TYPE OF INSTITUTION / TYPE D'ETABLISSEMENT / TIPO DE ESTABLECIMIENTO	YEAR / ANNEE / AÑO	TEACHING STAFF / PERSONNEL ENSEIGNANT / PERSONAL DOCENTE TOTAL	FEMALE / FEMININ / FEMENINO	% F	STUDENTS ENROLLED / ETUDIANTS INSCRITS / ESTUDIANTES MATRICULADOS TOTAL	FEMALE / FEMININ / FEMENINO	% F
			(1)	(2)	(3)	(4)	(5)	(6)
UGANDA (CONT)	OTHER THIRD LEVEL INSTS.	1975	173	25	14	1 560	369	24
		1980	...	...	...	1 821	528	29
		1981	207	23	11	1 940	559	29
		1982	271	18	7	2 458	909	37
UNITED REPUBLIC OF TANZANIA‡	ALL INSTITUTIONS	1975	...	...	...	3 064	420	14
		1981	...	...	...	...	...	...
		1982	...	...	...	...	...	...
		1983	...	...	...	...	...	...
		1984	...	...	...	...	...	...
	UNIVERSITIES & EQ. INSTS.	1975	434	...	...	2 644	270	10
		1981	893	31	3	3 662	770	21
		1982	795	39	5	3 817	673	18
		1983	974	31	3	3 943	649	16
		1984	...	...	...	3 232	576	18
	OTHER THIRD LEVEL INSTS.	1975	...	...	...	420	150	36
ZAIRE	ALL INSTITUTIONS	1975	2 010	...	...	24 853	...	...
		1980	...	...	...	28 493	...	...
		1981	...	...	...	25 223	...	...
		1982	...	...	...	31 643	...	...
ZAMBIA	ALL INSTITUTIONS	1975	...	...	...	8 403	*1 170	*14
		1980	...	...	...	...	...	...
		1981	...	...	...	7 541	1 566	21
		1982	...	...	...	8 062	1 759	22
		1983	...	...	...	8 781	...	...
		1984	...	...	...	...	...	...
	UNIVERSITIES & EQ. INSTS.	1975	...	...	...	2 354	*395	*17
		1980	...	...	...	3 425	...	...
		1981	329	...	...	3 646	707	19
		1982	...	...	...	4 236	866	20
		1983	574	15	3	4 330	798	18
	OTHER THIRD LEVEL INSTS.	1975	...	...	...	6 049	775	13
		1981	...	...	...	3 895	859	22
		1982	...	...	...	3 826	893	23
		1983	...	...	...	4 451	...	...
		1984	...	...	...	4 214	...	...
ZIMBABWE	ALL INSTITUTIONS	1975	...	...	...	8 479	...	...
		1980	...	...	...	8 339	...	...
		1981	...	...	...	12 226	...	...
		1982	...	...	...	14 926	...	...
		1983	...	...	...	17 892	...	...
		1984	...	...	...	...	...	...
	UNIVERSITIES & EQ. INSTS.	1975	...	...	...	1 355	...	...
		1980	...	...	...	1 873	...	...
		1981	...	...	...	2 525	...	...
		1982	325	56	17	3 091	680	22
		1983	...	...	...	3 620	805	22
		1984	342	68	20	4 131	933	23
	OTHER THIRD LEVEL INSTS.	1975	...	...	...	7 124	...	...
		1980	262	...	...	6 466	...	...
		1981	417	102	24	9 701	...	...
		1982	...	...	...	11 835	...	...
		1983	376	87	23	14 272	...	...
AMERICA, NORTH								
BAHAMAS	ALL INSTITUTIONS	1976	128	...	...	5 660	...	...
		1980	127	...	...	4 093	...	...
		1981	126	...	...	3 963	...	...
		1982	128	...	...	3 097	...	...
BARBADOS	ALL INSTITUTIONS	1975	...	...	...	...	...	...
		1980	317	90	28	4 033	2 170	54
		1981	...	...	...	4 938	...	...
		1982	...	...	...	...	...	...
		1983	446	122	27	5 133	2 409	47
		1984	544	...	...	5 227	2 565	49
	UNIVERSITIES & EQ. INSTS.	1975	...	...	...	1 065	...	...
		1980	140	32	23	1 606	778	48
		1981	...	...	...	1 601	...	...
		1982	...	...	...	1 564	...	...
		1983	200	50	25	1 664	899	54
		1984	242	...	...	1 767	967	55

3.11 **Third level: teachers and students by type of institution**
Troisième degré: professeurs et étudiants par type d'établissement
Tercer grado: profesores y estudiantes por tipo de establecimiento

COUNTRY / PAYS / PAIS	TYPE OF INSTITUTION / TYPE D'ETABLISSEMENT / TIPO DE ESTABLECIMIENTO	YEAR / ANNEE / AÑO	TEACHING STAFF / PERSONNEL ENSEIGNANT / PERSONAL DOCENTE: TOTAL	FEMALE / FEMININ / FEMENINO	% F	STUDENTS ENROLLED / ETUDIANTS INSCRITS / ESTUDIANTES MATRICULADOS: TOTAL	FEMALE / FEMININ / FEMENINO	% F
			(1)	(2)	(3)	(4)	(5)	(6)
BARBADOS (CONT)	OTHER THIRD LEVEL INSTS.	1980	177	58	33	2 427	1 392	57
		1981	...	...	...	3 337	1 476	44
		1983	246	72	29	3 469	1 510	44
		1984	302	...	...	3 460	1 598	46
BERMUDA‡	ALL INSTITUTIONS	1980	67	22	33	608	312	51
		1981	118	44	37	3 368	...	...
		1982	110	40	36	2 667	...	...
	OTHER THIRD LEVEL INSTS.	1980	67	22	33	608	312	51
		1981	118	44	37	3 368	...	...
		1982	110	40	36	2 667	...	...
CANADA‡	ALL INSTITUTIONS	1975	...	...	...	818 153	367 270	45
		1980	53 434	12 565	24	888 444	445 242	50
		1981	53 964	9 238	21	924 445	467 165	51
		1982	57 147	9 496	21	988 334	502 609	51
		1983	58 277	13 890	24	1 192 925	617 802	52
	UNIVERSITIES & EQ. INSTS.	1975	30 732	4 304	14	546 769	234 270	43
		1980	33 015	5 105	15	627 617	312 169	50
		1981	33 500	5 180	15	649 166	325 836	50
		1982	33 900	5 250	15	692 775	350 340	51
		1983	34 965	5 645	16	729 217	370 866	51
	OTHER THIRD LEVEL INSTS.	1975	...	...	...	271 384	133 000	49
		1980	20 419	7 460	37	260 827	133 073	51
		1981	10 964	4 058	37	275 279	141 329	51
		1982	11 447	4 246	37	295 559	152 269	52
		1983	23 312	8 245	35	463 708	246 936	53
COSTA RICA‡	ALL INSTITUTIONS	1975	...	...	...	33 239	...	...
		1980	...	...	...	55 593	...	...
		1981	...	...	...	58 961	...	...
		1982	...	...	...	58 974	...	...
		1983	...	...	...	58 927	...	...
		1984	...	...	...	60 288	...	...
	UNIVERSITIES & EQ. INSTS.	1975	...	...	...	32 794	...	...
		1980	4 382	...	...	50 812	...	...
		1981	4 317	...	...	53 915	...	...
		1982	4 343	...	...	54 334	...	...
		1983	...	...	...	54 257	...	...
		1984	...	...	...	54 456	...	...
	OTHER THIRD LEVEL INSTS.	1975	...	...	...	445	...	...
		1980	...	...	...	4 781	...	...
		1981	...	...	...	5 046	...	...
		1982	...	...	...	4 640	...	...
		1983	...	...	...	4 670	...	...
		1984	...	...	...	5 832	...	...
CUBA	ALL INSTITUTIONS	1975	5 380	...	...	82 688	...	...
		1980	10 680	...	...	151 733	73 413	48
		1981	12 068	4 564	38	165 496	85 462	52
		1982	12 222	4 843	40	173 403	90 758	52
		1983	15 894	5 749	36	192 958	101 711	53
		1984	17 717	7 043	40	212 155	113 956	54
	UNIVERSITIES & EQ. INSTS.	1975	5 380	...	...	82 688	...	...
		1980	10 680	...	...	151 733	73 413	48
		1981	12 068	4 564	38	165 496	85 462	52
		1982	12 222	4 843	40	173 403	90 758	52
		1983	15 894	5 749	36	192 958	101 711	53
		1984	17 717	7 043	40	212 155	113 956	54
DOMINICA	ALL INSTITUTIONS	1980	17	12	71	63	14	22
		1983	17	11	65	58	50	86
		1984	*17	*11	*65	60	40	67
	OTHER THIRD LEVEL INSTS.	1980	17	12	71	63	14	22
		1983	17	11	65	58	50	86
		1984	*17	*11	*65	60	40	67
DOMINICAN REPUBLIC	ALL INSTITUTIONS	1975	...	...	...	...	...	...
		1978	...	...	...	...	...	...
	UNIVERSITIES & EQ. INSTS.	1975	1 435	...	...	28 628	11 773	41
		1978	...	...	...	42 412	...	...
EL SALVADOR‡	ALL INSTITUTIONS	1975	2 137	485	23	28 281	9 468	33
		1980	893	208	23	16 838	5 202	31
		1981	1 220	289	24	25 783	7 842	30
		1982	...	...	...	46 976	18 017	38
		1983	2 888	846	29	57 374	24 635	43

COUNTRY / PAYS / PAIS	TYPE OF INSTITUTION / TYPE D'ETABLISSEMENT / TIPO DE ESTABLECIMIENTO	YEAR / ANNEE / AÑO	TEACHING STAFF / PERSONNEL ENSEIGNANT / PERSONAL DOCENTE			STUDENTS ENROLLED / ETUDIANTS INSCRITS / ESTUDIANTES MATRICULADOS		
			TOTAL	FEMALE FEMININ FEMENINO	% F	TOTAL	FEMALE FEMININ FEMENINO	% F
			(1)	(2)	(3)	(4)	(5)	(6)
EL SALVADOR (CONT)‡	UNIVERSITIES & EQ. INSTS.	1975	1 880	379	20	26 909	8 931	33
		1980	445	72	16	12 740	3 999	31
		1981	802	185	23	18 434	4 960	27
		1983	2 202	499	23	46 941	19 692	42
	OTHER THIRD LEVEL INSTS.	1975	257	106	41	1 372	537	39
		1980	448	136	30	4 098	1 203	29
		1981	418	104	25	7 349	2 882	39
		1983	686	347	51	10 433	4 943	47
GRENADA‡	ALL INSTITUTIONS	1981	71	19	27	926	569	61
		1982	40	14	35	519	256	49
	OTHER THIRD LEVEL INSTS.	1981	71	19	27	926	569	61
		1982	40	14	35	519	256	49
GUATEMALA‡	ALL INSTITUTIONS	1975	1 411	...	...	22 881	5 277	23
		1980	...	...	...	50 890	...	...
		1982	...	...	...	*47 433	...	...
	UNIVERSITIES & EQ. INSTS.	1975	1 411	...	...	22 881	5 277	23
		1980	...	...	...	50 890	...	...
		1982	...	...	...	*47 433	...	...
HAITI	ALL INSTITUTIONS	1975	408	48	12	2 881	691	24
		1980	690	75	11	4 671	1 410	30
		1982	817	104	13	5 300	...	...
		1983	...	...	...	6 289	2 119	34
	UNIVERSITIES & EQ. INSTS.	1975	366	47	13	2 467	665	27
		1980	523	66	13	3 441	1 209	35
		1982	...	...	...	3 618	...	...
	OTHER THIRD LEVEL INSTS.	1975	42	1	2	414	26	6
		1980	167	9	5	1 230	201	16
		1982	...	...	...	1 682	517	31
HONDURAS	ALL INSTITUTIONS	1975	817	...	...	11 907	4 060	34
		1980	1 653	...	...	25 825	9 736	38
		1981	1 789	518	29	30 653	...	...
		1982	2 039	...	...	33 279	...	...
		1983	2 269	...	...	34 468	...	...
		1984	...	...	...	33 742	...	...
	UNIVERSITIES & EQ. INSTS.	1975	648	116	18	10 635	3 408	32
		1980	1 439	...	...	24 021	9 025	38
		1981	1 518	431	28	27 503	10 464	38
		1982	1 760	...	...	29 195	11 396	39
		1983	1 940	...	...	30 119	12 127	40
		1984	2 127	...	...	30 417	...	...
	OTHER THIRD LEVEL INSTS.	1975	169	...	...	1 272	652	51
		1980	214	...	...	1 804	711	39
		1981	271	87	32	3 150	...	...
		1982	279	...	...	4 084	...	...
		1983	329	97	29	4 349	...	...
		1984	...	...	...	3 325	...	...
JAMAICA	ALL INSTITUTIONS	1975	...	...	...	...	...	...
		1980	...	...	...	13 999	...	...
		1981	...	...	...	...	...	...
		1982	...	...	...	...	...	...
	UNIVERSITIES & EQ. INSTS.	1975	...	...	...	3 963	...	...
		1980	397	...	...	4 548	...	...
		1981	...	...	...	4 798	...	...
		1982	...	...	...	4 884	...	...
	OTHER THIRD LEVEL INSTS.	1980	...	...	...	9 451	...	...
MEXICO	ALL INSTITUTIONS	1975	47 529	...	...	562 056	...	...
		1980	77 653	...	...	897 726	296 781	33
		1981	82 967	...	...	966 228	330 897	34
		1982	85 943	...	...	1 013 117	360 486	36
		1983	99 127	...	...	1 071 676	385 710	36
	UNIVERSITIES & EQ. INSTS.	1975	45 025	...	...	520 194	...	...
		1980	72 742	...	...	785 419	239 791	31
		1981	77 209	...	...	840 368	266 904	32
		1982	79 934	...	...	879 240	291 876	33
		1983	92 926	...	...	939 513	317 276	34

COUNTRY / PAYS / PAIS	TYPE OF INSTITUTION / TYPE D'ETABLISSEMENT / TIPO DE ESTABLECIMIENTO	YEAR / ANNEE / AÑO	TEACHING STAFF / PERSONNEL ENSEIGNANT / PERSONAL DOCENTE TOTAL	FEMALE / FEMININ / FEMENINO	% F	STUDENTS ENROLLED / ETUDIANTS INSCRITS / ESTUDIANTES MATRICULADOS TOTAL	FEMALE / FEMININ / FEMENINO	% F
			(1)	(2)	(3)	(4)	(5)	(6)
MEXICO (CONT)	OTHER THIRD LEVEL INSTS.	1975	2 504	...	...	41 862	...	...
		1980	4 911	...	...	112 307	56 990	51
		1981	5 758	...	...	125 860	63 993	51
		1982	6 009	...	...	133 877	68 610	51
		1983	6 201	...	...	132 163	68 434	52
NICARAGUA	ALL INSTITUTIONS	1975	1 066	...	...	18 282	6 216	34
		1980	...	...	...	35 268	...	...
		1982	1 369	...	...	32 838	15 374	47
		1983	1 715	496	29	35 588	16 107	45
		1984	1 887	613	32	31 725	15 115	48
		1985	2 526	...	...	29 001	16 355	56
	UNIVERSITIES & EQ. INSTS.	1975	911	...	...	15 579	5 920	38
		1980	...	...	...	32 958	...	...
		1982	1 087	...	...	28 049	13 371	48
		1983	1 293	389	30	29 633	13 606	46
		1984	1 450	486	34	25 663	12 643	49
		1985	2 151	...	...	24 430	14 009	57
	OTHER THIRD LEVEL INSTS.	1975	155	...	...	2 703	296	11
		1980	...	...	...	2 310	...	...
		1982	282	...	...	4 789	2 003	42
		1983	422	107	25	5 955	2 501	42
		1984	437	127	29	6 062	2 472	41
		1985	385	...	...	4 571	2 346	51
PANAMA	ALL INSTITUTIONS	1975	1 519	...	...	26 289	*13 090	*50
		1980	2 673	...	...	40 369	22 168	55
		1981	2 911	922	32	42 425	22 924	54
		1982	...	...	...	45 060	24 758	55
		1983	3 475	...	...	44 568	26 131	59
		1984	3 272	...	...	52 224	29 246	56
	UNIVERSITIES & EQ. INSTS.	1975	1 519	...	...	26 289	*13 090	*50
		1980	2 673	...	...	40 369	22 168	55
		1981	2 911	922	32	42 425	22 924	54
		1982	...	...	...	45 060	24 758	55
		1983	3 475	...	...	44 568	26 131	59
		1984	3 272	...	...	52 224	29 246	56
FORMER CANAL ZONE	ALL INSTITUTIONS	1975	...	...	...	1 590	796	50
	UNIVERSITIES & EQ. INSTS.	1975	...	...	...	1 590	796	50
PUERTO RICO	ALL INSTITUTIONS	1975	...	...	...	97 517	52 138	53
		1979	...	...	...	129 708	75 116	58
	UNIVERSITIES & EQ. INSTS.	1975	...	...	...	91 254	48 383	53
		1979	...	...	...	97 379	56 290	58
	OTHER THIRD LEVEL INSTS.	1975	...	...	...	6 263	3 755	60
		1979	...	...	...	32 329	18 826	58
ST. LUCIA	ALL INSTITUTIONS	1980	...	...	...	301	157	52
		1981	73	29	40	367	220	60
		1982	71	27	38	411	192	47
		1983	90	31	34	402	198	49
		1984	76	28	37	346	158	46
	OTHER THIRD LEVEL INSTS.	1980	...	...	...	301	157	52
		1981	73	29	40	367	220	60
		1982	71	27	38	411	192	47
		1983	90	31	34	402	198	49
		1984	76	28	37	346	158	46
TRINIDAD AND TOBAGO‡	ALL INSTITUTIONS	1975	...	...	...	4 940	1 885	38
		1980	...	...	...	5 649	2 389	42
		1981	...	...	...	5 754	2 285	40
		1982	...	...	...	5 470	2 343	43
	UNIVERSITIES & EQ. INSTS.	1975	178	...	...	2 229	702	31
		1980	...	...	...	2 923	1 099	38
		1981	...	...	...	3 144	1 179	38
		1982	...	...	...	3 483	1 624	47
	OTHER THIRD LEVEL INSTS.	1975	...	...	...	2 711	1 183	44
		1980	...	...	...	2 726	1 290	47
		1981	...	...	...	2 610	1 106	42
		1982	...	...	...	1 987	719	36

COUNTRY / PAYS / PAIS	TYPE OF INSTITUTION / TYPE D'ETABLISSEMENT / TIPO DE ESTABLECIMIENTO	YEAR / ANNEE / AÑO	TEACHING STAFF / PERSONNEL ENSEIGNANT / PERSONAL DOCENTE: TOTAL	FEMALE / FEMININ / FEMENINO	% F	STUDENTS ENROLLED / ETUDIANTS INSCRITS / ESTUDIANTES MATRICULADOS: TOTAL	FEMALE / FEMININ / FEMENINO	% F
			(1)	(2)	(3)	(4)	(5)	(6)
UNITED STATES‡	ALL INSTITUTIONS	1975	670 000	...	...	11 184 859	5 035 862	45
		1980	395 992	104 663	26	12 096 895	6 222 521	51
		1981	...	...	...	12 371 672	6 396 616	52
		1982	391 594	105 545	27	12 425 780	6 394 396	51
		1983	...	...	...	12 393 700	...	...
		1984	...	...	...	12 467 740	...	...
	UNIVERSITIES & EQ. INSTS.	1975	...	...	...	7 223 037	3 235 908	45
		1980	305 982	71 980	24	7 572 657	3 745 958	49
		1981	...	...	...	7 741 564	3 821 328	49
		1982	301 943	72 352	24	7 654 074	3 792 852	50
	OTHER THIRD LEVEL INSTS.	1975	...	...	...	3 961 822	1 799 954	45
		1980	90 010	32 683	36	4 524 238	2 476 563	55
		1981	...	...	...	4 630 108	2 575 288	56
		1982	89 651	33 193	37	4 771 706	2 601 544	55
U.S. VIRGIN ISLANDS	ALL INSTITUTIONS	1975	...	...	...	2 069	1 301	63
		1981	245	89	36	2 608	1 861	71
		1982	210	90	43	2 744	1 980	72
	UNIVERSITIES & EQ. INSTS.	1975	...	...	...	2 069	1 301	63
		1981	245	89	36	2 608	1 861	71
		1982	210	90	43	2 744	1 980	72
AMERICA, SOUTH								
ARGENTINA	ALL INSTITUTIONS	1975	45 204	17 665	39	596 736	283 762	48
		1980	46 267	20 039	43	491 473	247 656	50
		1982	53 166	23 194	44	550 556	292 396	53
		1983	56 089	25 728	46	580 626	311 772	54
		1984	64 230	29 715	46	677 535	360 860	53
		1985	70 699	32 694	46	846 145	444 636	53
	UNIVERSITIES & EQ. INSTS.	1975	33 176	9 770	29	536 959	231 715	43
		1980	30 602	9 273	30	397 828	169 412	43
		1982	33 322	9 447	28	411 113	176 677	43
		1983	33 450	9 910	30	416 571	181 592	44
		1984	39 296	12 403	32	507 994	227 329	45
		1985	44 038	14 222	32	664 200	302 509	46
	OTHER THIRD LEVEL INSTS.	1975	12 028	7 895	66	59 777	52 047	87
		1980	15 665	10 766	69	93 645	78 244	84
		1982	19 844	13 747	69	139 443	115 719	83
		1983	22 639	15 818	70	164 055	130 180	79
		1984	24 934	17 312	69	169 541	133 531	79
		1985	26 661	18 472	69	181 945	142 127	78
BOLIVIA‡	ALL INSTITUTIONS	1975	...	...	...	*49 850	...	...
		1980	...	...	...	...	...	...
		1981	...	...	...	...	...	...
		1982	...	...	...	...	...	...
	UNIVERSITIES & EQ. INSTS.	1975	2 178	...	...	34 350	...	...
		1980	...	...	...	60 900	...	...
		1981	2 635	...	...	52 888	...	...
		1982	3 480	...	...	56 632	...	...
	OTHER THIRD LEVEL INSTS.	1975	...	...	...	*15 500	...	...
BRAZIL‡	ALL INSTITUTIONS	1975	92 546	...	...	1 089 808	...	...
		1980	109 788	33 238	30	1 409 243	680 445	48
		1981	120 217	...	...	1 419 426	...	...
		1982	121 954	...	...	1 436 287	...	...
		1983	122 697	52 935	43	1 479 397	740 327	50
	UNIVERSITIES & EQ. INSTS.	1975	92 546	...	...	1 089 808	...	...
		1980	109 788	33 238	30	1 409 243	680 445	48
		1981	120 217	...	...	1 419 426	...	...
		1982	121 954	...	...	1 436 287	...	...
		1983	122 697	52 935	43	1 479 397	740 327	50
CHILE‡	ALL INSTITUTIONS	1975	11 419	...	...	149 647	*67 400	*45
		1980	...	...	...	145 497	62 804	43
		1982	...	...	...	158 117	...	...
		1983	13 767	2 939	21	178 332	75 492	42
		1984	15 131	3 350	22	188 665	80 652	43
		1985	...	...	...	196 937	...	...
	UNIVERSITIES & EQ. INSTS.	1975	11 419	...	...	149 647	*67 400	*45
		1980	...	...	...	120 168	48 462	40
		1982	10 372	2 038	20	121 138	47 590	39
		1983	10 299	1 959	19	130 877	52 047	40
		1984	11 603	2 209	19	132 254	52 565	40

3.11 Third level: teachers and students by type of institution
Troisième degré: professeurs et étudiants par type d'établissement
Tercer grado: profesores y estudiantes por tipo de establecimiento

COUNTRY / PAYS / PAIS	TYPE OF INSTITUTION / TYPE D'ETABLISSEMENT / TIPO DE ESTABLECIMIENTO	YEAR / ANNEE / AÑO	TEACHING STAFF / PERSONNEL ENSEIGNANT / PERSONAL DOCENTE			STUDENTS ENROLLED / ETUDIANTS INSCRITS / ESTUDIANTES MATRICULADOS		
			TOTAL	FEMALE / FEMININ / FEMENINO	% F	TOTAL	FEMALE / FEMININ / FEMENINO	% F
			(1)	(2)	(3)	(4)	(5)	(6)
CHILE (CONT)‡	OTHER THIRD LEVEL INSTS.	1980	804	264	33	25 329	14 342	57
		1982	...	...	...	36 979	...	...
		1983	3 468	980	28	47 455	23 445	49
		1984	3 528	1 141	32	56 411	28 087	50
COLOMBIA‡	ALL INSTITUTIONS	1975	21 153	2 934	14	176 098	64 039	36
		1980	31 136	6 184	20	271 630	121 115	45
		1982	38 464	8 232	21	335 833	153 828	46
		1983	39 292	...	...	356 000	...	...
		1984	41 636	9 465	23	378 586	180 909	48
		1985	42 344	9 819	23	389 075	...	...
	UNIVERSITIES & EQ. INSTS.	1975	19 821	2 585	13	167 503	59 309	35
		1980	26 930	5 181	19	234 705	100 587	43
		1982	33 210	...	...	296 030	131 048	44
		1983	...	...	...	312 371	...	...
		1984	35 466	7 726	22	331 758	153 612	46
		1985	36 335	8 090	22	340 165	...	...
	OTHER THIRD LEVEL INSTS.	1975	1 332	349	26	8 595	4 730	55
		1980	4 206	1 003	24	36 925	20 528	56
		1982	5 254	...	...	39 803	22 780	57
		1983	...	...	...	43 629	...	...
		1984	6 170	1 739	28	46 828	27 297	58
		1985	6 009	1 729	29	48 910	...	...
ECUADOR‡	ALL INSTITUTIONS	1975	...	...	...	170 173	...	...
		1980	...	...	...	269 775	...	...
		1981	...	...	...	261 075	...	...
		1982	...	...	...	254 148	...	...
		1983	...	...	...	266 222	103 371	39
		1984	...	...	...	280 594	...	...
	UNIVERSITIES & EQ. INSTS.	1975	...	...	...	170 173	...	...
		1980	11 326	...	...	264 136	97 350	37
		1981	11 679	...	...	258 054	93 623	36
		1982	10 536	...	...	251 614	...	...
		1983	11 099	...	...	264 181	102 138	39
		1984	11 495	...	...	277 799	...	...
	OTHER THIRD LEVEL INSTS.	1980	...	65	...	5 639	...	...
		1981	...	68	...	3 021	...	...
		1982	...	...	...	2 534	1 576	62
		1983	...	...	...	2 041	1 233	60
		1984	...	...	...	2 795	...	...
GUYANA	ALL INSTITUTIONS	1975	...	...	...	2 852	1 012	35
		1980	442	118	27	2 465	1 078	44
		1981	...	...	...	2 746	1 232	45
		1982	449	127	28	2 049	845	41
		1983	534	156	29	2 111	1 012	48
	UNIVERSITIES & EQ. INSTS.	1975	172	37	22	1 749	486	28
		1980	322	68	21	1 681	535	32
		1981	...	...	...	1 995	681	34
		1982	340	77	23	1 567	502	32
		1983	447	114	26	1 580	597	38
	OTHER THIRD LEVEL INSTS.	1975	...	...	...	1 103	526	48
		1980	120	50	42	784	543	69
		1981	117	54	46	751	551	73
		1982	109	50	46	482	343	71
		1983	87	42	48	531	415	78
PARAGUAY	ALL INSTITUTIONS	1975	...	...	...	18 302	...	...
		1980	...	...	...	26 915	...	...
		1981	...	...	...	28 792	...	...
		1982	...	...	...	30 207	...	...
		1983	...	...	...	34 199	...	...
		1984	...	...	...	33 203	...	...
	UNIVERSITIES & EQ. INSTS.	1975	1 741	...	...	17 153	...	...
		1980	1 893	...	...	25 333	...	...
		1981	2 014	...	...	27 041	...	...
		1982	2 448	...	...	27 916	...	...
		1983	2 694	...	...	31 317	...	...
		1984	2 694	...	...	30 222	...	...
	OTHER THIRD LEVEL INSTS.	1975	...	...	...	1 149	...	...
		1980	...	...	...	1 582	...	...
		1981	...	...	...	1 751	...	...
		1982	...	...	...	2 291	...	...
		1983	...	...	...	2 882	...	...
		1984	...	...	...	2 981	...	...

COUNTRY / PAYS / PAIS	TYPE OF INSTITUTION / TYPE D'ETABLISSEMENT / TIPO DE ESTABLECIMIENTO	YEAR / ANNEE / AÑO	TEACHING STAFF / PERSONNEL ENSEIGNANT / PERSONAL DOCENTE			STUDENTS ENROLLED / ETUDIANTS INSCRITS / ESTUDIANTES MATRICULADOS		
			TOTAL	FEMALE / FEMININ / FEMENINO	% F	TOTAL	FEMALE / FEMININ / FEMENINO	% F
			(1)	(2)	(3)	(4)	(5)	(6)
PERU	ALL INSTITUTIONS	1975	11 598	1 669	14	195 641	62 850	32
		1980	17 853	...	...	306 353	107 980	35
		1981	...	...	...	...	...	...
		1982	...	...	...	...	...	...
	UNIVERSITIES & EQ. INSTS.	1975	10 844	1 321	12	186 511	59 684	32
		1980	14 727	2 343	16	246 510	83 791	34
		1981	15 958	2 727	17	279 476	96 530	35
		1982	16 913	2 991	18	305 390	105 968	35
	OTHER THIRD LEVEL INSTS.	1975	754	348	46	9 130	3 166	35
		1980	3 126	...	...	59 843	24 189	40
SURINAME	ALL INSTITUTIONS	1975	...	...	...	...	...	...
		1980	...	...	...	2 374	...	...
		1981	...	...	...	2 684	...	...
		1982	...	...	...	2 987	...	...
		1983	...	...	...	3 002	...	...
		1984	373	52	14	2 914	1 497	51
	UNIVERSITIES & EQ. INSTS.	1975	...	...	...	465	54	12
		1980	...	...	...	1 217	...	...
		1981	195	...	...	1 526	...	...
		1982	...	...	...	1 671	...	...
		1983	...	...	...	1 227	...	...
		1984	190	20	11	1 274	500	39
	OTHER THIRD LEVEL INSTS.	1980	...	...	...	1 161	...	...
		1981	...	...	...	1 158	...	...
		1982	176	...	...	1 316	...	...
		1983	224	...	...	1 775	...	...
		1984	183	32	17	1 640	997	61
URUGUAY	ALL INSTITUTIONS	1975	2 332	530	23	32 627	14 313	44
		1980	3 847	1 141	30	36 298	19 236	53
		1982	...	...	...	48 234	26 782	56
		1983	4 349	...	...	50 151	28 389	57
		1984	4 537	...	...	63 734	...	...
		1985	...	...	...	77 480	...	...
	UNIVERSITIES & EQ. INSTS.	1975	2 332	530	23	32 627	14 313	44
		1980	3 847	1 141	30	36 298	19 236	53
		1982	...	...	...	48 234	26 782	56
		1983	4 349	...	...	50 151	28 389	57
		1984	4 537	...	...	63 734	...	...
		1985	...	...	...	77 480	...	...
VENEZUELA	ALL INSTITUTIONS	1975	15 792	...	...	213 542	...	...
		1980	28 052	...	...	307 133	...	...
		1981	28 567	...	...	331 115	...	...
		1982	28 892	...	...	349 773	...	...
		1983	28 705	...	...	384 717	...	...
		1984	30 122	...	...	381 575	...	...
	UNIVERSITIES & EQ. INSTS.	1975	12 849	...	...	185 518	...	...
		1980	23 984	...	...	271 583	...	...
		1981	24 263	...	...	289 323	...	...
		1982	24 186	...	...	298 483	...	...
		1983	23 394	...	...	326 666	...	...
		1984	23 570	...	...	318 727	...	...
	OTHER THIRD LEVEL INSTS.	1975	2 943	...	...	28 024	...	...
		1980	4 068	...	...	35 550	...	...
		1981	4 304	...	...	41 792	...	...
		1982	4 706	...	...	51 290	...	...
		1983	5 311	...	...	58 051	...	...
		1984	5 790	...	...	62 848	...	...
ASIA								
AFGHANISTAN	ALL INSTITUTIONS	1975	...	...	...	*12 256	*1 681	*14
		1979	1 448	101	7	22 974	3 489	15
		1982	1 724	...	...	19 652	...	...
	UNIVERSITIES & EQ. INSTS.	1975	...	...	...	8 681	800	9
		1979	818	63	8	13 204	2 303	17
		1982	1 212	...	...	13 611	...	...
	OTHER THIRD LEVEL INSTS.	1975	258	17	7	*3 575	*881	*25
		1979	630	38	6	9 770	1 186	12
		1982	512	...	...	6 041	...	...

COUNTRY / PAYS / PAIS	TYPE OF INSTITUTION / TYPE D'ETABLISSEMENT / TIPO DE ESTABLECIMIENTO	YEAR / ANNEE / AÑO	TEACHING STAFF / PERSONNEL ENSEIGNANT / PERSONAL DOCENTE			STUDENTS ENROLLED / ETUDIANTS INSCRITS / ESTUDIANTES MATRICULADOS		
			TOTAL	FEMALE FEMININ FEMENINO	% F	TOTAL	FEMALE FEMININ FEMENINO	% F
			(1)	(2)	(3)	(4)	(5)	(6)
BAHRAIN	ALL INSTITUTIONS	1975	79	11	14	703	371	53
		1980	159	21	13	1 908	786	41
		1981	230	47	20	2 348	1 093	47
		1982	...	...	...	...	...	...
		1983	...	...	...	...	...	...
		1984	...	...	...	4 235	2 377	56
	UNIVERSITIES & EQ. INSTS.	1980	70	18	26	317	260	82
		1981	127	33	26	490	414	84
		1982	225	40	18	1 577	633	40
		1983	220	76	35	2 098	1 498	71
		1984	287	107	37	2 085	1 529	73
	OTHER THIRD LEVEL INSTS.	1975	79	11	14	703	371	53
		1980	89	3	3	1 591	526	33
		1981	103	14	14	1 858	679	37
		1984	...	...	...	2 150	848	39
BANGLADESH	ALL INSTITUTIONS	1976	13 503	1 370	10	158 604	19 827	13
		1980	12 428	1 305	11	240 181	33 348	14
		1981	12 775	1 569	12	244 091	33 898	14
		1982	15 023	1 624	11	297 930	63 361	21
		1983	14 685	1 752	12	386 542	70 942	18
		1984	15 205	1 907	13	436 615	78 289	18
	UNIVERSITIES & EQ. INSTS.	1976	2 103	175	8	27 553	4 703	17
		1980	2 421	191	8	36 530	6 552	18
		1981	2 400	209	9	37 108	6 637	18
		1982	2 484	218	9	39 699	7 361	19
		1983	2 626	226	9	40 527	7 596	19
		1984	2 636	224	8	36 166	6 388	18
	OTHER THIRD LEVEL INSTS.	1976	11 400	1 195	10	131 051	15 124	12
		1980	10 007	1 114	11	203 651	26 796	13
		1981	10 375	1 360	13	206 983	27 261	13
		1982	12 539	1 406	11	258 231	56 000	22
		1983	12 059	1 526	13	346 015	63 346	18
		1984	12 569	1 683	13	364 938	71 901	20
BHUTAN‡	ALL INSTITUTIONS	1980	37	10	27	322	70	22
		1983	18	1	6	55	3	5
	UNIVERSITIES & EQ. INSTS.	1980	15	3	20	180	14	8
		1983	9	1	11	38	–	–
	OTHER THIRD LEVEL INSTS.	1980	22	7	32	142	56	39
		1983	9	–	–	17	3	18
BRUNEI DARUSSALAM	ALL INSTITUTIONS	1980	57	18	32	143	72	50
		1981	61	21	34	181	118	65
		1983	64	17	27	218	99	45
	OTHER THIRD LEVEL INSTS.	1980	57	18	32	143	72	50
		1981	61	21	34	181	118	65
		1983	64	17	27	218	99	45
BURMA	ALL INSTITUTIONS	1975	...	...	...	56 083	...	...
		1978	45 222	...	...	121 609	61 206	50
		1981	...	...	...	165 000	...	...
	UNIVERSITIES & EQ. INSTS.	1978	2 260	...	...	27 830	13 692	49
	OTHER THIRD LEVEL INSTS.	1978	2 262	...	...	93 779	47 514	51
CHINA‡	ALL INSTITUTIONS	1975	155 723	37 988	24	500 993	163 290	33
		1980	246 862	62 469	25	1 161 440	270 255	23
		1981	249 876	64 455	26	1 295 047	314 671	24
		1982	286 908	73 826	26	1 175 238	308 375	26
		1983	302 919	78 324	26	1 237 394	329 393	27
		1984	315 021	82 509	26	1 443 605	407 814	28
CYPRUS	ALL INSTITUTIONS	1975	69	17	25	602	241	40
		1980	227	57	25	1 940	806	42
		1981	247	57	23	1 977	752	38
		1982	255	68	27	1 804	787	44
		1983	271	66	24	2 201	989	45
		1984	290	77	27	2 580	1 147	44
	OTHER THIRD LEVEL INSTS.	1975	69	17	25	602	241	40
		1980	227	57	25	1 940	806	42
		1981	247	57	23	1 977	752	38
		1982	255	68	27	1 804	787	44
		1983	271	66	24	2 201	989	45
		1984	290	77	27	2 580	1 147	44

COUNTRY / PAYS / PAIS	TYPE OF INSTITUTION / TYPE D'ETABLISSEMENT / TIPO DE ESTABLECIMIENTO	YEAR / ANNEE / AÑO	TEACHING STAFF / PERSONNEL ENSEIGNANT / PERSONAL DOCENTE: TOTAL	FEMALE / FEMININ / FEMENINO	% F	STUDENTS ENROLLED / ETUDIANTS INSCRITS / ESTUDIANTES MATRICULADOS: TOTAL	FEMALE / FEMININ / FEMENINO	% F
			(1)	(2)	(3)	(4)	(5)	(6)
DEMOCRATIC YEMEN	ALL INSTITUTIONS	1975	185	...	...	1 262	273	22
		1980	386	45	12	3 292	1 705	52
		1981	403	45	11	3 645	1 907	52
	UNIVERSITIES & EQ. INSTS.	1975	185	...	...	1 262	273	22
		1980	386	45	12	3 292	1 705	52
		1981	403	45	11	3 645	1 907	52
HONG KONG‡	ALL INSTITUTIONS	1975	3 043	446	15	44 482	11 194	25
		1980	3 060	...	...	38 153	9 743	26
		1981	4 992	777	16	63 971	20 087	31
		1982	5 659	899	16	71 382	23 717	33
		1983	6 224	1 085	17	74 563	25 589	34
		1984	5 928	1 438	24	76 844	26 542	35
	UNIVERSITIES & EQ. INSTS.	1975	814	138	17	8 264	2 435	29
		1980	1 073	208	19	11 689	4 021	34
		1981	1 237	206	17	11 975	4 136	35
		1982	1 369	212	15	12 618	4 390	35
		1983	1 418	255	18	13 362	4 666	35
		1984	1 569	287	18	14 436	5 101	35
	OTHER THIRD LEVEL INSTS.	1975	2 229	308	14	36 218	8 759	24
		1980	1 987	...	...	26 464	5 722	22
		1981	3 755	571	15	51 996	15 951	31
		1982	4 290	687	16	58 764	19 327	33
		1983	4 806	830	17	61 201	20 923	34
		1984	4 359	1 151	26	62 408	21 441	34
INDIA‡	ALL INSTITUTIONS	1975	235 822	39 272	17	4 615 992	1 070 962	23
		1979	277 468	50 562	18	5 345 580	1 396 466	26
INDONESIA	ALL INSTITUTIONS	1975	...	...	...	278 200	...	...
		1981	60 584	...	...	565 501	176 195	31
		1982	74 470	12 779	17	616 117	197 336	32
		1983	73 839	13 233	18	831 625	258 942	31
		1984	75 589	13 634	18	980 162	316 273	32
	UNIVERSITIES & EQ. INSTS.	1981	...	...	...	526 110	159 455	30
		1982	...	...	...	570 392	177 790	31
		1983	...	...	...	768 582	232 654	30
		1984	...	...	...	852 104	271 406	32
	OTHER THIRD LEVEL INSTS.	1981	...	...	...	39 391	16 740	42
		1982	...	...	...	45 725	19 546	43
		1983	...	...	...	63 043	26 288	42
		1984	...	...	...	128 058	44 867	35
IRAN, ISLAMIC REPUBLIC OF‡	ALL INSTITUTIONS	1975	13 392	1 831	14	151 905	42 789	28
		1982	9 395	2 016	21	135 717	40 443	30
		1983	10 334	1 856	18	151 333	45 418	30
		1984	8 240	1 660	20	177 286	45 216	26
	UNIVERSITIES & EQ. INSTS.	1975	6 253	893	14	57 264	17 368	30
		1982	8 823	1 751	20	107 896	33 300	31
		1983	7 214	1 176	16	113 993	35 201	31
		1984	7 513	1 323	18	133 302	41 334	31
	OTHER THIRD LEVEL INSTS.	1975	7 139	938	13	94 641	25 421	27
		1982	572	265	46	27 821	7 143	26
		1983	3 120	680	22	37 340	10 217	27
		1984	727	337	46	43 984	3 882	9
IRAQ	ALL INSTITUTIONS	1975	3 801	748	20	86 111	28 267	33
		1980	6 703	1 107	17	106 709	33 869	32
		1981	7 058	1 153	16	116 294	36 036	31
		1982	6 893	1 265	18	122 743	38 943	32
		1983	7 176	1 341	19	126 715	40 915	32
	UNIVERSITIES & EQ. INSTS.	1975	2 965	383	13	71 456	20 956	29
		1980	4 627	738	16	81 782	26 496	32
		1981	...	...	...	84 657	...	...
		1982	4 624	802	17	85 573	28 386	33
		1983	4 907	856	17	84 751	28 366	33
	OTHER THIRD LEVEL INSTS.	1975	836	365	44	14 655	7 311	50
		1980	2 076	369	18	24 927	7 373	30
		1981	...	...	...	31 637	...	...
		1982	2 269	463	20	37 170	10 557	28

3.11 **Third level: teachers and students by type of institution**
Troisième degré: professeurs et étudiants par type d'établissement
Tercer grado: profesores y estudiantes por tipo de establecimiento

COUNTRY / PAYS / PAIS	TYPE OF INSTITUTION / TYPE D'ETABLISSEMENT / TIPO DE ESTABLECIMIENTO	YEAR / ANNEE / AÑO	TEACHING STAFF / PERSONNEL ENSEIGNANT / PERSONAL DOCENTE			STUDENTS ENROLLED / ETUDIANTS INSCRITS / ESTUDIANTES MATRICULADOS		
			TOTAL	FEMALE FEMININ FEMENINO	% F	TOTAL	FEMALE FEMININ FEMENINO	% F
			(1)	(2)	(3)	(4)	(5)	(6)
ISRAEL‡	ALL INSTITUTIONS	1976	...	...	...	85 081	39 368	46
		1980	...	...	...	97 097	49 861	51
		1981	...	...	...	107 583	49 607	46
		1982	...	...	...	110 309	51 091	46
		1983	...	...	...	112 901	53 051	47
		1984	...	...	...	101 641	46 833	46
	UNIVERSITIES & EQ. INSTS.	1976	...	...	...	52 980	23 258	44
		1980	10 237	*3 275	*32	67 746	*32 586	*48
		1981	...	...	...	70 810	32 446	46
		1982	...	...	...	72 481	33 658	46
		1983	...	...	...	74 228	35 992	48
		1984	...	...	...	61 155	29 293	48
	OTHER THIRD LEVEL INSTS.	1976	*5 631			32 101	16 110	50
		1980	...	...	...	29 351	*17 275	*59
		1981	...	...	...	36 773	17 161	47
		1982	...	...	...	37 828	17 433	46
		1983	...	...	...	38 673	17 059	44
		1984	...	...	...	40 486	17 540	43
JAPAN‡	ALL INSTITUTIONS	1975	191 551	23 508	12	2 248 903	727 256	32
		1980	213 537	29 389	14	2 412 117	791 264	33
		1981	221 091	29 997	14	2 402 725	791 398	33
		1982	225 507	30 937	14	2 391 915	797 801	33
		1983	230 022	32 306	14	2 409 983	812 988	34
		1984	237 884	33 875	14	2 403 371	825 911	34
	UNIVERSITIES & EQ. INSTS.	1975	149 349	12 375	8	1 840 708	412 072	22
		1980	168 739	16 002	9	1 937 124	447 256	23
		1981	174 429	16 136	9	1 921 914	444 114	23
		1982	178 097	16 756	9	1 916 792	446 561	23
		1983	181 286	17 490	10	1 935 033	458 517	24
		1984	187 342	18 528	10	1 938 939	466 559	24
	OTHER THIRD LEVEL INSTS.	1975	42 202	11 133	26	408 195	315 184	77
		1980	44 798	13 387	30	474 993	344 008	72
		1981	46 662	13 861	30	480 811	347 284	72
		1982	47 410	14 181	30	475 123	351 240	74
		1983	48 736	14 816	30	474 950	354 471	75
		1984	50 542	15 347	30	464 432	359 352	77
JORDAN	ALL INSTITUTIONS	1975	*797	*169	*21	11 873	3 969	33
		1980	...	...	...	36 549	16 682	46
		1981	2 289	368	16	45 196	18 194	40
		1982	2 465	392	16	49 416	20 722	42
		1983	2 358	367	16	56 253	24 108	43
	UNIVERSITIES & EQ. INSTS.	1975	344	30	9	5 307	1 694	32
		1980	...	...	...	17 103	7 068	41
		1981	1 162	121	10	19 852	7 593	38
		1982	1 011	121	12	22 305	8 706	39
		1983	1 155	145	13	23 862	9 417	39
	OTHER THIRD LEVEL INSTS.	1975	*453	*139	*31	6 566	2 275	35
		1980	...	...	...	19 446	9 614	49
		1981	1 127	247	22	25 344	10 601	42
		1982	1 454	271	19	27 111	12 016	44
		1983	1 203	222	18	32 391	14 691	45
KOREA, REPUBLIC OF	ALL INSTITUTIONS	1975	15 317	2 266	15	297 219	81 228	27
		1980	21 173	3 270	15	615 452	148 076	24
		1981	24 357	3 899	16	786 354	194 951	25
		1982	27 616	4 609	17	954 066	245 791	26
		1983	30 049	5 127	17	1 075 969	296 449	28
		1984	32 215	5 596	17	1 193 006	340 896	29
	UNIVERSITIES & EQ. INSTS.	1975	11 578	1 654	14	222 856	57 717	26
		1980	14 969	2 289	15	436 918	96 420	22
		1981	17 728	2 737	15	580 607	129 913	22
		1982	20 424	3 246	16	715 333	169 271	24
		1983	23 040	3 688	16	839 748	215 278	26
		1984	24 835	4 047	16	933 032	243 986	26
	OTHER THIRD LEVEL INSTS.	1975	3 739	612	16	74 363	23 511	32
		1980	6 204	981	16	178 534	51 656	29
		1981	6 629	1 162	18	205 747	65 038	32
		1982	7 192	1 363	19	238 733	76 520	32
		1983	7 009	1 439	21	236 221	81 171	34
		1984	7 380	1 549	21	259 974	96 910	37

COUNTRY / PAYS / PAIS	TYPE OF INSTITUTION / TYPE D'ETABLISSEMENT / TIPO DE ESTABLECIMIENTO	YEAR / ANNEE / AÑO	TEACHING STAFF / PERSONNEL ENSEIGNANT / PERSONAL DOCENTE			STUDENTS ENROLLED / ETUDIANTS INSCRITS / ESTUDIANTES MATRICULADOS		
			TOTAL	FEMALE / FEMININ / FEMENINO	% F	TOTAL	FEMALE / FEMININ / FEMENINO	% F
			(1)	(2)	(3)	(4)	(5)	(6)
KUWAIT	ALL INSTITUTIONS	1975	596	164	28	8 104	4 608	57
		1980	1 151	270	23	13 630	7 807	57
		1981	1 279	291	23	15 725	8 551	54
		1982	1 355	282	21	17 909	10 038	56
		1983	1 502	331	22	19 185	10 346	54
		1984	1 534	378	25	21 924	11 639	53
	UNIVERSITIES & EQ. INSTS.	1975	327	16	5	6 246	3 499	56
		1980	608	61	10	9 388	5 466	58
		1981	671	69	10	10 683	5 781	54
		1982	735	74	10	12 085	6 900	57
		1983	848	125	15	13 233	7 335	55
		1984	798	88	11	15 512	8 555	55
	OTHER THIRD LEVEL INSTS.	1975	269	148	55	1 858	1 109	60
		1980	543	209	38	4 242	2 341	55
		1981	608	222	37	5 042	2 770	55
		1982	620	208	34	5 824	3 138	54
		1983	654	206	31	5 952	3 011	51
		1984	736	290	39	6 412	3 084	48
LAO PEOPLE'S DEMOCRATIC REPUBLIC‡	ALL INSTITUTIONS	1980	140	25	18	1 408	441	31
		1981	260	64	25	2 894	924	32
		1982	320	71	22	3 924	1 227	31
		1983	452	...	...	4 790	...	...
	UNIVERSITIES & EQ. INSTS.	1980	140	25	18	1 408	441	31
		1981	232	60	26	2 417	794	33
		1982	268	66	25	3 268	1 067	33
		1983	320	...	...	3 658	...	...
	OTHER THIRD LEVEL INSTS.	1981	28	4	14	477	130	27
		1982	52	5	10	656	160	24
		1983	132	...	...	1 132	...	...
LEBANON	ALL INSTITUTIONS	1980	...	...	...	79 073	28 531	36
		1981	...	...	...	70 314	26 284	37
		1982	7 976	2 478	31	73 052	27 225	37
	UNIVERSITIES & EQ. INSTS.	1980	...	...	...	79 073	28 531	36
		1981	...	...	...	70 314	26 284	37
		1982	7 976	2 478	31	73 052	27 225	37
MALAYSIA	ALL INSTITUTIONS	1980	5 541	1 415	26	57 650	22 199	39
		1981	...	...	...	67 368	28 703	43
		1982	...	...	...	68 687	30 729	45
		1983	7 431	2 127	29	77 750	33 357	43
		1984	8 213	1 801	22	93 249	41 468	44
	UNIVERSITIES & EQ. INSTS.	1980	3 299	766	23	26 287	9 105	35
		1981	3 064	851	28	33 030	12 615	38
		1982	4 020	991	25	31 018	12 210	39
		1983	4 380	1 134	26	36 744	13 726	37
		1984	4 718	1 149	24	43 295	17 066	39
	OTHER THIRD LEVEL INSTS.	1980	2 242	649	29	31 363	13 094	42
		1981	...	...	...	34 338	16 088	47
		1982	...	...	...	37 669	18 519	49
		1983	3 051	993	33	41 006	19 631	48
		1984	3 495	652	19	49 954	24 402	49
PENINSULAR MALAYSIA	ALL INSTITUTIONS	1975	...	...	...	31 529	...	...
		1978	4 929	1 192	24	49 734	18 239	37
	UNIVERSITIES & EQ. INSTS.	1975	...	...	...	18 388	...	...
		1978	3 045	642	21	22 297	7 168	32
	OTHER THIRD LEVEL INSTS.	1975	...	...	...	13 141	...	...
		1978	1 884	550	29	27 437	11 071	40
SARAWAK	ALL INSTITUTIONS	1978	113	35	31	1 467	688	47
	OTHER THIRD LEVEL INSTS.	1978	113	35	31	1 467	688	47
MONGOLIA	ALL INSTITUTIONS	1975	807	...	...	9 861	5 054	51
		1979	1 033	242	23	11 826	7 209	61
		1981	2 400	900	38	38 200	24 000	63
	UNIVERSITIES & EQ. INSTS.	1975	625	...	...	7 677	3 777	49
		1979	834	179	22	9 970	7 086	71
		1981	1 300	400	31	18 700	11 000	59

3.11 Third level: teachers and students by type of institution
Troisième degré: professeurs et étudiants par type d'établissement
Tercer grado: profesores y estudiantes por tipo de establecimiento

COUNTRY / PAYS / PAIS	TYPE OF INSTITUTION / TYPE D'ETABLISSEMENT / TIPO DE ESTABLECIMIENTO	YEAR / ANNEE / AÑO	TEACHING STAFF / PERSONNEL ENSEIGNANT / PERSONAL DOCENTE			STUDENTS ENROLLED / ETUDIANTS INSCRITS / ESTUDIANTES MATRICULADOS		
			TOTAL	FEMALE FEMININ FEMENINO	% F	TOTAL	FEMALE FEMININ FEMENINO	% F
			(1)	(2)	(3)	(4)	(5)	(6)
MONGOLIA (CONT)	OTHER THIRD LEVEL INSTS.	1975	182	...	...	2 184	1 277	58
		1979	199	63	32	1 856	123	7
		1981	1 100	500	45	19 500	13 000	67
NEPAL‡	ALL INSTITUTIONS	1975	1 516	...	...	23 504	...	...
		1980	2 918	480	16	38 450	7 358	19
		1981	...	...	...	60 296	11 672	19
		1982	...	...	...	52 070	...	...
		1983	3 795	...	...	48 229	*9 549	*20
	UNIVERSITIES & EQ. INSTS.	1975	1 516	...	...	23 504	...	...
		1980	2 918	480	16	38 450	7 358	19
		1981	...	...	...	60 296	11 672	19
		1982	...	...	...	52 070	...	...
		1983	3 795	...	...	48 229	*9 549	*20
PAKISTAN‡	ALL INSTITUTIONS	1975	5 327	750	14	127 932	30 096	24
		1979	7 042	813	12	156 558	42 046	27
	UNIVERSITIES & EQ. INSTS.	1975	5 327	750	14	127 932	30 096	24
		1979	7 042	813	12	156 558	42 046	27
PHILIPPINES	ALL INSTITUTIONS	1975	31 783	...	...	769 749	...	...
		1980	43 770	23 381	53	1 276 016	681 140	53
		1981	44 506	...	...	1 335 889	714 113	53
		1982	...	...	...	1 411 515	...	...
	UNIVERSITIES & EQ. INSTS.	1980	...	...	...	1 143 702	613 197	54
		1981	...	...	...	1 201 872	645 296	54
	OTHER THIRD LEVEL INSTS.	1980	...	...	...	132 314	67 943	51
		1981	...	...	...	134 017	68 817	51
QATAR	ALL INSTITUTIONS	1975	69	13	19	779	447	57
		1980	283	87	31	2 269	1 403	62
		1981	198	17	9	2 981	1 701	57
		1982	215	21	10	4 015	2 260	56
		1983	235	27	11	4 627	2 370	51
		1984	401	152	38	4 624	2 822	61
	UNIVERSITIES & EQ. INSTS.	1975	69	13	19	779	447	57
		1980	283	87	31	2 269	1 403	62
		1981	198	17	9	2 981	1 701	57
		1982	215	21	10	4 015	2 260	56
		1983	235	27	11	4 627	2 370	51
		1984	401	152	38	4 624	2 822	61
SAUDI ARABIA	ALL INSTITUTIONS	1975	2 133	325	15	26 437	5 310	20
		1980	7 448	1 419	19	62 074	17 311	28
		1981	8 043	1 692	21	70 657	21 003	30
		1982	8 943	2 107	24	82 132	26 172	32
		1983	9 713	2 373	24	87 821	30 948	35
	UNIVERSITIES & EQ. INSTS.	1975	2 133	325	15	26 437	5 310	20
		1980	6 598	1 306	20	56 552	16 472	29
		1981	6 943	1 533	22	64 290	19 922	31
		1982	7 928	1 824	23	75 110	24 480	33
		1983	8 559	2 001	23	80 469	28 472	35
	OTHER THIRD LEVEL INSTS.	1980	850	113	13	5 822	839	14
		1981	1 100	159	14	6 367	1 081	17
		1982	1 015	283	28	7 022	1 692	24
		1983	1 154	372	32	7 352	2 476	34
SINGAPORE	ALL INSTITUTIONS	1975	1 448	254	18	22 607	8 933	40
		1980	2 270	422	19	23 256	9 087	39
		1981	2 474	477	19	25 705	10 190	40
		1982	3 052	601	20	30 966	12 491	40
		1983	3 141	653	21	35 192	14 759	42
	UNIVERSITIES & EQ. INSTS.	1975	927	164	18	8 539	3 768	44
		1980	1 433	244	17	9 078	4 011	44
		1981	1 436	307	21	10 485	4 738	45
		1982	1 737	323	19	12 424	5 754	46
		1983	1 613	328	20	14 179	6 909	49
	OTHER THIRD LEVEL INSTS.	1975	521	90	17	14 068	5 165	37
		1980	837	178	21	14 178	5 076	36
		1981	1 038	170	16	15 220	5 452	36
		1982	1 315	278	21	18 542	6 737	36
		1983	1 528	325	21	21 013	7 850	37

COUNTRY / PAYS / PAIS	TYPE OF INSTITUTION / TYPE D'ETABLISSEMENT / TIPO DE ESTABLECIMIENTO	YEAR / ANNEE / AÑO	TEACHING STAFF / PERSONNEL ENSEIGNANT / PERSONAL DOCENTE			STUDENTS ENROLLED / ETUDIANTS INSCRITS / ESTUDIANTES MATRICULADOS		
			TOTAL	FEMALE FEMININ FEMENINO	% F	TOTAL	FEMALE FEMININ FEMENINO	% F
			(1)	(2)	(3)	(4)	(5)	(6)
SRI LANKA‡	ALL INSTITUTIONS	1975	2 000	338	17	15 426	5 506	36
		1980	4 818	...	...	42 694	18 514	43
		1981	4 652	...	...	44 247	18 877	43
		1982	4 120	...	...	57 352	...	...
		1983	5 629	...	...	63 460	...	...
	UNIVERSITIES & EQ. INSTS.	1975	2 000	338	17	15 426	5 506	36
		1980	1 827	...	...	18 111	7 214	40
		1981	1 609	...	...	17 657	7 617	43
		1982	1 913	...	...	30 164	...	...
		1983	2 234	577	26	34 725	13 596	39
	OTHER THIRD LEVEL INSTS.	1980	2 991	...	...	24 583	11 300	46
		1981	3 043	921	30	26 590	11 260	42
		1982	2 207	...	...	27 188	...	...
		1983	3 395	...	...	28 735	...	...
SYRIAN ARAB REPUBLIC	ALL INSTITUTIONS	1975	...	...	...	73 660	18 641	25
		1980	...	...	...	135 077	40 161	30
		1981	...	...	...	139 041	43 810	32
		1982	...	...	...	141 392	45 410	32
		1983	...	...	...	153 530	50 082	33
	UNIVERSITIES & EQ. INSTS.	1975	1 332	106	8	65 348	14 647	22
		1980	...	...	...	110 832	29 565	27
		1981	...	...	...	113 507	32 311	28
		1982	...	...	...	115 229	34 292	30
		1983	...	...	...	123 735	36 741	30
	OTHER THIRD LEVEL INSTS.	1975	...	...	...	8 312	3 994	48
		1980	...	...	...	24 245	10 596	44
		1981	...	...	...	25 534	11 499	45
		1982	...	...	...	26 163	11 118	42
		1983	...	...	...	29 795	13 341	45
THAILAND‡	ALL INSTITUTIONS	1975	9 070	5 121	56	130 965	52 112	40
		1980	*19 594	...	...	361 400	...	...
		1981	35 731	...	...	911 166	...	...
		1982	26 443	...	...	1 056 809	...	...
		1983	28 865	...	...	1 120 084	...	...
	UNIVERSITIES & EQ. INSTS.	1975	9 070	5 121	56	130 965	52 112	40
		1980	10 350	...	...	182 540	...	...
		1981	17 116	...	...	712 650	...	...
		1982	16 245	...	...	795 970	...	...
		1983	16 329	...	...	805 285	...	...
	OTHER THIRD LEVEL INSTS.	1980	9 244	...	...	178 860	...	...
		1981	18 165	...	...	198 516	...	...
		1982	10 198	...	...	260 839	...	...
		1983	12 536	...	...	314 799	...	...
TURKEY‡	ALL INSTITUTIONS	1975	15 560	3 759	24	327 082	52 954	16
		1980	21 577	5 312	25	246 183	61 557	25
		1981	23 364	5 783	25	254 446	66 206	26
		1982	21 814	5 839	27	281 929	85 214	30
		1983	20 492	...	...	335 080	113 008	34
		1984	21 949	...	...	417 225	131 356	31
	UNIVERSITIES & EQ. INSTS.	1975	9 596	2 279	24	183 019	21 160	12
		1980	16 162	3 734	23	175 389	42 839	24
		1981	17 413	4 026	23	171 896	43 127	25
		1982	21 814	5 839	27	281 929	85 214	30
		1983	20 492	...	...	335 080	113 008	34
		1984	21 949	...	...	417 225	131 356	31
	OTHER THIRD LEVEL INSTS.	1975	5 964	1 480	25	144 063	31 794	22
		1980	5 415	1 578	29	70 794	18 718	26
		1981	5 951	1 757	30	82 550	23 079	28
UNITED ARAB EMIRATES	ALL INSTITUTIONS	1980	...	...	...	2 734	1 306	48
		1981	...	...	...	3 407	1 770	52
		1982	...	...	...	4 408	2 293	52
		1983	...	...	...	5 867	2 999	51
		1984	599	76	13	6 856	3 975	58
	UNIVERSITIES & EQ. INSTS.	1980	208	11	5	2 519	1 126	45
		1981	...	...	...	3 185	1 570	49
		1982	279	14	5	4 227	2 123	50
		1983	...	...	...	5 615	2 761	49
		1984	449	46	10	6 326	3 475	55

3.11 Third level: teachers and students by type of institution
Troisième degré: professeurs et étudiants par type d'établissement
Tercer grado: profesores y estudiantes por tipo de establecimiento

COUNTRY / PAYS / PAIS	TYPE OF INSTITUTION / TYPE D'ETABLISSEMENT / TIPO DE ESTABLECIMIENTO	YEAR / ANNEE / AÑO	TEACHING STAFF / PERSONNEL ENSEIGNANT / PERSONAL DOCENTE: TOTAL (1)	FEMALE / FEMININ / FEMENINO (2)	% F (3)	STUDENTS ENROLLED / ETUDIANTS INSCRITS / ESTUDIANTES MATRICULADOS: TOTAL (4)	FEMALE / FEMININ / FEMENINO (5)	% F (6)
UNITED ARAB EMIRATES (CONT)	OTHER THIRD LEVEL INSTS.	1980	...	...	...	215	180	84
		1981	...	...	...	222	200	90
		1982	...	...	...	181	170	94
		1983	50	10	20	252	238	94
		1984	150	30	20	530	500	94
VIET-NAM‡	ALL INSTITUTIONS	1975	9 642	1 705	18	80 323	31 702	39
		1980	17 242	3 857	22	114 701	27 090	24
	UNIVERSITIES & EQ. INSTS.	1975	9 642	1 705	18	80 323	31 702	39
		1980	17 242	3 857	22	114 701	27 090	24
YEMEN	ALL INSTITUTIONS	1975	...	...	...	2 408	246	10
		1980	157	7	4	4 519	508	11
	UNIVERSITIES & EQ. INSTS.	1975	...	...	...	2 408	246	10
		1980	157	7	4	4 519	508	11
EUROPE								
ALBANIA‡	ALL INSTITUTIONS	1980	1 103	222	20	14 568	7 221	50
		1982	1 240	280	23	17 500	8 350	48
		1983	1 360	308	23	19 670	9 130	46
		1984	1 502	333	22	21 285	9 580	45
	UNIVERSITIES & EQ. INSTS.	1980	1 103	222	20	14 568	7 221	50
		1982	1 240	280	23	17 500	8 350	48
		1983	1 360	308	23	19 670	9 130	46
		1984	1 502	333	22	21 285	9 580	45
AUSTRIA‡	ALL INSTITUTIONS	1975	...	...	...	96 736	36 527	38
		1980	...	...	...	136 774	57 491	42
		1981	...	...	...	140 720	60 268	43
		1982	...	...	...	146 351	64 127	44
		1983	...	...	...	154 126	68 163	44
		1984	11 744	2 308	20	165 313	74 116	45
	UNIVERSITIES & EQ. INSTS.	1975	10 001	1 282	13	86 123	28 931	34
		1980	12 572	1 599	13	127 423	50 200	39
		1981	9 387	1 520	16	129 037	51 751	40
		1982	9 414	1 567	17	134 621	55 626	41
		1983	9 644	1 656	17	142 159	59 442	42
		1984	9 945	1 737	17	151 934	64 647	43
	OTHER THIRD LEVEL INSTS.	1975	...	...	...	10 613	7 596	72
		1980	...	...	...	9 351	7 291	78
		1981	...	...	...	11 683	8 517	73
		1982	...	...	...	11 730	8 501	72
		1983	...	...	...	11 967	8 721	73
		1984	1 799	571	32	13 379	9 469	71
BELGIUM‡	ALL INSTITUTIONS	1975	...	...	...	159 660	66 167	41
		1980	...	...	...	196 153	86 947	44
		1981	...	...	...	213 281	94 648	44
		1982	...	...	...	219 591	99 443	45
		1983	...	...	...	225 378	103 499	46
		1984	...	...	...	245 762	111 349	45
	UNIVERSITIES & EQ. INSTS.	1975	...	...	...	83 360	27 773	33
		1980	...	...	...	95 246	35 107	37
		1981	...	...	...	95 882	36 100	38
		1982	...	...	...	96 795	37 405	39
		1983	...	...	...	100 362	39 816	40
		1984	...	...	...	102 354	41 231	40
	OTHER THIRD LEVEL INSTS.	1975	...	...	...	76 300	38 394	50
		1980	...	...	...	100 907	51 840	51
		1981	...	...	...	117 399	58 548	50
		1982	...	...	...	122 796	62 038	51
		1983	...	...	...	125 016	63 683	51
		1984	...	...	...	143 408	70 118	49
BULGARIA‡	ALL INSTITUTIONS	1975	12 230	3 937	32	128 593	73 806	57
		1980	14 412	5 592	39	101 359	56 946	56
		1981	13 910	4 788	34	97 785	52 672	54
		1982	14 227	5 316	37	95 723	50 775	53
		1983	14 171	5 179	37	98 612	52 779	54
		1984	14 918	5 370	36	104 333	56 084	54

COUNTRY / PAYS / PAIS	TYPE OF INSTITUTION / TYPE D'ETABLISSEMENT / TIPO DE ESTABLECIMIENTO	YEAR / ANNEE / AÑO	TEACHING STAFF / PERSONNEL ENSEIGNANT / PERSONAL DOCENTE			STUDENTS ENROLLED / ETUDIANTS INSCRITS / ESTUDIANTES MATRICULADOS		
			TOTAL	FEMALE / FEMININ / FEMENINO	% F	TOTAL	FEMALE / FEMININ / FEMENINO	% F
			(1)	(2)	(3)	(4)	(5)	(6)
BULGARIA (CONT)‡	UNIVERSITIES & EQ. INSTS.	1975	11 248	3 411	30	108 814	57 957	53
		1980	12 622	4 638	37	87 335	46 491	53
		1981	12 820	4 253	33	87 033	45 101	52
		1982	13 254	4 798	36	85 824	43 682	51
		1983	13 205	4 656	35	88 637	45 438	51
		1984	14 005	4 886	35	95 207	49 457	52
	OTHER THIRD LEVEL INSTS.	1975	982	526	54	19 779	15 849	80
		1980	1 790	954	53	14 024	10 455	75
		1981	1 090	535	49	10 752	7 571	70
		1982	973	518	53	9 899	7 093	72
		1983	966	523	54	9 975	7 341	74
		1984	913	484	53	9 126	6 627	73
CZECHOSLOVAKIA	ALL INSTITUTIONS	1975	21 298	5 230	25	155 059	62 514	40
		1980	22 478	5 816	26	197 041	81 975	42
		1981	21 842	5 915	27	198 784	83 660	42
		1982	21 863	5 891	27	192 397	82 111	43
		1983	20 574	5 763	28	181 524	78 024	43
		1984	23 274	6 390	27	174 843	74 535	43
	UNIVERSITIES & EQ. INSTS.	1975	21 298	5 230	25	155 059	62 514	40
		1980	22 478	5 816	26	197 041	81 975	42
		1981	21 842	5 915	27	198 784	83 660	42
		1982	21 863	5 891	27	192 397	82 111	43
		1983	20 574	5 763	28	181 524	78 024	43
		1984	23 274	6 390	27	174 843	74 535	43
DENMARK‡	ALL INSTITUTIONS	1975	...	...	...	110 271	48 837	44
		1980	...	...	...	106 241	51 923	49
		1981	...	...	...	106 669	52 914	50
		1982	...	...	...	110 731	54 184	49
		1983	...	...	...	113 157	55 765	49
	UNIVERSITIES & EQ. INSTS.	1975	4 777	...	...	60 106	21 870	36
		1980	...	...	...	85 388	36 318	43
		1981	...	...	...	85 145	36 765	43
		1982	...	...	...	86 235	37 320	43
		1983	...	...	...	87 308	37 930	43
	OTHER THIRD LEVEL INSTS.	1975	1 551	...	...	50 165	26 967	54
		1980	...	...	...	20 853	15 605	75
		1981	...	...	...	21 524	16 149	75
		1982	...	...	...	24 496	16 864	69
		1983	...	...	...	25 849	17 835	69
FINLAND	ALL INSTITUTIONS	1975	...	...	...	114 272	...	...
		1980	...	...	...	123 165	59 356	48
		1981	...	...	...	124 831	60 897	49
		1982	...	...	...	127 657	62 837	49
		1983	...	...	...	119 982	57 231	48
		1984	...	...	...	119 519	...	...
	UNIVERSITIES & EQ. INSTS.	1975	5 225	...	...	75 765	37 151	49
		1980	6 194	...	...	84 176	41 746	50
		1981	6 471	...	...	86 026	43 171	50
		1982	6 618	...	...	87 488	44 034	50
		1983	6 938	...	...	88 295	44 524	50
	OTHER THIRD LEVEL INSTS.	1975	...	...	...	38 507	...	...
		1980	...	...	...	38 989	17 610	45
		1981	...	...	...	38 805	17 726	46
		1982	...	...	...	40 169	18 803	47
		1983	...	...	...	31 687	12 707	40
FRANCE‡	ALL INSTITUTIONS	1975	...	...	...	1 038 576	*496 049	*48
		1980	...	...	...	1 076 717	...	...
		1981	...	...	...	1 150 055	556 990	48
		1982	...	...	...	1 179 268	579 459	49
		1983	...	...	...	1 144 080	...	...
	UNIVERSITIES & EQ. INSTS.	1975	40 512	...	...	811 258	*386 000	*48
		1980	...	...	...	869 788	...	...
		1981	...	...	...	900 529	454 889	51
		1982	...	...	...	923 547	471 614	51
		1983	...	...	...	942 069	...	...
	OTHER THIRD LEVEL INSTS.	1975	...	...	...	227 318	110 049	48
		1980	...	...	...	206 929	80 104	39
		1981	...	...	...	249 526	102 101	41
		1982	...	...	...	255 721	107 845	42
		1983	...	...	...	202 020	...	...

3.11 Third level: teachers and students by type of institution
Troisième degré: professeurs et étudiants par type d'établissement
Tercer grado: profesores y estudiantes por tipo de establecimiento

COUNTRY / PAYS / PAIS	TYPE OF INSTITUTION / TYPE D'ETABLISSEMENT / TIPO DE ESTABLECIMIENTO	YEAR / ANNEE / AÑO	TEACHING STAFF / PERSONNEL ENSEIGNANT / PERSONAL DOCENTE			STUDENTS ENROLLED / ETUDIANTS INSCRITS / ESTUDIANTES MATRICULADOS		
			TOTAL	FEMALE / FEMININ / FEMENINO	% F	TOTAL	FEMALE / FEMININ / FEMENINO	% F
			(1)	(2)	(3)	(4)	(5)	(6)
GERMAN DEMOCRATIC REPUBLIC‡	ALL INSTITUTIONS	1975	34 566	8 784	25	386 000	...	...
		1980	38 699	10 498	27	400 799	232 336	58
		1981	40 835	12 926	32	404 618	235 955	58
		1982	41 385	13 584	33	403 388	235 994	59
		1983	41 655	13 617	33	434 326	240 569	55
		1984	41 755	13 622	33	431 774	237 564	55
	UNIVERSITIES & EQ. INSTS.	1975	26 115	5 822	22	142 567	66 899	47
		1980	28 848	6 509	23	137 554	65 297	47
		1981	29 380	7 466	25	139 293	66 212	48
		1982	29 460	7 763	26	139 699	66 809	48
		1983	29 678	7 730	26	147 376	69 917	47
		1984	29 818	7 749	26	147 432	69 425	47
	OTHER THIRD LEVEL INSTS.	1975	8 451	2 962	35	243 433	...	...
		1980	9 851	3 989	40	263 245	167 039	63
		1981	11 455	5 460	48	265 325	169 743	64
		1982	11 925	5 821	49	263 689	169 185	64
		1983	11 977	5 887	49	286 950	170 652	59
		1984	11 937	5 873	49	284 342	168 139	59
GERMANY, FEDERAL REPUBLIC OF	ALL INSTITUTIONS	1975	144 834	...	...	1 041 225	400 986	39
		1980	171 708	...	...	1 223 221	503 448	41
		1981	177 202	...	...	1 325 179	552 783	42
		1982	177 146	...	...	1 405 478	589 646	42
		1983	...	...	...	1 471 964	613 622	42
		1984	182 310	...	...	1 503 035	627 505	42
	UNIVERSITIES & EQ. INSTS.	1975	103 578	...	...	836 002	282 113	34
		1980	127 383	...	...	1 031 590	378 556	37
		1981	129 781	19 743	15	1 121 434	422 179	38
		1982	130 743	20 010	15	1 198 330	456 391	38
		1983	...	...	...	1 266 488	479 256	38
		1984	134 566	...	...	1 311 475	494 831	38
	OTHER THIRD LEVEL INSTS.	1975	41 256	...	...	205 223	118 873	58
		1980	44 325	13 847	31	191 631	124 892	65
		1981	47 421	...	...	203 745	130 604	64
		1982	46 403	...	...	207 148	133 255	64
		1983	46 944	...	...	205 476	134 366	65
		1984	47 744	15 732	33	191 560	132 674	69
GREECE	ALL INSTITUTIONS	1975	...	...	...	117 246	43 361	37
		1980	10 542	3 372	32	121 116	50 204	41
		1981	11 310	3 695	33	124 694	53 376	43
	UNIVERSITIES & EQ. INSTS.	1975	5 956	2 092	35	95 385	35 701	37
		1980	6 924	2 444	35	85 718	36 335	42
		1981	7 489	2 646	35	87 476	37 660	43
	OTHER THIRD LEVEL INSTS.	1975	...	...	...	21 861	7 660	35
		1980	3 618	928	26	35 398	13 869	39
		1981	3 821	1 049	27	37 218	15 716	42
HOLY SEE‡	ALL INSTITUTIONS	1975	1 280	37	3	7 758	2 099	27
		1980	1 349	90	7	9 104	3 538	39
		1981	974	70	7	7 417	2 727	37
		1982	1 113	81	7	8 239	3 001	36
		1983	1 427	87	6	9 211	3 079	33
		1984	1 464	87	6	9 656	3 354	35
	UNIVERSITIES & EQ. INSTS.	1975	1 280	37	3	7 758	2 099	27
		1980	1 349	90	7	9 104	3 538	39
		1981	974	70	7	7 417	2 727	37
		1982	1 113	81	7	8 239	3 001	36
		1983	1 427	87	6	9 211	3 079	33
		1984	1 464	87	6	9 656	3 354	35
HUNGARY‡	ALL INSTITUTIONS	1975	12 135	3 244	27	107 555	51 952	48
		1980	13 890	4 046	29	101 166	50 314	50
		1981	13 843	4 012	29	102 564	52 322	51
		1982	14 011	4 234	30	100 564	51 869	52
		1983	14 452	4 339	30	99 865	52 720	53
		1984	14 545	4 551	31	99 986	52 977	53
	UNIVERSITIES & EQ. INSTS.	1975	9 494	2 382	25	67 983	33 081	49
		1980	10 616	2 872	27	61 767	29 099	47
		1981	10 554	2 807	27	61 140	28 932	47
		1982	10 610	2 992	28	60 168	28 670	48
		1983	11 121	3 047	27	60 084	29 389	49
		1984	11 136	3 244	29	60 648	29 683	49

COUNTRY / PAYS / PAIS	TYPE OF INSTITUTION / TYPE D'ETABLISSEMENT / TIPO DE ESTABLECIMIENTO	YEAR / ANNEE / AÑO	TEACHING STAFF / PERSONNEL ENSEIGNANT / PERSONAL DOCENTE TOTAL	FEMALE FEMININ FEMENINO	% F	STUDENTS ENROLLED / ETUDIANTS INSCRITS / ESTUDIANTES MATRICULADOS TOTAL	FEMALE FEMININ FEMENINO	% F
			(1)	(2)	(3)	(4)	(5)	(6)
HUNGARY (CONT)‡	OTHER THIRD LEVEL INSTS.	1975	2 641	862	33	39 572	18 871	48
		1980	3 274	1 174	36	39 399	21 215	54
		1981	3 289	1 205	37	41 424	23 390	56
		1982	3 401	1 242	37	40 396	23 199	57
		1983	3 331	1 292	39	39 781	23 331	59
		1984	3 409	1 307	38	39 338	23 294	59
ICELAND	ALL INSTITUTIONS	1975	575	68	12	2 970	1 094	37
		1980	...	...	...	5 219	2 071	40
		1981	...	...	...	4 383	2 179	50
		1982	...	...	...	5 053	2 563	51
		1983	...	...	...	5 212	2 699	52
		1984	...	...	...	5 125	...	...
	UNIVERSITIES & EQ. INSTS.	1975	527	54	10	2 789	965	35
	OTHER THIRD LEVEL INSTS.	1975	48	14	29	181	129	71
IRELAND	ALL INSTITUTIONS	1975	4 088	...	...	46 174	15 842	34
		1980	...	...	...	54 746	22 248	41
		1981	5 572	...	...	59 824	24 085	40
		1982	4 806	...	...	64 116	26 427	41
	UNIVERSITIES & EQ. INSTS.	1975	2 261	...	...	24 976	10 172	41
		1980	...	...	...	33 173	15 819	48
		1981	2 897	...	...	33 982	16 185	48
		1982	2 427	...	...	35 315	16 835	48
	OTHER THIRD LEVEL INSTS.	1975	1 827	...	...	21 198	5 670	27
		1980	2 688	...	...	21 573	6 429	30
		1981	2 675	...	...	25 842	7 900	31
		1982	2 379	...	...	28 801	9 592	33
ITALY‡	ALL INSTITUTIONS	1975	...	...	...	976 712	380 408	39
		1980	...	...	...	1 117 742	476 028	43
		1981	...	...	...	...	...	...
		1982	48 787	...	...	1 090 775	480 616	44
		1983	49 071	...	...	1 120 342	498 725	45
		1984	49 997	...	...	1 181 953	534 595	45
	UNIVERSITIES & EQ. INSTS.	1975	41 824	...	...	968 119	376 323	39
		1980	42 531	...	...	1 110 547	471 919	42
		1981	...	...	...	1 024 681	449 149	44
		1982	47 936	...	...	1 083 403	476 134	44
		1983	48 590	...	...	1 112 487	493 894	44
		1984	49 472	...	...	1 173 910	529 503	45
	OTHER THIRD LEVEL INSTS.	1975	...	...	...	8 593	4 085	48
		1980	...	...	...	7 195	4 109	57
		1982	851	...	...	7 372	4 482	61
		1983	481	77	16	7 855	4 831	62
		1984	525	...	...	8 043	5 092	63
LUXEMBOURG‡	ALL INSTITUTIONS	1975	137	11	8	483	204	42
		1980	250	...	...	748	264	35
		1981	236	...	...	699	244	35
		1982	236	...	...	941	301	32
		1983	318	...	...	982	351	36
	OTHER THIRD LEVEL INSTS.	1975	137	11	8	483	204	42
		1980	250	...	...	748	264	35
		1981	236	...	...	699	244	35
		1982	236	...	...	941	301	32
		1983	318	...	...	982	351	36
MALTA	ALL INSTITUTIONS	1975	236	13	6	1 425	401	28
		1980	129	7	5	947	231	24
		1981	125	8	6	934	198	21
		1982	146	6	4	1 010	218	22
		1983	156	7	4	1 337	337	25
		1984	156	8	5	1 411	424	30
	UNIVERSITIES & EQ. INSTS.	1975	179	9	5	844	256	30
		1980	129	7	5	947	231	24
		1981	125	8	6	934	198	21
		1982	146	6	4	1 010	218	22
		1983	156	7	4	1 337	337	25
		1984	156	8	5	1 411	424	30
	OTHER THIRD LEVEL INSTS.	1975	57	4	7	581	145	25

3.11 Third level: teachers and students by type of institution
Troisième degré: professeurs et étudiants par type d'établissement
Tercer grado: profesores y estudiantes por tipo de establecimiento

COUNTRY / PAYS / PAIS	TYPE OF INSTITUTION / TYPE D'ETABLISSEMENT / TIPO DE ESTABLECIMIENTO	YEAR / ANNEE / AÑO	TEACHING STAFF / PERSONNEL ENSEIGNANT / PERSONAL DOCENTE			STUDENTS ENROLLED / ETUDIANTS INSCRITS / ESTUDIANTES MATRICULADOS		
			TOTAL	FEMALE / FEMININ / FEMENINO	% F	TOTAL	FEMALE / FEMININ / FEMENINO	% F
			(1)	(2)	(3)	(4)	(5)	(6)
NETHERLANDS‡	ALL INSTITUTIONS	1975	...	...	...	288 026	94 021	33
		1980	...	...	...	360 033	143 083	40
		1981	...	...	...	371 515	152 918	41
		1982	...	...	...	379 047	158 878	42
		1983	...	...	...	384 131	161 515	42
		1984	...	...	...	...	...	...
	UNIVERSITIES & EQ. INSTS.	1975	...	...	...	120 134	29 995	25
		1980	...	...	...	149 524	46 227	31
		1981	...	...	...	152 141	48 929	32
		1982	...	...	...	155 025	51 498	33
		1983	...	...	...	162 567	56 111	35
		1984	...	...	...	174 525	62 055	36
	OTHER THIRD LEVEL INSTS.	1975	...	...	...	167 892	64 026	38
		1980	...	...	...	210 509	96 856	46
		1981	...	...	...	219 374	103 989	47
		1982	...	...	...	224 022	107 380	48
		1983	...	...	...	221 564	105 404	48
NORWAY	ALL INSTITUTIONS	1975	6 650	1 071	16	66 628	25 088	38
		1980	7 763	1 490	19	79 117	37 831	48
		1981	9 555	2 483	26	82 511	40 092	49
		1982	10 093	...	...	88 510	43 200	49
		1983	10 206	...	...	91 330	45 135	49
	UNIVERSITIES & EQ. INSTS.	1975	3 757	446	12	40 774	14 695	36
		1980	3 903	511	13	40 620	16 642	41
		1981	4 001	559	14	39 827	16 811	42
		1982	...	...	...	41 002	18 043	44
		1983	...	...	...	41 367	18 588	45
	OTHER THIRD LEVEL INSTS.	1975	2 893	625	22	25 854	10 393	40
		1980	3 860	979	25	38 497	21 189	55
		1981	5 554	1 924	35	42 684	23 281	55
		1982	...	...	...	47 508	25 157	53
		1983	...	...	...	49 963	26 547	53
POLAND‡	ALL INSTITUTIONS	1975	...	...	...	575 499	311 867	54
		1980	...	...	...	589 134	328 416	56
		1981	...	...	...	544 895	303 959	56
		1982	...	...	...	495 902	273 505	55
		1983	...	...	...	475 816	262 999	55
		1984	...	...	...	456 661	253 246	55
	UNIVERSITIES & EQ. INSTS.	1975	50 272	17 068	34	468 129	230 503	49
		1980	57 083	19 726	35	453 652	226 658	50
		1981	56 997	19 806	35	426 466	215 626	51
		1982	58 933	20 369	35	396 629	199 750	50
		1983	58 750	19 471	33	384 429	194 126	50
		1984	59 913	19 727	33	365 310	184 242	50
	OTHER THIRD LEVEL INSTS.	1975	...	...	...	107 370	81 364	76
		1980	...	...	...	135 482	101 758	75
		1981	...	...	...	118 429	88 333	75
		1982	...	...	...	99 273	73 755	74
		1983	...	...	...	91 387	68 873	75
		1984	...	...	...	91 351	69 004	76
PORTUGAL‡	ALL INSTITUTIONS	1975	7 891	2 527	32	79 702	35 854	45
		1980	10 695	3 364	31	92 152	44 549	48
		1981	11 366	3 217	28	94 958	47 182	50
		1982	12 608	4 083	32	99 165	49 785	50
	UNIVERSITIES & EQ. INSTS.	1975	4 168	1 060	25	51 489	23 854	46
		1980	6 906	2 038	30	67 652	32 269	48
		1981	7 423	1 795	24	69 371	34 211	49
		1982	8 211	2 384	29	71 697	35 205	49
	OTHER THIRD LEVEL INSTS.	1975	3 723	1 467	39	28 213	12 000	43
		1980	3 789	1 326	35	24 500	12 280	50
		1981	3 943	1 422	36	25 587	12 971	51
		1982	4 397	1 699	39	27 468	14 580	53
ROMANIA‡	ALL INSTITUTIONS	1975	14 066	4 105	29	164 567	73 690	45
		1980	14 592	4 364	30	192 769	82 113	43
		1981	14 354	4 339	30	190 903	81 677	43
		1982	13 931	4 137	30	181 081	76 889	42
		1983	13 344	3 975	30	174 042	75 255	43
		1984	13 250	3 799	29	166 328	72 583	44

COUNTRY PAYS PAIS	TYPE OF INSTITUTION TYPE D'ETABLISSEMENT TIPO DE ESTABLECIMIENTO	YEAR ANNEE AÑO	TEACHING STAFF PERSONNEL ENSEIGNANT PERSONAL DOCENTE TOTAL	 FEMALE FEMININ FEMENINO	 % F	STUDENTS ENROLLED ETUDIANTS INSCRITS ESTUDIANTES MATRICULADOS TOTAL	 FEMALE FEMININ FEMENINO	 % F
			(1)	(2)	(3)	(4)	(5)	(6)
ROMANIA (CONT)‡	UNIVERSITIES & EQ. INSTS.	1975	14 066	4 105	29	164 567	73 690	45
		1980	14 592	4 364	30	192 769	82 113	43
		1981	14 354	4 339	30	190 903	81 677	43
		1982	13 931	4 137	30	181 081	76 889	42
		1983	13 344	3 975	30	174 042	75 255	43
		1984	13 250	3 799	29	166 328	72 583	44
SPAIN‡	ALL INSTITUTIONS	1975	29 701	5 538	19	540 238	195 616	36
		1980	42 831	8 997	21	681 022	298 983	44
		1981	44 241	10 285	23	704 310	318 805	45
		1982	45 689	10 995	24	731 053	341 853	47
		1983	47 087	11 630	25	787 864	379 407	48
	UNIVERSITIES & EQ. INSTS.	1975	22 848	3 924	17	405 869	144 699	36
		1980	31 163	5 636	18	498 874	211 940	42
		1981	32 040	6 640	21	517 215	227 099	44
		1982	32 838	7 031	21	543 873	248 592	46
		1983	34 171	7 607	22	594 245	281 591	47
	OTHER THIRD LEVEL INSTS.	1975	6 853	1 614	24	134 369	50 917	38
		1980	11 668	3 361	29	182 148	87 043	48
		1981	12 201	3 389	28	187 095	91 706	49
		1982	12 851	3 964	31	187 180	93 261	50
		1983	12 916	4 023	31	193 619	97 816	51
SWEDEN	ALL INSTITUTIONS	1975	...	...	...	162 640	65 626	40
		1980	...	...	...	203 699	...	...
		1981	...	...	...	205 431	94 584	46
		1982	...	...	...	216 412	...	...
		1983	...	...	...	223 295	103 839	47
		1984	...	...	...	221 005	...	...
	UNIVERSITIES & EQ. INSTS.	1975	...	...	...	113 348	41 529	37
	OTHER THIRD LEVEL INSTS.	1975	...	...	...	49 292	24 097	49
SWITZERLAND	ALL INSTITUTIONS	1975	...	...	...	64 720	...	...
		1980	...	...	...	85 127	25 766	30
		1981	...	...	...	88 385	27 562	31
		1982	...	...	...	90 568	29 246	32
		1983	...	...	...	95 661	31 358	33
		1984	...	...	...	105 897	33 785	32
	UNIVERSITIES & EQ. INSTS.	1975	5 414	356	7	52 623	14 088	27
		1980	5 942	457	8	61 374	19 915	32
		1981	6 050	...	...	63 899	21 428	34
		1982	5 882	...	...	66 206	22 761	34
		1983	5 827	...	...	69 839	24 484	35
		1984	5 982	...	...	72 604	25 709	35
	OTHER THIRD LEVEL INSTS.	1975	...	...	...	12 097	...	...
		1980	...	...	...	23 753	5 851	25
		1981	...	...	...	24 486	6 134	25
		1982	...	...	...	24 362	6 485	27
		1983	...	...	...	25 822	6 874	27
		1984	...	...	...	33 293	8 076	24
UNITED KINGDOM‡	ALL INSTITUTIONS	1975	...	...	...	732 947	264 254	36
		1980	...	...	...	827 146	302 972	37
		1981	*63 000	...	...	858 416	320 237	37
		1982	...	...	...	*875 000	*336 000	*38
		1983	...	...	...	*897 000	350 000	*39
	UNIVERSITIES & EQ. INSTS.	1975	...	...	...	346 066	117 682	34
		1980	...	...	...	407 665	156 439	38
		1981	39 377	5 016	13	414 508	162 409	39
		1982	...	...	...	*413 000	*165 000	*40
		1983	...	...	...	*413 000	*167 000	*40
	OTHER THIRD LEVEL INSTS.	1975	...	...	...	386 881	146 572	38
		1980	...	...	...	419 481	146 533	35
		1981	*23 623	...	...	443 908	157 828	36
		1982	...	...	...	*462 000	*171 000	*37
		1983	...	...	...	*484 000	*183 000	*38
YUGOSLAVIA	ALL INSTITUTIONS	1975	...	...	...	394 992	157 514	40
		1980	24 449	5 785	24	411 995	186 991	45
		1981	24 824	5 909	24	403 029	183 580	46
		1982	25 118	6 015	24	387 337	175 804	45
		1983	25 235	6 274	25	375 393	168 592	45

3.11 Third level: teachers and students by type of institution
Troisième degré: professeurs et étudiants par type d'établissement
Tercer grado: profesores y estudiantes por tipo de establecimiento

COUNTRY / PAYS / PAIS	TYPE OF INSTITUTION / TYPE D'ETABLISSEMENT / TIPO DE ESTABLECIMIENTO	YEAR / ANNEE / AÑO	TEACHING STAFF / PERSONNEL ENSEIGNANT / PERSONAL DOCENTE: TOTAL	FEMALE / FEMININ / FEMENINO	% F	STUDENTS ENROLLED / ETUDIANTS INSCRITS / ESTUDIANTES MATRICULADOS: TOTAL	FEMALE / FEMININ / FEMENINO	% F
			(1)	(2)	(3)	(4)	(5)	(6)
YUGOSLAVIA (CONT)	UNIVERSITIES & EQ. INSTS.	1975	...	...	...	271 517	109 450	40
		1980	19 981	4 799	24	310 650	142 517	46
		1981	20 478	4 951	24	312 916	143 155	46
		1982	20 718	5 036	24	303 392	138 226	46
		1983	21 218	5 375	25	294 492	133 707	45
	OTHER THIRD LEVEL INSTS.	1975	...	...	...	123 475	48 064	39
		1980	4 468	986	22	101 345	44 474	44
		1981	4 346	958	22	90 113	40 425	45
		1982	4 400	979	22	83 945	37 578	45
		1983	4 017	899	22	80 901	34 885	43
OCEANIA								
AMERICAN SAMOA	ALL INSTITUTIONS	1975	...	...	...	689	337	49
		1982	...	...	...	1 007	516	51
	OTHER THIRD LEVEL INSTS.	1975	...	...	...	689	337	49
		1982	...	...	...	1 007	516	51
AUSTRALIA‡	ALL INSTITUTIONS	1975	19 920	...	...	274 738	111 596	41
		1980	20 822	...	...	323 716	146 676	45
		1981	20 687	...	...	334 030	150 825	45
		1982	19 377	...	...	337 953	154 133	46
		1983	20 783	...	...	349 243	161 419	46
		1984	22 234	...	...	358 498	166 797	47
	UNIVERSITIES & EQ. INSTS.	1975	19 920	...	...	274 738	111 596	41
		1980	20 822	...	...	323 716	146 676	45
		1981	20 687	...	...	334 030	150 825	45
		1982	19 377	...	...	337 953	154 133	46
		1983	20 783	...	...	349 243	161 419	46
		1984	22 234	...	...	358 498	166 797	47
COOK ISLANDS	ALL INSTITUTIONS	1980	41	10	24	360	163	45
	UNIVERSITIES & EQ. INSTS.	1980	32	8	25	303	134	44
	OTHER THIRD LEVEL INSTS.	1980	9	2	22	57	29	51
FIJI‡	ALL INSTITUTIONS	1975	166	29	17	1 653	478	29
		1980	...	...	...	1 814	...	...
		1981	...	...	...	2 003	699	35
		1982	...	...	...	2 299	...	...
	UNIVERSITIES & EQ. INSTS.	1975	105	17	16	1 229	385	31
		1980	...	...	...	1 814	...	...
		1981	...	...	...	2 003	699	35
		1982	...	...	...	2 299	...	...
	OTHER THIRD LEVEL INSTS.	1975	61	12	20	424	93	22
FRENCH POLYNESIA	ALL INSTITUTIONS	1980	14	1	7	27	7	26
		1981	...	...	...	37	...	...
		1982	12	4	33	68	33	49
		1983	...	...	...	180	...	...
	OTHER THIRD LEVEL INSTS.	1980	14	1	7	27	7	26
		1981	...	...	...	37	...	...
		1982	12	4	33	68	33	49
		1983	...	...	...	180	...	...
GUAM	ALL INSTITUTIONS	1975	...	...	...	3 800	1 616	43
		1979	...	...	...	3 168	1 703	54
	UNIVERSITIES & EQ. INSTS.	1975	...	...	...	3 800	1 616	43
		1979	...	...	...	3 168	1 703	54
NEW CALEDONIA	ALL INSTITUTIONS	1975	23	3	13	178	62	35
		1980	97	47	48	438	169	39
		1981	72	...	...	421	...	...
		1982	65	...	...	715	192	27
		1983	54	...	...	580	194	33
		1984	59	20	34	660	252	38
	OTHER THIRD LEVEL INSTS.	1975	23	3	13	178	62	35
		1980	97	47	48	438	169	39
		1981	72	...	...	421	...	...
		1982	65	...	...	715	192	27
		1983	54	...	...	580	194	33
		1984	59	20	34	660	252	38

COUNTRY / PAYS / PAIS	TYPE OF INSTITUTION / TYPE D'ETABLISSEMENT / TIPO DE ESTABLECIMIENTO	YEAR / ANNEE / AÑO	TEACHING STAFF / PERSONNEL ENSEIGNANT / PERSONAL DOCENTE			STUDENTS ENROLLED / ETUDIANTS INSCRITS / ESTUDIANTES MATRICULADOS		
			TOTAL	FEMALE FEMININ FEMENINO	% F	TOTAL	FEMALE FEMININ FEMENINO	% F
			(1)	(2)	(3)	(4)	(5)	(6)
NEW ZEALAND	ALL INSTITUTIONS	1975	...	...	...	66 178	24 146	36
		1980	7 694	1 377	18	76 643	31 101	41
		1981	7 683	1 531	20	80 715	33 492	41
		1982	7 753	1 796	23	82 666	33 930	41
		1983	7 676	1 669	22	84 764	35 231	42
	UNIVERSITIES & EQ. INSTS.	1975	4 108	454	11	36 931	13 801	37
		1980	4 780	647	14	43 933	18 379	42
		1981	4 670	752	16	44 736	19 063	43
		1982	4 727	786	17	45 311	19 900	44
		1983	4 699	873	19	46 470	20 870	45
	OTHER THIRD LEVEL INSTS.	1975	...	...	...	29 247	10 345	35
		1980	2 914	730	25	32 710	12 722	39
		1981	3 013	779	26	35 979	14 429	40
		1982	3 026	816	27	37 355	14 030	38
		1983	2 977	796	27	38 294	14 361	38
PACIFIC ISLANDS	ALL INSTITUTIONS	1980	...	...	...	2 129	514	24
		1981	174	81	47	1 602	733	46
		1982	189	69	37	*1 964	608	*31
	OTHER THIRD LEVEL INSTS.	1980	...	...	...	2 129	514	24
		1981	174	81	47	1 602	733	46
		1982	189	69	37	*1 964	608	*31
PAPUA NEW GUINEA	ALL INSTITUTIONS	1975	...	...	...	...	...	...
		1980	*638	...	...	*5 040	*1 112	*22
		1982	...	...	...	...	...	...
		1983	...	...	...	4 846	1 127	23
		1984	...	...	...	6 062	1 376	23
	UNIVERSITIES & EQ. INSTS.	1975	353	...	...	2 869	338	12
		1980	473	...	...	2 872	305	11
		1982	589	...	...	3 458	525	15
		1983	660	...	...	3 386	562	17
		1984	...	...	...	3 167	517	16
	OTHER THIRD LEVEL INSTS.	1980	*165	...	...	*2 168	*807	*37
		1983	...	...	...	1 460	565	39
		1984	...	...	...	2 895	859	30
SAMOA‡	ALL INSTITUTIONS	1975	*40	–	–	249	*13	*5
		1981	79	...	...	644	45	7
		1983	37	11	30	562	264	47
	UNIVERSITIES & EQ. INSTS.	1981	22	...	...	295	10	3
		1983	11	3	27	134	67	50
	OTHER THIRD LEVEL INSTS.	1975	*40	–	–	249	*13	*5
		1981	57	11	19	349	35	10
		1983	26	8	31	428	197	46
TONGA	ALL INSTITUTIONS	1980	...	...	...	...	...	...
		1981	64	25	39	693	298	43
		1984	...	...	...	680	382	56
	UNIVERSITIES & EQ. INSTS.	1981	13	6	46	79	11	14
		1984	15	3	20	45	8	18
	OTHER THIRD LEVEL INSTS.	1980	36	14	39	371	180	49
		1981	51	19	37	614	287	47
		1984	...	...	...	635	374	59
U.S.S.R.								
U.S.S.R.‡	ALL INSTITUTIONS	1975	317 152	118 298	37	4 853 958	2 448 551	50
		1980	365 300	...	...	5 235 200	...	...
		1981	...	...	...	5 284 500	...	...
		1982	375 600	...	...	5 315 200	...	...
		1983	...	...	...	5 301 300	...	...
		1984	...	...	...	5 280 100	...	...
BYELORUSSIAN S.S.R.‡	ALL INSTITUTIONS	1975	...	...	...	159 903	...	...
		1980	12 900	...	...	177 000	...	...
		1981	...	...	...	178 800	...	...
		1982	13 500	...	...	182 200	...	...
		1983	...	...	...	183 800	...	...
		1984	...	...	...	185 100	...	...

3.11 Third level: teachers and students by type of institution
Troisième degré: professeurs et étudiants par type d'établissement
Tercer grado: profesores y estudiantes por tipo de establecimiento

COUNTRY / PAYS / PAIS	TYPE OF INSTITUTION / TYPE D'ETABLISSEMENT / TIPO DE ESTABLECIMIENTO	YEAR / ANNEE / AÑO	TEACHING STAFF / PERSONNEL ENSEIGNANT / PERSONAL DOCENTE			STUDENTS ENROLLED / ETUDIANTS INSCRITS / ESTUDIANTES MATRICULADOS		
			TOTAL	FEMALE FEMININ FEMENINO	% F	TOTAL	FEMALE FEMININ FEMENINO	% F
			(1)	(2)	(3)	(4)	(5)	(6)
UKRAINIAN S.S.R. ‡	ALL INSTITUTIONS	1975	...	...	...	831 300	408 800	49
		1980	...	...	...	880 400	...	...
		1981	...	...	...	882 900	...	...
		1982	...	...	...	884 900	...	...
		1983	...	...	...	880 900	...	...
		1984	...	...	...	878 500	...	...

The data in this table refer in principle to teaching staff and students enrolled in all institutions, both public and private, at the third level of education for 1975, 1980, 1981, 1982, 1983 and 1984. For most countries and territories data are shown separately by type of institution: (a) universities and equivalent degree-granting institutions; (b) other third level educational institutions - these include all other education at the third level in non-university institutions (teacher training colleges, technical colleges, etc.).

It should be noted, however, that the criteria applied for determining the two types of institutions may not be exactly the same in each of the countries and territories covered. Moreover, following reforms in the educational system, a number of non-university institutions in a given country may be attached to universities or recognized as equivalent institutions from one yea to the next. This will tend to impair international comparability an the breakdown by type of institution must therefore be used wit caution.

As far as possible, the figures include both full-time and par time teachers and students. Although as a general rule thes figures do not cover correspondence courses, they do includ them in certain well-defined cases (indicated by a note) in whic such courses provide recognized third-level education leading t the same diplomas as intra-mural studies. Figures referring t teaching staff include, in principle, auxiliary teachers (assistants demonstrators, etc.) but exclude staff with no teaching dutie (administrators, laboratory technicians, etc.).

Ces données se rapportent en principe au personnel enseignant et aux étudiants inscrits dans tous les établissements, publics et privés, d'enseignement du troisième degré pour 1975, 1980, 1981, 1982, 1983 et 1984. Pour la plupart des pays et territoires, les données sont présentées séparément par type d'établissement: (a) universités et établissements conférant des grades équivalents; (b) autres établissements du troisième degré. Ceux-ci incluent l'ensemble des autres formes d'enseignement du troisième degré dispensées dans des établissements non-universitaires (écoles normales supérieures, écoles techniques supérieures, etc.).

Il faut cependant souligner que le critère appliqué pour déterminer les deux types d'établissements peut ne pas être exactement le même dans chacun des pays et territoires concernés. De plus, il se peut que dans un même pays, à la suite des réformes du système d'enseignement, plusieurs établissements non universitaires soient, d'une année à l'autre, rattachés aux universités ou considérés comme de établissements équivalents. Cela rend difficile la comparabilit internationale et c'est pourquoi cette répartition par typ d'établissement doit être utilisée avec précaution.

Dans la mesure du possible, ces statistiques couvrent aussi bie les professeurs et étudiants à plein temps que ceux à temp partiel. Bien que d'une manière générale, les statistiques n couvrent pas les cours par correspondance, elles en tiennen compte dans certains cas bien déterminés (indiqués par une note où ces cours dispensent un enseignement reconnu comme étan du troisième degré et sanctionné par les mêmes diplômes qu l'enseignement intra-muros. Les chiffres relatifs au personne enseignant incluent en principe le personnel auxiliaire (assistants chefs de travaux, etc.) mais non le personnel qui n'exerce pas d fonctions d'enseignement (administrateurs, techniciens d laboratoire, etc.).

En principio, los datos de este cuadro se refieren al personal docente y a los estudiantes inscritos en todos los establecimientos, públicos y privados, de la enseñanza de tercer grado, para 1975, 1980, 1981, 1982, 1983 y 1984. Para la mayoría de los países y territorios, los datos se presentan separadamente por tipo de establecimiento: a) universidades e instituciones que conceden títulos equivalentes; b) todas las otras modalidades de enseñanza de tercer grado, dispensada en centros no universitarios (escuelas normales superiores, escuelas técnicas superiores, etc.)

Procede señalar, sin embargo, que los criterios aplicados para determinar los dos tipos de establecimiento pueden no ser exactamente los mismos en cada uno de los países y territorios. Es posible que, en un mismo país, debido a una reforma del sistema de enseñanza, ciertos establecimientos no universitarios queden, de un año para otro, adscritos a unas universidades o considerados como establecimientos docentes equivalentes. Po todo ello, resulta difícil la comparabilidad internacional, y convendría utilizar con precaución esta distribución por tipo d establecimientos de enseñanza.

En la medida de lo posible, estas estadísticas abarcan a la ve a los profesores y estudiantes de jornada completa y de jornada parcial. Aunque, en general, las estadísticas no comprenden la enseñanza por correspondencia, se le tiene en cuenta en ciertos casos muy precisos (indicados en una nota), a saber, cuando se trata de una enseñanza reconocida como de tercer grado y que desemboca en la obtención de los mismos diplomas que los estudios intramuros. Las cifras relativas al personal docente comprenden, en principio, el personal auxiliar (adjuntos encargados de prácticas, etc.) pero no el personal que no ejerce funciones docentes (administradores, técnicos de laboratorio etc.).

AFRICA:

Algeria:

E--> In 1984, data on female students exclude post-graduate students.

FR-> En 1984, les données relatives aux étudiants excluent celles du niveau universitaire supérieur.

ESP> En 1984, los datos relativos a las estudiantes excluyen los del nivel postuniversitario.

Cameroon:

E--> Data revised and exclude 'ENAM' between 1980 to 1982.

FR-> Les données revisées excluent 'ENAM' entre 1980 et 1982.

ESP> Los datos revisados excluyen 'ENAM' entre 1980 y 1982.

Côte d'Ivoire:

E--> Data for 1975 refer to institutions under the Ministry o Education.

FR-> En 1975, les données se réfèrent aux établissements relevant du

Côte d'Ivoire: (Cont):
Ministère de l'Education seulement.

ESP> En 1975, los datos se refieren a los establecimientos dependientes del Ministerio de Educación.

Egypt:

E--> Revised data. Data exclude Al Azhar University, in 1975 on students and from 1981 on teaching staff.

FR-> Données révisées. En 1975 les données relatives aux étudiants et à partir de 1981 celles relatives au personnel enseignant excluent l'Université Al Azhar.

ESP> Datos revisados. En 1975, los datos relativos a los estudiantes y a partir de 1981 los del personal docente excluyen la universidad Al Azhar.

Equatorial Guinea:

E--> Data include 'la universidad de educación a distancia'.

FR-> Les données incluent 'la universidad de educación a distancia'.

ESP> Los datos incluyen la universidad de educación a distancia.

Kenya:

E--> Data for 1975 to 1981 refer to institutions under the Ministry of Education. In 1983, data on other education include adult education.

FR-> De 1975 à 1981, les données se réfèrent aux établissements relevant du Ministère de l'Education seulement. En 1983, les données incluent l'éducation des adultes.

ESP> De 1975 a 1981, los datos se refieren a los establecimientos dependientes del Ministerio de Educación. En 1983, los datos incluyen la educación de los adultos.

Mali:

E--> In 1980, data exclude students who were suspended from courses.

FR-> En 1980, les données excluent les étudiants suspendus des cours.

ESP> En 1980, los datos excluyen los estudiantes suspendidos de los cursos.

Morocco:

E--> In 1983, data on students exclude post-graduate students.

FR-> En 1983, les données excluent les étudiants du niveau universitaire supérieur.

ESP> En 1983, los datos excluyen los estudiantes del nivel postuniversitario.

Mozambique:

E--> In 1980 and 1981, data on female enrolment refer to full-time national students only.

FR-> En 1980 et 1981, les données relatives aux étudiantes se réfèrent aux effectifs nationaux à plein temps seulement.

ESP> En 1980 y 1981, los datos relativos a las estudiantes se refieren a los efectivos nacionales de jornada completa solamente.

Seychelles:

E--> From 1981, teacher training is included at the second level of education.

FR-> A partir de 1981, l'enseignement normal est inclus dans l'enseignement du second degré.

ESP> A partir de 1981, la enseñanza normal se incluye en la enseñanza de segundo grado.

Swaziland:

E--> Data on students include students abroad. In 1982, students at 'other third level institutions' refer to teacher training only.

FR-> Les données relatives aux étudiants incluent les étudiants à l'étranger. En 1982, les données relatives aux étudiants dans les 'autres établissements du troisième degré' se réfèrent à l'enseignement normal seulement.

ESP> Los datos relativos a los estudiantes incluyen los estudiantes en el extranjero. En 1982, los datos relativos a los estudiantes en los 'otros establecimientos de tercer grado' se refieren a la enseñanza normal solamente.

Togo:

E--> Data on teaching staff in 'other third level institutions' are included with teacher training at the second level.

FR-> Les données relatives au personnel enseignant des 'autres établissements du troisième degré' sont incluses dans l'enseignement normal du second degré.

ESP> Los datos relativos al personal docente de los 'otros establecimientos de tercer grado' se incluyen en la enseñanza normal de segundo grado.

United Republic of Tanzania:

E--> Data exclude female students in 1982 and 1983 and also post-graduate students in 1984.

FR-> Les données de 1982 et 1983 excluent les étudiantes du niveau supérieur universitaire, et en 1984 excluent tous les étudiants.

ESP> Los datos de 1982 y 1983 excluyen las estudiantes del nivel postuniversitario y en 1984 excluyen todos los estudiantes.

AMERICA, NORTH:

Bermuda:

E--> In 1981 and 1982, data include adult education.

FR-> En 1981 et 1982, les données incluent l'éducation des adultes.

ESP> En 1981 y 1982, los datos incluyen la educación de los adultos.

Canada:

E--> Except in 1975 and 1983, data on students at 'other third level institutions' and on teaching staff for all the years and for all institutions refer to full-time only. In 1981 and 1982, they exclude female teaching staff in Community Colleges in the Province of Quebec.

FR-> A l'exception de 1975 et de 1983, les données relatives aux étudiants dans les 'autres établissements du troisième degré, ainsi que celles relatives aux professeurs pour toutes les années et pour tous les établissements, se réfèrent à plein temps seulement. En 1981 et 1982, les données relatives aux 'Community Colleges' excluent le personnel enseignant féminin de la Province du Québec.

ESP> A la excepción de 1975 y 1983, los datos relativos a los estudiantes en los 'otros establecimientos de tercer grado', y los relativos a los profesores para todos los años y para todos los establecimientos se refieren a jornada parcial solamente. En 1981 y 1982, en 'otra enseñanza del tercer grado' los datos relativos a los 'Community Colleges' excluyen los profesores femeninos de la Provincia del 'Quebec'.

Costa Rica:

E--> From 1980, data refer only to institutions recognized by the National Council for Higher Education.

FR-> A partir de 1980, les données se réfèrent seulement aux institutions reconnues par le Conseil National pour l'Education supérieure.

ESP> A partir de 1980, los datos se refieren solamente a las instituciones reconocidas por el Consejo nacional para la educación superior.

El Salvador:

E--> In 1980 and 1981, data exclude the National University which was closed.

FR-> En 1980 et 1981, les données excluent l'université nationale qui était fermée.

ESP> En 1980 y 1981, los datos excluyen la universidad nacional que cerró.

Grenada:

E--> In 1982, data exclude Grenada Teachers' College.

FR-> En 1982, les données excluent *Grenada Teachers' College*.

ESP> En 1982, los datos excluyen *Grenada teachers' College*.

Guatemala:

E--> Data for 1975 refer to the University of San Carlos only.

FR-> En 1975, les données se réfèrent à l'Université de San Carlos seulement.

ESP> En 1975, los datos se refieren a la Universidad de San Carlos solamente.

Trinidad and Tobago:

E--> From 1975 to 1981, data on female students in universities refer to nationals only.

FR-> De 1975 à 1981, les données relatives aux étudiantes des universités se réfèrent aux étudiantes nationales seulement.

ESP> De 1975 a 1981, los datos relativos a las estudiantes de las universidades se refieren a las estudiantes nacionales solamente.

United States:

E--> In 1980 and 1982, data on teaching staff refer to full-time teachers only.

FR-> En 1980 et 1982, les données relatives au personnel enseignant se réfèrent aux professeurs à plein temps seulement.

ESP> En 1980 y 1982, los datos relativos al personal docente se refieren a los profesores de jornada completa solamente.

AMERICA, SOUTH:

Bolivia:

E--> In 1981 and 1982, data exclude 'la Universidad católica Boliviana'.

FR-> En 1981 et 1982, les données excluent 'la Universidad Católica Boliviana'.

ESP> En 1981 y 1982, los datos excluyen la Universidad Católica Boliviana.

Brazil:

E--> In 1980, data on female students exclude post-graduate students.

FR-> En 1980, les données relatives aux étudiantes excluent celles du niveau universitaire supérieur.

ESP> En 1980, los datos relativos a las estudiantes excluyen las del nivel postuniversitario.

Chile:

E--> In 1975, data on teaching staff refer to full-time teachers only.

FR-> En 1975, les données relatives au personnel enseignant se réfèrent aux professeurs à plein temps seulement.

ESP> En 1975, los datos relativos al personal docente se refieren a los profesores de jornada completa solamente.

Colombia:

E--> From 1980, data include 'Educación a distancia' and on teaching staff, refer to teaching posts only.

FR-> A partir de 1980, les données incluent 'Educación a distancia', et le personnel enseignant se réfère aux postes d'enseignants.

ESP> A partir de 1980, los datos incluyen 'Educación a distancia', y el personal docente se refiere a los puestos de enseñanza.

Ecuador:
E--> Revised data.
FR-> Données révisées.
ESP> Datos revisados.

ASIA:

Bhutan:
E--> In 1983, data on teacher training and on vocational education are included at the second level.
FR-> En 1983, les données relatives à l'enseignement normal et à l'enseignement technique sont incluses au second degré.
ESP> En 1983, los datos relativos a la enseñanza normal y a la enseñanza técnica están incluídos al segundo grado.

China:
E--> Data refer to full-time education only.
FR-> Les données se réfèrent à l'enseignement à plein temps seulement.
ESP> Los datos se refieren a la enseñanza de jornada completa solamente.

Hong Kong:
E--> In 1980, data on 'other third level institutions' refer to Hong Kong Polytechnic only.
FR-> En 1980, les données relatives à 'l'autre enseignement du troisième degré' se réfèrent à 'Hong Kong Polytechnic' seulement.
ESP> En 1980, los datos relativos a la 'otra enseñanza de tercer grado' se refieren a 'Hong Kong Polytechnic' solamente.

India:
E--> Data include intermediate and pre-university courses.
FR-> Les données incluent les cours intermédiaires et pré-universitaires.
ESP> Los datos incluyen los cursos intermedios y preuniversitarios.

Iran, Islamic Republic of:
E--> Data on teaching staff in 1982 and 1984 and on female students in 1984 exclude teacher training colleges.
FR-> Les données relatives au personnel enseignant en 1982 et 1984 ainsi que celles des étudiantes en 1984 excluent les collèges d'enseignement normal.
ESP> Los datos relativos al personal docente en 1982 y 1984 y los relativos a las estudiantes en 1984 excluyen los colegios del enseñanza normal.

Israel:
E--> Except in 1984, data include open university and in 1980 data on 'other third level institutions' exclude Jewish studies institutes.
FR-> A l'exception de 1984, les données incluent 'Open University' et en 1980 les données relatives aux 'autres établissements du troisième degré' excluent 'Jewish studies'.
ESP> A la excepción de 1984, los datos incluyen 'Open University' y en 1980 los datos relativos a 'los otros establecimientos de tercer grado' excluyen 'Jewish studies'.

Japan:
E--> Including correspondence courses.
FR-> Y compris les cours par correspondance.
ESP> Incluídos los cursos por correspondencia.

Lao People's Democratic Republic:
E--> Revised data.
FR-> Données révisées.
ESP> Datos revisados.

Nepal:
E--> In 1982 and 1983 data refer to public universities only.
FR-> En 1982 et 1983 les données se réfèrent aux universités publiques seulement.
ESP> En 1982 y 1983 los datos se refieren a las universidades públicas solamente.

Pakistan:
E--> Excluding data on teaching staff in arts and sciences colleges.
FR-> Non compris les données relatives au personnel enseignant des 'Arts and sciences colleges'.
ESP> Excluídos los datos relativos al personal docente de los 'Arts and sciences colleges'.

Sri Lanka:
E--> From 1980, data on universities refer to full-time students only. In 1982 and 1983, data include open university.
FR-> A partir de 1980, les données relatives aux universités se réfèrent aux étudiants à plein temps seulement. En 1982 et 1983, les données incluent l'*Open University*.
ESP> A partir de 1980, los datos relativos a las universidades se refieren a los estudiantes de jornada completa solamente. En 1982 y 1983, los datos incluyen la *Open University*.

Thailand:
E--> In 1980, data exclude one Open university with teaching staff of 717 and enrolment of 243,825 in 1979.
FR-> En 1980, les données excluent une 'Open university' qui comptait 717 professeurs et 243 825 étudiants en 1979.
ESP> En 1980, los datos excluyen una 'Open University' que tenía 717 profesores y 243 825 estudiantes en 1979.

Turkey:
E--> In 1975 and those on female students up to 1981, data exclude Open University.
FR-> En 1975 et jusqu'en 1981 pour les étudiantes, les données

Turkey: (Cont):
excluent 'Open University'.
ESP> En 1975 y hasta 1981 para las estudiantes, los datos exclu
'Open University'.

Viet-Nam:
E--> In 1980, data include correspondence courses.
FR-> En 1980, les données incluent les cours par correspondanc
ESP> En 1980, los datos incluyen los cursos por correspondenci

EUROPE:

Albania:
E--> Including evening and correspondence courses.
FR-> Y compris les cours du soir et par correspondance.
ESP> Incluídos los cursos nocturnos y por correspondencia.

Austria:
E--> Data on universities from 1981 refer to full-time teach only.
FR-> A partir de 1981, les données relatives aux universités réfèrent aux professeurs à plein temps seulement.
ESP> A partir de 1981, los datos relativos a las universidades refieren a los profesores de jornada completa solamente.

Belgium:
E--> In 1975 and 1980, data refer to full-time students only.
FR-> En 1975 et 1980, les données se réfèrent aux étudiants à p temps seulement.
ESP> En 1975 y 1980, los datos se refieren a los estudiantes jornada completa solamente.

Bulgaria:
E--> Including evening and correspondence courses.
FR-> Y compris les cours du soir et par correspondance.
ESP> Incluídos los cursos nocturnos y por correspondencia.

Denmark:
E--> Data on teaching staff refer to full-time teachers only. F 1980 data on students are not comparable with those of the previous y due to classification changes.
FR-> Les données relatives au personnel enseignant se réfère professeurs à plein temps seulement. A partir de 1980 les donn relatives aux étudiants ne sont pas comparables avec celles des ann antérieures à la suite d'un changement de classification.
ESP> Los datos relativos al personal docente se refiere a los profeso de jornada completa solamente. A partir de 1980 los datos relativos a estudiantes no son comparables con los de los años anteriores debido a cambio de clasificación.

France:
E--> The total number of students (all institutions) is overestima due to some students enrolled at institutions, considered here as n university ('grandes écoles, classes préparatoires aux grandes écoles' 'sections de techniciens supérieurs') being enrolled also at the universit Their number is unknown.
FR-> Le nombre total d'étudiants (ensemble d'établissements) surestimé du fait que certains étudiants inscrits dans les établisseme considérés ici comme non-universitaires (grandes écoles, clas préparatoires aux grandes écoles et sections de techniciens supérie sont également inscrits dans les universités, sans que l'on puisse en indic le nombre exact.
ESP> El número total de estudiantes (todos los establecimientos) e sobrestimado debido a que ciertos estudiantes inscritos en establecimientos considerados aqui como no universitarios (gran écoles, classes préparatoires aux grandes écoles et sections de technici supérieurs) están inscritos igualmente en las universidades, sin que posible precisar su número con exactitud.

German Democratic Republic:
E--> Including evening and correspondence courses. Due to application of ISCED, data from 1975 include preparatory studies higher education, extended secondary school (data also included at second level) and vocational training (including University entra examination).
FR-> Y compris les cours du soir et par correspondance. D l'application de la CITE, les donnéés à partir de 1975 comprennent études préparatoires à l'enseignement supérieur, les écoles seconda prolongées (données également incluses au second degré) l'enseignement technique (y compris l'examen d'entrée à l'université).
ESP> Incluídos los cursos nocturnos y por correspondencia. Debid la aplicación de la CINE a partir de 1975, los datos incluyen los estu preparatorios a la enseñanza superior, les escuelas secunda prolongadas (datos igualmente incluídos en el segundo grado) y enseñanza técnica (incluyendo el examen de entrada a la universidad)

Holy See:
E--> Data refer to teaching staff and students enrolled in hig institutions under the authority of the Holy See.
FR-> Les données se réfèrent aux enseignants et étudiants dans institutions du troisième degré sous l'autorité du Saint-Siège.
ESP> Los datos se refieren al personal docente y a los estudiantes los institutos del tercer grado bajo la autoridad del Santa Sede.

Hungary:
E--> Including evening and correspondence courses.
FR-> Y compris les cours du soir et par correspondance.
ESP> Incluídos los cursos nocturnos y por correspondencia.

Italy:
E--> In 1981, data exclude post-graduate students.
FR-> En 1981, les données excluent les étudiants du niveau universitaire supérieur.
ESP> En 1981, los datos excluyen los estudiantes del nivel postuniversitario.
Luxembourg:
E--> Data refer to students enrolled in institutions located in Luxembourg. At university level, the majority of the students pursue their studies in the following countries: Austria, Belgium, France, Federal Republic of Germany and Switzerland.
FR-> Les données se réfèrent seulement aux étudiants inscrits dans les institutions du Luxembourg. La plus grande partie des étudiants luxembourgeois poursuivent leurs études universitaires dans les universités des pays suivants: Autriche, Belgique, France, République fédérale d'Allemagne et Suisse.
ESP> Los datos se refieren solamente a los estudiantes matriculados en las instituciones en Luxemburgo. La mayoría de los estudiantes de Luxemburgo cursan sus estudios universitarios en las universidades de los países siguientes: Austria, Bélgica, Francia, República Federal de Alemania y Suiza.
Netherlands:
E--> In 1984, data include Open University.
FR-> En 1984, les données incluent 'Open University'.
ESP> En 1984, los datos incluyen 'Open University'.
Poland:
E--> Including evening and correspondence courses.
FR-> Y compris les cours du soir et par correspondance.
ESP> Incluídos los cursos nocturnos y por correspondencia.
Portugal:
E--> In 1981, data on female teachers exclude the University of Porto.
FR-> En 1981, les données relatives aux professeurs féminins excluent l'Université de Porto.
ESP> En 1981, los datos relativos a los profesores femeninos excluyen la universidad de Porto.
Romania:
E--> Including evening and correspondence courses.
FR-> Y compris les cours du soir et par correspondance.
ESP> Incluídos los cursos nocturnos y por correspondencia.

Spain:
E--> From 1975, data include 'universidad de educación a distancia'.
FR-> A partir de 1975, l''universidad de educación a distancia' est incluse.
ESP> A partir de 1975 se incluye la universidad de educación a distancia.
United Kingdom:
E--> From 1975, data include students at the Open University.
FR-> A partir de 1975, les effectifs de l''Open University' sont inclus.
ESP> A partir de 1975, se incluyen los estudiantes a la 'Open University'.
OCEANIA:
Australia:
E--> Excluding part-time teachers.
FR-> Les professeurs à temps partiel sont exclus.
ESP> Excluídos los profesores de jornada parcial.
Fiji:
E--> Data refer to University of South Pacific.
FR-> Les données se réfèrent à l''University of South Pacific'.
ESP> Los datos se refieren a la 'University of South Pacific'.
Samoa:
E--> In 1983, data exclude school of agriculture.
FR-> En 1983, les données excluent l'école d'agriculture.
ESP> En 1983, los datos excluyen la escuela de agricultura.
U.S.S.R.:
U.S.S.R.:
E--> Including evening and correspondence courses.
FR-> Y compris les cours du soir et par correspondance.
ESP> Incluídos los cursos nocturnos y por correspondencia.
Byelorussian S.S.R.:
E--> Including evening and correspondence courses.
FR-> Y compris les cours du soir et par correspondance.
ESP> Incluídos los cursos nocturnos y por correspondencia.
Ukrainian S.S.R.:
E--> Including evening and correspondence courses.
FR-> Y compris les cours du soir et par correspondance.
ESP> Incluídos los cursos nocturnos y por correspondencia.

3.12 Education at the third level: enrolment by sex and field of study (1980, 1983 and 1984)

Enseignement du troisième degré: nombre d'étudiants par sexe d'après les domaines d'études (1980, 1983 et 1984)

Enseñanza de tercer grado: número de estudiantes por sexo según los sectores de estudios (1980, 1983 y 1984)

EDUCATION SCIENCE AND TEACHER TRAINING	=	SCIENCES DE L'EDUCATION ET FORMATION D'ENSEIGNANTS	=	CIENCIAS DE LA EDUCACION Y FORMACION DE PERSONAL DOCENTE
HUMANITIES, RELIGION AND THEOLOGY	=	LETTRES, RELIGION ET THEOLOGIE	=	HUMANIDADES, RELIGION Y TEOLOGIA
FINE AND APPLIED ARTS	=	BEAUX-ARTS ET ARTS APPLIQUES	=	BELLAS ARTES Y ARTES APLICADAS
LAW	=	DROIT	=	DERECHO
SOCIAL AND BEHAVIOURAL SCIENCE	=	SCIENCES SOCIALES ET SCIENCES DU COMPORTEMENT	=	CIENCIAS SOCIALES Y DEL COMPORTAMIENTO
COMMERCIAL AND BUSINESS ADMINISTRATION	=	FORMATION AU COMMERCE ET A L'ADMINISTRATION DES ENTREPRISES	=	ENSEÑANZA COMERCIAL Y DE ADMINISTRACION DE EMPRESAS
MASS COMMUNICATION AND DOCUMENTATION	=	INFORMATION ET DOCUMENTATION	=	DOCUMENTACION Y COMUNICACION SOCIAL
HOME ECONOMICS (DOMESTIC SCIENCE)	=	ENSEIGNEMENT MENAGER	=	ECONOMIA DOMESTICA (ENSEÑANZA DEL HOGAR)
SERVICE TRADES	=	FORMATION POUR LE SECTEUR TERTIAIRE	=	FORMACION PARA EL SECTOR DE LOS SERVICIOS
NATURAL SCIENCE	=	SCIENCES EXACTES ET NATURELLES	=	CIENCIAS NATURALES
MATHEMATICS AND COMPUTER SCIENCE	=	MATHEMATIQUES ET INFORMATIQUE	=	MATEMATICAS E INFORMATICA
MEDICAL SCIENCE AND HEALTH-RELATED	=	SCIENCES MEDICALES, SANTE ET HYGIENE	=	CIENCIAS MEDICAS, SANIDAD E HIGIENE
ENGINEERING	=	SCIENCES DE L'INGENIEUR	=	INGENIERIA Y TECNOLOGIA
ARCHITECTURE & TOWN PLANNING	=	ARCHITECTURE ET URBANISME	=	ARQUITECTURA Y URBANISMO
TRADE, CRAFT & INDUSTRIAL PROGRAMMES	=	METIERS DE LA PRODUCTION INDUSTRIELLE	=	ARTES Y OFICIOS INDUSTRIALES
TRANSPORT AND COMMUNICATIONS	=	TRANSPORTS ET TELECOMMUNICATIONS	=	TRANSPORTES Y COMUNICACIONES
AGRICULTURE, FORESTRY AND FISHERY	=	AGRICULTURE, SYLVICULTURE ET HALIEUTIQUE	=	ENSEÑANZA AGRONOMICA, DASONOMICA Y PESQUERA
OTHER AND NOT SPECIFIED	=	AUTRES PROGRAMMES	=	OTROS PROGRAMAS

PLEASE REFER TO EXPLANATORY TEXT AT END OF TABLE

Ø DATA FOR 1983 FOR COUNTRIES SHOWN WITH THIS SYMBOL ARE FOR 1982.

NUMBER OF COUNTRIES AND TERRITORIES PRESENTED IN THIS TABLE: 141

PRIERE DE SE REFERER AU TEXTE EXPLICATIF A LA FIN DU TABLEAU

Ø LES DONNEES DE 1983 RELATIVES AUX PAYS ACCOMPAGNES DE CE SYMBOLE SE REFERENT A 1982.

NOMBRE DE PAYS ET DE TERRITOIRES PRESENTES DANS CE TABLEAU: 141

REFERIRSE AL TEXTO EXPLICATIVO AL FINAL DEL CUADRO

Ø LOS DATOS DE 1983 RELATIVOS A LOS PAISES EN LOS QUE APARECE ESTO SIMBOLO SE REFIEREN A 1982.

NUMERO DE PAISES Y DE TERRITORIOS PRESENTADOS EN ESTE CUADRO: 141

COUNTRY / PAYS / PAIS	FIELD OF STUDY / DOMAINES D'ETUDES / SECTORES DE ESTUDIOS	1980		1983		1984	
		MF	F	MF	F	MF	F
		(1)	(2)	(3)	(4)	(5)	(6)
AFRICA							
ALGERIA‡ Ø	TOTAL	79 351	21 014	95 867	...	111 507	...
	EDUCATION SCIENCE & TEACHER TRAINING	2 057	412	16 247	...	5 261	...
	HUMANITIES, RELIGION & THEOLOGY	8 648	2 958	./.	...	9 800	...
	FINE AND APPLIED ARTS	–	–	–	–	–	–
	LAW	11 938	2 750	10 253	...	10 817	...
	SOCIAL AND BEHAVIOURAL SCIENCE	9 989	2 464	8 536	...	9 564	...
	COMMERCIAL & BUSINESS ADMINISTRATION	496	165	490	...	825	...
	MASS COMMUNICATION & DOCUMENTATION	332	123	319	...	1 047	...
	HOME ECONOMICS (DOMESTIC SCIENCE)	–	–	–	–	–	–
	SERVICE TRADES	–	–	–	–	–	–
	NATURAL SCIENCE	22 645	5 689	23 177	...	5 639	...
	MATHEMATICS & COMPUTER SCIENCE	1 660	387	1 981	...	3 745	...
	MEDICAL SCIENCE & HEALTH-RELATED	12 501	4 814	18 989	...	32 766	...
	ENGINEERING	5 959	617	6 805	...	3 899	...
	ARCHITECTURE & TOWN PLANNING	1 971	330	4 501	...	3 935	...
	TRADE, CRAFT & INDUSTRIAL PROGRAMMES	33	21	2 468	...	2 009	...
	TRANSPORT AND COMMUNICATIONS	–	–	604	...	727	...
	AGRICULTURE, FORESTRY & FISHERY	1 018	206	1 324	...	2 503	...
	OTHER AND NOT SPECIFIED	104	78	173	...	18 970	...
ANGOLA Ø	TOTAL	2 183	...	2 674	...	...	...
	EDUCATION SCIENCE & TEACHER TRAINING	78	...	40	...	...	...
	HUMANITIES, RELIGION & THEOLOGY	–	–	25	...	...	...
	FINE AND APPLIED ARTS	–	–	–	–	...	...
	LAW	289	...	467	...	...	...
	SOCIAL AND BEHAVIOURAL SCIENCE	632	...	426	...	...	...
	COMMERCIAL & BUSINESS ADMINISTRATION	–	–	–	–	...	...
	MASS COMMUNICATION & DOCUMENTATION	–	–	–	–	...	...
	HOME ECONOMICS (DOMESTIC SCIENCE)	–	–	–	–	...	...
	SERVICE TRADES	–	–	–	–	...	...
	NATURAL SCIENCE	164	...	177	...	...	...
	MATHEMATICS & COMPUTER SCIENCE	–	–	3	...	...	...
	MEDICAL SCIENCE & HEALTH-RELATED	407	...	542	...	...	...
	ENGINEERING	367	...	722	...	...	...
	ARCHITECTURE & TOWN PLANNING	–	–	106	...	...	...
	TRADE, CRAFT & INDUSTRIAL PROGRAMMES	–	–	–	–	...	...
	TRANSPORT AND COMMUNICATIONS	–	–	–	–	...	...
	AGRICULTURE, FORESTRY & FISHERY	246	...	166	...	...	...
	OTHER AND NOT SPECIFIED	–	–	–	–	...	...
BENIN Ø	TOTAL	...	...	6 302	1 035	...	...
	EDUCATION SCIENCE & TEACHER TRAINING	...	...	880	141	...	...
	HUMANITIES, RELIGION & THEOLOGY	...	...	366	79	...	...
	FINE AND APPLIED ARTS	...	...	–	–	...	...
	LAW	...	...	1 244	249	...	...
	SOCIAL AND BEHAVIOURAL SCIENCE	...	...	1 373	236	...	...
	COMMERCIAL & BUSINESS ADMINISTRATION	...	...	764	143	...	...
	MASS COMMUNICATION & DOCUMENTATION	...	...	–	–	...	...
	HOME ECONOMICS (DOMESTIC SCIENCE)	...	...	–	–	...	...
	SERVICE TRADES	...	...	–	–	...	...
	NATURAL SCIENCE	...	...	311	58	...	...
	MATHEMATICS & COMPUTER SCIENCE	...	...	288	18	...	...
	MEDICAL SCIENCE & HEALTH-RELATED	...	...	494	74	...	...
	ENGINEERING	...	...	243	9	...	...
	ARCHITECTURE & TOWN PLANNING	...	...	–	–	...	...
	TRADE, CRAFT & INDUSTRIAL PROGRAMMES	...	...	–	–	...	...
	TRANSPORT AND COMMUNICATIONS	...	...	–	–	...	...
	AGRICULTURE, FORESTRY & FISHERY	...	...	339	28	...	...
	OTHER AND NOT SPECIFIED	...	...	–	–	...	...

3.12 Third level: students by field of study (1980,1983,1984)
Troisième degré: étudiants par domaine d'études (1980,1983,1984)
Tercer grado: estudiantes por sector de estudios (1980,1983,1984)

COUNTRY / PAYS / PAIS	FIELD OF STUDY / DOMAINES D'ETUDES / SECTORES DE ESTUDIOS	1980		1983		1984	
		MF	F	MF	F	MF	F
		(1)	(2)	(3)	(4)	(5)	(6)
BOTSWANA‡	TOTAL	928	372	1 435	632	1 773	...
	EDUCATION SCIENCE & TEACHER TRAINING	235	112	401	193	501	...
	HUMANITIES, RELIGION & THEOLOGY	170	65	287	129	319	...
	FINE AND APPLIED ARTS	–	–	–	–	–	–
	LAW	–	–	32	9	62	...
	SOCIAL AND BEHAVIOURAL SCIENCE	244	96	222	87	697	...
	COMMERCIAL & BUSINESS ADMINISTRATION	30	13	334	188	./.	...
	MASS COMMUNICATION & DOCUMENTATION	42	29	–	–	–	–
	HOME ECONOMICS (DOMESTIC SCIENCE)	–	–	–	–	–	–
	SERVICE TRADES	–	–	–	–	–	–
	NATURAL SCIENCE	184	48	159	26	194	...
	MATHEMATICS & COMPUTER SCIENCE	23	9	–	–	–	–
	MEDICAL SCIENCE & HEALTH–RELATED	–	–	–	–	–	–
	ENGINEERING	–	–	–	–	–	–
	ARCHITECTURE & TOWN PLANNING	–	–	–	–	–	–
	TRADE, CRAFT & INDUSTRIAL PROGRAMMES	–	–	–	–	–	–
	TRANSPORT AND COMMUNICATIONS	–	–	–	–	–	–
	AGRICULTURE, FORESTRY & FISHERY	–	–	–	–	–	–
	OTHER AND NOT SPECIFIED	–	–	–	–	–	–
BURKINA FASO‡	TOTAL	1 643	354	3 406	757	...	...
	EDUCATION SCIENCE & TEACHER TRAINING	–	–	./.	./.	...	...
	HUMANITIES, RELIGION & THEOLOGY	595	144	1 063	282	...	...
	FINE AND APPLIED ARTS	–	–	85	19	...	...
	LAW	160	33	577	186	...	...
	SOCIAL AND BEHAVIOURAL SCIENCE	386	71	567	79	...	...
	COMMERCIAL & BUSINESS ADMINISTRATION	124	69	170	85	...	...
	MASS COMMUNICATION & DOCUMENTATION	53	12	–	–	...	...
	HOME ECONOMICS (DOMESTIC SCIENCE)	–	–	–	–	...	...
	SERVICE TRADES	–	–	–	–	...	...
	NATURAL SCIENCE	325	25	178	30	...	...
	MATHEMATICS & COMPUTER SCIENCE	./.	./.	178	8	...	...
	MEDICAL SCIENCE & HEALTH–RELATED	–	–	188	37	...	...
	ENGINEERING	–	–	–	–	...	...
	ARCHITECTURE & TOWN PLANNING	–	–	–	–	...	...
	TRADE, CRAFT & INDUSTRIAL PROGRAMMES	–	–	–	–	...	...
	TRANSPORT AND COMMUNICATIONS	–	–	–	–	...	...
	AGRICULTURE, FORESTRY & FISHERY	–	–	400	31	...	...
	OTHER AND NOT SPECIFIED	–	–	–	–	...	...
BURUNDI‡	TOTAL	1 879	464	2 411	648	...	...
	EDUCATION SCIENCE & TEACHER TRAINING	162	52	225	58	...	...
	HUMANITIES, RELIGION & THEOLOGY	359	100	506	151	...	...
	FINE AND APPLIED ARTS	–	–	–	–	...	...
	LAW	380	104	331	118	...	...
	SOCIAL AND BEHAVIOURAL SCIENCE	./.	./.	251	86	...	...
	COMMERCIAL & BUSINESS ADMINISTRATION	333	105	245	92	...	...
	MASS COMMUNICATION & DOCUMENTATION	33	15	40	17	...	...
	HOME ECONOMICS (DOMESTIC SCIENCE)	–	–	–	–	...	...
	SERVICE TRADES	–	–	–	–	...	...
	NATURAL SCIENCE	423	55	291	57	...	...
	MATHEMATICS & COMPUTER SCIENCE	–	–	43	3	...	...
	MEDICAL SCIENCE & HEALTH–RELATED	160	32	181	38	...	...
	ENGINEERING	–	–	126	2	...	...
	ARCHITECTURE & TOWN PLANNING	–	–	51	6	...	...
	TRADE, CRAFT & INDUSTRIAL PROGRAMMES	–	–	–	–	...	...
	TRANSPORT AND COMMUNICATIONS	–	–	–	–	...	...
	AGRICULTURE, FORESTRY & FISHERY	–	–	66	4	...	...
	OTHER AND NOT SPECIFIED	29	1	55	16	...	...

COUNTRY / PAYS / PAIS	FIELD OF STUDY / DOMAINES D'ETUDES / SECTORES DE ESTUDIOS	1980		1983		1984	
		MF	F	MF	F	MF	F
		(1)	(2)	(3)	(4)	(5)	(6)
CAMEROON‡	TOTAL	10 631	...	...	...	...	...
	EDUCATION SCIENCE & TEACHER TRAINING	823	112	...	...	...	...
	HUMANITIES, RELIGION & THEOLOGY	765	–	...	...	...	...
	FINE AND APPLIED ARTS	–	–	...	...	...	...
	LAW	2 217	518	...	...	...	...
	SOCIAL AND BEHAVIOURAL SCIENCE	858	140	...	...	...	...
	COMMERCIAL & BUSINESS ADMINISTRATION	2 609	465	...	...	...	...
	MASS COMMUNICATION & DOCUMENTATION	73	4	...	...	...	...
	HOME ECONOMICS (DOMESTIC SCIENCE)	–	–	...	...	...	...
	SERVICE TRADES	117	...	...	...	...	...
	NATURAL SCIENCE	1 237	182	...	...	...	...
	MATHEMATICS & COMPUTER SCIENCE	373	14	...	...	...	...
	MEDICAL SCIENCE & HEALTH-RELATED	319	67	...	...	...	...
	ENGINEERING	373	...	...	...	...	...
	ARCHITECTURE & TOWN PLANNING	–	–	...	...	...	...
	TRADE, CRAFT & INDUSTRIAL PROGRAMMES	–	–	...	...	...	...
	TRANSPORT AND COMMUNICATIONS	–	–	...	...	...	...
	AGRICULTURE, FORESTRY & FISHERY	825	...	...	...	...	...
	OTHER AND NOT SPECIFIED	42	2	...	...	...	...
CENTRAL AFRICAN REPUBLIC‡	TOTAL	1 719	143	2 413	240	...	...
	EDUCATION SCIENCE & TEACHER TRAINING	224	6	568	76	...	...
	HUMANITIES, RELIGION & THEOLOGY	365	15	./.	./.	...	...
	FINE AND APPLIED ARTS	–	–	–	–	...	...
	LAW	524	64	733	64	...	...
	SOCIAL AND BEHAVIOURAL SCIENCE	./.	./.	616	47	...	...
	COMMERCIAL & BUSINESS ADMINISTRATION	307	42	165	36	...	...
	MASS COMMUNICATION & DOCUMENTATION	–	–	–	–	...	...
	HOME ECONOMICS (DOMESTIC SCIENCE)	–	–	–	–	...	...
	SERVICE TRADES	–	–	–	–	...	...
	NATURAL SCIENCE	54	4	84	3	...	...
	MATHEMATICS & COMPUTER SCIENCE	–	–	–	–	...	...
	MEDICAL SCIENCE & HEALTH-RELATED	116	10	122	14	...	...
	ENGINEERING	51	2	51	–	...	...
	ARCHITECTURE & TOWN PLANNING	–	–	–	–	...	...
	TRADE, CRAFT & INDUSTRIAL PROGRAMMES	–	–	–	–	...	...
	TRANSPORT AND COMMUNICATIONS	–	–	–	–	...	...
	AGRICULTURE, FORESTRY & FISHERY	78	–	74	–	...	...
	OTHER AND NOT SPECIFIED	–	–	–	–	...	...
CHAD	TOTAL	...	...	...	...	1 643	142
	EDUCATION SCIENCE & TEACHER TRAINING	...	...	...	...	173	3
	HUMANITIES, RELIGION & THEOLOGY	...	...	...	...	316	31
	FINE AND APPLIED ARTS	...	...	...	...	–	–
	LAW	...	...	...	...	460	46
	SOCIAL AND BEHAVIOURAL SCIENCE	...	...	...	...	499	52
	COMMERCIAL & BUSINESS ADMINISTRATION	...	...	...	...	–	–
	MASS COMMUNICATION & DOCUMENTATION	...	...	...	...	–	–
	HOME ECONOMICS (DOMESTIC SCIENCE)	...	...	...	...	–	–
	SERVICE TRADES	...	...	...	...	–	–
	NATURAL SCIENCE	...	...	...	...	195	10
	MATHEMATICS & COMPUTER SCIENCE	...	...	...	...	–	–
	MEDICAL SCIENCE & HEALTH-RELATED	...	...	...	...	–	–
	ENGINEERING	...	...	...	...	–	–
	ARCHITECTURE & TOWN PLANNING	...	...	...	...	–	–
	TRADE, CRAFT & INDUSTRIAL PROGRAMMES	...	...	...	...	–	–
	TRANSPORT AND COMMUNICATIONS	...	...	...	...	–	–
	AGRICULTURE, FORESTRY & FISHERY	...	...	...	...	–	–
	OTHER AND NOT SPECIFIED	...	...	...	...	–	–

3.12 Third level: students by field of study (1980,1983,1984)
Troisième degré: étudiants par domaine d'études (1980,1983,1984)
Tercer grado: estudiantes por sector de estudios (1980,1983,1984)

COUNTRY PAYS PAIS	FIELD OF STUDY DOMAINES D'ETUDES SECTORES DE ESTUDIOS	1980		1983		1984	
		MF	F	MF	F	MF	F
		(1)	(2)	(3)	(4)	(5)	(6)
CONGO‡	TOTAL	7 255	1 079	8 886	1 182	...	...
	EDUCATION SCIENCE & TEACHER TRAINING	1 601	259	1 436	182	...	...
	HUMANITIES, RELIGION & THEOLOGY	938	101	2 072	254	...	...
	FINE AND APPLIED ARTS	–	–	–	–	...	...
	LAW	1 260	209	1 622	223	...	...
	SOCIAL AND BEHAVIOURAL SCIENCE	1 889	291	2 145	365	...	...
	COMMERCIAL & BUSINESS ADMINISTRATION	186	86	./.	./.	...	...
	MASS COMMUNICATION & DOCUMENTATION	60	7	./.	./.	...	...
	HOME ECONOMICS (DOMESTIC SCIENCE)	–	–	–	–	...	...
	SERVICE TRADES	–	–	–	–	...	...
	NATURAL SCIENCE	601	44	793	63	...	...
	MATHEMATICS & COMPUTER SCIENCE	242	9	270	11	...	...
	MEDICAL SCIENCE & HEALTH–RELATED	362	68	414	78	...	...
	ENGINEERING	–	–	–	–	...	...
	ARCHITECTURE & TOWN PLANNING	–	–	–	–	...	...
	TRADE, CRAFT & INDUSTRIAL PROGRAMMES	–	–	–	–	...	...
	TRANSPORT AND COMMUNICATIONS	–	–	–	–	...	...
	AGRICULTURE, FORESTRY & FISHERY	116	5	134	6	...	...
	OTHER AND NOT SPECIFIED	–	–	–	–	...	...
COTE D'IVOIRE	TOTAL	19 633	...	18 872	...	...	...
	EDUCATION SCIENCE & TEACHER TRAINING	3 564	...	3 746	...	...	...
	HUMANITIES, RELIGION & THEOLOGY	3 132	373	2 779	665	...	...
	FINE AND APPLIED ARTS	179	36	244	53	...	...
	LAW	3 676	619	3 246	511	...	...
	SOCIAL AND BEHAVIOURAL SCIENCE	2 583	335	2 648	463	...	...
	COMMERCIAL & BUSINESS ADMINISTRATION	1 059	307	322	33	...	...
	MASS COMMUNICATION & DOCUMENTATION	–	–	–	–	...	...
	HOME ECONOMICS (DOMESTIC SCIENCE)	–	–	–	–	...	...
	SERVICE TRADES	–	–	–	–	...	...
	NATURAL SCIENCE	1 363	99	1 464	221	...	...
	MATHEMATICS & COMPUTER SCIENCE	244	...	293	13	...	...
	MEDICAL SCIENCE & HEALTH–RELATED	1 325	...	2 488	895	...	...
	ENGINEERING	57	1	101	15	...	...
	ARCHITECTURE & TOWN PLANNING	926	36	645	23	...	...
	TRADE, CRAFT & INDUSTRIAL PROGRAMMES	162	4	290	10	...	...
	TRANSPORT AND COMMUNICATIONS	366	39	335	30	...	...
	AGRICULTURE, FORESTRY & FISHERY	848	61	271	11	...	...
	OTHER AND NOT SPECIFIED	149	...	–	–	...	...
EGYPT‡	TOTAL	528 751	168 402	613 570	206 376	...	...
	EDUCATION SCIENCE & TEACHER TRAINING	64 787	27 137	85 222	38 604	...	...
	HUMANITIES, RELIGION & THEOLOGY	72 903	32 911	91 425	42 319	...	...
	FINE AND APPLIED ARTS	6 839	2 715	7 120	3 063	...	...
	LAW	64 123	14 159	83 470	18 227	...	...
	SOCIAL AND BEHAVIOURAL SCIENCE	5 268	2 001	5 467	2 283	...	...
	COMMERCIAL & BUSINESS ADMINISTRATION	120 887	35 931	150 581	45 942	...	...
	MASS COMMUNICATION & DOCUMENTATION	1 505	758	1 527	821	...	...
	HOME ECONOMICS (DOMESTIC SCIENCE)	1 553	1 463	1 709	1 404	...	...
	SERVICE TRADES	469	259	965	570	...	...
	NATURAL SCIENCE	22 990	7 289	26 265	9 072	...	...
	MATHEMATICS & COMPUTER SCIENCE	1 267	325	1 137	309	...	...
	MEDICAL SCIENCE & HEALTH–RELATED	60 169	20 919	51 850	20 316	...	...
	ENGINEERING	54 837	7 939	54 859	7 123	...	...
	ARCHITECTURE & TOWN PLANNING	./.	./.	./.	./.	...	...
	TRADE, CRAFT & INDUSTRIAL PROGRAMMES	./.	./.	./.	./.	...	...
	TRANSPORT AND COMMUNICATIONS	./.	./.	./.	./.	...	...
	AGRICULTURE, FORESTRY & FISHERY	46 358	12 517	45 649	14 137	...	...
	OTHER AND NOT SPECIFIED	4 796	2 079	6 324	2 186	...	...

COUNTRY / PAYS / PAIS	FIELD OF STUDY / DOMAINES D'ETUDES / SECTORES DE ESTUDIOS	1980		1983		1984	
		MF	F	MF	F	MF	F
		(1)	(2)	(3)	(4)	(5)	(6)
ETHIOPIA‡	TOTAL	14 368	...	16 030	1 761	...	...
	EDUCATION SCIENCE & TEACHER TRAINING	1 763	...	2 179	169	...	...
	HUMANITIES, RELIGION & THEOLOGY	490	...	555	90	...	...
	FINE AND APPLIED ARTS	–	–	–	–	...	...
	LAW	207	...	236	21	...	...
	SOCIAL AND BEHAVIOURAL SCIENCE	3 769	...	3 314	321	...	...
	COMMERCIAL & BUSINESS ADMINISTRATION	./.	...	1 067	421	...	...
	MASS COMMUNICATION & DOCUMENTATION	./.	...	89	25	...	...
	HOME ECONOMICS (DOMESTIC SCIENCE)	./.	...	–	–	...	...
	SERVICE TRADES	–	–	–	–	...	...
	NATURAL SCIENCE	3 117	...	3 105	242	...	...
	MATHEMATICS & COMPUTER SCIENCE	./.	...	./.	./.	...	...
	MEDICAL SCIENCE & HEALTH-RELATED	1 002	...	1 206	208	...	...
	ENGINEERING	1 570	...	1 316	59	...	...
	ARCHITECTURE & TOWN PLANNING	./.	...	104	8	...	...
	TRADE, CRAFT & INDUSTRIAL PROGRAMMES	./.	...	–	–	...	...
	TRANSPORT AND COMMUNICATIONS	./.	...	–	–	...	...
	AGRICULTURE, FORESTRY & FISHERY	2 450	...	2 828	189	...	...
	OTHER AND NOT SPECIFIED	–	–	31	8	...	...
GABON	TOTAL	...	...	3 228	873	...	...
	EDUCATION SCIENCE & TEACHER TRAINING	...	...	291	43	...	...
	HUMANITIES, RELIGION & THEOLOGY	...	...	342	100	...	...
	FINE AND APPLIED ARTS	...	...	–	–	...	...
	LAW	...	...	435	122	...	...
	SOCIAL AND BEHAVIOURAL SCIENCE	...	...	715	202	...	...
	COMMERCIAL & BUSINESS ADMINISTRATION	...	...	349	170	...	...
	MASS COMMUNICATION & DOCUMENTATION	...	...	120	29	...	...
	HOME ECONOMICS (DOMESTIC SCIENCE)	...	...	–	–	...	...
	SERVICE TRADES	...	...	–	–	...	...
	NATURAL SCIENCE	...	...	113	18	...	...
	MATHEMATICS & COMPUTER SCIENCE	...	...	258	49	...	...
	MEDICAL SCIENCE & HEALTH-RELATED	...	...	290	122	...	...
	ENGINEERING	...	...	210	10	...	...
	ARCHITECTURE & TOWN PLANNING	...	...	43	2	...	...
	TRADE, CRAFT & INDUSTRIAL PROGRAMMES	...	...	–	–	...	...
	TRANSPORT AND COMMUNICATIONS	...	...	–	–	...	...
	AGRICULTURE, FORESTRY & FISHERY	...	...	62	6	...	...
	OTHER AND NOT SPECIFIED	...	...	–	–	...	...
GHANA‡	TOTAL	7 981	1 389	...	...	7 649	1 309
	EDUCATION SCIENCE & TEACHER TRAINING	250	64	...	...	206	53
	HUMANITIES, RELIGION & THEOLOGY	2 144	460	...	...	./.	./.
	FINE AND APPLIED ARTS	183	51	...	...	261	80
	LAW	95	14	...	...	./.	./.
	SOCIAL AND BEHAVIOURAL SCIENCE	979	195	...	...	2 882	623
	COMMERCIAL & BUSINESS ADMINISTRATION	563	87	...	...	648	93
	MASS COMMUNICATION & DOCUMENTATION	78	22	...	...	45	13
	HOME ECONOMICS (DOMESTIC SCIENCE)	44	44	...	...	52	47
	SERVICE TRADES	–	–	...	...	–	–
	NATURAL SCIENCE	1 293	161	...	...	1 269	154
	MATHEMATICS & COMPUTER SCIENCE	./.	./.	...	...	./.	./.
	MEDICAL SCIENCE & HEALTH-RELATED	769	170	...	...	650	136
	ENGINEERING	717	13	...	...	774	14
	ARCHITECTURE & TOWN PLANNING	337	53	...	...	244	37
	TRADE, CRAFT & INDUSTRIAL PROGRAMMES	–	–	...	...	–	–
	TRANSPORT AND COMMUNICATIONS	–	–	...	...	–	–
	AGRICULTURE, FORESTRY & FISHERY	529	55	...	...	618	59
	OTHER AND NOT SPECIFIED	–	–	...	...	–	–

3.12 Third level: students by field of study (1980,1983,1984)
Troisième degré: étudiants par domaine d'études (1980,1983,1984)
Tercer grado: estudiantes por sector de estudios (1980,1983,1984)

COUNTRY / PAYS / PAIS	FIELD OF STUDY / DOMAINES D'ETUDES / SECTORES DE ESTUDIOS	1980		1983		1984	
		MF	F	MF	F	MF	F
		(1)	(2)	(3)	(4)	(5)	(6)
GUINEA‡	TOTAL	18 270	3 497	12 304	...	10 664	2 737
	EDUCATION SCIENCE & TEACHER TRAINING	2 407	461	266	...	236	10
	HUMANITIES, RELIGION & THEOLOGY	./.	./.	–	–	./.	./.
	FINE AND APPLIED ARTS	–	–	–	–	./.	./.
	LAW	./.	./.	–	–	122	39
	SOCIAL AND BEHAVIOURAL SCIENCE	./.	./.	./.	...	1 950	702
	COMMERCIAL & BUSINESS ADMINISTRATION	2 601	1 048	911	...	413	210
	MASS COMMUNICATION & DOCUMENTATION	–	–	–	–	–	–
	HOME ECONOMICS (DOMESTIC SCIENCE)	–	–	–	–	–	–
	SERVICE TRADES	–	–	–	–	–	–
	NATURAL SCIENCE	405	99	2 971	...	3 617	1 047
	MATHEMATICS & COMPUTER SCIENCE	./.	./.	./.	...	./.	./.
	MEDICAL SCIENCE & HEALTH–RELATED	1 049	372	585	...	596	126
	ENGINEERING	734	46	928	...	512	23
	ARCHITECTURE & TOWN PLANNING	./.	./.	./.	...	186	10
	TRADE, CRAFT & INDUSTRIAL PROGRAMMES	./.	./.	26	...	67	24
	TRANSPORT AND COMMUNICATIONS	–	–	160	...	139	21
	AGRICULTURE, FORESTRY & FISHERY	10 898	1 447	6 457	...	2 661	506
	OTHER AND NOT SPECIFIED	176	24	–	–	165	19
KENYA‡	TOTAL	9 155	2 302	22 157	...	...	...
	EDUCATION SCIENCE & TEACHER TRAINING	2 520	891	2 748	1 199	...	...
	HUMANITIES, RELIGION & THEOLOGY	248	68	./.	./.	...	...
	FINE AND APPLIED ARTS	48	23	4	1	...	...
	LAW	259	91	340	138	...	...
	SOCIAL AND BEHAVIOURAL SCIENCE	1 411	520	1 432	485	...	...
	COMMERCIAL & BUSINESS ADMINISTRATION	613	170	1 691	...	...	...
	MASS COMMUNICATION & DOCUMENTATION	14	2	150	...	...	...
	HOME ECONOMICS (DOMESTIC SCIENCE)	–	–	–	–	...	...
	SERVICE TRADES	–	–	163	...	...	...
	NATURAL SCIENCE	1 184	65	1 091	141	...	...
	MATHEMATICS & COMPUTER SCIENCE	9	2	15	2	...	...
	MEDICAL SCIENCE & HEALTH–RELATED	942	272	1 373	295	...	...
	ENGINEERING	589	8	2 376	...	...	...
	ARCHITECTURE & TOWN PLANNING	362	37	288	...	...	...
	TRADE, CRAFT & INDUSTRIAL PROGRAMMES	–	–	985	...	...	...
	TRANSPORT AND COMMUNICATIONS	–	–	–	–	...	...
	AGRICULTURE, FORESTRY & FISHERY	956	153	4 399	...	...	...
	OTHER AND NOT SPECIFIED	–	–	5 102	...	...	...
LESOTHO	TOTAL	1 889	...	...	...	2 303	1 461
	EDUCATION SCIENCE & TEACHER TRAINING	1 094	...	...	...	1 399	1 069
	HUMANITIES, RELIGION & THEOLOGY	163	...	...	...	99	51
	FINE AND APPLIED ARTS	6	...	...	...	47	26
	LAW	121	...	...	...	158	58
	SOCIAL AND BEHAVIOURAL SCIENCE	46	...	...	...	36	18
	COMMERCIAL & BUSINESS ADMINISTRATION	241	...	...	...	209	116
	MASS COMMUNICATION & DOCUMENTATION	–	–	...	...	–	–
	HOME ECONOMICS (DOMESTIC SCIENCE)	–	–	...	...	–	–
	SERVICE TRADES	–	–	...		–	–
	NATURAL SCIENCE	200	...	...	...	205	56
	MATHEMATICS & COMPUTER SCIENCE	6	...	...	...	63	13
	MEDICAL SCIENCE & HEALTH–RELATED	12	...	...	...	24	15
	ENGINEERING	–	–	...	...	–	–
	ARCHITECTURE & TOWN PLANNING	–	–	...	...	–	–
	TRADE, CRAFT & INDUSTRIAL PROGRAMMES	–	–	...	...	–	–
	TRANSPORT AND COMMUNICATIONS	–	–	...	...	–	–
	AGRICULTURE, FORESTRY & FISHERY	–	–	...	...	63	39
	OTHER AND NOT SPECIFIED	–	–	...	...	–	–

COUNTRY / PAYS / PAIS	FIELD OF STUDY / DOMAINES D'ETUDES / SECTORES DE ESTUDIOS	1980		1983		1984	
		MF	F	MF	F	MF	F
		(1)	(2)	(3)	(4)	(5)	(6)
MADAGASCAR Ø	TOTAL	22 632	...	32 599	...	...	...
	EDUCATION SCIENCE & TEACHER TRAINING	275	...	766	...	...	...
	HUMANITIES, RELIGION & THEOLOGY	4 596	...	5 433	...	...	...
	FINE AND APPLIED ARTS	–	–	–	–	...	...
	LAW	2 993	...	4 480	...	...	...
	SOCIAL AND BEHAVIOURAL SCIENCE	3 868	...	5 150	...	...	...
	COMMERCIAL & BUSINESS ADMINISTRATION	1 502	...	2 242	...	...	...
	MASS COMMUNICATION & DOCUMENTATION	–	–	–	–	...	...
	HOME ECONOMICS (DOMESTIC SCIENCE)	–	–	–	–	...	...
	SERVICE TRADES	–	–	–	–	...	...
	NATURAL SCIENCE	3 139	...	4 515	...	...	...
	MATHEMATICS & COMPUTER SCIENCE	812	...	1 625	...	...	...
	MEDICAL SCIENCE & HEALTH-RELATED	3 645	...	5 657	...	...	...
	ENGINEERING	1 526	...	2 333	...	...	...
	ARCHITECTURE & TOWN PLANNING	–	–	–	–	...	...
	TRADE, CRAFT & INDUSTRIAL PROGRAMMES	–	–	–	–	...	...
	TRANSPORT AND COMMUNICATIONS	–	–	36	...	...	...
	AGRICULTURE, FORESTRY & FISHERY	–	–	362	...	...	...
	OTHER AND NOT SPECIFIED	276	...	–	–	...	...
MALAWI‡ Ø	TOTAL	1 722	427	1 849	...	...	...
	EDUCATION SCIENCE & TEACHER TRAINING	250	48	321	...	...	...
	HUMANITIES, RELIGION & THEOLOGY	171	37	–	–	...	...
	FINE AND APPLIED ARTS	–	–	–	–	...	...
	LAW	40	–	43	...	...	...
	SOCIAL AND BEHAVIOURAL SCIENCE	–	–	–	...	...	...
	COMMERCIAL & BUSINESS ADMINISTRATION	288	45	216	...	...	...
	MASS COMMUNICATION & DOCUMENTATION	–	–	–	–	...	...
	HOME ECONOMICS (DOMESTIC SCIENCE)	–	–	–	–	...	...
	SERVICE TRADES	–	–	85	...	...	...
	NATURAL SCIENCE	–	–	–	–	...	...
	MATHEMATICS & COMPUTER SCIENCE	–	–	–	–	...	...
	MEDICAL SCIENCE & HEALTH-RELATED	–	–	181	...	...	...
	ENGINEERING	159	–	211	...	...	...
	ARCHITECTURE & TOWN PLANNING	–	–	–	–	...	...
	TRADE, CRAFT & INDUSTRIAL PROGRAMMES	–	–	14	...	...	...
	TRANSPORT AND COMMUNICATIONS	–	–	–	–	...	...
	AGRICULTURE, FORESTRY & FISHERY	427	93	403	...	...	...
	OTHER AND NOT SPECIFIED	387	204	375	...	...	...
MALI‡ Ø	TOTAL	1 631	184	5 792	708	...	...
	EDUCATION SCIENCE & TEACHER TRAINING	23	10	1 880	183	...	...
	HUMANITIES, RELIGION & THEOLOGY	–	–	–	–	...	...
	FINE AND APPLIED ARTS	–	–	–	–	...	...
	LAW	–	–	430	62	...	...
	SOCIAL AND BEHAVIOURAL SCIENCE	–	–	769	137	...	...
	COMMERCIAL & BUSINESS ADMINISTRATION	408	71	1 052	185	...	...
	MASS COMMUNICATION & DOCUMENTATION	–	–	–	–	...	...
	HOME ECONOMICS (DOMESTIC SCIENCE)	–	–	–	–	...	...
	SERVICE TRADES	–	–	–	–	...	...
	NATURAL SCIENCE	–	–	–	–	...	...
	MATHEMATICS & COMPUTER SCIENCE	–	–	–	–	...	...
	MEDICAL SCIENCE & HEALTH-RELATED	258	33	339	71	...	...
	ENGINEERING	339	7	714	15	...	...
	ARCHITECTURE & TOWN PLANNING	–	–	–	–	...	...
	TRADE, CRAFT & INDUSTRIAL PROGRAMMES	–	–	–	–	...	...
	TRANSPORT AND COMMUNICATIONS	52	8		–	...	...
	AGRICULTURE, FORESTRY & FISHERY	534	55	608	55	...	...
	OTHER AND NOT SPECIFIED	17	–	–	–	...	...

3.12 Third level: students by field of study (1980,1983,1984)
Troisième degré: étudiants par domaine d'études (1980,1983,1984)
Tercer grado: estudiantes por sector de estudios (1980,1983,1984)

COUNTRY / PAYS / PAIS	FIELD OF STUDY / DOMAINES D'ETUDES / SECTORES DE ESTUDIOS	1980 MF	1980 F	1983 MF	1983 F	1984 MF	1984 F
		(1)	(2)	(3)	(4)	(5)	(6)
MAURITIUS	TOTAL	1 038	317	702	208	794	216
	EDUCATION SCIENCE & TEACHER TRAINING	568	229	272	97	450	150
	HUMANITIES, RELIGION & THEOLOGY	–	–	–	–	–	–
	FINE AND APPLIED ARTS	–	–	–	–	–	–
	LAW	–	–	–	–	–	–
	SOCIAL AND BEHAVIOURAL SCIENCE	54	31	38	25	12	2
	COMMERCIAL & BUSINESS ADMINISTRATION	147	31	111	32	140	31
	MASS COMMUNICATION & DOCUMENTATION	8	4	42	18	12	8
	HOME ECONOMICS (DOMESTIC SCIENCE)	–	–	–	–	–	–
	SERVICE TRADES	–	–	–	–	–	–
	NATURAL SCIENCE	–	–	–	–	–	–
	MATHEMATICS & COMPUTER SCIENCE	–	–	11	2	10	2
	MEDICAL SCIENCE & HEALTH–RELATED	24	9	16	7	28	7
	ENGINEERING	195	–	90	1	101	4
	ARCHITECTURE & TOWN PLANNING	–	–	–	–	–	–
	TRADE, CRAFT & INDUSTRIAL PROGRAMMES	–	–	–	–	–	–
	TRANSPORT AND COMMUNICATIONS	–	–	–	–	–	–
	AGRICULTURE, FORESTRY & FISHERY	42	13	73	16	41	12
	OTHER AND NOT SPECIFIED	–	–	49	10	–	–
MOROCCO‡	TOTAL	86 731	21 663	99 637	31 649	126 481	41 073
	EDUCATION SCIENCE & TEACHER TRAINING	444	128	453	151	530	151
	HUMANITIES, RELIGION & THEOLOGY	33 212	10 150	45 015	18 184	43 556	19 481
	FINE AND APPLIED ARTS	–	–	–	–	–	–
	LAW	33 666	6 822	20 521	4 293	21 017	4 114
	SOCIAL AND BEHAVIOURAL SCIENCE	./.	./.	./.	./.	12 494	3 161
	COMMERCIAL & BUSINESS ADMINISTRATION	./.	./.	./.	./.	–	–
	MASS COMMUNICATION & DOCUMENTATION	–	–	–	–	–	–
	HOME ECONOMICS (DOMESTIC SCIENCE)	–	–	–	–	–	–
	SERVICE TRADES	–	–	–	–	–	–
	NATURAL SCIENCE	12 272	2 650	26 236	6 900	32 826	8 850
	MATHEMATICS & COMPUTER SCIENCE	–	–	–	–	./.	./.
	MEDICAL SCIENCE & HEALTH–RELATED	6 556	1 841	6 815	2 058	6 767	2 027
	ENGINEERING	581	72	597	63	580	58
	ARCHITECTURE & TOWN PLANNING	–	–	–	–	–	–
	TRADE, CRAFT & INDUSTRIAL PROGRAMMES	–	–	–	–	–	–
	TRANSPORT AND COMMUNICATIONS	–	–	–	–	–	–
	AGRICULTURE, FORESTRY & FISHERY	–	–	–	–	–	–
	OTHER AND NOT SPECIFIED	–	–	–	–	8 711	3 231
MOZAMBIQUE‡	TOTAL	1 000	*212	...	...	1 442	332
	EDUCATION SCIENCE & TEACHER TRAINING	142	62	...	...	91	30
	HUMANITIES, RELIGION & THEOLOGY	71	16	...	...	11	4
	FINE AND APPLIED ARTS	–	–	...	...	–	–
	LAW	150	20	...	...	–	–
	SOCIAL AND BEHAVIOURAL SCIENCE	167	25	...	...	247	56
	COMMERCIAL & BUSINESS ADMINISTRATION	–	–	...	...	–	–
	MASS COMMUNICATION & DOCUMENTATION	–	–	...	...	–	–
	HOME ECONOMICS (DOMESTIC SCIENCE)	–	–	...	...	–	–
	SERVICE TRADES	–	–	...	...	–	–
	NATURAL SCIENCE	67	14	...	...	69	21
	MATHEMATICS & COMPUTER SCIENCE	15	5	...	...	–	–
	MEDICAL SCIENCE & HEALTH–RELATED	86	28	...	...	162	82
	ENGINEERING	232	13	...	...	541	42
	ARCHITECTURE & TOWN PLANNING	–	–	...	...	–	–
	TRADE, CRAFT & INDUSTRIAL PROGRAMMES	–	–	...	...	–	–
	TRANSPORT AND COMMUNICATIONS	–	–	...	...	–	–
	AGRICULTURE, FORESTRY & FISHERY	70	29	...	...	321	97
	OTHER AND NOT SPECIFIED	–	–	...	...	–	–

COUNTRY / PAYS / PAIS	FIELD OF STUDY / DOMAINES D'ETUDES / SECTORES DE ESTUDIOS	1980		1983		1984	
		MF	F	MF	F	MF	F
		(1)	(2)	(3)	(4)	(5)	(6)
NIGER	TOTAL	1 435	285	2 450	526	2 863	526
	EDUCATION SCIENCE & TEACHER TRAINING	275	44	316	71	351	72
	HUMANITIES, RELIGION & THEOLOGY	291	67	440	110	598	169
	FINE AND APPLIED ARTS	–	–	–	–	–	–
	LAW	139	81	435	144	439	91
	SOCIAL AND BEHAVIOURAL SCIENCE	102	28	458	104	618	106
	COMMERCIAL & BUSINESS ADMINISTRATION	–	–	–	–	–	–
	MASS COMMUNICATION & DOCUMENTATION	–	–	–	–	–	–
	HOME ECONOMICS (DOMESTIC SCIENCE)	–	–	–	–	–	–
	SERVICE TRADES	–	–	–	–	–	–
	NATURAL SCIENCE	140	8	202	17	237	18
	MATHEMATICS & COMPUTER SCIENCE	134	5	179	13	209	12
	MEDICAL SCIENCE & HEALTH-RELATED	213	38	282	58	267	49
	ENGINEERING	–	–	–	–	–	–
	ARCHITECTURE & TOWN PLANNING	–	–	–	–	–	–
	TRADE, CRAFT & INDUSTRIAL PROGRAMMES	–	–	–	–	–	–
	TRANSPORT AND COMMUNICATIONS	–	–	–	–	–	–
	AGRICULTURE, FORESTRY & FISHERY	141	14	138	9	144	9
	OTHER AND NOT SPECIFIED	–	–	–	–	–	–
NIGERIA‡	TOTAL	70 395	...	...	...	...	...
	EDUCATION SCIENCE & TEACHER TRAINING	11 420	...	...	...	...	...
	HUMANITIES, RELIGION & THEOLOGY	10 908	...	...	...	...	...
	FINE AND APPLIED ARTS	–	–	...	...	...	...
	LAW	3 745	...	...	...	...	...
	SOCIAL AND BEHAVIOURAL SCIENCE	9 233	...	...	...	...	...
	COMMERCIAL & BUSINESS ADMINISTRATION	4 008	...	...	...	...	...
	MASS COMMUNICATION & DOCUMENTATION	–	–	...	...	...	...
	HOME ECONOMICS (DOMESTIC SCIENCE)	–	–	...	...	...	...
	SERVICE TRADES	–	–	...	...	...	...
	NATURAL SCIENCE	9 868	...	...	...	...	...
	MATHEMATICS & COMPUTER SCIENCE	–	–	...	...	...	...
	MEDICAL SCIENCE & HEALTH-RELATED	7 826	...	...	...	...	...
	ENGINEERING	4 974	...	...	...	...	...
	ARCHITECTURE & TOWN PLANNING	2 147	...	...	...	...	...
	TRADE, CRAFT & INDUSTRIAL PROGRAMMES	–	–	...	...	...	...
	TRANSPORT AND COMMUNICATIONS	–	–	...	...	...	...
	AGRICULTURE, FORESTRY & FISHERY	3 931	...	...	...	...	...
	OTHER AND NOT SPECIFIED	2 335	...	...	...	...	...
RWANDA‡	TOTAL	1 243	122	1 705	229	...	...
	EDUCATION SCIENCE & TEACHER TRAINING	188	21	146	30	...	...
	HUMANITIES, RELIGION & THEOLOGY	328	20	358	25	...	...
	FINE AND APPLIED ARTS	–	–	–	–	...	...
	LAW	74	10	129	22	...	...
	SOCIAL AND BEHAVIOURAL SCIENCE	224	41	297	85	...	...
	COMMERCIAL & BUSINESS ADMINISTRATION	–	–	./.	./.	...	...
	MASS COMMUNICATION & DOCUMENTATION	–	–	–	–	...	...
	HOME ECONOMICS (DOMESTIC SCIENCE)	–	–	19	6	...	...
	SERVICE TRADES	–	–	–	–	...	...
	NATURAL SCIENCE	105	6	95	11	...	...
	MATHEMATICS & COMPUTER SCIENCE	–	–	./.	./.	...	...
	MEDICAL SCIENCE & HEALTH-RELATED	155	11	194	23	...	...
	ENGINEERING	29	–	65	–	...	...
	ARCHITECTURE & TOWN PLANNING	–	–	–	–	...	...
	TRADE, CRAFT & INDUSTRIAL PROGRAMMES	–	–	15	15	...	...
	TRANSPORT AND COMMUNICATIONS	–	–	–	–	...	...
	AGRICULTURE, FORESTRY & FISHERY	128	6	123	4	...	...
	OTHER AND NOT SPECIFIED	12	7	264	8	...	...

COUNTRY / PAYS / PAIS	FIELD OF STUDY / DOMAINES D'ETUDES / SECTORES DE ESTUDIOS	1980		1983		1984	
		MF	F	MF	F	MF	F
		(1)	(2)	(3)	(4)	(5)	(6)
ST. HELENA‡	TOTAL	36	9	37	5	...	...
	EDUCATION SCIENCE & TEACHER TRAINING	8	8	5	5	...	...
	HUMANITIES, RELIGION & THEOLOGY	–	–	–	–	...	...
	FINE AND APPLIED ARTS	–	–	–	–	...	...
	LAW	–	–	–	–	...	...
	SOCIAL AND BEHAVIOURAL SCIENCE	–	–	–	–	...	...
	COMMERCIAL & BUSINESS ADMINISTRATION	–	–	–	–	...	...
	MASS COMMUNICATION & DOCUMENTATION	–	–	–	–	...	...
	HOME ECONOMICS (DOMESTIC SCIENCE)	–	–	–	–	...	...
	SERVICE TRADES	–	–	–	–	...	...
	NATURAL SCIENCE	–	–	–	–	...	...
	MATHEMATICS & COMPUTER SCIENCE	–	–	–	–	...	...
	MEDICAL SCIENCE & HEALTH-RELATED	–	–	–	–	...	...
	ENGINEERING	–	–	–	–	...	...
	ARCHITECTURE & TOWN PLANNING	–	–	–	–	...	...
	TRADE, CRAFT & INDUSTRIAL PROGRAMMES	28	1	32	–	...	...
	TRANSPORT AND COMMUNICATIONS	–	–	–	–	...	...
	AGRICULTURE, FORESTRY & FISHERY	–	–	–	–	...	...
	OTHER AND NOT SPECIFIED	–	–	–	–	...	...
SENEGAL	TOTAL	13 560	2 507	11 809	2 434	...	...
	EDUCATION SCIENCE & TEACHER TRAINING	680	79	483	62	...	...
	HUMANITIES, RELIGION & THEOLOGY	2 532	607	2 142	530	...	...
	FINE AND APPLIED ARTS	–	–	–	–	...	...
	LAW	2 055	383	1 473	302	...	...
	SOCIAL AND BEHAVIOURAL SCIENCE	3 063	603	1 925	325	...	...
	COMMERCIAL & BUSINESS ADMINISTRATION	379	22	290	24	...	...
	MASS COMMUNICATION & DOCUMENTATION	248	51	272	79	...	...
	HOME ECONOMICS (DOMESTIC SCIENCE)	–	–	–	–	...	...
	SERVICE TRADES	152	49	525	98	...	...
	NATURAL SCIENCE	1 610	115	1 648	171	...	...
	MATHEMATICS & COMPUTER SCIENCE	56	12	324	19	...	...
	MEDICAL SCIENCE & HEALTH-RELATED	1 997	554	2 308	757	...	...
	ENGINEERING	518	24	–	–	...	...
	ARCHITECTURE & TOWN PLANNING	8	1	15	1	...	...
	TRADE, CRAFT & INDUSTRIAL PROGRAMMES	–	–	–	–	...	...
	TRANSPORT AND COMMUNICATIONS	–	–	–	–	...	...
	AGRICULTURE, FORESTRY & FISHERY	262	7	318	19	...	...
	OTHER AND NOT SPECIFIED	–	–	86	47	...	...
SEYCHELLES	TOTAL	144	128	–	–	–	–
	EDUCATION SCIENCE & TEACHER TRAINING	144	128	–	–	–	–
	HUMANITIES, RELIGION & THEOLOGY	–	–	–	–	–	–
	FINE AND APPLIED ARTS	–	–	–	–	–	–
	LAW	–	–	–	–	–	–
	SOCIAL AND BEHAVIOURAL SCIENCE	–	–	–	–	–	–
	COMMERCIAL & BUSINESS ADMINISTRATION	–	–	–	–	–	–
	MASS COMMUNICATION & DOCUMENTATION	–	–	–	–	–	–
	HOME ECONOMICS (DOMESTIC SCIENCE)	–	–	–	–	–	–
	SERVICE TRADES	–	–	–	–	–	–
	NATURAL SCIENCE	–	–	–	–	–	–
	MATHEMATICS & COMPUTER SCIENCE	–	–	–	–	–	–
	MEDICAL SCIENCE & HEALTH-RELATED	–	–	–	–	–	–
	ENGINEERING	–	–	–	–	–	–
	ARCHITECTURE & TOWN PLANNING	–	–	–	–	–	–
	TRADE, CRAFT & INDUSTRIAL PROGRAMMES	–	–	–	–	–	–
	TRANSPORT AND COMMUNICATIONS	–	–	–	–	–	–
	AGRICULTURE, FORESTRY & FISHERY	–	–	–	–	–	–
	OTHER AND NOT SPECIFIED	–	–	–	–	–	–

COUNTRY PAYS PAIS	FIELD OF STUDY DOMAINES D'ETUDES SECTORES DE ESTUDIOS	1980		1983		1984	
		MF	F	MF	F	MF	F
		(1)	(2)	(3)	(4)	(5)	(6)
SUDAN‡	TOTAL	33 527	10 240	...	...	...	...
	EDUCATION SCIENCE & TEACHER TRAINING	885	294	...	...	...	...
	HUMANITIES, RELIGION & THEOLOGY	7 777	2 482	...	...	...	...
	FINE AND APPLIED ARTS	355	72	...	...	...	...
	LAW	5 149	1 742	...	...	...	...
	SOCIAL AND BEHAVIOURAL SCIENCE	1 776	645	...	...	...	...
	COMMERCIAL & BUSINESS ADMINISTRATION	7 862	2 124	...	...	...	...
	MASS COMMUNICATION & DOCUMENTATION	–	–	...	...	...	...
	HOME ECONOMICS (DOMESTIC SCIENCE)	–	–	...	...	...	...
	SERVICE TRADES	–	–	...	...	...	...
	NATURAL SCIENCE	489	186	...	...	...	...
	MATHEMATICS & COMPUTER SCIENCE	351	70	...	...	...	...
	MEDICAL SCIENCE & HEALTH-RELATED	2 128	681	...	...	...	...
	ENGINEERING	2 418	180	...	...	...	...
	ARCHITECTURE & TOWN PLANNING	171	27	...	...	...	...
	TRADE, CRAFT & INDUSTRIAL PROGRAMMES	–	–	...	...	...	...
	TRANSPORT AND COMMUNICATIONS	–	–	...	...	...	...
	AGRICULTURE, FORESTRY & FISHERY	2 959	556	...	...	...	...
	OTHER AND NOT SPECIFIED	1 207	1 181	...	...	...	...
SWAZILAND‡ Ø	TOTAL	1 875	751	1 201	459	...	...
	EDUCATION SCIENCE & TEACHER TRAINING	442	201	159	78	...	...
	HUMANITIES, RELIGION & THEOLOGY	–	–	123	80	...	...
	FINE AND APPLIED ARTS	–	–	–	–	...	...
	LAW	104	28	107	29	...	...
	SOCIAL AND BEHAVIOURAL SCIENCE	120	45	100	48	...	...
	COMMERCIAL & BUSINESS ADMINISTRATION	272	167	180	73	...	...
	MASS COMMUNICATION & DOCUMENTATION	–	–	–	–	...	...
	HOME ECONOMICS (DOMESTIC SCIENCE)	87	83	50	50	...	...
	SERVICE TRADES	86	17	–	–	...	...
	NATURAL SCIENCE	–	–	244	65	...	...
	MATHEMATICS & COMPUTER SCIENCE	–	–	./.	./.	...	...
	MEDICAL SCIENCE & HEALTH-RELATED	211	176	–	–	...	...
	ENGINEERING	137	1	–	–	...	...
	ARCHITECTURE & TOWN PLANNING	–	–	–	–	...	...
	TRADE, CRAFT & INDUSTRIAL PROGRAMMES	189	2	–	–	...	...
	TRANSPORT AND COMMUNICATIONS	–	–	–	–	...	...
	AGRICULTURE, FORESTRY & FISHERY	227	31	238	36	...	...
	OTHER AND NOT SPECIFIED	–	–	–	–	...	...
TOGO‡	TOTAL	4 750	703	4 234	661	4 192	628
	EDUCATION SCIENCE & TEACHER TRAINING	344	36	1 479	327	1 205	265
	HUMANITIES, RELIGION & THEOLOGY	748	150	./.	./.	./.	./.
	FINE AND APPLIED ARTS	./.	./.	./.	./.	./.	./.
	LAW	942	181	661	121	735	146
	SOCIAL AND BEHAVIOURAL SCIENCE	861	129	761	93	883	101
	COMMERCIAL & BUSINESS ADMINISTRATION	./.	./.	./.	./.	./.	./.
	MASS COMMUNICATION & DOCUMENTATION	37	2	./.	./.	./.	./.
	HOME ECONOMICS (DOMESTIC SCIENCE)	–	–	–	–	–	–
	SERVICE TRADES	–	–	–	–	–	–
	NATURAL SCIENCE	531	43	370	29	602	36
	MATHEMATICS & COMPUTER SCIENCE	./.	./.	193	3	./.	./.
	MEDICAL SCIENCE & HEALTH-RELATED	537	95	383	80	347	74
	ENGINEERING	121	1	143	1	149	–
	ARCHITECTURE & TOWN PLANNING	105	1	92	3	90	1
	TRADE, CRAFT & INDUSTRIAL PROGRAMMES	–	–	–	–	–	–
	TRANSPORT AND COMMUNICATIONS	–	–	–	–	–	–
	AGRICULTURE, FORESTRY & FISHERY	274	23	152	4	181	5
	OTHER AND NOT SPECIFIED	250	42	–	–	–	–

3.12 Third level: students by field of study (1980,1983,1984)
Troisième degré: étudiants par domaine d'études (1980,1983,1984)
Tercer grado: estudiantes por sector de estudios (1980,1983,1984)

COUNTRY / PAYS / PAIS	FIELD OF STUDY / DOMAINES D'ETUDES / SECTORES DE ESTUDIOS	1980 MF	1980 F	1983 MF	1983 F	1984 MF	1984 F
		(1)	(2)	(3)	(4)	(5)	(6)
TUNISIA Ø	TOTAL	31 827	9 437	34 077	11 209	...	...
	EDUCATION SCIENCE & TEACHER TRAINING	2 180	545	2 617	684	...	...
	HUMANITIES, RELIGION & THEOLOGY	6 330	2 676	6 308	2 872	...	...
	FINE AND APPLIED ARTS	120	72	201	103	...	...
	LAW	2 199	720	2 307	844	...	...
	SOCIAL AND BEHAVIOURAL SCIENCE	130	53	2 322	653	...	...
	COMMERCIAL & BUSINESS ADMINISTRATION	4 974	1 331	3 869	1 210	...	...
	MASS COMMUNICATION & DOCUMENTATION	403	130	439	204	...	...
	HOME ECONOMICS (DOMESTIC SCIENCE)	210	121	197	106	...	...
	SERVICE TRADES	534	49	342	83	...	...
	NATURAL SCIENCE	5 325	1 414	5 143	1 494	...	...
	MATHEMATICS & COMPUTER SCIENCE	125	27	233	46	...	...
	MEDICAL SCIENCE & HEALTH-RELATED	4 982	1 848	5 005	2 297	...	...
	ENGINEERING	1 858	105	2 396	147	...	...
	ARCHITECTURE & TOWN PLANNING	332	58	353	65	...	...
	TRADE, CRAFT & INDUSTRIAL PROGRAMMES	216	48	1 106	203	...	...
	TRANSPORT AND COMMUNICATIONS	926	137	110	12	...	...
	AGRICULTURE, FORESTRY & FISHERY	983	103	1 129	186	...	...
	OTHER AND NOT SPECIFIED	–	–	–	–	...	...
UGANDA Ø	TOTAL	5 856	1 323	7 312	1 964	...	...
	EDUCATION SCIENCE & TEACHER TRAINING	1 396	356	1 638	488	...	...
	HUMANITIES, RELIGION & THEOLOGY	519	176	440	115	...	...
	FINE AND APPLIED ARTS	60	13	99	30	...	...
	LAW	189	35	188	52	...	...
	SOCIAL AND BEHAVIOURAL SCIENCE	84	25	1 013	259	...	...
	COMMERCIAL & BUSINESS ADMINISTRATION	849	359	1 271	632	...	...
	MASS COMMUNICATION & DOCUMENTATION	39	18	38	18	...	...
	HOME ECONOMICS (DOMESTIC SCIENCE)	–	–	–	–	...	...
	SERVICE TRADES	44	30	50	33	...	...
	NATURAL SCIENCE	823	83	733	84	...	...
	MATHEMATICS & COMPUTER SCIENCE	55	6	92	3	...	...
	MEDICAL SCIENCE & HEALTH-RELATED	496	113	498	117	...	...
	ENGINEERING	856	28	781	37	...	...
	ARCHITECTURE & TOWN PLANNING	–	–	–	–	...	...
	TRADE, CRAFT & INDUSTRIAL PROGRAMMES	–	–	–	–	...	...
	TRANSPORT AND COMMUNICATIONS	–	–	–	–	...	...
	AGRICULTURE, FORESTRY & FISHERY	446	81	471	96	...	...
	OTHER AND NOT SPECIFIED	–	–	–	–	...	...
UNITED REPUBLIC OF TANZANIA	TOTAL	3 662	770	...	...	...	...
	EDUCATION SCIENCE & TEACHER TRAINING	1 166	381	...	...	...	...
	HUMANITIES, RELIGION & THEOLOGY	92	8	...	...	...	...
	FINE AND APPLIED ARTS	156	23	...	...	...	...
	LAW	305	71	...	...	...	...
	SOCIAL AND BEHAVIOURAL SCIENCE	118	12	...	...	...	...
	COMMERCIAL & BUSINESS ADMINISTRATION	366	84	...	...	...	...
	MASS COMMUNICATION & DOCUMENTATION	–	–	...	...	...	...
	HOME ECONOMICS (DOMESTIC SCIENCE)	–	–	...	...	...	...
	SERVICE TRADES	–	–	...	...	...	...
	NATURAL SCIENCE	58	10	...	...	...	...
	MATHEMATICS & COMPUTER SCIENCE	–	–	...	...	...	...
	MEDICAL SCIENCE & HEALTH-RELATED	500	108	...	...	...	...
	ENGINEERING	579	23	...	...	...	...
	ARCHITECTURE & TOWN PLANNING	–	–	...	...	...	...
	TRADE, CRAFT & INDUSTRIAL PROGRAMMES	–	–	...	...	...	...
	TRANSPORT AND COMMUNICATIONS	–	–	...	...	...	...
	AGRICULTURE, FORESTRY & FISHERY	305	47	...	...	...	...
	OTHER AND NOT SPECIFIED	17	3	...	...	...	...

COUNTRY / PAYS / PAIS	FIELD OF STUDY / DOMAINES D'ETUDES / SECTORES DE ESTUDIOS	1980 MF	1980 F	1983 MF	1983 F	1984 MF	1984 F
		(1)	(2)	(3)	(4)	(5)	(6)
ZAMBIA‡	TOTAL	...	...	8 781	...	4 214	...
	EDUCATION SCIENCE & TEACHER TRAINING	...	...	2 112	...	1 200	...
	HUMANITIES, RELIGION & THEOLOGY	...	...	./.	...	–	–
	FINE AND APPLIED ARTS	...	...	188	...	197	...
	LAW	...	...	144	41	–	–
	SOCIAL AND BEHAVIOURAL SCIENCE	...	...	776	257	–	–
	COMMERCIAL & BUSINESS ADMINISTRATION	...	...	1 939	...	1 311	...
	MASS COMMUNICATION & DOCUMENTATION	...	...	./.	...	–	–
	HOME ECONOMICS (DOMESTIC SCIENCE)	...	...	–	–	–	–
	SERVICE TRADES	...	...	–	–	–	–
	NATURAL SCIENCE	...	...	681	60	–	–
	MATHEMATICS & COMPUTER SCIENCE	...	...	–	–	–	–
	MEDICAL SCIENCE & HEALTH-RELATED	...	...	525	...	272	...
	ENGINEERING	...	...	1 586	...	832	...
	ARCHITECTURE & TOWN PLANNING	...	...	–	–	–	–
	TRADE, CRAFT & INDUSTRIAL PROGRAMMES	...	...	–	–	–	–
	TRANSPORT AND COMMUNICATIONS	...	...	124	...	120	...
	AGRICULTURE, FORESTRY & FISHERY	...	...	233	13	–	–
	OTHER AND NOT SPECIFIED	...	...	473	...	282	...
ZIMBABWE‡	TOTAL	...	...	10 101	3 451	4 131	...
	EDUCATION SCIENCE & TEACHER TRAINING	...	...	7 047	2 763	533	...
	HUMANITIES, RELIGION & THEOLOGY	...	...	–	–	610	...
	FINE AND APPLIED ARTS	...	...	478	133	./.	...
	LAW	...	...	871	177	927	...
	SOCIAL AND BEHAVIOURAL SCIENCE	...	...	627	168	766	...
	COMMERCIAL & BUSINESS ADMINISTRATION	...	...	./.	./.	./.	...
	MASS COMMUNICATION & DOCUMENTATION	...	...	–	–	–	–
	HOME ECONOMICS (DOMESTIC SCIENCE)	...	...	–	–	–	–
	SERVICE TRADES	...	...	–	–	–	–
	NATURAL SCIENCE	...	...	250	51	309	...
	MATHEMATICS & COMPUTER SCIENCE	...	...	./.	./.	./.	...
	MEDICAL SCIENCE & HEALTH-RELATED	...	...	419	115	484	...
	ENGINEERING	...	...	232	4	262	...
	ARCHITECTURE & TOWN PLANNING	...	...	–	–	–	–
	TRADE, CRAFT & INDUSTRIAL PROGRAMMES	...	...	–	–	–	–
	TRANSPORT AND COMMUNICATIONS	...	...	–	–	–	–
	AGRICULTURE, FORESTRY & FISHERY	...	...	177	40	240	...
	OTHER AND NOT SPECIFIED	...	...	–	–	–	–
AMERICA, NORTH							
BAHAMAS Ø	TOTAL	...	...	3 097	...	...	...
	EDUCATION SCIENCE & TEACHER TRAINING	...	...	116	...	...	...
	HUMANITIES, RELIGION & THEOLOGY	...	...	154	...	...	...
	FINE AND APPLIED ARTS	...	...	–	–	...	...
	LAW	...	...	–	–	...	...
	SOCIAL AND BEHAVIOURAL SCIENCE	...	...	138	...	...	...
	COMMERCIAL & BUSINESS ADMINISTRATION	...	...	1 472	...	...	...
	MASS COMMUNICATION & DOCUMENTATION	...	...	–	–	...	...
	HOME ECONOMICS (DOMESTIC SCIENCE)	...	...	–	–	...	...
	SERVICE TRADES	...	...	–	–	...	...
	NATURAL SCIENCE	...	...	325	...	...	...
	MATHEMATICS & COMPUTER SCIENCE	...	...	–	–	...	...
	MEDICAL SCIENCE & HEALTH-RELATED	...	...	–	–	...	...
	ENGINEERING	...	...	–	–	...	...
	ARCHITECTURE & TOWN PLANNING	...	...	–	–	...	...
	TRADE, CRAFT & INDUSTRIAL PROGRAMMES	...	...	61	...	...	...
	TRANSPORT AND COMMUNICATIONS	...	...	–	–	...	...
	AGRICULTURE, FORESTRY & FISHERY	...	...	–	–	...	...
	OTHER AND NOT SPECIFIED	...	...	831	...	...	...

3.12 Third level: students by field of study (1980,1983,1984)
Troisième degré: étudiants par domaine d'études (1980,1983,1984)
Tercer grado: estudiantes por sector de estudios (1980,1983,1984)

COUNTRY PAYS PAIS	FIELD OF STUDY DOMAINES D'ETUDES SECTORES DE ESTUDIOS	1980		1983		1984	
		MF	F	MF	F	MF	F
		(1)	(2)	(3)	(4)	(5)	(6)
BARBADOS‡	TOTAL	4 033	2 170	5 133	2 407	5 227	2 565
	EDUCATION SCIENCE & TEACHER TRAINING	412	280	368	233	373	234
	HUMANITIES, RELIGION & THEOLOGY	783	546	668	464	706	472
	FINE AND APPLIED ARTS	102	64	59	39	66	43
	LAW	290	122	299	152	297	165
	SOCIAL AND BEHAVIOURAL SCIENCE	387	164	1 324	894	1 344	898
	COMMERCIAL & BUSINESS ADMINISTRATION	649	424	./.	./.	./.	./.
	MASS COMMUNICATION & DOCUMENTATION	–	–	–	–	–	–
	HOME ECONOMICS (DOMESTIC SCIENCE)	–	–	39	38	47	47
	SERVICE TRADES	283	173	203	132	265	174
	NATURAL SCIENCE	751	275	722	293	773	312
	MATHEMATICS & COMPUTER SCIENCE	./.	./.	./.	./.	./.	./.
	MEDICAL SCIENCE & HEALTH–RELATED	–	–	95	52	142	89
	ENGINEERING	–	–	122	5	117	4
	ARCHITECTURE & TOWN PLANNING	–	–	–	–	–	–
	TRADE, CRAFT & INDUSTRIAL PROGRAMMES	–	–	1 150	69	1 003	78
	TRANSPORT AND COMMUNICATIONS	–	–	–	–	–	–
	AGRICULTURE, FORESTRY & FISHERY	–	–	36	6	40	12
	OTHER AND NOT SPECIFIED	376	122	48	30	54	37
BERMUDA‡ Ø	TOTAL	608	312	2 667	...	...	...
	EDUCATION SCIENCE & TEACHER TRAINING	–	–	30	...	...	...
	HUMANITIES, RELIGION & THEOLOGY	95	51	401	...	...	...
	FINE AND APPLIED ARTS	–	–	./.	...	...	...
	LAW	–	–	–	–	...	...
	SOCIAL AND BEHAVIOURAL SCIENCE	–	–	./.	...	...	...
	COMMERCIAL & BUSINESS ADMINISTRATION	195	144	1 417	...	...	...
	MASS COMMUNICATION & DOCUMENTATION	–	–	–	–	...	...
	HOME ECONOMICS (DOMESTIC SCIENCE)	–	–	–	–	...	...
	SERVICE TRADES	154	68	374	...	...	...
	NATURAL SCIENCE	–	–	./.	...	...	...
	MATHEMATICS & COMPUTER SCIENCE	–	–	./.	...	...	...
	MEDICAL SCIENCE & HEALTH–RELATED	–	–	–	–	...	...
	ENGINEERING	–	–	–	–	...	...
	ARCHITECTURE & TOWN PLANNING	–	–	–	–	...	...
	TRADE, CRAFT & INDUSTRIAL PROGRAMMES	70	5	372	...	...	...
	TRANSPORT AND COMMUNICATIONS	–	–	–	–	...	...
	AGRICULTURE, FORESTRY & FISHERY	–	–	–	–	...	...
	OTHER AND NOT SPECIFIED	94	44	73	...	...	...
CANADA‡	TOTAL	888 444	445 242	1 192 925	617 802	...	...
	EDUCATION SCIENCE & TEACHER TRAINING	67 955	47 399	73 617	53 355	...	...
	HUMANITIES, RELIGION & THEOLOGY	118 348	60 679	185 280	100 928	...	...
	FINE AND APPLIED ARTS	32 927	20 419	43 562	26 811	...	...
	LAW	11 328	4 352	11 913	5 301	...	...
	SOCIAL AND BEHAVIOURAL SCIENCE	87 713	51 493	95 763	55 388	...	...
	COMMERCIAL & BUSINESS ADMINISTRATION	136 396	63 402	167 047	85 452	...	...
	MASS COMMUNICATION & DOCUMENTATION	11 140	6 601	13 829	8 123	...	...
	HOME ECONOMICS (DOMESTIC SCIENCE)	4 021	3 864	4 450	4 243	...	...
	SERVICE TRADES	–	–	2 871	1 457	...	...
	NATURAL SCIENCE	25 361	8 459	30 478	10 787	...	...
	MATHEMATICS & COMPUTER SCIENCE	25 519	8 926	52 069	18 975	...	...
	MEDICAL SCIENCE & HEALTH–RELATED	63 862	45 213	74 102	54 171	...	...
	ENGINEERING	76 020	5 973	92 701	8 114	...	...
	ARCHITECTURE & TOWN PLANNING	9 593	1 877	9 646	2 060	...	...
	TRADE, CRAFT & INDUSTRIAL PROGRAMMES	–	–	–	–	...	...
	TRANSPORT AND COMMUNICATIONS	1 198	72	1 395	145	...	...
	AGRICULTURE, FORESTRY & FISHERY	17 609	5 458	18 961	6 101	...	...
	OTHER AND NOT SPECIFIED	199 454	111 055	315 241	176 391	...	...

COUNTRY / PAYS / PAIS	FIELD OF STUDY / DOMAINES D'ETUDES / SECTORES DE ESTUDIOS	1980		1983		1984	
		MF	F	MF	F	MF	F
		(1)	(2)	(3)	(4)	(5)	(6)
COSTA RICA‡	TOTAL	50 812	...	54 257	...	54 456	...
	EDUCATION SCIENCE & TEACHER TRAINING	6 838	...	5 570	...	5 738	...
	HUMANITIES, RELIGION & THEOLOGY	7 947	...	15 318	...	11 152	...
	FINE AND APPLIED ARTS	924	...	1 036	...	1 227	...
	LAW	2 428	...	2 613	...	3 153	...
	SOCIAL AND BEHAVIOURAL SCIENCE	4 622	...	4 471	...	5 830	...
	COMMERCIAL & BUSINESS ADMINISTRATION	5 778	...	4 950	...	6 053	...
	MASS COMMUNICATION & DOCUMENTATION	636	...	1 071	...	1 208	...
	HOME ECONOMICS (DOMESTIC SCIENCE)	–	–	–	–	–	–
	SERVICE TRADES	–	–	115	...	188	...
	NATURAL SCIENCE	1 952	...	1 578	...	1 530	...
	MATHEMATICS & COMPUTER SCIENCE	2 065	...	2 119	...	2 440	...
	MEDICAL SCIENCE & HEALTH–RELATED	2 824	...	2 886	...	3 323	...
	ENGINEERING	4 319	...	4 361	...	4 799	...
	ARCHITECTURE & TOWN PLANNING	1 161	...	1 038	...	984	...
	TRADE, CRAFT & INDUSTRIAL PROGRAMMES	–	–	–	–	–	–
	TRANSPORT AND COMMUNICATIONS	–	–	–	–	–	–
	AGRICULTURE, FORESTRY & FISHERY	3 169	...	2 328	...	2 296	...
	OTHER AND NOT SPECIFIED	6 149	...	4 803	...	4 535	...
CUBA‡	TOTAL	151 733	...	192 958	101 711	212 155	113 956
	EDUCATION SCIENCE & TEACHER TRAINING	60 942	...	82 567	52 032	92 535	58 196
	HUMANITIES, RELIGION & THEOLOGY	2 795	...	3 371	2 381	2 815	2 678
	FINE AND APPLIED ARTS	902	...	615	261	1 222	627
	LAW	3 175	...	3 047	1 687	2 898	1 738
	SOCIAL AND BEHAVIOURAL SCIENCE	1 727	...	14 281	7 588	13 385	6 310
	COMMERCIAL & BUSINESS ADMINISTRATION	15 340	...	5 717	3 421	8 166	5 300
	MASS COMMUNICATION & DOCUMENTATION	1 222	...	1 542	833	1 443	847
	HOME ECONOMICS (DOMESTIC SCIENCE)	–	–	–	–	–	–
	SERVICE TRADES	–	–	–	–	–	–
	NATURAL SCIENCE	3 791	...	2 570	1 574	2 715	1 715
	MATHEMATICS & COMPUTER SCIENCE	1 475	...	1 588	891	1 619	901
	MEDICAL SCIENCE & HEALTH–RELATED	15 559	...	22 689	13 609	25 793	15 321
	ENGINEERING	18 893	...	28 101	8 682	24 177	7 651
	ARCHITECTURE & TOWN PLANNING	4 876	...	1 910	991	6 606	2 990
	TRADE, CRAFT & INDUSTRIAL PROGRAMMES	./.	...	339	244	351	254
	TRANSPORT AND COMMUNICATIONS	1 987	...	2 730	414	2 988	484
	AGRICULTURE, FORESTRY & FISHERY	14 538	...	14 336	5 440	16 790	7 032
	OTHER AND NOT SPECIFIED	4 511	...	7 555	1 663	8 652	1 912
DOMINICA	TOTAL	63	14	58	50	60	40
	EDUCATION SCIENCE & TEACHER TRAINING	63	14	58	50	60	40
	HUMANITIES, RELIGION & THEOLOGY	–	–	–	–	–	–
	FINE AND APPLIED ARTS	–	–	–	–	–	–
	LAW	–	–	–	–	–	–
	SOCIAL AND BEHAVIOURAL SCIENCE	–	–	–	–	–	–
	COMMERCIAL & BUSINESS ADMINISTRATION	–	–	–	–	–	–
	MASS COMMUNICATION & DOCUMENTATION	–	–	–	–	–	–
	HOME ECONOMICS (DOMESTIC SCIENCE)	–	–	–	–	–	–
	SERVICE TRADES	–	–	–	–	–	–
	NATURAL SCIENCE	–	–	–	–	–	–
	MATHEMATICS & COMPUTER SCIENCE	–	–	–	–	–	–
	MEDICAL SCIENCE & HEALTH–RELATED	–	–	–	–	–	–
	ENGINEERING	–	–	–	–	–	–
	ARCHITECTURE & TOWN PLANNING	–	–	–	–	–	–
	TRADE, CRAFT & INDUSTRIAL PROGRAMMES	–	–	–	–	–	–
	TRANSPORT AND COMMUNICATIONS	–	–	–	–	–	–
	AGRICULTURE, FORESTRY & FISHERY	–	–	–	–	–	–
	OTHER AND NOT SPECIFIED	–	–	–	–	–	–

3.12 Third level: students by field of study (1980,1983,1984)
Troisième degré: étudiants par domaine d'études (1980,1983,1984)
Tercer grado: estudiantes por sector de estudios (1980,1983,1984)

COUNTRY PAYS PAIS	FIELD OF STUDY DOMAINES D'ETUDES SECTORES DE ESTUDIOS	1980		1983		1984	
		MF	F	MF	F	MF	F
		(1)	(2)	(3)	(4)	(5)	(6)
EL SALVADOR‡	TOTAL	16 838	5 202	57 374	24 635	...	...
	EDUCATION SCIENCE & TEACHER TRAINING	698	236	9 074	5 342	...	...
	HUMANITIES, RELIGION & THEOLOGY	158	44	1 025	567	...	...
	FINE AND APPLIED ARTS	339	240	357	241	...	...
	LAW	592	250	3 261	1 170	...	...
	SOCIAL AND BEHAVIOURAL SCIENCE	1 959	952	4 371	2 221	...	...
	COMMERCIAL & BUSINESS ADMINISTRATION	4 198	1 277	14 284	5 847	...	...
	MASS COMMUNICATION & DOCUMENTATION	–	–	467	329	...	...
	HOME ECONOMICS (DOMESTIC SCIENCE)	–	–	74	69	...	...
	SERVICE TRADES	99	75	117	65	...	...
	NATURAL SCIENCE	29	8	344	157	...	...
	MATHEMATICS & COMPUTER SCIENCE	–	–	205	68	...	...
	MEDICAL SCIENCE & HEALTH-RELATED	479	479	6 679	3 930	...	...
	ENGINEERING	6 308	1 156	10 682	1 448	...	...
	ARCHITECTURE & TOWN PLANNING	945	398	2 259	1 168	...	...
	TRADE, CRAFT & INDUSTRIAL PROGRAMMES	551	87	195	120	...	...
	TRANSPORT AND COMMUNICATIONS	–	–	–	–	...	...
	AGRICULTURE, FORESTRY & FISHERY	483	–	1 940	183	...	...
	OTHER AND NOT SPECIFIED	–	–	2 040	1 710	...	...
GRENADA Ø	TOTAL	...	...	519	256	...	...
	EDUCATION SCIENCE & TEACHER TRAINING	...	...	–	–	...	...
	HUMANITIES, RELIGION & THEOLOGY	...	...	–	–	...	...
	FINE AND APPLIED ARTS	...	...	–	–	...	...
	LAW	...	...	–	–	...	...
	SOCIAL AND BEHAVIOURAL SCIENCE	...	...	–	–	...	...
	COMMERCIAL & BUSINESS ADMINISTRATION	...	...	78	78	...	...
	MASS COMMUNICATION & DOCUMENTATION	...	...	–	–	...	...
	HOME ECONOMICS (DOMESTIC SCIENCE)	...	...	–	–	...	...
	SERVICE TRADES	...	...	–	–	...	...
	NATURAL SCIENCE	...	...	–	–	...	...
	MATHEMATICS & COMPUTER SCIENCE	...	...	–	–	...	...
	MEDICAL SCIENCE & HEALTH-RELATED	...	...	89	84	...	...
	ENGINEERING	...	...	129	13	...	...
	ARCHITECTURE & TOWN PLANNING	...	...	./.	./.	...	...
	TRADE, CRAFT & INDUSTRIAL PROGRAMMES	...	...	–	–	...	...
	TRANSPORT AND COMMUNICATIONS	...	...	–	–	...	...
	AGRICULTURE, FORESTRY & FISHERY	...	...	39	12	...	...
	OTHER AND NOT SPECIFIED	...	...	184	69	...	...
HAITI‡	TOTAL	4 671	1 410	6 289	2 119	...	...
	EDUCATION SCIENCE & TEACHER TRAINING	324	79	1 016	623	...	...
	HUMANITIES, RELIGION & THEOLOGY	./.	./.	226	30	...	...
	FINE AND APPLIED ARTS	–	–	–	–	...	...
	LAW	1 039	432	958	222	...	...
	SOCIAL AND BEHAVIOURAL SCIENCE	769	209	731	224	...	...
	COMMERCIAL & BUSINESS ADMINISTRATION	–	–	1 313	555	...	...
	MASS COMMUNICATION & DOCUMENTATION	–	–	–	–	...	...
	HOME ECONOMICS (DOMESTIC SCIENCE)	–	–	–	–	...	...
	SERVICE TRADES	–	–	–	–	...	...
	NATURAL SCIENCE	175	20	159	4	...	...
	MATHEMATICS & COMPUTER SCIENCE	./.	./.	./.	./.	...	...
	MEDICAL SCIENCE & HEALTH-RELATED	1 112	506	767	323	...	...
	ENGINEERING	908	68	896	108	...	...
	ARCHITECTURE & TOWN PLANNING	–	–	–	–	...	...
	TRADE, CRAFT & INDUSTRIAL PROGRAMMES	–	–	–	–	...	...
	TRANSPORT AND COMMUNICATIONS	–	–	–	–	...	...
	AGRICULTURE, FORESTRY & FISHERY	174	24	223	30	...	...
	OTHER AND NOT SPECIFIED	170	72	–	–	...	...

COUNTRY / PAYS / PAIS	FIELD OF STUDY / DOMAINES D'ETUDES / SECTORES DE ESTUDIOS	1980		1983		1984	
		MF	F	MF	F	MF	F
		(1)	(2)	(3)	(4)	(5)	(6)
HONDURAS	TOTAL	25 825	9 736	34 468	...	33 742	...
	EDUCATION SCIENCE & TEACHER TRAINING	491	343	4 220	...	3 407	...
	HUMANITIES, RELIGION & THEOLOGY	204	114	178	...	211	...
	FINE AND APPLIED ARTS	16	3	31	...	21	...
	LAW	2 222	766	3 087	...	2 978	...
	SOCIAL AND BEHAVIOURAL SCIENCE	3 345	1 575	4 000	...	3 850	...
	COMMERCIAL & BUSINESS ADMINISTRATION	6 171	2 626	6 894	...	6 216	...
	MASS COMMUNICATION & DOCUMENTATION	147	56	339	...	340	...
	HOME ECONOMICS (DOMESTIC SCIENCE)	61	61	–	–	–	–
	SERVICE TRADES	–	–	–	–	–	–
	NATURAL SCIENCE	232	120	287	...	1 891	...
	MATHEMATICS & COMPUTER SCIENCE	215	107	111	...	92	...
	MEDICAL SCIENCE & HEALTH-RELATED	4 432	2 300	5 307	...	4 239	...
	ENGINEERING	6 389	1 009	6 319	...	6 364	...
	ARCHITECTURE & TOWN PLANNING	–	–	484	...	323	...
	TRADE, CRAFT & INDUSTRIAL PROGRAMMES	–	–	–	–	–	–
	TRANSPORT AND COMMUNICATIONS	–	–	–	–	–	–
	AGRICULTURE, FORESTRY & FISHERY	707	–	3 133	...	2 850	...
	OTHER AND NOT SPECIFIED	1 193	656	78	...	960	...
JAMAICA	TOTAL	13 999	...	...	...	...	...
	EDUCATION SCIENCE & TEACHER TRAINING	4 984	...	...	...	...	...
	HUMANITIES, RELIGION & THEOLOGY	1 078	...	...	...	...	...
	FINE AND APPLIED ARTS	633	...	...	...	...	...
	LAW	37	...	...	...	...	...
	SOCIAL AND BEHAVIOURAL SCIENCE	845	...	...	...	...	...
	COMMERCIAL & BUSINESS ADMINISTRATION	2 354	...	...	...	...	...
	MASS COMMUNICATION & DOCUMENTATION	66	...	...	...	...	...
	HOME ECONOMICS (DOMESTIC SCIENCE)	343	...	...	...	...	...
	SERVICE TRADES	–	–	...	...	...	...
	NATURAL SCIENCE	1 137	...	...	...	...	...
	MATHEMATICS & COMPUTER SCIENCE	46	...	...	...	...	...
	MEDICAL SCIENCE & HEALTH-RELATED	1 026	...	...	...	...	...
	ENGINEERING	671	...	...	...	...	...
	ARCHITECTURE & TOWN PLANNING	378	...	...	...	...	...
	TRADE, CRAFT & INDUSTRIAL PROGRAMMES	–	–	...	...	...	...
	TRANSPORT AND COMMUNICATIONS	–	–	...	...	...	...
	AGRICULTURE, FORESTRY & FISHERY	383	...	...	...	...	...
	OTHER AND NOT SPECIFIED	18	...	...	...	...	...
MEXICO‡	TOTAL	785 419	239 791	939 513	317 276	...	...
	EDUCATION SCIENCE & TEACHER TRAINING	10 528	5 308	11 505	7 939	...	...
	HUMANITIES, RELIGION & THEOLOGY	9 894	5 115	10 632	5 853	...	...
	FINE AND APPLIED ARTS	5 825	2 922	8 647	4 536	...	...
	LAW	65 726	19 892	101 280	32 423	...	...
	SOCIAL AND BEHAVIOURAL SCIENCE	55 600	29 026	83 728	45 663	...	...
	COMMERCIAL & BUSINESS ADMINISTRATION	162 402	61 600	181 465	76 738	...	...
	MASS COMMUNICATION & DOCUMENTATION	13 188	7 270	19 291	11 748	...	...
	HOME ECONOMICS (DOMESTIC SCIENCE)	–	–	–	–	...	...
	SERVICE TRADES	7 394	4 712	11 409	7 643	...	...
	NATURAL SCIENCE	21 024	7 095	24 242	9 937	...	...
	MATHEMATICS & COMPUTER SCIENCE	7 855	1 871	12 917	5 341	...	...
	MEDICAL SCIENCE & HEALTH-RELATED	155 100	66 839	133 685	63 384	...	...
	ENGINEERING	160 522	14 586	257 537	28 484	...	...
	ARCHITECTURE & TOWN PLANNING	31 409	5 735	39 298	8 692	...	...
	TRADE, CRAFT & INDUSTRIAL PROGRAMMES	2 268	818	–	–	...	...
	TRANSPORT AND COMMUNICATIONS	467	33	274	–	...	...
	AGRICULTURE, FORESTRY & FISHERY	75 038	6 763	39 049	7 828	...	...
	OTHER AND NOT SPECIFIED	1 179	206	4 554	1 067	...	...

3.12 Third level: students by field of study (1980,1983,1984)
Troisième degré: étudiants par domaine d'études (1980,1983,1984)
Tercer grado: estudiantes por sector de estudios (1980,1983,1984)

COUNTRY / PAYS / PAIS	FIELD OF STUDY / DOMAINES D'ETUDES / SECTORES DE ESTUDIOS	1980 MF	1980 F	1983 MF	1983 F	1984 MF	1984 F
		(1)	(2)	(3)	(4)	(5)	(6)
NICARAGUA‡	TOTAL	35 268	...	31 725	15 115	29 001	16 355
	EDUCATION SCIENCE & TEACHER TRAINING	2 253	...	5 696	3 935	5 856	4 150
	HUMANITIES, RELIGION & THEOLOGY	675	...	1 342	1 044	112	105
	FINE AND APPLIED ARTS	–	–	–	–	142	105
	LAW	1 145	...	606	285	446	235
	SOCIAL AND BEHAVIOURAL SCIENCE	2 957	...	./.	./.	2 760	1 650
	COMMERCIAL & BUSINESS ADMINISTRATION	3 871	...	7 438	3 456	3 528	2 068
	MASS COMMUNICATION & DOCUMENTATION	346	...	./.	./.	360	294
	HOME ECONOMICS (DOMESTIC SCIENCE)	129	...	./.	./.	244	239
	SERVICE TRADES	–	–	–	–	–	–
	NATURAL SCIENCE	1 239	...	1 184	764	712	486
	MATHEMATICS & COMPUTER SCIENCE	759	...	162	81	395	255
	MEDICAL SCIENCE & HEALTH-RELATED	1 987	...	4 273	2 540	4 339	2 728
	ENGINEERING	3 538	...	5 208	1 138	4 013	1 290
	ARCHITECTURE & TOWN PLANNING	497	...	535	254	404	246
	TRADE, CRAFT & INDUSTRIAL PROGRAMMES	66	...	–	–	69	57
	TRANSPORT AND COMMUNICATIONS	–	–	–	–	46	4
	AGRICULTURE, FORESTRY & FISHERY	933	...	5 281	1 618	4 477	2 039
	OTHER AND NOT SPECIFIED	14 873	...	–	–	1 098	404
PANAMA‡	TOTAL	31 277	16 852	44 568	26 131	52 224	29 229
	EDUCATION SCIENCE & TEACHER TRAINING	1 210	996	2 367	1 885	3 033	2 346
	HUMANITIES, RELIGION & THEOLOGY	1 293	966	2 210	1 689	2 029	1 494
	FINE AND APPLIED ARTS	553	257	429	265	409	254
	LAW	1 739	641	2 047	801	2 163	858
	SOCIAL AND BEHAVIOURAL SCIENCE	3 156	1 653	3 399	1 880	3 672	2 008
	COMMERCIAL & BUSINESS ADMINISTRATION	8 968	5 368	14 804	9 575	17 228	10 808
	MASS COMMUNICATION & DOCUMENTATION	968	620	1 168	802	1 514	976
	HOME ECONOMICS (DOMESTIC SCIENCE)	319	319	239	239	253	253
	SERVICE TRADES	–	–	–	–	16	4
	NATURAL SCIENCE	2 278	914	1 303	606	1 329	659
	MATHEMATICS & COMPUTER SCIENCE	284	141	1 019	521	1 106	562
	MEDICAL SCIENCE & HEALTH-RELATED	3 200	2 296	3 482	2 720	3 609	2 842
	ENGINEERING	1 747	401	6 865	1 894	9 607	2 489
	ARCHITECTURE & TOWN PLANNING	764	205	778	293	830	250
	TRADE, CRAFT & INDUSTRIAL PROGRAMMES	1 984	326	324	150	509	242
	TRANSPORT AND COMMUNICATIONS	–	–	–	–	–	–
	AGRICULTURE, FORESTRY & FISHERY	457	110	229	68	332	61
	OTHER AND NOT SPECIFIED	2 357	1 639	3 905	2 743	4 585	3 123
ST. LUCIA	TOTAL	...	...	402	198	346	158
	EDUCATION SCIENCE & TEACHER TRAINING	...	...	109	88	112	70
	HUMANITIES, RELIGION & THEOLOGY	...	...	–	–	–	–
	FINE AND APPLIED ARTS	...	...	–	–	–	–
	LAW	...	...	–	–	–	–
	SOCIAL AND BEHAVIOURAL SCIENCE	...	...	–	–	–	–
	COMMERCIAL & BUSINESS ADMINISTRATION	...	...	52	51	61	42
	MASS COMMUNICATION & DOCUMENTATION	...	...	–	–	–	–
	HOME ECONOMICS (DOMESTIC SCIENCE)	...	...	–	–	–	–
	SERVICE TRADES	...	...	30	26	25	25
	NATURAL SCIENCE	...	...	–	–	–	–
	MATHEMATICS & COMPUTER SCIENCE	...	...	–	–	–	–
	MEDICAL SCIENCE & HEALTH-RELATED	...	...	20	8	–	–
	ENGINEERING	...	...	59	9	–	–
	ARCHITECTURE & TOWN PLANNING	...	...	–	–	27	8
	TRADE, CRAFT & INDUSTRIAL PROGRAMMES	...	...	99	10	97	8
	TRANSPORT AND COMMUNICATIONS	...	...	–	–	–	–
	AGRICULTURE, FORESTRY & FISHERY	...	...	33	6	24	5
	OTHER AND NOT SPECIFIED	...	...	–	–	–	–

COUNTRY / PAYS / PAIS	FIELD OF STUDY / DOMAINES D'ETUDES / SECTORES DE ESTUDIOS	1980 MF	1980 F	1983 MF	1983 F	1984 MF	1984 F
		(1)	(2)	(3)	(4)	(5)	(6)
TRINIDAD AND TOBAGO‡ Ø	TOTAL	...	...	5 470	2 343	...	...
	EDUCATION SCIENCE & TEACHER TRAINING	...	...	446	362	...	...
	HUMANITIES, RELIGION & THEOLOGY	...	...	860	578	...	...
	FINE AND APPLIED ARTS	...	...	–	–	...	...
	LAW	...	...	56	33	...	...
	SOCIAL AND BEHAVIOURAL SCIENCE	...	...	766	370	...	...
	COMMERCIAL & BUSINESS ADMINISTRATION	...	...	469	274	...	...
	MASS COMMUNICATION & DOCUMENTATION	...	...	–	–	...	...
	HOME ECONOMICS (DOMESTIC SCIENCE)	...	...	35	35	...	...
	SERVICE TRADES	...	...	–	–	...	...
	NATURAL SCIENCE	...	...	697	290	...	...
	MATHEMATICS & COMPUTER SCIENCE	...	...	./.	./.	...	...
	MEDICAL SCIENCE & HEALTH-RELATED	...	...	–	–	...	...
	ENGINEERING	...	...	1 246	216	...	...
	ARCHITECTURE & TOWN PLANNING	...	...	–	–	...	...
	TRADE, CRAFT & INDUSTRIAL PROGRAMMES	...	...	486	21	...	...
	TRANSPORT AND COMMUNICATIONS	...	...	50	4	...	...
	AGRICULTURE, FORESTRY & FISHERY	...	...	329	141	...	...
	OTHER AND NOT SPECIFIED	...	...	30	19	...	...
AMERICA, SOUTH							
ARGENTINA‡	TOTAL	491 473	247 656	403 978	175 392	...	...
	EDUCATION SCIENCE & TEACHER TRAINING	84 727	74 588	7 681	6 622	...	...
	HUMANITIES, RELIGION & THEOLOGY	24 738	18 746	26 178	19 487	...	...
	FINE AND APPLIED ARTS	7 214	5 372	4 194	2 940	...	...
	LAW	60 981	28 416	59 165	27 296	...	...
	SOCIAL AND BEHAVIOURAL SCIENCE	10 749	7 690	10 075	7 245	...	...
	COMMERCIAL & BUSINESS ADMINISTRATION	74 963	25 606	78 646	30 768	...	...
	MASS COMMUNICATION & DOCUMENTATION	1 788	1 062	–	–	...	...
	HOME ECONOMICS (DOMESTIC SCIENCE)	–	–	–	–	...	...
	SERVICE TRADES	–	–	–	–	...	...
	NATURAL SCIENCE	18 877	11 473	22 969	13 495	...	...
	MATHEMATICS & COMPUTER SCIENCE	20 022	13 874	20 849	14 151	...	...
	MEDICAL SCIENCE & HEALTH-RELATED	57 460	31 583	51 112	26 683	...	...
	ENGINEERING	68 861	8 235	69 323	7 730	...	...
	ARCHITECTURE & TOWN PLANNING	29 920	12 206	30 320	12 515	...	...
	TRADE, CRAFT & INDUSTRIAL PROGRAMMES	6 139	2 028	–	–	...	...
	TRANSPORT AND COMMUNICATIONS	–	–	–	–	...	...
	AGRICULTURE, FORESTRY & FISHERY	25 034	6 777	23 466	6 460	...	...
	OTHER AND NOT SPECIFIED	–	–	–	–	...	...
BOLIVIA Ø	TOTAL	...	...	56 632	...	...	...
	EDUCATION SCIENCE & TEACHER TRAINING	...	...	366	...	...	...
	HUMANITIES, RELIGION & THEOLOGY	...	...	1 543	...	...	...
	FINE AND APPLIED ARTS	...	...	77	...	...	...
	LAW	...	...	6 239	...	...	...
	SOCIAL AND BEHAVIOURAL SCIENCE	...	...	1 107	...	...	...
	COMMERCIAL & BUSINESS ADMINISTRATION	...	...	16 529	...	...	...
	MASS COMMUNICATION & DOCUMENTATION	...	...	98	...	...	...
	HOME ECONOMICS (DOMESTIC SCIENCE)	...	...	–	–	...	...
	SERVICE TRADES	...	...	–	–	...	...
	NATURAL SCIENCE	...	...	720	...	...	...
	MATHEMATICS & COMPUTER SCIENCE	...	...	564	...	...	...
	MEDICAL SCIENCE & HEALTH-RELATED	...	...	11 146	...	...	...
	ENGINEERING	...	...	12 179	...	...	...
	ARCHITECTURE & TOWN PLANNING	...	...	3 058	...	...	...
	TRADE, CRAFT & INDUSTRIAL PROGRAMMES	...	...	–	–	...	...
	TRANSPORT AND COMMUNICATIONS	...	...	–	–	...	...
	AGRICULTURE, FORESTRY & FISHERY	...	...	3 006	...	...	...
	OTHER AND NOT SPECIFIED	...	...	–	–	...	...

3.12 Third level: students by field of study (1980,1983,1984)
Troisième degré: étudiants par domaine d'études (1980,1983,1984)
Tercer grado: estudiantes por sector de estudios (1980,1983,1984)

COUNTRY / PAYS / PAIS	FIELD OF STUDY / DOMAINES D'ETUDES / SECTORES DE ESTUDIOS	1980		1983		1984	
		MF	F	MF	F	MF	F
		(1)	(2)	(3)	(4)	(5)	(6)
BRAZIL‡	TOTAL	1 409 243	...	1 479 397	740 327	...	...
	EDUCATION SCIENCE & TEACHER TRAINING	403 949	...	113 294	...	...	...
	HUMANITIES, RELIGION & THEOLOGY	77 696	...	149 302	108 377	...	...
	FINE AND APPLIED ARTS	13 849	...	30 664	22 483	...	...
	LAW	137 373	...	139 870	53 868	...	...
	SOCIAL AND BEHAVIOURAL SCIENCE	87 696	...	177 713	103 023	...	...
	COMMERCIAL & BUSINESS ADMINISTRATION	208 620	...	220 067	74 325	...	...
	MASS COMMUNICATION & DOCUMENTATION	34 486	...	40 527	25 230	...	...
	HOME ECONOMICS (DOMESTIC SCIENCE)	1 956	...	1 948	1 805	...	...
	SERVICE TRADES	6 331	...	4 494	3 422	...	...
	NATURAL SCIENCE	51 374	...	120 903	...	...	...
	MATHEMATICS & COMPUTER SCIENCE	12 710	...	38 197	15 979	...	...
	MEDICAL SCIENCE & HEALTH-RELATED	110 123	...	132 094	81 216	...	...
	ENGINEERING	156 726	...	164 607	20 290	...	...
	ARCHITECTURE & TOWN PLANNING	24 287	...	24 801	13 146	...	...
	TRADE, CRAFT & INDUSTRIAL PROGRAMMES	13 891	...	13 357	1 942	...	...
	TRANSPORT AND COMMUNICATIONS	–	–	–	–	...	...
	AGRICULTURE, FORESTRY & FISHERY	33 162	...	40 616	8 965	...	...
	OTHER AND NOT SPECIFIED	35 014	...	66 943	43 300	...	...
CHILE	TOTAL	145 497	62 804	178 332	75 492	188 665	80 652
	EDUCATION SCIENCE & TEACHER TRAINING	11 732	9 538	16 137	11 957	19 278	15 222
	HUMANITIES, RELIGION & THEOLOGY	12 097	7 361	15 460	8 999	13 961	8 725
	FINE AND APPLIED ARTS	5 738	3 176	7 317	4 153	7 614	4 335
	LAW	2 757	838	3 921	1 028	4 314	1 235
	SOCIAL AND BEHAVIOURAL SCIENCE	1 743	916	4 477	2 139	5 087	2 714
	COMMERCIAL & BUSINESS ADMINISTRATION	17 188	5 929	34 272	14 991	36 430	14 701
	MASS COMMUNICATION & DOCUMENTATION	2 825	1 996	631	413	652	428
	HOME ECONOMICS (DOMESTIC SCIENCE)	756	573	531	432	528	440
	SERVICE TRADES	7 176	4 468	295	208	298	213
	NATURAL SCIENCE	9 015	4 335	9 583	4 680	9 535	4 623
	MATHEMATICS & COMPUTER SCIENCE	8 674	3 793	7 444	2 782	8 051	3 017
	MEDICAL SCIENCE & HEALTH-RELATED	14 531	8 701	14 862	8 448	15 485	8 729
	ENGINEERING	33 508	4 175	50 480	10 155	54 412	11 211
	ARCHITECTURE & TOWN PLANNING	2 797	737	2 463	717	2 554	741
	TRADE, CRAFT & INDUSTRIAL PROGRAMMES	3 391	938	1 020	77	1 575	441
	TRANSPORT AND COMMUNICATIONS	1 594	901	–	–	–	–
	AGRICULTURE, FORESTRY & FISHERY	3 023	1 090	4 574	1 776	3 888	1 288
	OTHER AND NOT SPECIFIED	6 952	3 339	4 865	2 537	5 003	2 589
COLOMBIA‡	TOTAL	271 630	...	378 586	180 909	389 075	...
	EDUCATION SCIENCE & TEACHER TRAINING	44 379	...	69 952	43 371	76 374	...
	HUMANITIES, RELIGION & THEOLOGY	2 755	...	2 860	1 372	2 675	...
	FINE AND APPLIED ARTS	./.	...	8 047	5 230	8 389	...
	LAW	25 646	...	42 918	20 601	46 425	...
	SOCIAL AND BEHAVIOURAL SCIENCE	14 069	...	./.	./.	./.	...
	COMMERCIAL & BUSINESS ADMINISTRATION	88 192	...	104 542	50 486	102 384	...
	MASS COMMUNICATION & DOCUMENTATION	./.	...	./.	./.	./.	...
	HOME ECONOMICS (DOMESTIC SCIENCE)	./.	...	./.	./.	./.	...
	SERVICE TRADES	./.	...	./.	./.	./.	...
	NATURAL SCIENCE	5 830	...	5 936	1 781	6 367	...
	MATHEMATICS & COMPUTER SCIENCE	./.	...	./.	./.	./.	...
	MEDICAL SCIENCE & HEALTH-RELATED	25 934	...	45 124	22 358	40 662	...
	ENGINEERING	36 657	...	88 944	32 631	95 630	...
	ARCHITECTURE & TOWN PLANNING	17 805	...	./.	./.	./.	...
	TRADE, CRAFT & INDUSTRIAL PROGRAMMES	./.	...	./.	./.	./.	...
	TRANSPORT AND COMMUNICATIONS	./.	...	./.	./.	./.	...
	AGRICULTURE, FORESTRY & FISHERY	10 363	...	10 263	3 079	10 169	...
	OTHER AND NOT SPECIFIED	–	–	–	–	–	–

COUNTRY PAYS PAIS	FIELD OF STUDY DOMAINES D'ETUDES SECTORES DE ESTUDIOS	1980		1983		1984	
		MF	F	MF	F	MF	F
		(1)	(2)	(3)	(4)	(5)	(6)
ECUADOR‡	TOTAL	269 775	97 350	266 222	...	280 594	...
	EDUCATION SCIENCE & TEACHER TRAINING	59 426	30 497	50 659	...	53 520	...
	HUMANITIES, RELIGION & THEOLOGY	13 379	8 210	14 076	...	14 264	...
	FINE AND APPLIED ARTS	1 394	406	2 798	...	2 634	...
	LAW	13 394	4 004	13 238	...	13 803	...
	SOCIAL AND BEHAVIOURAL SCIENCE	21 219	8 526	19 915	...	21 116	...
	COMMERCIAL & BUSINESS ADMINISTRATION	35 307	15 791	38 527	...	41 993	...
	MASS COMMUNICATION & DOCUMENTATION	1 377	523	1 812	...	1 882	...
	HOME ECONOMICS (DOMESTIC SCIENCE)	225	223	389	...	389	...
	SERVICE TRADES	357	221	392	...	314	...
	NATURAL SCIENCE	6 194	2 270	7 263	...	8 797	...
	MATHEMATICS & COMPUTER SCIENCE	4 679	409	8 215	...	5 255	...
	MEDICAL SCIENCE & HEALTH-RELATED	30 233	12 556	27 304	...	28 824	...
	ENGINEERING	47 244	5 194	50 787	...	54 876	...
	ARCHITECTURE & TOWN PLANNING	10 456	2 527	10 345	...	10 672	...
	TRADE, CRAFT & INDUSTRIAL PROGRAMMES	1 800	483	900	...	900	...
	TRANSPORT AND COMMUNICATIONS	–	–	–	–	–	–
	AGRICULTURE, FORESTRY & FISHERY	16 584	2 898	5 197	...	4 043	...
	OTHER AND NOT SPECIFIED	6 507	2 612	14 405	...	17 312	...
GUYANA‡	TOTAL	1 681	535	2 111	1 012	...	...
	EDUCATION SCIENCE & TEACHER TRAINING	216	96	804	557	...	...
	HUMANITIES, RELIGION & THEOLOGY	200	115	125	88	...	...
	FINE AND APPLIED ARTS	–	–	–	–	...	...
	LAW	19	5	23	9	...	...
	SOCIAL AND BEHAVIOURAL SCIENCE	289	80	246	100	...	...
	COMMERCIAL & BUSINESS ADMINISTRATION	193	68	226	80	...	...
	MASS COMMUNICATION & DOCUMENTATION	27	4	18	7	...	...
	HOME ECONOMICS (DOMESTIC SCIENCE)	–	–	–	–	...	...
	SERVICE TRADES	–	–	32	3	...	...
	NATURAL SCIENCE	145	32	120	38	...	...
	MATHEMATICS & COMPUTER SCIENCE	51	12	45	13	...	...
	MEDICAL SCIENCE & HEALTH-RELATED	58	28	41	21	...	...
	ENGINEERING	248	6	192	5	...	...
	ARCHITECTURE & TOWN PLANNING	21	5	17	2	...	...
	TRADE, CRAFT & INDUSTRIAL PROGRAMMES	–	–	–	–	...	...
	TRANSPORT AND COMMUNICATIONS	–	–	–	–	...	...
	AGRICULTURE, FORESTRY & FISHERY	54	4	72	11	...	...
	OTHER AND NOT SPECIFIED	160	80	150	78	...	...
PERU‡ Ø	TOTAL	306 353	...	305 390	105 968	...	...
	EDUCATION SCIENCE & TEACHER TRAINING	23 314	...	24 034	15 535	...	...
	HUMANITIES, RELIGION & THEOLOGY	3 513	...	4 367	2 278	...	...
	FINE AND APPLIED ARTS	441	...	275	159	...	...
	LAW	14 534	...	20 614	5 659	...	...
	SOCIAL AND BEHAVIOURAL SCIENCE	37 388	...	46 572	15 471	...	...
	COMMERCIAL & BUSINESS ADMINISTRATION	76 026	...	57 657	20 335	...	...
	MASS COMMUNICATION & DOCUMENTATION	5 670	...	6 169	3 020	...	...
	HOME ECONOMICS (DOMESTIC SCIENCE)	1 425	...	611	477	...	...
	SERVICE TRADES	403	...	1 283	1 038	...	...
	NATURAL SCIENCE	8 373	...	10 484	4 196	...	...
	MATHEMATICS & COMPUTER SCIENCE	4 201	...	5 680	1 484	...	...
	MEDICAL SCIENCE & HEALTH-RELATED	23 781	...	27 913	15 302	...	...
	ENGINEERING	53 338	...	57 718	5 500	...	...
	ARCHITECTURE & TOWN PLANNING	5 049	...	5 253	1 611	...	...
	TRADE, CRAFT & INDUSTRIAL PROGRAMMES	10 523	...	–	–	...	...
	TRANSPORT AND COMMUNICATIONS	–	–	–	–	...	...
	AGRICULTURE, FORESTRY & FISHERY	24 018	...	20 736	3 529	...	...
	OTHER AND NOT SPECIFIED	14 356	...	16 094	10 374	...	...

3.12 Third level: students by field of study (1980,1983,1984)
Troisième degré: étudiants par domaine d'études (1980,1983,1984)
Tercer grado: estudiantes por sector de estudios (1980,1983,1984)

COUNTRY / PAYS / PAIS	FIELD OF STUDY / DOMAINES D'ETUDES / SECTORES DE ESTUDIOS	1980 MF (1)	1980 F (2)	1983 MF (3)	1983 F (4)	1984 MF (5)	1984 F (6)
SURINAME‡	TOTAL	...	...	...	...	2 914	1 497
	EDUCATION SCIENCE & TEACHER TRAINING	...	...	...	...	1 640	997
	HUMANITIES, RELIGION & THEOLOGY	...	...	...	...	–	–
	FINE AND APPLIED ARTS	...	...	...	...	–	–
	LAW	...	...	...	...	./.	./.
	SOCIAL AND BEHAVIOURAL SCIENCE	...	...	...	...	760	369
	COMMERCIAL & BUSINESS ADMINISTRATION	...	...	...	...	–	–
	MASS COMMUNICATION & DOCUMENTATION	...	...	...	...	–	–
	HOME ECONOMICS (DOMESTIC SCIENCE)	...	...	...	...	–	–
	SERVICE TRADES	...	...	...	...	–	–
	NATURAL SCIENCE	...	...	...	...	–	–
	MATHEMATICS & COMPUTER SCIENCE	...	...	...	...	–	–
	MEDICAL SCIENCE & HEALTH-RELATED	...	...	...	...	206	72
	ENGINEERING	...	...	...	...	308	59
	ARCHITECTURE & TOWN PLANNING	...	...	...	...	–	–
	TRADE, CRAFT & INDUSTRIAL PROGRAMMES	...	...	...	...	–	–
	TRANSPORT AND COMMUNICATIONS	...	...	...	...	–	–
	AGRICULTURE, FORESTRY & FISHERY	...	...	...	...	–	–
	OTHER AND NOT SPECIFIED	...	...	...	...	–	–
URUGUAY‡	TOTAL	36 298	19 236	63 734	...	77 480	...
	EDUCATION SCIENCE & TEACHER TRAINING	253	199	681	540	1 048	834
	HUMANITIES, RELIGION & THEOLOGY	582	435	1 894	1 339	2 704	1 877
	FINE AND APPLIED ARTS	312	175	264	137	1 677	...
	LAW	10 812	6 641	13 871	9 570	15 840	...
	SOCIAL AND BEHAVIOURAL SCIENCE	1 310	1 018	5 530	4 084	7 823	...
	COMMERCIAL & BUSINESS ADMINISTRATION	4 183	2 055	11 784	6 338	12 902	...
	MASS COMMUNICATION & DOCUMENTATION	156	145	380	346	816	...
	HOME ECONOMICS (DOMESTIC SCIENCE)	–	–	–	–	151	...
	SERVICE TRADES	–	–	–	–	–	–
	NATURAL SCIENCE	627	348	3 749	1 968	2 423	1 255
	MATHEMATICS & COMPUTER SCIENCE	496	178	2 141	777	3 058	...
	MEDICAL SCIENCE & HEALTH-RELATED	10 324	5 788	11 768	7 609	15 723	...
	ENGINEERING	1 303	116	3 544	408	4 121	...
	ARCHITECTURE & TOWN PLANNING	1 850	712	2 791	...	*3 316	...
	TRADE, CRAFT & INDUSTRIAL PROGRAMMES	74	–	179	–	278	–
	TRANSPORT AND COMMUNICATIONS	–	–	–	–	–	–
	AGRICULTURE, FORESTRY & FISHERY	3 600	1 042	4 511	1 491	4 792	...
	OTHER AND NOT SPECIFIED	416	384	647	587	808	...
VENEZUELA	TOTAL	307 133	...	349 773	...	381 575	...
	EDUCATION SCIENCE & TEACHER TRAINING	44 875	...	51 373	...	55 416	...
	HUMANITIES, RELIGION & THEOLOGY	3 478	...	3 897	...	5 051	...
	FINE AND APPLIED ARTS	410	...	516	...	679	...
	LAW	18 975	...	23 395	...	32 060	...
	SOCIAL AND BEHAVIOURAL SCIENCE	21 699	...	28 095	...	51 730	...
	COMMERCIAL & BUSINESS ADMINISTRATION	42 286	...	49 673	...	64 304	...
	MASS COMMUNICATION & DOCUMENTATION	3 667	...	4 060	...	4 317	...
	HOME ECONOMICS (DOMESTIC SCIENCE)	–	–	–	–	–	–
	SERVICE TRADES	1 419	...	1 105	...	–	–
	NATURAL SCIENCE	5 912	...	6 401	...	6 899	...
	MATHEMATICS & COMPUTER SCIENCE	6 221	...	7 528	...	11 731	...
	MEDICAL SCIENCE & HEALTH-RELATED	35 650	...	40 585	...	40 879	...
	ENGINEERING	51 306	...	62 074	...	65 068	...
	ARCHITECTURE & TOWN PLANNING	5 858	...	6 210	...	6 397	...
	TRADE, CRAFT & INDUSTRIAL PROGRAMMES	1 175	...	673	...	–	–
	TRANSPORT AND COMMUNICATIONS	–	–	–	–	–	–
	AGRICULTURE, FORESTRY & FISHERY	12 813	...	14 740	...	14 868	...
	OTHER AND NOT SPECIFIED	51 389	...	49 448	...	22 052	...

COUNTRY / PAYS / PAIS	FIELD OF STUDY / DOMAINES D'ETUDES / SECTORES DE ESTUDIOS	1980		1983		1984	
		MF	F	MF	F	MF	F
		(1)	(2)	(3)	(4)	(5)	(6)
ASIA							
AFGHANISTAN Ø	TOTAL	...	...	19 652	...	...	...
	EDUCATION SCIENCE & TEACHER TRAINING	...	...	4 637	...	...	...
	HUMANITIES, RELIGION & THEOLOGY	...	...	1 595	...	...	...
	FINE AND APPLIED ARTS	...	...	–	–	...	...
	LAW	...	...	624	–	...	...
	SOCIAL AND BEHAVIOURAL SCIENCE	...	...	1 427	...	...	...
	COMMERCIAL & BUSINESS ADMINISTRATION	...	...	420	...	...	...
	MASS COMMUNICATION & DOCUMENTATION	...	...	–	–	...	...
	HOME ECONOMICS (DOMESTIC SCIENCE)	...	...	–	–	...	...
	SERVICE TRADES	...	...	–	–	...	...
	NATURAL SCIENCE	...	...	1 218	...	...	...
	MATHEMATICS & COMPUTER SCIENCE	...	...	–	–	...	...
	MEDICAL SCIENCE & HEALTH-RELATED	...	...	3 279	...	...	...
	ENGINEERING	...	...	3 462	...	...	...
	ARCHITECTURE & TOWN PLANNING	...	...	–	–	...	...
	TRADE, CRAFT & INDUSTRIAL PROGRAMMES	...	...	–	–	...	...
	TRANSPORT AND COMMUNICATIONS	...	...	263	...	...	...
	AGRICULTURE, FORESTRY & FISHERY	...	...	1 546	...	...	...
	OTHER AND NOT SPECIFIED	...	...	1 181	...	...	...
BAHRAIN‡	TOTAL	1 908	786	...	...	4 235	2 377
	EDUCATION SCIENCE & TEACHER TRAINING	317	260	...	...	1 153	879
	HUMANITIES, RELIGION & THEOLOGY	–	–	...	...	–	–
	FINE AND APPLIED ARTS	–	–	...	...	–	–
	LAW	–	–	...	...	–	–
	SOCIAL AND BEHAVIOURAL SCIENCE	–	–	...	...	–	–
	COMMERCIAL & BUSINESS ADMINISTRATION	797	351	...	...	1 095	301
	MASS COMMUNICATION & DOCUMENTATION	–	–	...	...	–	–
	HOME ECONOMICS (DOMESTIC SCIENCE)	–	–	...	...	–	–
	SERVICE TRADES	–	–	...	...	–	–
	NATURAL SCIENCE	–	–	...	...	–	–
	MATHEMATICS & COMPUTER SCIENCE	–	–	...	...	225	108
	MEDICAL SCIENCE & HEALTH-RELATED	–	–	...	...	932	650
	ENGINEERING	794	175	...	...	830	439
	ARCHITECTURE & TOWN PLANNING	–	–	...	...	–	–
	TRADE, CRAFT & INDUSTRIAL PROGRAMMES	./.	./.	...	...	./.	./.
	TRANSPORT AND COMMUNICATIONS	–	–	...	...	–	–
	AGRICULTURE, FORESTRY & FISHERY	–	–	...	...	–	–
	OTHER AND NOT SPECIFIED	–	–	...	...	–	–
BANGLADESH‡	TOTAL	240 181	33 348	386 542	70 942	436 615	78 289
	EDUCATION SCIENCE & TEACHER TRAINING	3 160	888	3 077	873	3 752	870
	HUMANITIES, RELIGION & THEOLOGY	70 702	10 353	127 395	26 696	144 083	29 750
	FINE AND APPLIED ARTS	46	17	–	–	–	–
	LAW	6 833	304	8 276	405	8 300	450
	SOCIAL AND BEHAVIOURAL SCIENCE	56 483	8 517	88 640	17 314	100 421	18 789
	COMMERCIAL & BUSINESS ADMINISTRATION	30 662	3 692	49 113	7 695	56 760	8 612
	MASS COMMUNICATION & DOCUMENTATION	–	–	852	151	–	–
	HOME ECONOMICS (DOMESTIC SCIENCE)	./.	./.	./.	./.	./.	./.
	SERVICE TRADES	–	–	–	–	–	–
	NATURAL SCIENCE	49 262	6 862	77 559	13 594	87 323	14 875
	MATHEMATICS & COMPUTER SCIENCE	5 325	625	7 863	1 282	8 732	1 566
	MEDICAL SCIENCE & HEALTH-RELATED	8 347	1 587	8 545	2 037	14 687	2 263
	ENGINEERING	3 707	47	5 089	84	4 593	118
	ARCHITECTURE & TOWN PLANNING	265	41	320	54	324	20
	TRADE, CRAFT & INDUSTRIAL PROGRAMMES	499	–	540	–	492	–
	TRANSPORT AND COMMUNICATIONS	–	–	–	–	–	–
	AGRICULTURE, FORESTRY & FISHERY	3 939	208	4 286	232	4 366	250
	OTHER AND NOT SPECIFIED	951	207	4 987	525	2 782	726

3.12 Third level: students by field of study (1980,1983,1984)
Troisième degré: étudiants par domaine d'études (1980,1983,1984)
Tercer grado: estudiantes por sector de estudios (1980,1983,1984)

COUNTRY / PAYS / PAIS	FIELD OF STUDY / DOMAINES D'ETUDES / SECTORES DE ESTUDIOS	1980		1983		1984	
		MF	F	MF	F	MF	F
		(1)	(2)	(3)	(4)	(5)	(6)
BHUTAN‡	TOTAL	322	70	55	3	...	...
	EDUCATION SCIENCE & TEACHER TRAINING	142	56	17	3	...	...
	HUMANITIES, RELIGION & THEOLOGY	–	–	–	–	...	...
	FINE AND APPLIED ARTS	–	–	–	–	...	...
	LAW	–	–	–	–	...	...
	SOCIAL AND BEHAVIOURAL SCIENCE	–	–	./.	–	...	...
	COMMERCIAL & BUSINESS ADMINISTRATION	–	–	38	–	...	...
	MASS COMMUNICATION & DOCUMENTATION	–	–	–	–	...	...
	HOME ECONOMICS (DOMESTIC SCIENCE)	–	–	–	–	...	...
	SERVICE TRADES	–	–	–	–	...	...
	NATURAL SCIENCE	–	–	–	–	...	...
	MATHEMATICS & COMPUTER SCIENCE	–	–	–	–	...	...
	MEDICAL SCIENCE & HEALTH–RELATED	–	–	–	–	...	...
	ENGINEERING	138	14	–	–	...	...
	ARCHITECTURE & TOWN PLANNING	–	–	–	–	...	...
	TRADE, CRAFT & INDUSTRIAL PROGRAMMES	–	–	–	–	...	...
	TRANSPORT AND COMMUNICATIONS	–	–	–	–	...	...
	AGRICULTURE, FORESTRY & FISHERY	42	–	–	–	...	...
	OTHER AND NOT SPECIFIED	–	–	–	–	...	...
BRUNEI DARUSSALAM	TOTAL	143	72	218	99	...	...
	EDUCATION SCIENCE & TEACHER TRAINING	143	72	218	99	...	...
	HUMANITIES, RELIGION & THEOLOGY	–	–	–	–	...	...
	FINE AND APPLIED ARTS	–	–	–	–	...	...
	LAW	–	–	–	–	...	...
	SOCIAL AND BEHAVIOURAL SCIENCE	–	–	–	–	...	...
	COMMERCIAL & BUSINESS ADMINISTRATION	–	–	–	–	...	...
	MASS COMMUNICATION & DOCUMENTATION	–	–	–	–	...	...
	HOME ECONOMICS (DOMESTIC SCIENCE)	–	–	–	–	...	...
	SERVICE TRADES	–	–	–	–	...	...
	NATURAL SCIENCE	–	–	–	–	...	...
	MATHEMATICS & COMPUTER SCIENCE	–	–	–	–	...	...
	MEDICAL SCIENCE & HEALTH–RELATED	–	–	–	–	...	...
	ENGINEERING	–	–	–	–	...	...
	ARCHITECTURE & TOWN PLANNING	–	–	–	–	...	...
	TRADE, CRAFT & INDUSTRIAL PROGRAMMES	–	–	–	–	...	...
	TRANSPORT AND COMMUNICATIONS	–	–	–	–	...	...
	AGRICULTURE, FORESTRY & FISHERY	–	–	–	–	...	...
	OTHER AND NOT SPECIFIED	–	–	–	–	...	...
CHINA‡	TOTAL	1 161 440	...	1 237 394	...	1 443 605	...
	EDUCATION SCIENCE & TEACHER TRAINING	339 901	...	313 683	...	362 432	...
	HUMANITIES, RELIGION & THEOLOGY	60 040	...	70 888	...	93 706	...
	FINE AND APPLIED ARTS	6 187	...	6 367	...	7 682	...
	LAW	6 169	...	19 183	...	26 849	...
	SOCIAL AND BEHAVIOURAL SCIENCE	./.	...	./.	...	./.	...
	COMMERCIAL & BUSINESS ADMINISTRATION	37 382	...	72 346	...	99 640	...
	MASS COMMUNICATION & DOCUMENTATION	–	–	–	–	–	–
	HOME ECONOMICS (DOMESTIC SCIENCE)	–	–	–	–	–	–
	SERVICE TRADES	–	–	–	–	–	–
	NATURAL SCIENCE	65 614	...	64 342	...	85 524	...
	MATHEMATICS & COMPUTER SCIENCE	30 174	...	36 553	...	30 644	...
	MEDICAL SCIENCE & HEALTH–RELATED	142 737	...	143 564	...	149 048	...
	ENGINEERING	363 146	...	395 831	...	455 215	...
	ARCHITECTURE & TOWN PLANNING	2 427	...	4 815	...	5 786	...
	TRADE, CRAFT & INDUSTRIAL PROGRAMMES	–	–	–	–	–	–
	TRANSPORT AND COMMUNICATIONS	15 247	...	16 492	...	19 894	...
	AGRICULTURE, FORESTRY & FISHERY	82 811	...	83 303	...	95 546	...
	OTHER AND NOT SPECIFIED	9 605	...	10 027	...	11 639	...

COUNTRY / PAYS / PAIS	FIELD OF STUDY / DOMAINES D'ETUDES / SECTORES DE ESTUDIOS	1980		1983		1984	
		MF	F	MF	F	MF	F
		(1)	(2)	(3)	(4)	(5)	(6)
CYPRUS	TOTAL	1 940	806	2 201	989	2 580	1 147
	EDUCATION SCIENCE & TEACHER TRAINING	117	103	270	219	341	264
	HUMANITIES, RELIGION & THEOLOGY	–	–	–	–	–	–
	FINE AND APPLIED ARTS	–	–	–	–	–	–
	LAW	–	–	–	–	–	–
	SOCIAL AND BEHAVIOURAL SCIENCE	–	–	–	–	–	–
	COMMERCIAL & BUSINESS ADMINISTRATION	641	287	749	369	895	432
	MASS COMMUNICATION & DOCUMENTATION	–	–	–	–	–	–
	HOME ECONOMICS (DOMESTIC SCIENCE)	–	–	–	–	–	–
	SERVICE TRADES	142	40	151	49	168	54
	NATURAL SCIENCE	–	–	–	–	–	–
	MATHEMATICS & COMPUTER SCIENCE	–	–	–	–	–	–
	MEDICAL SCIENCE & HEALTH-RELATED	252	219	205	163	230	181
	ENGINEERING	450	112	496	123	507	105
	ARCHITECTURE & TOWN PLANNING	–	–	–	–	–	–
	TRADE, CRAFT & INDUSTRIAL PROGRAMMES	306	45	297	66	402	111
	TRANSPORT AND COMMUNICATIONS	–	–	–	–	–	–
	AGRICULTURE, FORESTRY & FISHERY	32	–	33	–	37	–
	OTHER AND NOT SPECIFIED	–	–	–	–	–	–
DEMOCRATIC YEMEN‡	TOTAL	3 292	1 705	3 645	1 907	...	...
	EDUCATION SCIENCE & TEACHER TRAINING	1 169	798	1 032	710	...	...
	HUMANITIES, RELIGION & THEOLOGY	./.	./.	310	229	...	...
	FINE AND APPLIED ARTS	–	–	–	–	...	...
	LAW	181	74	208	82	...	...
	SOCIAL AND BEHAVIOURAL SCIENCE	793	340	1 009	434	...	...
	COMMERCIAL & BUSINESS ADMINISTRATION	–	–	–	–	...	...
	MASS COMMUNICATION & DOCUMENTATION	–	–	–	–	...	...
	HOME ECONOMICS (DOMESTIC SCIENCE)	–	–	–	–	...	...
	SERVICE TRADES	–	–	–	–	...	...
	NATURAL SCIENCE	–	–	–	–	...	...
	MATHEMATICS & COMPUTER SCIENCE	–	–	–	–	...	...
	MEDICAL SCIENCE & HEALTH-RELATED	403	197	459	228	...	...
	ENGINEERING	560	208	445	133	...	...
	ARCHITECTURE & TOWN PLANNING	–	–	./.	./.	...	...
	TRADE, CRAFT & INDUSTRIAL PROGRAMMES	–	–	–	–	...	...
	TRANSPORT AND COMMUNICATIONS	–	–	–	–	...	...
	AGRICULTURE, FORESTRY & FISHERY	186	88	182	91	...	...
	OTHER AND NOT SPECIFIED	–	–	–	–	...	...
HONG KONG‡	TOTAL	38 153	9 743	74 563	25 589	76 844	26 542
	EDUCATION SCIENCE & TEACHER TRAINING	1 321	593	5 367	3 403	6 007	3 808
	HUMANITIES, RELIGION & THEOLOGY	2 412	1 439	4 860	2 956	4 657	2 854
	FINE AND APPLIED ARTS	768	321	1 569	720	1 546	718
	LAW	248	117	319	149	373	197
	SOCIAL AND BEHAVIOURAL SCIENCE	2 476	1 234	4 981	2 546	3 882	1 913
	COMMERCIAL & BUSINESS ADMINISTRATION	9 109	3 895	18 116	9 579	19 194	10 177
	MASS COMMUNICATION & DOCUMENTATION	108	60	1 192	747	1 007	614
	HOME ECONOMICS (DOMESTIC SCIENCE)	–	–	–	–	–	–
	SERVICE TRADES	–	–	1 414	536	1 787	552
	NATURAL SCIENCE	2 379	409	3 087	652	2 863	618
	MATHEMATICS & COMPUTER SCIENCE	1 524	392	2 488	653	2 508	648
	MEDICAL SCIENCE & HEALTH-RELATED	1 721	455	2 334	704	2 459	792
	ENGINEERING	13 927	371	21 768	565	22 146	547
	ARCHITECTURE & TOWN PLANNING	253	46	1 687	175	1 589	186
	TRADE, CRAFT & INDUSTRIAL PROGRAMMES	1 652	397	3 238	1 180	3 911	1 411
	TRANSPORT AND COMMUNICATIONS	–	–	251	10	–	–
	AGRICULTURE, FORESTRY & FISHERY	–	–	–	–	–	–
	OTHER AND NOT SPECIFIED	255	14	1 892	1 014	2 915	1 507

3.12 Third level: students by field of study (1980,1983,1984)
Troisième degré: étudiants par domaine d'études (1980,1983,1984)
Tercer grado: estudiantes por sector de estudios (1980,1983,1984)

COUNTRY / PAYS / PAIS	FIELD OF STUDY / DOMAINES D'ETUDES / SECTORES DE ESTUDIOS	1980		1983		1984	
		MF	F	MF	F	MF	F
		(1)	(2)	(3)	(4)	(5)	(6)
INDIA‡	TOTAL	5 345 580	1 396 466	...	...	...	...
	EDUCATION SCIENCE & TEACHER TRAINING	160 026	78 467	...	...	...	...
	HUMANITIES, RELIGION & THEOLOGY	2 652 315	832 149	...	...	...	...
	FINE AND APPLIED ARTS	19 961	10 261	...	...	...	...
	LAW	163 263	10 631	...	...	...	...
	SOCIAL AND BEHAVIOURAL SCIENCE	867 538	158 245	...	...	...	...
	COMMERCIAL & BUSINESS ADMINISTRATION	./.	./.	...	...	...	...
	MASS COMMUNICATION & DOCUMENTATION	2 584	987	...	...	...	...
	HOME ECONOMICS (DOMESTIC SCIENCE)	./.	./.	...	...	...	...
	SERVICE TRADES	–	–	...	...	...	...
	NATURAL SCIENCE	872 936	226 436	...	...	...	...
	MATHEMATICS & COMPUTER SCIENCE	./.	./.	...	...	...	...
	MEDICAL SCIENCE & HEALTH–RELATED	146 472	42 305	...	...	...	...
	ENGINEERING	396 974	32 260	...	...	...	...
	ARCHITECTURE & TOWN PLANNING	./.	./.	...	...	...	...
	TRADE, CRAFT & INDUSTRIAL PROGRAMMES	./.	./.	...	...	...	...
	TRANSPORT AND COMMUNICATIONS	./.	./.	...	...	...	...
	AGRICULTURE, FORESTRY & FISHERY	47 970	1 474	...	...	...	...
	OTHER AND NOT SPECIFIED	15 541	3 251	...	...	...	...
INDONESIA	TOTAL	...	...	831 625	258 942	980 162	316 273
	EDUCATION SCIENCE & TEACHER TRAINING	...	...	205 512	72 568	236 324	89 907
	HUMANITIES, RELIGION & THEOLOGY	...	...	25 898	10 349	28 098	10 274
	FINE AND APPLIED ARTS	...	...	3 534	974	4 152	1 421
	LAW	...	...	102 188	29 439	109 989	30 055
	SOCIAL AND BEHAVIOURAL SCIENCE	...	...	159 986	45 346	218 173	72 709
	COMMERCIAL & BUSINESS ADMINISTRATION	...	...	122 300	49 558	136 425	54 728
	MASS COMMUNICATION & DOCUMENTATION	...	...	4 997	1 827	5 281	1 999
	HOME ECONOMICS (DOMESTIC SCIENCE)	...	...	1 663	1 360	1 982	1 602
	SERVICE TRADES	...	...	1 842	800	2 215	974
	NATURAL SCIENCE	...	...	10 450	2 955	21 411	8 337
	MATHEMATICS & COMPUTER SCIENCE	...	...	4 878	385	6 441	791
	MEDICAL SCIENCE & HEALTH–RELATED	...	...	24 124	8 819	24 855	7 978
	ENGINEERING	...	...	106 703	15 722	109 472	18 008
	ARCHITECTURE & TOWN PLANNING	...	...	4 809	775	12 410	2 430
	TRADE, CRAFT & INDUSTRIAL PROGRAMMES	...	...	2 219	362	3 694	935
	TRANSPORT AND COMMUNICATIONS	...	...	430	69	474	108
	AGRICULTURE, FORESTRY & FISHERY	...	...	48 444	16 502	54 643	13 587
	OTHER AND NOT SPECIFIED	...	...	1 648	132	4 123	430
IRAN, ISLAMIC REPUBLIC OF‡	TOTAL	...	...	151 333	45 418	177 286	45 216
	EDUCATION SCIENCE & TEACHER TRAINING	...	...	43 110	11 555	46 095	5 976
	HUMANITIES, RELIGION & THEOLOGY	...	...	12 547	5 206	14 247	5 909
	FINE AND APPLIED ARTS	...	...	1 091	404	1 421	561
	LAW	...	...	2 509	560	3 242	592
	SOCIAL AND BEHAVIOURAL SCIENCE	...	...	7 957	3 330	12 881	4 891
	COMMERCIAL & BUSINESS ADMINISTRATION	...	...	8 336	2 351	5 699	1 711
	MASS COMMUNICATION & DOCUMENTATION	...	...	465	253	586	340
	HOME ECONOMICS (DOMESTIC SCIENCE)	...	...	646	470	859	585
	SERVICE TRADES	...	...	126	65	134	70
	NATURAL SCIENCE	...	...	11 878	4 339	11 900	4 287
	MATHEMATICS & COMPUTER SCIENCE	...	...	6 198	1 518	6 224	1 520
	MEDICAL SCIENCE & HEALTH–RELATED	...	...	25 197	12 619	32 598	15 770
	ENGINEERING	...	...	22 839	1 451	31 507	1 704
	ARCHITECTURE & TOWN PLANNING	...	...	1 834	520	2 106	528
	TRADE, CRAFT & INDUSTRIAL PROGRAMMES	...	...	237	47	533	139
	TRANSPORT AND COMMUNICATIONS	...	...	156	12	93	7
	AGRICULTURE, FORESTRY & FISHERY	...	...	5 159	354	5 664	229
	OTHER AND NOT SPECIFIED	...	...	1 048	364	1 497	397

COUNTRY / PAYS / PAIS	FIELD OF STUDY / DOMAINES D'ETUDES / SECTORES DE ESTUDIOS	1980 MF (1)	1980 F (2)	1983 MF (3)	1983 F (4)	1984 MF (5)	1984 F (6)
ISRAEL‡	TOTAL	85 191	...	99 283	45 672	101 641	46 810
	EDUCATION SCIENCE & TEACHER TRAINING	31 419	...	40 622	24 304	41 145	24 723
	HUMANITIES, RELIGION & THEOLOGY	./.	...	./.	./.	./.	./.
	FINE AND APPLIED ARTS	./.	...	./.	./.	./.	./.
	LAW	2 176	...	2 560	998	2 612	1 036
	SOCIAL AND BEHAVIOURAL SCIENCE	17 901	...	19 704	8 336	19 176	8 177
	COMMERCIAL & BUSINESS ADMINISTRATION	./.	...	./.	./.	./.	./.
	MASS COMMUNICATION & DOCUMENTATION	./.	...	./.	./.	./.	./.
	HOME ECONOMICS (DOMESTIC SCIENCE)	./.	...	./.	./.	./.	./.
	SERVICE TRADES	./.	...	./.	./.	./.	./.
	NATURAL SCIENCE	7 618	...	4 715	2 379	5 144	2 629
	MATHEMATICS & COMPUTER SCIENCE	./.	...	4 308	1 405	4 506	1 465
	MEDICAL SCIENCE & HEALTH-RELATED	5 705	...	6 570	4 060	6 539	4 049
	ENGINEERING	16 958	...	17 779	2 662	19 873	3 319
	ARCHITECTURE & TOWN PLANNING	./.	...	./.	./.	./.	./.
	TRADE, CRAFT & INDUSTRIAL PROGRAMMES	./.	...	./.	./.	./.	./.
	TRANSPORT AND COMMUNICATIONS	./.	...	./.	./.	./.	./.
	AGRICULTURE, FORESTRY & FISHERY	1 690	...	1 588	534	1 181	416
	OTHER AND NOT SPECIFIED	1 724	...	1 437	994	1 465	996
JAPAN‡	TOTAL	2 412 117	791 264	2 409 983	812 988	2 403 371	825 911
	EDUCATION SCIENCE & TEACHER TRAINING	237 421	171 509	235 812	165 885	228 685	161 648
	HUMANITIES, RELIGION & THEOLOGY	345 474	229 690	354 449	235 779	358 831	239 946
	FINE AND APPLIED ARTS	68 708	48 720	68 443	49 070	67 544	48 616
	LAW	./.	./.	./.	./.	./.	./.
	SOCIAL AND BEHAVIOURAL SCIENCE	788 980	88 225	764 320	92 905	760 132	97 013
	COMMERCIAL & BUSINESS ADMINISTRATION	./.	./.	./.	./.	./.	./.
	MASS COMMUNICATION & DOCUMENTATION	./.	./.	./.	./.	./.	./.
	HOME ECONOMICS (DOMESTIC SCIENCE)	135 775	135 388	138 219	137 813	137 798	137 386
	SERVICE TRADES	–	–	–	–	–	–
	NATURAL SCIENCE	45 863	6 251	47 643	7 095	48 391	7 402
	MATHEMATICS & COMPUTER SCIENCE	15 202	3 016	16 814	3 669	17 192	3 897
	MEDICAL SCIENCE & HEALTH-RELATED	135 575	49 396	144 266	54 544	147 601	57 016
	ENGINEERING	396 856	7 513	401 515	11 665	406 145	12 780
	ARCHITECTURE & TOWN PLANNING	./.	./.	./.	./.	./.	./.
	TRADE, CRAFT & INDUSTRIAL PROGRAMMES	./.	./.	./.	./.	./.	./.
	TRANSPORT AND COMMUNICATIONS	2 862	5	2 571	38	2 629	54
	AGRICULTURE, FORESTRY & FISHERY	61 525	7 814	63 166	9 581	63 583	10 055
	OTHER AND NOT SPECIFIED	177 876	43 737	172 765	44 944	164 840	50 098
JORDAN‡	TOTAL	36 549	16 682	56 253	24 108	...	...
	EDUCATION SCIENCE & TEACHER TRAINING	11 514	8 428	12 677	10 111	...	...
	HUMANITIES, RELIGION & THEOLOGY	4 342	2 638	5 686	3 232	...	...
	FINE AND APPLIED ARTS	–	–	278	144	...	...
	LAW	381	108	407	124	...	...
	SOCIAL AND BEHAVIOURAL SCIENCE	2 485	849	./.	./.	...	...
	COMMERCIAL & BUSINESS ADMINISTRATION	7 482	1 419	17 250	4 720	...	...
	MASS COMMUNICATION & DOCUMENTATION	161	28	./.	./.	...	...
	HOME ECONOMICS (DOMESTIC SCIENCE)	–	–	–	–	...	...
	SERVICE TRADES	–	–	–	–	...	...
	NATURAL SCIENCE	3 000	1 333	5 391	2 312	...	...
	MATHEMATICS & COMPUTER SCIENCE	327	165	./.	./.	...	...
	MEDICAL SCIENCE & HEALTH-RELATED	1 230	571	3 074	1 594	...	...
	ENGINEERING	3 548	257	8 577	1 035	...	...
	ARCHITECTURE & TOWN PLANNING	146	104	./.	./.	...	...
	TRADE, CRAFT & INDUSTRIAL PROGRAMMES	–	–	–	–	...	...
	TRANSPORT AND COMMUNICATIONS	–	–	–	–	...	...
	AGRICULTURE, FORESTRY & FISHERY	757	256	1 044	366	...	...
	OTHER AND NOT SPECIFIED	1 176	526	1 869	470	...	...

3.12 Third level: students by field of study (1980,1983,1984)
Troisième degré: étudiants par domaine d'études (1980,1983,1984)
Tercer grado: estudiantes por sector de estudios (1980,1983,1984)

COUNTRY / PAYS / PAIS	FIELD OF STUDY / DOMAINES D'ETUDES / SECTORES DE ESTUDIOS	1980		1983		1984	
		MF	F	MF	F	MF	F
		(1)	(2)	(3)	(4)	(5)	(6)
KOREA, REPUBLIC OF‡	TOTAL	615 452	148 076	1 075 969	296 449	...	...
	EDUCATION SCIENCE & TEACHER TRAINING	74 376	36 511	134 424	82 245	...	...
	HUMANITIES, RELIGION & THEOLOGY	59 646	18 604	134 007	53 309	...	...
	FINE AND APPLIED ARTS	25 819	18 972	53 741	37 002	...	...
	LAW	–	–	22 034	883	...	...
	SOCIAL AND BEHAVIOURAL SCIENCE	111 685	12 496	64 105	12 600	...	...
	COMMERCIAL & BUSINESS ADMINISTRATION	./.	./.	109 450	13 127	...	...
	MASS COMMUNICATION & DOCUMENTATION	./.	./.	9 711	4 033	...	...
	HOME ECONOMICS (DOMESTIC SCIENCE)	./.	./.	20 542	18 616	...	...
	SERVICE TRADES	./.	./.	831	68	...	...
	NATURAL SCIENCE	52 146	28 184	46 758	16 976	...	...
	MATHEMATICS & COMPUTER SCIENCE	./.	./.	19 433	4 816	...	...
	MEDICAL SCIENCE & HEALTH–RELATED	41 420	18 900	65 824	30 716	...	...
	ENGINEERING	209 636	10 103	277 361	8 197	...	...
	ARCHITECTURE & TOWN PLANNING	./.	./.	4 395	398	...	...
	TRADE, CRAFT & INDUSTRIAL PROGRAMMES	./.	./.	27 298	2 883	...	...
	TRANSPORT AND COMMUNICATIONS	./.	./.	4 792	639	...	...
	AGRICULTURE, FORESTRY & FISHERY	40 092	4 246	65 746	5 934	...	...
	OTHER AND NOT SPECIFIED	632	60	15 517	4 007	...	...
KUWAIT‡	TOTAL	13 630	7 807	19 185	10 346	21 924	11 639
	EDUCATION SCIENCE & TEACHER TRAINING	707	392	3 939	2 349	2 990	2 086
	HUMANITIES, RELIGION & THEOLOGY	1 613	1 095	2 622	1 610	3 261	1 889
	FINE AND APPLIED ARTS	166	87	–	–	204	112
	LAW	624	225	946	313	1 034	336
	SOCIAL AND BEHAVIOURAL SCIENCE	2 742	1 829	2 889	1 663	3 174	1 702
	COMMERCIAL & BUSINESS ADMINISTRATION	2 748	1 525	3 153	1 823	3 178	1 835
	MASS COMMUNICATION & DOCUMENTATION	70	–	–	–	–	–
	HOME ECONOMICS (DOMESTIC SCIENCE)	–	–	–	–	132	132
	SERVICE TRADES	–	–	–	–	–	–
	NATURAL SCIENCE	1 338	823	1 821	939	2 264	1 184
	MATHEMATICS & COMPUTER SCIENCE	765	498	732	490	1 113	701
	MEDICAL SCIENCE & HEALTH–RELATED	654	504	944	734	835	573
	ENGINEERING	1 148	400	1 070	425	2 288	579
	ARCHITECTURE & TOWN PLANNING	77	–	–	–	–	–
	TRADE, CRAFT & INDUSTRIAL PROGRAMMES	–	–	1 069	–	./.	./.
	TRANSPORT AND COMMUNICATIONS	–	–	–	–	–	–
	AGRICULTURE, FORESTRY & FISHERY	–	–	–	–	–	–
	OTHER AND NOT SPECIFIED	978	429	–	–	1 451	510
LAO PEOPLE'S DEMOCRATIC REPUBLIC	TOTAL	1 408	441	4 790	...	...	...
	EDUCATION SCIENCE & TEACHER TRAINING	1 408	441	2 780		...	...
	HUMANITIES, RELIGION & THEOLOGY	–	–	–	–	...	...
	FINE AND APPLIED ARTS	–	–	–	–	...	...
	LAW	–	–	–	–	...	...
	SOCIAL AND BEHAVIOURAL SCIENCE	–	–	–	–	...	...
	COMMERCIAL & BUSINESS ADMINISTRATION	–	–	–	–	...	...
	MASS COMMUNICATION & DOCUMENTATION	–	–	–	–	...	...
	HOME ECONOMICS (DOMESTIC SCIENCE)	–	–	–	–	...	...
	SERVICE TRADES	–	–	–	–	...	...
	NATURAL SCIENCE	–	–	–	–	...	...
	MATHEMATICS & COMPUTER SCIENCE	–	–	–	–	...	...
	MEDICAL SCIENCE & HEALTH–RELATED	–	–	878	...	...	...
	ENGINEERING	–	–	–	–	...	...
	ARCHITECTURE & TOWN PLANNING	–	–	719	...	...	...
	TRADE, CRAFT & INDUSTRIAL PROGRAMMES	–	–	–	–	...	...
	TRANSPORT AND COMMUNICATIONS	–	–	327	...	...	...
	AGRICULTURE, FORESTRY & FISHERY	–	–	–	–	...	...
	OTHER AND NOT SPECIFIED	–	–	86	...	...	...

COUNTRY / PAYS / PAIS	FIELD OF STUDY / DOMAINES D'ETUDES / SECTORES DE ESTUDIOS	1980 MF	1980 F	1983 MF	1983 F	1984 MF	1984 F
		(1)	(2)	(3)	(4)	(5)	(6)
LEBANON Ø	TOTAL	79 073	28 531	73 052	27 225	...	...
	EDUCATION SCIENCE & TEACHER TRAINING	455	223	450	150	...	...
	HUMANITIES, RELIGION & THEOLOGY	12 929	7 426	17 529	9 201	...	...
	FINE AND APPLIED ARTS	1 439	824	1 270	762	...	...
	LAW	12 117	3 017	12 870	2 960	...	...
	SOCIAL AND BEHAVIOURAL SCIENCE	17 700	7 617	10 241	4 508	...	...
	COMMERCIAL & BUSINESS ADMINISTRATION	16 829	3 593	12 988	3 276	...	...
	MASS COMMUNICATION & DOCUMENTATION	691	491	581	430	...	...
	HOME ECONOMICS (DOMESTIC SCIENCE)	–	–	–	–	...	...
	SERVICE TRADES	161	112	233	117	...	...
	NATURAL SCIENCE	5 056	2 232	4 791	2 347	...	...
	MATHEMATICS & COMPUTER SCIENCE	2 906	801	2 049	655	...	...
	MEDICAL SCIENCE & HEALTH-RELATED	2 326	1 180	2 553	1 276	...	...
	ENGINEERING	2 548	189	4 685	515	...	...
	ARCHITECTURE & TOWN PLANNING	3 136	446	1 580	395	...	...
	TRADE, CRAFT & INDUSTRIAL PROGRAMMES	–	–	–	–	...	...
	TRANSPORT AND COMMUNICATIONS	–	–	–	–	...	...
	AGRICULTURE, FORESTRY & FISHERY	349	133	–	–	...	...
	OTHER AND NOT SPECIFIED	431	247	1 232	630	...	...
MALAYSIA	TOTAL	57 650	22 199	77 750	32 289	93 249	41 468
	EDUCATION SCIENCE & TEACHER TRAINING	16 842	8 321	17 926	10 436	24 121	15 256
	HUMANITIES, RELIGION & THEOLOGY	1 467	543	2 369	1 177	1 597	733
	FINE AND APPLIED ARTS	585	169	720	317	700	295
	LAW	1 014	482	1 152	615	956	478
	SOCIAL AND BEHAVIOURAL SCIENCE	8 112	3 668	6 529	3 353	9 797	4 482
	COMMERCIAL & BUSINESS ADMINISTRATION	5 542	2 550	10 464	5 148	14 310	6 807
	MASS COMMUNICATION & DOCUMENTATION	891	744	165	100	410	166
	HOME ECONOMICS (DOMESTIC SCIENCE)	98	39	82	82	174	88
	SERVICE TRADES	329	201	710	241	3 042	2 293
	NATURAL SCIENCE	8 281	2 758	6 541	3 364	6 300	2 583
	MATHEMATICS & COMPUTER SCIENCE	579	297	2 625	1 224	2 238	1 000
	MEDICAL SCIENCE & HEALTH-RELATED	1 639	599	1 580	992	2 920	1 373
	ENGINEERING	6 833	847	9 930	2 893	11 767	1 646
	ARCHITECTURE & TOWN PLANNING	2 270	572	11 835	564	3 484	706
	TRADE, CRAFT & INDUSTRIAL PROGRAMMES	506	32	–	–	912	265
	TRANSPORT AND COMMUNICATIONS	901	180	439	230	618	138
	AGRICULTURE, FORESTRY & FISHERY	1 682	143	1 795	281	2 242	454
	OTHER AND NOT SPECIFIED	79	54	2 888	1 272	7 661	2 705
MONGOLIA‡	TOTAL	38 200	...	...	...	...	...
	EDUCATION SCIENCE & TEACHER TRAINING	4 200	...	...	...	...	...
	HUMANITIES, RELIGION & THEOLOGY	1 800	...	...	...	...	...
	FINE AND APPLIED ARTS	1 400	...	...	...	...	...
	LAW	800	...	...	...	...	...
	SOCIAL AND BEHAVIOURAL SCIENCE	1 500	...	...	...	...	...
	COMMERCIAL & BUSINESS ADMINISTRATION	1 900	...	...	...	...	...
	MASS COMMUNICATION & DOCUMENTATION	100	...	...	...	...	...
	HOME ECONOMICS (DOMESTIC SCIENCE)	1 300	...	...	...	...	...
	SERVICE TRADES	100	...	...	...	...	...
	NATURAL SCIENCE	1 800	...	...	...	...	...
	MATHEMATICS & COMPUTER SCIENCE	400	...	...	...	...	...
	MEDICAL SCIENCE & HEALTH-RELATED	5 200	...	...	...	...	...
	ENGINEERING	5 300	...	...	...	...	...
	ARCHITECTURE & TOWN PLANNING	100	...	...	...	...	...
	TRADE, CRAFT & INDUSTRIAL PROGRAMMES	3 400	...	...	...	...	...
	TRANSPORT AND COMMUNICATIONS	3 100	...	...	...	...	...
	AGRICULTURE, FORESTRY & FISHERY	5 300	...	...	...	...	...
	OTHER AND NOT SPECIFIED	500	...	...	...	...	...

3.12 Third level: students by field of study (1980,1983,1984)
Troisième degré: étudiants par domaine d'études (1980,1983,1984)
Tercer grado: estudiantes por sector de estudios (1980,1983,1984)

COUNTRY PAYS PAIS	FIELD OF STUDY DOMAINES D'ETUDES SECTORES DE ESTUDIOS	1980		1983		1984	
		MF	F	MF	F	MF	F
		(1)	(2)	(3)	(4)	(5)	(6)
NEPAL‡	TOTAL	38 450	7 358	48 229	*9 549	...	...
	EDUCATION SCIENCE & TEACHER TRAINING	2 826	850	3 535	581	...	...
	HUMANITIES, RELIGION & THEOLOGY	16 163	4 423	18 293	5 945	...	...
	FINE AND APPLIED ARTS	56	17	./.	./.	...	...
	LAW	2 066	102	3 184	173	...	...
	SOCIAL AND BEHAVIOURAL SCIENCE	./.	./.	./.	./.	...	...
	COMMERCIAL & BUSINESS ADMINISTRATION	9 182	861	10 783	1 286	...	...
	MASS COMMUNICATION & DOCUMENTATION	–	–	–	–	...	...
	HOME ECONOMICS (DOMESTIC SCIENCE)	–	–	–	–	...	...
	SERVICE TRADES	–	–	–	–	...	...
	NATURAL SCIENCE	4 043	494	8 281	1 227	...	...
	MATHEMATICS & COMPUTER SCIENCE	./.	./.	./.	./.	...	...
	MEDICAL SCIENCE & HEALTH-RELATED	1 293	574	817	247	...	...
	ENGINEERING	1 504	36	1 940	76	...	...
	ARCHITECTURE & TOWN PLANNING	–	–	–	–	...	...
	TRADE, CRAFT & INDUSTRIAL PROGRAMMES	–	–	–	–	...	...
	TRANSPORT AND COMMUNICATIONS	–	–	–	–	...	...
	AGRICULTURE, FORESTRY & FISHERY	1 317	1	1 396	14	...	...
	OTHER AND NOT SPECIFIED	–	–	–	–	...	...
PAKISTAN‡	TOTAL	156 558	42 046	...	...	...	...
	EDUCATION SCIENCE & TEACHER TRAINING	5 675	2 211	...	...	...	...
	HUMANITIES, RELIGION & THEOLOGY	46 482	22 152	...	...	...	...
	FINE AND APPLIED ARTS	424	107	...	...	...	...
	LAW	10 299	248	...	...	...	...
	SOCIAL AND BEHAVIOURAL SCIENCE	–	–	...	...	...	...
	COMMERCIAL & BUSINESS ADMINISTRATION	11 909	706	...	...	...	...
	MASS COMMUNICATION & DOCUMENTATION	–	–	...	...	...	...
	HOME ECONOMICS (DOMESTIC SCIENCE)	1 316	1 316	...	...	...	...
	SERVICE TRADES	–	–	...	...	...	...
	NATURAL SCIENCE	23 681	7 146	...	...	...	...
	MATHEMATICS & COMPUTER SCIENCE	–	–	...	...	...	...
	MEDICAL SCIENCE & HEALTH-RELATED	24 427	6 067	...	...	...	...
	ENGINEERING	18 221	108	...	...	...	...
	ARCHITECTURE & TOWN PLANNING	./.	./.	...	...	...	...
	TRADE, CRAFT & INDUSTRIAL PROGRAMMES	–	–	...	...	...	...
	TRANSPORT AND COMMUNICATIONS	–	–	...	...	...	...
	AGRICULTURE, FORESTRY & FISHERY	6 137	454	...	...	...	...
	OTHER AND NOT SPECIFIED	8 047	1 531	...	...	...	...
PHILIPPINES‡	TOTAL	1 276 016	681 140	1 335 889	714 113	...	...
	EDUCATION SCIENCE & TEACHER TRAINING	92 585	73 744	109 524	87 236	...	...
	HUMANITIES, RELIGION & THEOLOGY	–	–	–	–	...	...
	FINE AND APPLIED ARTS	9 612	2 437	9 982	2 531	...	...
	LAW	24 451	5 709	26 751	6 246	...	...
	SOCIAL AND BEHAVIOURAL SCIENCE	–	–	–	–	...	...
	COMMERCIAL & BUSINESS ADMINISTRATION	444 643	266 697	473 396	283 943	...	...
	MASS COMMUNICATION & DOCUMENTATION	–	–	–	–	...	...
	HOME ECONOMICS (DOMESTIC SCIENCE)	13 899	13 394	14 306	13 786	...	...
	SERVICE TRADES	–	–	–	–	...	...
	NATURAL SCIENCE	91 254	58 853	88 984	57 330	...	...
	MATHEMATICS & COMPUTER SCIENCE	–	–	–	–	...	...
	MEDICAL SCIENCE & HEALTH-RELATED	123 367	106 096	125 971	108 335	...	...
	ENGINEERING	225 254	35 815	229 002	36 411	...	...
	ARCHITECTURE & TOWN PLANNING	–	–	–	–	...	...
	TRADE, CRAFT & INDUSTRIAL PROGRAMMES	132 314	67 943	134 017	68 817	...	...
	TRANSPORT AND COMMUNICATIONS	–	–	–	–	...	...
	AGRICULTURE, FORESTRY & FISHERY	55 007	26 986	54 513	26 744	...	...
	OTHER AND NOT SPECIFIED	63 630	23 466	69 443	22 734	...	...

COUNTRY / PAYS / PAIS	FIELD OF STUDY / DOMAINES D'ETUDES / SECTORES DE ESTUDIOS	1980		1983		1984	
		MF	F	MF	F	MF	F
		(1)	(2)	(3)	(4)	(5)	(6)
QATAR‡	TOTAL	2 269	1 403	4 627	2 830	4 624	2 822
	EDUCATION SCIENCE & TEACHER TRAINING	1 693	1 146	3 245	2 220	2 965	1 920
	HUMANITIES, RELIGION & THEOLOGY	327	156	850	400	874	415
	FINE AND APPLIED ARTS	–	–	–	–	59	59
	LAW	–	–	–	–	–	–
	SOCIAL AND BEHAVIOURAL SCIENCE	–	–	–	–	./.	./.
	COMMERCIAL & BUSINESS ADMINISTRATION	–	–	–	–	–	–
	MASS COMMUNICATION & DOCUMENTATION	–	–	–	–	./.	./.
	HOME ECONOMICS (DOMESTIC SCIENCE)	./.	./.	./.	./.	240	240
	SERVICE TRADES	–	–	–	–	–	–
	NATURAL SCIENCE	176	101	377	210	347	188
	MATHEMATICS & COMPUTER SCIENCE	./.	./.	./.	./.	./.	./.
	MEDICAL SCIENCE & HEALTH-RELATED	–	–	–	–	–	–
	ENGINEERING	73	–	155	–	139	–
	ARCHITECTURE & TOWN PLANNING	–	–	–	–	–	–
	TRADE, CRAFT & INDUSTRIAL PROGRAMMES	–	–	–	–	–	–
	TRANSPORT AND COMMUNICATIONS	–	–	–	–	–	–
	AGRICULTURE, FORESTRY & FISHERY	–	–	–	–	–	–
	OTHER AND NOT SPECIFIED	–	–	–	–	–	–
SAUDI ARABIA‡	TOTAL	62 074	17 311	87 821	30 948	...	...
	EDUCATION SCIENCE & TEACHER TRAINING	12 094	3 935	21 840	10 252	...	...
	HUMANITIES, RELIGION & THEOLOGY	27 532	9 828	34 500	13 439	...	...
	FINE AND APPLIED ARTS	–	–	–	–	...	...
	LAW	–	–	./.	./.	...	...
	SOCIAL AND BEHAVIOURAL SCIENCE	8 347	1 211	10 976	2 488	...	...
	COMMERCIAL & BUSINESS ADMINISTRATION	./.	./.	./.	./.	...	...
	MASS COMMUNICATION & DOCUMENTATION	–	–	–	–	...	...
	HOME ECONOMICS (DOMESTIC SCIENCE)	–	–	./.	./.	...	...
	SERVICE TRADES	–	–	–	–	...	...
	NATURAL SCIENCE	3 367	808	7 241	2 626	...	...
	MATHEMATICS & COMPUTER SCIENCE	./.	./.	./.	./.	...	...
	MEDICAL SCIENCE & HEALTH-RELATED	2 936	1 222	4 491	1 787	...	...
	ENGINEERING	4 934	–	7 135	73	...	...
	ARCHITECTURE & TOWN PLANNING	./.	./.	./.	./.	...	...
	TRADE, CRAFT & INDUSTRIAL PROGRAMMES	95	–	–	–	...	...
	TRANSPORT AND COMMUNICATIONS	–	–	–	–	...	...
	AGRICULTURE, FORESTRY & FISHERY	1 060	75	1 638	283	...	...
	OTHER AND NOT SPECIFIED	1 709	232	–	–	...	...
SINGAPORE‡	TOTAL	23 256	9 087	35 192	14 759	...	...
	EDUCATION SCIENCE & TEACHER TRAINING	3 428	2 653	5 188	3 754	...	...
	HUMANITIES, RELIGION & THEOLOGY	1 908	1 273	2 828	2 123	...	...
	FINE AND APPLIED ARTS	–	–	–	–	...	...
	LAW	368	195	602	321	...	...
	SOCIAL AND BEHAVIOURAL SCIENCE	./.	./.	./.	./.	...	...
	COMMERCIAL & BUSINESS ADMINISTRATION	2 380	1 321	4 170	2 772	...	...
	MASS COMMUNICATION & DOCUMENTATION	–	–	–	–	...	...
	HOME ECONOMICS (DOMESTIC SCIENCE)	–	–	–	–	...	...
	SERVICE TRADES	–	–	–	–	...	...
	NATURAL SCIENCE	1 628	891	2 375	1 522	...	...
	MATHEMATICS & COMPUTER SCIENCE	./.	./.	350	218	...	...
	MEDICAL SCIENCE & HEALTH-RELATED	937	372	1 121	370	...	...
	ENGINEERING	10 704	1 792	15 374	2 574	...	...
	ARCHITECTURE & TOWN PLANNING	1 113	475	1 725	825	...	...
	TRADE, CRAFT & INDUSTRIAL PROGRAMMES	–	–	–	–	...	...
	TRANSPORT AND COMMUNICATIONS	122	–	107	–	...	...
	AGRICULTURE, FORESTRY & FISHERY	–	–	–	–	...	...
	OTHER AND NOT SPECIFIED	668	115	1 352	280	...	...

COUNTRY PAYS PAIS	FIELD OF STUDY DOMAINES D'ETUDES SECTORES DE ESTUDIOS	1980		1983		1984	
		MF	F	MF	F	MF	F
		(1)	(2)	(3)	(4)	(5)	(6)
SRI LANKA‡	TOTAL	...	...	63 460	18 504	...	...
	EDUCATION SCIENCE & TEACHER TRAINING	...	...	8 824	5 757	...	...
	HUMANITIES, RELIGION & THEOLOGY	...	...	–	–	...	...
	FINE AND APPLIED ARTS	...	...	8 008	4 287	...	...
	LAW	...	...	372	154	...	...
	SOCIAL AND BEHAVIOURAL SCIENCE	...	...	–	–	...	...
	COMMERCIAL & BUSINESS ADMINISTRATION	...	...	13 380	1 205	...	...
	MASS COMMUNICATION & DOCUMENTATION	...	...	–	–	...	...
	HOME ECONOMICS (DOMESTIC SCIENCE)	...	...	–	–	...	...
	SERVICE TRADES	...	...	–	–	...	...
	NATURAL SCIENCE	...	...	4 791	1 994	...	...
	MATHEMATICS & COMPUTER SCIENCE	...	...	./.	./.	...	...
	MEDICAL SCIENCE & HEALTH-RELATED	...	...	2 600	1 154	...	...
	ENGINEERING	...	...	6 674	1 461	...	...
	ARCHITECTURE & TOWN PLANNING	...	...	114	21	...	...
	TRADE, CRAFT & INDUSTRIAL PROGRAMMES	...	...	11 394	–	...	...
	TRANSPORT AND COMMUNICATIONS	...	...	–	–	...	...
	AGRICULTURE, FORESTRY & FISHERY	...	...	997	302	...	...
	OTHER AND NOT SPECIFIED	...	...	6 306	2 169	...	...
SYRIAN ARAB REPUBLIC	TOTAL	135 077	40 161	153 530	50 082	...	...
	EDUCATION SCIENCE & TEACHER TRAINING	14 886	9 044	16 627	10 066	...	...
	HUMANITIES, RELIGION & THEOLOGY	30 412	12 058	29 906	14 383	...	...
	FINE AND APPLIED ARTS	892	260	810	211	...	...
	LAW	12 717	1 754	16 038	2 239	...	...
	SOCIAL AND BEHAVIOURAL SCIENCE	2 138	386	11 052	2 761	...	...
	COMMERCIAL & BUSINESS ADMINISTRATION	8 898	2 948	4 339	1 848	...	...
	MASS COMMUNICATION & DOCUMENTATION	84	22	21	–	...	...
	HOME ECONOMICS (DOMESTIC SCIENCE)	–	–	–	–	...	...
	SERVICE TRADES	28	–	195	32	...	...
	NATURAL SCIENCE	11 836	3 741	14 515	5 314	...	...
	MATHEMATICS & COMPUTER SCIENCE	–	–	77	39	...	...
	MEDICAL SCIENCE & HEALTH-RELATED	13 262	4 109	15 862	5 330	...	...
	ENGINEERING	26 277	4 010	27 196	4 604	...	...
	ARCHITECTURE & TOWN PLANNING	–	–	2 669	756	...	...
	TRADE, CRAFT & INDUSTRIAL PROGRAMMES	3 134	88	4 141	266	...	...
	TRANSPORT AND COMMUNICATIONS	–	–	–	–	...	...
	AGRICULTURE, FORESTRY & FISHERY	10 003	1 486	7 894	1 221	...	...
	OTHER AND NOT SPECIFIED	510	255	2 188	1 012	...	...
TURKEY‡	TOTAL	236 441	61 557	335 080	113 008	417 225	131 356
	EDUCATION SCIENCE & TEACHER TRAINING	28 080	9 685	51 481	21 534	58 335	24 675
	HUMANITIES, RELIGION & THEOLOGY	17 604	5 125	20 548	6 993	25 533	9 145
	FINE AND APPLIED ARTS	4 112	1 748	4 525	2 188	4 755	2 288
	LAW	11 624	2 200	14 343	8 206	19 074	4 814
	SOCIAL AND BEHAVIOURAL SCIENCE	21 489	6 578	24 506	9 312	91 155	26 684
	COMMERCIAL & BUSINESS ADMINISTRATION	37 217	7 946	78 726	22 796	47 750	14 373
	MASS COMMUNICATION & DOCUMENTATION	4 318	1 693	4 066	1 830	4 590	2 123
	HOME ECONOMICS (DOMESTIC SCIENCE)	777	738	799	721	579	565
	SERVICE TRADES	274	86	2 444	582	3 368	813
	NATURAL SCIENCE	10 688	4 098	14 206	5 772	15 386	6 722
	MATHEMATICS & COMPUTER SCIENCE	5 161	1 803	7 380	2 984	7 373	2 989
	MEDICAL SCIENCE & HEALTH-RELATED	25 988	9 057	32 124	13 158	39 050	15 237
	ENGINEERING	57 711	7 873	58 514	10 210	76 745	13 202
	ARCHITECTURE & TOWN PLANNING	7 150	2 177	6 956	2 846	7 406	3 564
	TRADE, CRAFT & INDUSTRIAL PROGRAMMES	484	212	1 756	601	1 007	428
	TRANSPORT AND COMMUNICATIONS	793	8	333	8	21	–
	AGRICULTURE, FORESTRY & FISHERY	1 576	176	12 373	3 267	15 098	3 734
	OTHER AND NOT SPECIFIED	1 395	354	–	–	–	–

COUNTRY / PAYS / PAIS	FIELD OF STUDY / DOMAINES D'ETUDES / SECTORES DE ESTUDIOS	1980		1983		1984	
		MF	F	MF	F	MF	F
		(1)	(2)	(3)	(4)	(5)	(6)
UNITED ARAB EMIRATES	TOTAL	2 734	1 306	5 867	2 999	6 856	3 975
	EDUCATION SCIENCE & TEACHER TRAINING	496	384	646	423	1 107	907
	HUMANITIES, RELIGION & THEOLOGY	152	80	1 035	332	–	–
	FINE AND APPLIED ARTS	–	–	–	–	2 165	1 315
	LAW	171	26	455	78	509	94
	SOCIAL AND BEHAVIOURAL SCIENCE	430	210	464	384	–	–
	COMMERCIAL & BUSINESS ADMINISTRATION	327	129	886	257	1 045	472
	MASS COMMUNICATION & DOCUMENTATION	169	106	197	150	–	–
	HOME ECONOMICS (DOMESTIC SCIENCE)	–	–	–	–	–	–
	SERVICE TRADES	–	–	–	–	–	–
	NATURAL SCIENCE	251	143	482	221	736	447
	MATHEMATICS & COMPUTER SCIENCE	62	42	100	68	–	–
	MEDICAL SCIENCE & HEALTH-RELATED	–	–	–	–	–	–
	ENGINEERING	101	20	152	–	274	89
	ARCHITECTURE & TOWN PLANNING	–	–	66	66	–	–
	TRADE, CRAFT & INDUSTRIAL PROGRAMMES	–	–	–	–	–	–
	TRANSPORT AND COMMUNICATIONS	–	–	–	–	–	–
	AGRICULTURE, FORESTRY & FISHERY	53	–	70	–	68	–
	OTHER AND NOT SPECIFIED	522	166	1 314	1 020	952	651
VIET-NAM‡	TOTAL	114 701	27 090	...	...	...	...
	EDUCATION SCIENCE & TEACHER TRAINING	42 363	12 169	...	...	...	...
	HUMANITIES, RELIGION & THEOLOGY	4 247	1 310	...	...	...	...
	FINE AND APPLIED ARTS	1 022	148	...	...	...	...
	LAW	1 005	48	...	...	...	...
	SOCIAL AND BEHAVIOURAL SCIENCE	818	169	...	...	...	...
	COMMERCIAL & BUSINESS ADMINISTRATION	14 030	3 527	...	...	...	...
	MASS COMMUNICATION & DOCUMENTATION	621	68	...	...	...	...
	HOME ECONOMICS (DOMESTIC SCIENCE)	–	–	...	...	...	...
	SERVICE TRADES	–	–	...	...	...	...
	NATURAL SCIENCE	2 487	505	...	...	...	...
	MATHEMATICS & COMPUTER SCIENCE	1 961	499	...	...	...	...
	MEDICAL SCIENCE & HEALTH-RELATED	11 462	1 839	...	...	...	...
	ENGINEERING	11 231	1 806	...	...	...	...
	ARCHITECTURE & TOWN PLANNING	2 432	653	...	...	...	...
	TRADE, CRAFT & INDUSTRIAL PROGRAMMES	8 374	1 724	...	...	...	...
	TRANSPORT AND COMMUNICATIONS	1 809	251	...	...	...	...
	AGRICULTURE, FORESTRY & FISHERY	10 839	2 374	...	...	...	...
	OTHER AND NOT SPECIFIED	–	–	...	...	...	...
YEMEN	TOTAL	4 519	508	...	...	...	...
	EDUCATION SCIENCE & TEACHER TRAINING	948	130	...	...	...	...
	HUMANITIES, RELIGION & THEOLOGY	344	81	...	...	...	...
	FINE AND APPLIED ARTS	–	–	...	...	...	...
	LAW	1 208	46	...	...	...	...
	SOCIAL AND BEHAVIOURAL SCIENCE	433	104	...	...	...	...
	COMMERCIAL & BUSINESS ADMINISTRATION	1 321	83	...	...	...	...
	MASS COMMUNICATION & DOCUMENTATION	–	–	...	...	...	...
	HOME ECONOMICS (DOMESTIC SCIENCE)	–	–	...	...	...	...
	SERVICE TRADES	–	–	...	...	...	...
	NATURAL SCIENCE	265	64	...	...	...	...
	MATHEMATICS & COMPUTER SCIENCE	–	–	...	...	...	...
	MEDICAL SCIENCE & HEALTH-RELATED	–	–	...	...	...	...
	ENGINEERING	–	–	...	...	...	...
	ARCHITECTURE & TOWN PLANNING	–	–	...	...	...	...
	TRADE, CRAFT & INDUSTRIAL PROGRAMMES	–	–	...	...	...	...
	TRANSPORT AND COMMUNICATIONS	–	–	...	...	...	...
	AGRICULTURE, FORESTRY & FISHERY	–	–	...	...	...	...
	OTHER AND NOT SPECIFIED	–	–	...	...	...	...

3.12 Third level: students by field of study (1980,1983,1984)
Troisième degré: étudiants par domaine d'études (1980,1983,1984)
Tercer grado: estudiantes por sector de estudios (1980,1983,1984)

COUNTRY / PAYS / PAIS	FIELD OF STUDY / DOMAINES D'ETUDES / SECTORES DE ESTUDIOS	1980		1983		1984	
		MF	F	MF	F	MF	F
		(1)	(2)	(3)	(4)	(5)	(6)
EUROPE							
ALBANIA‡	TOTAL	14 568	7 221	19 670	9 130	21 285	9 580
	EDUCATION SCIENCE & TEACHER TRAINING	1 530	808	2 150	1 125	3 090	1 577
	HUMANITIES, RELIGION & THEOLOGY	1 041	591	817	466	1 010	590
	FINE AND APPLIED ARTS	301	103	385	130	500	165
	LAW	311	119	415	178	423	194
	SOCIAL AND BEHAVIOURAL SCIENCE	2 225	1 572	3 418	2 372	3 034	2 072
	COMMERCIAL & BUSINESS ADMINISTRATION	–	–	–	–	–	–
	MASS COMMUNICATION & DOCUMENTATION	–	–	–	–	–	–
	HOME ECONOMICS (DOMESTIC SCIENCE)	–	–	–	–	–	–
	SERVICE TRADES	–	–	–	–	–	–
	NATURAL SCIENCE	636	348	980	528	1 100	627
	MATHEMATICS & COMPUTER SCIENCE	./.	./.	./.	./.	./.	./.
	MEDICAL SCIENCE & HEALTH-RELATED	810	457	868	388	997	473
	ENGINEERING	2 725	861	4 365	1 283	4 728	1 382
	ARCHITECTURE & TOWN PLANNING	–	–	–	–	–	–
	TRADE, CRAFT & INDUSTRIAL PROGRAMMES	–	–	–	–	–	–
	TRANSPORT AND COMMUNICATIONS	–	–	–	–	–	–
	AGRICULTURE, FORESTRY & FISHERY	4 581	2 227	5 850	2 525	5 913	2 350
	OTHER AND NOT SPECIFIED	408	135	422	135	490	150
AUSTRIA‡	TOTAL	136 774	57 491	157 560	64 826	168 865	70 599
	EDUCATION SCIENCE & TEACHER TRAINING	11 402	8 329	4 056	2 310	4 535	2 695
	HUMANITIES, RELIGION & THEOLOGY	23 643	14 459	27 690	17 061	28 698	17 767
	FINE AND APPLIED ARTS	7 450	3 856	9 121	4 890	9 677	5 263
	LAW	14 112	4 384	15 757	5 369	16 324	5 673
	SOCIAL AND BEHAVIOURAL SCIENCE	13 092	5 891	16 377	7 540	18 238	8 611
	COMMERCIAL & BUSINESS ADMINISTRATION	13 217	3 812	21 274	7 466	24 397	8 833
	MASS COMMUNICATION & DOCUMENTATION	1 572	678	2 229	1 055	2 485	1 230
	HOME ECONOMICS (DOMESTIC SCIENCE)	27	27	129	124	178	170
	SERVICE TRADES	–	–	–	–	–	–
	NATURAL SCIENCE	7 523	2 773	9 375	3 521	10 001	3 787
	MATHEMATICS & COMPUTER SCIENCE	5 146	1 443	6 417	1 635	6 807	1 759
	MEDICAL SCIENCE & HEALTH-RELATED	19 580	8 448	21 743	10 124	22 204	10 616
	ENGINEERING	9 695	750	13 607	651	14 460	749
	ARCHITECTURE & TOWN PLANNING	5 360	828	4 020	1 060	4 327	1 180
	TRADE, CRAFT & INDUSTRIAL PROGRAMMES	–	–	–	–	–	–
	TRANSPORT AND COMMUNICATIONS	–	–	–	–	–	–
	AGRICULTURE, FORESTRY & FISHERY	2 363	633	4 973	1 683	5 453	1 928
	OTHER AND NOT SPECIFIED	2 592	1 180	792	337	1 081	338
BELGIUM‡	TOTAL	95 246	35 107	100 362	39 816	245 762	111 349
	EDUCATION SCIENCE & TEACHER TRAINING	5 812	3 375	6 015	3 664	31 788	20 489
	HUMANITIES, RELIGION & THEOLOGY	14 419	8 235	15 281	8 801	15 050	8 687
	FINE AND APPLIED ARTS	–	–	–	–	4 199	2 227
	LAW	11 397	4 216	12 536	5 083	13 203	5 610
	SOCIAL AND BEHAVIOURAL SCIENCE	8 820	2 637	9 415	3 016	28 077	13 049
	COMMERCIAL & BUSINESS ADMINISTRATION	5 787	1 196	7 918	2 008	46 333	22 426
	MASS COMMUNICATION & DOCUMENTATION	2	1	–	–	–	–
	HOME ECONOMICS (DOMESTIC SCIENCE)	–	–	–	–	–	–
	SERVICE TRADES	–	–	–	–	699	62
	NATURAL SCIENCE	7 101	2 674	10 353	3 999	31 706	12 453
	MATHEMATICS & COMPUTER SCIENCE	2 545	999	./.	./.	./.	./.
	MEDICAL SCIENCE & HEALTH-RELATED	25 959	9 893	20 280	8 780	28 345	19 133
	ENGINEERING	7 163	499	8 072	740	20 951	2 468
	ARCHITECTURE & TOWN PLANNING	–	–	–	–	3 358	928
	TRADE, CRAFT & INDUSTRIAL PROGRAMMES	–	–	–	–	15 654	1 687
	TRANSPORT AND COMMUNICATIONS	–	–	–	–	149	45
	AGRICULTURE, FORESTRY & FISHERY	5 660	1 263	5 895	1 664	4 432	1 151
	OTHER AND NOT SPECIFIED	581	119	4 597	2 061	1 818	934

COUNTRY / PAYS / PAIS	FIELD OF STUDY / DOMAINES D'ETUDES / SECTORES DE ESTUDIOS	1980		1983		1984	
		MF	F	MF	F	MF	F
		(1)	(2)	(3)	(4)	(5)	(6)
BULGARIA‡	TOTAL	101 359	56 946	98 612	52 779	104 333	56 084
	EDUCATION SCIENCE & TEACHER TRAINING	10 199	6 461	14 093	10 339	12 829	10 255
	HUMANITIES, RELIGION & THEOLOGY	12 993	10 050	9 791	7 207	10 334	7 038
	FINE AND APPLIED ARTS	2 376	1 056	2 993	1 464	2 785	1 442
	LAW	1 284	568	1 413	644	2 022	966
	SOCIAL AND BEHAVIOURAL SCIENCE	1 279	856	950	544	995	534
	COMMERCIAL & BUSINESS ADMINISTRATION	13 655	7 902	12 405	6 712	14 021	7 442
	MASS COMMUNICATION & DOCUMENTATION	597	362	396	201	306	152
	HOME ECONOMICS (DOMESTIC SCIENCE)	–	–	–	–	–	–
	SERVICE TRADES	1 457	1 036	932	631	925	624
	NATURAL SCIENCE	3 647	2 351	3 622	2 743	5 954	3 729
	MATHEMATICS & COMPUTER SCIENCE	2 647	1 763	2 490	1 578	2 212	1 409
	MEDICAL SCIENCE & HEALTH-RELATED	15 461	10 245	12 287	6 089	12 357	5 804
	ENGINEERING	29 044	11 310	30 331	11 568	32 229	13 426
	ARCHITECTURE & TOWN PLANNING	742	327	543	221	555	215
	TRADE, CRAFT & INDUSTRIAL PROGRAMMES	–	–	–	–	–	–
	TRANSPORT AND COMMUNICATIONS	1 298	541	1 297	584	1 329	648
	AGRICULTURE, FORESTRY & FISHERY	4 680	2 118	5 069	2 254	5 480	2 400
	OTHER AND NOT SPECIFIED	–	–	–	–	–	–
CZECHOSLOVAKIA	TOTAL	197 041	81 975	181 524	78 024	174 843	74 535
	EDUCATION SCIENCE & TEACHER TRAINING	29 984	22 397	31 014	23 473	30 390	22 859
	HUMANITIES, RELIGION & THEOLOGY	1 973	1 183	1 699	851	1 758	856
	FINE AND APPLIED ARTS	3 172	1 416	2 417	1 061	2 301	1 006
	LAW	8 655	4 392	6 989	3 500	6 142	3 004
	SOCIAL AND BEHAVIOURAL SCIENCE	2 561	1 428	1 821	1 110	1 532	774
	COMMERCIAL & BUSINESS ADMINISTRATION	24 835	13 528	23 246	13 497	21 927	12 700
	MASS COMMUNICATION & DOCUMENTATION	1 512	983	1 217	757	1 134	668
	HOME ECONOMICS (DOMESTIC SCIENCE)	–	–	–	–	–	–
	SERVICE TRADES	–	–	–	–	–	–
	NATURAL SCIENCE	3 338	1 697	2 916	1 405	2 690	1 290
	MATHEMATICS & COMPUTER SCIENCE	2 913	971	2 845	940	2 752	878
	MEDICAL SCIENCE & HEALTH-RELATED	15 566	9 068	12 680	7 546	12 427	7 429
	ENGINEERING	74 496	16 027	71 096	15 826	69 663	15 610
	ARCHITECTURE & TOWN PLANNING	1 723	601	1 128	458	1 021	406
	TRADE, CRAFT & INDUSTRIAL PROGRAMMES	–	–	–	–	–	–
	TRANSPORT AND COMMUNICATIONS	5 077	1 039	4 644	1 059	4 277	1 025
	AGRICULTURE, FORESTRY & FISHERY	20 484	7 100	17 272	6 381	16 358	5 877
	OTHER AND NOT SPECIFIED	752	145	540	160	471	153
DENMARK	TOTAL	106 241	51 923	113 157	55 765	...	...
	EDUCATION SCIENCE & TEACHER TRAINING	23 987	15 576	21 299	14 591	...	...
	HUMANITIES, RELIGION & THEOLOGY	16 428	9 772	15 818	10 065	...	...
	FINE AND APPLIED ARTS	3 408	1 880	3 616	2 079	...	...
	LAW	3 947	1 584	4 258	1 925	...	...
	SOCIAL AND BEHAVIOURAL SCIENCE	9 902	3 878	10 811	4 380	...	...
	COMMERCIAL & BUSINESS ADMINISTRATION	4 188	646	6 349	1 294	...	...
	MASS COMMUNICATION & DOCUMENTATION	1 857	1 092	1 684	982	...	...
	HOME ECONOMICS (DOMESTIC SCIENCE)	–	–	–	–	...	...
	SERVICE TRADES	240	228	212	199	...	...
	NATURAL SCIENCE	3 683	997	3 871	1 068	...	...
	MATHEMATICS & COMPUTER SCIENCE	2 942	551	3 537	739	...	...
	MEDICAL SCIENCE & HEALTH-RELATED	17 618	12 356	18 582	14 219	...	...
	ENGINEERING	9 414	676	12 352	1 156	...	...
	ARCHITECTURE & TOWN PLANNING	2 576	797	2 184	828	...	...
	TRADE, CRAFT & INDUSTRIAL PROGRAMMES	832	74	960	89	...	...
	TRANSPORT AND COMMUNICATIONS	820	10	1 149	11	...	...
	AGRICULTURE, FORESTRY & FISHERY	2 279	704	2 661	903	...	...
	OTHER AND NOT SPECIFIED	2 120	1 102	3 814	1 237	...	...

3.12 Third level: students by field of study (1980,1983,1984)
Troisième degré: étudiants par domaine d'études (1980,1983,1984)
Tercer grado: estudiantes por sector de estudios (1980,1983,1984)

COUNTRY / PAYS / PAIS	FIELD OF STUDY / DOMAINES D'ETUDES / SECTORES DE ESTUDIOS	1980		1983		1984	
		MF	F	MF	F	MF	F
		(1)	(2)	(3)	(4)	(5)	(6)
FINLAND	TOTAL	123 165	59 356	119 982	57 231	...	...
	EDUCATION SCIENCE & TEACHER TRAINING	7 856	5 766	10 424	7 554	...	...
	HUMANITIES, RELIGION & THEOLOGY	16 522	11 875	17 042	12 298	...	...
	FINE AND APPLIED ARTS	1 433	788	1 874	1 120	...	...
	LAW	3 866	1 523	4 038	1 591	...	...
	SOCIAL AND BEHAVIOURAL SCIENCE	9 300	5 498	9 087	5 382	...	...
	COMMERCIAL & BUSINESS ADMINISTRATION	20 793	11 672	12 278	5 725	...	...
	MASS COMMUNICATION & DOCUMENTATION	251	148	250	131	...	...
	HOME ECONOMICS (DOMESTIC SCIENCE)	244	239	213	204	...	...
	SERVICE TRADES	312	247	395	294	...	...
	NATURAL SCIENCE	7 905	3 772	8 318	3 985	...	...
	MATHEMATICS & COMPUTER SCIENCE	5 251	1 942	4 401	1 571	...	...
	MEDICAL SCIENCE & HEALTH-RELATED	13 164	10 360	14 354	11 639	...	...
	ENGINEERING	30 245	2 714	30 856	2 836	...	...
	ARCHITECTURE & TOWN PLANNING	1 660	596	1 769	658	...	...
	TRADE, CRAFT & INDUSTRIAL PROGRAMMES	–	–	–	–	...	...
	TRANSPORT AND COMMUNICATIONS	64	4	101	5	...	...
	AGRICULTURE, FORESTRY & FISHERY	2 924	1 136	3 440	1 313	...	...
	OTHER AND NOT SPECIFIED	1 375	1 076	1 142	925	...	...
FRANCE‡ Ø	TOTAL	869 788	...	1 179 268	579 459	...	...
	EDUCATION SCIENCE & TEACHER TRAINING	–	–	47 934	29 926	...	...
	HUMANITIES, RELIGION & THEOLOGY	272 327	...	282 236	189 339	...	...
	FINE AND APPLIED ARTS	–	–	12 033	6 466	...	...
	LAW	135 390	...	143 088	75 035	...	...
	SOCIAL AND BEHAVIOURAL SCIENCE	78 994	...	84 834	36 330	...	...
	COMMERCIAL & BUSINESS ADMINISTRATION	...	...	84 996	51 079	...	...
	MASS COMMUNICATION & DOCUMENTATION	...	...	6 151	4 874	...	...
	HOME ECONOMICS (DOMESTIC SCIENCE)	...	...	2 834	2 812	...	...
	SERVICE TRADES	...	...	./.	./.	...	...
	NATURAL SCIENCE	130 388	...	149 184	48 417	...	...
	MATHEMATICS & COMPUTER SCIENCE	...	...	34 548	8 220	...	...
	MEDICAL SCIENCE & HEALTH-RELATED	189 589	...	186 970	88 125	...	...
	ENGINEERING	...	...	38 822	6 261	...	...
	ARCHITECTURE & TOWN PLANNING	...	...	14 347	3 798	...	...
	TRADE, CRAFT & INDUSTRIAL PROGRAMMES	...	...	47 692	7 974	...	...
	TRANSPORT AND COMMUNICATIONS	...	...	1 400	209	...	...
	AGRICULTURE, FORESTRY & FISHERY	–	–	9 303	2 348	...	...
	OTHER AND NOT SPECIFIED	63 100	...	32 896	18 247	...	...
GERMAN DEMOCRATIC REPUBLIC‡	TOTAL	400 799	232 336	434 326	240 569	431 774	237 564
	EDUCATION SCIENCE & TEACHER TRAINING	53 165	41 230	55 534	43 006	55 007	42 781
	HUMANITIES, RELIGION & THEOLOGY	8 656	4 432	9 355	4 800	9 345	4 790
	FINE AND APPLIED ARTS	4 423	2 144	4 580	2 259	4 607	2 243
	LAW	3 906	1 309	4 735	1 634	4 102	1 442
	SOCIAL AND BEHAVIOURAL SCIENCE	22 105	14 936	22 626	15 551	22 895	15 959
	COMMERCIAL & BUSINESS ADMINISTRATION	42 362	31 539	40 132	30 307	38 518	29 071
	MASS COMMUNICATION & DOCUMENTATION	2 694	2 071	2 758	2 067	2 752	2 056
	HOME ECONOMICS (DOMESTIC SCIENCE)	–	–	–	–	–	–
	SERVICE TRADES	–	–	1 734	1 236	2 505	1 822
	NATURAL SCIENCE	6 309	2 643	7 127	3 220	7 302	3 169
	MATHEMATICS & COMPUTER SCIENCE	3 176	1 220	4 088	2 036	4 418	2 175
	MEDICAL SCIENCE & HEALTH-RELATED	61 353	54 384	63 274	55 491	62 387	54 508
	ENGINEERING	81 971	23 636	85 656	24 406	84 953	23 654
	ARCHITECTURE & TOWN PLANNING	1 125	575	1 375	595	1 315	561
	TRADE, CRAFT & INDUSTRIAL PROGRAMMES	–	–	47 866	10 878	47 028	10 526
	TRANSPORT AND COMMUNICATIONS	–	–	3 486	1 429	3 941	1 393
	AGRICULTURE, FORESTRY & FISHERY	18 842	8 874	24 138	12 312	23 942	11 774
	OTHER AND NOT SPECIFIED	90 712	43 343	55 862	29 342	56 757	29 640

COUNTRY / PAYS / PAIS	FIELD OF STUDY / DOMAINES D'ETUDES / SECTORES DE ESTUDIOS	1980		1983		1984	
		MF	F	MF	F	MF	F
		(1)	(2)	(3)	(4)	(5)	(6)
GERMANY, FEDERAL REPUBLIC OF	TOTAL	1 223 221	503 448	1 471 964	613 622	...	...
	EDUCATION SCIENCE & TEACHER TRAINING	87 089	59 951	94 950	68 505	...	...
	HUMANITIES, RELIGION & THEOLOGY	169 062	98 900	195 575	117 848	...	...
	FINE AND APPLIED ARTS	39 908	19 979	46 622	23 857	...	...
	LAW	69 778	22 437	86 117	32 161	...	...
	SOCIAL AND BEHAVIOURAL SCIENCE	204 722	75 861	265 461	103 727	...	...
	COMMERCIAL & BUSINESS ADMINISTRATION	30 706	11 414	32 850	12 627	...	...
	MASS COMMUNICATION & DOCUMENTATION	4 572	2 210	7 150	3 761	...	...
	HOME ECONOMICS (DOMESTIC SCIENCE)	16 257	15 242	16 091	15 068	...	...
	SERVICE TRADES	458	336	419	345	...	...
	NATURAL SCIENCE	90 934	28 406	110 257	34 822	...	...
	MATHEMATICS & COMPUTER SCIENCE	45 948	13 508	55 488	14 629	...	...
	MEDICAL SCIENCE & HEALTH-RELATED	184 868	115 884	208 061	133 166	...	...
	ENGINEERING	178 238	9 053	237 269	14 494	...	...
	ARCHITECTURE & TOWN PLANNING	31 582	10 054	40 896	14 980	...	...
	TRADE, CRAFT & INDUSTRIAL PROGRAMMES	5 469	486	4 865	491	...	...
	TRANSPORT AND COMMUNICATIONS	–	–	–	–	...	...
	AGRICULTURE, FORESTRY & FISHERY	37 011	8 495	43 387	11 446	...	...
	OTHER AND NOT SPECIFIED	26 619	11 232	26 506	11 695	...	...
GREECE‡	TOTAL	121 116	50 204	124 694	53 376	...	...
	EDUCATION SCIENCE & TEACHER TRAINING	6 368	3 366	7 070	3 740	...	...
	HUMANITIES, RELIGION & THEOLOGY	12 238	8 885	12 934	9 524	...	...
	FINE AND APPLIED ARTS	1 177	687	1 247	688	...	...
	LAW	9 919	5 344	12 801	7 169	...	...
	SOCIAL AND BEHAVIOURAL SCIENCE	15 910	7 684	12 346	5 764	...	...
	COMMERCIAL & BUSINESS ADMINISTRATION	17 157	6 369	18 057	7 425	...	...
	MASS COMMUNICATION & DOCUMENTATION	291	160	360	232	...	...
	HOME ECONOMICS (DOMESTIC SCIENCE)	220	220	183	183	...	...
	SERVICE TRADES	1 309	586	1 402	796	...	...
	NATURAL SCIENCE	7 449	2 271	7 578	2 441	...	...
	MATHEMATICS & COMPUTER SCIENCE	5 901	2 212	5 860	1 883	...	...
	MEDICAL SCIENCE & HEALTH-RELATED	13 249	6 602	14 017	7 216	...	...
	ENGINEERING	21 831	3 217	21 893	3 484	...	...
	ARCHITECTURE & TOWN PLANNING	965	497	1 092	542	...	...
	TRADE, CRAFT & INDUSTRIAL PROGRAMMES	427	212	468	220	...	...
	TRANSPORT AND COMMUNICATIONS	670	119	2 200	107	...	...
	AGRICULTURE, FORESTRY & FISHERY	4 957	1 725	5 186	1 962	...	...
	OTHER AND NOT SPECIFIED	1 078	48			...	...
HOLY SEE‡	TOTAL	9 104	3 538	9 211	3 079	9 656	3 354
	EDUCATION SCIENCE & TEACHER TRAINING	554	394	371	162	514	242
	HUMANITIES, RELIGION & THEOLOGY	7 864	3 016	8 103	2 778	8 305	2 967
	FINE AND APPLIED ARTS	90	35	77	30	61	23
	LAW	383	28	484	39	579	34
	SOCIAL AND BEHAVIOURAL SCIENCE	172	24	152	46	159	50
	COMMERCIAL & BUSINESS ADMINISTRATION	–	–	–	–	–	–
	MASS COMMUNICATION & DOCUMENTATION	–	–	–	–	–	–
	HOME ECONOMICS (DOMESTIC SCIENCE)	–	–	–	–	–	–
	SERVICE TRADES	–	–	–	–	–	–
	NATURAL SCIENCE	–	–	–	–	–	–
	MATHEMATICS & COMPUTER SCIENCE	–	–	–	–	–	–
	MEDICAL SCIENCE & HEALTH-RELATED	–	–	–	–	–	–
	ENGINEERING	–	–	–	–	–	–
	ARCHITECTURE & TOWN PLANNING	–	–	–	–	–	–
	TRADE, CRAFT & INDUSTRIAL PROGRAMMES	–	–	–	–	–	–
	TRANSPORT AND COMMUNICATIONS	–	–	–	–	–	–
	AGRICULTURE, FORESTRY & FISHERY	–	–	–	–	–	–
	OTHER AND NOT SPECIFIED	41	41	24	24	38	38

3.12 Third level: students by field of study (1980,1983,1984)
Troisième degré: étudiants par domaine d'études (1980,1983,1984)
Tercer grado: estudiantes por sector de estudios (1980,1983,1984)

COUNTRY PAYS PAIS	FIELD OF STUDY DOMAINES D'ETUDES SECTORES DE ESTUDIOS	1980		1983		1984	
		MF	F	MF	F	MF	F
		(1)	(2)	(3)	(4)	(5)	(6)
HUNGARY‡	TOTAL	101 166	50 314	99 865	52 720	99 986	52 977
	EDUCATION SCIENCE & TEACHER TRAINING	33 544	25 088	35 387	26 610	37 070	27 601
	HUMANITIES, RELIGION & THEOLOGY	3 136	1 818	2 586	1 601	2 570	1 746
	FINE AND APPLIED ARTS	1 183	508	1 168	524	1 195	544
	LAW	6 609	3 270	6 357	3 411	6 102	3 301
	SOCIAL AND BEHAVIOURAL SCIENCE	3 220	1 500	3 048	1 400	3 044	1 442
	COMMERCIAL & BUSINESS ADMINISTRATION	6 859	4 528	7 082	4 683	6 989	4 616
	MASS COMMUNICATION & DOCUMENTATION	–	–	–	–	–	–
	HOME ECONOMICS (DOMESTIC SCIENCE)	–	–	–	–	–	–
	SERVICE TRADES	791	431	838	479	844	477
	NATURAL SCIENCE	1 200	404	1 325	396	1 091	367
	MATHEMATICS & COMPUTER SCIENCE	1 418	514	1 025	404	1 183	403
	MEDICAL SCIENCE & HEALTH–RELATED	9 197	5 630	10 866	7 337	10 500	6 915
	ENGINEERING	11 467	1 527	10 001	1 231	9 837	1 200
	ARCHITECTURE & TOWN PLANNING	5 328	1 310	4 345	1 033	5 223	1 119
	TRADE, CRAFT & INDUSTRIAL PROGRAMMES	9 079	1 668	7 804	1 334	6 339	1 060
	TRANSPORT AND COMMUNICATIONS	1 460	306	1 413	310	1 318	311
	AGRICULTURE, FORESTRY & FISHERY	6 022	1 677	5 985	1 806	6 006	1 721
	OTHER AND NOT SPECIFIED	653	135	635	161	675	154
ICELAND	TOTAL	5 219	...	5 212	2 699	...	...
	EDUCATION SCIENCE & TEACHER TRAINING	613	...	840	688	...	...
	HUMANITIES, RELIGION & THEOLOGY	746	...	974	545	...	...
	FINE AND APPLIED ARTS	71	...	14	3	...	...
	LAW	245	...	327	124	...	...
	SOCIAL AND BEHAVIOURAL SCIENCE	205	...	257	158	...	...
	COMMERCIAL & BUSINESS ADMINISTRATION	537	...	676	167	...	...
	MASS COMMUNICATION & DOCUMENTATION	53	...	85	76	...	...
	HOME ECONOMICS (DOMESTIC SCIENCE)	–	–	–	–	...	...
	SERVICE TRADES	19	...	–	–	...	...
	NATURAL SCIENCE	232	...	260	105	...	...
	MATHEMATICS & COMPUTER SCIENCE	84	...	196	39	...	...
	MEDICAL SCIENCE & HEALTH–RELATED	963	...	1 116	737	...	...
	ENGINEERING	347	...	379	34	...	...
	ARCHITECTURE & TOWN PLANNING	–	–	–	–	...	...
	TRADE, CRAFT & INDUSTRIAL PROGRAMMES	870	...	48	–	...	...
	TRANSPORT AND COMMUNICATIONS	111	...	–	–	...	...
	AGRICULTURE, FORESTRY & FISHERY	22	...	40	23	...	...
	OTHER AND NOT SPECIFIED	101	...	–	–	...	...
IRELAND Ø	TOTAL	54 746	22 248	64 116	26 427	...	...
	EDUCATION SCIENCE & TEACHER TRAINING	5 707	4 379	5 199	3 930	...	...
	HUMANITIES, RELIGION & THEOLOGY	9 050	5 139	9 412	5 358	...	...
	FINE AND APPLIED ARTS	1 958	1 172	2 491	1 564	...	...
	LAW	1 021	390	1 017	416	...	...
	SOCIAL AND BEHAVIOURAL SCIENCE	2 008	1 059	1 880	1 049	...	...
	COMMERCIAL & BUSINESS ADMINISTRATION	7 934	2 470	11 291	4 282	...	...
	MASS COMMUNICATION & DOCUMENTATION	198	71	461	238	...	...
	HOME ECONOMICS (DOMESTIC SCIENCE)	171	171	158	157	...	...
	SERVICE TRADES	–	–	–	–	...	...
	NATURAL SCIENCE	6 604	3 027	8 645	4 212	...	...
	MATHEMATICS & COMPUTER SCIENCE	1 136	329	1 403	407	...	...
	MEDICAL SCIENCE & HEALTH–RELATED	4 001	1 655	3 973	1 777	...	...
	ENGINEERING	9 333	545	12 600	961	...	...
	ARCHITECTURE & TOWN PLANNING	1 341	238	1 496	257	...	...
	TRADE, CRAFT & INDUSTRIAL PROGRAMMES	252	147	291	161	...	...
	TRANSPORT AND COMMUNICATIONS	–	–	–	–	...	...
	AGRICULTURE, FORESTRY & FISHERY	1 410	197	1 123	233	...	...
	OTHER AND NOT SPECIFIED	2 622	1 259	2 676	1 425	...	...

COUNTRY / PAYS / PAIS	FIELD OF STUDY / DOMAINES D'ETUDES / SECTORES DE ESTUDIOS	1980		1983		1984	
		MF	F	MF	F	MF	F
		(1)	(2)	(3)	(4)	(5)	(6)
ITALY	TOTAL	1 117 742	476 028	1 120 342	498 725	1 181 953	534 595
	EDUCATION SCIENCE & TEACHER TRAINING	62 125	45 474	39 006	33 055	38 917	33 648
	HUMANITIES, RELIGION & THEOLOGY	155 487	116 436	154 137	118 966	161 723	126 762
	FINE AND APPLIED ARTS	11 131	5 876	13 107	7 500	13 135	7 923
	LAW	146 970	60 032	160 328	71 217	173 642	79 073
	SOCIAL AND BEHAVIOURAL SCIENCE	81 882	38 088	187 849	76 534	209 177	86 748
	COMMERCIAL & BUSINESS ADMINISTRATION	105 904	32 454	14 058	3 835	15 852	4 388
	MASS COMMUNICATION & DOCUMENTATION	–	–	83	29	95	35
	HOME ECONOMICS (DOMESTIC SCIENCE)	–	–	–	–	–	–
	SERVICE TRADES	–	–	–	–	–	–
	NATURAL SCIENCE	67 933	39 580	75 934	40 333	79 572	42 519
	MATHEMATICS & COMPUTER SCIENCE	40 143	17 583	37 522	16 969	39 817	17 226
	MEDICAL SCIENCE & HEALTH-RELATED	256 408	90 646	226 611	85 773	230 471	89 085
	ENGINEERING	90 295	3 671	91 034	4 679	96 886	5 304
	ARCHITECTURE & TOWN PLANNING	57 306	17 293	62 403	21 485	64 706	22 825
	TRADE, CRAFT & INDUSTRIAL PROGRAMMES	–	–	–	–	–	–
	TRANSPORT AND COMMUNICATIONS	–	–	–	–	–	–
	AGRICULTURE, FORESTRY & FISHERY	41 841	8 867	39 956	9 473	39 047	9 870
	OTHER AND NOT SPECIFIED	317	28	18 314	8 877	18 913	9 189
LUXEMBOURG‡	TOTAL	748	264	982	351	...	...
	EDUCATION SCIENCE & TEACHER TRAINING	101	60	89	55	...	...
	HUMANITIES, RELIGION & THEOLOGY	67	39	130	79	...	...
	FINE AND APPLIED ARTS	–	–	–	–	...	...
	LAW	24	8	32	12	...	...
	SOCIAL AND BEHAVIOURAL SCIENCE	83	57	228	109	...	...
	COMMERCIAL & BUSINESS ADMINISTRATION	59	24	./.	./.	...	...
	MASS COMMUNICATION & DOCUMENTATION	–	–	–	–	...	...
	HOME ECONOMICS (DOMESTIC SCIENCE)	–	–	–	–	...	...
	SERVICE TRADES	–	–	–	–	...	...
	NATURAL SCIENCE	34	11	64	25	...	...
	MATHEMATICS & COMPUTER SCIENCE	./.	./.	./.	./.	...	...
	MEDICAL SCIENCE & HEALTH-RELATED	99	37	70	31	...	...
	ENGINEERING	221	5	299	8	...	...
	ARCHITECTURE & TOWN PLANNING	–	–	–	–	...	...
	TRADE, CRAFT & INDUSTRIAL PROGRAMMES	–	–	–	–	...	...
	TRANSPORT AND COMMUNICATIONS	–	–	–	–	...	...
	AGRICULTURE, FORESTRY & FISHERY	–	–	–	–	...	...
	OTHER AND NOT SPECIFIED	60	23	70	32	...	...
MALTA	TOTAL	947	231	1 337	337	1 411	424
	EDUCATION SCIENCE & TEACHER TRAINING	214	91	216	121	293	170
	HUMANITIES, RELIGION & THEOLOGY	197	50	12	1	7	1
	FINE AND APPLIED ARTS	–	–	–	–	–	–
	LAW	91	12	151	35	95	26
	SOCIAL AND BEHAVIOURAL SCIENCE	–	–	–	–	–	–
	COMMERCIAL & BUSINESS ADMINISTRATION	112	10	294	49	313	68
	MASS COMMUNICATION & DOCUMENTATION	–	–	–	–	–	–
	HOME ECONOMICS (DOMESTIC SCIENCE)	–	–	–	–	–	–
	SERVICE TRADES	–	–	–	–	–	–
	NATURAL SCIENCE	4	2	–	–	–	–
	MATHEMATICS & COMPUTER SCIENCE	–	–	–	–	–	–
	MEDICAL SCIENCE & HEALTH-RELATED	225	60	398	115	409	143
	ENGINEERING	42	5	160	9	194	10
	ARCHITECTURE & TOWN PLANNING	62	1	106	7	100	6
	TRADE, CRAFT & INDUSTRIAL PROGRAMMES	–	–	–	–	–	–
	TRANSPORT AND COMMUNICATIONS	–	–	–	–	–	–
	AGRICULTURE, FORESTRY & FISHERY	–	–	–	–	–	–
	OTHER AND NOT SPECIFIED	–	–	–	–	–	–

3.12 Third level: students by field of study (1980,1983,1984)
Troisième degré: étudiants par domaine d'études (1980,1983,1984)
Tercer grado: estudiantes por sector de estudios (1980,1983,1984)

COUNTRY / PAYS / PAIS	FIELD OF STUDY / DOMAINES D'ETUDES / SECTORES DE ESTUDIOS	1980 MF	1980 F	1983 MF	1983 F	1984 MF	1984 F
		(1)	(2)	(3)	(4)	(5)	(6)
NETHERLANDS‡	TOTAL	360 033	143 083	384 131	161 515	166 858	59 561
	EDUCATION SCIENCE & TEACHER TRAINING	90 428	51 786	81 373	49 056	–	–
	HUMANITIES, RELIGION & THEOLOGY	28 820	13 612	29 906	15 795	30 109	16 380
	FINE AND APPLIED ARTS	15 752	7 249	19 463	10 004	–	–
	LAW	20 865	6 731	25 966	9 881	27 833	11 008
	SOCIAL AND BEHAVIOURAL SCIENCE	57 783	23 747	60 540	26 898	36 170	11 485
	COMMERCIAL & BUSINESS ADMINISTRATION	10 014	1 487	19 448	4 414	2 620	519
	MASS COMMUNICATION & DOCUMENTATION	2 913	1 970	3 667	2 329	–	–
	HOME ECONOMICS (DOMESTIC SCIENCE)	903	659	1 699	1 270	–	–
	SERVICE TRADES	1 159	547	1 256	614	–	–
	NATURAL SCIENCE	12 043	2 292	12 609	2 546	11 505	2 500
	MATHEMATICS & COMPUTER SCIENCE	1 963	243	1 401	225	2 489	363
	MEDICAL SCIENCE & HEALTH-RELATED	36 917	17 741	39 478	21 096	17 949	6 697
	ENGINEERING	53 045	4 950	20 396	1 406	21 341	1 618
	ARCHITECTURE & TOWN PLANNING	–	–	–	–	–	–
	TRADE, CRAFT & INDUSTRIAL PROGRAMMES	./.	./.	37 113	4 084	–	–
	TRANSPORT AND COMMUNICATIONS	3 296	58	3 600	114	–	–
	AGRICULTURE, FORESTRY & FISHERY	11 372	2 509	13 490	3 449	7 514	2 535
	OTHER AND NOT SPECIFIED	12 760	7 502	12 726	8 334	9 328	6 456
NORWAY	TOTAL	79 117	37 831	91 330	45 135	...	...
	EDUCATION SCIENCE & TEACHER TRAINING	14 138	9 750	13 410	9 892	...	...
	HUMANITIES, RELIGION & THEOLOGY	9 993	5 497	8 500	5 053	...	...
	FINE AND APPLIED ARTS	1 195	668	1 142	671	...	...
	LAW	3 591	1 308	4 486	2 097	...	...
	SOCIAL AND BEHAVIOURAL SCIENCE	6 709	3 055	7 698	4 069	...	...
	COMMERCIAL & BUSINESS ADMINISTRATION	7 115	2 427	15 979	5 725	...	...
	MASS COMMUNICATION & DOCUMENTATION	501	369	546	391	...	...
	HOME ECONOMICS (DOMESTIC SCIENCE)	55	49	40	37	...	...
	SERVICE TRADES	–	–	–	–	...	...
	NATURAL SCIENCE	5 416	1 430	6 256	1 878	...	...
	MATHEMATICS & COMPUTER SCIENCE	130	42	938	247	...	...
	MEDICAL SCIENCE & HEALTH-RELATED	10 408	7 423	10 980	8 260	...	...
	ENGINEERING	10 610	1 372	11 452	2 094	...	...
	ARCHITECTURE & TOWN PLANNING	571	188	601	238	...	...
	TRADE, CRAFT & INDUSTRIAL PROGRAMMES	251	110	276	141	...	...
	TRANSPORT AND COMMUNICATIONS	796	87	941	138	...	...
	AGRICULTURE, FORESTRY & FISHERY	1 130	319	1 158	418	...	...
	OTHER AND NOT SPECIFIED	6 508	3 737	6 927	3 786	...	...
POLAND‡	TOTAL	589 134	328 416	475 816	262 999	456 661	253 246
	EDUCATION SCIENCE & TEACHER TRAINING	73 988	59 316	82 996	66 955	82 415	66 477
	HUMANITIES, RELIGION & THEOLOGY	32 001	23 689	34 470	23 438	35 403	23 746
	FINE AND APPLIED ARTS	8 651	4 398	8 070	4 053	8 243	4 174
	LAW	13 097	6 079	14 883	6 974	14 207	6 715
	SOCIAL AND BEHAVIOURAL SCIENCE	12 308	7 525	12 789	7 387	12 288	7 024
	COMMERCIAL & BUSINESS ADMINISTRATION	117 178	81 267	72 261	46 145	66 689	42 427
	MASS COMMUNICATION & DOCUMENTATION	5 935	4 914	3 663	3 172	3 097	2 653
	HOME ECONOMICS (DOMESTIC SCIENCE)	–	–	400	356	407	367
	SERVICE TRADES	–	–	–	–	–	–
	NATURAL SCIENCE	13 700	8 835	14 470	8 964	14 583	9 014
	MATHEMATICS & COMPUTER SCIENCE	6 259	4 301	5 803	3 821	5 575	3 649
	MEDICAL SCIENCE & HEALTH-RELATED	62 349	47 698	59 432	44 291	62 037	46 190
	ENGINEERING	155 445	40 393	88 455	17 932	79 904	14 840
	ARCHITECTURE & TOWN PLANNING	4 084	1 973	4 145	2 031	3 865	1 830
	TRADE, CRAFT & INDUSTRIAL PROGRAMMES	–	–	13 860	3 117	12 989	2 703
	TRANSPORT AND COMMUNICATIONS	5 624	640	4 552	292	3 853	205
	AGRICULTURE, FORESTRY & FISHERY	65 019	31 889	44 217	19 950	38 814	16 782
	OTHER AND NOT SPECIFIED	13 496	5 499	11 350	4 121	12 292	4 450

COUNTRY / PAYS / PAIS	FIELD OF STUDY / DOMAINES D'ETUDES / SECTORES DE ESTUDIOS	1980		1983		1984	
		MF	F	MF	F	MF	F
		(1)	(2)	(3)	(4)	(5)	(6)
PORTUGAL‡ Ø	TOTAL	92 152	44 549	99 165	49 785	...	...
	EDUCATION SCIENCE & TEACHER TRAINING	11 101	8 644	12 666	9 651	...	...
	HUMANITIES, RELIGION & THEOLOGY	14 442	10 382	15 293	10 900	...	...
	FINE AND APPLIED ARTS	1 178	705	3 025	1 303	...	...
	LAW	9 584	3 355	10 239	4 260	...	...
	SOCIAL AND BEHAVIOURAL SCIENCE	10 613	4 872	19 056	9 091	...	...
	COMMERCIAL & BUSINESS ADMINISTRATION	6 798	2 174	./.	./.	...	...
	MASS COMMUNICATION & DOCUMENTATION	676	499	./.	./.	...	...
	HOME ECONOMICS (DOMESTIC SCIENCE)	182	102	–	–	...	...
	SERVICE TRADES	–	–	–	–	...	...
	NATURAL SCIENCE	45	25	975	542	...	...
	MATHEMATICS & COMPUTER SCIENCE	113	26	./.	./.	...	...
	MEDICAL SCIENCE & HEALTH–RELATED	13 739	8 202	12 941	8 392	...	...
	ENGINEERING	15 940	2 715	18 217	3 094	...	...
	ARCHITECTURE & TOWN PLANNING	1 600	525	./.	./.	...	...
	TRADE, CRAFT & INDUSTRIAL PROGRAMMES	374	107	./.	./.	...	...
	TRANSPORT AND COMMUNICATIONS	–	–	–	–	...	...
	AGRICULTURE, FORESTRY & FISHERY	2 100	781	2 738	1 132	...	...
	OTHER AND NOT SPECIFIED	3 667	1 435	4 015	1 420	...	...
ROMANIA‡	TOTAL	192 769	...	174 042	...	166 328	...
	EDUCATION SCIENCE & TEACHER TRAINING	8 970	...	7 607	...	6 876	...
	HUMANITIES, RELIGION & THEOLOGY	./.	...	./.	...	./.	...
	FINE AND APPLIED ARTS	2 207	...	1 103	...	986	...
	LAW	3 863	...	2 574	...	2 438	...
	SOCIAL AND BEHAVIOURAL SCIENCE	21 919	...	19 219	...	17 940	...
	COMMERCIAL & BUSINESS ADMINISTRATION	–	–	./.	...	./.	...
	MASS COMMUNICATION & DOCUMENTATION	–	–	./.	...	./.	...
	HOME ECONOMICS (DOMESTIC SCIENCE)	–	–	./.	...	./.	...
	SERVICE TRADES	–	–	./.	...	./.	...
	NATURAL SCIENCE	5 689	...	7 357	...	7 627	...
	MATHEMATICS & COMPUTER SCIENCE	2 734	...	./.	...	./.	...
	MEDICAL SCIENCE & HEALTH–RELATED	23 381	...	21 093	...	19 953	...
	ENGINEERING	109 958	...	103 745	...	99 734	...
	ARCHITECTURE & TOWN PLANNING	1 488	...	./.	...	./.	...
	TRADE, CRAFT & INDUSTRIAL PROGRAMMES	–	–	./.	...	./.	...
	TRANSPORT AND COMMUNICATIONS	1 877	...	3 434	...	3 425	...
	AGRICULTURE, FORESTRY & FISHERY	10 683	...	7 910	...	7 349	...
	OTHER AND NOT SPECIFIED	–	–	–	–	–	–
SPAIN‡	TOTAL	681 022	298 983	787 864	379 407		
	EDUCATION SCIENCE & TEACHER TRAINING	116 261	78 057	106 231	76 247	...	...
	HUMANITIES, RELIGION & THEOLOGY	37 214	23 725	50 139	34 651	...	...
	FINE AND APPLIED ARTS	7 627	4 126	9 790	5 361	...	...
	LAW	83 443	31 144	113 288	49 232	...	...
	SOCIAL AND BEHAVIOURAL SCIENCE	107 125	47 657	138 689	69 406	...	...
	COMMERCIAL & BUSINESS ADMINISTRATION	22 774	7 472	31 999	12 929	...	...
	MASS COMMUNICATION & DOCUMENTATION	7 043	3 180	13 771	6 974	...	...
	HOME ECONOMICS (DOMESTIC SCIENCE)	–	–	–	–	...	...
	SERVICE TRADES	4 877	3 288	8 157	5 773	...	...
	NATURAL SCIENCE	45 437	20 323	53 497	25 165	...	...
	MATHEMATICS & COMPUTER SCIENCE	14 260	5 008	21 477	8 027	...	...
	MEDICAL SCIENCE & HEALTH–RELATED	107 174	56 170	93 663	54 565	...	...
	ENGINEERING	72 555	5 303	78 687	7 319	...	...
	ARCHITECTURE & TOWN PLANNING	25 638	3 776	24 208	4 595	...	...
	TRADE, CRAFT & INDUSTRIAL PROGRAMMES	–	–	–	–	...	...
	TRANSPORT AND COMMUNICATIONS	–	–	–	–	...	...
	AGRICULTURE, FORESTRY & FISHERY	6 612	1 998	10 995	3 997	...	...
	OTHER AND NOT SPECIFIED	22 982	7 756	33 273	15 166	...	...

3.12 Third level: students by field of study (1980,1983,1984)
Troisième degré: étudiants par domaine d'études (1980,1983,1984)
Tercer grado: estudiantes por sector de estudios (1980,1983,1984)

COUNTRY / PAYS / PAIS	FIELD OF STUDY / DOMAINES D'ETUDES / SECTORES DE ESTUDIOS	1980		1983		1984	
		MF	F	MF	F	MF	F
		(1)	(2)	(3)	(4)	(5)	(6)
SWEDEN‡	TOTAL	216 182	...	223 295	103 839	...	...
	EDUCATION SCIENCE & TEACHER TRAINING	24 824	...	28 266	21 120	...	...
	HUMANITIES, RELIGION & THEOLOGY	27 326	...	25 831	16 544	...	...
	FINE AND APPLIED ARTS	5 917	...	5 908	3 634	...	...
	LAW	10 369	...	9 168	4 105	...	...
	SOCIAL AND BEHAVIOURAL SCIENCE	21 783	...	16 388	8 470	...	...
	COMMERCIAL & BUSINESS ADMINISTRATION	19 490	...	21 069	9 298	...	...
	MASS COMMUNICATION & DOCUMENTATION	1 672	...	1 899	1 252	...	...
	HOME ECONOMICS (DOMESTIC SCIENCE)	482	...	354	341	...	...
	SERVICE TRADES	–	–	692	155	...	...
	NATURAL SCIENCE	7 462	...	7 126	2 675	...	...
	MATHEMATICS & COMPUTER SCIENCE	7 374	...	9 258	2 456	...	...
	MEDICAL SCIENCE & HEALTH-RELATED	25 124	...	24 979	17 456	...	...
	ENGINEERING	50 058	...	58 621	9 049	...	...
	ARCHITECTURE & TOWN PLANNING	1 685	...	1 621	682	...	...
	TRADE, CRAFT & INDUSTRIAL PROGRAMMES	686	...	1 112	59	...	...
	TRANSPORT AND COMMUNICATIONS	566	...	685	59	...	...
	AGRICULTURE, FORESTRY & FISHERY	2 197	...	2 422	834	...	...
	OTHER AND NOT SPECIFIED	9 167	...	7 896	5 650	...	...
SWITZERLAND	TOTAL	85 127	25 766	95 661	31 359	105 897	33 785
	EDUCATION SCIENCE & TEACHER TRAINING	5 466	3 274	5 573	3 392	5 589	3 417
	HUMANITIES, RELIGION & THEOLOGY	14 203	7 130	15 156	7 977	15 557	8 214
	FINE AND APPLIED ARTS	1 635	1 003	2 838	1 875	3 175	2 123
	LAW	7 574	2 035	8 827	2 715	9 098	2 913
	SOCIAL AND BEHAVIOURAL SCIENCE	11 905	3 808	16 331	6 098	17 550	6 582
	COMMERCIAL & BUSINESS ADMINISTRATION	3 386	489	4 212	950	9 308	1 767
	MASS COMMUNICATION & DOCUMENTATION	149	127	61	29	65	34
	HOME ECONOMICS (DOMESTIC SCIENCE)	956	328	1 271	505	1 303	543
	SERVICE TRADES	237	49	–	–	–	–
	NATURAL SCIENCE	7 709	1 583	18 963	2 352	8 886	2 041
	MATHEMATICS & COMPUTER SCIENCE	1 349	255	1 982	298	2 482	371
	MEDICAL SCIENCE & HEALTH-RELATED	9 861	3 466	10 329	3 935	10 285	4 022
	ENGINEERING	11 733	257	4 730	202	15 825	527
	ARCHITECTURE & TOWN PLANNING	2 236	338	1 734	484	1 928	569
	TRADE, CRAFT & INDUSTRIAL PROGRAMMES	3 060	243	1 452	59	2 481	20
	TRANSPORT AND COMMUNICATIONS	136	–	25	–	27	–
	AGRICULTURE, FORESTRY & FISHERY	1 896	387	2 135	488	2 338	642
	OTHER AND NOT SPECIFIED	1 636	994	42	–	–	–
UNITED KINGDOM‡	TOTAL	832 106	302 820	858 416	320 237	...	...
	EDUCATION SCIENCE & TEACHER TRAINING	82 861	50 585	75 938	46 458	...	...
	HUMANITIES, RELIGION & THEOLOGY	85 605	51 912	88 953	54 418	...	...
	FINE AND APPLIED ARTS	45 567	26 463	30 944	14 705	...	...
	LAW	20 745	8 017	21 510	8 620	...	...
	SOCIAL AND BEHAVIOURAL SCIENCE	82 038	37 715	89 512	40 200	...	...
	COMMERCIAL & BUSINESS ADMINISTRATION	124 379	37 854	109 979	34 160	...	...
	MASS COMMUNICATION & DOCUMENTATION	2 174	1 683	1 769	1 323	...	...
	HOME ECONOMICS (DOMESTIC SCIENCE)	2 167	1 919	1 672	1 434	...	...
	SERVICE TRADES	8 424	4 351	7 608	3 905	...	...
	NATURAL SCIENCE	97 013	31 386	91 331	30 056	...	...
	MATHEMATICS & COMPUTER SCIENCE	39 772	9 904	29 731	7 668	...	...
	MEDICAL SCIENCE & HEALTH-RELATED	52 551	25 538	53 742	27 172	...	...
	ENGINEERING	155 926	7 152	151 739	6 235	...	...
	ARCHITECTURE & TOWN PLANNING	13 866	2 582	17 194	4 747	...	...
	TRADE, CRAFT & INDUSTRIAL PROGRAMMES	3 369	631	3 194	830	...	...
	TRANSPORT AND COMMUNICATIONS	1 673	58	1 742	64	...	...
	AGRICULTURE, FORESTRY & FISHERY	8 666	2 701	8 995	2 881	...	...
	OTHER AND NOT SPECIFIED	5 310	2 369	72 863	32 661	...	...

COUNTRY / PAYS / PAIS	FIELD OF STUDY / DOMAINES D'ETUDES / SECTORES DE ESTUDIOS	1980 MF	1980 F	1983 MF	1983 F	1984 MF	1984 F
		(1)	(2)	(3)	(4)	(5)	(6)
YUGOSLAVIA‡	TOTAL	411 995	186 991	375 393	168 592	...	...
	EDUCATION SCIENCE & TEACHER TRAINING	38 029	21 166	34 625	20 256	...	...
	HUMANITIES, RELIGION & THEOLOGY	33 377	20 313	28 553	18 920	...	...
	FINE AND APPLIED ARTS	3 463	1 524	3 794	1 913	...	...
	LAW	58 385	31 520	41 895	22 420	...	...
	SOCIAL AND BEHAVIOURAL SCIENCE	93 498	49 088	65 146	34 163	...	...
	COMMERCIAL & BUSINESS ADMINISTRATION	11 388	4 228	5 485	2 043	...	...
	MASS COMMUNICATION & DOCUMENTATION	453	218	380	182	...	...
	HOME ECONOMICS (DOMESTIC SCIENCE)	528	424	304	247	...	...
	SERVICE TRADES	6 795	2 983	5 158	2 211	...	...
	NATURAL SCIENCE	14 874	8 049	16 369	8 924	...	...
	MATHEMATICS & COMPUTER SCIENCE	./.	./.	./.	./.	...	...
	MEDICAL SCIENCE & HEALTH-RELATED	29 751	19 336	31 622	20 074	...	...
	ENGINEERING	83 059	14 934	94 489	21 327	...	...
	ARCHITECTURE & TOWN PLANNING	4 551	2 320	4 863	2 581	...	...
	TRADE, CRAFT & INDUSTRIAL PROGRAMMES	3 131	1 579	2 703	1 365	...	...
	TRANSPORT AND COMMUNICATIONS	8 110	1 306	9 532	1 517	...	...
	AGRICULTURE, FORESTRY & FISHERY	17 105	5 680	27 114	9 530	...	...
	OTHER AND NOT SPECIFIED	5 498	2 323	3 361	919	...	...
OCEANIA							
AMERICAN SAMOA Ø	TOTAL	...	...	1 007	...	...	...
	EDUCATION SCIENCE & TEACHER TRAINING	...	...	52	...	...	...
	HUMANITIES, RELIGION & THEOLOGY	...	...	239	...	...	...
	FINE AND APPLIED ARTS	...	...	41	...	...	...
	LAW	...	...	–	...	...	...
	SOCIAL AND BEHAVIOURAL SCIENCE	...	...	44	...	...	...
	COMMERCIAL & BUSINESS ADMINISTRATION	...	...	163	...	...	...
	MASS COMMUNICATION & DOCUMENTATION	...	...	–	...	...	...
	HOME ECONOMICS (DOMESTIC SCIENCE)	...	...	–	...	...	...
	SERVICE TRADES	...	...	–	...	...	...
	NATURAL SCIENCE	...	...	51	...	...	...
	MATHEMATICS & COMPUTER SCIENCE	...	...	38	...	...	...
	MEDICAL SCIENCE & HEALTH-RELATED	...	...	59	...	...	...
	ENGINEERING	...	...	–	...	...	...
	ARCHITECTURE & TOWN PLANNING	...	...	–	...	...	...
	TRADE, CRAFT & INDUSTRIAL PROGRAMMES	...	...	83	...	...	...
	TRANSPORT AND COMMUNICATIONS	...	...	–	...	...	...
	AGRICULTURE, FORESTRY & FISHERY	...	...	–	...	...	...
	OTHER AND NOT SPECIFIED	...	...	237	...	...	...
AUSTRALIA‡	TOTAL	323 716	146 676	349 243	161 419	358 498	166 797
	EDUCATION SCIENCE & TEACHER TRAINING	56 720	39 014	72 292	47 764	71 586	47 184
	HUMANITIES, RELIGION & THEOLOGY	45 525	28 296	51 840	33 513	53 976	34 657
	FINE AND APPLIED ARTS	13 780	8 024	11 686	7 143	11 962	7 424
	LAW	10 074	3 319	10 271	4 093	10 079	4 146
	SOCIAL AND BEHAVIOURAL SCIENCE	12 033	7 178	23 146	14 849	24 478	15 937
	COMMERCIAL & BUSINESS ADMINISTRATION	57 946	14 599	63 561	18 785	66 188	20 239
	MASS COMMUNICATION & DOCUMENTATION	24 007	15 431	./.	./.	./.	./.
	HOME ECONOMICS (DOMESTIC SCIENCE)	–	–	–	–	–	–
	SERVICE TRADES	–	–	–	–	–	–
	NATURAL SCIENCE	41 784	14 106	47 256	16 483	49 642	17 516
	MATHEMATICS & COMPUTER SCIENCE	./.	./.	./.	./.	./.	./.
	MEDICAL SCIENCE & HEALTH-RELATED	23 486	12 280	20 553	10 968	21 285	11 729
	ENGINEERING	22 595	750	27 875	1 396	28 709	1 511
	ARCHITECTURE & TOWN PLANNING	8 704	1 659	7 981	1 656	8 106	1 732
	TRADE, CRAFT & INDUSTRIAL PROGRAMMES	–	–	–	–	–	–
	TRANSPORT AND COMMUNICATIONS	–	–	–	–	–	–
	AGRICULTURE, FORESTRY & FISHERY	6 641	1 835	7 838	2 385	8 100	2 578
	OTHER AND NOT SPECIFIED	421	185	4 944	2 384	4 387	2 144

3.12 Third level: students by field of study (1980,1983,1984)
Troisième degré: étudiants par domaine d'études (1980,1983,1984)
Tercer grado: estudiantes por sector de estudios (1980,1983,1984)

COUNTRY / PAYS / PAIS	FIELD OF STUDY / DOMAINES D'ETUDES / SECTORES DE ESTUDIOS	1980		1983		1984	
		MF	F	MF	F	MF	F
		(1)	(2)	(3)	(4)	(5)	(6)
COOK ISLANDS	TOTAL	360	163	...	...	...	...
	EDUCATION SCIENCE & TEACHER TRAINING	57	29	...	...	...	...
	HUMANITIES, RELIGION & THEOLOGY	–	–	...	...	...	...
	FINE AND APPLIED ARTS	–	–	...	...	...	...
	LAW	–	–	...	...	...	...
	SOCIAL AND BEHAVIOURAL SCIENCE	233	113	...	...	...	...
	COMMERCIAL & BUSINESS ADMINISTRATION	–	–	...	...	...	...
	MASS COMMUNICATION & DOCUMENTATION	–	–	...	...	...	...
	HOME ECONOMICS (DOMESTIC SCIENCE)	–	–	...	...	...	...
	SERVICE TRADES	–	–	...	...	...	...
	NATURAL SCIENCE	22	1	...	...	...	...
	MATHEMATICS & COMPUTER SCIENCE	48	20	...	...	...	...
	MEDICAL SCIENCE & HEALTH–RELATED	–	–	...	...	...	...
	ENGINEERING	–	–	...	...	...	...
	ARCHITECTURE & TOWN PLANNING	–	–	...	...	...	...
	TRADE, CRAFT & INDUSTRIAL PROGRAMMES	–	–	...	...	...	...
	TRANSPORT AND COMMUNICATIONS	–	–	...	...	...	...
	AGRICULTURE, FORESTRY & FISHERY	–	–	...	...	...	...
	OTHER AND NOT SPECIFIED	–	–	...	...	...	...
FIJI‡	TOTAL	2 003	...	...	...	...	...
	EDUCATION SCIENCE & TEACHER TRAINING	820	...	...	...	...	...
	HUMANITIES, RELIGION & THEOLOGY	–	–	...	...	...	...
	FINE AND APPLIED ARTS	–	–	...	...	...	...
	LAW	–	–	...	...	...	...
	SOCIAL AND BEHAVIOURAL SCIENCE	687	...	...	...	...	...
	COMMERCIAL & BUSINESS ADMINISTRATION	./.	...	...	...	...	...
	MASS COMMUNICATION & DOCUMENTATION	–	–	...	...	...	...
	HOME ECONOMICS (DOMESTIC SCIENCE)	–	–	...	...	...	...
	SERVICE TRADES	–	–	...	...	...	...
	NATURAL SCIENCE	272	...	...	...	...	...
	MATHEMATICS & COMPUTER SCIENCE	–	–	...	...	...	...
	MEDICAL SCIENCE & HEALTH–RELATED	–	–	...	...	...	...
	ENGINEERING	–	–	...	...	...	...
	ARCHITECTURE & TOWN PLANNING	–	–	...	...	...	...
	TRADE, CRAFT & INDUSTRIAL PROGRAMMES	–	–	...	...	...	...
	TRANSPORT AND COMMUNICATIONS	–	–	...	...	...	...
	AGRICULTURE, FORESTRY & FISHERY	190	...	...	...	...	...
	OTHER AND NOT SPECIFIED	34	...	...	...	...	...
FRENCH POLYNESIA Ø	TOTAL	27	7	68	33	...	...
	EDUCATION SCIENCE & TEACHER TRAINING	–	–	–	–	...	...
	HUMANITIES, RELIGION & THEOLOGY	–	–	–	–	...	...
	FINE AND APPLIED ARTS	–	–	–	–	...	...
	LAW	–	–	–	–	...	...
	SOCIAL AND BEHAVIOURAL SCIENCE	–	–	–	–	...	...
	COMMERCIAL & BUSINESS ADMINISTRATION	17	7	52	33	...	...
	MASS COMMUNICATION & DOCUMENTATION	–	–	–	–	...	...
	HOME ECONOMICS (DOMESTIC SCIENCE)	–	–	–	–	...	...
	SERVICE TRADES	–	–	–	–	...	...
	NATURAL SCIENCE	–	–	–	–	...	...
	MATHEMATICS & COMPUTER SCIENCE	–	–	–	–	...	...
	MEDICAL SCIENCE & HEALTH–RELATED	–	–	–	–	...	...
	ENGINEERING	10	–	16	–	...	...
	ARCHITECTURE & TOWN PLANNING	–	–	–	–	...	...
	TRADE, CRAFT & INDUSTRIAL PROGRAMMES	–	–	–	–	...	...
	TRANSPORT AND COMMUNICATIONS	–	–	–	–	...	...
	AGRICULTURE, FORESTRY & FISHERY	–	–	–	–	...	...
	OTHER AND NOT SPECIFIED	–	–	–	–	...	...

COUNTRY / PAYS / PAIS	FIELD OF STUDY / DOMAINES D'ETUDES / SECTORES DE ESTUDIOS	1980		1983		1984	
		MF	F	MF	F	MF	F
		(1)	(2)	(3)	(4)	(5)	(6)
NEW CALEDONIA‡	TOTAL	438	169	580	194	660	252
	EDUCATION SCIENCE & TEACHER TRAINING	155	103	142	92	124	90
	HUMANITIES, RELIGION & THEOLOGY	–	–	–	–	–	–
	FINE AND APPLIED ARTS	–	–	–	–	–	–
	LAW	126	45	184	77	174	66
	SOCIAL AND BEHAVIOURAL SCIENCE	–	–	1	–	1	–
	COMMERCIAL & BUSINESS ADMINISTRATION	25	13	30	24	30	18
	MASS COMMUNICATION & DOCUMENTATION	–	–	–	–	–	–
	HOME ECONOMICS (DOMESTIC SCIENCE)	–	–	–	–	–	–
	SERVICE TRADES	36	8	–	–	–	–
	NATURAL SCIENCE	16	–	./.	–	./.	./.
	MATHEMATICS & COMPUTER SCIENCE	61	–	182	–	283	77
	MEDICAL SCIENCE & HEALTH-RELATED	–	–	–	–	–	–
	ENGINEERING	19	–	33	1	33	–
	ARCHITECTURE & TOWN PLANNING	–	–	–	–	–	–
	TRADE, CRAFT & INDUSTRIAL PROGRAMMES	–	–	8	–	15	1
	TRANSPORT AND COMMUNICATIONS	–	–	–	–	–	–
	AGRICULTURE, FORESTRY & FISHERY	–	–	–	–	–	–
	OTHER AND NOT SPECIFIED	–	–	–	–	–	–
NEW ZEALAND‡	TOTAL	78 001	31 510	86 666	36 125	...	...
	EDUCATION SCIENCE & TEACHER TRAINING	8 617	6 540	5 807	4 608	...	...
	HUMANITIES, RELIGION & THEOLOGY	1 417	684	12 325	8 062	...	...
	FINE AND APPLIED ARTS	11 240	7 354	903	541	...	...
	LAW	3 808	1 456	4 355	1 996	...	...
	SOCIAL AND BEHAVIOURAL SCIENCE	756	433	1 074	705	...	...
	COMMERCIAL & BUSINESS ADMINISTRATION	19 262	5 619	21 842	8 089	...	...
	MASS COMMUNICATION & DOCUMENTATION	286	171	313	178	...	...
	HOME ECONOMICS (DOMESTIC SCIENCE)	325	324	292	292	...	...
	SERVICE TRADES	–	–	124	77	...	...
	NATURAL SCIENCE	8 831	2 730	9 716	3 522	...	...
	MATHEMATICS & COMPUTER SCIENCE	602	146	1 113	325	...	...
	MEDICAL SCIENCE & HEALTH-RELATED	5 069	2 806	5 036	3 318	...	...
	ENGINEERING	8 714	377	8 774	491	...	...
	ARCHITECTURE & TOWN PLANNING	1 496	323	1 451	407	...	...
	TRADE, CRAFT & INDUSTRIAL PROGRAMMES	538	118	3 869	188	...	...
	TRANSPORT AND COMMUNICATIONS	193	14	353	23	...	...
	AGRICULTURE, FORESTRY & FISHERY	3 643	960	4 744	1 307	...	...
	OTHER AND NOT SPECIFIED	3 204	1 455	4 575	1 996	...	...
PACIFIC ISLANDS Ø	TOTAL	2 129	514	1 964	608	...	...
	EDUCATION SCIENCE & TEACHER TRAINING	1 203	297	75	18	...	...
	HUMANITIES, RELIGION & THEOLOGY	35	10	–	–	...	...
	FINE AND APPLIED ARTS	–	–	–	–	...	...
	LAW	73	7	–	–	...	...
	SOCIAL AND BEHAVIOURAL SCIENCE	68	4	–	–	...	...
	COMMERCIAL & BUSINESS ADMINISTRATION	189	89	112	78	...	...
	MASS COMMUNICATION & DOCUMENTATION	15	2	–	–	...	...
	HOME ECONOMICS (DOMESTIC SCIENCE)	28	22	–	–	...	...
	SERVICE TRADES	11	1	15	9	...	...
	NATURAL SCIENCE	–	–	–	–	...	...
	MATHEMATICS & COMPUTER SCIENCE	7	1	–	–	...	...
	MEDICAL SCIENCE & HEALTH-RELATED	98	41	19	14	...	...
	ENGINEERING	15	–	–	–	...	...
	ARCHITECTURE & TOWN PLANNING	203	4	–	–	...	...
	TRADE, CRAFT & INDUSTRIAL PROGRAMMES	7	2	191	13	...	...
	TRANSPORT AND COMMUNICATIONS	4	–	–	–	...	...
	AGRICULTURE, FORESTRY & FISHERY	56	7	–	–	...	...
	OTHER AND NOT SPECIFIED	117	27	1 552	476	...	...

3.12 Third level: students by field of study (1980,1983,1984)
Troisième degré: étudiants par domaine d'études (1980,1983,1984)
Tercer grado: estudiantes por sector de estudios (1980,1983,1984)

COUNTRY / PAYS / PAIS	FIELD OF STUDY / DOMAINES D'ETUDES / SECTORES DE ESTUDIOS	1980 MF (1)	1980 F (2)	1983 MF (3)	1983 F (4)	1984 MF (5)	1984 F (6)
PAPUA NEW GUINEA‡	TOTAL	5 039	1 112	4 846	1 127	6 062	1 376
	EDUCATION SCIENCE & TEACHER TRAINING	538	143	657	206	749	230
	HUMANITIES, RELIGION & THEOLOGY	–	–	–	–	578	79
	FINE AND APPLIED ARTS	–	–	66	4	31	–
	LAW	239	18	247	24	254	35
	SOCIAL AND BEHAVIOURAL SCIENCE	529	68	172	28	289	38
	COMMERCIAL & BUSINESS ADMINISTRATION	849	522	349	75	797	160
	MASS COMMUNICATION & DOCUMENTATION	132	33	40	20	115	58
	HOME ECONOMICS (DOMESTIC SCIENCE)	96	37	–	–	–	–
	SERVICE TRADES	26	12	–	–	–	–
	NATURAL SCIENCE	243	32	224	27	328	39
	MATHEMATICS & COMPUTER SCIENCE	./.	./.	–	–	3	–
	MEDICAL SCIENCE & HEALTH–RELATED	384	73	911	527	904	540
	ENGINEERING	486	6	517	14	539	18
	ARCHITECTURE & TOWN PLANNING	95	2	109	7	91	3
	TRADE, CRAFT & INDUSTRIAL PROGRAMMES	–	–	–	–	–	–
	TRANSPORT AND COMMUNICATIONS	24	6	117	2	156	21
	AGRICULTURE, FORESTRY & FISHERY	807	86	892	105	639	39
	OTHER AND NOT SPECIFIED	591	74	545	88	589	116
SAMOA‡	TOTAL	644	45	562	264	...	...
	EDUCATION SCIENCE & TEACHER TRAINING	54	21	98	65	...	...
	HUMANITIES, RELIGION & THEOLOGY	155	14	77	30	...	...
	FINE AND APPLIED ARTS	–	–	–	–	...	...
	LAW	–	–	–	–	...	...
	SOCIAL AND BEHAVIOURAL SCIENCE	–	–	7	3	...	...
	COMMERCIAL & BUSINESS ADMINISTRATION	290	–	341	144	...	...
	MASS COMMUNICATION & DOCUMENTATION	–	–	–	–	...	...
	HOME ECONOMICS (DOMESTIC SCIENCE)	–	–	15	15	...	...
	SERVICE TRADES	–	–	–	–	...	...
	NATURAL SCIENCE	–	–	–	–	...	...
	MATHEMATICS & COMPUTER SCIENCE	–	–	24	7	...	...
	MEDICAL SCIENCE & HEALTH–RELATED	–	–	–	–	...	...
	ENGINEERING	–	–	–	–	...	...
	ARCHITECTURE & TOWN PLANNING	–	–	–	–	...	...
	TRADE, CRAFT & INDUSTRIAL PROGRAMMES	–	–	–	–	...	...
	TRANSPORT AND COMMUNICATIONS	–	–	–	–	...	...
	AGRICULTURE, FORESTRY & FISHERY	145	10	–	–	...	...
	OTHER AND NOT SPECIFIED	–	–	–	–	...	...
TONGA‡	TOTAL	693	298	...	...	680	382
	EDUCATION SCIENCE & TEACHER TRAINING	202	123	...	...	183	92
	HUMANITIES, RELIGION & THEOLOGY	103	19	...	...	94	17
	FINE AND APPLIED ARTS	–	–	...	...	–	–
	LAW	144	28	...	...	–	–
	SOCIAL AND BEHAVIOURAL SCIENCE	17	4	...	...	–	–
	COMMERCIAL & BUSINESS ADMINISTRATION	87	22	...	...	58	58
	MASS COMMUNICATION & DOCUMENTATION	–	–	...	...	–	–
	HOME ECONOMICS (DOMESTIC SCIENCE)	–	–	...	...	132	132
	SERVICE TRADES	–	–	...	...	–	–
	NATURAL SCIENCE	27	3	...	...	–	–
	MATHEMATICS & COMPUTER SCIENCE	16	2	...	...	–	–
	MEDICAL SCIENCE & HEALTH–RELATED	97	97	...	...	79	79
	ENGINEERING	–	–	...	...	16	–
	ARCHITECTURE & TOWN PLANNING	–	–	...	...	–	–
	TRADE, CRAFT & INDUSTRIAL PROGRAMMES	–	–	...	...	–	–
	TRANSPORT AND COMMUNICATIONS	–	–	...	...	–	–
	AGRICULTURE, FORESTRY & FISHERY	–	–	...	...	93	–
	OTHER AND NOT SPECIFIED	–	–	...	...	25	4

COUNTRY / PAYS / PAIS	FIELD OF STUDY / DOMAINES D'ETUDES / SECTORES DE ESTUDIOS	1980		1983		1984	
		MF	F	MF	F	MF	F
		(1)	(2)	(3)	(4)	(5)	(6)
U.S.S.R.							
U.S.S.R.‡	TOTAL	5 235 200	...	5 301 300	...	5 280 100	...
	EDUCATION SCIENCE & TEACHER TRAINING	1 509 000	...	1 528 500	...	1 529 100	...
	HUMANITIES, RELIGION & THEOLOGY	...	...	...	...	...	...
	FINE AND APPLIED ARTS	48 000	...	49 800	...	49 300	...
	LAW	377 000	...	385 000	...	385 600	...
	SOCIAL AND BEHAVIOURAL SCIENCE	...	...	...	...	...	...
	COMMERCIAL & BUSINESS ADMINISTRATION	...	...	...	...	...	...
	MASS COMMUNICATION & DOCUMENTATION	...	...	...	...	...	...
	HOME ECONOMICS (DOMESTIC SCIENCE)	...	...	...	...	...	...
	SERVICE TRADES	...	...	...	...	...	...
	NATURAL SCIENCE	...	...	...	...	...	...
	MATHEMATICS & COMPUTER SCIENCE	...	...	...	...	...	...
	MEDICAL SCIENCE & HEALTH-RELATED	378 700	...	390 800	...	388 300	...
	ENGINEERING	2 388 700	...	2 395 700	...	2 375 200	...
	ARCHITECTURE & TOWN PLANNING	...	...	...	...	...	...
	TRADE, CRAFT & INDUSTRIAL PROGRAMMES	...	...	...	...	...	...
	TRANSPORT AND COMMUNICATIONS	./.	...	./.	...	./.	...
	AGRICULTURE, FORESTRY & FISHERY	533 800	...	551 500	...	552 600	...
	OTHER AND NOT SPECIFIED	./.	...	./.	...	./.	...
BYELORUSSIAN S.S.R.‡	TOTAL	177 000	...	183 800	...	185 100	...
	EDUCATION SCIENCE & TEACHER TRAINING	54 600	...	57 500	...	58 600	...
	HUMANITIES, RELIGION & THEOLOGY	...	...	...	...	...	...
	FINE AND APPLIED ARTS	1 500	...	1 600	...	1 500	...
	LAW	16 300	...	18 300	...	18 700	...
	SOCIAL AND BEHAVIOURAL SCIENCE	...	...	...	...	...	...
	COMMERCIAL & BUSINESS ADMINISTRATION	...	...	...	...	...	...
	MASS COMMUNICATION & DOCUMENTATION	...	...	...	...	...	...
	HOME ECONOMICS (DOMESTIC SCIENCE)	...	...	...	...	...	...
	SERVICE TRADES	...	...	...	...	...	...
	NATURAL SCIENCE	...	...	...	...	...	...
	MATHEMATICS & COMPUTER SCIENCE	...	...	...	...	...	...
	MEDICAL SCIENCE & HEALTH-RELATED	12 000	...	12 900	...	13 200	...
	ENGINEERING	68 200	...	68 700	...	68 300	...
	ARCHITECTURE & TOWN PLANNING	...	...	...	...	...	...
	TRADE, CRAFT & INDUSTRIAL PROGRAMMES	...	...	...	...	...	...
	TRANSPORT AND COMMUNICATIONS	./.	...	./.	...	./.	...
	AGRICULTURE, FORESTRY & FISHERY	24 400	...	24 800	...	24 800	...
	OTHER AND NOT SPECIFIED	./.	...	./.	...	./.	...
UKRAINIAN S.S.R.‡	TOTAL	880 400	...	880 900	...	878 500	...
	EDUCATION SCIENCE & TEACHER TRAINING	224 400	...	228 200	...	230 600	...
	HUMANITIES, RELIGION & THEOLOGY	...	...	...	...	...	...
	FINE AND APPLIED ARTS	7 100	...	6 800	...	6 700	...
	LAW	77 900	...	76 200	...	75 600	...
	SOCIAL AND BEHAVIOURAL SCIENCE	...	...	...	...	...	...
	COMMERCIAL & BUSINESS ADMINISTRATION	...	...	...	...	...	...
	MASS COMMUNICATION & DOCUMENTATION	...	...	...	...	...	...
	HOME ECONOMICS (DOMESTIC SCIENCE)	...	...	...	...	...	...
	SERVICE TRADES	...	...	...	...	...	...
	NATURAL SCIENCE	...	...	...	...	...	...
	MATHEMATICS & COMPUTER SCIENCE	...	...	...	...	...	...
	MEDICAL SCIENCE & HEALTH-RELATED	60 200	...	61 600	...	61 300	...
	ENGINEERING	424 400	...	418 200	...	414 000	...
	ARCHITECTURE & TOWN PLANNING	...	...	...	...	...	...
	TRADE, CRAFT & INDUSTRIAL PROGRAMMES	...	...	...	...	...	...
	TRANSPORT AND COMMUNICATIONS	./.	...	./.	...	./.	...
	AGRICULTURE, FORESTRY & FISHERY	86 400	...	89 900	...	90 300	...
	OTHER AND NOT SPECIFIED	./.	...	./.	...	./.	...

3.12 Third level: students by field of study (1980,1983,1984)
Troisième degré: étudiants par domaine d'études (1980,1983,1984)
Tercer grado: estudiantes por sector de estudios (1980,1983,1984)

This table, intended to supplement the data provided in Table 3.11, presents enrolment at the third level of education by field of study and by sex.

Ce tableau, qui complète le tableau 3.11, présente la répartition des étudiants inscrits dans l'enseignement du troisième degré par domaine d'études et par sexe.

Este cuadro que completa el cuadro 3.11, presenta los estudiantes inscritos en la enseñanza de tercer grado por sector de estudios y por sexo.

AFRICA:

Algeria:

E--> In 1982, education science and teacher training includes humanities, religion and theology.

FR-> En 1982, les sciences de l'éducation et formation d'enseignants incluent les lettres, religion et théologie.

ESP> En 1982, las ciencias de la educación y formación de personal docente incluyen las humanidades, religión y teología.

Botswana:

E--> In 1984, social and behavioural science include commercial and business administration.

FR-> En 1984, les sciences sociales et sciences du comportement incluent la formation au commerce et à l'administration des entreprises.

ESP> En 1984, las ciencias sociales y del comportamiento incluyen la enseñanza comercial y de administración de empresas.

Burkina Faso:

E--> In 1980, natural science includes mathematics and computer science. In 1983, humanities, religion and theology include education science and teacher training.

FR-> En 1980, les sciences exactes et naturelles comprennent les mathématiques et l'informatique. En 1983, les lettres, la religion et la théologie incluent les sciences de l'éducation et la formation d'enseignants.

ESP> En 1980, las ciencias naturales comprenden las matemáticas y la informática. En 1983, las humanidades, la religión y la teología incluyen las ciencias de la educación y formación de personal docente.

Burundi:

E--> In 1980, commercial and business administration includes social and behavioural science.

FR-> En 1980, la formation au commerce et à l'administration des entreprises inclut les sciences sociales et sciences du comportement.

ESP> En 1980, la enseñanza comercial y de administración de empresas incluye las ciencias sociales y del comportamiento.

Cameroon:

E--> Revised data and refer to universities and equivalent degree-granting institutions only.

FR-> Les données révisées se réfèrent aux universités et établissements conférant des grades équivalents seulement.

ESP> Los datos revisados se refieren a las universidades y establecimientos que otorguen grados equivalentes solamente.

Central African Republic:

E--> In 1980, law includes social and behavioural science. In 1983, education science and teacher training include humanities, religion and theology.

FR-> En 1980, le droit comprend les sciences sociales et les sciences du comportement. En 1983, les sciences de l'éducation et formation d'enseignants incluent les lettres, la religion et la théologie.

ESP> En 1980, el derecho comprende las ciencias sociales y del comportamiento. En 1983, las ciencias de la educación y formación de personal docente incluyen las humanidades, la religión y la teología.

Congo:

E--> Data for 1983 refer to 1981; social and behavioural science include commercial and business administration and mass communication and documentation.

FR-> Les données de 1983 se réfèrent à 1981; les sciences sociales et sciences du comportement incluent la formation au commerce et à l'administration des entreprises et l'information et la documentation.

ESP> Los datos de 1983 se refieren a 1981; las ciencias sociales y del comportamiento comprenden la enseñanza comercial y de administración de empresas y la documentación y comunicación social.

Egypt

E--> Data refer to universities and equivalent degree-granting institutions, excluding Al Azhar University. Engineering includes architecture and town planning, trade, craft and industrial programmes and transport and communications.

FR-> Les données se réfèrent aux universités et établissements conférant des grades équivalents seulement, non compris l'Université d'Al Azhar. Les sciences de l'ingénieur comprennent l'architecture et l'urbanisme, les métiers de la production industrielle, les transports et les télécommunications.

Egypt (Cont):

ESP> Los datos se refieren a las universidades y establecimientos que otorguen grados equivalentes solamente pero no comprenden la universidad de Al Azhar. La ingeniería y tecnología comprenden la arquitectura y el urbanismo, las artes y oficios industriales además de los transportes y comunicaciones.

Ethiopia:

E--> Natural science includes mathematics and computer science. In 1980, social and behavioural science include commercial and business administration, mass communication and documentation and home economics; engineering includes architecture and town planning, trade craft and industrial programmes, transport and communications.

FR-> Les sciences exactes et naturelles comprennent les mathématiques et l'informatique. En 1980, les sciences sociales et sciences du comportement comprennent la formation au commerce et à l'administration des entreprises, l'information et la documentation et l'enseignement ménager; les sciences de l'ingénieur incluent l'architecture et l'urbanisme, les métiers de la production industrielle et les transports et télécommunications.

ESP> Las ciencias naturales comprenden las matemáticas y la informática. En 1980, las ciencias sociales y del comportamiento comprenden la enseñanza comercial y de administración de empresas, la documentación y comunicación social y la economía doméstica; la ingeniería y tecnología incluyen la arquitectura y el urbanismo, las artes y oficios industriales y los transportes y comunicaciones.

Ghana:

E--> Data refer to universities only. Natural science includes mathematics and computer science. Data for 1980 refer to 1981. In 1984, social and behavioural science include law, humanities, religion and theology.

FR-> Les données se réfèrent aux universités seulement. Les sciences exactes et naturelles incluent les mathématiques et l'informatique. Les données de 1980 se réfèrent à 1981. En 1984, les sciences sociales et sciences du comportement incluent le droit les lettres, religion et théologie.

ESP> Los datos se refieren a las universidades solamente. Las ciencias naturales comprenden las matemáticas y la informática. Los datos de 1980 se refieren a 1981. En 1984, las ciencias sociales y del comportamiento incluyen el derecho, las humanidades, religión y teología.

Guinea:

E--> In 1980, education science and teacher training include humanities, religion and theology, social and behavioural science and mathematics and computer science; commercial and business administration includes law; engineering includes architecture and town planning and trade, craft and industrial programmes. In 1983, natural science includes mathematics and computer science and social and behavioural sciences. Engineering includes architecture and town planning. In 1984, social and behavioural sciences include humanities, religion and theology; natural science includes mathematics and computer science.

FR-> En 1980, les sciences de l'éducation et la formation d'enseignants incluent les lettres, la religion et la théologie, les sciences sociales et sciences du comportement et les mathématiques et l'informatique; la formation au commerce et à l'administration des entreprises inclut le droit; les sciences de l'ingénieur incluent l'architecture et l'urbanisme et les métiers de la production industrielle. En 1983, les sciences exactes et naturelles incluent les mathématiques et l'informatique et les sciences sociales et sciences du comportement; les sciences de l'ingénieur incluent l'architecture et l'urbanisme. En 1984, les sciences sociales et sciences du comportement incluent les lettres, la religion et la théologie; les sciences exactes et naturelles incluent les mathématiques et l'informatique.

ESP> En 1980, las ciencias de la educación y formación de personal docente incluyen las humanidades, la religión y la teología, las ciencias sociales y del comportamiento y las matemáticas y la informática; la enseñanza comercial y de administración de empresas incluye el derecho; la ingeniería y tecnología incluyen la arquitectura y urbanismo y las artes y oficios industriales. En 1983, las ciencias naturales incluyen las matemáticas e informática y las ciencias sociales y del comportamiento; la ingeniería y tecnología incluyen la arquitectura y urbanismo. En 1984, las ciencias sociales y del comportamiento incluyen las humanidades,

Guinea: (Cont):
religión y la teología; las ciencias naturales incluyen las matemáticas e informática.

Kenya:

E--> In 1980, data refer to universities and equivalent degree-granting institutions. In 1983, education science and teacher training includes humanities, religion and theology and 'Other and not specified' include adult education.

FR-> En 1980, les données se réfèrent aux universités et aux établissements conférant des grades équivalents. En 1983, les sciences de l'éducation et la formation d'enseignants incluent les lettres, la religion et la théologie et la rubrique 'Autres programmes' inclut l'éducation des adultes.

ESP> En 1980, los datos se refieren a las universidades y establecimientos que otorguen grados equivalentes. En 1983, las ciencias de la educación y formación de personal docente incluyen las humanidades, la religión y la teología, y la rúbrica 'otros programas' incluye la educación de adultos.

Malawi:

E--> Data refer to the university only.

FR-> Les données se réfèrent à l'université seulement.

ESP> Los datos se refieren a la universidad solamente.

Mali:

E--> In 1980, data exclude students who were suspended from courses.

FR-> En 1980, les données excluent les étudiants suspendus des cours.

ESP> En 1980, los datos excluyen los estudiantes suspendidos de los cursos.

Morocco:

E--> Data refer to universities only. In 1980 and 1983, law includes social and behavioural science and commercial and business administration. In 1983, data exclude post-graduate students. In 1984, natural sciences includes mathematics and computer science.

FR-> Les données se réfèrent aux universités seulement. En 1980 et 1983, le droit comprend les sciences sociales et sciences du comportement et la formation au commerce et à l'administration des entreprises. En 1983, les données excluent les étudiants du niveau universitaire supérieur. En 1984, les sciences exactes et naturelles incluent les mathématiques et l'informatique.

ESP> Los datos se refieren a las universidades solamente. En 1980 y 1983, el derecho comprende las ciencias sociales y del comportamiento y la enseñanza comercial y de administración de empresas. En 1983, los datos excluyen los estudiantes del nivel postuniversitario. En 1984, las ciencias naturales incluyen las matemáticas y la informática.

Mozambique:

E--> In 1980, data on female enrolment refer to full-time national students only. Data for 1984 refer to 1985.

FR-> En 1980, les données relatives aux étudiantes se réfèrent aux effectifs nationaux à plein temps seulement. Les données de 1984 se réfèrent à 1985.

ESP> En 1980, los datos relativos a las estudiantes se refieren a los efectivos nacionales de jornada completa solamente. Los datos de 1984 se refieren a 1985.

Nigeria:

E--> Data refer to universities only.

FR-> Les données se réfèrent aux universités seulement.

ESP> Los datos se refieren a las universidades solamente.

Rwanda:

E--> In 1983, social and behavioural science include commercial and business administration. Natural sciences includes mathematics and computer sciences.

FR-> En 1983, les sciences sociales et sciences du comportement incluent la formation au commerce et à l'administration des entreprises. Les sciences exactes et naturelles incluent les mathématiques et l'informatique.

ESP> En 1983, las ciencias sociales y del comportamiento incluyen la enseñanza comercial y del administración de empresas. Las ciencias naturales incluyen las matemáticas e informática.

St. Helena:

E--> Data for 1983 refer to 1981.

FR-> Les données de 1983 se réfèrent à 1981.

ESP> Los datos de 1983 se refieren a 1981.

Sudan:

E--> Revised data and refer to 1981.

FR-> Les données révisées se réfèrent à 1981.

ESP> Los datos revisados se refieren a 1981.

Swaziland:

E--> In 1982, data refer to universities and equivalent degree-granting institutions and teacher training colleges only. Natural science includes mathematics and computer science.

FR-> En 1982, les données se réfèrent aux universités et établissements conférant des grades equivalents, et aux collèges d'enseignement normal. Les sciences exactes et naturelles comprennent les mathématiques et l'informatique.

ESP> En 1982, los datos se refieren a las universidades y establecimientos que otorguen grados equivalentes, y a los colegios de

Swaziland: (Cont):
enseñanza normal. Las ciencas naturales comprenden las matemáticas y la informática.

Togo:

E--> In 1980 and 1984, natural science includes mathematics and computer science. In 1980, humanities, religion and theology include fine and applied arts. In 1980, social and behavioural science includes commercial and business administration and in 1983 and 1984 also mass communication and documentation. In 1983 and 1984, education science and teacher training includes humanities, religion and theology and fine and applied arts. In 1984, data refer to the university only.

FR-> En 1980 et 1984, les sciences exactes et naturelles incluent les mathématiques et l'informatique. En 1980, les lettres, la religion et la théologie incluent les beaux-arts et les arts appliqués. En 1980, les sciences sociales et sciences du comportement incluent la formation au commerce et à l'administration des entreprises et en 1983 et 1984 également l'information et la documentation. En 1983 et 1984 les sciences de l'éducation et la formation d'enseignants incluent les lettres, la religion et la théologie et les beaux-arts et arts appliqués. En 1984, les données se réfèrent à l'université seulement.

ESP> En 1980 y 1984, las ciencias naturales incluyen las matemáticas y la informática. En 1980, las humanidades, la religión y la teología incluyen las bellas artes y artes aplicadas. En 1980 las ciencias sociales y del comportamiento incluyen la enseñanza comercial y de administración de empresas y en 1983 y 1984 igualmente la documentación y comunicación social. En 1983 et 1984 las ciencias de la educación y formación de personal docente incluyen las humanidades, la religión y la teología y las bellas artes y artes aplicadas. En 1984, los datos se refieren a la universidad solamente.

Zambia:

E--> In 1983, social and behavioural science include humanities, religion and theology and mass communication and documentation. In 1984, data refer only to other education in non-university institutions.

FR-> En 1983, les sciences sociales et sciences du comportement incluent les lettres, religion et théologie et l'information et la documentation. En 1984, les données se réfèrent seulement à l'autre enseignement dans les institutions non-universitaires.

ESP> En 1983, las ciencias de la educación y formación de personal docente incluyen las humanidades, religión y teología y la documentación y comunicación social. En 1984, los datos se refieren solamente a la otra enseñanza en las instituciones no-universitarias.

Zimbabwe:

E--> Law includes commercial and business administration. Natural science includes mathematics and computer science. In 1983, data refer to universities and equivalent degree-granting institutions and to teacher training colleges. In 1984, data refer to universities and equivalent degree-granting institutions only; humanities, religion and theology include fine and applied arts.

FR-> Le droit inclut la formation au commerce et à l'administration des entreprises. Les sciences exactes et naturelles incluent les mathématiques et l'informatique. En 1983, les données se réfèrent aux universités et établissements conférant des grades équivalents et aux écoles normales. En 1984, les données se réfèrent aux universités et établissements conférant des grades équivalents seulement; les lettres, la religion et la théologie incluent les beaux-arts et les arts appliqués.

ESP> El derecho incluye la enseñanza comercial y de administración de empresas. Las ciencias naturales incluyen las matemáticas e informática. En 1983, los datos se refieren a las universidades y establecimientos que otorguen grados equivalentes y a las escuelas normales. En 1984, los datos se refieren a las universidades y establecimientos que otorguen grados equivalentes solamente; las humanidades, religión y teología incluyen las bellas artes y artes aplicadas.

AMERICA, NORTH:

Barbados:

E--> Natural science includes mathematics and computer science. In 1983 and 1984, social and behavioural science includes commercial and business administration.

FR-> Les sciences exactes et naturelles incluent les mathématiques et l'informatique. En 1983 et 1984, les sciences sociales et sciences du comportement incluent la formation au commerce et à l'administration des entreprises.

ESP> Las ciencias naturales incluyen las matemáticas e informática. En 1983 y 1984, las ciencias sociales y del comportamiento incluyen la enseñanza comercial y de administración de empresas.

Bermuda:

E--> In 1982, data include adult education; humanities, religion and theology include fine and applied arts, social and behavioural science, natural science and mathematics and computer science.

FR-> En 1982, les données incluent l'éducation des adultes; les lettres, la religion et la théologie incluent les beaux arts et les arts appliqués, les sciences sociales et sciences du comportement, les sciences exactes et naturelles, les mathématiques et l'informatique.

ESP> En 1982, los datos incluyen la educación de los adultos; las humanidades, la religión y la teología incluyen las bellas artes y artes aplicadas, las ciencias sociales y del comportamiento, las ciencias naturales y las matemáticas e informática.

Canada:

E--> In 1980, data on enrolment at 'other third level institutions' refer

Canada: (Cont):
to full-time students only.

FR–> En 1980, les données relatives aux 'autres établissements du troisième degré' se réfèrent aux étudiants à plein temps seulement.

ESP> En 1980, los datos relativos a los 'otros establecimientos de tercer grado' se refieren a los estudiantes de jornada completa solamente.

Costa Rica:

E--> Data refer to universities only.

FR–> Les données se réfèrent aux universités seulement.

ESP> Los datos se refieren a las universidades solamente.

Cuba:

E--> In 1980, engineering includes trade, craft and industrial programmes.

FR–> En 1980, les sciences de l'ingénieur incluent les métiers de la production industrielle.

ESP> En 1980, la ingeniería y tecnología incluyen las artes y oficios industriales.

El Salvador:

E--> In 1980, data exclude figures for the National University which was closed in 1979.

FR–> En 1980 les données excluent les chiffres de l'université nationale qui était fermée depuis 1979.

ESP> En 1980, los datos excluyen las cifras de la universidad nacional que cerró en 1979.

Grenada:

E--> Data exclude Grenada teachers' college. Engineering includes architecture and town planning.

FR–> Les données excluent 'Grenada teachers' college'. Les sciences de l'ingénieur incluent l'architecture et l'urbanisme.

ESP> Los datos excluyen 'Grenada teachers' college'. La ingeniería incluyen la arquitectura y urbanismo.

Haiti:

E--> Natural science includes mathematics and computer science. Law includes economics. In 1980, education science and teacher-training includes humanities, religion and theology.

FR–> Les sciences exactes et naturelles incluent les mathématiques et l'informatique. Le droit inclut les sciences économiques. En 1980, les sciences de l'éducation et la formation d'enseignants comprennent les lettres, la religion et la théologie.

ESP> Las ciencias naturales incluyen las matemáticas y la informática. El derecho incluye las ciencias económicas. En 1980, las ciencias de la educación y formación de personal docente comprenden las humanidades, la religión y la teología.

Mexico:

E--> Data refer to universities and equivalent degree-granting institutions only.

FR–> Les données se réfèrent aux universités et établissements conférant des grades équivalents seulement.

ESP> Los datos se refieren a las universidades y establecimientos que otorguen grados equivalentes solamente. Nicaragua:

E--> Data for 1983 and 1984 refer respectively to 1984 and 1985. In 1984, commercial and business administration includes social and behavioural science, mass communication and documentation and home economics.

FR–> Les données de 1983 et 1984 se réfèrent respectivement à 1984 et 1985. En 1984, la formation au commerce et à l'administration des entreprises incluent les sciences sociales et sciences du comportement, l'information et documentation et l'enseignement ménager.

ESP> Los datos de 1983 y 1984 se refieren respectivamente a 1984 y 1985. En 1984, la enseñanza comercial y de administración de empresas incluye las ciencias sociales y del comportamiento, la documentación y comunicación social y la economía doméstica.

Panama:

E--> In 1980 data exclude regional centers.

FR–> En 1980, les données excluent les centres régionaux.

ESP> En 1980, los datos excluyen los centros regionales.

Trinidad and Tobago:

E--> Natural science includes mathematics and computer science.

FR–> Les sciences exactes et naturelles incluent les mathématiques et l'informatique.

ESP> Las ciencas naturales incluyen las matemáticas y la informática.

AMERICA, SOUTH:

Argentina:

E--> Data for 1983 refer to 1981 and to universities and equivalent degree-granting institutions only.

FR–> Les données de 1983 se réfèrent à 1981 et aux universités et établissements conférant des grades équivalents seulement.

ESP> Los datos de 1983 se refieren a 1981 y a las universidades y establecimientos que otorguen grados equivalentes solamente.

Bolivia:

E--> Data refer to universities and equivalent degree-granting institutions only and exclude 'la universidad católica boliviana'.

FR–> Les données se réfèrent aux universités et établissements conférant des grades équivalents seulement et excluent 'la universidad católica boliviana'.

ESP> Los datos se refieren a las universidades y establecimientos que

Bolivia: (Cont):
otorguen grados equivalentes solamente y excluyen la universidad católic boliviana.

Brazil:

E--> In 1980, data on education science and teacher training includ part of natural science, and of humanities, religion and theology.

FR–> En 1980, les sciences de l'éducation et la formatio d'enseignants incluent une partie des sciences naturelles et des lettre religion et théologie.

ESP> En 1980, las ciencias de la educación y formación de person docente incluyen una parte de las ciencias naturales y de las humanidade religión y teología.

Colombia:

E--> Natural science includes mathematics and computer scienc Data for 1983 and 1984 refer respectively to 1984 and 1985. In 198 architecture and town planning includes fine and applied arts; social an behavioural science include mass communication and documentatio Commercial and business administration includes home economics ar service trades. Engineering includes trade, craft and industrial programm and transport and communications. In 1984 and 1985, law includes soci and behavioural science. Commercial and business administration include mass communication and documentation, home economics and servic trades; engineering includes architecture and town planning, trade, cra and industrial programmes, transport and communications.

FR–> Les sciences exactes et naturelles comprennent l mathématiques et l'informatique. Les données de 1983 et 1984 référent à 1984 et 1985 respectivement. En 1980, l'architecture l'urbanisme incluent les beaux arts et arts appliqués; les sciences social et sciences du comportement incluent l'information et la documentation. formation au commerce et à l'administration des entreprises compre l'enseignement ménager et la formation pour le secteur tertiaire. L sciences de l'ingénieur comprennent les métiers de la producti industrielle et les transports et télécommunications. En 1984 et 1985, droit inclut les sciences sociales et sciences du comportement; formation au commerce et à l'administration des entreprises inc l'information et la documentation, l'enseignement ménager et la formati pour le secteur tertiaire; les sciences de l'ingénieur incluent l'architectu et l'urbanisme, les métiers de la production industrielle et les transports télécommunications.

ESP> Las ciencias naturales comprenden las matemáticas y informática. Los datos de 1983 y 1984 se refieren a 1984 y 19 respectivamente. En 1980, la arquitectura y urbanismo incluyen las bell artes y artes aplicadas; las ciencias sociales y del comportamiento incluy la documentación y comunicación social. La enseñanza comercial y administración de empresas comprenden la economía doméstica y formación para el sector de los servicios. La ingeniería y la tecnolog comprenden las artes y oficios industriales y los transportes comunicaciones. En 1984 y 1985 el derecho incluye las ciencias socia y del comportamiento; la enseñanza comercial y de administración empresas incluye la documentación y comunicación social, la econon doméstica y la formación para el sector de los servicios; la ingenie incluye la arquitectura y urbanismo, las artes y oficios industriales y transportes y comunicación.

Ecuador:

E--> In 1980, data on female students refer to universities a equivalent degree-granting institutions only.

FR–> En 1980, les données relatives aux étudiantes se réfèrent a universités et établissements conférant des grades équivale seulement.

ESP> En 1980, los datos relativos a las estudiantes se refieren a universidades y establecimientos que otorguen grados equivalen solamente.

Guyana:

E--> In 1980, data refer to the University of Guyana only.

FR–> En 1980, les données se réfèrent à l'université de la Guya seulement.

ESP> En 1980, los datos se refieren a la universidad de la Guya solamente.

Peru:

E--> In 1982, data refer to universities only.

FR–> En 1982, les données se réfèrent aux universités seulement

ESP> En 1982, los datos se refieren a las universidades solament

Surinam:

E--> Social and behavioural science include law.

FR–> Les sciences sociales et sciences du comportement incluen droit.

ESP> Las ciencias sociales y del comportamiento incluyen derecho.

Uruguay:

E--> Data for 1983 and 1984 refer respectively to 1984 a 1985.

FR–> Les données de 1983 et 1984 se réfèrent respectivemen 1984 et 1985.

ESP> Los datos de 1983 y 1984 se refieren respectivamente a 19 y 1985.

ASIA:

Bahrain:

E--> Engineering includes trade, craft and industrial programmes

Bahrain: (Cont):

FR-> Les sciences de l'ingénieur incluent les métiers de la production industrielle.

ESP> La ingeniería y tecnología incluyen las artes y oficios industriales.

Bangladesh:

E--> Natural science includes home economics.

FR-> Les sciences exactes et naturelles incluent l'enseignement ménager.

ESP> Las ciencias naturales incluyen la economía doméstica.

Bhutan:

E--> In 1983, commercial and business administration includes social and behavioural science.

FR-> En 1983, la formation au commerce et à l'administration des entreprises inclut les sciences sociales et sciences du comportement.

ESP> En 1983, la enseñanza comercial y de administración de empresas incluye las ciencias sociales y del comportamiento.

China:

E--> Data refer to full-time students only. Commercial and business administration includes social and behavioural science.

FR-> Les données se réfèrent aux étudiants à plein temps seulement. La formation au commerce et à l'administration des entreprises inclut les sciences sociales et sciences du comportement.

ESP> Los datos se refieren a los estudiantes de jornada completa solamente. La enseñanza comercial y de administración de empresas incluye las ciencias sociales y del comportamiento.

Democratic Yemen:

E--> In 1980, education science and teacher training includes humanities, religion and theology Data for 1983 refer to 1981, and engineering includes architecture and town planning.

FR-> En 1980, les sciences de l'éducation et la formation d'enseignants comprennent les lettres, la religion et la théologie. Les données de 1983 se réfèrent à 1981, et les sciences de l'ingénieur incluent l'architecture et l'urbanisme.

ESP> En 1980, las ciencias de la educación y formación de personal docente comprenden las humanidades, religión y teología. Los datos de 1983 se refieren a 1981, y la ingeniería y tecnología incluyen la arquitectura y urbanismo.

Hong Kong:

E--> In 1980, data refer to universities and to Hong Kong Polytechnic.

FR-> En 1980, les données se réfèrent aux universités et à 'Hong Kong Polytechnic'.

ESP> En 1980, los datos se refieren a las universidades y a 'Hong Kong Polytechnic'.

India:

E--> Data refer to 1979. Social and behavioural science includes commercial and business administration. Natural science includes mathematics and computer science and home economics. Engineering includes architecture and town planning, trade, craft and industrial programmes, transport and communications.

FR-> Les données se réfèrent à 1979. Les sciences sociales et sciences du comportement comprennent la formation au commerce et à l'administration des entreprises. Les sciences exactes et naturelles comprennent les mathématiques et l'informatique et l'enseignement ménager. Les sciences de l'ingénieur comprennent l'architecture et l'urbanisme, les métiers de la production industrielle et les transports et télécommunications.

ESP> Los datos se refieren al año 1979. Las ciencias sociales y del comportamiento comprenden la enseñanza comercial y de administración de empresas. Las ciencias naturales comprenden las matemáticas y la informática y la economía doméstica. La ingeniería y tecnología comprenden la arquitectura y el urbanismo, las artes y oficios industriales además de los transportes y comunicaciones.

Iran, Islamic Republic of:

E--> In 1984, data on female students exclude teacher training colleges.

FR-> En 1984, les données relatives aux étudiantes excluent les collèges d'enseignement normal.

ESP> En 1984, los datos relativos a las estudiantes excluyen los colegios del enseñanza normal.

Israel:

E--> Data exclude open university. Education science and teacher training includes humanities, religion and theology, fine and applied arts. Social and behavioural science include commercial and business administration, mass communication and documentation, home economics and service trades. Engineering includes architecture and town planning, trade, craft and industrial programmes, transport and communications. In 1980, natural science includes mathematics and computer science.

FR-> Les données excluent 'Open University'. Les sciences de l'éducation et la formation d'enseignants comprennent les lettres, la religion et la théologie, les beaux-arts et les arts appliqués. Les sciences sociales et sciences du comportement comprennent la formation au commerce et à l'administration des entreprises, l'information et la documentation, l'enseignement ménager et la formation pour le secteur tertiaire. Les sciences de l'ingénieur comprennent l'architecture et l'urbanisme, les métiers de la production industrielle et les transports et télécommunications. En 1980, les sciences exactes et naturelles

Israel: (Cont):

comprennent les mathématiques et l'informatique.

ESP> Los datos excluyen 'open university'. Las ciencias de la educación y formación de personal docente comprenden las humanidades, la religión y la teología, las bellas artes y las artes aplicadas. Las ciencias sociales y del comportamiento comprenden la enseñanza comercial y de administración de empresas, la documentación y comunicación social, la economía doméstica y la formación para el sector de los servicios. La ingeniería y tecnología comprenden la arquitectura y el urbanismo, las artes y oficios industriales además de los transportes y comunicaciones. En 1980, las ciencias naturales comprenden las matemáticas y la informática.

Japan:

E--> Including correspondence courses. Humanities, religion and theology include mass communication and documentation. Social and behavioural science includes law, commercial and business administration. Engineering includes architecture and town planning, trade, craft and industrial programmes.

FR-> Y compris les cours par correspondance. Les lettres, la religion et la théologie comprennent l'information et la documentation. Les sciences sociales et sciences du comportement comprennent le droit et la formation au commerce et à l'administration des entreprises. Les sciences de l'ingénieur comprennent l'architecture et l'urbanisme et les métiers de la production industrielle.

ESP> Incluídos los cursos por correspondencia. Las humanidades, la religión y la teología comprenden la documentación y comunicación social. Las ciencias sociales y del comportamiento comprenden el derecho y la enseñanza comercial y de administración de empresas. La ingeniería y tecnología comprenden la arquitectura y el urbanismo además de las artes y oficios industriales.

Jordan:

E--> In 1983, commercial and business administration includes economics and mass communication and documentation; natural science includes mathematics and computer science and engineering includes architecture and town planning. Humanities, religion and theology include social and behavioural science.

FR-> En 1983, la formation au commerce et à l'administration des entreprises inclut les sciences économiques et l'information et la documentation. Les sciences exactes et naturelles incluent les mathématiques et l'informatique et les sciences de l'ingénieur incluent l'architecture et l'urbanisme; les lettres, la religion et la théologie incluent les sciences sociales et sciences du comportement.

ESP> En 1983, la enseñanza comercial y de administración de empresas incluye las ciencias ecońomicas y la documentación y comunicación social. Las ciencias naturales incluyen las matemáticas e informática, la ingeniería incluye la arquitectura y el urbanismo; las humanidades, la religión y la teología incluyen las ciencias sociales y del comportamiento.

Korea, Republic of:

E--> In 1980, social and behavioural science include commercial and business administration, mass communication and documentation, home economics and service trades; natural science includes mathematics and computer science; engineering includes architecture and town planning, trade, craft and industrial programmes, transport and communications.

FR-> En 1980, les sciences sociales et sciences du comportement incluent la formation au commerce et à l'administration des entreprises, l'information et la documentation, l'enseignement ménager et la formation pour le secteur tertiaire; les sciences exactes et naturelles incluent les mathématiques et l'informatique; les sciences de l'ingénieur comprennent l'architecture et l'urbanisme, les métiers de la production industrielle et les transports et télécommunications.

ESP> En 1980, las ciencias sociales y del comportamiento comprenden la enseñanza comercial y de administración de empresas, la documentación y comunicación social, la econom
ia doméstica y la formación para el sector de los servicios; las ciencias naturales incluyen las matemáticas y la informática; la ingeniería y tecnología comprenden la arquitectura y el urbanismo, las artes y oficios industriales además de los transportes y comunicaciones.

Kuwait:

E--> In 1984, engineering includes trade, craft and industrial programmes.

FR-> En 1984, les sciences de l'ingénieur comprennent l'architecture et l'urbanisme et les métiers de la production industrielle.

ESP> En 1984, la ingeniería y tecnología comprenden la arquitectura y el urbanismo.

Mongolia:

E--> Data for 1980 refer to 1981.

FR-> Les données de 1980 se réfèrent à 1981.

ESP> Los datos de 1980 se refieren a 1981.

Nepal:

E--> Humanities, religion and theology include social and behavioural science. Natural science includes mathematics and computer science. In 1983, data refer to public universities only and humanities, religion and theology include fine and applied arts.

FR-> Les lettres, religion et théologie comprennent les sciences sociales et sciences du comportement. Les sciences exactes et naturelles comprennent les mathématiques et l'informatique. En 1983 les données se réfèrent aux universités publiques seulement et les lettres, la

Nepal: (Cont):
religion et la théologie incluent les beaux-arts et arts appliqués.

ESP> Las humanidades, la religión y la teología comprenden las ciencias sociales y del comportamiento. Las ciencias naturales comprenden las matemáticas y la informática. En 1983, los datos se refieren a las universidades públicas solamente y las humanidades, la religión y la teología incluyen las bellas artes y artes aplicadas.

Pakistan:

E--> Data refer to 1979. Engineering includes architecture and town planning.

FR-> Les données se réfèrent à 1979. Les sciences de l'ingénieur incluent l'architecture et l'urbanisme.

ESP> Los datos se refieren a 1979. La ingeniería incluye la arquitectura y el urbanismo.

Philippines:

E--> Data for 1983 refer to 1981.

FR-> Les données de 1983 se réfèrent à 1981.

ESP> Los datos de 1983 se refieren a 1981.

Qatar:

E--> Natural science includes mathematics and computer science. In 1980 and 1983, education science and teacher training includes home economics. In 1984, humanities, religion and theology include social and behavioural science and mass communication and information.

FR-> Les sciences exactes et naturelles incluent les mathématiques et l'informatique. En 1980 et 1983, les sciences de l'éducation et la formation d'enseignants incluent l'enseignement ménager. En 1984, les lettres, religion et théologie incluent les sciences sociales et sciences du comportement et l'information et documentation.

ESP> Las ciencias naturales incluyen las matemáticas y informática. En 1980 y 1983, las ciencias de la educación y formación de personal docente incluyen la enseñanza doméstica. En 1984, las humanidades, la religión y la teología incluyen las ciencias sociales y del comportamiento y la documentación y comunicación social.

Saudi Arabia:

E--> Social and behavioural science include commercial and business administration. Natural science includes mathematics and computer science. Engineering includes architecture and town planning. The figures shown under 'other and not specified' refer mainly to students enrolled either in the first year or in the preparatory year (general studies). In 1983, humanities, religion and theology include law and home economics.

FR-> Les sciences sociales et sciences du comportement incluent la formation au commerce et à l'administration des entreprises. Les sciences exactes et naturelles incluent les mathématiques et l'informatique. Les sciences de l'ingénieur incluent l'architecture et l'urbanisme. Les chiffres montrés sous la rubrique 'autres programmes' se réfèrent pour la plupart aux étudiants inscrits soit en première année soit en année préparatoire (études générales). En 1983, les lettres, religion et théologie incluent le droit et l'enseignement ménager.

ESP> Las ciencias sociales y del comportamiento incluyen la enseñanza comercial y de administración de empresas. Las ciencias naturales incluyen las matemáticas y la informática. La ingeniería y tecnología incluyen la arquitectura y urbanismo. Las cifras que figuran bajo la rúbrica 'otros programas' se refieren en su mayor parte, a los estudiantes inscritos en el primer año de estudios o en el año preparatorio (estudios generales). En 1983, las bellas artes y artes aplicadas incluyen el derecho y la economía doméstica.

Singapore:

E--> Humanities, religion and theology include social and behavioural science. In 1980, natural science includes mathematics and computer science.

FR-> Les lettres, la religion et la théologie comprennent les sciences sociales et sciences du comportement. En 1980, les sciences exactes et naturelles comprennent les mathématiques et l'informatique.

ESP> Las humanidades, la religión y la teología comprenden las ciencias sociales y del comportamiento. En 1980, las ciencias naturales comprenden las matemáticas y la informática.

Sri Lanka:

E--> Data include Open University and natural science includes mathematics and computer science.

FR-> Les données incluent 'Open University' et les sciences exactes et naturelles incluent les mathématiques et l'informatique.

ESP> Los datos incluyen 'Open university' y las ciencias naturales incluyen las matemáticas y la informática.

Turkey:

E--> In 1983 and 1984, data include open university.

FR-> En 1983 et 1984, les données incluent 'open university'.

ESP> En 1983 y 1984, los datos incluyen 'open university'.

Viet-Nam:

E--> Including correspondence courses.

FR-> Y compris les cours par correspondance.

ESP> Incluídos los cursos por corespondencia.

EUROPE:

Albania:

E--> Including evening and correspondence courses. Natural science includes mathematics and computer science.

FR-> Y compris les cours du soir et par correspondance. Les sciences exactes et naturelles incluent les mathématiques et l'informatique.

ESP> Incluídos los cursos nocturnos y por correspondencia. Las ciencias naturales incluyen las matemáticas e informática.

Austria:

E--> In 1983 and 1984, data include multiple counting of studen enrolled in more than one field of study.

FR-> En 1983 et 1984, les données incluent les étudiants inscr dans plusieurs domaines d'études.

ESP> En 1983 y 1984, los datos incluyen los estudiantes inscrit en diversos sectores de estudios.

Belgium:

E--> In 1980 and 1983, data refer to universities and equivale degree-granting institutions only. In 1983 and 1984, natural scien includes mathematics and computer science.

FR-> En 1980 et 1983, les données se réfèrent aux universités établissements conférant des grades équivalents seulement. En 1983 1984, les sciences exactes et naturelles incluent les mathématiques l'informatique.

ESP> En 1980 y 1983, los datos se refieren a las universidades establecimientos que otorguen grados equivalentes solamente. En 198 1984, las ciencias naturales incluyen las matemáticas e informática.

Bulgaria:

E--> Including evening and correspondence courses.

FR-> Y compris les cours du soir et par correspondance.

ESP> Incluídos los cursos nocturnos y por correspondencia.

France:

E--> In 1980, universities only; the heading 'humanities, religion a theology' refers to 'lettres et sciences humaines' which include the major of the social sciences (except economics); the natural science categ refers to sciences which also include certain fields of engineering. T heading 'other and not specified' refers to the university institutes technology (I.U.T.), and in 1982, includes service trades.

FR-> En 1980, universités seulement. La rubrique 'lettres, religion théologie' comprend les lettres et sciences humaines qui incluent majorité des sciences sociales, excepté les sciences économiques. sciences exactes et naturelles comprennent également certai disciplines des sciences de l'ingénieur. La rubrique 'autres programmes' réfère aux instituts universitaires de technologie (I.U.T.) et en 1982, inc la formation pour le secteur tertiaire.

ESP> En 1980, universidades solamente. El epigrafe 'humanidad religión y teología' se refiere al grupo de humanidades y cienc humanas, que comprenden las disciplinas dependientes de las cienc sociales, salvo las ciencias económicas. La rúbrica 'ciencias natural incluye algunos estudios relativos a la ingeniería. La rúbrica 'ot programas' se refiere a los institutos universitarios de tecnología (I.U. y en 1982, incluye la formación para el sector de los servicios.

German Democratic Republic:

E--> Including evening and correspondence courses.

FR-> Y compris les cours du soir et par correspondance.

ESP> Incluídos los cursos nocturnos y por correspondencia.

Greece:

E--> Data for 1983 refer to 1981.

FR-> Les données de 1983 se réfèrent à 1981.

ESP> Los datos de 1983 se refieren a 1981.

Holy See:

E--> Data refer to students enrolled in higher institutions under authority of the Holy See.

FR-> Les données se réfèrent aux étudiants dans les institutions troisième degré sous l'autorité du Saint-Siège.

ESP> Los datos se refieren a los estudiantes en los institutos del te grado bajo la autoridad del Santa Sede.

Hungary:

E--> Including evening and correspondence courses.

FR-> Y compris les cours du soir et par corespondance.

ESP> Incluídos los cursos nocturnos y por correspondencia.

Luxembourg:

E--> Data refer only to students enrolled in institutions locate Luxembourg. At university level, the majority of the students pursue t studies in the following countries: Austria, Belgium, France, Fed Republic of Germany and Switzerland. Natural science inclu mathematics and computer science. In 1983, social and behavio science includes commercial and business administration.

FR-> Les données se réfèrent seulement aux étudiants inscrits dans institutions du Luxembourg. La plus grande partie des étudi Luxembourgeois poursuivent leurs études universitaires dans les univers des pays suivants: Autriche, Belgique, France, République fédé d'Allemagne et Suisse. Les sciences exactes et naturelles comprenn les mathématiques et l'informatique. En 1983, les sciences sociale sciences du comportement incluent la formation au commerce e l'administration des entreprises.

ESP> Los datos se refieren solamente a los estudiantes matriculado las instituciones en Luxemburgo. La mayoría de los estudiantes Luxemburgo cursan sus estudios universitarios en las universidades los países siguientes: Austria, Bélgica, Francia, República Federal Alemania y Suiza. Las ciencias naturales comprenden las matemáticas informática. En 1983, las ciencias sociales y del comportamiento inclu la documentación y comunicación social.

Netherlands:

E--> In 1980, engineering includes trade, craft and indus programmes. In 1984, data refer to universities and equivalent deg granting institutions.

FR-> En 1980 les sciences de l'ingénieur comprennent les métier la production industrielle. En 1984, les données se réfèrent aux univer

Netherlands: (Cont):
et établissements conférant des grades équivalents seulement.
ESP> En 1980 la ingeniería y tecnología comprenden las artes y oficios industriales. En 1984, los datos se refieren a las universidades y establecimientos que otorguen grados equivalentes.
Poland:
E--> Including evening and correspondence courses.
FR-> Y compris les cours du soir et par correspondance.
ESP> Incluídos los cursos nocturnos y por correspondencia.
Portugal:
E--> In 1982, social and behavioural science include commercial and business administration and mass communication and documentation; natural science includes mathematics and computer science; engineering includes architecture and town planning and trade, craft and industrial programmes.
FR-> En 1982, les sciences sociales et sciences du comportment incluent la formation au commerce et à l'administration des entreprises et l'information et documentation; les sciences exactes et naturelles incluent les mathématiques et l'informatique; les sciences de l'ingénieur incluent l'architecture et l'urbanisme et les métiers de la production industrielle.
ESP> En 1982, las ciencias sociales y del comportamiento incluyen la enseñanza comercial y de administración de empresas y la documentación y comunicación social; las ciencias naturales incluyen las matemáticas e informática; la ingeniería y tecnología incluyen la arquitectura y urbanismo y las artes y oficios industriales.
Romania:
E--> Including evening and correspondence courses. Education science and teacher training includes humanities, religion and theology. In 1983 and 1984, social and behavioural science include commercial and business administration, mass communication and documentation, home economics and service trades; natural science includes mathematics and computer science and engineering includes architecture and town planning and trade, craft and industrial programmes.
FR-> Y compris les cours du soir et par correspondance. Les sciences de l'éducation et la formation d'enseignants comprennent les lettres, la religion et la théologie. En 1983 et 1984, les sciences sociales et sciences du comportement incluent la formation au commerce et à l'administration des entreprises, l'information et la documentation, l'enseignement ménager et la formation pour le secteur tertiaire; les sciences exactes et naturelles incluent les mathématiques et l'informatique et les sciences de l'ingénieur incluent l'architecture et l'urbanisme et les métiers de la production industrielle.
ESP> Incluídos los cursos nocturnos y por corespondencia. Las ciencias de la educación y formación de personal docente comprenden las humanidades, la religión y la teología. En 1983 y 1984, las ciencias sociales y del comportamiento incluyen la enseñanza comercial y de administración de empresas, la documentación y comunicación social, la economía doméstica y la formación para el sector de los servicios; las ciencias naturales incluyen las matemáticas e informática y la ingeniería y tecnología incluyen la arquitectura y urbanismo y las artes y oficios industriales.
Spain:
E--> Including 'Universidad de educación a distancia'.
FR-> Y compris la 'Universidad de educación a distancia'.
ESP> Incluída la Universidad de educación a distancia.
Sweden:
E--> In 1980, data include multiple counting of students enrolled in more than one field of study.
FR-> En 1980, les données incluent les étudiants inscrits dans plusieurs domaines d'études.
ESP> En 1980, los datos incluyen los estudiantes inscritos en diversos sectores de estudios.
United Kingdom:
E--> Data include open university and in 1980 include multiple counting of students enrolled in more than one field of study. In 1983 data refer to 1981.
FR-> Les données comprennent l'*Open University* et en 1980 incluent également les étudiants inscrits dans plusieurs domaines d'études. En 1983 les données se réfèrent à 1981.
ESP> Los datos incluyen la 'Open university' y en 1980 incluyen igualmente los estudiantes inscritos en diversos sectores de estudios. En 1983 los datos se refieren a 1981.
Yugoslavia:
E--> Natural science includes mathematics and computer science.
FR-> Les sciences exactes et naturelles comprennent les mathématiques et l'informatique.
ESP> Las ciencias naturales comprenden las matemáticas y la informática.
OCEANIA:
Australia:
E--> Natural science includes mathematics and computer science. In 1983 and 1984, social and behavioural science include mass communication and documentation.
FR-> Les sciences exactes et naturelles comprennent les mathématiques et l'informatique. En 1983 et 1984, les sciences sociales et sciences du comportement incluent l'information et la documentation.
ESP> Las ciencias naturales comprenden las matemáticas y la informática. En 1983 y 1984, las ciencias sociales y del comportamiento incluyen la documentación y comunicación social.
Fiji:
E--> Data refer to 1981. Social and behavioural science includes commercial and business administration.
FR-> Les données se réfèrent à 1981. Les sciences sociales et sciences du comportement incluent la formation au commerce et à l'administration des entreprises.
ESP> Los datos se refieren a 1981. Las ciencias sociales y del comportamiento incluyen la enseñanza comercial y de administración de empresas.
New Caledonia:
E--> In 1983 and 1984, mathematics and computer science includes natural science.
FR-> En 1983 et 1984, les mathématiques et l'informatique incluent les sciences exactes et naturelles.
ESP> En 1983 y 1984, las matemáticas e informática incluyen las ciencias naturales.
New Zealand:
E--> Data include multiple counting of students enrolled in more than one field of study.
FR-> Y compris les étudiants inscrits dans plusieurs domaines d'études.
ESP> Incluídos los estudiantes inscritos en diversos sectores de estudios.
Papua New Guinea:
E--> In 1980, commercial and business administration includes mathematics and computer science.
FR-> En 1980, la formation au commerce et à l'administration des entreprises comprennent les mathématiques et l'informatique.
ESP> En 1980, la enseñanza comercial y de administración de empresas incluyen las matemáticas y la informática.
Samoa:
E--> Data for 1980 refer to 1981. In 1983 data exclude the school of Agriculture.
FR-> Les données de 1980 se réfèrent à 1981. En 1983 les données excluent l'école d'Agriculture.
ESP> Los datos de 1980 se refieren a 1981. En 1983 los datos excluyen la escuela de Agricultura.
Tonga:
E--> Data for 1980 refer to 1981.
FR-> Les données de 1980 se réfèrent à 1981.
ESP> Los datos de 1980 se refieren a 1981.
U.S.S.R.:
U.S.S.R.:
E--> The figures have been provided by the U.S.S.R., according to their own system of classification. Law and economics are combined. Medical science and health-related includes physical culture and sport. Engineering includes transport and communications.
FR-> Ces chiffres sont fournis par l'U.R.S.S. selon son propre système de classification. Le droit comprend les sciences économiques. Les sciences médicales, la santé et l'hygiène comprennent la culture physique et le sport. Les sciences de l'ingénieur comprennent les transports et télécommunications.
ESP> Estas cifras han sido facilitadas por la U.R.S.S. con arreglo a su propio sistema de clasificación. El derecho comprende las ciencias económicas. Las ciencias médicas, la sanidad y la higiene incluyen la cultura física y el deporte. La ingeniería y tecnología comprenden los transportes y comunicaciones.
Byelorussian S.S.R.:
E--> The figures have been provided by the Byelorussian S.S.R., according to their own system of classification. Law and economics are combined. Medical science and health-related includes physical culture and sport. Engineering includes transport and communication.
FR-> Ces chiffres sont fournis par la R.S.S. de Biélorussie selon son propre système de classification. Le droit comprend les sciences économiques. Les sciences médicales, la santé et l'hygiène comprennent la culture physique et le sport. Les sciences de l'ingénieur comprennent les transports et télécommunications.
ESP> Estas cifras han sido facilitadas por la R.S.S. de Bielorrusia con arreglo a su propio sistema de clasificación. El derecho comprende las ciencias económicas. Las ciencias médicas, la sanidad y la higiene incluyen la cultura física y el deporte. La ingeniería y tecnología comprenden los transportes y comunicaciones.
Ukrainian S.S.R.:
E--> The figures have been provided by the Ukrainian S.S.R., according to their own system of classification. Law and economics are combined. Medical science and health-related includes physical culture and sport. Engineering includes transport and communication.
FR-> Ces chiffres sont fournis par la R.S.S. d'Ukraine selon son propre système de classification. Le droit comprend les sciences économiques. Les sciences médicales, la santé et l'hygiène comprennent la culture physique et le sport. Les sciences de l'ingénieur comprennent les transports et télécommunications.
ESP> Estas cifras han sido facilitadas por la R.S.S. de Ucrania con arreglo a su propio sistema de clasificación. El derecho comprende las ciencias económicas. Las ciencias médicas, la sanidad y la higiene incluyen la cultura física y el deporte. La ingeniería y tecnología comprenden los transportes y comunicaciones.

3.13 Education at the third level: enrolment by ISCED level of programme and field of study

Enseignement du troisième degré: nombre d'étudiants par niveau de programmes et domaine d'études de la CITE

Enseñanza de tercer grado: número de estudiantes por nivel de programas y sector de estudios de la CINE

EDUCATION SCIENCE AND TEACHER TRAINING	=	SCIENCES DE L'EDUCATION ET FORMATION D'ENSEIGNANTS	=	CIENCIAS DE LA EDUCACION Y FORMACION DE PERSONAL DOCENTE
HUMANITIES, RELIGION AND THEOLOGY	=	LETTRES, RELIGION ET THEOLOGIE	=	HUMANIDADES, RELIGION Y TEOLOGIA
FINE AND APPLIED ARTS	=	BEAUX-ARTS ET ARTS APPLIQUES	=	BELLAS ARTES Y ARTES APLICADAS
LAW	=	DROIT	=	DERECHO
SOCIAL AND BEHAVIOURAL SCIENCE	=	SCIENCES SOCIALES ET SCIENCES DU COMPORTEMENT	=	CIENCIAS SOCIALES Y DEL COMPORTAMIENTO
COMMERCIAL AND BUSINESS ADMINISTRATION	=	FORMATION AU COMMERCE ET A L'ADMINISTRATION DES ENTREPRISES	=	ENSEÑANZA COMERCIAL Y DE ADMINISTRACION DE EMPRESAS
MASS COMMUNICATION AND DOCUMENTATION	=	INFORMATION ET DOCUMENTATION	=	DOCUMENTACION Y COMUNICACION SOCIAL
HOME ECONOMICS (DOMESTIC SCIENCE)	=	ENSEIGNEMENT MENAGER	=	ECONOMIA DOMESTICA (ENSEÑANZA DEL HOGAR)
SERVICE TRADES	=	FORMATION POUR LE SECTEUR TERTIAIRE	=	FORMACION PARA EL SECTOR DE LOS SERVICIOS
NATURAL SCIENCE	=	SCIENCES EXACTES ET NATURELLES	=	CIENCIAS NATURALES
MATHEMATICS AND COMPUTER SCIENCE	=	MATHEMATIQUES ET INFORMATIQUE	=	MATEMATICAS E INFORMATICA
MEDICAL SCIENCE AND HEALTH-RELATED	=	SCIENCES MEDICALES, SANTE ET HYGIENE	=	CIENCIAS MEDICAS, SANIDAD E HIGIENE
ENGINEERING	=	SCIENCES DE L'INGENIEUR	=	INGENIERIA Y TECNOLOGIA
ARCHITECTURE & TOWN PLANNING	=	ARCHITECTURE ET URBANISME	=	ARQUITECTURA Y URBANISMO
TRADE, CRAFT & INDUSTRIAL PROGRAMMES	=	METIERS DE LA PRODUCTION INDUSTRIELLE	=	ARTES Y OFICIOS INDUSTRIALES
TRANSPORT AND COMMUNICATIONS	=	TRANSPORTS ET TELECOMMUNICATIONS	=	TRANSPORTES Y COMUNICACIONES
AGRICULTURE, FORESTRY AND FISHERY	=	AGRICULTURE, SYLVICULTURE ET HALIEUTIQUE	=	ENSEÑANZA AGRONOMICA, DASONOMICA Y PESQUERA
OTHER AND NOT SPECIFIED	=	AUTRES PROGRAMMES	=	OTROS PROGRAMAS

LEVEL 5	PROGRAMMES LEADING TO AN AWARD NOT EQUIVALENT TO A FIRST UNIVERSITY DEGREE	NIVEAU 5	PROGRAMMES CONDUISANT A UN DIPLOME N'EQUIVALANT PAS A UN PREMIER GRADE UNIVERSITAIRE	NIVEL 5	PROGRAMAS QUE CONDUCEN A UN DIPLOMA QUE NO EQUIVALE A UN PRIMER GRADO UNIVERSITARIO
LEVEL 6	PROGRAMMES LEADING TO A FIRST UNIVERSITY DEGREE OR EQUIVALENT QUALIFICATION	NIVEAU 6	PROGRAMMES CONDUISANT A UN PREMIER GRADE UNIVERSITAIRE OU A UN DIPLOME EQUIVALENT	NIVEL 6	PROGRAMAS QUE CONDUCEN A UN PRIMER GRADO UNIVERSITARIO O A UN DIPLOMA EQUIVALENTE
LEVEL 7	PROGRAMMES LEADING TO A POST-GRADUATE UNIVERSITY DEGREE OR EQUIVALENT QUALIFICATION	NIVEAU 7	PROGRAMMES CONDUISANT A UN GRADE UNIVERSITAIRE SUPERIEUR OU A UN DIPLOME EQUIVALENT	NIVEL 7	PROGRAMAS QUE CONDUCEN A UN GRADO UNIVERSITARIO SUPERIOR O A UN DIPLOMA EQUIVALENTE

PLEASE REFER TO EXPLANATORY TEXT AT END OF TABLE

PRIERE DE SE REFERER AU TEXTE EXPLICATIF A LA FIN DU TABLEAU

REFERIRSE AL TEXTO EXPLICATIVO AL FINAL DEL CUADRO

NUMBER OF COUNTRIES AND TERRITORIES PRESENTED IN THIS TABLE: 115

NOMBRE DE PAYS ET DE TERRITOIRES PRESENTES DANS CE TABLEAU: 115

NUMERO DE PAISES Y DE TERRITORIOS PRESENTADOS EN ESTE CUADRO: 115

COUNTRY / YEAR PAYS / ANNEE PAIS / AÑO	FIELD OF STUDY DOMAINES D'ETUDES SECTORES DE ESTUDIOS	INTERNATIONAL STANDARD CLASSIFICATION OF EDUCATION BY LEVEL CLASSIFICATION INTERNATIONALE TYPE DE L'EDUCATION PAR NIVEAUX CLASIFICACION INTERNACIONAL NORMALIZADA DE LA EDUCACION POR NIVELES							
		ALL LEVELS TOUS NIVEAUX TODOS LOS NIVELES		LEVEL 5 NIVEAU 5 NIVEL 5		LEVEL 6 NIVEAU 6 NIVEL 6		LEVEL 7 NIVEAU 7 NIVEL 7	
		MF	F	MF	F	MF	F	MF	F
		(1)	(2)	(3)	(4)	(5)	(6)	(7)	(8)
AFRICA									
ALGERIA 1984	TOTAL	111 507	...	3 326	...	99 484	...	8 697	...
	EDUCATION SCIENCE & TEACHER TRNG.	5 261	...	–	–	5 261	...	–	–
	HUMANITIES, RELIGION & THEOLOGY	9 800	...	–	–	8 954	...	846	...
	FINE AND APPLIED ARTS	–	–	–	–	–	–	–	–
	LAW	10 817	...	–	–	10 021	...	796	...
	SOCIAL AND BEHAVIOURAL SCIENCE	9 564	...	–	–	8 732	...	832	...
	COMMERCIAL & BUSINESS ADMIN.	825	...	–	–	825	...	–	–
	MASS COMMUNICATION & DOCUMENT.	1 047	...	183	...	738	...	126	...
	HOME ECONOMICS (DOMESTIC SCIENCE)	–	–	–	–	–	–	–	–
	SERVICE TRADES	–	–	–	–	–	–	–	–
	NATURAL SCIENCE	5 639	...	151	...	4 583	...	905	...
	MATHEMATICS & COMPUTER SCIENCE	3 745	...	420	...	3 110	...	215	...
	MEDICAL SCIENCE AND HEALTH–RELATED	32 766	...	–	–	28 527	...	4 239	...
	ENGINEERING	3 899	...	981	...	2 671	...	247	...
	ARCHITECTURE & TOWN PLANNING	3 935	...	–	–	3 851	...	84	...
	TRADE, CRAFT & INDUSTRIAL PGMS.	2 009	...	552	...	1 247	...	210	...
	TRANSPORT AND COMMUNICATIONS	727	...	501	...	226	...	–	–
	AGRICULTURE, FORESTRY & FISHERY	2 503	...	437	...	1 879	...	187	...
	OTHER AND NOT SPECIFIED	18 970	...	101	...	18 859	...	10	...
BENIN 1982	TOTAL	6 302	1 035	111	12	1 458	237	4 733	786
	EDUCATION SCIENCE & TEACHER TRNG.	880	141	75	6	632	105	173	30
	HUMANITIES, RELIGION & THEOLOGY	366	79	–	–	–	–	366	79
	FINE AND APPLIED ARTS	–	–	–	–	–	–	–	–
	LAW	1 244	249	–	–	35	11	1 209	238
	SOCIAL AND BEHAVIOURAL SCIENCE	1 373	236	–	–	85	28	1 288	208
	COMMERCIAL & BUSINESS ADMIN.	764	143	–	–	282	49	482	94
	MASS COMMUNICATION & DOCUMENT.	–	–	–	–	–	–	–	–
	HOME ECONOMICS (DOMESTIC SCIENCE)	–	–	–	–	–	–	–	–
	SERVICE TRADES	–	–	–	–	–	–	–	–
	NATURAL SCIENCE	311	58	–	–	19	2	292	56
	MATHEMATICS & COMPUTER SCIENCE	288	18	–	–	50	6	238	12
	MEDICAL SCIENCE AND HEALTH–RELATED	494	74	36	6	85	19	373	49
	ENGINEERING	243	9	–	–	243	9	–	–
	ARCHITECTURE & TOWN PLANNING	–	–	–	–	–	–	–	–
	TRADE, CRAFT & INDUSTRIAL PGMS.	–	–	–	–	–	–	–	–
	TRANSPORT AND COMMUNICATIONS	–	–	–	–	–	–	–	–
	AGRICULTURE, FORESTRY & FISHERY	339	28	–	–	27	8	312	20
	OTHER AND NOT SPECIFIED	–	–	–	–	–	–	–	–
BOTSWANA‡ 1984	TOTAL	1 773	...	708	...	1 006	...	59	...
	EDUCATION SCIENCE & TEACHER TRNG.	501	...	275	...	170	...	56	...
	HUMANITIES, RELIGION & THEOLOGY	319	...	67	...	249	...	3	...
	FINE AND APPLIED ARTS	–	–	–	–	–	–	–	–
	LAW	62	...	–	–	62	...	–	–
	SOCIAL AND BEHAVIOURAL SCIENCE	697	...	366	...	331	...	–	–
	COMMERCIAL & BUSINESS ADMIN.	./.	...	./.	...	./.	...	–	–
	MASS COMMUNICATION & DOCUMENT.	–	–	–	–	–	–	–	–
	HOME ECONOMICS (DOMESTIC SCIENCE)	–	–	–	–	–	–	–	–
	SERVICE TRADES	–	–	–	–	–	–	–	–
	NATURAL SCIENCE	194	...	–	–	194	...	–	–
	MATHEMATICS & COMPUTER SCIENCE	–	–	–	–	–	–	–	–
	MEDICAL SCIENCE AND HEALTH–RELATED	–	–	–	–	–	–	–	–
	ENGINEERING	–	–	–	–	–	–	–	–
	ARCHITECTURE & TOWN PLANNING	–	–	–	–	–	–	–	–
	TRADE, CRAFT & INDUSTRIAL PGMS.	–	–	–	–	–	–	–	–
	TRANSPORT AND COMMUNICATIONS	–	–	–	–	–	–	–	–
	AGRICULTURE, FORESTRY & FISHERY	–	–	–	–	–	–	–	–
	OTHER AND NOT SPECIFIED	–	–	–	–	–	–	–	–

3.13 Third level: students by level and field of study
Troisième degré: étudiants par niveau de programmes et domaine d'études
Tercer grado: estudiantes por nivel de programas y sector de estudios

COUNTRY / YEAR PAYS / ANNEE PAIS / AÑO	FIELD OF STUDY DOMAINES D'ETUDES SECTORES DE ESTUDIOS	INTERNATIONAL STANDARD CLASSIFICATION OF EDUCATION BY LEVEL / CLASSIFICATION INTERNATIONALE TYPE DE L'EDUCATION PAR NIVEAUX / CLASIFICACION INTERNACIONAL NORMALIZADA DE LA EDUCACION POR NIVELES							
		ALL LEVELS TOUS NIVEAUX TODOS LOS NIVELES		LEVEL 5 NIVEAU 5 NIVEL 5		LEVEL 6 NIVEAU 6 NIVEL 6		LEVEL 7 NIVEAU 7 NIVEL 7	
		MF	F	MF	F	MF	F	MF	F
		(1)	(2)	(3)	(4)	(5)	(6)	(7)	(8)
CAMEROON‡									
1980	TOTAL	10 631	...	...	...	...	...	...	...
	EDUCATION SCIENCE & TEACHER TRNG.	823	112	480	70	135	18	208	24
	HUMANITIES, RELIGION & THEOLOGY	765	–	488	149	157	38	120	36
	FINE AND APPLIED ARTS	–	–	–	–	–	–	–	–
	LAW	2 217	518	1 268	287	608	155	341	76
	SOCIAL AND BEHAVIOURAL SCIENCE	858	140	565	100	154	20	139	20
	COMMERCIAL & BUSINESS ADMIN.	2 609	465	1 437	288	652	98	520	79
	MASS COMMUNICATION & DOCUMENT.	73	4	50	3	23	1	–	–
	HOME ECONOMICS (DOMESTIC SCIENCE)	–	–	–	–	–	–	–	–
	SERVICE TRADES	117	...	...	...	...	...	...	...
	NATURAL SCIENCE	1 237	182	1 020	159	150	15	67	8
	MATHEMATICS & COMPUTER SCIENCE	373	14	336	11	27	3	10	–
	MEDICAL SCIENCE AND HEALTH-RELATED	319	67	93	17	50	12	176	38
	ENGINEERING	373	...	...	...	...	...	...	...
	ARCHITECTURE & TOWN PLANNING	–	–	–	–	–	–	–	–
	TRADE, CRAFT & INDUSTRIAL PGMS.	–	–	–	–	–	–	–	–
	TRANSPORT AND COMMUNICATIONS	–	–	–	–	–	–	–	–
	AGRICULTURE, FORESTRY & FISHERY	825	...	...	...	...	...	...	...
	OTHER AND NOT SPECIFIED	42	2	11	–	–	–	31	2
CHAD‡									
1984	TOTAL	1 643	142	./.	./.	1 643	142	–	–
	EDUCATION SCIENCE & TEACHER TRNG.	173	3	./.	./.	173	3	–	–
	HUMANITIES, RELIGION & THEOLOGY	316	31	./.	./.	316	31	–	–
	FINE AND APPLIED ARTS	–	–	–	–	–	–	–	–
	LAW	460	46	./.	./.	460	46	–	–
	SOCIAL AND BEHAVIOURAL SCIENCE	499	52	./.	./.	499	52	–	–
	COMMERCIAL & BUSINESS ADMIN.	–	–	–	–	–	–	–	–
	MASS COMMUNICATION & DOCUMENT.	–	–	–	–	–	–	–	–
	HOME ECONOMICS (DOMESTIC SCIENCE)	–	–	–	–	–	–	–	–
	SERVICE TRADES	–	–	–	–	–	–	–	–
	NATURAL SCIENCE	195	10	./.	./.	195	10	–	–
	MATHEMATICS & COMPUTER SCIENCE	–	–	–	–	–	–	–	–
	MEDICAL SCIENCE AND HEALTH-RELATED	–	–	–	–	–	–	–	–
	ENGINEERING	–	–	–	–	–	–	–	–
	ARCHITECTURE & TOWN PLANNING	–	–	–	–	–	–	–	–
	TRADE, CRAFT & INDUSTRIAL PGMS.	–	–	–	–	–	–	–	–
	TRANSPORT AND COMMUNICATIONS	–	–	–	–	–	–	–	–
	AGRICULTURE, FORESTRY & FISHERY	–	–	–	–	–	–	–	–
	OTHER AND NOT SPECIFIED	–	–	–	–	–	–	–	–
COTE D'IVOIRE									
1983	TOTAL	18 872	...	6 832	...	9 738	...	2 302	544
	EDUCATION SCIENCE & TEACHER TRNG.	3 746	...	3 302	...	444	...	–	–
	HUMANITIES, RELIGION & THEOLOGY	2 779	665	180	99	2 161	454	438	112
	FINE AND APPLIED ARTS	244	53	244	53	–	–	–	–
	LAW	3 246	511	990	27	1 692	348	564	136
	SOCIAL AND BEHAVIOURAL SCIENCE	2 648	463	219	39	1 652	256	777	168
	COMMERCIAL & BUSINESS ADMIN.	322	33	226	10	96	23	–	–
	MASS COMMUNICATION & DOCUMENT.	–	–	–	–	–	–	–	–
	HOME ECONOMICS (DOMESTIC SCIENCE)	–	–	–	–	–	–	–	–
	SERVICE TRADES	–	–	–	–	–	–	–	–
	NATURAL SCIENCE	1 464	221	–	–	1 348	198	116	23
	MATHEMATICS & COMPUTER SCIENCE	293	13	34	3	193	5	66	5
	MEDICAL SCIENCE AND HEALTH-RELATED	2 488	895	864	368	1 283	427	341	100
	ENGINEERING	101	15	–	–	101	15	–	–
	ARCHITECTURE & TOWN PLANNING	645	23	298	5	347	18	–	–
	TRADE, CRAFT & INDUSTRIAL PGMS.	290	10	217	4	73	6	–	–
	TRANSPORT AND COMMUNICATIONS	335	30	258	24	77	6	–	–
	AGRICULTURE, FORESTRY & FISHERY	271	11	–	–	271	11	–	–
	OTHER AND NOT SPECIFIED	–	–	–	–	–	–	–	–

COUNTRY YEAR / PAYS ANNEE / PAIS AÑO	FIELD OF STUDY / DOMAINES D'ETUDES / SECTORES DE ESTUDIOS	INTERNATIONAL STANDARD CLASSIFICATION OF EDUCATION BY LEVEL / CLASSIFICATION INTERNATIONALE TYPE DE L'EDUCATION PAR NIVEAUX / CLASIFICACION INTERNACIONAL NORMALIZADA DE LA EDUCACION POR NIVELES							
		ALL LEVELS / TOUS NIVEAUX / TODOS LOS NIVELES		LEVEL 5 / NIVEAU 5 / NIVEL 5		LEVEL 6 / NIVEAU 6 / NIVEL 6		LEVEL 7 / NIVEAU 7 / NIVEL 7	
		MF	F	MF	F	MF	F	MF	F
		(1)	(2)	(3)	(4)	(5)	(6)	(7)	(8)
EGYPT‡ 1983	TOTAL	613 570	206 376	–	–	552 512	191 245	61 058	15 131
	EDUCATION SCIENCE & TEACHER TRNG.	85 222	38 604	–	–	77 557	36 141	7 665	2 463
	HUMANITIES, RELIGION & THEOLOGY	91 425	42 319	–	–	84 223	39 581	7 202	2 738
	FINE AND APPLIED ARTS	7 120	3 063	–	–	6 397	2 847	723	216
	LAW	83 470	18 227	–	–	76 495	17 513	6 975	714
	SOCIAL AND BEHAVIOURAL SCIENCE	5 467	2 283	–	–	4 111	1 935	1 356	348
	COMMERCIAL & BUSINESS ADMIN.	150 581	45 942	–	–	142 481	44 681	8 100	1 261
	MASS COMMUNICATION & DOCUMENT.	1 527	821	–	–	1 286	726	241	95
	HOME ECONOMICS (DOMESTIC SCIENCE)	1 709	1 404	–	–	1 610	1 310	99	94
	SERVICE TRADES	965	570	–	–	740	488	225	82
	NATURAL SCIENCE	26 265	9 072	–	–	22 397	7 586	3 868	1 486
	MATHEMATICS & COMPUTER SCIENCE	1 137	309	–	–	342	128	795	181
	MEDICAL SCIENCE AND HEALTH-RELATED	51 850	20 316	–	–	40 271	17 280	11 579	3 036
	ENGINEERING	54 859	7 123	–	–	49 167	6 276	5 692	847
	ARCHITECTURE & TOWN PLANNING	./.	./.	–	–	./.	./.	./.	./.
	TRADE, CRAFT & INDUSTRIAL PGMS.	./.	./.	–	–	./.	./.	./.	./.
	TRANSPORT AND COMMUNICATIONS	./.	./.	–	–	./.	./.	./.	./.
	AGRICULTURE, FORESTRY & FISHERY	45 649	14 137	–	–	39 686	12 773	5 963	1 364
	OTHER AND NOT SPECIFIED	6 324	2 186	–	–	5 749	1 980	575	206
ETHIOPIA‡ 1983	TOTAL	16 030	1 761	5 504	844	10 303	908	223	9
	EDUCATION SCIENCE & TEACHER TRNG.	2 179	169	1 643	141	536	28	–	–
	HUMANITIES, RELIGION & THEOLOGY	555	90	–	–	517	89	38	1
	FINE AND APPLIED ARTS	–	–	–	–	–	–	–	–
	LAW	236	21	–	–	236	21	–	–
	SOCIAL AND BEHAVIOURAL SCIENCE	3 314	321	–	–	3 279	321	35	–
	COMMERCIAL & BUSINESS ADMIN.	1 067	421	1 067	421	–	–	–	–
	MASS COMMUNICATION & DOCUMENT.	89	25	89	25	–	–	–	–
	HOME ECONOMICS (DOMESTIC SCIENCE)	–	–	–	–	–	–	–	–
	SERVICE TRADES	–	–	–	–	–	–	–	–
	NATURAL SCIENCE	3 105	242	–	–	3 042	237	63	5
	MATHEMATICS & COMPUTER SCIENCE	./.	./.	–	–	./.	./.	./.	./.
	MEDICAL SCIENCE AND HEALTH-RELATED	1 206	208	181	54	973	153	52	1
	ENGINEERING	1 316	59	772	48	544	11	–	–
	ARCHITECTURE & TOWN PLANNING	104	8	–	–	104	8	–	–
	TRADE, CRAFT & INDUSTRIAL PGMS.	–	–	–	–	–	–	–	–
	TRANSPORT AND COMMUNICATIONS	–	–	–	–	–	–	–	–
	AGRICULTURE, FORESTRY & FISHERY	2 828	189	1 721	147	1 072	40	35	2
	OTHER AND NOT SPECIFIED	31	8	31	8	./.	./.	–	–
GABON‡ 1983	TOTAL	3 228	873	872	282	2 356	591	./.	./.
	EDUCATION SCIENCE & TEACHER TRNG.	291	43	26	3	265	40	–	–
	HUMANITIES, RELIGION & THEOLOGY	342	100	–	–	342	100	./.	./.
	FINE AND APPLIED ARTS	–	–	–	–	–	–	–	–
	LAW	435	122	–	–	435	122	–	–
	SOCIAL AND BEHAVIOURAL SCIENCE	715	202	63	18	652	184	./.	./.
	COMMERCIAL & BUSINESS ADMIN.	349	170	185	142	164	28	./.	./.
	MASS COMMUNICATION & DOCUMENT.	120	29	57	19	63	10	–	–
	HOME ECONOMICS (DOMESTIC SCIENCE)	–	–	–	–	–	–	–	–
	SERVICE TRADES	–	–	–	–	–	–	–	–
	NATURAL SCIENCE	113	18	113	18	–	–	–	–
	MATHEMATICS & COMPUTER SCIENCE	258	49	201	37	57	12	./.	./.
	MEDICAL SCIENCE AND HEALTH-RELATED	290	122	46	32	244	90	./.	./.
	ENGINEERING	210	10	119	7	91	3	./.	./.
	ARCHITECTURE & TOWN PLANNING	43	2	–	–	43	2	–	–
	TRADE, CRAFT & INDUSTRIAL PGMS.	–	–	–	–	–	–	–	–
	TRANSPORT AND COMMUNICATIONS	–	–	–	–	–	–	–	–
	AGRICULTURE, FORESTRY & FISHERY	62	6	62	6	–	–	–	–
	OTHER AND NOT SPECIFIED	–	–	–	–	–	–	–	–

3.13 **Third level: students by level and field of study**
Troisième degré: étudiants par niveau de programmes et domaine d'études
Tercer grado: estudiantes por nivel de programas y sector de estudios

COUNTRY / YEAR PAYS / ANNEE PAIS / AÑO	FIELD OF STUDY DOMAINES D'ETUDES SECTORES DE ESTUDIOS	ALL LEVELS / TOUS NIVEAUX / TODOS LOS NIVELES MF	F	LEVEL 5 / NIVEAU 5 / NIVEL 5 MF	F	LEVEL 6 / NIVEAU 6 / NIVEL 6 MF	F	LEVEL 7 / NIVEAU 7 / NIVEL 7 MF	F
		(1)	(2)	(3)	(4)	(5)	(6)	(7)	(8)
GHANA‡ 1984	TOTAL	7 649	1 309	833	200	6 660	1 089	156	20
	EDUCATION SCIENCE & TEACHER TRNG.	206	53	35	20	163	33	8	–
	HUMANITIES, RELIGION & THEOLOGY	./.	./.	–	–	./.	./.	–	–
	FINE AND APPLIED ARTS	261	80	87	33	174	47	–	–
	LAW	./.	./.	./.	./.	./.	./.	./.	./.
	SOCIAL AND BEHAVIOURAL SCIENCE	2 882	623	130	48	2 662	565	90	10
	COMMERCIAL & BUSINESS ADMIN.	648	93	127	19	501	72	20	2
	MASS COMMUNICATION & DOCUMENT.	45	13	23	5	–	–	22	8
	HOME ECONOMICS (DOMESTIC SCIENCE)	52	47	19	19	33	28	–	–
	SERVICE TRADES	–	–	–	–	–	–	–	–
	NATURAL SCIENCE	1 269	154	149	35	1 109	119	11	–
	MATHEMATICS & COMPUTER SCIENCE	./.	./.	./.	./.	./.	./.	./.	–
	MEDICAL SCIENCE AND HEALTH–RELATED	650	136	6	14	644	122	–	–
	ENGINEERING	774	14	132	–	642	14	–	–
	ARCHITECTURE & TOWN PLANNING	244	37	–	–	244	37	–	–
	TRADE, CRAFT & INDUSTRIAL PGMS.	–	–	–	–	–	–	–	–
	TRANSPORT AND COMMUNICATIONS	–	–	–	–	–	–	–	–
	AGRICULTURE, FORESTRY & FISHERY	618	59	125	7	488	52	5	–
	OTHER AND NOT SPECIFIED	–	–	–	–	–	–	–	–
GUINEA‡ 1984	TOTAL	10 664	2 737	–	–	7 394	1 975	3 270	762
	EDUCATION SCIENCE & TEACHER TRNG.	236	10	–	–	–	–	236	10
	HUMANITIES, RELIGION & THEOLOGY	./.	./.	–	–	./.	./.	./.	./.
	FINE AND APPLIED ARTS	./.	./.	–	–	./.	./.	./.	./.
	LAW	122	39	–	–	34	18	88	21
	SOCIAL AND BEHAVIOURAL SCIENCE	1 950	702	–	–	1 704	606	246	96
	COMMERCIAL & BUSINESS ADMIN.	413	210	–	–	119	66	294	144
	MASS COMMUNICATION & DOCUMENT.	–	–	–	–	–	–	–	–
	HOME ECONOMICS (DOMESTIC SCIENCE)	–	–	–	–	–	–	–	–
	SERVICE TRADES	–	–	–	–	–	–	–	–
	NATURAL SCIENCE	3 617	1 047	–	–	3 389	966	228	81
	MATHEMATICS & COMPUTER SCIENCE	./.	./.	–	–	./.	./.	./.	./.
	MEDICAL SCIENCE AND HEALTH–RELATED	596	126	–	–	324	53	272	73
	ENGINEERING	512	23	–	–	402	19	110	4
	ARCHITECTURE & TOWN PLANNING	186	10	–	–	151	10	35	–
	TRADE, CRAFT & INDUSTRIAL PGMS.	67	24	–	–	47	16	20	8
	TRANSPORT AND COMMUNICATIONS	139	21	–	–	119	18	20	3
	AGRICULTURE, FORESTRY & FISHERY	2 661	506	–	–	977	188	1 684	318
	OTHER AND NOT SPECIFIED	165	19	–	–	128	15	37	4
KENYA‡ 1983	TOTAL	22 157	...	12 999	...	7 328	2 211	1 830	402
	EDUCATION SCIENCE & TEACHER TRNG.	2 748	1 199	–	–	2 140	1 032	608	167
	HUMANITIES, RELIGION & THEOLOGY	./.	./.	–	–	./.	./.	./.	./.
	FINE AND APPLIED ARTS	4	1	–	–	4	1	–	–
	LAW	340	138	–	–	325	133	15	5
	SOCIAL AND BEHAVIOURAL SCIENCE	1 432	485	–	–	1 150	403	282	82
	COMMERCIAL & BUSINESS ADMIN.	1 691	...	1 120	...	507	174	64	9
	MASS COMMUNICATION & DOCUMENT.	150	...	128	...	–	–	22	5
	HOME ECONOMICS (DOMESTIC SCIENCE)	–	–	–	–	–	–	–	–
	SERVICE TRADES	163	...	163	...	–	–	–	–
	NATURAL SCIENCE	1 091	141	–	–	817	98	274	43
	MATHEMATICS & COMPUTER SCIENCE	15	2	–	–	–	–	15	2
	MEDICAL SCIENCE AND HEALTH–RELATED	1 373	295	39	32	1 021	205	313	58
	ENGINEERING	2 376	...	1 815	...	519	12	42	3
	ARCHITECTURE & TOWN PLANNING	288	...	12	...	226	29	50	4
	TRADE, CRAFT & INDUSTRIAL PGMS.	985	...	985	...	–	–	–	–
	TRANSPORT AND COMMUNICATIONS	–	–	–	–	–	–	–	–
	AGRICULTURE, FORESTRY & FISHERY	4 399	...	3 786	...	468	86	145	24
	OTHER AND NOT SPECIFIED	5 102	...	4 951	...	151	38	–	–

Header: INTERNATIONAL STANDARD CLASSIFICATION OF EDUCATION BY LEVEL / CLASSIFICATION INTERNATIONALE TYPE DE L'EDUCATION PAR NIVEAUX / CLASIFICACION INTERNACIONAL NORMALIZADA DE LA EDUCACION POR NIVELES

COUNTRY YEAR / PAYS ANNEE / PAIS AÑO	FIELD OF STUDY / DOMAINES D'ETUDES / SECTORES DE ESTUDIOS	INTERNATIONAL STANDARD CLASSIFICATION OF EDUCATION BY LEVEL / CLASSIFICATION INTERNATIONALE TYPE DE L'EDUCATION PAR NIVEAUX / CLASIFICACION INTERNACIONAL NORMALIZADA DE LA EDUCACION POR NIVELES							
		ALL LEVELS / TOUS NIVEAUX / TODOS LOS NIVELES		LEVEL 5 / NIVEAU 5 / NIVEL 5		LEVEL 6 / NIVEAU 6 / NIVEL 6		LEVEL 7 / NIVEAU 7 / NIVEL 7	
		MF	F	MF	F	MF	F	MF	F
		(1)	(2)	(3)	(4)	(5)	(6)	(7)	(8)
LESOTHO‡ 1984	TOTAL	2 303	1 461	1 170	922	1 091	516	42	23
	EDUCATION SCIENCE & TEACHER TRNG.	1 399	1 069	1 070	889	293	158	36	22
	HUMANITIES, RELIGION & THEOLOGY	99	51	–	–	93	50	6	1
	FINE AND APPLIED ARTS	47	26	–	–	47	26	–	–
	LAW	158	58	–	–	158	58	–	–
	SOCIAL AND BEHAVIOURAL SCIENCE	36	18	–	–	36	18	–	–
	COMMERCIAL & BUSINESS ADMIN.	209	116	–	–	209	116	–	–
	MASS COMMUNICATION & DOCUMENT.	–	–	–	–	–	–	–	–
	HOME ECONOMICS (DOMESTIC SCIENCE)	–	–	–	–	–	–	–	–
	SERVICE TRADES	–	–	–	–	–	–	–	–
	NATURAL SCIENCE	205	56	–	–	205	56	–	–
	MATHEMATICS & COMPUTER SCIENCE	63	13	44	–	19	13	–	–
	MEDICAL SCIENCE AND HEALTH-RELATED	24	15	./.	./.	24	15	–	–
	ENGINEERING	–	–	–	–	–	–	–	–
	ARCHITECTURE & TOWN PLANNING	–	–	–	–	–	–	–	–
	TRADE, CRAFT & INDUSTRIAL PGMS.	–	–	–	–	–	–	–	–
	TRANSPORT AND COMMUNICATIONS	–	–	–	–	–	–	–	–
	AGRICULTURE, FORESTRY & FISHERY	63	39	56	33	7	6	–	–
	OTHER AND NOT SPECIFIED	–	–	–	–	–	–	–	–
MALAWI‡ 1980	TOTAL	1 722	427	1 419	369	303	58	–	–
	EDUCATION SCIENCE & TEACHER TRNG.	250	48	250	48	–	–	–	–
	HUMANITIES, RELIGION & THEOLOGY	171	37	–	–	171	37	–	–
	FINE AND APPLIED ARTS	–	–	–	–	–	–	–	–
	LAW	40	–	40	–	–	–	–	–
	SOCIAL AND BEHAVIOURAL SCIENCE	–	–	–	–	–	–	–	–
	COMMERCIAL & BUSINESS ADMIN.	288	45	243	36	45	9	–	–
	MASS COMMUNICATION & DOCUMENT.	–	–	–	–	–	–	–	–
	HOME ECONOMICS (DOMESTIC SCIENCE)	–	–	–	–	–	–	–	–
	SERVICE TRADES	–	–	–	–	–	–	–	–
	NATURAL SCIENCE	–	–	–	–	–	–	–	–
	MATHEMATICS & COMPUTER SCIENCE	–	–	–	–	–	–	–	–
	MEDICAL SCIENCE AND HEALTH-RELATED	–	–	–	–	–	–	–	–
	ENGINEERING	159	–	144	–	15	–	–	–
	ARCHITECTURE & TOWN PLANNING	–	–	–	–	–	–	–	–
	TRADE, CRAFT & INDUSTRIAL PGMS.	–	–	–	–	–	–	–	–
	TRANSPORT AND COMMUNICATIONS	–	–	–	–	–	–	–	–
	AGRICULTURE, FORESTRY & FISHERY	427	93	355	81	72	12	–	–
	OTHER AND NOT SPECIFIED	387	204	387	204	–	–	–	–
MAURITIUS 1984	TOTAL	794	216	630	185	40	4	124	27
	EDUCATION SCIENCE & TEACHER TRNG.	450	150	334	125	–	–	116	25
	HUMANITIES, RELIGION & THEOLOGY	–	–	–	–	–	–	–	–
	FINE AND APPLIED ARTS	–	–	–	–	–	–	–	–
	LAW	–	–	–	–	–	–	–	–
	SOCIAL AND BEHAVIOURAL SCIENCE	12	2	12	2	–	–	–	–
	COMMERCIAL & BUSINESS ADMIN.	140	31	140	31	–	–	–	–
	MASS COMMUNICATION & DOCUMENT.	12	8	12	8	–	–	–	–
	HOME ECONOMICS (DOMESTIC SCIENCE)	–	–	–	–	–	–	–	–
	SERVICE TRADES	–	–	–	–	–	–	–	–
	NATURAL SCIENCE	–	–	–	–	–	–	–	–
	MATHEMATICS & COMPUTER SCIENCE	10	2	10	2	–	–	–	–
	MEDICAL SCIENCE AND HEALTH-RELATED	28	7	28	7	–	–	–	–
	ENGINEERING	101	4	69	4	29	–	3	–
	ARCHITECTURE & TOWN PLANNING	–	–	–	–	–	–	–	–
	TRADE, CRAFT & INDUSTRIAL PGMS.	–	–	–	–	–	–	–	–
	TRANSPORT AND COMMUNICATIONS	–	–	–	–	–	–	–	–
	AGRICULTURE, FORESTRY & FISHERY	41	12	25	6	11	4	5	2
	OTHER AND NOT SPECIFIED	–	–	–	–	–	–	–	–

3.13 Third level: students by level and field of study
Troisième degré: étudiants par niveau de programmes et domaine d'études
Tercer grado: estudiantes por nivel de programas y sector de estudios

COUNTRY YEAR / PAYS ANNEE / PAIS AÑO	FIELD OF STUDY / DOMAINES D'ETUDES / SECTORES DE ESTUDIOS	INTERNATIONAL STANDARD CLASSIFICATION OF EDUCATION BY LEVEL / CLASSIFICATION INTERNATIONALE TYPE DE L'EDUCATION PAR NIVEAUX / CLASIFICACION INTERNACIONAL NORMALIZADA DE LA EDUCACION POR NIVELES							
		ALL LEVELS / TOUS NIVEAUX / TODOS LOS NIVELES		LEVEL 5 / NIVEAU 5 / NIVEL 5		LEVEL 6 / NIVEAU 6 / NIVEL 6		LEVEL 7 / NIVEAU 7 / NIVEL 7	
		MF	F	MF	F	MF	F	MF	F
		(1)	(2)	(3)	(4)	(5)	(6)	(7)	(8)
MOROCCO‡ 1984	TOTAL	126 481	41 073	–	–	119 920	39 669	6 561	1 404
	EDUCATION SCIENCE & TEACHER TRNG.	530	151	–	–	530	151	–	–
	HUMANITIES, RELIGION & THEOLOGY	43 556	19 481	–	–	41 942	19 110	1 614	371
	FINE AND APPLIED ARTS	–	–	–	–	–	–	–	–
	LAW	21 017	4 114	–	–	17 897	3 569	3 120	545
	SOCIAL AND BEHAVIOURAL SCIENCE	12 494	3 161	–	–	11 198	2 845	1 296	316
	COMMERCIAL & BUSINESS ADMIN.	–	–	–	–	–	–	–	–
	MASS COMMUNICATION & DOCUMENT.	–	–	–	–	–	–	–	–
	HOME ECONOMICS (DOMESTIC SCIENCE)	–	–	–	–	–	–	–	–
	SERVICE TRADES	–	–	–	–	–	–	–	–
	NATURAL SCIENCE	32 826	8 850	–	–	32 295	8 678	531	172
	MATHEMATICS & COMPUTER SCIENCE	./.	./.	–	–	./.	./.	./.	./.
	MEDICAL SCIENCE AND HEALTH-RELATED	6 767	2 027	–	–	6 767	2 027	–	–
	ENGINEERING	580	58	–	–	580	58	–	–
	ARCHITECTURE & TOWN PLANNING	–	–	–	–	–	–	–	–
	TRADE, CRAFT & INDUSTRIAL PGMS.	–	–	–	–	–	–	–	–
	TRANSPORT AND COMMUNICATIONS	–	–	–	–	–	–	–	–
	AGRICULTURE, FORESTRY & FISHERY	–	–	–	–	–	–	–	–
	OTHER AND NOT SPECIFIED	8 711	3 231	–	–	8 711	3 231	–	–
MOZAMBIQUE 1985	TOTAL	1 442	332	–	–	1 442	332	–	–
	EDUCATION SCIENCE & TEACHER TRNG.	91	30	–	–	91	30	–	–
	HUMANITIES, RELIGION & THEOLOGY	11	4	–	–	11	4	–	–
	FINE AND APPLIED ARTS	–	–	–	–	–	–	–	–
	LAW	–	–	–	–	–	–	–	–
	SOCIAL AND BEHAVIOURAL SCIENCE	247	56	–	–	247	56	–	–
	COMMERCIAL & BUSINESS ADMIN.	–	–	–	–	–	–	–	–
	MASS COMMUNICATION & DOCUMENT.	–	–	–	–	–	–	–	–
	HOME ECONOMICS (DOMESTIC SCIENCE)	–	–	–	–	–	–	–	–
	SERVICE TRADES	–	–	–	–	–	–	–	–
	NATURAL SCIENCE	69	21	–	–	69	21	–	–
	MATHEMATICS & COMPUTER SCIENCE	–	–	–	–	–	–	–	–
	MEDICAL SCIENCE AND HEALTH-RELATED	162	82	–	–	162	82	–	–
	ENGINEERING	541	42	–	–	541	42	–	–
	ARCHITECTURE & TOWN PLANNING	–	–	–	–	–	–	–	–
	TRADE, CRAFT & INDUSTRIAL PGMS.	–	–	–	–	–	–	–	–
	TRANSPORT AND COMMUNICATIONS	–	–	–	–	–	–	–	–
	AGRICULTURE, FORESTRY & FISHERY	321	97	–	–	321	97	–	–
	OTHER AND NOT SPECIFIED	–	–	–	–	–	–	–	–
NIGER 1984	TOTAL	2 863	526	1 291	224	819	143	753	159
	EDUCATION SCIENCE & TEACHER TRNG.	351	72	172	33	158	36	21	3
	HUMANITIES, RELIGION & THEOLOGY	598	169	262	83	229	43	107	43
	FINE AND APPLIED ARTS	–	–	–	–	–	–	–	–
	LAW	439	91	209	35	92	20	138	36
	SOCIAL AND BEHAVIOURAL SCIENCE	618	106	284	49	157	30	177	27
	COMMERCIAL & BUSINESS ADMIN.	–	–	–	–	–	–	–	–
	MASS COMMUNICATION & DOCUMENT.	–	–	–	–	–	–	–	–
	HOME ECONOMICS (DOMESTIC SCIENCE)	–	–	–	–	–	–	–	–
	SERVICE TRADES	–	–	–	–	–	–	–	–
	NATURAL SCIENCE	237	18	115	11	52	3	70	4
	MATHEMATICS & COMPUTER SCIENCE	209	12	114	3	64	7	31	2
	MEDICAL SCIENCE AND HEALTH-RELATED	267	49	70	7	44	4	153	38
	ENGINEERING	–	–	–	–	–	–	–	–
	ARCHITECTURE & TOWN PLANNING	–	–	–	–	–	–	–	–
	TRADE, CRAFT & INDUSTRIAL PGMS.	–	–	–	–	–	–	–	–
	TRANSPORT AND COMMUNICATIONS	–	–	–	–	–	–	–	–
	AGRICULTURE, FORESTRY & FISHERY	144	9	65	3	23	–	56	6
	OTHER AND NOT SPECIFIED	–	–	–	–	–	–	–	–

COUNTRY YEAR / PAYS ANNEE / PAIS AÑO	FIELD OF STUDY / DOMAINES D'ETUDES / SECTORES DE ESTUDIOS	INTERNATIONAL STANDARD CLASSIFICATION OF EDUCATION BY LEVEL / CLASSIFICATION INTERNATIONALE TYPE DE L'EDUCATION PAR NIVEAUX / CLASIFICACION INTERNACIONAL NORMALIZADA DE LA EDUCACION POR NIVELES							
		ALL LEVELS / TOUS NIVEAUX / TODOS LOS NIVELES		LEVEL 5 / NIVEAU 5 / NIVEL 5		LEVEL 6 / NIVEAU 6 / NIVEL 6		LEVEL 7 / NIVEAU 7 / NIVEL 7	
		MF	F	MF	F	MF	F	MF	F
		(1)	(2)	(3)	(4)	(5)	(6)	(7)	(8)
NIGERIA‡ 1980	TOTAL	70 395	...	–	–	70 395	...	–	–
	EDUCATION SCIENCE & TEACHER TRNG.	11 420	...	–	–	11 420	...	–	–
	HUMANITIES, RELIGION & THEOLOGY	10 908	...	–	–	10 908	...	–	–
	FINE AND APPLIED ARTS	–	–	–	–	–	–	–	–
	LAW	3 745	...	–	–	3 745	...	–	–
	SOCIAL AND BEHAVIOURAL SCIENCE	9 233	...	–	–	9 233	...	–	–
	COMMERCIAL & BUSINESS ADMIN.	4 008	...	–	–	4 008	...	–	–
	MASS COMMUNICATION & DOCUMENT.	–	–	–	–	–	–	–	–
	HOME ECONOMICS (DOMESTIC SCIENCE)	–	–	–	–	–	–	–	–
	SERVICE TRADES	–	–	–	–	–	–	–	–
	NATURAL SCIENCE	9 868	...	–	–	9 868	...	–	–
	MATHEMATICS & COMPUTER SCIENCE	–	–	–	–	–	–	–	–
	MEDICAL SCIENCE AND HEALTH-RELATED	7 826	...	–	–	7 826	...	–	–
	ENGINEERING	4 974	...	–	–	4 974	...	–	–
	ARCHITECTURE & TOWN PLANNING	2 147	...	–	–	2 147	...	–	–
	TRADE, CRAFT & INDUSTRIAL PGMS.	–	–	–	–	–	–	–	–
	TRANSPORT AND COMMUNICATIONS	–	–	–	–	–	–	–	–
	AGRICULTURE, FORESTRY & FISHERY	3 931	...	–	–	3 931	...	–	–
	OTHER AND NOT SPECIFIED	2 335	...	–	–	2 335	...	–	–
ST. HELENA 1981	TOTAL	37	5	37	5	–	–	–	–
	EDUCATION SCIENCE & TEACHER TRNG.	5	5	5	5	–	–	–	–
	HUMANITIES, RELIGION & THEOLOGY	–	–	–	–	–	–	–	–
	FINE AND APPLIED ARTS	–	–	–	–	–	–	–	–
	LAW	–	–	–	–	–	–	–	–
	SOCIAL AND BEHAVIOURAL SCIENCE	–	–	–	–	–	–	–	–
	COMMERCIAL & BUSINESS ADMIN.	–	–	–	–	–	–	–	–
	MASS COMMUNICATION & DOCUMENT.	–	–	–	–	–	–	–	–
	HOME ECONOMICS (DOMESTIC SCIENCE)	–	–	–	–	–	–	–	–
	SERVICE TRADES	–	–	–	–	–	–	–	–
	NATURAL SCIENCE	–	–	–	–	–	–	–	–
	MATHEMATICS & COMPUTER SCIENCE	–	–	–	–	–	–	–	–
	MEDICAL SCIENCE AND HEALTH-RELATED	–	–	–	–	–	–	–	–
	ENGINEERING	–	–	–	–	–	–	–	–
	ARCHITECTURE & TOWN PLANNING	–	–	–	–	–	–	–	–
	TRADE, CRAFT & INDUSTRIAL PGMS.	32	–	32	–	–	–	–	–
	TRANSPORT AND COMMUNICATIONS	–	–	–	–	–	–	–	–
	AGRICULTURE, FORESTRY & FISHERY	–	–	–	–	–	–	–	–
	OTHER AND NOT SPECIFIED	–	–	–	–	–	–	–	–
SENEGAL 1983	TOTAL	11 809	2 434	7 046	1 566	2 584	501	2 179	367
	EDUCATION SCIENCE & TEACHER TRNG.	483	62	338	42	24	3	121	17
	HUMANITIES, RELIGION & THEOLOGY	2 142	530	1 188	336	492	106	462	88
	FINE AND APPLIED ARTS	–	–	–	–	–	–	–	–
	LAW	1 473	302	1 106	246	225	38	142	18
	SOCIAL AND BEHAVIOURAL SCIENCE	1 925	325	960	161	574	104	391	60
	COMMERCIAL & BUSINESS ADMIN.	290	24	110	11	66	8	114	5
	MASS COMMUNICATION & DOCUMENT.	272	79	–	–	260	75	12	4
	HOME ECONOMICS (DOMESTIC SCIENCE)	–	–	–	–	–	–	–	–
	SERVICE TRADES	525	98	–	–	525	98	–	–
	NATURAL SCIENCE	1 648	171	1 200	119	177	16	271	36
	MATHEMATICS & COMPUTER SCIENCE	324	19	206	12	78	5	40	2
	MEDICAL SCIENCE AND HEALTH-RELATED	2 308	757	1 734	628	–	–	574	129
	ENGINEERING	–	–	–	–	–	–	–	–
	ARCHITECTURE & TOWN PLANNING	15	1	–	–	15	1	–	–
	TRADE, CRAFT & INDUSTRIAL PGMS.	–	–	–	–	–	–	–	–
	TRANSPORT AND COMMUNICATIONS	–	–	–	–	–	–	–	–
	AGRICULTURE, FORESTRY & FISHERY	318	19	204	11	62	–	52	8
	OTHER AND NOT SPECIFIED	86	47	–	–	86	47	–	–

COUNTRY YEAR / PAYS ANNEE / PAIS AÑO	FIELD OF STUDY / DOMAINES D'ETUDES / SECTORES DE ESTUDIOS	ALL LEVELS / TOUS NIVEAUX / TODOS LOS NIVELES MF	F	LEVEL 5 / NIVEAU 5 / NIVEL 5 MF	F	LEVEL 6 / NIVEAU 6 / NIVEL 6 MF	F	LEVEL 7 / NIVEAU 7 / NIVEL 7 MF	F
		(1)	(2)	(3)	(4)	(5)	(6)	(7)	(8)
SEYCHELLES 1980	TOTAL	144	128	144	128	–	–	–	–
	EDUCATION SCIENCE & TEACHER TRNG.	144	128	144	128	–	–	–	–
	HUMANITIES, RELIGION & THEOLOGY	–	–	–	–	–	–	–	–
	FINE AND APPLIED ARTS	–	–	–	–	–	–	–	–
	LAW	–	–	–	–	–	–	–	–
	SOCIAL AND BEHAVIOURAL SCIENCE	–	–	–	–	–	–	–	–
	COMMERCIAL & BUSINESS ADMIN.	–	–	–	–	–	–	–	–
	MASS COMMUNICATION & DOCUMENT.	–	–	–	–	–	–	–	–
	HOME ECONOMICS (DOMESTIC SCIENCE)	–	–	–	–	–	–	–	–
	SERVICE TRADES	–	–	–	–	–	–	–	–
	NATURAL SCIENCE	–	–	–	–	–	–	–	–
	MATHEMATICS & COMPUTER SCIENCE	–	–	–	–	–	–	–	–
	MEDICAL SCIENCE AND HEALTH-RELATED	–	–	–	–	–	–	–	–
	ENGINEERING	–	–	–	–	–	–	–	–
	ARCHITECTURE & TOWN PLANNING	–	–	–	–	–	–	–	–
	TRADE, CRAFT & INDUSTRIAL PGMS.	–	–	–	–	–	–	–	–
	TRANSPORT AND COMMUNICATIONS	–	–	–	–	–	–	–	–
	AGRICULTURE, FORESTRY & FISHERY	–	–	–	–	–	–	–	–
	OTHER AND NOT SPECIFIED	–	–	–	–	–	–	–	–
SUDAN‡ 1981	TOTAL	33 527	10 240	4 109	1 666	29 418	8 574	./.	./.
	EDUCATION SCIENCE & TEACHER TRNG.	885	294	22	3	863	291	./.	./.
	HUMANITIES, RELIGION & THEOLOGY	7 777	2 482	–	–	7 777	2 482	./.	./.
	FINE AND APPLIED ARTS	355	72	355	72	–	–	–	–
	LAW	5 149	1 742	–	–	5 149	1 742	./.	./.
	SOCIAL AND BEHAVIOURAL SCIENCE	1 776	645	–	–	1 776	645	./.	./.
	COMMERCIAL & BUSINESS ADMIN.	7 862	2 124	294	81	7 568	2 043	./.	./.
	MASS COMMUNICATION & DOCUMENT.	–	–	–	–	–	–	–	–
	HOME ECONOMICS (DOMESTIC SCIENCE)	–	–	–	–	–	–	–	–
	SERVICE TRADES	–	–	–	–	–	–	–	–
	NATURAL SCIENCE	489	186	–	–	489	186	./.	./.
	MATHEMATICS & COMPUTER SCIENCE	351	70	–	–	351	70	./.	./.
	MEDICAL SCIENCE AND HEALTH-RELATED	2 128	681	317	177	1 811	504	./.	./.
	ENGINEERING	2 418	180	1 061	108	1 357	72	./.	./.
	ARCHITECTURE & TOWN PLANNING	171	27	–	–	171	27	./.	./.
	TRADE, CRAFT & INDUSTRIAL PGMS.	–	–	–	–	–	–	–	–
	TRANSPORT AND COMMUNICATIONS	–	–	–	–	–	–	–	–
	AGRICULTURE, FORESTRY & FISHERY	2 959	556	853	44	2 106	512	./.	./.
	OTHER AND NOT SPECIFIED	1 207	1 181	1 207	1 181	–	–	–	–
SWAZILAND‡ 1982	TOTAL	1 201	459	456	173	745	286	–	–
	EDUCATION SCIENCE & TEACHER TRNG.	159	78	137	64	22	14	–	–
	HUMANITIES, RELIGION & THEOLOGY	123	80	–	–	123	80	–	–
	FINE AND APPLIED ARTS	–	–	–	–	–	–	–	–
	LAW	107	29	–	–	107	29	–	–
	SOCIAL AND BEHAVIOURAL SCIENCE	100	48	–	–	100	48	–	–
	COMMERCIAL & BUSINESS ADMIN.	180	73	93	33	87	40	–	–
	MASS COMMUNICATION & DOCUMENT.	–	–	–	–	–	–	–	–
	HOME ECONOMICS (DOMESTIC SCIENCE)	50	50	50	50	–	–	–	–
	SERVICE TRADES	–	–	–	–	–	–	–	–
	NATURAL SCIENCE	244	65	–	–	244	65	–	–
	MATHEMATICS & COMPUTER SCIENCE	./.	./.	–	–	./.	./.	–	–
	MEDICAL SCIENCE AND HEALTH-RELATED	–	–	–	–	–	–	–	–
	ENGINEERING	–	–	–	–	–	–	–	–
	ARCHITECTURE & TOWN PLANNING	–	–	–	–	–	–	–	–
	TRADE, CRAFT & INDUSTRIAL PGMS.	–	–	–	–	–	–	–	–
	TRANSPORT AND COMMUNICATIONS	–	–	–	–	–	–	–	–
	AGRICULTURE, FORESTRY & FISHERY	238	36	176	26	62	10	–	–
	OTHER AND NOT SPECIFIED	–	–	–	–	–	–	–	–

COUNTRY / YEAR PAYS / ANNEE PAIS / AÑO	FIELD OF STUDY DOMAINES D'ETUDES SECTORES DE ESTUDIOS	INTERNATIONAL STANDARD CLASSIFICATION OF EDUCATION BY LEVEL / CLASSIFICATION INTERNATIONALE TYPE DE L'EDUCATION PAR NIVEAUX / CLASIFICACION INTERNACIONAL NORMALIZADA DE LA EDUCACION POR NIVELES							
		ALL LEVELS TOUS NIVEAUX TODOS LOS NIVELES		LEVEL 5 NIVEAU 5 NIVEL 5		LEVEL 6 NIVEAU 6 NIVEL 6		LEVEL 7 NIVEAU 7 NIVEL 7	
		MF	F	MF	F	MF	F	MF	F
		(1)	(2)	(3)	(4)	(5)	(6)	(7)	(8)
TUNISIA 1982	TOTAL	34 077	11 209	4 569	1 922	25 174	8 347	4 334	940
	EDUCATION SCIENCE & TEACHER TRNG.	2 617	684	–	–	2 571	680	46	4
	HUMANITIES, RELIGION & THEOLOGY	6 308	2 872	–	–	5 615	2 671	693	201
	FINE AND APPLIED ARTS	201	103	29	7	143	78	29	18
	LAW	2 307	844	–	–	2 068	763	239	81
	SOCIAL AND BEHAVIOURAL SCIENCE	2 322	653	–	–	2 149	597	173	56
	COMMERCIAL & BUSINESS ADMIN.	3 869	1 210	804	349	1 716	569	1 349	292
	MASS COMMUNICATION & DOCUMENT.	439	204	99	48	340	156	–	–
	HOME ECONOMICS (DOMESTIC SCIENCE)	197	106	197	106	–	–	–	–
	SERVICE TRADES	342	83	342	83	–	–	–	–
	NATURAL SCIENCE	5 143	1 494	–	–	4 872	1 386	271	108
	MATHEMATICS & COMPUTER SCIENCE	233	46	25	7	85	14	123	25
	MEDICAL SCIENCE AND HEALTH-RELATED	5 005	2 297	1 492	1 107	3 513	1 190	–	–
	ENGINEERING	2 396	147	748	32	1 052	80	596	35
	ARCHITECTURE & TOWN PLANNING	353	65	–	–	–	–	353	65
	TRADE, CRAFT & INDUSTRIAL PGMS.	1 106	203	454	139	561	62	91	2
	TRANSPORT AND COMMUNICATIONS	110	12	110	12	–	–	–	–
	AGRICULTURE, FORESTRY & FISHERY	1 129	186	269	32	489	101	371	53
	OTHER AND NOT SPECIFIED	–	–	–	–	–	–	–	–
UGANDA‡ 1982	TOTAL	7 312	1 964	2 892	1 012	4 420	952	./.	./.
	EDUCATION SCIENCE & TEACHER TRNG.	1 638	488	1 126	331	512	157	./.	./.
	HUMANITIES, RELIGION & THEOLOGY	440	115	–	–	440	115	./.	./.
	FINE AND APPLIED ARTS	99	30	28	9	71	21	./.	./.
	LAW	188	52	–	–	188	52	–	–
	SOCIAL AND BEHAVIOURAL SCIENCE	1 013	259	–	–	1 013	259	./.	./.
	COMMERCIAL & BUSINESS ADMIN.	1 271	632	1 079	588	192	44	–	–
	MASS COMMUNICATION & DOCUMENT.	38	18	38	18	–	–	–	–
	HOME ECONOMICS (DOMESTIC SCIENCE)	–	–	–	–	–	–	–	–
	SERVICE TRADES	50	33	50	33	–	–	–	–
	NATURAL SCIENCE	733	84	–	–	733	84	./.	./.
	MATHEMATICS & COMPUTER SCIENCE	92	3	–	–	92	3	–	–
	MEDICAL SCIENCE AND HEALTH-RELATED	498	117	–	–	498	117	./.	./.
	ENGINEERING	781	37	571	33	210	4	–	–
	ARCHITECTURE & TOWN PLANNING	–	–	–	–	–	–	–	–
	TRADE, CRAFT & INDUSTRIAL PGMS.	–	–	–	–	–	–	–	–
	TRANSPORT AND COMMUNICATIONS	–	–	–	–	–	–	–	–
	AGRICULTURE, FORESTRY & FISHERY	471	96	–	–	471	96	./.	./.
	OTHER AND NOT SPECIFIED	–	–	–	–	–	–	–	–
UNITED REPUBLIC OF TANZANIA‡ 1981	TOTAL	3 662	770	282	28	2 852	686	528	56
	EDUCATION SCIENCE & TEACHER TRNG.	1 166	381	–	–	1 166	381	–	–
	HUMANITIES, RELIGION & THEOLOGY	92	8	–	–	–	–	92	8
	FINE AND APPLIED ARTS	156	23	–	–	–	–	156	23
	LAW	305	71	117	7	164	60	24	4
	SOCIAL AND BEHAVIOURAL SCIENCE	118	12	–	–	–	–	118	12
	COMMERCIAL & BUSINESS ADMIN.	366	84	–	–	350	82	16	2
	MASS COMMUNICATION & DOCUMENT.	–	–	–	–	–	–	–	–
	HOME ECONOMICS (DOMESTIC SCIENCE)	–	–	–	–	–	–	–	–
	SERVICE TRADES	–	–	–	–	–	–	–	–
	NATURAL SCIENCE	58	10	–	–	53	9	5	1
	MATHEMATICS & COMPUTER SCIENCE	–	–	–	–	–	–	–	–
	MEDICAL SCIENCE AND HEALTH-RELATED	500	108	148	18	295	89	57	1
	ENGINEERING	579	23	–	–	572	23	7	–
	ARCHITECTURE & TOWN PLANNING	–	–	–	–	–	–	–	–
	TRADE, CRAFT & INDUSTRIAL PGMS.	–	–	–	–	–	–	–	–
	TRANSPORT AND COMMUNICATIONS	–	–	–	–	–	–	–	–
	AGRICULTURE, FORESTRY & FISHERY	305	47	–	–	252	42	53	5
	OTHER AND NOT SPECIFIED	17	3	17	3	–	–	–	–

3.13 Third level: students by level and field of study
Troisième degré: étudiants par niveau de programmes et domaine d'études
Tercer grado: estudiantes por nivel de programas y sector de estudios

COUNTRY / YEAR PAYS / ANNEE PAIS / AÑO	FIELD OF STUDY DOMAINES D'ETUDES SECTORES DE ESTUDIOS	INTERNATIONAL STANDARD CLASSIFICATION OF EDUCATION BY LEVEL / CLASSIFICATION INTERNATIONALE TYPE DE L'EDUCATION PAR NIVEAUX / CLASIFICACION INTERNACIONAL NORMALIZADA DE LA EDUCACION POR NIVELES							
		ALL LEVELS / TOUS NIVEAUX / TODOS LOS NIVELES		LEVEL 5 / NIVEAU 5 / NIVEL 5		LEVEL 6 / NIVEAU 6 / NIVEL 6		LEVEL 7 / NIVEAU 7 / NIVEL 7	
		MF	F	MF	F	MF	F	MF	F
		(1)	(2)	(3)	(4)	(5)	(6)	(7)	(8)
ZIMBABWE‡ 1984	TOTAL	4 131	...	234	...	3 191	...	706	...
	EDUCATION SCIENCE & TEACHER TRNG.	533	...	61	...	191	...	281	...
	HUMANITIES, RELIGION & THEOLOGY	610	...	15	...	489	...	106	...
	FINE AND APPLIED ARTS	./.	...	./.	...	./.	...	./.	...
	LAW	927	...	112	...	751	...	64	...
	SOCIAL AND BEHAVIOURAL SCIENCE	766	...	46	...	648	...	72	...
	COMMERCIAL & BUSINESS ADMIN.	./.	...	./.	...	./.	...	./.	...
	MASS COMMUNICATION & DOCUMENT.	–	–	–	–	–	–	–	–
	HOME ECONOMICS (DOMESTIC SCIENCE)	–	–	–	–	–	–	–	–
	SERVICE TRADES	–	–	–	–	–	–	–	–
	NATURAL SCIENCE	309	...	–	–	234	...	75	...
	MATHEMATICS & COMPUTER SCIENCE	–	–	–	–	–	–	–	–
	MEDICAL SCIENCE AND HEALTH–RELATED	484	...	–	–	410	...	74	...
	ENGINEERING	262	...	–	–	257	...	5	...
	ARCHITECTURE & TOWN PLANNING	–	–	–	–	–	–	–	–
	TRADE, CRAFT & INDUSTRIAL PGMS.	–	–	–	–	–	–	–	–
	TRANSPORT AND COMMUNICATIONS	–	–	–	–	–	–	–	–
	AGRICULTURE, FORESTRY & FISHERY	240	...	–	–	211	...	29	...
	OTHER AND NOT SPECIFIED	–	–	–	–	–	–	–	–
AMERICA, NORTH									
BAHAMAS 1982	TOTAL	3 097	...	3 097	...	–	–	–	–
	EDUCATION SCIENCE & TEACHER TRNG.	116	...	116	...	–	–	–	–
	HUMANITIES, RELIGION & THEOLOGY	154	...	154	...	–	–	–	–
	FINE AND APPLIED ARTS	–	–	–	–	–	–	–	–
	LAW	–	–	–	–	–	–	–	–
	SOCIAL AND BEHAVIOURAL SCIENCE	138	...	138	...	–	–	–	–
	COMMERCIAL & BUSINESS ADMIN.	1 472	...	1 472	...	–	–	–	–
	MASS COMMUNICATION & DOCUMENT.	–	–	–	–	–	–	–	–
	HOME ECONOMICS (DOMESTIC SCIENCE)	–	–	–	–	–	–	–	–
	SERVICE TRADES	–	–	–	–	–	–	–	–
	NATURAL SCIENCE	325	...	325	...	–	–	–	–
	MATHEMATICS & COMPUTER SCIENCE	–	–	–	–	–	–	–	–
	MEDICAL SCIENCE AND HEALTH–RELATED	–	–	–	–	–	–	–	–
	ENGINEERING	–	–	–	–	–	–	–	–
	ARCHITECTURE & TOWN PLANNING	–	–	–	–	–	–	–	–
	TRADE, CRAFT & INDUSTRIAL PGMS.	61	...	61	...	–	–	–	–
	TRANSPORT AND COMMUNICATIONS	–	–	–	–	–	–	–	–
	AGRICULTURE, FORESTRY & FISHERY	–	–	–	–	–	–	–	–
	OTHER AND NOT SPECIFIED	831	...	831	...	–	–	–	–
BARBADOS‡ 1984	TOTAL	5 227	2 565	3 527	1 634	1 617	892	83	39
	EDUCATION SCIENCE & TEACHER TRNG.	373	234	355	224	18	10	–	–
	HUMANITIES, RELIGION & THEOLOGY	706	472	262	164	413	292	31	16
	FINE AND APPLIED ARTS	66	43	66	43	–	–	–	–
	LAW	297	165	./.	./.	270	155	27	10
	SOCIAL AND BEHAVIOURAL SCIENCE	1 344	898	804	615	528	277	12	6
	COMMERCIAL & BUSINESS ADMIN.	./.	./.	./.	./.	–	–	–	–
	MASS COMMUNICATION & DOCUMENT.	–	–	–	–	–	–	–	–
	HOME ECONOMICS (DOMESTIC SCIENCE)	47	47	47	47	–	–	–	–
	SERVICE TRADES	265	174	254	167	11	7	–	–
	NATURAL SCIENCE	773	312	383	154	377	151	13	7
	MATHEMATICS & COMPUTER SCIENCE	./.	./.	./.	./.	./.	./.	./.	./.
	MEDICAL SCIENCE AND HEALTH–RELATED	142	89	142	89	–	–	–	–
	ENGINEERING	117	4	117	4	–	–	–	–
	ARCHITECTURE & TOWN PLANNING	–	–	–	–	–	–	–	–
	TRADE, CRAFT & INDUSTRIAL PGMS.	1 003	78	1 003	78	–	–	–	–
	TRANSPORT AND COMMUNICATIONS	–	–	–	–	–	–	–	–
	AGRICULTURE, FORESTRY & FISHERY	40	12	40	12	–	–	–	–
	OTHER AND NOT SPECIFIED	54	37	54	37	–	–	–	–

COUNTRY YEAR / PAYS ANNEE / PAIS AÑO	FIELD OF STUDY / DOMAINES D'ETUDES / SECTORES DE ESTUDIOS	INTERNATIONAL STANDARD CLASSIFICATION OF EDUCATION BY LEVEL / CLASSIFICATION INTERNATIONALE TYPE DE L'EDUCATION PAR NIVEAUX / CLASIFICACION INTERNACIONAL NORMALIZADA DE LA EDUCACION POR NIVELES							
		ALL LEVELS / TOUS NIVEAUX / TODOS LOS NIVELES		LEVEL 5 / NIVEAU 5 / NIVEL 5		LEVEL 6 / NIVEAU 6 / NIVEL 6		LEVEL 7 / NIVEAU 7 / NIVEL 7	
		MF	F	MF	F	MF	F	MF	F
		(1)	(2)	(3)	(4)	(5)	(6)	(7)	(8)
BERMUDA‡ 1982	TOTAL	2 667	...	2 667	...	–	–	–	–
	EDUCATION SCIENCE & TEACHER TRNG.	30	...	30	...	–	–	–	–
	HUMANITIES, RELIGION & THEOLOGY	401	...	401	...	–	–	–	–
	FINE AND APPLIED ARTS	./.	...	./.	...	–	–	–	–
	LAW	–	–	–	–	–	–	–	–
	SOCIAL AND BEHAVIOURAL SCIENCE	./.	...	./.	...	–	–	–	–
	COMMERCIAL & BUSINESS ADMIN.	1 417	...	1 417	...	–	–	–	–
	MASS COMMUNICATION & DOCUMENT.	–	–	–	–	–	–	–	–
	HOME ECONOMICS (DOMESTIC SCIENCE)	–	–	–	–	–	–	–	–
	SERVICE TRADES	374	...	374	...	–	–	–	–
	NATURAL SCIENCE	./.	...	./.	...	–	–	–	–
	MATHEMATICS & COMPUTER SCIENCE	./.	...	./.	...	–	–	–	–
	MEDICAL SCIENCE AND HEALTH-RELATED	–	–	–	–	–	–	–	–
	ENGINEERING	–	–	–	–	–	–	–	–
	ARCHITECTURE & TOWN PLANNING	–	–	–	–	–	–	–	–
	TRADE, CRAFT & INDUSTRIAL PGMS.	372	...	372	...	–	–	–	–
	TRANSPORT AND COMMUNICATIONS	–	–	–	–	–	–	–	–
	AGRICULTURE, FORESTRY & FISHERY	–	–	–	–	–	–	–	–
	OTHER AND NOT SPECIFIED	73	...	73	...	–	–	–	–
CANADA 1983	TOTAL	1 192 525	617 802	328 560	175 542	777 303	407 248	87 062	35 012
	EDUCATION SCIENCE & TEACHER TRNG.	73 617	53 355	6 775	5 890	53 497	39 521	13 345	7 944
	HUMANITIES, RELIGION & THEOLOGY	185 280	100 928	4 703	2 957	171 194	93 293	9 383	4 678
	FINE AND APPLIED ARTS	43 562	26 811	19 287	11 737	22 664	14 192	1 611	882
	LAW	11 913	5 301	–	–	11 105	4 991	808	310
	SOCIAL AND BEHAVIOURAL SCIENCE	95 763	55 388	22 154	14 599	62 514	35 861	11 095	4 928
	COMMERCIAL & BUSINESS ADMIN.	167 047	85 452	69 245	44 235	86 057	37 680	11 745	3 537
	MASS COMMUNICATION & DOCUMENT.	13 829	8 123	6 490	3 648	5 801	3 408	1 538	1 067
	HOME ECONOMICS (DOMESTIC SCIENCE)	4 450	4 243	91	86	4 080	3 926	279	231
	SERVICE TRADES	2 871	1 457	2 871	1 457	–	–	–	–
	NATURAL SCIENCE	30 478	10 787	–	–	23 807	9 126	6 671	1 661
	MATHEMATICS & COMPUTER SCIENCE	52 069	18 975	18 692	8 465	31 071	10 026	2 306	484
	MEDICAL SCIENCE AND HEALTH-RELATED	74 102	54 171	33 506	29 062	29 385	20 625	11 211	4 484
	ENGINEERING	92 701	8 114	41 923	3 163	42 967	4 265	7 811	686
	ARCHITECTURE & TOWN PLANNING	9 646	2 060	6 210	978	2 960	938	476	144
	TRADE, CRAFT & INDUSTRIAL PGMS.	–	–	–	–	–	–	–	–
	TRANSPORT AND COMMUNICATIONS	1 395	145	1 395	145	–	–	–	–
	AGRICULTURE, FORESTRY & FISHERY	18 961	6 101	11 870	3 171	5 661	2 478	1 430	452
	OTHER AND NOT SPECIFIED	315 241	176 391	83 348	45 949	224 540	126 918	7 353	3 524
COSTA RICA‡ 1984	TOTAL	54 456	...	./.	...	54 456	...	–	–
	EDUCATION SCIENCE & TEACHER TRNG.	5 738	...	./.	...	5 738	...	–	–
	HUMANITIES, RELIGION & THEOLOGY	11 152	...	./.	...	11 152	...	–	–
	FINE AND APPLIED ARTS	1 227	...	./.	...	1 227	...	–	–
	LAW	3 153	...	–	–	3 153	...	–	–
	SOCIAL AND BEHAVIOURAL SCIENCE	5 830	...	–	–	5 830	...	–	–
	COMMERCIAL & BUSINESS ADMIN.	6 053	...	./.	...	6 053	...	–	–
	MASS COMMUNICATION & DOCUMENT.	1 208	...	–	–	1 208	...	–	–
	HOME ECONOMICS (DOMESTIC SCIENCE)	–	–	–	–	–	–	–	–
	SERVICE TRADES	188	...	–	–	188	...	–	–
	NATURAL SCIENCE	1 530	...	–	–	1 530	...	–	–
	MATHEMATICS & COMPUTER SCIENCE	2 440	...	–	–	2 440	...	–	–
	MEDICAL SCIENCE AND HEALTH-RELATED	3 323	...	./.	...	3 323	...	–	–
	ENGINEERING	4 799	...	./.	...	4 799	...	–	–
	ARCHITECTURE & TOWN PLANNING	984	...	–	–	984	...	–	–
	TRADE, CRAFT & INDUSTRIAL PGMS.	–	–	–	–	–	–	–	–
	TRANSPORT AND COMMUNICATIONS	–	–	–	–	–	–	–	–
	AGRICULTURE, FORESTRY & FISHERY	2 296	...	–	–	2 296	...	–	–
	OTHER AND NOT SPECIFIED	4 535	...	–	–	4 535	...	–	–

3.13 Third level: students by level and field of study
Troisième degré: étudiants par niveau de programmes et domaine d'études
Tercer grado: estudiantes por nivel de programas y sector de estudios

COUNTRY / YEAR PAYS / ANNEE PAIS / AÑO	FIELD OF STUDY DOMAINES D'ETUDES SECTORES DE ESTUDIOS	INTERNATIONAL STANDARD CLASSIFICATION OF EDUCATION BY LEVEL / CLASSIFICATION INTERNATIONALE TYPE DE L'EDUCATION PAR NIVEAUX / CLASIFICACION INTERNACIONAL NORMALIZADA DE LA EDUCACION POR NIVELES							
		ALL LEVELS TOUS NIVEAUX TODOS LOS NIVELES		LEVEL 5 NIVEAU 5 NIVEL 5		LEVEL 6 NIVEAU 6 NIVEL 6		LEVEL 7 NIVEAU 7 NIVEL 7	
		MF	F	MF	F	MF	F	MF	F
		(1)	(2)	(3)	(4)	(5)	(6)	(7)	(8)
CUBA 1984	TOTAL	212 155	113 956	–	–	212 155	113 956	–	–
	EDUCATION SCIENCE & TEACHER TRNG.	92 535	58 196	–	–	92 535	58 196	–	–
	HUMANITIES, RELIGION & THEOLOGY	2 815	2 678	–	–	2 815	2 678	–	–
	FINE AND APPLIED ARTS	1 222	627	–	–	1 222	627	–	–
	LAW	2 898	1 738	–	–	2 898	1 738	–	–
	SOCIAL AND BEHAVIOURAL SCIENCE	13 385	6 310	–	–	13 385	6 310	–	–
	COMMERCIAL & BUSINESS ADMIN.	8 166	5 300	–	–	8 166	5 300	–	–
	MASS COMMUNICATION & DOCUMENT.	1 443	847	–	–	1 443	847	–	–
	HOME ECONOMICS (DOMESTIC SCIENCE)	–	–	–	–	–	–	–	–
	SERVICE TRADES	–	–	–	–	–	–	–	–
	NATURAL SCIENCE	2 715	1 715	–	–	2 715	1 715	–	–
	MATHEMATICS & COMPUTER SCIENCE	1 619	901	–	–	1 619	901	–	–
	MEDICAL SCIENCE AND HEALTH–RELATED	25 793	15 321	–	–	25 793	15 321	–	–
	ENGINEERING	24 177	7 651	–	–	24 177	7 651	–	–
	ARCHITECTURE & TOWN PLANNING	6 606	2 990	–	–	6 606	2 990	–	–
	TRADE, CRAFT & INDUSTRIAL PGMS.	351	254	–	–	351	254	–	–
	TRANSPORT AND COMMUNICATIONS	2 988	484	–	–	2 988	484	–	–
	AGRICULTURE, FORESTRY & FISHERY	16 790	7 032	–	–	16 790	7 032	–	–
	OTHER AND NOT SPECIFIED	8 652	1 912	–	–	8 652	1 912	–	–
DOMINICA 1984	TOTAL	60	40	60	40	–	–	–	–
	EDUCATION SCIENCE & TEACHER TRNG.	60	40	60	40	–	–	–	–
	HUMANITIES, RELIGION & THEOLOGY	–	–	–	–	–	–	–	–
	FINE AND APPLIED ARTS	–	–	–	–	–	–	–	–
	LAW	–	–	–	–	–	–	–	–
	SOCIAL AND BEHAVIOURAL SCIENCE	–	–	–	–	–	–	–	–
	COMMERCIAL & BUSINESS ADMIN.	–	–	–	–	–	–	–	–
	MASS COMMUNICATION & DOCUMENT.	–	–	–	–	–	–	–	–
	HOME ECONOMICS (DOMESTIC SCIENCE)	–	–	–	–	–	–	–	–
	SERVICE TRADES	–	–	–	–	–	–	–	–
	NATURAL SCIENCE	–	–	–	–	–	–	–	–
	MATHEMATICS & COMPUTER SCIENCE	–	–	–	–	–	–	–	–
	MEDICAL SCIENCE AND HEALTH–RELATED	–	–	–	–	–	–	–	–
	ENGINEERING	–	–	–	–	–	–	–	–
	ARCHITECTURE & TOWN PLANNING	–	–	–	–	–	–	–	–
	TRADE, CRAFT & INDUSTRIAL PGMS.	–	–	–	–	–	–	–	–
	TRANSPORT AND COMMUNICATIONS	–	–	–	–	–	–	–	–
	AGRICULTURE, FORESTRY & FISHERY	–	–	–	–	–	–	–	–
	OTHER AND NOT SPECIFIED	–	–	–	–	–	–	–	–
EL SALVADOR 1983	TOTAL	57 374	24 635	10 433	4 943	46 876	19 684	65	8
	EDUCATION SCIENCE & TEACHER TRNG.	9 074	5 342	4 371	2 401	4 703	2 941	–	–
	HUMANITIES, RELIGION & THEOLOGY	1 025	567	–	–	1 025	567	–	–
	FINE AND APPLIED ARTS	357	241	30	13	327	228	–	–
	LAW	3 261	1 170	–	–	3 261	1 170	–	–
	SOCIAL AND BEHAVIOURAL SCIENCE	4 371	2 221	–	–	4 349	2 219	22	2
	COMMERCIAL & BUSINESS ADMIN.	14 284	5 847	1 253	269	12 991	5 574	40	4
	MASS COMMUNICATION & DOCUMENT.	467	329	–	–	467	329	–	–
	HOME ECONOMICS (DOMESTIC SCIENCE)	74	69	–	–	74	69	–	–
	SERVICE TRADES	117	65	88	58	29	7	–	–
	NATURAL SCIENCE	344	157	–	–	344	157	–	–
	MATHEMATICS & COMPUTER SCIENCE	205	68	–	–	205	68	–	–
	MEDICAL SCIENCE AND HEALTH–RELATED	6 679	3 930	878	849	5 801	3 081	–	–
	ENGINEERING	10 682	1 448	1 422	110	9 257	1 336	3	2
	ARCHITECTURE & TOWN PLANNING	2 259	1 168	167	62	2 092	1 106	–	–
	TRADE, CRAFT & INDUSTRIAL PGMS.	195	120	164	103	31	17	–	–
	TRANSPORT AND COMMUNICATIONS	–	–	–	–	–	–	–	–
	AGRICULTURE, FORESTRY & FISHERY	1 940	183	825	26	1 115	157	–	–
	OTHER AND NOT SPECIFIED	2 040	1 710	1 235	1 052	805	658	–	–

COUNTRY YEAR PAYS ANNEE PAIS AÑO	FIELD OF STUDY DOMAINES D'ETUDES SECTORES DE ESTUDIOS	INTERNATIONAL STANDARD CLASSIFICATION OF EDUCATION BY LEVEL CLASSIFICATION INTERNATIONALE TYPE DE L'EDUCATION PAR NIVEAUX CLASIFICACION INTERNACIONAL NORMALIZADA DE LA EDUCACION POR NIVELES							
		ALL LEVELS TOUS NIVEAUX TODOS LOS NIVELES		LEVEL 5 NIVEAU 5 NIVEL 5		LEVEL 6 NIVEAU 6 NIVEL 6		LEVEL 7 NIVEAU 7 NIVEL 7	
		MF	F	MF	F	MF	F	MF	F
		(1)	(2)	(3)	(4)	(5)	(6)	(7)	(8)
GRENADA‡ 1982	TOTAL	519	256	519	256	–	–	–	–
	EDUCATION SCIENCE & TEACHER TRNG.	–	–	–	–	–	–	–	–
	HUMANITIES, RELIGION & THEOLOGY	–	–	–	–	–	–	–	–
	FINE AND APPLIED ARTS	–	–	–	–	–	–	–	–
	LAW	–	–	–	–	–	–	–	–
	SOCIAL AND BEHAVIOURAL SCIENCE	–	–	–	–	–	–	–	–
	COMMERCIAL & BUSINESS ADMIN.	78	78	78	78	–	–	–	–
	MASS COMMUNICATION & DOCUMENT.	–	–	–	–	–	–	–	–
	HOME ECONOMICS (DOMESTIC SCIENCE)	–	–	–	–	–	–	–	–
	SERVICE TRADES	–	–	–	–	–	–	–	–
	NATURAL SCIENCE	–	–	–	–	–	–	–	–
	MATHEMATICS & COMPUTER SCIENCE	–	–	–	–	–	–	–	–
	MEDICAL SCIENCE AND HEALTH-RELATED	89	84	89	84	–	–	–	–
	ENGINEERING	129	13	129	13	–	–	–	–
	ARCHITECTURE & TOWN PLANNING	./.	./.	./.	./.	–	–	–	–
	TRADE, CRAFT & INDUSTRIAL PGMS.	–	–	–	–	–	–	–	–
	TRANSPORT AND COMMUNICATIONS	–	–	–	–	–	–	–	–
	AGRICULTURE, FORESTRY & FISHERY	39	12	39	12	–	–	–	–
	OTHER AND NOT SPECIFIED	184	69	184	69	–	–	–	–
HONDURAS 1984	TOTAL	33 742	...	3 325	...	30 417	...	–	–
	EDUCATION SCIENCE & TEACHER TRNG.	3 407	...	2 683	...	724	...	–	–
	HUMANITIES, RELIGION & THEOLOGY	211	...	–	–	211	...	–	–
	FINE AND APPLIED ARTS	21	...	–	–	21	...	–	–
	LAW	2 978	...	–	–	2 978	...	–	–
	SOCIAL AND BEHAVIOURAL SCIENCE	3 850	...	–	–	3 850	...	–	–
	COMMERCIAL & BUSINESS ADMIN.	6 216	...	–	–	6 216	...	–	–
	MASS COMMUNICATION & DOCUMENT.	340	...	–	–	340	...	–	–
	HOME ECONOMICS (DOMESTIC SCIENCE)	–	–	–	–	–	–	–	–
	SERVICE TRADES	–	–	–	–	–	–	–	–
	NATURAL SCIENCE	1 891	...	–	–	1 891	...	–	–
	MATHEMATICS & COMPUTER SCIENCE	92	...	–	–	92	...	–	–
	MEDICAL SCIENCE AND HEALTH-RELATED	4 239	...	–	–	4 239	...	–	–
	ENGINEERING	6 364	...	–	–	6 364	...	–	–
	ARCHITECTURE & TOWN PLANNING	323	...	–	–	323	...	–	–
	TRADE, CRAFT & INDUSTRIAL PGMS.	–	–	–	–	–	–	–	–
	TRANSPORT AND COMMUNICATIONS	–	–	–	–	–	–	–	–
	AGRICULTURE, FORESTRY & FISHERY	2 850	...	642	...	2 208	...	–	–
	OTHER AND NOT SPECIFIED	960	...	–	–	960	...	–	–
MEXICO‡ 1983	TOTAL	939 513	317 276	–	–	939 513	317 276	–	–
	EDUCATION SCIENCE & TEACHER TRNG.	11 505	7 939	–	–	11 505	7 939	–	–
	HUMANITIES, RELIGION & THEOLOGY	10 632	5 853	–	–	10 632	5 853	–	–
	FINE AND APPLIED ARTS	8 647	4 536	–	–	8 647	4 536	–	–
	LAW	101 280	32 423	–	–	101 280	32 423	–	–
	SOCIAL AND BEHAVIOURAL SCIENCE	83 728	45 663	–	–	83 728	45 663	–	–
	COMMERCIAL & BUSINESS ADMIN.	181 465	76 738	–	–	181 465	76 738	–	–
	MASS COMMUNICATION & DOCUMENT.	19 291	11 748	–	–	19 291	11 748	–	–
	HOME ECONOMICS (DOMESTIC SCIENCE)	–	–	–	–	–	–	–	–
	SERVICE TRADES	11 409	7 643	–	–	11 409	7 643	–	–
	NATURAL SCIENCE	24 242	9 937	–	–	24 242	9 937	–	–
	MATHEMATICS & COMPUTER SCIENCE	12 917	5 341	–	–	12 917	5 341	–	–
	MEDICAL SCIENCE AND HEALTH-RELATED	133 685	63 384	–	–	133 685	63 384	–	–
	ENGINEERING	257 537	28 484	–	–	257 537	28 484	–	–
	ARCHITECTURE & TOWN PLANNING	39 298	8 692	–	–	39 298	8 692	–	–
	TRADE, CRAFT & INDUSTRIAL PGMS.	–	–	–	–	–	–	–	–
	TRANSPORT AND COMMUNICATIONS	274	–	–	–	274	–	–	–
	AGRICULTURE, FORESTRY & FISHERY	39 049	7 828	–	–	39 049	7 828	–	–
	OTHER AND NOT SPECIFIED	4 554	1 067	–	–	4 554	1 067	–	–

3.13 Third level: students by level and field of study
Troisième degré: étudiants par niveau de programmes et domaine d'études
Tercer grado: estudiantes por nivel de programas y sector de estudios

COUNTRY / YEAR PAYS / ANNEE PAIS / AÑO	FIELD OF STUDY DOMAINES D'ETUDES SECTORES DE ESTUDIOS	INTERNATIONAL STANDARD CLASSIFICATION OF EDUCATION BY LEVEL / CLASSIFICATION INTERNATIONALE TYPE DE L'EDUCATION PAR NIVEAUX / CLASIFICACION INTERNACIONAL NORMALIZADA DE LA EDUCACION POR NIVELES							
		ALL LEVELS TOUS NIVEAUX TODOS LOS NIVELES		LEVEL 5 NIVEAU 5 NIVEL 5		LEVEL 6 NIVEAU 6 NIVEL 6		LEVEL 7 NIVEAU 7 NIVEL 7	
		MF	F	MF	F	MF	F	MF	F
		(1)	(2)	(3)	(4)	(5)	(6)	(7)	(8)
NICARAGUA 1985	TOTAL	29 001	16 355	5 558	2 690	23 443	13 665	–	–
	EDUCATION SCIENCE & TEACHER TRNG.	5 856	4 150	–	–	5 856	4 150	–	–
	HUMANITIES, RELIGION & THEOLOGY	112	105	–	–	112	105	–	–
	FINE AND APPLIED ARTS	142	105	84	63	58	42	–	–
	LAW	446	235	–	–	446	235	–	–
	SOCIAL AND BEHAVIOURAL SCIENCE	2 760	1 650	–	–	2 760	1 650	–	–
	COMMERCIAL & BUSINESS ADMIN.	3 528	2 068	662	449	2 866	1 619	–	–
	MASS COMMUNICATION & DOCUMENT.	360	294	–	–	360	294	–	–
	HOME ECONOMICS (DOMESTIC SCIENCE)	244	239	66	65	178	174	–	–
	SERVICE TRADES	–	–	–	–	–	–	–	–
	NATURAL SCIENCE	712	486	–	–	712	486	–	–
	MATHEMATICS & COMPUTER SCIENCE	395	255	201	126	194	129	–	–
	MEDICAL SCIENCE AND HEALTH–RELATED	4 339	2 728	850	800	3 489	1 928	–	–
	ENGINEERING	4 013	1 290	1 361	276	2 652	1 014	–	–
	ARCHITECTURE & TOWN PLANNING	404	246	–	–	404	246	–	–
	TRADE, CRAFT & INDUSTRIAL PGMS.	69	57	69	57	–	–	–	–
	TRANSPORT AND COMMUNICATIONS	46	4	46	4	–	–	–	–
	AGRICULTURE, FORESTRY & FISHERY	4 477	2 039	1 121	446	3 356	1 593	–	–
	OTHER AND NOT SPECIFIED	1 098	404	1 098	404	–	–	–	–
PANAMA 1984	TOTAL	52 224	29 229	7 826	3 188	43 856	25 779	542	262
	EDUCATION SCIENCE & TEACHER TRNG.	3 033	2 346	–	–	2 756	2 182	277	164
	HUMANITIES, RELIGION & THEOLOGY	2 029	1 494	–	–	2 029	1 494	–	–
	FINE AND APPLIED ARTS	409	254	48	10	361	244	–	–
	LAW	2 163	858	–	–	2 163	858	–	–
	SOCIAL AND BEHAVIOURAL SCIENCE	3 672	2 008	–	–	3 672	2 008	–	–
	COMMERCIAL & BUSINESS ADMIN.	17 228	10 808	1 909	1 682	15 183	9 085	136	41
	MASS COMMUNICATION & DOCUMENT.	1 514	976	34	16	1 480	960	–	–
	HOME ECONOMICS (DOMESTIC SCIENCE)	253	253	–	–	253	253	–	–
	SERVICE TRADES	16	4	–	–	16	4	–	–
	NATURAL SCIENCE	1 329	659	32	20	1 297	639	–	–
	MATHEMATICS & COMPUTER SCIENCE	1 106	562	–	–	1 090	555	16	7
	MEDICAL SCIENCE AND HEALTH–RELATED	3 609	2 842	59	52	3 538	2 790	12	–
	ENGINEERING	9 607	2 489	5 665	1 373	3 942	1 116	–	–
	ARCHITECTURE & TOWN PLANNING	830	250	–	–	830	250	–	–
	TRADE, CRAFT & INDUSTRIAL PGMS.	509	242	79	35	430	207	–	–
	TRANSPORT AND COMMUNICATIONS	–	–	–	–	–	–	–	–
	AGRICULTURE, FORESTRY & FISHERY	332	61	–	–	332	61	–	–
	OTHER AND NOT SPECIFIED	4 585	3 123	–	–	4 484	3 073	101	50
ST. LUCIA 1984	TOTAL	346	158	346	158	–	–	–	–
	EDUCATION SCIENCE & TEACHER TRNG.	112	70	112	70	–	–	–	–
	HUMANITIES, RELIGION & THEOLOGY	–	–	–	–	–	–	–	–
	FINE AND APPLIED ARTS	–	–	–	–	–	–	–	–
	LAW	–	–	–	–	–	–	–	–
	SOCIAL AND BEHAVIOURAL SCIENCE	–	–	–	–	–	–	–	–
	COMMERCIAL & BUSINESS ADMIN.	61	42	61	42	–	–	–	–
	MASS COMMUNICATION & DOCUMENT.	–	–	–	–	–	–	–	–
	HOME ECONOMICS (DOMESTIC SCIENCE)	–	–	–	–	–	–	–	–
	SERVICE TRADES	25	25	25	25	–	–	–	–
	NATURAL SCIENCE	–	–	–	–	–	–	–	–
	MATHEMATICS & COMPUTER SCIENCE	–	–	–	–	–	–	–	–
	MEDICAL SCIENCE AND HEALTH–RELATED	–	–	–	–	–	–	–	–
	ENGINEERING	–	–	–	–	–	–	–	–
	ARCHITECTURE & TOWN PLANNING	27	8	27	8	–	–	–	–
	TRADE, CRAFT & INDUSTRIAL PGMS.	97	8	97	8	–	–	–	–
	TRANSPORT AND COMMUNICATIONS	–	–	–	–	–	–	–	–
	AGRICULTURE, FORESTRY & FISHERY	24	5	24	5	–	–	–	–
	OTHER AND NOT SPECIFIED	–	–	–	–	–	–	–	–

COUNTRY YEAR / PAYS ANNEE / PAIS AÑO	FIELD OF STUDY / DOMAINES D'ETUDES / SECTORES DE ESTUDIOS	INTERNATIONAL STANDARD CLASSIFICATION OF EDUCATION BY LEVEL / CLASSIFICATION INTERNATIONALE TYPE DE L'EDUCATION PAR NIVEAUX / CLASIFICACION INTERNACIONAL NORMALIZADA DE LA EDUCACION POR NIVELES							
		ALL LEVELS / TOUS NIVEAUX / TODOS LOS NIVELES		LEVEL 5 / NIVEAU 5 / NIVEL 5		LEVEL 6 / NIVEAU 6 / NIVEL 6		LEVEL 7 / NIVEAU 7 / NIVEL 7	
		MF	F	MF	F	MF	F	MF	F
		(1)	(2)	(3)	(4)	(5)	(6)	(7)	(8)
TRINIDAD AND TOBAGO‡									
1982	TOTAL	5 470	2 343	2 863	1 291	2 607	1 052	./.	./.
	EDUCATION SCIENCE & TEACHER TRNG.	446	362	326	282	120	80	./.	./.
	HUMANITIES, RELIGION & THEOLOGY	860	578	788	532	72	46	./.	./.
	FINE AND APPLIED ARTS	–	–	–	–	–	–	–	–
	LAW	56	33	–	–	56	33	–	–
	SOCIAL AND BEHAVIOURAL SCIENCE	766	370	–	–	766	370	./.	./.
	COMMERCIAL & BUSINESS ADMIN.	469	274	469	274	–	–	–	–
	MASS COMMUNICATION & DOCUMENT.	–	–	–	–	–	–	–	–
	HOME ECONOMICS (DOMESTIC SCIENCE)	35	35	35	35	–	–	–	–
	SERVICE TRADES	–	–	–	–	–	–	–	–
	NATURAL SCIENCE	697	290	30	13	667	277	./.	./.
	MATHEMATICS & COMPUTER SCIENCE	./.	./.	./.	./.	./.	./.	./.	./.
	MEDICAL SCIENCE AND HEALTH-RELATED	–	–	–	–	–	–	–	–
	ENGINEERING	1 246	216	649	111	597	105	./.	./.
	ARCHITECTURE & TOWN PLANNING	–	–	–	–	–	–	–	–
	TRADE, CRAFT & INDUSTRIAL PGMS.	486	21	486	21	–	–	–	–
	TRANSPORT AND COMMUNICATIONS	50	4	50	4	–	–	–	–
	AGRICULTURE, FORESTRY & FISHERY	329	141	–	–	329	141	./.	./.
	OTHER AND NOT SPECIFIED	30	19	30	19	–	–	–	–
AMERICA, SOUTH									
BOLIVIA‡									
1982	TOTAL	56 632	...	1 135	...	55 497	...	–	–
	EDUCATION SCIENCE & TEACHER TRNG.	366	...	–	–	366	...	–	–
	HUMANITIES, RELIGION & THEOLOGY	1 543	...	–	–	1 543	...	–	–
	FINE AND APPLIED ARTS	77	...	–	–	77	...	–	–
	LAW	6 239	...	–	–	6 239	...	–	–
	SOCIAL AND BEHAVIOURAL SCIENCE	1 107	...	–	–	1 107	...	–	–
	COMMERCIAL & BUSINESS ADMIN.	16 529	...	–	–	16 529	...	–	–
	MASS COMMUNICATION & DOCUMENT.	98	...	–	–	98	...	–	–
	HOME ECONOMICS (DOMESTIC SCIENCE)	–	–	–	–	–	–	–	–
	SERVICE TRADES	–	–	–	–	–	–	–	–
	NATURAL SCIENCE	720	...	–	–	720	...	–	–
	MATHEMATICS & COMPUTER SCIENCE	564	...	–	–	564	...	–	–
	MEDICAL SCIENCE AND HEALTH-RELATED	11 146	...	–	–	11 146	...	–	–
	ENGINEERING	12 179	...	1 135	...	11 044	...	–	–
	ARCHITECTURE & TOWN PLANNING	3 058	...	–	–	3 058	...	–	–
	TRADE, CRAFT & INDUSTRIAL PGMS.	–	–	–	–	–	–	–	–
	TRANSPORT AND COMMUNICATIONS	–	–	–	–	–	–	–	–
	AGRICULTURE, FORESTRY & FISHERY	3 006	...	–	–	3 006	...	–	–
	OTHER AND NOT SPECIFIED	–	–	–	–	–	–	–	–
BRAZIL									
1983	TOTAL	1 479 397	740 327	–	–	1 438 992	723 119	40 405	17 208
	EDUCATION SCIENCE & TEACHER TRNG.	113 294	...	–	–	110 686	...	2 608	1 883
	HUMANITIES, RELIGION & THEOLOGY	149 302	108 377	–	–	145 195	105 687	4 107	2 690
	FINE AND APPLIED ARTS	30 664	22 483	–	–	30 454	22 366	210	117
	LAW	139 870	53 868	–	–	137 901	53 139	1 969	729
	SOCIAL AND BEHAVIOURAL SCIENCE	177 713	103 023	–	–	172 642	100 048	5 071	2 975
	COMMERCIAL & BUSINESS ADMIN.	220 067	74 325	–	–	218 221	73 945	1 846	380
	MASS COMMUNICATION & DOCUMENT.	40 527	25 230	–	–	39 849	24 817	678	413
	HOME ECONOMICS (DOMESTIC SCIENCE)	1 948	1 805	–	–	1 948	1 805	–	–
	SERVICE TRADES	4 494	3 422	–	–	4 494	3 422	–	–
	NATURAL SCIENCE	120 903	...	–	–	114 978	...	5 925	2 602
	MATHEMATICS & COMPUTER SCIENCE	38 197	15 979	–	–	36 617	15 379	1 580	600
	MEDICAL SCIENCE AND HEALTH-RELATED	132 094	81 216	–	–	127 168	79 123	4 926	2 093
	ENGINEERING	164 607	20 290	–	–	157 278	18 967	7 329	1 323
	ARCHITECTURE & TOWN PLANNING	24 801	13 146	–	–	24 303	12 940	498	206
	TRADE, CRAFT & INDUSTRIAL PGMS.	13 357	1 942	–	–	13 357	1 942	–	–
	TRANSPORT AND COMMUNICATIONS	–	–	–	–	–	–	–	–
	AGRICULTURE, FORESTRY & FISHERY	40 616	8 965	–	–	37 230	7 832	3 386	1 133
	OTHER AND NOT SPECIFIED	66 943	43 300	–	–	66 671	43 236	272	64

3.13 Third level: students by level and field of study
Troisième degré: étudiants par niveau de programmes et domaine d'études
Tercer grado: estudiantes por nivel de programas y sector de estudios

COUNTRY / YEAR PAYS / ANNEE PAIS / AÑO	FIELD OF STUDY DOMAINES D'ETUDES SECTORES DE ESTUDIOS	INTERNATIONAL STANDARD CLASSIFICATION OF EDUCATION BY LEVEL / CLASSIFICATION INTERNATIONALE TYPE DE L'EDUCATION PAR NIVEAUX / CLASIFICACION INTERNACIONAL NORMALIZADA DE LA EDUCACION POR NIVELES							
		ALL LEVELS TOUS NIVEAUX TODOS LOS NIVELES		LEVEL 5 NIVEAU 5 NIVEL 5		LEVEL 6 NIVEAU 6 NIVEL 6		LEVEL 7 NIVEAU 7 NIVEL 7	
		MF	F	MF	F	MF	F	MF	F
		(1)	(2)	(3)	(4)	(5)	(6)	(7)	(8)
CHILE 1984	TOTAL	188 665	80 652	53 398	23 994	132 896	55 776	2 371	882
	EDUCATION SCIENCE & TEACHER TRNG.	19 278	15 222	2 324	1 781	16 531	13 239	423	202
	HUMANITIES, RELIGION & THEOLOGY	13 961	8 725	1 171	924	12 440	7 642	350	159
	FINE AND APPLIED ARTS	7 614	4 335	2 745	1 589	4 863	2 744	6	2
	LAW	4 314	1 235	–	–	4 194	1 215	120	20
	SOCIAL AND BEHAVIOURAL SCIENCE	5 087	2 714	1 351	785	3 494	1 856	242	73
	COMMERCIAL & BUSINESS ADMIN.	36 430	14 701	18 810	9 459	17 611	5 241	9	1
	MASS COMMUNICATION & DOCUMENT.	652	428	–	–	617	405	35	23
	HOME ECONOMICS (DOMESTIC SCIENCE)	528	440	–	–	495	418	33	22
	SERVICE TRADES	298	213	298	213	–	–	–	–
	NATURAL SCIENCE	9 535	4 623	218	110	8 748	4 295	569	218
	MATHEMATICS & COMPUTER SCIENCE	8 051	3 017	615	194	7 295	2 780	141	43
	MEDICAL SCIENCE AND HEALTH-RELATED	15 485	8 729	2 832	1 479	12 501	7 190	152	60
	ENGINEERING	54 412	11 211	20 244	6 631	33 971	4 558	197	22
	ARCHITECTURE & TOWN PLANNING	2 554	741	–	–	2 514	724	40	17
	TRADE, CRAFT & INDUSTRIAL PGMS.	1 575	441	1 575	441	–	–	–	–
	TRANSPORT AND COMMUNICATIONS	–	–	–	–	–	–	–	–
	AGRICULTURE, FORESTRY & FISHERY	3 888	1 288	1 098	341	2 751	936	39	11
	OTHER AND NOT SPECIFIED	5 003	2 589	117	47	4 871	2 533	15	9
COLOMBIA‡ 1984	TOTAL	378 586	180 909	62 195	35 420	308 812	142 641	7 579	2 848
	EDUCATION SCIENCE & TEACHER TRNG.	69 952	43 371	5 614	3 981	62 894	38 994	1 444	396
	HUMANITIES, RELIGION & THEOLOGY	2 860	1 372	157	115	1 850	888	853	369
	FINE AND APPLIED ARTS	8 047	5 230	4 831	3 740	3 216	1 490	–	–
	LAW	42 918	20 601	1 128	741	40 892	19 629	898	231
	SOCIAL AND BEHAVIOURAL SCIENCE	./.	./.	./.	./.	./.	./.	./.	./.
	COMMERCIAL & BUSINESS ADMIN.	104 542	50 486	26 073	14 615	76 464	35 009	2 005	862
	MASS COMMUNICATION & DOCUMENT.	./.	./.	./.	./.	./.	./.	./.	./.
	HOME ECONOMICS (DOMESTIC SCIENCE)	./.	./.	./.	./.	./.	./.	./.	./.
	SERVICE TRADES	./.	./.	./.	./.	./.	./.	./.	./.
	NATURAL SCIENCE	5 936	1 781	1 380	414	4 169	1 251	387	116
	MATHEMATICS & COMPUTER SCIENCE	./.	./.	./.	./.	./.	./.	./.	./.
	MEDICAL SCIENCE AND HEALTH-RELATED	45 124	22 358	2 201	1 346	41 547	20 352	1 376	660
	ENGINEERING	88 944	32 631	18 659	9 823	69 714	22 608	571	200
	ARCHITECTURE & TOWN PLANNING	./.	./.	./.	./.	./.	./.	./.	./.
	TRADE, CRAFT & INDUSTRIAL PGMS.	./.	./.	./.	./.	./.	./.	./.	./.
	TRANSPORT AND COMMUNICATIONS	./.	./.	./.	./.	./.	./.	./.	./.
	AGRICULTURE, FORESTRY & FISHERY	10 263	3 079	2 152	645	8 066	2 420	45	14
	OTHER AND NOT SPECIFIED	–	–	–	–	–	–	–	–
GUYANA 1983	TOTAL	2 111	1 012	1 169	630	921	377	21	5
	EDUCATION SCIENCE & TEACHER TRNG.	804	557	646	465	158	92	–	–
	HUMANITIES, RELIGION & THEOLOGY	125	88	–	–	120	87	5	1
	FINE AND APPLIED ARTS	–	–	–	–	–	–	–	–
	LAW	23	9	23	9	–	–	–	–
	SOCIAL AND BEHAVIOURAL SCIENCE	246	100	–	–	235	98	11	2
	COMMERCIAL & BUSINESS ADMIN.	226	80	128	41	98	39	–	–
	MASS COMMUNICATION & DOCUMENT.	18	7	18	7	–	–	–	–
	HOME ECONOMICS (DOMESTIC SCIENCE)	–	–	–	–	–	–	–	–
	SERVICE TRADES	32	3	32	3	–	–	–	–
	NATURAL SCIENCE	120	38	–	–	115	36	5	2
	MATHEMATICS & COMPUTER SCIENCE	45	13	–	–	45	13	–	–
	MEDICAL SCIENCE AND HEALTH-RELATED	41	21	41	21	–	–	–	–
	ENGINEERING	192	5	118	4	74	1	–	–
	ARCHITECTURE & TOWN PLANNING	17	2	13	2	4	–	–	–
	TRADE, CRAFT & INDUSTRIAL PGMS.	–	–	–	–	–	–	–	–
	TRANSPORT AND COMMUNICATIONS	–	–	–	–	–	–	–	–
	AGRICULTURE, FORESTRY & FISHERY	72	11	–	–	72	11	–	–
	OTHER AND NOT SPECIFIED	150	78	150	78	–	–	–	–

COUNTRY YEAR / PAYS ANNEE / PAIS AÑO	FIELD OF STUDY / DOMAINES D'ETUDES / SECTORES DE ESTUDIOS	INTERNATIONAL STANDARD CLASSIFICATION OF EDUCATION BY LEVEL / CLASSIFICATION INTERNATIONALE TYPE DE L'EDUCATION PAR NIVEAUX / CLASIFICACION INTERNACIONAL NORMALIZADA DE LA EDUCACION POR NIVELES							
		ALL LEVELS / TOUS NIVEAUX / TODOS LOS NIVELES		LEVEL 5 / NIVEAU 5 / NIVEL 5		LEVEL 6 / NIVEAU 6 / NIVEL 6		LEVEL 7 / NIVEAU 7 / NIVEL 7	
		MF	F	MF	F	MF	F	MF	F
		(1)	(2)	(3)	(4)	(5)	(6)	(7)	(8)
SURINAME‡ 1984	TOTAL	2 914	1 497	1 640	997	1 274	500	–	–
	EDUCATION SCIENCE & TEACHER TRNG.	1 640	997	1 640	997	–	–	–	–
	HUMANITIES, RELIGION & THEOLOGY	–	–	–	–	–	–	–	–
	FINE AND APPLIED ARTS	–	–	–	–	–	–	–	–
	LAW	./.	./.	–	–	./.	./.	–	–
	SOCIAL AND BEHAVIOURAL SCIENCE	760	369	–	–	760	369	–	–
	COMMERCIAL & BUSINESS ADMIN.	–	–	–	–	–	–	–	–
	MASS COMMUNICATION & DOCUMENT.	–	–	–	–	–	–	–	–
	HOME ECONOMICS (DOMESTIC SCIENCE)	–	–	–	–	–	–	–	–
	SERVICE TRADES	–	–	–	–	–	–	–	–
	NATURAL SCIENCE	–	–	–	–	–	–	–	–
	MATHEMATICS & COMPUTER SCIENCE	–	–	–	–	–	–	–	–
	MEDICAL SCIENCE AND HEALTH-RELATED	206	72	–	–	206	72	–	–
	ENGINEERING	308	59	–	–	308	59	–	–
	ARCHITECTURE & TOWN PLANNING	–	–	–	–	–	–	–	–
	TRADE, CRAFT & INDUSTRIAL PGMS.	–	–	–	–	–	–	–	–
	TRANSPORT AND COMMUNICATIONS	–	–	–	–	–	–	–	–
	AGRICULTURE, FORESTRY & FISHERY	–	–	–	–	–	–	–	–
	OTHER AND NOT SPECIFIED	–	–	–	–	–	–	–	–
URUGUAY 1985	TOTAL	77 480	...	17 894	...	59 586	...	–	–
	EDUCATION SCIENCE & TEACHER TRNG.	1 048	834	–	–	1 048	834	–	–
	HUMANITIES, RELIGION & THEOLOGY	2 704	1 877	54	34	2 650	1 843	–	–
	FINE AND APPLIED ARTS	1 677	...	1 311	...	366	...	–	–
	LAW	15 840	...	–	–	15 840	...	–	–
	SOCIAL AND BEHAVIOURAL SCIENCE	7 823	...	4 694	...	3 129	...	–	–
	COMMERCIAL & BUSINESS ADMIN.	12 902	...	*4 760	...	8 142	...	–	–
	MASS COMMUNICATION & DOCUMENT.	816	...	441	...	375	...	–	–
	HOME ECONOMICS (DOMESTIC SCIENCE)	151	...	151	...	–	–	–	–
	SERVICE TRADES	–	–	–	–	–	–	–	–
	NATURAL SCIENCE	2 423	1 255	–	–	2 423	1 255	–	–
	MATHEMATICS & COMPUTER SCIENCE	3 058	...	695	...	2 363	...	–	–
	MEDICAL SCIENCE AND HEALTH-RELATED	15 723	...	4 552	...	11 171	...	–	–
	ENGINEERING	4 121	...	150	...	3 971	...	–	–
	ARCHITECTURE & TOWN PLANNING	*3 316	...	–	–	3 316	...	–	–
	TRADE, CRAFT & INDUSTRIAL PGMS.	278	...	278	...	–	–	–	–
	TRANSPORT AND COMMUNICATIONS	–	–	–	–	–	–	–	–
	AGRICULTURE, FORESTRY & FISHERY	4 792	...	–	–	4 792	...	–	–
	OTHER AND NOT SPECIFIED	808	...	808	...	–	–	–	–
VENEZUELA‡ 1984	TOTAL	381 575	...	./.	...	381 575	...	–	–
	EDUCATION SCIENCE & TEACHER TRNG.	55 416	...	./.	...	55 416	...	–	–
	HUMANITIES, RELIGION & THEOLOGY	5 051	...	./.	...	5 051	...	–	–
	FINE AND APPLIED ARTS	679	...	–	–	679	...	–	–
	LAW	32 060	...	–	–	32 060	...	–	–
	SOCIAL AND BEHAVIOURAL SCIENCE	51 730	...	./.	...	51 730	...	–	–
	COMMERCIAL & BUSINESS ADMIN.	64 304	...	./.	...	64 304	...	–	–
	MASS COMMUNICATION & DOCUMENT.	4 317	...	./.	...	4 317	...	–	–
	HOME ECONOMICS (DOMESTIC SCIENCE)	–	–	–	–	–	–	–	–
	SERVICE TRADES	–	–	–	–	–	–	–	–
	NATURAL SCIENCE	6 899	...	–	–	6 899	...	–	–
	MATHEMATICS & COMPUTER SCIENCE	11 731	...	./.	...	11 731	...	–	–
	MEDICAL SCIENCE AND HEALTH-RELATED	40 879	...	./.	...	40 879	...	–	–
	ENGINEERING	65 068	...	./.	...	65 068	...	–	–
	ARCHITECTURE & TOWN PLANNING	6 397	...	–	–	6 397	...	–	–
	TRADE, CRAFT & INDUSTRIAL PGMS.	–	–	–	–	–	–	–	–
	TRANSPORT AND COMMUNICATIONS	–	–	–	–	–	–	–	–
	AGRICULTURE, FORESTRY & FISHERY	14 868	...	./.	...	14 868	...	–	–
	OTHER AND NOT SPECIFIED	22 052	...	./.	...	22 052	...	–	–

3.13 Third level: students by level and field of study
Troisième degré: étudiants par niveau de programmes et domaine d'études
Tercer grado: estudiantes por nivel de programas y sector de estudios

COUNTRY YEAR / PAYS ANNEE / PAIS AÑO	FIELD OF STUDY / DOMAINES D'ETUDES / SECTORES DE ESTUDIOS	INTERNATIONAL STANDARD CLASSIFICATION OF EDUCATION BY LEVEL / CLASSIFICATION INTERNATIONALE TYPE DE L'EDUCATION PAR NIVEAUX / CLASIFICACION INTERNACIONAL NORMALIZADA DE LA EDUCACION POR NIVELES							
		ALL LEVELS / TOUS NIVEAUX / TODOS LOS NIVELES		LEVEL 5 / NIVEAU 5 / NIVEL 5		LEVEL 6 / NIVEAU 6 / NIVEL 6		LEVEL 7 / NIVEAU 7 / NIVEL 7	
		MF	F	MF	F	MF	F	MF	F
		(1)	(2)	(3)	(4)	(5)	(6)	(7)	(8)
ASIA									
AFGHANISTAN 1982	TOTAL	19 652	...	6 041	...	13 611	...	–	–
	EDUCATION SCIENCE & TEACHER TRNG.	4 637	...	4 109	...	528	...	–	–
	HUMANITIES, RELIGION & THEOLOGY	1 595	...	...	...	1 595	...	–	–
	FINE AND APPLIED ARTS	–	–	–	–	–	–	–	–
	LAW	624	...	–	–	624	...	–	–
	SOCIAL AND BEHAVIOURAL SCIENCE	1 427	...	–	–	1 427	...	–	–
	COMMERCIAL & BUSINESS ADMIN.	420	...	420	...	–	–	–	–
	MASS COMMUNICATION & DOCUMENT.	–	–	–	–	–	–	–	–
	HOME ECONOMICS (DOMESTIC SCIENCE)	–	–	–	–	–	–	–	–
	SERVICE TRADES	–	–	–	–	–	–	–	–
	NATURAL SCIENCE	1 218	...	–	–	1 218	...	–	–
	MATHEMATICS & COMPUTER SCIENCE	–	–	–	–	–	–	–	–
	MEDICAL SCIENCE AND HEALTH-RELATED	3 279	...	528	...	2 751	...	–	–
	ENGINEERING	3 462	...	–	–	3 462	...	–	–
	ARCHITECTURE & TOWN PLANNING	–	–	–	–	–	–	–	–
	TRADE, CRAFT & INDUSTRIAL PGMS.	–	–	–	–	–	–	–	–
	TRANSPORT AND COMMUNICATIONS	263	...	263	...	–	–	–	–
	AGRICULTURE, FORESTRY & FISHERY	1 546	...	332	...	1 214	...	–	–
	OTHER AND NOT SPECIFIED	1 181	...	389	...	792	...	–	–
BANGLADESH‡ 1984	TOTAL	436 615	78 289	287	–	410 431	73 592	25 897	4 697
	EDUCATION SCIENCE & TEACHER TRNG.	3 752	870	–	–	3 752	870	–	–
	HUMANITIES, RELIGION & THEOLOGY	144 083	29 750	–	–	130 441	27 128	13 642	2 622
	FINE AND APPLIED ARTS	–	–	–	–	–	–	–	–
	LAW	8 300	450	–	–	8 122	419	178	31
	SOCIAL AND BEHAVIOURAL SCIENCE	100 421	18 789	–	–	95 400	17 474	5 021	1 315
	COMMERCIAL & BUSINESS ADMIN.	56 760	8 612	–	–	53 922	8 439	2 838	173
	MASS COMMUNICATION & DOCUMENT.	–	–	–	–	–	–	–	–
	HOME ECONOMICS (DOMESTIC SCIENCE)	./.	./.	–	–	./.	./.	./.	./.
	SERVICE TRADES	–	–	–	–	–	–	–	–
	NATURAL SCIENCE	87 323	14 875	–	–	84 703	14 429	2 620	446
	MATHEMATICS & COMPUTER SCIENCE	8 732	1 566	–	–	8 121	1 503	611	63
	MEDICAL SCIENCE AND HEALTH-RELATED	14 687	2 263	–	–	14 540	2 240	147	23
	ENGINEERING	4 593	118	–	–	4 317	110	276	8
	ARCHITECTURE & TOWN PLANNING	324	20	–	–	240	14	84	6
	TRADE, CRAFT & INDUSTRIAL PGMS.	492	–	287	–	205	–	–	–
	TRANSPORT AND COMMUNICATIONS	–	–	–	–	–	–	–	–
	AGRICULTURE, FORESTRY & FISHERY	4 366	250	–	–	3 886	240	480	10
	OTHER AND NOT SPECIFIED	2 782	726	–	–	2 782	726	–	–
BHUTAN‡ 1983	TOTAL	55	3	55	3	–	–	–	–
	EDUCATION SCIENCE & TEACHER TRNG.	17	3	17	3	–	–	–	–
	HUMANITIES, RELIGION & THEOLOGY	–	–	–	–	–	–	–	–
	FINE AND APPLIED ARTS	–	–	–	–	–	–	–	–
	LAW	–	–	–	–	–	–	–	–
	SOCIAL AND BEHAVIOURAL SCIENCE	./.	–	./.	–	–	–	–	–
	COMMERCIAL & BUSINESS ADMIN.	38	–	38	–	–	–	–	–
	MASS COMMUNICATION & DOCUMENT.	–	–	–	–	–	–	–	–
	HOME ECONOMICS (DOMESTIC SCIENCE)	–	–	–	–	–	–	–	–
	SERVICE TRADES	–	–	–	–	–	–	–	–
	NATURAL SCIENCE	–	–	–	–	–	–	–	–
	MATHEMATICS & COMPUTER SCIENCE	–	–	–	–	–	–	–	–
	MEDICAL SCIENCE AND HEALTH-RELATED	–	–	–	–	–	–	–	–
	ENGINEERING	–	–	–	–	–	–	–	–
	ARCHITECTURE & TOWN PLANNING	–	–	–	–	–	–	–	–
	TRADE, CRAFT & INDUSTRIAL PGMS.	–	–	–	–	–	–	–	–
	TRANSPORT AND COMMUNICATIONS	–	–	–	–	–	–	–	–
	AGRICULTURE, FORESTRY & FISHERY	–	–	–	–	–	–	–	–
	OTHER AND NOT SPECIFIED	–	–	–	–	–	–	–	–

COUNTRY YEAR / PAYS ANNEE / PAIS AÑO	FIELD OF STUDY / DOMAINES D'ETUDES / SECTORES DE ESTUDIOS	INTERNATIONAL STANDARD CLASSIFICATION OF EDUCATION BY LEVEL / CLASSIFICATION INTERNATIONALE TYPE DE L'EDUCATION PAR NIVEAUX / CLASIFICACION INTERNACIONAL NORMALIZADA DE LA EDUCACION POR NIVELES							
		ALL LEVELS / TOUS NIVEAUX / TODOS LOS NIVELES		LEVEL 5 / NIVEAU 5 / NIVEL 5		LEVEL 6 / NIVEAU 6 / NIVEL 6		LEVEL 7 / NIVEAU 7 / NIVEL 7	
		MF	F	MF	F	MF	F	MF	F
		(1)	(2)	(3)	(4)	(5)	(6)	(7)	(8)
BRUNEI DARUSSALAM 1983	TOTAL	218	99	218	99	–	–	–	–
	EDUCATION SCIENCE & TEACHER TRNG.	218	99	218	99	–	–	–	–
	HUMANITIES, RELIGION & THEOLOGY	–	–	–	–	–	–	–	–
	FINE AND APPLIED ARTS	–	–	–	–	–	–	–	–
	LAW	–	–	–	–	–	–	–	–
	SOCIAL AND BEHAVIOURAL SCIENCE	–	–	–	–	–	–	–	–
	COMMERCIAL & BUSINESS ADMIN.	–	–	–	–	–	–	–	–
	MASS COMMUNICATION & DOCUMENT.	–	–	–	–	–	–	–	–
	HOME ECONOMICS (DOMESTIC SCIENCE)	–	–	–	–	–	–	–	–
	SERVICE TRADES	–	–	–	–	–	–	–	–
	NATURAL SCIENCE	–	–	–	–	–	–	–	–
	MATHEMATICS & COMPUTER SCIENCE	–	–	–	–	–	–	–	–
	MEDICAL SCIENCE AND HEALTH-RELATED	–	–	–	–	–	–	–	–
	ENGINEERING	–	–	–	–	–	–	–	–
	ARCHITECTURE & TOWN PLANNING	–	–	–	–	–	–	–	–
	TRADE, CRAFT & INDUSTRIAL PGMS.	–	–	–	–	–	–	–	–
	TRANSPORT AND COMMUNICATIONS	–	–	–	–	–	–	–	–
	AGRICULTURE, FORESTRY & FISHERY	–	–	–	–	–	–	–	–
	OTHER AND NOT SPECIFIED	–	–	–	–	–	–	–	–
CHINA‡ 1984	TOTAL	1 443 605	...	387 935	...	1 007 721	...	47 949	...
	EDUCATION SCIENCE & TEACHER TRNG.	362 432	...	192 841	...	168 986	...	605	...
	HUMANITIES, RELIGION & THEOLOGY	93 706	...	27 343	...	61 803	...	4 560	...
	FINE AND APPLIED ARTS	7 682	...	1 732	...	5 769	...	181	...
	LAW	26 849	...	6 496	...	18 741	...	1 612	...
	SOCIAL AND BEHAVIOURAL SCIENCE	./.	...	./.	...	./.	...	./.	...
	COMMERCIAL & BUSINESS ADMIN.	99 640	...	39 132	...	58 273	...	2 235	...
	MASS COMMUNICATION & DOCUMENT.	–	–	–	–	–	–	–	–
	HOME ECONOMICS (DOMESTIC SCIENCE)	–	–	–	–	–	–	–	–
	SERVICE TRADES	–	–	–	–	–	–	–	–
	NATURAL SCIENCE	85 524	...	3 438	...	74 840	...	7 246	...
	MATHEMATICS & COMPUTER SCIENCE	30 644	...	3 864	...	23 324	...	3 456	...
	MEDICAL SCIENCE AND HEALTH-RELATED	149 048	...	18 955	...	124 900	...	5 193	...
	ENGINEERING	455 215	...	67 476	...	369 835	...	17 904	...
	ARCHITECTURE & TOWN PLANNING	5 786	...	1 002	...	4 476	...	308	...
	TRADE, CRAFT & INDUSTRIAL PGMS.	–	–	–	–	–	–	–	–
	TRANSPORT AND COMMUNICATIONS	19 894	...	3 713	...	14 453	...	1 728	...
	AGRICULTURE, FORESTRY & FISHERY	95 546	...	19 881	...	72 744	...	2 921	...
	OTHER AND NOT SPECIFIED	11 639	...	2 062	...	9 577	...	–	–
CYPRUS 1984	TOTAL	2 580	1 147	2 580	1 147	–	–	–	–
	EDUCATION SCIENCE & TEACHER TRNG.	341	264	341	264	–	–	–	–
	HUMANITIES, RELIGION & THEOLOGY	–	–	–	–	–	–	–	–
	FINE AND APPLIED ARTS	–	–	–	–	–	–	–	–
	LAW	–	–	–	–	–	–	–	–
	SOCIAL AND BEHAVIOURAL SCIENCE	–	–	–	–	–	–	–	–
	COMMERCIAL & BUSINESS ADMIN.	895	432	895	432	–	–	–	–
	MASS COMMUNICATION & DOCUMENT.	–	–	–	–	–	–	–	–
	HOME ECONOMICS (DOMESTIC SCIENCE)	–	–	–	–	–	–	–	–
	SERVICE TRADES	168	54	168	54	–	–	–	–
	NATURAL SCIENCE	–	–	–	–	–	–	–	–
	MATHEMATICS & COMPUTER SCIENCE	–	–	–	–	–	–	–	–
	MEDICAL SCIENCE AND HEALTH-RELATED	230	181	230	181	–	–	–	–
	ENGINEERING	507	105	507	105	–	–	–	–
	ARCHITECTURE & TOWN PLANNING	–	–	–	–	–	–	–	–
	TRADE, CRAFT & INDUSTRIAL PGMS.	402	111	402	111	–	–	–	–
	TRANSPORT AND COMMUNICATIONS	–	–	–	–	–	–	–	–
	AGRICULTURE, FORESTRY & FISHERY	37	–	37	–	–	–	–	–
	OTHER AND NOT SPECIFIED	–	–	–	–	–	–	–	–

3.13 Third level: students by level and field of study
Troisième degré: étudiants par niveau de programmes et domaine d'études
Tercer grado: estudiantes por nivel de programas y sector de estudios

COUNTRY YEAR / PAYS ANNEE / PAIS AÑO	FIELD OF STUDY / DOMAINES D'ETUDES / SECTORES DE ESTUDIOS	INTERNATIONAL STANDARD CLASSIFICATION OF EDUCATION BY LEVEL / CLASSIFICATION INTERNATIONALE TYPE DE L'EDUCATION PAR NIVEAUX / CLASIFICACION INTERNACIONAL NORMALIZADA DE LA EDUCACION POR NIVELES							
		ALL LEVELS / TOUS NIVEAUX / TODOS LOS NIVELES		LEVEL 5 / NIVEAU 5 / NIVEL 5		LEVEL 6 / NIVEAU 6 / NIVEL 6		LEVEL 7 / NIVEAU 7 / NIVEL 7	
		MF	F	MF	F	MF	F	MF	F
		(1)	(2)	(3)	(4)	(5)	(6)	(7)	(8)
HONG KONG 1984	TOTAL	76 844	26 542	60 324	20 799	11 455	4 056	5 065	1 687
	EDUCATION SCIENCE & TEACHER TRNG.	6 007	3 808	4 470	3 117	–	–	1 537	691
	HUMANITIES, RELIGION & THEOLOGY	4 657	2 854	2 169	1 273	2 211	1 478	277	103
	FINE AND APPLIED ARTS	1 546	718	1 328	602	210	110	8	6
	LAW	373	197	4	3	275	153	94	41
	SOCIAL AND BEHAVIOURAL SCIENCE	3 882	1 913	1 936	984	1 612	794	334	135
	COMMERCIAL & BUSINESS ADMIN.	19 194	10 177	16 503	9 380	1 140	363	1 551	434
	MASS COMMUNICATION & DOCUMENT.	1 007	614	877	540	123	70	7	4
	HOME ECONOMICS (DOMESTIC SCIENCE)	–	–	–	–	–	–	–	–
	SERVICE TRADES	1 787	552	933	401	798	141	56	10
	NATURAL SCIENCE	2 863	618	1 238	269	1 427	297	198	52
	MATHEMATICS & COMPUTER SCIENCE	2 508	648	2 099	572	404	75	5	1
	MEDICAL SCIENCE AND HEALTH–RELATED	2 459	792	1 172	496	1 105	211	182	85
	ENGINEERING	22 146	547	20 127	468	1 365	45	654	34
	ARCHITECTURE & TOWN PLANNING	1 589	186	1 270	123	285	52	34	11
	TRADE, CRAFT & INDUSTRIAL PGMS.	3 911	1 411	3 817	1 353	–	–	94	58
	TRANSPORT AND COMMUNICATIONS	–	–	–	–	–	–	–	–
	AGRICULTURE, FORESTRY & FISHERY	–	–	–	–	–	–	–	–
	OTHER AND NOT SPECIFIED	2 915	1 507	2 381	1 218	500	267	34	22
INDIA‡ 1979	TOTAL	5 345 580	1 396 466	2 374 425	582 701	2 635 390	723 968	335 765	89 797
	EDUCATION SCIENCE & TEACHER TRNG.	160 026	78 467	88 042	44 738	64 136	30 296	7 848	3 433
	HUMANITIES, RELIGION & THEOLOGY	2 652 315	832 149	1 488 059	382 017	1 021 960	403 097	142 296	47 035
	FINE AND APPLIED ARTS	19 961	10 261	11 942	5 852	6 332	3 309	1 687	1 100
	LAW	163 263	10 631	88	–	159 441	10 319	3 734	312
	SOCIAL AND BEHAVIOURAL SCIENCE	867 538	158 245	103 287	17 273	682 880	124 618	81 371	16 354
	COMMERCIAL & BUSINESS ADMIN.	./.	./.	./.	./.	./.	./.	./.	./.
	MASS COMMUNICATION & DOCUMENT.	2 584	987	416	202	1 684	658	484	127
	HOME ECONOMICS (DOMESTIC SCIENCE)	./.	./.	./.	./.	./.	./.	./.	./.
	SERVICE TRADES	–	–	–	–	–	–	–	–
	NATURAL SCIENCE	872 936	226 436	363 233	87 320	452 714	122 999	56 989	16 117
	MATHEMATICS & COMPUTER SCIENCE	./.	./.	./.	./.	./.	./.	./.	./.
	MEDICAL SCIENCE AND HEALTH–RELATED	146 472	42 305	29 498	15 921	101 932	22 898	15 042	3 486
	ENGINEERING	396 974	32 260	278 161	27 978	105 339	3 620	13 474	662
	ARCHITECTURE & TOWN PLANNING	./.	./.	./.	./.	./.	./.	./.	./.
	TRADE, CRAFT & INDUSTRIAL PGMS.	./.	./.	./.	./.	./.	./.	./.	./.
	TRANSPORT AND COMMUNICATIONS	./.	./.	./.	./.	./.	./.	./.	./.
	AGRICULTURE, FORESTRY & FISHERY	47 970	1 474	3 634	109	34 357	920	9 979	445
	OTHER AND NOT SPECIFIED	15 541	3 251	8 065	1 291	4 615	1 234	2 861	726
INDONESIA 1984	TOTAL	980 162	316 273	128 058	44 867	104 702	42 570	747 402	228 836
	EDUCATION SCIENCE & TEACHER TRNG.	236 324	89 907	58 565	26 085	–	–	177 759	63 822
	HUMANITIES, RELIGION & THEOLOGY	28 098	10 274	4 485	1 895	5 511	3 093	18 102	5 286
	FINE AND APPLIED ARTS	4 152	1 421	67	11	2 094	839	1 991	571
	LAW	109 989	30 055	1 461	451	939	235	107 589	29 369
	SOCIAL AND BEHAVIOURAL SCIENCE	218 173	72 709	6 336	1 563	5 125	1 570	206 712	69 576
	COMMERCIAL & BUSINESS ADMIN.	136 425	54 728	27 958	11 507	68 686	31 574	39 781	11 647
	MASS COMMUNICATION & DOCUMENT.	5 281	1 999	174	53	871	327	4 236	1 619
	HOME ECONOMICS (DOMESTIC SCIENCE)	1 982	1 602	199	199	1 783	1 403	–	–
	SERVICE TRADES	2 215	974	760	191	1 455	783	–	–
	NATURAL SCIENCE	21 411	8 337	43	11	–	–	21 368	8 326
	MATHEMATICS & COMPUTER SCIENCE	6 441	791	3 577	75	–	–	2 864	716
	MEDICAL SCIENCE AND HEALTH–RELATED	24 855	7 978	447	204	932	827	23 476	6 947
	ENGINEERING	109 472	18 008	16 263	1 239	10 131	659	83 078	16 110
	ARCHITECTURE & TOWN PLANNING	12 410	2 430	1 168	221	576	59	10 666	2 150
	TRADE, CRAFT & INDUSTRIAL PGMS.	3 694	935	1 347	306	2 347	629	–	–
	TRANSPORT AND COMMUNICATIONS	474	108	–	–	294	63	180	45
	AGRICULTURE, FORESTRY & FISHERY	54 643	13 587	4 160	830	1 518	340	48 965	12 417
	OTHER AND NOT SPECIFIED	4 123	430	1 048	26	2 440	169	635	235

COUNTRY / YEAR PAYS / ANNEE PAIS / AÑO	FIELD OF STUDY DOMAINES D'ETUDES SECTORES DE ESTUDIOS	INTERNATIONAL STANDARD CLASSIFICATION OF EDUCATION BY LEVEL CLASSIFICATION INTERNATIONALE TYPE DE L'EDUCATION PAR NIVEAUX CLASIFICACION INTERNACIONAL NORMALIZADA DE LA EDUCACION POR NIVELES							
		ALL LEVELS TOUS NIVEAUX TODOS LOS NIVELES		LEVEL 5 NIVEAU 5 NIVEL 5		LEVEL 6 NIVEAU 6 NIVEL 6		LEVEL 7 NIVEAU 7 NIVEL 7	
		MF	F	MF	F	MF	F	MF	F
		(1)	(2)	(3)	(4)	(5)	(6)	(7)	(8)
IRAN, ISLAMIC REPUBLIC OF‡ 1984	TOTAL	177 286	45 216	66 840	10 602	91 053	28 581	19 393	6 033
	EDUCATION SCIENCE & TEACHER TRNG.	46 095	5 976	35 840	1 338	10 111	4 568	144	70
	HUMANITIES, RELIGION & THEOLOGY	14 247	5 909	294	70	13 568	5 714	385	125
	FINE AND APPLIED ARTS	1 421	561	55	55	1 334	496	32	10
	LAW	3 242	592	–	–	3 145	578	97	14
	SOCIAL AND BEHAVIOURAL SCIENCE	12 881	4 891	615	59	11 886	4 735	380	97
	COMMERCIAL & BUSINESS ADMIN.	5 699	1 711	411	106	4 750	1 498	538	107
	MASS COMMUNICATION & DOCUMENT.	586	340	374	246	71	28	141	66
	HOME ECONOMICS (DOMESTIC SCIENCE)	859	585	345	233	474	322	40	30
	SERVICE TRADES	134	70	134	70	–	–	–	–
	NATURAL SCIENCE	11 900	4 287	321	91	11 347	4 137	232	59
	MATHEMATICS & COMPUTER SCIENCE	6 224	1 520	640	129	5 435	1 369	149	22
	MEDICAL SCIENCE AND HEALTH-RELATED	32 598	15 770	14 208	7 903	3 986	2 777	14 404	5 090
	ENGINEERING	31 507	1 704	9 854	149	20 685	1 498	968	57
	ARCHITECTURE & TOWN PLANNING	2 106	528	325	50	908	284	873	194
	TRADE, CRAFT & INDUSTRIAL PGMS.	533	139	31	–	491	139	11	–
	TRANSPORT AND COMMUNICATIONS	93	7	93	7	–	–	–	–
	AGRICULTURE, FORESTRY & FISHERY	5 664	229	2 976	26	1 735	122	953	81
	OTHER AND NOT SPECIFIED	1 497	397	324	70	1 127	316	46	11
ISRAEL‡ 1984	TOTAL	101 641	46 810	40 486	17 540	44 264	21 360	16 891	7 910
	EDUCATION SCIENCE & TEACHER TRNG.	41 145	24 723	23 433	12 106	13 143	9 536	4 569	3 081
	HUMANITIES, RELIGION & THEOLOGY	./.	./.	./.	./.	./.	./.	./.	./.
	FINE AND APPLIED ARTS	./.	./.	./.	./.	./.	./.	./.	./.
	LAW	2 612	1 036	–	–	2 408	977	204	59
	SOCIAL AND BEHAVIOURAL SCIENCE	19 176	8 177	2 603	722	12 035	5 327	4 538	2 128
	COMMERCIAL & BUSINESS ADMIN.	./.	./.	./.	./.	./.	./.	./.	./.
	MASS COMMUNICATION & DOCUMENT.	./.	./.	./.	./.	./.	./.	./.	./.
	HOME ECONOMICS (DOMESTIC SCIENCE)	./.	./.	./.	./.	./.	./.	./.	./.
	SERVICE TRADES	./.	./.	./.	./.	./.	./.	./.	./.
	NATURAL SCIENCE	5 144	2 629	–	–	2 563	1 396	2 581	1 233
	MATHEMATICS & COMPUTER SCIENCE	4 506	1 465	–	–	3 801	1 273	705	192
	MEDICAL SCIENCE AND HEALTH-RELATED	6 539	4 049	2 315	1 889	2 637	1 542	1 587	618
	ENGINEERING	19 873	3 319	11 261	2 170	6 657	876	1 955	273
	ARCHITECTURE & TOWN PLANNING	./.	./.	./.	./.	./.	./.	./.	./.
	TRADE, CRAFT & INDUSTRIAL PGMS.	./.	./.	./.	./.	./.	./.	./.	./.
	TRANSPORT AND COMMUNICATIONS	./.	./.	./.	./.	./.	./.	./.	./.
	AGRICULTURE, FORESTRY & FISHERY	1 181	416	–	–	735	267	446	149
	OTHER AND NOT SPECIFIED	1 465	996	874	653	285	166	306	177
JAPAN‡ 1984	TOTAL	2 403 371	825 911	410 290	349 042	1 819 651	443 059	65 692	8 587
	EDUCATION SCIENCE & TEACHER TRNG.	228 685	161 648	84 252	83 504	140 821	77 031	3 612	1 113
	HUMANITIES, RELIGION & THEOLOGY	358 831	239 946	83 717	82 059	266 352	155 170	8 762	2 717
	FINE AND APPLIED ARTS	67 544	48 616	21 091	19 193	45 133	28 828	1 320	595
	LAW	./.	./.	./.	./.	./.	./.	./.	./.
	SOCIAL AND BEHAVIOURAL SCIENCE	760 132	97 013	45 131	28 062	708 320	67 934	6 681	1 017
	COMMERCIAL & BUSINESS ADMIN.	./.	./.	./.	./.	./.	./.	./.	./.
	MASS COMMUNICATION & DOCUMENT.	./.	./.	./.	./.	./.	./.	./.	./.
	HOME ECONOMICS (DOMESTIC SCIENCE)	137 798	137 386	101 096	100 966	36 353	36 093	349	327
	SERVICE TRADES	–	–	–	–	–	–	–	–
	NATURAL SCIENCE	48 391	7 402	–	–	42 560	6 946	5 831	456
	MATHEMATICS & COMPUTER SCIENCE	17 192	3 897	291	275	15 886	3 541	1 015	81
	MEDICAL SCIENCE AND HEALTH-RELATED	147 601	57 016	20 145	17 831	117 071	38 170	10 385	1 015
	ENGINEERING	406 145	12 780	36 953	3 542	347 869	8 865	21 323	373
	ARCHITECTURE & TOWN PLANNING	./.	./.	./.	./.	./.	./.	./.	./.
	TRADE, CRAFT & INDUSTRIAL PGMS.	./.	./.	./.	./.	./.	./.	./.	./.
	TRANSPORT AND COMMUNICATIONS	2 629	54	1 031	–	1 539	54	59	–
	AGRICULTURE, FORESTRY & FISHERY	63 583	10 055	3 617	818	54 364	8 468	5 602	769
	OTHER AND NOT SPECIFIED	164 840	50 098	12 966	12 792	43 383	11 959	753	124

COUNTRY / YEAR — PAYS / ANNEE — PAIS / AÑO	FIELD OF STUDY — DOMAINES D'ETUDES — SECTORES DE ESTUDIOS	INTERNATIONAL STANDARD CLASSIFICATION OF EDUCATION BY LEVEL / CLASSIFICATION INTERNATIONALE TYPE DE L'EDUCATION PAR NIVEAUX / CLASIFICACION INTERNACIONAL NORMALIZADA DE LA EDUCACION POR NIVELES							
		ALL LEVELS / TOUS NIVEAUX / TODOS LOS NIVELES		LEVEL 5 / NIVEAU 5 / NIVEL 5		LEVEL 6 / NIVEAU 6 / NIVEL 6		LEVEL 7 / NIVEAU 7 / NIVEL 7	
		MF	F	MF	F	MF	F	MF	F
		(1)	(2)	(3)	(4)	(5)	(6)	(7)	(8)
JORDAN‡ 1983	TOTAL	56 253	24 108	32 442	14 732	22 312	9 032	1 499	344
	EDUCATION SCIENCE & TEACHER TRNG.	12 677	10 111	11 000	9 278	935	646	742	187
	HUMANITIES, RELIGION & THEOLOGY	5 686	3 232	–	–	5 475	3 169	211	63
	FINE AND APPLIED ARTS	278	144	–	–	278	144	–	–
	LAW	407	124	–	–	377	120	30	4
	SOCIAL AND BEHAVIOURAL SCIENCE	./.	./.	–	–	./.	./.	./.	./.
	COMMERCIAL & BUSINESS ADMIN.	17 250	4 720	12 557	3 438	4 612	1 261	81	21
	MASS COMMUNICATION & DOCUMENT.	./.	./.	–	–	./.	./.	./.	./.
	HOME ECONOMICS (DOMESTIC SCIENCE)	–	–	–	–	–	–	–	–
	SERVICE TRADES	–	–	–	–	–	–	–	–
	NATURAL SCIENCE	5 391	2 312	1 307	659	3 885	1 598	199	55
	MATHEMATICS & COMPUTER SCIENCE	./.	./.	./.	./.	./.	./.	./.	./.
	MEDICAL SCIENCE AND HEALTH–RELATED	3 074	1 594	1 554	770	1 451	815	69	9
	ENGINEERING	8 577	1 035	5 982	587	2 466	447	129	1
	ARCHITECTURE & TOWN PLANNING	./.	./.	./.	./.	./.	./.	./.	./.
	TRADE, CRAFT & INDUSTRIAL PGMS.	–	–	–	–	–	–	–	–
	TRANSPORT AND COMMUNICATIONS	–	–	–	–	–	–	–	–
	AGRICULTURE, FORESTRY & FISHERY	1 044	366	42	–	964	362	38	4
	OTHER AND NOT SPECIFIED	1 869	470	–	–	1 869	470	–	–
KOREA, REPUBLIC OF 1983	TOTAL	1 075 969	296 449	236 221	81 171	779 466	205 030	60 282	10 248
	EDUCATION SCIENCE & TEACHER TRNG.	134 424	82 245	19 913	18 667	103 238	60 761	11 273	2 817
	HUMANITIES, RELIGION & THEOLOGY	134 007	53 309	8 766	3 033	117 960	48 452	7 281	1 824
	FINE AND APPLIED ARTS	53 741	37 002	16 680	10 909	34 731	24 585	2 330	1 508
	LAW	22 034	883	954	171	19 744	663	1 336	49
	SOCIAL AND BEHAVIOURAL SCIENCE	64 105	12 600	6 169	2 550	54 731	9 568	3 205	482
	COMMERCIAL & BUSINESS ADMIN.	109 450	13 127	25 623	7 011	74 244	5 861	9 583	255
	MASS COMMUNICATION & DOCUMENT.	9 711	4 033	1 744	1 397	7 434	2 461	533	175
	HOME ECONOMICS (DOMESTIC SCIENCE)	20 542	18 616	7 469	6 352	12 274	11 745	799	519
	SERVICE TRADES	831	68	569	62	–	–	262	6
	NATURAL SCIENCE	46 758	16 976	2 554	2 550	41 335	13 700	2 869	726
	MATHEMATICS & COMPUTER SCIENCE	19 433	4 816	–	–	18 327	4 641	1 106	175
	MEDICAL SCIENCE AND HEALTH–RELATED	65 824	30 716	26 617	19 062	33 246	10 442	5 961	1 212
	ENGINEERING	277 361	8 197	88 272	5 479	180 440	2 595	8 649	123
	ARCHITECTURE & TOWN PLANNING	4 395	398	410	71	3 612	308	373	19
	TRADE, CRAFT & INDUSTRIAL PGMS.	27 298	2 883	4 851	1 189	21 004	1 667	1 443	27
	TRANSPORT AND COMMUNICATIONS	4 792	639	4 228	628	558	11	6	–
	AGRICULTURE, FORESTRY & FISHERY	65 746	5 934	16 782	1 528	46 575	4 234	2 389	172
	OTHER AND NOT SPECIFIED	15 517	4 007	4 620	512	10 013	3 336	884	159
KUWAIT‡ 1984	TOTAL	21 924	11 639	6 412	3 084	15 471	8 522	41	33
	EDUCATION SCIENCE & TEACHER TRNG.	2 990	2 086	755	537	2 235	1 549	–	–
	HUMANITIES, RELIGION & THEOLOGY	3 261	1 889	–	–	3 260	1 889	1	–
	FINE AND APPLIED ARTS	204	112	204	112	–	–	–	–
	LAW	1 034	336	–	–	1 034	336	–	–
	SOCIAL AND BEHAVIOURAL SCIENCE	3 174	1 702	–	–	3 174	1 702	–	–
	COMMERCIAL & BUSINESS ADMIN.	3 178	1 835	1 918	1 200	1 260	635	–	–
	MASS COMMUNICATION & DOCUMENT.	–	–	–	–	–	–	–	–
	HOME ECONOMICS (DOMESTIC SCIENCE)	132	132	132	132	–	–	–	–
	SERVICE TRADES	–	–	–	–	–	–	–	–
	NATURAL SCIENCE	2 264	1 184	295	133	1 951	1 037	18	14
	MATHEMATICS & COMPUTER SCIENCE	1 113	701	223	113	883	583	7	5
	MEDICAL SCIENCE AND HEALTH–RELATED	835	573	405	269	415	290	15	14
	ENGINEERING	2 288	579	1 029	78	1 259	501	–	–
	ARCHITECTURE & TOWN PLANNING	–	–	–	–	–	–	–	–
	TRADE, CRAFT & INDUSTRIAL PGMS.	./.	./.	./.	./.	./.	./.	–	–
	TRANSPORT AND COMMUNICATIONS	–	–	–	–	–	–	–	–
	AGRICULTURE, FORESTRY & FISHERY	–	–	–	–	–	–	–	–
	OTHER AND NOT SPECIFIED	1 451	510	1 451	510	–	–	–	–

COUNTRY YEAR / PAYS ANNEE / PAIS AÑO	FIELD OF STUDY / DOMAINES D'ETUDES / SECTORES DE ESTUDIOS	INTERNATIONAL STANDARD CLASSIFICATION OF EDUCATION BY LEVEL / CLASSIFICATION INTERNATIONALE TYPE DE L'EDUCATION PAR NIVEAUX / CLASIFICACION INTERNACIONAL NORMALIZADA DE LA EDUCACION POR NIVELES							
		ALL LEVELS / TOUS NIVEAUX / TODOS LOS NIVELES		LEVEL 5 / NIVEAU 5 / NIVEL 5		LEVEL 6 / NIVEAU 6 / NIVEL 6		LEVEL 7 / NIVEAU 7 / NIVEL 7	
		MF	F	MF	F	MF	F	MF	F
		(1)	(2)	(3)	(4)	(5)	(6)	(7)	(8)
LAO PEOPLE'S DEMOCRATIC REPUBLIC									
1983	TOTAL	4 790	...	2 028	...	2 762	...	–	–
	EDUCATION SCIENCE & TEACHER TRNG.	2 780	...	896	...	1 884	...	–	–
	HUMANITIES, RELIGION & THEOLOGY	–	–	–	–	–	–	–	–
	FINE AND APPLIED ARTS	–	–	–	–	–	–	–	–
	LAW	–	–	–	–	–	–	–	–
	SOCIAL AND BEHAVIOURAL SCIENCE	–	–	–	–	–	–	–	–
	COMMERCIAL & BUSINESS ADMIN.	–	–	–	–	–	–	–	–
	MASS COMMUNICATION & DOCUMENT.	–	–	–	–	–	–	–	–
	HOME ECONOMICS (DOMESTIC SCIENCE)	–	–	–	–	–	–	–	–
	SERVICE TRADES	–	–	–	–	–	–	–	–
	NATURAL SCIENCE	–	–	–	–	–	–	–	–
	MATHEMATICS & COMPUTER SCIENCE	–	–	–	–	–	–	–	–
	MEDICAL SCIENCE AND HEALTH-RELATED	878	...	–	–	878	...	–	–
	ENGINEERING	–	–	–	–	–	–	–	–
	ARCHITECTURE & TOWN PLANNING	719	...	719	...	–	–	–	–
	TRADE, CRAFT & INDUSTRIAL PGMS.	–	–	–	–	–	–	–	–
	TRANSPORT AND COMMUNICATIONS	327	...	327	...	–	–	–	–
	AGRICULTURE, FORESTRY & FISHERY	–	–	–	–	–	–	–	–
	OTHER AND NOT SPECIFIED	86	...	86	...	–	–	–	–
LEBANON‡									
1982	TOTAL	73 052	27 225	1 358	732	71 694	26 493	./.	./.
	EDUCATION SCIENCE & TEACHER TRNG.	450	153	–	–	450	153	./.	./.
	HUMANITIES, RELIGION & THEOLOGY	17 529	9 201	177	104	17 352	9 097	./.	./.
	FINE AND APPLIED ARTS	1 270	762	–	–	1 270	762	./.	./.
	LAW	12 870	2 960	–	–	12 870	2 960	./.	./.
	SOCIAL AND BEHAVIOURAL SCIENCE	10 241	4 508	–	–	10 241	4 508	./.	./.
	COMMERCIAL & BUSINESS ADMIN.	12 988	3 276	–	–	12 988	3 276	./.	./.
	MASS COMMUNICATION & DOCUMENT.	581	430	–	–	581	430	./.	./.
	HOME ECONOMICS (DOMESTIC SCIENCE)	–	–	–	–	–	–	–	–
	SERVICE TRADES	233	117	233	117	–	–	–	–
	NATURAL SCIENCE	4 791	2 347	–	–	4 791	2 347	./.	./.
	MATHEMATICS & COMPUTER SCIENCE	2 049	655	–	–	2 049	655	./.	./.
	MEDICAL SCIENCE AND HEALTH-RELATED	2 553	1 276	–	–	2 553	1 276	./.	./.
	ENGINEERING	4 685	515	–	–	4 685	515	./.	./.
	ARCHITECTURE & TOWN PLANNING	1 580	395	–	–	1 580	395	./.	./.
	TRADE, CRAFT & INDUSTRIAL PGMS.	–	–	–	–	–	–	–	–
	TRANSPORT AND COMMUNICATIONS	–	–	–	–	–	–	–	–
	AGRICULTURE, FORESTRY & FISHERY	–	–	–	–	–	–	–	–
	OTHER AND NOT SPECIFIED	1 232	630	948	511	284	119	–	–
MALAYSIA									
1984	TOTAL	93 249	41 468	59 348	27 581	32 598	13 459	1 303	428
	EDUCATION SCIENCE & TEACHER TRNG.	24 121	15 256	20 443	12 996	3 482	2 190	196	70
	HUMANITIES, RELIGION & THEOLOGY	1 597	733	724	325	840	405	33	3
	FINE AND APPLIED ARTS	700	295	700	295	–	–	–	–
	LAW	956	478	295	164	655	312	6	2
	SOCIAL AND BEHAVIOURAL SCIENCE	9 797	4 482	209	146	9 209	4 221	379	115
	COMMERCIAL & BUSINESS ADMIN.	14 310	6 807	11 141	5 321	3 099	1 461	70	25
	MASS COMMUNICATION & DOCUMENT.	410	166	410	166	–	–	–	–
	HOME ECONOMICS (DOMESTIC SCIENCE)	174	88	82	52	92	36	–	–
	SERVICE TRADES	3 042	2 293	2 933	2 238	80	34	29	21
	NATURAL SCIENCE	6 300	2 583	486	293	5 621	2 213	193	77
	MATHEMATICS & COMPUTER SCIENCE	2 238	1 000	1 557	714	645	271	36	15
	MEDICAL SCIENCE AND HEALTH-RELATED	2 920	1 373	160	32	2 615	1 290	145	51
	ENGINEERING	11 767	1 646	7 470	1 043	4 263	595	34	8
	ARCHITECTURE & TOWN PLANNING	3 484	706	2 482	522	980	179	22	5
	TRADE, CRAFT & INDUSTRIAL PGMS.	912	265	897	264	–	–	15	1
	TRANSPORT AND COMMUNICATIONS	618	138	332	13	286	125	–	–
	AGRICULTURE, FORESTRY & FISHERY	2 242	454	1 511	327	731	127	–	–
	OTHER AND NOT SPECIFIED	7 661	2 705	7 516	2 670	–	–	145	35

3.13 Third level: students by level and field of study
Troisième degré: étudiants par niveau de programmes et domaine d'études
Tercer grado: estudiantes por nivel de programas y sector de estudios

COUNTRY / YEAR PAYS / ANNEE PAIS / AÑO	FIELD OF STUDY DOMAINES D'ETUDES SECTORES DE ESTUDIOS	INTERNATIONAL STANDARD CLASSIFICATION OF EDUCATION BY LEVEL / CLASSIFICATION INTERNATIONALE TYPE DE L'EDUCATION PAR NIVEAUX / CLASIFICACION INTERNACIONAL NORMALIZADA DE LA EDUCACION POR NIVELES							
		ALL LEVELS / TOUS NIVEAUX / TODOS LOS NIVELES		LEVEL 5 / NIVEAU 5 / NIVEL 5		LEVEL 6 / NIVEAU 6 / NIVEL 6		LEVEL 7 / NIVEAU 7 / NIVEL 7	
		MF	F	MF	F	MF	F	MF	F
		(1)	(2)	(3)	(4)	(5)	(6)	(7)	(8)
MONGOLIA 1981	TOTAL	38 200	...	19 500	...	18 700	...	–	–
	EDUCATION SCIENCE & TEACHER TRNG.	4 200	...	2 300	...	1 900	...	–	–
	HUMANITIES, RELIGION & THEOLOGY	1 800	...	–	–	1 800	...	–	–
	FINE AND APPLIED ARTS	1 400	...	900	...	500	...	–	–
	LAW	800	...	300	...	500	...	–	–
	SOCIAL AND BEHAVIOURAL SCIENCE	1 500	...	–	–	1 500	...	–	–
	COMMERCIAL & BUSINESS ADMIN.	1 900	...	1 300	...	600	...	–	–
	MASS COMMUNICATION & DOCUMENT.	100	...	–	–	100	...	–	–
	HOME ECONOMICS (DOMESTIC SCIENCE)	1 300	...	1 200	...	100	...	–	–
	SERVICE TRADES	100	...	–	–	100	...	–	–
	NATURAL SCIENCE	1 800	...	–	–	1 800	...	–	–
	MATHEMATICS & COMPUTER SCIENCE	400	...	–	–	400	...	–	–
	MEDICAL SCIENCE AND HEALTH-RELATED	5 200	...	3 000	...	2 200	...	–	–
	ENGINEERING	5 300	...	2 600	...	2 700	...	–	–
	ARCHITECTURE & TOWN PLANNING	100	...	–	–	100	...	–	–
	TRADE, CRAFT & INDUSTRIAL PGMS.	3 400	...	2 900	...	500	...	–	–
	TRANSPORT AND COMMUNICATIONS	3 100	...	2 300	...	800	...	–	–
	AGRICULTURE, FORESTRY & FISHERY	5 300	...	2 700	...	2 600	...	–	–
	OTHER AND NOT SPECIFIED	500	...	–	–	500	...	–	–
NEPAL‡ 1983	TOTAL	48 229	*9 549	34 448	6 780	12 191	2 379	1 590	390
	EDUCATION SCIENCE & TEACHER TRNG.	3 535	581	2 222	339	1 238	220	75	22
	HUMANITIES, RELIGION & THEOLOGY	18 293	5 945	11 940	4 068	5 543	1 602	810	275
	FINE AND APPLIED ARTS	./.	./.	./.	./.	./.	./.	./.	./.
	LAW	3 184	173	2 236	141	948	32	–	–
	SOCIAL AND BEHAVIOURAL SCIENCE	./.	./.	./.	./.	./.	./.	–	–
	COMMERCIAL & BUSINESS ADMIN.	10 783	1 286	7 416	913	2 801	315	566	58
	MASS COMMUNICATION & DOCUMENT.	–	–	–	–	–	–	–	–
	HOME ECONOMICS (DOMESTIC SCIENCE)	–	–	–	–	–	–	–	–
	SERVICE TRADES	–	–	–	–	–	–	–	–
	NATURAL SCIENCE	8 281	1 227	7 073	1 022	1 069	170	139	35
	MATHEMATICS & COMPUTER SCIENCE	./.	./.	./.	./.	./.	./.	./.	./.
	MEDICAL SCIENCE AND HEALTH-RELATED	817	247	685	211	132	36	–	–
	ENGINEERING	1 940	76	1 872	75	68	1	–	–
	ARCHITECTURE & TOWN PLANNING	–	–	–	–	–	–	–	–
	TRADE, CRAFT & INDUSTRIAL PGMS.	–	–	–	–	–	–	–	–
	TRANSPORT AND COMMUNICATIONS	–	–	–	–	–	–	–	–
	AGRICULTURE, FORESTRY & FISHERY	1 396	14	1 004	11	392	3	–	–
	OTHER AND NOT SPECIFIED	–	–	–	–	–	–	–	–
PAKISTAN‡ 1979	TOTAL	156 558	42 046	21 372	2 430	119 992	35 254	15 194	4 362
	EDUCATION SCIENCE & TEACHER TRNG.	5 675	2 211	781	231	3 851	1 723	1 043	257
	HUMANITIES, RELIGION & THEOLOGY	46 422	22 152	1 531	243	38 721	19 324	6 170	2 585
	FINE AND APPLIED ARTS	424	107	424	107	–	–	–	–
	LAW	10 299	248	–	–	10 221	244	78	4
	SOCIAL AND BEHAVIOURAL SCIENCE	–	–	–	–	–	–	–	–
	COMMERCIAL & BUSINESS ADMIN.	11 909	706	123	4	9 638	595	2 148	107
	MASS COMMUNICATION & DOCUMENT.	–	–	–	–	–	–	–	–
	HOME ECONOMICS (DOMESTIC SCIENCE)	1 316	1 316	–	–	1 164	1 164	152	152
	SERVICE TRADES	–	–	–	–	–	–	–	–
	NATURAL SCIENCE	23 681	7 146	240	39	19 366	5 957	4 075	1 150
	MATHEMATICS & COMPUTER SCIENCE	–	–	–	–	–	–	–	–
	MEDICAL SCIENCE AND HEALTH-RELATED	24 427	6 067	160	52	24 228	6 009	39	6
	ENGINEERING	18 221	108	8 870	–	8 957	108	394	–
	ARCHITECTURE & TOWN PLANNING	./.	./.	./.	–	./.	./.	./.	–
	TRADE, CRAFT & INDUSTRIAL PGMS.	–	–	–	–	–	–	–	–
	TRANSPORT AND COMMUNICATIONS	–	–	–	–	–	–	–	–
	AGRICULTURE, FORESTRY & FISHERY	6 137	454	1 844	326	3 198	27	1 095	101
	OTHER AND NOT SPECIFIED	8 047	1 531	7 399	1 428	648	103	–	–

COUNTRY / YEAR PAYS / ANNEE PAIS / AÑO	FIELD OF STUDY DOMAINES D'ETUDES SECTORES DE ESTUDIOS	INTERNATIONAL STANDARD CLASSIFICATION OF EDUCATION BY LEVEL CLASSIFICATION INTERNATIONALE TYPE DE L'EDUCATION PAR NIVEAUX CLASIFICACION INTERNACIONAL NORMALIZADA DE LA EDUCACION POR NIVELES							
		ALL LEVELS TOUS NIVEAUX TODOS LOS NIVELES		LEVEL 5 NIVEAU 5 NIVEL 5		LEVEL 6 NIVEAU 6 NIVEL 6		LEVEL 7 NIVEAU 7 NIVEL 7	
		MF	F	MF	F	MF	F	MF	F
		(1)	(2)	(3)	(4)	(5)	(6)	(7)	(8)
QATAR‡ 1984	TOTAL	4 624	2 822	730	382	3 638	2 354	256	86
	EDUCATION SCIENCE & TEACHER TRNG.	2 965	1 920	730	382	1 979	1 452	256	86
	HUMANITIES, RELIGION & THEOLOGY	874	415	–	–	874	415	–	–
	FINE AND APPLIED ARTS	59	59	–	–	59	59	–	–
	LAW	–	–	–	–	–	–	–	–
	SOCIAL AND BEHAVIOURAL SCIENCE	./.	./.	–	–	./.	./.	–	–
	COMMERCIAL & BUSINESS ADMIN.	–	–	–	–	–	–	–	–
	MASS COMMUNICATION & DOCUMENT.	./.	./.	–	–	./.	./.	–	–
	HOME ECONOMICS (DOMESTIC SCIENCE)	240	240	–	–	240	240	–	–
	SERVICE TRADES	–	–	–	–	–	–	–	–
	NATURAL SCIENCE	347	188	–	–	347	188	–	–
	MATHEMATICS & COMPUTER SCIENCE	./.	./.	–	–	./.	./.	–	–
	MEDICAL SCIENCE AND HEALTH–RELATED	–	–	–	–	–	–	–	–
	ENGINEERING	139	–	–	–	139	–	–	–
	ARCHITECTURE & TOWN PLANNING	–	–	–	–	–	–	–	–
	TRADE, CRAFT & INDUSTRIAL PGMS.	–	–	–	–	–	–	–	–
	TRANSPORT AND COMMUNICATIONS	–	–	–	–	–	–	–	–
	AGRICULTURE, FORESTRY & FISHERY	–	–	–	–	–	–	–	–
	OTHER AND NOT SPECIFIED	–	–	–	–	–	–	–	–
SAUDI ARABIA‡ 1983	TOTAL	87 821	30 948	8 465	2 543	75 577	27 540	3 779	865
	EDUCATION SCIENCE & TEACHER TRNG.	21 840	10 252	7 352	2 476	13 559	7 234	929	542
	HUMANITIES, RELIGION & THEOLOGY	34 500	13 439	1 113	67	31 463	13 100	1 924	272
	FINE AND APPLIED ARTS	–	–	–	–	–	–	–	–
	LAW	./.	./.	./.	./.	./.	./.	./.	./.
	SOCIAL AND BEHAVIOURAL SCIENCE	10 976	2 488	–	–	10 580	2 485	396	3
	COMMERCIAL & BUSINESS ADMIN.	./.	./.	–	–	./.	./.	./.	./.
	MASS COMMUNICATION & DOCUMENT.	–	–	–	–	–	–	–	–
	HOME ECONOMICS (DOMESTIC SCIENCE)	./.	./.	./.	./.	./.	./.	./.	./.
	SERVICE TRADES	–	–	–	–	–	–	–	–
	NATURAL SCIENCE	7 241	2 626	–	–	7 010	2 585	231	41
	MATHEMATICS & COMPUTER SCIENCE	./.	./.	–	–	./.	./.	./.	./.
	MEDICAL SCIENCE AND HEALTH–RELATED	4 491	1 787	–	–	4 475	1 780	16	7
	ENGINEERING	7 135	73	–	–	6 880	73	255	–
	ARCHITECTURE & TOWN PLANNING	./.	./.	–	–	./.	./.	./.	–
	TRADE, CRAFT & INDUSTRIAL PGMS.	–	–	–	–	–	–	–	–
	TRANSPORT AND COMMUNICATIONS	–	–	–	–	–	–	–	–
	AGRICULTURE, FORESTRY & FISHERY	1 638	283	–	–	1 610	283	28	–
	OTHER AND NOT SPECIFIED	–	–	–	–	–	–	–	–
SINGAPORE‡ 1983	TOTAL	35 192	14 759	16 677	4 791	16 646	9 108	1 869	860
	EDUCATION SCIENCE & TEACHER TRNG.	5 188	3 754	827	683	3 440	2 392	921	679
	HUMANITIES, RELIGION & THEOLOGY	2 828	2 123	–	–	2 722	2 061	106	62
	FINE AND APPLIED ARTS	–	–	–	–	–	–	–	–
	LAW	602	321	–	–	596	320	6	1
	SOCIAL AND BEHAVIOURAL SCIENCE	./.	./.	–	–	./.	./.	./.	./.
	COMMERCIAL & BUSINESS ADMIN.	4 170	2 772	1 357	912	2 524	1 820	289	40
	MASS COMMUNICATION & DOCUMENT.	–	–	–	–	–	–	–	–
	HOME ECONOMICS (DOMESTIC SCIENCE)	–	–	–	–	–	–	–	–
	SERVICE TRADES	–	–	–	–	–	–	–	–
	NATURAL SCIENCE	2 375	1 522	–	–	2 301	1 492	74	30
	MATHEMATICS & COMPUTER SCIENCE	350	218	350	218	–	–	–	–
	MEDICAL SCIENCE AND HEALTH–RELATED	1 121	370	–	–	1 051	347	70	23
	ENGINEERING	15 374	2 574	11 827	2 223	3 159	329	388	22
	ARCHITECTURE & TOWN PLANNING	1 725	825	857	475	853	347	15	3
	TRADE, CRAFT & INDUSTRIAL PGMS.	–	–	–	–	–	–	–	–
	TRANSPORT AND COMMUNICATIONS	107	–	107	–	–	–	–	–
	AGRICULTURE, FORESTRY & FISHERY	–	–	–	–	–	–	–	–
	OTHER AND NOT SPECIFIED	1 352	280	1 352	280	–	–	–	–

3.13 Third level: students by level and field of study
Troisième degré: étudiants par niveau de programmes et domaine d'études
Tercer grado: estudiantes por nivel de programas y sector de estudios

COUNTRY / YEAR PAYS / ANNEE PAIS / AÑO	FIELD OF STUDY DOMAINES D'ETUDES SECTORES DE ESTUDIOS	ALL LEVELS / TOUS NIVEAUX / TODOS LOS NIVELES MF	F	LEVEL 5 / NIVEAU 5 / NIVEL 5 MF	F	LEVEL 6 / NIVEAU 6 / NIVEL 6 MF	F	LEVEL 7 / NIVEAU 7 / NIVEL 7 MF	F
		(1)	(2)	(3)	(4)	(5)	(6)	(7)	(8)
SRI LANKA‡ 1983	TOTAL	63 460	18 504	39 886	8 296	20 891	9 143	2 683	1 065
	EDUCATION SCIENCE & TEACHER TRNG.	8 824	5 757	7 045	4 908	–	–	1 779	849
	HUMANITIES, RELIGION & THEOLOGY	–	–	–	–	–	–	–	–
	FINE AND APPLIED ARTS	8 008	4 287	77	12	7 721	4 214	210	61
	LAW	372	154	–	–	322	146	50	8
	SOCIAL AND BEHAVIOURAL SCIENCE	–	–	–	–	–	–	–	–
	COMMERCIAL & BUSINESS ADMIN.	13 380	1 205	10 381	100	2 895	1 089	104	16
	MASS COMMUNICATION & DOCUMENT.	–	–	–	–	–	–	–	–
	HOME ECONOMICS (DOMESTIC SCIENCE)	–	–	–	–	–	–	–	–
	SERVICE TRADES	–	–	–	–	–	–	–	–
	NATURAL SCIENCE	4 791	1 994	234	74	4 462	1 890	95	30
	MATHEMATICS & COMPUTER SCIENCE	./.	./.	./.	./.	./.	./.	./.	./.
	MEDICAL SCIENCE AND HEALTH–RELATED	2 600	1 154	–	–	2 374	1 060	226	94
	ENGINEERING	6 674	1 461	4 820	1 173	1 827	282	27	6
	ARCHITECTURE & TOWN PLANNING	114	21	–	–	95	20	19	1
	TRADE, CRAFT & INDUSTRIAL PGMS.	11 394	–	11 394	–	–	–	–	–
	TRANSPORT AND COMMUNICATIONS	–	–	–	–	–	–	–	–
	AGRICULTURE, FORESTRY & FISHERY	997	302	–	–	824	302	173	–
	OTHER AND NOT SPECIFIED	6 306	2 169	5 935	2 029	371	140	–	–
TURKEY‡ 1984	TOTAL	417 225	131 356	45 642	13 865	352 543	111 292	19 040	6 199
	EDUCATION SCIENCE & TEACHER TRNG.	58 335	24 675	16 010	6 606	41 370	17 609	955	460
	HUMANITIES, RELIGION & THEOLOGY	25 533	9 145	–	–	24 125	8 664	1 408	481
	FINE AND APPLIED ARTS	4 755	2 288	455	243	3 879	1 836	421	209
	LAW	19 074	4 814	820	325	17 998	4 422	256	67
	SOCIAL AND BEHAVIOURAL SCIENCE	91 155	26 684	991	669	87 403	25 168	2 761	847
	COMMERCIAL & BUSINESS ADMIN.	47 750	14 373	9 159	3 572	36 713	10 340	1 878	461
	MASS COMMUNICATION & DOCUMENT.	4 590	2 123	–	–	4 323	2 014	267	109
	HOME ECONOMICS (DOMESTIC SCIENCE)	579	565	–	–	529	522	50	43
	SERVICE TRADES	3 368	813	1 345	459	2 023	354	–	–
	NATURAL SCIENCE	15 386	6 722	–	–	14 091	6 269	1 295	453
	MATHEMATICS & COMPUTER SCIENCE	7 373	2 989	212	103	7 161	2 886	–	–
	MEDICAL SCIENCE AND HEALTH–RELATED	39 050	15 237	157	53	35 258	13 804	3 635	1 380
	ENGINEERING	76 745	13 202	15 966	1 686	56 916	10 691	3 863	825
	ARCHITECTURE & TOWN PLANNING	7 406	3 564	58	35	6 463	3 113	885	416
	TRADE, CRAFT & INDUSTRIAL PGMS.	1 007	428	340	108	667	320	–	–
	TRANSPORT AND COMMUNICATIONS	21	–	21	–	–	–	–	–
	AGRICULTURE, FORESTRY & FISHERY	15 098	3 734	108	6	13 624	3 280	1 366	448
	OTHER AND NOT SPECIFIED	–	–	–	–	–	–	–	–
UNITED ARAB EMIRATES 1984	TOTAL	6 856	3 975	530	500	6 326	3 475	–	–
	EDUCATION SCIENCE & TEACHER TRNG.	1 107	907	530	500	577	407	–	–
	HUMANITIES, RELIGION & THEOLOGY	–	–	–	–	–	–	–	–
	FINE AND APPLIED ARTS	2 165	1 315	–	–	2 165	1 315	–	–
	LAW	509	94	–	–	509	94	–	–
	SOCIAL AND BEHAVIOURAL SCIENCE	–	–	–	–	–	–	–	–
	COMMERCIAL & BUSINESS ADMIN.	1 045	472	–	–	1 045	472	–	–
	MASS COMMUNICATION & DOCUMENT.	–	–	–	–	–	–	–	–
	HOME ECONOMICS (DOMESTIC SCIENCE)	–	–	–	–	–	–	–	–
	SERVICE TRADES	–	–	–	–	–	–	–	–
	NATURAL SCIENCE	736	447	–	–	736	447	–	–
	MATHEMATICS & COMPUTER SCIENCE	–	–	–	–	–	–	–	–
	MEDICAL SCIENCE AND HEALTH–RELATED	–	–	–	–	–	–	–	–
	ENGINEERING	274	89	–	–	274	89	–	–
	ARCHITECTURE & TOWN PLANNING	–	–	–	–	–	–	–	–
	TRADE, CRAFT & INDUSTRIAL PGMS.	–	–	–	–	–	–	–	–
	TRANSPORT AND COMMUNICATIONS	–	–	–	–	–	–	–	–
	AGRICULTURE, FORESTRY & FISHERY	68	–	–	–	68	–	–	–
	OTHER AND NOT SPECIFIED	952	651	–	–	952	651	–	–

International Standard Classification of Education by level / Classification internationale type de l'education par niveaux / Clasificacion internacional normalizada de la educacion por niveles

COUNTRY YEAR / PAYS ANNEE / PAIS AÑO	FIELD OF STUDY / DOMAINES D'ETUDES / SECTORES DE ESTUDIOS	ALL LEVELS / TOUS NIVEAUX / TODOS LOS NIVELES MF	F	LEVEL 5 / NIVEAU 5 / NIVEL 5 MF	F	LEVEL 6 / NIVEAU 6 / NIVEL 6 MF	F	LEVEL 7 / NIVEAU 7 / NIVEL 7 MF	F
		(1)	(2)	(3)	(4)	(5)	(6)	(7)	(8)
VIET-NAM‡ 1980	TOTAL	114 701	27 090	–	–	114 701	27 090	–	–
	EDUCATION SCIENCE & TEACHER TRNG.	42 363	12 169	–	–	42 363	12 169	–	–
	HUMANITIES, RELIGION & THEOLOGY	4 247	1 310	–	–	4 247	1 310	–	–
	FINE AND APPLIED ARTS	1 022	148	–	–	1 022	148	–	–
	LAW	1 005	48	–	–	1 005	48	–	–
	SOCIAL AND BEHAVIOURAL SCIENCE	818	169	–	–	818	169	–	–
	COMMERCIAL & BUSINESS ADMIN.	14 030	3 527	–	–	14 030	3 527	–	–
	MASS COMMUNICATION & DOCUMENT.	621	68	–	–	621	68	–	–
	HOME ECONOMICS (DOMESTIC SCIENCE)	–	–	–	–	–	–	–	–
	SERVICE TRADES	–	–	–	–	–	–	–	–
	NATURAL SCIENCE	2 487	505	–	–	2 487	505	–	–
	MATHEMATICS & COMPUTER SCIENCE	1 961	499	–	–	1 961	499	–	–
	MEDICAL SCIENCE AND HEALTH-RELATED	11 462	1 839	–	–	11 462	1 839	–	–
	ENGINEERING	11 231	1 806	–	–	11 231	1 806	–	–
	ARCHITECTURE & TOWN PLANNING	2 432	653	–	–	2 432	653	–	–
	TRADE, CRAFT & INDUSTRIAL PGMS.	8 374	1 724	–	–	8 374	1 724	–	–
	TRANSPORT AND COMMUNICATIONS	1 809	251	–	–	1 809	251	–	–
	AGRICULTURE, FORESTRY & FISHERY	10 839	2 374	–	–	10 839	2 374	–	–
	OTHER AND NOT SPECIFIED	–	–	–	–	–	–	–	–
YEMEN 1980	TOTAL	4 519	508	–	–	4 519	508	–	–
	EDUCATION SCIENCE & TEACHER TRNG.	948	130	–	–	948	130	–	–
	HUMANITIES, RELIGION & THEOLOGY	344	81	–	–	344	81	–	–
	FINE AND APPLIED ARTS	–	–	–	–	–	–	–	–
	LAW	1 208	46	–	–	1 208	46	–	–
	SOCIAL AND BEHAVIOURAL SCIENCE	433	104	–	–	433	104	–	–
	COMMERCIAL & BUSINESS ADMIN.	1 321	83	–	–	1 321	83	–	–
	MASS COMMUNICATION & DOCUMENT.	–	–	–	–	–	–	–	–
	HOME ECONOMICS (DOMESTIC SCIENCE)	–	–	–	–	–	–	–	–
	SERVICE TRADES	–	–	–	–	–	–	–	–
	NATURAL SCIENCE	265	64	–	–	265	64	–	–
	MATHEMATICS & COMPUTER SCIENCE	–	–	–	–	–	–	–	–
	MEDICAL SCIENCE AND HEALTH-RELATED	–	–	–	–	–	–	–	–
	ENGINEERING	–	–	–	–	–	–	–	–
	ARCHITECTURE & TOWN PLANNING	–	–	–	–	–	–	–	–
	TRADE, CRAFT & INDUSTRIAL PGMS.	–	–	–	–	–	–	–	–
	TRANSPORT AND COMMUNICATIONS	–	–	–	–	–	–	–	–
	AGRICULTURE, FORESTRY & FISHERY	–	–	–	–	–	–	–	–
	OTHER AND NOT SPECIFIED	–	–	–	–	–	–	–	–
EUROPE									
ALBANIA‡ 1984	TOTAL	21 285	9 580	–	–	21 285	9 580	–	–
	EDUCATION SCIENCE & TEACHER TRNG.	3 090	1 577	–	–	3 090	1 577	–	–
	HUMANITIES, RELIGION & THEOLOGY	1 010	590	–	–	1 010	590	–	–
	FINE AND APPLIED ARTS	500	165	–	–	500	165	–	–
	LAW	423	194	–	–	423	194	–	–
	SOCIAL AND BEHAVIOURAL SCIENCE	3 034	2 072	–	–	3 034	2 072	–	–
	COMMERCIAL & BUSINESS ADMIN.	–	–	–	–	–	–	–	–
	MASS COMMUNICATION & DOCUMENT.	–	–	–	–	–	–	–	–
	HOME ECONOMICS (DOMESTIC SCIENCE)	–	–	–	–	–	–	–	–
	SERVICE TRADES	–	–	–	–	–	–	–	–
	NATURAL SCIENCE	1 100	627	–	–	1 100	627	–	–
	MATHEMATICS & COMPUTER SCIENCE	./.	./.	–	–	./.	./.	–	–
	MEDICAL SCIENCE AND HEALTH-RELATED	997	473	–	–	997	473	–	–
	ENGINEERING	4 728	1 382	–	–	4 728	1 382	–	–
	ARCHITECTURE & TOWN PLANNING	–	–	–	–	–	–	–	–
	TRADE, CRAFT & INDUSTRIAL PGMS.	–	–	–	–	–	–	–	–
	TRANSPORT AND COMMUNICATIONS	–	–	–	–	–	–	–	–
	AGRICULTURE, FORESTRY & FISHERY	5 913	2 350	–	–	5 913	2 350	–	–
	OTHER AND NOT SPECIFIED	490	150	–	–	490	150	–	–

3.13 Third level: students by level and field of study
Troisième degré: étudiants par niveau de programmes et domaine d'études
Tercer grado: estudiantes por nivel de programas y sector de estudios

COUNTRY / YEAR PAYS / ANNEE PAIS / AÑO	FIELD OF STUDY DOMAINES D'ETUDES SECTORES DE ESTUDIOS	INTERNATIONAL STANDARD CLASSIFICATION OF EDUCATION BY LEVEL / CLASSIFICATION INTERNATIONALE TYPE DE L'EDUCATION PAR NIVEAUX / CLASIFICACION INTERNACIONAL NORMALIZADA DE LA EDUCACION POR NIVELES							
		ALL LEVELS TOUS NIVEAUX TODOS LOS NIVELES		LEVEL 5 NIVEAU 5 NIVEL 5		LEVEL 6 NIVEAU 6 NIVEL 6		LEVEL 7 NIVEAU 7 NIVEL 7	
		MF	F	MF	F	MF	F	MF	F
		(1)	(2)	(3)	(4)	(5)	(6)	(7)	(8)
AUSTRIA‡ 1984	TOTAL	168 865	70 599	1 311	487	162 112	68 660	5 442	1 452
	EDUCATION SCIENCE & TEACHER TRNG.	4 535	2 695	–	–	4 353	2 623	182	72
	HUMANITIES, RELIGION & THEOLOGY	28 698	17 767	95	89	27 695	17 206	908	472
	FINE AND APPLIED ARTS	9 677	5 263	–	–	9 638	5 244	39	19
	LAW	16 324	5 673	–	–	16 313	5 673	11	–
	SOCIAL AND BEHAVIOURAL SCIENCE	18 238	8 611	–	–	17 798	8 478	440	133
	COMMERCIAL & BUSINESS ADMIN.	24 397	8 833	1 216	398	21 741	8 047	1 440	388
	MASS COMMUNICATION & DOCUMENT.	2 485	1 230	–	–	2 480	1 229	5	1
	HOME ECONOMICS (DOMESTIC SCIENCE)	178	170	–	–	178	170	–	–
	SERVICE TRADES	–	–	–	–	–	–	–	–
	NATURAL SCIENCE	10 001	3 787	–	–	9 558	3 667	443	120
	MATHEMATICS & COMPUTER SCIENCE	6 807	1 759	–	–	6 431	1 708	376	51
	MEDICAL SCIENCE AND HEALTH-RELATED	22 204	10 616	–	–	22 094	10 563	110	53
	ENGINEERING	14 460	749	–	–	13 536	723	924	26
	ARCHITECTURE & TOWN PLANNING	4 327	1 180	–	–	4 132	1 149	195	31
	TRADE, CRAFT & INDUSTRIAL PGMS.	–	–	–	–	–	–	–	–
	TRANSPORT AND COMMUNICATIONS	–	–	–	–	–	–	–	–
	AGRICULTURE, FORESTRY & FISHERY	5 453	1 928	–	–	5 162	1 858	291	70
	OTHER AND NOT SPECIFIED	1 081	338	–	–	1 003	322	78	16
BELGIUM‡ 1984	TOTAL	245 762	111 349	125 621	65 536	120 141	45 813	./.	./.
	EDUCATION SCIENCE & TEACHER TRNG.	31 788	20 489	26 876	17 664	4 912	2 825	./.	./.
	HUMANITIES, RELIGION & THEOLOGY	15 050	8 687	–	–	15 050	8 687	./.	./.
	FINE AND APPLIED ARTS	4 199	2 227	4 199	2 227	–	–	–	–
	LAW	13 203	5 610	–	–	13 203	5 610	./.	./.
	SOCIAL AND BEHAVIOURAL SCIENCE	28 077	13 049	9 526	6 443	18 551	6 606	./.	./.
	COMMERCIAL & BUSINESS ADMIN.	46 333	22 426	36 393	18 416	9 940	4 010	./.	./.
	MASS COMMUNICATION & DOCUMENT.	–	–	–	–	–	–	–	–
	HOME ECONOMICS (DOMESTIC SCIENCE)	–	–	–	–	–	–	–	–
	SERVICE TRADES	699	62	699	62	–	–	–	–
	NATURAL SCIENCE	31 706	12 453	7 622	2 369	24 084	10 084	./.	./.
	MATHEMATICS & COMPUTER SCIENCE	./.	./.	./.	./.	./.	./.	./.	./.
	MEDICAL SCIENCE AND HEALTH-RELATED	28 345	19 133	19 305	15 044	9 040	4 089	./.	./.
	ENGINEERING	20 951	2 468	1 007	39	19 944	2 429	./.	./.
	ARCHITECTURE & TOWN PLANNING	3 358	928	2 176	620	1 182	308	./.	./.
	TRADE, CRAFT & INDUSTRIAL PGMS.	15 654	1 687	15 654	1 687	–	–	–	–
	TRANSPORT AND COMMUNICATIONS	149	45	149	45	–	–	–	–
	AGRICULTURE, FORESTRY & FISHERY	4 432	1 151	1 241	287	3 191	864	./.	./.
	OTHER AND NOT SPECIFIED	1 818	934	774	633	1 044	301	./.	./.
BULGARIA‡ 1984	TOTAL	104 333	56 084	9 126	6 627	92 636	48 359	2 571	1 098
	EDUCATION SCIENCE & TEACHER TRNG.	12 829	10 255	6 602	4 972	6 189	5 259	38	24
	HUMANITIES, RELIGION & THEOLOGY	10 334	7 038	458	454	9 764	6 503	112	81
	FINE AND APPLIED ARTS	2 785	1 442	72	18	2 667	1 398	46	26
	LAW	2 022	966	–	–	1 980	947	42	19
	SOCIAL AND BEHAVIOURAL SCIENCE	995	534	–	–	544	302	451	232
	COMMERCIAL & BUSINESS ADMIN.	14 021	7 442	–	–	14 021	7 442	–	–
	MASS COMMUNICATION & DOCUMENT.	306	152	–	–	294	146	12	6
	HOME ECONOMICS (DOMESTIC SCIENCE)	–	–	–	–	–	–	–	–
	SERVICE TRADES	925	624	925	624	–	–	–	–
	NATURAL SCIENCE	5 954	3 729	–	–	5 462	3 505	492	224
	MATHEMATICS & COMPUTER SCIENCE	2 212	1 409	–	–	2 042	1 363	170	46
	MEDICAL SCIENCE AND HEALTH-RELATED	12 357	5 804	–	–	12 283	5 760	74	44
	ENGINEERING	32 229	13 426	–	–	31 292	13 124	937	302
	ARCHITECTURE & TOWN PLANNING	555	215	–	–	513	196	42	19
	TRADE, CRAFT & INDUSTRIAL PGMS.	–	–	–	–	–	–	–	–
	TRANSPORT AND COMMUNICATIONS	1 329	648	1 069	559	245	86	15	3
	AGRICULTURE, FORESTRY & FISHERY	5 480	2 400	–	–	5 340	2 328	140	72
	OTHER AND NOT SPECIFIED	–	–	–	–	–	–	–	–

COUNTRY / YEAR PAYS / ANNEE PAIS / AÑO	FIELD OF STUDY DOMAINES D'ETUDES SECTORES DE ESTUDIOS	INTERNATIONAL STANDARD CLASSIFICATION OF EDUCATION BY LEVEL CLASSIFICATION INTERNATIONALE TYPE DE L'EDUCATION PAR NIVEAUX CLASIFICACION INTERNACIONAL NORMALIZADA DE LA EDUCACION POR NIVELES							
		ALL LEVELS TOUS NIVEAUX TODOS LOS NIVELES		LEVEL 5 NIVEAU 5 NIVEL 5		LEVEL 6 NIVEAU 6 NIVEL 6		LEVEL 7 NIVEAU 7 NIVEL 7	
		MF	F	MF	F	MF	F	MF	F
		(1)	(2)	(3)	(4)	(5)	(6)	(7)	(8)
CZECHOSLOVAKIA 1984	TOTAL	174 843	74 535	–	–	174 843	74 535	–	–
	EDUCATION SCIENCE & TEACHER TRNG.	30 390	22 859	–	–	30 390	22 859	–	–
	HUMANITIES, RELIGION & THEOLOGY	1 758	856	–	–	1 758	856	–	–
	FINE AND APPLIED ARTS	2 301	1 006	–	–	2 301	1 006	–	–
	LAW	6 142	3 004	–	–	6 142	3 004	–	–
	SOCIAL AND BEHAVIOURAL SCIENCE	1 532	774	–	–	1 532	774	–	–
	COMMERCIAL & BUSINESS ADMIN.	21 927	12 700	–	–	21 927	12 700	–	–
	MASS COMMUNICATION & DOCUMENT.	1 134	668	–	–	1 134	668	–	–
	HOME ECONOMICS (DOMESTIC SCIENCE)	–	–	–	–	–	–	–	–
	SERVICE TRADES	–	–	–	–	–	–	–	–
	NATURAL SCIENCE	2 690	1 290	–	–	2 690	1 290	–	–
	MATHEMATICS & COMPUTER SCIENCE	2 752	878	–	–	2 752	878	–	–
	MEDICAL SCIENCE AND HEALTH–RELATED	12 427	7 429	–	–	12 427	7 429	–	–
	ENGINEERING	69 663	15 610	–	–	69 663	15 610	–	–
	ARCHITECTURE & TOWN PLANNING	1 021	406	–	–	1 021	406	–	–
	TRADE, CRAFT & INDUSTRIAL PGMS.	–	–	–	–	–	–	–	–
	TRANSPORT AND COMMUNICATIONS	4 277	1 025	–	–	4 277	1 025	–	–
	AGRICULTURE, FORESTRY & FISHERY	16 358	5 877	–	–	16 358	5 877	–	–
	OTHER AND NOT SPECIFIED	471	153	–	–	471	153	–	–
DENMARK‡ 1983	TOTAL	113 157	55 765	29 155	20 659	84 002	35 106	./.	./.
	EDUCATION SCIENCE & TEACHER TRNG.	21 299	14 591	9 578	7 848	11 721	6 743	./.	./.
	HUMANITIES, RELIGION & THEOLOGY	15 818	10 065	2 740	2 452	13 078	7 613	./.	./.
	FINE AND APPLIED ARTS	3 616	2 079	983	646	2 633	1 433	./.	./.
	LAW	4 258	1 925	–	–	4 258	1 925	./.	./.
	SOCIAL AND BEHAVIOURAL SCIENCE	10 811	4 380	8	2	10 803	4 378	./.	./.
	COMMERCIAL & BUSINESS ADMIN.	6 349	1 294	299	86	6 050	1 208	./.	./.
	MASS COMMUNICATION & DOCUMENT.	1 684	982	55	38	1 629	944	./.	./.
	HOME ECONOMICS (DOMESTIC SCIENCE)	–	–	–	–	–	–	–	–
	SERVICE TRADES	212	199	212	199	–	–	–	–
	NATURAL SCIENCE	3 871	1 068	–	–	3 871	1 068	./.	./.
	MATHEMATICS & COMPUTER SCIENCE	3 537	739	–	–	3 537	739	./.	./.
	MEDICAL SCIENCE AND HEALTH–RELATED	18 582	14 219	9 428	8 852	9 154	5 367	./.	./.
	ENGINEERING	12 352	1 156	1 315	200	11 037	956	./.	./.
	ARCHITECTURE & TOWN PLANNING	2 184	828	–	–	2 184	828	./.	./.
	TRADE, CRAFT & INDUSTRIAL PGMS.	960	89	960	89	–	–	–	–
	TRANSPORT AND COMMUNICATIONS	1 149	11	1 149	11	–	–	–	–
	AGRICULTURE, FORESTRY & FISHERY	2 661	903	364	42	2 297	861	./.	./.
	OTHER AND NOT SPECIFIED	3 814	1 237	2 064	194	1 750	1 043	./.	./.
FINLAND‡ 1983	TOTAL	119 982	57 231	32 725	13 319	87 257	43 912	./.	./.
	EDUCATION SCIENCE & TEACHER TRNG.	10 424	7 554	1 959	1 757	8 465	5 797	./.	./.
	HUMANITIES, RELIGION & THEOLOGY	17 042	12 298	–	–	17 042	12 298	./.	./.
	FINE AND APPLIED ARTS	1 874	1 120	640	505	1 234	615	./.	./.
	LAW	4 038	1 591	–	–	4 038	1 591	./.	./.
	SOCIAL AND BEHAVIOURAL SCIENCE	9 087	5 382	–	–	9 087	5 382	./.	./.
	COMMERCIAL & BUSINESS ADMIN.	12 278	5 725	2 055	1 291	10 223	4 434	./.	./.
	MASS COMMUNICATION & DOCUMENT.	250	131	246	128	4	3	./.	./.
	HOME ECONOMICS (DOMESTIC SCIENCE)	213	204	–	–	213	204	./.	./.
	SERVICE TRADES	395	294	395	294	–	–	–	–
	NATURAL SCIENCE	8 318	3 985	–	–	8 318	3 985	./.	./.
	MATHEMATICS & COMPUTER SCIENCE	4 401	1 571	–	–	4 401	1 571	./.	./.
	MEDICAL SCIENCE AND HEALTH–RELATED	14 354	11 639	8 293	7 690	6 061	3 949	./.	./.
	ENGINEERING	30 856	2 836	17 939	1 317	12 917	1 519	./.	./.
	ARCHITECTURE & TOWN PLANNING	1 769	658	–	–	1 769	658	./.	./.
	TRADE, CRAFT & INDUSTRIAL PGMS.	–	–	–	–	–	–	–	–
	TRANSPORT AND COMMUNICATIONS	101	5	101	5	–	–	–	–
	AGRICULTURE, FORESTRY & FISHERY	3 440	1 313	910	184	2 530	1 129	./.	./.
	OTHER AND NOT SPECIFIED	1 142	925	187	148	955	777	./.	./.

3.13 Third level: students by level and field of study
Troisième degré: étudiants par niveau de programmes et domaine d'études
Tercer grado: estudiantes por nivel de programas y sector de estudios

COUNTRY / YEAR PAYS / ANNEE PAIS / AÑO	FIELD OF STUDY DOMAINES D'ETUDES SECTORES DE ESTUDIOS	ALL LEVELS / TOUS NIVEAUX / TODOS LOS NIVELES MF (1)	ALL LEVELS F (2)	LEVEL 5 / NIVEAU 5 / NIVEL 5 MF (3)	LEVEL 5 F (4)	LEVEL 6 / NIVEAU 6 / NIVEL 6 MF (5)	LEVEL 6 F (6)	LEVEL 7 / NIVEAU 7 / NIVEL 7 MF (7)	LEVEL 7 F (8)
		INTERNATIONAL STANDARD CLASSIFICATION OF EDUCATION BY LEVEL / CLASSIFICATION INTERNATIONALE TYPE DE L'EDUCATION PAR NIVEAUX / CLASIFICACION INTERNACIONAL NORMALIZADA DE LA EDUCACION POR NIVELES							
FRANCE‡ 1982	TOTAL	1 179 268	579 459	190 283	95 758	843 151	426 480	145 834	57 221
	EDUCATION SCIENCE & TEACHER TRNG.	47 934	29 926	24 199	15 712	15 084	9 033	8 651	5 181
	HUMANITIES, RELIGION & THEOLOGY	282 236	189 339	258	243	252 864	174 818	29 114	14 278
	FINE AND APPLIED ARTS	12 033	6 466	612	309	11 421	6 157	–	–
	LAW	143 088	75 034	22 776	12 243	104 068	56 544	16 244	6 247
	SOCIAL AND BEHAVIOURAL SCIENCE	84 834	36 330	1 121	777	70 966	32 065	12 747	3 488
	COMMERCIAL & BUSINESS ADMIN.	84 996	51 079	61 679	42 257	23 317	8 822	–	–
	MASS COMMUNICATION & DOCUMENT.	6 151	4 874	5 550	4 600	601	274	–	–
	HOME ECONOMICS (DOMESTIC SCIENCE)	2 834	2 812	2 834	2 812	–	–	–	–
	SERVICE TRADES	./.	./.	./.	./.	–	–	–	–
	NATURAL SCIENCE	149 184	48 417	–	–	118 893	40 234	30 291	8 183
	MATHEMATICS & COMPUTER SCIENCE	34 548	8 220	8 005	3 706	26 543	4 514	–	–
	MEDICAL SCIENCE AND HEALTH-RELATED	186 970	88 125	886	733	139 011	67 907	47 073	19 485
	ENGINEERING	38 822	6 261	–	–	37 861	6 150	961	111
	ARCHITECTURE & TOWN PLANNING	14 347	3 798	2 615	212	11 732	3 586	–	–
	TRADE, CRAFT & INDUSTRIAL PGMS.	47 692	7 974	47 692	7 974	–	–	–	–
	TRANSPORT AND COMMUNICATIONS	1 400	209	534	159	866	50	–	–
	AGRICULTURE, FORESTRY & FISHERY	9 303	2 348	6 796	1 604	2 507	744	–	–
	OTHER AND NOT SPECIFIED	32 896	18 247	4 726	2 417	27 417	15 582	753	248
GERMAN DEMOCRATIC REPUBLIC‡ 1984	TOTAL	431 774	237 564	116 801	46 838	167 541	121 301	147 432	69 425
	EDUCATION SCIENCE & TEACHER TRNG.	55 007	42 781	–	–	25 627	21 937	29 380	20 844
	HUMANITIES, RELIGION & THEOLOGY	9 345	4 790	–	–	1 172	611	8 173	4 179
	FINE AND APPLIED ARTS	4 607	2 243	192	82	1 038	699	3 377	1 462
	LAW	4 102	1 442	–	–	–	–	4 102	1 442
	SOCIAL AND BEHAVIOURAL SCIENCE	22 895	15 959	–	–	11 661	10 290	11 234	5 669
	COMMERCIAL & BUSINESS ADMIN.	38 518	29 071	392	324	25 388	20 626	12 738	8 121
	MASS COMMUNICATION & DOCUMENT.	2 752	2 056	–	–	1 724	1 510	1 028	546
	HOME ECONOMICS (DOMESTIC SCIENCE)	–	–	–	–	–	–	–	–
	SERVICE TRADES	2 505	1 822	2 505	1 822	–	–	–	–
	NATURAL SCIENCE	7 302	3 169	–	–	–	–	7 302	3 169
	MATHEMATICS & COMPUTER SCIENCE	4 418	2 175	637	451	1 002	566	2 779	1 158
	MEDICAL SCIENCE AND HEALTH-RELATED	62 387	54 508	–	–	47 765	46 293	14 622	8 215
	ENGINEERING	84 953	23 654	–	–	42 628	13 727	42 325	9 927
	ARCHITECTURE & TOWN PLANNING	1 315	561	–	–	–	–	1 315	561
	TRADE, CRAFT & INDUSTRIAL PGMS.	47 028	10 526	47 028	10 526	–	–	–	–
	TRANSPORT AND COMMUNICATIONS	3 941	1 393	3 941	1 393	–	–	–	–
	AGRICULTURE, FORESTRY & FISHERY	23 942	11 774	5 349	2 600	9 536	5 042	9 057	4 132
	OTHER AND NOT SPECIFIED	56 757	29 640	56 757	29 640	–	–	–	–
GERMANY, FEDERAL REPUBLIC OF 1983	TOTAL	1 471 964	613 622	205 476	134 366	1 245 817	472 487	20 671	6 769
	EDUCATION SCIENCE & TEACHER TRNG.	94 950	68 505	25 979	22 585	67 098	45 049	1 873	871
	HUMANITIES, RELIGION & THEOLOGY	195 575	117 848	3 013	2 431	188 483	113 497	4 079	1 920
	FINE AND APPLIED ARTS	46 622	23 857	2 779	1 510	43 548	22 224	295	123
	LAW	86 117	32 161	–	–	85 189	31 946	928	215
	SOCIAL AND BEHAVIOURAL SCIENCE	265 461	103 727	–	–	260 797	102 430	4 664	1 297
	COMMERCIAL & BUSINESS ADMIN.	32 850	12 627	8 249	2 979	24 582	9 645	19	3
	MASS COMMUNICATION & DOCUMENT.	7 150	3 761	–	–	6 972	3 675	178	86
	HOME ECONOMICS (DOMESTIC SCIENCE)	16 091	15 068	7 828	7 816	8 207	7 215	56	37
	SERVICE TRADES	419	345	419	345	–	–	–	–
	NATURAL SCIENCE	110 257	34 822	–	–	105 573	33 716	4 684	1 106
	MATHEMATICS & COMPUTER SCIENCE	55 488	14 629	–	–	55 031	14 562	457	67
	MEDICAL SCIENCE AND HEALTH-RELATED	208 061	133 166	106 152	91 373	100 372	41 187	1 537	606
	ENGINEERING	237 269	14 494	29 880	1 606	206 683	12 853	706	35
	ARCHITECTURE & TOWN PLANNING	40 896	14 980	–	–	40 746	14 948	150	32
	TRADE, CRAFT & INDUSTRIAL PGMS.	4 865	491	4 865	491	–	–	–	–
	TRANSPORT AND COMMUNICATIONS	–	–	–	–	–	–	–	–
	AGRICULTURE, FORESTRY & FISHERY	43 387	11 446	12 449	511	30 081	10 607	857	328
	OTHER AND NOT SPECIFIED	26 506	11 695	3 863	2 719	22 455	8 933	188	43

COUNTRY YEAR / PAYS ANNEE / PAIS AÑO	FIELD OF STUDY / DOMAINES D'ETUDES / SECTORES DE ESTUDIOS	INTERNATIONAL STANDARD CLASSIFICATION OF EDUCATION BY LEVEL / CLASSIFICATION INTERNATIONALE TYPE DE L'EDUCATION PAR NIVEAUX / CLASIFICACION INTERNACIONAL NORMALIZADA DE LA EDUCACION POR NIVELES							
		ALL LEVELS / TOUS NIVEAUX / TODOS LOS NIVELES		LEVEL 5 / NIVEAU 5 / NIVEL 5		LEVEL 6 / NIVEAU 6 / NIVEL 6		LEVEL 7 / NIVEAU 7 / NIVEL 7	
		MF	F	MF	F	MF	F	MF	F
		(1)	(2)	(3)	(4)	(5)	(6)	(7)	(8)
GREECE 1981	TOTAL	124 694	53 376	37 218	15 716	87 476	37 660	...	...
	EDUCATION SCIENCE & TEACHER TRNG.	7 070	3 740	7 070	3 740	–	–	...	...
	HUMANITIES, RELIGION & THEOLOGY	12 934	9 524	399	–	12 535	9 524	...	...
	FINE AND APPLIED ARTS	1 247	688	908	496	339	192	...	...
	LAW	12 801	7 169	–	–	12 801	7 169	...	...
	SOCIAL AND BEHAVIOURAL SCIENCE	12 346	5 764	613	533	11 733	5 231	...	...
	COMMERCIAL & BUSINESS ADMIN.	18 057	7 425	4 945	2 773	13 112	4 652	...	...
	MASS COMMUNICATION & DOCUMENT.	360	232	360	232	–	–	...	...
	HOME ECONOMICS (DOMESTIC SCIENCE)	183	183	183	183	–	–	...	...
	SERVICE TRADES	1 402	796	1 402	796	–	–	...	...
	NATURAL SCIENCE	7 578	2 441	–	–	7 578	2 441	...	...
	MATHEMATICS & COMPUTER SCIENCE	5 860	1 883	–	–	5 860	1 883	...	...
	MEDICAL SCIENCE AND HEALTH–RELATED	14 017	7 216	4 358	3 615	9 659	3 601	...	...
	ENGINEERING	21 893	3 484	11 991	1 917	9 902	1 567	...	...
	ARCHITECTURE & TOWN PLANNING	1 092	542	–	–	1 092	542	...	...
	TRADE, CRAFT & INDUSTRIAL PGMS.	468	220	468	220	–	–	...	...
	TRANSPORT AND COMMUNICATIONS	2 200	107	2 200	107	–	–	...	...
	AGRICULTURE, FORESTRY & FISHERY	5 186	1 962	2 321	1 104	2 865	858	...	...
	OTHER AND NOT SPECIFIED	–	–	–	–	–	–	...	...
HOLY SEE‡ 1984	TOTAL	9 656	3 354	2 359	1 611	3 325	864	3 972	879
	EDUCATION SCIENCE & TEACHER TRNG.	514	242	50	30	159	83	305	129
	HUMANITIES, RELIGION & THEOLOGY	8 305	2 967	2 288	1 574	2 796	712	3 221	681
	FINE AND APPLIED ARTS	61	23	–	–	61	23	–	–
	LAW	579	34	6	–	227	14	346	20
	SOCIAL AND BEHAVIOURAL SCIENCE	159	50	15	7	82	32	62	11
	COMMERCIAL & BUSINESS ADMIN.	–	–	–	–	–	–	–	–
	MASS COMMUNICATION & DOCUMENT.	–	–	–	–	–	–	–	–
	HOME ECONOMICS (DOMESTIC SCIENCE)	–	–	–	–	–	–	–	–
	SERVICE TRADES	–	–	–	–	–	–	–	–
	NATURAL SCIENCE	–	–	–	–	–	–	–	–
	MATHEMATICS & COMPUTER SCIENCE	–	–	–	–	–	–	–	–
	MEDICAL SCIENCE AND HEALTH–RELATED	–	–	–	–	–	–	–	–
	ENGINEERING	–	–	–	–	–	–	–	–
	ARCHITECTURE & TOWN PLANNING	–	–	–	–	–	–	–	–
	TRADE, CRAFT & INDUSTRIAL PGMS.	–	–	–	–	–	–	–	–
	TRANSPORT AND COMMUNICATIONS	–	–	–	–	–	–	–	–
	AGRICULTURE, FORESTRY & FISHERY	–	–	–	–	–	–	–	–
	OTHER AND NOT SPECIFIED	38	38	–	–	–	–	38	38
HUNGARY‡ 1984	TOTAL	99 986	52 977	42 204	24 386	15 488	10 810	42 294	17 781
	EDUCATION SCIENCE & TEACHER TRNG.	37 070	27 601	15 913	12 944	14 032	9 930	7 125	4 727
	HUMANITIES, RELIGION & THEOLOGY	2 570	1 746	–	–	781	726	1 789	1 020
	FINE AND APPLIED ARTS	1 195	544	130	85	–	–	1 065	459
	LAW	6 102	3 301	1 801	1 234	–	–	4 301	2 067
	SOCIAL AND BEHAVIOURAL SCIENCE	3 044	1 442	–	–	–	–	3 044	1 442
	COMMERCIAL & BUSINESS ADMIN.	6 989	4 616	5 608	3 918	–	–	1 381	698
	MASS COMMUNICATION & DOCUMENT.	–	–	–	–	–	–	–	–
	HOME ECONOMICS (DOMESTIC SCIENCE)	–	–	–	–	–	–	–	–
	SERVICE TRADES	844	477	844	477	–	–	–	–
	NATURAL SCIENCE	1 091	367	–	–	–	–	1 091	367
	MATHEMATICS & COMPUTER SCIENCE	1 183	403	786	315	–	–	397	88
	MEDICAL SCIENCE AND HEALTH–RELATED	10 500	6 915	2 913	2 752	–	–	7 587	4 163
	ENGINEERING	9 837	1 200	1 875	216	–	–	7 962	984
	ARCHITECTURE & TOWN PLANNING	5 223	1 119	3 199	639	–	–	2 024	480
	TRADE, CRAFT & INDUSTRIAL PGMS.	6 339	1 060	6 339	1 060	–	–	–	–
	TRANSPORT AND COMMUNICATIONS	1 318	311	1 044	275	–	–	274	36
	AGRICULTURE, FORESTRY & FISHERY	6 006	1 721	1 752	471	–	–	4 254	1 250
	OTHER AND NOT SPECIFIED	675	154	–	–	675	154	–	–

3.13 **Third level: students by level and field of study**
Troisième degré: étudiants par niveau de programmes et domaine d'études
Tercer grado: estudiantes por nivel de programas y sector de estudios

COUNTRY YEAR / PAYS ANNEE / PAIS AÑO	FIELD OF STUDY / DOMAINES D'ETUDES / SECTORES DE ESTUDIOS	INTERNATIONAL STANDARD CLASSIFICATION OF EDUCATION BY LEVEL / CLASSIFICATION INTERNATIONALE TYPE DE L'EDUCATION PAR NIVEAUX / CLASIFICACION INTERNACIONAL NORMALIZADA DE LA EDUCACION POR NIVELES							
		ALL LEVELS / TOUS NIVEAUX / TODOS LOS NIVELES		LEVEL 5 / NIVEAU 5 / NIVEL 5		LEVEL 6 / NIVEAU 6 / NIVEL 6		LEVEL 7 / NIVEAU 7 / NIVEL 7	
		MF	F	MF	F	MF	F	MF	F
		(1)	(2)	(3)	(4)	(5)	(6)	(7)	(8)
IRELAND 1982	TOTAL	64 116	26 427	26 836	9 955	32 110	14 213	5 170	2 259
	EDUCATION SCIENCE & TEACHER TRNG.	5 199	3 930	370	297	3 231	2 600	1 598	1 033
	HUMANITIES, RELIGION & THEOLOGY	9 412	5 358	1 297	702	7 570	4 426	545	230
	FINE AND APPLIED ARTS	2 491	1 564	2 104	1 349	352	195	35	20
	LAW	1 017	416	3	1	805	335	209	80
	SOCIAL AND BEHAVIOURAL SCIENCE	1 880	1 049	33	16	1 391	789	456	244
	COMMERCIAL & BUSINESS ADMIN.	11 291	4 282	7 011	3 065	3 941	1 169	339	48
	MASS COMMUNICATION & DOCUMENT.	461	238	179	50	251	174	31	14
	HOME ECONOMICS (DOMESTIC SCIENCE)	158	157	44	44	114	113	–	–
	SERVICE TRADES	–	–	–	–	–	–	–	–
	NATURAL SCIENCE	8 645	4 212	3 915	2 013	3 973	1 926	757	273
	MATHEMATICS & COMPUTER SCIENCE	1 403	407	394	122	687	197	322	88
	MEDICAL SCIENCE AND HEALTH-RELATED	3 973	1 777	276	251	3 367	1 391	330	135
	ENGINEERING	12 600	961	7 644	525	4 634	410	322	26
	ARCHITECTURE & TOWN PLANNING	1 496	257	1 084	169	376	76	36	12
	TRADE, CRAFT & INDUSTRIAL PGMS.	291	161	241	143	48	16	2	2
	TRANSPORT AND COMMUNICATIONS	–	–	–	–	–	–	–	–
	AGRICULTURE, FORESTRY & FISHERY	1 123	233	75	16	914	192	134	25
	OTHER AND NOT SPECIFIED	2 676	1 425	2 166	1 192	456	204	54	29
ITALY 1984	TOTAL	1 181 953	534 595	31 194	17 328	1 083 016	495 346	67 743	21 921
	EDUCATION SCIENCE & TEACHER TRNG.	38 917	33 648	2 577	2 200	35 036	30 367	1 304	1 081
	HUMANITIES, RELIGION & THEOLOGY	161 723	126 762	–	–	159 984	125 416	1 739	1 346
	FINE AND APPLIED ARTS	13 135	7 923	8 150	5 158	4 985	2 765	–	–
	LAW	173 642	79 073	–	–	172 267	78 637	1 375	436
	SOCIAL AND BEHAVIOURAL SCIENCE	209 177	86 748	–	–	208 831	86 666	346	82
	COMMERCIAL & BUSINESS ADMIN.	15 852	4 388	–	–	15 852	4 388	–	–
	MASS COMMUNICATION & DOCUMENT.	95	35	–	–	–	–	95	35
	HOME ECONOMICS (DOMESTIC SCIENCE)	–	–	–	–	–	–	–	–
	SERVICE TRADES	–	–	–	–	–	–	–	–
	NATURAL SCIENCE	79 572	42 519	–	–	78 474	41 888	1 098	631
	MATHEMATICS & COMPUTER SCIENCE	39 817	17 226	2 142	920	37 247	16 121	428	185
	MEDICAL SCIENCE AND HEALTH-RELATED	230 471	89 085	–	–	170 827	71 472	59 644	17 613
	ENGINEERING	96 886	5 304	–	–	96 473	5 227	413	77
	ARCHITECTURE & TOWN PLANNING	64 706	22 825	–	–	64 271	22 616	435	209
	TRADE, CRAFT & INDUSTRIAL PGMS.	–	–	–	–	–	–	–	–
	TRANSPORT AND COMMUNICATIONS	–	–	–	–	–	–	–	–
	AGRICULTURE, FORESTRY & FISHERY	39 047	9 870	–	–	38 377	9 727	670	143
	OTHER AND NOT SPECIFIED	18 913	9 189	18 325	9 050	392	56	196	83
LUXEMBOURG‡ 1983	TOTAL	982	351	982	351	–	–	–	–
	EDUCATION SCIENCE & TEACHER TRNG.	89	55	89	55	–	–	–	–
	HUMANITIES, RELIGION & THEOLOGY	130	79	130	79	–	–	–	–
	FINE AND APPLIED ARTS	–	–	–	–	–	–	–	–
	LAW	32	12	32	12	–	–	–	–
	SOCIAL AND BEHAVIOURAL SCIENCE	228	109	228	109	–	–	–	–
	COMMERCIAL & BUSINESS ADMIN.	./.	./.	./.	./.	–	–	–	–
	MASS COMMUNICATION & DOCUMENT.	–	–	–	–	–	–	–	–
	HOME ECONOMICS (DOMESTIC SCIENCE)	–	–	–	–	–	–	–	–
	SERVICE TRADES	–	–	–	–	–	–	–	–
	NATURAL SCIENCE	64	25	64	25	–	–	–	–
	MATHEMATICS & COMPUTER SCIENCE	./.	./.	./.	./.	–	–	–	–
	MEDICAL SCIENCE AND HEALTH-RELATED	70	31	70	31	–	–	–	–
	ENGINEERING	299	8	299	8	–	–	–	–
	ARCHITECTURE & TOWN PLANNING	–	–	–	–	–	–	–	–
	TRADE, CRAFT & INDUSTRIAL PGMS.	–	–	–	–	–	–	–	–
	TRANSPORT AND COMMUNICATIONS	–	–	–	–	–	–	–	–
	AGRICULTURE, FORESTRY & FISHERY	–	–	–	–	–	–	–	–
	OTHER AND NOT SPECIFIED	70	32	70	32	–	–	–	–

COUNTRY / YEAR PAYS / ANNEE PAIS / AÑO	FIELD OF STUDY DOMAINES D'ETUDES SECTORES DE ESTUDIOS	INTERNATIONAL STANDARD CLASSIFICATION OF EDUCATION BY LEVEL / CLASSIFICATION INTERNATIONALE TYPE DE L'EDUCATION PAR NIVEAUX / CLASIFICACION INTERNACIONAL NORMALIZADA DE LA EDUCACION POR NIVELES							
		ALL LEVELS / TOUS NIVEAUX / TODOS LOS NIVELES		LEVEL 5 / NIVEAU 5 / NIVEL 5		LEVEL 6 / NIVEAU 6 / NIVEL 6		LEVEL 7 / NIVEAU 7 / NIVEL 7	
		MF	F	MF	F	MF	F	MF	F
		(1)	(2)	(3)	(4)	(5)	(6)	(7)	(8)
MALTA 1984	TOTAL	1 411	424	–	–	1 411	424	–	–
	EDUCATION SCIENCE & TEACHER TRNG.	293	170	–	–	293	170	–	–
	HUMANITIES, RELIGION & THEOLOGY	7	1	–	–	7	1	–	–
	FINE AND APPLIED ARTS	–	–	–	–	–	–	–	–
	LAW	95	26	–	–	95	26	–	–
	SOCIAL AND BEHAVIOURAL SCIENCE	–	–	–	–	–	–	–	–
	COMMERCIAL & BUSINESS ADMIN.	313	68	–	–	313	68	–	–
	MASS COMMUNICATION & DOCUMENT.	–	–	–	–	–	–	–	–
	HOME ECONOMICS (DOMESTIC SCIENCE)	–	–	–	–	–	–	–	–
	SERVICE TRADES	–	–	–	–	–	–	–	–
	NATURAL SCIENCE	–	–	–	–	–	–	–	–
	MATHEMATICS & COMPUTER SCIENCE	–	–	–	–	–	–	–	–
	MEDICAL SCIENCE AND HEALTH–RELATED	409	143	–	–	409	143	–	–
	ENGINEERING	194	10	–	–	194	10	–	–
	ARCHITECTURE & TOWN PLANNING	100	6	–	–	100	6	–	–
	TRADE, CRAFT & INDUSTRIAL PGMS.	–	–	–	–	–	–	–	–
	TRANSPORT AND COMMUNICATIONS	–	–	–	–	–	–	–	–
	AGRICULTURE, FORESTRY & FISHERY	–	–	–	–	–	–	–	–
	OTHER AND NOT SPECIFIED	–	–	–	–	–	–	–	–
NETHERLANDS‡ 1984	TOTAL	166 858	59 561	–	–	166 858	59 561	./.	./.
	EDUCATION SCIENCE & TEACHER TRNG.	–	–	–	–	–	–	–	–
	HUMANITIES, RELIGION & THEOLOGY	30 109	16 380	–	–	30 109	16 380	./.	./.
	FINE AND APPLIED ARTS	–	–	–	–	–	–	–	–
	LAW	27 833	11 008	–	–	27 833	11 008	./.	./.
	SOCIAL AND BEHAVIOURAL SCIENCE	36 170	11 485	–	–	36 170	11 485	./.	./.
	COMMERCIAL & BUSINESS ADMIN.	2 620	519	–	–	2 620	519	./.	./.
	MASS COMMUNICATION & DOCUMENT.	–	–	–	–	–	–	–	–
	HOME ECONOMICS (DOMESTIC SCIENCE)	–	–	–	–	–	–	–	–
	SERVICE TRADES	–	–	–	–	–	–	–	–
	NATURAL SCIENCE	11 505	2 500	–	–	11 505	2 500	./.	./.
	MATHEMATICS & COMPUTER SCIENCE	2 489	363	–	–	2 489	363	./.	./.
	MEDICAL SCIENCE AND HEALTH–RELATED	17 949	6 697	–	–	17 949	6 697	./.	./.
	ENGINEERING	21 341	1 618	–	–	21 341	1 618	./.	./.
	ARCHITECTURE & TOWN PLANNING	–	–	–	–	–	–	–	–
	TRADE, CRAFT & INDUSTRIAL PGMS.	–	–	–	–	–	–	–	–
	TRANSPORT AND COMMUNICATIONS	–	–	–	–	–	–	–	–
	AGRICULTURE, FORESTRY & FISHERY	7 514	2 535	–	–	7 514	2 535	./.	./.
	OTHER AND NOT SPECIFIED	9 328	6 456	–	–	9 328	6 456	./.	./.
NORWAY 1983	TOTAL	91 330	45 135	42 146	21 753	23 698	13 976	25 486	9 406
	EDUCATION SCIENCE & TEACHER TRNG.	13 410	9 892	912	627	12 151	9 070	347	195
	HUMANITIES, RELIGION & THEOLOGY	8 500	5 053	3 460	2 235	1 852	1 289	3 188	1 529
	FINE AND APPLIED ARTS	1 142	671	573	411	524	241	45	19
	LAW	4 486	2 097	–	–	–	–	4 486	2 097
	SOCIAL AND BEHAVIOURAL SCIENCE	7 698	4 069	2 920	1 814	1 201	628	3 577	1 627
	COMMERCIAL & BUSINESS ADMIN.	15 979	5 725	11 602	4 520	4 330	1 195	47	10
	MASS COMMUNICATION & DOCUMENT.	546	391	341	206	205	185	–	–
	HOME ECONOMICS (DOMESTIC SCIENCE)	40	37	–	–	40	37	–	–
	SERVICE TRADES	–	–	–	–	–	–	–	–
	NATURAL SCIENCE	6 256	1 878	1 184	469	1 233	438	3 839	971
	MATHEMATICS & COMPUTER SCIENCE	938	247	888	232	36	8	14	7
	MEDICAL SCIENCE AND HEALTH–RELATED	10 980	8 260	7 933	6 928	–	–	3 047	1 332
	ENGINEERING	11 452	2 094	6 296	1 085	641	154	4 515	855
	ARCHITECTURE & TOWN PLANNING	601	238	93	13	–	–	508	225
	TRADE, CRAFT & INDUSTRIAL PGMS.	276	141	276	141	–	–	–	–
	TRANSPORT AND COMMUNICATIONS	941	138	941	138	–	–	–	–
	AGRICULTURE, FORESTRY & FISHERY	1 158	418	50	13	107	14	1 001	391
	OTHER AND NOT SPECIFIED	6 927	3 786	4 677	2 921	1 378	717	872	148

3.13 Third level: students by level and field of study
Troisième degré: étudiants par niveau de programmes et domaine d'études
Tercer grado: estudiantes por nivel de programas y sector de estudios

COUNTRY / YEAR PAYS / ANNEE PAIS / AÑO	FIELD OF STUDY DOMAINES D'ETUDES SECTORES DE ESTUDIOS	INTERNATIONAL STANDARD CLASSIFICATION OF EDUCATION BY LEVEL / CLASSIFICATION INTERNATIONALE TYPE DE L'EDUCATION PAR NIVEAUX / CLASIFICACION INTERNACIONAL NORMALIZADA DE LA EDUCACION POR NIVELES							
		ALL LEVELS TOUS NIVEAUX TODOS LOS NIVELES		LEVEL 5 NIVEAU 5 NIVEL 5		LEVEL 6 NIVEAU 6 NIVEL 6		LEVEL 7 NIVEAU 7 NIVEL 7	
		MF	F	MF	F	MF	F	MF	F
		(1)	(2)	(3)	(4)	(5)	(6)	(7)	(8)
POLAND‡ 1984	TOTAL	456 661	253 246	91 351	69 004	336 974	172 172	28 336	12 070
	EDUCATION SCIENCE & TEACHER TRNG.	82 415	66 477	26 299	23 333	54 189	41 842	1 927	1 302
	HUMANITIES, RELIGION & THEOLOGY	35 403	23 746	–	–	31 631	21 568	3 772	2 178
	FINE AND APPLIED ARTS	8 243	4 174	363	197	7 859	3 964	21	13
	LAW	14 207	6 715	–	–	14 129	6 695	78	20
	SOCIAL AND BEHAVIOURAL SCIENCE	12 288	7 024	–	–	11 709	6 881	579	143
	COMMERCIAL & BUSINESS ADMIN.	66 689	42 427	20 517	16 816	35 495	20 376	10 677	5 235
	MASS COMMUNICATION & DOCUMENT.	3 097	2 653	–	–	3 097	2 653	–	–
	HOME ECONOMICS (DOMESTIC SCIENCE)	407	367	–	–	400	362	7	5
	SERVICE TRADES	–	–	–	–	–	–	–	–
	NATURAL SCIENCE	14 583	9 014	–	–	12 147	7 876	2 436	1 138
	MATHEMATICS & COMPUTER SCIENCE	5 575	3 649	–	–	5 530	3 643	45	6
	MEDICAL SCIENCE AND HEALTH–RELATED	62 037	46 190	28 001	24 780	33 881	21 349	155	61
	ENGINEERING	79 904	14 840	–	–	75 210	14 268	4 694	572
	ARCHITECTURE & TOWN PLANNING	3 865	1 830	–	–	3 865	1 830	–	–
	TRADE, CRAFT & INDUSTRIAL PGMS.	12 989	2 703	12 989	2 703	–	–	–	–
	TRANSPORT AND COMMUNICATIONS	3 853	205	–	–	3 743	200	110	5
	AGRICULTURE, FORESTRY & FISHERY	38 814	16 782	3 182	1 175	32 308	14 405	3 324	1 202
	OTHER AND NOT SPECIFIED	12 292	4 450	–	–	11 781	4 260	511	190
PORTUGAL‡ 1982	TOTAL	99 165	49 785	8 990	8 048	89 746	41 603	429	134
	EDUCATION SCIENCE & TEACHER TRNG.	12 666	9 651	5 377	4 966	7 289	4 685	–	–
	HUMANITIES, RELIGION & THEOLOGY	15 293	10 900	–	–	15 293	10 900	–	–
	FINE AND APPLIED ARTS	3 025	1 303	–	–	3 025	1 303	–	–
	LAW	10 239	4 260	–	–	10 239	4 260	–	–
	SOCIAL AND BEHAVIOURAL SCIENCE	18 995	9 046	–	–	18 995	9 046	61	45
	COMMERCIAL & BUSINESS ADMIN.	./.	./.	–	–	./.	./.	–	–
	MASS COMMUNICATION & DOCUMENT.	./.	./.	–	–	./.	./.	./.	./.
	HOME ECONOMICS (DOMESTIC SCIENCE)	–	–	–	–	–	–	–	–
	SERVICE TRADES	–	–	–	–	–	–	–	–
	NATURAL SCIENCE	975	542	–	–	975	542	–	–
	MATHEMATICS & COMPUTER SCIENCE	./.	./.	–	–	./.	./.	–	–
	MEDICAL SCIENCE AND HEALTH–RELATED	12 941	8 392	3 613	3 082	9 328	5 310	–	–
	ENGINEERING	18 060	3 005	–	–	18 060	3 005	–	–
	ARCHITECTURE & TOWN PLANNING	157	89	–	–	–	–	157	89
	TRADE, CRAFT & INDUSTRIAL PGMS.	–	–	–	–	–	–	–	–
	TRANSPORT AND COMMUNICATIONS	–	–	–	–	–	–	–	–
	AGRICULTURE, FORESTRY & FISHERY	2 738	1 132	–	–	2 738	1 132	–	–
	OTHER AND NOT SPECIFIED	4 015	1 420	–	–	3 804	1 420	211	–
ROMANIA‡ 1984	TOTAL	166 328	...	–	–	166 328	...	–	–
	EDUCATION SCIENCE & TEACHER TRNG.	6 876	...	–	–	6 876	...	–	–
	HUMANITIES, RELIGION & THEOLOGY	./.	...	–	–	./.	...	–	–
	FINE AND APPLIED ARTS	986	...	–	–	986	...	–	–
	LAW	2 438	...	–	–	2 438	...	–	–
	SOCIAL AND BEHAVIOURAL SCIENCE	17 940	...	–	–	17 940	...	–	–
	COMMERCIAL & BUSINESS ADMIN.	./.	...	–	–	./.	...	–	–
	MASS COMMUNICATION & DOCUMENT.	./.	...	–	–	./.	...	–	–
	HOME ECONOMICS (DOMESTIC SCIENCE)	./.	...	–	–	./.	...	–	–
	SERVICE TRADES	./.	...	–	–	./.	...	–	–
	NATURAL SCIENCE	7 627	...	–	–	7 627	...	–	–
	MATHEMATICS & COMPUTER SCIENCE	./.	...	–	–	./.	...	–	–
	MEDICAL SCIENCE AND HEALTH–RELATED	19 953	...	–	–	19 953	...	–	–
	ENGINEERING	99 734	...	–	–	99 734	...	–	–
	ARCHITECTURE & TOWN PLANNING	./.	...	–	–	./.	...	–	–
	TRADE, CRAFT & INDUSTRIAL PGMS.	./.	...	–	–	./.	...	–	–
	TRANSPORT AND COMMUNICATIONS	3 425	...	–	–	3 425	...	–	–
	AGRICULTURE, FORESTRY & FISHERY	7 349	...	–	–	7 349	...	–	–
	OTHER AND NOT SPECIFIED	–	–	–	–	–	–	–	–

COUNTRY YEAR / PAYS ANNEE / PAIS AÑO	FIELD OF STUDY / DOMAINES D'ETUDES / SECTORES DE ESTUDIOS	INTERNATIONAL STANDARD CLASSIFICATION OF EDUCATION BY LEVEL / CLASSIFICATION INTERNATIONALE TYPE DE L'EDUCATION PAR NIVEAUX / CLASIFICACION INTERNACIONAL NORMALIZADA DE LA EDUCACION POR NIVELES							
		ALL LEVELS / TOUS NIVEAUX / TODOS LOS NIVELES		LEVEL 5 / NIVEAU 5 / NIVEL 5		LEVEL 6 / NIVEAU 6 / NIVEL 6		LEVEL 7 / NIVEAU 7 / NIVEL 7	
		MF	F	MF	F	MF	F	MF	F
		(1)	(2)	(3)	(4)	(5)	(6)	(7)	(8)
SPAIN‡ 1983	TOTAL	787 864	379 407	192 670	96 977	595 194	282 430	./.	./.
	EDUCATION SCIENCE & TEACHER TRNG.	106 231	76 247	75 695	56 881	30 536	19 366	./.	./.
	HUMANITIES, RELIGION & THEOLOGY	50 139	34 651	899	677	49 240	33 974	./.	./.
	FINE AND APPLIED ARTS	9 790	5 361	45	31	9 745	5 330	./.	./.
	LAW	113 288	49 232	–	–	113 288	49 232	./.	./.
	SOCIAL AND BEHAVIOURAL SCIENCE	138 689	69 406	–	–	138 689	69 406	./.	./.
	COMMERCIAL & BUSINESS ADMIN.	31 999	12 929	31 999	12 929	–	–	–	–
	MASS COMMUNICATION & DOCUMENT.	13 771	6 974	458	372	13 313	6 602	./.	./.
	HOME ECONOMICS (DOMESTIC SCIENCE)	–	–	–	–	–	–	–	–
	SERVICE TRADES	8 157	5 773	–	–	8 157	5 773	–	–
	NATURAL SCIENCE	53 497	25 165	–	–	53 497	25 165	./.	./.
	MATHEMATICS & COMPUTER SCIENCE	21 477	8 027	6 102	1 741	15 375	6 286	./.	./.
	MEDICAL SCIENCE AND HEALTH-RELATED	93 663	54 565	18 130	14 253	75 533	40 312	./.	./.
	ENGINEERING	78 687	7 319	45 575	4 518	33 112	2 801	./.	./.
	ARCHITECTURE & TOWN PLANNING	24 208	4 595	9 323	1 550	14 885	3 045	./.	./.
	TRADE, CRAFT & INDUSTRIAL PGMS.	–	–	–	–	–	–	–	–
	TRANSPORT AND COMMUNICATIONS	–	–	–	–	–	–	–	–
	AGRICULTURE, FORESTRY & FISHERY	10 995	3 997	–	–	10 995	3 997	./.	./.
	OTHER AND NOT SPECIFIED	33 273	15 166	4 444	4 025	28 829	11 141	./.	./.
SWITZERLAND 1984	TOTAL	105 897	33 785	34 792	8 989	60 341	21 852	10 764	2 944
	EDUCATION SCIENCE & TEACHER TRNG.	5 589	3 417	3 940	2 365	1 457	965	192	87
	HUMANITIES, RELIGION & THEOLOGY	15 557	8 214	819	571	13 063	6 962	1 675	681
	FINE AND APPLIED ARTS	3 175	2 123	1 989	1 380	1 077	683	109	60
	LAW	9 098	2 913	6	3	7 674	2 550	1 418	360
	SOCIAL AND BEHAVIOURAL SCIENCE	17 550	6 582	3 163	1 773	12 141	4 141	2 246	668
	COMMERCIAL & BUSINESS ADMIN.	9 308	1 767	9 308	1 767	–	–	–	–
	MASS COMMUNICATION & DOCUMENT.	65	34	57	29	6	4	2	1
	HOME ECONOMICS (DOMESTIC SCIENCE)	1 303	543	1 303	543	–	–	–	–
	SERVICE TRADES	–	–	–	–	–	–	–	–
	NATURAL SCIENCE	8 886	2 041	–	–	6 291	1 522	2 595	519
	MATHEMATICS & COMPUTER SCIENCE	2 482	371	2	–	2 232	312	248	59
	MEDICAL SCIENCE AND HEALTH-RELATED	10 285	4 022	163	104	8 626	3 500	1 496	418
	ENGINEERING	15 825	527	11 065	321	4 307	186	453	20
	ARCHITECTURE & TOWN PLANNING	1 928	569	–	–	1 876	558	52	11
	TRADE, CRAFT & INDUSTRIAL PGMS.	2 481	20	2 481	20	–	–	–	–
	TRANSPORT AND COMMUNICATIONS	27	–	27	–	–	–	–	–
	AGRICULTURE, FORESTRY & FISHERY	2 338	642	469	113	1 591	469	278	60
	OTHER AND NOT SPECIFIED	–	–	–	–	–	–	–	–
UNITED KINGDOM‡ 1981	TOTAL	858 416	320 237	251 267	73 184	502 885	213 715	104 264	33 338
	EDUCATION SCIENCE & TEACHER TRNG.	75 938	46 458	17 768	10 163	33 660	24 185	24 510	12 110
	HUMANITIES, RELIGION & THEOLOGY	88 953	54 418	5 866	4 007	73 709	46 737	9 378	3 674
	FINE AND APPLIED ARTS	30 944	17 405	4 790	2 678	23 492	13 543	2 662	1 184
	LAW	21 510	8 620	2 631	1 137	16 967	6 935	1 912	548
	SOCIAL AND BEHAVIOURAL SCIENCE	89 512	40 200	21 280	9 499	57 608	26 531	10 624	4 170
	COMMERCIAL & BUSINESS ADMIN.	109 979	34 160	67 958	21 452	28 940	10 016	13 081	2 692
	MASS COMMUNICATION & DOCUMENT.	1 769	1 323	205	154	1 081	840	483	329
	HOME ECONOMICS (DOMESTIC SCIENCE)	1 672	1 434	335	333	1 277	1 072	60	29
	SERVICE TRADES	7 608	3 905	5 809	3 113	1 694	754	105	38
	NATURAL SCIENCE	91 331	30 056	13 812	4 585	63 749	22 303	13 770	3 168
	MATHEMATICS & COMPUTER SCIENCE	29 731	7 668	7 106	1 702	19 561	5 473	3 064	493
	MEDICAL SCIENCE AND HEALTH-RELATED	53 742	27 172	13 782	9 650	32 844	14 948	7 116	2 574
	ENGINEERING	151 739	6 235	78 973	1 778	60 999	3 662	11 767	795
	ARCHITECTURE & TOWN PLANNING	17 194	4 747	4 656	1 584	9 287	2 463	3 251	700
	TRADE, CRAFT & INDUSTRIAL PGMS.	3 194	830	2 644	660	480	151	70	19
	TRANSPORT AND COMMUNICATIONS	1 742	64	1 375	44	256	15	111	5
	AGRICULTURE, FORESTRY & FISHERY	8 995	2 881	2 096	547	5 359	1 959	1 540	375
	OTHER AND NOT SPECIFIED	72 863	32 661	181	98	71 922	32 128	760	435

3.13 Third level: students by level and field of study
Troisième degré: étudiants par niveau de programmes et domaine d'études
Tercer grado: estudiantes por nivel de programas y sector de estudios

COUNTRY YEAR / PAYS ANNEE / PAIS AÑO	FIELD OF STUDY / DOMAINES D'ETUDES / SECTORES DE ESTUDIOS	INTERNATIONAL STANDARD CLASSIFICATION OF EDUCATION BY LEVEL / CLASSIFICATION INTERNATIONALE TYPE DE L'EDUCATION PAR NIVEAUX / CLASIFICACION INTERNACIONAL NORMALIZADA DE LA EDUCACION POR NIVELES							
		ALL LEVELS / TOUS NIVEAUX / TODOS LOS NIVELES		LEVEL 5 / NIVEAU 5 / NIVEL 5		LEVEL 6 / NIVEAU 6 / NIVEL 6		LEVEL 7 / NIVEAU 7 / NIVEL 7	
		MF	F	MF	F	MF	F	MF	F
		(1)	(2)	(3)	(4)	(5)	(6)	(7)	(8)
YUGOSLAVIA‡									
1983	TOTAL	375 393	168 592	81 119	34 895	294 274	133 697	...	...
	EDUCATION SCIENCE & TEACHER TRNG.	34 625	20 256	23 206	14 072	11 419	6 184	...	...
	HUMANITIES, RELIGION & THEOLOGY	28 553	18 920	–	–	28 553	18 920	...	...
	FINE AND APPLIED ARTS	3 794	1 913	–	–	3 794	1 913	...	...
	LAW	41 895	22 420	1 153	643	40 742	21 777	...	...
	SOCIAL AND BEHAVIOURAL SCIENCE	65 146	34 163	12 647	7 114	52 499	27 049	...	...
	COMMERCIAL & BUSINESS ADMIN.	5 485	2 043	1 470	593	4 015	1 450	...	...
	MASS COMMUNICATION & DOCUMENT.	380	182	1	–	379	182	...	...
	HOME ECONOMICS (DOMESTIC SCIENCE)	304	247	304	247		–	...	...
	SERVICE TRADES	5 158	2 211	3 600	1 437	1 558	774	...	...
	NATURAL SCIENCE	16 369	8 924	398	223	15 971	8 701	...	...
	MATHEMATICS & COMPUTER SCIENCE	./.	./.	./.	./.	./.	./.	...	...
	MEDICAL SCIENCE AND HEALTH–RELATED	31 622	20 074	4 284	3 361	27 338	16 713	...	...
	ENGINEERING	94 489	21 327	21 606	3 594	72 883	17 733	...	...
	ARCHITECTURE & TOWN PLANNING	4 863	2 581	–	–	4 863	2 581	...	...
	TRADE, CRAFT & INDUSTRIAL PGMS.	2 703	1 365	2 703	1 365	–	–	...	...
	TRANSPORT AND COMMUNICATIONS	9 532	1 517	4 252	701	5 280	816	...	...
	AGRICULTURE, FORESTRY & FISHERY	27 114	9 530	2 273	709	24 841	8 821	...	...
	OTHER AND NOT SPECIFIED	3 361	919	3 222	836	139	83	...	...
OCEANIA									
AMERICAN SAMOA									
1982	TOTAL	1 007	...	1 007	...	–	–	–	–
	EDUCATION SCIENCE & TEACHER TRNG.	52	...	52	...	–	–	–	–
	HUMANITIES, RELIGION & THEOLOGY	239	...	239	...	–	–	–	–
	FINE AND APPLIED ARTS	41	...	41	...	–	–	–	–
	LAW	–	–	–	–	–	–	–	–
	SOCIAL AND BEHAVIOURAL SCIENCE	44	...	44	...	–	–	–	–
	COMMERCIAL & BUSINESS ADMIN.	163	...	163	...	–	–	–	–
	MASS COMMUNICATION & DOCUMENT.	–	–	–	–	–	–	–	–
	HOME ECONOMICS (DOMESTIC SCIENCE)	–	–	–	–	–	–	–	–
	SERVICE TRADES	–	–	–	–	–	–	–	–
	NATURAL SCIENCE	51	...	51	...	–	–	–	–
	MATHEMATICS & COMPUTER SCIENCE	38	...	38	...	–	–	–	–
	MEDICAL SCIENCE AND HEALTH–RELATED	59	...	59	...	–	–	–	–
	ENGINEERING	–	–	–	–	–	–	–	–
	ARCHITECTURE & TOWN PLANNING	–	–	–	–	–	–	–	–
	TRADE, CRAFT & INDUSTRIAL PGMS.	83	...	83	...	–	–	–	–
	TRANSPORT AND COMMUNICATIONS	–	–	–	–	–	–	–	–
	AGRICULTURE, FORESTRY & FISHERY	–	–	–	–	–	–	–	–
	OTHER AND NOT SPECIFIED	237	...	237	...	–	–	–	–
AUSTRALIA‡									
1984	TOTAL	358 498	166 797	95 426	51 116	237 284	107 480	25 788	8 201
	EDUCATION SCIENCE & TEACHER TRNG.	71 586	47 184	40 373	27 321	26 994	17 939	4 219	1 924
	HUMANITIES, RELIGION & THEOLOGY	53 976	34 657	5 248	3 430	45 544	29 570	3 184	1 657
	FINE AND APPLIED ARTS	11 962	7 424	5 100	3 210	6 541	4 069	321	145
	LAW	10 079	4 146	666	235	8 609	3 694	804	217
	SOCIAL AND BEHAVIOURAL SCIENCE	24 478	15 937	5 689	3 845	16 397	10 855	2 392	1 237
	COMMERCIAL & BUSINESS ADMIN.	66 188	20 239	11 789	3 514	50 246	15 917	4 153	808
	MASS COMMUNICATION & DOCUMENT.	./.	./.	./.	./.	./.	./.	./.	./.
	HOME ECONOMICS (DOMESTIC SCIENCE)	–	–	–	–	–		–	–
	SERVICE TRADES	–	–	–	–	–	–	–	–
	NATURAL SCIENCE	49 642	17 516	9 070	2 764	35 956	13 715	4 616	1 037
	MATHEMATICS & COMPUTER SCIENCE	./.	./.	./.	./.	./.	./.	./.	./.
	MEDICAL SCIENCE AND HEALTH–RELATED	21 285	11 729	4 731	3 537	14 823	7 609	1 731	583
	ENGINEERING	28 709	1 511	4 160	154	22 039	1 217	2 510	140
	ARCHITECTURE & TOWN PLANNING	8 106	1 732	1 397	191	6 053	1 381	656	160
	TRADE, CRAFT & INDUSTRIAL PGMS.	–	–	–	–	–	–	–	–
	TRANSPORT AND COMMUNICATIONS	–	–	–	–	–	–	–	–
	AGRICULTURE, FORESTRY & FISHERY	8 100	2 578	3 037	900	3 990	1 465	1 073	213
	OTHER AND NOT SPECIFIED	4 387	2 144	4 166	2 015	92	49	129	80

COUNTRY / YEAR PAYS / ANNEE PAIS / AÑO	FIELD OF STUDY DOMAINES D'ETUDES SECTORES DE ESTUDIOS	INTERNATIONAL STANDARD CLASSIFICATION OF EDUCATION BY LEVEL / CLASSIFICATION INTERNATIONALE TYPE DE L'EDUCATION PAR NIVEAUX / CLASIFICACION INTERNACIONAL NORMALIZADA DE LA EDUCACION POR NIVELES							
		ALL LEVELS / TOUS NIVEAUX / TODOS LOS NIVELES		LEVEL 5 / NIVEAU 5 / NIVEL 5		LEVEL 6 / NIVEAU 6 / NIVEL 6		LEVEL 7 / NIVEAU 7 / NIVEL 7	
		MF	F	MF	F	MF	F	MF	F
		(1)	(2)	(3)	(4)	(5)	(6)	(7)	(8)
FIJI‡ 1981	TOTAL	2 003	...	933	...	1 036	...	34	...
	EDUCATION SCIENCE & TEACHER TRNG.	820	...	445	...	375	...	–	–
	HUMANITIES, RELIGION & THEOLOGY	–	–	–	–	–	–	–	–
	FINE AND APPLIED ARTS	–	–	–	–	–	–	–	–
	LAW	–	–	–	–	–	–	–	–
	SOCIAL AND BEHAVIOURAL SCIENCE	687	...	124	...	563	...	–	–
	COMMERCIAL & BUSINESS ADMIN.	./.	...	./.	...	./.	...	–	–
	MASS COMMUNICATION & DOCUMENT.	–	–	–	–	–	–	–	–
	HOME ECONOMICS (DOMESTIC SCIENCE)	–	–	–	–	–	–	–	–
	SERVICE TRADES	–	–	–	–	–	–	–	–
	NATURAL SCIENCE	272	...	210	...	62	...	–	–
	MATHEMATICS & COMPUTER SCIENCE	–	–	–	–	–	–	–	–
	MEDICAL SCIENCE AND HEALTH-RELATED	–	–	–	–	–	–	–	–
	ENGINEERING	–	–	–	–	–	–	–	–
	ARCHITECTURE & TOWN PLANNING	–	–	–	–	–	–	–	–
	TRADE, CRAFT & INDUSTRIAL PGMS.	–	–	–	–	–	–	–	–
	TRANSPORT AND COMMUNICATIONS	–	–	–	–	–	–	–	–
	AGRICULTURE, FORESTRY & FISHERY	190	...	154	...	36	...	–	–
	OTHER AND NOT SPECIFIED	34	...	–	–	–	–	34	...
NEW CALEDONIA‡ 1984	TOTAL	660	252	469	181	174	67	17	4
	EDUCATION SCIENCE & TEACHER TRNG.	124	90	124	90	–	–	–	–
	HUMANITIES, RELIGION & THEOLOGY	–	–	–	–	–	–	–	–
	FINE AND APPLIED ARTS	–	–	–	–	–	–	–	–
	LAW	174	66	62	14	96	48	16	4
	SOCIAL AND BEHAVIOURAL SCIENCE	1	–	–	–	–	–	1	–
	COMMERCIAL & BUSINESS ADMIN.	30	18	–	–	30	18	–	–
	MASS COMMUNICATION & DOCUMENT.	–	–	–	–	–	–	–	–
	HOME ECONOMICS (DOMESTIC SCIENCE)	–	–	–	–	–	–	–	–
	SERVICE TRADES	–	–	–	–	–	–	–	–
	NATURAL SCIENCE	./.	./.	./.	./.	–	–	–	–
	MATHEMATICS & COMPUTER SCIENCE	283	77	283	77	–	–	–	–
	MEDICAL SCIENCE AND HEALTH-RELATED	–	–	–	–	–	–	–	–
	ENGINEERING	33	–	–	–	33	–	–	–
	ARCHITECTURE & TOWN PLANNING	–	–	–	–	–	–	–	–
	TRADE, CRAFT & INDUSTRIAL PGMS.	15	1	–	–	15	1	–	–
	TRANSPORT AND COMMUNICATIONS	–	–	–	–	–	–	–	–
	AGRICULTURE, FORESTRY & FISHERY	–	–	–	–	–	–	–	–
	OTHER AND NOT SPECIFIED	–	–	–	–	–	–	–	–
NEW ZEALAND‡ 1983	TOTAL	86 666	36 125	42 193	16 282	38 678	17 655	5 795	2 188
	EDUCATION SCIENCE & TEACHER TRNG.	5 807	4 608	3 670	2 921	1 796	1 481	341	206
	HUMANITIES, RELIGION & THEOLOGY	12 325	8 062	37	28	10 861	7 214	1 427	820
	FINE AND APPLIED ARTS	903	541	291	165	558	343	54	33
	LAW	4 355	1 996	731	463	3 142	1 354	482	179
	SOCIAL AND BEHAVIOURAL SCIENCE	1 074	705	40	70	759	488	275	147
	COMMERCIAL & BUSINESS ADMIN.	21 842	8 089	14 294	5 715	6 871	2 209	677	165
	MASS COMMUNICATION & DOCUMENT.	313	178	238	136	–	–	75	42
	HOME ECONOMICS (DOMESTIC SCIENCE)	292	292	153	153	136	136	3	3
	SERVICE TRADES	124	77	124	77	–	–	–	–
	NATURAL SCIENCE	9 716	3 522	1 527	807	6 828	2 388	1 361	327
	MATHEMATICS & COMPUTER SCIENCE	1 113	325	1 107	322	./.	./.	6	3
	MEDICAL SCIENCE AND HEALTH-RELATED	5 036	3 318	2 859	2 549	1 802	671	375	98
	ENGINEERING	8 774	491	6 231	355	2 369	129	174	7
	ARCHITECTURE & TOWN PLANNING	1 451	407	576	177	801	207	74	23
	TRADE, CRAFT & INDUSTRIAL PGMS.	3 869	188	3 869	188	–	–	–	–
	TRANSPORT AND COMMUNICATIONS	353	23	353	23	–	–	–	–
	AGRICULTURE, FORESTRY & FISHERY	4 744	1 307	2 077	498	2 322	736	345	73
	OTHER AND NOT SPECIFIED	4 575	1 996	4 016	1 635	433	299	126	62

3.13 Third level: students by level and field of study
Troisième degré: étudiants par niveau de programmes et domaine d'études
Tercer grado: estudiantes por nivel de programas y sector de estudios

COUNTRY YEAR / PAYS ANNEE / PAIS AÑO	FIELD OF STUDY / DOMAINES D'ETUDES / SECTORES DE ESTUDIOS	INTERNATIONAL STANDARD CLASSIFICATION OF EDUCATION BY LEVEL / CLASSIFICATION INTERNATIONALE TYPE DE L'EDUCATION PAR NIVEAUX / CLASIFICACION INTERNACIONAL NORMALIZADA DE LA EDUCACION POR NIVELES							
		ALL LEVELS / TOUS NIVEAUX / TODOS LOS NIVELES		LEVEL 5 / NIVEAU 5 / NIVEL 5		LEVEL 6 / NIVEAU 6 / NIVEL 6		LEVEL 7 / NIVEAU 7 / NIVEL 7	
		MF	F	MF	F	MF	F	MF	F
		(1)	(2)	(3)	(4)	(5)	(6)	(7)	(8)
PACIFIC ISLANDS 1982	TOTAL	1 964	608	1 964	608	–	–	–	–
	EDUCATION SCIENCE & TEACHER TRNG.	75	18	75	18	–	–	–	–
	HUMANITIES, RELIGION & THEOLOGY	–	–	–	–	–	–	–	–
	FINE AND APPLIED ARTS	–	–	–	–	–	–	–	–
	LAW	–	–	–	–	–	–	–	–
	SOCIAL AND BEHAVIOURAL SCIENCE	–	–	–	–	–	–	–	–
	COMMERCIAL & BUSINESS ADMIN.	112	78	112	78	–	–	–	–
	MASS COMMUNICATION & DOCUMENT.	–	–	–	–	–	–	–	–
	HOME ECONOMICS (DOMESTIC SCIENCE)	–	–	–	–	–	–	–	–
	SERVICE TRADES	15	9	15	9	–	–	–	–
	NATURAL SCIENCE	–	–	–	–	–	–	–	–
	MATHEMATICS & COMPUTER SCIENCE	–	–	–	–	–	–	–	–
	MEDICAL SCIENCE AND HEALTH–RELATED	19	14	19	14	–	–	–	–
	ENGINEERING	–	–	–	–	–	–	–	–
	ARCHITECTURE & TOWN PLANNING	–	–	–	–	–	–	–	–
	TRADE, CRAFT & INDUSTRIAL PGMS.	191	13	191	13	–	–	–	–
	TRANSPORT AND COMMUNICATIONS	–	–	–	–	–	–	–	–
	AGRICULTURE, FORESTRY & FISHERY	–	–	–	–	–	–	–	–
	OTHER AND NOT SPECIFIED	1 552	476	1 552	476	–	–	–	–
PAPUA NEW GUINEA 1984	TOTAL	6 062	1 376	3 740	1 090	2 247	279	75	7
	EDUCATION SCIENCE & TEACHER TRNG.	749	230	555	186	188	43	6	1
	HUMANITIES, RELIGION & THEOLOGY	578	79	325	56	252	22	1	1
	FINE AND APPLIED ARTS	31	–	31	–	–	–	–	–
	LAW	254	35	32	3	186	30	36	2
	SOCIAL AND BEHAVIOURAL SCIENCE	289	38	16	1	272	36	1	1
	COMMERCIAL & BUSINESS ADMIN.	797	160	670	142	127	18	–	–
	MASS COMMUNICATION & DOCUMENT.	115	58	115	58	–	–	–	–
	HOME ECONOMICS (DOMESTIC SCIENCE)	–	–	–	–	–	–	–	–
	SERVICE TRADES	–	–	–	–	–	–	–	–
	NATURAL SCIENCE	328	39	–	–	327	39	1	–
	MATHEMATICS & COMPUTER SCIENCE	3	–	–	–	3	–	–	–
	MEDICAL SCIENCE AND HEALTH–RELATED	904	540	752	509	135	30	17	1
	ENGINEERING	539	18	148	2	391	16	–	–
	ARCHITECTURE & TOWN PLANNING	91	3	20	–	71	3	–	–
	TRADE, CRAFT & INDUSTRIAL PGMS.	–	–	–	–	–	–	–	–
	TRANSPORT AND COMMUNICATIONS	156	21	156	21	–	–	–	–
	AGRICULTURE, FORESTRY & FISHERY	639	39	510	35	129	4	–	–
	OTHER AND NOT SPECIFIED	589	116	410	77	166	38	13	1
SAMOA‡ 1983	TOTAL	562	264	532	255	30	9	–	–
	EDUCATION SCIENCE & TEACHER TRNG.	98	65	96	63	2	2	–	–
	HUMANITIES, RELIGION & THEOLOGY	77	30	77	30	–	–	–	–
	FINE AND APPLIED ARTS	–	–	–	–	–	–	–	–
	LAW	–	–	–	–	–	–	–	–
	SOCIAL AND BEHAVIOURAL SCIENCE	7	3	–	–	7	3	–	–
	COMMERCIAL & BUSINESS ADMIN.	341	144	322	141	19	3	–	–
	MASS COMMUNICATION & DOCUMENT.	–	–	–	–	–	–	–	–
	HOME ECONOMICS (DOMESTIC SCIENCE)	15	15	15	15	–	–	–	–
	SERVICE TRADES	–	–	–	–	–	–	–	–
	NATURAL SCIENCE	–	–	–	–	–	–	–	–
	MATHEMATICS & COMPUTER SCIENCE	24	7	22	6	2	1	–	–
	MEDICAL SCIENCE AND HEALTH–RELATED	–	–	–	–	–	–	–	–
	ENGINEERING	–	–	–	–	–	–	–	–
	ARCHITECTURE & TOWN PLANNING	–	–	–	–	–	–	–	–
	TRADE, CRAFT & INDUSTRIAL PGMS.	–	–	–	–	–	–	–	–
	TRANSPORT AND COMMUNICATIONS	–	–	–	–	–	–	–	–
	AGRICULTURE, FORESTRY & FISHERY	–	–	–	–	–	–	–	–
	OTHER AND NOT SPECIFIED	–	–	–	–	–	–	–	–

COUNTRY / YEAR PAYS / ANNEE PAIS / AÑO	FIELD OF STUDY DOMAINES D'ETUDES SECTORES DE ESTUDIOS	INTERNATIONAL STANDARD CLASSIFICATION OF EDUCATION BY LEVEL / CLASSIFICATION INTERNATIONALE TYPE DE L'EDUCATION PAR NIVEAUX / CLASIFICACION INTERNACIONAL NORMALIZADA DE LA EDUCACION POR NIVELES							
		ALL LEVELS TOUS NIVEAUX TODOS LOS NIVELES		LEVEL 5 NIVEAU 5 NIVEL 5		LEVEL 6 NIVEAU 6 NIVEL 6		LEVEL 7 NIVEAU 7 NIVEL 7	
		MF	F	MF	F	MF	F	MF	F
		(1)	(2)	(3)	(4)	(5)	(6)	(7)	(8)
TONGA 1984	TOTAL	680	382	635	374	45	8	–	–
	EDUCATION SCIENCE & TEACHER TRNG.	183	92	138	84	45	8	–	–
	HUMANITIES, RELIGION & THEOLOGY	94	17	94	17	–	–	–	–
	FINE AND APPLIED ARTS	–	–	–	–	–	–	–	–
	LAW	–	–	–	–	–	–	–	–
	SOCIAL AND BEHAVIOURAL SCIENCE	–	–	–	–	–	–	–	–
	COMMERCIAL & BUSINESS ADMIN.	58	58	58	58	–	–	–	–
	MASS COMMUNICATION & DOCUMENT.	–	–	–	–	–	–	–	–
	HOME ECONOMICS (DOMESTIC SCIENCE)	132	132	132	132	–	–	–	–
	SERVICE TRADES	–	–	–	–	–	–	–	–
	NATURAL SCIENCE	–	–	–	–	–	–	–	–
	MATHEMATICS & COMPUTER SCIENCE	–	–	–	–	–	–	–	–
	MEDICAL SCIENCE AND HEALTH-RELATED	79	79	79	79	–	–	–	–
	ENGINEERING	16	–	16	–	–	–	–	–
	ARCHITECTURE & TOWN PLANNING	–	–	–	–	–	–	–	–
	TRADE, CRAFT & INDUSTRIAL PGMS.	–	–	–	–	–	–	–	–
	TRANSPORT AND COMMUNICATIONS	–	–	–	–	–	–	–	–
	AGRICULTURE, FORESTRY & FISHERY	93	–	93	–	–	–	–	–
	OTHER AND NOT SPECIFIED	25	4	25	4	–	–	–	–

This table, also intended to supplement the data provided in Table 3.11, gives the breakdown by field of study and by level of programmes of enrolment at the third level of education.

In both Tables 3.12 and 3.13 the definitions used are based on the International Standard Classification of Education (ISCED). Sometimes the coverage of these tables is less complete than that of Table 3.11, because the distribution by field of study is not always available for the total number of students enrolled.

The different level categories presented in Table 3.13 by their ISCED codes (5, 6, and 7) may be defined as follows:

Level 5: Programmes leading to an award not equivalent to a first university degree. Programmes of this type are usually practical in orientation in that they are designed to prepare students for particular vocational fields in which they can qualify as high-level technicians, teachers, nurses, production supervisors, etc.

Level 6: Programmes leading to a first university degree or equivalent qualification. Programmes of this type comprise those leading to typical first university degrees such as a Bachelors degree , a *Licence*, etc., as well as those which lead to first professional degrees such as *Doctorates* awarded after completion of studies in medicine, engineering, law, etc.

Level 7: Programmes leading to a post-graduate university degree or equivalent qualification. Programmes of this type generally require a first university degree or equivalent qualification for admission. They are intended to reflect specialization within a given subject area.

Field of Study should be taken to mean the student's main area of specialization. The subjects falling within each of the major fields according to the ISCED classification are shown in the introductory text to this chapter.

Ce tableau complète aussi le tableau 3.11 et présente la répartition de l'effectif du troisième degré d'enseignement par niveau de programmes et domaine d'études.

Dans les tableaux 3.12 et 3.13, les critères de classification utilisés sont ceux de la Classification Internationale Type de l'Education (CITE).

Il arrive parfois que les renseignements fournis dans les tableaux 3.12 et 3.13 soient moins complets que dans le tableau 3.11, la répartition par domaine d'études n'étant pas toujours disponible pour l'ensemble des étudiants.

Les différents niveaux, désignés dans le tableau 3.13 par leurs codes (5, 6 et 7) de la CITE, peuvent être définis comme suit:

Niveau 5: Programmes conduisant à un diplôme n'équivalant pas à un premier grade universitaire. Ces programmes ont généralement un caractère *pratique* en ce sens qu'ils ont pour objectif la formation professionnelle des étudiants dans des domaines précis où ils pourront se qualifier, par exemple, comme techniciens, enseignants, infirmiers, contrôleurs de la production, etc.

Niveau 6: Programmes conduisant à un premier grade universitaire ou à un diplôme équivalent. Sont compris ici les programmes qui conduisent à un premier grade universitaire tels que le *bachelors' degree*, la licence, ainsi que les programmes qui conduisent aux titres de caractère professionnel, tels que les *doctorats* décernés à la fin des études de médecine, de sciences de l'ingénieur, de droit, etc.

Niveau 7: Programmes conduisant à un grade universitaire supérieur ou à un diplôme équivalent. Ces programmes s'adressent en général aux personnes déjà titulaires d'un premier grade universitaire ou d'un diplôme équivalent. IL s'agit de programmes d'études post-universitaires qui prévoient habituellement une spécialisation à l'intérieur même de la discipline choisie.

Par *domaine d'études* il faut entendre le domaine principal de spécialisation de l'étudiant. Les sujets compris dans chacune des disciplines principales en accord avec la classification de la CITE sont précisés dans l'introduction de ce chapitre.

Este cuadro, que también completa el cuadro 3.11, contiene la distribución de la matrícula en la enseñanza de tercer grado por sector de estudios y por nivel de programas.

En los cuadros 3.12 y 3.13 las definiciones utilizadas se basan en los criterios de la Clasificación Internacional Normalizada de la Educación (CINE).

Ocurre a veces que los datos en ambos cuadros 3.12 y 3.13 son menos completos que los del cuadro 3.11, ya que no siempre se dispone de la distribución de todos los estudiantes inscritos por sector de estudios.

Los diferentes niveles, que se designan en el cuadro 3.13 según codificación (5, 6 y 7) en la CINE, pueden definirse como sigue:

Nivel 5: Programas que conducen a un diploma que no equivale a un primer grado universitario. Los programas de este tipo suelen ser de orientación *práctica*, y están destinados a preparar los estudiantes para determinadas ramas profesionales en las que podrán calificarse, como por ejemplo técnicos, maestros, enfermeros, supervisores de producción, etc.

Nivel 6: Programas que conducen a un primer grado universitario o a un diploma equivalente. Figuran igualmente aquí los programas que conducen a los títulos de carácter profesional, tales como el de *doctor* obtenido al terminar los estudios de medicina, ingeniería, derecho, etc.

Nivel 7: Programas que conducen a un grado universitario superior o a un diploma equivalente. Estos programas se destinan en general a las personas titulares de un primer grado universitario o calificación equivalente. Se trata de programas de postgraduación que tienden a la especialización dentro del sector de estudio.

Por *sector de estudios* se comprende el campo principal c especialización del estudiante. Las materias que figuran e cada una de las ramas principales de acuerdo con la clasificaci de la CINE se muestran en la introducción de este capítulo.

AFRICA:

Botswana:

E--> Social and behavioural science include commercial and business administration.

FR-> Les sciences sociales et sciences du comportement incluent la formation au commerce et à l'administration des entreprises.

ESP> Las ciencias sociales y del comportamiento incluyen la enseñanza comercial y de administración de empresas.

Cameroon:

E--> Data revised and refer to universities and equivalent degree-granting institutions only.

FR-> Les données révisées se réfèrent aux universités et établissements conférant des grades équivalents seulement.

ESP> Los datos revisados se refieren a las universidades y establecimientos que otorguen grados equivalentes solamente.

Chad:

E--> Programmes of levels 5 and 6 are combined.

FR-> Les données relatives aux programmes des niveaux 5 et 6 sont regroupées.

ESP> Los datos relativos a los programas de los niveles 5 y 6 están agrupados.

Egypt:

E--> Data refer to universities and equivalent degree-granting institutions, excluding Al Azhar University. Engineering includes architecture and town planning, trade, craft and industrial programmes and transport and communications.

FR-> Les données se réfèrent aux universités et établissements conférant des grades équivalents seulement, non compris l'Université d'Al Azhar. Les sciences de l'ingénieur comprennent l'architecture et l'urbanisme, les métiers de la production industrielle et les transports et télécommunications.

ESP> Los datos se refieren a las universidades y establecimientos equivalentes solamente, pero no comprenden la Universidad de Al Azhar. La ingeniería y la tecnología comprenden la arquitectura y el urbanismo, las artes y oficios industriales, además de los transportes y comunicaciones.

Ethiopia:

E--> Natural science includes mathematics and computer science. In 'Other and not specified' data of levels 5 and 6 are combined.

FR-> Les sciences exactes et naturelles comprennent les mathématiques et l'informatique. Dans la rubrique 'Autres programmes' les données des niveaux 5 et 6 sont regroupées.

ESP> Las ciencias naturales comprenden las matemáticas y la informática. En la rúbrica 'Otros programas' los datos de los niveles 5 y 6 están agrupados.

Gabon:

E--> Programmes of levels 6 and 7 are combined.

FR-> Les donn

es relatives aux programmes des niveaux 6 et 7 sont regroupées.

ESP> Los datos relativos a los programas de los niveles 6 y 7 están agrupados.

Ghana:

E--> Data refer to universities only. Social and behavioural science include law, humanities, religion and theology. Natural science includes mathematics and computer science.

FR-> Les données se réfèrent aux universités seulement. Les sciences sociales et sciences du comportement incluent le droit, les lettres, religion et théologie. Les sciences exactes et naturelles comprennent les mathématiques et l'informatique.

ESP> Los datos se refieren a las universidades solamente. Las ciencias sociales y del comportamiento incluyen el derecho, las humanidades, religión y teología. Las ciencias naturales comprenden las matemáticas y la informática.

Guinea:

E--> Social and behavioural science include humanities, religion and theology and fine and applied arts. Natural science includes mathematics and computer science.

Guinea: (Cont):

FR-> Les sciences sociales et sciences du comportement incluent l lettres, religion et théologie et les beaux-arts et arts appliqués. Les scienc exactes et naturelles comprennent les mathématiques et l'informatique.

ESP> Las ciencias sociales y del comportamiento incluyen l humanidades, religion y teología y las bellas artes y artes aplicadas. L ciencias naturales comprenden las matemáticas y la informática.

Kenya:

E--> Education science and teacher training include humaniti religion and theology. 'Other and not specified' includes adult educatio

FR-> Les sciences de l'éducation et la formation d'enseignan incluent les lettres, religion et théologie. La rubrique 'Autres programme inclut l'éducation des adultes.

ESP> Las ciencias de la educación y formación de personal docen incluyen las humanidades, religión y teología. La rúbrica 'Otros programa incluye la educación de los adultos.

Lesotho:

E--> Medical science and health-related at level 6 include level 5.

FR-> Les sciences médicales, santé et hygiène au niveau 6 incluent niveau 5.

ESP> Las ciencias médicas, sanidad e higiene al nivel 6 incluyen el niv 5.

Malawi:

E--> Data refer to the university only.

FR-> Les données se réfèrent à l'université seulement.

ESP> Los datos se refieren a la universidad solamente.

Morocco:

E--> Data refer to universities only. Natural sciences includ mathematics and computer science.

FR-> Les données se réfèrent aux universités seulement. Les scienc exactes et naturelles incluent les mathématiques et l'informatique.

ESP> Los datos se refieren a las universidades solamente. Las cienci naturales incluyen las matemáticas e informática.

Nigeria:

E--> Data refer to universities only.

FR-> Les données se réfèrent aux universités seulement.

ESP> Los datos se refieren a las universidades solamente.

Sudan:

E--> Programmes of levels 6 and 7 are combined.

FR-> Les données relatives aux programmes des niveaux 6 et 7 so regroupées.

ESP> Los datos relativos a los programas de los niveles 6 y 7 está agrupados.

Swaziland:

E--> Data refer to universities and equivalent degree-grantir institutions, and to teacher training colleges. Natural science includ mathematics and computer science.

FR-> Les données se réfèrent aux universités et aux établissemen conférant des grades équivalents et aux colleges d'enseignement norm Les sciences exactes et naturelles incluent les mathématiques l'informatique.

ESP> Los datos se refieren a las universidades y establecimientos qu otorguen grados equivalentes y a los colegios de enseñanza normal. L ciencias naturales incluyen las matemáticas y la informática.

Uganda:

E--> Programmes of levels 6 and 7 are combined.

FR-> Les données relatives aux programmes des niveaux 6 et 7 so regroupées.

ESP> Los datos relativos a los programas de los niveles 6 y 7 está agrupados.

United Republic of Tanzania:

E--> Data refer to universities and equivalent degree-grantir institutions only.

FR-> Les données se réfèrent aux universités et établissemen conférant des grades équivalents seulement.

ESP> Los datos se refieren a las universidades y establecimient

United Republic of Tanzania: (Cont):
que otorguen grados equivalentes solamente.

Zimbabwe:

E--> Data refer to universities and equivalent degree-granting institutions. Humanities, religion and theology include fine and applied arts. Law includes commercial and business administration.

FR-> Les données se réfèrent aux universités et aux établissements conférant des grades équivalents. Les lettres, la religion et la théologie incluent les beaux-arts et arts appliqués. Le droit inclut la formation au commerce et à l'administration des entreprises.

ESP> Los datos se refieren a las universidades y establecimientos que otorguen grados equivalentes. Las humanidades, religión y teología incluyen las bellas artes y artes aplicadas. El derecho incluye la enseñanza comercial y de administración de empresas.

AMERICA, NORTH:

Barbados:

E--> At level 5, social and behavioural science include law and commercial and business administration. Natural science includes mathematics and computer science.

FR-> Au niveau 5, les sciences sociales et sciences du comportement incluent le droit et la formation au commerce et à l'administration des entreprises. Les sciences exactes et naturelles incluent les mathématiques et l'informatique.

ESP> Al nivel 5, las ciencias sociales y del comportamiento incluyen el derecho y la enseñanza comercial y de administración de empresas. Las ciencias naturales incluyen las matemáticas y la informática.

Bermuda:

E--> Data include adult education. Humanities, religion and theology include fine and applied arts, social and behavioural science, natural science and mathematics and computer science.

FR-> Les données incluent l'éducation des adultes. Les lettres, la religion et la théologie incluent les beaux arts et les arts appliqués, les sciences sociales et sciences du comportement, les sciences exactes et naturelles, les mathématiques et l'informatique.

ESP> Los datos incluyen la educación de los adultos. Las humanidades, la religión y la teología incluyen las bellas artes y artes aplicadas, las ciencias sociales y del comportamiento, las ciencias naturales y las matemáticas e informática.

Costa Rica:

E--> Data refer to universities only. Programmes of levels 5 and 6 are combined.

FR-> Les données se réfèrent aux universités seulement. Les données relatives aux programmes des niveaux 5 et 6 sont regroupées.

ESP> Los datos se refieren a las universidades solamente. Los datos relativos a los programas de los niveles 5 y 6 están agrupados.

Grenada:

E--> Data exclude Grenada Teacher's College. Engineering includes architecture and town planning.

FR-> Les données excluent 'Grenada Teacher's College'. Les sciences de l'ingénieur incluent l'architecture et l'urbanisme.

ESP> Los datos excluyen 'Grenada Teacher's College'. La ingeniería y tecnología incluyen la arquitectura y urbanismo.

Mexico:

E--> Data refer to universities and equivalent degree-granting institutions only.

FR-> Les données se réfèrent aux universités et établissements conférant des grades équivalents seulement.

ESP> Los datos se refieren a las universidades y establecimientos que otorguen grados equivalentes solamente.

Trinidad and Tobago:

E--> Natural science includes mathematics and computer science. Programmes of levels 6 and 7 are combined.

FR-> Les sciences exactes et naturelles incluent les mathématiques et l'informatique. Les données relatives aux programmes des niveaux 6 et 7 sont regroupées.

ESP> Las ciencias naturales incluyen las matemáticas e informática. Los datos relativos a los programas de los niveles 6 y 7 están agrupados.

AMERICA, SOUTH:

Bolivia:

E--> Data refer to universities and equivalent degree-granting institutions only and exclude 'la universidad católica boliviana'.

FR-> Les données se réfèrent aux universités et établissements conférant des grades équivalents seulement et excluent 'la universidad católica boliviana'.

ESP> Los datos se refieren a las universidades y establecimientos que otorguen grados equivalentes solamente y excluyen la universidad católica boliviana.

Colombia:

E--> Law includes social and behavioural science. Commercial and business administration includes mass communication and documentation, home economics and service trades. Natural science includes mathematics and computer science. Engineering includes architecture and town planning, trade, craft and industrial programmes and transport and communications.

FR-> Le droit inclut les sciences sociales et sciences du comportement. La formation au commerce et à l'administration des entreprises inclut l'information et la documentation, l'enseignement ménager et la formation pour le secteur tertiaire. Les sciences exactes et naturelles incluent les mathématiques et l'informatique. Les sciences de l'ingénieur comprennent l'architecture et l'urbanisme, les métiers de la production industrielle et les transports et télécommunications.

ESP> El derecho incluye las ciencias sociales y del comportamiento. La enseñanza comercial y de administración de empresas incluye la documentación y comunicación social, la economía doméstica y la formación para el sector de los servicios. Las ciencias naturales incluyen las matemáticas e informática. La ingeniería y tecnología comprenden la arquitectura y urbanismo, las artes y oficios industriales y los transportes y comunicaciones.

Suriname:

E--> Social and behavioural science include law.

FR-> Les sciences sociales et sciences du comportement incluent le droit.

ESP> Las ciencias sociales y del comportamiento incluyen el derecho.

Venezuela:

E--> Programmes of levels 5 and 6 are combined.

FR-> Les données relatives aux programmes des niveaux 5 et 6 sont regroupées.

ESP> Los datos relativos a los programas de los niveles 5 y 6 están agrupados.

ASIA:

Bangladesh:

E--> Natural science includes home economics.

FR-> Les sciences exactes et naturelles incluent l'enseignement ménager.

ESP> Las ciencias naturales incluyen la economía doméstica.

Bhutan:

E--> Commercial and business administration includes social and behavioural science.

FR-> La formation au commerce et à l'administration des entreprises inclut les sciences sociales et sciences du comportement.

ESP> La enseñanza comercial y de administración de empresas incluye las ciencias sociales y del comportamiento.

China:

E--> Data refer to full-time students only. Commercial and business administration includes social and behavioural science.

FR-> Les données se réfèrent aux étudiants à plein temps seulement. La formation au commerce et à l'administration des entreprises inclut les sciences sociales et sciences du comportement.

ESP> Los datos se refieren a los estudiantes de jornada completa solamente. La enseñanza comercial y de administración de empresas incluye las ciencias sociales y del comportamiento.

India:

E--> Social and behavioural science include commercial and business administration. Natural science includes mathematics and computer science and home economics. Engineering includes architecture and town planning, trade, craft and industrial programmes, transport and communications.

FR-> Les sciences sociales et sciences du comportement comprennent la formation au commerce et à l'administration des entreprises. Les sciences exactes et naturelles incluent les mathématiques et l'informatique et l'enseignement ménager. Les sciences de l'ingénieur comprennent l'architecture et l'urbanisme, les métiers de la production industrielle et les transports et télécommunications.

ESP> Las ciencias sociales y del comportamiento comprenden la enseñanza comercial y de administración de empresas. Las ciencias naturales comprenden las matemáticas y la informática y la economía doméstica. La ingeniería y tecnología comprenden la arquitectura y el urbanismo, las artes y oficios industriales además de los transportes y comunicaciones.

Iran, Islamic Rep. of:

E--> Data on female students do not include teacher training colleges.

FR-> Les données relatives aux étudiantes n'incluent pas les collèges d'enseignement normal.

ESP> Los datos relativos a las estudiantes no incluyen los colegios de la enseñanza normal.

Israel:

E--> Data exclude open university. Education science and teacher training includes humanities, religion and theology, fine and applied arts. Social and behavioural science include commercial and business administration, mass communication and documentation, home economics and service trades. Engineering includes architecture and town planning, trade, craft and industrial programmes, transport and communications.

FR-> Les données excluent 'open university'. Les sciences de l'éducation et la formation d'enseignants comprennent les lettres, la religion et la théologie, les beaux-arts et les arts appliqués. Les sciences sociales et sciences du comportement comprennent la formation au commerce et à l'administration des entreprises, l'information et la documentation, l'enseignement ménager et la formation pour le secteur tertiaire. Les sciences de l'ingénieur comprennent l'architecture et l'urbanisme, les métiers de la production industrielle et les transports et télécommunications.

ESP> Los datos excluyen 'open university'. Las ciencias de la

Israel: (Cont):
educación y formación de personal docente comprenden las humanidades, la religión y la teología, las bellas artes y las artes aplicadas. Las ciencias sociales y del comportamiento comprenden la enseñanza comercial y de administración de empresas, la documentación y comunicación social, la economía doméstica y la formación para el sector de los servicios. La ingeniería y tecnología comprenden la arquitectura y el urbanismo y las artes y oficios industriales, además de los transportes y comunicaciones.

Japan:

E--> Including correspondence courses. Humanities, religion and theology include mass communication and documentation. Social and behavioural science includes law, commercial and business administration. Engineering includes architecture and town planning, trade, craft and industrial programmes. 'Other and not specified' includes 107,738 (F 25,223) students for which the breakdown by ISCED level is not available.

FR-> Y compris les cours par correspondance. Les lettres, la religion et la théologie comprennent l'information et la documentation. Les sciences sociales et les sciences du comportement comprennent le droit et la formation au commerce et à l'administration des entreprises. Les sciences de l'ingénieur comprennent l'architecture et l'urbanisme et les métiers de la production industrielle. La rubrique 'Autres programmes' comprend 107 738 (F 25 223) étudiants pour lesquels la répartition par type de programmes de la CITE n'est pas disponible.

ESP> Incluídos los cursos por correspondencia. Las humanidades, la religión y la teología comprenden la documentación y comunicación social. Las ciencias sociales y del comportamiento comprenden el derecho y la enseñanza comercial y de administración de empresas. La ingeniería y tecnología comprenden la arquitectura y el urbanismo además de las artes y oficios industriales. La rúbrica 'otros programas' incluye 107 738 (F 25 223) estudiantes para los cuales la repartición según los tipos de programas de la CINE se desconoce.

Jordan:

E--> Humanities, religion and theology include social and behavioural science. Commercial and business administration includes economics. Natural science includes mathematics and computer science. Engineering includes architecture and town planning.

FR-> Les lettres, la religion et la théologie incluent les sciences sociales et sciences du comportement. La formation au commerce et à l'administration des entreprises incluent les sciences économiques. Les sciences exactes et naturelles incluent les mathématiques et l'informatique. Les sciences de l'ingénieur incluent l'architecture et l'urbanisme.

ESP> Las humanidades, religion y teología incluyen las ciencias sociales y del comportamiento. La enseñan
a comercial y de administración de empresas incluye las ciencias económicas. Las ciencias naturales incluyen las matemáticas e informática. La ingeniería y tecnología incluyen la arquitectura y urbanismo.

Kuwait:

E--> Engineering includes trade, craft and industrial programmes.

FR-> Les sciences de l'ingénieur incluent les métiers de la production industrielle.

ESP> La ingeniería y tecnología incluyen las artes y oficios industriales.

Lebanon:

E--> Programmes of levels 6 and 7 are combined.

FR-> Les données relatives aux programmes des niveaux 6 et 7 sont regroupées.

ESP> Los datos relativos a los programas de los niveles 6 y 7 están agrupados.

Nepal:

E--> Data refer to public universities only. Humanities, religion and theology include social and behavioural science and fine and applied arts. Natural science includes mathematics and computer science.

FR-> Les données se réfèrent aux universités publiques seulement. Les lettres, religion et théologie incluent les sciences sociales et sciences du comportement et les beaux-arts et arts appliqués. Les sciences naturelles incluent les mathématiques et l'informatique.

ESP> Los datos se refieren a las universidades públicas solamente. Las humanidades, religión y teología incluyen las ciencias sociales y del comportamiento y las bellas artes y artes aplicadas. Las ciencias naturales incluyen las matemáticas e informática.

Pakistan:

E--> Engineering includes architecture and town planning.

FR-> Les sciences de l'ingénieur incluent l'architecture et l'urbanisme.

ESP> La ingeniería y tecnología incluyen la arquitectura y urbanismo.

Qatar:

E--> Humanities, religion and theology include social and behavioural science and mass communication and documentation. Natural science includes mathematics and computer science.

FR-> Les lettres, religion et théologie incluent les sciences sociales et sciences du comportement et l'information et la documentation. Les sciences exactes et naturelles incluent les mathématiques et l'informatique.

ESP> Las humanidades, religión y teología incluyen las ciencias sociales y del comportamiento y la documentación y communicación social. Las ciencias naturales incluyen las matemáticas y la informática.

Saudi Arabia:

E--> Humanities, religion and theology include law and hom economics. Social and behavioural science includes commercial ar business administration. Natural science includes mathematics ar computer science. Engineering includes architecture and town planning

FR-> Les lettres, religion et théologie incluent le droit l'enseignement ménager. Les sciences sociales et sciences c comportement incluent la formation au commerce et à l'administratio des entreprises. Les sciences exactes et naturelles incluent l mathématiques et l'informatique. Les sciences de l'ingénieur inclue l'architecture et l'urbanisme.

ESP> Las humanidades, religión y telolgía incluyen el derecho y economía doméstica. Las ciencias sociales y del comportamien incluyen la enseñanza comercial y de administración de empresas. La ciencias naturales incluyen las matemáticas y la informática. La ingenier y tecnología incluyen la arquitectura y urbanismo.

Singapore:

E--> Humanities, religion and theology include social and behaviour science.

FR-> Les lettres, la religion et la théologie comprennent les science sociales et sciences du comportement.

ESP> Las humanidades, la religión y la teología comprenden la ciencias sociales y del comportamiento.

Sri Lanka:

E--> Data include Open University. Natural science include mathematics and computer science.

FR-> Les données incluent 'Open University'. Les sciences exactes naturelles incluent les mathématiques et l'informatique.

ESP> Los datos incluyen 'Open University'. Las ciencias naturale incluyen las matemáticas y la informática.

Turkey:

E--> Data include Open University.

FR-> Les données incluent 'Open University'.

ESP> Los datos incluyen 'Open University'.

Viet-nam:

E--> Including correspondence courses.

FR-> Y compris les cours par correspondance.

ESP> Incluídos los cursos por correspondencia.

EUROPE:

Albania:

E--> Including evening and correspondence courses. Natural scienc includes mathematics and computer science.

FR-> Y compris les cours du soir et par correspondance. Les science exactes et naturelles incluent les mathématiques et l'informatique.

ESP> Incluídos los cursos nocturnos y por correspondencia. La ciencias naturales incluyen las matemáticas y la informática.

Austria:

E--> Data include multiple counting of students enrolled in more tha one field of study.

FR-> Les données incluent les étudiants inscrits dans plusieu domaines d'études.

ESP> Los datos incluyen los estudiantes inscritos en diversos sectore de estudios.

Belgium:

E--> Natural science incudes mathematics and computer scienc Programmes of levels 6 and 7 are combined.

FR-> Les sciences exactes et naturelles incluent les mathématiques e l'informatique. Les données relatives aux programmes des niveaux 6 et sont regroupées.

ESP> Las ciencias naturales incluyen las matemáticas e informátic Los datos relativos a los programas de los niveles 6 y 7 está agrupados.

Bulgaria:

E--> Including evening and correspondence courses.

FR-> Y compris les cours du soir et par correspondance.

ESP> Incluídos los cursos nocturnos y por corespondencia.

Denmark:

E--> Programmes of levels 6 and 7 are combined.

FR-> Les données relatives aux programmes des niveaux 6 et 7 sor regroupées.

ESP> Los datos relativos a los programas de los niveles 6 y 7 está agrupados.

Finland:

E--> Programmes of levels 6 and 7 are combined.

FR-> Les données relatives aux programmes des niveaux 6 et 7 sor regroupées.

ESP> Los datos relativos a los programas de los niveles 6 y 7 está agrupados.

France:

E--> The heading 'humanities, religion and theology' refers to 'lettre et sciences humaines' which includes the majority of the social scienc (except economics); the natural science category refers to science whic also includes certain fields of engineering. The heading 'other and no specified' refers to the university institutes of technology (I.U.T.). an includes service trades.

FR-> La rubrique 'lettres, religion et théologie' comprend les lettres e sciences humaines qui incluent la majorité des sciences sociale excepté les sciences économiques. Les sciences exactes et naturelle

France: (Cont):
comprennent également certaines disciplines des sciences de l'ingénieur. La rubrique 'autres programmes' se réfère aux instituts universitaires de technologie (I.U.T.) et inclut la formation pour le secteur tertiaire.

ESP> El epígrafe 'humanidades, religión y teología' se refiere al grupo de humanidades y ciencias humanas, que comprenden las disciplinas dependientes de las ciencias sociales, salvo las ciencias económicas. La rúbrica 'ciencias naturales' incluye algunos estudios relativos a la ingeniería. La rúbrica 'otros programas' se refiere a los institutos universitarios de tecnología (I.U.T.) y incluye la formación para el sector de los servicios.

German Democratic Republic:

E--> Including evening and correspondence courses.

FR-> Y compris les cours du soir et par correspondance.

ESP> Incluídos los cursos nocturnos y por corespondencia.

Holy See:

E--> Data refer to students enrolled in higher institutions under the authority of the Holy See.

FR-> Les données se réfèrent aux étudiants dans les institutions du troisième degré sous l'autorité du Saint-Siège.

ESP> Los datos se refieren a los estudiantes en los institutos del tercer grado bajo la autoridad del Santa Sede.

Hungary:

E--> Including evening and correspondence courses.

FR-> Y compris les cours du soir et par correspondance.

ESP> Incluídos los cursos nocturnos y por correspondencia.

Luxembourg:

E--> Data refer only to students enrolled in institutions located in Luxembourg. At university level, the majority of the students pursue their studies in the following countries: Austria, Belgium, France, Federal Republic of Germany and Switzerland. Social and behavioural science include commercial and business administration. Natural science includes mathematics and computer science.

FR-> Les données se réfèrent aux étudiants inscrits dans les institutions du Luxembourg. La plus grande partie des étudiants luxembourgeois poursuivent leurs études universitaires dans les universités des pays suivants: Autriche, Belgique, France, République fédérale d'Allemagne et Suisse. Les sciences sociales et sciences du comportement incluent la formation au commerce et à l'administration des entreprises. Les sciences exactes et naturelles comprennent également les mathématiques et l'informatique.

ESP> Los datos se refieren solamente a los estudiantes matriculados en las instituciones en Luxemburgo. La mayoría de los estudiantes de Luxemburgo cursan sus estudios universitarios en las universidades de los países siguientes: Austria, Bélgica, Francia, Républica Federal de Alemania y Suiza. Las ciencias sociales y del comportamiento incluyen la enseñanza comercial y de administración de empresas. Las ciencias naturales comprenden las matemáticas y la informática.

Netherlands:

E--> Data refer to universities and equivalent degree-granting institutions. Programmes of levels 6 and 7 are combined.

FR-> Les données se réfèrent aux universités et établissements conférant des grades équivalents seulement. Les données relatives aux programmes des niveaux 6 et 7 sont regroupées.

ESP> Los datos se refieren a las universidades y establecimientos que otorguen grados equivalentes. Los datos relativos a los programas de los niveles 6 y 7 están agrupados.

Poland:

E--> Including evening and correspondence courses.

FR-> Y compris les cours du soir et par correspondance.

ESP> Incluídos los cursos nocturnos y por correspondencia.

Portugal:

E--> Social and behavioural science include commercial and business administration and mass communication and documentation. Natural science includes mathematics and computer science.

FR-> Les sciences sociales et sciences du comportement comprennent la formation au commerce et à l'administration des entreprises et l'information et la documentation. Les sciences exactes et naturelles incluent les mathématiques et l'informatique.

ESP> Las ciencias sociales y del comportamiento comprenden la enseñanza comercial y de administración de empresas y la documentación y comunicación social. Las ciencias naturales comprenden las matemáticas y la informática.

Romania:

E--> Including evening and correspondence courses. Education science and teacher training includes humanities, religion and theology. Social and behavioural science include commercial and business administration, mass communication and documentation, home economics and service trades. Natural science includes mathematics and computer science. Engineering includes architecture and town planning and trade, craft and industrial programmes.

FR-> Y compris les cours du soir et par correspondance. Les sciences de l'éducation et la formation d'enseignants incluent les lettres, la religion et la théologie. Les sciences sociales et sciences du comportement comprennent la formation au commerce et à l'administration des entreprises, l'information et la documentation, l'enseignement ménager et la formation pour le secteur tertiaire. Les sciences exactes et naturelles incluent les mathématiques et l'informatique. Les sciences de l'ingénieur incluent l'architecture et l'urbanisme et les métiers de la production industrielle.

ESP> Incluídos los cursos nocturnos y por corespondencia. Las ciencias de la educación y formación de personal docente comprenden las humanidades, la religión y la teología. Las ciencias sociales y del comportamiento comprenden la enseñanza comercial y de administration de empresas, la documentación y comunicación social, la economía doméstica y la formación para el sector de los servicios. Las ciencias naturales incluyen las matemáticas y informática. La ingeniería y la tecnología incluyen la arquitectura y urbanismo y las artes y oficios industriales.

Spain:

E--> Programmes of levels 6 and 7 are combined. Including 'Universidad de Educación a distancia'.

FR-> Les données relatives aux programmes des niveaux 6 et 7 sont regroupées. Y compris la 'Universidad de educación a distancia'.

ESP> Los datos relativos a los programas de los niveles 6 y 7 están agrupados. Incluída la universidad de educación a distancia.

United Kingdom:

E--> Data on 'other and not specified' include students enrolled at the Open University.

FR-> Les données sur la rubrique 'autres programmes' incluent les étudiants inscrits à l'*Open University*.

ESP> Los datos en la rúbrica 'otros programas' incluyen los estudiantes inscritos en la 'Open University'.

Yugoslavia:

E--> Natural science includes mathematics and computer science.

FR-> Les sciences exactes et naturelles comprennent les mathématiques et l'informatique.

ESP> Las ciencias naturales comprenden las matemáticas y la informática.

OCEANIA:

Australia:

E--> Social and behavioural science include mass communication and documentation. Natural science includes mathematics and computer science.

FR-> Les sciences sociales et sciences du comportement incluent l'information et la documentation. Les sciences exactes et naturelles comprennent les mathématiques et l'informatique.

ESP> Las ciencias sociales y del comportamiento incluyen la documentación y comunicación social. Las ciencias naturales comprenden las matemáticas y la informática.

Fiji:

E--> Social and behavioural science include commercial and business administration.

FR-> Les sciences sociales et sciences du comportement incluent la formation au commerce et à l'administration des entreprises.

ESP> Las ciencias sociales y del comportamiento incluyen la enseñanza comercial y de administración de empresas.

New Caledonia:

E--> Mathematics and computer science include natural science.

FR-> Les mathématiques et l'informatique comprennent les sciences exactes et naturelles.

ESP> Las matemáticas y la informática incluyen las ciencias naturales.

New Zealand:

E--> Including multiple counting of students enrolled in more than one field of study. Natural science at level 6 includes mathematics and computer science.

FR-> Y compris les étudiants inscrits dans plusieurs domaines d'études. Les sciences exactes et naturelles au niveau 6 incluent les mathématiques et l'informatique.

ESP> Incluídos los estudiantes inscritos en diversos sectores de estudios. Las ciencias naturales en el grado 6 incluyen las matemáticas e informática.

Samoa:

E--> Data exclude the school of agriculture.

FR-> Les données excluent l'école d'agriculture.

ESP> Los datos excluyen la escuela de agricultura.

3.14 Education at the third level: graduates by ISCED level of programme and field of study

Enseignement du troisième degré: nombre de diplômés par niveau de programmes et domaine d'études de la CITE

Enseñanza de tercer grado: número de diplomados por nivel de programas y sector de estudios de la CINE

EDUCATION SCIENCE AND TEACHER TRAINING	=	SCIENCES DE L'EDUCATION ET FORMATION D'ENSEIGNANTS	=	CIENCIAS DE LA EDUCACION Y FORMACION DE PERSONAL DOCENTE
HUMANITIES, RELIGION AND THEOLOGY	=	LETTRES, RELIGION ET THEOLOGIE	=	HUMANIDADES, RELIGION Y TEOLOGIA
FINE AND APPLIED ARTS	=	BEAUX-ARTS ET ARTS APPLIQUES	=	BELLAS ARTES Y ARTES APLICADAS
LAW	=	DROIT	=	DERECHO
SOCIAL AND BEHAVIOURAL SCIENCE	=	SCIENCES SOCIALES ET SCIENCES DU COMPORTEMENT	=	CIENCIAS SOCIALES Y DEL COMPORTAMIENTO
COMMERCIAL AND BUSINESS ADMINISTRATION	=	FORMATION AU COMMERCE ET A L'ADMINISTRATION DES ENTREPRISES	=	ENSEÑANZA COMERCIAL Y DE ADMINISTRACION DE EMPRESAS
MASS COMMUNICATION AND DOCUMENTATION	=	INFORMATION ET DOCUMENTATION	=	DOCUMENTACION Y COMUNICACION SOCIAL
HOME ECONOMICS (DOMESTIC SCIENCE)	=	ENSEIGNEMENT MENAGER	=	ECONOMIA DOMESTICA (ENSEÑANZA DEL HOGAR)
SERVICE TRADES	=	FORMATION POUR LE SECTEUR TERTIAIRE	=	FORMACION PARA EL SECTOR DE LOS SERVICIOS
NATURAL SCIENCE	=	SCIENCES EXACTES ET NATURELLES	=	CIENCIAS NATURALES
MATHEMATICS AND COMPUTER SCIENCE	=	MATHEMATIQUES ET INFORMATIQUE	=	MATEMATICAS E INFORMATICA
MEDICAL SCIENCE AND HEALTH-RELATED	=	SCIENCES MEDICALES, SANTE ET HYGIENE	=	CIENCIAS MEDICAS, SANIDAD E HIGIENE
ENGINEERING	=	SCIENCES DE L'INGENIEUR	=	INGENIERIA Y TECNOLOGIA
ARCHITECTURE & TOWN PLANNING	=	ARCHITECTURE ET URBANISME	=	ARQUITECTURA Y URBANISMO
TRADE, CRAFT & INDUSTRIAL PROGRAMMES	=	METIERS DE LA PRODUCTION INDUSTRIELLE	=	ARTES Y OFICIOS INDUSTRIALES
TRANSPORT AND COMMUNICATIONS	=	TRANSPORTS ET TELECOMMUNICATIONS	=	TRANSPORTES Y COMUNICACIONES
AGRICULTURE, FORESTRY AND FISHERY	=	AGRICULTURE, SYLVICULTURE ET HALIEUTIQUE	=	ENSEÑANZA AGRONOMICA, DASONOMICA Y PESQUERA
OTHER AND NOT SPECIFIED	=	AUTRES PROGRAMMES	=	OTROS PROGRAMAS

LEVEL 5	DIPLOMAS AND CERTIFICATES NOT EQUIVALENT TO A FIRST UNIVERSITY DEGREE	NIVEAU 5	DIPLOMES ET CERTIFICATS NON EQUIVALENTS A UN PREMIER GRADE UNIVERSITAIRE	NIVEL 5	DIPLOMAS Y CERTIFICADOS NO EQUIVALENTES A UN PRIMER TITULO UNIVERSITARIO
LEVEL 6	FIRST UNIVERSITY DEGREES OR EQUIVALENT QUALIFICATIONS	NIVEAU 6	PREMIERS GRADES UNIVERSITAIRES OU DIPLOMES EQUIVALENTS	NIVEL 6	PRIMEROS TITULOS UNIVERSITARIOS O DIPLOMAS EQUIVALENTES
LEVEL 7	POST-GRADUATE UNIVERSITY DEGREES OR EQUIVALENT QUALIFICATIONS	NIVEAU 7	GRADES UNIVERSITAIRES SUPERIEURS OU DIPLOMES EQUIVALENTS	NIVEL 7	TITULOS UNIVERSITARIOS SUPERIORES O DIPLOMAS EQUIVALENTES

PLEASE REFER TO EXPLANATORY TEXT AT END OF TABLE

PRIERE DE SE REFERER AU TEXTE EXPLICATIF A LA FIN DU TABLEAU

REFERIRSE AL TEXTO EXPLICATIVO AL FINAL DEL CUADRO

NUMBER OF COUNTRIES AND TERRITORIES PRESENTED IN THIS TABLE: 131

NOMBRE DE PAYS ET DE TERRITOIRES PRESENTES DANS CE TABLEAU: 131

NUMERO DE PAISES Y DE TERRITORIOS PRESENTADOS EN ESTE CUADRO: 131

COUNTRY / YEAR PAYS / ANNEE PAIS / AÑO	FIELD OF STUDY DOMAINES D'ETUDES SECTORES DE ESTUDIOS	INTERNATIONAL STANDARD CLASSIFICATION OF EDUCATION BY LEVEL / CLASSIFICATION INTERNATIONALE TYPE DE L'EDUCATION PAR NIVEAU / CLASIFICACION INTERNACIONAL NORMALIZADA DE LA EDUCACION POR NIVEL							
		ALL LEVELS TOUS NIVEAUX TODOS LOS NIVELES		LEVEL 5 NIVEAU 5 NIVEL 5		LEVEL 6 NIVEAU 6 NIVEL 6		LEVEL 7 NIVEAU 7 NIVEL 7	
		MF	F	MF	F	MF	F	MF	F
		(1)	(2)	(3)	(4)	(5)	(6)	(7)	(8)
AFRICA									
ALGERIA 1984	TOTAL	10 727	...	396	...	10 331	...	...	...
	EDUCATION SCIENCE & TEACHER TRNG.	2 942	...	–	–	2 942	...	...	...
	HUMANITIES, RELIGION & THEOLOGY	673	...	–	–	673	...	...	...
	FINE AND APPLIED ARTS	–	–	–	–	–	–	...	...
	LAW	1 217	...	–	–	1 217	...	...	...
	SOCIAL AND BEHAVIOURAL SCIENCE	1 194	...	–	–	1 194	...	...	...
	COMMERCIAL & BUSINESS ADMIN.	35	...	–	–	35	...	...	...
	MASS COMMUNICATION & DOCUMENT.	76	...	–	–	76	...	...	...
	HOME ECONOMICS (DOMESTIC SCIENCE)	–	–	–	–	–	–	...	...
	SERVICE TRADES	–	–	–	–	–	–	...	...
	NATURAL SCIENCE	486	...	–	–	486	...	...	...
	MATHEMATICS & COMPUTER SCIENCE	447	...	79	...	368	...	...	...
	MEDICAL SCIENCE & HEALTH-RELATED	1 836	...	–	–	1 836	...	...	...
	ENGINEERING	713	...	120	...	593	...	...	...
	ARCHITECTURE & TOWN PLANNING	380	...	–	–	380	...	...	...
	TRADE, CRAFT & INDUSTRIAL PGMS.	320	...	139	...	181	...	...	...
	TRANSPORT AND COMMUNICATIONS	104	...	–	–	104	...	...	...
	AGRICULTURE, FORESTRY & FISHERY	231	...	25	...	206	...	...	...
	OTHER AND NOT SPECIFIED	73	...	33	...	40	...	...	...
BOTSWANA 1984	TOTAL	458	...	228	...	182	...	48	...
	EDUCATION SCIENCE & TEACHER TRNG.	164	...	89	...	28	...	47	...
	HUMANITIES, RELIGION & THEOLOGY	112	...	61	...	50	...	1	...
	FINE AND APPLIED ARTS	–	–	–	–	–	–	–	–
	LAW	11	...	–	–	11	...	–	–
	SOCIAL AND BEHAVIOURAL SCIENCE	65	...	25	...	40	...	–	–
	COMMERCIAL & BUSINESS ADMIN.	92	...	53	...	39	...	–	–
	MASS COMMUNICATION & DOCUMENT.	–	–	–	–	–	–	–	–
	HOME ECONOMICS (DOMESTIC SCIENCE)	–	–	–	–	–	–	–	–
	SERVICE TRADES	–	–	–	–	–	–	–	–
	NATURAL SCIENCE	14	...	–	–	14	...	–	–
	MATHEMATICS & COMPUTER SCIENCE	–	–	–	–	–	–	–	–
	MEDICAL SCIENCE & HEALTH-RELATED	–	–	–	–	–	–	–	–
	ENGINEERING	–	–	–	–	–	–	–	–
	ARCHITECTURE & TOWN PLANNING	–	–	–	–	–	–	–	–
	TRADE, CRAFT & INDUSTRIAL PGMS.	–	–	–	–	–	–	–	–
	TRANSPORT AND COMMUNICATIONS	–	–	–	–	–	–	–	–
	AGRICULTURE, FORESTRY & FISHERY	–	–	–	–	–	–	–	–
	OTHER AND NOT SPECIFIED	–	–	–	–	–	–	–	–
BURKINA FASO‡ 1982	TOTAL	1 671	...	...	...	...	...	...	...
	EDUCATION SCIENCE & TEACHER TRNG.	./.	...	...	...	...	...	...	...
	HUMANITIES, RELIGION & THEOLOGY	439	...	...	...	...	...	...	...
	FINE AND APPLIED ARTS	–	–	...	...	...	...	...	...
	LAW	311	...	...	...	...	...	...	...
	SOCIAL AND BEHAVIOURAL SCIENCE	364	...	...	...	...	...	...	...
	COMMERCIAL & BUSINESS ADMIN.	–	–	...	...	...	...	...	...
	MASS COMMUNICATION & DOCUMENT.	–	–	...	...	...	...	...	...
	HOME ECONOMICS (DOMESTIC SCIENCE)	–	–	...	...	...	...	...	...
	SERVICE TRADES	–	–	...	...	...	...	...	...
	NATURAL SCIENCE	135	...	...	...	...	...	...	...
	MATHEMATICS & COMPUTER SCIENCE	123	...	...	...	...	...	...	...
	MEDICAL SCIENCE & HEALTH-RELATED	–	–	...	...	...	...	...	...
	ENGINEERING	–	–	...	...	...	...	...	...
	ARCHITECTURE & TOWN PLANNING	–	–	...	...	...	...	...	...
	TRADE, CRAFT & INDUSTRIAL PGMS.	–	–	...	...	...	...	...	...
	TRANSPORT AND COMMUNICATIONS	–	–	...	...	...	...	...	...
	AGRICULTURE, FORESTRY & FISHERY	299	...	...	...	...	...	...	...
	OTHER AND NOT SPECIFIED	–	–	...	...	...	...	...	...

3.14 **Third level: graduates by ISCED level and field of study**
Troisième degré: diplômés par niveau de la CITE et domaine d'études
Tercer grado: diplomados por nivel de la CINE y sector de estudios

COUNTRY YEAR / PAYS ANNEE / PAIS AÑO	FIELD OF STUDY / DOMAINES D'ETUDES / SECTORES DE ESTUDIOS	INTERNATIONAL STANDARD CLASSIFICATION OF EDUCATION BY LEVEL / CLASSIFICATION INTERNATIONALE TYPE DE L'EDUCATION PAR NIVEAU / CLASIFICACION INTERNACIONAL NORMALIZADA DE LA EDUCACION POR NIVEL							
		ALL LEVELS / TOUS NIVEAUX / TODOS LOS NIVELES		LEVEL 5 / NIVEAU 5 / NIVEL 5		LEVEL 6 / NIVEAU 6 / NIVEL 6		LEVEL 7 / NIVEAU 7 / NIVEL 7	
		MF	F	MF	F	MF	F	MF	F
		(1)	(2)	(3)	(4)	(5)	(6)	(7)	(8)
BURUNDI 1983	TOTAL	695	170	...	...	...	...	...	...
	EDUCATION SCIENCE & TEACHER TRNG.	73	19	...	...	...	...	...	...
	HUMANITIES, RELIGION & THEOLOGY	191	42	...	...	...	...	...	...
	FINE AND APPLIED ARTS	–	–	...	...	...	...	...	...
	LAW	105	34	...	...	...	...	...	...
	SOCIAL AND BEHAVIOURAL SCIENCE	66	18	...	...	...	...	...	...
	COMMERCIAL & BUSINESS ADMIN.	107	34	...	...	...	...	...	...
	MASS COMMUNICATION & DOCUMENT.	17	6	...	...	...	...	...	...
	HOME ECONOMICS (DOMESTIC SCIENCE)	–	–	...	...	...	...	...	...
	SERVICE TRADES	–	–	...	...	...	...	...	...
	NATURAL SCIENCE	57	7	...	...	...	...	...	...
	MATHEMATICS & COMPUTER SCIENCE	14	1	...	...	...	...	...	...
	MEDICAL SCIENCE & HEALTH-RELATED	47	9	...	...	...	...	...	...
	ENGINEERING	–	–	...	...	...	...	...	...
	ARCHITECTURE & TOWN PLANNING	–	–	...	...	...	...	...	...
	TRADE, CRAFT & INDUSTRIAL PGMS.	–	–	...	...	...	...	...	...
	TRANSPORT AND COMMUNICATIONS	–	–	...	...	...	...	...	...
	AGRICULTURE, FORESTRY & FISHERY	–	–	...	...	...	...	...	...
	OTHER AND NOT SPECIFIED	18	–	...	...	...	...	...	...
CAMEROON‡ 1981	TOTAL	1 804	...	179	...	1 329	...	296	...
	EDUCATION SCIENCE & TEACHER TRNG.	193	...	–	–	113	...	80	...
	HUMANITIES, RELIGION & THEOLOGY	460	...	–	–	294	...	166	...
	FINE AND APPLIED ARTS	–	–	–	–	–	–	–	–
	LAW	750	...	–	–	750	...	–	–
	SOCIAL AND BEHAVIOURAL SCIENCE	29	...	29	...	–	...	–	–
	COMMERCIAL & BUSINESS ADMIN.	–	–	–	–	–	–	–	–
	MASS COMMUNICATION & DOCUMENT.	23	...	23	...	–	...	–	–
	HOME ECONOMICS (DOMESTIC SCIENCE)	–	–	–	–	–	–	–	–
	SERVICE TRADES	–	–	–	–	–	–	–	–
	NATURAL SCIENCE	./.	...	–	–	./.	...	./.	...
	MATHEMATICS & COMPUTER SCIENCE	162	...	–	–	112	...	50	...
	MEDICAL SCIENCE & HEALTH-RELATED	121	...	70	...	51	...	–	–
	ENGINEERING	66	...	57	...	9	...	–	–
	ARCHITECTURE & TOWN PLANNING	–	–	–	–	–	–	–	–
	TRADE, CRAFT & INDUSTRIAL PGMS.	–	–	–	–	–	–	–	–
	TRANSPORT AND COMMUNICATIONS	–	–	–	–	–	–	–	–
	AGRICULTURE, FORESTRY & FISHERY	–	–	–	–	–	–	–	–
	OTHER AND NOT SPECIFIED	–	–	–	–	–	–	–	–
CENTRAL AFRICAN REPUBLIC‡ 1983	TOTAL	398	...	...	...	...	...	...	...
	EDUCATION SCIENCE & TEACHER TRNG.	226	...	...	...	...	...	...	...
	HUMANITIES, RELIGION & THEOLOGY	./.	...	...	...	...	...	...	...
	FINE AND APPLIED ARTS	–	–	...	...	...	...	...	...
	LAW	47	...	...	...	...	...	...	...
	SOCIAL AND BEHAVIOURAL SCIENCE	20	...	...	...	...	...	...	...
	COMMERCIAL & BUSINESS ADMIN.	12	...	...	...	...	...	...	...
	MASS COMMUNICATION & DOCUMENT.	–	–	...	...	...	...	...	...
	HOME ECONOMICS (DOMESTIC SCIENCE)	–	–	...	...	...	...	...	...
	SERVICE TRADES	–	–	...	...	...	...	...	...
	NATURAL SCIENCE	11	...	...	...	...	...	...	...
	MATHEMATICS & COMPUTER SCIENCE	–	–	...	...	...	...	...	...
	MEDICAL SCIENCE & HEALTH-RELATED	56	...	...	...	...	...	...	...
	ENGINEERING	3	...	...	...	...	...	...	...
	ARCHITECTURE & TOWN PLANNING	6	...	...	...	...	...	...	...
	TRADE, CRAFT & INDUSTRIAL PGMS.	–	–	...	...	...	...	...	...
	TRANSPORT AND COMMUNICATIONS	–	–	...	...	...	...	...	...
	AGRICULTURE, FORESTRY & FISHERY	17	...	...	...	...	...	...	...
	OTHER AND NOT SPECIFIED	–	–	...	...	...	...	...	...

COUNTRY YEAR / PAYS ANNEE / PAIS AÑO	FIELD OF STUDY / DOMAINES D'ETUDES / SECTORES DE ESTUDIOS	INTERNATIONAL STANDARD CLASSIFICATION OF EDUCATION BY LEVEL / CLASSIFICATION INTERNATIONALE TYPE DE L'EDUCATION PAR NIVEAU / CLASIFICACION INTERNACIONAL NORMALIZADA DE LA EDUCACION POR NIVEL							
		ALL LEVELS / TOUS NIVEAUX / TODOS LOS NIVELES		LEVEL 5 / NIVEAU 5 / NIVEL 5		LEVEL 6 / NIVEAU 6 / NIVEL 6		LEVEL 7 / NIVEAU 7 / NIVEL 7	
		MF	F	MF	F	MF	F	MF	F
		(1)	(2)	(3)	(4)	(5)	(6)	(7)	(8)
CHAD 1984	TOTAL	335	25	335	25	–	–	–	–
	EDUCATION SCIENCE & TEACHER TRNG.	74	–	74	–	–	–	–	–
	HUMANITIES, RELIGION & THEOLOGY	84	7	84	7	–	–	–	–
	FINE AND APPLIED ARTS	–	–	–	–	–	–	–	–
	LAW	63	5	63	5	–	–	–	–
	SOCIAL AND BEHAVIOURAL SCIENCE	77	10	77	10	–	–	–	–
	COMMERCIAL & BUSINESS ADMIN.	–	–	–	–	–	–	–	–
	MASS COMMUNICATION & DOCUMENT.	–	–	–	–	–	–	–	–
	HOME ECONOMICS (DOMESTIC SCIENCE)	–	–	–	–	–	–	–	–
	SERVICE TRADES	–	–	–	–	–	–	–	–
	NATURAL SCIENCE	37	3	37	3	–	–	–	–
	MATHEMATICS & COMPUTER SCIENCE	–	–	–	–	–	–	–	–
	MEDICAL SCIENCE & HEALTH-RELATED	–	–	–	–	–	–	–	–
	ENGINEERING	–	–	–	–	–	–	–	–
	ARCHITECTURE & TOWN PLANNING	–	–	–	–	–	–	–	–
	TRADE, CRAFT & INDUSTRIAL PGMS.	–	–	–	–	–	–	–	–
	TRANSPORT AND COMMUNICATIONS	–	–	–	–	–	–	–	–
	AGRICULTURE, FORESTRY & FISHERY	–	–	–	–	–	–	–	–
	OTHER AND NOT SPECIFIED	–	–	–	–	–	–	–	–
CONGO‡ 1981	TOTAL	1 129	...	...	...	...	...	...	...
	EDUCATION SCIENCE & TEACHER TRNG.	527	...	...	...	...	...	...	...
	HUMANITIES, RELIGION & THEOLOGY	171	...	...	...	...	...	...	...
	FINE AND APPLIED ARTS	–	–	...	...	...	...	...	...
	LAW	115	...	...	...	...	...	...	...
	SOCIAL AND BEHAVIOURAL SCIENCE	140	...	...	...	...	...	...	...
	COMMERCIAL & BUSINESS ADMIN.	./.	...	...	...	...	...	...	...
	MASS COMMUNICATION & DOCUMENT.	./.	...	...	...	...	...	...	...
	HOME ECONOMICS (DOMESTIC SCIENCE)	–	–	...	...	...	...	...	...
	SERVICE TRADES	–	–	...	...	...	...	...	...
	NATURAL SCIENCE	96	...	...	...	...	...	...	...
	MATHEMATICS & COMPUTER SCIENCE	./.	...	...	...	...	...	...	...
	MEDICAL SCIENCE & HEALTH-RELATED	55	...	...	...	...	...	...	...
	ENGINEERING	–	–	...	...	...	...	...	...
	ARCHITECTURE & TOWN PLANNING	–	–	...	...	...	...	...	...
	TRADE, CRAFT & INDUSTRIAL PGMS.	–	–	...	...	...	...	...	...
	TRANSPORT AND COMMUNICATIONS	–	–	...	...	...	...	...	...
	AGRICULTURE, FORESTRY & FISHERY	25	...	...	...	...	...	...	...
	OTHER AND NOT SPECIFIED	–	–	...	...	...	...	...	...
COTE D'IVOIRE‡ 1983	TOTAL	5 243	...	2 481	...	2 036	...	726	...
	EDUCATION SCIENCE & TEACHER TRNG.	–	–	–	–	–	–	–	–
	HUMANITIES, RELIGION & THEOLOGY	1 117	...	700	...	364	...	53	...
	FINE AND APPLIED ARTS	–	–	–	–	–	–	–	–
	LAW	672	...	359	...	216	...	97	...
	SOCIAL AND BEHAVIOURAL SCIENCE	1 220	...	403	...	399	...	418	...
	COMMERCIAL & BUSINESS ADMIN.	./.	...	./.	...	./.	...	./.	...
	MASS COMMUNICATION & DOCUMENT.	–	–	–	–	–	–	–	–
	HOME ECONOMICS (DOMESTIC SCIENCE)	–	–	–	–	–	–	–	–
	SERVICE TRADES	–	–	–	–	–	–	–	–
	NATURAL SCIENCE	614	...	524	...	61	...	29	...
	MATHEMATICS & COMPUTER SCIENCE	173	...	124	...	31	...	18	...
	MEDICAL SCIENCE & HEALTH-RELATED	1 399	...	345	...	944	...	110	...
	ENGINEERING	–	–	–	–	–	–	–	–
	ARCHITECTURE & TOWN PLANNING	–	–	–	–	–	–	–	–
	TRADE, CRAFT & INDUSTRIAL PGMS.	48	...	26	...	21	...	1	...
	TRANSPORT AND COMMUNICATIONS	–	–	–	–	–	–	–	–
	AGRICULTURE, FORESTRY & FISHERY	–	–	–	–	–	–	–	–
	OTHER AND NOT SPECIFIED	–	–	–	–	–	–	–	–

3.14 Third level: graduates by ISCED level and field of study
Troisième degré: diplômés par niveau de la CITE et domaine d'études
Tercer grado: diplomados por nivel de la CINE y sector de estudios

COUNTRY YEAR / PAYS ANNEE / PAIS AÑO	FIELD OF STUDY / DOMAINES D'ETUDES / SECTORES DE ESTUDIOS	INTERNATIONAL STANDARD CLASSIFICATION OF EDUCATION BY LEVEL / CLASSIFICATION INTERNATIONALE TYPE DE L'EDUCATION PAR NIVEAU / CLASIFICACION INTERNACIONAL NORMALIZADA DE LA EDUCACION POR NIVEL							
		ALL LEVELS / TOUS NIVEAUX / TODOS LOS NIVELES		LEVEL 5 / NIVEAU 5 / NIVEL 5		LEVEL 6 / NIVEAU 6 / NIVEL 6		LEVEL 7 / NIVEAU 7 / NIVEL 7	
		MF	F	MF	F	MF	F	MF	F
		(1)	(2)	(3)	(4)	(5)	(6)	(7)	(8)
EGYPT‡ 1983	TOTAL	94 602	32 075	–	–	85 973	29 631	8 629	2 444
	EDUCATION SCIENCE & TEACHER TRNG.	13 234	5 700	–	–	12 100	5 290	1 134	410
	HUMANITIES, RELIGION & THEOLOGY	12 574	6 159	–	–	11 883	5 890	691	269
	FINE AND APPLIED ARTS	1 383	505	–	–	1 057	423	326	82
	LAW	9 060	2 118	–	–	8 613	2 062	447	56
	SOCIAL AND BEHAVIOURAL SCIENCE	717	303	–	–	581	265	136	38
	COMMERCIAL & BUSINESS ADMIN.	23 357	7 191	–	–	22 492	7 047	865	144
	MASS COMMUNICATION & DOCUMENT.	247	129	–	–	204	113	43	16
	HOME ECONOMICS (DOMESTIC SCIENCE)	366	366	–	–	300	300	66	66
	SERVICE TRADES	130	80	–	–	109	69	21	11
	NATURAL SCIENCE	4 671	1 627	–	–	4 092	1 407	579	220
	MATHEMATICS & COMPUTER SCIENCE	259	83	–	–	116	32	143	51
	MEDICAL SCIENCE & HEALTH–RELATED	10 607	3 856	–	–	8 157	3 112	2 450	744
	ENGINEERING	8 133	1 077	–	–	8 133	1 077	–	–
	ARCHITECTURE & TOWN PLANNING	182	35	–	–	–	–	182	35
	TRADE, CRAFT & INDUSTRIAL PGMS.	295	31	–	–	–	–	295	31
	TRANSPORT AND COMMUNICATIONS	55	8	–	–	–	–	55	8
	AGRICULTURE, FORESTRY & FISHERY	8 262	2 353	–	–	7 280	2 175	982	178
	OTHER AND NOT SPECIFIED	1 070	454	–	–	856	369	214	85
ETHIOPIA‡ 1983	TOTAL	4 177	...	2 477	...	1 633	...	67	–
	EDUCATION SCIENCE & TEACHER TRNG.	862	...	798		64	...	–	–
	HUMANITIES, RELIGION & THEOLOGY	149	...	–	–	143	...	6	–
	FINE AND APPLIED ARTS	–	–	–	–	–	–	–	–
	LAW	66	...	–	–	66	...	–	–
	SOCIAL AND BEHAVIOURAL SCIENCE	418	...	–	–	404	...	14	–
	COMMERCIAL & BUSINESS ADMIN.	367	...	367	...	–	–	–	–
	MASS COMMUNICATION & DOCUMENT.	20	...	20	...	–	–	–	–
	HOME ECONOMICS (DOMESTIC SCIENCE)	–	–	–	–	–	–	–	–
	SERVICE TRADES	–	–	–	–	–	–	–	–
	NATURAL SCIENCE	461	...	–	–	443	...	18	–
	MATHEMATICS & COMPUTER SCIENCE	./.	...	–	–	./.	...	./.	–
	MEDICAL SCIENCE & HEALTH–RELATED	299	...	101		181	...	17	–
	ENGINEERING	388	...	334	...	54	...	–	–
	ARCHITECTURE & TOWN PLANNING	21	...	–	...	21	...	–	–
	TRADE, CRAFT & INDUSTRIAL PGMS.	–	–	–	–	–	–	–	–
	TRANSPORT AND COMMUNICATIONS	–	–	–	–	–	–	–	–
	AGRICULTURE, FORESTRY & FISHERY	1 126	...	857	...	257	...	12	–
	OTHER AND NOT SPECIFIED	–	–	–	–	–	–	–	–
GABON‡ 1983	TOTAL	602	128	290	62	162	45	150	21
	EDUCATION SCIENCE & TEACHER TRNG.	55	8	55	8	–	–	–	–
	HUMANITIES, RELIGION & THEOLOGY	109	33	23	6	60	21	26	6
	FINE AND APPLIED ARTS	–	–	–	–	–	–	–	–
	LAW	16	6	1	–	15	6	–	–
	SOCIAL AND BEHAVIOURAL SCIENCE	147	33	39	11	82	18	26	4
	COMMERCIAL & BUSINESS ADMIN.	73	20	28	14	–	–	45	6
	MASS COMMUNICATION & DOCUMENT.	9	–	9	–	–	–	–	–
	HOME ECONOMICS (DOMESTIC SCIENCE)	–	–	–	–	–	–	–	–
	SERVICE TRADES	–	–	–	–	–	–	–	–
	NATURAL SCIENCE	29	8	29	8	–	–	–	–
	MATHEMATICS & COMPUTER SCIENCE	61	3	51	3	–	–	10	–
	MEDICAL SCIENCE & HEALTH–RELATED	34	16	17	11	–	–	17	5
	ENGINEERING	56	–	30	–	–	–	26	–
	ARCHITECTURE & TOWN PLANNING	5	–	–	–	5	–	–	–
	TRADE, CRAFT & INDUSTRIAL PGMS.	–	–	–	–	–	–	–	–
	TRANSPORT AND COMMUNICATIONS	–	–	–	–	–	–	–	–
	AGRICULTURE, FORESTRY & FISHERY	8	1	8	1	–	–	–	–
	OTHER AND NOT SPECIFIED	–	–	–	–	–	–	–	–

COUNTRY YEAR / PAYS ANNEE / PAIS AÑO	FIELD OF STUDY / DOMAINES D'ETUDES / SECTORES DE ESTUDIOS	INTERNATIONAL STANDARD CLASSIFICATION OF EDUCATION BY LEVEL / CLASSIFICATION INTERNATIONALE TYPE DE L'EDUCATION PAR NIVEAU / CLASIFICACION INTERNACIONAL NORMALIZADA DE LA EDUCACION POR NIVEL							
		ALL LEVELS / TOUS NIVEAUX / TODOS LOS NIVELES		LEVEL 5 / NIVEAU 5 / NIVEL 5		LEVEL 6 / NIVEAU 6 / NIVEL 6		LEVEL 7 / NIVEAU 7 / NIVEL 7	
		MF	F	MF	F	MF	F	MF	F
		(1)	(2)	(3)	(4)	(5)	(6)	(7)	(8)
GHANA‡ 1981	TOTAL	2 212	...	335	...	1 591	...	286	...
	EDUCATION SCIENCE & TEACHER TRNG.	50	8	–	–	32	4	18	4
	HUMANITIES, RELIGION & THEOLOGY	570	...	34	...	509	...	27	...
	FINE AND APPLIED ARTS	75	11	10	1	56	10	9	–
	LAW	38	...	–	–	38	...	–	–
	SOCIAL AND BEHAVIOURAL SCIENCE	289	...	105	...	136	25	48	...
	COMMERCIAL & BUSINESS ADMIN.	161	...	25	...	115	...	21	...
	MASS COMMUNICATION & DOCUMENT.	89	...	53	...	–	–	36	...
	HOME ECONOMICS (DOMESTIC SCIENCE)	20	20	11	11	9	9	–	–
	SERVICE TRADES	–	–	–	–	–	–	–	–
	NATURAL SCIENCE	305	...	23	5	274	...	8	...
	MATHEMATICS & COMPUTER SCIENCE	./.	...	./.	./.	./.	...	./.	...
	MEDICAL SCIENCE & HEALTH–RELATED	148	...	12	...	136	...	–	–
	ENGINEERING	175	2	–	–	175	2	–	–
	ARCHITECTURE & TOWN PLANNING	115	15	–	–	–	–	115	15
	TRADE, CRAFT & INDUSTRIAL PGMS.	–	–	–	–	–	–	–	–
	TRANSPORT AND COMMUNICATIONS	–	–	–	–	–	–	–	–
	AGRICULTURE, FORESTRY & FISHERY	177	...	62	...	111	...	4	...
	OTHER AND NOT SPECIFIED	–	–	–	–	–	–	–	–
GUINEA‡ 1984	TOTAL	1 929	...	–	–	1 165	...	764	98
	EDUCATION SCIENCE & TEACHER TRNG.	337	45	–	–	292	45	45	–
	HUMANITIES, RELIGION & THEOLOGY	./.	./.	–	–	./.	./.	./.	–
	FINE AND APPLIED ARTS	./.	./.	–	–	./.	./.	./.	–
	LAW	265	...	–	–	265	...	–	–
	SOCIAL AND BEHAVIOURAL SCIENCE	./.	./.	–	–	./.	./.	./.	–
	COMMERCIAL & BUSINESS ADMIN.	./.	...	–	–	./.	...	–	–
	MASS COMMUNICATION & DOCUMENT.	–	–	–	–	–	–	–	–
	HOME ECONOMICS (DOMESTIC SCIENCE)	–	–	–	–	–	–	–	–
	SERVICE TRADES	–	–	–	–	–	–	–	–
	NATURAL SCIENCE	192	55	–	–	47	–	145	55
	MATHEMATICS & COMPUTER SCIENCE	./.	./.	–	–	./.	–	./.	./.
	MEDICAL SCIENCE & HEALTH–RELATED	200	10	–	–	55	5	145	5
	ENGINEERING	86	12	–	–	54	6	32	6
	ARCHITECTURE & TOWN PLANNING	37	4	–	–	22	–	15	4
	TRADE, CRAFT & INDUSTRIAL PGMS.	./.	./.	–	–	./.	./.	./.	./.
	TRANSPORT AND COMMUNICATIONS	22	5	–	–	22	5	–	–
	AGRICULTURE, FORESTRY & FISHERY	790	76	–	–	408	48	382	28
	OTHER AND NOT SPECIFIED	–	–	–	–	–	–	–	–
KENYA‡ 1983	TOTAL	2 386	749	23	19	2 363	730	–	–
	EDUCATION SCIENCE & TEACHER TRNG.	838	384	–	–	838	384	–	–
	HUMANITIES, RELIGION & THEOLOGY	./.	./.	–	–	./.	./.	–	–
	FINE AND APPLIED ARTS	1	1	–	–	1	1	–	–
	LAW	88	41	–	–	88	41	–	–
	SOCIAL AND BEHAVIOURAL SCIENCE	357	123	–	–	357	123	–	–
	COMMERCIAL & BUSINESS ADMIN.	160	51	–	–	160	51	–	–
	MASS COMMUNICATION & DOCUMENT.	–	–	–	–	–	–	–	–
	HOME ECONOMICS (DOMESTIC SCIENCE)	–	–	–	–	–	–	–	–
	SERVICE TRADES	–	–	–	–	–	–	–	–
	NATURAL SCIENCE	282	25	–	–	282	25	–	–
	MATHEMATICS & COMPUTER SCIENCE	–	–	–	–	–	–	–	–
	MEDICAL SCIENCE & HEALTH–RELATED	278	78	23	19	255	59	–	–
	ENGINEERING	167	4	–	–	167	4	–	–
	ARCHITECTURE & TOWN PLANNING	48	6	–	–	48	6	–	–
	TRADE, CRAFT & INDUSTRIAL PGMS.	–	–	–	–	–	–	–	–
	TRANSPORT AND COMMUNICATIONS	–	–	–	–	–	–	–	–
	AGRICULTURE, FORESTRY & FISHERY	111	24	–	–	111	24	–	–
	OTHER AND NOT SPECIFIED	56	12	–	–	56	12	–	–

3.14 Third level: graduates by ISCED level and field of study
Troisième degré: diplômés par niveau de la CITE et domaine d'études
Tercer grado: diplomados por nivel de la CINE y sector de estudios

COUNTRY YEAR / PAYS ANNEE / PAIS AÑO	FIELD OF STUDY / DOMAINES D'ETUDES / SECTORES DE ESTUDIOS	INTERNATIONAL STANDARD CLASSIFICATION OF EDUCATION BY LEVEL / CLASSIFICATION INTERNATIONALE TYPE DE L'EDUCATION PAR NIVEAU / CLASIFICACION INTERNACIONAL NORMALIZADA DE LA EDUCACION POR NIVEL							
		ALL LEVELS / TOUS NIVEAUX / TODOS LOS NIVELES		LEVEL 5 / NIVEAU 5 / NIVEL 5		LEVEL 6 / NIVEAU 6 / NIVEL 6		LEVEL 7 / NIVEAU 7 / NIVEL 7	
		MF	F	MF	F	MF	F	MF	F
		(1)	(2)	(3)	(4)	(5)	(6)	(7)	(8)
LESOTHO 1983	TOTAL	730	...	466	...	256	...	8	...
	EDUCATION SCIENCE & TEACHER TRNG.	492	...	421	...	63	...	8	...
	HUMANITIES, RELIGION & THEOLOGY	51	...	–	–	51	...	–	–
	FINE AND APPLIED ARTS	3	...	3	...	–	–	–	–
	LAW	58	...	12	...	46	...	–	–
	SOCIAL AND BEHAVIOURAL SCIENCE	69	...	–	–	69	...	–	–
	COMMERCIAL & BUSINESS ADMIN.	27	...	–	–	27	...	–	–
	MASS COMMUNICATION & DOCUMENT.	–	–	–	–	–	–	–	–
	HOME ECONOMICS (DOMESTIC SCIENCE)	–	–	–	–	–	–	–	–
	SERVICE TRADES	–	–	–	–	–	–	–	–
	NATURAL SCIENCE	–	–	–	–	–	–	–	–
	MATHEMATICS & COMPUTER SCIENCE	4	...	4	...	–	–	–	–
	MEDICAL SCIENCE & HEALTH-RELATED	7	...	7	...	–	–	–	–
	ENGINEERING	–	–	–	–	–	–	–	–
	ARCHITECTURE & TOWN PLANNING	–	–	–	–	–	–	–	–
	TRADE, CRAFT & INDUSTRIAL PGMS.	–	–	–	–	–	–	–	–
	TRANSPORT AND COMMUNICATIONS	–	–	–	–	–	–	–	–
	AGRICULTURE, FORESTRY & FISHERY	19	7	19	7	–	–	–	–
	OTHER AND NOT SPECIFIED	–	–	–	–	–	–	–	–
MADAGASCAR 1982	TOTAL	1 411	...	–	–	785	...	626	...
	EDUCATION SCIENCE & TEACHER TRNG.	–	–	–	–	–	–	–	–
	HUMANITIES, RELIGION & THEOLOGY	209	...	–	–	200	...	9	...
	FINE AND APPLIED ARTS	–	–	–	–	–	–	–	–
	LAW	88	...	–	–	63	...	25	...
	SOCIAL AND BEHAVIOURAL SCIENCE	206	...	–	–	180	...	26	...
	COMMERCIAL & BUSINESS ADMIN.	212	...	–	–	123	...	89	...
	MASS COMMUNICATION & DOCUMENT.	–	–	–	–	–	–	–	–
	HOME ECONOMICS (DOMESTIC SCIENCE)	–	–	–	–	–	–	–	–
	SERVICE TRADES	–	–	–	–	–	–	–	–
	NATURAL SCIENCE	195	...	–	–	130	...	65	...
	MATHEMATICS & COMPUTER SCIENCE	113	...	–	–	89	...	24	...
	MEDICAL SCIENCE & HEALTH-RELATED	135	...	–	–	–	–	135	...
	ENGINEERING	167	...	–	–	–	–	167	...
	ARCHITECTURE & TOWN PLANNING	–	–	–	–	–	–	–	–
	TRADE, CRAFT & INDUSTRIAL PGMS.	–	–	–	–	–	–	–	–
	TRANSPORT AND COMMUNICATIONS	–	–	–	–	–	–	–	–
	AGRICULTURE, FORESTRY & FISHERY	86	...	–	–	–	–	86	...
	OTHER AND NOT SPECIFIED	–	–	–	–	–	–	–	–
MALAWI 1984	TOTAL	620	...	360	...	256	...	4	...
	EDUCATION SCIENCE & TEACHER TRNG.	141	...	98	...	40	...	3	...
	HUMANITIES, RELIGION & THEOLOGY	17	...	–	–	16	...	1	...
	FINE AND APPLIED ARTS	–	–	–	–	–	–	–	–
	LAW	14	...	–	–	14	...	–	–
	SOCIAL AND BEHAVIOURAL SCIENCE	64	...	–	–	64	...	–	–
	COMMERCIAL & BUSINESS ADMIN.	114	...	63	...	51	...	–	–
	MASS COMMUNICATION & DOCUMENT.	–	–	–	–	–	–	–	–
	HOME ECONOMICS (DOMESTIC SCIENCE)	–	–	–	–	–	–	–	–
	SERVICE TRADES	–	–	–	–	–	–	–	–
	NATURAL SCIENCE	31	...	–	–	31	...	–	–
	MATHEMATICS & COMPUTER SCIENCE	–	–	–	–	–	–	–	–
	MEDICAL SCIENCE & HEALTH-RELATED	57	...	57	–	–	–	–	–
	ENGINEERING	68	...	55	...	13	...	–	–
	ARCHITECTURE & TOWN PLANNING	–	–	–	–	–	–	–	–
	TRADE, CRAFT & INDUSTRIAL PGMS.	–	–	–	–	–	–	–	–
	TRANSPORT AND COMMUNICATIONS	–	–	–	–	–	–	–	–
	AGRICULTURE, FORESTRY & FISHERY	114	...	87	...	27	...	–	–
	OTHER AND NOT SPECIFIED	–	–	–	–	–	–	–	–

COUNTRY YEAR / PAYS ANNEE / PAIS AÑO	FIELD OF STUDY / DOMAINES D'ETUDES / SECTORES DE ESTUDIOS	INTERNATIONAL STANDARD CLASSIFICATION OF EDUCATION BY LEVEL / CLASSIFICATION INTERNATIONALE TYPE DE L'EDUCATION PAR NIVEAU / CLASIFICACION INTERNACIONAL NORMALIZADA DE LA EDUCACION POR NIVEL							
		ALL LEVELS / TOUS NIVEAUX / TODOS LOS NIVELES		LEVEL 5 / NIVEAU 5 / NIVEL 5		LEVEL 6 / NIVEAU 6 / NIVEL 6		LEVEL 7 / NIVEAU 7 / NIVEL 7	
		MF	F	MF	F	MF	F	MF	F
		(1)	(2)	(3)	(4)	(5)	(6)	(7)	(8)
MALI‡ 1980	TOTAL	420	69	–	–	180	39	240	30
	EDUCATION SCIENCE & TEACHER TRNG.	23	10	–	–	–	–	23	10
	HUMANITIES, RELIGION & THEOLOGY	–	–	–	–	–	–	–	–
	FINE AND APPLIED ARTS	–	–	–	–	–	–	–	–
	LAW	–	–	–	–	–	–	–	–
	SOCIAL AND BEHAVIOURAL SCIENCE	–	–	–	–	–	–	–	–
	COMMERCIAL & BUSINESS ADMIN.	167	35	–	–	163	35	4	–
	MASS COMMUNICATION & DOCUMENT.	–	–	–	–	–	–	–	–
	HOME ECONOMICS (DOMESTIC SCIENCE)	–	–	–	–	–	–	–	–
	SERVICE TRADES	–	–	–	–	–	–	–	–
	NATURAL SCIENCE	–	–	–	–	–	–	–	–
	MATHEMATICS & COMPUTER SCIENCE	–	–	–	–	–	–	–	–
	MEDICAL SCIENCE & HEALTH–RELATED	37	7	–	–	–	–	37	7
	ENGINEERING	51	3	–	–	–	–	51	3
	ARCHITECTURE & TOWN PLANNING	–	–	–	–	–	–	–	–
	TRADE, CRAFT & INDUSTRIAL PGMS.	–	–	–	–	–	–	–	–
	TRANSPORT AND COMMUNICATIONS	17	4	–	–	17	4	–	–
	AGRICULTURE, FORESTRY & FISHERY	108	10	–	–	–	–	108	10
	OTHER AND NOT SPECIFIED	17	–	–	–	–	–	17	–
MAURITIUS 1984	TOTAL	307	107	294	106	–	–	13	1
	EDUCATION SCIENCE & TEACHER TRNG.	246	88	234	87	–	–	12	1
	HUMANITIES, RELIGION & THEOLOGY	–	–	–	–	–	–	–	–
	FINE AND APPLIED ARTS	–	–	–	–	–	–	–	–
	LAW	–	–	–	–	–	–	–	–
	SOCIAL AND BEHAVIOURAL SCIENCE	12	2	12	2	–	–	–	–
	COMMERCIAL & BUSINESS ADMIN.	25	9	25	9	–	–	–	–
	MASS COMMUNICATION & DOCUMENT.	9	6	9	6	–	–	–	–
	HOME ECONOMICS (DOMESTIC SCIENCE)	–	–	–	–	–	–	–	–
	SERVICE TRADES	–	–	–	–	–	–	–	–
	NATURAL SCIENCE	–	–	–	–	–	–	–	–
	MATHEMATICS & COMPUTER SCIENCE	8	2	8	2	–	–	–	–
	MEDICAL SCIENCE & HEALTH–RELATED	–	–	–	–	–	–	–	–
	ENGINEERING	1	–	–	–	–	–	1	–
	ARCHITECTURE & TOWN PLANNING	6	–	6	–	–	–	–	–
	TRADE, CRAFT & INDUSTRIAL PGMS.	–	–	–	–	–	–	–	–
	TRANSPORT AND COMMUNICATIONS	–	–	–	–	–	–	–	–
	AGRICULTURE, FORESTRY & FISHERY	–	–	–	–	–	–	–	–
	OTHER AND NOT SPECIFIED	–	–	–	–	–	–	–	–
MOROCCO‡ 1983	TOTAL	9 332	2 808	51	33	9 281	2 775	...	...
	EDUCATION SCIENCE & TEACHER TRNG.	553	166	51	33	502	133	...	...
	HUMANITIES, RELIGION & THEOLOGY	3 836	1 466	–	–	3 836	1 466	...	...
	FINE AND APPLIED ARTS	–	–	–	–	–	–	...	...
	LAW	1 466	241	–	–	1 466	241	...	...
	SOCIAL AND BEHAVIOURAL SCIENCE	1 296	341	–	–	1 296	341	...	...
	COMMERCIAL & BUSINESS ADMIN.	–	–	–	–	–	–	...	...
	MASS COMMUNICATION & DOCUMENT.	–	–	–	–	–	–	...	...
	HOME ECONOMICS (DOMESTIC SCIENCE)	–	–	–	–	–	–	...	...
	SERVICE TRADES	–	–	–	–	–	–	...	...
	NATURAL SCIENCE	1 315	350	–	–	1 315	350	...	...
	MATHEMATICS & COMPUTER SCIENCE	./.	./.	–	–	./.	./.	...	...
	MEDICAL SCIENCE & HEALTH–RELATED	750	231	–	–	750	231	...	...
	ENGINEERING	116	13	–	–	116	13	...	...
	ARCHITECTURE & TOWN PLANNING	–	–	–	–	–	–	...	...
	TRADE, CRAFT & INDUSTRIAL PGMS.	–	–	–	–	–	–	...	...
	TRANSPORT AND COMMUNICATIONS	–	–	–	–	–	–	...	...
	AGRICULTURE, FORESTRY & FISHERY	–	–	–	–	–	–	...	...
	OTHER AND NOT SPECIFIED	–	–	–	–	–	–	...	...

3.14 Third level: graduates by ISCED level and field of study
Troisième degré: diplômés par niveau de la CITE et domaine d'études
Tercer grado: diplomados por nivel de la CINE y sector de estudios

COUNTRY YEAR / PAYS ANNEE / PAIS AÑO	FIELD OF STUDY / DOMAINES D'ETUDES / SECTORES DE ESTUDIOS	INTERNATIONAL STANDARD CLASSIFICATION OF EDUCATION BY LEVEL / CLASSIFICATION INTERNATIONALE TYPE DE L'EDUCATION PAR NIVEAU / CLASIFICACION INTERNACIONAL NORMALIZADA DE LA EDUCACION POR NIVEL							
		ALL LEVELS / TOUS NIVEAUX / TODOS LOS NIVELES		LEVEL 5 / NIVEAU 5 / NIVEL 5		LEVEL 6 / NIVEAU 6 / NIVEL 6		LEVEL 7 / NIVEAU 7 / NIVEL 7	
		MF	F	MF	F	MF	F	MF	F
		(1)	(2)	(3)	(4)	(5)	(6)	(7)	(8)
MOZAMBIQUE 1984	TOTAL	165	...	–	–	165	...	–	–
	EDUCATION SCIENCE & TEACHER TRNG.	43	...	–	–	43	...	–	–
	HUMANITIES, RELIGION & THEOLOGY	11	...	–	–	11	...	–	–
	FINE AND APPLIED ARTS	–	–	–	–	–	–	–	–
	LAW	–	–	–	–	–	–	–	–
	SOCIAL AND BEHAVIOURAL SCIENCE	61	...	–	–	61	...	–	–
	COMMERCIAL & BUSINESS ADMIN.	–	–	–	–	–	–	–	–
	MASS COMMUNICATION & DOCUMENT.	–	–	–	–	–	–	–	–
	HOME ECONOMICS (DOMESTIC SCIENCE)	–	–	–	–	–	–	–	–
	SERVICE TRADES	–	–	–	–	–	–	–	–
	NATURAL SCIENCE	–	–	–	–	–	–	–	–
	MATHEMATICS & COMPUTER SCIENCE	–	–	–	–	–	–	–	–
	MEDICAL SCIENCE & HEALTH-RELATED	15	...	–	–	15	...	–	–
	ENGINEERING	18	...	–	–	18	...	–	–
	ARCHITECTURE & TOWN PLANNING	–	–	–	–	–	–	–	–
	TRADE, CRAFT & INDUSTRIAL PGMS.	–	–	–	–	–	–	–	–
	TRANSPORT AND COMMUNICATIONS	–	–	–	–	–	–	–	–
	AGRICULTURE, FORESTRY & FISHERY	17	...	–	–	17	...	–	–
	OTHER AND NOT SPECIFIED	–	–	–	–	–	–	–	–
NIGER 1984	TOTAL	849	164	423	88	228	40	198	36
	EDUCATION SCIENCE & TEACHER TRNG.	175	46	161	44	14	2	–	–
	HUMANITIES, RELIGION & THEOLOGY	276	63	133	34	81	17	62	12
	FINE AND APPLIED ARTS	–	–	–	–	–	–	–	–
	LAW	97	20	30	2	42	10	25	8
	SOCIAL AND BEHAVIOURAL SCIENCE	153	27	46	5	56	11	51	11
	COMMERCIAL & BUSINESS ADMIN.	–	–	–	–	–	–	–	–
	MASS COMMUNICATION & DOCUMENT.	–	–	–	–	–	–	–	–
	HOME ECONOMICS (DOMESTIC SCIENCE)	–	–	–	–	–	–	–	–
	SERVICE TRADES	–	–	–	–	–	–	–	–
	NATURAL SCIENCE	55	–	13	–	27	–	15	–
	MATHEMATICS & COMPUTER SCIENCE	43	3	28	3	8	–	7	–
	MEDICAL SCIENCE & HEALTH-RELATED	–	–	–	–	–	–	–	–
	ENGINEERING	–	–	–	–	–	–	–	–
	ARCHITECTURE & TOWN PLANNING	–	–	–	–	–	–	–	–
	TRADE, CRAFT & INDUSTRIAL PGMS.	–	–	–	–	–	–	–	–
	TRANSPORT AND COMMUNICATIONS	–	–	–	–	–	–	–	–
	AGRICULTURE, FORESTRY & FISHERY	50	5	12	–	–	–	38	5
	OTHER AND NOT SPECIFIED	–	–	–	–	–	–	–	–
NIGERIA‡ 1981	TOTAL	17 215	...	–	–	15 951	...	1 264	...
	EDUCATION SCIENCE & TEACHER TRNG.	4 495	...	–	–	4 495	...	–	–
	HUMANITIES, RELIGION & THEOLOGY	2 746	...	–	–	2 746	...	–	–
	FINE AND APPLIED ARTS	–	–	–	–	–	–	–	–
	LAW	727	...	–	–	727	...	–	–
	SOCIAL AND BEHAVIOURAL SCIENCE	2 800	...	–	–	2 800	...	–	–
	COMMERCIAL & BUSINESS ADMIN.	1 291	...	–	–	1 291	...	–	–
	MASS COMMUNICATION & DOCUMENT.	–	–	–	–	–	–	–	–
	HOME ECONOMICS (DOMESTIC SCIENCE)	–	–	–	–	–	–	–	–
	SERVICE TRADES	–	–	–	–	–	–	–	–
	NATURAL SCIENCE	1 889	...	–	–	1 889	...	–	–
	MATHEMATICS & COMPUTER SCIENCE	–	–	–	–	–	–	–	–
	MEDICAL SCIENCE & HEALTH-RELATED	1 157	...	–	–	–	–	1 157	...
	ENGINEERING	841	...	–	–	841	...	–	–
	ARCHITECTURE & TOWN PLANNING	460	...	–	–	460	...	–	–
	TRADE, CRAFT & INDUSTRIAL PGMS.	–	–	–	–	–	–	–	–
	TRANSPORT AND COMMUNICATIONS	–	–	–	–	–	–	–	–
	AGRICULTURE, FORESTRY & FISHERY	809	...	–	–	702	...	107	...
	OTHER AND NOT SPECIFIED	–	–	–	–	–	–	–	–

COUNTRY / YEAR PAYS / ANNEE PAIS / AÑO	FIELD OF STUDY DOMAINES D'ETUDES SECTORES DE ESTUDIOS	INTERNATIONAL STANDARD CLASSIFICATION OF EDUCATION BY LEVEL CLASSIFICATION INTERNATIONALE TYPE DE L'EDUCATION PAR NIVEAU CLASIFICACION INTERNACIONAL NORMALIZADA DE LA EDUCACION POR NIVEL							
		ALL LEVELS TOUS NIVEAUX TODOS LOS NIVELES		LEVEL 5 NIVEAU 5 NIVEL 5		LEVEL 6 NIVEAU 6 NIVEL 6		LEVEL 7 NIVEAU 7 NIVEL 7	
		MF	F	MF	F	MF	F	MF	F
		(1)	(2)	(3)	(4)	(5)	(6)	(7)	(8)
RWANDA‡ 1983	TOTAL	332	48	–	–	234	41	98	7
	EDUCATION SCIENCE & TEACHER TRNG.	39	7	–	–	29	6	10	1
	HUMANITIES, RELIGION & THEOLOGY	89	7	–	–	54	7	35	–
	FINE AND APPLIED ARTS	–	–	–	–	–	–	–	–
	LAW	43	5	–	–	43	5	–	–
	SOCIAL AND BEHAVIOURAL SCIENCE	38	13	–	–	28	9	10	4
	COMMERCIAL & BUSINESS ADMIN.	./.	./.	–	–	./.	./.	./.	./.
	MASS COMMUNICATION & DOCUMENT.	–	–	–	–	–	–	–	–
	HOME ECONOMICS (DOMESTIC SCIENCE)	5	1	–	–	5	1	–	–
	SERVICE TRADES	–	–	–	–	–	–	–	–
	NATURAL SCIENCE	24	3	–	–	14	2	10	1
	MATHEMATICS & COMPUTER SCIENCE	./.	./.	–	–	./.	./.	./.	./.
	MEDICAL SCIENCE & HEALTH-RELATED	49	7	–	–	27	7	22	–
	ENGINEERING	16	–	–	–	16	–	–	–
	ARCHITECTURE & TOWN PLANNING	–	–	–	–	–	–	–	–
	TRADE, CRAFT & INDUSTRIAL PGMS.	3	3	–	–	3	3	–	–
	TRANSPORT AND COMMUNICATIONS	–	–	–	–	–	–	–	–
	AGRICULTURE, FORESTRY & FISHERY	26	2	–	–	15	1	11	1
	OTHER AND NOT SPECIFIED	–	–	–	–	–	–	–	–
ST. HELENA 1981	TOTAL	13	5	13	5	–	–	–	–
	EDUCATION SCIENCE & TEACHER TRNG.	5	5	5	5	–	–	–	–
	HUMANITIES, RELIGION & THEOLOGY	–	–	–	–	–	–	–	–
	FINE AND APPLIED ARTS	–	–	–	–	–	–	–	–
	LAW	–	–	–	–	–	–	–	–
	SOCIAL AND BEHAVIOURAL SCIENCE	–	–	–	–	–	–	–	–
	COMMERCIAL & BUSINESS ADMIN.	–	–	–	–	–	–	–	–
	MASS COMMUNICATION & DOCUMENT.	–	–	–	–	–	–	–	–
	HOME ECONOMICS (DOMESTIC SCIENCE)	–	–	–	–	–	–	–	–
	SERVICE TRADES	–	–	–	–	–	–	–	–
	NATURAL SCIENCE	–	–	–	–	–	–	–	–
	MATHEMATICS & COMPUTER SCIENCE	–	–	–	–	–	–	–	–
	MEDICAL SCIENCE & HEALTH-RELATED	–	–	–	–	–	–	–	–
	ENGINEERING	–	–	–	–	–	–	–	–
	ARCHITECTURE & TOWN PLANNING	–	–	–	–	–	–	–	–
	TRADE, CRAFT & INDUSTRIAL PGMS.	8	–	8	–	–	–	–	–
	TRANSPORT AND COMMUNICATIONS	–	–	–	–	–	–	–	–
	AGRICULTURE, FORESTRY & FISHERY	–	–	–	–	–	–	–	–
	OTHER AND NOT SPECIFIED	–	–	–	–	–	–	–	–
SENEGAL 1983	TOTAL	1 955	...	310	...	746	...	899	...
	EDUCATION SCIENCE & TEACHER TRNG.	291	...	–	–	129	...	162	...
	HUMANITIES, RELIGION & THEOLOGY	240	...	–	–	117	...	123	...
	FINE AND APPLIED ARTS	–	–	–	–	–	–	–	–
	LAW	172	...	–	–	93	...	79	...
	SOCIAL AND BEHAVIOURAL SCIENCE	429	...	–	–	243	...	186	...
	COMMERCIAL & BUSINESS ADMIN.	200	...	81	6	37	4	82	...
	MASS COMMUNICATION & DOCUMENT.	88	...	88	...	–	–	–	–
	HOME ECONOMICS (DOMESTIC SCIENCE)	–	–	–	–	–	–	–	–
	SERVICE TRADES	141	...	141	...	–	–	–	–
	NATURAL SCIENCE	98	...	–	–	52	...	46	...
	MATHEMATICS & COMPUTER SCIENCE	44	...	–	–	39	...	5	...
	MEDICAL SCIENCE & HEALTH-RELATED	152	...	–	–	–	–	152	...
	ENGINEERING	–	–	–	–	–	–	–	–
	ARCHITECTURE & TOWN PLANNING	–	–	–	–	–	–	–	–
	TRADE, CRAFT & INDUSTRIAL PGMS.	–	–	–	–	–	–	–	–
	TRANSPORT AND COMMUNICATIONS	–	–	–	–	–	–	–	–
	AGRICULTURE, FORESTRY & FISHERY	64	...	–	–	–	–	64	–
	OTHER AND NOT SPECIFIED	36	20	–	–	36	20	–	–

3.14 Third level: graduates by ISCED level and field of study
Troisième degré: diplômés par niveau de la CITE et domaine d'études
Tercer grado: diplomados por nivel de la CINE y sector de estudios

COUNTRY / YEAR PAYS / ANNEE PAIS / AÑO	FIELD OF STUDY DOMAINES D'ETUDES SECTORES DE ESTUDIOS	ALL LEVELS / TOUS NIVEAUX / TODOS LOS NIVELES MF (1)	F (2)	LEVEL 5 / NIVEAU 5 / NIVEL 5 MF (3)	F (4)	LEVEL 6 / NIVEAU 6 / NIVEL 6 MF (5)	F (6)	LEVEL 7 / NIVEAU 7 / NIVEL 7 MF (7)	F (8)
SEYCHELLES 1980	TOTAL	23	19	23	19	–	–	–	–
	EDUCATION SCIENCE & TEACHER TRNG.	23	19	23	19	–	–	–	–
	HUMANITIES, RELIGION & THEOLOGY	–	–	–	–	–	–	–	–
	FINE AND APPLIED ARTS	–	–	–	–	–	–	–	–
	LAW	–	–	–	–	–	–	–	–
	SOCIAL AND BEHAVIOURAL SCIENCE	–	–	–	–	–	–	–	–
	COMMERCIAL & BUSINESS ADMIN.	–	–	–	–	–	–	–	–
	MASS COMMUNICATION & DOCUMENT.	–	–	–	–	–	–	–	–
	HOME ECONOMICS (DOMESTIC SCIENCE)	–	–	–	–	–	–	–	–
	SERVICE TRADES	–	–	–	–	–	–	–	–
	NATURAL SCIENCE	–	–	–	–	–	–	–	–
	MATHEMATICS & COMPUTER SCIENCE	–	–	–	–	–	–	–	–
	MEDICAL SCIENCE & HEALTH-RELATED	–	–	–	–	–	–	–	–
	ENGINEERING	–	–	–	–	–	–	–	–
	ARCHITECTURE & TOWN PLANNING	–	–	–	–	–	–	–	–
	TRADE, CRAFT & INDUSTRIAL PGMS.	–	–	–	–	–	–	–	–
	TRANSPORT AND COMMUNICATIONS	–	–	–	–	–	–	–	–
	AGRICULTURE, FORESTRY & FISHERY	–	–	–	–	–	–	–	–
	OTHER AND NOT SPECIFIED	–	–	–	–	–	–	–	–
SUDAN‡ 1981	TOTAL	4 667	...	919	...	3 748	...	./.	./.
	EDUCATION SCIENCE & TEACHER TRNG.	245	...	15	3	230	54	./.	./.
	HUMANITIES, RELIGION & THEOLOGY	1 261	...	–	–	1 261	...	–	–
	FINE AND APPLIED ARTS	88	13	88	13	–	–	–	–
	LAW	361	...	–	–	361	...	–	–
	SOCIAL AND BEHAVIOURAL SCIENCE	409	...	–	–	409	46	./.	./.
	COMMERCIAL & BUSINESS ADMIN.	710	...	94	...	616	...	–	–
	MASS COMMUNICATION & DOCUMENT.	–	–	–	–	–	–	–	–
	HOME ECONOMICS (DOMESTIC SCIENCE)	–	–	–	–	–	–	–	–
	SERVICE TRADES	–	–	–	–	–	–	–	–
	NATURAL SCIENCE	95	39	–	–	95	39	–	–
	MATHEMATICS & COMPUTER SCIENCE	45	...	–	–	45	...	–	–
	MEDICAL SCIENCE & HEALTH-RELATED	297	98	89	53	208	45	–	–
	ENGINEERING	489	42	264	39	225	3	–	–
	ARCHITECTURE & TOWN PLANNING	46	7	–	–	46	7	–	–
	TRADE, CRAFT & INDUSTRIAL PGMS.	–	–	–	–	–	–	–	–
	TRANSPORT AND COMMUNICATIONS	–	–	–	–	–	–	–	–
	AGRICULTURE, FORESTRY & FISHERY	540	53	288	16	252	37	–	–
	OTHER AND NOT SPECIFIED	81	62	81	62	–	–	–	–
SWAZILAND‡ 1982	TOTAL	400	158	262	99	138	59	–	–
	EDUCATION SCIENCE & TEACHER TRNG.	70	39	58	29	12	10	–	–
	HUMANITIES, RELIGION & THEOLOGY	22	11	–	–	22	11	–	–
	FINE AND APPLIED ARTS	–	–	–	–	–	–	–	–
	LAW	19	5	–	–	19	5	–	–
	SOCIAL AND BEHAVIOURAL SCIENCE	20	10	–	–	20	10	–	–
	COMMERCIAL & BUSINESS ADMIN.	77	30	54	19	23	11	–	–
	MASS COMMUNICATION & DOCUMENT.	–	–	–	–	–	–	–	–
	HOME ECONOMICS (DOMESTIC SCIENCE)	32	32	32	32	–	–	–	–
	SERVICE TRADES	–	–	–	–	–	–	–	–
	NATURAL SCIENCE	42	12	–	–	42	12	–	–
	MATHEMATICS & COMPUTER SCIENCE	./.	./.	–	–	./.	./.	–	–
	MEDICAL SCIENCE & HEALTH-RELATED	–	–	–	–	–	–	–	–
	ENGINEERING	–	–	–	–	–	–	–	–
	ARCHITECTURE & TOWN PLANNING	–	–	–	–	–	–	–	–
	TRADE, CRAFT & INDUSTRIAL PGMS.	–	–	–	–	–	–	–	–
	TRANSPORT AND COMMUNICATIONS	–	–	–	–	–	–	–	–
	AGRICULTURE, FORESTRY & FISHERY	118	19	118	19	–	–	–	–
	OTHER AND NOT SPECIFIED	–	–	–	–	–	–	–	–

COUNTRY / YEAR PAYS / ANNEE PAIS / AÑO	FIELD OF STUDY DOMAINES D'ETUDES SECTORES DE ESTUDIOS	INTERNATIONAL STANDARD CLASSIFICATION OF EDUCATION BY LEVEL / CLASSIFICATION INTERNATIONALE TYPE DE L'EDUCATION PAR NIVEAU / CLASIFICACION INTERNACIONAL NORMALIZADA DE LA EDUCACION POR NIVEL							
		ALL LEVELS TOUS NIVEAUX TODOS LOS NIVELES		LEVEL 5 NIVEAU 5 NIVEL 5		LEVEL 6 NIVEAU 6 NIVEL 6		LEVEL 7 NIVEAU 7 NIVEL 7	
		MF	F	MF	F	MF	F	MF	F
		(1)	(2)	(3)	(4)	(5)	(6)	(7)	(8)
TUNISIA 1982	TOTAL	4 938	...	...	...	...	...	...	...
	EDUCATION SCIENCE & TEACHER TRNG.	414	...	...	...	...	...	...	...
	HUMANITIES, RELIGION & THEOLOGY	638	...	...	...	...	...	...	...
	FINE AND APPLIED ARTS	21	13	...	...	...	...	...	...
	LAW	116	28	...	...	...	...	...	...
	SOCIAL AND BEHAVIOURAL SCIENCE	184	62	...	...	...	...	...	...
	COMMERCIAL & BUSINESS ADMIN.	956	...	...	...	...	...	...	...
	MASS COMMUNICATION & DOCUMENT.	69	16	...	...	...	...	...	...
	HOME ECONOMICS (DOMESTIC SCIENCE)	64	38	...	...	...	...	...	...
	SERVICE TRADES	78	15	...	...	...	...	...	...
	NATURAL SCIENCE	398	113	...	...	...	...	...	...
	MATHEMATICS & COMPUTER SCIENCE	34	12	...	...	...	...	...	...
	MEDICAL SCIENCE & HEALTH-RELATED	886	...	...	...	...	...	...	...
	ENGINEERING	445	28	...	...	...	...	...	...
	ARCHITECTURE & TOWN PLANNING	44	9	...	...	...	...	...	...
	TRADE, CRAFT & INDUSTRIAL PGMS.	31	2	...	...	...	...	...	...
	TRANSPORT AND COMMUNICATIONS	308	64	...	...	...	...	...	...
	AGRICULTURE, FORESTRY & FISHERY	252	29	...	...	...	...	...	...
	OTHER AND NOT SPECIFIED	–	–	...	...	...	...	...	...
UGANDA 1982	TOTAL	1 529	386	391	139	1 113	243	25	4
	EDUCATION SCIENCE & TEACHER TRNG.	350	126	239	92	106	33	5	1
	HUMANITIES, RELIGION & THEOLOGY	136	42	–	–	132	41	4	1
	FINE AND APPLIED ARTS	36	9	13	5	21	4	2	–
	LAW	58	13	–	–	58	13	–	–
	SOCIAL AND BEHAVIOURAL SCIENCE	279	64	–	–	278	64	1	–
	COMMERCIAL & BUSINESS ADMIN.	177	50	115	33	62	17	–	–
	MASS COMMUNICATION & DOCUMENT.	14	7	14	7	–	–	–	–
	HOME ECONOMICS (DOMESTIC SCIENCE)	–	–	–	–	–	–	–	–
	SERVICE TRADES	–	–	–	–	–	–	–	–
	NATURAL SCIENCE	189	29	–	–	188	28	1	1
	MATHEMATICS & COMPUTER SCIENCE	19	2	–	–	19	2	–	–
	MEDICAL SCIENCE & HEALTH-RELATED	102	29	10	2	81	26	11	1
	ENGINEERING	47	–	–	–	47	–	–	–
	ARCHITECTURE & TOWN PLANNING	–	–	–	–	–	–	–	–
	TRADE, CRAFT & INDUSTRIAL PGMS.	–	–	–	–	–	–	–	–
	TRANSPORT AND COMMUNICATIONS	–	–	–	–	–	–	–	–
	AGRICULTURE, FORESTRY & FISHERY	122	15	–	–	121	15	1	–
	OTHER AND NOT SPECIFIED	–	–	–	–	–	–	–	–
UNITED REPUBLIC OF TANZANIA‡ 1983	TOTAL	938	192	65	12	742	161	131	19
	EDUCATION SCIENCE & TEACHER TRNG.	50	15	–	–	50	15	–	–
	HUMANITIES, RELIGION & THEOLOGY	311	71	–	–	263	61	48	10
	FINE AND APPLIED ARTS	./.	./.	–	–	./.	./.	./.	./.
	LAW	67	21	–	–	57	20	10	1
	SOCIAL AND BEHAVIOURAL SCIENCE	./.	./.	–	–	./.	./.	./.	./.
	COMMERCIAL & BUSINESS ADMIN.	113	22	–	–	96	20	17	2
	MASS COMMUNICATION & DOCUMENT.	–	–	–	–	–	–	–	–
	HOME ECONOMICS (DOMESTIC SCIENCE)	–	–	–	–	–	–	–	–
	SERVICE TRADES	–	–	–	–	–	–	–	–
	NATURAL SCIENCE	62	21	–	–	41	18	21	3
	MATHEMATICS & COMPUTER SCIENCE	./.	./.	–	–	./.	./.	./.	./.
	MEDICAL SCIENCE & HEALTH-RELATED	128	24	65	12	51	11	12	1
	ENGINEERING	119	4	–	–	118	4	1	–
	ARCHITECTURE & TOWN PLANNING	–	–	–	–	–	–	–	–
	TRADE, CRAFT & INDUSTRIAL PGMS.	–	–	–	–	–	–	–	–
	TRANSPORT AND COMMUNICATIONS	–	–	–	–	–	–	–	–
	AGRICULTURE, FORESTRY & FISHERY	59	10	–	–	50	10	9	–
	OTHER AND NOT SPECIFIED	29	4	–	–	16	2	13	2

3.14 Third level: graduates by ISCED level and field of study
Troisième degré: diplômés par niveau de la CITE et domaine d'études
Tercer grado: diplomados por nivel de la CINE y sector de estudios

COUNTRY / YEAR — PAYS / ANNEE — PAIS / AÑO	FIELD OF STUDY — DOMAINES D'ETUDES — SECTORES DE ESTUDIOS	INTERNATIONAL STANDARD CLASSIFICATION OF EDUCATION BY LEVEL / CLASSIFICATION INTERNATIONALE TYPE DE L'EDUCATION PAR NIVEAU / CLASIFICACION INTERNACIONAL NORMALIZADA DE LA EDUCACION POR NIVEL							
		ALL LEVELS / TOUS NIVEAUX / TODOS LOS NIVELES		LEVEL 5 / NIVEAU 5 / NIVEL 5		LEVEL 6 / NIVEAU 6 / NIVEL 6		LEVEL 7 / NIVEAU 7 / NIVEL 7	
		MF	F	MF	F	MF	F	MF	F
		(1)	(2)	(3)	(4)	(5)	(6)	(7)	(8)
ZAMBIA‡ 1984	TOTAL	2 186	...	1 475	...	696	...	15	...
	EDUCATION SCIENCE & TEACHER TRNG.	502	...	361	...	139	...	2	...
	HUMANITIES, RELIGION & THEOLOGY	./.	...	./.	...	./.	...	./.	...
	FINE AND APPLIED ARTS	79	...	79	...	–	–	–	–
	LAW	53	...	8	...	38	...	7	...
	SOCIAL AND BEHAVIOURAL SCIENCE	133	...	11	...	118	...	4	...
	COMMERCIAL & BUSINESS ADMIN.	524	...	447	...	77	...	–	–
	MASS COMMUNICATION & DOCUMENT.	21	...	8	...	13	...	–	–
	HOME ECONOMICS (DOMESTIC SCIENCE)	–	–	–	–	–	–	–	–
	SERVICE TRADES	–	–	–	–	–	–	–	–
	NATURAL SCIENCE	124	...	–	–	122	...	2	...
	MATHEMATICS & COMPUTER SCIENCE	–	–	–	–	–	–	–	–
	MEDICAL SCIENCE & HEALTH-RELATED	168	...	126	...	42	...	–	–
	ENGINEERING	436	...	337	...	99	...	–	–
	ARCHITECTURE & TOWN PLANNING	–	–	–	–	–	–	–	–
	TRADE, CRAFT & INDUSTRIAL PGMS.	–	–	–	–	–	–	–	–
	TRANSPORT AND COMMUNICATIONS	76	...	76	...	–	–	–	–
	AGRICULTURE, FORESTRY & FISHERY	48	...	–	–	48	...	–	–
	OTHER AND NOT SPECIFIED	22	...	22	...	–	–	–	–
ZIMBABWE‡ 1983	TOTAL	2 444	...	1 531	...	874	...	39	...
	EDUCATION SCIENCE & TEACHER TRNG.	1 604	...	1 432	...	153	...	19	...
	HUMANITIES, RELIGION & THEOLOGY	162	...	4	...	156	...	2	...
	FINE AND APPLIED ARTS	./.	...	./.	...	./.	...	./.	...
	LAW	97	...	–	–	97	...	–	–
	SOCIAL AND BEHAVIOURAL SCIENCE	211	...	32	...	171	...	8	...
	COMMERCIAL & BUSINESS ADMIN.	165	...	9	...	156	...	...	–
	MASS COMMUNICATION & DOCUMENT.	–	–	–	–	–	–	–	–
	HOME ECONOMICS (DOMESTIC SCIENCE)	–	–	–	–	–	–	–	–
	SERVICE TRADES	–	–	–	–	–	–	–	–
	NATURAL SCIENCE	62	...	–	–	58	...	4	...
	MATHEMATICS & COMPUTER SCIENCE	./.	...	–	–	./.	...	./.	...
	MEDICAL SCIENCE & HEALTH-RELATED	71	...	54	...	17	...	–	–
	ENGINEERING	31	...	–	–	30	...	1	...
	ARCHITECTURE & TOWN PLANNING	–	–	–	–	–	–	–	–
	TRADE, CRAFT & INDUSTRIAL PGMS.	–	–	–	–	–	–	–	–
	TRANSPORT AND COMMUNICATIONS	–	–	–	–	–	–	–	–
	AGRICULTURE, FORESTRY & FISHERY	41	...	–	–	36	...	5	...
	OTHER AND NOT SPECIFIED	–	–	–	–	–	–	–	–
AMERICA, NORTH									
BARBADOS‡ 1984	TOTAL	1 764	...	1 452	...	310	...	2	1
	EDUCATION SCIENCE & TEACHER TRNG.	174	...	173	...	1	...	–	–
	HUMANITIES, RELIGION & THEOLOGY	141	...	61	44	80	...	–	–
	FINE AND APPLIED ARTS	20	14	20	14	–	–	–	–
	LAW	138	...	37	...	101	...	–	–
	SOCIAL AND BEHAVIOURAL SCIENCE	360	...	285	...	75	...	–	–
	COMMERCIAL & BUSINESS ADMIN.	./.	...	./.	...	./.	...	–	–
	MASS COMMUNICATION & DOCUMENT.	–	–	–	–	–	–	–	–
	HOME ECONOMICS (DOMESTIC SCIENCE)	30	30	30	30	–	–	–	–
	SERVICE TRADES	163	102	163	102	–	–	–	–
	NATURAL SCIENCE	123	...	68	31	53	...	2	1
	MATHEMATICS & COMPUTER SCIENCE	./.	...	./.	./.	./.	...	./.	./.
	MEDICAL SCIENCE & HEALTH-RELATED	61	36	61	36	–	–	–	–
	ENGINEERING	16	...	16	...	–	–	–	–
	ARCHITECTURE & TOWN PLANNING	–	–	–	–	–	–	–	–
	TRADE, CRAFT & INDUSTRIAL PGMS.	495	41	495	41	–	–	–	–
	TRANSPORT AND COMMUNICATIONS	–	–	–	–	–	–	–	–
	AGRICULTURE, FORESTRY & FISHERY	11	5	11	5	–	–	–	–
	OTHER AND NOT SPECIFIED	32	29	32	29	–	–	–	–

COUNTRY / YEAR / PAYS / ANNEE / PAIS / AÑO	FIELD OF STUDY / DOMAINES D'ETUDES / SECTORES DE ESTUDIOS	INTERNATIONAL STANDARD CLASSIFICATION OF EDUCATION BY LEVEL / CLASSIFICATION INTERNATIONALE TYPE DE L'EDUCATION PAR NIVEAU / CLASIFICACION INTERNACIONAL NORMALIZADA DE LA EDUCACION POR NIVEL							
		ALL LEVELS / TOUS NIVEAUX / TODOS LOS NIVELES		LEVEL 5 / NIVEAU 5 / NIVEL 5		LEVEL 6 / NIVEAU 6 / NIVEL 6		LEVEL 7 / NIVEAU 7 / NIVEL 7	
		MF	F	MF	F	MF	F	MF	F
		(1)	(2)	(3)	(4)	(5)	(6)	(7)	(8)
BERMUDA‡ 1982	TOTAL	167	105	167	105	–	–	–	–
	EDUCATION SCIENCE & TEACHER TRNG.	20	20	20	20	–	–	–	–
	HUMANITIES, RELIGION & THEOLOGY	33	19	33	19	–	–	–	–
	FINE AND APPLIED ARTS	./.	./.	./.	./.	–	–	–	–
	LAW	–	–	–	–	–	–	–	–
	SOCIAL AND BEHAVIOURAL SCIENCE	./.	./.	./.	./.	–	–	–	–
	COMMERCIAL & BUSINESS ADMIN.	58	46	58	46	–	–	–	–
	MASS COMMUNICATION & DOCUMENT.	–	–	–	–	–	–	–	–
	HOME ECONOMICS (DOMESTIC SCIENCE)	–	–	–	–	–	–	–	–
	SERVICE TRADES	23	15	23	15	–	–	–	–
	NATURAL SCIENCE	./.	./.	./.	./.	–	–	–	–
	MATHEMATICS & COMPUTER SCIENCE	./.	./.	./.	./.	–	–	–	–
	MEDICAL SCIENCE & HEALTH–RELATED	–	–	–	–	–	–	–	–
	ENGINEERING	–	–	–	–	–	–	–	–
	ARCHITECTURE & TOWN PLANNING	–	–	–	–	–	–	–	–
	TRADE, CRAFT & INDUSTRIAL PGMS.	33	5	33	5	–	–	–	–
	TRANSPORT AND COMMUNICATIONS	–	–	–	–	–	–	–	–
	AGRICULTURE, FORESTRY & FISHERY	–	–	–	–	–	–	–	–
	OTHER AND NOT SPECIFIED	–	–	–	–	–	–	–	–
CANADA 1983	TOTAL	179 081	93 477	56 574	32 162	105 107	54 465	17 400	6 850
	EDUCATION SCIENCE & TEACHER TRNG.	22 652	16 062	1 313	1 223	17 917	12 967	3 422	1 872
	HUMANITIES, RELIGION & THEOLOGY	10 901	6 596	203	134	9 071	5 714	1 627	748
	FINE AND APPLIED ARTS	7 686	5 101	4 160	2 753	3 231	2 196	295	152
	LAW	3 663	1 464	–	–	3 343	1 344	320	120
	SOCIAL AND BEHAVIOURAL SCIENCE	23 809	13 520	6 954	4 587	14 708	8 070	2 147	863
	COMMERCIAL & BUSINESS ADMIN.	33 099	16 653	14 242	9 874	15 492	5 770	3 365	1 009
	MASS COMMUNICATION & DOCUMENT.	3 375	1 994	1 551	890	1 266	697	558	407
	HOME ECONOMICS (DOMESTIC SCIENCE)	876	845	25	25	806	783	45	37
	SERVICE TRADES	591	324	591	324	–	–	–	–
	NATURAL SCIENCE	6 151	2 103	–	–	4 850	1 794	1 301	309
	MATHEMATICS & COMPUTER SCIENCE	8 136	2 969	3 731	1 595	3 953	1 281	452	93
	MEDICAL SCIENCE & HEALTH–RELATED	17 765	13 815	9 944	8 767	6 812	4 537	1 009	511
	ENGINEERING	18 113	1 490	8 658	704	7 987	676	1 468	110
	ARCHITECTURE & TOWN PLANNING	2 080	416	1 354	206	660	194	66	16
	TRADE, CRAFT & INDUSTRIAL PGMS.	–	–	–	–	–	–	–	–
	TRANSPORT AND COMMUNICATIONS	333	9	333	9	–	–	–	–
	AGRICULTURE, FORESTRY & FISHERY	4 866	1 569	3 331	987	1 238	500	297	82
	OTHER AND NOT SPECIFIED	14 985	8 547	184	84	13 773	7 942	1 028	521
COSTA RICA‡ 1984	TOTAL	3 054	...	168	...	2 670	...	216	...
	EDUCATION SCIENCE & TEACHER TRNG.	237	...	–	–	237	...	–	–
	HUMANITIES, RELIGION & THEOLOGY	139	...	19	...	120	...	–	–
	FINE AND APPLIED ARTS	162	...	14	...	148	...	–	–
	LAW	212	...	–	–	212	...	–	–
	SOCIAL AND BEHAVIOURAL SCIENCE	231	...	–	–	231	...	–	–
	COMMERCIAL & BUSINESS ADMIN.	344	...	22	...	322	...	–	–
	MASS COMMUNICATION & DOCUMENT.	83	...	–	–	82	...	1	...
	HOME ECONOMICS (DOMESTIC SCIENCE)	–	–	–	–	–	–	–	–
	SERVICE TRADES	–	–	–	–	–	–	–	–
	NATURAL SCIENCE	92	...	–	–	92	...	–	–
	MATHEMATICS & COMPUTER SCIENCE	76	...	–	–	76	...	–	–
	MEDICAL SCIENCE & HEALTH–RELATED	592	...	44	...	488	...	60	...
	ENGINEERING	276	...	10	...	266	...	–	–
	ARCHITECTURE & TOWN PLANNING	63	...	–	...	63	...	–	–
	TRADE, CRAFT & INDUSTRIAL PGMS.	–	–	–	–	–	–	–	–
	TRANSPORT AND COMMUNICATIONS	–	–	–	–	–	–	–	–
	AGRICULTURE, FORESTRY & FISHERY	234	...	...	...	234	...	–	–
	OTHER AND NOT SPECIFIED	313	...	59	...	99	...	155	...

COUNTRY YEAR PAYS ANNEE PAIS AÑO	FIELD OF STUDY DOMAINES D'ETUDES SECTORES DE ESTUDIOS	INTERNATIONAL STANDARD CLASSIFICATION OF EDUCATION BY LEVEL / CLASSIFICATION INTERNATIONALE TYPE DE L'EDUCATION PAR NIVEAU / CLASIFICACION INTERNACIONAL NORMALIZADA DE LA EDUCACION POR NIVEL							
		ALL LEVELS TOUS NIVEAUX TODOS LOS NIVELES		LEVEL 5 NIVEAU 5 NIVEL 5		LEVEL 6 NIVEAU 6 NIVEL 6		LEVEL 7 NIVEAU 7 NIVEL 7	
		MF	F	MF	F	MF	F	MF	F
		(1)	(2)	(3)	(4)	(5)	(6)	(7)	(8)
CUBA									
1983	TOTAL	19 429	...	–	–	19 429	...	–	–
	EDUCATION SCIENCE & TEACHER TRNG.	6 806	...	–	–	6 806	...	–	–
	HUMANITIES, RELIGION & THEOLOGY	487	...	–	–	487	...	–	–
	FINE AND APPLIED ARTS	85	...	–	–	85	...	–	–
	LAW	723	...	–	–	723	...	–	–
	SOCIAL AND BEHAVIOURAL SCIENCE	1 104	...	–	–	1 104	...	–	–
	COMMERCIAL & BUSINESS ADMIN.	703	...	–	–	703	...	–	–
	MASS COMMUNICATION & DOCUMENT.	206	...	–	–	206	...	–	–
	HOME ECONOMICS (DOMESTIC SCIENCE)	–	–	–	–	–	–	–	–
	SERVICE TRADES	–	–	–	–	–	–	–	–
	NATURAL SCIENCE	244	...	–	–	244	...	–	–
	MATHEMATICS & COMPUTER SCIENCE	163	...	–	–	163	...	–	–
	MEDICAL SCIENCE & HEALTH-RELATED	2 582	...	–	–	2 582	...	–	–
	ENGINEERING	3 039	...	–	–	3 039	...	–	–
	ARCHITECTURE & TOWN PLANNING	207	...	–	–	207	...	–	–
	TRADE, CRAFT & INDUSTRIAL PGMS.	28	...	–	–	28	...	–	–
	TRANSPORT AND COMMUNICATIONS	290	...	–	–	290	...	–	–
	AGRICULTURE, FORESTRY & FISHERY	1 871	...	–	–	1 871	...	–	–
	OTHER AND NOT SPECIFIED	891	...	–	–	891	...	–	–
DOMINICA									
1980	TOTAL	3	1	3	1	–	–	–	–
	EDUCATION SCIENCE & TEACHER TRNG.	3	1	3	1	–	–	–	–
	HUMANITIES, RELIGION & THEOLOGY	–	–	–	–	–	–	–	–
	FINE AND APPLIED ARTS	–	–	–	–	–	–	–	–
	LAW	–	–	–	–	–	–	–	–
	SOCIAL AND BEHAVIOURAL SCIENCE	–	–	–	–	–	–	–	–
	COMMERCIAL & BUSINESS ADMIN.	–	–	–	–	–	–	–	–
	MASS COMMUNICATION & DOCUMENT.	–	–	–	–	–	–	–	–
	HOME ECONOMICS (DOMESTIC SCIENCE)	–	–	–	–	–	–	–	–
	SERVICE TRADES	–	–	–	–	–	–	–	–
	NATURAL SCIENCE	–	–	–	–	–	–	–	–
	MATHEMATICS & COMPUTER SCIENCE	–	–	–	–	–	–	–	–
	MEDICAL SCIENCE & HEALTH-RELATED	–	–	–	–	–	–	–	–
	ENGINEERING	–	–	–	–	–	–	–	–
	ARCHITECTURE & TOWN PLANNING	–	–	–	–	–	–	–	–
	TRADE, CRAFT & INDUSTRIAL PGMS.	–	–	–	–	–	–	–	–
	TRANSPORT AND COMMUNICATIONS	–	–	–	–	–	–	–	–
	AGRICULTURE, FORESTRY & FISHERY	–	–	–	–	–	–	–	–
	OTHER AND NOT SPECIFIED	–	–	–	–	–	–	–	–
EL SALVADOR									
1983	TOTAL	5 083	2 382	3 872	1 839	1 211	543	–	–
	EDUCATION SCIENCE & TEACHER TRNG.	2 117	1 175	1 952	1 044	165	131	–	–
	HUMANITIES, RELIGION & THEOLOGY	20	11	–	–	20	11	–	–
	FINE AND APPLIED ARTS	–	–	–	–	–	–	–	–
	LAW	83	27	–	–	83	27	–	–
	SOCIAL AND BEHAVIOURAL SCIENCE	104	57	–	–	104	57	–	–
	COMMERCIAL & BUSINESS ADMIN.	579	221	321	102	258	119	–	–
	MASS COMMUNICATION & DOCUMENT.	2	1	–	–	2	1	–	–
	HOME ECONOMICS (DOMESTIC SCIENCE)	–	–	–	–	–	–	–	–
	SERVICE TRADES	43	30	43	30	–	–	–	–
	NATURAL SCIENCE	23	16	–	–	23	16	–	–
	MATHEMATICS & COMPUTER SCIENCE	5	1	–	–	5	1	–	–
	MEDICAL SCIENCE & HEALTH-RELATED	330	281	217	207	113	74	–	–
	ENGINEERING	779	99	475	43	304	56	–	–
	ARCHITECTURE & TOWN PLANNING	137	59	61	22	76	37	–	–
	TRADE, CRAFT & INDUSTRIAL PGMS.	52	32	49	30	3	2	–	–
	TRANSPORT AND COMMUNICATIONS	–	–	–	–	–	–	–	–
	AGRICULTURE, FORESTRY & FISHERY	387	18	340	12	47	6	–	–
	OTHER AND NOT SPECIFIED	422	354	414	349	8	5	–	–

COUNTRY YEAR / PAYS ANNEE / PAIS AÑO	FIELD OF STUDY / DOMAINES D'ETUDES / SECTORES DE ESTUDIOS	INTERNATIONAL STANDARD CLASSIFICATION OF EDUCATION BY LEVEL / CLASSIFICATION INTERNATIONALE TYPE DE L'EDUCATION PAR NIVEAU / CLASIFICACION INTERNACIONAL NORMALIZADA DE LA EDUCACION POR NIVEL							
		ALL LEVELS / TOUS NIVEAUX / TODOS LOS NIVELES		LEVEL 5 / NIVEAU 5 / NIVEL 5		LEVEL 6 / NIVEAU 6 / NIVEL 6		LEVEL 7 / NIVEAU 7 / NIVEL 7	
		MF	F	MF	F	MF	F	MF	F
		(1)	(2)	(3)	(4)	(5)	(6)	(7)	(8)
GRENADA‡ 1982	TOTAL	...	...	...	...	–	–	–	–
	EDUCATION SCIENCE & TEACHER TRNG.	–	–	–	–	–	–	–	–
	HUMANITIES, RELIGION & THEOLOGY	–	–	–	–	–	–	–	–
	FINE AND APPLIED ARTS	–	–	–	–	–	–	–	–
	LAW	–	–	–	–	–	–	–	–
	SOCIAL AND BEHAVIOURAL SCIENCE	–	–	–	–	–	–	–	–
	COMMERCIAL & BUSINESS ADMIN.	39	39	39	39	–	–	–	–
	MASS COMMUNICATION & DOCUMENT.	–	–	–	–	–	–	–	–
	HOME ECONOMICS (DOMESTIC SCIENCE)	–	–	–	–	–	–	–	–
	SERVICE TRADES	–	–	–	–	–	–	–	–
	NATURAL SCIENCE	–	–	–	–	–	–	–	–
	MATHEMATICS & COMPUTER SCIENCE	–	–	–	–	–	–	–	–
	MEDICAL SCIENCE & HEALTH-RELATED	60	59	60	59	–	–	–	–
	ENGINEERING	29	3	29	3	–	–	–	–
	ARCHITECTURE & TOWN PLANNING	34	4	34	4	–	–	–	–
	TRADE, CRAFT & INDUSTRIAL PGMS.	–	–	–	–	–	–	–	–
	TRANSPORT AND COMMUNICATIONS	–	–	–	–	–	–	–	–
	AGRICULTURE, FORESTRY & FISHERY	...	...	...	...	–	–	–	–
	OTHER AND NOT SPECIFIED	70	26	70	26	–	–	–	–
HAITI‡ 1982	TOTAL	831	276	...	...	...	...	...	...
	EDUCATION SCIENCE & TEACHER TRNG.	68	20	...	...	...	...	...	...
	HUMANITIES, RELIGION & THEOLOGY	./.	./.	...	...	...	...	...	...
	FINE AND APPLIED ARTS	–	–	...	...	...	...	...	...
	LAW	108	25	...	...	...	...	...	...
	SOCIAL AND BEHAVIOURAL SCIENCE	116	34	...	...	...	...	...	...
	COMMERCIAL & BUSINESS ADMIN.	–	–	...	...	...	...	...	...
	MASS COMMUNICATION & DOCUMENT.	–	–	...	...	...	...	...	...
	HOME ECONOMICS (DOMESTIC SCIENCE)	–	–	...	...	...	...	...	...
	SERVICE TRADES	–	–	...	...	...	...	...	...
	NATURAL SCIENCE	33	10	...	...	...	...	...	...
	MATHEMATICS & COMPUTER SCIENCE	./.	./.	...	...	...	...	...	...
	MEDICAL SCIENCE & HEALTH-RELATED	264	166	...	...	...	...	...	...
	ENGINEERING	200	13	...	...	...	...	...	...
	ARCHITECTURE & TOWN PLANNING	–	–	...	...	...	...	...	...
	TRADE, CRAFT & INDUSTRIAL PGMS.	–	–	...	...	...	...	...	...
	TRANSPORT AND COMMUNICATIONS	–	–	...	...	...	...	...	...
	AGRICULTURE, FORESTRY & FISHERY	42	8	...	...	...	...	...	...
	OTHER AND NOT SPECIFIED	–	–	...	...	...	...	...	...
HONDURAS‡ 1983	TOTAL	1 350	...	...	...	...	...	...	...
	EDUCATION SCIENCE & TEACHER TRNG.	136	...	...	...	...	...	...	...
	HUMANITIES, RELIGION & THEOLOGY	15	8	...	...	...	...	...	...
	FINE AND APPLIED ARTS	2	1	...	...	...	...	...	...
	LAW	87	25	...	...	...	...	...	...
	SOCIAL AND BEHAVIOURAL SCIENCE	260	150	...	...	...	...	...	...
	COMMERCIAL & BUSINESS ADMIN.	174	...	...	...	...	...	...	...
	MASS COMMUNICATION & DOCUMENT.	1	...	...	...	...	...	...	...
	HOME ECONOMICS (DOMESTIC SCIENCE)	–	–	...	...	...	...	...	...
	SERVICE TRADES	–	–	...	...	...	...	...	...
	NATURAL SCIENCE	5	1	...	...	...	...	...	...
	MATHEMATICS & COMPUTER SCIENCE	16	1	...	...	...	...	...	...
	MEDICAL SCIENCE & HEALTH-RELATED	262	170	...	...	...	...	...	...
	ENGINEERING	119	33	...	...	...	...	...	...
	ARCHITECTURE & TOWN PLANNING	–	–	...	...	...	...	...	...
	TRADE, CRAFT & INDUSTRIAL PGMS.	–	–	...	...	...	...	...	...
	TRANSPORT AND COMMUNICATIONS	–	–	...	...	...	...	...	...
	AGRICULTURE, FORESTRY & FISHERY	273	...	...	...	...	...	...	...
	OTHER AND NOT SPECIFIED	–	–	...	...	...	...	...	...

3.14 Third level: graduates by ISCED level and field of study
Troisième degré: diplômés par niveau de la CITE et domaine d'études
Tercer grado: diplomados por nivel de la CINE y sector de estudios

COUNTRY / YEAR PAYS / ANNEE PAIS / AÑO	FIELD OF STUDY DOMAINES D'ETUDES SECTORES DE ESTUDIOS	INTERNATIONAL STANDARD CLASSIFICATION OF EDUCATION BY LEVEL / CLASSIFICATION INTERNATIONALE TYPE DE L'EDUCATION PAR NIVEAU / CLASIFICACION INTERNACIONAL NORMALIZADA DE LA EDUCACION POR NIVEL							
		ALL LEVELS TOUS NIVEAUX TODOS LOS NIVELES		LEVEL 5 NIVEAU 5 NIVEL 5		LEVEL 6 NIVEAU 6 NIVEL 6		LEVEL 7 NIVEAU 7 NIVEL 7	
		MF	F	MF	F	MF	F	MF	F
		(1)	(2)	(3)	(4)	(5)	(6)	(7)	(8)
JAMAICA 1980	TOTAL	4 266	...	3 320	...	879	...	67	...
	EDUCATION SCIENCE & TEACHER TRNG.	1 887	...	1 782	...	89	...	16	...
	HUMANITIES, RELIGION & THEOLOGY	278	...	6	...	267	...	5	...
	FINE AND APPLIED ARTS	91	...	2	...	89	...	–	–
	LAW	31	...	–	–	31	...	–	–
	SOCIAL AND BEHAVIOURAL SCIENCE	289	...	157	...	126	...	6	...
	COMMERCIAL & BUSINESS ADMIN.	327	...	295	...	11	...	21	...
	MASS COMMUNICATION & DOCUMENT.	19	...	19	...	–	–	–	–
	HOME ECONOMICS (DOMESTIC SCIENCE)	48	...	48	...	–	–	–	–
	SERVICE TRADES	–	–	–	–	–	–	–	–
	NATURAL SCIENCE	159	...	–	–	154	...	5	...
	MATHEMATICS & COMPUTER SCIENCE	1	...	1	...	–	–	–	–
	MEDICAL SCIENCE & HEALTH-RELATED	816	...	693	...	109	...	14	...
	ENGINEERING	157	...	157	...	–	–	–	–
	ARCHITECTURE & TOWN PLANNING	97	...	94	...	3	...	–	–
	TRADE, CRAFT & INDUSTRIAL PGMS.	–	–	–	–	–	–	–	–
	TRANSPORT AND COMMUNICATIONS	–	–	–	–	–	–	–	–
	AGRICULTURE, FORESTRY & FISHERY	66	...	66	...	–	–	–	–
	OTHER AND NOT SPECIFIED	–	–	–	–	–	–	–	–
MEXICO‡ 1982	TOTAL	96 572	...	–	–	96 572	...	–	–
	EDUCATION SCIENCE & TEACHER TRNG.	1 758	...	–	–	1 758	...	–	–
	HUMANITIES, RELIGION & THEOLOGY	907	...	–	–	907	...	–	–
	FINE AND APPLIED ARTS	829	...	–	–	829	...	–	–
	LAW	8 342	...	–	–	8 342	...	–	–
	SOCIAL AND BEHAVIOURAL SCIENCE	8 148	...	–	–	8 148	...	–	–
	COMMERCIAL & BUSINESS ADMIN.	19 499	...	–	–	19 499	...	–	–
	MASS COMMUNICATION & DOCUMENT.	2 053	...	–	–	2 053	...	–	–
	HOME ECONOMICS (DOMESTIC SCIENCE)	–	–	–	–	–	–	–	–
	SERVICE TRADES	1 264	...	–	–	1 264	...	–	–
	NATURAL SCIENCE	2 142	...	–	–	2 142	...	–	–
	MATHEMATICS & COMPUTER SCIENCE	760	...	–	–	760	...	–	–
	MEDICAL SCIENCE & HEALTH-RELATED	19 761	...	–	–	19 761	...	–	–
	ENGINEERING	23 866	...	–	–	23 866	...	–	–
	ARCHITECTURE & TOWN PLANNING	3 047	...	–	–	3 047	...	–	–
	TRADE, CRAFT & INDUSTRIAL PGMS.	–	–	–	–	–	–	–	–
	TRANSPORT AND COMMUNICATIONS	92	...	–	–	92	...	–	–
	AGRICULTURE, FORESTRY & FISHERY	3 452	...	–	–	3 452	...	–	–
	OTHER AND NOT SPECIFIED	652	...	–	–	652	...	–	–
NICARAGUA 1985	TOTAL	1 636	810	635	226	1 001	584	–	–
	EDUCATION SCIENCE & TEACHER TRNG.	214	139	–	–	214	139	–	–
	HUMANITIES, RELIGION & THEOLOGY	29	19	–	–	29	19	–	–
	FINE AND APPLIED ARTS	3	2	–	–	3	2	–	–
	LAW	86	30	–	–	86	30	–	–
	SOCIAL AND BEHAVIOURAL SCIENCE	122	80	–	–	122	80	–	–
	COMMERCIAL & BUSINESS ADMIN.	218	142	4	2	214	140	–	–
	MASS COMMUNICATION & DOCUMENT.	15	9	–	–	15	9	–	–
	HOME ECONOMICS (DOMESTIC SCIENCE)	32	21	32	21	–	–	–	–
	SERVICE TRADES	–	–	–	–	–	–	–	–
	NATURAL SCIENCE	96	62	–	–	96	62	–	–
	MATHEMATICS & COMPUTER SCIENCE	16	10	5	3	11	7	–	–
	MEDICAL SCIENCE & HEALTH-RELATED	265	208	163	152	102	56	–	–
	ENGINEERING	217	76	120	42	97	34	–	–
	ARCHITECTURE & TOWN PLANNING	10	4	–	–	10	4	–	–
	TRADE, CRAFT & INDUSTRIAL PGMS.	–	–	–	–	–	–	–	–
	TRANSPORT AND COMMUNICATIONS	–	–	–	–	–	–	–	–
	AGRICULTURE, FORESTRY & FISHERY	311	7	309	5	2	2	–	–
	OTHER AND NOT SPECIFIED	2	1	2	1	–	–	–	–

COUNTRY YEAR / PAYS ANNEE / PAIS AÑO	FIELD OF STUDY / DOMAINES D'ETUDES / SECTORES DE ESTUDIOS	INTERNATIONAL STANDARD CLASSIFICATION OF EDUCATION BY LEVEL / CLASSIFICATION INTERNATIONALE TYPE DE L'EDUCATION PAR NIVEAU / CLASIFICACION INTERNACIONAL NORMALIZADA DE LA EDUCACION POR NIVEL							
		ALL LEVELS / TOUS NIVEAUX / TODOS LOS NIVELES		LEVEL 5 / NIVEAU 5 / NIVEL 5		LEVEL 6 / NIVEAU 6 / NIVEL 6		LEVEL 7 / NIVEAU 7 / NIVEL 7	
		MF	F	MF	F	MF	F	MF	F
		(1)	(2)	(3)	(4)	(5)	(6)	(7)	(8)
PANAMA 1984	TOTAL	3 284	1 841	1 088	674	1 905	1 004	291	163
	EDUCATION SCIENCE & TEACHER TRNG.	279	244	172	160	95	78	12	6
	HUMANITIES, RELIGION & THEOLOGY	151	116	–	–	132	101	19	15
	FINE AND APPLIED ARTS	52	31	39	18	13	13	–	–
	LAW	128	51	–	–	120	46	8	5
	SOCIAL AND BEHAVIOURAL SCIENCE	247	132	–	–	203	112	44	20
	COMMERCIAL & BUSINESS ADMIN.	799	502	176	133	572	339	51	30
	MASS COMMUNICATION & DOCUMENT.	47	28	4	4	35	21	8	3
	HOME ECONOMICS (DOMESTIC SCIENCE)	20	20	–	–	19	19	1	1
	SERVICE TRADES	–	–	–	–	–	–	–	–
	NATURAL SCIENCE	139	60	8	5	89	36	42	19
	MATHEMATICS & COMPUTER SCIENCE	92	48	–	–	34	15	58	33
	MEDICAL SCIENCE & HEALTH-RELATED	381	323	231	227	140	89	10	7
	ENGINEERING	614	139	415	101	199	38	–	–
	ARCHITECTURE & TOWN PLANNING	78	31	13	8	64	23	1	–
	TRADE, CRAFT & INDUSTRIAL PGMS.	22	16	19	14	3	2	–	–
	TRANSPORT AND COMMUNICATIONS	–	–	–	–	–	–	–	–
	AGRICULTURE, FORESTRY & FISHERY	109	27	11	4	88	19	10	4
	OTHER AND NOT SPECIFIED	126	73	–	–	99	53	27	20
ST. LUCIA 1984	TOTAL	194	88	194	88	–	–	–	–
	EDUCATION SCIENCE & TEACHER TRNG.	66	40	66	40	–	–	–	–
	HUMANITIES, RELIGION & THEOLOGY	–	–	–	–	–	–	–	–
	FINE AND APPLIED ARTS	–	–	–	–	–	–	–	–
	LAW	–	–	–	–	–	–	–	–
	SOCIAL AND BEHAVIOURAL SCIENCE	–	–	–	–	–	–	–	–
	COMMERCIAL & BUSINESS ADMIN.	16	10	16	10	–	–	–	–
	MASS COMMUNICATION & DOCUMENT.	–	–	–	–	–	–	–	–
	HOME ECONOMICS (DOMESTIC SCIENCE)	–	–	–	–	–	–	–	–
	SERVICE TRADES	25	25	25	25	–	–	–	–
	NATURAL SCIENCE	–	–	–	–	–	–	–	–
	MATHEMATICS & COMPUTER SCIENCE	–	–	–	–	–	–	–	–
	MEDICAL SCIENCE & HEALTH-RELATED	–	–	–	–	–	–	–	–
	ENGINEERING	–	–	–	–	–	–	–	–
	ARCHITECTURE & TOWN PLANNING	12	4	12	4	–	–	–	–
	TRADE, CRAFT & INDUSTRIAL PGMS.	51	4	51	4	–	–	–	–
	TRANSPORT AND COMMUNICATIONS	–	–	–	–	–	–	–	–
	AGRICULTURE, FORESTRY & FISHERY	24	5	24	5	–	–	–	–
	OTHER AND NOT SPECIFIED	–	–	–	–	–	–	–	–
TRINIDAD AND TOBAGO‡ 1982	TOTAL	376	188	–	–	376	188	–	–
	EDUCATION SCIENCE & TEACHER TRNG.	–	–	–	–	–	–	–	–
	HUMANITIES, RELIGION & THEOLOGY	115	79	–	–	115	79	–	–
	FINE AND APPLIED ARTS	–	–	–	–	–	–	–	–
	LAW	–	–	–	–	–	–	–	–
	SOCIAL AND BEHAVIOURAL SCIENCE	70	41	–	–	70	41	–	–
	COMMERCIAL & BUSINESS ADMIN.	–	–	–	–	–	–	–	–
	MASS COMMUNICATION & DOCUMENT.	–	–	–	–	–	–	–	–
	HOME ECONOMICS (DOMESTIC SCIENCE)	–	–	–	–	–	–	–	–
	SERVICE TRADES	–	–	–	–	–	–	–	–
	NATURAL SCIENCE	73	31	–	–	73	31	–	–
	MATHEMATICS & COMPUTER SCIENCE	./.	./.	–	–	./.	./.	–	–
	MEDICAL SCIENCE & HEALTH-RELATED	–	–	–	–	–	–	–	–
	ENGINEERING	89	24	–	–	89	24	–	–
	ARCHITECTURE & TOWN PLANNING	–	–	–	–	–	–	–	–
	TRADE, CRAFT & INDUSTRIAL PGMS.	–	–	–	–	–	–	–	–
	TRANSPORT AND COMMUNICATIONS	–	–	–	–	–	–	–	–
	AGRICULTURE, FORESTRY & FISHERY	29	13	–	–	29	13	–	–
	OTHER AND NOT SPECIFIED	–	–	–	–	–	–	–	–

3.14 Third level: graduates by ISCED level and field of study
Troisième degré: diplômés par niveau de la CITE et domaine d'études
Tercer grado: diplomados por nivel de la CINE y sector de estudios

COUNTRY / YEAR PAYS / ANNEE PAIS / AÑO	FIELD OF STUDY DOMAINES D'ETUDES SECTORES DE ESTUDIOS	ALL LEVELS / TOUS NIVEAUX / TODOS LOS NIVELES MF	F	LEVEL 5 / NIVEAU 5 / NIVEL 5 MF	F	LEVEL 6 / NIVEAU 6 / NIVEL 6 MF	F	LEVEL 7 / NIVEAU 7 / NIVEL 7 MF	F
		(1)	(2)	(3)	(4)	(5)	(6)	(7)	(8)
UNITED STATES‡									
1982	TOTAL	1 810 732	911 518	445 390	243 225	969 510	490 370	395 832	177 923
	EDUCATION SCIENCE & TEACHER TRNG.	197 915	144 898	7 520	5 169	97 991	74 321	92 404	65 408
	HUMANITIES, RELIGION & THEOLOGY	73 448	41 371	1 809	942	54 964	32 531	16 675	7 898
	FINE AND APPLIED ARTS	55 050	33 643	6 365	3 965	39 251	24 659	9 434	5 019
	LAW	78 140	24 448	1 742	1 475	1 099	642	75 299	22 331
	SOCIAL AND BEHAVIOURAL SCIENCE	168 680	85 787	3 749	2 087	138 423	71 510	26 508	12 190
	COMMERCIAL & BUSINESS ADMIN.	409 300	187 722	116 279	73 549	226 893	95 175	66 128	18 998
	MASS COMMUNICATION & DOCUMENT.	50 761	29 873	4 052	1 920	38 860	22 647	7 849	5 306
	HOME ECONOMICS (DOMESTIC SCIENCE)	28 410	24 885	9 044	6 779	16 705	15 751	2 661	2 355
	SERVICE TRADES	–	–	–	–	–	–	–	–
	NATURAL SCIENCE	85 067	31 553	4 084	1 598	63 387	24 807	17 596	5 148
	MATHEMATICS & COMPUTER SCIENCE	56 528	22 182	10 447	5 183	36 963	14 362	9 118	2 637
	MEDICAL SCIENCE & HEALTH–RELATED	148 586	125 857	65 749	58 105	64 614	54 410	18 223	13 342
	ENGINEERING	160 991	17 854	49 611	4 981	89 199	10 951	22 181	1 922
	ARCHITECTURE & TOWN PLANNING	14 731	5 720	1 454	1 144	9 823	3 420	3 454	1 156
	TRADE, CRAFT & INDUSTRIAL PGMS.	–	–	–	–	–	–	–	–
	TRANSPORT AND COMMUNICATIONS	–	–	–	–	–	–	–	–
	AGRICULTURE, FORESTRY & FISHERY	33 957	10 572	7 645	2 478	20 909	6 824	5 403	1 270
	OTHER AND NOT SPECIFIED	249 168	125 153	155 840	73 850	70 429	38 360	22 899	12 943
U.S. VIRGIN ISLANDS									
1982	TOTAL	144	102	37	29	91	63	16	10
	EDUCATION SCIENCE & TEACHER TRNG.	41	36	–	–	29	28	12	8
	HUMANITIES, RELIGION & THEOLOGY	–	–	–	–	–	–	–	–
	FINE AND APPLIED ARTS	–	–	–	–	–	–	–	–
	LAW	–	–	–	–	–	–	–	–
	SOCIAL AND BEHAVIOURAL SCIENCE	13	10	–	–	11	9	2	1
	COMMERCIAL & BUSINESS ADMIN.	66	42	26	20	38	21	2	1
	MASS COMMUNICATION & DOCUMENT.	–	–	–	–	–	–	–	–
	HOME ECONOMICS (DOMESTIC SCIENCE)	–	–	–	–	–	–	–	–
	SERVICE TRADES	–	–	–	–	–	–	–	–
	NATURAL SCIENCE	10	4	–	–	10	4	–	–
	MATHEMATICS & COMPUTER SCIENCE	3	1	–	–	3	1	–	–
	MEDICAL SCIENCE & HEALTH–RELATED	10	9	10	9	–	–	–	–
	ENGINEERING	–	–	–	–	–	–	–	–
	ARCHITECTURE & TOWN PLANNING	–	–	–	–	–	–	–	–
	TRADE, CRAFT & INDUSTRIAL PGMS.	–	–	–	–	–	–	–	–
	TRANSPORT AND COMMUNICATIONS	–	–	–	–	–	–	–	–
	AGRICULTURE, FORESTRY & FISHERY	1	–	1	–	–	–	–	–
	OTHER AND NOT SPECIFIED	–	–	–	–	–	–	–	–
AMERICA, SOUTH									
BOLIVIA‡									
1981	TOTAL	1 272	...	...	...	...	...	...	...
	EDUCATION SCIENCE & TEACHER TRNG.	./.	...	...	...	...	...	...	...
	HUMANITIES, RELIGION & THEOLOGY	139	...	...	...	...	...	...	...
	FINE AND APPLIED ARTS	–	–	...	...	...	...	...	...
	LAW	192	...	...	...	...	...	...	...
	SOCIAL AND BEHAVIOURAL SCIENCE	222	...	...	...	...	...	...	...
	COMMERCIAL & BUSINESS ADMIN.	–	–	...	...	...	...	...	...
	MASS COMMUNICATION & DOCUMENT.	–	–	...	...	...	...	...	...
	HOME ECONOMICS (DOMESTIC SCIENCE)	–	–	...	...	...	...	...	...
	SERVICE TRADES	–	–	...	...	...	...	...	...
	NATURAL SCIENCE	51	...	...	...	...	...	...	...
	MATHEMATICS & COMPUTER SCIENCE	–	–	...	...	...	...	...	...
	MEDICAL SCIENCE & HEALTH–RELATED	359	...	...	...	...	...	...	...
	ENGINEERING	235	...	...	...	...	...	...	...
	ARCHITECTURE & TOWN PLANNING	23	...	...	...	...	...	...	...
	TRADE, CRAFT & INDUSTRIAL PGMS.	13	...	...	...	...	...	...	...
	TRANSPORT AND COMMUNICATIONS	–	–	...	...	...	...	...	...
	AGRICULTURE, FORESTRY & FISHERY	38	...	...	...	...	...	...	...
	OTHER AND NOT SPECIFIED	–	–	...	...	...	...	...	...

COUNTRY YEAR / PAYS ANNEE / PAIS AÑO	FIELD OF STUDY / DOMAINES D'ETUDES / SECTORES DE ESTUDIOS	INTERNATIONAL STANDARD CLASSIFICATION OF EDUCATION BY LEVEL / CLASSIFICATION INTERNATIONALE TYPE DE L'EDUCATION PAR NIVEAU / CLASIFICACION INTERNACIONAL NORMALIZADA DE LA EDUCACION POR NIVEL							
		ALL LEVELS / TOUS NIVEAUX / TODOS LOS NIVELES		LEVEL 5 / NIVEAU 5 / NIVEL 5		LEVEL 6 / NIVEAU 6 / NIVEL 6		LEVEL 7 / NIVEAU 7 / NIVEL 7	
		MF	F	MF	F	MF	F	MF	F
		(1)	(2)	(3)	(4)	(5)	(6)	(7)	(8)
BRAZIL 1982	TOTAL	253 553	151 391	–	–	244 639	147 501	8 914	3 890
	EDUCATION SCIENCE & TEACHER TRNG.	48 932	41 170	–	–	48 208	40 632	724	538
	HUMANITIES, RELIGION & THEOLOGY	20 621	17 944	–	–	19 865	16 993	756	951
	FINE AND APPLIED ARTS	6 890	5 567	–	–	6 871	5 556	19	11
	LAW	21 983	8 723	–	–	21 287	8 470	696	253
	SOCIAL AND BEHAVIOURAL SCIENCE	34 499	24 314	–	–	33 598	24 188	901	126
	COMMERCIAL & BUSINESS ADMIN.	32 596	12 087	–	–	32 322	12 035	274	52
	MASS COMMUNICATION & DOCUMENT.	7 173	5 015	–	–	7 033	4 958	140	57
	HOME ECONOMICS (DOMESTIC SCIENCE)	253	246	–	–	253	246	–	–
	SERVICE TRADES	624	504	–	–	624	504	–	–
	NATURAL SCIENCE	7 726	4 127	–	–	5 927	3 376	1 799	751
	MATHEMATICS & COMPUTER SCIENCE	4 369	2 311	–	–	4 020	2 192	349	119
	MEDICAL SCIENCE & HEALTH–RELATED	23 528	14 470	–	–	22 222	13 895	1 306	575
	ENGINEERING	21 025	2 678	–	–	19 992	2 498	1 033	180
	ARCHITECTURE & TOWN PLANNING	2 954	1 695	–	–	2 873	1 661	81	34
	TRADE, CRAFT & INDUSTRIAL PGMS.	1 716	225	–	–	1 716	225	–	–
	TRANSPORT AND COMMUNICATIONS	–	–	–	–	–	–	–	–
	AGRICULTURE, FORESTRY & FISHERY	6 832	1 374	–	–	6 033	1 142	799	232
	OTHER AND NOT SPECIFIED	11 832	8 941	–	–	11 795	8 930	37	11
CHILE 1984	TOTAL	20 256	9 945	1 462	350	18 581	9 505	213	90
	EDUCATION SCIENCE & TEACHER TRNG.	4 391	3 238	–	–	4 367	3 225	24	13
	HUMANITIES, RELIGION & THEOLOGY	2 038	1 314	34	30	1 996	1 280	8	4
	FINE AND APPLIED ARTS	770	437	–	–	770	437	–	–
	LAW	377	149	1	1	360	144	16	4
	SOCIAL AND BEHAVIOURAL SCIENCE	591	298	–	–	580	294	11	4
	COMMERCIAL & BUSINESS ADMIN.	1 897	506	92	42	1 803	463	2	1
	MASS COMMUNICATION & DOCUMENT.	153	79	38	14	115	65	–	–
	HOME ECONOMICS (DOMESTIC SCIENCE)	142	111	–	–	109	86	33	25
	SERVICE TRADES	36	29	36	29	–	–	–	–
	NATURAL SCIENCE	1 197	605	38	22	1 127	577	32	6
	MATHEMATICS & COMPUTER SCIENCE	625	271	41	17	565	249	19	5
	MEDICAL SCIENCE & HEALTH–RELATED	2 704	1 602	–	–	2 668	1 579	36	23
	ENGINEERING	3 580	612	779	88	2 790	522	11	2
	ARCHITECTURE & TOWN PLANNING	330	83	12	3	312	79	6	1
	TRADE, CRAFT & INDUSTRIAL PGMS.	330	94	330	94	–	–	–	–
	TRANSPORT AND COMMUNICATIONS	–	–	–	–	–	–	–	–
	AGRICULTURE, FORESTRY & FISHERY	357	105	61	10	282	93	14	2
	OTHER AND NOT SPECIFIED	738	412	–	–	737	412	1	–
COLOMBIA‡ 1984	TOTAL	42 006	21 657	11 086	6 939	29 062	13 962	1 858	756
	EDUCATION SCIENCE & TEACHER TRNG.	7 206	4 297	1 073	777	5 840	3 362	293	158
	HUMANITIES, RELIGION & THEOLOGY	319	189	36	28	219	135	64	26
	FINE AND APPLIED ARTS	1 261	1 045	1 012	858	249	187	–	–
	LAW	5 896	2 979	236	183	5 402	2 693	258	103
	SOCIAL AND BEHAVIOURAL SCIENCE	./.	./.	./.	./.	./.	./.	./.	./.
	COMMERCIAL & BUSINESS ADMIN.	13 143	7 689	5 082	3 882	7 180	3 446	881	361
	MASS COMMUNICATION & DOCUMENT.	./.	./.	./.	./.	./.	./.	./.	./.
	HOME ECONOMICS (DOMESTIC SCIENCE)	./.	./.	./.	./.	./.	./.	./.	./.
	SERVICE TRADES	./.	./.	./.	./.	./.	./.	./.	./.
	NATURAL SCIENCE	666	247	233	114	346	111	87	22
	MATHEMATICS & COMPUTER SCIENCE	./.	./.	./.	./.	./.	./.	./.	./.
	MEDICAL SCIENCE & HEALTH–RELATED	4 608	2 520	418	284	3 993	2 173	197	63
	ENGINEERING	7 988	2 311	2 709	623	5 211	1 668	68	20
	ARCHITECTURE & TOWN PLANNING	./.	./.	./.	./.	./.	./.	./.	./.
	TRADE, CRAFT & INDUSTRIAL PGMS.	./.	./.	./.	./.	./.	./.	./.	./.
	TRANSPORT AND COMMUNICATIONS	./.	./.	./.	./.	./.	./.	./.	./.
	AGRICULTURE, FORESTRY & FISHERY	919	380	287	190	622	187	10	3
	OTHER AND NOT SPECIFIED	–	–	–	–	–	–	–	–

3.14 **Third level: graduates by ISCED level and field of study**
Troisième degré: diplômés par niveau de la CITE et domaine d'études
Tercer grado: diplomados por nivel de la CINE y sector de estudios

COUNTRY YEAR / PAYS ANNEE / PAIS AÑO	FIELD OF STUDY / DOMAINES D'ETUDES / SECTORES DE ESTUDIOS	INTERNATIONAL STANDARD CLASSIFICATION OF EDUCATION BY LEVEL / CLASSIFICATION INTERNATIONALE TYPE DE L'EDUCATION PAR NIVEAU / CLASIFICACION INTERNACIONAL NORMALIZADA DE LA EDUCACION POR NIVEL							
		ALL LEVELS / TOUS NIVEAUX / TODOS LOS NIVELES		LEVEL 5 / NIVEAU 5 / NIVEL 5		LEVEL 6 / NIVEAU 6 / NIVEL 6		LEVEL 7 / NIVEAU 7 / NIVEL 7	
		MF	F	MF	F	MF	F	MF	F
		(1)	(2)	(3)	(4)	(5)	(6)	(7)	(8)
ECUADOR‡ 1981	TOTAL	15 441	6 262	...	...	...	...	...	...
	EDUCATION SCIENCE & TEACHER TRNG.	6 892	3 603	...	...	...	...	...	...
	HUMANITIES, RELIGION & THEOLOGY	179	92	...	...	...	...	...	...
	FINE AND APPLIED ARTS	86	43	...	...	...	...	...	...
	LAW	858	225	...	...	...	...	...	...
	SOCIAL AND BEHAVIOURAL SCIENCE	1 445	603	...	...	...	...	...	...
	COMMERCIAL & BUSINESS ADMIN.	991	350	...	...	...	...	...	...
	MASS COMMUNICATION & DOCUMENT.	93	32	...	...	...	...	...	...
	HOME ECONOMICS (DOMESTIC SCIENCE)	61	61	...	...	...	...	...	...
	SERVICE TRADES	–	–	...	...	...	...	...	...
	NATURAL SCIENCE	–	–	...	...	...	...	...	...
	MATHEMATICS & COMPUTER SCIENCE	–	–	...	...	...	...	...	...
	MEDICAL SCIENCE & HEALTH–RELATED	2 077	883	...	...	...	...	...	...
	ENGINEERING	1 074	100	...	...	...	...	...	...
	ARCHITECTURE & TOWN PLANNING	397	71	...	...	...	...	...	...
	TRADE, CRAFT & INDUSTRIAL PGMS.	./.	./.	...	...	...	...	...	...
	TRANSPORT AND COMMUNICATIONS	–	–	...	...	...	...	...	...
	AGRICULTURE, FORESTRY & FISHERY	1 252	187	...	...	...	...	...	...
	OTHER AND NOT SPECIFIED	36	12	...	...	...	...	...	...
GUYANA‡ 1982	TOTAL	791	413	609	359	163	47	19	7
	EDUCATION SCIENCE & TEACHER TRNG.	413	306	362	282	32	17	19	7
	HUMANITIES, RELIGION & THEOLOGY	./.	./.	./.	./.	./.	./.	./.	./.
	FINE AND APPLIED ARTS	–	–	–	–	–	–	–	–
	LAW	16	6	16	6	–	–	–	–
	SOCIAL AND BEHAVIOURAL SCIENCE	49	13	–	–	49	13	–	–
	COMMERCIAL & BUSINESS ADMIN.	40	13	16	3	24	10	–	–
	MASS COMMUNICATION & DOCUMENT.	12	3	12	3	–	–	–	–
	HOME ECONOMICS (DOMESTIC SCIENCE)	–	–	–	–	–	–	–	–
	SERVICE TRADES	–	–	–	–	–	–	–	–
	NATURAL SCIENCE	12	3	–	–	12	3	–	–
	MATHEMATICS & COMPUTER SCIENCE	7	2	–	–	7	2	–	–
	MEDICAL SCIENCE & HEALTH–RELATED	70	30	70	30	–	–	–	–
	ENGINEERING	88	6	61	5	27	1	–	–
	ARCHITECTURE & TOWN PLANNING	10	–	6	–	4	–	–	–
	TRADE, CRAFT & INDUSTRIAL PGMS.	–	–	–	–	–	–	–	–
	TRANSPORT AND COMMUNICATIONS	–	–	–	–	–	–	–	–
	AGRICULTURE, FORESTRY & FISHERY	8	1	–	–	8	1	–	–
	OTHER AND NOT SPECIFIED	66	30	66	30	–	–	–	–
PERU‡ 1982	TOTAL	10 449	4 197	...	...	...	...	...	...
	EDUCATION SCIENCE & TEACHER TRNG.	1 973	1 213	...	...	...	...	...	...
	HUMANITIES, RELIGION & THEOLOGY	17	8	...	...	...	...	...	...
	FINE AND APPLIED ARTS	2	1	...	...	...	...	...	...
	LAW	898	193	...	...	...	...	...	...
	SOCIAL AND BEHAVIOURAL SCIENCE	754	323	...	...	...	...	...	...
	COMMERCIAL & BUSINESS ADMIN.	1 815	566	...	...	...	...	...	...
	MASS COMMUNICATION & DOCUMENT.	47	26	...	...	...	...	...	...
	HOME ECONOMICS (DOMESTIC SCIENCE)	1	1	...	...	...	...	...	...
	SERVICE TRADES	–	–	...	...	...	...	...	...
	NATURAL SCIENCE	179	75	...	...	...	...	...	...
	MATHEMATICS & COMPUTER SCIENCE	52	12	...	...	...	...	...	...
	MEDICAL SCIENCE & HEALTH–RELATED	2 177	1 148	...	...	...	...	...	...
	ENGINEERING	947	86	...	...	...	...	...	...
	ARCHITECTURE & TOWN PLANNING	180	52	...	...	...	...	...	...
	TRADE, CRAFT & INDUSTRIAL PGMS.	–	–	...	...	...	...	...	...
	TRANSPORT AND COMMUNICATIONS	–	–	...	...	...	...	...	...
	AGRICULTURE, FORESTRY & FISHERY	788	63	...	...	...	...	...	...
	OTHER AND NOT SPECIFIED	619	430	...	...	...	...	...	...

COUNTRY YEAR / PAYS ANNEE / PAIS AÑO	FIELD OF STUDY / DOMAINES D'ETUDES / SECTORES DE ESTUDIOS	INTERNATIONAL STANDARD CLASSIFICATION OF EDUCATION BY LEVEL / CLASSIFICATION INTERNATIONALE TYPE DE L'EDUCATION PAR NIVEAU / CLASIFICACION INTERNACIONAL NORMALIZADA DE LA EDUCACION POR NIVEL							
		ALL LEVELS / TOUS NIVEAUX / TODOS LOS NIVELES		LEVEL 5 / NIVEAU 5 / NIVEL 5		LEVEL 6 / NIVEAU 6 / NIVEL 6		LEVEL 7 / NIVEAU 7 / NIVEL 7	
		MF	F	MF	F	MF	F	MF	F
		(1)	(2)	(3)	(4)	(5)	(6)	(7)	(8)
URUGUAY 1985	TOTAL	2 628	1 479	644	519	1 976	956	8	4
	EDUCATION SCIENCE & TEACHER TRNG.	11	6	–	–	11	6	–	–
	HUMANITIES, RELIGION & THEOLOGY	45	37	33	30	12	7	–	–
	FINE AND APPLIED ARTS	4	3	–	–	4	3	–	–
	LAW	422	275	–	–	422	275	–	–
	SOCIAL AND BEHAVIOURAL SCIENCE	146	114	125	104	21	10	–	–
	COMMERCIAL & BUSINESS ADMIN.	276	129	–	–	276	129	–	–
	MASS COMMUNICATION & DOCUMENT.	40	40	40	40	–	–	–	–
	HOME ECONOMICS (DOMESTIC SCIENCE)	23	23	23	23	–	–	–	–
	SERVICE TRADES	–	–	–	–	–	–	–	–
	NATURAL SCIENCE	27	13	–	–	27	13	–	–
	MATHEMATICS & COMPUTER SCIENCE	92	37	77	35	15	2	–	–
	MEDICAL SCIENCE & HEALTH–RELATED	1 008	638	295	250	705	384	8	4
	ENGINEERING	134	13	–	–	134	13	–	–
	ARCHITECTURE & TOWN PLANNING	98	49	–	–	98	49	–	–
	TRADE, CRAFT & INDUSTRIAL PGMS.	8	–	8	–	–	–	–	–
	TRANSPORT AND COMMUNICATIONS	–	–	–	–	–	–	–	–
	AGRICULTURE, FORESTRY & FISHERY	251	65	–	–	251	65	–	–
	OTHER AND NOT SPECIFIED	43	37	43	37	–	–	–	–
VENEZUELA 1983	TOTAL	24 147	...	5 082	...	19 065	...	–	–
	EDUCATION SCIENCE & TEACHER TRNG.	6 719	...	306	...	6 413	...	–	–
	HUMANITIES, RELIGION & THEOLOGY	272	...	–	–	272	...	–	–
	FINE AND APPLIED ARTS	30	...	–	–	30	...	–	–
	LAW	1 104	...	–	–	1 104	...	–	–
	SOCIAL AND BEHAVIOURAL SCIENCE	1 602	...	255	...	1 347	...	–	–
	COMMERCIAL & BUSINESS ADMIN.	3 547	...	1 841	...	1 706	...	–	–
	MASS COMMUNICATION & DOCUMENT.	311	...	48	...	263	...	–	–
	HOME ECONOMICS (DOMESTIC SCIENCE)	–	–	–	–	–	–	–	–
	SERVICE TRADES	183	...	183	...	–	–	–	–
	NATURAL SCIENCE	404	...	–	–	404	...	–	–
	MATHEMATICS & COMPUTER SCIENCE	688	...	415	...	273	...	–	–
	MEDICAL SCIENCE & HEALTH–RELATED	2 770	...	57	...	2 713	...	–	–
	ENGINEERING	4 316	...	1 071	...	3 245	...	–	–
	ARCHITECTURE & TOWN PLANNING	469	...	–	–	469	...	–	–
	TRADE, CRAFT & INDUSTRIAL PGMS.	151	...	151	...	–	–	–	–
	TRANSPORT AND COMMUNICATIONS	–	–	–	–	–	–	–	–
	AGRICULTURE, FORESTRY & FISHERY	1 400	...	687	...	713	...	–	–
	OTHER AND NOT SPECIFIED	181	...	68	...	113	...	–	–
ASIA									
AFGHANISTAN 1982	TOTAL	2 989	...	1 253	...	1 736	...	–	–
	EDUCATION SCIENCE & TEACHER TRNG.	1 037	...	1 026	...	11	...	–	–
	HUMANITIES, RELIGION & THEOLOGY	175	...	–	–	175	...	–	–
	FINE AND APPLIED ARTS	–	–	–	–	–	–	–	–
	LAW	147	...	–	–	147	...	–	–
	SOCIAL AND BEHAVIOURAL SCIENCE	154	...	–	–	154	...	–	–
	COMMERCIAL & BUSINESS ADMIN.	106	...	106	...	–	–	–	–
	MASS COMMUNICATION & DOCUMENT.	–	–	–	–	–	–	–	–
	HOME ECONOMICS (DOMESTIC SCIENCE)	–	–	–	–	–	–	–	–
	SERVICE TRADES	–	–	–	–	–	–	–	–
	NATURAL SCIENCE	153	...	–	–	153	...	–	–
	MATHEMATICS & COMPUTER SCIENCE	–	–	–	–	–	–	–	–
	MEDICAL SCIENCE & HEALTH–RELATED	355	...	108	...	247	...	–	–
	ENGINEERING	595	...	–	–	595	...	–	–
	ARCHITECTURE & TOWN PLANNING	–	–	–	–	–	–	–	–
	TRADE, CRAFT & INDUSTRIAL PGMS.	–	–	–	–	–	–	–	–
	TRANSPORT AND COMMUNICATIONS	13	...	13	...	–	–	–	–
	AGRICULTURE, FORESTRY & FISHERY	133	...	–	–	133	...	–	–
	OTHER AND NOT SPECIFIED	121	...	–	–	121	...	–	–

3.14 Third level: graduates by ISCED level and field of study
Troisième degré: diplômés par niveau de la CITE et domaine d'études
Tercer grado: diplomados por nivel de la CINE y sector de estudios

COUNTRY YEAR / PAYS ANNEE / PAIS AÑO	FIELD OF STUDY / DOMAINES D'ETUDES / SECTORES DE ESTUDIOS	INTERNATIONAL STANDARD CLASSIFICATION OF EDUCATION BY LEVEL / CLASSIFICATION INTERNATIONALE TYPE DE L'EDUCATION PAR NIVEAU / CLASIFICACION INTERNACIONAL NORMALIZADA DE LA EDUCACION POR NIVEL							
		ALL LEVELS / TOUS NIVEAUX / TODOS LOS NIVELES		LEVEL 5 / NIVEAU 5 / NIVEL 5		LEVEL 6 / NIVEAU 6 / NIVEL 6		LEVEL 7 / NIVEAU 7 / NIVEL 7	
		MF	F	MF	F	MF	F	MF	F
		(1)	(2)	(3)	(4)	(5)	(6)	(7)	(8)
BAHRAIN‡ 1984	TOTAL	608	356	...	...	...	...	...	...
	EDUCATION SCIENCE & TEACHER TRNG.	88	64	...	...	...	...	...	...
	HUMANITIES, RELIGION & THEOLOGY	–	–	...	...	...	...	...	...
	FINE AND APPLIED ARTS	–	–	...	...	...	...	...	...
	LAW	–	–	...	...	...	...	...	...
	SOCIAL AND BEHAVIOURAL SCIENCE	–	–	...	...	...	...	...	...
	COMMERCIAL & BUSINESS ADMIN.	141	106	...	...	...	...	...	...
	MASS COMMUNICATION & DOCUMENT.	–	–	...	...	...	...	...	...
	HOME ECONOMICS (DOMESTIC SCIENCE)	–	–	...	...	...	...	...	...
	SERVICE TRADES	–	–	...	...	...	...	...	...
	NATURAL SCIENCE	–	–	...	...	...	...	...	...
	MATHEMATICS & COMPUTER SCIENCE	110	54	...	...	...	...	...	...
	MEDICAL SCIENCE & HEALTH-RELATED	159	104	...	...	...	...	...	...
	ENGINEERING	110	28	...	...	...	...	...	...
	ARCHITECTURE & TOWN PLANNING	–	–	...	...	...	...	...	...
	TRADE, CRAFT & INDUSTRIAL PGMS.	./.	./.	...	...	...	...	...	...
	TRANSPORT AND COMMUNICATIONS	–	–	...	...	...	...	...	...
	AGRICULTURE, FORESTRY & FISHERY	–	–	...	...	...	...	...	...
	OTHER AND NOT SPECIFIED	–	–	...	...	...	...	...	...
BANGLADESH‡ 1983	TOTAL	42 337	...	465	...	36 704	...	5 168	...
	EDUCATION SCIENCE & TEACHER TRNG.	3 098	...	–	–	2 993	...	105	...
	HUMANITIES, RELIGION & THEOLOGY	10 422	...	–	–	10 422	...	–	–
	FINE AND APPLIED ARTS	60	...	–	–	60	...	–	–
	LAW	2 612	...	–	–	2 473	...	139	...
	SOCIAL AND BEHAVIOURAL SCIENCE	6 994	...	–	–	4 215	...	2 779	...
	COMMERCIAL & BUSINESS ADMIN.	6 771	...	–	–	5 719	...	1 052	...
	MASS COMMUNICATION & DOCUMENT.	–	–	–	–	–	–	–	–
	HOME ECONOMICS (DOMESTIC SCIENCE)	./.	...	–	–	./.	...	./.	...
	SERVICE TRADES	–	–	–	–	–	–	–	–
	NATURAL SCIENCE	9 047	...	–	–	8 100	...	947	...
	MATHEMATICS & COMPUTER SCIENCE	./.	...	–	–	./.	...	./.	...
	MEDICAL SCIENCE & HEALTH-RELATED	1 662	...	–	–	1 636	...	26	...
	ENGINEERING	816	...	–	–	800	...	16	...
	ARCHITECTURE & TOWN PLANNING	–	–	–	–	–	–	–	–
	TRADE, CRAFT & INDUSTRIAL PGMS.	–	–	–	–	–	–	–	–
	TRANSPORT AND COMMUNICATIONS	–	–	–	–	–	–	–	–
	AGRICULTURE, FORESTRY & FISHERY	390	...	–	–	286	...	104	...
	OTHER AND NOT SPECIFIED	465	...	465	...	–	–	–	–
BHUTAN 1980	TOTAL	82	15	82	15	–	–	–	–
	EDUCATION SCIENCE & TEACHER TRNG.	48	15	48	15	–	–	–	–
	HUMANITIES, RELIGION & THEOLOGY	–	–	–	–	–	–	–	–
	FINE AND APPLIED ARTS	–	–	–	–	–	–	–	–
	LAW	–	–	–	–	–	–	–	–
	SOCIAL AND BEHAVIOURAL SCIENCE	–	–	–	–	–	–	–	–
	COMMERCIAL & BUSINESS ADMIN.	–	–	–	–	–	–	–	–
	MASS COMMUNICATION & DOCUMENT.	–	–	–	–	–	–	–	–
	HOME ECONOMICS (DOMESTIC SCIENCE)	–	–	–	–	–	–	–	–
	SERVICE TRADES	–	–	–	–	–	–	–	–
	NATURAL SCIENCE	–	–	–	–	–	–	–	–
	MATHEMATICS & COMPUTER SCIENCE	–	–	–	–	–	–	–	–
	MEDICAL SCIENCE & HEALTH-RELATED	–	–	–	–	–	–	–	–
	ENGINEERING	34	–	34	–	–	–	–	–
	ARCHITECTURE & TOWN PLANNING	–	–	–	–	–	–	–	–
	TRADE, CRAFT & INDUSTRIAL PGMS.	–	–	–	–	–	–	–	–
	TRANSPORT AND COMMUNICATIONS	–	–	–	–	–	–	–	–
	AGRICULTURE, FORESTRY & FISHERY	–	–	–	–	–	–	–	–
	OTHER AND NOT SPECIFIED	–	–	–	–	–	–	–	–

COUNTRY / YEAR PAYS / ANNEE PAIS / AÑO	FIELD OF STUDY DOMAINES D'ETUDES SECTORES DE ESTUDIOS	INTERNATIONAL STANDARD CLASSIFICATION OF EDUCATION BY LEVEL / CLASSIFICATION INTERNATIONALE TYPE DE L'EDUCATION PAR NIVEAU / CLASIFICACION INTERNACIONAL NORMALIZADA DE LA EDUCACION POR NIVEL							
		ALL LEVELS TOUS NIVEAUX TODOS LOS NIVELES		LEVEL 5 NIVEAU 5 NIVEL 5		LEVEL 6 NIVEAU 6 NIVEL 6		LEVEL 7 NIVEAU 7 NIVEL 7	
		MF	F	MF	F	MF	F	MF	F
		(1)	(2)	(3)	(4)	(5)	(6)	(7)	(8)
BRUNEI DARUSSALAM 1983	TOTAL	194	90	194	90	–	–	–	–
	EDUCATION SCIENCE & TEACHER TRNG.	194	90	194	90	–	–	–	–
	HUMANITIES, RELIGION & THEOLOGY	–	–	–	–	–	–	–	–
	FINE AND APPLIED ARTS	–	–	–	–	–	–	–	–
	LAW	–	–	–	–	–	–	–	–
	SOCIAL AND BEHAVIOURAL SCIENCE	–	–	–	–	–	–	–	–
	COMMERCIAL & BUSINESS ADMIN.	–	–	–	–	–	–	–	–
	MASS COMMUNICATION & DOCUMENT.	–	–	–	–	–	–	–	–
	HOME ECONOMICS (DOMESTIC SCIENCE)	–	–	–	–	–	–	–	–
	SERVICE TRADES	–	–	–	–	–	–	–	–
	NATURAL SCIENCE	–	–	–	–	–	–	–	–
	MATHEMATICS & COMPUTER SCIENCE	–	–	–	–	–	–	–	–
	MEDICAL SCIENCE & HEALTH-RELATED	–	–	–	–	–	–	–	–
	ENGINEERING	–	–	–	–	–	–	–	–
	ARCHITECTURE & TOWN PLANNING	–	–	–	–	–	–	–	–
	TRADE, CRAFT & INDUSTRIAL PGMS.	–	–	–	–	–	–	–	–
	TRANSPORT AND COMMUNICATIONS	–	–	–	–	–	–	–	–
	AGRICULTURE, FORESTRY & FISHERY	–	–	–	–	–	–	–	–
	OTHER AND NOT SPECIFIED	–	–	–	–	–	–	–	–
BURMA 1978	TOTAL	23 141	...	–	–	22 266	...	875	...
	EDUCATION SCIENCE & TEACHER TRNG.	954	...	–	–	453	...	501	...
	HUMANITIES, RELIGION & THEOLOGY	3 188	...	–	–	3 108	...	80	...
	FINE AND APPLIED ARTS	–	–	–	–	–	–	–	–
	LAW	272	...	–	–	265	...	7	...
	SOCIAL AND BEHAVIOURAL SCIENCE	2 657	...	–	–	2 625	...	32	...
	COMMERCIAL & BUSINESS ADMIN.	554	...	–	–	544	...	10	...
	MASS COMMUNICATION & DOCUMENT.	20	...	–	–	–	–	20	...
	HOME ECONOMICS (DOMESTIC SCIENCE)	–	–	–	–	–	–	–	–
	SERVICE TRADES	–	–	–	–	–	–	–	–
	NATURAL SCIENCE	11 600	...	–	–	11 445	...	155	...
	MATHEMATICS & COMPUTER SCIENCE	2 265	...	–	–	2 243	...	22	...
	MEDICAL SCIENCE & HEALTH-RELATED	614	...	–	–	591	...	23	...
	ENGINEERING	575	...	–	–	566	...	9	...
	ARCHITECTURE & TOWN PLANNING	13	...	–	–	13	...	–	–
	TRADE, CRAFT & INDUSTRIAL PGMS.	–	–	–	–	–	–	–	–
	TRANSPORT AND COMMUNICATIONS	–	–	–	–	–	–	–	–
	AGRICULTURE, FORESTRY & FISHERY	429	...	–	–	413	...	16	...
	OTHER AND NOT SPECIFIED	–	–	–	–	–	–	–	–
CHINA‡ 1984	TOTAL	289 241	...	82 689	...	204 248	...	2 304	...
	EDUCATION SCIENCE & TEACHER TRNG.	84 842	...	50 946	...	33 875	...	21	...
	HUMANITIES, RELIGION & THEOLOGY	14 596	...	1 972	...	12 442	...	182	...
	FINE AND APPLIED ARTS	1 343	...	182	...	1 152	...	9	...
	LAW	3 163	...	575	...	2 528	...	60	...
	SOCIAL AND BEHAVIOURAL SCIENCE	./.	...	./.	...	./.	...	./.	...
	COMMERCIAL & BUSINESS ADMIN.	15 036	...	4 580	...	10 396	...	60	...
	MASS COMMUNICATION & DOCUMENT.	–	–	–	–	–	–	–	–
	HOME ECONOMICS (DOMESTIC SCIENCE)	–	–	–	–	–	–	–	–
	SERVICE TRADES	–	–	–	–	–	–	–	–
	NATURAL SCIENCE	16 433	...	346	...	15 856	...	231	...
	MATHEMATICS & COMPUTER SCIENCE	5 178	...	370	...	4 610	...	198	...
	MEDICAL SCIENCE & HEALTH-RELATED	32 257	...	6 496	...	25 403	...	358	...
	ENGINEERING	90 917	...	12 518	...	77 388	...	1 011	...
	ARCHITECTURE & TOWN PLANNING	855	...	28	...	811	...	16	...
	TRADE, CRAFT & INDUSTRIAL PGMS.	–	–	–	–	–	–	–	–
	TRANSPORT AND COMMUNICATIONS	3 631	...	809	...	2 717	...	105	...
	AGRICULTURE, FORESTRY & FISHERY	18 569	...	3 501	...	15 015	...	53	...
	OTHER AND NOT SPECIFIED	2 421	...	366	...	2 055	...	–	–

3.14 Third level: graduates by ISCED level and field of study
Troisième degré: diplômés par niveau de la CITE et domaine d'études
Tercer grado: diplomados por nivel de la CINE y sector de estudios

COUNTRY / YEAR PAYS / ANNEE PAIS / AÑO	FIELD OF STUDY DOMAINES D'ETUDES SECTORES DE ESTUDIOS	INTERNATIONAL STANDARD CLASSIFICATION OF EDUCATION BY LEVEL / CLASSIFICATION INTERNATIONALE TYPE DE L'EDUCATION PAR NIVEAU / CLASIFICACION INTERNACIONAL NORMALIZADA DE LA EDUCACION POR NIVEL							
		ALL LEVELS / TOUS NIVEAUX / TODOS LOS NIVELES		LEVEL 5 / NIVEAU 5 / NIVEL 5		LEVEL 6 / NIVEAU 6 / NIVEL 6		LEVEL 7 / NIVEAU 7 / NIVEL 7	
		MF	F	MF	F	MF	F	MF	F
		(1)	(2)	(3)	(4)	(5)	(6)	(7)	(8)
CYPRUS 1983	TOTAL	797	350	797	350	–	–	–	–
	EDUCATION SCIENCE & TEACHER TRNG.	25	25	25	25	–	–	–	–
	HUMANITIES, RELIGION & THEOLOGY	–	–	–	–	–	–	–	–
	FINE AND APPLIED ARTS	–	–	–	–	–	–	–	–
	LAW	–	–	–	–	–	–	–	–
	SOCIAL AND BEHAVIOURAL SCIENCE	–	–	–	–	–	–	–	–
	COMMERCIAL & BUSINESS ADMIN.	196	122	196	122	–	–	–	–
	MASS COMMUNICATION & DOCUMENT.	–	–	–	–	–	–	–	–
	HOME ECONOMICS (DOMESTIC SCIENCE)	–	–	–	–	–	–	–	–
	SERVICE TRADES	110	42	110	42	–	–	–	–
	NATURAL SCIENCE	–	–	–	–	–	–	–	–
	MATHEMATICS & COMPUTER SCIENCE	–	–	–	–	–	–	–	–
	MEDICAL SCIENCE & HEALTH-RELATED	75	63	75	63	–	–	–	–
	ENGINEERING	137	44	137	44	–	–	–	–
	ARCHITECTURE & TOWN PLANNING	–	–	–	–	–	–	–	–
	TRADE, CRAFT & INDUSTRIAL PGMS.	221	49	221	49	–	–	–	–
	TRANSPORT AND COMMUNICATIONS	11	5	11	5	–	–	–	–
	AGRICULTURE, FORESTRY & FISHERY	22	–	22	–	–	–	–	–
	OTHER AND NOT SPECIFIED	–	–	–	–	–	–	–	–
DEMOCRATIC YEMEN 1981	TOTAL	743	324	...	...	...	...	...	...
	EDUCATION SCIENCE & TEACHER TRNG.	53	29	...	...	...	...	...	...
	HUMANITIES, RELIGION & THEOLOGY	239	143	...	...	...	...	...	...
	FINE AND APPLIED ARTS	–	–	...	...	...	...	...	...
	LAW	52	16	...	...	...	...	...	...
	SOCIAL AND BEHAVIOURAL SCIENCE	248	93	...	...	...	...	...	...
	COMMERCIAL & BUSINESS ADMIN.	–	–	...	...	...	...	...	...
	MASS COMMUNICATION & DOCUMENT.	–	–	...	...	...	...	...	...
	HOME ECONOMICS (DOMESTIC SCIENCE)	–	–	...	...	...	...	...	...
	SERVICE TRADES	–	–	...	...	...	...	...	...
	NATURAL SCIENCE	–	–	...	...	...	...	...	...
	MATHEMATICS & COMPUTER SCIENCE	–	–	...	...	...	...	...	...
	MEDICAL SCIENCE & HEALTH-RELATED	52	14	...	...	...	...	...	...
	ENGINEERING	62	16	...	...	...	...	...	...
	ARCHITECTURE & TOWN PLANNING	–	–	...	...	...	...	...	...
	TRADE, CRAFT & INDUSTRIAL PGMS.	–	–	...	...	...	...	...	...
	TRANSPORT AND COMMUNICATIONS	–	–	...	...	...	...	...	...
	AGRICULTURE, FORESTRY & FISHERY	37	13	...	...	...	...	...	...
	OTHER AND NOT SPECIFIED	–	–	...	...	...	...	...	...
HONG KONG 1984	TOTAL	20 004	7 302	15 322	5 579	3 405	1 245	1 277	478
	EDUCATION SCIENCE & TEACHER TRNG.	2 621	1 511	1 927	1 218	–	–	694	293
	HUMANITIES, RELIGION & THEOLOGY	840	557	161	105	609	419	70	33
	FINE AND APPLIED ARTS	479	199	454	183	23	14	2	2
	LAW	155	74	–	–	73	37	82	37
	SOCIAL AND BEHAVIOURAL SCIENCE	783	403	157	74	536	279	90	50
	COMMERCIAL & BUSINESS ADMIN.	5 042	3 077	4 258	2 804	628	239	156	34
	MASS COMMUNICATION & DOCUMENT.	85	57	59	43	26	14	–	–
	HOME ECONOMICS (DOMESTIC SCIENCE)	–	–	–	–	–	–	–	–
	SERVICE TRADES	332	142	332	142	–	–	–	–
	NATURAL SCIENCE	495	108	320	80	153	23	22	5
	MATHEMATICS & COMPUTER SCIENCE	780	251	439	155	316	92	25	4
	MEDICAL SCIENCE & HEALTH-RELATED	566	221	237	130	321	89	8	2
	ENGINEERING	5 894	133	5 219	105	610	27	65	1
	ARCHITECTURE & TOWN PLANNING	616	100	497	73	56	10	63	17
	TRADE, CRAFT & INDUSTRIAL PGMS.	1 004	306	970	304	34	2	–	–
	TRANSPORT AND COMMUNICATIONS	–	–	–	–	–	–	–	–
	AGRICULTURE, FORESTRY & FISHERY	–	–	–	–	–	–	–	–
	OTHER AND NOT SPECIFIED	312	163	292	163	20	–	–	–

COUNTRY / YEAR — PAYS / ANNEE — PAIS / AÑO	FIELD OF STUDY — DOMAINES D'ETUDES — SECTORES DE ESTUDIOS	INTERNATIONAL STANDARD CLASSIFICATION OF EDUCATION BY LEVEL / CLASSIFICATION INTERNATIONALE TYPE DE L'EDUCATION PAR NIVEAU / CLASIFICACION INTERNACIONAL NORMALIZADA DE LA EDUCACION POR NIVEL							
		ALL LEVELS / TOUS NIVEAUX / TODOS LOS NIVELES		LEVEL 5 / NIVEAU 5 / NIVEL 5		LEVEL 6 / NIVEAU 6 / NIVEL 6		LEVEL 7 / NIVEAU 7 / NIVEL 7	
		MF	F	MF	F	MF	F	MF	F
		(1)	(2)	(3)	(4)	(5)	(6)	(7)	(8)
INDIA‡									
1978	TOTAL	1 095 682	...	291 481	...	675 478	...	128 723	...
	EDUCATION SCIENCE & TEACHER TRNG.	108 898	...	42 796	...	63 702	...	2 400	...
	HUMANITIES, RELIGION & THEOLOGY	18 306	...	14 555	...	2 691	...	1 060	...
	FINE AND APPLIED ARTS	581	...	–	–	283	...	298	...
	LAW	36 664	...	–	–	36 291	...	373	...
	SOCIAL AND BEHAVIOURAL SCIENCE	501 349	...	96 413	...	320 109	...	84 827	...
	COMMERCIAL & BUSINESS ADMIN.	149 910	...	24 220	...	111 354	...	14 336	...
	MASS COMMUNICATION & DOCUMENT.	1 692	...	–	–	1 487	...	205	...
	HOME ECONOMICS (DOMESTIC SCIENCE)	3 073	...	–	–	2 566	...	507	...
	SERVICE TRADES	–	–	–	–	–	–	–	–
	NATURAL SCIENCE	165 263	...	49 719	...	98 736	...	16 808	...
	MATHEMATICS & COMPUTER SCIENCE	./.	...	./.	...	./.	...	./.	...
	MEDICAL SCIENCE & HEALTH-RELATED	21 020	...	2 400	...	15 260	...	3 360	...
	ENGINEERING	27 889	...	13 815	...	13 054	...	1 020	...
	ARCHITECTURE & TOWN PLANNING	./.	...	./.	...	./.	...	./.	...
	TRADE, CRAFT & INDUSTRIAL PGMS.	./.	...	./.	...	./.	...	./.	...
	TRANSPORT AND COMMUNICATIONS	./.	...	./.	...	./.	...	./.	...
	AGRICULTURE, FORESTRY & FISHERY	11 714	...	999	...	7 892	...	2 823	...
	OTHER AND NOT SPECIFIED	49 323	...	46 564	...	2 053	...	706	...
INDONESIA									
1984	TOTAL	73 627	24 907	16 178	7 553	31 224	9 067	26 225	8 287
	EDUCATION SCIENCE & TEACHER TRNG.	30 000	12 459	12 923	6 794	7 858	2 572	9 219	3 093
	HUMANITIES, RELIGION & THEOLOGY	1 711	456	122	52	1 024	209	565	195
	FINE AND APPLIED ARTS	87	22	–	–	35	13	52	9
	LAW	7 531	1 763	12	1	4 407	846	3 112	916
	SOCIAL AND BEHAVIOURAL SCIENCE	13 616	4 091	165	54	7 917	2 363	5 534	1 674
	COMMERCIAL & BUSINESS ADMIN.	7 199	2 634	935	384	5 563	2 098	701	152
	MASS COMMUNICATION & DOCUMENT.	307	84	–	–	268	71	39	13
	HOME ECONOMICS (DOMESTIC SCIENCE)	138	125	–	–	138	125	–	–
	SERVICE TRADES	152	62	34	13	118	49	–	–
	NATURAL SCIENCE	913	287	–	–	147	37	766	250
	MATHEMATICS & COMPUTER SCIENCE	140	46	27	13	7	4	106	29
	MEDICAL SCIENCE & HEALTH-RELATED	2 385	624	42	25	911	168	1 432	431
	ENGINEERING	4 495	977	1 275	137	1 408	203	1 812	637
	ARCHITECTURE & TOWN PLANNING	505	104	26	5	122	22	357	77
	TRADE, CRAFT & INDUSTRIAL PGMS.	54	11	37	11	17	–	–	–
	TRANSPORT AND COMMUNICATIONS	6	–	–	–	6	–	–	–
	AGRICULTURE, FORESTRY & FISHERY	4 264	1 133	580	64	1 188	269	2 496	800
	OTHER AND NOT SPECIFIED	124	29	–	–	90	18	34	11
IRAN, ISLAMIC REPUBLIC OF‡									
1983	TOTAL	12 831	3 750	5 011	1 288	6 565	2 095	1 255	367
	EDUCATION SCIENCE & TEACHER TRNG.	489	131	33	21	450	106	6	4
	HUMANITIES, RELIGION & THEOLOGY	1 100	514	46	13	1 020	491	34	10
	FINE AND APPLIED ARTS	25	7	13	4	8	2	4	1
	LAW	96	23	4	2	86	21	6	–
	SOCIAL AND BEHAVIOURAL SCIENCE	885	372	39	22	836	346	10	4
	COMMERCIAL & BUSINESS ADMIN.	1 009	300	679	204	228	80	102	16
	MASS COMMUNICATION & DOCUMENT.	43	26	1	–	40	24	2	2
	HOME ECONOMICS (DOMESTIC SCIENCE)	39	30	–	–	38	29	1	1
	SERVICE TRADES	7	3	7	3	–	–	–	–
	NATURAL SCIENCE	785	247	121	41	660	205	4	1
	MATHEMATICS & COMPUTER SCIENCE	313	70	67	29	238	40	8	1
	MEDICAL SCIENCE & HEALTH-RELATED	2 751	1 626	976	794	760	514	1 015	318
	ENGINEERING	4 133	153	2 605	75	1 519	78	9	–
	ARCHITECTURE & TOWN PLANNING	266	80	238	74	27	6	1	–
	TRADE, CRAFT & INDUSTRIAL PGMS.	87	3	63	1	23	2	1	–
	TRANSPORT AND COMMUNICATIONS	–	–	–	–	–	–	–	–
	AGRICULTURE, FORESTRY & FISHERY	700	119	116	5	532	105	52	9
	OTHER AND NOT SPECIFIED	103	46	3	–	100	46	–	–

3.14 Third level: graduates by ISCED level and field of study
Troisième degré: diplômés par niveau de la CITE et domaine d'études
Tercer grado: diplomados por nivel de la CINE y sector de estudios

COUNTRY / YEAR PAYS / ANNEE PAIS / AÑO	FIELD OF STUDY DOMAINES D'ETUDES SECTORES DE ESTUDIOS	INTERNATIONAL STANDARD CLASSIFICATION OF EDUCATION BY LEVEL / CLASSIFICATION INTERNATIONALE TYPE DE L'EDUCATION PAR NIVEAU / CLASIFICACION INTERNACIONAL NORMALIZADA DE LA EDUCACION POR NIVEL							
		ALL LEVELS TOUS NIVEAUX TODOS LOS NIVELES		LEVEL 5 NIVEAU 5 NIVEL 5		LEVEL 6 NIVEAU 6 NIVEL 6		LEVEL 7 NIVEAU 7 NIVEL 7	
		MF	F	MF	F	MF	F	MF	F
		(1)	(2)	(3)	(4)	(5)	(6)	(7)	(8)
ISRAEL‡ 1984	TOTAL	11 218	5 443	–	–	8 113	3 977	3 105	1 466
	EDUCATION SCIENCE & TEACHER TRNG.	3 312	2 392	–	–	2 281	1 653	1 031	739
	HUMANITIES, RELIGION & THEOLOGY	./.	./.	–	–	./.	./.	./.	./.
	FINE AND APPLIED ARTS	./.	./.	–	–	./.	./.	./.	./.
	LAW	505	194	–	–	489	190	16	4
	SOCIAL AND BEHAVIOURAL SCIENCE	2 879	1 318	–	–	2 260	1 074	619	244
	COMMERCIAL & BUSINESS ADMIN.	./.	./.	–	–	./.	./.	./.	./.
	MASS COMMUNICATION & DOCUMENT.	./.	./.	–	–	./.	./.	./.	./.
	HOME ECONOMICS (DOMESTIC SCIENCE)	./.	./.	–	–	./.	./.	./.	./.
	SERVICE TRADES	./.	./.	–	–	./.	./.	./.	./.
	NATURAL SCIENCE	1 066	553	–	–	556	313	510	240
	MATHEMATICS & COMPUTER SCIENCE	750	278	–	–	656	244	94	34
	MEDICAL SCIENCE & HEALTH-RELATED	822	381	–	–	380	248	442	133
	ENGINEERING	1 485	178	–	–	1 174	132	311	46
	ARCHITECTURE & TOWN PLANNING	./.	./.	–	–	./.	./.	./.	./.
	TRADE, CRAFT & INDUSTRIAL PGMS.	./.	./.	–	–	./.	./.	./.	./.
	TRANSPORT AND COMMUNICATIONS	./.	./.	–	–	./.	./.	./.	./.
	AGRICULTURE, FORESTRY & FISHERY	399	149	–	–	317	123	82	26
	OTHER AND NOT SPECIFIED	–	–	–	–	–	–	–	–
JAPAN‡ 1983	TOTAL	576 487	254 515	181 561	159 797	374 408	92 333	20 518	2 385
	EDUCATION SCIENCE & TEACHER TRNG.	66 985	54 719	39 446	39 181	26 508	15 208	1 031	330
	HUMANITIES, RELIGION & THEOLOGY	94 922	72 390	38 721	38 208	54 207	33 518	1 994	664
	FINE AND APPLIED ARTS	19 814	15 635	9 152	8 624	10 107	6 749	555	262
	LAW	./.	./.	./.	./.	./.	./.	./.	./.
	SOCIAL AND BEHAVIOURAL SCIENCE	166 123	24 308	14 220	10 590	150 270	13 509	1 633	209
	COMMERCIAL & BUSINESS ADMIN.	./.	./.	./.	./.	./.	./.	./.	./.
	MASS COMMUNICATION & DOCUMENT.	./.	./.	./.	./.	./.	./.	./.	./.
	HOME ECONOMICS (DOMESTIC SCIENCE)	55 715	55 607	47 942	47 901	7 666	7 608	107	98
	SERVICE TRADES	–	–	–	–	–	–	–	–
	NATURAL SCIENCE	10 958	1 591	–	–	9 054	1 453	1 904	138
	MATHEMATICS & COMPUTER SCIENCE	3 580	819	115	112	3 180	682	285	25
	MEDICAL SCIENCE & HEALTH-RELATED	29 091	13 740	6 769	6 192	20 408	7 317	1 914	231
	ENGINEERING	94 967	2 983	14 587	1 362	71 640	1 506	8 740	115
	ARCHITECTURE & TOWN PLANNING	./.	./.	./.	./.	./.	./.	./.	./.
	TRADE, CRAFT & INDUSTRIAL PGMS.	./.	./.	./.	./.	./.	./.	./.	./.
	TRANSPORT AND COMMUNICATIONS	617	5	300	–	304	5	13	–
	AGRICULTURE, FORESTRY & FISHERY	16 138	2 501	1 490	374	12 545	1 846	2 103	281
	OTHER AND NOT SPECIFIED	17 577	10 217	8 819	7 253	8 519	2 932	239	32
JORDAN‡ 1983	TOTAL	4 118	1 538	17	13	3 695	1 465	406	60
	EDUCATION SCIENCE & TEACHER TRNG.	539	187	–	–	235	141	304	46
	HUMANITIES, RELIGION & THEOLOGY	1 276	675	–	–	1 237	669	39	6
	FINE AND APPLIED ARTS	–	–	–	–	–	–	–	–
	LAW	88	20	–	–	83	20	5	–
	SOCIAL AND BEHAVIOURAL SCIENCE	./.	./.	–	–	./.	./.	./.	./.
	COMMERCIAL & BUSINESS ADMIN.	1 003	229	–	–	996	228	7	1
	MASS COMMUNICATION & DOCUMENT.	./.	./.	–	–	./.	./.	./.	./.
	HOME ECONOMICS (DOMESTIC SCIENCE)	–	–	–	–	–	–	–	–
	SERVICE TRADES	–	–	–	–	–	–	–	–
	NATURAL SCIENCE	664	288	17	13	633	273	14	2
	MATHEMATICS & COMPUTER SCIENCE	./.	./.	./.	./.	./.	./.	./.	./.
	MEDICAL SCIENCE & HEALTH-RELATED	115	47	–	–	100	44	15	3
	ENGINEERING	271	38	–	–	261	38	10	–
	ARCHITECTURE & TOWN PLANNING	./.	./.	–	–	./.	./.	./.	–
	TRADE, CRAFT & INDUSTRIAL PGMS.	–	–	–	–	–	–	–	–
	TRANSPORT AND COMMUNICATIONS	–	–	–	–	–	–	–	–
	AGRICULTURE, FORESTRY & FISHERY	106	45	–	–	94	43	12	2
	OTHER AND NOT SPECIFIED	56	9	–	–	56	9	–	–

COUNTRY / YEAR — PAYS / ANNEE — PAIS / AÑO	FIELD OF STUDY — DOMAINES D'ETUDES — SECTORES DE ESTUDIOS	INTERNATIONAL STANDARD CLASSIFICATION OF EDUCATION BY LEVEL / CLASSIFICATION INTERNATIONALE TYPE DE L'EDUCATION PAR NIVEAU / CLASIFICACION INTERNACIONAL NORMALIZADA DE LA EDUCACION POR NIVEL							
		ALL LEVELS / TOUS NIVEAUX / TODOS LOS NIVELES		LEVEL 5 / NIVEAU 5 / NIVEL 5		LEVEL 6 / NIVEAU 6 / NIVEL 6		LEVEL 7 / NIVEAU 7 / NIVEL 7	
		MF	F	MF	F	MF	F	MF	F
		(1)	(2)	(3)	(4)	(5)	(6)	(7)	(8)
KOREA, REPUBLIC OF									
1983	TOTAL	171 926	53 727	80 674	27 885	78 038	23 369	13 214	2 473
	EDUCATION SCIENCE & TEACHER TRNG.	20 939	13 235	6 285	5 819	12 351	6 939	2 303	477
	HUMANITIES, RELIGION & THEOLOGY	11 077	4 874	1 109	593	8 337	3 679	1 631	602
	FINE AND APPLIED ARTS	11 049	8 681	5 899	4 507	4 617	3 810	533	364
	LAW	2 138	109	321	35	1 817	74	–	–
	SOCIAL AND BEHAVIOURAL SCIENCE	8 421	1 780	1 782	969	4 083	662	2 556	149
	COMMERCIAL & BUSINESS ADMIN.	15 502	3 459	8 289	2 485	7 213	974	–	–
	MASS COMMUNICATION & DOCUMENT.	1 386	974	875	747	511	227	–	–
	HOME ECONOMICS (DOMESTIC SCIENCE)	4 706	4 356	2 681	2 348	2 025	2 008	–	–
	SERVICE TRADES	83	8	83	8	–	–	–	–
	NATURAL SCIENCE	6 093	3 405	1 636	1 636	3 150	1 343	1 307	426
	MATHEMATICS & COMPUTER SCIENCE	1 616	667	–	–	1 616	667	–	–
	MEDICAL SCIENCE & HEALTH-RELATED	13 042	6 815	7 381	4 894	3 861	1 581	1 800	340
	ENGINEERING	56 963	2 265	34 176	2 029	20 395	201	2 392	35
	ARCHITECTURE & TOWN PLANNING	399	55	14	–	385	55	–	–
	TRADE, CRAFT & INDUSTRIAL PGMS.	4 100	591	1 925	381	2 175	210	–	–
	TRANSPORT AND COMMUNICATIONS	1 822	265	1 738	264	84	1	–	–
	AGRICULTURE, FORESTRY & FISHERY	10 722	1 617	5 613	984	4 603	591	506	42
	OTHER AND NOT SPECIFIED	1 868	571	867	186	815	347	186	38
KUWAIT‡									
1984	TOTAL	3 715	2 174	1 920	1 065	1 795	1 109	–	–
	EDUCATION SCIENCE & TEACHER TRNG.	345	249	281	211	64	38	–	–
	HUMANITIES, RELIGION & THEOLOGY	250	188	–	–	250	188	–	–
	FINE AND APPLIED ARTS	103	58	103	58	–	–	–	–
	LAW	126	49	–	–	126	49	–	–
	SOCIAL AND BEHAVIOURAL SCIENCE	551	368	–	–	551	368	–	–
	COMMERCIAL & BUSINESS ADMIN.	754	454	507	328	247	126	–	–
	MASS COMMUNICATION & DOCUMENT.	–	–	–	–	–	–	–	–
	HOME ECONOMICS (DOMESTIC SCIENCE)	61	61	61	61	–	–	–	–
	SERVICE TRADES	–	–	–	–	–	–	–	–
	NATURAL SCIENCE	229	155	96	50	133	105	–	–
	MATHEMATICS & COMPUTER SCIENCE	202	123	81	33	121	90	–	–
	MEDICAL SCIENCE & HEALTH-RELATED	237	162	143	98	94	64	–	–
	ENGINEERING	373	101	164	20	209	81	–	–
	ARCHITECTURE & TOWN PLANNING	–	–	–	–	–	–	–	–
	TRADE, CRAFT & INDUSTRIAL PGMS.	./.	./.	./.	./.	./.	./.	–	–
	TRANSPORT AND COMMUNICATIONS	–	–	–	–	–	–	–	–
	AGRICULTURE, FORESTRY & FISHERY	–	–	–	–	–	–	–	–
	OTHER AND NOT SPECIFIED	484	206	484	206	–	–	–	–
LAO PEOPLE'S DEMOCRATIC REPUBLIC									
1983	TOTAL	1 021	...	619	...	402	...	–	–
	EDUCATION SCIENCE & TEACHER TRNG.	717	...	419	...	298	...	–	–
	HUMANITIES, RELIGION & THEOLOGY	–	–	–	–	–	–	–	–
	FINE AND APPLIED ARTS	–	–	–	–	–	–	–	–
	LAW	–	–	–	–	–	–	–	–
	SOCIAL AND BEHAVIOURAL SCIENCE	–	–	–	–	–	–	–	–
	COMMERCIAL & BUSINESS ADMIN.	–	–	–	–	–	–	–	–
	MASS COMMUNICATION & DOCUMENT.	–	–	–	–	–	–	–	–
	HOME ECONOMICS (DOMESTIC SCIENCE)	–	–	–	–	–	–	–	–
	SERVICE TRADES	–	–	–	–	–	–	–	–
	NATURAL SCIENCE	–	–	–	–	–	–	–	–
	MATHEMATICS & COMPUTER SCIENCE	–	–	–	–	–	–	–	–
	MEDICAL SCIENCE & HEALTH-RELATED	104	...	–	–	104	...	–	–
	ENGINEERING	–	–	–	–	–	–	–	–
	ARCHITECTURE & TOWN PLANNING	200	...	200	...	–	–	–	–
	TRADE, CRAFT & INDUSTRIAL PGMS.	–	–	–	–	–	–	–	–
	TRANSPORT AND COMMUNICATIONS	–	–	–	–	–	–	–	–
	AGRICULTURE, FORESTRY & FISHERY	–	–	–	–	–	–	–	–
	OTHER AND NOT SPECIFIED	–	–	–	–	–	–	–	–

3.14 Third level: graduates by ISCED level and field of study
Troisième degré: diplômés par niveau de la CITE et domaine d'études
Tercer grado: diplomados por nivel de la CINE y sector de estudios

COUNTRY / YEAR PAYS / ANNEE PAIS / AÑO	FIELD OF STUDY DOMAINES D'ETUDES SECTORES DE ESTUDIOS	INTERNATIONAL STANDARD CLASSIFICATION OF EDUCATION BY LEVEL / CLASSIFICATION INTERNATIONALE TYPE DE L'EDUCATION PAR NIVEAU / CLASIFICACION INTERNACIONAL NORMALIZADA DE LA EDUCACION POR NIVEL							
		ALL LEVELS / TOUS NIVEAUX / TODOS LOS NIVELES		LEVEL 5 / NIVEAU 5 / NIVEL 5		LEVEL 6 / NIVEAU 6 / NIVEL 6		LEVEL 7 / NIVEAU 7 / NIVEL 7	
		MF	F	MF	F	MF	F	MF	F
		(1)	(2)	(3)	(4)	(5)	(6)	(7)	(8)
LEBANON 1982	TOTAL	6 662	2 834	199	99	6 097	2 603	366	132
	EDUCATION SCIENCE & TEACHER TRNG.	79	62	1	1	34	28	44	33
	HUMANITIES, RELIGION & THEOLOGY	1 458	767	6	5	1 452	762	–	–
	FINE AND APPLIED ARTS	149	77	–	–	149	77	–	–
	LAW	624	191	–	–	599	185	25	6
	SOCIAL AND BEHAVIOURAL SCIENCE	946	460	–	–	907	446	39	14
	COMMERCIAL & BUSINESS ADMIN.	1 311	502	95	38	1 195	460	21	4
	MASS COMMUNICATION & DOCUMENT.	143	95	10	10	133	85	–	–
	HOME ECONOMICS (DOMESTIC SCIENCE)	–	–	–	–	–	–	–	–
	SERVICE TRADES	–	–	–	–	–	–	–	–
	NATURAL SCIENCE	452	178	–	–	435	170	17	8
	MATHEMATICS & COMPUTER SCIENCE	138	63	8	5	117	55	13	3
	MEDICAL SCIENCE & HEALTH-RELATED	498	328	24	20	267	244	207	64
	ENGINEERING	528	24	–	–	528	24	–	–
	ARCHITECTURE & TOWN PLANNING	171	27	–	–	171	27	–	–
	TRADE, CRAFT & INDUSTRIAL PGMS.	–	–	–	–	–	–	–	–
	TRANSPORT AND COMMUNICATIONS	–	–	–	–	–	–	–	–
	AGRICULTURE, FORESTRY & FISHERY	160	60	50	20	110	40	–	–
	OTHER AND NOT SPECIFIED	5	–	5	–	–	–	–	–
MALAYSIA 1984	TOTAL	24 853	11 823	17 988	8 863	6 806	2 950	59	10
	EDUCATION SCIENCE & TEACHER TRNG.	8 399	5 474	7 663	5 015	735	459	1	–
	HUMANITIES, RELIGION & THEOLOGY	1 336	705	188	69	1 143	636	5	–
	FINE AND APPLIED ARTS	140	51	140	51	–	–	–	–
	LAW	160	87	44	21	116	66	–	–
	SOCIAL AND BEHAVIOURAL SCIENCE	1 712	800	437	203	1 273	597	2	–
	COMMERCIAL & BUSINESS ADMIN.	2 488	1 184	2 118	1 029	354	152	16	3
	MASS COMMUNICATION & DOCUMENT.	126	107	126	107	–	–	–	–
	HOME ECONOMICS (DOMESTIC SCIENCE)	91	44	70	40	21	4	–	–
	SERVICE TRADES	796	542	762	519	34	23	–	–
	NATURAL SCIENCE	1 778	797	813	436	948	358	17	3
	MATHEMATICS & COMPUTER SCIENCE	468	205	315	142	145	59	8	4
	MEDICAL SCIENCE & HEALTH-RELATED	1 148	491	61	26	1 087	465	–	–
	ENGINEERING	2 830	402	2 325	355	505	47	–	–
	ARCHITECTURE & TOWN PLANNING	416	115	282	90	127	25	7	–
	TRADE, CRAFT & INDUSTRIAL PGMS.	788	164	788	164	–	–	–	–
	TRANSPORT AND COMMUNICATIONS	49	28	–	–	49	28	–	–
	AGRICULTURE, FORESTRY & FISHERY	868	88	596	57	269	31	3	–
	OTHER AND NOT SPECIFIED	1 260	539	1 260	539	–	–	–	–
MONGOLIA 1981	TOTAL	8 000	...	...	...	...	...	...	...
	EDUCATION SCIENCE & TEACHER TRNG.	800	...	...	...	...	...	...	...
	HUMANITIES, RELIGION & THEOLOGY	400	...	...	...	...	...	...	...
	FINE AND APPLIED ARTS	200	...	...	...	...	...	...	...
	LAW	200	...	...	...	...	...	...	...
	SOCIAL AND BEHAVIOURAL SCIENCE	300	...	...	...	...	...	...	...
	COMMERCIAL & BUSINESS ADMIN.	1 300	...	...	...	...	...	...	...
	MASS COMMUNICATION & DOCUMENT.	–	–	...	...	...	...	...	...
	HOME ECONOMICS (DOMESTIC SCIENCE)	–	–	...	...	...	...	...	...
	SERVICE TRADES	100	...	...	...	...	...	...	...
	NATURAL SCIENCE	300	...	...	...	...	...	...	...
	MATHEMATICS & COMPUTER SCIENCE	100	...	...	...	...	...	...	...
	MEDICAL SCIENCE & HEALTH-RELATED	1 300	...	...	...	...	...	...	...
	ENGINEERING	600	...	...	...	...	...	...	...
	ARCHITECTURE & TOWN PLANNING	600	...	...	...	...	...	...	...
	TRADE, CRAFT & INDUSTRIAL PGMS.	–	–	...	...	...	...	...	...
	TRANSPORT AND COMMUNICATIONS	600	...	...	...	...	...	...	...
	AGRICULTURE, FORESTRY & FISHERY	1 200	...	...	...	...	...	...	...
	OTHER AND NOT SPECIFIED	–	–	...	...	...	...	...	...

COUNTRY / YEAR PAYS / ANNEE PAIS / AÑO	FIELD OF STUDY DOMAINES D'ETUDES SECTORES DE ESTUDIOS	INTERNATIONAL STANDARD CLASSIFICATION OF EDUCATION BY LEVEL / CLASSIFICATION INTERNATIONALE TYPE DE L'EDUCATION PAR NIVEAU / CLASIFICACION INTERNACIONAL NORMALIZADA DE LA EDUCACION POR NIVEL							
		ALL LEVELS TOUS NIVEAUX TODOS LOS NIVELES		LEVEL 5 NIVEAU 5 NIVEL 5		LEVEL 6 NIVEAU 6 NIVEL 6		LEVEL 7 NIVEAU 7 NIVEL 7	
		MF	F	MF	F	MF	F	MF	F
		(1)	(2)	(3)	(4)	(5)	(6)	(7)	(8)
NEPAL‡									
1983	TOTAL	3 142	...	2 227	...	639	...	276	...
	EDUCATION SCIENCE & TEACHER TRNG.	31	...	31	...	–	–	–	–
	HUMANITIES, RELIGION & THEOLOGY	1 696	...	1 157	...	360	...	179	...
	FINE AND APPLIED ARTS	–	–	–	–	–	–	–	–
	LAW	243	...	140	...	103	...	–	–
	SOCIAL AND BEHAVIOURAL SCIENCE	./.	...	./.	...	./.	...	./.	...
	COMMERCIAL & BUSINESS ADMIN.	488	...	307	...	129	...	52	...
	MASS COMMUNICATION & DOCUMENT.	–	–	–	–	–	–	–	–
	HOME ECONOMICS (DOMESTIC SCIENCE)	–	–	–	–	–	–	–	–
	SERVICE TRADES	–	–	–	–	–	–	–	–
	NATURAL SCIENCE	373	...	307	...	23	...	43	...
	MATHEMATICS & COMPUTER SCIENCE	./.	...	./.	...	./.	...	./.	...
	MEDICAL SCIENCE & HEALTH-RELATED	127	...	127	...	–	–	–	–
	ENGINEERING	64	...	48	...	16	...	–	–
	ARCHITECTURE & TOWN PLANNING	–	–	–	–	–	–	–	–
	TRADE, CRAFT & INDUSTRIAL PGMS.	–	–	–	–	–	–	–	–
	TRANSPORT AND COMMUNICATIONS	–	–	–	–	–	–	–	–
	AGRICULTURE, FORESTRY & FISHERY	101	...	100	...	1	...	–	–
	OTHER AND NOT SPECIFIED	19	...	10	...	7	...	2	...
PAKISTAN‡									
1979	TOTAL	37 488	...	17	...	30 689	...	6 782	...
	EDUCATION SCIENCE & TEACHER TRNG.	1 808	...	–	–	1 500	...	308	...
	HUMANITIES, RELIGION & THEOLOGY	21 118	...	–	–	16 700	...	4 418	...
	FINE AND APPLIED ARTS	17	...	17	...	–	–	–	–
	LAW	2 728	...	–	–	2 728	...	–	–
	SOCIAL AND BEHAVIOURAL SCIENCE	–	–	–	–	–	–	–	–
	COMMERCIAL & BUSINESS ADMIN.	1 669	...	–	...	1 459	...	210	...
	MASS COMMUNICATION & DOCUMENT.	–	–	–	–	–	–	–	–
	HOME ECONOMICS (DOMESTIC SCIENCE)	190	...	–	–	161	...	29	...
	SERVICE TRADES	–	–	–	–	–	–	–	–
	NATURAL SCIENCE	4 215	...	–	–	3 343	...	872	...
	MATHEMATICS & COMPUTER SCIENCE	188	...	–	–	–	–	188	...
	MEDICAL SCIENCE & HEALTH-RELATED	2 695	...	–	–	2 664	...	31	...
	ENGINEERING	1 673	...	–	–	1 599	...	74	...
	ARCHITECTURE & TOWN PLANNING	./.	...	–	–	./.	...	./.	...
	TRADE, CRAFT & INDUSTRIAL PGMS.	–	–	–	–	–	–	–	–
	TRANSPORT AND COMMUNICATIONS	–	–	–	–	–	–	–	–
	AGRICULTURE, FORESTRY & FISHERY	1 068	...	–	–	535	...	533	...
	OTHER AND NOT SPECIFIED	119	...	–	–	–	–	119	...
PHILIPPINES									
1982	TOTAL	242 242	...	...	...	...	...	...	...
	EDUCATION SCIENCE & TEACHER TRNG.	21 306	...	...	...	...	...	...	...
	HUMANITIES, RELIGION & THEOLOGY	–	–	...	...	...	...	...	...
	FINE AND APPLIED ARTS	14 502	...	...	...	...	...	...	...
	LAW	2 245	...	...	...	...	...	...	...
	SOCIAL AND BEHAVIOURAL SCIENCE	–	–	...	...	...	...	...	...
	COMMERCIAL & BUSINESS ADMIN.	65 092	...	...	...	...	...	...	...
	MASS COMMUNICATION & DOCUMENT.	–	–	...	...	...	...	...	...
	HOME ECONOMICS (DOMESTIC SCIENCE)	2 170	...	...	...	...	...	...	...
	SERVICE TRADES	–	–	...	...	...	...	...	...
	NATURAL SCIENCE	568	...	...	...	...	...	...	...
	MATHEMATICS & COMPUTER SCIENCE	–	–	...	...	...	...	...	...
	MEDICAL SCIENCE & HEALTH-RELATED	20 356	...	...	...	...	...	...	...
	ENGINEERING	25 032	...	...	...	...	...	...	...
	ARCHITECTURE & TOWN PLANNING	–	–	...	...	...	...	...	...
	TRADE, CRAFT & INDUSTRIAL PGMS.	78 158	...	...	...	...	...	...	...
	TRANSPORT AND COMMUNICATIONS	–	–	...	...	...	...	...	...
	AGRICULTURE, FORESTRY & FISHERY	6 952	...	...	...	...	...	...	...
	OTHER AND NOT SPECIFIED	5 861	...	...	...	...	...	...	...

3.14 Third level: graduates by ISCED level and field of study
Troisième degré: diplômés par niveau de la CITE et domaine d'études
Tercer grado: diplomados por nivel de la CINE y sector de estudios

COUNTRY YEAR / PAYS ANNEE / PAIS AÑO	FIELD OF STUDY / DOMAINES D'ETUDES / SECTORES DE ESTUDIOS	INTERNATIONAL STANDARD CLASSIFICATION OF EDUCATION BY LEVEL / CLASSIFICATION INTERNATIONALE TYPE DE L'EDUCATION PAR NIVEAU / CLASIFICACION INTERNACIONAL NORMALIZADA DE LA EDUCACION POR NIVEL							
		ALL LEVELS / TOUS NIVEAUX / TODOS LOS NIVELES		LEVEL 5 / NIVEAU 5 / NIVEL 5		LEVEL 6 / NIVEAU 6 / NIVEL 6		LEVEL 7 / NIVEAU 7 / NIVEL 7	
		MF	F	MF	F	MF	F	MF	F
		(1)	(2)	(3)	(4)	(5)	(6)	(7)	(8)
QATAR‡ 1984	TOTAL	774	465	53	17	640	430	81	18
	EDUCATION SCIENCE & TEACHER TRNG.	381	247	53	17	247	212	81	18
	HUMANITIES, RELIGION & THEOLOGY	226	128	–	–	226	128	–	–
	FINE AND APPLIED ARTS	–	–	–	–	–	–	–	–
	LAW	–	–	–	–	–	–	–	–
	SOCIAL AND BEHAVIOURAL SCIENCE	./.	./.	–	–	./.	./.	–	–
	COMMERCIAL & BUSINESS ADMIN.	–	–	–	–	–	–	–	–
	MASS COMMUNICATION & DOCUMENT.	–	–	–	–	–	–	–	–
	HOME ECONOMICS (DOMESTIC SCIENCE)	20	20	–	–	20	20	–	–
	SERVICE TRADES	–	–	–	–	–	–	–	–
	NATURAL SCIENCE	125	70	–	–	125	70	–	–
	MATHEMATICS & COMPUTER SCIENCE	./.	./.	–	–	./.	./.	–	–
	MEDICAL SCIENCE & HEALTH-RELATED	–	–	–	–	–	–	–	–
	ENGINEERING	22	–	–	–	22	–	–	–
	ARCHITECTURE & TOWN PLANNING	–	–	–	–	–	–	–	–
	TRADE, CRAFT & INDUSTRIAL PGMS.	–	–	–	–	–	–	–	–
	TRANSPORT AND COMMUNICATIONS	–	–	–	–	–	–	–	–
	AGRICULTURE, FORESTRY & FISHERY	–	–	–	–	–	–	–	–
	OTHER AND NOT SPECIFIED	–	–	–	–	–	–	–	–
SAUDI ARABIA‡ 1982	TOTAL	10 336	...	2 128	...	7 636	2 595	572	88
	EDUCATION SCIENCE & TEACHER TRNG.	3 168	...	1 815	...	1 223	572	130	50
	HUMANITIES, RELIGION & THEOLOGY	4 027	1 300	313	–	3 380	1 264	334	36
	FINE AND APPLIED ARTS	–	–	–	–	–	–	–	–
	LAW	./.	./.	./.	–	./.	./.	./.	./.
	SOCIAL AND BEHAVIOURAL SCIENCE	1 377	310	–	–	1 308	310	69	–
	COMMERCIAL & BUSINESS ADMIN.	./.	./.	–	–	./.	./.	./.	–
	MASS COMMUNICATION & DOCUMENT.	–	–	–	–	–	–	–	–
	HOME ECONOMICS (DOMESTIC SCIENCE)	./.	./.	–	–	./.	./.	./.	./.
	SERVICE TRADES	–	–	–	–	–	–	–	–
	NATURAL SCIENCE	588	306	–	–	577	304	11	2
	MATHEMATICS & COMPUTER SCIENCE	./.	./.	–	–	./.	./.	./.	./.
	MEDICAL SCIENCE & HEALTH-RELATED	287	116	–	–	287	116	–	–
	ENGINEERING	681	–	–	–	653	–	28	–
	ARCHITECTURE & TOWN PLANNING	./.	–	–	–	./.	–	./.	–
	TRADE, CRAFT & INDUSTRIAL PGMS.	–	–	–	–	–	–	–	–
	TRANSPORT AND COMMUNICATIONS	–	–	–	–	–	–	–	–
	AGRICULTURE, FORESTRY & FISHERY	208	29	–	–	208	29	–	–
	OTHER AND NOT SPECIFIED	–	–	–	–	–	–	–	–
SINGAPORE‡ 1983	TOTAL	8 551	3 504	4 411	1 408	3 409	1 742	731	354
	EDUCATION SCIENCE & TEACHER TRNG.	876	687	460	394	–	–	416	293
	HUMANITIES, RELIGION & THEOLOGY	865	534	–	–	839	516	26	18
	FINE AND APPLIED ARTS	–	–	–	–	–	–	–	–
	LAW	107	54	–	–	106	54	1	–
	SOCIAL AND BEHAVIOURAL SCIENCE	./.	./.	–	–	./.	./.	./.	./.
	COMMERCIAL & BUSINESS ADMIN.	1 195	771	397	273	735	494	63	4
	MASS COMMUNICATION & DOCUMENT.	–	–	–	–	–	–	–	–
	HOME ECONOMICS (DOMESTIC SCIENCE)	–	–	–	–	–	–	–	–
	SERVICE TRADES	–	–	–	–	–	–	–	–
	NATURAL SCIENCE	696	485	–	–	688	479	8	6
	MATHEMATICS & COMPUTER SCIENCE	./.	./.	–	–	./.	./.	./.	./.
	MEDICAL SCIENCE & HEALTH-RELATED	312	131	–	–	245	107	67	24
	ENGINEERING	3 494	572	2 761	527	585	36	148	9
	ARCHITECTURE & TOWN PLANNING	471	207	258	151	211	56	2	–
	TRADE, CRAFT & INDUSTRIAL PGMS.	–	–	–	–	–	–	–	–
	TRANSPORT AND COMMUNICATIONS	106	–	106	–	–	–	–	–
	AGRICULTURE, FORESTRY & FISHERY	–	–	–	–	–	–	–	–
	OTHER AND NOT SPECIFIED	429	63	429	63	–	–	–	–

COUNTRY / YEAR PAYS / ANNEE PAIS / AÑO	FIELD OF STUDY DOMAINES D'ETUDES SECTORES DE ESTUDIOS	INTERNATIONAL STANDARD CLASSIFICATION OF EDUCATION BY LEVEL / CLASSIFICATION INTERNATIONALE TYPE DE L'EDUCATION PAR NIVEAU / CLASIFICACION INTERNACIONAL NORMALIZADA DE LA EDUCACION POR NIVEL							
		ALL LEVELS TOUS NIVEAUX TODOS LOS NIVELES		LEVEL 5 NIVEAU 5 NIVEL 5		LEVEL 6 NIVEAU 6 NIVEL 6		LEVEL 7 NIVEAU 7 NIVEL 7	
		MF	F	MF	F	MF	F	MF	F
		(1)	(2)	(3)	(4)	(5)	(6)	(7)	(8)
SRI LANKA‡ 1982	TOTAL	17 598	...	12 526	...	4 503	...	569	...
	EDUCATION SCIENCE & TEACHER TRNG.	4 346	...	3 934	...	9	...	403	...
	HUMANITIES, RELIGION & THEOLOGY	–	–	–	–	–	–	–	–
	FINE AND APPLIED ARTS	2 290	...	–	–	2 251	...	39	...
	LAW	14	...	–	–	12	...	2	...
	SOCIAL AND BEHAVIOURAL SCIENCE	–	–	–	–	–	–	–	–
	COMMERCIAL & BUSINESS ADMIN.	3 989	...	3 323	...	666	...	–	–
	MASS COMMUNICATION & DOCUMENT.	–	–	–	–	–	–	–	–
	HOME ECONOMICS (DOMESTIC SCIENCE)	120	...	120	...	–	–	–	–
	SERVICE TRADES	–	–	–	–	–	–	–	–
	NATURAL SCIENCE	641	...	–	–	603	...	38	...
	MATHEMATICS & COMPUTER SCIENCE	./.	...	–	–	./.	...	./.	...
	MEDICAL SCIENCE & HEALTH-RELATED	568	...	–	–	529	...	39	...
	ENGINEERING	1 894	...	1 621	...	273	...	–	–
	ARCHITECTURE & TOWN PLANNING	51	...	–	–	29	...	22	...
	TRADE, CRAFT & INDUSTRIAL PGMS.	1 015	...	1 015	...	–	–	–	–
	TRANSPORT AND COMMUNICATIONS	–	–	–	–	–	–	–	–
	AGRICULTURE, FORESTRY & FISHERY	157	...	–	–	131	...	26	...
	OTHER AND NOT SPECIFIED	2 513	...	2 513	...	–	–	–	–
SYRIAN ARAB REPUBLIC‡ 1983	TOTAL	16 606	5 072	...	...	...	...	...	...
	EDUCATION SCIENCE & TEACHER TRNG.	996	490	...	...	...	...	...	...
	HUMANITIES, RELIGION & THEOLOGY	2 430	1 146	...	...	...	...	...	...
	FINE AND APPLIED ARTS	96	38	...	...	...	...	...	...
	LAW	636	50	...	...	...	...	...	...
	SOCIAL AND BEHAVIOURAL SCIENCE	965	264	...	...	...	...	...	...
	COMMERCIAL & BUSINESS ADMIN.	961	459	...	...	...	...	...	...
	MASS COMMUNICATION & DOCUMENT.	21	–	...	...	...	...	...	...
	HOME ECONOMICS (DOMESTIC SCIENCE)	–	–	...	...	...	...	...	...
	SERVICE TRADES	111	24	...	...	...	...	...	...
	NATURAL SCIENCE	1 152	458	...	...	...	...	...	...
	MATHEMATICS & COMPUTER SCIENCE	31	23	...	...	...	...	...	...
	MEDICAL SCIENCE & HEALTH-RELATED	2 186	823	...	...	...	...	...	...
	ENGINEERING	3 070	623	...	...	...	...	...	...
	ARCHITECTURE & TOWN PLANNING	324	97	...	...	...	...	...	...
	TRADE, CRAFT & INDUSTRIAL PGMS.	1 795	99	...	...	...	...	...	...
	TRANSPORT AND COMMUNICATIONS	–	–	...	...	...	...	...	...
	AGRICULTURE, FORESTRY & FISHERY	1 230	241	...	...	...	...	...	...
	OTHER AND NOT SPECIFIED	602	237	...	...	...	...	...	...
TURKEY‡ 1983	TOTAL	42 746	13 650	8 920	3 013	30 960	9 781	2 866	856
	EDUCATION SCIENCE & TEACHER TRNG.	10 401	4 313	4 721	1 977	5 586	2 298	94	38
	HUMANITIES, RELIGION & THEOLOGY	2 893	734	–	–	2 764	716	129	18
	FINE AND APPLIED ARTS	626	294	69	48	433	196	124	50
	LAW	1 648	464	175	64	1 446	392	27	8
	SOCIAL AND BEHAVIOURAL SCIENCE	2 536	941	167	103	2 224	780	145	58
	COMMERCIAL & BUSINESS ADMIN.	5 747	1 645	1 269	459	4 273	1 117	205	69
	MASS COMMUNICATION & DOCUMENT.	563	249	–	–	530	236	33	13
	HOME ECONOMICS (DOMESTIC SCIENCE)	42	32	–	–	33	24	9	8
	SERVICE TRADES	391	100	241	78	150	22	–	–
	NATURAL SCIENCE	1 257	595	–	–	1 059	525	198	70
	MATHEMATICS & COMPUTER SCIENCE	564	244	30	23	534	221	–	–
	MEDICAL SCIENCE & HEALTH-RELATED	4 559	1 707	–	–	3 782	1 458	777	249
	ENGINEERING	9 031	1 458	2 192	246	6 071	1 071	768	141
	ARCHITECTURE & TOWN PLANNING	954	451	–	–	806	370	148	81
	TRADE, CRAFT & INDUSTRIAL PGMS.	208	77	56	15	152	62	–	–
	TRANSPORT AND COMMUNICATIONS	–	–	–	–	–	–	–	–
	AGRICULTURE, FORESTRY & FISHERY	1 326	346	–	–	1 117	293	209	53
	OTHER AND NOT SPECIFIED	–	–	–	–	–	–	–	–

3.14 Third level: graduates by ISCED level and field of study
Troisième degré: diplômés par niveau de la CITE et domaine d'études
Tercer grado: diplomados por nivel de la CINE y sector de estudios

COUNTRY YEAR / PAYS ANNEE / PAIS AÑO	FIELD OF STUDY / DOMAINES D'ETUDES / SECTORES DE ESTUDIOS	INTERNATIONAL STANDARD CLASSIFICATION OF EDUCATION BY LEVEL / CLASSIFICATION INTERNATIONALE TYPE DE L'EDUCATION PAR NIVEAU / CLASIFICACION INTERNACIONAL NORMALIZADA DE LA EDUCACION POR NIVEL							
		ALL LEVELS / TOUS NIVEAUX / TODOS LOS NIVELES		LEVEL 5 / NIVEAU 5 / NIVEL 5		LEVEL 6 / NIVEAU 6 / NIVEL 6		LEVEL 7 / NIVEAU 7 / NIVEL 7	
		MF	F	MF	F	MF	F	MF	F
		(1)	(2)	(3)	(4)	(5)	(6)	(7)	(8)
UNITED ARAB EMIRATES 1984	TOTAL	1 663	981	530	500	1 133	481	–	–
	EDUCATION SCIENCE & TEACHER TRNG.	648	586	530	500	118	86	–	–
	HUMANITIES, RELIGION & THEOLOGY	–	–	–	–	–	–	–	–
	FINE AND APPLIED ARTS	393	210	–	–	393	210	–	–
	LAW	142	27	–	–	142	27	–	–
	SOCIAL AND BEHAVIOURAL SCIENCE	–	–	–	–	–	–	–	–
	COMMERCIAL & BUSINESS ADMIN.	239	73	–	–	239	73	–	–
	MASS COMMUNICATION & DOCUMENT.	–	–	–	–	–	–	–	–
	HOME ECONOMICS (DOMESTIC SCIENCE)	–	–	–	–	–	–	–	–
	SERVICE TRADES	–	–	–	–	–	–	–	–
	NATURAL SCIENCE	176	85	–	–	176	85	–	–
	MATHEMATICS & COMPUTER SCIENCE	–	–	–	–	–	–	–	–
	MEDICAL SCIENCE & HEALTH-RELATED	–	–	–	–	–	–	–	–
	ENGINEERING	34	–	–	–	34	–	–	–
	ARCHITECTURE & TOWN PLANNING	–	–	–	–	–	–	–	–
	TRADE, CRAFT & INDUSTRIAL PGMS.	–	–	–	–	–	–	–	–
	TRANSPORT AND COMMUNICATIONS	–	–	–	–	–	–	–	–
	AGRICULTURE, FORESTRY & FISHERY	31	–	–	–	31	–	–	–
	OTHER AND NOT SPECIFIED	–	–	–	–	–	–	–	–
YEMEN 1980	TOTAL	374	35	–	–	374	35	–	–
	EDUCATION SCIENCE & TEACHER TRNG.	95	9	–	–	95	9	–	–
	HUMANITIES, RELIGION & THEOLOGY	23	5	–	–	23	5	–	–
	FINE AND APPLIED ARTS	–	–	–	–	–	–	–	–
	LAW	94	8	–	–	94	8	–	–
	SOCIAL AND BEHAVIOURAL SCIENCE	25	6	–	–	25	6	–	–
	COMMERCIAL & BUSINESS ADMIN.	120	3	–	–	120	3	–	–
	MASS COMMUNICATION & DOCUMENT.	–	–	–	–	–	–	–	–
	HOME ECONOMICS (DOMESTIC SCIENCE)	–	–	–	–	–	–	–	–
	SERVICE TRADES	–	–	–	–	–	–	–	–
	NATURAL SCIENCE	17	4	–	–	17	4	–	–
	MATHEMATICS & COMPUTER SCIENCE	–	–	–	–	–	–	–	–
	MEDICAL SCIENCE & HEALTH-RELATED	–	–	–	–	–	–	–	–
	ENGINEERING	–	–	–	–	–	–	–	–
	ARCHITECTURE & TOWN PLANNING	–	–	–	–	–	–	–	–
	TRADE, CRAFT & INDUSTRIAL PGMS.	–	–	–	–	–	–	–	–
	TRANSPORT AND COMMUNICATIONS	–	–	–	–	–	–	–	–
	AGRICULTURE, FORESTRY & FISHERY	–	–	–	–	–	–	–	–
	OTHER AND NOT SPECIFIED	–	–	–	–	–	–	–	–
EUROPE									
ALBANIA‡ 1984	TOTAL	3 248	1 661	–	–	3 248	1 661	–	–
	EDUCATION SCIENCE & TEACHER TRNG.	288	162	–	–	288	162	–	–
	HUMANITIES, RELIGION & THEOLOGY	179	124	–	–	179	124	–	–
	FINE AND APPLIED ARTS	85	28	–	–	85	28	–	–
	LAW	108	52	–	–	108	52	–	–
	SOCIAL AND BEHAVIOURAL SCIENCE	478	391	–	–	478	391	–	–
	COMMERCIAL & BUSINESS ADMIN.	–	–	–	–	–	–	–	–
	MASS COMMUNICATION & DOCUMENT.	–	–	–	–	–	–	–	–
	HOME ECONOMICS (DOMESTIC SCIENCE)	–	–	–	–	–	–	–	–
	SERVICE TRADES	–	–	–	–	–	–	–	–
	NATURAL SCIENCE	127	77	–	–	127	77	–	–
	MATHEMATICS & COMPUTER SCIENCE	./.	./.	–	–	./.	./.	–	–
	MEDICAL SCIENCE & HEALTH-RELATED	186	95	–	–	186	95	–	–
	ENGINEERING	582	183	–	–	582	183	–	–
	ARCHITECTURE & TOWN PLANNING	–	–	–	–	–	–	–	–
	TRADE, CRAFT & INDUSTRIAL PGMS.	–	–	–	–	–	–	–	–
	TRANSPORT AND COMMUNICATIONS	–	–	–	–	–	–	–	–
	AGRICULTURE, FORESTRY & FISHERY	1 099	512	–	–	1 099	512	–	–
	OTHER AND NOT SPECIFIED	116	37	–	–	116	37	–	–

COUNTRY YEAR / PAYS ANNEE / PAIS AÑO	FIELD OF STUDY / DOMAINES D'ETUDES / SECTORES DE ESTUDIOS	INTERNATIONAL STANDARD CLASSIFICATION OF EDUCATION BY LEVEL / CLASSIFICATION INTERNATIONALE TYPE DE L'EDUCATION PAR NIVEAU / CLASIFICACION INTERNACIONAL NORMALIZADA DE LA EDUCACION POR NIVEL							
		ALL LEVELS / TOUS NIVEAUX / TODOS LOS NIVELES		LEVEL 5 / NIVEAU 5 / NIVEL 5		LEVEL 6 / NIVEAU 6 / NIVEL 6		LEVEL 7 / NIVEAU 7 / NIVEL 7	
		MF	F	MF	F	MF	F	MF	F
		(1)	(2)	(3)	(4)	(5)	(6)	(7)	(8)
AUSTRIA‡ 1983	TOTAL	10 070	3 701	49	35	9 415	3 534	606	132
	EDUCATION SCIENCE & TEACHER TRNG.	206	118	–	–	196	114	10	4
	HUMANITIES, RELIGION & THEOLOGY	1 464	869	21	20	1 349	813	94	36
	FINE AND APPLIED ARTS	710	332	–	–	708	332	2	–
	LAW	2 238	721	–	–	2 238	721	–	–
	SOCIAL AND BEHAVIOURAL SCIENCE	550	237	–	–	482	221	68	16
	COMMERCIAL & BUSINESS ADMIN.	1 067	324	28	15	943	285	96	24
	MASS COMMUNICATION & DOCUMENT.	38	15	–	–	37	15	1	–
	HOME ECONOMICS (DOMESTIC SCIENCE)	–	–	–	–	–	–	–	–
	SERVICE TRADES	–	–	–	–	–	–	–	–
	NATURAL SCIENCE	473	162	–	–	387	144	86	18
	MATHEMATICS & COMPUTER SCIENCE	363	112	–	–	325	106	38	6
	MEDICAL SCIENCE & HEALTH-RELATED	1 672	670	–	–	1 666	667	6	3
	ENGINEERING	810	21	–	–	679	16	131	5
	ARCHITECTURE & TOWN PLANNING	174	43	–	–	170	43	4	–
	TRADE, CRAFT & INDUSTRIAL PGMS.	–	–	–	–	–	–	–	–
	TRANSPORT AND COMMUNICATIONS	–	–	–	–	–	–	–	–
	AGRICULTURE, FORESTRY & FISHERY	290	74	–	–	220	54	70	20
	OTHER AND NOT SPECIFIED	15	3	–	–	15	3	–	–
BELGIUM‡ 1982	TOTAL	18 135	7 463	...	...	...	...	...	...
	EDUCATION SCIENCE & TEACHER TRNG.	1 050	607	...	...	...	...	...	...
	HUMANITIES, RELIGION & THEOLOGY	4 058	2 387	...	...	...	...	...	...
	FINE AND APPLIED ARTS	–	–	...	...	...	...	...	...
	LAW	1 777	662	...	...	...	...	...	...
	SOCIAL AND BEHAVIOURAL SCIENCE	1 343	436	...	...	...	...	...	...
	COMMERCIAL & BUSINESS ADMIN.	1 213	317	...	...	...	...	...	...
	MASS COMMUNICATION & DOCUMENT.	–	–	...	...	...	...	...	...
	HOME ECONOMICS (DOMESTIC SCIENCE)	–	–	...	...	...	...	...	...
	SERVICE TRADES	–	–	...	...	...	...	...	...
	NATURAL SCIENCE	2 268	1 016	...	...	...	...	...	...
	MATHEMATICS & COMPUTER SCIENCE	./.	./.	...	...	...	...	...	...
	MEDICAL SCIENCE & HEALTH-RELATED	3 160	1 173	...	...	...	...	...	...
	ENGINEERING	1 312	106	...	...	...	...	...	...
	ARCHITECTURE & TOWN PLANNING	–	–	...	...	...	...	...	...
	TRADE, CRAFT & INDUSTRIAL PGMS.	–	–	...	...	...	...	...	...
	TRANSPORT AND COMMUNICATIONS	–	–	...	...	...	...	...	...
	AGRICULTURE, FORESTRY & FISHERY	797	185	...	...	...	...	...	...
	OTHER AND NOT SPECIFIED	1 157	574	...	...	...	...	...	...
BULGARIA 1983	TOTAL	18 652	10 723	4 039	3 044	14 322	7 566	291	113
	EDUCATION SCIENCE & TEACHER TRNG.	4 245	3 147	3 099	2 431	1 143	716	3	–
	HUMANITIES, RELIGION & THEOLOGY	1 708	1 222	192	187	1 501	1 023	15	12
	FINE AND APPLIED ARTS	809	396	148	65	660	330	1	1
	LAW	265	126	–	–	260	124	5	2
	SOCIAL AND BEHAVIOURAL SCIENCE	242	125	–	–	204	107	38	18
	COMMERCIAL & BUSINESS ADMIN.	2 143	1 227	–	–	2 143	1 227	–	–
	MASS COMMUNICATION & DOCUMENT.	71	48	–	–	65	43	6	5
	HOME ECONOMICS (DOMESTIC SCIENCE)	–	–	–	–	–	–	–	–
	SERVICE TRADES	335	240	335	240	–	–	–	–
	NATURAL SCIENCE	692	470	–	–	646	454	46	16
	MATHEMATICS & COMPUTER SCIENCE	444	236	–	–	427	234	17	2
	MEDICAL SCIENCE & HEALTH-RELATED	1 904	1 176	–	–	1 879	1 161	25	15
	ENGINEERING	4 523	1 735	–	–	4 419	1 709	104	26
	ARCHITECTURE & TOWN PLANNING	130	53	–	–	127	50	3	3
	TRADE, CRAFT & INDUSTRIAL PGMS.	–	–	–	–	–	–	–	–
	TRANSPORT AND COMMUNICATIONS	326	140	265	121	56	18	5	1
	AGRICULTURE, FORESTRY & FISHERY	815	382	–	–	792	370	23	12
	OTHER AND NOT SPECIFIED	–	–	–	–	–	–	–	–

3.14 Third level: graduates by ISCED level and field of study
Troisième degré: diplômés par niveau de la CITE et domaine d'études
Tercer grado: diplomados por nivel de la CINE y sector de estudios

COUNTRY / YEAR PAYS / ANNEE PAIS / AÑO	FIELD OF STUDY DOMAINES D'ETUDES SECTORES DE ESTUDIOS	INTERNATIONAL STANDARD CLASSIFICATION OF EDUCATION BY LEVEL / CLASSIFICATION INTERNATIONALE TYPE DE L'EDUCATION PAR NIVEAU / CLASIFICACION INTERNACIONAL NORMALIZADA DE LA EDUCACION POR NIVEL							
		ALL LEVELS TOUS NIVEAUX TODOS LOS NIVELES		LEVEL 5 NIVEAU 5 NIVEL 5		LEVEL 6 NIVEAU 6 NIVEL 6		LEVEL 7 NIVEAU 7 NIVEL 7	
		MF	F	MF	F	MF	F	MF	F
		(1)	(2)	(3)	(4)	(5)	(6)	(7)	(8)
CZECHOSLOVAKIA 1983	TOTAL	35 241	15 971	–	–	35 241	15 971	–	–
	EDUCATION SCIENCE & TEACHER TRNG.	5 821	4 501	–	–	5 821	4 501	–	–
	HUMANITIES, RELIGION & THEOLOGY	422	232	–	–	422	232	–	–
	FINE AND APPLIED ARTS	605	263	–	–	605	263	–	–
	LAW	1 345	859	–	–	1 345	859	–	–
	SOCIAL AND BEHAVIOURAL SCIENCE	658	257	–	–	658	257	–	–
	COMMERCIAL & BUSINESS ADMIN.	4 766	2 830	–	–	4 766	2 830	–	–
	MASS COMMUNICATION & DOCUMENT.	279	205	–	–	279	205	–	–
	HOME ECONOMICS (DOMESTIC SCIENCE)	–	–	–	–	–	–	–	–
	SERVICE TRADES	–	–	–	–	–	–	–	–
	NATURAL SCIENCE	542	266	–	–	542	266	–	–
	MATHEMATICS & COMPUTER SCIENCE	465	148	–	–	465	148	–	–
	MEDICAL SCIENCE & HEALTH-RELATED	2 293	1 360	–	–	2 293	1 360	–	–
	ENGINEERING	12 800	3 266	–	–	12 800	3 266	–	–
	ARCHITECTURE & TOWN PLANNING	221	81	–	–	221	81	–	–
	TRADE, CRAFT & INDUSTRIAL PGMS.	–	–	–	–	–	–	–	–
	TRANSPORT AND COMMUNICATIONS	1 069	240	–	–	1 069	240	–	–
	AGRICULTURE, FORESTRY & FISHERY	3 817	1 433	–	–	3 817	1 433	–	–
	OTHER AND NOT SPECIFIED	138	30	–	–	138	30	–	–
DENMARK‡ 1982	TOTAL	19 112	10 257	8 341	5 512	10 771	4 745	./.	./.
	EDUCATION SCIENCE & TEACHER TRNG.	5 710	4 037	2 895	2 428	2 815	1 609	./.	./.
	HUMANITIES, RELIGION & THEOLOGY	1 326	984	632	590	694	394	./.	./.
	FINE AND APPLIED ARTS	319	186	166	115	153	71	./.	./.
	LAW	423	189	–	–	423	189	./.	./.
	SOCIAL AND BEHAVIOURAL SCIENCE	683	254	–	–	683	254	./.	./.
	COMMERCIAL & BUSINESS ADMIN.	957	142	17	13	940	129	./.	./.
	MASS COMMUNICATION & DOCUMENT.	422	242	2	–	420	242	./.	./.
	HOME ECONOMICS (DOMESTIC SCIENCE)	–	–	–	–	–	–	–	–
	SERVICE TRADES	89	82	89	82	–	–	–	–
	NATURAL SCIENCE	182	48	–	–	182	48	./.	./.
	MATHEMATICS & COMPUTER SCIENCE	147	29	–	–	147	29	./.	./.
	MEDICAL SCIENCE & HEALTH-RELATED	4 107	3 237	2 239	2 089	1 868	1 148	./.	./.
	ENGINEERING	1 662	150	464	77	1 198	73	./.	./.
	ARCHITECTURE & TOWN PLANNING	304	87	7	2	297	85	./.	./.
	TRADE, CRAFT & INDUSTRIAL PGMS.	538	48	538	48	–	–	–	–
	TRANSPORT AND COMMUNICATIONS	261	3	261	3	–	–	–	–
	AGRICULTURE, FORESTRY & FISHERY	531	128	250	21	281	107	./.	./.
	OTHER AND NOT SPECIFIED	1 451	411	781	44	670	367	./.	./.
FINLAND 1982	TOTAL	24 736	13 177	15 096	8 268	8 977	4 740	663	169
	EDUCATION SCIENCE & TEACHER TRNG.	1 615	1 316	890	821	710	489	15	6
	HUMANITIES, RELIGION & THEOLOGY	1 923	1 390	–	–	1 836	1 353	87	37
	FINE AND APPLIED ARTS	174	97	81	53	91	44	2	–
	LAW	497	205	–	–	483	203	14	2
	SOCIAL AND BEHAVIOURAL SCIENCE	857	565	–	–	782	536	75	29
	COMMERCIAL & BUSINESS ADMIN.	5 422	3 668	4 614	3 261	790	403	18	4
	MASS COMMUNICATION & DOCUMENT.	51	33	14	5	37	28	–	–
	HOME ECONOMICS (DOMESTIC SCIENCE)	24	24	–	–	23	23	1	1
	SERVICE TRADES	197	154	197	154	–	–	–	–
	NATURAL SCIENCE	1 179	527	–	–	1 017	488	162	39
	MATHEMATICS & COMPUTER SCIENCE	507	202	–	–	480	199	27	3
	MEDICAL SCIENCE & HEALTH-RELATED	4 725	4 060	3 726	3 485	888	546	111	29
	ENGINEERING	6 089	477	4 898	318	1 083	153	108	6
	ARCHITECTURE & TOWN PLANNING	113	47	–	–	107	44	6	3
	TRADE, CRAFT & INDUSTRIAL PGMS.	–	–	–	–	–	–	–	–
	TRANSPORT AND COMMUNICATIONS	67	9	67	9	–	–	–	–
	AGRICULTURE, FORESTRY & FISHERY	557	176	291	79	237	88	29	9
	OTHER AND NOT SPECIFIED	739	227	318	83	413	143	8	1

COUNTRY YEAR PAYS ANNEE PAIS AÑO	FIELD OF STUDY DOMAINES D'ETUDES SECTORES DE ESTUDIOS	INTERNATIONAL STANDARD CLASSIFICATION OF EDUCATION BY LEVEL CLASSIFICATION INTERNATIONALE TYPE DE L'EDUCATION PAR NIVEAU CLASIFICACION INTERNACIONAL NORMALIZADA DE LA EDUCACION POR NIVEL							
		ALL LEVELS TOUS NIVEAUX TODOS LOS NIVELES		LEVEL 5 NIVEAU 5 NIVEL 5		LEVEL 6 NIVEAU 6 NIVEL 6		LEVEL 7 NIVEAU 7 NIVEL 7	
		MF	F	MF	F	MF	F	MF	F
		(1)	(2)	(3)	(4)	(5)	(6)	(7)	(8)
FRANCE‡ 1981	TOTAL	269 841	118 866	51 473	...	164 430	...	53 938	...
	EDUCATION SCIENCE & TEACHER TRNG.	14 500	8 345	4 590	2 683	8 659	5 173	1 251	489
	HUMANITIES, RELIGION & THEOLOGY	61 113	40 710	357	305	51 780	35 996	8 976	4 409
	FINE AND APPLIED ARTS	2 708	1 233	185	92	2 523	1 141	–	–
	LAW	36 606	...	1 758	...	28 904	15 319	5 944	2 342
	SOCIAL AND BEHAVIOURAL SCIENCE	17 903	...	486	...	12 692	5 030	4 725	1 254
	COMMERCIAL & BUSINESS ADMIN.	23 545	...	17 676	...	5 869	2 069	–	–
	MASS COMMUNICATION & DOCUMENT.	2 132	...	1 851	...	281	149	–	–
	HOME ECONOMICS (DOMESTIC SCIENCE)	1 020	1 019	1 020	1 019	–	–	–	–
	SERVICE TRADES	./.	./.	./.	./.	–	–	–	–
	NATURAL SCIENCE	36 982	12 369	–	–	26 495	9 554	10 487	2 815
	MATHEMATICS & COMPUTER SCIENCE	2 621	...	2 483	...	138	51	–	–
	MEDICAL SCIENCE & HEALTH-RELATED	26 705	11 848	255	174	3 895	2 428	22 555	9 246
	ENGINEERING	15 002	2 053	–	–	15 002	2 053	./.	./.
	ARCHITECTURE & TOWN PLANNING	2 050	...	1 115	...	935	231	–	–
	TRADE, CRAFT & INDUSTRIAL PGMS.	16 822	...	16 822	...	–	–	–	–
	TRANSPORT AND COMMUNICATIONS	540	...	158	...	382	15	–	–
	AGRICULTURE, FORESTRY & FISHERY	3 364	...	2 530	...	834	213	–	–
	OTHER AND NOT SPECIFIED	6 228	3 332	187	49	6 041	3 283	–	–
GERMAN DEMOCRATIC REPUBLIC 1983	TOTAL	129 760	70 300	48 754	20 108	46 557	34 604	34 449	15 588
	EDUCATION SCIENCE & TEACHER TRNG.	15 133	11 297	–	–	7 825	6 291	7 308	5 006
	HUMANITIES, RELIGION & THEOLOGY	2 508	1 307	–	–	261	141	2 247	1 166
	FINE AND APPLIED ARTS	1 038	465	76	12	222	156	740	297
	LAW	1 128	370	–	–	–	–	1 128	370
	SOCIAL AND BEHAVIOURAL SCIENCE	4 955	3 310	–	–	2 398	2 192	2 557	1 118
	COMMERCIAL & BUSINESS ADMIN.	9 879	7 248	229	193	6 434	5 310	3 216	1 745
	MASS COMMUNICATION & DOCUMENT.	668	496	–	–	448	388	220	108
	HOME ECONOMICS (DOMESTIC SCIENCE)	–	–	–	–	–	–	–	–
	SERVICE TRADES	736	445	736	445	–	–	–	–
	NATURAL SCIENCE	1 870	665	–	–	–	–	1 870	665
	MATHEMATICS & COMPUTER SCIENCE	914	410	188	138	214	117	512	155
	MEDICAL SCIENCE & HEALTH-RELATED	18 896	16 586	–	–	15 240	14 637	3 656	1 949
	ENGINEERING	19 366	5 886	–	–	10 645	3 850	8 721	2 036
	ARCHITECTURE & TOWN PLANNING	298	119	–	–	–	–	298	119
	TRADE, CRAFT & INDUSTRIAL PGMS.	15 981	3 712	15 981	3 712	–	–	–	–
	TRANSPORT AND COMMUNICATIONS	1 298	446	1 298	446	–	–	–	–
	AGRICULTURE, FORESTRY & FISHERY	6 622	3 345	1 776	969	2 870	1 522	1 976	854
	OTHER AND NOT SPECIFIED	28 470	14 193	28 470	14 193	–	–	–	–
GERMANY, FEDERAL REPUBLIC OF 1982	TOTAL	217 401	100 312	79 737	49 846	124 027	47 418	13 637	3 048
	EDUCATION SCIENCE & TEACHER TRNG.	30 171	17 815	–	–	29 805	17 683	366	132
	HUMANITIES, RELIGION & THEOLOGY	5 591	2 631	–	–	4 678	2 358	913	273
	FINE AND APPLIED ARTS	3 334	1 742	–	–	3 259	1 714	75	28
	LAW	6 637	2 000	–	–	6 143	1 934	494	66
	SOCIAL AND BEHAVIOURAL SCIENCE	26 489	10 982	–	–	25 523	10 801	966	181
	COMMERCIAL & BUSINESS ADMIN.	7 006	2 657	–	–	7 003	2 657	3	–
	MASS COMMUNICATION & DOCUMENT.	627	413	–	–	598	403	29	10
	HOME ECONOMICS (DOMESTIC SCIENCE)	744	639	–	–	697	606	47	33
	SERVICE TRADES	–	–	–	–	–	–	–	–
	NATURAL SCIENCE	7 951	1 749	–	–	5 712	1 418	2 239	331
	MATHEMATICS & COMPUTER SCIENCE	2 739	502	–	–	2 465	480	274	22
	MEDICAL SCIENCE & HEALTH-RELATED	58 449	40 349	40 516	34 471	11 471	4 143	6 462	1 735
	ENGINEERING	19 789	840	–	–	18 837	821	952	19
	ARCHITECTURE & TOWN PLANNING	3 494	1 203	–	–	3 426	1 196	68	7
	TRADE, CRAFT & INDUSTRIAL PGMS.	–	–	–	–	–	–	–	–
	TRANSPORT AND COMMUNICATIONS	–	–	–	–	–	–	–	–
	AGRICULTURE, FORESTRY & FISHERY	4 446	1 284	–	–	3 708	1 073	738	211
	OTHER AND NOT SPECIFIED	39 934	15 506	39 221	15 375	702	131	11	–

3.14 Third level: graduates by ISCED level and field of study
Troisième degré: diplômés par niveau de la CITE et domaine d'études
Tercer grado: diplomados por nivel de la CINE y sector de estudios

COUNTRY / YEAR PAYS / ANNEE PAIS / AÑO	FIELD OF STUDY DOMAINES D'ETUDES SECTORES DE ESTUDIOS	ALL LEVELS / TOUS NIVEAUX / TODOS LOS NIVELES MF	F	LEVEL 5 / NIVEAU 5 / NIVEL 5 MF	F	LEVEL 6 / NIVEAU 6 / NIVEL 6 MF	F	LEVEL 7 / NIVEAU 7 / NIVEL 7 MF	F
		(1)	(2)	(3)	(4)	(5)	(6)	(7)	(8)
GREECE 1981	TOTAL	24 184	10 418	9 896	4 389	13 921	5 943	367	86
	EDUCATION SCIENCE & TEACHER TRNG.	2 217	1 317	2 217	1 317	–	–	–	–
	HUMANITIES, RELIGION & THEOLOGY	2 199	1 697	82	–	2 077	1 679	40	18
	FINE AND APPLIED ARTS	213	123	182	102	31	21	–	–
	LAW	1 955	1 034	–	–	1 944	1 033	11	1
	SOCIAL AND BEHAVIOURAL SCIENCE	1 966	983	221	188	1 745	795	–	–
	COMMERCIAL & BUSINESS ADMIN.	3 479	1 501	1 363	635	2 111	865	5	1
	MASS COMMUNICATION & DOCUMENT.	60	41	60	41	–	–	–	–
	HOME ECONOMICS (DOMESTIC SCIENCE)	68	68	68	68	–	–	–	–
	SERVICE TRADES	452	182	452	182	–	–	–	–
	NATURAL SCIENCE	1 271	376	–	–	1 214	359	57	17
	MATHEMATICS & COMPUTER SCIENCE	1 146	286	–	–	1 135	286	11	–
	MEDICAL SCIENCE & HEALTH-RELATED	3 339	1 746	1 472	1 195	1 686	515	181	36
	ENGINEERING	3 800	583	2 443	416	1 335	162	22	5
	ARCHITECTURE & TOWN PLANNING	189	101	–	–	183	100	6	1
	TRADE, CRAFT & INDUSTRIAL PGMS.	147	96	147	96	–	–	–	–
	TRANSPORT AND COMMUNICATIONS	911	42	911	42	–	–	–	–
	AGRICULTURE, FORESTRY & FISHERY	772	242	278	107	460	128	34	7
	OTHER AND NOT SPECIFIED	–	–	–	–	–	–	–	–
HOLY SEE‡ 1984	TOTAL	2 869	1 080	1 614	924	890	136	365	20
	EDUCATION SCIENCE & TEACHER TRNG.	172	80	93	41	77	39	2	–
	HUMANITIES, RELIGION & THEOLOGY	1 778	348	829	256	656	82	293	10
	FINE AND APPLIED ARTS	36	18	13	6	12	6	11	6
	LAW	214	4	46	–	123	3	45	1
	SOCIAL AND BEHAVIOURAL SCIENCE	58	19	22	10	22	6	14	3
	COMMERCIAL & BUSINESS ADMIN.	–	–	–	–	–	–	–	–
	MASS COMMUNICATION & DOCUMENT.	–	–	–	–	–	–	–	–
	HOME ECONOMICS (DOMESTIC SCIENCE)	–	–	–	–	–	–	–	–
	SERVICE TRADES	–	–	–	–	–	–	–	–
	NATURAL SCIENCE	–	–	–	–	–	–	–	–
	MATHEMATICS & COMPUTER SCIENCE	–	–	–	–	–	–	–	–
	MEDICAL SCIENCE & HEALTH-RELATED	–	–	–	–	–	–	–	–
	ENGINEERING	–	–	–	–	–	–	–	–
	ARCHITECTURE & TOWN PLANNING	–	–	–	–	–	–	–	–
	TRADE, CRAFT & INDUSTRIAL PGMS.	–	–	–	–	–	–	–	–
	TRANSPORT AND COMMUNICATIONS	–	–	–	–	–	–	–	–
	AGRICULTURE, FORESTRY & FISHERY	–	–	–	–	–	–	–	–
	OTHER AND NOT SPECIFIED	611	611	611	611	–	–	–	–
HUNGARY 1984	TOTAL	25 089	13 997	12 782	7 777	3 435	2 445	8 872	3 775
	EDUCATION SCIENCE & TEACHER TRNG.	9 705	7 323	4 732	4 045	3 083	2 242	1 890	1 036
	HUMANITIES, RELIGION & THEOLOGY	679	426	–	–	208	156	471	270
	FINE AND APPLIED ARTS	235	104	–	–	–	–	235	104
	LAW	1 387	778	569	380	–	–	818	398
	SOCIAL AND BEHAVIOURAL SCIENCE	508	259	–	–	–	–	508	259
	COMMERCIAL & BUSINESS ADMIN.	1 863	1 227	1 540	1 066	–	–	323	161
	MASS COMMUNICATION & DOCUMENT.	–	–	–	–	–	–	–	–
	HOME ECONOMICS (DOMESTIC SCIENCE)	–	–	–	–	–	–	–	–
	SERVICE TRADES	218	143	218	143	–	–	–	–
	NATURAL SCIENCE	308	106	–	–	–	–	308	106
	MATHEMATICS & COMPUTER SCIENCE	289	120	173	83	–	–	116	37
	MEDICAL SCIENCE & HEALTH-RELATED	2 496	1 904	1 195	1 134	–	–	1 301	770
	ENGINEERING	2 276	334	704	111	–	–	1 572	223
	ARCHITECTURE & TOWN PLANNING	980	267	600	157	–	–	380	110
	TRADE, CRAFT & INDUSTRIAL PGMS.	2 219	426	2 219	426	–	–	–	–
	TRANSPORT AND COMMUNICATIONS	361	79	299	74	–	–	62	5
	AGRICULTURE, FORESTRY & FISHERY	1 421	454	533	158	–	–	888	296
	OTHER AND NOT SPECIFIED	144	47	–	–	144	47	–	–

The column headings span: INTERNATIONAL STANDARD CLASSIFICATION OF EDUCATION BY LEVEL / CLASSIFICATION INTERNATIONALE TYPE DE L'EDUCATION PAR NIVEAU / CLASIFICACION INTERNACIONAL NORMALIZADA DE LA EDUCACION POR NIVEL

COUNTRY YEAR / PAYS ANNEE / PAIS AÑO	FIELD OF STUDY / DOMAINES D'ETUDES / SECTORES DE ESTUDIOS	INTERNATIONAL STANDARD CLASSIFICATION OF EDUCATION BY LEVEL / CLASSIFICATION INTERNATIONALE TYPE DE L'EDUCATION PAR NIVEAU / CLASIFICACION INTERNACIONAL NORMALIZADA DE LA EDUCACION POR NIVEL							
		ALL LEVELS / TOUS NIVEAUX / TODOS LOS NIVELES		LEVEL 5 / NIVEAU 5 / NIVEL 5		LEVEL 6 / NIVEAU 6 / NIVEL 6		LEVEL 7 / NIVEAU 7 / NIVEL 7	
		MF	F	MF	F	MF	F	MF	F
		(1)	(2)	(3)	(4)	(5)	(6)	(7)	(8)
IRELAND‡ 1982	TOTAL	8 736	3 963	642	345	5 400	2 312	2 694	1 306
	EDUCATION SCIENCE & TEACHER TRNG.	1 544	1 037	33	25	118	104	1 393	908
	HUMANITIES, RELIGION & THEOLOGY	1 743	1 036	100	71	1 513	912	130	53
	FINE AND APPLIED ARTS	108	64	23	14	79	47	6	3
	LAW	308	132	–	–	253	107	55	25
	SOCIAL AND BEHAVIOURAL SCIENCE	555	319	11	5	446	257	98	57
	COMMERCIAL & BUSINESS ADMIN.	938	254	74	19	726	219	138	16
	MASS COMMUNICATION & DOCUMENT.	48	38	40	31	–	–	8	7
	HOME ECONOMICS (DOMESTIC SCIENCE)	28	28	–	–	28	28	–	–
	SERVICE TRADES	–	–	–	–	–	–	–	–
	NATURAL SCIENCE	784	332	–	–	628	284	156	48
	MATHEMATICS & COMPUTER SCIENCE	500	148	91	32	167	49	242	67
	MEDICAL SCIENCE & HEALTH-RELATED	924	392	114	108	603	205	207	79
	ENGINEERING	759	32	73	4	556	22	130	6
	ARCHITECTURE & TOWN PLANNING	83	19	–	–	50	13	33	6
	TRADE, CRAFT & INDUSTRIAL PGMS.	11	7	–	–	11	7	–	–
	TRANSPORT AND COMMUNICATIONS	–	–	–	–	–	–	–	–
	AGRICULTURE, FORESTRY & FISHERY	270	43	36	2	188	40	46	1
	OTHER AND NOT SPECIFIED	133	82	47	34	34	18	52	30
ITALY 1983	TOTAL	90 645	38 995	5 065	2 893	69 367	31 067	16 213	5 035
	EDUCATION SCIENCE & TEACHER TRNG.	2 730	2 167	226	190	2 172	1 775	332	202
	HUMANITIES, RELIGION & THEOLOGY	10 482	8 272	–	–	10 246	8 102	236	170
	FINE AND APPLIED ARTS	1 493	894	1 292	801	201	93	–	–
	LAW	8 417	3 492	–	–	8 220	3 433	197	59
	SOCIAL AND BEHAVIOURAL SCIENCE	9 141	3 578	–	–	9 054	3 555	87	23
	COMMERCIAL & BUSINESS ADMIN.	927	232	–	–	927	232	–	–
	MASS COMMUNICATION & DOCUMENT.	1	1	–	–	–	–	1	1
	HOME ECONOMICS (DOMESTIC SCIENCE)	–	–	–	–	–	–	–	–
	SERVICE TRADES	–	–	–	–	–	–	–	–
	NATURAL SCIENCE	5 994	3 642	–	–	5 994	3 642	–	–
	MATHEMATICS & COMPUTER SCIENCE	2 639	1 626	122	71	2 228	1 340	289	215
	MEDICAL SCIENCE & HEALTH-RELATED	31 701	10 860	–	–	17 089	6 572	14 612	4 288
	ENGINEERING	6 145	294	–	–	6 103	283	42	11
	ARCHITECTURE & TOWN PLANNING	4 301	1 364	–	–	4 287	1 356	14	8
	TRADE, CRAFT & INDUSTRIAL PGMS.	–	–	–	–	–	–	–	–
	TRANSPORT AND COMMUNICATIONS	–	–	–	–	–	–	–	–
	AGRICULTURE, FORESTRY & FISHERY	3 182	728	–	–	2 840	683	342	45
	OTHER AND NOT SPECIFIED	3 492	1 845	3 425	1 831	6	1	61	13
MALTA 1982	TOTAL	145	42	50	5	95	37	–	–
	EDUCATION SCIENCE & TEACHER TRNG.	49	21	2	–	47	21	–	–
	HUMANITIES, RELIGION & THEOLOGY	2	1	–	–	2	1	–	–
	FINE AND APPLIED ARTS	–	–	–	–	–	–	–	–
	LAW	48	5	48	5	–	–	–	–
	SOCIAL AND BEHAVIOURAL SCIENCE	–	–	–	–	–	–	–	–
	COMMERCIAL & BUSINESS ADMIN.	–	–	–	–	–	–	–	–
	MASS COMMUNICATION & DOCUMENT.	–	–	–	–	–	–	–	–
	HOME ECONOMICS (DOMESTIC SCIENCE)	–	–	–	–	–	–	–	–
	SERVICE TRADES	–	–	–	–	–	–	–	–
	NATURAL SCIENCE	–	–	–	–	–	–	–	–
	MATHEMATICS & COMPUTER SCIENCE	–	–	–	–	–	–	–	–
	MEDICAL SCIENCE & HEALTH-RELATED	25	15	–	–	25	15	–	–
	ENGINEERING	–	–	–	–	–	–	–	–
	ARCHITECTURE & TOWN PLANNING	21	–	–	–	21	–	–	–
	TRADE, CRAFT & INDUSTRIAL PGMS.	–	–	–	–	–	–	–	–
	TRANSPORT AND COMMUNICATIONS	–	–	–	–	–	–	–	–
	AGRICULTURE, FORESTRY & FISHERY	–	–	–	–	–	–	–	–
	OTHER AND NOT SPECIFIED	–	–	–	–	–	–	–	–

3.14 **Third level: graduates by ISCED level and field of study**
Troisième degré: diplômés par niveau de la CITE et domaine d'études
Tercer grado: diplomados por nivel de la CINE y sector de estudios

COUNTRY / YEAR PAYS / ANNEE PAIS / AÑO	FIELD OF STUDY DOMAINES D'ETUDES SECTORES DE ESTUDIOS	INTERNATIONAL STANDARD CLASSIFICATION OF EDUCATION BY LEVEL / CLASSIFICATION INTERNATIONALE TYPE DE L'EDUCATION PAR NIVEAU / CLASIFICACION INTERNACIONAL NORMALIZADA DE LA EDUCACION POR NIVEL							
		ALL LEVELS TOUS NIVEAUX TODOS LOS NIVELES		LEVEL 5 NIVEAU 5 NIVEL 5		LEVEL 6 NIVEAU 6 NIVEL 6		LEVEL 7 NIVEAU 7 NIVEL 7	
		MF	F	MF	F	MF	F	MF	F
		(1)	(2)	(3)	(4)	(5)	(6)	(7)	(8)
NETHERLANDS‡									
1984	TOTAL	14 835	4 545	–	–	14 835	4 545	./.	./.
	EDUCATION SCIENCE & TEACHER TRNG.	–	–	–	–	–	–	–	–
	HUMANITIES, RELIGION & THEOLOGY	2 277	1 089	–	–	2 277	1 089	./.	./.
	FINE AND APPLIED ARTS	–	–	–	–	–	–	–	–
	LAW	2 348	774	–	–	2 348	774	./.	./.
	SOCIAL AND BEHAVIOURAL SCIENCE	2 723	799	–	–	2 723	799	./.	./.
	COMMERCIAL & BUSINESS ADMIN.	384	62	–	–	384	62	./.	./.
	MASS COMMUNICATION & DOCUMENT.	–	–	–	–	–	–	–	–
	HOME ECONOMICS (DOMESTIC SCIENCE)	–	–	–	–	–	–	–	–
	SERVICE TRADES	–	–	–	–	–	–	–	–
	NATURAL SCIENCE	1 360	271	–	–	1 360	271	./.	./.
	MATHEMATICS & COMPUTER SCIENCE	174	21	–	–	174	21	./.	./.
	MEDICAL SCIENCE & HEALTH-RELATED	2 035	594	–	–	2 035	594	./.	./.
	ENGINEERING	1 727	66	–	–	1 727	66	./.	./.
	ARCHITECTURE & TOWN PLANNING	–	–	–	–	–	–	–	–
	TRADE, CRAFT & INDUSTRIAL PGMS.	–	–	–	–	–	–	–	–
	TRANSPORT AND COMMUNICATIONS	–	–	–	–	–	–	–	–
	AGRICULTURE, FORESTRY & FISHERY	774	201	–	–	774	201	./.	./.
	OTHER AND NOT SPECIFIED	1 033	668	–	–	1 033	668	./.	./.
POLAND									
1983	TOTAL	112 917	68 757	38 227	29 787	59 569	32 561	15 121	6 409
	EDUCATION SCIENCE & TEACHER TRNG.	22 914	19 813	12 193	11 315	9 431	7 693	1 290	805
	HUMANITIES, RELIGION & THEOLOGY	5 045	3 400	–	–	2 877	2 195	2 168	1 205
	FINE AND APPLIED ARTS	1 436	725	87	46	1 340	673	9	6
	LAW	1 933	947	–	–	1 857	932	76	15
	SOCIAL AND BEHAVIOURAL SCIENCE	1 618	1 008	–	–	1 467	979	151	29
	COMMERCIAL & BUSINESS ADMIN.	21 024	14 548	8 165	6 901	8 404	5 480	4 455	2 167
	MASS COMMUNICATION & DOCUMENT.	659	582	–	–	659	582	–	–
	HOME ECONOMICS (DOMESTIC SCIENCE)	69	59	–	–	68	58	1	1
	SERVICE TRADES	–	–	–	–	–	–	–	–
	NATURAL SCIENCE	3 196	1 875	–	–	1 660	1 148	1 536	727
	MATHEMATICS & COMPUTER SCIENCE	771	503	–	–	685	477	86	26
	MEDICAL SCIENCE & HEALTH-RELATED	16 183	13 250	10 204	9 318	5 488	3 732	491	200
	ENGINEERING	16 971	3 847	–	–	14 271	3 425	2 700	422
	ARCHITECTURE & TOWN PLANNING	436	248	–	–	436	248	–	–
	TRADE, CRAFT & INDUSTRIAL PGMS.	5 761	1 428	5 761	1 428	–	–	–	–
	TRANSPORT AND COMMUNICATIONS	881	94	–	–	875	94	6	–
	AGRICULTURE, FORESTRY & FISHERY	11 635	5 483	1 817	779	8 054	4 034	1 764	670
	OTHER AND NOT SPECIFIED	2 385	947	–	–	1 997	811	388	136
PORTUGAL									
1982	TOTAL	11 760	6 832	...	...	...	...	...	...
	EDUCATION SCIENCE & TEACHER TRNG.	2 382	2 070	...	...	...	...	...	...
	HUMANITIES, RELIGION & THEOLOGY	2 026	1 517	...	...	...	...	...	...
	FINE AND APPLIED ARTS	313	141	...	...	...	...	...	...
	LAW	814	286	...	...	...	...	...	...
	SOCIAL AND BEHAVIOURAL SCIENCE	1 844	814	...	...	...	...	...	...
	COMMERCIAL & BUSINESS ADMIN.	–	–	...	...	...	...	...	...
	MASS COMMUNICATION & DOCUMENT.	12	8	...	...	...	...	...	...
	HOME ECONOMICS (DOMESTIC SCIENCE)	–	–	...	...	...	...	...	...
	SERVICE TRADES	–	–	...	...	...	...	...	...
	NATURAL SCIENCE	73	36	...	...	...	...	...	...
	MATHEMATICS & COMPUTER SCIENCE	–	–	...	...	...	...	...	...
	MEDICAL SCIENCE & HEALTH-RELATED	2 164	1 464	...	...	...	...	...	...
	ENGINEERING	1 309	220	...	...	...	...	...	...
	ARCHITECTURE & TOWN PLANNING	6	3	...	...	...	...	...	...
	TRADE, CRAFT & INDUSTRIAL PGMS.	–	–	...	...	...	...	...	...
	TRANSPORT AND COMMUNICATIONS	–	–	...	...	...	...	...	...
	AGRICULTURE, FORESTRY & FISHERY	178	47	...	...	...	...	...	...
	OTHER AND NOT SPECIFIED	639	226	...	...	...	...	...	...

COUNTRY YEAR / PAYS ANNEE / PAIS AÑO	FIELD OF STUDY / DOMAINES D'ETUDES / SECTORES DE ESTUDIOS	INTERNATIONAL STANDARD CLASSIFICATION OF EDUCATION BY LEVEL / CLASSIFICATION INTERNATIONALE TYPE DE L'EDUCATION PAR NIVEAU / CLASIFICACION INTERNACIONAL NORMALIZADA DE LA EDUCACION POR NIVEL — ALL LEVELS / TOUS NIVEAUX / TODOS LOS NIVELES		LEVEL 5 / NIVEAU 5 / NIVEL 5		LEVEL 6 / NIVEAU 6 / NIVEL 6		LEVEL 7 / NIVEAU 7 / NIVEL 7	
		MF	F	MF	F	MF	F	MF	F
		(1)	(2)	(3)	(4)	(5)	(6)	(7)	(8)
ROMANIA‡ 1979	TOTAL	37 834	...	–	–	37 834	...	–	–
	EDUCATION SCIENCE & TEACHER TRNG.	3 918	...	–	–	3 918	...	–	–
	HUMANITIES, RELIGION & THEOLOGY	./.	...	–	–	./.	...	–	–
	FINE AND APPLIED ARTS	951	...	–	–	951	...	–	–
	LAW	1 867	...	–	–	1 867	...	–	–
	SOCIAL AND BEHAVIOURAL SCIENCE	4 953	...	–	–	4 953	...	–	–
	COMMERCIAL & BUSINESS ADMIN.	–	–	–	–	–	–	–	–
	MASS COMMUNICATION & DOCUMENT.	–	–	–	–	–	–	–	–
	HOME ECONOMICS (DOMESTIC SCIENCE)	–	–	–	–	–	–	–	–
	SERVICE TRADES	–	–	–	–	–	–	–	–
	NATURAL SCIENCE	1 744	...	–	–	1 744	...	–	–
	MATHEMATICS & COMPUTER SCIENCE	786	...	–	–	786	...	–	–
	MEDICAL SCIENCE & HEALTH-RELATED	3 447	...	–	–	3 447	...	–	–
	ENGINEERING	16 499	...	–	–	16 499	...	–	–
	ARCHITECTURE & TOWN PLANNING	278	...	–	–	278	...	–	–
	TRADE, CRAFT & INDUSTRIAL PGMS.	–	–	–	–	–	–	–	–
	TRANSPORT AND COMMUNICATIONS	301	...	–	–	301	...	–	–
	AGRICULTURE, FORESTRY & FISHERY	3 090	...	–	–	3 090	...	–	–
	OTHER AND NOT SPECIFIED	–	–	–	–	–	–	–	–
SPAIN‡ 1983	TOTAL	81 193	43 390	36 533	23 228	44 660	20 162	./.	./.
	EDUCATION SCIENCE & TEACHER TRNG.	25 640	18 671	23 307	17 222	2 333	1 449	./.	./.
	HUMANITIES, RELIGION & THEOLOGY	3 177	2 142	107	79	3 070	2 063	./.	./.
	FINE AND APPLIED ARTS	1 043	392	18	11	1 025	381	./.	./.
	LAW	5 011	1 956	–	–	5 011	1 956	./.	./.
	SOCIAL AND BEHAVIOURAL SCIENCE	9 710	5 126	–	–	9 710	5 126	./.	./.
	COMMERCIAL & BUSINESS ADMIN.	2 630	1 002	2 630	1 002	–	–	–	–
	MASS COMMUNICATION & DOCUMENT.	881	359	14	14	867	345	./.	./.
	HOME ECONOMICS (DOMESTIC SCIENCE)	–	–	–	–	–	–	–	–
	SERVICE TRADES	931	661	–	–	931	661	–	–
	NATURAL SCIENCE	3 444	1 627	–	–	3 444	1 627	./.	./.
	MATHEMATICS & COMPUTER SCIENCE	693	258	22	8	671	250	./.	./.
	MEDICAL SCIENCE & HEALTH-RELATED	16 735	9 150	4 847	3 840	11 888	5 310	./.	./.
	ENGINEERING	6 160	442	3 930	317	2 230	125	./.	./.
	ARCHITECTURE & TOWN PLANNING	1 914	247	988	115	926	132	./.	./.
	TRADE, CRAFT & INDUSTRIAL PGMS.	–	–	–	–	–	–	–	–
	TRANSPORT AND COMMUNICATIONS	–	–	–	–	–	–	–	–
	AGRICULTURE, FORESTRY & FISHERY	456	121	–	–	456	121	–	–
	OTHER AND NOT SPECIFIED	2 768	1 236	670	620	2 098	616	./.	./.
SWITZERLAND 1984	TOTAL	8 699	2 656	444	305	6 134	1 942	2 121	409
	EDUCATION SCIENCE & TEACHER TRNG.	239	157	74	66	115	76	50	15
	HUMANITIES, RELIGION & THEOLOGY	1 347	717	305	218	872	445	170	54
	FINE AND APPLIED ARTS	52	32	1	1	42	27	9	4
	LAW	1 019	303	1	–	857	287	161	16
	SOCIAL AND BEHAVIOURAL SCIENCE	1 665	537	8	3	1 410	474	247	60
	COMMERCIAL & BUSINESS ADMIN.	–	–	–	–	–	–	–	–
	MASS COMMUNICATION & DOCUMENT.	18	7	18	7	–	–	–	–
	HOME ECONOMICS (DOMESTIC SCIENCE)	–	–	–	–	–	–	–	–
	SERVICE TRADES	–	–	–	–	–	–	–	–
	NATURAL SCIENCE	1 078	198	32	8	656	140	390	50
	MATHEMATICS & COMPUTER SCIENCE	193	31	5	2	152	23	36	6
	MEDICAL SCIENCE & HEALTH-RELATED	1 929	544	–	–	1 064	358	865	186
	ENGINEERING	673	19	–	–	552	15	121	4
	ARCHITECTURE & TOWN PLANNING	193	47	–	–	189	45	4	2
	TRADE, CRAFT & INDUSTRIAL PGMS.	–	–	–	–	–	–	–	–
	TRANSPORT AND COMMUNICATIONS	–	–	–	–	–	–	–	–
	AGRICULTURE, FORESTRY & FISHERY	293	64	–	–	225	52	68	12
	OTHER AND NOT SPECIFIED	–	–	–	–	–	–	–	–

3.14 Third level: graduates by ISCED level and field of study
Troisième degré: diplômés par niveau de la CITE et domaine d'études
Tercer grado: diplomados por nivel de la CINE y sector de estudios

COUNTRY YEAR PAYS ANNEE PAIS AÑO	FIELD OF STUDY DOMAINES D'ETUDES SECTORES DE ESTUDIOS	INTERNATIONAL STANDARD CLASSIFICATION OF EDUCATION BY LEVEL / CLASSIFICATION INTERNATIONALE TYPE DE L'EDUCATION PAR NIVEAU / CLASIFICACION INTERNACIONAL NORMALIZADA DE LA EDUCACION POR NIVEL							
		ALL LEVELS TOUS NIVEAUX TODOS LOS NIVELES		LEVEL 5 NIVEAU 5 NIVEL 5		LEVEL 6 NIVEAU 6 NIVEL 6		LEVEL 7 NIVEAU 7 NIVEL 7	
		MF	F	MF	F	MF	F	MF	F
		(1)	(2)	(3)	(4)	(5)	(6)	(7)	(8)
UNITED KINGDOM‡									
1981	TOTAL	164 301	...	30 755	...	105 586	40 906	27 960	8 476
	EDUCATION SCIENCE & TEACHER TRNG.	15 491	8 741	5 420	2 665	5 914	4 026	4 157	2 050
	HUMANITIES, RELIGION & THEOLOGY	17 810	10 343	139	74	15 321	9 332	2 350	937
	FINE AND APPLIED ARTS	6 360	3 514	1	–	6 044	3 357	315	157
	LAW	5 617	2 102	9	4	4 757	1 856	851	242
	SOCIAL AND BEHAVIOURAL SCIENCE	19 000	8 359	94	58	15 791	7 036	3 115	1 265
	COMMERCIAL & BUSINESS ADMIN.	16 143	...	6 971	...	6 668	1 778	2 504	567
	MASS COMMUNICATION & DOCUMENT.	489	378	–	–	489	378	–	–
	HOME ECONOMICS (DOMESTIC SCIENCE)	212	141	–	–	181	124	31	17
	SERVICE TRADES	./.	./.	–	–	./.	./.	./.	./.
	NATURAL SCIENCE	22 932	...	3 741	...	15 290	4 797	3 901	789
	MATHEMATICS & COMPUTER SCIENCE	5 700	1 379	10	1	4 705	1 224	985	154
	MEDICAL SCIENCE & HEALTH–RELATED	9 434	...	258	...	7 342	3 048	1 834	636
	ENGINEERING	32 070	...	13 578	...	14 695	705	3 797	289
	ARCHITECTURE & TOWN PLANNING	2 786	567	41	4	2 095	428	650	135
	TRADE, CRAFT & INDUSTRIAL PGMS.	554	22	–	–	554	22	–	–
	TRANSPORT AND COMMUNICATIONS	–	–	–	–	–	–	–	–
	AGRICULTURE, FORESTRY & FISHERY	2 582	...	493	...	1 430	492	659	142
	OTHER AND NOT SPECIFIED	7 121	3 399	–	–	4 310	2 303	2 811	1 096
YUGOSLAVIA‡									
1982	TOTAL	58 799	26 594	23 767	11 699	32 095	14 116	2 937	779
	EDUCATION SCIENCE & TEACHER TRNG.	7 694	4 968	5 767	4 170	1 886	790	41	8
	HUMANITIES, RELIGION & THEOLOGY	3 720	2 465	291	277	3 146	2 071	283	117
	FINE AND APPLIED ARTS	645	290	19	15	547	243	79	32
	LAW	5 543	2 817	1 142	607	4 256	2 185	145	25
	SOCIAL AND BEHAVIOURAL SCIENCE	13 602	7 113	5 637	3 223	7 536	3 802	429	88
	COMMERCIAL & BUSINESS ADMIN.	1 785	519	1 076	325	669	186	40	8
	MASS COMMUNICATION & DOCUMENT.	61	21	6	1	55	20	–	–
	HOME ECONOMICS (DOMESTIC SCIENCE)	87	61	87	61	–	–	–	–
	SERVICE TRADES	1 005	385	881	342	120	43	4	–
	NATURAL SCIENCE	2 254	1 187	214	120	1 702	945	338	122
	MATHEMATICS & COMPUTER SCIENCE	./.	./.	./.	./.	./.	./.	./.	./.
	MEDICAL SCIENCE & HEALTH–RELATED	5 385	3 395	1 309	1 095	3 500	2 079	576	221
	ENGINEERING	10 655	1 698	3 867	552	6 141	1 048	647	98
	ARCHITECTURE & TOWN PLANNING	670	295	31	14	601	270	38	11
	TRADE, CRAFT & INDUSTRIAL PGMS.	440	197	440	197	–	–	–	–
	TRANSPORT AND COMMUNICATIONS	1 918	248	1 624	210	283	37	11	1
	AGRICULTURE, FORESTRY & FISHERY	2 310	550	395	122	1 653	397	262	31
	OTHER AND NOT SPECIFIED	1 025	385	981	368	–	–	44	17
OCEANIA									
AMERICAN SAMOA									
1982	TOTAL	131	53	131	53	–	–	–	–
	EDUCATION SCIENCE & TEACHER TRNG.	–	–	–	–	–	–	–	–
	HUMANITIES, RELIGION & THEOLOGY	52	32	52	32	–	–	–	–
	FINE AND APPLIED ARTS	9	3	9	3	–	–	–	–
	LAW	–	–	–	–	–	–	–	–
	SOCIAL AND BEHAVIOURAL SCIENCE	–	–	–	–	–	–	–	–
	COMMERCIAL & BUSINESS ADMIN.	37	13	37	13	–	–	–	–
	MASS COMMUNICATION & DOCUMENT.	–	–	–	–	–	–	–	–
	HOME ECONOMICS (DOMESTIC SCIENCE)	–	–	–	–	–	–	–	–
	SERVICE TRADES	–	–	–	–	–	–	–	–
	NATURAL SCIENCE	–	–	–	–	–	–	–	–
	MATHEMATICS & COMPUTER SCIENCE	–	–	–	–	–	–	–	–
	MEDICAL SCIENCE & HEALTH–RELATED	5	4	5	4	–	–	–	–
	ENGINEERING	–	–	–	–	–	–	–	–
	ARCHITECTURE & TOWN PLANNING	–	–	–	–	–	–	–	–
	TRADE, CRAFT & INDUSTRIAL PGMS.	20	–	20	–	–	–	–	–
	TRANSPORT AND COMMUNICATIONS	–	–	–	–	–	–	–	–
	AGRICULTURE, FORESTRY & FISHERY	–	–	–	–	–	–	–	–
	OTHER AND NOT SPECIFIED	8	1	8	1	–	–	–	–

COUNTRY YEAR / PAYS ANNEE / PAIS AÑO	FIELD OF STUDY / DOMAINES D'ETUDES / SECTORES DE ESTUDIOS	INTERNATIONAL STANDARD CLASSIFICATION OF EDUCATION BY LEVEL / CLASSIFICATION INTERNATIONALE TYPE DE L'EDUCATION PAR NIVEAU / CLASIFICACION INTERNACIONAL NORMALIZADA DE LA EDUCACION POR NIVEL							
		ALL LEVELS / TOUS NIVEAUX / TODOS LOS NIVELES		LEVEL 5 / NIVEAU 5 / NIVEL 5		LEVEL 6 / NIVEAU 6 / NIVEL 6		LEVEL 7 / NIVEAU 7 / NIVEL 7	
		MF	F	MF	F	MF	F	MF	F
		(1)	(2)	(3)	(4)	(5)	(6)	(7)	(8)
AUSTRALIA‡ 1984	TOTAL	68 939	19 501	16 320	8 352	41 015	7 282	11 604	3 867
	EDUCATION SCIENCE & TEACHER TRNG.	21 629	11 599	9 875	5 574	7 024	3 550	4 730	2 475
	HUMANITIES, RELIGION & THEOLOGY	1 094	773	165	102	669	467	260	204
	FINE AND APPLIED ARTS	11 764	1 259	1 412	608	9 266	539	1 086	112
	LAW	2 039	...	59	...	1 877	...	103	...
	SOCIAL AND BEHAVIOURAL SCIENCE	2 028	1 407	712	551	919	589	397	267
	COMMERCIAL & BUSINESS ADMIN.	10 465	1 801	1 001	359	7 144	933	2 320	509
	MASS COMMUNICATION & DOCUMENT.	–	–	–	–	–	–	–	–
	HOME ECONOMICS (DOMESTIC SCIENCE)	–	–	–	–	–	–	–	–
	SERVICE TRADES	–	–	–	–	–	–	–	–
	NATURAL SCIENCE	8 644	1 053	835	212	6 477	678	1 332	163
	MATHEMATICS & COMPUTER SCIENCE	–	–	–				–	–
	MEDICAL SCIENCE & HEALTH–RELATED	4 500	1 288	951	733	3 098	439	451	116
	ENGINEERING	3 996	35	499	6	2 918	22	579	7
	ARCHITECTURE & TOWN PLANNING	1 188	73	164	11	869	52	155	10
	TRADE, CRAFT & INDUSTRIAL PGMS.	–	–	–	–	–	–	–	–
	TRANSPORT AND COMMUNICATIONS	–	–	–	–	–	–	–	–
	AGRICULTURE, FORESTRY & FISHERY	1 587	213	647	196	754	13	186	4
	OTHER AND NOT SPECIFIED	5	–	–	–	–	–	5	–
FIJI‡ 1981	TOTAL	356	108	203	70	153	38	–	–
	EDUCATION SCIENCE & TEACHER TRNG.	210	83	147	68	63	15	–	–
	HUMANITIES, RELIGION & THEOLOGY	–	–	–	–	–	–	–	–
	FINE AND APPLIED ARTS	–	–	–	–	–	–	–	–
	LAW	–	–	–	–	–	–	–	–
	SOCIAL AND BEHAVIOURAL SCIENCE	67	17	1	–	66	17	–	–
	COMMERCIAL & BUSINESS ADMIN.	./.	./.	./.	–	./.	./.	–	–
	MASS COMMUNICATION & DOCUMENT.	–	–	–	–	–	–	–	–
	HOME ECONOMICS (DOMESTIC SCIENCE)	–	–	–	–	–	–	–	–
	SERVICE TRADES	–	–	–	–	–	–	–	–
	NATURAL SCIENCE	9	2	–	–	9	2	–	–
	MATHEMATICS & COMPUTER SCIENCE	–	–	–	–	–	–	–	–
	MEDICAL SCIENCE & HEALTH–RELATED	–	–	–	–	–	–	–	–
	ENGINEERING	–	–	–	–	–	–	–	–
	ARCHITECTURE & TOWN PLANNING	–	–	–	–	–	–	–	–
	TRADE, CRAFT & INDUSTRIAL PGMS.	–	–	–	–	–	–	–	–
	TRANSPORT AND COMMUNICATIONS	–	–	–	–	–	–	–	–
	AGRICULTURE, FORESTRY & FISHERY	70	6	55	2	15	4	–	–
	OTHER AND NOT SPECIFIED	–	–	–	–	–	–	–	–
FRENCH POLYNESIA 1982	TOTAL	15	4	–	–	15	4	–	–
	EDUCATION SCIENCE & TEACHER TRNG.	–	–	–	–	–	–	–	–
	HUMANITIES, RELIGION & THEOLOGY	–	–	–	–	–	–	–	–
	FINE AND APPLIED ARTS	–	–	–	–	–	–	–	–
	LAW	–	–	–	–	–	–	–	–
	SOCIAL AND BEHAVIOURAL SCIENCE	–	–	–	–	–	–	–	–
	COMMERCIAL & BUSINESS ADMIN.	11	4	–	–	11	4	–	–
	MASS COMMUNICATION & DOCUMENT.	–	–	–	–	–	–	–	–
	HOME ECONOMICS (DOMESTIC SCIENCE)	–	–	–	–	–	–	–	–
	SERVICE TRADES	–	–	–	–	–	–	–	–
	NATURAL SCIENCE	–	–	–	–	–	–	–	–
	MATHEMATICS & COMPUTER SCIENCE	–	–	–	–	–	–	–	–
	MEDICAL SCIENCE & HEALTH–RELATED	4	–	–	–	4	–	–	–
	ENGINEERING	–	–	–	–	–	–	–	–
	ARCHITECTURE & TOWN PLANNING	–	–	–	–	–	–	–	–
	TRADE, CRAFT & INDUSTRIAL PGMS.	–	–	–	–	–	–	–	–
	TRANSPORT AND COMMUNICATIONS	–	–	–	–	–	–	–	–
	AGRICULTURE, FORESTRY & FISHERY	–	–	–	–	–	–	–	–
	OTHER AND NOT SPECIFIED	–	–	–	–	–	–	–	–

3.14 Third level: graduates by ISCED level and field of study
Troisième degré: diplômés par niveau de la CITE et domaine d'études
Tercer grado: diplomados por nivel de la CINE y sector de estudios

COUNTRY YEAR / PAYS ANNEE / PAIS AÑO	FIELD OF STUDY / DOMAINES D'ETUDES / SECTORES DE ESTUDIOS	INTERNATIONAL STANDARD CLASSIFICATION OF EDUCATION BY LEVEL / CLASSIFICATION INTERNATIONALE TYPE DE L'EDUCATION PAR NIVEAU / CLASIFICACION INTERNACIONAL NORMALIZADA DE LA EDUCACION POR NIVEL							
		ALL LEVELS / TOUS NIVEAUX / TODOS LOS NIVELES		LEVEL 5 / NIVEAU 5 / NIVEL 5		LEVEL 6 / NIVEAU 6 / NIVEL 6		LEVEL 7 / NIVEAU 7 / NIVEL 7	
		MF	F	MF	F	MF	F	MF	F
		(1)	(2)	(3)	(4)	(5)	(6)	(7)	(8)
NEW CALEDONIA‡									
1984	TOTAL	273	98	230	82	36	14	7	2
	EDUCATION SCIENCE & TEACHER TRNG.	45	32	45	32	–	–	–	–
	HUMANITIES, RELIGION & THEOLOGY	–	–	–	–	–	–	–	–
	FINE AND APPLIED ARTS	–	–	–	–	–	–	–	–
	LAW	24	10	4	–	14	8	6	2
	SOCIAL AND BEHAVIOURAL SCIENCE	1	–	–	–	–	–	1	–
	COMMERCIAL & BUSINESS ADMIN.	8	6	–	–	8	6	–	–
	MASS COMMUNICATION & DOCUMENT.	–	–	–	–	–	–	–	–
	HOME ECONOMICS (DOMESTIC SCIENCE)	–	–	–	–	–	–	–	–
	SERVICE TRADES	–	–	–	–	–	–	–	–
	NATURAL SCIENCE	./.	./.	./.	./.	–	–	–	–
	MATHEMATICS & COMPUTER SCIENCE	181	50	181	50	–	–	–	–
	MEDICAL SCIENCE & HEALTH-RELATED	–	–	–	–	–	–	–	–
	ENGINEERING	12	–	–	–	12	–	–	–
	ARCHITECTURE & TOWN PLANNING	–	–	–	–	–	–	–	–
	TRADE, CRAFT & INDUSTRIAL PGMS.	2	–	–	–	2	–	–	–
	TRANSPORT AND COMMUNICATIONS	–	–	–	–	–	–	–	–
	AGRICULTURE, FORESTRY & FISHERY	–	–	–	–	–	–	–	–
	OTHER AND NOT SPECIFIED	–	–	–	–	–	–	–	–
NEW ZEALAND‡									
1982	TOTAL	11 536	5 315	2 937	1 907	6 718	2 702	1 881	706
	EDUCATION SCIENCE & TEACHER TRNG.	2 401	1 819	1 977	1 553	254	180	170	86
	HUMANITIES, RELIGION & THEOLOGY	2 463	1 452	–	–	1 834	1 163	629	289
	FINE AND APPLIED ARTS	134	77	18	7	86	52	30	18
	LAW	410	148	–	–	393	141	17	7
	SOCIAL AND BEHAVIOURAL SCIENCE	181	91	9	6	121	65	51	20
	COMMERCIAL & BUSINESS ADMIN.	1 456	349	69	10	1 163	288	224	51
	MASS COMMUNICATION & DOCUMENT.	66	48	–	–	–	–	66	48
	HOME ECONOMICS (DOMESTIC SCIENCE)	76	76	51	51	25	25	–	–
	SERVICE TRADES	–	–	–	–	–	–	–	–
	NATURAL SCIENCE	1 671	498	–	–	1 338	434	333	64
	MATHEMATICS & COMPUTER SCIENCE	5	3	1	–	./.	./.	4	3
	MEDICAL SCIENCE & HEALTH-RELATED	654	251	12	–	471	177	171	67
	ENGINEERING	480	12	–	–	450	11	30	1
	ARCHITECTURE & TOWN PLANNING	179	43	–	–	155	32	24	11
	TRADE, CRAFT & INDUSTRIAL PGMS.	–	–	–	–	–	–	–	–
	TRANSPORT AND COMMUNICATIONS	–	–	–	–	–	–	–	–
	AGRICULTURE, FORESTRY & FISHERY	1 074	255	584	136	385	95	105	24
	OTHER AND NOT SPECIFIED	286	193	216	137	43	39	27	17
PACIFIC ISLANDS									
1982	TOTAL	540	243	540	243	–	–	–	–
	EDUCATION SCIENCE & TEACHER TRNG.	360	167	360	167	–	–	–	–
	HUMANITIES, RELIGION & THEOLOGY	–	–	–	–	–	–	–	–
	FINE AND APPLIED ARTS	–	–	–	–	–	–	–	–
	LAW	–	–	–	–	–	–	–	–
	SOCIAL AND BEHAVIOURAL SCIENCE	–	–	–	–	–	–	–	–
	COMMERCIAL & BUSINESS ADMIN.	–	–	–	–	–	–	–	–
	MASS COMMUNICATION & DOCUMENT.	55	36	55	36	–	–	–	–
	HOME ECONOMICS (DOMESTIC SCIENCE)	–	–	–	–	–	–	–	–
	SERVICE TRADES	7	5	7	5	–	–	–	–
	NATURAL SCIENCE	–	–	–	–	–	–	–	–
	MATHEMATICS & COMPUTER SCIENCE	–	–	–	–	–	–	–	–
	MEDICAL SCIENCE & HEALTH-RELATED	14	10	14	10	–	–	–	–
	ENGINEERING	–	–	–	–	–	–	–	–
	ARCHITECTURE & TOWN PLANNING	–	–	–	–	–	–	–	–
	TRADE, CRAFT & INDUSTRIAL PGMS.	53	3	53	3	–	–	–	–
	TRANSPORT AND COMMUNICATIONS	–	–	–	–	–	–	–	–
	AGRICULTURE, FORESTRY & FISHERY	7	1	7	1	–	–	–	–
	OTHER AND NOT SPECIFIED	44	21	44	21	–	–	–	–

COUNTRY / YEAR PAYS / ANNEE PAIS / AÑO	FIELD OF STUDY DOMAINES D'ETUDES SECTORES DE ESTUDIOS	INTERNATIONAL STANDARD CLASSIFICATION OF EDUCATION BY LEVEL / CLASSIFICATION INTERNATIONALE TYPE DE L'EDUCATION PAR NIVEAU / CLASIFICACION INTERNACIONAL NORMALIZADA DE LA EDUCACION POR NIVEL							
		ALL LEVELS TOUS NIVEAUX TODOS LOS NIVELES		LEVEL 5 NIVEAU 5 NIVEL 5		LEVEL 6 NIVEAU 6 NIVEL 6		LEVEL 7 NIVEAU 7 NIVEL 7	
		MF	F	MF	F	MF	F	MF	F
		(1)	(2)	(3)	(4)	(5)	(6)	(7)	(8)
PAPUA NEW GUINEA									
1983	TOTAL	1 520	390	1 143	351	352	37	25	2
	EDUCATION SCIENCE & TEACHER TRNG.	193	68	164	60	26	8	3	–
	HUMANITIES, RELIGION & THEOLOGY	105	37	70	35	35	2	–	–
	FINE AND APPLIED ARTS	4	1	4	1	–	–	–	–
	LAW	42	2	–	–	22	1	20	1
	SOCIAL AND BEHAVIOURAL SCIENCE	35	4	–	–	34	3	1	1
	COMMERCIAL & BUSINESS ADMIN.	173	29	95	20	78	9	–	–
	MASS COMMUNICATION & DOCUMENT.	37	21	37	21	–	–	–	–
	HOME ECONOMICS (DOMESTIC SCIENCE)	–	–	–	–	–	–	–	–
	SERVICE TRADES	–	–	–	–	–	–	–	–
	NATURAL SCIENCE	23	1	–	–	23	1	–	–
	MATHEMATICS & COMPUTER SCIENCE	7	2	–	–	7	2	–	–
	MEDICAL SCIENCE & HEALTH–RELATED	261	171	241	164	20	7	–	–
	ENGINEERING	95	1	32	–	63	1	–	–
	ARCHITECTURE & TOWN PLANNING	30	–	13	–	17	–	–	–
	TRADE, CRAFT & INDUSTRIAL PGMS.	–	–	–	–	–	–	–	–
	TRANSPORT AND COMMUNICATIONS	–	–	–	–	–	–	–	–
	AGRICULTURE, FORESTRY & FISHERY	380	38	359	37	21	1	–	–
	OTHER AND NOT SPECIFIED	135	15	128	13	6	2	1	–
TONGA‡									
1981	TOTAL	300	91	246	83	54	8	–	–
	EDUCATION SCIENCE & TEACHER TRNG.	69	38	69	38	–	–	–	–
	HUMANITIES, RELIGION & THEOLOGY	18	2	6	–	12	2	–	–
	FINE AND APPLIED ARTS	–	–	–	–	–	–	–	–
	LAW	144	28	144	28	–	–	–	–
	SOCIAL AND BEHAVIOURAL SCIENCE	18	3	–	–	18	3	–	–
	COMMERCIAL & BUSINESS ADMIN.	11	1	11	1	–	–	–	–
	MASS COMMUNICATION & DOCUMENT.	–	–	–	–	–	–	–	–
	HOME ECONOMICS (DOMESTIC SCIENCE)	–	–	–	–	–	–	–	–
	SERVICE TRADES	–	–	–	–	–	–	–	–
	NATURAL SCIENCE	18	3	–	–	18	3	–	–
	MATHEMATICS & COMPUTER SCIENCE	6	–	–	–	6	–	–	–
	MEDICAL SCIENCE & HEALTH–RELATED	16	16	16	16	–	–	–	–
	ENGINEERING	–	–	–	–	–	–	–	–
	ARCHITECTURE & TOWN PLANNING	–	–	–	–	–	–	–	–
	TRADE, CRAFT & INDUSTRIAL PGMS.	–	–	–	–	–	–	–	–
	TRANSPORT AND COMMUNICATIONS	–	–	–	–	–	–	–	–
	AGRICULTURE, FORESTRY & FISHERY	–	–	–	–	–	–	–	–
	OTHER AND NOT SPECIFIED	–	–	–	–	–	–	–	–
U.S.S.R.									
U.S.S.R.‡									
1983	TOTAL	855 000	...	...	...	...	...	...	...
	EDUCATION SCIENCE & TEACHER TRNG.	272 500	...	...	...	...	...	...	...
	HUMANITIES, RELIGION & THEOLOGY	...	...	...	...	...	...	...	...
	FINE AND APPLIED ARTS	9 100	...	...	...	...	...	...	...
	LAW	69 300	...	...	...	...	...	...	...
	SOCIAL AND BEHAVIOURAL SCIENCE	...	...	...	...	...	...	...	...
	COMMERCIAL & BUSINESS ADMIN.	...	...	...	...	...	...	...	...
	MASS COMMUNICATION & DOCUMENT.	...	...	...	...	...	...	...	...
	HOME ECONOMICS (DOMESTIC SCIENCE)	...	...	...	...	...	...	...	...
	SERVICE TRADES	...	...	...	...	...	...	...	...
	NATURAL SCIENCE	...	...	...	...	...	...	...	...
	MATHEMATICS & COMPUTER SCIENCE	...	...	...	...	...	...	...	...
	MEDICAL SCIENCE & HEALTH–RELATED	64 000	...	...	...	...	...	...	...
	ENGINEERING	356 800	...	...	...	...	...	...	...
	ARCHITECTURE & TOWN PLANNING	...	...	...	...	...	...	...	...
	TRADE, CRAFT & INDUSTRIAL PGMS.	...	...	...	...	...	...	...	...
	TRANSPORT AND COMMUNICATIONS	./.	...	...	...	...	...	...	...
	AGRICULTURE, FORESTRY & FISHERY	83 300	...	...	...	...	...	...	...
	OTHER AND NOT SPECIFIED	./.	...	...	...	...	...	...	...

3.14 Third level: graduates by ISCED level and field of study
Troisième degré: diplômés par niveau de la CITE et domaine d'études
Tercer grado: diplomados por nivel de la CINE y sector de estudios

COUNTRY / YEAR — PAYS / ANNEE — PAIS / AÑO	FIELD OF STUDY — DOMAINES D'ETUDES — SECTORES DE ESTUDIOS	INTERNATIONAL STANDARD CLASSIFICATION OF EDUCATION BY LEVEL / CLASSIFICATION INTERNATIONALE TYPE DE L'EDUCATION PAR NIVEAU / CLASIFICACION INTERNACIONAL NORMALIZADA DE LA EDUCACION POR NIVEL							
		ALL LEVELS / TOUS NIVEAUX / TODOS LOS NIVELES		LEVEL 5 / NIVEAU 5 / NIVEL 5		LEVEL 6 / NIVEAU 6 / NIVEL 6		LEVEL 7 / NIVEAU 7 / NIVEL 7	
		MF	F	MF	F	MF	F	MF	F
		(1)	(2)	(3)	(4)	(5)	(6)	(7)	(8)
BYELORUSSIAN S.S.R.‡									
1983	TOTAL	31 300	...	...	...	...	...	...	...
	EDUCATION SCIENCE & TEACHER TRNG.	10 300	...	...	...	...	...	...	...
	HUMANITIES, RELIGION & THEOLOGY	...	...	...	...	...	...	...	...
	FINE AND APPLIED ARTS	300	...	...	...	...	...	...	...
	LAW	3 300	...	...	...	...	...	...	...
	SOCIAL AND BEHAVIOURAL SCIENCE	...	...	...	...	...	...	...	...
	COMMERCIAL & BUSINESS ADMIN.	...	...	...	...	...	...	...	...
	MASS COMMUNICATION & DOCUMENT.	...	...	...	...	...	...	...	...
	HOME ECONOMICS (DOMESTIC SCIENCE)	...	...	...	...	...	...	...	...
	SERVICE TRADES	...	...	...	...	...	...	...	...
	NATURAL SCIENCE	...	...	...	...	...	...	...	...
	MATHEMATICS & COMPUTER SCIENCE	...	...	...	...	...	...	...	...
	MEDICAL SCIENCE & HEALTH-RELATED	2 100	...	...	...	...	...	...	...
	ENGINEERING	11 300	...	...	...	...	...	...	...
	ARCHITECTURE & TOWN PLANNING	...	...	...	...	...	...	...	...
	TRADE, CRAFT & INDUSTRIAL PGMS.	...	...	...	...	...	...	...	...
	TRANSPORT AND COMMUNICATIONS	./.	...	...	...	...	...	...	...
	AGRICULTURE, FORESTRY & FISHERY	4 000	...	...	...	...	...	...	...
	OTHER AND NOT SPECIFIED	./.	...	...	...	...	...	...	...
UKRAINIAN S.S.R.‡									
1983	TOTAL	150 200	...	...	...	...	...	...	...
	EDUCATION SCIENCE & TEACHER TRNG.	42 500	...	...	...	...	...	...	...
	HUMANITIES, RELIGION & THEOLOGY	...	...	...	...	...	...	...	...
	FINE AND APPLIED ARTS	1 300	...	...	...	...	...	...	...
	LAW	15 100	...	...	...	...	...	...	...
	SOCIAL AND BEHAVIOURAL SCIENCE	...	...	...	...	...	...	...	...
	COMMERCIAL & BUSINESS ADMIN.	...	...	...	...	...	...	...	...
	MASS COMMUNICATION & DOCUMENT.	...	...	...	...	...	...	...	...
	HOME ECONOMICS (DOMESTIC SCIENCE)	...	...	...	...	...	...	...	...
	SERVICE TRADES	...	...	...	...	...	...	...	...
	NATURAL SCIENCE	...	...	...	...	...	...	...	...
	MATHEMATICS & COMPUTER SCIENCE	...	...	...	...	...	...	...	...
	MEDICAL SCIENCE & HEALTH-RELATED	10 100	...	...	...	...	...	...	...
	ENGINEERING	66 500	...	...	...	...	...	...	...
	ARCHITECTURE & TOWN PLANNING	...	...	...	...	...	...	...	...
	TRADE, CRAFT & INDUSTRIAL PGMS.	...	...	...	...	...	...	...	...
	TRANSPORT AND COMMUNICATIONS	./.	...	...	...	...	...	...	...
	AGRICULTURE, FORESTRY & FISHERY	14 700	...	...	...	...	...	...	...
	OTHER AND NOT SPECIFIED	./.	...	...	...	...	...	...	...

This table shows the number of students who have successfully completed their studies by level of degree or diploma obtained and by field of study.

In general, these degrees or diplomas were awarded at the end of the academic year which began during the calendar year indicated. For example, where the academic year does not coincide with the calendar year the data shown as 1984 refer to degrees awarded at the end of the academic year 1984/1985. More information on this point is given in the general introduction to the *Education* section.

The three level categories, represented here by their ISCED codes (5, 6 and 7) are defined as follows:

Level 5: Diplomas and certificates not equivalent to a first university degree. These correspond to higher studies of reduced duration (generally less than three years). They include, for instance, certificates awarded to certain types of technicians, nursing diplomas, land-surveying diplomas, associate degrees, certificates of competence in law, etc.

Level 6: First university degrees or equivalent qualifications. These represent higher studies of normal duration (generally three to five years and, in certain cases, seven years). These are the most numerous. They include typical first degrees such as the Bachelor's degree, the *Licence* etc., as well as in certain countries first professional degrees such as *Doctorates* awarded after completion of studies in medicine, engineering, law, etc.

Level 7: Post-graduate university degrees or equivalent qualifications. These are qualifications which persons who already possess a first university degree (or equivalent qualification) can obtain by continuing their studies. For example, the various diplomas obtained after completion of a first university degree (post-graduate diploma), the Master's degree, the various types of Doctorates, etc.

The classification according to level is intended to establish distinction between the different degrees and diplomas and facilitate international comparability on third-level qualifications. should be noted that the classification by ISCED level category no way implies an equivalence of the degrees and diplomas eith within a country or between countries and that any comparativ studies should be made with caution.

With regard to the subjects included in the various fields study, see the definitions in the introductory text to th chapter.

Ce tableau présente le nombre d'étudiants qui ont terminé leurs études avec succès, selon le niveau du grade ou diplôme obtenu et par domaine d'études.

En principe, ces grades et diplômes ont été décernés à la fin de l'année universitaire commencée pendant l'année civile indiquée. Par exemple, dans le cas où l'année universitaire ne coïncide pas avec l'année civile, les données indiquées pour 1984 se réfèrent aux diplômes décernés à la fin de l'année universitaire 1984/1985. Pour plus de détails, se reporter à l'introduction générale de la partie *Education*.

Les trois niveaux indiqués ici par leurs codes (5, 6 et 7) de la CITE sont définis comme suit:

Niveau 5: Les diplômes et certificats non équivalents à un premier grade universitaire sont ceux décernés à la fin d'études supérieures de durée réduite (en général, moins de trois ans). Ils comprennent, par exemple, les certificats délivrés à certains types de techniciens, les diplômes d'infirmière, d'arpenteur, les grades d'associés, les certificats de capacité en droit, etc.

Niveau 6: Les premiers grades universitaires ou diplômes équivalents sont ceux qui sanctionnent des études supérieures de durée normale (en général, trois à cinq ans et parfois sept ans). Ce sont les plus nombreux. Ils comprennent non seulement les grades bien connus tels que la licence, le *Bachelor's degree*, etc., mais aussi les titres de caractère professionnel tels que les doctorats décernés dans certains pays à la fin des études de médecine, sciences de l'ingénieur, droit, etc.

Niveau 7: Les grades universitaires supérieurs ou diplômes équivalents sont ceux que peuvent obtenir, en poursuivant leurs études, les personnes déjà titulaires d'un premier grade universitaire (ou d'un diplôme équivalent). Par exemple les divers diplômes obtenus après la préparation d'un premier grade universitaire (diplôme de *post-graduate*), la maîtrise (*master's degree*), les divers types de doctorats, etc.

Le classement selon le niveau a été effectué afin d'établir une distinction entre les différents grades et diplômes et dans l'espoir de faciliter la comparabilité internationale des statistiques sur les diplômes de l'enseignement du troisième degré. Il faut néanmoins souligner qu'il n'est pas souhaitable de procéder à des comparaisons approfondies, étant donné que le classement par niveau n'implique en aucune manière une équivalence des grades et diplômes, que ce soit à l'intérieur du pays considéré ou par rapport à d'autres pays.

En ce qui concerne les sujets inclus dans les divers domaines d'études, voir les définitions présentées dans la texte d'introduction à ce chapitre.

Este cuadro presenta el número de estudiantes que terminaron sus estudios con éxito, según el nivel del título o diploma obtenido y por sectores de estudio.

En principio, estos títulos y diplomas han sido concedidos al finalizar el año universitario empezado durante el año civil indicado. Por ejemplo, cuando el año universitario no coincide con el año civil, los datos que se indican para 1984 se refieren a los diplomas concedidos al finalizar el año universitario 1984/1985. Para más detalles, referirse a la introducción general del sección *Educación*.

Los tres niveles que aquí se indican según codificación (5, 6 y 7) en la CINE se definen como sigue:

Nivel 5. Diplomas y certificados no equivalentes a un primer título universitario, concedidos al final de unos estudios superiores de breve duración (en general, menos de tres años). Comprenden, por ejemplo, los certificados concedidos a ciertos tipos de técnicos, los diplomas de enfermera o enfermero, los *associate degrees*, los certificados de competencia jurídica, etc.

Nivel 6. Primeros títulos universitarios o diplomas equivalentes, que sancionan unos estudios superiores de duración normal (en general de 3 a 5 años, y a veces 7). Son los más frecuentes. Comprenden no solamente títulos tan conocidos como la licenciatura, el Bachelor's degree, etc., sino también títulos de carácter profesional, como ciertos doctorados que se pueden obtener en algunos países al final de los estudios de medicina, ingeniería, derecho, etc.

Nivel 7. Títulos universitarios superiores o diplomas equivalentes, que pueden obtener, continuando sus estudios, quienes tienen ya un primer título universitario (o un diploma equivalente). Por ejemplo, los diversos diplomas obtenidos después de la preparación de un primer título universitario (diploma de postgraduado), la *maîtrise* (master's degree), los diversos tipos de doctorado, etc.

La clasificación según el nivel se ha efectuado con vistas a establecer una distinción entre los diferentes títulos y diplomas y con la esperanza de facilitar la comparabilidad internacional de las estadísticas relativas a los diplomados de la enseñanza de tercer grado. Sin embargo, conviene subrayar que no es indicado proceder a comparaciones excesivas, ya que la clasificación por nivel no implica necesariamente una equivalencia de los títulos o diplomas, ya sea en el propio país o con respecto a otros países.

En lo que se refiere a las materias incluídas en las diversas disciplinas, véase la nota de definiciones en el texto de introducción de este capítulo.

AFRICA:

Burkina Faso:

E--> Humanities, religion and theology include education science and teacher training.

FR-> Les lettres, religion et théologie incluent les sciences de l'éducation et la formation d'enseignants.

ESP> Las humanidades, religión y teología incluyen las ciencias de la educación y formación de personal docente.

Cameroon:

E--> Data refer to universities and equivalent degree-granting institutions only. Mathematics and computer science includes natural science.

FR-> Les données se réfèrent aux universités et établissements conférant des grades équivalents seulement. Les mathématiques et l'informatique incluent les sciences exactes et naturelles.

ESP> Los datos se refieren a las universidades y establecimientos que otorguen grados equivalentes solamente. Las matemáticas e informática incluyen las ciencias naturales.

Central African Republic:

E--> Education science and teacher training includes humanities, religion and theology.

FR-> Les sciences de l'éducation et formation d'enseignants incluent les lettres, religion et théologie.

ESP> Las ciencias de la educación y formación de personal docente incluyen las humanidades, religión y teología.

Congo:

E--> Social and behavioural science include commercial and business administration and mass communication and documentation. Natural science includes mathematics and computer science.

FR-> Les sciences sociales et sciences du comportement incluent la formation au commerce et à l'administration des entreprises et l'information et documentation. Les sciences exactes et naturelles incluent les mathématiques et l'informatique.

ESP> Las ciencias sociales y del comportamiento incluyen la enseñanza comercial y de administración de empresas y la documentación y comunicación social. Las ciencias naturales incluyen las matemáticas y la informática.

Côte d'Ivoire:

E--> Data exclude teacher training colleges. Social and behavioural science include commercial and business administration.

FR-> Les données excluent les collèges d'enseignement normal. Les sciences sociales et sciences du comportement incluent la formation au commerce et à l'administration des entreprises.

ESP> Los datos excluyen los colegios de la enseñanza normal. Las ciencias sociales y del comportamiento incluyen la enseñanza comercial y de administración de empresas.

Egypt:

E--> Universities and equivalent degree-granting institutions only. Excluding Al Azhar University.

FR-> Universités et établissements conférant des grades équivalents seulement. L'Université d'Al Azhar n'est pas incluse.

ESP> Universidades y establecimientos que otorguen grados equivalentes solamente. Excluída la Universidad de Al Azhar.

Ethiopia:

E--> Natural science includes mathematics and computer science.

Ethiopia: (Cont):
FR-> Les sciences exactes et naturelles comprennent les mathématiques et l'informatique.
ESP> Las ciencias naturales comprenden las matemáticas y la informática.
Ghana:
E--> Data refer to universities. Natural science includes mathematics and computer science.
FR-> Les données se réfèrent aux universités. Les sciences exactes et naturelles incluent les mathématiques et l'informatique.
ESP> Los datos se refieren a las universidades. Las ciencias naturales incluyen las matemáticas e informática.
Guinea:
E--> Education science and teacher training includes humanities, religion and theology, fine and applied arts and social and behavioural science. Law includes commercial and business administration. Natural science includes mathematics and computer science. Engineering includes trade, craft and industrial programmes.
FR-> Les sciences de l'éducation et formation d'enseignants incluent les lettres, la religion et la théologie, les beaux-arts et arts appliqués et les sciences sociales et sciences du comportement. Le droit inclut la formation au commerce et à l'administration des entreprises. Les sciences exactes et naturelles incluent les mathématiques et l'informatique. Les sciences de 'ingénieur incluent les métiers de la production industrielle.
ESP> Las ciencias de la educación y formación de personal docente incluyen las humanidades, la religión y teología, las bellas artes y artes aplicadas y las ciencias sociales y del comportamiento. El derecho incluye la enseñanza comercial y de administración de empresas. Las ciencias naturales incluyen las matemáticas e informática. La ingeniería y tecnología incluyen las artes y oficios industriales.
Kenya:
E--> Data refer to universities only. Education science and teacher training include humanities, religion and theology.
FR-> Les données se réfèrent aux universités seulement. Les sciences de l'éducation et la formation d'enseignants incluent les lettres, la religion et la théologie.
ESP> Los datos se refieren a las universidades solamente. Las ciencias de la educación y formación de personal docente incluyen las humanidades, la religión y la teología.
Mali:
E--> Data exclude students who were suspended from courses.
FR-> Les données excluent les étudiants suspendus des cours.
ESP> Los datos excluyen los estudiantes suspendidos de los cursos.
Morocco:
E--> Data refer to universities only. Natural science includes mathematics and computer science.
FR-> Les données se réfèrent aux universités seulement. Les sciences exactes et naturelles incluent les mathématiques et l'informatique.
ESP> Los datos se refieren a las universidades solamente. Las ciencias naturales incluyen las matemáticas e informática.
Nigeria:
E--> Data refer to universities only.
FR-> Les données se réfèrent aux universités seulement.
ESP> Los datos se refieren a las universidades solamente.
Rwanda:
E--> Data refer to universities. Social and behavioural science include commercial and business administration. Natural science includes mathematics and computer science.
FR-> Les données se réfèrent aux universités. Les sciences sociales et sciences du comportement incluent la formation au commerce et à l'administration des entreprises. Les sciences exactes et naturelles incluent les mathématiques et l'informatique.
ESP> Los datos se refieren a las universidades. Las ciencias sociales y del comportamiento incluyen la enseñanza comercial y de administración de empresas. Las ciencias naturales incluyen las matemáticas e informática.
Sudan:
E--> Data at ISCED levels 6 and 7 on education science and teacher training and social and behavioural science are combined.
FR-> Les données relatives aux niveaux 6 et 7 de la CITE dans les programmes des sciences de l'éducation et formation d'enseignants ainsi que dans ceux des sciences sociales et sciences du comportement sont regroupées.
ESP> Los datos relativos a los niveles 6 y 7 de la CINE en los programas de las ciencias de la educación y formación de personal docente y en los de las ciencias sociales y del comportamiento están agrupados.
Swaziland:
E--> Data refer to universities and equivalent degree-granting institutions and to teacher training colleges. Natural science includes mathematics and computer science.
FR-> Les données se réfèrent aux universités et établissements conférant des grades équivalents et aux collèges d'enseignement normal. Les sciences exactes et naturelles incluent les mathématiques et l'informatique.
ESP> Los datos se refieren a las universidades y establecimientos que otorguen grados equivalentes y a los colegios de enseñanza normal. Las ciencias naturales incluyen las matemáticas e informática.

United Republic of Tanzania:
E--> Humanities, religion and theology include fine and applied a Commercial and business administration include social and behavio science. Natural science includes mathematics and computer science
FR-> Les lettres, la religion et la théologie incluent les beaux arts et arts appliqués. La formation au commerce et à l'administration entreprises incluent les sciences sociales et sciences du comportement. sciences exactes et naturelles incluent les mathématiques l'informatique.
ESP> Las humanidades, la religión y la teología incluyen las bellas a y artes aplicadas. La enseñanza comercial y de administración empresas incluyen las ciencias sociales y del comportamiento. Las cien naturales incluyen las matemáticas e informática.
Zambia:
E--> Social and behavioural science include humanities, religion theology.
FR-> Les sciences sociales et sciences du comportement incluent lettres, religion et théologie.
ESP> Las ciencias sociales y del comportamiento incluyen humanidades, religión y teología.
Zimbabwe:
E--> Humanities , religion and theology include fine and applied a Natural science includes mathematics and computer science.
FR-> Les lettres, religion et théologie incluent les beaux arts et appliqués. Les sciences exactes et naturelles incluent les mathématique l'informatique.
ESP> Las humanidades, religión y teología incluyen las bellas arte artes aplicadas. Las ciencias naturales incluyen las matemáticas informática.
AMERICA, NORTH:
Barbados:
E--> Social and behavioural science includes commercial business administration. Natural science includes mathematics computer science.
FR-> Les sciences sociales et sciences du comportement incluen formation au commerce et à l'administration des entreprises. Les scien exactes et naturelles incluent les mathématiques et l'informatique.
ESP> Las ciencias sociales y del comportamiento incluyen enseñanza comercial y de administración de empresas. Las cien naturales incluyen las matemáticas y la informática.
Bermuda:
E--> Humanities, religion and theology include fine and applied a social and behavioural science, natural science and mathematics computer science.
FR-> Les lettres, la religion et la théologie incluent les beaux arts et arts appliqués, les sciences sociales et sciences du comportement, sciences exactes et naturelles, les mathématiques et l'informatique.
ESP> Las humanidades, la religión y la teología incluyen las bellas a y artes aplicadas, las ciencias sociales y del comportamiento, ciencias naturales y las matemáticas e informática.
Costa Rica:
E--> Data refer to universities only.
FR-> Les données se réfèrent aux universités seulement.
ESP> Los datos se refieren a las universidades solamente.
Grenada:
E--> Data exclude Grenada Teachers' College.
FR-> Les données excluent 'Grenada Teachers' College'.
ESP> Los datos excluyen 'Grenada Teachers' College'.
Haiti:
E--> Education science and teacher training include humanit religion and theology. Law includes economics. Natural science inclu mathematics and computer science.
FR-> Les sciences de l'éducation et la formation d'enseigna incluent les lettres, la religion et la théologie. Le droit inclut les scien économiques. Les sciences exactes et naturelles incluent mathématiques et l'informatique.
ESP> Las ciencias de la educación y formación de personal doce incluyen las humanidades, religión y teología. El derecho incluye ciencias económicas. Las ciencias naturales incluyen las matemática informática.
Mexico:
E--> Universities and equivalent degree-granting institutions only
FR-> Universités et établissements conférant des grades équivale seulement.
ESP> Universidades y establecimientos que otorguen gra equivalentes solamente.
Trinidad and Tobago:
E--> Data refer to Tobago national students at the university o Natural science includes mathematics and computer science.
FR-> Les données se réfèrent aux étudiants nationaux de Tobag l'université seulement. Les sciences exactes et naturelles incluent mathématiques et l'informatique.
ESP> Los datos se refieren a los estudiantes nationales de Tob en la universidad solamente. Las ciencias naturales incluyen matemáticas e informática.
United States:
E--> At ISCED level 7, law includes a part of humanities, religion theology and medical sciences and health-related.

United States: (Cont):

FR-> Au niveau 7 de la CITE, les données relatives au droit incluent une partie des lettres, religion et théologie ainsi que celles des sciences médicales, santé et hygiène.

ESP> Al nivel 7 de la CINE, los datos relativos al derecho incluyen una parte de las humanidades, religión y teología y los de las ciencias médicas, sanidad e higiene.

AMERICA, SOUTH:

Bolivia:

E--> Data refer to universities and equivalent degree-granting institutions only and exclude 'la universidad católica boliviana'. Humanities, religion and theology include education science and teacher training.

FR-> Les données se réfèrent aux universités et établissements conférant des grades équivalents seulement et excluent 'la universidad católica boliviana'. Les lettres, la religion et la théologie incluent les sciences de l'éducation et la formation d'enseignants.

ESP> Los datos se refieren a las universidades y establecimientos que otorguen grados equivalentes solamente y excluyen la universidad católica boliviana. Las humanidades, religión y teología incluyen las ciencias de la educación y formación de personal docente.

Colombia:

E--> Law includes social and behavioural science. Commercial and business administration include mass communication and documentation, home economics and service trades. Natural science includes mathematics and computer science. Engineering includes architecture and town planning, trade, craft and industrial programmes and transport and communications.

FR-> Le droit inclut les sciences sociales et sciences du comportement. La formation au commerce et à l'administration des entreprises inclut l'information et la documentation, l'enseignement ménager et la formation pour le secteur tertiaire. Les sciences exactes et naturelles incluent les mathématiques et l'informatique. Les sciences de l'ingénieur incluent l'architecture et l'urbanisme, les métiers de la production industrielle et les transports et télécommunications.

ESP> El derecho incluye las ciencias sociales y del comportamiento. La enseñanza comercial y de administración de empresas incluye la documentación y comunicación social, la economía doméstica y la formación para el sector de los servicios. Las ciencias naturales incluyen las matemáticas e informática. La ingeniería y tecnología incluyen la arquitectura y urbanismo, las artes y oficios industriales y los transportes y comunicaciones.

Ecuador:

E--> Data refer to universities and equivalent degree-granting institutions only. Engineering includes trade, craft and industrial programmes.

FR-> Les données se réfèrent aux universités et établissements conférant des grades équivalents seulement. Les sciences de l'ingénieur incluent les métiers de la production industrielle.

ESP> Los datos se refieren a las universidades y establecimientos que otorguen grados equivalentes solamente. La ingeniería y tecnología incluyen las artes y oficios industriales.

Guyana:

E--> Education science and teacher training includes humanities, religion and theology.

FR-> Les sciences de l'éducation et formation d'enseignants incluent les lettres, religion et théologie.

ESP> Las ciencias de la educación y formación de personal docente incluyen las humanidades, religión y teología.

Peru:

E--> Data refer to universities and equivalent degree-granting institutions only.

FR-> Les données se réfèrent aux universités et établissements conférant des grades équivalents seulement.

ESP> Los datos se refieren a las universidades y establecimientos que otorguen grados equivalentes solamente.

ASIA:

Bahrain:

E--> Engineering includes trade, craft and industrial programmes.

FR-> Les sciences de l'ingénieur incluent les métiers de la production industrielle.

ESP> La ingeniería y tecnología incluyen las artes y oficios industriales.

Bangladesh:

E--> Natural science includes home economics and mathematics and computer science.

FR-> Les sciences exactes et naturelles incluent l'enseignement ménager et les mathématiques et l'informatique.

ESP> Las ciencias naturales incluyen la economía doméstica y las matemáticas e informática.

China:

E--> Commercial and business administration includes social and behavioural science.

FR-> La formation au commerce et à l'administration des entreprises incluent les sciences sociales et sciences du comportement.

ESP> La enseñanza comercial y de administración de empresas incluyen las ciencias sociales y del comportamiento.

India:

E--> Natural science includes mathematics and computer science.

India: (Cont):

Engineering includes architecture and town planning, trade, craft and industrial programmes and transport and communications.

FR-> Les sciences exactes et naturelles incluent les mathématiques et l'informatique. Les sciences de l'ingénieur comprennent l'architecture et l'urbanisme, les métiers de la production industrielle, les transports et télécommunications.

ESP> Las ciencias naturales incluyen las matemáticas y la informática. La ingeniería y tecnología comprenden la arquitectura y el urbanismo, las artes y oficios industriales y los transportes y comunicaciones.

Iran, Islamic Republic of:

E--> Data exclude teacher training colleges.

FR-> Les données excluent les établissements d'enseignement normal.

ESP> Los datos excluyen los establecimientos de enseñanza normal.

Israel:

E--> Education science and teacher training includes humanities, religion and theology, fine and applied arts. Social and behavioural science include commercial and business administration, mass communication and documentation, home economics and service trades. Engineering includes architecture and town planning, trade, craft and industrial programmes, transport and communications.

FR-> Les sciences de l'éducation et la formation d'enseignants comprennent les lettres, la religion et la théologie, les beaux-arts et les arts appliqués. Les sciences sociales et sciences du comportement incluent la formation au commerce et à l'administration des entreprises, l'information et la documentation, l'enseignement ménager et la formation pour le secteur tertiaire. Les sciences de l'ingénieur comprennent l'architecture et l'urbanisme, les métiers de la production industrielle et les transports et télécommunications.

ESP> Las ciencias de la educación y formación de personal docente comprenden las humanidades, la religión y la teología, las bellas artes y las artes aplicadas. Las ciencias sociales y del comportamiento comprenden la enseñanza comercial y de administración de empresas, la documentación y comunicación social, la economía doméstica y la formación para el sector de los servicios. La ingeniería y tecnología comprenden la arquitectura y el urbanismo y las artes y oficios industriales, además de los transportes y comunicaciones.

Japan:

E--> Including correspondence courses. Humanities, religion and theology include mass communication and documentation. Social and behavioural science include law, commercial and business administration. Engineering includes architecture and town planning, trade, craft and industrial programmes.

FR-> Y compris les cours par correspondance. Les lettres, la religion et la théologie comprennent l'information et la documentation. Les sciences sociales et les sciences du comportement comprennent le droit, la formation au commerce et à l'administration des entreprises. Les sciences de l'ingénieur comprennent l'architecture et l'urbanisme et les métiers de la production industrielle.

ESP> Incluídos los cursos por correspondencia. Las humanidades, la religión y la teología comprenden la documentación y comunicación social. Las ciencias sociales y del comportamiento comprenden el derecho, la enseñanza comercial y de administración de empresas. La ingeniería y tecnología comprenden la arquitectura y el urbanismo y las artes y oficios industriales.

Jordan:

E--> Data refer to universities only. Humanities, religion and theology include social and behavioural science. Commercial and business administration includes economics. Natural science includes mathematics and computer science. Engineering includes architecture and town planning.

FR-> Les données se réfèrent aux universités seulement. Les lettres, la religion et la théologie incluent les sciences sociales et sciences du comportement. La formation au commerce et à l'administration des entreprises inclut les sciences économiques. Les sciences exactes et naturelles incluent les mathématiques et l'informatique. Les sciences de l'ingénieur incluent l'architecture et l'urbanisme.

ESP> Los datos se refieren a las universidades solamente. Las humanidades, religión y teología incluyen las ciencias sociales y del comportamiento. La enseñanza comercial y de administración de empresas incluye las ciencias económicas. Las ciencias naturales incluyen las matemáticas e informática. La ingeniería y tecnología incluyen la arquitectura y urbanismo.

Kuwait:

E--> Engineering includes trade, craft and industrial programmes.

FR-> Les sciences de l'ingénieur incluent les métiers de la production industrielle.

ESP> La ingeniería y tecnología incluyen las artes y oficios industriales.

Nepal:

E--> Humanities, religion and theology include social and behavioural science. Natural science includes mathematics and computer science.

FR-> Les lettres, religion et théologie incluent les sciences sociales et sciences du comportement. Les sciences exactes et naturelles incluent les mathématiques et l'informatique.

ESP> Las humanidades, religión y teología incluyen las ciencias sociales y del comportamiento. Las ciencias naturales incluyen las

Nepal: (Cont):
matemáticas e informática.
Pakistan:
E--> Engineering includes architecture and town planning.
FR-> Les sciences de l'ingénieur incluent l'architecture et l'urbanisme.
ESP> La ingeniería y tecnología incluyen la arquitectura y urbanismo.
Qatar:
E--> Humanities, religion and theology include social and behavioural science. Natural science includes mathematics and computer science.
FR-> Les lettres, religion et théologie incluent les sciences sociales et sciences du comportement. Les sciences exactes et naturelles incluent les mathématiques et l'informatique.
ESP> Las humanidades, religión y teología incluyen las ciencias sociales y del comportamiento. Las ciencias naturales incluyen las matemáticas y la informática.
Saudi Arabia:
E--> Humanities, religion and theology include law and home economics. Social and behavioural science include commercial and business administration. Natural science includes mathematics and computer science. Engineering includes architecture and town planning.
FR-> Les lettres, religion et théologie incluent le droit et l'enseignement ménager. Les sciences sociales et sciences du comportement incluent la formation au commerce et à l'administration des entreprises. Les sciences exactes et naturelles incluent les mathématiques et l'informatique. Les sciences de l'ingénieur incluent l'architecture et l'urbanisme.
ESP> Las humanidades, religión y teología incluyen el derecho y la economía doméstica. Las ciencias sociales y del comportamiento incluyen la enseñanza comercial y de administración de empresas. Las ciencias naturales incluyen las matemáticas y la informática. La ingeniería y tecnología incluyen la arquitectura y urbanismo.
Singapore:
E--> Humanities, religion and theology include social and behavioural science. Natural science includes mathematics and computer science.
FR-> Les lettres, la religion et la théologie comprennent les sciences sociales et sciences du comportement. Les sciences exactes et naturelles comprennent les mathématiques et l'informatique.
ESP> Las humanidades, la religión y la teología comprenden las ciencias sociales y del comportamiento. Las ciencias naturales incluyen las matemáticas y la informática.
Sri Lanka:
E--> Natural science includes mathematics and computer science.
FR-> Les sciences exactes et naturelles comprennent les mathématiques et l'informatique.
ESP> Las ciencias naturales comprenden las matemáticas y la informática.
Syrian Arab Republic:
E--> Education science and teacher training excludes data on teacher training colleges.
FR-> Les sciences de l'éducation et formation d'enseignants n'incluent pas les données relatives à la formation d'enseignants.
ESP> Las ciencias de la educación y formación de personal docente excluyen los datos relativos a la formación de personal docente.
Turkey:
E--> Data include students graduating from the Open University.
FR-> Les données incluent les étudiants diplômés de l'*Open University*.
ESP> Los datos incluyen los estudiantes graduados de la *Open University*.
EUROPE:
Albania:
E--> Natural science includes mathematics and computer science.
FR-> Les sciences exactes et naturelles incluent les mathématiques et l'informatique.
ESP> Las ciencias naturales incluyen las matemáticas e informática.
Austria:
E--> Data refer to universities and equivalent degree-granting institutions only.
FR-> Les données se réfèrent aux universités et établissements conférant des grades équivalents seulement.
ESP> Los datos se refieren a las universidades y establecimientos que otorguen grados equivalentes solamente.
Belgium:
E--> Data refer to universities and equivalent degree-granting institutions only. Natural science includes mathematics and computer science.
FR-> Les données se réfèrent aux universités et établissements conférant des grades équivalents seulement. Les sciences exactes et naturelles incluent les mathématiques et l'informatique.
ESP> Los datos se refieren a las universidades y establecimientos que otorguen grados equivalentes solamente. Las ciencias naturales incluyen las matemáticas e informática.
Denmark:
E--> Programmes at levels 6 and 7 are combined.
FR-> Les données relatives aux programmes des niveaux 6 et 7 sont regroupées.

Denmark: (Cont):
ESP> Los datos relativos a los programas de los niveles 6 y 7 están agrupados.
France:
E--> 'Other and not specified' includes service trades. In engineering programmes at levels 6 and 7 are combined.
FR-> La rubrique 'autres programmes' inclut la formation pour le secteur tertiaire. Dans la rubrique 'sciences de l'ingénieur' les données de niveaux 6 et 7 sont regroupées.
ESP> La rúbrica 'otros programas' incluye la formación para el sector de los servicios. En la rúbrica 'ingeniería y tecnología' los datos relativos los programas de los niveles 6 y 7 están agrupados.
Holy See:
E--> Data refer to students enrolled in higher institutions under the authority of the Holy See.
FR-> Les données se réfèrent aux étudiants dans les institutions du troisième degré sous l'autorité du Saint-Siège.
ESP> Los datos se refieren a los estudiantes en los institutos del tercer grado bajo la autoridad del Santa Sede.
Ireland:
E--> Data refer to universities and equivalent degree-granting institutions only.
FR-> Les données se réfèrent aux universités et établissements conférant des grades équivalents seulement.
ESP> Los datos se refieren a las universidades y establecimientos que otorguen grados equivalentes solamente.
Netherlands:
E--> Data refer to universities and equivalent degree-granting institutions only. Programmes at levels 6 and 7 are combined.
FR-> Les données se réfèrent aux universités et établissements conférant des grades équivalents seulement. Les données relatives au niveaux 6 et 7 sont regroupées.
ESP> Los datos se refieren a las universidades y establecimientos que otorguen grados equivalentes solamente. Los datos relativos a los programas de los niveles 6 y 7 están agrupados.
Romania:
E--> Education science and teacher training includes humanities religion and theology.
FR-> Les sciences de l'éducation et formation d'enseignants incluent les lettres, religion et théologie.
ESP> Las ciencias de la educación y formación de personal docente incluyen las humanidades, religión y teologia.
Spain:
E--> Programmes at levels 6 and 7 are combined. Including 'Universidad de educación a distancia'.
FR-> Les données relatives aux programmes des niveaux 6 et 7 sont regroupées. Y compris la 'Universidad de educación a distancia'.
ESP> Los datos relativos a los programas de los niveles 6 y 7 están agrupados. Incluída la Universidad de educación a distancia.
United Kingdom:
E--> Data include students graduating from Open University. Home economics includes service trades.
FR-> Les données incluent les étudiants diplômés de l''Open University'. L'enseignement ménager inclut la formation pour le secteur tertiaire.
ESP> Los datos incluyen los estudiantes graduados de la 'Open University'. La economía doméstica incluye la formación para el sector de los servicios.
Yugoslavia:
E--> Natural science includes mathematics and computer science.
FR-> Les sciences exactes et naturelles comprennent les mathématiques et l'informatique.
ESP> Las ciencias naturales comprenden las matemáticas y informática.
OCEANIA:
Australia:
E--> Data on female students refer to Advanced education only.
FR-> Les données relatives aux étudiantes se réfèrent à 'Advanced education' seulement.
ESP> Los datos relativos a las estudiantes se refieren a 'Advanced education' solamente.
Fiji:
E--> Social and behavioural science include commercial and business administration.
FR-> Les sciences sociales et sciences du comportement incluent la formation au commerce et à l'administration des entreprises.
ESP> Las ciencias sociales y del comportamiento incluyen la enseñanza comercial y de administración de empresas.
New Caledonia:
E--> Mathematics and computer science include natural science.
FR-> Les mathématiques et l'informatique incluent les sciences exactes et naturelles.
ESP> Las matemáticas e informática incluyen las ciencias naturales.
New Zealand:
E--> Data refer to universities and teacher training colleges only. Natural science, at level 6, includes mathematics and computer science.
FR-> Les données se réfèrent aux universités et aux écoles normales supérieures seulement. Les sciences exactes et naturelles,

New Zealand: (Cont):
niveau 6, incluent les mathématiques et l'informatique.

ESP> Los datos se refieren a las universidades y a las escuelas normales superiores solamente. Las ciencias naturales al nivel 6, incluyen las matemáticas y la informática.

Tonga:

E--> Data at level 6 refer to the academic years 1977 to 1982 for Atenesi University only.

FR-> Les données au niveau 6 se réfèrent aux années académiques 1977 à 1982 pour l'université Atenesi seulement.

ESP> Los datos al nivel 6 se refieren a los años académicos 1977 a 1982 para la universidad Atenesi solamente.

U.S.S.R.:

U.S.S.R.:

E--> These figures are provided by the U.S.S.R. according to their own system of classification. Law and economics are combined. Medical science and health-related includes physical culture and sport. Engineering includes transport and communications.

FR-> Ces chiffres sont fournis par l'U.R.S.S., selon son propre système de classification. Le droit comprend les sciences économiques. Les sciences médicales, la santé et l'hygiène comprennent la culture physique et le sport. Les sciences de l'ingénieur comprennent les transports et télécommunications.

ESP> Estas cifras han sido facilitadas por la U.R.S.S. con arreglo a su propio sistema de clasificación. El derecho y la economía figuran clasificados bajo la misma rúbrica. Las ciencias médicas, la sanidad y la higiene comprenden la cultura física y el deporte. La ingeniería y tecnología comprenden los transportes y comunicaciones.

Byelorussian S.S.R.:

E--> These figures are provided by the Byelorussian S.S.R. according to their own system of classification. Law and economics are combined. Medical science and health-related includes physical culture and sport. Engineering includes transport and communications.

FR-> Ces chiffres sont fournis par la R.S.S. de Biélorussie selon son propre système de classification. Le droit comprend les sciences économiques. Les sciences médicales, la santé et l'hygiène comprennent la culture physique et le sport. Les sciences de l'ingénieur comprennent les transports et télécommunications.

ESP> Estas cifras han sido facilitadas por la R.S.S. de Bielorrusia con arreglo a su propio sistema de clasificación. El derecho y la economía figuran clasificados bajo la misma rúbrica. Las ciencias médicas, la sanidad y la higiene comprenden la cultura física y el deporte. La ingeniería y tecnología comprenden los transportes y comunicaciones.

Ukrainian S.S.R.:

E--> These figures are provided by the Ukrainian S.S.R. according to their own system of classification. Law and economics are combined. Medical science and health-related includes physical culture and sport. Engineering includes transport and communications.

FR-> Ces chiffres sont fournis par la R.S.S. d'Ukraine selon son propre système de classification. Le droit comprend les sciences économiques. Les sciences médicales, la santé et l'hygiène comprennent la culture physique et le sport. Les sciences de l'ingénieur comprennent les transports et télécommunications.

ESP> Estas cifras han sido facilitadas por la R.S.S. de Ucrania con arreglo a su propio sistema de clasificación. El derecho y la economía figuran clasificados bajo la misma rúbrica. Las ciencias médicas, la sanidad y la higiene comprenden la cultura física y el deporte. La ingeniería y tecnología comprenden los transportes y comunicaciones.

3.15 Education at the third level: number of foreign students enrolled

Enseignement du troisième degré: nombre d'étudiants étrangers inscrits

Enseñanza de tercer grado: número de estudiantes extranjeros matriculados

Ø DATA FOR 1982 FOR COUNTRIES SHOWN WITH THIS SYMBOL ARE FOR 1981.

Ø LES DONNEES DE 1982 RELATIVES AUX PAYS ACCOMPAGNES DE CE SYMBOLE SE REFERENT A 1981.

Ø LOS DATOS DE 1982 RELATIVOS A LOS PAISES EN LOS QUE APARECE ESTO SIMBOLO SE REFIEREN A 1981.

NUMBER OF COUNTRIES AND TERRITORIES PRESENTED IN THIS TABLE: 115

NOMBRE DE PAYS ET DE TERRITOIRES PRESENTES DANS CE TABLEAU: 115

NUMERO DE PAISES Y DE TERRITORIOS PRESENTADOS EN ESTE CUADRO: 115

HOST COUNTRY / PAYS D'ACCUEIL / PAIS HUESPED	FOREIGN STUDENTS ENROLLED (MF) / ETUDIANTS ETRANGERS INSCRITS (MF) / ESTUDIANTES EXTRANJEROS MATRICULADOS (MF)				
	1975	1980	1982	1983	1984
AFRICA					
ALGERIA‡	1 574	1 810	1 084	2 209	...
BENIN	26	...	139	216	...
BOTSWANA	121	204	120	109	102
BURKINA FASO	134	85	...	...	233
BURUNDI	174	471	...	340	...
CAMEROON	...	173	...	...	...
CENTRAL AFRICAN REPUBLIC	26	...	91	360	...
CHAD	57	...	...	...	...
CONGO Ø	275	544	736	...	...
COTE D'IVOIRE‡ Ø	1 383	2 314	2 039	1 749	...
EGYPT‡	...	21 751	17 062	...	...
ETHIOPIA Ø	...	...	46	31	...
GABON	...	...	531	374	...
GHANA‡	356	...	...	...	54
GUINEA	...	...	18	...	...
KENYA‡	483	556	...	827	...
LESOTHO‡	...	200	195	224	214
LIBYAN ARAB JAMAHIRIYA	1 262	...	...	...	...
MADAGASCAR	...	40	...	...	...
MALAWI	10	5	...	...	...
MALI	...	161	216	...	...
MAURITIUS‡	...	5	...	...	9
MOROCCO‡	1 804	1 641	1 978	1 834	1 905
MOZAMBIQUE‡	...	183	165	...	149
NIGER	247	229	211	246	287
NIGERIA Ø	446	...	329	...	...
RWANDA‡	...	87	40	95	...
SENEGAL Ø	2 118	3 065	2 880	2 433	...
SIERRA LEONE	354	...	...	...	...
SUDAN Ø	1 828	1 679	1 790	...	...
SWAZILAND‡	...	...	194	...	...
TOGO‡	478	1 114	559	679	675
TUNISIA	446	781	1 042	1 291	1 409
UGANDA‡	482	...	42	...	...
UNITED REP. OF TANZANIA‡	...	...	167	135	...
ZAMBIA‡	344	...	64	...	...
ZIMBABWE	...	...	38	...	66
AMERICA, NORTH					
BARBADOS	...	621	...	692	...
BERMUDA‡	...	10	15	...	...
CANADA‡	*22 700	28 443	35 556	35 365	...
CUBA	...	2 026	2 733	2 858	3 435
EL SALVADOR	336	...	...	...	...

HOST COUNTRY / PAYS D'ACCUEIL / PAIS HUESPED	FOREIGN STUDENTS ENROLLED (MF) / ETUDIANTS ETRANGERS INSCRITS (MF) / ESTUDIANTES EXTRANJEROS MATRICULADOS (MF)				
	1975	1980	1982	1983	1984
GUATEMALA‡	1 038	1 017	...	...	...
HAITI	...	...	28	...	...
HONDURAS	...	493	737	726	...
JAMAICA	...	837	...	...	...
NICARAGUA	...	...	275	170	248
PANAMA	477	848	897	833	...
ST. LUCIA	...	...	57	...	...
TRINIDAD AND TOBAGO	443	420	419	...	...
UNITED STATES	179 350	311 882	336 985	338 894	342 113
AMERICA, SOUTH					
ARGENTINA‡	14 526	7 882	...	...	...
BRAZIL	...	12 800	10 829	...	...
CHILE‡	940	534	625	524	501
ECUADOR Ø	...	800	781	...	...
GUYANA‡	...	11	6	19	...
ASIA					
BAHRAIN Ø	48	102	106	...	254
BANGLADESH	...	240	246	246	318
CHINA‡	...	1 381	1 759	2 066	2 593
CYPRUS	20	331	179	332	351
HONG KONG‡	135	142	165	176	208
INDIA‡	8 880	14 710	...	...	...
INDONESIA‡	...	...	...	116	258
IRAN, ISLAMIC REPUBLIC OF	650	...	176	182	144
IRAQ	4 476	...	...	...	...
JAPAN	5 541	6 543	8 117	9 523	10 697
JORDAN‡ Ø	197	722	754	985	...
KOREA, REPUBLIC OF	469	1 015	1 040	1 037	978
KUWAIT‡	2 871	2 892	2 585	3 612	5 622
LAO PEOPLE'S DEMOCRATIC REP.	...	2	...	...	...
LEBANON	...	31 028	29 480	...	...
PAKISTAN‡	1 582	2 229	...	...	...
PHILIPPINES	...	7 901	4 687	...	...
QATAR‡	...	1 099	1 430	1 003	1 320
SAUDI ARABIA‡	4 026	14 298	17 275	16 529	...
SINGAPORE	...	1 709	3 241	3 992	...
SYRIAN ARAB REPUBLIC‡	7 032	6 267	6 293	7 658	...
THAILAND	101	...	...	...	...
TURKEY	5 907	...	6 030	5 524	6 732
UNITED ARAB EMIRATES	...	660	1 071	1 147	1 111
VIET–NAM	140	...	...	...	...
YEMEN	348	192	...	...	...
EUROPE					
AUSTRIA‡	10 320	...	13 515	13 943	14 858
BELGIUM‡	9 748	12 875	11 871	12 528	21 188
BULGARIA‡	2 533	3 988	5 587	5 459	6 060
CZECHOSLOVAKIA	3 370	3 642	3 878	3 868	4 007
DENMARK	1 958	3 035	3 055	3 084	...
FINLAND‡	529	610	690	766	...
FRANCE‡	93 750	110 763	134 566	130 244	128 350
GERMAN DEMOCRATIC REPUBLIC	5 386	7 106	7 987	8 472	9 143
GERMANY, FEDERAL REPUBLIC OF	53 560	61 841	71 393	74 267	76 918
GREECE	10 049	7 673	6 683	...	...
HOLY SEE‡	5 740	9 104	8 239	9 211	9 656
HUNGARY	2 572	2 742	2 659	2 528	2 520
ICELAND	120	...	...	...	...
IRELAND‡	1 513	2 845	2 839	...	...
ITALY	18 921	29 447	29 221	28 068	27 548
LUXEMBOURG	38	49	81	83	...
MALTA	16	36	20	26	30
NETHERLANDS‡	...	4 128	4 634	4 915	3 453
NORWAY	931	...	...	...	...
POLAND	2 438	2 912	2 773	2 913	2 885
PORTUGAL	672	1 318	1 994	...	...
ROMANIA	4 971	15 888	16 251	14 808	13 068
SPAIN	8 909	10 997	...	...	...
SWEDEN‡	2 723	...	...	...	...
SWITZERLAND‡	10 113	14 716	15 657	16 277	16 830
UNITED KINGDOM‡	49 032	56 003	*46 000	42 267	...
YUGOSLAVIA	2 358	4 426	5 610	6 694	7 982

HOST COUNTRY / PAYS D'ACCUEIL / PAIS HUESPED	FOREIGN STUDENTS ENROLLED (MF) / ETUDIANTS ETRANGERS INSCRITS (MF) / ESTUDIANTES EXTRANJEROS MATRICULADOS (MF)				
	1975	1980	1982	1983	1984
OCEANIA					
AMERICAN SAMOA	...	...	251	...	...
AUSTRALIA‡	8 356	8 777	12 104	10 797	12 028
FIJI Ø	...	...	39	...	16
NEW ZEALAND‡	2 965	2 464	2 344	2 265	...
PAPUA NEW GUINEA‡	360	292	318	...	...
SAMOA	...	21	...	...	...
U.S.S.R.					
U.S.S.R.‡	43 287	62 942	...	...	...

According to the Unesco definition, a foreign student is defined as *a person enrolled at an institution of higher education in a country or territory in which he is not a permanent resident.* It should, however, be noted that most of the countries have established their statistics concerning foreign students on the basis of nationality. The differences resulting from the application of these two cri can, in certain countries, be quite appreciable; for exampl concerns those immigrants who have not taken the nationali the host country but who are permanent residents.

Selon la définition de l'Unesco, un étudiant étranger se définit comme une *personne inscrite dans un établissement d'enseignement supérieur d'un pays ou d'un territoire où elle n'a pas son domicile permanent.* Il faut signaler cependant que la plupart des pays ont établi leurs statistiques concernant les étudiants étrangers d'après le concept de nationalité. Les différences résultant de l'applica de ce concept peuvent être importantes dans certains pay les statistiques tiennent compte, par exemple, des immigrants n'ayant pas acquis la nationalité du pays hôte, y rési cependant de façon permanente.

De acuerdo con la definición de la Unesco, un estudiante extranjero es una *persona matriculada en un establecimiento de enseñanza superior de un país o territorio en el que no tiene su domicilio fijo.* Sin embargo, es necesario señalar que la mayoría de países han establecido sus estadísticas sobre los estudiantes extranjeros ateniéndose al concepto de nacionalidad. Las diferencias motivadas por la aplicación de este concepto pueden importantes en ciertos países donde las estadísticas toma consideración, por ejemplo, los inmigrantes que no habi adquirido la nacionalidad del país huésped residen sin embarg el mismo de manera permanente.

AFRICA:

Algeria:
E--> In 1982 data refer only to students holding government scholarships.
FR-> En 1982, les données se réfèrent aux étudiants boursiers seulement.
ESP> En 1982, los datos se refieren a los becarios solamente.

Côte d'Ivoire:
E--> Data refer to University of Abidjan only.
FR-> Les données se réfèrent à l'Université d'Abidjan seulement.
ESP> Los datos se refieren a la Universidad de Abidjan solamente.

Egypt:
E--> Data exclude Al Azhar University.
FR-> Les données n'incluent pas l'université Al Azhar.
ESP> Excluídos los datos relativos a la universidad Al Azhar.

Ghana:
E--> In 1984, data refer to universities only.
FR-> En 1984, les données se réfèrent aux universités seulement.
ESP> En 1984, los datos se refieren a las universidades solamente.

Kenya:
E--> Data refer to the University of Nairobi only.
FR-> Les données se réfèrent à l'Université de Nairobi seulement.
ESP> Los datos se refieren a la Universidad de Nairobi solamente.

Lesotho:
E--> Data refer to university only.
FR-> Les données se réfèrent à l'université seulement.
ESP> Los datos se refieren a la universidad solamente.

Mauritius:
E--> Data refer to university only.
FR-> Les données se réfèrent à l'Université seulement.
ESP> Los datos se refieren a la universidad solamente.

Morocco:
E--> From 1980 data refer to universities only.
FR-> A partir de 1980, les données se réfèrent aux universités seulement.
ESP> A partir de 1980, los datos se refieren a las universidades solamente.

Mozambique:
E--> Data for 1984 refer to 1985.
FR-> Les données de 1984 se réfèrent à 1985.
ESP> Los datos de 1984 se refieren a 1985.

Rwanda:
E--> Data refer to university only.
FR-> Les données se réfèrent à l'université seulement.
ESP> Los datos se refieren a la universidad solamente.

Swaziland:
E--> Data refer to universities and equivalent degree-gra institutions only.
FR-> Les données se réfèrent aux universités et établisser conférant des grades équivalents seulement.
ESP> Los datos se refieren a las universidades, y establecimiento otorguen grados equivalentes solamente.

Togo:
E--> From 1982, data refer to university only.
FR-> A partir de 1982, les données se réfèrent à l'Univ seulement.
ESP> A partir de 1982, los datos se refieren a la univer solamente.

Uganda:
E--> Data refer to universities and equivalent degree-gra institutions only.
FR-> Les données se réfèrent aux universités et établisser conférant des grades équivalents seulement.
ESP> Los datos se refieren a las universidades, y establecimiento otorguen grados equivalentes solamente.

United Republic of Tanzania:
E--> Data refer to university only.
FR-> Les données se réfèrent à l'Université seulement.
ESP> Los datos se refieren a la universidad solamente.

Zambia:
E--> In 1982, data refer to technical education only.
FR-> En 1982, les données se réfèrent à l'enseignement tech seulement.
ESP> En 1982, los datos se refieren a la enseñanza té

Zambia: (Cont):
solamente.

AMERICA, NORTH:

Bermuda:

E--> Data refer to full-time students only.

FR-> Les données se réfèrent aux étudiants à plein temps seulement.

ESP> Los datos se refieren a los estudiantes de jornada completa solamente.

Canada:

E--> Data for 1975 are estimates of full-time and part-time students in universities. From 1980, data refer to universities only.

FR-> En 1975 il s'agit d'une estimation des étudiants inscrits à plein temps et à temps partiel dans les universités. A partir de 1980, les données se réfèrent aux universités seulement.

ESP> En 1975 se trata de una estimación de los estudiantes de jornada completa y de jornada parcial inscritos en las universidades. A partir de 1980, los datos se refieren a las universidades solamente.

Guatemala:

E--> In 1975, data refer to University of San Carlos only.

FR-> En 1975, les données se réfèrent à l'Université de San Carlos seulement.

ESP> En 1975, los datos se refieren a la Universidad de San Carlos solamente.

AMERICA, SOUTH:

Argentina:

E--> Data for 1980 refer to the year 1979.

FR-> En 1980, les données se réfèrent à l'année 1979.

ESP> En 1980, los datos se refieren al año 1979.

Chile:

E--> In 1983 and 1984, data refer to public universities only.

FR-> En 1983 et 1984, les données se réfèrent aux universités seulement.

ESP> En 1983 y 1984, los datos se refieren a las universidades públicas solamente.

Guyana:

E--> In 1980 and 1982 data refer to the university only.

FR-> En 1980 et 1982 les données se réfèrent à l'université de la Guyana seulement.

ESP> En 1980 y 1982 los datos se refieren a la universidad de la Guyana solamente.

ASIA:

China:

E--> Data refer to full-time students only.

FR-> Les données se réfèrent aux étudiants à plein temps seulement.

ESP> Los datos se refieren a los estudiantes de jornada completa solamente.

Hong Kong:

E--> From 1980 data refer to universities and Hong Kong Polytechnic only.

FR-> A partir de 1980, des données se réfèrent aux universités et à 'Hong Kong Polytechnic seulement.

ESP> A partir de 1980 los datos se refieren a las universidades y a Hong Kong Polytechnic solamente.

India:

E--> Data for 1980 refer to the year 1979.

FR-> En 1980 les données se réfèrent à l'année 1979.

ESP> En 1980 los datos se refieren al año 1979.

Indonesia:

E--> Dat refer to public education only.

FR-> Les données se réfèrent à l'enseignement public seulement.

ESP> Los datos se refieren a la enseñanza pública solamente.

Jordan:

E--> Data refer to universities only.

FR-> Les données se réfèrent aux universités seulement.

ESP> Los datos se refieren a las universidades solamente.

Kuwait:

E--> Data refer to university only.

FR-> Les données se réfèrent à l'Université seulement.

ESP> Los datos se refieren a la universidad solamente.

Pakistan:

E--> Data for 1980 refer to the year 1979.

FR-> En 1980 les données se réfèrent à l'année 1979.

ESP> En 1980 los datos se refieren al año 1979.

Qatar:

E--> In 1983, data refer to students enrolled at ISCED level 6.

FR-> En 1983, les données se réfèrent aux étudiants inscrits au niveau 6 de la CITE.

ESP> En 1983, los datos se refieren a los estudiantes inscritos en el nivel 6 de la CINE.

Saudi Arabia:

E--> In 1983, data refer to university only.

FR-> En 1983, les données se réfèrent à l'Université seulement.

ESP> En 1983, los datos se refieren a la universidad solamente.

Syrian Arab Republic:

E--> From 1980, data refer to university only.

FR-> A partir de 1980, les données se réfèrent à l'Université seulement.

Syrian Arab Republic: (Cont):

ESP> A partir de 1980, los datos se refieren a la universidad solamente.

EUROPE:

Austria:

E--> Data refer to universities and equivalent degree-granting institutions only.

FR-> Les données se réfèrent aux universités et établissements conférant des grades équivalents seulement.

ESP> Los datos se refieren a las universidades, y establecimientos que otorguen grados equivalentes solamente.

Belgium:

E--> Except for 1984, data refer to universities and equivalent degree-granting institutions only.

FR-> A l'exception de 1984, les données se réfèrent aux universités et établissements conférant des grades équivalents seulement.

ESP> A la excepción de 1984, los datos se refieren a las universidades, y establecimientos que otorguen grados equivalentes solamente.

Bulgaria:

E--> From 1980, data refer to universities only.

FR-> A partir de 1980 les données se réfèrent aux universités seulement.

ESP> A partir de 1980, los datos se refieren a las universidades solamente.

Finland:

E--> Data refer to universities and equivalent degree-granting institutions only.

FR-> Les données se réfèrent aux universités et établissements conférant des grades équivalents seulement.

ESP> Los datos se refieren a las universidades, y establecimientos que otorguen grados equivalentes solamente.

France:

E--> Except for 1982, data refer to universities only.

FR-> A l'exception de 1982, les données se réfèrent aux universités seulement.

ESP> A la excepción de 1982, los datos se refieren a las universidades solamente.

Holy See:

E--> Data refer to foreign students enrolled in higher institutions under the authority of the Holy See.

FR-> Les données se réfèrent aux étudiants étrangers dans les institutions du troisième degré sous l'autorité du Saint-Siège.

ESP> Los datos se refieren a los estudiantes extranjeros en los institutos del tercer grado bajo la autoridad del Santa Sede.

Ireland:

E--> Data refer to full-time students only.

FR-> Les données se réfèrent aux étudiants à plein temps seulement.

ESP> Los datos se refieren a los estudiantes de jornada completa solamente.

Netherlands:

E--> Data refer to full-time students only and for 1984, to universities only.

FR-> Les données se réfèrent aux étudiants à plein temps seulement et en 1984, aux universités seulement.

ESP> Los datos se refieren a los estudiantes de jornada completa solamente y en 1984, a las universidades solamente.

Sweden:

E--> In 1975 data refer to first year university students only.

FR-> En 1975 les données se réfèrent aux nouveaux entrants dans les universités seulement.

ESP> En 1975 los datos se refieren a los nuevos entrantes en las universidades solamente.

Switzerland:

E--> In 1975 data refer to universities and equivalent degree-granting institutions only.

FR-> En 1975 les données se réfèrent aux universités et établissements conférant des grades équivalents seulement.

ESP> En 1975 los datos se refieren a las universidades y establecimientos que otorguen grados equivalentes solamente.

United Kingdom:

E--> Data refer to foreign students enrolled at universities (for full-time study or research), technical colleges (advanced courses) and colleges of education.

FR-> Les données se réfèrent aux étudiants étrangers inscrits dans les universités (pour études ou recherches à plein temps), 'technical colleges (advanced courses)' et 'colleges of education'.

ESP> Los datos se refieren a los estudiantes extranjeros matriculados en universidades (para realizar estudios o investigaciones en régimen de jornada completa) en los 'technical colleges (advanced courses)' y en los 'colleges of education'.

OCEANIA:

Australia:

E--> In 1983, data refer to universities only.

FR-> En 1983, les données se réfèrent aux universités seulement.

ESP> En 1983, los datos se refieren a las universidades solamente.

HOST COUNTRY‡	YEAR	COUNTRY OF ORIGIN / PAYS D'ORIGINE / PAIS DE ORIGEN						
PAYS D'ACCUEIL‡ / PAIS HUESPED‡	ANNEE / AÑO	OCEANIA– OTHER AND NOT SPECIFIED		U.S.S.R.			NOT SPECIFIED	
UNITED STATES	1984	–		196			49 914	
FRANCE‡	1983	153		–			1 478	
GERMANY, FEDERAL REPUBLIC OF	1983	9		86			1 305	
UNITED KINGDOM	1983	25		7			608	
CANADA‡	1983	4		6			378	
LEBANON‡	1982	–		–			2 397	
ITALY‡	1983	–		8			17	
BELGIUM	1984	–		3			454	
EGYPT‡	1982	–		–			–	
SWITZERLAND	1984	1		7			132	
SAUDI ARABIA‡	1983	–		–			1 441	
AUSTRIA‡	1984	–		9			390	
INDIA	1979	–		8			429	
AUSTRALIA	1984	–		4			178	
SPAIN	1980	–		–			4 328	
JAPAN	1984	–		6			6	
HOLY SEE‡	1984	7		–			–	
GERMAN DEMOCRATIC REPUBLIC	1984	8		268			–	
GREECE	1981	–		5			8	
TURKEY	1984	–		3			113	
YUGOSLAVIA	1983	–		24			22	
KUWAIT	1984	–		–			1 103	
PHILIPPINES	1982	–		–			401	
CZECHOSLOVAKIA	1984	–		149			22	
SINGAPORE	1983	–		–			112	
NETHERLANDS‡	1984	–		3			54	
CUBA	1984	–		85			–	
DENMARK	1983	–		4			13	
POLAND	1984	–		9			–	
IRELAND‡	1982	–		–			17	
CHINA‡	1984	–		69			–	
HUNGARY	1984	–		151			–	
SENEGAL	1983	–		1			–	
NEW ZEALAND‡	1983	7		–			–	
PAKISTAN	1979	–		–			–	
ALGERIA	1984	–		4			–	
PORTUGAL	1982	3		–			20	
MOROCCO‡	1983	–		–			–	
COTE D'IVOIRE‡	1983	–		–			1	
TUNISIA	1984	–		9			–	
QATAR	1984	–		–			–	
UNITED ARAB EMIRATES	1984	–		–			13	
GUATEMALA‡	1980	–		–			6	
JORDAN	1983	–		2			–	
KOREA, REPUBLIC OF	1984	–		–			–	
PANAMA	1983	–		1			–	
FINLAND‡	1983	–		18			3	
HONDURAS	1983	–		1			–	
BARBADOS	1983	–		–			–	
CHILE‡	1984	–		–			–	
TOTAL (50 COUNTRIES)		217		1 146			65 363	

This table indicates the country or territory of origin of foreign students enrolled in institutions at the third level in fifty selected host countries.

The choice of these fifty countries was governed by the number of foreign students enrolled; the last year for which their distribution by country of origin was available (1984 for most countries) was taken as a basis. The following countries, whilst host to many foreign students, have not been listed in the 50 selected countries as a distribution by country of origin was not communicated: Romania (13,068 students in 1984), Brazil (10,829 students in 1982), Bulgaria (6,060 students in 1984) and Sudan (1,790 students in 1981). The U.S.S.R. (62,94[illegible] foreign students in 1978) has also been excluded due to lack [illegible] more recent information.

It should be noted that for a few countries, foreign studen[illegible] have been distributed by continent of origin instead of country [illegible] origin.

Foreign students enrolled in these 50 countries represe[illegible] about 95 per cent of the known world total.

A special study on students abroad (*Statistics of Studen[illegible] Abroad, 1974-1978*) has been published by Unesco as No. 27 in th[illegible] series *Statistical Reports and Studies.*

Ce tableau présente, pour cinquante pays d'accueil sélectionnés, le nombre d'étudiants étrangers inscrits dans les établissements d'enseignement du troisième degré avec l'indication du pays ou territoire d'origine.

Ces cinquante pays ont été choisis en fonction de l'importance du nombre d'étudiants étrangers inscrits et sur la base de la dernière année pour laquelle la distribution par pays d'origine était disponible (pour la majorité des pays, l'année 1984). Les pays indiqués ci-après auraient dû figurer parmi les cinquante pays sélectionnés, mais il n'a pas été possible d'en tenir compte parce que la répartition des étudiants étrangers par pays d'origine n'avait pas été communiquée. Il s'agit de la Roumanie (13 068 étudiants en 1984), le Brésil (10 829 étudiants en 1982), la Bulgarie (6 060 étudiants en 1984) et le Souda[illegible] (1 790 étudiants en 1981). L'U.R.S.S. (62 942 étudian[illegible] étrangers en 1978) a été également exclue faute [illegible] renseignements plus récents.

Il convient de noter que pour quelques pays, les étudian[illegible] étrangers sont répartis par continent d'origine et non pas p[illegible] pays d'origine .

Les étudiants étrangers inscrits dans ces 50 pays représente[illegible] environ 95% du total mondial connu.

Une étude spéciale portant sur les étudiants à l'étrang[illegible] (*Statistiques des étudiants à l'étranger, 1974-1978*) a été publiée da[illegible] le numéro 27 de la collection *Rapports et études statistiques* [illegible] l'Unesco.

Este cuadro presenta, para cincuenta países huéspedes seleccionados, el número de estudiantes extranjeros matriculados en establecimientos de enseñanza de tercer grado, señalando los países o territorios de orígen.

Esos cincuenta países fueron escogidos en función de la importancia del número de estudiantes extranjeros matriculados; el último año para el que se disponía de la distribución por países de orígen (en el caso de la mayoría de ellos, se trata de 1984), se tomó como base. Los países que se indican a continuación deberían haber figurado entre esos cincuenta países, pero no fue posible tomarlos en consideración por no conocerse la distribución de los estudiantes extranjeros por país de orígen. Se trata de Rumania (13 068 estudiantes en 1984), Brasil (10 829 estudiantes en 1982), Bulgaria (6 060 estudiantes en 1984) y Sudán (1 790 estudiantes en 1981). Asimismo, la U.R.S.S. (6[illegible] 942 estudiantes extranjeros en 1978) fue excluída por falta [illegible] datos más recientes.

Conviene señalar que para algunos países, los estudiant[illegible] extranjeros son repartidos por continente de orígen y no por pa[illegible] de orígen.

Los estudiantes extranjeros matriculados en esos 50 país[illegible] equivalen aproximadamente al 95% del total mundi[illegible] conocido.

Véase también la nota de introducción al cuadro 3.14. U[illegible] estudio especial relativo a los estudiantes en el extranje[illegible] *Statistiques des étudiants à l'étranger, 1974-1978* ha sido publicado e[illegible] inglés y en francés en el número 27 de la colección *Informes* [illegible] *Estudios Estadísticos* de la Unesco.

Host country / Pays d'accueil / País huésped:

E--> The data provided in this table are to be considered as indicative. Foreign students enrolled in these 50 countries represent almost 95% of the known foreign students. The following countries, whilst host to many foreign students, have not been listed in the 50 selected countries because the distribution by country of origin was not provided: Romania (13,068 students in 1984), Brazil (10,829 students in 1982), Bulgaria (6,060 students in 1984) and Sudan (1,790 students in 1981).

FR-> Les données présentées dans ce tableau doivent être considérées à titre indicatif. Les étudiants inscrits dans ces 50 pays représentent presque 95% des étudiants étrangers connus. Les pays indiqués ci-après auraient dû figurer parmi les 50 pays sélectionnés, mais, il n'a pas été possible d'en tenir compte, parce que la répartition des étudiants étrangers par pays d'origine n'a pas été communiquée: la Roumanie (13 068 étudiants en 1984), le Brésil (10 829 étudiants en 1982), la Bulgarie (6 060 étudiants en 1984) et le Soudan (1 790 étudiants en 1981).

ESP> Los datos presentados en este cuadro deben considerarse como indicativos. Los estudiantes extranjeros matriculados en éstos 50 países representan casi 95% de los estudiantes extranjeros conocidos. Los países indicados a continuación deberían haber figurado entre los 50 países seleccionados, pero no pudieron tomarse en consideración debido a que la distribución por país de orígen no fue comunicada: la Rumania (13 068 estudiantes en 1984), el Brasil (10 829 estudiantes en 1982), la Bulgaria (6 060 estudiantes en 1984) y el Sudán (1 790 estudiantes en 1981).

France:

E--> Universities only. Foreign students from South America are included with those from North America.

FR-> Universités seulement. Les étudiants étrangers de l'Amérique du Sud sont inclus avec ceux de l'Amérique du Nord.

ESP> Universidades solamente. Los estudiantes extranjeros del América del Sur están incluídos con los del América del Norte.

Canada:

E--> Universities only.

FR-> Universités seulement.

ESP> Universidades solamente.

Lebanon:

E--> Data in column 'Asia - other and not specified' refer to studen[illegible] from unspecified arab countries.

FR-> Les données de la colonne 'Asia - other and not specified' [illegible] réfèrent aux étudiants des pays arabes non spécifiés.

ESP> Los datos de la columna 'Asia - other and not specified' [illegible] refieren a los estudiantes de los países árabes no especificados.

Italy:

E--> Data in column 'America, South - Other and Not specifie[illegible] include foreign students from North America.

FR-> Les données de la colonne 'America, South - Other and n[illegible] specified' incluent les étudiants étrangers de l'Amérique du Nord.

ESP> Los datos de la columna 'America, South - Other and n[illegible] specified' incluyen los estudiantes extranjeros de América del Norte.

Egypt:

E--> Data refer to students enrolled at ISCED level 6.

FR-> Les données se réfèrent aux étudiants inscrits au niveau 6 de CITE.

ESP> Los datos se refieren a los estudiantes inscritos al nivel 6 de CINE.

Saudi Arabia:

E--> Universities only.

FR-> Universités seulement.

ESP> Universidades solamente.

Austria:

E--> Universities only.

FR-> Universités seulement.

ESP> Universidades solamente.

Holy See:
E--> Data refer to foreign students enrolled in higher education institutions under the authority of the Holy See.
FR-> Les données se réfèrent aux étudiants étrangers dans les institutions d'enseignement du troisième degré sous l'autorité du Saint-Siège.
ESP> Los datos se refieren a los estudiantes extranjeros en los institutos de enseñanza del tercer grado bajo la autoridad del Santa Sede.

Netherlands:
E--> Data refer to full-time students and to universities only.
FR-> Les données se réfèrent aux étudiants à plein temps, et aux universités seulement.
ESP> Los datos se refieren a los estudiantes de jornada completa, y a las universidades solamente.

Ireland:
E--> Data refer to full-time students.
FR-> Les données se réfèrent aux étudiants à plein temps.
ESP> Los datos se refieren a los estudiantes de jornada completa.

China:
E--> Data refer to full-time students only.
FR-> Les données se réfèrent aux étudiants à plein temps seulement.
ESP> Los datos se refieren a los estudiantes de jornada completa solamente.

New Zealand:
E--> Data exclude part-time students enrolled at technical institutes, community colleges and senior technical divisions.
FR-> Les données excluent les étudiants à temps partiel inscrits dans les instituts techniques, les 'community colleges' et les unités techniques supérieures.
ESP> Los datos excluyen los estudiantes de jornada parcial inscritos en los institutos técnicos, los 'community colleges' y los unidades técnicos

New Zealand: (Cont):
superiores.

Morocco:
E--> Universities only.
FR-> Universités seulement.
ESP> Universidades solamente.

Côte d'Ivoire:
E--> University only.
FR-> Université seulement.
ESP> Universidad solamente.

Guatemala:
E--> Data refer to university of San Carlos only.
FR-> Les données se réfèrent à l'Université de San Carlos seulement.
ESP> Los datos se refieren a la Universidad de San Carlos solamente.

Finland:
E--> Universities only.
FR-> Universités seulement.
ESP> Universidades solamente.

Chile:
E--> Universities only.
FR-> Universités seulement.
ESP> Universidades solamente.

Total (50 countries):
E--> It should be noted that for a few countries, foreign students have been distributed by continent of origin instead of country of origin.
FR-> Il faut noter que pour quelques pays, la distribution des étudiants étrangers a été faite par continent et non par pays d'origine.
ESP> Debe notarse que para algunos países, la distribución de estudiantes extranjeros fue hecha por continente y no por país de orígen.

4 Educational expenditure

Dépenses de l'enseignement

Gastos de la educación

This chapter consists of four tables on educational expenditure. The expenditure is divided into two main categories.

Current expenditure includes expenditure on administration, emoluments of teachers and supporting teaching staff, school books and other teaching materials, scholarships, welfare services and maintenance of school buildings.

Capital expenditure refers to expenditure on land, buildings, construction, equipment etc. This item also includes loan transactions.

The data presented in this chapter refer solely to *public expenditure on education* i.e. public expenditure on public education plus subsidies for private education. It has not been possible to show private expenditure on education due to lack of data for a great number of countries.

Public expenditure on education includes, unless otherwise indicated, educational expenditure at every level of administration according to the constitution of the States, i.e. central or federal government, State governments, provincial or regional authorities, local authorities.

In general, these statistics do not take into account foreign aid received for education. However, whenever information on the inclusion of foreign aid is available it is indicated in a footnote.

Data are expressed in national currency at current market prices. Exchange rates between national currencies and the United States dollar can be found in Appendix C.

The years stated indicate the calendar year in which the financial year begins. Although in the majority of countries and territories the financial year begins in January, i.e. actually coincides with the calendar year, in some seventy countries it overlaps to a greater or lesser extent into the following calendar year. Appendix B gives information on the dates of commencement of the financial year in each country and territory.

Data presented in this edition of the *Yearbook* which differ from the corresponding data for the same year given in earlier editions should be taken to reflect revisions made as a result of the receipt of further information.

Table 4.1

This table presents total public expenditure on education distributed between current and capital.

Educational expenditure is also expressed as a percentage of the Gross National Product (GNP) and of total public expenditure. For some countries with centrally-planned economies, use was made of the Material Product.

For almost the totality of countries, data on GNP are supplied by the World Bank. These data being revised every year by the World Bank, the percentages of educational expenditure in relation to GNP may sometimes differ from those shown in previous editions of the *Yearbook*.

Table 4.2

Public current expenditure on education in this table is divided into the following categories:

Administration: emoluments of administrative staff and other expenditure of the central and local administration.

Emoluments of teachers: salaries and all additional benefits paid to teachers as well as to other auxiliary teaching staff.

Teaching materials: expenditure directly related to instructional activities such as the purchase of textbooks, books and other scholastic supplies.

Scholarships: scholarships and all other forms of financial aid granted to students for studies in the country or abroad.

Welfare services: boarding costs, school meals, transport, medical services, etc.

Not distributed: expenditure which cannot be classified in one of the above categories and other expenditure attached to the operation and maintenance of buildings and equipment.

As concerns the presentation of this table, two observations must be made. When in a category the symbol ./. is shown without explanatory note, the corresponding data are included with expenditure *not distributed*. Secondly, several categories in this table are shown with the symbol ..., due to the questionnaire reply not clearly showing whether the relevant expenditure is nil or included with other categories.

Table 4.3

This table presents the percentage breakdown of public current expenditure by level of education.

The column *other types* includes special, adult and other types of education which can not be classified by level.

The column *not distributed* while generally covering unspecified expenditure may sometimes include expenditure on administration for which there is no breakdown by level of education.

Table 4.4

This table gives a cross classification of public current expenditure by level of education and by purpose, for the latest year available. The categories used for the breakdown of expenditure by purpose are those defined in the note to Table 4.2. Unless otherwise specified by a footnote, when administrative expenditure is not shown separately, it is included with expenditure not distributed.

When the data supplied did not cover all the categories of expenditure used in this table, only the relevant categories have been shown for the countries concerned.

Ce chapitre contient quatre tableaux sur les dépenses de l'enseignement. Ces dépenses sont réparties selon deux grandes catégories:

Dépenses ordinaires: dépenses d'administration, émoluments du personnel enseignant et auxiliaire, manuels scolaires et autre matériel pour l'enseignement, bourses d'études, services sociaux et entretien et fonctionnement des établissements scolaires.

Dépenses en capital: dépenses relatives aux terrains, bâtiments, constructions, équipements, etc. Cette rubrique comprend également les transactions afférentes aux prêts.

Les données présentées dans ce chapitre se réfèrent uniquement aux *dépenses publiques d'éducation*, c'est-à-dire, aux dépenses publiques pour l'enseignement public plus les subventions à l'enseignement privé. Faute de données pour la plupart des pays, il n'a pas été tenu compte des dépenses privées d'éducation.

Les dépenses publiques d'éducation comprennent, sauf indication contraire, toutes les dépenses effectuées à quelque échelon administratif que ce soit, en fonction de l'organisation politique des Etats: gouvernement central ou fédéral, gouvernements d'Etat, autorités de province ou régionales, autorités municipales et locales.

D'une manière générale, ces statistiques ne tiennent pas compte de l'aide étrangère reçue pour l'éducation. Cependant, une note signale tous les cas pour lesquels les informations disponibles indiquent expressément l'inclusion de l'aide étrangère.

Les données sont exprimées en monnaie nationale aux prix courants du marché. Les taux de change des monnaies nationales en dollars des Etats-Unis sont indiqués dans l'Annexe C.

Les années indiquées sont les années civiles pendant lesquelles commencent les exercices financiers. Bien que dans la plupart des pays et territoires l'exercice financier commence en Janvier (c'est-à-dire coincide avec l'année civile), dans quelque soixante dix pays il empiète plus ou moins largement sur l'année civile qui suit. L'annexe B fournit des renseignements sur le commencement de l'exercice financier dans chaque pays et territoire.

Lorsque les données présentées dans cette édition de l'*Annuaire* diffèrent des données correspondant à la même année qui figuraient dans les éditions précédentes, on doit considérer qu'il s'agit de chiffres révisés à la suite de nouveaux renseignements reçus.

Tableau 4.1

Ce tableau présente le total des dépenses publiques d'éducation réparties entre dépenses ordinaires et en capital.

Les dépenses d'éducation sont aussi exprimées en pourcentage du Produit National Brut (PNB) et de l'ensemble des dépenses publiques. Pour certains pays dont l'économie est soumise à une planification centralisée, on a dû utiliser le Produit Matériel.

Pour la presque totalité des pays, les données relatives au PNB sont fournies par la Banque Mondiale. Comme ces données sont révisées tous les ans par la Banque Mondiale, les pourcentages des dépenses d'éducation par rapport au PNB peuvent parfois différer des pourcentages parus dans les éditions précédentes de l'*Annuaire*.

Tableau 4.2

Les dépenses publiques ordinaires d'éducation sont répartie dans ce tableau selon les catégories suivantes:

Administration: émoluments du personnel administratif et autres dépenses de l'administration centrale et locale.

Emoluments du personnel enseignant: traitements et toutes sortes de primes additionnelles du personnel enseignant ainsi que du personnel auxiliaire apportant un concours direct à l'enseignement.

Matériel pour l'enseignement: dépenses directement liées à l'enseignement telles que l'achat des manuels, livres et autres fournitures scolaires.

Bourses d'études: bourses et toute autre forme d'aide financière accordée aux élèves pour étudier dans le pays et à l'étranger.

Services sociaux: frais d'internat, repas scolaires, transport scolaire, services médicaux, etc.

Non réparties: dépenses ne pouvant pas être classées dans l'une des rubriques ci-dessus mentionnées et autres dépenses liées au fonctionnement et à l'entretien des bâtiments et du matériel.

En ce qui concerne la présentation de ce tableau, deu observations doivent être faites. Lorsque le symbole ./. est utilis dans une rubrique sans aucune note explicative, les donnée correspondant à cette rubrique sont comptées avec les dépense *non réparties*. D'autre part, plusieurs rubriques de ce tableau sor présentées avec le symbole ... parce que les réponses reçues a questionnaire ne précisent pas si ces rubriques ont été classée avec d'autres rubriques ou si les dépenses correspondantes sor nulles.

Tableau 4.3

Ce tableau présente la répartition en pourcentage de dépenses publiques ordinaires par degré d'enseignement.

La colonne intitulée *autres types* regroupe l'éducation spécial l'éducation des adultes et autres types d'enseignement n pouvant pas être classés par degré.

La colonne intitulée *non réparties*, qui regroupe généralemer les diverses dépenses non spécifiées, peut parfois inclure le dépenses d'administration quand celles-ci ne sont pas dé réparties par degré.

Tableau 4.4

Ce tableau indique, pour la dernière année disponible, répartition croisée des dépenses publiques ordinaires par degr d'enseignement et selon leur destination.

Les catégories utilisées pour la répartition des dépense selon leur destination sont définies dans la note relative au tablea 4.2. Sauf indication contraire signalée par une note, lorsque le dépenses relatives à l'administration ne sont pas présentée séparément, elles sont incluses avec les dépenses nc réparties.

Lorsque les données communiquées ne couvraient pas toute les catégories de dépenses figurant dans ce tableau, seules le catégories pertinentes ont été présentées, pour les pay concernés.

Este capítulo comprende cuatro cuadros relativos a los gastos destinados a la educación. Estos gastos se distribuyen según las dos categorías principales siguientes:

Gastos ordinarios: gastos de administración, emolumentos del personal docente y auxiliar, manuales escolares y otro material educativo, becas de estudios, servicios sociales y todos los otros gastos de funcionamiento de los establecimientos escolares.

Gastos de capital: gastos relativos a los terrenos, edificios, construcciones, equipo, etc. Esta rúbrica comprende igualmente las operaciones de préstamos.

Los datos presentados en este capítulo se refieren únicamente a *los gastos públicos destinados a la educación*, es decir, a los gastos públicos para la enseñanza pública más las subvenciones para la enseñanza privada. Careciendo de datos para la mayoría de países, no se han tenido en cuenta los gastos privados destinados a la educación.

Los gastos públicos destinados a la educación comprenden, salvo indicación contraria, todos los gastos efectuados a cualquier nivel administrativo, en función de la organización política de los Estados: Gobierno Central o Federal, Gobiernos de Estado, autoridades de provincia o de región, autoridades municipales y locales.

En general, estas estadísticas no toman en cuenta la ayuc extranjera recibida para la educación. Sin embargo, en una no se señalan todos los casos para los que las informacion disponibles indican expresamente la inclusión de la ayuc extranjera.

Los datos se presentan en moneda nacional a preci corrientes del mercado. Los tipos de cambio entre las moned nacionales y el dólar de los Estados Unidos se indican en el Ane C.

Los años indicados son los años civiles durante los cual empiezan los ejercicios economicos. A pesar de que la mayoría d los países y territorios el ejercicio economico empieza en ene (es dicir coincide con el año civil), en unos setenta países extiende, en forma más o menos pronunciada, sobre el año ci siguiente. En el apendice B se presentan datos sobre el comien del ejercicio economico en cada país y territorio.

Cuando los datos presentados en esta edición del *Anua* difieren de los datos correspondientes al mismo año qu figuraban en las ediciones anteriores, debe considerarse que trata de cifras revisadas de acuerdo con las nuevas informacion recibidas.

Cuadro 4.1

Este cuadro presenta el total de los gastos públicos destinados a la educación, distribuídos entre gastos ordinarios y gastos de capital.

El total de los gastos en educación también se expresa en porcentaje del Producto Nacional Bruto (PNB) y del total de los gastos públicos. En ciertos países cuya economía está sometida a una planificación centralizada, se ha utilizado el Producto Material.

Para casi todos los países, los datos relativos al PNB son proporcionados por el Banco Mundial. Como estos datos son revisados cada año por el mismo Banco Mundial, los porcentajes de gastos de educación con respecto al PNB pueden ser diferentes de los porcentajes indicados en ediciones anteriores del *Anuario*.

Cuadro 4.2

Los gastos públicos ordinarios destinados a la educación, se distribuyen en este cuadro de acuerdo con las siguientes categorías:

Administración: emolumentos del personal administrativo y otros gastos de la administración central y local.

Emolumentos del personal docente: sueldos y toda clase de primas adicionales del personal docente y del personal auxiliar que aporta una ayuda directa a la enseñanza.

Material educativo: gastos directamente relacionados con la enseñanza, como la adquisición de libros de texto, libros y otros suministros escolares.

Becas de estudios: becas y toda otra forma de ayuda financiera concedida a los alumnos para estudiar en el país y en el extranjero.

Servicios sociales: gastos de internado, cantinas escolares, transportes escolares, servicios médicos, etc.

Sin distribución: gastos que no pueden ser clasificados en las categorías que preceden y otros gastos relacionados con el funcionamiento y la conservación de los edificios y del material.

En lo que concierne a la presentación de este cuadro, dos observaciones deben ser precisadas: cuando el símbolo ./. aparece sin nota explicativa, los datos correspondientes son presentados con gastos *sin distribucíon*. También, varias categorías en este cuadro aparecen con el símbolo ... puesto que las respuestas al cuestionario no muestran claramente si estas categorías han sido incluídas junto con otras categorías o si los gastos correspondientes son nulos.

Cuadro 4.3

Este cuadro presenta la distribución en porcentaje de los gastos públicos ordinarios por grado de enseñanza.

La columna titulada *Otros tipos* agrupa la educación especial, la educación de adultos y los otros tipos de enseñanza que no pueden clasificarse por grado.

La columna titulada *Sin distribución* comprende en general los diversos gastos no especificados e incluye a veces los gastos de administración, cuando no han sido distribuidos por grado.

Cuadro 4.4

Este cuadro da la distribución cruzada de los gastos públicos ordinarios por grados de enseñanza y según su destino, para el ultimo año disponible.

Las categorías utilizadas para la distribución de los gastos según su destino, se definen en la nota relativa al cuadro 4.2. A menos que sea precisado por una nota explicativa, cuando los gastos administrativos no están mostrados separadamente, están incluídos junto con los gastos no distribuídos.

Cuando los datos que nos han sido comunicados no cubren todas las categorías de gastos que figuran en este cuadro, sólo las categorías pertinentes han sido presentadas, para los países correspondientes.

4.1 Public expenditure on education: total and as percentage of the GNP and of all public expenditure

Dépenses publiques afférentes à l'enseignement: total et pourcentage par rapport au PNB et à l'ensemble des dépenses publiques

Gastos públicos destinados a la educación: total y porcentaje en relación con el PNB y el conjunto de gastos públicos

NUMBER OF COUNTRIES AND TERRITORIES PRESENTED IN THIS TABLE: 182

NOMBRE DE PAYS ET DE TERRITOIRES PRESENTES DANS CE TABLEAU: 182

NUMERO DE PAISES Y DE TERRITORIOS PRESENTADOS EN ESTE CUADRO: 182

COUNTRY CURRENCY PAYS MONNAIE PAIS MONEDA	YEAR ANNEE AÑO	TOTAL EDUCATIONAL EXPENDITURE DEPENSES TOTALES D'EDUCATION GASTOS TOTALES DE EDUCACION			CURRENT EDUCATIONAL EXPENDITURE DEPENSES ORDINAIRES D'EDUCATION GASTOS ORDINARIOS DE EDUCACION				CAPITAL EXPENDITURE DEPENSES EN CAPITAL GASTOS EN CAPITAL (000)
		AMOUNT MONTANT IMPORTE (000)	AS % OF GROSS NATIONAL PRODUCT EN % DU PRODUIT NATIONAL BRUT EN % DEL PRODUCTO NACIONAL BRUTO (%)	AS % OF TOTAL GOVERNMENT EXPENDITURE EN % DES DEPENSES TOTALES DU GOUVERNEMENT EN % DE LOS GASTOS TOTALES DEL GOBIERNO (%)	AMOUNT MONTANT IMPORTE (000)	AS % OF THE TOTAL EN % DU TOTAL EN % DEL TOTAL (%)	AS % OF GROSS NATIONAL PRODUCT EN % DU PRODUIT NATIONAL BRUT EN % DEL PRODUCTO NACIONAL BRUTO (%)	AS % OF CURRENT GOVERNMENT EXPENDITURE EN % DES DEPENSES ORDINAIRES DU GOUVERNEMENT EN % DE LOS GASTOS ORDINARIOS DEL GOBIERNO (%)	
		(1)	(2)	(3)	(4)	(5)	(6)	(7)	(8)
AFRICA									
ALGERIA‡ DINAR	1975	4 080 500	7.1	23.0	2 951 000	72.3	5.1	23.9	1 129 500
	1980	12 354 500	8.2	24.3	8 259 100	66.9	5.5	29.8	4 095 400
	1982	8 979 428	4.7	...	8 189 328	91.2	4.2	...	790 100
ANGOLA KWANSA	1979	...	...	...	6 706 231	...	4.7	...	...
	1982	11 187 818	5.5	...	10 955 768	97.9	5.4	...	232 050
	1983	10 039 394	5.0	12.0	9 639 794	96.0	4.8	16.5	399 600
	1984	10 879 326	5.2	11.5	10 501 156	96.5	5.1	15.6	378 170
BENIN FRANC C.F.A.	1975	...	...	...	5 627 477	...	4.9	38.9	...
	1980	...	...	...	12 426 246	...	5.1	36.8	...
BOTSWANA PULA	1975	15 927	8.5	18.8	8 688	54.5	4.6	17.6	7 239
	1980	46 825	7.1	16.0	35 495	75.8	5.4	20.8	11 330
	1982	53 971	7.5	13.7	45 243	83.8	6.2	19.4	8 728
	1983	64 669	7.2	18.5	54 235	83.9	6.1	23.4	10 434
	1984	91 696	...	...	75 572	82.4	...	...	16 124
BURKINA FASO FRANC C.F.A.	1976	4 020 947	2.4	19.0	3 674 455	91.4	2.2	22.0	346 492
	1980	7 994 307	2.6	19.8	7 435 813	93.0	2.4	21.1	558 494
	1982	10 987 910	2.8	23.0	10 387 910	94.5	2.7	22.9	600 000
	1983	12 812 360	3.2	23.9	12 706 470	99.2	3.2	25.3	105 890
	1984	11 982 276	2.9	23.0	11 962 276	99.8	2.9	24.3	20 000
BURUNDI FRANC	1975	...	...	...	721 831	...	2.2	22.7	...
	1979	2 066 175	3.0	17.5	1 796 482	86.9	2.6	...	269 693
	1981	2 956 024	3.4	15.6	2 634 658	89.1	3.0	20.8	321 366
CAMEROON FRANC C.F.A.	1975	21 924 800	3.9	21.3	18 310 000	83.5	3.2	22.7	3 614 800
	1980	45 099 400	3.3	20.3	36 653 400	81.3	2.6	...	8 446 000
	1981	56 581 000	3.2	18.3	40 978 000	72.4	2.3	20.6	15 603 000
	1982	79 313 000	3.8	19.3	56 710 000	71.5	2.7	22.1	22 603 000
	1983	89 335 000	3.6	17.2	70 644 000	79.1	2.8	21.7	18 691 000
CAPE VERDE ESCUDO	1976	...	...	...	99 660	...	5.1	20.2	...
	1978	205 455	7.5	10.6	125 245	61.0	4.5	19.1	80 210
CENTRAL AFRICAN REPUBLIC FRANC C.F.A.	1975	3 905 000	4.9	20.1	3 393 000	86.9	4.2	...	512 000
	1980	...	...	...	6 282 843	...	3.7	21.5	...
	1982	...	...	...	8 532 482	...	3.9	25.9	...
	1983	...	...	...	8 863 462	...	3.8	26.5	...
	1984	15 083 971	5.7	...	14 912 971	98.9	5.6	...	171 000

COUNTRY CURRENCY PAYS MONNAIE PAIS MONEDA	YEAR ANNEE AÑO	TOTAL EDUCATIONAL EXPENDITURE / DEPENSES TOTALES D'EDUCATION / GASTOS TOTALES DE EDUCACION			CURRENT EDUCATIONAL EXPENDITURE / DEPENSES ORDINAIRES D'EDUCATION / GASTOS ORDINARIOS DE EDUCACION				
		AMOUNT MONTANT IMPORTE (000)	AS % OF GROSS NATIONAL PRODUCT EN % DU PRODUIT NATIONAL BRUT EN % DEL PRODUCTO NACIONAL BRUTO (%)	AS % OF TOTAL GOVERNMENT EXPENDITURE EN % DES DEPENSES TOTALES DU GOUVERNEMENT EN % DE LOS GASTOS TOTALES DEL GOBIERNO (%)	AMOUNT MONTANT IMPORTE (000)	AS % OF THE TOTAL EN % DU TOTAL EN % DEL TOTAL (%)	AS % OF GROSS NATIONAL PRODUCT EN % DU PRODUIT NATIONAL BRUT EN % DEL PRODUCTO NACIONAL BRUTO (%)	AS % OF CURRENT GOVERNMENT EXPENDITURE EN % DES DEPENSES ORDINAIRES DU GOUVERNEMENT EN % DE LOS GASTOS ORDINARIOS DEL GOBIERNO (%)	CAPITAL EXPENDITURE DEPENSES EN CAPITAL GASTOS EN CAPITAL (000)
		(1)	(2)	(3)	(4)	(5)	(6)	(7)	(8)
CHAD	1975	...	...	...	2 297 200	...	2.2	11.9	...
FRANC C.F.A.	1983	...	...	...	4 099 374	...	...	...	...
COMOROS FRANC C.F.A.	1982	1 878 956	5.4	36.0	1 773 956	94.4	5.1	40.6	105 000
CONGO	1975	12 752 237	8.1	18.2	10 537 237	82.6	6.7	24.7	2 215 000
FRANC C.F.A	1980	22 941 531	6.9	23.6	21 517 291	93.8	6.4	24.1	1 424 240
	1981	30 635 724	6.0	19.2	28 795 018	94.0	5.6	25.8	1 840 706
COTE D'IVOIRE	1975	50 879 000	6.3	19.0	43 076 000	84.7	5.3	33.7	7 803 000
FRANC C.F.A.	1979	160 092 300	8.4	29.8	124 616 400	77.8	6.5	39.8	35 475 900
DJIBOUTI	1974	1 624 821	...	...	1 479 821	91.1	...	...	145 000
FRANC	1979	1 367 509	3.0	11.5	1 045 949	76.5	2.3	9.6	321 560
	1982	2 236 309	3.9	12.1	...	...	...	...	...
EGYPT‡	1975	262 328	5.0	...	226 668	86.4	4.3	...	35 660
POUND	1980	...	...	...	505 330	...	2.8	8.5	...
	1981	918 679	4.5	9.4	722 108	78.6	3.5	10.1	196 571
	1982	1 033 500	4.3	8.6	...	...	...	...	...
	1983	1 186 500	4.1	8.9	...	...	...	...	...
ETHIOPIA‡	1976	196 965	3.3	13.4	164 528	83.5	2.7	16.7	32 437
BIRR	1980	247 923	2.9	9.3	221 504	89.3	2.6	12.7	26 419
	1981	290 292	3.3	10.1	256 439	88.3	2.9	13.9	33 853
	1982	375 625	4.1	11.3	290 229	77.3	3.2	14.2	85 396
GABON	1975	8 902 838	2.1	...	7 569 838	85.0	1.8	...	1 333 000
FRANC C.F.A	1980	22 203 707	2.8	...	16 054 707	72.3	2.0	...	6 149 000
	1984	59 285 000	4.6	9.9	34 297 000	57.9	2.6	...	24 988 000
GAMBIA	1975	7 007	3.2	...	5 471	78.1	2.5	...	1 536
DALASI	1980	12 869	3.2	...	11 336	88.1	2.9	...	1 533
	1981	23 984	6.0	...	16 460	68.6	4.1	...	7 524
	1983	25 796	5.0	...	24 119	93.5	4.7	...	1 677
	1984	24 993	4.4	...	23 994	96.0	4.2	...	999
GHANA	1975	309 024	5.9	21.5	240 682	77.9	4.6	24.1	68 342
CEDI	1980	1 318 860	3.1	...	...	...	...	...	...
	1981	1 775 772	2.4	...	...	...	...	...	...
	1984	4 007 439	1.5	...	3 843 913	95.9	1.4	...	163 526
GUINEA	1979	...	...	...	1 185 500	...	4.2	...	...
SYLI	1984	1 491 077	3.3	15.3	1 486 054	98.5	3.2	17.2	5 023
GUINEA-BISSAU	1976	...	...	...	175 917	...	3.9	...	...
PESO	1980	...	...	...	207 512	...	4.0	...	...
	1981	...	...	...	241 804	...	3.7	...	...
	1982	...	...	...	260 000	...	3.2	...	...
	1983	...	...	...	276 194	...	2.9	...	...
KENYA	1975	1 444 760	6.3	19.4	1 378 580	95.4	6.0	27.7	66 180
SHILLING	1980	3 526 420	6.9	18.1	3 247 000	92.1	6.4	23.6	279 420
	1981	3 976 780	6.8	17.7	3 592 140	90.3	6.1	22.5	384 640
	1982	4 307 060	6.7	16.5	3 905 520	90.7	6.0	20.5	401 540
	1984	4 649 320	5.6	18.3	4 429 160	95.3	5.3	20.8	220 160
LESOTHO	1975	8 912	4.2	23.5	6 777	76.0	3.2	26.8	2 135
MALOTI	1980	25 074	5.0	14.8	20 037	79.9	4.0	19.0	5 037
	1981	...	...	...	25 174	...	4.3	18.9	...
	1982	46 903	7.2	...	28 082	59.9	4.3	...	18 821
	1983	27 695	3.9	...	25 939	93.7	3.7	...	1 756
LIBERIA	1975	13 866	2.4	11.6	...	...	...	...	...
DOLLAR	1980	61 778	6.3	24.3	53 074	85.9	5.4	27.0	8 704
LIBYAN ARAB JAMAHIRIYA	1975	224 908	6.7	14.5	122 485	54.5	3.7	...	102 423
DINAR	1980	356 131	3.7	...	224 431	63.0	2.3	...	131 700

COUNTRY / CURRENCY PAYS / MONNAIE PAIS / MONEDA	YEAR ANNEE AÑO	TOTAL EDUCATIONAL EXPENDITURE DEPENSES TOTALES D'EDUCATION GASTOS TOTALES DE EDUCACION			CURRENT EDUCATIONAL EXPENDITURE DEPENSES ORDINAIRES D'EDUCATION GASTOS ORDINARIOS DE EDUCACION				CAPITAL EXPENDITURE DEPENSES EN CAPITAL GASTOS EN CAPITAL (000)
		AMOUNT MONTANT IMPORTE (000)	AS % OF GROSS NATIONAL PRODUCT EN % DU PRODUIT NATIONAL BRUT EN % DEL PRODUCTO NACIONAL BRUTO (%)	AS % OF TOTAL GOVERNMENT EXPENDITURE EN % DES DEPENSES TOTALES DU GOUVERNEMENT EN % DE LOS GASTOS TOTALES DEL GOBIERNO (%)	AMOUNT MONTANT IMPORTE (000)	AS % OF THE TOTAL EN % DU TOTAL EN % DEL TOTAL (%)	AS % OF GROSS NATIONAL PRODUCT EN % DU PRODUIT NATIONAL BRUT EN % DEL PRODUCTO NACIONAL BRUTO (%)	AS % OF CURRENT GOVERNMENT EXPENDITURE EN % DES DEPENSES ORDINAIRES DU GOUVERNEMENT EN % DE LOS GASTOS ORDINARIOS DEL GOBIERNO (%)	
		(1)	(2)	(3)	(4)	(5)	(6)	(7)	(8)
MADAGASCAR	1975	12 313 747	3.2	18.5	11 726 747	95.2	3.0	23.0	587 000
FRANC	1980	36 895 761	5.5	...	31 547 842	85.5	4.7	...	5 347 919
	1982	38 854 626	4.0	...	34 775 654	89.5	3.6	...	4 078 972
	1983	40 123 887	3.3	...	38 810 098	96.7	3.2	...	1 313 789
	1984	49 653 156	3.9	...	47 519 440	95.7	3.7	...	2 133 716
MALAWI	1975	13 052	2.5	9.6	11 992	91.9	2.3	18.3	1 060
KWACHA	1980	31 208	3.2	...	23 595	75.6	2.4	...	7 613
	1981	39 125	3.5	14.7	27 363	69.9	2.5	11.1	11 762
	1982	35 522	2.7	11.7	31 475	88.6	2.4	11.5	4 047
	1983	38 571	2.5	8.5	34 754	90.1	2.3	11.3	3 817
MALI	1975	...	...	...	5 852 452	...	4.4	30.6	...
FRANC C.F.A.	1980	12 903 455	4.6	30.8	12 752 393	98.8	4.5	...	151 062
	1981	14 418 838	4.7	33.7	14 165 477	98.2	4.7	...	253 361
	1982	14 370 523	4.2	32.2	14 219 340	98.9	4.2	...	151 183
	1984	15 179 302	3.5	30.2	15 124 302	99.6	3.5	...	55 000
MAURITANIA	1975	...	...	...	723 100	...	3.7	16.1	...
OUGUIYA	1980	...	...	...	1 546 000	...	5.0	...	...
	1981	...	...	...	2 062 153	...	5.9	...	...
	1982	...	...	...	2 503 687	...	6.9	...	...
	1983	...	...	...	3 006 217	...	7.4	29.7	...
MAURITIUS	1975	144 000	3.6	9.6	125 800	87.4	3.1	11.7	18 200
RUPEE	1980	453 901	5.3	11.6	407 926	89.9	4.7	15.5	45 975
	1982	537 900	4.7	11.1	517 000	96.1	4.5	13.4	20 900
	1983	538 400	4.3	10.3	532 000	98.8	4.3	12.6	6 400
	1984	587 400	4.2	10.3	539 800	91.9	3.9	12.7	47 600
MOROCCO	1975	1 846 709	4.8	14.3	1 591 988	86.2	4.2	20.4	254 721
DIRHAM	1980	4 358 718	6.1	18.5	3 528 566	81.0	4.9	23.3	830 152
	1981	4 791 398	6.1	18.9	3 991 948	83.3	5.1	26.0	799 450
	1982	6 524 387	7.2	18.7	4 692 083	71.9	5.2	25.9	1 832 304
	1983	7 136 000	7.4	22.0	5 174 600	72.5	5.4	27.4	1 961 400
NAMIBIA	1981	24 700	1.5	...	...	...	...	...	...
SOUTH AFRICAN RAND	1982	34 781	1.9	4.1	31 042	89.3	1.7	4.7	3 739
NIGER	1975	5 249 700	3.8	18.7	4 566 400	87.0	3.3	17.9	683 300
FRANC C.F.A.	1980	16 532 722	4.3	22.9	7 762 522	47.0	2.0	16.8	8 770 200
	1981	...	...	...	16 585 807	...	3.7	...	...
NIGERIA‡	1976	1 157 389	4.3	16.5	590 312	51.0	2.2	27.3	567 077
NAIRA	1979	1 551 600	3.9	16.2	1 020 380	65.8	2.5	32.8	531 220
	1981	...	...	...	2 522 740	...	5.3	68.7	...
	1982	1 049 430	2.1	9.6	549 430	52.4	1.1	15.6	500 000
	1983	1 054 078	2.2	9.3	620 786	58.9	1.3	16.2	433 292
REUNION									
FRENCH FRANC	1980	1 314 343	15.6	...	1 263 595	96.1	15.0	...	50 748
RWANDA	1975	1 198 064	2.3	25.3	1 197 164	99.9	2.3	28.4	*900
FRANC	1980	2 880 120	2.7	21.6	2 438 563	84.7	2.3	21.5	441 557
	1981	5 471 735	4.7	28.6	4 497 308	82.2	3.8	27.4	974 427
	1983	4 560 953	3.1	24.0	4 527 718	99.3	3.0	27.7	33 235
ST. HELENA	1975	...	...	...	79	...	...	6.3	...
POUND STERLING	1980	...	...	...	262	...	...	...	...
	1981	...	...	...	314	...	...	...	...
	1982	...	...	...	275	...	...	...	...
	1983	...	...	...	337	...	...	...	...
SAO TOME AND									
PRINCIPE	1981	90 639	6.2	...	...	...	...	...	...
DOBRA	1982	91 169	5.9	...	...	...	...	...	...
SENEGAL	1975	...	...	...	15 949 600	...	4.0	21.4	
FRANC C.F.A.	1980	...	...	...	27 485 411	...	4.5	23.5	...
	1981	...	...	...	*30 195 000	...	*4.7	...	...
SEYCHELLES‡	1975	12 632	4.4	9.5	11 202	88.7	3.9	15.1	1 430
RUPEE	1980	52 485	5.8	14.4	50 215	95.7	5.5	14.0	2 270
	1982	88 086	9.0	21.1	79 435	90.2	8.1	19.4	8 651
	1984	128 481	...	22.1	111 391	86.7	...	26.5	17 090

COUNTRY CURRENCY PAYS MONNAIE PAIS MONEDA	YEAR ANNEE AÑO	TOTAL EDUCATIONAL EXPENDITURE / DEPENSES TOTALES D'EDUCATION / GASTOS TOTALES DE EDUCACION			CURRENT EDUCATIONAL EXPENDITURE / DEPENSES ORDINAIRES D'EDUCATION / GASTOS ORDINARIOS DE EDUCACION				CAPITAL EXPENDITURE DEPENSES EN CAPITAL GASTOS EN CAPITAL (000)
		AMOUNT MONTANT IMPORTE (000)	AS % OF GROSS NATIONAL PRODUCT EN % DU PRODUIT NATIONAL BRUT EN % DEL PRODUCTO NACIONAL BRUTO (%)	AS % OF TOTAL GOVERNMENT EXPENDITURE EN % DES DEPENSES TOTALES DU GOUVERNEMENT EN % DE LOS GASTOS TOTALES DEL GOBIERNO (%)	AMOUNT MONTANT IMPORTE (000)	AS % OF THE TOTAL EN % DU TOTAL EN % DEL TOTAL (%)	AS % OF GROSS NATIONAL PRODUCT EN % DU PRODUIT NATIONAL BRUT EN % DEL PRODUCTO NACIONAL BRUTO (%)	AS % OF CURRENT GOVERNMENT EXPENDITURE EN % DES DEPENSES ORDINAIRES DU GOUVERNEMENT EN % DE LOS GASTOS ORDINARIOS DEL GOBIERNO (%)	
		(1)	(2)	(3)	(4)	(5)	(6)	(7)	(8)
SIERRA LEONE	1975	19 300	3.4	...	17 410	90.2	3.1	16.3	1 890
LEONE	1980	42 734	3.8	...	40 731	95.3	3.6	14.5	2 003
SOMALIA‡	1975	92 400	2.1	12.5	77 300	83.7	1.8	12.8	15 100
SHILLING	1980	169 384	1.7	8.7	154 384	91.1	1.5	...	15 000
	1981	239 813	1.5	8.1	209 813	87.5	1.3	...	30 000
	1982	271 963	1.5	6.9	224 076	82.4	1.2	...	47 887
	1983	327 521	1.4	6.3	281 246	85.9	1.2	...	46 275
SUDAN	1974	68 257	5.5	14.8	61 157	89.6	4.9	...	7 100
POUND	1980	187 005	4.6	9.1	172 399	92.2	4.2	12.6	14 606
SWAZILAND‡	1975	7 920	3.7	...	6 186	78.1	2.9	...	1 734
LILANGENI	1980	25 697	5.7	...	19 627	76.4	4.4	23.1	6 070
	1981	31 707	5.9	...	22 562	71.2	4.2	23.0	9 145
	1982	31 295	5.3	...	26 679	85.3	4.5	19.7	4 616
TOGO	1975	4 622 873	3.5	15.2	4 450 794	96.3	3.4	21.3	172 079
FRANC C.F.A.	1980	13 049 223	5.6	19.4	12 574 743	96.4	5.4	21.0	474 480
	1981	15 381 640	6.1	21.8	14 880 824	96.7	5.9	22.3	500 816
	1982	14 859 236	5.6	19.6	14 591 364	98.2	5.5	...	267 872
	1983	15 974 576	5.9	20.8	15 563 576	97.4	5.8	...	411 000
TUNISIA‡	1975	87 533	5.0	16.4	78 045	89.2	4.5	22.5	9 488
DINAR	1980	185 351	5.2	16.4	162 291	87.6	4.6	23.5	23 060
	1982	253 963	5.2	14.2	230 255	90.7	4.8	20.4	23 708
	1983	245 191	4.4	...	222 578	90.8	4.0	...	22 613
	1984	282 406	4.5	...	256 956	91.0	4.1	...	25 450
UGANDA‡	1975	568 638	2.5	17.0	529 014	93.0	2.4	22.0	39 624
SHILLING	1980	1 547 500	0.7	11.3	1 366 700	88.3	0.6	12.8	180 800
	1981	6 728 000	1.5	12.3	5 691 000	84.6	1.3	15.9	1 037 000
	1982	7 356 000	0.8	12.3	6 743 000	91.7	0.7	16.7	613 000
	1983	16 321 000	1.3	...	12 402 000	76.0	1.0	...	3 919 000
UNITED REPUBLIC OF TANZANIA‡	1975	1 029 100	5.4	17.8	827 800	80.4	4.4	22.5	201 300
SHILLING	1980	2 148 704	5.4	14.3	...	...	...	...	...
	1981	2 226 205	5.0	15.1	1 858 175	83.5	4.2	...	368 030
	1982	2 500 715	5.3	15.0	2 211 972	88.5	4.7	...	288 743
	1983	2 843 585	5.8	15.3	2 480 200	87.2	5.1	...	363 385
ZAIRE	1975	...	...	...	107 794	...	6.1	27.0	...
ZAIRE	1980	...	...	...	947 891	...	5.9	32.3	...
ZAMBIA	1975	98 020	6.5	11.9	75 420	76.9	5.0	13.0	22 600
KWACHA	1980	126 637	4.5	7.6	120 377	95.1	4.2	11.1	6 260
	1982	185 647	5.5	11.3	185 495	99.9	5.5	14.0	152
	1983	225 561	5.7	...	209 166	92.7	5.3	...	16 395
	1984	246 706	5.7	16.3	230 681	93.5	5.3	17.5	16 025
ZIMBABWE	1975	70 827	3.6	...	65 015	91.8	3.3	14.2	5 812
DOLLAR	1980	223 845	6.6	13.7	218 037	97.4	6.5	14.1	5 808
	1982	358 112	7.4	12.8	...	...	...	...	...
	1983	449 656	8.3	...	432 547	96.2	8.0	...	17 109
	1984	...	...	...	456 000	...	7.5	...	...
AMERICA, NORTH									
ANTIGUA AND BARBUDA	1975	6 346	4.5	14.4	5 681	89.5	4.0	15.9	665
E.CARIBBEAN DOLLAR	1980	8 621	3.1	...	8 529	98.9	3.1	...	92
	1982	11 312	3.3	...	10 983	97.1	3.2	...	329
	1983	11 598	3.3	...	10 885	93.9	3.1	...	713
	1984	11 870	3.0	...	11 371	95.8	2.9	...	499
BAHAMAS	1975	32 495	8.0	...	29 938	92.1	7.4	22.2	2 557
DOLLAR	1980	...	...	...	53 386	...	7.3	22.1	...
	1981	...	...	...	62 148	...	8.0	22.3	...
	1982	...	...	...	66 128	...	7.9	25.5	...
BARBADOS	1975	48 827	6.0	20.9	42 256	86.5	5.2	...	6 571
DOLLAR	1981	126 902	6.7	19.6	97 143	76.6	5.1	20.5	29 759
	1982	112 826	5.7	17.6	95 245	84.4	4.8	18.0	17 581

COUNTRY CURRENCY PAYS MONNAIE PAIS MONEDA	YEAR ANNEE AÑO	TOTAL EDUCATIONAL EXPENDITURE / DEPENSES TOTALES D'EDUCATION / GASTOS TOTALES DE EDUCACION AMOUNT MONTANT IMPORTE (000)	AS % OF GROSS NATIONAL PRODUCT EN % DU PRODUIT NATIONAL BRUT EN % DEL PRODUCTO NACIONAL BRUTO (%)	AS % OF TOTAL GOVERNMENT EXPENDITURE EN % DES DEPENSES TOTALES DU GOUVERNEMENT EN % DE LOS GASTOS TOTALES DEL GOBIERNO (%)	CURRENT EDUCATIONAL EXPENDITURE / DEPENSES ORDINAIRES D'EDUCATION / GASTOS ORDINARIOS DE EDUCACION AMOUNT MONTANT IMPORTE (000)	AS % OF THE TOTAL EN % DU TOTAL EN % DEL TOTAL (%)	AS % OF GROSS NATIONAL PRODUCT EN % DU PRODUIT NATIONAL BRUT EN % DEL PRODUCTO NACIONAL BRUTO (%)	AS % OF CURRENT GOVERNMENT EXPENDITURE EN % DES DEPENSES ORDINAIRES DU GOUVERNEMENT EN % DE LOS GASTOS ORDINARIOS DEL GOBIERNO (%)	CAPITAL EXPENDITURE DEPENSES EN CAPITAL GASTOS EN CAPITAL (000)
		(1)	(2)	(3)	(4)	(5)	(6)	(7)	(8)
BERMUDA DOLLAR	1975	10 877	3.0	...	10 417	95.8	2.9	...	460
	1980	26 247	4.1	...	25 713	98.0	4.0	...	534
	1981	21 723	2.8	15.7	21 201	97.6	2.7	17.0	522
	1982	25 550	3.2	15.9	25 031	98.0	3.1	16.9	519
	1983	28 542	3.1	15.9	27 510	96.4	3.0	17.4	1 032
BRITISH VIRGIN ISLANDS UNITED STATES DOLLAR	1975	1 002	4.7	...	967	96.5	4.5	...	35
	1980	...	...	...	1 622	...	...	13.3	...
	1983	3 384	...	...	3 361	99.3	...	...	23
	1984	4 161	...	15.3	4 161	100.0	...	16.9	–
CANADA DOLLAR	1975	12 790 683	7.8	17.8	11 526 821	90.1	7.0	...	1 263 862
	1980	22 100 070	7.7	17.3	20 450 870	92.5	7.1	...	1 649 200
	1982	28 430 054	8.0	...	26 264 997	92.4	7.4	...	2 165 057
	1983	29 957 545	7.7	...	27 702 373	92.5	7.2	...	2 255 172
	1984	30 987 959	7.4	15.2	28 692 121	92.6	6.9	...	2 295 838
CAYMAN ISLANDS JAMAICAN DOLLAR	1975	1 625	...	12.0	1 384	85.2	...	14.6	241
	1980	4 895	...	...	3 398	69.4	...	...	1 497
COSTA RICA COLON	1975	1 113 826	6.9	31.1	1 041 297	93.5	6.4	39.7	72 529
	1980	3 069 078	7.8	22.2	2 802 162	91.3	7.1	26.7	266 916
	1982	4 800 089	5.7	...	4 328 004	90.2	5.2	...	472 085
	1983	6 462 562	5.7	...	5 853 136	90.6	5.2	...	609 426
	1984	8 650 583	6.3	18.9	8 070 432	93.3	5.9	23.6	580 151
CUBA‡ PESO	1975	808 500	5.7	30.1	...	...	...	...	...
	1980	1 267 000	7.2	...	1 134 500	89.5	6.5	...	132 500
	1981	1 397 200	6.3	...	1 275 300	91.3	5.7	...	121 900
	1982	1 457 100	6.3	...	1 396 000	95.8	6.0	...	61 100
	1983	1 435 900	5.9	...	1 335 800	93.0	5.5	...	100 100
DOMINICAN REPUBLIC‡ PESO	1976	75 977	2.0	14.3	62 595	82.4	1.6	19.7	13 382
	1980	138 515	2.3	16.0	104 387	75.4	1.8	...	10 408
	1982	160 111	2.2	17.2	136 507	85.3	1.9	...	4 364
	1983	175 853	2.3	16.0	165 477	94.1	2.1	19.0	10 376
	1984	193 212	2.0	16.8	187 141	96.9	1.9	20.1	6 071
EL SALVADOR COLON	1975	150 893	3.4	22.2	138 364	91.7	3.1	28.1	12 529
	1980	340 136	3.9	17.1	320 009	94.1	3.6	22.9	20 127
	1981	331 445	3.9	14.6	321 814	97.1	3.8	20.4	9 631
	1982	333 863	3.8	8.5	322 158	96.5	3.7	10.8	11 705
	1984	335 535	3.0	...	292 928	87.3	2.6	...	42 607
GRENADA‡ E.CARIBBEAN DOLLAR	1975	5 507	7.6	12.5	5 478	99.5	7.6	23.4	29
	1979	...	...	...	11 096	...	7.2	20.9	...
	1983	9 830	4.6	...	9 561	97.3	4.5	...	269
GUADELOUPE FRENCH FRANC	1980	862 034	14.3	...	818 124	94.9	13.6	...	43 910
GUATEMALA QUETZAL	1975	56 200	1.6	15.7	...	...	...	...	...
	1981	156 706	1.8	10.7	149 714	95.5	1.7	22.5	6 992
	1982	162 262	1.9	11.0	129 226	79.6	1.5	17.1	33 036
	1983	162 884	1.8	12.4	153 750	94.4	1.7	...	9 134
	1984	163 367	1.8	12.4	159 778	97.8	1.7	23.1	3 589
HAITI GOURDE	1975	...	...	...	34 138	...	1.0	15.8	...
	1980	107 136	1.5	10.7	85 781	80.1	1.2	15.3	21 355
	1981	83 763	1.2	...	83 452	99.6	1.1	...	311
	1982	87 164	1.2	9.5	87 076	99.9	1.2	16.1	88
	1983	94 799	1.2	...	92 943	98.0	1.2	13.6	1 856
HONDURAS LEMPIRA	1975	80 078	3.7	20.3	...	...	...	...	...
	1980	155 003	3.3	14.2	141 075	91.0	3.0	19.5	13 928
	1981	188 735	3.8	15.3	168 689	89.4	3.4	20.4	20 046
	1982	224 921	4.3	16.9	206 880	92.0	4.0	24.0	18 041
JAMAICA‡ DOLLAR	1975	154 676	5.9	16.0	121 854	78.8	4.7	...	32 822
	1980	303 837	6.9	13.1	302 669	99.6	6.8	19.4	1 168
	1981	...	...	...	349 102	...	7.0	20.5	...
	1982	...	...	...	375 200	...	6.8	19.8	...
	1983	497 160	7.5	14.6	456 377	91.8	6.9	18.9	40 783
MARTINIQUE FRENCH FRANC	1980	930 613	15.2	...	886 861	95.3	14.5	...	43 752

4.1 **Public expenditure on education**
Dépenses publiques afférentes à l'enseignement
Gastos públicos destinados a la educación

COUNTRY / CURRENCY PAYS / MONNAIE PAIS / MONEDA	YEAR ANNEE AÑO	TOTAL EDUCATIONAL EXPENDITURE / DEPENSES TOTALES D'EDUCATION / GASTOS TOTALES DE EDUCACION			CURRENT EDUCATIONAL EXPENDITURE / DEPENSES ORDINAIRES D'EDUCATION / GASTOS ORDINARIOS DE EDUCACION				CAPITAL EXPENDITURE DEPENSES EN CAPITAL GASTOS EN CAPITAL (000)
		AMOUNT MONTANT IMPORTE (000)	AS % OF GROSS NATIONAL PRODUCT EN % DU PRODUIT NATIONAL BRUT EN % DEL PRODUCTO NACIONAL BRUTO (%)	AS % OF TOTAL GOVERNMENT EXPENDITURE EN % DES DEPENSES TOTALES DU GOUVERNEMENT EN % DE LOS GASTOS TOTALES DEL GOBIERNO (%)	AMOUNT MONTANT IMPORTE (000)	AS % OF THE TOTAL EN % DU TOTAL EN % DEL TOTAL (%)	AS % OF GROSS NATIONAL PRODUCT EN % DU PRODUIT NATIONAL BRUT EN % DEL PRODUCTO NACIONAL BRUTO (%)	AS % OF CURRENT GOVERNMENT EXPENDITURE EN % DES DEPENSES ORDINAIRES DU GOUVERNEMENT EN % DE LOS GASTOS ORDINARIOS DEL GOBIERNO (%)	
		(1)	(2)	(3)	(4)	(5)	(6)	(7)	(8)
MEXICO‡	1975	41 185 400	3.8	...	26 783 400	...	2.5	...	3 768 500
PESO	1980	125 354 205	3.0	16.7	114 913 003	91.7	2.8	...	10 441 202
	1981	248 092 000	4.4	...	181 262 144	...	3.2	...	15 229 856
	1982	380 222 900	4.3	...	282 559 038	...	3.2	...	23 963 862
	1983	443 829 058	2.8	6.4	416 192 879	93.8	2.6	7.5	27 636 179
NICARAGUA‡	1975	258 448	2.4	13.1	206 346	79.8	1.9	...	52 102
CORDOBA	1980	662 132	3.2	10.4	579 693	87.5	2.8	...	82 439
	1982	1 146 547	4.0	10.3	1 079 240	94.1	3.8	...	67 307
	1983	1 555 936	4.6	...	1 177 728	75.7	3.5	...	378 208
	1984	2 692 300	6.0	10.0	2 458 200	91.3	5.5	...	234 100
PANAMA	1975	103 316	5.7	21.3	96 693	93.6	5.3	31.6	6 623
BALBOA	1980	166 140	4.9	19.0	155 716	93.7	4.6	19.8	10 424
	1982	202 440	5.0	16.7	174 375	86.1	4.3	15.9	28 065
	1983	216 126	5.3	17.5	198 413	91.8	4.9	17.7	17 713
	1984	220 914	5.5	16.6	210 998	95.5	5.2	17.8	9 916
ST. CHRISTOPHER									
AND NEVIS	1975	2 752	4.0	10.5	2 732	99.3	4.0	12.5	20
E.CARIBBEAN DOLLAR	1980	6 595	5.1	9.4	6 563	99.5	5.0	13.6	32
	1982	9 879	6.1	13.4	9 839	99.6	6.1	15.7	40
	1983	10 576	6.6	...	10 536	99.6	6.6	...	40
	1984	11 266	6.7	...	11 226	99.6	6.7	...	40
ST. LUCIA‡	1975	8 338	7.7	16.8	7 321	87.8	6.8	20.0	1 017
E.CARIBBEAN DOLLAR	1980	...	...	...	18 596	...	6.3	...	...
	1982	27 466	7.8	...	23 045	83.9	6.5	...	4 421
ST. PIERRE AND									
MIQUELON	1980	18 432	...	...	16 725	90.7	...	...	1 707
FRENCH FRANC	1982	24 250	...	...	24 006	99.0	...	...	244
	1983	29 388	...	...	29 037	98.8	...	...	351
	1984	32 514	...	...	32 306	99.4	...	...	208
ST. VINCENT AND THE									
GRENADINES	1975	...	...	...	5 196	...	7.3	...	...
E.CARIBBEAN DOLLAR	1978	5 931	5.0	...	5 931	100.0	5.0	...	–
TRINIDAD AND TOBAGO	1975	157 055	3.0	14.7	138 295	88.1	2.7	17.7	18 760
DOLLAR	1980	563 931	3.8	11.5	430 831	76.4	2.9	17.6	133 100
	1982	1 066 212	6.1	11.8	888 080	83.3	5.1	18.6	178 132
	1983	1 074 491	5.4	12.3	867 816	80.8	4.3	16.3	206 675
	1984	1 094 771	5.1	...	901 433	82.3	4.2	...	193 338
TURKS AND CAICOS									
ISLANDS	1975	718	...	14.4	601	83.7	...	16.2	117
UNITED STATES DOLLAR	1980	1 018	...	...	832	81.7	...	...	186
	1983	1 394	...	10.3	1 287	92.3	...	12.4	107
UNITED STATES	1975	100 700 000	6.5	18.1	90 800 000	90.2	5.8	29.8	9 900 000
DOLLAR	1980	181 300 000	6.9	...	...	...	...	...	...
	1981	199 800 000	6.7	...	...	...	...	...	...
U.S. VIRGIN ISLANDS	1975	40 575	9.2	...	40 138	98.9	9.1	...	437
UNITED STATES DOLLAR	1980	57 541	7.9	...	56 774	98.7	7.8	...	767
AMERICA, SOUTH									
ARGENTINA	1975	3 577	2.5	9.5	3 356	93.8	2.3	10.9	221
PESO	1980	1 017 675	3.6	15.1	859 892	84.5	3.1	18.8	157 783
	1982	3 517 710	2.5	14.5	3 155 063	89.7	2.2	18.2	362 647
	1983	17 826 476	2.5	11.4	15 212 677	85.3	2.2	14.6	2 613 799
	1984	204 577 422	4.3	...	180 530 252	88.2	3.8	...	24 047 170
BOLIVIA‡	1975	1 660 734	3.4	...	1 658 659	99.9	3.4	...	2 075
PESO	1980	5 122 191	4.2	25.3	4 919 122	96.0	4.1	27.0	203 069
	1981	5 109 345	3.3	18.7	4 621 655	90.5	3.0	18.8	487 690
	1982	10 214 739	3.0	25.8	10 211 808	100.0	3.0	...	2 931
BRAZIL‡	1975	30 207	3.0	...	...	...	...	...	...
CRUZEIRO	1980	431 194	3.4	...	...	...	...	...	...
	1981	963 546	3.9	...	...	...	...	...	...
	1982	2 087 281	4.3	...	...	...	...	...	...
	1983	3 709 515	3.3	18.4	...	...	...	...	...

COUNTRY / CURRENCY PAYS / MONNAIE PAIS / MONEDA	YEAR ANNEE AÑO	TOTAL EDUCATIONAL EXPENDITURE / DEPENSES TOTALES D'EDUCATION / GASTOS TOTALES DE EDUCACION			CURRENT EDUCATIONAL EXPENDITURE / DEPENSES ORDINAIRES D'EDUCATION / GASTOS ORDINARIOS DE EDUCACION				
		AMOUNT MONTANT IMPORTE (000)	AS % OF GROSS NATIONAL PRODUCT EN % DU PRODUIT NATIONAL BRUT EN % DEL PRODUCTO NACIONAL BRUTO (%)	AS % OF TOTAL GOVERNMENT EXPENDITURE EN % DES DEPENSES TOTALES DU GOUVERNEMENT EN % DE LOS GASTOS TOTALES DEL GOBIERNO (%)	AMOUNT MONTANT IMPORTE (000)	AS % OF THE TOTAL EN % DU TOTAL EN % DEL TOTAL (%)	AS % OF GROSS NATIONAL PRODUCT EN % DU PRODUIT NATIONAL BRUT EN % DEL PRODUCTO NACIONAL BRUTO (%)	AS % OF CURRENT GOVERNMENT EXPENDITURE EN % DES DEPENSES ORDINAIRES DU GOUVERNEMENT EN % DE LOS GASTOS ORDINARIOS DEL GOBIERNO (%)	CAPITAL EXPENDITURE DEPENSES EN CAPITAL GASTOS EN CAPITAL (000)
		(1)	(2)	(3)	(4)	(5)	(6)	(7)	(8)
CHILE	1975	1 399 626	4.1	12.0	1 321 482	94.4	3.9	16.0	78 144
PESO	1980	47 960 718	4.6	...	45 503 514	94.9	4.4	...	2 457 204
	1982	65 336 340	5.8	...	...	...	...	...	...
	1983	70 576 749	5.0	...	70 243 488	99.5	5.0	...	333 261
	1984	82 275 895	4.8	...	81 651 572	99.2	4.8	...	624 323
COLOMBIA‡	1975	8 763 702	2.2	16.4	7 486 158	85.4	1.9	25.0	1 277 544
PESO	1980	29 240 258	1.9	14.3	27 286 015	93.3	1.7	19.9	1 954 243
	1981	51 777 416	2.7	...	49 004 771	94.6	2.5	...	2 772 645
	1983	86 528 000	2.9	21.5	83 436 200	96.4	2.8	27.7	3 091 800
	1984	117 065 000	3.3	24.8	108 896 000	93.0	3.1	33.2	8 169 000
ECUADOR‡	1975	3 386 500	3.2	25.9	...	...	...	...	...
SUCRE	1980	15 579 992	5.6	33.3	14 649 139	94.0	5.2	36.0	930 853
	1982	18 990 758	4.9	...	16 715 998	88.0	4.3	...	2 274 160
	1983	19 455 000	3.7	...	17 794 352	91.5	3.4	...	1 660 648
	1984	26 976 567	3.9	...	25 126 365	93.1	3.6	...	1 850 202
FALKLAND ISLANDS (MALVINAS)	1975	137	...	13.5	128	93.4	...	...	9
POUND STERLING	1979	207	...	...	204	98.6	...	...	3
FRENCH GUIANA FRENCH FRANC	1980	158 509	17.6	...	152 333	96.1	16.9	...	6 176
GUYANA	1975	57 064	4.9	9.8	47 944	84.0	4.2	14.9	9 120
DOLLAR	1981	144 757	10.1	...	110 827	76.6	7.7	13.3	33 930
	1982	119 363	9.1	7.3	96 509	80.9	7.3	11.4	22 854
	1983	121 231	8.9	9.6	105 299	86.9	7.7	11.6	15 932
	1984	120 263	7.4	6.4	112 361	93.4	6.9	8.9	7 902
PARAGUAY‡	1975	2 963 772	1.6	14.0	2 292 296	...	1.2	...	417 704
GUARANI	1980	8 793 247	1.6	16.4	6 267 238	...	...	...	1 157 830
	1982	16 412 296	2.2	17.4	10 833 407	...	...	...	2 278 940
	1983	16 642 924	2.0	17.6	12 461 417	...	...	...	1 774 638
	1984	16 988 000	1.6	...	14 049 200	82.7	1.3	...	2 938 800
PERU‡	1975	21 756	3.5	16.6	20 970	96.4	3.4	23.2	786
SOL	1980	175 915	3.3	15.2	166 040	94.4	3.1	18.5	9 875
	1982	484 616	3.3	15.8	478 168	98.7	3.3	23.8	6 448
	1983	888 229	3.3	14.7	873 165	98.3	3.2	17.3	15 064
	1984	1 922 834	3.2	...	1 892 284	98.4	3.1	...	30 550
SURINAME	1975	50 700	5.5	14.1	44 800	88.4	4.9	17.9	5 900
GUILDER	1980	105 193	6.0	18.1	105 193	100.0	6.0	...	–
	1983	159 200	7.0	...	...	...	...	...	...
URUGUAY	1980	2 035 103	2.2	10.0	1 926 769	94.7	2.1	...	108 334
PESO	1981	2 958 337	2.4	12.8	2 771 237	93.7	2.3	13.7	187 100
	1984	6 581 085	2.4	9.8	6 328 453	96.2	2.3	10.3	252 632
VENEZUELA	1975	6 225 161	5.2	...	5 965 747	95.8	5.0	...	259 414
BOLIVAR	1980	13 162 451	5.2	14.7	12 523 608	95.1	5.0	24.3	638 843
	1981	17 018 635	6.0	15.0	16 265 045	95.6	5.7	21.8	753 590
	1982	18 985 128	6.7	21.2	18 007 971	94.9	6.3	29.3	977 157
	1983	22 678 100	8.1	28.3	21 035 800	92.8	7.5	39.1	1 642 300
ASIA									
AFGHANISTAN	1974	1 264 216	1.3	...	1 142 630	90.4	1.2	15.3	121 586
AFGHANI	1980	3 205 456	2.0	12.7	2 886 301	90.0	1.8	14.4	319 155
	1981	3 115 782	1.8	8.8	2 891 136	92.8	1.6	10.0	224 646
	1982	2 362 753	...	6.4	2 191 353	92.7	...	6.9	171 400
BAHRAIN	1975	10 541	...	8.8	9 606	91.1	...	14.2	935
DINAR	1980	32 674	2.8	10.3	28 166	86.4	2.4	14.7	4 408
	1982	...	...	...	37 195	...	2.7	...	...
	1983	45 160	3.1	...	43 529	96.4	3.0	...	1 631
	1984	50 978	3.3	...	45 978	90.2	2.9	...	5 000
BANGLADESH‡	1975	1 379 862	1.1	13.6	929 862	67.4	0.7	18.9	450 000
TAKA	1980	3 009 311	1.7	8.2	2 010 009	66.8	1.1	15.4	999 302
	1982	3 834 867	1.7	...	2 942 897	76.7	1.3	...	891 970
	1983	5 117 246	1.9	8.6	3 626 348	70.9	1.4	15.4	1 490 898
	1984	6 191 904	1.9	...	4 932 264	79.7	1.5	...	1 259 640

4.1 Public expenditure on education
Dépenses publiques afférentes à l'enseignement
Gastos públicos destinados a la educación

COUNTRY / CURRENCY PAYS / MONNAIE PAIS / MONEDA	YEAR ANNEE AÑO	TOTAL EDUCATIONAL EXPENDITURE / DEPENSES TOTALES D'EDUCATION / GASTOS TOTALES DE EDUCACION			CURRENT EDUCATIONAL EXPENDITURE / DEPENSES ORDINAIRES D'EDUCATION / GASTOS ORDINARIOS DE EDUCACION				
		AMOUNT MONTANT IMPORTE (000)	AS % OF GROSS NATIONAL PRODUCT EN % DU PRODUIT NATIONAL BRUT EN % DEL PRODUCTO NACIONAL BRUTO (%)	AS % OF TOTAL GOVERNMENT EXPENDITURE EN % DES DEPENSES TOTALES DU GOUVERNEMENT EN % DE LOS GASTOS TOTALES DEL GOBIERNO (%)	AMOUNT MONTANT IMPORTE (000)	AS % OF THE TOTAL EN % DU TOTAL EN % DEL TOTAL (%)	AS % OF GROSS NATIONAL PRODUCT EN % DU PRODUIT NATIONAL BRUT EN % DEL PRODUCTO NACIONAL BRUTO (%)	AS % OF CURRENT GOVERNMENT EXPENDITURE EN % DES DEPENSES ORDINAIRES DU GOUVERNEMENT EN % DE LOS GASTOS ORDINARIOS DEL GOBIERNO (%)	CAPITAL EXPENDITURE DEPENSES EN CAPITAL GASTOS EN CAPITAL (000)
		(1)	(2)	(3)	(4)	(5)	(6)	(7)	(8)
BHUTAN / NGULTRUM	1974	23 275	...	...	12 853	55.2	...	...	10 422
	1978	26 796	...	...	18 426	68.8	...	...	8 370
BRUNEI DARUSSALAM / DOLLAR	1975	55 908	2.0	12.2	47 354	84.7	1.7	12.8	8 554
	1980	129 428	1.2	11.8	114 917	88.8	1.1	12.5	14 511
	1981	155 179	1.7	11.7	143 926	92.7	1.6	12.8	11 253
	1982	161 401	1.8	...	148 330	91.9	1.7	...	13 071
BURMA / KYAT	1975	405 257	1.7	15.3	385 990	95.2	1.6	16.3	19 267
	1977	486 818	1.6	12.2	470 430	96.6	1.6	14.6	16 388
CHINA / YUAN	1975	5 193 000	1.8	4.2	4 826 000	92.9	1.7	5.9	367 000
	1980	10 822 000	2.5	6.1	9 418 000	87.0	2.2	7.8	1 404 000
	1981	11 762 000	2.6	7.6	10 248 000	87.1	2.2	9.2	1 514 000
	1982	13 332 000	2.7	7.8	11 578 000	86.8	2.3	10.0	1 754 000
	1983	15 192 000	2.8	8.1	12 785 000	84.2	2.3	9.9	2 407 000
CYPRUS‡ / POUND	1975	11 421	4.3	14.3	10 325	90.4	3.9	15.2	1 096
	1980	27 066	3.5	12.9	25 452	94.0	3.3	16.2	1 614
	1981	34 512	3.9	13.5	32 600	94.5	3.7	15.3	1 912
	1982	39 756	3.9	13.1	37 835	95.2	3.7	14.5	1 921
	1983	43 468	3.9	11.9	42 181	97.0	3.8	13.4	1 287
DEMOCRATIC YEMEN / DINAR	1975	4 324	4.0	14.7	...	...	...	...	...
	1980	17 461	6.2	16.9	...	...	...	...	...
	1981	21 037	6.7	...	17 938	85.3	5.7	...	3 099
	1982	24 136	7.4	...	19 298	80.0	5.9	...	4 838
HONG KONG / DOLLAR	1975	1 246 272	2.7	20.7	1 144 538	91.8	2.5	25.7	101 734
	1980	3 446 432	2.5	14.6	3 036 139	88.1	2.2	25.5	410 293
	1982	5 315 959	2.8	15.0	4 749 727	89.3	2.5	24.4	566 232
	1983	5 901 440	2.8	17.6	5 348 983	90.6	2.6	23.0	552 457
	1984	6 990 588	2.8	18.7	6 189 691	88.5	2.5	23.0	800 897
INDIA / RUPEE	1975	21 036 400	2.8	8.6	20 852 100	99.1	2.8	15.1	184 300
	1980	37 924 238	3.0	10.0	37 461 638	98.8	2.9	...	462 600
	1981	44 102 000	3.0	9.6	43 543 500	98.7	3.0	13.7	558 500
	1982	51 859 000	3.2	...	...	...	...	...	...
INDONESIA‡ / RUPIAH	1975	357 110	3.0	13.1	277 076	77.6	2.3	...	80 034
	1980	808 087	1.9	8.9	...	...	...	...	...
	1981	1 147 785	2.2	9.3	...	...	...	...	...
IRAN, ISLAMIC REPUBLIC OF / RIAL	1975	...	...	...	165 723 000	...	4.6	...	...
	1980	498 268 000	...	15.7	440 298 000	88.4	...	20.1	57 970 000
	1982	447 102 000	...	15.6	394 119 000	88.2	...	18.0	52 983 000
	1983	521 688 000	...	15.5	452 014 000	86.6	...	18.4	69 674 000
	1984	529 969 000	...	13.6	462 785 000	87.3	...	16.9	67 184 000
IRAQ / DINAR	1976	204 493	4.3	6.9	155 763	76.2	3.3	10.5	48 730
	1980	298 000	...	...	...	...	...	...	...
	1981	272 100	...	...	...	...	...	...	...
	1982	...	...	...	457 378	...	...	8.5	...
ISRAEL / SHEKEL	1975	551 100	6.7	7.6	464 100	84.2	5.7	8.3	87 000
	1980	8 861 000	8.4	7.3	8 182 000	92.3	7.7	8.9	679 000
	1981	19 766 000	7.9	6.8	18 290 000	92.5	7.3	8.0	1 476 000
	1982	48 159 000	8.4	9.2	44 845 000	93.1	7.9	9.3	3 314 000
JAPAN‡ / YEN	1975	8 156 673	5.5	22.4	5 826 604	...	3.9	...	1 990 370
	1980	13 908 111	5.9	19.6	9 416 591	...	4.0	...	3 920 843
	1981	14 906 759	5.9	19.4	10 174 793	...	4.0	...	4 103 492
	1982	15 050 949	5.7	19.1	10 376 852	...	3.9	...	4 020 708
JORDAN‡ / DINAR	1975	16 698	5.1	8.1	13 900	83.2	4.3	11.1	2 798
	1980	63 822	6.6	11.3	50 543	79.2	5.2	15.0	13 279
	1982	84 226	6.2	12.1	64 129	76.1	4.7	14.8	20 097
	1983	88 575	6.0	12.5	79 530	89.8	5.4	16.2	9 045
	1984	113 859	7.1	14.8	82 655	72.6	5.2	18.3	31 204
KOREA, REPUBLIC OF‡ / WON	1975	220 282	2.2	13.9	163 800	74.4	1.6	...	56 482
	1980	1 374 736	3.7	23.7	1 158 967	84.3	3.1	...	215 769
	1982	2 061 867	4.0	21.5	1 619 449	78.5	3.1	...	442 418
	1983	2 942 892	5.0	24.2	2 231 377	75.8	3.8	...	711 515
	1984	3 155 013	4.8	...	2 501 253	79.3	3.8	...	653 760

COUNTRY / CURRENCY PAYS / MONNAIE PAIS / MONEDA	YEAR ANNEE AÑO	TOTAL EDUCATIONAL EXPENDITURE / DEPENSES TOTALES D'EDUCATION / GASTOS TOTALES DE EDUCACION AMOUNT MONTANT IMPORTE (000)	AS % OF GROSS NATIONAL PRODUCT EN % DU PRODUIT NATIONAL BRUT EN % DEL PRODUCTO NACIONAL BRUTO (%)	AS % OF TOTAL GOVERNMENT EXPENDITURE EN % DES DEPENSES TOTALES DU GOUVERNEMENT EN % DE LOS GASTOS TOTALES DEL GOBIERNO (%)	CURRENT EDUCATIONAL EXPENDITURE / DEPENSES ORDINAIRES D'EDUCATION / GASTOS ORDINARIOS DE EDUCACION AMOUNT MONTANT IMPORTE (000)	AS % OF THE TOTAL EN % DU TOTAL EN % DEL TOTAL (%)	AS % OF GROSS NATIONAL PRODUCT EN % DU PRODUIT NATIONAL BRUT EN % DEL PRODUCTO NACIONAL BRUTO (%)	AS % OF CURRENT GOVERNMENT EXPENDITURE EN % DES DEPENSES ORDINAIRES DU GOUVERNEMENT EN % DE LOS GASTOS ORDINARIOS DEL GOBIERNO (%)	CAPITAL EXPENDITURE DEPENSES EN CAPITAL GASTOS EN CAPITAL (000)
		(1)	(2)	(3)	(4)	(5)	(6)	(7)	(8)
KUWAIT DINAR	1975	112 023	2.9	10.0	90 069	80.4	2.4	10.8	21 954
	1980	218 910	2.5	8.1	203 758	93.1	2.3	11.2	15 152
	1982	316 223	4.3	10.2	289 168	91.4	4.0	...	27 055
	1983	313 229	4.1	14.1	296 966	94.8	3.9	15.8	16 263
	1984	332 981	4.2	9.3	317 386	95.3	4.0	12.1	15 595
LAO PEOPLE'S DEMOCRATIC REPUBLIC KIP	1980	23 500	...	1.3	...	...	...	...	...
MALAYSIA RINGGIT	1975	1 362 900	6.3	19.3	1 157 500	84.9	5.4	23.6	205 400
	1980	3 104 258	6.2	14.7	2 575 488	83.0	5.1	18.4	528 770
	1981	3 863 936	7.1	14.3	3 159 495	81.8	5.8	20.1	704 441
	1982	4 409 491	7.5	15.7	3 473 997	78.8	5.9	20.8	935 494
	1984	4 510 191	6.4	...	3 676 580	81.5	5.2	...	833 611
PENINSULAR MALAYSIA RINGGIT	1975	1 158 845	...	...	992 192	85.6	...	...	166 653
	1980	2 692 962	...	...	2 225 908	82.7	...	...	467 054
	1981	3 362 453	...	...	2 723 305	81.0	...	...	639 148
	1982	3 856 342	...	...	2 988 685	77.5	...	...	867 657
	1984	3 947 275	...	...	3 179 989	80.6	...	...	767 286
SABAH RINGGIT	1975	105 848	...	...	89 559	84.6	...	...	16 289
	1980	145 350	...	...	145 350	100.0	...	...	–
	1981	162 646	...	...	162 646	100.0	...	...	–
	1982	185 728	...	...	185 728	100.0	...	...	–
	1983	183 287	...	...	183 287	100.0	...	...	–
SARAWAK RINGGIT	1975	97 747	...	...	74 491	76.2	...	...	23 256
	1980	265 946	...	...	204 230	76.8	...	...	61 716
	1981	338 837	...	...	273 544	80.7	...	...	65 293
	1982	367 421	...	...	299 584	81.5	...	...	67 837
	1984	379 629	...	...	313 304	82.5	...	...	66 325
MALDIVES RUFIYAA	1975	...	...	...	1 115	...	0.7	11.5	...
	1978	1 279	0.6	3.1	1 221	95.5	0.6	8.0	58
NEPAL RUPEE	1975	245 990	1.5	11.5	...	...	...	...	...
	1980	429 681	1.8	...	...	...	...	...	...
	1981	568 896	2.1	...	...	...	...	...	...
	1982	839 902	2.8	...	...	...	...	...	...
OMAN RIAL	1975	9 396	1.6	1.9	6 605	70.3	1.1	2.0	2 791
	1980	38 235	2.0	4.1	31 067	81.3	1.6	4.6	7 168
	1981	54 300	2.3	4.6	44 600	82.1	1.9	5.2	9 700
	1984	95 890	3.9	...	68 972	71.9	2.8	...	26 918
PAKISTAN RUPEE	1975	2 488 206	2.2	5.2	1 731 089	69.6	1.5	...	757 117
	1980	4 619 071	1.8	5.0	3 378 591	73.1	1.3	5.2	1 240 480
	1981	5 601 957	1.8	5.1	3 914 601	69.9	1.3	4.9	1 687 356
	1982	6 469 479	1.9	4.9	4 529 003	70.0	1.3	4.6	1 940 476
	1983	8 165 100	2.1	...	6 197 000	75.9	1.6	...	1 968 100
PHILIPPINES‡ PESO	1975	2 149 896	1.9	11.4	1 753 958	...	1.5	13.8	31 938
	1980	4 190 750	1.6	10.3	4 022 850	96.0	1.5	...	167 900
	1982	6 581 205	2.0	...	5 356 174	81.4	1.6	...	1 225 031
	1983	6 778 951	1.8	9.9	5 996 256	88.5	1.6	13.2	782 695
	1984	6 902 622	1.3	7.0	6 284 788	91.0	1.2	8.0	617 834
QATAR RIYAL	1975	177 124	2.0	4.0	123 524	69.7	1.4	4.1	53 600
	1980	792 200	3.3	7.2	598 000	75.5	2.5	7.8	194 200
	1981	808 557	3.1	5.5	642 307	79.4	2.5	5.8	166 250
	1983	1 084 599	5.0	...	863 891	79.7	4.0	...	220 708
	1984	1 004 997	4.7	...	812 798	80.9	3.8	...	192 199
SAUDI ARABIA RIYAL	1975	12 940 937	10.3	11.7	5 528 566	42.7	4.4	15.1	7 412 371
	1980	21 294 465	5.5	8.7	13 526 367	63.5	3.5	...	7 768 098
	1981	25 823 287	4.8	8.7	16 116 847	62.4	3.0	...	9 706 440
	1982	31 404 295	6.0	10.0	20 369 004	64.9	3.9	...	11 035 291
	1983	27 266 265	7.1	10.5	20 500 792	75.2	5.4	15.6	6 765 473
SINGAPORE DOLLAR	1975	391 264	2.9	8.6	339 870	86.9	2.5	11.4	51 394
	1980	686 380	2.9	7.3	587 469	85.6	2.5	10.3	98 911
	1981	1 011 596	3.7	8.5	712 733	70.5	2.6	9.3	298 863
	1982	1 358 429	4.4	9.6	983 750	72.4	3.2	10.8	374 679

4.1 Public expenditure on education
Dépenses publiques afférentes à l'enseignement
Gastos públicos destinados a la educación

COUNTRY / CURRENCY — PAYS / MONNAIE — PAIS / MONEDA	YEAR / ANNEE / AÑO	TOTAL EDUCATIONAL EXPENDITURE / DEPENSES TOTALES D'EDUCATION / GASTOS TOTALES DE EDUCACION — AMOUNT / MONTANT / IMPORTE (000)	AS % OF GROSS NATIONAL PRODUCT / EN % DU PRODUIT NATIONAL BRUT / EN % DEL PRODUCTO NACIONAL BRUTO (%)	AS % OF TOTAL GOVERNMENT EXPENDITURE / EN % DES DEPENSES TOTALES DU GOUVERNEMENT / EN % DE LOS GASTOS TOTALES DEL GOBIERNO (%)	CURRENT EDUCATIONAL EXPENDITURE / DEPENSES ORDINAIRES D'EDUCATION / GASTOS ORDINARIOS DE EDUCACION — AMOUNT / MONTANT / IMPORTE (000)	AS % OF THE TOTAL / EN % DU TOTAL / EN % DEL TOTAL (%)	AS % OF GROSS NATIONAL PRODUCT / EN % DU PRODUIT NATIONAL BRUT / EN % DEL PRODUCTO NACIONAL BRUTO (%)	AS % OF CURRENT GOVERNMENT EXPENDITURE / EN % DES DEPENSES ORDINAIRES DU GOUVERNEMENT / EN % DE LOS GASTOS ORDINARIOS DEL GOBIERNO (%)	CAPITAL EXPENDITURE / DEPENSES EN CAPITAL / GASTOS EN CAPITAL (000)
		(1)	(2)	(3)	(4)	(5)	(6)	(7)	(8)
SRI LANKA	1975	729 590	2.8	10.1	682 680	93.6	2.6	13.0	46 910
RUPEE	1980	2 073 012	3.1	8.8	1 736 787	83.8	2.6	15.3	336 225
	1981	2 485 499	3.0	8.7	2 360 108	95.0	2.8	15.0	125 391
	1983	3 603 742	3.0	7.1	3 208 859	89.0	2.7	12.3	394 883
	1984	4 275 550	2.9	8.5	3 445 123	80.6	2.3	12.0	830 427
SYRIAN ARAB REPUBLIC‡	1975	813 245	3.9	7.8	462 514	...	2.2	10.1	188 625
POUND	1980	2 346 984	4.5	8.1	1 272 481	...	2.4	8.7	457 411
	1982	4 058 679	5.7	12.2	2 220 219	...	3.1	13.3	893 202
	1983	4 512 089	6.1	12.1	2 441 825	...	3.3	13.1	843 612
	1984	4 644 309	6.1	11.2	2 562 936	...	3.4	10.9	794 926
THAILAND	1975	10 605 251	3.6	21.0	7 775 347	73.3	2.6	18.9	2 829 904
BAHT	1980	22 489 450	3.3	20.6	15 867 328	70.6	2.4	19.1	6 622 122
	1981	27 932 500	3.7	20.0	21 464 829	76.8	2.8	...	6 467 671
	1982	32 364 600	3.9	20.1	24 575 384	75.9	3.0	...	7 789 216
	1983	35 300 074	3.9	...	28 127 463	79.7	3.1	...	7 172 611
TURKEY	1980	117 744 353	2.7	10.5	98 592 809	83.7	2.2	...	19 151 544
LIRA	1982	253 575 968	2.9	...	210 254 579	82.9	2.4	...	43 321 389
	1983	383 098 853	3.3	...	324 182 424	84.6	2.8	...	58 916 429
	1984	459 742 000	2.5	...	382 385 000	83.2	2.1	...	77 357 000
UNITED ARAB EMIRATES	1975	346 585	1.0	...	271 382	78.3	0.8	...	75 203
DIRHAM	1980	1 459 688	1.4	...	1 153 063	79.0	1.1	...	306 625
	1982	1 495 443	1.4	6.6	1 442 423	96.5	1.3	7.6	53 020
	1983	1 800 443	1.8	9.8	1 606 019	89.2	1.6	9.9	194 424
	1984	1 683 473	1.7	9.8	1 537 253	91.3	1.5	9.7	146 220
YEMEN	1976	...	...	...	63 300	...	1.1	7.5	...
RIAL	1980	932 782	6.6	13.7	694 400	74.4	4.9	22.3	238 382
EUROPE									
ANDORRA	1975	41 315	...	...	39 185	94.8	...	...	2 130
PESETA	1982	628 134	...	10.0	495 836	78.9	...	16.5	132 298
AUSTRIA	1975	37 409 300	5.7	8.5	29 366 500	78.5	4.5	9.8	8 042 800
SCHILLING	1980	55 016 300	5.6	8.0	46 955 400	85.3	4.8	8.4	8 060 900
	1982	67 157 100	6.0	8.1	60 043 800	89.4	5.3	8.8	7 113 300
	1983	70 874 800	6.0	8.0	63 476 700	89.6	5.3	8.7	7 398 100
	1984	74 262 000	5.9	8.0	66 453 600	85.5	5.0	8.8	7 808 400
BELGIUM‡	1975	143 856 800	6.2	22.2	131 906 200	91.7	5.7	23.0	11 950 600
FRANC	1980	208 469 200	6.0	16.3	206 226 600	98.9	6.0	18.6	2 242 600
	1982	238 273 400	6.2	13.6	236 391 500	99.2	6.1	15.0	1 881 900
	1983	256 884 000	6.3	14.2	243 807 200	94.9	6.0	15.3	13 076 800
	1984	261 038 300	6.0	13.8	247 337 900	94.8	5.7	14.5	13 700 400
BULGARIA‡	1975	787 599	5.5	8.5	725 259	92.1	5.1	...	62 340
LEV	1980	1 145 118	5.6	...	1 097 806	95.9	5.4	...	47 312
	1982	1 541 175	6.7	...	1 345 425	87.3	5.9	...	195 750
	1983	1 543 507	6.6	...	1 367 567	88.6	5.8	...	175 940
	1984	1 651 568	6.6	...	1 480 646	89.7	5.9	...	170 922
CZECHOSLOVAKIA‡	1975	19 104 801	4.7	7.0	17 288 021	90.5	4.3	...	1 816 780
KORUNA	1980	23 180 783	4.8	...	21 801 883	94.1	4.5	...	1 378 900
	1982	25 569 580	5.2	...	24 166 099	94.5	4.9	...	1 403 481
	1983	25 798 118	5.1	...	24 495 059	94.9	4.9	...	1 303 059
	1984	27 131 589	5.1	...	25 814 818	95.1	4.8	...	1 316 771
DENMARK	1975	16 801 000	7.8	15.2	14 600 000	86.9	6.8	...	2 201 000
KRONE	1980	25 020 000	6.9	9.5	22 188 000	88.7	6.1	9.0	2 832 000
	1982	32 442 000	7.1	...	...	...	...	...	...
	1983	34 654 000	7.0	...	...	...	...	...	...
	1984	35 589 000	6.5	...	...	...	...	...	...
FINLAND	1975	6 497 103	6.5	13.0	5 596 511	86.1	5.6	14.3	900 592
MARKKA	1980	10 434 855	5.7	...	9 565 205	91.7	5.2	12.5	869 650
	1981	12 053 168	5.8	...	11 213 594	93.0	5.4	12.4	839 574
	1982	13 535 225	5.6	12.8	12 545 795	92.7	5.2	14.3	989 430
	1983	15 355 425	5.7	13.1	14 222 522	92.6	5.3	14.3	1 132 903

COUNTRY / CURRENCY PAYS / MONNAIE PAIS / MONEDA	YEAR ANNEE AÑO	TOTAL EDUCATIONAL EXPENDITURE / DEPENSES TOTALES D'EDUCATION / GASTOS TOTALES DE EDUCACION			CURRENT EDUCATIONAL EXPENDITURE / DEPENSES ORDINAIRES D'EDUCATION / GASTOS ORDINARIOS DE EDUCACION				CAPITAL EXPENDITURE DEPENSES EN CAPITAL GASTOS EN CAPITAL (000)
		AMOUNT MONTANT IMPORTE (000)	AS % OF GROSS NATIONAL PRODUCT EN % DU PRODUIT NATIONAL BRUT EN % DEL PRODUCTO NACIONAL BRUTO (%)	AS % OF TOTAL GOVERNMENT EXPENDITURE EN % DES DEPENSES TOTALES DU GOUVERNEMENT EN % DE LOS GASTOS TOTALES DEL GOBIERNO (%)	AMOUNT MONTANT IMPORTE (000)	AS % OF THE TOTAL EN % DU TOTAL EN % DEL TOTAL (%)	AS % OF GROSS NATIONAL PRODUCT EN % DU PRODUIT NATIONAL BRUT EN % DEL PRODUCTO NACIONAL BRUTO (%)	AS % OF CURRENT GOVERNMENT EXPENDITURE EN % DES DEPENSES ORDINAIRES DU GOUVERNEMENT EN % DE LOS GASTOS ORDINARIOS DEL GOBIERNO (%)	
		(1)	(2)	(3)	(4)	(5)	(6)	(7)	(8)
FRANCE‡ FRANC	1975	76 357 000	5.2	...	66 873 000	87.6	4.6	...	9 484 000
	1980	142 099 000	5.1	...	131 441 000	92.5	4.7	...	10 658 000
	1981	175 433 000	5.6	...	163 300 000	93.1	5.3	...	12 133 000
	1982	208 230 000	5.8	...	194 708 000	93.5	5.4	...	13 522 000
GERMAN DEMOCRATIC REPUBLIC‡ DDR MARK	1975	...	...	...	8 276 353	...	5.4	...	...
	1980	...	...	...	9 836 257	...	5.3	...	...
	1982	...	...	...	10 959 400	...	5.5	...	...
	1983	...	...	...	11 118 900	...	5.3	...	...
	1984	...	...	...	11 838 400	...	5.3	...	...
GERMANY, FEDERAL REPUBLIC OF DEUTSCHE MARK	1975	52 860 900	5.1	10.7	42 456 700	80.3	4.1	9.4	10 404 200
	1980	70 098 600	4.7	10.1	60 557 900	86.4	4.1	9.5	9 540 700
	1981	73 499 800	4.7	...	64 408 400	87.6	4.1	...	9 091 400
	1982	74 183 600	4.6	...	66 078 100	89.1	4.1	...	8 105 500
	1983	74 449 300	4.5	8.8	67 382 800	90.5	4.0	9.0	7 066 500
GIBRALTAR POUND STERLING	1975	997	3.3	...	909	91.2	3.1	...	88
	1980	5 421	9.0	...	3 305	61.0	5.5	...	2 116
	1981	8 811	13.4	...	3 749	42.5	5.7	...	5 062
	1982	5 501	7.9	...	4 083	74.2	5.8	...	1 418
	1983	4 865	6.0	...	4 502	92.5	5.6	...	363
GREECE DRACHMA	1975	13 559 508	2.0	8.0	12 336 357	91.0	1.8	9.0	1 223 151
	1979	31 754 307	2.2	8.4	29 950 864	94.3	2.0	9.6	1 803 443
	1981	54 666 621	2.6	...	51 962 470	95.1	2.5	...	2 704 151
	1982	68 081 928	2.6	...	65 621 662	96.4	2.5	...	2 460 266
HUNGARY FORINT	1975	19 325 492	4.1	4.2	16 719 792	86.5	3.5	5.3	2 605 700
	1980	33 099 379	4.7	5.2	27 516 379	83.1	3.9	6.4	5 583 000
	1982	41 384 905	5.0	5.8	35 722 905	86.3	4.3	7.2	5 662 000
	1983	51 099 888	5.8	6.6	45 205 888	88.5	5.2	8.2	5 894 000
	1984	51 361 490	5.4	6.4	45 725 490	89.0	4.8	7.9	5 636 000
ICELAND‡ KRONA	1975	78 100	4.1	12.2	...	...	...	...	...
IRELAND POUND	1975	230 483	6.2	10.8	199 666	86.6	5.3	12.8	30 817
	1980	594 520	7.1	...	515 000	86.6	6.1	...	79 520
	1981	759 279	7.2	10.9	663 136	87.3	6.3	12.6	96 143
	1982	840 369	7.0	9.7	734 997	87.5	6.1	11.1	105 372
	1983	912 050	6.9	9.7	813 873	89.2	6.1	11.0	98 177
ITALY‡ LIRA	1975	5 675 784	4.5	9.4	5 060 156	89.2	4.1	12.6	615 628
	1979	13 633 022	5.0	11.1	11 791 069	86.5	4.4	10.7	1 841 953
	1983	30 230 337	5.7	9.6	28 040 275	92.8	5.3	10.0	2 190 062
LUXEMBOURG FRANC	1975	5 023 200	4.8	15.0	3 903 300	77.7	3.8	15.8	1 119 900
	1980	9 791 500	5.7	14.9	9 305 300	95.0	5.4	19.8	486 200
	1981	10 822 300	5.9	14.6	10 239 400	94.6	5.6	18.9	582 900
	1982	13 198 700	6.1	16.1	12 550 200	95.1	5.8	20.4	648 500
	1983	13 114 700	5.3	14.1	12 315 800	93.9	5.0	18.8	798 900
MALTA LIRA	1975	7 105	3.9	7.6	6 881	96.8	3.7	11.9	224
	1980	12 558	3.0	7.8	12 475	99.3	3.0	9.7	83
	1982	17 393	3.4	8.0	16 951	97.5	3.3	9.5	442
	1983	17 179	3.5	...	16 882	98.3	3.4	...	297
	1984	16 100	3.2	...	15 545	96.6	3.1	...	555
MONACO FRENCH FRANC	1974	35 282	...	10.4	20 538	58.2	...	...	14 744
	1980	...	...	...	42 629	...	...	...	...
	1981	...	...	...	50 234	...	...	...	...
	1982	...	...	...	60 248	...	...	...	...
NETHERLANDS GUILDER	1975	18 096 000	8.2	...	14 881 000	82.2	6.8	...	3 215 000
	1980	26 606 000	7.9	...	23 079 000	86.7	6.9	...	3 527 000
	1981	27 569 000	7.9	...	23 968 000	86.9	6.9	...	3 601 000
	1982	28 124 000	7.7	...	24 484 000	87.1	6.7	...	3 640 000
NORWAY KRONE	1975	10 456 000	7.1	14.7	8 427 000	80.6	5.7	13.9	2 029 000
	1980	19 731 000	7.2	13.8	16 448 000	83.4	6.0	14.5	3 283 000
	1981	21 756 000	6.9	13.5	18 601 000	85.5	5.9	14.2	3 155 000
	1982	24 646 000	7.0	13.5	21 250 000	86.2	6.1	14.4	3 396 000
	1983	27 167 000	7.0	12.9	23 522 000	86.6	6.0	14.3	3 645 000

COUNTRY / CURRENCY PAYS / MONNAIE PAIS / MONEDA	YEAR ANNEE AÑO	TOTAL EDUCATIONAL EXPENDITURE / DEPENSES TOTALES D'EDUCATION / GASTOS TOTALES DE EDUCACION			CURRENT EDUCATIONAL EXPENDITURE / DEPENSES ORDINAIRES D'EDUCATION / GASTOS ORDINARIOS DE EDUCACION				
		AMOUNT MONTANT IMPORTE (000)	AS % OF GROSS NATIONAL PRODUCT EN % DU PRODUIT NATIONAL BRUT EN % DEL PRODUCTO NACIONAL BRUTO (%)	AS % OF TOTAL GOVERNMENT EXPENDITURE EN % DES DEPENSES TOTALES DU GOUVERNEMENT EN % DE LOS GASTOS TOTALES DEL GOBIERNO (%)	AMOUNT MONTANT IMPORTE (000)	AS % OF THE TOTAL EN % DU TOTAL EN % DEL TOTAL (%)	AS % OF GROSS NATIONAL PRODUCT EN % DU PRODUIT NATIONAL BRUT EN % DEL PRODUCTO NACIONAL BRUTO (%)	AS % OF CURRENT GOVERNMENT EXPENDITURE EN % DES DEPENSES ORDINAIRES DU GOUVERNEMENT EN % DE LOS GASTOS ORDINARIOS DEL GOBIERNO (%)	CAPITAL EXPENDITURE DEPENSES EN CAPITAL GASTOS EN CAPITAL (000)
		(1)	(2)	(3)	(4)	(5)	(6)	(7)	(8)
POLAND‡ ZLOTY	1975	...	...	...	50 449 000	...	3.7	8.7	...
	1980	...	...	...	79 984 000	...	4.0	7.0	...
	1982	...	...	...	192 966 000	...	4.1	8.9	...
	1983	...	...	...	255 298 000	...	4.3	11.2	...
	1984	...	...	...	333 055 000	...	4.6	11.4	...
PORTUGAL‡ ESCUDO	1975	15 214 700	4.0	11.2	14 269 981	93.8	3.8	13.9	944 719
	1980	53 233 500	4.4	...	45 442 800	85.4	3.8	...	7 790 700
	1981	65 983 200	4.7	...	57 032 900	86.4	4.0	...	8 950 300
	1982	84 697 800	4.8	...	72 884 100	86.1	4.2	...	11 813 700
ROMANIA LEU	1975	15 194 700	3.5	6.4	12 892 700	84.9	3.0	...	2 302 000
	1980	19 930 200	3.3	6.7	17 691 200	88.8	2.9	...	2 239 000
	1982	19 991 300	2.7	...	18 438 300	92.2	2.5	...	1 553 000
	1983	17 749 700	2.3	7.5	17 005 700	95.8	2.2	...	744 000
	1984	17 465 100	2.1	...	16 903 100	96.8	2.1	...	562 000
SAN MARINO LIRA	1975	2 775 902	...	13.1	2 499 565	90.0	...	15.0	276 337
	1980	7 251 937	...	7.5	6 263 207	86.4	...	9.5	988 730
	1981	9 535 948	...	8.1	7 685 931	80.6	...	9.9	1 850 017
	1982	11 523 447	...	10.6	9 546 420	82.8	...	12.4	1 977 027
	1983	16 877 433	...	15.5	15 358 869	91.0	...	16.2	1 518 564
SPAIN PESETA	1976	154 003 000	2.1	16.8	134 391 000	87.3	1.9	...	19 612 000
	1979	342 376 000	2.6	16.4	295 443 000	86.3	2.3	16.7	46 933 000
	1981	444 078 000	2.6	...	...	...	...	...	...
	1982	485 365 000	2.5	...	...	...	...	...	...
SWEDEN KRONA	1975	21 230 200	7.1	13.4	19 281 100	90.8	6.4	13.9	1 949 100
	1980	47 322 300	9.1	14.1	40 885 700	86.4	7.9	...	6 436 600
	1982	54 954 200	9.0	13.0	46 823 900	85.2	7.7	...	8 130 300
	1983	57 624 000	8.4	12.5	49 262 200	85.5	7.2	...	8 361 800
	1984	61 539 800	8.0	12.2	54 190 500	88.1	7.1	...	7 349 300
SWITZERLAND FRANC	1975	7 392 300	5.1	19.4	5 978 800	80.9	4.1	19.8	1 413 500
	1980	8 872 700	5.0	18.8	7 936 800	89.5	4.5	20.0	935 900
	1981	9 439 300	4.9	18.9	8 371 600	88.7	4.3	20.2	1 067 700
	1982	10 198 600	5.0	18.8	9 097 100	89.2	4.4	20.0	1 101 500
	1983	10 796 700	5.1	18.8	9 756 600	90.4	4.6	20.2	1 040 100
UNITED KINGDOM POUND STERLING	1975	7 020 000	6.7	14.3	6 292 000	89.6	6.0	...	728 000
	1980	12 856 000	5.7	13.9	12 094 000	94.1	5.4	...	762 000
	1981	13 962 000	5.5	12.2	13 310 000	95.3	5.2	12.4	652 000
	1982	14 922 000	5.4	11.9	14 240 000	95.4	5.1	12.0	682 000
	1983	15 824 000	5.3	11.5	15 108 000	95.5	5.0	11.8	716 000
YUGOSLAVIA DINAR	1975	28 897 000	5.4	24.4	25 515 000	88.3	4.8	...	3 382 000
	1980	84 051 000	5.1	32.5	71 514 000	85.1	4.3	...	12 537 000
	1981	105 307 000	4.5	...	90 367 000	85.8	3.8	...	14 940 000
	1982	131 809 000	4.4	...	116 886 000	88.7	3.9	...	14 923 000
	1983	160 204 000	3.9	...	145 149 000	90.6	3.6	...	15 055 000
OCEANIA									
AMERICAN SAMOA UNITED STATES DOLLAR	1975	9 642	14.2	...	7 962	82.6	11.8	...	1 680
	1981	11 470	8.6	16.0	11 248	98.1	8.4	17.9	222
AUSTRALIA DOLLAR	1975	4 495 000	6.2	14.8	3 735 000	83.1	5.2	18.4	760 000
	1980	7 592 000	5.9	14.8	6 899 000	90.9	5.3	16.8	693 000
	1981	8 580 000	5.9	14.5	7 882 000	91.9	5.4	16.6	698 000
	1982	9 846 000	6.2	14.0	9 110 000	92.5	5.7	16.2	736 000
	1983	10 897 000	6.0	13.6	10 081 000	92.5	5.6	15.7	816 000
COOK ISLANDS NEW ZEALAND DOLLAR	1981	2 768	...	13.1	2 712	98.0	...	...	56
	1984	3 481	...	10.2	3 474	99.8	...	...	7
FIJI DOLLAR	1975	26 032	4.7	*19.5	24 039	92.3	4.3	23.2	1 993
	1980	49 641	5.1	...	47 861	96.4	4.9	21.5	1 780
	1981	61 472	5.9	11.3	57 758	94.0	5.5	22.4	3 714
	1983	74 091	6.4	...	73 404	99.1	6.3	24.1	687
FRENCH POLYNESIA FRANC C.F.P.	1975	3 740 422	8.3	...	3 268 311	87.4	7.3	...	472 111
	1983	16 286 000	9.9	17.2	14 778	90.7	9.0	...	1 508 000
GUAM UNITED STATES DOLLAR	1975	52 874	12.4	...	52 723	99.7	12.4	...	151
	1981	48 761	7.5	...	47 888	98.2	7.3	...	873

COUNTRY CURRENCY / PAYS MONNAIE / PAIS MONEDA	YEAR / ANNEE / AÑO	TOTAL EDUCATIONAL EXPENDITURE / DEPENSES TOTALES D'EDUCATION / GASTOS TOTALES DE EDUCACION: AMOUNT / MONTANT / IMPORTE (000)	AS % OF GROSS NATIONAL PRODUCT / EN % DU PRODUIT NATIONAL BRUT / EN % DEL PRODUCTO NACIONAL BRUTO (%)	AS % OF TOTAL GOVERNMENT EXPENDITURE / EN % DES DEPENSES TOTALES DU GOUVERNEMENT / EN % DE LOS GASTOS TOTALES DEL GOBIERNO (%)	CURRENT EDUCATIONAL EXPENDITURE / DEPENSES ORDINAIRES D'EDUCATION / GASTOS ORDINARIOS DE EDUCACION: AMOUNT / MONTANT / IMPORTE (000)	AS % OF THE TOTAL / EN % DU TOTAL / EN % DEL TOTAL (%)	AS % OF GROSS NATIONAL PRODUCT / EN % DU PRODUIT NATIONAL BRUT / EN % DEL PRODUCTO NACIONAL BRUTO (%)	AS % OF CURRENT GOVERNMENT EXPENDITURE / EN % DES DEPENSES ORDINAIRES DU GOUVERNEMENT / EN % DE LOS GASTOS ORDINARIOS DEL GOBIERNO (%)	CAPITAL EXPENDITURE / DEPENSES EN CAPITAL / GASTOS EN CAPITAL (000)
		(1)	(2)	(3)	(4)	(5)	(6)	(7)	(8)
KIRIBATI AUSTRALIAN DOLLAR	1975	2 077	4.9	...	2 022	97.4	4.8	6.7	55
	1980	2 550	12.3	...	2 550	100.0	12.3	17.4	–
	1981	2 939	12.8	13.0	2 939	100.0	12.8	16.8	–
	1984	2 703	8.7	16.8	2 703	100.0	8.7	...	–
NEW CALEDONIA FRENCH FRANC	1981	627 856	11.9	...	595 836	94.9	11.2	...	32 020
	1982	712 022	12.0	...	662 363	93.0	11.1	...	49 659
	1983	799 047	12.1	...	736 197	92.1	11.1	...	62 850
	1984	915 765	12.5	...	835 410	91.2	11.4	...	80 355
NEW ZEALAND DOLLAR	1975	631 751	5.6	17.1	503 643	79.7	4.5	...	128 108
	1980	1 302 324	5.5	14.5	1 171 226	89.9	5.0	...	131 098
	1982	1 639 000	5.3	12.9	...	...	...	...	...
	1983	1 690 488	5.1	11.9	1 541 429	91.2	4.6	...	149 059
	1984	1 746 868	4.9	...	1 598 765	91.5	4.4	...	148 103
NIUE NEW ZEALAND DOLLAR	1975	631	...	18.6	595	94.3	...	28.7	36
	1980	777	...	13.2	755	97.2	...	15.9	22
	1981	717	...	...	717	100.0	...	...	–
	1982	664	...	10.9	664	100.0	...	10.9	–
NORFOLK ISLAND AUSTRALIAN DOLLAR	1975	220	...	13.7	209	95.0	...	17.7	11
	1980	425	...	15.1	425	100.0	...	17.3	–
	1981	728	...	19.8	722	99.2	...	21.5	6
	1982	455	...	14.0	455	100.0	...	14.9	–
PACIFIC ISLANDS UNITED STATES DOLLAR	1975	23 469	27.0	*24.3	21 501	91.6	24.7	...	1 968
	1979	25 837	24.2	...	25 837	100.0	24.2	...	–
	1981	26 129	19.0	...	26 129	100.0	19.0	...	–
	1982	27 710	19.0	...	27 710	100.0	19.0	...	–
PAPUA NEW GUINEA KINA	1976	89 159	7.7	...	80 426	90.2	6.9	...	8 733
	1979	74 329	4.7	14.2	71 852	96.7	4.5	...	2 477
SAMOA TALA	1975		...	...	1 939		...	20.5	...
	1978	3 012	...	...	2 701	89.7		...	311
SOLOMON ISLANDS‡ AUSTRALIAN DOLLAR	1979	3 959	3.6	10.6	3 473	87.7	3.2	15.6	486
TOKELAU NEW ZEALAND DOLLAR	1981	669	...	...	630	94.2	...	...	39
	1982	614	...	...	579	94.3	...	...	35
TONGA PA'ANGA	1975	709	2.8	12.7	686	96.8	2.7	14.4	23
	1980	1 558	2.8	11.9	1 399	89.8	2.5	13.3	159
	1981	1 909	2.7	11.6	1 892	99.1	2.7	16.1	17
	1983	6 990	7.8	34.4	2 974	42.5	3.3	17.5	4 016
	1984	6 448	...	37.1	2 448	38.0	...	...	4 000
U.S.S.R.									
U.S.S.R.‡ ROUBLE	1975	27 747 100	7.6	12.9	23 415 900	84.4	6.4	...	4 331 200
	1980	33 026 200	7.1	11.2	28 098 600	85.1	6.1	...	4 927 600
	1982	35 323 300	6.7	10.3	30 156 300	85.4	5.8	...	5 167 000
	1983	36 221 000	6.6	10.2	30 913 600	85.3	5.6	...	5 307 400
	1984	37 932 800	...	10.2	31 735 800	83.7	...	...	6 197 000
BYELORUSSIAN S.S.R. ROUBLE	1975	1 040 600	...	...	859 300	82.6	...	...	181 300
	1980	1 253 300	...	...	1 051 300	83.9	...	...	202 000
	1982	1 327 000	...	...	1 145 900	86.4	...	...	181 100
	1983	1 345 600	...	...	1 158 000	86.1	...	...	187 600
	1984	1 424 700	...	...	1 210 100	84.9	...	...	214 600
UKRAINIAN S.S.R. ROUBLE	1975	5 014 000	...	27.4	4 312 200	86.0	...	...	701 800
	1980	5 926 700	...	24.5	5 114 300	86.3	...	...	812 400
	1982	6 191 600	...	21.6	5 402 200	87.3	...	...	789 400
	1983	6 200 900	...	20.6	5 391 400	86.9	...	...	809 500
	1984	6 428 500	...	20.7	5 487 700	85.4	...	...	940 800

AFRICA

Algeria:

E--> For 1982, expenditure on third level education is not included.

FR-> En 1982, les dépenses relatives à l'enseignement du troisième degré ne sont pas incluses.

Algeria: (Cont):

ESP> En 1982, no se incluyen los gastos relativos a la enseñanza de tercer grado.

Egypt:

E--> For 1982 and 1983, expenditure of Al-Azhar education is not included.

Egypt: (Cont):
FR-> En 1982 et 1983, les dépenses relatives à l'enseignement Al-Azhar ne sont pas incluses.
ESP> En 1982 y 1983, no se incluyen los gastos relativos a la enseñanza Al-Azhar.

Ethiopia:
E--> For 1982, data include foreign aid.
FR-> En 1982, les données incluent l'aide étrangère.
ESP> En 1982, los datos incluyen la ayuda extranjera.

Nigeria:
E--> Except for 1981, data refer to expenditure of the Federal government only.
FR-> Sauf pour 1981, les données se réfèrent aux dépenses du gouvernement fédéral seulement.
ESP> Salvo por 1981, los datos se refieren a los gastos del gobierno federal solamente.

Seychelles:
E--> For 1984, expenditure on third level education is not included.
FR-> En 1984, les dépenses relatives à l'enseignement du troisième degré ne sont pas incluses.
ESP> En 1984, no se incluyen los gastos relativos a la enseñanza de tercer grado.

Somalia:
E--> From 1980 to 1983, expenditure on third level education is not included.
FR-> De 1980 à 1983, les dépenses relatives à l'enseignement du troisième degré ne sont pas incluses.
ESP> De 1980 a 1983, no se incluyen los gastos relativos a la enseñanza de tercer grado.

Swaziland:
E--> For 1975, data refer to expenditure of the Ministry of Education only.
FR-> En 1975, les données se réfèrent aux dépenses du Ministère de l'Education seulement.
ESP> En 1975, los datos se refieren a los gastos del Ministerio de Educación solamente.

Tunisia:
E--> For 1983 and 1984, expenditure on third level education is not included.
FR-> En 1983 et 1984, les dépenses relatives à l'enseignement du troisième degré ne sont pas incluses.
ESP> En 1983 y 1984, no se incluyen los gastos relativos a la enseñanza de tercer grado.

Uganda:
E--> Data refer to expenditure of the Ministry of Education only.
FR-> Les données se réfèrent aux dépenses du Ministère de l'Education seulement.
ESP> Los datos se refieren a los gastos del Ministerio de Educación solamente.

United Republic of Tanzania:
E--> From 1980 to 1983, data refer to expenditure of the Ministry of Education only.
FR-> De 1980 à 1983, les données se réfèrent aux dépenses du Ministère de l'Education seulement.
ESP> De 1980 a 1983, los datos se refieren a los gastos del Ministerio de Educación solamente.

AMERICA, NORTH

Cuba:
E--> Expenditure on education is calculated as percentage of global social product.
FR-> Les dépenses de l'enseignement sont calculées en pourcentage du produit social global.
ESP> Los gastos relativos a la enseñanza se calculan como porcentaje del producto social global.

Dominican Republic:
E--> For 1980 and 1982, data on current and capital expenditure (columns 4 to 8) refer to the Ministry of Education only.
FR-> En 1980 et 1982, les données relatives aux dépenses ordinaires et en capital (colonnes 4 à 8) se réfèrent au Ministère de l'Education seulement.
ESP> En 1980 y 1982, los datos relativos a los gastos ordinarios y de capital (columnas 4 a 8) se refieren al Ministerio de Educación solamente.

Grenada:
E--> For 1983, expenditure on third level education is not included.
FR-> En 1983, les dépenses relatives à l'enseignement du troisième degré ne sont pas incluses.
ESP> En 1983, no se incluyen los gastos relativos a la enseñanza de tercer grado.

Jamaica:
E--> For 1975 and 1980, data refer to expenditure of the Ministry of Education only.
FR-> En 1975 et 1980, les données se réfèrent aux dépenses du Ministère de l'Education seulement.
ESP> En 1975 y 1980, los datos se refieren a los gastos del Ministerio de Educación solamente.

Mexico:
E--> Data on current and capital expenditure (columns 4 to 8) refer to the Ministry of Education only. For 1980 and 1983, this applies to total expenditure as well (column 1). Percentages shown in columns 3 and 7 have therefore been calculated using expenditure of the central government only.
FR-> Les données relatives aux dépenses ordinaires et en capital (colonnes 4 à 8) se réfèrent au Ministère de l'Education seulement. En 1980 et 1983, cela se réfère aussi aux dépenses totales (colonne 1). Les pourcentages présentés dans les colonnes 3 et 7 ont été par conséquent calculés en utilisant les dépenses du gouvernement central seulement.
ESP> Los datos relativos a los gastos ordinarios y en capital (columnas 4 a 8) se refieren al Ministerio de Educación solamente. En 1980 y 1983, eso también se refiere a los gastos totales (columna 1). Por lo que procede, los porcentages de las columnas 3 y 7 han sido calculados utilizando los gastos del gobierno central solamente.

Nicaragua:
E--> For 1983, data refer to expenditure of the Ministry of Education only.
FR-> En 1983, les données se réfèrent aux dépenses du Ministère de l'Education seulement.
ESP> En 1983, los datos se refieren a los gastos del Ministerio de Educación solamente.

St. Lucia:
E--> For 1982, data refer to expenditure of the Ministry of Education only.
FR-> En 1982, les données se réfèrent aux dépenses du Ministère de l'Education seulement.
ESP> En 1982, los datos se refieren a los gastos del Ministerio de Educación solamente.

AMERICA, SOUTH

Bolivia:
E--> For 1981 and 1982, expenditure on universities is not included.
FR-> En 1981 et 1982, les dépenses des universités ne sont pas incluses.
ESP> En 1981 y 1982, no se incluyen los gastos relativos a las universidades.

Brazil:
E--> Figures are in millions.
FR-> Les chiffres sont exprimés en millions.
ESP> Las cifras expresadas son millones.

Colombia:
E--> Data refer to expenditure of the Ministry of Education only.
FR-> Les données se réfèrent aux dépenses du Ministère de l'Education seulement.
ESP> Los datos se refieren a los gastos del Ministerio de Educación solamente.

Ecuador:
E--> For 1975, data refer to the expenditure of the Ministry of Education only.
FR-> En 1975, les données se réfèrent aux dépenses du Ministère de l'Education seulement.
ESP> En 1975, los datos se refieren a los gastos del Ministerio de Educación solamente.

Paraguay:
E--> Except for 1984, data on current and capital expenditure (columns 4 to 8) refer to the Ministry of Education only.
FR-> Sauf pour 1984, les données relatives aux dépenses ordinaires et en capital (colonnes 4 à 8) se réfèrent aux dépenses du Ministère de l'Education seulement.
ESP> Salvo por 1984, los datos relativos a los gastos ordinarios y en capital (columnas 4 a 8) se refieren a los gastos del Ministerio de Educación solamente.

Peru:
E--> Figures are in millions.
FR-> Les chiffres sont exprimés en millions.
ESP> Las cifras expresadas son millones.

ASIA

Bangladesh:
E--> Except for 1975, data refer to the expenditure of the Ministry of Education only.
FR-> Sauf pour 1975, les données se réfèrent aux dépenses du Ministère de l'Education seulement.
ESP> Salvo por 1975, los datos se refieren a los gastos del Ministerio de Educación solamente.

Cyprus:
E--> Expenditure by the Office of Greek Education only.
FR-> Dépenses du bureau grec de l'Education seulement.
ESP> Gastos del servicio griego de Educación solamente.

Indonesia:
E--> Figures are in millions.
FR-> Les chiffres sont exprimés en millions.
ESP> Las cifras expresadas son millones.

Japan:
E--> Figures are in millions. Data on current and capital expenditure (columns 4 to 8) do not include public subsidies to private education.
FR-> Les chiffres sont exprimés en millions. Les données relatives a

Japan: (Cont):
dépenses ordinaires et en capital (colonnes 4 à 8) ne comprennent pas les subventions publiques à l'enseignement privé.
ESP> Las cifras expresadas son millones. Los datos relativos a los gastos ordinarios y de capital (columnas 4 a 8) no incluyen las subvenciones publicas a la enseñanza privada.
Jordan:
E--> For 1975, expenditure on universities is not included.
FR-> En 1975, les dépenses relatives aux universités ne sont pas incluses.
ESP> En 1975, no se incluyen los datos relativos a las universidades.
Korea, Republic of:
E--> Figures are in millions.
FR-> Les chiffres sont exprimés en millions.
ESP> Las cifras expresadas son millones.
Philippines:
E--> For 1975, data on current and capital expenditure (columns 4 to 8) do not include state universities and colleges.
FR-> En 1975, les données relatives aux dépenses ordinaires et en capital (colonnes 4 à 8) ne comprennent pas les universités et collèges d'état.
ESP> En 1975, los datos relativos a los gastos ordinarios y de capital (columnas 4 a 8) no incluyen las universidades y los colegios de estado.
Syrian Arab Republic:
E--> Data on current and capital expenditure (columns 4 to 8) do not include education at the third level.
FR-> Les données relatives aux dépenses ordinaires et en capital (colonnes 4 à 8) ne comprennent pas l'enseignement du troisième degré.
ESP> Los datos relativos a los gastos ordinarios y de capital (columnas 4 a 8) no incluyen la enseñanza de tercer grado.
EUROPE
Belgium:
E--> Expenditure of the Ministry of Education only.
FR-> Dépenses du Ministère de l'Education seulement.
ESP> Gastos del Ministerio de Educación solamente.
Bulgaria:
E--> Expenditure on education is calculated as percentage of net material product.
FR-> Les dépenses d'enseignement sont calculées en pourcentage du produit matériel net.
ESP> Los gastos relativos a la enseñanza se han calculado como porcentaje del producto material neto.
Czechoslovakia:
E--> Expenditure on education is calculated as percentage of net material product.
FR-> Les dépenses d'enseignement sont calculées en pourcentage du produit matériel net.

Czechoslovakia: (Cont):
ESP> Los gastos relativos a la enseñanza se han calculado como porcentaje del producto material neto.
France:
E--> Metropolitan France.
FR-> France métropolitaine.
ESP> Francia metropolitana.
German Democratic Republic:
E--> Expenditure on education is calculated as percentage of net material product.
FR-> Les dépenses d'enseignement sont calculées en pourcentage du produit matériel net.
ESP> Los gastos relativos a la enseñanza se han calculado como porcentaje del producto material neto.
Iceland:
E--> Expenditure of the Central Government only.
FR-> Dépenses du gouvernement central seulement.
ESP> Gastos del gobierno central solamente.
Italy:
E--> Figures are in millions.
FR-> Les chiffres sont exprimés en millions.
ESP> Las cifras expresadas son millones.
Poland:
E--> Expenditure on education is calculated as percentage of net material product.
FR-> Les dépenses d'enseignement sont calculées en pourcentage du produit matériel net.
ESP> Los gastos relativos a la enseñanza se han calculado como porcentaje del producto material neto.
Portugal:
E--> For 1975, data refer to the expenditure of the Ministry of Education only.
FR-> En 1975, les données se réfèrent aux dépenses du Ministère de l'Education seulement.
ESP> En 1975, los datos se refieren a los gastos del Ministerio de Educación solamente.
OCEANIA:
Solomon Islands:
E--> Data include foreign aid.
FR-> Les données incluent l'aide étrangère.
ESP> Los datos incluyen la ayuda extranjera.
U.S.S.R.:
U.S.S.R.:
E--> Expenditure on education is calculated as percentage of net material product.
FR-> Les dépenses d'enseignement sont calculées en pourcentage du produit matériel net.
ESP> Los gastos relativos a la enseñanza se han calculado como porcentaje del producto material neto.

4.2 Public current expenditure on education: distribution according to purpose

Dépenses publiques ordinaires afférentes à l'enseignement: répartition selon leur destination

Gastos públicos ordinarios destinados a la educación: distribución según su destino

NUMBER OF COUNTRIES AND TERRITORIES PRESENTED IN THIS TABLE: 146

NOMBRE DE PAYS ET DE TERRITOIRES PRESENTES DANS CE TABLEAU: 146

NUMERO DE PAISES Y DE TERRITORIOS PRESENTADOS EN ESTE CUADRO: 146

COUNTRY CURRENCY / PAYS MONNAIE / PAIS MONEDA	YEAR / ANNEE / AÑO	TOTAL / TOTAL / TOTAL (000)	ADMINISTRATION / ADMINISTRATION / ADMINISTRACION (%)	TEACHERS' EMOLUMENTS / EMOLUMENTS DU PERSONNEL ENSEIGNANT / EMOLUMENTOS DEL PERSONAL DOCENTE (%)	TEACHING MATERIALS / MATERIEL POUR L'ENSEIGNEMENT / MATERIAL EDUCATIVO (%)	SCHOLARSHIPS / BOURSES D'ETUDES / BECAS DE ESTUDIOS (%)	WELFARE SERVICES / SERVICES SOCIAUX / SERVICIOS SOCIALES (%)	NOT DISTRIBUTED / NON REPARTIES / SIN DISTRIBUCION (%)
		(1)	(2)	(3)	(4)	(5)	(6)	(7)
AFRICA								
ALGERIA‡ DINAR	1974	1 609 900	4.4	79.1	3.0	8.3	5.2	–
	1980	8 259 100		63.6	0.3	8.9	3.0	24.2
	1982	8 189 328	14.1	69.1	0.7	4.2	10.2	1.7
ANGOLA KWANSA	1979	6 706 231	<——	72.8	11.9	...	12.7	2.6
	1982	10 955 768	19.3	62.2	0.1	1.0	5.5	11.8
	1983	9 639 794	13.6	67.2	–	1.0	4.8	13.5
BENIN FRANC C.F.A.	1975	5 627 477	<——	66.5	0.5	26.3	0.5	6.3
	1978	8 324 906	<——	72.5	0.3	20.3	0.2	6.7
BOTSWANA‡ PULA	1975	8 688	6.5	52.8	./.	14.9	7.0	18.7
	1979	27 483	5.6	57.6	./.	14.2	3.5	19.2
	1984	75 572	18.2	51.9	5.2	9.5	–	15.2
BURKINA FASO FRANC C.F.A.	1975	3 171 371	2.2	56.3	5.1	29.6	6.1	0.8
	1980	7 435 813	<——	61.0	0.4	29.9	6.8	1.8
	1983	12 706 470	11.2	56.1	2.6	20.5	4.5	5.0
	1984	11 962 276	3.4	68.0	1.0	23.5	1.7	2.4
BURUNDI FRANC	1975	721 831	0.7	71.9	10.9	4.1	11.8	0.6
	1979	1 796 482	<——	63.0	0.4	9.8	21.3	5.4
	1981	2 634 658	0.6	74.3	1.2	9.6	8.6	5.6
CAMEROON‡ FRANC C.F.A.	1975	10 298 000	0.9	80.9	...	4.6	...	13.7
	1981	40 978 000	./.	82.9	./.	2.6	./.	14.4
	1982	56 710 000	./.	84.0	./.	2.4	./.	13.6
	1983	70 644 000	./.	83.8	./.	2.4	./.	13.8
CENTRAL AFRICAN REPUBLIC FRANC C.F.A.	1975	3 393 000	6.2	63.5	./.	13.3	...	17.0
	1979	5 509 867	...	69.4	./.	25.9	...	4.8
CHAD FRANC C.F.A.	1975	2 297 200	...	59.2	9.9	24.1	...	6.9
	1983	4 099 374	<——	83.6	12.3	0.3	1.1	2.7
COMOROS FRANC C.F.A.	1982	1 773 956	8.6	54.0	3.9	30.7	0.8	1.9
CONGO FRANC C.F.A	1975	10 537 237	4.3	56.5	./.	30.4	...	8.9
	1980	21 517 291	<——	70.8	5.5	19.0	1.2	3.6
	1981	28 795 018	<——	65.2	./.	21.4	1.5	11.9
COTE D'IVOIRE‡ FRANC C.F.A.	1975	48 123 000	4.4	68.4	12.2	10.8	4.3	–
	1979	124 616 400	5.0	58.4	2.3	8.5	15.7	10.1
DJIBOUTI‡ FRANC	1974	1 479 821	1.1	89.9	./.	3.1	1.4	4.5
	1979	1 045 949	0.1	61.0	6.3	24.9	5.3	2.5
	1982	1 309 034	1.1	78.1	14.7	6.1	–	–
EGYPT POUND	1975	226 668	<——	81.2	...	...	...	18.8
	1980	505 330	<——	75.8	0.7	–	–	23.4
	1981	722 108	<——	81.0	0.6	–	–	18.4

COUNTRY CURRENCY PAYS MONNAIE PAIS MONEDA	YEAR ANNEE AÑO	TOTAL TOTAL TOTAL (000)	ADMINIS–TRATION ADMINIS–TRATION ADMINIS–TRACION (%)	TEACHERS' EMOLUMENTS EMOLUMENTS DU PERSONNEL ENSEIGNANT EMOLUMENTOS DEL PERSONAL DOCENTE (%)	TEACHING MATERIALS MATERIEL POUR L'ENSEIGNEMENT MATERIAL EDUCATIVO (%)	SCHOLARSHIPS BOURSES D'ETUDES BECAS DE ESTUDIOS (%)	WELFARE SERVICES SERVICES SOCIAUX SERVICIOS SOCIALES (%)	NOT DIS–TRIBUTED NON REPARTIES SIN DISTRI–BUCION (%)
		(1)	(2)	(3)	(4)	(5)	(6)	(7)
ETHIOPIA‡	1975	112 859	...	84.9	5.3	<——	4.8	5.0
BIRR	1981	210 098	8.1	83.4	5.8	–	1.7	0.9
GABON	1976	10 506 571	...	43.9	<——	34.0	7.3	14.9
FRANC C.F.A	1980	16 054 707	...	56.7	...	27.0	...	16.4
GAMBIA	1975	5 471	4.4	69.1	3.5	10.0	2.9	10.0
DALASI	1981	16 460	2.4	74.2	4.1	1.0	2.6	15.7
	1983	24 119	3.2	71.4	4.1	2.8	2.1	16.4
	1984	23 994	12.5	72.7	4.8	6.0	2.0	2.1
GHANA‡	1975	240 682	8.9	72.3	./.	–	<——	18.8
CEDI	1980	734 256	23.6	60.0	10.6	...	...	5.8
	1981	1 332 170	9.8	74.3	15.4	...	...	0.5
	1984	3 843 913	4.2	64.0	21.6	–	7.7	2.4
GUINEA	1979	1 185 500	8.3	62.8	<——	<——	<——	28.9
SYLI	1984	1 486 054	9.8	82.5	2.6	0.2	4.5	0.4
GUINEA–BISSAU	1980	207 512	10.8	73.5	...	...	...	15.7
PESO	1982	260 000	10.0	76.7	...	...	...	13.2
LESOTHO‡	1982	28 082	<——	81.6	0.2	6.4	–	11.5
MALOTI	1983	25 939	<——	93.0	3.5	0.5	0.9	2.1
LIBERIA DOLLAR	1980	53 074	9.0	48.9	8.6	8.0	1.4	24.1
MADAGASCAR‡	1975	11 726 747	9.9	77.8	4.5	5.7	0.4	1.7
FRANC	1981	32 515 056	5.2	78.6	1.7	6.5	1.2	6.7
	1983	38 810 098	4.2	73.8	0.3	8.1	0.9	12.7
	1984	47 519 440	3.9	77.2	0.2	7.3	0.7	10.5
MALAWI‡	1975	11 992	7.5	78.3	1.9	6.1	6.3	–
KWACHA	1981	27 363	12.6	73.1	4.3	–	./.	10.1
	1982	31 475	9.7	75.6	4.2	–	./.	10.4
	1983	34 754	14.1	74.1	3.8	–	./.	8.0
MALI	1975	5 852 452	<——	63.0	6.6	19.4	–	11.0
FRANC C.F.A.	1980	12 752 392	9.7	51.0	4.2	35.1	–	–
	1982	14 219 340	13.1	58.5	5.5	23.0	–	–
	1984	15 124 302	10.5	61.5	4.0	24.1	–	–
MAURITANIA OUGUIYA	1983	3 006 217	19.2	52.1	3.8	24.9	——>	–
MAURITIUS‡	1976	197 000	./.	78.4	1.3	./.	4.5	15.8
RUPEE	1980	407 926	22.8	69.2	0.1	./.	3.1	4.8
	1983	532 000	10.9	81.5	0.1	./.	3.7	3.9
	1984	539 800	32.4	61.6	0.1	./.	3.2	2.6
MOROCCO‡	1975	1 154 752	<——	91.1	0.7	...	...	8.2
DIRHAM	1980	3 528 566	<——	83.4	...	...	...	16.6
	1981	3 991 948	<——	85.4	0.5	11.8	1.0	1.4
	1982	4 692 083	<——	85.8	0.3	11.6	0.0	2.3
NIGER	1975	4 566 400	...	51.5	24.9	13.9	...	9.8
FRANC C.F.A.	1980	7 762 522	<——	68.2	13.1	9.4	9.4	–
REUNION FRENCH FRANC	1980	1 263 595	7.1	71.0	0.2	5.1	2.1	14.4
RWANDA‡	1975	1 197 164	3.6	80.2	2.9	5.0	6.8	1.5
FRANC	1980	2 438 563	6.5	80.6	3.6	3.9	5.4	0.0
	1981	4 497 308	5.3	85.9	3.3	2.4	2.6	0.6
	1983	4 527 718	<——	80.4	3.1	3.5	3.1	9.8
ST. HELENA	1975	79	16.5	49.4	17.7	2.5	10.1	3.8
POUND STERLING	1980	262	15.3	58.8	10.7	2.3	2.3	10.7
	1982	275	20.4	49.1	16.4	2.5	2.2	9.5
	1983	337	20.5	48.1	16.6	2.1	2.4	10.4
SENEGAL‡	1975	15 949 600	<——	67.8	9.7	22.5	——>	–
FRANC C.F.A.	1980	27 485 411	4.1	60.1	5.4	19.1	——>	11.3
	1981	21 694 900	<——	85.2	6.9	5.3	2.5	–
SEYCHELLES‡	1975	11 202	6.3	77.7	5.7	2.1	3.4	4.7
RUPEE	1980	50 215	12.6	64.4	9.8	1.4	2.7	9.0
	1982	79 435	24.7	51.4	8.1	1.7	3.5	10.6
	1984	111 391	25.4	44.7	5.5	4.2	17.8	2.3
SOMALIA‡	1976	90 314	...	62.2	18.4	...	10.2	9.2
SHILLING	1980	154 384	<——	80.9	16.6	...	...	2.5
	1983	281 246	<——	82.2	15.1	...	...	2.8

4.2 **Public current expenditure by purpose**
Dépenses publiques ordinaires selon leur destination
Gastos públicos ordinarios según su destino

COUNTRY CURRENCY / PAYS MONNAIE / PAIS MONEDA	YEAR / ANNEE / AÑO	TOTAL / TOTAL / TOTAL (000)	ADMINISTRATION / ADMINISTRATION / ADMINISTRACION (%)	TEACHERS' EMOLUMENTS / EMOLUMENTS DU PERSONNEL ENSEIGNANT / EMOLUMENTOS DEL PERSONAL DOCENTE (%)	TEACHING MATERIALS / MATERIEL POUR L'ENSEIGNEMENT / MATERIAL EDUCATIVO (%)	SCHOLARSHIPS / BOURSES D'ETUDES / BECAS DE ESTUDIOS (%)	WELFARE SERVICES / SERVICES SOCIAUX / SERVICIOS SOCIALES (%)	NOT DISTRIBUTED / NON REPARTIES / SIN DISTRIBUCION (%)
		(1)	(2)	(3)	(4)	(5)	(6)	(7)
SWAZILAND								
LILANGENI	1981	22 562	6.0	86.5	7.5	...	...	...
TOGO	1975	4 450 794	...	47.5	10.3	13.8	——>	28.4
FRANC C.F.A.	1980	12 574 743	12.6	68.3	1.5	15.6	...	2.0
	1981	14 880 824	4.6	58.5	1.3	15.7	0.2	19.8
TUNISIA‡	1980	162 291	<——	81.3	4.9	6.5	2.3	5.0
DINAR	1983	222 578	<——	84.9	4.8	1.2	0.6	8.5
	1984	256 956	1.4	84.8	4.5	1.0	0.5	7.9
UNITED REPUBLIC OF TANZANIA								
SHILLING	1979	1 769 328	9.2	35.2	15.9	13.2	7.6	19.0
ZAMBIA‡	1975	75 420	14.1	63.7	6.9	0.5	8.5	6.2
KWACHA	1980	120 377	17.1	63.3	2.6	2.0	5.5	9.6
	1981	135 749	16.5	69.1	1.4	4.7	6.0	2.2
	1982	185 495	9.0	71.1	2.6	3.3	6.1	7.8
ZIMBABWE‡	1975	65 015	6.4	80.9	0.5	1.9	7.2	3.2
DOLLAR	1980	218 037	3.5	80.0	0.5	0.5	4.0	11.4
	1982	354 712	...	89.8	9.8	...	...	0.4
	1983	432 547	2.9	83.1	8.3	0.9	2.1	2.6
AMERICA, NORTH								
ANTIGUA AND BARBUDA‡	1975	5 681	6.1	58.9	3.8	16.7	2.0	12.4
E.CARIBBEAN DOLLAR	1979	8 678	3.6	64.8	3.0	6.5	0.9	21.3
BERMUDA	1975	10 417	5.6	79.4	2.6	8.4	0.6	3.4
DOLLAR	1980	25 713	5.0	59.7	16.6	2.7	–	16.0
	1982	25 031	6.6	71.6	7.2	2.8	–	11.8
	1983	27 510	6.5	71.4	7.0	3.3	–	11.8
BRITISH VIRGIN ISLANDS	1975	967	4.0	74.0	3.1	6.3	2.6	9.9
UNITED STATES DOLLAR	1980	1 622	5.9	75.0	1.6	4.3	1.2	12.1
	1983	3 361	11.4	57.3	2.0	6.0	1.9	21.5
	1984	4 161	10.9	59.0	4.5	8.4	1.6	15.6
CANADA	1975	11 526 821	6.3	54.0	10.4	4.6	4.1	20.6
DOLLAR	1980	20 450 870	6.9	52.2	10.0	3.9	3.8	23.3
	1983	27 702 373	8.4	51.9	10.4	4.4	4.0	21.0
	1984	28 692 121	8.1	53.5	9.3	4.3	5.3	19.6
CAYMAN ISLANDS	1975	1 384	6.4	76.3	5.6	3.3	8.1	0.4
JAMAICAN DOLLAR	1980	3 398	13.1	68.8	6.4	6.9	4.1	0.7
COSTA RICA‡	1975	1 041 297	11.9	82.6	...	1.9	...	3.6
COLON	1980	2 802 162	./.	76.2	0.2	<——	2.0	21.6
	1982	4 328 004	./.	74.8	0.5	<——	1.5	23.1
	1983	5 853 136	./.	72.1	0.4	<——	1.6	25.9
CUBA	1980	1 134 500	3.8	38.8	6.6	2.5	45.1	3.1
PESO	1981	1 275 300	4.0	38.7	5.9	1.9	38.7	10.7
	1982	1 396 000	4.0	37.6	5.9	1.6	43.1	7.9
DOMINICAN REPUBLIC‡	1976	62 595	5.4	77.9	3.3	...	...	13.4
PESO	1980	104 387	6.6	86.1	–	2.0	–	5.3
	1983	146 813	6.3	86.6	–	1.5	–	5.6
	1984	170 322	5.5	90.3	–	0.9	–	3.3
GRENADA‡								
E. CARIBBEAN DOLLAR	1983	9 561	5.5	90.4	0.3	–	1.1	2.7
GUADELOUPE								
FRENCH FRANC	1980	818 124	8.8	69.2	0.2	4.2	1.9	15.7
GUATEMALA‡	1976	67 193	7.5	79.5	11.3	1.6	...	–
QUETZAL	1979	116 780	6.2	69.1	0.5	0.6	22.2	1.3
	1984	159 778	7.7	85.5	0.3	0.7	0.7	5.1
HAITI	1976	37 191	2.9	85.4	4.4	...	...	7.3
GOURDE	1980	85 781	11.2	66.9	2.2	1.2	0.2	18.2
	1982	87 076	20.5	64.7	2.0	1.0	0.8	11.0
	1983	92 943	19.3	61.6	1.7	1.9	1.2	14.3
HONDURAS‡	1980	141 075	6.5	88.6	2.6	1.6	0.6	0.1
LEMPIRA	1981	168 689	6.5	86.8	1.2	1.4	1.0	3.1
	1982	206 880	6.6	85.0	1.3	1.3	0.1	5.6
JAMAICA‡	1975	121 854	3.7	69.0	6.1	18.1	1.1	2.0
DOLLAR	1980	302 669	12.5	65.6	2.2	0.0	3.9	15.7
	1983	456 377	11.3	70.4	3.8	0.2	6.3	8.0

COUNTRY CURRENCY / PAYS MONNAIE / PAIS MONEDA	YEAR / ANNEE / AÑO	TOTAL / TOTAL / TOTAL (000)	ADMINIS–TRATION / ADMINIS–TRATION / ADMINIS–TRACION (%)	TEACHERS' EMOLUMENTS / EMOLUMENTS DU PERSONNEL ENSEIGNANT / EMOLUMENTOS DEL PERSONAL DOCENTE (%)	TEACHING MATERIALS / MATERIEL POUR L'ENSEIGNEMENT / MATERIAL EDUCATIVO (%)	SCHOLARSHIPS / BOURSES D'ETUDES / BECAS DE ESTUDIOS (%)	WELFARE SERVICES / SERVICES SOCIAUX / SERVICIOS SOCIALES (%)	NOT DIS–TRIBUTED / NON REPARTIES / SIN DISTRI–BUCION (%)
		(1)	(2)	(3)	(4)	(5)	(6)	(7)
MARTINIQUE FRENCH FRANC	1980	886 861	9.2	78.0	0.2	3.9	2.4	6.4
MEXICO‡ PESO	1975	26 783 400	./.	85.1	./.	0.4	0.8	13.7
	1980	114 913 003	7.5	67.3	./.	0.2	./.	25.1
	1982	282 559 038	11.7	61.5	1.1	0.1	0.2	25.5
	1983	416 192 879	15.6	61.1	0.7	0.0	0.1	22.5
NICARAGUA‡ CORDOBA	1980	579 693	10.8	69.7	2.2	0.7	10.7	5.9
	1982	1 007 895	9.0	78.4	6.9	0.4	0.0	5.3
	1984	2 458 200	20.4	69.7	6.6	0.2	0.0	3.2
PANAMA‡ BALBOA	1975	96 693	4.1	83.7	...	3.9	–	8.3
	1980	155 716	13.8	80.6	1.8	3.8	–	–
	1983	198 413	14.7	80.5	0.9	3.8	–	–
	1984	210 998	14.1	84.9	1.0	–	–	–
ST. CHRISTOPHER AND NEVIS‡ E. CARIBBEAN DOLLAR	1984	8 701	9.0	82.8	2.3	2.0	4.0	–
ST. LUCIA‡ E.CARIBBEAN DOLLAR	1975	7 321	4.8	69.3	3.9	2.9	2.3	16.9
	1980	18 596	7.2	66.9	2.8	7.7	4.0	11.4
	1982	23 045	<——	78.0	5.8	1.0	5.2	9.9
ST. PIERRE AND MIQUELON FRENCH FRANC	1980	16 725	4.7	72.0	5.6	–	–	17.6
	1982	24 006	<——	79.9	5.5	6.3	0.4	7.9
	1983	29 037	3.5	75.6	5.2	7.0	0.2	8.5
TRINIDAD AND TOBAGO‡ DOLLAR	1980	430 831	7.1	82.6	7.3	0.3	1.0	1.6
	1983	867 816	4.9	77.1	1.7	6.2	5.9	4.1
	1984	901 433	5.0	76.6	1.9	6.1	5.9	4.4
TURKS AND CAICOS ISLANDS UNITED STATES DOLLAR	1975	601	*11.8	*74.0	4.2	9.7	0.3	–
	1980	832	3.6	72.7	7.2	9.4	0.1	7.0
	1983	1 287	14.1	76.8	3.6	4.7	0.9	–
UNITED STATES DOLLAR	1979	158 149 000	9.1	52.5	2.5	1.4	6.6	27.9
U.S. VIRGIN ISLANDS UNITED STATES DOLLAR	1980	56 774	16.7	45.0	2.1	0.0	11.3	24.8
AMERICA, SOUTH								
ARGENTINA PESO	1975	3 356	<——	93.3	...	0.7	...	6.0
	1980	859 892	<——	86.7	7.9	5.0	...	0.3
	1983	15 212 677	<——	88.9	...	0.1	...	11.0
	1984	180 530 252	<——	89.6	...	0.3	...	10.1
BOLIVIA‡ PESO	1980	4 919 122	6.5	89.5	–	0.2	2.9	0.9
	1981	4 621 655	5.1	84.9	0.8	0.4	1.9	7.0
	1982	10 211 808	6.2	93.3	–	0.1	–	0.4
CHILE‡ PESO	1975	1 321 482	5.8	73.2	0.9	...	...	20.1
	1980	45 503 514	2.5	84.1	5.1	<——	5.9	2.4
	1981	62 609 745	2.8	83.8	6.0	<——	5.9	1.6
COLOMBIA‡ PESO	1980	27 286 015	...	90.7	...	...	...	9.3
	1983	83 436 200	<——	98.3	0.2	0.0	0.0	1.5
	1984	108 896 000	0.5	94.5	0.1	./.	0.6	4.2
ECUADOR SUCRE	1980	14 649 139	2.2	77.4	0.8	0.2	<——	19.3
FALKLAND ISLANDS (MALVINAS) POUND STERLING	1974	105	...	57.1	3.8	15.2	23.8	–
	1979	204	4.9	56.4	6.9	4.9	8.3	18.6
FRENCH GUIANA FRENCH FRANC	1980	152 333	10.8	63.6	1.3	2.7	4.3	17.4
GUYANA‡ DOLLAR	1975	45 277	4.8	79.9	6.5	1.3	2.1	5.3
	1979	89 369	8.8	66.5	6.0	3.2	5.9	9.6
	1983	105 299	15.3	69.7	0.4	4.3	0.3	10.0
	1984	112 361	10.5	65.1	0.8	8.4	0.9	14.4
PERU‡ SOL	1975	20 970	4.9	65.1	2.7	...	...	27.4
	1980	166 040	8.4	59.4	0.9	...	...	31.3
	1983	873 165	10.8	58.0	0.8	...	...	30.4
	1984	1 892 284	7.9	57.4	0.5	...	...	34.3

4.2 Public current expenditure by purpose
Dépenses publiques ordinaires selon leur destination
Gastos públicos ordinarios según su destino

COUNTRY CURRENCY PAYS MONNAIE PAIS MONEDA	YEAR ANNEE AÑO	TOTAL TOTAL TOTAL (000)	ADMINISTRATION ADMINISTRATION ADMINISTRACION (%)	TEACHERS' EMOLUMENTS EMOLUMENTS DU PERSONNEL ENSEIGNANT EMOLUMENTOS DEL PERSONAL DOCENTE (%)	TEACHING MATERIALS MATERIEL POUR L'ENSEIGNEMENT MATERIAL EDUCATIVO (%)	SCHOLARSHIPS BOURSES D'ETUDES BECAS DE ESTUDIOS (%)	WELFARE SERVICES SERVICES SOCIAUX SERVICIOS SOCIALES (%)	NOT DISTRIBUTED NON REPARTIES SIN DISTRIBUCION (%)
		(1)	(2)	(3)	(4)	(5)	(6)	(7)
SURINAME‡ GUILDER	1980	67 284	23.3	41.8	7.2	5.5	2.8	19.3
URUGUAY PESO	1980	1 926 769	20.5	56.9	5.1	<——	7.5	10.1
VENEZUELA‡ BOLIVAR	1975	5 965 747	./.	66.5	0.3	11.7	...	21.5
	1980	12 523 608	13.7	60.7	1.0	7.4	3.2	14.0
	1982	18 007 971	13.6	56.9	1.1	2.7	10.5	15.2
	1983	21 035 800	13.3	57.6	1.1	2.7	10.2	15.0
ASIA								
AFGHANISTAN AFGHANI	1980	2 886 301	32.8	46.8	12.7	–	6.1	1.5
	1981	2 891 136	31.5	48.2	12.6	–	6.1	1.5
	1982	2 191 353	32.6	50.6	10.4	–	5.2	1.2
BAHRAIN DINAR	1975	9 605	<——	67.4	8.5	14.1	2.7	7.4
	1980	28 166	7.7	69.2	6.5	6.7	2.4	7.5
	1983	43 529	<——	80.1	3.0	4.3	0.9	11.7
	1984	45 978	7.0	80.5	6.2	3.3	0.2	2.8
BANGLADESH‡ TAKA	1980	2 010 009	6.8	70.7	0.1	0.0	16.6	5.8
	1983	3 626 348	5.8	65.4	0.0	–	25.4	3.3
	1984	4 932 264	<——	59.8	0.2	0.3	33.1	6.7
BHUTAN NGULTRUM	1974	12 853	9.6	26.1	21.9	20.5	21.8	–
	1978	18 426	7.6	46.4	6.0	34.8	1.9	3.2
BRUNEI DARUSSALAM DOLLAR	1975	47 354	9.6	49.5	8.3	9.9	20.1	2.6
	1980	114 917	6.3	43.5	5.1	15.3	20.8	9.1
	1981	143 926	5.7	43.7	4.3	16.7	20.7	9.0
	1982	148 330	5.8	48.9	3.9	12.7	21.6	7.1
CYPRUS‡ POUND	1975	10 325	6.5	79.1	3.3	1.9	2.5	6.7
	1980	25 452	8.1	80.0	2.4	1.0	2.3	6.3
	1982	37 835	8.1	81.2	1.8	0.8	1.9	6.3
	1983	42 181	7.8	82.4	1.9	0.7	2.1	5.1
DEMOCRATIC YEMEN‡ DINAR	1976	5 288	7.1	84.4	3.5	0.9	4.1	–
	1980	15 596	15.2	58.3	0.2	0.8	5.9	19.6
HONG KONG DOLLAR	1975	1 144 538	4.8	79.4	1.4	4.4	1.9	8.2
	1980	3 036 139	15.2	72.9	1.3	0.7	0.8	9.0
	1983	5 348 983	10.5	76.8	1.9	0.3	1.0	9.5
	1984	6 189 691	10.6	76.5	1.9	0.4	1.1	9.5
ISRAEL‡ SHEKEL	1975	464 100	3.9	45.7	...	...	...	50.4
	1980	8 182 000	4.1	88.9	5.6	1.5	–	–
	1981	18 290 000	4.0	89.5	5.3	1.1	–	–
	1982	44 845 000	3.9	89.7	5.4	1.0	–	–
JAPAN‡ YEN	1975	5 826 604	4.8	67.7	8.0	0.9	5.0	13.6
	1980	9 416 591	7.1	49.8	6.5	1.2	5.0	30.3
	1981	10 174 793	7.4	48.4	6.3	1.2	5.1	31.7
	1982	10 376 852	7.2	48.1	6.4	1.2	5.1	32.0
JORDAN‡ DINAR	1975	13 900	6.8	73.9	7.6	3.0	...	8.7
	1980	50 543	7.3	69.6	7.5	5.2	2.4	8.1
	1983	79 530	10.0	63.3	6.3	6.3	5.4	8.7
	1984	82 655	<——	77.9	4.3	4.8	3.0	9.9
KOREA, REPUBLIC OF‡ WON	1975	163 800	...	99.4	...	0.6	...	–
	1980	1 158 967	./.	81.0	./.	./.	./.	19.0
	1983	2 231 377	4.0	55.1	1.1	0.5	1.0	38.2
	1984	2 501 253	3.9	52.0	1.7	0.5	3.5	38.4
KUWAIT DINAR	1975	90 069	9.8	53.8	3.9	6.2	12.8	13.4
	1980	203 758	32.2	46.5	5.1	4.0	5.5	6.7
	1983	296 966	31.6	48.7	2.1	3.5	5.2	8.8
	1984	317 386	29.5	52.6	1.9	3.1	5.4	7.5
MALAYSIA‡ RINGGIT	1980	2 575 488	16.4	68.7	5.8	2.5	2.7	3.9
	1982	3 473 997	14.4	70.9	5.5	3.1	3.1	3.0
	1984	3 676 580	7.0	82.4	4.3	2.2	2.0	2.2
PENINSULAR MALAYSIA‡ RINGGIT	1980	2 225 908	18.0	72.1	4.5	2.6	1.5	1.3
	1982	2 988 685	16.2	69.9	5.3	3.3	1.8	3.4
	1984	3 179 989	7.6	81.2	4.2	2.3	2.2	2.5
SABAH RINGGIT	1975	89 559	3.7	81.3	9.1	5.4	0.0	0.5
	1980	145 350	8.0	77.5	11.2	2.7	–	0.6
	1982	185 728	9.0	72.8	15.0	2.2	–	1.0
	1983	183 287	8.4	78.3	10.5	1.7	–	1.1

COUNTRY CURRENCY PAYS MONNAIE PAIS MONEDA	YEAR ANNEE AÑO	TOTAL TOTAL TOTAL (000)	ADMINIS-TRATION ADMINIS-TRATION ADMINIS-TRACION (%)	TEACHERS' EMOLUMENTS EMOLUMENTS DU PERSONNEL ENSEIGNANT EMOLUMENTOS DEL PERSONAL DOCENTE (%)	TEACHING MATERIALS MATERIEL POUR L'ENSEIGNEMENT MATERIAL EDUCATIVO (%)	SCHOLARSHIPS BOURSES D'ETUDES BECAS DE ESTUDIOS (%)	WELFARE SERVICES SERVICES SOCIAUX SERVICIOS SOCIALES (%)	NOT DIS-TRIBUTED NON REPARTIES SIN DISTRI-BUCION (%)
		(1)	(2)	(3)	(4)	(5)	(6)	(7)
SARAWAK RINGGIT	1975	74 491	4.7	76.3	6.6	...	12.0	0.4
	1980	204 230	3.5	62.1	16.5	1.1	16.8	–
	1982	299 584	<——	79.5	1.0	1.5	18.0	–
	1984	313 304	<——	97.7	1.2	0.7	0.3	–
NEPAL‡ RUPEE	1980	429 681	11.7	59.2	7.1	3.4	–	18.6
OMAN RIAL	1975	6 605	15.8	67.2	2.6	10.0	3.2	1.2
	1980	31 067	16.1	60.3	6.4	8.6	4.4	4.2
	1984	68 972	8.1	70.5	4.7	10.9	3.4	2.3
PHILIPPINES‡ PESO	1980	4 022 850	<——	78.4	0.3	7.5	2.1	11.7
	1983	4 766 638	<——	74.5	4.4	1.2	4.1	15.9
	1984	4 987 464	<——	77.7	1.2	1.2	2.1	17.8
QATAR RIYAL	1975	123 524	21.5	51.8	12.1	9.5	5.1	–
	1980	598 000	<——	68.7	3.7	14.4	9.9	3.3
	1983	863 891	<——	68.2	4.3	9.4	–	18.1
	1984	812 798	25.5	45.5	3.5	9.8	8.0	7.6
SAUDI ARABIA RIYAL	1975	5 528 566	<——	52.2	20.7	./.	./.	27.2
	1980	13 526 367	<——	65.5	./.	./.	./.	34.5
	1982	20 369 004	<——	73.6	./.	./.	./.	26.4
	1983	20 500 792	<——	72.2	./.	./.	./.	27.8
SINGAPORE‡ DOLLAR	1975	339 870	2.9	90.5	...	1.1	0.0	5.5
	1980	587 469	1.6	90.6	0.0	0.3	<——	7.5
	1981	712 733	2.8	88.4	0.0	0.1	<——	8.7
	1982	983 750	2.7	90.1	0.0	1.1	<——	6.1
SRI LANKA‡ RUPEE	1975	682 680	4.5	78.2	1.6	0.0	2.3	13.4
	1980	1 397 461	4.4	80.0	0.9	0.5	7.1	7.0
	1983	2 577 987	4.9	80.3	3.0	0.3	2.5	9.0
	1984	2 850 141	2.4	82.5	2.2	0.2	5.4	7.3
SYRIAN ARAB REPUBLIC‡ POUND	1975	462 514	4.8	77.0	5.9	2.5	3.9	5.9
	1980	1 272 481	4.3	85.9	2.0	0.8	2.2	4.8
	1983	2 441 825	./.	85.1	2.1	0.4	<——	12.4
	1984	2 562 936	./.	84.9	1.3	0.4	<——	13.4
THAILAND BAHT	1975	7 775 347	3.8	77.2	3.7	3.3	6.7	5.3
	1980	15 867 328	4.5	80.3	4.6	4.3	5.3	0.9
	1982	24 575 384	2.9	71.5	5.2	3.6	2.5	14.2
	1983	28 127 463	<——	78.0	4.9	5.3	2.7	9.1
TURKEY LIRA	1980	98 592 809	<——	89.7	0.5	0.5	2.0	7.3
	1983	324 182 424	<——	86.6	0.9	0.4	4.0	8.1
	1984	382 385 000	<——	85.3	1.3	0.4	4.7	8.3
UNITED ARAB EMIRATES DIRHAM	1975	271 382	...	66.4	3.7	10.0	9.8	10.1
	1981	1 157 696	9.7	51.9	11.8	7.8	11.3	7.5
	1983	1 606 019	7.2	53.9	6.6	7.6	6.8	18.0
	1984	1 537 253	7.3	55.6	5.2	6.5	5.9	19.6
EUROPE								
ANDORRA PESETA	1975	39 185	...	86.3	5.5	2.8	5.5	–
	1982	495 836	3.9	38.1	3.6	1.7	26.4	26.3
AUSTRIA SCHILLING	1975	29 366 500	35.0	48.1	./.	3.2	2.3	11.4
	1980	46 955 400	32.1	53.1	./.	2.9	2.7	9.3
	1983	63 476 700	29.0	49.3	1.6	2.7	2.5	14.8
	1984	66 453 600	28.9	50.0	1.3	2.7	2.5	14.6
BELGIUM‡ FRANC	1975	131 906 200	2.8	72.3	./.	1.9	...	22.9
	1980	206 226 600	3.0	73.0	0.1	0.8	0.6	22.4
	1983	243 807 200	4.0	75.0	0.1	./.	0.7	20.2
	1984	247 337 900	2.2	78.4	0.1	./.	0.8	18.5
BULGARIA LEV	1975	725 259	...	47.6	...	4.1	...	48.3
	1980	1 097 806	...	44.4	...	6.9	...	48.7
	1983	1 367 567	...	38.5	...	5.0	...	56.6
	1984	1 480 646	...	37.3	...	4.6	...	58.1
CZECHOSLOVAKIA KORUNA	1975	17 288 021	0.2	53.8	12.0	1.9	10.9	21.2
	1980	21 801 883	0.2	50.0	18.9	2.1	13.4	15.5
	1983	24 495 059	0.2	48.8	20.9	1.8	14.0	14.3
	1984	25 814 818	0.2	47.3	21.2	1.7	14.8	14.8
DENMARK KRONE	1980	22 188 000	15.6	49.3	4.8	2.7	3.9	23.7

4.2 Public current expenditure by purpose
Dépenses publiques ordinaires selon leur destination
Gastos públicos ordinarios según su destino

COUNTRY CURRENCY PAYS MONNAIE PAIS MONEDA	YEAR ANNEE AÑO	TOTAL TOTAL TOTAL (000)	ADMINIS- TRATION ADMINIS- TRATION ADMINIS- TRACION (%)	TEACHERS' EMOLUMENTS EMOLUMENTS DU PERSONNEL ENSEIGNANT EMOLUMENTOS DEL PERSONAL DOCENTE (%)	TEACHING MATERIALS MATERIEL POUR L'ENSEIGNEMENT MATERIAL EDUCATIVO (%)	SCHOLARSHIPS BOURSES D'ETUDES BECAS DE ESTUDIOS (%)	WELFARE SERVICES SERVICES SOCIAUX SERVICIOS SOCIALES (%)	NOT DIS- TRIBUTED NON REPARTIES SIN DISTRI- BUCION (%)
		(1)	(2)	(3)	(4)	(5)	(6)	(7)
FINLAND MARKKA	1975	5 596 511	2.2	61.9	3.9	1.8	9.8	20.3
	1980	9 565 205	6.3	50.5	5.7	4.1	14.4	19.0
	1982	12 545 795	6.4	49.0	5.1	3.7	15.6	20.1
	1983	14 222 522	6.5	49.6	5.1	4.2	15.1	19.6
FRANCE‡ FRANC	1975	66 873 000	3.3	68.5	0.1	3.2	8.2	16.8
	1980	131 441 000	3.5	68.1	0.1	2.1	8.9	17.3
	1981	163 300 000	3.4	69.7	0.1	1.8	8.6	16.4
	1982	194 708 000	3.4	69.3	0.1	1.8	8.7	16.7
GERMANY, FED. REP. OF DEUTSCHE MARK	1975	42 456 700	1.4	71.5	./.	6.7	3.0	17.4
	1980	60 557 900	1.3	71.3	./.	5.3	2.8	19.3
	1982	66 078 100	1.3	71.6	./.	4.7	3.0	19.4
	1983	67 382 800	1.3	72.1	./.	3.7	3.0	19.9
GIBRALTAR POUND STERLING	1975	909	4.8	52.4	8.1	10.3	0.8	23.5
	1980	3 305	5.6	56.4	4.2	11.2	0.7	21.9
	1982	4 083	5.4	59.2	4.3	6.8	0.7	23.7
	1983	4 502	5.3	58.0	3.7	7.0	0.7	25.4
GREECE DRACHMA	1975	12 336 357	5.6	74.2	./.	0.2	3.1	16.8
	1979	29 950 864	10.7	82.2	2.6	0.4	1.3	2.8
HUNGARY FORINT	1975	16 719 792	0.2	44.4	./.	4.5	13.7	37.3
	1980	27 516 379	0.3	45.2	./.	3.4	16.3	34.8
	1983	45 205 888	0.3	33.3	./.	3.4	13.9	49.1
	1984	45 725 490	0.3	33.1	./.	3.7	15.6	47.4
IRELAND POUND	1975	199 666	3.8	70.4	2.3	1.2	4.1	18.3
	1980	515 000	4.1	67.6	0.4	1.5	4.7	21.7
	1982	734 997	4.3	73.2	0.1	2.0	4.2	16.1
	1984	813 873	2.7	72.8	0.2	1.4	4.3	18.6
ITALY‡ LIRA	1975	5 060 156	...	73.4	...	3.6	3.4	19.6
	1979	11 791 069	16.9	68.2	./.	0.6	2.0	12.3
	1983	28 040 275	15.6	67.5	0.0	0.9	2.5	13.5
LUXEMBOURG‡ FRANC	1975	3 903 300	./.	80.8	./.	1.6	./.	17.6
	1980	6 122 500	./.	87.8	1.0	1.0	./.	10.2
	1982	9 053 900	./.	90.0	0.8	1.0	./.	8.1
	1983	7 900 300	./.	87.2	1.0	1.6	./.	10.2
MALTA‡ LIRA	1975	6 881	4.9	79.2	0.2	6.2	2.5	7.0
	1980	12 475	28.0	62.3	0.2	4.7	2.4	2.4
	1983	16 882	28.0	57.0	0.0	3.1	2.9	8.9
	1984	15 545	24.1	60.1	0.1	1.5	3.0	11.3
MONACO FRENCH FRANC	1974	20 538	...	70.9	...	...	...	29.1
	1980	42 629	3.7	81.3	–	2.6	1.5	10.8
	1981	50 234	3.7	82.6	–	2.5	1.6	9.6
	1982	60 248	4.1	82.5	–	2.4	1.6	9.4
NETHERLANDS GUILDER	1975	14 881 000	2.8	75.5	0.7	2.0	1.3	17.7
	1980	23 079 000	3.2	73.5	1.1	3.2	1.5	17.6
	1981	23 968 000	3.5	72.2	1.2	3.6	1.5	17.9
	1982	24 484 000	3.5	72.7	1.1	4.4	1.6	16.7
NORWAY KRONE	1975	8 427 000	2.0	71.3	...	7.2	...	19.4
	1980	16 448 000	2.7	64.3	6.0	5.2	2.4	19.4
	1982	21 250 000	2.9	64.5	5.9	4.4	2.1	20.1
	1983	23 522 000	2.8	63.6	6.0	4.8	2.4	20.3
PORTUGAL‡ ESCUDO	1975	14 269 981	5.0	78.8	2.7	1.3	6.8	5.5
	1980	45 442 800	3.7	82.8	0.8	3.9	3.7	5.1
	1981	57 032 900	3.8	84.0	0.2	3.6	4.1	4.3
	1982	72 884 100	3.8	82.3	0.3	3.7	5.3	4.7
SAN MARINO LIRA	1975	2 499 565	...	79.6	...	8.2	5.7	6.5
	1980	6 263 207	...	84.7	2.8	2.7	6.0	3.8
	1982	9 546 420	...	89.8	1.9	1.4	1.2	5.6
	1983	15 358 869	...	91.2	1.3	2.5	0.8	4.3
SPAIN PESETA	1974	71 688 000	4.8	78.4	6.2	10.1	0.6	–
	1979	295 443 000	2.1	88.1	./.	5.7	0.3	3.8
SWEDEN KRONA	1975	19 281 100	3.5	52.4	...	2.9	13.3	27.9
	1980	40 885 700	2.7	46.5	2.4	3.8	15.4	29.1
	1983	49 262 200	3.7	46.7	2.7	4.0	10.1	32.8
	1984	54 190 500	3.3	45.0	2.1	4.1	7.1	38.4
SWITZERLAND FRANC	1975	5 978 800	13.0	61.5	...	2.4	...	23.1
	1980	7 936 800	13.3	61.0	3.5	2.4	...	19.7
	1982	9 097 100	13.6	62.2	3.1	2.2	...	18.9
	1983	9 756 600	12.8	62.3	3.1	2.0	...	19.7

COUNTRY CURRENCY	YEAR	TOTAL	ADMINISTRATION	TEACHERS' EMOLUMENTS	TEACHING MATERIALS	SCHOLARSHIPS	WELFARE SERVICES	NOT DISTRIBUTED
PAYS MONNAIE	ANNEE	TOTAL	ADMINISTRATION	EMOLUMENTS DU PERSONNEL ENSEIGNANT	MATERIEL POUR L'ENSEIGNEMENT	BOURSES D'ETUDES	SERVICES SOCIAUX	NON REPARTIES
PAIS MONEDA	AÑO	TOTAL (000)	ADMINISTRACION (%)	EMOLUMENTOS DEL PERSONAL DOCENTE (%)	MATERIAL EDUCATIVO (%)	BECAS DE ESTUDIOS (%)	SERVICIOS SOCIALES (%)	SIN DISTRIBUCION (%)
		(1)	(2)	(3)	(4)	(5)	(6)	(7)
UNITED KINGDOM POUND STERLING	1980	12 094 000	./.	52.1	3.6	9.1	5.7	29.4
	1982	14 240 000	./.	51.3	4.0	8.2	5.3	31.2
	1983	15 108 000	./.	50.8	4.0	8.4	5.1	31.8
YUGOSLAVIA DINAR	1975	25 515 000	...	64.9	...	2.9	4.6	27.6
	1980	71 514 000	...	63.9	6.2	1.5	8.4	20.1
	1982	116 886 000	...	60.7	6.9	1.5	9.5	21.4
	1983	145 149 000	...	61.5	7.8	1.4	9.3	20.0
OCEANIA								
AMERICAN SAMOA UNITED STATES DOLLAR	1981	11 248	14.5	44.0	4.7	6.4	5.3	25.1
COOK ISLANDS NEW ZEALAND DOLLAR	1981	2 712	17.5	72.3	10.2	–	–	–
	1984	3 474	12.3	74.5	6.9	0.9	4.5	0.9
FIJI‡ DOLLAR	1979	42 224	7.9	84.0	1.1	1.7	0.5	4.8
	1981	57 758	6.4	88.4	0.2	2.0	0.7	2.3
KIRIBATI AUSTRALIAN DOLLAR	1975	2 022	6.4	87.2	...	6.4	...	–
	1980	2 550	9.1	45.2	5.1	5.9	12.4	22.4
	1982	2 694	20.4	43.1	11.5	./.	15.7	9.2
	1984	2 703	9.7	52.9	8.3	./.	21.3	7.9
NEW CALEDONIA FRENCH FRANC	1981	595 836	...	85.8	6.9	3.5	–	3.7
	1983	736 197	...	88.1	7.1	4.8	–	–
	1984	835 410	...	88.1	7.3	4.6	–	–
NEW ZEALAND‡ DOLLAR	1980	1 171 226	1.5	82.7	5.6	3.7	2.0	4.5
	1983	1 541 429	1.3	81.4	6.1	4.4	2.5	4.3
	1984	1 598 765	4.9	72.0	6.0	4.8	3.5	8.7
NIUE NEW ZEALAND DOLLAR	1975	595	<——	87.2	9.7	...	3.0	–
	1980	755	20.1	74.2	2.8	...	2.6	0.3
	1981	717	16.3	74.1	9.6	...	–	–
	1982	664	14.9	79.1	6.0	...	–	–
NORFOLK ISLAND AUSTRALIAN DOLLAR	1975	209	2.9	74.6	4.8	1.9	6.2	9.6
	1980	425	3.3	76.5	4.5	2.4	4.7	8.7
	1981	722	3.6	84.5	2.8	1.1	2.4	5.7
	1982	455	2.0	78.2	2.6	2.6	2.6	11.9
PACIFIC ISLANDS UNITED STATES DOLLAR	1976	20 205	11.5	55.5	6.5	7.6	9.4	9.6
	1981	26 129	22.7	59.3	3.3	4.0	–	10.8
	1982	27 710	25.5	52.3	3.4	6.6	–	12.2
PAPUA NEW GUINEA KINA	1976	80 426	4.6	81.6	5.9	6.7	1.1	–
	1978	86 773	14.2	68.8	4.2	5.7	5.8	1.3
SAMOA TALA	1975	1 939	2.6	89.8	...	...	3.6	4.0
	1978	2 701	2.2	77.9	0.5	0.0	4.1	15.3
SOLOMON ISLANDS‡ AUSTRALIAN DOLLAR	1979	3 473	5.7	62.9	8.8	11.1	9.3	2.2
TOKELAU NEW ZEALAND DOLLAR	1981	630	2.2	21.9	4.1	71.1	–	0.6
	1982	579	3.5	28.5	2.9	64.4	–	0.7
TONGA PA'ANGA	1975	686	12.8	68.4	1.6	17.2	...	–
	1980	1 399	2.4	76.6	3.5	8.4	<——	9.1
	1983	2 974	4.4	58.8	15.8	4.3	<——	16.7
	1984	2 448	7.4	72.1	2.7	5.2	<——	12.6

AFRICA

Algeria:

E--> For 1974 and 1982, expenditure on third level education is not included.

FR-> En 1974 et 1982, les dépenses relatives à l'enseignement du troisième degré ne sont pas incluses.

ESP> En 1974 y 1982, no se incluyen los gastos relativos a la enseñanza de tercer grado.

Botswana:

E--> For 1975 and 1979, transfers to universities and other third level institutions are included with scholarships.

FR-> En 1975 et 1979, les transferts aux universités et autres établissements du troisième degré sont inclus avec les bourses d'études.

ESP> En 1975 y 1979, las transferencias a las universidades y otros establecimientos de tercer grado quedan incluídas en las becas de estudios.

Cameroon:

E--> For 1975, data refer to the expenditure of the Ministry of Education only. For 1981 and 1982, the totality of transfers to universities is included with teachers' emoluments.

FR-> En 1975, les données se réfèrent aux dépenses du Ministère de l'Education seulement. En 1981 et 1982, la totalité des transferts aux universités est incluse avec les émoluments du personnel enseignant.

ESP> En 1975, los datos se refieren a los gastos del Ministerio de Educación solamente. En 1981 y 1982, la totalidad de las transferencias a las universidades queda incluída en los emolumentos del personal docente.

Côte d'Ivoire:

E--> For 1975, data include foreign aid.

FR-> En 1975, les données incluent l'aide étrangère.

ESP> En 1975, los datos incluyen la ayuda extranjera.

Djibouti:

E--> For 1982, data refer to the expenditure of the Ministry of

Djibouti: (Cont):
Education only.

FR-> En 1982, les données se réfèrent aux dépenses du Ministère de l'Education seulement.

ESP> En 1982, los datos se refieren a los gastos del Ministerio de Educación solamente.

Ethiopia:

E--> Expenditure on third level education is not included.

FR-> Les dépenses relatives à l'enseignement du troisième degré ne sont pas incluses.

ESP> No se incluyen los gastos relativos a la enseñanza de tercer grado.

Ghana:

E--> For 1975 and 1984, the totality of transfers to universities is included with teachers' emoluments. For 1980 and 1981, expenditure on universities is not included.

FR-> En 1975 et 1984, la totalité des transferts aux universités est incluse avec les émoluments du personnel enseignant. En 1980 et 1981, les dépenses des universités ne sont pas incluses.

ESP> En 1975 y 1984, la totalidad de las transferencias a las universidades queda incluída en los emolumentos del personal docente. En 1980 y 1981, no se incluyen los gastos relativos a las universidades.

Lesotho:

E--> For 1982, with the exception of scolarships transfers to universities are included with teachers' emoluments. For 1983, the totality of transfers to universities is included with teachers emoluments.

FR-> En 1982, à l'exception des bourses d'études les transferts aux universités sont inclus avec les émoluments du personnel enseignant. En 1983, la totalité des transferts aux universités est incluse avec les émoluments du personnel enseignant.

ESP> En 1982, salvo las becas de estudios las transferencias a las universidades quedan incluídas en los emolumentos del personal docente. En 1983, la totalidad de las transferencias a las universidades queda incluída en los emolumentos del personal docente.

Madagascar:

E--> Except for 1975, expenditure on third level education is not included.

FR-> Sauf pour 1975, les dépenses relatives à l'enseignement du troisième degré ne sont pas incluses.

ESP> Salvo por 1975, no se incluyen los gastos relativos a la enseñanza de tercer grado.

Malawi:

E--> The totality of transfers to universities is included with teachers' emoluments. From 1981, subsidies to second level schools are also included with teachers' emoluments, and welfare services are included with teaching materials.

FR-> La totalité des transferts aux universités est incluse avec les émoluments du personnel enseignant. A partir de 1981, les subventions aux écoles secondaires sont incluses avec les émoluments du personnel enseignant et les services sociaux sont inclus avec le matériel pour l'enseignement.

ESP> La totalidad de las transferencias a las universidades queda incluía en los emolumentos del personal docente. A partir de 1981, las subvenciones a las escuelas secundarias quedan incluídas en los emolumentos del personal docente y los servicios sociales quedan incluídos en el material educativo.

Mauritius:

E--> Scholarhips and transfers to all types of education are included with teachers' emoluments.

FR-> Les bourses d'études et les transferts à tout type d'enseignement sont inclus avec les émoluments du personnel enseignant.

ESP> Las becas de estudios y las transferencias a todos tipos de enseñanza quedan incluídas en los emolumentos del personal docente.

Morocco:

E--> For 1975, data refer to the expenditure of the Ministry of Primary and Secondary Education only.

FR-> En 1975, les données se réfèrent aux dépenses du Ministère des enseignements primaire et secondaire seulement.

ESP> En 1975, los datos se refieren a los gastos del Ministerio de las enseñanzas de primer y segundo grado solamente.

Rwanda:

E--> From 1975 to 1981, with the exception of scholarships, transfers to third level institutions are included with teachers' emoluments.

FR-> De 1975 à 1981, à l'exception des bourses d'études, les transferts aux établissements d'enseignement du troisième degré, sont inclus avec les émoluments du personnel enseignant.

ESP> De 1975 a 1981, salvo las becas de estudios, las transferencias a los establecimientos de enseñanza de tercer grado quedan incluídas en los emolumentos del personal docente.

Senegal:

E--> For 1981, data refer to expenditure of the Ministry of Primary and Secondary Education only.

FR-> En 1981, les données se réfèrent aux dépenses du Ministère des enseignements primaire et secondaire seulement.

ESP> En 1981, los datos se refieren a los gastos del Ministerio de las enseñanzas de primer y segundo grado solamente.

Seychelles:

E--> For 1984, expenditure on third level education is nc included.

FR-> En 1984, les dépenses relatives à l'enseignement du troisièm degré ne sont pas incluses.

ESP> En 1984, no se incluyen los gastos relativos a la enseñanza d tercer grado.

Somalia:

E--> For 1980 and 1983, expenditure on third level education is nc included.

FR-> En 1980 et 1983, les dépenses relatives à l'enseignement d troisième degré ne sont pas incluses.

ESP> En 1980 y 1983, no se incluyen los gastos relativos a enseñanza de tercer grado.

Tunisia:

E--> For 1983 and 1984, expenditure on third level education is nc included.

FR-> En 1983 et 1984, les dépenses relatives à l'enseignement d troisième degré ne sont pas incluses.

ESP> En 1983 y 1984, no se incluyen los gastos relativos a enseñanza de tercer grado.

Zambia:

E--> For 1980, the totality of transfers to universities is included wi teachers' emoluments. For 1981 and 1982, with the exception scholarships transfers to universities are included with teacher emoluments.

FR-> En 1980, la totalité des transferts aux universités est incluse ave les émoluments du personnel enseignant. En 1981 et 1982, à l'exceptic des bourses d'études les transferts aux universités sont inclus avec le émoluments du personnel enseignant.

ESP> En 1980, la totalidad de las transferencias a las universidade queda incluída en los emolumentos del personal docente. En 1981 y 198 salvo las becas de estudios, las transferencias a las universidades queda incluídas en los emolumentos del personal docente.

Zimbabwe:

E--> Except for 1983, the totality of transfers to universities and othe third level institutions is included with teachers' emoluments.

FR-> Sauf pour 1983, la totalité des transferts aux universités et autre établissements de l'enseignement du troisième degré est incluse avec le émoluments du personnel enseignant.

ESP> Salvo por 1983, la totalidad de las transferencias a la universidades y otros establecimientos de enseñanza de tercer grado quec incluída en los emolumentos del personal docente.

AMERICA, NORTH

Antigua and Barbuda:

E--> For 1975, contributions for the University of the West Indies ar included with scholarships.

FR-> En 1975, les subventions à l'Université de *West Indies* sor incluses avec les bourses d'études.

ESP> En 1975, las subvenciones a la Universidad de *West Indi* quedan incluídas en las becas de estudios.

Costa Rica:

E--> The totality of transfers to universities is included with teacher emoluments.

FR-> La totalité des transferts aux universités est incluse avec le émoluments du personnel enseignant.

ESP> La totalidad de las transferencias a las universidades qued incluída en los emolumentos del personal docente.

Dominican Republic:

E--> The totality of transfers to universities is included with teacher emoluments. Except for 1976, data refer to expenditure of the Ministry c Education only.

FR-> La totalité des transferts aux universités, est incluse avec le émoluments du personnel enseignant. Sauf pour 1976, les données s réfèrent aux dépenses du Ministère de l'Education seulement.

ESP> La totalidad de las transferencias a las universidades qued incluída en los emolumentos del personal docente. Salvo por 1976, lo datos se refieren a los gastos del Ministerio de Educación solamente.

Grenada:

E--> Expenditure on third level education is not included.

FR-> Les dépenses relatives à l'enseignement du troisième degré n sont pas incluses.

ESP> No se incluyen los gastos relativos a la enseñanza de terce grado.

Guatemala:

E--> Except for 1979, the totality of transfers to universities i included with teachers' emoluments.

FR-> Sauf pour 1979, la totalité des transferts aux universités es incluse avec les émoluments du personnel enseignant.

ESP> Salvo por 1979, la totalidad de las transferencias a la universidades queda incluída en los emolumentos del personal docente.

Honduras:

E--> The totality of transfers to universities is included with teacher emoluments.

FR-> La totalité des transferts aux universités est incluse avec le émoluments du personnel enseignant.

ESP> La totalidad de las transferencias a las universidades qued incluída en los emolumentos del personal docente.

Jamaica:
E--> Except for 1983, data refer to expenditure of the Ministry of Education only. For 1975, the totality of transfers to universities is included with teachers' emoluments.
FR-> Sauf pour 1983, les données se réfèrent aux dépenses du Ministère de l'Education seulement. En 1975, la totalité des transferts aux universités est incluse avec les émoluments du personnel enseignant.
ESP> Salvo por 1983, los datos se refieren a los gastos del Ministerio de Educación solamente. En 1975, la totalidad de las transferencias a las universidades queda incluída en los emolumentos del personal docente.
Mexico:
E--> Expenditure of the Ministry of Education only.
FR-> Dépenses du Ministère de l'Education seulement.
ESP> Gastos del Ministerio de Educación solamente.
Nicaragua:
E--> For 1982, data refer to expenditure of Ministry of Education only and the totality of transfers to universities is included with teachers' emoluments.
FR-> En 1982, les données se réfèrent aux dépenses du Ministère de l'Education seulement et la totalité des transferts aux universités est incluse avec les émoluments du personnel enseignant.
ESP> En 1982, los datos se refieren a los gastos del Ministerio de Educación solamente y la totalidad de las transferencias a las universidades queda incluída en los emolumentos del personal docente.
Panama:
E--> The totality of transfers to universities is included with teachers' emoluments.
FR-> La totalité des transferts aux universités est incluse avec les émoluments du personnel enseignant.
ESP> La totalidad de las transferencias a las universidades queda incluída en los emolumentos del personal docente.
St. Christopher and Nevis:
E--> Expenditure on education at the third level is not included.
FR-> Les dépenses relatives à l'enseignement du troisième degré ne sont pas incluses.
ESP> No se incluyen los gastos relativos a la enseñanza de tercer grado.
St. Lucia:
E--> For 1980, contributions to the University of West Indies are included with scholarships. For 1982, data refer to expenditure of the Ministry of Education only.
FR-> En 1980, les subventions à l'Université de *West Indies* sont incluses avec les bourses d'études. En 1982, les données se réfèrent aux dépenses du Ministère de l'Education seulement.
ESP> En 1980, las subvenciones a la Universidad de *West Indies* quedan incluídas en las becas de estudios. En 1982, los datos se refieren a los gastos del Ministerio de Educación solamente.
Trinidad and Tobago:
E--> The totality of transfers to universities is included with teachers' emoluments.
FR-> La totalité des transferts aux universités est incluse avec les émoluments du personnel enseignant.
ESP> La totalidad de las transferencias a las universidades queda incluída en los emolumentos del personal docente.
AMERICA, SOUTH
Bolivia:
E--> For 1980, the totality of transfers to universities is included with teachers' emoluments. For 1981 and 1982, expenditure on universities is not included.
FR-> En 1980, la totalité des transferts aux universités est incluse avec les émoluments du personnel enseignant. En 1981 et 1982, les dépenses relatives aux universités ne sont pas incluses.
ESP> En 1980, la totalidad de las transferencias a las universidades queda incluída en los emolumentos del personal docente. En 1981 y 1982, no se incluyen los gastos relativos a las universidades.
Chile:
E--> For 1975, the totality of transfers to universities is included with teachers' emoluments.
FR-> En 1975, la totalité des transferts aux universités est incluse avec les émoluments du personnel enseignant.
ESP> En 1975, la totalidad de las transferencias a las universidades queda incluída en los emolumentos del personal docente.
Colombia:
E--> Expenditure of the Ministry of Education only.
FR-> Dépenses du Ministère de l'Education seulement.
ESP> Gastos del Ministerio de Educación solamente.
Guyana:
E--> Except for 1979, the totality of transfers to universities is included with teachers' emoluments. For 1975, data refer to the expenditure of the Ministry of Education only.
FR-> Sauf pour 1979, la totalité des transferts aux universités est incluse avec les émoluments du personnel enseignant. En 1975, les données se réfèrent aux dépenses du Ministère de l'Education seulement.
ESP> Salvo por 1979, la totalidad de las transferencias a las universidades queda incluída en los emolumentos del personal docente. En 1975, los datos se refieren a los gastos del Ministerio de Educación solamente.
Peru:
E--> Figures in column 1 are in millions. Transfers to universities and to other types of institutions as well as some types of pensions and staff benefits are shown in column 7.
FR-> Les chiffres de la colonne 1 sont exprimés en millions. Les transferts aux universités et à certains autres établissements ainsi que différents types de pensions et indemnités du personnel sont présentés dans la colonne 7.
ESP> Las cifras de la columna 1 se expresan en millones. Las transferencias a las universidades y otros establecimientos así como diferentes tipos de pensiones y indemnizaciones del personal quedan incluídos en la columna 7.
Suriname:
E--> Subsidies to private education are not included.
FR-> Les subventions à l'enseignement privé ne sont pas incluses.
ESP> No se incluyen las subvenciones relativas a la enseñanza privada.
Venezuela:
E--> For 1975, transfers to universities and other third level institutions are included with teachers' emoluments.
FR-> En 1975, les transferts aux universités et autres établissements d'enseignement du troisième degré sont inclus avec les émoluments du personnel enseignant.
ESP> En 1975, las transferencias a las universidades y otros establecimientos de enseñanza de tercer grado quedan incluídas en los emolumentos del personal docente.
ASIA
Bangladesh:
E--> Expenditure of the Ministry of Education only.
FR-> Dépenses du Ministère de l'Education seulement.
ESP> Gastos del Ministerio de Educación solamente.
Cyprus:
E--> Expenditure of the Office of Greek Education only.
FR-> Dépenses du bureau grec de l'Education seulement.
ESP> Gastos del servicio griego de Educación solamente.
Democratic Yemen:
E--> For 1980, expenditure on third level education is not included.
FR-> En 1980, les dépenses relatives à l'enseignement du troisième degré ne sont pas incluses.
ESP> En 1980, no se incluyen los gastos relativos a la enseñanza de tercer grado.
Israel:
E--> Transfers to universities and public subsidies to private educational institutions are included with teachers' emoluments.
FR-> Les transferts aux universités et les subventions publiques aux établissements d'enseignement privé sont inclus avec les émoluments du personnel enseignant.
ESP> Las transferencias a las universidades y las subvenciones públicas a los establecimientos de enseñanza privada quedan incluídas en los emolumentos del personal docente.
Japan:
E--> Figures in column 1 are in millions. Data do not include public subsidies to private education.
FR-> Les chiffres de la colonne 1 sont exprimés en millions. Les données ne comprennent pas les subventions publiques à l'enseignement privé.
ESP> Las cifras de la columna 1 se expresan en millones. Los datos no comprenden las subvenciones públicas a la enseñanza privada.
Jordan:
E--> For 1975 expenditure on universities is not included.
FR-> En 1975 les dépenses relatives aux universités ne sont pas incluses.
ESP> En 1975 no se incluyen los gastos relativos a las universidades.
Korea, Republic of:
E--> Figures in column 1 are in millions.
FR-> Les chiffres de la colonne 1 sont exprimés en millions.
ESP> Las cifras de la columna 1 se expresan en millones.
Malaysia:
E--> With the exception of scholarships, transfers to third level institutions are included with teachers' emoluments.
FR-> A l'exception des bourses d'études, les transferts aux établissements d'enseignement du troisième degré sont inclus avec les émoluments du personnel enseignant.
ESP> Salvo las becas de estudios, las transferencias a los establecimientos de enseñanza de tercer grado quedan incluídas en los emolumentos del personal docente.
Peninsular Malaysia:
E--> With the exception of scholarhips, transfers to third level institutions are included with teachers' emoluments.
FR-> A l'excéption des bourses d'études, les transferts aux établissements d'enseignement du troisième degré sont inclus avec les émoluments du personnel enseignant.
ESP> Salvo las becas de estudios, las transferencias a los establecimientos de enseñanza de tercer grado quedan incluídas en los emolumentos del personal docente.

4.2 Public current expenditure by purpose
Dépenses publiques ordinaires selon leur destination
Gastos públicos ordinarios según su destino

Nepal:
E--> Data refer to 'regular' and 'development' expenditure.
FR-> Les données se réfèrent aux dépenses 'ordinaires' et 'de développement'.
ESP> Los datos se refieren a los gastos 'ordinarios' y 'de desarrollo'.
Philippines:
E--> For 1983 and 1984, expenditure on state universities and colleges is not included.
FR-> En 1983 et 1984, les dépenses des universités et collèges d'Etat ne sont pas incluses.
ESP> En 1983 y 1984, no se incluyen los gastos de las universidades y los colegios del Estado.
Singapore:
E--> Transfers to third level institutions (namely universities), industrial training board and other educational organizations are included with teachers' emoluments.
FR-> Les transferts aux établissements d'enseignement du troisième degré (notamment aux universités), à l'*industrial training board* et à d'autres organismes d'enseignement sont inclus avec les émoluments du personnel enseignant.
ESP> Las transferencias a los establecimientos de enseñanza de tercer grado (en particular las universidades), al *industrial training board* y a otros organismos de enseñanza quedan incluídas en los emolumentos del personal docente.
Sri Lanka:
E--> For 1975, the totality of transfers to universities is included with teachers' emoluments. From 1980 to 1984, data refer to expenditure of the Ministry of Education only.
FR-> En 1975, la totalité des transferts aux universités est incluse avec les émoluments du personnel enseignant. De 1980 à 1984, les données se réfèrent aux dépenses du Ministère de l'Education seulement.
ESP> En 1975, la totalidad de las transferencias a las universidades queda incluída en los emolumentos del personal docente. De 1980 a 1984, los datos se refieren a los gastos del Ministerio de Educación solamente.
Syrian Arab Republic:
E--> Expenditure on education at the third level is not included.
FR-> Les dépenses relatives à l'enseignement du troisième degré ne sont pas incluses.
ESP> No se incluyen los gastos relativos a la enseñanza de tercer grado.
EUROPE
Belgium:
E--> Expenditure of the Ministry of Education only.
FR-> Dépenses du Ministère de l'Education seulement.
ESP> Gastos del Ministerio de Educación solamente.
France:
E--> Metropolitan France.
FR-> France métropolitaine.
ESP> Francia metropolitana.
Italy:
E--> Figures in column 1 are in millions.
FR-> Les chiffres de la colonne 1 sont exprimés en millions.
ESP> Las cifras de la columna 1 se expresan en millones.
Luxembourg:
E--> Except for 1975, expenditure of the Central Government on
FR-> Sauf pour 1975, dépenses du gouvernement cent seulement.
ESP> Salvo por 1975, gastos del gobierno central solamente.
Malta:
E--> The totality of transfers to the university is included w teachers' emoluments.
FR-> La totalité des transferts à l'université est incluse avec émoluments du personnel enseignant.
ESP> La totalidad de las transferencias a la universidad queda incluí en los emolumentos del personal docente.
Portugal:
E--> For 1975, data refer to expenditure of the Ministry of Educati only.
FR-> En 1975, les données se réfèrent aux dépenses du Ministère l'Education seulement.
ESP> En 1975, los datos se refieren a los gastos del Ministerio Educación solamente.
OCEANIA
Fiji:
E--> The totality of transfers to universities is included with teache emoluments.
FR-> La totalité des transferts aux universités est incluse avec émoluments du personnel enseignant.
ESP> La totalidad de las transferencias a las universidades que incluída en los emolumentos del personal docente.
New Zealand:
E--> With the exception of scholarships, transfers to universities a included with teachers' emoluments.
FR-> A l'exception des bourses d'études, les transferts aux universit sont inclus avec les émoluments du personnel enseignant.
ESP> Salvo las becas de estudios, las transferencias a las universidad quedan incluídas en los emolumentos del personal docente.
Solomon Islands:
E--> Data include foreign aid.
FR-> Les données incluent l'aide étrangère.
ESP> Los datos incluyen la ayuda extranjera.

4.3 Public current expenditure on education: distribution by level of education

Dépenses publiques ordinaires afférentes à l'enseignement: répartition par degré d'enseignement

Gastos públicos ordinarios destinados a la educación: distribución por grado de enseñanza

NUMBER OF COUNTRIES AND TERRITORIES PRESENTED IN THIS TABLE: 143

NOMBRE DE PAYS ET DE TERRITOIRES PRESENTES DANS CE TABLEAU: 143

NUMERO DE PAISES Y DE TERRITORIOS PRESENTADOS EN ESTE CUADRO: 143

COUNTRY CURRENCY	YEAR	TOTAL	PRE-PRIMARY	1ST LEVEL	SECOND LEVEL				3RD LEVEL	OTHER TYPES	NOT DISTRIBUTED
PAYS MONNAIE	ANNEE	TOTAL	PRE-PRIMAIRE	1ER DEGRE	SECOND DEGRE				3EME DEGRE	AUTRES TYPES	NON REPARTIES
PAIS MONEDA	AÑO	TOTAL	PRE-PRIMARIA	1ER GRADO	SEGUNDO GRADO				3ER GRADO	OTROS TIPOS	SIN DISTRIBUCION
					TOTAL / TOTAL / TOTAL	GENERAL / GENERAL / GENERAL	TEACHER TRAINING / NORMAL / NORMAL	VOCATIONAL / TECHNIQUE / TECNICA			
		(000)	(%)	(%)	(%)	(%)	(%)	(%)	(%)	(%)	(%)
		(1)	(2)	(3)	(4)	(5)	(6)	(7)	(8)	(9)	(10)
AFRICA											
ALGERIA DINAR	1980	8 259 100	–	28.5	25.2	...	...	...	17.3	19.8	9.3
BENIN	1975	5 627 477	–	44.9	26.1	20.9	–	5.2	18.5	4.8	5.8
FRANC C.F.A.	1978	8 324 906	–	46.2	23.3	18.7	–	4.7	18.5	4.6	7.4
BOTSWANA	1975	8 688	–	46.5	33.5	25.7	3.4	4.3	13.6	–	6.5
PULA	1979	27 483	–	52.1	29.2	23.3	2.8	3.0	13.2	–	5.6
	1983	54 235	–	43.0	29.1	22.5	2.5	4.1	23.7	0.9	3.4
	1984	75 572	–	43.2	34.2	24.2	2.5	7.5	9.3	0.9	12.4
BURKINA FASO‡	1975	3 171 371	–	43.3	26.2	...	...	...	24.8	0.0	5.6
FRANC C.F.A.	1980	7 435 813	–	32.3	19.8	17.4	1.2	1.1	33.7	9.2	5.1
	1983	12 706 470	–	31.4	16.6	...	...	...	25.9	16.6	9.5
	1984	11 962 276	–	35.3	20.2	...	...	...	27.5	17.0	–
BURUNDI	1975	721 831	–	45.0	33.3	13.0	12.4	7.9	19.5	0.9	1.2
FRANC	1979	1 796 482	–	42.7	31.0	...	...	...	20.6	5.1	0.6
	1981	2 634 658	–	38.8	35.3	...	...	9.5	23.8	1.4	0.7
CENTRAL AFRICAN REPUBLIC	1975	3 393 000	–	56.9	14.5	...	...	...	9.9	1.1	17.7
FRANC C.F.A.	1981	8 441 464	–	54.9	13.9	...	...	...	16.3	0.2	14.7
	1982	8 532 482	–	58.8	11.6	...	...	...	19.3	0.1	10.2
	1983	8 863 462	–	55.4	14.8	...	...	...	18.1	0.1	11.5
CHAD FRANC C.F.A.	1983	4 099 374	<——	82.9	——>	...	...	...	16.3	...	0.9
COMOROS FRANC C.F.A.	1982	1 773 956	5.1	36.4	20.0	18.5	1.0	0.5	23.8	–	14.7
CONGO	1975	10 537 237	0.8	34.3	31.9	20.1	3.0	8.8	28.6	0.2	4.3
FRANC C.F.A	1980	21 517 291	<——	35.8	29.1	21.9	2.3	4.9	24.3	0.1	10.7
COTE D'IVOIRE‡	1975	48 123 000	–	37.0	38.6	36.4	2.1	...	18.7	–	5.7
FRANC C.F.A.	1979	124 616 400	–	39.0	45.6	29.7	4.4	11.5	15.4	–	–
DJIBOUTI‡	1974	1 479 821	–	47.5	43.3	...	...	...	–	–	9.2
FRANC	1982	1 309 034	–	71.9	27.0	...	...	...	–	–	1.1
EGYPT	1975	226 668	<——	70.0	——>	...	...	...	30.0	–	–
POUND	1980	505 330	<——	69.1	——>	...	...	...	30.9	–	–
	1981	722 108	<——	68.0	——>	...	...	...	32.0	–	–
ETHIOPIA	1976	164 528	–	38.6	40.9	35.8	2.6	2.5	14.7	1.7	4.2
BIRR	1980	221 504	–	42.0	29.8	25.9	2.6	1.3	19.0	4.0	5.2
	1981	256 439	–	45.1	28.8	25.3	2.3	1.1	18.1	3.5	4.6
	1982	290 229	–	45.5	29.4	25.9	2.3	1.2	17.5	3.1	4.5
GAMBIA‡	1975	5 471	–	44.0	21.3	16.9	1.7	2.7	–	–	34.6
DALASI	1980	11 336	–	49.2	31.9	23.5	<——	8.5	–	1.5	17.5
	1983	24 119	–	50.2	49.8	31.0	6.5	12.4	–	–	–
	1984	23 994	–	49.3	34.8	21.2	5.4	8.1	–	–	15.9

4.3 Public current expenditure by level of education
Dépenses publiques ordinaires par degrés d'enseignement
Gastos públicos ordinarios por grados de enseñanza

COUNTRY CURRENCY PAYS MONNAIE PAIS MONEDA	YEAR ANNEE AÑO	TOTAL TOTAL TOTAL (000)	PRE-PRIMARY PRE-PRIMAIRE PRE-PRIMARIA (%)	1ST LEVEL 1ER DEGRE 1ER GRADO (%)	SECOND LEVEL / SECOND DEGRE / SEGUNDO GRADO TOTAL TOTAL TOTAL (%)	GENERAL GENERAL GENERAL (%)	TEACHER TRAINING NORMAL NORMAL (%)	VOCATIONAL TECHNIQUE TECNICA (%)	3RD LEVEL 3EME DEGRE 3ER GRADO (%)	OTHER TYPES AUTRES TYPES OTROS TIPOS (%)	NOT DISTRIBUTED NON REPARTIES SIN DISTRIBUCION (%)
		(1)	(2)	(3)	(4)	(5)	(6)	(7)	(8)	(9)	(10)
GHANA‡	1975	240 682	–	24.5	37.0	28.7	5.6	2.7	16.8	0.5	21.3
CEDI	1980	734 256	–	29.3	38.7	31.5	4.7	2.5	1.8	0.9	29.3
	1981	1 332 170	–	33.7	42.7	35.1	4.7	2.9	2.1	0.9	20.6
	1984	3 843 913	–	24.5	29.5	26.4	1.7	1.4	12.5	0.8	32.7
GUINEA	1979	1 185 500	–	24.7	28.9	...	...	...	31.9	0.7	13.8
SYLI	1984	1 486 054	–	30.8	36.9	31.3	–	5.6	23.5	0.3	8.5
GUINEA-BISSAU	1980	207 512	0.5	75.8	16.2	12.7	1.9	1.5	–	–	7.5
PESO	1981	241 804	1.8	65.0	17.2	8.8	4.8	3.5	1.6	1.0	13.4
	1982	260 000	1.5	67.2	14.5	7.5	3.5	3.4	1.5	0.9	14.5
KENYA‡	1975	1 331 734	–	65.4	18.8	14.3	3.3	1.2	11.0	0.4	4.4
SHILLING	1980	3 049 526	–	63.4	16.0	11.9	3.2	1.0	12.4	2.3	5.8
	1983	3 484 470	0.1	64.8	14.6	10.9	2.7	1.0	12.9	2.7	5.0
	1984	4 429 160	0.1	60.4	18.8	14.5	4.3	–	13.3	0.5	6.9
LESOTHO	1975	6 777	–	47.7	23.1	18.2	2.7	2.2	20.6	–	8.6
MALOTI	1980	20 037	–	38.6	33.4	25.1	6.0	2.4	21.8	1.9	4.3
	1982	28 082	–	36.8	29.2	21.9	5.2	2.1	24.2	3.3	6.5
	1983	25 939	–	39.7	35.1	27.7	4.2	3.1	19.5	...	5.7
LIBERIA											
DOLLAR	1979	41 803	←	17.6	26.6	13.7	2.6	10.3	19.0	33.4	3.4
MADAGASCAR	1975	11 726 747	–	42.9	30.5	19.1	4.2	7.2	13.9	–	12.7
FRANC	1980	31 547 842	–	41.4	25.5	15.1	3.3	7.1	27.5	–	5.6
	1983	38 810 098	–	41.5	25.9	19.8	0.9	5.2	28.6	–	4.0
	1984	47 519 440	–	46.5	23.3	18.9	0.9	3.5	26.4	–	3.8
MALAWI	1975	11 992	–	44.6	23.2	17.7	4.1	1.5	22.8	1.8	7.5
KWACHA	1980	23 595	–	38.9	15.7	14.4	–	1.4	30.2	–	15.2
	1982	31 475	–	38.5	16.0	14.5	–	1.5	27.6	3.9	13.9
	1983	34 754	–	40.9	14.8	13.4	–	1.4	27.3	4.2	12.9
MALI‡	1975	5 852 452	0.1	39.7	25.5	17.7	4.4	3.5	22.9	0.9	11.0
FRANC C.F.A.	1980	12 752 392	0.2	38.8	25.1	13.3	4.3	7.5	24.9	–	11.0
	1982	14 219 340	0.2	43.5	22.3	9.2	5.3	7.7	18.7	–	15.2
	1984	15 124 302	←	47.2	23.4	9.4	5.9	8.0	13.8	0.6	15.0
MAURITANIA	1975	723 100	–	45.3	39.5	25.7	6.0	7.7	14.6	0.3	0.3
OUGUIYA	1980	1 546 000	–	35.4	50.3	...	...	...	13.5	–	0.8
	1982	2 503 687	–	27.9	36.1	...	...	...	22.6	–	13.4
	1983	3 006 217	–	29.8	31.9	20.5	3.5	7.8	24.5	–	13.8
MAURITIUS	1976	197 000	–	50.5	31.1	25.9	2.8	2.4	9.7	3.5	5.2
RUPEE	1980	407 926	–	44.1	36.5	34.5	1.3	0.7	7.7	3.5	8.1
	1983	532 000	–	46.2	35.7	35.0	–	0.7	6.9	3.2	8.0
	1984	539 800	0.0	46.4	36.9	35.9	–	1.1	6.9	3.4	6.4
MOROCCO	1976	1 801 546	–	39.5	47.1	...	...	...	13.4	–	0.0
DIRHAM	1980	3 528 566	–	35.4	46.3	...	...	...	18.3	–	–
	1982	4 692 083	–	35.4	45.8	...	...	...	18.7	–	–
	1983	5 174 600	–	36.5	44.7	...	...	...	18.9	–	–
NIGER											
FRANC C.F.A.	1981	16 585 807	–	36.8	46.2	...	...	...	17.0	0.0	–
NIGERIA	1974	326 361	–	22.7	15.6	...	...	...	42.0	0.4	19.4
NAIRA	1981	2 522 740	–	17.2	39.8	28.4	8.6	2.8	25.0	0.6	17.4
RWANDA	1975	1 197 164	–	69.0	16.6	...	...	...	10.8	–	3.7
FRANC	1980	2 438 563	–	67.1	19.9	...	...	...	9.6	0.0	3.3
	1981	4 497 308	–	73.9	14.1	...	...	...	7.5	1.9	2.7
	1983	4 527 718	–	78.2	→	...	...	...	12.7	0.9	8.1
SENEGAL‡	1976	16 310 900	–	47.8	29.1	...	...	...	20.7	–	2.4
FRANC C.F.A.	1980	27 485 411	–	43.8	27.2	21.6	2.8	2.7	26.9	–	2.2
	1981	21 694 900	–	56.8	37.6	27.8	4.1	5.7	–	0.1	5.5
SEYCHELLES‡	1975	11 202	–	53.1	39.1	33.9	...	5.2	6.8	1.0	–
RUPEE	1984	111 391	←	38.0	58.5	...	...	...	–	...	3.5
SUDAN											
POUND	1980	172 399	–	48.0	31.0	29.0	0.1	1.9	20.7	0.3	–
SWAZILAND‡	1975	6 186	–	32.2	40.6	34.6	6.0	–	18.7	0.0	8.5
LILANGENI	1980	19 627	–	45.8	34.3	32.0	2.3	–	10.7	1.8	7.4
	1981	22 562	0.1	46.5	35.0	33.1	1.8	–	10.2	1.8	6.5
	1982	26 679	0.0	47.3	32.5	30.8	1.7	–	12.2	2.1	5.8

COUNTRY CURRENCY / PAYS MONNAIE / PAIS MONEDA	YEAR / ANNEE / AÑO	TOTAL / TOTAL / TOTAL (000)	PRE-PRIMARY / PRE-PRIMAIRE / PRE-PRIMARIA (%)	1ST LEVEL / 1ER DEGRE / 1ER GRADO (%)	SECOND LEVEL / SECOND DEGRE / SEGUNDO GRADO: TOTAL / TOTAL / TOTAL (%)	GENERAL / GENERAL / GENERAL (%)	TEACHER TRAINING / NORMAL / NORMAL (%)	VOCATIONAL / TECHNIQUE / TECNICA (%)	3RD LEVEL / 3EME DEGRE / 3ER GRADO (%)	OTHER TYPES / AUTRES TYPES / OTROS TIPOS (%)	NOT DISTRIBUTED / NON REPARTIES / SIN DISTRIBUCION (%)
		(1)	(2)	(3)	(4)	(5)	(6)	(7)	(8)	(9)	(10)
TOGO	1980	12 574 743	0.7	29.5	31.0	26.8	1.9	2.3	29.8	0.2	8.7
FRANC C.F.A.	1981	14 880 824	0.7	25.4	25.9	22.9	1.2	1.8	28.2	5.1	14.7
TUNISIA	1975	78 045	–	42.3	38.2	...	...	...	17.7	–	1.9
DINAR	1980	162 291	–	41.2	36.6	...	...	...	20.5	–	1.8
	1982	230 255	–	41.2	38.1	...	...	...	19.2	–	1.5
UGANDA‡	1975	529 014	–	41.1	33.4	25.4	5.9	2.1	21.9	0.0	3.6
SHILLING	1981	5 691 000	–	16.2	58.0	46.9	6.0	5.1	18.0	–	7.8
	1982	6 743 000	–	16.3	55.7	40.2	9.9	5.6	17.5	–	10.4
	1983	12 402 000	–	25.6	40.2	24.8	10.2	5.1	19.9	–	14.4
UNITED REPUBLIC OF											
TANZANIA‡	1975	827 800	–	37.3	22.3	17.1	5.2	./.	12.8	5.0	22.6
SHILLING	1979	1 769 328	–	45.0	13.6	7.4	3.6	2.5	26.7	1.6	13.1
ZAIRE	1975	107 794	...	44.1	35.3	...	...	...	20.6	...	–
ZAIRE	1980	947 891	...	47.1	27.5	...	...	...	25.4	...	–
ZAMBIA	1975	75 420	–	45.3	25.0	22.2	2.8	<——	16.7	–	13.0
KWACHA	1980	120 377	0.0	45.3	25.5	18.8	3.1	3.6	18.0	0.2	11.0
	1983	209 166	–	46.5	35.4	26.8	2.5	6.1	12.6	0.1	5.4
	1984	230 681	–	44.2	36.0	27.7	2.7	5.6	12.1	0.3	7.3
ZIMBABWE	1975	65 015	–	49.4	33.7	33.7	–	–	8.4	–	8.4
DOLLAR	1980	218 037	–	66.5	21.4	21.4	–	–	7.5	–	4.6
	1981	290 070	–	60.0	25.7	25.7	–	–	8.9	–	5.4
	1983	432 547	–	65.2	24.3	24.3	–	–	6.5	–	4.0
AMERICA, NORTH											
ANTIGUA AND BARBUDA	1975	5 681	–	29.2	35.2	24.4	3.2	7.7	16.7	3.5	15.3
E.CARIBBEAN DOLLAR	1980	8 529	0.2	33.2	24.1	...	...	...	13.8	...	28.8
	1983	10 885	–	40.0	31.8	...	...	...	7.5	...	20.8
	1984	11 371	–	36.6	30.6	...	...	...	12.7	...	20.1
BARBADOS	1975	42 256	<——	27.3	29.7	27.7	–	2.0	18.5	1.3	23.2
DOLLAR	1981	97 143	<——	42.6	36.0	32.2	–	3.8	17.3	0.8	3.2
	1982	95 245	<——	44.3	37.6	34.0	–	3.6	15.3	0.6	2.2
BRITISH VIRGIN											
ISLANDS	1975	967	–	43.4	40.0	...	...	...	6.3	0.3	9.9
UNITED STATES DOLLAR	1980	1 622	–	45.1	42.7	...	...	...	4.3	–	8.0
	1983	3 361	<——	34.8	35.1	...	...	...	9.2	–	20.9
	1984	4 161	0.1	37.2	38.0	36.2	1.8	–	6.6	–	18.0
CANADA	1975	11 526 821	<——	<——	63.3	...	...	...	28.9	7.9	–
DOLLAR	1980	20 450 870	<——	<——	65.3	...	...	...	27.4	7.4	–
	1983	27 702 373	<——	<——	63.8	...	...	...	28.7	7.5	–
	1984	28 692 121	<——	<——	63.8	...	...	...	27.9	8.3	–
COSTA RICA	1975	1 041 297	<——	37.2	22.4	16.9	–	5.5	24.4	1.0	15.1
COLON	1980	2 802 162	<——	28.0	21.5	14.7	–	6.8	26.1	1.0	23.4
	1982	4 328 004	<——	25.5	17.1	11.9	–	5.2	31.5	0.9	25.0
	1983	5 853 136	<——	26.6	18.9	13.0	–	5.9	25.8	0.9	27.9
CUBA	1980	1 134 500	5.1	24.4	40.8	28.6	2.2	10.0	6.9	5.9	16.9
PESO	1982	1 396 000	5.7	22.8	43.3	28.1	2.5	12.7	10.6	5.0	12.5
	1983	1 335 800	6.2	24.5	48.5	...	...	...	12.4	5.8	2.6
DOMINICAN REPUBLIC	1976	62 595	–	37.5	20.4	15.1	1.7	3.5	19.6	3.8	18.6
PESO‡	1980	104 387	–	36.8	22.9	17.7	1.9	3.3	23.9	10.6	5.8
	1983	146 813	<——	43.5	19.9	16.0	1.2	2.7	22.2	10.1	4.4
	1984	170 322	0.4	44.6	19.6	15.9	1.1	2.6	18.8	10.2	6.3
EL SALVADOR	1975	138 364	–	57.5	6.6	6.3	–	0.3	23.7	1.3	10.9
COLON	1980	320 009	–	61.9	6.2	5.9	–	0.3	14.2	1.9	15.9
	1981	321 814	–	60.3	6.0	5.7	–	0.3	15.7	1.9	16.2
GRENADA‡	1975	5 478	–	53.5	19.9	...	...	...	19.3	...	7.3
E.CARIBBEAN DOLLAR	1983	9 561	3.3	71.9	21.7	16.4	3.7	1.6	–	3.1	–
GUATEMALA	1976	67 193	2.5	51.3	15.5	8.9	2.9	3.6	19.9	3.3	7.5
QUETZAL	1982	129 226	1.8	38.2	17.2	8.8	2.6	5.8	19.7	14.2	8.9
HAITI‡	1975	34 138	–	63.0	17.5	11.1	<——	6.5	11.4	<——	8.1
GOURDE	1980	85 781	–	59.3	20.4	8.8	2.3	9.3	9.6	4.7	6.0
	1982	87 076	–	65.7	15.6	9.5	./.	6.2	7.9	4.8	6.0
	1983	92 943	–	63.2	15.8	9.5	./.	6.4	9.4	5.6	5.9
HONDURAS	1980	141 075	–	61.9	17.9	...	...	...	19.3	0.9	–
LEMPIRA	1981	168 689	–	57.5	19.4	...	...	...	22.2	1.0	–
	1982	206 880	–	54.0	18.2	...	...	...	26.5	1.0	0.3

Public current expenditure by level of education
Dépenses publiques ordinaires par degrés d'enseignement
Gastos públicos ordinarios por grados de enseñanza

COUNTRY CURRENCY / PAYS MONNAIE / PAIS MONEDA	YEAR / ANNEE / AÑO	TOTAL / TOTAL / TOTAL (000)	PRE-PRIMARY / PRE-PRIMAIRE / PRE-PRIMARIA (%)	1ST LEVEL / 1ER DEGRE / 1ER GRADO (%)	SECOND LEVEL / SECOND DEGRE / SEGUNDO GRADO: TOTAL / TOTAL / TOTAL (%)	GENERAL / GENERAL / GENERAL (%)	TEACHER TRAINING / NORMAL / NORMAL (%)	VOCATIONAL / TECHNIQUE / TECNICA (%)	3RD LEVEL / 3EME DEGRE / 3ER GRADO (%)	OTHER TYPES / AUTRES TYPES / OTROS TIPOS (%)	NOT DISTRIBUTED / NON REPARTIES / SIN DISTRIBUCION (%)
		(1)	(2)	(3)	(4)	(5)	(6)	(7)	(8)	(9)	(10)
JAMAICA‡	1975	121 854	2.2	33.5	32.3	28.9	–	3.5	19.8	1.9	10.3
DOLLAR	1980	302 669	1.0	33.7	36.9	26.9	5.9	4.1	19.2	4.3	5.0
	1983	456 377	1.4	27.1	33.0	29.6	–	3.4	24.9	3.4	10.2
MEXICO‡	1975	26 783 400	2.3	42.9	31.1	...	...	...	12.6	0.8	10.3
PESO	1980	114 913 003	2.3	39.7	18.8	9.9	1.8	7.1	26.5	4.2	8.5
	1982	282 559 038	3.9	33.3	17.4	9.5	2.0	6.0	27.5	6.7	11.1
	1983	416 192 879	4.1	30.8	15.7	9.1	1.5	5.0	28.8	6.3	14.4
NICARAGUA	1975	206 346	–	55.1	22.4	12.6	2.1	7.7	16.5	6.0	–
CORDOBA	1980	579 693	0.4	44.7	25.1	19.2	1.8	4.2	10.5	7.7	11.5
	1981	872 260	1.3	41.3	23.1	16.3	1.8	5.0	16.9	9.1	8.3
	1984	2 458 200	1.9	31.5	14.4	9.9	1.5	2.9	18.3	8.6	25.3
PANAMA	1975	96 693	–	39.1	23.5	14.3	3.1	6.1	12.6	<——	24.8
BALBOA	1980	155 716	–	46.3	22.0	12.3	2.5	7.2	13.4	1.9	16.4
	1983	198 413	–	37.2	24.9	15.6	0.2	9.0	18.5	2.9	16.4
	1984	210 998	–	39.8	25.4	15.7	0.2	9.5	19.4	3.0	12.3
ST. CHRISTOPHER AND NEVIS	1975	2 732	–	48.0	42.5	...	...	...	3.1	0.1	6.3
E.CARIBBEAN DOLLAR	1980	6 563	0.4	49.6	40.6	...	...	...	2.9	0.2	6.3
	1983	10 536	1.2	48.3	41.1	...	...	...	2.1	0.2	7.0
	1984	11 226	1.2	47.3	41.9	...	...	...	2.1	0.2	7.3
ST. LUCIA‡	1975	7 321	–	46.6	34.9	...	...	...	10.0	0.1	8.4
E.CARIBBEAN DOLLAR	1980	18 596	–	45.6	23.7	...	...	...	14.7	0.7	15.3
	1982	23 045	–	58.2	40.6	27.5	8.5	4.6	0.9	0.2	0.1
ST. PIERRE AND MIQUELON	1982	24 006	10.2	26.0	62.9	...	...	...	–	1.0	–
FRENCH FRANC	1983	29 037	<——	35.3	50.1	38.1	–	11.9	–	–	14.6
TRINIDAD AND TOBAGO	1980	430 831	–	46.7	33.1	...	...	...	12.0	–	8.2
DOLLAR	1983	867 816	–	42.6	34.7	33.0	–	1.7	10.1	–	12.6
	1984	901 433	–	42.3	36.3	34.4	–	1.8	8.7	0.1	12.6
TURKS AND CAICOS ISL.	1975	601	–	52.2	22.8	22.6	0.2	–	–	–	25.0
UNITED STATES DOLLAR	1980	832	–	58.2	40.6	...	...	...	1.2	–	–
UNITED STATES‡	1975	90 800 000	<——	67.5	——>	...	...	...	32.5	–	–
DOLLAR	1979	158 149 000	<——	63.7	——>	...	...	...	36.0	0.3	–
	1981	199 800 000	<——	63.4	——>	...	...	...	36.6	–	–
AMERICA, SOUTH											
ARGENTINA	1975	3 356	<——	27.0	30.5	...	...	...	30.2	–	12.3
PESO	1980	859 892	<——	40.1	25.6	18.1	–	7.5	22.7	1.9	9.7
	1983	15 212 677	<——	40.0	27.7	...	...	...	18.1	0.8	13.3
	1984	180 530 252	<——	37.7	27.4	...	...	...	19.2	0.7	15.0
BOLIVIA‡	1975	1 658 659	2.1	60.4	7.3	...	...	...	15.0	2.3	13.0
PESO	1980	4 919 122	<——	58.9	11.4	...	...	...	17.1	2.9	9.7
	1981	4 621 655	<——	61.3	11.8	10.2	–	1.7	3.4	3.0	20.4
	1982	10 211 808	<——	71.9	13.0	...	...	...	3.2	3.3	8.5
BRAZIL‡	1976	47 800	<——	45.4	10.9	...	...	...	22.8	2.1	18.8
CRUZEIRO	1980	431 194	<——	44.8	7.1	...	...	...	18.9	1.8	27.5
	1982	2 087 281	0.2	40.8	6.6	...	...	...	17.7	2.3	32.4
	1983	3 709 515	<——	44.2	7.2	...	...	...	19.9	1.3	27.4
CHILE	1975	1 321 482	<——	34.9	13.5	7.7	–	5.8	25.2	4.1	22.4
PESO	1980	45 503 514	1.9	42.7	18.0	11.2	–	6.8	33.2	0.4	3.8
	1983	70 243 488	<——	55.4	16.3	11.2	–	5.1	24.5	–	3.8
	1984	81 651 572	<——	54.5	16.7	11.8	–	4.9	24.3	–	4.5
COLOMBIA‡	1980	27 286 015	0.2	44.4	27.0	...	...	...	24.1	4.3	0.1
PESO	1981	49 004 771	<——	47.4	26.9	...	...	...	23.2	0.6	2.0
	1984	108 896 000	<——	43.1	29.3	...	...	...	21.2	1.1	5.3
ECUADOR SUCRE	1980	14 649 139	<——	20.6	18.5	14.7	0.4	3.5	15.6	2.5	42.7
GUYANA‡	1975	45 277	–	44.8	33.3	29.5	–	3.8	15.9	1.5	4.5
DOLLAR	1981	110 827	8.7	31.5	28.5	24.4	1.8	2.3	*12.6	...	18.8
	1983	105 299	7.5	38.3	27.2	22.6	2.0	2.6	15.2	0.1	11.6
	1984	112 361	7.2	34.8	24.0	21.0	1.6	1.4	20.8	0.1	13.1
PARAGUAY‡ GUARANI	1984	12 629 900	–	41.5	25.3	20.7	2.1	2.5	22.2	4.0	7.0
PERU‡	1975	20 970	2.0	40.7	20.8	15.0	–	5.8	1.8	4.4	30.3
SOL	1980	166 040	2.8	45.1	19.9	19.9	–	./.	3.1	3.8	25.2
	1983	873 165	3.3	36.5	23.2	...	...	...	1.9	4.8	30.4

COUNTRY CURRENCY / PAYS MONNAIE / PAIS MONEDA	YEAR / ANNEE / AÑO	TOTAL / TOTAL / TOTAL (000)	PRE-PRIMARY / PRE-PRIMAIRE / PRE-PRIMARIA (%)	1ST LEVEL / 1ER DEGRE / 1ER GRADO (%)	SECOND LEVEL / SECOND DEGRE / SEGUNDO GRADO: TOTAL / TOTAL / TOTAL (%)	GENERAL / GENERAL / GENERAL (%)	TEACHER TRAINING / NORMAL / NORMAL (%)	VOCATIONAL / TECHNIQUE / TECNICA (%)	3RD LEVEL / 3EME DEGRE / 3ER GRADO (%)	OTHER TYPES / AUTRES TYPES / OTROS TIPOS (%)	NOT DISTRIBUTED / NON REPARTIES / SIN DISTRIBUCION (%)
		(1)	(2)	(3)	(4)	(5)	(6)	(7)	(8)	(9)	(10)
	1984	1 892 284	3.5	34.1	20.4	...	...	...	2.4	5.2	34.3
SURINAME GUILDER	1980	105 193	–	64.0	8.4	6.1	0.6	1.6	7.4	1.1	19.1
URUGUAY PESO	1980	1 926 769	–	48.4	33.2	20.4	–	12.7	16.1	2.3	–
VENEZUELA‡ BOLIVAR	1975	5 965 747	<——	22.1	18.4	11.4	0.5	6.5	37.0	1.4	21.0
	1980	11 052 734	3.6	17.5	15.0	9.0	0.6	5.5	39.2	4.6	20.2
	1982	14 284 337	5.9	27.9	9.5	...	...	...	43.1	4.7	8.9
	1983	16 758 800	5.9	28.2	10.0	6.2	0.6	3.2	42.6	4.8	8.4
ASIA											
AFGHANISTAN AFGHANI	1974	1 142 630		38.3	34.0	22.3	6.5	5.3	17.7	–	9.9
	1980	2 886 301	1.6	41.9	22.3	14.3	3.2	4.8	18.4	4.8	11.0
	1981	2 891 136	1.6	42.3	20.7	15.6	–	5.1	21.9	4.7	8.8
	1982	2 191 353	1.7	43.2	22.0	15.9	–	6.1	19.3	4.8	9.0
BANGLADESH‡ TAKA	1975	929 862	–	57.0	16.5	...	...	...	17.4	9.1	–
	1980	2 010 009	–	45.3	29.2	19.8	0.5	8.8	23.0	0.0	2.5
	1983	3 626 348	–	45.8	30.8	28.4	0.2	2.2	20.8	0.0	2.6
	1984	4 932 264	–	46.2	30.1	21.9	0.2	8.0	19.1	3.6	0.9
BRUNEI DARUSSALAM DOLLAR	1975	47 354	–	33.0	53.2	36.2	10.4	6.5	8.9	3.3	1.6
	1980	114 917	–	31.4	46.0	30.4	8.6	7.1	16.7	3.2	2.6
	1981	143 926	–	32.0	44.9	30.2	7.3	7.3	17.9	4.2	1.0
	1982	148 330	–	33.2	47.9	31.4	7.4	9.1	13.5	4.4	1.0
CHINA YUAN	1975	4 826 000	<——	<——	85.2	...	...	...	14.8	...	–
	1980	9 418 000	<——	<——	79.7	...	...	...	20.3	...	–
	1981	10 248 000	<——	<——	78.3	...	...	...	21.7	...	–
	1982	11 578 000	<——	<——	79.4	...	...	...	20.6	...	–
CYPRUS‡ POUND	1975	10 325	0.5	42.7	48.8	40.3	–	8.5	3.4	2.7	1.9
	1980	25 452	2.5	35.4	50.5	41.5	–	9.0	4.1	4.0	3.5
	1982	37 835	2.7	34.3	51.5	42.2	–	9.3	3.7	4.0	3.7
	1983	42 181	3.2	34.3	51.5	42.4	–	9.1	3.7	4.2	3.1
DEMOCRATIC YEMEN‡ DINAR	1976	5 288	1.3	73.0	——>	...	...	...	2.5	0.6	22.7
	1980	17 461	1.6	63.2	——>	...	...	...	11.6	...	23.6
HONG KONG DOLLAR	1975	1 144 538	–	48.7	26.3	20.4	1.4	4.4	20.7	3.5	0.9
	1980	3 036 139	–	33.7	35.7	33.4	1.3	1.0	24.6	6.1	–
	1983	5 348 983	0.3	31.2	36.7	31.4	1.1	4.2	24.9	5.5	1.5
	1984	6 189 691	0.1	31.4	37.9	33.0	1.2	3.7	25.1	4.6	0.9
INDIA RUPEE	1975	20 852 100	<——	40.0	26.6	...	...	...	12.1	2.0	19.3
	1980	37 461 638	<——	36.9	24.2	...	...	...	13.5	3.0	22.4
IRAN, ISLAMIC REPUBLIC OF RIAL	1976	230 748 564	1.4	19.0	19.8	13.1	4.0	2.7	43.1	–	16.7
	1980	440 298 000	2.0	41.7	38.1	18.6	13.1	6.4	7.1	3.8	7.4
	1983	452 014 000	1.4	38.5	34.0	28.5	1.3	4.2	17.9	0.7	7.5
	1984	462 785 000	1.3	41.1	35.6	29.9	1.6	4.1	11.8	3.0	7.3
IRAQ DINAR	1976	155 763	<——	45.3	16.2	...	...	...	18.1	1.5	18.9
	1979	*306 000	<——	*40.5	*18.9	*15.1	*0.1	*3.7	*22.6	*14.4	*3.6
ISRAEL SHEKEL	1975	464 100	6.1	32.7	25.5	...	...	...	30.1	0.8	4.8
	1980	8 182 000	6.6	33.7	29.2	...	...	...	24.8	1.5	4.1
	1981	18 290 000	7.0	33.3	29.8	24.5	–	5.3	24.0	1.8	4.0
	1982	44 845 000	7.7	33.0	28.8	23.8	–	5.0	25.0	1.6	3.9
JAPAN‡ YEN	1975	5 826 604	1.3	39.1	37.2	...	...	...	10.2	5.3	6.9
	1980	9 416 591	1.3	38.2	34.6	...	...	...	11.1	6.8	8.0
	1981	10 174 793	1.3	37.9	34.6	...	...	...	11.0	7.0	8.3
	1982	10 376 852	1.3	37.7	35.1	...	...	...	10.5	7.4	8.1
JORDAN‡ DINAR	1975	13 900	–	<——	85.8	81.7	–	4.1	4.1	2.1	8.0
	1980	50 543	–	<——	75.1	72.8	–	2.4	22.8	1.3	0.7
	1983	79 530	–	<——	66.4	64.9	–	1.5	32.9	0.7	–
	1984	82 655	–	<——	67.1	65.5	–	1.6	32.4	0.6	–
KOREA, REPUBLIC OF‡ WON	1975	163 800	–	62.4	25.5	...	...	...	12.2	–	–
	1980	1 158 967	–	49.9	33.2	...	...	...	8.7	0.1	8.2
	1983	2 231 377	0.4	51.4	37.0	29.9	0.1	7.0	10.9	0.2	0.1
	1984	2 501 253	0.4	48.8	38.1	31.5	–	6.6	12.3	0.3	0.0
KUWAIT DINAR	1976	113 750	5.5	26.8	35.8	...	...	...	16.0	2.7	13.2
	1980	203 758	6.3	29.5	41.9	...	...	...	16.5	4.1	1.6
	1983	296 966	6.7	25.3	42.5	...	...	<——	17.9	3.9	3.7
	1984	317 386	6.7	68.7	——>	...	...	<——	17.3	3.6	3.8

4.3 Public current expenditure by level of education
Dépenses publiques ordinaires par degrés d'enseignement
Gastos públicos ordinarios por grados de enseñanza

COUNTRY / CURRENCY PAYS / MONNAIE PAIS / MONEDA	YEAR ANNEE AÑO	TOTAL TOTAL TOTAL (000)	PRE-PRIMARY PRE-PRIMAIRE PRE-PRIMARIA (%)	1ST LEVEL 1ER DEGRE 1ER GRADO (%)	SECOND LEVEL / SECOND DEGRE / SEGUNDO GRADO TOTAL TOTAL TOTAL (%)	GENERAL GENERAL GENERAL (%)	TEACHER TRAINING NORMAL NORMAL (%)	VOCATIONAL TECHNIQUE TECNICA (%)	3RD LEVEL 3EME DEGRE 3ER GRADO (%)	OTHER TYPES AUTRES TYPES OTROS TIPOS (%)	NOT DISTRIBUTED NON REPARTIES SIN DISTRIBUCION (%)
		(1)	(2)	(3)	(4)	(5)	(6)	(7)	(8)	(9)	(10)
MALAYSIA	1980	2 575 488	–	35.0	34.0	28.0	3.4	2.7	12.4	2.0	16.5
RINGGIT	1982	3 473 997	–	33.6	34.0	...	...	...	14.0	0.2	18.1
	1984	3 676 580	–	39.7	39.1	...	...	...	14.0	0.1	7.1
PENINSULAR MALAYSIA	1975	992 192	–	41.4	33.8	32.7	...	1.1	13.1	0.2	11.5
RINGGIT	1980	2 225 908	–	33.2	31.9	27.0	3.4	1.6	14.4	0.3	20.2
	1982	2 988 685	–	30.8	32.2	26.8	3.8	1.6	16.3	0.2	20.5
	1984	3 179 989	–	37.6	38.4	32.6	4.2	1.6	16.2	0.1	7.7
SABAH	1975	89 559	–	49.1	45.6	39.3	5.1	1.1	–	–	5.3
RINGGIT	1980	145 350	–	50.6	40.8	35.1	4.3	1.4	–	–	8.6
	1982	185 728	–	50.3	39.7	34.7	2.9	2.1	–	–	10.0
	1983	183 287	–	51.0	39.6	34.9	2.4	2.3	–	–	9.5
SARAWAK	1975	74 491	–	56.2	38.8	35.0	3.3	0.5	–	0.4	4.7
RINGGIT	1980	204 230	–	44.2	52.3	33.6	3.3	15.4	–	–	3.5
	1982	299 584	–	50.9	49.1	...	...	...	–	0.0	–
	1984	313 304	–	54.7	45.3	...	...	...	–	–	–
NEPAL‡	1975	245 990	–	48.8	——>	...	...	...	40.7	1.5	9.0
RUPEE	1980	429 681	–	58.8	——>	...	...	...	35.0	2.1	4.2
	1981	568 896	–	55.8	——>	...	...	...	35.6	4.0	4.7
	1982	839 902	–	48.6	——>	...	...	...	44.2	3.1	4.1
PAKISTAN	1975	1 731 089	–	41.1	30.3	19.9	1.3	9.1	17.2	–	11.5
RUPEE	1980	3 378 591	–	39.4	31.0	22.6	1.3	7.2	*19.7	–	*9.8
	1981	3 914 601	–	38.9	32.6	21.8	1.3	9.5	19.7	–	8.8
	1982	4 529 003	–	38.3	32.2	21.4	1.2	9.5	20.1	–	9.4
PHILIPPINES‡	1976	2 266 373	–	65.7	6.7	...	...	...	22.4	–	5.3
PESO	1980	4 022 850	–	61.4	15.7	...	...	...	22.1	0.1	0.7
	1983	5 996 256	–	62.7	10.2	...	...	...	22.7	0.4	4.0
	1984	6 284 788	–	63.5	10.0	...	...	...	22.5	0.4	3.6
SINGAPORE	1975	339 870	–	38.1	34.3	26.2	–	8.0	17.6	6.4	3.7
DOLLAR	1980	587 469	–	35.8	41.1	36.1	–	5.1	17.1	3.1	3.0
	1981	712 733	–	33.9	39.8	34.4	–	5.5	20.2	2.8	3.3
	1982	983 750	–	34.3	34.4	29.1	0.5	4.8	26.4	1.7	3.2
SRI LANKA	1975	682 680	–	<——	84.5	81.9	1.5	1.1	6.5	0.0	9.0
RUPEE	1978	959 025	–	<——	86.1	84.8	1.3	–	8.7	0.1	5.1
SYRIAN ARAB REPUBLIC‡	1975	623 400	–	38.4	30.0	26.4	0.6	3.0	25.8	0.3	5.6
POUND	1980	1 889 573	–	38.8	28.5	25.6	0.4	2.4	32.7	0.1	–
	1983	3 662 191	–	40.5	22.7	17.8	0.6	4.3	33.3	0.2	3.3
	1984	3 849 383	–	39.0	23.5	18.8	——>	4.7	33.4	0.6	3.5
THAILAND‡	1975	7 775 347	0.6	62.5	16.2	9.4	2.5	4.3	11.1	2.0	7.7
BAHT	1980	15 867 328	0.7	57.8	16.7	15.0	–	1.8	19.3	3.6	1.9
	1982	24 575 384	<——	61.1	21.1	14.5	–	6.6	14.5	1.9	1.5
	1983	28 127 463	<——	60.2	21.1	15.6	–	5.4	13.8	4.8	0.2
TURKEY	1980	98 592 809	–	43.7	22.9	16.0	1.0	5.9	28.3	2.3	2.8
LIRA	1983	324 182 424	<——	41.5	28.0	18.5	0.9	8.5	22.6	4.6	3.3
	1984	382 385 000	<——	46.8	21.8	11.2	0.8	9.9	23.7	3.5	4.2
EUROPE											
ANDORRA‡	1975	41 315	–	69.4	26.6	26.6	–	–	2.0	1.9	–
PESETA	1982	495 836	13.3	24.3	28.5	...	...	...	1.0	2.7	30.3
AUSTRIA	1975	29 366 500	1.2	23.0	50.8	33.6	1.4	15.8	14.7	6.1	4.1
SCHILLING	1980	46 955 400	6.1	17.9	53.2	29.0	1.6	22.6	14.5	4.4	3.8
	1983	63 476 700	5.8	15.5	49.8	26.4	1.5	21.9	14.6	3.9	10.4
	1984	66 453 600	5.8	17.7	47.1	28.5	0.4	18.2	16.2	3.9	93
BELGIUM‡	1975	131 906 200	<——	25.5	47.7	...	...	...	15.3	4.4	7.1
FRANC	1980	206 226 600	<——	25.3	47.3	...	...	...	17.3	6.4	3.7
	1983	243 807 200	<——	24.3	46.5	...	...	...	17.1	7.2	4.9
	1984	247 337 900	<——	25.1	47.8	...	...	...	16.2	7.3	3.7
BULGARIA	1975	725 259	18.5	45.4	——>	...	...	15.6	12.9	23.2	–
LEV	1980	1 097 806	19.7	45.3	——>	...	...	14.9	13.6	21.4	–
	1983	1 367 567	<——	65.3	——>	...	...	...	12.1	22.5	–
	1984	1 480 646	19.3	46.7	——>	...	...	...	12.0	22.0	–
CZECHOSLOVAKIA	1975	17 288 021	9.5	41.2	16.0	2.9	<——	13.1	19.1	14.0	0.2
KORUNA	1980	21 801 883	12.3	40.9	14.2	2.9	<——	11.3	16.1	16.2	0.2
	1983	24 495 059	11.8	43.6	14.1	3.0	<——	11.0	14.3	16.1	0.2
	1984	25 814 818	11.3	43.3	13.6	3.0	<——	10.6	14.8	16.3	0.6
DENMARK	1975	146 000 000	<——	71.0	——>	...	...	...	20.8	8.1	–
KRONE	1980	221 880 000	<——	53.5	18.6	...	...	...	17.6	6.0	4.4

COUNTRY CURRENCY / PAYS MONNAIE / PAIS MONEDA	YEAR / ANNEE / AÑO	TOTAL / TOTAL / TOTAL (000)	PRE-PRIMARY / PRE-PRIMAIRE / PRE-PRIMARIA (%)	1ST LEVEL / 1ER DEGRE / 1ER GRADO (%)	SECOND LEVEL / SECOND DEGRE / SEGUNDO GRADO: TOTAL / TOTAL / TOTAL (%)	SECOND LEVEL: GENERAL / GENERAL / GENERAL (%)	SECOND LEVEL: TEACHER TRAINING / NORMAL / NORMAL (%)	SECOND LEVEL: VOCATIONAL / TECHNIQUE / TECNICA (%)	3RD LEVEL / 3EME DEGRE / 3ER GRADO (%)	OTHER TYPES / AUTRES TYPES / OTROS TIPOS (%)	NOT DISTRIBUTED / NON REPARTIES / SIN DISTRIBUCION (%)
		(1)	(2)	(3)	(4)	(5)	(6)	(7)	(8)	(9)	(10)
FINLAND MARKKA	1975	5 596 511	–	46.1	31.3	13.5	0.1	17.7	12.8	7.6	2.3
	1980	9 565 205	–	31.8	40.7	26.6	0.0	14.1	18.9	8.0	0.6
	1982	12 545 795	–	29.4	41.2	26.9	0.0	14.3	18.1	10.8	0.5
	1983	14 222 522	–	29.5	41.9	26.1	0.0	15.8	17.2	10.9	0.5
FRANCE‡ FRANC	1975	66 873 000	7.8	23.0	38.7	...	...	...	13.4	11.7	5.4
	1980	131 441 000	8.4	22.0	40.3	...	...	...	12.5	11.0	5.8
	1981	163 300 000	8.4	21.9	40.9	...	...	...	12.9	10.5	5.4
	1982	194 708 000	8.4	21.4	41.1	...	...	...	12.6	11.2	5.5
GERMAN DEMOCRATIC REPUBLIC DDR MARK	1975	8 276 353	8.1	<——	57.4	49.0	–	8.4	20.8	–	13.7
	1980	9 836 257	7.2	<——	54.8	45.7	–	9.1	20.5	–	17.5
	1983	11 118 900	11.2	<——	53.7	45.2	–	8.5	21.6	–	13.4
	1984	11 838 400	11.9	<——	56.2	47.1	–	9.1	21.3	–	10.6
GERMANY, FED. REP. OF DEUTSCHE MARK	1975	42 456 700	3.0	18.2	50.2	41.9	–	8.3	17.5	6.3	4.7
	1980	60 557 900	3.5	16.0	53.6	...	...	...	15.1	7.3	4.5
	1982	66 078 100	3.7	15.3	54.0	...	...	...	14.8	7.5	4.7
	1983	67 382 800	3.9	15.1	53.7	...	...	...	14.6	7.9	4.7
GIBRALTAR POUND STERLING	1975	909	–	47.6	36.6	31.7	–	5.0	10.3	0.6	4.8
	1980	3 305	–	47.6	40.8	31.7	6.2	2.9	5.6	0.5	5.6
	1982	4 083	–	50.3	37.8	33.5	0.8	3.5	6.0	0.6	5.4
	1983	4 502	–	49.8	35.9	33.2	0.3	2.3	6.7	2.4	5.2
GREECE DRACHMA	1975	12 336 357	3.2	36.7	28.6	22.8	–	5.8	20.0	0.3	11.2
	1979	29 950 864	4.8	36.9	36.8	29.4	–	7.3	21.0	0.6	–
HUNGARY FORINT	1975	16 719 792	11.6	38.0	25.0	6.7	–	18.2	21.4	3.8	0.2
	1981	32 654 689	14.1	38.3	21.6	6.2	–	15.4	19.3	6.5	0.3
	1983	45 205 888	11.8	38.0	24.0	10.9	–	13.1	20.2	5.7	0.3
	1984	45 725 490	12.5	38.5	18.7	8.6	–	10.1	24.2	6.1	–
IRELAND POUND	1975	199 666	<——	35.9	37.0	24.7	–	12.2	17.7	2.2	7.3
	1980	515 000	8.7	26.1	39.2	26.5	–	12.7	17.6	6.1	2.3
	1982	734 997	<——	36.8	40.3	26.7	–	13.6	17.4	3.4	2.1
	1983	813 873	9.8	28.5	40.8	39.2	–	1.6	17.4	0.2	3.2
ITALY‡ LIRA	1975	5 060 156	4.8	30.0	42.4	29.0	——>	13.4	13.3	3.0	6.4
	1979	11 791 069	6.0	29.2	41.0	23.9	——>	17.0	9.1	0.0	14.8
	1983	28 040 275	5.7	21.3	37.3	21.1	——>	16.2	10.1	0.0	25.5
LUXEMBOURG‡ FRANC	1975	3 517 600	<——	41.9	40.1	26.6	–	13.4	2.3	4.2	11.5
	1980	9 305 300	<——	49.3	29.1	13.7	–	15.4	1.5	19.1	1.0
	1982	12 550 200	<——	55.5	25.4	11.6	–	13.8	1.5	16.7	0.9
	1983	7 900 300	<——	38.9	44.3	20.1	–	24.2	2.5	12.9	1.5
MALTA LIRA	1975	6 881	<——	25.4	49.1	37.8	–	11.2	13.5	1.6	10.5
	1980	12 475	<——	31.4	44.3	33.9	–	10.4	9.3	1.5	13.5
	1983	16 882	<——	28.8	40.2	30.0	–	10.2	8.0	2.8	20.2
	1984	15 545	<——	28.2	44.0	32.3	–	11.8	8.8	3.0	16.1
NETHERLANDS GUILDER	1975	14 881 000	5.7	20.3	36.2	20.0	0.3	15.9	28.3	5.0	4.5
	1980	23 079 000	5.5	19.2	33.8	19.1	0.3	14.4	27.5	8.7	5.3
	1981	23 968 000	5.7	19.2	34.1	19.3	0.3	14.6	26.8	8.9	5.3
	1982	24 484 000	5.4	19.0	35.6	19.7	0.3	15.6	26.4	9.2	4.5
NORWAY KRONE	1975	8 427 000	–	48.8	24.7	11.6	<——	13.1	13.3	10.9	2.3
	1980	16 448 000	–	47.9	24.3	...	...	...	13.6	8.1	6.0
	1982	21 250 000	–	47.1	25.2	...	...	...	13.6	7.9	6.2
	1983	23 522 000	–	46.3	26.8	...	...	...	13.5	7.6	5.9
POLAND ZLOTY	1975	50 449 000	7.0	27.6	23.4	4.3	0.3	18.7	25.4	15.8	0.9
	1980	79 984 000	8.2	28.7	21.0	4.4	...	16.6	23.6	17.8	0.7
	1983	255 298 000	10.0	32.1	18.4	3.8	...	14.6	21.6	17.2	0.7
	1984	333 055 000	10.2	33.4	17.8	3.7	...	14.1	20.0	18.4	0.2
PORTUGAL ESCUDO	1980	45 422 800	0.1	32.4	45.7	...	...	...	10.5	6.0	5.3
	1981	57 032 900	0.2	31.6	47.6	...	...	...	10.4	5.7	4.4
	1982	72 884 100	0.0	31.2	47.7	...	...	...	11.3	5.4	4.4
SAN MARINO‡ LIRA	1975	2 499 565	<——	52.0	33.3	...	...	...	8.2	–	6.5
	1981	7 685 931	<——	60.4	31.6	...	...	...	2.1	2.1	3.8
	1982	9 546 420	23.8	36.5	32.2	...	...	...	1.4	2.3	3.7
	1983	15 358 869	22.8	36.7	33.1	...	...	...	2.5	2.4	2.5
SPAIN PESETA	1976	134 391 000	<——	61.2	17.5	13.2	–	4.2	15.1	2.3	3.9
	1979	295 443 000	3.5	58.9	19.3	14.1	–	5.1	14.0	1.7	2.6
SWEDEN‡ KRONA	1975	19 281 100	–	38.3	13.3	...	...	...	12.3	6.6	29.6
	1980	40 885 700	0.1	44.6	13.6	...	...	...	9.3	16.1	16.4
	1983	49 262 200	0.1	45.9	16.8	...	...	...	8.8	12.3	16.1
	1984	54 190 500	0.1	47.1	20.0	...	...	...	12.8	12.2	7.9

4.3 Public current expenditure by level of education
Dépenses publiques ordinaires par degrés d'enseignement
Gastos públicos ordinarios por grados de enseñanza

COUNTRY CURRENCY	YEAR	TOTAL	PRE-PRIMARY	1ST LEVEL	SECOND LEVEL / SECOND DEGRE / SEGUNDO GRADO				3RD LEVEL	OTHER TYPES	NOT DISTRIBUTED
					TOTAL	GENERAL	TEACHER TRAINING	VOCATIONAL			
PAYS MONNAIE	ANNEE	TOTAL	PRE-PRIMAIRE	1ER DEGRE	TOTAL	GENERAL	NORMAL	TECHNIQUE	3EME DEGRE	AUTRES TYPES	NON REPARTIES
PAIS MONEDA	AÑO	TOTAL (000)	PRE-PRIMARIA (%)	1ER GRADO (%)	TOTAL (%)	GENERAL (%)	NORMAL (%)	TECNICA (%)	3ER GRADO (%)	OTROS TIPOS (%)	SIN DISTRIBUCION (%)
		(1)	(2)	(3)	(4)	(5)	(6)	(7)	(8)	(9)	(10)
SWITZERLAND FRANC	1975	5 978 800	3.2	<——	77.9	54.1	10.3	13.6	17.0	–	1.8
	1980	7 936 800	2.8	<——	73.7	50.4	10.3	13.0	18.6	2.2	2.7
	1982	9 097 100	2.9	<——	73.3	48.8	11.2	13.3	18.6	2.6	2.6
	1983	9 756 600	2.9	<——	73.1	47.8	11.4	13.9	18.7	3.0	2.3
UNITED KINGDOM POUND STERLING	1975	6 292 000	<——	28.5	39.5	...	...	...	20.7	11.3	——>
	1980	12 094 000	<——	26.6	40.1	...	...	...	22.4	10.8	——>
	1982	14 240 000	2.4	23.3	41.2	...	...	...	22.0	11.1	——>
	1983	15 108 000	2.6	22.3	41.5	...	...	...	21.7	11.9	——>
YUGOSLAVIA DINAR	1975	25 515 000	–	74.3	——>	...	–	20.1	15.2	1.7	8.7
	1980	71 514 000	–	73.0	——>	...	–	22.8	18.5	1.8	6.8
	1982	116 886 000	–	74.1	——>	...	–	22.4	17.9	1.5	6.5
	1983	145 149 000	–	73.7	——>	...	–	22.2	17.7	1.9	6.7
OCEANIA											
AUSTRALIA DOLLAR	1980	6 899 000	1.7	<——	67.0	...	...	...	22.6	2.7	6.0
	1982	9 110 000	1.6	<——	61.3	...	...	...	29.5	4.5	3.1
	1983	10 081 000	1.6	<——	60.9	...	...	...	29.4	4.9	3.2
COOK ISLANDS NEW ZEALAND DOLLAR	1981	2 712	1.8	38.9	27.5	...	...	...	4.5	–	27.3
	1984	3 474	2.7	37.2	36.1	...	...	...	5.4	–	18.6
FIJI DOLLAR	1975	24 039	–	43.0	41.6	31.4	5.1	5.1	6.7	–	8.8
	1981	57 758	–	53.0	45.1	36.2	1.7	7.2	1.9	–	–
	1983	73 404	–	51.2	32.7	...	...	...	10.1	–	6.0
KIRIBATI AUSTRALIAN DOLLAR	1974	1 015	–	48.3	35.2	23.4	8.6	3.3	10.6	–	5.9
	1981	2 939	–	37.6	44.8	14.3	6.4	24.2	–	–	17.6
	1982	2 694	–	43.2	36.7	12.8	7.7	16.3	–	–	20.0
NEW CALEDONIA FRENCH FRANC	1981	595 836	–	24.0	75.6	...	...	...	0.4	–	–
	1983	736 197	–	45.3	54.0	...	...	...	0.7	–	–
	1984	835 410	–	45.4	53.9	...	...	...	0.7	–	–
NEW ZEALAND DOLLAR	1975	503 643	1.4	35.6	29.7	24.3	–	5.4	23.4	2.1	7.9
	1980	1 171 226	1.4	35.4	34.8	29.7	5.1	<——	23.2	2.6	2.6
	1983	1 541 429	1.5	38.9	31.2	28.3	2.9	<——	23.9	2.2	2.4
	1984	1 598 765	1.5	38.2	39.1	28.9	2.2	8.0	16.3	2.2	2.6
NIUE NEW ZEALAND DOLLAR	1975	595	0.3	35.1	39.3	...	...	...	–	–	25.2
	1980	755	–	32.2	48.1	...	...	...	–	1.1	18.7
	1981	717	–	30.4	52.0	...	...	...	–	1.3	16.3
	1982	664	–	38.3	37.0	...	...	...	–	–	24.7
SAMOA TALA	1975	1 939	–	65.2	18.8	13.7	2.7	2.4	–	3.5	12.6
	1978	2 701	–	60.6	24.6	...	...	...	–	1.6	13.2
PACIFIC ISLANDS UNITED STATES DOLLAR	1975	21 501	–	30.7	18.9	...	...	...	13.6	3.0	33.9
	1981	26 129	–	27.7	48.3	...	...	...	12.6	6.9	4.6
	1982	27 710	–	29.6	43.7	...	...	...	18.0	5.3	3.4
SOLOMON ISLANDS‡ AUSTRALIAN DOLLAR	1979	3 473	...	44.1	42.2	11.3	9.4	21.5	13.3	0.4	–
TOKELAU NEW ZEALAND DOLLAR	1981	630	1.4	26.8	71.7	...	...	...	–	–	–
	1982	579	1.7	33.2	65.1	...	...	...	–	–	–
TONGA‡ PA'ANGA	1974	692	–	50.0	35.1	23.6	7.4	4.2	1.3	–	13.6
	1980	1 399	–	55.0	25.4	19.4	6.1	–	14.7	–	4.9
	1981	1 892	–	58.3	22.8	16.8	5.6	0.4	12.1	–	6.8
	1983	2 974	–	40.3	43.3	18.6	5.1	19.6	11.9	–	4.4
U.S.S.R.											
U.S.S.R.‡ ROUBLE	1975	23 415 900	21.4	38.2	16.2	./.	./.	16.2	13.2	11.0	–
	1980	28 098 600	23.6	33.9	16.4	./.	./.	16.4	13.8	12.4	–
	1983	30 913 600	24.0	33.2	14.9	./.	./.	14.9	13.5	14.4	–
	1984	31 735 800	23.9	34.0	14.9	./.	./.	14.9	13.5	13.6	–
BYELORUSSIAN S.S.R.‡ ROUBLE	1975	859 300	19.1	40.5	17.7	./.	./.	17.7	13.4	9.3	–
	1980	1 051 300	21.1	35.2	18.0	./.	./.	18.0	13.9	11.8	–
	1983	1 158 000	21.8	34.1	16.9	./.	./.	16.9	14.8	12.3	–
	1984	1 210 100	22.3	34.4	16.8	./.	./.	16.8	13.2	13.4	–
UKRAINIAN S.S.R.‡ ROUBLE	1975	4 312 200	22.9	35.5	16.0	./.	./.	16.0	13.4	12.3	–
	1980	5 114 300	24.8	31.5	16.3	./.	./.	16.3	14.0	13.4	–
	1983	5 391 400	24.9	31.7	15.0	./.	./.	15.0	13.5	14.9	–
	1984	5 487 700	25.0	32.6	15.3	./.	./.	15.3	14.1	13.0	–

AFRICA

Burkina Faso:

E--> For 1975, expenditure on third level also includes a part of scholarships for second level education.

FR-> En 1975, les dépenses relatives au troisième degré comprennent également une partie des bourses d'études pour le second degré.

ESP> En 1975, los gastos relativos al tercer grado incluyen también una parte de las becas de estudios del segundo grado.

Côte d'Ivoire:

E--> For 1975, data include foreign aid.

FR-> Pour 1975, les données comprennent l'aide étrangère.

ESP> En 1975, los datos incluyen la ayuda extranjera.

Djibouti:

E--> For 1982, expenditure of the Ministry of Education only.

FR-> En 1982, dépenses du Ministère de l'Education seulement.

ESP> En 1982, gastos del Ministerio de Educación solamente.

Gambia:

E--> For 1975, only teachers' emoluments are distributed by level of education. All other expenditure is shown in column 10.

FR-> En 1975, seuls les émoluments du personnel enseignant sont distribués par degré d'enseignement. Toutes les autres dépenses sont présentées dans la colonne 10.

ESP> En 1975, solo se distribuyen por grado de enseñanza los emolumentos del personal docente. Todos los otros gastos figuran en la columna 10.

Ghana:

E--> For 1980 and 1981, expenditure on universities is not included.

FR-> En 1980 et 1981, les dépenses des universités ne sont pas incluses.

ESP> En 1980 y 1981, no se incluyen los gastos relativos a las universidades.

Kenya:

E--> Expenditure of the Ministries of Basic Education and Higher Education. For 1980 and 1984, teacher training at the third level is included with second level.

FR-> Dépenses des Ministères de l'Education de base et de l'enseignement supérieur. En 1980 et 1984, l'enseignement normal du troisième degré est inclus avec l'enseignement du second degré.

ESP> Gastos de los Ministerios de Educación de base y de la enseñanza superior. En 1980 y 1984, la enseñanza normal del tercer grado queda incluída en el segundo grado.

Mali:

E--> For 1980 and 1982, scholarships and allocations for study abroad for all levels of education is included with third level education.

FR-> En 1980 et 1982, les bourses et allocations d'études à l'étranger pour tous les degrés d'enseignement sont incluses avec l'enseignement du troisième degré.

ESP> En 1980 y 1982, las becas y los subsidios para los estudios en el extranjero en todos los niveles de enseñanza quedan incluídos en la enseñanza de tercer grado.

Senegal:

E--> For 1981, expenditure of the Ministry of Primary and Secondary Education only.

FR-> En 1981, les données se réfèrent aux dépenses du Ministère des enseignements primaire et secondaire seulement.

ESP> En 1981, los datos se refieren a los gastos del Ministerio de las enseñanzas de primer y segundo grado solamente.

Seychelles:

E--> Expenditure on third level education is not included.

FR-> Les dépenses relatives à l'enseignement du troisième degré ne sont pas incluses.

ESP> No se incluyen los gastos relativos a la enseñanza de tercer grado.

Swaziland:

E--> For 1975, expenditure of the Ministry of Education only.

FR-> En 1975, dépenses du Ministère de l'Education seulement.

ESP> En 1975, gastos del Ministerio de Educación solamente.

Uganda:

E--> Expenditure of the Ministry of Education only.

FR-> Dépenses du Ministère de l'Education seulement.

ESP> Gastos del Ministerio de Educación solamente.

United Republic of Tanzania:

E--> For 1975, data for column 7 are included in column 5.

FR-> En 1975, les données de la colonne 7 sont incluses dans la colonne 5.

ESP> En 1975, los datos de la columna 7 quedan incluídos en la columna 5.

AMERICA, NORTH

Dominican Republic:

E--> For 1980 and 1984, expenditure of the Ministry of Education only.

FR-> En 1980 et 1984, dépenses du Ministère de l'Education seulement.

ESP> En 1980 y 1984, gastos del Ministerio de Educación solamente.

Grenada:

E--> For 1983, expenditure on third level education is not included.

FR-> En 1983, les dépenses relatives à l'enseignement du troisième degré ne sont pas incluses.

ESP> En 1983, no se incluyen los gastos relativos a la enseñanza de tercer grado.

Haiti:

E--> For 1982 and 1983, teacher training at the second level is included with first level.

FR-> En 1982 et 1983, l'enseignement normal du second degré est inclus avec le premier degré.

ESP> En 1982 y 1983, la enseñanza normal del segundo grado queda incluída en el primer grado.

Jamaica:

E--> Except for 1983, expenditure of the Ministry of Education only.

FR-> Sauf en 1983, dépenses du Ministère de l'Education seulement.

ESP> Salvo por 1983, gastos del Ministerio de Educación solamente.

Mexico:

E--> Expenditure of the Ministry of Education only.

FR-> Dépenses du Ministère de l'Education seulement.

ESP> Gastos del Ministerio de Educación solamente.

St. Lucia:

E--> For 1982, expenditure of the Ministry of Education only.

FR-> En 1982, dépenses du Ministère de l'Education seulement.

ESP> En 1982, gastos del Ministerio de Educación solamente.

United States:

E--> For 1981, capital expenditure is included.

FR-> En 1981, les dépenses en capital sont incluses.

ESP> En 1981, se incluyen los gastos de capital.

AMERICA, SOUTH

Bolivia:

E--> For 1981 and 1982, expenditure on universities is not included.

FR-> En 1981 et 1982, les dépenses des universités ne sont pas incluses.

ESP> En 1981 y 1982, no se incluyen los gastos de las universidades.

Brazil:

E--> Figures in column 1 are in millions. Data include capital expenditure.

FR-> Les chiffres de la colonne 1 sont exprimés en millions. Les données comprennent les dépenses en capital.

ESP> Las cifras de la columna 1 se expresan en millones. Los datos incluyen los gastos de capital.

Colombia:

E--> Expenditure of the Ministry of Education only.

FR-> Dépenses du Ministère de l'Education seulement.

ESP> Gastos del Ministerio de Educación solamente.

Guyana:

E--> For 1975, expenditure of the Ministry of Education only.

FR-> En 1975, dépenses du Ministère de l'Education seulement.

ESP> En 1975, gastos del Ministerio de Educación solamente.

Paraguay:

E--> Expenditure of the Ministry of Education only.

FR-> Dépenses du Ministère de l'Education seulement.

ESP> Gastos del Ministerio de Educación solamente.

Peru:

E--> Figures in column 1 are in millions. Transfers to universities and to other types of institutions as well as some types of pensions and staff benefits are included in column 10.

FR-> Les chiffres de la colonne 1 sont exprimés en millions. Les transferts aux universités et à certains autres établissements ainsi que différents types de pensions et d'indemnités du personnel sont incluses dans la colonne 10.

ESP> Las cifras de la columna 1 se expresan en millones. Los datos no incluyen las transferencias a las universidades y otros establecimientos así como diferentes tipos de pensiones y indemnizaciones del personal quedan incluídos en la columna 10.

Venezuela:

E--> From 1980 to 1983, expenditure of the central government only.

FR-> De 1980 à 1983, dépenses du gouvernement central seulement.

ESP> De 1980 a 1983, gastos del gobierno central solamente.

ASIA

Bangladesh:

E--> Expenditure on intermediate colleges and intermediate sections of degree colleges (grades XI and XII) is included with third level education. From 1980 to 1984, expenditure of the Ministry of Education only.

FR-> Les dépenses des collèges intermédiaires et des sections intermédiaires des 'degree colleges' (XI ème et XII ème années d'études) sont classées avec l'enseignement du troisième degré. De 1980 à 1984, dépenses du Ministère de l'Education seulement.

ESP> Los gastos de los colegios intermediarios y de las secciones

Bangladesh: (Cont):
intermediarias de los 'degree colleges' (XI y XII años de estudios), se clasifican con los de la enseñanza de tercer grado. De 1980 a 1984 gastos del Ministerio de Educación solamente.

Cyprus:
E--> Expenditure by the Office of Greek Education only.
FR-> Dépenses du bureau grec de l'Education seulement.
ESP> Gastos del servicio griego de Educación solamente.

Democratic Yemen:
E--> For 1980, data include capital expenditure.
FR-> En 1980, les données comprennent les dépenses en capital.
ESP> En 1980, los datos incluyen los gastos de capital.

Japan:
E--> Figures in column 1 are in millions. Data do not include public subsidies to private education.
FR-> Les chiffres de la colonne 1 sont exprimés en millions. Les données ne comprennent pas les subventions publiques à l'enseignement privé.
ESP> Las cifras de la columna 1 se expresan en millones. Los datos no incluyen las subvenciones públicas a la enseñanza privada.

Jordan:
E--> For 1975, expenditure on universities is not included.
FR-> En 1975, les dépenses des universités ne sont pas incluses.
ESP> En 1975, no se incluyen los gastos de las universidades.

Korea, Republic of:
E--> Figures in column 1 are in millions.
FR-> Les chiffres de la colonne 1 sont exprimés en millions.
ESP> Las cifras de la columna 1 se expresan en millones.

Nepal:
E--> Data refer to 'regular' and 'development' expenditure.
FR-> Les données se réfèrent aux dépenses 'ordinaires' et 'de développement'.
ESP> Los datos se refieren a los gastos 'ordinarios' y 'de desarrollo'.

Philippines:
E--> For 1976, capital expenditure on state universities and colleges is included.
FR-> En 1976, les dépenses en capital des universités et collèges d'Etat sont incluses.
ESP> En 1976, se incluyen los gastos de capital de las universidades y los colegios del Estado.

Syrian Arab Republic:
E--> Capital expenditure for education at the third level is included.
FR-> Les dépenses en capital de l'enseignement du troisième degré sont incluses.
ESP> Se incluyen los gastos de capital relativos a la enseñanza de tercer grado.

Thailand:
E--> For 1975 and 1980, public subsidies to private education at the first and second levels are included with first level.
FR-> En 1975 et 1980, les subventions publiques à l'enseignement privé des premier et second degrés sont incluses avec le premier degré.
ESP> En 1975 y 1980, las subvenciones públicas a la enseñanza privada de primer y segundo grado quedan incluídas en el primer grado.

EUROPE

Andorra:
E--> For 1975, capital expenditure is included.
FR-> En 1975, les dépenses en capital sont incluses.
ESP> En 1975, se incluyen los gastos de capital.

Belgium:
E--> Expenditure of the Ministry of Education only.
FR-> Dépenses du Ministère de l'Education seulement.
ESP> Gastos del Ministerio de Educación solamente.

France:
E--> France metropolitan.
FR-> France métropolitaine.
ESP> Francia metropolitana.

Italy:
E--> Figures in column 1 are in millions.

Italy: (Cont):
FR-> Les chiffres de la colonne 1 sont exprimés en millions.
ESP> Las cifras de la columna 1 se expresan en millones.

Luxembourg:
E--> For 1975 and 1983, expenditure of the Central Governme only.
FR-> En 1975 et 1983, dépenses du gouvernement cent seulement.
ESP> En 1975 y 1983, gastos del gobierno central solamente.

San Marino:
E--> Data in column 8 refer to scholarships for the students at t second and third levels of education.
FR-> Les données de la colonne 8 se réfèrent aux bourses pour étudiants des enseignements du second et du troisième degré.
ESP> Los datos de la columna 8 se refieren a las becas para l estudiantes de las enseñanzas de segundo y tercer grado.

Sweden:
E--> Expenditure on first level (column 3) refers to compulso education which covers six grades of primary education and the first thr grades of secondary education. Expenditure on second level educatio therefore, covers only the last three grades (upper secondary school).
FR-> Les dépenses relatives au premier degré (colonne 3) se réfère à l'enseignement obligatoire qui comprend six années de l'enseigneme primaire et les trois premières années de l'enseignement secondaire. L dépenses relatives à l'enseignement du second degré, donc, comprennent que les trois dernières années (école seconda supérieure).
ESP> Los gastos relativos al primer grado (columna 3) se refieren a enseñanza obligatoria que incluye seis años de la enseñanza primaria y l tres primeros años de la enseñanza secundaria. Los gastos relativos segundo grado, por consiguiente, incluyen solamente los tres ultimos añ (escuela secundaria superior).

OCEANIA:

Solomon Islands:
E--> Data include foreign aid.
FR-> Les données incluent l'aide étrangère.
ESP> Los gastos incluyen la ayuda extranjera.

Tonga:
E--> For 1974, expenditure of the Ministry of of Education only.
FR-> En 1974, dépenses du Ministère de l'Education seulement.
ESP> En 1974, gastos del Ministerio de Educación solamente.

U.S.S.R.

U.S.S.R.:
E--> Expenditure on pre-primary education includes plays centre General education at the second level is included with first level (column 3 Total second level (column 4) therefore, refers to technical and vocation education only (column 7) which includes teacher-training (column 6 Special education is included partly in column 3 and partly in column 7
FR-> Les dépenses de l'enseignement préprimaire comprennent l garderies d'enfants. L'enseignement général du second degré est incl avec l'enseignement du premier degré (colonne 3). Le total d l'enseignement du second degré (colonne 4) se réfère donc uniquement l'enseignement technique et professionnel (colonne 7) qui comprer l'enseignement normal (colonne 6). L'enseignement spécial est compris e partie dans la colonne 3 et en partie dans la colonne 7.
ESP> Los gastos de la enseñanza preprimaria comprenden la guarderías. La enseñanza general de segundo grado se incluye en enseñanza de primer grado (columna 3). El total de la enseñanza de segund grado (columna 4) se refiere pues unicamente a la enseñanza tecnica profesional (columna 7) que comprende la enseñanza normal (columna 6 La educación especial se distribuye entre las columnas 3 y 7.

Byelorussian S.S.R.:
E--> See the note for the U.S.S.R.
FR-> Voir la note pour l'U.R.S.S.
ESP> Véase la nota de la U.R.S.S.

Ukrainian S.S.R.:
E--> See the note for the U.S.S.R.
FR-> Voir la note pour l'U.R.S.S.
ESP> Véase la nota de la U.R.S.S.

4.4 Public current expenditure on education: distribution by level of education and purpose

Dépenses publiques ordinaires afférentes à l'enseignement: répartition par degré d'enseignement et selon leur destination

Gastos públicos ordinarios destinados a la educación: distribución por grado de enseñanza y según su destino

TOTAL CURRENT EXPENDITURE = TOTAL DES DEPENSES ORDINAIRES / TOTAL DE GASTOS ORDINARIOS
ADMINISTRATION = ADMINISTRATION / ADMINISTRACION
TEACHERS' EMOLUMENTS = EMOLUMENTS DU PERSONNEL ENSEIGNANT / EMOLUMENTOS DEL PERSONAL DOCENTE
TEACHING MATERIALS = MATERIEL POUR L'ENSEIGNEMENT / MATERIAL EDUCATIVO
SCHOLARSHIPS = BOURSES D'ETUDES / BECAS DE ESTUDIOS
WELFARE SERVICES = SERVICES SOCIAUX / SERVICIOS SOCIALES
NOT DISTRIBUTED = NON REPARTIES / SIN DISTRIBUCION

NUMBER OF COUNTRIES AND TERRITORIES PRESENTED IN THIS TABLE: 100

NOMBRE DE PAYS ET DE TERRITOIRES PRESENTES DANS CE TABLEAU: 100

NUMERO DE PAISES Y DE TERRITORIOS PRESENTADOS EN ESTE CUADRO: 100

COUNTRY / CURRENCY PAYS / MONNAIE PAIS / MONEDA	YEAR ANNEE AÑO	PURPOSE DESTINATION DESTINO	TOTAL CURRENT EXPENDITURE TOTAL DES DEPENSES ORDINAIRES TOTAL DE GASTOS ORDINARIOS (000)	PRE-PRIMARY PRE-PRIMAIRE PRE-PRIMARIA (000)	FIRST LEVEL PREMIER DEGRE PRIMER GRADO (000)	SECOND LEVEL SECOND DEGRE SEGUNDO GRADO (000)	THIRD LEVEL TROISIEME DEGRE TERCER GRADO (000)	OTHER TYPES AND NOT DISTRIBUTED AUTRES TYPES ET NON REPARTIES OTROS TIPOS Y SIN DISTRIBUCION (000)
			(1)	(2)	(3)	(4)	(5)	(6)
AFRICA								
ALGERIA DINAR	1980	TOTAL	8 259 100	–	2 349 700	2 077 700	1 425 900	2 405 800
		TEACHERS' EMOLUMENTS	5 256 100	–	2 303 500	1 716 900	400 800	834 900
		TEACHING MATERIALS	25 100	–	25 100	–	–	–
		SCHOLARSHIPS	733 800	–	5 500	194 500	415 700	118 100
		WELFARE SERVICES	246 400	–	2 000	–	244 400	–
		NOT DISTRIBUTED	1 997 700	–	13 600	166 300	365 000	1 452 800
BOTSWANA‡ PULA	1984	TOTAL	75 572	–	32 670	25 850	7 029	10 023
		ADMINISTRATION	13 713	–	1 376	8 544	–	3 793
		TEACHERS' EMOLUMENTS	39 268	–	27 003	12 120	145	–
		TEACHING MATERIALS	3 935	–	2 804	1 116	–	15
		SCHOLARSHIPS	7 186	–	–	302	6 884	–
		NOT DISTRIBUTED	11 470	–	1 487	3 768	–	6 215
BURKINA FASO FRANC C.F.A.	1984	TOTAL	11 962 276	–	4 224 563	2 413 568	3 291 012	2 033 133
		ADMINISTRATION	408 236	–	–	332 161	76 075	–
		TEACHERS' EMOLUMENTS	8 137 377	–	4 187 586	1 723 815	371 030	1 854 946
		TEACHING MATERIALS	119 899	–	35 637	29 437	15 791	39 034
		SCHOLARSHIPS	2 812 704	–	–	273 144	2 400 407	139 153
		WELFARE SERVICES	201 942	–	–	54 661	147 281	–
		NOT DISTRIBUTED	282 118	–	1 340	350	280 428	–
BURUNDI‡ FRANC	1981	TOTAL	2 504 253	–	1 023 330	798 771	627 257	54 895
		ADMINISTRATION	16 624	–	–	–	–	16 624
		TEACHERS' EMOLUMENTS	1 957 518	–	1 006 480	541 290	375 071	34 677
		TEACHING MATERIALS	32 300	–	14 000	18 300	–	–
		SCHOLARSHIPS	251 866	–	–	–	251 866	–
		WELFARE SERVICES	227 581	–	–	227 581	–	–
		NOT DISTRIBUTED	18 364	–	2 850	11 600	320	3 594
COMOROS FRANC C.F.A	1982	TOTAL	1 773 956	89 978	646 358	354 724	422 054	260 842
		ADMINISTRATION	153 276	–	–	–	19 035	134 241
		TEACHERS' EMOLUMENTS	957 624	89 978	630 310	237 336	–	–
		TEACHING MATERIALS	69 700	–	2 000	6 500	1 200	60 000
		SCHOLARSHIPS	545 247	–	–	85 000	393 646	66 601
		NOT DISTRIBUTED	48 109	–	14 048	25 888	8 173	–
CONGO‡ FRANC C.F.A	1980	TOTAL	21 517 291	<——	7 706 503	6 255 736	5 238 676	2 316 376
		TEACHERS' EMOLUMENTS	15 228 932	<——	7 659 942	5 249 410	904 283	1 415 297
		TEACHING MATERIALS	1 175 380	<——	6 938	110 685	559 910	497 847
		SCHOLARSHIPS	4 093 374	<——	39 623	620 517	3 426 257	6 977
		WELFARE SERVICES	253 124	–	–	253 124	–	–
		NOT DISTRIBUTED	766 481	–	–	22 000	348 226	396 255

4.4 Public current expenditure by level and purpose
Dépenses publiques ordinaires par degré d'enseignement et destination
Gastos públicos ordinarios por grado de enseñanza y destino

COUNTRY CURRENCY PAYS MONNAIE PAIS MONEDA	YEAR ANNEE AÑO	PURPOSE DESTINATION DESTINO	TOTAL CURRENT EXPENDITURE TOTAL DES DEPENSES ORDINAIRES TOTAL DE GASTOS ORDINARIOS (000)	PRE-PRIMARY PRE-PRIMAIRE PRE-PRIMARIA (000)	FIRST LEVEL PREMIER DEGRE PRIMER GRADO (000)	SECOND LEVEL SECOND DEGRE SEGUNDO GRADO (000)	THIRD LEVEL TROISIEME DEGRE TERCER GRADO (000)	OTHER TYPES AND NOT DISTRIBUTED AUTRES TYPES ET NON REPARTIES OTROS TIPOS Y SIN DISTRIBUCION (000)
			(1)	(2)	(3)	(4)	(5)	(6)
EGYPT‡ POUND	1981	TOTAL	722 108	<——	<——	490 925	231 183	–
		TEACHERS' EMOLUMENTS	584 924	<——	<——	424 900	160 024	–
		TEACHING MATERIALS	4 346	<——	<——	2 596	1 750	–
		NOT DISTRIBUTED	132 838	<——	<——	63 429	69 409	–
ETHIOPIA‡ BIRR	1981	TOTAL	210 098	–	115 716	73 794	–	20 588
		ADMINISTRATION	17 047	–	1 603	2 281	–	13 163
		TEACHERS' EMOLUMENTS	175 267	–	110 150	64 283	–	834
		TEACHING MATERIALS	12 286	–	2 917	4 408	–	4 961
		WELFARE SERVICES	3 568	–	761	2 382	–	425
		NOT DISTRIBUTED	1 930	–	285	440	–	1 205
GAMBIA DALASI	1984	TOTAL	23 994	–	11 834	8 350	–	3 810
		ADMINISTRATION	2 989	–	3	624	–	2 362
		TEACHERS' EMOLUMENTS	17 436	–	11 190	6 245	–	1
		TEACHING MATERIALS	1 155	–	461	248	–	446
		SCHOLARSHIPS	1 433	–	–	1 073	–	360
		WELFARE SERVICES	486	–	–	8	–	478
		NOT DISTRIBUTED	495	–	180	152	–	163
GHANA‡ CEDI	1984	TOTAL	3 843 913	–	940 899	1 132 623	481 255	1 289 136
		ADMINISTRATION	163 141	–	–	–	–	163 141
		TEACHERS' EMOLUMENTS	2 460 628	–	925 454	1 050 103	467 593	17 478
		TEACHING MATERIALS	832 083	–	9 862	39 046	9 282	773 893
		WELFARE SERVICES	295 744	–	–	–	–	295 744
		NOT DISTRIBUTED	92 317	–	5 583	43 474	4 380	38 880
GUINEA-BISSAU PESO	1982	TOTAL	260 000	3 786	174 742	37 655	3 817	40 000
		ADMINISTRATION	26 078	–	–	–	–	26 078
		TEACHERS' EMOLUMENTS	199 525	3 336	161 722	29 926	2 589	1 952
		NOT DISTRIBUTED	34 397	450	13 020	7 729	1 228	11 970
LESOTHO‡ MALOTI	1983	TOTAL	25 939	–	10 300	9 101	5 067	1 471
		TEACHERS' EMOLUMENTS	24 121	–	10 287	8 625	5 067	142
		TEACHING MATERIALS	908	–	–	–	–	908
		SCHOLARSHIPS	139	–	13	–	–	126
		WELFARE SERVICES	225	–	–	47	–	178
		NOT DISTRIBUTED	546	–	–	429	–	117
MADAGASCAR FRANC	1984	TOTAL	47 519 440	–	22 112 279	11 052 897	12 538 964	1 815 300
		ADMINISTRATION	1 868 026	–	78 282	305 587	620 634	863 523
		TEACHERS' EMOLUMENTS	36 674 501	–	22 033 697	10 201 225	3 495 942	943 637
		TEACHING MATERIALS	116 400	–	160	111 050	–	5 190
		SCHOLARSHIPS	3 547 588	–	–	91 495	3 456 093	–
		WELFARE SERVICES	343 540	–	–	343 540	–	–
		NOT DISTRIBUTED	4 969 385	–	140	–	4 966 295	2 950
MALAWI‡ KWACHA	1983	TOTAL	34 754	–	14 198	5 155	9 476	5 925
		ADMINISTRATION	4 908	–	1 120	205	53	3 530
		TEACHERS' EMOLUMENTS	25 746	–	12 678	3 781	8 628	659
		TEACHING MATERIALS	1 320	–	–	470	385	465
		NOT DISTRIBUTED	2 780	–	400	699	410	1 271
MALI FRANC C.F.A.	1984	TOTAL	15 124 302	<——	7 139 442	3 539 225	2 088 805	2 356 830
		ADMINISTRATION	1 585 366	<——	282 183	53 297	26 660	1 223 226
		TEACHERS' EMOLUMENTS	9 298 448	<——	6 529 866	2 042 100	713 087	13 395
		TEACHING MATERIALS	600 488	<——	327 393	127 753	42 240	103 102
		SCHOLARSHIPS	3 640 000	–	–	1 316 075	1 306 818	1 017 107
MAURITANIA OUGUIYA	1983	TOTAL	3 006 217	–	896 000	957 692	737 138	415 387
		ADMINISTRATION	578 074	–	1 354	65 680	95 653	415 387
		TEACHERS' EMOLUMENTS	1 565 158	–	877 566	558 950	128 642	–
		TEACHING MATERIALS	115 148	–	17 080	43 045	55 023	–
		SCHOLARSHIPS	747 837	–	–	290 017	457 820	–
MAURITIUS‡ RUPEE	1984	TOTAL	539 800	200	250 500	199 400	37 100	52 600
		ADMINISTRATION	175 100	–	126 700	28 800	–	19 600
		TEACHERS' EMOLUMENTS	332 700	200	109 400	167 700	37 100	18 300
		TEACHING MATERIALS	600	–	400	100	–	100
		WELFARE SERVICES	17 300	–	12 900	1 500	–	2 900
		NOT DISTRIBUTED	14 100	–	1 100	1 300	–	11 700
MOROCCO‡ DIRHAM	1982	TOTAL	4 692 083	–	1 663 303	2 150 179	878 601	–
		TEACHERS' EMOLUMENTS	4 024 201	–	1 626 694	2 043 133	354 374	–
		TEACHING MATERIALS	16 040	–	3 200	12 840	–	–
		SCHOLARSHIPS	543 840	–	11 000	80 800	452 040	–
		WELFARE SERVICES	1 947	–	925	340	682	–
		NOT DISTRIBUTED	106 055	–	21 484	13 066	71 505	–

COUNTRY CURRENCY / PAYS MONNAIE / PAIS MONEDA	YEAR / ANNEE / AÑO	PURPOSE / DESTINATION / DESTINO	TOTAL CURRENT EXPENDITURE / TOTAL DES DEPENSES ORDINAIRES / TOTAL DE GASTOS ORDINARIOS (000)	PRE-PRIMARY / PRE-PRIMAIRE / PRE-PRIMARIA (000)	FIRST LEVEL / PREMIER DEGRE / PRIMER GRADO (000)	SECOND LEVEL / SECOND DEGRE / SEGUNDO GRADO (000)	THIRD LEVEL / TROISIEME DEGRE / TERCER GRADO (000)	OTHER TYPES AND NOT DISTRIBUTED / AUTRES TYPES ET NON REPARTIES / OTROS TIPOS Y SIN DISTRIBUCION (000)
			(1)	(2)	(3)	(4)	(5)	(6)
RWANDA‡ FRANC	1983	TOTAL	4 527 718	–	3 541 310	——>	576 518	409 890
		TEACHERS' EMOLUMENTS	3 638 038	–	3 222 441	——>	415 597	
		TEACHING MATERIALS	141 689	–	140 496	——>	–	1 193
		SCHOLARSHIPS	160 362	–		–	159 502	860
		WELFARE SERVICES	142 200	–	142 200	——>	–	
		NOT DISTRIBUTED	445 429	–	36 173	——>	1 419	407 837
SENEGAL‡ FRANC C.F.A.	1981	TOTAL	21 694 900	–	12 320 257	8 164 902	–	1 209 741
		TEACHERS' EMOLUMENTS	18 484 500	–	11 255 105	6 212 269	–	1 017 126
		TEACHING MATERIALS	1 500 100	–	442 350	898 696	–	159 054
		SCHOLARSHIPS	1 160 236	–	72 738	1 053 937	–	33 561
		WELFARE SERVICES	550 064	–	550 064	–	–	–
		NOT DISTRIBUTED	–	–	–	–	–	–
SEYCHELLES‡ RUPEE	1984	TOTAL	111 391	<——	42 321	65 150	–	3 920
		ADMINISTRATION	28 340	<——	15 000	13 340	–	–
		TEACHERS' EMOLUMENTS	49 752	<——	24 852	24 900	–	–
		TEACHING MATERIALS	6 123	<——	2 400	3 723	–	–
		SCHOLARSHIPS	4 720	–		800	–	3 920
		WELFARE SERVICES	19 878	<——	69	19 809	–	–
		NOT DISTRIBUTED	2 578	–	–	2 578	–	–
SWAZILAND‡ LILANGENI	1981	TOTAL	22 562	16	10 499	7 886	2 291	1 870
		ADMINISTRATION	1 345	–			–	1 345
		TEACHERS' EMOLUMENTS	19 522	–	10 440	6 893	2 062	127
		TEACHING MATERIALS	1 695	16	59	993	229	398
TOGO FRANC C.F.A.	1981	TOTAL	14 880 824	110 702	3 786 529	3 851 333	4 189 990	2 942 270
		ADMINISTRATION	686 137	13 332	24 038	203 237	144 018	301 512
		TEACHERS' EMOLUMENTS	8 709 199	97 370	3 682 516	3 080 756	1 848 557	–
		TEACHING MATERIALS	186 607	–		170 331	16 276	–
		SCHOLARSHIPS	2 333 605	–		256 000	2 077 605	–
		WELFARE SERVICES	25 344	–	–	11 810	13 534	–
		NOT DISTRIBUTED	2 939 932	–	79 975	129 199	90 000	2 640 758
TUNISIA‡ DINAR	1984	TOTAL	256 956	–	134 340	118 728	–	3 888
		TEACHERS' EMOLUMENTS	221 324	–	123 178	95 858	–	2 288
		TEACHING MATERIALS	11 438	–	2 268	8 150	–	1 020
		SCHOLARSHIPS	2 640	–	–	2 640	–	–
		WELFARE SERVICES	1 360	–	1 200	80	–	80
		NOT DISTRIBUTED	20 194	–	7 694	12 000	–	500
ZAMBIA‡ KWACHA	1982	TOTAL	185 495	40	89 052	62 626	33 463	314
		ADMINISTRATION	16 728	–	6 373	10 355	–	–
		TEACHERS' EMOLUMENTS	131 959	40	79 797	24 551	27 257	314
		TEACHING MATERIALS	4 816	–	2 746	2 070	–	–
		SCHOLARSHIPS	6 206	–			6 206	–
		WELFARE SERVICES	11 296	–	136	11 160	–	–
		NOT DISTRIBUTED	14 490	–	–	14 490	–	–
ZIMBABWE DOLLAR	1983	TOTAL	432 547	–	281 973	104 894	28 304	17 376
		ADMINISTRATION	12 750	–	218	527	1 606	10 399
		TEACHERS' EMOLUMENTS	359 648	–	251 610	88 052	19 986	–
		TEACHING MATERIALS	35 954	–	26 531	8 927	496	–
		SCHOLARSHIPS	3 989	–		–	94	3 895
		WELFARE SERVICES	9 166	–	1 904	5 358	1 904	–
		NOT DISTRIBUTED	11 040	–	1 710	2 030	4 218	3 082
AMERICA, NORTH								
BRITISH VIRGIN ISLANDS UNITED STATES DOLLAR	1984	TOTAL	4 161	6	1 549	1 583	275	748
		ADMINISTRATION	454	–		–	–	454
		TEACHERS' EMOLUMENTS	2 454	–	1 232	1 222	–	–
		TEACHING MATERIALS	186	6	77	103	–	–
		SCHOLARSHIPS	350	–	–	75	275	–
		WELFARE SERVICES	67	–	9	58	–	–
		NOT DISTRIBUTED	650	–	231	125	–	294
CANADA DOLLAR	1984	TOTAL	28 692 121	<——	<——	18 295 242	8 003 230	2 393 649
		ADMINISTRATION	2 310 628	<——	<——	1 314 555	761 403	234 670
		TEACHERS' EMOLUMENTS	15 341 825	<——	<——	11 184 908	3 182 863	974 054
		TEACHING MATERIALS	2 675 672	<——	<——	1 258 027	1 103 221	314 424
		SCHOLARSHIPS	1 240 128	–		–	837 937	402 191
		WELFARE SERVICES	1 509 076	<——	<——	1 151 189	301 871	56 016
		NOT DISTRIBUTED	5 614 792	<——	<——	3 386 563	1 815 935	412 294

4.4 Public current expenditure by level and purpose
Dépenses publiques ordinaires par degré d'enseignement et destination
Gastos públicos ordinarios por grado de enseñanza y destino

COUNTRY CURRENCY / PAYS MONNAIE / PAIS MONEDA	YEAR / ANNEE / AÑO	PURPOSE / DESTINATION / DESTINO	TOTAL CURRENT EXPENDITURE / TOTAL DES DEPENSES ORDINAIRES / TOTAL DE GASTOS ORDINARIOS (000)	PRE-PRIMARY / PRE-PRIMAIRE / PRE-PRIMARIA (000)	FIRST LEVEL / PREMIER DEGRE / PRIMER GRADO (000)	SECOND LEVEL / SECOND DEGRE / SEGUNDO GRADO (000)	THIRD LEVEL / TROISIEME DEGRE / TERCER GRADO (000)	OTHER TYPES AND NOT DISTRIBUTED / AUTRES TYPES ET NON REPARTIES / OTROS TIPOS Y SIN DISTRIBUCION (000)
			(1)	(2)	(3)	(4)	(5)	(6)
COSTA RICA‡ COLON	1983	TOTAL	5 853 136	<——	1 554 615	1 106 800	1 507 832	1 683 889
		TEACHERS' EMOLUMENTS	4 217 715	<——	1 529 656	1 011 266	1 507 832	168 961
		TEACHING MATERIALS	24 139	<——	22 704	–	–	1 435
		WELFARE SERVICES	95 445	–	–	95 445	–	–
		NOT DISTRIBUTED	1 515 837	<——	2 255	89	–	1 513 493
CUBA PESO	1982	TOTAL	1 396 000	80 200	318 500	604 500	147 600	245 200
		ADMINISTRATION	55 300	–	–	–	–	55 300
		TEACHERS' EMOLUMENTS	524 200	29 600	186 700	225 000	36 200	46 700
		TEACHING MATERIALS	82 500	2 700	19 000	36 600	10 900	13 300
		SCHOLARSHIPS	22 900	200	3 200	7 300	11 500	700
		WELFARE SERVICES	601 300	47 700	109 600	335 600	89 000	19 400
		NOT DISTRIBUTED	109 800	–	–	–	–	109 800
DOMINICAN REPUBLIC‡ PESO	1984	TOTAL	170 322	764	75 972	33 435	31 987	28 164
		ADMINISTRATION	9 341	–	338	477	–	8 526
		TEACHERS' EMOLUMENTS	153 798	764	73 909	31 957	31 987	15 181
		SCHOLARSHIPS	1 561	–	284	785	–	492
		NOT DISTRIBUTED	5 622	–	1 441	216	–	3 965
GRENADA‡ E.CARIBBEAN DOLLAR	1983	TOTAL	9 561	314	6 875	2 072	–	300
		TEACHERS' EMOLUMENTS	9 163	314	6 569	2 002	–	278
		TEACHING MATERIALS	33	–	–	18	–	15
		WELFARE SERVICES	108	–	108	–	–	
		NOT DISTRIBUTED	257	–	198	52	–	7
HAITI‡ GOURDE	1983	TOTAL	92 943	–	58 744	14 706	8 743	10 750
		ADMINISTRATION	17 968	–	11 666	1 578	1 938	2 786
		TEACHERS' EMOLUMENTS	57 284	–	40 086	10 700	3 860	2 638
		TEACHING MATERIALS	1 576	–	75	952	267	282
		SCHOLARSHIPS	1 732	–	1 272	158	248	54
		WELFARE SERVICES	1 126	–	547	382	121	76
		NOT DISTRIBUTED	13 257	–	5 098	936	2 309	4 914
HONDURAS‡ LEMPIRA	1982	TOTAL	206 880	–	111 747	37 714	54 734	2 685
		ADMINISTRATION	13 752	–	1 929	11 338	256	229
		TEACHERS' EMOLUMENTS	175 920	–	103 568	18 748	52 464	1 140
		TEACHING MATERIALS	2 724	–	1 998	519	29	178
		SCHOLARSHIPS	2 745	–	4	1 542	916	283
		WELFARE SERVICES	187	–	–		77	110
		NOT DISTRIBUTED	11 552	–	4 248	5 567	992	745
JAMAICA DOLLAR	1983	TOTAL	456 377	6 590	123 448	150 638	113 662	62 039
		ADMINISTRATION	51 410	1 566	9 962	13 194	3 547	23 141
		TEACHERS' EMOLUMENTS	321 328	4 740	106 409	109 194	96 320	4 665
		TEACHING MATERIALS	17 526	156	2 225	13 173	1 540	432
		SCHOLARSHIPS	718	–	–	–	718	–
		WELFARE SERVICES	28 937	–	2 466	7 300	6 537	12 634
		NOT DISTRIBUTED	36 458	128	2 386	7 777	5 000	21 167
MEXICO‡ PESO	1983	TOTAL	416 192 879	16 929 682	128 275 330	65 320 805	119 715 969	85 951 093
		ADMINISTRATION	64 820 958	314 122	550 660	5 113 883	–	58 842 293
		TEACHERS' EMOLUMENTS	254 357 916	10 849 872	105 940 929	47 322 370	71 881 293	18 363 452
		TEACHING MATERIALS	2 841 211	–	2 841 211	–	–	–
		SCHOLARSHIPS	65 515	–	8 622	21 651	34 568	674
		WELFARE SERVICES	532 366	–	–	–	–	532 366
		NOT DISTRIBUTED	93 574 913	5 765 688	18 933 908	12 862 901	47 800 108	8 212 308
NICARAGUA CORDOBA	1984	TOTAL	2 458 200	46 030	773 760	353 190	450 800	834 420
		ADMINISTRATION	500 600	2 100	5 500	9 300	–	483 700
		TEACHERS' EMOLUMENTS	1 712 310	42 700	730 560	329 330	450 800	158 920
		TEACHING MATERIALS	161 000	1 230	37 700	9 570	–	112 500
		SCHOLARSHIPS	4 770	–	–	4 770	–	
		WELFARE SERVICES	220	–	–	220	–	–
		NOT DISTRIBUTED	79 300	–	–	–	–	79 300
PANAMA‡ BALBOA	1984	TOTAL	210 998	–	84 041	53 697	40 962	32 298
		ADMINISTRATION	29 696	–	1 034	2 507	–	26 155
		TEACHERS' EMOLUMENTS	179 127	–	81 328	50 724	40 962	6 113
		TEACHING MATERIALS	2 175	–	1 679	466	–	30
ST. LUCIA‡ E.CARIBBEAN DOLLAR	1982	TOTAL	23 045	–	13 415	9 358	197	75
		TEACHERS' EMOLUMENTS	17 969	–	12 206	5 714	–	49
		TEACHING MATERIALS	1 344	–	410	934	–	–
		SCHOLARSHIPS	240	–	–	43	197	–
		WELFARE SERVICES	1 209	–	12	1 197	–	–
		NOT DISTRIBUTED	2 283	–	787	1 470	–	26

COUNTRY / CURRENCY PAYS / MONNAIE PAIS / MONEDA	YEAR ANNEE AÑO	PURPOSE DESTINATION DESTINO	TOTAL CURRENT EXPENDITURE TOTAL DES DEPENSES ORDINAIRES TOTAL DE GASTOS ORDINARIOS (000)	PRE-PRIMARY PRE-PRIMAIRE PRE-PRIMARIA (000)	FIRST LEVEL PREMIER DEGRE PRIMER GRADO (000)	SECOND LEVEL SECOND DEGRE SEGUNDO GRADO (000)	THIRD LEVEL TROISIEME DEGRE TERCER GRADO (000)	OTHER TYPES AND NOT DISTRIBUTED AUTRES TYPES ET NON REPARTIES OTROS TIPOS Y SIN DISTRIBUCION (000)
			(1)	(2)	(3)	(4)	(5)	(6)
ST. PIERRE AND MIQUELON FRENCH FRANC	1983	TOTAL	29 037	<——	10 252	14 545	–	4 240
		ADMINISTRATION	1 012	–	–	–	–	1 012
		TEACHERS' EMOLUMENTS	21 963	<——	9 429	12 534	–	–
		TEACHING MATERIALS	1 517	<——	205	832	–	480
		SCHOLARSHIPS	2 027	–	–	–	–	2 027
		WELFARE SERVICES	60	–	–	–	–	60
		NOT DISTRIBUTED	2 458	<——	618	1 179	–	661
TRINIDAD AND TOBAGO‡ DOLLAR	1984	TOTAL	901 433	–	381 102	326 808	78 524	114 999
		ADMINISTRATION	45 479	–	667	1 933	494	42 385
		TEACHERS' EMOLUMENTS	690 641	–	339 899	271 808	77 709	1 225
		TEACHING MATERIALS	17 086	–	2 656	14 309	121	–
		SCHOLARSHIPS	55 241	–	25 159	30 082	–	–
		WELFARE SERVICES	53 062	–	–	–	–	53 062
		NOT DISTRIBUTED	39 924	–	12 721	8 676	200	18 327
TURKS AND CAICOS ISLANDS UNITED STATES DOLLAR	1980	TOTAL	832	–	484	338	10	–
		ADMINISTRATION	30	–	15	15	–	–
		TEACHERS' EMOLUMENTS	605	–	405	200	–	–
		TEACHING MATERIALS	60	–	20	40	–	–
		SCHOLARSHIPS	78	–	–	68	10	–
		WELFARE SERVICES	1	–	1	–	–	–
		NOT DISTRIBUTED	58	–	43	15	–	–
AMERICA, SOUTH								
ARGENTINA‡ PESO	1984	TOTAL	180 530 252	<——	68 147 102	49 448 094	34 574 198	28 360 858
		TEACHERS' EMOLUMENTS	161 745 705	<——	64 394 707	48 159 035	32 507 619	16 684 344
		SCHOLARSHIPS	465 970	–	–	–	465 970	–
		NOT DISTRIBUTED	18 318 577	<——	3 752 395	1 289 059	1 600 609	11 676 514
BOLIVIA‡ PESO	1982	TOTAL	10 211 808	<——	7 341 144	1 330 541	329 420	1 210 703
		ADMINISTRATION	630 424	–	–	–	–	630 424
		TEACHERS' EMOLUMENTS	9 526 564	<——	7 339 373	1 330 094	319 684	537 413
		SCHOLARSHIPS	8 939	–	–	–	8 939	–
		NOT DISTRIBUTED	45 881	<——	1 771	447	797	42 866
CHILE‡ PESO	1981	TOTAL	62 609 745	1 396 544	28 479 709	9 719 091	20 995 476	2 018 925
		ADMINISTRATION	1 782 815	–	–	–	–	1 782 815
		TEACHERS' EMOLUMENTS	52 445 285	1 286 815	25 091 077	9 492 741	16 574 652	–
		TEACHING MATERIALS	3 733 358	–	110 000	–	3 623 358	–
		WELFARE SERVICES	3 665 068	109 729	2 987 775	37 622	529 942	–
		NOT DISTRIBUTED	983 219	–	290 857	188 728	267 524	236 110
COLOMBIA‡ PESO	1981	TOTAL	49 004 771	<——	23 228 287	13 179 129	11 352 789	1 244 566
		ADMINISTRATION	858 700	<——	79 650	126 300	2 110	650 640
		TEACHERS' EMOLUMENTS	45 754 000	<——	22 486 000	12 572 000	10 696 000	–
		NOT DISTRIBUTED	2 392 071	<——	662 637	480 829	654 679	593 926
GUYANA‡ DOLLAR	1984	TOTAL	112 361	8 062	39 157	26 952	23 396	14 794
		ADMINISTRATION	11 742	891	7 547	2 747	–	557
		TEACHERS' EMOLUMENTS	73 128	6 773	30 383	21 902	14 000	70
		TEACHING MATERIALS	911	13	618	280	–	–
		SCHOLARSHIPS	9 396	–	–	–	9 396	–
		WELFARE SERVICES	971	147	79	404	–	341
		NOT DISTRIBUTED	16 213	238	530	1 619	–	13 826
PERU‡ SOL	1984	TOTAL	1 892 284	66 826	646 032	386 546	45 851	747 029
		ADMINISTRATION	148 687	10 408	81 778	31 224	13 381	11 896
		TEACHERS' EMOLUMENTS	1 085 217	55 967	559 772	351 872	31 744	85 862
		TEACHING MATERIALS	10 030	451	4 482	3 450	726	921
		NOT DISTRIBUTED	648 350	–	–	–	–	648 350
URUGUAY‡ PESO	1980	TOTAL	1 926 769	–	933 414	638 787	310 616	43 952
		ADMINISTRATION	395 179	–	149 226	117 133	114 461	14 359
		TEACHERS' EMOLUMENTS	1 095 723	–	570 946	400 356	103 215	21 206
		TEACHING MATERIALS	97 343	–	54 163	40 213	–	2 967
		WELFARE SERVICES	143 966	–	48 959	2 067	92 940	–
		NOT DISTRIBUTED	194 558	–	110 120	79 018	–	5 420
VENEZUELA‡ BOLIVAR	1983	TOTAL	16 758 800	994 000	4 733 700	1 677 000	7 146 600	2 207 500
		ADMINISTRATION	2 383 900	96 600	166 000	80 500	944 300	1 096 500
		TEACHERS' EMOLUMENTS	9 906 300	516 200	3 961 300	1 108 100	3 830 700	490 000
		TEACHING MATERIALS	171 900	2 600	7 300	11 700	131 700	18 600
		SCHOLARSHIPS	247 200	20 300	116 800	30 800	79 300	–
		WELFARE SERVICES	1 770 700	–	189 600	68 100	1 296 000	217 000
		NOT DISTRIBUTED	2 278 800	358 300	292 700	377 800	864 600	385 400

4.4 Public current expenditure by level and purpose
Dépenses publiques ordinaires par degré d'enseignement et destination
Gastos públicos ordinarios por grado de enseñanza y destino

COUNTRY / CURRENCY PAYS / MONNAIE PAIS / MONEDA	YEAR ANNEE AÑO	PURPOSE DESTINATION DESTINO	TOTAL CURRENT EXPENDITURE TOTAL DES DEPENSES ORDINAIRES TOTAL DE GASTOS ORDINARIOS (000)	PRE-PRIMARY PRE-PRIMAIRE PRE-PRIMARIA (000)	FIRST LEVEL PREMIER DEGRE PRIMER GRADO (000)	SECOND LEVEL SECOND DEGRE SEGUNDO GRADO (000)	THIRD LEVEL TROISIEME DEGRE TERCER GRADO (000)	OTHER TYPES AND NOT DISTRIBUTED AUTRES TYPES ET NON REPARTIES OTROS TIPOS Y SIN DISTRIBUCION (000)
			(1)	(2)	(3)	(4)	(5)	(6)
ASIA								
AFGHANISTAN AFGHANI	1982	TOTAL	2 191 353	36 183	946 242	482 091	423 827	303 010
		ADMINISTRATION	713 813	15 921	104 086	193 937	165 048	234 821
		TEACHERS' EMOLUMENTS	1 109 748	8 322	775 919	218 615	96 023	10 869
		TEACHING MATERIALS	226 829	5 789	47 312	49 169	118 015	6 544
		WELFARE SERVICES	114 402	6 151	18 925	18 180	26 379	44 767
		NOT DISTRIBUTED	26 561	–	–	2 190	18 362	6 009
BANGLADESH‡ TAKA	1984	TOTAL	4 932 264	–	2 280 207	1 485 991	944 091	221 975
		TEACHERS' EMOLUMENTS	2 948 556	–	997 814	1 378 506	517 694	54 542
		TEACHING MATERIALS	8 527	–	–	–	–	8 527
		SCHOLARSHIPS	13 860	–	–	3 832	3 448	6 580
		WELFARE SERVICES	1 632 723	–	1 241 253	81 139	226 701	83 630
		NOT DISTRIBUTED	328 598	–	41 140	22 514	196 248	68 696
BRUNEI DARUSSALAM DOLLAR	1982	TOTAL	148 330	–	49 182	71 090	20 028	8 030
		ADMINISTRATION	8 559	–	1 454	3 835	128	3 142
		TEACHERS' EMOLUMENTS	72 573	–	33 394	38 716	–	463
		TEACHING MATERIALS	5 784	–	2 079	2 905	–	800
		SCHOLARSHIPS	18 864	–	–	255	18 609	–
		WELFARE SERVICES	32 030	–	10 872	21 158	–	–
		NOT DISTRIBUTED	10 520	–	1 383	4 221	1 291	3 625
CYPRUS‡ POUND	1983	TOTAL	42 181	1 367	14 483	21 712	1 541	3 078
		ADMINISTRATION	3 285	–	308	1 610	114	1 253
		TEACHERS' EMOLUMENTS	34 737	1 080	12 900	18 426	881	1 450
		TEACHING MATERIALS	799	20	305	440	8	26
		SCHOLARSHIPS	302	–	–	51	250	1
		WELFARE SERVICES	892	27	110	580	100	75
		NOT DISTRIBUTED	2 166	240	860	605	188	273
HONG KONG DOLLAR	1984	TOTAL	6 189 691	6 786	1 942 157	2 344 915	1 554 451	341 382
		ADMINISTRATION	655 757	–	16 160	298 034	199 451	142 112
		TEACHERS' EMOLUMENTS	4 737 511	–	1 867 234	1 922 642	765 127	182 508
		TEACHING MATERIALS	118 598	–	6 472	26 737	84 619	770
		SCHOLARSHIPS	23 661	–	–	8 639	12 929	2 093
		WELFARE SERVICES	67 223	6 786	1 612	3 798	52 870	2 157
		NOT DISTRIBUTED	586 941	–	50 679	85 065	439 455	11 742
ISRAEL‡ SHEKEL	1982	TOTAL	44 845	3 439	14 777	12 915	11 230	2 484
		ADMINISTRATION	1 755	–	–	–	–	1 755
		TEACHERS' EMOLUMENTS	40 217	3 434	13 290	12 206	10 861	426
		TEACHING MATERIALS	2 443	–	1 445	637	214	147
		SCHOLARSHIPS	430	5	42	72	155	156
JAPAN‡ YEN	1982	TOTAL	10 376 852	134 235	3 907 435	3 642 095	1 091 782	1 601 305
		ADMINISTRATION	744 723	–	–	–	–	744 723
		TEACHERS' EMOLUMENTS	4 987 898	85 950	2 151 330	2 208 155	362 917	179 546
		TEACHING MATERIALS	666 994	6 013	187 121	326 979	121 975	24 906
		SCHOLARSHIPS	126 123	478	13 007	18 594	3	94 041
		WELFARE SERVICES	529 884	6 600	352 431	139 240	5 553	26 060
		NOT DISTRIBUTED	3 321 230	35 194	1 203 546	949 127	601 334	532 029
JORDAN‡ DINAR	1984	TOTAL	82 655	–	←	55 434	26 740	481
		TEACHERS' EMOLUMENTS	64 409	–	←	49 830	14 480	99
		TEACHING MATERIALS	3 553	–	←	1 735	1 770	48
		SCHOLARSHIPS	3 998	–	–	–	3 998	–
		WELFARE SERVICES	2 491	–	←	894	1 597	–
		NOT DISTRIBUTED	8 204	–	←	2 975	4 895	334
KOREA, REPUBLIC OF‡ WON	1984	TOTAL	2 501 253	10 588	1 221 759	952 980	308 007	7 919
		ADMINISTRATION	96 531	356	44 294	14 026	36 286	1 569
		TEACHERS' EMOLUMENTS	1 301 344	4 428	699 210	434 869	161 566	1 271
		TEACHING MATERIALS	41 881	2 105	25 255	7 867	6 598	56
		SCHOLARSHIPS	12 786	–	–	9 409	3 377	–
		WELFARE SERVICES	89 035	88	16 168	58 688	14 091	–
		NOT DISTRIBUTED	959 676	3 611	436 832	428 121	86 089	5 023
KUWAIT‡ DINAR	1984	TOTAL	317 386	21 137	218 000	→	54 772	23 477
		ADMINISTRATION	93 659	10 248	80 860	→	–	2 551
		TEACHERS' EMOLUMENTS	166 885	10 002	120 246	→	33 668	2 969
		TEACHING MATERIALS	6 037	530	4 732	→	–	775
		SCHOLARSHIPS	9 729	–	–	–	2 815	6 914
		WELFARE SERVICES	17 171	357	12 162	→	3 874	778
		NOT DISTRIBUTED	23 905	–	–	–	14 415	9 490

COUNTRY CURRENCY / PAYS MONNAIE / PAIS MONEDA	YEAR / ANNEE / AÑO	PURPOSE / DESTINATION / DESTINO	TOTAL CURRENT EXPENDITURE / TOTAL DES DEPENSES ORDINAIRES / TOTAL DE GASTOS ORDINARIOS (000)	PRE-PRIMARY / PRE-PRIMAIRE / PRE-PRIMARIA (000)	FIRST LEVEL / PREMIER DEGRE / PRIMER GRADO (000)	SECOND LEVEL / SECOND DEGRE / SEGUNDO GRADO (000)	THIRD LEVEL / TROISIEME DEGRE / TERCER GRADO (000)	OTHER TYPES AND NOT DISTRIBUTED / AUTRES TYPES ET NON REPARTIES / OTROS TIPOS Y SIN DISTRIBUCION (000)
			(1)	(2)	(3)	(4)	(5)	(6)
MALAYSIA‡ RINGGIT	1984	TOTAL	3 676 580	–	1 459 813	1 436 818	515 133	264 816
		ADMINISTRATION	255 772	–	53 312	77 807	–	124 653
		TEACHERS' EMOLUMENTS	3 031 206	–	1 305 832	1 245 503	469 500	10 371
		TEACHING MATERIALS	157 125	–	73 583	82 756	–	786
		SCHOLARSHIPS	79 144	–	–	30 752	45 633	2 759
		WELFARE SERVICES	72 474	–	27 086	–	–	45 388
		NOT DISTRIBUTED	80 859	–	–	–	–	80 859
PENINSULAR MALAYSIA‡ RINGGIT	1984	TOTAL	3 179 989	–	1 194 916	1 222 503	515 133	247 437
		ADMINISTRATION	240 456	–	53 312	77 807	–	109 337
		TEACHERS' EMOLUMENTS	2 581 477	–	1 049 491	1 052 115	469 500	10 371
		TEACHING MATERIALS	134 033	–	66 016	67 231	–	786
		SCHOLARSHIPS	73 742	–	–	25 350	45 633	2 759
		WELFARE SERVICES	71 485	–	26 097	–	–	45 388
		NOT DISTRIBUTED	78 796	–	–	–	–	78 796
SABAH RINGGIT	1983	TOTAL	183 287	–	93 387	72 521	–	17 379
		ADMINISTRATION	15 316	–	–	–	–	15 316
		TEACHERS' EMOLUMENTS	143 525	–	88 678	54 847	–	–
		TEACHING MATERIALS	19 238	–	4 709	14 529	–	–
		SCHOLARSHIPS	3 145	–	–	3 145	–	–
		NOT DISTRIBUTED	2 063	–	–	–	–	2 063
SARAWAK‡ RINGGIT	1984	TOTAL	313 304	–	171 510	141 794	–	–
		TEACHERS' EMOLUMENTS	306 204	–	167 663	138 541	–	–
		TEACHING MATERIALS	3 854	–	2 858	996	–	–
		SCHOLARSHIPS	2 257	–	–	2 257	–	–
		WELFARE SERVICES	989	–	989	–	–	–
NEPAL‡ RUPEE	1980	TOTAL	429 681	–	252 445	——>	150 279	26 957
		ADMINISTRATION	50 349	–	24 287	——>	26 062	–
		TEACHERS' EMOLUMENTS	254 502	–	193 773	——>	60 729	–
		TEACHING MATERIALS	30 482	–	18 252	——>	12 230	–
		SCHOLARSHIPS	14 534	–	2 526	——>	12 008	–
		WELFARE SERVICES	–	–	–	–	–	–
		NOT DISTRIBUTED	79 814	–	13 607	——>	39 250	26 957
SINGAPORE‡ DOLLAR	1982	TOTAL	983 750	–	337 339	338 572	259 844	47 995
		ADMINISTRATION	26 223	–	–	–	–	26 223
		TEACHERS' EMOLUMENTS	885 960	–	329 263	279 729	259 546	17 422
		TEACHING MATERIALS	154	–	34	33	81	6
		SCHOLARSHIPS	11 195	–	3 365	5 589	217	2 024
		NOT DISTRIBUTED	60 218	–	4 677	53 221	–	2 320
SYRIAN ARAB REPUBLIC‡ POUND	1984	TOTAL	2 562 936	–	1 500 699	905 454	–	156 783
		ADMINISTRATION	320 104	–	112 328	109 475	–	98 301
		TEACHERS' EMOLUMENTS	2 176 134	–	1 388 371	756 667	–	31 096
		TEACHING MATERIALS	34 162	–	–	32 879	–	1 283
		SCHOLARSHIPS	9 195	–	–	6 088	–	3 107
		NOT DISTRIBUTED	23 341	–	–	345	–	22 996
THAILAND‡ BAHT	1983	TOTAL	28 127 463	<——	16 929 243	5 922 673	3 889 867	1 385 680
		TEACHERS' EMOLUMENTS	21 948 983	<——	15 108 700	4 385 524	2 231 808	222 951
		TEACHING MATERIALS	1 365 748	<——	265 286	451 730	554 540	94 192
		SCHOLARSHIPS	1 499 993	<——	679 045	13 754	46 016	761 178
		WELFARE SERVICES	749 276	<——	153 091	257 155	194 130	144 900
		NOT DISTRIBUTED	2 563 463	<——	723 121	814 510	863 373	162 459
TURKEY‡ LIRA	1984	TOTAL	382 385	<——	178 854	83 359	90 777	29 395
		TEACHERS' EMOLUMENTS	326 045	<——	169 183	72 035	60 896	23 931
		TEACHING MATERIALS	5 152	<——	408	273	3 068	1 403
		SCHOLARSHIPS	1 564	–	–	54	–	1 510
		WELFARE SERVICES	17 893	<——	3 116	3 940	9 763	1 074
		NOT DISTRIBUTED	31 731	<——	6 147	7 057	17 050	1 477
EUROPE								
ANDORRA PESETA	1982	TOTAL	495 836	65 833	120 443	141 436	4 768	163 356
		ADMINISTRATION	19 512	–	–	–	–	19 512
		TEACHERS' EMOLUMENTS	189 059	43 384	61 307	72 414	–	11 954
		TEACHING MATERIALS	17 684	3 984	7 680	5 927	–	93
		SCHOLARSHIPS	8 194	–	–	3 426	4 768	–
		WELFARE SERVICES	130 786	18 465	51 456	59 669	–	1 196
		NOT DISTRIBUTED	130 601	–	–	–	–	130 601
AUSTRIA SCHILLING	1984	TOTAL	66 453 600	3 875 200	11 754 100	31 268 700	10 796 300	8 759 300
		ADMINISTRATION	19 227 800	3 263 200	3 207 800	7 768 200	2 443 500	2 545 100
		TEACHERS' EMOLUMENTS	33 196 600	–	8 435 300	20 766 200	3 614 800	380 300
		TEACHING MATERIALS	887 700	–	–	–	–	887 700
		SCHOLARSHIPS	1 767 500	32 600	12 100	229 200	569 900	923 700
		WELFARE SERVICES	1 671 000	162 000	8 400	299 300	999 100	202 200
		NOT DISTRIBUTED	9 703 000	417 400	90 500	2 205 800	3 169 000	3 820 300

4.4 Public current expenditure by level and purpose
Dépenses publiques ordinaires par degré d'enseignement et destination
Gastos públicos ordinarios por grado de enseñanza y destino

COUNTRY CURRENCY PAYS MONNAIE PAIS MONEDA	YEAR ANNEE AÑO	PURPOSE DESTINATION DESTINO	TOTAL CURRENT EXPENDITURE TOTAL DES DEPENSES ORDINAIRES TOTAL DE GASTOS ORDINARIOS (000)	PRE-PRIMARY PRE-PRIMAIRE PRE-PRIMARIA (000)	FIRST LEVEL PREMIER DEGRE PRIMER GRADO (000)	SECOND LEVEL SECOND DEGRE SEGUNDO GRADO (000)	THIRD LEVEL TROISIEME DEGRE TERCER GRADO (000)	OTHER TYPES AND NOT DISTRIBUTED AUTRES TYPES ET NON REPARTIES OTROS TIPOS Y SIN DISTRIBUCION (000)
			(1)	(2)	(3)	(4)	(5)	(6)
BELGIUM‡ FRANC	1984	TOTAL	247 337 900	<——	62 018 600	118 119 700	39 955 000	27 244 600
		ADMINISTRATION	5 400 100	<——	257 200	2 629 900	707 300	1 805 700
		TEACHERS' EMOLUMENTS	193 930 800	<——	53 840 700	99 662 300	20 502 900	19 924 900
		TEACHING MATERIALS	275 400	<——	88 500	105 400	33 600	47 900
		WELFARE SERVICES	1 956 500	<——	117 200	–	1 116 800	722 500
		NOT DISTRIBUTED	45 775 100	<——	7 715 000	15 722 100	17 594 400	4 743 600
BULGARIA LEV	1984	TOTAL	1 480 646	286 150	691 092	——>	177 842	325 562
		TEACHERS' EMOLUMENTS	552 754	117 125	327 400	——>	69 827	38 402
		SCHOLARSHIPS	68 255	–	34 338	——>	32 435	1 482
		NOT DISTRIBUTED	859 637	169 025	329 354	——>	75 580	285 678
CZECHOSLOVAKIA KORUNA	1984	TOTAL	25 814 818	2 925 935	11 188 906	3 504 196	3 819 368	4 376 413
		ADMINISTRATION	47 332	–	–	–	–	47 332
		TEACHERS' EMOLUMENTS	12 217 410	1 913 960	4 790 210	2 175 828	1 500 723	1 836 689
		TEACHING MATERIALS	5 483 437	641 372	2 621 859	739 801	752 139	728 266
		SCHOLARSHIPS	427 247	–	–	40 021	387 226	–
		WELFARE SERVICES	3 820 493	1	2 881 724	295 736	643 029	3
		NOT DISTRIBUTED	3 818 899	370 602	895 113	252 810	536 251	1 764 123
DENMARK‡ KRONE	1980	TOTAL	22 188	<——	11 879	4 116	3 895	2 298
		ADMINISTRATION	3 470	<——	1 932	421	580	537
		TEACHERS' EMOLUMENTS	10 942	<——	6 221	2 213	1 916	592
		TEACHING MATERIALS	1 068	<——	510	409	124	25
		SCHOLARSHIPS	596	<——	2	1	114	479
		WELFARE SERVICES	856	<——	533	152	160	11
		NOT DISTRIBUTED	5 256	<——	2 681	920	1 001	654
FINLAND MARKKA	1983	TOTAL	14 222 522	–	4 192 221	5 958 370	2 443 403	1 628 528
		ADMINISTRATION	926 541	–	192 411	360 743	140 057	233 330
		TEACHERS' EMOLUMENTS	7 051 803	–	2 245 433	2 980 106	1 299 596	526 668
		TEACHING MATERIALS	722 801	–	226 619	360 483	47 297	88 402
		SCHOLARSHIPS	596 051	–	–	216 431	368 363	11 257
		WELFARE SERVICES	2 142 437	–	723 526	908 828	87 337	422 746
		NOT DISTRIBUTED	2 782 889	–	804 232	1 131 779	500 753	346 125
FRANCE‡ FRANC	1982	TOTAL	194 708	16 272	41 618	79 987	24 444	32 387
		ADMINISTRATION	6 685	–	–	–	448	6 237
		TEACHERS' EMOLUMENTS	135 008	11 123	31 824	62 806	17 465	11 790
		TEACHING MATERIALS	177	–	–	176	–	1
		SCHOLARSHIPS	3 410	–	–	1 668	961	781
		WELFARE SERVICES	16 860	1 050	1 990	8 044	1 229	4 547
		NOT DISTRIBUTED	32 568	4 099	7 804	7 293	4 341	9 031
GERMANY, FEDERAL REPUBLIC OF DEUTSCHE MARK	1983	TOTAL	67 382 800	2 639 300	10 205 700	36 213 500	9 860 900	8 463 400
		ADMINISTRATION	843 300	–	–	–	–	843 300
		TEACHERS' EMOLUMENTS	48 610 500	1 085 900	8 834 200	28 779 000	6 695 100	3 216 300
		SCHOLARSHIPS	2 513 000	–	–	1 297 800	1 215 200	–
		WELFARE SERVICES	1 993 500	–	–	58 800	94 200	1 840 500
		NOT DISTRIBUTED	13 422 500	1 553 400	1 371 500	6 077 900	1 856 400	2 563 300
HUNGARY FORINT	1984	TOTAL	45 725 490	5 705 810	17 582 842	8 569 793	11 067 179	2 799 866
		TEACHERS' EMOLUMENTS	15 127 404	2 025 176	6 463 932	2 806 554	2 701 624	1 130 118
		SCHOLARSHIPS	1 699 397	–	–	46 032	1 653 365	–
		WELFARE SERVICES	7 110 433	–	238 347	1 134 146	5 737 940	
		NOT DISTRIBUTED	21 788 256	3 680 634	10 880 563	4 583 061	974 250	1 669 748
IRELAND POUND	1983	TOTAL	813 873	79 518	232 318	332 104	141 675	28 258
		ADMINISTRATION	22 330	118	344	5 554	428	15 886
		TEACHERS' EMOLUMENTS	592 300	68 505	200 141	246 700	76 954	–
		TEACHING MATERIALS	1 541	159	465	863	–	54
		SCHOLARSHIPS	11 405	–	–	–	11 401	4
		WELFARE SERVICES	35 005	5 574	16 285	12 216	–	930
		NOT DISTRIBUTED	151 292	5 162	15 083	66 771	52 892	11 384
ITALY‡ LIRA	1983	TOTAL	28 040 275	1 611 654	5 985 371	10 463 067	2 839 071	7 141 112
		ADMINISTRATION	4 383 189	80 550	196 905	448 568	993 518	2 663 648
		TEACHERS' EMOLUMENTS	18 940 597	1 206 307	5 430 723	8 441 359	920 081	2 942 127
		TEACHING MATERIALS	6 160	–	6 160	–	–	–
		SCHOLARSHIPS	244 542	–	–	106 586	81 997	55 959
		WELFARE SERVICES	688 931	53 700	62 700	53 545	–	518 986
		NOT DISTRIBUTED	3 776 856	271 097	288 883	1 413 009	843 475	960 392
LUXEMBOURG‡ FRANC	1983	TOTAL	7 900 300	<——	3 070 300	3 499 100	198 700	1 132 200
		TEACHERS' EMOLUMENTS	6 888 600	<——	2 978 600	3 179 900	68 100	662 000
		TEACHING MATERIALS	75 400	<——	10 500	40 500	6 500	17 900
		SCHOLARSHIPS	129 800	<——	600	300	93 300	35 600
		NOT DISTRIBUTED	806 500	<——	80 600	278 400	30 800	416 700

COUNTRY CURRENCY / PAYS MONNAIE / PAIS MONEDA	YEAR / ANNEE / AÑO	PURPOSE / DESTINATION / DESTINO	TOTAL CURRENT EXPENDITURE / TOTAL DES DEPENSES ORDINAIRES / TOTAL DE GASTOS ORDINARIOS (000)	PRE-PRIMARY / PRE-PRIMAIRE / PRE-PRIMARIA (000)	FIRST LEVEL / PREMIER DEGRE / PRIMER GRADO (000)	SECOND LEVEL / SECOND DEGRE / SEGUNDO GRADO (000)	THIRD LEVEL / TROISIEME DEGRE / TERCER GRADO (000)	OTHER TYPES AND NOT DISTRIBUTED / AUTRES TYPES ET NON REPARTIES / OTROS TIPOS Y SIN DISTRIBUCION (000)
			(1)	(2)	(3)	(4)	(5)	(6)
MALTA‡ LIRA	1984	TOTAL	15 545	<——	4 378	6 845	1 366	2 956
		ADMINISTRATION	3 742	<——	992	1 494	–	1 256
		TEACHERS' EMOLUMENTS	9 341	<——	3 045	4 714	1 366	216
		TEACHING MATERIALS	18	<——	10	3	–	5
		SCHOLARSHIPS	230	–	–	14	–	216
		WELFARE SERVICES	465	<——	230	221	–	14
		NOT DISTRIBUTED	1 749	<——	101	399	–	1 249
NETHERLANDS‡ GUILDER	1982	TOTAL	24 484	1 314	4 646	8 709	6 452	3 363
		ADMINISTRATION	848	–	189	60	53	546
		TEACHERS' EMOLUMENTS	17 795	1 046	3 534	7 129	4 314	1 772
		TEACHING MATERIALS	271	8	70	39	126	28
		SCHOLARSHIPS	1 086	–	–	349	485	252
		WELFARE SERVICES	387	1	10	–	94	282
		NOT DISTRIBUTED	4 097	259	843	1 132	1 380	483
NORWAY‡ KRONE	1983	TOTAL	23 522	–	10 887	6 299	3 164	3 172
		ADMINISTRATION	658	–	414	149	48	47
		TEACHERS' EMOLUMENTS	14 967	–	7 963	3 812	2 196	996
		TEACHING MATERIALS	1 408	–	194	330	804	80
		SCHOLARSHIPS	1 136	–	–	211	13	912
		WELFARE SERVICES	568	–	568	–	–	–
		NOT DISTRIBUTED	4 785	–	1 748	1 797	103	1 137
PORTUGAL ESCUDO	1982	TOTAL	72 884 100	17 600	22 766 000	34 737 600	8 267 600	7 095 300
		ADMINISTRATION	2 798 200	–	27 100	118 300	65 700	2 587 100
		TEACHERS' EMOLUMENTS	59 961 200	8 100	21 430 800	29 882 100	6 053 500	2 586 700
		TEACHING MATERIALS	182 200	200	32 500	102 300	5 600	41 600
		SCHOLARSHIPS	2 684 800	–	322 900	1 381 900	442 800	537 200
		WELFARE SERVICES	3 839 700	9 300	816 100	1 968 800	795 500	250 000
		NOT DISTRIBUTED	3 418 000	–	136 600	1 284 200	904 500	1 092 700
SAN MARINO‡ LIRA	1983	TOTAL	15 358 869	3 499 289	5 639 166	5 076 529	385 971	757 914
		TEACHERS' EMOLUMENTS	14 001 887	3 408 482	5 543 755	4 871 200	–	178 450
		TEACHING MATERIALS	198 449	27 491	44 528	126 430	–	–
		SCHOLARSHIPS	385 971	–	–	–	385 971	–
		WELFARE SERVICES	117 031	–	–	–	–	117 031
		NOT DISTRIBUTED	655 531	63 316	50 883	78 899	–	462 433
SWEDEN‡ KRONA	1984	TOTAL	54 190 500	31 100	25 539 700	10 825 600	6 936 100	10 858 000
		ADMINISTRATION	1 778 000	–	976 600	426 500	137 200	237 700
		TEACHERS' EMOLUMENTS	24 400 300	–	14 843 200	4 468 600	2 450 300	2 638 200
		TEACHING MATERIALS	1 148 900	–	656 800	439 000	–	53 100
		SCHOLARSHIPS	2 195 700	–	–	–	–	2 195 700
		WELFARE SERVICES	3 834 500	–	2 716 200	1 109 500	–	8 800
		NOT DISTRIBUTED	20 833 100	31 100	6 346 900	4 382 000	4 348 600	5 724 500
SWITZERLAND FRANC	1983	TOTAL	9 756 600	287 500	<——	7 131 200	1 827 700	510 200
		ADMINISTRATION	1 250 800	14 700	<——	601 200	470 400	164 500
		TEACHERS' EMOLUMENTS	6 083 100	239 600	<——	4 897 900	816 400	129 200
		TEACHING MATERIALS	299 600	4 200	<——	197 400	90 500	7 500
		SCHOLARSHIPS	198 900	–	<——	113 400	76 900	8 600
		NOT DISTRIBUTED	1 924 200	29 000	<——	1 321 300	373 500	200 400
UNITED KINGDOM‡ POUND STERLING	1983	TOTAL	15 108	399	3 366	6 272	3 281	1 790
		TEACHERS' EMOLUMENTS	7 668	272	2 058	4 122	911	305
		TEACHING MATERIALS	605	16	103	286	171	29
		SCHOLARSHIPS	1 268	1	8	54	1 079	126
		WELFARE SERVICES	766	33	311	323	19	80
		NOT DISTRIBUTED	4 801	77	886	1 487	1 101	1 250
YUGOSLAVIA‡ DINAR	1983	TOTAL	145 149	–	107 022	——>	25 643	12 484
		TEACHERS' EMOLUMENTS	89 303	–	71 305	——>	14 689	3 309
		TEACHING MATERIALS	11 324	–	7 163	——>	2 255	1 906
		SCHOLARSHIPS	2 004	–	–	–	–	2 004
		WELFARE SERVICES	13 497	–	7 533	——>	2 653	3 311
		NOT DISTRIBUTED	29 021	–	21 021	——>	6 046	1 954
OCEANIA								
COOK ISLANDS NEW ZEALAND DOLLAR	1984	TOTAL	3 474	94	1 291	1 255	187	647
		ADMINISTRATION	429	–	–	–	–	429
		TEACHERS' EMOLUMENTS	2 587	94	1 189	1 130	174	–
		TEACHING MATERIALS	239	–	74	71	13	81
		SCHOLARSHIPS	31	–	–	31	–	–
		WELFARE SERVICES	157	–	–	20	–	137
		NOT DISTRIBUTED	31	–	28	3	–	–

COUNTRY CURRENCY / PAYS MONNAIE / PAIS MONEDA	YEAR / ANNEE / AÑO	PURPOSE / DESTINATION / DESTINO	TOTAL CURRENT EXPENDITURE / TOTAL DES DEPENSES ORDINAIRES / TOTAL DE GASTOS ORDINARIOS (000)	PRE-PRIMARY / PRE-PRIMAIRE / PRE-PRIMARIA (000)	FIRST LEVEL / PREMIER DEGRE / PRIMER GRADO (000)	SECOND LEVEL / SECOND DEGRE / SEGUNDO GRADO (000)	THIRD LEVEL / TROISIEME DEGRE / TERCER GRADO (000)	OTHER TYPES AND NOT DISTRIBUTED / AUTRES TYPES ET NON REPARTIES / OTROS TIPOS Y SIN DISTRIBUCION (000)
			(1)	(2)	(3)	(4)	(5)	(6)
FIJI DOLLAR	1981	TOTAL	57 758	–	30 614	26 063	1 081	–
		ADMINISTRATION	3 696	–	2 194	1 502	–	...
		TEACHERS' EMOLUMENTS	49 960	–	28 319	21 641	–	...
		TEACHING MATERIALS	128	–	9	119	–	...
		SCHOLARSHIPS	1 151	–	–	1 151	–	...
		WELFARE SERVICES	401	–	–	401	–	...
		NOT DISTRIBUTED	2 422	–	92	1 249	1 081	...
KIRIBATI AUSTRALIAN DOLLAR	1982	TOTAL	2 694	–	1 164	990	–	540
		ADMINISTRATION	550	–	2	8	–	540
		TEACHERS' EMOLUMENTS	1 161	–	779	382	–	–
		TEACHING MATERIALS	311	–	237	74	–	–
		WELFARE SERVICES	424	–	121	303	–	–
		NOT DISTRIBUTED	248	–	25	223	–	–
NEW CALEDONIA FRENCH FRANC	1984	TOTAL	835 410	–	379 342	450 537	5 531	–
		TEACHERS' EMOLUMENTS	735 817	–	343 159	392 293	365	–
		TEACHING MATERIALS	61 368	–	21 832	39 536	–	–
		SCHOLARSHIPS	38 225	–	14 351	18 708	5 166	–
NEW ZEALAND DOLLAR	1984	TOTAL	1 598 765	23 835	611 285	624 753	261 304	77 588
		ADMINISTRATION	78 957	961	15 423	36 680	–	25 893
		TEACHERS' EMOLUMENTS	1 151 109	18 894	459 536	443 902	204 390	24 387
		TEACHING MATERIALS	96 204	2 968	47 644	40 834	–	4 758
		SCHOLARSHIPS	77 066	–	–	20 152	56 914	–
		WELFARE SERVICES	55 836	–	35 493	20 343	–	–
		NOT DISTRIBUTED	139 593	1 012	53 189	62 842	–	22 550
NIUE NEW ZEALAND DOLLAR	1982	TOTAL	664	–	254	246	–	164
		ADMINISTRATION	99	–	22	41	–	36
		TEACHERS' EMOLUMENTS	525	–	224	190	–	111
		TEACHING MATERIALS	40	–	8	15	–	17
PACIFIC ISLANDS UNITED STATES DOLLAR	1982	TOTAL	27 710	–	8 196	12 112	4 979	2 423
		ADMINISTRATION	7 068	–	216	4 111	1 575	1 166
		TEACHERS' EMOLUMENTS	14 494	–	7 959	3 703	1 934	898
		TEACHING MATERIALS	933	–	14	842	52	25
		SCHOLARSHIPS	1 829	–	7	371	1 418	33
		NOT DISTRIBUTED	3 386	–	–	3 085	–	301
TOKELAU NEW ZEALAND DOLLAR	1982	TOTAL	579	10	192	377	–	–
		ADMINISTRATION	20	–	20	–	–	–
		TEACHERS' EMOLUMENTS	165	8	157	–	–	–
		TEACHING MATERIALS	17	2	15	–	–	–
		SCHOLARSHIPS	373	–	–	373	–	–
		NOT DISTRIBUTED	4	–	–	4	–	–
TONGA‡ PA'ANGA	1981	TOTAL	1 892	–	1 103	431	229	129
		TEACHERS' EMOLUMENTS	1 300	–	956	344	–	–
		TEACHING MATERIALS	22	–	7	15	–	–
		SCHOLARSHIPS	358	–	–	–	229	129
		WELFARE SERVICES	212	–	140	72	–	–

AFRICA

Botswana:

E--> Public subsidies to private education not included.

FR-> Non compris les subventions publiques à l'enseignement privé.

ESP> No se incluyen las subvenciones públicas a la enseñanza privada.

Burundi:

E--> Expenditure of the Ministry of Education only.

FR-> Dépenses du Ministère de l'Education seulement.

ESP> Gastos del Ministerio de Educación solamente.

Congo:

E--> Expenditure on administration is included with teachers' emoluments.

FR-> Les dépenses relatives à l'administration sont incluses avec les émoluments du personnel enseignant.

ESP> Los gastos relativos a la administración quedan incluídos en los emolumentos del personal docente.

Egypt:

E--> Expenditure on administration is included with teachers' emoluments.

FR-> Les dépenses d'administration sont incluses avec les émoluments du personnel enseignant.

ESP> Los gastos de administración se incluyen en los emolumentos del personal docente.

Ethiopia:

E--> Expenditure on third level education is not included.

FR-> Les dépenses relatives à l'enseignement du troisième degré ne sont pas incluses.

ESP> No se incluyen los gastos relativos a la enseñanza de tercer grado.

Ghana:

E--> The totality of transfers to universities is included with teachers' emoluments.

FR-> La totalité des transferts aux universités est incluse avec les émoluments du personnel enseignant.

ESP> La totalidad de las transferencias a las universidades queda incluída en los emolumentos del personal docente.

Lesotho:

E--> The totality of transfers to universities is included with teachers' emoluments.

FR-> La totalité des transferts aux universités est incluse avec les émoluments du personnel enseignant.

ESP> La totalidad de las transferencias a las universidades queda incluída en los emolumentos del personal docente.

Malawi:

E--> Transfers to universities and other higher education institutions as well as subsidies to second level schools are included with teachers' emoluments. Welfare services are included with teaching materials.

Malawi: (Cont):

FR-> Les transferts aux universités et autres établissements d'enseignement supérieur ainsi que les subventions aux écoles secondaires sont inclus avec les émoluments du personnel enseignant. Les services sociaux sont inclus avec les matériels pour l'enseignement.

ESP> Las transferencias a las universidades y otros establecimientos de enseñanza superior así como subvenciones a las escuelas secundarias quedan incluídas en los emolumentos del personal docente. Los servicios sociales quedan incluídos en los materiales educativos.

Mauritius:

E--> Scholarships and transfers to all types of education are included with teachers' emoluments.

FR-> Les bourses d'études et les transferts à tout type d'enseignement sont inclus avec les émoluments du personnel enseignant.

ESP> Las becas de estudios y las transferencias a todos tipos de enseñanza quedan incluídas en los emolumentos del personal docente.

Morocco:

E--> Expenditure on administration is included with teachers' emoluments.

FR-> Les dépenses de l'administration sont incluses avec les émoluments du personnel enseignant.

ESP> Los gastos de la administración quedan incluídos en los emolumentos del personal docente.

Rwanda:

E--> Expenditure on administration is included with teachers' emoluments.

FR-> Les dépenses d'administration sont incluses avec les émoluments du personnel enseignant.

ESP> Los gastos de administración quedan incluídos en los emolumentos del personal docente.

Senegal:

E--> Data refer to expenditure of the Ministry of Primary and Secondary Education only. Expenditure on administration is included with teachers' emoluments.

FR-> Les données se réfèrent aux dépenses du Ministère des enseignements primaire et secondaire seulement. Les dépenses de l'administration sont incluses avec les émoluments du personnel enseignant.

ESP> Los datos se refieren a los gastos del Ministerio de las enseñanzas de primer y segundo grado solamente. Los gastos de administración quedan incluídos en los emolumentos del personal docente.

Seychelles:

E--> Expenditure on third level education is not included.

FR-> Les dépenses relatives à l'enseignement du troisième degré ne sont pas incluses.

ESP> No se incluyen los gastos relativos a la enseñanza de tercer grado.

Swaziland:

E--> Expenditure of the Ministry of Education only.

FR-> Dépenses du Ministère de l'Education seulement.

ESP> Gastos del Ministerio de Educación solamente.

Tunisia:

E--> Expenditure on third level is not included. Expenditure on administration is included with teachers' emoluments.

FR-> Les dépenses relatives a l'enseignement du troisième degré ne sont pas incluses. Les dépenses de l'administration sont incluses avec les émoluments du personnel enseignant.

ESP> No se incluyen los gastos relativos a la enseñanza de tercer grado. Los gastos de la administración quedan incluídos en los emolumentos del personal docente.

Zambia:

E--> With the exception of scholarships, transfers to universities are included with teachers' emoluments.

FR-> A l'exception des bourses d'études, les transferts aux universités sont inclus avec les émoluments du personnel enseignant.

ESP> Salvo las becas de estudios, las transferencias a las universidades quedan incluídas en los emolumentos del personal docente.

AMERICA, NORTH

Costa Rica:

E--> The totality of transfers to universities is included with teachers' emoluments. Scholarships are included with welfare services.

FR-> La totalité des transferts aux universités est incluse avec les émoluments du personnel enseignant. Les bourses d'études sont incluses avec les services sociaux.

ESP> La totalidad de las transferencias a las universidades queda incluída en los emolumentos del personal docente. Las becas de estudios quedan incluídas en los servicios sociales.

Dominican Republic:

E--> Expenditure of the Ministry of Education only. Transfers to universities and other third level institutions are included with teachers' emoluments.

FR-> Dépenses du Ministère de l'Education seulement. Les transferts aux universités et autres établissements du troisième degré sont inclus avec les émoluments du personnel enseignant.

ESP> Gastos del Ministerio de Educación solamente. Las transferencias a las universidades y otros establecimientos de tercer grado quedan incluídas en los emolumentos del personal docente.

Grenada:

E--> Expenditure on third level education is not included. Expenditure on administration is included with teachers' emoluments.

FR-> Les dépenses relatives à l'enseignement du troisième degré ne sont pas incluses. Les dépenses de l'administration sont incluses avec les émoluments du personnel enseignant.

ESP> No se incluyen los gastos relativos a la enseñanza de tercer grado. Los gastos de administración quedan incluídos en los emolumentos del personal docente.

Haiti:

E--> Expenditure on teacher training at second level is included with first level.

FR-> Les dépenses de l'enseignement normal du second degré sont incluses avec le premier degré.

ESP> Los gastos de la enseñanza normal del segundo grado quedan incluídos en el primer grado.

Honduras:

E--> The totality of transfers to universities is included with teachers' emoluments.

FR-> La totalité des transferts aux universités est incluse avec les émoluments du personnel enseignant.

ESP> La totalidad de las transferencias a las universidades queda incluída en los emolumentos del personal docente.

Mexico:

E--> Expenditure of the Ministry of Education only.

FR-> Dépenses du Ministère de l'Education seulement.

ESP> Gastos del Ministerio de Educación solamente.

Panama:

E--> Transfers to universities are included with teachers' emoluments.

FR-> Les transferts aux universités sont inclus avec les émoluments du personnel enseignant.

ESP> Las transferencias a las universidades quedan incluídas en los emolumentos del personal docente.

St. Lucia:

E--> Expenditure of the Ministry of Education only. Expenditure on administration is included with teachers' emoluments.

FR-> Dépenses du Ministère de l'Education seulement. Les dépenses d'administration sont incluses avec les émoluments du personnel enseignant.

ESP> Gastos del Ministerio de Educación solamente. Los gastos de administración quedan incluídos en los emolumentos del personal docente.

Trinidad and Tobago:

E--> Transfers to universities are included with teachers' emoluments.

FR-> Les transferts aux universités sont inclus avec les émoluments du personnel enseignant.

ESP> Las transferencias a las universidades quedan incluídas en los emolumentos del personal docente.

AMERICA, SOUTH

Argentina:

E--> Expenditure on administration is included with teachers' emoluments.

FR-> Les dépenses d'administration sont incluses avec les émoluments du personnel enseignant.

ESP> Los gastos de administración quedan incluídos en los emolumentos del personal docente.

Bolivia:

E--> Expenditure on universities is not included.

FR-> Les dépenses relatives aux universités ne sont pas incluses.

ESP> No se incluyen los gastos relativos a las universidades.

Chile:

E--> Scholarships are included with welfare services.

FR-> Les bourses d'études sont incluses avec les services sociaux.

ESP> Las becas de estudios quedan incluídas en los servicios sociales.

Colombia:

E--> Expenditure of the Ministry of Education only.

FR-> Dépenses du Ministère de l'Education seulement.

ESP> Gastos del Ministerio de Educación solamente.

Guyana:

E--> With the exception of scholarships, transfers to universities and other third level institutions are included with teachers' emoluments.

FR-> A l'exception des bourses d'études, les transferts aux universités et autres établissements du troisième degré sont inclus avec les émoluments du personnel enseignant.

ESP> Salvo las becas de estudios, las transferencias a las universidades y otros establecimientos de tercer grado quedan incluídas en los emolumentos del personal docente.

Peru:

E--> Figures are in millions. Transfers to universities and to other types of institutions as well as some types of pensions and staff benefits are included in column 6.

FR-> Les chiffres sont exprimés en millions. Les transferts aux universités et à certains autres établissements ainsi que différents types de pensions et d'indemnités du personnel sont inclus dans la colonne 6.

ESP> Las cifras se expresan en millones. Las transferencias a las

Peru: (Cont):
universidades y otros establecimientos así como diferentes tipos de pensiones y indemnizaciones del personal quedan incluídos en la columna 6.

Uruguay:
E--> Expenditure on scholarships is included with welfare services.
FR-> Les dépenses relatives aux bourses d'études sont incluses avec les services sociaux.
ESP> Los gastos relativos a las becas de estudios quedan incluídos en los servicios sociales.

Venezuela:
E--> Expenditure of the Central government only.
FR-> Dépenses du gouvernement central seulement.
ESP> Gastos del gobierno central solamente.

ASIA

Bangladesh:
E--> Expenditure of the Ministry of Education only. Administration is included with teachers' emoluments. Expenditure on intermediate colleges and intermediate sections of degree colleges (grades XI and XII) is included with third level education.
FR-> Dépenses du Ministère de l'Education seulement. Les dépenses d'administration sont incluses avec les émoluments du personnel. enseignant. Les dépenses des collèges intermédiaires et des sections intermédiaires des degree colleges (XI ème et XII ème années d'études) sont incluses avec l'enseignement du troisième degré.
ESP> Gastos del Ministerio de Educación solamente. Los gastos de administración quedan incluídos en los emolumentos del personal docente. Los gastos de los colegios intermediarios y de las secciones intermediarias de los 'degree colleges' (onceavo y doceavo años de estudios) están incluídos en la enseñanza de tercer grado.

Cyprus:
E--> Expenditure of the Office of Greek Education only.
FR-> Dépenses du bureau grec de l'Education seulement.
ESP> Gastos del servicio griego de Educación solamente.

Israel:
E--> Figures are in millions. Transfers to universities and public subsidies to private educational institutions are included with teachers' emoluments.
FR-> Les chiffres sont exprimés en millions. Les transferts aux universités et les subventions publiques aux établissements d'enseignement privé sont inclus avec les émoluments du personnel enseignant.
ESP> Las cifras se expresan en millones. Las transferencias a las universidades y las subvenciones públicas a los establecimientos de enseñanza privada quedan incluídas en los emolumentos del personal docente.

Japan:
E--> Figures are in millions. Public subsidies to private education are not included.
FR-> Les chiffres sont exprimés en millions. Les subventions publiques à l'enseignement privé ne sont pas incluses.
ESP> Las cifras se expresan en millones. No se incluyen las subvenciones públicas a la enseñanza privada.

Jordan:
E--> Expenditure on administration is included with teachers' emoluments.
FR-> Les dépenses d'administration sont incluses avec les émoluments du personnel enseignant.
ESP> Los gastos de administración quedan incluídos en los emolumentos del personal docente.

Korea, Republic of:
E--> Figures are in millions.
FR-> Les chiffres sont exprimés en millions.
ESP> Las cifras se expresan en millones.

Kuwait:
E--> Vocational education at the second level is included with third level education.
FR-> L'enseignement technique du second degré est inclus avec l'enseignement du troisième degré.
ESP> La enseñanza técnica del segundo grado queda incluída en la enseñanza de tercer grado.

Malaysia
E--> With the exception of scholarships, transfers to institutions of education at the third level are included with teachers' emoluments.
FR-> A l'exception des bourses d'études, les transferts aux établissements d'enseignement du troisième degré sont inclus avec les émoluments du personnel enseignant.
ESP> Salvo las becas de estudios, las transferencias a los establecimientos de enseñanza de tercer grado quedan incluídas en los emolumentos del personal docente.

Peninsular Malaysia:
E--> With the exception of scholarships, transfers to institutions of education at the third level are included with teachers' emoluments.
FR-> A l'exception des bourses d'études, les transferts aux établissements d'enseignement du troisième degré sont inclus avec les émoluments du personnel enseignant.
ESP> Salvo las becas de estudios, las transferencias a los establecimientos de enseñanza de tercer grado quedan incluídas en los emolumentos del personel docente.

Sarawak:
E--> Expenditure on administration is included with teach emoluments.
FR-> Les dépenses de l'administration sont incluses avec émoluments du personnel enseignant.
ESP> Los gastos de la administración quedan incluídos en emolumentos del personal docente.

Nepal:
E--> Data refer to 'regular' and 'development' expenditure.
FR-> Les données se réfèrent aux dépenses 'ordinaires' et développement'.
ESP> Los gastos se refieren a los gastos 'ordinarios' y desarrollo'.

Singapore:
E--> Transfers to third level institutions (namely universities), indust training board and other educational organizations are included v teachers' emoluments.
FR-> Les transferts aux établissements du troisième degré (notamm les universités), à l''industrial training board', et à d'autres organism d'enseignement sont inclus avec les émoluments du persor enseignant.
ESP> Las transferencias a los establecimientos de tercer gra (especialmente las universidades) al consejo de formación indust 'industrial training board' y otros organismos de enseñanza, que incluídas en los emolumentos del personal docente.

Syrian Arab Republic:
E--> Expenditure on education at the third level is not includ Welfare services are included with administration.
FR-> Les dépenses de l'enseignement du troisième degré ne sont incluses. Les services sociaux sont inclus avec l'administration.
ESP> No se incluyen los gastos relativos a la enseñanza de ter grado. Los servicios sociales quedan incluídos en la administración.

Thailand:
E--> Expenditure on administration is included with teach emoluments.
FR-> Les dépenses de l'administration sont incluses avec émoluments du personnel enseignant.
ESP> Los gastos de la administración quedan incluídos en emolumentos del personal docente.

Turkey:
E--> Figures are in millions. Expenditure on administration included with teachers' emoluments.
FR-> Les chiffres sont exprimés en millions. Les dépenses l'administration sont incluses avec les émoluments du person enseignant.
ESP> Las cifras se expresan en millones. Los gastos de administración quedan incluídos en los emolumentos del perso docente.

EUROPE

Belgium:
E--> Expenditure of the Ministry of Education only.
FR-> Dépenses du Ministère de l'Education seulement.
ESP> Gastos del Ministerio de Educación solamente.

Denmark:
E--> Figures are in millions.
FR-> Les chiffres sont exprimés en millions.
ESP> Las cifras se expresan en millones.

France:
E--> Figures are in millions. Data refer to France Metropolitan.
FR-> Les chiffres sont exprimés en millions. Les données se réfèrer la France métropolitaine.
ESP> Las cifras se expresan en millones. Los datos se refieren a Francia metropolitana.

Italy:
E--> Figures are in millions.
FR-> Les chiffres sont exprimés en millions.
ESP> Las cifras se expresan en millones.

Luxembourg:
E--> Expenditure of Central Government only.
FR-> Dépenses du gouvernement central seulement.
ESP> Gastos del gobierno central solamente.

Malta:
E--> Transfers to universities are included with teache emoluments.
FR-> Les transferts aux universités sont inclus avec les émoluments personnel enseignant.
ESP> Las transferencias a las universidades quedan incluídas en emolumentos del personal docente.

Netherlands:
E--> Figures are in millions.
FR-> Les chiffres sont exprimés en millions.
ESP> Las cifras se expresan en millones.

Norway:
E--> Figures are in millions.
FR-> Les chiffres sont exprimés en millions.
ESP> Las cifras se expresan en millones.

San Marino:
E--> Data in column 5 refer to scholarships for second and third le

San Marino: (Cont):
students.
FR-> Les données de la colonne 5 se réfèrent aux bourses pour les étudiants des enseignements du second et du troisième degrés.
ESP> Los datos de la columna 5 se refieren a las becas para los estudiantes de las enseñanzas de segundo y tercer grado.
Sweden:
E--> Expenditure on first level (column 3) refers to compulsory education which covers six grades of primary education and the first three grades of secondary education. Expenditure on second level education, therefore, covers only the last three grades (upper secondary school).
FR-> Les dépenses relatives au premier degré (colonne 3) se réfèrent à l'enseignement obligatoire qui comprend six années de l'enseignement primaire et les trois premières années de l'enseignement secondaire. Les dépenses relatives à l'enseignement du second degré, par conséquent, ne comprennent que les trois dernières années (école secondaire supérieure).
ESP> Los gastos relativos al primer grado (columna 3) se refieren a la enseñanza obligatoria que incluye seis años de la enseñanza primaria y los

Sweden: (Cont):
tres primeros años de la enseñanza secundaria. Los gastos relativos al segundo grado, por consiguiente, incluyen solamente los tres ultimos años (escuela secundaria superior).
United Kingdom:
E--> Figures are in millions.
FR-> Les chiffres sont exprimés en millions.
ESP> Las cifras se expresan en millones.
Yugoslavia:
E--> Figures are in millions.
FR-> Les chiffres sont exprimés en millions.
ESP> Las cifras se expresan en millones.
OCEANIA
Tonga:
E--> Expenditure on administration is included with teachers' emoluments.
FR-> Les dépenses de l'administration sont incluses avec les émoluments du personnel enseignant.
ESP> Los gastos de la administración quedan incluídos en los emolumentos del personal docente.

5 Science and technology

Science et technologie

Ciencia y tecnología

This chapter presents selected results of the world-wide data collection effort by Unesco in the field of science and technology. Most of the data were obtained from replies to the annual statistical questionnaires on manpower and expenditure for research and experimental development sent to the Member States of Unesco during recent years, completed or supplemented by data collected in the earlier surveys and from official reports and publications.

The definitions and concepts suggested for use in the *Statistical Questionnaire on Scientific Research and Experimental Development* (most recent docs. Unesco STS/Q/841 and Unesco STS/Q/851) are based on the *Recommendation concerning the International Standardization of Statistics on Science and Technology* and can be found in the *Manual for Statistics on Scientific and Technological Activities* (doc. Unesco ST-84/WS/12). They can also be found in previous editions of this *Yearbook*.

Abridged versions of the definitions set out in the above-mentioned Recommendation are given below.

Type of personnel.

The following three categories of scientific and technical personnel are defined according to the work they are engaged in and their qualifications:

(1) *Scientists and engineers*, comprising persons working in those capacities, i.e. as persons with scientific or technological training (usually completion of third level education) in any field of science as defined below, who are engaged in professional work on R&D activities, administrators and other high-level personnel who direct the execution of R&D activities.

(2) *Technicians* comprising persons engaged in that capacity in R&D activities who have received vocational or technical training in any branch of knowledge or technology of a specified standard (usually at least three years after the first stage of second-level education).

(3) *Auxiliary personnel*, comprising persons whose work is *directly* associated with the performance of R&D activities, i.e. clerical, secretarial and administrative personnel, skilled, semi-skilled and unskilled workers in the various trades and all other auxiliary personnel.

Scientific and technical manpower potential

An indication of the total numerical strength of the most qualified human resources is obtained either from the total stock or the number of economically active persons who possess the necessary qualifications to be scientists, engineers or technicians.

Full- and part-time scientific and technical personnel and full-time equivalent.

Data concerning personnel are normally calculated in FTE, especially in the case of scientists and engineers.

Full-time equivalent (FTE). This is a measurement unit representing one person working full-time for a given period; this unit is used to convert figures relating to the number of part-time workers into the equivalent number of full-time workers.

Research and experimental development (R&D).

In general R&D is defined as any creative systematic activity undertaken in order to increase the stock of knowledge, including knowledge of man, culture and society, and the use of this knowledge to devise new applications. It includes fundamental research ((i.e. experimental or theoretical work undertaken with no immediate practical purpose in mind), applied research in such fields as agriculture, medicine, industrial chemistry, etc., (i.e. research directed primarily towards a special practical aim or objective), and experimental development work leading to new devices, products or processes.

Field of study.

The broad fields of study in science and technology are correlated with the following groups of programmes of ISCED fields:

Natural sciences, engineering and technology, medical sciences, agricultural sciences, social sciences and humanities, and other fields.

Sectors of performance.

The sectors of performance identify those areas of the economy in which R&D work is performed. The term 'sector of performance' distinguishes the execution or the performance of R&D activities from their financing.

Three major sectors of performance can be distinguished: the productive sector, the higher education sector and the general service sector, the productive sector being measured on two 'levels' - R&D activities 'integrated' and those 'not integrated' with production. The productive sector thus covers industrial and trading establishments which produce and distribute goods and services for sale; the higher education sector relates to establishments of education at the third level and also includes those research institutes, experimental stations, etc. serving them, whilst the general service sector includes various public or government establishments serving the community as a whole.

Field of activity.

For more detailed analysis of R&D activities within a given sector of performance, subsectoral classifications are often used in national practice.

For institutions belonging to the *productive sector* (integrated or non-integrated activities) the human and financial resources devoted to R&D activities are subdivided by branch of economic activity in accordance with the *International Standard Industrial Classification of all Economic Activities* (ISIC), under the following industry groupings:

(i) Agriculture, hunting, forestry and fishing
(ii) Mining, and quarrying (extracting industries)
(iii) Manufacturing industries
(iv) Utilities

(v) Construction
(vi) Transport, storage and communication
(vii) Other (ISIC:6, 8 and that part of 9 which includes those activities which are not included in the *general service* or *higher education sectors*).

In institutions belonging to the *higher education sector* and to the *general service sector* the human and financial resources devoted to R&D activities are subdivided by field of science and technology as follows:

Natural sciences, engineering and technology, medical sciences, agricultural sciences and social sciences and humanities.

R&D expenditure.

The measurement of R&D expenditure is calculated on the basis of intramural current expenditure, including overheads, and intramural capital expenditure. The sum of the intramural expenditures incurred by the national institutions provides the total domestic expenditure which is the information presented at the international level.

Total domestic expenditure on R&D activities refers to all expenditure made for this purpose in the course of a reference year in institutions and installations established in the national territory, as well as installations physically situated abroad.

The total *expenditure for R&D* as defined above comprises *current expenditure*, including overheads, and *capital expenditure*. Current intramural expenditure is further separated into labour costs and other current costs.

Source of funds.

The following sources of finance for domestic expenditure on R&D activities permit the identification of the financial supporters of such activities:

Government funds: include funds provided by the central (federal) State or local authorities.

Productive enterprise funds and special funds: funds allocated to R&D activities by institutions classified in the productive sector and all sums received from the 'Technical and Economic Progress Fund' and other similar funds.

Foreign funds: funds received from abroad for national R&D activities.

Other funds: funds that cannot be classified under any of the preceding headings.

Major socio-economic aims

The classification of data on *national activities in R&D* by socio-economic aims or objectives is based on the ultimate aim or purpose for which these activities are carried out.

I Exploration and assessment of the earth, the seas and atmosphere
II Civil space
III Development of agriculture, forestry and fishing
IV Promotion of industrial development
V Production, conservation and distribution of energy
VI Development of transport and communication
VII Development of educational services
VIII Development of health services
IX Social development and socio-economic services
X Protection of the environment
XI General advancement of knowledge
XII Other aims
XIII Defence

Table Notes

The tables in this chapter are presented in four sections. The first section (A) comprises 9 figures and two tables (5.1 and 5.2) which provide a summary presentation of data relating to R&D scientists and engineers and expenditures.

The first 6 figures, based on world and regional estimates of R&D scientists and engineers and R&D expenditure in 1970, 1975 and 1980, illustrate the distribution of human and financial resources devoted to R&D in the developed and developing countries and by groups of countries.

The remaining 3 figures, which are based on the historical data contained in tables 5.16 and 5.17 of this *Yearbook* (and the preceding editions) show the 'density' of R&D scientists and engineers, i.e., their number per million population, and the expenditure for R&D as a percentage of the gross national product (G.N.P.) for selected developed and developing countries and those with centrally-planned economies.

The following three sections comprise 17 tables presenting information obtained from the Unesco statistical surveys. The reader will find in each table an indication of the number of countries and territories included. The total number of countries covered in the seventeen tables is 150.

The second section (B) consists of 6 tables relating to scientifi and technical manpower. The scientific and technical manpowe potential is shown in ***Table 5.3***. The total numerical strength c the most qualified human resources, namely the stock and numb of economically active persons who possess the necessa qualifications to become scientists, engineers or technicians, essential information for the planning and formulation of scienc policy. Data relating to stock are usually obtained through th population census so that they are not readily available eve year and, where possible, the number of economically activ qualified manpower is shown, with stock given as an alternativ when such data are lacking. The corresponding number of wome is also shown. In some countries and territories the number non-national qualified manpower is relatively significant and whe the situation is known it has been indicated in a footnote.

Table 5.4 provides corresponding data for the scientist engineers and technicians engaged in research and experimen development activities, with some data for women when they a available. Unlike Table 5.3 which reports the actual number persons, in this table, unless otherwise indicated, the data a shown in full-time equivalent.

In ***Table 5.5*** only data for scientists and engineers engaged research and experimental development are presente distributed by the field of study, i.e. the field of science of th qualification, and according to whether they are occupied fu time or part-time. Their full-time equivalent is also shown ar where possible separate data are given for women.

Table 5.6 covers all personnel engaged in R&D and show their distribution according to the three sectors of performan (Productive, Higher education and General service), providi both the absolute numbers (in full-time equivalent unle otherwise indicated) and the percentage distribution. Because the different structure of the Productive sector in countri with different socio-economic systems, to facilitate compariso two 'integration levels' are also shown within this sector. Th provides an indication of the degree of linkage between R&D ar production in the different socio-economic systems. The differe types of personnel performing in these sectors are also shown

Tables 5.7 and ***5.8*** provide an indication of the orientation national R&D efforts in a limited number of countries, showi scientists and engineers engaged in R&D according to their fie of activity, i.e. the industry group or field of investigation of th enterprise, or institution, or their present field of investigation. T absolute number of scientists and engineers (in full-tin equivalent unless otherwise indicated) and their percenta distribution are provided. In the Productive sector (***Table 5.7***) t data are distributed by branch of economic activity according industry groupings. For the Higher education and General servi sectors (***Table 5.8***) the data refer to field of science technology.

The third section (C), comprises 7 tables and provides a gene picture of the cost of R&D activities. The data are given in natior currencies.

The absolute figures for R&D expenditure should not compared country by country. Such comparisons would requ the conversion of national currencies into a common currency means of the official exchange rates, since special R&D exchan rates do not exist. Official exchange rates do not always reflect t real costs of R&D activities and comparisons based on such rat can result in misleading conclusions. However, they do have sor limited value in indicating at least a gross order of magnitude expenditure on R&D. For the rates of exchange betwe national currencies and the United States dollar, the reader referred to Appendix C.

In ***Table 5.9*** total expenditure for R&D is subdivided by ty of expenditure - total, capital and current, further subdivided in labour and other current costs - and the current as percentage total expenditure is provided.

The structure of the financing of R&D can be seen in ***Tab 5.10*** which gives the distribution of total expenditure alternatively current expenditure) by four main categories sources of funds. Again, the data are presented in natio currencies and in percentages where the information considered sufficiently complete to enable the reader to compa between countries the efforts of different financial supporters R&D activities.

In ***Table 5.11*** the absolute figures and the percenta distribution of current expenditure according to type of R& activity - fundamental research, applied research experimental development - are presented, thus showing t relative importance in terms of financial resources devoted each of the types of such activity.

Table 5.12 shows the distribution of total and current expenditure by the three sectors of performance. As in Table 5.6 the Productive sector is further broken down into two 'integration levels'. The expenditures are presented in absolute numbers and to facilitate country-wise comparisons, where sufficiently complete data are available, the percentage distribution among the sectors is also given.

Analagous to Tables 5.7 and 5.8 for scientists and engineers, ***Tables 5.13*** and ***5.14*** aim at showing the financial resources devoted to R&D in different fields of activity within each sector of performance setting out both the amounts expended in national currency and the percentage distribution. For the Productive sector (***Table 5.13***) the total expenditure for R&D is distributed by branch of economic activity showing different industry groupings. For the Higher education and General service sectors (***Table 5.14***), the total expenditure for R&D is subdivided by field of science or technology.

Table 5.15 presents the distribution (both in absolute figures and in percentages) of public (government) funds or alternatively total national expenditure for R&D according to thirteen major aims; this is an analytical breakdown of R&D expenditures classified 'functionally' (in Table 5.12 the classification is 'institutional' or 'sectoral'), providing summary information on the broad pattern of national R&D efforts.

The last section (D) has been provided to convey a general picture of the development of R&D activities and to include additional indicators. Two tables present historical data, showing the growth in human and financial resources devoted to R&D activities, whilst the last two provide indications of the efforts made in the area of R&D activities.

Table 5.16 is concerned with trends in total personnel and the three types of personnel - scientists and engineers, technicians and auxiliary personnel - engaged in R&D and presents selected years, normally between 1969 and 1984; the information for scientists and engineers is also expressed in index numbers using as far as possible the base 1969 equal to 100 to show more clearly their variation.

In ***Table 5.17*** a time series of total and current expenditures devoted to R&D activities covers the same period, generally around 1969 and selected years to 1984. The relationship between current and total expenditures is also shown in percentage form thus indicating any variations in the structure of R&D expenditure.

The last two tables provide selected indicators on the human and financial resources for R&D. ***Table 5.18*** is devoted to scientific and technical manpower. It shows both the scientific and technical manpower potential, i.e. those who possess the necessary qualifications to become scientists, engineers or technicians, and the scientists, engineers and technicians engaged in R&D related to the total population; the relationship between potential scientists and engineers and those engaged in R&D is also provided as well as the support ratio for scientists and engineers, i.e. the number of technicians per scientist or engineer engaged in R&D.

The indicators presented in ***Table 5.19*** are concerned with the financial resources for R&D showing expenditure for R&D related to the total population and to the number of scientists and engineers engaged in R&D and also given as a percentage of gross national product (G.N.P.).

Research workers interested in obtaining further details or clarification pertaining to particular countries as regards national definitions, coverage or limitations of the data presented in the tables may address their enquiries to the Division of Statistics on Science and Technology of the Office of Statistics.

Le lecteur trouvera consignés dans ce chapitre quelques résultats sélectionnés des efforts que l'Unesco a déployés pour rassembler à l'échelon mondial des données statistiques concernant la science et la technologie. Les données proviennent pour la plupart des réponses aux questionnaires statistiques annuels sur le personnel et les dépenses de recherche et de développement expérimental que l'Unesco a adressés aux Etats membres ces dernières années. Elles ont été complétées par des renseignements recueillis auparavant à l'aide des précédentes enquêtes et des rapports officiels et publications.

Les définitions et concepts proposés pour être utilisés dans le *Questionnaire statistique sur la recherche scientifique et le développement expérimental* (docs. Unesco STS/Q/841 et Unesco STS/Q/851) sont basés sur la *Recommandation concernant la normalisation internationale des statistiques relatives à la science et à la technologie* et figurent dans le *Manuel pour les statistiques relatives aux activités scientifiques et techniques* (doc. Unesco ST-84/WS/12). Ces définitions ont déjà été publiées dans des éditions précédentes de cet *Annuaire*.

On trouvera ci-dessous des versions abrégées des définitions proposées dans la Recommandation sus-mentionnée.

Catégories du personnel.

Les trois catégories de personnel scientifique et technique suivantes sont définies d'après leurs fonctions et qualifications:

(1) *Scientifiques et ingénieurs* comprenant les personnes qui travaillent en tant que tels, c'est-à-dire comme personnel de conception dans les activités de R-D et qui ont reçu une formation scientifique ou technique (d'ordinaire des études complètes du troisième degré) dans n'importe quel domaine de la science, cité ci-dessous, les administrateurs et autres personnel de haut niveau qui dirigent l'exécution des activités de R-D.

(2) *Techniciens* comprenant les personnes qui travaillent en tant que tels dans des activités de R-D et qui ont reçu une formation professionnelle ou technique dans n'importe quelle branche du savoir ou de la technologie d'un niveau specifié (d'ordinaire au moins trois années d'études après achèvement du premier cycle de l'enseignement du second degré).

(3) *Personnel auxiliaire* comprenant les personnes dont les fonctions sont *directement* associées à l'exécution des activités de R-D à savoir le personnel de bureau, de secrétariat et d'administration, les ouvriers qualifiés, semi-qualifiés et non qualifiés dans les divers métiers et tout autre personnel auxiliaire.

Potentiel humain scientifique et technique

Une indication du potentiel des ressources humaines les plus qualifiées est obtenue d'après le stock total du personnel ou du nombre de personnes économiquement actives qui possèdent les qualifications requises pour être classées dans les catégories de 'scientifiques et ingénieurs' et 'techniciens'.

Personnel scientifique et technique travaillant à plein temps et à temps partiel et équivalent plein temps.

En principe, les données concernant le personnel sont calculées en EPT, surtout dans le cas des scientifiques et ingénieurs.

Equivalent plein temps (EPT). Unité d'évaluation qui correspond à une personne travaillant à plein temps pendant une période donnée. On se sert de cette unité pour convertir en nombre de personnes à plein temps le nombre de celles qui travaillent à temps partiel.

Recherche et développement expérimental (R-D).

En général, la recherche scientifique et le développement expérimental (R-D) englobent tous les travaux systématiques et créateurs entrepris afin d'accroître le stock de connaissances, y compris celles qui concernent l'homme, la culture et la société, et l'utilisation de ce stock de connaissances pour imaginer de nouvelles applications. Elle comprend la recherche fondamentale (c'est-à-dire, travaux expérimentaux ou théoriques entrepris principalement sans qu'une application ou utilisation particulière ou spécifique soit recherchée), la recherche appliquée dans des domaines tels que l'agriculture, la médecine, la chimie industrielle, etc. (c'est-à-dire, recherche originale visant principalement un but ou objectif pratique spécifique), et le développement expérimental conduisant à la mise au point de nouveaux produits, dispositifs ou procédés.

Domaine d'études

La concordance entre les grands domaines d'études de science et de technologie et la classification des domaines d'études de la CITE doit être la suivante:

> Sciences exactes et naturelles, sciences de l'ingénieur et technologiques, sciences médicales, sciences agricoles, sciences sociales et humaines, et autres domaines.

Secteurs d'exécution.

Les secteurs d'exécution sont les secteurs de l'économie dans lesquels s'exercent les activités de R-D. La notion de 'secteur d'exécution' permet de distinguer entre l'exécution des activités de R-D et leur financement. On peut distinguer trois grands secteurs d'exécution: le secteur de la production, le secteur de l'enseignement supérieur et le secteur de service général, le secteur de la production se subdivisant en deux 'niveau d'integration' - les activités de R-D 'intégrées' à la production et les activités 'non-intégrées' à la production. Le secteur de la production comprend donc les entreprises industrielles et commerciales qui produisent et distribuent des biens et des services contre rémunération, le secteur de l'enseignement supérieur comprend tous les établissements d'enseignement du troisième degré ainsi que les instituts de recherche, stations d'essais, etc. qui desservent ces établissements, et le secteur de service général comprend tous les organismes, ministères et établissements des administrations publiques - administrations centrales ou administrations des Etats - qui desservent l'ensemble de la communauté.

Domaine d'activité

Pour une analyse plus détaillée des activités de R-D d'un secteur d'exécution donné, on a souvent recours, dans la pratique nationale, à des classifications par sous-secteur.

En ce qui concerne les institutions appartenant au *secteur de la production* (activités intégrées ou non), les ressources humaines et financières consacrées aux activités de R-D sont subdivisées par branche d'activité économique suivant la 'Classification internationale type, par industrie, de toutes les branches de l'activité économique' (CITI), et selon les groupements d'industries suivants:

(i) Agriculture, chasse, sylviculture et pêche
(ii) Industries extractives
(iii) Industries manufacturières
(iv) Services publics
(v) Bâtiment et travaux publics
(vi) Transports, entrepôts et communication
(vii) Activités diverses (CITI: 6, 8 et la partie de 9 qui comprend les activités non incluses dans le *secteur de service général* ou celui de *l'enseignement supérieur*).

Dans les institutions appartenant aux *secteurs de l'enseignement supérieur* et *de service général* les ressources humaines et financières consacrées aux activités de R-D sont subdivisées d'après les domaines de la science et de la technologie, comme suit:

Sciences exactes et naturelles, sciences de l'ingénieur et technologiques, sciences médicales, sciences agricoles, sciences sociales et humaines.

Dépenses de R-D. Le coût des activités de R-D est calculé sur la base des dépenses courantes intra-muros y compris les frais généraux, et les dépenses en capital intra-muros. La somme des dépenses intra-muros effectuées par toutes les institutions nationales conduit à un agrégat total des dépenses intérieures, qui est l'information présentée à l'échelon international.

Total des dépenses intérieures pour des activités de R-D peut être défini comme l'ensemble des dépenses effectuées à ce titre, au cours d'une année de référence, dans les institutions et installations situées sur le territoire national, y compris dans les installations qui sont géographiquement situées à l'étranger.

Les *dépenses totales pour les activités de R-D*, telles qu'elles sont définies ci-dessus, comprennent toutes les dépenses courantes, y compris les frais généraux et les dépenses en capital. Les dépenses courantes intramuros sont subdivisées en dépenses totales de personnel et autres dépenses courantes.

Sources de financement.

Afin de pouvoir identifier l'origine du financement des activités de R-D, les catégories de sources de financement pour les dépenses de R-D se définissent comme suit:

Fonds publics comprend les fonds fournis par le gouvernement central ou par les autorités locales.

Fonds provenant des entreprises de production et fonds spéciaux: comprend les fonds affectés aux activités de R-D par les institutions classées dans le secteur de la production comme des établissements ou des entreprises de production et tous les fonds provenant des 'Fonds de développement technique et économique' et d'autres fonds analogues.

Fonds étrangers comprend les fonds reçus de l'étranger pour les activités de R-D nationales.

Fonds divers: comprend les fonds qui ne peuvent être classés dans l'une des rubriques précédentes.

Finalités socio-économiques principales

La classification des données relatives aux *activités nationales de R-D* par finalités ou objectifs socio-économiques repose sur le but final de ces travaux.

I Exploration et évaluation de la terre, des mers et de l'atmosphère
II Espace civil
III Développement de l'agriculture, de la sylviculture et de la pêche
IV Promotion du développement industriel
V Production, conservation et distribution de l'énergie
VI Développement des transports et des communications
VII Développement des services d'enseignement
VIII Développement des services de santé
IX Développement social et services socio-économiques
X Protection de l'environnement
XI Promotion générale des connaissances
XII Autres finalités
XIII Défense

Notes sur les tableaux

Les tableaux de ce chapitre sont classés en quatre sections. première section (A) comprend 9 graphiques et 2 tableaux (5.1 5.2) qui fournissent une présentation sommaire de donné relatives aux scientifiques et ingénieurs et aux dépenses de D.

Les 6 premiers graphiques basés sur les estimations mondial et régionales des scientifiques et ingénieurs employés dans d activités de R-D et des dépenses de R-D en 1970, 1975 1980 illustrent la distribution des ressources humaines financières consacrées à la R-D dans les pays développés et développement et par groupes de pays.

Les 3 derniers graphiques, qui sont basés sur les donné historiques présentées dans les tableaux 5.16 et 5.17 de c *Annuaire* (et dans les éditions précédentes), montrent la 'densi des scientifiques et ingénieurs employés á des travaux de R c'est à dire leur nombre par million d'habitants et les dépens consacrées à la R-D exprimées en pourcentage du produit natio brut (P.N.B), rassemblant des pays développés, des pays développement et ceux d'une économie planifiée.

Les trois sections suivantes comprennent 17 tableaux c présentent les données recueillies au moyen des enquêt statistiques de l'Unesco. Le lecteur trouvera le nombre des pa et territoires considérés indiqué en tête de chaque tableau. Po ces dix-sept tableaux, le total des pays est de 150.

La deuxième section (B) comprend 6 tableaux concernant personnel scientifique et technique. Le potentiel huma scientifique et technique est présenté dans le ***tableau 5.3***. potentiel des ressources humaines les plus qualifiées, à savoir stock total ou le nombre économiquement actif de personnes c possèdent les qualifications requises pour être scientifiqu ingénieurs ou techniciens est une information essentielle po planifier et formuler la politique scientifique. Les données relativ à l'effectif total (stock) sont généralement obtenues lors d recensements de la population, ce qui fait qu'elles ne sont p disponibles tous les ans. Dans la mesure du possible, le nombre personnes qualifiées économiquement actives est presenté, 'stock' étant donné comme une alternative lorsque nous disposons pas de cette information. Le nombre correspondant femmes est également indiqué. Pour certains pays ou territoi le nombre de personnes qualifiées mais ressortissants étrange est assez significatif; lorsque l'information a été indiquée, le f est signalé par une note.

Le ***tableau 5.4*** présente les données relatives a scientifiques, ingénieurs et techniciens qui sont employés à d travaux de recherche et de développement expérimental, avec nombre correspondant de femmes lorsque cette information connue. Dans ce tableau, sauf indication contraire, les donné sont exprimées en 'équivalent plein temps' (dans le table précédent les chiffres se réfèrent au nombre de personn physiques).

Seules figurent au ***tableau 5.5*** les données concernant scientifiques et ingénieurs employés à des travaux de recherc et de développement expérimental classés selon le domai d'études, c'est-à-dire, la discipline scientifique correspondan leur qualification et selon qu'ils sont employés à plein temps à temps partiel. On donne aussi leur équivalent plein temps et, possible, séparément, des données concernant les femmes.

Le ***tableau 5.6*** concerne tout le personnel employé à c travaux de R-D et montre leur répartition entre les trois secte d'exécution (secteurs de la production, de l'enseigneme supérieur et de service général). Il donne à la fois les chiff absolus (exprimés en équivalent plein temps, sauf indicati contraire) et la distribution en pourcentage du personnel. Comp tenu des différentes structures du secteur de la production da des pays aux systèmes socio-économiques différents et pour faciliter la comparaison, les données de ce secteur sont classe suivant deux 'niveaux d'intégration', qui indiquent le degré du l existant entre la R-D et la production dans les différents systèm socio-économiques. Les différentes catégories de person employé dans ces secteurs sont aussi présentées.

Les ***tableaux 5.7*** et ***5.8*** montrent l'orientation donnée a efforts nationaux de R-D pour un nombre limité de pays.

nombre de scientifiques et d'ingénieurs employés à des travaux de R-D est exprimé en équivalent plein temps ainsi qu'en pourcentage, ventilé par domaine d'activité, c'est-à-dire, par groupes d'industries ou le domaine de recherche auquel appartient leur entreprise, leur établissement ou leur institution ou selon leur domaine actuel de recherche. Pour le secteur de la production (***tableau 5.7***) les données sont présentées par les principales branches d'activité économique selon des regroupements des industries. Pour les secteurs de l'enseignement supérieur et de service général (***tableau 5.8***) les données se réfèrent au domaine de la science et de la technologie.

La troisième section (C) comprend 7 tableaux et donne un profil du coût des activités de R-D. Les données sont présentées en monnaie nationale.

Il faut éviter de comparer, d'un pays à l'autre, les chiffres absolus qui concernent les dépenses de R-D. On ne pourrait procéder à de telles comparaisons qu'en convertissant en une même monnaie les sommes libellées en monnaie nationale et, comme il n'existe pas de taux de change qui soit spécialement applicable aux activités de R-D, il faudrait nécessairement se fonder, pour cela, sur les taux de change officiels. Or ces taux ne reflètent pas toujours le coût réel des activités de R-D et les comparaisons risquent alors d'être trompeuses. De telles comparaisons ne sont cependant pas totalement dénuées d'intérêt, car elles donnent au moins une idée de l'ordre de grandeur des dépenses de R-D. Le lecteur trouvera dans l'Annexe C les taux de change applicables à la conversion des monnaies nationales en dollars des Etats-Unis.

Dans le ***tableau 5.9***, les dépenses totales de R-D sont subdivisées par type de dépenses (totales, en capital et courantes - ces dernières à leur tour subdivisées en dépenses de personnel et autres dépenses courantes) et les dépenses courantes en pourcentage du total sont aussi présentés.

Quant à la structure du financement de la R-D, elle est présentée dans le ***tableau 5.10*** où les dépenses totales (ou à défaut les dépenses courantes) sont distribuées d'après les quatre grandes catégories de sources de financement. Les données sont toujours présentées en monnaie nationale et en pourcentages, lorsque des informations complètes sont disponibles, pour permettre au lecteur de comparer les efforts réalisés dans les différents pays par ceux qui assurent le financement des activités de R-D.

Le ***tableau 5.11*** montre la distribution des dépenses courantes en chiffres absolus et en pourcentage par type d'activité de R-D - recherche fondamentale, recherche appliquée ou développement expérimental - afin de faire ressortir l'importance relative des ressources financières consacrées à chacun des types de cette activité.

Le ***tableau 5.12*** présente la distribution des dépenses totales et courantes selon les trois secteurs d'exécution. Comme dans le tableau 5.6, les données pour le secteur de la production sont réparties selon les deux niveaux d'intégration. Les dépenses sont présentées en chiffres absolus et, pour faciliter les comparaisons entre les pays, lorsque des données complètes sont disponibles, leur distribution en pourcentage selon les secteurs est indiquée.

De façon analogue aux tableaux 5.7 et 5.8 qui concerne les scientifiques et ingénieurs, les ***tableaux 5.13*** et ***5.14*** ont pour objectif de présenter les ressources financières investies dans la R-D dans les différents domaines d'activités suivant les secteurs d'exécution montrant leur répartition en monnaie nationale et en pourcentage. Pour le secteur de la production (***tableau 5.13***) les dépenses totales consacrées à la R-D sont réparties par les principales branches d'activité économique selon des regroupements des industries. Pour les secteurs de l'enseignement supérieur et de service général (***tableau 5.14***), les dépenses totales consacrées à la R-D sont subdivisées d'après les domaines de la science et de la technologie.

Le ***tableau 5.15*** donne la distribution (tant en chiffres absolus qu'en pourcentage) des fonds publics, ou alternativement les dépenses totales nationales, consacrées aux activités de R-D selon treize finalités principales; il s'agit là d'une ventilation analytique des dépenses de R-D d'après une classification 'fonctionnelle' (dans le tableau 5.12, la classification est 'institutionnelle ou sectorielle'); cette ventilation montre la structure générale des efforts nationaux de R-D.

La dernière section (D) donne une vue générale du développement des activités de R-D et comprend également des indicateurs supplémentaires. Deux tableaux présentent des données rétrospectives montrant la croissance des ressources humaines et financières consacrées à la R-D, tandis que les deux derniers tableaux fournissent des indications des efforts réalisés pour consacrer des ressources financières et en main d'oeuvre à ces activités.

Le ***tableau 5.16*** montre les tendances en ce qui concerne l'ensemble du personnel ainsi que les trois catégories de personnel - scientifiques et ingénieurs, techniciens et personnel auxiliaire - employés à des travaux de R-D pendant les dernières années, période couvrant, en général 1969 et des années selectionnées jusqu'à 1984. Les informations concernant les scientifiques et ingénieurs sont également exprimées sous forme d'indices en utilisant, dans toute la mesure du possible, la base 1969=100 pour que les variations apparaissent plus clairement.

Le ***tableau 5.17*** présente une série chronologique des dépenses totales et courantes consacrées à des activités de R-D pour la même période, en général à partir de 1969 et pour des années sélectionnées jusqu'à 1984. On trouvera aussi en pourcentage le rapport entre les dépenses totales et courantes, permettant de déceler les variations dans la structure des dépenses de R-D.

Les deux derniers tableaux fournissent des indicateurs sélectionnés sur les ressources humaines et financières consacrées à la R-D. Le ***tableau 5.18*** concerne le personnel scientifique et technique et présente le potentiel humain scientifique et technique, c'est à dire les personnes ayant les qualifications requises pour être scientifique, ingénieur ou technicien ainsi que les scientifiques, ingénieurs et techniciens employés à des travaux de R-D par rapport à la population totale. On trouvera aussi le rapport entre les scientifiques et ingénieurs potentiels et ceux employés à des travaux de R-D ainsi que le rapport entre le nombre de techniciens et celui des scientifiques et ingénieurs employés à des travaux de R-D.

Les indicateurs présentés dans le ***tableau 5.19*** concernent les ressources financières consacrées á la R-D et montrent les dépenses de R-D rapportées, elles aussi, à la population totale et au nombre de scientifiques et ingénieurs employés à la R-D, et exprimées en pourcentage du produit national brut (P.N.B.).

Les chercheurs qui souhaiteraient obtenir d'autres détails ou des éclaircissements sur un pays particulier en ce qui concerne les définitions nationales, la portée ou les limitations des données présentées dans les tableaux, peuvent adresser leur demande à l'Office des Statistiques, Division des Statistiques relatives à la Science et à la Technologie.

El presente capítulo contiene una selección de los resultados alcanzados por la Unesco gracias al esfuerzo hecho, a escala mundial, para reunir datos estadísticos relativos a la ciencia y la tecnología. Los datos proceden, en su mayor parte, de las respuestas al cuestionario estadístico anual sobre el personal y gastos de investigación y desarrollo experimental, que la Unesco envió a los Estados Miembros en años recientes, habiendo sido completados con informaciones procedentes de las anteriores encuestas, de informes oficiales y publicaciones.

Las definiciones propuestas para su empleo en el *Cuestionario Estadístico sobre la Investigación Científica y el Desarrollo Experimental* (docs. Unesco STS/Q/841 y Unesco STS/Q/851) están basadas en la *Recomendación sobre la normalización internacional de las estadísticas relativas a la ciencia y la tecnología* y que pueden encontrarse en el *Manual de Estadísticas sobre las Actividades Científicas y Tecnológicas* (doc. Unesco ST-84/WS/12). Pueden también encontrarse estas definiciones en las ediciones precedentes de esto *Anuario*.

A continuación encontrarán las versiones resumidas de las definiciones propuestas en la Recomendación arriba mencionada.

Categoría de personal.

Las tres categorías siguientes de personal científico y técnico se definen según su función y calificaciones.

(1) *Científicos e ingenieros*, que son las personas que trabajan como tales, es decir, como personal de concepción en las actividades de I y D y que han recibido formación científica o técnica (normalmente enseñanza de tercer grado completa) en no importa que campo de la ciencia, que se indica más abajo, los administradores y demás personal de categoría superior que dirigen la ejecución de las actividades de I y D.

(2) *Técnicos*, que son las personas que trabajan como tales en

actividades de I y D y que han recibido formación profesional técnica en cualquiera de las ramas del saber o de la tecnología, (normalmente con un mínimo de tres años de estudios después de haber terminado el primer ciclo de la enseñanza de segundo grado).

(3) *Personal auxiliar*, que son las personas cuyas funciones están directamente asociadas a la ejecución de las actividades de I y D, a saber, el personal administrativo, de secretaría y de oficina, los obreros especializados, semiespecializados y no especializados en los diversos oficios y los demás tipos de personal auxiliar.

Recursos humanos científicos y técnicos potenciales.

Una indicación del potencial de los recursos humanos más capacitados se obtiene según el número total del personal o el número de personas económicamente activas que poseen las calificaciones necesarias para quedar clasificadas como 'científicos, ingenieros y técnicos'.

Personal científico y técnico que trabaja a jornada completa, a jornada parcial y en equivalente de jornada completa.

En principio, los datos relativos al personal se calculan en EJC sobre todo en el caso de los científicos e ingenieros.

Equivalente de jornada completa (EJC). Unidad de evaluación que corresponde a una persona que trabaja en régimen de plena dedicación durante un período dado. Se emplea esta unidad para convertir las cifras relativas al número de personas que trabajan en régimen de jornada parcial en un número equivalente de personas que trabajan a jornada completa.

Investigación y desarrollo experimental (I y D).

Por I y D se entiende, en general, cualquier trabajo sistemático y creador realizado con el fin de aumentar el caudal de conocimientos, inclusive el conocimiento del hombre, la cultura y la sociedad, y de utilizar estos conocimientos para descubrir nuevas aplicaciones. Comprende la investigación fundamental (es decir, trabajo experimental o téorico efectuado principalmente sin prever ninguna aplicación determinada o específica), la investigación aplicada en ramas tales como la agricultura, la medicina, la química industrial, etc., (es decir, investigación original encaminada principalmente hacia una finalidad u objetivo práctico determinado), y el desarrollo experimental que conduce a la creación de nuevos dispositivos o procedimientos.

Sector de estudios

La clasificación según el sector de estudios en materia de ciencia y tecnología debe relacionarse con los siguientes grupos de sectores de la CINE:

Ciencias exactas y naturales, ingeniería y tecnología, ciencias médicas, ciencias agrícolas, ciencias sociales y humanas, y otros campos.

Sectores de ejecución.

Los sectores de ejecución son aquellos sectores de la economía en los que se realizan actividades de I y D. El término 'Sector de Ejecución' distingue la realización o ejecución de actividades de I y D y de su financiamiento. Se pueden distinguir tres grandes sectores de ejecución: el sector productivo, el sector de enseñanza superior y el sector de servicio general, el sector productivo se reparten según dos 'niveles' de integración - actividades de I y D 'integradas' a la producción y las actividades 'no integradas' a la producción. El sector productivo engloba las empresas industriales y comerciales nacionales y extranjeras, situadas en el país, que producen y distribuyen bienes y servicios a cambio de una remuneración. El sector de enseñanza superior comprende todos los centros de enseñanza de tercer grado así como los institutos de investigación, estaciones de ensayo, etc. que prestan servicios a esos centros. El sector de servicio general comprende todos los organismos, ministerios y establecimientos de la administración pública - administración central o administración de los Estados de una federación que prestan servicios a toda la comunidad.

Campos de actuación

Con miras a un análisis más detallado de las actividades de I y D en un determinado sector de ejecución, se utilizan a menudo en la práctica nacional clasificaciones subsectoriales.

En el caso de las instituciones pertenecientes al *sector productivo* (actividades integradas o no), procede subdividir los recursos humanos y financieros dedicados a las actividades de I y D según la rama de actividad económica, en consonancia con la Clasificación Industrial Internacional Uniforme (CIIU), y los siguientes grupos industriales:

(i) Agricultura, silvicultura, caza y pesca
(ii) Industrias extractivas
(iii) Industrias manufactureras
(iv) Servicios públicos
(v) Construcción
(vi) Transportes, almacenamiento y comunicaciones
(vii) Otros grupos industriales (CIIU: 6, 8 y 9 en parte, que comprende las actividades no incluídas en el *sector de servicio general* o de *enseñanza superior*).

En las instituciones del *sector de enseñanza superior* y en el *sec. de servicio general* convendrá subdividir los recursos humanos financieros dedicados a las actividades de I y D, según l campos de la ciencia y la tecnología a saber:

Ciencias exactas y naturales, ingeniería y tecnología, ciencias médicas, ciencias agrícolas, ciencias sociales y humanas.

Gastos de I y D.

El cálculo de los gastos relativos a las actividades de I y D efectuará sobre la base de los gastos ordinarios intramur incluídos los gastos generales y los gastos de capital intramur La suma de los gastos intramuros de todas las institucion nacionales constituye un total final que recibe el nombre 'gastos interiores totales' que se utilizan cuando se preser información a escala internacional.

Total de los gastos interiores para actividades de I y D pued definirse como todos los gastos efectuados a este respec durante el año de referencia, en las instituciones instalaciones situadas en el territorio nacional, comprendidos l relativos a las instalaciones situadas geográficamente en extranjero.

Los *gastos totales para I y D* tal como se definen en el párra anterior, comprenden los gastos corrientes intramuros, incluíd los gastos generales, y los gastos de capital intramuros. Los gast corrientes intramuros se distribuirán en gastos totales de perso y gastos corrientes varios.

Origen de los fondos.

Con el fin de poder identificar el origen de financiamiento las actividades de I y D, las categorías de fuentes financiamiento para los gastos interiores de I y D se defin como sigue:

Fondos públicos comprende los fondos proporcionados por autoridades centrales (federales), estatales o locales.

Fondos procedentes de empresas de producción y fondos especia comprende los fondos asignados a actividades de I y D por instituciones clasificadas en el sector productivo con establecimientos o empresas de producción y todos los fond procedentes de los 'Fondos de Desarrollo Técnico y Económic y otros fondos análogos.

Fondos extranjeros comprende los fondos recibidos extranjero para la realización de actividades nacionales de I D.

Fondos varios comprende los fondos que no queda clasificar ninguna de las categorías anteriores.

Principales finalidades socioeconómicas

La clasificación de los datos sobre las *actividades nacionales I y D* según las finalidades u objetivos socioeconómicos se ba en definitiva, en la finalidad última para la que se llevan a ca esas actividades.

I Exploración y evaluación de la tierra, los mares, la atmósfera y el espacio
II Espacio civil
III Desarrollo de la agricultura, la silvicultura y la pesca
IV Fomento del desarollo industrial
V Producción, conservación y distribución de la energía
VI Desarrollo de los transportes y las comunicaciones
VII Desarrollo de los servicios educativos
VIII Desarrollo de los servicios de sanidad
IX Desarrollo social y los servicios socioeconómicos
X Protección del medio ambiente
XI Adelanto general del saber
XII Otras finalidades
XIII Defensa nacional

Notas sobre los cuadros

Los cuadros en este capítulo se han clasificado en cuat secciones. La primera sección (A) consiste de 9 gráficos y cuadros (5.1 y 5.2) que muestran una presentación somera datos relativos a científicos e ingenieros y a los gastos en I D.

Los primeros 6 gráficos, basados en las estimacion mundiales y regionales de los científicos e ingenieros emplead en actividades de I y D y de los gastos de I y D en 1970, 19 y 1980, ilustran la distribución de los recursos humanos financieros dedicados a la I y D en los países desarrollados y desarrollo y por grupos de países.

Los últimos 3 gráficos, que están basados en los datos históricos presentados en los cuadros 5.16 y 5.17 de este *Anuario* (y en sus ediciones precedentes) muestran la 'densidad' de científicos e ingenieros empleados en trabajos de I y D; es decir el total por millón de habitantes y los gastos consagrados a la I y D presentados en porcentaje del Producto Nacional Bruto (PNB) para países desarrollados, en desarrollo, y los de planificación centralizada.

Las tres secciones siguientes comprenden 17 cuadros y muestran datos obtenidos por las encuestas estadísticas de la Unesco. El lector encontrará el número de países y de territorios considerados en el encabezamiento de cada cuadro. El número total de países cubiertos en los diecisiete cuadros asciende a 150.

La segunda sección (B) comprende 6 cuadros que se refieren al personal científico y técnico. El potencial humano científico y técnico se presenta en el ***cuadro 5.3***. El potencial de los recursos humanos más capacitados, es decir, el número total o el número de personas económicamente activas que poseen las calificaciones necesarias para ser científicos, ingenieros o técnicos, es una información esencial para planificar y formular la política científica. Los datos relativos al número total (stock) se obtiene generalmente a través de los censos de población, no disponiéndose por consiguiente de este dato todos los años. En la medida de lo posible, se presenta el número de personas calificadas económicamente activas, el número total (stock) dándose como una alternativa. El número correspondiente de mujeres figura igualmente en el cuadro. En algunos países y territorios el número de personas calificadas extranjeras es relativamente alto, y cada vez que tal situación ha llegado a nuestro conocimiento lo hemos indicado en una nota.

El ***cuadro 5.4*** indica los datos que se refieren a los científicos e ingenieros empleados en trabajos de investigación y de desarrollo experimental con algunos datos sobre mujeres empleadas, cuando éstos nos son proporcionados. Contrariamente al cuadro 5.3 que indica el número actual de personas, en este cuadro, salvo cuando se indica lo contrario, los datos figuran en equivalente de jornada completa.

El ***cuadro 5.5*** indica solamente los datos que se refieren a los científicos e ingenieros empleados en trabajos de investigación y de desarrollo experimental clasificados según el sector de estudios, es decir, la disciplina científica correspondiente a su calificación, y teniendo en cuenta su calidad de empleados de jornada completa o jornada parcial. Se da también su equivalente de jornada completa y, en la medida de lo posible, datos separados relativos a las mujeres.

El ***cuadro 5.6*** se refiere a todo el personal empleado en trabajos de I y D repartido entre los tres sectores de ejecución (sectores productivo, de enseñanza superior y de servicio general). Da a la vez las cifras absolutas (indicadas en equivalente de jornada completa salvo cuando se indica lo contrario) y la repartición en porcentaje del personal. Teniendo en cuenta las diversas estructuras del sector productivo en países con sistemas socio-económicos diferentes y con vistas a facilitar su comparación, los datos de este sector se han clasificado siguiendo dos 'niveles de integración', que indican el grado de relación existente entre la I y D y la producción en los diferentes sistemas socio-económicos. Se presentan igualmente las diferentes categorías de personal empleado en esos sectores.

Los ***cuadros 5.7*** y ***5.8*** muestran la orientación dada a los esfuerzos nacionales de I y D para un número limitado de países. El número de científicos e ingenieros ocupados en trabajos de I y D se indica según su campo de actuación, es decir, por grupos de industrias o por el campo de investigación a que pertenece su empresa, establecimiento o institución, o según su campo actual de investigación. Se indica tanto el número absoluto de científicos e ingenieros (en su equivalente de jornada completa, salvo cuando se señala lo contrario) como el porcentaje de distribución de éstos. Para el sector productivo (***cuadro 5.7***), los datos se presentan de acuerdo con las principales ramas de actividad económica, por agrupaciones de actividades industriales. Para los sectores de enseñanza superior y de servicio general (***cuadro 5.8***) los datos refieren al campo de la ciencia y de la tecnología.

La tercera sección (C) comprende 7 cuadros y da una idea del costo de las actividades de I y D. Los datos se presentan en moneda nacional.

Debe evitarse comparar, de un país a otro, las cifras absolutas referentes a los gastos de I y D. Sólo se podrían efectuar comparaciones semejantes convirtiendo en una misma moneda las sumas que figuran en moneda nacional, y como no existe un tipo de cambio especialmente aplicable a las actividades de I y D, sería necesario basarse para ello en los tipos de cambio oficiales. Como sea que tales tipos no siempre reflejan el costo real de las actividades de I y D, se corre el riesgo de que dichas comparaciones sean erróneas. Sin embargo, no carecen totalmente de interés ya que como mínimo dan una idea del orden de magnitud de los gastos de I y D. En el Anexo C pueden verse los tipos de cambio aplicables a la conversión de las monedas nacionales en dólares de los Estados Unidos.

En el ***cuadro 5.9***, los gastos totales de I y D se desglosan por tipo de gastos (total, de capital y corrientes - estos últimos subdividos a su vez en gastos de personal y gastos corrientes varios), estableciéndose una relación en porcentaje entre los gastos corrientes y los gastos totales.

En cuanto a la estructura del financiamiento de la I y D, se indica en el ***cuadro 5.10***, donde los gastos totales (o en su defecto los gastos corrientes) se desglosan según las cuatro grandes categorías de fuentes de financiamiento. Los datos se presentan como siempre en moneda nacional y en porcentaje cuando se dispone de datos completos, para que el lector pueda comparar los esfuerzos realizados en los diferentes países por parte de quienes aseguran el financiamiento de las actividades de I y D.

El ***cuadro 5.11*** muestra la repartición de los gastos corrientes en cifras absolutas y en porcentaje por tipo de actividad de I y D - investigación fundamental, investigación aplicada o desarrollo experimental - con objeto de indicar la importancia relativa de los recursos financieros destinados a cado uno de estos tipos de actividades.

El ***cuadro 5.12*** presenta la repartición de los gastos totales y corrientes para los tres sectores de ejecución. Como en el cuadro 5.6 los datos para el sector productivo se reparten según dos niveles de integración. Los gastos se presentan en cifras absolutas y, para facilitar las comparaciones entre los países cuando se dispone de datos completos, se indica su repartición entre los sectores en porcentaje.

Al igual que los cuadros 5.7 y 5.8 que conciernen a los científicos e ingenieros, los ***cuadros 5.13*** y ***5.14*** tienen por objeto indicar los recursos financieros dedicados a las actividades de I y D en los diferentes campos de actividad, según el sector de ejecución, haciendo resaltar tanto los gastos en moneda nacional así como su repartición en porcentaje. Para el sector productivo (***cuadro 5.13***) los datos se presentan de acuerdo con las principales ramas de actividad económica por agrupaciones de actividades industriales. Para los sectores de enseñanza superior y de servicio general (***cuadro 5.14***), los gastos totales dedicados a la I y D se subdividen de acuerdo con los campos de la ciencia y la tecnología.

El ***cuadro 5.15*** da la repartición de los fondos públicos, en cifras absolutas así como en porcentajes, o alternativamente de los gastos totales nacionales destinados a las actividades de I y D de acuerdo con doce finalidades principales; se trata de una ventilación analítica de los gastos de I y D según una clasificación 'funcional' (en el cuadro 5.12, la clasificación es 'institucional o sectorial'); esta ventilación pone de relieve la estructura general de los esfuerzos nacionales de I y D.

La última sección (D) da una visión general del desarrollo de las actividades de I y D, y comprende igualmente indicadores adicionales. Dos cuadros procuran datos retrospectivos mostrando el crecimiento de los recursos humanos y financieros dedicados a la I y D, mientras que los dos ultimos cuadros demuestran los esfuerzos realizados en I y D.

El ***cuadro 5.16*** muestra las tendencias en lo que concierne el total del personal, así como los tres tipos de personal, científicos e ingenieros, técnicos y personal auxiliar, empleados en trabajos de I y D durante los últimos años; en general a partir de 1969 y para años seleccionados hasta 1984. Las informaciones que se refieren a los científicos e ingenieros están traducidas en números índices utilizando en la medida de lo posible la base de 1969 igual a 100, para que las variaciones se aprecien más claramente.

El ***cuadro 5.17*** presenta una serie cronológica de los gastos totales y corrientes dedicados a la I y D para el mismo período; en general a partir de 1969 y para años seleccionados hasta 1984. También se indica la relación en porcentaje entre los gastos totales y corrientes, indicando además cualquier tipo de cambio en la estructura de los gastos de I y D.

Los dos últimos cuadros procuran indicadores seleccionados sobre los recursos humanos y financieros consagrados a la I y D. El ***cuadro 5.18*** comprende el personal científico y técnico y presenta el potencial humano científico y técnico, es decir, las personas que poseen las calificaciones necesarias para ser científicos, ingenieros o técnicos, así como también de los científicos, ingenieros y técnicos empleados en trabajos de I y D en relación con la población total. También se encontrará la relación entre los científicos e ingenieros potenciales y los empleados en trabajos de I y D así como la relación del número de técnicos, científicos e ingenieros con respecto al total de los empleados en trabajos de I y D.

Los indicadores en el ***cuadro 5.19*** se refieren a los recursos financieros consagrados a la I y D y presentan los gastos de I y D, relacionados a su vez con la población total y con el número de científicos e ingenieros empleados en la I y D, y están también expresados en porcentaje del Producto Nacional Bruto (P.N.B.).

Los investigadores que deseen obtener otros detalles y aclaraciones sobre un país en particular en lo que se refiere a las definiciones nacionales, el alcance o las limitaciones de los datos presentados en los cuadros, pueden dirigir su petición a la Oficina de Estadística, División de Estadísticas relativas a la Ciencia y la Tecnología.

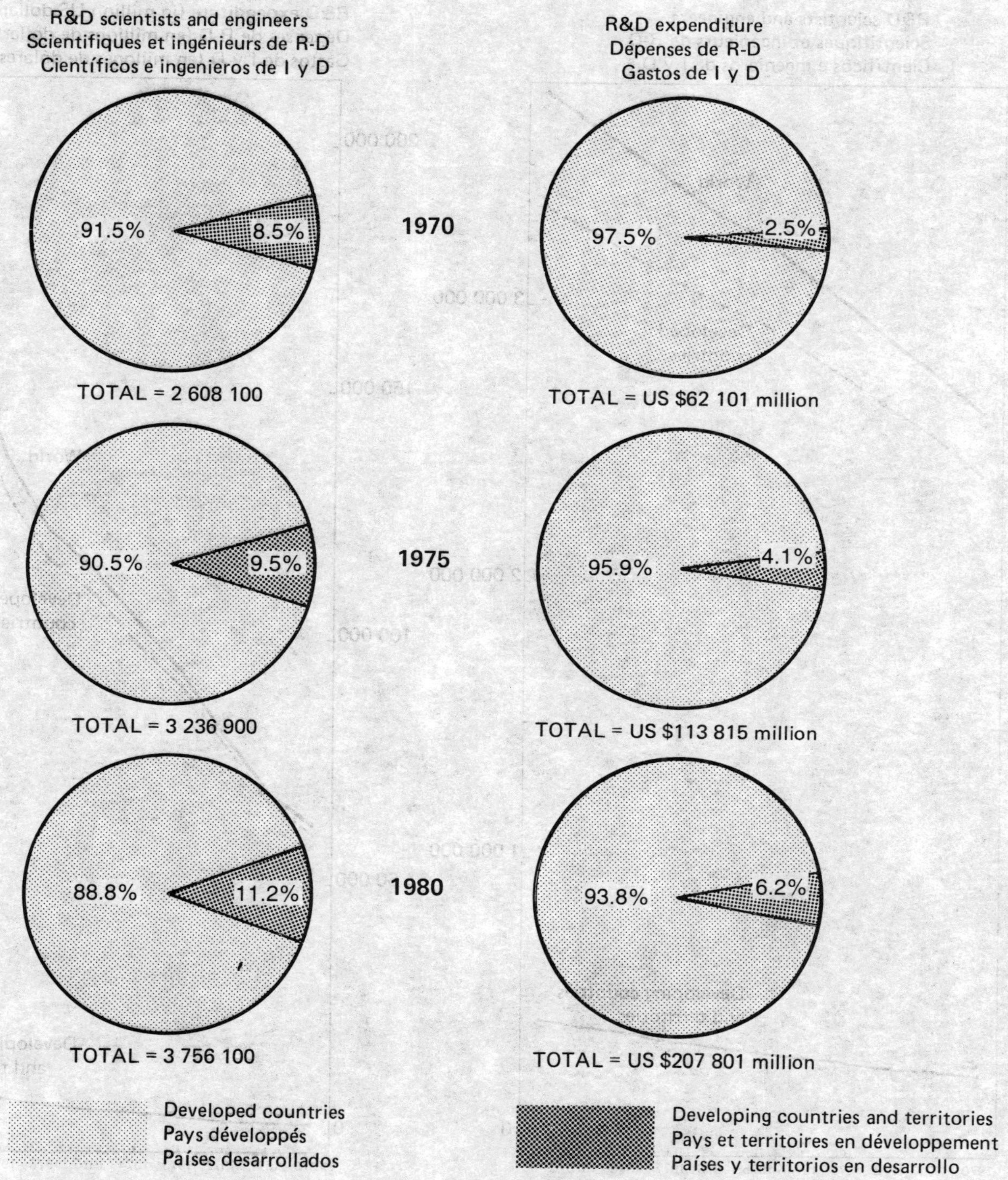

For USSR, data for R&D scientists and engineers and expenditure refer respectively to scientific workers and "expenditure on science".

Pour l'URSS, les données relatives aux scientifiques et ingénieurs et les dépenses de R-D se réfèrent respectivement aux travailleurs scientifiques et aux "dépenses pour la science".

Para la URSS, los datos relativos a los científicos e ingenieros y los gastos de I y D se refieren respectivamente a los trabajadores científicos y a "los gastos efectuados para la ciencia".

Figure 4: Distribution of R&D scientists and engineers and expenditure. Estimated percentages for 1970, 1975 and 1980.

Graphique 4 : Répartition des scientifiques et ingénieurs et des dépenses de R-D. Estimations en pourcentage pour 1970, 1975 et 1980.

Gráfico 4: Distribución de los científicos e ingenieros y de los gastos de I y D. Estimaciones en porcentaje para 1970, 1975 y 1980.

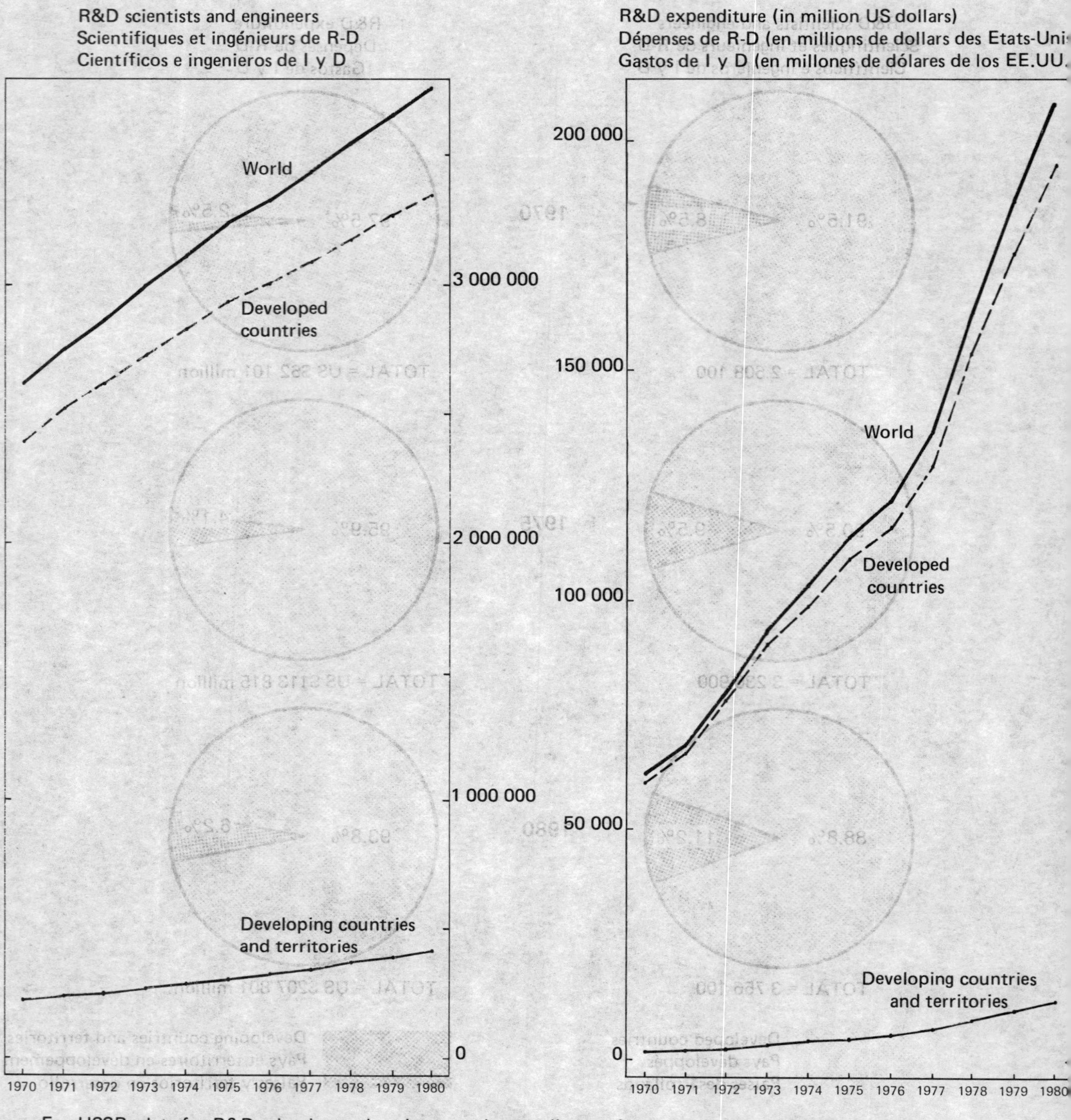

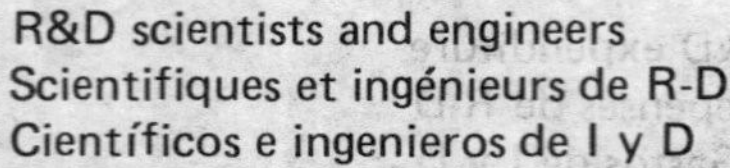

For USSR, data for R&D scientists and engineers and expenditure refer respectively to scientific workers and "expenditure on science".

Pour l'URSS, les données relatives aux scientifiques et ingénieurs et les dépenses de R-D se réfèrent respectivement aux travailleurs scientifiques et aux "dépenses pour la science".

Para la URSS, los datos relativos a los científicos e ingenieros y los gastos de I y D se refieren respectivamente a los trabajadores científicos y a "los gastos efectuados para la ciencia".

Figure 5: **World trends in R&D scientists and engineers and R&D expenditure. Estimates for 1970-1980.**

Graphique 5 : **Tendances mondiales des scientifiques et ingénieurs de R-D et des dépenses de R-D. Estimations pour 1970-1980.**

Gráfico 5: **Tendencias mundiales de los científicos e ingenieros en I y D y de los gastos de IyD. Estimaciones para 1970-1980.**

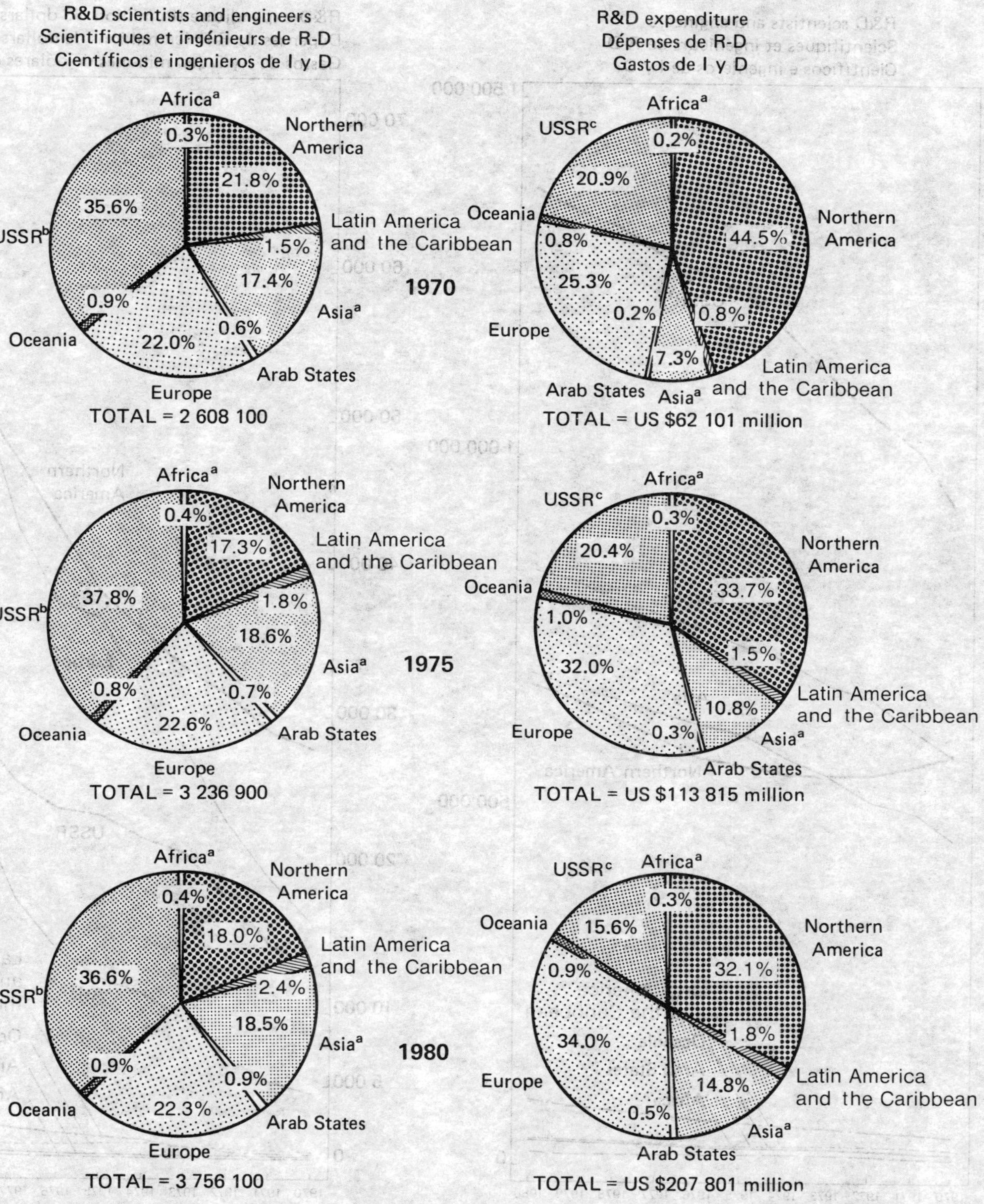

a. Excluding Arab States.
Non compris les Etats Arabes.
Excluídos los Estados Arabes.

b. Data refer to scientific workers.
Les données se réfèrent aux travailleurs scientifiques.
Los datos se refieren a los trabajadores científicos.

c. Data refer to "expenditure on science".
Les données se réfèrent aux « dépenses pour la science ».
Los datos se refieren a los "gastos efectuados para la ciencia".

Figure 6 : **Distribution of R&D scientists and engineers and expenditure by groups of countries. Estimated percentages for 1970, 1975 and 1980**

Graphique 6 : **Répartition des scientifiques et ingénieurs et des dépenses de R-D par groupes de pays. Estimations en pourcentage pour 1970, 1975 et 1980**

Gráfico 6 : **Distribución de los científicos e ingenieros y de los gastos de I y D por grupos de países. Estimaciones en porcentaje para 1970, 1975 y 1980**

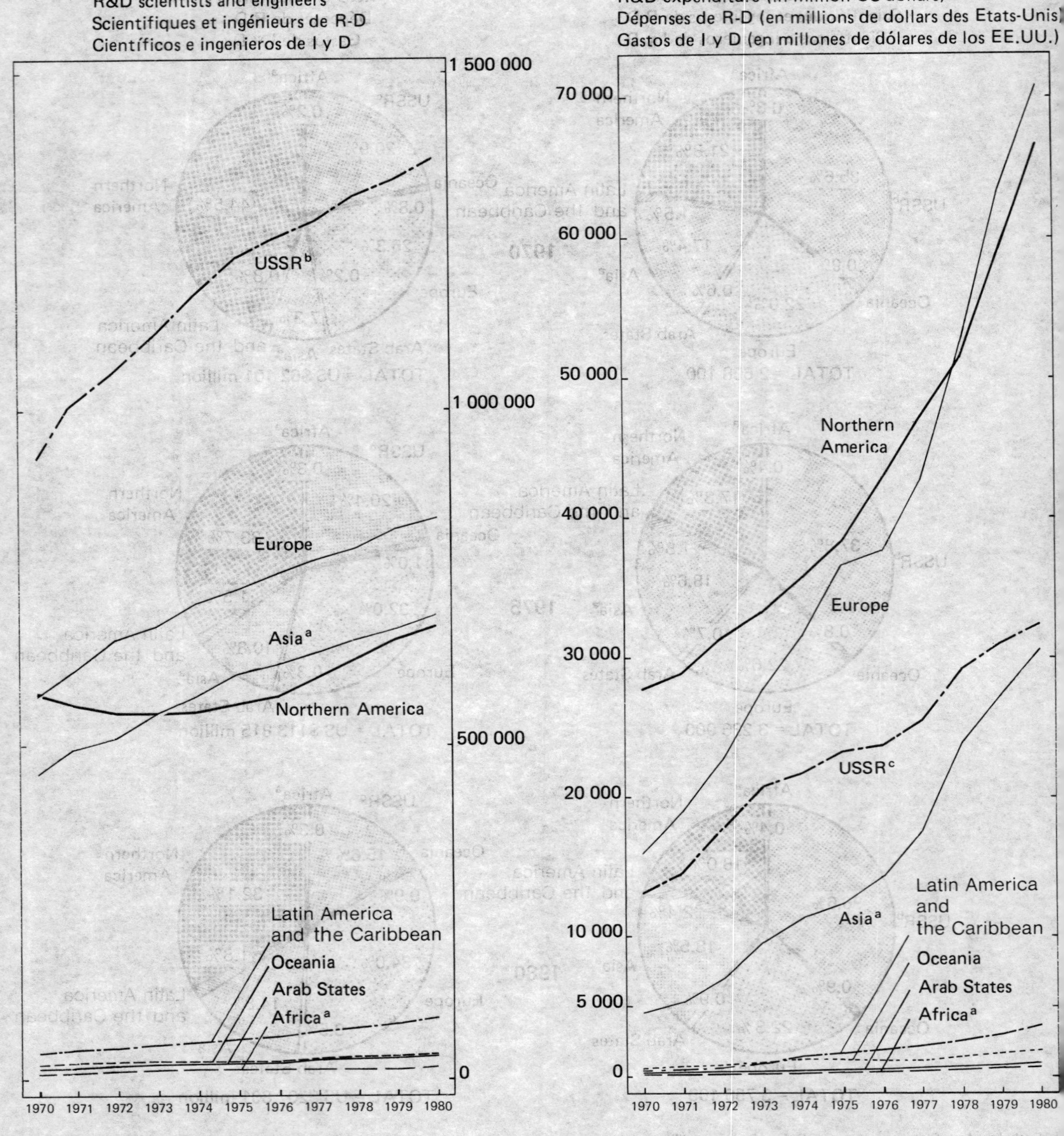

a. Excluding Arab States.
Non compris les Etats Arabes.
Excluidos los Estados Arabes.

b. Data refer to scientific workers.
Les données se réfèrent aux travailleurs scientifiques.
Los datos se refieren a los trabajadores científicos.

c. Data refer to "expenditure on science".
Les données se réfèrent aux « dépenses pour la science ».
Los datos se refieren a los "gastos efectuados para la ciencia".

Figure 7: Regional trends in R&D scientists and engineers and R&D expenditure. Estimates for 1970-1980.

Graphique 7 : Tendances régionales des scientifiques et ingénieurs de R-D et des dépenses de R-D. Estimations pour 1970-1980.

Gráfico 7: Tendencias regionales de los científicos e ingenieros de I y D y de los gastos de I y D. Estimaciones para 1970-1980.

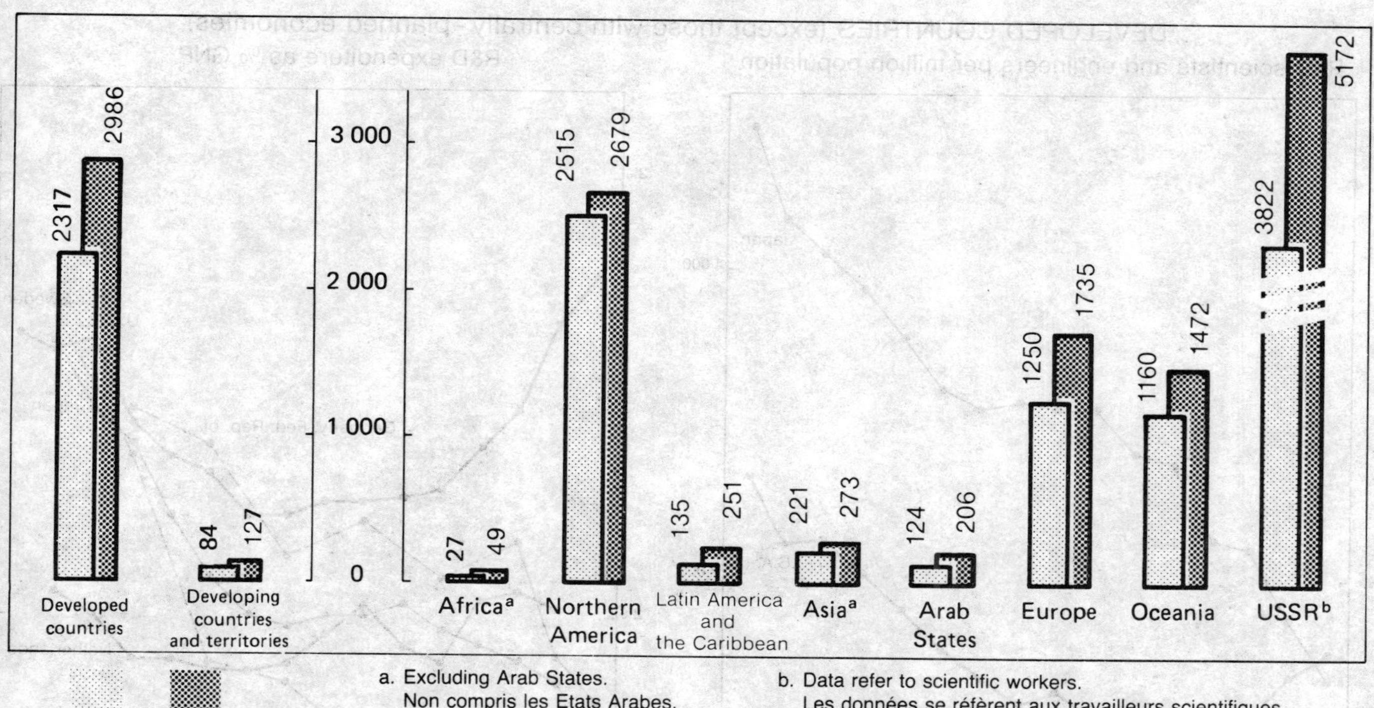

a. Excluding Arab States.
Non compris les Etats Arabes.
Excluídos los Estados Arabes.

b. Data refer to scientific workers.
Les données se réfèrent aux travailleurs scientifiques.
Los datos se refieren a los trabajadores científicos.

Figure 8: **Number of R&D scientists and engineers per million population. Estimates for 1970 and 1980.**

Graphique 8 : **Nombre de scientifiques et d'ingénieurs de R-D par million d'habitants. Estimations pour 1970 et 1980.**

Gráfico 8: **Número de científicos y de ingenieros de I y D por millón de habitantes. Estimaciones para 1970 y 1980.**

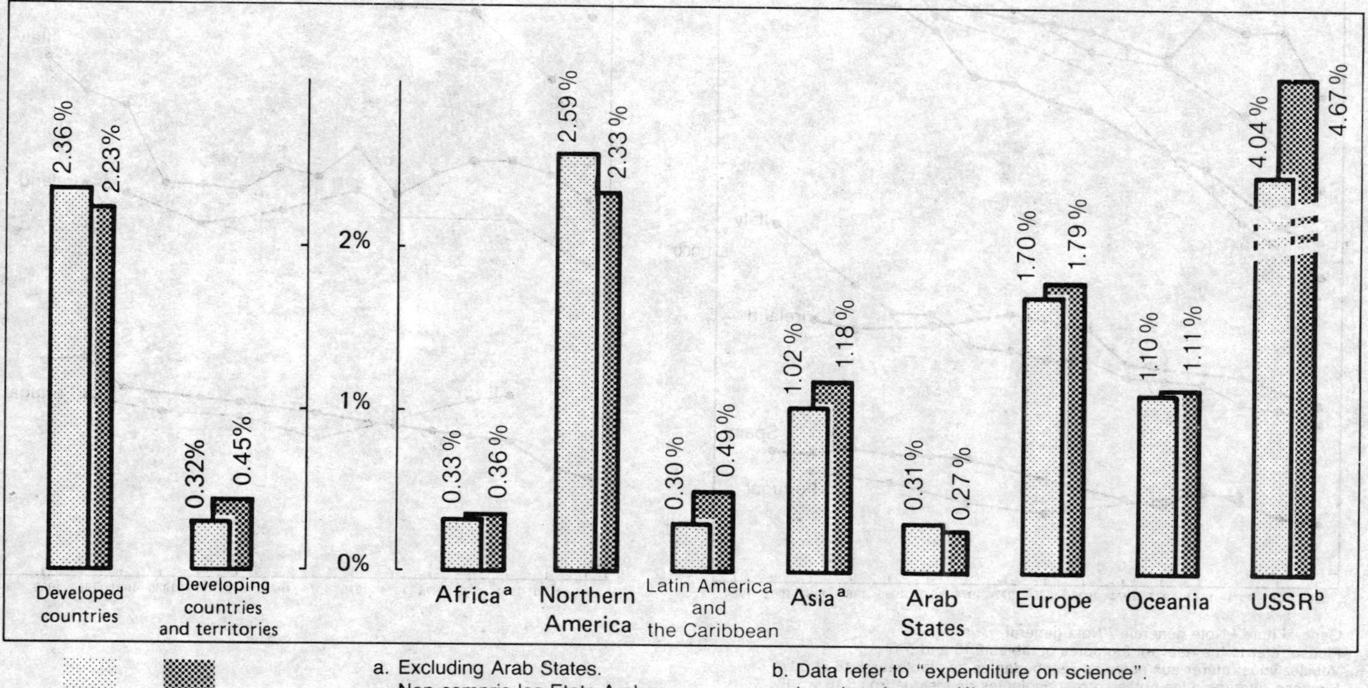

a. Excluding Arab States.
Non compris les Etats Arabes.
Excluídos los Estados Arabes.

b. Data refer to "expenditure on science".
Les données se réfèrent aux « dépenses pour la science ».
Los datos se refieren a los "gastos efectuados para la ciencia".

Figure 9: **Expenditure for R&D as percentage of Gross National Product (GNP). Estimates for 1970 and 1980.**

Graphique 9 : **Dépenses de R-D en pourcentage du produit national brut (PNB). Estimations pour 1970 et 1980.**

Gráfico 9: **Gastos de I y D en porcentaje del producto nacional bruto (PNB). Estimaciones para 1970 y 1980.**

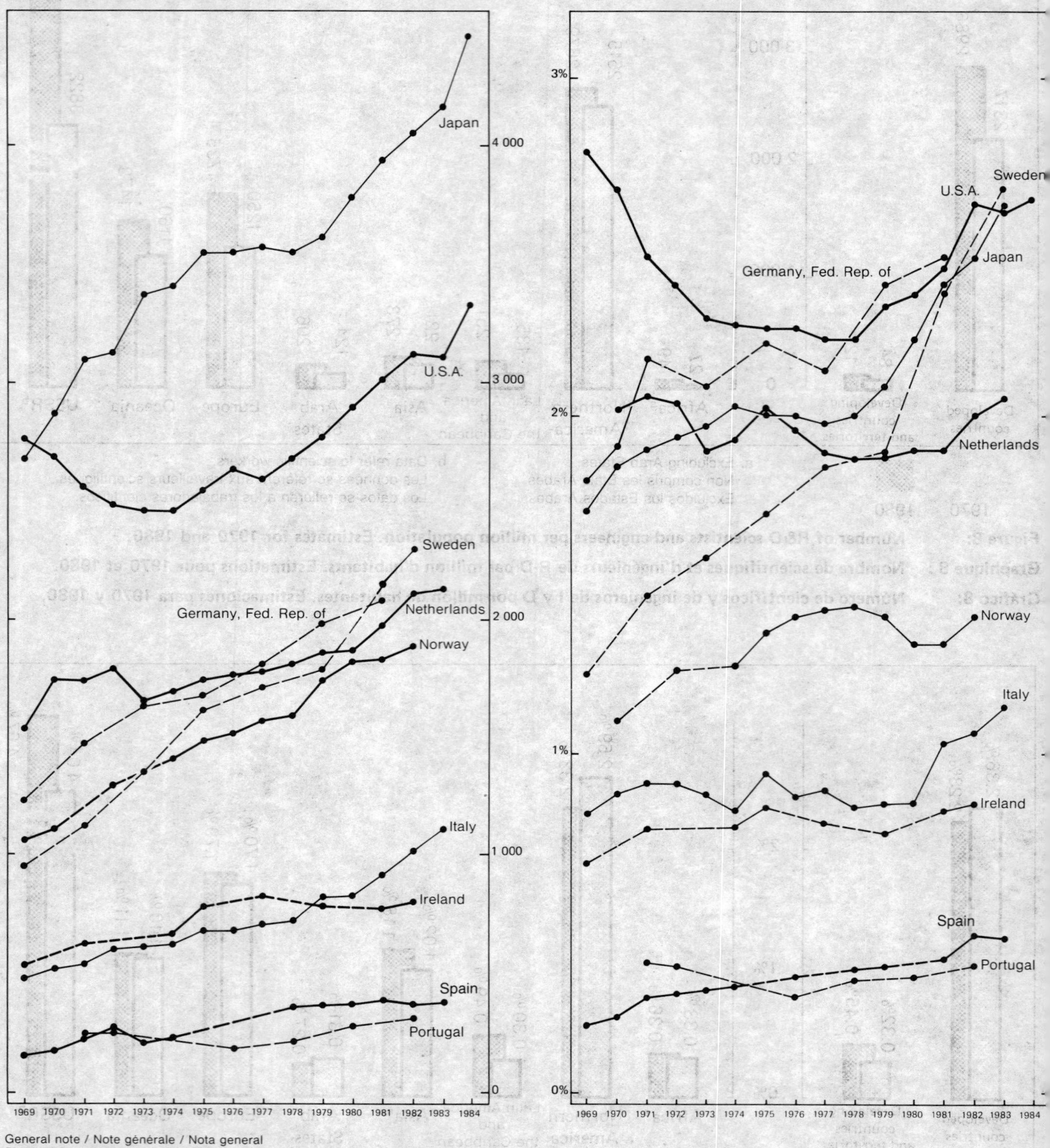

General note / Note générale / Nota general
Please refer to the relevant footnotes of tables 5.16 and 5.17
Veuillez vous référer aux notes correspondantes des tableaux 5.16 et 5.17
Sírvanse referirse a las notas correspondientes de los cuadros 5.16 y 5.17

Figure 10 : Number of R&D scientists and engineers per million population and total expenditure for R&D as a percentage of GNP in 10 selected developed countries : trends since 1969

Graphique 10 : Nombre de scientifiques et ingénieurs de R-D par million d'habitants et dépenses totales de R-D en pourcentage du PNB dans 10 pays développés choisis : tendances depuis 1969

Gráfico 10 : Numero de científicos e ingenieros de I y D por millón de habitantes y gastos totales de I y D en porcentaje del PNB en 10 países desarrollados seleccionados : tendencias desde 1969

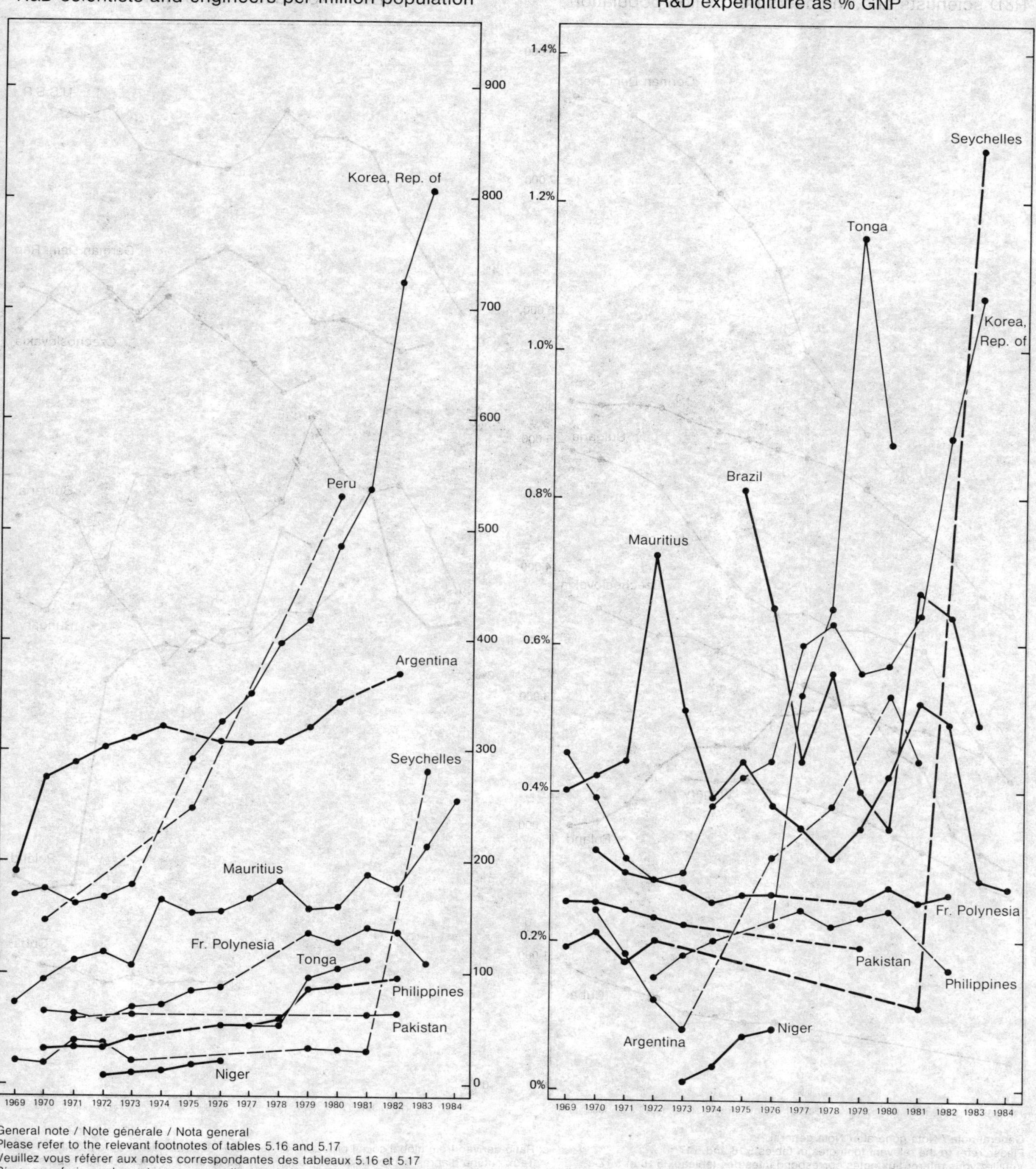

General note / Note générale / Nota general
Please refer to the relevant footnotes of tables 5.16 and 5.17
Veuillez vous référer aux notes correspondantes des tableaux 5.16 et 5.17
Sirvanse referirse a las notas correspondientes de los cuadros 5.16 y 5.17

Figure 11 : Number of R&D scientists and engineers per million population and total expenditure for R&D as a percentage of GNP in 10 selected developing countries : trends since 1969

Graphique 11 : Nombre de scientifiques et ingénieurs de R-D par million d'habitants et dépenses totales de R-D en pourcentage du PNB dans 10 pays en développement choisis : tendances depuis 1969

Gráfico 11 : Numero de científicos e ingenieros de I y D por millón de habitantes y gastos totales de I y D en porcentaje del PNB en 10 países en desarrollo seleccionados : tendencias desde 1969

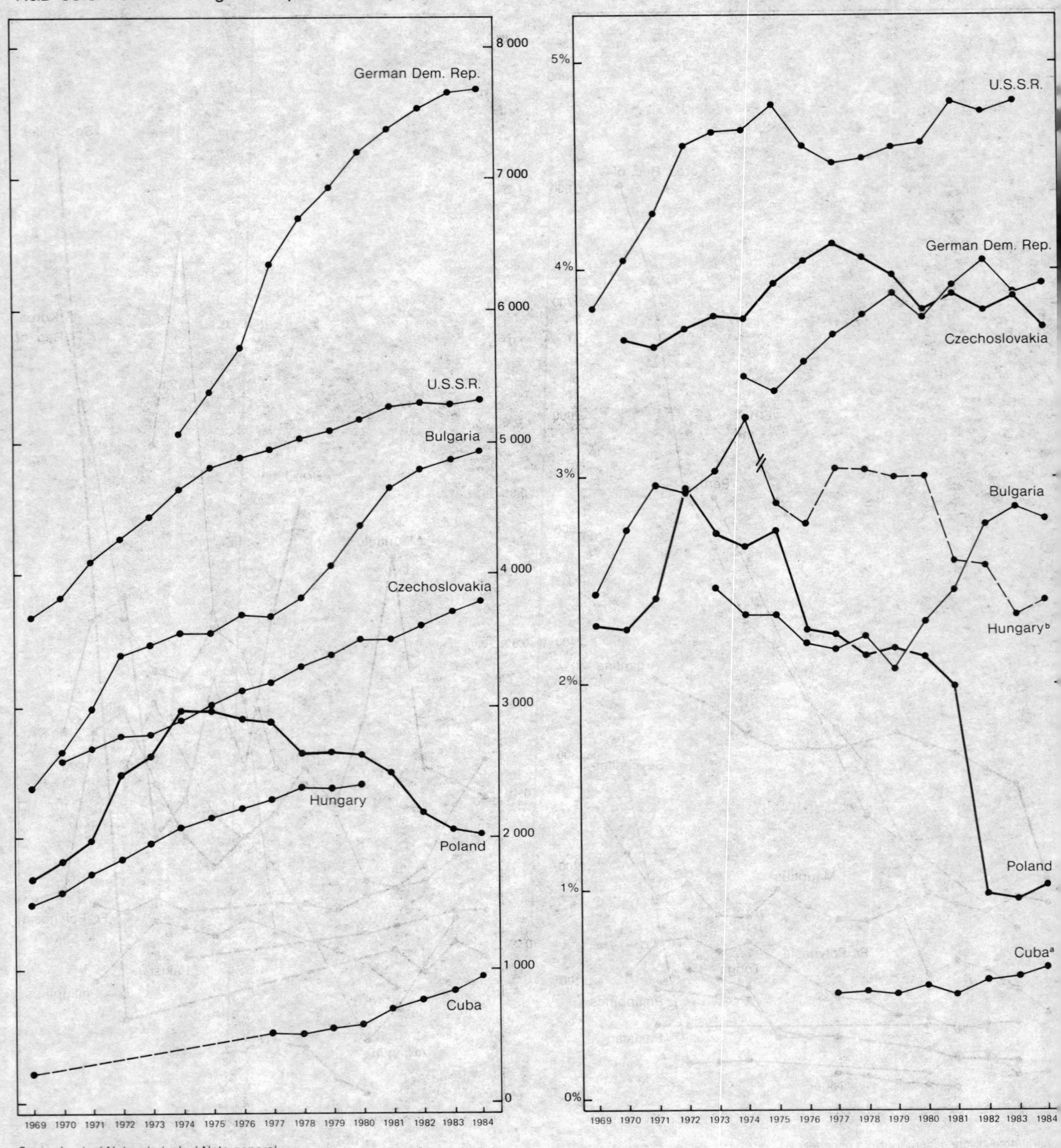

General note / Note générale / Nota general
Please refer to the relevant footnotes of tables 5.16 and 5.17
Veuillez vous référer aux notes correspondantes des tableaux 5.16 et 5.17
Sirvanse referirse a las notas correspondientes de los cuadros 5.16 y 5.17

a. Ratio derived from global social product
Taux obtenu d'après le produit social global
Tasa obtenida del producto social global

b. From 1975 ratio derived from GNP
A partir de 1975, taux obtenu d'après le PNB
Desde 1975, tasas obtenidas del PNB

Figure 12 : **Number of R&D scientists and engineers per million population and total expenditure for R&D as a percentage of NMP in 7 selected countries with centrally-planned economies : trends since 1969**

Graphique 12 : **Nombre de scientifiques et ingénieurs de R-D par million d'habitants et dépenses totales de R-D en pourcentage du PMN dans 7 pays à économie planifiée choisis : tendances depuis 1969**

Gráfico 12 : **Numero de científicos e ingenieros de I y D por millón de habitantes y gastos totales de I y D en porcentaje del PMN en 7 países de planificación centralizada seleccionados : tendencias desde 1969**

5.1 Estimated number of scientists and engineers engaged in R&D for 1970 and 1980

Nombre de scientifiques et ingénieurs employés à des travaux de R-D pour 1970 et 1980 (estimation)

Número de científicos y ingenieros empleados en trabajos de I y D para 1970 y 1980 (estimación)

CONTINENTS, MAJOR AREAS AND GROUPS OF COUNTRIES CONTINENTS, GRANDES REGIONS ET GROUPES DE PAYS CONTINENTES, GRANDES REGIONES Y GRUPOS DE PAISES	YEAR ANNEE AÑO	ESTIMATED NUMBER NOMBRE (ESTIMATION) NUMERO (ESTIMACION)	ESTIMATED NUMBER PER MILLION POPULATION NOMBRE PAR MILLION DE POPULATION (ESTIMATION) NUMERO POR MILLON DE POBLACION (ESTIMACION)
WORLD TOTAL	1970	2 608 100	712
	1980	3 756 100	848
AFRICA	1970	18 589	56
	1980	40 812	91
AMERICA	1970	608 247	1 192
	1980	765 661	1 247
ASIA	1970	458 028	219
	1980	702 920	271
EUROPE	1970	573 083	1 250
	1980	839 473	1 735
OCEANIA	1970	22 420	1 160
	1980	33 889	1 472
U.S.S.R.	1970	927 709	3 822
	1980	1 373 300	5 172
DEVELOPED COUNTRIES	1970	2 386 482	2 317
	1980	3 336 072	2 986
DEVELOPING COUNTRIES	1970	221 618	84
	1980	420 028	127
AFRICA (EXCLUDING ARAB STATES)	1970	6 754	27
	1980	16 387	49
ASIA (EXCLUDING ARAB STATES)	1970	454 731	221
	1980	693 659	273
ARAB STATES	1970	15 132	124
	1980	33 686	206
NORTHERN AMERICA	1970	569 836	2 515
	1980	674 725	2 679
LATIN AMERICA AND THE CARIBBEAN	1970	38 411	135
	1980	90 936	251

5.2 Estimated expenditure for research and experimental development, 1970 and 1980, in United States dollars

Dépenses consacrées à la recherche et au développement experimental, 1970 et 1980, en dollars des Etats-unis (estimation)

Gastos dedicados a la investigación y el desarrollo experimental, 1970 y 1980, en dólares de los Estados Unidos (estimación)

CONTINENTS, MAJOR AREAS AND GROUPS OF COUNTRIES CONTINENTS, GRANDES REGIONS ET GROUPES DE PAYS CONTINENTES, GRANDES REGIONES Y GRUPOS DE PAISES	YEAR ANNEE AÑO	ESTIMATED AMOUNT (IN MILLIONS OF DOLLARS) MONTANT (EN MILLIONS DE DOLLARS) (ESTIMATION) IMPORTE (EN MILLONES DE DOLARES (ESTIMACION)	AS % OF GNP EN % DU PNB EN % DEL PNB
WORLD TOTAL	1970	62 101	2.04
	1980	207 801	1.78
AFRICA	1970	188	0.34
	1980	1 156	0.36
AMERICA	1970	28 118	2.28
	1980	70 391	1.94
ASIA	1970	4 572	0.99
	1980	31 230	1.08
EUROPE	1970	15 739	1.70
	1980	70 649	1.79
OCEANIA	1970	497	1.10
	1980	1 953	1.11
U.S.S.R.	1970	12 987	4.04
	1980	32 421	4.67
DEVELOPED COUNTRIES	1970	60 545	2.36
	1980	194 852	2.23
DEVELOPING COUNTRIES	1970	1 556	0.32
	1980	12 949	0.45
AFRICA (EXCLUDING ARAB STATES)	1970	105	0.33
	1980	698	0.36
ASIA (EXCLUDING ARAB STATES)	1970	4 540	1.02
	1980	30 661	1.18
ARAB STATES	1970	115	0.31
	1980	1 027	0.27
NORTHERN AMERICA	1970	27 620	2.59
	1980	66 646	2.33
LATIN AMERICA AND THE CARIBBEAN	1970	498	0.30
	1980	3 745	0.49

5.3 Scientific and technical manpower potential

Potentiel humain scientifique et technique

Recursos humanos científicos y técnicos potenciales

PLEASE REFER TO INTRODUCTION FOR DEFINITIONS OF CATEGORIES INCLUDED IN THIS TABLE.

EA = ECONOMICALLY ACTIVE QUALIFIED MANPOWER

ST = STOCK OF QUALIFIED MANPOWER

NUMBER OF COUNTRIES AND TERRITORIES PRESENTED IN THIS TABLE: 125

POUR LES DEFINITIONS DES CATEGORIES PRESENTEES DANS CE TABLEAU, SE REFERER A L'INTRODUCTION.

EA = PERSONNES QUALIFIEES ECONOMIQUEMENT ACTIVES

ST = NOMBRE TOTAL DE PERSONNES QUALIFIEES

NOMBRE DE PAYS ET DE TERRITOIRES PRESENTES DANS CE TABLEAU: 125

EN LA INTRODUCCION SE DAN LAS DEFINICIONES DE LAS CATEGORIAS QUE FIGURAN EN ESTE CUADRO.

EA = PERSONAS CALIFICADAS ECONOMICAMENTE ACTIVAS

ST = TOTAL DE PERSONAS CALIFICADAS

NUMERO DE PAISES Y DE TERRITORIOS PRESENTADOS EN ESTE CUADRO: 125

COUNTRY PAYS PAIS	YEAR ANNEE AÑO	TYPE OF DATA TYPE DE DONNEES TIPO DE DATOS	TOTAL TOTAL TOTAL	POTENTIAL SCIENTISTS AND ENGINEERS SCIENTIFIQUES ET INGENIEURS POTENTIELS CIENTIFICOS E INGENIEROS POTENCIALES		POTENTIAL TECHNICIANS TECHNICIENS POTENTIELS TECNICOS POTENCIALES	
				TOTAL	F	TOTAL	F
			(1)	(2)	(3)	(4)	(5)
AFRICA							
BOTSWANA‡	1972	EA	1 527	786	...	741	...
CAMEROON‡	1976	ST	...	11 785	2 053	...	...
CONGO	1977	EA	...	...	...	3 461	...
DJIBOUTI	1973	EA	35	35	4	—	—
EGYPT‡	1976	ST	...	492 470	96 200	...	...
GAMBIA‡	1973	ST	...	445	...	...	...
GHANA‡	1970	EA	21 993	6 897	789	15 096	7 944
KENYA	1982	EA	62 203	16 241	...	45 962	...
LIBYAN ARAB JAMAHIRIYA‡	1980	EA	52 757	43 737	1 142	9 020	439
MALAWI‡	1977	ST	...	3 981	933	...	...
MAURITIUS	1983	ST	26 754	7 256	1 732	19 498	7 177
NIGERIA	1980	ST	133 750	22 050	...	111 700	...
RWANDA‡	1978	ST	1 762	1 762	221	./.	./.
SEYCHELLES‡	1983	EA	...	900	...	...	...
SUDAN	1971	EA	11 229	9 708	...	1 521	...
SWAZILAND‡	1977	EA	...	1 384	...	...	...
TOGO	1971	EA	672	461	...	211	...
TUNISIA‡	1974	EA	11 135	3 421	...	7 714	...
ZAMBIA	1973	ST	37 000	11 000	...	26 000	...
AMERICA, NORTH							
ANTIGUA AND BARBUDA‡	1970	EA	*780	*480	*410	*300	./.
BAHAMAS	1970	EA	*6 600	*3 000	*800	*3 600	*2 100
BARBADOS	1970	ST	3 039	1 163	309	1 876	833
BELIZE	1970	ST	1 062	419	114	643	287
BERMUDA	1970	EA	3 603	1 626	569	1 977	808
BRITISH VIRGIN ISLANDS	1980	EA	...	355	131	...	...
CANADA	1981	EA	7 042 555	1 240 420	428 090	5 802 135	2 426 460
CAYMAN ISLANDS	1971	EA	450	150	15	300	30
CUBA	1981	ST	...	139 469	55 924	...	...
DOMINICA	1970	ST	459	162	49	297	114
DOMINICAN REPUBLIC‡	1970	ST	...	7 837	...	...	...
EL SALVADOR	1974	EA	7 262	5 489	...	1 773	...
GRENADA	1970	ST	562	233	61	329	106
GUATEMALA	1974	EA	12 656	5 551	...	7 105	...
HAITI‡	1982	EA	32 209	14 189	4 530	18 020	8 639

COUNTRY / PAYS / PAIS	YEAR / ANNEE / AÑO	TYPE OF DATA / TYPE DE DONNEES / TIPO DE DATOS	TOTAL / TOTAL / TOTAL	POTENTIAL SCIENTISTS AND ENGINEERS / SCIENTIFIQUES ET INGENIEURS POTENTIELS / CIENTIFICOS E INGENIEROS POTENCIALES		POTENTIAL TECHNICIANS / TECHNICIENS POTENTIELS / TECNICOS POTENCIALES	
				TOTAL	F	TOTAL	F
			(1)	(2)	(3)	(4)	(5)
HONDURAS	1974	EA	9 885	6 702	...	3 183	...
JAMAICA	1970	ST	15 753	5 963	2 004	9 790	5 015
MONTSERRAT	1970	ST	236	101	34	135	74
NETHERLANDS ANTILLES‡	1971	ST	...	3 387	...	...	...
PANAMA	1976	EA	19 267	5 415	651	13 852	89
FORMER CANAL ZONE	1976	EA	1 437	1 268	678	169	47
PUERTO RICO‡	1970	ST	...	72 998	...	...	...
ST. CHRISTOPHER–NEVIS AND ANGUILLA	1970	ST	445	135	31	310	138
ST. LUCIA	1970	ST	621	259	64	362	147
ST. VINCENT AND THE GRENADINES	1970	ST	486	152	29	334	134
TRINIDAD AND TOBAGO	1970	ST	10 899	3 314	854	7 585	3 162
TURKS AND CAICOS ISLANDS	1980	ST	302	176	45	126	65
UNITED STATES‡	1982	EA	...	3 431 800	418 700	...	...
AMERICA, SOUTH							
ARGENTINA‡	1980	EA	2 232 053	535 656	233 982	1 696 397	703 164
BOLIVIA‡	1976	ST	...	58 090	19 511	...	...
BRAZIL	1980	ST	4 436 564	1 362 206	668 911	3 074 358	1 615 947
CHILE‡	1970	ST	...	69 946	20 496	...	...
ECUADOR	1974	ST	98 130	48 559	...	49 571	...
GUYANA	1980	EA	1 848	1 512	...	336	...
PERU	1981	ST	1 689 763	291 812	...	1 397 951	579 871
URUGUAY‡	1975	ST	...	*56 400	*33 300	...	...
VENEZUELA	1982	EA	1 881 000	347 000	...	1 534 000	...
ASIA							
BANGLADESH	1973	EA	*63 500	23 500	...	*40 000	...
BRUNEI DARUSSALAM‡	1981	EA	6 515	2 214	390	4 301	1 770
BURMA‡	1975	EA	...	18 500	...	...	...
CHINA‡	1984	EA	7 466 000	...	...	...	...
HONG KONG	1981	EA	826 519	98 561	22 939	727 958	278 980
INDIA‡	1980	EA	1 949 000	...	...	...	...
INDONESIA	1980	ST	2 104 780	193 262	...	1 911 518	...
IRAN, ISLAMIC REPUBLIC OF‡	1982	ST	465 541	294 647	...	170 894	...
IRAQ‡	1972	EA	68 334	*43 645	*10 901	*24 689	*2 950
ISRAEL‡	1974	EA	146 100	82 300	28 900	63 800	16 300
JAPAN‡	1982	EA	37 050 000	7 046 000	881 000	30 004 000	13 057 000
JORDAN	1977	EA	17 232	11 575	1 623	5 657	704
KOREA, REPUBLIC OF	1981	EA	*2 025 639	*94 171	...	*1 931 468	...
KUWAIT‡	1980	ST	181 923	78 795	...	103 128	...
LEBANON‡	1972	ST	...	*28 530	...	...	...
MALAYSIA‡	1982	ST	...	26 000	3 562	...	...
MONGOLIA	1972	ST	2 040	1 908	603	132	...
NEPAL‡	1980	EA	*11 004	3 668	...	*7 336	...
PAKISTAN‡	1973	EA	...	*100 500	...	...	...
PHILIPPINES	1980	ST	...	1 758 614	998 965	...	...
QATAR‡	1983	EA	15 236	6 302	1 701	8 934	2 346
SAUDI ARABIA‡	1974	ST	...	*33 376	...	...	...
SINGAPORE	1980	EA	64 179	38 259	10 246	25 920	4 769
SRI LANKA	1972	EA	18 454	7 457	...	10 997	...
SYRIAN ARAB REPUBLIC	1970	EA	44 909	24 523	3 473	20 386	7 176
THAILAND‡	1975	EA	67 632	20 288	...	47 344	...
TURKEY‡	1980	ST	1 538 000	708 000	163 000	830 000	285 000
YEMEN	1974	EA	2 074	1 394	18	680	18
EUROPE							
AUSTRIA‡	1981	ST	153 923	153 923	42 128	./.	./.
BULGARIA‡	1983	EA	931 802	302 809	144 273	628 993	358 846
CZECHOSLOVAKIA‡	1980	EA	...	542 706	191 256	...	...
DENMARK	1980	ST	323 738	83 529	17 922	240 209	154 344
FINLAND	1982	ST	1 616 621	172 244	79 710	1 444 377	725 204
FRANCE	1975	EA	...	1 251 610	409 910	...	...
GERMAN DEMOCRATIC REPUBLIC‡	1984	EA	1 594 200	571 500	214 400	1 022 700	623 500
GERMANY, FEDERAL REPUBLIC OF	1980	EA	8 374 000	2 278 000	641 000	6 096 000	1 933 000
GIBRALTAR	1970	ST	164	41	–	123	2
GREECE	1981	ST	1 602 088	329 489	100 528	1 272 599	652 412

COUNTRY / PAYS / PAIS	YEAR / ANNEE / AÑO	TYPE OF DATA / TYPE DE DONNEES / TIPO DE DATOS	TOTAL / TOTAL / TOTAL	POTENTIAL SCIENTISTS AND ENGINEERS / SCIENTIFIQUES ET INGENIEURS POTENTIELS / CIENTIFICOS E INGENIEROS POTENCIALES		POTENTIAL TECHNICIANS / TECHNICIENS POTENTIELS / TECNICOS POTENCIALES	
				TOTAL	F	TOTAL	F
			(1)	(2)	(3)	(4)	(5)
HUNGARY‡	1980	EA	1 860 086	412 219	161 529	1 447 867	461 080
ICELAND	1975	ST	...	5 024	900	...	...
IRELAND	1971	EA	*258 966	*56 420	*17 146	*202 546	*83 643
ITALY	1981	EA	4 703 361	1 175 418	420 694	3 527 943	1 436 119
MONACO‡	1982	ST	3 125	3 125	1 334		...
NETHERLANDS‡	1981	EA	2 660 600	773 100	236 400	1 887 500	597 800
NORWAY	1981	ST	...	97 450	17 200	...	...
POLAND‡	1978	EA	5 088 000	1 075 000	440 000	4 013 000	2 230 000
SAN MARINO‡	1983	EA	2 458	400	133	2 058	1 058
SPAIN‡	1983	EA	4 634 800	1 152 000	454 300	3 482 800	1 282 600
SWEDEN	1979	EA	2 178 400	335 900	125 200	1 842 500	835 200
SWITZERLAND‡	1980	EA	...	348 167	61 729	...	...
YUGOSLAVIA	1981	EA	3 986 034	402 041	150 831	3 583 993	1 248 636
OCEANIA							
AMERICAN SAMOA	1973	EA	422	327		95	...
AUSTRALIA	1981	EA	2 092 998	383 368	119 629	1 709 630	493 251
COOK ISLANDS	1970	EA	305	164	78	141	34
FIJI	1976	ST	9 734	...		...	...
FRENCH POLYNESIA	1973	EA	...	95	11	...	...
KIRIBATI	1971	EA	177	112	30	65	–
NEW CALEDONIA	1973	ST	145	69	...	76	...
NEW ZEALAND	1971	EA	139 521	47 249	6 554	92 272	48 782
NIUE	1971	ST	6	2	–	4	–
NORFOLK ISLAND	1981	EA	...	140	72	...	...
PACIFIC ISLANDS	1973	ST	1 103	161	9	942	361
PAPUA NEW GUINEA‡	1973	EA	12 798	2 646	...	10 152	...
SAMOA	1977	ST	514	350	140	164	36
SOLOMON ISLANDS	1971	EA	894	129	...	765	...
VANUATU‡	1973	EA	476	71	...	405	...
U.S.S.R.							
U.S.S.R.‡	1983	EA	31 628 000	13 487 000	7 197 000	18 141 000	11 636 000
BYELORUSSIAN S.S.R.‡	1983	EA	1 191 000	519 000	283 000	672 000	436 000
UKRAINIAN S.S.R.‡	1983	EA	5 958 000	2 528 000	1 332 000	3 430 000	2 184 000

AFRICA:

Botswana:

E--> 557 of the potential scientists and engineers in column 2 and 171 of the technicians in column 4 are foreigners.

FR-> 557 des scientifiques et ingénieurs potentiels de la colonne 2 et 171 des techniciens de la colonne 4 sont ressortissants étrangers.

ESP> 557 científicos e ingenieros potenciales de la columna 2 y 171 técnicos de la columna 4 son extranjeros.

Cameroon:

E--> Data refer to persons aged 15 years and over with a university education.

FR-> Les données se réfèrent aux personnes âgées de 15 ans et plus ayant une formation universitaire.

ESP> Los datos se refieren a las personas de 15 años y más que poseen una formación universitaria.

Egypt:

E--> Data refer to persons aged 25 years and over with an education at the third level.

FR-> Les données se réfèrent aux personnes âgées de 25 ans et plus ayant suivi un enseignement du troisième degré.

ESP> Los datos se refieren a las personas de 25 años y más que poseen una formación de enseñanza de tercer grado.

Gambia:

E--> Data refer to persons aged 25 years and over having completed education at the third level.

FR-> Les données se réfèrent aux personnes âgées de 25 ans et plus ayant complété l'enseignement du troisième degré.

ESP> Los datos se refieren a las personas de 25 años y más que completaron la enseñanza de tercer grado.

Ghana:

E--> 1,761 of the potential scientists and engineers in column 2 and 317 of the technicians in column 4 are foreigners. The figures in columns 4 and 5 do not include social sciences and humanities.

FR-> 1 761 des scientifiques et ingénieurs potentiels de la colonne 2 et 317 des techniciens de la colonne 4 sont ressortissants étrangers. Les

Ghana: (Cont):

chiffres des colonnes 4 et 5 ne comprennent pas les sciences sociales et humaines.

ESP> 1 761 científicos e ingenieros potenciales de la columna 2 y 317 técnicos de la columna 4 son extranjeros. Las cifras de las columnas 4 y 5 excluyen las ciencias sociales y humanas.

Libyan Arab Jamahiriya:

E--> 32,135 of the potential scientists and engineers in column 2 and 5,673 of the technicians in column 4 are foreigners.

FR-> 32 135 des scientifiques et ingénieurs potentiels de la colonne 2 et 5 673 des techniciens de la colonne 4 sont ressortissants étrangers.

ESP> 32 135 científicos e ingenieros potenciales de la columna 2 y 5 673 técnicos de la columna 4 son extranjeros.

Malawi:

E--> Data refer to persons aged 25 years and over having completed more than 5 years education at the third level.

FR-> Les données se réfèrent aux personnes âgées de 25 ans et plus ayant complété plus de 5 années dans l'enseignement du troisième degré.

ESP> Los datos se refieren a las personas de 25 años y más que completaron más de 5 años de enseñanza de tercer grado.

Rwanda:

E--> Data for columns 4 and 5 are included under columns 2 and 3.

FR-> Les données des colonnes 4 et 5 sont incluses dans les colonnes 2 et 3.

ESP> Los datos de las columnas 4 y 5 están incluídos en los de las columnas 2 y 3.

Seychelles:

E--> 600 of the potential scientists and engineers in column 2 are foreigners.

FR-> 600 des scientifiques et ingénieurs potentiels de la colonne 2 sont ressortissants étrangers.

ESP> 600 científicos e ingenieros potenciales de la columna 2 son

Seychelles: (Cont):
extranjeros.
Swaziland:
E--> Data relate to university degree-holders of which 972 are foreigners.
FR-> Les données se réfèrent aux diplômés des universités, dont 972 sont ressortissants étrangers.
ESP> Los datos se refieren a los diplomados de las universidades, de los cuales 972 son extranjeros.
Tunisia:
E--> Data are under-estimated.
FR-> Les données sont sous-estimées.
ESP> Los datos son subestimados.
AMERICA, NORTH:
Antigua and Barbuda:
E--> Data for column 5 are included under column 3.
FR-> Les données de la colonne 5 sont incluses dans la colonne 3.
ESP> Los datos de la columna 5 están incluídos en la columna 3.
Dominican Republic:
E--> Data refer to persons aged 25 years and over having completed education at the third level.
FR-> Les données se réfèrent aux personnes âgées de 25 ans et plus ayant complété l'enseignement du troisième degré.
ESP> Los datos se refieren a las personas de 25 años y más que completaron la enseñanza de tercer grado.
Haiti:
E--> Data are based on a 2 1/2% sample of the 1982 census; the figures in columns 2 and 3 refer to persons having completed education at the third level and those in columns 4 and 5 to those having completed post-secondary education.
FR-> Les données sont basées sur un sondage portant sur 2 1/2% du recensement de 1982; les chiffres des colonnes 2 et 3 concernent les personnes ayant complété l'enseignement du troisième degré et ceux des colonnes 4 et 5 celles qui ont complété l'enseignement post-secondaire.
ESP> Datos basados en un sondeo que abarcó el 2 1/2% del censo de 1982; las cifras de las columnas 2 y 3 conciernen las personas que han terminado la enseñanza de tercer grado y las de las columnas 4 y 5 las que completaron la enseñanza post-secundaria.
Netherlands Antilles:
E--> Data refer to persons aged 25 years and over having completed education at the third level.
FR-> Les données se réfèrent aux personnes âgées de 25 ans et plus ayant complété l'enseignement du troisième degré.
ESP> Los datos se refieren a las personas de 25 años y más que completaron la enseñanza de tercer grado.
Puerto Rico:
E--> Data refer to persons aged 25 years and over having completed education at the third level.
FR-> Les données se réfèrent aux personnes âgées de 25 ans et plus ayant complété l'enseignement du troisième degré.
ESP> Los datos se refieren a las personas de 25 años y más que completaron la enseñanza de tercer grado.
United States:
E--> Not including data for law, humanities and education.
FR-> Non compris les données pour le droit, les sciences humaines et l'éducation.
ESP> Excluídos los datos relativos al derecho, las ciencias humanas y la educación.
AMERICA, SOUTH:
Argentina:
E--> Data for technicians with qualifications at ISCED level 5 are included with those for potential scientists and engineers.
FR-> Les données relatives aux techniciens ayant des qualifications de la CITE niveau 5, sont comprises avec celles des scientifiques et ingénieurs potentiels.
ESP> Los datos relativos a los técnicos con una calificación de la CINE nivel 5, están incluidos con los de los científicos e ingenieros potenciales.
Bolivia:
E--> Data refer to persons aged 20 years and over with 4 years or more university education.
FR-> Les données se réfèrent aux personnes âgées de 20 ans et plus ayant 4 ans et plus de formation universitaire.
ESP> Los datos se refieren a las personas de 20 años y más con una formación universitaria de 4 años o más.
Chile:
E--> Data refer to persons aged 25 years and over with 5 to 8 years education at the third level.
FR-> Les données se réfèrent aux personnes âgées de 25 ans et plus ayant accompli de cinq à huit années dans l'enseignement du troisième degré.
ESP> Los datos se refieren a las personas de 25 a
nos y más que completaron de cinco a ocho años en la enseñanza de tercer grado.
Uruguay:
E--> Data refer to persons aged 25 years and over having completed education at the third level.

Uruguay: (Cont):
FR-> Les données se réfèrent aux personnes âgées de 25 ans et pl ayant complété l'enseignement du troisième degré.
ESP> Los datos se refieren a las personas de 25 años y más qu completaron la enseñanza de tercer grado.
ASIA:
Brunei Darussalam:
E--> 1,495 of the potential scientists and engineers in column 2 a 919 of the technicians in column 4 are foreigners.
FR-> 1 495 des scientifiques et ingénieurs potentiels de la colonne et 919 des techniciens de la colonne 4 sont ressortissants étrangers.
ESP> 1 495 des científicos e ingenieros potenciales de la columna y 919 técnicos de la columna 4 son extranjeros.
Burma:
E--> Not including data for social sciences and humanities.
FR-> Non compris les données pour les sciences sociales humaines.
ESP> Excluídos los datos relativos a las ciencias sociales y humana
China:
E--> Not including data either for social sciences and humanities or f collective organizations.
FR-> Les données ne sont pas comprises pour les sciences sociales humaines ni pour les collectivités.
ESP> Excluídos los datos relativos a las ciencias sociales y humanas a las colectividades.
India:
E--> Not including data either for social sciences and humanities or f technicians with qualifications at ISCED level 3.
FR-> Non compris les données relatives aux sciences sociales humaines ni les techniciens ayant des qualifications de la CITE niveau
ESP> Excluídos los datos relativos a las ciencias sociales y humanos los técnicos con una calificación de la CINE nivel 3.
Iran, Islamic Republic of:
E--> Data in columns 1 and 4 do not include technicians wi qualifications at ISCED level 3.
FR-> Les données des colonnes 1 et 4 ne comprennent pas l techniciens ayant des qualifications de la CITE niveau 3.
EPS> Los datos de las columnas 1 y 4 no incluyen los técnicos c una calificación de la CINE nivel 3.
Iraq:
E--> Data relate to persons employed in government institutio only.
FR-> Les données ne concernent que les personnes employées da les institutions gouvernementales.
ESP> Los datos sólo se refieren a las personas empleadas en l instituciones gubernamentales.
Israel:
E--> Data refer to the annual civilian labour force.
FR-> Los données se réfèrent au nombre de travailleurs civils po l'année considérée.
ESP> Los datos se refieren a los trabajaderos civiles durante el a considerado.
Japan:
E--> Data refer to persons in gainful employment.
FR-> Les données se réfèrent aux personnes qui occupent un emp rémunéré.
ESP> Los datos se refieren a las personas que ocupan un emple remunerado.
Kuwait:
E--> 63,339 of the potential scientists and engineers in column and 77,188 of the technicians in column 4 are foreigners.
FR-> 63 339 des scientifiques et ingénieurs potentiels de la colonn 2 et 77 188 des techniciens de la colonne 4 sont resortissan étrangers.
ESP> 63 339 de los científicos e ingenieros potenciales de la column 2 y 77 188 de los técnicos de la columna 4 son extranjeros.
Lebanon:
E--> Data are based on a sample survey.
FR-> Les données sont basées sur une enquête par sondage.
ESP> Datos basados en una encuesta por sondeo.
Malaysia:
E--> Not including data for social sciences and humanities.
FR-> Non compris les données pour les sciences sociales humaines.
ESP> Excluídos los datos relativos a las ciencias sociales y humana
Nepal:
E--> Not including data either for social sciences and humanities or f technicians with qualifications at ISCED level 3.
FR-> Non compris les données relatives aux sciences sociales humaines ni les techniciens ayant des qualifications de la CITE niveau
ESP> Excluídos los datos relativos a las ciencias sociales y humanos los técnicos con una calificación de la CINE nivel 3.
Pakistan:
E--> Not including data for social sciences and humanities.
FR-> Non compris les données pour les sciences sociales humaines.
ESP> Excluídos los datos relativos a las ciencias sociales y humana

Qatar:
E--> 4,782 of the potential scientists and engineers in column 2 and 6,032 of the technicians in column 4 are foreigners.
FR-> 4 782 des scientifiques et ingénieurs potentiels de la colonne 2 et 6 032 des techniciens de la colonne 4 sont ressortissants étrangers.
ESP> 4 782 de los científicos e ingenieros potenciales de la columna 2 y 6 032 de los técnicos de la columna 4 son extranjeros.
Saudi Arabia:
E--> The figure refers to potential scientists and engineers with qualifications at the third level of education.
FR-> Le chiffre se réfère aux scientifiques et ingénieurs potentiels avec une qualification dans l'enseignement du troisième degré.
ESP> La cifra se refiere a los científicos e ingenieros potenciales con una calificación en la enseñanza de tercer grado.
Thailand:
E--> Data for potential scientists and engineers in column 2 do not include social sciences and humanities.
FR-> Les données relatives aux scientifiques et ingénieurs potentiels de la colonne 2 ne comprennent pas les sciences sociales et humaines.
ESP> Los datos relativos a los científicos e ingenieros potenciales de la columna 2 no incluyen las ciencias sociales y humanas.
Turkey:
E--> Data are based on a 1% sample. The figures in columns 2 and 3 refer to persons having completed faculty and other higher education; the figures in columns 4 and 5 refer to persons having completed vocational education.
FR-> Les données sont basées sur un sondage portant sur 1%. Les chiffres des colonnes 2 et 3 se réfèrent aux personnes ayant complété leurs études en faculté et autres institutions de l'enseignement supérieur; les chiffres des colonnes 4 et 5 se réfèrent aux personnes ayant complété l'enseignement technique.
ESP> Datos basados en un sondeo que abarcó el 1%. Las cifras de las columnas 2 y 3 se refieren a las personas que completaron sus estudios en facultades y otras instituciones de enseñanza superior; las cifras de las columnas 4 y 5 se refieren a las personas que completaron la enseñanza técnica.
EUROPE:
Austria:
E--> Data for technicians with qualifications at ISCED level 5 are included with those for potential scientists and engineers.
FR-> Les données relatives aux techniciens ayant des qualifications de la CITE niveau 5, sont comprises avec celles des scientifiques et ingénieurs potentiels.
ESP> Los datos relativos a los técnicos con una calificación de la CINE nivel 5, están incluídos con los de los científicos e ingenieros potenciales.
Bulgaria:
E--> Data refer to employed persons in the national economy.
FR-> Les données se réfèrent aux personnes employées dans l'économie nationale.
ESP> Los datos se refieren a las personas empleadas en la economía nacional.
Czechoslovakia:
E--> Data refer to persons aged 15 years and over with an education at the third level.
FR-> Les données se réfèrent aux personnes âgées de 15 ans et plus ayant suivi un enseignement du troisième degré.
ESP> Los datos se refieren a las personas de 15 años y más que poseen una formación de enseñanza de tercer grado.
German Democratic Republic:
E--> The figures in columns 2 and 3 refer to university graduates; the figures in columns 4 and 5 to technical college graduates.
FR-> Les chiffres des colonnes 2 et 3 se réfèrent aux diplômés des universités; les chiffres des colonnes 4 et 5 se réfèrent aux diplômés des collèges techniques.
ESP> Las cifras de las columnas 2 y 3 se refieren a los diplomados de las universidades; las cifras de las columnas 4 y 5 se refieren a los diplomados de los colegios técnicos.
Hungary:
E--> Data for technicians with qualifications at ISCED level 5 are included with those for potential scientists and engineers.
FR-> Les données relatives aux techniciens ayant des qualifications de la CITE niveau 5, sont comprises avec celles des scientifiques et ingénieurs potentiels.
ESP> Los datos relativos a los técnicos con una calificación de la CINE nivel 5, están incluídos con los de los científicos e ingenieros potenciales.
Monaco:
E--> Data for columns 4 and 5 are included under columns 2 and 3.
FR-> Les données des colonnes 4 et 5 sont incluses dans les colonnes 2 et 3.
ESP> Los datos de las columnas 4 y 5 están incluídos en los de las columnas 2 y 3.
Netherlands:
E--> Data for technicians with qualifications at ISCED level 5 are included with those for potential scientists and engineers.
FR-> Les données relatives aux techniciens ayant des qualifications de la CITE niveau 5, sont comprises avec celles des scientifiques et ingénieurs potentiels.
ESP> Los datos relativos a los tecnicos con una calificación de la CINE nivel 5, están incluídos con los de los científicos e ingenieros potenciales.
Poland:
E--> Data refer to employed persons in the national economy.
FR-> Les données se réfèrent aux personnes employées dans l'économie nationale.
ESP> Los datos se refieren a las personas empleadas en la economía nacional.
San Marino:
E--> 85 of the potential scientists and engineers in column 2 and 475 of the technicians in column 4 are foreigners.
FR-> 85 scientifiques et ingénieurs potentiels de la colonne 2 et 475 techniciens de la colonne 4 sont ressortissants étrangers.
ESP> 85 científicos e ingenieros potenciales de la columna 2 y 475 técnicos de la columna 4 son extranjeros.
Spain:
E--> Data for technicians with qualifications at ISCED level 5 are included with those for potential scientists and engineers.
FR-> Les données relatives aux techniciens ayant des qualifications de la CITE niveau 5, sont comprises avec celles des scientifiques et ingénieurs potentiels.
ESP> Los datos relativos a los tecnicos con una calificación de la CINE nivel 5, están incluídos con los de los científicos e ingenieros potenciales.
Switzerland:
E--> Data refer to persons in gainful employment aged 25 years and over with an education at the third level.
FR-> Les données se réfèrent aux personnes qui occupent un emploi remunéré âgées de 25 ans et plus ayant suivi un enseignement du troisième degré.
ESP> Los datos se refieren a las personas de 25 años y más que ocupan un empleo remunerado y que poseen una formación de enseñanza de tercer grado.
OCEANIA:
Papua New Guinea:
E--> 2,501 of the potential scientists and engineers in column 2 and 7,213 of the technicians in column 4 are foreigners.
FR-> 2 501 scientifiques et ingénieurs potentiels de la colonne 2 et 7 213 techniciens de la colonne 4 sont ressortissants étrangers.
ESP> 2 501 científicos e ingenieros potenciales de la columna 2 y 7 213 técnicos de la columna 4 son extranjeros.
Vanuatu:
E--> 67 of the potential scientists and engineers in column 2 and 350 of the technicians in column 4 are foreigners.
FR-> 67 scientifiques et ingénieurs potentiels de la colonne 2 et 350 techniciens de la colonne 4 sont ressortissants étrangers.
ESP> 67 científicos e ingenieros potenciales de la columna 2 y 350 técnicos de la columna 4 son extranjeros.
U.S.S.R.:
U.S.S.R.:
E--> Refers to specialists in the national economy, i.e. persons having completed education at the third level for potential scientists and engineers and secondary specialized education for technicians.
FR-> Les chiffres se réfèrent aux spécialistes employés dans l'économie nationale, c.-à-d., aux personnes ayant complété les études du troisième degré pour les scientifiques et ingénieurs potentiels et l'enseignement secondaire spécialisé pour les techniciens.
ESP> Se trata de especialistas empleados en la economía nacional, es decir, de las personas que completaron los estudios de tercer grado para los científicos e ingenieros potenciales y la enseñanza secundaria especializada para los técnicos.
Byelorussian S.S.R.:
E--> See note for the U.S.S.R.
FR-> Voir la note pour l'U.R.S.S.
ESP> Véase la nota de la U.R.S.S.
Ukrainian S.S.R.:
E--> See note for the U.S.S.R.
FR-> Voir la note pour l'U.R.S.S.
ESP> Véase la nota de la U.R.S.S.

5.4 Number of scientists, engineers and technicians engaged in research and experimental development

Nombre de scientifiques, d'ingénieurs et de techniciens employés à des travaux de recherche et de développement expérimental

Número de científicos, ingenieros y técnicos empleados en trabajos de investigación y de desarrollo experimental

PLEASE REFER TO INTRODUCTION FOR DEFINITIONS OF CATEGORIES INCLUDED IN THIS TABLE.

SET = SCIENTISTS, ENGINEERS AND TECHNICIANS

DATA ARE IN FULL-TIME EQUIVALENT (FTE)

NUMBER OF COUNTRIES AND TERRITORIES PRESENTED IN THIS TABLE: 100

POUR LES DEFINITIONS DES CATEGORIES PRESENTEES DANS CE TABLEAU, SE REFERER A L'INTRODUCTION.

SET = SCIENTIFIQUES, INGENIEURS ET TECHNICIENS

LES DONNEES SONT EN EQUIVALENT PLEIN TEMPS (EPT)

NOMBRE DE PAYS ET DE TERRITOIRES PRESENTES DANS CE TABLEAU: 100

EN LA INTRODUCCION SE DAN LAS DEFINICIONES DE LAS CATEGORIAS QUE FIGURAN EN ESTE CUADRO.

SET = CIENTIFICOS, INGENIEROS Y TECNICOS

DATOS EN EQUIVALENTE DE JORNADA COMPLETA (EJC)

NUMERO DE PAISES Y DE TERRITORIOS PRESENTADOS EN ESTE CUADRO: 100

COUNTRY / PAYS / PAIS	YEAR / ANNEE / AÑO	TOTAL (FTE) / TOTAL (EPT) / TOTAL (EJC)	SCIENTISTS AND ENGINEERS / SCIENTIFIQUES ET INGENIEURS / CIENTIFICOS E INGENIEROS		TECHNICIANS / TECHNICIENS / TECNICOS	
		SET	TOTAL	F	TOTAL	F
		(1)	(2)	(3)	(4)	(5)
AFRICA						
BURUNDI	1984	333	218	...	115	...
CENTRAL AFRICAN REPUBLIC‡	1984	579	196	...	383	...
CONGO‡	1984	2 335	862	...	1 473	...
COTE D'IVOIRE‡	1975	502	502	...	...	...
EGYPT‡	1982	26 617	19 939	11 503	6 678	3 947
GHANA‡	1976	9 819	4 084	...	5 735	...
GUINEA	1984	1 893	1 282	...	611	...
KENYA‡	1975	544	361	...	183	...
LIBYAN ARAB JAMAHIRIYA	1980	2 600	1 100	...	1 500	...
MADAGASCAR‡	1980	479	112	...	367	...
MALAWI‡	1977	431	189	7	242	4
MAURITIUS	1984	439	263	20	176	26
NIGER‡	1976	94	93	18	1	–
NIGERIA‡	1977	3 545	2 200	...	1 345	...
RWANDA‡	1981	*245	*245	...	...	...
SENEGAL‡	1976	522	522	...	...	...
SEYCHELLES‡	1983	24	18	...	6	...
SUDAN	1978	7 077	3 806	...	3 271	...
TOGO‡	1976	445	261	...	184	...
ZAMBIA‡	1976	400	250	24	150	9
AMERICA, NORTH						
BRITISH VIRGIN ISLANDS	1984	–	–	–	–	–
CANADA‡	1982	*50 490	*31 950	...	*18 540	...
COSTA RICA	1982	411	411	...	...	...
CUBA‡	1984	18 391	9 548	...	8 843	...
EL SALVADOR‡	1984	1 601	...	...	...	...
GUATEMALA‡	1984	2 699	...	...	...	...
PANAMA‡	1975	505	204	67	301	*49
ST. LUCIA	1979	8	3	...	5	...
ST. PIERRE AND MIQUELON	1984	13	6	–	7	–
TURKS AND CAICOS ISLANDS	1984	–	–	–	–	–
UNITED STATES‡	1983	...	728 600	...	...	...

COUNTRY / PAYS / PAIS	YEAR / ANNEE / AÑO	TOTAL (FTE) / TOTAL (EPT) / TOTAL (EJC)	SCIENTISTS AND ENGINEERS / SCIENTIFIQUES ET INGENIEURS / CIENTIFICOS E INGENIEROS		TECHNICIANS / TECHNICIENS / TECNICOS	
		SET	TOTAL	F	TOTAL	F
		(1)	(2)	(3)	(4)	(5)
AMERICA, SOUTH						
ARGENTINA‡	1982	10 486	10 486	6 705	...	...
BRAZIL	1982	...	32 508	...	...	...
CHILE	1983	2 005	...	...	...	...
COLOMBIA‡	1982	2 107	1 083	...	1 024	...
ECUADOR‡	1979	3 301	2 049	...	1 252	...
GUYANA‡	1982	267	89	...	178	
PARAGUAY‡	1981	807	...	...	...	...
PERU‡	1981	...	4 858	...	...	...
VENEZUELA‡	1983	7 260	4 568	1 479	2 692	...
ASIA						
BRUNEI DARUSSALAM‡	1984	136	20	...	116	...
BURMA	1975	2 220	1 720	...	500	...
CYPRUS‡	1984	131	51	...	80	...
INDIA‡	1982	93 698	...	...	...	...
INDONESIA‡	1984	29 020	24 895	...	4 125	...
IRAN, ISLAMIC REPUBLIC OF‡	1980	2 337	2 132		205	...
ISRAEL‡	1978	14 722	14 722		...	...
JAPAN‡	1984	628 686	531 612	...	97 074	...
JORDAN‡	1982	1 261	1 241	...	20	...
KOREA, REPUBLIC OF‡	1983	51 610	32 117	1 816	19 493	5 195
KUWAIT‡	1984	2 072	1 511	334	561	113
LEBANON‡	1980	186	180		6	...
MALAYSIA‡	1983	2 697	...	...	...	...
MALDIVES	1980	–	–	–	–	–
NEPAL‡	1980	409	334	...	75	...
PAKISTAN‡	1982	12 535	5 397	418	7 138	...
PHILIPPINES‡	1982	*7 474	*5 146	...	*2 328	...
QATAR‡	1984	48	33	–	15	–
SINGAPORE‡	1981	1 259	724	...	535	...
SRI LANKA	1983	3 359	1 939	...	1 420	...
TURKEY‡	1983	10 436	7 747	...	2 689	...
VIET-NAM‡	1978	19 090	13 050	...	6 040	...
EUROPE						
AUSTRIA	1981	12 857	6 712	...	6 145	...
BELGIUM	1977	21 579	13 883	...	7 696	...
BULGARIA‡	1984	57 609	45 125	21 070	12 484	8 347
CZECHOSLOVAKIA‡	1984	105 620	58 820	...	46 800	...
DENMARK‡	1983	17 759	7 508	...	10 251	...
FINLAND‡	1983	20 218	10 951	...	9 267	...
FRANCE‡	1979	230 766	72 889	...	157 877	...
GERMAN DEMOCRATIC REPUBLIC‡	1984	197 288	127 595	...	69 693	...
GERMANY, FEDERAL REPUBLIC OF‡	1981	243 680	128 162	...	115 518	...
GREECE‡	1983	3 508	2 441	...	1 067	...
HUNGARY‡	1984	40 956	22 518	10 528	18 438	...
ICELAND	1979	531	304	...	227	...
IRELAND	1982	4 044	2 773	...	1 271	...
ITALY	1983	91 715	63 021	...	28 694	...
MALTA‡	1984	39	34	...	5	...
NETHERLANDS‡	1983	57 630	30 530	...	27 100	...
NORWAY‡	1982	15 218	7 754	...	7 464	...
POLAND‡	1984	109 800	74 700	...	35 100	...
PORTUGAL	1982	6 119	3 019	...	3 100	...
SAN MARINO	1982	–	–	–	–	–
SPAIN‡	1983	19 369	14 229	2 510	5 140	535
SWEDEN‡	1983	47 758	19 081	...	28 677	...
SWITZERLAND‡	1983	13 350	13 350	...	...	...
UNITED KINGDOM‡	1978	163 100	86 500	...	76 600	...
YUGOSLAVIA‡	1981	38 611	24 882	...	13 729	...
OCEANIA						
AUSTRALIA	1981	36 215	24 208	...	12 007	...
FRENCH POLYNESIA‡	1983	33	17	...	16	...
GUAM‡	1979	40	21	...	19	...
KIRIBATI	1980	3	2	–	1	–
NEW CALEDONIA	1983	12	7	–	5	–

COUNTRY / PAYS / PAIS	YEAR / ANNEE / AÑO	TOTAL (FTE) / TOTAL (EPT) / TOTAL (EJC)	SCIENTISTS AND ENGINEERS / SCIENTIFIQUES ET INGENIEURS / CIENTIFICOS E INGENIEROS		TECHNICIANS / TECHNICIENS / TECNICOS	
		SET	TOTAL	F	TOTAL	F
		(1)	(2)	(3)	(4)	(5)
NEW ZEALAND‡	1979	8 080	...	...	...	...
PACIFIC ISLANDS	1979	15	4	...	11	...
SAMOA‡	1978	232	140	...	92	...
TONGA‡	1981	15	11	–	4	1
VANUATU	1975	4	3	.5	1	–
U.S.S.R.						
U.S.S.R.‡	1984	...	1 463 800	585 200	...	...
BYELORUSSIAN S.S.R.‡	1984	...	40 200	16 000	...	...
UKRAINIAN S.S.R.‡	1984	...	204 900	77 600	...	...

AFRICA:

Central African Republic:

E--> Data relate to the number of full-time plus part-time scientists and engineers and technicians.

FR-> Les données se réfèrent au nombre des scientifiques et ingénieurs et techniciens à plein temps et à temps partiel.

ESP> Los datos se refieren al número de científicos e ingenieros y técnicos de jornada completa y de jornada parcial.

Congo:

E--> Data relate to the number of full-time plus part-time scientists and engineers of whom 206 are foreigners. Not including military and defence R&D.

FR-> Les données se réfèrent au nombre de scientifiques et ingénieurs à plein temps et à temps partiel dont 206 sont ressortissants étrangers. Non compris les activités de R-D de caractère militaire ou relevant de la défense nationale.

ESP> Los datos se refieren al número de científicos e ingenieros de jornada completa y de jornada parcial de los cuales 206 son extranjeros. Excluídas las actividades militares y de defensa de I y D.

Côte d'Ivoire:

E--> Data refer to full-time scientists and engineers of whom 362 are foreigners.

FR-> Les données se réfèrent aux scientifiques et ingénieurs à plein temps dont 362 sont ressortissants étrangers.

ESP> Los datos se refieren a los científicos e ingenieros de jornada completa de los cuales 362 son extranjeros.

Egypt:

E--> In columns 3 and 5 the numbers relating to female scientists and engineers are counted in full-time plus part-time. Not including military and defence R&D.

FR-> Dans les colonnes 3 et 5 les scientifiques et ingénieurs de sexe féminin sont comptés en plein temps et temps partiel. Non compris les activités de R-D de caractère militaire ou relevant de la défense nationale.

ESP> En las columnas 3 y 5 las cifras que se refieren a los científicos e ingenieros de sexo femenino se cuentan en jornada completa y jornada parcial. Excluídas las actividades militares y de defense de I y D.

Ghana:

E--> Data in columns 1 and 4 include auxiliary personnel.

FR-> Les chiffres des colonnes 1 et 4 comprennent le personnel auxiliaire.

ESP> Las cifras de las columnas 1 y 4 incluyen el personal auxiliar.

Kenya:

E--> Not including data for humanities.

FR-> Non compris les données pour les sciences humaines.

ESP> Excluídos los datos relativos a las ciencias humanas.

Madagascar:

E--> Data relate to the number of full-time plus part-time scientists and engineers and technicians at 4 research institutes only but do not include those engaged in the administration of R&D.

FR-> Les données se réfèrent au nombre de scientifiques et ingénieurs et techniciens, à plein temps et à temps partiel dans 4 instituts de recherche seulement mais ne comprennent pas ceux qui sont employés dans les services administratifs de R-D.

ESP> Los datos se refieren al número de científicos e ingenieros y técnicos de jornada completa y de jornada parcial en 4 centros de investigación solamente pero no incluyen los que están empleados en los servicios administrativos de I y D.

Malawi:

E--> 115 (F. 7) of the scientists and engineers in column 2 and 2 (F. -) of the technicians in column 4 are foreigners.

FR-> 115 (F. 7) scientifiques et ingénieurs de la colonne 2 et 2 (F. -) techniciens de la colonne 4 sont ressortissants étrangers.

ESP> 115 (F. 7) científicos e ingenieros de la columna 2 y 2 (F. técnicos de la columna 4 son extranjeros.

Niger:

E--> Data refer to the higher education sector only. 59 (F. 18) of th scientists and engineers in columns 2 and 3 are foreigners.

FR-> Les données ne concernent que le secteur de l'enseigneme supérieur. 59 (F. 18) scientifiques et ingénieurs des colonnes 2 et sont ressortissants étrangers.

ESP> Los datos sólo incluyen el sector de enseñanza superior. 5 (F. 18) científicos e ingenieros de las columnas 2 y 3 son extranjeros.

Nigeria:

E--> Data refer to the number of full-time plus part-time scientists ar engineers and do not include social sciences and humanities.

FR-> Les données se réfèrent au nombre de scientifiques et ingénieu à plein temps et à temps partiel et ne comprennent pas les sciences sociale et humaines.

ESP> Para los científicos e ingenieros los datos se refieren a lo efectivos de jornada completa y de jornada parcial y no incluyen la ciencias sociales y humanas.

Rwanda:

E--> Partial data. 76 of the scientists and engineers in column 2 ar foreigners.

FR-> Données partielles. 76 scientifiques et ingénieurs de la colonn 2 sont ressortissants étrangers.

ESP> Datos parciales. 76 científicos e ingenieros de la columna 2 so extranjeros.

Senegal:

E--> Data refer to the number of full-time plus part-time scientists an engineers of whom 70% are foreigners.

FR-> Les données se réfèrent au nombre de scientifiques et ingénieu à plein temps et à temps partiel dont 70% sont ressortissants étranger

ESP> Los datos se refieren al número de científicos e ingenieros d jornada completa y de jornada parcial, de los cuales 70% so extranjeros.

Seychelles:

E--> Not including military and defence R&D.

FR-> Non compris les activités de R-D de caractère militaire o relevant de la défense nationale.

ESP> Excluídas las actividades militares y de defensa de I y D.

Togo:

E--> Data for scientists and engineers refer only to full-time.

FR-> Pour les scientifiques et ingénieurs, les données se réfèren seulement aux effectifs à plein temps.

ESP> Para los científicos e ingenieros los datos se refieren solament a los efectivos de jornada completa.

Zambia:

E--> Partial data for 9 institutes only. 222 of the scientists an engineers in column 2 are foreigners.

FR-> Données partielles pour 9 instituts seulement. 222 scientifique et ingénieurs de la colonne 2 sont ressortissants étrangers.

ESP> Datos parciales para 9 institutos solamente. 222 científicos ingenieros de la columna 2 son extranjeros.

AMERICA, NORTH:

Canada:

E--> Not including social sciences and humanities in the productiv sector (integrated R&D).

FR-> Non compris les sciences sociales et humaines dans le secteur d la production (activités de R-D intégrées).

ESP> Excluídas las ciencias sociales y humanas del secto productivo (actividades de I y D integradas).

Cuba:

E--> Not including military and defence R&D.

FR-> Non compris les activités de R-D de caractère militaire ou relevant de la défense nationale.

ESP> Excluídas las actividades militares y de defensa de I y D.

El Salvador:

E--> Data refer to the number of full-time plus part-time scientists and engineers and technicians engaged in public enterprises.

FR-> Les données se réfèrent au nombre de scientifiques et ingénieurs et techniciens à plein temps et à temps partiel employés dans les entreprises publiques.

ESP> Los datos se refieren al número de científicos e ingenieros y técnicos de jornada completa y de jornada parcial empleados en las empresas públicas.

Guatemala:

E--> Data relate to the number of full-time plus part-time scientists and engineers and technicians.

FR-> Les données se réfèrent au nombre des scientifiques et ingénieurs et techniciens à plein temps et à temps partiel.

ESP> Los datos se refieren al número de científicos e ingenieros y técnicos de jornada completa y de jornada parcial.

Panama:

E--> Data also include scientific and technological services (STS). The total number of technicians includes 60 persons for whom a distribution by sex is not available.

FR-> Les données comprennent en plus les services scientifiques et techniques (SST). Le nombre total de techniciens comprend 60 personnes pour lesquelles la répartition par sexe n'est pas disponible.

ESP> Los datos también incluyen los servicios científicos y tecnológicos (SCT). El nùmero total de técnicos comprende 60 personas para las que se desconoce la repartición por sexo.

United States:

E--> Not including data for law, humanities and education.

FR-> Non compris les données pour le droit, les sciences humaines et l'éducation.

ESP> Excluídos los datos relativos al derecho, las ciencias humanas y la educación.

AMERICA, SOUTH:

Argentina:

E--> In column 3 the number relating to female scientists and engineers is counted in full-time plus part-time.

FR-> Dans la colonne 3 les scientifiques et ingénieurs de sexe féminin sont comptés en plein temps et temps partiel.

ESP> En la columna 3 la cifra que se refiere a los científicos e ingenieros de sexo feminino se cuenta en jornada completa y jornada parcial.

Colombia:

E--> Not including data for the productive sector (non-integrated R&D).

FR-> Non compris les données relatives au secteur de la production (activités de R-D non intégrées).

ESP> Excluídos los datos relativos al sector productivo (actividades de I y D no integradas).

Ecuador:

E--> Data also include scientific and technological services (STS) and refer to the number of full-time plus part-time scientists and engineers and technicians.

FR-> Les données comprennent en plus les services scientifiques et techniques (SST) et se réfèrent au nombre de scientifiques et ingénieurs et techniciens à plein temps et à temps partiel.

ESP> Los datos también incluyen los servicios científicos y tecnológicos (SCT) y se refieren al número de científicos e ingenieros y técnicos de jornada completa y de jornada parcial.

Guyana:

E--> Not including military and defence R&D. Data for the general service sector and for medical sciences in the higher education sector are also excluded.

FR-> Non compris les activités de R-D de caractère militaire ou relevant de la défense nationale. Les données relatives au secteur de service général et les sciences médicales du secteur de l'enseignement supérieur sont aussi exclues.

ESP> Excluídas las actividades militares y de defensa de I y D. Se excluyen tambíen los datos relativos al sector de servicio general y las ciencias médicas al sector de enseñanza superior.

Paraguay:

E--> Data refer to the number of full-time plus part-time scientists and engineers and technicians.

FR-> Les données se réfèrent au nombre de scientifiques et ingénieurs et techniciens à plein temps et à temps partiel.

ESP> Los datos se refieren al número de científicos e ingenieros y técnicos de jornada completa y de jornada parcial.

Peru:

E--> Data for scientists and engineers refer only to full-time.

FR-> Pour les scientifiques et ingénieurs, les données se réfèrent seulement aux effectifs à plein temps.

ESP> Para los científicos e ingenieros los datos se refieren solamente a los efectivos de jornada completa.

Venezuela:

E--> Not including military and defence R&D. Data refer to the number of full-time plus part-time scientists and engineers and technicians.

FR-> Non compris les activités de R-D de caractère militaire ou relevant de la défense nationale. Les données se réfèrent au nombre de scientifiques et ingénieurs et techniciens à plein temps et à temps partiel.

ESP> Excluídas las actividades militares y de defensa de I y D. Los datos se refieren al número de científicos e ingenieros y técnicos de jornada completa y de jornada parcial.

ASIA:

Brunei Darussalam:

E--> Data relate to the number of full-time plus part-time scientists and engineers and technicians at 2 research institutes only.

FR-> Les données se réfèrent au nombre de scientifiques et ingénieurs et techniciens, à plein temps et à temps partiel, dans 2 instituts de recherche seulement.

ESP> Los datos se refieren al número de científicos y ingenieros y técnicos de jornada completa y de jornada parcial en 2 centros de investigación solamente.

Cyprus:

E--> Not including data for the productive sector. Data in columns 1 and 4 include auxiliary personnel.

FR-> Non compris les données relatives au secteur de la production. Les chiffres des colonnes 1 et 4 comprennent le personnel auxiliaire.

ESP> Excluídos los datos relativos al sector productivo. Las cifras de las columnas 1 y 4 incluyen el personal auxiliar.

India:

E--> The figure in column 1 includes auxiliary personnel.

FR-> Le chiffre de la colonne 1 comprend le personnel auxiliaire.

ESP> La cifra de la columna 1 incluye el personal auxiliar.

Indonesia:

E--> Data refer to the number of full-time plus part-time scientists and engineers and technicians.

FR-> Les données se réfèrent au nombre de scientifiques et ingénieurs et techniciens à plein temps et à temps partiel.

ESP> Para los científicos e ingenieros y técnicos, los datos se refieren a los efectivos de jornada completa y de jornada parcial.

Iran, Islamic Republic of:

E--> Data relate to the number of full-time plus part-time scientists and engineers and technicians at 64 research institutes.

FR-> Les données se réfèrent au nombre de scientifiques et ingénieurs et techniciens à plein temps et à temps partiel dans 64 centres de recherche.

ESP> Los datos se refieren al número de científicos y ingenieros y técnicos de jornada completa y de jornada parcial en 64 centros de investigación.

Israel:

E--> Data for scientists and engineers are full-time and some part-time.

FR-> Pour les scientifiques et ingénieurs les données se réfèrent aux effectifs à plein temps et à un certain nombre à temps partiel.

ESP> Para los científicos e ingenieros los datos se refieren a los efectivos de jornada completa y a un cierto número de jornada parcial.

Japan:

E--> Data refer to full-time scientists and engineers and technicians. Not including social sciences and humanities in the productive sector.

FR-> Les données se réfèrent aux scientifiques et ingénieurs et techniciens à plein temps. Non compris les sciences sociales et humaines dans le secteur de la production.

ESP> Los datos se refieren a los científicos e ingenieros y técnicos de jornada completa. Excluídas las ciencias sociales y humanas en el sector productivo.

Jordan:

E--> Data refer to the number of full-time plus part-time scientists and engineers. Not including military and defence R&D.

FR-> Les données se réfèrent au nombre de scientifiques et ingénieurs à plein temps et à temps partiel. Non compris les activités de R-D de caractère militaire ou relevant de la défense nationale.

ESP> Para los científicos e ingenieros los datos se refieren a los efectivos de jornada completa y de jornada parcial. Excluídas las actividades militares y de defensa de I y D.

Korea, Republic of:

E--> Not including either military and defence R&D or social sciences and humanities. Data relate to the number of full-time plus part-time scientists and engineers and technicians.

FR-> Non compris les activités de R-D de. caractère militaire ou relevant de la défense nationale ni les sciences sociales et humaines. Les données se réfèrent au nombre de scientifiques et ingénieurs et techniciens à plein temps et à temps partiel.

ESP> Excluídas las actividades militares y de defensa de I y D y las ciencias sociales y humanas. Los datos se refieren al número de científicos e ingenieros y técnicos de jornada completa y de jornada parcial.

Kuwait:

E--> Data refer to scientific and technological activities (STA) and relate to the number of full-time plus part-time scientists and engineers and

Kuwait: (Cont):
technicians. 1,027 (F. 179) of the scientists and engineers in columns 2 and 3, and 113 (F. 67) of the technicians in columns 4 and 5 are foreigners.

FR-> Les données se réfèrent aux activités scientifiques et techniques (AST) et au nombre de scientifiques et ingénieurs et techniciens à plein temps et à temps partiel. 1,027 (F. 179) scientifiques et ingénieurs des colonnes 2 et 3, et 113 (F. 67) techniciens des colonnes 4 et 5 sont ressortissants étrangers.

ESP> Los datos se refieren a las actividades científicas y tecnológicas (ACT) y al número de científicos e ingenieros y técnicos de jornada completa y de jornada parcial. 1,027 (F. 179) científicos e ingenieros de las columnas 2 y 3, y 113 (F. 67) técnicos de las columnas 4 y 5 son extranjeros.

Lebanon:
E--> Data refer to the Faculty of Science at the University of Lebanon only.

FR-> Les données ne se réfèrent qu'à la Faculté des Sciences de l'Université du Liban.

ESP> Los datos se refieren a la Facultad de Ciencias de la Universidad del Líbano solamente.

Malaysia:
E--> Data refer to the number of full-time plus part-time scientists and engineers and technicians. Not including social sciences and humanities.

FR-> Les données se réfèrent au nombre de scientifiques et ingénieurs et techniciens à plein temps et à temps partiel. Non compris les sciences sociales et humaines.

ESP> Los datos se refieren al número de científicos e ingenieros y técnicos de jornada completa y de jornada parcial. Excluídas las ciencias sociales y humanas.

Nepal:
E--> Data refer to scientific and technological activities (STA) and do not include social sciences and humanities. Data relate to full-time scientists and engineers and technicians.

FR-> Les données se réfèrent aux activités scientifiques et techniques (AST) et ne comprennent pas les sciences sociales et humaines. Les données se réfèrent aux scientifiques et ingénieurs et techniciens à plein temps.

ESP> Los datos se refieren a las actividades científicas y tecnológicas (ACT) y no incluyen las ciencias sociales y humanas. Los datos se refieren a los científicos y ingenieros y técnicos de jornada completa.

Pakistan:
E--> Data relate to R&D activities concentrated mainly in government-financed research establishments only; social sciences and humanities in the higher education and general service sectors are excluded. Not including the productive sector (integrated R&D) or military and defence R&D. Data in column 4 refer to the number of full-time plus part-time technicians.

FR-> Les données se réfèrent aux activités de R-D se trouvant pour la plupart dans les établissements de recherche financés par le gouvernement; les sciences sociales et humaines dans les secteurs de l'enseignement supérieur et de service général sont exclues. Compte non tenu du secteur de la production (activités de R-D intégrées) ni des activités de R-D de caractère militaire ou relevant de la défense nationale. Les données de la colonne 4 se réfèrent au nombre de techniciens à plein temps et à temps partiel.

ESP> Los datos se refieren a las actividades de I y D concentradas principalmente en los establecimientos de investigación subvencionados por el gobierno; se excluyen las ciencias sociales y humanas de los sectores de enseñanza superior y de servicio general. Excluídos el sector productivo (actividades de I y D integradas) y las actividades militares y de defensa de I y D. Los datos de la columna 4 se refieren a los técnicos de jornada completa y de jornada parcial.

Philippines:
E--> Data do not include the higher education sector.

FR-> Les données ne comprennent pas le secteur de l'enseignement supérieur.

ESP> Los datos no comprenden el sector de enseñanza superior.

Qatar:
E--> Data do not include the higher education sector.

FR-> Les données ne comprennent pas le secteur de l'enseignement supérieur.

ESP> Los datos no comprenden el sector de enseñanza superior.

Singapore:
E--> Not including either military and defence R&D or social sciences and humanities.

FR-> Non compris les activités de R-D de caractère militaire ou relevant de la défense nationale ni les sciences sociales et humaines.

ESP> Excluídas las actividades militares y de defensa de I y D y las ciencias sociales y humanas.

Turkey:
E--> Not including data for social sciences and humanities in the general service sector.

FR-> Compte non tenu des sciences sociales et humaines dans le secteur de service général.

ESP> Excluídas las ciencias sociales y humanas en el sector de servicio general.

Viet-nam:
E--> The figures in columns 1 and 4 do not include data technicians in the higher education sector.

FR-> Les chiffres des colonnes 1 et 4 ne comprennent pas les don relatives aux techniciens du secteur de l'enseignement supérieur.

ESP> Las cifras de las columnas 1 y 4 no incluyen los datos relat a los técnicos del sector de enseñanza superior.

EUROPE:

Bulgaria:
E--> The figures in columns 1, 4 and 5 do not include data technicians in the higher education sector.

FR-> Les chiffres des colonnes 1, 4 et 5 ne comprennent pas données relatives aux techniciens du secteur de l'enseigner supérieur.

ESP> Las cifras des las columnas 1, 4 y 5 no incluyen los datos relat a los técnicos del sector de enseñanza superior.

Czechoslovakia:
E--> Not including scientists and engineers engaged in administration of R&D; of military R&D only that part carried out in establishments is included.

FR-> Non compris les scientifiques et ingénieurs employés dans services administratifs de R-D; pour la R-D de caractère militaire, s la partie effectuée dans les établissements civils a été considérée.

ESP> Excluídos los científicos e ingenieros empleados en los servi administrativos de I y D; para las actividades de I y D de cará militar sólo se ha considerado la parte correspondiente a establecimientos civiles.

Denmark:
E--> The figures in columns 1 and 4 include auxiliary personnel

FR-> Les chiffres des colonnes 1 et 4 comprennent le perso auxiliaire.

ESP> Las cifras de las columnas 1 y 4 incluyen el personal auxili

Finland:
E--> Data in columns 1 and 4 include auxiliary personnel.

FR-> Les chiffres des colonnes 1 et 4 comprennent le perso auxiliaire.

ESP> Las cifras de las columnas 1 y 4 incluyen el personal auxili

France:
E--> Data in columns 1 and 4 include auxiliary personnel.

FR-> Les chiffres des colonnes 1 et 4 comprennent le perso auxiliaire.

ESP> Las cifras de las columnas 1 y 4 incluyen el personal auxili

German Democratic Republic:
E--> Data in columns 1 and 4 include auxiliary personnel.

FR-> Les chiffres des colonnes 1 et 4 comprennent le perso auxiliaire.

ESP> Las cifras de las columnas 1 y 4 incluyen el personal auxili

Germany, Federal Republic of:
E--> Not including social sciences and humanities in the produc sector.

FR-> Non compris les sciences sociales et humaines dans le sec de la production.

ESP> Excluídas las ciencias sociales y humanas del se productivo.

Greece:
E--> Data relate to government activities only.

FR-> Les données se réfèrent aux activités gouvernement seulement.

ESP> Los datos se refieren a las actividades gubernament solamente.

Hungary:
E--> Not including scientists and engineers engaged in administration of R&D; figures in columns 1 and 4 include sk workers.

FR-> Non compris les scientifiques et ingénieurs employés dans services administratifs de R-D; les chiffres des colonnes 1 et 4 comprenr les ouvriers qualifiés.

ESP> No incluye los científicos e ingenieros empleados en los servi administrativos de I y D; las cifras de las columnas 1 y 4 comprenden obreros calificados.

Malta:
E--> Data relate to the higher education sector only.

FR-> Les données ne concernent que le secteur de l'enseignem supérieur.

ESP> Los datos se refieren exclusivamente al sector de enseña superior.

Netherlands:
E--> Not including data for social sciences and humanities in productive sector (integrated R&D). The figures in columns 1 anc include auxiliary personnel.

FR-> Non compris les sciences sociales et humaines du secteur d production (activités de R-D intégrées). Les chiffres des colonnes 1 e comprennent le personnel auxiliaire.

ESP> Excluídas las ciencias sociales y humanas del sector produc (actividades de I y D integradas). Las cifras de las columnas 1 y 4 inclu el personal auxiliar.

Norway:
E--> Data in columns 1 and 4 include auxiliary personnel.

Norway: (Cont):
FR-> Les chiffres des colonnes 1 et 4 comprennent le personnel auxiliaire.
ESP> Las cifras de las columnas 1 y 4 incluyen el personal auxiliar.
Poland:
E--> Not including military and defence R&D. The figure in column 4 refers to persons with a vocational education at the second level; not including technicians in the higher education sector.
FR-> Non compris les activités de R-D de caractère militaire ou relevant de la défense nationale. Le chiffre de la colonne 4 concerne les personnes ayant suivi un enseignement technique du second degré; compte non tenu des techniciens dans le secteur de l'enseignement supérieur.
ESP> Excluídas las actividades militares y de defensa de I y D. La cifra de la columna 4 se refiere a las personas que han recibido una formación técnica de segundo grado; excluídos los técnicos del sector de enseñanza superior.
Spain:
E--> The figures in columns 1 and 4 do not include data for technicians in the higher education sector.
FR-> Les chiffres des colonnes 1 et 4 ne comprennent pas les données relatives aux techniciens du secteur de l'enseignement supérieur.
ESP> Las cifras de las columnas 1 y 4 no comprenden los técnicos del sector de enseñanza superior.
Sweden:
E--> Not including social sciences and humanities in the productive and general service sectors. The figures in columns 1 and 4 include auxiliary personnel.
FR-> Compte non tenu des sciences sociales et humaines dans les secteurs de la production et du service général. Les chiffres des colonnes 1 et 4 comprennent le personnel auxiliaire.
ESP> Excluídas las ciencias sociales y humanas en los sectores productivo y de servicio general. Las cifras de las columnas 1 y 4 incluyen el personal auxiliar.
Switzerland:
E--> Data do not include the higher education sector.
FR-> Les données ne comprennent pas le secteur de l'enseignement supérieur.
ESP> Los datos no comprenden el sector de enseñanza superior.
United Kingdom:
E--> Data do not include the higher education sector.
FR-> Les données ne comprennent pas le secteur de l'enseignement supérieur.
ESP> Los datos no comprenden el sector de enseñanza superior.
Yugoslavia:
E--> Not including military and defence R&D.
FR-> Non compris les activités de R-D de caractère militaire ou relevant de la défense nationale.
ESP> Excluídas las actividades militares y de defensa de I y D.
OCEANIA:
French Polynesia:
E--> Data relate to one research institute only.
FR-> Les données ne concernent qu'un institut de recherche.
ESP> Los datos se refieren a un centro de investigación solamente.
Guam:
E--> Data relate to the higher education sector only.

Guam: (Cont):
FR-> Les données ne concernent que le secteur de l'enseignement supérieur.
ESP> Los datos se refieren exclusivamente al sector de enseñanza superior.
New Zealand:
E--> The figure in column 1 includes auxiliary personnel.
FR-> Le chiffre de la colonnne 1 comprend le personnel auxiliaire.
ESP> La cifra de la columna 1 incluye el personal auxiliar.
Samoa:
E--> Data for scientists and engineers refer only to full-time.
FR-> Pour les scientifiques et ingénieurs, les données se réfèrent seulement aux effectifs à plein temps.
ESP> Para los científicos e ingenieros los datos se refieren solamente a los efectivos de jornada completa.
Tonga:
E--> Data relate to one research institute only. Data refer to the number of full-time plus part-time scientists and engineers of whom 8 are foreigners.
FR-> Les données ne concernent qu'un institut de recherche. Les données se réfèrent au nombre de scientifiques et ingénieurs à plein temps et à temps partiel dont 8 sont ressortissants étrangers.
ESP> Los datos se refieren a un centro de investigación solamente. Los datos se refieren al número de científicos e ingenieros de jornada completa y de jornada parcial de los cuales 8 son extranjeros.
U.S.S.R.:
U.S.S.R.:
E--> The figures in columns 2 and 3 refer to scientific workers, i.e. all persons with a higher scientific degree or scientific title, regardless of the nature of their work, persons undertaking research work in scientific establishments and scientific teaching staff in institutions of higher education; also includes persons undertaking scientific work in industrial enterprises.
FR-> Les chiffres des colonnes 2 et 3 se réfèrent aux travailleurs scientifiques, c.-à-d., à toutes les personnes ayant un diplôme scientifique supérieur ou un titre scientifique, sans considération de la nature de leur travail, aux personnes qui effectuent un travail de recherche dans des institutions scientifiques et au personnel scientifique enseignant dans des établissements d'enseignement supérieur; sont incluses aussi les personnes qui effectuent des travaux scientifiques dans les entreprises industrielles.
ESP> Las cifras de las columnas 2 y 3 se refieren a los trabajadores científicos, es decir, a todas las personas que poseen un diploma científico superior o un título científico, sin tener en cuenta la naturaleza de su trabajo, a las personas que efectuan un trabajo de investigación en las instituciones científicas y al personal científico que ejerce funciones docentes en los establecimientos de enseñanza superior; también se incluyen las personas que efectuan trabajos científicos en las empresas industriales.
Byelorussian S.S.R.:
E--> See note for the U.S.S.R.
FR-> Voir la note pour l'U.R.S.S.
ESP> Véase la nota de la U.R.S.S.
Ukrainian S.S.R.:
E--> See note for the U.S.S.R.
FR-> Voir la note pour l'U.R.S.S.
ESP> Véase la nota de la U.R.S.S.

5.5 Number of scientists and engineers engaged in research and experimental development by their field of study

Nombre de scientifiques et d'ingénieurs employés à des travaux de recherche et de développement expérimental, par leur domaine d'études

Número de científicos e ingenieros empleados en trabajos de investigación y de desarrollo experimental, según su sector de estudios

PLEASE REFER TO INTRODUCTION FOR DEFINITIONS OF CATEGORIES IN THIS TABLE.

FT = FULL-TIME
PT = PART-TIME
FT+PT = FULL-TIME PLUS PART-TIME

FTE = FULL-TIME EQUIVALENT

NUMBER OF COUNTRIES AND TERRITORIES PRESENTED IN THIS TABLE: 54

POUR LES DEFINITIONS DES CATEGORIES PRESENTEES DANS CE TABLEAU, SE REFERER A L'INTRODUCTION.

FT = A PLEIN TEMPS
PT = A TEMPS PARTIEL
FT+PT = A PLEIN TEMPS ET A TEMPS PARTIEL

FTE = EQUIVALENT PLEIN TEMPS

NOMBRE DE PAYS ET DE TERRITOIRES PRESENTES DANS CE TABLEAU: 54

EN LA INTRODUCCION SE DAN LAS DEFINICIONES DE LAS CATEGORIAS QUE FIGURAN EN ESTE CUADRO.

FT = JORNADA COMPLETA
PT = JORNADA PARCIAL
FT+PT = JORNADA COMPLETA MAS JORNADA PARCIAL

FTE = EQUIVALENTE DE JORNADA COMPLETA

NUMERO DE PAISES Y DE TERRITORIOS PRESENTADOS EN ESTE CUADRO: 54

COUNTRY / PAYS / PAIS	YEAR / ANNEE / AÑO	SEX / SEXE / SEXO	TYPE OF DATA / TYPE DE DONNEES / TIPO DE DATOS	TOTAL / TOTAL / TOTAL	FIELD OF STUDY / DOMAINE D'ETUDES / SECTOR DE ESTUDIOS					
					NATURAL SCIENCES / SCIENCES EXACTES ET NATURELLES / CIENCIAS EXACTAS Y NATURALES	ENGINEERING AND TECHNOLOGY / SCIENCES DE L'INGENIEUR ET TECHNOLOGIQUES / INGENIERIA Y TECNOLOGIA	MEDICAL SCIENCES / SCIENCES MEDICALES / CIENCIAS MEDICAS	AGRICULTURAL SCIENCES / SCIENCES AGRICOLES / CIENCIAS AGRICOLAS	SOCIAL SCIENCES AND HUMANITIES / SCIENCES SOCIALES ET HUMAINES / CIENCIAS SOCIALES Y HUMANAS	OTHER FIELDS / AUTRES DOMAINES / OTROS SECTORES
				(1)	(2)	(3)	(4)	(5)	(6)	(7)
AFRICA										
CENTRAL AFRICAN REPUBLIC‡	1975	MF	FT	62	35	5	–	4	18	–
		MF	PT	29	–	10	–	–	19	–
		MF	FTE	76	35	9	–	4	28	–
		F	FTE	8	1	3	–	–	4	–
CONGO‡	1983	MF	FT+PT	789	129	31	43	292	225	69
EGYPT	1982	MF	FT	9 950	1 605	2 605	2 050	3 143	547	–
		MF	PT	29 967	8 152	3 735	6 390	2 782	8 908	–
		MF	FTE	19 939	4 322	3 850	4 180	4 070	3 517	–
		F	FT+PT	11 503	3 075	1 189	3 109	1 186	2 944	–
KENYA‡	1975	MF	FTE	361	99	28	16	183	35	–
LIBYAN ARAB JAMAHIRIYA	1980	MF	FTE	1 100	230	198	130	221	321	–
MALAWI	1977	MF	FT	118	35	1	–	63	19	–
		MF	PT	145	42	38	4	16	45	–
		MF	FTE	189	56	20	2	71	40	–
		F	FTE	7	2	–	–	–	5	–
MAURITIUS	1983	MF	FT	202	31	24	1	139	7	–
		MF	PT	17	–	4	–	13	–	–
		MF	FTE	211	31	26	1	146	7	–
		F	FT+PT	13	1	–	–	11	1	–
NIGER‡	1976	MF	FT	93	46	–	4	9	34	–
		MF	PT	–	–	–	–	–	–	–
		MF	FTE	93	46	–	4	9	34	–
		F	FTE	18	9	–	–	–	9	–

COUNTRY / PAYS / PAIS	YEAR / ANNEE / AÑO	SEX / SEXE / SEXO	TYPE OF DATA / TYPE DE DONNEES / TIPO DE DATOS	TOTAL / TOTAL / TOTAL	NATURAL SCIENCES / SCIENCES EXACTES ET NATURELLES / CIENCIAS EXACTAS Y NATURALES	ENGINEERING AND TECHNOLOGY / SCIENCES DE L'INGENIEUR ET TECHNOLOGIQUES / INGENIERIA Y TECNOLOGIA	MEDICAL SCIENCES / SCIENCES MEDICALES / CIENCIAS MEDICAS	AGRICULTURAL SCIENCES / SCIENCES AGRICOLES / CIENCIAS AGRICOLAS	SOCIAL SCIENCES AND HUMANITIES / SCIENCES SOCIALES ET HUMAINES / CIENCIAS SOCIALES Y HUMANAS	OTHER FIELDS / AUTRES DOMAINES / OTROS SECTORES
					FIELD OF STUDY / DOMAINE D'ETUDES / SECTOR DE ESTUDIOS					
				(1)	(2)	(3)	(4)	(5)	(6)	(7)
RWANDA‡	1981	MF	FT+PT	*335	*42	*57	*23	*66	*147	–
		MF	FTE	*245	*37	*40	*14	*64	*90	–
SEYCHELLES‡	1981	MF	FT	2	2	–	–	–	–	–
		MF	PT	–	–	–	–	–	–	–
		MF	FTE	2	2	–	–	–	–	–
		F	FTE	–	–	–	–	–	–	–
SUDAN	1978	MF	FT	3 266	513	686	222	560	1 218	67
TOGO	1976	MF	FT	261	44	29	32	16	140	–
ZAMBIA‡	1976	MF	FTE	250	83	112	10	21	24	–
		F	FTE	24	6	10	2	2	4	–
AMERICA, NORTH										
CUBA‡	1983	MF	FT	6 903	666	1 773	1 187	1 741	1 209	327
		MF	PT	5 387	20	885	513	518	253	3198
		MF	FTE	8 247	686	1 938	1 379	1 896	1 310	1038
		F	FT+PT	5 089	298	969	650	789	808	1575
PANAMA‡	1975	MF	FT	193	39	41	31	33	28	21
		MF	PT	34	1	2	21	–	–	10
		MF	FTE	204	39	41	40	33	28	23
		F	FTE	67	19	9	23	3	8	5
ST. PIERRE AND MIQUELON	1983	MF	FT	5	–	–	–	5	–	–
		MF	PT	3	–	–	–	3	–	–
		MF	FTE	6	–	–	–	6	–	–
		F	FTE	–	–	–	–	–	–	–
TURKS AND CAICOS ISLANDS	1976	MF	FT	2	2	–	–	–	–	–
		MF	PT	–	–	–	–	–	–	–
		MF	FTE	2	2	–	–	–	–	–
		F	FTE	1	1	–	–	–	–	–
AMERICA, SOUTH										
ARGENTINA	1982	MF	FTE	10 486	4 024	1 971	856	1 835	1 076	724
		F	FT+PT	6 705	3 107	452	797	645	1 275	429
CHILE	1975	MF	FTE	5 948	1 885	1 367	1 562	411	723	–
COLOMBIA‡	1982	MF	FT	831	288	49	21	334	139	–
		MF	PT	3 938	1 238	544	1 088	358	710	–
		MF	FTE	1 083	341	150	299	98	195	–
GUYANA‡	1982	MF	FT	89	43	22	...	21	3	–
		MF	PT	–	–	–	–	–	–	–
		MF	FTE	89	43	22	...	21	3	–
VENEZUELA‡	1983	MF	FT+PT	4 568	1 457	727	558	874	802	150
		MF	FTE	2 175	786	300	204	437	388	60
		F	FT+PT	1 479	438	134	302	171	375	59
ASIA										
BURMA	1975	MF	FTE	1 720	900	300	120	100	300	–
INDONESIA	1983	MF	FT+PT	18 533	5 317	3 285	1 615	4 083	4 233	–
JAPAN‡	1981	MF	FT	379 405	80 442	142 316	64 408	26 598	41 316	24325
		F	FT+PT	22 475	2 277	775	7 850	904	4 108	6561
JORDAN‡	1982	MF	FT+PT	1 241	310	340	118	92	381	–
KOREA, REPUBLIC OF‡	1983	MF	FT	30 309	4 706	16 371	3 964	3 589	...	1679
		MF	PT	1 808	171	1 373	101	130	...	33
KUWAIT	1977	MF	FTE	606	109	165	9	52	271	–
		F	FTE	96	30	13	–	15	38	–
PAKISTAN‡	1982	MF	FT	4 505	–	929	821	2 149	...	606
		MF	PT	2 670	1 211	730	–	729	...	–
		MF	FTE	5 397	406	1 172	821	2 392	...	606
		F	FTE	418	152	114	80	56	...	16

COUNTRY / PAYS / PAIS	YEAR / ANNEE / AÑO	SEX / SEXE / SEXO	TYPE OF DATA / TYPE DE DONNEES / TIPO DE DATOS	TOTAL / TOTAL / TOTAL	FIELD OF STUDY / DOMAINE D'ETUDES / SECTOR DE ESTUDIOS: NATURAL SCIENCES / SCIENCES EXACTES ET NATURELLES / CIENCIAS EXACTAS Y NATURALES	ENGINEERING AND TECHNOLOGY / SCIENCES DE L'INGENIEUR ET TECHNOLOGIQUES / INGENIERIA Y TECNOLOGIA	MEDICAL SCIENCES / SCIENCES MEDICALES / CIENCIAS MEDICAS	AGRICULTURAL SCIENCES / SCIENCES AGRICOLES / CIENCIAS AGRICOLAS	SOCIAL SCIENCES AND HUMANITIES / SCIENCES SOCIALES ET HUMAINES / CIENCIAS SOCIALES Y HUMANAS	OTHER FIELDS / AUTRES DOMAINES / OTROS SECTORES
				(1)	(2)	(3)	(4)	(5)	(6)	(7)
PHILIPPINES‡	1982	MF	FT	4 642	722	1 352	121	1 584	863	–
		MF	PT	534	116	142	38	57	181	–
		MF	FTE	4 816	753	1 404	131	1 599	929	–
SINGAPORE‡	1981	MF	FTE	1 193	346	648	149	30	...	20
SRI LANKA	1977	MF	FT	422	...	...	...	...	...	...
		MF	PT	547	...	...	...	...	...	...
		MF	FTE	604	213	199	17	175	...	–
TURKEY‡	1983	MF	FTE	7 309	891	1 040	1 350	1 590	531	1907
EUROPE										
AUSTRIA‡	1981	MF	FT+PT	10 839	2 994	1 679	2 131	613	3 422	–
BULGARIA	1983	MF	FTE	43 462	4 073	9 161	4 107	2 033	4 901	19187
		F	FTE	19 890	1 781	2 493	1 739	588	2 338	10951
DENMARK‡	1979	MF	FT+PT	12 130	2 022	1 050	2 670	650	2 868	2870
		MF	FTE	6 011	1 008	569	827	401	1 227	1979
FINLAND	1983	MF	FTE	10 951	2 291	5 211	890	572	1 947	40
HUNGARY‡	1982	MF	FT+PT	37 302	3 621	18 357	3 472	2 876	8 757	219
		F	FT+PT	10 354	1 139	3 433	1 235	729	3 735	83
ICELAND	1979	MF	FT+PT	558	119	166	76	104	93	–
		MF	FTE	304	66	98	29	75	36	–
IRELAND	1975	MF	FTE	2 545	804	549	134	452	606	–
MALTA‡	1983	MF	FTE	34	3	7	10	–	14	–
NORWAY	1981	MF	FT+PT	12 867	2 225	5 024	1 757	659	3 202	–
		MF	FTE	7 496	1 332	3 442	809	436	1 477	–
POLAND‡	1983	MF	FT	57 400	4 600	44 100	2 500	3 600	2 600	–
		MF	PT	59 000	14 500	20 900	10 000	6 800	6 800	–
		MF	FTE	75 000	8 900	50 400	5 500	5 600	4 600	–
PORTUGAL‡	1980	MF	FT	1 790	529	246	123	307	300	285
		MF	PT	2 023	561	410	304	162	293	293
		MF	FTE	2 663	808	416	251	383	430	375
SPAIN	1983	MF	FT+PT	27 870	4 885	8 052	4 777	2 104	8 052	–
		MF	FTE	14 229	2 417	5 134	2 153	1 305	3 220	–
		F	FT+PT	4 728	1 159	515	870	326	1 858	–
SWITZERLAND	1975	MF	FT	21 900	6 800	9 330	2 490	890	2 390	–
		MF	FTE	16 230	5 140	8 370	1 300	330	1 090	–
YUGOSLAVIA‡	1980	MF	FT+PT	27 135	4 988	8 357	2 982	3 098	5 014	2696
OCEANIA										
AUSTRALIA‡	1981	MF	FTE	24 209	6 575	3 449	1 887	3 108	5 718	3472
FRENCH POLYNESIA‡	1983	MF	FT	17	8	1	7	–	1	–
		MF	PT	–	–	–	–	–	–	–
		MF	FTE	17	8	1	7	–	1	–
GUAM	1977	MF	FTE	213	50	120	15	10	18	–
NEW CALEDONIA	1983	MF	FT	7	4	2	–	–	–	1
		MF	PT	–	–	–	–	–	–	–
		MF	FTE	7	4	2	–	–	–	1
		F	FTE	–	–	–	–	–	–	–
SAMOA	1977	MF	FT	140	33	60	34	5	8	–
		MF	PT	30	8	14	6	1	1	–
TONGA‡	1981	MF	FT+PT	11	–	–	–	11	–	–
VANUATU	1975	MF	FT	2	–	–	–	2	–	–
		MF	PT	2	–	–	–	2	–	–
		MF	FTE	3	–	–	–	3	–	–
		F	FTE	0.5	–	–	–	0.5	–	–

AFRICA:

Central African Republic:

E--> Data relate to the higher education sector.

FR-> Les données ne concernent que le secteur de l'enseignement supérieur.

ESP> Los datos se refieren exclusivamente al sector de enseñanza superior.

Congo:

E--> Not including military and defence R&D. Data for the general service sector are also excluded.

FR-> Non compris les activités de R-D de caractère militaire ou relevant de la défense nationale. Les données relatives au secteur de service général sont également exclues.

ESP> Excluídas las actividades militares y de defensa de I y D. Se excluyen igualmente los datos relativos al sector de servicio general.

Kenya:

E--> Not including data for humanities.

FR-> Non compris les données pour les sciences humaines.

ESP> Excluídos los datos relativos a las ciencias humanas.

Niger:

E--> Data relate to the higher education sector only.

FR-> Les données ne concernent que le secteur de l'enseignement supérieur.

ESP> Los datos se refieren exclusivamente al sector de enseñanza superior.

Rwanda:

E--> Partial data.

FR-> Données partielles.

ESP> Datos parciales.

Seychelles:

E--> Not including military and defence R&D.

FR-> Non compris les activités de R-D de caractère militaire ou relevant de la défense nationale.

ESP> Excluídas las actividades militares y de defensa de I y D.

Zambia:

E--> Partial data for 9 institutes only.

FR-> Données partielles pour 9 instituts seulement.

ESP> Datos parciales para 9 institutos solamente.

AMERICA, NORTH:

Cuba:

E--> Not including military and defence R&D.

FR-> Non compris les activités de R-D de caractère militaire ou relevant de la défense nationale.

ESP> Excluídas las actividades militares y de defensa de I y D.

Panama:

E--> Data also include scientific and technological services (STS).

FR-> Les données comprennent en plus les services scientifiques et techniques (SST).

ESP> Los datos también incluyen los servicios científicos y tecnológicos (SCT).

AMERICA, SOUTH:

Colombia:

E--> Not including data for the productive sector (non-integrated R&D).

FR-> Non compris les données relatives au secteur de la production (activités de R-D non intégrées).

ESP> Excluídos los datos relativos al sector productivo (actividades de I y D no integradas).

Guyana:

E--> Not including military and defence R&D. Data for the general service sector and for medical sciences in the higher education sector are also excluded.

FR-> Non compris les activités de R-D de caractère militaire ou relevant de la défense nationale. Les données relatives au secteur de service général et les sciences médicales du secteur de l'enseignement supérieur sont également exclues.

ESP> Excluídas las actividades militares y de defensa de I y D. Se excluyen igualmente los datos relativos al sector de servicio general y las ciencias médicas en el sector de enseñanza superior.

Venezuela:

E--> Not including military and defence R&D.

FR-> Non compris les activités de R-D de caractère militaire ou relevant de la défense nationale.

ESP> Excluídas las actividades militares y de defensa de I y D.

ASIA:

Japan:

E--> Data relate to regular research workers only. Not including social sciences and humanities in the productive sector.

FR-> Les données se réfèrent aux chercheurs réguliers seulement. Non compris les sciences sociales et humaines dans le secteur de la production.

ESP> Los datos sólo se refieren a las personas que trabajan regularmente en actividades de investigación. Excluídas las ciencias sociales y humanas en el sector productivo.

Jordan:

E--> Not including military and defence R&D.

FR-> Non compris les activités de R-D de caractère militaire ou relevant de la défense nationale.

Jordan: (Cont):

ESP> Excluídas las actividades militares y de defensa de I y D.

Korea, Republic of:

E--> Not including military and defence R&D and social sciences and humanities.

FR-> Non compris les activités de R-D de caractère militaire ou relevant de la défense nationale ni les sciences sociales et humaines.

ESP> Excluídas las actividades militares y de defensa de I y D y las ciencias sociales y humanas.

Pakistan:

E--> Data relate to R&D activities concentrated mainly in government-financed research establishments only; social sciences and humanities in the higher education and general service sectors are excluded. Not including the productive sector (integrated R&D) nor military and defence R&D.

FR->Les données se réfèrent aux activités de R-D se trouvant pour la plupart dans les établissements de recherche financés par le gouvernement; les sciences sociales et humaines dans les secteurs de l'enseignement supérieur et de service général sont exclues. Compte non tenu du secteur de la production (activités de R-D intégrées) ni des activités de caractère militaire ou relevant de la défense nationale.

ESP> Los datos se refieren a las actividades de I y D concentrados principalmente en los establecimientos de investigación subvencionados por el gobierno; se excluyen las ciencias sociales y humanas de los sectores de enseñanza superior y de servicio general. Excluídos el sector productivo (actividades de I y D integradas) y las actividades militares y de defensa de I y D.

Philippines:

E--> Data relate to the general service sector only.

FR-> Les données ne se réfèrent qu'au secteur de service général.

ESP> Los datos se refieren solamente al sector de servicio general.

Singapore:

E--> Not including either military and defence R&D or social sciences and humanities.

FR-> Non compris les activités de R-D de caractère militaire ou relevant de la défense nationale ni les sciences sociales et humaines.

ESP> Excluídas las actividades militares y de defensa de I y D y las ciencias sociales y humanas.

Turkey:

E--> Not including data for the productive sector. Social sciences and humanities in the general service sector are excluded.

FR-> Non compris les données relatives au secteur de la production. Compte non tenu des sciences sociales et humaines du secteur de service général.

ESP> Excluídos los datos relativos al sector productivo. Se excluyen las ciencias sociales y humanas del sector de servico general.

EUROPE:

Austria:

E--> Not including data for the productive sector (integrated R&D).

FR-> Non compris les données relatives au secteur de la production (activités de R-D intégrées).

ESP> Excluidos los datos relativos al sector productivo (actividades de I y D no integradas).

Denmark:

E--> Data in column 7 (other fields of study) refer to scientists and engineers engaged in the productive sector for whom a distribution by field of study is unknown.

FR-> Les données de la colonne 7 (autres domaines d'études) se réfèrent aux scientifiques et ingénieurs employés dans le secteur de la production pour lesquels une répartition par domaine d'études n'est pas connue.

ESP> Los datos de la columna 7 (otros sectores de estudios) se refieren a los científicos e ingenieros empleados en el sector productivo para los cuales no se conoce la distribución por sector de estudios.

Hungary:

E--> Not including scientists and engineers in the administration of R&D.

FR-> Compte non tenu des scientifiques et ingénieurs employés dans les services administratifs de R-D.

ESP> Excluídos los científicos e ingenieros empleados en los servicios administrativos de I y D.

Malta:

E--> Data relate to the higher education sector.

FR-> Les données ne concernent que le secteur de l'enseignement supérieur.

ESP> Los datos se refieren exclusivamente al sector de enseñanza superior.

Poland:

E--> Not including military and defence R&D.

FR-> Non compris les activités de R-D de caractère militaire ou relevant de la défense nationale.

ESP> Excluídas las actividades militares y de defensa de I y D.

Portugal:

E--> Data in column 7 (other fields of study) refer to scientists and engineers engaged in the productive sector (integrated R&D) for whom a distribution by field of study is unknown.

FR-> Les données de la colonne 7 (autres domaines d'études) se réfèrent aux scientifiques et ingénieurs employés dans le secteur de la

Portugal: (Cont):
production (activités de R-D intégrées) pour lesquels une répartition par domaine d'études n'est pas connue.
ESP> Los datos de la columna 7 (otros sectores de estudios) se refieren a los científicos e ingenieros empleados en el sector productivo (actividades de I y D integradas) para los cuales no se conoce la distribución por sector de estudios.
Yugoslavia:
E--> Not including military and defence R&D.
FR-> Non compris les activités de R-D de caractère militaire ou relevant de la défense nationale.
ESP> Excluídas las actividades militares y de defensa de I y D.
OCEANIA:
Australia:
E--> Data in column 7 (other fields of study) refer to scientists and engineers engaged in the productive sector (integrated R&D) for whom a distribution by field of study is unknown.

Australia: (Cont):
FR-> Les données de la colonne 7 (autres domaines d'études) réfèrent aux scientifiques et ingénieurs employés dans le secteur de production (activités de R-D intégrées) pour lesquels une répartition p[ar] domaine d'études n'est pas connue.
ESP> Los datos de la columna 7 (otros sectores de estudios) se refie[ren] a los científicos e ingenieros empleados en el sector producti[vo] (actividades de I y D integradas) para los cuales no se conoce [la] distribución por sector de estudios.
French Polynesia:
E--> Data relate to one research institute only.
FR-> Les données ne concernent qu'un seul institut de recherche.
ESP> Los datos se refieren a un centro de investigación solamente.
Tonga:
E--> Data relate to one research institute only.
FR-> Les données ne concernent qu'un seul institut de recherche.
ESP> Los datos se refieren a un centro de investigación solamente.

5.6 Total personnel engaged in research and experimental development by sector of performance and by category of personnel

Total du personnel employé à des travaux de recherche et de développement expérimental, par secteur d'exécution et par categorie de personnel

Personal empleado en trabajos de investigación y de desarrollo experimental, por sector de ejecución y por categoría de personal

PLEASE REFER TO INTRODUCTION FOR DEFINITIONS OF CATEGORIES INCLUDED IN THIS TABLE.

DATA ARE IN FULL-TIME EQUIVALENT (FTE)

NUMBER OF COUNTRIES AND TERRITORIES PRESENTED IN THIS TABLE: 79

POUR LES DEFINITIONS DES CATEGORIES PRESENTEES DANS CE TABLEAU, SE REFERER A L'INTRODUCTION.

LES DONNEES SONT EN EQUIVALENT PLEIN TEMPS (EPT)

NOMBRE DE PAYS ET DE TERRITOIRES PRESENTES DANS CE TABLEAU: 79

EN LA INTRODUCCION SE DAN LAS DEFINICIONES DE LAS CATEGORIAS QUE FIGURAN EN ESTE CUADRO.

DATOS EN EQUIVALENTE DE JORNADA COMPLETA (EJC)

NUMERO DE PAISES Y DE TERRITORIOS PRESENTADOS EN ESTE CUADRO: 79

COUNTRY / PAYS / PAIS	YEAR / ANNEE / AÑO	CATEGORY OF PERSONNEL / CATEGORIE DE PERSONNEL / CATEGORIA DE PERSONAL	SECTOR OF PERFORMANCE/SECTEUR D'EXECUTION/SECTOR DE EJECUCION: ALL SECTORS (FTE) / TOUS LES SECTEURS (EPT) / TODOS LOS SECTORES (EJC)	PRODUCTIVE SECTOR / SECTEUR DE LA PRODUCTION / SECTOR PRODUCTIVO: INTEGRATED R&D / ACTIVITES DE R-D INTEGREES / ACTIVIDADES DE I Y D INTEGRADAS	NON INTEGRATED R&D / ACTIVITES DE R-D NON INTEGREES / ACTIVIDADES DE I Y D NO INTEGRADAS	HIGHER EDUCATION / ENSEIGNEMENT SUPERIEUR / ENSEÑANZA SUPERIOR	GENERAL SERVICE / SERVICE GENERAL / SERVICIO GENERAL
			(1)	(2)	(3)	(4)	(5)
AFRICA							
BURUNDI	1984	TOTAL IN R&D	666	–	–	56	610
		% BY SECTOR	100	–	–	8.4	91.6
		SCIENTISTS AND ENGINEERS	218	–	–	42	176
		TECHNICIANS	115	–	–	10	105
		AUXILIARY PERSONNEL	333	–	–	4	329
CENTRAL AFRICAN REPUBLIC‡	1984	TOTAL IN R&D	1 290	196	–	166	928
		% BY SECTOR	100	15.2	–	12.9	71.9
		SCIENTISTS AND ENGINEERS	196	35	–	69	92
		TECHNICIANS	383	76	–	–	307
		AUXILIARY PERSONNEL	711	85	–	97	529
CONGO‡	1984	TOTAL IN R&D	2 335	790	991	525	29
		% BY SECTOR	100	33.8	42.4	22.5	1.2
		SCIENTISTS AND ENGINEERS	862	205	163	473	21
		TECHNICIANS	1 473	585	828	52	8
EGYPT‡	1982	TOTAL IN R&D	47 069	2 733	14 591	22 060	7 685
		% BY SECTOR	100	5.8	31.0	46.9	16.3
		SCIENTISTS AND ENGINEERS	19 941	1 015	4 512	9 989	4 425
		TECHNICIANS	6 727	597	2 298	2 791	1 041
		AUXILIARY PERSONNEL	20 401	1 121	7 781	9 280	2 219
GUINEA	1984	TOTAL IN R&D	2 357	562	627	780	388
		% BY SECTOR	100	23.8	26.6	33.1	16.5
		SCIENTISTS AND ENGINEERS	1 282	210	235	634	203
		TECHNICIANS	611	182	255	75	99
		AUXILIARY PERSONNEL	464	170	137	71	86
KENYA‡	1975	TOTAL IN R&D	544	61	335	148	–
		% BY SECTOR	100	11.2	61.6	27.2	–
		SCIENTISTS AND ENGINEERS	361	29	210	122	–
		TECHNICIANS	183	32	125	26	–
LIBYAN ARAB JAMAHIRIYA	1980	SCIENTISTS AND ENGINEERS	1 100	200	——>	800	100
		% BY SECTOR	100	18.2	——>	72.7	9.1

COUNTRY / PAYS / PAIS	YEAR / ANNEE / AÑO	CATEGORY OF PERSONNEL / CATEGORIE DE PERSONNEL / CATEGORIA DE PERSONAL	ALL SECTORS (FTE) / TOUS LES SECTEURS (EPT) / TODOS LOS SECTORES (EJC)	SECTOR OF PERFORMANCE/SECTEUR D'EXECUTION/SECTOR DE EJECUCION — PRODUCTIVE SECTOR / SECTEUR DE LA PRODUCTION / SECTOR PRODUCTIVO: INTEGRATED R&D / ACTIVITES DE R–D INTEGREES / ACTIVIDADES DE I Y D INTEGRADAS	NON INTEGRATED R&D / ACTIVITES DE R–D NON INTEGREES / ACTIVIDADES DE I Y D NO INTEGRADAS	HIGHER EDUCATION / ENSEIGNEMENT SUPERIEUR / ENSEÑANZA SUPERIOR	GENERAL SERVICE / SERVICE GENERAL / SERVICIO GENERAL
			(1)	(2)	(3)	(4)	(5)
MADAGASCAR‡	1980	TOTAL IN R&D	...	...	...	...	816
		SCIENTISTS AND ENGINEERS	...	...	...	...	112
		TECHNICIANS	...	...	...	...	367
		AUXILIARY PERSONNEL	...	...	...	...	337
MALAWI	1977	TOTAL IN R&D	1 909	752	874	217	66
		% BY SECTOR	100	39.4	45.8	11.4	3.5
		SCIENTISTS AND ENGINEERS	189	39	62	77	11
		TECHNICIANS	242	118	92	22	10
		AUXILIARY PERSONNEL	1 478	595	720	118	45
MAURITIUS	1984	TOTAL IN R&D	1 224	73	–	131	1 020
		% BY SECTOR	100	6.0	–	10.7	83.3
		SCIENTISTS AND ENGINEERS	263	8	–	60	195
		TECHNICIANS	176	12	–	25	139
		AUXILIARY PERSONNEL	785	53	–	46	686
NIGER	1976	TOTAL IN R&D	...	...	...	94	...
		SCIENTISTS AND ENGINEERS	...	...	...	93	...
		TECHNICIANS	...	...	...	1	...
		AUXILIARY PERSONNEL	...	...	...	–	...
SEYCHELLES‡	1983	TOTAL IN R&D	33	–	7	–	26
		% BY SECTOR	100	–	21.2	–	78.8
		SCIENTISTS AND ENGINEERS	18	–	2	–	16
		TECHNICIANS	6	–	5	–	10
		AUXILIARY PERSONNEL	9	–	./.	–	./.
SUDAN	1978	TOTAL IN R&D	22 136	7 738	1 981	3 535	8 882
		% BY SECTOR	100	35.0	8.9	16.0	40.1
		SCIENTISTS AND ENGINEERS	3 806	724	243	1 474	1 365
		TECHNICIANS	3 271	1 174	204	351	1 542
		AUXILIARY PERSONNEL	15 059	5 840	1 534	1 710	5 975
TOGO‡	1976	TOTAL IN R&D	445	./.	–	184	261
		% BY SECTOR	100	./.	–	41.3	58.7
		SCIENTISTS AND ENGINEERS	261	./.	–	160	101
		TECHNICIANS	184	./.	–	24	160
ZAMBIA‡	1976	TOTAL IN R&D	931	451	–	189	291
		% BY SECTOR	100	48.4	–	20.3	31.3
		SCIENTISTS AND ENGINEERS	250	112	–	54	84
		TECHNICIANS	150	21	–	74	55
		AUXILIARY PERSONNEL	531	318	–	61	152
AMERICA, NORTH							
CANADA‡	1982	TOTAL IN R&D	*68 560	*32 980	./.	*14 010	*21 570
		% BY SECTOR	100	*48.1	./.	*20.4	*31.5
		SCIENTISTS AND ENGINEERS	*31 950	*15 900	./.	*7 870	*8 180
		TECHNICIANS	*18 540	*10 775	./.	*2 040	*5 725
		AUXILIARY PERSONNEL	*18 070	*6 305	./.	*4 100	*7 665
COSTA RICA	1982	SCIENTISTS AND ENGINEERS	411	32	——>	237	142
		% BY SECTOR	100	7.8	——>	57.7	34.5
CUBA‡	1984	TOTAL IN R&D	32 937	341	17 386	2 621	12 589
		% BY SECTOR	100	1.0	52.8	8.0	38.2
		SCIENTISTS AND ENGINEERS	9 548	135	4 011	1 821	3 581
		TECHNICIANS	8 843	115	4 456	281	3 991
		AUXILIARY PERSONNEL	14 546	91	8 919	519	5 017
EL SALVADOR‡	1981	TOTAL IN R&D	2 535	1 656	–	454	425
		% BY SECTOR	100	65.3	–	17.9	16.8
		SCIENTISTS AND ENGINEERS	564	421	–	115	28
		TECHNICIANS	1 971	1 235	–	339	397
PANAMA‡	1975	TOTAL IN R&D	982	–	600	249	133
		% BY SECTOR	100	–	61.1	25.4	13.5
		SCIENTISTS AND ENGINEERS	204	–	116	62	26
		TECHNICIANS	301	–	194	80	27
		AUXILIARY PERSONNEL	477	–	290	107	80
ST. LUCIA	1979	TOTAL IN R&D	8	–	–	–	8
		% BY SECTOR	100	–	–	–	100.0
		SCIENTISTS AND ENGINEERS	3	–	–	–	3
		TECHNICIANS	5	–	–	–	5
		AUXILIARY PERSONNEL	–	–	–	–	–

COUNTRY / PAYS / PAIS	YEAR / ANNEE / AÑO	CATEGORY OF PERSONNEL / CATEGORIE DE PERSONNEL / CATEGORIA DE PERSONAL	SECTOR OF PERFORMANCE/SECTEUR D'EXECUTION/SECTOR DE EJECUCION				
			ALL SECTORS (FTE) / TOUS LES SECTEURS (EPT) / TODOS LOS SECTORES (EJC)	PRODUCTIVE SECTOR / SECTEUR DE LA PRODUCTION / SECTOR PRODUCTIVO		HIGHER EDUCATION / ENSEIGNEMENT SUPERIEUR / ENSEÑANZA SUPERIOR	GENERAL SERVICE / SERVICE GENERAL / SERVICIO GENERAL
				INTEGRATED R&D / ACTIVITES DE R-D INTEGREES / ACTIVIDADES DE I Y D INTEGRADAS	NON INTEGRATED R&D / ACTIVITES DE R-D NON INTEGREES / ACTIVIDADES DE I Y D NO INTEGRADAS		
			(1)	(2)	(3)	(4)	(5)
ST. PIERRE AND MIQUELON	1984	TOTAL IN R&D	15	–	15	–	–
		% BY SECTOR	100	–	100.0	–	–
		SCIENTISTS AND ENGINEERS	6	–	6	–	–
		TECHNICIANS	7	–	7	–	–
		AUXILIARY PERSONNEL	2	–	2	–	–
TURKS AND CAICOS ISLANDS	1976	TOTAL IN R&D	2	–	2	–	–
		% BY SECTOR	100	–	100.0	–	–
		SCIENTISTS AND ENGINEERS	2	–	2	–	–
		TECHNICIANS	–	–	–	–	–
		AUXILIARY PERSONNEL	–	–	–	–	–
UNITED STATES‡	1983	SCIENTISTS AND ENGINEERS	728 600	535 600	——>	100 000	93 000
		% BY SECTOR	100	73.5	——>	13.7	12.8
AMERICA, SOUTH							
ARGENTINA	1982	SCIENTISTS AND ENGINEERS	10 486	476	2 466	3 497	4 047
		% BY SECTOR	100	4.5	23.5	33.3	38.6
BRAZIL	1978	TOTAL IN R&D	...	43 056	——>		...
		SCIENTISTS AND ENGINEERS	...	8 497	——>	15 518	...
		TECHNICIANS	...	5 392	——>	...	...
		AUXILIARY PERSONNEL	...	29 167	——>	...	...
CHILE‡	1983	TOTAL IN R&D	2 005	22	497	1 399	87
		% BY SECTOR	100	1.1	24.8	69.8	4.3
COLOMBIA‡	1982	TOTAL IN R&D	3 709	91	...	1 474	2 144
		% BY SECTOR	100	2.5	...	39.7	57.8
		SCIENTISTS AND ENGINEERS	1 083	33	...	687	363
		TECHNICIANS	1 024	34	...	388	602
		AUXILIARY PERSONNEL	1 602	24	...	399	1 179
ECUADOR‡	1979	TOTAL IN R&D	5 297	270	——>	1 202	3 825
		% BY SECTOR	100	5.1	——>	22.7	72.2
		SCIENTISTS AND ENGINEERS	2 049	52	——>	599	1 398
		TECHNICIANS	1 252	44	——>	283	925
		AUXILIARY PERSONNEL	1 996	174	——>	320	1 502
GUYANA‡	1982	TOTAL IN R&D	623	469	——>	154	...
		% BY SECTOR	100	75.3	——>	24.7	...
		SCIENTISTS AND ENGINEERS	89	67	——>	22	...
		TECHNICIANS	178	134	——>	44	...
		AUXILIARY PERSONNEL	356	268	——>	88	...
PERU‡	1981	TOTAL IN R&D	12 528	1 269	——>	4 753	6 506
		% BY SECTOR	100	10.1	——>	37.9	51.9
		SCIENTISTS AND ENGINEERS	7 464	896	——>	3 600	2 968
		TECHNICIANS	5 064	373	——>	1 153	3 538
VENEZUELA‡	1983	TOTAL IN R&D	10 687	903	337	5 913	3 534
		% BY SECTOR	100	8.4	3.2	55.3	33.1
		SCIENTISTS AND ENGINEERS	4 568	347	117	2 921	1 183
		TECHNICIANS	2 692	97	126	1 297	1 172
		AUXILIARY PERSONNEL	3 427	459	94	1 695	1 179
ASIA							
CYPRUS‡	1984	TOTAL IN R&D	131	...	...	18	113
		% BY SECTOR	100	...	...	13.7	86.3
		SCIENTISTS AND ENGINEERS	51	...	...	10	41
		TECHNICIANS	80	...	...	8	72
		AUXILIARY PERSONNEL	./.	...	...	./.	./.
INDIA	1982	TOTAL IN R&D	93 698	22 233	——>	*22 100	49 365
		% BY SECTOR	100	23.7	——>	*23.6	52.7
JAPAN‡	1984	TOTAL IN R&D	710 872	410 860	——>	228 331	71 681
		% BY SECTOR	100	57.8	——>	32.1	10.1
		SCIENTISTS AND ENGINEERS	531 612	300 730	——>	187 350	43 532
		TECHNICIANS	97 074	72 389	——>	12 955	11 730
		AUXILIARY PERSONNEL	82 186	37 741	——>	28 026	16 419
JORDAN‡	1982	SCIENTISTS AND ENGINEERS	1 241	279	——>	669	293
		% BY SECTOR	100	22.5	——>	53.9	23.6

5.6 R&D personnel by sector of performance
Personnel de R-D par secteur d'exécution
Personal de I y D por sector de ejecución

COUNTRY / PAYS / PAIS	YEAR / ANNEE / AÑO	CATEGORY OF PERSONNEL / CATEGORIE DE PERSONNEL / CATEGORIA DE PERSONAL	SECTOR OF PERFORMANCE/SECTEUR D'EXECUTION/SECTOR DE EJECUCION: ALL SECTORS (FTE) / TOUS LES SECTEURS (EPT) / TODOS LOS SECTORES (EJC)	PRODUCTIVE SECTOR / SECTEUR DE LA PRODUCTION / SECTOR PRODUCTIVO: INTEGRATED R&D / ACTIVITES DE R–D INTEGREES / ACTIVIDADES DE I Y D INTEGRADAS	NON INTEGRATED R&D / ACTIVITES DE R–D NON INTEGREES / ACTIVIDADES DE I Y D NO INTEGRADAS	HIGHER EDUCATION / ENSEIGNEMENT SUPERIEUR / ENSEÑANZA SUPERIOR	GENERAL SERVICE / SERVICE GENERAL / SERVICIO GENERAL
			(1)	(2)	(3)	(4)	(5)
KOREA, REPUBLIC OF‡	1983	TOTAL IN R&D	58 720	25 099	——>	20 504	13 117
		% BY SECTOR	100	42.7	——>	34.9	22.3
		SCIENTISTS AND ENGINEERS	32 117	12 586	——>	13 137	6 394
		TECHNICIANS	19 493	10 226	——>	5 495	3 772
		AUXILIARY PERSONNEL	7 110	2 287	——>	1 872	2 951
KUWAIT‡	1984	TOTAL IN R&D	2 539	298	148	448	1 645
		% BY SECTOR	100	11.7	5.8	17.6	64.8
		SCIENTISTS AND ENGINEERS	1 511	194	102	414	801
		TECHNICIANS	561	72	8	25	456
		AUXILIARY PERSONNEL	467	32	38	9	388
LEBANON‡	1980	TOTAL IN R&D	...	...	...	206	...
		SCIENTISTS AND ENGINEERS	...	...	...	180	...
		TECHNICIANS	...	...	...	6	...
		AUXILIARY PERSONNEL	...	...	...	20	...
PAKISTAN‡	1982	TOTAL IN R&D	24 723	...	17 067	5 295	2 361
		% BY SECTOR	100	...	69.0	21.4	9.6
		SCIENTISTS AND ENGINEERS	5 397	...	3 684	892	821
		TECHNICIANS	7 138	...	5 307	1 016	815
		AUXILIARY PERSONNEL	12 188	...	8 076	3 387	725
PHILIPPINES‡	1982	TOTAL IN R&D	11 625	*785	–	...	10 840
		% BY SECTOR	100	*6.8	–	...	93.2
		SCIENTISTS AND ENGINEERS	5 146	*330	–	...	4 816
		TECHNICIANS	2 328	*199	–	...	2 129
		AUXILIARY PERSONNEL	4 151	*256	–	...	3 895
QATAR‡	1984	TOTAL IN R&D	48	–	36	...	12
		% BY SECTOR	100	–	75.0	...	25.0
		SCIENTISTS AND ENGINEERS	33	–	25	...	8
		TECHNICIANS	15	–	11	...	4
SINGAPORE‡	1981	TOTAL IN R&D	1 814	883	——>	322	609
		% BY SECTOR	100	48.7	——>	17.8	33.6
		SCIENTISTS AND ENGINEERS	724	424	——>	177	123
		TECHNICIANS	535	300	——>	98	137
		AUXILIARY PERSONNEL	555	159	——>	47	349
SRI LANKA‡	1983	TOTAL IN R&D	3 359	867	——>	224	2 268
		% BY SECTOR	100	25.8	——>	6.7	67.5
		SCIENTISTS AND ENGINEERS	1 939	497	——>	173	1 269
		TECHNICIANS	1 420	370	——>	51	999
TURKEY‡	1983	TOTAL IN R&D	12 004	1 088	——>	7 314	3 602
		% BY SECTOR	100	9.1	——>	60.9	30.0
		SCIENTISTS AND ENGINEERS	7 747	438	——>	5 660	1 649
		TECHNICIANS	2 689	650	——>	1 185	854
		AUXILIARY PERSONNEL	1 568	...	...	469	1 099
VIET–NAM‡	1978	TOTAL IN R&D	25 050	8 100	7 650	3 830	5 470
		% BY SECTOR	100	32.3	30.5	15.3	21.8
		SCIENTISTS AND ENGINEERS	13 050	4 200	1 750	3 830	3 270
		TECHNICIANS	6 040	1 900	2 640	...	1 500
		AUXILIARY PERSONNEL	5 960	2 000	3 260	...	700
EUROPE							
AUSTRIA	1981	TOTAL IN R&D	18 599	10 228	1 408	4 778	2 185
		% BY SECTOR	100	55.0	7.6	25.7	11.7
		SCIENTISTS AND ENGINEERS	6 711	2 486	399	3 051	775
		TECHNICIANS	6 145	4 613	387	813	332
		AUXILIARY PERSONNEL	5 742	3 129	621	915	1 077
BELGIUM	1977	TOTAL IN R&D	30 186	17 969	1 117	8 290	2 810
		% BY SECTOR	100	59.5	3.7	27.5	9.3
		SCIENTISTS AND ENGINEERS	13 883	6 302	413	5 862	1 306
		TECHNICIANS	7 696	4 834	302	1 742	818
		AUXILIARY PERSONNEL	8 607	6 833	402	686	686
BULGARIA‡	1984	TOTAL IN R&D	87 329	59 662	——>	11 821	15 846
		% BY SECTOR	100	68.3	——>	13.5	18.1
		SCIENTISTS AND ENGINEERS	45 125	23 850	——>	11 821	9 454
		TECHNICIANS	12 484	11 111	——>	...	1 373
		AUXILIARY PERSONNEL	29 720	24 701	——>	...	5 019

COUNTRY / PAYS / PAIS	YEAR / ANNEE / AÑO	CATEGORY OF PERSONNEL / CATEGORIE DE PERSONNEL / CATEGORIA DE PERSONAL	SECTOR OF PERFORMANCE/SECTEUR D'EXECUTION/SECTOR DE EJECUCION: ALL SECTORS (FTE) / TOUS LES SECTEURS (EPT) / TODOS LOS SECTORES (EJC)	PRODUCTIVE SECTOR / SECTEUR DE LA PRODUCTION / SECTOR PRODUCTIVO: INTEGRATED R&D / ACTIVITES DE R-D INTEGREES / ACTIVIDADES DE I Y D INTEGRADAS	NON INTEGRATED R&D / ACTIVITES DE R-D NON INTEGREES / ACTIVIDADES DE I Y D NO INTEGRADAS	HIGHER EDUCATION / ENSEIGNEMENT SUPERIEUR / ENSEÑANZA SUPERIOR	GENERAL SERVICE / SERVICE GENERAL / SERVICIO GENERAL
			(1)	(2)	(3)	(4)	(5)
CZECHOSLOVAKIA‡	1984	TOTAL IN R&D	176 219	64 919	76 455	5 168	29 677
		% BY SECTOR	100	36.8	43.4	2.9	16.8
		SCIENTISTS AND ENGINEERS	58 820	20 369	21 836	3 128	13 487
		TECHNICIANS	46 800	21 192	12 098	1 608	11 902
		AUXILIARY PERSONNEL	70 599	23 358	42 521	432	4 288
DENMARK‡	1983	TOTAL IN R&D	17 759	9 021	907	4 116	3 715
		% BY SECTOR	100	50.8	5.1	23.2	20.9
		SCIENTISTS AND ENGINEERS	7 508	2 516	324	2 719	1 949
		TECHNICIANS	10 251	6 505	583	1 397	1 766
		AUXILIARY PERSONNEL	./.	./.	./.	./.	./.
FINLAND‡	1983	TOTAL IN R&D	20 218	9 334	326	5 483	5 075
		% BY SECTOR	100	46.2	1.6	27.1	25.1
		SCIENTISTS AND ENGINEERS	10 951	4 507	155	3 773	2 516
		TECHNICIANS	9 267	4 827	171	1 710	2 559
		AUXILIARY PERSONNEL	./.	./.	./.	./.	./.
FRANCE‡	1979	TOTAL IN R&D	230 766	122 484	5 853	45 997	56 432
		% BY SECTOR	100	53.1	2.5	19.9	24.5
		SCIENTISTS AND ENGINEERS	72 889	31 649	2 014	23 888	15 338
		TECHNICIANS	157 877	90 835	3 839	22 109	41 094
		AUXILIARY PERSONNEL	./.	./.	./.	./.	./.
GERMANY, FEDERAL REPUBLIC OF‡	1981	TOTAL IN R&D	371 548	242 544	→	73 134	55 870
		% BY SECTOR	100	65.3	→	19.7	15.0
		SCIENTISTS AND ENGINEERS	128 162	77 017	→	30 299	20 846
		TECHNICIANS	115 518	73 039	→	27 794	14 685
		AUXILIARY PERSONNEL	127 868	92 488	→	15 041	20 339
GREECE‡	1979	TOTAL IN R&D	4 308	128	...	1 382	2 798
		% BY SECTOR	100	3.0	...	32.1	64.9
		SCIENTISTS AND ENGINEERS	2 634	50	...	1 270	1 314
		TECHNICIANS	984	42	...	112	830
		AUXILIARY PERSONNEL	690	36	...	...	654
HUNGARY‡	1984	TOTAL IN R&D	49 360	23 819	5 386	7 878	12 277
		% BY SECTOR	100	48.3	10.9	16.0	24.9
		SCIENTISTS AND ENGINEERS	22 518	9 775	2 578	4 601	5 564
		TECHNICIANS	18 438	11 240	1 689	2 032	3 477
		AUXILIARY PERSONNEL	8 404	2 804	1 119	1 245	3 236
ICELAND	1979	TOTAL IN R&D	614	41	192	202	179
		% BY SECTOR	100	6.7	31.3	32.9	29.2
		SCIENTISTS AND ENGINEERS	304	24	77	119	84
		TECHNICIANS	227	17	83	62	65
		AUXILIARY PERSONNEL	84	0.9	32	21	30
IRELAND‡	1982	TOTAL IN R&D	5 449	1 549	./.	1 608	2 292
		% BY SECTOR	100	28.4	./.	29.5	42.1
		SCIENTISTS AND ENGINEERS	2 773	655	./.	1 383	735
		TECHNICIANS	1 271	494	./.	201	576
		AUXILIARY PERSONNEL	1 405	400	./.	24	981
ITALY	1983	TOTAL IN R&D	112 743	51 504	9 437	39 368	12 434
		% BY SECTOR	100	45.7	8.4	34.9	11.0
		SCIENTISTS AND ENGINEERS	63 021	20 976	3 602	32 308	6 135
		TECHNICIANS	28 694	18 602	3 157	2 584	4 351
		AUXILIARY PERSONNEL	21 028	11 926	2 678	4 476	1 948
MALTA	1984	TOTAL IN R&D	...	...	...	46	...
		SCIENTISTS AND ENGINEERS	...	...	...	34	...
		TECHNICIANS	...	...	...	5	...
		AUXILIARY PERSONNEL	...	...	...	7	...
NETHERLANDS‡	1983	TOTAL IN R&D	57 630	26 790	410	15 880	14 550
		% BY SECTOR	100	46.5	0.7	27.6	25.2
		SCIENTISTS AND ENGINEERS	30 530	14 190	230	7 410	8 700
		TECHNICIANS	27 100	6 680	70	8 470	2 590
		AUXILIARY PERSONNEL	./.	5 920	110	./.	3 260
NORWAY‡	1982	TOTAL IN R&D	15 218	4 405	2 455	4 975	3 383
		% BY SECTOR	100	28.9	16.1	32.7	22.2
		SCIENTISTS AND ENGINEERS	7 754	1 723	1 603	2 928	1 500
		TECHNICIANS	7 464	2 682	852	2 047	1 883
		AUXILIARY PERSONNEL	./.	./.	./.	./.	./.

COUNTRY / PAYS / PAIS	YEAR / ANNEE / AÑO	CATEGORY OF PERSONNEL / CATEGORIE DE PERSONNEL / CATEGORIA DE PERSONAL	ALL SECTORS (FTE) / TOUS LES SECTEURS (EPT) / TODOS LOS SECTORES (EJC)	PRODUCTIVE SECTOR / SECTEUR DE LA PRODUCTION / SECTOR PRODUCTIVO: INTEGRATED R&D / ACTIVITES DE R-D INTEGREES / ACTIVIDADES DE I Y D INTEGRADAS	NON INTEGRATED R&D / ACTIVITES DE R-D NON INTEGREES / ACTIVIDADES DE I Y D NO INTEGRADAS	HIGHER EDUCATION / ENSEIGNEMENT SUPERIEUR / ENSEÑANZA SUPERIOR	GENERAL SERVICE / SERVICE GENERAL / SERVICIO GENERAL
			(1)	(2)	(3)	(4)	(5)
POLAND‡	1984	TOTAL IN R&D	173 500	34 400	93 400	17 500	28 200
		% BY SECTOR	100	19.8	53.8	10.1	16.3
		SCIENTISTS AND ENGINEERS	74 700	12 000	32 600	17 500	12 600
		TECHNICIANS	35 100	10 900	19 400	...	4 800
		AUXILIARY PERSONNEL	63 700	11 500	41 400	...	10 800
PORTUGAL	1982	TOTAL IN R&D	8 552	1 891	278	2 330	4 053
		% BY SECTOR	100	22.1	3.3	27.2	47.4
		SCIENTISTS AND ENGINEERS	3 019	655	110	1 267	987
		TECHNICIANS	3 100	704	97	564	1 735
		AUXILIARY PERSONNEL	2 433	532	71	499	1 331
SPAIN‡	1983	TOTAL IN R&D	30 948	12 905	./.	7 830	10 213
		% BY SECTOR	100	41.7	./.	25.3	33.0
		SCIENTISTS AND ENGINEERS	14 229	3 527	./.	7 830	2 872
		TECHNICIANS	5 140	3 884	./.	...	1 256
		AUXILIARY PERSONNEL	11 579	5 494	./.	...	6 085
SWEDEN‡	1983	TOTAL IN R&D	47 758	25 359	4 679	14 300	3 420
		% BY SECTOR	100	53.1	9.8	29.9	7.2
		SCIENTISTS AND ENGINEERS	19 081	8 467	1 859	7 200	1 555
		TECHNICIANS	28 677	16 892	2 820	7 100	1 865
		AUXILIARY PERSONNEL	./.	./.	./.	./.	./.
SWITZERLAND	1979	TOTAL IN R&D	37 945	28 700	⟶	7 000	2 245
		% BY SECTOR	100	75.6	⟶	18.4	5.9
		SCIENTISTS AND ENGINEERS	16 410	11 000	⟶	4 300	1 110
		TECHNICIANS	15 840	13 300	⟶	1 800	740
		AUXILIARY PERSONNEL	5 695	4 400	⟶	900	395
UNITED KINGDOM‡	1978	TOTAL IN R&D	261 400	184 300	5 800	...	71 300
		% BY SECTOR	100	70.5	2.2	...	27.3
		SCIENTISTS AND ENGINEERS	86 500	65 900	2 200	...	18 400
		TECHNICIANS	76 600	62 100	1 700	...	12 800
		AUXILIARY PERSONNEL	98 300	56 300	1 900	...	40 100
YUGOSLAVIA‡	1981	TOTAL IN R&D	56 552	14 285	10 090	17 634	14 543
		% BY SECTOR	100	25.3	17.8	31.2	25.7
		SCIENTISTS AND ENGINEERS	24 882	5 691	3 890	7 568	7 733
		TECHNICIANS	13 729	4 900	2 653	3 015	3 161
		AUXILIARY PERSONNEL	17 941	3 694	3 547	7 051	3 649
OCEANIA							
AUSTRALIA	1981	TOTAL IN R&D	44 532	7 923	12 420	18 239	5 950
		% BY SECTOR	100	17.8	27.9	41.0	13.4
		SCIENTISTS AND ENGINEERS	24 208	3 472	4 869	13 610	2 257
		TECHNICIANS	12 007	2 928	3 791	3 438	1 850
		AUXILIARY PERSONNEL	8 317	1 523	3 760	1 191	1 843
FRENCH POLYNESIA‡	1983	TOTAL IN R&D	97	–	–	–	97
		% BY SECTOR	100	–	–	–	100.0
		SCIENTISTS AND ENGINEERS	17	–	–	–	17
		TECHNICIANS	16	–	–	–	16
		AUXILIARY PERSONNEL	64	–	–	–	64
GUAM	1979	TOTAL IN R&D	...	...	...	52	...
		SCIENTISTS AND ENGINEERS	...	...	...	21	...
		TECHNICIANS	...	...	...	19	...
		AUXILIARY PERSONNEL	...	...	...	12	...
KIRIBATI	1980	TOTAL IN R&D	3	–	3	–	–
		% BY SECTOR	100	–	100.0	–	–
		SCIENTISTS AND ENGINEERS	2	–	2	–	–
		TECHNICIANS	1	–	1	–	–
		AUXILIARY PERSONNEL	–	–	–	–	–
NEW CALEDONIA	1983	TOTAL IN R&D	17	–	14	–	3
		% BY SECTOR	100	–	82.4	–	17.6
		SCIENTISTS AND ENGINEERS	7	–	5	–	2
		TECHNICIANS	5	–	4	–	1
		AUXILIARY PERSONNEL	5	–	5	–	–
NEW ZEALAND‡	1979	TOTAL IN R&D	8 080	1 849	./.	1 409	4 822
		% BY SECTOR	100	22.9	./.	17.4	59.7

COUNTRY / PAYS / PAIS	YEAR / ANNEE / AÑO	CATEGORY OF PERSONNEL / CATEGORIE DE PERSONNEL / CATEGORIA DE PERSONAL	SECTOR OF PERFORMANCE/SECTEUR D'EXECUTION/SECTOR DE EJECUCION				
			ALL SECTORS (FTE) / TOUS LES SECTEURS (EPT) / TODOS LOS SECTORES (EJC)	PRODUCTIVE SECTOR / SECTEUR DE LA PRODUCTION / SECTOR PRODUCTIVO		HIGHER EDUCATION / ENSEIGNEMENT SUPERIEUR / ENSEÑANZA SUPERIOR	GENERAL SERVICE / SERVICE GENERAL / SERVICIO GENERAL
				INTEGRATED R&D / ACTIVITES DE R-D INTEGREES / ACTIVIDADES DE I Y D INTEGRADAS	NON INTEGRATED R&D / ACTIVITES DE R-D NON INTEGREES / ACTIVIDADES DE I Y D NO INTEGRADAS		
			(1)	(2)	(3)	(4)	(5)
PACIFIC ISLANDS	1979	TOTAL IN R&D	23	–	18	–	5
		% BY SECTOR	100	–	78.3	–	21.7
		SCIENTISTS AND ENGINEERS	4	–	3	–	1
		TECHNICIANS	11	–	9	–	2
		AUXILIARY PERSONNEL	8	–	6	–	2
SAMOA‡	1978	TOTAL IN R&D	280	73	65	85	57
		% BY SECTOR	100	26.1	23.2	30.4	20.4
		SCIENTISTS AND ENGINEERS	140	30	25	60	25
		TECHNICIANS	92	18	25	21	28
		AUXILIARY PERSONNEL	48	25	15	4	4
TONGA‡	1981	TOTAL IN R&D	15	–	–	–	15
		% BY SECTOR	100	–	–	–	100.0
		SCIENTISTS AND ENGINEERS	11	–	–	–	11
		TECHNICIANS	4	–	–	–	4
VANUATU	1975	TOTAL IN R&D	39	–	39	–	–
		% BY SECTOR	100	–	100.0	–	–
		SCIENTISTS AND ENGINEERS	3	–	3	–	–
		TECHNICIANS	1	–	1	–	–
		AUXILIARY PERSONNEL	35	–	35	–	–

AFRICA:

Central African Republic:

E--> Data relate to the number of full-time plus part-time scientists and engineers and technicians.

FR-> Les données se réfèrent au nombre de scientifiques et ingénieurs et techniciens à plein temps et à temps partiel.

ESP> Los datos se refieren al número de científicos e ingenieros y técnicos de jornada completa y de jornada parcial.

Congo:

E--> Data refer to the number of full-time plus part-time scientists and engineers and technicians. Not including either military and defence R&D or auxiliary personnel.

FR-> Les données se réfèrent au nombre de scientifiques et ingénieurs et techniciens à plein temps et à temps partiel. Non compris les activités de R-D de caractère militaire ou relevant de la défense nationale ni le personnel auxiliaire.

ESP> Los datos se refieren al número de científicos e ingenieros y técnicos de jornada completa y de jornada parcial. Excluídas las actividades militares y de defensa de I y D y al personal auxiliar.

Egypt:

E--> Not including military and defence R&D.

FR-> Non compris les activités de R-D de caractère militaire ou relevant de la défense nationale.

ESP> Excluídas la actividades militares y de defensa de I y D.

Kenya:

E--> Not including auxiliary personnel. Data for humanities are also excluded.

FR-> Non compris le personnel auxiliaire. Les données relatives aux sciences humaines sont également exclues.

ESP> No incluye el personal auxiliar. Se excluyen igualmente los datos relativos a las ciencias humanas.

Madagascar:

E--> Data relate to the number of full-time plus part-time personnel at 4 research institutes only but do not include those engaged in the administration of R&D.

FR-> Les données se réfèrent au personnel à plein temps et à temps partiel de 4 instituts de recherche seulement, mais ne comprennent pas ceux qui sont employés dans les services administratifs de R-D.

ESP> Los datos se refieren al personal de jornada completa y de jornada parcial de 4 centros de investigación solamente, pero no incluye el que está empleado en los servicios administrativos de I y D.

Seychelles:

E--> Auxiliary personnel and technicians in columns 3 and 5 are counted together. Not including military and defence R&D.

FR-> Le personnel auxiliaire et les techniciens des colonnes 3 et 5 sont comptés ensemble. Non compris les activités de R-D de caractère militaire ou relevant de la défense nationale.

ESP> El personal auxiliar y los técnicos de las columnas 3 y 5 se cuentan conjuntamente. Excluídas las actividades militares y de defensa de I y D.

Togo:

E--> Not including auxiliary personnel. Data referring to the productive sector (integrated R&D) are included with the general service sector. Scientists and engineers are full-time.

FR-> Non compris le personnel auxiliaire. Les données relatives au secteur de la production (activités de R-D intégrées) sont comprises avec celles du secteur de service général. Pour les scientifiques et ingénieurs, les données se réfèrent aux effectifs à plein temps.

ESP> Excluído el personal auxiliar. Los datos correspondientes al sector productivo (actividades de I y D integradas) figuran en el sector de servicio general. Para los científicos e ingenieros los datos se refieren a los efectivos de jornada completa.

Zambia:

E--> Partial data for 9 institutes only.

FR-> Données partielles pour 9 instituts seulement.

ESP> Datos parciales para 9 institutos solamente.

AMERICA, NORTH:

Canada:

E--> Not including social sciences and humanities in the productive sector (integrated R&D). Data for the productive sector (non-integrated R&D) are included with the general service sector.

FR-> Non compris les sciences sociales et humaines dans le secteur de la production (activités de R-D intégrées). Les données relatives au secteur de la production (activités de R-D non intégrées) sont comprises avec celles du secteur de service général.

ESP> Excluídas las ciencias sociales y humanas del sector productivo (actividades de R y D integradas). Los datos correspondientes al sector productivo (actividades de I y D no integradas) están incluídos en el sector de servicio general.

Cuba:

E--> Not including military and defence R&D.

FR-> Non compris les activités de R-D de caractère militaire ou relevant de la défense nationale.

ESP> Excluídas las actividades militares y de defensa de I y D.

El Salvador:

E--> Not including auxiliary personnel. Data relate to the number of full-time plus part-time scientists and engineers and technicians engaged in public enterprises.

FR-> Non compris le personnel auxiliaire. Les données se réfèrent au nombre de scientifiques et ingénieurs et techniciens à plein temps et à temps partiel employés dans les entreprises publiques.

ESP> Excluído el personal auxiliar. Los datos se refieren al número de científicos e ingenieros y técnicos de jornada completa y de jornada parcial empleados en las empresas públicas.

Panama:

E--> Data also include scientific and technological services (STS).

FR-> Les données comprennent en plus les services scientifiques et

Panama: (Cont):
techniques (SST).

ESP> Los datos también incluyen los servicios científicos y tecnológicos (SCT).

United States:

E--> Not including data for law, humanities and education. Data referring to private non-profit organizations are included with the general service sector.

FR-> Non compris les données pour le droit, les sciences humaines et l'éducation. Le secteur de service général comprend les données relatives aux organisations privées à but non lucratif.

ESP> Excluídos los datos relativos al derecho, las ciencias humanas y la educación. El sector de servicio general incluye los datos correspondientes a las organizaciones privadas de carácter no lucrativo.

AMERICA, SOUTH:

Chile:

E--> Not including auxiliary personnel.

FR-> Non compris le personnel auxiliaire.

ESP> Excluído el personal auxiliar.

Colombia:

E--> Not including data for the productive sector (non-integrated R&D).

FR-> Non compris les données relatives au secteur de la production (activités de R-D non intégrées).

ESP> Excluídos los datos relativos al sector productivo (actividades de I y D no integradas).

Ecuador:

E--> Data also include scientific and technological services (STS) and refer to the number of full-time plus part-time scientists and engineers and technicians.

FR-> Les données comprennent en plus les services scientifiques et techniques (SST) et se réfèrent au nombre de scientifiques et ingénieurs et techniciens à plein temps et à temps partiel.

ESP> Los datos también incluyen los servicios científicos y tecnológicos (SCT) y se refieren al número de científicos e ingenieros y técnicos de jornada completa y de jornada parcial.

Guyana:

E--> Not including military and defence R&D. Data for the general service sector and for medical sciences in the higher education sector are also excluded.

FR-> Non compris les activités de R-D de caractère militaire ou relevant de la défense nationale. Les données relatives au secteur du service général et les sciences médicales du secteur de l'enseignement supérieur sont aussi exclues.

ESP> Excluídas las actividades militares y de defensa de I y D. Se excluyen también los datos relativos al sector de servicio general y las ciencias médicas del sector de enseñanza superior.

Peru:

E--> Not including auxiliary personnel. Data refer to full-time scientists and engineers and technicians engaged in scientific and technological activities (STA).

FR-> Non compris le personnel auxiliaire. Les données se réfèrent aux scientifiques et ingénieurs et techniciens à plein temps employés dans les activités scientifiques et techniques (AST).

ESP> Excluído el personal auxiliar. Los datos se refieren a los científicos e ingenieros y técnicos de jornada completa empleados a las actividades científicos y tecnológicas (ACT).

Venezuela:

E--> Data relate to the number of full-time plus part-time scientists and engineers and technicians. Not including military and defence R&D.

FR-> Les données se réfèrent au nombre de scientifiques et ingénieurs et techniciens à plein temps et à temps partiel. Non compris les activités de R-D de caractère militaire ou relevant de la défense nationale.

ESP> Los datos se refieren al número de científicos e ingenieros y técnicos de jornada completa y de jornada parcial. Excluídas las actividades militares y de defense de I y D.

ASIA:

Cyprus:

E--> Not including data for the productive sector. Auxiliary personnel and technicians are counted together.

FR-> Non compris les données pour le secteur de la production. Le personnel auxiliaire et les techniciens sont comptés ensemble.

ESP> Excluídos los datos relativos al sector productivo. El personal auxiliar y los técnicos se cuentan conjuntamente.

Japan:

E--> Data refer to full-time personnel. Not including social sciences and humanities in the productive sector.

FR-> Les données se réfèrent aux effectifs à plein temps. Compte non tenu des sciences sociales et humaines dans le secteur de la production.

ESP> Los datos se refieren a los efectivos de jornada completa. Excluídas las ciencias sociales y humanas del sector productivo.

Jordan:

E--> Data refer to the number of full-time plus part-time scientists and engineers.

FR-> Les données se réfèrent au nombre de scientifiques et ingénieurs à plein temps et à temps partiel.

ESP> Los datos se refieren al número de científicos e ingenieros de jornada completa y de jornada parcial.

Korea, Republic of:

E--> Not including either military and defence R&D or social scienc and humanities. Data refer to the number of full-time plus part-tin personnel.

FR-> Non compris les activités de R-D de caractère militaire relevant de la défense nationale ni les sciences sociales et humaines. L données se réfèrent au personnel à plein temps et à temps partiel.

ESP> Excluídas las actividades militares y de defensa de I y D y l ciencias sociales y humanas. Los datos se refieren al personal de jorna completa y de jornada parcial.

Kuwait:

E--> Data relate to scientific and technological activities (STA) and the number of full-time plus part-time scientists and engineers a technicians.

FR-> Les données se réfèrent aux activités scientifiques et techniqu (AST) et au nombre de scientifiques et ingénieurs et techniciens à ple temps et à temps partiel.

ESP> Los datos se refieren a las actividades científicos y tecnológic (ACT) y al número de científicos e ingenieros y técnicos de jorna completa y de jornada parcial.

Lebanon:

E--> Data refer to the Faculty of Science at the University of Leban only.

FR-> Les données ne se réfèrent qu'à la Faculté des Sciences l'Université du Liban.

ESP> Los datos se refieren a la Facultad de Ciencias de la Universid del Líbano solamente.

Pakistan:

E--> Not including military and defence R&D nor the producti sector (integrated R&D). Data relate to R&D activities concentrated mair in government-financed research establishments only; social sciences a humanities in the higher education and general service sectors a excluded. Data for technicians and auxiliary personnel are full-time pl part-time.

FR-> Compte non tenu du secteur de la production (activités de R intégrées) ni des activités de R-D de caractère militaire ou relevant de défense nationale. Les données se réfèrent aux activités de R-D se trouva pour la plupart dans les établissements de recherche financés par gouvernement; les sciences sociales et humaines dans les secteurs l'enseignement supérieur et de service général sont exclues. Pour techniciens et le personnel auxiliaire, les données se réfèrent aux effect à plein temps et à temps partiel.

ESP> Excluídos el sector productivo (actividades de I y D integrad y las actividades militares y de defensa de I y D. Los datos se refieren a actividades de I y D concentradas principalmente en los establecimient de investigación subvencionados por el gobierno; se excluyen las cienc sociales y humanas de los sectores de enseñanza superior y de servic general. Para los científicos e ingenieros, los datos se refieren a l efectivos de jornada completa y de jornada parcial.

Philippines:

E--> Data do not include the higher education sector.

FR-> Les données ne comprennent pas le secteur de l'enseigneme supérieur.

ESP> Los datos no comprenden el sector de enseñanza superior.

Qatar:

E--> Data do not include the higher education sector. Not includi auxiliary personnel.

FR-> Les données ne comprennent pas le secteur de l'enseigneme supérieur. Non compris le personnel auxiliaire.

ESP> Los datos no comprenden el sector de enseñanza superi Excluído el personal auxiliar.

Singapore:

E--> Not including either military and defence R&D or social scienc and humanities.

FR-> Non compris les activités de R-D de caractère militaire relevant de la défense nationale ni les sciences sociales et humaines.

ESP> Excluídas las actividades militares y de defensa de I y D y l ciencias sociales y humanas.

Sri Lanka:

E--> Not including auxiliary personnel.

FR-> Non compris le personnel auxiliaire.

ESP> Excluído el personal auxiliar.

Turkey:

E--> Not including auxiliary personnel in the productive sector a social sciences and humanities in the general service sector.

FR-> Non compris le personnel auxiliaire dans le secteur de production et les sciences sociales et humaines dans le secteur de servi général.

ESP> Excluídos el personal auxiliar del sector productivo y las cienci sociales y humanas del sector de servicio general.

Viet-nam:

E--> Not including data for technicians and auxiliary personnel in t higher education sector.

FR-> Non compris les données relatives aux techniciens et personnel auxiliaire du secteur de l'enseignement supérieur.

ESP> No incluye los datos relativos a los técnicos y al personal auxil del sector de enseñanza superior.

EUROPE:

Bulgaria:
E--> Not including data for technicians and auxiliary personnel in the higher education sector.
FR-> Non compris les données relatives aux techniciens et au personnel auxiliaire du secteur de l'enseignement supérieur.
ESP> No incluye los datos relativos a los técnicos y al personal auxiliar del sector de enseñanza superior.
Czechoslovakia:
E--> Of military R&D only that part carried out in civil establishments is included; scientists and engineers engaged in the administration of R&D are included with auxiliary personnel.
FR-> Pour la R-D de caractère militaire seule la partie effectuée dans les établissements civils a été considérée. Les scientifiques et ingénieurs employés dans les services administratifs de R-D sont compris avec le personnel auxiliaire.
ESP> Para la I y D de carácter militar sólo se ha considerado la parte correspondiente a los establecimientos civiles. Los científicos e ingenieros empleados en los servicios administrativos de I y D figuran con el personal auxiliar.
Denmark:
E--> Auxiliary personnel and technicians are counted together.
FR-> Le personnel auxiliaire et les techniciens sont comptés ensemble.
ESP> El personal auxiliar y los técnicos se cuentan conjuntamente.
Finland:
E--> Auxiliary personnel and technicians are counted together.
FR-> Le personnel auxiliaire et les techniciens sont comptés ensemble.
ESP> El personal auxiliar y los técnicos se cuentan conjuntamente.
France:
E--> Auxiliary personnel and technicians are counted together.
FR-> Le personnel auxiliaire et les techniciens sont comptés ensemble.
ESP> El personal auxiliar y los técnicos se cuentan conjuntamente.
Germany, Federal Republic of:
E--> Not including social sciences and humanities in the productive sector.
FR-> Non compris les sciences sociales et humaines du secteur de la production.
ESP> Excluídas las ciencias sociales y humanas del sector productivo.
Greece:
E--> Data relate to government activities only. Not including auxiliary personnel in the higher education sector.
FR-> Les données se réfèrent aux activités gouvernementales. Non compris le personnel auxiliaire du secteur de l'enseignement supérieur.
ESP> Los datos se refieren a las actividades gubernamentales. Excluído el personal auxiliar del sector de enseñanza superior.
Hungary:
E--> Not including personnel engaged in the administration of R&D. Skilled workers are included with technicians rather than with auxiliary personnel.
FR-> Compte non tenu du personnel employé dans les services administratifs de R-D. Les ouvriers qualifiés sont compris avec les techniciens plutôt qu'avec le personnel auxiliaire.
ESP> Excluído el personal empleado en los servicios administrativos de I y D. Los trabajadores calificados están más bien incluídos con los técnicos que con el personal auxiliar.
Ireland:
E--> Data for the productive sector (non-integrated R&D) are included with the general service sector.
FR-> Les données relatives au secteur de la production (activités de R-D non intégrées) sont comprises avec celles du secteur de service général.
ESP> Los datos correspondientes al sector productivo (actividades de I y D no integradas) están incluídos en el sector de servicio general.
Netherlands:
E--> Not including social sciences and humanities in the productive sector (integrated R&D). Auxiliary personnel and technicians in columns 1 and 4 are counted together.
FR-> Non compris les données pour les sciences sociales et humaines du secteur de la production (activités de R-D intégrées). Le personnel auxiliaire et les techniciens des colonnes 1 et 4 sont comptés ensemble.
ESP> Excluídos los datos relativos a las ciencias sociales y humanas del sector productivo (actividades de I y D integradas). El personal auxiliar y los técnicos de las columnas 1 y 4 se cuentan conjuntamente.
Norway:
E--> Auxiliary personnel and technicians are counted together.

Norway: (Cont):
FR-> Le personnel auxiliaire et les techniciens sont comptés ensemble.
ESP> El personal auxiliar y los técnicos se cuentan conjuntamente.
Poland:
E--> Not including military and defence R&D. Not including data for technicians and auxiliary personnel in the higher education sector; data relating to technicians refer only to those persons with a vocational education at the second level.
FR-> Non compris les activités de R-D de caractère militaire ou relevant de la défense nationale. Non compris les données relatives aux techniciens et au personnel auxiliaire du secteur de l'enseignement supérieur; les techniciens ne comprennent que des personnes ayant suivi un enseignement technique du second degré.
ESP> Excluídas las actividades militares y de defensa de I y D. Excluídos los datos relativos a los técnicos y al personal auxiliar del sector de enseñanza superior; los técnicos sólo comprenden las personas que han recibido una formación técnica de segundo grado.
Spain:
E--> Data for the productive sector (non-integrated R&D) are included with the general service sector. Not including data for technicians and auxiliairy personnel in the higher education sector.
FR-> Les données relatives au secteur de la production (activités de R-D non intégrées) sont comprises avec celles du secteur de service général. Non compris les données relatives aux techniciens et personnel auxiliaire du secteur de l'enseignement supérieur.
ESP> Los datos correspondientes al sector productivo (actividades de I y D no integradas) están incluídos en el sector de servicio general. Excluídos los datos relativos a los técnicos y al personal auxiliar del sector de enseñanza superior.
Sweden:
E--> Not including data for social sciences and humanities in the productive and general service sector. Auxiliary personnel and technicians are counted together.
FR-> Non compris les données pour les sciences sociales et humaines dans les secteurs de la production et de service général. Le personnel auxiliaire et les techniciens sont comptés ensemble.
ESP> Excluídas las ciencias sociales y humanas en los sectores productivo y de servicio general. El personal auxiliar y los técnicos se cuentan conjuntamente.
United Kingdom:
E--> Data do not include the higher education sector.
FR-> Les données ne comprennent pas le secteur de l'enseignement supérieur.
ESP> Los datos no comprenden el sector de enseñanza superior.
Yugoslavia:
E--> Not including military and defence R&D.
FR-> Non compris les activités de R-D de caractère militaire ou relevant de la défense nationale.
ESP> Excluídas las actividades militares y de defensa de I y D.
OCEANIA:
French Polynesia:
E--> Data relate to one research institute only.
FR-> Les données ne concernent qu'un seul institut de recherche.
ESP> Los datos se refieren a un centro de investigación solamente.
New Zealand:
E--> Data for the productive sector (non-integrated R&D) are included with the general service sector.
FR-> Les données relatives au secteur de la production (activités de R-D non intégrées) sont comprises avec celles de service général.
ESP> Los datos correspondientes al sector productivo (actividades de I y D no integradas) están incluídos en el sector de servicio general.
Samoa:
E--> Data for scientists and engineers refer only to full-time.
FR-> Pour les scientifiques et ingénieurs, les données se réfèrent seulement aux effectifs à plein temps.
ESP> Para los científicos e ingenieros, los datos se refieren solamente a los efectivos de jornada completa.
Tonga:
E--> Data refer to one research institute only. Not including auxiliary personnel. Data refer to the number of full-time plus part-time scientists and engineers.
FR-> Les données ne concernent qu'un seule institut de recherche. Non compris le personnel auxiliaire. Les données se réfèrent au nombre de scientifiques et ingénieurs à plein temps et à temps partiel.
ESP> Los datos se refieren a un centro de investigación solamente. No incluye el personal auxiliar. Los datos se refieren al número de científicos e ingenieros de jornada completa y de jornada parcial.

5.7 Number of scientists and engineers engaged in research and experimental development performed in the productive sector, by branch of economic activity

Nombre de scientifiques et d'ingénieurs employés à des travaux de recherche et de développement expérimental effectués dans le secteur de la production, par branche d'activité économique

Número de científicos e ingenieros empleados en trabajos de investigación y de desarrollo experimental efectuados en el sector productivo, por rama de actividad económica

PLEASE REFER TO INTRODUCTION FOR DEFINITIONS OF CATEGORIES INCLUDED IN THIS TABLE.

POUR LES DEFINITIONS DES CATEGORIES PRESENTEES DANS CE TABLEAU, SE REFERER A L'INTRODUCTION.

EN LA INTRODUCCION SE DAN LAS DEFINICIONES DE LAS CATEGORIAS QUE FIGURAN EN ESTE CUADRO.

SCIENTISTS AND ENGINEERS ENGAGED IN R&D ARE GIVEN IN FULL-TIME EQUIVALENT (FTE).

LE NOMBRE DE SCIENTIFIQUES ET INGENIEURS EMPLOYES A DES TRAVAUX DE R-D EST EN EQUIVALENT PLEIN TEMPS (EPT).

EL NUMERO DE CIENTIFICOS E INGENIEROS EMPLEADOS EN TRABAJOS DE I Y D SE DA EN EQUIVALENTE DE JORNADA COMPLETA (EJC).

NUMBER OF COUNTRIES AND TERRITORIES PRESENTED IN THIS TABLE: 47

NOMBRE DE PAYS ET DE TERRITOIRES PRESENTES DANS CE TABLEAU: 47

NUMERO DE PAISES Y DE TERRITORIOS PRESENTADOS EN ESTE CUADRO: 47

COUNTRY / PAYS / PAIS	YEAR / ANNEE / AÑO		TOTAL / TOTAL / TOTAL	AGRICULTURE FORESTRY HUNTING AND FISHING / AGRICULTURE SYLVICULTURE CHASSE ET PECHE / AGRICULTURA SILVICULTURA CAZA Y PESCA	EXTRACTING INDUSTRIES / INDUSTRIES EXTRACTIVES / INDUSTRIAS EXTRACTIVAS	MANUFACTURING INDUSTRIES / INDUSTRIES MANUFACTURIERES / INDUSTRIAS MANUFACTURERAS	UTILITIES / SERVICES PUBLICS / SERVICIOS PUBLICOS	CONSTRUCTION / BATIMENTS ET TRAVAUX PUBLICS / CONSTRUCCION	TRANSPORT AND COMMUNICATION / TRANSPORTS ET COMMUNICATIONS / TRANSPORTES Y COMUNICACIONES	OTHER ACTIVITIES / ACTIVITES DIVERSES / OTRAS ACTIVIDADES
				BRANCH OF ECONOMIC ACTIVITY/BRANCHE D'ACTIVITE ECONOMIQUE/RAMA DE ACTIVIDAD ECONOMICA						
			(1)	(2)	(3)	(4)	(5)	(6)	(7)	(8)
AFRICA										
CONGO‡	1984		368	290	–	–	–	37	–	41
		%	100	78.8	–	–	–	10.1	–	11.1
EGYPT‡	1982		5 527	3 194	651	1 327	210	111	34	–
		%	100	57.8	11.8	24.0	3.8	2.0	0.6	–
MALAWI	1977		101	101	–	–	–	–	–	–
		%	100	100.0	–	–	–	–	–	–
MAURITIUS	1983		8	–	–	–	8	–	–	–
		%	100	–	–	–	100.0	–	–	–
ZAMBIA‡	1976		112	10	102	–	–	–	–	–
		%	100	8.9	91.1	–	–	–	–	–
AMERICA, NORTH										
CANADA‡	1982		*15 900	–	*650	*12 235	./.	./.	*1 860	*1 155
		%	100	–	*4.1	*77.0	./.	./.	*11.7	*7.3
CUBA‡	1983		3 672	1 735	83	1 053	–	239	225	337
		%	100	47.2	2.3	28.7	–	6.5	6.1	9.2
PANAMA‡	1975		116	7	8	–	./.	–	–	101
		%	100	6.0	6.9	–	./.	–	–	87.1
ST. PIERRE AND MIQUELON	1983		6	6	–	–	–	–	–	–
		%	100	100.0	–	–	–	–	–	–
TURKS AND CAICOS ISLANDS	1976		2	2	–	–	–	–	–	–
		%	100	100.0	–	–	–	–	–	–

COUNTRY / PAYS / PAIS	YEAR / ANNEE / AÑO		TOTAL / TOTAL / TOTAL (1)	AGRICULTURE FORESTRY HUNTING AND FISHING / AGRICULTURE SYLVICULTURE CHASSE ET PECHE / AGRICULTURA SILVICULTURA CAZA Y PESCA (2)	EXTRACTING INDUSTRIES / INDUSTRIES EXTRACTIVES / INDUSTRIAS EXTRACTIVAS (3)	MANUFACTURING INDUSTRIES / INDUSTRIES MANUFACTURIERES / INDUSTRIAS MANUFACTURERAS (4)	UTILITIES / SERVICES PUBLICS / SERVICIOS PUBLICOS (5)	CONSTRUCTION / BATIMENTS ET TRAVAUX PUBLICS / CONSTRUCCION (6)	TRANSPORT AND COMMUNICATION / TRANSPORTS ET COMMUNICATIONS / TRANSPORTES Y COMUNICACIONES (7)	OTHER ACTIVITIES / ACTIVITES DIVERSES / OTRAS ACTIVIDADES (8)
			BRANCH OF ECONOMIC ACTIVITY/BRANCHE D'ACTIVITE ECONOMIQUE/RAMA DE ACTIVIDAD ECONOMICA							
AMERICA, SOUTH										
ARGENTINA	1980		*1 700	*675	*30	*450	*370	*25	*115	*35
		%	100	*39.7	*26.4	*26.5	*1.4	*1.5	*6.8	*2.1
CHILE	1975		627	–	–	627	–	–	–	–
		%	100	–	–	100.0	–	–	–	–
GUYANA‡	1982		67	20	25	13	–	9	–	–
		%	100	29.9	37.3	19.4	–	13.4	–	–
PERU‡	1981		896	6	144	149	–	–	–	597
		%	100	0.7	16.1	16.6	–	–	–	66.6
VENEZUELA‡	1983		310	18	151	129	10	–	1	1
		%	100	5.8	48.7	41.6	3.2	–	0.3	0.3
ASIA										
JAPAN‡	1984		300 730	429	850	287 775	./.	6 629	5 047	–
		%	100	0.1	0.3	95.7	./.	2.2	1.7	–
KOREA, REPUBLIC OF‡	1983		12 586	123	49	11 224	131	315	89	655
		%	100	1.0	0.4	89.2	1.0	2.5	0.7	5.2
PAKISTAN‡	1982		3 684	2 149	44	781	413	31	73	193
		%	100	58.3	1.2	21.2	11.2	0.8	2.0	5.2
PHILIPPINES	1982		*330	*2	–	*213	*78	*30	–	*7
		%	100	*0.6	–	*64.5	*23.6	*9.1	–	*2.1
EUROPE										
AUSTRIA	1981		2 885	9	25	2 588	6	21	–	236
		%	100	0.3	0.9	89.7	0.2	0.7	–	8.2
BULGARIA	1983		23 184	4 060	1 764	14 534	356	1 345	963	162
		%	100	17.5	7.6	62.7	1.5	5.8	4.2	0.7
CZECHOSLOVAKIA‡	1983		41 861	4 030	1 705	29 033	./.	2 477	1 481	3 135
		%	100	9.6	4.1	69.4	./.	5.9	3.5	7.5
DENMARK‡	1981		2 003	./.	–	1 723	./.	20	54	206
		%	100	./.	–	86.0	./.	1.0	2.7	10.3
FINLAND	1983		4 662	50	43	4 141	100	32	137	159
		%	100	1.1	0.9	88.8	2.1	0.7	2.9	3.4
FRANCE	1979		33 663	330	304	30 798	725	454	844	208
		%	100	1.0	0.9	91.5	2.2	1.3	2.5	0.6
GERMANY, FEDERAL REPUBLIC OF‡	1981		77 017	56	804	73 528	259	424	621	1 325
		%	100	0.1	1.0	95.5	0.3	0.6	0.8	1.7
GREECE	1976		678	180	110	160	./.	40	68	120
		%	100	26.5	16.2	23.6	./.	5.9	10.0	17.7
HUNGARY‡	1983		12 482	741	611	8 528	206	629	323	1 444
		%	100	5.9	4.9	68.3	1.7	5.0	2.6	11.6
ICELAND	1979		101	53	4	33	–	6	–	5
		%	100	52.5	4.0	32.7	–	5.9	–	5.0
IRELAND‡	1982		655	4	8	580	12	1	25	25
		%	100	0.6	1.2	88.6	1.8	0.2	3.8	3.8
ITALY‡	1983		20 976	28	46	18 334	458	87	139	1 884
		%	100	0.1	0.2	87.4	2.2	0.4	0.7	9.0
NETHERLANDS‡	1982		14 290	150	./.	12 720	50	220	940	210
		%	100	1.1	./.	89.0	0.4	1.5	6.6	1.5
NORWAY	1981		3 079	86	553	1 965	104	104	136	131
		%	100	2.8	18.0	63.8	3.4	3.4	4.4	4.3

COUNTRY	YEAR		TOTAL	BRANCH OF ECONOMIC ACTIVITY/BRANCHE D'ACTIVITE ECONOMIQUE/RAMA DE ACTIVIDAD ECONOMICA						
				AGRICULTURE FORESTRY HUNTING AND FISHING	EXTRACTING INDUSTRIES	MANUFACTURING INDUSTRIES	UTILITIES	CONSTRUC-TION	TRANSPORT AND COMMUNI-CATION	OTHER ACTIVITIES
PAYS	ANNEE		TOTAL	AGRICULTURE SYLVICULTURE CHASSE ET PECHE	INDUSTRIES EXTRACTIVES	INDUSTRIES MANU-FACTURIERES	SERVICES PUBLICS	BATIMENTS ET TRAVAUX PUBLICS	TRANSPORTS ET COMMU-NICATIONS	ACTIVITES DIVERSES
PAIS	AÑO		TOTAL	AGRICULTURA SILVICULTURA CAZA Y PESCA	INDUSTRIAS EXTRACTIVAS	INDUSTRIAS MANU-FACTURERAS	SERVICIOS PUBLICOS	CONSTRUC-CION	TRANSPORTES Y COMUNI-CACIONES	OTRAS ACTIVI-DADES
			(1)	(2)	(3)	(4)	(5)	(6)	(7)	(8)
POLAND‡	1983		45 400	3 400	35 500	——>	–	3 700	1 600	1 200
		%	100	7.5	78.2	——>	–	8.2	3.5	2.6
PORTUGAL‡	1982		655	–	6	333	182	–	105	29
		%	100	–	0.9	50.8	27.8	–	16.0	4.4
SPAIN‡	1983		3 527	5	14	2 730	97	70	377	234
		%	100	0.1	0.4	77.4	2.8	2.0	10.7	6.6
SWEDEN‡	1979		9 422	172	52	8 577	312	./.	./.	309
		%	100	1.8	0.6	91.0	3.3	./.	./.	3.3
SWITZERLAND	1975		10 590	–	–	10 320	./.	110	90	70
		%	100	–	–	97.5	./.	1.0	0.9	0.7
UNITED KINGDOM	1975		59 700	–	1 000	53 400	./.	300	2 800	2 200
		%	100	–	1.7	89.4	./.	0.5	4.7	3.7
YUGOSLAVIA‡	1981		9 581	1 211	1 535	5 564	–	756	138	377
		%	100	12.6	16.0	58.1	–	7.9	1.4	3.9
OCEANIA										
AUSTRALIA‡	1981		8 341	2 321	449	2 840	./.	87	./.	2 644
		%	100	27.8	5.4	34.0	./.	1.0	./.	31.7
GUAM	1977		5	5	–	–	–	–	–	–
		%	100	100.0	–	–	–	–	–	–
NEW CALEDONIA	1983		5	4	–	–	1	–	–	–
		%	100	80.0	–	–	20.0	–	–	–
NEW ZEALAND	1975		1 982	793	69	954	–	93	49	24
		%	100	40.0	3.5	48.1	–	4.7	2.5	1.2
SAMOA‡	1977		60	22	3	4	–	12	14	5
		%	100	36.7	5.0	6.7	–	20.0	23.3	8.3
TONGA	1981		–	–	–	–	–	–	–	–
		%	–	–	–	–	–	–	–	–
VANUATU	1975		3	3	–	–	–	–	–	–
		%	100	100.0	–	–	–	–	–	–

AFRICA:
Congo:
E--> Scientists and engineers are full-time plus part time. Not including military and defence R&D.
FR-> Les scientifiques et ingénieurs sont à plein temps et à temps partiel. Non compris les activités de R-D de caractère militaire ou relevant de la défense nationale.
ESP> Los científicos e ingenieros son de jornada completa et de jornada parcial. Excluídas las actividades militares y de defensa de I y D.
Egypt:
E--> Not including military and defence R&D.
FR-> Non compris les activités de R-D de caractère militaire ou relevant de la défense nationale.
ESP> Excluídas las actividades militares y de defensa de I y D.
Zambia:
E--> Partial data.
FR-> Données partielles.
ESP> Datos parciales.
AMERICA, NORTH:
Canada:
E--> Data relate only to integrated R&D in the productive sector and do not include social sciences and humanities. Data for utilities are included with transport and communication, those for construction are included with 'other' activities.
FR-> Les données ne se réfèrent qu'aux activités de R-D intégrées dans le secteur de la production et ne comprennent pas les sciences sociales et humaines. Les données relatives aux services publics sont comptées avec celles des transports et communications, celles des bâtiments et travaux publics sont comptées avec les activités 'diverses'.
ESP> Los datos sólo se refieren a las actividades de I y D integradas
Canada: (Cont):
en el sector productivo y no incluyen las ciencias sociales y humanas. datos relativos a los servicios públicos quedan incluídos con los transportes y comunicaciones y las de la construcción quedan incluídos las 'otras' actividades.
Cuba:
E--> Not including military and defence R&D.
FR-> Non compris les activités de R-D de caractère militaire relevant de la défense nationale.
ESP> Excluídas las actividades militares y de defensa de I y D.
Panama:
E--> Data also include scientific and technological services (STS
FR-> Les données comprennent en plus les services scientifique techniques (SST).
ESP> Los datos también incluyen los servicios científicos tecnológicos (SCT).
AMERICA, SOUTH:
Guyana:
E--> Not including military and defence R&D.
FR-> Non compris les activités de R-D de caractère militaire relevant de la défense nationale.
ESP> Excluídas las actividades militares y de defensa de I y D.
Peru:
E--> Data refer to full-time scientists and engineers employe scientific and technological activities (STA).
FR-> Les données se réfèrent aux scientifiques et ingénieurs à p temps employés dans les activités scientifiques et techniques (ACT).
ESP> Los datos se refieren a los científicos e ingenieros de jorn completa empleados a las actividades científicas y tecnológicas (ACT
Venezuela:
E--> Not including military and defence R&D.

Venezuela: (Cont):

FR-> Non compris les activités de R-D de caractère militaire ou relevant de la défense nationale.

ESP> Excluídas las actividades militares y de defensa de I y D.

ASIA:

Japan:

E--> Data refer to full-time scientists and engineers. Not including social sciences and humanities. Data for utilities are included with transport and communication.

FR-> Les données se réfèrent aux scientifiques et ingénieurs à plein temps. Non compris les sciences sociales et humaines. Les données relatives aux services publics sont comptées avec celles des transports et communications.

ESP> Los datos se refieren a los científicos e ingenieros de jornada completa. Excluídas las ciencias sociales y humanas. Los datos relativos a los servicios públicos quedan incluídos con los de transportes y comunicaciones.

Korea, Republic of:

E--> Scientists and engineers are full-time plus part-time. Not including military and defence R&D. Not including social sciences and humanities.

FR-> Les scientifiques et ingénieurs sont à plein temps et à temps partiel. Non compris les activités de R-D de caractère militaire ou relevant de la défense nationale. Non compris les sciences sociales et humaines.

ESP> Los científicos e ingenieros son de jornada completa y de jornada parcial. Excluídas las actividades militares y de defensa de I y D. Excluídas las ciencias sociales y humanas.

Pakistan:

E--> Data relate to R&D activities concentrated mainly in government-financed research establishments only. Not including the productive sector (integrated R&D) or military and defence R&D.

FR-> Les données se réfèrent aux activités de R-D se trouvant pour la plupart dans les établissements de recherche financés par le gouvernement. Compte non tenu du secteur de la production (activités de R-D intégrées) ni des activités de caractère militaire ou relevant de la défense nationale.

ESP> Los datos se refieren a las actividades de I y D concentradas principalmente en los establecimientos de investigación subvencionados par el gobierno. Excluídos el sector productivo (actividades de I y D integradas) y las actividades militares y de defensa de I y D.

EUROPE:

Czechoslovakia:

E--> Of military R&D only that part carried out in civil establishments is included. Not including scientists and engineers engaged in the administration of R&D.

FR-> Pour la R-D de caractère militaire seule la partie effectuée dans les établissements civils a été considérée. Compte non tenu des scientifiques et ingénieurs employés dans les services administratifs de R-D.

ESP> Para la I y D de carácter militar sólo se ha considerado la parte correspondiente a los establecimientos civiles. Excluídos los científicos e ingenieros empleados en los servicios administrativos de I y D.

Denmark:

E--> Not including 321 scientists and engineers engaged in the productive sector (non-integrated R&D) for whom a distribution by branch of economic activity is not available. Data for utilities are included with transport and communication.

FR-> Non compris 321 scientifiques et ingénieurs employés dans le secteur de la production (activités de R-D non intégrées) pour lesquels la répartition par branche d'activité économique n'est pas disponible. Les données relatives aux services publics sont comptées avec celles des transports et communications.

ESP> No se incluyen 321 científicos e ingenieros empleados en el sector productivo (actividades de I y D no integradas) cuya repartición por rama de actividad económica se desconoce. Los datos relativos al servicio público quedan incluídos con los de transportes y comunicaciones.

Germany, Federal Republic of:

E--> Not including social sciences and humanities.

FR-> Non compris les sciences sociales et humaines.

ESP> Excluídas las ciencias sociales y humanas.

Hungary:

E--> Not including scientists and engineers engaged in the administration of R&D.

FR-> Compte non tenu des scientifiques et ingénieurs employés dans les services administratifs de R-D.

ESP> Excluídos los científicos e ingenieros empleados en los servicios administrativos de I y D.

Ireland:

E--> Data relate only to integrated R&D in the productive sector (non-integrated R&D is included with the general service sector.)

FR-> Les données ne se réfèrent qu'aux activités de R-D intégrées dans le secteur de la production (les activités de R-D non intégrées sont comptées avec le secteur de service général).

ESP> Los datos sólo se refieren a las actividades de I y D en el sector productivo (las actividades de I y D no integradas quedan incluídas en el sector de servicio general).

Italy:

E--> Data relate only to integrated R&D in the productive sector.

FR-> Les données ne se réfèrent qu'aux activités de R-D intégrées dans le secteur de la production.

ESP> Los datos sólo se refieren a las actividades de I y D en el sector productivo.

Netherlands:

E--> Not including data for social sciences and humanities in the productive sector (integrated R&D). Data for extracting industries are included with 'other' activities.

FR-> Non compris les données pour les sciences sociales et humaines du secteur de la production (activités de R-D intégrées). Les données relatives aux industries extractives sont comptées avec les activités 'diverses'.

ESP> Excluídos los datos relativos a las ciencias sociales y humanas del sector productivo (actividades de I y D integradas). Los datos relativos a las industrias extractivas quedan incluídos con las 'otras' actividades.

Poland:

E--> Not including military and defence R&D.

FR-> Non compris les activités de R-D de caractère militaire ou relevant de la défense nationale.

ESP> Excluídas las actividades militares y de defensa de I y D.

Portugal:

E--> Not including 110 scientists and engineers engaged in the productive sector (non-integrated R&D) for whom a distribution by branch of economic activity is not available.

FR-> Non compris 110 scientifiques et ingénieurs employés dans le secteur de la production (activités de R-D non intégrées) pour lesquels la répartition par branche d'activité économique n'est pas disponible.

ESP> No se incluyen 110 científicos e ingenieros empleados en el sector productivo (actividades de I y D no integradas) cuya repartición por rama de actividad económica se desconoce.

Spain:

E--> Data relate only to integrated R&D in the productive sector (non-integrated R&D is included with the general service sector).

FR-> Les données ne se réfèrent qu'aux activités de R-D intégrées dans le secteur de la production (les activités de R-D non-intégrées sont comptées avec le secteur de service général).

ESP> Los datos sólo se refieren a las actividades de I y D en el sector productivo (las actividades de I y D no integradas quedan incluídas en el sector de servicio general).

Sweden:

E--> Not including data for social sciences and humanities.

FR-> Non compris les données pour les sciences sociales et humaines.

ESP> Excluídos los datos correspondientes a las ciencias sociales y humanas.

Yugoslavia:

E--> Not including military and defence R&D.

FR-> Non compris les activités de R-D de caractère militaire ou relevant de la défense nationale.

ESP> Excluídas las actividades militares y de defensa de I y D.

OCEANIA:

Australia:

E--> Data for utilities and transport and communication are incuded with 'other' activities.

FR-> Les données relatives aux services publics et aux transports et communications sont comptées avec les activités 'diverses'.

ESP> Los datos relativos al servicio público y a los transportes y comunicaciones quedan incluídos con las 'otras' actividades.

Samoa:

E--> Data refer to full-time scientists and engineers.

FR-> Les données se réfèrent aux scientifiques et ingénieurs à plein temps.

ESP> Los datos se refieren a los científicos e ingenieros de jornada completa.

5.8 Number of scientists and engineers engaged in research and experimental development performed in the higher education and the general service sectors, by field of science and technology

Nombre de scientifiques et d'ingénieurs employés à des travaux de recherche et de développement expérimental effectués dans les secteurs de l'enseignement supérieur et de service général, par domaine de la science et de la technologie

Número de científicos e ingenieros empleados en trabajos de investigación y de desarrollo experimental efectuados en los sectores de enseñanza superior y de servicio general, por campo de la ciencia y de la tecnología

PLEASE REFER TO INTRODUCTION FOR DEFINITIONS OF CATEGORIES INCLUDED IN THIS TABLE.

HES = HIGHER EDUCATION SECTOR
GSS = GENERAL SERVICE SECTOR

SCIENTISTS AND ENGINEERS ENGAGED IN R&D ARE GIVEN IN FULL-TIME EQUIVALENT (FTE).

NUMBER OF COUNTRIES AND TERRITORIES PRESENTED IN THIS TABLE: 54

POUR LES DEFINITIONS DES CATEGORIES PRESENTEES DANS CE TABLEAU, SE REFERER A L'INTRODUCTION.

HES = SECTEUR DE L'ENSEIGNEMENT SUPERIEUR
GSS = SECTEUR DE SERVICE GENERAL

LE NOMBRE DE SCIENTIFIQUES ET INGENIEURS EMPLOYES A DES TRAVAUX DE R-D EST EN EQUIVALENT PLEIN TEMPS (EPT).

NOMBRE DE PAYS ET DE TERRITOIRES PRESENTES DANS CE TABLEAU: 54

EN LA INTRODUCCION SE DAN LAS DEFINICIONES DE LAS CATEGORIAS QUE FIGURAN EN ESTE CUADRO.

HES = SECTOR DE ENSEÑANZA SUPERIOR
GSS = SECTOR DE SERVICIO GENERAL

EL NUMERO DE CIENTIFICOS E INGENIEROS EMPLEADOS EN TRABAJOS DE I Y D SE DA EN EQUIVALENTE DE JORNADA COMPLETA (EJC).

NUMERO DE PAISES Y DE TERRITORIOS PRESENTADOS EN ESTE CUADRO: 54

COUNTRY	YEAR	SECTOR OF PERFORMANCE	TOTAL (FTE)	FIELD OF SCIENCE AND TECHNOLOGY / DOMAINE DE LA SCIENCE ET DE LA TECHNOLOGIE / CAMPO DE LA CIENCIA Y DE LA TECNOLOGIA					
				NATURAL SCIENCES	ENGINEERING AND TECHNOLOGY	MEDICAL SCIENCES	AGRICULTURAL SCIENCES	SOCIAL SCIENCES AND HUMANITIES	OTHER FIELDS
PAYS	ANNEE	SECTEUR D'EXECUTION	TOTAL (EPT)	SCIENCES EXACTES ET NATURELLES	SCIENCES DE L'INGENIEUR ET TECHNOLOGIQUES	SCIENCES MEDICALES	SCIENCES AGRICOLES	SCIENCES SOCIALES ET HUMAINES	DOMAINES DIVERS
PAIS	AÑO	SECTOR DE EJECUCION	TOTAL (EJC)	CIENCIAS EXACTAS Y NATURALES	INGENIERIA Y TECNOLOGIA	CIENCIAS MEDICAS	CIENCIAS AGRICOLAS	CIENCIAS SOCIALES Y HUMANAS	CAMPOS DIVERSOS
			(1)	(2)	(3)	(4)	(5)	(6)	(7)
AFRICA									
CENTRAL AFRICAN REPUBLIC	1975	HES	76	35	9	–	4	28	–
		%	100	46.1	11.8	–	5.3	36.8	–
CONGO‡	1984	HES	473	96	30	41	–	237	69
		%	100	20.3	6.3	8.7	–	50.1	14.6
		GSS	21	11	1	2	4	3	–
		%	100	52.4	4.8	9.5	19.0	14.3	–
EGYPT‡	1982	HES	9 989	2 717	1 245	2 130	927	2 970	–
		%	100	27.2	12.5	21.3	9.3	29.7	–
		GSS	4 425	1 446	842	1 379	235	523	–
		%	100	32.7	19.0	31.2	5.3	11.8	–
KENYA‡	1975	HES	122	26	23	16	24	33	–
		%	100	21.3	18.9	13.1	19.7	27.0	–
		GSS	–	–	–	–	–	–	–
		%	–	–	–	–	–	–	–
MALAWI	1977	HES	77	21	19	2	6	29	–
		%	100	27.3	24.7	2.6	7.8	37.7	–
		GSS	11	–	–	–	–	11	–
		%	100	–	–	–	–	100.0	–

COUNTRY PAYS PAIS	YEAR ANNEE AÑO	SECTOR OF PERFORMANCE SECTEUR D'EXECUTION SECTOR DE EJECUCION		TOTAL (FTE) TOTAL (EPT) TOTAL (EJC)	FIELD OF SCIENCE AND TECHNOLOGY DOMAINE DE LA SCIENCE ET DE LA TECHNOLOGIE CAMPO DE LA CIENCIA Y DE LA TECNOLOGIA					
					NATURAL SCIENCES SCIENCES EXACTES ET NATURELLES CIENCIAS EXACTAS Y NATURALES	ENGINEERING AND TECHNOLOGY SCIENCES DE L'INGENIEUR ET TECHNO-LOGIQUES INGENIERIA Y TECNOLOGIA	MEDICAL SCIENCES SCIENCES MEDICALES CIENCIAS MEDICAS	AGRICULTURAL SCIENCES SCIENCES AGRICOLES CIENCIAS AGRICOLAS	SOCIAL SCIENCES AND HUMANITIES SCIENCES SOCIALES ET HUMAINES CIENCIAS SOCIALES Y HUMANAS	OTHER FIELDS DOMAINES DIVERS CAMPOS DIVERSOS
				(1)	(2)	(3)	(4)	(5)	(6)	(7)
MAURITIUS	1983	HES		47	2	23	–	16	6	–
			%	100	4.3	48.9	–	34.0	12.8	–
		GSS		156	13	–	–	143	–	–
			%	100	8.3	–	–	91.7	–	–
NIGER	1976	HES		93	46	–	4	9	34	–
			%	100	49.5	–	4.3	9.7	36.6	–
SUDAN‡	1978	HES		1 065	174	133	140	139	454	25
			%	100	16.3	12.5	13.1	13.1	42.6	2.3
		GSS		1 341	203	169	76	287	585	21
			%	100	15.1	12.6	5.7	21.4	43.6	1.6
TOGO‡	1976	HES		160	42	–	23	8	87	–
			%	100	26.3	–	14.4	5.0	54.4	–
		GSS		101	2	29	9	8	53	–
			%	100	2.0	28.7	8.9	7.9	52.5	–
ZAMBIA‡	1976	HES		54	12	6	10	6	20	–
			%	100	22.2	11.1	18.5	11.1	37.0	–
		GSS		84	70	4	–	6	4	–
			%	100	83.3	4.8	–	7.1	4.8	–
AMERICA, NORTH										
CANADA‡	1977	HES		*7 350	*1 760	*710	*1 280	*220	*3 380	–
			%	100	*23.9	*9.7	*17.4	*3.0	*46.0	–
		GSS		7 555	...	...	...	...	1 086	...
			%	100	...	...	...	...	14.4	...
CUBA‡	1983	HES		1 355	–	205	192	161	49	748
			%	100	–	15.1	14.2	11.9	3.6	55.2
		GSS		3 220	686	93	1 180	–	1 261	–
			%	100	21.3	2.9	36.6	–	39.2	–
PANAMA‡	1975	HES		62	–	16	14	32	–	–
			%	100	–	25.8	22.6	51.6	–	–
		GSS		26	–	–	25	–	1	–
			%	100	–	–	96.2	–	3.8	–
UNITED STATES‡	1983	HES		100 000	45 700	20 500	16 300	8 800	8 700	–
			%	100	45.7	20.5	16.3	8.8	8.7	–
		GSS		93 000	...	...	...	...	...	...
			%	100	...	...	...	...	...	...
AMERICA, SOUTH										
ARGENTINA	1980	HES		*5 200	*2 000	*500	*1 400	*400	*870	*30
			%	100	*38.5	*9.6	*26.9	*7.7	*16.7	*0.6
		GSS		*2 600	*900	*350	*420	*600	*310	*20
			%	100	*34.6	*13.5	*16.2	*23.1	*11.9	0.8
CHILE	1975	HES		4 975	1 758	808	1 493	211	705	–
			%	100	35.3	16.2	30.0	4.2	14.2	–
		GSS		346	127	108	69	24	18	–
			%	100	36.7	31.2	19.9	6.9	5.2	–
GUYANA‡	1982	HES		22	16	2	...	1	3	–
			%	100	72.7	9.1	...	4.5	13.6	–

5.8 R&D scientists and engineers - higher education & general service
Scientifiques et ingénieurs de R-D - enseignement supérieur & service général
Científicos e ingenieros de I y D - enseñanza superior y servicio general

COUNTRY / PAYS / PAIS	YEAR / ANNEE / AÑO	SECTOR OF PERFORMANCE / SECTEUR D'EXECUTION / SECTOR DE EJECUCION		TOTAL (FTE) / TOTAL (EPT) / TOTAL (EJC)	FIELD OF SCIENCE AND TECHNOLOGY / DOMAINE DE LA SCIENCE ET DE LA TECHNOLOGIE / CAMPO DE LA CIENCIA Y DE LA TECNOLOGIA: NATURAL SCIENCES / SCIENCES EXACTES ET NATURELLES / CIENCIAS EXACTAS Y NATURALES	ENGINEERING AND TECHNOLOGY / SCIENCES DE L'INGENIEUR ET TECHNOLOGIQUES / INGENIERIA Y TECNOLOGIA	MEDICAL SCIENCES / SCIENCES MEDICALES / CIENCIAS MEDICAS	AGRICULTURAL SCIENCES / SCIENCES AGRICOLES / CIENCIAS AGRICOLAS	SOCIAL SCIENCES AND HUMANITIES / SCIENCES SOCIALES ET HUMAINES / CIENCIAS SOCIALES Y HUMANAS	OTHER FIELDS / DOMAINES DIVERS / CAMPOS DIVERSOS
				(1)	(2)	(3)	(4)	(5)	(6)	(7)
PERU‡	1981	HES		3 600	...	...	...	...	...	...
			%	100	...	...	...	...	...	...
		GSS		2 968	417	131	180	1 273	416	551
			%	100	14.1	4.4	6.1	42.9	14.0	18.6
VENEZUELA‡	1983	HES		1 001	316	99	110	190	250	36
			%	100	31.6	9.9	11.0	19.0	25.0	3.6
		GSS		864	321	74	87	231	135	16
			%	100	37.2	8.6	10.1	26.7	15.6	1.8
ASIA										
JAPAN‡	1984	HES		187 350	12 709	30 776	71 834	7 554	34 783	29 694
			%	100	6.8	16.4	38.3	4.0	18.6	15.8
		GSS		43 532	6 854	16 038	4 263	12 113	2 431	1 833
			%	100	15.7	36.8	9.8	27.8	5.6	4.2
JORDAN	1976	HES		75	17	1	4	7	46	–
			%	100	22.7	1.3	5.3	9.3	61.3	–
		GSS		117	18	33	1	35	30	–
			%	100	15.4	28.2	0.9	29.9	25.6	–
KOREA, REPUBLIC OF‡	1983	HES		13 137	2 470	4 711	3 446	1 582	...	928
			%	100	18.8	35.9	26.2	12.0	...	7.1
		GSS		6 394	1 178	2 464	564	1 866	...	322
			%	100	18.4	38.5	8.8	29.2	...	5.0
KUWAIT	1977	HES		111	11	1	1	–	98	–
			%	100	9.9	0.9	0.9	–	88.3	–
		GSS		312	76	36	3	38	159	–
			%	100	24.4	11.5	1.0	12.2	51.0	–
PHILIPPINES	1982	GSS		4 816	753	1 404	131	1 599	929	–
			%	100	15.6	29.2	2.7	33.2	19.3	–
SINGAPORE‡	1981	HES		177	53	61	63	–	...	–
			%	100	29.9	34.5	35.6	–	...	–
		GSS		123	...	...	...	...	...	...
			%	100	...	...	...	...	...	...
TURKEY‡	1983	HES		5 660	851	797	1 235	350	531	1 896
			%	100	15.0	14.1	21.8	6.2	9.4	33.5
		GSS		1 649	40	243	115	1 240	...	11
			%	100	2.4	14.7	7.0	75.2	...	0.7
EUROPE										
AUSTRIA	1981	HES		3 051	869	451	649	96	986	–
			%	100	28.5	14.8	21.3	3.1	32.3	–
		GSS		775	104	32	60	153	426	–
			%	100	13.4	4.1	7.7	19.7	55.0	–
BULGARIA	1983	HES		11 334	1 777	2 887	2 949	453	3 268	–
			%	100	15.7	25.5	26.0	4.0	28.8	–
		GSS		8 944	1 686	860	1 042	280	1 146	3 930
			%	100	18.9	9.6	11.7	3.1	12.8	43.9
CZECHOSLOVAKIA‡	1980	HES		2 872	335	1 089	590	426	432	–
			%	100	11.7	37.9	20.5	14.8	15.0	–
		GSS		10 528	3 004	1 356	2 673	177	3 318	–
			%	100	28.5	12.9	25.4	1.7	31.5	–

COUNTRY / PAYS / PAIS	YEAR / ANNEE / AÑO	SECTOR OF PERFORMANCE / SECTEUR D'EXECUTION / SECTOR DE EJECUCION	TOTAL (FTE) / TOTAL (EPT) / TOTAL (EJC)	FIELD OF SCIENCE AND TECHNOLOGY / DOMAINE DE LA SCIENCE ET DE LA TECHNOLOGIE / CAMPO DE LA CIENCIA Y DE LA TECNOLOGIA					
				NATURAL SCIENCES / SCIENCES EXACTES ET NATURELLES / CIENCIAS EXACTAS Y NATURALES	ENGINEERING AND TECHNOLOGY / SCIENCES DE L'INGENIEUR ET TECHNOLOGIQUES / INGENIERIA Y TECNOLOGIA	MEDICAL SCIENCES / SCIENCES MEDICALES / CIENCIAS MEDICAS	AGRICULTURAL SCIENCES / SCIENCES AGRICOLES / CIENCIAS AGRICOLAS	SOCIAL SCIENCES AND HUMANITIES / SCIENCES SOCIALES ET HUMAINES / CIENCIAS SOCIALES Y HUMANAS	OTHER FIELDS / DOMAINES DIVERS / CAMPOS DIVERSOS
			(1)	(2)	(3)	(4)	(5)	(6)	(7)
DENMARK	1979	HES	2 397	726	346	304	119	902	–
		%	100	30.3	14.4	12.7	5.0	37.6	–
		GSS	1 635	282	223	523	282	325	–
		%	100	17.2	13.6	32.0	17.2	19.9	–
FINLAND	1983	HES	3 773	973	894	653	106	1 147	–
		%	100	25.8	23.7	17.3	2.8	30.4	–
		GSS	2 580	354	1 029	259	425	513	–
		%	100	13.7	39.9	10.0	16.5	19.9	–
FRANCE	1977	HES	22 636	14 725	→	4 929	→	2 982	–
		%	100	65.1	→	21.8	→	13.2	–
		GSS	13 256	7 810	→	3 516	1 280	650	–
		%	100	58.9	→	26.5	9.7	4.9	–
GERMANY, FEDERAL REPUBLIC OF	1981	HES	30 299	9 284	5 665	4 822	991	9 537	–
		%	100	30.6	18.7	15.9	3.3	31.5	–
		GSS	20 846	10 598	3 737	1 991	1 338	3 182	–
		%	100	50.8	17.9	9.6	6.4	15.3	–
GREECE	1976	HES	843	289	183	243	58	70	–
		%	100	34.3	21.7	28.8	6.9	8.3	–
		GSS	1 048	380	→	73	450	145	–
		%	100	36.3	→	7.0	42.9	13.8	–
HUNGARY‡	1983	HES	4 569	1 040	738	1 041	532	1 218	–
		%	100	22.8	16.2	22.8	11.6	26.7	–
		GSS	5 081	1 744	836	442	438	1 621	–
		%	100	34.3	16.5	8.7	8.6	31.9	–
ICELAND	1979	HES	119	49	7	18	15	30	–
		%	100	41.2	5.9	15.1	12.6	25.2	–
		GSS	84	13	47	11	7	6	–
		%	100	15.5	56.0	13.1	8.3	7.1	–
IRELAND‡	1982	HES	1 383	529	155	80	131	488	–
		%	100	38.3	11.2	5.8	9.5	35.3	–
		GSS	735	81	206	81	162	161	44
		%	100	11.0	28.0	11.0	22.0	21.9	6.0
ITALY	1983	HES	32 308	9 324	4 788	7 812	3 276	7 108	–
		%	100	28.9	14.8	24.2	10.1	22.0	–
		GSS	6 114	1 823	2 368	662	793	468	–
		%	100	29.8	38.7	10.8	13.0	7.7	–
MALTA	1983	HES	34	3	7	10	–	14	–
		%	100	8.8	20.6	29.4	–	41.2	–
NETHERLANDS	1982	HES	7 450	1 480	1 010	1 680	300	2 980	–
		%	100	19.9	13.6	22.6	4.0	40.0	–
		GSS	8 420	...	...	...	...	...	...
		%	100	...	...	...	...	...	...
NORWAY	1981	HES	2 899	867	295	620	150	967	–
		%	100	29.9	10.2	21.4	5.2	33.4	–
		GSS	1 518	330	339	185	200	464	–
		%	100	21.7	22.3	12.2	13.2	30.6	–
POLAND‡	1983	HES	17 100	4 300	5 900	2 900	2 000	2 000	–
		%	100	25.1	34.5	17.0	11.7	11.7	–
		GSS	12 500	4 600	2 500	2 500	200	2 700	–
		%	100	36.8	20.0	20.0	1.6	21.6	–

5.8 R&D scientists and engineers - higher education & general service
Scientifiques et ingénieurs de R-D - enseignement supérieur & service général
Científicos e ingenieros de I y D - enseñanza superior y servicio general

COUNTRY / PAYS / PAIS	YEAR / ANNEE / AÑO	SECTOR OF PERFORMANCE / SECTEUR D'EXECUTION / SECTOR DE EJECUCION	TOTAL (FTE) / TOTAL (EPT) / TOTAL (EJC)	FIELD OF SCIENCE AND TECHNOLOGY / DOMAINE DE LA SCIENCE ET DE LA TECHNOLOGIE / CAMPO DE LA CIENCIA Y DE LA TECNOLOGIA					
				NATURAL SCIENCES / SCIENCES EXACTES ET NATURELLES / CIENCIAS EXACTAS Y NATURALES	ENGINEERING AND TECHNOLOGY / SCIENCES DE L'INGENIEUR ET TECHNOLOGIQUES / INGENIERIA Y TECNOLOGIA	MEDICAL SCIENCES / SCIENCES MEDICALES / CIENCIAS MEDICAS	AGRICULTURAL SCIENCES / SCIENCES AGRICOLES / CIENCIAS AGRICOLAS	SOCIAL SCIENCES AND HUMANITIES / SCIENCES SOCIALES ET HUMAINES / CIENCIAS SOCIALES Y HUMANAS	OTHER FIELDS / DOMAINES DIVERS / CAMPOS DIVERSOS
			(1)	(2)	(3)	(4)	(5)	(6)	(7)
PORTUGAL	1980	HES	1 380	601	191	230	79	279	–
		%	100	43.6	13.8	16.7	5.7	20.2	–
		GSS	836	167	215	17	304	133	–
		%	100	20.0	25.7	2.0	36.4	15.9	–
SPAIN‡	1983	HES	7 830	1 837	1 271	1 357	335	3 030	–
		%	100	23.5	16.2	17.3	4.3	38.7	–
		GSS	2 872	504	975	315	889	189	–
		%	100	17.5	33.9	11.0	31.0	6.6	–
SWEDEN	1981	HES	*7 000	1 200	1 600	2 200	600	1 400	–
		%	*100	*17.1	*22.9	*31.4	*8.6	*20.0	–
		GSS	1 509	...	...	...	...	...	...
		%	100	...	...	...	...	...	...
SWITZERLAND	1975	HES	4 670	1 980	660	900	210	920	–
		%	100	42.4	14.1	19.3	4.5	19.7	–
		GSS	1 138	360	569	14	136	41	18
		%	100	31.6	50.0	1.2	12.0	3.6	1.6
YUGOSLAVIA‡	1981	HES	7 568	731	2 572	1 352	1 109	1 804	–
		%	100	9.7	34.0	17.9	14.7	23.8	–
		GSS	7 733	1 998	731	1 449	163	3 049	343
		%	100	25.8	9.5	18.7	2.1	39.4	4.4
OCEANIA									
AUSTRALIA	1981	HES	13 610	4 565	1 548	1 410	951	5 136	–
		%	100	33.5	11.4	10.4	7.0	37.7	–
		GSS	2 257	512	1 062	300	9	374	–
		%	100	22.7	47.1	13.3	0.4	16.6	–
FRENCH POLYNESIA‡	1983	GSS	17	8	–	9	–	–	–
		%	100	47.1	–	52.9	–	–	–
GUAM	1977	HES	88	40	20	5	5	18	–
		%	100	45.5	22.7	5.7	5.7	20.5	–
		GSS	120	10	100	10	–	–	–
		%	100	8.3	83.3	8.3	–	–	–
NEW CALEDONIA	1983	HES	–	–	–	–	–	–	–
		%		–	–	–	–	–	–
		GSS	2	–	2	–	–	–	–
		%	100	–	100.0	–	–	–	–
NEW ZEALAND	1975	HES	1 048	270	59	135	106	478	–
		%	100	25.8	5.6	12.9	10.1	45.6	–
		GSS	629	354	./.	89	./.	119	67
		%	100	56.3	./.	14.1	./.	18.9	10.7
SAMOA‡	1977	HES	58	25	15	10	6	2	–
		%	100	43.1	25.9	17.2	10.3	3.4	–
		GSS	22	10	8	2	1	1	–
		%	100	45.5	36.4	9.1	4.5	4.5	–
TONGA‡	1981	HES	–	–	–	–	–	–	–
		%	–	–	–	–	–	–	–
		GSS	11	–	–	–	11	–	–
		%	100	–	–	–	100.0	–	–

AFRICA:

Congo:

E--> Data refer to the number of full-time plus part-time scientists and engineers. Not including military and defence R&D.

FR-> Les données se réfèrent au nombre de scientifiques et ingénieurs à plein temps et à temps partiel. Non compris les activités de R-D de caractère militaire ou relevant de la défense nationale.

Congo: (Cont):

ESP> Los datos se refieren a los científicos e ingenieros de jornada completa y de jornada parcial. Excluídas las actividades militares y de defensa de I y D.

Egypt:
E--> Not including military and defence R&D.
FR-> Non compris les activités de R-D de caractère militaire ou relevant de la défense nationale.
ESP> Excluídas las actividades militares y de defensa de I y D.
Kenya:
E--> Data for the higher education sector do not include humanities.
FR-> Les données relatives au secteur de l'enseignement supérieur ne comprennent pas les sciences humaines.
ESP> Los datos correspondientes al sector de enseñanza superior no incluyen las ciencias humanas.
Sudan:
E--> Data refer to full-time scientists and engineers.
FR-> Les données se réfèrent aux scientifiques et ingénieurs à plein temps.
ESP> Los datos se refieren a los científicos e ingenieros de jornada completa.
Togo:
E--> Data refer to full-time scientists and engineers. The general service sector also includes data for the productive sector (integrated R&D).
FR-> Les données se réfèrent aux scientifiques et ingénieurs à plein temps. Le secteur de service général comprend aussi les données relatives au secteur de la production (activités de R-D intégrées).
ESP> Los datos se refieren a los científicos e ingenieros de jornada completa. El sector de servicio general también comprende los datos relativos al sector productivo (actividades de I y D integradas).
Zambia:
E--> Partial data.
FR-> Données partielles.
ESP> Datos parciales.
AMERICA, NORTH:
Canada:
E--> The general service sector also includes data for the productive sector (non-integrated R&D).
FR-> Le secteur de service général comprend aussi les données relatives au secteur de la production (activités de R-D non intégrées).
ESP> El sector de servicio general también comprende los datos relativos al sector productivo (actividades de I y D no integradas).
Cuba:
E--> Not including military and defence R&D.
FR-> Non compris les activités de R-D de caractère militaire ou relevant de la défense nationale.
ESP> Excluídas las actividades militares y de defensa de I y D.
Panama:
E--> Data also include scientific and technological services (STS).
FR-> Les données comprennent en plus les services scientifiques et techniques (SST).
ESP> Los datos también incluyen los servicios científicos y tecnológicos (SCT).
United States:
E--> Not including data for law, humanities and education.
FR-> Non compris les données pour le droit, les sciences humaines et l'éducation.
ESP> Excluídos los datos relativos al derecho, las ciencias humanas y la educación.
AMERICA, SOUTH:
Guyana:
E--> Not including military and defence R&D nor medical sciences.
FR-> Non compris les activités de R-D de caractère militaire ou relevant de la défense nationale ni les sciences médicales.
ESP> Excluídas las actividades militares y de defensa de I y D. y las ciencias médicas.
Peru:
E--> Data refer to full-time scientists and engineers employed in scientific and technological activities (STA).
FR-> Les données se réfèrent aux scientifiques et ingénieurs à plein temps employés dans les activités scientifiques et techniques (ACT).
ESP> Los datos se refieren a los científicos e ingenieros de jornada completa empleados a las actividades científicas y tecnológicas (ACT).
Venezuela:
E--> Not including military and defence R&D.
FR-> Non compris les activités de R-D de caractère militaire ou relevant de la défense nationale.
ESP> Excluídas las actividades militares y de defensa de I y D.
ASIA:
Japan:
E--> Data refer to full-time scientists and engineers.
FR-> Les données se réfèrent aux scientifiques et ingénieurs à plein temps.
ESP> Los datos se refieren a los científicos e ingenieros de jornada completa.
Korea, Republic of:
E--> Scientists and engineers are full-time plus part-time. Not including military and defence R&D. Not including social sciences and humanities.

Korea, Republic of: (Cont):
FR-> Les scientifiques et ingénieurs sont à plein temps et à temps partiel. Non compris les activités de R-D de caractère militaire ou relevant de la défense nationale. Non compris les sciences sociales et humaines.
ESP> Los científicos e ingenieros son de jornada completa y de jornada parcial. Excluídas las actividades militares y de defensa de I y D. Excluídas las ciencias sociales y humanas.
Singapore:
E--> Not including either military and defence R&D or social sciences and humanities.
FR-> Compte non tenu des scientifiques et ingénieurs employés dans les services administratifs de R-D ni les sciences sociales et humaines.
ESP> Excluídos los científicos e ingenieros empleados en los servicios administrativos de I y D y las ciencias sociales y humanas.
Turkey:
E--> Not including social sciences and humanities in the general service sector.
FR-> Non compris les sciences sociales et humaines dans le secteur de service général.
ESP> Excluídas las ciencias sociales y humanas en el sector de servicio general.
EUROPE:
Czechoslovakia:
E--> Of military R&D only that part carried out in civil establishments is included. Not including scientists and engineers engaged in the administration of R&D.
FR-> Pour la R-D de caractère militaire seule la partie effectuée dans les établissements civils a été considérée. Compte non tenu des scientifiques et ingénieurs employés dans les services administratifs de R-D.
ESP> Para la I y D de carácter militar sólo se ha considerado la parte correspondiente a los establecimientos civiles. Excluídos los científicos e ingenieros empleados en los servicios administrativos de I y D.
Hungary:
E--> Not including scientists and engineers engaged in the administration of R&D.
FR-> Compte non tenu des scientifiques et ingénieurs employés dans les services administratifs de R-D.
ESP> Excluídos los científicos e ingenieros empleados en los servicios administrativos de I y D.
Ireland:
E--> The general service sector also includes data for the productive sector (non-integrated R&D).
FR-> Le secteur de service général comprend aussi les données relatives au secteur de la production (activités de R-D non intégrées).
ESP> El sector de servicio general también comprende los datos relativos al sector productivo (actividades de I y D no integradas).
Poland:
E--> Not including military and defence R&D.
FR-> Non compris les activités de R-D de caractère militaire ou relevant de la défense nationale.
ESP> Excluídas las actividades militares y de defensa de I y D.
Spain:
E--> The general service sector also includes data for the productive sector (non-integrated R&D).
FR-> Le secteur de service général comprend aussi les données relatives au secteur de la production (activités de R-D non intégrées).
ESP> El sector de servicio general también comprende los datos relativos al sector productivo (actividades de I y D no integradas).
Yugoslavia:
E--> Not including military and defence R&D.
FR-> Non compris les activités de R-D de caractère militaire ou relevant de la défense nationale.
ESP> Excluídas las actividades militares y de defensa de I y D.
OCEANIA:
French Polynesia:
E--> Data relate to one research institute only.
FR-> Les données ne concernent qu'un institut de recherche.
ESP> Los datos se refieren a un centro de investigación.
Samoa:
E--> Data refer to full-time scientists and engineers.
FR-> Les données se réfèrent aux scientifiques et ingénieurs à plein temps.
ESP> Los datos se refieren a los científicos e ingenieros de jornada completa.
Tonga:
E--> Data refer to the number of full-time plus part-time scientists and engineers at one research institute only.
FR-> Les données se réfèrent au nombre de scientifiques et ingénieurs à plein temps et à temps partiel d'un institut de recherche.
ESP> Los datos se refieren a los científicos e ingenieros de jornada completa y de jornada parcial de un centre de investigación.

5.9 Total expenditure for research and experimental development by type of expenditure

Dépenses totales consacrées à la recherche et au développement expérimental, par type de dépenses

Gastos totales dedicados a la investigación y al desarrollo experimental, por tipo de gastos

PLEASE REFER TO INTRODUCTION FOR DEFINITIONS OF CATEGORIES INCLUDED IN THIS TABLE.

POUR LES DEFINITIONS DES CATEGORIES PRESENTEES DANS CE TABLEAU, SE REFERER A L'INTRODUCTION.

EN LA INTRODUCCION SE DAN LAS DEFINICIONES DE LAS CATEGORIAS QUE FIGURAN EN ESTE CUADRO.

NUMBER OF COUNTRIES AND TERRITORIES PRESENTED IN THIS TABLE: 86

NOMBRE DE PAYS ET DE TERRITOIRES PRESENTES DANS CE TABLEAU: 86

NUMERO DE PAISES Y DE TERRITORIOS PRESENTADOS EN ESTE CUADRO: 86

COUNTRY PAYS PAIS	REFERENCE YEAR ANNEE DE REFERENCE AÑO DE REFERENCIA	CURRENCY MONNAIE MONEDA	TOTAL TOTAL TOTAL (000)	TYPE OF EXPENDITURE / TYPE DE DEPENSES / TIPO DE GASTOS CAPITAL EN CAPITAL DE CAPITAL (000)	CURRENT / COURANTES / CORRIENTES TOTAL TOTAL TOTAL (000)	LABOUR COSTS DEPENSES DE PERSONNEL GASTOS DE PERSONAL (000)	OTHER CURRENT COSTS AUTRES DEPENSES COURANTES GASTOS CORRIENTES VARIOS (000)	CURRENT AS % OF TOTAL COURANTES EN % DU TOTAL CORRIENTES EN % DEL TOTAL
			(1)	(2)	(3)	(4)	(5)	(6)
AFRICA								
BURUNDI	1984	FRANC	405 561	77 657	327 904	...	...	80.9
CENTRAL AFRICAN REPUBLIC‡	1984	FRANC C.F.A.	680 791	...	...	...	...	...
CONGO‡	1984	FRANC C.F.A.	25 530	14 263	11 267	...	...	44.1
EGYPT‡	1982	POUND	40 378	6 136	34 242	28 055	6 187	84.8
LIBYAN ARAB JAMAHIRIYA	1980	DINAR	22 875	...	...	...	...	...
MADAGASCAR‡	1980	FRANC	1 391 879	...	...	...	...	...
MALAWI‡	1977	KWACHA	1 290	282	1 008	357	451	78.1
MAURITIUS	1984	RUPEE	38 700	7 700	31 000	...	...	80.1
NIGER‡	1976	FRANC C.F.A.	141 703	–	141 703	103 653	38 050	100.0
NIGERIA‡	1977	NAIRA	*102 000	*64 000	*38 000	...	...	*37.3
SENEGAL‡	1976	FRANC C.F.A.	4 485 000	...	...	...	...	...
SEYCHELLES‡	1983	RUPEE	12 854	6 771	6 083	...	...	47.3
SUDAN	1978	POUND	5 115	821	4 294	913	3 381	83.9
AMERICA, NORTH								
BRITISH VIRGIN ISLANDS	1984	U.S. DOLLAR	–	–	–	–	–	–
CANADA‡	1983	DOLLAR	5 365 000	...	...	...	...	...
COSTA RICA	1982	COLON	81 333	...	...	...	...	...
CUBA‡	1984	PESO	164 202	32 401	131 801	...	...	80.3
EL SALVADOR‡	1984	COLON	97 009	...	...	...	...	...
GUATEMALA	1983	QUETZAL	44 797	...	...	...	...	...
PANAMA	1975	BALBOA	3 296	...	...	...	...	...
ST. LUCIA	1979	E.C. DOLLAR	77	–	77	...	...	100.0
ST. PIERRE AND MIQUELON	1984	FR. FRANC	*2 719	*672	*2 047	...	...	*75.3
TURKS AND CAICOS ISLANDS	1984	U.S. DOLLAR	–	–	–	–	–	–
UNITED STATES‡	1983	DOLLAR	...	...	86 204 900	...	...	...

COUNTRY PAYS PAIS	REFERENCE YEAR ANNEE DE REFERENCE AÑO DE REFERENCIA	CURRENCY MONNAIE MONEDA	TOTAL TOTAL TOTAL (000)	TYPE OF EXPENDITURE / TYPE DE DEPENSES / TIPO DE GASTOS CAPITAL EN CAPITAL DE CAPITAL (000)	CURRENT / COURANTES / CORRIENTES TOTAL TOTAL TOTAL (000)	LABOUR COSTS DEPENSES DE PERSONNEL GASTOS DE PERSONAL (000)	OTHER CURRENT COSTS AUTRES DEPENSES COURANTES GASTOS CORRIENTES VARIOS (000)	CURRENT AS % OF TOTAL COURANTES EN % DU TOTAL CORRIENTES EN % DEL TOTAL
			(1)	(2)	(3)	(4)	(5)	(6)
AMERICA, SOUTH								
ARGENTINA‡	1981	PESO	2 321 932					
BRAZIL	1982	CRUZEIRO	*305 500 000	...	...	...	...	...
CHILE	1980	PESO	4 665 400	992 700	3 672 700	...	...	78.7
COLOMBIA‡	1982	PESO	2 754 273	...	...	...	...	...
ECUADOR‡	1979	SUCRE	856 090	280 915	575 175	380 012	195 163	67.2
GUYANA‡	1982	DOLLAR	2 800	...	...	...	...	...
PERU‡	1984	SOL	159 024 000	...	...	...	...	...
VENEZUELA‡	1984	BOLIVAR	1 361 640	...	...	...	...	...
ASIA								
BRUNEI DARUSSALAM‡	1984	DOLLAR	10 880	2 660	8 220	3 840	4 380	75.6
CYPRUS‡	1984	POUND	1 173	...		...	...	...
INDIA	1982	RUPEE	*11 586 360	*3 823 500	*7 762 860	...	...	*67.0
INDONESIA‡	1983	RUPIAH	270 313 000	35 146 000	235 167 000	...	...	87.0
IRAN, ISLAMIC REPUBLIC OF‡	1984	RIAL	21 527 000	9 943 000	11 584 000	...	...	53.8
ISRAEL‡	1978	POUND	6 154 300	211 300	5 943 000	...	...	96.6
JAPAN‡	1983	YEN	7 180 782	1 226 855	5 953 927	3 373 051	2 580 876	82.9
JORDAN‡	1979	DINAR	*7 565	*3 917	*3 647	...	...	*48.2
KOREA, REPUBLIC OF‡	1983	WON	621 749 314	223 171 955	398 577 359	212 376 732	186 200 627	64.1
KUWAIT‡	1984	DINAR	71 163	8 147	63 016	...	...	88.6
LEBANON‡	1980	POUND	22 000	...	...	...	...	...
MALDIVES	1979	RUFIYAA	–		–	–		–
PAKISTAN‡	1979	RUPEE	391 059	192 556	198 503			50.8
PHILIPPINES‡	1982	PESO	*522 970	*52 469	*470 501	*263 250	*197 650	*90.0
QATAR‡	1984	RIYAL	12 300	9 500	2 800	...	...	22.8
SINGAPORE‡	1981	DOLLAR	81 900	22 600	59 300	...	...	72.4
SRI LANKA	1983	RUPEE	206 528	96 629	109 899	...	...	53.2
TURKEY‡	1983	LIRA	27 220 500	11 161 300	16 054 000	10 148 200	5 905 800	59.0
VIET-NAM	1979	DONG	108 300	39 500	68 800	...	...	63.5
EUROPE								
AUSTRIA	1981	SCHILLING	12 331 026	2 129 499	10 201 527	6 436 529	3 764 998	82.7
BELGIUM	1977	FRANC	38 894 080	3 976 863	34 917 217	...	...	89.8
BULGARIA	1984	LEV	696 900	92 700	604 200	...	...	86.7
CZECHOSLOVAKIA‡	1984	KORUNA	19 875 000	2 407 000	17 468 000	...	...	87.9
DENMARK	1983	KRONE	5 970 400	802 400	5 168 000	...	...	86.6
FINLAND	1984	MARKKA	4 381 000	...	...	...	...	...
FRANCE	1979	FRANC	44 123 000	3 854 000	40 269 000	...	...	91.3
GERMAN DEMOCRATIC REPUBLIC‡	1984	DDR MARK	*8 750 000	...	...	...	...	...
GERMANY, FEDERAL REPUBLIC OF‡	1981	D. MARK	38 352 000	4 382 000	33 520 000	22 549 000	10 971 000	88.4
GREECE‡	1983	DRACHMA	6 067 000	...	...	...	...	...
HUNGARY	1984	FORINT	22 686 000	3 137 000	19 549 000	...	...	86.2
ICELAND	1979	KRONA	6 427 500	764 500	5 663 000	3 704 400	1 958 600	88.1
IRELAND	1982	POUND	97 582	12 095	85 487	54 837	30 650	87.6
ITALY‡	1983	LIRA	6 027 005	1 027 088	4 999 917	2 888 074	2 111 843	83.0
MALTA‡	1984	LIRA	10	1	9	...	...	90.0
NETHERLANDS‡	1983	GUILDER	7 699 000	470 000	7 029 000	...	...	91.3
NORWAY	1982	KRONE	4 952 500	479 400	4 473 100	...	...	90.3
POLAND‡	1984	ZLOTY	73 728 300	*10 000 000	*63 700 000	...	...	*86.4
PORTUGAL	1982	ESCUDO	6 541 200	1 170 600	5 370 600	4 102 500	1 268 100	82.1
SAN MARINO	1982	LIRA	–	–	–	–	–	–
SPAIN	1983	PESETA	100 697 093	17 376 947	83 320 146	64 028 225	19 291 921	82.7
SWEDEN‡	1983	KRONA	18 189 000	1 714 000	16 475 000	...	...	90.6
SWITZERLAND	1983	FRANC	...		4 643 000	...	...	...
UNITED KINGDOM‡	1981	POUND STG.	5 921 000	...	...	...	...	...
YUGOSLAVIA‡	1981	DINAR	18 235 000	...	...	...	...	...

COUNTRY / PAYS / PAIS	REFERENCE YEAR / ANNEE DE REFERENCE / AÑO DE REFERENCIA	CURRENCY / MONNAIE / MONEDA	TOTAL / TOTAL / TOTAL (000)	TYPE OF EXPENDITURE / TYPE DE DEPENSES / TIPO DE GASTOS: CAPITAL / EN CAPITAL / DE CAPITAL (000)	CURRENT / COURANTES / CORRIENTES: TOTAL / TOTAL / TOTAL (000)	LABOUR COSTS / DEPENSES DE PERSONNEL / GASTOS DE PERSONAL (000)	OTHER CURRENT COSTS / AUTRES DEPENSES COURANTES / GASTOS CORRIENTES VARIOS (000)	CURRENT AS % OF TOTAL / COURANTES EN % DU TOTAL / CORRIENTES EN % DEL TOTAL
			(1)	(2)	(3)	(4)	(5)	(6)
OCEANIA								
AUSTRALIA	1981	DOLLAR	1 522 247	190 456	1 331 791	1 014 972	316 819	87.5
FRENCH POLYNESIA‡	1983	FRANC C.F.P.	324 720	16 280	308 440	253 750	54 690	95.0
GUAM‡	1979	U.S. DOLLAR	1 256	...		...	...	
NEW CALEDONIA	1983	FRANC C.F.P.	83 000	27 200	55 800	...	...	67.2
NEW ZEALAND	1979	DOLLAR	175 373	17 605	157 768	...	...	90.0
PACIFIC ISLANDS	1979	U.S. DOLLAR	185	–	185	...	...	100.0
SAMOA	1978	TALA	2 500	2 000	500	...	...	20.0
TONGA‡	1980	PA'ANGA	426	147	279	237	42	65.5
VANUATU	1975	FRANC	21 603	–	21 603	12 480	9 123	100.0
U.S.S.R.								
U.S.S.R.‡	1984	ROUBLE	27 600 000	...	...	...	...	...

AFRICA:

Central African Republic:

E--> Not including data for the general service sector.

FR-> Non compris les données pour le secteur de service général.

ESP> Excluídos los datos relativos al sector de servicio general.

Congo:

E--> Not including military and defence R&D.

FR-> Non compris les activités de R-D de caractère militaire ou relevant de la défense nationale.

ESP> Excluídas las actividades militares y de defensa de I y D.

Egypt:

E--> Not including military and defence R&D.

FR-> Non compris les activités de R-D de caractère militaire ou relevant de la défense nationale.

ESP> Excluídas las actividades militares y de defensa de I y D.

Madagascar:

E--> Data relate to 4 research institutes only.

FR-> Les données ne concernent que 4 instituts de recherche.

ESP> Los datos se refieren a 4 centros de investigación solamente.

Malawi:

E--> Data in column 3 include 200 thousand kwachas for which a distribution between labour and other current costs is not available.

FR-> Les données de la colonne 3 comprennent 200 milliers de kwachas dont la répartition entre dépenses de personnel et autres dépenses courantes n'est pas disponible.

ESP> Los datos de la columna 3 incluyen 200 millares de kwachas cuya repartición entre gastos de personal y gastos corrientes varios se desconoce.

Niger:

E--> Data relate to the higher education sector only.

FR-> Les données ne concernent que le secteur de l'enseignement supérieur.

ESP> Los datos se refieren al sector de enseñanza superior solamente.

Nigeria:

E--> Not including data for social sciences and humanities.

FR-> Non compris les données pour les sciences sociales et humaines.

ESP> Excluídos los datos relativos a las ciencias sociales y humanas.

Senegal:

E--> Labour costs represent 82% of the total expenditure shown in column 1.

FR-> Les dépenses de personnel représentent 82% des dépenses totales de la colonne 1.

ESP> Los gastos de personal representan 82% de los gastos totales de la columna 1.

Seychelles:

E--> Not including military and defence R&D.

FR-> Non compris les activités de R-D de caractère militaire ou relevant de la défense nationale.

ESP> Excluídas las actividades militares y de defensa de I y D.

AMERICA NORTH:

Canada:

Canada: (Cont):

E--> Not including social sciences and humanities in the productiv sector (integrated R&D).

FR-> Non compris les données pour les sciences sociales et humaine du secteur de la production (activités de R-D intégrées).

ESP> Excluídos los datos relativos a las ciencias sociales y humanas d sector productivo (actividades de I y D integradas).

Cuba:

E--> Not including military and defence R&D.

FR-> Non compris les activités de R-D de caractère miitaire ou relevar de la défense nationale.

ESP> Excluídas las actividades militares y de defensa de I y D.

El Salvador:

E--> Data refer to funds originating from public sources.

FR-> Les données se réfèrent aux fonds provenant des source publiques.

ESP> Los datos se refieren a los fondos procedentes de fuente públicos.

United States:

E--> Not including data for law, humanities and education.

FR-> Non compris les données pour le droit, les sciences humaines e l'éducation.

ESP> Excluídos los datos relativos al derecho, las ciencias humanas la educación.

AMERICA SOUTH:

Argentina:

E--> Figures in millions.

FR-> Chiffres en millions.

ESP> Cifras en millones.

Colombia:

E--> Not including data for the productive sector (non-integrate R&D).

FR-> Non compris les données pour le secteur de la productio (activités de R-D non intégrées).

ESP> Excluídos los datos relativos al sector productivo (actividades d I y D no integradas).

Ecuador:

E--> Data also include expenditure for scientific and technologica services (STS).

FR-> Les données comprennent en plus les dépenses relatives au services scientifiques et techniques (SST).

ESP> Los datos también incluyen los gastos relativos a las servicio científicos y tecnológicos (SCT).

Guyana:

E--> Not including military and defence R&D. Data for the genera service sector and for medical sciences in the higher education sector ar also excluded.

FR-> Non compris les activités de R-D de caractère militaire o relevant de la défense nationale. Les données relatives au secteur de servic général et les sciences médicales du secteur de l'enseignement supérieu sont aussi exclues.

ESP> Excluídas las actividades militares y de defensa de I y D. S excluyen también los datos relativos al sector de servicio general y la

Guyana: (Cont):
ciencias médicas al sector de enseñanza superior.
Peru:
E--> Data refer to the budget allotment for science and technology.
FR-> Les données se réfèrent aux crédits budgétaires relatifs à la science et à la technologie.
ESP> Los datos se refieren a las consignaciones presupuestarias relativas a la ciencia y la tecnología.
Venezuela:
E--> Data relate to government expenditure only and do not include military and defence R&D.
FR-> Les données ne concernent que les dépenses du gouvernement et ne comprennent pas les activités de R-D de caractère militaire ou relevant de la défense nationale.
ESP> Los datos se refieren a los gastos del gobierno solamente y excluyen las actividades militares y de defensa de I y D.
ASIA:
Brunei Darussalam:
E--> Data relate to 2 research institutes only.
FR-> Les données se réfèrent à 2 instituts de recherche seulement.
ESP> Los datos se refieren a 2 centros de investigación solamente.
Cyprus:
E--> Not including data for the productive sector.
FR-> Non compris les données pour le secteur de la production.
ESP> Excluídos los datos relativos al sector productivo.
Indonesia:
E--> Data relate to government expenditure only and do not include the productive sector.
FR-> Les données ne concernent que les dépenses du gouvernenent et ne comprennent pas le secteur de la production.
ESP> Los datos se refieren a los gastos del gobierno solamente y excluyen el sector productivo.
Iran, Islamic Republic of:
E--> Data refer to the budget allotment.
FR-> Les données se réfèrent aux crédits budgétaires.
ESP> Los datos se refieren a las consignaciones presupuestarias.
Israel:
E--> Data refer to expenditure in the fields of natural sciences and engineering only.
FR-> Les données se réfèrent aux dépenses dans les domaines des sciences exactes et naturelles et des sciences de l'ingénieur seulement.
ESP> Los datos sólo se refieren a los gastos relativos a las ciencias exactas y naturales y a la ingeniería.
Japan:
E--> Figures in millions. Not including data for social sciences and humanities in the productive sector.
FR-> Chiffres en millions. Non compris les données pour les sciences sociales et humaines dans le secteur de la production.
ESP> Cifras en millones. Excluídos los datos relativos a las ciencias sociales y humanas del sector productivo.
Jordan:
E--> Not including military and defence R&D.
FR-> Non compris les activités de R-D de caractère militaire ou relevant de la défense nationale.
ESP> Excluídas las actividades militares y de defensa de I y D.
Korea, Republic of:
E--> Not including military and defence R&D and social sciences and humanities.
FR-> Non compris les activités de R-D de caractère militaire ou relevant de la défense nationale ni les sciences sociales et humaines.
ESP> Excluídas las actividades militares y de defensa de I y D y las ciencias sociales y humanas.
Kuwait:
E--> Data refer to scientific and technological activities (STA).
FR-> Les données se réfèrent aux activités scientifiques et technologiques (AST).
ESP> Los datos se refieren a las actividades científicas y tecnológicas (ACT).
Lebanon:
E--> Data refer to the Faculty of Science at the University of the Lebanon only.
FR-> Les données ne se réfèrent qu'à la Faculté des Sciences de l'Université du Liban.
ESP> Los datos se refieren a la Facultad de Ciencias de la Universidad del Líbano solamente.
Pakistan:
E--> Data relate to R&D activities concentrated mainly in government-financed research establishments only; social sciences and humanities in the higher education and general service sectors are excluded. Not including the productive sector (integrated R&D) or military and defence R&D.
FR-> Les données se réfèrent aux activités de R-D se trouvant pour la plupart dans les établissements de recherche financés par le gouvernement; les sciences sociales et humaines dans les secteurs de l'enseignement supérieur et de service général sont exclues. Compte non tenu du secteur de la production (activités de R-D intégrées) ni des activités de R-D de caractère militaire ou relevant de la défense nationale.
ESP> Los datos se refieren a las actividades de I y D concentradas

Pakistan: (Cont):
principalmente en los establecimientos de investigación subvencionados por el gobierno; se excluyen las ciencias sociales y humanas de los sectores de enseñanza superior y de servicio general. Excluídos el sector productivo (actividades de I y D integradas) y las actividades militares y de defensa de I y D.
Philippines:
E--> The figure in column 3 does not include 9,601 thousand pesos for which a distribution between labour and other current costs is not available.
FR-> Le chiffre de la colonne 3 ne comprend pas 9 601 milliers de pesos dont la répartition entre dépenses de personnel et autres dépenses courantes n'est pas disponible.
ESP> La cifra de la columna 3 excluye 9 601 millares de pesos cuya repartición entre gastos de personal y gastos corrientes varios se desconoce.
Qatar:
E--> Not including data for the higher education sector.
FR-> Non compris les données pour le secteur de l'enseignement supérieur.
ESP> Excluídos los datos relativos al sector de enseñanza superior.
Singapore:
E--> Not including either military and defence R&D or social science and humanities.
FR-> Non compris les activités de R-D de caractère militaire ou relevant de la défense nationale ni les sciences sociales et humaines.
ESP> Excluídas las actividades militares y de defensa de I y D y las ciencias sociales y humanas.
Turkey:
E--> Data in column 1 include 5.2 million lira for which a distribution by type of expenditure is not available; this figure has been excluded from the percentage distribution in column 6. Not including data for social sciences and humanities in the general service sector.
FR-> Les données de la colonne 1 comprennent 5.2 millions de livres dont la répartition par type de dépenses n'est pas disponible; on n'a pas tenu compte de ce chiffre pour calculer le pourcentage de la colonne 6. Non compris les données pour les sciences sociales et humaines du secteur de service général.
ESP> Los datos de la columna 1 incluyen 5.2 millones de liras cuya repartición por tipo de gastos se desconoce; esta cifra no se ha tenido en cuenta para calcular el porcentaje de la columna 6. No se incluyen las ciencias sociales y humanas del sector de servicio general.
EUROPE:
Czechoslovakia:
E--> Of military R&D only that part carried out in civil establishments is included.
FR-> Pour la R-D de caractère militaire, seule la partie effectuée dans les établissements civils a été considérée.
ESP> Para las actividades de I y D de carácter militar sólo se ha considerado la parte correspondiente a los establecimientos civiles.
German Democratic Republic:
E--> Data refer to 'expenditure for science and technology'.
FR-> Les données se réfèrent aux 'dépenses relatives à la science et à la technologie'.
ESP> Los datos se refieren a los 'gastos relativos a la ciencia y la tecnología'.
Germany, Federal Republic of:
E--> Data in column 1 include 450 million Deutsche marks for which a distribution by type of expenditure is not available; this figure has been excluded from the percentage distribution in column 6. Not including data for social sciences and humanities in the productive sector.
FR-> Les données de la colonne 1 comprennent 450 millions de deutsche marks dont la répartition par type de dépenses n'est pas disponible; on n'a pas tenu compte de ce chiffre pour calculer le pourcentage de la colonne 6. Non compris les sciences sociales et humaines dans le secteur de la production.
ESP> Los datos de la columna 1 incluyen 450 millones de marcos cuya repartición por tipo de gastos se deconoce; esta cifra no se ha tenido en cuenta para calcular el porcentaje de la columna 6. No se incluyen las ciencias sociales y humanas del sector productivo.
Greece:
E--> Data relate to government activities only.
FR-> Les données se réfèrent aux activités gouvernementales seulement.
ESP> Los datos se refieren a las actividades gubernamentales solamente.
Italy:
E--> Figures in millions.
FR-> Chiffres en millions.
ESP> Cifras en millones.
Malta:
E--> Data relate to the higher education sector only.
FR-> Les données ne concernent que le secteur de l'enseignement supérieur.
ESP> Los datos se refieren al sector de enseñanza superior solamente.
Netherlands:
E--> Not including data for social sciences and humanities in the

Netherlands: (Cont):
productive sector (integrated R&D).

FR-> Non compris les données pour les sciences sociales et humaines du secteur de la production (activités de R-D intégrées).

ESP> Excluídos los datos relativos a las ciencias sociales y humanas del sector productivo (actividades de I y D integradas).

Poland:

E--> Not including military and defence R&D.

FR-> Non compris les activités de R-D de caractère militaire ou relevant de la défense nationale.

ESP> Excluídas las actividades militares y de defensa de I y D.

Sweden:

E--> Not including data for social sciences and humanities in the productive and general service sectors.

FR-> Non compris les données pour les sciences sociales et humaines dans les secteurs de la production et de service général.

ESP> No se incluyen los datos relativos a las ciencias sociales y humanas en los sectores productivo y de servicio general.

United Kingdom:

E--> Not including data either for social sciences and humanities or funds for R&D performed abroad.

FR-> Non compris les sciences sociales et humaines ni les fonds de R-D exécutés à l'étranger.

ESP> Excluídos las ciencias sociales y humanas y los fondos de I y D que se executan en el extranjero.

Yugoslavia:

E--> Data refer to total revenue rather than total expenditure. Not including military and defence R&D.

Yugoslavia: (Cont):

FR-> Les données se réfèrent au total des revenus au lieu des dépenses totales. Non compris les activités de R-D de caractère militaire ou relevant de la défense nationale.

ESP> Los datos se refieren a los ingresos totales en lugar de los gastos totales. Excluídas las actividades militares y de defensa de I y D.

OCEANIA:

French Polynesia:

E--> Data relate to one research institute only.

FR-> Les données ne concernent qu'un institut de recherche.

ESP> Los datos se refieren a un centro de investigación solamente.

Guam:

E--> Data relate to the higher education sector only.

FR-> Les données ne concernent que le secteur de l'enseignement supérieur.

ESP> Los datos se refieren al sector de enseñanza superior solamente.

Tonga:

E--> Data relate to one research institute only.

FR-> Les données ne concernent qu'un centre de recherche.

ESP> Los datos se refieren a un centro de investigación solamente.

U.S.S.R.:

U.S.S.R.:

E--> *Expenditure on Science* from the national budget and other sources.

FR-> Montant total des sommes *dépensées pour la science* d'après le budget national et autres sources.

ESP> Importe total de los *gastos efectuados para la ciencia*, según el presupuesto nacional y otras fuentes.

5.10 Total expenditure for the performance of research and experimental development by source of funds

Dépenses totales consacrées à la recherche et au développement expérimental, selon la source de financement

Gastos totales dedicados a la investigación y al desarrollo experimental, según la fuente de financiación

PLEASE REFER TO INTRODUCTION FOR DEFINITIONS OF CATEGORIES INCLUDED IN THIS TABLE.

AMOUNTS SHOWN ARE IN THOUSANDS.

NUMBER OF COUNTRIES AND TERRITORIES PRESENTED IN THIS TABLE: 60

POUR LES DEFINITIONS DES CATEGORIES PRESENTEES DANS CE TABLEAU, SE REFERER A L'INTRODUCTION.

LES MONTANTS SONT EXPRIMES EN MILLIERS.

NOMBRE DE PAYS ET DE TERRITOIRES PRESENTES DANS CE TABLEAU: 60

EN LA INTRODUCCION SE DAN LAS DEFINICIONES DE LAS CATEGORIAS QUE FIGURAN EN ESTE CUADRO.

LOS IMPORTES ESTAN EXPRESADOS EN MILLARES.

NUMERO DE PAISES Y DE TERRITORIOS PRESENTADOS EN ESTE CUADRO: 60

COUNTRY / PAYS / PAIS	REFERENCE YEAR / ANNEE DE REFERENCE / AÑO DE REFERENCIA	CURRENCY / MONNAIE / MONEDA		ALL SOURCES OF FUNDS / TOUTES LES SOURCES DE FINANCEMENT / TODAS LAS FUENTES DE FINANCIACION (000)	SOURCE OF FUNDS / SOURCE DE FINANCEMENT / FUENTE DE FINANCIACION			
					GOVERNMENT FUNDS / FONDS PUBLICS / FONDOS PUBLICOS (000)	PRODUCTIVE ENTERPRISE FUNDS AND SPECIAL FUNDS / FONDS DES ENTREPRISES DE PRODUCTION ET FONDS SPECIAUX / FONDOS DE EMPRESAS DE PRODUCCION Y FONDOS ESPECIALES (000)	FOREIGN FUNDS / FONDS ETRANGERS / FONDOS EXTRANJEROS (000)	OTHER FUNDS / FONDS DIVERS / FONDOS VARIOS (000)
				(1)	(2)	(3)	(4)	(5)
AFRICA								
BURUNDI	1984	FRANC		405 561	213 478	–	156 181	35 902
			%	100	52.6	–	38.5	8.9
CENTRAL AFRICAN REPUBLIC‡	1984	FRANC C.F.A.		680 791	406 684	144 515	75 592	54 000
			%	100	59.7	21.2	11.1	7.9
CONGO‡	1984	FRANC C.F.A		25 530	17 575	6 500	1 455	–
			%	100	68.8	25.5	5.7	–
MAURITIUS	1984	RUPEE		38 700	16 000	600	1 500	20 600
			%	100	41.3	1.6	3.9	53.2
NIGER‡	1976	FRANC C.F.A.		141 703	141 703	–	–	–
			%	100	100.0	–	–	–
SEYCHELLES‡	1983	RUPEE		12 854	6 274	–	6 580	–
			%	100	48.8	–	51.2	–
SUDAN	1978	POUND		5 115	4 809	30	35	241
			%	100	94.0	0.6	0.7	4.7
AMERICA, NORTH								
CANADA‡	1983	DOLLAR		5 365 000	2 353 000	2 069 000	224 000	719 000
			%	100	43.9	38.6	4.2	13.4
CUBA‡	1984	PESO		164 202	158 212	–	5 990	–
			%	100	96.4	–	3.6	–

5.10 R&D expenditure by source of funds
Dépenses de R-D selon la source de financement
Gastos de I y D según la fuente de financiación

COUNTRY PAYS PAIS	REFERENCE YEAR ANNEE DE REFERENCE AÑO DE REFERENCIA	CURRENCY MONNAIE MONEDA	ALL SOURCES OF FUNDS TOUTES LES SOURCES DE FINANCEMENT TODAS LAS FUENTES DE FINANCIACION (000)	SOURCE OF FUNDS / SOURCE DE FINANCEMENT / FUENTE DE FINANCIACION GOVERNMENT FUNDS FONDS PUBLICS FONDOS PUBLICOS (000)	PRODUCTIVE ENTERPRISE FUNDS AND SPECIAL FUNDS FONDS DES ENTREPRISES DE PRODUCTION ET FONDS SPECIAUX FONDOS DE EMPRESAS DE PRODUCCION Y FONDOS ESPECIALES (000)	FOREIGN FUNDS FONDS ETRANGERS FONDOS EXTRANJEROS (000)	OTHER FUNDS FONDS DIVERS FONDOS VARIOS (000)
			(1)	(2)	(3)	(4)	(5)
EL SALVADOR‡	1980	COLON	202 694	115 242	–	87 452	–
			% 100	56.9	–	43.1	–
PANAMA	1975	BALBOA	3 296	1 764	330	942	260
			% 100	53.5	10.0	28.6	7.9
ST. LUCIA	1979	E. CARIBBEAN DOLLAR	77	77	–	–	–
			% 100	100.0	–	–	–
ST. PIERRE AND MIQUELON	1984	FRENCH FRANC	*2 719	*2 719	–	–	–
			% 100	*100.0	–	–	–
UNITED STATES‡	1983	DOLLAR	86 204 600	40 433 200	42 784 000	–	2 987 400
			% 100	46.9	49.6	–	3.5
AMERICA, SOUTH							
ARGENTINA‡	1981	PESO	2 321 932	2 200 591	——>	33 521	87 820
			% 100	94.8	——>	1.4	3.8
BRAZIL	1982	CRUZEIRO	*305 500 000	*204 300 000	*60 500 000	16 100 000	24 600 000
			% 100	*66.9	*19.8	*5.3	*8.1
COLOMBIA‡	1978	PESO	735 783	529 043	434	70 106	136 200
			% 100	71.9	0.1	9.5	18.5
ECUADOR‡	1979	SUCRE	856 090	590 704	46 314	133 892	85 180
			% 100	69.0	5.4	15.6	10.0
PERU ‡	1984	SOL	159 024 000	76 289 000	43 255 000	33 367 000	6 113 000
			% 100	48.0	27.2	21.0	3.8
ASIA							
CYPRUS‡	1984	POUND	1 173	1 159	–	14	–
			% 100	98.8	–	1.2	–
INDIA	1982	RUPEE	*11 586 360	*9 972 560	*1 613 800	–	–
			% 100	*86.1	*13.9	–	–
ISRAEL‡	1978	POUND	6 154 300	3 887 500	1 783 600	./.	483 300
			% 100	63.2	29.0	./.	7.9
JAPAN‡	1983	YEN	7 180 782	1 721 433	5 451 130	8 220	–
			% 100	24.0	75.9	0.1	–
JORDAN‡	1979	DINAR	*7 565	*4 516	*1 556	*1 493	–
			% 100	*59.7	*20.6	*19.7	–
KOREA, REPUBLIC OF‡	1983	WON	621 749 314	169 554 309	451 046 817	1 148 188	–
			% 100	27.3	72.5	0.2	–
KUWAIT‡	1984	DINAR	71 163	24 437	45 736	–	990
			% 100	34.3	64.3	–	1.4
PAKISTAN‡	1979	RUPEE	391 059	391 059	–	–	–
			% 100	100.0	–	–	–
PHILIPPINES	1982	PESO	*522 970	*401 846	*78 146	39 769	3 209
			% 100	*76.8	*14.9	*7.6	*.6
SINGAPORE‡	1978	DOLLAR	27 775	10 446	15 534	1 442	353
			% 100	37.6	55.9	5.2	1.3
SRI LANKA	1983	RUPEE	206 528	162 651	32 029	11 848	–
			% 100	78.8	15.5	5.7	–

COUNTRY PAYS PAIS	REFERENCE YEAR ANNEE DE REFERENCE AÑO DE REFERENCIA	CURRENCY MONNAIE MONEDA	ALL SOURCES OF FUNDS TOUTES LES SOURCES DE FINANCEMENT TODAS LAS FUENTES DE FINANCIACION (000)	SOURCE OF FUNDS / SOURCE DE FINANCEMENT / FUENTE DE FINANCIACION GOVERNMENT FUNDS FONDS PUBLICS FONDOS PUBLICOS (000)	PRODUCTIVE ENTERPRISE FUNDS AND SPECIAL FUNDS FONDS DES ENTREPRISES DE PRODUCTION ET FONDS SPECIAUX FONDOS DE EMPRESAS DE PRODUCCION Y FONDOS ESPECIALES (000)	FOREIGN FUNDS FONDS ETRANGERS FONDOS EXTRANJEROS (000)	OTHER FUNDS FONDS DIVERS FONDOS VARIOS (000)
			(1)	(2)	(3)	(4)	(5)
EUROPE							
AUSTRIA	1981	SCHILLING	12 331 026	5 779 297	6 194 909	304 959	51 861
			% 100	46.9	50.2	2.5	0.4
BELGIUM	1977	FRANC	38 894 080	13 509 945	24 405 896	345 634	632 605
			% 100	34.7	62.8	0.9	1.6
BULGARIA	1984	LEV	696 900	256 800	440 100	–	–
			% 100	36.8	63.2	–	–
CZECHOSLOVAKIA‡	1984	KORUNA	19 875 000	7 991 000	11 884 000	–	–
			% 100	40.2	59.8	–	–
DENMARK	1983	KRONE	5 970 400	2 976 500	2 777 400	124 000	92 500
			% 100	49.9	46.5	2.1	1.5
FINLAND	1983	MARKKA	3 626 730	1 532 970	2 015 730	33 990	44 040
			% 100	42.3	55.6	0.9	1.2
FRANCE	1979	FRANC	44 123 000	22 607 000	18 943 000	2 292 000	281 000
			% 100	51.2	42.9	5.2	0.6
GERMANY, FEDERAL REPUBLIC OF‡	1981	DEUTSCHE MARK	38 352 000	15 832 000	21 860 000	364 000	296 000
			% 100	41.3	57.0	0.9	0.8
HUNGARY	1984	FORINT	22 686 000	4 846 000	17 751 000	89 000	–
			% 100	21.4	78.2	0.4	–
ICELAND	1979	KRONA	6 427 500	4 863 900	1 165 900	307 200	90 500
			% 100	75.7	18.1	4.8	1.4
IRELAND	1982	POUND	97 582	55 104	36 803	4 638	1 037
			% 100	56.5	37.7	4.8	1.1
ITALY‡	1983	LIRA	4 602 225	1 775 908	2 677 245	149 072	–
			% 100	38.6	58.2	3.2	–
MALTA‡	1983	LIRA	10	10	–	–	–
			% 100	100.0	–	–	–
NETHERLANDS‡	1983	GUILDER	7 699 000	3 652 000	3 569 000	386 000	92 000
			% 100	47.4	46.4	5.0	1.2
NORWAY	1982	KRONE	4 952 500	2 651 900	2 061 000	125 300	114 300
			% 100	53.5	41.6	2.5	2.3
PORTUGAL	1982	ESCUDO	6 541 200	4 051 300	1 959 800	218 400	311 700
			% 100	61.9	30.0	3.3	4.8
SPAIN	1983	PESETA	100 697 093	49 899 583	49 477 440	1 234 095	85 975
			% 100	49.6	49.1	1.2	0.1
SWEDEN‡	1983	KRONA	18 189 000	7 144 000	10 739 000	271 000	35 000
			% 100	39.3	59.0	1.5	0.2
SWITZERLAND‡	1983	FRANC	4 643 000	1 015 000	3 628 000	–	–
			% 100	21.9	78.1	–	–
UNITED KINGDOM‡	1981	POUND STERLING	5 921 200	2 825 900	2 529 300	411 400	154 600
			% 100	47.7	42.7	6.9	2.6
YUGOSLAVIA‡	1981	DINAR	18 235 000	5 790 000	10 422 000	334 000	1 690 000
			% 100	31.8	57.2	1.8	9.3
OCEANIA							
AUSTRALIA	1981	DOLLAR	1 522 247	1 154 266	319 496	16 055	32 430
			% 100	75.8	21.0	1.1	2.1

COUNTRY / PAYS / PAIS	REFERENCE YEAR / ANNEE DE REFERENCE / AÑO DE REFERENCIA	CURRENCY / MONNAIE / MONEDA		ALL SOURCES OF FUNDS / TOUTES LES SOURCES DE FINANCEMENT / TODAS LAS FUENTES DE FINANCIACION (000)	SOURCE OF FUNDS / SOURCE DE FINANCEMENT / FUENTE DE FINANCIACION: GOVERNMENT FUNDS / FONDS PUBLICS / FONDOS PUBLICOS (000)	PRODUCTIVE ENTERPRISE FUNDS AND SPECIAL FUNDS / FONDS DES ENTREPRISES DE PRODUCTION ET FONDS SPECIAUX / FONDOS DE EMPRESAS DE PRODUCCION Y FONDOS ESPECIALES (000)	FOREIGN FUNDS / FONDS ETRANGERS / FONDOS EXTRANJEROS (000)	OTHER FUNDS / FONDS DIVERS / FONDOS VARIOS (000)
				(1)	(2)	(3)	(4)	(5)
FRENCH POLYNESIA‡	1983	FRANC C.F.P.		324 720	269 950	3 820	–	50 950
			%	100	83.1	1.2	–	15.7
GUAM‡	1979	UNITED STATES DOLLAR		1 256	615	–	–	641
			%	100	49.0	–	–	51.0
NEW CALEDONIA	1983	FRANC C.F.P.		83 000	61 500	21 500	–	–
			%	100	74.1	25.9	–	–
NEW ZEALAND	1975	DOLLAR		99 776	79 974	18 768	–	1 034
			%	100	80.2	18.8	–	1.0
PACIFIC ISLANDS	1979	UNITED STATES DOLLAR		185	185	–	–	–
			%	100	100.0	–	–	–
SAMOA	1978	TALA		2 500	1 500	500	200	300
			%	100	60.0	20.0	8.0	12.0
TONGA‡	1980	PA'ANGA		426	106	–	320	–
			%	100	24.9	–	75.1	–
VANUATU	1975	FRANC		21 603	19 941	1 662	–	–
			%	100	92.3	7.7	–	–

AFRICA:

Central African Republic:

E--> Not including data for the general service sector.

FR-> Non compris les données pour le secteur de service général.

ESP> Excluídos los datos relativos al sector de servicio general.

Congo:

E--> Not including military and defence R&D.

FR-> Non compris les activités de R-D de caractère militaire ou relevant de la défense nationale.

ESP> Excluídas las actividades militares y de defensa de I y D.

Niger:

E--> Data relate to the higher education sector only.

FR-> Les données ne concernent que le secteur de l'enseignement supérieur.

ESP> Los datos se refieren al sector de enseñanza superior solamente.

Seychelles:

E--> Not including military and defence R&D.

FR-> Non compris les activités de R-D de caractère militaire ou relevant de la défense nationale.

ESP> Excluídas las actividades militares y de defensa de I y D.

AMERICA, NORTH:

Canada:

E--> Not including data for social sciences and humanities in the productive sector (integrated R&D).

FR-> Non compris les données pour les sciences sociales et humaines dans le secteur de la production (activités de R-D intégrées).

ESP> Excluídos los datos relativos a las ciencias sociales y humanas del sector productivo (actividades de I y D integradas).

Cuba:

E--> Not including military and defence R&D.

FR-> Non compris les activités de R-D de caractère militaire ou relevant de la défense nationale.

ESP> Excluídas las actividades militares y de defensa de I y D.

El Salvador:

E--> Data refer to funds originating from public sources.

FR-> Les données se réfèrent aux fonds provenant des sources publiques.

ESP> Los datos se refieren a los fondos procedentes de fuentes públicas.

United States:

E--> Data refer to current expenditure only. Not including data for law, humanities and education.

FR-> Les données se réfèrent aux dépenses courantes seulement. N compris les données pour le droit, les sciences humaines et l'éducatio

ESP> Los datos se refieren a los gastos corrientes solamente. Excluíc los datos relativos al derecho, las ciencias humanas y la educación.

AMERICA, SOUTH:

Argentina:

E--> Figures in millions.

FR-> Chiffres en millions.

ESP> Cifras en millones.

Colombia:

E--> Not including data for private enterprises.

FR-> Non compris les données relatives aux entreprises privées.

ESP> Excluídos los datos relativos a las empresas privadas.

Ecuador:

E--> Data also include expenditure for scientific and technologi services (STS).

FR-> Les données comprennent en plus les dépenses relatives a services scientifiques et techniques (SST).

ESP> Los datos también incluyen los gastos relativos a los servic científicos y tecnológicos (SCT).

Peru:

E--> Data refer to the budget allotment for science and technolo

FR-> Les données se réfèrent aux crédits budgétaires relatifs à science et à la technologie.

ESP> Los datos se refieren a las consignaciones presupuestar relativas a la ciencia y la tecnología.

ASIA:

Cyprus:

E--> Not including data for the productive sector.

FR-> Non compris les données pour le secteur de la production.

ESP> Excluídos los datos relativos al sector productivo.

Israel:

E--> Data refer to expenditure in the fields of natural sciences a engineering only. Foreign funds (column 4) are included with different sources of funds.

FR-> Les données se réfèrent aux dépenses dans les domaines c sciences exactes et naturelles et des sciences de l'ingénieur seulement. L fonds étrangers (colonne 4) sont comptés avec les différentes sources financement.

ESP> Los datos sólo se refieren a los gastos relativos a las cienc

Israel: (Cont):
exactas y naturales y a la ingeniería. Los fondos extranjeros (columna 4) están incluídos en las diferentes fuentes de financiación.

Japan:
E--> Figures in millions. Not including data for social sciences and humanities in the productive sector.
FR-> Chiffres en millions. Non compris les données pour les sciences sociales et humaines dans le secteur de la production.
ESP> Cifras en millones. Excluídos los datos relativos a las ciencias sociales y humanas del sector productivo.

Jordan:
E--> Not including military and defence R&D.
FR-> Non compris les activités de R-D de caractère militaire ou relevant de la défense nationale.
ESP> Excluídas las actividades militares y de defensa de I y D.

Korea, Republic of:
E--> Not including military and defence R&D and social sciences and humanities.
FR-> Non compris les activités de R-D de caractère militaire ou relevant de la défense nationale et les sciences sociales et humaines.
ESP> Excluídas las actividades militares y de defensa de I y D y las ciencias sociales y humanas.

Kuwait:
E--> Data refer to scientific and technological activities (STA).
FR-> Les données se réfèrent aux activités scientifiques et techniques (AST).
ESP> Los datos se refieren a las actividades científicas y tecnologícas (ACT).

Pakistan:
E--> Data relate to R&D activities concentrated mainly in government-financed research establishments only; social sciences and humanities in the higher education and general service sectors are excluded. Not including the productive sector or military and defence R&D.
FR-> Les données se réfèrent aux activités de R-D se trouvant pour la plupart dans les établissements de recherche financés par le gouvernement; les sciences sociales et humaines dans les secteurs de l'enseignement supérieur et de service général sont exclues. Compte non tenu du secteur de la production (activités de R-D intégrées) ni les activités de R-D de caractère militaire ou relevant de la défense nationale.
ESP> Los datos se refieren a las actividades de I y D concentradas principalmente en los establecimientos de investigación subvencionados por el gobierno; se excluyen las ciencias sociales y humanas de los sectores de enseñanza superior y de servicio general. Excluídos el sector productivo (actividades de I y D integradas) y las actividades militares y de defensa de I y D.

Singapore:
E--> Not including military and defence R&D.
FR-> Non compris les activités de R-D de caractère militaire ou relevant de la défense nationale.
ESP> Excluídas las actividades militares y de defensa de I y D.

EUROPE:

Czechoslovakia:
E--> Of military R&D only that part carried out in civil establishments is included.
FR-> Pour la R-D de caractère militaire seule la partie effectuée dans les établissements civils a été considérée.
ESP> Para las actividades de I y D de carácter militar sólo se ha considerado la parte correspondiente a los establecimientos civiles.

Germany, Federal Republic of:
E--> Not including data for social sciences and humanities in the productive sector.
FR-> Non compris les données relatives aux sciences sociales et humaines dans le secteur de la production.
ESP> No incluye los datos relativos a las ciencias sociales y humanas del sector productivo.

Italy:
E--> Figures in millions. Data relate to the productive sector (integrated R&D) and the higher education sector only.
FR-> Chiffres en millions. Les données se réfèrent aux secteurs de la production (activités de R-D intégrées) et de l'enseignement supérieur seulement.
ESP> Cifras en millones. Los datos se refieren a los sectores productivos (actividades de IyD integradas) y de enseñanza superior solamente.

Malta:
E--> Data relate to the higher education sector only.
FR-> Les données ne concernent que le secteur de l'enseignement supérieur.
ESP> Los datos se refieren al sector de enseñanza superior solamente.

Netherlands:
E--> Not including data for social sciences and humanities in the productive sector (integrated R&D).
FR-> Non compris les données pour les sciences sociales et humaines du secteur de la production (activités de R-D intégrées).
ESP> Excluídos los datos relativos a las ciencias sociales y humanas del sector productivo (actividades de I y D integradas).

Sweden:
E--> Not including data for social sciences and humanities in the productive and general service sectors.
FR-> Non compris les données pour les sciences sociales et humaines dans les secteurs de la production et de service général.
ESP> Excluídos los datos relativos a las ciencias sociales y humanas en los sectores productivo y de servicio general.

Switzerland:
E--> Data refer to current expenditure only.
FR-> Les données ne concernent que les dépenses courantes.
ESP> Los datos sólo se refieren a los gastos corrientes.

United Kingdom:
E--> Not including either social sciences and humanities or funds for R&D performed abroad.
FR-> Non compris les sciences sociales et humaines ni les fonds de R-D exécuté à l'étranger.
ESP> Excluídas las ciencias sociales y humanas y los fondos de I y D que se ejecutan en el extranjero.

Yugoslavia:
E--> Data refer to total revenue rather than total expenditure. Not including military and defence R&D.
FR-> Les données se réfèrent au total des revenus au lieu des dépenses totales. Non compris les activités de R-D de caractère militaire ou relevant de la défense nationale.
ESP> Los datos se refieren a los ingresos totales en lugar de los gastos totales. Excluídas las actividades militares y de defensa de I y D.

OCEANIA:

French Polynesia:
E--> Data relate to one research institute only.
FR-> Les données ne concernent qu'un institut de recherche.
ESP> Los datos se refieren a un centro de investigación solamente.

Guam:
E--> Data relate to the higher education sector only.
FR-> Les données ne concernent que le secteur de l'enseignement supérieur.
ESP> Los datos se refieren al sector de enseñanza superior solamente.

Tonga:
E--> Data relate to one research institute only.
FR-> Les données ne concernent qu'un institut de recherche.
ESP> Los datos se refieren a un centro de investigación solamente.

5.11 Current expenditure for research and experimental development by type of R&D activity

Dépenses courantes consacrées à la recherche et au développement expérimental, par type d'activité de R-D

Gastos corrientes dedicados a la investigación y al desarrollo experimental, por tipo de actividad de I y D

PLEASE REFER TO INTRODUCTION FOR DEFINITIONS OF CATEGORIES INCLUDED IN THIS TABLE.

POUR LES DEFINITIONS DES CATEGORIES PRESENTEES DANS CE TABLEAU, SE REFERER A L'INTRODUCTION.

EN LA INTRODUCCION SE DAN LAS DEFINICIONES DE LAS CATEGORIAS QUE FIGURAN EN ESTE CUADRO.

AMOUNTS SHOWN ARE IN THOUSANDS.

LES MONTANTS SONT EXPRIMES EN MILLIERS.

LOS IMPORTES ESTAN EXPRESADOS EN MILLARES.

NUMBER OF COUNTRIES AND TERRITORIES PRESENTED IN THIS TABLE: 40

NOMBRE DE PAYS ET DE TERRITOIRES PRESENTES DANS CE TABLEAU: 40

NUMERO DE PAISES Y DE TERRITORIOS PRESENTADOS EN ESTE CUADRO: 40

COUNTRY / PAYS / PAIS	REFERENCE YEAR / ANNEE DE REFERENCE / AÑO DE REFERENCIA	CURRENCY / MONNAIE / MONEDA		CURRENT EXPENDITURE BY TYPE OF R&D ACTIVITY / DEPENSES COURANTES PAR TYPE D'ACTIVITE DE R–D / GASTOS CORRIENTES POR TIPO DE ACTIVIDAD DE I Y D			
				ALL TYPES OF R&D ACTIVITY / TOUTES LES ACTIVITES DE R–D / TODAS LAS ACTIVIDADES DE I Y D	FUNDAMENTAL RESEARCH / RECHERCHE FONDAMENTALE / INVESTIGACION FUNDAMENTAL	APPLIED RESEARCH / RECHERCHE APPLIQUEE / INVESTIGACION APLICADA	EXPERIMENTAL DEVELOPMENT / DEVELOPPEMENT EXPERIMENTAL / DESARROLLO EXPERIMENTAL
				(1)	(2)	(3)	(4)
AFRICA							
MALAWI	1977	KWACHA		1 008	272	694	42
			%	100	27.0	68.8	4.2
MAURITIUS	1977	RUPEE		12 700	–	11 200	1 500
			%	100	–	88.2	11.8
NIGER‡	1976	FRANC C.F.A.		141 703	141 703	–	–
			%	100	100.0	–	–
SEYCHELLES‡	1983	RUPEE		6 083	–	5 400	683
			%	100	–	88.8	11.2
SUDAN‡	1978	POUND		5 115	917	3 920	278
			%	100	17.9	76.6	5.4
AMERICA, NORTH							
CUBA‡	1983	PESO		106 476	17 036	81 987	7 453
			%	100	16.0	77.0	7.0
ST. PIERRE AND MIQUELON‡	1983	FRENCH FRANC		3 803	–	*2 697	*1 106
			%	100	–	*70.9	*29.1
UNITED STATES‡	1983	DOLLAR		86 204 600	10 787 900	21 949 700	53 467 000
			%	100	12.5	25.5	62.0
AMERICA, SOUTH							
ARGENTINA‡	1980	PESO		1 480 800	*377 300	*674 900	*428 600
			%	100	*25.5	*45.6	*28.9
VENEZUELA‡	1977	BOLIVAR		755 561	290 122	446 831	18 608
			%	100	38.4	59.1	2.5
ASIA							
ISRAEL‡	1975	POUND		803 000	387 000	416 000	——>
			%	100	48.2	51.8	——>
JAPAN‡	1983	YEN		6 478 369	944 858	1 642 246	3 891 265
			%	100	14.6	25.4	60.1

COUNTRY PAYS PAIS	REFERENCE YEAR ANNEE DE REFERENCE AÑO DE REFERENCIA	CURRENCY MONNAIE MONEDA		CURRENT EXPENDITURE BY TYPE OF R&D ACTIVITY / DEPENSES COURANTES PAR TYPE D'ACTIVITE DE R-D / GASTOS CORRIENTES POR TIPO DE ACTIVIDAD DE I Y D ALL TYPES OF R&D ACTIVITY TOUTES LES ACTIVITES DE R-D TODAS LAS ACTIVIDADES DE I Y D	FUNDAMENTAL RESEARCH RECHERCHE FONDAMENTALE INVESTIGACION FUNDAMENTAL	APPLIED RESEARCH RECHERCHE APPLIQUEE INVESTIGACION APLICADA	EXPERIMENTAL DEVELOPMENT DEVELOPPEMENT EXPERIMENTAL DESARROLLO EXPERIMENTAL
				(1)	(2)	(3)	(4)
KOREA, REPUBLIC OF‡	1981	WON		293 131 000	70 367 000	84 283 000	138 481 000
			%	100	24.0	28.8	47.2
KUWAIT‡	1977	DINAR		6 284	506	5 076	702
			%	100	8.1	80.8	11.2
PHILIPPINES‡	1975	PESO		176 930	33 499	126 984	16 447
			%	100	18.9	71.8	9.3
SINGAPORE‡	1981	DOLLAR		81 896	8 022	30 925	42 949
			%	100	9.8	37.8	52.4
EUROPE							
AUSTRIA‡	1981	SCHILLING		4 520 861	1 923 075	2 008 435	589 351
			%	100	42.5	44.4	13.0
BULGARIA	1983	LEV		603 200	80 000	523 200	——>
			%	100	13.3	86.7	——>
CZECHOSLOVAKIA‡	1983	KORUNA		17 111 000	2 101 000	15 010 000	——>
			%	100	12.3	87.7	——>
FRANCE‡	1979	FRANC		44 123 000	9 200 000	14 579 000	20 344 000
			%	100	20.9	33.0	46.1
GERMANY, FEDERAL REPUBLIC OF‡	1981	DEUTSCHE MARK		33 520 000	7 412 000	26 108 000	——>
			%	100	22.1	77.9	——>
HUNGARY‡	1983	FORINT		15 445 000	1 743 000	5 344 000	8 358 000
			%	100	11.3	34.6	54.1
ICELAND	1979	KRONA		5 663 000	1 399 000	2 865 300	1 398 700
			%	100	24.7	50.6	24.7
IRELAND	1982	POUND		85 487	10 351	39 790	35 346
			%	100	12.1	46.5	41.3
ITALY‡	1982	LIRA		4 108 706	649 670	1 605 388	1 853 648
			%	100	15.8	39.1	45.1
MALTA‡	1983	LIRA		10	–	10	–
			%	100	–	100.0	–
NETHERLANDS‡	1982	GUILDER		4 852 000	840 000	1 635 000	2 377 000
			%	100	17.3	33.7	49.0
NORWAY	1981	KRONE		3 812 300	667 300	1 463 000	1 682 000
			%	100	17.5	38.4	44.1
POLAND‡	1983	ZLOTY		50 435 900	8 507 500	16 820 200	25 108 200
			%	100	16.9	33.4	49.8
PORTUGAL	1976	ESCUDO		1 146 353	*156 142	*487 556	*502 655
			%	100	*13.6	*42.5	*43.8
SPAIN	1983	PESETA		83 320 146	16 514 878	38 321 577	28 483 691
			%	100	19.8	46.0	34.2
SWEDEN‡	1981	KRONA		12 240 000	3 016 000	2 131 000	7 093 000
			%	100	24.6	17.4	57.9
SWITZERLAND	1976	FRANC		3 212 000	*1 570 000	*1 549 000	*93 000
			%	100	*48.9	*48.2	*2.9
UNITED KINGDOM‡	1978	POUND STERLING		2 792 800	198 500	650 600	1 943 700
			%	100	7.1	23.3	69.6
OCEANIA							
AUSTRALIA‡	1981	DOLLAR		1 522 247	550 639	623 997	347 611
			%	100	36.2	41.0	22.8
FRENCH POLYNESIA‡	1983	FRANC C.F.P.		324 720	–	324 720	–
			%	100	–	100.0	–
NEW CALEDONIA‡	1983	FRANC C.F.P.		83 000	1 500	–	81 500
			%	100	1.8	–	98.2

5.11 Current expenditure by type of R&D activity
Dépenses courantes par type d'activité de R-D
Gastos corrientes por tipo de actividad de I y D

COUNTRY PAYS PAIS	REFERENCE YEAR ANNEE DE REFERENCE AÑO DE REFERENCIA	CURRENCY MONNAIE MONEDA		CURRENT EXPENDITURE BY TYPE OF R&D ACTIVITY / DEPENSES COURANTES PAR TYPE D'ACTIVITE DE R–D / GASTOS CORRIENTES POR TIPO DE ACTIVIDAD DE I Y D			
				ALL TYPES OF R&D ACTIVITY TOUTES LES ACTIVITES DE R–D TODAS LAS ACTIVIDADES DE I Y D	FUNDAMENTAL RESEARCH RECHERCHE FONDAMENTALE INVESTIGACION FUNDAMENTAL	APPLIED RESEARCH RECHERCHE APPLIQUEE INVESTIGACION APLICADA	EXPERIMENTAL DEVELOPMENT DEVELOPPEMENT EXPERIMENTAL DESARROLLO EXPERIMENTAL
				(1)	(2)	(3)	(4)
SAMOA	1977	TALA		341	62	49	230
			%	100	18.2	14.4	67.4
TONGA‡	1980	PA'ANGA		279	–	279	–
			%	100	–	100.0	–
VANUATU	1975	FRANC		21 603	–	21 603	–
			%	100	–	100.0	–

AFRICA:

Niger:

E--> Data refer to the higher education sector only.

FR-> Les données ne concernent que le secteur de l'enseignement supérieur.

ESP> Los datos sólo incluyen el sector de enseñanza superior.

Seychelles:

E--> Not including military and défence R&D.

FR-> Non compris les activités de R-D de caractère militaire ou relevant de la défense nationale.

ESP> Excluídas las actividades militares y de defensa de I y D.

Sudan:

E--> Data refer to total expenditure by type of R&D activity.

FR-> Les données correspondent aux dépenses totales réparties par type d'activité de R-D.

ESP> Los datos se refieren a los gastos totales repartidos por tipo de actividad de I y D.

AMERICA, NORTH:

Cuba:

E--> The total in column 1 does not include 9.4 million pesos for which a breakdown by type of R&D activity is not available. Not including military and defence R&D.

FR-> Le total de la colonne 1 ne comprend pas 9.4 millions de pesos dont la répartition par type d'activité de R-D n'est pas disponible. Non compris les activités de R-D de caractère militaire ou relevant de la défense nationale.

ESP> El total de la colonne 1 no incluye 9.4 millones de pesos dont la repartición por tipo de actividad de I y D se desconoce. Excluídas las actividades militares y de defensa de I y D.

St. Pierre et Miquelon:

E--> Data refer to total expenditure by type of R&D activity.

FR-> Les données correspondent aux dépenses totales réparties par type d'activité de R-D.

ESP> Los datos se refieren a los gastos totales repartidos por tipo de actividad de I y D.

United States:

E--> Not including data for law, humanities and education.

FR-> Non compris les données pour le droit, les sciences humaines et l'éducation.

ESP> Excluídos los datos relativos al derecho, las ciencias humanas y la educación.

AMERICA, SOUTH:

Argentina:

E--> Figures in millions. Data refer to total expenditure by type of R&D activity.

FR-> Chiffres en millions. Les données correspondent aux dépenses totales réparties par type d'activité de R-D.

ESP> Cifras en millones. Los datos se refieren a los gastos totales repartidos por tipo de actividad de I y D.

Venezuela:

E--> Data concern 167 institutes out of a total of 406 which perform R&D.

FR-> Les données ne concernent que 167 instituts sur un total de 406 qui exécutent des activités de R-D.

ESP> Los datos sólo se refieren a 167 centros sobre un total de 406 que ejecutan actividades de I y D.

ASIA:

Israel:

E--> Data refer to the civilian sector only and do not include social sciences and humanities.

FR-> Les données ne concernent que le secteur civil et ne comprennent pas les sciences sociales et humaines.

ESP> Los datos sólo se refieren al sector civil y no incluyen las ciencias sociales y humanas.

Japan:

E--> Figures in millions. Data refer to total expenditure by type of R& activity and do not include social sciences and humanities.

FR-> Chiffres en millions. Les données correspondent aux dépen totales réparties par type d'activité de R-D et ne comprennent pas sciences sociales et humaines.

ESP> Cifras en millones. Los datos se refieren a los gastos tota repartidos por tipo de actividad de I y D y no incluyen las ciencias socia y humanas.

Korea, Republic of:

E--> Data refer to total expenditure by type of R&D activity. N including military and defence R&D and social sciences and humaniti

FR-> Les données correspondent aux dépenses totales réparties type d'activité de R-D. Non compris les activités de R-D de caract militaire ou relevant de la défense nationale ni les sciences sociales humaines.

ESP> Los datos se refieren a los gastos totales repartidos por ti de actividad de I y D. Excluídas las actividades militares y de defensa I y D y las ciencias sociales y humanas.

Kuwait:

E--> Data relate to total expenditure by type of R&D activity.

FR-> Les données correspondent aux dépenses totales réparties type d'activité de R-D.

ESP> Los datos se refieren a los gastos totales repartidos por tipo actividad de I y D.

Philippines:

E--> Data relate to total expenditure by type of R&D activity in general service sector only.

FR-> Les données correspondent aux dépenses totales réparties type d'activité de R-D dans le secteur de service général seulement.

ESP> Los datos se refieren a los gastos totales repartidos por t de actividad de I y D en el sector de servicio general solamente.

Singapore:

E--> Data relate to total expenditure by type of R&D activity and not include military and defence R&D.

FR-> Les données correspondent aux dépenses totales réparties type d'activité de R-D et ne comprennent pas les activités de R-D caractère militaire ou relevant de la défense nationale.

ESP> Los datos se refieren a los gastos totales repartidos por tipo actividad de I y D y excluyen las actividades militares y de defensa I y D.

EUROPE:

Austria:

E--> Not including data for the productive sector (integrated R&D) r the relevant part of 375.9 million schillings for which a breakdown betwe current and capital expenditure is not known.

FR-> Non compris les données pour le secteur de la product (activités de R-D intégrées) ni la partie de la somme de 375.9 millions schillings dont la ventilation entre dépenses courantes et dépenses capital n'a pas été précisée.

ESP> Excluídos los datos relativos al sector productivo (actividades I y D integradas) y la parte correspondiente de la suma de 375.9 millor de chelinas cuya repartición entre gastos corrientes y gastos en capital se ha precisado.

Czechoslovakia:

E--> Of military R&D only that part carried out in c establishments is included.

FR-> Pour la R-D de caractère militaire, seule la partie effectuée da les établissements civils a été considérée.

ESP> Para las actividades de I y D de carácter militar sólo se considerado la parte correspondiente a los establecimientos civiles.

France:

E--> Data refer to total expenditure by type of R&D activity.

FR-> Les données correspondent aux dépenses totales réparties type d'activité de R-D.

France: (Cont):

ESP> Los datos se refieren a los gastos totales repartidos por tipo de actividad de I y D.

Germany, Federal Republic of:

E--> Not including the relevant part of 450 million Deutsche marks for which a breakdown between current and capital expenditure is not known. Not including social sciences and humanities in the productive sector.

FR-> Non compris la partie de la somme de 450 millions de deutsche marks dont la ventilation entre dépenses courantes et dépenses en capital n'a pas été précisée. Non compris les sciences sociales et humaines dans le secteur de la production.

ESP> Excluída la parte correspondiente de la suma de 450 millones de marcos cuya repartición entre gastos corrientes y gastos en capital no se ha precisado. No se incluyen las ciencias sociales y humanas del sector productivo.

Hungary:

E--> The total in column 1 does not include 2,316 million forints for which a breakdown by type of R&D activity is not available.

FR-> Le total de la colonne 1 ne comprend pas 2 316 millions de forints dont la répartition par type d'activité de R-D n'est pas disponible.

ESP> El total de la columna 1 no incluye 2 316 millones de forints, cuya repartición por tipo de actividad de I y D se desconoce.

Italy:

E--> Figures in millions.

FR-> Chiffres en millions.

ESP> Cifras en millones.

Malta:

E--> Data refer to the higher education sector only.

FR-> Les données ne concernent que le secteur de l'enseignement supérieur.

ESP> Los datos sólo incluyen el sector de enseñanza superior.

Netherlands:

E--> Data do not include the higher education sector. Not including social sciences and humanities in the productive sector (integrated R&D).

FR-> Les données ne comprennent pas le secteur de l'enseignement supérieur. Non compris les sciences sociales et humaines dans le secteur de la production (activités de R-D).

ESP> Los datos no comprenden el sector de enseñanza superior. Excluídas las ciencias sociales y humanas del sector productivo (actividades de I y D integradas).

Poland:

E--> Not including military and defence R&D.

FR-> Non compris les activités de R-D de caractère militaire ou relevant de la défense nationale.

Poland: (Cont):

ESP> Excluídas las actividades militares y de defensa de I y D.

Sweden:

E--> Not including social sciences and humanities in the productive and general service sectors.

FR-> Non compris les données pour les sciences sociales et humaines dans les secteurs de la production et de service général.

ESP> No se incluyen los datos relativos a las ciencias sociales y humanas en los sectores productivo y de servicio general.

United Kingdom:

E--> Not including the relevant part of 387.7 million pounds sterling for which a breakdown between current and capital expenditure is not known. Excluding data for social sciences and humanities.

FR-> Non compris la partie de la somme de 387.7 millions de livres sterling dont la ventilation entre dépenses courantes et dépenses en capital n'a pas été précisée. Non compris les données pour les sciences sociales et humaines.

ESP> Excluída la parte correspondiente de la suma de 387.7 millones de libras esterlinas cuya repartición entre gastos corrientes y gastos de capital no se ha precisado. No se incluyen los datos relativos a las ciencias sociales y humanas.

OCEANIA:

Australia:

E--> Data relate to total expenditure by type of R&D activity.

FR-> Les données correspondent aux dépenses totales réparties par type d'activité de R-D.

ESP> Los datos se refieren a los gastos totales repartidos por tipo de actividad de I y D.

French Polynesia:

E--> Data refer to total expenditure by type of R&D activity at one research institute.

FR-> Les données correspondent aux dépenses totales réparties par type d'activité de R-D dans un institut de recherche.

ESP> Los datos se refieren a los gastos totales repartidos por tipo de actividad de I y D en un centro de investigación.

New Caledonia:

E--> Data refer to total expenditure by type of R&D activity.

FR-> Les données correspondent aux dépenses totales réparties par type d'activité de R-D dans un institut de recherche.

ESP> Los datos se refieren a los gastos totales repartidos por tipo de actividad de I y D en un centro de investigación.

Tonga:

E--> Data relate to one research institute only.

FR-> Les données ne concernent qu'un institut de recherche.

ESP> Los datos se refieren a un centro de investigación solamente.

5.12 Total and current expenditure for research and experimental development by sector of performance

Dépenses totales et courantes consacrées à la recherche et au développement expérimental, par secteur d'exécution

Gastos totales y corrientes dedicados a la investigación y al desarrollo experimental, por sector de ejecución

PLEASE REFER TO INTRODUCTION FOR DEFINITIONS OF CATEGORIES INCLUDED IN THIS TABLE.

POUR LES DEFINITIONS DES CATEGORIES PRESENTEES DANS CE TABLEAU, SE REFERER A L'INTRODUCTION.

EN LA INTRODUCCION SE DAN LAS DEFINICIONES DE LAS CATEGORIAS QUE FIGURAN EN ESTE CUADRO.

CURRENT EXPENDITURE = DEPENSES COURANTES = GASTOS CORRIENTES

AMOUNTS SHOWN ARE IN THOUSANDS.

LES MONTANTS SONT EXPRIMES EN MILLIERS.

LOS IMPORTES ESTAN EXPRESADOS EN MILLARES.

NUMBER OF COUNTRIES AND TERRITORIES PRESENTED IN THIS TABLE: 74

NOMBRE DE PAYS ET DE TERRITOIRES PRESENTES DANS CE TABLEAU: 74

NUMERO DE PAISES Y DE TERRITORIOS PRESENTADOS EN ESTE CUADRO: 74

COUNTRY / PAYS / PAIS	REFERENCE YEAR / ANNEE DE REFERENCE / AÑO DE REFERENCIA	CURRENCY / MONNAIE / MONEDA	TYPE OF EXPENDITURE / TYPE DE DEPENSES / TIPO DE GASTOS	SECTOR OF PERFORMANCE/SECTEUR D'EXECUTION/SECTOR DE EJECUCION: ALL SECTORS / TOUS LES SECTEURS / TODOS LOS SECTORES	PRODUCTIVE SECTOR / SECTEUR DE LA PRODUCTION / SECTOR PRODUCTIVO: INTEGRATED R&D / ACTIVITES DE R-D INTEGREES / ACTIVIDADES DE I Y D INTEGRADAS	NON INTEGRATED R&D / ACTIVITES DE R-D NON-INTEGREES / ACTIVIDADES DE I Y D NO INTEGRADAS	HIGHER EDUCATION / ENSEIGNEMENT SUPERIEUR / ENSEÑANZA SUPERIOR	GENERAL SERVICE / SERVICE GENERAL / SERVICIO GENERAL
				(1)	(2)	(3)	(4)	(5)
AFRICA								
BURUNDI	1984	FRANC	TOTAL	405 561	–	–	10 446	395 116
			%	100	–	–	2.6	97.4
CENTRAL AFRICAN REPUBLIC‡	1984	FRANC C.F.A.	TOTAL	680 791	616 312	–	64 479	...
			%	100	90.5	–	9.5	...
CONGO‡	1984	FRANC C.F.A.	TOTAL	25 530	20 394	4 106	622	408
			%	100	79.9	16.1	2.4	1.6
			CURRENT	11 267	6 831	3 925	372	139
			%	100	60.6	34.8	3.3	1.2
EGYPT	1982	POUND	TOTAL	40 378	1 285	6 239	31 385	1 469
			%	100	3.2	15.5	77.7	3.6
			CURRENT	34 242	116	3 642	29 434	1 050
			%	100	0.3	10.6	86.0	3.1
MALAWI	1977	KWACHA	TOTAL	1 290	366	898	13	13
			%	100	28.4	69.6	1.0	1.0
			CURRENT	1 008	360	635	5	8
			%	100	35.7	63.0	0.5	0.8
MAURITIUS	1984	RUPEE	TOTAL	38 700	–	–	700	38 000
			%	100	–	–	1.8	98.2
NIGER	1976	FRANC C.F.A.	TOTAL	...	...	...	141 703	...
			CURRENT	...	...	...	141 703	...
NIGERIA‡	1977	NAIRA	TOTAL	*102 000	...	...	*10 300	...
			%	100	...	...	*10.1	...
	1977		CURRENT	*38 000	...	...	*10 300	...
			%	100	...	...	*27.1	...
SEYCHELLES‡	1983	RUPEE	TOTAL	12 854	–	730	–	12 124
			%	100	–	5.7	–	94.3
			CURRENT	6 083	–	400	–	5 683
			%	100	–	6.6	–	93.4

COUNTRY / PAYS / PAIS	REFERENCE YEAR / ANNEE DE REFERENCE / AÑO DE REFERENCIA	CURRENCY / MONNAIE / MONEDA	TYPE OF EXPENDITURE / TYPE DE DEPENSES / TIPO DE GASTOS	SECTOR OF PERFORMANCE/SECTEUR D'EXECUTION/SECTOR DE EJECUCION				
				ALL SECTORS / TOUS LES SECTEURS / TODOS LOS SECTORES	PRODUCTIVE SECTOR / SECTEUR DE LA PRODUCTION / SECTOR PRODUCTIVO		HIGHER EDUCATION / ENSEIGNEMENT SUPERIEUR / ENSEÑANZA SUPERIOR	GENERAL SERVICE / SERVICE GENERAL / SERVICIO GENERAL
					INTEGRATED R&D / ACTIVITES DE R-D INTEGREES / ACTIVIDADES DE I Y D INTEGRADAS	NON INTEGRATED R&D / ACTIVITES DE R-D NON-INTEGREES / ACTIVIDADES DE I Y D NO INTEGRADAS		
				(1)	(2)	(3)	(4)	(5)
SUDAN	1978	POUND	TOTAL	5 115	153	2 195	779	1 988
			%	100	3.0	42.9	15.2	38.9
			CURRENT	4 294	140	1 663	709	1 782
			%	100	3.3	38.7	16.5	41.5
AMERICA, NORTH								
CANADA‡	1983	DOLLAR	TOTAL	5 365 000	2 518 000	./.	1 341 000	1 506 000
			%	100	46.9	./.	25.0	28.1
COSTA RICA	1982	COLON	TOTAL	81 333	10 333	——>	37 368	33 632
			%	100	12.7	——>	45.9	41.4
CUBA‡	1984	PESO	TOTAL	164 202	1 118	97 312	6 845	58 927
			%	100	0.7	59.3	4.2	35.9
EL SALVADOR‡	1984	COLON	TOTAL	97 007	52 521	–	31 769	12 719
			%	100	54.1	–	32.7	13.1
GUATEMALA	1977	QUETZAL	TOTAL	13 526	...	...	2 294	...
			%	100	...	...	17.0	...
PANAMA	1975	BALBOA	TOTAL	3 296	–	1 429	503	1 364
			%	100	–	43.4	15.3	41.4
ST. LUCIA	1979	E.C. DOLLAR	TOTAL	77	–	–	–	77
			%	100	–	–	–	100.0
			CURRENT	77	–	–	–	77
			%	100	–	–	–	100.0
ST. PIERRE AND MIQUELON	1984	FR. FRANC	TOTAL	*2 719	–	*2 719	–	–
			%	100	–	*100.0	–	–
UNITED STATES‡	1983	DOLLAR	CURRENT	86 204 900	*62 920 000	——>	10 481 600	12 803 300
			%	100	*73.0	——>	12.2	14.9
AMERICA, SOUTH								
ARGENTINA‡	1982	PESO	TOTAL	2 321 932	472 441	478 469	509 570	861 452
			%	100	20.3	20.6	21.9	37.1
BRAZIL	1982	CRUZEIRO	TOTAL	*305 500 000	*91 900 000	——>	*50 400 000	*163 200 000
			%	100	*30.1	——>	*16.5	*53.4
CHILE	1980	PESO	TOTAL	4 665 400	117 100	2 611 600	1 705 900	230 800
			%	100	2.5	56.0	36.6	4.9
			CURRENT	3 672 700	110 200	1 820 500	1 513 100	228 900
			%	100	3.0	49.6	41.2	6.2
COLOMBIA‡	1982	PESO	TOTAL	2 754 273	42 579	...	422 272	2 289 422
			%	100	1.5	...	15.3	83.1
ECUADOR‡	1979	SUCRE	TOTAL	856 090	25 253	——>	124 448	706 389
			%	100	3.0	——>	14.5	82.5
			CURRENT	575 175	...	...	*85 965	...
			%	100	...	...	*14.9	...
GUYANA‡	1982	DOLLAR	TOTAL	2 800	900	——>	1 900	...
			%	100	32.1	——>	67.9	...
VENEZUELA‡	1977	BOLIVAR	TOTAL	883 545	9 599	608 637	248 829	16 480
			%	100	1.1	68.9	28.2	1.9
	1977		CURRENT	755 561	9 523	496 641	234 665	14 732
			%	100	1.3	65.7	31.1	2.0
ASIA								
BRUNEI DARUSSALAM‡	1984	DOLLAR	TOTAL	10 880	9 440	–	–	1 440
			%	100	86.8	–	–	13.2
			CURRENT	8 220	7 130	–	–	1 090
			%	100	86.7	–	–	13.3
CYPRUS‡	1984	POUND	TOTAL	1 173	...	...	5	1 168
			%	100	...	...	0.4	99.6

5.12 R&D expenditure by sector of performance
Dépenses de R-D par secteur d'exécution
Gastos de I y D por sector de ejecución

COUNTRY / PAYS / PAIS	REFERENCE YEAR / ANNEE DE REFERENCE / AÑO DE REFERENCIA	CURRENCY / MONNAIE / MONEDA	TYPE OF EXPENDITURE / TYPE DE DEPENSES / TIPO DE GASTOS	SECTOR OF PERFORMANCE/SECTEUR D'EXECUTION/SECTOR DE EJECUCION				
					PRODUCTIVE SECTOR / SECTEUR DE LA PRODUCTION / SECTOR PRODUCTIVO			
				ALL SECTORS / TOUS LES SECTEURS / TODOS LOS SECTORES	INTEGRATED R&D / ACTIVITES DE R-D INTEGREES / ACTIVIDADES DE I Y D INTEGRADAS	NON INTEGRATED R&D / ACTIVITES DE R-D NON-INTEGREES / ACTIVIDADES DE I Y D NO INTEGRADAS	HIGHER EDUCATION / ENSEIGNEMENT SUPERIEUR / ENSEÑANZA SUPERIOR	GENERAL SERVICE / SERVICE GENERAL / SERVICIO GENERAL
				(1)	(2)	(3)	(4)	(5)
INDIA	1982	RUPEE	TOTAL	*11 586 360	*2 856 120	–	*386 400	*8 343 840
			%	100	*24.7	–	*3.3	*72.0
			CURRENT	*7 762 860	*1 913 600	–	*258 890	*5 590 370
			%	100	*24.7	–	*3.3	*72.0
IRAN, ISLAMIC REPUBLIC OF‡	1984	RIAL	TOTAL	21 527 000	17 534 000	——>	3 298 000	695 000
			%	100	81.5	——>	15.3	3.2
			CURRENT	11 584 000	8 325 000	——>	2 564 000	695 000
			%	100	71.9	——>	22.1	6.0
ISRAEL‡	1978	POUND	TOTAL	6 154 300	3 845 000	./.	1 839 700	469 700
			%	100	62.5	./.	29.9	7.6
JAPAN‡	1983	YEN	TOTAL	7 180 782	4 560 127	——>	1 649 646	971 010
			%	100	63.5	——>	23.0	13.5
			CURRENT	5 953 927	3 856 242	——>	1 368 551	729 134
			%	100	64.8	——>	23.0	12.2
JORDAN‡	1979	DINAR	TOTAL	*7 565	*876	——>	*78	*6 611
			%	100	*11.6	——>	*1.0	*87.4
KOREA, REPUBLIC OF‡	1983	WON	TOTAL	621 749 314	375 809 962	——>	64 251 213	181 688 139
			%	100	60.4	——>	10.3	29.2
			CURRENT	398 577 359	198 152 489	——>	51 339 078	149 085 792
			%	100	49.7	——>	12.9	37.4
KUWAIT‡	1984	DINAR	TOTAL	71 163	43 324	1 543	1 480	24 816
			%	100	60.9	2.2	2.0	34.9
LEBANON‡	1980	POUND	TOTAL	...	...	...	22 000	...
PAKISTAN‡	1979	RUPEE	TOTAL	391 059	...	321 722	24 953	44 384
			%	100	...	82.3	6.4	11.4
			CURRENT	198 503	...	154 803	17 218	26 482
			%	100	...	78.0	8.7	13.3
PHILIPPINES	1982	PESO	TOTAL	*522 970	*51 047	–	55 241	416 682
			%	100	*9.8	–	*10.6	*79.7
			CURRENT	*470 501	*49 516	–	48 877	372 108
			%	100	*10.5	–	*10.4	*79.1
QATAR‡	1984	RIYAL	TOTAL	12 300	–	10 300	...	2 000
			%	100	–	83.7	...	16.3
SINGAPORE‡	1981	DOLLAR	TOTAL	81 900	44 400	——>	24 600	12 900
			%	100	54.2	——>	30.0	15.8
			CURRENT	59 300	29 500	——>	18 200	11 600
			%	100	49.7	——>	30.7	19.6
SRI LANKA	1983	RUPEE	TOTAL	206 528	20 528	——>	8 458	177 542
			%	100	9.9	——>	4.1	86.0
TURKEY‡	1983	LIRA	TOTAL	27 220 500	4 415 200	——>	15 083 100	7 722 200
			%	100	16.2	——>	55.4	28.4
			CURRENT	16 054 000	2 715 000	——>	9 026 100	4 312 900
			%	100	16.9	——>	56.2	26.9
VIET-NAM	1979	DONG	TOTAL	108 300	76 500	——>	8 300	23 500
			%	100	70.6	——>	7.7	21.7
EUROPE								
AUSTRIA	1981	SCHILLING	TOTAL	12 331 026	6 122 341	764 296	4 044 607	1 399 782
			%	100	49.7	6.2	32.8	11.4
			CURRENT	10 201 527	5 367 336	681 607	2 942 306	1 210 278
			%	100	52.6	6.7	28.8	11.9
BELGIUM	1977	FRANC	TOTAL	38 894 080	25 770 213	1 667 566	7 553 410	3 902 891
			%	100	66.3	4.3	19.4	10.0
BULGARIA	1984	LEV	TOTAL	696 900	440 500	——>	45 400	211 000
			%	100	63.2	——>	6.5	30.3
DENMARK	1983	KRONE	TOTAL	5 970 400	2 923 200	328 600	1 442 600	1 276 000
			%	100	49.0	5.5	24.2	21.4
FINLAND	1984	MARKKA	TOTAL	4 381 000	2 574 000	64 000	849 000	894 000
			%	100	58.8	1.5	19.4	20.4

COUNTRY / PAYS / PAIS	REFERENCE YEAR / ANNEE DE REFERENCE / AÑO DE REFERENCIA	CURRENCY / MONNAIE / MONEDA	TYPE OF EXPENDITURE / TYPE DE DEPENSES / TIPO DE GASTOS	SECTOR OF PERFORMANCE/SECTEUR D'EXECUTION/SECTOR DE EJECUCION				
				ALL SECTORS / TOUS LES SECTEURS / TODOS LOS SECTORES	PRODUCTIVE SECTOR / SECTEUR DE LA PRODUCTION / SECTOR PRODUCTIVO		HIGHER EDUCATION / ENSEIGNEMENT SUPERIEUR / ENSEÑANZA SUPERIOR	GENERAL SERVICE / SERVICE GENERAL / SERVICIO GENERAL
					INTEGRATED R&D / ACTIVITES DE R-D INTEGREES / ACTIVIDADES DE I Y D INTEGRADAS	NON INTEGRATED R&D / ACTIVITES DE R-D NON-INTEGREES / ACTIVIDADES DE I Y D NO INTEGRADAS		
				(1)	(2)	(3)	(4)	(5)
FRANCE	1979	FRANC	TOTAL	44 123 000	25 941 000	1 114 000	6 846 000	10 222 000
			%	100	58.8	2.5	15.5	23.2
			CURRENT	40 269 000	24 033 000	1 031 000	6 329 000	8 876 000
			%	100	59.7	2.6	15.7	22.0
GERMANY, FEDERAL REPUBLIC OF‡	1981	D. MARK	TOTAL	38 352 000	26 196 000	——>	6 462 000	5 694 000
			%	100	68.3	——>	16.8	14.8
			CURRENT	33 520 000	23 207 000	——>	5 605 000	4 708 000
			%	100	69.2	——>	16.7	14.0
GREECE‡	1979	DRACHMA	TOTAL	2 640 000	64 000	...	368 000	2 208 000
			%	100	2.4	...	13.9	83.6
HUNGARY‡	1984	FORINT	TOTAL	20 037 000	10 853 000	3 072 000	2 506 000	3 606 000
			%	100	54.2	15.3	12.5	18.0
ICELAND	1979	KRONA	TOTAL	6 427 500	596 600	2 391 000	1 743 200	1 696 700
			%	100	9.3	37.2	27.1	26.4
			CURRENT	5 663 000	433 000	2 064 800	1 589 700	1 575 400
			%	100	7.6	36.5	28.1	27.8
IRELAND‡	1982	POUND	TOTAL	97 582	42 528	./.	15 643	39 411
			%	100	43.6	./.	16.0	40.4
			CURRENT	85 487	32 453	./.	14 662	38 372
			%	100	38.0	./.	17.2	44.9
ITALY‡	1983	LIRA	TOTAL	6 027 005	3 440 994	379 161	1 161 231	1 045 619
			%	100	57.1	6.3	19.3	17.3
			CURRENT	4 999 917	3 111 903	314 842	990 525	582 647
			%	100	62.2	6.3	19.8	11.7
MALTA	1984	LIRA	TOTAL	...	...	...	10	...
			CURRENT	...	...	...	9	...
NETHERLANDS‡	1983	GUILDER	TOTAL	7 699 000	4 069 000	55 000	1 946 000	1 629 000
			%	100	52.9	0.7	25.3	21.2
NORWAY	1982	KRONE	TOTAL	4 952 500	1 658 100	1 014 500	1 333 800	946 100
			%	100	33.5	20.5	26.9	19.1
			CURRENT	4 473 100	1 537 300	879 600	1 209 900	846 300
			%	100	34.4	19.7	27.0	18.9
POLAND‡	1984	ZLOTY	TOTAL	73 728 300	9 065 100	38 736 000	14 403 200	11 524 000
			%	100	12.3	52.5	19.5	15.6
PORTUGAL	1982	ESCUDO	TOTAL	6 541 200	2 043 600	298 000	1 347 700	2 851 900
			%	100	31.2	4.6	20.6	43.6
			CURRENT	5 370 600	1 711 600	240 300	1 194 900	2 223 800
			%	100	31.9	4.5	22.2	41.4
SPAIN‡	1983	PESETA	TOTAL	100 697 093	52 142 859	./.	17 804 758	30 749 476
			%	100	51.8	./.	17.7	30.5
SWEDEN‡	1983	KRONA	TOTAL	18 189 000	11 733 000	——>	5 496 000	960 000
			%	100	64.5	——>	30.2	5.3
SWITZERLAND	1983	FRANC	CURRENT	4 643 000	3 597 000	——>	*810 000	*236 000
			%	100	77.5	——>	*17.4	*5.1
UNITED KINGDOM‡	1981	POUND STG.	TOTAL	5 921 000	3 704 300	88 100	629 600	1 499 000
			%	100	62.6	1.5	10.6	25.3
YUGOSLAVIA‡	1981	DINAR	TOTAL	18 235 000	5 108 000	5 186 000	3 454 000	4 487 000
			%	100	28.0	28.4	18.9	24.6
OCEANIA								
AUSTRALIA	1981	DOLLAR	TOTAL	1 522 247	340 507	505 133	452 489	224 118
			%	100	22.4	33.2	29.7	14.7
	1981		CURRENT	1 331 791	295 940	412 019	420 428	203 404
			%	100	22.2	30.9	31.6	15.3
FRENCH POLYNESIA‡	1983	FRANC C.F.P.	TOTAL	324 720	–	–	–	324 720
			%	100	–	–	–	100.0
			CURRENT	308 440	–	–	–	308 440
			%	100	–	–	–	100.0

5.12 R&D expenditure by sector of performance
Dépenses de R-D par secteur d'exécution
Gastos de I y D por sector de ejecución

COUNTRY / PAYS / PAIS	REFERENCE YEAR / ANNEE DE REFERENCE / AÑO DE REFERENCIA	CURRENCY / MONNAIE / MONEDA	TYPE OF EXPENDITURE / TYPE DE DEPENSES / TIPO DE GASTOS	SECTOR OF PERFORMANCE/SECTEUR D'EXECUTION/SECTOR DE EJECUCION				
				ALL SECTORS / TOUS LES SECTEURS / TODOS LOS SECTORES	PRODUCTIVE SECTOR / SECTEUR DE LA PRODUCTION / SECTOR PRODUCTIVO		HIGHER EDUCATION / ENSEIGNEMENT SUPERIEUR / ENSEÑANZA SUPERIOR	GENERAL SERVICE / SERVICE GENERAL / SERVICIO GENERAL
					INTEGRATED R&D / ACTIVITES DE R-D INTEGREES / ACTIVIDADES DE I Y D INTEGRADAS	NON INTEGRATED R&D / ACTIVITES DE R-D NON-INTEGREES / ACTIVIDADES DE I Y D NO INTEGRADAS		
				(1)	(2)	(3)	(4)	(5)
GUAM	1979	U.S. DOLLAR	TOTAL	...	...	...	1 256	...
NEW CALEDONIA	1983	FRANC C.F.P.	TOTAL	83 000	–	81 500	–	1 500
			%	100	–	98.2	–	1.8
			CURRENT	55 800	–	54 300	–	1 500
			%	100	–	97.3	–	2.7
NEW ZEALAND‡	1979	DOLLAR	TOTAL	175 373	37 041	./.	21 744	116 588
			%	100	21.1	./.	12.4	66.5
PACIFIC ISLANDS	1979	U.S.DOLLAR	TOTAL	185	–	120	–	65
			%	100	–	64.9	–	35.1
	1979		CURRENT	185	–	120	–	65
			%	100	–	64.9	–	35.1
SAMOA	1978	TALA	TOTAL	2 500	1 251	556	482	211
			%	100	50.0	22.2	19.3	8.4
TONGA‡	1980	PA'ANGA	TOTAL	426	–	–	–	426
			%	100	–	–	–	100.0
			CURRENT	279	–	–	–	279
			%	100	–	–	–	100.0
VANUATU	1975	FRANC	TOTAL	21 603	–	21 603	–	–
			%	100	–	100.0	–	–
			CURRENT	21 603	–	21 603	–	–
			%	100	–	100.0	–	–

AFRICA:

Central African Republic:

E--> Not including data for the general service sector.

FR-> Non compris les données pour le secteur du service général.

ESP> Excluídos los datos relativos al sector de servicio general.

Congo:

E--> Not including military and defence R&D.

FR-> Non compris les activités de R-D de caractère militaire ou relevant de la défense nationale.

ESP> Excluídas las actividades militares y de defensa de I y D.

Nigeria:

E--> Not including data for social sciences and humanities.

FR-> Non compris les données pour les sciences sociales et humaines.

ESP> Excluídos los datos relativos a las ciencias sociales y humanas.

Seychelles:

E--> Not including data for military and defence R&D.

FR-> Non compris les activités de R-D de caractère militaire ou relevant de la défense nationale.

ESP> Excluídas las actividades militares y de defensa de I y D.

AMERICA, NORTH:

Canada:

E--> Not including social sciences and humanities in the productive sector (integrated R&D). Data relating to the productive sector (non-integrated R&D) are included with the general service sector.

FR-> Non compris les sciences sociales et humaines dans le secteur de la production (activités de R-D intégrées). Les données relatives au secteur de la production (activités de R-D non intégrées) sont comprises avec celles du secteur de service général.

ESP> Excluídas las ciencias sociales y humanas del sector de la production (actividades de I y D integradas). Los datos relativos al sector productivo (actividades de I y D no integradas) se incluyen en el sector de servicio general.

Cuba:

E--> Not including military and defence R&D.

FR-> Non compris les activités de R-D de caractère militaire ou relevant de la défense nationale.

ESP> Excluídas las actividades militares y de defensa de I y D.

El Salvador:

E--> Data relate to funds originating from public sources.

FR-> Les données se réfèrent aux fonds provenant des sources publiques.

ESP> Los datos se refieren a los fondos procedentes de fuentes públicos.

United States:

E--> Not including data for law, humanities and education. The figu in column 5 includes 2,575 million dollars from private non-pro organizations.

FR-> Non compris les données pour le droit, les sciences humaines l'éducation. Le chiffre de la colonne 5 comprend 2 575 millions dollars provenant des organisations privées à but non lucratif.

ESP> Excluídos los datos relativos al derecho, las ciencias humanas la educación. La cifra de la columna 5 comprende 2 575 millones dólares procedentes de organizaciones privadas de carácter lucrativo.

AMERICA, SOUTH:

Argentina:

E--> Figures in millions.

FR-> Chiffres en millions.

ESP> Cifras en millones.

Colombia:

E--> Not including data for the productive sector (non-integrat R&D).

FR-> Non compris les données pour le secteur de la producti (activités de R-D non intégrées).

ESP> Excluídos los datos relativos al sector productivo (actividades I y D no integradas).

Ecuador:

E--> Data also include expenditure for scientific and technologic services (STS).

FR-> Les données comprennent en plus les dépenses relatives a services scientifiques et techniques (SST).

ESP> Los datos también incluyen los gastos relativos a los servici científicos y tecnológicos (SCT).

Guyana:

E--> Not including military and defence R&D. Data for the gene service sector and for medical sciences in the higher education sector a also excluded.

FR-> Non compris les activités de R-D de caractère militaire relevant de la défense nationale. Les données relatives au secteur de servi général et les sciences médicales du secteur de l'enseignement supérie sont aussi exclues.

ESP> Excluídas las actividades militares y de defensa de I y D. excluyen también los datos relativos al sector de servicio general y ciencias médicas al sector de enseñanza superior.

Venezuela:

E--> Data concern 167 institutes out of a total of 406 which perfo R&D.

Venezuela: (Cont):
FR-> Les données ne concernent que 167 instituts sur un total de 406 qui exécutent des activités de R-D.
ESP> Los datos sólo se refieren a 167 centros sobre un total de 406 que ejecutan actividades de I y D.

ASIA:

Brunei Darussalam:
E--> Data relate to 2 research institutes only.
FR-> Les données se réfèrent à 2 instituts de recherche seulement.
ESP> Los datos se refieren a 2 centros de investigación solamente.

Cyprus:
E--> Not including data for the productive sector.
FR-> Non compris les données pour le secteur de la production.
ESP> Excluídos los datos relativos al sector productivo.

Iran, Islamic Republic of:
E--> Data relate to the budget allotment.
FR-> Les données se réfèrent aux crédits budgétaires.
ESP> Los datos se refieren a las consignaciones presupuestarias.

Israel:
E--> Data refer to expenditure in the fields of natural sciences and engineering only. Data relating to the productive sector (non-integrated R&D) are included with the general service sector.
FR-> Les données se réfèrent aux dépenses dans les domaines des sciences exactes et naturelles et des sciences de l'ingénieur seulement. Les données relatives au secteur de la production (activités de R-D non intégrées) sont comprises avec celles du secteur de service général.
ESP> Los datos sólo se refieren a los gastos relativos a las ciencias exactas y naturales y a la ingeniería. Los datos relativos al sector productivo (actividades de I y D no integradas) se incluyen en el sector de servicio general.

Japan:
E--> Figures in millions. Not including data for social sciences and humanities in the productive sector.
FR-> Chiffres en millions. Non compris les données pour les sciences sociales et humaines dans le secteur de la production.
ESP> Cifras en millones. Excluídos los datos relativos a las ciencias sociales y humanas del sector productivo.

Jordan:
E--> Not including military and defence R&D.
FR-> Non compris les activités de R-D de caractère militaire ou relevant de la défense nationale.
ESP> Excluídas las actividades militares y de defensa de I y D.

Korea, Republic of:
E--> Not including military and defence R&D and social sciences and humanities.
FR-> Non compris les activités de R-D de caractère militaire ou relevant de la défense nationale ni les sciences sociales et humaines.
ESP> Excluídas las actividades militares y de defensa de I y D y las ciencias sociales y humanas.

Kuwait:
E--> Data refer to scientific and technological activities (STA).
FR-> Les données se réfèrent aux activités scientifiques et technologiques (AST).
ESP> Los datos se refieren a las actividades científicas y tecnológicas (ACT).

Lebanon:
E--> Data refer to the Faculty of Science at the University of Lebanon only.
FR-> Les données ne se réfèrent qu'à la Faculté des Sciences de l'Université du Liban.
ESP> Los datos se refieren a la Facultad de Ciencias de la Universidad del Líbano solamente.

Pakistan:
E--> Data relate to R&D activities concentrated mainly in government-financed research establishments only; social sciences and humanities in the higher education and general service sectors are excluded. Not including the productive sector (integrated R&D) or military and defence R&D.
FR-> Les données se réfèrent aux activités de R-D se trouvant pour la plupart dans les établissements de recherche financés par le gouvernement; les sciences sociales et humaines dans les secteurs de l'enseignement supérieur et de service général sont exclues. Compte non tenu du secteur de la production (activités de R-D intégrées) ni des activités de R-D de caractère militaire ou relevant de la défense nationale.
ESP> Los datos se refieren a las actividades de I y D concentradas principalmente en los establecimientos de investigación subvencionados por el gobierno; se excluyen las ciencias sociales y humanas de los sectores de enseñanza superior y de servicio general. Excluídos el sector productivo (actividades de I y D integradas) y las actividades militares y de defensa de I y D.

Qatar:
E--> Not including data for the higher education sector.
FR-> Non compris les données pour le secteur de l'enseignement supérieur.
ESP> Excluídos los datos para el sector de enseñanza superior.

Singapore:
E--> Not including either military and defence R&D or social sciences and humanities.

Singapore: (Cont):
FR-> Non compris les activités de R-D de caractère militaire ou relevant de la défense nationale ni les sciences sociales et humaines.
ESP> Excluídas las actividades militares y de defensa de I y D y las ciencias sociales y humanas.

Turkey:
E--> Data relating to current expenditure do not include the relevant portion of 5.2 million lira by the productive sector for which a distribution between current and capital expenditure is unknown. Not including data for social sciences and humanities in the general service sector.
FR-> Les données relatives aux dépenses courantes ne comprennent pas la partie de la somme de 5.2 millions de livres du secteur de la production dont la répartition entre dépenses en capital et les dépenses courantes n'a pas été précisée. Non compris les données pour les sciences sociales et humaines du secteur de service général.
ESP> Los datos relativos a los gastos corrientes excluyen 5.2 millones de liras en el sector productivo cuya repartición entre gastos corrientes y gastos de capital no se ha precisado. Excluídos los datos relativos a las ciencias sociales y humanas del sector de servicio general.

EUROPE:

Germany, Federal Republic of:
E--> Data relating to current expenditure do not include the relevant part of 450 million Deutsche marks by the productive sector for which a distribution between capital and current expenditure is unknown. Not including data for social sciences and humanities in the productive sector.
FR-> Les données relatives aux dépenses courantes ne comprennent pas la partie de la somme de 450 millions de deutsche marks du secteur de la production dont la répartition entre les dépenses en capital et les dépenses courantes n'a pas été précisée. Non compris les données pour les sciences sociales et humaines dans le secteur de la production.
ESP> Los datos relativos a los gastos corrientes excluyen la parte correspondiente de la suma de 450 millones de marcos en el sector productivo, cuya repartición entre gastos corrientes y gastos de capital no se ha precisado. Excluídos los datos relativos a las ciencias sociales y humanas del sector productivo.

Greece:
E--> Data relate to government activities only.
FR-> Les données se réfèrent aux activités gouvernementales seulement.
ESP> Los datos se refieren a las actividades gubernamentales solamente.

Hungary:
E--> Not including 2,649 million forints (all current expenditure) for which a breakdown by sector is not available.
FR-> Compte non tenu de 2 649 millions de forints (dépenses courantes) dont la répartition par secteur n'est pas disponible.
ESP> Excluídos 2 649 millones de forints (gastos corrientes) cuya repartición por sector se desconoce.

Ireland:
E--> Data relating to the productive sector (non-integrated R&D) are included with the general service sector.
FR-> Les données relatives au secteur de la production (activités de R-D non intégrées) sont comprises avec celles du secteur de service général.
ESP> Los datos relativos al sector productivo (actividades de I y D no integradas) se incluyen en el sector de servicio general.

Italy:
E--> Figures in millions.
FR-> Chiffres en millions.
ESP> Cifras en millones.

Netherlands:
E--> Not including data for social sciences and humanities in the productive sector (integrated R&D).
FR-> Non compris les données pour les sciences sociales et humaines du secteur de la production (activités de R-D intégrées).
ESP> Excluídos los datos relativos a las ciencias sociales y humanas del sector productivo (actividades de I y D integradas).

Poland:
E--> Not including military and defence R&D.
FR-> Non compris les activités de R-D de caractère militaire ou relevant de la défense nationale.
ESP> Excluídas las actividades militares y de defensa de I y D.

Spain:
E--> Data relating to the productive sector (non-integrated R&D) are included with the general service sector.
FR-> Les données relatives au secteur de la production (activités de R-D non intégrées) sont comprises avec celles du secteur de service général.
ESP> Los datos relativos al sector productivo (actividades de I y D no integradas) se incluyen en el sector de servicio general.

Sweden:
E--> Not including social sciences and humanities in the productive and general service sectors.
FR-> Non compris les sciences sociales et humaines dans les secteurs de la production et de service général.
ESP> Excluídas las ciencias sociales y humanas en los sectores productivo y de servicio general.

United Kingdom:

E--> Not including social sciences and humanities or funds for R&D performed abroad.

FR-> Non compris les sciences sociales et humaines ni les fonds de R-D exécuté à l'étranger.

ESP> Excluídos los datos relativos a las ciencias sociales y humanas y los fondos de I y D que se executan en el extranjero.

Yugoslavia:

E--> Data refer to total revenue rather than total expenditure. Not including military and defence R&D.

FR-> Les données se réfèrent au total des revenus au lieu des dépenses totales. Non compris les activités de R-D de caractère militaire ou relevant de la défense nationale.

ESP> Los datos se refieren a los ingresos totales en lugar de los gastos totales. Excluídas las actividades militares y de defensa de I y D.

OCEANIA:

French Polynesia:

E--> Data refer to one research institute only.

FR-> Les données ne concernent qu'un institut de recherche.

ESP> Los datos se refieren a un centro de investigación solamente.

New Zealand:

E--> Data relating to the productive sector (non-integrated R&D) are included with the general service sector.

FR-> Les données relatives au secteur de la production (activités de R-D non intégrées) sont comprises avec celles du secteur de service général.

ESP> Los datos relativos al sector productivo (actividades de I y D no integradas) se incluyen en el sector de servicio general.

Tonga:

E--> Data refer to one research institute only.

FR-> Les données ne concernent qu'un institut de recherche.

ESP> Los datos se refieren a un centro de investigación solamente.

5.13 Total expenditure for the performance of research and experimental development in the productive sector, by branch of economic activity

Dépenses totales pour l'exécution de travaux de recherche et de développement expérimental dans le secteur de la production, par branche d'activité économique

Gastos totales para la ejecución de trabajos de investigación y de desarrollo experimental en el sector productivo, por rama de actividad económica

PLEASE REFER TO INTRODUCTION FOR DEFINITIONS OF CATEGORIES INCLUDED IN THIS TABLE.

AMOUNTS SHOWN ARE IN THOUSANDS.

NUMBER OF COUNTRIES AND TERRITORIES PRESENTED IN THIS TABLE: 42

POUR LES DEFINITIONS DES CATEGORIES PRESENTEES DANS CE TABLEAU, SE REFERER A L'INTRODUCTION.

LES MONTANTS SONT EXPRIMES EN MILLIERS.

NOMBRE DE PAYS ET DE TERRITOIRES PRESENTES DANS CE TABLEAU: 42

EN LA INTRODUCCION SE DAN LAS DEFINICIONES DE LAS CATEGORIAS QUE FIGURAN EN ESTE CUADRO.

LOS IMPORTES ESTAN EXPRESADOS EN MILLARES.

NUMERO DE PAISES Y DE TERRITORIOS PRESENTADOS EN ESTE CUADRO: 42

			BRANCH OF ECONOMIC ACTIVITY/BRANCHE D'ACTIVITE ECONOMIQUE/RAMA DE ACTIVIDAD ECONOMICA						
COUNTRY CURRENCY	REFERENCE YEAR	TOTAL EXPENDITURE	AGRICULTURE FORESTRY HUNTING AND FISHING	EXTRACTING INDUSTRIES	MANUFACTURING INDUSTRIES	UTILITIES	CONSTRUCTION	TRANSPORT AND COMMUNICATION	OTHER ACTIVITIES
PAYS MONNAIE	ANNEE DE REFERENCE	DEPENSES TOTALES	AGRICULTURE SYLVICULTURE CHASSE ET PECHE	INDUSTRIES EXTRACTIVES	INDUSTRIES MANUFACTURIERES	SERVICES PUBLICS	BATIMENTS ET TRAVAUX PUBLICS	TRANSPORTS ET COMMUNICATIONS	ACTIVITES DIVERSES
PAIS MONEDA	AÑO DE REFERENCIA	GASTOS TOTALES	AGRICULTURA SILVICULTURA CAZA Y PESCA	INDUSTRIAS EXTRACTIVAS	INDUSTRIAS MANUFACTURERAS	SERVICIOS PUBLICOS	CONSTRUCCION	TRANSPORTES Y COMUNICACIONES	OTRAS ACTIVIDADES
		(000)	(000)	(000)	(000)	(000)	(000)	(000)	(000)
		(1)	(2)	(3)	(4)	(5)	(6)	(7)	(8)
AFRICA									
CONGO‡	1984	24 500	23 330	–	–	–	47	–	1 123
FRANC C.F.A	%	100	95.2	–	–	–	0.2	–	4.6
MALAWI	1977	1 264	1 264	–	–	–	–	–	–
KWACHA	%	100	100.0	–	–	–	–	–	–
MAURITIUS	1983	3 100	–	–	–	3 100	–	–	–
RUPEE	%	100	–	–	–	100.0	–	–	–
AMERICA, NORTH									
CANADA‡	1982	2 381 000	–	*168 000	1 879 000	*118 000	./.	*90 000	*126 000
DOLLAR	%	100	–	*7.1	78.9	*5.0	./.	*3.8	*5.3
CUBA‡	1983	81 620	38 414	2 583	24 907	–	5 693	3 622	6 402
PESO	%	100	47.1	3.2	30.5	–	7.0	4.4	7.8
PANAMA	1975	1 429	49	297	–	–	–	–	1 083
BALBOA	%	100	3.4	20.8	–	–	–	–	75.8
ST. PIERRE AND MIQUELON	1983	*3 803	*3 803	–	–	–	–	–	–
FRENCH FRANC	%	100	*100.0	–	–	–	–	–	–
AMERICA, SOUTH									
ARGENTINA‡	1980	*784 800	251 800	*90 100	*132 200	*166 200	*30 000	44 900	*69 600
PESO	%	100	*32.1	*11.5	*16.8	*21.2	*3.8	*5.7	*8.9
BRAZIL	1977	6 580 300	1 499 100	701 800	1 236 000	./.	50 200	625 400	2 467 800
CRUZEIRO	%	100	22.8	10.7	18.8	./.	0.8	9.5	37.5
VENEZUELA‡	1977	506 164	187 399	4 776	22 935	–	630	836	289 588
BOLIVAR	%	100	37.0	0.9	4.5	–	0.1	0.2	57.2

5.13 R&D expenditure - productive sector
Dépenses de R-D - secteur de la production
Gastos de I y D - sector productivo

COUNTRY / CURRENCY PAYS / MONNAIE PAIS / MONEDA	REFERENCE YEAR ANNEE DE REFERENCE AÑO DE REFERENCIA	TOTAL EXPENDITURE DEPENSES TOTALES GASTOS TOTALES (000)	BRANCH OF ECONOMIC ACTIVITY/BRANCHE D'ACTIVITE ECONOMIQUE/RAMA DE ACTIVIDAD ECONOMICA AGRICULTURE FORESTRY HUNTING AND FISHING AGRICULTURE SYLVICULTURE CHASSE ET PECHE AGRICULTURA SILVICULTURA CAZA Y PESCA (000)	EXTRACTING INDUSTRIES INDUSTRIES EXTRACTIVES INDUSTRIAS EXTRACTIVAS (000)	MANUFACTURING INDUSTRIES INDUSTRIES MANUFACTURIERES INDUSTRIAS MANUFACTURERAS (000)	UTILITIES SERVICES PUBLICS SERVICIOS PUBLICOS (000)	CONSTRUCTION BATIMENTS ET TRAVAUX PUBLICS CONSTRUCCION (000)	TRANSPORT AND COMMUNICATION TRANSPORTS ET COMMUNICATIONS TRANSPORTES Y COMUNICACIONES (000)	OTHER ACTIVITIES ACTIVITES DIVERSES OTRAS ACTIVIDADES (000)
		(1)	(2)	(3)	(4)	(5)	(6)	(7)	(8)
ASIA									
INDIA	1978	1 352 000	2 000	15 000	1 158 000	./.	./.	177 000	–
RUPEE		% 100	0.1	1.1	85.7	./.	./.	13.1	–
IRAN, ISLAMIC REPUBLIC OF‡	1984	17 534 000	8 600 000	–	1 128 000	7 016 000	200 000	590 000	–
RIAL		% 100	49.0	–	6.4	40.0	1.1	3.4	–
JAPAN‡	1983	4 560 127	5 652	15 622	4 257 191	./.	101 342	180 321	–
YEN		% 100	0.1	0.3	93.4	./.	2.2	4.0	–
KOREA, REPUBLIC OF‡	1983	375 809 962	2 647 243	1 938 804	342 840 791	2 355 000	12 004 574	2 115 383	11 908 167
WON		% 100	0.7	0.5	91.2	0.6	3.2	0.6	3.2
PAKISTAN‡	1979	337 378	184 989	15 235	34 849	29 896	1 269	9 704	61 436
RUPEE		% 100	54.8	4.5	10.3	8.9	0.4	2.9	18.2
PHILIPPINES	1982	*51 047	*521	*71	*39 541	*9 755	*541	–	*618
PESO		% 100	*1.0	*0.1	*77.5	*19.1	*1.1	–	*1.2
SRI LANKA	1975	36 970	26 974	–	7 105	./.	2 812	79	–
RUPEE		% 100	73.0	–	19.2	./.	7.6	0.2	–
TURKEY	1983	4 415 200	222 500	24 200	4 151 400	–	17 100	–	–
LIRA		% 100	5.0	0.5	94.0	–	0.4	–	–
EUROPE									
AUSTRIA	1981	6 886 637	21 314	53 231	6 313 193	10 260	62 867	–	425 772
SCHILLING		% 100	0.3	0.8	91.7	0.1	0.9	–	6.2
DENMARK‡	1981	1 988 100	./.	–	1 788 000	./.	16 300	39 200	144 600
KRONE		% 100	./.	–	89.9	./.	0.8	2.0	7.3
FINLAND	1983	2 060 640	25 780	20 170	1 854 010	64 410	12 020	37 390	46 860
MARKKA		% 100	1.3	1.0	90.0	3.1	0.6	1.8	2.3
FRANCE	1979	27 055 000	181 000	291 000	24 869 000	791 000	273 000	562 000	88 000
FRANC		% 100	0.7	1.1	91.9	2.9	1.0	2.1	0.3
GERMANY, FEDERAL REPUBLIC OF‡	1981	25 746 000	17 000	757 000	24 351 000	138 000	102 000	107 000	274 000
DEUTSCHE MARK		% 100	0.1	2.9	94.6	0.5	0.4	0.4	1.1
GREECE	1976	575 000	95 000	222 000	155 000	./.	6 000	32 500	64 500
DRACHMA		% 100	16.5	38.6	27.0	./.	1.0	5.7	11.2
HUNGARY‡	1983	12 598 000	531 000	456 000	9 376 000	206 000	287 000	163 000	1 579 000
FORINT		% 100	4.2	3.6	74.4	1.6	2.3	1.3	12.5
ICELAND	1979	2 987 600	1 882 700	235 900	642 400	–	96 800	–	129 800
KRONA		% 100	63.0	7.9	21.5	–	3.2	–	4.3
IRELAND‡	1982	42 528	253	441	37 909	1 973	108	666	1 178
POUND		% 100	0.6	1.0	89.1	4.6	0.3	1.6	2.8
ITALY‡	1983	3 440 994	2 230	6 092	3 040 812	138 808	34 958	20 639	197 455
LIRA		% 100	0.1	0.2	88.4	4.0	1.0	0.6	5.7
NETHERLANDS‡	1982	3 757 000	79 000	./.	3 388 000	11 000	46 000	182 000	51 000
GUILDER		% 100	2.1	./.	90.2	0.3	1.2	4.8	1.4
NORWAY	1981	2 196 900	20 400	396 400	1 527 100	50 300	63 300	87 300	52 100
KRONE		% 100	0.9	18.0	69.5	2.3	2.9	4.0	2.4
POLAND‡	1983	33 808 300	3 188 300	26 849 500	——>	–	2 053 800	1 144 700	572 000
ZLOTY		% 100	9.4	79.4	——>	–	6.1	3.4	1.7
PORTUGAL‡	1982	2 043 600	–	226 600	1 141 900	481 300	4 900	105 000	83 900
ESCUDO		% 100	–	11.1	55.9	23.6	0.2	5.1	4.1
SPAIN‡	1983	52 142 859	20 417	428 792	44 410 784	1 276 816	773 290	3 255 101	1 977 659
PESETA		% 100	0.0	0.8	85.2	2.4	1.5	6.2	3.8
SWEDEN‡	1979	6 001 900	97 100	30 600	5 506 800	230 800	./.	./.	136 600
KRONA		% 100	1.6	0.5	91.8	3.8	./.	./.	2.3

COUNTRY CURRENCY	REFERENCE YEAR	TOTAL EXPENDITURE	BRANCH OF ECONOMIC ACTIVITY/BRANCHE D'ACTIVITE ECONOMIQUE/RAMA DE ACTIVIDAD ECONOMICA							
			AGRICULTURE FORESTRY HUNTING AND FISHING	EXTRACTING INDUSTRIES	MANUFACTURING INDUSTRIES	UTILITIES	CONSTRUCTION	TRANSPORT AND COMMUNICATION	OTHER ACTIVITIES
PAYS MONNAIE	ANNEE DE REFERENCE	DEPENSES TOTALES	AGRICULTURE SYLVICULTURE CHASSE ET PECHE	INDUSTRIES EXTRACTIVES	INDUSTRIES MANUFACTURIERES	SERVICES PUBLICS	BATIMENTS ET TRAVAUX PUBLICS	TRANSPORTS ET COMMUNICATIONS	ACTIVITES DIVERSES
PAIS MONEDA	AÑO DE REFERENCIA	GASTOS TOTALES	AGRICULTURA SILVICULTURA CAZA Y PESCA	INDUSTRIAS EXTRACTIVAS	INDUSTRIAS MANUFACTURERAS	SERVICIOS PUBLICOS	CONSTRUCCION	TRANSPORTES Y COMUNICACIONES	OTRAS ACTIVIDADES
		(000)	(000)	(000)	(000)	(000)	(000)	(000)	(000)
		(1)	(2)	(3)	(4)	(5)	(6)	(7)	(8)
SWITZERLAND‡	1975	2 381 000	–	–	2 342 000	./.	17 000	13 000	9 000
FRANC		% 100	–	–	98.4	./.	0.7	0.5	0.4
UNITED KINGDOM‡	1975	1 340 100	./.	18 000	1 218 100	./.	6 000	45 400	52 500
POUND STERLING		% 100	./.	1.3	90.9	./.	0.4	3.4	3.9
YUGOSLAVIA‡	1981	10 294 000	1 424 000	1 837 000	5 702 000	–	1 022 000	125 000	184 000
DINAR		% 100	13.8	17.8	55.4	–	9.9	1.2	1.8
OCEANIA									
AUSTRALIA	1981	845 640	275 467	46 332	272 513	./.	7 863	4 605	238 860
DOLLAR		% 100	32.6	5.5	32.2	./.	0.9	0.5	28.2
NEW CALEDONIA	1983	81 500	81 500	–	–	–	–	–	–
FRANC C.F.P.		% 100	100.0	–	–	–	–	–	–
NEW ZEALAND	1975	61 620	29 360	1 487	23 115	./.	2 698	930	4 030
DOLLAR		% 100	47.6	2.4	37.5	./.	4.4	1.5	6.5
SAMOA‡	1977	116	72	23	19	./.	1	1	–
TALA		% 100	62.1	19.8	16.4	./.	0.9	0.9	–
VANUATU	1975	21 603	21 603	–	–	–	–	–	–
FRANC		% 100	100.0	–	–	–	–	–	–

AFRICA:

Congo:

E--> Not including military and defence R&D.

FR-> Non compris les activités de R-D de caractère militaire ou relevant de la défense nationale.

ESP> Excluídas las actividades militares y de defensa de I y D.

AMERICA, NORTH:

Canada:

E--> Data relate only to integrated R&D in the productive sector and do not include social sciences and humanities.

FR-> Les données ne se réfèrent qu'aux activités de R-D intégrées dans le secteur de la production et ne comprennent pas les sciences sociales et humaines.

ESP> Los datos sólo se refieren a las actividades de I y D integradas en el sector productivo y no incluyen las ciencias sociales y humanas.

Cuba:

E--> Not including military and defence R&D.

FR-> Non compris les activités de R-D de caractère militaire ou relevant de la défense nationale.

ESP> Excluídas las actividades militares y de defensa de I y D.

AMERICA, SOUTH:

Argentina:

E--> Figures in millions.

FR-> Chiffres en millions.

ESP> Cifras en millones.

Venezuela:

E--> Data relate to current expenditure for the relevant number of 167 institutes out of a total of 406 which perform R&D.

FR-> Les données ne se réfèrent qu'aux dépenses courantes pour une partie des 167 instituts sur un total de 406 qui exécutent les activités de R-D.

ESP> Los datos sólo se refieren a los gastos corrientes para una parte de los 167 centros sobre un total de 406 que ejecutan actividades de I y D.

ASIA:

Iran, Islamic Republic of:

E--> Data refer to the budget allotment.

FR-> Les données se réfèrent aux crédits budgétaires.

ESP> Los datos se refieren a las consignaciones presupuestarias.

Japan:

E--> Figures in millions. Not including social sciences and humanities. Data for utilities are included with transport and communication.

Japan: (Cont):

FR-> Chiffres en millions. Non compris les sciences sociales et humaines. Les données relatives aux services publics sont comptées avec celles des transports et communications.

ESP> Cifras en millones. No se incluyen las ciencias sociales y humanas. Los datos relativos a los servicios públicos quedan incluídos con los de transportes y communicaciones.

Korea, Republic of:

E--> Not including military and defence R&D and social sciences and humanities.

FR-> Non compris les activités de R-D de caractère militaire ou relevant de la défense nationale ni les sciences sociales et humaines.

ESP> Excluídas las actividades militares y de defensa de I y D y las ciencias sociales y humanas.

Pakistan:

E--> Data relate to R&D activities concentrated mainly in government-financed research establishments only. Not including the productive sector (integrated R&D) or military and defence R&D.

FR-> Les données se réfèrent aux activités de R-D se trouvant pour la plupart dans les établissements de recherche financés par le gouvernement. Compte non tenu du secteur de la production (activités de R-D intégrées) ni les activités de R-D de caractère militaire ou relevant de la défense nationale.

ESP> Los datos se refieren a las actividades de I y D concentradas principalmente en los establecimientos de investigación subvencionados por el gobierno. Excluídos el sector productivo (actividades de I y D integradas) y las actividades militares y de defensa de I y D.

EUROPE:

Denmark:

E--> Not including the productive sector (non-integrated R&D). Data for utilities are included with transport and communication.

FR-> Non compris le secteur de la production (activités de R-D non intégrées). Les données relatives aux services publics sont comptées avec celles des transports et communications.

ESP> No se incluye el sector productivo (actividades de I y D no integradas). Los datos relativos a los servicios públicos quedan incluídos con los de transportes y communicaciones.

Germany, Federal Republic of:

E--> Not including 450 million Deutsche marks for which a distribution by branch of economic activity is not available. Not including social sciences and humanities.

FR-> Non compris 450 millions de deutsche marks dont la répartition par branche d'activité économique n'est pas disponible. Non compris les

Germany, Federal Republic of: (Cont):
sciences sociales et humaines.

ESP> No se incluyen 450 millones de marcos cuya repartición por rama de actividad económica se desconoce. Excluídas las ciencias sociales y humanas.

Hungary:

E--> Not including the relevant part of 2,316 million forints (all current expenditure) for which a distribution by sector of performance and branch of economic activity is not available.

FR-> Non compris la part correspondante d'un montant de 2 316 millions de forints (dépenses courantes) dont la ventilation par secteur d'exécution et branche d'activité économique n'est pas disponible.

ESP> Excluída la parte correspondiente de la suma de 2 316 millones de forints (gastos corrientes) cuya repartición por sector de ejecución y rama de actividad económica se desconoce.

Ireland:

E--> Data relate only to integrated R&D in the productive sector.

FR-> Les données ne se réfèrent qu'aux activités de R-D intégrées dans le secteur de la production..

ESP> Los datos sólo se refieren a las actividades de I y D integradas en el sector productivo.

Italy:

E--> Figures in millions. Not including the productive sector (non-integrated R&D).

FR-> Chiffres en millions. Non compris le secteur de la production (activités de R-D non intégrées).

ESP> Cifras en millones. No se incluye el sector productivo (actividades de I y D no integradas).

Netherlands:

E--> Not including data for social sciences and humanities in the productive sector (integrated R&D). Data for extracting industries are included with 'other' industries.

FR-> Non compris les données pour les sciences sociales et humaines du secteur de la production (activités de R-D intégrées). Les données relatives aux industries extractives sont comptées avec les activités 'diverses'.

ESP> Excluídos los datos relativos a las ciencias sociales y humanas del sector productivo (actividades de I y D integradas). Los datos relativos a las industrias extractivas quedan incluídos con las 'otras' actividades.

Poland:

E--> Data relate to current expenditure only. Not including military and defence R&D.

FR-> Les données ne se réfèrent qu'aux dépenses courantes. Non compris les activités de R-D de caractère militaire ou relevant de la défense nationale.

ESP> Los datos se refieren a los gastos corrientes solamente. Excluídas las actividades militares y de defensa de I y D.

Portugal:

E--> Not including 298 million escudos in the productive sec (non-integrated R&D) for which a distribution by branch of econon activity is not available.

FR-> Non compris 298 millions d'escudos dans le secteur de production (activités de R-D non intégrées) dont la répartition par branc d'activité économique n'est pas disponible.

ESP> No se incluyen 298 millones de escudos en el sector producti (actividades de I y D no integradas) cuya repartición por rama de activid económica se desconoce.

Spain:

E--> Data relate only to integrated R&D in the productive sector.

FR-> Les données ne se réfèrent qu'aux activités de R-D intégrées da le secteur de la production.

ESP> Los datos sólo se refieren a las actividades de I y D integrad en el sector productivo.

Sweden:

E--> Not including data for social sciences and humanities.

FR-> Non compris les données pour les sciences sociales humaines.

ESP> Excluídos los datos relativos a las ciencias sociales y human

Switzerland:

E--> Data relate to current expenditure only and do not include soc sciences and humanities.

FR-> Les données ne se réfèrent qu'aux dépenses courantes et comprennent pas les sciences sociales et humaines.

ESP> Los datos se refieren a los gastos corrientes solamente excluyen las ciencias sociales y humanas.

United Kingdom:

E--> Not including data for social sciences and humanities.

FR-> Non compris les données pour les sciences sociales humaines.

ESP> Excluídos los datos relativos a las ciencias sociales y human

Yugoslavia:

E--> Not including military and defence R&D. Data refer to to revenue rather than total expenditure.

FR-> Non compris les activités de R-D de caractère militaire relevant de la défense nationale. Les données se réfèrent au total d revenus au lieu des dépenses totales.

ESP> Excluídas las actividades militares y de defensa de I y D. L datos se refieren a los ingresos totales en lugar de los gastos totales.

OCEANIA:

Samoa:

E--> Data relate to current expenditure only.

FR-> Les données ne se réfèrent qu'aux dépenses courantes.

ESP> Los datos se refieren a los gastos corrientes solamente.

5.14 Total expenditure for the performance of research and experimental development in the higher education and the general service sectors, by field of science and technology

Dépenses totales pour l'exécution de travaux de recherche et de développement expérimental dans les secteurs de l'enseignement supérieur et de service général, par domaine de la science et de la technologie

Gastos totales para la ejecución de trabajos de investigación y de desarrollo experimental en los sectores de enseñanza superior y de servicio general, por campo de la ciencia y de la tecnología

PLEASE REFER TO INTRODUCTION FOR DEFINITIONS OF CATEGORIES INCLUDED IN THIS TABLE.

HES = HIGHER EDUCATION SECTOR
GSS = GENERAL SERVICE SECTOR

AMOUNTS SHOWN ARE IN THOUSANDS.

NUMBER OF COUNTRIES AND TERRITORIES PRESENTED IN THIS TABLE: 43

POUR LES DEFINITIONS DES CATEGORIES PRESENTEES DANS CE TABLEAU, SE REFERER A L'INTRODUCTION.

HES = SECTEUR DE L'ENSEIGNEMENT SUPERIEUR
GSS = SECTEUR DE SERVICE GENERAL

LES MONTANTS SONT EXPRIMES EN MILLIERS.

NOMBRE DE PAYS ET DE TERRITOIRES PRESENTES DANS CE TABLEAU: 43

EN LA INTRODUCCION SE DAN LAS DEFINICIONES DE LAS CATEGORIAS QUE FIGURAN EN ESTE CUADRO.

HES = SECTOR DE ENSEÑANZA SUPERIOR
GSS = SECTOR DE SERVICIO GENERAL

LOS IMPORTES ESTAN EXPRESADOS EN MILLARES.

NUMERO DE PAISES Y DE TERRITORIOS PRESENTADOS EN ESTE CUADRO: 43

COUNTRY / CURRENCY PAYS / MONNAIE PAIS / MONEDA	REFERENCE YEAR ANEEE DE REFERENCE AÑO DE REFERENCIA	SECTOR OF PERFORMANCE SECTEUR DE EXECUTION SECTOR DE EJECUTION		TOTAL EXPENDITURE DEPENSES TOTALES GASTOS TOTALES (000)	FIELD OF SCIENCE AND TECHNOLOGY / DOMAINE DE LA SCIENCE ET DE LA TECHNOLOGIE / CAMPO DE LA CIENCIA Y DE LA TECNOLOGIA NATURAL SCIENCES SCIENCES EXACTES ET NATURELLES CIENCIAS EXACTAS Y NATURALES (000)	ENGINEERING AND TECHNOLOGY SCIENCES DE L'INGENIEUR ET TECHNO-LOGIQUES INGENIERIA Y TECNOLOGIA (000)	MEDICAL SCIENCES SCIENCES MEDICALES CIENCIAS MEDICAS (000)	AGRICULTURAL SCIENCES SCIENCES AGRICOLES CIENCIAS AGRICOLAS (000)	SOCIAL SCIENCES AND HUMANITIES SCIENCES SOCIALES ET HUMAINES CIENCIAS SOCIALES Y HUMANAS (000)	OTHER FIELDS DOMAINES DIVERS CAMPOS DIVERSOS (000)
				(1)	(2)	(3)	(4)	(5)	(6)	(7)
AFRICA										
CONGO‡	1984	HES		622	./.	./.	./.	./.	372	250
FRANC C.F.A			%	100	./.	./.	./.	./.	59.8	40.2
		GSS		407	./.	./.	./.	./.	./.	407
			%	100	./.	./.	./.	./.	./.	100.0
MALAWI‡	1977	HES		5	–	–	–	2	3	–
KWACHA			%	100		–	–	40.0	60.0	–
		GSS		13	–	–	–	–	13	–
			%	100	–	–	–	–	100.0	–
MAURITIUS	1983	HES		300	–	200	–	100	–	–
RUPEE			%	100	–	66.7	–	33.3	–	–
		GSS		34 700	–	–	–	34 700	–	–
			%	100	–	–	–	100.0	–	–
NIGER	1976	HES		141 703	55 786	–	16 571	12 257	57 089	–
FRANC C.F.A.			%	100	39.4	–	11.7	8.7	40.3	–
AMERICA, NORTH										
CANADA	1977	HES		*710 100	*210 700	*99 700	*165 200	*38 500	*196 000	–
DOLLAR			%	100	*29.7	*14.0	*23.3	*5.4	*27.6	–
	1982	GSS		*1 340 000	...	...	...	...	*83 000	...
			%	100	...	...	...	...	*6.2	...

COUNTRY CURRENCY / PAYS MONNAIE / PAIS MONEDA	REFERENCE YEAR / ANEEE DE REFERENCE / AÑO DE REFERENCIA	SECTOR OF PERFORMANCE / SECTEUR DE EXECUTION / SECTOR DE EJECUTION	TOTAL EXPENDITURE / DEPENSES TOTALES / GASTOS TOTALES (000)	FIELD OF SCIENCE AND TECHNOLOGY / DOMAINE DE LA SCIENCE ET DE LA TECHNOLOGIE / CAMPO DE LA CIENCIA Y DE LA TECNOLOGIA: NATURAL SCIENCES / SCIENCES EXACTES ET NATURELLES / CIENCIAS EXACTAS Y NATURALES (000)	ENGINEERING AND TECHNOLOGY / SCIENCES DE L'INGENIEUR ET TECHNO-LOGIQUES / INGENIERIA Y TECNOLOGIA (000)	MEDICAL SCIENCES / SCIENCES MEDICALES / CIENCIAS MEDICAS (000)	AGRICULTURAL SCIENCES / SCIENCES AGRICOLES / CIENCIAS AGRICOLAS (000)	SOCIAL SCIENCES AND HUMANITIES / SCIENCES SOCIALES ET HUMAINES / CIENCIAS SOCIALES Y HUMANAS (000)	OTHER FIELDS / DOMAINES DIVERS / CAMPOS DIVERSOS (000)
			(1)	(2)	(3)	(4)	(5)	(6)	(7)
CUBA‡ PESO	1983	HES	6 135	–	696	316	860	292	3 971
			% 100	–	11.3	5.2	14.0	4.8	64.7
		GSS	55 433	17 008	944	22 260	–	15 221	–
			% 100	30.7	1.7	40.2	–	27.5	–
PANAMA BALBOA	1975	HES	503	–	14	16	473	–	–
			% 100	–	2.8	3.2	94.0	–	–
		GSS	1 364	–	–	942	–	422	–
			% 100	–	–	69.1	–	30.9	–
UNITED STATES‡ DOLLAR	1983	HES	10 481 600	5 039 900	2 045 900	1 807 700	893 900	503 800	190 500
			% 100	48.1	19.5	17.3	8.5	4.8	1.8
AMERICA, SOUTH									
ARGENTINA‡ PESO	1980	HES	*222 100	*66 700	*33 300	*55 500	*33 300	*22 200	*11 100
			% 100	*30.0	*15.0	*25.0	*15.0	*10.0	*5.0
		GSS	*473 900	*161 100	*52 100	*80 600	*28 400	*61 600	*90 100
			% 100	*34.0	*11.0	*17.0	*6.0	*13.0	*19.0
BRAZIL CRUZEIRO	1977	HES	2 781 000	...	...	...	...	...	...
		GSS	1 236 900	67 900	156 000	66 100	25 100	921 800	–
			% 100	5.5	12.6	5.3	2.0	74.5	–
VENEZUELA‡ BOLIVAR	1977	HES	234 664	29 657	128 057	20 036	24 717	11 686	20 511
			% 100	12.6	54.6	8.5	10.5	5.0	8.7
		GSS	14 732	4 572	–	–	7 488	1 383	1 289
			% 100	31.0	–	–	50.8	9.4	8.8
ASIA									
INDIA RUPEE	1978	HES	92 000	...	...	...	...	...	...
		GSS	3 760 000	252 000	2 474 000	67 000	820 000	94 000	53 000
			% 100	6.7	65.8	1.8	21.8	2.5	1.4
IRAN, ISLAMIC REPUBLIC OF‡ RIAL	1984	HES	3 298 000	...	...	...	...	...	...
		GSS	695 000	./.	./.	./.	./.	95 000	600 000
			% 100	./.	./.	./.	./.	13.7	86.3
JAPAN‡ YEN	1983	HES	1 649 645	147 984	358 749	440 951	80 672	621 290	–
			% 100	9.0	21.7	26.7	4.9	37.7	–
		GSS	971 010	270 066	418 865	60 423	165 900	55 756	–
			% 100	27.8	43.1	6.2	17.1	5.7	–
KOREA, REPUBLIC OF‡ WON	1983	HES	64 251 213	13 310 195	19 896 428	21 124 514	6 466 559	...	3 453517
			% 100	20.7	31.0	32.9	10.1	...	5.4
		GSS	181 688 139	46 807 843	77 290 132	11 771 930	38 069 933	...	7 748301
			% 100	25.8	42.5	6.5	21.0	...	4.3
KUWAIT DINAR	1977	HES	616	324	70	25	–	197	–
			% 100	52.6	11.4	4.1	–	32.0	–
		GSS	4 166	2 324	459	40	546	797	–
			% 100	55.8	11.0	1.0	13.1	19.1	–
PHILIPPINES PESO	1982	HES	55 241	5 188	8 181	2 097	22 033	17 742	–
			% 100	9.4	14.8	3.8	39.9	32.1	–
		GSS	416 682	53 600	123 780	5 670	139 745	93 887	–
			% 100	12.9	29.7	1.4	33.5	22.5	–
SINGAPORE‡ DOLLAR	1981	HES	24 600	9 000	12 200	3 400	–	...	–
			% 100	36.6	49.6	13.8	–	...	–

COUNTRY CURRENCY PAYS MONNAIE PAIS MONEDA	REFERENCE YEAR ANEEE DE REFERENCE AÑO DE REFERENCIA	SECTOR OF PERFORMANCE SECTEUR DE EXECUTION SECTOR DE EJECUTION	TOTAL EXPENDITURE DEPENSES TOTALES GASTOS TOTALES (000)	FIELD OF SCIENCE AND TECHNOLOGY / DOMAINE DE LA SCIENCE ET DE LA TECHNOLOGIE / CAMPO DE LA CIENCIA Y DE LA TECNOLOGIA NATURAL SCIENCES SCIENCES EXACTES ET NATURELLES CIENCIAS EXACTAS Y NATURALES (000)	ENGINEERING AND TECHNOLOGY SCIENCES DE L'INGENIEUR ET TECHNO-LOGIQUES INGENIERIA Y TECNOLOGIA (000)	MEDICAL SCIENCES SCIENCES MEDICALES CIENCIAS MEDICAS (000)	AGRICULTURAL SCIENCES SCIENCES AGRICOLES CIENCIAS AGRICOLAS (000)	SOCIAL SCIENCES AND HUMANITIES SCIENCES SOCIALES ET HUMAINES CIENCIAS SOCIALES Y HUMANAS (000)	OTHER FIELDS DOMAINES DIVERS CAMPOS DIVERSOS (000)
			(1)	(2)	(3)	(4)	(5)	(6)	(7)
SRI LANKA‡	1975	HES	1 382	415	138	484	276	69	–
RUPEE			% 100	30.0	10.0	35.0	20.0	5.0	–
		GSS	6 745	645	232	1 256	./.	4 612	–
			% 100	9.6	3.4	18.6	./.	68.4	–
TURKEY‡	1983	HES	15 083 100	2 126 300	1 522 300	5 673 200	1 942 300	627 400	3 191600
LIRA			% 100	14.1	10.1	37.6	12.9	4.2	21.2
		GSS	7 722 200	160 200	2 028 100	1 071 400	4 355 100	...	107 400
			% 100	2.1	26.3	13.9	56.4	...	1.4
EUROPE									
AUSTRIA	1981	HES	4 044 607	990 407	462 003	1 499 683	154 709	937 805	–
SCHILLING			% 100	24.5	11.4	37.1	3.8	23.2	–
		GSS	1 399 782	136 984	65 406	464 104	244 197	489 091	–
			% 100	9.8	4.7	33.2	17.4	34.9	–
DENMARK	1979	HES	881 300	283 500	118 000	190 200	37 600	252 000	–
KRONE			% 100	32.2	13.4	21.6	4.3	28.6	–
		GSS	765 400	130 300	117 100	281 000	127 800	109 200	–
			% 100	17.0	15.3	36.7	16.7	14.3	–
FINLAND	1983	HES	775 310	208 330	170 150	173 530	21 840	201 460	–
MARKKA			% 100	26.9	21.9	22.4	2.8	26.0	–
	1981	GSS	656 140	116 340	272 180	57 320	134 280	76 020	–
			% 100	17.7	41.5	8.7	20.5	11.6	–
FRANCE	1977	HES	5 176 000	3 549 000	→	1 133 000	→	494 000	–
FRANC			% 100	68.6	→	21.9	→	9.5	–
	1975	GSS	5 901 700	4 429 600	→	640 000	705 400	126 700	–
			% 100	75.1	→	10.8	12.0	2.1	–
GERMANY, FEDERAL REPUBLIC OF	1981	HES	6 462 000	2 007 000	1 219 000	1 739 000	250 000	1 247 000	–
DEUTSCHE MARK			% 100	31.1	18.9	26.9	3.9	19.3	–
		GSS	5 694 000	3 301 000	907 000	545 000	338 000	603 000	–
			% 100	58.0	15.9	9.6	5.9	10.6	–
HUNGARY‡	1983	HES	2 339 000	569 000	793 000	360 000	330 000	287 000	–
FORINT			% 100	24.3	33.9	15.4	14.1	12.3	–
		GSS	3 166 000	1 323 000	762 000	342 000	299 000	440 000	–
			% 100	41.8	24.1	10.8	9.4	13.9	–
ICELAND	1979	HES	1 743 200	815 300	60 500	278 900	226 700	361 800	–
KRONA			% 100	46.8	3.5	16.0	13.0	20.8	–
		GSS	1 696 600	227 100	979 400	311 800	137 200	41 100	–
			% 100	13.4	57.7	18.4	8.1	2.4	–
IRELAND‡	1982	HES	15 643	5 434	2 727	1 989	1 676	3 817	–
POUND			% 100	34.7	17.4	12.7	10.7	24.4	–
		GSS	39 411	4 970	10 496	1 710	14 953	5 827	1 455
			% 100	12.6	26.6	4.3	37.9	14.8	3.7
ITALY‡	1983	HES	1 161 231	336 757	174 185	278 695	116 124	255 470	–
LIRA			% 100	29.0	15.0	24.0	10.0	22.0	–
NETHERLANDS	1982	HES	1 939 000	400 000	309 000	583 000	87 000	560 000	–
GUILDER			% 100	20.6	15.9	30.1	4.5	28.9	–
		GSS	1 588 000	./.	./.	./.	./.	251 000	–
			% 100	./.	./.	./.	./.	15.8	–

COUNTRY CURRENCY / PAYS MONNAIE / PAIS MONEDA	REFERENCE YEAR / ANEEE DE REFERENCE / AÑO DE REFERENCIA	SECTOR OF PERFORMANCE / SECTEUR DE EXECUTION / SECTOR DE EJECUTION	TOTAL EXPENDITURE / DEPENSES TOTALES / GASTOS TOTALES (000)	FIELD OF SCIENCE AND TECHNOLOGY / DOMAINE DE LA SCIENCE ET DE LA TECHNOLOGIE / CAMPO DE LA CIENCIA Y DE LA TECNOLOGIA: NATURAL SCIENCES / SCIENCES EXACTES ET NATURELLES / CIENCIAS EXACTAS Y NATURALES (000)	ENGINEERING AND TECHNOLOGY / SCIENCES DE L'INGENIEUR ET TECHNO-LOGIQUES / INGENIERIA Y TECNOLOGIA (000)	MEDICAL SCIENCES / SCIENCES MEDICALES / CIENCIAS MEDICAS (000)	AGRICULTURAL SCIENCES / SCIENCES AGRICOLES / CIENCIAS AGRICOLAS (000)	SOCIAL SCIENCES AND HUMANITIES / SCIENCES SOCIALES ET HUMAINES / CIENCIAS SOCIALES Y HUMANAS (000)	OTHER FIELDS / DOMAINES DIVERS / CAMPOS DIVERSOS (000)
			(1)	(2)	(3)	(4)	(5)	(6)	(7)
NORWAY KRONE	1981	HES	1 220 000	369 100	130 500	332 800	79 000	308 600	–
			% 100	30.3	10.7	27.3	6.5	25.3	–
		GSS	796 900	211 000	223 500	71 800	119 700	170 900	–
			% 100	26.5	28.0	9.0	15.0	21.4	–
POLAND‡ ZLOTY	1983	HES	8 228 400	...	...	...	...	...	...
		GSS	8 399 200	4 178 500	1 626 900	1 537 500	211 100	845 200	–
			% 100	49.7	19.4	18.3	2.5	10.1	–
PORTUGAL ESCUDO	1976	HES	224 085	108 374	43 066	34 653	11 376	26 616	–
			% 100	48.4	19.2	15.5	5.1	11.9	–
		GSS	726 783	75 508	213 046	44 683	336 138	57 408	–
			% 100	10.4	29.3	6.1	46.3	7.9	–
SPAIN‡ PESETA	1983	HES	17 804 758	4 992 097	2 841 300	3 513 764	948 595	5 509 002	–
			% 100	28.0	16.0	19.7	5.3	30.9	–
		GSS	30 749 476	5 888 941	13 314 326	2 903 859	7 380 380	1 261 970	–
			% 100	19.2	43.3	9.4	24.0	4.1	–
SWEDEN KRONA	1981	HES	3 995 000	621 000	829 000	1 638 000	327 000	580 000	–
			% 100	15.5	20.8	41.0	8.2	14.5	–
SWITZERLAND‡ FRANC	1976	HES	*523 000	*210 000	*80 000	*140 000	*20 000	*73 000	–
			% 100	*40.2	*15.3	*26.8	*3.8	*14.0	–
		GSS	*189 000	*90 000	*30 000	*15 000	*50 000	*4 000	–
			% 100	*47.6	*15.9	*7.9	*26.5	*2.1	–
YUGOSLAVIA‡ DINAR	1981	HES	3 454 000	182 000	1 394 000	658 000	891 000	329 000	–
			% 100	5.3	40.4	19.1	25.8	9.5	–
		GSS	4 487 000	1 681 000	658 000	558 000	88 000	1 450 000	52 000
			% 100	37.5	14.7	12.4	2.0	32.3	1.2
OCEANIA									
AUSTRALIA DOLLAR	1981	HES	452 489	170 193	51 407	59 721	33 746	137 422	
			% 100	37.6	11.4	13.2	7.5	30.4	–
		GSS	224 118	65 255	121 686	21 579	485	15 113	–
			% 100	29.1	54.3	9.6	.2	6.7	–
FRENCH POLYNESIA‡ FRANC C.F.P.	1983	GSS	324 720	103 020	–	221 700	–	–	–
			% 100	31.7	–	68.3	–	–	–
NEW CALEDONIA FRANC C.F.P.	1983	HES	–	–	–	–	–	–	–
			% 100	–	–	–	–	–	–
		GSS	1 500	1 500	–	–	–	–	–
			% 100	100.0	–	–	–	–	–
NEW ZEALAND‡ DOLLAR	1975	HES	17 033	3 588	785	4 797	1 421	4 980	1 462
			% 100	21.1	4.6	28.2	8.3	29.2	8.6
		GSS	19 377	15 113	——>	2 266	./.	1 998	–
			% 100	78.0	——>	11.7	./.	10.3	–
SAMOA‡ TALA	1977	HES	152	28	32	48	20	24	–
			% 100	18.4	21.1	31.6	13.2	15.8	–
		GSS	73	25	20	3	22	3	–
			% 100	34.2	27.4	4.1	30.1	4.1	–
TONGA‡ PA'ANGA	1980	HES	–	–	–	–	–	–	–
			% 100	–	–	–	–	–	–
		GSS	426	–	–	–	426	–	–
			% 100	–	–	–	100.0	–	–

AFRICA:

Congo:

E--> Not including military and defence R&D.

FR--> Non compris les activités de R-D de caractère militaire ou relevant de la défense nationale.

ESP> Excluídas las actividades militares y de defensa de I y D.

Malawi:

E--> Data for the higher education sector relate to current expenditure only.

FR--> Les données relatives au secteur de l'enseignement supérieur ne se réfèrent qu'aux dépenses courantes.

ESP> Los datos relativos al sector del enseñanza superior se refieren a los gastos corrientes solamente.

AMERICA, NORTH:

Cuba:

E--> Not including military and defence R&D.

FR--> Non compris les activités de R-D de caractère militaire ou relevant de la défense nationale.

ESP> Excluídas las actividades militares y de defensa de I y D.

United States:

E--> Data relate to current expenditure only. Not including data for law, humanities and education.

FR--> Les données ne se réfèrent qu'aux dépenses courantes. Non compris les données pour le droit, les sciences humaines et l'éducation.

ESP> Los datos se refieren a los gastos corrientes solamente. Excluídos los datos relativos al derecho, las ciencias humanas y la educación.

AMERICA, SOUTH:

Argentina;

E--> Figures in millions.

FR--> Chiffres en millions.

ESP> Cifras en millones.

Venezuela:

E--> Data relate to current expenditure only for the relevant number of the 167 institutes out of a total of 406 which perform R&D.

FR--> Les données ne se réfèrent qu'aux dépenses courantes pour une partie des 167 instituts sur un total de 406 qui exécutent les activités de R-D.

ESP> Los datos se refieren a los gastos corrientes para una parte de los 167 centros sobre un total de 406 que ejecutan actividades de I y D.

ASIA:

Iran, Republic Islamic of:

E--> Data refer to the budget allotment.

FR--> Les données se réfèrent aux crédits budgétaires.

ESP> Los datos se refieren a las consignaciones presupuestarias.

Japan:

E--> Figures in millions.

FR--> Chiffres en millions

ESP> Cifras en millones.

Korea, Republic of:

E--> Not including military and defence R&D and social sciences and humanities.

FR--> Non compris les activités de R-D de caractère militaire ou relevant de la défense nationale ni les sciences sociales et humaines.

ESP> Excluídas las actividades militares y de defensa de I y D y las ciencias sociales y humanas.

Singapore:

E--> Not including military and defence R&D and social sciences and humanities.

FR--> Non compris les activités de R-D de caractère militaire ou relevant de la défense nationale ni les sciences sociales et humaines.

ESP> Excluídas las actividades militares y de defensa de I y D y las ciencias sociales y humanas.

Sri Lanka:

E--> Data relate to current expenditure only.

FR--> Les données ne se réfèrent qu'aux dépenses courantes.

ESP> Los datos se refieren a los gastos corrientes solamente.

Turkey:

E--> Not including data for social sciences and humanities in the general service sector.

FR--> Non compris les données pour les sciences sociales et humaines du secteur de service général.

ESP> Excluídos los datos relativos a las ciencias sociales y humanos al sector de servicio general.

EUROPE:

Hungary:

E--> Not including the relevant part of 2 316 million forints (all current expenditure) for which a distribution by sector of performance and field of science and technology is not available.

FR--> Non compris la part correspondante d'un montant de 2 316 millions de forints (dépenses courantes) dont la ventilation par secteur d'exécution et domaine de la science et de la technologie n'est pas disponible.

ESP> Excluída la parte correspondiente de la suma de 2 316 millones de forints (gastos corrientes) cuya repartición por sector de ejecución y campo de la ciencia y la tecnología se desconoce.

Ireland:

E--> Data for the productive sector (non-integrated R&D) are included with the general service sector.

FR--> Les données relatives au secteur de la production (activités de R-D non intégrées) sont comptées avec celles de service général.

ESP> Los datos relativos al sector productivo (actividades de I y D no integradas) quedan incluídos con los del servicio general.

Italy:

E--> Figures in millions.

FR--> Chiffres en millions.

ESP> Cifras en millones.

Poland:

E--> Data relate to current expenditure only. Not including military and defence R&D.

FR--> Les données ne se réfèrent qu'aux dépenses courantes. Non compris les activités de R-D de caractère militaire ou relevant de la défense nationale.

ESP> Los datos se refieren a los gastos corrientes solamente. Excluídas las actividades militares y de defensa de I y D.

Spain:

E--> Data for the productive sector (non-integrated R&D) are included with the general service sector.

FR--> Les données relatives au secteur de la production (activités de R-D non intégrées) sont comptées avec celles de service général.

ESP> Los datos relativos al sector productivo (actividades de I y D no integradas) quedan incluídos con los del servicio general.

Switzerland:

E--> Data relate to current expenditure only.

FR--> Les données ne se réfèrent qu'aux dépenses courantes.

ESP> Los datos se refieren a los gastos corrientes solamente.

Yugoslavia:

E--> Not including military and defence R&D. Data refer to total revenue rather than total expenditure.

FR--> Non compris les activités de R-D de caractère militaire ou relevant de la défense nationale. Les données se réfèrent au total des revenus au lieu des dépenses totales.

ESP> Excluídas las actividades militares y de defensa de I y D. Los datos se refieren a los ingresos totales en lugar de los gastos totales.

OCEANIA:

French Polynesia:

E--> Data refer to one research institute only.

FR--> Les données ne concernent qu'un institut de recherche seulement.

ESP> Los datos se refieren a un centro de investigación solamente.

New Zealand:

E--> Data for the general service sector relate to current expenditure only. Agricultural sciences are included with natural sciences.

FR--> Les données pour le secteur de service général ne se réfèrent qu'aux dépenses courantes. Les sciences de l'agriculture sont comptées avec les sciences exactes et naturelles.

ESP> Los datos para el sector de servicio general se refieren a los gastos corrientes solamente. Las ciencias agrícolas quedan incluídas con las ciencias exactas y naturales.

Samoa:

E--> Data relate to current expenditure only.

FR--> Les données ne se réfèrent qu'aux dépenses courantes.

ESP> Los datos se refieren a los gastos corrientes solamente.

Tonga:

E--> Data refer to one research institute only.

FR--> Les données ne concernent qu'un institut de recherche seulement.

ESP> Los datos se refieren a un centro de investigación solamente.

5.15 Expenditure for national research and experimental development activities by major socio-economic aim

Dépenses afférentes aux activités nationales de recherche et de développement expérimental, par finalités socio-économiques principales

Gastos destinados a las actividades nacionales de investigación y de desarrollo experimental, por finalidades socio-económicas principales

PLEASE REFER TO INTRODUCTION FOR DEFINITIONS OF CATEGORIES INCLUDED IN THIS TABLE.

T = TOTAL EXPENDITURE
P = EXPENDITURE FINANCED FROM PUBLIC FUNDS

AMOUNTS SHOWN ARE IN THOUSANDS.

NUMBER OF COUNTRIES AND TERRITORIES PRESENTED IN THIS TABLE: 40

POUR LES DEFINITIONS DES CATEGORIES PRESENTEES DANS CE TABLEAU, SE REFERER A L'INTRODUCTION.

T = DEPENSES TOTALES
P = DEPENSES FINANCEES AVEC DES FONDS PUBLICS

LES MONTANTS SONT EXPRIMES EN MILLIERS.

NOMBRE DE PAYS ET DE TERRITOIRES PRESENTES DANS CE TABLEAU: 40

COUNTRY CURRENCY PAYS MONNAIE PAIS MONEDA	REFERENCE YEAR ANNEE DE REFERENCE AÑO DE REFERENCIA	TYPE OF EXPENDITURE TYPE DE DEPENSES TIPO DE GASTOS		TOTAL TOTAL TOTAL	DISTRIBUTION BY MAJOR AIM / DISTRIBUTION				
					I EARTH, SEAS AND THE ATMOSPHERE LA TERRE, LES MERS ET L'ATMOSPHERE LA TIERRA, LOS MARES Y LA ATMOSFERA	II CIVIL SPACE ESPACE CIVIL ESPACIO CIVIL	III DEVELOPMENT OF AGRICULTURE DEVELOPPEMENT DE L'AGRICULTURE DESARROLLO DE LA AGRICULTURA	IV INDUSTRIAL DEVELOPMENT DEVELOPPEMENT INDUSTRIEL DESARROLLO INDUSTRIAL	V ENERGY ENERGIE ENERGIA
				(1)	(2)	(3)	(4)	(5)	(6)
AFRICA									
CONGO (FRANC C.F.A.)	1984	P	 %	17 575 100	– –	– –	16 164 92.0	– –	– –
SUDAN (POUND)	1977	T	 %	5 115 100	– –	– –	1 854 36.2	481 9.4	– –
AMERICA, NORTH									
CANADA‡ (DOLLAR)	1983	P	 %	*2 281 900 100	*170 000 *7.5	– –	*465 100 *20.4	*274 900 *12.0	*172 900 *7.6
CUBA‡ (PESO)	1983	T	 %	143 188 100	– –	– –	43 587 30.4	38 516 26.9	599 0.4
PANAMA (BALBOA)	1975	P	 %	1 765 100	241 13.6	——> ——>	176 9.9	253 14.4	327 18.6
ST. PIERRE AND MIQUELON (FRENCH FRANC)	1983	T	 %	*3 803 100	– –	– –	*3 803 *100.0	– –	– –
UNITED STATES‡ (DOLLAR)	1982	P	 %	38 768 000 100	477 000 1.2	2 134 000 5.5	1 012 000 2.6	151 000 0.4	2 578 000 6.7
AMERICA, SOUTH									
ARGENTINA‡ (PESO)	1981	T	 %	2 321 932 100	194 346 8.4	15 325 0.7	393 103 16.9	218 494 9.4	153 248 6.6
BRAZIL (CRUZEIRO)	1977	P	 %	10 337 400 100	547 300 5.3	——> ——>	1 382 700 13.4	1 487 400 14.4	2 303 700 22.3
COLOMBIA‡ (PESO)	1982	T	 %	2 754 273 100	208 909 7.6	167 0.0	1 426 728 51.8	140 188 5.1	338 693 12.3
ASIA									
INDIA (RUPEE)	1982	T	 %	9 972 570 100	911 180 9.1	860 520 8.6	2 387 240 23.9	1 630 650 16.4	1 348 490 13.5

EN LA INTRODUCCION SE DAN LAS DEFINICIONES DE LAS CATEGORIAS QUE FIGURAN EN ESTE CUADRO.

T = GASTOS TOTALES
P = GASTOS FINANCIADOS CON FONDOS PUBLICOS

LOS IMPORTES ESTAN EXPRESADOS EN MILLARES.

NUMERO DE PAISES Y DE TERRITORIOS PRESENTADOS EN ESTE CUADRO: 40

PAR FINALITES PRINCIPALES / REPARTICION POR PRINCIPALES FINALIDADES

VI	VII	VIII	IX	X	XI	XII	XIII	
TRANSPORT AND COMMUNICATION	EDUCATION SERVICES	HEALTH SERVICES	SOCIO-ECONOMIC SERVICES	ENVIRONMENT	ADVANCEMENT OF KNOWLEDGE	OTHER AIMS	DEFENCE	COUNTRY
TRANSPORTS ET COMMUNICATIONS	SERVICES D'ENSEIGNEMENT	SERVICES DE SANTE	SERVICES SOCIO-ECONOMIQUES	ENVIRONNEMENT	PROMOTION DES CONNAISSANCES	AUTRES FINALITES	DEFENSE	PAYS
TRANSPORTES Y COMUNICACIONES	SERVICIOS EDUCATIVOS	SERVICIOS DE SANIDAD	SERVICIOS SOCIO-ECONOMICOS	MEDIO AMBIENTE	ADELANTO DEL SABER	OTRAS FINALIDADES	DEFENSA	PAIS
(7)	(8)	(9)	(10)	(11)	(12)	(13)	(14)	
								AFRICA
–	622	90	104	–	595	–	...	CONGO
–	3.5	0.5	0.6	–	3.4	–	...	
–	–	–	–	–	291	2 489	–	SUDAN
–	–	–	–	–	5.7	48.7	–	
								AMERICA, NORTH
*132 200	–	*171 500	*106 400	*42 400	*586 900	*9 100	*150 500	CANADA‡
*5.8	–	*7.5	*4.7	*1.9	*25.7	*0.4	*6.6	
3 622	123	22 491	5 036	493	18 045	10 676	...	CUBA‡
2.5	0.1	15.7	3.5	0.3	12.6	7.5	...	
–	–	11	718	–	–	39	–	PANAMA
–	–	0.6	40.7	–	–	2.2	–	
–	–	–	–	–	–	–	–	ST. PIERRE AND MIQUELON
–	–	–	–	–	–	–	–	
876 000	102 000	4 455 000	339 000	208 000	1 502 000	–	24 936 000	UNITED STATES‡
2.3	0.3	11.5	0.9	0.5	3.9	–	64.3	
								AMERICA, SOUTH
136 758	65 478	509 664	./.	./.	278 400	330 414	26 702	ARGENTINA‡
5.9	2.8	22.0	./.	./.	12.0	14.2	1.1	
584 900	162 600	65 200	395 400	85 200	2 781 800	541 200	./.	BRAZIL
5.7	1.6	0.6	3.8	0.8	26.9	5.2	./.	
12 833	64 217	261 363	134 153	64 669	26 120	68 064	8 169	COLOMBIA‡
0.5	2.3	9.5	4.9	2.3	0.9	2.5	0.3	
								ASIA
315 670	./.	277 540	33 520	47 400	675 320	78 320	1 406 720	INDIA
3.2	./.	2.8	0.3	0.5	6.8	0.8	14.1	

COUNTRY CURRENCY PAYS MONNAIE PAIS MONEDA	REFERENCE YEAR ANNEE DE REFERENCE AÑO DE REFERENCIA	TYPE OF EXPENDI-TURE TYPE DE DEPENSES TIPO DE GASTOS		TOTAL TOTAL TOTAL	DISTRIBUTION BY MAJOR AIM / DISTRIBUTION I EARTH, SEAS AND THE ATMOSPHERE LA TERRE, LES MERS ET L'ATMOSPHERE LA TIERRA, LOS MARES Y LA ATMOSFERA	II CIVIL SPACE ESPACE CIVIL ESPACIO CIVIL	III DEVELOPMENT OF AGRICULTURE DEVELOPPE-MENT DE L'-AGRICULTURE DESARROLLO DE LA AGRICULTURA	IV INDUSTRIAL DEVELOPMENT DEVELOPPE-MENT INDUSTRIEL DESARROLLO INDUSTRIAL	V ENERGY ENERGIE ENERGIA
				(1)	(2)	(3)	(4)	(5)	(6)
JAPAN‡	1983	P		691 359	15 516	63 370	156 781	87 135	201 127
(YEN)			%	100	2.2	9.2	22.7	12.6	29.1
PHILIPPINES‡	1975	T		176 930	6 236	→	81 766	21 784	9 926
(PESO)			%	100	3.5	→	46.2	12.3	5.6
SINGAPORE‡	1981	P		12 900	–	–	7 900	3 500	–
(DOLLAR)			%	100	–	–	61.2	27.1	–
SRI LANKA‡	1975	P		24 140	–	–	11 787	2 613	–
(RUPEE)			%	100	–	–	48.8	10.8	–
THAILAND‡	1975	P		33 587 313	–	–	4 248 461	188 284	298 296
(BAHT)			%	100	–	–	12.6	0.6	0.9
EUROPE									
AUSTRIA‡	1981	P		5 587 544	153 096	9 629	342 023	645 985	124 033
(SCHILLING)			%	100	2.7	0.2	6.1	11.6	2.2
DENMARK‡	1979	T		1 496 900	64 800	6 000	158 700	92 200	93 200
(KRONE)			%	100	4.3	0.4	10.6	6.2	6.2
FINLAND‡	1984	P		1 880 600	131 100	→	189 700	447 800	95 100
(MARKKA)			%	100	7.0	→	10.1	23.8	5.1
FRANCE‡	1980	P		31 100 000	929 000	1 927 000	1 214 000	2 902 000	2 340 000
(FRANC)			%	100	3.0	6.2	3.9	9.3	7.5
GERMANY, FEDERAL REPUBLIC OF‡	1981	P		18 067 000	514 000	710 000	357 000	1 834 000	2 700 000
(DEUTSCHE MARK)			%	100	2.8	3.9	2.0	10.2	14.9
GREECE	1979	P		2 640 000	137 700	8 100	810 000	132 000	185 500
(DRACHMA)			%	100	5.2	0.3	30.7	5.0	7.0
HUNGARY‡	1976	T		9 030 000	./.	./.	463 000	6 010 000	→
(FORINT)			%	100	./.	./.	5.1	66.6	→
ICELAND	1979	T		6 427 525	59 205	18 997	2 144 532	1 043 620	858 554
(KRONA)			%	100	0.9	0.3	33.4	16.2	13.4
IRELAND	1982	T		97 582	1 937	–	19 462	31 399	4 921
(POUND)			%	100	2.0	–	19.9	32.2	5.0
ITALY‡	1976	P		582 807	60 940	→	18 066	60 350	121 134
(LIRA)			%	100	10.5	→	3.1	10.4	20.8
NETHERLANDS‡	1982	P		3 893 000	36 000	200 000	279 000	260 000	207 000
(GUILDER)			%	100	0.9	5.1	7.2	6.7	5.3
NORWAY‡	1981	T		3 812 300	295 500	10 500	269 500	1 377 800	247 200
(KRONE)			%	100	7.8	0.3	7.1	36.1	6.5
PORTUGAL	1982	T		6 541 200	573 600	–	765 900	*1 801 500	*226 600
(ESCUDO)			%	100	8.8	–	11.7	*27.5	*3.5
SPAIN‡	1983	T		82 892 334	546 340	–	6 656 270	37 921 679	3 204 362
(PESETA)			%	100	0.6	–	8.0	45.7	3.9
SWEDEN‡	1981	T		12 240 000	33 000	7 000	154 000	6 401 000	338 000
(KRONA)			%	100	0.3	0.1	1.3	52.3	2.8
SWITZERLAND‡	1975	P		638 000	13 000	→	67 000	23 000	47 000
(FRANC)			%	100	2.0	→	10.5	3.6	7.4
UNITED KINGDOM‡	1981	P		3 563 600	63 900	69 000	190 900	224 400	226 700
(POUND STERLING)			%	100	1.8	1.9	5.4	6.3	6.4
OCEANIA									
AUSTRALIA‡	1981	P		1 120 919	69 697	–	300 776	95 074	78 999
(DOLLAR)			%	100	6.2	–	26.8	8.5	7.0
FRENCH POLYNESIA‡	1983	P		269 950	–	–	*15 000	–	–
(FRANC C.F.P.)			%	100	–	–	*5.6	–	–
NEW CALEDONIA	1983	P		61 500	–	–	60 000	–	–
(FRANC C.F.P.)			%	100	–	–	97.6	–	–

PAR FINALITES PRINCIPALES / REPARTICION POR PRINCIPALES FINALIDADES

VI	VII	VIII	IX	X	XI	XII	XIII	
TRANSPORT AND COMMUNICATION	EDUCATION SERVICES	HEALTH SERVICES	SOCIO-ECONOMIC SERVICES	ENVIRONMENT	ADVANCEMENT OF KNOWLEDGE	OTHER AIMS	DEFENCE	COUNTRY
TRANSPORTS ET COMMUNICATIONS	SERVICES D'ENSEIGNEMENT	SERVICES DE SANTE	SERVICES SOCIO-ECONOMIQUES	ENVIRONNEMENT	PROMOTION DES CONNAISSANCES	AUTRES FINALITES	DEFENSE	PAYS
TRANSPORTES Y COMUNICACIONES	SERVICIOS EDUCATIVOS	SERVICIOS DE SANIDAD	SERVICIOS SOCIO-ECONOMICOS	MEDIO AMBIENTE	ADELANTO DEL SABER	OTRAS FINALIDADES	DEFENSA	PAIS
(7)	(8)	(9)	(10)	(11)	(12)	(13)	(14)	
20 320 2.9	./. ./.	36 282 5.2	9 826 1.6	20 439 3.0	24 594 3.6	15 636 2.3	40 331 5.8	JAPAN‡
1 143 0.6	10 572 6.0	17 087 9.7	9 928 5.6	3 702 2.1	3 709 2.1	2 654 1.5	8 423 4.8	PHILIPPINES‡
700 5.4	... ...	400 3.1	300 2.3	100 0.8	– –	– –	... ...	SINGAPORE‡
31 0.1	– –	1 256 5.2	3 602 14.9	– –	2 259 9.4	2 592 10.7	– –	SRI LANKA‡
5 341 728 15.9	10 011 284 29.8	1 526 322 4.5	3 725 081 11.1	– –	– –	– –	8 247 857 24.6	THAILAND‡
								EUROPE
80 613 1.4	106 906 1.9	1 945 321 34.8	474 256 8.5	117 329 2.1	1 511 212 27.0	76 434 1.4	707 0.0	AUSTRIA‡
54 600 3.6	174 300 11.6	389 200 26.0	./. ./.	./. ./.	458 300 30.6	– –	5 600 0.4	DENMARK‡
85 300 4.5	14 400 0.8	70 100 3.7	45 200 2.4	51 700 2.7	713 200 37.9	./. ./.	37 000 2.0	FINLAND‡
844 000 2.7	./. ./.	1 377 000 4.4	402 000 1.3	342 000 1.1	6 917 000 22.2	556 000 1.8	11 350 000 36.5	FRANCE‡
385 000 2.1	./. ./.	704 000 3.9	683 000 3.8	308 000 1.7	8 037 000 44.5	307 000 1.7	1 527 000 8.5	GERMANY, FEDERAL REPUBLIC OF‡
42 000 1.6	./. ./.	130 000 4.9	216 400 8.2	32 000 1.2	839 000 31.8	12 300 0.5	95 000 3.6	GREECE
138 000 1.5	100 000 1.1	——> ——>	./. ./.	./. ./.	1 431 000 15.8	888 000 9.8	... ...	HUNGARY‡
35 842 0.6	20 325 0.3	345 139 5.4	30 289 0.5	69 448 1.1	1 801 574 28.0	– –	– –	ICELAND
680 0.7	./. ./.	6 272 6.4	6 329 6.5	./. ./.	16 371 16.8	10 211 10.5	– –	IRELAND
2 353 0.4	492 0.1	17 413 3.0	5 887 1.0	4 137 0.7	260 099 44.6	5 612 1.0	26 324 4.5	ITALY‡
51 000 1.3	24 000 0.6	170 000 4.4	107 000 2.7	./. ./.	2 153 000 55.3	282 000 7.2	124 000 3.2	NETHERLANDS‡
186 200 4.9	51 900 1.3	246 400 6.5	301 400 7.9	115 900 3.0	558 700 14.7	– –	151 300 4.0	NORWAY‡
*269 500 *4.1	– –	608 800 9.3	383 200 5.9	*481 300 *7.4	1 346 900 20.6	*83 900 *1.3	– –	PORTUGAL
7 345 068 8.9	./. ./.	5 456 427 6.6	13 656 0.0	183 370 0.2	18 334 0.0	17 089 742 20.6	4 457 086 5.4	SPAIN‡
200 000 1.6	2 000 0.0	30 000 0.2	132 000 1.1	84 000 0.7	3 901 000 31.9	– –	958 000 7.8	SWEDEN‡
29 000 4.5	8 000 1.3	114 000 17.9	9 000 1.4	20 000 3.1	257 000 40.3	20 000 3.1	31 000 4.9	SWITZERLAND‡
./. ./.	./. ./.	132 900 3.7	86 800 2.4	42 400 1.2	540 000 15.2	247 100 6.9	1 739 400 48.8	UNITED KINGDOM‡
								OCEANIA
12 492 1.1	20 547 1.8	106 941 9.5	70 698 6.3	41 049 3.7	210 797 18.8	– –	113 849 10.2	AUSTRALIA‡
– –	– –	*174 950 *64.8	*30 000 *11.1	*10 000 *3.7	*40 000 *14.8	– –	– –	FRENCH POLYNESIA‡
– –	– –	– –	– –	– –	1 500 2.4	– –	– –	NEW CALEDONIA

COUNTRY CURRENCY / PAYS MONNAIE / PAIS MONEDA	REFERENCE YEAR / ANNEE DE REFERENCE / AÑO DE REFERENCIA	TYPE OF EXPENDITURE / TYPE DE DEPENSES / TIPO DE GASTOS		TOTAL / TOTAL / TOTAL	DISTRIBUTION BY MAJOR AIM / DISTRIBUTION: I EARTH, SEAS AND THE ATMOSPHERE / LA TERRE, LES MERS ET L'ATMOSPHERE / LA TIERRA, LOS MARES Y LA ATMOSFERA	II CIVIL SPACE / ESPACE CIVIL / ESPACIO CIVIL	III DEVELOPMENT OF AGRICULTURE / DEVELOPPEMENT DE L'AGRICULTURE / DESARROLLO DE LA AGRICULTURA	IV INDUSTRIAL DEVELOPMENT / DEVELOPPEMENT INDUSTRIEL / DESARROLLO INDUSTRIAL	V ENERGY / ENERGIE / ENERGIA
				(1)	(2)	(3)	(4)	(5)	(6)
NEW ZEALAND‡	1975	P		79 974	15 474	⟶	32 027	7 152	–
(DOLLAR)			%	100	19.3	⟶	40.0	8.9	–
SAMOA	1975	P		217	–	–	19	19	15
(TALA)			%	100	–	–	8.8	8.8	6.9
TONGA‡	1980	P		106	–	–	106	–	–
(PA'ANGA)			%	100	–	–	100.0	–	–
VANUATU	1975	P		19 941	–	–	19 941	–	–
(FRANC)			%	100	–	–	100.0	–	–

PAR FINALITES PRINCIPALES / REPARTICION POR PRINCIPALES FINALIDADES								
VI	VII	VIII	IX	X	XI	XII	XIII	
TRANSPORT AND COM- MUNICATION	EDUCATION SERVICES	HEALTH SERVICES	SOCIO- ECONOMIC SERVICES	ENVIRON- MENT	ADVANCE- MENT OF KNOWLEDGE	OTHER AIMS	DEFENCE	COUNTRY
TRANSPORTS ET COMMUNI- CATIONS	SERVICES D'EN- SEIGNEMENT	SERVICES DE SANTE	SERVICES SOCIO- ECONOMIQUES	ENVIRON- NEMENT	PROMOTION DES CON- NAISSANCES	AUTRES FINALITES	DEFENSE	PAYS
TRANSPORTES Y COMUNICA- CIONES	SERVICIOS EDUCATIVOS	SERVICIOS DE SANIDAD	SERVICIOS SOCIO- ECONOMICOS	MEDIO AMBIENTE	ADELANTO DEL SABER	OTRAS FINALI- DADES	DEFENSA	PAIS
(7)	(8)	(9)	(10)	(11)	(12)	(13)	(14)	
934	./.	5 124	2 377	–	12 929	3 957	–	NEW ZEALAND‡
1.2	./.	6.4	3.0	–	16.2	4.9	–	
62	20	61	–	–	6	15	–	SAMOA
28.6	9.2	28.1	–	–	2.8	6.9	–	
–	–	–	–	–	–	–	–	TONGA‡
–	–	–	–	–	–	–	–	
–	–	–	–	–	–	–	–	VANUATU
–	–	–	–	–	–	–	–	

AMERICA, NORTH:

Canada:

E--> Data relate to the federal government budget only.

FR-> Les données ne concernent que le budget du gouvernement fédéral.

ESP> Los datos sólo se refieren al presupuesto del gobierno federal.

Cuba:

E--> Data relate to current expenditure only.

FR-> Les données ne se réfèrent qu'aux dépenses courantes.

ESP> Los datos sólo se refieren a los gastos corrientes.

United States:

E--> Data are based on federal obligations by function.

FR-> Données basées sur les engagements fédéraux de R-D par fonctions.

ESP> Los datos se basan en las obligaciones federales de I y D por funciones.

AMERICA, SOUTH:

Argentina:

E--> Figures in millions. Data for column 10 are included under column 7 and for column 11 under column 9.

FR-> Chiffres en millions. Les données relatives à la colonne 10 sont comprises dans la colonne 7 et celles de la colonne 11 dans la colonne 9.

ESP> Cifras en millones. Los datos correspondientes a la columna 10 están incluídos en la columna 11 y los da la columna 11 en la columna 9.

Colombia:

E--> Not including data for the productive sector (non-integrated R-D).

FR-> Non compris les données relatives au secteur de la production (activités de R-D non integrées).

ESP> Excluídos los datos relativos al sector productivo (actividades de I y D no integradas).

ASIA:

Japan:

E--> Figures in millions. Data relate to the expenditure of public institutes and corporations in the general service sector.

FR-> Chiffres en millions. Les données se réfèrent aux dépenses des instituts et sociétés publics dans le secteur de service général.

ESP> Cifras en millones. Los datos se refieren a los fondos de los institutos y sociedades públicos del sector de servicio general.

Philippines:

E--> Data relate to total expenditure in the general service sector only and cover a period of 18 months from July 1975 to December 1976.

FR-> Les données se réfèrent aux dépenses totales du secteur de service général et couvrent une période de 18 mois de juillet 1975 à décembre 1976.

ESP> Los datos se refieren únicamente a los gastos totales del sector de servicio general y cubren un período de 18 meses de julio de 1975 a diciembre de 1976.

Singapore:

E--> Data relate to total expenditure in the general service sector only and do not include social sciences and humanities.

FR-> Les données se réfèrent aux dépenses totales du secteur de service général et ne comprennent pas les sciences sociales et humaines.

ESP> Los datos se refieren únicamente a los gastos totales del sector de servicio general y excluyen las ciencias sociales y humanas.

Sri Lanka:

E--> Not including capital expenditure for the higher education sector.

FR-> Non compris les dépenses en capital dans le secteur de l'enseignement supérieur.

ESP> Excluídos los gastos de capital del sector de enseñanza superior.

Thailand:

E--> Data are based on the provisional budget for 1975.

FR-> Les données sont fondées sur le budget provisoire pour 1975.

ESP> Los datos están basados en el presupuesto provisional para 1975.

EUROPE:

Austria:

E--> Not including data for the productive sector (integrated R-D).

FR-> Non compris les données relatives au secteur de la production (activités de R-D intégrées).

ESP> Excluídos los datos relativos al sector productivo (actividades de I y D integradas).

Denmark:

E--> Data relate to current expenditure for the higher education and general service sectors only. Data for column 11 are included under column 7 and for column 10 under column 8.

FR-> Les données se réfèrent aux dépenses courantes dans les secteurs de l'enseignement supérieur et de service général seulement. Les données relatives à la colonne 11 sont comprises dans la colonne 7 et celles de la colonne 10 dans la colonne 8.

ESP> Los datos se refieren a los gastos corrientes en los sectores de enseñanza superior y de servicio general. Los datos correspondientes a la columna 11 están incluídos en la columna 7 y los de la columna 10 en la columna 8.

Finland:

E--> Data are based on a budget analysis.

FR-> Les données sont basées sur une analyse du budget.

ESP> Los datos están basados en un análisis del presupuesto.

France:

E--> Data are based on a budget allotment. Data for column 8 are included under column 10.

FR-> Les données sont basées sur les crédits budgétaires. Les données relatives à la colonne 8 sont comprises dans la colonne 10.

ESP> Los datos están basados en consignaciones presupuestarias. Los datos corespondientes a la columna 8 están incluídos en la columna 10.

Germany, Federal Republic of:

E--> Data include funds disbursed abroad and contributions to international organizations. Data for column 8 are included under column 10.

FR-> Les données comprennent les sommes déboursées à l'étranger et les contributions aux organisations internationales. Les données relatives à la colonne 8 sont comprises dans la colonne 10.

ESP> Los datos incluyen las sumas desembolsadas en el extranjero y las contribuciones a las organizaciones internacionales. Los datos correspondientes a la columna 8 están incluídos en la columna 10.

Hungary:

E--> Data refer only to direct expenditure on research. Data for columns 2, 3, 10 and 11 are included under column 13.

FR-> Les données concernent seulement les dépenses directes destinées à la recherche; les chiffres relatifs aux colonnes 2, 3, 10 et 11 sont compris dans la colonne 13.

Hungary: (Cont):

ESP> Los datos se refieren a los gastos directos correspondientes únicamente a la investigación. Los datos relativos a las columnas 2, 3, 10 y 11 están incluídos en la columna 13.

Italy:

E--> Figures in millions.

FR-> Chiffres en millions.

ESP> Cifras en millones.

Netherlands:

E--> Including contributions to international organizations. Data for column 11 are included under column 9.

FR-> Y compris les contributions aux organisations internationales. Les données relatives à la colonne 11 sont comprises dans la colonne 9.

ESP> Incluídas las contribuciones a las organizaciones internacionales. Los datos correspondientes a la columna 11 están incluídos en la columna 9.

Norway:

E--> Data relate to current expenditure only.

FR-> Les données ne concernent que les dépenses courantes.

ESP> Los datos sólo se refieren a los gastos corrientes.

Spain:

E--> Not including data for the higher education sector. Data for column 8 are included under column 10.

FR-> Non compris les données relatives au secteur de l'enseignement supérieur. Les données relatives à la colonne 8 sont comprises dans la colonne 10.

ESP> Excluídos los datos relativos al sector de enseñanza superior. Los datos correspondientes a la columna 8 están incluídos en la columna 10.

Sweden:

E--> Data relate to current expenditure only and do not include social sciences and humanities in the productive and general service sectors.

FR-> Les données se réfèrent aux dépenses courantes seulement et ne comprennent pas les sciences sociales et humaines dans les secteurs de la production et de service général.

ESP> Los datos sólo se refieren a los gastos corrientes y excluyen las ciencias sociales y humanas en los sectores productivo y de servicio general.

Switzerland:

E--> Data refer to the federal administration and 'hautes écoles'. Not including capital expenditure amounting to 87 million francs for the 'hautes écoles'.

FR-> Les données se réfèrent à l'administration fédérale et aux hautes écoles. Compte non tenu des dépenses en capital d'un montant de 87 millions de francs pour les hautes écoles.

ESP> Los datos se refieren a la administracion federal y a las 'hautes écoles'. Excluídos los gastos de capital que ascienden a 87 millones de francos para las 'hautes écoles'.

United Kingdom:

E--> Data relate to government net expenditure.

FR-> Les données se réfèrent aux dépenses nettes du gouvernement.

ESP> Los datos se refieren a los gastos netos del gobierno.

OCEANIA:

Australia:

E--> Not including data for the productive sector (integrated R&D).

FR-> Non compris les données relatives au secteur de la production (activités de R-D intégrées).

ESP> Excluídos los datos relativos al sector productivo (actividades I y D integradas).

French Polynesia:

E--> Data relate to one research institute only.

FR-> Les données ne concernent qu'un institut de recherche.

ESP> Los datos se refieren a un centro de investigación solamente.

New Zealand:

E--> Data for column 8 are included under column 10.

FR-> Les données relatives à la colonne 8 sont comprises dans la colonne 10.

ESP> Los datos relativos a la columna 8 están incluídos en la columna 10.

Tonga:

E--> Data relate to one research institute only.

FR-> Les données ne concernent qu'un institut de recherche.

ESP> Los datos se refieren a un centro de investigación solamente.

5.16 Personnel engaged in research and experimental development: selected data for recent years

Personnel employé à des travaux de recherche et de développement expérimental: données sélectionnées pour des années récentes

Personal empleado en actividades de investigación y de desarrollo experimental: datos seleccionados sobre los últimos años

PLEASE REFER TO INTRODUCTION FOR DEFINITIONS OF CATEGORIES INCLUDED IN THIS TABLE.

DATA ARE IN FULL-TIME EQUIVALENT (FTE).

NUMBER OF COUNTRIES AND TERRITORIES PRESENTED IN THIS TABLE: 85

POUR LES DEFINITIONS DES CATEGORIES PRESENTEES DANS CE TABLEAU, SE REFERER A L'INTRODUCTION.

LES DONNEES SONT EN EQUIVALENT PLEIN TEMPS (EPT).

NOMBRE DE PAYS ET DE TERRITOIRES PRESENTES DANS CE TABLEAU: 85

EN LA INTRODUCCION SE DAN LAS DEFINICIONES DE LAS CATEGORIAS QUE FIGURAN EN ESTE CUADRO.

DATOS EN EQUIVALENTE DE JORNADA COMPLETA (EJC).

NUMERO DE PAISES Y DE TERRITORIOS PRESENTADOS EN ESTE CUADRO: 85

COUNTRY / PAYS / PAIS	YEAR / ANNEE / AÑO	PERSONNEL ENGAGED IN R&D / PERSONNEL EMPLOYE A DES TRAVAUX DE R-D / PERSONAL DEDICADO A ACTIVIDADES DE I Y D				
		TOTAL (FTE) / TOTAL (EPT) / TOTAL (EJC)	SCIENTISTS AND ENGINEERS / SCIENTIFIQUES ET INGENIEURS / CIENTIFICOS E INGENIEROS: NUMBER / NOMBRE / NUMERO	INDEXES (1969 = 100) / INDICES (1969 = 100) / INDICES (1969 = 100)	NUMBER OF TECHNICIANS / NOMBRE DE TECHNICIENS / NUMERO DE TECNICOS	NUMBER OF AUXILIARY PERSONNEL / NOMBRE DE PERSONNEL AUXILIAIRE / NUMERO DE PERSONAL AUXILIAR
		(1)	(2)	(3)	(4)	(5)
AFRICA						
COTE D'IVOIRE‡	1970	...	319	100	222	...
	1973	...	368	115	...	...
	1974	877	463	145	92	322
	1975	...	502	157	...	...
EGYPT‡	1973	...	10 665	100	...	...
	1982	46 796	19 939	187	6 678	20 179
GABON‡	1969	84	6	100	20	58
	1970	86	8	133	20	58
GHANA‡	1971	7 610	3 067	100	4 543	——>
	1972	8 559	3 559	116	5 000	——>
	1974	8 906	3 704	121	5 202	——>
	1975	9 351	3 889	127	5 462	——>
	1976	9 819	4 084	133	5 735	——>
MAURITIUS	1969	335	61	100	65	209
	1970	364	78	128	58	228
	1982	1 388	173	284	169	1 046
	1983	1 191	211	346	165	815
	1984	1 224	263	431	176	785
NIGER‡	1972	...	28	100	...	...
	1973	...	42	150	...	...
	1974	...	53	189	...	...
	1975	...	79	282	...	...
	1976	94	93	332	1	–
NIGERIA‡	1970	...	1 429	100	...	...
	1971	...	1 922	135	...	...
	1972	...	2 210	155	...	...
	1977	9 545	2 200	154	1 345	6 000
SENEGAL‡	1971	...	416	100	...	...
	1972	...	609	146	516	...
	1976	...	522	125	...	...

COUNTRY / PAYS / PAIS	YEAR / ANNEE / AÑO	PERSONNEL ENGAGED IN R&D / PERSONNEL EMPLOYE A DES TRAVAUX DE R-D / PERSONAL DEDICADO A ACTIVIDADES DE I Y D: TOTAL (FTE) / TOTAL (EPT) / TOTAL (EJC)	SCIENTISTS AND ENGINEERS / SCIENTIFIQUES ET INGENIEURS / CIENTIFICOS E INGENIEROS: NUMBER / NOMBRE / NUMERO	SCIENTISTS AND ENGINEERS: INDEXES (1969 = 100) / INDICES (1969 = 100) / INDICES (1969 = 100)	NUMBER OF TECHNICIANS / NOMBRE DE TECHNICIENS / NUMERO DE TECNICOS	NUMBER OF AUXILIARY PERSONNEL / NOMBRE DE PERSONNEL AUXILIAIRE / NUMERO DE PERSONAL AUXILIAR
		(1)	(2)	(3)	(4)	(5)
SEYCHELLES‡	1969	1	1	100	–	–
	1970	1	1	100	–	–
	1980	3	2	200	1	–
	1981	3	2	200	1	–
	1983	33	18	1 800	6	9
SUDAN‡	1971	6 378	1 299	100	222	4 857
	1974	16 598	3 324	256	1 798	11 476
	1978	22 675	4 345	334	3 271	15 059
TOGO‡	1971	...	118	100	18	...
	1976	...	261	229	184	...
ZAMBIA	1969	...	*60	100	*180	...
	1970	...	*75	125	*210	...
	1973	1 060	260	433	800	——>
AMERICA, NORTH						
BERMUDA‡	1969	10	4	100	6	——>
	1970	10	4	100	3	3
CANADA‡	1969	*53 258	*21 052	100	*15 779	*16 427
	1970	*52 255	*20 425	97	*16 330	*15 500
	1980	*57 330	*24 760	118	*17 210	*15 370
	1981	*59 660	*25 730	122	*18 510	*15 420
	1982	*68 560	*31 950	152	*18 540	*18 070
COSTA RICA‡	1978	334	156	100	178	——>
	1979	351	171	110	180	——>
	1980	389	175	112	214	——>
	1982	...	411	263	...	...
CUBA‡	1969	12 361	1 850	100	2 453	8 058
	1977	19 659	4 959	268	6 075	8 625
	1982	26 574	7 497	405	8 066	11 011
	1983	29 064	8 247	446	8 406	12 409
	1984	32 937	9 548	516	8 843	14 546
EL SALVADOR‡	1980	...	533		1 547	...
	1981	...	564		1 971	...
GUATEMALA‡	1970	...	*230	100	*134	...
	1972	...	*267	116	*255	...
	1974	...	310	135	439	...
MEXICO‡	1969	4 222	3 665	100	557	...
	1970	12 456	3 743	102	8 713	——>
	1971	*13 525	*4 064	111	*7 181	*2 280
	1974	...	8 446	230	...	...
ST. PIERRE AND MIQUELON	1969	...	5	100	1	...
	1970	14	7	140	4	3
	1982	16	7	140	7	2
	1983	15	6	120	7	2
	1984	15	6	120	7	2
TURKS AND CAICOS ISLANDS‡	1974	3	3	100	–	–
	1975	3	3	100	–	–
	1976	2	2	67	–	–
	1984	–	–	–	–	–
UNITED STATES‡	1969	...	559 400	100	232 000	...
	1970	...	549 400	98	226 600	...
	1982	...	723 000	129	...	...
	1983	...	728 600	130	...	...
	1984	...	*785 000	140	...	...
AMERICA, SOUTH						
ARGENTINA‡	1970	*21 250	*6 500	100	*14 750	——>
	1971	*22 550	*6 900	106	*15 650	——>
	1979	...	*8 750	135	*12 500	...
	1980	...	*9 500	146	*13 300	...
	1982	...	10 486	161	...	...

COUNTRY / PAYS / PAIS	YEAR / ANNEE / AÑO	PERSONNEL ENGAGED IN R&D / PERSONNEL EMPLOYE A DES TRAVAUX DE R–D / PERSONAL DEDICADO A ACTIVIDADES DE I Y D				
		TOTAL (FTE) / TOTAL (EPT) / TOTAL (EJC)	SCIENTISTS AND ENGINEERS / SCIENTIFIQUES ET INGENIEURS / CIENTIFICOS E INGENIEROS: NUMBER / NOMBRE / NUMERO	SCIENTISTS AND ENGINEERS: INDEXES (1969 = 100) / INDICES (1969 = 100) / INDICES (1969 = 100)	NUMBER OF TECHNICIANS / NOMBRE DE TECHNICIENS / NUMERO DE TECNICOS	NUMBER OF AUXILIARY PERSONNEL / NOMBRE DE PERSONNEL AUXILIAIRE / NUMERO DE PERSONAL AUXILIAR
		(1)	(2)	(3)	(4)	(5)
CHILE	1981	1 481	...	...	...	...
	1982	1 893	...	...	...	...
	1983	2 005	...	...	...	...
ECUADOR‡	1970	...	595	100	508	...
	1973	...	544	91	217	...
FALKLAND ISLANDS (MALVINAS)	1969	6	5	100	–	1
	1970	–	–	–	–	–
	1971	–	–	–	–	–
GUYANA‡	1980	720	94		250	376
	1982	623	89		178	356
PERU‡	1970	...	1 925	100	...	...
	1975	...	3 750	195	...	...
	1980	...	9 171	476	5 218	...
VENEZUELA‡	1980	...	3 673	100	...	...
	1983	10 687	4 568	124	2 692	3 427
ASIA						
BRUNEI DARUSSALAM‡	1980	89	18	100	71	–
	1981	93	19	106	74	–
	1982	104	23	128	81	–
	1983	188	21	117	70	97
	1984	243	20	...	116	107
CYPRUS‡	1980	121	45	100	76	——>
	1981	122	46	102	76	——>
	1982	125	47	104	78	——>
	1983	129	49	109	80	——>
	1984	131	51	113	80	——>
INDIA‡	1973	40 497	...	...	...	...
	1974	48 328	...	...	...	...
	1976	54 105	28 233	...	25 872	——>
	1980	60 875	...	...	...	...
	1982	71 598	...	...	...	...
INDONESIA‡	1979	19 042	...	...	...	...
	1980	22 505	...	...	...	...
	1982	28 464	17 287	...	3 234	7 943
	1983	29 857	18 533	...	3 405	7 919
	1984	36 185	24 895	...	4 125	7 165
IRAN, ISLAMIC REPUBLIC OF‡	1970	6 432	3 007	100	482	2 943
	1971	8 223	3 584	119	712	3 927
	1972	9 865	4 896	163	857	4 112
IRAQ‡	1969	201	116	100	27	58
	1970	167	124	107	43	——>
	1972	248	170	147	78	——>
	1973	316	205	177	111	——>
	1974	365	240	207	125	——>
ISRAEL‡	1970	...	2 800	100	...	...
	1971	...	2 960	106	...	...
	1972	...	2 900	104	...	...
	1973	...	3 100	111	...	...
	1974	...	3 350	120	...	...
JAPAN‡	1969	427 950	275 686	100	86 147	66 117
	1970	459 274	298 814	108	90 088	70 372
	1982	648 977	479 954	174	91 169	77 854
	1983	668 939	496 145	180	93 326	79 468
	1984	710 872	531 612	193	97 074	82 186
JORDAN‡	1973	...	180	100	41	...
	1975	...	235	131	213	...
	1976	417	208	116	146	63
KOREA, REPUBLIC OF‡	1969	12 145	5 337	100	2 614	4 194
	1970	12 922	5 628	105	2 637	4 657
	1981	35 805	20 718	388	8 815	6 272
	1982	46 390	28 448	533	11 663	6 279
	1983	58 720	32 117	602	19 493	7 110

5.16 Historical data for R&D personnel
Données rétrospectives pour le personnel de R-D
Datos retrospectivos sobre el personal de I y D

COUNTRY / PAYS / PAIS	YEAR / ANNEE / AÑO	PERSONNEL ENGAGED IN R&D / PERSONNEL EMPLOYE A DES TRAVAUX DE R–D / PERSONAL DEDICADO A ACTIVIDADES DE I Y D				
		TOTAL (FTE) / TOTAL (EPT) / TOTAL (EJC)	SCIENTISTS AND ENGINEERS / SCIENTIFIQUES ET INGENIEURS / CIENTIFICOS E INGENIEROS		NUMBER OF TECHNICIANS / NOMBRE DE TECHNICIENS / NUMERO DE TECNICOS	NUMBER OF AUXILIARY PERSONNEL / NOMBRE DE PERSONNEL AUXILIAIRE / NUMERO DE PERSONAL AUXILIAR
			NUMBER / NOMBRE / NUMERO	INDEXES (1969 = 100) / INDICES (1969 = 100) / INDICES (1969 = 100)		
		(1)	(2)	(3)	(4)	(5)
KUWAIT‡	1980	787	582	100	125	90
	1982	1 864	1 013	174	443	408
	1983	2 064	1 157	199	470	437
	1984	2 539	1 511	260	561	467
LEBANON‡	1977	133	133	100	–	–
	1978	160	160	120	–	–
	1979	175	170	128	5	——>
	1980	206	180	135	6	20
PAKISTAN‡	1981	22 922	5 144	100	6 476	11 302
	1982	24 723	5 397	105	7 138	12 188
PHILIPPINES‡	1970	2 124	1 108	100	278	738
	1971	2 548	1 265	114	338	945
	1979	7 505	4 011	362	3 494	——>
	1980	8 509	4 200	379	4 309	——>
	1982	*10 840	*4 816	435	*2 129	*3 895
VIET–NAM‡	1972	15 630	7 780	100	7 850	——>
	1974	16 490	9 160	118	7 330	——>
	1976	24 560	11 230	144	13 330	——>
	1978	25 050	13 050	168	6 040	5 960
EUROPE						
AUSTRIA‡	1970	10 734	3 894	100	3 358	3 482
	1975	15 392	5 387	138	4 944	5 061
	1981	18 599	6 712	172	6 145	5 742
BELGIUM	1969	25 165	10 070	100	12 854	2 241
	1971	...	11 961	119	...	...
	1973	29 235	12 932	128	9 990	6 313
	1975	30 131	13 883	138	6 570	9 677
	1977	30 186	13 883	138	7 696	8 607
BULGARIA‡	1969	39 468	19 990	100	8 933	10 545
	1970	46 633	22 452	112	11 459	12 722
	1982	81 207	42 756	214	12 519	25 932
	1983	83 291	43 462	217	12 429	27 400
	1984	87 329	45 125	226	12 484	29 720
CZECHOSLOVAKIA‡	1970	137 667	36 927	100	58 852	41 888
	1971	137 407	38 572	104	57 906	40 929
	1982	173 292	55 463	150	48 284	69 565
	1983	174 844	57 247	155	47 590	70 007
	1984	176 219	58 820	159	46 800	70 599
DENMARK‡	1970	11 669	4 552	100	7 117	——>
	1973	12 092	4 850	107	7 242	——>
	1979	15 274	6 011	132	9 263	——>
	1981	16 428	6 785	149	9 643	——>
	1983	17 759	7 508	165	10 251	——>
FINLAND‡	1971	10 244	4 885	100	5 359	——>
	1975	13 450	6 772	139	6 678	——>
	1981	17 651	9 722	199	8 282	——>
	1983	20 218	10 951	224	9 267	——>
	1984	10 997	...	...	...	...
FRANCE	1969	201 100	57 200	100	143 900	——>
	1970	202 869	59 004	103	143 865	——>
	1977	222 100	68 000	119	154 100	——>
	1978	225 000	70 900	124	154 100	——>
	1979	230 800	72 900	127	157 900	——>
GERMAN DEMOCRATIC REPUBLIC‡	1974	153 032	85 748	100	67 284	——>
	1975	158 573	90 836	106	67 737	——>
	1982	197 686	125 637	147	72 049	——>
	1983	199 220	127 538	149	71 682	——>
	1984	197 288	127 595	149	69 693	——>
GERMANY, FEDERAL REPUBLIC‡	1969	*247 176	*74 943	100	172 233	——>
	1971	297 118	90 206	120	206 912	——>
	1977	319 347	110 972	148	104 377	103 998
	1979	363 208	121 978	163	115 513	125 717
	1981	371 548	128 162	171	115 518	127 868

COUNTRY / PAYS / PAIS	YEAR / ANNEE / AÑO	PERSONNEL ENGAGED IN R&D / PERSONNEL EMPLOYE A DES TRAVAUX DE R–D / PERSONAL DEDICADO A ACTIVIDADES DE I Y D				
		SCIENTISTS AND ENGINEERS / SCIENTIFIQUES ET INGENIEURS / CIENTIFICOS E INGENIEROS			NUMBER OF TECHNICIANS / NOMBRE DE TECHNICIENS / NUMERO DE TECNICOS	NUMBER OF AUXILIARY PERSONNEL / NOMBRE DE PERSONNEL AUXILIAIRE / NUMERO DE PERSONAL AUXILIAR
		TOTAL (FTE) / TOTAL (EPT) / TOTAL (EJC)	NUMBER / NOMBRE / NUMERO	INDEXES (1969 = 100) / INDICES (1969 = 100) / INDICES (1969 = 100)		
		(1)	(2)	(3)	(4)	(5)
GREECE‡	1969	2 470	1 032	100	785	653
	1976	5 345	2 569	249	1 759	1 017
HUNGARY‡	1969	48 800	15 304	100	23 375	10 121
	1970	50 749	16 282	106	23 811	10 656
	1982	49 236	21 970	.	18 354	8 912
	1983	48 740	22 132	.	18 477	8 131
	1984	49 360	22 518	.	18 438	8 404
ICELAND‡	1971	241	129	100	112	→
	1973	314	156	121	158	→
	1975	509	215	167	294	→
	1977	564	273	212	291	→
	1979	614	304	236	227	83
IRELAND‡	1969	3 847	1 549	100	1 006	1 292
	1971	4 475	1 857	120	2 618	→
	1979	6 153	2 620	169	1 848	1 685
	1981	5 474	2 635	170	1 408	1 431
	1982	5 449	2 773	179	1 271	1 405
ITALY	1969	70 009	25 363	100	44 646	→
	1970	75 376	27 618	109	47 758	→
	1981	102 836	52 060	205	29 385	21 391
	1982	105 927	56 707	224	28 027	21 193
	1983	112 743	63 021	248	28 694	21 028
MALTA‡	1973	73	39	100	22	12
	1981	46	34	87	5	7
	1983	46	34	87	5	7
	1984	46	34	87	5	7
NETHERLANDS‡	1969	56 120	19 860	100	36 260	→
	1970	54 750	22 708	114	32 042	→
	1981	54 470	28 110	142	26 360	→
	1982	57 450	30 160	152	27 290	→
	1983	57 630	30 530	154	27 100	→
NORWAY	1969	9 268	4 058	100	5 210	→
	1970	9 730	4 280	105	5 450	→
	1980	15 005	7 427	183	7 578	→
	1981	14 843	7 496	185	7 347	→
	1982	15 218	7 754	191	7 464	→
POLAND‡	1969	184 500	54 500	100	52 900	77 100
	1970	196 200	59 000	108	55 100	82 100
	1982	188 000	79 000	145	41 000	68 000
	1983	176 000	75 000	138	37 000	64 000
	1984	174 000	75 000	138	35 000	64 000
PORTUGAL‡	1971	7 165	2 187	100	4 978	→
	1972	7 653	2 216	101	1 838	3 599
	1978	6 543	2 061	94	2 088	2 394
	1980	7 711	2 663	122	2 867	2 181
	1982	8 552	3 019	138	3 100	2 433
ROMANIA	1969	43 021	18 711	100	8 392	15 918
	1970	46 382	20 764	111	8 001	17 617
	1971	51 200	22 888	122	9 175	19 137
	1972	55 283	23 133	124	11 057	21 093
	1973	62 918	26 107	140	12 651	24 160
SPAIN‡	1969	14 522	5 135	100	1 322	8 065
	1970	16 187	5 842	114	1 526	8 819
	1981	31 329	14 376	280	4 969	11 984
	1982	30 510	13 762	268	5 142	11 606
	1983	30 948	14 229	278	5 140	11 579
SWEDEN‡	1969	25 038	7 537	100	17 501	→
	1971	29 844	9 066	120	20 778	→
	1977	36 283	14 102	187	22 181	→
	1979	36 434	14 766	196	21 668	→
	1981	44 314	17 896	237	26 418	→
	1983	47 758	19 081	253	28 677	→

COUNTRY / PAYS / PAIS	YEAR / ANNEE / AÑO	PERSONNEL ENGAGED IN R&D / PERSONNEL EMPLOYE A DES TRAVAUX DE R–D / PERSONAL DEDICADO A ACTIVIDADES DE I Y D				
		TOTAL (FTE) / TOTAL (EPT) / TOTAL (EJC)	SCIENTISTS AND ENGINEERS / SCIENTIFIQUES ET INGENIEURS / CIENTIFICOS E INGENIEROS		NUMBER OF TECHNICIANS / NOMBRE DE TECHNICIENS / NUMERO DE TECNICOS	NUMBER OF AUXILIARY PERSONNEL / NOMBRE DE PERSONNEL AUXILIAIRE / NUMERO DE PERSONAL AUXILIAR
			NUMBER / NOMBRE / NUMERO	INDEXES (1969 = 100) / INDICES (1969 = 100) / INDICES (1969 = 100)		
		(1)	(2)	(3)	(4)	(5)
SWITZERLAND‡	1972	*23 800	*8 800	100	*15 000	——>
	1973	*26 100	*9 100	103	*17 000	——>
	1977	*36 920	*16 000	182	*20 920	——>
	1978	38 530	16 150	184	22 380	——>
	1979	37 945	16 410	186	15 840	——>
UNITED KINGDOM‡	1972	258 746	77 086	100	80 220	101 440
	1975	259 100	79 300	103	75 800	104 000
	1978	261 400	86 500	112	76 600	98 300
YUGOSLAVIA‡	1969	36 294	14 453	100	10 279	11 562
	1970	36 467	15 118	105	9 601	11 748
	1979	51 305	22 430	155	12 262	16 613
	1980	53 699	22 951	159	13 431	17 317
	1981	56 552	24 882	172	13 729	17 941
OCEANIA						
AMERICAN SAMOA‡	1969	14	2	100	12	——>
	1970	14	2	100	12	——>
	1971	15	3	150	2	10
AUSTRALIA‡	1968	42 200	17 700	100	12 600	11 900
	1973	51 400	24 600	139	16 700	10 100
	1976	43 745	22 561	127	12 637	8 547
	1978	43 642	22 458	127	12 289	8 895
	1981	44 537	24 210	137	12 007	8 320
COOK ISLANDS	1969	12	12	100	–	–
	1970	9	9	75	–	–
FRENCH POLYNESIA‡	1970	72	7	100	65	——>
	1971	72	7	100	65	——>
	1981	102	21	300	13	68
	1982	101	21	300	14	66
	1983	97	17	243	16	64
GUAM‡	1973	16	10	100	3	3
	1974	*10	*3	30	7	——>
	1977	*37	*10	100	27	——>
	1978	*46	*12	120	*20	14
	1979	52	21	210	19	12
KIRIBATI	1969	16	4	100	2	10
	1980	3	2	50	1	–
	1981	3	2	50	1	–
NEW CALEDONIA	1969	1	0.25	100	0.50	0.25
	1970	1	0.25	100	0.50	0.25
	1981	12	4	1 600	3	5
	1982	15	5	2 000	4	6
	1983	17	7	2 800	5	5
NEW ZEALAND‡	1973	...	*2 950	100	...	...
	1975	8 003	3 659	124	3 164	1 180
	1979	8 080	...	...	...	...
PACIFIC ISLANDS‡	1973	66	23	100	24	19
	1978	22	5	22	11	6
	1979	23	4	17	11	8
PAPUA NEW GUINEA‡	1971	...	*110	100	...	...
	1972	...	*115	105	...	...
	1973	...	131	119	...	...
SAMOA‡	1975	698	234	100	124	340
	1976	254	135	58	82	37
	1977	266	140	60	87	39
	1978	280	140	60	92	48
TONGA‡	1977	...	5	100	1	...
	1978	...	5	100	1	...
	1979	...	9	180	1	...
	1980	...	10	200	4	...
	1981	...	11	220	4	...

COUNTRY / PAYS / PAIS	YEAR / ANNEE / AÑO	TOTAL (FTE) / TOTAL (EPT) / TOTAL (EJC)	PERSONNEL ENGAGED IN R&D / PERSONNEL EMPLOYE A DES TRAVAUX DE R–D / PERSONAL DEDICADO A ACTIVIDADES DE I Y D — SCIENTISTS AND ENGINEERS / SCIENTIFIQUES ET INGENIEURS / CIENTIFICOS E INGENIEROS: NUMBER / NOMBRE / NUMERO	INDEXES (1969 = 100) / INDICES (1969 = 100) / INDICES (1969 = 100)	NUMBER OF TECHNICIANS / NOMBRE DE TECHNICIENS / NUMERO DE TECNICOS	NUMBER OF AUXILIARY PERSONNEL / NOMBRE DE PERSONNEL AUXILIAIRE / NUMERO DE PERSONAL AUXILIAR
		(1)	(2)	(3)	(4)	(5)
VANUATU	1969	26	1	100	25	--->
	1970	25	3	300	22	--->
	1973	29	2	200	1	26
	1974	39	4	400	1	34
	1975	39	3	300	1	35
U.S.S.R.						
U.S.S.R.‡	1969	...	883 420	100	...	...
	1970	...	927 709	105	...	...
	1982	...	1 431 696	162	...	...
	1983	...	1 440 000	163	...	...
	1984	...	1 463 800	166	...	...
BYELORUSSIAN S.S.R.‡	1969	...	20 631	100	...	...
	1970	...	21 863	106	...	...
	1982	...	38 963	189	...	...
	1983	...	39 134	190	...	...
	1984	...	40 200	195	...	...
UKRAINIAN S.S.R.‡	1969	...	122 754	100	...	...
	1970	...	129 781	106	...	...
	1982	...	205 400	167	...	...
	1983	...	203 300	166	...	...
	1984	...	204 900	167	...	...

AFRICA:

Côte d'Ivoire:

E--> Base year: 1970=100. Not including military and defence R&D.

FR-> Année de base: 1970=100. Non compris les activités de R-D de caractère militaire ou relevant de la défense nationale.

ESP> Año de base: 1970=100. Excluídas las actividades militares y de defensa de I y D.

Egypt:

E--> Base year: 1973=100.

FR-> Année de base: 1973=100.

ESP> Año de base: 1973=100.

Gabon:

E--> Data relate to the (French) *Office de la Recherche Scientifique et Technique Outre-Mer* (ORSTOM) only; scientists and engineers in column 2 are all foreigners.

FR-> Les données ne concernent que l'Office francÇais de la recherche scientifique et technique outre-mer (ORSTOM); les scientifiques et ingénieurs de la colonne 2 sont tous ressortissants étrangers.

ESP> Los datos sólo se refieren al *Office (francais) de la recherche scientifique et technique outre-mer* (ORSTOM); los científicos e ingenieros de la columna 2 son todos extranjeros.

Ghana:

E--> Base year: 1971=100.

FR-> Année de base: 1971=100.

ESP> Año de base: 1971=100.

Niger:

E--> Base year: 1972=100. Data relate to the higher education sector only.

FR-> Année de base: 1972=100. Les données ne concernent que le secteur de l'enseignement supérieur.

ESP> Año de base: 1972=100. Los datos sólo se refieren al sector de enseñanza superior.

Nigeria:

E--> Base year: 1970=100. Data referring to scientists and engineers are full-time plus part-time; not including data for social sciences and humanities.

FR-> Année de base: 1970=100. Les données relatives aux scientifiques et ingénieurs sont à plein temps et à temps partiel; les données ne comprennent pas les sciences sociales et humaines.

ESP> Año de base: 1970=100. Les datos relativos a los científicos e ingenieros se refieren al personal de jornada completa y de jornada parcial; no se incluyen los datos relativos a las ciencias sociales y humanas.

Senegal:

E--> Base year: 1971=100. Data for scientists and engineers are full-time plus part-time.

Senegal: (Cont):

FR-> Année de base: 1971=100. Les données relatives aux scientifiques et ingénieurs sont à plein temps et à temps partiel.

ESP> Año de base: 1971=100. Los datos relativos a los científicos e ingenieros son de jornada completa y de jornada parcial.

Seychelles:

E--> Not including military and defence R&D.

FR-> Non compris les activités de R-D de caractère militaire ou relevant de la défense nationale.

ESP> Excluídas las actividades militares y de defensa de I y D.

Sudan:

E--> Base year: 1971=100. Data referring to scientists and engineers are full-time plus part-time.

FR-> Année de base: 1971=100. Les données relatives aux scientifiques et ingénieurs sont à plein temps et à temps partiel.

ESP> Año de base: 1971=100. Los datos relativos a los científicos e ingenieros se refieren al personal de jornada completa y de jornada parcial.

Togo:

E--> Base year: 1971=100. Data for scientists and engineers refer only to full-time.

FR-> Année de base: 1971=100. Les données relatives aux scientifiques et ingénieurs sont à plein temps seulement.

ESP> Año de base: 1971=100. Los datos relativos a los científicos e ingenieros son de jornada completa solamente.

AMERICA, NORTH:

Bermuda:

E--> Not including data for the productive sector and excluding law, humanities and education.

FR-> Non compris les données pour le secteur de la production et compte non tenu des données relatives au droit, aux sciences humaines et à l'éducation.

ESP> Excluídos los datos relativos al sector productivo y los que se refieren al derecho, las ciencias humanas y la educación.

Canada:

E--> Data for 1969 and 1970 do not include social sciences and humanities; from 1980 these are only excluded from the productive sector (integrated R&D).

FR-> Les données pour 1969 et 1970 ne comprennent pas les sciences sociales et humaines; à partir de 1980 celles-ci sont exclues seulement du secteur de la production (activités de R-D intégrées).

ESP> Los datos para 1969 y 1970 no incluyen las ciencias sociales y humanas; a partir de 1980 se excluyen solamente del sector productivo (actividades de I y D integradas).

Costa Rica:

Costa Rica: (Cont):
E--> Base year: 1978=100. Data relate to the University of Costa Rica only.
FR-> Année de base: 1978=100. Les données se réfèrent à l'Université de Costa Rica seulement.
ESP> Año de base: 1978=100. Los datos se refieren a la Universidad de Costa Rica solamente.
Cuba:
E--> Not including military and defence R&D.
FR-> Non compris les activités de R-D de caractère militaire ou relevant de la défense nationale.
ESP> Excluídas las actividades militares y de defensa de I y D.
El Salvador:
E--> Data refer to the number of full-time plus part-time scientists and engineers and technicians engaged in public enterprises.
FR-> Les données se réfèrent au nombre de scientifiques et ingénieurs et techniciens à plein temps et à temps partiel employés dans les entreprises publiques.
ESP> Los datos se refieren al número de científicos e ingenieros y técnicos de jornada completa y de jornada parcial empleados en las empresas públicas.
Guatemala:
E--> Base year: 1970=100.
FR-> Année de base: 1970=100.
ESP> Año de base: 1970=100.
Mexico:
E--> Data are for full-time plus part-time personnel.
FR-> Les données se réfèrent au personnel à plein temps et à temps partiel.
ESP> Los datos se refieren al personal de jornada completa y de jornada parcial.
Turks and Caicos Islands:
E--> Base year: 1974=100.
FR-> Année de base: 1974=100.
ESP> Año de base: 1974=100.
United States:
E--> Not including data for law, humanities and education.
FR-> Non compris les données pour le droit, les sciences humaines et l'éducation.
ESP> Excluídos los datos relativos al derecho, las ciencias humanas y la educación.
AMERICA, SOUTH:
Argentina:
E--> Base year: 1970=100.
FR-> Année de base: 1970=100.
ESP> Año de base: 1970=100.
Ecuador:
E--> Base year: 1970=100.
FR-> Année de base: 1970=100.
ESP> Año de base: 1970=100.
Guyana:
E--> Not including military and defence R&D. Data for the general service sector and for medical sciences in the higher education sector are also excluded.
FR-> Non compris les activités de R-D de caractère militaire ou relevant de la défense nationale. Les données relatives au secteur de service général et les sciences médicales du secteur de l'enseignement supérieur sont aussi exclues.
ESP> Excluídas las actividades militares y de defensa de I y D. Se excluyen también los datos relativos al sector de servicio general y las ciencias médicas al sector de enseñanza superior.
Peru:
E--> Base year: 1970=100. Data also include scientific and technological services (STS) and refer to the number of full-time plus part-time scientists and engineers.
FR-> Année de base: 1970=100. Les données comprennent en plus les services scientifiques et techniques (SST) et se réfèrent au nombre de scientifiques et ingénieurs à plein temps et à temps partiel.
ESP> Año de base: 1970=100. Los datos también incluyen los servicios científicos y tecnológicos (SCT) y se refieren al número de científicos e ingenieros de jornada completa y de jornada parcial.
Venezuela:
E--> Base year: 1980=100. Not including military and defence R&D. Data relate to full-time plus part-time personnel.
FR-> Année de base: 1980=100. Non compris les activités de R-D de caractère militaire ou relevant de la défense nationale. Les données se réfèrent au personnel à plein temps et à temps partiel.
ESP> Año de base: 1980=100. Excluídas las actividades militares y de defensa de I y D. Los datos se refieren al personal de jornada completa y de jornada parcial.
ASIA:
Brunei Darussalem:
E--> Base year: 1980=100. Data relate to full-time plus part-time personnel at 2 research institutes only.
FR-> Année de base: 1980=100. Les données se réfèrent au personnel à plein temps et à temps partiel dans 2 instituts de recherche seulement.
ESP> Año de base: 1980=100. Los datos se refieren al personal de

Brunei Darussalem: (Cont):
jornada completa y de jornada parcial en 2 centros de investigaci solamente.
Cyprus:
E--> Base year: 1980=100. Not including data for the producti sector.
FR-> Année de base: 1980=100. Non compris les données pour secteur de la production.
ESP> Año de base: 1980=100. Excluídos los datos relativos sector productivo.
India:
E--> Not including data for the higher education sector in 197 1980 and 1982.
FR-> Compte non tenu, en 1976, 1980 et 1982 des donné relatives au secteur de l'enseignement supérieur.
ESP> En 1976, 1980 y 1982 se excluyen los datos relativos al sec de enseñanza superior.
Indonesia:
E--> Data relate to full-time plus part-time personnel.
FR-> Les données se réfèrent au personnel à plein temps et à tem partiel.
ESP> Los datos se refieren al personal de jornada completa y jornada parcial.
Iran, Islamic Republic of:
E--> Base year: 1970=100.
FR-> Année de base: 1970=100.
ESP> Año de base: 1970=100.
Iraq:
E--> Data relate to the Foundation of Scientific Research only. 1974 there were 1,862 persons (of whom 1,486 scientists and enginee working in government departments concerned with scientific activitie
FR-> Les données ne concernent que la 'Foundation of Scienti Research'. Il y avait en 1974, 1 862 personnes (dont 1 486 scientifiqu et ingénieurs), employées dans les départements gouvernementa concernés par les activités scientifiques.
ESP> Los datos se refieren a la 'Foundation of Scientific Research'. 1974 había 1 862 personas (de las cuales 1 486 eran científicos ingenieros), empleadas en los servicios gubernamentales que se ocupan las actividades científicas.
Israel:
E--> Base year: 1970=100. Data refer to the civilian sector only a do not include social sciences and humanities.
FR-> Année de base: 1970=100. Les données ne concernent que secteur civil et ne comprennent pas les sciences sociales et humaines.
ESP> Año de base: 1970=100. Los datos se refieren solamente sector civil y no incluyen las ciencias sociales y humanas.
Japan:
E--> Data refer to full-time personnel. Not including data for soc sciences and humanities in the productive sector.
FR-> Les données se réfèrent au personnel à plein temps. Non comp les données relatives aux sciences sociales et humaines dans le secteur la production.
ESP> Los datos se refieren al personal de jornada completa. Excluí los datos relativos a las ciencias sociales y humanas del sec productivo.
Jordan:
E--> Base year: 1973=100.
FR-> Année de base: 1973=100.
ESP> Año de base: 1973=100.
Korea, Republic of:
E--> Not including military and defence R&D. From 1969 to 19 data exclude law, humanities and education; from 1980 not includ social sciences and humanities. Data refer to full-time plus part-ti personnel.
FR-> Non compris les activités de R-D de caractère militaire relevant de la défense nationale. De 1969 à 1979, les données comprennent pas le droit, les sciences humaines et l'éducation; à partir 1980 les sciences sociales et humaines sont exclues. Les données réfèrent au personnel à plein temps et à temps partiel.
ESP> Excluídas las actividades militares y de defensa de I y D. 1969 a 1979 los datos no incluyen el derecho, las ciencias humanas y educación; a partir de 1980 se excluyen las ciencias sociales y human Los datos se refieren al personal de jornada completa y de jorna parcial.
Kuwait:
E--> Base year: 1980=100. Data refer to scientific and technologi activities (STA) and relate to the number of full-time plus part-time scienti and engineers and technicians.
FR-> Année de base: 1980=100. Les données se réfèrent a activités scientifiques et techniques (AST) et au nombre de scientifiques ingénieurs et techniciens à plein temps et à temps partiel.
ESP> Año de base: 1980=100. Los datos se refieren a las activida científicas y tecnológicas (ACT) y al número de científicos y ingeniero técnicos de jornada completa yk de jornada parcial.
Lebanon:
E--> Base year: 1977=100. Partial data referring to the Faculty Science at the University of Lebanon only.
FR-> Année de base: 1977=100. Données partielles pour la Facu

Lebanon: (Cont):
des Sciences de l'Université du Liban seulement.
ESP> Año de base: 1977=100. Datos parciales para la Facultad de Ciencias de la Universidad del Líbano solamente.
Pakistan:
E--> Base year 1981=100. Data relate to R&D activities concentrated mainly in government-financed research establishments; social sciences and humanities in the higher education and general service sectors are excluded.
FR-> Année de base: 1981=100. Les données se réfèrent aux activités de R-D se trouvant pour la plupart dans les établissements de recherche financés par le gouvernement. Les sciences sociales et humaines dans les secteurs de l'enseignement supérieur et de service général sont exclues.
ESP> Año de base: 1981=100. Los datos se refieren a las actividades de I y D concentradas principalmente en los establecimientos de investigación subvencionados por el gobierno. Se excluyen las ciencias sociales y humanas de los sectores de enseñanza superior y de servicio general.
Philippines:
E--> Base year: 1970=100. Data refer to the general service sector only.
FR-> Année de base: 1970=100. Les données ne concernent que le secteur de service général.
ESP> Año de base: 1970=100. Los datos sólo se refieren al sector de servicio general.
Viet-nam:
E--> Base year: 1972=100. The figures in columns 1 and 4 do not include data for technicians and auxiliary personal in the higher education sector.
FR-> Année de base: 1972=100. Les totaux des colonnes 1 et 4 ne comprennent pas les techniciens ni le personnel auxiliaire du secteur de l'enseignement supérieur.
ESP> Año de base: 1972=100. Los totales de las columnas 1 y 4 no incluyen el personal auxiliar ni los técnicos del sector de enseñanza superior.
EUROPE:
Austria:
E--> Base year: 1970=100.
FR-> Année de base: 1970=100.
ESP> Año de base: 1970=100.
Bulgaria:
E--> Data for 1982, 1983 and 1984 in columns 1, 4 and 5 do not include technicians and auxiliary personnel in the higher education sector.
FR-> Les données des colonnes 1, 4 et 5 pour 1982, 1983 et 1984, ne comprennent pas les techniciens ni le personnel auxiliaire dans le secteur de l'enseignement supérieur.
ESP> Para 1982, 1983 y 1984, los datos de las columnas 1, 4 y 5 no incluyen los técnicos ni el personal auxiliar en el sector de enseñanza superior.
Czechoslovakia:
E--> Base year: 1970=100. Due to methodological changes in 1981 these data are not strictly comparable with earlier years. Scientists and engineers engaged in the administration of R&D are included with auxiliary personnel; of military R&D only that part carried out in civil establishments is included.
FR-> Année de base: 1970=100. Suite à des changements de méthodologie en 1981 ces données ne sont pas strictement comparables avec celles des années précédentes. Les scientifiques et ingénieurs employés dans les services administratifs de R-D sont compris avec le personnel auxiliaire; pour la R-D de caractère militaire seule la partie effectuée dans les établissements civils a été considérée.
ESP> Año de base: 1970=100. Debido a los cambios de metodología en 1981 estos datos no son directamente comparables con los de los años anteriores. Los científicos e ingenieros empleados en los servicios administrativos de I y D están incluídos con el personal auxiliar; para la I y D de carácter militar sólo se ha considerado la parte correspondiente a los establecimientos civiles.
Denmark:
E--> Base year: 1970=100.
FR-> Année de base: 1970=100.
ESP> Año de base: 1970=100.
Finland:
E--> Base year: 1971=100.
FR-> Année de base: 1971=100.
ESP> Año de base: 1971=100.
German Democratic Republic:
E--> Base year: 1974=100.
FR-> Année de base: 1974=100.
ESP> Año de base: 1974=100.
Germany, Federal Republic of:
E--> Not including data for social sciences and humanities in the productive sector. In 1979, coverage extended to include small and medium-sized enterprises employing 31,949 persons.
FR-> Non compris les données relatives aux sciences sociales et humaines dans le secteur de la production. En 1979, la portée de l'enquête englobait également les petites et moyennes entreprises employant 31 949 personnes.
ESP> Excluídos los datos relativos a las ciencias sociales y humanas del sector productivo. En 1979, la encuesta cubría igualmente las pequeñas y medianas empresas que empleaban 31 949 personas.
Greece:
E--> Data in 1969 do not include social sciences and humanities.
FR-> Les données pour 1969 ne comprennent pas les sciences sociales et humaines.
ESP> Los datos para 1969 no incluyen las ciencias sociales y humanas.
Hungary:
E--> Due to methodological changes in 1981 data since then are not comparable with the previous years. Not including personnel engaged in the administration of R&D. Skilled workers are included with technicians rather than with auxiliary personnel.
FR-> Suite à des changements de méthodologie en 1981 les données ne sont pas comparables avec celles des années précédentes. Non compris le personnel employé dans les services administratifs de R-D. Les ouvriers qualifiés sont compris avec les techniciens plutôt qu'avec le personnel auxiliaire.
ESP> Debido a los cambios de metodología en 1981 los datos no son comparables con los de los años anteriores. Excluído el personal empleado en los servicios administrativos de I y D. Los trabajadores calificados están incluídos con el personal técnico y no con el personal auxiliar.
Iceland:
E--> Base year: 1971=100.
FR-> Année de base: 1971=100.
ESP> Año de base: 1971=100.
Ireland:
E--> Data for 1969 and 1971 do not include humanities.
FR-> Les données pour 1969 et 1971 ne comprennent pas les sciences humaines.
ESP> Los datos relativos a 1969 y 1971 no incluyen las ciencias humanas.
Malta:
E--> Base year: 1973=100. Data relate to the higher education sector only.
FR-> Année de base: 1973=100. Les données ne concernent que le secteur de l'enseignement supérieur.
ESP> Año de base: 1973=100. Los datos sólo se refieren al sector de enseñanza superior.
Netherlands:
E--> Due to methodological changes in 1981 these data are not strictly comparable with earlier years. Not including social sciences and humanities in the productive sector (integrated R&D).
FR-> Suite à des changements de méthodologie en 1981 ces données ne sont pas strictement comparables avec celles des années précédentes. Non compris les données pour les sciences sociales et humaines dans le secteur de la production (activités de R-D intégrées).
ESP> Debido a los cambios de metodología en 1981 estos datos no son directamente comparables con los de los años anteriores. Excluídos los datos relativos a las ciencias sociales y humanas del sector productivo (actividades de I y D integradas).
Poland:
E--> Not including military and defence R&D. Data for 1982, 1983 and 1984 do not include technicians and auxiliary personnel in the higher education sector.
FR-> Non compris les activités de caractère militaire ou relevant de la défense nationale. Les données pour 1982, 1983 et 1984 ne comprennent pas les techniciens ni le personnel auxiliaire du secteur de l'enseignement supérieur.
ESP> Excluídas las actividades militares y de defensa de I y D. Los datos para 1982, 1983 y 1984 no incluyen ni los técnicos ni el personal auxiliar del sector de enseñanza superior.
Portugal:
E--> Base year: 1971=100.
FR-> Année de base: 1971=100.
ESP> Año de base: 1971=100.
Spain:
E--> Data for 1981, 1982 and 1983 do not include technicians and auxiliary personnel in the higher education sector.
FR-> Les données de 1981, 1982 et 1983 ne comprennent pas les techniciens ni le personnel auxiliaire du secteur de l'enseignement supérieur.
ESP> Para 1981, 1982 y 1983, los datos no incluyen el personal auxiliar ni los técnicos del sector de enseñanza superior.
Sweden:
E--> From 1969 to 1979, data exclude social sciences and humanities whilst in 1981 these fields are included only for the productive and general service sectors.
FR-> De 1969 à 1979 les données ne comprennent pas les sciences sociales et humaines tandis qu'en 1981 ces domaines sont comptés seulement pour les secteurs de la production et de service général.
ESP> De 1969 a 1979 los datos se excluyen las ciencias sociales y humanas mientras que en 1981 estos campos fueron incluídos solamente para los sectores productivo y de servicio general.

Switzerland:
E--> Base year: 1972=100.
FR-> Année de base: 1972=100.
ESP> Año de base: 1972=100.

United Kingdom:
E--> Base year: 1972=100. Data do not include the higher education sector.
FR-> Année de base: 1972=100. Les données ne comprennent pas le secteur de l'enseignement supérieur.
ESP> Año de base: 1972=100. Los datos no incluyen el sector de enseñanza superior.

Yugoslavia:
E--> Not including military and defence R&D.
FR-> Non compris les activités de R-D de caractère militaire ou relevant de la défense nationale.
ESP> Excluídas las actividades militares y de defensa de I y D.

OCEANIA:

American Samoa:
E--> Data relate to one research institute only.
FR-> Les données ne concernent qu'un institut de recherche.
ESP> Los datos se refieren a un centro de investigación solamente.

Australia:
E--> Base year: 1968=100.
FR-> Année de base: 1968=100.
ESP> Año de base: 1968=100.

French Polynesia:
E--> Base year: 1970=100. Data relate to one research institute only.
FR-> Année de base: 1970=100. Les données ne concernent qu'un institut de recherche.
ESP> Año de base: 1970=100. Los datos sólo se refieren a un instituto de investigación.

Guam:
E--> Base year: 1973=100. Data relate to the higher education sector only.
FR-> Année de base: 1973=100. Les données ne concernent que le secteur de l'enseignement supérieur.
ESP> Año de base: 1973=100. Los datos sólo se refieren al sector de enseñanza superior.

New Zealand:
E--> Base year: 1973=100. The total in 1975 in column 1 does not include auxiliary personnel in the higher education sector.
FR-> Année de base: 1973=100. Le total en 1975 de la colonne 1 ne comprend pas le personnel auxiliaire du secteur de l'enseignement supérieur.
ESP> Año de base: 1973=100. El total en 1975 de la columna 1 no incluye el personal auxiliar del sector de enseñanza superior.

Pacific Islands:
E--> Base year: 1973=100.
FR-> Année de base: 1973=100.
ESP> Año de base: 1973=100.

Papua New Guinea: (Cont):
E--> Base year: 1971=100.
FR-> Année de base: 1971=100.
ESP> Año de base: 1971=100.

Samoa:
E--> Base year: 1975=100. Data for scientists and engineers ref only to full-time. Data for 1975 do not include social sciences a humanities.
FR-> Année de base: 1975=100. Les données pour les scientifiqu et ingénieurs sont à plein temps seulement. Les données pour 1975 comprennent pas les sciences sociales et humaines.
ESP> Año de base: 1975=100. Los datos para los científicos ingenieros son de jornada completa solamente. Los datos para 1975 incluyen las ciencias sociales y humanas.

Tonga:
E--> Base year: 1977=100. Data relate to one research institu only. Data for scientists and engineers are full-time plus part-time.
FR-> Année de base: 1977=100. Les données ne concernent qu' institut de recherche. Les données relatives aux scientifiques et ingénie sont à plein temps et à temps partiel.
ESP> Año de base: 1977=100. Los datos sólo se refieren a instituto de investigación. Los datos relativos a los científicos e ingenie son de jornada completa y de jornada parcial.

U.S.S.R.:

U.S.S.R.:
E--> Data refer to all persons with a higher scientific degree scientific title, regardless of the nature of their work, perso undertaking research work in scientific establishments and scient teaching staff in institutions of higher education; also includes perso undertaking scientific work in industrial enterprises.
FR-> Les données se réfèrent aux travailleurs scientifiques, c.a.d. toutes les personnes ayant un diplôme scientifique supérieur ou un t scientifique, sans considération de la nature de leur travail, aux person qui effectuent un travail de recherche dans des institutions scientifiques au personnel scientifique enseignant dans des établisseme d'enseignement supérieur; sont inclues aussi les personnes qui effectu des travaux scientifiques dans les entreprises industrielles.
ESP> Los datos se refieren a los trabajadores científicos, es deci todas las personas que poseen un diploma científico superior o un tít científico, sin tener en cuenta la naturaleza de su trabajo, a las personas efectuan un trabajo de investigación en las instituciones científicas y personal científico que ejerce funciones docentes en los establecimien de enseñanza superior; también se incluyen las personas que efect trabajos científicos en las empresas industriales.

Byelorussian S.S.R.:
E--> See note for the U.S.S.R.
FR-> Voir la note pour l'U.R.S.S.
ESP> Véase la nota de la U.R.S.S.

Ukrainian S.S.R.:
E--> See note for the U.S.S.R.
FR-> Voir la note pour l'U.R.S.S.
ESP> Véase la nota de la U.R.S.S.

5.17 Expenditure for research and experimental development: selected data for recent years

Dépenses consacrées à la recherche et au développement expérimental: données sélectionnées pour des années récentes

Gastos dedicados a la investigación y al desarrollo experimental: datos seleccionados sobre los últimos años

PLEASE REFER TO INTRODUCTION FOR DEFINITIONS OF CATEGORIES INCLUDED IN THIS TABLE.

POUR LES DEFINITIONS DES CATEGORIES PRESENTEES DANS CE TABLEAU, SE REFERER A L'INTRODUCTION.

EN LA INTRODUCCION SE DAN LAS DEFINICIONES DE LAS CATEGORIAS QUE FIGURAN EN ESTE CUADRO.

NUMBER OF COUNTRIES AND TERRITORIES PRESENTED IN THIS TABLE: 85

NOMBRE DE PAYS ET DE TERRITOIRES PRESENTES DANS CE TABLEAU: 85

NUMERO DE PAISES Y DE TERRITORIOS PRESENTADOS EN ESTE CUADRO: 85

COUNTRY / PAYS / PAIS	REFERENCE YEAR / ANNEE DE REFERENCE / AÑO DE REFERENCIA	CURRENCY / MONNAIE / MONEDA	EXPENDITURE FOR R&D / DEPENSES CONSACREES A R–D / GASTOS DEDICADOS A I Y D: TOTAL / TOTAL / TOTAL (000)	CURRENT EXPENDITURE / DEPENSES COURANTES / GASTOS CORRIENTES: AMOUNT / MONTANT / IMPORTE (000)	PERCENTAGE OF TOTAL / POURCENTAGE DU TOTAL / PORCENTAJE DEL TOTAL %
			(1)	(2)	(3)
AFRICA					
ALGERIA‡	1971	DINAR	77 500	67 500	87.1
	1972		78 000	68 000	87.2
CAMEROON	1969	FRANC C.F.A.	*1 443 000	...	...
	1970		*1 765 000	...	...
GABON‡	1969	FRANC C.F.A	1 647	1 603	97.3
	1970		1 895	1 882	99.3
MADAGASCAR‡	1969	FRANC	1 480 000	1 438 000	97.2
	1970		2 043 000	2 015 000	98.6
	1971		2 294 000	2 294 000	100.0
MAURITIUS	1969	RUPEE	*4 187	*3 621	*86.5
	1970		*5 124	*4 290	*83.7
	1982		56 300	49 200	87.4
	1983		38 100	31 900	83.7
	1984		38 700	31 000	80.1
NIGER‡	1973	FRANC C.F.A.	7 900	7 900	100.0
	1974		40 140	40 140	100.0
	1975		92 794	92 794	100.0
	1976		141 703	141 703	100.0
NIGERIA‡	1970	NAIRA	...	8 750	...
	1971		...	12 563	...
	1972		...	17 574	...
	1977		*102 000	*38 000	*37.3
SEYCHELLES‡	1969	RUPEE	161	...	...
	1970		209	209	100.0
	1973		402	290	72.1
	1981		1 037	337	32.5
	1983		12 854	6 083	47.3
SUDAN	1972	POUND	2 291	...	...
	1973		3 012	2 444	81.1
	1978		5 115	4 294	83.9

COUNTRY / PAYS / PAIS	REFERENCE YEAR / ANNEE DE REFERENCE / AÑO DE REFERENCIA	CURRENCY / MONNAIE / MONEDA	EXPENDITURE FOR R&D / DEPENSES CONSACREES A R-D / GASTOS DEDICADOS A I Y D — TOTAL / TOTAL / TOTAL (000)	CURRENT EXPENDITURE / DEPENSES COURANTES / GASTOS CORRIENTES — AMOUNT / MONTANT / IMPORTE (000)	PERCENTAGE OF TOTAL / POURCENTAGE DU TOTAL / PORCENTAJE DEL TOTAL %
			(1)	(2)	(3)
ZAMBIA	1969	KWACHA	...	*1 500	...
	1970		...	*1 980	...
	1972		6 261	4 726	75.5
AMERICA, NORTH					
BERMUDA‡	1969	DOLLAR	221	216	97.7
	1970		240	205	85.4
CANADA‡	1969	DOLLAR	1 057 000	841 000	79.6
	1970		*1 103 000	*865 000	*78.4
	1981		*4 332 000	...	...
	1982		5 089 000	...	...
	1983		5 365 000	...	...
COSTA RICA‡	1974	COLON	...	35 201	...
	1975		...	39 113	...
	1977		...	48 288	...
	1978		...	53 653	...
	1979		...	62 000	...
CUBA	1969	PESO	91 735	35 786	39.0
	1977		74 258	62 442	84.1
	1982		131 064	103 124	78.7
	1983		143 188	115 850	80.9
	1984		164 202	131 801	80.3
GUATEMALA	1970	QUETZAL	3 008	1 534	51.0
	1972		*3 932	*2 390	*60.8
	1974		*5 139	*3 721	*72.4
	1977		13 526	...	...
	1983		44 797	...	...
JAMAICA	1969	DOLLAR	...	833	...
	1970		...	1 060	...
	1971		...	1 095	...
MEXICO‡	1969	PESO	...	519 134	...
	1970		761 611	...	...
	1971		*1 034 124	570 172	*55.1
	1973		1 277 618	1 150 593	90.1
PANAMA	1974	BALBOA	2 908	2 707	93.1
	1975		3 296	...	...
ST. PIERRE AND MIQUELON	1976	FRENCH FRANC	*706	*666	*94.3
	1977		*710	*670	*94.4
	1982		*2 615	*2 065	*79.0
	1983		*3 803	*2 938	*77.3
	1984		*2 719	*2 047	*75.3
TRINIDAD AND TOBAGO‡	1969	DOLLAR	4 180	3 923	93.9
	1970		5 171	4 371	84.5
TURKS AND CAICOS ISLANDS	1970	UNITED STATES DOLLAR	25	...	...
	1971		25	...	...
	1972		41	...	...
	1973		51	...	...
	1974		8	...	...
UNITED STATES‡	1969	DOLLAR	...	26 169 000	...
	1970		...	26 545 000	...
	1982		...	80 317 000	...
	1983		...	86 204 900	...
	1984		...	*96 975 000	...
AMERICA, SOUTH					
ARGENTINA‡	1970	PESO	207	...	...
	1972		246	194	79.0
	1978		195 278	136 550	69.9
	1980		1 480 800	1 006 900	68.0
	1981		2 321 932	...	...
BRAZIL‡	1975	CRUZEIRO	8 020 500	...	...
	1976		10 346 500	...	...
	1981		*165 100 000	...	...
	1982		*309 400 000	...	...
	1983		*559 700 000	...	...

COUNTRY	REFERENCE YEAR	CURRENCY	EXPENDITURE FOR R&D / DEPENSES CONSACREES A R–D / GASTOS DEDICADOS A I Y D		
			TOTAL	CURRENT EXPENDITURE / DEPENSES COURANTES / GASTOS CORRIENTES	
PAYS	ANNEE DE REFERENCE	MONNAIE	TOTAL	AMOUNT	PERCENTAGE OF TOTAL
				MONTANT	POURCENTAGE DU TOTAL
PAIS	AÑO DE REFERENCIA	MONEDA	TOTAL	IMPORTE	PORCENTAJE DEL TOTAL
			(000)	(000)	%
			(1)	(2)	(3)
ECUADOR	1970	SUCRE	90 515	...	...
	1973		142 310	...	...
FALKLAND ISLANDS (MALVINAS)	1969	POUND STERLING	4	...	...
	1970		–	–	–
	1971		–	–	–
PERU‡	1971	SOL	525 000	...	...
	1973		733 000	...	...
	1982		43 413 000	...	...
	1983		83 742 000	...	...
	1984		159 024 000	...	...
URUGUAY	1971	PESO	*1 673	*1 401	*83.7
	1972		1 858	...	...
VENEZUELA‡	1970	BOLIVAR	102 270	97 150	95.0
	1973		289 697	...	...
	1982		1 151 820	...	...
	1983		1 196 500	...	...
	1984		1 361 820	...	...
ASIA					
BRUNEI DARUSSALAM‡	1971	DOLLAR	...	2 425	...
	1974		3 055	2 933	96.0
	1982		7 130	4 460	62.6
	1983		7 560	4 560	60.3
	1984		10 880	8 220	75.6
CYPRUS‡	1969	POUND	922	806	87.4
	1970		909	810	89.1
	1982		937	...	...
	1983		1 044	...	...
	1984		1 159	...	...
INDIA	1969	RUPEE	1 166 200	...	...
	1970		1 396 400	...	...
	1980		7 605 200	...	...
	1981		9 407 300	...	...
	1982		*11 586 360	...	...
INDONESIA‡	1978	RUPIAH	82 730 000	...	...
	1979		102 762 000	...	...
	1981		200 674 000	...	...
	1982		295 481 000	...	...
	1983		270 313 000	235 167 000	87.0
IRAN, ISLAMIC REPUBLIC OF‡	1970	RIAL	4 414 595	3 966 820	89.9
	1971		4 856 054	4 322 745	89.0
	1972		3 531 807	2 246 789	63.6
IRAQ‡	1971	DINAR	1 839	1 448	78.7
	1972		2 361	1 794	76.0
	1973		2 310	1 791	77.5
	1974		3 471	2 743	79.0
ISRAEL‡	1969	POUND	...	175 000	...
	1970		...	242 000	...
	1976		2 333 500	2 227 100	95.4
	1978		6 154 300	5 943 000	96.6
JAPAN‡	1969	YEN	1 064 653	839 784	78.9
	1970		1 355 505	1 058 154	78.1
	1981		5 982 356	4 886 784	81.7
	1982		6 528 700	5 365 711	82.2
	1983		7 180 782	5 953 927	82.9
JORDAN‡	1975	DINAR	1 540	...	...
	1976		2 074	1 242	59.9
	1979		7 565	3 647	48.2
KOREA, REPUBLIC OF‡	1969	WON	9 773 985	5 203 400	53.2
	1970		10 547 753	7 586 539	71.9
	1981		293 131 465	207 853 799	70.9
	1982		457 688 485	340 071 460	74.3
	1983		621 749 314	398 577 359	64.1

5.17 **Historical data on R&D expenditure**
Données rétrospectives sur les dépenses de R-D
Datos retrospectivos sobre los gastos de I y D

COUNTRY / PAYS / PAIS	REFERENCE YEAR / ANNEE DE REFERENCE / AÑO DE REFERENCIA	CURRENCY / MONNAIE / MONEDA	EXPENDITURE FOR R&D / DEPENSES CONSACREES A R–D / GASTOS DEDICADOS A I Y D — TOTAL / TOTAL / TOTAL (000)	CURRENT EXPENDITURE / DEPENSES COURANTES / GASTOS CORRIENTES — AMOUNT / MONTANT / IMPORTE (000)	PERCENTAGE OF TOTAL / POURCENTAGE DU TOTAL / PORCENTAJE DEL TOTAL %
			(1)	(2)	(3)
KUWAIT‡	1980	DINAR	40 459	34 504	85.3
	1981		40 361	37 045	91.8
	1982		43 746	40 500	92.6
	1983		67 250	60 616	90.1
	1984		71 163	63 016	88.6
LEBANON‡	1977	POUND	...	7 200	...
	1978		...	9 400	...
	1979		...	11 500	...
	1980		22 000	...	...
PAKISTAN‡	1969	RUPEE	104 280	...	...
	1970		116 980	...	...
	1972		123 250	...	...
	1973		150 430	...	...
	1979		391 059	198 503	50.8
PHILIPPINES‡	1972	PESO	80 406	55 519	75.9
	1973		126 046	85 911	78.4
	1979		510 739	366 342	71.7
	1980		623 000	474 026	76.1
	1982		*522 970	*470 500	*90.0
SINGAPORE‡	1978	DOLLAR	27 775	20 326	73.2
	1981		81 900	59 350	72.5
SRI LANKA‡	1969	RUPEE	21 517	16 689	77.6
	1970		21 887	18 332	83.8
	1974		35 797	26 961	75.3
	1975		45 097	32 662	72.4
	1983		206 528	109 898	53.2
TURKEY‡	1969	LIRA	434 700	...	...
	1970		492 000	...	...
	1977		6 466 409	...	...
	1978		7 601 531	...	...
	1979		12 572 229	...	...
VIET–NAM	1976	DONG	101 000	38 000	37.6
	1977		77 000	44 000	57.1
	1978		117 000	56 000	47.9
	1979		108 300	68 800	63.5
EUROPE					
AUSTRIA	1970	SCHILLING	2 286 474	1 834 170	80.2
	1975		6 039 416	4 877 257	80.7
	1981		12 331 026	10 201 527	82.7
BELGIUM	1969	FRANC	14 474 727	11 915 282	82.3
	1971		20 626 163	...	...
	1973		25 026 578	20 713 379	82.8
	1975		29 829 603	26 787 654	89.8
	1977		38 894 080	34 917 217	89.8
BULGARIA	1973	LEV	298 400	265 500	89.0
	1974		305 600	265 900	87.0
	1982		631 800	547 300	86.6
	1983		669 800	603 200	90.1
	1984		696 900	604 200	86.7
CZECHOSLOVAKIA‡	1970	KORUNA	11 391 000	9 524 000	83.6
	1971		11 789 000	10 104 000	85.7
	1982		18 688 000	16 627 000	89.0
	1983		19 455 000	17 111 000	88.0
	1984		19 875 000	17 468 000	87.9
DENMARK	1970	KRONE	1 140 000	992 000	87.0
	1973		1 677 000	1 507 000	89.9
	1979		3 367 000	3 027 000	89.9
	1981		4 379 000	...	...
	1983		5 970 400	5 168 000	86.6
FINLAND	1969	MARKKA	298 630	247 480	82.9
	1971		435 590	354 850	81.5
	1981		2 595 000	2 310 000	89.0
	1983		3 626 730	3 190 550	88.0
	1984		4 381 000	...	...

COUNTRY / PAYS / PAIS	REFERENCE YEAR / ANNEE DE REFERENCE / AÑO DE REFERENCIA	CURRENCY / MONNAIE / MONEDA	EXPENDITURE FOR R&D / DEPENSES CONSACREES A R–D / GASTOS DEDICADOS A I Y D — TOTAL / TOTAL / TOTAL (000) (1)	CURRENT EXPENDITURE / DEPENSES COURANTES / GASTOS CORRIENTES — AMOUNT / MONTANT / IMPORTE (000) (2)	PERCENTAGE OF TOTAL / POURCENTAGE DU TOTAL / PORCENTAJE DEL TOTAL % (3)
FRANCE	1969	FRANC	14 210 000	11 464 000	80.7
	1970		14 955 200	...	...
	1977		33 185 000	30 258 000	91.2
	1978		37 671 000	34 372 000	91.2
	1979		44 123 000	40 269 000	91.3
GERMAN DEMOCRATIC REPUBLIC‡	1981	DDR MARK	7 686 000	...	...
	1982		8 120 000	...	...
	1983		8 165 000	...	...
	1984		*8 750 000	...	...
GERMANY, FEDERAL REPUBLIC OF‡	1969	DEUTSCHE MARK	10 866 900	8 940 200	82.3
	1970		*12 950 000	...	...
	1977		25 733 000	22 664 000	89.2
	1979		33 457 000	29 041 000	88.4
	1981		38 352 000	33 520 000	88.4
GREECE‡	1979	DRACHMA	2 663 000	...	...
	1980		3 042 000	...	...
	1981		4 039 000	...	...
	1982		5 019 000	...	...
	1983		6 067 000	...	...
HUNGARY‡	1969	FORINT	6 308 500	5 076 100	80.5
	1970		7 525 000	5 862 000	77.9
	1982		21 215 000	18 529 000	87.3
	1983		20 419 000	17 761 000	87.0
	1984		22 686 000	19 549 000	86.2
ICELAND‡	1969	KRONA	*159 700	*128 300	*80.3
	1970		*164 500	*135 800	*82.6
	1975		1 791 800	1 208 900	67.5
	1977		2 582 600	2 281 200	88.3
	1979		6 427 500	5 663 000	88.1
IRELAND‡	1969	POUND	9 950	8 403	84.5
	1971		14 425	12 515	86.8
	1979		55 266	48 196	87.2
	1981		83 332	73 003	87.6
	1982		97 582	85 487	87.6
ITALY‡	1969	LIRA	464 214	391 503	84.3
	1970		554 671	461 208	83.2
	1981		4 055 335	3 304 380	81.5
	1982		4 915 678	4 108 706	83.6
	1983		6 027 005	4 999 917	83.0
MALTA‡	1973	LIRA	149	131	87.9
	1981		10	...	...
	1983		10	9	90.0
	1984		10	9	90.0
NETHERLANDS‡	1970	GUILDER	2 441 000	2 075 000	85.0
	1971		2 818 000	2 391 000	84.8
	1981		6 643 000	5 981 000	90.0
	1982		7 284 000	6 632 000	91.0
	1983		7 699 000	7 029 000	91.3
NORWAY	1970	KRONE	873 000	786 000	90.0
	1972		1 220 000	1 110 000	91.0
	1980		3 629 800	3 307 200	91.1
	1981		4 213 800	3 812 300	90.5
	1982		4 952 500	4 473 100	90.3
POLAND‡	1969	ZLOTY	15 900 000	12 000 000	75.5
	1970		16 900 000	13 200 000	78.1
	1982		46 400 000	39 600 000	85.3
	1983		57 400 000	50 400 000	87.8
	1984		73 700 000	63 700 000	86.4
PORTUGAL	1971	ESCUDO	751 189	...	...
	1972		854 150	738 916	86.5
	1978		2 521 100	2 120 200	84.1
	1980		4 118 500	3 160 600	76.7
	1982		6 541 200	5 370 600	82.1

5.17 Historical data on R&D expenditure
Données rétrospectives sur les dépenses de R-D
Datos retrospectivos sobre los gastos de I y D

COUNTRY / PAYS / PAIS	REFERENCE YEAR / ANNEE DE REFERENCE / AÑO DE REFERENCIA	CURRENCY / MONNAIE / MONEDA	EXPENDITURE FOR R&D / DEPENSES CONSACREES A R-D / GASTOS DEDICADOS A I Y D: TOTAL / TOTAL / TOTAL (000)	CURRENT EXPENDITURE / DEPENSES COURANTES / GASTOS CORRIENTES: AMOUNT / MONTANT / IMPORTE (000)	CURRENT EXPENDITURE / DEPENSES COURANTES / GASTOS CORRIENTES: PERCENTAGE OF TOTAL / POURCENTAGE DU TOTAL / PORCENTAJE DEL TOTAL %
			(1)	(2)	(3)
ROMANIA	1969	LEU	2 033 441	1 641 450	80.7
	1970		2 181 390	1 719 332	78.8
	1971		2 750 870	2 114 142	76.9
	1972		3 074 995	2 430 833	79.1
	1973		3 354 196	2 631 161	78.4
SPAIN	1969	PESETA	4 621 185	3 669 853	79.4
	1970		5 547 957	4 360 120	78.6
	1981		67 126 042	59 617 936	88.8
	1982		89 724 436	74 198 736	82.7
	1983		100 697 093	83 320 146	82.7
SWEDEN‡	1969	KRONA	1 896 000	1 738 000	91.7
	1971		2 725 700	2 514 100	92.2
	1979		8 611 000	7 962 900	92.5
	1981		13 320 000	12 240 000	91.9
	1983		18 189 000	16 475 000	90.6
SWITZERLAND	1972	FRANC	*2 610 000	*2 320 000	*88.9
	1973		*2 900 000	*2 580 000	*89.0
	1980		...	3 611 100	...
	1981		...	3 789 100	...
	1983		...	4 643 000	...
UNITED KINGDOM‡	1969	POUND STERLING	1 045 362	923 032	88.3
	1972		1 313 400	1 175 600	89.5
	1975		2 151 300	1 935 000	89.9
	1978		3 510 300	3 102 900	88.4
	1981		5 921 200	...	...
YUGOSLAVIA‡	1969	DINAR	1 316 300	...	...
	1970		1 646 000	...	...
	1979		11 129 000	...	...
	1980		14 105 000	...	...
	1981		18 235 000	...	...
OCEANIA					
AMERICAN SAMOA‡	1969	UNITED STATES DOLLAR	80	70	87.5
	1970		100	80	80.0
	1971		120	100	83.3
AUSTRALIA	1976	DOLLAR	873 400	790 300	90.5
	1978		1 053 800	933 300	88.6
	1981		1 522 200	1 331 800	87.5
COOK ISLANDS	1969	NEW ZEALAND DOLLAR	61	...	...
	1970		112	...	...
FRENCH POLYNESIA‡	1970	FRANC C.F.P.	69 322	61 423	88.6
	1971		73 332	63 002	85.9
	1981		255 200	250 150	98.0
	1982		304 320	301 650	99.1
	1983		324 720	308 440	95.0
GUAM‡	1973	UNITED STATES DOLLAR	579	330	57.0
	1978		1 295	...	...
	1979		1 256	...	...
NEW CALEDONIA	1969	FRANC C.F.P.	1 440	1 240	86.1
	1970		1 440	1 240	86.1
	1981		40 200	28 600	71.1
	1982		57 800	52 700	91.2
	1983		83 000	55 800	67.2
NEW ZEALAND‡	1969	DOLLAR	21 010	...	...
	1970		24 270	...	...
	1975		*99 776	*91 449	*91.7
	1977		117 322	110 936	94.6
	1979		175 373	157 768	90.0
PACIFIC ISLANDS	1978	UNITED STATES DOLLAR	185	185	100.0
	1979		185	185	100.0
SAMOA	1975	TALA	1 437	785	54.6
	1976		1 385	380	27.4
	1977		2 341	341	14.6
	1978		2 500	500	20.0

COUNTRY PAYS PAIS	REFERENCE YEAR ANNEE DE REFERENCE AÑO DE REFERENCIA	CURRENCY MONNAIE MONEDA	EXPENDITURE FOR R&D / DEPENSES CONSACREES A R–D / GASTOS DEDICADOS A I Y D TOTAL TOTAL TOTAL (000)	CURRENT EXPENDITURE / DEPENSES COURANTES / GASTOS CORRIENTES AMOUNT MONTANT IMPORTE (000)	 PERCENTAGE OF TOTAL POURCENTAGE DU TOTAL PORCENTAJE DEL TOTAL %
			(1)	(2)	(3)
TONGA‡	1976	PA'ANGA	55	51	92.7
	1977		165	112	67.9
	1978		240	226	94.2
	1979		475	256	53.9
	1980		426	279	65.5
VANUATU	1969	FRANC	6 759	...	...
	1970		8 667	...	...
	1973		13 119	13 119	100.0
	1974		20 925	20 925	100.0
	1975		21 603	21 603	100.0
U.S.S.R.					
U.S.S.R.‡	1969	ROUBLE	9 970 000	8 640 000	86.7
	1970		11 690 000	10 130 000	86.7
	1982		24 900 000	...	...
	1983		26 400 000	...	...
	1984		27 600 000	...	...
BYELORUSSIAN S.S.R.‡	1969	ROUBLE	45 444	34 295	75.5
	1970		46 399	33 380	71.9

AFRICA:

Algeria:

E--> Data relate to the higher education sector only.

FR-> Les données ne concernent que le secteur de l'enseignement supérieur.

ESP> Los datos se refieren al sector de enseñanza superior solamente.

Gabon:

E--> Data refer to the (French) 'Office de la Recherche Scientifique et Technique Outre-Mer' (ORSTOM).

FR-> Les données ne concernent que l'Office franc¢ais de la recherche scientifique et technique outre-mer (ORSTOM).

ESP> Los datos se refieren al 'Office (franc¢ais) de la recherche scientifique et technique outre-mer' (ORSTOM) solamente.

Madagascar:

E--> Not including data for humanities and education for 1969 and 1970; not including the productive sector for 1969; not including the productive sector (integrated R&D) for 1970 and 1971.

FR-> Non compris les données pour les sciences humaines et l'éducation en 1969 et 1970; non compris les données pour le secteur de la production en 1969; non compris les données pour le secteur de la production (activites de R-D intégrées) en 1970 et 1971.

ESP> Para 1969 y 1970, excluídos los datos relativos a las ciencias humanas y a la educación; en 1969 no se incluye el sector productivo y en 1970 y 1971, queda excluído el sector productivo (actividades de I y D integradas).

Niger:

E--> Data relate to the higher education sector only.

FR-> Les données ne concernent que le secteur de l'enseignement supérieur.

ESP> Los datos se refieren al sector de enseñanza superior solamente.

Nigeria:

E--> Not including data for social sciences and humanities.

FR-> Non compris les données pour les sciences sociales et humaines.

ESP> Excluídos los datos relativos a las ciencias sociales y humanas.

Seychelles:

E--> Not including military and defence R&D.

FR-> Non compris les activités de R-D de caractère militaire ou relevant de la défense nationale.

ESP> Excluídas las actividades militares y de defensa de I y D.

AMERICA, NORTH:

Bermuda:

E--> Not including data for the productive sector and excluding law, humanities and education.

FR-> Non compris les données pour le secteur de la production et compte non tenu des données relatives au droit, aux sciences humaines et à l'éducation.

Bermuda: (Cont):

ESP> Excluídos los datos relativos al sector productivo y los que se refieren al derecho, las ciencias humanas y la educación.

Canada:

E--> Data for 1969 and 1970 do not include social sciences and humanities; from 1981 these are only excluded from the productive sector (integrated R&D).

FR-> Les données pour 1969 et 1970 ne comprennent pas les sciences sociales et humaines; à partir de 1981 celles-ci sont exclues seulement du secteur de la production (activités de R-D intégrées).

ESP> Los datos para 1969 y 1970 no incluyen las ciencias sociales y humanas; a partir de 1981 se excluyen solamente del sector productivo (actividades de I y D integradas).

Costa Rica:

E--> Data refer to government expenditure only.

FR-> Les données se réfèrent aux dépenses publiques seulement.

ESP> Los datos sólo se refieren a los gastos públicos.

Mexico:

E--> Data for current expenditure for 1969 (column 2) include some capital expenditure and do not include law, humanities and education; for 1971 figures in columns 2 and 3 refer to labour costs only.

FR-> Les données relatives aux dépenses courantes (colonne 2) pour 1969 comprennent certaines dépenses en capital et n'incluent pas le droit, les sciences humaines et l'éducation; pour 1971, les chiffres des colonnes 2 et 3 ne concernent que les dépenses de personnel.

ESP> Los datos relativos a los gastos corrientes (columna 2) incluyen en 1969 ciertos gastos de capital y no comprenden el derecho, las ciencias humanas y la educación; en 1971, las cifras de las columnas 2 y 3 sólo conciernen los gastos de personal.

Trinidad and Tobago:

E--> Not including data for law, education and arts.

FR-> Non compris les données pour le droit, l'éducation et les arts.

ESP> Excluídos los datos relativos al derecho, la educación y las artes.

United States:

E--> Not including data for law, humanities and education.

FR-> Non compris les données pour le droit, les sciences humaines et l'éducation.

ESP> Excluídos los datos relativos al derecho, las ciencias humanas y la educación.

AMERICA, SOUTH:

Argentina:

E--> Figures in millions.

FR-> Chiffres en millions.

ESP> Cifras en millones.

Brazil:

E--> Not including military and defence R&D.

FR-> Non compris les activités de R-D de caractère militaire ou relevant de la défense nationale.

Brazil: (Cont):
ESP> Excluídas las actividades militares y de defensa de I y D.

Peru:
E--> Data refer to the budget allotment for science and technology.
FR-> Les données se réfèrent aux crédits budgétaires relatifs à la science et à la technologie.
ESP> Los datos se refieren a las consignaciones presupuestarias relativas a la ciencia y la tecnología.

Venezuela:
E--> Data for 1982, 1983 and 1984 refer to government funds only and do not include military and defence R&D.
FR-> Les données de 1982, 1983 et 1984 se réfèrent aux dépenses publiques seulement et ne comprennent pas les activités de R-D de caractère militaire ou relevant de la défense nationale.
ESP> Los datos de 1982, 1983 y 1984 sólo se refieren a los gastos públicos y excluyen las actividades militares y de defensa de I y D.

ASIA:

Brunei Darussalem:
E--> Data for 1982, 1983 and 1984 relate to 2 research institutes only.
FR-> Les données de 1982, 1983 et 1984 se réfèrent à 2 instituts de recherche seulement.
ESP> Para 1982, 1983 y 1984 los datos se refieren a 2 centros de investigación solamente.

Cyprus:
E--> Data for 1982, 1983 and 1984 do not include the productive sector and refer to government funds.
FR-> Les données de 1982, 1983 et 1984 ne comprennent pas le secteur de la production et ne concernent que les dépenses du gouvernement.
ESP> Los datos de 1982, 1983 y 1984 no incluyen el sector productivo y sólo se refieren a los gastos del gobierno.

Indonesia:
E--> Change in series. Data do not include the productive sector and refer to government funds.
FR-> Changement de série. Les données ne comprennent pas le secteur de la production et ne concernent que les dépenses du gouvernement.
ESP> Cambio de serie. Los datos no incluyen el sector productivo y sólo se refieren a los gastos del gobierno.

Iran, Islamic Republic of:
E--> Data for 1972 refer to government expenditure only.
FR-> Les données pour 1972 ne se réfèrent qu'aux fonds publics.
ESP> Los datos para 1972 sólo se refieren a los fondos públicos.

Iraq:
E--> Partial data. In 1974 expenditure for R&D in government departments concerned only with scientific activities was 7,409 thousand dinars of which 4,909 thousand dinars were current expenditure.
FR-> Données partielles. En 1974, les dépenses consacrées à la R-D dans les départements gouvernementaux concernés par les activités scientifiques s'élevaient à 7 409 milliers de dinars dont 4 909 milliers correspondaient aux dépenses courantes.
ESP> Datos parciales. En 1974 los gastos destinados a la I y D en los servicios gubernamentales que se ocupan de las actividades científicas alcanzaron la suma de 7 409 millares de dinares, de los cuales 4 909 millares correspondían a los gastos corrientes.

Israel:
E--> For 1969, 1970 and 1975 data refer to the civilian sector only and do not include social sciences and humanities. For 1976 and 1978, data refer to expenditure in the fields of natural sciences and engineering.
FR-> Pour 1969, 1970 et 1975 les données ne se réfèrent qu'au secteur civil et ne comprennent pas les données pour les sciences sociales et humaines. Pour 1976 et 1978, les données se réfèrent aux dépenses dans les domaines des sciences exactes et naturelles et des sciences de l'ingénieur seulement.
ESP> Para 1969, 1970 y 1975 los datos sólo se refieren al sector civil y no incluyen las ciencias sociales y humanas. Para 1976 y 1978, los datos se refieren a los gastos relativos a las ciencias exactas y naturales y a la ingeniería solamente.

Japan:
E--> Figures in millions. Not including data for social sciences and humanities in the productive sector.
FR-> Chiffres en millions. Non compris les données pour les sciences sociales et humaines dans le secteur de la production.
ESP> Cifras en millones. Excluídos los datos relativos a las ciencias sociales y humanas del sector productivo.

Jordan:
E--> Not including military and defence R&D.
FR-> Non compris les activités de R-D de caractère militaire ou relevant de la défense nationale.
ESP> Excluídas las actividades militares y de defensa de I y D.

Korea, Republic of:
E--> Not including military and defence R&D. From 1969 to 1979 data exclude law, humanities and education; from 1981 not including social sciences and humanities.
FR-> Non compris les activités de R-D de caractère militaire ou relevant de la défense nationale. De 1969 à 1979 les données ne comprennent pas le droit, les sciences humaines et l'éducation; à partir d 1981 les sciences sociales et humaines sont exclues.
ESP> Excluídas las actividades militares y de defensa de I y D. D 1969 a 1979 los datos no incluyen el derecho, las ciencias humanas y l educación; a partir de 1981 se excluyen las ciencias sociales humanas.

Kuwait:
E--> Data refer to scientific and technological activities (STA).
FR-> Les données se réfèrent aux activités scientifiques technologiques (AST).
ESP> Los datos se refieren a las actividades científicas y tecnológica (ACT).

Lebanon:
E--> Partial data referring to the Faculty of Science at the Universi of Lebanon only.
FR-> Données partielles pour la Faculté des Sciences de l'Universi du Liban seulement.
ESP> Datos parciales para la Facultad de Ciencias de la Universidad d Líbano solamente.

Pakistan:
E--> Data refer to R&D activities which are concentrated mainly government-financed research establishements. Social sciences ar humanities in the higher education and general service sectors are n included. Not including the productive sector or military and defen R&D.
FR-> Les données se réfèrent aux activités de R-D se trouvant pour plupart dans les établissements de recherche financés par le gouverneme Les sciences sociales et humaines dans les secteurs de l'enseigneme supérieur et de service général sont exclues. Compte non tenu du secte de la production (activités de R-D intégrées) ni des activités de R-D caractère militaire ou relevant de la défense nationale.
ESP> Los datos se refieren a las actividades de I y D concentrad principalmente en los establecimientos de investigación subvencionad por el gobierno. No se incluyen los datos relativos a las ciencias sociales humanas, en los sectores de enseñanza superior y de servicio gener Excluídos el sector productivo (actividades de I y D integradas) y actividades militares y de defensa de I y D.

Philippines:
E--> In 1972 and 1973 total expenditure includes respectively 8,27 and 16,466 thousand pesos for which a distribution between current a capital expenditure is not available. These figures have been excluded fro the percentage calculations shown in column 3.
FR-> En 1972 et 1973, les dépenses totales de la colonne comprennent respectivement 8 274 et 16 466 milliers de pesos dont répartition entre dépenses courantes et dépenses en capital n'a pas é précisée. On n'a pas tenu compte de ces chiffres pour calculer pourcentages de la colonne 3.
ESP> En 1972 y 1973, los gastos totales de la columna 1 incluy respectivamente 8 274 y 16 466 miles de pesos cuya repartición en gastos corrientes y gastos de capital no se ha precisado. Dichas cifras se han tenido en cuenta para calcular los porcentajes de la columna 3

Singapore:
E--> Not including either military and defence R&D or social scienc and humanities.
FR-> Non compris les activités de R-D de caractère militaire relevant de la défense nationale ni les sciences sociales et humaines.
ESP> Excluídas las actividades militares y de defensa de I y D y ciencias sociales y humanas.

Sri Lanka:
E--> For 1969, 1970, 1974 and 1975 data do not include cap expenditure in the higher education sector.
FR-> Pour 1969, 1970, 1974 et 1975 les données ne comprenn pas les dépenses en capital du secteur de l'enseignement supérieur.
ESP> Para 1969, 1970, 1974 y 1975 los datos no incluyen los gas de capital del sector de enseñanza superior.

Turkey:
E--> Data relate to government expenditure only and do not inclu the productive sector. Not including data for social sciences a humanities.
FR-> Les données ne concernent que les dépenses du gouvernem et ne comprennent pas le secteur de la production. Non compris données pour les sciences sociales et humaines.
ESP> Los datos sólo se refieren a los gastos del gobierno y no incluy el sector productivo. No se incluyen las ciencias sociales y humanas.

EUROPE:

Czechoslovakia:
E--> Of military R&D only that part carried out in civil establishme is included.
FR-> Pour la R-D de caractère militaire seule la partie effectuée da les établissements civils a été considérée.
ESP> Para la I y D de carácter militar sólo se ha considerado la pa correspondiente a los establecimientos civiles.

German Democratic Republic:
E--> Data refer to 'expenditure for science and technology'.
FR-> Les données se réfèrent aux 'dépenses relatives à la scier et à la technologie'.
ESP> Los datos se refieren a los 'gastos relativos a la ciencias y

German Democratic Republic: (Cont):
tecnología'.

Germany, Federal Republic of:

E--> For 1977, 1979 and 1981 total expenditure in column 1 includes respectively 320, 615 and 450 million Deutsche marks for which a distribution between current and capital expenditure is not available. These figures have been excluded from the percentage calculations shown in column 3. Not including social sciences and humanities in the productive sector. In 1979 coverage extended to include small and medium-sized enterprises accounting for 2,800 million Deutsche marks.

FR-> Pour 1977, 1979 et 1981 les dépenses totales de la colonne 1 comprennent respectivement 320, 615 et 450 millions de deutsche marks dont la répartition entre dépenses courantes et dépenses en capital n'a pas été précisée. On n'a pas tenu compte de ces chiffres pour calculer les pourcentages de la colonne 3. Non compris les sciences sociales et humaines dans le secteur de la production. En 1979, la portée de l'enquête englobait également les petites et moyennes entreprises pour un montant de 2 800 millions de deutsche marks.

ESP> En 1977, 1979 y 1981 los gastos totales de la columna 1 incluyen respectivamente 320, 615 y 450 millones de marcos cuya repartición entre gastos corrientes y gastos de capital no se ha precisado. Dichas cifras no se han tenido en cuenta para calcular los porcentajes de la columna 3. Excluídos los datos relativos a las ciencias sociales y humanas del sector productivo. En 1979 la encuesta cubría igualmente las pequeñas y medianas empresas con un gasto de 2 800 millones de marcos.

Greece:

E--> Data relate to government activities only.

FR-> Les données se réfèrent aux activités gouvernementales seulement.

ESP> Los datos se refieren a las actividades gubernamentales solamente.

Hungary:

E--> Due to methodological changes in 1981 data since then are not comparable with the previous years.

FR-> Suite à des changements de méthodologie en 1981 les données ne sont pas comparables avec celles des années précédentes.

ESP> Debido a los cambios de metodología en 1981, los datos no son comparables con los de los años anteriores.

Iceland:

E--> In 1969 and 1970 data do not include social sciences and humanities.

FR-> Les données pour 1969 et 1970 ne comprennent pas les sciences sociales et humaines.

ESP> Los datos para 1969 y 1970 no comprenden las ciencias sociales y humanas.

Ireland:

E--> Data for 1969 and 1971 do not include humanities.

FR-> Les données pour 1969 et 1971 ne comprennent pas les sciences humaines.

ESP> Los datos para 1969 y 1971 no incluyen las ciencias humanas.

Italy:

E--> Figures in millions.

FR-> Chiffres en millions.

ESP> Cifras en millones.

Malta:

E--> Data relate to the higher education sector only.

FR-> Les données ne concernent que le secteur de l'enseignement supérieur.

ESP> Los datos se refieren al sector de enseñanza superior solamente.

Netherlands:

E--> Not including social sciences and humanities in the productive sector (integrated R&D).

FR-> Non compris les données pour les sciences sociales et humaines du secteur de la production (activités de R-D intégrées).

ESP> Excluídos los datos relativos a las ciencias sociales y humanas del sector productivo (actividades de I y D integradas).

Poland:

E--> Not including military and defence R&D.

FR-> Non compris les activités de R-D de caractère militaire ou relevant de la défense nationale.

ESP> Excluídas las actividades militares y de defensa de I y D.

Sweden:

E--> From 1969 to 1979, data exclude social sciences and humanities whilst in 1981 and 1983 these fields are included only for the productive and general service sectors.

FR-> De 1969 à 1979 les données ne comprennent pas les sciences sociales et humaines tandis qu'en 1981 et 1983 ces domaines sont comptés seulement pour les secteurs de la production et de service

Sweden: (Cont):
général.

ESP> De 1969 a 1979 los datos se excluyen las ciencias sociales y humanas mientras que en 1981 y 1983 estos campos fueron incluídos para los sectores productivo y de servicio general.

United Kingdom:

E--> For 1969, 1972, 1975 and 1978, the total expenditure in column 1 includes respectively 5,666, 25,700, 43,500 and 77,400 thousand pounds sterling for which a distribution between current and capital expenditure is not available; current expenditure in column 2 does not therefore include the relevant portions of these sums. These figures have been excluded from the percentage calculations shown in column 3. Not including data for social sciences and humanities.

FR-> Les dépenses totales de la colonne 1 comprennent pour 1969, 1972, 1975 et 1978 respectivement 5 666, 25 700, 43 500 et 77 400 milliers de livres sterling dont la répartition entre dépenses courantes et dépenses en capital n'a pas été précisée; les dépenses courantes de la colonne 2 ne comprennent donc pas une partie de ces sommes. On n'a pas tenu compte de ces chiffres pour calculer les pourcentages de la colonne 3. Non compris les données pour les sciences sociales et humaines.

ESP> Los gastos totales de la columna 1 comprenden para 1969, 1972, 1975 y 1978 respectivamente 5 666, 25 700, 43 500 y 77 400 millares de libras esterlinas, cuya repartición entre gastos corrientes y gastos de capital no se ha precisado; los gastos corrientes de la columna 2 no incluyen por consiguiente una parte de dicha suma. Dichas cifras no se han tenido en cuenta para calcular los porcentajes de la columna 3. No se incluyen los datos relativos a las ciencias sociales y humanas.

Yugoslavia:

E--> Not including military and defence R&D. In 1981 data refer to total revenue rather than total expenditure.

FR-> Non compris les activités de R-D de caractère militaire ou relevant de la défense nationale. En 1981, les données se réfèrent au total des revenus au lieu des dépenses totales.

ESP> Excluídas las actividades militares y de defensa de I y D. En 1981 los datos se refieren a los ingresos totales en lugar de los gastos totales.

OCEANIA:

American Samoa:

E--> Data relate to one research institute only.

FR-> Les données ne concernent qu'un institut de recherche.

ESP> Los datos se refieren a un centro de investigación solamente.

French Polynesia:

E--> Data relate to one research institute only.

FR-> Les données ne concernent qu'un institut de recherche.

ESP> Los datos se refieren a un centro de investigación solamente.

Guam:

E--> Data relate to the higher education sector only.

FR-> Les données ne concernent que le secteur de l'enseignement supérieur.

ESP> Los datos se refieren al sector de enseñanza superior solamente.

New Zealand:

E--> For 1969 and 1970, data do not include funds from overseas, for 1977 total expenditure in column 1 excludes capital expenditure for buildings.

FR-> Pour 1969 et 1970, les données ne comprennent pas les fonds en provenance de l'étranger, en 1977 les dépenses totales de la colonne 1 ne comprennent pas les dépenses en capital destinées aux bâtiments.

ESP> Para 1969 y 1970, los datos no incluyen los fondos procedentes del extranjero, en 1977 los gastos totales de la columna 1 no incluyen los gastos de capital destinados a los edificios.

Tonga:

E--> Data relate to one research institute only.

FR-> Les données ne concernent qu'un institut de recherche.

ESP> Los datos se refieren a un centro de investigación solamente.

U.S.S.R.:

U.S.S.R.:

E--> *Expenditure on Science* from the national budget and other sources.

FR-> Montant total des *sommes dépensées pour la science* d'après le budget national et autres sources.

ESP> Importe total de los *gastos dedicados a la ciencia*, según el presupuesto nacional y otras fuentes.

Byelorussian S.S.R.:

E--> R&D expenditure relates to research institutions administered by the Council of Ministers of the Byelorussian S.S.R.

FR-> Les données se réfèrent aux instituts de recherche administrés par le Conseil des Ministres de la R.S.S. de Biélorussie.

ESP> Los datos se refieren a los centros de investigación administrados por el Consejo de ministros de la RSS de Bielorrusia.

5.18 Selected indicators for scientific and technical manpower potential and personnel engaged in research and experimental development

Indicateurs sélectionnés pour le potentiel scientifique et technique et le personnel employé à des travaux de recherche et de développement expérimental

Indicadores seleccionados para los recursos científicos y técnicos y el personal dedicado a actividades de investigación y de desarrollo experimental

PLEASE REFER TO INTRODUCTION FOR DEFINITIONS OF CATEGORIES INCLUDED IN THIS TABLE.

FOR FURTHER DETAILS CONCERNING THE COVERAGE AND THE LIMITATIONS OF THE BASIC DATA USED FOR THE INDICATORS, PLEASE REFER TO TABLES RELATING TO SCIENTIFIC AND TECHNICAL MANPOWER (TABLES 5.3 AND 5.4) AS APPROPRIATE.

DATA FOR PERSONNEL ENGAGED IN R&D ARE IN FULL-TIME EQUIVALENT.

EA = ECONOMICALLY ACTIVE QUALIFIED MANPOWER
ST = STOCK OF QUALIFIED MANPOWER
S&E = SCIENTISTS AND ENGINEERS

NUMBER OF COUNTRIES AND TERRITORIES PRESENTED IN THIS TABLE: 110

POUR LES DEFINITIONS DES CATEGORIES PRESENTEES DANS CE TABLEAU, SE REFERER A L'INTRODUCTION.

POUR DES DETAILS PLUS COMPLETS EN CE QUI CONCERNE LA PORTEE DES DONNEES DE BASE ET LES ELEMENTS PRIS EN CONSIDERATION POUR LE CALCUL DES INDICATEURS, SE REFERER SELON LE CAS, AUX TABLEAUX 5.3 ET 5.4 CONCERNANT LE PERSONNEL SCIENTIFIQUE ET TECHNIQUE.

POUR LE PERSONNEL EMPLOYE A DES TRAVAUX DE R-D LES DONNEES SONT EN EQUIVALENT PLEIN TEMPS.

EA = PERSONNES QUALIFIEES ECONOMIQUEMENT ACTIVES
ST = NOMBRE DE PERSONNES QUALIFIEES
S&I = SCIENTIFIQUES ET INGENIEURS

NOMBRE DE PAYS ET DE TERRITOIRES PRESENTES DANS CE TABLEAU: 110

EN LA INTRODUCCION SE DAN LAS DEFINICIONES DE LAS CATEGORIAS QUE FIGURAN EN ESTE CUADRO.

PARA UNA INFORMACION MAS COMPLETA EN LO QUE SE REFIERE AL ALCANCE DE LOS DATOS DE BASE Y DE LOS ELEMENTOS QUE SE TOMARON EN CONSIDERACION PARA EL CALCULO DE LOS INDICADORES, SIRVANSE REFERIRSE, SEGUN EL CASO, A LOS CUADROS 5.3 Y 5.4 RELATIVOS AL PERSONAL CIENTIFICO Y TECNICO.

LOS DATOS DEL PERSONAL DEDICADO A ACTIVIDADES DE I Y D SE DAN EN EQUIVALENTE DE JORNADA COMPLETA.

EA = PERSONAS CALIFICADAS ECONOMICAMENTE ACTIVAS
ST = TOTAL DE PERSONAS CALIFICADAS
C&I = CIENTIFICOS E INGENIEROS

NUMERO DE PAISES Y DE TERRITORIOS PRESENTADOS EN ESTE CUADRO: 110

COUNTRY / PAYS / PAIS	YEAR / ANNEE / AÑO	TYPE OF DATA / TYPE DE DONNEES / TIPO DE DATOS	QUALIFIED MANPOWER / PERSONNES QUALIFIEES / PERSONAS CALIFICADAS: POTENTIAL SCIENTISTS AND ENGINEERS PER MILLION POPULATION / SCIENTIFIQUES ET INGENIEURS POTENTIELS PAR MILLION D'HABITANTS / CIENTIFICOS E INGENIEROS POTENCIALES POR MILLON DE HABITANTES	POTENTIAL TECHNICIANS PER MILLION POPULATION / TECHNICIENS POTENTIELS PAR MILLION D'HABITANTS / TECNICOS POTENCIALES POR MILLON DE HABITANTES	PERSONNEL ENGAGED IN R&D / PERSONNEL EMPLOYE A DES TRAVAUX DE R-D / PERSONAL DEDICADO A ACTIVIDADES DE I Y D: SCIENTISTS AND ENGINEERS PER MILLION POPULATION / SCIENTIFIQUES ET INGENIEURS PAR MILLION D'HABITANTS / CIENTIFICOS E INGENIEROS POR MILLON DE HABITANTES	TECHNICIANS PER MILLION POPULATION / TECHNICIENS PAR MILLION D'HABITANTS / TECNICOS POR MILLON DE HABITANTES	NUMBER OF TECHNICIANS PER SCIENTIST OR ENGINEER / NOMBRE DE TECHNICIENS PAR SCIENTIFIQUE OU INGENIEUR / NUMERO DE TECNICOS POR CIENTIFICO O INGENIERO	S&E IN R&D AS % OF POTENTIAL S&E / S&I EN R-D EN % DES S&I POTENTIELS / C&I EN I Y D EN % DE LOS C&I POTENCIALES
			(1)	(2)	(3)	(4)	(5)	(6)
AFRICA								
BURUNDI	1984	.	...	...	48	25	0.5	...
CAMEROON	1976	ST	1 516	...	...	...	...	...
CENTRAL AFRICAN REPUBLIC	1984	.	...	...	78	152	2.0	...
CONGO‡	1984	EA	...	2 441	509	869	1.7	...
COTE D'IVOIRE	1975	.		...	74	...	...	...
EGYPT‡	1982	ST	13 196	...	458	153	0.3	...
GHANA‡	1976	.	...	...	403	566	1.4	...
GUINEA	1984	.	...	...	216	103	0.5	...
KENYA‡	1982	EA	892	2 526	26	13	0.5	...
LIBYAN ARAB JAMAHIRIYA	1980	EA	14 711	3 034	370	505	1.4	2.5
MADAGASCAR	1980	.	...	...	13	42	3.3	...
MALAWI	1977	ST	729	...	35	44	1.3	4.7

COUNTRY / PAYS / PAIS	YEAR / ANNEE / AÑO	TYPE OF DATA / TYPE DE DONNEES / TIPO DE DATOS	QUALIFIED MANPOWER / PERSONNES QUALIFIEES / PERSONAS CALIFICADAS: POTENTIAL SCIENTISTS AND ENGINEERS PER MILLION POPULATION / SCIENTIFIQUES ET INGENIEURS POTENTIELS PAR MILLION D'HABITANTS / CIENTIFICOS E INGENIEROS POTENCIALES POR MILLON DE HABITANTES	POTENTIAL TECHNICIANS PER MILLION POPULATION / TECHNICIENS POTENTIELS PAR MILLION D'HABITANTS / TECNICOS POTENCIALES POR MILLON DE HABITANTES	PERSONNEL ENGAGED IN R&D / PERSONNEL EMPLOYE A DES TRAVAUX DE R-D / PERSONAL DEDICADO A ACTIVIDADES DE I Y D: SCIENTISTS AND ENGINEERS PER MILLION POPULATION / SCIENTIFIQUES ET INGENIEURS PAR MILLION D'HABITANTS / CIENTIFICOS E INGENIEROS POR MILLON DE HABITANTES	TECHNICIANS PER MILLION POPULATION / TECHNICIENS PAR MILLION D'HABITANTS / TECNICOS POR MILLON DE HABITANTES	NUMBER OF TECHNICIANS PER SCIENTIST OR ENGINEER / NOMBRE DE TECHNICIENS PAR SCIENTIFIQUE OU INGENIEUR / NUMERO DE TECNICOS POR CIENTIFICO O INGENIERO	S&E IN R&D AS % OF POTENTIAL S&E / S&I EN R-D EN % DES S&I POTENTIELS / C&I EN I Y D EN % DE LOS C&I POTENCIALES
			(1)	(2)	(3)	(4)	(5)	(6)
MAURITIUS‡	1984	ST	7 175	19 280	255	171	0.7	3.6
NIGER	1976	.	...	...	19	0	0.0	...
NIGERIA‡	1980	ST	274	1 387	30	19	0.6	...
RWANDA‡	1981	ST	366	——>	*46	...	...	...
SENEGAL	1976	.	...	...	106	...	...	...
SEYCHELLES	1983	.	...	...	254	85	0.3	...
SUDAN	1978	.	...	...	217	186	0.9	...
SWAZILAND	1977	EA	2 730	...	...	...	...	...
TOGO	1976	.	...	...	113	80	0.7	...
ZAMBIA	1976	.	...	...	50	30	0.6	...
AMERICA, NORTH								
BRITISH VIRGIN ISLANDS	1982	EA	29 583	...	–	–	–	–
CANADA‡	1982	EA	50 959	238 362	*1 298	*753	*0.6	*2.6
COSTA RICA	1982	.	...	...	171	...	...	...
CUBA‡	1984	ST	14 349	...	955	885	0.9	...
EL SALVADOR	1984	.	...	...	397	——>	...	...
GUATEMALA	1984	.	...	...	348	——>	...	...
HAITI	1982	EA	2 320	2 947	...	...	...	...
PANAMA‡	1976	EA	3 150	8 058	121	179	1.5	3.8
FORMER CANAL ZONE	1976	EA	30 190	4 024	...	...	...	...
ST. LUCIA	1979	.	...	...	25	42	1.7	...
ST. PIERRE AND MIQUELON	1984	.	...	...	1 000	1 167	1.2	...
TURKS AND CAICOS ISLANDS‡	1980	ST	25 143	18 000	333	–	–	...
UNITED STATES‡	1983	EA	14 777	...	3 111	...	...	21.2
AMERICA, SOUTH								
ARGENTINA‡	1982	EA	18 970	60 077	360	...	...	...
BOLIVIA	1976	ST	11 562	...	...	...	...	...
BRAZIL‡	1982	EA	11 231	25 348	256	...	...	...
CHILE	1983	.	...	...	172	——>	...	...
COLOMBIA	1982	.	...	...	40	38	0.9	...
ECUADOR	1979	.	...	...	259	158	0.6	...
GUYANA‡	1982	EA	1 749	389	99	198	2.0	...
PARAGUAY	1981	.	...	...	247	——>	...	...
PERU	1981	ST	16 426	78 690	420	285	0.7	2.6
URUGUAY	1975	ST	19 939	...	...	...	...	...
VENEZUELA‡	1983	EA	21 819	96 456	279	165	0.6	1.3
ASIA								
BRUNEI DARUSSALAM‡	1984	EA	11 472	22 285	91	527	5.8	...
BURMA	1975	EA	608	...	57	16	0.3	9.3
CHINA	1984	EA	7 129	——>	...	...	...	...
CYPRUS	1984	.	...	...	77	121	1.6	...
HONG KONG	1981	EA	19 137	141 340	...	...	...	...
INDIA‡	1982	ST	2 829	——>	131	——>	...	...
INDONESIA‡	1983	ST	1 280	12 663	152	25	0.2	...
IRAN, ISLAMIC REPUBLIC OF‡	1982	ST	7 196	4 174	55	5	0.1	...
ISRAEL	1978	.	...	...	3 960	...	...	...
JAPAN‡	1984	EA	59 636	253 941	4 436	810	0.2	...
JORDAN‡	1982	EA	4 194	2 050	394	6	0.0	...
KOREA, REP. OF‡	1983	EA	2 426	49 762	801	486	0.6	...
KUWAIT‡	1984	ST	57 310	75 008	887	329	0.4	...
LEBANON	1980	.	...	...	67	2	0.0	...
MALAYSIA‡	1983	ST	1 796	...	182	——>	...	...
NEPAL	1980	EA	250	*500	23	5	0.2	9.1

COUNTRY / PAYS / PAIS	YEAR / ANNEE / AÑO	QUALIFIED MANPOWER / PERSONNES QUALIFIEES / PERSONAS CALIFICADAS			PERSONNEL ENGAGED IN R&D / PERSONNEL EMPLOYE A DES TRAVAUX DE R–D / PERSONAL DEDICADO A ACTIVIDADES DE I Y D			
		TYPE OF DATA / TYPE DE DONNEES / TIPO DE DATOS	POTENTIAL SCIENTISTS AND ENGINEERS PER MILLION POPULATION / SCIENTIFIQUES ET INGENIEURS POTENTIELS PAR MILLION D'HABITANTS / CIENTIFICOS E INGENIEROS POTENCIALES POR MILLON DE HABITANTES	POTENTIAL TECHNICIANS PER MILLION POPULATION / TECHNICIENS POTENTIELS PAR MILLION D'HABITANTS / TECNICOS POTENCIALES POR MILLON DE HABITANTES	SCIENTISTS AND ENGINEERS PER MILLION POPULATION / SCIENTIFIQUES ET INGENIEURS PAR MILLION D'HABITANTS / CIENTIFICOS E INGENIEROS POR MILLON DE HABITANTES	TECHNICIANS PER MILLION POPULATION / TECHNICIENS PAR MILLION D'HABITANTS / TECNICOS POR MILLON DE HABITANTES	NUMBER OF TECHNICIANS PER SCIENTIST OR ENGINEER / NOMBRE DE TECHNICIENS PAR SCIENTIFIQUE OU INGENIEUR / NUMERO DE TECNICOS POR CIENTIFICO O INGENIERO	S&E IN R&D AS % OF POTENTIAL S&E / S&I EN R–D EN % DES S&I POTENTIELS / C&I EN I Y D EN % DE LOS C&I POTENCIALES
			(1)	(2)	(3)	(4)	(5)	(6)
PAKISTAN	1982	.	...	...	59	78	1.3	...
PHILIPPINES‡	1982	.	...	...	101	46	0.5	...
QATAR	1984	EA	23 315	33 052	113	52	0.5	0.5
SINGAPORE‡	1981	EA	15 846	10 735	296	219	0.7	1.9
SRI LANKA	1983	.	...	...	124	91	0.7	...
THAILAND	1975	EA	490	1 144	...	...	...	...
TURKEY‡	1983	ST	15 922	18 665	163	57	0.3	...
VIET–NAM	1978	.	...	...	252	116	0.5	...
EUROPE								
AUSTRIA	1981	ST	20 506	——>	894	819	0.9	4.4
BELGIUM	1977	.	...	...	1 414	784	0.6	...
BULGARIA‡	1984	EA	33 780	70 167	5 006	1 385	0.3	14.9
CZECHOSLOVAKIA‡	1984	EA	35 445	...	3 797	3 021	0.8	...
DENMARK‡	1983	ST	16 305	46 888	1 466	2 001	1.4	7.2
FINLAND‡	1983	ST	35 798	300 193	2 265	1 917	0.8	6.4
FRANCE‡	1979	EA	23 747	...	1 364	2 955	2.2	...
GERMAN DEMOCRATIC REPUBLIC‡	1984	EA	34 181	61 168	7 631	4 168	0.5	22.3
GERMANY, FEDERAL REPUBLIC OF‡	1981	EA	37 001	99 015	2 084	1 879	0.9	5.6
GREECE‡	1983	ST	34 002	131 328	250	109	0.4	...
HUNGARY‡	1983	EA	38 485	135 174	2 108	1 726	0.8	...
ICELAND‡	1979	ST	23 056	...	1 343	1 003	0.7	...
IRELAND	1982	.	...	...	795	364	0.5	...
ITALY‡	1983	EC	20 596	61 817	1 102	502	0.5	...
MALTA	1984	.	...	...	90	13	0.1	...
NETHERLANDS‡	1983	EA	54 358	132 713	2 126	1 887	0.9	...
NORWAY‡	1982	ST	23 787	...	1 888	1 817	1.0	8.0
POLAND‡	1984	EA	30 773	114 876	2 030	954	0.5	...
PORTUGAL	1982	.	...	...	301	309	1.0	...
SAN MARINO	1983	EA	18 182	93 545	–	–	–	–
SPAIN	1983	EA	30 228	91 388	373	135	0.4	1.2
SWEDEN‡	1983	EA	40 597	222 686	2 292	3 445	1.5	...
SWITZERLAND‡	1983	EA	55 031	...	2 101	...	...	...
UNITED KINGDOM	1978	.	...	...	1 545	1 368	0.9	...
YUGOSLAVIA	1981	EA	17 918	159 729	1 109	612	0.6	6.2
OCEANIA								
AUSTRALIA	1981	EA	25 739	114 785	1 625	806	0.5	6.3
FIJI	1976	ST	16 532	——>	...	...	...	...
FRENCH POLYNESIA	1983	.	...	...	108	102	0.9	...
GUAM	1979	.	...	...	210	190	0.9	...
KIRIBATI	1980	.	...	...	34	17	0.5	...
NEW CALEDONIA	1983	.	...	...	47	34	0.7	...
NEW ZEALAND	1979	.	...	...	2 558	——>	...	...
NORFOLK ISLAND	1981	EA	70 000	...	–	–	–	–
PACIFIC ISLANDS	1979	.	...	...	29	79	2.8	...
SAMOA‡	1978	ST	2 288	1 072	909	597	0.7	40.0
TONGA	1981	.	...	...	111	40	0.4	...
VANUATU	1975	.	...	...	31	11	0.3	...
U.S.S.R.								
U.S.S.R.‡	1984	EA	49 507	66 590	5 316	...	...	10.8
BYELORUSSIAN S.S.R.	1983	EA	52 927	68 529	...	...	...	...
UKRAINIAN S.S.R.	1983	EA	50 014	67 859	...	...	...	...

AFRICA:
Congo:
E--> Data for qualified manpower relate to 1977.
FR-
Les données pour les personnes qualifiées se réfèrent à 1977.
ESP> Los datos relativos a las personas calificadas se refieren a 1977.
Egypt:
E--> Data for qualified manpower relate to 1976.
FR-> Les données pour les personnes qualifiées se réfèrent à 1976.
ESP> Los datos relativos a las personas calificadas se refieren a 1976.
Ghana:
E--> The number of technicians used to calculate columns 4 and 5 includes auxiliary personnel.
FR-> Le nombre de techniciens utilisé pour le calcul des colonnes 4 et 5 comprend le personnel auxiliaire.
ESP> El número de técnicos que sirvió para el cálculo de las columnas 4 y 5 incluye el personal auxiliar.
Kenya:
E--> Data for personnel engaged in R&D relate to 1975.
FR-> Les données relatives au personnel employé à des travaux de R-D se réfèrent à 1975.
ESP> Los datos relativos al personal empleado en trabajos de I y D se refieren a 1975.
Mauritius:
E--> Data for qualified manpower relate to 1983.
FR-> Les données pour les personnes qualifiés se réfèrent à 1983.
ESP> Los datos relativos a las personas calificadas se refieren a 1983.
Nigeria:
E--> Data for personnel engaged in R&D relate to 1977.
FR-> Les données relatives au personnel employé à des travaux de R-D se réfèrent à 1977.
ESP> Los datos relativos al personal empleado en trabajos de I y D se refieren a 1977.
Rwanda:
E--> Data for qualified manpower relate to 1978.
FR-> Les données pour les personnes qualifiées se réfèrent à 1978.
ESP> Los datos relativos a las personas calificadas se refieren a 1978.
AMERICA, NORTH:
Canada:
E--> Data for qualified manpower relate to 1981.
FR-> Les données pour les personnes qualifiées se réfèrent a 1981.
ESP> Los datos relativos a las personas calificadas se refieren a 1981.
Cuba:
E--> Data for qualified manpower relate to 1981.
FR-> Les données pour les personnes qualifiées se réfèrent à 1981.
ESP> Los datos relativos a las personas calificadas se refieren a 1981.
Panama:
E--> Data for personnel engaged in R&D relate to 1975.
FR-> Les données relatives au personnel employé à des travaux de R-D se réfèrent à 1975.
ESP> Los datos relativos al personal empleado en trabajos de I y D se refieren a 1975.
Turks and Caicos Islands:
E--> Data for personnel engaged in R&D relate to 1976.
FR-> Les données relatives au personnel employé à des travaux de R-D se réfèrent à 1976.
ESP> Los datos relativos al personal empleado en trabajos de I y D se refieren a 1976.
United States:
E--> Data for qualified manpower relate to 1982.
FR-> Les données pour les personnes qualifiées se réfèrent à l'année 1982.
ESP> Los datos relativos a las personas calificadas se refieren a 1982.
AMERICA, SOUTH:
Argentina:
E--> Data for qualified manpower relate to 1980.
FR-> Les données pour les personnes qualifiées se réfèrent à 1980.
ESP> Los datos relativos a las personas calificadas se refieren a 1980.
Brazil:
E--> Data for qualified manpower relate to 1980.
FR-> Les données pour les personnes qualifiées se réfèrent à 1980.
ESP> Los datos relativos a las personas calificadas se refieren a 1980.
Guyana:
E--> Data for qualified manpower relate to 1980.
FR-> Les données pour les personnes qualifiées se réfèrent à 1980.
ESP> Los datos relativos a las personas calificadas se refieren a 1980.
Venezuela:
E--> Data for qualified manpower relate to 1982.
Venezuela: (Cont):
FR-> Les données pour les personnes qualifiées se réfèrent à 1982.
ESP> Los datos relativos a las personas calificadas se refieren a 1982.
ASIA:
Brunei Darussalam:
E--> Data for qualified manpower relate to 1981.
FR-> Les données pour les personnes qualifiées se réfèrent à 1981.
ESP> Los datos relativos a las personas calificadas se refieren a 1981.
India:
E--> Data for qualified manpower relate to 1980.
FR-> Les données pour les personnes qualifiées se réfèrent à 1980.
ESP> Los datos relativos a las personas calificadas se refieren a 1980.
Indonesia:
E--> Data for qualified manpower relate to 1980.
FR-> Les données pour les personnes qualifiées se réfèrent à 1980.
ESP> Los datos relativos a las personas calificadas se refieren a 1980.
Iran, Islamic Republic of:
E--> Data for personnel engaged in R&D relate to 1980.
FR-> Les données relatives au personnel employé à des travaux de R-D se réfèrent à 1980.
ESP> Los datos relativos al personal empleado en trabajos de I y D se refieren a 1980.
Japan:
E--> Data for qualified manpower relate to 1982.
FR-> Les données pour les personnes qualifiées se réfèrent à 1982.
ESP> Los datos relativos a las personas calificadas se refieren a 1982.
Jordan:
E--> Data for qualified manpower relate to 1977.
FR-> Les données pour les personnes qualifiées se réfèrent à 1977.
ESP> Los datos relativos a las personas calificadas se refieren a 1977.
Korea, Republic of:
E--> Data for qualified manpower relate to 1981.
FR-> Les données pour les personnes qualifiées se réfèrent à 1981.
ESP> Los datos relativos a las personas calificadas se refieren a 1981.
Kuwait:
E--> Data for qualified manpower relate to 1980.
FR-> Les données pour les personnes qualifiées se réfèrent à 1980
ESP> Los datos relativos a las personas calificadas se refieren a 1980.
Malaysia:
E--> Data for qualified manpower relate to 1982.
FR-> Les données pour les personnes qualifiées se réfèrent à 1982.
ESP> Los datos relativos a las personas calificadas se refieren a 1982.
Philippines:
E--> Data for qualified manpower relate to 1980.
FR-> Les données pour les personnes qualifiées se réfèrent à 1980.
ESP> Los datos relativos a las personas calificadas se refieren a 1980.
Qatar:
E--> Data for qualified manpower relate to 1983.
FR-> Les données pour les personnes qualifiées se réfèrent à 1983.
ESP> Los datos relativos a las personas calificadas se refieren a 1983.
Singapore:
E--> Data for qualified manpower relate to 1980.
FR-> Les données pour les personnes qualifiées se réfèrent à 1980.
ESP> Los datos relativos a las personas calificadas se refieren a 1980.
Turkey:
E--> Data for qualified manpower relate to 1980.
FR-> Les données pour les personnes qualifiées se réfèrent à 1980.
ESP> Los datos relativos a las personas calificadas se refieren a 1980.
EUROPE:
Bulgaria:
E--> Data for qualified manpower relate to 1983.
FR-> Les données pour les personnes qualifiées se réfèrent à 1983.
ESP> Los datos relativos a las personas calificadas se refieren a 1983.
Czechoslovakia:
E--> Data for qualified manpower relate to 1980.
FR-> Les données pour les personnes qualifiées se réfèrent à 1980.
ESP> Los datos relativos a las personas calificadas se refieren a 1980.
Denmark:
E--> Data for qualified manpower relate to 1980. The number of technicians used to calculate columns 4 and 5 includes auxiliary personnel.
FR-> Les données pour les personnes qualifiées se réfèrent à 1980. Le nombre de techniciens utilisé pour le calcul des colonnes 4 et 5 comprend

Denmark: (Cont):
le personnel auxiliaire.
ESP> Los datos relativos a las personas calificadas se refieren a 1980. El número de técnicos que sirvió para el cálculo de las columnas 4 y 5 incluye el personal auxiliar.
Finland:
E--> Data for qualified manpower relate to 1982. The number of technicians used to calculate columns 4 and 5 includes auxiliary personnel.
FR-> Les données pour les personnes qualifiées se réfèrent à 1982. Le nombre de techniciens utilisé pour le calcul des colonnes 4 et 5 comprend le personnel auxiliaire.
ESP> Los datos relativos a las personas calificadas se refieren a 1982. El número de técnicos qui sirvió para el cálculo de las columnas 4 y 5 incluye el personal auxiliar.
France:
E--> Data for qualified manpower relate to 1975. The number of technicians used to calculate columns 4 and 5 includes auxiliary personnel.
FR-> Les données pour les personnes qualifiées se réfèrent à 1975. Le nombre de techniciens utilisé pour le calcul des colonnes 4 et 5 comprend le personnel auxiliaire.
ESP> Los datos relativos a las personas calificadas se refieren a 1975. El número de técnicos que sirvió para el cálculo de las columnas 4 y 5 incluye el personal auxiliar.
German Democratic Republic:
E--> The number of technicians used to calculate columns 4 and 5 includes auxiliary personnel.
FR-> Le nombre de techniciens utilisé pour le calcul des colonnes 4 et 5 comprend le personnel auxiliaire.
ESP> El número de técnicos que sirvió para el cálculo de las columnas 4 y 5 incluye el personal auxiliar.
Germany, Federal Republic of:
E--> Data for qualified manpower relate to 1980.
FR-> Les données pour les personnes qualifiées se réfèrent à 1980.
ESP> Los datos relativos a las personas calificadas se refieren a 1980.
Greece:
E--> Data for qualified manpower relate to 1981.
FR-> Les données pour les personnes qualifiées se réfèrent à 1981.
ESP> Los datos relativos a las personas calificadas se refieren a 1981.
Hungary:
E--> Data for qualified manpower relate to 1980.
FR-> Les données pour les personnes qualifiées se réfèrent à 1980.
ESP> Los datos relativos a las personas calificadas se refieren a 1980.
Iceland:
E--> Data for qualified manpower relate to 1975.
FR-> Les données pour les personnes qualifiées se réfèrent à 1975.
ESP> Los datos relativos a las personas calificadas se refieren a 1975.
Italy:
E--> Data for qualified manpower relate to 1981.
FR-> Les données pour les personnes qualifiées se réfèrent à 1981.
ESP> Los datos relativos a las personas calificadas se refieren a 1981.
Netherlands:
E--> Data for qualified manpower relate to 1981. The number of technicians used to calculate columns 4 and 5 includes auxiliary personnel.
FR-> Les données pour les personnes qualifiées se réfèrent à 1981. Le nombre de techniciens utilisé pour le calcul des colonnes 4 et 5 comprend le personnel auxiliaire.
ESP> Los datos relativos a las personas calificadas se refieren a 1981. El número de técnicos que sirvió para el cálculo de las columnas 4 y 5 incluye el personal auxiliar.
Norway:
E--> Data for qualified manpower relate to 1981. The number of technicians used to calculate columns 4 and 5 includes auxiliary personnel.
FR-> Les données pour les personnes qualifiées se réfèrent à 1981. Le nombre de techniciens utilisé pour le calcul des colonnes 4 et 5 comprend le personnel auxiliaire.
ESP> Los datos relativos a las personas calificadas se refieren a 1981. El número de técnicos que sirvió para el cálculo de las columnas 4 y 5 incluye el personal auxiliar.
Poland:
E--> Data for qualified manpower relate to 1978.
FR-> Les données pour les personnes qualifiées se réfèrent à 1978.
ESP> Los datos relativos a las personas calificadas se refieren a 1978.
Sweden:
E--> Data for qualified manpower relate to 1979.
FR-> Les données pour les personnes qualifiées se réfèrent à 1979.
ESP> Los datos relativos a las personas calificadas se refieren a 1979.
Switzerland:
E--> Data for qualified manpower relate to 1980.
FR-> Les données pour les personnes qualifiées se réfèrent à 1980.
ESP> Los datos relativos a las personas calificadas se refieren a 1980.
OCEANIA:
Samoa:
E--> Data for qualified manpower relate to 1977.
FR-> Les données pour les personnes qualifiées se réfèrent à l'année 1977.
ESP> Los datos relativos a las personas calificadas se refieren a 1977.
U.S.S.R.:
U.S.S.R.:
E--> Data for qualified manpower relate to 1983.
FR-> Les données pour les personnes qualifiées se réfèrent à 1983.
ESP> Los datos relativos a las personas calificadas se refieren a 1983.

5.19 Selected indicators for expenditure for research and experimental development

Indicateurs sélectionnés pour les dépenses de recherche et de développement expérimental

Indicadores seleccionados para los gastos de investigación y de desarrollo experimental

PLEASE REFER TO INTRODUCTION FOR DEFINITIONS OF CATEGORIES INCLUDED IN THIS TABLE.

FOR FURTHER DETAILS CONCERNING THE COVERAGE AND THE LIMITATIONS OF THE BASIC DATA USED FOR THE INDICATORS, PLEASE REFER TO TABLES RELATING TO R&D PERSONNEL (TABLE 5.4) AND TO R&D EXPENDITURE (TABLE 5.9) AS APPROPRIATE.

NUMBER OF COUNTRIES AND TERRITORIES PRESENTED IN THIS TABLE: 81

POUR LES DEFINITIONS DES CATEGORIES PRESENTEES DANS CE TABLEAU, SE REFERER A L'INTRODUCTION.

POUR DES DETAILS PLUS COMPLETS EN CE QUI CONCERNE LA PORTEE DES DONNEES DE BASE ET LES ELEMENTS PRIS EN CONSIDERATION POUR LE CALCUL DES INDICATEURS, SE REFERER SELON LE CAS, AU TABLEAU 5.4 CONCERNANT LE PERSONNEL SCIENTIFIQUE ET TECHNIQUE ET AU TABLEAU 5.9 CONCERNANT LES DEPENSES AFFERENTES A LA R-D.

NOMBRE DE PAYS ET DE TERRITOIRES PRESENTES DANS CE TABLEAU: 81

EN LA INTRODUCCION SE DAN LAS DEFINICIONES DE LAS CATEGORIAS QUE FIGURAN EN ESTE CUADRO.

PARA UNA INFORMACION MAS COMPLETA EN LO QUE SE REFIERE AL ALCANCE DE LOS DATOS DE BASE Y DE LOS ELEMENTOS QUE SE TOMARON EN CONSIDERACION PARA EL CALCULO DE LOS INDICADORES, SIRVANSE REFERIRSE, SEGUN EL CASO, AL CUADRO 5.4 RELATIVO AL PERSONAL CIENTIFICO Y TECNICO Y AL CUADRO 5.9 SOBRE LOS GASTOS DEDICADOS A LA I Y D.

NUMERO DE PAISES Y DE TERRITORIOS PRESENTADOS EN ESTE CUADRO: 81

COUNTRY / PAYS / PAIS	YEAR / ANNEE / AÑO	CURRENCY / MONNAIE / MONEDA	EXPENDITURE FOR R&D / DEPENSES CONSACREES A R-D / GASTOS DEDICADOS A I Y D		
			AS PERCENTAGE OF GROSS NATIONAL PRODUCT (GNP) / EN POURCENTAGE DU PRODUIT NATIONAL BRUT (PNB) / EN PORCENTAJE DEL PRODUCTO NACIONAL BRUTO (PNB) %	PER CAPITA (IN NATIONAL CURRENCY) / PAR HABITANT (EN MONNAIE NATIONALE) / POR PERSONA (EN MONEDA NACIONAL)	ANNUAL AVERAGE PER R&D SCIENTIST OR ENGINEER (IN NATIONAL CURRENCY / MOYENNE ANNUELLE PAR SCIENTIFIQUE OU INGENIEUR DE R-D (EN MONNAIE NATIONALE) / PROMEDIO ANUAL POR CIENTIFICO O INGENIERO DE I Y D (EN MONEDA NACIONAL)
			(1)	(2)	(3)
AFRICA					
CENTRAL AFRICAN REPUBLIC	1984	FRANC C.F.A.	0.3	270.6	3 473 400
CONGO	1984	FRANC C.F.A	0.0	15.1	29 700
EGYPT	1982	POUND	0.2	0.9	2 000
LIBYAN ARAB JAMAHIRIYA	1980	DINAR	0.2	7.7	20 800
MADAGASCAR	1980	FRANC	0.2	159.9	12 427 500
MALAWI	1977	KWACHA	0.2	0.2	6 800
MAURITIUS	1984	RUPEE	0.3	37.6	147 100
NIGER	1976	FRANC C.F.A.	0.1	29.6	1 523 700
NIGERIA	1977	NAIRA	*0.3	*1.4	*46 400
SENEGAL	1976	FRANC C.F.A.	1.0	909.5	8 592 000
SEYCHELLES	1983	RUPEE	1.3	181.0	714 100
SUDAN	1978	POUND	0.2	0.3	1 300
AMERICA, NORTH					
BRITISH VIRGIN ISLANDS	1984	UNITED STATES DOLLAR	–	–	–
CANADA	1983	DOLLAR	1.4	215.6	*169 700
COSTA RICA	1982	COLON	0.1	33.8	197 900
CUBA	1984	PESO	0.6	16.4	17 200

COUNTRY PAYS PAIS	YEAR ANNEE AÑO	CURRENCY MONNAIE MONEDA	EXPENDITURE FOR R&D / DEPENSES CONSACREES A R-D / GASTOS DEDICADOS A I Y D		
			AS PERCENTAGE OF GROSS NATIONAL PRODUCT (GNP) EN POURCENTAGE DU PRODUIT NATIONAL BRUT (PNB) EN PORCENTAJE DEL PRODUCTO NACIONAL BRUTO (PNB) %	PER CAPITA (IN NATIONAL CURRENCY) PAR HABITANT (EN MONNAIE NATIONALE) POR PERSONA (EN MONEDA NACIONAL)	ANNUAL AVERAGE PER R&D SCIENTIST OR ENGINEER (IN NATIONAL CURRENCY MOYENNE ANNUELLE PAR SCIENTIFIQUE OU INGENIEUR DE R-D (EN MONNAIE NATIONALE) PROMEDIO ANUAL POR CIENTIFICO O INGENIERO DE I Y D (EN MONEDA NACIONAL)
			(1)	(2)	(3)
EL SALVADOR	1984	COLON	0.9	18.0	...
GUATEMALA	1983	QUETZAL	0.5	5.9	...
PANAMA	1975	BALBOA	0.2	1.9	16 200
ST. LUCIA	1979	E.CARIBBEAN DOLLAR	0.0	0.6	25 700
ST. PIERRE AND MIQUELON	1984	FRENCH FRANC	...	*453.2	*453 200
UNITED STATES	1983	DOLLAR	2.7	376.1	120 900
AMERICA, SOUTH					
ARGENTINA	1981	PESO	0.4	80 959.4	221 431 600
BRAZIL	1982	CRUZEIRO	*0.6	*2407.1	*9 397 700
CHILE	1983	PESO	0.3	388.9	...
COLOMBIA	1982	PESO	0.1	102.1	2 543 200
ECUADOR	1979	SUCRE	0.4	108.3	417 800
GUYANA	1982	DOLLAR	0.2	3.1	31 500
PERU	1984	SOL	0.3	8 282.2	...
VENEZUELA	1984	BOLIVAR	0.4	80.9	*298 100
ASIA					
BRUNEI DARUSSALAM	1984	DOLLAR	...	49.5	544 000
CYPRUS	1984	POUND	0.1	1.8	23 000
INDIA	1982	RUPEE	*0.7	*16.2	...
INDONESIA	1983	RUPIAH	0.4	1 685.0	14 585 500
ISRAEL	1978	POUND	2.5	1 655.5	418 000
JAPAN	1983	YEN	2.6	60 361.0	14 473 200
JORDAN	1979	DINAR	*1.0	*2.6	...
KOREA, REPUBLIC OF	1983	WON	1.1	15 499.6	19 358 900
KUWAIT	1984	DINAR	0.9	41.8	47 100
LEBANON	1980	POUND	...	8.2	122 200
PAKISTAN	1979	RUPEE	0.2	4.7	...
PHILIPPINES	1982	PESO	*0.2	*10.3	*101 600
QATAR	1984	RIYAL	0.1	42.2	372 700
SINGAPORE	1981	DOLLAR	0.3	33.5	113 100
SRI LANKA	1983	RUPEE	0.2	13.2	106 500
TURKEY	1983	LIRA	0.2	574.0	3 513 700
VIET-NAM	1979	DONG	...	2.0	8 300
EUROPE					
AUSTRIA	1981	SCHILLING	1.2	1 642.8	1 837 200
BELGIUM	1977	FRANC	1.4	3 961.3	2 801 600
BULGARIA	1984	LEV	2.8	77.3	15 400
CZECHOSLOVAKIA	1984	KORUNA	3.7	1 283.0	337 900
DENMARK	1983	KRONE	1.2	1 165.7	795 200
FINLAND	1984	MARKKA	1.5	901.2	*400 100
FRANCE	1979	FRANC	1.8	825.8	605 300
GERMAN DEMOCRATIC REPUBLIC	1984	DDR MARK	*3.9	*523.3	*68 600
GERMANY, FEDERAL REPUBLIC OF	1981	DEUTSCHE MARK	2.5	623.7	299 200
GREECE	1979	DRACHMA	0.2	277.2	1 002 300
HUNGARY	1984	FORINT	2.4	2 123.7	1 007 500
ICELAND	1979	KRONA	76.0	28 402.6	21 143 100
IRELAND	1982	POUND	0.8	28.0	35 200
ITALY	1983	LIRA	1.1	105 418.8	95 634 900
MALTA	1984	LIRA	0.0	0.0	300
NETHERLANDS	1983	GUILDER	2.0	536.2	252 200
NORWAY	1982	KRONE	1.4	1 205.8	638 700
POLAND	1984	ZLOTY	1.0	2 003.6	987 000
PORTUGAL	1982	ESCUDO	0.4	652.7	2 166 700
SPAIN	1983	PESETA	0.5	2 642.3	7 076 400

COUNTRY / PAYS / PAIS	YEAR / ANNEE / AÑO	CURRENCY / MONNAIE / MONEDA	EXPENDITURE FOR R&D / DEPENSES CONSACREES A R–D / GASTOS DEDICADOS A I Y D		
			AS PERCENTAGE OF GROSS NATIONAL PRODUCT (GNP) / EN POURCENTAGE DU PRODUIT NATIONAL BRUT (PNB) / EN PORCENTAJE DEL PRODUCTO NACIONAL BRUTO (PNB) %	PER CAPITA (IN NATIONAL CURRENCY) / PAR HABITANT (EN MONNAIE NATIONALE) / POR PERSONA (EN MONEDA NACIONAL)	ANNUAL AVERAGE PER R&D SCIENTIST OR ENGINEER (IN NATIONAL CURRENCY / MOYENNE ANNUELLE PAR SCIENTIFIQUE OU INGENIEUR DE R–D (EN MONNAIE NATIONALE) / PROMEDIO ANUAL POR CIENTIFICO O INGENIERO DE I Y D (EN MONEDA NACIONAL)
			(1)	(2)	(3)
SWEDEN	1983	KRONA	2.6	2 184.8	953 300
SWITZERLAND	1983	FRANC	2.2	730.8	347 800
UNITED KINGDOM	1981	POUND STERLING	2.3	105.7	...
YUGOSLAVIA	1981	DINAR	0.8	812.7	732 900
OCEANIA					
AUSTRALIA	1981	DOLLAR	1.0	102.2	62 900
FRENCH POLYNESIA	1983	FRANC C.F.P.	0.2	2 068.3	19 101 200
GUAM	1979	UNITED STATES DOLLAR	0.2	12.6	59 800
NEW CALEDONIA	1983	FRANC C.F.P.	1.3	560.8	11 857 100
NEW ZEALAND	1979	DOLLAR	0.9	55.5	...
NORFOLK ISLAND	1982	AUSTRALIAN DOLLAR	–	–	–
PACIFIC ISLANDS	1979	UNITED STATES DOLLAR	0.2	1.3	46 300
SAMOA	1978	TALA	...	16.2	17 900
TONGA	1980	PA'ANGA	0.8	4.4	*38 700
VANUATU	1975	FRANC	...	225.0	7 201 000
U.S.S.R.					
U.S.S.R.	1984	ROUBLE	...	100.2	18 900

General note / Note générale / Nota general:

E--> In the absence of R&D exchange rates those data which are set out in national currency can be compared, one country with another, by the use of the official exchange rates between national currencies and the United States dollar given in appendix C. It should be understood, of course, that these exchange rates do not always reflect the real costs of R&D activities. For the following countries, the figures in column 1 refer to expenditure as percentage of the net material product: Bulgaria, Czechoslovakia, German Democratic Republic, Poland and the U.S.S.R.

FR-> En l'absence de taux de change applicables aux activités de R-D pour comparer d'un pays à l'autre les données établies en monnaie nationale, il faudra nécessairement se baser sur les taux de change officiels de conversion des monnaies nationales en dollars des Etats-Unis, tels qu'ils figurent dans l'annexe C. Il va sans dire que ces taux de change ne

General note / Note générale / Nota general: (Cont):

reflètent pas toujours le coût réel des activités de R-D. Pour les pays suivants les chiffres de la colonne 1 sont exprimés en pourcentage du produit matériel net: Bulgarie, Tchécoslovaquie, République démocratique allemande, Pologne et l'URSS.

ESP> No disponiendo de tipos de cambio aplicables a las actividades de I y D para comparar de un país a otro los datos establecidos en moneda nacional, será necesario basarse en los tipos de cambio oficiales de conversión de las monedas nacionales en dólares de los Estados Unidos, tal y como figuran en el anexo C. Es inútil señalar que esos tipos de cambio no siempre reflejan el costo real de las actividades de I y D. Para los países siguentes las cifras de la columna 1 corresponden a los gastos en porcentaje del producto material neto: Bulgaria, Checoslovaquia, República Democrática Alemana, Polonia y el URSS.

6 Summary tables for culture and communication subjects by continents, major areas and groups of countries

Tableaux récapitulatifs pour la culture et la communication, par continents, grandes régions et groupes de pays

Cuadros recapitulativos para la cultura y la comunicación, por continentes, grandes regiones y grupos de países

This chapter provides a number of summary tables on some selected subjects of culture and communication. The statistics contained in these tables are distributed by continents, major areas and groups of countries the composition of which is given in the headnote to Table 1.2 of this *Yearbook.* The subjects dealt with are the following: book production, daily newspapers, cultural paper, production of long films, number and seating capacity of fixed cinemas, cinema attendance and radio as well as television transmitters and receivers.

It has to be pointed out that due to the difficulties of assessing the reliability of the statistics available and the lack of information for many countries the calculated world and regional figures given in this chapter represent a very rough approximation of the existing situation.

Table 6.1

The object of this table is to show the evolution of book production (in terms of titles) in the world from 1955 to 1984.

Table 6.2

This table gives world and regional estimates for daily newspapers in 1975 and 1984. The statistics relate to the number of newspapers, their circulation and the circulation per 1,000 inhabitants.

Tables 6.3 and 6.4

On the basis of the statistics made available to Unesco by the Food and Agriculture Organization of the United Nations (FAO), world and regional estimates have been calculated for the production and consumption of 'cultural paper' (newsprint and other printing and writing paper) for the years 1970, 1975, 1980 and 1983.

Table 6.5

This table shows world and regional estimates for the production of long or feature films for the years 1965, 1970, 1975, 1980 and 1983.

Table 6.6

This table shows the number of cinemas, their seating capacity and the seating capacity per 1,000 inhabitants for the years 1970 and 1983.

Table 6.7

Table 6.7 shows trends in cinema attendance for the years 1965, 1970, 1975, 1980 and 1983.

Table 6.8

This table gives the number of radio broadcasting transmitters for around 1965, 1970, 1975, 1980 and 1983.

Table 6.9

Total figures for radio receivers in the world for 1965, 1970, 1975, 1980 and 1983 respectively are shown in this table. It should be pointed out that many countries have reported the number of licences issued rather than the number of receivers in use. This has led to a certain under-enumeration of the number of receivers for those countries and regions where one licence covers the possession of several receivers.

Table 6.10

This table gives the number of television broadcasting transmitters for around 1965, 1970, 1975, 1980 and 1983. The figures which have been supplied to the Secretariat are sometimes incomplete due to the fact that not all countries include relay or re-broadcast transmitters in their statistics.

Table 6.11

Table 6.11 shows the number of television receivers for 1965, 1970, 1975, 1980 and 1983.

The summary tables in this chapter are preceded by eight charts which present the statistical information in a more attractive form.

Ce chapitre présente une série de tableaux récapitulatifs sur quelques sujets sélectionnés relatifs à la culture et à la communication. Les statistiques qui figurent dans ces tableaux sont distribuées par continents, grandes régions et groupes de pays, dont la composition est indiquée dans la note en-tête du tableau 1.2 de cet *Annuaire*. Les sujets considérés sont les suivants: édition de livres, journaux quotidiens, papier culturel, production de films de long métrage, nombre de cinémas fixes et de sièges, fréquentation des cinémas, émetteurs et récepteurs de radio ainsi qu'émetteurs et récepteurs de télévision.

Il faut préciser que les difficultés qui existent pour déterminer la fiabilité des statistiques disponibles et les lacunes qui se manifestent dans les informations communiquées par plusieurs pays, font que les calculs sur les données mondiales et régionales qui figurent dans ce chapitre ne représentent tout au plus qu'une approximation très grossière de la situation réelle.

Tableau 6.1

Ce tableau a pour objet de présenter l'évolution de l'édition de livres (en nombre de titres) dans le monde, entre 1955 et 1984.

Tableau 6.2

Ce tableau présente des estimations mondiales et régionales sur les journaux quotidiens en 1975 et 1984. Les statistiques se réfèrent au nombre de journaux, à leur tirage et au tirage pour 1 000 habitants.

Tableaux 6.3 et 6.4

Sur la base des statistiques disponibles, procurées à l'Unesco par l'Organisation des Nations Unies pour l'Agriculture et l'Alimentation (FAO), des estimations mondiales et régionales ont été effectuées sur la production et la consommation de 'papier culturel' (papier journal et papier d'impression et d'écriture) pour les années 1970, 1975, 1980 et 1983.

Tableau 6.5

Ce tableau présente des estimations mondiales et régionales sur la production de films de long métrage ou de 'films vedettes' pour les années 1965, 1970, 1975, 1980 et 1983.

Tableau 6.6

Ce tableau présente le nombre de cinémas, le nombre de sièges, et le nombre de sièges pour 1 000 habitants pour les années 1970 et 1983.

Tableau 6.7

Le tableau 6.7 présente l'évolution de la fréquentation des cinémas pour les années 1965, 1970, 1975, 1980 et 1983.

Tableau 6.8

Dans ce tableau figure le nombre d'émetteurs de radiodiffusion sonore autour de 1965, 1970, 1975, 1980 et 1983.

Tableau 6.9

Ce tableau présente le nombre total de récepteurs de radio dans le monde pour 1965, 1970, 1975, 1980 et 1983. Il faut préciser que plusieurs pays ont communiqué le nombre de licences délivrées plutôt que le nombre de récepteurs en service. Ceci explique qu'il y ait un certain sous dénombrement dans le nombre de récepteurs des pays et régions où une seule licence permet d'avoir plusieurs récepteurs.

Tableau 6.10

Ce tableau indique le nombre d'émetteurs de télévision autour de 1965, 1970, 1975, 1980 et 1983. Les chiffres communiqués au Secrétariat sont souvent incomplets, puisque tous les pays n'incluent pas dans leurs statistiques les réémetteurs.

Tableau 6.11

Le tableau 6.11 présente le nombre de récepteurs de télévision pour 1965, 1970, 1975, 1980 et 1983.

Avant les tableaux récapitulatifs de ce chapitre se trouvent huit graphiques qui présentent les statistiques d'une manière plus attrayante.

Este capítulo presenta una serie de cuadros recapitulativos sobre algunas materias seleccionadas relativas a la cultura y la comunicación. Las estadísticas que figuran en estos cuadros se distribuyen por continentes, grandes regiones y grupos de países cuya composición se indica en la nota de encabezamiento del cuadro 1.2. de este *Anuario*. Las materias consideradas son las siguientes: edición de libros, periódicos diarios, papel cultural, producción de películas de largo metraje, número de cines fijos y de asientos, frecuentación anual en los cines, transmisores y receptores de radio y transmisores y receptores de televisión.

Es necesario precisar que debido a las dificultades que existen para determinar la fiabilidad de las estadísticas disponibles y las lagunas que se manifiestan en la información proporcionada por varios países, los cálculos de los datos mundiales y regionales que figuran en este capítulo no constituyen a lo sumo más que una aproximación muy relativa de la situación real.

Cuadro 6.1

El propósito de este cuadro es el de presentar la evolución de la edición de libros (en número de títulos) en el mundo entre 1955 y 1984.

Cuadro 6.2

Este cuadro presenta estimaciones mundiales y regionales sobre los periódicos diarios en 1975 y 1984. Las estadísticas se refieren al número de periódicos, su tirada y la tirada por 1 000 habitantes.

Cuadros 6.3 y 6.4

Sobre la base de las estadísticas disponibles, proporcionadas a la Unesco por la Organización de las Naciones Unidas para la Agricultura y la Alimentación (FAO), se han efectuado estimaciones mundiales y regionales de la producción y el consumo de 'papel cultural' (papel de periódico y papel de imprenta y de escribir) para los años 1970, 1975, 1980 y 1983.

Cuadro 6.5

Este cuadro presenta estimaciones mundiales y regionales sobre la producción de películas de largo metraje, o de 'películas principales', para los años 1965, 1970, 1975, 1980 y 1983.

Cuadro 6.6

Este cuadro presenta el número de cines, el número de asientos y el número de asientos por 1 000 habitantes para los años 1970 y 1983.

Cuadro 6.7

El cuadro 6.7 presenta la evolución de la frecuentación en los cines para las años 1965, 1970, 1975, 1980 y 1983.

Cuadro 6.8

En este cuadro figura el número de transmisores de radiodifusión sonora alrededor de 1965, 1970, 1975, 1980 y 1983.

Cuadro 6.9

El total de receptores de radio en el mundo para 1965, 1970, 1975, 1980 y 1983 figura en este cuadro. Es necesario precisar que varios países han comunicado el número de permisos concedidos en lugar del número de receptores en funcionamiento. Esto motiva que haya una cierta subenumeración en el número de receptores de los países y regiones donde un solo permiso autoriza a tener varios receptores.

Cuadro 6.10

Este cuadro indica el número de transmisores de televisión alrededor de 1965, 1970, 1975, 1980 y 1983. Las cifras que han sido comunicadas al Secretariado son con frecuencia incompletas, ya que no todos los países incluyen en sus estadísticas los retransmisores.

Cuadro 6.11

El cuadro 6.11 presenta el número de receptores de televisión para 1965, 1970, 1975, 1980 y 1983.

Antes de los cuadros recapitulativos de este capítulo figuran ocho gráficos que presentan las estadísticas de una forma más atractiva.

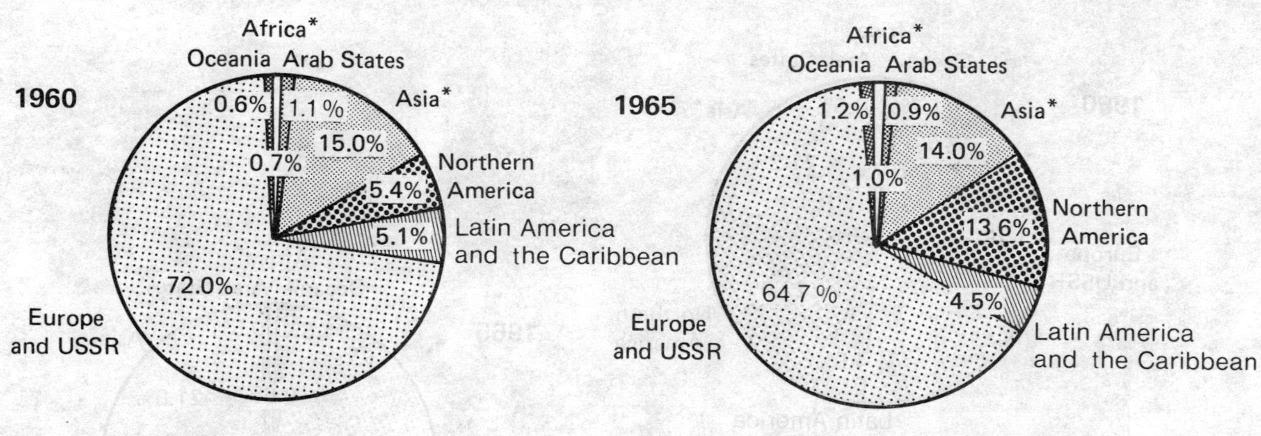

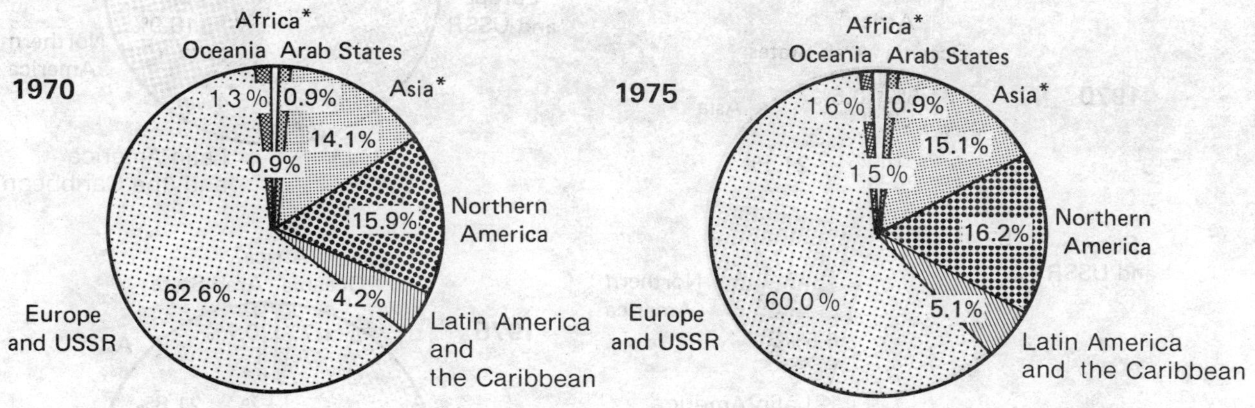

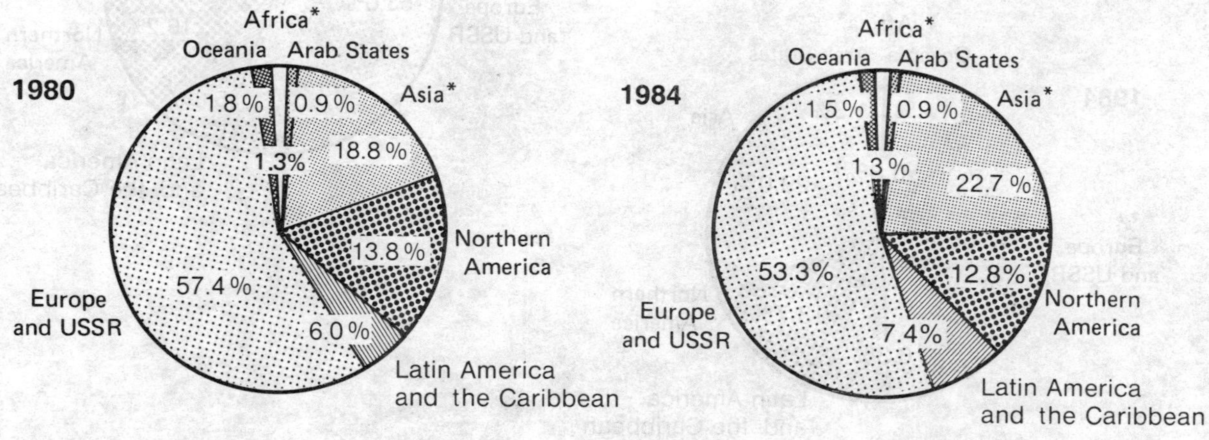

Data prior to 1980 do not include China.
Les données antérieures à 1980 n'incluent pas la Chine.
Los datos anteriores a 1980 excluyen China.

* Excluding Arab States
* Non compris les Etats Arabes
* Excluídos los Estados Arabes

Figure 13: **Distribution of book production (in number of titles) by continents and major areas: estimated percentage 1960, 1965, 1970, 1975, 1980 and 1984**

Graphique 13 : **Répartition de l'édition de livres (en nombre de titres) par continents et grandes régions : estimations en pourcentage pour 1960, 1965, 1970, 1975, 1980 et 1984**

Gráfico 13: **Distribución de la edición de libros (en número de titulos) por continentes y grandes regiones: estimaciones en porcentaje para 1960, 1965, 1970, 1975, 1980 y 1984**

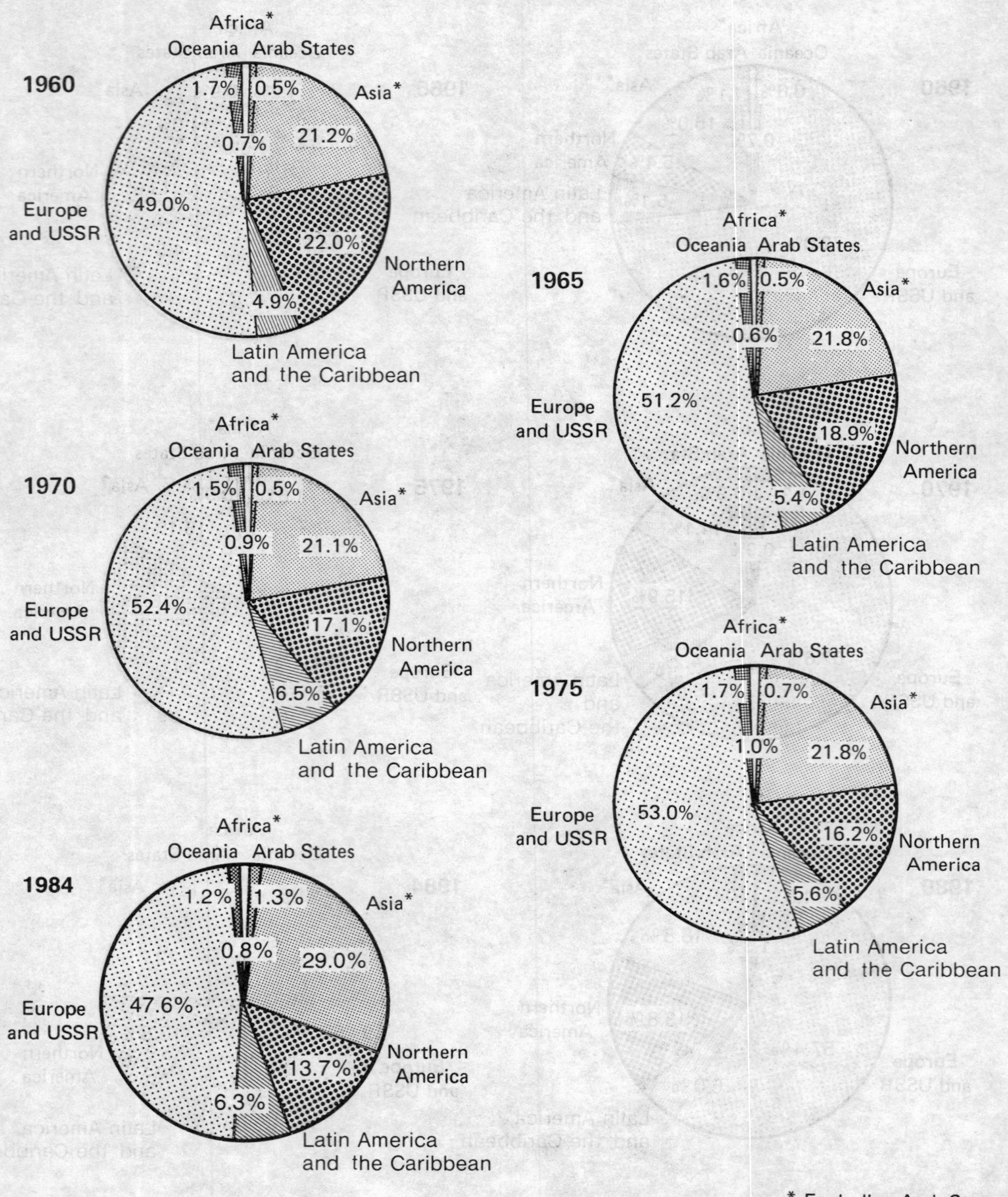

Figure 14: **Distribution of circulation of daily general-interest newspapers by continents and major areas: estimated percentage 1960, 1965, 1970, 1975 and 1984**

Graphique 14 : **Répartition du tirage des journaux quotidiens d'information générale par continents et grandes régions : estimations en pourcentage pour 1960, 1965, 1970, 1975 et 1984**

Gráfico 14: **Distribución de la tirada de periódicos diarios de información general por continentes y grandes regiones: estimaciones en porcentaje para 1960, 1965, 1970, 1975 y 1984**

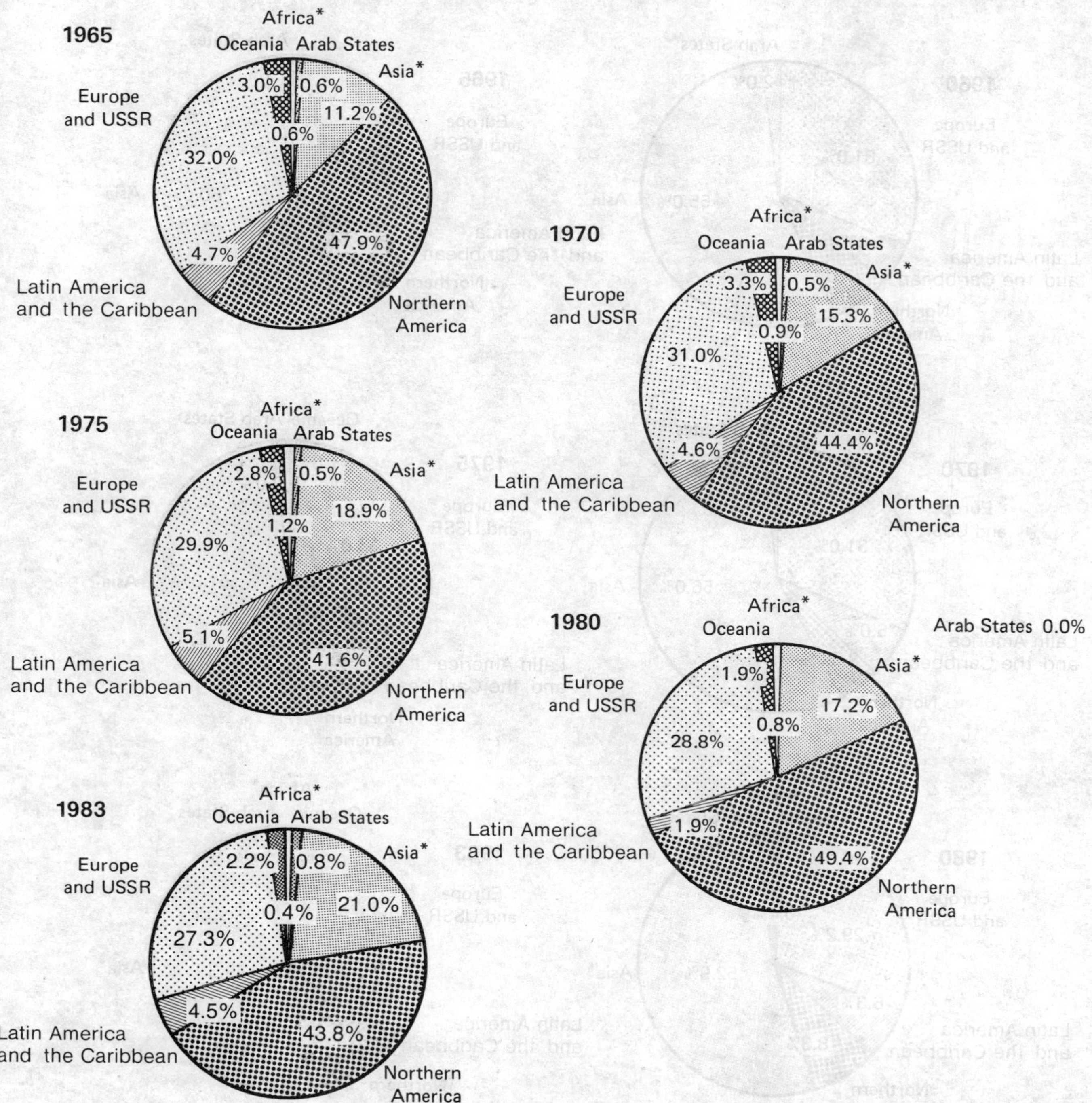

* Excluding Arab States
* Non compris les Etats Arabes
* Excluídos los Estados Arabes

Figure 15: **Distribution of newsprint consumption by continents and major areas: estimated percentage 1965, 1970, 1975, 1980 and 1983**

Graphique 15 : **Répartition de la consommation de papier journal par continents et grandes régions : estimations en pourcentage pour 1965, 1970, 1975, 1980 et 1983**

Gráfico 15: **Distribución del consumo de papel de periódico por continentes y grandes regiones: estimaciones en porcentaje para 1965, 1970, 1975, 1980 y 1983**

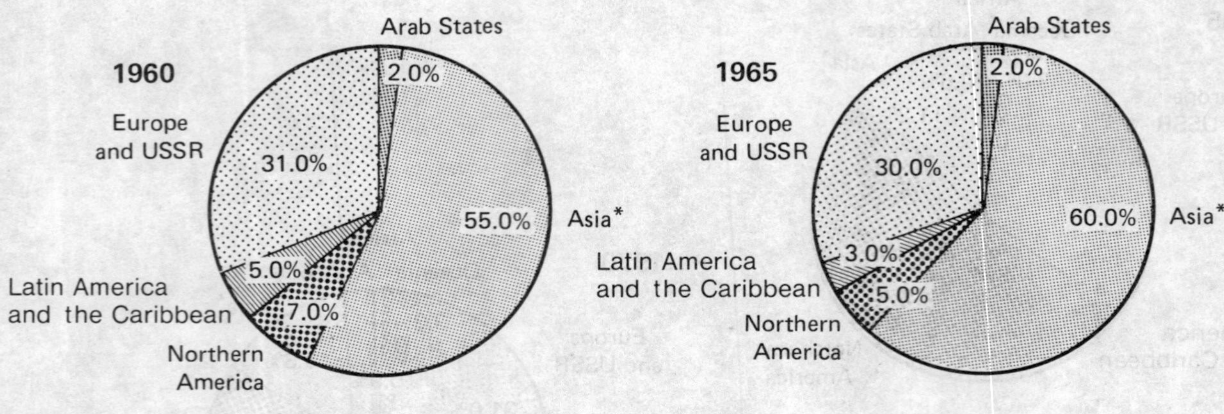

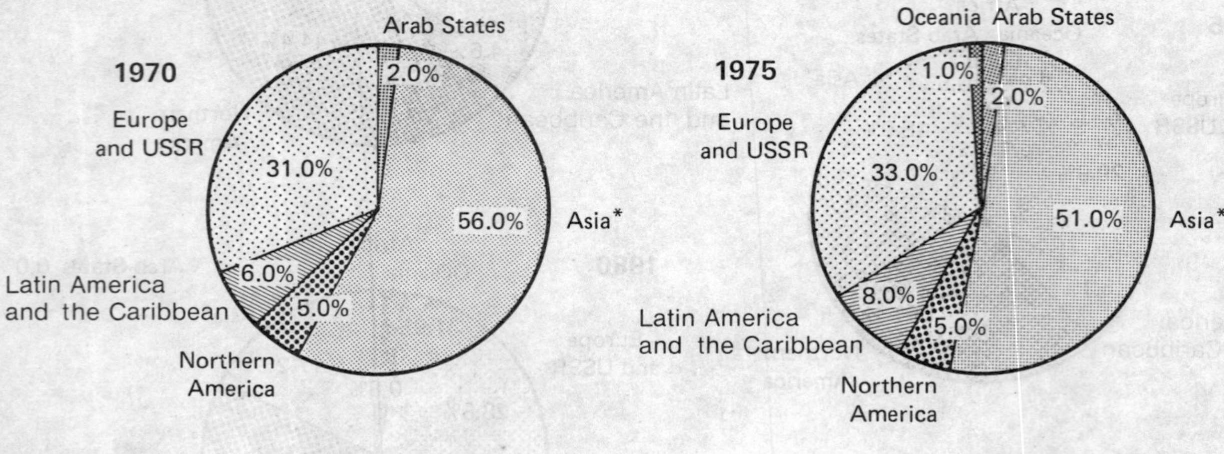

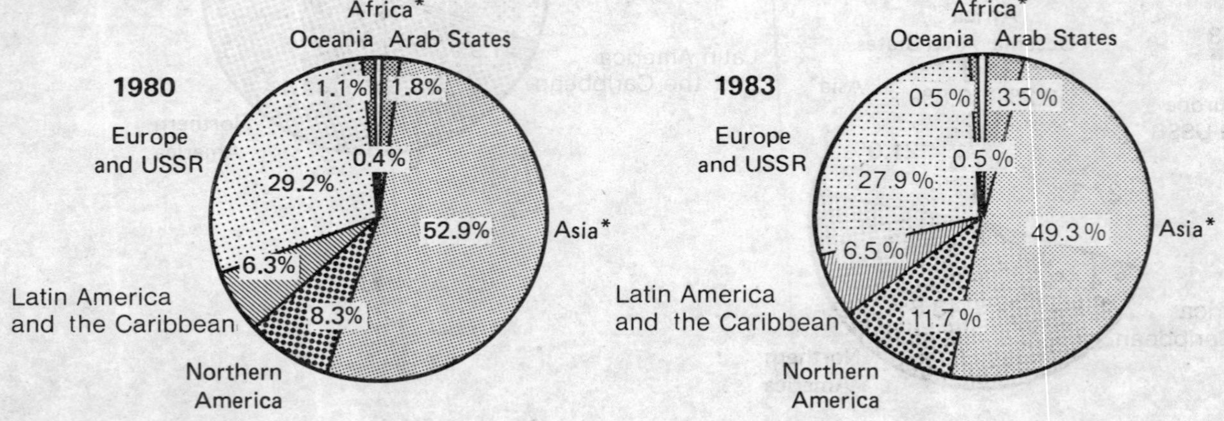

Data do not include China
Les données n'incluent pas la Chine
Los datos excluyen China

* Excluding Arab States
* Non compris les Etats Arabes
* Excluídos los Estados Arabes

Figure 16: Distribution of world long-film production by continents and major areas: estimated percentage 1960, 1965, 1970, 1975, 1980 and 1983

Graphique 16 : Répartition de la production mondiale de films de long métrage par continents et grandes régions: estimations en pourcentage pour 1960, 1965, 1970, 1975, 1980 et 1983

Gráfico 16: Distribución de la producción mundial de películas de largo metraje por continentes y grandes regiones: estimaciones en porcentaje para 1960, 1965, 1970, 1975, 1980 y 1983

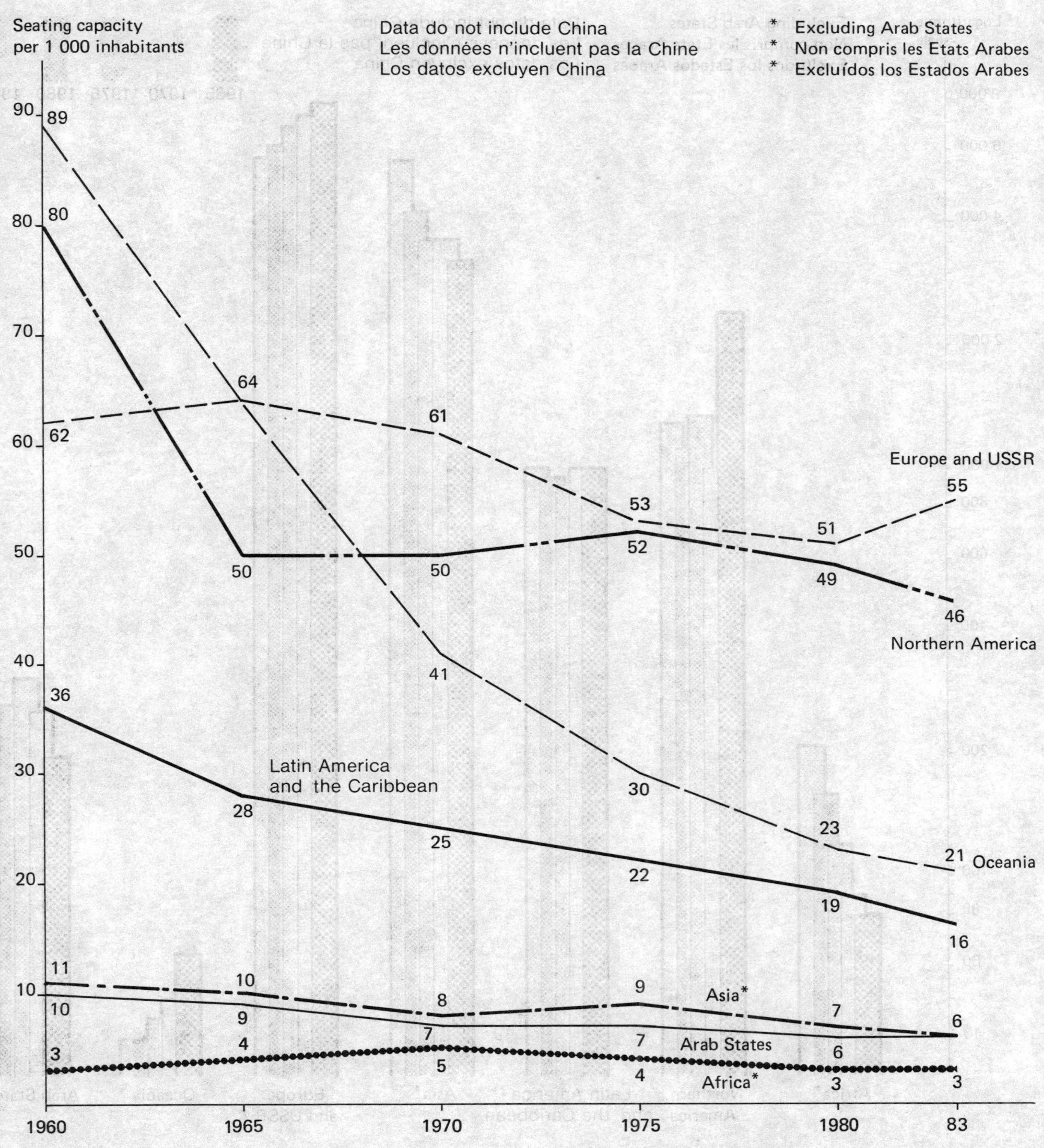

Figure 17: Estimated cinema seating capacity per 1,000 inhabitants by continents and major areas: 1960, 1965, 1970, 1975, 1980 and 1983.

Graphique 17 : Cinémas : estimations du nombre de sièges pour 1 000 habitants, par continents et grandes régions : 1960, 1965, 1970, 1975, 1980 et 1983.

Gráfico 17: Cines: estimaciones del número de asientos por 1 000 habitantes, por continentes y grandes regiones: 1960, 1965, 1970, 1975, 1980 y 1983.

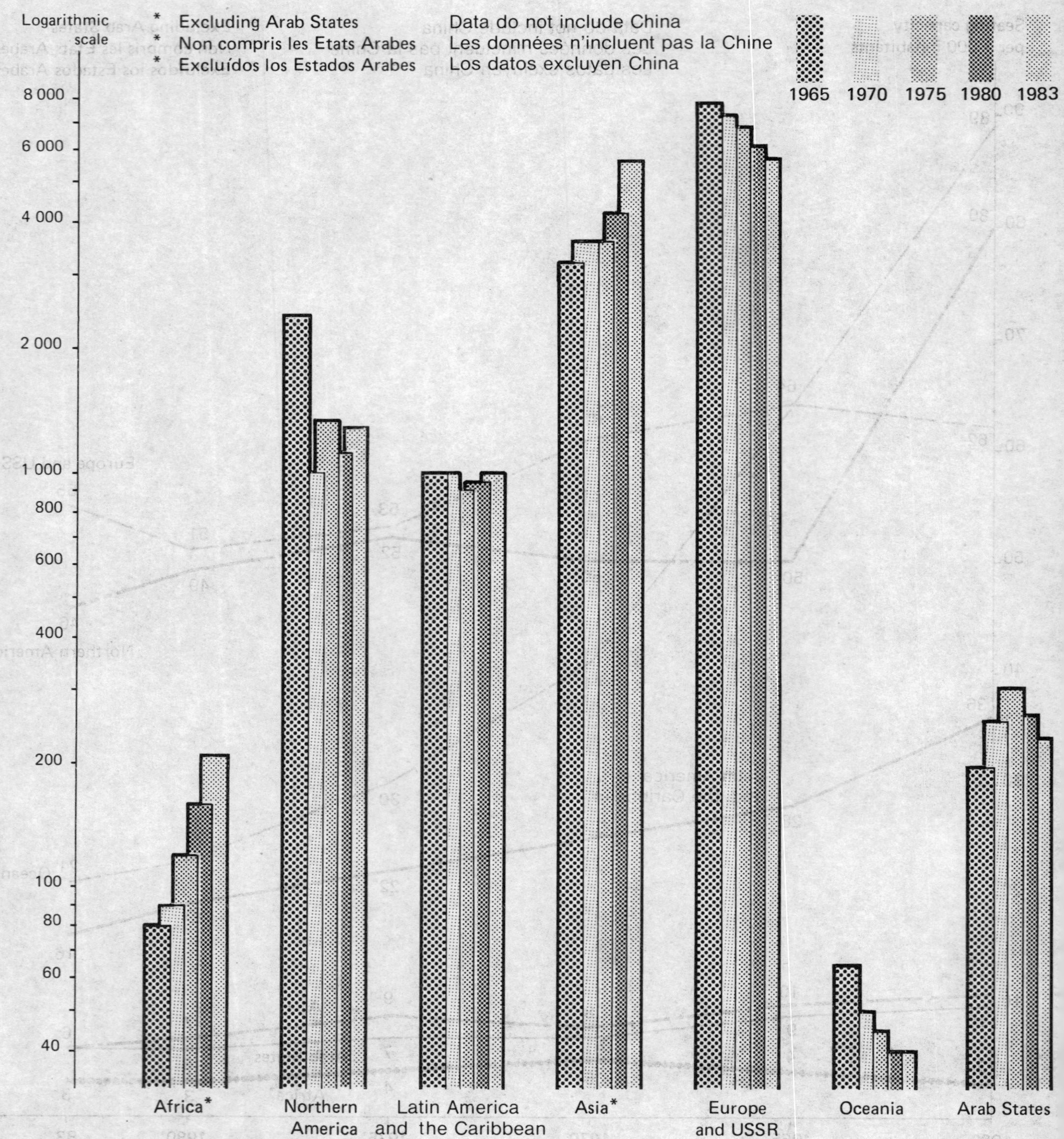

Figure 18: **Estimated annual cinema attendance by continents and major areas: 1965, 1970, 1975, 1980 and 1983**

Graphique 18: **Cinémas : estimations de la fréquentation annuelle par continents et grandes régions : 1965, 1970, 1975, 1980 et 1983**

Gráfico 18: **Cines: estimaciones de la frecuentación anual por continentes y grandes regiones: 1965, 1970, 1975, 1980 y 1983**

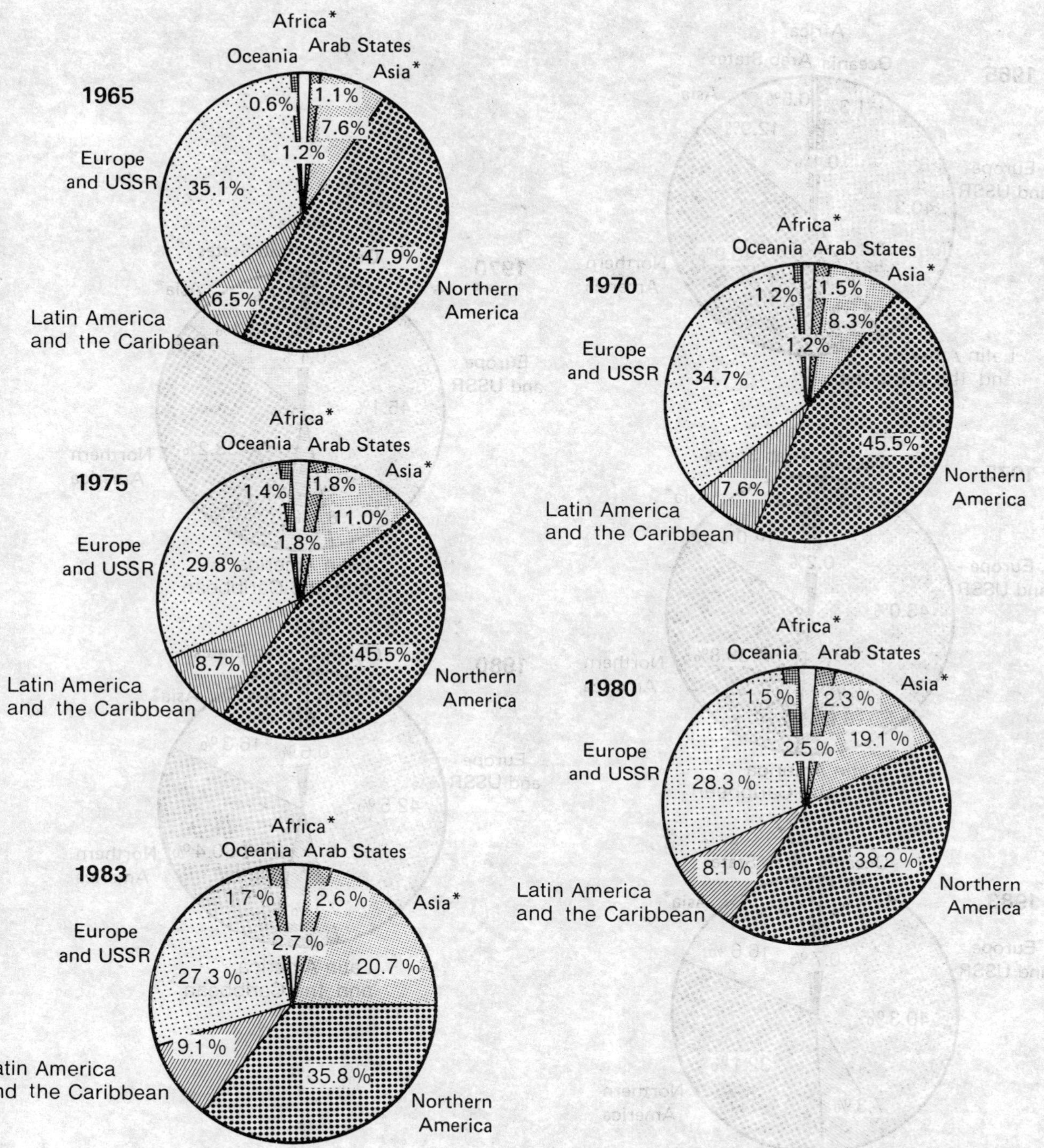

* Excluding Arab States
* Non compris les Etats Arabes
* Excluídos los Estados Arabes

Figure 19: **Distribution of radio receivers by continents and major areas: estimated percentage 1965, 1970, 1975, 1980 and 1983**

Graphique 19: **Répartition des récepteurs de radio par continents et grandes régions : estimations en pourcentage pour 1965, 1970, 1975, 1980 et 1983**

Gráfico 19: **Distribución de los receptores de radio por continentes y grandes regiones: Estimaciones en porcentaje para 1965, 1970, 1975, 1980 y 1983**

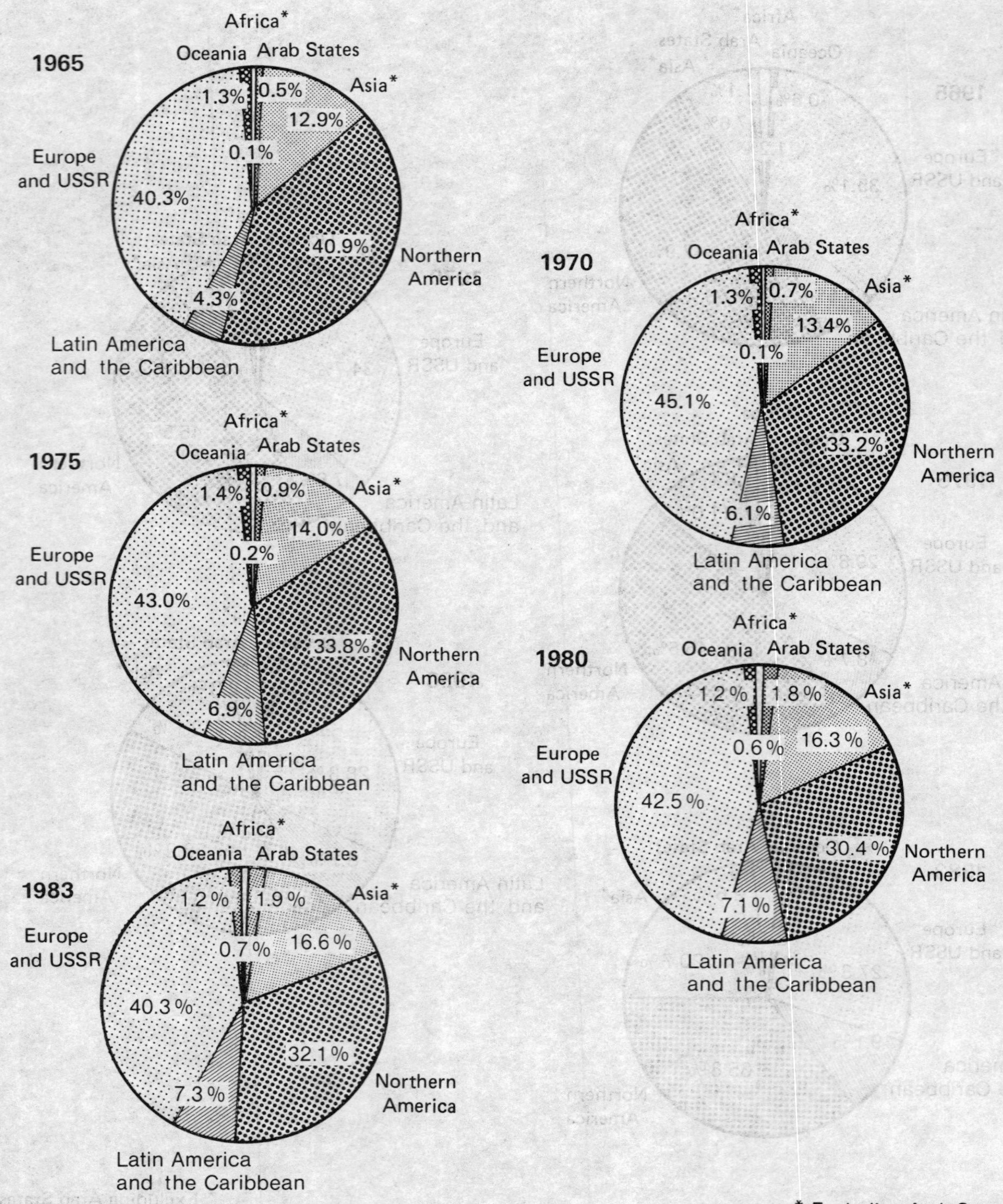

* Excluding Arab States
* Non compris les Etats Arabes
* Excluídos los Estados Arabes

Figure 20: **Distribution of television receivers by continents and major areas: estimated percentage 1965, 1970, 1975, 1980 and 1983**

Graphique 20: **Répartition des récepteurs de télévision par continents et grandes régions : estimations en pourcentage pour 1965, 1970, 1975, 1980 et 1983**

Gráfico 20: **Distribución de los receptores de televisión por continentes y grandes regiones: estimaciones en porcentaje para 1965, 1970, 1975, 1980 y 1983**

6.1 Number of book titles published
Nombre de titres de livres publiés
Número de títulos de libros publicados

CONTINENTS, MAJOR AREAS, AND GROUPS OF COUNTRIES / CONTINENTS. GRANDES REGIONS ET GROUPES DE PAYS / CONTINENTES, GRANDES REGIONES Y GRUPOS DE PAISES	BOOK PRODUCTION: NUMBER OF TITLES / EDITION DE LIVRES: NOMBRE DE TITRES / EDICION DE LIBROS: NUMERO DE TITULOS						
	1955	1960	1965	1970	1975	1980	1984
WORLD TOTAL	269 000	332 000	426 000	521 000	572 000	715 500	780 000
AFRICA	3 000	5 000	7 000	8 000	11 000	12 000	13 000
AMERICA	25 000	35 000	77 000	105 000	121 000	142 000	158 000
ASIA	54 000	51 000	61 000	75 000	88 000	138 000	181 000
EUROPE (INCL. U.S.S.R.)	186 000	239 000	260 000	317 000	343 000	411 000	416 000
OCEANIA	1 000	2 000	5 000	7 000	9 000	12 500	12 000
DEVELOPED COUNTRIES	225 000	285 000	366 000	451 000	484 000	570 000	573 000
DEVELOPING COUNTRIES	44 000	47 000	60 000	70 000	88 000	145 500	207 000
AFRICA (EXCLUDING ARAB STATES)	1 600	2 400	4 300	4 600	8 300	9 000	10 000
ASIA (EXCLUDING ARAB STATES)	53 200	49 900	59 700	73 700	85 800	134 500	177 000
ARAB STATES	2 200	3 700	4 000	4 700	4 900	6 500	7 000
NORTHERN AMERICA	14 000	18 000	58 000	83 000	92 000	99 000	100 000
LATIN AMERICA AND THE CARIBBEAN	11 000	17 000	19 000	22 000	29 000	43 000	58 000
	NUMBER OF TITLES PER MILLION INHABITANTS / NOMBRE DE TITRES PAR MILLION D'HABITANTS / NUMERO DE TITULOS POR MILLON DE HABITANTES						
	1955	1960	1965	1970	1975	1980	1984
WORLD TOTAL	131	144	168	187	184	161	164
AFRICA	13	19	23	23	27	25	24
AMERICA	68	84	167	206	216	231	240
ASIA	64	53	57	62	65	53	65
EUROPE (INCL. U.S.S.R.)	307	374	385	464	471	549	543
OCEANIA	68	121	286	361	428	543	494
DEVELOPED COUNTRIES	249	296	357	420	431	488	477
DEVELOPING COUNTRIES	38	35	40	41	45	44	58
AFRICA (EXCLUDING ARAB STATES)	10	12	18	17	27	25	24
ASIA (EXCLUDING ARAB STATES)	65	53	58	63	65	53	65
ARAB STATES	27	40	38	38	35	40	38
NORTHERN AMERICA	77	91	271	367	389	393	383
LATIN AMERICA AND THE CARIBBEAN	60	79	77	78	89	119	146

CONTINENTS, MAJOR AREAS, AND GROUPS OF COUNTRIES / CONTINENTS. GRANDES REGIONS ET GROUPES DE PAYS / CONTINENTES, GRANDES REGIONES Y GRUPOS DE PAISES	1955	1960	1965	1970	1975	1980	1984
PERCENTAGE DISTRIBUTION OF BOOK PRODUCTION / REPARTITION DE L'EDITION DE LIVRES EN POURCENTAGE / DISTRIBUCION PORCENTUAL DE LA EDICION DE LIBROS							
WORLD TOTAL	100.0	100.0	100.0	100.0	100.0	100.0	100.0
AFRICA	1.1	1.5	1.6	1.5	1.9	1.7	1.7
AMERICA	9.3	10.5	18.1	20.2	21.2	19.8	20.3
ASIA	20.1	15.4	14.3	14.4	15.3	19.3	23.2
EUROPE (INCL. U.S.S.R.)	69.1	72.0	64.7	62.6	60.0	57.4	53.3
OCEANIA	0.4	0.6	1.2	1.3	1.6	1.8	1.5
DEVELOPED COUNTRIES	83.6	85.8	85.9	86.6	84.6	79.7	73.5
DEVELOPING COUNTRIES	16.4	14.2	14.1	13.4	15.4	20.3	26.5
AFRICA (EXCLUDING ARAB STATES)	0.6	0.7	1.0	0.9	1.5	1.3	1.3
ASIA (EXCLUDING ARAB STATES)	19.8	15.0	14.0	14.1	15.1	18.8	22.7
ARAB STATES	0.8	1.1	0.9	0.9	0.9	0.9	0.9
NORTHERN AMERICA	5.2	5.4	13.6	15.9	16.2	13.8	12.8
LATIN AMERICA AND THE CARIBBEAN	4.1	5.1	4.5	4.2	5.1	6.0	7.4
PERCENTAGE DISTRIBUTION OF POPULATION / REPARTITION DE LA POPULATION EN POURCENTAGE / DISTRIBUCION PORCENTUAL DE LA POBLACION	1955	1960	1965	1970	1975	1980	1984
WORLD TOTAL	100.0	100.0	100.0	100.0	100.0	100.0	100.0
AFRICA	10.8	11.8	12.2	12.6	13.1	10.7	11.3
AMERICA	17.8	17.9	18.2	18.3	18.3	13.8	13.8
ASIA	41.1	41.9	42.2	43.2	44.2	58.2	58.3
EUROPE (INCL. U.S.S.R.)	29.5	27.7	26.7	25.2	23.7	16.8	16.1
OCEANIA	0.7	0.7	0.7	0.7	0.7	0.5	0.5
DEVELOPED COUNTRIES	44.0	41.6	40.5	38.5	36.9	26.2	25.2
DEVELOPING COUNTRIES	56.0	58.4	59.5	61.5	63.1	73.8	74.8
AFRICA (EXCLUDING ARAB STATES)	8.0	9.0	9.3	9.5	9.9	8.1	8.7
ASIA (EXCLUDING ARAB STATES)	40.0	40.7	40.9	41.9	42.8	57.1	57.1
ARAB STATES	4.0	4.1	4.2	4.4	4.6	3.7	3.8
NORTHERN AMERICA	8.8	8.6	8.4	8.1	7.7	5.7	5.5
LATIN AMERICA AND THE CARIBBEAN	9.0	9.3	9.8	10.2	10.6	8.1	8.3

General note/Note générale/Nota general:
E--> Data prior to 1980 for: World total, Asia, Developing countries, and Asia (excluding Arab States) do not include China.
FR-> Les données antérieures à 1980 pour: le monde, Asie, Pays en développement, et Asie (sans les Etats arabes) n'incluent pas la Chine.
ESP> Los datos anteriores a 1980 para: el mundo, Asia, Países en desarrollo, y Asia (sin los Estados árabes) excluyen China.

6.2 Number and circulation of daily newspapers
Nombre et tirage des journaux quotidiens
Número y tirada de los periódicos diarios

CONTINENTS, MAJOR AREAS AND GROUPS OF COUNTRIES / CONTINENTS, GRANDES REGIONS ET GROUPES DE PAYS / CONTINENTES, GRANDES REGIONES Y GRUPOS DE PAISES	NUMBER OF DAILIES / NOMBRE DE QUOTIDIENS / NUMERO DE DIARIOS		ESTIMATED CIRCULATION / TIRAGE (ESTIMATION) / TIRADA (ESTIMACION)			
			TOTAL (MILLIONS) (MILLONES)		PER 1,000 INHABITANTS / POUR 1 000 HABITANTS / POR 1 000 HABITANTES	
	1975	1984	1975	1984	1975	1984
WORLD TOTAL	7 870	8 230	451	502	110	104
AFRICA	180	160	6	9	14	17
AMERICA	3 000	2 970	90	101	160	153
ASIA	2 200	2 570	128	147	54	53
EUROPE (INCLUDING U.S.S.R.)	2 380	2 420	220	239	302	312
OCEANIA	120	110	7	6	308	255
DEVELOPED COUNTRIES	4 600	4 490	355	384	316	319
DEVELOPING COUNTRIES	3 270	3 740	96	118	32	33
AFRICA (EXCLUDING ARAB STATES)	150	120	4	4	12	10
ASIA (EXCLUDING ARAB STATES)	2 120	2 500	127	146	55	54
ARAB STATES	110	110	3	6	23	35
NORTHERN AMERICA	1 900	1 800	66	69	275	263
LATIN AMERICA AND THE CARIBBEAN	1 100	1 170	24	32	75	80

6.3 Newsprint production and consumption

Production et consommation de papier journal

Producción y consumo de papel de periódico

MT = MILLIONS OF METRIC TONS

MT = MILLIONS DE TONNES METRIQUES

MT = MILLONES DE TONELADAS METRICAS

CONTINENTS, MAJOR AREAS AND GROUPS OF COUNTRIES / CONTINENTS, GRANDES REGIONS ET GROUPES DE PAYS / CONTINENTES, GRANDES REGIONES Y GRUPOS DE PAISES	NEWSPRINT / PAPIER JOURNAL / PAPEL DE PERIODICO					
	PRODUCTION PRODUCTION PRODUCCION (MT)	CONSUMPTION / CONSOMMATION / CONSUMO				
		TOTAL (MT)	PER INHABITANT (KG) PAR HABITANT (KG) POR HABITANTE (KG)			
	1983	1983	1970	1975	1980	1983
WORLD TOTAL	26.3	26.7	5.8	5.3	5.9	5.7
AFRICA	0.3	0.2	0.9	0.8	0.5	0.4
AMERICA	13.8	12.9	20.9	17.6	20.9	20.0
ASIA	4.4	5.6	1.5	1.6	2.0	2.1
EUROPE (INCLUDING U.S.S.R.)	7.5	7.3	9.6	9.2	9.7	9.6
OCEANIA	0.6	0.6	28.7	30.4	27.7	25.0
DEVELOPED COUNTRIES	23.8	22.4	17.8	16.6	19.4	19.2
DEVELOPING COUNTRIES	2.5	4.3	0.9	0.9	1.2	1.2
AFRICA (EXCLUDING ARAB STATES)	0.3	0.1	1.0	0.9	0.5	0.3
ASIA (EXCLUDING ARAB STATES)	4.4	5.6	1.5	1.6	2.1	2.1
ARAB STATES	–	0.2	0.4	0.6	0.7	1.1
NORTHERN AMERICA	13.2	11.7	42.4	38.0	45.6	45.2
LATIN AMERICA AND THE CARIBBEAN	0.6	1.2	3.8	2.7	3.6	3.1

6.4 Production and consumption of other printing and writing paper

Production et consommation des autres papiers d'impression et d'écriture

Producción y consumo de otros papeles de imprenta y de escribir

MT = MILLIONS OF METRIC TONS

MT = MILLIONS DE TONNES METRIQUES

MT = MILLONES DE TONELADAS METRICAS

CONTINENTS, MAJOR AREAS AND GROUPS OF COUNTRIES / CONTINENTS, GRANDES REGIONS ET GROUPES DE PAYS / CONTINENTES, GRANDES REGIONES Y GRUPOS DE PAISES	OTHER PRINTING AND WRITING PAPER / AUTRES PAPIERS D'IMPRESSION ET D'ECRITURE / OTROS PAPELES DE IMPRENTA Y DE ESCRIBIR					
	PRODUCTION / PRODUCTION / PRODUCCION (MT)	CONSUMPTION / CONSOMMATION / CONSUMO				
		TOTAL (MT)	PER INHABITANT (KG) / PAR HABITANT (KG) / POR HABITANTE (KG)			
	1983	1983	1970	1975	1980	1983
WORLD TOTAL	44.7	44.3	7.3	7.0	9.1	9.5
AFRICA	0.1	0.3	1.1	0.9	1.2	0.6
AMERICA	19.0	19.3	22.9	21.1	27.9	29.9
ASIA	8.2	8.4	1.9	2.3	2.9	3.1
EUROPE (INCLUDING U.S.S.R.)	17.2	15.8	14.8	14.4	20.0	20.8
OCEANIA	0.2	0.4	14.7	17.1	18.9	16.7
DEVELOPED COUNTRIES	38.6	37.5	22.2	21.2	29.8	32.1
DEVELOPING COUNTRIES	6.1	6.8	1.1	1.4	1.9	1.9
AFRICA (EXCLUDING ARAB STATES)	0.3	0.1	1.0	0.8	1.1	0.3
ASIA (EXCLUDING ARAB STATES)	8.2	8.3	1.9	2.3	2.9	3.1
ARAB STATES	0.1	0.3	1.3	1.5	2.3	1.7
NORTHERN AMERICA	17.1	17.4	47.4	44.6	60.1	67.2
LATIN AMERICA AND THE CARIBBEAN	1.8	1.9	3.3	3.9	5.4	4.9

6.5 Production of long films

Production de films de long métrage

Producción de películas de largo metraje

CONTINENTS, MAJOR AREAS AND GROUPS OF COUNTRIES CONTINENTS, GRANDES REGIONS ET GROUPES DE PAYS CONTINENTES, GRANDES REGIONES Y GRUPOS DE PAISES	ESTIMATED PRODUCTION OF LONG FILMS PRODUCTION DE FILMS DE LONG METRAGE (ESTIMATION) PRODUCCION DE PELICULAS DE LARGO METRAJE (ESTIMACION)				
	1965	1970	1975	1980	1983
WORLD TOTAL	3 850	4 170	3 920	3 630	3 690
AFRICA	50	60	100	70	130
AMERICA	360	480	530	530	670
ASIA	2 300	2 315	2 000	1 930	1 840
EUROPE (INCLUDING U.S.S.R.)	1 140	1 300	1 250	1 060	1 030
OCEANIA	.	15	40	40	20
DEVELOPED COUNTRIES	1 840	2 000	1 860	1 750	1 830
DEVELOPING COUNTRIES	2 010	2 170	2 060	1 880	1 860
AFRICA (EXCLUDING ARAB STATES)	.	5	5	15	20
ASIA (EXCLUDING ARAB STATES)	2 280	2 300	1 990	1 920	1 820
ARAB STATES	70	70	105	65	130
NORTHERN AMERICA	200	250	220	300	430
LATIN AMERICA AND THE CARIBBEAN	160	230	310	230	240

General note/Note générale/Nota general:
E--> Data do not include China.

General note/Note générale/Nota general: (Cont):
FR-> Les données n'incluent pas la Chine.
ESP> Los datos excluyen China.

6.6 Number and seating capacity of fixed cinemas

Nombre de cinémas fixes et de sièges

Número de cines fijos y de asientos

CONTINENTS, MAJOR AREAS AND GROUPS OF COUNTRIES / CONTINENTS, GRANDES REGIONS ET GROUPES DE PAYS / CONTINENTES, GRANDES REGIONES Y GRUPOS DE PAISES	FIXED CINEMAS / CINEMAS FIXES / CINES FIJOS — NUMBER (THOUSANDS) / NOMBRE (MILLIERS) / NUMERO (MILES)		SEATING CAPACITY / NOMBRE DE SIEGES / NUMERO DE ASIENTOS — TOTAL (MILLIONS) / TOTAL (MILLIONS) / TOTAL (MILLONES)		PER 1,000 INHABITANTS / POUR 1 000 HABITANTS / POR 1 000 HABITANTES	
	1970	1983	1970	1983	1970	1983
WORLD TOTAL	261	238	72	73	26	20
AFRICA	3.0	2.5	1.9	2.0	6	4
AMERICA	28	29	18	18	36	28
ASIA	15	16	9.7	10	8	6
EUROPE (INCLUDING U.S.S.R.)	213	190	42	42	61	55
OCEANIA	1.5	1.0	0.8	0.5	41	21
DEVELOPED COUNTRIES	235	214	56	56	48	47
DEVELOPING COUNTRIES	26	24	16	17	9	7
AFRICA (EXCLUDING ARAB STATES)	1.8	1.5	1.2	1.2	5	3
ASIA (EXCLUDING ARAB STATES)	14	16	9.4	10	8	6
ARAB STATES	1.6	1.4	0.9	1.1	7	6
NORTHERN AMERICA	16	20	11	12	50	46
LATIN AMERICAN AND THE CARIBBEAN	12	9	7.1	6	25	16

General note/Note générale/Nota general:
E--> Data do not include China.

General note/Note générale/Nota general: (Cont):
FR-> Les données n'incluent pas la Chine.
ESP> Los datos excluyen China.

6.7 Annual cinema attendance

Frequentation annuelle de cinémas

Frecuentación anual de cines

CONTINENTS, MAJOR AREAS AND GROUPS OF COUNTRIES CONTINENTS, GRANDES REGIONS ET GROUPES DE PAYS CONTINENTES, GRANDES REGIONES Y GRUPOS DE PAISES	ESTIMATED ANNUAL CINEMA ATTENDANCE (MILLIONS) FREQUENTATION ANNUELLE DE CINEMAS (ESTIMATION) (MILLIONS) FRECUENTACION ANUAL DE CINES (ESTIMACION) (MILLONES))				
	1965	1970	1975	1980	1983
WORLD TOTAL	14 700	13 300	13 100	12 900	14 100
AFRICA	215	250	300	320	350
AMERICA	3 400	2 000	2 250	2 100	2 300
ASIA	3 260	3 690	3 720	4 300	5 700
EUROPE (INCLUDING U.S.S.R.)	7 750	7 300	6 800	6 100	5 700
OCEANIA	65	50	45	40	40
DEVELOPED COUNTRIES	10 640	8 640	8 400	7 500	7 200
DEVELOPING COUNTRIES	4 060	4 660	4 700	5 400	6 900
AFRICA (EXCLUDING ARAB STATES)	80	90	120	160	210
ASIA (EXCLUDING ARAB STATES)	3 200	3 600	3 600	4 200	5 600
ARAB STATES	195	250	300	260	240
NORTHERN AMERICA	2 400	1 000	1 350	1 130	1 300
LATIN AMERICA AND THE CARIBBEAN	1 000	1 000	900	950	1 000

General note/Note générale/Nota general:
E--> Data do not include China.

General note/Note générale/Nota general: (Cont):
FR-> Les données n'incluent pas la Chine.
ESP> Los datos excluyen China.

6.8 Number of radio broadcasting transmitters

Nombre d'émetteurs de radiodiffusion sonore

Número de transmisores de radiodifusión sonora

CONTINENTS, MAJOR AREAS AND GROUPS OF COUNTRIES CONTINENTS, GRANDES REGIONS ET GROUPES DE PAYS CONTINENTES, GRANDES REGIONES Y GRUPOS DE PAISES	TOTAL NUMBER OF RADIO BROADCASTING TRANSMITTERS NOMBRE TOTAL D'EMETTEURS DE RADIODIFFUSION SONORE NUMERO TOTAL DE TRANSMISORES DE RADIODIFUSION SONORA				
	1965	1970	1975	1980	1983
WORLD TOTAL	16 400	22 100	25 800	28 480	30 010
AFRICA	500	680	730	900	970
AMERICA	9 640	10 910	12 730	14 300	15 300
ASIA	1 390	1 930	2 730	2 950	3 050
EUROPE (INCLUDING U.S.S.R.)	4 580	8 270	9 280	9 900	10 240
OCEANIA	290	310	330	430	450
DEVELOPED COUNTRIES	11 670	16 200	19 100	21 000	21 640
DEVELOPING COUNTRIES	4 730	5 900	6 700	7 480	8 370
AFRICA (EXCLUDING ARAB STATES)	400	560	580	680	700
ASIA (EXCLUDING ARAB STATES)	1 330	1 830	2 630	2 810	2 870
ARAB STATES	160	220	250	360	450
NORTHERN AMERICA	6 170	6 770	8 530	9 700	10 000
LATIN AMERICA AND THE CARIBBEAN	3 470	4 140	4 200	4 600	5 300

General note/Note générale/Nota general:
E--> Data do not include China.

General note/Note générale/Nota general: (Cont):
FR-> Les données n'incluent pas la Chine.
ESP> Los datos excluyen China.

6.9 Number of radio broadcasting receivers and receivers per 1,000 inhabitants

Nombre de récepteurs de radiodiffusion sonore et de récepteurs pour 1 000 habitants

Número de receptores de radiodifusión sonora y de receptores por 1 000 habitantes

CONTINENTS, MAJOR AREAS AND GROUPS OF COUNTRIES CONTINENTS, GRANDES REGIONS ET GROUPES DE PAYS CONTINENTES, GRANDES REGIONES Y GRUPOS DE PAISES	NUMBER OF RADIO BROADCASTING RECEIVERS NOMBRE DE RECEPTEURS DE RADIODIFFUSION SONORE NUMERO DE RECEPTORES DE RADIODIFUSION SONORA TOTAL (MILLIONS/MILLONES)					PER 1,000 INHABITANTS POUR 1 000 HABITANTS POR 1 000 HABITANTES				
	1965	1970	1975	1980	1983	1965	1970	1975	1980	1983
WORLD TOTAL	535	684	961	1 233	1 390	159	186	238	277	296
AFRICA	10	16	28	49	60	32	45	69	103	116
AMERICA	285	357	505	571	625	617	701	903	930	966
ASIA	53	70	138	245	301	28	30	60	95	110
EUROPE (INCLUDING U.S.S.R.)	184	233	277	349	380	272	331	380	466	500
OCEANIA	3	8	13	19	24	171	421	619	826	1 006
DEVELOPED COUNTRIES	460	572	770	926	996	449	532	686	793	835
DEVELOPING COUNTRIES	75	112	191	307	394	32	43	66	94	113
AFRICA (EXCLUDING ARAB STATES)	6	8	17	31	37	26	30	56	86	93
ASIA (EXCLUDING ARAB STATES)	51	68	132	235	288	27	33	58	93	107
ARAB STATES	6	10	17	28	36	56	81	121	172	200
NORTHERN AMERICA	251	306	424	471	498	1 173	1 354	1 797	1 869	1 923
LATIN AMERICA AND THE CARIBBEAN	34	51	81	100	127	137	180	251	276	327

6.10 Number of television transmitters

Nombre d'émetteurs de télévision

Número de transmisores de televisión

CONTINENTS, MAJOR AREAS AND GROUPS OF COUNTRIES CONTINENTS, GRANDES REGIONS ET GROUPES DE PAYS CONTINENTES, GRANDES REGIONES Y GRUPOS DE PAISES	NUMBER OF REGULAR TELEVISION TRANSMITTERS NOMBRE D'EMETTEURS DE TELEVISION FONCTIONNANT REGULIEREMENT NUMERO DE TRANSMISORES DE TELEVISION QUE FUNCIONAN REGULARMENTE				
	1965	1970	1975	1980	1983
WORLD TOTAL	8 550	17 700	29 000	38 800	45 370
AFRICA	100	140	230	270	370
AMERICA	3 070	4 310	5 000	5 400	6 600
ASIA	1 100	3 780	6 700	11 600	13 200
EUROPE (INCLUDING U.S.S.R.)	4 200	9 240	16 700	21 000	24 200
OCEANIA	80	230	370	500	1 000
DEVELOPED COUNTRIES	8 100	16 900	27 580	36 800	41 800
DEVELOPING COUNTRIES	450	800	1 420	2 000	3 570
AFRICA (EXCLUDING ARAB STATES)	55	70	120	160	180
ASIA (EXCLUDING ARAB STATES)	1 070	3 730	6 630	11 100	12 960
ARAB STATES	75	120	180	310	430
NORTHERN AMERICA	2 820	3 850	4 360	4 700	5 200
LATIN AMERICA AND THE CARIBBEAN	250	460	640	700	1 400

General note/Note générale/Nota general:
E--> Data do not include China.

General note/Note générale/Nota general: (Cont):
FR-> Les données n'incluent pas la Chine.
ESP> Los datos excluyen China.

6.11 Number of television receivers and receivers per 1,000 inhabitants

Nombre de récepteurs de télévision et de récepteurs pour 1 000 habitants

Número de receptores de televisión y de receptores por 1 000 habitantes

CONTINENTS, MAJOR AREAS AND GROUPS OF COUNTRIES CONTINENTS, GRANDES REGIONS ET GROUPES DE PAYS CONTINENTES, GRANDES REGIONES Y GRUPOS DE PAISES	NUMBER OF TELEVISION RECEIVERS NOMBRE DE RECEPTEURS DE TELEVISION NUMERO DE RECEPTORES DE TELEVISION TOTAL (MILLIONS/MILLONES)					PER 1,000 INHABITANTS POUR 1 000 HABITANTS POR 1 000 HABITANTES				
	1965	1970	1975	1980	1983	1965	1970	1975	1980	1983
WORLD TOTAL	186	278	394	547	613	55	76	98	123	131
AFRICA	0.6	1.2	2.5	7.9	9.8	1.9	3.4	6.2	17	19
AMERICA	84	109	160	205	241	182	214	286	335	373
ASIA	24	39	57	95	107	13	19	25	37	39
EUROPE (INCLUDING U.S.S.R.)	75	125	169	232	247	111	178	232	309	324
OCEANIA	2.4	3.5	5.5	6.6	7.6	137	184	262	275	316
DEVELOPED COUNTRIES	175	255	353	471	521	171	237	315	403	437
DEVELOPING COUNTRIES	11	23	41	76	92	4.7	9	14	23	26
AFRICA (EXCLUDING ARAB STATES)	0.1	0.3	0.6	3.5	4.0	0.4	1.1	2.0	9.7	10
ASIA (EXCLUDING ARAB STATES)	24	38	56	89	102	13	18	25	37	38
ARAB STATES	0.9	1.9	3.4	9.7	11.4	8.4	15	24	60	64
NORTHERN AMERICA	76	92	133	166	197	355	407	564	660	760
LATIN AMERICA AND THE CARIBBEAN	8	17	27	39	45	32	60	84	108	115

7 Printed material

Imprimés

Impresos

This chapter is divided into four sections. Section 1 (Tables 7.1 to 7.6) gives statistics on libraries. The second section (Tables 7.7 to 7.18) deals with statistics on book production, including translations. The third section is concerned with statistics on newspapers and other periodical publications (Tables 7.19 to 7.21), while the last section, consisting of a single table, presents data on the production, importation, exportation, and consumption of newsprint and other printing and writing paper (Table 7.22).

The following text is divided into four sections in accordance with the different subject matters indicated above.

Section 1.

This first section contains six tables, the first of which shows national statistics on different categories of libraries and their collections. The other five tables provide more detailed statistics on acquisitions, loans, expenditure, personnel, etc. of the following types of libraries: national libraries, public libraries, libraries of institutions of higher education, school libraries and special libraries. Since 1950 Unesco has collected library statistics every other year. This periodicity was changed to three years following the Recommendation on the International Standardization of Library Statistics, adopted by the General Conference of Unesco at its sixteenth session in 1970. The first three surveys conducted after the adoption of the 1970 Recommendation requested data for 1971, 1974 and 1977 respectively. In order to facilitate the collection of data and improve the response rate from Member States, it was decided as from 1980 to survey not more than two categories of library at any one time. The questionnaire was therefore divided into three parts dealing respectively with (1) national and public libraries, (2) libraries of institutions of higher education and school libraries and (3) special libraries, each part being sent out in turn. Thus, the 1981 and 1985 surveys dealt with national and public libraries, the one carried out in early 1983 concentrated on libraries of institutions of higher education and school libraries, and statistics on special libraries have been obtained from the 1984 survey.

For the compilation of library statistics, the following definitions are used:

1. *Library*: irrespective of its title, any organized collection of printed books and periodicals or any other graphic or audio-visual materials, with a staff to provide and facilitate the use of such materials as are required to meet the informational, research, educational or recreational needs of its users. Libraries should be counted in numbers of administrative units and service points, as follows: (a) *administrative unit*, any independent library, or a group of libraries, under a single director or a single administration; (b) *service point*, any library serving users in premises of its own, whether the library itself be independent or one of a group of libraries forming an administrative unit. Independent libraries, central libraries and branch libraries (both static and mobile, library vans, ship libraries or train libraries) are considered to be service points provided there is direct service to users in them. The stops of library vans are not counted as service points.

Libraries thus defined are classified as follows:

2. *National libraries*: libraries which, irrespective of their title, are responsible for acquiring and conserving copies of all significant publications published in the country and functioning as 'deposit' libraries, either by law or under special agreements. Libraries described as 'national' but which do not conform to the above definition should not be placed in the *national libraries* category.

3. *Libraries of institutions of higher education*: those primarily serving students and teachers in universities and other institutions of education at the third level. They can also be open to the general public. A distinction should be made between:

(a) The main or central university library, or a group of libraries which may be in different places but under one librarian;
(b) The libraries of university institutes or departments which are neither technically nor administratively under the main or central university library;
(c) Libraries attached to institutes of higher education which are not part of a university.

4. *Other major non-specialized libraries*: non-specialized libraries of a learned character which are neither libraries of institutions of higher education nor national libraries, though they may fulfil the functions of a national library for a specified geographical area.

5. *School libraries*: those attached to all types of schools below the level of education at the third level and serving primarily the pupils and teachers of such schools, even though they may also be open to the general public. Separate collections for the use of several classes in the same school should be regarded as a single library, which should be counted both as an administrative unit and as a service point.

6. *Special libraries*: those maintained by an association, government service, parliament, research institution (excluding university institutes), learned society, professional association, museum, business firm, industrial enterprise, chamber of commerce, etc., or other organized group, the greater part of their collection being in a specific field or subject, e.g. natural sciences, social sciences, agriculture, chemistry, medicine, economics, engineering, law, history. A distinction should be made between:

(a) Libraries which provide materials and services to all members of the public who need them;
(b) Those libraries whose collections and services are for the most part designed to provide for the information needs of their primary users, even if in some cases they serve the information needs of specialists outside the group responsible for their maintenance.

7. *Public (or popular) libraries*: those which serve the

population of a community or region free of charge or for a nominal fee; they may serve the general public or special categories of users such as children, members of the armed forces, hospital patients, prisoners, workers and employees. A distinction should be made between:

(a) Public libraries proper, i.e. those libraries receiving financial support, in whole or in large part from the public authorities (municipal or regional libraries);

(b) Libraries financed from private sources.

Each library should appear in one only of the foregoing categories, according to its primary function.

With respect to library holdings, acquisitions, lendings, expenditure, personnel etc., the following definitions and classifications are given:

8. *Collection*: all library materials provided by the library for its users.

Statistics relating to library collections should cover only the following *documents available to users* and including an allowance for material on loan: (a) books and (bound) periodicals, by metres of occupied shelves, volumes and titles; (b) manuscripts, by metres of occupied shelves and volumes; (c) microforms of books, periodicals, manuscripts and other library materials, by number of physical units; (d) audio-visual documents, by number of physical units; (e) other library materials, by number of physical units.

9. *Annual additions:* all materials added to collections during the year whether by purchase, donation, exchange or any other method. Statistics relating to additions to collections should cover the following materials only (available to users): (a) books and (bound) periodicals by titles, volumes and metres of shelves added ; (b) manuscripts, by number of units and metres of shelves added; (c) microforms of books, periodicals, manuscripts and other library materials by number of physical units added; (d) audio-visual materials, by number of physical units added; (e) other library materials, by number of physical units added.

10. *Printed*: this term covers all methods of reproduction whatever their nature, with the exception of microprinting.

11. *Periodicals*: publications constituting one issue in a continuous series under the same title published at regular or irregular intervals, over an indefinite period, individual issues in the series being numbered consecutively or each issue being dated. Newspapers as well as publications appearing annually or less frequently are included in the definition.

12. *Title*: the term used to describe a printed item which forms a separate whole, whether issued in one or several volumes.

13. *Volume*: a physical unit of any printed or manuscript work contained in one binding or portfolio.

14. *Audio-visual materials*: non-book, non-microform library materials which require the use of special equipment to be seen and/or heard. This includes materials such as records, tapes, cassettes, motion pictures, slides, transparencies, video recordings, etc.

15. *Other library materials*: all materials other than books, periodicals, manuscripts, microforms and audio-visual materials. This includes materials such as maps, charts, art prints, photographs, dioramas, etc.

16. *Library user*: any person utilizing the services of a library.

17. *Registered borrower*: any person registered with a library in order to borrow the materials of the collection for use outside the library. Only borrowers registered for the year under report should be counted.

18. *Ordinary expenditure*: expenditure incurred in the running of the library. Within the total ordinary expenditure the following only are shown separately:

(a) *Employees*: the total amount of money spent on salaries and wages, allowances and other related costs:

(b) *Acquisitions*: the cost of all items (printed, manuscript and audio-visual materials) added to the library.

19. *Trained librarians*: all persons employed in libraries who have received a general training in librarianship or information science. The training may be by formal methods or by means of an extended period of work in a library under supervision.

20. *Population served*: (a) by *public libraries*: the total number of inhabitants in the districts served by public libraries proper (libraries financed wholly or largely by the authorities): (b) by *school libraries*: the total number of pupils and teachers of primary and secondary schools served by school libraries; (c) by *libraries of institutions of higher education*: the total number of students and teachers in institutions of higher education served by this category of library.

Some items in the Unesco questionnaire do not figure in the tables due to lack of response. Even in this abridged form as compared with the programme of the Recommendation, tables 7.2 to 7.6 often show lacunae which in themselves are revelatory of the state of these statistics in the countries in question. The fact is that for a good many countries the statistics reported leave much to be desired and caution is called for if comparisons between countries are to be made.

Table 7.1

Table 7.1 presents for the different categories of libraries selected statistics on collections, annual additions and borrowers.

Tables 7.2 to 7.6

The tables 7.2 to 7.6 refer to national libraries, public libraries, libraries of institutions of higher education, school libraries and special libraries. These five tables include only those countries whose statistics give more information than shown in the appropriate columns of table 7.1.

Section 2

In general, national book production statistics up to 1985 were compiled in accordance with the definitions and classifications set forth in the Recommendation concerning the International Standardization of Statistics relating to Book Production and Periodicals adopted in 1964 by the General Conference of Unesco. From 1986 onwards, the international collection and reporting of statistics on books (as well as on newspapers and periodicals) will be guided by a revised version of the 1964 Recommendation which was adopted by the General Conference of Unesco at its twenty-third session in November 1985. Statistics collected according to this new international instrument will be published in the 1987 yearbook.

In line with the 1964 Recommendation, book production statistics should cover printed non-periodical publications which are published in a particular country and made available to the public and which, in general, should be included in the national bibliographies of the various countries, with the exception of the following categories:

a) *Publications issued for advertising purposes*, provided that the literary or scientific text is subsidiary and that the publications are distributed free of charge (trade catalogues, prospectuses and other types of commercial, industrial and tourist advertising; publications describing activities or technical progress in some branch of industry or commerce and drawing attention to the products or services supplied by the publisher);

b) *Publications belonging to the following categories, when they are considered to be of a transitory character*: time-tables, price lists, telephone directories, etc.; programmes of entertainment, exhibitions, fairs, etc.; regulations and reports of business firms, company directives, circulars, etc.; calendars, almanacs, etc.;

c) *Publications belonging to the following categories in which the text is not the most important part*: musical works (scores or music books), provided that the music is more important than the words; maps and charts, with the exception of atlases.

The following types of publication, *inter alia*, should be included in book production statistics:

1. *Government publications*, i.e. publications issued by public administrations or their subsidiary bodies, except for those which are confidential or designed for internal distribution only.
2. *School textbooks*, i.e. books prescribed for pupils receiving education at the first and second levels.
3. *University theses.*
4. *Offprints*, i.e. reprints of a part of a book or a periodical already published, provided that they have a title and a separate pagination and that they constitute a distinct work.
5. *Publications which form part of a series*, but which constitute separate bibliographical units.
6. *Illustrated works*: (i) collections of prints, reproductions of works of art, drawings, etc. when such collections form complete paginated volumes and when the illustrations are accompanied by an explanatory text, however short, referring to these works or to the artists themselves; (ii) albums, illustrated books and pamphlets written in the form of continuous narratives, with pictures illustrating certain episodes; (iii) albums and picture books for children.

In compiling these statistics, the following definitions should be used:

a) A publication is considered to be *non-periodical* if it is published at one time, or at intervals, by volumes, the number of which is generally determined in advance;

b) The term *printed* includes reproduction by any

method of mechanical impression, whatever it may be;

c) A publication is considered to be *published in a particular country* if the publisher has his registered office in the country where the statistics are compiled, the place of printing or place of circulation here being irrelevant. When a publication is issued by one or more publishers who have registered offices in two or more countries, it is considered as having been published in the country or countries where it is issued;

d) A publication is considered as being *made available to the public* when it is obtainable either by purchase or by distribution free of charge. Publications intended for a restricted readership, such as certain government publications, those of learned societies, political or professional organizations, etc., are also considered as being available to the public;

e) A *book* is a non-periodical printed publication of at least 49 pages, exclusive of the cover pages, published in the country and made available to the public;

f) A *pamphlet* is a non-periodical printed publication of at least 5 but not more than 48 pages, exclusive of the cover pages, published in a particular country and made available to the public;

g) A *first edition* is the first publication of an original or translated manuscript;

h) A *re-edition* is a publication distinguished from previous editions by a change made in the contents (revised edition) or layout (new edition);

i) A *reprint* is unchanged in contents and layout, apart from correction of typographical errors in the previous edition. A reprint by any publisher other than the original publisher is regarded as a re-edition;

j) A *translation* is a publication which reproduces a work in a language other than the original language;

k) A *title* is a term used to designate a printed publication which forms a separate whole, whether issued in one or several volumes.

This section comprises thirteen tables, the first six of which cover production as a whole, while the remaining seven tables are limited exclusively to reproductions of translations.

Tables 7.7 to 7.13 present data collected each year by questionnaires sent to Member States. Unless otherwise indicated it may be assumed that these data cover books and pamphlet, of original works or of translations. However, certain categories of publications which, according to the Recommendation, should be included in book production statistics (e.g. government publications, school textbooks, university theses, offprints, illustrated works) or excluded from such statistics (e.g. publications issued for advertising purposes, publications of a transitory nature, publications in which the text is not the most important part) are classified differently, for statistical purposes, in different countries. In the absence of complete and precise information, it has not been possible to indicate certain differences of this kind between the various national statistics and the Recommendation.

Only those countries are included in Tables 7.8 and 7.11 which were able to present statistics in accordance with the classification by subject set forth in the 1964 Recommendation. The classification given below, which is based upon the Universal Decimal Classification (UDC) is taken from this Recommendation (the corresponding UDC headings are shown in parentheses):

1. Generalities (0)
2. Philosophy, Psychology (1)
3. Religion,Theology (2)
4. Sociology, Statistics (30-31)
5. Politics, Economics (32-33)
6. Law, Public Administration, Social Relief and Welfare, Insurance (34,351-354,36)
7. Military Art and Science (335-359)
8. Education, Teaching, Training, Leisure (37)
9. Trade, Communication, Transport, Tourism (38)
10. Ethnography, Cultural Anthropology, (customs, folklore, mores, tradition) (39)
11. Philology, Languages, Linguistics (4)
12. Mathematics (51)
13. Natural Science (52-59)
14. Medical Sciences, Public Health (61)
15. Engineering, Technology, Industries, Trades and Crafts (62, 66-69)
16. Agriculture, Forestry, Stockbreeding, Hunting and Fisheries (63)
17. Domestic Science (64)
18. Management, Administration and Organization (65)
19. Physical Planning, Town and Country Planning, Architecture (70-72)
20. Plastic and Graphic Arts, Photography, (73-77)
21. Music, Performing Art, Theatre, Film and Cinema (78, 791-792)
22. Games and Sport (793-799)
23. Literature (8)
(a) History of Literature and Literary Criticism
(b) Literary Texts
24. Geography (91)
25. History, biography (92-99)

Whenever an indicated total does not correspond to the sum of its component items, the difference either represents the number of works not distributed among the nine main branches of the Universal Decimal Classification (Tables 7.7 and 7.10) or is explained by the rounding off of figures (Tables 7.8 and 7.11). These tables present for each country figures on books (A), pamphlets (B), and the total of the two groups (A+B). The figures received sometimes refer to the two groups separately, or to their total, or to only one group. The tables show the different cases.

Table 7.7

Table 7.7 presents, for the years 1982 to 1984, data on the number of titles of *first editions* and *re-editions* of original works (or translations) by UDC classes. It contains only those countries for which Unesco can produce statistics relating to at least one of the three years under review.

This table indicates that from data available for the years 1982 to 1984 the ten countries with the largest book production (in terms of titles) are the following: U.S.S.R., U.S.A., Federal Republic of Germany, United Kingdom, Japan, France, Spain, Republic of Korea, China and Canada.

Table 7.8

The figures given in Table 7.8 refer to the number of titles by subject groups of both *first editions* and *re-editions*. For countries where the total number of editions is identical to that of first editions, it should be taken that either there are no re-editions or that their number is unknown. Similarly, where the total number of titles and that of the number of books do not differ, it may be assumed that either no pamphlets were published or that their number is unknown.

Table 7.9

Unless otherwise stated, the data in this table refer to the total number of titles (*first editions* and *re-editions* of original works or of translations) by language of publication.

Table 7.10

Table 7.10 presents data for the years 1982 to 1984 on the number of copies of *first editions, re-editions* and *reprints* of original works (or translations) by UDC classes.

Table 7.11

The figures given in Table 7.11 refer to the number of copies by subject group of *first editions, re-editions* and *reprints*. The comments concerning total editions and first editions, and total editions and books only in Table 7.8 also apply to this table.

Table 7.12

The figures in this table refer to both *first editions* and *re-editions* of school textbooks which are defined in the Recommendation as books prescribed for pupils receiving education at the first and second levels.

Table 7.13

The figures in Table 7.13 refer to both *first editions* and *re-editions* of children's books.

Tables 7.14 to 7.18

Tables 7.14 to 7.17 give information on translations published in 1979, 1980 and 1981, while Table 7.18 contains statistics on the authors most frequently translated during the period 1961-1981. These statistics are based on information contained in the *Index Translationum*, the international bibliography of translations published by Unesco. It should be noted that the year shown in the tables corresponds to the reference year of the *Index Translationum* from which the data have been compiled. Thus, data shown for a given year may in certain instances represent in part translations published in previous years and at the same time omit in part translations published during the year under reference.

Section 3

The statistics in Tables 7.19 to 7.21 cover daily as well as non-daily newspapers of general interest and other periodicals.

In general, national statistics on newspapers and other periodicals should be drawn up in accordance with the definitions and classifications set out in the Recommendation concerning the International Standardization of Statistics relating to Book Production and Periodicals adopted by the General Conference of Unesco in 1964 (for the revised version of this Recommendation see first paragraph of Section 2 of this chapter). According to the 1984 Recommendation, national statistics on the press should cover printed periodical publications which are published in a particular country and made available to the public, with the exception of publications issued for advertising purposes, those of a transitory character, and those in which the text is not the most important part. However, the following types of publications, *inter alia*, should be included in statistics on periodicals: government periodicals, academic and scientific journals, periodicals of professional, trade union, political or sports organizations, etc., publications appearing annually or less frequently, parish magazines, school magazines and school newspapers, and 'house organs'.

In compiling these statistics, the following definitions should be used:

1. A publication is considered to be a *periodical* if it constitutes one issue in a continuous series under the same title, published at regular or irregular intervals over an indefinite period, individual issues in the series being numbered consecutively or each issue being dated.
2. Periodical publications are subdivided into two categories:
   a) *General-interest newspapers* are periodicals intended for the general public and mainly designed to be a primary source of written information on current events connected with public affairs, international questions, politics, etc. A newspaper thus defined, issued at least four times a week, is considered to be a daily newspaper; those appearing three times a week or less frequently are considered as non-daily newspapers;
   b) *Other periodicals* are those which either are concerned with subjects of very general interest or else mainly publish studies and factual information on such specialized subjects as legislation, finance, trade, medicine, fashion, sports, etc. This category covers specialized journals, reviews, magazines and all other periodicals apart from general-interest newspapers.
3. *Circulation* figures should show the average daily circulation, or the average circulation per issue in the case of non-daily publications. These figures should include the number of copies sold, either directly or by subscription, plus the number of free copies regularly distributed, both inside the country and abroad, except unsold copies. When circulation data are not available, the number of copies printed should be indicated. In interpreting data in the following tables, it should be borne in mind that in some cases, methods of enumeration, definitions and classifications applied by the different countries do not entirely conform to the standards recommended by Unesco. For example, circulation data refer either to the circulation itself as defined above or to the number of printed copies, and the corresponding figures are only estimates, usually official, of varying degrees of accuracy.

Table 7.19.

Table 7.19 presents data on the number, total circulation and circulation per 1,000 inhabitants of daily general-interest newspapers for the years 1970, 1975, 1979 and 1984.

For the purpose of this table, a *daily general-interest newspaper* is defined as a publication devoted primarily to recording news of current events in public affairs, international affairs, politics, etc., and which is published at least four times a week.

When the circulation figures do not correspond to the total number of daily newspapers (this is indicated by a footnote) the number of copies per 1,000 inhabitants is not shown.

Table 7.20

This table gives data, for the latest year available, on the number, total circulation and circulation per 1,000 inhabitants of non-daily newspapers of general interest, as well as of other periodicals.

For the purpose of this table, a 'non-daily general-interest newspaper' is defined as a publication devoted primarily to recording news of current events in public affairs, international affairs, politics, etc., and which is published three times or less a week. Under the category of 'other periodicals' are included publications of periodic issue other than general interest newspapers.

Table 7.21

Table 7.21 presents data concerning the number and circulation of periodicals other than general-interest newspapers, classified by subject groups. This classification is shown below:

A. Total
1. Generalities (0)
2. Philosophy, Psychology (1)
3. Religion, Theology (2)
4. Sociology, Statistics (30-31)
5. Political science ... (32-33)
6. Law ... (34, 351-354, 36)
7. Military art (355-359)
8. Education (37)
9. Trade, Transport (38)
10. Ethnography, Folklore ... (39)
11. Linguistics, Philology (4)
12. Mathematics (51)
13. Natural sciences (52-59)
14. Medical sciences ... (61)
15. Industries...(62, 66-69)
16. Agriculture (63)
17. Domestic science (64)
18. Commercial techniques (65)
19. Arts ... (70-78, 791-792)
20. Games, Sports (790, 793-799)
21. Literature (8)
22. Geography, Travel (91)
23. History, Biography (92-99)

B. Total
1. Children's and adolescents' magazines
2. Comics and humour magazines
3. Parish magazines
4. School magazines and newspapers
5. 'House organs'.

The data in this table refer to a given year in the period 1979-1984.

The reader's attention is drawn to the fact that the addition of the two subtotals shown in this table should be identical to the total shown for *other periodicals* in Table 7.20. This is not always the case, probably because data originate from different sources or because it is not yet possible for certain countries to apply the international standardization. However, it has been considered preferable to publish data for as many countries as possible rather than restrict the number to those for which statistics are complete and consistent. For this reason the information provided in this table should be interpreted and used with caution not forgetting that in many cases the figures represent at the most a very rough approximation of the existing situation.

Section 4

The data given in Table 7.22 relate to the consumption, production, export and import of *cultural paper*, i.e. newsprint as well as printing paper (other than newsprint) and writing paper for the years 1970, 1975, 1980 and 1983. As in preceding years, these data have been furnished by the *Food and Agriculture Organization of the United Nations* (FAO). Readers needing additional information should refer to the *Yearbook of Forest Products* published by the FAO.

The term *newsprint* (item 641.1 of the Standard International Trade Classification, Revised) designates the bleached, unsized or slack-sized printing paper, without coating, of the type usually used for newspapers. Newsprint weighs from 45 to 60 grammes per square metre, at least 70 per cent of the weight of fibrous material usually being derived from mechanical pulp.

The expression *other printing and writing paper* (item 641.2 of the Standard International Trade Classification, Revised) covers paper other than newsprint in rolls or sheets, suitable for use in printing and writing. It does not cover articles manufactured from printing and writing paper, such as stationery, exercise books, registers, etc.

For countries where no separate information for the two above-mentioned categories of paper is available, the totals are shown under the category *newsprint*.

Ce chapitre est divisé en quatre sections. La section 1 (tableaux 7.1 à 7.6) présente les statistiques relatives aux bibliothèques. La section 2 (tableaux 7.7 à 7.18) se réfère aux statistiques sur l'édition de livres, y compris les traductions La section 3 concerne les statistiques relatives aux journaux et autres périodiques (tableaux 7.19 à 7.21); la dernière section présente des données sur la production, l'importation, l'exportation et la consommation de papier journal et autre papier d'impression et d'écriture (tableau 7.22).

Le texte suivant se compose donc de quatre sections, en accord avec les différentes matières indiquées ci-dessus.

Section 1

Cette première section comprend six tableaux dont le premier présente les statistiques nationales sur les différents types de bibliothèques et leurs collections. Les cinq autres tableaux contiennent des statistiques plus détaillées sur les acquisitions, les prêts, les dépenses, le personnel, etc., des différents types de bibliothèques: bibliothèques nationales, bibliothèques publiques, bibliothèques d'établissements d'enseignement supérieur, bibliothèques scolaires et bibliothèques spécialisées.

Depuis 1950, l'Unesco a rassemblé des statistiques sur les bibliothèques tous les deux ans. Conformément à la Recommandation concernant la normalisation internationale des statistiques relatives aux bibliothèques, adoptée par la Conférence générale de l'Unesco à sa seizième session, en 1970, la périodicité a été portée à trois ans. Dans les trois premières enquêtes qui ont été effectuées après l'adoption de la Recommendatin de 1970, les données demandées concernaient respectivement les années 1971, 1974 et 1977. Il a été décidé en 1980 de n'enquêter que sur deux catégories de bibliothèques à la fois, afin de faciliter la collecte des données et d'améliorer le taux de réponse des Etats membres. Le questionnaire sur les bibliothèques a été par conséquent divisé en trois parties séparées, comme suit: (1) bibliothèques nationales et publiques, (2) bibliothèques d'établissements d'enseignement supérieur et bibliothèques scolaires et (3) bibliothèques spécialisées, chacune d'entre elles étant envoyée à tour de rôle. Les enquêtes de 1981 et 1985 concernaient les bibliothèques nationales et publiques, celle réalisée au début de 1982 a été axée sur les bibliothèques d'établissements d'enseignement supérieur et les bibliothèques scolaires alors que les statistiques relatives aux bibliothèques spécialisées ont été recueillies dans l'enquête de 1984.

Pour le rassemblement des statistiques relatives aux bibliothèques les définitions suivantes sont utilisées:

1. *Bibliothèque*: est considérée comme bibliothèque, quelle que soit sa dénomination, toute collection organisée de livres et de périodiques imprimés ou de tous autres documents, notamment graphiques et audiovisuels, ainsi que les services du personnel chargé de faciliter l'utilisation de ces documents par les usagers à des fins d'information, de recherche, d'éducation ou de récréation. Les bibliothèques sont comptées en nombre d'unités administratives et de points de desserte.

Est considérée comme: (a) *unité administrative*, toute bibliothèque indépendante ou tout groupe de bibliothèque ayant un directeur ou une administration uniques; (b) *point de desserte*, toute bibliothèque desservant les usagers dans un local séparé, qu'elle soit indépendante ou fasse partie d'un groupe de bibliothèques constituant une unité administrative. Sont considérées comme *points de desserte* les bibliothèques indépendantes, les bibliothèques centrales, les succursales (qu'elles soient fixes ou mobiles, bibliobus, bibliothèques-navires, bibliothèques-trains), à condition que le service direct aux usagers y soit pratiqué. Les haltes de bibliobus ne sont pas des points de desserte.

Les bibliothèques ainsi définies sont classées comme suit:

2. *Bibliothèques nationales*: bibliothèques, quelle que soit leur appellation, qui sont responsables de l'acquisition et de la conservation d'exemplaires de toutes les publications éditées dans le pays et fonctionnant comme bibliothèques de 'dépôt', soit en vertu d'une loi, soit en vertu d'accords particuliers. Les bibliothèques appelées 'nationales' mais ne répondant pas à la définition ci-dessus ne devraient pas être classées dans la catégorie des *bibliothèques nationales*.

3. *Bibliothèques d'établissements d'enseignement supérieur*: bibliothèques qui sont, en premier lieu, au service des étudiants et du personnel enseignant des universités et autres établissements d'enseignement du troisième degré. Elles peuvent aussi être ouvertes au public. Une distinction devrait être faite entre:

(a) La bibliothèque universitaire principale, ou centrale, ou encore un groupe de bibliothèques pouvant avoir des localisations distinctes, mais placées sous la responsabilité d'un directeur unique;
(b) les bibliothèques d'instituts ou de départements universitaires qui ne sont ni dirigées ni administrées par la bibliothèque universitaire principale ou centrale;
(c) les bibliothèques d'établissements d'enseignement supérieur ne faisant pas partie d'une université.

4. *Autres bibliothèques importantes non spécialisées*: bibliothèques non spécialisées de caractère savant qui ne sont ni des bibliothèques d'établissements d'enseignement supérieur, ni des bibliothèques nationales, même si certaines remplissent les fonctions d'une bibliothèque nationale pour une aire géographique déterminée.

5. *Bibliothèques scolaires*: bibliothèques qui dépendent d'établissements d'enseignement de tout type, à l'exception des établissements d'enseignement du troisième degré et qui doivent avant tout être au service des élèves et des professeurs de ces établissements même si elles sont, par ailleurs, ouvertes au public. Les collections séparées des classes d'une même école devront être considérées comme constituant une seule bibliothèque, qui sera comptée comme une unité administrative et un point de desserte.

6. *Bibliothèques spécialisées*: bibliothèques qui relèvent d'une association, d'un service gouvernemental, d'un parlement, d'une institution de recherche (à l'exclusion des instituts d'université), d'une société savante, d'une association professionnelle, d'un musée, d'une entreprise commerciale ou industrielle, d'une chambre de commerce, etc., ou d'un autre organisme, la plus grande partie de leurs collections concernant une discipline ou un domaine particuliers, par exemple: sciences naturelles, sciences sociales, agriculture, chimie, médecine, sciences économiques, sciences de l'ingénieur, droit, histoire. Une distinction devrait être faite entre:

(a) les bibliothèques qui fournissent documentation et services à toute personne faisant appel à elles;
(b) les bibliothèques dont les collections et les services sont essentiellement prévus pour répondre aux besoins d'information de leur clientèle particulière, même si, dans certains cas, elles sont utilisées par des spécialistes n'appartenant pas à l'organisme dont elles relèvent.

7. *Bibliothèques publiques (ou populaires)*: bibliothèques servant gratuitement ou contre une cotisation de principe une collectivité et, notamment, une collectivité locale ou régionale, et s'adressant soit à l'ensemble du public, soit à certaines catégories d'usagers, telles que les enfants, les membres des forces armées, les malades des hôpitaux, les prisonniers, les ouvriers et les employés. Une distinction devrait être faite entre:

(a) les bibliothèques publiques proprement dites, c'est-à-dire les bibliothèques financées en totalité ou en majeure partie par les pouvoirs publics (bibliothèques municipales ou régionales);
(b) Les bibliothèques financées par des fonds privés.

Chaque bibliothèque ne devra figurer que dans une seule des catégories précitées, compte tenu de sa fonction principale.

En ce qui concerne les collections, acquisitions, prêts, dépenses, personnel etc., les définitions et classifications sont les suivantes:

8. *Collection d'une bibliothèque*: l'ensemble des documents mis à la disposition des usagers.

Les statistiques concernant les collections des bibliothèques ne devraient porter que sur les documents suivants mis à la disposition des usagers, y compris les documents prêtés au dehors: (a) livres et périodiques (reliés), comptés en mètres de rayonnages occupés, par volumes et par titres; (b) manuscrits, comptés en mètres de rayonnages occupés et par volumes; (c) microcopies de livres, périodiques, manuscrits et autres matériels de bibliothèque, comptés par nombre d'unités matérielles; (d) matériels audiovisuels, comptés par nombre d'unités matérielles; (e) autres matériels de bibliothèque, comptés par nombre d'unités matérielles.

9. *Acquisitions annuelles*: ensemble des documents qui sont venus enrichir les collections au cours de l'année, par voie d'achat, de don, d'échange ou de toute autre manière.

Les statistiques sur les acquisitions de collections ne devraient tenir compte que des documents suivants (mis à la disposition des usagers): (a) livres et périodiques (reliés), comptés par titres, par volumes et par mètres de rayonnages ajoutés; (b) manuscrits, comptés par nombre d'unités acquises et par mètre de rayonnages ajoutés; (c) microcopies de livres, périodiques, manuscrits et autres matériels de bibliothèque, comptés par nombre d'unités matérielles acquises; autres matériels de bibliothèque, comptés par nombre d'unités matérielles acquises.

10. *Imprimé*: ce terme recouvre tous les divers procédés d'impression quels qu'ils soient, à l'exception de la microcopie imprimée ('microprinting').

11. *Périodiques*: les publications qui paraissent en série continue sous un même titre, à intervalles réguliers ou irréguliers pendant une période indéterminée, les différents numéros de la série étant numerotés consécutivement ou chaque numéro étant daté. Sont compris dans cette définition les journaux ainsi que les publications annuelles ou à périodicité plus espacée.

12. *Titre*: terme utilisé pour désigner un document imprimé constituant un tout distinct, qu'il soit en un ou plusieurs volumes.

13. *Volume*: une unité matérielle de documents imprimés ou manuscrits contenus dans une reliure ou un carton.

14. *Matériels audiovisuels*: matériel de bibliothèque autre que

les livres et les microcopies qui ont besoin d'un équipement spécial pour être vus et/ou entendus. Ceci comprend des matériels tels que disques, bandes, cassettes, films, diapositives, transparences, enregistrements video, etc.

15. *Autres matériels de bibliothèque*: tous les matériels de bibliothèque autres que les livres, périodiques, manuscrits, microcopies et matériels audiovisuels. Ceci comprend des matériels tels que cartes, graphiques, reproductions artistiques, photographies, dioramas, etc.

16. *Usager de bibliothèque*: toute personne qui utilise les services de la bibliothèque.

17. *Emprunteur inscrit*: toute personne inscrite à une bibliothèque pour y emprunter les documents de la collection et en faire usage au dehors. Ne devraient être comptés que les emprunteurs dont l'inscription est valable pour l'année considérée.

18. *Dépenses ordinaires*: toutes dépenses qui résultent du fonctionnement de la bibliothèque. Du total de ces dépenses on distingue seulement:

(a) *Dépenses pour le personnel*: montant des dépenses pour les salaires, les indemnités et les charges diverses du même type;

(b) *Dépenses pour les acquisitions*: montant des dépenses pour tous les documents (imprimés, manuscrits et audiovisuels) acquis par la bibliothèque.

19. Bibliothécaire professionnel: toute personne employée dans une bibliothèque ayant reçu une formation générale en bibliothéconomie ou en science de l'information. Cette formation peut consister en un enseignement théorique ou en un stage prolongé sous contrôle dans une bibliothèque.

20. *Population desservie*: (a) *par les bibliothèques publiques*: nombre total d'habitants des localités desservies par les bibliothèques publiques proprement dites (bibliothèques financées en totalité ou en majeure partie par les pouvoirs publics); (b) *par les bibliothèques scolaires*: nombre total d'élèves et de professeurs des écoles du premier et du second degré (écoles primaires et secondaires) desservis par les bibliothèques scolaires; (c) *par les bibliothèques des établissements d'enseignement supérieur*: nombre total d'étudiants et d'enseignants dans les établissements d'enseignement supérieur desservis par cette catégorie de bibliothèques.

Quelques questions figurant au questionnaire de l'Unesco ne se trouvent pas dans les tableaux, faute de réponses. Même ainsi réduits par rapport au programme de la Recommandation, les tableaux 7.2 à 7.6 comportent souvent des lacunes, qui, par elles-mêmes, illustrent l'état de ces statistiques dans les pays considérés. En effet, pour bon nombre de pays, les statistiques communiquées laissent beaucoup à désirer et il importe de procéder avec prudence si l'on cherche à établir des comparaisons entre pays.

Tableau 7.1

Le tableau 7.1 présente pour les différentes catégories de bibliothèques des statistiques sélectionnées sur les collections, les acquisitions annuelles et les emprunteurs.

Tableaux 7.2 à 7.6

Les tableaux 7.2 à 7.6 se réfèrent aux bibliothèques nationales, aux bibliothèques publiques, aux bibliothèques d'établissements d'enseignement supérieur, aux bibliothèques scolaires et aux bibliothèques spécialisées. Ces cinq tableaux ne comprennent que les pays dont les statistiques contiennent plus de données que celles qui figurent dans les colonnes concernées du tableau 7. 1.

Section 2

D'une manière générale, les statistiques nationales de l'édition de livres jusqu'en 1985 ont été établies conformément aux définitions et aux classifications figurant dans la Recommandation concernant la normalisation internationale des statistiques de l'édition de livres et de périodiques adoptée en 1964 par la Conférence Générale de l'Unesco. A partir de 1986, la collecte internationale de la presentation de statistiques des livres (et également des journaux et périodiques) sera guidée par une version révisée de la Recommendation de 1964 qui a été adoptée par la Conférence générale de l'Unesco à sa vingt-troisième session en novembre 1985. Les statistiques recueillies conformément à ce nouvel instrument international seront publiées dans l'Annuaire de 1987.

Selon les termes de la Recommandation, les statistiques de l'édition de livres devraient porter sur les publications non périodiques imprimées qui sont éditées dans le pays et offertes au public et qui devraient, en général, figurer dans les bibliographies nationales des différents pays, à l'exception des catégories suivantes:

a) *Publications éditées à des fins publicitaires*, à condition que le texte littéraire ou scientifique ne prédomine pas et que ces publications soient distribuées gratuitement (catalogues, prospectus et autres publications de propagande commerciale, industrielle et touristique; publications traitant de l'activité ou de l'évolution technique d'une branche de l'industrie ou du commerce en attirant l'attention sur les produits ou les services fournis par l'éditeur).

b) *Publications appartenant aux catégories suivantes, lorsqu'elles sont jugées comme ayant un caractère éphémère*: horaires, tarifs, annuaires téléphoniques, etc.; programmes de spectacles, d'expositions, de foires, etc.; statuts et bilans de sociétés, directives des entreprises, circulaires, etc.; calendriers, almanachs, etc.;

c) *Publications appartenant aux catégories suivantes dont le contenu prédominant n'est pas le texte*: les oeuvres musicales (partitions, cahiers de musique), à condition que la notation musicale soit plus importante que le texte; la production cartographique, excepté les atlas.

Les catégories suivantes de publications, notamment, devraient être comptées dans les statistiques de l'édition de livres:

1. *Publications officielles*, c'est-à-dire ouvrages publiés par les administrations publiques ou les organismes qui en dépendent, à l'exception de ceux qui sont confidentiels ou réservés à la distribution intérieure;
2. *Livres de classe* (manuels scolaires), c'est-à-dire ouvrages prescrits aux élèves de l'enseignement du premier degré et du second degré;
3. *Thèses universitaires*;
4) *Tirages à part* (c'est-à-dire réimpressions d'une partie d'un livre ou d'une publication périodique déjà parus), à condition qu'ils aient un titre et une pagination distincts et qu'ils constituent un ouvrage distinct;
5. *Publications faisant partie d'une série*, mais dont chacune constitue une unité bibliographique;
6. *Ouvrages illustrés*: (i) recueils de gravures, de reproductions d'oeuvres d'art, de dessins, etc., pour autant que ces collections constituent des ouvrages complets et paginés et que les illustrations soient accompagnées d'un texte explicatif, même sommaire, se rapportant à ces oeuvres ou à leurs auteurs; (ii) albums, livres et brochures illustrés, rédigés sous la forme d'une narration continue et ornés d'images illustrant certains épisodes; (iii) albums et livres d'images pour les enfants.

Pour l'établissement de ces statistiques, les définitions ci-après devraient être utilisées:

a) Une publication est considérée comme *non périodique* si elle est publiée en une seule fois, ou à intervalles, par volumes dont le nombre est généralement déterminé d'avance;

b) Le terme *imprimé* recouvre tous les divers procédés d'impression, quels qu'ils soient;

c) Est considérée comme *éditée dans le pays* toute publication dont l'éditeur a son siège social dans le pays établissant les statistiques, sans qu'il soit tenu compte ni du lieu d'impression ni du lieu de distribution. Lorsqu'une publication est faite par un ou des éditeurs ayant leur siège social dans deux ou plusieurs pays, elle est considérée comme étant éditée dans celui ou ceux de ces pays où elle est distribuée;

d) Une publication est considérée comme *offerte au public* lorsqu'il peut se la procurer soit en la payant, soit gratuitement. Sont également considérées comme offertes au public les publications destinées à un nombre restreint de personnes, telles que certaines publications officielles, de sociétés savantes, d'organisations politiques ou professionnelles, etc.;

e) Un *livre* est une publication non périodique imprimée comptant au moins 49 pages (pages de couverture non comprises), éditée dans le pays et offerte au public;

f) Une *brochure* est une publication non périodique imprimée comptant au moins 5, mais pas plus de 48 pages (pages de couverture non comprises), éditée dans le pays et offerte au public;

g) Une *première édition* est la première publication d'un manuscrit original ou traduit;

h) Une *réédition* est une édition qui se distingue des éditions antérieures par des modifications apportées au contenu ou à la présentation;

i) Une *réimpression* ne comporte pas de modifications de contenu ou de présentation autres que des corrections typographiques par rapport à l'édition antérieure. Une réimpression faite par un éditeur autre que l'éditeur précédent est considérée comme une réédition;

j) Une *traduction* est une publication qui reproduit un ouvrage dans une langue autre que la langue originale;

k) Un *titre* est un terme utilisé pour désigner une publication imprimée, constituant un tout distinct, qu'elle soit en un ou en plusieurs volumes.

La présente section comprend treize tableaux, dont les six premiers se rapportent à la totalité de l'édition, tandis que les sept derniers se réfèrent exclusivement à l'édition de traductions.

Les données présentées dans les tableaux 7.7 à 7.13 sont rassemblées chaque année au moyen de questionnaires adressés aux Etats membres. Sauf indication contraire, elles sont censées englober les livres et les brochures d'ouvrages originaux ou de traductions. Toutefois, certaines catégories de publications qui, selon la Recommandation, devraient être soit comprises dans les statistiques de l'édition de livres - par exemple les publications officielles, les livres de classe (manuels scolaires), les thèses universitaires, les tirages à part, les ouvrages illustrés - soit exclues de ces statistiques (telles les publications éditées à des fins publicitaires, les publications de caractère éphémère et celles dont le contenu prédominant n'est pas le texte) sont traitées différemment, suivant les pays, lorsqu'il s'agit d'établir les statistiques. Faute de renseignements complets et précis, il n'a pas été possible d'indiquer dans quelle mesure les différentes statistiques nationales s'écartent, à cet égard, des normes formulées dans la Recommandation.

Seuls figurent dans les tableaux 7.8 et 7.11 les pays qui ont été en mesure de présenter des statistiques établies selon la classification par catégories de sujets préconisée dans la Recommandation de 1964. La classification ci-après, fondée sur la Classification Décimale Universelle (CDU) est extraite de cette Recommandation (entre parenthèses : indices correspondants de la CDU):

1. Généralités (0)
2. Philosophie, psychologie (1)
3. Religion, théologie (2)
4. Sociologie, statistique (30-31)
5. Sciences politiques, sciences économiques (32-33)
6. Droit, administration publique, prévoyance et aide sociale, assurance (34, 351-354, 36)
7. Art et science militaire (355-359)
8. Education, enseignement, formation, loisirs (37)
9. Commerce, communication, transport, tourisme (38)
10. Ethnographie, anthropologie culturelle (coutumes, folklore, moeurs, tradition) (39)
11. Philologie, langues, linguistique (4)
12. Mathématiques (51)
13. Sciences naturelles (52-59)
14. Sciences médicales, santé publique (61)
15. Art de l'ingénieur, technologie, industries, métiers (62, 66-69)
16. Agriculture, sylviculture, élevage, chasse et pêche (63)
17. Science ménagère (64)
18. Gestion, administration et organisation (65)
19. Aménagement du territoire, urbanisme, architecture (70-72)
20. Arts graphiques et plastiques, photographie (73-77)
21. Musique, arts du spectacle, théatre, film et cinéma (78, 791-792)
22. Jeux et sports (793-799)
23. Littérature (8)
(a) Histoire et critique littéraires
(b) Textes littéraires
24. Géographie (91)
25. Histoire, biographie (92-99)

La différence éventuelle entre les totaux et la somme des chiffres correspondant aux neuf catégories de la Classification Décimale Universelle représente le nombre d'ouvrages qui n'ont pas été classés dans ces catégories (tableaux 7.7 et 7.10) ou s'explique par le fait que les chiffres ont été arrondis (tableaux 7.8 et 7.11). Ces tableaux sont conçus pour donner pour chaque pays les chiffres sur les livres (A), les brochures (B), et le total des deux groupes (A+B). Les chiffres reçus se réfèrent parfois aux deux groupes séparément, ou au total des deux groupes, ou à l'un ou l'autre groupe seulement. Les tableaux reflètent les différents cas.

Tableau 7.7

Dans le tableau 7.7 les données sont présentées pour les années 1982 à 1984 et ne se réfèrent qu'aux pays pour lesquels l'Unesco dispose de statistiques concernant au moins l'une des trois années considérées. Sauf indication contraire, les données de ce tableau comprennent le nombre de titres des *premières éditions* et des *rééditions* d'ouvrages originaux ou de traductions par catégorie de la CDU.

Il ressort de ce tableau, d'après les données disponibles pour les années 1982 à 1984, que les dix premiers pays producteurs de livres (d'après le nombre de titres) sont les suivants: U.R.S.S., Etats-Unis, République fédérale d'Allemagne, Royaume-Uni, Japon , France, Espagne, République de Corée, Chine et Canada.

Tableau 7.8

Les chiffres du tableau 7.8 se rapportent au nombre de titres par groupes de sujets des *premières éditions* et des *re-editions*. Pour les pays où le nombre total des éditions et le nombre des premières éditions sont identiques, on doit considérer qu'il n'y a pas de rééditions ou que leur nombre est inconnu. De même lorsque le nombre de titres est égal au nombre de livres, on peut supposer qu'aucune brochure n'a été publiée ou que leur nombre est inconnu.

Tableau 7.9 Sauf indication contraire, les données de ce tableau comprennent le nombre de titres des *premières éditions* et des *rééditions* d'ouvrages originaux ou de traductions d'après la langue de publication.

Tableau 7.10

Le tableau 7.10 présente pour les années 1982 à 1984 les données sur le nombre d'exemplaires des *premières éditions, rééditions* et *réimpressions* d'ouvrages originaux (ou de traductions) classés d'après la C.D.U.

Tableau 7.11

Les chiffres du tableau 7.11 se rapportent au nombre d'exemplaires par groupes de sujets des *premières éditions*, des *rééditions* et aux *réimpressions*. Les observations concernant le total d'éditions et les premières éditions ainsi que celles qui concernent le total d'éditions et les livres seulement du tableau 7.8 s'appliquent également à ce tableau.

Tableau 7.12

Les données de ce tableau se réfèrent aux *premières éditions* et aux *rééditions* de manuels scolaires qui, dans la Recommandation, sont définis comme ouvrages prescrits aux élèves de l'enseignement du premier degré et du second degré.

Tableau 7.13

Les données du tableau 7.13 se réfèrent aux *premières éditions* et aux *rééditions* de livres pour enfants.

Tableaux 7.14 à 7.18

Les tableaux 7.14 à 7.17 présentent des données concernant les traductions publiées en 1979, 1980 et 1981, tandis que le tableau 7.18 contient des renseignements sur les auteurs les plus traduits durant la période 1961-1981. Ces statistiques ont été établies sur la base des renseignements publiés dans l'*Index Translationum*, bibliographie internationale des traductions, publiée par l'Unesco. Il faut noter que l'année qui figure dans les tableaux correspond à l'année de référence de l'édition de l'*Index Translationum* dont les données ont été tirées. Néanmoins, les données pour l'année de référence peuvent comprendre dans certains cas une partie de traductions publiées dans des années antérieures et omettre en même temps des traductions publiées pendant l'année de référence.

Section 3

Les tableaux 7.19 à 7.21 contiennent des données relatives aux journaux quotidiens et non quotidiens d'information générale, ainsi qu'aux autres périodiques.

D'une manière générale, les statistiques nationales des journaux et des autres périodiques devraient être établies conformément aux définitions et aux classifications figurant dans la Recommandation concernant la normalisation internationale des statistiques de l'édition de livres et de périodiques adoptée par la Conférence Générale de l'Unesco en 1964 (pour la version révisée de cette Recommandation, voir le premier paragraphe de la Section 2 de ce Chapitre). Selon les termes de la Recommandation de 1964, les statistiques nationales sur la presse devraient porter sur les publications périodiques imprimées qui sont éditées dans le pays et offertes au public, à l'exception des publications éditées à des fins publicitaires, de celles de caractère éphémère et de celles dont le contenu prédominant n'est pas le texte. Par contre, les catégories de publications ci-après, notamment, devraient être comptées dans les statistiques des périodiques: périodiques officiels, périodiques académiques et scientifiques, périodiques des organisations professionnelles, syndicales, politiques, sportives, etc., publications annuelles ou à périodicité plus espacée, bulletins paroissiaux, bulletins des écoles, journaux d'entreprise.

Pour l'établissement de ces statistiques, les définitions ci-après devraient être utilisées:

1. Une publication est considérée comme *périodique* si elle est publiée en série continue sous un même titre à intervalles réguliers ou irréguliers pendant une période indéterminée, les différents numéros de la série étant numérotés consécutivement ou chaque numéro étant daté.

2. Les publications périodiques sont subdivisées en deux catégories:

a) Les *journaux d'information générale* sont des publications périodiques destinées au grand public, qui ont essentiellement pour objet de constituer une source originale d'information écrite sur les événements d'actualité intéressant les affaires publiques, les questions internationales, la politique, etc. Un journal répondant à cette définition qui paraît au moins quatre fois par semaine est considéré comme un quotidien, un journal paraîssant trois fois par semaine ou moins fréquemment est classé dans la catégorie des journaux non quotidiens;

b) Les *autres périodiques* sont ceux qui traitent des sujets d'intérêt général ou qui sont spécialement consacrés à des études et informations documentaires sur des questions particulières: législation, finances, commerce, médecine, mode, sports, etc. Cette catégorie englobe les journaux spécialisés, les revues, les magazines et tous les périodiques autres que les journaux d'information générale.

3. Les chiffres concernant la *diffusion* devraient représenter la diffusion quotidienne moyenne, ou la diffusion moyenne par numéro dans le cas des publications non quotidiennes. Ces chiffres devraient comprendre le nombre d'exemplaires vendus soit directement, soit par abonnement, plus le nombre d'exemplaires faisant l'objet d'un service gratuit régulier dans le pays et à l'étranger, à l'exclusion des invendus. A défaut de données sur la diffusion, le nombre d'exemplaires imprimés devrait être indiqué.

En interprétant les données des tableaux ci-après, il ne faut pas perdre de vue que dans certains cas les méthodes de recensement, les définitions et les classifications utilisées par les pays ne s'ajustent pas entièrement aux normes préconisées par l'Unesco. Ainsi, par exemple, les tirages mentionnés se réfèrent soit à la diffusion, soit au nombre d'exemplaires imprimés et les chiffres correspondants ne représentent que des estimations, généralement officielles, mais d'exactitude variable.

Tableau 7.19

On trouvera dans le tableau 7.19 des données sur le nombre, le tirage total et le tirage pour 1.000 habitants des journaux quotidiens d'information générale en 1970, 1975, 1979 et 1984.

Dans ce tableau, on entend par *journal quotidien d'information générale* toute publication qui a essentiellement pour objet de rendre compte des événements d'actualité dans les domaines des affaires publiques, des questions internationales, de la politique, etc., et qui paraît au moins quatre fois par semaine.

Lorsque le tirage ne correspond pas au total des journaux quotidiens (ce qui est indiqué par une note), le nombre d'exemplaires par 1,000 habitants ne figure pas sur le tableau.

Tableau 7.20

Ce tableau indique le nombre, le tirage total et le tirage pour 1,000 habitants des journaux non quotidiens d'information générale ainsi que le nombre et le tirage total des autres périodiques au cours de la dernière année pour laquelle on possède des chiffres.

Dans ce tableau, on entend par *journal non quotidien d'information générale* toute publication qui a essentiellement pour objet de rendre compte des évènements d'actualité dans les domaines des affaires publiques, des questions internationales, de la politique, etc., et qui paraît trois fois par semaine ou moins fréquemment. La catégorie *autres périodiques* comprend les publications périodiques - autres que les journaux d'information générale.

Tableau 7.21

Le tableau 7.21 présente des données relatives aux périodiques autres que les journaux d'information générale classés par groupes de sujets. Cette classification est indiquée ci-dessous:

A. Total
1. Généralités (0)
2. Philosophie, psychologie (1)
3. Religion, théologie (2)
4. Sociologie, statistique (30-31)
5. Sciences politiques ... (32-33)
6. Droit ... (34, 351-354, 36)
7. Art militaire ... (355-359)
8. Enseignement, éducation (37)
9. Commerce, transports ... (38)
10. Ethnographie, folklore ... (39)
11. Linguistique, philologie (4)
12. Mathématiques (51)
13. Sciences naturelles (52-59)
14. Sciences médicales ... (61)
15. Industries ... (62, 66-69)
16. Agriculture ... (63)
17. Economie domestique (64)
18. Organisation du commerce ... (65)
19. Beaux-arts ... (70-78, 791-792)
20. Jeux, sports ... (790, 793-799)
21. Littérature (8)
22. Géographie, voyages (91)
23. Histoire, biographies (92-99)

B. Total
1. Périodiques pour enfants et adolescents
2. Périodiques humoristiques et bandes dessinées
3. Bulletins paroissiaux
4. Bulletins des écoles
5. Journaux d'entreprise

Les données de ce tableau se réfèrent à une des années de la période 1979-1984.

Il faut souligner à l'attention des lecteurs que la somme des deux totaux partiels qui figurent dans ce tableau doit correspondre au total indiqué sous la rubrique *autres périodiques* du tableau 7.20. On constatera que ce n'est pas toujours le cas, probablement parce que les données proviennent de sources différentes ou qu'il n'a pas encore été possible à certains pays d'appliquer les normes internationales. Néanmoins, il a été jugé préférable d'inclure dans ce tableau le plus grand nombre de pays possible, plutôt que de limiter leur nombre aux seuls pays pour lesquels nous possédons des statistiques complètes et conséquentes. Pour cette raison, il est évident que les données publiées doivent être utilisées et interprétées avec circonspection, sans oublier que les chiffres ne représentent souvent tout au plus qu'une approximation très grossière de la situation réelle.

Section 4

Les données qui figurent dans le tableau 7.22 se rapportent à la consommation, à la production, à l'exportation et à l'importation de *papier culturel*, c'est-à-dire, de papier journal, de papier d'impression (autre que le papier journal) et de papier d'écriture pour les années 1970, 1975, 1980 et 1983. Comme pour les années précédentes, ces données nous ont été fournies par l'*Organisation des Nations Unies pour l'Alimentation et l'Agriculture* (FAO). Les lecteurs qui souhaiteraient obtenir des renseignements complémentaires doivent se réferer à l'*Annuaire des Produits Forestiers* publié par la FAO.

Le terme *papier journal* (sous-groupe 641.1 de la Classification Type pour le Commerce International, révisée) désigne le papier d'impression blanchi, non collé ou peu encollé, non couché, du type utilisé d'ordinaire pour les journaux. Le papier journal a un poids de 45 à 60 grammes au mètre carré et contient en général au moins 70 pour cent en poids de matière fibreuse tirée de la pâte mécanique.

L'expression *autres papiers d'impression et papier d'écriture* (sous-groupe 641.2 de la Classification Type pour le Commerce International, révisée) désigne les différents types de papiers (en feuilles ou en rouleaux) autres que le papier journal qui sont destinés à l'impression ainsi qu'à l'écriture. N'entrent pas dans cette catégorie les produits manufacturés tels que fournitures de bureau, cahiers, registres, etc.

Pour les pays sur lesquels on ne dispose pas de données séparées pour les deux catégories de papier définies ci-dessus, les chiffres globaux sont présentés sous la rubrique *papier journal*.

Este capítulo se divide en cuatro secciones. La sección 1 (Cuadro 7.1 a 7.6) se refiere a las estadísticas de bibliotecas. La segunda sección se refiere a las estadísticas de la edición de libros, incluídas las traducciones (cuadros 7.7 a 7.18). La sección 3 concierne las estadísticas relativas a los periódicos diarios y otras publicaciones periódicas (cuadros 7.19 a 7.21); la última sección presenta datos sobre la producción, la importación, la exportación y el consumo de papel de periódico y otro papel de imprenta y de escribir (cuadro 7.22).

El texto que figura a continuación consta por consiguiente de cuatro secciones, de acuerdo con las diferentes materias más arriba indicadas.

Sección 1.

Esta primera sección contiene seis cuadros, figurando en el primero las estadísticas nacionales sobre los diferentes categorías de bibliotecas y sus fondos. En los otros cinco cuadros se facilitan estadísticas más detalladas sobre las adquisiciones, préstamos, gastos, personal, etc. de los varios tipos de bibliotecas: bibliotecas nacionales, bibliotecas públicas, bibliotecas de instituciones de enseñanza superior, bibliotecas escolares y bibliotecas especializadas.

Desde 1950, la Unesco ha compilado estadísticas sobre bibliotecas cada dos años. De acuerdo con la Recomendación sobre la normalización internacional de las estadísticas relativas a las bibliotecas, aprobada por la Conferencia General de la Unesco en su décimosexta reunión en 1970, la periodicidad ha sido fijada a tres años. En las tres primeras encuestas que han sido efectuadas después de la adopción de la Recommendación de 1970, se han solicitado datos para 1971, 1974 y 1977 respectivamente. En 1980 se decidió que sólo se efectuarían encuestas sobre dos categorías de bibliotecas a la vez, con el fin de facilitar la recolección de datos y de mejorar la tasa de repuestas de los Estados Miembros. Por consiguiente, el cuestionario sobre las bibliotecas se dividió en tres partes separadas como sigue: (1) bibliotecas nacionales y públicas, (2) bibliotecas de instituciones de enseñanza superior y bibliotecas escolares y (3) bibliotecas especializadas, enviándose cada una de ellos por turno. Las encuestas de 1981 y 1985 se referían a las bibliotecas nacionales y públicas; la encuesta llevada a cabo en 1983 estaba orientada a las bibliotecas de instituciones de enseñanza superior y a las bibliotecas escolares y las estadísticas sobre las bibliotecas especializadas fueron obtenidas a partir de la encuesta de 1984.

Para la recolección de las estadísticas relativas a las bibliotecas, deben tenerse en cuenta las siguientes definiciones:

1. *Biblioteca*: Se entenderá por biblioteca, sea cual fuere su denominación, toda colección organizada de libros y publicaciones periódicas impresas o de cualesquiera otros documentos, en especial gráficos y audiovisuales, así como los servicios del personal que facilite a los usuarios la utilización de estos documentos, con fines informativos, de investigación, de educación o recreativos. Las bibliotecas deberían contarse según el número de unidades administrativas y de puntos de servicio.

Se entenderá por: a) *unidad administrativa*, toda biblioteca independiente, o todo grupo de bibliotecas que tengan una misma dirección o una administración única; b) *punto de servicio*, toda biblioteca que preste servicio a usuarios en un local aparte, tanto si es independiente, como si forma parte de un grupo de bibliotecas que constituyan una unidad administrativa.

Se considerarán *puntos de servicio* las bibliotecas independientes, las bibliotecas centrales, las filiales (tanto fijas como móviles: bibliobuses, bibliotecas de buque, bibliotecas de tren) siempre que sirvan directamente a usarios. No se considerarán puntos de servicio las paradas de los bibliobuses.

Las bibliotecas así definidas se clasifican como sigue:

2. *Bibliotecas nacionales*: bibliotecas que cualquiera que sea su denominación, son responsables de la adquisición y conservación de ejemplares de todas las publicaciones impresas en el país y que funcionan como bibliotecas de 'depósito', en virtud de disposiciones sobre el depósito legal o de otras disposiciones. Las bibliotecas tituladas 'nacionales' que no correspondan a esta definición no deberían clasificarse en la categoría de *bibliotecas nacionales*.

3. *Bibliotecas de instituciones de enseñanza superior*: bibliotecas dedicadas primordialmente al servicio de los estudiantes y del personal docente de las universidades y demás instituciones de enseñanza superior. Pueden también estar abiertas al público . Conviene distinguir entre:

a) la biblioteca universitaria principal o central, o incluso un grupo de bibliotecas que pueden tener locales distintos pero que no dependen de un director único;
b) Las bibliotecas de centros o de departamentos universitarios que no están dirigidas o administradas por la biblioteca universitaria principal o central;
c) las bibliotecas de instituciones de enseñanza superior que no formen parte de la universidad.

4. *Otras bibliotecas importantes no especializadas*: bibliotecas no especializadas, de carácter científico o erudito, que no son ni universitarias ni nacionales, aunque puedan ejercer funciones de biblioteca nacional en un área geográfica determinada.

5. *Bibliotecas escolares*: bibliotecas que dependen de instituciones de enseñanza de cualquier categoría inferior a la enseñanza superior y que, ante todo, están al servicio de los alumnos y profesores de esos establecimientos, aunque estén abiertas al público. Los fondos particulares de las aulas de una misma escuela deberían considerarse como una sola biblioteca, que se contará como una unidad administritiva y un punto de servicio.

6. *Bibliotecas especializadas*: bibliotecas que dependen de una asociación, servicio oficial, parlamento, centro de investigación (excluídos los centros universitarios), sociedad erudita, asociación profesional, museo, empresa comercial o industrial, cámara de comercio, etc., o de cualquier otro organismo y cuyos fondos pertenezcan en su mayor parte a una disciplina o una rama particular, por ejemplo: ciencias naturales, ciencias sociales, agricultura, química, medicina, ciencias económicas, derecho, historia. Conviene distinguir entre:

a) las bibliotecas que proporcionan documentación y servicios a todas las personas que lo pidan;
b) las bibliotecas cuyos fondos y servicios están esencialmente destinados a responder a las necesidades de información de su clientela particular, aunque en algunos casos las utilicen especialistas que no pertenecen al organismo del que ellas dependen.

7. *Bibliotecas públicas (o populares)*: bibliotecas que están, gratuitamente o por una módica suma, al servicio de una comunidad, especialmente de una comunidad local o regional, para atender al público en general o a cierta categoría de usuarios como niños, militares, enfermos de los hospitales y empleados. Conviene distinguir entre:

a) las bibliotecas públicas propiamente dichas, es decir, las bibliotecas financiadas totalmente o en su mayor parte por los poderes públicos (bibliotecas municipales o regionales);
b) las bibliotecas financiadas con fondos privados.

Cada biblioteca debe figurar en una sola de las categorías mencionadas, teniendo en cuenta su función principal.

En lo que se refiere a los fondos, adquisiciones, préstamos, gastos, personal, etc., las definiciones y clasificaciones son las siguientes:

8. *Fondos de una biblioteca*: conjunto de documentos puestos a disposición de los usarios.

Los datos referentes a los fondos de las bibliotecas sólo deberían comprender los documentos siguientes puestos a disposición de los usarios, incluídos los préstamos: a) libros y publicaciones periódicas (encuadernadas) por metros de estantes ocupados, por número de volúmenes y por títulos; b) manuscritos, por metros de estantes ocupados y número de volúmenes; c) microcopias de libros, publicaciones periódicas, manuscritos y otros materiales de biblioteca, por número de unidades materiales; d) materiales audiovisuales, por número de unidades materiales; e) otros materiales de biblioteca, por número de unidades materiales.

9. *Adquisiciones anuales*: conjunto de documentos que han ido enriqueciendo el fondo durante el año, por compra, donación, intercambio o de cúalquier otro modo.

Las estadísticas referentes a las adquisiciones sólo deberían tener en cuenta los documentos siguientes (puestos a disposición de los usarios): a) libros y publicaciones periódicas (encuadernadas), por número de títulos, de volúmenes y por metros de estantes añadidos; b) manuscritos, por número de unidades adquiridas y por metros de estantes añadidos; c) microcopias de libros, publicaciones periódicas, manuscritos y otros materiales de biblioteca, por número de unidades materiales adquiridas; d) materiales audiovisuales, por número de unidades materiales adquiridas; e) otros materiales de biblioteca, por número de unidades materiales adquiridas.

10. *Impresos*: este término abarca todos los procedimientos de impresión sean cuales fueren, excepto la microcopia (microprinting).

11. *Publicaciones periódicas*: publicaciónes editadas en serie contínua con el mismo título, a intervalos regulares o irregulares, durante un período indeterminado, estando numerados consecutivamente los números de la serie o fechaedo cada uno de ellos. Están comprendidos en esta definición los períodicos diarios, así como las publicaciones anuales o las de periodicidad más amplia.

12. *Título*: término utilizado para designar un documento impreso que constituye un todo único, tanto si consta de uno como de varios volúmenes.

13. *Volumen*: la unidad material de documentos impresos o manuscritos contenidos en una encuadernación o carpeta.

14. *Materiales audiovisuales*: materiales de biblioteca otros que libros y microcopias que precisan de un equipo especial para ser vistas y/o óidas. Comprende materiales tales como discos, cintas,

cassettes, películas, diapositivas, proyecciones de transparencia, grabaciones, vidéo, etc.

15. *Otros materiales de biblioteca*: materiales de biblioteca otros que libros, publicaciones periódicas, manuscritos, microcopias y material audio-visual. Comprende materiales tales como mapas, gráficos, reproducciones artísticas, fotografías, diorama, etc.

16. *Usario de la biblioteca*: toda persona que utiliza los servicios de la biblioteca.

17. *Prestatario inscrito*: toda persona inscrita en una biblioteca con el fin de tomar en préstamo documentos para utilizarlos fuera de ella. Sólo deben tenerse en cuenta los prestatarios cuya inscripción es válida para el año de que se trata.

18. *Gastos ordinarios*: todos los gastos que ocasione el funcionamiento de la biblioteca. Del total de estos gastos, sólo se distingue entre:

a) *Gastos de personal*: total de gastos por concepto de sueldos, subsidios y otras atenciones de la misma índole;

b) *Gastos de adquisiciones*: total de gastos para todos los documentos (impresos, manuscritos y audiovisuales) adquiridos por la biblioteca.

19. *Bibliotecario profesional*: toda persona empleada en una biblioteca que ha adquirido una formación general en biblioteconomía o en ciencia de la información. Esta formación puede haberla adquirido mediante una enseñanza teórica or trabajando durante un tiempo prolongado, bajo control, en una biblioteca.

20. *Población servida*: a) *Por las bibliotecas públicas*: es decir, el número total de habitantes de las localidades servidas por las bibliotecas públicas propiamente dichas (bibliotecas financiadas totalmente o en su mayor parte por los poderes públicos): b) *por las bibliotecas escolares*: es decir, el número total de alumnos y el personal docente de las escuelas de primero y segundo grado (escuelas primarias y secundarias) provistas de servicios de bibliotecas escolares: c) *por las bibliotecas de instituciones de enseñanza superior*: es decir, el número total de estudiantes y personal docente de las instituciones de enseñanza superior servidos por esta categoría de bibliotecas.

Algunas de las preguntas que figuran en el cuestionario de la Unesco no se ven reflejadas en ellos por no haberse recibido las respuestas esperadas. Aún en esta forma, reducida en relación con el programa de la Recomendación, los cuadros 7.2 a 7.6 tienen a menudo lagunas que por sí solas ponen de manifiesto el estado de dichas estadísticas en los países considerados. En hecho es que, en el caso de un buen número de países, las estadísticas dejan mucho que desear, y será preciso proceder con prudencia si se desean establecer comparaciones entre países.

Cuadro 7.1

El cuadro 7.1 presenta para las diferentes categorías de bibliotecas, estadísticas seleccionadas sobre los fondos, las adquisiciones anuales y los prestatarios.

Cuadros 7.2 a 7.6

Los cuadros 7.2 a 7.6 se refieren a las bibliotecas nacionales, las bibliotecas públicas, las bibliotecas de instituciones de enseñanza superior, las bibliotecas escolares y las bibliotecas especializadas. Estos cinco cuadros sólo incluyen los países cuyas informaciones estadísticas contienen más datos que los que figuran en el cuadro 7.1.

Sección 2

En general, las estadísticas nacionales de edición de libros hasta 1985, fueron calculadas de acuerdo con las definiciones y clasificaciones que figuran en la Recomendación sobre la Normalización Internacional de las Estadísticas Relativas a la Edición de Libros y Publicaciones Periódicas aprobada en 1964 por la Conferencia General de la Unesco. A partir de 1986, la recolección y presentación de estadísticas de libros (así como periódicos diarios y otros periódicos), sera guiada por la versión de la Recomendación de 1964 que fué adoptada por la Conferencia General de la Unesco en su vigésima tercera sessión, en Noviembre de 1985. Las estadísticas recolectadas de acuerdo con este nuevo instrumento internacional, serán publicadas en el *Anuario Estadístico* de 1987.

De acuerdo con la Recomendación de 1964, las Estadísticas de Edición de Libros deberían referirse a las publicaciones no periódicas impresas, editadas en el país y puestas a la disposición del público, y que, en general, son publicaciones que deberían figurar en las bibliotecas nacionales de los diferentes países, con excepción de las siguientes categorías:

a) *Publicaciones editadas con fines publicitarios*, siempre que no predomine en ellas el texto literario o científico, y que su distribución sea gratuita (catálogos, prospectos y otras publicaciones de propaganda comercial, industrial y turística; publicaciones sobre la actividad o evolución técnica de una rama de la industria o del comercio y en las que se señalen a la atención de los lectores los productos o servicios suministrados por su editor);

b) *Publicaciones pertenecientes a las siguientes categorías, siempre que sean consideradas de carácter efímero*: horarios, tarifas, guías telefónicas, etc.; programas de espectáculos, exposiciones, ferias, etc.; estatutos y balances de sociedades, instrucciones formuladas por empresas, circulares, etc; calendarios, almanaques, etc.;

c) *Publicaciones pertenecientes a las siguientes categorías, cuya parte más importante no es el texto*: las obras musicales (partituras, cuadernos de música) siempre que la música sea más importante que el texto; la producción cartográfica, excepto los atlas.

En las estadísticas relativas a la edición de libros, no deberían omitirse las siguientes categorías de publicaciones:

1. *Publicaciones oficiales*: es decir, las obras editadas por las administraciones públicas o los organismos que de ellas dependen, excepto las que tengan carácter confidencial o sean distribuidas únicamente en el servicio interesado;
2. *Libros de texto*: es decir, obras prescritas a los alumnos que reciben enseñanza de primero o de segundo grado;
3. *Tesis universitarias*;
4. *Separatas*: es decir, las reimpresiones de partes de un libro o de una publicación periódica ya editados, siempre que tengan título y paginación propios y que constituyan una obra independiente;
5. *Publicaciones que forman parte de una serie* pero que constituyen una unidad bibliográfica diferente;
6. *Obras ilustradas*: (i) colecciones de grabados, reproducciones de obras de arte, dibujos, etc., siempre que tales colecciones constituyan obras completas y paginadas, y que los grabados vayan acompañados de un texto explicativo, por breve que sea, referente a esas obras o a sus autores; (ii) álbumes, libros y folletos ilustrados cuyo texto se presente como narración continua acompañada de imágenes para ilustrar determinados episodios: (iii) álbumes y libros de imágenes para niños.

Al compilar las estadísticas deberían utilizarse las siguientes definiciones:

a) Se entiende por publicación *no periódica* la obra editada, de una sola vez o a intervalos en varios volúmenes, cuyo número se determina generalmente con antelación;

b) El término *impreso* comprende los diversos procedimientos de impresión que se puedan utilizar;

c) Se considera como *editada en el país* cualquier publicación cuyo editor tenga su domicilio social en el país en que se compilen las estadísticas; no se toman en consideración el lugar de impresión ni el de distribución. Las publicaciones hechas por uno o varios editores con domicilio social en dos o mas países se considerarán como editadas en el país o países donde se distribuyan;

d) Se considerarán como *puestas a disposición del público* las publicaciones que éste pueda obtener pagando o gratuitamente. Se considerarán también como puestas a disposición del público las publicaciones destinadas a un número restringido de personas, por ejemplo, ciertas publicaciones oficiales de sociedades eruditas, de organizaciones políticas o profesionales, etc.;

e) Se entiende por *libro* una publicación impresa no periódica que consta como mínimo de 49 páginas sin contar las de cubierta, editada en el país y puesta a disposición del público;

f) Se entiende por *folleto* una publicación impresa no periódica que consta de 5 a 48 páginas sin las de cubierta, impresa, editada en el país y puesta a disposición del público;

g) Se entiende por *primera edición* la primera publicación de un manuscrito original o traducido;

h) Se entiende por *reedición* una edición que se distingue de las ediciones anteriores por algunas modificaciones introducidas en el contenido o en la presentación;

i) Una *reimpresión* no contiene otras modificaciones de contenido o de presentación sino las correcciones tipográficas realizadas en el texto de la edición anterior. Toda reimpresión hecha por un editor diferente al editor anterior se considera como una reedición;

j) Se entiende por *traducción* la publicación en que se reproduce una obra en un idioma distinto del original;

k) Un *título* es un término utilizado para designar una publicación impresa que constituye un todo único, tanto si consta de uno como de varios volúmenes.

Esta sección comprende trece cuadros, de los cuales, los seis primeros se refieren a la edición de libros en su totalidad, y los siete últimos a las traducciones exclusivamente.

En los cuadros 7.7 a 7.13 figuran los datos que se compilan todos los años mediante los cuestionarios que se envían a los Estados Miembros. Salvo indicación contraria, cabe suponer que esos datos abarcan a la vez libros y folletos de obras originales o de traducciones. Ahora bien, ciertas categorías de publicaciones que, según la Recomendación, deberían quedar comprendidas en las estadísticas de edición de libros (por ejemplo, las publicaciones oficiales, los libros de texto, las tesis universitarias, las separatas, las obras ilustradas) o excluidas de esas estadísticas (por ejemplo, las publicaciones editadas con fines publicitarios, las de carácter efímero y aquellas otras cuyo contenido predominante no es un texto escrito) reciben un trato distinto según los países, cuando se trata de preparar las estadísticas. Al no disponerse de datos completos y precisos, no ha sido posible indicar en que medida las diferentes estadísticas nacionales se apartan a este respecto de las normas formuladas en la Recomendación.

Sólo figuran en los cuadros 7.8 y 7.11 los países que han podido proporcionarnos estadísticas establecidas de acuerdo con la clasificación por categorías de materias preconizada en la Recomendación de 1964. La siguiente clasificación, basada en la Clasificación Decimal Universal (CDU), está tomada de esta Recomendación (se indican entre paréntesis los índices correspondientes de la CDU) :

1. Generalidades (0)
2. Filosofía, psicología (1)
3. Religión, teología (2)
4. Sociología, estadística (30-31)
5. Ciencias políticas, ciencias económicas (32-33)
6. Derecho, administración pública, previsión y asistencia social, seguros (34, 351-354, 36)
7. Arte y ciencia militar (355-359)
8. Educación, enseñanza, formación, distracciones (37)
9. Comercio, comunicaciones, transportes, turismo (38)
10. Etnografía, antropología cultural (costumbres, folklore, hábitos, tradición) (39)
11 Filología, idiomas, linguistica (4)
12. Matemáticas (51)
13. Ciencias naturales (52-59)
14. Ciencias médicas, sanidad (61)
15. Ingeniería, tecnología, industrias, oficios (62, 66-69)
16. Agricultura, silvicultura, ganadería, caza y pesca (63)
17. Ciencia doméstica (64)
18. Gestión, administración y organización (65)
19. Acondicionamiento del territorio, urbanismo, arquitectura (70-72)
20. Artes plásticas y gráficas, fotografía (73-77)
21. Música, artes del espectáculo, teatro, películas y cine (78, 791-792)
22. Juegos y deportes (793-799)
23. Literatura (8)
(a) Historia y crítica literarias
(b) Textos literarios
24. Geografía (91)
25. Historia, biografía (92-99)

Las posibles diferencias entre los totales y la suma de las cifras correspondientes a las nueve categorías de la Clasificación Decimal Universal equivalen al número de obras que no han quedado clasificadas en esas categorías (cuadros 7.7 y 7.10) o se explican debido a que las cifras han sido redondeadas (cuadros 7.8 y 7.11). Estos cuadros se prepararon con vistas a ofrecer para cada país las cifras relativas a los libros (A), los folletos (B), y el total de los dos grupos (A+B). Las cifras recibidas se refieren algunas veces a los dos grupos por separado, o al total de los dos grupos, o a uno grupo solamente. Los diferentes casos quedan reflejados en los cuadros.

Cuadro 7.7

El cuadro 7.7 presenta los datos relativos a los años 1982 a 1984 y sólo incluye los países con respecto a los cuales la Unesco dispone de estadísticas relativas por lo menos a uno de esos tres años. Cuando no se indica otra cosa, los datos de este cuadro comprenden el número de títulos de las *primeras ediciones* y de las *reediciones* de obras originales y de traducciones clasificadas por materias (C.D.U.).

De este cuadro se desprende igualmente a partir de datos disponibles para los años 1982 a 1984 que los diez países mas importantes como productores de libros (según el número de títulos) son los siguientes: U.S.S.R., Estados Unidos, República Federal de Alemania, Reino-Unido, Japón, Francia, España, República de Corea, China y Canadá.

Cuadro 7.8 Las cifras del cuadro 7.8 se refieren al número de títulos por categorias de temas de las *primeras ediciones* y a las *reediciones*. Para los países en los que el número total de ediciones y el número de primeras ediciones son idénticos, se deberá considerar que no hay reediciones o que el número de reediciones no es conocido. De la misma forma, cuando el número de títulos es igual al número de libros, se supondrá que ningún folleto fue publicado, o que su número no es conocido.

Cuadro 7.9

Cuando no se indica otra cosa, los datos de este cuadro comprenden el número total de títulos (*primeras ediciones* y *reediciones*) de obras originales o de traducciones según la lengua en que se publican.

Cuadro 7.10

El cuadro 7.10 presenta para los años 1982 a 1984, datos sobre el número de ejemplares de las *primeras ediciones, reediciones* y *reimpresiones* de obras originales (o de traducciones) clasificados por materias (C.D.U.).

Cuadro 7.11

Las cifras del cuadro 7.11 se refieren al número de ejemplares por categorias de temas de las *primeras ediciones*, las *reediciones* y a las *reimpresiones*. Las observaciones sobre el total de ediciones y de primeras ediciones, así como aquellas que conciernen al total de ediciones y de libros solamente del cuadro 7.8, también deben ser tomadas en cuenta para este cuadro.

Cuadro 7.12

Los datos de este cuadro se refieren a las *primeras ediciones* y a las *reediciones* de los libros de texto escolares que, en la Recomendación, se definen como obras prescritas a los alumnos que reciben enseñanza de primero o de segundo grado.

Cuadro 7.13

Los datos del cuadro 7.13 se refieren a las *primeras ediciones* y a las *reediciones* de libros para niños.

Cuadro 7.14 a 7.18

Los cuadros 7.14 a 7.17 presentan datos referentes a las traducciones publicadas en 1979, 1980 y 1981, y el cuadro 7.18 proporciona información sobre los autores mas traducidos de 1961 a 1981. Estas estadísticas se basan en los datos publicados en el *Index Translationum*, bibliografía internacional de las traducciones, que publica la Unesco. Es de notar que el año que figura en los cuadros corresponde al año de referencia de la edición del *Index Translationum* en la que se obtuvieron los datos. Sin embargo, los datos para el año de referencia pueden reunir en ciertos casos una parte de traducciones publicadas en años anteriores y omitir al mismo tiempo traducciones publicadas durante el año de referencia.

Sección 3

Los cuadros 7.19 a 7.21 contienen datos relativos a los periódicos diarios y no diarios de información general, así como a las otras publicaciones periódicas.

En general, las estadísticas nacionales de los diarios y otras publicaciones periódicas deberían establecerse de conformidad con las definiciones y las clasificaciones que figuran en la Recomendación sobre la normalización internacional de las estadísticas relativas a la edición de libros y publicaciones periódicas, aprobada por la Conferencia General de la Unesco en 1964. (La versión revisada de esta Recomendación referimos al lector al primer párrafo de la Sección 2 de este Capítulo). De acuerdo con la Recomendación de 1964, las estadísticas nacionales relativas a la prensa deberían referirse a las publicaciones periódicas impresas en el país y ofrecidas al público, a excepción de las publicaciones editadas con fines publicitarios de carácter efímero y de aquéllas cuyo contenido predominante no es el texto. En cambio, las categorías de publicaciones siguientes, entre otras, no deberían omitirse en las estadísticas de publicaciones periódicas: publicaciones periódicas oficiales, publicaciones periódicas académicas y científicas, publicaciones periódicas de entidades profesionales, sindicales, políticas, deportivas, etc., publicaciones anuales o de menor frecuencia de aparición, boletines parroquiales, boletines escolares y periódicos de empresa.

Para calcular esas estadísticas, deberían utilizarse las definiciones siguientes:

1. Se entiende por publicación *periódica* la editada en serie continua con el mismo título, a intervalos regulares o irregulares durante un período indeterminado de forma que los números de la serie lleven una numeración consecutiva o cada número esté fechado.

2. Las publicaciones periódicas se subdividen en dos categorías:

a) *Periódicos de información general*: son las publicaciones periódicas destinadas al gran público y que tengan esencialmente por objeto constituir una fuente de información escrita sobre los acontecimientos de actualidad relacionados con asuntos públicos, cuestiones internacionales, políticas, etc. Un periódico que responda a esa definición y que se publique al menos cuatro veces por semana se considerará como un diario; un periódico que aparezca tres veces por semana o con menor frecuencia, se clasificará en la categoría de los periódicos no diarios;

b) *Otras publicaciones periódicas*: son las que tratan de temas muy amplios o las dedicadas especialmente a estudios e informaciones documentales sobre determinadas cuestiones: legislación, hacienda, comercio, medicina, modas, deportes, etc. Esta definición abarca los periódicos especializados, las revistas ilustradas y todas las demás publicaciones periódicas que no sean de información general.

3. Las cifras concernientes a la *difusión* deberían expresar el promedio de difusión cotidiana y comprenden el número de ejemplares vendidos, tanto directamente como por suscripción, sumado al número de ejemplares distribuidos regularmente en forma gratuita, en el país y en el extranjero, con exclusión de los ejemplares no vendidos. En caso de que no sea posible proporcionar los datos correspondientes al promedio de la difusión, debería indicarse el número total de ejemplares tirados.

Al interpretar los datos de los cuadros que figuran a continuación, no hay que perder de vista que en ciertos casos los métodos de compilación, y las definiciones y clasificaciones que aplican los países no se ajustan enteramente a las normas preconizadas por la Unesco. Por ejemplo, las tiradas que se mencionan se refieren ora a la difusión, ora al número de ejemplares impresos, y las cifras correspondientes no representan sino estimaciones, generalmente oficiales, pero de exactitud variable.

Cuadro 7.19

En el cuadro 7.19 figuran datos sobre el número, la tirada total y la tirada por 1.000 habitantes de los periódicos diarios de información general en 1970, 1975, 1979 y 1984.

En este cuadro, se entiende por *periódico diario de información general* toda publicación que tenga esencialmente por objeto dar cuenta de acontecimientos de actualidad relacionados con asuntos públicos, cuestiones internacionales, política, etc. y que aparezca cuatro veces por semana como mínimo.

Cuando la tirada no corresponde al total de los periódicos diarios (circunstancia que se indica en una nota) el número de ejemplares por 1,000 habitantes no figura en el cuadro.

Cuadro 7.20

Este cuadro indica el número, la tirada total y la tirada por 1 000 habitantes de los periódicos no diarios de información general, asi como el número y la tirada total de las otras publicaciones periódicas durante el último año para el cual se poseen cifras.

En este cuadro se entiende por *periódico no diario de información general* toda publicación que tenga esencialmente por objeto dar cuenta de acontecimientos de actualidad relacionados con asuntos públicos, cuestiones internacionales, política, y que aparezca tres veces por semana o con menor frecuencia. La categoría *otras publicaciones periódicas* comprende las publicaciones periódicas distintas de los diarios de información general.

Cuadro 7.21

El cuadro 7.21 presenta datos relativos a las publicaciones periódicas distintas de los diarios de información general, clasificadas por grupos de materias. Esta clasificación se indica a continuación.

A. Total
1. Generalidades (0)
2. Filosofía, psycología (1)
3. Religion, teología (2)
4. Sociología, estadística (30-31)
5. Ciencias políticas ... (32-33)
6. Derecho ... (34, 351-354, 36)
7. Arte y ciencia militar...(355-359)
8. Enseñanza, educación (37)
9. Comercio, comunicaciones, transportes (38)
10. Etnografía, usos y costumbres, folklore (39)
11. Linguística, filología (4)
12. Matemáticas (51)
13. Ciencias naturales (52-59)
14. Ciencias médicas ... (61)
15. Industrias ... (62, 66-69)
16. Agricultura ... (63)
17. Economía doméstica (64)
18. Organización, administración y técnica comercio ... (65)
19. Artes plásticas ... (70-78, 791-792)
20. Juegos, deportes ... (790, 793-799)
21. Literatura (8)
22. Geografía, viajes (91)
23. Historia, biografia (92-99)

B. Total
1. Periódicos para niños y jovenes
2. Periódicos humoristicos, historietas ilustradas
3. Boletines parroquiales
4. Boletines escolares y periódicos
5. Periódicos de empresa

Los datos de ese cuadro se refieren a uno de los años del período 1979-84.

Hay que señalar a la atención de los lectores que la suma de los dos totales parciales que figuran en ese cuadro debe corresponder al total indicado bajo el epígrafe *Otras publicaciones periódicas* del cuadro 7.20. Se observará que no es ese siempre el caso, probablemente porque las fuentes nacionales utilizadas son diferentes o porque en algunos países no ha sido todavía posible aplicar las normas internacionales. No obstante, se ha estimado preferible incluir en ese cuadro el mayor número posible de países, en lugar de limitarlo únicamente a los países cuyas estadísticas son completas y seguras. Por esta razón, los datos publicados deberán utilizarse e interpretarse con circunspección, sin olvidar que, con frecuencia, las cifras no constituyen a lo sumo más que una aproximación muy relativa de la situación real.

Sección 4

Los datos que figuran en el cuadro 7.22 se refieren al consumo, a la producción, a la exportación y a la importación de 'papel cultural', es decir, de papel de periódico, de papel de imprenta (distinto al papel de periódico) y de papel de escribir para los años 1970, 1975, 1980 y 1983. Como para los años anteriores, estos datos nos han sido procurados por la *Organización de las Naciones Unidas para la Alimentación y la Agricultura* (FAO). Los lectores deseosos de obtener información complementaria deben referirse al *Anuario de Productos Forestales* publicado por la FAO.

El término *papel de periódico* (subgrupo 641.1 de la Clasificación Tipo para el Comercio Internacional, revisada) se refiere al papel de imprenta blanqueado, no encolado o poco encolado, no cuché, del tipo utilizado corrientemente para los periódicos. El papel de periódico tiene un peso de 45 a 60 gramos por metro cuadrado y contiene, en general, al menos un 70% en peso de materia fibrosa extraída de la pasta mecánica.

La expresión *otros papeles de imprenta y papel de escribir* (subgrupo 641.2 de la Clasificación Tipo para el Comercio Internacional, Revisada) designa las diferentes clases de papel en hojas o en rollo que no sean el papel periódico y que se destinan a la impresión y escritura. No se incluyen en esa categoría los productos manufacturados tales como material de oficina, cuadernos, libros de registro, etc.

Para los países sobre los cuales no se dispone de datos separados relativos a las dos categorías de papel arriba definidas, las cifras globales se presentan bajo la rúbrica *papel de periódico.*

7.1 Libraries and their holdings by category of library

Bibliothèques, et leurs collections, classées par catégorie

Bibliotecas, con sus fondos, clasificadas por categoría

CATEGORY OF LIBRARIES:

A. NATIONAL
B. PUBLIC
C. HIGHER EDUCATION
D. SCHOOL
E. SPECIAL
F. NON-SPECIALIZED

CATEGORIE DE BIBLIOTHEQUES:

A. NATIONALES
B. PUBLIQUES
C. ENSEIGNEMENT SUPERIEUR
D. SCOLAIRES
E. SPECIALISEES
F. NON-SPECIALISEES

CATEGORIA DE BIBLIOTECAS:

A. NACIONALES
B. PUBLICAS
C. ENSEÑANZA SUPERIOR
D. ESCOLARES
E. ESPECIALIZADAS
F. NO ESPECIALIZADAS

NUMBER OF COUNTRIES AND TERRITORIES PRESENTED IN THIS TABLE: 148

NOMBRE DE PAYS ET DE TERRITOIRES PRESENTES DANS CE TABLEAU: 148

NUMERO DE PAISES Y DE TERRITORIOS PRESENTADOS EN ESTE CUADRO: 148

COUNTRY / PAYS / PAIS	YEAR / ANNEE / AÑO	CATEGORY OF LIBRARIES / CATEGORIE DE BIBLIOTHEQUES / CATEGORIA DE BIBLIOTECAS	NUMBER OF LIBRARIES / NOMBRE DE BIBLIOTHEQUES / NUMERO DE BIBLIOTECAS	COLLECTIONS: NUMBER OF VOLUMES (000) / NOMBRE DE VOLUMES (000) / NUMERO DE VOLUMENES (000)	COLLECTIONS: METRES OF SHELVING / METRES DE RAYONNAGE / METROS DE ESTANTES	ANNUAL ADDITIONS (VOLUMES) / ACQUISITIONS ANNUELLES (VOLUMES) / ADQUISICIONES ANUALES (VOLUMENES)	REGISTERED BORROWERS / EMPRUNTEURS INSCRITS / PRESTATARIOS INSCRITOS
			(1)	(2)	(3)	(4)	(5)
AFRICA							
ALGERIA‡	1980	A. NATIONAL	1	34 100	600	19 045	11 881
	1981	C. HIGHER EDUCATION	1	...	5	3 650	
	1983	E. SPECIAL	1	...	5	402	191
BENIN	1980	A. NATIONAL	1	...	32	...	15 427
	1982	C. HIGHER EDUCATION	12	...	49	...	...
	1984	E. SPECIAL	1	43	2	263	...
	1983	F. NON-SPECIALIZED	6	...	30	...	3 250
BOTSWANA‡	1984	A. NATIONAL	1	...	337	10 148	48 472
	1980	B. PUBLIC	1	3 454	108	7 654	30 000
BURUNDI	1978	C. HIGHER EDUCATION	4	2 660	92	4 000	1 890
CAMEROON	1980	A. NATIONAL	1	641	22	4 450	...
	1981	C. HIGHER EDUCATION	1	...	85	1 965	...
CENTRAL AFRICAN REPUBLIC	1980	C. HIGHER EDUCATION	4	25 000	30	587	1 500
CHAD	1985	B. PUBLIC	1	19	4	1 500	250
	1984	E. SPECIAL	1	...	4	1 500	250
	1984	F. NON-SPECIALIZED	2	56	3	86	50
CONGO	1984	A. NATIONAL	1	125	6	400	603
	1984	B. PUBLIC	1	360	11	...	13 550
	1981	C. HIGHER EDUCATION	1	2 800	70	3 561	12 000
COTE D'IVOIRE	1981	A. NATIONAL	1	450	65	574	12 000
	1981	B. PUBLIC	1	714	25	2 900	2 120
	1981	F. NON-SPECIALIZED	1	6 055	12	585	60
EGYPT	1980	A. NATIONAL	1	38 360	1 000	24 490	...
	1980	B. PUBLIC	223	...	1 329	...	6 000
	1979	C. HIGHER EDUCATION	...	...	2 755	...	...
	1982	D. SCHOOL	4 565	...	8 150	430 440	1 100 000
	1983	E. SPECIAL	380	...	1 639	...	...
ETHIOPIA‡	1982	A. NATIONAL	1	...	59	1 300	...

7.1 Libraries by category
Bibliothèques classées par catégorie
Bibliotecas clasificadas por categoría

COUNTRY / PAYS / PAIS	YEAR / ANNEE / AÑO	CATEGORY OF LIBRARIES / CATEGORIE DE BIBLIOTHEQUES / CATEGORIA DE BIBLIOTECAS	NUMBER OF LIBRARIES / NOMBRE DE BIBLIOTHEQUES / NUMERO DE BIBLIOTECAS	COLLECTIONS: NUMBER OF VOLUMES (000) / NOMBRE DE VOLUMES (000) / NUMERO DE VOLUMENES (000)	COLLECTIONS: METRES OF SHELVING / METRES DE RAYONNAGE / METROS DE ESTANTES	ANNUAL ADDITIONS (VOLUMES) / ACQUISITIONS ANNUELLES (VOLUMES) / ADQUISICIONES ANUALES (VOLUMENES)	REGISTERED BORROWERS / EMPRUNTEURS INSCRITS / PRESTATARIOS INSCRITOS
			(1)	(2)	(3)	(4)	(5)
GABON	1981	C. HIGHER EDUCATION	4	2 380	34	1 751	788
	1981	D. SCHOOL	5	...	17	630	2 846
GAMBIA‡	1983	A. NATIONAL	1	220	4	67	950
	1983	B. PUBLIC	1	...	89	7 946	1 735
	1978	D. SCHOOL	129	700	...	500	35 196
	1978	E. SPECIAL	17	1 120	24	500	...
GHANA	1983	A. NATIONAL	1	...	30	822	...
	1983	B. PUBLIC	9	...	1 119	4 828	54 514
GUINEA	1980	A. NATIONAL	1	615	66	1 500	...
KENYA‡	1981	A. NATIONAL	1	...	19	5 500	...
	1981	B. PUBLIC	2	2 700	511	60 586	97 387
	1981	C. HIGHER EDUCATION	1	...	270	14 343	6 700
LESOTHO	1984	A. NATIONAL	1	...	36	500	23
	1983	B. PUBLIC	1	...	...	120	3 016
LIBERIA‡	1983	C. HIGHER EDUCATION	6	...	108	2 628	3 241
MADAGASCAR	1983	A. NATIONAL	1	3 843	240	3 093	...
	1983	B. PUBLIC	56	1 209	76	1 346	...
	1981	C. HIGHER EDUCATION	2	...	174	1 343	14 086
	1981	D. SCHOOL	3	36 266	19	2 397	2 349
	1983	E. SPECIAL	23	941	51	...	6 442
MALAWI	1981	C. HIGHER EDUCATION	1	11 368	269	...	4 624
	1983	E. SPECIAL	5	531	24	352	963
MAURITIUS	1984	D. SCHOOL	27	...	149	8 843	21 907
NIGERIA	1980	A. NATIONAL	1	...	251	28 596	208
	1979	B. PUBLIC	18	2 019	481	59 099	205 678
REUNION‡	1981	C. HIGHER EDUCATION	1	1 665	30	1 635	...
RWANDA	1981	C. HIGHER EDUCATION	2	3 786	132	5 236	1 417
	1984	E. SPECIAL	5	607	30	2 551	270
SENEGAL‡	1983	A. NATIONAL	191	...	25	484	2 132
	1981	C. HIGHER EDUCATION	1	7 440	227	5 988	7 103
SEYCHELLES	1983	B. PUBLIC	1	583	35	1 853	...
	1982	C. HIGHER EDUCATION	2	...	11	1 144	170
	1982	D. SCHOOL	11	...	11	...	3 621
	1984	E. SPECIAL	1	...	11	862	...
SOMALIA	1983	C. HIGHER EDUCATION	1	905	40	152	1 162
TOGO‡	1980	A. NATIONAL	1	...	6	1 575	...
	1982	C. HIGHER EDUCATION	1	1 428	50	3 600	4 904
TUNISIA	1983	B. PUBLIC	280	...	1 315	300 000	65 077
UGANDA	1980	B. PUBLIC	1	...	73	6 232	156 891
UNITED REPUBLIC OF TANZANIA	1980	B. PUBLIC	1	...	404	21 362	10 225
ZAIRE	1980	A. NATIONAL	1	...	146	...	...
ZAMBIA	1981	C. HIGHER EDUCATION	4	...	274	7 972	9 465
	1983	D. SCHOOL	1	...	9	210	1 305
ZIMBABWE	1981	A. NATIONAL	1	...	45	912	...
	1983	B. PUBLIC	6	...	...	8 115	18 000
	1982	C. HIGHER EDUCATION	10	...	485	24 459	7 380
	1980	D. SCHOOL	100	...	261	78 300	27 423
	1984	F. NON-SPECIALIZED	1	...	86	2 772	...
AMERICA, NORTH							
BARBADOS‡	1983	B. PUBLIC	1	2 514	173	8 802	63 822
	1981	C. HIGHER EDUCATION	3	...	95	5 100	3 679
BERMUDA‡	1980	B. PUBLIC	1	1 818	140	4 000	3 318
	1982	C. HIGHER EDUCATION	1	360	18	2 645	500
	1982	D. SCHOOL	22	1 294	52	...	6 862
	1980	F. NON-SPECIALIZED	3	594	2	...	840

COUNTRY / PAYS / PAIS	YEAR / ANNEE / AÑO	CATEGORY OF LIBRARIES / CATEGORIE DE BIBLIOTHEQUES / CATEGORIA DE BIBLIOTECAS	NUMBER OF LIBRARIES / NOMBRE DE BIBLIOTHEQUES / NUMERO DE BIBLIOTECAS	COLLECTIONS: NUMBER OF VOLUMES (000) / NOMBRE DE VOLUMES (000) / NUMERO DE VOLUMENES (000)	COLLECTIONS: METRES OF SHELVING / METRES DE RAYONNAGE / METROS DE ESTANTES	ANNUAL ADDITIONS (VOLUMES) / ACQUISITIONS ANNUELLES (VOLUMES) / ADQUISICIONES ANUALES (VOLUMENES)	REGISTERED BORROWERS / EMPRUNTEURS INSCRITS / PRESTATARIOS INSCRITOS
			(1)	(2)	(3)	(4)	(5)
BRITISH VIRGIN ISLANDS‡	1983	B. PUBLIC	1	498	35	1 484	9 886
	1982	D. SCHOOL	2	160	7	50	720
CANADA‡	1984	A. NATIONAL	1	58 958	1 005	58 345	...
	1983	B. PUBLIC	1 014	...	51 812	3 793 927	...
	1980	C. HIGHER EDUCATION	168	...	43 750	1 725 749	...
	1981	D. SCHOOL	7 982	...	47 606	5 306 732	...
CAYMAN ISLANDS	1981	B. PUBLIC	1	362	6	115	1 630
	1982	C. HIGHER EDUCATION	1	900	20	1 100	175
	1981	D. SCHOOL	1	298	10	862	800
	1980	F. NON-SPECIALIZED	1	...	9	581	700
COSTA RICA	1983	C. HIGHER EDUCATION	1	6 826	227	10 687	17 000
CUBA	1983	A. NATIONAL	1	...	1 396	158 626	30 259
	1983	B. PUBLIC	296	...	3 711	517 918	553 111
	1982	C. HIGHER EDUCATION	56	...	1 438	69 827	204 568
	1982	D. SCHOOL	2 432	...	11 508	113 859	...
DOMINICA	1981	B. PUBLIC	1	250	15	300	4 000
DOMINICAN REPUBLIC‡	1980	B. PUBLIC	68	...	...	...	532 852
EL SALVADOR	1980	A. NATIONAL	1	2 442	80	1 000	22 780
GRENADA	1980	B. PUBLIC	1	400	15	2 857	841
	1984	E. SPECIAL	1	74	3	400	40
GUADELOUPE‡	1980	B. PUBLIC	1	1 800	90	9 000	15 000
	1980	F. NON-SPECIALIZED	1	510	24	2 500	2 100
GUATEMALA	1981	C. HIGHER EDUCATION	1	818	120	...	45 000
JAMAICA	1980	A. NATIONAL	1	1 465	40	1 800	...
	1980	B. PUBLIC	1	...	1 108	68 738	614 911
MEXICO‡	1983	A. NATIONAL	2	...	1 548	...	...
	1983	B. PUBLIC	557	...	3 720	...	8 492 000
	1981	C. HIGHER EDUCATION	263	...	2 698	...	8 427 513
	1981	D. SCHOOL	1 880	...	5 403	...	15 932 421
	1983	E. SPECIAL	171	...	2 300	...	2 829 264
NETHERLANDS ANTILLES	1981	B. PUBLIC	1	295	100	11 050	9 543
PANAMA	1980	A. NATIONAL	...	6 784	221	13 572	49 794
	1980	B. PUBLIC	18	...	26	450	...
	1983	E. SPECIAL	1	...	55	1 500	530
ST. LUCIA	1981	C. HIGHER EDUCATION	1	247	24	811	605
ST. PIERRE AND MIQUELON‡	1984	E. SPECIAL	1	135	7	200	100
TRINIDAD AND TOBAGO‡	1983	B. PUBLIC	3	...	246	22 294	72 538
	1981	C. HIGHER EDUCATION	1	9 707	222	5 948	2 264
TURKS AND CAICOS ISLANDS‡	1983	B. PUBLIC	1	906	26	400	2 684
	1982	D. SCHOOL	1	213	6	...	...
UNITED STATES‡	1978	A. NATIONAL	3	...	20 799	359 656	...
	1978	B. PUBLIC	8 456	5 679 317	439 486	26 007 296	...
	1979	C. HIGHER EDUCATION	3 122	...	519 895	21 608 010	...
	1978	D. SCHOOL	85 096	24 646 328	591 261	32 717 838	...
	1978	F. NON-SPECIALIZED	1 877	...	36 348	1 591 752	...
U.S. VIRGIN ISLANDS	1984	B. PUBLIC	1	...	90	9 000	10 000
AMERICA, SOUTH							
ARGENTINA	1984	E. SPECIAL	63	...	1 645	...	654 288
BOLIVIA	1980	A. NATIONAL	2	1 200	135	600	...
	1980	B. PUBLIC	...	33 622	125	599	1 119 618
	1983	C. HIGHER EDUCATION	17	...	220	3 000	...
	1982	F. NON-SPECIALIZED	13	6 220	220	1 890	...

COUNTRY PAYS PAIS	YEAR ANNEE AÑO	CATEGORY OF LIBRARIES CATEGORIE DE BIBLIOTHEQUES CATEGORIA DE BIBLIOTECAS	NUMBER OF LIBRARIES NOMBRE DE BIBLIOTHEQUES NUMERO DE BIBLIOTECAS	COLLECTIONS: NUMBER OF VOLUMES (000) NOMBRE DE VOLUMES (000) NUMERO DE VOLUMENES (000)	COLLECTIONS: METRES OF SHELVING METRES DE RAYONNAGE METROS DE ESTANTES	ANNUAL ADDITIONS (VOLUMES) ACQUISITIONS ANNUELLES (VOLUMES) ADQUISICIONES ANUALES (VOLUMENES)	REGISTERED BORROWERS EMPRUNTEURS INSCRITS PRESTATARIOS INSCRITOS
			(1)	(2)	(3)	(4)	(5)
BRAZIL	1982	B. PUBLIC	3 600	...	18 106	...	2 919 155
	1979	C. HIGHER EDUCATION	1 029	...	11 496	1 176 253	1 115 408
	1982	D. SCHOOL	9 169	...	26 048	...	4 038 811
	1982	E. SPECIAL	1 494	...	12 854	...	424 425
	1982	F. NON-SPECIALIZED	763	...	2 175	...	276 169
CHILE	1984	A. NATIONAL	1	...	2 766	8 380	1 694
	1983	B. PUBLIC	179	...	783	...	18 345
	1981	D. SCHOOL	...	...	1 458	...	...
COLOMBIA	1980	A. NATIONAL	1	18 000	540	26 027	...
ECUADOR	1983	E. SPECIAL	1	60	2	330	230
FRENCH GUIANA‡	1980	B. PUBLIC	1	406	19	1 568	704
	1981	C. HIGHER EDUCATION	1	2 054	43	2 176	2 382
GUYANA	1980	A. NATIONAL	1	...	179	10 191	46 112
PERU	1983	A. NATIONAL	1	19 507	2 690	69 155	39 672
	1983	B. PUBLIC	557	...	1 950	...	...
	1982	C. HIGHER EDUCATION	3	...	58	2 888	...
	1981	D. SCHOOL	292	...	516	102 500	447 000
SURINAME	1978	B. PUBLIC	2	3 070	268	2 100	53 637
	1978	C. HIGHER EDUCATION	2	1 027	29	1 720	...
	1978	D. SCHOOL	3	1 425	60	5 039	20 447
	1978	E. SPECIAL	27	1 586	63	2 531	967
URUGUAY	1983	A. NATIONAL	1	25 356	879	17 451	...
	1984	F. NON-SPECIALIZED	1	2 700	115	...	...
VENEZUELA	1980	A. NATIONAL	1	3 830	765	7 077	...
	1980	B. PUBLIC	23	31 315	977	87 120	66 250
	1978	D. SCHOOL	46	...	105	8 187	...
ASIA							
AFGHANISTAN	1984	B. PUBLIC	55	...	350	...	11 331
BAHRAIN	1981	B. PUBLIC	1	...	140	10 000	50 000
	1983	E. SPECIAL	1	600	14	1 877	1 800
BHUTAN	1983	E. SPECIAL	1	182	10	1 303	150
BRUNEI DARUSSALAM	1980	B. PUBLIC	1	2 205	97	9 113	6 422
	1981	C. HIGHER EDUCATION	5	1 140	48	...	828
	1981	D. SCHOOL	2	2 822	191	17 138	13 099
	1983	E. SPECIAL	2	454	9	568	31
	1980	F. NON-SPECIALIZED	2	2 468	176	...	8 889
CYPRUS	1983	E. SPECIAL	68	8 570	300	19 000	...
HONG KONG‡	1983	B. PUBLIC	2	11 329	1 693	311 822	1 287 186
	1981	C. HIGHER EDUCATION	12	549	1 750	80 338	63 166
	1981	D. SCHOOL	191	...	1 422	...	216 440
INDIA	1978	A. NATIONAL	1	48 000	1 608	24 984	25 357
INDONESIA	1981	A. NATIONAL	1	9 126	525	6 420	5 548
	1979	B. PUBLIC	30	4 485	460	63 320	2 768 100
IRAN, ISLAMIC REPUBLIC OF	1980	A. NATIONAL	1	...	160	2 000	6 000
	1980	B. PUBLIC	385	20 000	2 161	...	...
	1982	C. HIGHER EDUCATION	198	33 272	3 993	199 638	...
IRAQ	1980	F. NON-SPECIALIZED	15	1 800	240	12 000	17 452
JAPAN‡	1984	A. NATIONAL	1	...	4 179	141 350	...
	1983	B. PUBLIC	1 028	...	97 172	10 645 000	10 947 000
	1982	C. HIGHER EDUCATION	893	...	131 499	7 282 023	2 205 290
	1981	D. SCHOOL	40 146	...	201 805	...	...
	1978	E. SPECIAL	2 019	...	31 164	...	...
	1980	F. NON-SPECIALIZED	928	...	80 206	9 104 000	8 621 000
JORDAN	1981	A. NATIONAL	1	500	17	3 000	350
	1983	B. PUBLIC	5	20 000	375	31 388	13 000
	1980	C. HIGHER EDUCATION	1	198	70	2 550	1 176
	1983	E. SPECIAL	7	...	419	64 388	13 752
	1983	F. NON-SPECIALIZED	1	450	26	10 000	650

COUNTRY PAYS PAIS	YEAR ANNEE AÑO	CATEGORY OF LIBRARIES CATEGORIE DE BIBLIOTHEQUES CATEGORIA DE BIBLIOTECAS	NUMBER OF LIBRARIES NOMBRE DE BIBLIOTHEQUES NUMERO DE BIBLIOTECAS	COLLECTIONS: NUMBER OF VOLUMES (000) NOMBRE DE VOLUMES (000) NUMERO DE VOLUMENES (000)	COLLECTIONS: METRES OF SHELVING METRES DE RAYONNAGE METROS DE ESTANTES	ANNUAL ADDITIONS (VOLUMES) ACQUISITIONS ANNUELLES (VOLUMES) ADQUISICIONES ANUALES (VOLUMENES)	REGISTERED BORROWERS EMPRUNTEURS INSCRITS PRESTATARIOS INSCRITOS
			(1)	(2)	(3)	(4)	(5)
KOREA, REPUBLIC OF‡	1983	A. NATIONAL	2	...	1 611	209 850	...
	1983	B. PUBLIC	130	...	2 254	...	...
	1981	C. HIGHER EDUCATION	222	...	11 025	820 717	...
	1981	D. SCHOOL	3 184	...	11 912	895 274	...
	1984	E. SPECIAL	229	...	3 565	284 931	1 417 480
KUWAIT‡	1981	B. PUBLIC	1	...	281	24 264	...
	1981	C. HIGHER EDUCATION	1	...	268	33 000	12 000
LAO PEOPLE'S DEMOCRATIC REPUBLIC	1983	F. NON-SPECIALIZED	1	1 328	145	500	400
MALAYSIA‡	1980	A. NATIONAL	1	4 800	194	15 755	8 534
	1984	B. PUBLIC	20	...	2 785	429 588	811 290
	1982	C. HIGHER EDUCATION	6	16 925	2 040	142 606	50 453
	1982	E. SPECIAL	162	...	1 319	...	...
PAKISTAN	1983	A. NATIONAL	1	3 025	126	4 511	–
	1980	B. PUBLIC	3	687	86	2 020	...
PHILIPPINES	1984	A. NATIONAL	1	14 108	720	12 820	370 136
	1984	B. PUBLIC	1	...	...	2 050	194 073
QATAR	1982	A. NATIONAL	1	...	...	...	4 795
	1982	B. PUBLIC	4	...	...	...	1 355
	1981	C. HIGHER EDUCATION	2	3 330	98	18 409	3 000
	1982	D. SCHOOL	122	5 628	214	35 169	13 608
SAUDI ARABIA	1984	E. SPECIAL	1	...	122	19 146	1 400
SINGAPORE‡	1984	A. NATIONAL	1	...	2 162	390 819	715 501
	1981	C. HIGHER EDUCATION	4	...	1 350	60 128	34 004
	1983	D. SCHOOL	405	...	4 087	427 433	471 072
	1984	E. SPECIAL	40	11 062	524	63 250	27 711
SRI LANKA	1984	A. NATIONAL	1	1 000	76	5 398	...
	1980	B. PUBLIC	650	...	...	191 500	197 200
	1984	E. SPECIAL	...	...	558	...	23 736
SYRIAN ARAB REPUBLIC	1980	A. NATIONAL	1	1 689	85	*2 000	...
	1983	E. SPECIAL	...	500	21	450	90
	1980	F. NON-SPECIALIZED	1	...	1	607	5 000
THAILAND	1983	A. NATIONAL	1	...	1 155	28 875	–
	1981	B. PUBLIC	375	...	1 599	168	30 530
	1983	E. SPECIAL	38	...	452	...	...
	1981	F. NON-SPECIALIZED	26	10 272	764	138 486	181 964
TURKEY	1983	A. NATIONAL	1	...	862	34 057	23 819
	1983	B. PUBLIC	...	...	6 045	309 320	510 700
UNITED ARAB EMIRATES	1982	C. HIGHER EDUCATION	1	2 380	95	31 246	3 953
EUROPE							
ALBANIA	1980	A. NATIONAL	1	...	803	22 138	9 003
	1980	B. PUBLIC	3 631	...	5 712	740 434	...
	1982	C. HIGHER EDUCATION	2	701 601	606	14 748	64 518
	1980	F. NON-SPECIALIZED	32	...	1 825	114 504	114 816
ANDORRA	1980	A. NATIONAL	1	...	9	2 839	...
AUSTRIA	1983	A. NATIONAL	1	58 177	2 435	30 646	...
	1984	B. PUBLIC	2 172	...	7 022	356 954	813 102
	1981	C. HIGHER EDUCATION	796	...	18 996	334 420	...
	1983	E. SPECIAL	1 434	...	26 034	622 409	...
	1983	F. NON-SPECIALIZED	9	...	1 809	42 422	...
BELGIUM	1980	A. NATIONAL	1	95 000	3 366	14 333	8 099
	1980	B. PUBLIC	2 351	...	24 140	...	1 731 256
BULGARIA	1983	A. NATIONAL	1	...	1 603	41 630	662 994
	1983	B. PUBLIC	5 664	...	52 977	2 664 511	2 224 502
	1981	C. HIGHER EDUCATION	56	...	4 949	259 262	119 580
	1981	D. SCHOOL	3 599	...	14 723	863 968	796 735
	1983	E. SPECIAL	676	...	8 360	354 795	205 496
	1983	F. NON-SPECIALIZED	27	...	8 901	438 713	335 506
CZECHOSLOVAKIA	1980	A. NATIONAL	15	...	17 185	467 631	292 822
	1983	B. PUBLIC	9 760	...	52 821	2 802 611	2 765 583
	1984	C. HIGHER EDUCATION	1 743	...	13 617	...	292 828

7.1 **Libraries by category**
Bibliothèques classées par catégorie
Bibliotecas clasificadas por categoría

COUNTRY / PAYS / PAIS	YEAR / ANNEE / AÑO	CATEGORY OF LIBRARIES / CATEGORIE DE BIBLIOTHEQUES / CATEGORIA DE BIBLIOTECAS	NUMBER OF LIBRARIES / NOMBRE DE BIBLIOTHEQUES / NUMERO DE BIBLIOTECAS	COLLECTIONS: NUMBER OF VOLUMES (000) / NOMBRE DE VOLUMES (000) / NUMERO DE VOLUMENES (000)	COLLECTIONS: METRES OF SHELVING / METRES DE RAYONNAGE / METROS DE ESTANTES	ANNUAL ADDITIONS (VOLUMES) / ACQUISITIONS ANNUELLES (VOLUMES) / ADQUISICIONES ANUALES (VOLUMENES)	REGISTERED BORROWERS / EMPRUNTEURS INSCRITS / PRESTATARIOS INSCRITOS
			(1)	(2)	(3)	(4)	(5)
DENMARK‡	1984	A. NATIONAL	1	...	2 700	...	...
	1984	B. PUBLIC	249	...	33 408	...	...
	1981	C. HIGHER EDUCATION	18	150 000	6 825	303 000	...
	1984	E. SPECIAL	23	...	5 352	...	...
FAEROE ISLANDS	1982	A. NATIONAL	1	...	91	1 789	2 809
	1982	B. PUBLIC	11	...	108	5 157	7 183
FINLAND	1984	A. NATIONAL	1	71 382	2 442	63 500	...
	1984	B. PUBLIC	461	...	29 900	2 400 000	2 100 000
	1984	C. HIGHER EDUCATION	29	...	8 731	...	...
	1984	D. SCHOOL	5 200	...	5 800	...	...
	1984	E. SPECIAL	23	...	2 037	...	...
FRANCE‡	1981	A. NATIONAL	1	700 000	10 000	60 000	...
	1983	B. PUBLIC	1 141	1 766 675	64 379	4 781 160	6 094 000
	1981	C. HIGHER EDUCATION	61	870 000	17 700	350 700	
	1979	F. NON-SPECIALIZED	6	...	3 482	13 666	7 600
GERMAN DEMOCRATIC REPUBLIC	1983	A. NATIONAL	2	...	10 290	169 105	56 905
	1983	B. PUBLIC	9 003	...	46 873	4 110 421	4 817 201
	1984	C. HIGHER EDUCATION	30	...	23 307	...	223 441
	1983	F. NON-SPECIALIZED	3	...	2 029	28 569	12 616
GERMANY, FEDERAL REPUBLIC OF‡	1983	A. NATIONAL	7	...	14 096	542 452	72 930
	1983	B. PUBLIC	...	...	75 600	...	6 174 357
	1981	C. HIGHER EDUCATION	145	...	66 778	2 730 796	820 142
	1983	E. SPECIAL	...	...	30 343	980 145	244 243
	1983	F. NON-SPECIALIZED	86	...	73 922	2 474 119	973 057
GIBRALTAR‡	1983	B. PUBLIC	1	358	20	...	...
	1978	C. HIGHER EDUCATION	1	66	5	18	385
	1978	D. SCHOOL	10	913	28	4 208	3 173
GREECE	1984	A. NATIONAL	1	26 400	2 000	270 000	...
HOLY SEE	1980	A. NATIONAL	1	4 500	160	1 950	...
	1980	B. PUBLIC	1	...	37	270	...
	1981	C. HIGHER EDUCATION	17	63 905	2 675	30 495	14 774
	1979	E. SPECIAL	2	...	700	52 200	7 500
	1980	F. NON-SPECIALIZED	3	5 650	597	14 657	9 971
HUNGARY	1983	A. NATIONAL	1	...	2 442	36 231	...
	1983	B. PUBLIC	2 069	...	46 370	2 642 203	2 251 283
	1982	C. HIGHER EDUCATION	221	...	10 958	364 211	142 614
	1981	D. SCHOOL	4 139	...	18 153	1 180 973	919 837
	1983	F. NON-SPECIALIZED	1	...	1 118	21 290	4 772
ICELAND	1982	A. NATIONAL	1	...	367	...	...
	1982	B. PUBLIC	240	...	1 395	...	...
	1982	C. HIGHER EDUCATION	1	...	223	...	...
IRELAND‡	1983	A. NATIONAL	1	14 100	790	7 000	...
	1983	B. PUBLIC	31	...	8 221	458 329	651 284
	1980	C. HIGHER EDUCATION	7	109 255	3 918	116 400	30 860
	1983	E. SPECIAL	21	3 987	131	9 661	3 149
ITALY	1983	A. NATIONAL	7	303 205	13 281	159 355	
LIECHTENSTEIN	1983	A. NATIONAL	1	...	120	2 674	8 930
LUXEMBOURG	1983	A. NATIONAL	1	19 500	640	8 500	19 500
MALTA	1983	A. NATIONAL	1	6 950	355	1 130	...
	1983	B. PUBLIC	1	6 500	196	17 000	60 600
	1981	C. HIGHER EDUCATION	1	7 100	240	5 247	1 950
	1981	D. SCHOOL	35	2 180	127	20 789	17 859
	1984	E. SPECIAL	8	809	35	3 157	2 916
MONACO	1980	A. NATIONAL	1	3 400	130	3 015	1 284
	1981	D. SCHOOL	4	290	12	760	1 149
NETHERLANDS‡	1982	A. NATIONAL	1	44 300	1 800	51 700	...
	1983	B. PUBLIC	471	...	36 112	379 000	4 160 000
	1981	C. HIGHER EDUCATION	690	500 000	17 536	641 500	...
	1982	E. SPECIAL	672	352 700	12 009	331 200	...
	1982	F. NON-SPECIALIZED	6	65 600	1 944	54 100	...

COUNTRY PAYS PAIS	YEAR ANNEE AÑO	CATEGORY OF LIBRARIES CATEGORIE DE BIBLIOTHEQUES CATEGORIA DE BIBLIOTECAS	NUMBER OF LIBRARIES NOMBRE DE BIBLIOTHEQUES NUMERO DE BIBLIOTECAS	COLLECTIONS: NUMBER OF VOLUMES (000) NOMBRE DE VOLUMES (000) NUMERO DE VOLUMENES (000)	COLLECTIONS: METRES OF SHELVING METRES DE RAYONNAGE METROS DE ESTANTES	ANNUAL ADDITIONS (VOLUMES) ACQUISITIONS ANNUELLES (VOLUMES) ADQUISICIONES ANUALES (VOLUMENES)	REGISTERED BORROWERS EMPRUNTEURS INSCRITS PRESTATARIOS INSCRITOS
			(1)	(2)	(3)	(4)	(5)
NORWAY‡	1984	A. NATIONAL	1	...	2 069	...	...
	1983	B. PUBLIC	454	...	15 966	583 000	1 198 000
	1981	C. HIGHER EDUCATION	82	209 481	7 148	286 009	...
	1981	D. SCHOOL	3 757	...	6 221	326 917	...
	1984	E. SPECIAL	242	...	5 072	...	...
POLAND	1983	A. NATIONAL	1	...	1 934	44 707	734
	1984	B. PUBLIC	9 700	...	113 900	...	7 397 000
	1980	C. HIGHER EDUCATION	1 064	...	34 220	1 241 000	...
	1983	E. SPECIAL	4 632	...	31 490	1 286	1 220
	1983	F. NON-SPECIALIZED	127	...	12 599	317 252	164 803
PORTUGAL‡	1983	A. NATIONAL	3	35 429	3 584	41 712	128 467
	1983	B. PUBLIC	178	226 384	7 546	305 076	...
	1981	C. HIGHER EDUCATION	219	75 998	2 193	53 622	817 990
	1981	D. SCHOOL	712	27 623	1 658	169 455	817 829
	1983	E. SPECIAL	126	365 815	2 000	101 218	81 905
	1983	F. NON-SPECIALIZED	9	2 206	735	13 864	55 050
ROMANIA‡	1984	A. NATIONAL	2	...	13 964	...	38 000
	1984	B. PUBLIC	6 821	...	66 672	...	4 507 000
	1984	C. HIGHER EDUCATION	43	...	22 106	...	389 000
	1984	D. SCHOOL	10 832	...	55 431	...	3 184 000
	1984	E. SPECIAL	3 452	...	20 829	...	800 000
SAN MARINO	1983	D. SCHOOL	5	553	22	1 968	3 300
	1983	E. SPECIAL	1	58	2	30	...
SPAIN‡	1980	A. NATIONAL	2	126 426	3 507	56 326	44 661
	1980	B. PUBLIC	1 396	279 824	11 730	601 650	1 307 938
	1981	C. HIGHER EDUCATION	332	275 211	8 462	376 099	319 740
	1981	D. SCHOOL	626	53 352	2 268	130 054	211 768
	1980	E. SPECIAL	435	283 883	8 641	224 914	175 618
SWEDEN	1984	A. NATIONAL	1	...	2 191	...	...
	1983	B. PUBLIC	414	...	42 886	2 356 000	...
	1984	C. HIGHER EDUCATION	15	...	15 445	...	...
	1983	D. SCHOOL	553	...	35 700	...	...
	1983	E. SPECIAL	38	84 165	3 859	82 056	33 594
	1983	F. NON-SPECIALIZED	51	524 982	...	384 765	...
SWITZERLAND‡	1983	A. NATIONAL	1	32 780	1 200	59 972	8 880
	1981	C. HIGHER EDUCATION	11	309 700	13 035	341 800	115 318
	1983	F. NON-SPECIALIZED	33	292 000	10 200	211 300	...
UNITED KINGDOM‡	1980	A. NATIONAL	3	...	20 550	481 851	...
	1980	B. PUBLIC	160	...	131 338	12 667 000	...
	1980	C. HIGHER EDUCATION	554	599 447	24 010	1 665 720	...
	1979	D. SCHOOL	...	...	31 000	2 170 000	...
YUGOSLAVIA	1983	A. NATIONAL	8	295 720	9 101	469 387	92 464
	1983	B. PUBLIC	803	543 743	27 141	1 177 926	...
	1980	C. HIGHER EDUCATION	398	207 225	10 647	295 692	682 643
	1980	D. SCHOOL	8 458	...	29 981	1 677 051	...
	1983	E. SPECIAL	1 038	261 213	14 048	558 405	1 035 942
	1983	F. NON-SPECIALIZED	18	42 395	3 007	94 383	54 467
OCEANIA							
AMERICAN SAMOA	1982	C. HIGHER EDUCATION	1	350	14	500	2 800
	1982	D. SCHOOL	1	1 900	76	6 000	8 000
AUSTRALIA	1983	A. NATIONAL	1	...	2 228	82 295	...
COOK ISLANDS	1980	B. PUBLIC	1	791	15	1 164	3 330
FIJI‡	1978	B. PUBLIC	9	...	91	10 469	33 044
	1983	E. SPECIAL	50	...	44	...	...
FRENCH POLYNESIA	1981	B. PUBLIC	1	*552	17	1 291	1 360
GUAM	1984	B. PUBLIC	8	7 900	188	3 098	17 202
	1981	D. SCHOOL	46	...	283	...	29 921
KIRIBATI	1984	A. NATIONAL	1	...	22	...	6 691
NEW ZEALAND‡	1984	A. NATIONAL	1	...	5 335	120 659	...
	1979	B. PUBLIC	209	*239 000	6 077	529 661	1 150 822
	1981	C. HIGHER EDUCATION	1	...	6	2 399	507
NIUE	1983	B. PUBLIC	1	85	6	420	1 312

COUNTRY PAYS PAIS	YEAR ANNEE AÑO	CATEGORY OF LIBRARIES CATEGORIE DE BIBLIOTHEQUES CATEGORIA DE BIBLIOTECAS	NUMBER OF LIBRARIES NOMBRE DE BIBLIOTHEQUES NUMERO DE BIBLIOTECAS	COLLECTIONS NUMBER OF VOLUMES (000) NOMBRE DE VOLUMES (000) NUMERO DE VOLUMENES (000)	COLLECTIONS METRES OF SHELVING METRES DE RAYONNAGE METROS DE ESTANTES	ANNUAL ADDITIONS (VOLUMES) ACQUISITIONS ANNUELLES (VOLUMES) ADQUISICIONES ANUALES (VOLUMENES)	REGISTERED BORROWERS EMPRUNTEURS INSCRITS PRESTATARIOS INSCRITOS
			(1)	(2)	(3)	(4)	(5)
NORFOLK ISLAND	1980	B. PUBLIC	1	130	5	386	231
	1982	D. SCHOOL	1	...	10	380	325
PACIFIC ISLANDS	1982	C. HIGHER EDUCATION	4	...	24	4 097	1 412
PAPUA NEW GUINEA‡	1982	C. HIGHER EDUCATION	1	15 204	50	4 737	2 615
SAMOA	1978	C. HIGHER EDUCATION	1	300	10	4	150
SOLOMON ISLANDS	1985	A. NATIONAL	1	...	68	5 400	4 150
	1985	B. PUBLIC	8	460	22	4 200	5 100
TOKELAU	1980	B. PUBLIC	1	10	0.2	210	...
TONGA	1981	C. HIGHER EDUCATION	1	168	6	2 400	507
	1978	D. SCHOOL	10	81	28	...	6 200
	1978	E. SPECIAL	2	...	4	...	...
U.S.S.R.							
U.S.S.R.‡	1983	A. NATIONAL	1	60	880	1 926 800	272 900
	1983	B. PUBLIC	109 821	...	2 000 100	...	109 111 900
	1980	D. SCHOOL	154 000	...	862 000	...	...
	1983	F. NON-SPECIALIZED	448	2 798	...	15 314 000	6 826 000
BYELORUSSIAN S.S.R.	1980	B. PUBLIC	6 957	...	87 145	...	5 416 000
UKRAINIAN S.S.R.	1980	B. PUBLIC	26 233	...	370 727	...	31 386 000

AFRICA:

Algeria:

E--> Data on libraries of institutions of higher education refer only to the 'Université des sciences et de la technologie d'Oran'.

FR-> Les données pour les bibliothèques d'établissements d'enseignement supérieur se réfèrent seulement à l'Université des sciences et de la technologie d'Oran.

ESP> Los datos para las bibliotecas de instituciones de enseñanza superior se refieren solamente a la 'Université des sciences et de la technologie d'Oran'.

Botwsana:

E--> The national library also serves as a public library.

FR-> La bibliothèque nationale sert également de bibliothèque publique.

ESP> La biblioteca nacional desempeña al mismo tiempo la función de biblioteca pública.

Ethiopia:

E--> Data refer only to the national library of Addis Ababa.

FR-> Les données se réfèrent seulement à la bibliothèque nationale d'Addis Abéba.

ESP> Los datos se refieren solamente a la biblioteca nacional de Addis Abeba.

Gambia:

E--> The National Library also serves as the public library.

FR-> La bibliothèque nationale remplit également la fonction de bibliothèque publique.

ESP> La biblioteca nacional también desempeña la función de biblioteca pública.

Kenya:

E--> The figure concerning the number of metres of shelving in public libraries (column 3) refers to only one library. Data on libraries of institutions of higher education refer to the central or main library of the University of Nairobi.

FR-> Le chiffre concernant le nombre de mètres de rayonnage dans les bibliothèques publiques (colonne 3) se réfère à une bibliothèque seulement. Les données pour les bibliothèques d'établissements d'enseignement supérieur se réfèrent à la bibliothèque principale ou centrale de l'université de Nairobi seulement.

ESP> La cifra relativa al número de metros de estantes en las bibliotecas públicas se refiere a una biblioteca solamente. Los datos para las bibliotecas de instituciones de enseñanza superior se refieren a la biblioteca principal o central de la universidad de Nairobi solamente.

Liberia:

E--> Data refer only to main or central university libraries.

FR-> Les données se réfèrent seulement aux bibliothèques universitaires principales ou centrales.

Liberia: (Cont):

ESP> Los datos se refieren solamente a las bibliotecas universitar principales o centrales.

Reunion:

E--> Data are also counted with those for France.

FR-> Les données sont également comprises avec celles de France.

ESP> Los datos se cuentan igualmente con los de Francia.

Senegal:

E--> Data refer to the main or central library of the University Dakar.

FR-> Les données se réfèrent à la bibliothèque principale ou centr de l'université de Dakar.

ESP> Los datos se refieren a la biblioteca principal o central de universidad de Dakar.

Togo:

E--> Data on libraries of institutions of higher education refer to t main or central university library.

FR-> Les données pour les bibliothèques d'établisseme d'enseignement supérieur se réfèrent à la bibliothèque universita principale ou centrale.

ESP> Los datos para las bibliotecas de instituciones de enseñar superior se refieren a la biblioteca universitaria principal o central.

AMERICA, NORTH:

Barbados:

E--> The public library also serves as a national library. Data do r include the library of Erdiston Teachers' Training College.

FR-> La bibliothèque publique sert également de bibliothè nationale. Les données des bibliothèques d'établissements d'enseigneme supérieur n'incluent pas la bibliothèque d''Erdiston Teachers' Traini College'.

ESP> La biblioteca pública desempeña al mismo tiempo la función biblioteca nacional. Los datos para las bibliotecas de instituciones enseñanza superior no incluyen la biblioteca de 'Erdiston Teachers' Traini College'.

Bermuda:

E--> Data on libraries of institutions of higher education refer to t library of Bermuda College.

FR-> Les données pour les bibliothèques d'établisseme d'enseignement supérieur se réfèrent à la bibliothèque de 'Bermu College'.

ESP> Los datos para las bibliotecas de instituciones de enseñar superior se refieren a la biblioteca de 'Bermuda College'.

British Virgin Islands:

E--> The public library also serves as a national library.

FR-> La bibliothèque publique sert également de bibliothè

British Virgin Islands: (Cont):
nationale.

ESP> La biblioteca pública desempeña al mismo tiempo la función de biblioteca nacional.

Canada:

E--> Data for public libraries refer to libraries financed by public authorities. Data on libraries of institutions of higher education include neither libraries attached to university institutes or departments nor libraries in the provinces of Quebec and British Colombia.

FR-> Les données relatives aux bibliothèques publiques se réfèrent aux bibliothèques financées par les pouvoirs publics seulement. Les données pour les bibliothèques d'établissements d'enseignement supérieur ne comprennent ni les bibliothèques relevant d'instituts ou de départements universitaires ni les bibliothèques des provinces du Québec et de la Colombie britannique.

ESP> Los datos relativos a las bibliotecas públicas se refieren sólo a las bibliotecas financiadas por los poderes públicos. Los datos para las bibliotecas de instituciones de enseñanza superior excluyen las bibliotecas dependientes de los instituciones o departamentos universitarios así como las bibliotecas en las provincias de Quebec y de Colombia británica.

Dominican Republic:

E--> The figure in column 5 shows the number of visits to reading rooms and not the number of registered borrowers.

FR-> Le chiffre de la colonne 5 se réfère au nombre de visites dans les salles de lecture et non au nombre d'emprunteurs inscrits.

ESP> La cifra de la columna 5 se refiere al número de visitas en las salas de lectura y no al número de los prestatarios inscritos.

Guadeloupe:

E--> Data are also counted with those for France.

FR-> Les données sont également comptées avec celles de la France.

ESP> Los datos se cuentan igualmente con los de Francia.

Mexico:

E--> The figures in column 5 refer to the number of visits to reading rooms and not to the number of registered borrowers.

FR-> Les chiffres de la colonne 5 se réfèrent au nombre de visites dans les salles de lecture et non au nombre d'emprunteurs inscrits.

ESP> Las cifras de la columna 5 se refieren al número de visitas en las salas de lectura y no al número de los prestatarios inscritos.

St. Pierre and Miquelon:

E--> Data are also counted with those for France.

FR-> Les données sont également comptées avec celles de la France.

ESP> Los datos se cuentan igualmente con los de Francia.

Trinidad and Tobago:

E--> Data refer to the main library of the 'University of the West Indies' at St. Augustine only.

FR-> Les données se réfèrent à la bibliothèque principale de l''University of the West Indies' à St-Augustine seulement.

ESP> Los datos se refieren a la biblioteca principal de la 'University of the West Indies' a San Augustino solamente.

Turks and Caicos Islands:

E--> The public library also serves as a national library.

FR-> La bibliothèque publique sert également de bibliothèque nationale.

ESP> La biblioteca pública desempeña al mismo tiempo la función de biblioteca nacional.

United States:

E--> The figure concerning the number of metres of shelving in school libraries (column 3) refers only to libraries financed by public authorities.

FR-> Le chiffre concernant le nombre de mètres de rayonnage dans les bibliothèques scolaires (colonne 3) se réfère seulement aux bibliothèques financées par les pouvoirs publics.

ESP> La cifra relativa al número de metros de estantes para las bibliotecas escolares (columna 3) se refiere solamente a las bibliotecas financiadas por los poderes públicos.

AMERICA, SOUTH:

French Guiana:

E--> Data are also counted with those of France.

FR-> Les données sont également comptées avec celles de la France.

ESP> Los datos se cuentan igualmente con los de Francia.

ASIA:

Hong Kong:

E--> The public library also serves as the national library.

FR-> La bibliothèque publique sert également de bibliothèque nationale.

ESP> La biblioteca pública desempeña al mismo tiempo al función de biblioteca nacional.

Japan:

E--> The figure on the number of volumes in the national library (column 2) does not include bound periodicals. The figure in column 5 for libraries of institutions of higher education refers only to main or central university libraries.

FR-> Le chiffre concernant le nombre de volumes dans la bibliothèque nationale (colonne 2) n'inclut pas les périodiques reliés. Le chiffre de la colonne 5 pour les bibliothèques d'établissements d'enseignement supérieur se réfère aux bibliothèques universitaires principales ou centrales seulement.

ESP> La cifra relativa al número de volumenes en la biblioteca nacional (columna 2) no incluye los periódicos encuadernos. La cifra de la columna 5 para las bibliotecas de instituciones de enseñanza superior se refiere a las bibliotecas universitarias principales o centrales solamente.

Korea, Republic of:

E--> Data on libraries of institutions of higher education refer only to main or central university libraries.

FR-> Les données pour les bibliothèques d'établissements d'enseignement supérieur se réfèrent aux bibliothèques universitaires principales ou centrales seulement.

ESP> Los datos relativos a las bibliotecas de instituciones de enseñanza superior se refieren a las bibliotecas universitarias solamente.

Kuwait:

E--> Data on libraries of institutions of higher education refer only to the main library of the University of Kuwait.

FR-> Les données relatives aux bibliothèques d'établissements d'enseignement supérieur se réfèrent à la bibliothèque principale de l'université de Koweit seulement.

ESP> Los datos relativos a las bibliotecas de instituciones de enseñanza superior se refieren a la biblioteca principal de la universidad de Kuweit solamente.

Malaysia:

E--> The figure in column 5 for public libraries refers only to libraries financed by public authorities.

FR-> Le chiffre de la colonne 5 pour les bibliothèques publiques se réfère seulement aux bibliothèques financées par les pouvoirs publics.

ESP> La cifra de la columna 5 para las bibliotecas públicas se refiere solamente a las bibliotecas financiadas por los poderes públicos.

Singapore:

E--> The national library also serves as a public library.

FR-> La bibliothèque nationale sert également de bibliothèque publique.

ESP> La biblioteca nacional desempeña al mismo tiempo al función de biblioteca pública.

EUROPE:

Denmark:

E--> The data on libraries of institutions of higher education do not include 400 libraries attached to university institutes or departments and 26 libraries of institutions of higher education which are not part of a university. In addition to the 26 special libraries shown in this table, there are 72 such libraries for which statistics have not been communicated.

FR-> Les données relatives aux bibliothèques d'établissements d'enseignement supérieur ne tiennent pas compte de 400 bibliothèques rattachées aux instituts ou aux départements universitaires et de 26 bibliothèques d'établissements d'enseignement supérieur ne faisant pas partie d'une université. Il y a en plus des 26 bibliothèques spécialisées, 72 autres bibliothèques spécialisées, pour lesquelles les statistiques n'ont pas été commmuniquées.

ESP> Los datos relativos a las bibliotecas de las instituciones de enseñanza superior no toman en consideración 400 bibliotecas dependientes de los institutos o departamentos universitarios y 26 bibliotecas de instituciones de enseñanza superior que no forman parte de una universidad. Además de las 26 bibliotecas especializadas, existen 72 otras bibliotecas especializadas, cuyos datos no nos han sido comunicados.

France:

E--> Data on libraries of institutions of higher education refer only to main or central university libraries. Data refer to Metropolitan France and overseas departments.

FR-> Les données relatives aux bibliothèques d'établissements d'enseignement supérieur se réfèrent seulement aux bibliothèques universitaires principales ou centrales. Les données se réfèrent à la France métropolitaine et aux départements d'Outre-Mer.

ESP> Los datos relativos a las bibliotecas de las instituciones de enseñanza superior se refieren solamente a las bibliotecas universitarias principales o centrales. Los datos se refieren a Francia metropolitana y a los departamentos de Ultramar.

Germany, Federal Republic of:

E--> Data on libraries of institutions of higher education do not include approximately 3,100 libraries attached to institutes or departments.

FR-> Les données relatives aux bibliothèques d'établissements d'enseignement supérieur excluent approximativement 3 100 bibliothèques attachées aux instituts ou aux départements.

ESP> Los datos relativos a las bibliotecas de las instituciones de enseñanza superior no incluyen approximadamente 3 100 bibliotecas de institutos y departamentos.

Gibraltar:

E--> The figure concerning the number of volumes in school libraries (column 2) refers to 6 libraries only.

FR-> Le chiffre qui concerne le nombre de volumes des bibliothèques scolaires (colonne 2) ne se réfère qu'à 6 bibliothèques.

ESP> La cifra sobre el número de volúmenes de las bibliotecas escolares (columna 2) sólo se refiere a 6 bibliotecas.

Ireland:

E--> Data relating to public libraries do not include libraries

Ireland: (Cont):
financed from private sources.

FR-> Les données relatives aux bibliothèques publiques ne comprennent pas les bibliothèques financées par des fonds privés.

ESP> Los datos relativos a las bibliotecas públicas no incluyen las bibliotecas financiadas con fondos privados.

Netherlands:

E--> Data relating to public libraries do not include libraries financed from private sources.

FR-> Les données relatives aux bibliothèques publiques ne comprennent pas les bibliothèques financées par des fonds privés.

ESP> Los datos relativos a las bibliotecas públicas no incluyen las bibliotecas financiadas con fondos privados.

Norway:

E--> Data for school libraries refer to libraries of primary schools only.

FR-> Les données pour les bibliothèques scolaires se réfèrent aux bibliothèques des écoles primaires seulement.

ESP> Los datos para las bibliotecas escolares se refieren a las bibliotecas de las escuelas primarias solamente.

Portugal:

E--> The figure concerning the number of borrowers in libraries of institutions of higher education (column 5) includes non-registered borrowers.

FR-> Le chiffre concernant le nombre d'emprunteurs aux bibliothèques d'établissements d'enseignement supérieur (colonne 5) comprend le nombre d'emprunteurs non inscrits.

ESP> La cifra relativa al número de prestatarios a las bibliotecas de instituciones de enseñanza superior (columna 5) incluye el número de los préstatarios non inscritos.

Romania:

E--> Data on libraries of institutions of higher education refer only to university libraries and do not include approximately 3,700 libraries attached to university institutes or departments.

FR-> Les données relatives aux bibliothèques d'établissements d'enseignement supérieur se réfèrent seulement aux bibliothèques universitaires, et excluent approximativement 3 700 bibliothèques attachées aux instituts ou aux départements universitaires.

ESP> Los datos relativos a las bibliotecas de las instituciones de enseñanza superior se refieren solamente a las bibliotecas universitarias, y no incluyen aproximadamente 3 700 bibliotecas de institutos y departamentos universitarios.

Spain:

E--> Data relating to public and special libraries are incomplete.

FR-> Les données relatives aux bibliothèques publiques et spécialisées sont incomplètes.

ESP> Los datos relativos a las bibliotecas públicas y especializadas son incompletos.

Switzerland:

E--> The figure on borrowers in libraries of institutions of higher education (column 5) does not include libraries of institutions of higher education which are not part of a university.

Switzerland: (Cont):

FR-> Le chiffre relatif aux emprunteurs des bibliothèque d'établissements d'enseignement supérieur (colonne 5) ne comprend pa les bibliothèques d'établissements d'enseignement supérieur ne faisant pa partie d'une université.

ESP> La cifra relativa a los prestatarios de las bibliotecas d instituciones de enseñanza superior no incluyen las bibliotecas d instituciones de enseñanza superior que no forman parte de un universidad.

United Kingdom:

E--> Data on libraries of institutions of higher education do no include Scotland.

FR-> Les données pour les bibliothèques d'établissement d'enseignement supérieur n'incluent pas l'Ecosse.

ESP> Los datos para las bibliotecas de instituciones de enseñanz superior no incluyen Escocia.

OCEANIA:

Fiji:

E--> The figure concerning the number of volumes in special librarie (column 2) refers only to 17 libraries and does not include boun periodicals.

FR-> Le chiffre relatif au nombre de volumes pour les bibliothèque spécialisées (colonne 2) se réfère à 17 bibliothèques seulement et n comprend pas les périodiques reliés.

ESP> La cifra relativa al número de volúmenes de las biblioteca especializadas (columna 2) se refiere a 17 bibliotecas solamente y n incluye los periódicos encuadernos.

New Zealand:

E--> Data on libraries of institutions of higher education refer only t university libraries.

FR-> Les données relatives aux bibliothèques d'établissement d'enseignement supérieur se réfèrent seulement aux bibliothèque universitaires.

ESP> Los datos relativos a las bibiotecas de las instituciones d enseñanza superior se refieren solamente a las bibliotecas universitarias.

Papua New Guinea:

E--> Data refer to the 'University of Technology' only.

FR-> Les données se réfèrent à l''université de technologie seulement.

ESP> Los datos se refieren a la 'universidad de tecnología solamente.

U.S.S.R.:

U.S.S.R.:

E--> The figures concerning the number of borrowers (column 5 refers to the number of visit to reading rooms and not to the number o registered borrowers for national and non-specialized libraries.

FR-> Les chiffres concernant le nombre d'emprunteurs (colonne 5) s réfèrent au nombre de visites dans les salles de lecture et non au nombr d'emprunteurs inscrits pour les bibliothèques nationales et non spécialisées.

ESP> Las cifras relativas al número de prestatarios (columna 5) s refieren al número de visitas en las salas de lectura y no al número de lo prestatarios inscritos para las bibliotecas nacionales y no especializadas.

7.2 National libraries: collections, borrowers, works loaned out, current expenditure, employees

Bibliothèques nationales: collections, emprunteurs inscrits, documents prêtés au-dehors, dépenses ordinaires, personnel

Bibliotecas nacionales: fondos, prestatarios inscritos, documentos prestados al exterior, gastos ordinarios, personal

NUMBER OF COUNTRIES AND TERRITORIES PRESENTED IN THIS TABLE: 84

NOMBRE DE PAYS ET DE TERRITOIRES PRESENTES DANS CE TABLEAU: 84

COUNTRY / PAYS / PAIS	YEAR / ANNEE / AÑO	ADMINISTRATIVE UNITS / UNITES ADMINISTRATIVES / UNIDADES ADMINISTRATIVAS	SERVICE POINTS / POINTS DE SERVICE / PUNTOS DE SERVICIO	COLLECTIONS / COLLECTIONS / FONDOS — BOOKS/LIVRES/LIBROS: METRES OF SHELVING / METRES DE RAYONNAGE / METROS DE ESTANTES	BOOKS/LIVRES/LIBROS: NUMBER OF VOLUMES (000) / NOMBRE DE VOLUMES (000) / NUMERO DE VOLUMENES (000)	MICROFORMS / MICROCOPIES / MICROCOPIAS	AUDIO-VISUAL DOCUMENTS / MATERIELS AUDIO-VISUELS / MATERIALES AUDIO-VISUALES	OTHER LIBRARY MATERIALS / AUTRES MATERIELS DE BIBLIOTHEQUE / OTROS MATERIALES DE BIBLIOTECA
		(1)	(2)	(3)	(4)	(5)	(6)	(7)
AFRICA								
ALGERIA	1980	1	1	34 100	600	1 750	6 000	...
BENIN	1980	1	8	...	32	...	...	...
BOTSWANA‡	1984	1	18	...	337	...	...	...
CAMEROON	1980	1	7	641	22	–	76	–
CONGO	1984	1	1	125	6	...	802	...
COTE D'IVOIRE	1981	1	1	450	65	–	–	–
EGYPT‡	1980	1	...	38 360	1 000	36 000	21 070	...
ETHIOPIA‡	1982	1	13	...	59	...	201	...
GAMBIA‡	1983	1	1	220	4	...	...	100
GHANA	1983	1	2	...	30	...	...	...
GUINEA	1980	1	3	615	66	...	1	...
KENYA	1981	1	1	...	19	450	3	500
LESOTHO	1984	1	7	...	36	...	...	...
MADAGASCAR‡	1983	1	1	3 843	240	...	4	1 512
NIGERIA	1980	1	8	...	251	–	...	...
SENEGAL‡	1983	1	...	...	25	...	21	...
TOGO	1980	1	...	...	6	...	...	6
ZAIRE	1980	1	1	...	146	...	...	...
ZIMBABWE	1981	1	2	...	45	3 100	1 762	31 000
AMERICA, NORTH								
CANADA‡	1984	1	...	58 958	1 005	2 216 066	63 500	...
CUBA	1983	1	1	...	1 396	...	...	...
EL SALVADOR	1980	1	1	2 442	80	–	–	–
GUATEMALA	1983	...	100	...	1 824	...	...	...
JAMAICA‡	1980	1	1	1 465	40	1 400	600	30 000
MEXICO	1983	2	2	...	1 548	415 315	20 000	...
PANAMA	1980	...	43	6 784	221	...	...	...
UNITED STATES‡	1978	3	...	...	20 799	3 448 150	9 599	50 162 930

NUMERO DE PAISES Y DE TERRITORIOS PRESENTADOS EN ESTE CUADRO: 84

ANNUAL ADDITIONS / ACQUISITIONS ANNUELLES / ADQUISICIONES ANUALES		REGISTERED BORROWERS	LOANS TO USERS	INTER-LIBRARY LOANS	CURRENT EXPENDITURE / DEPENSES ORDINAIRES / GASTOS ORDINARIOS		LIBRARY EMPLOYEES / PERSONNEL DES BIBLIOTHEQUES / PERSONAL DE LAS BIBLIOTECAS		
VOLUMES / VOLUMES / VOLUMENES	OTHER MATERIALS / AUTRES MATERIELS / OTROS MATERIALES	EMPRUNTEURS INSCRITS / PRESTATARIOS INSCRITOS	PRETS AUX USAGERS / PRESTAMOS A LOS USUARIOS	PRETS ENTRE BIBLIOTHEQUES / PRESTAMOS ENTRE BIBLIOTECAS	TOTAL (000) / TOTAL (000) / TOTAL (000)	STAFF (%) / PERSONNEL (%) / PERSONAL (%)	TOTAL / TOTAL / TOTAL	HOLDING A DIPLOMA / DIPLOME / DIPLOMADO	TRAINED ON THE JOB / FORME SUR LE TAS / FORMADO EN EJERCICIO
(8)	(9)	(10)	(11)	(12)	(13)	(14)	(15)	(16)	(17)
19 045	531	11 881	80 061	92	2 725	66	82	9	3
...	...	15 427	123 265	...	16 657	85	42	2	10
10 148	...	48 472	137 096	...	797	62	190	48	–
4 450	...	...	936	–	20 338	68	22	4	–
400	...	603	6 500	...	...	...	8	3	5
574	–	12 000	...	...	...	...	90	10	30
24 490	7 471	...	...	...	83	...	800	160	300
1 300	...	...	...	...	311	78	70	20	10
67	...	950	100	...	12 068	90	24	4	13
822	...	...	...	...	...	...	...	...	...
1 500	...	...	...	21	693	80	17	5	...
5 500	450	...	500	27	765	24	300	26	50
500	...	23	40 000	30	2	...	20	5	1
3 093	...	...	20 843	...	...	...	19	2	7
28 596	...	208	313	11	3 303	22	514	58	–
484	...	2 132	1 507	...	4 286	...	4	4	–
1 575	–	...	–	–	33 262	82	40	9	7
...	...	...	...	...	...	...	17	...	8
912	1 951	...	118	...	...	...	10	5	2
58 345	127 353	...	130 010	111 592	30 963	57	540	183	...
158 626	...	30 259	295 000	...	...	...	379	189	190
1 000	...	22 780	295 544	...	529	92	63	2	...
30 377	...	...	...	...	30 482	58	...	...	...
1 800	706	...	12 560	20	551	69	58	10	–
...	...	...	207 573	...	35 761	41	393	...	...
13 572	...	49 794	257 252	...	218 351	96	145	6	5
359 656	451 732	...	2 290 260	300 738	185 111	52	5 194	...	...

7.2 National libraries
Bibliothèques nationales
Bibliotecas nacionales

COUNTRY / PAYS / PAIS	YEAR / ANNEE / AÑO	ADMINISTRATIVE UNITS / UNITES ADMINISTRATIVES / UNIDADES ADMINISTRATIVAS	SERVICE POINTS / POINTS DE SERVICE / PUNTOS DE SERVICIO	COLLECTIONS / COLLECTIONS / FONDOS — BOOKS/LIVRES/LIBROS: METRES OF SHELVING / METRES DE RAYONNAGE / METROS DE ESTANTES	BOOKS/LIVRES/LIBROS: NUMBER OF VOLUMES (000) / NOMBRE DE VOLUMES (000) / NUMERO DE VOLUMENES (000)	MICROFORMS / MICROCOPIES / MICROCOPIAS	AUDIO-VISUAL DOCUMENTS / MATERIELS AUDIO-VISUELS / MATERIALES AUDIO-VISUALES	OTHER LIBRARY MATERIALS / AUTRES MATERIELS DE BIBLIOTHEQUE / OTROS MATERIALES DE BIBLIOTECA
		(1)	(2)	(3)	(4)	(5)	(6)	(7)
AMERICA, SOUTH								
BOLIVIA	1980	2	5	1 200	135	...	3 280	...
CHILE‡	1984	1	3	...	2 766	...	774	8 565
COLOMBIA	1980	1	...	18 000	540	...	663	...
GUYANA	1980	1	28	...	179	...	1 323	52 079
PERU	1983	1	...	19 507	2 690	24 166	10 180	36 398
URUGUAY	1983	1	1	25 356	879	410	4 413	30 288
VENEZUELA	1980	1	8	3 830	765	...	122 351	–
ASIA								
INDIA‡	1978	1	3	48 000	1 608	...	...	72 201
INDONESIA	1981	1	...	9 126	525	...	...	...
IRAN, ISLAMIC REPUBLIC OF	1980	1	1	...	160	...	–	20 000
JAPAN‡	1984	1	3	...	4 179	134 790	265 941	442 346
JORDAN	1981	1	...	500	17	1	–	2 777
KOREA, REPUBLIC OF‡	1983	2	3	...	1 611	25 988	3 412	...
MALAYSIA	1980	1	2	4 800	194	5 103	235	1 727
PAKISTAN	1983	1	2	3 025	126	...	...	
PHILIPPINES	1984	1	10	14 108	720	5 173	13 649	8 701
QATAR	1982	1	...	...	...	...	...	...
SINGAPORE‡	1984	1	18	...	2 162	55 206	44 588	20 937
SRI LANKA	1984	1	2	1 000	76	103	25	594
SYRIAN ARAB REPUBLIC	1980	1	1	1 689	85	–	–	–
THAILAND	1983	1	9	...	1 155	8 051	30 026	4 644
TURKEY	1983	1	1	...	862	9 370	2 936	103 089
EUROPE								
ALBANIA	1980	1	2	...	803	5 496	–	...
ANDORRA‡	1980	1	...	...	9	–	–	–
AUSTRIA	1983	1	1	58 177	2 435	188 568	2 386 307	1 583 179
BELGIUM	1980	1	1	95 000	3 366	15 000	38	–
BULGARIA	1983	1	...	...	1 603	209 743	...	641 844
CZECHOSLOVAKIA‡	1980	15	427	...	17 185	77 853	...	10 919 753
DENMARK	1980	1	...	75 000	2 300	63 191	4 382	3 191 522
FAEROE ISLANDS	1982	1	...	...	91	196	...	655
FINLAND	1984	1	5	71 382	2 442	128 229	21 949	1 600 000
FRANCE‡	1981	1	8	700 000	10 000	...	400 000	...
GERMAN DEMOCRATIC REPUBLIC‡	1983	2	...	...	10 290	50 398	37 815	3 581 061
GERMANY, FEDERAL REPUBLIC OF‡	1983	7	...	...	14 096	1 452 453	5 248 307	1 936 663
GREECE	1984	1	1	26 400	2 000	5 000	...	...
HUNGARY‡	1983	1	4	...	2 442	3 214 717	./.	./.
IRELAND‡	1983	1	2	14 100	790	12 200	–	20 300
ITALY‡	1983	7	7	303 205	13 281	52 344	3 890	251 001
LIECHTENSTEIN‡	1983	1	1	...	120	150	–	–
LUXEMBOURG‡	1983	1	1	19 500	640	...	640	...
MALTA	1983	1	2	6 950	355	–	–	–
MONACO	1980	1	1	3 400	130	–	–	–
NETHERLANDS	1982	1	4	44 300	1 800	76 000	20 100	5 900
NORWAY‡	1983	1	3	56 790	1 994	405 029	167 229	298 447
POLAND‡	1983	1	1	...	1 934	126 500	14 105	1 983 535
PORTUGAL	1983	3	...	35 429	3 584	2 438	5 784	...
ROMANIA	1984	2	...	...	13 964	...	...	...
SPAIN‡	1980	2	3	126 426	3 507	4 408	...	...
SWEDEN	1983	1	7	62 992	...	112 770	./.	./.
SWITZERLAND	1983	1	1	32 780	1 200	201 273	237 842	...
UNITED KINGDOM‡	1980	3	17	...	20 550	5 967 000	9 567	8 860 000
YUGOSLAVIA‡	1983	8	8	295 720	9 101	16 106	327 027	1 333 742
OCEANIA								
AUSTRALIA‡	1983	1	1	...	2 228	1 567 000	1 352 500	106 000
KIRIBATI	1984	1	18	...	22	200	...	...
NEW ZEALAND‡	1984	1	33	...	5 335	1 411 120	578 379	53 435
SOLOMON ISLANDS	1985	1	10	...	68	–	–	–
U.S.S.R.								
U.S.S.R.‡	1983	1	1	60	880	...	17 300	...

ANNUAL ADDITIONS ACQUISITIONS ANNUELLES ADQUISICIONES ANUALES		REGISTERED BORROWERS	LOANS TO USERS	INTER-LIBRARY LOANS	CURRENT EXPENDITURE DEPENSES ORDINAIRES GASTOS ORDINARIOS		LIBRARY EMPLOYEES PERSONNEL DES BIBLIOTHEQUES PERSONAL DE LAS BIBLIOTECAS		
VOLUMES VOLUMES VOLUMENES	OTHER MATERIALS AUTRES MATERIELS OTROS MATERIALES	EMPRUNTEURS INSCRITS PRESTATARIOS INSCRITOS	PRETS AUX USAGERS PRESTAMOS A LOS USUARIOS	PRETS ENTRE BIBLIOTHEQUES PRESTAMOS ENTRE BIBLIOTECAS	TOTAL (000) TOTAL (000) TOTAL (000)	STAFF (%) PERSONNEL (%) PERSONAL (%)	TOTAL TOTAL TOTAL	HOLDING A DIPLOMA DIPLOME DIPLOMADO	TRAINED ON THE JOB FORME SUR LE TAS FORMADO EN EJERCICIO
(8)	(9)	(10)	(11)	(12)	(13)	(14)	(15)	(16)	(17)
600	...	...	...	...			40	–	8
8 380	2 833	1 694	506 528	274	...	...	128	37	7
26 027	...	...	178 209	...	14 750	82	100	10	40
10 191	1 191	46 112	522 581	17	892	42	75	4	9
69 155	12 995	39 672	719 338	...	...	...	237	65	...
17 451	4 214	...	449 316	1 000	19 272	80	180	53	3
7 077	13 066	...	152 435	–	5 894	96	110	32	67
24 984	...	25 357	80 671	21	7 418	61	632	161	–
6 420	...	5 548	8 520	...	368 816	16	105	57	1
2 000	340	6 000	22 696	–	43 000	59	60	4	45
141 350	47 882		...	17 988	8 292 794	73	877	132	...
3 000	...	350		...	...		20	...	5
209 850	4 352	...	1 104 666	...	4 248 022	52	447	134	–
15 755	–	8 534	167 969	490	2 418	58	145	36	–
4 511	...	–	–	...	15 849	9	90	16	...
12 820	5 885	370 136		...	9 933	44	258	92	52
...	...	4 795	14 504	...			...		...
390 819	29 064	715 501	6 093 392	942	11 485	57	398	62	...
5 398	163			...	...	...	81		...
*2 000	–	...	46 470	...	...	...	14	1	...
28 875	23 799		–	45	19 030	53	229	62	...
34 057	1 704	23 819	...	299	136 177	34	182	23	86
22 138	...	9 003	294 086	2 148	...	...	57	32	21
2 839	–		...	...	1 300	...	1	–	1
30 646	67 685	...	53 388	8 297	43 166	...	207	166	27
14 333	...	8 099	220 000	21 918	345 952	58	265	–	38
41 630	114 039	662 994	6 070 616	...	5 435	39	785	662	123
467 631	772 725	292 822	6 083 682	150 553	167 072	35	2 548	1 288	...
113 423	38 045	...	67 272	53 054	57 589	75	357	142	...
1 789	...	2 809	11 681	29	2 000	72	10	6	...
63 500	91 200	...	419 547	20 961	18 849	69	187	81	–
60 000	4 000	...	...	...	200 000	...	1 300	300	...
169 105	76 149	56 905	1 549 925	29 696	...	...	998	474	–
542 452	254 249	72 930	1 476 086	694 236	119 512	63	1 522	...	...
270 000	...	...	...	...	26 000	...	70	17	11
36 231	95 803	...	6 556	12 141	7 435	...	457	254	58
7 000	2 100	...	...	...	600	...	55	5	7
159 355	376	...	55 682	...	6 756 169	...	1 444	...	...
2 674	–	8 930	25 375	69	563	42	7	1	...
8 500	215	19 500	91 000	132	38 230	62	28	5	8
1 130	38		...	32	86	86	26	2	2
3 015	–	1 284	21 725	31	999 760	68	8	2	2
51 700	16 300	...	60 200	...	19 244	63	214	20	45
83 001	50 501	33 000	113 833	22 603	8 867	...	179	106	73
44 707	66 882	734	16 735	12 969	154 144	...	754	...	...
41 712	6 578	128 467	12 125	...	202 476	74	397	47	102
...	...	38 000	1 436 000	...	...	...	...	...	...
56 326	180	44 661	112 937	1 238	269 120	80	507	7	...
...	5 812	3 100	113 232	8 434	47 042	57	175	49	
59 972	13 071	8 880	113 241	62 600	7 069	75	79	18	12
481 851	190 750	...	20 774	2 055 505	48 763	41	2 650	...	...
469 387	209 237	92 464	...	...	41 187 000	...	1 159	433	726
82 295	180 500	...	197 000	80 000	21 824	61	653	167	–
...	...	6 691	20 000	...	51	53	9	1	3
120 659	401 339	...	2 172 003	283	20 950	34	400	194	...
5 400	–	4 150	...	...	...	...	22	3	10
1 926 800	65 500	272 900	11 800 000	169 900	...	...	...	2 318	...

AFRICA:

Botswana:

E--> The national library also serves as a public library.

FR-> La bibliothèque nationale sert également de bibliothèque publique.

ESP> La biblioteca nacional desempeña al mismo tiempo la función de biblioteca pública.

Egypt:

E--> The figure in column 13 refers only to expenditure for acquisitions.

FR-> Le chiffre de la colonne 13 se réfère seulement aux dépenses pour les acquisitions.

ESP> La cifra de la columna 13 incluye solamente los gastos destinados a las adquisiciones.

Ethiopia:

E--> Data refer to the National Library of Addis Ababa.

FR-> Les données se réfèrent à la bibliothèque nationale d'Addis Abéba.

ESP> Los datos se refieren a las bibliotecas nacionales de Addis Abeba.

Gambia:

E--> The national library also serves as the public library.

FR-> La bibliothèque nationale remplit également la fonction de bibliothèque publique.

ESP> La biblioteca nacional tambíen desempeña la función de biblioteca pública.

Madagascar:

E--> The figure in column 13 refers only to expenditure for the employees.

FR-> Le chiffre de la colonne 13 se réfère seulement aux dépenses pour le personnel.

ESP> La cifra de la columna 13 se refiere solamente a los gastos de personal.

Senegal:

E--> The figure in column 13 does not include expenditure for employees.

FR-> Le chiffre de la colonne 13 n'inclut pas les dépenses pour le personnel.

ESP> La cifra de la columna 13 no incluye los gastos de personel.

AMERICA, NORTH:

Canada:

E--> The figure in column 6 refers only to auditory materials.

FR-> Le chiffre de la colonne 6 prend en considération seulement les matériels auditifs.

ESP> La cifra de la columna 6 toma solamente en consideración los materiales auditivos.

Jamaica:

E--> The figure in column 12 refers only to loan transactions on the international level.

FR-> Le chiffre de la colonne 12 se rapporte aux prêts internationaux seulement.

ESP> La cifra de la columna 12 se refiere a los prestamos a nivel internacional solamente.

United States:

E--> The figures in columns 5 and 9 also include books and periodicals on microforms. The figure in column 6 refers only to 2 libraries.

FR-> Les chiffres des colonnes 5 et 9 comprennent également les livres et périodiques sur microcopies. Le chiffre de la colonne 6 se réfère à 2 bibliothèques seulement.

ESP> Las cifras de las columnas 5 y 9 incluyen igualmente los libros y publicaciones periódicas en microcopias. La cifra de la columna 6 se refiere a 2 bibliotecas solamente.

AMERICA, SOUTH:

Chile:

E--> The figure in column 15 includes part-time employees but not calculated in full-time equivalent.

FR-> Le chiffre de la colonne 15 comprend le personnel employé à temps partiel non calculé en équivalent plein temps.

ESP> La cifra de la columna 15 incluye el personal de jornada parcial que no se ha calculado en equivalente de jornada completa.

ASIA:

India:

E--> The figure in column 12 refers to loan transactions on the international level only.

FR-> Le chiffre de la colonne 12 se réfère aux prêts internationaux seulement.

ESP> La cifra de la columna 12 incluye los prestamos a nivel internacional solamente.

Japan:

E--> The figure in column 4 does not include bound periodicals; the figure in column 6 refers only to gramophone records.

FR-> Le chiffre de la colonne 4 n'inclut pas les périodiques reliés; le chiffre de la colonne 6 se rapporte uniquement aux disques.

ESP> La cifra de la columna 4 no incluye los periódicos encuadernados; la cifra de la columna 6 se refiere únicamente a los discos.

Korea, Republic of:

E--> The figure in column 6 refers only to auditory materials and t audio-visual documents.

FR-> Le chiffre de la colonne 6 prend en considération seulement le matériels auditifs et les matériels audiovisuels.

ESP> La cifra de la columna 6 toma solamente en consideración lo materiales auditivos y los materiales audiovisuales.

Singapore:

E--> The national library also serves as the public library.

FR-> La bibliothèque nationale remplit également la fonction d bibliothèque publique.

ESP> La biblioteca nacional también desempeña la función d biblioteca pública.

EUROPE:

Andorra:

E--> The figure in column 13 refers only to expenditure fo acquisitions.

FR-> Le chiffre de la colonne 13 se réfère seulement aux dépense pour les acquisitions.

ESP> La cifra de la columna 13 incluye solamente los gasto destinados a las adquisiciones.

Czechoslovakia:

E--> Data on acquisitions in column 9 do not include audio-visu documents.

FR-> Les données concernant les acquisitions, colonne 9, n'inclue pas les matériels audiovisuels.

ESP> Los datos de la columna 9 relativos a las adquisiciones n incluyen los materiales audiovisuales.

France:

E--> Data on acquisitions in column 9 refer only to audio-visu documents. Data refer to Metropolitan France and overse departments.

FR-> Les données relatives aux acquisitions dans la colonne 9 n concernent que les matériels audiovisuels. Les données se réfèrent à France métropolitaine et aux départements d'Outre-Mer.

ESP> Los datos de la columna 9 relativos a las adquisiciones se refiere a los materiales audiovisuales solamente. Los datos se refieren a Franci metropolitana y a los departamentos de ultramar.

German Democratic Republic:

E--> The figure in column 6 refers only to auditory materials.

FR-> Le chiffre de la colonne 6 prend en considération seulemen les matériels auditifs.

ESP> La cifra de la columna 6 toma solamente en consideración lo materiales auditivos.

Germany, Federal Republic of:

E--> The figure in column 12 does not include inter-library loa transactions on the international level.

FR-> Le chiffre de la colonne 12 n'inclut pas les prêts entr bibliothèques au niveau international.

ESP> La cifra de la columna 12 no incluye los prestamos entr bibliotecas a nivel internacional.

Hungary:

E--> The figure in column 13 refers only to expenditure fo acquisitions.

FR-> Le chiffre de la colonne 13 se réfère seulement aux dépense pour les acquisitions.

ESP> La cifra de la columna 13 incluye solamente los gasto destinados a las adquisiciones.

Ireland:

E--> The figure in column 13 includes only expenditure for employee and for acquisitions.

FR-> Le chiffre de la colonne 13 comprend seulement les dépense pour le personnel et les acquisitions.

ESP> La cifra da la columna 13 comprende únicamente los gastos d personal y de adquisiciones.

Italy:

E--> The figure in column 6 refers only to auditory materials. Data i column 13 refer only to expenditure for acquisitions.

FR-> Le chiffre de la colonne 6 prend en considération seulement le matériels auditifs. Le chiffre de la colonne 13 se réfère seulement au dépenses pour les acquisitions.

ESP> La cifra de la columna 6 toma solamente en consideración lo materiales auditivos. La cifra de la columna 13 incluye solamente los gasto destinados a las adquisiciones.

Liechtenstein:

E--> The figure in column 12 refers to inter-library loa transactions on the international level only.

FR-> Le chiffre de la colonne 12 se réfère seulement aux prêt entre bibliothèques au niveau international.

ESP> La cifra de la columna 12 sólo se refiere a los prestamos entr bibliotecas a nivel internacional.

Luxembourg:

E--> The figure in column 12 refers to inter-library loan transaction on the international level only.

FR-> Le chiffre de la colonne 12 se réfère seulement aux prêts entr bibliothèques au niveau international.

ESP> La cifra de la columna 12 sólo se refiere a los prestamos entr bibliotecas a nivel internacional.

Norway:
E--> The figure in column 13 does not include expenditure for employees.
FR-> Le chiffre de la colonne 13 n'inclut pas les dépenses pour le personnel.
ESP> La cifra de la coluna 13 no incluye los gastos de personal.

Poland:
E--> The figure in column 13 does not include expenditure for employees.
FR-> Le chiffre de la colonne 13 n'inclut pas les dépenses pour le personnel.
ESP> La cifra de la columna 13 no incluye los gastos de personal.

Spain:
E--> The figure in column 9 refers to manuscripts and microforms only.
FR-> Le chiffre de la colonne 9 se réfère aux manuscrits et aux microcopies seulement.
ESP> La cifra de la columna 9 solo se refiere a los manuscritos y a las microcopias.

United Kingdom:
E--> The figure in column 15 refers to full-time employees only.
FR-> Le chiffre de la colonne 15 ne comprend que le personnel employé à plein temps.
ESP> La cifra de la columna 15 sólo incluye el personal de jornada completa.

Yugoslavia:
E--> The figure in column 13 shows only expenditure (in millions) for acquisitions.
FR-> Le chiffre de la colonne 13 ne tient compte que des dépenses (en millions) pour les acquisitions.

Yugoslavia: (Cont):
ESP> La cifra de la columna 13 incluye únicamente los gastos (en millones) para las adquisiciones.

OCEANIA:

Australia:
E--> The figure in column 11 refers only to works consulted in reading rooms, and the one in column 12 to inter-library loan transactions on the national level.
FR-> Le chiffre de la colonne 11 se réfère seulement au nombre d'ouvrages consultés dans les salles de lecture; celui de la colonne 12 se réfère aux prêts entre bibliothèques au niveau national.
ESP> La cifra de la columna 11 se refiere solamente a las publicaciones consideradas en las salas de lectura; la columna 12 se refiere a los prestamos entre las bibliotecas a nivel nacional.

New Zealand:
E--> The figure in column 12 does not include inter-library loan transactions on the national level.
FR-> Le chiffre de la colonne 12 n'inclut pas les prêts entre bibliothèques au niveau national.
ESP> La cifra de la columna 12 no incluye los prestamos entre bibliotecas a nivel nacional.

U.S.S.R.:

U.S.S.R.:
E--> Data in columns 10 and 11 refer to the number of visits to reading rooms and not to the number of registered borrowers.
FR-> Les données des colonnes 10 et 11 se réfèrent au nombre de visites dans les salles de lecture et non au nombre d'emprunteurs inscrits.
ESP> Los datos de las columnas 10 y 11 se refieren al número de visitas en las salas de lectura y no al número de los prestatarios inscritos.

7.3 Public libraries: collections, borrowers, works loaned out, current expenditure, employees

Bibliothèques publiques: collections, emprunteurs inscrits, documents prêtés au-dehors, dépenses ordinaires, personnel

Bibliotecas públicas: fondos, prestatarios inscritos, documentos prestados al exterior, gastos ordinarios, personal

NUMBER OF COUNTRIES AND TERRITORIES PRESENTED IN THIS TABLE: 96

NOMBRE DE PAYS ET DE TERRITOIRES PRESENTES DANS CE TABLEAU: 96

COUNTRY / PAYS / PAIS	YEAR / ANNEE / AÑO	ADMINISTRATIVE UNITS / UNITES ADMINISTRATIVES / UNIDADES ADMINISTRATIVAS	SERVICE POINTS / POINTS DE SERVICE / PUNTOS DE SERVICIO	COLLECTIONS / COLLECTIONS / FONDOS — BOOKS/LIVRES/LIBROS: METRES OF SHELVING / METRES DE RAYONNAGE / METROS DE ESTANTES	BOOKS/LIVRES/LIBROS: NUMBER OF VOLUMES (000) / NOMBRE DE VOLUMES (000) / NUMERO DE VOLUMENES (000)	MICROFORMS / MICROCOPIES / MICROCOPIAS	AUDIO-VISUAL DOCUMENTS / MATERIELS AUDIO-VISUELS / MATERIALES AUDIO-VISUALES	OTHER LIBRARY MATERIALS / AUTRES MATERIELS DE BIBLIOTHEQUE / OTROS MATERIALES DE BIBLIOTECA
		(1)	(2)	(3)	(4)	(5)	(6)	(7)
AFRICA								
BOTSWANA	1980	1	17	3 454	108	–	–	–
CHAD	1985	1	...	19	4	172	21	...
CONGO	1984	1	4	360	11	...	4	...
COTE D'IVOIRE	1981	1	...	714	25	...	...	...
EGYPT‡	1980	223	...	...	1 329	–	2 000	–
GAMBIA	1983	1	4	...	89	...	155	...
GHANA	1983	9	42	...	1 119	...	...	...
KENYA‡	1981	2	14	2 700	511	–	1 372	3 031
LESOTHO	1983	1	1	...	...	...	921	...
MADAGASCAR‡	1983	56	56	1 209	76	...	...	...
NIGERIA	1979	18	52	2 019	481	–	116	6 511
SEYCHELLES	1983	1	6	583	35	...	...	...
TUNISIA	1983	280	1 558	...	1 315	...	34	17
UGANDA	1980	1	18	...	73	–	–	90
UNITED REPUBLIC OF TANZANIA	1980	1	20	...	404	400	6	1 984
ZIMBABWE‡	1983	6	6	...	...	...	...	...
AMERICA, NORTH								
BARBADOS‡	1983	1	10	2 514	173	432	2 019	17 763
BERMUDA	1980	1	4	1 818	140	296	1 096	...
BRITISH VIRGIN ISLANDS‡	1983	1	5	498	35	12	766	25
CANADA‡	1983	1 014	3 136	...	51 812	694 607	3 194 792	760 878
CAYMAN ISLANDS	1981	1	2	362	6	3 000	–	25
CUBA	1983	296	2 713	...	3 711	...	...	...
DOMINICA	1981	1	2	250	15	–	26	–
DOMINICAN REPUBLIC‡	1980	68	...	...	...	...	...	...
GRENADA	1980	1	1	400	15	–	–	–
GUADELOUPE‡	1980	1	2	1 800	90	–	–	–
JAMAICA	1980	1	216	...	1 108	...	188	...
MEXICO‡	1983	557	557	...	3 720	135 719	4 478	...
NETHERLANDS ANTILLES	1981	1	3	295	100	300	2 500	...
PANAMA	1980	18	18	...	26	–	–	–
TRINIDAD AND TOBAGO	1983	3	18	...	246	...	...	2 080

NUMERO DE PAISES Y DE TERRITORIOS
PRESENTADOS EN ESTE CUADRO: 96

ANNUAL ADDITIONS / ACQUISITIONS ANNUELLES / ADQUISICIONES ANUALES		REGISTERED BORROWERS	LOANS TO USERS	CURRENT EXPENDITURE / DEPENSES ORDINAIRES / GASTOS ORDINARIOS		LIBRARY EMPLOYEES / PERSONNEL DES BIBLIOTHEQUES / PERSONAL DE LAS BIBLIOTECAS			POPULATION SERVED
VOLUMES / VOLUMES / VOLUMENES	OTHER MATERIALS / AUTRES MATERIELS / OTROS MATERIALES	EMPRUNTEURS INSCRITS / PRESTATARIOS INSCRITOS	PRETS AUX USAGERS / PRESTAMOS A LOS USUARIOS	TOTAL (000) / TOTAL (000) / TOTAL (000)	STAFF (%) / PERSONNEL (%) / PERSONAL (%)	TOTAL / TOTAL / TOTAL	HOLDING A DIPLOMA / DIPLOME / DIPLOMADO	TRAINED ON THE JOB / FORME SUR LE TAS / FORMADO EN EJERCICIO	POPULATION DESSERVIE / POBLACION SERVIDA
(8)	(9)	(10)	(11)	(12)	(13)	(14)	(15)	(16)	(17)
7 654	125	30 000	175 000	544	61	66	18	1	3
1 500	93	250	...	...	...	4	1	3	...
...	...	13 550	43 500	...	...	21	4	17	...
2 900	...	2 120	24 200	20	77	7	1	6	...
...	...	6 000	...	...	...	1 029	...	...	...
7 946	...	1 735	20 345	156	70	24	4	13	45
4 828	...	54 514	658 597	49 465	32	471	45	...	...
60 586	22	97 387	582 000	835	28	349	28	50	6
120	60	3 016	21 000	...	...	6	2	3	...
1 346	...	...	18 817	...	...	84	...	75	13
59 099	988	205 678	180 709	1 767	58	1 045	128	–	...
1 853	...	...	107 583	454	78	15	–	10	97
300 000	6	65 077	1 189 579	1 204	80	534	60	333	...
6 232	...	156 891	397 950	...	...	103	15	8	...
21 362	–	10 225	158 989	9 300	44	341	47	–	10
8 115	...	18 000	570 667	93	...	25	3	22	...
8 802	...	63 822	555 767	1 243	69	69	10	21	25
4 000	...	3 318	...	321	70	20	6	–	100
1 484	849	9 886	33 947	156	52	14	4	2	82
3 793 927	...	...	154 807 607	373 108	64	11 355	1 954	...	...
115	–	1 630	40 205	22	69	2	2	–	47
517 918	...	553 111	10 298 200	...	...	1 420	992	428	...
300	20	4 000	50 000	166	42	8	2	–	33
...	...	532 852	645 886	...	...	...	...	...	...
2 857	...	841	...	138	54	11	1	–	100
9 000	–	15 000	130 000	810	62	8	2	1	30
68 738	–	614 911	2 477 254	5 856	69	1 057	43	–	28
...	...	8 492 000	13 040 000	103 928	35	1 933	...	...	...
11 050	1 075	9 543	236 259	2 337	74	56	14	–	10
450	–	...	56 550	...	...	37	...	...	17
22 294	...	72 538	395 258	12 966	54	313	35	–	84

COUNTRY / PAYS / PAIS	YEAR / ANNEE / AÑO	ADMINISTRATIVE UNITS / UNITES ADMINISTRATIVES / UNIDADES ADMINISTRATIVAS	SERVICE POINTS / POINTS DE SERVICE / PUNTOS DE SERVICIO	COLLECTIONS / COLLECTIONS / FONDOS — BOOKS/LIVRES/LIBROS: METRES OF SHELVING / METRES DE RAYONNAGE / METROS DE ESTANTES	NUMBER OF VOLUMES (000) / NOMBRE DE VOLUMES (000) / NUMERO DE VOLUMENES (000)	MICROFORMS / MICROCOPIES / MICROCOPIAS	AUDIO-VISUAL DOCUMENTS / MATERIELS AUDIO-VISUELS / MATERIALES AUDIO-VISUALES	OTHER LIBRARY MATERIALS / AUTRES MATERIELS DE BIBLIOTHEQUE / OTROS MATERIALES DE BIBLIOTECA
		(1)	(2)	(3)	(4)	(5)	(6)	(7)
TURKS AND CAICOS ISLANDS‡	1983	1	3	906	26	1	6	...
UNITED STATES‡	1978	8 456	...	5 679 317	439 486	15 285 872	9 490 702	29 650 807
U.S. VIRGIN ISLANDS	1984	1	12	...	90	2 000	1 000	30 000
AMERICA, SOUTH								
BOLIVIA	1980	...	99	33 622	125	...	545	100
BRAZIL	1982	3 600	...	...	18 106	...	...	...
CHILE	1983	179	...	...	783	...	...	...
FRENCH GUIANA‡	1980	1	2	406	19	–	–	–
PERU	1983	557	...	...	1 950	...	2 250	...
SURINAME	1978	2	68	3 070	268	–	–	–
VENEZUELA	1980	23	373	31 315	977	...	5 984	4 867
ASIA								
AFGHANISTAN	1984	55	55	...	350	...	...	...
BAHRAIN	1981	1	10	...	140	...	720	...
BRUNEI DARUSSALAM	1980	1	8	2 205	97	...	...	...
CYPRUS	1981	...	103	6 201	236	...	...	...
HONG KONG‡	1983	2	34	11 329	1 693	3 934	55 191	–
INDONESIA‡	1979	30	44	4 485	460	–	1	–
IRAN, ISLAMIC REPUBLIC OF‡	1980	385	385	20 000	2 161	...	3 000	...
JAPAN	1983	1 028	2 017	...	97 172	...	...	...
JORDAN	1980	1	3	198	70	–	443	89
KOREA, REPUBLIC OF	1983	130	130	...	2 254	...	7 115	...
KUWAIT	1981	1	23	...	281	1 588	1 421	279
MALAYSIA‡	1984	20	159	...	2 785	...	1 255	7 554
PAKISTAN	1980	3	3	687	86	–	–	–
PHILIPPINES	1984	1	507	...	...	...	...	978
QATAR	1982	4	...	...	...	...	...	...
SRI LANKA‡	1980	650	684	...	...	...	...	...
THAILAND	1981	375	402	...	1 599	–	2 414	...
TURKEY	1983	...	762	...	6 045	...	133	...
EUROPE								
ALBANIA	1980	3 631	3 633	...	5 712	–	–	...
AUSTRIA	1984	2 172	2 313	...	7 022	...	...	...
BELGIUM	1980	2 351	...	...	24 140	...	...	...
BULGARIA	1983	5 664	...	...	52 977	214 093	...	1 371 788
CZECHOSLOVAKIA	1983	9 760	12 095	...	52 821	./.	./.	910 576
DENMARK	1984	249	...	...	33 408	...	...	...
FAEROE ISLANDS‡	1982	11	...	...	108	...	...	443
FINLAND	1984	461	1 785	...	29 900	...	550 000	...
FRANCE‡	1983	1 141	2 422	1 766 675	64 379	...	1 725 230	...
GERMAN DEMOCRATIC REPUBLIC‡	1983	9 003	18 813	...	46 873	...	3 731 105	...
GERMANY, FEDERAL REPUBLIC OF	1983	...	13 806	...	75 660	...	1 701 817	...
GIBRALTAR‡	1983	1	1	358	20	...	...	...
HOLY SEE	1980	1	...	...	37	...	...	...
HUNGARY‡	1983	2 069	10 080	...	46 370	1 396 402	./.	./.
IRELAND‡	1983	31	...	...	8 221	7 303	74 437	–
MALTA	1983	1	43	6 500	196	–	1 200	–
NETHERLANDS‡	1983	471	1 069	...	36 112	...	1 583 000	984 000
NORWAY‡	1983	454	1 395	...	15 966	32 108	137 260	111 346
POLAND‡	1984	9 700	23 000	...	113 900	...	...	...
PORTUGAL	1983	178	454	226 384	7 546	499	1 281	4 510
ROMANIA	1984	6 821	...	...	66 672	...	...	...
SPAIN‡	1980	1 396	1 662	279 824	11 730	25 877	16 528	...
SWEDEN	1983	404	2 096	...	42 886	161 000	1 282 000	...
UNITED KINGDOM‡	1980	160	16 244	...	131 338	834 825	3 267 000	822 765
YUGOSLAVIA‡	1983	803	1 972	543 743	27 141	36 920	107 899	226 971
OCEANIA								
COOK ISLANDS	1980	1	1	791	15	–	–	–
FIJI	1978	9	9	...	91	...	...	...
FRENCH POLYNESIA	1981	1	2	*552	17	–	–	–
GUAM	1984	8	9	7 900	188	5 852	23 752	...
NEW ZEALAND‡	1979	209	291	*239 000	6 077	9 223	60 606	...

ANNUAL ADDITIONS / ACQUISITIONS ANNUELLES / ADQUISICIONES ANUALES		REGISTERED BORROWERS	LOANS TO USERS	CURRENT EXPENDITURE / DEPENSES ORDINAIRES / GASTOS ORDINARIOS		LIBRARY EMPLOYEES / PERSONNEL DES BIBLIOTHEQUES / PERSONAL DE LAS BIBLIOTECAS			POPULATION SERVED
VOLUMES / VOLUMES / VOLUMENES	OTHER MATERIALS / AUTRES MATERIELS / OTROS MATERIALES	EMPRUNTEURS INSCRITS / PRESTATARIOS INSCRITOS	PRETS AUX USAGERS / PRESTAMOS A LOS USUARIOS	TOTAL (000) / TOTAL (000) / TOTAL (000)	STAFF (%) / PERSONNEL (%) / PERSONAL (%)	TOTAL / TOTAL / TOTAL	HOLDING A DIPLOMA / DIPLOME / DIPLOMADO	TRAINED ON THE JOB / FORME SUR LE TAS / FORMADO EN EJERCICIO	POPULATION DESSERVIE / POBLACION SERVIDA
(8)	(9)	(10)	(11)	(12)	(13)	(14)	(15)	(16)	(17)
400	...	2 684	13 127	25	65	7	1	...	...
26 007 296	2 555 540	...	986 714 576	1 467 891	54	93 335	27 900	...	...
9 000	5 000	10 000	76 000	1 247	72	82	13	3	100
599	–	1 119 618	...	9 664	99.6	110	1	54	–
...	...	2 919 155	7 728 684	...	...	10 533	...	...	
...	...	18 345	4 292 364	66 141	84	476	82	4	
1 568	–	704	14 636	66	...	6	–	–	...
...	8 000	...	2 293 846	...	...	...	6	577	...
2 100	...	53 637	769 000	376	66	52	18	34	77
87 120	...	66 250	2 374 219	13 072	44	1 102	29	1 073	19
...	...	11 331	...	12 944	91	457	71	...	...
10 000	...	50 000	29 000	323	94	70	4	7	30
9 113	...	6 422	43 503	598	78	53	1	...	67
...	...	...	144 000	...	...	115	1	114	...
311 822	20 143	1 287 186	7 590 033	42 780	52	441	51	–	68
63 320	...	2 768 100	...	291 272	...	317	...	...	...
...	2 000	...	300 000	...	...	900	20	...	75
10 645 000	...	10 947 000	188 280 000	69 756 800	56	12 336	5 502	...	...
2 550	14	1 176	12 793	42	72	26	2	8	...
...	...	...	...	5 280 031	...	1 515	...	...	...
24 264	903	...	74 671	790	64	170	8	–	60
429 588	440	811 290	5 022 808	13 152	34	672	64	11	...
2 020	–	...	70	600	83	550	13	3	...
2 050	485	194 073	...	...	...	764	180	180	51
...	...	1 355	6 185	...	...	...	...	...	...
191 500	...	197 200	...	5 498	...	952	7	239	...
168	102	30 530	...	1 055	59	238	238	–	...
309 320	...	510 700	2 142 733	1 176 428	82	2 992	135	747	44
740 434	...	...	...	...	...	7 182	33	86	95
356 954	...	813 102	...	...	...	5 011	...	...	...
...	...	1 731 256	42 059 745	...	...	...	...	...	...
2 664 511	83 114	2 224 502	34 360 750	20 490	47	3 298	2 414	884	38
2 802 611	89 862	2 765 583	95 256 845	293 176	48	13 704	368	9 893	...
...	...	...	87 344 000	...	...	...	...	...	...
5 157	...	7 183	125 670	2 952	...	22	6	–	75
2 400 000	...	2 100 000	76 000 000	553 000	52	3 536	1 326	1 586	100
4 781 160	453 800	6 094 000	107 115 000	1 594 467	60	10 996	4 072	...	88
4 110 421	...	4 817 201	97 674 903	102 700	...	7 131	5 103	2 651	100
...	...	6 174 357	196 253 123	680 656	63	8 941	...	...	...
...	...	...	45 000	10	...	4	1	3	100
270	...	...	...	...	...	3	1		...
2 642 203	273 955	2 251 283	50 553 902	136 596	...	5 052	...	...	100
458 329	20 298	651 284	14 948 000	15 746	53	1 040	206	–	100
17 000	300	60 600	...	111	85	44	1	–	70
379 000	68 000	4 160 000	179 735 000	658 625	51	6 040	2 708	...	86
583 000	6 856 000	1 198 000	17 889 000	364 836	59	2 819	...	...	100
...	...	7 397 000	148 000 000	...	...	...	...	...	...
305 076	4 630	...	5 139 352	1 018 699	47	815	104	182	...
...	...	4 507 000	52 229 000	...	...	...	...	...	...
601 650	1 724	1 307 938	6 278 955	1 226 082	70	4 648	805	3 843	61
2 356 000	84 227	...	77 144 000	1 415 435	53	5 820	2 227		100
12 667 000	1 137 386	...	637 367 000	309 373	54	27 624	...	...	100
1 177 926	14 309	...	...	395 157	...	3 905	1 377	2 528	98
1 164	–	3 330	20 154	22	64	2	1	1	...
10 469	...	33 044	313 698	...	...	35	3	6	26
1 291	...	1 360	34 817	...	...	3	–	3	38
3 098	3 745	17 202	...	873	61	37	2	3	38
529 661	2 146	1 150 822	29 366 000	16 371	62	1 349	350	59	92

COUNTRY / PAYS / PAIS	YEAR / ANNEE / AÑO	ADMINISTRATIVE UNITS / UNITES ADMINISTRATIVES / UNIDADES ADMINISTRATIVAS	SERVICE POINTS / POINTS DE SERVICE / PUNTOS DE SERVICIO	COLLECTIONS / COLLECTIONS / FONDOS — BOOKS/LIVRES/LIBROS — METRES OF SHELVING / METRES DE RAYONNAGE / METROS DE ESTANTES	NUMBER OF VOLUMES (000) / NOMBRE DE VOLUMES (000) / NUMERO DE VOLUMENES (000)	MICROFORMS / MICROCOPIES / MICROCOPIAS	AUDIO-VISUAL DOCUMENTS / MATERIELS AUDIO-VISUELS / MATERIALES AUDIO-VISUALES	OTHER LIBRARY MATERIALS / AUTRES MATERIELS DE BIBLIOTHEQUE / OTROS MATERIALES DE BIBLIOTECA
		(1)	(2)	(3)	(4)	(5)	(6)	(7)
NIUE	1983	1	5	85	6	...	...	...
NORFOLK ISLAND	1980	1	1	130	5	–	–	–
SOLOMON ISLANDS	1985	8	8	460	22	–	–	–
TOKELAU	1980	1	3	10	.2	...	–	–
U.S.S.R.								
U.S.S.R.‡	1983	109 821	...	...	2 000 100	...	...	...
BYELORUSSIAN S.S.R.	1980	6 957	...	...	87 145	...	...	...
UKRAINIAN S.S.R.	1980	26 233	...	...	370 727	...	...	...

ANNUAL ADDITIONS ACQUISITIONS ANNUELLES ADQUISICIONES ANUALES		REGISTERED BORROWERS	LOANS TO USERS	CURRENT EXPENDITURE DEPENSES ORDINAIRES GASTOS ORDINARIOS		LIBRARY EMPLOYEES PERSONNEL DES BIBLIOTHEQUES PERSONAL DE LAS BIBLIOTECAS			POPULATION SERVED
VOLUMES VOLUMES VOLUMENES	OTHER MATERIALS AUTRES MATERIELS OTROS MATERIALES	EMPRUNTEURS INSCRITS PRESTATARIOS INSCRITOS	PRETS AUX USAGERS PRESTAMOS A LOS USUARIOS	TOTAL (000) TOTAL (000) TOTAL (000)	STAFF (%) PERSONNEL (%) PERSONAL (%)	TOTAL TOTAL TOTAL	HOLDING A DIPLOMA DIPLOME DIPLOMADO	TRAINED ON THE JOB FORME SUR LE TAS FORMADO EN EJERCICIO	POPULATION DESSERVIE POBLACION SERVIDA
(8)	(9)	(10)	(11)	(12)	(13)	(14)	(15)	(16)	(17)
420	...	1 312	10 183	...	...	2	1	1	...
386	–	231	12 065	8	55	1	–	–	100
4 200	–	5 100	...	...	...	14	–	9	...
210	–	...	...	1	–	...	...	...	...
...	...	109 111 900	2 382 613	...	...	...	121 820	...	55
...	...	5 416 000	114 084 000	...	...	...	...	...	...
...	...	31 386 000	665 542 000	...	...	...	...	...	...

AFRICA:

Egypt:

E--> The figure in column 6 refers to auditory materials only.

FR-> Le chiffre de la colonne 6 prend en considération les matériels auditifs seulement.

ESP> La cifra de la columna 6 toma en consideración los materiales auditivos solamente.

Kenya:

E--> The data in column 3 refer to only 1 library. The figure in column 9 refers only to cassettes.

FR-> Les données de la colonne 3 se réfèrent à 1 bibliothèque seulement. Le chiffre de la colonne 9 se réfère seulement aux cassettes.

ESP> Los datos de la columna 3 se refieren a 1 biblioteca solamente. La cifra de la columna 9 se refiere únicamente a los cassettes.

Madagascar:

E--> The figure in column 12 refers to acquisitions only.

FR-> Le chiffre de la colonne 12 se réfère aux acquisitions seulement.

ESP> La cifra de la columna 12 se refiere a las adquisiciones solamente.

Zimbabwe:

E--> The figure in column 12 represents expenditure for employees and for acquisitions.

FR-> Le chiffre de la colonne 12 représente les dépenses pour le personnel et les acquisitions.

ESP> La cifra de la columna 12 representa los gastos de personal y de adquisiciones.

AMERICA, NORTH:

Barbados:

E--> Data do not include the library of Erdiston Teacher Training College. The public library also serves as the national library.

FR-> Les données n'incluent pas la bibliothèque d''Erdiston Teacher training College'. La bibliothèque publique remplit également la fonction de bibliothèque nationale.

ESP> Los datos no incluyen la biblioteca del 'Erdiston Teacher Training College'. La biblioteca pública también desempeña la función de biblioteca nacional.

British Virgin Islands:

E--> The public library also serves as the national library.

FR-> La bibliothèque publique remplit également la fonction de bibliothèque nationale.

ESP> La biblioteca pública también desempeña la función de biblioteca nacional.

Canada:

E--> Data refer only to libraries financed by public authorities.

FR-> Les données se réfèrent seulement aux bibliothèques financées par les pouvoirs publics.

ESP> Los datos se refieren solamente a las bibliotecas financiados por los poderes públicos.

Dominican Republic:

E--> The figure in column 10 refers to the number of visits to reading rooms and not to the number of registered borrowers.

FR-> Le chiffre de la colonne 10 se réfère au nombre de visites dans les salles de lecture et non au nombre d'emprunteurs inscrits.

ESP> La cifra de la columna 10 se refiere al número de visitas en las salas de lectura y no al número de prestatarios inscritos.

Guadeloupe:

E--> Data are also counted with those for France.

FR-> Les données sont également comptées avec celles de la France.

Guadeloupe: (Cont):

ESP> Los datos se cuentan con los de Francia.

Mexico:

E--> The figure in column 10 refers to the number of visits to reading rooms and not to the number of registered borrowers.

FR-> Le chiffre de la colonne 10 se réfère au nombre de visites dans les salles de lecture et non au nombre d'emprunteurs inscrits.

ESP> La cifra de la columna 10 se refiere al número de visitas en las salas de lectura y no al número de prestatarios inscritos.

Turks and Caicos Islands:

E--> The public library also serves as the national library.

FR-> La bibliothèque publique remplit également la fonction de bibliothèque nationale.

ESP> La biblioteca pública desempeña al mismo tiempo la función de biblioteca nacional.

United States:

E--> The figure relative to acquisitions in column 9 refers to microforms and audiovisual materials only.

FR-> Les données relatives aux acquisitions dans la colonne 9 se réfèrent aux microcopies et aux matériels audiovisuels seulement.

ESP> Los datos de la columna 9 relativos a las adquisiciones sólo se refieren a las microcopias y a los materiales audiovisuales.

AMERICA, SOUTH:

French Guiana:

E--> The figure in column 12 does not include expenditure for employees. Data are also counted with those for France.

FR-> Le chiffre de la colonne 12 n'inclut pas les dépenses pour le personnel. Les données sont également comptées avec celles de la France.

ESP> La cifra de la columna 12 no incluye los gastos de personal. Los datos se cuentan con los de Francia.

ASIA:

Hong Kong:

E--> The public library also serves as the national library.

FR-> La bibliothèque publique remplit également la fonction de biblothèque nationale.

ESP> La biblioteca pública desempeña al misco tiempo al función de biblioteca nacional.

Indonesia:

E--> The figure in column 12 refers to acquisitions only.

FR-> Le chiffre de la colonne 12 se réfère aux acquisitions seulement.

ESP> La cifra de la columna 12 sólo incluye los gastos relativos a las adquisiciones.

Iran, Islamic Republic of:

E--> The figure in column 9 refers to audiovisual materials only.

FR-> Le chiffre de la colonne 9 se réfère aux matériels audiovisuels seulement.

ESP> La cifra de la columna 9 se refiere a los materiales audiovisuales solamente.

Malaysia:

E--> The figures in columns 10 and 12 refer only to libraries financed by public authorities.

FR-> Les chiffres des colonnes 10 et 12 se réfèrent seulement aux bibliothèques financées par les pouvoirs publics.

ESP> Las cifras de las columnas 10 y 12 se refieren solamente a las bibliotecas financiadas por los poderes públicos.

Sri Lanka:

E--> The figure in column 12 represents only expenditure for employees.

Sri Lanka: (Cont):

FR-> Le chiffre de la colonne 12 représente seulement les dépenses pour le personnel.

ESP> La cifra de la columna 12 representa únicamente los gastos de personal.

EUROPE:

Faeroe Islands:

E--> The figure in column 12 represents expenditure for employees and for acquisitions.

FR-> Le chiffre de la colonne 12 représente les dépenses pour le personnel et les acquisitions.

ESP> La cifra de la columna 12 representa los gastos de personal y de adquisiciones.

France:

E--> Data refer to Metropolitan France and overseas departments. The figure in column 9 refers only to auditory materials.

FR-> Les données se réfèrent à la France métropolitaine et aux départements d'Outre-Mer. Le chiffre de la colonne 9 ne concerne que les matériels auditifs.

ESP> Los datos se refieren a Francia metropolitana y a los departamentos de Ultramar. La cifra de la columna 9 se refiere a los materiales auditivos solamente.

German Democratic Republic:

E--> The figure in column 12 represents expenditure for employees and for acquisitions.

FR-> Le chiffre de la colonne 12 représente les dépenses pour le personnel et les acquisitions.

ESP> La cifra de la columna 12 representa los gastos de personal y de adquisiciones.

Gibraltar:

E--> The figure in column 12 refers only to expenditure for acquisitions.

FR-> Le chiffre de la colonne 12 réfère aux dépenses pour les acquisitions seulement.

ESP> La cifra de la columna 12 se refiere a los gastos destinados a las adquisiciones solamente.

Hungary:

E--> The figure in column 12 represents only expenditure for acquisitions.

FR-> Le chiffre de la colonne 12 représente seulement les dépenses pour les acquisitions.

ESP> La cifra de la columna 12 representa únicamente los gastos de adquisiciones.

Ireland:

E--> Data refer only to libraries financed by public authorities. The figure in column 9 refers to microforms and audio-visual materials only.

FR-> Les données se réfèrent seulement aux bibliothèques financées par les pouvoirs publics seulement. Le chiffre de la colonne 9 se réfère aux microcopies et aux matériels audiovisuels seulement.

ESP> Los datos se refieren solamente a las bibliotecas financiadas por los poderes públicos. La cifra de la columna 9 se refiere a las microcopias y a los materiales audiovisuales solamente.

Netherlands:

E--> Data refer only to libraries financed by public authorities. The figure in column 14 includes part-time employees but not in full-time equivalent.

Netherlands: (Cont):

FR-> Les données se réfèrent seulement aux bibliothèques financées par les pouvoirs publics. Le chiffre de la colonne 14 comprend le personnel employé à temps partiel non calculé en équivalent plein temps.

ESP> Los datos se refieren solamente a las bibliotecas financiadas por los poderes públicos. La cifra de la columna 14 incluye el personal de jornada parcial, que no se ha calculado en equivalente de jornada completa.

Norway:

E--> The figure in column 9 refers to microforms only. Column 14 includes part-time employees but not in full-time equivalent.

FR-> Le chiffre de la colonne 9 se réfère aux microcopies seulement. La colonne 14 comprend le personnel employé à temps partiel non calculé en équivalent plein temps.

ESP> La cifra de la columna 9 se refiere a las microcopias solamente. La columna 14 incluye el personal de jornada parcial que no se ha calculado en equivalente de jornada completa.

Poland:

E--> The figure in column 12 does not include expenditure for employees.

FR-> Le chiffre de la colonne 12 ne comprend pas les dépenses pour le personnel.

ESP> La cifra de la columna 12 no incluye los gastos de personal.

Spain:

E--> Data are incomplete. The figure in column 9 refers to microforms and audiovisual materials only.

FR-> Les données sont incomplètes. Le chiffre de la colonne 9 se réfère aux microcopies et aux matériels audiovisuels seulement.

ESP> Los datos están incompletos. La cifra de la columna 9 se refiere a las microcopias y a los materiales audiovisuales solamente.

United Kingdom:

E--> The figure in column 6 refers to auditory materials only.

FR-> Le chiffre de la colonne 6 se rapporte aux matériels auditifs seulement.

ESP> La cifra de la columna 6 se refiere a los materiales auditivos solamente.

Yugoslavia:

E--> The figure in column 12 refers to expenditure for acquisitions.

FR-> Le chiffre de la colonne 12 se réfère aux dépenses pour les acquisitions.

ESP> La cifra de la columna 12 se refiere a los gastos relativos a las adquisiciones.

OCEANIA:

New Zealand:

E--> The figure in column 9 refers to microforms only.

FR-> Le chiffre de la colonne 9 se réfère aux microcopies seulement.

ESP> La cifra de la columna 9 se refiere a las microcopias solamente.

U.S.S.R.:

U.S.S.R.:

E--> The figure in column 11 is shown in millions.

FR-> Le chiffre de la colonne 11 est présenté en millions.

ESP> La cifra de la columna 11 está presentada en millones.

7.4 Libraries of institutions of higher education: collections, borrowers, works loaned out, current expenditure, employees

Bibliothèques d'établissements d'enseignement supérieur: collections, emprunteurs inscrits, documents prêtés au-dehors, dépenses ordinaires, personnel

Bibliotecas de instituciones de enseñanza superior: fondos, prestatarios inscritos, documentos prestados al exterior, gastos ordinarios, personal

NUMBER OF COUNTRIES AND TERRITORIES PRESENTED IN THIS TABLE: 78

NOMBRE DE PAYS ET DE TERRITOIRES PRESENTES DANS CE TABLEAU: 78

COUNTRY / PAYS / PAIS	YEAR / ANNEE / AÑO	ADMINISTRATIVE UNITS / UNITES ADMINISTRATIVES / UNIDADES ADMINISTRATIVAS	SERVICE POINTS / POINTS DE SERVICE / PUNTOS DE SERVICIO	COLLECTIONS / COLLECTIONS / FONDOS — BOOKS/LIVRES/LIBROS: METRES OF SHELVING / METRES DE RAYONNAGE / METROS DE ESTANTES	NUMBER OF VOLUMES (000) / NOMBRE DE VOLUMES (000) / NUMERO DE VOLUMENES (000)	MICROFORMS / MICROCOPIES / MICROCOPIAS	AUDIO-VISUAL DOCUMENTS / MATERIELS AUDIO-VISUELS / MATERIALES AUDIO-VISUALES	OTHER LIBRARY MATERIALS / AUTRES MATERIELS DE BIBLIOTHEQUE / OTROS MATERIALES DE BIBLIOTECA
		(1)	(2)	(3)	(4)	(5)	(6)	(7)
AFRICA								
ALGERIA‡	1981	1	...	...	5	...	...	5
BENIN‡	1982	12	12	...	49	...	...	...
BURUNDI‡	1978	4	6	2 660	92	100	3	4
CAMEROON‡	1981	1	...	...	85	...	...	...
CENTRAL AFRICAN REPUBLIC	1980	4	–	25 000	30	–	–	–
CONGO	1981	1	10	2 800	70	...	...	...
EGYPT	1979	...	163	...	2 755	...	4 000	18 000
GABON‡	1981	4	4	2 380	34	...	2	...
KENYA‡	1981	1	8	...	270	400	–	–
LIBERIA‡	1983	6	6	...	108	2 804	–	–
MADAGASCAR	1981	2	6	...	174	250	213	331
MALAWI	1981	1	4	11 368	269	1 271	1 735	...
REUNION‡	1981	1	1	1 665	30	120	...	...
RWANDA	1981	2	3	3 786	132	1 337	7 414	*2 500
SENEGAL‡	1981	1	4	7 440	227	1 070	1 071	–
SEYCHELLES	1982	2	2	...	11	...	...	...
SOMALIA	1983	1	3	905	40	–	–	15
TOGO‡	1982	1	6	1 428	50	...	–	–
ZAMBIA	1981	4	6	...	274	50 055	2 013	–
ZIMBABWE‡	1982	10	10	...	485	269	...	144
AMERICA, NORTH								
BARBADOS‡	1981	3	5	...	95	...	...	...
BERMUDA‡	1982	1	1	360	18	117	325	5
CANADA‡	1980	168	...	...	43 750	22 731 050	1 444 549	...
CAYMAN ISLANDS	1982	1	1	900	20	3 000	3 030	360
COSTA RICA	1983	1	3	6 826	227	...	19 220	3 149
CUBA	1982	56	56	...	1 438	...	...	...
GUATEMALA	1981	1	7	818	120	...	...	141 834
MEXICO‡	1981	263	263	...	2 698	...	...	...
ST. LUCIA	1981	1	1	247	24	3 120	1 665	–
TRINIDAD AND TOBAGO‡	1981	1	1	9 707	222	4 476	6 388	...
UNITED STATES‡	1979	3 122	3 122	...	519 895	224 334 739	20 929 651	118 967 622

NUMERO DE PAISES Y DE TERRITORIOS
PRESENTADOS EN ESTE CUADRO: 78

ANNUAL ADDITIONS / ACQUISITIONS ANNUELLES / ADQUISICIONES ANUALES		REGISTERED BORROWERS	LOANS TO USERS	INTER-LIBRARY LOANS	CURRENT EXPENDITURE / DEPENSES ORDINAIRES / GASTOS ORDINARIOS		LIBRARY EMPLOYEES / PERSONNEL DES BIBLIOTHEQUES / PERSONAL DE LAS BIBLIOTECAS		
VOLUMES / VOLUMES / VOLUMENES	OTHER MATERIALS / AUTRES MATERIELS / OTROS MATERIALES	EMPRUNTEURS INSCRITS / PRESTATARIOS INSCRITOS	PRETS AUX USAGERS / PRESTAMOS A LOS USUARIOS	PRETS ENTRE BIBLIOTHEQUES / PRESTAMOS ENTRE BIBLIOTECAS	TOTAL (000) / TOTAL (000) / TOTAL (000)	STAFF (%) / PERSONNEL (%) / PERSONAL (%)	TOTAL / TOTAL / TOTAL	HOLDING A DIPLOMA / DIPLOME / DIPLOMADO	TRAINED ON THE JOB / FORME SUR LE TAS / FORMADO EN EJERCICIO
(8)	(9)	(10)	(11)	(12)	(13)	(14)	(15)	(16)	(17)
3 650	...	...	32 640	...	250	...	13	1	...
...	...	...	...	...	8 000	...	50	3	...
4 000	4	1 890	45 360	118	92	...	36	7	...
1 965	...	...	...	100	...	...	40	7	–
587	...	1 500	...	–	3 750	...	12	3	–
3 561	...	12 000	...	...	28 000	10	53	9	–
...	...	...	...	...	...	...	1 476	...	...
1 751	...	788	20 826	526	34 890	48	20	8	7
14 343	...	6 700	250 800	–	69	...	127	–	24
2 628	–	3 241	121 152	11 262	346	8	65	7	16
1 343	50	14 086	...	185	84 530	82	127	3	10
...	...	4 624	40 619	856	305	51	105	13	...
1 635	...	...	...	...	...	...	12	5	...
5 236	12	1 417	24 819	–	17 030	59	50	3	–
5 988	1 250	7 103	48 881	...	72 500	...	67	18	–
1 144	...	170	1 639	...	...	...	...	...	...
152	–	1 162	27 600	55	165	...	13	–	–
3 600	–	4 904	23 145	22	34 383	68	41	7	–
7 972	–	9 465	107 409	5	625	16	106	35	5
24 459	8	7 380	304 239	3 232	...	...	99	6	25
5 100	...	3 679	75 696	...	9 858	29	40	9	–
2 645	...	500	5 994	...	128	26	5	1	2
1 725 749	...	...	20 405 339	159 325	216 309	64	7 928	1 701	...
1 100	...	175	4 200	–	11	84	3	–	3
10 687	446	17 000	558 315	...	...	...	...	70	–
69 827	...	204 568	6 896	...	...	...	314	95	131
...	...	45 000	69 792	...	272	95	58	16	16
...	...	8 427 513	9 938 439	...	191 955	14	1 818	...	...
811	–	605	16 670	...	5 410	44	10	1	1
5 948	429	2 264	83 699	11	3 644	67	91	20	...
21 608 010	29 099 451	...	201 306 592	3 088 626	1 502 157	61	58 414	...	...

7.4 Libraries of institutions of higher education
Bibliothèques d'établissements d'enseignement supérieur
Bibliotecas de instituciones de enseñanza superior

COUNTRY / PAYS / PAIS	YEAR / ANNEE / AÑO	ADMINISTRATIVE UNITS / UNITES ADMINISTRATIVES / UNIDADES ADMINISTRATIVAS	SERVICE POINTS / POINTS DE SERVICE / PUNTOS DE SERVICIO	COLLECTIONS / COLLECTIONS / FONDOS: BOOKS/LIVRES/LIBROS: METRES OF SHELVING / METRES DE RAYONNAGE / METROS DE ESTANTES	BOOKS/LIVRES/LIBROS: NUMBER OF VOLUMES (000) / NOMBRE DE VOLUMES (000) / NUMERO DE VOLUMENES (000)	MICROFORMS / MICROCOPIES / MICROCOPIAS	AUDIO-VISUAL DOCUMENTS / MATERIELS AUDIO-VISUELS / MATERIALES AUDIO-VISUALES	OTHER LIBRARY MATERIALS / AUTRES MATERIELS DE BIBLIOTHEQUE / OTROS MATERIALES DE BIBLIOTECA
		(1)	(2)	(3)	(4)	(5)	(6)	(7)
AMERICA, SOUTH								
BOLIVIA‡	1983	17	...	...	220	...	...	...
BRAZIL‡	1979	1 029	...	...	11 496	152 668	...	...
FRENCH GUIANA‡	1981	1	2	2 054	43	648	233	–
PERU‡	1982	3	7	...	58	...	...	2 342
SURINAME	1978	2	5	1 027	29	–	–	–
ASIA								
BRUNEI DARUSSALAM	1981	5	3	1 140	48	...	...	...
HONG KONG	1981	12	25	549	1 750	112 567	26 794	50
IRAN, ISLAMIC REPUBLIC OF‡	1982	198	198	33 272	3 993	...	...	...
JAPAN‡	1982	893	1 317	...	131 499	...	...	...
JORDAN‡	1983	5	12	20 000	375	4 831	2 448	–
KOREA, REPUBLIC OF‡	1981	222	...	...	11 025	...	...	
KUWAIT‡	1981	1	11	...	268	21 170	40 086	...
MALAYSIA	1982	6	18	16 925	2 040	248 206	126 151	30 506
QATAR	1981	2	5	3 330	98	648	–	–
SINGAPORE‡	1981	4	15	...	1 350	116 861	13 709	10
UNITED ARAB EMIRATES	1982	1	14	2 380	95	1 893	1 927	–
EUROPE								
ALBANIA‡	1982	2	14	701 601	606	...	2 900	...
AUSTRIA	1981	796	796	...	18 996	...	...	...
BULGARIA	1981	56	...	...	4 949	1 855	...	410 234
CZECHOSLOVAKIA	1984	1 743	1 743	...	13 617	...	...	...
DENMARK‡	1981	18	23	150 000	6 825	1 146 814	850 000	...
FINLAND	1982	26	147	...	7 423	694 998	...	...
FRANCE‡	1981	61	184	870 000	17 700	178 000	29 900	3 059 000
GERMAN DEMOCRATIC REPUBLIC	1981	29	505	...	21 341	144 248	80 141	4 587 789
GERMANY, FEDERAL REPUBLIC OF‡	1981	145	...	...	66 778	4 618 304	240 180	11 336 818
GIBRALTAR‡	1978	1	1	66	5	...	1 000	...
HOLY SEE	1981	17	19	63 905	2 675	1 099	208	5
HUNGARY‡	1982	221	221	...	10 958	3 197 090	./.	./.
ICELAND	1982	1	...	...	223	...	...	...
IRELAND	1980	7	38	109 255	3 918	...	...	...
MALTA	1981	1	2	7 100	240	420	179	400
NETHERLANDS	1981	690	1 016	500 000	17 536	947 200	788 000	729 000
NORWAY‡	1981	82	281	209 481	7 148	...	...	...
POLAND‡	1980	1 064	...	...	34 220	...	717 000	7 404 000
PORTUGAL‡	1981	219	219	75 998	2 193	6 122	...	...
ROMANIA‡	1984	43	...	...	22 106	...	...	...
SPAIN	1981	332	626	275 211	8 462	12 952	32 288	–
SWEDEN	1983	10	10	331 048	...	62 100	123 002	125 844
SWITZERLAND‡	1981	11	...	309 700	13 035	1 340 000	591 000	...
UNITED KINGDOM‡	1980	554	937	599 447	24 010	736 966	...	...
YUGOSLAVIA‡	1980	398	411	207 225	10 647	6 719	20 602	226 656
OCEANIA								
AMERICAN SAMOA	1982	1	1	350	14	1 000	540	...
NEW ZEALAND‡	1981	1	4	...	6	...	86	103
PACIFIC ISLANDS	1982	4	7	...	24	1 219	9 378	217
PAPUA NEW GUINEA‡	1982	1	1	15 204	50	110	1 083	580
SAMOA	1978	1	1	300	10	10	3	4
TONGA	1981	1	4	168	6	–	86	103

ANNUAL ADDITIONS / ACQUISITIONS ANNUELLES / ADQUISICIONES ANUALES		REGISTERED BORROWERS	LOANS TO USERS	INTER-LIBRARY LOANS	CURRENT EXPENDITURE / DEPENSES ORDINAIRES / GASTOS ORDINARIOS		LIBRARY EMPLOYEES / PERSONNEL DES BIBLIOTHEQUES / PERSONAL DE LAS BIBLIOTECAS		
VOLUMES / VOLUMES / VOLUMENES	OTHER MATERIALS / AUTRES MATERIELS / OTROS MATERIALES	EMPRUNTEURS INSCRITS / PRESTATARIOS INSCRITOS	PRETS AUX USAGERS / PRESTAMOS A LOS USUARIOS	PRETS ENTRE BIBLIOTHEQUES / PRESTAMOS ENTRE BIBLIOTECAS	TOTAL (000) / TOTAL (000) / TOTAL (000)	STAFF (%) / PERSONNEL (%) / PERSONAL (%)	TOTAL / TOTAL / TOTAL	HOLDING A DIPLOMA / DIPLOME / DIPLOMADO	TRAINED ON THE JOB / FORME SUR LE TAS / FORMADO EN EJERCICIO
(8)	(9)	(10)	(11)	(12)	(13)	(14)	(15)	(16)	(17)
3 000	...	...	750 000	...	20	...	70	1	30
1 176 253	14 876	1 115 408	7 888 019	107 478	...	...	6 160	1 725	736
2 176	617	2 382	25 422	41	795	–	21	7	...
2 888	591	...	366 742	...	40 200	...	41	1	14
1 720	...	...	4 579	...	...	...	11	8	3
...	...	828	...	...	...	...	10	...	5
80 338	22 735	63 166	1 643 646	616	40 279	66	412	73	1
199 638	...	...	1 109 616	...	449 446	...	1 196	156	...
7 282 023	...	2 205 290	14 871 039	...	99 200 960	40	11 519	...	...
31 388	450	13 000	377 500	1 100	250	...	110	10	40
820 717	...	...	...	...	9 100 385	...	1 969	462	483
33 000	...	12 000	133 962	...	1 288	55	177	28	27
142 606	293	50 453	1 631 904	4 804	18 057	32	1 007	133	62
18 409	–	3 000	17 184	...	7 328	25	38	–	–
60 128	5 063	34 004	975 965	1 643	12 537	70	262	47	20
31 246	418	3 953	36 522	...	12 894	30	101	11	5
14 748	102	64 518	750	1 333	385	...	54	...	34
334 420	...	...	675 107	...	...	...	...	485	...
259 262	12 029	119 580	2 737 756	...	3 379	31	427	297	130
...	...	292 828	5 326 660	...	...	...	...	...	...
303 000	118 036	...	1 430 590	244 268	193 796	62	864	385	–
291 511	...	...	1 222 720	112 390	57 947	48	588	260	–
350 700	64 950	...	3 576 000	239 770	106 126	6	3 178	1 233	...
436 800	214 947	209 724	4 670 162	109 194	...	...	1 905	1 032	22
2 730 796	354 803	820 142	24 013 590	1 037 570	355 276	57	6 645	...	...
18	50	385	1 190	...	1	...	...	...	...
30 495	193	14 774	78 374	...	809 263	26	75	32	43
364 211	106 942	142 614	4 391 019	43 722	129 837	...	1 336	517	231
...	...	...	25 000	...	...	...	...	...	...
116 400	...	30 860	932 680	...	5 126	62	399	137	...
5 247	87	1 950	64 429	59	124	44	21	4	14
641 500	14 500	...	3 883 000	344 900	37 093	...	1 982	898	544
286 009	...	...	...	...	35 490	...	564	381	183
1 241 000	...	...	6 352 000	2 300	475 662	...	4 936	903	...
53 622	1 355	817 990	265 395	20 786	115 473	35	197	48	344
...	...	389 000	13 322 000	...	...	...	...	...	...
376 099	...	319 740	1 172 939	8 634	837 422	52	2 713	803	1 910
180 186	132 080	...	1 242 592	...	135 220	69	787	258	...
341 800	105 936	115 318	1 494 600	...	59 824	64	661	204	...
1 665 720	90 851	...	...	380 000	36 009	56	4 009	...	...
295 692	7 618	682 643	...	...	226 476	...	1 030	861	37
500	215	2 800	...	...	...	...	5	2	3
2 399	...	507	...	...	3 921	57	2	1	1
4 097	72	1 412	970	170	95	80	9	2	6
4 737	...	2 615	49 867	252	466	40	30	9	–
4	80	150	350	...	...	...	...	...	...
2 400	...	507	1 960	...	...	...	...	...	...

AFRICA:

Algeria:

E--> Data refer only to the *Université des sciences et de la technologie d'Oran*. The figure in column 13 does not include expenditure for employees.

FR-> Les données se réfèrent seulement à l'Université des sciences et de la technologie d'Oran. Le chiffre de la colonne 13 n'inclut pas les dépenses pour le personnel.

ESP> Los datos se refieren solamente a la *Université des sciences et de la technologie d'Oran*. La cifra de la columna 13 no comprende los gastos de personal.

Benin:

E--> The figure in column 13 refers only to expenditure for acquisitions.

FR-> Le chiffre de la colonne 13 se réfère seulement aux dépenses pour les acquisitions.

ESP> La cifra de la columna 13 se refiere a los gastos relativos a las adquisiciones solamente.

Burundi:

E--> The figure in column 13 does not include expenditure for employees.

FR-> Le chiffre de la colonne 13 ne comprend pas les dépenses pour le personnel.

Burundi: (Cont):

ESP> La cifra de la columna 13 no comprende los gastos de personal.

Cameroon:

E--> The figure in column 12 refers only to loan transactions on the international level.

FR-> Le chiffre de la colonne 12 se réfère aux prêts internationaux seulement.

ESP> La cifra de la columna 12 se refiere a los prestamos internacionales solamente.

Gabon:

E--> The figure in column 12 refers only to loan transactions on the national level.

FR-> Le chiffre de la colonne 12 se réfère aux prêts nationaux seulement.

ESP> La cifra de la columna 12 se refiere a los préstamos nacionales solamente.

Kenya:

E--> Data refer to the main or central library of the University of Nairobi. The figure in column 13 refers only to expenditure for acquisitions.

FR-> Les données se réfèrent à la bibliothèque principale ou centrale de l'université de Nairobi. Le chiffre de la colonne 13 se réfère seulement aux dépenses pour les acquisitions.

ESP> Los datos se refieren a la biblioteca principal o central de la universidad de Nairobi. La cifra de la columna 13 se refiere a los gastos relativos a las adquisiciones solamente.

Liberia:

E--> Data refer only to main or central university libraries.

FR-> Les données se réfèrent seulement aux bibliothèques universitaires principales ou centrales.

ESP> Los datos se refieren solamente a las bibliotecas universitarias principales o centrales.

Reunion:

E--> Data are also counted with those for France.

FR-> Les données sont également comptées avec celles de la France.

ESP> Los datos se cuentan con los de Francia.

Senegal:

E--> Data refer to the main or central library of the University of Dakar. The figure in column 13 does not include expenditure for employees.

FR-> Les données se réfèrent à la bibliothèque principale ou centrale de l'université de Dakar. Le chiffre de la colonne 13 n'inclut pas les dépenses pour le personnel.

ESP> Los datos se refieren a la biblioteca principal o central de la universidad de Dakar. La cifra de la columna 13 no comprende los gastos de personal.

Togo:

E--> Data refer to the main or central university library.

FR-> Les données se réfèrent à la bibliothèque principale ou centrale.

ESP> Los datos se refieren a la biblioteca principal o central.

Zimbabwe:

E--> The figures in columns 7 and 9 refer to main or central university libraries only.

FR-> Les chiffres des colonnes 7 et 9 se réfèrent aux bibliothèques universitaires principales ou centrales seulement.

ESP> Las cifras de las columnas 7 y 9 se refieren a las bibliotecas universitarias principales o centrales solamente.

AMERICA, NORTH:

Barbados:

E--> Data do not include the library of Erdiston Teacher Training College.

FR-> Les données ne comprennent pas la bibliothèque d''Erdiston Teacher Training College'.

ESP> Los datos no incluyen la biblioteca del *Erdiston Teacher Training College.*

Bermuda:

E--> Data refer to the library of Bermuda College.

FR-> Les données se réfèrent à la bibliothèque de *Bermuda College.*

ESP> Los datos se refieren a la biblioteca de *Bermuda College.*

Canada:

E--> Data include neither libraries attached to university institutes or departments nor libraries in the provinces of Quebec and British Colombia.

FR-> Les données ne comprennent ni les bibliothèques relevant d'Instituts ou de départements universitaires ni les bibliothèques des provinces du Québec et de la Colombie britannique.

ESP> Los datos excluyen las bibliotecas dependientes de los instituciones o departamentos universitarios así como las bibliotecas en las provincias de Quebec y de Colombia británica.

Mexico:

E--> The figure in column 10 refers to the number of visits to reading rooms and not to the number of registered borrowers.

FR-> Le chiffre de la colonne 10 se réfère au nombre de visites dans les salles de lecture et non au nombre d'emprunteurs inscrits.

ESP> La cifra de la columna 10 se refiere al número de visitas en las salas de lectura y no al número de los prestatarios inscritos.

Trinidad and Tobago:

E--> Data refer to the main library of the University of the West Indies at St. Augustine.

FR-> Les données se réfèrent à la bibliothèque principale de l'*University of the West Indies* à St-Augustine.

ESP> Los datos se refieren a la biblioteca principal de la *University of the West Indies* a San Augustino. United States:

E--> The figure in column 12 refers only to loan transactions on the national level.

FR-> Le chiffre de la colonne 12 se réfère aux prêts nationaux seulement.

ESP> La cifra de la columna 12 se refiere a los préstamos nacionales solamente.

AMERICA, SOUTH:

Bolivia:

E--> The figure in column 13 does not include expenditure fo employees.

FR-> Le chiffre de la colonne 13 ne comprend pas les dépenses pou le personnel.

ESP> La cifra de la columna 13 no comprende los gastos de personal.

Brazil:

E--> Data on acquisitions in column 9 refer to microforms and manuscripts only. Column 12 refers only to loan transactions on the national level.

FR-> Les données de la colonne 9 concernant les acquisitions se réfèrent aux microcopies et aux manuscrits seulement. La colonne 12 se réfère aux prêts nationaux seulement.

ESP> Los datos de la columna 9 relativos a las adquisiciones se refieren a las microcopias y a los manuscritos solamente. La columna 12 se refiere a los préstamos nacionales solamente.

French Guiana:

E--> Data are also counted with those for France.

FR-> Les données sont également comptées avec celles de la France.

ESP> Los datos se cuentan igualmente con los de Francia.

Peru:

E--> The figures in columns 7, 9 and 13 refer only to the Universit of Santa Maria. The figure in column 13 includes only expenditure fo employees and for acquisitions.

FR-> Les chiffres des colonnes 7, 9 et 13 se réfèrent seulement à l'université de Santa Maria. Le chiffre de la colonne 13 compren seulement les dépenses pour le personnel et les acquisitions.

ESP> Las cifras de las columnas 7, 9 y 13 se refieren solamente a la universidad de Santa Maria. La cifra de la columna 13 comprend únicamente los gastos de personal y de adquisiciones.

ASIA:

Iran, Islamic Republic of:

E--> The figure in column 13 refers only to expenditure fo acquisitions.

FR-> Le chiffre de la colonne 13 se réfère seulement aux dépense pour les acquisitions.

ESP> La cifra de la columna 13 se refiere a los gastos relativos a la adquisiciones solamente.

Japan:

E--> The figure in column 10 refers only to main or central universit libraries.

FR-> Le chiffre de la colonne 10 se réfère aux bibliothèque universitaires principales ou centrales seulement.

ESP> La cifra de la columna 10 se refiere a las bibliotecas universitaria principales o centrales solamente.

Jordan:

E--> The figure in column 13 refers only to expenditure fo acquisitions.

FR-> Le chiffre de la colonne 13 se réfère seulement aux dépense pour les acquisitions.

ESP> La cifra de la columna 13 se refiere a los gastos relativos a la adquisiciones solamente.

Korea, Republic of:

E--> Data refer only to the main or central university libraries.

FR-> Les données se réfèrent aux bibliothèques universitaire principales ou centrales seulement.

ESP> Los datos se refieren a las bibliotecas universitarias principales centrales solamente.

Kuwait:

E--> Data refer to the main library of the University of Kuwait.

FR-> Les données se réfèrent à la bibliothèque principale d l'université de Koweit.

ESP> Los datos se refieren a la biblioteca principal de la universidad d Kuweit.

Singapore:

E--> The figures in columns 13 and 14 refer to main or centr university libraries only.

FR-> Les chiffres des colonnes 13 et 14 se réfèrent au bibliothèques universitaires principales ou centrales seulement.

ESP> Las cifras de las columnas 13 y 14 se refieren a las bibliotec

Singapore: (Cont):
universitarias principales o centrales solamente.

EUROPE:

Albania:

E--> Column 9 concerns only microforms. Loans to users in column 11 concern only cassettes. Column 13 refers only to expenditure for acquisitions.

FR-> Le chiffre de la colonne 9 concerne les microcopies seulement. Les prêts aux usagers de la colonne 11 concernent les cassettes seulement. La colonne 13 se réfère seulement aux dépenses pour les acquisitions.

ESP> La cifra de la columna 9 se refiere a las microcopias solamente. Los préstamos a los usarios en la columna 11 se refieren a las cassettes solamente. La columna 13 se refiere a los gastos relativos a las adquisiciones solamente.

Denmark:

E--> Data do not include 400 libraries attached to university institutes or departments and 26 libraries of institutions of higher education which are not part of a university.

FR-> Les données n'incluent pas 400 bibliothèques d'instituts ou de départements universitaires ainsi que 26 bibliothèques d'établissements d'enseignement supérieur ne faisant pas partie d'une université.

ESP> Los datos no incluyen 400 bibliotecas de institutos o de departamentos universitarios y 26 bibliotecas de instituciones de enseñanza superior que no pertenecen a una universidad.

France:

E--> Data refer only to main or central university libraries. Data refer to Metropolitan France and overseas departments.

FR-> Les données se réfèrent seulement aux bibliothèques universitaires principales ou centrales. Les données se réfèrent à la France métropolitaine et aux départements d'Outre-Mer.

ESP> Los datos se refieren solamente a las bibliotecas universitarias principales o centrales. Los datos se refieren a Francia metropolitana y a los departamentos de Ultramar.

Germany, Federal Republic of:

E--> Data do not include approximately 3,100 libraries attached to university institutes or departments. Column 12 refers only to loan transactions on the national level. Column 13 includes only expenditure for employees and for aqcuisitions.

FR-> Les données excluent approximativement 3 100 bibliothèques attachées aux instituts ou aux départements universitaires. La colonne 12 se réfère aux prêts nationaux seulement. La colonne 13 comprend seulement les dépenses pour le personnel et les acquisitions.

ESP> Los datos no incluyen aproximadamente 3 100 bibliotecas de institutos y departamentos universitarios. La columna 12 se refiere a los préstamos nacionales solamente. La columna 13 se refiere únicamente a los gastos de personal y de adquisiciones.

Gibraltar:

E--> The figure in column 13 refers only to expenditure for acquisitions.

FR-> Le chiffre de la colonne 13 se réfère seulement aux dépenses pour les acquisitions.

ESP> La cifra de la columna 13 se refiere a los gastos relativos a las adquisiciones solamente.

Hungary:

E--> The figure in column 13 refers only to expenditure for acquisitions.

FR-> Le chiffre de la colonne 13 se réfère seulement aux dépenses pour les acquisitions.

ESP> La cifra de la columna 13 se refiere a los gastos relativos a las adquisiciones solamente.

Norway:

E--> The figure in column 13 refers only to expenditure for acquisitions.

FR-> Le chiffre de la colonne 13 se réfère seulement aux dépenses pour les acquisitions.

ESP> La cifra de la columna 13 se refiere a los gastos relativos a las adquisiciones solamente.

Poland:

E--> The figure in column 6 includes microfilms and microfiches. Column 12 refers only to loan transactions on an international level. Column 13 refers only to expenditure for acquisitions.

Poland: (Cont):

FR-> Les données de la colonne 6 incluent les microfilms et les microfiches. La colonne 12 se réfère aux prêts internationaux seulement. La colonne 13 se réfère seulement aux dépenses pour les acquisitions.

ESP> Los datos de la columna 6 incluyen los microfilmos y las microfichas. La columna 12 se refiere a los préstamos internacionales solamente. La columna 13 se refiere a los gastos relativos a las adquisiciones solamente.

Portugal:

E--> The figure in column 9 refers only to manuscripts and microforms. Column 10 includes the number of non-registered borrowers. Column 11 includes books consulted in reading rooms. Column 12 refers only to loan transactions on the national level.

FR-> Le chiffre de la colonne 9 se réfère aux manuscrits et aux microcopies seulement. La colonne 10 comprend le nombre d'emprunteurs non-inscrits. La colonne 11 comprend les livres consultés dans les salles de lecture. La colonne 12 se réfère aux prêts nationaux seulement.

ESP> La cifra de la columna 9 se refiere a los manuscritos y las microcopias solamente. La columna 10 incluye el número de los prestatarios non-inscritos. La columna 11 incluye los libros consultados dentro de las salas de lectura. La columna 12 incluye los préstamos nacionales solamente.

Romania:

E--> Data do not include approximately 3,700 libraries attached to university institutes or departments.

FR-> Les données excluent approximativement 3 700 bibliothèques attachées aux instituts ou aux départements universitaires.

ESP> Los datos no incluyen aproximadamente 3 700 bibliotecas de institutos y departmentos universitarios.

Switzerland:

E--> The figure in column 10 does not include borrowers in libraries of institutions of higher education which are not part of a university.

FR-> Le chiffre de la colonne 10 ne comprend pas les emprunteurs aux bibliothèques d'établissements d'enseignement supérieur ne faisant pas partie d'une université.

ESP> La cifra de la columna 10 no incluye los prestatarios en las bibliotecas de instituciones de enseñanza superior que no forman parte de una universidad.

United Kingdom:

E--> Not including Scotland. The figure in column 12 refers only to loan transactions on the national level.

FR-> On ne tient pas compte des données pour l'Ecosse. Le chiffre de la colonne 12 se réfère aux prêts nationaux seulement.

ESP> No se toma en consideración los datos por Escocia. La cifra de la columna 12 se refiere a los préstamos nacionales solamente.

Yugoslavia:

E--> Column 6 refers to auditory materials only. Column 9 concerns only microforms. The data in column 13 refer to expenditure for acquisitions (in millions). Columns 15, 16 and 17 do not include part-time staff.

FR-> La colonne 6 se rapporte aux matériels auditifs seulement. la colonne 9 ne tient compte que des microcopies. Les données de la colonne 13 se réfèrent aux dépenses pour les acquisitions (en millions). Les colonnes 15, 16 et 17 n'incluent pas le personnel employé à temps partiel.

ESP> Los datos de la columna 6 se refieren solamente a los materiales auditivos. En la columna 9 sólo se toman en consideración las microcopias. La cifra de la columna 13 se refiere a los gastos relativos a las adquisiciones (en millones). Las columnas 15, 16 y 17 no incluyen el personal de jornada parcial.

OCEANIA:

New Zealand:

E--> Data refer only to main or central university libraries.

FR-> Les données se réfèrent seulement aux bibliothèques universitaires principales ou centrales.

ESP> Los datos se refieren solamente a las bibliotecas universitarias principales o centrales.

Papua New Guinea:

E--> Data refer to the University of Technology only.

FR-> Les données se réfèrent à l'université de technologie seulement.

ESP> Los datos se refieren a la universidad de tecnología solamente.

7.5 School libraries: collections, borrowers, works loaned out, current expenditure, employees

Bibliothèques scolaires: collections, emprunteurs inscrits, documents prêtés au-dehors, dépenses ordinaires, personnel

Bibliotecas escolares: fondos, prestatarios inscritos, documentos prestados al exterior, gastos ordinarios, personal

NUMBER OF COUNTRIES AND TERRORIES PRESENTED IN THIS TABLE: 39

NOMBRE DE PAYS ET DE TERRITOIRES PRESENTES DANS CE TABLEAU: 39

COUNTRY / PAYS / PAIS	YEAR / ANNEE / AÑO	ADMINISTRATIVE UNITS / UNITES ADMINISTRATIVES / UNIDADES ADMINISTRATIVAS	SERVICE POINTS / POINTS DE SERVICE / PUNTOS DE SERVICIO	COLLECTIONS / COLLECTIONS / FONDOS — BOOKS/LIVRES/LIBROS: METRES OF SHELVING / METRES DE RAYONNAGE / METROS DE ESTANTES	BOOKS/LIVRES/LIBROS: NUMBER OF VOLUMES (000) / NOMBRE DE VOLUMES (000) / NUMERO DE VOLUMENES (000)	MICROFORMS / MICROCOPIES / MICROCOPIAS	AUDIO-VISUAL DOCUMENTS / MATERIELS AUDIO-VISUELS / MATERIALES AUDIO-VISUALES	OTHER LIBRARY MATERIALS / AUTRES MATERIELS DE BIBLIOTHEQUE / OTROS MATERIALES DE BIBLIOTECA
		(1)	(2)	(3)	(4)	(5)	(6)	(7)
AFRICA								
GABON‡	1981	5	5	...	17	–	8	2
GAMBIA‡	1978	129	129	700	...	...	...	...
MADAGASCAR‡	1981	3	5	36 266	19	...	714	–
MAURITIUS‡	1984	27	27	...	149	...	...	...
SEYCHELLES	1982	11	11	...	11	...	...	...
ZAMBIA‡	1983	1	1	...	9	...	1 430	140
ZIMBABWE	1980	100	...	...	261	...	...	...
AMERICA, NORTH								
BERMUDA	1982	22	...	1 294	52	...	...	...
BRITISH VIRGIN ISLANDS	1982	2	2	160	7	...	22	...
CANADA‡	1981	7 982	7 982	...	47 606	919 862	5 084 967	5 044 575
CAYMAN ISLANDS	1981	1	1	298	10	–	107	–
CUBA	1982	2 432	2 432	...	11 508	...	...	...
MEXICO‡	1981	1 880	1 880	...	5 403	...	...	...
TURKS AND CAICOS ISLANDS	1982	1	17	213	6			...
UNITED STATES‡	1978	85 096	...	24 646 328	591 261	10 254 750	83 493 940	32 800 006
AMERICA, SOUTH								
BRAZIL‡	1979	9 479	...	...	14 495	8 803	...	...
CHILE	1981	...	551	...	1 458	...	...	...
PERU	1981	292	311	...	516	...	7 040	...
SURINAME	1978	3	49	1 425	60	–	–	–
VENEZUELA	1978	46	...	...	105	...	144	1 820
ASIA								
BRUNEI DARUSSALAM	1981	2	15	2 822	191	24	139	20
HONG KONG	1981	191	191	...	1 422	...	...	...
JAPAN‡	1981	40 146	40 146	...	201 805	...	...	...
KOREA, REPUBLIC OF	1981	3 184	...	...	11 912	...	...	...
QATAR	1982	122	...	5 628	214	...	...	...
SINGAPORE	1983	405	...	...	4 087	...	...	...

NUMERO DE PAISES Y TERRITORIOS
PRESENTADOS EN ESTE CUADRO: 39

ANNUAL ADDITIONS / ACQUISITIONS ANNUELLES / ADQUISICIONES ANUALES		REGISTERED BORROWERS	LOANS TO USERS	CURRENT EXPENDITURE / DEPENSES ORDINAIRES / GASTOS ORDINARIOS		LIBRARY EMPLOYEES / PERSONNEL DES BIBLIOTHEQUES / PERSONAL DE LAS BIBLIOTECAS			POPULATION SERVED
VOLUMES / VOLUMES / VOLUMENES	OTHER MATERIALS / AUTRES MATERIELS / OTROS MATERIALES	EMPRUNTEURS INSCRITS / PRESTATARIOS INSCRITOS	PRETS AUX USAGERS / PRESTAMOS A LOS USUARIOS	TOTAL (000) / TOTAL (000) / TOTAL (000)	STAFF (%) / PERSONNEL (%) / PERSONAL (%)	TOTAL / TOTAL / TOTAL	HOLDING A DIPLOMA / DIPLOME / DIPLOMADO	TRAINED ON THE JOB / FORME SUR LE TAS / FORMADO EN EJERCICIO	POPULATION DESSERVIE / POBLACION SERVIDA
(8)	(9)	(10)	(11)	(12)	(13)	(14)	(15)	(16)	(17)
630	5	2 846	...	1 220	...	6	...	2	28
500	...	35 196	5 525	9	...	...	2	100	100
2 397	–	2 349	8 121	600	...	29	–	29	...
8 843	–	21 907	255 229	300	...	30	1	7	...
...	...	3 621	47 696	317	50	11	–	11	...
210	–	1 305	138 640	25	...	4	2	1	...
78 300	...	27 423	...	...	...	40	5	35	...
...	...	6 862	...	...	...	6	3	3	88
50	...	720	11 000	14	67	1	–	1	...
5 306 732	...	...	...	30 616	...	4 633	425	...	...
862	–	800	3 358	...	...	2	1	–	...
113 859	...	...	5 857 300	...	...	3 015	227	2 129	...
...	...	15 932 421	15 224 489	111 950	30	3 786	...	...	...
...	...	...	...	...	...	5	...	...	...
32 717 838	3 910 754	...	18 828 123	1 472 218	71	159 851	38 328	68 036	93
1 630 162	3 804	3 628 273	7 999 232	...	...	14 883	817	3 579	...
...	...	...	2 516 497	...	...	758	14	322	...
102 500	...	447 000	894 000	...	...	316	41	–	...
5 039	...	20 447	330 844	200	72	62	8	54	74
8 187	30	...	...	2 166	...	92	–	92	...
17 138	...	13 099	20 571	644	68	64	1	18	...
...	...	216 440	962 920	...	...	191	...	...	...
...	...	...	...	17 909 343	...	...	...	...	...
895 274	...	...	31 623 895	2 424 600	...	1 852	...	749	...
35 169	...	13 608	...	...	...	127	30	40	...
427 433	...	471 072	5 012 030	6 005	...	18	7	2	...

COUNTRY / PAYS / PAIS	YEAR / ANNEE / AÑO	ADMINISTRATIVE UNITS / UNITES ADMINISTRATIVES / UNIDADES ADMINISTRATIVAS	SERVICE POINTS / POINTS DE SERVICE / PUNTOS DE SERVICIO	COLLECTIONS / COLLECTIONS / FONDOS — BOOKS/LIVRES/LIBROS: METRES OF SHELVING / METRES DE RAYONNAGE / METROS DE ESTANTES	NUMBER OF VOLUMES (000) / NOMBRE DE VOLUMES (000) / NUMERO DE VOLUMENES (000)	MICROFORMS / MICROCOPIES / MICROCOPIAS	AUDIO-VISUAL DOCUMENTS / MATERIELS AUDIO-VISUELS / MATERIALES AUDIO-VISUALES	OTHER LIBRARY MATERIALS / AUTRES MATERIELS DE BIBLIOTHEQUE / OTROS MATERIALES DE BIBLIOTECA
		(1)	(2)	(3)	(4)	(5)	(6)	(7)
EUROPE								
BULGARIA‡	1981	3 599	...	...	14 723	620	...	98 341
GIBRALTAR‡	1978	10	12	913	28	...	–	...
HUNGARY‡	1981	4 139	4 139	...	18 153	...	...	...
MALTA	1981	35	35	2 180	127	–	–	–
MONACO	1981	4	7	290	12	...	96	1 606
NORWAY‡	1981	3 757	3 757	...	6 221	...	...	...
ROMANIA	1984	10 832	...	...	55 431	...	...	...
SAN MARINO	1983	5	17	553	22	...	2 056	635
SPAIN	1981	626	626	53 352	2 268	3 949	45 925	...
OCEANIA								
AMERICAN SAMOA	1982	1	26	1 900	76	...	5 000	...
GUAM	1981	46	46	...	283	392	86 178	3 359
NORFOLK ISLAND‡	1982	1	1	...	10	...	502	...
TONGA	1978	10	–	81	28	–	...	–

ANNUAL ADDITIONS / ACQUISITIONS ANNUELLES / ADQUISICIONES ANUALES		REGISTERED BORROWERS	LOANS TO USERS	CURRENT EXPENDITURE / DEPENSES ORDINAIRES / GASTOS ORDINARIOS		LIBRARY EMPLOYEES / PERSONNEL DES BIBLIOTHEQUES / PERSONAL DE LAS BIBLIOTECAS			POPULATION SERVED
VOLUMES / VOLUMES / VOLUMENES	OTHER MATERIALS / AUTRES MATERIELS / OTROS MATERIALES	EMPRUNTEURS INSCRITS / PRESTATARIOS INSCRITOS	PRETS AUX USAGERS / PRESTAMOS A LOS USUARIOS	TOTAL (000) / TOTAL (000) / TOTAL (000)	STAFF (%) / PERSONNEL (%) / PERSONAL (%)	TOTAL / TOTAL / TOTAL	HOLDING A DIPLOMA / DIPLOME / DIPLOMADO	TRAINED ON THE JOB / FORME SUR LE TAS / FORMADO EN EJERCICIO	POPULATION DESSERVIE / POBLACION SERVIDA
(8)	(9)	(10)	(11)	(12)	(13)	(14)	(15)	(16)	(17)
863 968	6 458	796 735	8 489 216	2 708	46	699	446	253	...
4 208	...	3 173	*64 580	5	...	6	1	5	...
1 180 973	...	919 837	6 457 945	44 149	...	...	...	...	...
20 789	–	17 859	107 562	24	38	23	–	18	41
760	78	1 149	...	538	79	5	–	4	...
326 917	...	...	5 756 161	15 558	...	...	...	...	...
...	...	3 184 000	2 506 000	...	...	...	...	...	...
1 968	202	3 300	...	15 050	...	6	–	6	...
130 054	...	211 768	271 233	87 837	32	1 752	154	1 598	...
6 000	13 000	8 000	84 000	140	87	25	–	19	30
...	...	29 921	...	...	...	58	21	10	100
380	24	325	14 650	762	...	1	–	1	...
...	–	6 200	...	...	...	20	3	10	...

AFRICA:

Gabon:

E--> The figure in column 12 does not include expenditure for employees.

FR-> Le chiffre de la colonne 12 n'inclut pas les dépenses pour le personnel.

ESP> La cifra de la columna 12 no incluye los gastos de personal.

Gambia:

E--> The figure in column 12 refers only to expenditure for acquisitions.

FR-> Le chiffre de la colonne 12 se réfère aux dépenses pour les acquisitions seulement.

ESP> La cifra de la columna 12 se refiere a los gastos destinados a las adquisiciones solamente.

Madagascar:

E--> The figure in column 12 does not include expenditure for employees.

FR-> Le chiffre de la colonne 12 n'inclut pas les dépenses pour le personnel.

ESP> La cifra de la columna 12 no incluye los gastos de personal.

Mauritius:

E--> The figure in column 12 refers only to expenditure for acquisitions.

FR-> Le chiffre de la colonne 12 se réfère aux dépenses pour les acquisitions seulement.

ESP> La cifra de la columna 12 se refiere a los gastos de las adquisiciones solamente.

Zambia:

E--> The figure in column 12 refers only to expenditure for acquisitions.

FR-> Le chiffre de la colonne 12 se réfère aux dépenses pour les acquisitions seulement.

ESP> La cifra de la columna 12 se refiere a los gastos destinados a las adquisiciones solamente.

AMERICA, NORTH:

Canada:

E--> The figure in column 12 refers only to expenditure for acquisitions.

FR-> Le chiffre de la colonne 12 se réfère aux dépenses pour les acquisitions seulement.

ESP> La cifra de la columna 12 se refiere a los gastos destinados a las adquisiciones solamente.

Mexico:

E--> The figure in column 10 refers to the number of visits to reading rooms and not to the number of registered borrowers.

FR-> Le chiffre de la colonne 10 se réfère au nombre de visites dans les salles de lecture et non au nombre d'emprunteurs inscrits.

ESP> La cifra de la columna 10 se refiere al número de visitas en las salas de lectura y no al número de los prestatarios inscritos.

United States:

E--> Data in columns 3 and 11 refer only to libraries financed by public authorities.

United States: (Cont):

FR-> Les données des colonnes 3 et 11 se réfèrent seulement aux bibliothèques financées par les pouvoirs publics.

ESP> Los datos de las columnas 3 y 11 se refieren solamente a las bibliotecas financiadas por los poderes públicos.

AMERICA, SOUTH:

Brazil:

E--> The figure in column 9 refers only to manuscripts and microforms.

FR-> Le chiffre de la colonne 9 se réfère aux manuscrits et aux microcopies seulement.

ESP> La cifra de la columna 9 se refiere a los manuscritos y a las microcopias solamente.

ASIA:

Japan:

E--> The figure in column 12 refers only to expenditure for acquisitions.

FR-> Le chiffre de la colonne 12 se réfère aux dépenses pour les acquisitions seulement.

ESP> La cifra de la columna 12 se refiere a los gastos destinados a las adquisiciones solamente.

EUROPE:

Bulgaria:

E--> Data in columns 14, 15 and 16 include library personnel of post-secondary schools.

FR-> Les données des colonnes 14, 15 et 16 incluent le personnel des bibliothèques des établissements post-secondaires.

ESP> Los datos de las columnas 14, 15 y 16 incluyen el personal de las bibliotecas de los establecimientos post-secundarios.

Gibraltar:

E--> Column 4 refers to 6 libraries only. The figure in column 12 does not include expenditure for employees.

FR-> Le chiffre de la colonne 4 se réfère à 6 bibliothèques seulement. La colonne 12 n'inclut pas les dépenses pour le personnel.

ESP> La cifra de la columna 4 se refiere a 6 bibliotecas solamente. La cifra de la columna 12 no incluye los gastos de personal.

Hungary:

E--> The figure in column 12 refers only to expenditure for acquisitions.

FR-> Le chiffre de la colonne 12 se réfère aux dépenses pour les acquisitions seulement.

ESP> La cifra de la columna 12 se refiere a los gastos destinados a las adquisiciones solamente.

Norway:

E--> Data refer to libraries of primary schools only. The figure in column 12 refers only to expenditure for acquisitions.

FR-> Les données se réfèrent aux bibliothèques des écoles primaires seulement. Le chiffre de la colonne 12 se réfère seulement aux dépenses pour les acquisitions.

ESP> Los datos se refieren a las bibliotecas de las escuelas primarias solamente. La cifra de la columna 12 incluye solamente los gastos destinados a las adquisiciones.

OCEANIA:
Norfolk Island:

E--> The figure in column 12 refers only to expenditure for employees and for acquisitions.

Norfolk Island: (Cont):

FR-> Le chiffre de la colonne 12 se réfère aux dépenses pour le personnel et les acquisitions seulement.

ESP> La cifra de la columna 12 se refiere a los gastos de personal y a las adquisiciones solamente.

7.6 Special libraries: collections, borrowers, works loaned out, current expenditure, employees

Bibliothèques spécialisées: collections, emprunteurs inscrits, documents prêtés au-dehors, dépenses ordinaires, personnel

Bibliotecas especializadas: colecciones, prestatarios inscritos, documentos prestados al exterior, gastos ordinarios, personal

NUMBER OF COUNTRIES AND TERRORIES PRESENTED IN THIS TABLE: 49

NOMBRE DE PAYS ET DE TERRITOIRES PRESENTES DANS CE TABLEAU: 49

COUNTRY / PAYS / PAIS	YEAR / ANNEE / AÑO	ADMINISTRATIVE UNITS / UNITES ADMINISTRATIVES / UNIDADES ADMINISTRATIVAS	SERVICE POINTS / POINTS DE SERVICE / PUNTOS DE SERVICIO	COLLECTIONS / COLLECTIONS / FONDOS					
				BOOKS/LIVRES/LIBROS					
				METRES OF SHELVING / METRES DE RAYONNAGE / METROS DE ESTANTES	NUMBER OF VOLUMES (000) / NOMBRE DE VOLUMES (000) / NUMERO DE VOLUMENES (000)	MICROFORMS / MICROCOPIES / MICROCOPIAS	AUDIO-VISUAL DOCUMENTS / MATERIELS AUDIO-VISUELS / MATERIALES AUDIO-VISUALES	OTHER LIBRARY MATERIALS / AUTRES MATERIELS DE BIBLIOTHEQUE / OTROS MATERIALES DE BIBLIOTECA
		(1)	(2)	(3)	(4)	(5)	(6)	(7)
AFRICA								
ALGERIA‡	1983	1	1	...	5	214	3	5
BENIN‡	1984	1	...	43	2	–	–	–
CHAD	1984	1	...	...	4	172	21	100
EGYPT	1983	380	...	...	1 639	52 900	1 800	29 000
GAMBIA	1978	17	20	1 120	24	–	–	–
MADAGASCAR	1983	23	23	941	51	5 216	16	2
MALAWI‡	1983	5	5	531	24	143	...	12
RWANDA	1984	5	13	607	30	...	42	841
SEYCHELLES‡	1984	1	1	...	11	...	7 495	...
AMERICA, NORTH								
GRENADA	1984	1	1	74	3	–	–	...
MEXICO‡	1983	171	171	...	2 300	1 481 908	31 700	...
PANAMA	1983	1	1	...	55	...	...	...
ST. PIERRE AND MIQUELON‡	1984	1	1	135	7	...	...	...
AMERICA, SOUTH								
ARGENTINA	1984	63	64	...	1 645	772	18 979	2 220
BRAZIL	1982	1 494	...	...	12 854	1 441 102	227 327	284 515
ECUADOR	1983	1	1	60	2	...	54	400
SURINAME	1978	27	27	1 586	63	–	–	–
ASIA								
BAHRAIN	1983	1	1	600	14	–	146	1 000
BHUTAN	1983	1	2	182	10	–	–	–
BRUNEI DARUSSALAM	1983	2	3	454	9	...	...	...
CYPRUS‡	1983	68	71	8 570	300	...	...	...
JAPAN	1978	2 019	...	...	31 164	2 242 649	...	...
JORDAN	1983	7	14	...	419	4 846	2 486	...
KOREA, REPUBLIC OF‡	1984	229	229	...	3 565	...	...	...
MALAYSIA	1982	162	...	...	1 319	74 148	2 912 246	689 310
SAUDI ARABIA	1984	1	4	...	122	2 434	329	38 510
SINGAPORE	1984	40	40	11 062	524	106 187	1 256 263	37 178

NUMERO DE PAISES Y DE TERRITORIOS
PRESENTADOS EN ESTE CUADRO: 49

ANNUAL ADDITIONS / ACQUISITIONS ANNUELLES / ADQUISICIONES ANUALES		REGISTERED BORROWERS	LOANS TO USERS	INTER-LIBRARY LOANS	CURRENT EXPENDITURE / DEPENSES ORDINAIRES / GASTOS ORDINARIOS		LIBRARY EMPLOYEES / PERSONNEL DES BIBLIOTHEQUES / PERSONAL DE LAS BIBLIOTECAS		
VOLUMES / VOLUMES / VOLUMENES	OTHER MATERIALS / AUTRES MATERIELS / OTROS MATERIALES	EMPRUNTEURS INSCRITS / PRESTATARIOS INSCRITOS	PRETS AUX USAGERS / PRESTAMOS A LOS USUARIOS	PRETS ENTRE BIBLIOTHEQUES / PRESTAMOS ENTRE BIBLIOTECAS	TOTAL (000) / TOTAL (000) / TOTAL (000)	STAFF (%) / PERSONNEL (%) / PERSONAL (%)	TOTAL / TOTAL / TOTAL	HOLDING A DIPLOMA / DIPLOME / DIPLOMADO	TRAINED ON THE JOB / FORME SUR LE TAS / FORMADO EN EJERCICIO
(8)	(9)	(10)	(11)	(12)	(13)	(14)	(15)	(16)	(17)
402	4	191	...	20	...	...	7	5	2
263	...	...	...	...	876	...	1	1	–
1 500	93	250	...	...	...	...	4	1	3
...	...	...	...	...	...	...	1 264	...	...
500	–	...	...	...	...	...	16	–	16
...	...	6 442	44	78	8 636	32	81	4	32
352	1 108	963	7 421	740	28	...	12	3	6
2 551	–	270	1 880	30	5 733	63	13	1	1
862	81	...	2 265	45	176	...	11	4	–
400	–	40	200	13	33	64	3	1	1
...	...	2 829 264	3 839 843	...	226 408	16	1 064	...	...
1 500	...	530	2 150	20	19	95	3	1	2
200	...	100	2 600	...	14 020	91	2	–	–
...	...	654 288	...	...	21 510	90	444	...	...
...	...	424 425	2 453 531	...	...	...	4 927	1 707	313
330	100	230	460	20	780	23	1	–	1
2 531	–	967	279	51	473	46	71	6	65
1 877	–	1 800	8 896	–	70	34	5	2	...
1 303	–	150	2 700	–	1 179	19	26	1	–
568	...	31	1 000	...	206	42	8	1	7
19 000	...	...	...	...	300	17	66	3	53
...	...	...	24 914 320	...	26 946 271	52	7 254	...	...
64 388	555	13 752	379 000	1 100	465	...	146	23	53
284 931	...	1 417 480	1 362 767	...	6 417 812	...	790	372	...
...	...	...	...	...	...	...	576	144	–
19 146	948	1 400	...	...	...	...	30	26	4
63 250	109 606	27 711	333 055	3 869	3 438	33	198	48	61

COUNTRY / PAYS / PAIS	YEAR / ANNEE / AÑO	ADMINISTRATIVE UNITS / UNITES ADMINISTRATIVES / UNIDADES ADMINISTRATIVAS	SERVICE POINTS / POINTS DE SERVICE / PUNTOS DE SERVICIO	COLLECTIONS / COLLECTIONS / FONDOS — BOOKS/LIVRES/LIBROS: METRES OF SHELVING / METRES DE RAYONNAGE / METROS DE ESTANTES	BOOKS/LIVRES/LIBROS: NUMBER OF VOLUMES (000) / NOMBRE DE VOLUMES (000) / NUMERO DE VOLUMENES (000)	MICROFORMS / MICROCOPIES / MICROCOPIAS	AUDIO-VISUAL DOCUMENTS / MATERIELS AUDIO-VISUELS / MATERIALES AUDIO-VISUALES	OTHER LIBRARY MATERIALS / AUTRES MATERIELS DE BIBLIOTHEQUE / OTROS MATERIALES DE BIBLIOTECA
		(1)	(2)	(3)	(4)	(5)	(6)	(7)
SRI LANKA	1984	...	84	...	558	1 974	174 592	–
SYRIAN ARAB REPUBLIC‡	1983	...	...	500	21	1 000	1	...
THAILAND‡	1983	38	38	...	452	...	...	...
EUROPE								
AUSTRIA	1983	1 434	1 434	...	26 034	1 113 636	3 346 489	...
BULGARIA	1983	676	...	...	8 360	4 135 242	16 569	16 355 661
DENMARK	1983	11	89	43 075	1 108	2 068 000	51 192	51 220
FINLAND	1983	19	56	47 300	1 770	173 355	2 500	...
GERMANY, FEDERAL REPUBLIC OF‡	1983	...	1 686	...	30 343	16 368 581	532 694	30 419 665
HOLY SEE	1979	2	2	...	700	350	...	...
IRELAND	1983	21	...	3 987	131	3 087	290	6 300
MALTA	1984	8	8	809	35	3 550	1 020	–
NETHERLANDS‡	1982	672	818	352 700	12 009	8 174 800	379 300	619 300
NORWAY‡	1983	144	156	67 405	3 041	1 889 595	466 097	15 740 729
POLAND	1983	4 632	...	...	31 490	...	...	...
PORTUGAL	1983	126	181	365 815	2 000	8 252	33 231	19 061
ROMANIA	1984	3 452	...	...	20 829	...	...	...
SAN MARINO‡	1983	1	1	58	2	...	...	...
SPAIN‡	1980	435	595	283 883	8 641	14 155	227 008	...
SWEDEN‡	1983	38	58	84 165	3 859	1 575 028	...	...
YUGOSLAVIA‡	1983	1 038	1 040	261 213	14 048	287 641	1 247 690	235 112
OCEANIA								
FIJI‡	1983	50	50	...	44	...	...	...
TONGA	1978	2	...	...	4	...	...	...

ANNUAL ADDITIONS / ACQUISITIONS ANNUELLES / ADQUISICIONES ANUALES		REGISTERED BORROWERS	LOANS TO USERS	INTER-LIBRARY LOANS	CURRENT EXPENDITURE / DEPENSES ORDINAIRES / GASTOS ORDINARIOS		LIBRARY EMPLOYEES / PERSONNEL DES BIBLIOTHEQUES / PERSONAL DE LAS BIBLIOTECAS		
VOLUMES / VOLUMES / VOLUMENES	OTHER MATERIALS / AUTRES MATERIELS / OTROS MATERIALES	EMPRUNTEURS INSCRITS / PRESTATARIOS INSCRITOS	PRETS AUX USAGERS / PRESTAMOS A LOS USUARIOS	PRETS ENTRE BIBLIO-THEQUES / PRESTAMOS ENTRE BIBLIOTECAS	TOTAL (000) / TOTAL (000) / TOTAL (000)	STAFF (%) / PERSONNEL (%) / PERSONAL (%)	TOTAL / TOTAL / TOTAL	HOLDING A DIPLOMA / DIPLOME / DIPLOMADO	TRAINED ON THE JOB / FORME SUR LE TAS / FORMADO EN EJERCICIO
(8)	(9)	(10)	(11)	(12)	(13)	(14)	(15)	(16)	(17)
...	...	23 736	615 482	...	10 582	39	297	54	–
450	–	90	1 000	30	...	...	7	4	...
...	...	...	...	...	2	...	195	65	128
622 409	...	...	...	...	...	...	1 891	...	...
354 795	1 274 972	205 496	6 510 380	...	6 104	28	803	544	259
28 372	135 143	...	149 483	30 996	21 125	66	117	44	57
68 032	67 320	...	106 839	19 872	23 621	61	191	95	–
980 145	2 557 717	244 243	3 650 101	1 421	111 495	46	1 911	...	...
52 200	...	7 500	...	...	320 000	19	23	8	...
9 661	14 404	3 149	14 438	2 944	1 332	65	89	26	35
3 157	549	2 916	20 700	100	...	...	16	2	7
331 200	990 600	...	1 934 000	231 400	51 018	...	1 973	989	663
116 470	426 391	...	475 205	46 306	20 551	...	409	179	154
1 286	2 855	1 220	8 678	226	...	...	10 638	...	...
101 218	1 177	81 905	146 485	2 378	339 599	53	580	148	120
...	...	800 000	5 835 000	...	...	...	...	...	...
30	...	...	...	...	2 000	...	1	...	...
224 914	50 387	175 618	...	...	...	...	...	...	...
82 056	61 529	33 594	212 135	74 729	64 012	61	299	125	...
558 405	95 338	1 035 942	...	...	465 632	...	1 258	621	637
...	...	...	...	...	...	...	32	16	1
...	...	...	...	...	2	79	3	–	1

AFRICA:

Algeria:

E--> The figure in column 12 refers only to loan transactions on the national level.

FR-> Le chiffre de la colonne 12 se rapportent aux prêts nationaux seulement.

ESP> La cifra de la columna 12 se refiere a los prestamos nacionales solamente.

Benin:

E--> The figure in column 13 refers only to expenditure for acquisitions.

FR-> Le chiffre de la colonne 13 se réfère seulement aux dépenses pour les acquisitions.

ESP> La cifra de la columna 13 incluye solamente los gastos relativos a las adquisiciones.

Malawi:

E--> The figure in column 13 does not include expenditure for employees.

FR-> Le chiffre de la colonne 13 ne comprend pas les dépenses pour le personnel.

ESP> La cifra de la columna 13 no comprende los gastos de personal.

Seychelles:

E--> The figure in column 12 refers only to loan transactions on the international level. The figure in column 13 refers only to expenditure for employees.

FR-> Le chiffre de la colonne 12 se rapportent aux prêts internationaux seulement. Le chiffre de la colonne 13 se réfère seulement aux dépenses pour le personnel.

ESP> La cifra de la columna 12 incluye los prestamos a nivel internacional solamente. La cifra de la columna 13 incluye solamente los gastos de personal.

AMERICA, NORTH:

Mexico:

E--> The figure in column 10 refers to the number of visits to reading rooms and not to the number of registered borrowers.

FR-> Le chiffre de la colonne 10 se réfère au nombre de visites dans les salles de lecture et non au nombre d'emprunteurs inscrits.

ESP> La cifra de la columna 10 se refiere al número de visitas en las salas de lectura y no al número de los prestatarios inscritos.

St. Pierre and Miquelon:

E--> Data are also counted with those for France.

St. Pierre and Miquelon: (Cont):

FR-> Les données sont également comptées avec celles de la France.

ESP> Los datos se cuentan igualmente con los de Francia.

ASIA:

Cyprus:

E--> The figure in column 13 includes only expenditure for employees and for acquisitions.

FR-> Le chiffre de la colonne 13 comprend seulement les dépenses pour le personnel et les acquisitions.

ESP> La cifra de la columna 13 comprende únicamente los gastos de personal y de adquisiciones.

Korea, Republic of:

E--> The figure in column 13 does not include expenditure for employees.

FR-> Le chiffre de la colonne 13 ne comprend pas les dépenses pour le personnel.

ESP> La cifra de la columna 13 no comprende los gastos de personal.

Syrian Arab Republic:

E--> The figure in column 12 refers only to loan transactions on the national level.

FR-> Le chiffre de la colonne 12 se réfère aux prêts nationaux seulement.

ESP> La cifra de la columna 12 se refiere a los prestamos nacionales solamente.

Thailand:

E--> The figure in column 13 represents only expenditure for employees.

FR-> Le chiffre de la colonne 13 représente seulement aux dépenses pour le personnel.

ESP> La cifra de la columna 13 representa únicamente los gastos de personal.

EUROPE:

Germany, Federal Republic of:

E--> The figure in column 12 refers only to loan transactions on the international level. Column 13 includes only expenditure for employees and for acquisitions.

FR-> Le chiffre de la colonne 12 se réfère aux prêts internationaux seulement. La colonne 13 comprend seulement les dépenses pour le personnel et les acquisitions.

ESP> La cifra de la columna 12 se refiere a los prestamos

Germany, Federal Republic of: (Cont):
internacionales solamente. La columna 13 se refiere únicamente a los gastos de personal y de adquisiciones.

Netherlands:
E--> The figure in column 13 does not include expenditure for employees.
FR-> Le chiffre de la colonne 13 ne comprend pas les dépenses pour le personnel.
ESP> La cifra de la columna 13 no comprende los gastos de personal.

Norway:
E--> The figure in column 13 refers only to expenditure for acquisitions.
FR-> Le chiffre de la colonne 13 se réfère seulement aux dépenses pour les acquisitions.
ESP> La cifra de la columna 13 se refiere a los gastos relativos a las adquisiciones solamente.

San Marino:
E--> The figure in column 13 refers only to expenditure for acquisitions.
FR-> Le chiffre de la colonne 13 se réfère seulement aux dépenses pour les acquisitions.
ESP> La cifra de la columna 13 se refiere a los gastos relativos a las adquisiciones solamente.

Spain:
E--> Dat are incomplete. The figure in column 9 refers to microforms only.

Spain: (Cont):
FR-> Les données sont incomplètes. Le chiffre de la colonne 9 se réfère aux microcopies seulement.
ESP> Los datos están incompletos. La cifra de la columna 9 se refiere a las microcopias solamente.

Sweden:
E--> The figure in column 13 refers only to expenditure for acquisitions.
FR-> Le chiffre de la colonne 13 se réfère seulement aux dépenses pour les acquisitions.
ESP> La cifra de la columna 13 se refiere a los gastos relativos a las adquisiciones solamente.

Yugoslavia:
E--> The figure in column 13 refers only to expenditure for acquisitions.
FR-> Le chiffre de la colonne 13 se réfère seulement aux dépenses pour les acquisitions.
ESP> La cifra de la columna 13 incluye solamente los gastos destinados a las adquisiciones.

OCEANIA:

Fiji:
E--> The figure in column 4 refers only to 17 libraries and does not include bound periodicals.
FR-> Le chiffre de la colonne 4 se réfère à 17 bibliothèques seulement et ne comprend pas les périodiques reliés.
ESP> La cifra de la columna 4 se refiere a 17 bibliotecas solamente y no incluye los periódicos encuadernos.

7.7 Book production: number of titles by UDC classes

Edition de livres: nombre de titres classés d'après la CDU

Edición de libros: número de títulos clasificados por materias según la CDU

NUMBER OF COUNTRIES AND TERRITORIES PRESENTED IN THIS TABLE: 84

NOMBRE DE PAYS ET DE TERRITOIRES PRESENTES DANS CE TABLEAU: 84

NUMERO DE PAISES Y DE TERRITORIOS PRESENTADOS EN ESTE CUADRO: 84

COUNTRY PAYS PAIS	YEAR ANNEE AÑO	TOTAL TOTAL TOTAL	GENERALITIES GENERALITES GENERALIDADES	PHILOSOPHY PHILOSOPHIE FILOSOFIA	RELIGION RELIGION RELIGION	SOCIAL SCIENCES SCIENCES SOCIALES CIENCIAS SOCIALES	PHILOLOGY PHILOLOGIE FILOLOGIA	PURE SCIENCES SCIENCES PURES CIENCIAS PURAS	APPLIED SCIENCES SCIENCES APPL. CIENCIAS APLICADAS	ARTS ARTS ARTES	LITERATURE LITTERATURE LITERATURA	GEOGR./HISTORY GEOGR./HISTOIRE GEOGR./HISTORIA
		(1)	(2)	(3)	(4)	(5)	(6)	(7)	(8)	(9)	(10)	(11)
AFRICA												
ALGERIA‡	1982	504	43	2	17	131	17	45	119	16	74	40
	1983	208	–	3	–	89	2	17	61	5	30	1
	1984	718	26	15	32	201	13	104	125	22	119	61
COTE D'IVOIRE‡	1983	46	–	–	–	18	–	–	4	3	4	6
ETHIOPIA	1983	457	9	–	66	180	21	37	88	6	26	24
	1984	349	1	–	31	202	24	25	35	10	14	7
GAMBIA‡	1983	101	12	–	3	40	2	6	18	7	3	10
	1984	146	15	–	4	49	7	11	30	11	3	16
GHANA	1982	145	5	2	38	37	2	11	8	8	30	4
	1983	350	–	1	31	130	16	13	65	33	38	23
KENYA‡	1983	235	10	2	50	48	18	23	17	20	23	24
MADAGASCAR	1982	351	6	4	46	55	22	32	142	8	21	15
	1983	418	2	2	48	67	29	29	216	5	13	7
	1984	321	3	8	48	41	14	20	161	7	13	6
MALI‡	1983	90	–	–	–	12	37	11	8	–	15	7
	1984	160	–	–	–	98	19	17	23	–	–	3
MAURITIUS	1982	80	–	2	11	27	–	2	6	1	25	6
	1984	124	1	–	10	30	25	8	13	11	13	13
MOZAMBIQUE	1983	88	–	–	–	60	–	6	3	2	12	5
NIGERIA	1982	1 666	58	6	176	812	48	88	212	34	132	100
	1983	1 495	28	11	188	852	34	72	108	33	29	140
	1984	1 836	64	14	138	888	98	86	284	44	156	64
REUNION	1982	73	2	2	5	18	3	3	9	3	21	7
	1983	79	–	–	8	22	1	3	9	14	16	6
SENEGAL‡	1983	42	–	2	3	9	4	2	–	–	14	8
UNITED REPUBLIC OF TANZANIA‡	1982	246	17	1	56	122	–	–	37	5	–	8
	1983	551	22	2	33	293	28	4	130	10	11	18
	1984	363	17	1	41	195	6	7	77	4	9	6
ZAMBIA	1983	454	143	–	–	231	–	15	13	18	–	34
ZIMBABWE‡	1982	32	–	–	3	–	6	5	–	–	13	5
	1983	533	10	1	19	178	108	58	52	15	64	28
	1984	193	1	–	14	14	40	19	14	–	40	10
AMERICA, NORTH												
BARBADOS	1982	139	3	–	1	99	–	–	14	14	4	4
	1983	87	4	–	–	43	–	2	21	10	3	4
BRITISH VIRGIN ISLANDS	1982	20	20	–	–	–	–	–	–	–	–	–

7.7 Number of titles by UDC classes
Nombre de titres classés d'après la CDU
Número de títulos clasificados por materias (CDU)

COUNTRY / PAYS / PAIS	YEAR / ANNEE / AÑO	TOTAL / TOTAL / TOTAL	GENERALITIES / GENERALITES / GENERALIDADES	PHILOSOPHY / PHILOSOPHIE / FILOSOFIA	RELIGION / RELIGION / RELIGION	SOCIAL SCIENCES / SCIENCES SOCIALES / CIENCIAS SOCIALES	PHILOLOGY / PHILOLOGIE / FILOLOGIA	PURE SCIENCES / SCIENCES PURES / CIENCIAS PURAS	APPLIED SCIENCES / SCIENCES APPL. / CIENCIAS APLICADAS	ARTS / ARTS / ARTES	LITERATURE / LITTERATURE / LITERATURA	GEOGR./HISTORY / GEOGR./HISTOIRE / GEOGR./HISTORIA
		(1)	(2)	(3)	(4)	(5)	(6)	(7)	(8)	(9)	(10)	(11)
COSTA RICA‡	1984	1 759	38	47	82	576	69	154	291	32	340	130
CUBA	1982	1 640	77	23	1	1 086	–	9	148	37	192	67
	1983	1 917	103	12	1	742	65	85	504	118	225	62
	1984	2 069	339	28	2	490	114	157	446	113	299	81
MEXICO‡	1982	2 818	259	128	71	840	141	310	467	92	287	223
	1984	4 505	569	276	114	1 202	129	357	458	151	971	278
NICARAGUA‡	1984	26	4	1	2	2	–	–	–	–	15	2
ST. CHRISTOPHER AND NEVIS‡	1982	5	–	–	–	3	–	–	1	–	–	1
AMERICA, SOUTH												
ARGENTINA‡	1982	4 962	242	616	——>	1 051	./.	188	749	1 166	924	26
	1983	4 216	189	536	——>	922	./.	199	659	702	992	17
BOLIVIA	1982	*301	8	1	13	93	11	11	12	27	64	61
BRAZIL	1982	19 179	1 160	732	2 251	5 483	606	1 462	2 238	1 924	2 588	735
CHILE	1983	1 326	31	36	97	604	34	52	120	31	224	97
	1984	1 653	30	24	112	606	28	68	160	49	450	126
COLOMBIA	1983	7 671	930	184	192	2 108	155	813	807	617	1 260	605
	1984	15 041	1 078	239	352	2 784	290	1 098	6 067	997	1 501	635
GUYANA	1982	92	3	–	7	47	9	1	10	2	12	1
	1983	55	2	–	–	27	–	3	7	4	7	5
PERU	1983	704	14	17	17	279	4	35	102	41	99	96
	1984	546	12	16	7	202	10	33	107	16	83	60
URUGUAY	1982	899	8	19	25	283	17	69	204	62	131	81
	1983	1 217	21	26	51	437	–	89	239	84	159	111
	1984	1 206	21	22	42	401	6	77	231	76	205	125
ASIA												
BAHRAIN‡	1982	78	–	–	9	5	11	24	14	–	–	15
BRUNEI DARUSSALAM	1982	72	25	–	6	–	13	22	2	1	–	3
CHINA‡	1983	31 602	./.	3 698	./.	5 641	./.	8 176	./.	./.	5 092	./.
	1984	34 920	./.	4 041	./.	6 216	./.	9 338	./.	./.	5 661	./.
HONG KONG	1982	3 560	57	78	177	555	344	259	747	312	635	396
	1983	5 681	231	67	451	1 485	553	442	778	213	1 066	395
INDIA‡	1982	10 649	268	333	754	3 194	156	581	805	124	3 634	800
	1984	9 954	285	378	814	2 580	132	409	1 114	297	3 161	784
INDONESIA	1982	5 488	685	147	264	1 927	142	285	852	344	518	324
	1983	5 731	436	86	258	2 266	211	421	1 152	216	256	429
	1984	5 254	429	76	344	1 894	152	273	1 342	134	366	244
IRAN, ISLAMIC REPUBLIC OF‡	1982	2 994	79	98	858	441	2	83	336	176	620	301
	1983	4 835	118	124	1 171	333	135	184	628	169	984	431
IRAQ‡	1983	82	6	–	–	15	–	1	–	–	54	6
ISRAEL‡	1982	1 892	17	72	163	246	55	79	79	39	846	289
JAPAN‡	1982	42 977	1 278	1 536	575	7 710	2 957	2 727	6 604	5 952	10 568	3 070
	1983	44 253	1 161	1 514	635	10 558	2 473	2 293	7 070	5 729	10 792	2 028
KOREA, REPUBLIC OF	1982	30 436	621	1 076	2 652	6 786	1 934	1 622	3 466	1 815	9 636	828
	1983	35 512	624	1 547	2 642	5 902	2 401	1 120	3 623	2 047	13 542	2 064
	1984	35 446	998	1 233	2 682	6 179	2 814	1 607	3 689	1 922	11 727	2 595
MALAYSIA	1982	2 801	53	22	90	695	379	304	414	147	454	243
	1983	3 534	91	16	157	1 049	413	400	444	97	622	245
	1984	3 975	135	36	231	1 346	463	304	596	99	479	286
MONGOLIA	1983	861	–	–	–	420	13	22	128	6	272	...
PHILIPPINES‡	1982	839	48	17	41	223	78	59	174	136	39	24
	1983	650	70	6	15	130	36	33	248	61	29	22
	1984	542	30	8	4	58	7	32	274	118	8	3
SINGAPORE‡	1982	1 530	38	12	105	470	148	74	181	116	266	120
	1983	1 927	34	12	216	623	154	123	261	77	376	51

COUNTRY PAYS PAIS	YEAR ANNEE AÑO	TOTAL TOTAL TOTAL	GENERALITIES GENERALITES GENERALIDADES	PHILOSOPHY PHILOSOPHIE FILOSOFIA	RELIGION RELIGION RELIGION	SOCIAL SCIENCES SCIENCES SOCIALES CIENCIAS SOCIALES	PHILOLOGY PHILOLOGIE FILOLOGIA	PURE SCIENCES SCIENCES PURES CIENCIAS PURAS	APPLIED SCIENCES SCIENCES APPL. CIENCIAS APLICADAS	ARTS ARTS ARTES	LITERATURE LITTERATURE LITERATURA	GEOGR./HISTORY GEOGR./HISTOIRE GEOGR./HISTORIA
		(1)	(2)	(3)	(4)	(5)	(6)	(7)	(8)	(9)	(10)	(11)
SRI LANKA	1983	1 951	23	32	302	935	52	54	193	30	262	68
SYRIAN ARAB REPUBLIC	1983	119	–	3	1	19	–	14	18	3	54	7
THAILAND	1982	5 645	741	98	280	2 252	321	385	1 005	223	23	317
	1983	6 819	842	102	285	2 778	244	457	1 195	253	371	292
	1984	8 633	952	193	486	3 498	382	530	1 325	288	567	412
TURKEY‡	1982	6 440	93	93	317	1 327	74	332	1 376	299	1 021	410
	1983	6 869	127	88	404	1 360	119	373	1 417	218	996	268
UNITED ARAB EMIRATES	1982	64	2	–	20	3	17	13	1	1	1	6
	1983	84	4	1	21	4	14	20	3	–	10	7
EUROPE												
ALBANIA	1982	1 149	27	2	1	190	65	251	437	32	107	37
	1983	997	12	3	1	203	70	151	340	32	134	51
	1984	1 130	25	7	1	234	88	175	315	49	178	58
AUSTRIA	1982	6 736	161	244	264	1 302	136	915	1 457	592	1 000	665
	1984	9 059	204	248	519	1 661	153	978	2 009	861	1 498	928
BELGIUM‡	1982	8 041	173	225	356	1 453	219	436	1 108	834	2 488	749
	1983	8 065	202	239	319	1 268	208	327	1 077	686	1 388	683
BULGARIA	1982	5 070	228	70	14	1 551	138	266	1 208	234	1 056	305
	1983	4 924	214	51	22	1 377	229	250	1 248	207	964	362
	1984	5 367	273	44	10	1 647	297	288	1 351	275	902	280
CZECHOSLOVAKIA	1982	10 519	834	138	93	1 983	408	1 102	3 088	747	1 771	355
	1983	9 574	659	135	82	1 794	236	981	2 764	747	1 851	325
	1984	9 911	650	113	49	1 704	359	1 025	3 056	685	1 887	383
DENMARK	1982	10 189	252	267	258	2 048	358	709	2 470	670	2 145	1 012
	1983	9 460	250	278	242	1 860	308	634	2 383	629	2 045	831
	1984	10 660	283	412	273	2 123	301	676	2 640	706	2 242	1 004
FINLAND	1982	7 436	356	202	322	1 970	272	807	1 847	307	1 022	331
	1983	8 594	372	178	318	2 171	310	868	2 463	454	1 044	416
	1984	8 563	361	193	333	2 192	342	974	2 347	408	1 016	397
FRANCE	1982	42 186	965	1 000	1 631	14 766	438	1 108	6 243	3 877	9 695	2 463
	1983	37 576	919	812	1 345	12 775	382	689	5 073	3 713	9 708	2 160
	1984	37 189	900	900	1 350	12 749	400	110	5 050	3 870	9 660	2 200
GERMAN DEMOCRATIC REPUBLIC‡	1982	5 938	92	154	327	736	253	469	876	449	1 315	275
	1983	6 175	93	125	336	747	287	450	910	491	1 428	298
	1984	6 175	85	141	308	738	301	447	925	452	1 449	306
GERMANY, FEDERAL REPUBLIC OF	1982	58 592	4 931	1 944	3 547	16 188	2 407	2 623	6 703	5 370	10 875	4 004
	1983	58 489	4 324	2 394	2 994	15 131	2 289	3 053	6 980	5 281	11 299	4 744
	1984	48 836	3 836	1 946	2 598	10 783	1 817	3 861	7 785	3 718	9 386	3 106
HOLY SEE‡	1982	194	23	14	117	28	1	–	–	3	2	6
	1983	191	22	12	121	20	1	–	–	4	2	9
HUNGARY	1982	8 836	325	97	79	2 046	388	665	2 653	787	1 324	472
	1983	8 469	289	114	89	1 756	395	724	2 597	730	1 272	503
	1984	10 421	310	97	106	2 356	495	938	3 277	771	1 488	583
IRELAND‡	1982	706	32	4	42	249	8	13	64	57	132	105
	1983	672	26	2	49	171	6	5	71	66	114	112
	1984	799	27	3	44	301	5	25	72	83	147	92
ITALY	1982	12 926	308	752	1 029	2 810	335	555	1 838	1 279	2 810	1 210
	1983	13 718	395	817	1 130	2 900	426	693	1 847	1 335	2 890	1 285
	1984	14 312	444	755	995	3 302	339	668	2 117	1 268	3 267	1 157
LUXEMBOURG‡	1982	305	11	5	4	95	4	7	19	60	50	50
	1983	359	13	2	5	138	–	8	18	63	53	59
	1984	341	17	8	5	114	2	5	32	70	44	44
MALTA	1982	247	6	1	37	114	7	–	16	3	51	12
	1983	278	4	3	70	107	11	6	10	17	43	7
	1984	313	6	–	56	121	16	5	15	17	64	13
MONACO	1982	105	77	–	–	4	–	–	–	13	10	1
NETHERLANDS‡	1982	13 324	229	501	558	2 389	1 351	975	1 623	934	3 866	898
	1984	13 209	119	452	707	1 346	212	561	1 634	854	2 792	973

7.7 Number of titles by UDC classes
Nombre de titres classés d'après la CDU
Número de títulos clasificados por materias (CDU)

COUNTRY / PAYS / PAIS	YEAR / ANNEE / AÑO	TOTAL / TOTAL / TOTAL	GENERALITIES / GENERALITES / GENERALIDADES	PHILOSOPHY / PHILOSOPHIE / FILOSOFIA	RELIGION / RELIGION / RELIGION	SOCIAL SCIENCES / SCIENCES SOCIALES / CIENCIAS SOCIALES	PHILOLOGY / PHILOLOGIE / FILOLOGIA	PURE SCIENCES / SCIENCES PURES / CIENCIAS PURAS	APPLIED SCIENCES / SCIENCES APPL. / CIENCIAS APLICADAS	ARTS / ARTS / ARTES	LITERATURE / LITTERATURE / LITERATURA	GEOGR./HISTORY / GEOGR./HISTOIRE / GEOGR./HISTORIA
		(1)	(2)	(3)	(4)	(5)	(6)	(7)	(8)	(9)	(10)	(11)
NORWAY‡	1982	5 175	152	66	257	1 190	77	532	813	268	1 399	421
	1983	5 540	209	131	218	1 437	88	514	978	326	1 253	386
POLAND	1982	9 814	335	176	377	1 844	453	871	2 805	588	1 629	736
	1983	8 789	306	163	372	1 615	382	796	2 403	442	1 606	704
	1984	9 195	317	173	399	1 889	336	806	2 504	474	1 582	715
PORTUGAL‡	1982	9 139	477	163	400	1 645	./.	548	1 102	2 198	2 017	589
	1983	8 647	498	121	309	1 122	./.	445	982	2 948	1 710	512
	1984	9 041	691	188	383	1 075	./.	460	684	3 065	1 936	559
ROMANIA	1982	6 702	179	116	65	1 288	267	887	1 933	375	1 355	237
	1983	5 771	124	74	45	771	225	720	1 752	330	1 434	296
	1984	5 632	124	94	39	627	201	808	1 814	299	1 346	280
SPAIN	1982	32 138	6 620	1 007	1 808	4 087	1 813	1 936	3 488	2 035	7 570	1 774
	1983	32 457	6 109	1 006	1 481	4 047	2 248	1 995	3 069	1 902	8 669	1 931
	1984	30 764	1 406	1 193	1 582	4 254	2 192	1 854	3 402	1 829	10 790	2 262
SWEDEN‡	1982	8 509	280	160	353	1 857	166	491	1 506	357	2 068	650
	1983	8 036	254	179	303	1 849	151	464	1 357	326	1 967	584
	1984	10 373	331	248	463	461	263	577	1 381	592	2 359	1 007
SWITZERLAND‡	1982	11 405	163	357	716	2 138	240	944	2 408	1 126	1 747	840
	1983	11 355	166	356	729	2 171	181	989	2 328	1 192	1 842	771
	1984	11 806	122	443	791	2 537	169	971	2 132	1 238	1 846	706
UNITED KINGDOM	1982	48 029	1 627	1 576	1 980	9 313	1 203	4 399	9 414	4 111	9 857	4 549
	1983	50 981	1 715	1 620	2 396	9 680	1 325	4 442	9 010	4 060	11 428	5 305
	1984	51 411	2 182	1 469	2 041	9 313	1 199	4 630	9 940	4 225	11 501	4 911
YUGOSLAVIA	1982	10 535	187	149	244	3 792	190	345	1 594	1 472	2 120	442
	1983	10 931	179	97	227	4 125	145	337	1 566	1 378	2 495	382
	1984	10 918	227	140	284	3 400	199	420	1 871	1 478	2 488	411
OCEANIA												
AUSTRALIA‡	1982	8 373	418	65	238	2 974	484	474	1 504	651	799	766
	1983	3 294	107	22	60	1 278	150	167	527	270	412	301
NEW CALEDONIA‡	1984	22	–	–	–	8	5	4	–	3	–	2
NEW ZEALAND	1983	2 944	94	12	63	1 059	94	234	653	280	210	245
	1984	3 452	102	16	91	1 262	18	319	799	348	300	197
U.S.S.R.												
U.S.S.R.‡	1982	80 674	3 099	1 335	237	20 900	1 626	7 011	30 879	2 476	10 750	2 008
	1983	82 589	2 561	1 444	275	21 685	1 604	7 485	31 148	2 859	11 152	1 980
	1984	82 790	2 493	1 503	301	21 818	1 720	7 373	30 871	2 744	11 611	1 966
BYELORUSSIAN S.S.R.	1982	2 923	126	33	4	900	83	140	1 175	74	348	40
	1983	3 264	134	49	13	1 073	109	187	1 215	82	372	30
	1984	3 264	122	53	7	1 100	104	191	1 156	107	377	47
UKRAINIAN S.S.R.‡	1982	8 239	321	182	44	2 341	161	749	2 886	208	1 095	188
	1983	8 882	359	179	50	2 389	197	790	3 251	226	1 191	175
	1984	8 403	324	191	53	2 472	163	734	2 774	210	1 205	207

AFRICA:

Algeria:

E--> For 1983, data do not include pamphlets and refer to school textbooks, government publications and university theses only.

FR-> Pour 1983, les données ne comprennent pas les brochures et se réfèrent seulement aux manuels scolaires, aux publications gouvernementales et aux thèses universitaires.

ESP> En 1983, los datos no incluyen los folletos y se refieren solamente a los manuales escolares, a las publicaciones oficiales y a las tesis universitarias.

Côte d'Ivoire:

E--> Data do not include pamphlets. Eleven school textbooks are included in the total but not identified in the 10 groups.

FR-> Les données ne comprennent pas les brochures. Onze manuels scolaires sont inclus dans le total mais ne sont pas répartis entre les 10 groupes.

ESP> Los datos no incluyen los folletos. Once manuales escolares quedan comprendidos en el total pero no están repartidos entre los 10 grupos.

Gambia:

E--> All first editions.

FR-> Tous les ouvrages recensés sont des premières éditions.

Gambia: (Cont):

ESP> Todas las obras consideradas son primeras ediciones.

Kenya:

E--> Data are incomplete.

FR-> Les données sont incomplètes.

ESP> Los datos están incompletos.

Mali:

E--> Pamphlets only. In 1983, data refer only to school textbook whilst in 1984, they refer also to government publications and univers theses.

FR-> Brochures seulement. En 1983, les données se réfère seulement aux manuels scolaires tandis qu'en 1984, elles se réfèrent aus aux publications gouvernementales et aux thèses universitaires.

ESP> Folletos solamente. En 1983, los datos se refieren solamente los manuales escolares, mientras que en 1984, se refieren igualmente a l publicaciones oficiales y a las tesis universitarias.

Senegal:

E--> All first editions.

FR-> Tous les ouvrages recensés sont des premières éditions.

ESP> Todas las obras consideradas son primeras ediciones.

United Republic of Tanzania:

E--> For 1984, all first editions.

United Republic of Tanzania: (Cont):

FR-> En 1984, tous les ouvrages recensés sont des premières éditions.

ESP> En 1984, todas las obras consideradas son primeras ediciones.

Zimbabwe:

E--> For 1982, data refer only to first editions of school textbooks and government publications. For 1984, school textbooks (41) are included in the total but are not identified in the 10 groups.

FR-> En 1982, les données se réfèrent seulement aux premières éditions des manuels scolaires et des publications gouvernementales. En 1984, les manuels scolaires (41) sont compris dans le total mais ne sont pas répartis entre les 10 groupes.

ESP> En 1982, los datos se refieren solamente a las primeras ediciones de los manuales escolares y de las publicaciones oficiales. En 1984, los manuales escolares (41) quedan comprendidos en el total pero no están repartidos entre los 10 grupos.

AMERICA, NORTH:

Costa Rica:

E--> Data do not include pamphlets.

FR-> Les données ne tiennent pas compte des brochures.

ESP> Los datos no incluyen los folletos.

Mexico:

E--> Data do not include pamphlets.

FR-> Les données ne tiennent pas compte des brochures.

ESP> Los datos no incluyen los folletos.

Nicaragua:

E--> Data do not include pamphlets.

FR-> Les données ne tiennent pas compte des brochures.

ESP> Los datos no incluyen los folletos.

St. Christopher and Nevis:

E--> All first editions.

FR-> Tous les ouvrages recensés sont des premières éditions.

ESP> Todas las obras consideradas son primeras ediciones.

AMERICA, SOUTH:

Argentina:

E--> Data on philology are included with those of literature.

FR-> Les données relatives à la philologie sont comprises avec celles de la littérature.

ESP> Los datos relativos a la filología quedan incluídos en los de la literatura.

ASIA:

Bahrain:

E--> Data refer to school textbooks only.

FR-> Les données se réfèrent aux manuels scolaires seulement.

ESP> Los datos se refieren a los manuales escolares solamente.

China:

E--> School textbooks (1983: 5,029, 1984: 5,574); and children's books (1983: 3,966, 1984: 4,090); are included in the total but not distributed in the 10 groups.

FR-> Les manuels scolaires (1983: 5 029, 1984: 5 574); et les livres pour enfants (1983: 3 966, 1984: 4 090); sont compris dans le total mais ne sont pas répartis entre les 10 groupes.

ESP> Los manuales escolares (1983: 5 029, 1984: 5 574); y los libros para niños (1983: 3 966, 1984: 4 090); quedan comprendidos en el total pero no están repartidos entre los 10 grupos.

India:

E--> In 1984, data do not include pamphlets.

FR-> En 1984, les données ne comprennent pas les brochures.

ESP> En 1984, los datos no incluyen los folletos.

Iran, Islamic Republic of:

E--> For 1983, children's books (558) are included in the total but not identified in the 10 groups.

FR-> Pour 1983, les livres pour enfants (558) sont compris dans le total mais ne sont pas répartis entre les 10 groupes.

ESP> En 1983, los libros para niños (558) quedan comprendidos en el total pero no están repartidos entre los 10 grupos.

Iraq:

E--> Data refer to first editions only and do not include pamphlets.

FR-> Les données se réfèrent aux premières éditions seulement et ne comprennent pas les brochures.

ESP> Los datos se refieren a las primeras ediciones solamente y no incluyen los folletos.

Israel:

E--> The total includes 7 titles for which a subject breakdown is not available.

FR-> Le total comprend 7 titres pour lesquels une répartition par sujets n'est pas disponible.

ESP> El total incluye 7 títulos cuya repartición por temas se desconoce.

Japan:

E--> Data do not include pamphlets.

FR-> Les données ne tiennent pas compte des brochures.

ESP> Los datos no incluyen los folletos.

Philippines:

E--> Data refer only to school textbooks, children's books and government publications. In 1983, university theses are included as well.

Philippines: (Cont):

FR-> Les données se réfèrent seulement aux manuels scolaires, aux livres pour enfants et aux publications gouvernementales. En 1983, les thèses universitaires sont aussi comprises.

ESP> Los datos se refieren solamente a los manuales escolares, a los libros para niños y a las publicaciones oficiales. En 1983, las tesis universitarias quedan comprendidas igualmente.

Singapore:

E--> Data do not include government publications.

FR-> Les données ne comprennent pas les publications officielles.

ESP> Los datos no incluyen las publicaciones oficiales.

Turkey:

E--> School textbooks (1982: 181; 1983: 387) and children's books (1982: 917; 1983: 1,112) are included in the total but are not identified in the 10 groups.

FR-> Les manuels scolaires (1982: 181; 1983: 387) et les livres pour enfants (1982: 917; 1983: 1 112) sont compris dans le total mais ne sont pas répartis entre les 10 groupes.

ESP> Los manuales escolares (1982: 181; 1983: 387) y los libros para niños (1982: 917; 1983: 1 112) quedan comprendidos en el total pero no están repartidos entre los 10 grupos.

EUROPE:

Belgium:

E--> For 1983, children's books (1,668) are included in the total but not distributed in the 10 groups.

FR-> Pour 1983, les livres pour enfants (1 668) sont compris dans le total mais non répartis entre les 10 groupes.

ESP> En 1983, los libros para niños (1 668) quedan comprendidos en el total pero no están repartidos entre los 10 grupos.

German Democratic Republic:

E--> Data include only books and pamphlets shown in series A of the German National Bibliography (publications of the book market) i.e., those of the series B (publications outside the book market) and C (books published by universities) are excluded. School textbooks (1982: 222; 1983: 208; 1984: 207) and children's books (1982: 770; 1983: 802; 1984: 816) are included in the total but not identified in the 10 groups.

FR-> Les données se réfèrent seulement aux livres et brochures de la série A de la Bibliographie nationale allemande (publications en vente dans le commerce). Les données relatives aux séries B (publications non vendues dans le commerce) et C (livres publiés par les universités) ne sont pas prises en compte. Les manuels scolaires (1982: 222; 1983: 208; 1984: 207) et les livres pour enfants (1982: 770; 1983: 802; 1984: 816) sont compris dans le total mais ne sont pas répartis entre les 10 groupes.

ESP> Los datos sólo se refieren a los libros y folletos de la serie A de la Bibliografía nacional alemana (publicaciones vendidas en el comercio). No se toman en consideración los datos relativos a las serias B (publicaciones que no se venden en el comercio) y C (libros publicados por las universidades). Los manuales escolares (1982: 222; 1983: 208; 1984: 207) y los libros para niños (1982: 770; 1983: 802; 1984: 816) quedan comprendidos en el total pero no están repartidos entre los 10 grupos.

Holy See:

E--> For 1983, data do not include pamphlets.

FR-> Pour 1983, les données ne comprennent pas les brochures.

ESP> En 1983, los datos no incluyen los folletos.

Ireland:

E--> For 1982, data do not include university theses. For 1983, data do not include pamphlets; school textbooks (35) and children's books (15) are included in the total but not identified in the 10 groups.

FR-> Pour 1982, les données n'incluent pas les thèses universitaires. Pour 1983, les données ne comprennent pas les brochures; les manuels scolaires (35) et les livres pour enfants (15) sont compris dans le total mais ne sont pas répartis entre les 10 groupes.

ESP> En 1982, los datos excluyen las tesis universitarias. En 1983, los datos no incluyen los folletos; los manuales escolares (35) y los libros para niños (15) quedan comprendidos en el total pero no están repartidos entre los 10 grupos.

Luxembourg:

E--> For 1983, all first editions.

FR-> Pour 1983, tous les ouvrages recensés sont des premières éditions.

ESP> En 1983, todas las obras consideradas son primeras ediciones.

Netherlands:

E--> Data do not include pamphlets. In 1984, school textbooks (2,039), children's books (1,369) and 151 other books are included in the total but not identified in the 10 groups.

FR-> Les données n'incluent pas les brochures. En 1984, les manuels scolaires (2 039), les livres pour enfants (1 369) et 151 autres livres sont compris dans le total mais ne sont pas répartis entre les 10 groupes.

ESP> Los datos no incluyen los folletos. En 1984, los manuales escolares (2 039), los libros para niños (1 369) y 151 otros libros quedan incluídos en el total pero no están repartidos entre los 10 grupos.

Norway:

E--> Data do not include school textbooks.

FR-> Les données n'incluent pas les manuels scolaires.

ESP> Los datos excluyen los manuales escolares.

Portugal:

E--> Data on philology are included with those of literature.

FR-> Les données relatives à la philologie sont comprises avec celles de la littérature.

ESP> Los datos relativos a la filología quedan incluídos con los de la literatura.

Sweden:

E--> Children's books (1982: 621; 1983: 602; 1984: 867) are included in the total but not distributed in the 10 groups. For 1984, the discrepancy between the total and the sum of the 25 groups is due to a variance in classification standards.

FR-> Les livres pour enfants (1982: 621; 1983: 602; 1984: 867) sont compris dans le total mais ne sont pas répartis entre les 10 groupes. En 1984, l'écart entre le total et la somme des 25 groupes est dû à une différence entre les normes de classification.

ESP> Los libros para niños (1982: 621; 1983: 602; 1984: 867) quedan comprendidos en el total pero no están repartidos entre los 10 grupos. En 1984, la diferencia entre el total y la suma de los 25 grupos se debe a una discordancia entre las normas de clasificación.

Switzerland:

E--> School textbooks (1982: 149; 1983: 145; 1984: 241) and children's books (1982: 577; 1983: 485; 1984: 610) are included in the total but not distributed in the 10 groups.

FR-> Les manuels scolaires (1982: 149; 1983: 145; 1984: 241) et les livres pour enfants (1982: 577; 1983: 485; 1984: 610) sont compris dans le total mais ne sont pas répartis entre les 10 groupes.

ESP> Los manuales escolares (1982: 149; 1983: 145; 1984: 241) y los libros para niños (1982: 577; 1983: 485; 1984: 610) quedan comprendidos en el total pero no están repartidos entre los 10 grupos.

OCEANIA:

Australia:

E--> Provisional data.

FR-> Les données sont provisoires.

ESP> Los datos son provisionales.

New Caledonia:

E--> All first editions.

FR-> Tous les ouvrages recensés sont des premières éditions.

ESP> Todas las obras consideradas son primeras ediciones.

U.S.S.R.:

U.S.S.R.:

E--> Books for the popularization of science for children (1982: 353 1983: 396; 1984: 390) are included in the total but not distributed in th 10 groups.

FR-> Les livres pour la vulgarisation des sciences pour les enfant (1982: 353; 1983: 396; 1984: 390) sont compris dans le total mais n sont pas répartis entre les 10 groupes.

ESP> Los libros para la vulgarización de las ciencias para niños (1982 353; 1983: 396; 1984: 390) quedan incluídos en el total pero no s desglosan entre los 10 grupos.

Ukrainian S.S.R.:

E--> Books for the popularization of science for children (1982: 64 1983: 75; 1984: 70) are included in the total but not distributed in the 1 groups.

FR-> Les livres pour la vulgarisation des sciences pour les enfant (1982: 64; 1983: 75; 1984: 70) sont compris dans le total mais ne sor pas répartis entre les 10 groupes.

ESP> Los libros para la vulgarización de las ciencias para niños (198 64; 1983: 75; 1984: 70) quedan incluídos en el total pero no se desglosa entre los 10 grupos.

7.8 Book production: number of titles by subject group

Edition de livres: nombre de titres par groupes de sujets

Edición de libros: número de títulos por categorías de temas

ALL EDITIONS: FIRST EDITIONS AND RE-EDITIONS PREMIERES EDITIONS ET REEDITIONS PRIMERAS EDICIONES Y REEDICIONES		FIRST EDITIONS ONLY PREMIERES EDITIONS SEULEMENT PRIMERAS EDICIONES SOLAMENTE	
TOTAL (BOOKS AND PAMPHLETS) TOTAL (LIVRES ET BROCHURES) TOTAL (LIBROS Y FOLLETOS)	OF WHICH: BOOKS DONT: LIVRES DEL CUAL: LIBROS	TOTAL (BOOKS AND PAMPHLETS) TOTAL (LIVRES ET BROCHURES) TOTAL (LIBROS Y FOLLETOS)	OF WHICH: BOOKS DONT: LIVRES DEL CUAL: LIBROS

FOR THE CLASSIFICATION, BASED UPON THE UNIVERSAL DECIMAL CLASSIFICATION (UDC), SEE SECTION 2 OF THE INTRODUCTORY TEXT TO THIS CHAPTER.

POUR LA CLASSIFICATION, FONDEE SUR LA CLASSIFICATION DECIMALE UNIVERSELLE (CDU), VOIR LA SECTION 2 DU TEXTE D'INTRODUCTION A CE CHAPITRE.

PARA LA CLASIFICACION, BASADA EN LA CLASIFICACION DECIMAL UNIVERSAL (CDU), VEASE LA SECCION 2 DEL TEXTO DE LA INTRODUCCION A ESTE CAPITULO.

NUMBER OF COUNTRIES AND TERRITORIES PRESENTED IN THIS TABLE: 84

NOMBRE DE PAYS ET DE TERRITOIRES PRESENTES DANS CE TABLEAU: 84

NUMERO DE PAISES Y DE TERRITORIOS PRESENTADOS EN ESTE CUADRO: 84

AFRICA

SUBJECT GROUP / GROUPE DE SUJETS / CATEGORIA DE TEMAS	ALGERIA (1984)				COTE D'IVOIRE‡ (1983)			
	ALL EDITIONS		FIRST EDITIONS		ALL EDITIONS		FIRST EDITIONS	
	TOTAL	OF WHICH: BOOKS	TOTAL	OF WHICH: BOOKS	TOTAL	OF WHICH: BOOKS	TOTAL	OF WHICH: BOOKS
TOTAL	718	551	710	544	46	46	32	32
1. GENERALITIES	26	18	26	18	–	–	–	–
2. PHILOSOPHY, PSYCHOLOGY	15	13	15	13	–	–	–	–
3. RELIGION, THEOLOGY	32	30	31	30	–	–	–	–
4. SOCIOLOGY, STATISTICS	87	36	86	35	–	–	–	–
5. POLITICAL SCIENCE	33	22	33	22	–	–	–	–
6. LAW, PUBLIC ADMINISTRATION	51	41	50	40	–	–	–	–
7. MILITARY ART	–	–	–	–	–	–	–	–
8. EDUCATION, LEISURE	25	24	25	24	17	17	11	11
9. TRADE, TRANSPORT	–	–	–	–	–	–	–	–
10. ETHNOGRAPHY, FOLKLORE	5	1	5	1	1	1	–	–
11. LINGUISTICS, PHILOLOGY	13	10	13	10	–	–	–	–
12. MATHEMATICS	26	19	23	16	–	–	–	–
13. NATURAL SCIENCES	78	54	78	54	–	–	–	–
14. MEDICAL SCIENCES	109	86	109	86	–	–	–	–
15. ENGINEERING, CRAFTS	12	7	12	7	–	–	–	–
16. AGRICULTURE	1	1	1	1	–	–	–	–
17. DOMESTIC SCIENCE	1	1	1	1	–	–	–	–
18. MANAGEMENT, ADMINISTRATION	2	–	2	–	4	4	4	4
19. PLANNING, ARCHITECTURE	9	9	9	9	–	–	–	–
20. PLASTIC ARTS	6	5	6	5	1	1	1	1
21. PERFORMING ARTS	3	3	3	3	2	2	2	2
22. GAMES, SPORTS	4	3	4	3	–	–	–	–
23. LITERATURE								
(A) HISTORY AND CRITICISM	19	15	19	15	–	–	–	–
(B) LITERARY TEXTS	100	95	99	94	4	4	4	4
24. GEOGRAPHY, TRAVEL	6	5	6	5	–	–	–	–
25. HISTORY, BIOGRAPHY	55	53	54	52	6	6	6	6

SUBJECT GROUP / GROUPE DE SUJETS / CATEGORIA DE TEMAS	ETHIOPIA (1984)				GAMBIA (1984)			
	ALL EDITIONS		FIRST EDITIONS		ALL EDITIONS		FIRST EDITIONS	
	TOTAL	OF WHICH: BOOKS	TOTAL	OF WHICH: BOOKS	TOTAL	OF WHICH: BOOKS	TOTAL	OF WHICH: BOOKS
TOTAL	349	192			146	21	146	21
1. GENERALITIES	1	1			15	3	15	3
2. PHILOSOPHY, PSYCHOLOGY	–	–			–	–	–	–
3. RELIGION, THEOLOGY	31	11			4	–	4	–
4. SOCIOLOGY, STATISTICS	–	–			7	2	7	2
5. POLITICAL SCIENCE	92	42			11	3	11	3
6. LAW, PUBLIC ADMINISTRATION	23	2			11	–	11	–
7. MILITARY ART	8	–			–	–	–	–
8. EDUCATION, LEISURE	67	45			15	3	15	3
9. TRADE, TRANSPORT	10	–			5	2	5	2
10. ETHNOGRAPHY, FOLKLORE	2	1			–	–	–	–
11. LINGUISTICS, PHILOLOGY	24	24			7	–	7	–
12. MATHEMATICS	13	13			4	–	4	–
13. NATURAL SCIENCES	12	12			7	1	7	1
14. MEDICAL SCIENCES	10	3			11	–	11	–
15. ENGINEERING, CRAFTS	4	1			4	–	4	–
16. AGRICULTURE	19	15			8	2	8	2
17. DOMESTIC SCIENCE	1	1			4	–	4	–
18. MANAGEMENT, ADMINISTRATION	1	–			3	–	3	–
19. PLANNING, ARCHITECTURE	2	–			7	1	7	1
20. PLASTIC ARTS	–	–			3	–	3	–
21. PERFORMING ARTS	3	1			–	–	–	–
22. GAMES, SPORTS	5	1			1	–	1	–
23. LITERATURE								
(A) HISTORY AND CRITICISM	8	8			–	–	–	–
(B) LITERARY TEXTS	6	6			3	–	3	–
24. GEOGRAPHY, TRAVEL	2	2			8	3	8	3
25. HISTORY, BIOGRAPHY	5	3			8	1	8	1

SUBJECT GROUP / GROUPE DE SUJETS / CATEGORIA DE TEMAS	GHANA (1983)				KENYA‡ (1983)			
	ALL EDITIONS		FIRST EDITIONS		ALL EDITIONS		FIRST EDITIONS	
	TOTAL	OF WHICH: BOOKS	TOTAL	OF WHICH: BOOKS	TOTAL	OF WHICH: BOOKS	TOTAL	OF WHICH: BOOKS
TOTAL	350	338	341	329	235	235		
1. GENERALITIES	–	–	–	–	10	10		
2. PHILOSOPHY, PSYCHOLOGY	1	1	1	1	2	2		
3. RELIGION, THEOLOGY	31	30	31	30	50	50		
4. SOCIOLOGY, STATISTICS	11	10	11	10	5	5		
5. POLITICAL SCIENCE	69	64	66	61	15	15		
6. LAW, PUBLIC ADMINISTRATION	10	10	10	10	6	6		
7. MILITARY ART	–	–	–	–	–	–		
8. EDUCATION, LEISURE	24	24	24	24	10	10		
9. TRADE, TRANSPORT	5	5	5	5	5	5		
10. ETHNOGRAPHY, FOLKLORE	11	11	11	11	7	7		
11. LINGUISTICS, PHILOLOGY	16	16	15	15	18	18		
12. MATHEMATICS	5	5	5	5	13	13		
13. NATURAL SCIENCES	8	8	7	7	10	10		
14. MEDICAL SCIENCES	16	16	15	15	4	4		
15. ENGINEERING, CRAFTS	8	8	8	8	–	–		
16. AGRICULTURE	34	34	33	33	5	5		
17. DOMESTIC SCIENCE	3	3	3	3	4	4		
18. MANAGEMENT, ADMINISTRATION	4	4	4	4	4	4		
19. PLANNING, ARCHITECTURE	3	3	3	3	–	–		
20. PLASTIC ARTS	3	3	3	3	3	3		
21. PERFORMING ARTS	18	18	18	18	12	12		
22. GAMES, SPORTS	9	4	9	4	5	5		
23. LITERATURE								
(A) HISTORY AND CRITICISM	13	13	13	13	7	7		
(B) LITERARY TEXTS	25	25	25	25	16	16		
24. GEOGRAPHY, TRAVEL	5	5	4	4	11	11		
25. HISTORY, BIOGRAPHY	18	18	17	17	13	13		

SUBJECT GROUP / GROUPE DE SUJETS / CATEGORIA DE TEMAS	MADAGASCAR (1984) ALL EDITIONS TOTAL	MADAGASCAR (1984) ALL EDITIONS OF WHICH: BOOKS	MADAGASCAR (1984) FIRST EDITIONS TOTAL	MADAGASCAR (1984) FIRST EDITIONS OF WHICH: BOOKS	MALI‡ (1984) ALL EDITIONS TOTAL	MALI‡ (1984) ALL EDITIONS OF WHICH: BOOKS	MALI‡ (1984) FIRST EDITIONS TOTAL	MALI‡ (1984) FIRST EDITIONS OF WHICH: BOOKS
TOTAL	321	242	308	231	160			
1. GENERALITIES	3	–	3	–	–			
2. PHILOSOPHY, PSYCHOLOGY	8	5	8	5	–			
3. RELIGION, THEOLOGY	48	21	45	20	–			
4. SOCIOLOGY, STATISTICS	1	1	1	1	20			
5. POLITICAL SCIENCE	5	2	5	2	–			
6. LAW, PUBLIC ADMINISTRATION	7	5	6	4	–			
7. MILITARY ART	3	1	3	1	–			
8. EDUCATION, LEISURE	20	13	16	9	78			
9. TRADE, TRANSPORT	2	1	2	1	–			
10. ETHNOGRAPHY, FOLKLORE	3	1	3	1	–			
11. LINGUISTICS, PHILOLOGY	14	11	12	9	19			
12. MATHEMATICS	9	9	8	8	13			
13. NATURAL SCIENCES	11	9	11	9	4			
14. MEDICAL SCIENCES	147	145	147	145	4			
15. ENGINEERING, CRAFTS	1	1	1	1	12			
16. AGRICULTURE	5	4	5	4	2			
17. DOMESTIC SCIENCE	1	0	1	0	1			
18. MANAGEMENT, ADMINISTRATION	7	2	7	2	4			
19. PLANNING, ARCHITECTURE	1	1	1	1	–			
20. PLASTIC ARTS	1	–	1	–	–			
21. PERFORMING ARTS	3	1	3	1	–			
22. GAMES, SPORTS	2	–	2	–	–			
23. LITERATURE								
(A) HISTORY AND CRITICISM	–	–	–	–	–			
(B) LITERARY TEXTS	13	6	11	4	–			
24. GEOGRAPHY, TRAVEL	3	1	3	1	3			
25. HISTORY, BIOGRAPHY	3	2	3	2	–			

SUBJECT GROUP / GROUPE DE SUJETS / CATEGORIA DE TEMAS	MAURITIUS (1984) ALL EDITIONS TOTAL	MAURITIUS (1984) ALL EDITIONS OF WHICH: BOOKS	MAURITIUS (1984) FIRST EDITIONS TOTAL	MAURITIUS (1984) FIRST EDITIONS OF WHICH: BOOKS	MOZAMBIQUE (1983) ALL EDITIONS TOTAL	MOZAMBIQUE (1983) ALL EDITIONS OF WHICH: BOOKS	MOZAMBIQUE (1983) FIRST EDITIONS TOTAL	MOZAMBIQUE (1983) FIRST EDITIONS OF WHICH: BOOKS
TOTAL	124	65	121	63	88	87	64	63
1. GENERALITIES	1	–	1	–	–	–	–	–
2. PHILOSOPHY, PSYCHOLOGY	–	–	–	–	–	–	–	–
3. RELIGION, THEOLOGY	10	3	10	3	–	–	–	–
4. SOCIOLOGY, STATISTICS	2	–	2	–	–	–	–	–
5. POLITICAL SCIENCE	7	4	7	4	17	17	17	17
6. LAW, PUBLIC ADMINISTRATION	16	7	15	7	–	–	–	–
7. MILITARY ART	–	–	–	–	1	1	1	1
8. EDUCATION, LEISURE	2	1	2	1	42	42	25	25
9. TRADE, TRANSPORT	1	–	1	–	–	–	–	–
10. ETHNOGRAPHY, FOLKLORE	2	1	2	1	–	–	–	–
11. LINGUISTICS, PHILOLOGY	25	19	25	19	–	–	–	–
12. MATHEMATICS	5	5	5	5	6	6	6	6
13. NATURAL SCIENCES	3	2	3	2	–	–	–	–
14. MEDICAL SCIENCES	4	2	4	2	3	3	2	2
15. ENGINEERING, CRAFTS	4	3	3	2	–	–	–	–
16. AGRICULTURE	–	–	–	–	–	–	–	–
17. DOMESTIC SCIENCE	3	–	3	–	–	–	–	–
18. MANAGEMENT, ADMINISTRATION	2	1	2	1	–	–	–	–
19. PLANNING, ARCHITECTURE	–	–	–	–	–	–	–	–
20. PLASTIC ARTS	1	1	1	1	–	–	–	–
21. PERFORMING ARTS	10	3	10	3	1	–	1	–
22. GAMES, SPORTS	–	–	–	–	1	1	1	1
23. LITERATURE								
(A) HISTORY AND CRITICISM	1	–	1	–	–	–	–	–
(B) LITERARY TEXTS	12	5	11	4	12	12	9	9
24. GEOGRAPHY, TRAVEL	1	1	1	1	–	–	–	–
25. HISTORY, BIOGRAPHY	12	7	12	7	5	5	2	2

7.8 **Number of titles by subject group**
Nombre de titres par groupes de sujets
Número de títulos por categorías de temas

SUBJECT GROUP / GROUPE DE SUJETS / CATEGORIA DE TEMAS	NIGERIA (1984)				REUNION (1983)			
	ALL EDITIONS		FIRST EDITIONS		ALL EDITIONS		FIRST EDITIONS	
	TOTAL	OF WHICH: BOOKS	TOTAL	OF WHICH: BOOKS	TOTAL	OF WHICH: BOOKS	TOTAL	OF WHICH: BOOKS
TOTAL	1 836	940	1 538	822	79	49	76	48
1. GENERALITIES	64	26	58	26	–	–	–	–
2. PHILOSOPHY, PSYCHOLOGY	14	8	14	8	–	–	–	–
3. RELIGION, THEOLOGY	138	68	118	68	8	3	6	2
4. SOCIOLOGY, STATISTICS	80	44	60	40	2	1	2	1
5. POLITICAL SCIENCE	322	154	304	140	3	2	3	2
6. LAW, PUBLIC ADMINISTRATION	178	84	120	60	7	4	7	4
7. MILITARY ART	–	–	–	–	–	–	–	–
8. EDUCATION, LEISURE	280	100	236	90	3	3	3	3
9. TRADE, TRANSPORT	16	8	10	6	6	2	6	2
10. ETHNOGRAPHY, FOLKLORE	12	4	12	4	1	1	1	1
11. LINGUISTICS, PHILOLOGY	98	72	72	46	1	1	1	1
12. MATHEMATICS	44	34	40	30	–	–	–	–
13. NATURAL SCIENCES	42	28	34	22	3	2	3	2
14. MEDICAL SCIENCES	44	26	28	12	2	2	2	2
15. ENGINEERING, CRAFTS	78	44	48	32	1	–	1	–
16. AGRICULTURE	102	24	92	24	4	4	4	4
17. DOMESTIC SCIENCE	2	2	2	2	2	1	1	1
18. MANAGEMENT, ADMINISTRATION	58	36	46	36	–	–	–	–
19. PLANNING, ARCHITECTURE	2	2	2	2	6	3	6	3
20. PLASTIC ARTS	14	4	14	4	2	1	2	1
21. PERFORMING ARTS	12	4	12	4	3	1	3	1
22. GAMES, SPORTS	16	6	12	6	3	1	3	1
23. LITERATURE								
(A) HISTORY AND CRITICISM	36	22	30	22	–	–	–	–
(B) LITERARY TEXTS	120	100	112	92	16	13	16	13
24. GEOGRAPHY, TRAVEL	6	4	6	4	–	–	–	–
25. HISTORY, BIOGRAPHY	58	36	56	42	6	4	6	4

SUBJECT GROUP / GROUPE DE SUJETS / CATEGORIA DE TEMAS	SENEGAL (1983)				UNITED REPUBLIC OF TANZANIA (1984)			
	ALL EDITIONS		FIRST EDITIONS		ALL EDITIONS		FIRST EDITIONS	
	TOTAL	OF WHICH: BOOKS	TOTAL	OF WHICH: BOOKS	TOTAL	OF WHICH: BOOKS	TOTAL	OF WHICH: BOOKS
TOTAL	42		42		363	166	363	166
1. GENERALITIES	–		–		17	3	17	3
2. PHILOSOPHY, PSYCHOLOGY	2		2		1	1	1	1
3. RELIGION, THEOLOGY	3		3		41	18	41	18
4. SOCIOLOGY, STATISTICS	3		3		13	6	13	6
5. POLITICAL SCIENCE	2		2		89	36	89	36
6. LAW, PUBLIC ADMINISTRATION	3		3		22	10	22	10
7. MILITARY ART	–		–		2	1	2	1
8. EDUCATION, LEISURE	1		1		53	31	53	31
9. TRADE, TRANSPORT	–		–		16	5	16	5
10. ETHNOGRAPHY, FOLKLORE	–		–		–	–	–	–
11. LINGUISTICS, PHILOLOGY	4		4		6	3	6	3
12. MATHEMATICS	–		–		5	2	5	2
13. NATURAL SCIENCES	2		2		2	2	2	2
14. MEDICAL SCIENCES	–		–		6	1	6	1
15. ENGINEERING, CRAFTS	–		–		4	–	4	–
16. AGRICULTURE	–		–		20	13	20	13
17. DOMESTIC SCIENCE	–		–		13	4	13	4
18. MANAGEMENT, ADMINISTRATION	–		–		34	15	34	15
19. PLANNING, ARCHITECTURE	–		–		1	1	1	1
20. PLASTIC ARTS	–		–		1	1	1	1
21. PERFORMING ARTS	–		–		1	–	1	–
22. GAMES, SPORTS	–		–		1	1	1	1
23. LITERATURE								
(A) HISTORY AND CRITICISM	5		5		1	1	1	1
(B) LITERARY TEXTS	9		9		8	6	8	6
24. GEOGRAPHY, TRAVEL	1		1		2	2	2	2
25. HISTORY, BIOGRAPHY	7		7		4	3	4	3

SUBJECT GROUP / GROUPE DE SUJETS / CATEGORIA DE TEMAS	ZAMBIA (1983)				ZIMBABWE‡ (1984)			
	ALL EDITIONS		FIRST EDITIONS		ALL EDITIONS		FIRST EDITIONS	
	TOTAL	OF WHICH: BOOKS	TOTAL	OF WHICH: BOOKS	TOTAL	OF WHICH: BOOKS	TOTAL	OF WHICH: BOOKS
TOTAL	454	454	373	373	193	183	155	147
1. GENERALITIES	143	143	109	109	1	1	1	1
2. PHILOSOPHY, PSYCHOLOGY	–	–	–	–	–	–	–	–
3. RELIGION, THEOLOGY	–	–	–	–	14	13	11	10
4. SOCIOLOGY, STATISTICS	15	15	9	9	5	5	4	4
5. POLITICAL SCIENCE	–	–	–	–	3	3	1	1
6. LAW, PUBLIC ADMINISTRATION	–	–	–	–	2	2	1	1
7. MILITARY ART	–	–	–	–	–	–	–	–
8. EDUCATION, LEISURE	210	210	189	189	3	3	2	2
9. TRADE, TRANSPORT	–	–	–	–	–	–	–	–
10. ETHNOGRAPHY, FOLKLORE	6	6	6	6	1	1	1	1
11. LINGUISTICS, PHILOLOGY	–	–	–	–	40	39	35	34
12. MATHEMATICS	12	12	12	12	7	6	5	5
13. NATURAL SCIENCES	3	3	3	3	12	12	8	8
14. MEDICAL SCIENCES	–	–	–	–	6	–	5	–
15. ENGINEERING, CRAFTS	–	–	–	–	–	–	–	–
16. AGRICULTURE	4	4	4	4	7	7	7	7
17. DOMESTIC SCIENCE	9	9	9	9	–	–	–	–
18. MANAGEMENT, ADMINISTRATION	–	–	–	–	1	1	–	–
19. PLANNING, ARCHITECTURE	–	–	–	–	–	–	–	–
20. PLASTIC ARTS	–	–	–	–	–	–	–	–
21. PERFORMING ARTS	18	18	18	18	–	–	–	–
22. GAMES, SPORTS	–	–	–	–	–	–	–	–
23. LITERATURE								
(A) HISTORY AND CRITICISM	–	–	–	–	3	3	2	2
(B) LITERARY TEXTS	–	–	–	–	37	37	24	24
24. GEOGRAPHY, TRAVEL	–	–	–	–	6	6	6	6
25. HISTORY, BIOGRAPHY	34	34	14	14	4	3	1	–

AMERICA, NORTH

SUBJECT GROUP / GROUPE DE SUJETS / CATEGORIA DE TEMAS	BARBADOS (1983)				BRITISH VIRGIN ISLANDS (1982)			
	ALL EDITIONS		FIRST EDITIONS		ALL EDITIONS		FIRST EDITIONS	
	TOTAL	OF WHICH: BOOKS	TOTAL	OF WHICH: BOOKS	TOTAL	OF WHICH: BOOKS	TOTAL	OF WHICH: BOOKS
TOTAL	87	18	63	15	20	20	–	–
1. GENERALITIES	4	–	4	–	20	20	–	–
2. PHILOSOPHY, PSYCHOLOGY	–	–	–	–	–	–	–	–
3. RELIGION, THEOLOGY	–	–	–	–	–	–	–	–
4. SOCIOLOGY, STATISTICS	1	–	–	–	–	–	–	–
5. POLITICAL SCIENCE	15	2	8	2	–	–	–	–
6. LAW, PUBLIC ADMINISTRATION	6	2	4	2	–	–	–	–
7. MILITARY ART	1	–	1	–	–	–	–	–
8. EDUCATION, LEISURE	11	2	11	2	–	–	–	–
9. TRADE, TRANSPORT	6	2	2	–	–	–	–	–
10. ETHNOGRAPHY, FOLKLORE	3	2	3	2	–	–	–	–
11. LINGUISTICS, PHILOLOGY	–	–	–	–	–	–	–	–
12. MATHEMATICS	–	–	–	–	–	–	–	–
13. NATURAL SCIENCES	2	–	2	–	–	–	–	–
14. MEDICAL SCIENCES	8	1	6	1	–	–	–	–
15. ENGINEERING, CRAFTS	7	–	6	–	–	–	–	–
16. AGRICULTURE	1	1	1	1	–	–	–	–
17. DOMESTIC SCIENCE	–	–	–	–	–	–	–	–
18. MANAGEMENT, ADMINISTRATION	5	–	2	–	–	–	–	–
19. PLANNING, ARCHITECTURE	6	2	5	2	–	–	–	–
20. PLASTIC ARTS	–	–	–	–	–	–	–	–
21. PERFORMING ARTS	3	–	3	–	–	–	–	–
22. GAMES, SPORTS	1	–	–	–	–	–	–	–
23. LITERATURE								
(A) HISTORY AND CRITICISM	–	–	–	–	–	–	–	–
(B) LITERARY TEXTS	3	2	2	1	–	–	–	–
24. GEOGRAPHY, TRAVEL	–	–	–	–	–	–	–	–
25. HISTORY, BIOGRAPHY	4	2	3	2	–	–	–	–

7.8 **Number of titles by subject group**
Nombre de titres par groupes de sujets
Número de títulos por categorías de temas

SUBJECT GROUP / GROUPE DE SUJETS / CATEGORIA DE TEMAS	COSTA RICA (1984)				CUBA (1984)			
	ALL EDITIONS		FIRST EDITIONS		ALL EDITIONS		FIRST EDITIONS	
	TOTAL	OF WHICH: BOOKS	TOTAL	OF WHICH: BOOKS	TOTAL	OF WHICH: BOOKS	TOTAL	OF WHICH: BOOKS
TOTAL	1 759	1 759	1 586	1 586	2 069	1 684	974	753
1. GENERALITIES	38	38	35	35	339	191	163	86
2. PHILOSOPHY, PSYCHOLOGY	47	47	45	45	28	27	7	7
3. RELIGION, THEOLOGY	82	82	76	76	2	2	–	–
4. SOCIOLOGY, STATISTICS	89	89	78	78	6	6	2	2
5. POLITICAL SCIENCE	197	197	168	168	44	44	18	18
6. LAW, PUBLIC ADMINISTRATION	191	191	189	189	20	18	6	6
7. MILITARY ART	1	1	1	1	10	9	3	3
8. EDUCATION, LEISURE	88	88	77	77	404	320	103	82
9. TRADE, TRANSPORT	3	3	3	3	5	5	4	4
10. ETHNOGRAPHY, FOLKLORE	7	7	6	6	1	1	1	1
11. LINGUISTICS, PHILOLOGY	69	69	63	63	114	112	18	18
12. MATHEMATICS	77	77	70	70	72	71	22	22
13. NATURAL SCIENCES	77	77	75	75	85	72	26	23
14. MEDICAL SCIENCES	18	18	16	16	221	113	169	64
15. ENGINEERING, CRAFTS	60	60	58	58	161	158	51	51
16. AGRICULTURE	185	185	183	183	47	44	17	17
17. DOMESTIC SCIENCE	4	4	4	4	9	9	5	5
18. MANAGEMENT, ADMINISTRATION	24	24	16	16	8	8	1	1
19. PLANNING, ARCHITECTURE	20	20	20	20	8	7	5	5
20. PLASTIC ARTS	6	6	6	6	10	9	2	2
21. PERFORMING ARTS	3	3	2	2	59	59	30	30
22. GAMES, SPORTS	3	3	3	3	36	22	33	19
23. LITERATURE								
(A) HISTORY AND CRITICISM	150	150	150	150	200	199	176	176
(B) LITERARY TEXTS	190	190	118	118	99	98	72	72
24. GEOGRAPHY, TRAVEL	49	49	48	48	24	24	9	9
25. HISTORY, BIOGRAPHY	81	81	76	76	57	56	31	30

SUBJECT GROUP / GROUPE DE SUJETS / CATEGORIA DE TEMAS	MEXICO‡ (1984)				NICARAGUA (1984)			
	ALL EDITIONS		FIRST EDITIONS		ALL EDITIONS		FIRST EDITIONS	
	TOTAL	OF WHICH: BOOKS	TOTAL	OF WHICH: BOOKS	TOTAL	OF WHICH: BOOKS	TOTAL	OF WHICH: BOOKS
TOTAL	4 505	4 505			26	26	17	17
1. GENERALITIES	569	569			4	4	4	4
2. PHILOSOPHY, PSYCHOLOGY	276	276			1	1	1	1
3. RELIGION, THEOLOGY	114	114			2	2	2	2
4. SOCIOLOGY, STATISTICS	292	292			–	–	–	–
5. POLITICAL SCIENCE	341	341			1	1	1	1
6. LAW, PUBLIC ADMINISTRATION	182	182			–	–	–	–
7. MILITARY ART	13	13			–	–	–	–
8. EDUCATION, LEISURE	338	338			–	–	–	–
9. TRADE, TRANSPORT	19	19			–	–	–	–
10. ETHNOGRAPHY, FOLKLORE	17	17			1	1	1	1
11. LINGUISTICS, PHILOLOGY	129	129			–	–	–	–
12. MATHEMATICS	119	119			–	–	–	–
13. NATURAL SCIENCES	238	238			–	–	–	–
14. MEDICAL SCIENCES	269	269			–	–	–	–
15. ENGINEERING, CRAFTS	67	67			–	–	–	–
16. AGRICULTURE	37	37			–	–	–	–
17. DOMESTIC SCIENCE	11	11			–	–	–	–
18. MANAGEMENT, ADMINISTRATION	74	74			–	–	–	–
19. PLANNING, ARCHITECTURE	24	24			–	–	–	–
20. PLASTIC ARTS	50	50			–	–	–	–
21. PERFORMING ARTS	46	46			–	–	–	–
22. GAMES, SPORTS	31	31			–	–	–	–
23. LITERATURE								
(A) HISTORY AND CRITICISM	971	971			1	1	1	1
(B) LITERARY TEXTS	./.	./.			14	14	5	5
24. GEOGRAPHY, TRAVEL	56	56			–	–	–	–
25. HISTORY, BIOGRAPHY	222	222			2	2	2	2

AMERICA, SOUTH

SUBJECT GROUP / GROUPE DE SUJETS / CATEGORIA DE TEMAS	ST. CHRISTOPHER AND NEVIS (1982)				ARGENTINA‡ (1983)			
	ALL EDITIONS		FIRST EDITIONS		ALL EDITIONS		FIRST EDITIONS	
	TOTAL	OF WHICH: BOOKS	TOTAL	OF WHICH: BOOKS	TOTAL	OF WHICH: BOOKS	TOTAL	OF WHICH: BOOKS
TOTAL	5	2	5	2	4 216			
1. GENERALITIES	–	–	–	–	189			
2. PHILOSOPHY, PSYCHOLOGY	–	–	–	–	536			
3. RELIGION, THEOLOGY	–	–	–	–	./.			
4. SOCIOLOGY, STATISTICS	–	–	–	–	337			
5. POLITICAL SCIENCE	–	–	–	–	./.			
6. LAW, PUBLIC ADMINISTRATION	–	–	–	–	342			
7. MILITARY ART	–	–	–	–	–			
8. EDUCATION, LEISURE	2	1	2	1	243			
9. TRADE, TRANSPORT	1	–	1	–	–			
10. ETHNOGRAPHY, FOLKLORE	–	–	–	–	–			
11. LINGUISTICS, PHILOLOGY	–	–	–	–	./.			
12. MATHEMATICS	–	–	–	–	179			
13. NATURAL SCIENCES	–	–	–	–	20			
14. MEDICAL SCIENCES	1	1	1	1	131			
15. ENGINEERING, CRAFTS	–	–	–	–	492			
16. AGRICULTURE	–	–	–	–	36			
17. DOMESTIC SCIENCE	–	–	–	–	–			
18. MANAGEMENT, ADMINISTRATION	–	–	–	–	–			
19. PLANNING, ARCHITECTURE	–	–	–	–	7			
20. PLASTIC ARTS	–	–	–	–	639			
21. PERFORMING ARTS	–	–	–	–	./.			
22. GAMES, SPORTS	–	–	–	–	56			
23. LITERATURE								
(A) HISTORY AND CRITICISM	–	–	–	–	58			
(B) LITERARY TEXTS	–	–	–	–	934			
24. GEOGRAPHY, TRAVEL	–	–	–	–	17			
25. HISTORY, BIOGRAPHY	1	–	1	–	./.			

SUBJECT GROUP / GROUPE DE SUJETS / CATEGORIA DE TEMAS	BOLIVIA‡ (1982)				BRAZIL‡ (1982)			
	ALL EDITIONS		FIRST EDITIONS		ALL EDITIONS		FIRST EDITIONS	
	TOTAL	OF WHICH: BOOKS	TOTAL	OF WHICH: BOOKS	TOTAL	OF WHICH: BOOKS	TOTAL	OF WHICH: BOOKS
TOTAL	*301	*274	*287	*260	19 179	15 410	11 447	8 987
1. GENERALITIES	8	8	8	8	1 160	826	839	559
2. PHILOSOPHY, PSYCHOLOGY	1	1	1	1	732	595	349	257
3. RELIGION, THEOLOGY	13	13	13	13	2 251	1 958	1 082	831
4. SOCIOLOGY, STATISTICS	14	13	14	13	327	236	210	161
5. POLITICAL SCIENCE	15	14	15	14	447	416	330	300
6. LAW, PUBLIC ADMINISTRATION	23	23	23	23	1 551	1 210	1 221	896
7. MILITARY ART	2	2	2	2	22	20	15	13
8. EDUCATION, LEISURE	16	14	16	14	2 679	2 001	1 081	674
9. TRADE, TRANSPORT	2	2	2	2	96	71	84	59
10. ETHNOGRAPHY, FOLKLORE	21	15	20	14	361	98	74	30
11. LINGUISTICS, PHILOLOGY	11	10	10	9	606	537	273	207
12. MATHEMATICS	1	1	1	1	613	558	279	256
13. NATURAL SCIENCES	10	10	10	10	849	587	493	392
14. MEDICAL SCIENCES	3	2	3	2	773	491	520	326
15. ENGINEERING, CRAFTS	2	–	2	–	902	556	563	299
16. AGRICULTURE	3	3	3	3	280	201	211	132
17. DOMESTIC SCIENCE	–	–	–	–	86	75	62	54
18. MANAGEMENT, ADMINISTRATION	4	4	4	4	197	191	69	64
19. PLANNING, ARCHITECTURE	1	1	1	1	52	52	35	35
20. PLASTIC ARTS	9	6	9	6	1 239	1 190	1 118	1 087
21. PERFORMING ARTS	13	13	13	13	–	–	–	–
22. GAMES, SPORTS	4	1	4	1	633	431	386	338
23. LITERATURE								
(A) HISTORY AND CRITICISM	64	61	54	51	2 588	2 406	1 644	1 532
(B) LITERARY TEXTS	./.	./.	./.	./.	./.	./.	./.	./.
24. GEOGRAPHY, TRAVEL	14	13	14	13	202	182	125	110
25. HISTORY, BIOGRAPHY	47	44	45	42	533	522	384	375

7.8 Number of titles by subject group
Nombre de titres par groupes de sujets
Número de títulos por categorías de temas

SUBJECT GROUP / GROUPE DE SUJETS / CATEGORIA DE TEMAS	CHILE (1984) ALL EDITIONS TOTAL	CHILE (1984) ALL EDITIONS OF WHICH: BOOKS	CHILE (1984) FIRST EDITIONS TOTAL	CHILE (1984) FIRST EDITIONS OF WHICH: BOOKS	COLOMBIA (1984) ALL EDITIONS TOTAL	COLOMBIA (1984) ALL EDITIONS OF WHICH: BOOKS	COLOMBIA (1984) FIRST EDITIONS TOTAL	COLOMBIA (1984) FIRST EDITIONS OF WHICH: BOOKS
TOTAL	1 653	1 207	1 432	1 000	15 041	6 500	11 848	4 738
1. GENERALITIES	30	25	27	22	1 078	708	780	470
2. PHILOSOPHY, PSYCHOLOGY	24	22	19	17	239	149	140	70
3. RELIGION, THEOLOGY	112	70	104	64	352	137	192	77
4. SOCIOLOGY, STATISTICS	73	51	70	48	205	125	140	80
5. POLITICAL SCIENCE	172	105	162	95	413	358	285	240
6. LAW, PUBLIC ADMINISTRATION	125	98	102	75	1 025	605	750	390
7. MILITARY ART	9	6	8	5	89	29	85	25
8. EDUCATION, LEISURE	180	135	135	92	517	382	345	240
9. TRADE, TRANSPORT	38	26	36	24	340	125	245	90
10. ETHNOGRAPHY, FOLKLORE	9	6	8	5	195	160	177	142
11. LINGUISTICS, PHILOLOGY	28	27	12	12	290	175	252	167
12. MATHEMATICS	15	15	12	12	530	405	364	249
13. NATURAL SCIENCES	53	46	41	35	568	293	423	203
14. MEDICAL SCIENCES	47	36	40	29	4 787	135	4 075	180
15. ENGINEERING, CRAFTS	56	31	55	30	365	265	312	212
16. AGRICULTURE	38	21	37	20	570	135	462	122
17. DOMESTIC SCIENCE	7	6	6	5	150	103	146	101
18. MANAGEMENT, ADMINISTRATION	12	8	7	3	195	135	152	122
19. PLANNING, ARCHITECTURE	12	10	11	9	135	105	120	90
20. PLASTIC ARTS	7	6	7	6	205	85	165	85
21. PERFORMING ARTS	19	11	19	11	332	170	290	150
22. GAMES, SPORTS	11	8	11	8	325	145	280	130
23. LITERATURE								
(A) HISTORY AND CRITICISM	7	7	7	7	340	180	306	146
(B) LITERARY TEXTS	443	336	388	286	1 161	821	978	638
24. GEOGRAPHY, TRAVEL	25	19	20	14	290	265	142	117
25. HISTORY, BIOGRAPHY	101	76	88	66	345	305	242	202

SUBJECT GROUP / GROUPE DE SUJETS / CATEGORIA DE TEMAS	GUYANA (1983) ALL EDITIONS TOTAL	GUYANA (1983) ALL EDITIONS OF WHICH: BOOKS	GUYANA (1983) FIRST EDITIONS TOTAL	GUYANA (1983) FIRST EDITIONS OF WHICH: BOOKS	PERU (1984) ALL EDITIONS TOTAL	PERU (1984) ALL EDITIONS OF WHICH: BOOKS	PERU (1984) FIRST EDITIONS TOTAL	PERU (1984) FIRST EDITIONS OF WHICH: BOOKS
TOTAL	55	17	52	16	546	481	451	389
1. GENERALITIES	2	1	2	1	12	12	11	11
2. PHILOSOPHY, PSYCHOLOGY	–	–	–	–	16	16	15	15
3. RELIGION, THEOLOGY	–	–	–	–	7	7	7	7
4. SOCIOLOGY, STATISTICS	1	–	1	–	26	25	24	23
5. POLITICAL SCIENCE	20	–	18	–	71	66	55	50
6. LAW, PUBLIC ADMINISTRATION	3	–	3	–	54	50	46	42
7. MILITARY ART	–	–	–	–	–	–	–	–
8. EDUCATION, LEISURE	2	1	2	1	29	26	24	21
9. TRADE, TRANSPORT	–	–	–	–	10	9	10	9
10. ETHNOGRAPHY, FOLKLORE	1	–	1	–	12	12	7	7
11. LINGUISTICS, PHILOLOGY	–	–	–	–	10	8	9	7
12. MATHEMATICS	2	1	2	1	17	17	11	11
13. NATURAL SCIENCES	1	–	1	–	16	15	9	8
14. MEDICAL SCIENCES	1	1	1	1	25	17	22	15
15. ENGINEERING, CRAFTS	–	–	–	–	22	18	17	13
16. AGRICULTURE	6	3	6	3	9	7	8	7
17. DOMESTIC SCIENCE	–	–	–	–	11	9	6	5
18. MANAGEMENT, ADMINISTRATION	–	–	–	–	40	39	35	34
19. PLANNING, ARCHITECTURE	4	4	4	4	1	–	1	–
20. PLASTIC ARTS	–	–	–	–	1	1	1	1
21. PERFORMING ARTS	–	–	–	–	7	6	7	6
22. GAMES, SPORTS	–	–	–	–	7	7	4	4
23. LITERATURE								
(A) HISTORY AND CRITICISM	1	1	1	1	15	13	13	11
(B) LITERARY TEXTS	6	3	5	2	68	47	67	46
24. GEOGRAPHY, TRAVEL	1	1	1	1	19	19	8	8
25. HISTORY, BIOGRAPHY	4	1	4	1	41	35	34	28

ASIA

SUBJECT GROUP / GROUPE DE SUJETS / CATEGORIA DE TEMAS	URUGUAY (1984)				BAHRAIN‡ (1982)			
	ALL EDITIONS		FIRST EDITIONS		ALL EDITIONS		FIRST EDITIONS	
	TOTAL	OF WHICH: BOOKS	TOTAL	OF WHICH: BOOKS	TOTAL	OF WHICH: BOOKS	TOTAL	OF WHICH: BOOKS
TOTAL	1 206	711	896	534	78	78	39	39
1. GENERALITIES	21	13	10	7	–	–	–	–
2. PHILOSOPHY, PSYCHOLOGY	22	13	9	6	–	–	–	–
3. RELIGION, THEOLOGY	42	12	24	5	9	9	2	2
4. SOCIOLOGY, STATISTICS	46	25	38	19	–	–	–	–
5. POLITICAL SCIENCE	69	49	37	32	–	–	–	–
6. LAW, PUBLIC ADMINISTRATION	112	69	76	52	–	–	–	–
7. MILITARY ART	11	6	3	2	–	–	–	–
8. EDUCATION, LEISURE	76	36	45	21	–	–	–	–
9. TRADE, TRANSPORT	84	53	75	47	5	5	5	5
10. ETHNOGRAPHY, FOLKLORE	3	2	3	2	–	–	–	–
11. LINGUISTICS, PHILOLOGY	6	5	8	6	11	11	1	1
12. MATHEMATICS	50	29	34	18	12	12	2	2
13. NATURAL SCIENCES	27	18	16	9	12	12	7	7
14. MEDICAL SCIENCES	52	29	39	22	–	–	–	–
15. ENGINEERING, CRAFTS	79	51	51	34	10	10	10	10
16. AGRICULTURE	59	31	46	27	–	–	–	–
17. DOMESTIC SCIENCE	4	–	3	–	4	4	4	4
18. MANAGEMENT, ADMINISTRATION	37	21	28	20	–	–	–	–
19. PLANNING, ARCHITECTURE	24	14	20	12	–	–	–	–
20. PLASTIC ARTS	15	6	10	4	–	–	–	–
21. PERFORMING ARTS	21	13	19	13	–	–	–	–
22. GAMES, SPORTS	16	11	13	9	–	–	–	–
23. LITERATURE					–	–	–	–
(A) HISTORY AND CRITICISM	36	25	29	20	–	–	–	–
(B) LITERARY TEXTS	169	92	164	87	–	–	–	–
24. GEOGRAPHY, TRAVEL	45	28	26	17	9	9	6	6
25. HISTORY, BIOGRAPHY	80	60	60	43	6	6	2	2

SUBJECT GROUP / GROUPE DE SUJETS / CATEGORIA DE TEMAS	BRUNEI DARUSSALAM (1982)				CHINA‡ (1984)			
	ALL EDITIONS		FIRST EDITIONS		ALL EDITIONS		FIRST EDITIONS	
	TOTAL	OF WHICH: BOOKS	TOTAL	OF WHICH: BOOKS	TOTAL	OF WHICH: BOOKS	TOTAL	OF WHICH: BOOKS
TOTAL	72	50	64	42	34 920		24 171	
1. GENERALITIES	25	22	23	20	./.		./.	
2. PHILOSOPHY, PSYCHOLOGY	–	–	–	–	4 041		3 163	
3. RELIGION, THEOLOGY	6	6	–	–	./.		./.	
4. SOCIOLOGY, STATISTICS	–	–	–	–	./.		./.	
5. POLITICAL SCIENCE	–	–	–	–	./.		./.	
6. LAW, PUBLIC ADMINISTRATION	–	–	–	–	./.		./.	
7. MILITARY ART	–	–	–	–	./.		./.	
8. EDUCATION, LEISURE	–	–	–	–	6 216		4 299	
9. TRADE, TRANSPORT	–	–	–	–	./.		./.	
10. ETHNOGRAPHY, FOLKLORE	–	–	–	–	./.		./.	
11. LINGUISTICS, PHILOLOGY	13	5	13	5	./.		./.	
12. MATHEMATICS	11	4	11	4	./.		./.	
13. NATURAL SCIENCES	11	10	11	10	9 338		6 950	
14. MEDICAL SCIENCES	1	–	1	–	./.		./.	
15. ENGINEERING, CRAFTS	–	–	–	–	./.		./.	
16. AGRICULTURE	1	1	1	1	./.		./.	
17. DOMESTIC SCIENCE	–	–	–	–	./.		./.	
18. MANAGEMENT, ADMINISTRATION	–	–	–	–	./.		./.	
19. PLANNING, ARCHITECTURE	–	–	–	–	./.		./.	
20. PLASTIC ARTS	–	–	–	–	./.		./.	
21. PERFORMING ARTS	1	–	1	–	./.		./.	
22. GAMES, SPORTS	–	–	–	–	./.		./.	
23. LITERATURE								
(A) HISTORY AND CRITICISM	–	–	–	–	5 661		4 277	
(B) LITERARY TEXTS	–	–	–	–	./.		./.	
24. GEOGRAPHY, TRAVEL	2	1	2	1	./.		./.	
25. HISTORY, BIOGRAPHY	1	1	1	1	./.		./.	

7.8 Number of titles by subject group
Nombre de titres par groupes de sujets
Número de títulos por categorías de temas

SUBJECT GROUP / GROUPE DE SUJETS / CATEGORIA DE TEMAS	HONG KONG (1983) ALL EDITIONS TOTAL	HONG KONG (1983) ALL EDITIONS OF WHICH: BOOKS	HONG KONG (1983) FIRST EDITIONS TOTAL	HONG KONG (1983) FIRST EDITIONS OF WHICH: BOOKS	INDIA (1984) ALL EDITIONS TOTAL	INDIA (1984) ALL EDITIONS OF WHICH: BOOKS	INDIA (1984) FIRST EDITIONS TOTAL	INDIA (1984) FIRST EDITIONS OF WHICH: BOOKS
TOTAL	5 681	3 642	4 358	3 065	9 954	9 954		
1. GENERALITIES	231	102	116	69	285	285		
2. PHILOSOPHY, PSYCHOLOGY	67	59	54	47	378	378		
3. RELIGION, THEOLOGY	451	309	317	192	814	814		
4. SOCIOLOGY, STATISTICS	389	193	230	114	379	379		
5. POLITICAL SCIENCE	330	281	277	233	1 496	1 496		
6. LAW, PUBLIC ADMINISTRATION	447	26	17	15	291	291		
7. MILITARY ART	55	22	52	20	24	24		
8. EDUCATION, LEISURE	212	98	137	105	244	244		
9. TRADE, TRANSPORT	16	8	11	6	84	84		
10. ETHNOGRAPHY, FOLKLORE	36	21	34	19	62	62		
11. LINGUISTICS, PHILOLOGY	553	358	492	324	132	132		
12. MATHEMATICS	230	152	200	127	144	144		
13. NATURAL SCIENCES	212	166	194	149	265	265		
14. MEDICAL SCIENCES	218	96	213	82	236	236		
15. ENGINEERING, CRAFTS	197	169	166	139	471	471		
16. AGRICULTURE	155	120	137	102	209	209		
17. DOMESTIC SCIENCE	176	156	155	137	79	79		
18. MANAGEMENT, ADMINISTRATION	32	31	21	20	119	119		
19. PLANNING, ARCHITECTURE	30	28	29	27	99	99		
20. PLASTIC ARTS	81	61	80	60	66	66		
21. PERFORMING ARTS	35	23	32	21	54	54		
22. GAMES, SPORTS	67	53	60	47	78	78		
23. LITERATURE								
(A) HISTORY AND CRITICISM	141	138	130	127	305	305		
(B) LITERARY TEXTS	925	653	847	600	2 856	2 856		
24. GEOGRAPHY, TRAVEL	191	165	175	150	103	103		
25. HISTORY, BIOGRAPHY	204	154	182	133	681	681		

SUBJECT GROUP / GROUPE DE SUJETS / CATEGORIA DE TEMAS	INDONESIA (1984) ALL EDITIONS TOTAL	INDONESIA (1984) ALL EDITIONS OF WHICH: BOOKS	INDONESIA (1984) FIRST EDITIONS TOTAL	INDONESIA (1984) FIRST EDITIONS OF WHICH: BOOKS	IRAN, ISLAMIC REPUBLIC OF‡ (1983) ALL EDITIONS TOTAL	IRAN, ISLAMIC REPUBLIC OF‡ (1983) ALL EDITIONS OF WHICH: BOOKS	IRAN, ISLAMIC REPUBLIC OF‡ (1983) FIRST EDITIONS TOTAL	IRAN, ISLAMIC REPUBLIC OF‡ (1983) FIRST EDITIONS OF WHICH: BOOKS
TOTAL	5 254	4 020	3 811	3 227	4 835	4 835	4 259	4 259
1. GENERALITIES	429	160	288	159	118	118	114	114
2. PHILOSOPHY, PSYCHOLOGY	76	68	60	47	124	124	102	102
3. RELIGION, THEOLOGY	344	299	268	248	1 171	1 171	1 125	1 125
4. SOCIOLOGY, STATISTICS	348	284	193	151	221	221	219	219
5. POLITICAL SCIENCE	210	118	157	105	52	52	44	44
6. LAW, PUBLIC ADMINISTRATION	270	252	232	220	36	36	34	34
7. MILITARY ART	227	197	115	100	2	2	2	2
8. EDUCATION, LEISURE	293	268	243	228	14	14	14	14
9. TRADE, TRANSPORT	209	181	207	180	4	4	4	4
10. ETHNOGRAPHY, FOLKLORE	337	301	314	300	4	4	4	4
11. LINGUISTICS, PHILOLOGY	152	92	91	82	135	135	119	119
12. MATHEMATICS	102	77	56	46	146	146	138	138
13. NATURAL SCIENCES	171	123	119	101	38	38	30	30
14. MEDICAL SCIENCES	146	72	78	48	268	268	256	256
15. ENGINEERING, CRAFTS	553	388	376	328	246	246	228	228
16. AGRICULTURE	309	270	265	250	62	62	58	58
17. DOMESTIC SCIENCE	86	54	55	39	38	38	30	30
18. MANAGEMENT, ADMINISTRATION	248	195	214	186	14	14	6	6
19. PLANNING, ARCHITECTURE	43	20	17	4	10	10	8	8
20. PLASTIC ARTS	22	16	12	8	104	104	98	98
21. PERFORMING ARTS	19	13	16	12	20	20	18	18
22. GAMES, SPORTS	50	42	35	31	35	35	35	35
23. LITERATURE								
(A) HISTORY AND CRITICISM	116	97	91	82	432	432	426	426
(B) LITERARY TEXTS	250	225	132	117	552	552	370	370
24. GEOGRAPHY, TRAVEL	63	43	44	32	173	173	167	167
25. HISTORY, BIOGRAPHY	181	165	133	123	258	258	222	222

SUBJECT GROUP / GROUPE DE SUJETS / CATEGORIA DE TEMAS	IRAQ (1983)				ISRAEL‡ (1982)			
	ALL EDITIONS		FIRST EDITIONS		ALL EDITIONS		FIRST EDITIONS	
	TOTAL	OF WHICH: BOOKS	TOTAL	OF WHICH: BOOKS	TOTAL	OF WHICH: BOOKS	TOTAL	OF WHICH: BOOKS
TOTAL	82	82	82	82	1 892	1 649	1 566	
1. GENERALITIES	6	6	6	6	17	17	15	
2. PHILOSOPHY, PSYCHOLOGY	–	–	–	–	72	71	55	
3. RELIGION, THEOLOGY	–	–	–	–	163	154	118	
4. SOCIOLOGY, STATISTICS	3	3	3	3	48	44	39	
5. POLITICAL SCIENCE	10	10	10	10	56	41	48	
6. LAW, PUBLIC ADMINISTRATION	2	2	2	2	46	41	44	
7. MILITARY ART	–	–	–	–	23	19	23	
8. EDUCATION, LEISURE	–	–	–	–	48	40	39	
9. TRADE, TRANSPORT	–	–	–	–	25	22	21	
10. ETHNOGRAPHY, FOLKLORE	–	–	–	–	./.	./.	./.	
11. LINGUISTICS, PHILOLOGY	–	–	–	–	55	52	34	
12. MATHEMATICS	–	–	–	–	27	26	16	
13. NATURAL SCIENCES	1	1	1	1	52	50	41	
14. MEDICAL SCIENCES	–	–	–	–	11	11	6	
15. ENGINEERING, CRAFTS	–	–	–	–	17	15	15	
16. AGRICULTURE	–	–	–	–	3	2	2	
17. DOMESTIC SCIENCE	–	–	–	–	48	46	41	
18. MANAGEMENT, ADMINISTRATION	–	–	–	–	./.	./.	./.	
19. PLANNING, ARCHITECTURE	–	–	–	–	./.	./.	./.	
20. PLASTIC ARTS	–	–	–	–	24	15	21	
21. PERFORMING ARTS	–	–	–	–	./.	./.	./.	
22. GAMES, SPORTS	–	–	–	–	15	13	12	
23. LITERATURE								
(A) HISTORY AND CRITICISM	3	3	3	3	32	32	24	
(B) LITERARY TEXTS	51	51	51	51	814	664	748	
24. GEOGRAPHY, TRAVEL	5	5	5	5	37	34	29	
25. HISTORY, BIOGRAPHY	1	1	1	1	252	233	174	

SUBJECT GROUP / GROUPE DE SUJETS / CATEGORIA DE TEMAS	JAPAN (1983)				KOREA, REPUBLIC OF (1984)			
	ALL EDITIONS		FIRST EDITIONS		ALL EDITIONS		FIRST EDITIONS	
	TOTAL	OF WHICH: BOOKS	TOTAL	OF WHICH: BOOKS	TOTAL	OF WHICH: BOOKS	TOTAL	OF WHICH: BOOKS
TOTAL	44 253	44 253	34 316	34 316	35 446	33 156	21 024	19 205
1. GENERALITIES	1 161	1 161	1 049	1 049	998	990	450	445
2. PHILOSOPHY, PSYCHOLOGY	1 514	1 514	1 154	1 154	1 233	1 217	531	518
3. RELIGION, THEOLOGY	635	635	531	531	2 682	2 546	1 547	1 428
4. SOCIOLOGY, STATISTICS	1 632	1 632	1 353	1 353	908	874	638	605
5. POLITICAL SCIENCE	2 209	2 209	1 993	1 993	687	682	467	462
6. LAW, PUBLIC ADMINISTRATION	941	941	807	807	1 285	1 175	968	858
7. MILITARY ART	–	–	–	–	22	22	15	15
8. EDUCATION, LEISURE	4 105	4 105	2 563	2 563	2 977	2 364	2 088	1 617
9. TRADE, TRANSPORT	1 302	1 302	899	899	203	199	135	134
10. ETHNOGRAPHY, FOLKLORE	369	369	307	307	97	96	60	59
11. LINGUISTICS, PHILOLOGY	2 473	2 473	1 547	1 547	2 814	2 559	1 895	1 704
12. MATHEMATICS	637	637	456	456	661	610	382	331
13. NATURAL SCIENCES	1 656	1 656	1 239	1 239	946	939	634	627
14. MEDICAL SCIENCES	1 077	1 077	973	973	307	303	178	174
15. ENGINEERING, CRAFTS	2 078	2 078	1 878	1 878	2 023	2 009	1 364	1 350
16. AGRICULTURE	423	423	349	349	254	254	142	142
17. DOMESTIC SCIENCE	1 802	1 802	1 374	1 374	470	435	177	142
18. MANAGEMENT, ADMINISTRATION	1 690	1 690	1 499	1 499	635	626	415	406
19. PLANNING, ARCHITECTURE	624	624	587	587	303	270	222	189
20. PLASTIC ARTS	2 340	2 340	2 013	2 013	373	356	232	218
21. PERFORMING ARTS	1 194	1 194	1 003	1 003	1 114	990	586	508
22. GAMES, SPORTS	1 571	1 571	1 067	1 067	132	132	95	95
23. LITERATURE								
(A) HISTORY AND CRITICISM	2 061	2 061	1 640	1 640	137	136	83	82
(B) LITERARY TEXTS	8 731	8 731	6 348	6 348	11 590	10 996	6 207	5 789
24. GEOGRAPHY, TRAVEL	324	324	251	251	243	219	214	191
25. HISTORY, BIOGRAPHY	1 704	1 704	1 436	1 436	2 352	2 157	1 299	1 116

7.8 Number of titles by subject group
Nombre de titres par groupes de sujets
Número de títulos por categorías de temas

SUBJECT GROUP / GROUPE DE SUJETS / CATEGORIA DE TEMAS	MALAYSIA (1984)				MONGOLIA‡ (1983)			
	ALL EDITIONS		FIRST EDITIONS		ALL EDITIONS		FIRST EDITIONS	
	TOTAL	OF WHICH: BOOKS	TOTAL	OF WHICH: BOOKS	TOTAL	OF WHICH: BOOKS	TOTAL	OF WHICH: BOOKS
TOTAL	3 975	2 348	3 944	2 318	861			
1. GENERALITIES	135	90	135	90	–			
2. PHILOSOPHY, PSYCHOLOGY	36	24	36	24	–			
3. RELIGION, THEOLOGY	231	159	230	158	–			
4. SOCIOLOGY, STATISTICS	124	99	122	97	–			
5. POLITICAL SCIENCE	140	85	138	83	269			
6. LAW, PUBLIC ADMINISTRATION	381	238	381	238	–			
7. MILITARY ART	14	10	14	10	–			
8. EDUCATION, LEISURE	157	117	154	114	151			
9. TRADE, TRANSPORT	187	119	186	118	–			
10. ETHNOGRAPHY, FOLKLORE	343	55	343	55	–			
11. LINGUISTICS, PHILOLOGY	463	233	463	233	13			
12. MATHEMATICS	124	86	120	82	22			
13. NATURAL SCIENCES	180	141	174	135	./.			
14. MEDICAL SCIENCES	45	28	45	28	19			
15. ENGINEERING, CRAFTS	111	50	109	48	11			
16. AGRICULTURE	265	57	265	57	98			
17. DOMESTIC SCIENCE	57	28	54	26	–			
18. MANAGEMENT, ADMINISTRATION	118	75	118	75	–			
19. PLANNING, ARCHITECTURE	15	7	15	7	–			
20. PLASTIC ARTS	27	16	27	16	./.			
21. PERFORMING ARTS	30	18	30	18	6			
22. GAMES, SPORTS	27	17	27	17	–			
23. LITERATURE								
(A) HISTORY AND CRITICISM	84	56	84	56	272			
(B) LITERARY TEXTS	395	298	395	298	./.			
24. GEOGRAPHY, TRAVEL	178	143	173	138	–			
25. HISTORY, BIOGRAPHY	108	99	106	97	–			

SUBJECT GROUP / GROUPE DE SUJETS / CATEGORIA DE TEMAS	PHILIPPINES‡ (1984)				SINGAPORE‡ (1983)			
	ALL EDITIONS		FIRST EDITIONS		ALL EDITIONS		FIRST EDITIONS	
	TOTAL	OF WHICH: BOOKS	TOTAL	OF WHICH: BOOKS	TOTAL	OF WHICH: BOOKS	TOTAL	OF WHICH: BOOKS
TOTAL	542	265	217	77	1 927	1 524	1 785	1 421
1. GENERALITIES	30	17	–	–	34	26	32	25
2. PHILOSOPHY, PSYCHOLOGY	8	8	–	–	12	5	12	5
3. RELIGION, THEOLOGY	4	4	–	–	216	150	188	130
4. SOCIOLOGY, STATISTICS	9	9	6	6	66	54	65	53
5. POLITICAL SCIENCE	13	7	–	–	66	39	63	38
6. LAW, PUBLIC ADMINISTRATION	18	15	–	–	53	43	48	38
7. MILITARY ART	–	–	–	–	1	1	1	1
8. EDUCATION, LEISURE	9	9	–	–	375	279	351	273
9. TRADE, TRANSPORT	9	9	–	–	46	25	42	22
10. ETHNOGRAPHY, FOLKLORE	–	–	–	–	16	14	13	11
11. LINGUISTICS, PHILOLOGY	7	7	3	3	154	146	140	133
12. MATHEMATICS	18	18	3	3	66	64	60	58
13. NATURAL SCIENCES	14	11	7	4	57	55	51	49
14. MEDICAL SCIENCES	99	25	82	8	106	102	104	101
15. ENGINEERING, CRAFTS	65	34	40	9	70	28	65	27
16. AGRICULTURE	74	46	72	44	4	4	4	4
17. DOMESTIC SCIENCE	1	1	–	–	20	18	17	15
18. MANAGEMENT, ADMINISTRATION	35	29	4	–	61	42	48	30
19. PLANNING, ARCHITECTURE	1	1	–	–	5	5	5	5
20. PLASTIC ARTS	113	–	–	–	21	19	21	19
21. PERFORMING ARTS	4	4	–	–	38	31	36	31
22. GAMES, SPORTS	–	–	–	–	13	11	13	11
23. LITERATURE								
(A) HISTORY AND CRITICISM	8	8	–	–	18	17	18	17
(B) LITERARY TEXTS	–	–	–	–	358	298	349	289
24. GEOGRAPHY, TRAVEL	1	1	–	–	20	19	14	13
25. HISTORY, BIOGRAPHY	2	2	–	–	31	29	25	23

SUBJECT GROUP / GROUPE DE SUJETS / CATEGORIA DE TEMAS	SRI LANKA (1983)				SYRIAN ARAB REPUBLIC (1983)			
	ALL EDITIONS		FIRST EDITIONS		ALL EDITIONS		FIRST EDITIONS	
	TOTAL	OF WHICH: BOOKS	TOTAL	OF WHICH: BOOKS	TOTAL	OF WHICH: BOOKS	TOTAL	OF WHICH: BOOKS
TOTAL	1 951	707	1 650	548	119	119	118	118
1. GENERALITIES	23	14	20	11	–	–	–	–
2. PHILOSOPHY, PSYCHOLOGY	32	22	23	14	3	3	3	3
3. RELIGION, THEOLOGY	302	107	251	80	1	1	1	1
4. SOCIOLOGY, STATISTICS	16	8	13	5	5	5	5	5
5. POLITICAL SCIENCE	119	56	117	55	12	12	12	12
6. LAW, PUBLIC ADMINISTRATION	574	115	567	122	–	–	–	–
7. MILITARY ART	–	–	–	–	–	–	–	–
8. EDUCATION, LEISURE	177	92	116	47	1	1	1	1
9. TRADE, TRANSPORT	47	10	45	8	–	–	–	–
10. ETHNOGRAPHY, FOLKLORE	2	1	2	1	1	1	1	1
11. LINGUISTICS, PHILOLOGY	52	38	33	20	–	–	–	–
12. MATHEMATICS	22	13	18	9	2	2	2	2
13. NATURAL SCIENCES	32	24	24	16	12	12	12	12
14. MEDICAL SCIENCES	37	13	36	12	1	1	–	–
15. ENGINEERING, CRAFTS	59	14	43	14	14	14	14	14
16. AGRICULTURE	38	13	37	12	3	3	3	3
17. DOMESTIC SCIENCE	3	3	2	2	–	–	–	–
18. MANAGEMENT, ADMINISTRATION	56	11	56	11	–	–	–	–
19. PLANNING, ARCHITECTURE	–	–	–	–	–	–	–	–
20. PLASTIC ARTS	–	–	–	–	1	1	1	1
21. PERFORMING ARTS	30	1	28	1	2	2	2	2
22. GAMES, SPORTS	–	–	–	–	–	–	–	–
23. LITERATURE								
(A) HISTORY AND CRITICISM	10	9	8	7	6	6	6	6
(B) LITERARY TEXTS	252	108	158	74	48	48	48	48
24. GEOGRAPHY, TRAVEL	10	6	2	1	2	2	2	2
25. HISTORY, BIOGRAPHY	58	29	51	26	5	5	5	5

SUBJECT GROUP / GROUPE DE SUJETS / CATEGORIA DE TEMAS	THAILAND‡ (1984)				TURKEY‡ (1983)			
	ALL EDITIONS		FIRST EDITIONS		ALL EDITIONS		FIRST EDITIONS	
	TOTAL	OF WHICH: BOOKS	TOTAL	OF WHICH: BOOKS	TOTAL	OF WHICH: BOOKS	TOTAL	OF WHICH: BOOKS
TOTAL	8 633	8 392	7 680	7 442	6 869	6 610	5 615	5 458
1. GENERALITIES	952	914	890	853	127	113	105	98
2. PHILOSOPHY, PSYCHOLOGY	193	193	159	159	88	85	77	76
3. RELIGION, THEOLOGY	486	466	428	409	404	336	314	263
4. SOCIOLOGY, STATISTICS	613	587	580	554	149	141	98	97
5. POLITICAL SCIENCE	599	577	575	554	491	474	396	385
6. LAW, PUBLIC ADMINISTRATION	462	453	423	414	326	313	295	288
7. MILITARY ART	57	56	55	54	15	13	14	12
8. EDUCATION, LEISURE	1 614	1 608	1 277	1 271	192	171	177	163
9. TRADE, TRANSPORT	73	71	71	69	73	69	65	61
10. ETHNOGRAPHY, FOLKLORE	80	79	73	72	114	106	104	98
11. LINGUISTICS, PHILOLOGY	382	377	301	296	119	113	93	87
12. MATHEMATICS	330	324	293	287	76	73	74	71
13. NATURAL SCIENCES	200	200	188	188	297	289	289	282
14. MEDICAL SCIENCES	490	425	453	388	429	412	396	394
15. ENGINEERING, CRAFTS	338	336	317	315	382	364	362	351
16. AGRICULTURE	254	242	235	223	475	456	411	403
17. DOMESTIC SCIENCE	77	75	58	56	47	47	39	39
18. MANAGEMENT, ADMINISTRATION	166	162	148	144	84	84	69	69
19. PLANNING, ARCHITECTURE	149	145	132	128	57	53	52	51
20. PLASTIC ARTS	23	23	22	22	45	42	45	42
21. PERFORMING ARTS	113	107	99	93	49	44	34	34
22. GAMES, SPORTS	3	3	2	2	67	63	51	48
23. LITERATURE								
(A) HISTORY AND CRITICISM	567	561	528	522	83	82	72	71
(B) LITERARY TEXTS	./.	./.	./.	./.	913	913	604	604
24. GEOGRAPHY, TRAVEL	161	158	144	141	98	89	69	65
25. HISTORY, BIOGRAPHY	251	250	229	228	170	166	152	148

7.8 Number of titles by subject group
Nombre de titres par groupes de sujets
Número de títulos por categorías de temas

EUROPE

SUBJECT GROUP / GROUPE DE SUJETS / CATEGORIA DE TEMAS	UNITED ARAB EMIRATES (1983)				ALBANIA (1984)			
	ALL EDITIONS		FIRST EDITIONS		ALL EDITIONS		FIRST EDITIONS	
	TOTAL	OF WHICH: BOOKS	TOTAL	OF WHICH: BOOKS	TOTAL	OF WHICH: BOOKS	TOTAL	OF WHICH: BOOKS
TOTAL	84	84	49	49	1 130	972	932	775
1. GENERALITIES	4	4	4	4	25	23	25	23
2. PHILOSOPHY, PSYCHOLOGY	1	1	1	1	7	7	4	4
3. RELIGION, THEOLOGY	21	21	7	7	1	1	1	1
4. SOCIOLOGY, STATISTICS	1	1	1	1	70	57	63	50
5. POLITICAL SCIENCE	3	3	3	3	88	56	70	38
6. LAW, PUBLIC ADMINISTRATION	–	–	–	–	15	13	15	13
7. MILITARY ART	–	–	–	–	4	3	4	3
8. EDUCATION, LEISURE	–	–	–	–	36	29	28	21
9. TRADE, TRANSPORT	–	–	–	–	8	7	7	6
10. ETHNOGRAPHY, FOLKLORE	–	–	–	–	13	10	10	7
11. LINGUISTICS, PHILOLOGY	14	14	4	4	88	87	60	59
12. MATHEMATICS	9	9	6	6	64	63	49	48
13. NATURAL SCIENCES	11	11	7	7	111	104	87	80
14. MEDICAL SCIENCES	1	1	1	1	70	69	54	53
15. ENGINEERING, CRAFTS	–	–	–	–	134	128	108	102
16. AGRICULTURE	–	–	–	–	86	63	74	51
17. DOMESTIC SCIENCE	2	2	1	1	3	3	2	2
18. MANAGEMENT, ADMINISTRATION	–	–	–	–	22	16	17	11
19. PLANNING, ARCHITECTURE	–	–	–	–	7	7	7	7
20. PLASTIC ARTS	–	–	–	–	5	4	3	2
21. PERFORMING ARTS	–	–	–	–	24	20	16	13
22. GAMES, SPORTS	–	–	–	–	13	11	12	10
23. LITERATURE								
(A) HISTORY AND CRITICISM	–	–	–	–	19	19	15	15
(B) LITERARY TEXTS	10	10	10	10	159	136	154	131
24. GEOGRAPHY, TRAVEL	4	4	2	2	5	5	2	2
25. HISTORY, BIOGRAPHY	3	3	2	2	53	31	45	23

SUBJECT GROUP / GROUPE DE SUJETS / CATEGORIA DE TEMAS	AUSTRIA (1984)				BELGIUM‡ (1983)			
	ALL EDITIONS		FIRST EDITIONS		ALL EDITIONS		FIRST EDITIONS	
	TOTAL	OF WHICH: BOOKS	TOTAL	OF WHICH: BOOKS	TOTAL	OF WHICH: BOOKS	TOTAL	OF WHICH: BOOKS
TOTAL	9 059	7 725	8 023	6 897	8 065		6 946	
1. GENERALITIES	204	170	181	149	202		179	
2. PHILOSOPHY, PSYCHOLOGY	248	242	232	226	239		199	
3. RELIGION, THEOLOGY	519	412	461	366	319		285	
4. SOCIOLOGY, STATISTICS	305	223	299	219	171		147	
5. POLITICAL SCIENCE	581	442	550	420	395		353	
6. LAW, PUBLIC ADMINISTRATION	279	232	195	153	407		300	
7. MILITARY ART	31	16	30	15	26		25	
8. EDUCATION, LEISURE	240	216	217	194	175		145	
9. TRADE, TRANSPORT	124	90	111	81	62		52	
10. ETHNOGRAPHY, FOLKLORE	101	86	87	73	32		27	
11. LINGUISTICS, PHILOLOGY	153	146	132	125	208		126	
12. MATHEMATICS	304	295	294	287	62		48	
13. NATURAL SCIENCES	674	644	634	605	265		213	
14. MEDICAL SCIENCES	215	152	195	136	346		280	
15. ENGINEERING, CRAFTS	645	573	628	562	312		264	
16. AGRICULTURE	203	174	189	166	101		93	
17. DOMESTIC SCIENCE	71	59	36	24	131		105	
18. MANAGEMENT, ADMINISTRATION	875	825	823	775	187		170	
19. PLANNING, ARCHITECTURE	139	112	123	102	483		451	
20. PLASTIC ARTS	360	236	344	222	./.		./.	
21. PERFORMING ARTS	253	204	240	192	./.		./.	
22. GAMES, SPORTS	109	82	84	59	203		176	
23. LITERATURE								
(A) HISTORY AND CRITICISM	213	197	211	196	124		108	
(B) LITERARY TEXTS	1 285	1 086	912	848	1 264		1 007	
24. GEOGRAPHY, TRAVEL	129	112	105	88	143		116	
25. HISTORY, BIOGRAPHY	799	699	710	614	540		474	

SUBJECT GROUP / GROUPE DE SUJETS / CATEGORIA DE TEMAS	BULGARIA‡ (1984)				CZECHOSLOVAKIA (1984)			
	ALL EDITIONS		FIRST EDITIONS		ALL EDITIONS		FIRST EDITIONS	
	TOTAL	OF WHICH: BOOKS	TOTAL	OF WHICH: BOOKS	TOTAL	OF WHICH: BOOKS	TOTAL	OF WHICH: BOOKS
TOTAL	5 367	4 440	4 947	4 026	9 911	8 581	8 071	6 914
1. GENERALITIES	273	162	273	162	650	292	595	283
2. PHILOSOPHY, PSYCHOLOGY	44	41	44	41	113	108	87	82
3. RELIGION, THEOLOGY	10	8	9	7	49	47	40	39
4. SOCIOLOGY, STATISTICS	166	132	160	126	60	53	53	46
5. POLITICAL SCIENCE	921	684	894	657	724	617	652	550
6. LAW, PUBLIC ADMINISTRATION	97	84	90	77	162	147	138	126
7. MILITARY ART	60	45	58	43	82	69	73	61
8. EDUCATION, LEISURE	349	294	288	235	558	491	391	341
9. TRADE, TRANSPORT	38	34	36	32	99	86	82	72
10. ETHNOGRAPHY, FOLKLORE	16	14	16	14	19	17	18	16
11. LINGUISTICS, PHILOLOGY	297	285	263	251	359	350	213	206
12. MATHEMATICS	65	63	60	58	303	296	193	189
13. NATURAL SCIENCES	223	209	193	179	722	696	550	526
14. MEDICAL SCIENCES	333	252	307	226	417	363	326	279
15. ENGINEERING, CRAFTS	610	541	560	492	1 880	1 785	1 571	1 483
16. AGRICULTURE	229	175	209	155	470	414	383	334
17. DOMESTIC SCIENCE	22	19	21	18	54	47	39	33
18. MANAGEMENT, ADMINISTRATION	157	115	146	105	235	222	193	180
19. PLANNING, ARCHITECTURE	163	129	157	123	91	79	79	67
20. PLASTIC ARTS	./.	./.	./.	./.	238	125	220	107
21. PERFORMING ARTS	./.	./.	./.	./.	158	133	139	116
22. GAMES, SPORTS	112	93	108	89	198	165	173	143
23. LITERATURE								
(A) HISTORY AND CRITICISM	902	822	801	723	150	140	132	122
(B) LITERARY TEXTS	./.	./.	./.	./.	1 737	1 520	1 393	1 233
24. GEOGRAPHY, TRAVEL	50	45	45	40	75	62	60	49
25. HISTORY, BIOGRAPHY	230	194	209	173	308	257	278	231

SUBJECT GROUP / GROUPE DE SUJETS / CATEGORIA DE TEMAS	DENMARK‡ (1984)				FINLAND (1984)			
	ALL EDITIONS		FIRST EDITIONS		ALL EDITIONS		FIRST EDITIONS	
	TOTAL	OF WHICH: BOOKS	TOTAL	OF WHICH: BOOKS	TOTAL	OF WHICH: BOOKS	TOTAL	OF WHICH: BOOKS
TOTAL	10 660	7 296	9 050	6 170	8 563	6 268	8 098	5 863
1. GENERALITIES	283	188	248	166	361	251	344	239
2. PHILOSOPHY, PSYCHOLOGY	412	306	349	276	193	165	185	159
3. RELIGION, THEOLOGY	273	192	238	164	333	273	314	258
4. SOCIOLOGY, STATISTICS	216	151	197	139	227	176	217	167
5. POLITICAL SCIENCE	646	384	582	368	800	560	763	532
6. LAW, PUBLIC ADMINISTRATION	564	352	378	265	602	437	568	409
7. MILITARY ART	54	36	46	31	69	51	64	46
8. EDUCATION, LEISURE	557	363	524	347	430	285	427	283
9. TRADE, TRANSPORT	./.	./.	./.	./.	–	–	–	–
10. ETHNOGRAPHY, FOLKLORE	86	63	70	51	64	51	60	48
11. LINGUISTICS, PHILOLOGY	301	209	248	167	342	310	308	277
12. MATHEMATICS	153	88	125	64	260	125	232	100
13. NATURAL SCIENCES	523	308	468	287	714	432	685	406
14. MEDICAL SCIENCES	614	423	525	368	368	279	339	265
15. ENGINEERING, CRAFTS	1 280	775	1 142	704	1 047	709	1 010	673
16. AGRICULTURE	262	175	224	146	405	235	388	221
17. DOMESTIC SCIENCE	134	107	101	83	92	71	83	63
18. MANAGEMENT, ADMINISTRATION	350	243	276	184	435	322	412	301
19. PLANNING, ARCHITECTURE	177	117	168	114	135	92	131	89
20. PLASTIC ARTS	181	111	175	106	93	81	92	80
21. PERFORMING ARTS	122	86	110	75	74	64	73	63
22. GAMES, SPORTS	226	152	204	134	106	83	99	76
23. LITERATURE								
(A) HISTORY AND CRITICISM	59	53	53	47	63	59	62	58
(B) LITERARY TEXTS	2 183	1 622	1 758	1 243	953	809	884	740
24. GEOGRAPHY, TRAVEL	334	237	264	174	83	69	75	62
25. HISTORY, BIOGRAPHY	670	555	577	467	314	279	283	248

7.8 Number of titles by subject group
Nombre de titres par groupes de sujets
Número de títulos por categorías de temas

SUBJECT GROUP / GROUPE DE SUJETS / CATEGORIA DE TEMAS	FRANCE (1984)				GERMAN DEMOCRATIC REPUBLIC‡ (1984)			
	ALL EDITIONS		FIRST EDITIONS		ALL EDITIONS		FIRST EDITIONS	
	TOTAL	OF WHICH: BOOKS	TOTAL	OF WHICH: BOOKS	TOTAL	OF WHICH: BOOKS	TOTAL	OF WHICH: BOOKS
TOTAL	37 189	25 448			6 175	5 398	3 429	2 986
1. GENERALITIES	900	400			85	85	80	80
2. PHILOSOPHY, PSYCHOLOGY	900	700			141	140	98	97
3. RELIGION, THEOLOGY	1 350	1 000			308	234	212	152
4. SOCIOLOGY, STATISTICS	740	500			89	84	55	53
5. POLITICAL SCIENCE	6 492	3 309			188	176	85	79
6. LAW, PUBLIC ADMINISTRATION	750	550			111	91	59	47
7. MILITARY ART	450	250			78	72	52	47
8. EDUCATION, LEISURE	2 417	1 609			208	179	74	69
9. TRADE, TRANSPORT	1 400	800			48	45	30	29
10. ETHNOGRAPHY, FOLKLORE	500	400			16	15	12	11
11. LINGUISTICS, PHILOLOGY	400	300			301	298	164	162
12. MATHEMATICS	110	100			108	107	67	66
13. NATURAL SCIENCES	–	–			339	324	217	206
14. MEDICAL SCIENCES	1 850	1 500			217	207	132	124
15. ENGINEERING, CRAFTS	1 600	1 100			540	508	255	240
16. AGRICULTURE	920	550			129	124	56	53
17. DOMESTIC SCIENCE	680	230			35	35	15	15
18. MANAGEMENT, ADMINISTRATION					4	4	–	–
19. PLANNING, ARCHITECTURE	900	580			212	178	135	114
20. PLASTIC ARTS	1 670	670			16	2	10	1
21. PERFORMING ARTS	850	650			123	116	82	77
22. GAMES ,SPORTS	450	350			101	98	66	65
23. LITERATURE								
(A) HISTORY AND CRITICISM	450	400			1 449	1 402	867	823
(B) LITERARY TEXTS	9 210	7 800			./.	./.	./.	./.
24. GEOGRAPHY, TRAVEL	800	500			143	122	55	51
25. HISTORY, BIOGRAPHY	1 400	1 200			163	152	114	106

SUBJECT GROUP / GROUPE DE SUJETS / CATEGORIA DE TEMAS	GERMANY, FEDERAL REPUBLIC OF‡ (1984)				HOLY SEE (1983)			
	ALL EDITIONS		FIRST EDITIONS		ALL EDITIONS		FIRST EDITIONS	
	TOTAL	OF WHICH: BOOKS	TOTAL	OF WHICH: BOOKS	TOTAL	OF WHICH: BOOKS	TOTAL	OF WHICH: BOOKS
TOTAL	48 836	42 012	37 879	32 212	191	191	166	166
1. GENERALITIES	3 836	2 788	3 032	2 146	22	22	22	22
2. PHILOSOPHY, PSYCHOLOGY	1 946	1 895	1 345	1 301	12	12	12	12
3. RELIGION, THEOLOGY	2 598	2 208	1 917	1 603	121	121	99	99
4. SOCIOLOGY, STATISTICS	2 247	1 818	1 747	1 524	3	3	3	3
5. POLITICAL SCIENCE	2 421	2 059	2 034	1 730	–	–	–	–
6. LAW, PUBLIC ADMINISTRATION	2 555	2 008	1 783	1 397	12	12	10	10
7. MILITARY ART	964	840	829	709	–	–	–	–
8. EDUCATION, LEISURE	2 250	1 952	1 793	1 525	5	5	4	4
9. TRADE, TRANSPORT	346	281	292	241	–	–	–	–
10. ETHNOGRAPHY, FOLKLORE	./.	./.	./.	./.	–	–	–	–
11. LINGUISTICS, PHILOLOGY	1 817	1 523	1 502	1 284	1	1	1	1
12. MATHEMATICS	1 690	1 371	1 438	1 141	–	–	–	–
13. NATURAL SCIENCES	2 171	1 731	1 876	1 444	–	–	–	–
14. MEDICAL SCIENCES	2 558	2 358	1 908	1 741	–	–	–	–
15. ENGINEERING, CRAFTS	3 493	2 795	3 020	2 343	–	–	–	–
16. AGRICULTURE	1 734	1 351	1 132	949	–	–	–	–
17. DOMESTIC SCIENCE	./.	./.	./.	./.	–	–	–	–
18. MANAGEMENT, ADMINISTRATION	./.	./.	./.	./.	–	–	–	–
19. PLANNING, ARCHITECTURE	./.	./.	./.	./.	2	2	2	2
20. PLASTIC ARTS	2 189	1 729	1 933	1 501	–	–	–	–
21. PERFORMING ARTS	979	875	792	692	2	2	2	2
22. GAMES ,SPORTS	550	525	381	358	–	–	–	–
23. LITERATURE								
(A) HISTORY AND CRITICISM	./.	./.	./.	./.	2	2	2	2
(B) LITERARY TEXTS	9 386	9 163	6 413	6 221	–	–	–	–
24. GEOGRAPHY, TRAVEL	1 335	1 078	1 265	1 011	–	–	–	–
25. HISTORY, BIOGRAPHY	1 771	1 664	1 447	1 351	9	9	9	9

SUBJECT GROUP / GROUPE DE SUJETS / CATEGORIA DE TEMAS	HUNGARY (1984)				IRELAND (1984)			
	ALL EDITIONS		FIRST EDITIONS		ALL EDITIONS		FIRST EDITIONS	
	TOTAL	OF WHICH: BOOKS	TOTAL	OF WHICH: BOOKS	TOTAL	OF WHICH: BOOKS	TOTAL	OF WHICH: BOOKS
TOTAL	10 421	9 128	8 115	6 992	799	609		
1. GENERALITIES	310	275	271	240	27	14		
2. PHILOSOPHY, PSYCHOLOGY	97	93	83	79	3	3		
3. RELIGION, THEOLOGY	106	102	83	81	44	24		
4. SOCIOLOGY, STATISTICS	459	416	425	382	35	23		
5. POLITICAL SCIENCE	629	492	580	445	130	66		
6. LAW, PUBLIC ADMINISTRATION	334	284	283	247	84	70		
7. MILITARY ART	23	22	22	21	–	–		
8. EDUCATION, LEISURE	680	588	591	502	28	21		
9. TRADE, TRANSPORT	156	141	144	130	18	14		
10. ETHNOGRAPHY, FOLKLORE	75	52	66	48	6	4		
11. LINGUISTICS, PHILOLOGY	495	426	248	210	5	5		
12. MATHEMATICS	214	190	116	100	10	10		
13. NATURAL SCIENCES	724	529	568	390	15	9		
14. MEDICAL SCIENCES	234	216	191	173	14	12		
15. ENGINEERING, CRAFTS	1 922	1 775	1 299	1 173	14	11		
16. AGRICULTURE	416	363	345	293	28	22		
17. DOMESTIC SCIENCE	103	91	78	68	6	5		
18. MANAGEMENT, ADMINISTRATION	602	539	467	408	10	9		
19. PLANNING, ARCHITECTURE	138	96	111	83	5	4		
20. PLASTIC ARTS	345	211	309	179	38	27		
21. PERFORMING ARTS	182	166	132	120	6	2		
22. GAMES ,SPORTS	106	103	92	89	34	32		
23. LITERATURE								
(A) HISTORY AND CRITICISM	207	196	144	134	19	18		
(B) LITERARY TEXTS	1 281	1 251	1 015	986	128	127		
24. GEOGRAPHY, TRAVEL	254	216	199	175	11	11		
25. HISTORY, BIOGRAPHY	329	295	253	236	81	66		

SUBJECT GROUP / GROUPE DE SUJETS / CATEGORIA DE TEMAS	ITALY (1984)				LUXEMBOURG (1984)			
	ALL EDITIONS		FIRST EDITIONS		ALL EDITIONS		FIRST EDITIONS	
	TOTAL	OF WHICH: BOOKS	TOTAL	OF WHICH: BOOKS	TOTAL	OF WHICH: BOOKS	TOTAL	OF WHICH: BOOKS
TOTAL	14 312	12 620	12 576	10 925	341	297	338	295
1. GENERALITIES	444	387	397	342	17	9	17	9
2. PHILOSOPHY, PSYCHOLOGY	755	700	655	600	8	7	8	7
3. RELIGION, THEOLOGY	995	848	896	755	5	3	5	3
4. SOCIOLOGY, STATISTICS	447	430	427	410	10	10	10	10
5. POLITICAL SCIENCE	615	597	531	516	24	22	24	22
6. LAW, PUBLIC ADMINISTRATION	1 409	1 269	1 128	996	53	52	53	52
7. MILITARY ART	33	32	29	29	–	–	–	–
8. EDUCATION, LEISURE	531	449	492	414	15	11	15	11
9. TRADE, TRANSPORT	90	85	70	65	10	9	10	9
10. ETHNOGRAPHY, FOLKLORE	177	172	162	157	2	2	2	2
11. LINGUISTICS, PHILOLOGY	339	331	271	263	2	2	2	2
12. MATHEMATICS	256	179	217	140	1	1	1	1
13. NATURAL SCIENCES	412	342	357	288	4	3	4	3
14. MEDICAL SCIENCES	1 109	577	1 051	519	5	3	5	3
15. ENGINEERING, CRAFTS	678	582	589	494	8	5	8	5
16. AGRICULTURE	137	111	120	96	5	5	5	5
17. DOMESTIC SCIENCE	88	88	80	80	14	14	14	14
18. MANAGEMENT, ADMINISTRATION	105	101	46	45	–	–	–	–
19. PLANNING, ARCHITECTURE	271	265	253	247	1	1	1	1
20. PLASTIC ARTS	488	450	454	417	15	13	15	13
21. PERFORMING ARTS	231	201	215	185	25	19	25	19
22. GAMES ,SPORTS	278	231	245	198	29	25	29	25
23. LITERATURE								
(A) HISTORY AND CRITICISM	362	344	334	316	2	2	2	2
(B) LITERARY TEXTS	2 905	2 728	2 506	2 336	42	36	42	36
24. GEOGRAPHY, TRAVEL	216	201	181	167	8	8	8	8
25. HISTORY, BIOGRAPHY	941	920	870	850	36	35	33	33

7.8 Number of titles by subject group
Nombre de titres par groupes de sujets
Número de títulos por categorías de temas

SUBJECT GROUP / GROUPE DE SUJETS / CATEGORIA DE TEMAS	MALTA (1984)				MONACO (1982)			
	ALL EDITIONS		FIRST EDITIONS		ALL EDITIONS		FIRST EDITIONS	
	TOTAL	OF WHICH: BOOKS	TOTAL	OF WHICH: BOOKS	TOTAL	OF WHICH: BOOKS	TOTAL	OF WHICH: BOOKS
TOTAL	313	220	304	211	105			
1. GENERALITIES	6	3	6	3	77			
2. PHILOSOPHY, PSYCHOLOGY	–	–	–	–	–			
3. RELIGION, THEOLOGY	56	34	56	34	–			
4. SOCIOLOGY, STATISTICS	7	6	7	6	–			
5. POLITICAL SCIENCE	32	23	32	23	–			
6. LAW, PUBLIC ADMINISTRATION	59	56	58	55	1			
7. MILITARY ART	–	–	–	–	–			
8. EDUCATION, LEISURE	10	8	10	8	3			
9. TRADE, TRANSPORT	3	3	3	3	–			
10. ETHNOGRAPHY, FOLKLORE	10	1	9	–	–			
11. LINGUISTICS, PHILOLOGY	16	11	16	11	–			
12. MATHEMATICS	4	3	4	3	–			
13. NATURAL SCIENCES	1	–	1	–	–			
14. MEDICAL SCIENCES	6	5	6	5	–			
15. ENGINEERING, CRAFTS	2	–	2	–	–			
16. AGRICULTURE	–	–	–	–	–			
17. DOMESTIC SCIENCE	5	4	4	3	–			
18. MANAGEMENT, ADMINISTRATION	2	2	2	2	–			
19. PLANNING, ARCHITECTURE	2	2	2	2	–			
20. PLASTIC ARTS	11	3	11	3	3			
21. PERFORMING ARTS	3	1	3	1	–			
22. GAMES ,SPORTS	1	1	1	1	10			
23. LITERATURE								
(A) HISTORY AND CRITICISM	1	1	1	1	2			
(B) LITERARY TEXTS	63	41	60	38	8			
24. GEOGRAPHY, TRAVEL	3	3	3	3	–			
25. HISTORY, BIOGRAPHY	10	9	7	6	1			

SUBJECT GROUP / GROUPE DE SUJETS / CATEGORIA DE TEMAS	NETHERLANDS‡ (1984)				NORWAY‡ (1983)			
	ALL EDITIONS		FIRST EDITIONS		ALL EDITIONS		FIRST EDITIONS	
	TOTAL	OF WHICH: BOOKS	TOTAL	OF WHICH: BOOKS	TOTAL	OF WHICH: BOOKS	TOTAL	OF WHICH: BOOKS
TOTAL	13 209	13 209	9 329	9 329	5 540	4 152	5 063	3 749
1. GENERALITIES	119	119	104	104	209	150	194	139
2. PHILOSOPHY, PSYCHOLOGY	452	452	312	312	131	104	123	97
3. RELIGION, THEOLOGY	707	707	477	477	218	169	198	155
4. SOCIOLOGY, STATISTICS	200	200	160	160	275	204	267	197
5. POLITICAL SCIENCE	286	286	257	257	501	300	477	281
6. LAW, PUBLIC ADMINISTRATION	518	518	368	368	284	194	261	175
7. MILITARY ART	33	33	27	27	20	12	20	12
8. EDUCATION, LEISURE	249	249	219	219	218	151	206	144
9. TRADE, TRANSPORT	22	22	20	20	103	67	99	64
10. ETHNOGRAPHY, FOLKLORE	38	38	28	28	36	20	32	16
11. LINGUISTICS, PHILOLOGY	212	212	163	163	88	73	76	61
12. MATHEMATICS	104	104	96	96	55	28	50	24
13. NATURAL SCIENCES	457	457	393	393	459	305	448	297
14. MEDICAL SCIENCES	544	544	416	416	291	222	282	216
15. ENGINEERING, CRAFTS	495	495	404	404	338	229	290	190
16. AGRICULTURE	173	173	131	131	206	124	189	118
17. DOMESTIC SCIENCE	240	240	172	172	58	47	52	42
18. MANAGEMENT, ADMINISTRATION	182	182	137	137	85	71	75	62
19. PLANNING, ARCHITECTURE	394	394	333	333	73	46	68	41
20. PLASTIC ARTS	./.	./.	./.	./.	101	68	86	55
21. PERFORMING ARTS	51	51	47	47	74	55	72	53
22. GAMES ,SPORTS	409	409	319	319	78	67	72	62
23. LITERATURE								
(A) HISTORY AND CRITICISM	147	147	133	133	45	40	44	39
(B) LITERARY TEXTS	2 645	2 645	1 807	1 807	1 208	1 102	1 025	931
24. GEOGRAPHY, TRAVEL	170	170	134	134	177	143	160	126
25. HISTORY, BIOGRAPHY	803	803	602	602	209	161	197	152

SUBJECT GROUP / GROUPE DE SUJETS / CATEGORIA DE TEMAS	POLAND‡ (1984)				PORTUGAL‡ (1984)			
	ALL EDITIONS		FIRST EDITIONS		ALL EDITIONS		FIRST EDITIONS	
	TOTAL	OF WHICH: BOOKS	TOTAL	OF WHICH: BOOKS	TOTAL	OF WHICH: BOOKS	TOTAL	OF WHICH: BOOKS
TOTAL	9 195	7 341	7 257	5 601	9 041	7 964	8 260	7 192
1. GENERALITIES	317	233	294	213	691	624	664	598
2. PHILOSOPHY, PSYCHOLOGY	173	163	139	129	188	162	161	135
3. RELIGION, THEOLOGY	399	342	317	262	383	281	338	237
4. SOCIOLOGY, STATISTICS	98	87	87	77	1 075	815	947	690
5. POLITICAL SCIENCE	827	542	782	501	./.	./.	./.	./.
6. LAW, PUBLIC ADMINISTRATION	342	264	291	221	./.	./.	./.	./.
7. MILITARY ART	66	62	61	57	./.	./.	./.	./.
8. EDUCATION, LEISURE	535	387	466	344	./.	./.	./.	./.
9. TRADE, TRANSPORT	1	1	1	1	./.	./.	./.	./.
10. ETHNOGRAPHY, FOLKLORE	20	13	16	9	./.	./.	./.	./.
11. LINGUISTICS, PHILOLOGY	336	329	189	182	./.	./.	./.	./.
12. MATHEMATICS	235	163	185	114	460	408	375	323
13. NATURAL SCIENCES	571	465	425	324	./.	./.	./.	./.
14. MEDICAL SCIENCES	378	317	264	215	684	537	624	478
15. ENGINEERING, CRAFTS	1 181	1 041	923	794	./.	./.	./.	./.
16. AGRICULTURE	495	304	374	196	./.	./.	./.	./.
17. DOMESTIC SCIENCE	87	68	56	38	./.	./.	./.	./.
18. MANAGEMENT, ADMINISTRATION	363	273	301	214	./.	./.	./.	./.
19. PLANNING, ARCHITECTURE	354	304	290	251	3 065	2 942	3 032	2 909
20. PLASTIC ARTS	./.	./.	./.	./.	./.	./.	./.	./.
21. PERFORMING ARTS	./.	./.	./.	./.	./.	./.	./.	./.
22. GAMES ,SPORTS	120	108	101	92	./.	./.	./.	./.
23. LITERATURE								
(A) HISTORY AND CRITICISM	201	188	173	160	1 936	1 748	1 629	1 443
(B) LITERARY TEXTS	1 381	1 085	941	730	./.	./.	./.	./.
24. GEOGRAPHY, TRAVEL	147	114	107	80	559	447	490	379
25. HISTORY, BIOGRAPHY	568	488	474	397	./.	./.	./.	./.

SUBJECT GROUP / GROUPE DE SUJETS / CATEGORIA DE TEMAS	ROMANIA‡ (1984)				SPAIN‡ (1984)			
	ALL EDITIONS		FIRST EDITIONS		ALL EDITIONS		FIRST EDITIONS	
	TOTAL	OF WHICH: BOOKS	TOTAL	OF WHICH: BOOKS	TOTAL	OF WHICH: BOOKS	TOTAL	OF WHICH: BOOKS
TOTAL	5 632				30 764	25 518	26 727	21 717
1. GENERALITIES	124				1 406	1 245	1 303	1 145
2. PHILOSOPHY, PSYCHOLOGY	94				1 193	1 095	1 043	949
3. RELIGION, THEOLOGY	39				1 582	1 320	1 359	1 115
4. SOCIOLOGY, STATISTICS	627				402	359	378	335
5. POLITICAL SCIENCE	./.				934	814	854	735
6. LAW, PUBLIC ADMINISTRATION	./.				1 191	1 048	1 061	920
7. MILITARY ART	./.				78	69	74	65
8. EDUCATION, LEISURE	./.				957	750	872	682
9. TRADE, TRANSPORT	./.				401	309	363	275
10. ETHNOGRAPHY, FOLKLORE	./.				291	244	278	233
11. LINGUISTICS, PHILOLOGY	201				2 192	1 858	1 923	1 597
12. MATHEMATICS	808				555	507	498	451
13. NATURAL SCIENCES	./.				1 299	1 025	199	932
14. MEDICAL SCIENCES	1 814				1 195	1 038	1 102	952
15. ENGINEERING, CRAFTS	./.				1 128	1 024	1 005	905
16. AGRICULTURE	./.				445	319	427	301
17. DOMESTIC SCIENCE	./.				348	320	316	290
18. MANAGEMENT, ADMINISTRATION	./.				286	274	256	244
19. PLANNING, ARCHITECTURE	299				236	221	222	207
20. PLASTIC ARTS	./.				880	746	823	697
21. PERFORMING ARTS	./.				359	333	336	312
22. GAMES ,SPORTS	./.				354	307	329	284
23. LITERATURE								
(A) HISTORY AND CRITICISM	1 346				10 790	8 288	8 759	6 370
(B) LITERARY TEXTS	./.				./.	./.	./.	./.
24. GEOGRAPHY, TRAVEL	280				761	652	625	520
25. HISTORY, BIOGRAPHY	./.				1 501	1 353	1 322	1 201

7.8 Number of titles by subject group
Nombre de titres par groupes de sujets
Número de títulos por categorías de temas

SUBJECT GROUP / GROUPE DE SUJETS / CATEGORIA DE TEMAS	SWEDEN‡ (1984) ALL EDITIONS TOTAL	ALL EDITIONS OF WHICH: BOOKS	FIRST EDITIONS TOTAL	FIRST EDITIONS OF WHICH: BOOKS	SWITZERLAND‡ (1984) ALL EDITIONS TOTAL	ALL EDITIONS OF WHICH: BOOKS	FIRST EDITIONS TOTAL	FIRST EDITIONS OF WHICH: BOOKS
TOTAL	10 373				11 806		11 525	
1. GENERALITIES	331				122		121	
2. PHILOSOPHY, PSYCHOLOGY	248				443		385	
3. RELIGION, THEOLOGY	463				791		756	
4. SOCIOLOGY, STATISTICS	./.				408		406	
5. POLITICAL SCIENCE	./.				652		642	
6. LAW, PUBLIC ADMINISTRATION	./.				523		515	
7. MILITARY ART	76				38		37	
8. EDUCATION, LEISURE	317				324		310	
9. TRADE, TRANSPORT	./.				384		384	
10. ETHNOGRAPHY, FOLKLORE	68				208		207	
11. LINGUISTICS, PHILOLOGY	263				169		167	
12. MATHEMATICS	48				98		93	
13. NATURAL SCIENCES	529				873		861	
14. MEDICAL SCIENCES	902				1 047		1 029	
15. ENGINEERING, CRAFTS	./.				692		688	
16. AGRICULTURE	./.				153		145	
17. DOMESTIC SCIENCE	230				77		73	
18. MANAGEMENT, ADMINISTRATION	249				163		157	
19. PLANNING, ARCHITECTURE	181				83		79	
20. PLASTIC ARTS	214				834		825	
21. PERFORMING ARTS	121				178		173	
22. GAMES ,SPORTS	76				143		143	
23. LITERATURE								
(A) HISTORY AND CRITICISM	167				338		337	
(B) LITERARY TEXTS	2 192				1 508		1 490	
24. GEOGRAPHY, TRAVEL	499				289		270	
25. HISTORY, BIOGRAPHY	508				417		413	

SUBJECT GROUP / GROUPE DE SUJETS / CATEGORIA DE TEMAS	UNITED KINGDOM (1984) ALL EDITIONS TOTAL	ALL EDITIONS OF WHICH: BOOKS	FIRST EDITIONS TOTAL	FIRST EDITIONS OF WHICH: BOOKS	YUGOSLAVIA (1984) ALL EDITIONS TOTAL	ALL EDITIONS OF WHICH: BOOKS	FIRST EDITIONS TOTAL	FIRST EDITIONS OF WHICH: BOOKS
TOTAL	51 411	47 571	40 161	36 959	10 918	8 546	8 853	6 625
1. GENERALITIES	2 182	2 081	1 892	1 800	227	181	209	170
2. PHILOSOPHY, PSYCHOLOGY	1 469	1 442	1 133	1 113	140	138	118	116
3. RELIGION, THEOLOGY	2 041	1 779	1 665	1 431	284	240	235	195
4. SOCIOLOGY, STATISTICS	1 042	989	889	843	210	168	199	157
5. POLITICAL SCIENCE	3 950	3 638	3 076	2 900	948	764	882	700
6. LAW, PUBLIC ADMINISTRATION	1 656	1 510	1 239	1 115	330	268	297	235
7. MILITARY ART	191	182	151	145	45	40	43	38
8. EDUCATION, LEISURE	1 556	1 382	1 174	1 031	1 768	1 581	786	678
9. TRADE, TRANSPORT	678	597	510	432	62	52	57	47
10. ETHNOGRAPHY, FOLKLORE	240	209	189	169	37	29	37	29
11. LINGUISTICS, PHILOLOGY	1 199	1 009	1 018	846	199	190	141	133
12. MATHEMATICS	1 734	1 552	1 529	1 360	185	170	125	112
13. NATURAL SCIENCES	2 896	2 748	2 434	2 313	235	219	175	160
14. MEDICAL SCIENCES	3 434	3 338	2 887	2 799	419	346	364	291
15. ENGINEERING, CRAFTS	2 939	2 777	2 480	2 331	649	519	544	415
16. AGRICULTURE	931	834	740	668	315	247	277	212
17. DOMESTIC SCIENCE	986	930	677	633	80	80	64	64
18. MANAGEMENT, ADMINISTRATION	1 650	1 583	1 213	1 152	408	321	373	287
19. PLANNING, ARCHITECTURE	505	436	361	314	121	74	115	70
20. PLASTIC ARTS	1 655	1 545	1 350	1 248	600	173	582	155
21. PERFORMING ARTS	1 166	1 079	711	631	602	183	567	159
22. GAMES ,SPORTS	899	816	800	731	155	112	148	106
23. LITERATURE								
(A) HISTORY AND CRITICISM	1 333	1 312	1 190	1 169	38	33	38	33
(B) LITERARY TEXTS	10 168	9 259	7 093	6 316	2 450	2 068	2 096	1 738
24. GEOGRAPHY, TRAVEL	1 480	1 335	1 006	905	108	86	99	79
25. HISTORY, BIOGRAPHY	3 431	3 209	2 754	2 564	303	264	282	246

OCEANIA

SUBJECT GROUP / GROUPE DE SUJETS / CATEGORIA DE TEMAS	AUSTRALIA‡ (1983)				NEW CALEDONIA (1984)			
	ALL EDITIONS		FIRST EDITIONS		ALL EDITIONS		FIRST EDITIONS	
	TOTAL	OF WHICH: BOOKS	TOTAL	OF WHICH: BOOKS	TOTAL	OF WHICH: BOOKS	TOTAL	OF WHICH: BOOKS
TOTAL	3 294	2 309	2 968	2 037	22	15	22	15
1. GENERALITIES	107	69	94	58	–	–	–	–
2. PHILOSOPHY, PSYCHOLOGY	22	15	19	12	–	–	–	–
3. RELIGION, THEOLOGY	60	35	54	31	–	–	–	–
4. SOCIOLOGY, STATISTICS	138	76	129	67	–	–	–	–
5. POLITICAL SCIENCE	439	250	414	229	–	–	–	–
6. LAW, PUBLIC ADMINISTRATION	381	281	321	229	–	–	–	–
7. MILITARY ART	14	7	12	6	–	–	–	–
8. EDUCATION, LEISURE	195	131	183	121	8	4	8	4
9. TRADE, TRANSPORT	103	54	99	52	–	–	–	–
10. ETHNOGRAPHY, FOLKLORE	8	6	7	6	–	–	–	–
11. LINGUISTICS, PHILOLOGY	150	75	137	67	5	5	5	5
12. MATHEMATICS	51	41	44	34	–	–	–	–
13. NATURAL SCIENCES	116	86	102	73	4	4	4	4
14. MEDICAL SCIENCES	93	77	80	65	–	–	–	–
15. ENGINEERING, CRAFTS	152	103	133	93	–	–	–	–
16. AGRICULTURE	125	82	108	71	–	–	–	–
17. DOMESTIC SCIENCE	78	66	68	56	–	–	–	–
18. MANAGEMENT, ADMINISTRATION	79	66	54	43	–	–	–	–
19. PLANNING, ARCHITECTURE	67	41	63	38	–	–	–	–
20. PLASTIC ARTS	85	68	80	63	1	–	1	–
21. PERFORMING ARTS	46	39	43	36	2	–	2	–
22. GAMES ,SPORTS	72	62	64	54	–	–	–	–
23. LITERATURE								
(A) HISTORY AND CRITICISM	35	25	31	21	–	–	–	–
(B) LITERARY TEXTS	377	306	365	296	–	–	–	–
24. GEOGRAPHY, TRAVEL	88	69	74	56	1	1	1	1
25. HISTORY, BIOGRAPHY	213	179	190	160	1	1	1	1

U.S.S.R.

SUBJECT GROUP / GROUPE DE SUJETS / CATEGORIA DE TEMAS	NEW ZEALAND (1984)				U.S.S.R.‡ (1984)			
	ALL EDITIONS		FIRST EDITIONS		ALL EDITIONS		FIRST EDITIONS	
	TOTAL	OF WHICH: BOOKS	TOTAL	OF WHICH: BOOKS	TOTAL	OF WHICH: BOOKS	TOTAL	OF WHICH: BOOKS
TOTAL	3 452	1 601	3 233	1 520	82 790	54 569	78 669	50 829
1. GENERALITIES	102	58	90	48	2 493	1 327	2 471	1 307
2. PHILOSOPHY, PSYCHOLOGY	16	6	15	6	1 503	1 188	1 475	1 160
3. RELIGION, THEOLOGY	91	47	87	45	301	202	287	188
4. SOCIOLOGY, STATISTICS	85	48	84	47	313	217	292	196
5. POLITICAL SCIENCE	466	203	454	197	10 553	6 453	10 213	6 183
6. LAW, PUBLIC ADMINISTRATION	377	188	321	165	1 808	1 116	1 747	1 086
7. MILITARY ART	5	4	4	3	1 735	1 483	1 710	1 458
8. EDUCATION, LEISURE	215	88	200	86	7 054	5 022	5 619	3 658
9. TRADE, TRANSPORT	102	45	98	44	355	224	335	205
10. ETHNOGRAPHY, FOLKLORE	12	5	10	3	./.	./.	./.	./.
11. LINGUISTICS, PHILOLOGY	18	9	17	8	15 991	15 455	8 267	7 759
12. MATHEMATICS	245	120	229	107	973	789	922	739
13. NATURAL SCIENCES	74	39	66	34	6 400	4 691	6 233	4 532
14. MEDICAL SCIENCES	289	123	260	114	3 938	2 287	3 769	2 141
15. ENGINEERING, CRAFTS	228	114	200	99	17 246	8 683	16 885	8 342
16. AGRICULTURE	86	49	78	40	5 276	3 179	5 118	3 058
17. DOMESTIC SCIENCE	90	33	73	28	525	275	500	250
18. MANAGEMENT, ADMINISTRATION	106	42	98	40	3 886	2 512	3 732	2 370
19. PLANNING, ARCHITECTURE	69	38	67	36	1 924	1 230	1 849	1 155
20. PLASTIC ARTS	12	6	11	6	./.	./.	./.	./.
21. PERFORMING ARTS	135	82	124	73	./.	./.	./.	./.
22. GAMES ,SPORTS	132	17	126	12	820	529	794	506
23. LITERATURE								
(A) HISTORY AND CRITICISM	36	14	34	13	1 180	1 043	1 133	1 000
(B) LITERARY TEXTS	264	128	238	110	10 431	8 624	9 781	8 061
24. GEOGRAPHY, TRAVEL	66	46	49	32	548	466	522	441
25. HISTORY, BIOGRAPHY	131	49	200	124	1 418	1 273	1 356	1 212

SUBJECT GROUP / GROUPE DE SUJETS / CATEGORIA DE TEMAS	BYELORUSSIAN S.S.R.‡ (1984) ALL EDITIONS TOTAL	OF WHICH: BOOKS	FIRST EDITIONS TOTAL	OF WHICH: BOOKS	UKRAINIAN S.S.R.‡ (1984) ALL EDITIONS TOTAL	OF WHICH: BOOKS	FIRST EDITIONS TOTAL	OF WHICH: BOOKS
TOTAL	3 264	1 866	3 127	1 735	8 403	5 236	7 768	4 673
1. GENERALITIES	122	56	122	56	324	139	321	136
2. PHILOSOPHY, PSYCHOLOGY	53	40	53	40	191	120	168	101
3. RELIGION, THEOLOGY	7	4	7	4	53	30	49	26
4. SOCIOLOGY, STATISTICS	6	3	5	2	15	7	14	6
5. POLITICAL SCIENCE	611	283	597	269	1 403	658	1 375	633
6. LAW, PUBLIC ADMINISTRATION	64	33	62	31	163	94	146	85
7. MILITARY ART	14	9	14	9	57	29	51	23
8. EDUCATION, LEISURE	352	232	276	158	736	465	593	323
9. TRADE, TRANSPORT	53	30	49	27	98	47	96	45
10. ETHNOGRAPHY, FOLKLORE	./.	./.	./.	./.	./.	./.	./.	./.
11. LINGUISTICS, PHILOLOGY	104	76	100	72	163	105	157	99
12. MATHEMATICS	30	22	28	20	129	88	125	84
13. NATURAL SCIENCES	161	118	157	114	605	444	602	441
14. MEDICAL SCIENCES	127	60	123	56	451	245	417	223
15. ENGINEERING, CRAFTS	517	247	513	246	1 512	919	1 487	894
16. AGRICULTURE	286	157	283	154	413	238	383	219
17. DOMESTIC SCIENCE	58	20	54	16	28	16	22	10
18. MANAGEMENT, ADMINISTRATION	168	80	164	76	370	199	350	183
19. PLANNING, ARCHITECTURE	15	9	15	9	135	85	127	77
20. PLASTIC ARTS	8	3	8	3	./.	./.	./.	./.
21. PERFORMING ARTS	40	26	40	26	./.	./.	./.	./.
22. GAMES ,SPORTS	44	21	43	20	75	42	73	40
23. LITERATURE								
(A) HISTORY AND CRITICISM	46	37	44	35	135	105	127	98
(B) LITERARY TEXTS	331	269	326	264	1 070	938	832	728
24. GEOGRAPHY, TRAVEL	8	6	8	6	72	48	60	36
25. HISTORY, BIOGRAPHY	39	25	36	22	135	114	130	109

AFRICA:

Côte d'Ivoire:

E--> Eleven school textbooks (of which 3 first editions) are included in the total but not distributed in the 25 groups.

FR-> Onze manuels scolaires (dont 3 premières éditions) sont compris dans le total mais ne sont pas répartis entre les 25 groupes.

ESP> Once manuales escolares (cuyas 3 primeras ediciones) quedan comprendidos en el total pero no están repartidos entre los 25 grupos.

Kenya:

E--> Data are incomplete.

FR-> Les données sont incomplètes.

ESP> Los datos están incompletos.

Mali:

E--> Pamphlets only. Data refer to school textbooks, government publications and university theses only.

FR-> Brochures seulement. Les données se réfèrent aux manuels scolaires, aux publications gouvernementales et aux thèses universitaires seulement.

ESP> Folletos solamente. Los datos se refieren a los manuales escolares, a las publicaciones oficiales y a las tesis universitarias solamente.

Zimbabwe:

E--> School textbooks (41) are included in the total but are not distributed in the 25 groups.

FR-> Les manuels scolaires (41) sont compris dans le total mais ne sont pas répartis entre les 25 groupes.

ESP> Los manuales escolares (41) quedan comprendidos en el total pero no están repartidos entre los 25 grupos.

AMERICA, NORTH:

Mexico:

E--> Works of group 23b are included in group 23a.

FR-> Les ouvrages du groupe 23b sont inclus dans le groupe 23a.

ESP> Las obras del grupo 23b quedan incluídas en el grupo 23a.

AMERICA, SOUTH:

Argentina:

E--> Works of group 3 are included in group 2; 5 in group 4; 21 in group 20; 11 and 25 in 23a.

FR-> Les ouvrages du groupe 3 sont inclus dans le groupe 2; 5 dans le groupe 4; 21 dans le groupe 20; 11 et 25 dans le groupe 23a.

ESP> Las obras del grupo 3 quedan incluídas en el grupo 2; las del grupo 5 en el grupo 4; las del grupo 21 en el grupo 20; las de los grupos 11 y 25 en el grupo 23a.

Bolivia:

E--> Works of group 23b are included in group 23a.

FR-> Les ouvrages du groupe 23b sont inclus dans le groupe 23a.

ESP> Las obras del grupo 23b quedan incluídas en el grupo 23a.

Brazil:

E--> Works of group 23b are included in group 23a.

FR-> Les ouvrages du groupe 23b sont inclus dans le groupe 23a.

ESP> Las obras del grupo 23b quedan incluidas en el grupo 23a.

ASIA:

Bahrain:

E--> Data refer to school textbooks only.

FR-> Les données se réfèrent aux manuels scolaires seulement.

ESP> Los datos se refieren a los manuales escolares solamente.

China:

E--> School textbooks (5,574 of which 2,164 first editions) and children's books (4,090 of which 3,318 first editions) are included in the total but not distributed in the 25 groups. Works of groups 3, 4, 5, 6, 7, 9 (trade), 10 (ethnography and anthropology), 18 and 25 are included in group 2; 1, 9 (tourism) and 10 (customs and habits), 17, 22, 11 and 24 in group 8; 10 (folklore), 20 and 21 in group 23; 12, 14, 15, 16 and 19 in group 13.

FR-> Les manuels scolaires (5 574 dont 2 164 premières éditions) et les livres pour enfants (4 090 dont 3 318 premières éditions) sont compris dans le total mais ne sont pas répartis entre les 25 groupes. Les ouvrages des groupes 3, 4, 5, 6, 7, 9 (commerce), 10 (ethnographie et anthropologie), 18 et 25 sont inclus dans le groupe 2; 1, 9 (tourisme) et 10 (coutumes et moeurs), 17, 22, 11 et 24 dans le groupe 8; 10 (folklore), 20 et 21 dans le groupe 23; 12, 14, 15, 16 et 19 dans le groupe 13.

ESP> Los manuales escolares (5 574 cuyas 2 164 primeras ediciones) y los libros para niños (4 090 cuyas 3 318 primeras ediciones) quedan comprendidos en el total pero no se desglosan entre los 25 grupos. Las obras de los grupos 3, 4, 5, 6, 7, 9 (comercio), 10 (etnografía y antropología), 18 y 25 quedan incluídos en el grupo 2; 1, 9 (turismo) y 10 (costumbres y hábitos) 17, 22, 11 y 24 en el grupo 8; 10 (folklore) 20 y 21 en el grupo 23; 12, 14, 15, 16 y 19 en el grupo 13.

Iran, Islamic Republic of:

E--> Children's books (558 of which 388 first editions) are included in the total but not distributed in the 25 groups.

FR-> Les livres pour enfants (558 dont 388 premières éditions) sont compris dans le total mais ne sont pas répartis entre les 25 groupes.

ESP> Los libros para niños (558 cuyas 388 primeras ediciones) quedan incluídos en el total pero no se desglosan entre los 25 grupos.

Israel:

E--> Works of group 4 include those of group 10. Works of group 6 include those of group 18. Works of group 15 include those of group 19, group 20 include those of group 21. The total includes 7 titles for which a subject breakdown is not available.

FR-> Les ouvrages du groupe 4 comprennent ceux du groupe 10. Les ouvrages du groupe 6 comprennent ceux du groupe 18. Les ouvrages du groupe 15 comprennent ceux du groupe 19, ceux du groupe 20

Israel: (Cont):
comprennent ceux du groupe 21. Le total comprend 7 titres pour lesquels une répartition par sujets n'est pas disponible.
ESP> Las obras del grupo 4 incluyen las del grupo 10. Las obras del grupo 6 incluyen las del grupo 18. Las obras del grupo 15 incluyen las del grupo 19, las del grupo 20 incluyen las del grupo 21. El total incluye 7 títulos para los cuales no se dispone de una repartición por temas.
Mongolia:
E--> Works of group 13 are included in group 12; 20 and 23b in 23a.
FR-> Les ouvrages du groupe 13 sont inclus dans le groupe 12; 20 et 23b dans le groupe 23a.
ESP> Las obras del grupo 13 quedan incluídas en el grupo 12; las del grupo 20 y 23b en el grupo 23a.
Philippines;
E--> Data refer to school textbooks, children's books and government publications only.
FR-> Les données se réfèrent aux manuels scolaires, aux livres pour enfants et aux publications gouvernementales seulement.
ESP> Los datos se refieren a los manuales escolares, a los libros para niños y a las publicaciones oficiales solamente.
Singapore:
E--> Data do not include government publications.
FR-> Les données ne tiennent pas compte des publications officielles.
ESP> Los datos excluyen las publicaciones oficiales.
Thailand:
E--> Works of group 23b are included in group 23a.
FR-> Les ouvrages du groupe 23b sont inclus dans le groupe 23a.
ESP> Las obras del grupo 23b quedan incluídas en el grupo 23a.
Turkey:
E--> School textbooks (387 of which 263 first editions) and children's books (1,112 of which 895 first editions) are included in the total but not identified in the 25 groups.
FR-> Les manuels scolaires (387 dont 263 premières éditions) et les livres pour enfants (1 112 dont 895 premières éditions) sont compris dans le total mais ne sont pas répartis entre les 25 groupes.
ESP> Los manuales escolares (387 cuyas 263 primeras ediciones) y los libros para niños (1 112 cuyas 895 primeras ediciones) quedan incluídos en el total pero no se desglosan entre los 25 grupos.
EUROPE:
Belgium:
E--> Children's books (1,668 of which 1,603 first editions) are included in the total but are not distributed in the 25 groups. Works of groups 20 and 21 are included in group 19.
FR-> Les livres pour enfants (1 668 dont 1 603 premières éditions) sont compris dans le total mais ne sont pas distribués entre les 25 groupes. Les ouvrages des groupes 20 et 21 sont inclus dans le groupe 19.
ESP> Los libros para niños (1 668 cuyas 1 603 primeras ediciones) quedan incluídos en el total pero no están repartidos entre los 25 grupos. Las obras de los grupos 20 y 21 quedan incluídas en el grupo 19.
Bulgaria:
E--> Works of groups 20 and 21 are included in group 19; 23b in group 23a.
FR-> Les ouvrages des groupes 20 et 21 sont inclus dans le groupe 19; 23b dans le groupe 23a.
ESP> Las obras de los grupos 20 y 21 quedan incluídas en el grupo 19; las del grupo 23b en el grupo 23a.
Denmark:
E--> Works of group 9 are included in group 18.
FR-> Les ouvrages du groupe 9 sont inclus dans le groupe 18.
ESP> Las obras del grupo 9 quedan incluídas en el grupo 18.
German Democratic Republic:
E--> Data include only books and pamphlets shown in series A of the German National Bibliography (publications of the book market) i.e., those of series B (publications outside the book market) and C (books published by universities) are excluded. School textbooks (207 of which 47 first editions) and children's books (816 of which 390 first editions) are included in the total but not identified in the 25 groups. Works of group 23b are included in group 23a.
FR-> Les données se réfèrent seulement aux livres et brochures de la série A de la Bibliographie nationale allemande (publications vendues dans le commerce). Les données relatives aux séries B (publications non vendues dans le commerce) et C (livres publiés par les universités) ne sont pas prises en compte. Les manuels scolaires (207 dont 47 premières éditions) et les livres pour enfants (816 dont 390 premières éditions) sont inclus dans le total mais ne sont pas répartis entre les 25 groupes. Les ouvrages du groupe 23b sont inclus dans le groupe 23a.
ESP> Los datos solo se refieren a los libros y folletos de la serie A de la Bibliografía nacional alemana (publicaciones que no se venden en el comercio). No se toman en consideración los datos relativos a las series B (publicaciones que no se venden en el comercio) y C (libros publicados por los universidades). Los manuales escolares (207 cuyas 47 primeras ediciones) y los libros para niños (816 cuyas 390 primeras ediciones) quedan incluídos en el total pero no se desglosan entre los 25 grupos. Las obras del grupo 23b quedan incluídas en el grupo 23a.
Germany, Federal Republic of:
E--> Works of group 10 are included in group 24; 17 in group 16; 18 in group 5; 19 in group 15; 23a in group 11.
FR-> Les ouvrages du groupe 10 sont inclus dans le groupe 24; 17 dans le groupe 16; 18 dans le groupe 5; 19 dans le groupe 15, 23a dans le groupe 11.
ESP> Las obras del grupo 10 quedan incluídas en el grupo 24; las del grupo 17 en el grupo 16; las del grupo 18 en el grupo 5; las del grupo 19 en el grupo 15; las del grupo 23a en el grupo 11.
Netherlands:
E--> Works of groups 20 are included in group 19; works of group 21 refer to theatre only. 2,039 school textbooks (of which 1,160 first editions), 1,369 children's books, (of which 788 first editions) and 151 other books (of which 122 first editions) are included in the total but not identified in the 25 groups.
FR-> Les ouvrages du groupe 20 sont compris dans le groupe 19; ceux du groupe 21 se réfèrent au théâtre seulement. 2 039 manuels scolaires (dont 1 160 premières éditions), 1 369 livres pour enfants (dont 788 premières éditions) et 151 autres livres (dont 122 premières éditions) sont compris dans le total mais ne sont pas répartis entre les 25 groupes.
ESP> Las obras del grupo 20 quedan incluídas en el grupo 19; las del grupo 21 se refieren al teatro solamente. 2 039 manuales escolares (de los cuales 1 160 primeras ediciones), 1 369 libros para niños (de los cuales 788 primeras ediciones) y 151 otros libros (de los cuales 122 primeras ediciones) quedan incluídos en el total pero no se desglosan entre los 25 grupos.
Norway:
E--> Data do not include school textbooks.
FR-> Les données ne comprennent pas les manuels scolaires.
ESP> Los datos excluyen los manuales escolares.
Poland:
E--> Works of groups 20 and 21 are included in group 19.
FR-> Les ouvrages des groupes 20 et 21 sont inclus dans le groupe 19.
ESP> Las obras de los grupos 20 y 21 quedan incluídas en el grupo 19.
Portugal:
E--> Works of groups 5 to 10 are included in group 4; 13 in group 12; 15 to 18 in group 14; 20 to 22 in group 19; 11 and 23b in group 23a; 25 in group 24.
FR-> Les ouvrages des groupes 5 à 10 sont inclus dans le groupe 4; 13 dans le groupe 12; 15 à 18 dans le groupe 14; 20 à 22 dans le groupe 19; 11 et 23b dans le groupe 23a; 25 dans le groupe 24.
ESP> Las obras de los grupos 5 a 10 quedan incluídas en el grupo 4; 13 en el grupo 12; 15 a 18 en el grupo 14; 20 a 22 en el grupo 19; 11 y 23b en el grupo 23a; 25 en el grupo 24.
Romania:
E--> Works of groups 5 to 10 are included in group 4; 13 in group 12; 15 to 18 in group 14; 20 to 22 in group 19; 23b in group 23a; 25 in group 24.
FR-> Les ouvrages des groupes 5 à 10 sont inclus dans le groupe 4; 13 dans le groupe 12; 15 à 18 dans le groupe 14; 20 à 22 dans le groupe 19; 23b dans le groupe 23a; 25 dans le groupe 24.
ESP> Las obras de los grupos 5 a 10 quedan incluídas en el grupo 4; 13 en el grupo 12; 15 a 18 en el grupo 14; 20 a 22 en el grupo 19; 23b en el grupo 23a; 25 en el grupo 24.
Spain:
E--> Works of group 23b are included in group 23a.
FR-> Les ouvrages du groupe 23b sont inclus dans le groupe 23a.
ESP> Las obras del grupo 23b quedan incluídas en el grupo 23a.
Sweden:
E--> Children's books (867 of which 716 first editions) are included in the total but not identified in the 25 groups. The discrepancy between the total and the sum made of the 25 groups is due to a variance in classification standards.
FR-> Les livres pour enfants (867 dont 716 premières éditions) sont compris dans le total mais ne sont pas répartis entre les 25 groupes. L'écart entre le total et la somme des 25 groupes est dû à une différence entre les normes de classification.
ESP> Los libros para niños (867 cuyas 716 primeras ediciones) quedan incluídos en el total pero no se desglosan entre los 25 grupos. La diferencia entre el total y la suma de los 25 grupos se debe a una discordancia entre las normas de clasificación.
Switzerland:
E--> School textbooks (241 of which 215 first editions) and children's books (610 of which 604 first editions) are included in the total but not identified in the 25 groups.
FR-> Les manuels scolaires (241 dont 215 premières éditions) et les livres pour enfants (610 dont 604 premières éditions) sont compris dans le total mais ne sont pas répartis entre les 25 groupes.
ESP> Los manuales escolares (241 cuyas 215 primeras ediciones) y los libros para niños (610 cuyas 604 primeras ediciones) quedan comprendidos en el total pero no se desglosan entre los 25 grupos.
OCEANIA:
Australia:
E--> Provisional data.
FR-> Les données sont provisoires.

Australia: (Cont):
ESP> Los datos son provisionales.
U.S.S.R.:
U.S.S.R.:
E--> Books for the popularization of science for children (390 of which 363 first editions) are included in the total, but not distributed in the 25 groups. Works of groups 20 and 21 are included in group 19, those of group 10 are distributed among other subjects not specified.
FR-> Les livres pour la vulgarisation des sciences pour les enfants (390 dont 363 premières éditions) sont inclus dans le total mais ne sont pas répartis entre les 25 groupes. Les ouvrages des groupes 20 et 21 sont inclus dans le groupe 19, ceux du groupe 10 sont répartis entre les autres sujets sans spécification.
ESP> Los libros por la vulgarización de las ciencias para niños (390 cuyas 363 primeras ediciones) quedan incluídos en el total pero no se desglosan entre los 25 grupos. Las obras de los grupos 20 y 21 quedan incluídas en el grupo 19, los del grupo 10 se desglosan entre los otros temas sin especificación.
Byelorussian S.S.R.:
E--> Works of group 10 are distributed among other subjects not specified.

Byelorussian S.S.R.: (Cont):
FR-> Les ouvrages du groupe 10 sont répartis entre les autres sujets sans spécification.
ESP> Las obras del grupo 10 se desglosan entre los otros temas sin especificación.
Ukrainian S.S.R.:
E--> Books for the popularization of science for children (70 of which 63 first editions) are included in the total, but are not distributed in the 25 groups. Works of groups 20 and 21 are included in group 19. those of group 10 are distributed among other subjects not specified.
FR-> Les livres pour la vulgarisation des sciences pour les enfants (70 dont 63 premières éditions) sont inclus dans le total mais ne sont pas répartis entre les 25 groupes. Les ouvrages des groupes 20 et 21 sont inclus dans le groupe 19. ceux du groupe 10 sont répartis entre les autres sujets sans spécification.
ESP> Los libros por la vulgarización de las ciencias para niños (70 cuyas 63 primeras ediciones) quedan incluídos en el total pero no se desglosan entre los 25 grupos. Las obras de los grupos 20 y 21 quedan incluídas en el grupo 19. los del grupo 10 se desglosan entre los otros temas sin especificación.

7.9 Book production: number of titles by language of publication

Edition de livres: nombre de titres classés d'après la langue de publication

Edición de libros: número de títulos clasificados según la lengua en que se publican

NUMBER OF COUNTRIES AND TERRITORIES PRESENTED IN THIS TABLE: 66

NOMBRE DE PAYS ET DE TERRITOIRES PRESENTES DANS CE TABLEAU: 66

NUMERO DE PAISES Y DE TERRITORIOS PRESENTADOS EN ESTE CUADRO: 66

COUNTRY / PAYS / PAIS	YEAR / ANNEE / AÑO	TOTAL	NATIONAL LANGUAGE / LANGUE NATIONALE / LENGUA NACIONAL	FOREIGN LANGUAGES / LANGUES ETRANGERES / LENGUAS EXTRANJERAS						TWO OR MORE LANGUAGES / DEUX LANGUES OU PLUS / DOS O MAS LENGUAS
				ENGLISH / ANGLAIS / INGLES	FRENCH / FRANCAIS / FRANCES	GERMAN / ALLEMAND / ALEMAN	SPANISH / ESPAGNOL / ESPAÑOL	RUSSIAN / RUSSE / RUSO	OTHERS / AUTRES LANGUES / OTRAS LENGUAS	
		(1)	(2)	(3)	(4)	(5)	(6)	(7)	(8)	(9)
AFRICA										
ALGERIA‡	1984	718	705	4	./.	–	–	–	–	1
ETHIOPIA	1984	349	166	20	–	–	–	–	163	–
GHANA‡	1983	350	350	./.	–	–	–	–	–	–
MADAGASCAR‡	1984	321	313	2	./.	–	–	2	–	4
MALI‡	1983	90	85	4	./.	1	–	–	–	–
MAURITIUS‡	1984	124	101	./.	./.	–	–	–	17	6
MOZAMBIQUE‡	1983	88	88	–	–	–	–	–	–	–
REUNION‡	1983	79	72	–	./.	–	–	–	–	4
SENEGAL‡	1983	42	42	–	./.	–	–	–	–	–
UNITED REPUBLIC OF TANZANIA‡	1982	246	246	./.	–	–	–	–	–	–
ZIMBABWE‡	1984	193	155	./.	–	–	–	–	–	–
AMERICA, NORTH										
BRITISH VIRGIN ISLANDS	1982	20	20	./.	–	–		–	–	–
COSTA RICA	1984	1 759	1 759	–	–	–	./.	–	–	–
CUBA	1984	2 069	1 955	54	3	–	./.	18	23	16
ST. CHRISTOPHER AND NEVIS‡	1982	5	5	./.	–	–	–	–		–
AMERICA, SOUTH										
ARGENTINA	1983	4 216	4 209	4	1	–	./.	–	2	–
BRAZIL	1982	19 179	18 357	455	40	13	42	–	139	133
CHILE	1983	1 326	1 309	16	1	–	./.	–	–	–
COLOMBIA	1984	15 041	14 933	60	12	–	–		36	–
GUYANA	1983	55	55	./.	–	–	–	–	–	–
PERU	1984	546	544	2	–	–	./.	–	–	–
URUGUAY‡	1984	1 206	892	3	1	–	./.	–	1	1
ASIA										
BAHRAIN‡	1982	78	73	1	–		–	–	–	4
BRUNEI DARUSSALAM‡	1982	72	64	./.	–	–	–	–	–	–
HONG KONG‡	1983	5 681	5 509	./.	22	9	1	–	109	31
INDIA‡	1982	10 649	10 618	./.	–	–	–		31	–
INDONESIA	1983	5 731	5 708	23	–	–	–		–	–

7.9 Number of titles by language of publication
Nombre de titres classés d'après la langue de publication
Número de títulos clasificados según la lengua en que se publican

COUNTRY / PAYS / PAIS	YEAR / ANNEE / AÑO	TOTAL	NATIONAL LANGUAGE / LANGUE NATIONALE / LENGUA NACIONAL	FOREIGN LANGUAGES / LANGUES ETRANGERES / LENGUAS EXTRANJERAS						TWO OR MORE LANGUAGES / DEUX LANGUES OU PLUS / DOS O MAS LENGUAS
				ENGLISH / ANGLAIS / INGLES	FRENCH / FRANCAIS / FRANCES	GERMAN / ALLEMAND / ALEMAN	SPANISH / ESPAGNOL / ESPAÑOL	RUSSIAN / RUSSE / RUSO	OTHERS / AUTRES LANGUES / OTRAS LENGUAS	
		(1)	(2)	(3)	(4)	(5)	(6)	(7)	(8)	(9)
IRAN, ISLAMIC REPUBLIC OF	1982	2 994	2 828	3	–	–	–	–	163	–
ISRAEL‡	1982	1 892	1 653	179	9	7	–	3	35	6
JAPAN‡	1983	44 253	44 253	–	–	–	–	–	–	–
KOREA, REPUBLIC OF	1984	35 446	34 632	409	10	29	–	–	9	357
MALAYSIA	1984	3 975	2 582	1 072	–	–	–	–	157	164
PHILIPPINES‡	1984	542	217	./.	–	–	–	–	–	–
SINGAPORE‡	1983	1 927	1 759	./.	–	–	–	–	10	158
SRI LANKA‡	1983	1 951	1 134	507	–	–	–	–	5	305
SYRIAN ARAB REPUBLIC	1983	119	119	–	–	–	–	–	–	–
THAILAND	1984	8 633	8 153	477	3	–	–	–	–	–
TURKEY	1983	6 869	6 574	78	56	34	–	–	113	14
UNITED ARAB EMIRATES	1983	84	84	–	–	–	–	–	–	–
EUROPE										
ALBANIA‡	1984	1 130	818	22	25	6	8	19	31	3
AUSTRIA	1984	9 059	8 591	279	50	./.	23	18	98	–
BELGIUM‡	1983	8 065	7 408	153	./.	./.	31	2	159	312
BULGARIA	1984	5 367	4 653	117	86	67	55	195	56	138
CZECHOSLOVAKIA‡	1984	9 911	9 272	129	30	73	12	82	304	9
DENMARK	1984	10 660	9 301	836	62	75	–	–	130	256
FINLAND‡	1984	8 563	7 378	1 091	9	38	5	11	27	4
HOLY SEE‡	1983	191	108	35	8	4	12	–	8	16
HUNGARY‡	1984	10 421	9 258	460	41	161	10	77	79	335
IRELAND‡	1984	799	781	./.	4	2	–	–	–	12
ITALY	1984	14 312	13 388	320	94	54	12	–	74	370
LUXEMBOURG‡	1984	341	251	–	./.	./.	–	–	11	79
MALTA‡	1984	313	309	./.	–	–	–	–	3	1
MONACO	1982	105	105	–	./.	–	–	–	–	–
NETHERLANDS‡	1982	13 324	11 142	1 211	73	236	–	–	19	643
NORWAY‡	1983	5 540	4 829	582	11	23	2	–	93	–
POLAND‡	1984	9 195	8 709	277	37	51	12	54	30	25
SPAIN‡	1984	30 764	28 215	869	681	166	./.	–	373	460
SWEDEN	1984	10 373	8 901	1 117	16	36	20	3	94	186
SWITZERLAND‡	1984	11 806	10 434	994	./.	./.	–	–	./.	378
YUGOSLAVIA‡	1984	10 918	9 865	68	12	26	–	5	695	247
OCEANIA										
AUSTRALIA‡	1982	2 358	2 340	./.	–	1	1	–	9	7
NEW CALEDONIA‡	1984	22	17	–	./.	–	–	–	5	–
NEW ZEALAND‡	1984	3 452	3 452	./.	–	–	–	–	–	–
U.S.S.R.										
U.S.S.R.‡	1984	82 790	78 651	1 231	445	396	506	./.	1 363	198
BYELORUSSIAN S.S.R.‡	1984	3 264	3 138	–	–	–	–	./.	126	–
UKRAINIAN S.S.R.‡	1984	8 403	8 139	78	29	43	16	./.	66	32

General note/Note générale/Nota general:

E--> The symbol ./. indicates that data are included in column 2 (national language).

FR-> Le signe ./. indique que les chiffres sont inclus dans la colonne 2 (langue nationale).

ESP> El signo ./. indica que los datos figuran en la columna 2 (lengua nacional).

AFRICA:

Algeria:

E--> The language breakdown refers to 710 first editions titles of which those in column 2 have been published in the following languages: Arabic (317), French (384), Arabic-French (4).

FR-> La répartition par langues se réfère aux 710 titres de premières éditions dont ceux de la colonne 2 ont été publiés dans les langues suivantes: (arabe (317), franc¢ais (384), arabe-franc¢ais (4).

ESP> La distribución por lenguas se refiere a los 710 títulos de las primeras ediciones de los cuales los de la columna 2 han sido publicados en las lenguas siguientes: árabe (314), francés (384), árabe-franc es (4).

Ghana:

E--> The titles in column 2 have been published in the following languages: English (312) and other national languages (38).

FR-> Les titres de la colonne 2 ont été publiés dans les langues

Ghana: (Cont):
suivantes: anglais (312) et autres langues nationales (38).

ESP> Los títulos de la columna 2 han sido publicados en las lenguas siguientes: inglés (312) y otras lenguas nacionales (38).

Madagascar:

E--> The titles in column 2 have been published in the following languages: Malagasy (114) and French (199).

FR-> Les titres de la colonne 2 ont été publiés dans les langues suivantes: malgache (114) et franc¢ais (199).

ESP> Los títulos en la columna 2 han sido publicados en las lenguas siguientes: malgache (114) y francés (199).

Mali:

E--> Data refer to school textbooks, government publications and university theses only. The titles in column 2 have been published in the following languages: French (63), Bambara (9), Peul (5), Tamasheq (7) and Sonrhai (1).

FR-> Les données se réfèrent aux manuels scolaires, publications gouvernementales et thèses universitaires seulement. Les titres de la colonne 2 ont été publiés dans les langues suivantes: franc¢ais (63), bambara (9), peul (5), tamasheq (7) et sonrhai (1).

ESP> Los datos se refieren solamente a los manuales escolares, a las publicaciones oficiales y a las tesis universitarias. Los títulos en la columna 2 han sido publicados en las lenguas siguientes: francés (63), bambara (9),

Mali: (Cont):
peul (5), tamasheq (7) y sonrhai (1).
Mauritius:
E--> The titles in column 2 have been published in the following languages: French (34), English (60), Creole (7).
FR-> Les titres de la colonne 2 ont été publiés dans les langues suivantes: franc¢ais (34), anglais (60), créole (7).
ESP> Los títulos de la columna 2 han sido publicados en las lenguas siguientes: francés (34), inglés (60), criolla (7).
Mozambique:
E--> The titles in column 2 have been published in the following languages: Portuguese (87) and Ronga (1).
FR-> Les titres de la colonne 2 ont été publiés dans les langues suivantes: portugais (87) et ronga (1).
ESP> Los títulos de la columna 2 han sido publicados en las lenguas siguientes: portugués (87) y ronga (1).
Reunion:
E--> Language breakdown refers to 76 titles of first editions only. The titles in column 2 have been published in the following languages: French (71) and Creole (1).
FR-> La répartition par langues se réfère aux 76 titres des premières éditions seulement. Les titres de la colonne 2 ont été publiés dans les langues suivantes: franc¢ais (71) et créole (1).
ESP> La distribución por lenguas se refiere a los 76 títulos de las primeras ediciones solamente. Los títulos de la columna 2 han sido publicados en las lenguas siguientes: francés (71) y criolla (1).
Senegal:
E--> All first editions.
FR-> Tous les ouvrages recensés sont des premières éditions seulement.
ESP> Todas las obras consideradas son primeras ediciones.
United Republic of Tanzania:
E--> The titles in column 2 have been published in the following languages: Swahili (142), English (103) and Kinyakyusa (1).
FR-> Les titres de la colonne 2 ont été publiés dans les langues suivantes: swahili (142), anglais (103) et kinyakyusa (1).
ESP> Los títulos de la columna 2 han sido publicados en las lenguas siguientes: swahili (142), inglés (103) y kinyakyusa (1).
Zimbabwe:
E--> The language breakdown refers to 155 first editions titles of which those in column 2 have been published in the following languages: English (88), Shona (42) and Ndebale (25).
FR-> La répartition par langues se réfère aux 155 titres de premières éditions dont ceux de la colonne 2 ont été publiés dans les langues suivantes: anglais (88), shona (42) et ndebale (25).
ESP> La distribución por lenguas se refiere a los 155 títulos de las primeras ediciones de los cuales los de la columna 2 han sido publicados en las lenguas siguientes: inglés (88), shona (42) y ndebale (25).
AMERICA, NORTH:
St. Christopher and Nevis:
E--> All first editions.
FR-> Tous les ouvrages recensés sont des premières éditions.
ESP> Todas las obras consideradas son primeras ediciones.
AMERICA, SOUTH:
Uruguay:
E--> Language breakdown refers to 896 titles of first editions only.
FR-> La répartition par langues se réfère aux 896 titres des premières éditions seulement.
ESP> La distribución por lenguas se refiere a los 896 títulos de las primeras ediciones solamente.
ASIA:
Bahrain:
E--> Data refer to school textbooks only.
FR-> Les données se réfèrent aux manuels scolaires seulement.
ESP> Los datos se refieren a los manuales escolares solamente.
Brunei Darussalam:
E--> Language breakdown refers to 64 titles of first editions only. The titles in column 2 have been published in the following languages: Malay (56), English (5), Malay/English (3).
FR-> La répartition par langues se réfère aux 64 titres des premières éditions seulement. Les titres de la colonne 2 ont été publiés dans les langues suivantes: malais (56), anglais (5), malais/anglais (3).
ESP> La distribución por lenguas se refiere a los 64 títulos de las primeras ediciones solamente. Los títulos de la columna 2 han sido publicados en las lenguas siguientes: malayo (56), inglés (5), malayo/inglés (3).
Hong Kong:
E--> The titles in column 2 have been published in the following languages: English (3,497), Chinese (2,012).
FR-> Les titres de la colonne 2 ont été publiés dans les langues suivantes: anglais (3 497), chinois (2 012).
ESP> Los títulos de la columna 2 han sido publicados en las lenguas siguientes: inglés (3 497), chino (2 012).
India:
E--> The titles in column 2 have been published in the following languages: English (4,313), Hindi (1,221), other national languages (5,084).
FR-> Les titres de la colonne 2 ont été publiés dans les langues

India: (Cont):
suivantes: anglais (4 313), hindi (1 221), autres langues nationales (5 084).
ESP> Los títulos de la columna 2 han sido publicados en las lenguas siguientes: inglés (4 313), hindi (1 221), otras lenguas nacionales (5 084).
Israel:
E--> The titles in column 2 have been published in the following languages: Hebrew (1,574), Arabic (48), Hebrew and other languages (31).
FR-> Les titres de la colonne 2 ont été publiés dans les langues suivantes: hébreu (1 574), arabe (48), hébreu et autres langues (31).
ESP> Los títulos de la columna 2 han sido publicados en las lenguas siguientes: (1 574), árabe (48) y hebreo y otras lenguas (31).
Japan:
E--> Data do not include pamphlets.
FR-> Les données ne tiennent pas compte des brochures.
ESP> Los datos no incluyen los folletos.
Philippines:
E--> Language breakdown refers to 217 titles of first editions of school textbooks, children's books and government publications only. The titles in column 2 have been published in the following languages: English (211), Pilipino (6).
FR-> La répartition par langues se réfère aux 217 titres des premières éditions des manuels scolaires, des livres d'enfants et des publications gouvernementales seulement. Les titres de la colonne 2 ont été publiés dans les langues suivantes: anglais (211), pilipino (6).
ESP> La distribución por lenguas se refiere a los 217 títulos de las primeras ediciones de los manuales escolares, de los libros para niños y de las publicaciones oficiales solamente. Los títulos de la columna 2 han sido publicados en las lenguas siguientes: inglés (211), pilipino (6).
Singapore:
E--> Not including government publications. The titles in column 2 have been published in the following languages: English (1,124), Chinese (587), Malay (38) and Tamil (10).
FR-> Non compris les publications officielles. Les titres de la colonne 2 ont été publiés dans les langues suivantes: anglais (1 124), chinois (587), malais (38) et tamoul (10).
ESP> Excluídas las publicaciones oficiales. Los títulos de la columna 2 han sido publicados en las lenguas siguientes: inglés (1 124), chino (587), malayo (38) y tamul (10).
Sri Lanka:
E--> The titles in column 2 have been published in the following languages: Sinhala (842) and Tamil (292).
FR-> Les titres de la colonne 2 ont été publiés dans les langues suivantes: sinhala (842) et tamoul (292).
ESP> Los títulos de la columna 2 han sido publicados en las lenguas siguientes: sinhala (842) y tamul (292).
EUROPE:
Albania:
E--> Language breakdown refers to 932 titles of first editions only.
FR-> La répartition par langue se réfère aux 932 titres de premières éditions seulement.
ESP> La distribución por lenguas se refiere a los 932 títulos de las primeras ediciones solamente.
Belgium:
E--> The titles in column 2 have been published in the following languages: Dutch (4,310), French (3,052) and German (46).
FR-> Les titres de la colonne 2 ont été publiés dans les langues suivantes: néerlandais (4 310), franc¢ais (3 052) et allemand (46).
ESP> Los títulos de la columna 2 han sido publicados en las lenguas siguientes: neerlandés (4 310), francés (3 052) y alemán (46).
Czechoslovakia:
E--> The titles in column 2 have been published in the following languages: Czech (6,208), Slovak (2,864), Czech and Slovak (153), Czech and/or Slovak and other languages (47).
FR-> Les titres de la colonne 2 ont été publiés dans les langues suivantes: tchèque (6 208), slovaque (2 864), tchèque et slovaque (153), tchèque et/ou slovaque et autres langues (47).
ESP> Los títulos de la columna 2 han sido publicados en las lenguas siguientes: checo (6 208) eslovaco (2 864), checo y eslovaco (153). checo y/o eslovaco y otro lengua (47).
Finland:
E--> The titles in column 2 have been published in the following languages: Finnish (6,784) and Swedish (594).
FR-> Les titres de la colonne 2 ont été publiés dans les langues suivantes: finnois (6 784) et suédois (594).
ESP> Los títulos de la columna 2 han sido publicados en las lenguas siguientes: finlandés (6 784) y sueco (594).
Holy See:
E--> Data do not include pamphlets.
FR-> Les données ne tiennent pas compte des brochures.
ESP> Los datos no incluyen los folletos.
Hungary:
E--> The titles in column 7 have been published in Russian and other languages of the U.S.S.R.
FR-> Les titres de la colonne 7 ont été publiés en russe et autres langues de l'U.R.S.S.

Hungary: (Cont):

ESP> Los títulos de la columna 7 han sido publicados en ruso y en otras lenguas de la U.R.S.S.

Ireland:

E--> The titles in column 2 have been published in the following languages: English (719) and Irish (62). Data do not include university theses.

FR-> Les titres de la colonne 2 ont été publiés dans les langues suivantes: anglais (719) et irlandais (62). Les données n'incluent pas les thèses universitaires.

ESP> Los títulos de la columna 2 han sido publicados en las lenguas siguientes: inglés (719) y irlandés (62). Los datos excluyen las tesis universitarias.

Luxembourg:

E--> The titles in column 2 have been published in the following languages: French (158), German (65) and Luxemburgish (28). The data in column 9 include other languages.

FR-> Les titres de la colonne 2 ont été publiés dans les langues suivantes: franc¢ais (158), allemand (65) et luxembourgeois (28). Les données de la colonne 9 comprennent les autres langues.

ESP> Los títulos de la columna 2 han sido publicados en las lenguas siguientes: francés (158), alemán (65) y luxemburgués (28). Los datos de la columna 9 incluyen las otras lenguas.

Malta:

E--> The titles in column 2 have been published in the following languages: Maltese (206) and and English (103).

FR-> Les titres de la colonne 2 ont été publiés dans les langues suivantes: maltais (206) et anglais (103).

ESP> Los títulos de la columna 2 han sido publicados en las lenguas siguientes: maltés (206) e inglés (103).

Netherlands:

E--> Data do not include pamphlets. The titles in column 2 have been published in the following languages: Dutch (11,059) and Frisian (83).

FR-> Les données ne tiennent pas compte des brochures. Les titres de la colonne 2 ont été publiés dans les langues suivantes: néerlandais (11 059) et frison (83).

ESP> Los datos no incluyen los folletos. Los títulos de la columna 2 han sido publicados en las lenguas siguientes: neerlandés (11 059) y frisiano (83).

Norway:

E--> Data do not include school textbooks. The titles in column 2 have been published in the following languages: Norwegian (4,507) and New-Norwegian (322).

FR-> Les manuels scolaires ne sont pas inclus dans les données. Les titres de la colonne 2 ont été publiés dans les langues suivantes: norvégien (4 507) et nouveau norvégien (322).

ESP> Los datos no incluyen los manuales escolares. Los títulos de la columna 2 han sido publicados en las lenguas siguientes: noruego (4 507) y nuevo-noruego (322).

Poland:

E--> The titles in column 7 have been published in Russian and other languages of the U.S.S.R.

FR-> Les titres de la colonne 7 ont été publiés en russe et autres langues de l'U.R.S.S.

ESP> Los títulos de la columna 7 han sido publicados en ruso y en otras lenguas de la U.R.S.S.

Spain:

E--> The titles in column 2 have been published in the following languages: Spanish (25,154), Galician (165), Catalan, Majorcan and Valencian (2,534) and Basque (362).

FR-> Les titres de la colonne 2 ont été publiés dans les langues suivantes: espagnol (25 154), galicien (165), catalan, majorquin et valencien (2 534), et basque (362).

ESP> Los títulos de la columna 2 han sido publicados en las lenguas siguientes: español (25 154), gallego (165), catalán, mallorquín y valenciano (2 534), y vascuence (362).

Switzerland:

E--> The titles in column 2 have been published in the following languages: German (7,215), French (2,934), Italian (232) and Romansh (53). The data in column 9 include other languages.

FR-> Les titres de la colonne 2 ont été publiés dans les langues

Switzerland: (Cont):

suivantes: allemand (7 215), franc¢ais (2 934), italien (232) et romanche (53). Les données de la colonne 9 comprennent les autres langues.

ESP> Los títulos de la columna 2 han sido publicados en las lenguas siguientes: alemán (7 215), francés (2 934), italiano (232) y romanche (53). Los datos de la columna 9 incluyen las otras lenguas.

Yugoslavia:

E--> The titles in column 2 have been published in the following languages: Serbo-Croat (7,418), Slovenian (1,889) and Macedonian (558).

FR-> Les titres de la colonne 2 ont été publiés dans les langues suivantes: serbo-croate (7 418), slovène (1 889) et macédonien (558).

ESP> Los títulos de la columna 2 han sido publicados en las lenguas siguientes: serbocroata (7 418), esloveno (1 889) y macedonio (558).

OCEANIA:

Australia:

E--> Provisional data. The titles in column 2 have been published in English (2,340).

FR-> Les données sont provisoires. Les titres de la colonne 2 ont été publiés en anglais (2 340).

ESP> Los datos son provisionales. Los títulos en la columna 2 han sido publicados en inglés (2 340).

New Caledonia:

E--> All first editions.

FR-> Tous les ouvrages recensés sont des premières éditions seulement.

ESP> Todas las obras consideradas son primeras ediciones.

New Zealand:

E--> The titles in column 2 have been published in the national languages of which breakdown is not known.

FR-> Les titres de la colonne 2 ont été publiés dans les langues nationales dont la ventilation n'est pas connue.

ESP> Los títulos de la columna 2 han sido publicados en las lenguas nacionales cuya distribución no se conoce.

U.S.S.R.:

U.S.S.R.:

E--> The titles in column 2 have been published in the following languages: Russian (63,502), Ukrainian (2,019), Lithuanian (1,940), Estonian (1,274), Georgian (1,714), Latvian (1,186), Uzbek (1,004), Kazakh (717), Azerbaidjan (860), Armenian (806), Moldavian (557), Kirghiz (456), Bielorussian (381), Turkoman (253), Tadzhik (375) and other languages of the U.S.S.R. (1,607).

FR-> Les titres de la colonne 2 ont été publiés dans les langues suivantes: russe (63 502), ukrainien (2 019), lituanien (1 940), estonien (1 274), géorgien (1 714), letton (1 186), ouzbek (1 004), kazakh (717), azerbaidjanais (860), arménien (806), moldave (557), kirghiz (456) biélorussien (381), turkmène (253), tadjik (375) et autres langues de l'U.R.S.S. (1 607).

ESP> Los títulos de la columna 2 han sido publicados en las lenguas siguientes: ruso (63 502), ucranio (2 019), lituano (1 940), estonio (1 274), georgiano (1 714), letón (1 186), uzbek (1 004), kazak (717), azerbaijanes (860), armenio (806), moldavo (557), kiriguiz (456), bieloruso (381), turcomano (253), takjik (375) y otras lenguas de la U.R.S.S. (1 607).

Byelorussian S.S.R.:

E--> The titles in column 2 have been published in the following languages: Russian (2,758) and Byelorussian (380).

FR-> Les titres de la colonne 2 ont été publiés dans les langues suivantes: russe (2 758) et biélorussien (380).

ESP> Los títulos de la columna 2 han sido publicados en las lenguas siguientes: ruso (2 758) y bieloruso (380).

Ukrainian S.S.R.:

E--> The titles in column 2 have been published in the following languages: Russian (6,104), Ukrainian (2,017), other languages of the U.S.S.R. (18).

FR-> Les titres de la colonne 2 ont été publiés dans les langues suivantes: russe (6 104), ukrainien (2 017), autres langues de l'U.R.S.S. (18).

ESP> Los títulos de la columna 2 han sido publicados en las lenguas siguientes: ruso (6 104), ucranio (2 017), otras lenguas de la U.R.S.S. (18).

7.10 Book production: number of copies by UDC classes

Edition de livres: nombre d'exemplaires classés d'après la CDU

Edición de libros: número de ejemplares clasificados por materias (CDU)

DATA ARE PRESENTED IN THOUSANDS

NUMBER OF COUNTRIES AND TERRITORIES PRESENTED IN THIS TABLE: 50

LES DONNEES SONT PRESENTEES EN MILLIERS

NOMBRE DE PAYS ET DE TERRITOIRES PRESENTES DANS CE TABLEAU: 50

LOS DATOS SE PRESENTAN EN MILLARES

NUMERO DE PAISES Y DE TERRITORIOS PRESENTADOS EN ESTE CUADRO: 50

COUNTRY	YEAR	TOTAL	GENERALITIES	PHILOSOPHY	RELIGION	SOCIAL SCIENCES	PHILOLOGY	PURE SCIENCES	APPLIED SCIENCES	ARTS	LITERATURE	GEOGR./HISTORY
PAYS	ANNEE	TOTAL	GENERALITES	PHILOSOPHIE	RELIGION	SCIENCES SOCIALES	PHILOLOGIE	SCIENCES PURES	SCIENCES APPL.	ARTS	LITTERATURE	GEOGR./HISTOIRE
PAIS	AÑO	TOTAL	GENERALIDADES	FILOSOFIA	RELIGION	CIENCIAS SOCIALES	FILOLOGIA	CIENCIAS PURAS	CIENCIAS APLICADAS	ARTES	LITERATURA	GEOGR./HISTORIA
		(1)	(2)	(3)	(4)	(5)	(6)	(7)	(8)	(9)	(10)	(11)
AFRICA												
ALGERIA‡	1983	1 300	–	10	–	380	10	192	582	23	100	3
COTE D'IVOIRE‡	1983	3 766	–	–	–	2 770	–	–	8	2	34	75
GAMBIA‡	1983	7	1	–	0	2	0	1	2	1	0	1
	1984	8	1	–	0	2	0	1	2	1	0	1
MADAGASCAR	1982	940	8	17	269	385	29	47	23	22	61	79
	1983	549	1	7	87	278	31	41	37	4	38	25
	1984	493	6	16	230	112	21	27	18	11	22	30
MALI‡	1983	9	–	–	–	2	1	0	0	–	4	2
	1984	92	–	–	–	49	20	12	10	–	–	1
MAURITIUS	1982	175	–	4	11	134	–	5	2	0	15	4
	1984	167	0	–	26	23	52	24	8	7	17	10
MOZAMBIQUE	1983	5 544	–	–	–	5 249	–	24	10	22	174	65
SENEGAL‡	1983	169	–	5	9	24	12	10	–	–	64	45
ZIMBABWE‡	1982	263	–	–	30	–	75	55	–	–	65	38
	1984	2 151	5	–	207	45	631	217	111	–	387	92
AMERICA, NORTH												
BRITISH VIRGIN ISLANDS	1982	3	3	–			–	–	–	–	–	–
COSTA RICA‡	1984	*641	*8	*8	*49	*222	*10	*69	*89	*6	*145	*35
CUBA	1982	44 437	1 763	339	18	33 669	–	319	952	1 114	5 352	911
	1983	41 080	2 106	187	9	15 281	1 610	3 962	7 663	3 747	3 245	3 270
	1984	44 622	5 274	328	2	16 100	2 280	4 494	3 023	1 586	8 560	2 975
NICARAGUA‡	1984	146	21	3	7	36	–	–	–	–	67	12
ST. CHRISTOPHER AND NEVIS‡	1982	1	–	–		0	–	–	0	–	–	1
AMERICA, SOUTH												
ARGENTINA‡	1982	14 763	948	2 456	——>	5 550	./.	268	605	772	4 114	50
	1983	13 526	1 984	1 872	——>	3 176	./.	122	692	558	5 090	32
BRAZIL	1982	396 355	55 527	7 552	78 170	100 204	16 542	25 260	40 005	24 804	27 388	20 903
CHILE	1983	19 888	465	540	1 455	9 058	510	780	1 800	465	3 360	1 455
COLOMBIA	1983	32 737	3 180	346	798	7 553	1 550	5 000	2 740	1 695	7 760	2 115
	1984	118 754	6 806	1 198	5 390	25 717	4 080	15 070	19 785	7 185	22 318	11 205

7.10 Number of copies by UDC classes
Nombre d'exemplaires classés d'après la CDU
Número de ejemplares clasificados por materias (CDU)

COUNTRY / PAYS / PAIS	YEAR / ANNEE / AÑO	TOTAL / TOTAL / TOTAL	GENERALITIES / GENERALITES / GENERALIDADES	PHILOSOPHY / PHILOSOPHIE / FILOSOFIA	RELIGION / RELIGION / RELIGION	SOCIAL SCIENCES / SCIENCES SOCIALES / CIENCIAS SOCIALES	PHILOLOGY / PHILOLOGIE / FILOLOGIA	PURE SCIENCES / SCIENCES PURES / CIENCIAS PURAS	APPLIED SCIENCES / SCIENCES APPL. / CIENCIAS APLICADAS	ARTS / ARTS / ARTES	LITERATURE / LITTERATURE / LITERATURA	GEOGR./HISTORY / GEOGR./HISTOIRE / GEOGR./HISTORIA
		(1)	(2)	(3)	(4)	(5)	(6)	(7)	(8)	(9)	(10)	(11)
ASIA												
BAHRAIN‡	1982	843	–	–	108	28	174	231	51	–	–	251
BRUNEI DARUSSALAM	1982	360	162	–	5	–	33	145	4	1	–	10
CHINA‡	1983	4 958 650	./.	370 530	./.	1 173 090	./.	208 590	./.	./.	214 890	./.
	1984	5 444 660	./.	285 780	./.	1 428 540	./.	220 620	./.	./.	243 460	./.
HONG KONG	1982	29 275	429	589	908	3 173	2 401	1 888	10 144	2 559	4 186	2 998
	1983	44 312	3 065	181	2 022	6 842	7 934	4 647	8 752	1 450	6 286	3 133
IRAQ‡	1983	452	34	–	–	138	–	6	–	–	244	30
ISRAEL‡	1982	11 654	209	186	1 612	824	1 317	1 301	619	113	3 831	1 634
JAPAN‡	1982	655 735	12 357	16 955	2 582	66 715	103 433	92 024	52 109	103 570	165 615	40 375
	1983	717 480	11 645	20 659	3 603	281 360	36 016	30 096	49 873	60 849	202 472	20 907
KOREA, REPUBLIC OF	1982	93 874	4 938	3 550	7 637	37 386	3 936	4 422	9 444	3 332	18 257	972
	1983	112 756	2 592	3 750	8 865	30 418	11 344	6 092	7 908	8 157	28 062	5 568
	1984	117 609	3 340	4 440	10 744	35 836	12 185	10 465	7 311	5 214	21 794	6 280
MALAYSIA	1982	8 203	48	2	303	2 788	1 748	1 027	248	140	1 332	567
	1983	14 104	99	44	883	4 070	2 602	1 626	1 353	293	1 948	1 186
	1984	14 073	239	89	1 062	3 997	2 879	1 277	1 151	281	2 187	911
MONGOLIA	1983	6 009	–	–	–	1 141	23	1 905	437	45	2 458	...
PHILIPPINES‡	1983	7 954	–	–	–	999	5 216	1 436	303	–	–	–
	1984	14 718	–	–	–	3 925	5 325	5 219	249	–	–	–
SINGAPORE‡	1982	8 396	108	48	454	4 447	820	420	644	318	877	260
	1983	11 126	189	230	1 027	5 373	661	576	1 027	381	1 283	379
SRI LANKA	1983	17 613	41	142	1 031	12 419	762	1 436	502	28	815	437
SYRIAN ARAB REPUBLIC	1983	553	–	10	3	248	–	27	25	9	206	25
UNITED ARAB EMIRATES	1982	809	20	–	104	17	358	206	14	5	5	80
	1983	1 590	27	9	180	4	426	654	29	–	26	235
EUROPE												
ALBANIA	1982	4 607	36	23	10	1 399	497	1 009	690	75	501	367
	1983	6 224	14	9	1	1 961	1 077	824	688	57	1 055	538
	1984	6 506	32	10	1	1 772	911	1 579	781	115	782	523
BULGARIA	1982	59 662	296	859	218	15 508	937	2 244	5 236	1 680	30 266	2 418
	1983	59 840	331	588	158	16 349	1 448	1 870	6 593	2 012	27 593	2 898
	1984	60 933	449	539	54	16 525	2 708	2 934	6 321	1 924	26 488	2 991
CZECHOSLOVAKIA	1982	92 454	4 273	863	258	26 444	2 717	2 567	15 566	4 941	31 907	2 918
	1983	94 223	4 254	611	318	21 924	3 255	7 694	10 596	4 816	35 616	5 139
	1984	98 325	4 003	667	184	19 671	3 957	8 261	11 093	4 907	40 231	5 351
GERMAN DEMOCRATIC REPUBLIC‡	1982	133 801	1 309	1 929	4 200	14 872	2 509	3 340	11 746	7 028	31 637	8 087
	1983	132 305	1 090	2 151	4 287	14 890	2 603	2 283	12 589	6 879	31 262	8 250
	1984	129 896	824	1 987	4 217	14 171	2 367	2 881	12 153	6 325	31 282	7 553
HOLY SEE‡	1982	169	22	16	96	25	2	–	–	2	0	6
	1983	178	22	23	98	19	2	–	–	5	0	9
HUNGARY	1982	103 735	3 952	651	1 034	9 267	7 095	9 020	10 836	7 947	43 798	10 135
	1983	107 975	6 189	866	1 143	8 635	8 739	10 237	10 785	8 899	41 274	11 208
	1984	115 593	3 916	703	984	15 918	7 867	13 380	16 483	8 205	38 021	10 116
ITALY	1982	148 199	8 852	3 518	10 772	29 381	6 841	8 913	12 284	11 623	39 544	16 471
	1983	147 787	10 297	4 215	10 858	26 369	6 970	10 575	11 967	15 347	34 244	16 945
	1984	132 802	9 210	3 166	11 018	26 343	5 482	8 988	11 212	8 866	34 540	13 977
MONACO	1982	792	486	–	–	18	–	–	–	248	39	1
POLAND	1982	178 050	1 218	1 677	6 597	14 157	16 801	20 522	23 226	7 504	71 790	14 558
	1983	194 922	1 577	1 127	7 297	17 676	16 925	19 029	23 350	8 149	82 401	17 391
	1984	229 755	1 827	1 941	6 913	30 665	13 239	13 442	34 965	11 809	95 023	19 931
PORTUGAL‡	1982	227 020	2 633	998	3 056	7 650	./.	2 569	2 679	192 289	13 096	2 050
	1983	57 942	3 993	443	1 946	6 273	./.	1 773	1 922	31 801	7 276	2 515
	1984	96 813	7 314	659	2 581	5 622	./.	2 973	2 564	64 143	8 750	2 207

COUNTRY / PAYS / PAIS	YEAR / ANNEE / AÑO	TOTAL / TOTAL / TOTAL	GENERALITIES / GENERALITES / GENERALIDADES	PHILOSOPHY / PHILOSOPHIE / FILOSOFIA	RELIGION / RELIGION / RELIGION	SOCIAL SCIENCES / SCIENCES SOCIALES / CIENCIAS SOCIALES	PHILOLOGY / PHILOLOGIE / FILOLOGIA	PURE SCIENCES / SCIENCES PURES / CIENCIAS PURAS	APPLIED SCIENCES / SCIENCES APPL. / CIENCIAS APLICADAS	ARTS / ARTS / ARTES	LITERATURE / LITTERATURE / LITERATURA	GEOGR./HISTORY / GEOGR./HISTOIRE / GEOGR./HISTORIA
		(1)	(2)	(3)	(4)	(5)	(6)	(7)	(8)	(9)	(10)	(11)
ROMANIA	1982	79 752	2 260	814	443	9 503	6 275	12 672	10 558	4 653	27 424	5 150
	1983	77 419	2 942	894	331	8 695	6 362	9 141	9 207	3 844	29 954	6 049
	1984	64 608	1 365	488	334	5 480	4 123	8 364	6 950	3 342	30 864	3 298
SPAIN	1982	273 391	67 035	5 713	12 749	27 426	19 622	20 470	18 856	13 717	76 327	11 476
	1983	262 790	66 730	4 930	11 716	17 237	20 787	14 109	14 436	11 658	88 712	12 475
	1984	250 526	10 586	8 941	11 559	21 582	24 214	14 658	15 939	10 319	117 208	15 520
YUGOSLAVIA	1982	58 325	427	494	1 207	30 733	883	629	4 918	6 533	10 922	1 579
	1983	65 954	458	362	1 111	33 904	939	788	6 453	6 190	13 805	1 944
	1984	56 412	635	776	1 378	27 254	953	1 087	5 868	5 113	11 840	1 508
OCEANIA												
NEW CALEDONIA‡	1984	8	–	–	–	2	5	1	–	0	–	0
U.S.S.R.												
U.S.S.R.‡	1982	1 925 084	45 032	21 289	4 865	583 133	18 005	34 520	232 171	36 000	891 675	31 596
	1983	1 969 433	34 199	20 994	5 715	613 105	14 787	38 970	218 421	37 960	925 574	32 092
	1984	2 085 344	25 158	21 736	6 714	608 161	15 991	36 193	229 818	43 772	‡‡‡‡‡‡‡‡	30 987
BYELORUSSIAN S.S.R.	1982	44 728	506	608	24	9 290	360	938	6 988	728	24 753	533
	1983	47 573	368	362	74	8 612	255	543	8 346	939	27 743	331
	1984	50 600	186	535	45	8 076	261	641	8 667	1 067	30 467	655
UKRAINIAN S.S.R.‡	1982	144 821	1 341	1 240	844	40 753	587	1 340	12 833	2 145	77 117	2 837
	1983	153 025	1 315	958	786	44 652	474	1 510	14 173	2 153	79 375	2 889
	1984	152 408	1 310	1 188	879	43 510	670	1 443	13 940	1 937	82 493	2 291

AFRICA:

Algeria:

E--> Data do not include pamphlets and refer to school textbooks, government publications and university theses only.

FR-> Les données ne comprennent pas les brochures et se réfèrent seulement aux manuels scolaires, aux publications gouvernementales et aux thèses universitaires.

ESP> Los datos no incluyen los folletos y se refieren solamente a los manuales escolares, a las publicaciones oficiales y a las tesis universitarias.

Côte d'Ivoire:

E--> Data do not include pamphlets. School textbooks (877,000) are included in the total but not identified in the 10 groups.

FR-> Les données ne comprennent pas les brochures. Les manuels scolaires (877 000) sont inclus dans le total mais ne sont pas répartis entre les 10 groupes.

ESP> Los datos no incluyen los folletos. Los manuales escolares (877 000) quedan comprendidos en el total pero no están repartidos entre los 10 grupos.

Gambia:

E--> All first editions.

FR-> Tous les ouvrages recensés sont des premières éditions.

ESP> Todas las obras consideradas son primeras ediciones.

Mali:

E--> Pamphlets only. In 1983, data refer to school textbooks only, whilst in 1984 they refer also to government publications and university theses.

FR-> Brochures seulement. En 1983, les données se réfèrent aux manuels scolaires seulement, tandis qu'en 1984, elles se réfèrent aussi aux publications gouvernementales et aux thèses universitaires.

ESP> Folletos solamente. En 1983, los datos se refieren a los manuales escolares solamente, mientras que en 1984, se refieren igualmente a las publicaciones oficiales y a las tesis universitarias.

Senegal:

E--> All first editions.

FR-> Tous les ouvrages recensés sont des premières éditions.

ESP> Todas las obras consideradas son primeras ediciones.

Zimbabwe:

E--> For 1982, data refer only to first editions of school textbooks and government publications. For 1984, school textbooks (456,000) are included in the total but are not identified in the 10 groups.

FR-> En 1982, les données se réfèrent seulement aux premières éditions des manuels scolaires et des publications gouvernementales. En 1984, les manuels scolaires (456 000) sont compris dans le total mais ne sont pas répartis entre les 10 groupes.

ESP> En 1982, los datos se referién solamente a las primeras ediciones de los manuales escolares y de las publicaciones oficiales. En 1984, los manuales escolares (456 000) quedan comprendidos en el total

Zimbabwe: (Cont):

pero no están repartidos entre los 10 grupos.

AMERICA, NORTH:

Costa Rica:

E--> Data do not include pamphlets.

FR-> Les données ne comprennent pas les brochures.

ESP> Los datos no incluyen los folletos.

Nicaragua:

E--> Data do not include pamphlets.

FR-> Les données ne comprennent pas les brochures.

ESP> Los datos no incluyen los folletos.

St. Christopher and Nevis:

E--> All first editions.

FR-> Tous les ouvrages recensés sont des premières éditions.

ESP> Todas las obras consideradas son primeras ediciones.

AMERICA,SOUTH:

Argentina:

E--> Data on philology are included with those of literature.

FR-> Les données relatives à la philologie sont comprises avec celles de la littérature.

ESP> Los datos relativos a la filología quedan incluídos con los de la literatura.

ASIA:

Bahrain:

E--> Data refer to school textbooks only.

FR-> Les données se réfèrent aux manuels scolaires seulement.

ESP> Los datos se refieren a los manuales escolares solamente.

China:

E--> School textbooks (2.270.4 million in 1983 and 2.358.7 million in 1984) and children's books (721.2 million in 1983 amd 907.5 million in 1984) are included in the total but not distributed in the 10 groups.

FR-> Les manuels scolaires (2 270.4 millions en 1983 et 2 358.7 millions en 1984), et les livres pour enfants (721.2 millions en 1983 et 907.5 millions en 1984) sont compris dans le total mais ne sont pas répartis entre les 10 groupes.

ESP> Los manuales escolares (2 270.4 millones en 1983 y 2 358.7 millones en 1984) y los libros para niños (721.2 millones en 1983 y 907.5 millones en 1984) quedan incluídos en el total pero no se desglosan entre los 10 grupos.

Iraq:

E--> Data refer to first editions only and do not include pamphlets.

FR-> Les données se réfèrent aux premières éditions seulement et ne comprennent pas les brochures.

ESP> Los datos se refieren a las primeras ediciones solamente y no incluyen los folletos.

Israel:

E--> The total includes 8,000 copies for which a subject breakdown is not available.

Israel: (Cont):

FR–> Le total comprend 8 000 exemplaires pour lesquels la répartition par sujets n'est pas disponible.

ESP> El total incluye 8 000 copias cuya repartición por témas se desconoce.

Japan:

E––> Data do not include pamphlets.

FR–> Les données ne tiennent pas compte des brochures.

ESP> Los datos no incluyen los folletos.

Philippines:

E––> Data refer only to school textbooks, children's books and government publications. In 1983, university theses are included as well.

FR–> Les données se réfèrent seulement aux manuels scolaires, aux livres pour enfants, aux publications gouvernementales. En 1983, les thèses universitaires sont aussi comprises.

ESP> Los datos se refieren solamente a los manuales escolares, a los libros para niños y a las publicaciones oficiales. En 1983, las tesis universitarias quedan comprendidas igualmente.

Singapore:

E––> Data do not include government publications.

FR–> Les données n'incluent pas les publications officielles.

ESP> Los datos no incluyen las publicaciones oficiales.

EUROPE:

German Democratic Republic:

E––> Data include only books and pamphlets shown in series A of the German National Bibliography (publications of the book market) i.e., those of the series B (publications outside the book market) and C (books published by universities) are excluded. School textbooks (24.2 million in 1982; 23 million in 1983 and 22.2 million in 1984) and children's books (22.9 million in 1982; 23 million in 1983 and 23.9 million in 1984) are included in the total but are not identified in the 10 groups.

FR–> Les données se réfèrent seulement aux livres et brochures de la série A de la Bibliographie nationale allemande (publications vendues dans le commerce). Les données relatives aux séries B (publications non vendues dans le commerce) et C (livres publiés par les universités) ne sont pas prises en compte. Les manuels scolaires (24.2 millions en 1982; 23 millions en 1983 et 22.2 millions en 1984) et les livres pour enfants (22.9 millions en 1982; 23 millions en 1983 et 23.9 millions en 1984) sont compris dans le total mais ne sont pas répartis entre les 10 groupes.

ESP> Los datos sólo se refieren a los libros y folletos de la serie A de la Bibliografía nacional alemana (publicaciones vendidas en el comercio). No se toman en consideración los datos relativos a las series B

German Democratic Republic: (Cont):

(publicaciones que no se venden en el comercio) y C (libros publicados por las universidades). Los manuales escolares (24.2 millones en 1982; 23 millones en 1983 y 22.2 millones en 1984) y los libros para niños (22.9 millones en 1982; 23 millones en 1983 y 23.9 millones en 1984) quedan comprendidos en el total pero no están repartidos entre los 10 grupos.

Holy See:

E––> For 1983, data do not include pamphlets.

FR–> Pour 1983, les données ne comprennent pas les brochures.

ESP> En 1983, los datos no incluyen los folletos.

Portugal:

E––> Data on philology are included with those of literature.

FR–> Les données relatives à la philologie sont comprises avec celles de la littérature.

ESP> Los datos relativos a la filología quedan incluídos con los de la literatura.

OCEANIA:

New Caledonia:

E––> All first editions.

FR–> Tous les ouvrages recensés sont des premières éditions.

ESP> Todas las obras consideradas son primeras ediciones.

U.S.S.R.:

U.S.S.R.:

E––> Books for the popularization of science for children (26.8 million in 1982; 27.6 million in 1983 and 25.7 million in 1984) are included in the total but are not distributed in the 10 groups.

FR–> Les livres pour la vulgarisation des sciences pour les enfants (26.8 millions en 1982; 27.6 millions en 1983 et 25.7 millions en 1984) sont inclus dans le total mais ne sont pas répartis entre les 10 groupes.

ESP> Los libros para la vulgarización de las ciencias para niños (26.8 millones en 1982; 27.6 millones en 1983 y 25.7 millones en 1984) quedan incluídos en el total pero no se desglosan entre los 10 grupos.

Ukrainian S.S.R.:

E––> Books for the popularization of science for children (3.8 million in 1982; 4.7 million in 1983 and 2.7 million in 1984) are included in the total, but are not distributed in the 10 groups.

FR–> Les livres pour la vulgarisation des sciences pour les enfants (3.8 millions en 1982; 4.7 millions en 1983 et 2.7 millions en 1984) sont inclus dans le total, mais ne sont pas répartis entre les 10 groupes.

ESP> Los libros para la vulgarización de las ciencias para niños (3.8 millones en 1982; 4.7 millones en 1983 y 2.7 millones en 1984) quedan incluídos en el total, pero no se desglosan entre les 10 grupos.

7.11 Book production: number of copies by subject group

Edition de livres: nombre d'exemplaires par groupes de sujets

Edición de libros: número de ejemplares por categorías de temas

ALL EDITIONS: FIRST EDITIONS AND RE-EDITIONS PREMIERES EDITIONS ET REEDITIONS PRIMERAS EDICIONES Y REEDICIONES		FIRST EDITIONS ONLY PREMIERES EDITIONS SEULEMENT PRIMERAS EDICIONES SOLAMENTE	
TOTAL (BOOKS AND PAMPHLETS) TOTAL (LIVRES ET BROCHURES) TOTAL (LIBROS Y FOLLETOS)	OF WHICH: BOOKS DONT: LIVRES DEL CUAL: LIBROS	TOTAL (BOOKS AND PAMPHLETS) TOTAL (LIVRES ET BROCHURES) TOTAL (LIBROS Y FOLLETOS)	OF WHICH: BOOKS DONT: LIVRES DEL CUAL: LIBROS

FOR THE CLASSIFICATION, BASED UPON THE UNIVERSAL DECIMAL CLASSIFICATION (UDC), SEE SECTION 2 OF THE INTRODUCTORY TEXT TO THIS CHAPTER.

POUR LA CLASSIFICATION, FONDEE SUR LA CLASSIFICATION DECIMALE UNIVERSELLE (CDU), VOIR LA SECTION 2 DU TEXTE D'INTRODUCTION A CE CHAPITRE.

PARA LA CLASIFICACION, BASADA EN LA CLASIFICACION DECIMAL UNIVERSAL (CDU), VEASE LA SECCION 2 DEL TEXTO DE LA INTRODUCCION A ESTE CAPITULO.

DATA ARE PRESENTED IN THOUSANDS

LES DONNEES SONT PRESENTEES EN MILLIERS

LOS DATOS SE PRESENTAN EN MILLARES

NUMBER OF COUNTRIES AND TERRITORIES PRESENTED IN THIS TABLE: 48

NOMBRE DE PAYS ET DE TERRITOIRES PRESENTES DANS CE TABLEAU: 48

NUMERO DE PAISES Y DE TERRITORIOS PRESENTADOS EN ESTE CUADRO: 48

AFRICA

SUBJECT GROUP GROUPE DE SUJETS CATEGORIA DE TEMAS	COTE D'IVOIRE‡ (1983)				GAMBIA (1984)			
	ALL EDITIONS		FIRST EDITIONS		ALL EDITIONS		FIRST EDITIONS	
	TOTAL	OF WHICH: BOOKS	TOTAL	OF WHICH: BOOKS	TOTAL	OF WHICH: BOOKS	TOTAL	OF WHICH: BOOKS
TOTAL	3 766	3 766	1 746	1 746	8		8	
1. GENERALITIES	–	–	–	–	1		1	
2. PHILOSOPHY, PSYCHOLOGY	–	–	–	–	–		–	
3. RELIGION, THEOLOGY	–	–	–	–	0		0	
4. SOCIOLOGY, STATISTICS	–	–	–	–	0		0	
5. POLITICAL SCIENCE	–	–	–	–	1		1	
6. LAW, PUBLIC ADMINISTRATION	–	–	–	–	0		0	
7. MILITARY ART	–	–	–	–	–		–	
8. EDUCATION, LEISURE	2 755	2 755	981	981	1		1	
9. TRADE, TRANSPORT	–	–	–	–	1		1	
10. ETHNOGRAPHY, FOLKLORE	15	15	–	–	–		–	
11. LINGUISTICS, PHILOLOGY	–	–	–	–	0		0	
12. MATHEMATICS	–	–	–	–	0		0	
13. NATURAL SCIENCES	–	–	–	–	1		1	
14. MEDICAL SCIENCES	–	–	–	–	0		0	
15. ENGINEERING, CRAFTS	–	–	–	–	0		0	
16. AGRICULTURE	–	–	–	–	1		1	
17. DOMESTIC SCIENCE	–	–	–	–	0		0	
18. MANAGEMENT, ADMINISTRATION	8	8	8	8	0		0	
19. PLANNING, ARCHITECTURE	–	–	–	–	1		1	
20. PLASTIC ARTS	1	1	1	1	0		0	
21. PERFORMING ARTS	1	1	1	1	–		–	
22. GAMES, SPORTS	–	–	–	–	0		0	
23. LITERATURE								
(A) HISTORY AND CRITICISM	–	–	–	–	–		–	
(B) LITERARY TEXTS	34	34	34	34	0		0	
24. GEOGRAPHY, TRAVEL	–	–	–	–	0		0	
25. HISTORY, BIOGRAPHY	75	75	75	75	1		1	

7.11 Number of copies by subject group
Nombre d'exemplaires par groupes de sujets
Número de ejemplares por categorías de temas

SUBJECT GROUP / GROUPE DE SUJETS / CATEGORIA DE TEMAS	MADAGASCAR (1984)				MALI‡ (1984)			
	ALL EDITIONS		FIRST EDITIONS		ALL EDITIONS		FIRST EDITIONS	
	TOTAL	OF WHICH: BOOKS	TOTAL	OF WHICH: BOOKS	TOTAL	OF WHICH: BOOKS	TOTAL	OF WHICH: BOOKS
TOTAL	493	335	438	282	92			
1. GENERALITIES	6	–	6	–	–			
2. PHILOSOPHY, PSYCHOLOGY	16	10	16	10	–			
3. RELIGION, THEOLOGY	230	176	226	174	–			
4. SOCIOLOGY, STATISTICS	0	0	0	0	2			
5. POLITICAL SCIENCE	11	5	11	5	–			
6. LAW, PUBLIC ADMINISTRATION	9	8	8	7	–			
7. MILITARY ART	1	0	1	0	–			
8. EDUCATION, LEISURE	84	56	51	23	47			
9. TRADE, TRANSPORT	1	0	1	0	–			
10. ETHNOGRAPHY, FOLKLORE	6	1	6	1	–			
11. LINGUISTICS, PHILOLOGY	21	18	15	12	20			
12. MATHEMATICS	14	14	12	12	11			
13. NATURAL SCIENCES	13	12	13	12	1			
14. MEDICAL SCIENCES	8	7	8	7	0			
15. ENGINEERING, CRAFTS	1	1	1	1	8			
16. AGRICULTURE	1	0	1	0	1			
17. DOMESTIC SCIENCE	1	–	1	–	1			
18. MANAGEMENT, ADMINISTRATION	7	2	7	2	0			
19. PLANNING, ARCHITECTURE	1	1	1	1	–			
20. PLASTIC ARTS	1	–	1	–	–			
21. PERFORMING ARTS	8	3	8	3	–			
22. GAMES, SPORTS	1	–	1	–	–			
23. LITERATURE								
(A) HISTORY AND CRITICISM	–	–	–	–	–			
(B) LITERARY TEXTS	22	15	13	6	–			
24. GEOGRAPHY, TRAVEL	7	3	7	3	1			
25. HISTORY, BIOGRAPHY	23	3	23	3	–			

SUBJECT GROUP / GROUPE DE SUJETS / CATEGORIA DE TEMAS	MAURITIUS (1984)				MOZAMBIQUE (1983)			
	ALL EDITIONS		FIRST EDITIONS		ALL EDITIONS		FIRST EDITIONS	
	TOTAL	OF WHICH: BOOKS	TOTAL	OF WHICH: BOOKS	TOTAL	OF WHICH: BOOKS	TOTAL	OF WHICH: BOOKS
TOTAL	167	104	164	102	5 544	5 542	4 501	4 499
1. GENERALITIES	0	–	0	–	–	–	–	–
2. PHILOSOPHY, PSYCHOLOGY	–	–	–	–	–	–	–	–
3. RELIGION, THEOLOGY	26	8	26	8	–	–	–	–
4. SOCIOLOGY, STATISTICS	1	–	1	–	–	–	–	–
5. POLITICAL SCIENCE	4	2	4	2	258	258	258	258
6. LAW, PUBLIC ADMINISTRATION	15	4	14	4	–	–	–	–
7. MILITARY ART	–	–	–	–	5	5	5	5
8. EDUCATION, LEISURE	2	0	2	0	4 986	4 986	4 026	4 026
9. TRADE, TRANSPORT	0	–	0	–	–	–	–	–
10. ETHNOGRAPHY, FOLKLORE	1	1	1	1	–	–	–	–
11. LINGUISTICS, PHILOLOGY	52	43	52	43	–	–	–	–
12. MATHEMATICS	22	22	22	22	24	24	24	24
13. NATURAL SCIENCES	2	1	2	1	–	–	–	–
14. MEDICAL SCIENCES	3	2	3	2	10	10	7	7
15. ENGINEERING, CRAFTS	1	1	1	1	–	–	–	–
16. AGRICULTURE	–	–	–	–	–	–	–	–
17. DOMESTIC SCIENCE	1	–	1	–	–	–	–	–
18. MANAGEMENT, ADMINISTRATION	3	1	3	1	–	–	–	–
19. PLANNING, ARCHITECTURE	–	–	–	–	–	–	–	–
20. PLASTIC ARTS	2	2	2	2	–	–	–	–
21. PERFORMING ARTS	5	4	5	4	2	–	2	–
22. GAMES, SPORTS	–	–	–	–	20	20	20	20
23. LITERATURE								
(A) HISTORY AND CRITICISM	0	–	0	–	–	–	–	–
(B) LITERARY TEXTS	17	7	15	5	174	174	114	114
24. GEOGRAPHY, TRAVEL	2	2	2	2	–	–	–	–
25. HISTORY, BIOGRAPHY	8	4	8	4	65	65	45	45

SUBJECT GROUP / GROUPE DE SUJETS / CATEGORIA DE TEMAS	SENEGAL (1983)				ZIMBABWE‡ (1984)			
	ALL EDITIONS		FIRST EDITIONS		ALL EDITIONS		FIRST EDITIONS	
	TOTAL	OF WHICH: BOOKS	TOTAL	OF WHICH: BOOKS	TOTAL	OF WHICH: BOOKS	TOTAL	OF WHICH: BOOKS
TOTAL	169		169		2 151	2 017	1 605	1 473
1. GENERALITIES	–		–		5	5	5	5
2. PHILOSOPHY, PSYCHOLOGY	5		5		–	–	–	–
3. RELIGION, THEOLOGY	9		9		207	107	195	95
4. SOCIOLOGY, STATISTICS	9		9		27	27	26	26
5. POLITICAL SCIENCE	6		6		5	5	1	1
6. LAW, PUBLIC ADMINISTRATION	6		6		1	1	1	1
7. MILITARY ART	–		–		–	–	–	–
8. EDUCATION, LEISURE	3		3		10	10	8	8
9. TRADE, TRANSPORT	–		–		–	–	–	–
10. ETHNOGRAPHY, FOLKLORE	–		–		2	2	2	2
11. LINGUISTICS, PHILOLOGY	12		12		631	626	484	479
12. MATHEMATICS	–		–		91	91	9	9
13. NATURAL SCIENCES	10		10		126	126	110	110
14. MEDICAL SCIENCES	–		–		28	–	26	–
15. ENGINEERING, CRAFTS	–		–		–	–	–	–
16. AGRICULTURE	–		–		80	80	80	80
17. DOMESTIC SCIENCE	–		–		–	–	–	–
18. MANAGEMENT, ADMINISTRATION	–		–		3	3	–	–
19. PLANNING, ARCHITECTURE	–		–		–	–	–	–
20. PLASTIC ARTS	–		–		–	–	–	–
21. PERFORMING ARTS	–		–		–	–	–	–
22. GAMES, SPORTS	–		–		–	–	–	–
23. LITERATURE								
(A) HISTORY AND CRITICISM	10		10		3	3	2	2
(B) LITERARY TEXTS	54		54		384	384	174	174
24. GEOGRAPHY, TRAVEL	10		10		61	61	25	25
25. HISTORY, BIOGRAPHY	35		35		31	30	1	–

AMERICA, NORTH

SUBJECT GROUP / GROUPE DE SUJETS / CATEGORIA DE TEMAS	BRITISH VIRGIN ISLANDS (1982)				COSTA RICA (1984)			
	ALL EDITIONS		FIRST EDITIONS		ALL EDITIONS		FIRST EDITIONS	
	TOTAL	OF WHICH: BOOKS	TOTAL	OF WHICH: BOOKS	TOTAL	OF WHICH: BOOKS	TOTAL	OF WHICH: BOOKS
TOTAL	3	3	–	–	*641	*641	*567	*567
1. GENERALITIES	3	3	–	–	*8	*8	*7	*7
2. PHILOSOPHY, PSYCHOLOGY	–	–	–	–	*8	*8	*8	*8
3. RELIGION, THEOLOGY	–	–	–	–	*49	*49	*46	*46
4. SOCIOLOGY, STATISTICS	–	–	–	–	*25	*25	*22	*22
5. POLITICAL SCIENCE	–	–	–	–	*84	*84	*72	*72
6. LAW, PUBLIC ADMINISTRATION	–	–	–	–	*64	*64	*63	*63
7. MILITARY ART	–	–	–	–	*3	*3	*3	*3
8. EDUCATION, LEISURE	–	–	–	–	*38	*38	*33	*33
9. TRADE, TRANSPORT	–	–	–	–	*4	*4	*4	*4
10. ETHNOGRAPHY, FOLKLORE	–	–	–	–	*4	*4	*3	*3
11. LINGUISTICS, PHILOLOGY	–	–	–	–	*10	*10	*9	*9
12. MATHEMATICS	–	–	–	–	*17	*17	*16	*16
13. NATURAL SCIENCES	–	–	–	–	*52	*52	*51	*51
14. MEDICAL SCIENCES	–	–	–	–	*9	*9	*8	*8
15. ENGINEERING, CRAFTS	–	–	–	–	*4	*4	*3	*3
16. AGRICULTURE	–	–	–	–	*60	*60	*59	*59
17. DOMESTIC SCIENCE	–	–	–	–	*2	*2	*2	*2
18. MANAGEMENT, ADMINISTRATION	–	–	–	–	*14	*14	*10	*10
19. PLANNING, ARCHITECTURE	–	–	–	–	*1	*1	*1	*1
20. PLASTIC ARTS	–	–	–	–	*1	*1	*1	*1
21. PERFORMING ARTS	–	–	–	–	*2	*2	*1	*1
22. GAMES, SPORTS	–	–	–	–	*2	*2	*2	*2
23. LITERATURE								
(A) HISTORY AND CRITICISM	–	–	–	–	*50	*50	*50	*50
(B) LITERARY TEXTS	–	–	–	–	*95	*95	*59	*59
24. GEOGRAPHY, TRAVEL	–	–	–	–	*15	*15	*15	*15
25. HISTORY, BIOGRAPHY	–	–	–	–	*20	*20	*19	*19

SUBJECT GROUP / GROUPE DE SUJETS / CATEGORIA DE TEMAS	CUBA (1984)				NICARAGUA (1984)			
	ALL EDITIONS		FIRST EDITIONS		ALL EDITIONS		FIRST EDITIONS	
	TOTAL	OF WHICH: BOOKS	TOTAL	OF WHICH: BOOKS	TOTAL	OF WHICH: BOOKS	TOTAL	OF WHICH: BOOKS
TOTAL	44 622	41 204	17 594	15 620	146	146	108	108
1. GENERALITIES	5 274	3 693	1 773	1 028	21	21	21	21
2. PHILOSOPHY, PSYCHOLOGY	328	324	34	34	3	3	3	3
3. RELIGION, THEOLOGY	2	2	–	–	7	7	7	7
4. SOCIOLOGY, STATISTICS	8	8	5	5	–	–	–	–
5. POLITICAL SCIENCE	870	870	591	591	30	30	30	30
6. LAW, PUBLIC ADMINISTRATION	431	427	337	337	–	–	–	–
7. MILITARY ART	123	21	15	15	–	–	–	–
8. EDUCATION, LEISURE	14 601	14 105	1 294	1 169	–	–	–	–
9. TRADE, TRANSPORT	59	59	58	58	–	–	–	–
10. ETHNOGRAPHY, FOLKLORE	8	8	8	8	6	6	6	6
11. LINGUISTICS, PHILOLOGY	2 280	2 247	358	358	–	–	–	–
12. MATHEMATICS	2 840	2 838	1 202	1 202	–	–	–	–
13. NATURAL SCIENCES	1 654	1 622	898	889	–	–	–	–
14. MEDICAL SCIENCES	1 387	1 155	1 010	799	–	–	–	–
15. ENGINEERING, CRAFTS	825	819	198	198	–	–	–	–
16. AGRICULTURE	315	314	51	51	–	–	–	–
17. DOMESTIC SCIENCE	439	439	78	78	–	–	–	–
18. MANAGEMENT, ADMINISTRATION	57	57	6	6	–	–	–	–
19. PLANNING, ARCHITECTURE	25	17	15	15	–	–	–	–
20. PLASTIC ARTS	56	53	9	9	–	–	–	–
21. PERFORMING ARTS	205	205	180	180	–	–	–	–
22. GAMES, SPORTS	1 300	416	1 276	392	–	–	–	–
23. LITERATURE								
(A) HISTORY AND CRITICISM	4 726	4 711	3 902	3 902	10	10	10	10
(B) LITERARY TEXTS	3 834	3 819	3 505	3 505	57	57	19	19
24. GEOGRAPHY, TRAVEL	1 473	1 473	243	243	–	–	–	–
25. HISTORY, BIOGRAPHY	1 502	1 502	548	548	12	12	12	12

AMERICA, SOUTH

SUBJECT GROUP / GROUPE DE SUJETS / CATEGORIA DE TEMAS	ST. CHRISTOPHER AND NEVIS (1982)				ARGENTINA‡ (1983)			
	ALL EDITIONS		FIRST EDITIONS		ALL EDITIONS		FIRST EDITIONS	
	TOTAL	OF WHICH: BOOKS	TOTAL	OF WHICH: BOOKS	TOTAL	OF WHICH: BOOKS	TOTAL	OF WHICH: BOOKS
TOTAL	1	0	1	0	13 526			
1. GENERALITIES	–	–	–	–	1 984			
2. PHILOSOPHY, PSYCHOLOGY	–	–	–	–	1 872			
3. RELIGION, THEOLOGY	–	–	–	–	./.			
4. SOCIOLOGY, STATISTICS	–	–	–	–	1 018			
5. POLITICAL SCIENCE	–	–	–	–	./.			
6. LAW, PUBLIC ADMINISTRATION	–	–	–	–	869			
7. MILITARY ART	–	–	–	–	–			
8. EDUCATION, LEISURE	0	0	0	0	1 289			
9. TRADE, TRANSPORT	0	–	0	–	–			
10. ETHNOGRAPHY, FOLKLORE	–	–	–	–	–			
11. LINGUISTICS, PHILOLOGY	–	–	–	–	./.			
12. MATHEMATICS	–	–	–	–	94			
13. NATURAL SCIENCES	–	–	–	–	28			
14. MEDICAL SCIENCES	0	0	0	0	432			
15. ENGINEERING, CRAFTS	–	–	–	–	195			
16. AGRICULTURE	–	–	–	–	65			
17. DOMESTIC SCIENCE	–	–	–	–	–			
18. MANAGEMENT, ADMINISTRATION	–	–	–	–	–			
19. PLANNING, ARCHITECTURE	–	–	–	–	3			
20. PLASTIC ARTS	–	–	–	–	409			
21. PERFORMING ARTS	–	–	–	–	./.			
22. GAMES, SPORTS	–	–	–	–	146			
23. LITERATURE								
(A) HISTORY AND CRITICISM	–	–	–	–	139			
(B) LITERARY TEXTS	–	–	–	–	4 951			
24. GEOGRAPHY, TRAVEL	–	–	–	–	32			
25. HISTORY, BIOGRAPHY	1	–	1	–	./.			

SUBJECT GROUP / GROUPE DE SUJETS / CATEGORIA DE TEMAS	BRAZIL‡ (1982)				COLOMBIA (1984)			
	ALL EDITIONS		FIRST EDITIONS		ALL EDITIONS		FIRST EDITIONS	
	TOTAL	OF WHICH: BOOKS	TOTAL	OF WHICH: BOOKS	TOTAL	OF WHICH: BOOKS	TOTAL	OF WHICH: BOOKS
TOTAL	396 355	206 999	266 212	121 221	118 754	48 005	88 804	29 935
1. GENERALITIES	55 527	29 380	41 396	25 207	6 806	4 956	4 854	3 304
2. PHILOSOPHY, PSYCHOLOGY	7 552	2 768	4 894	1 187	1 198	298	898	198
3. RELIGION, THEOLOGY	78 170	21 592	62 260	10 412	5 390	2 740	3 370	1 830
4. SOCIOLOGY, STATISTICS	1 047	991	687	635	775	375	550	250
5. POLITICAL SCIENCE	3 908	3 455	2 834	2 385	2 340	1 790	1 644	1 194
6. LAW, PUBLIC ADMINISTRATION	58 768	6 677	53 901	5 085	4 520	2 420	3 420	1 620
7. MILITARY ART	642	160	527	45	687	87	660	60
8. EDUCATION, LEISURE	33 121	26 559	13 654	9 690	11 656	306	9 045	225
9. TRADE, TRANSPORT	892	556	845	509	5 175	375	3 710	250
10. ETHNOGRAPHY, FOLKLORE	1 826	520	302	111	564	389	450	275
11. LINGUISTICS, PHILOLOGY	16 542	16 468	3 817	3 756	4 080	1 780	2 860	1 160
12. MATHEMATICS	12 932	12 115	6 098	5 314	6 550	4 050	5 000	2 700
13. NATURAL SCIENCES	12 328	10 568	7 495	5 800	8 520	4 395	6 230	2 930
14. MEDICAL SCIENCES	19 359	2 992	3 001	1 990	6 040	540	4 880	360
15. ENGINEERING, CRAFTS	8 882	3 650	8 319	3 109	2 325	1 325	1 885	885
16. AGRICULTURE	2 150	976	1 983	809	9 140	440	7 060	260
17. DOMESTIC SCIENCE	8 185	1 603	6 431	1 144	1 207	267	935	170
18. MANAGEMENT, ADMINISTRATION	1 429	1 394	417	410	1 073	473	610	310
19. PLANNING, ARCHITECTURE	214	214	146	146	563	263	474	174
20. PLASTIC ARTS	19 440	16 212	15 707	15 531	1 412	212	940	140
21. PERFORMING ARTS	–	–	–	–	1 960	340	1 630	230
22. GAMES, SPORTS	5 150	3 532	3 333	2 816	3 250	1 450	2 460	960
23. LITERATURE								
(A) HISTORY AND CRITICISM	27 388	25 053	12 693	10 827	4 009	720	3 769	480
(B) LITERARY TEXTS	./.	./.	./.	./.	18 309	8 109	13 600	3 400
24. GEOGRAPHY, TRAVEL	6 782	6 117	4 772	4 269	5 830	5 330	4 020	3 520
25. HISTORY, BIOGRAPHY	14 121	13 447	10 700	10 034	5 375	4 575	3 850	3 050

ASIA

SUBJECT GROUP / GROUPE DE SUJETS / CATEGORIA DE TEMAS	BAHRAIN‡ (1982)				BRUNEI DARUSSALAM (1982)			
	ALL EDITIONS		FIRST EDITIONS		ALL EDITIONS		FIRST EDITIONS	
	TOTAL	OF WHICH: BOOKS	TOTAL	OF WHICH: BOOKS	TOTAL	OF WHICH: BOOKS	TOTAL	OF WHICH: BOOKS
TOTAL	843	843	289	289	360	341	350	331
1. GENERALITIES	–	–	–	–	162	159	157	154
2. PHILOSOPHY, PSYCHOLOGY	–	–	–	–	–	–	–	–
3. RELIGION, THEOLOGY	108	108	36	36	5	5	–	–
4. SOCIOLOGY, STATISTICS	–	–	–	–	–	–	–	–
5. POLITICAL SCIENCE	–	–	–	–	–	–	–	–
6. LAW, PUBLIC ADMINISTRATION	–	–	–	–	–	–	–	–
7. MILITARY ART	–	–	–	–	–	–	–	–
8. EDUCATION, LEISURE	–	–	–	–	–	–	–	–
9. TRADE, TRANSPORT	28	28	28	28	–	–	–	–
10. ETHNOGRAPHY, FOLKLORE	–	–	–	–	–	–	–	–
11. LINGUISTICS, PHILOLOGY	174	174	16	16	33	25	33	25
12. MATHEMATICS	131	131	8	8	44	40	44	40
13. NATURAL SCIENCES	100	100	26	26	101	100	101	100
14. MEDICAL SCIENCES	–	–	–	–	1	–	1	–
15. ENGINEERING, CRAFTS	20	20	20	20	–	–	–	–
16. AGRICULTURE	–	–	–	–	3	3	3	3
17. DOMESTIC SCIENCE	31	31	31	31	–	–	–	–
18. MANAGEMENT, ADMINISTRATION	–	–	–	–	–	–	–	–
19. PLANNING, ARCHITECTURE	–	–	–	–	–	–	–	–
20. PLASTIC ARTS	–	–	–	–	–	–	–	–
21. PERFORMING ARTS	–	–	–	–	1	–	1	–
22. GAMES, SPORTS	–	–	–	–	–	–	–	–
23. LITERATURE	–	–	–	–				
(A) HISTORY AND CRITICISM	–	–	–	–	–	–	–	–
(B) LITERARY TEXTS	–	–	–	–	–	–	–	–
24. GEOGRAPHY, TRAVEL	211	211	104	104	6	5	6	5
25. HISTORY, BIOGRAPHY	40	40	20	20	4	4	4	4

7.11 Number of copies by subject group
Nombre d'exemplaires par groupes de sujets
Número de ejemplares por categorías de temas

SUBJECT GROUP / GROUPE DE SUJETS / CATEGORIA DE TEMAS	CHINA‡ (1984) ALL EDITIONS TOTAL	CHINA‡ (1984) ALL EDITIONS OF WHICH: BOOKS	CHINA‡ (1984) FIRST EDITIONS TOTAL	CHINA‡ (1984) FIRST EDITIONS OF WHICH: BOOKS	HONG KONG (1983) ALL EDITIONS TOTAL	HONG KONG (1983) ALL EDITIONS OF WHICH: BOOKS	HONG KONG (1983) FIRST EDITIONS TOTAL	HONG KONG (1983) FIRST EDITIONS OF WHICH: BOOKS
TOTAL	5 444 660				44 312	27 483	40 779	24 690
1. GENERALITIES	./.				3 065	2 490	2 859	2 412
2. PHILOSOPHY, PSYCHOLOGY	285 780				181	141	146	118
3. RELIGION, THEOLOGY	./.				2 022	1 399	1 481	926
4. SOCIOLOGY, STATISTICS	./.				1 403	1 249	3 438	1 174
5. POLITICAL SCIENCE	./.				1 862	1 564	1 049	755
6. LAW, PUBLIC ADMINISTRATION	./.				213	66	59	48
7. MILITARY ART	./.				368	213	358	209
8. EDUCATION, LEISURE	1 428 540				2 726	322	752	310
9. TRADE, TRANSPORT	./.				44	36	38	33
10. ETHNOGRAPHY, FOLKLORE	./.				226	156	221	151
11. LINGUISTICS, PHILOLOGY	./.				7 934	4 453	7 499	4 309
12. MATHEMATICS	./.				2 827	1 612	2 605	1 407
13. NATURAL SCIENCES	220 620				1 820	787	1 756	724
14. MEDICAL SCIENCES	./.				2 543	413	2 478	370
15. ENGINEERING, CRAFTS	./.				1 180	839	1 078	742
16. AGRICULTURE	./.				1 625	1 371	1 505	1 251
17. DOMESTIC SCIENCE	./.				3 222	2 556	3 044	2 393
18. MANAGEMENT, ADMINISTRATION	./.				182	182	129	129
19. PLANNING, ARCHITECTURE	./.				237	195	197	193
20. PLASTIC ARTS	./.				400	352	395	347
21. PERFORMING ARTS	./.				344	216	332	207
22. GAMES, SPORTS	./.				469	192	426	180
23. LITERATURE								
(A) HISTORY AND CRITICISM	243 460				725	598	691	564
(B) LITERARY TEXTS	./.				5 561	3 570	5 308	3 425
24. GEOGRAPHY, TRAVEL	./.				1 885	1 554	1 754	1 423
25. HISTORY, BIOGRAPHY	./.				1 248	957	1 181	890

SUBJECT GROUP / GROUPE DE SUJETS / CATEGORIA DE TEMAS	IRAQ (1983) ALL EDITIONS TOTAL	IRAQ (1983) ALL EDITIONS OF WHICH: BOOKS	IRAQ (1983) FIRST EDITIONS TOTAL	IRAQ (1983) FIRST EDITIONS OF WHICH: BOOKS	ISRAEL‡ (1982) ALL EDITIONS TOTAL	ISRAEL‡ (1982) ALL EDITIONS OF WHICH: BOOKS	ISRAEL‡ (1982) FIRST EDITIONS TOTAL	ISRAEL‡ (1982) FIRST EDITIONS OF WHICH: BOOKS
TOTAL	452	452	452	452	11 654			
1. GENERALITIES	34	34	34	34	209			
2. PHILOSOPHY, PSYCHOLOGY	–	–	–	–	186			
3. RELIGION, THEOLOGY	–	–	–	–	1 612			
4. SOCIOLOGY, STATISTICS	12	12	12	12	79			
5. POLITICAL SCIENCE	112	112	112	112	170			
6. LAW, PUBLIC ADMINISTRATION	14	14	14	14	121			
7. MILITARY ART	–	–	–	–	161			
8. EDUCATION, LEISURE	–	–	–	–	197			
9. TRADE, TRANSPORT	–	–	–	–	96			
10. ETHNOGRAPHY, FOLKLORE	–	–	–	–	./.			
11. LINGUISTICS, PHILOLOGY	–	–	–	–	1 317			
12. MATHEMATICS	–	–	–	–	847			
13. NATURAL SCIENCES	6	6	6	6	454			
14. MEDICAL SCIENCES	–	–	–	–	45			
15. ENGINEERING, CRAFTS	–	–	–	–	160			
16. AGRICULTURE	–	–	–	–	42			
17. DOMESTIC SCIENCE	–	–	–	–	372			
18. MANAGEMENT, ADMINISTRATION	–	–	–	–	./.			
19. PLANNING, ARCHITECTURE	–	–	–	–	./.			
20. PLASTIC ARTS	–	–	–	–	59			
21. PERFORMING ARTS	–	–	–	–	./.			
22. GAMES, SPORTS	–	–	–	–	54			
23. LITERATURE								
(A) HISTORY AND CRITICISM	14	14	14	14	41			
(B) LITERARY TEXTS	230	230	230	230	3 790			
24. GEOGRAPHY, TRAVEL	26	26	26	26	553			
25. HISTORY, BIOGRAPHY	4	4	4	4	1 081			

SUBJECT GROUP / GROUPE DE SUJETS / CATEGORIA DE TEMAS	JAPAN (1983)				KOREA, REPUBLIC OF (1984)			
	ALL EDITIONS		FIRST EDITIONS		ALL EDITIONS		FIRST EDITIONS	
	TOTAL	OF WHICH: BOOKS	TOTAL	OF WHICH: BOOKS	TOTAL	OF WHICH: BOOKS	TOTAL	OF WHICH: BOOKS
TOTAL	717 480	717 480	323 932	323 932	117 609	110 498	76 262	69 951
1. GENERALITIES	11 645	11 645	7 094	7 094	3 340	3 323	1 242	1 232
2. PHILOSOPHY, PSYCHOLOGY	20 659	20 659	12 275	12 275	4 440	4 427	2 359	2 352
3. RELIGION, THEOLOGY	3 603	3 603	2 701	2 701	10 744	10 470	3 707	3 485
4. SOCIOLOGY, STATISTICS	17 554	17 554	8 877	8 877	3 326	3 144	2 492	2 310
5. POLITICAL SCIENCE	12 146	12 146	9 468	9 468	1 129	1 126	948	945
6. LAW, PUBLIC ADMINISTRATION	3 747	3 747	2 945	2 945	2 267	1 792	1 886	1 411
7. MILITARY ART	–	–	–	–	22	22	18	18
8. EDUCATION, LEISURE	233 009	233 009	35 535	35 535	28 605	24 359	24 768	20 792
9. TRADE, TRANSPORT	11 758	11 758	7 778	7 778	351	346	317	316
10. ETHNOGRAPHY, FOLKLORE	3 146	3 146	2 435	2 435	136	135	89	88
11. LINGUISTICS, PHILOLOGY	36 016	36 016	11 352	11 352	12 185	11 821	8 634	8 333
12. MATHEMATICS	13 338	13 338	3 315	3 315	4 802	4 719	3 869	3 786
13. NATURAL SCIENCES	16 758	16 758	7 288	7 288	5 663	5 627	4 640	4 604
14. MEDICAL SCIENCES	2 525	2 525	2 217	2 217	298	296	158	156
15. ENGINEERING, CRAFTS	10 383	10 383	8 730	8 730	3 262	3 254	2 453	2 445
16. AGRICULTURE	2 177	2 177	1 662	1 662	588	588	459	459
17. DOMESTIC SCIENCE	25 821	25 821	16 293	16 293	2 373	2 307	1 169	1 103
18. MANAGEMENT, ADMINISTRATION	8 967	8 967	7 086	7 086	790	786	516	512
19. PLANNING, ARCHITECTURE	1 546	1 546	1 319	1 319	277	211	225	159
20. PLASTIC ARTS	29 098	29 098	21 282	21 282	837	795	633	593
21. PERFORMING ARTS	13 040	13 040	8 548	8 548	3 853	3 629	2 126	1 995
22. GAMES, SPORTS	17 165	17 165	11 923	11 923	247	247	181	181
23. LITERATURE								
(A) HISTORY AND CRITICISM	22 972	22 972	14 846	14 846	152	152	113	113
(B) LITERARY TEXTS	179 500	179 500	106 890	106 890	21 642	20 780	9 826	9 235
24. GEOGRAPHY, TRAVEL	3 290	3 290	1 500	1 500	803	785	708	690
25. HISTORY, BIOGRAPHY	17 617	17 617	10 573	10 573	5 477	5 357	2 726	2 638

SUBJECT GROUP / GROUPE DE SUJETS / CATEGORIA DE TEMAS	MALAYSIA (1984)				MONGOLIA‡ (1983)			
	ALL EDITIONS		FIRST EDITIONS		ALL EDITIONS		FIRST EDITIONS	
	TOTAL	OF WHICH: BOOKS	TOTAL	OF WHICH: BOOKS	TOTAL	OF WHICH: BOOKS	TOTAL	OF WHICH: BOOKS
TOTAL	14 073	7 951	13 992	7 873	6 009			
1. GENERALITIES	239	204	239	204	–			
2. PHILOSOPHY, PSYCHOLOGY	89	53	89	53	–			
3. RELIGION, THEOLOGY	1 062	535	1 059	532	–			
4. SOCIOLOGY, STATISTICS	247	97	246	96	–			
5. POLITICAL SCIENCE	581	259	576	254	1 094			
6. LAW, PUBLIC ADMINISTRATION	1 033	317	1 033	317	–			
7. MILITARY ART	26	20	26	20	–			
8. EDUCATION, LEISURE	571	295	564	288	47			
9. TRADE, TRANSPORT	329	238	327	236	–			
10. ETHNOGRAPHY, FOLKLORE	1 210	248	1 210	248	–			
11. LINGUISTICS, PHILOLOGY	2 879	1 433	2 879	1 433	23			
12. MATHEMATICS	671	549	660	538	1 905			
13. NATURAL SCIENCES	606	579	595	568	./.			
14. MEDICAL SCIENCES	85	55	85	55	33			
15. ENGINEERING, CRAFTS	155	107	150	102	137			
16. AGRICULTURE	515	54	515	54	267			
17. DOMESTIC SCIENCE	303	195	293	188	–			
18. MANAGEMENT, ADMINISTRATION	93	74	93	74	–			
19. PLANNING, ARCHITECTURE	24	17	24	17	–			
20. PLASTIC ARTS	65	53	65	53	./.			
21. PERFORMING ARTS	152	108	152	108	45			
22. GAMES, SPORTS	40	9	40	9	–			
23. LITERATURE								
(A) HISTORY AND CRITICISM	393	368	393	368	2 458			
(B) LITERARY TEXTS	1 794	1 300	1 794	1 300	./.			
24. GEOGRAPHY, TRAVEL	413	388	393	368	–			
25. HISTORY, BIOGRAPHY	498	396	492	390	–			

7.11 Number of copies by subject group
Nombre d'exemplaires par groupes de sujets
Número de ejemplares por categorías de temas

SUBJECT GROUP / GROUPE DE SUJETS / CATEGORIA DE TEMAS	PHILIPPINES‡ (1984) ALL EDITIONS TOTAL	PHILIPPINES‡ (1984) ALL EDITIONS OF WHICH: BOOKS	PHILIPPINES‡ (1984) FIRST EDITIONS TOTAL	PHILIPPINES‡ (1984) FIRST EDITIONS OF WHICH: BOOKS	SINGAPORE‡ (1983) ALL EDITIONS TOTAL	SINGAPORE‡ (1983) ALL EDITIONS OF WHICH: BOOKS	SINGAPORE‡ (1983) FIRST EDITIONS TOTAL	SINGAPORE‡ (1983) FIRST EDITIONS OF WHICH: BOOKS
TOTAL	14 718	14 516	14 718	14 516	11 126	8 947	8 826	6 954
1. GENERALITIES	–	–	–	–	189	162	88	81
2. PHILOSOPHY, PSYCHOLOGY	–	–	–	–	230	100	230	100
3. RELIGION, THEOLOGY	–	–	–	–	1 027	745	514	370
4. SOCIOLOGY, STATISTICS	3 925	3 925	3 925	3 925	140	112	106	78
5. POLITICAL SCIENCE	–	–	–	–	294	117	240	69
6. LAW, PUBLIC ADMINISTRATION	–	–	–	–	388	232	327	171
7. MILITARY ART	–	–	–	–	12	12	12	12
8. EDUCATION, LEISURE	–	–	–	–	4 105	3 356	3 448	2 785
9. TRADE, TRANSPORT	–	–	–	–	322	148	255	113
10. ETHNOGRAPHY, FOLKLORE	–	–	–	–	112	110	67	65
11. LINGUISTICS, PHILOLOGY	5 325	5 325	5 325	5 325	661	635	600	583
12. MATHEMATICS	5 216	5 216	5 216	5 216	334	331	273	270
13. NATURAL SCIENCES	3	2	3	2	242	241	159	158
14. MEDICAL SCIENCES	63	6	63	6	303	294	239	237
15. ENGINEERING, CRAFTS	125	5	125	5	228	81	214	71
16. AGRICULTURE	59	37	59	37	16	16	16	16
17. DOMESTIC SCIENCE	–	–	–	–	297	280	231	214
18. MANAGEMENT, ADMINISTRATION	2	–	2	–	183	136	146	103
19. PLANNING, ARCHITECTURE	–	–	–	–	18	18	18	18
20. PLASTIC ARTS	–	–	–	–	111	107	111	107
21. PERFORMING ARTS	–	–	–	–	149	143	148	143
22. GAMES, SPORTS	–	–	–	–	103	98	102	97
23. LITERATURE								
(A) HISTORY AND CRITICISM	–	–	–	–	164	142	164	142
(B) LITERARY TEXTS	–	–	–	–	1 119	962	879	722
24. GEOGRAPHY, TRAVEL	–	–	–	–	190	187	163	160
25. HISTORY, BIOGRAPHY	–	–	–	–	189	182	76	69

SUBJECT GROUP / GROUPE DE SUJETS / CATEGORIA DE TEMAS	SRI LANKA (1983) ALL EDITIONS TOTAL	SRI LANKA (1983) ALL EDITIONS OF WHICH: BOOKS	SRI LANKA (1983) FIRST EDITIONS TOTAL	SRI LANKA (1983) FIRST EDITIONS OF WHICH: BOOKS	SYRIAN ARAB REPUBLIC (1983) ALL EDITIONS TOTAL	SYRIAN ARAB REPUBLIC (1983) ALL EDITIONS OF WHICH: BOOKS	SYRIAN ARAB REPUBLIC (1983) FIRST EDITIONS TOTAL	SYRIAN ARAB REPUBLIC (1983) FIRST EDITIONS OF WHICH: BOOKS
TOTAL	17 613	12 340	7 332	3 933	553	553	552	552
1. GENERALITIES	41	27	35	21	–	–	–	–
2. PHILOSOPHY, PSYCHOLOGY	142	100	124	87	10	10	10	10
3. RELIGION, THEOLOGY	1 031	548	486	160	3	3	3	3
4. SOCIOLOGY, STATISTICS	4 053	4 047	10	4	13	13	13	13
5. POLITICAL SCIENCE	286	110	283	109	230	230	230	230
6. LAW, PUBLIC ADMINISTRATION	2 072	235	2 067	230	–	–	–	–
7. MILITARY ART	–	–	–	–	–	–	–	–
8. EDUCATION, LEISURE	5 913	4 443	2 160	2 023	2	2	2	2
9. TRADE, TRANSPORT	91	38	83	30	–	–	–	–
10. ETHNOGRAPHY, FOLKLORE	4	4	2	2	3	3	3	3
11. LINGUISTICS, PHILOLOGY	762	565	196	149	–	–	–	–
12. MATHEMATICS	691	676	499	484	2	2	2	2
13. NATURAL SCIENCES	745	732	323	310	25	25	25	25
14. MEDICAL SCIENCES	150	53	147	50	1	1	1	–
15. ENGINEERING, CRAFTS	60	11	45	11	21	21	21	21
16. AGRICULTURE	221	42	221	42	3	3	3	3
17. DOMESTIC SCIENCE	8	8	3	3	–	–	–	–
18. MANAGEMENT, ADMINISTRATION	63	10	63	10	–	–	–	–
19. PLANNING, ARCHITECTURE	–	–	–	–	–	–	–	–
20. PLASTIC ARTS	–	–	–	–	2	2	2	2
21. PERFORMING ARTS	28	0	24	0	7	7	7	7
22. GAMES, SPORTS	–	–	–	–	–	–	–	–
23. LITERATURE								
(A) HISTORY AND CRITICISM	90	87	13	10	17	17	17	17
(B) LITERARY TEXTS	725	301	363	131	189	189	189	189
24. GEOGRAPHY, TRAVEL	241	232	3	2	8	8	8	8
25. HISTORY, BIOGRAPHY	196	71	182	65	17	17	17	17

EUROPE

SUBJECT GROUP / GROUPE DE SUJETS / CATEGORIA DE TEMAS	UNITED ARAB EMIRATES (1983)				ALBANIA (1984)			
	ALL EDITIONS		FIRST EDITIONS		ALL EDITIONS		FIRST EDITIONS	
	TOTAL	OF WHICH: BOOKS	TOTAL	OF WHICH: BOOKS	TOTAL	OF WHICH: BOOKS	TOTAL	OF WHICH: BOOKS
TOTAL	1 590	1 590	587	587	6 506	6 012	3 876	3 383
1. GENERALITIES	27	27	27	27	32	30	32	30
2. PHILOSOPHY, PSYCHOLOGY	9	9	5	5	10	10	7	7
3. RELIGION, THEOLOGY	180	180	81	81	1	1	1	1
4. SOCIOLOGY, STATISTICS	1	1	1	1	958	861	957	860
5. POLITICAL SCIENCE	3	3	3	3	262	182	246	166
6. LAW, PUBLIC ADMINISTRATION	–	–	–	–	14	12	14	12
7. MILITARY ART	–	–	–	–	5	2	5	2
8. EDUCATION, LEISURE	–	–	–	–	476	471	60	55
9. TRADE, TRANSPORT	–	–	–	–	8	6	7	5
10. ETHNOGRAPHY, FOLKLORE	–	–	–	–	49	18	46	15
11. LINGUISTICS, PHILOLOGY	426	426	177	177	911	841	504	434
12. MATHEMATICS	171	171	78	78	1 001	991	225	215
13. NATURAL SCIENCES	483	483	98	98	578	572	189	183
14. MEDICAL SCIENCES	3	3	3	3	213	208	194	189
15. ENGINEERING, CRAFTS	–	–	–	–	128	125	101	98
16. AGRICULTURE	–	–	–	–	248	186	152	90
17. DOMESTIC SCIENCE	26	26	14	14	124	124	74	74
18. MANAGEMENT, ADMINISTRATION	–	–	–	–	68	27	65	24
19. PLANNING, ARCHITECTURE	–	–	–	–	14	14	14	14
20. PLASTIC ARTS	–	–	–	–	18	17	10	9
21. PERFORMING ARTS	–	–	–	–	70	68	13	12
22. GAMES, SPORTS	–	–	–	–	13	11	13	11
23. LITERATURE								
(A) HISTORY AND CRITICISM	–	–	–	–	52	52	10	10
(B) LITERARY TEXTS	26	26	26	26	730	688	640	598
24. GEOGRAPHY, TRAVEL	149	149	52	52	123	123	4	4
25. HISTORY, BIOGRAPHY	86	86	22	22	400	372	293	265

SUBJECT GROUP / GROUPE DE SUJETS / CATEGORIA DE TEMAS	BULGARIA‡ (1984)				CZECHOSLOVAKIA (1984)			
	ALL EDITIONS		FIRST EDITIONS		ALL EDITIONS		FIRST EDITIONS	
	TOTAL	OF WHICH: BOOKS	TOTAL	OF WHICH: BOOKS	TOTAL	OF WHICH: BOOKS	TOTAL	OF WHICH: BOOKS
TOTAL	60 933	54 423	45 946	39 621	98 325	79 700	65 453	52 655
1. GENERALITIES	449	372	449	372	4 003	954	2 798	829
2. PHILOSOPHY, PSYCHOLOGY	539	451	539	451	667	601	498	432
3. RELIGION, THEOLOGY	54	49	51	46	184	181	154	152
4. SOCIOLOGY, STATISTICS	668	427	620	379	130	97	121	88
5. POLITICAL SCIENCE	5 669	4 795	5 068	4 194	7 835	5 741	6 917	4 899
6. LAW, PUBLIC ADMINISTRATION	770	704	730	664	960	781	789	652
7. MILITARY ART	421	377	388	344	1 147	1 056	920	836
8. EDUCATION, LEISURE	8 805	8 223	5 155	4 628	8 570	6 256	2 226	1 997
9. TRADE, TRANSPORT	73	66	67	60	940	849	823	753
10. ETHNOGRAPHY, FOLKLORE	119	117	119	117	89	88	88	87
11. LINGUISTICS, PHILOLOGY	2 708	2 675	1 421	1 388	3 957	3 914	1 684	1 645
12. MATHEMATICS	1 107	1 104	645	642	3 906	3 880	1 710	1 696
13. NATURAL SCIENCES	1 827	1 704	1 173	1 050	4 355	4 193	2 948	2 792
14. MEDICAL SCIENCES	2 092	1 601	1 825	1 334	1 647	1 213	1 214	844
15. ENGINEERING, CRAFTS	2 018	1 949	1 547	1 479	4 632	4 295	3 911	3 609
16. AGRICULTURE	436	379	285	228	2 795	2 492	1 712	1 431
17. DOMESTIC SCIENCE	979	961	859	841	1 436	1 184	1 067	840
18. MANAGEMENT, ADMINISTRATION	796	724	361	289	583	546	465	428
19. PLANNING, ARCHITECTURE	1 065	921	908	764	654	612	572	529
20. PLASTIC ARTS	./.	./.	./.	./.	2 094	1 645	1 791	1 342
21. PERFORMING ARTS	./.	./.	./.	./.	842	718	723	604
22. GAMES, SPORTS	859	603	826	570	1 317	1 153	1 056	903
23. LITERATURE								
(A) HISTORY AND CRITICISM	26 488	23 453	20 942	18 036	1 183	1 151	823	791
(B) LITERARY TEXTS	./.	./.	./.	./.	39 048	32 003	26 423	21 485
24. GEOGRAPHY, TRAVEL	682	660	468	446	2 546	1 882	1 717	1 247
25. HISTORY, BIOGRAPHY	2 309	2 108	1 500	1 299	2 805	2 215	2 303	1 744

7.11 Number of copies by subject group
Nombre d'exemplaires par groupes de sujets
Número de ejemplares por categorías de temas

SUBJECT GROUP / GROUPE DE SUJETS / CATEGORIA DE TEMAS	GERMAN DEMOCRATIC REPUBLIC‡ (1984)				HOLY SEE (1983)			
	ALL EDITIONS		FIRST EDITIONS		ALL EDITIONS		FIRST EDITIONS	
	TOTAL	OF WHICH: BOOKS	TOTAL	OF WHICH: BOOKS	TOTAL	OF WHICH: BOOKS	TOTAL	OF WHICH: BOOKS
TOTAL	129 896	103 766	62 993	47 276	178	178	167	167
1. GENERALITIES	824	824	702	702	22	22	22	22
2. PHILOSOPHY, PSYCHOLOGY	1 987	1 986	901	900	23	23	23	23
3. RELIGION, THEOLOGY	4 217	2 109	3 333	1 421	98	98	90	90
4. SOCIOLOGY, STATISTICS	1 440	1 362	609	586	2	2	2	2
5. POLITICAL SCIENCE	4 326	3 975	2 450	2 237	–	–	–	–
6. LAW, PUBLIC ADMINISTRATION	3 255	2 804	1 371	1 076	10	10	8	8
7. MILITARY ART	1 639	1 416	1 237	1 094	–	–	–	–
8. EDUCATION, LEISURE	2 529	2 135	1 111	937	7	7	6	6
9. TRADE, TRANSPORT	776	733	329	316	–	–	–	–
10. ETHNOGRAPHY, FOLKLORE	206	146	136	76	–	–	–	–
11. LINGUISTICS, PHILOLOGY	2 367	2 360	627	625	2	2	2	2
12. MATHEMATICS	381	380	152	151	–	–	–	–
13. NATURAL SCIENCES	2 500	2 437	921	908	–	–	–	–
14. MEDICAL SCIENCES	1 526	1 292	689	605	–	–	–	–
15. ENGINEERING, CRAFTS	5 434	5 123	2 109	1 937	–	–	–	–
16. AGRICULTURE	2 350	2 326	625	621	–	–	–	–
17. DOMESTIC SCIENCE	2 792	2 792	691	691	–	–	–	–
18. MANAGEMENT, ADMINISTRATION	51	51	–	–	–	–	–	–
19. PLANNING, ARCHITECTURE	2 504	1 933	1 359	930	1	1	1	1
20. PLASTIC ARTS	148	48	68	15	–	–	–	–
21. PERFORMING ARTS	1 202	887	651	490	4	4	4	4
22. GAMES, SPORTS	2 471	2 426	1 351	1 346	–	–	–	–
23. LITERATURE								
(A) HISTORY AND CRITICISM	31 282	27 912	19 696	16 372	0	0	0	0
(B) LITERARY TEXTS					–	–	–	–
24. GEOGRAPHY, TRAVEL	3 389	3 024	855	804	–	–	–	–
25. HISTORY, BIOGRAPHY	4 164	3 773	3 274	3 000	9	9	9	9

SUBJECT GROUP / GROUPE DE SUJETS / CATEGORIA DE TEMAS	HUNGARY (1984)				ITALY (1984)			
	ALL EDITIONS		FIRST EDITIONS		ALL EDITIONS		FIRST EDITIONS	
	TOTAL	OF WHICH: BOOKS	TOTAL	OF WHICH: BOOKS	TOTAL	OF WHICH: BOOKS	TOTAL	OF WHICH: BOOKS
TOTAL	115 593	100 490	65 037	53 743	132 802	123 529	65 560	58 313
1. GENERALITIES	3 916	3 754	2 580	2 435	9 210	8 945	4 766	4 540
2. PHILOSOPHY, PSYCHOLOGY	703	593	605	495	3 166	3 126	1 756	1 718
3. RELIGION, THEOLOGY	984	941	648	625	11 018	6 619	7 054	3 443
4. SOCIOLOGY, STATISTICS	796	762	721	687	1 635	1 590	1 278	1 233
5. POLITICAL SCIENCE	9 179	3 405	8 840	3 076	1 706	1 651	1 078	1 041
6. LAW, PUBLIC ADMINISTRATION	1 664	1 017	1 541	924	4 868	4 172	3 023	2 384
7. MILITARY ART	473	472	458	457	104	102	79	79
8. EDUCATION, LEISURE	3 299	2 406	2 880	1 991	16 598	15 063	6 852	5 889
9. TRADE, TRANSPORT	149	130	128	109	779	665	344	232
10. ETHNOGRAPHY, FOLKLORE	358	183	296	171	653	643	491	481
11. LINGUISTICS, PHILOLOGY	7 867	6 768	850	835	5 482	5 463	1 090	1 075
12. MATHEMATICS	5 926	5 871	495	461	3 481	3 447	598	582
13. NATURAL SCIENCES	7 454	6 743	2 324	2 121	5 507	5 446	2 087	2 031
14. MEDICAL SCIENCES	2 606	2 280	1 661	1 335	3 006	2 817	2 001	1 821
15. ENGINEERING, CRAFTS	6 781	6 621	3 193	3 055	5 001	4 903	3 001	2 905
16. AGRICULTURE	1 690	1 311	1 395	1 016	595	567	307	289
17. DOMESTIC SCIENCE	3 961	3 543	3 223	2 814	1 411	1 411	715	715
18. MANAGEMENT, ADMINISTRATION	1 445	1 265	918	744	1 199	1 191	135	135
19. PLANNING, ARCHITECTURE	1 418	991	646	498	705	703	442	440
20. PLASTIC ARTS	1 986	1 436	1 348	1 147	3 217	3 130	1 712	1 654
21. PERFORMING ARTS	3 285	3 154	1 053	1 047	1 675	1 636	789	769
22. GAMES, SPORTS	1 516	1 441	1 315	1 240	3 269	2 918	2 525	2 194
23. LITERATURE								
(A) HISTORY AND CRITICISM	3 138	3 095	810	782	3 338	3 322	882	866
(B) LITERARY TEXTS	34 883	34 074	21 979	21 176	31 202	30 105	17 017	16 320
24. GEOGRAPHY, TRAVEL	4 846	3 797	2 774	2 242	7 409	7 342	2 953	2 905
25. HISTORY, BIOGRAPHY	5 270	4 437	2 356	2 260	6 568	6 552	2 585	2 572

SUBJECT GROUP / GROUPE DE SUJETS / CATEGORIA DE TEMAS	MONACO (1982)				POLAND‡ (1984)			
	ALL EDITIONS		FIRST EDITIONS		ALL EDITIONS		FIRST EDITIONS	
	TOTAL	OF WHICH: BOOKS	TOTAL	OF WHICH: BOOKS	TOTAL	OF WHICH: BOOKS	TOTAL	OF WHICH: BOOKS
TOTAL	792				229 755	155 288	129 790	79 417
1. GENERALITIES	486				1 827	1 285	1 116	677
2. PHILOSOPHY, PSYCHOLOGY	–				1 941	1 666	1 170	895
3. RELIGION, THEOLOGY	–				6 913	6 046	4 188	3 343
4. SOCIOLOGY, STATISTICS	–				1 082	756	1 006	695
5. POLITICAL SCIENCE	–				14 387	4 108	13 851	3 655
6. LAW, PUBLIC ADMINISTRATION	1				8 579	4 896	7 019	3 920
7. MILITARY ART	–				1 900	1 610	1 279	989
8. EDUCATION, LEISURE	17				4 510	2 511	3 687	2 059
9. TRADE, TRANSPORT	–				5	5	5	5
10. ETHNOGRAPHY, FOLKLORE	–				202	192	89	80
11. LINGUISTICS, PHILOLOGY	–				13 239	13 238	3 806	3 805
12. MATHEMATICS	–				5 223	5 206	1 853	1 837
13. NATURAL SCIENCES	–				8 219	7 240	2 024	1 698
14. MEDICAL SCIENCES	–				12 984	7 244	7 778	4 336
15. ENGINEERING, CRAFTS	–				6 051	5 167	2 771	2 174
16. AGRICULTURE	–				6 058	3 671	3 267	1 229
17. DOMESTIC SCIENCE	–				7 907	6 134	5 559	3 886
18. MANAGEMENT, ADMINISTRATION	–				1 965	1 293	1 468	799
19. PLANNING, ARCHITECTURE	–				8 718	7 860	3 805	3 429
20. PLASTIC ARTS	3				./.	./.	./.	./.
21. PERFORMING ARTS	–				./.	./.	./.	./.
22. GAMES, SPORTS	245				3 091	2 463	2 469	2 051
23. LITERATURE								
(A) HISTORY AND CRITICISM	9				2 983	2 908	1 761	1 686
(B) LITERARY TEXTS	30				92 040	53 284	49 429	27 153
24. GEOGRAPHY, TRAVEL	–				7 999	5 397	3 153	2 602
25. HISTORY, BIOGRAPHY	1				11 932	11 108	7 237	6 414

SUBJECT GROUP / GROUPE DE SUJETS / CATEGORIA DE TEMAS	PORTUGAL‡ (1984)				ROMANIA‡ (1984)			
	ALL EDITIONS		FIRST EDITIONS		ALL EDITIONS		FIRST EDITIONS	
	TOTAL	OF WHICH: BOOKS	TOTAL	OF WHICH: BOOKS	TOTAL	OF WHICH: BOOKS	TOTAL	OF WHICH: BOOKS
TOTAL	96 813	92 395	92 196	87 963	64 608			
1. GENERALITIES	7 314	7 024	7 193	6 903	1 365			
2. PHILOSOPHY, PSYCHOLOGY	659	648	491	480	488			
3. RELIGION, THEOLOGY	2 581	2 341	2 188	2 023	334			
4. SOCIOLOGY, STATISTICS	5 622	4 160	5 069	3 713	5 480			
5. POLITICAL SCIENCE	./.	./.	./.	./.	./.			
6. LAW, PUBLIC ADMINISTRATION	./.	./.	./.	./.	./.			
7. MILITARY ART	./.	./.	./.	./.	./.			
8. EDUCATION, LEISURE	./.	./.	./.	./.	./.			
9. TRADE, TRANSPORT	./.	./.	./.	./.	./.			
10. ETHNOGRAPHY, FOLKLORE	./.	./.	./.	./.	./.			
11. LINGUISTICS, PHILOLOGY	./.	./.	./.	./.	4 123			
12. MATHEMATICS	2 973	2 748	2 227	2 002	8 364			
13. NATURAL SCIENCES	./.	./.	./.	./.	./.			
14. MEDICAL SCIENCES	2 564	1 768	2 161	1 366	6 950			
15. ENGINEERING, CRAFTS	./.	./.	./.	./.	./.			
16. AGRICULTURE	./.	./.	./.	./.	./.			
17. DOMESTIC SCIENCE	./.	./.	./.	./.	./.			
18. MANAGEMENT, ADMINISTRATION	./.	./.	./.	./.	./.			
19. PLANNING, ARCHITECTURE	64 143	63 801	63 921	63 579	3 342			
20. PLASTIC ARTS	./.	./.	./.	./.	./.			
21. PERFORMING ARTS	./.	./.	./.	./.	./.			
22. GAMES, SPORTS	./.	./.	./.	./.	./.			
23. LITERATURE								
(A) HISTORY AND CRITICISM	8 750	8 519	7 255	7 027	30 864			
(B) LITERARY TEXTS	./.	./.	./.	./.	./.			
24. GEOGRAPHY, TRAVEL	2 207	1 386	1 691	870	3 298			
25. HISTORY, BIOGRAPHY	./.	./.	./.	./.	./.			

7.11 Number of copies by subject group
Nombre d'exemplaires par groupes de sujets
Número de ejemplares por categorías de temas

SUBJECT GROUP / GROUPE DE SUJETS / CATEGORIA DE TEMAS	SPAIN‡ (1984)				YUGOSLAVIA (1984)			
	ALL EDITIONS		FIRST EDITIONS		ALL EDITIONS		FIRST EDITIONS	
	TOTAL	OF WHICH: BOOKS	TOTAL	OF WHICH: BOOKS	TOTAL	OF WHICH: BOOKS	TOTAL	OF WHICH: BOOKS
TOTAL	250 526	212 874	217 165	180 881	56 412	46 034	32 792	24 570
1. GENERALITIES	10 586	9 487	9 770	8 678	635	515	477	392
2. PHILOSOPHY, PSYCHOLOGY	8 941	8 880	8 185	8 130	776	772	668	664
3. RELIGION, THEOLOGY	11 559	10 513	9 197	8 218	1 378	1 126	990	774
4. SOCIOLOGY, STATISTICS	772	724	695	647	260	228	229	197
5. POLITICAL SCIENCE	4 010	3 656	3 700	3 346	3 390	2 732	3 142	2 494
6. LAW, PUBLIC ADMINISTRATION	3 565	3 301	2 933	2 676	620	531	531	442
7. MILITARY ART	501	361	486	346	574	169	570	165
8. EDUCATION, LEISURE	10 054	5 645	9 586	5 340	22 206	19 869	5 749	5 023
9. TRADE, TRANSPORT	1 607	1 254	1 487	1 151	116	109	106	99
10. ETHNOGRAPHY, FOLKLORE	1 073	956	1 032	917	88	83	88	83
11. LINGUISTICS, PHILOLOGY	24 214	20 864	20 857	17 897	953	925	567	542
12. MATHEMATICS	6 127	5 908	5 664	5 447	427	399	242	225
13. NATURAL SCIENCES	8 531	8 075	7 727	7 307	660	630	444	415
14. MEDICAL SCIENCES	5 164	4 874	4 735	4 468	1 380	1 081	1 184	885
15. ENGINEERING, CRAFTS	4 363	4 019	3 836	3 496	1 194	972	935	716
16. AGRICULTURE	2 008	1 431	1 878	1 301	1 346	1 188	1 094	948
17. DOMESTIC SCIENCE	3 473	3 275	3 259	3 096	851	851	666	666
18. MANAGEMENT, ADMINISTRATION	931	921	859	849	1 097	926	1 003	832
19. PLANNING, ARCHITECTURE	751	727	706	682	286	148	214	111
20. PLASTIC ARTS	4 517	4 098	4 244	3 858	1 123	781	935	593
21. PERFORMING ARTS	2 876	2 793	2 705	2 624	3 113	368	2 955	287
22. GAMES, SPORTS	2 175	1 849	2 080	1 760	591	499	500	413
23. LITERATURE								
(A) HISTORY AND CRITICISM	117 208	94 556	97 920	75 791	127	115	127	115
(B) LITERARY TEXTS	./.	./.	./.	./.	11 713	9 811	8 069	6 441
24. GEOGRAPHY, TRAVEL	6 739	6 385	5 826	5 476	461	377	394	313
25. HISTORY, BIOGRAPHY	8 781	8 322	7 798	7 380	1 047	829	913	735

OCEANIA | U.S.S.R.

SUBJECT GROUP / GROUPE DE SUJETS / CATEGORIA DE TEMAS	NEW CALEDONIA (1984)				U.S.S.R.‡ (1984)			
	ALL EDITIONS		FIRST EDITIONS		ALL EDITIONS		FIRST EDITIONS	
	TOTAL	OF WHICH: BOOKS	TOTAL	OF WHICH: BOOKS	TOTAL	OF WHICH: BOOKS	TOTAL	OF WHICH: BOOKS
TOTAL	8	7	8	7	2 085 344	1 465 747	1 715 416	1 147 841
1. GENERALITIES	–	–	–	–	25 158	20 390	24 173	19 406
2. PHILOSOPHY, PSYCHOLOGY	–	–	–	–	21 736	17 688	18 991	14 943
3. RELIGION, THEOLOGY	–	–	–	–	6 714	6 042	5 516	4 844
4. SOCIOLOGY, STATISTICS	–	–	–	–	1 437	1 159	1 164	886
5. POLITICAL SCIENCE	–	–	–	–	179 772	105 016	154 747	88 092
6. LAW, PUBLIC ADMINISTRATION	–	–	–	–	27 651	16 587	24 597	15 134
7. MILITARY ART	–	–	–	–	26 593	23 145	24 242	20 794
8. EDUCATION, LEISURE	2	1	2	1	371 535	333 809	174 499	152 979
9. TRADE, TRANSPORT	–	–	–	–	1 173	1 055	988	871
10. ETHNOGRAPHY, FOLKLORE	–	–	–	–	./.	./.	./.	./.
11. LINGUISTICS, PHILOLOGY	5	5	5	5	1 720	1 411	1 563	1 262
12. MATHEMATICS	–	–	–	–	9 154	8 707	8 267	7 759
13. NATURAL SCIENCES	1	1	1	1	27 039	25 112	21 587	19 693
14. MEDICAL SCIENCES	–	–	–	–	45 983	39 228	37 477	31 332
15. ENGINEERING, CRAFTS	–	–	–	–	86 036	46 763	74 169	35 223
16. AGRICULTURE	–	–	–	–	32 594	26 730	26 934	21 251
17. DOMESTIC SCIENCE	–	–	–	–	10 107	9 540	6 960	6 393
18. MANAGEMENT, ADMINISTRATION	–	–	–	–	55 098	30 162	46 037	22 705
19. PLANNING, ARCHITECTURE	–	–	–	–	21 160	18 601	18 255	15 696
20. PLASTIC ARTS	0	–	0	–	./.	./.	./.	./.
21. PERFORMING ARTS	0	–	0	–	./.	./.	./.	./.
22. GAMES, SPORTS	–	–	–	–	22 612	19 812	20 648	18 050
23. LITERATURE								
(A) HISTORY AND CRITICISM	–	–	–	–	12 166	11 240	10 522	9 604
(B) LITERARY TEXTS	–	–	–	–	1 028 982	636 478	962 164	592 732
24. GEOGRAPHY, TRAVEL	0	0	0	0	10 277	9 628	9 353	8 708
25. HISTORY, BIOGRAPHY	0	0	0	0	20 710	19 873	15 729	14 893

SUBJECT GROUP / GROUPE DE SUJETS / CATEGORIA DE TEMAS	BYELORUSSIAN S.S.R.‡ (1984)				UKRAINIAN S.S.R.‡ (1984)			
	ALL EDITIONS		FIRST EDITIONS		ALL EDITIONS		FIRST EDITIONS	
	TOTAL	OF WHICH: BOOKS	TOTAL	OF WHICH: BOOKS	TOTAL	OF WHICH: BOOKS	TOTAL	OF WHICH: BOOKS
TOTAL	50 600	41 575	44 516	35 528	152 408	109 402	83 679	57 821
1. GENERALITIES	186	123	186	123	1 310	962	1 229	881
2. PHILOSOPHY, PSYCHOLOGY	535	407	535	407	1 188	827	913	560
3. RELIGION, THEOLOGY	45	27	45	27	879	585	687	393
4. SOCIOLOGY, STATISTICS	30	29	4	3	23	10	20	7
5. POLITICAL SCIENCE	1 492	1 120	1 360	988	6 090	3 524	5 269	2 821
6. LAW, PUBLIC ADMINISTRATION	602	354	535	287	4 115	1 893	2 241	1 221
7. MILITARY ART	317	314	317	314	1 077	924	793	640
8. EDUCATION, LEISURE	5 595	5 442	2 119	2 001	31 986	29 726	11 419	9 360
9. TRADE, TRANSPORT	40	29	31	20	219	174	198	153
10. ETHNOGRAPHY, FOLKLORE	./.	./.	./.	./.	./.	./.	./.	./.
11. LINGUISTICS, PHILOLOGY	261	250	246	235	670	648	354	332
12. MATHEMATICS	133	129	112	108	341	310	211	180
13. NATURAL SCIENCES	508	489	404	385	1 102	932	992	822
14. MEDICAL SCIENCES	1 812	1 348	1 471	1 007	3 714	2 925	2 722	2 195
15. ENGINEERING, CRAFTS	2 337	605	2 326	596	3 513	3 159	2 455	2 101
16. AGRICULTURE	1 866	1 623	1 710	1 467	2 197	1 709	1 373	991
17. DOMESTIC SCIENCE	1 385	1 319	414	348	1 036	1 024	376	364
18. MANAGEMENT, ADMINISTRATION	1 267	1 028	1 130	891	3 480	2 075	995	855
19. PLANNING, ARCHITECTURE	22	14	22	14	749	607	473	331
20. PLASTIC ARTS	45	39	45	39	./.	./.	./.	./.
21. PERFORMING ARTS	122	102	122	102	./.	./.	./.	./.
22. GAMES, SPORTS	878	823	828	773	1 188	1 029	1 148	989
23. LITERATURE								
(A) HISTORY AND CRITICISM	365	356	160	151	950	727	836	621
(B) LITERARY TEXTS	30 102	25 073	29 858	24 829	81 543	51 001	45 042	28 478
24. GEOGRAPHY, TRAVEL	71	66	71	66	1 357	1 254	877	774
25. HISTORY, BIOGRAPHY	584	466	465	347	934	784	819	669

AFRICA:

Côte d'Ivoire:

E--> School textbooks (872,000 of which 641,000 first editions) are included in the total but not distributed in the 25 groups.

FR-> Les manuels scolaires (872 000 dont 641 000 premières éditions) sont inclus dans le total mais ne sont pas répartis entre les 25 groupes.

ESP> Los manuales escolares (872 000 cuyas 641 000 primeras ediciones) quedan comprendidos en el total pero no están repartidos entre los 25 grupos.

Mali:

E--> Pamphlets only. Data refer only to school textbooks, government publications and university theses.

FR-> Brochures seulement. Les données se réfèrent seulement aux manuels scolaires, aux publications gouvernementales et aux thèses universitaires.

ESP> Folletos solamente. Los datos se refieren a los manuales escolares solamente, a las publicaciones oficiales y a las tesis universitarias.

Zimbabwe:

E--> School textbooks (456,000) are included in the total but are not identified in the 25 groups.

FR-> Les manuels scolaires (456 000) sont compris dans le total mais ne sont pas répartis entre les 25 groupes.

ESP> Los manuales escolares (456 000) quedan incluídos en el total pero no están repartidos entre los 25 grupos.

AMERICA, SOUTH:

Argentina:

E--> Works of group 3 are included in group 2; 5 in group 4; 21 in group 20; 11 and 25 in group 23a.

FR-> Les ouvrages du groupe 3 sont inclus dans le groupe 2; 5 dans le groupe 4; 21 dans le groupe 20; 11 et 25 dans le groupe 23a.

ESP> Las obras del grupo 3 quedan incluídas en el grupo 2; las del grupo 5 en el grupo 4; las del grupo 21 en el grupo 20; las de los grupos 11 y 25 en el grupo 23a.

Brazil:

E--> Works of group 23b are included in group 23a.

FR-> Les ouvrages du groupe 23b sont inclus dans le groupe 23a.

ESP> Las obras del grupo 23b quedan incluídas en el grupo 23a.

ASIA:

Bahrain:

E--> Data refer to school textbooks only.

FR-> Les données se réfèrent aux manuels scolaires seulement.

ESP> Los datos se refieren a los manuales escolares solamente.

China:

E--> School textbooks (2,358.7 million) and children's books (907.5 million) are included in the total but are not identified in the 25 groups. Works of groups 3, 4, 5, 6, 7, 9 (trade), 10 (ethnography and anthropology), 18 and 25 are included in group 2; 1, 9 (tourism), 10 (customs and habits), 17, 22, 11 and 24 in group 8; 10 (folklore), 20 and 21 in group 23; 12, 14, 15, 16 and 19 are included in group 13.

FR-> Les manuels scolaires (2 358.7 millions) et les livres pour enfants (907.5 millions) sont compris dans le total mais ne sont pas répartis entre les 25 groupes. Les ouvrages des groupes 3, 4, 5, 6, 7, 9 (commerce), 10 (ethnographie et anthropologie) 18 et 25 sont compris dans le groupe 2; 1, 9 (tourisme), 10 (coutumes et moeurs), 17, 22, 11 et 24 dans le groupe 8; 10 (folklore), 20 et 21 dans le groupe 23; 12, 14, 15, 16 et 19 dans le groupe 13.

ESP> Los manuales escolares (2 358.7 millones) y los libros para niños (907.5 millones) quedan incluídos en el total pero no se desglosan entre los 25 grupos. Las obras de los grupos 3, 4, 5, 6, 7, 9 (comercio), 10 (etnografía y antropología), 18 y 25 quedan incluídas en el grupo 2; 1, 9 (turismo), 10 (costumbres y hábitos), 17, 22, 11 y 24 en el grupo 8; 10 (folklore), 20 y 21 en el grupo 23; 12, 14, 15, 16 y 19 en el grupo 13.

Israel:

E--> Works of group 4 include those of group 10; 6 include those of group 18; 15 include those of group 19, and 20 include those of group 21. The total includes 8,000 copies for which a subject breakdown is not available.

FR-> Les ouvrages du groupe 4 comprennent ceux du groupe 10; groupe 6 ceux du groupe 18, 15 ceux du groupe 19 et 20 ceux du groupe 21. Le total comprend 8 000 exemplaires pour lesquels une répartition par sujets n'est pas disponible.

ESP> Las obras del grupo 4 incluyen las del grupo 10; el grupo 6 las del grupo 18, el grupo 15 las del grupo 19 y grupo 20 las del grupo 21. El total incluye 8 000 ejamplares para los cuales no se dispone de una repartición por temas.

Mongolia:

E--> Works of group 13 are included in group 12; 20 and 23b in group 23a.

FR-> Les ouvrages du groupe 13 sont inclus dans le groupe 12; 20 et 23b dans le groupe 23a.

ESP> Las obras del grupo 13 quedan incluídas en el grupo 12; las del grupo 20 y 23b en el grupo 23a.

Philippines:

E--> Data refer only to school textbooks, children's books and government publications.

FR-> Les données se réfèrent seulement aux manuels scolaires, aux livres pour enfants et aux publications gouvernementales.

ESP> Los datos se refieren solamente a los manuales escolares, a los libros para niños y a las publicaciones oficiales.

Singapore:
E--> Data do not include government publications.
FR-> Les données ne tiennent pas compte des publications officielles.
ESP> Los datos excluyen las publicaciones oficiales.
EUROPE:
Bulgaria:
E--> Works of groups 20 and 21 are included in group 19; 23b in group 23a.
FR-> Les ouvrages des groupes 20 et 21 sont inclus dans le groupe 19; ceux du groupe 23b dans le groupe 23a.
ESP> Las obras de los grupos 20 y 21 quedan incluídas en el grupo 19; las del grupo 23b en el grupo 23a.
German Democratic Republic:
E--> Data only include books and pamphlets shown in series A of the German National Bibliography (publications of the book market) i.e., those of the series B (publications outside the book market) and C (books published by the universities) are excluded. School textbooks (22.2 million of which 5.5 million first editions) and children's books (23.9 million of which 12.2 million first editions) are included in the total but not identified in the 25 groups. Works of group 23b are included in group 23a.
FR-> Les données se réfèrent seulement aux livres et brochures de la série A de la Bibliographie nationale allemande (publications vendues dans le commerce). Les données relatives aux séries B (publications non vendues dans le commerce) et C (livres publiés par les universités) ne sont pas prises en compte. Les manuels scolaires (22.2 millions dont 5.5 millions premières éditions) et les livres pour enfants (23.9 millions dont 12.2 millions premières éditions) sont compris dans le total mais ne sont pas répartis entre les 25 groupes.Les ouvrages du groupe 23b sont inclus dans le groupe 23a.
ESP> Los datos sólo se refieren a los libros y folletos de la serie A de la Bibliografía nacional alemana (publicaciones vendidas en el comercio). No se toman en consideración los datos relativos a las series B (publicaciones non vendidas en el comercio) y C (libros publicados por las universidades). Los manuales escolares (22.2 millones cuyas 5.5 millones primeras ediciones) y los libros para niños (23.9 millones cuyas 12.2 millones primeras ediciones) quedan comprendidos en el total pero no se desglosan entre los 25 grupos. Las obras del grupo 23b quedan incluídas en el grupo 23a.
Poland:
E--> Works of groups 20 and 21 are included in group 19.
FR-> Les ouvrages des groupes 20 et 21 sont inclus dans le groupe 19.
ESP> Las obras de los grupos 20 y 21 quedan incluídas en el grupo 19.
Portugal:
E--> Works of groups 5 to 10 are included in group 4; 13 in group 12; 15 to 18 in group 14; 20 to 22 in group 19; 11 and 23b in group 23a; 25 in group 24.
FR-> Les ouvrages des groupes 5 à 10 sont inclus dans le groupe 4; ceux du groupe 13 dans le groupe 12; 15 à 18 dans le groupe 14; 20 à 22 dans le groupe 19; 11 et 23b dans le groupe 23a; 25 dans le groupe 24.
ESP> Las obras de los grupos 5 a 10 quedan incluídas en el grupo 4; las del grupo 13 en el grupo 12; 15 a 18 en el grupo 14; 20 a 22 en el grupo 19; 11 y 23b en el grupo 23a; 25 en el grupo 24.
Portugal: (Cont):
Romania:
E--> Works of groups 5 to 10 are included in group 4; 13 in group 12; 15 to 18 in group 14; 20 to 22 in group 19; 23b in group 23a; 25 in group 24.
FR-> Les ouvrages des groupes 5 à 10 sont inclus dans le groupe 4; 13 dans le groupe 12; 15 à 18 dans le groupe 14; 20 à 22 dans le groupe 19; 23b dans le groupe 23a; 25 dans le groupe 24;
ESP> Las obras de los grupos 5 a 10 se incluyen en el grupo 4; 13 en el grupo 12; 15 a 18 en el grupo 14; 20 a 22 en el grupo 19; 23b en el grupo 23a; 25 en el grupo 24.
Spain:
E--> Works of group 23b are included in group 23a.
FR-> Les ouvrages du groupe 23b sont inclus dans le groupe 23a.
ESP> Las obras del grupo 23b quedan incluídas en el grupo 23a.
U.S.S.R.:
U.S.S.R.:
E--> Books for the popularization of science for children (25.7 million of which 23.3 million first editions) are included in the total but are not distributed in the 25 groups. Works of groups 20 and 21 are included in group 19, those of group 10 are distributed among other subjects not specified.
FR-> Les livres pour la vulgarisation des sciences pour les enfants (25.7 millions dont 23.3 millions premières éditions) sont inclus dans le total, mais ne sont pas répartis entre les 25 groupes. Les ouvrages des groupes 20 et 21 sont inclus dans le groupe 19, ceux du groupe 10 sont répartis entre les autres sujets sans spécification.
ESP> Los libros para la vulgarización de las ciencias para niños (25.7 millones cuyas 23.3 millones primeras ediciones) quedan incluídos en el total pero no se desglosan entre los 25 grupos. Las obras de los grupos 20 y 21 quedan incluídas en el grupo 19, las del grupo 10 se desglosan entre los otros temas sin especificación.
Byelorussian S.S.R.:
E--> Works of group 10 are distributed among other subjects not specified.
FR-> Les ouvrages du groupe 10 sont répartis entre les autres sujets sans spécification.
ESP> Las obras del grupo 10 se desglosan entre los otros temas sin especificación.
Ukrainian S.S.R.:
E--> Books for the popularization of science for children (2.7 million of which 2.2 million first editions) are included in the total but are not distributed in the 25 groups. Works of groups 20 and 21 are included in group 19, those of group 10 are distributed among other subjects not specified.
FR-> Les livres pour la vulgarisation des sciences pour les enfants (2.7 millions dont 2.2 millions premières éditions) sont inclus dans le total, mais ne sont pas répartis entre les 25 groupes. Les ouvrages des groupes 20 et 21 sont inclus dans le groupe 19, ceux du groupe 10 sont répartis entre les autres sujets sans spécification.
ESP> Los libros para la vulgarización de las ciencias para niños (2.7 millones cuyas 2.2 millones primeras ediciones) quedan incluídos en el total pero no se desglosan entre los 25 grupos. Las obras de los grupos 20 y 21 quedan incluídas en el grupo 19, las del grupo 10 se desglosan entre los otros temas sin especificación.

7.12 Production of school textbooks: number of titles and copies

Edition de manuels scolaires: nombre de titres et d'exemplaires

Edición de libros de texto escolares: número de títulos y de ejemplares

DATA FOR COUNTRIES SHOWN WITH THIS SYMBOL ARE ALL FIRST EDITIONS.

NUMBER OF COUNTRIES AND TERRITORIES PRESENTED IN THIS TABLE: 68

TOUTES LES DONNEES RELATIVES AUX PAYS ACCOMPAGNES DE CE SYMBOLE SONT DES PREMIERES EDITIONS.

NOMBRE DE PAYS ET DE TERRITOIRES PRESENTES DANS CE TABLEAU: 68

TODOS LOS DATOS RELATIVOS A LOS PAISES EN LOS QUE APARECE ESTO SIMBOLO SON PRIMERAS EDICIONES.

NUMERO DE PAISES Y DE TERRITORIOS PRESENTADOS EN ESTE CUADRO: 68

COUNTRY PAYS PAIS	YEAR ANNEE AÑO	NUMBER OF TITLES NOMBRE DE TITRES NUMERO DE TITULOS			NUMBER OF COPIES NOMBRE D'EXEMPLAIRES NUMERO DE EJEMPLARES		
		BOOKS LIVRES LIBROS	PAMPHLETS BROCHURES FOLLETOS	TOTAL	BOOKS LIVRES LIBROS (000)	PAMPHLETS BROCHURES FOLLETOS (000)	TOTAL (000)
AFRICA							
ALGERIA	1984	39	–	39	...	–	...
COTE D'IVOIRE	1983	13	...	13	3 517	...	3 517
ETHIOPIA	1984	57	–	57	...	–	...
GAMBIA #	1984	30	–	30	...	–	...
GHANA	1983	27	–	27	...	–	...
MADAGASCAR	1984	44	9	53	100	35	135
MALI	1984	–	76	76	–	56	56
MAURITIUS #	1984	27	5	32	69	7	76
MOZAMBIQUE	1983	41	–	41	4 985	–	4 985
NIGERIA	1984	360	...	360	...	...	...
REUNION #	1983	1	–	1	...	–	...
SENEGAL #	1983	...	...	8	...	...	70
UNITED REPUBLIC OF TANZANIA #	1984	12	3	15	...	...	...
ZAMBIA #	1983	215	–	215	...	–	...
ZIMBABWE	1984	41	–	41	456	–	456
AMERICA, NORTH							
COSTA RICA	1984	825	...	825	...	...	...
CUBA	1984	851	15	866	22 522	118	22 640
ST. CHRISTOPHER AND NEVIS	1982	–	–	–	–	–	–
AMERICA, SOUTH							
ARGENTINA	1983	...	...	243	...	...	...
BOLIVIA #	1982	4	–	4	...	–	...
CHILE	1984	90	13	103	...	...	...
COLOMBIA	1984	2 570	...	2 570	25 750	...	25 750
GUYANA	1983	–	–	–	–	–	–
PERU	1984	41	–	41	...	–	...
URUGUAY	1984	152	91	243	...	...	...
ASIA							
BAHRAIN	1982	78	–	78	843	–	843
BRUNEI DARUSSALAM #	1982	25	–	25	249	–	249
CHINA	1984	...	...	5 574	...	...	2 358 720
HONG KONG	1983	538	611	1 149	7 771	12 551	20 322
INDIA	1984	362	...	362	...	...	...
INDONESIA	1984	265	116	381	...	...	...
ISRAEL	1982	232	23	255	...	...	5 263
JAPAN	1983	2 044	–	2 044	224 169	–	224 169
KOREA, REPUBLIC OF	1984	3 497	370	3 867	43 991	3 685	47 676
MALAYSIA	1984	392	4	396	3 040	187	3 227
PHILIPPINES‡	1984	175	10	185	14 464	–	14 464
SINGAPORE	1983	389	36	425	4 081	252	4 333
SRI LANKA	1983	111	31	142	10 895	1 642	12 537
SYRIAN ARAB REPUBLIC #	1983	1	–	1	...	–	...
THAILAND	1984	319	–	319	...	–	...
TURKEY	1983	387	–	387	...	...	...
UNITED ARAB EMIRATES	1983	63	–	63	1 535	–	1 535

COUNTRY / PAYS / PAIS	YEAR / ANNEE / AÑO	NUMBER OF TITLES / NOMBRE DE TITRES / NUMERO DE TITULOS			NUMBER OF COPIES / NOMBRE D'EXEMPLAIRES / NUMERO DE EJEMPLARES		
		BOOKS LIVRES LIBROS	PAMPHLETS BROCHURES FOLLETOS	TOTAL	BOOKS LIVRES LIBROS (000)	PAMPHLETS BROCHURES FOLLETOS (000)	TOTAL (000)
EUROPE							
ALBANIA	1984	497	8	505	3 547	121	3 668
AUSTRIA	1984	86	6	92	...	...	...
BULGARIA	1984	1 076	117	1 193	13 874	755	14 629
CZECHOSLOVAKIA‡	1984	2 981	75	3 056	19 871	2 492	22 363
DENMARK	1984	...	...	903	...	...	...
FINLAND	1984	604	66	670			
GERMAN DEMOCRATIC REPUBLIC	1984	163	44	207	17 892	4 342	22 234
GERMANY, FEDERAL REPUBLIC OF	1984	429	84	513	...	...	...
HOLY SEE	1983	10	...	10	9	...	9
HUNGARY	1984	959	74	1 033	29 052	3 126	32 178
IRELAND	1984	20	3	23	...	...	...
ITALY	1984	1 103	28	1 131	45 940	319	46 259
LUXEMBOURG #	1984	6	–	6	...	–	...
MALTA #	1984	17	4	21	...	...	...
NETHERLANDS	1984	2 039	...	2 039	...	...	...
POLAND	1984	321	8	329	32 478	3 047	35 525
PORTUGAL	1984	...	...	775	...	...	11 072
SPAIN	1984	2 465	371	2 836	37 556	7 334	44 890
SWITZERLAND	1984	...	...	241	...	...	...
UNITED KINGDOM	1984	1 354	539	1 893	...	...	...
YUGOSLAVIA	1984	1 387	124	1 511	19 769	2 113	21 882
OCEANIA							
AUSTRALIA‡	1983	190	99	289	...	...	...
NEW ZEALAND	1984	14	40	54	...	...	...
U.S.S.R.							
U.S.S.R.	1984	...	...	2 836	...	...	293 085
BYELORUSSIAN S.S.R.	1984	71	1	72	3 381	35	3 416
UKRAINIAN S.S.R.	1984	182	5	187	24 933	665	25 598

ASIA:
Philippines:
E--> Data for copies refer only to first editions.
FR-> Les données pour les exemplaires se réfèrent seulement aux premières éditions.
ESP> Los datos para los ejemplares se refieren solamente a las primeras ediciones.
EUROPE:
Czechoslovakia:
E--> University theses are included with school textbooks.

Czechoslovakia: (Cont):
FR-> Les thèses universitaires sont comprises avec les manuels scolaires.
ESP> Las tesis universitarias quedan incluídas en los manuales escolares.
OCEANIA:
Australia:
E--> Provisional data.
FR-> Les données snt provisoires.
ESP> Los datos son provisionales.

7.13 Production of children's books: number of titles and copies

Edition de livres pour enfants: nombre de titres et d'exemplaires

Edición de libros para niños: número de títulos y de ejemplares

DATA FOR COUNTRIES SHOWN WITH THIS SYMBOL ARE ALL FIRST EDITIONS.

TOUTES LES DONNEES RELATIVES AUX PAYS ACCOMPAGNES DE CE SYMBOLE SONT DES PREMIERES EDITIONS.

TODOS LOS DATOS RELATIVOS A LOS PAISES EN LOS QUE APARECE ESTO SIMBOLO SON PRIMERAS EDICIONES.

NUMBER OF COUNTRIES AND TERRITORIES PRESENTED IN THIS TABLE: 69

NOMBRE DE PAYS ET DE TERRITOIRES PRESENTES DANS CE TABLEAU: 69

NUMERO DE PAISES Y DE TERRITORIOS PRESENTADOS EN ESTE CUADRO: 69

COUNTRY PAYS PAIS	YEAR ANNEE AÑO	NUMBER OF TITLES NOMBRE DE TITRES NUMERO DE TITULOS			NUMBER OF COPIES NOMBRE D'EXEMPLAIRES NUMERO DE EJEMPLARES		
		BOOKS LIVRES LIBROS	PAMPHLETS BROCHURES FOLLETOS	TOTAL	BOOKS LIVRES LIBROS (000)	PAMPHLETS BROCHURES FOLLETOS (000)	TOTAL (000)
AFRICA							
ALGERIA	1984	13	–	13	...	–	...
GAMBIA #	1984	10	–	10	...	–	...
GHANA	1983	11	–	11	...	–	...
MADAGASCAR	1984	–	–	–	–	–	–
MALI	1984	...	–	–	...	–	–
MAURITIUS #	1984	1	1	2	0	0	0
MOZAMBIQUE	1983	7	–	7	115	–	115
NIGERIA	1984	56	...	56	...	...	...
REUNION #	1983	–	2	2	–	...	...
SENEGAL #	1983	...	...	9	...	...	45
UNITED REPUBLIC OF TANZANIA	1984	–	–	–	–	–	–
ZAMBIA #	1983	11	–	11	...	–	...
AMERICA, NORTH							
COSTA RICA	1984	40	...	40	*320		*320
CUBA	1984	67	9	76	5 796	510	6 306
NICARAGUA #	1984	4	...	4	13	...	13
ST. CHRISTOPHER AND NEVIS	1982	–	–	–	–	–	–
AMERICA, SOUTH							
ARGENTINA	1983	...	...	302	...	...	...
BOLIVIA #	1982	6	–	6	...	–	...
CHILE	1984	60	38	98	...	...	...
COLOMBIA	1984	300	...	300	2 100	...	2 100
GUYANA	1983	–	–	–	–	–	–
PERU	1984	6	4	10	...	...	...
URUGUAY	1984	84	44	128	...	...	...
ASIA							
BRUNEI DARUSSALAM #	1982	14	–	14	75	–	75
CHINA	1984	...	...	4 090	...	...	907 540
HONG KONG	1983	228	250	478	1 823	1 821	3 644
INDIA	1984	544	...	544	...	...	...
INDONESIA	1984	196	148	344	...	...	...
IRAN, ISLAMIC REPUBLIC OF	1983	558	–	558	...	–	...
ISRAEL	1982	101	57	158	...	...	1 561
JAPAN	1983	3 509	–	3 509	52 681	–	52 681
KOREA, REPUBLIC OF	1984	5 553	1 629	7 182	14 793	3 733	18 526
MALAYSIA #	1984	270	619	889	1 470	2 549	4 019
PHILIPPINES‡	1984	5	7	12	–	100	100
SINGAPORE	1983	267	64	331	1 298	439	1 737
SRI LANKA	1983	13	109	122	50	404	454
SYRIAN ARAB REPUBLIC #	1983	13	–	13	...	–	...
THAILAND	1984	456	–	456	...	–	...
TURKEY	1983	1 112	–	1 112	...	–	...
UNITED ARAB EMIRATES	1983	–	–	–	–	–	–

COUNTRY / PAYS / PAIS	YEAR / ANNEE / AÑO	NUMBER OF TITLES / NOMBRE DE TITRES / NUMERO DE TITULOS			NUMBER OF COPIES / NOMBRE D'EXEMPLAIRES / NUMERO DE EJEMPLARES		
		BOOKS LIVRES LIBROS	PAMPHLETS BROCHURES FOLLETOS	TOTAL	BOOKS LIVRES LIBROS (000)	PAMPHLETS BROCHURES FOLLETOS (000)	TOTAL (000)
EUROPE							
ALBANIA	1984	46	16	62	268	170	438
AUSTRIA	1984	182	99	281	...	...	...
BELGIUM	1983	...	...	1 668	...	...	...
BULGARIA	1984	181	58	239	7 046	3 527	10 573
CZECHOSLOVAKIA	1984	397	383	780	10 942	8 900	19 842
DENMARK	1984	...	...	1 017	...	...	...
FINLAND	1984	201	117	318	...	...	...
GERMAN DEMOCRATIC REPUBLIC	1984	437	379	816	11 620	12 282	23 902
GERMANY, FEDERAL REPUBLIC OF	1984	2 223	875	3 098	...	...	...
HOLY SEE	1983	–	...	–	–	...	–
HUNGARY	1984	283	17	300	13 196	700	13 896
IRELAND	1984	14	2	16	...	...	...
ITALY	1984	429	215	644	8 593	2 847	11 440
LUXEMBOURG #	1984	11	1	12	...	...	...
MALTA #	1984	4	30	34	...	...	...
NETHERLANDS #	1984	1 369	...	1 369	...	...	...
NORWAY	1983	131	73	204	...	...	...
POLAND	1984	199	181	380	16 993	34 357	51 350
PORTUGAL	1984	...	...	487	...	...	6 704
SPAIN	1984	1 632	2 310	3 942	21 523	22 267	43 790
SWEDEN	1984	...	...	867	...	...	...
SWITZERLAND	1984	...	...	610	...	...	...
UNITED KINGDOM	1984	3 641	789	4 430	...	...	...
YUGOSLAVIA	1984	420	178	598	3 226	1 529	4 755
OCEANIA							
AUSTRALIA‡	1983	50	58	108	...	...	...
NEW ZEALAND	1984	29	103	132	...	...	...
U.S.S.R.							
U.S.S.R.	1984	...	...	4 055	...	...	587 517
BYELORUSSIAN S.S.R.	1984	92	59	151	6 980	5 170	12 150
UKRAINIAN S.S.R.	1984	244	117	361	19 265	30 628	49 893

ASIA:
Philippines:
E--> Data for copies refer only to first editions.
FR-> Les données pour les exemplaires se réfèrent seulement aux premières éditions.
ESP> Los datos para los ejemplares se refieren solamente a las primeras ediciones.

OCEANIA:
Australia:
E--> Provisional data.
FR-> Les données sont provisoires.
ESP> Los datos son provisionales.

7.14 Translations by country of publication and by UDC classes

Traductions classées par pays de publication et d'après les groupes de sujets de la CDU

Traducciones clasificadas según el país de publicación y según los grupos de materias de la CDU

PHILOLOGY IS INCLUDED WITH LITERATURE.

NUMBER OF COUNTRIES AND TERRITORIES PRESENTED IN THIS TABLE : 69

LA PHILOLOGIE EST COMPRISE DANS LA LITTERATURE.

NOMBRE DE PAYS ET DE TERRITOIRES PRESENTES DANS CE TABLEAU: 69

LA FILOLOGIA QUEDA COMPRENDIDA EN LA LITERATURA.

NUMERO DE PAISES Y DE TERRITORIOS PRESENTADOS EN ESTE CUADRO: 69

COUNTRY / PAYS / PAIS	YEAR / ANNEE / AÑO	TOTAL / TOTAL / TOTAL	GENERALITIES / GENERALITES / GENERALIDADES	PHILOSOPHY / PHILOSOPHIE / FILOSOFIA	RELIGION / RELIGION / RELIGION	SOCIAL SCIENCES / SCIENCES SOCIALES / CIENCIAS SOCIALES	PURE SCIENCES / SCIENCES PURES / CIENCIAS PURAS	APPLIED SCIENCES / SCIENCES APPL. / CIENCIAS APLICADAS	ARTS / BEAUX-ARTS / ARTES PLASTICAS	LITERATURE / LITTERATURE / LITERATURA	GEOGR./HISTORY / GEOGR./HISTOIRE / GEOGR./HISTORIA
		(1)	(2)	(3)	(4)	(5)	(6)	(7)	(8)	(9)	(10)
WORLD TOTAL	1979	54 413	366	2 697	3 151	7 088	3 412	5 185	3 179	24 874	4 461
	1980	53 167	374	2 805	3 116	6 071	3 257	4 965	2 973	25 529	4 077
	1981	43 841	330	2 372	2 425	5 126	2 725	4 167	2 519	20 777	3 400
ALBANIA	1979	116	2	–	–	63	–	–	7	36	8
	1980	173	2	–	–	102	4	–	6	53	6
	1981	125	1	–	–	91	–	–	2	29	2
ALGERIA	1979	–	–	–	–	–	–	–	–	–	–
	1980	–	–	–	–	–	–	–	–	–	–
	1981	13	–	1	–	3	3	1	1	3	1
ANGOLA	1979	11	–	–	–	–	–	–	–	11	–
	1980	–	–	–	–	–	–	–	–	–	–
	1981	–	–	–	–	–	–	–	–	–	–
ARGENTINA	1979	335	–	123	32	38	4	40	16	78	4
	1980	248	–	70	19	22	1	29	3	101	3
	1981	318	–	90	54	8	–	14	2	146	4
AUSTRALIA	1979	208	–	2	47	25	10	6	8	72	38
	1980	113	–	–	14	5	2	9	3	59	21
	1981	39	–	–	–	–	1	3	–	22	13
AUSTRIA	1979	289	–	11	8	9	17	16	14	179	35
	1980	327	–	7	18	11	21	20	14	197	39
	1981	390	–	16	30	17	36	36	26	198	31
BANGLADESH	1979	–	–	–	–	–	–	–	–	–	–
	1980	–	–	–	–	–	–	–	–	–	–
	1981	27	1	4	–	4	2	–	–	16	–
BELGIUM	1979	1 294	5	42	38	61	88	206	71	704	79
	1980	1 149	1	52	87	34	54	135	76	651	59
	1981	1 071	2	45	38	38	46	133	79	619	71
BRAZIL	1979	1 094	7	169	95	181	43	128	19	365	87
	1980	716	7	89	60	98	36	113	16	253	44
	1981	844	11	93	65	103	40	96	17	379	40
BULGARIA	1979	725	9	15	–	128	22	84	36	369	62
	1980	656	6	20	3	96	30	86	19	330	66
	1981	737	4	11	3	86	52	90	19	384	88
BURMA	1979	47	2	2	7	1	–	–	1	30	4
	1980	–	–	–	–	–	–	–	–	–	–
	1981	–	–	–	–	–	–	–	–	–	–
CANADA	1979	409	4	36	24	77	24	81	31	74	58
	1980	360	6	33	32	56	24	71	16	79	43
	1981	364	7	45	31	38	21	86	21	72	43
COLOMBIA	1979	91	–	3	4	15	7	7	–	48	7
	1980	48	1	7	1	14	5	4	–	14	2
	1981	60	1	9	–	6	3	5	1	30	5
CYPRUS	1979	–	–	–	–	–	–	–	–	–	–
	1980	22	1	9	–	4	–	2	–	2	4
	1981	3	–	2	–	–	–	–	–	1	–

7.14 Translations by country and by UDC classes
Traductions classées par pays et d'après la CDU
Traducciones clasificadas según el país y por materias (CDU)

COUNTRY / PAYS / PAIS	YEAR / ANNEE / AÑO	TOTAL / TOTAL / TOTAL	GENERALITIES / GENERALITES / GENERALIDADES	PHILOSOPHY / PHILOSOPHIE / FILOSOFIA	RELIGION / RELIGION / RELIGION	SOCIAL SCIENCES / SCIENCES SOCIALES / CIENCIAS SOCIALES	PURE SCIENCES / SCIENCES PURES / CIENCIAS PURAS	APPLIED SCIENCES / SCIENCES APPL. / CIENCIAS APLICADAS	ARTS / BEAUX-ARTS / ARTES PLASTICAS	LITERATURE / LITTERATURE / LITERATURA	GEOGR./HISTORY / GEOGR./HISTOIRE / GEOGR./HISTORIA
		(1)	(2)	(3)	(4)	(5)	(6)	(7)	(8)	(9)	(10)
CZECHOSLOVAKIA	1979	1 855	35	47	9	309	114	172	60	1 049	60
	1980	1 190	8	40	6	138	90	125	52	689	42
	1981	729	16	46	2	138	47	62	32	367	19
DENMARK	1979	2 015	5	47	82	116	81	128	75	1 349	132
	1980	1 913	7	53	91	86	64	155	56	1 312	89
	1981	1 120	4	32	64	71	21	91	38	728	71
DOMINICAN REPUBLIC	1979	–	–	–	–	–	–	–	–	–	–
	1980	1	–	–	–	–	–	–	–	–	1
	1981	–	–	–	–	–	–	–	–	–	–
EGYPT	1979	133	–	12	29	23	9	3	4	42	11
	1980	123	1	11	18	17	12	8	3	46	7
	1981	142	3	14	20	25	12	12	4	43	9
ETHIOPIA	1979	–	–	–	–	–	–	–	–	–	–
	1980	–	–	–	–	–	–	–	–	–	–
	1981	13	–	–	–	10	–	–	–	–	3
FINLAND	1979	1 027	6	41	81	60	57	62	31	643	46
	1980	1 476	19	78	172	84	25	132	36	842	88
	1981	1 454	8	58	145	119	35	126	73	817	73
FRANCE	1979	1 448	14	93	59	95	75	62	81	766	203
	1980	5 691	28	267	305	233	244	351	316	3 373	574
	1981	2 794	13	129	117	132	106	137	171	1 702	287
GERMAN DEMOCRATIC REPUBLIC	1979	834	1	20	22	63	49	55	39	537	48
	1980	929	5	25	23	71	48	34	43	621	59
	1981	707	4	12	27	50	31	30	38	470	45
GERMANY, FEDERAL REPUBLIC OF	1979	7 726	22	405	561	441	295	593	711	3 956	742
	1980	6 752	9	371	559	440	229	595	468	3 567	514
	1981	4 904	14	340	372	187	195	473	460	2 309	554
GREECE	1979	358	–	41	10	64	6	11	14	191	21
	1980	–	–	–	–	–	–	–	–	–	–
	1981	482	4	17	5	51	9	15	12	341	28
GUYANA	1979	–	–	–	–	–	–	–	–	–	–
	1980	–	–	–	–	–	–	–	–	–	–
	1981	3	–	–	2	–	–	–	–	1	–
HOLY SEE	1979	39	–	–	39	–	–	–	–	–	–
	1980	–	–	–	–	–	–	–	–	–	–
	1981	–	–	–	–	–	–	–	–	–	–
HUNGARY	1979	1 623	37	25	16	257	136	239	169	625	119
	1980	1 121	22	28	11	199	82	151	99	447	82
	1981	419	10	4	8	66	45	59	89	113	25
ICELAND	1979	–	–	–	–	–	–	–	–	–	–
	1980	435	2	7	19	18	3	15	20	323	28
	1981	–	–	–	–	–	–	–	–	–	–
INDIA	1979	843	4	46	167	92	21	21	18	366	108
	1980	685	–	51	113	53	18	31	13	310	96
	1981	577	2	37	141	30	14	13	3	272	65
INDONESIA	1979	591	4	40	65	51	49	62	8	285	27
	1980	372	6	47	18	56	18	84	11	113	19
	1981	–	–	–	–	–	–	–	–	–	–
IRAN, ISLAMIC REPUBLIC OF	1979	–	–	–	–	–	–	–	–	–	–
	1980	7	3	–	2	1	–	–	1	–	–
	1981	–	–	–	–	–	–	–	–	–	–
ISRAEL	1979	445	5	21	32	55	20	6	12	227	67
	1980	330	–	10	27	42	10	9	18	157	57
	1981	387	5	15	32	39	7	16	13	179	81
ITALY	1979	2 291	22	226	174	287	106	219	147	867	243
	1980	2 055	22	195	204	283	92	197	129	729	204
	1981	1 871	21	162	139	233	82	177	123	770	164
JAPAN	1979	2 184	4	151	53	364	216	278	156	807	155
	1980	1 968	15	152	54	357	247	253	117	659	114
	1981	2 754	37	161	54	427	248	423	186	1 014	204
JORDAN	1979	12	–	–	–	3	4	1	–	3	1
	1980	10	1	–	–	2	2	4	–	1	–
	1981	–	–	–	–	–	–	–	–	–	–

COUNTRY / PAYS / PAIS	YEAR / ANNEE / AÑO	TOTAL / TOTAL / TOTAL	GENERALITIES / GENERALITES / GENERALIDADES	PHILOSOPHY / PHILOSOPHIE / FILOSOFIA	RELIGION / RELIGION / RELIGION	SOCIAL SCIENCES / SCIENCES SOCIALES / CIENCIAS SOCIALES	PURE SCIENCES / SCIENCES PURES / CIENCIAS PURAS	APPLIED SCIENCES / SCIENCES APPL. / CIENCIAS APLICADAS	ARTS / BEAUX-ARTS / ARTES PLASTICAS	LITERATURE / LITTERATURE / LITERATURA	GEOGR./HISTORY / GEOGR./HISTOIRE / GEOGR./HISTORIA
		(1)	(2)	(3)	(4)	(5)	(6)	(7)	(8)	(9)	(10)
KOREA, REPUBLIC OF	1979	389	2	37	98	65	7	9	26	113	32
	1980	363	–	38	110	63	8	12	34	76	22
	1981	181	4	20	31	49	13	22	17	14	11
KUWAIT	1979	19	–	1	–	–	–	–	–	18	–
	1980	2	–	1	–	1	–	–	–	–	–
	1981	–	–	–	–	–	–	–	–	–	–
LEBANON	1979	7	–	–	–	7	–	–	–	–	–
	1980	10	–	–	2	4	–	–	–	3	1
	1981	–	–	–	–	–	–	–	–	–	–
LUXEMBOURG	1979	–	–	–	–	–	–	–	–	–	–
	1980	–	–	–	–	–	–	–	–	–	–
	1981	2	–	–	–	–	–	–	1	1	–
MALAWI	1979	3	–	–	3	–	–	–	–	–	–
	1980	–	–	–	–	–	–	–	–	–	–
	1981	–	–	–	–	–	–	–	–	–	–
MALAYSIA	1979	–	–	–	–	–	–	–	–	–	–
	1980	331	2	1	11	37	86	11	–	155	28
	1981	78	–	1	1	6	7	–	1	59	3
MALTA	1979	–	–	–	–	–	–	–	–	–	–
	1980	3	–	–	1	–	–	–	–	2	–
	1981	4	–	–	1	–	–	–	–	3	–
MAURITIUS	1979	–	–	–	–	–	–	–	–	–	–
	1980	–	–	–	–	–	–	–	–	–	–
	1981	5	–	1	2	2	–	–	–	–	–
MEXICO	1979	269	1	34	–	39	37	103	–	42	13
	1980	2	–	–	–	1	–	1	–	–	–
	1981	–	–	–	–	–	–	–	–	–	–
NETHERLANDS	1979	1 846	22	72	105	142	79	264	108	872	182
	1980	3	–	–	–	–	–	–	–	3	–
	1981	–	–	–	–	–	–	–	–	–	–
NEW ZEALAND	1979	21	–	–	–	5	–	–	2	4	10
	1980	1	–	–	–	–	1	–	–	–	–
	1981	1	–	–	–	1	–	–	–	–	–
NIGERIA	1979	–	–	–	–	–	–	–	–	–	–
	1980	9	–	–	9	–	–	–	–	–	–
	1981	10	–	–	3	1	4	–	–	2	–
NORWAY	1979	1 108	4	19	73	45	41	78	47	727	74
	1980	1 176	4	18	67	52	32	56	49	839	59
	1981	983	6	16	41	42	21	58	42	722	35
PAKISTAN	1979	83	–	4	29	17	1	–	–	16	16
	1980	79	1	4	42	7	1	4	–	12	8
	1981	–	–	–	–	–	–	–	–	–	–
PANAMA	1979	–	–	–	–	–	–	–	–	–	–
	1980	9	–	–	1	–	1	–	–	1	6
	1981	–	–	–	–	–	–	–	–	–	–
PERU	1979	25	–	–	1	7	–	6	1	7	3
	1980	19	–	1	2	3	1	1	1	7	3
	1981	16	–	1	–	5	–	2	–	6	2
POLAND	1979	931	9	27	55	102	69	106	62	402	99
	1980	883	24	38	37	115	70	99	59	383	58
	1981	591	22	29	58	97	43	67	33	211	31
PORTUGAL	1979	–	–	–	–	–	–	–	–	–	–
	1980	939	20	127	33	188	22	118	38	354	39
	1981	449	2	44	18	57	13	45	24	220	26
ROMANIA	1979	617	5	18	6	154	27	42	54	256	55
	1980	609	3	13	8	140	38	34	49	265	59
	1981	604	6	15	4	108	67	39	61	273	31
SAUDI ARABIA	1979	2	2	–	–	–	–	–	–	–	–
	1980	–	–	–	–	–	–	–	–	–	–
	1981	–	–	–	–	–	–	–	–	–	–
SINGAPORE	1979	12	–	–	2	2	1	1	–	2	4
	1980	70	–	–	2	16	4	4	1	40	3
	1981	72	1	–	10	6	–	5	3	40	7
SPAIN	1979	5 883	60	441	475	683	314	916	371	2 255	368
	1980	5 366	70	426	388	482	321	826	402	2 130	321
	1981	6 361	81	408	445	387	254	894	391	3 180	321

7.14 Translations by country and by UDC classes
Traductions classées par pays et d'après la CDU
Traducciones clasificadas según el país y por materias (CDU)

COUNTRY	YEAR	TOTAL	GENER-ALITIES	PHILO-SOPHY	RELIGION	SOCIAL SCIENCES	PURE SCIENCES	APPLIED SCIENCES	ARTS	LITERA-TURE	GEOGR./ HISTORY
PAYS	ANNEE	TOTAL	GENERA-LITES	PHILO-SOPHIE	RELIGION	SCIENCES SOCIALES	SCIENCES PURES	SCIENCES APPL.	BEAUX-ARTS	LITTERA-TURE	GEOGR./ HISTOIRE
PAIS	AÑO	TOTAL	GENERA-LIDADES	FILO-SOFIA	RELIGION	CIENCIAS SOCIALES	CIENCIAS PURAS	CIENCIAS APLICADAS	ARTES PLASTICAS	LITERA-TURA	GEOGR./ HISTORIA
		(1)	(2)	(3)	(4)	(5)	(6)	(7)	(8)	(9)	(10)
SRI LANKA	1979	30	–	–	4	11	2	1	1	9	2
	1980	–	–	–	–	–	–	–	–	–	–
	1981	17	–	1	–	1	–	2	–	11	2
SWEDEN	1979	1 555	6	28	24	96	59	112	56	1 105	69
	1980	2 189	14	44	53	91	45	156	82	1 611	93
	1981	840	4	21	22	28	28	40	36	617	44
SWITZERLAND	1979	1 031	7	54	91	72	67	90	84	458	108
	1980	811	4	62	100	50	34	83	70	296	112
	1981	897	3	73	84	72	35	100	58	377	95
SYRIAN ARAB REPUBLIC	1979	51	–	1	–	9	1	3	2	32	3
	1980	44	–	2	–	16	–	1	2	22	1
	1981	55	1	2	–	13	5	5	1	25	3
THAILAND	1979	64	–	–	1	6	–	2	1	49	5
	1980	95	–	2	3	14	–	1	–	62	13
	1981	33	–	1	–	4	2	2	–	24	–
TUNISIA	1979	10	–	2	–	3	–	–	–	1	4
	1980	7	–	–	1	1	–	–	–	4	1
	1981	15	–	–	–	1	–	1	2	9	2
TURKEY	1979	694	3	22	28	172	9	39	12	371	38
	1980	–	–	–	–	–	–	–	–	–	–
	1981	–	–	–	–	–	–	–	–	–	–
U.S.S.R.	1979	7 235	26	127	30	1 873	958	566	223	2 810	622
	1980	7 200	28	228	31	1 655	977	633	290	2 718	640
	1981	7 171	10	211	20	1 806	973	533	146	2 896	576
UNITED KINGDOM	1979	1 278	6	59	136	148	138	97	139	429	126
	1980	1 348	10	51	118	168	135	114	138	495	119
	1981	1 035	4	58	109	115	91	91	137	320	110
UNITED STATES	1979	1 894	11	80	296	234	120	153	203	592	205
	1980	1 390	5	81	183	150	94	125	160	432	160
	1981	1 086	2	57	185	141	75	116	93	311	106
URUGUAY	1979	13	–	–	–	3	–	1	1	8	–
	1980	11	1	–	–	–	–	–	–	10	–
	1981	7	–	1	1	1	–	–	2	1	1
YUGOSLAVIA	1979	1 300	14	53	40	315	29	116	58	617	58
	1980	1 328	16	46	58	295	26	73	63	681	70
	1981	981	16	69	41	211	38	47	61	430	68

7.15 Translations by original language and by UDC classes

Traductions classées d'après la langue originale et les groupes de sujets de la CDU

Traducciones clasificadas según la lengua original y los grupos de materias de la CDU

LANGUAGES ARE ARRANGED IN DECREASING ORDER OF NUMBER OF TRANSLATIONS IN 1981.

LES LANGUES SONT CLASSEES DANS UN ORDRE CORRESPONDANT AU NOMBRE DECROISSANT DES TRADUCTIONS EN 1981.

LOS IDIOMAS QUEDAN CLASIFICADOS POR ORDEN DECRECIENTE DEL NUMERO DE TRADUCCIONES EN 1981.

LANGUAGE / LANGUE / IDIOMA	YEAR / ANNEE / AÑO	TOTAL / TOTAL / TOTAL	GENERALITIES / GENERALITES / GENERALIDADES	PHILOSOPHY / PHILOSOPHIE / FILOSOFIA	RELIGION / RELIGION / RELIGION	SOCIAL SCIENCES / SCIENCES SOCIALES / CIENCIAS SOCIALES	PURE SCIENCES / SCIENCES PURES / CIENCIAS PURAS	APPLIED SCIENCES / SCIENCES APPL. / CIENCIAS APLICADAS	ARTS / BEAUX-ARTS / ARTES PLASTICAS	LITERATURE / LITTERATURE / LITERATURA	GEOGR./HISTORY / GEOGR./HISTOIRE / GEOGR./HISTORIA
		(1)	(2)	(3)	(4)	(5)	(6)	(7)	(8)	(9)	(10)
TOTAL	1979	54 412	366	2 697	3 151	7 088	3 412	5 185	3 179	24 874	4 460
TOTAL	1980	53 167	374	2 805	3 116	6 071	3 257	4 965	2 973	25 529	4 077
TOTAL	1981	43 841	330	2 372	2 425	5 126	2 725	4 167	2 519	20 777	3 400
ENGLISH	1979	21 518	128	1 289	972	1 752	1 359	2 379	917	11 163	1 559
ANGLAIS	1980	22 416	135	1 253	1 047	1 536	1 357	2 272	969	12 450	1 397
INGLES	1981	18 445	157	1 097	700	1 219	1 107	2 059	913	10 015	1 178
RUSSIAN	1979	6 834	42	188	46	2 053	951	501	283	2 070	700
RUSSE	1980	6 450	37	263	53	1 758	922	512	336	1 867	702
RUSO	1981	5 919	22	226	27	1 884	927	407	191	1 646	589
FRENCH	1979	6 371	33	431	422	688	215	498	470	2 992	622
FRANCAIS	1980	5 972	48	430	395	642	206	514	423	2 758	556
FRANCES	1981	4 977	27	373	319	480	139	459	395	2 322	463
GERMAN	1979	5 230	37	415	399	676	259	751	489	1 721	483
ALLEMAND	1980	4 823	50	417	347	521	243	723	419	1 680	423
ALEMAN	1981	3 964	37	345	317	395	184	533	340	1 438	375
ITALIAN	1979	1 570	19	36	131	154	105	159	349	497	120
ITALIEN	1980	1 477	15	48	124	135	84	130	246	561	134
ITALIANO	1981	1 327	28	44	133	87	54	128	220	538	95
SWEDISH	1979	1 229	4	20	31	79	61	113	59	805	57
SUEDOIS	1980	1 225	3	24	52	66	56	127	47	792	58
SUECO	1981	813	2	16	25	51	22	99	51	510	37
SPANISH	1979	809	2	14	61	88	19	38	50	462	75
ESPAGNOL	1980	851	14	22	72	87	19	39	51	468	79
ESPAÑOL	1981	619	1	26	49	68	15	21	25	364	50
POLISH‡	1979	618	6	15	28	72	18	55	54	294	76
POLONAIS‡	1980	608	19	21	17	91	22	47	45	296	50
POLACO‡	1981	481	18	14	31	63	16	53	29	209	48
DANISH	1979	493	–	24	9	34	35	49	28	289	25
DANOIS	1980	649	1	23	6	30	32	55	35	438	29
DANES	1981	439	–	13	7	18	15	39	19	306	22
LATIN	1979	535	3	41	197	18	13	19	12	157	75
LATIN	1980	537	2	59	217	32	11	11	14	130	61
LATIN	1981	383	–	41	152	13	10	13	7	88	59
HUNGARIAN	1979	868	22	6	13	137	88	139	115	265	83
HONGROIS	1980	633	12	11	3	124	55	89	78	201	60
HUNGARO	1981	379	9	10	–	53	31	43	73	138	22
CZECH‡	1979	833	15	7	2	177	112	157	51	264	48
TCHEQUE‡	1980	667	7	8	5	111	99	132	52	223	30
CHECO‡	1981	376	3	6	7	53	38	58	30	150	31
ROMANIAN‡	1979	397	3	3	4	144	32	23	23	124	41
ROUMAIN‡	1980	392	1	2	2	130	31	31	24	126	45
RUMANO‡	1981	365	3	1	3	96	53	35	33	120	21
CLASSICAL GREEK	1979	478	–	71	152	9	8	1	2	204	31
GREC CLASSIQUE	1980	458	–	69	152	10	5	2	4	189	27
GRIEGO CLASICO	1981	349	–	57	120	10	2	–	1	137	22

7.15 Translations by original language and by UDC classes
Traductions classées d'après la langue originale et la CDU
Traducciones clasificadas según la lengua original y por materias (CDU)

LANGUAGE / LANGUE / IDIOMA	YEAR / ANNEE / AÑO	TOTAL / TOTAL / TOTAL	GENERALITIES / GENERALITES / GENERALIDADES	PHILOSOPHY / PHILOSOPHIE / FILOSOFIA	RELIGION / RELIGION / RELIGION	SOCIAL SCIENCES / SCIENCES SOCIALES / CIENCIAS SOCIALES	PURE SCIENCES / SCIENCES PURES / CIENCIAS PURAS	APPLIED SCIENCES / SCIENCES APPL. / CIENCIAS APLICADAS	ARTS / BEAUX-ARTS / ARTES PLASTICAS	LITERATURE / LITTERATURE / LITERATURA	GEOGR./HISTORY / GEOGR./HISTOIRE / GEOGR./HISTORIA
		(1)	(2)	(3)	(4)	(5)	(6)	(7)	(8)	(9)	(10)
SERBO-CROATIAN‡	1979	430	6	2	1	233	7	25	12	107	37
SERBO-CROATE‡	1980	382	4	2	5	211	1	9	11	104	35
SERVIOCROATA‡	1981	316	3	2	4	177	3	2	14	75	36
DUTCH	1979	439	2	13	70	38	28	62	58	130	38
NEERLANDAIS	1980	409	3	20	49	39	32	65	41	137	23
NEERLANDES	1981	304	4	8	52	8	15	51	49	94	23
BULGARIAN‡	1979	299	4	2	1	88	8	15	13	151	17
BULGARE‡	1980	239	–	5	1	59	11	14	9	118	22
BULGARO‡	1981	214	1	3	1	37	21	17	4	100	30
HEBREW‡	1979	218	5	–	83	28	–	–	7	65	30
HEBREU‡	1980	181	–	1	76	22	–	1	7	49	25
HEBREO‡	1981	207	2	1	89	20	1	3	10	43	38
UKRAINIAN	1979	220	–	1	–	41	4	1	12	141	20
UKRAINIEN	1980	158	–	–	1	17	5	3	2	117	13
UCRANIANO	1981	193	1	–	2	34	7	4	1	120	24
NORWEGIAN	1979	294	1	5	17	27	2	9	8	197	28
NORWEGIEN	1980	358	–	4	27	24	1	21	9	244	28
NORUEGO	1981	193	1	4	17	12	1	16	3	122	17
ARABIC	1979	253	2	8	93	37	1	8	1	86	17
ARABE	1980	230	–	4	79	15	1	9	–	107	15
ARABE	1981	169	–	6	39	9	–	8	2	89	16
PORTUGUESE	1979	189	–	6	27	20	–	4	3	119	10
PORTUGAIS	1980	198	–	3	24	24	4	3	5	120	15
PORTUGUES	1981	154	–	8	46	13	2	2	2	75	6
SANSKRIT‡	1979	163	–	20	83	2	1	–	2	54	1
SANSCRIT‡	1980	204	–	38	93	3	2	8	4	53	3
SANSCRITO‡	1981	154	–	17	77	2	3	4	–	51	–
FINNISH‡	1979	109	1	1	6	25	2	5	2	65	2
FINNOIS‡	1980	165	6	1	5	25	4	14	4	80	26
FINLANDES‡	1981	149	–	–	15	34	–	13	13	67	7
JAPANESE	1979	206	–	3	7	12	15	12	25	120	12
JAPONAIS	1980	199	1	7	15	12	11	21	23	97	12
JAPONES	1981	141	1	3	7	9	8	9	18	75	11
ESTONIAN	1979	130	–	–	–	22	1	4	11	74	18
ESTONIEN	1980	124	2	–	–	18	1	9	12	66	16
ESTONIO	1981	121	–	–	–	23	3	5	5	64	21
SLOVAK‡	1979	211	7	2	1	40	16	26	9	96	14
SLOVAQUE‡	1980	148	–	1	2	19	7	21	8	78	12
ESLOVACO‡	1981	109	1	4	–	20	5	14	7	56	2
CHINESE	1979	204	–	14	14	35	1	14	5	105	16
CHINOIS	1980	187	2	27	7	14	3	14	4	101	15
CHINO	1981	103	1	13	8	9	–	9	4	48	11
BIELORUSSIAN	1979	86	–	–	–	4	–	1	–	78	3
BIELORUSSE	1980	99	–	–	–	18	–	–	–	78	3
BIELORRUSO	1981	97	–	–	–	2	1	–	2	87	5
LATVIAN	1979	102	1	1	–	12	–	3	6	62	17
LETTON	1980	77	1	–	–	14	–	1	8	45	8
LETON	1981	88	1	–	–	11	1	4	2	57	12
GEORGIAN	1979	88	–	–	–	6	–	1	5	62	14
GEORGIEN	1980	71	–	–	–	8	–	3	5	50	5
GEORGIANO	1981	84	–	–	–	4	1	1	1	72	5
LITHUANIAN	1979	121	–	–	1	12	2	4	1	78	23
LITUANIEN	1980	99	1	–	–	12	2	9	5	61	9
LITUANO	1981	81	–	–	2	8	4	3	2	57	5
KAZAKH	1979	70	–	–	–	5	–	–	–	65	–
KAZAKH	1980	66	–	–	–	5	1	1	–	55	4
KAZAK	1981	80	–	–	–	9	–	–	1	69	1
ALBANIAN	1979	115	2	1	–	75	–	2	7	22	6
ALBANAIS	1980	118	2	–	–	75	–	–	6	30	5
ALBANES	1981	78	1	–	–	55	–	–	2	17	3
BENGALI‡	1979	101	–	2	5	2	–	1	–	83	8
BENGALI‡	1980	77	–	4	3	–	–	–	2	62	6
BENGALI‡	1981	76	–	1	8	3	–	–	–	57	7
ARMENIAN	1979	71	–	1	–	4	1	–	–	61	4
ARMENIEN	1980	54	–	–	–	–	–	–	5	47	2
ARMENIO	1981	68	–	–	–	4	–	–	3	52	9

LANGUAGE LANGUE IDIOMA	YEAR ANNEE AÑO	TOTAL TOTAL TOTAL	GENER-ALITIES GENERA-LITES GENERA-LIDADES	PHILO-SOPHY PHILO-SOPHIE FILO-SOFIA	RELIGION RELIGION RELIGION	SOCIAL SCIENCES SCIENCES SOCIALES CIENCIAS SOCIALES	PURE SCIENCES SCIENCES PURES CIENCIAS PURAS	APPLIED SCIENCES SCIENCES APPL. CIENCIAS APLICADAS	ARTS BEAUX-ARTS ARTES PLASTICAS	LITERA-TURE LITTERA-TURE LITERA-TURA	GEOGR./HISTORY GEOGR./HISTOIRE GEOGR./HISTORIA
		(1)	(2)	(3)	(4)	(5)	(6)	(7)	(8)	(9)	(10)
YIDDISH‡	1979	106	–	–	4	2	–	–	3	91	6
YIDDISH‡	1980	69	–	–	1	1	–	–	–	57	10
YIDDISH‡	1981	67	–	–	–	1	–	–	1	59	6
MODERN GREEK	1979	98	1	1	2	5	–	1	13	67	8
GREC MODERNE	1980	86	1	–	1	1	–	–	2	73	8
GRIEGO MODERNO	1981	67	1	1	–	2	–	1	1	52	9
USBEK	1979	85	–	–	–	4	–	–	–	81	–
OUSBEK	1980	63	–	1	–	4	–	1	3	50	4
UZBECO	1981	61	–	–	–	8	–	–	–	49	4
HINDUSTANI‡	1979	66	–	11	7	1	2	1	1	33	10
HINDOUSTANI‡	1980	64	–	1	10	3	1	1	–	36	12
HINDUSTANI‡	1981	61	–	2	24	1	1	2	–	26	5
TURKISH	1979	62	–	–	1	1	–	1	4	49	6
TURC	1980	52	–	–	–	3	–	–	–	45	4
TURCO	1981	54	–	–	1	–	–	–	1	45	7
KIRGHIZ	1979	52	–	–	–	3	–	–	1	48	–
KIRGHIZ	1980	67	–	–	–	2	–	–	–	64	1
KIRGUIZ	1981	51	–	–	–	1	–	–	–	50	–
AZERBAIJANI	1979	52	–	–	–	4	–	–	–	48	–
AZERBAIDJANAIS	1980	47	–	1	–	3	–	–	1	39	3
AZERBAIJAN	1981	49	–	–	–	5	–	1	1	41	1
PERSIAN	1979	66	–	1	18	7	–	–	1	37	2
PERSAN	1980	96	–	–	26	7	–	–	–	56	7
PERSA	1981	47	–	1	6	2	–	–	–	36	2
CATALAN	1979	51	1	–	6	4	–	1	5	29	5
CATALAN	1980	27	–	1	5	–	–	4	1	15	1
CATALAN	1981	42	–	1	1	1	–	–	6	31	2
MOLDAVIAN	1979	43		–	–	–	–	1	2	39	1
MOLDAVE	1980	45	–	–	–	3	–	1	2	37	2
MOLDAVO	1981	37	–	–	–	2	–	–	1	33	1
SLOVENE‡	1979	61	2	–	3	10	–	3	–	37	6
SLOVENE‡	1980	41	–	–	–	4	–	2	3	28	4
ESLOVENO‡	1981	34	–	1	–	2	–	2	1	24	4
TATAR	1979	31	–	–	–	–	–	–	–	31	–
TATAR	1980	32	–	–	–	–	–	–	–	32	–
TARTARO	1981	34	–	–	–	1	–	–	–	33	–
TURKOMAN	1979	30	–	–	–	–	–	–	–	29	1
TURKMENE	1980	30	–	–	–	–	–	–	–	30	–
TURCOMANO	1981	32	–	–	–	2	–	–	–	29	1
MACEDONIAN	1979	49	–	–	–	27	–	–	–	21	1
MACEDONIEN	1980	36	–	–	–	18	–	–	–	16	2
MACEDONIO	1981	31	–	–	–	10	–	–	–	13	8
BASKIR	1979	27	–	–	–	–	–	–	–	27	–
BASKIR	1980	18	–	–	–	–	–	–	–	18	–
BASKIR	1981	29	–	–	–	–	–	–	–	28	1
ICELANDIC	1979	35	–	–	1	–	–	1	–	30	3
ISLANDAIS	1980	39	–	–	–	1	–	–	2	36	–
ISLANDES	1981	27	–	–	–	–	–	1	–	25	1
TADZHIK	1979	26	–	–	–	–	–	1	–	25	–
TADJIK	1980	22	–	–	–	1	–	–	–	21	–
TADZIK	1981	27	–	1	–	3	–	–	–	23	–
PUNJABI	1979	26	–	–	11	1	–	–	–	14	–
PENDJABI	1980	11	–	–	3	1	–	–	–	7	–
PANJABI	1981	24	–	–	9	–	–	–	–	15	–
VIETNAMESE	1979	28	–	–	1	5	–	–	–	18	4
VIETNAMIEN	1980	17	–	–	–	4	–	1	–	11	1
VIETNAMITA	1981	21	–	–	–	1	–	2	–	15	3
TIBETAN	1979	16	–	2	10	–	–	1	–	2	1
TIBETAIN	1980	17	–	3	11	–	–	–	–	3	–
TIBETANO	1981	20	–	6	11	–	–	–	–	2	1
MIDDLE HIGH GERMAN	1979	21	–	–	2	–	–	–	–	18	1
MOYEN ALLEMAND	1980	20	–	–	3	–	–	–	–	17	–
ALTO ALEMAN MEDIO	1981	18	–	–	4	–	–	–	–	14	–
MALAYSIAN	1979	2	–	–	–	–	–	–	–	2	–
MALAIS	1980	31	–	1	6	10	–	–	–	12	2
MALAYO	1981	15	–	–	–	–	–	–	–	15	–

LANGUAGE / LANGUE / IDIOMA	YEAR / ANNEE / AÑO	TOTAL / TOTAL / TOTAL	GENERALITIES / GENERALITES / GENERALIDADES	PHILOSOPHY / PHILOSOPHIE / FILOSOFIA	RELIGION / RELIGION / RELIGION	SOCIAL SCIENCES / SCIENCES SOCIALES / CIENCIAS SOCIALES	PURE SCIENCES / SCIENCES PURES / CIENCIAS PURAS	APPLIED SCIENCES / SCIENCES APPL. / CIENCIAS APLICADAS	ARTS / BEAUX-ARTS / ARTES PLASTICAS	LITERATURE / LITTERATURE / LITERATURA	GEOGR./HISTORY / GEOGR./HISTOIRE / GEOGR./HISTORIA
		(1)	(2)	(3)	(4)	(5)	(6)	(7)	(8)	(9)	(10)
URDU	1979	41	–	–	22	3	–	–	–	15	1
OURDOU	1980	37	–	–	23	1	–	–	–	10	3
URDU	1981	12	–	1	5	–	–	–	–	4	2
TAMIL	1979	19	–	1	–	–	–	–	2	16	–
TAMOUL	1980	24	–	1	2	–	–	–	–	20	1
TAMUL	1981	10	–	1	1	1	–	–	–	7	–
KOREAN	1979	16	–	–	1	6	–	1	–	5	3
COREEN	1980	21	–	–	1	12	–	–	–	6	2
COREANO	1981	9	–	–	1	2	–	–	–	4	2
MARATHI	1979	21	–	1	2	3	–	–	1	14	–
MAHRATTE	1980	26	–	–	2	2	–	–	–	20	2
MAHRATTE	1981	7	–	–	–	–	–	–	–	6	1
OLD FRENCH	1979	31	–	1	–	–	–	–	–	24	6
VIEUX FRANCAIS	1980	19	–	1	–	–	–	–	–	15	3
FRANCES ANTIGUO	1981	7	–	–	1	–	–	–	–	5	1
OCCITAN	1979	2	–	–	–	–	–	–	1	1	–
OCCITAN	1980	23	–	–	1	–	–	–	–	22	–
OCCITAN	1981	–	–	–	–	–	–	–	–	–	–
OTHER LANGUAGES	1979	545	3	5	60	27	–	3	3	421	23
AUTRES LANGUES	1980	513	1	10	38	19	2	7	3	410	23
OTROS IDIOMAS	1981	438	–	5	14	24	–	2	3	368	22
TWO OR MORE LANGUAGES	1979	802	14	32	124	126	46	91	53	274	42
DEUX LANGUES OU PLUS	1980	573	6	18	104	64	26	38	43	245	29
DOS IDIOMAS O MAS	1981	495	5	13	90	64	35	44	32	197	15

General note/Note générale/Nota general:

E--> Most of the works originally written in languages spoken in the U.S.S.R. were translated and published in the country itself; the following are the figures for such works: In 1979: 3,997 titles from Russian, 182 from Ukrainian, 116 from Estonian, 101 from Lithuanian, 92 from Latvian, 82 from Uzbek, 78 from Georgian, 69 from Kazakh, 68 from Byelorussian, 60 from Armenian, 48 from Azerbaijani, 44 from Kirghiz, 36 from Moldavian, 30 from Tatar, 30 from Turkoman, 27 from Baskir, 22 from Tadzhik, 13 from Chuvash and 12 from Abhaz. In 1980: 4,039 titles from Russian, 131 from Ukrainian, 107 from Estonian, 92 from Byelorussian, 86 from Lithuanian, 72 from Latvian, 64 from Georgian, 65 from Kazakh, 60 from Uzbek, 43 from Azerbaijani, 56 from Kirghiz, 47 from Armenian, 43 from Moldavian, 43 from Azerbaijani, 32 from Tatar, 30 from Turkoman, 22 from Tadzhik, 18 from Baskir, 15 from Abhaz, and 14 from Chuvash. In 1981: 4,035 titles from Russian, 165 from Ukrainian, 103 from Estonian, 83 from Byelorussian, 79 from Lastvian, 79 from Kazakh, 73 from Georgian, 69 from Lithvanian, 59 from Hzbek, 55 from Armenian, 36 from Azerbaijani, 45 from Kirghiz, 37 from Moldavian, 34 from Tatar, 32 from Turkoman, 29 from Baskir, 27 from Tadzhik, 17 from Chuvash and 7 from Abhaz.

FR-> Les oeuvres rédigées dans les langues parlées en U.R.S.S. ont été, pour la plupart, traduites et publiées dans ce pays; voici le relevé de ces traductions: En 1979: 3 997 titres traduits du russe, 182 de l'ukranien, 116 de l'estonien, 101 du lituanien, 92 du letton, 82 de l'ouzbek, 78 du géorgien, 69 du kazakh, 68 du biélorusse, 60 de l'arménien, 48 de l'azerbaidjanais, 44 du kirkgiz, 36 du moldave, 30 du tatar, 27 du baskir, 22 du tadjik, 13 de l'abhaz et 12 du tchouvache. En 1980: 4 039 titres traduits du russe, 131 de l'ukrainien, 107 de l'estonien, 92 du biélorusse, 86 du lituanien, 72 du letton, 64 du géorgien, 65 du kazakh, 60 de l'ouzbek, 47 de l'arménien, 56 du kirghiz, 43 du moldave, 43 de l'azerbaidjanais, 32 du tatar, 30 du turkmène, 22 du tadjik, 18 du baskir, 15 de l'abhaz, et 14 du tchouvache. En 1981: 4 035 titres traduits du russe, 165 de l'ukrainien, 103 de l'estonien, 83 du biélorusse, 79 de letton, 79 du kazakh, 73 du géorgien, 69 du lituanien, 59 du l'ouzbek, 55 de l'arménien, 46 de l'azerbaidjanais, 45 du kirghiz, 37 du moldave, 34 du tatar, 32 du turkmène, 29 du baskir, 27 du tadjik, 17 du tchouvache et 7 de l'abhaz.

ESP> La mayoría de las obras escritas originalmente en los idiomas que se hablan en la U.R.S.S. fueron traducidas y publicadas en este país. A continuación se indican las cifras correspondientes a esas traducciones: En 1979: 3 997 títulos traducidos del ruso, 182 del ucraniano, 116 del estonio, 101 del lituano, 92 del leton, 82 del uzbek, 78 del georgiano, 69 del kazak, 68 del bielorruso, 60 del armenio, 48 del azerbaijan, 44 del kirguiz, 36 del moldavo, 30 del tartaro, 27 del baskir, 22 del tadzik, 13 del abhaz y 12 del chuvashe. En 1980: 4 039 títulos traducidos del ruso, 131 del ucraniano, 107 del estonio, 92 del bielorusso, 86 del lituano, 72 del leton, 64 del georgiano, 65 del kazak, 60 del uzbeco, 47 del armenio, 56 del kirguiz, 43 del moldavo, 43 del azerbaijan, 32 del tartaro, 30 del turcomano, 18 del baskir, 22 del tadzik, 15 del abhaz y 14 del chuvashe. En 1981: 4 035 títulos traducidos del ruso, 165 del ucranio, 103 del estonio, 83 del bielorruso, 79 del leton, 79 del kuzak, 73 del georgiano, 69 del lituano, 59 del uzbeco, 55 del moldavo, 34 del t., 32 del turcomano, 29 del baskir, 27 del tadzik, 17 del chuvash y 7 del abhaz.

Polish/Polonais/Polaco:

E--> Including titles published in Poland: 1979, 159; 1980, 160; 1981: 106.

FR-> Y compris les traductions publiées en Pologne: 1979, 159; 1980, 160; 1981: 106.

ESP> Incluídas las traducciones publicadas en Polonia: 1979, 159; 1980, 160; 1981: 106.

Czech/Tchèque/Checo:

E--> Including titles published in Czechoslovakia: 1979, 465; 1980, 321; 1981: 115.

FR-> Y compris les traductions publiées en Tchécoslovaquie: 1979, 465; 1980, 321; 1981: 115.

ESP> Incluídas las traducciones publicadas en Checoslovaquia: 1979, 465; 1980, 321; 1981: 115.

Romanian/Roumain/Rumano:

E--> Including titles published in Romania: 1979, 296; 1980, 303; 1981: 283.

FR-> Y compris les traductions publiées en Roumanie: 1979, 296; 1980, 303; 1981: 283.

ESP> Incluídas las traducciones publicadas en Rumania: 1979, 296; 1980, 303; 1981: 283.

Serbo-Croatian/Serbo-Croate/Serviocroata:

E--> Including titles published in Yugoslavia: 1979, 334; 1980, 280; 1981: 232.

FR-> Y compris les traductions publiées en Yougoslavie: 1979, 334; 1980, 280; 1981: 232.

ESP> Incluídas las traducciones publicadas en Yugoslavia: 1979, 334; 1980, 280; 1981: 232.

Bulgarian/Bulgare/Búlgaro:

E--> Including titles published in Bulgaria: 1979, 120; 1980, 92.; 1981: 107.

FR-> Y compris les traductions publiées en Bulgarie: 1979, 120; 1980, 92; 1981: 107.

ESP> Incluídas las traducciones publicadas en Bulgaria: 1979, 120; 1980, 92; 1981: 107.

Hebrew/Hébreu/Hebreo:

E--> Including titles published in Israel: 1979, 95; 1980, 67; 1981: 93.

FR-> Y compris les traductions publiées en Israel: 1979, 95; 1980, 67; 1981: 93.

ESP> Incluídas las traducciones publicadas en Israel: 1979, 95; 1980, 67; 1981: 93.

Sanskrit/Sanscrit/Sánscrito:
E--> Including titles published in India: 1979, 115; 1980, 129; 1981: 110.
FR-> Y compris les traductions publiées en Inde: 1979, 115; 1980, 129; 1981: 110.
ESP> Incluídas las traducciones publicadas en la India: 1979, 115; 1980, 129; 1981: 110.
Finnish/Finnois/Finlandes:
E--> Including tiles published in Finland: 1979, 27; 1980, 79; 1981: 76.
FR-> Y compris les traductions publiées en Finlande: 1979, 27; 1980, 79; 1981: 76.
ESP> Incluídas las traducciones publicadas en Finlandia: 1979, 27, 1980, 79; 1981: 76.
Slovak/Slovaque/Eslovaco:
E--> Including titles published in Czechoslovakia: 1979, 128; 1980, 75; 1981: 54.
FR-> Y compris les traductions publiées en Tchécoslovaquie: 1979, 128; 1980, 75; 1981: 54.
ESP> Incluídas las traducciones publicadas en Checoslovaquia: 1979, 128; 1980, 75; 1981: 54
Bengali/Bengali/Bengalí:
E--> Including titles published in India: 1979, 71; 1980, 65; 1981: 53.
FR-> Y compris les traductions publiées en Inde: 1979, 71; 1980, 65; 1981: 53.
ESP> Incluídas las traducciones publicadas en la India: 1979, 71; 1980, 65; 1981: 53.
Yiddish/Yiddish/Yiddish:
E--> Including titles published in Israel: 1979, 26; 1980, 15; 1981: 21.
FR-> Y compris les traductions publiées en Israel: 1979, 26; 1980, 15; 1981: 21.
ESP> Incluídas las traducciones publicadas en Israel: 1979, 26; 1980, 15; 1981: 21.
Hindustani/Hindoustani/Hindustani:
E--> Including titles published in India: 1979, 43; 1980, 47; 1981: 51.
FR-> Y compris les traductions publiées en Inde: 1979, 43; 1980, 47; 1981: 51.
ESP> Incluídas las traducciones publicadas en la India: 1979, 43; 1980, 47; 1981: 51.
Slovene/Slovène/Esloveno:
E--> Including titles published in Yugoslavia: 1979, 41; 1980, 34; 1981: 24.
FR-> Y compris les traductions publiées en Yougoslavie: 1979, 41; 1980, 34; 1981: 24.
ESP> Incluídas las traducciones publicadas en Yugoslavia: 1979, 41; 1980, 34; 1981: 24.

7.16 Translations by country of publication and by selected languages from which translated

Traductions classées par pays de publication et d'après les langues sélectionnées à partir desquelles elles sont traduites

Traducciones clasificadas por país de publicación y según las lenguas seleccionadas a partir de las cuales fueron traducidas

SCANDINAVIAN LANGUAGES INCLUDE DANISH, NORWEGIAN AND SWEDISH. CLASSICS INCLUDE CLASSICAL GREEK AND LATIN. VALUES ARE GIVEN SEPARATELY FOR THESE LANGUAGES IN TABLE 7.15.

NUMBER OF COUNTRIES AND TERRITORIES PRESENTED IN THIS TABLE: 69

LES LANGUES SCANDINAVES COMPRENNENT LE DANOIS, LE NORVEGIEN ET LE SUEDOIS. LES LANGUES CLASSIQUES COMPRENNENT LE GREC CLASSIQUE ET LE LATIN. CES LANGUES SONT MONTREES SEPAREMENT DANS LE TABLEAU 7.15.

NOMBRE DE PAYS ET DE TERRITOIRES PRESENTES DANS CE TABLEAU: 69

COUNTRY PAYS PAIS	YEAR ANNEE AÑO	TOTAL TOTAL TOTAL	ENGLISH ANGLAIS INGLES	FRENCH FRANCAIS FRANCES	GERMAN ALLEMAND ALEMAN	RUSSIAN RUSSE RUSO
WORLD TOTAL	1979	54 413	21 519	6 371	5 230	6 834
	1980	53 167	22 416	5 972	4 823	6 450
	1981	43 841	18 445	4 977	3 964	5 919
ALBANIA	1979	116	3	7	8	4
	1980	173	8	12	8	37
	1981	125	5	5	7	32
ALGERIA	1981	13	4	9	–	–
ANGOLA	1979	11	3	7	–	1
ARGENTINA	1979	335	191	66	28	2
	1980	248	169	33	20	1
	1981	318	182	51	28	1
AUSTRALIA	1979	208	93	20	16	4
	1980	113	60	6	4	2
	1981	39	15	1	5	2
AUSTRIA	1979	289	178	40	12	14
	1980	327	159	81	19	7
	1981	390	231	52	12	14
BANGLADESH	1981	27	16	4	–	1
BELGIUM	1979	1 294	763	175	242	7
	1980	1 149	643	122	208	9
	1981	1 071	598	147	203	9
BRAZIL	1979	1 094	717	150	124	–
	1980	716	488	94	54	1
	1981	844	565	106	56	–
BULGARIA	1979	725	76	43	48	284
	1980	656	87	53	52	233
	1981	737	114	38	61	255
BURMA	1979	47	17	–	–	2
CANADA	1979	409	298	49	9	3
	1980	360	269	26	13	3
	1981	364	277	25	7	1
COLOMBIA	1979	91	64	10	3	1
	1980	48	38	3	3	1
	1981	60	37	5	4	–
CYPRUS	1980	22	15	–	1	–
	1981	3	3	–	–	–
CZECHOSLOVAKIA	1979	1 855	201	95	148	442
	1980	1 190	115	63	105	266
	1981	729	82	35	56	220
DENMARK	1979	2 015	995	178	220	20
	1980	1 913	1 007	195	187	18
	1981	1 120	605	69	118	19

LAS LENGUAS ESCANDINAVAS INCLUYEN EL DANES, EL NORUEGO Y EL SUECO. LAS LENGUAS CLASICAS INCLUYEN EL GRIEGO CLASICO Y EL LATIN. LAS LENGUAS SE PRESENTAN SEPARADAMENTE EN EL CUADRO 7.15.

NUMERO DE PAISES Y DE TERRITORIOS PRESENTADOS EN ESTE CUADRO: 69

ITALIAN ITALIEN ITALIANO	SCANDINAVIAN LANGUAGES LANGUES SCANDINAVES LENGUAS ESCANDINAVAS	SPANISH ESPAGNOL ESPAÑOL	CLASSICS LANGUES CLASSIQUES LENGUAS CLASICAS	ARABIC ARABE ARABE	JAPANESE JAPONAIS JAPONES	CHINESE CHINOIS CHINO	OTHER LANGUAGES AUTRES LANGUES OTROS IDIOMAS
1 570	2 020	809	1 013	253	206	204	8 384
1 477	2 236	851	995	23	199	187	7 331
1 327	1 446	619	732	169	141	103	5 999
3	3	–	2	–	–	–	86
1	4	2	3	–	–	–	98
4	–	2	–	–	–	–	70
–	–	–	–	–	–	–	–
–	–	–	–	–	–	–	–
2	1	–	2	–	1	1	41
4	–	–	7	–	–	–	14
13	–	–	3	1	–	1	38
2	1	–	25	1	6	–	40
3	–	–	11	–	–	1	26
1	–	–	–	–	–	–	15
5	19	1	–	1	2	1	16
8	16	2	5	1	2	–	27
19	9	2	12	1	1	–	37
–	–	–	2	1	–	–	3
23	22	9	18	7	1	–	27
29	36	8	32	4	–	1	57
13	36	7	10	1	1	–	46
31	2	52	8	3	–	1	6
29	2	42	2	–	1	–	3
19	2	85	4	–	–	1	6
14	3	29	5	–	1	–	222
10	8	14	8	–	1	–	190
13	6	20	8	–	2	–	220
–	–	–	–	1	1	16	10
7	2	5	4	3	–	6	23
4	4	2	13	2	–	–	24
10	1	13	11	1	–	–	18
7	1	–	–	–	–	1	4
2	–	–	–	–	–	–	1
9	2	–	1	1	–	–	1
–	–	–	–	–	–	–	6
–	–	–	–	–	–	–	–
27	31	35	20	1	4	3	848
22	19	26	9	1	2	–	562
18	16	16	8	–	2	–	276
24	437	43	22	2	2	6	66
18	357	22	19	5	9	4	72
9	227	10	18	2	1	3	39

7.16 **Translations from languages most frequently translated**
Traductions à partir des langues les plus traduites
Traducciones a partir de las lenguas más traducidas

COUNTRY / PAYS / PAIS	YEAR / ANNEE / AÑO	TOTAL / TOTAL / TOTAL	ENGLISH / ANGLAIS / INGLES	FRENCH / FRANCAIS / FRANCES	GERMAN / ALLEMAND / ALEMAN	RUSSIAN / RUSSE / RUSO
DOMINICAN REPUBLIC	1980	1	1	–	–	–
EGYPT	1979	133	106	10	7	6
	1980	123	98	11	6	4
	1981	142	116	5	7	7
ETHIOPIA	1981	13	5	–	–	5
FINLAND	1979	1 027	568	59	90	37
	1980	1 476	708	76	120	60
	1981	1 454	686	75	142	48
FRANCE	1979	1 448	855	37	161	50
	1980	5 691	3 491	112	659	162
	1981	2 794	1 834	57	300	80
GERMAN DEMOCRATIC REPUBLIC	1979	834	106	76	–	323
	1980	929	136	88	2	333
	1981	707	103	75	1	266
GERMANY, FEDERAL REPUBLIC OF	1979	7 726	4 460	1 073	459	213
	1980	6 752	4 099	881	325	175
	1981	4 904	3 028	667	209	119
GREECE	1979	358	112	98	37	35
	1981	482	243	125	27	33
GUYANA	1981	3	–	–	–	–
HOLY SEE	1979	39	2	–	–	–
HUNGARY	1979	1 623	181	102	156	227
	1980	1 121	141	70	115	177
	1981	419	44	26	39	50
ICELAND	1980	435	223	60	16	5
INDIA	1979	843	325	20	9	42
	1980	685	215	12	12	25
	1981	577	199	8	8	16
INDONESIA	1979	591	377	31	19	5
	1980	372	297	16	11	1
IRAN, ISLAMIC REPUBLIC OF	1980	7	5	1	–	–
ISRAEL	1979	445	203	24	34	17
	1980	330	141	26	32	10
	1981	387	165	23	25	10
ITALY	1979	2 291	1 065	520	288	74
	1980	2 055	975	506	274	63
	1981	1 871	917	436	241	50
JAPAN	1979	2 184	1 484	242	234	95
	1980	1 968	1 421	213	163	76
	1981	2 754	2 011	241	246	100
JORDAN	1979	12	9	1	–	–
	1980	10	9	–	–	1
KOREA, REPUBLIC OF	1979	389	289	50	37	3
	1980	363	291	36	27	1
	1981	181	154	13	8	1
KUWAIT	1979	19	6	7	1	–
	1980	2	2	–	–	–
LEBANON	1979	7	3	2	–	–
	1980	10	2	4	–	1
LUXEMBOURG	1981	2	–	–	–	–
MALAWI	1979	3	3	–	–	–
MALAYSIA	1980	331	297	1	1	–
	1981	78	62	–	–	–
MALTA	1980	3	2	–	–	–
	1981	4	2	–	–	–
MAURITIUS	1981	5	–	1	–	–
MEXICO	1979	269	243	12	6	–
	1980	2	1	–	1	–
NETHERLANDS	1979	1 846	1 109	133	367	18
	1980	3	1	1	–	–

ITALIAN ITALIEN ITALIANO	SCANDINAVIAN LANGUAGES LANGUES SCANDINAVES LENGUAS ESCANDINAVAS	SPANISH ESPAGNOL ESPAÑOL	CLASSICS LANGUES CLASSIQUES LENGUAS CLASICAS	ARABIC ARABE ARABE	JAPANESE JAPONAIS JAPONES	CHINESE CHINOIS CHINO	OTHER LANGUAGES AUTRES LANGUES OTROS IDIOMAS
–	–	–	–	–	–	–	–
1	–	–	2	–	–	–	1
–	1	–	2	–	–	–	1
1	1	2	–	–	–	1	2
–	–	–	–	–	–	–	3
4	185	7	5	1	3	–	68
18	298	19	11	3	6	1	156
26	294	22	15	1	7	–	138
84	18	47	42	5	10	12	127
280	90	158	168	46	21	48	456
154	33	70	56	16	9	14	171
17	25	21	28	5	1	6	226
20	38	28	39	2	5	1	237
18	23	20	12	1	2	4	182
277	270	95	215	9	20	22	613
187	259	115	187	14	26	34	450
150	144	65	128	10	13	16	355
19	10	7	–	–	1	2	37
11	4	8	1	1	–	–	29
–	–	–	2	–	–	–	1
8	–	–	29	–	–	–	–
44	14	19	10	1	2	1	866
23	14	20	16	–	6	3	536
9	2	3	2	1	1	–	242
–	119	1	3	–	–	2	6
3	2	1	8	6	–	3	424
4	5	2	8	1	–	1	400
1	4	–	5	5	–	–	331
3	3	1	7	60	10	2	73
3	–	–	2	13	–	–	29
–	–	–	–	–	–	–	1
3	4	4	4	5	1	2	144
2	6	4	4	5	1	2	97
7	3	3	2	6	1	1	141
37	24	87	86	4	4	8	94
13	17	50	68	3	4	6	76
14	17	33	71	3	7	5	77
29	26	23	12	3	–	9	27
20	15	12	8	2	–	7	31
28	26	28	10	1	–	15	48
1	–	–	–	–	–	–	1
–	–	–	–	–	–	–	–
1	2	3	–	–	1	–	3
2	2	2	–	–	–	–	2
3	–	–	–	–	–	–	2
–	–	5	–	–	–	–	–
–	–	–	–	–	–	–	–
–	–	–	–	–	–	–	2
–	–	2	–	–	–	–	1
2	–	–	–	–	–	–	–
–	–	–	–	–	–	–	–
–	–	–	–	5	1	–	26
–	–	–	–	1	–	–	15
–	–	1	–	–	–	–	–
–	–	–	1	–	–	–	1
–	–	–	2	1	–	–	1
2	–	3	1	–	–	–	2
–	–	–	–	–	–	–	–
63	60	20	22	5	3	3	43
–	1	–	–	–	–	–	–

7.16 **Translations from languages most frequently translated**
Traductions à partir des langues les plus traduites
Traducciones a partir de las lenguas más traducidas

COUNTRY / PAYS / PAIS	YEAR / ANNEE / AÑO	TOTAL / TOTAL / TOTAL	ENGLISH / ANGLAIS / INGLES	FRENCH / FRANCAIS / FRANCES	GERMAN / ALLEMAND / ALEMAN	RUSSIAN / RUSSE / RUSO
NEW ZEALAND	1979	21	16	1	1	–
	1980	1	–	–	–	1
	1981	1	–	1	–	–
NIGERIA	1980	9	9	–	–	–
	1981	10	10	–	–	–
NORWAY	1979	1 108	592	43	77	13
	1980	1 176	681	54	81	17
	1981	983	627	28	53	11
PAKISTAN	1979	83	30	1	–	–
	1980	79	29	–	1	2
PANAMA	1980	9	7	–	–	–
PERU	1979	25	11	–	–	–
	1980	19	7	1	1	–
	1981	16	8	–	2	–
POLAND	1979	931	184	72	123	176
	1980	883	164	76	113	158
	1981	591	104	50	72	107
PORTUGAL	1980	939	312	412	80	13
	1981	449	196	143	48	3
ROMANIA	1979	617	49	79	30	24
	1980	609	56	75	26	28
	1981	604	54	75	42	26
SAUDI ARABIA	1979	2	2	–	–	–
SINGAPORE	1979	12	9	–	–	–
	1980	70	50	–	1	–
	1981	72	48	2	–	–
SPAIN	1979	5 883	2 702	1 396	656	141
	1980	5 366	2 528	1 258	632	90
	1981	6 361	3 240	1 300	675	101
SRI LANKA	1979	30	12	1	–	12
	1981	17	5	4	1	1
SWEDEN	1979	1 555	1 011	117	95	27
	1980	2 189	1 414	163	170	36
	1981	840	524	74	74	11
SWITZERLAND	1979	1 031	502	189	171	35
	1980	811	377	130	163	20
	1981	897	385	168	166	28
SYRIAN ARAB REPUBLIC	1979	51	24	15	–	3
	1980	44	9	21	1	5
	1981	55	11	27	1	10
THAILAND	1979	64	49	4	–	5
	1980	95	77	4	1	9
	1981	33	31	–	–	1
TUNISIA	1979	10	–	6	1	–
	1980	7	–	6	–	–
	1981	15	–	10	–	–
TURKEY	1979	694	280	98	84	81
U.S.S.R.	1979	7 235	614	176	308	3 997
	1980	7 200	709	177	299	4 039
	1981	7 171	624	171	319	4 035
UNITED KINGDOM	1979	1 278	34	298	321	116
	1980	1 348	45	363	307	126
	1981	1 035	19	276	278	84
UNITED STATES	1979	1 894	20	398	433	184
	1980	1 390	26	296	313	126
	1981	1 086	10	257	287	91
URUGUAY	1979	13	4	6	–	1
	1980	11	1	4	–	1
	1981	7	3	2	–	–
YUGOSLAVIA	1979	1 300	269	134	167	90
	1980	1 328	301	130	196	107
	1981	981	243	90	136	71

ITALIAN ITALIEN ITALIANO	SCANDINAVIAN LANGUAGES LANGUES SCANDINAVES LENGUAS ESCANDINAVAS	SPANISH ESPAGNOL ESPAÑOL	CLASSICS LANGUES CLASSIQUES LENGUAS CLASICAS	ARABIC ARABE ARABE	JAPANESE JAPONAIS JAPONES	CHINESE CHINOIS CHINO	OTHER LANGUAGES AUTRES LANGUES OTROS IDIOMAS
–	–	–	–	–	1	–	2
–	–	–	–	–	–	–	–
–	–	–	–	–	–	–	–
–	–	–	–	–	–	–	–
–	–	–	–	–	–	–	–
26	305	12	2	–	2	3	33
9	280	11	3	3	1	3	33
5	211	8	4	1	–	–	35
1	–	–	–	15	1	–	35
–	–	–	–	27	1	–	19
–	–	–	–	–	–	–	2
–	–	7	–	–	–	–	7
1	–	1	–	–	–	–	8
–	–	2	–	–	–	–	4
16	14	17	22	–	1	–	306
19	21	23	15	–	1	–	293
10	16	14	18	1		–	199
34	10	57	6	1	1	–	13
17	8	24	2	–	–	–	8
10	2	13	9	–	2	1	398
12	1	15	12	1	1	1	381
17	–	13	7	3	1	1	365
–	–	–	–	–	–	–	–
–	–	–	–	2	–	–	1
1	–	–	–	5	–	7	6
–	–	–	–	12	–	7	3
452	75	1	166	26	10	14	244
392	96	–	138	26	10	12	184
457	119	–	177	38	5	6	243
–	–	–	–	–	1	1	3
–	1	–	–	–	–	–	5
27	158	18	8	–	3	3	88
18	271	8	10	1	2	3	93
9	82	13	4	1	1	–	47
51	19	7	14	2	1	–	40
33	18	10	19	1	1	2	37
50	10	6	16	1	1	–	66
1	–	–	–	–	–	–	8
1	1	–	–	–	–	–	6
1	–	1	–	–	–	–	4
–	–	–	–	1	3	–	2
–	–	–	–	–	1	–	3
–	–	–	1	–	–	–	–
–	–	–	–	3	–	–	–
–	–	–	–	1	–	–	–
–	2	–	–	3	–	–	–
3	15	12	6	23	2	7	83
21	55	49	17	21	18	15	1 944
24	46	54	21	27	16	9	1 779
27	37	48	13	21	10	4	1 862
88	104	28	56	12	30	16	175
81	101	40	51	9	24	13	188
61	62	21	34	14	22	7	157
95	86	103	119	21	57	38	340
91	65	68	84	16	52	21	232
57	41	47	55	16	54	16	155
–	–	–	–	–	–	–	2
–	–	–	–	–	–	–	5
1	–	–	–	–	–	–	1
38	22	25	17	4	–	1	533
59	15	32	11	5	3	5	464
63	7	13	17	3		1	337

7.17 Translations by original language and by selected languages into which translated

Traductions classées, pour des langues sélectionnées, d'après la langue originale et la langue dans laquelle elles sont traduites

Traducciones clasificadas, por idiomas seleccionados, según la lengua original y la lengua en que han sido traducidas

ORIGINAL LANGUAGE LANGUE ORIGINALE LENGUA ORIGINAL	YEAR ANNEE AÑO	TRANSLATIONS BY LANGUAGE INTO WHICH TRANSLATED TRADUCTIONS SELON LA LANGUE DANS LAQUELLE ELLES SONT TRADUITES TRADUCCIONES SEGUN LA LENGUA EN QUE HAN SIDO TRADUCIDAS						
		ENGLISH ANGLAIS INGLES	FRENCH FRANCAIS FRANCES	SPANISH ESPAGNOL ESPAÑOL	RUSSIAN RUSSE RUSO	ARABIC ARABE ARABE	GERMAN ALLEMAND ALEMAN	ITALIAN ITALIEN ITALIANO
ALBANIAN	1979	13	17	10	5	–	13	11
ALBANAIS	1980	28	25	12	7	1	16	7
ALBANES	1981	12	17	11	8	1	9	9
ARABIC	1979	39	14	26	8	–	18	4
ARABE	1980	32	49	26	23	–	15	3
ARABE	1981	32	22	40	12	–	13	3
ARMENIAN	1979	8	1	–	41	–	–	–
ARMENIEN	1980	3	1	–	36	–	–	–
ARMENIO	1981	12	–	–	35	1	–	–
AZERBAIJANI	1979	–	–	–	27	–	1	–
AZERBAIDJANAIS	1980	–	–	–	21	2	3	–
AZERBAIJAN	1981	2	–	–	31	1	1	–
BASKIR	1979	–	–	–	23	–	–	–
BASKIR	1980	–	–	–	16	–	–	–
BASKIR	1981	–	–	–	21	–	–	–
BENGALI	1979	10	–	5	–	–	4	3
BENGALI	1980	16	1	–	1	–	1	2
BENGALI	1981	10	1	9	3	–	–	2
BIELORUSSIAN	1979	4	3	1	42	–	2	–
BIELORUSSE	1980	11	4	6	43	–	9	–
BIELORRUSO	1981	6	1	2	46	–	3	–
BULGARIAN	1979	24	13	13	93	2	24	3
BULGARE	1980	16	20	8	84	–	22	4
BULGARO	1981	19	17	9	83	2	25	3
CATALAN	1979	2	–	43	–	–	2	2
CATALAN	1980	4	2	19	–	–	–	–
CATALAN	1981	2	2	33	1	–	1	1
CHINESE	1979	58	12	19	9	–	29	8
CHINOIS	1980	41	46	12	7	–	38	6
CHINO	1981	31	14	7	2	1	20	5
CZECH	1979	84	34	14	53	1	139	6
TCHEQUE	1980	73	47	5	49	3	109	10
CHECO	1981	45	23	10	46	–	81	6
DANISH	1979	58	3	39	18	–	98	6
DANOIS	1980	73	49	50	14	–	89	3
DANES	1981	42	15	90	7	2	54	5
DUTCH	1979	87	33	29	1	1	170	7
NEERLANDAIS	1980	71	65	25	3	–	120	7
NEERLANDES	1981	58	41	33	1	–	109	4
ENGLISH	1979	–	1 338	3 146	527	153	5 120	1 046
ANGLAIS	1980	–	3 785	2 697	609	121	4 686	948
INGLES	1981	–	2 247	3 357	521	136	3 642	892

JAPANESE JAPONAIS JAPONES	DUTCH NEERLANDAIS NEERLANDES	DANISH DANOIS DANES	NORWEGIAN NORVEGIEN NORUEGO	SWEDISH SUEDOIS SUECO	HUNGARIAN HONGROIS HUNGARO	POLISH POLONAIS POLACO	SLOVAK SLOVAQUE ESLOVAKO	TURKISH TURC TURCO	ORIGINAL LANGUAGE / LANGUE ORIGINALE / LENGUA ORIGINAL
TRANSLATIONS BY LANGUAGE INTO WHICH TRANSLATED / TRADUCTIONS SELON LA LANGUE DANS LAQUELLE ELLES SONT TRADUITES / TRADUCCIONES SEGUN LA LENGUA EN QUE HAN SIDO TRADUCIDAS									
— — —	— — —	3 2 3	— — —	1 2 —	1 — —	— — —	— — —	15 1 —	ALBANIAN ALBANAIS ALBANES
3 2 1	8 4 —	2 5 2	— 3 1	— 1 1	1 — 1	1 — 1	— — —	22 1 —	ARABIC ARABE ARABE
— — —	— — —	— — —	— — —	— 1 —	— — —	1 1 2	1 1 —	— — —	ARMENIAN ARMENIEN ARMENIO
— — —	— — —	— — —	— — —	— — —	1 — 1	— 1 1	— — —	1 — 1	AZERBAIJANI AZERBAIDJANAIS AZERBAIJAN
— — —	— — —	— — —	— — —	— — —	— — 1	— — —	— — —	— — —	BASKIR BASKIR BASKIR
— — —	— — —	— — 1	— — —	— — —	— 1 —	— — —	1 — —	— — —	BENGALI BENGALI BENGALI
1 — —	— — —	— — —	— — —	— — —	2 — —	5 3 6	1 1 —	— — —	BIELORUSSIAN BIELORUSSE BIELORRUSO
1 1 —	3 — 1	1 1 —	— — —	— 1 —	14 9 4	9 14 2	9 8 7	24 — —	BULGARIAN BULGARE BULGARO
— — —	— 1 —	— 1 1	— — —	— — —	— — —	— — —	1 — —	— — —	CATALAN CATALAN CATALAN
10 7 15	3 1 —	6 4 3	3 3 —	3 3 —	1 3 —	— — —	1 — —	7 — —	CHINESE CHINOIS CHINO
9 2 4	11 4 3	10 2 1	2 5 3	16 14 6	72 53 17	29 24 22	264 203 59	3 — —	CZECH TCHEQUE CHECO
4 1 11	22 9 9	— — —	76 61 61	89 154 55	5 4 2	4 4 5	2 3 1	6 — —	DANISH DANOIS DANES
1 4 2	— — —	13 22 4	6 5 9	9 18 13	5 3 1	2 9 —	— — —	2 — —	DUTCH NEERLANDAIS NEERLANDES
1 487 1 420 2 008	1 716 585 528	980 1 006 602	588 679 627	1 004 1 400 523	187 155 52	184 165 103	68 33 27	295 1 —	ENGLISH ANGLAIS INGLES

7.17 Translations by original language and by new language
Translations d'après la langue originale et la nouvelle langue
Traducciones según la lengua original y la lengua nueva

ORIGINAL LANGUAGE / LANGUE ORIGINALE / LENGUA ORIGINAL	YEAR / ANNEE / AÑO	TRANSLATIONS BY LANGUAGE INTO WHICH TRANSLATED / TRADUCTIONS SELON LA LANGUE DANS LAQUELLE ELLES SONT TRADUITES / TRADUCCIONES SEGUN LA LENGUA EN QUE HAN SIDO TRADUCIDAS						
		ENGLISH ANGLAIS INGLES	FRENCH FRANCAIS FRANCES	SPANISH ESPAGNOL ESPAÑOL	RUSSIAN RUSSE RUSO	ARABIC ARABE ARABE	GERMAN ALLEMAND ALEMAN	ITALIAN ITALIEN ITALIANO
ESTONIAN	1979	17	2	–	55	–	17	–
ESTONIEN	1980	21	2	–	49	–	12	–
ESTONIO	1981	20	1	1	39	–	20	–
FINNISH	1979	8	1	1	15	1	16	–
FINNOIS	1980	23	7	2	11	–	22	–
FINLANDES	1981	14	5	1	21	–	16	2
FRENCH	1979	800	–	1 420	120	39	1 320	517
FRANCAIS	1980	768	–	1 252	119	44	1 155	493
FRANCES	1981	613	–	1 282	110	54	937	444
OLD FRENCH	1979	9	2	6	–	–	10	1
VIEUX FRANCAIS	1980	1	7	2	1	–	5	–
FRANCES ANTIGUO	1981	1	–	3	–	–	1	–
GEORGIAN	1979	7	4	–	53	–	2	–
GEORGIEN	1980	1	1	–	40	–	4	–
GEORGIANO	1981	2	2	–	51	–	1	–
GERMAN	1979	982	371	703	164	10	–	315
ALLEMAND	1980	870	851	664	169	16	–	293
ALEMAN	1981	763	462	685	180	12	–	262
MIDDLE HIGH GERMAN	1979	3	1	–	–	–	16	–
MOYEN ALLEMAND	1980	2	2	1	–	–	13	–
ALTO ALEMAN MEDIO	1981	1	–	–	–	–	17	–
CLASSICAL GREEK	1979	66	16	76	3	1	103	31
GREC CLASSIQUE	1980	56	69	67	7	2	104	26
GRIEGO CLASICO	1981	38	34	88	3	–	62	28
MODERN GREEK	1979	20	7	4	3	–	16	8
GREC MODERNE	1980	17	8	4	2	–	8	5
GRIEGO MODERNO	1981	12	5	3	2	–	13	5
HEBREW	1979	104	14	38	22	–	65	6
HEBREU	1980	76	37	28	10	7	41	8
HEBREO	1981	94	39	48	10	–	56	1
HINDUSTANI	1979	17	–	–	3	–	7	–
HINDOUSTANI	1980	20	3	–	2	–	7	–
HINDUSTANI	1981	12	1	–	–	–	2	1
HUNGARIAN	1979	273	53	16	103	–	195	8
HONGROIS	1980	190	51	20	76	1	149	9
HUNGARO	1981	74	25	12	54	1	90	5
ICELANDIC	1979	6	2	–	–	–	9	–
ISLANDAIS	1980	9	3	–	1	–	6	1
ISLANDES	1981	2	1	–	–	–	6	–
ITALIAN	1979	209	130	455	12	3	336	–
ITALIEN	1980	189	300	389	17	1	240	–
ITALIANO	1981	133	185	460	13	2	215	–
JAPANESE	1979	92	10	11	12	–	22	5
JAPONAIS	1980	78	22	10	13	–	31	4
JAPONES	1981	76	9	5	9	–	17	7
KAZAKH	1979	–	–	1	50	1	3	–
KAZAKH	1980	1	–	1	47	–	2	–
KAZAK	1981	1	–	–	53	1	3	–
KIRGHIZ	1979	2	1	–	27	–	4	–
KIRGHIZE	1980	3	1	2	29	–	10	–
KIRIGUIZ	1981	–	1	1	30	1	3	–
LATIN	1979	99	36	63	2	1	134	59
LATIN	1980	85	108	70	4	–	142	31
LATIN	1981	56	36	66	2	–	98	42
LATVIAN	1979	12	–	–	53	–	8	–
LETTON	1980	8	1	–	41	–	9	–
LETON	1981	11	1	1	47	–	5	–
LITHUANIAN	1979	18	1	–	49	–	11	–
LITUANIEN	1980	16	7	1	31	–	8	–
LITUANO	1981	9	2	–	36	–	4	–
MACEDONIAN	1979	1	–	–	2	–	–	–
MACEDONIEN	1980	3	3	–	–	–	–	–
MACEDONIO	1981	2	2	1	1	–	1	–
MALAYSIAN	1979	1	–	–	–	–	–	–
MALAIS	1980	16	–	–	–	–	–	–
MALAYO	1981	15	–	–	–	–	–	–

TRANSLATIONS BY LANGUAGE INTO WHICH TRANSLATED / TRADUCTIONS SELON LA LANGUE DANS LAQUELLE ELLES SONT TRADUITES / TRADUCCIONES SEGUN LA LENGUA EN QUE HAN SIDO TRADUCIDAS									ORIGINAL LANGUAGE / LANGUE ORIGINALE / LENGUA ORIGINAL
JAPANESE JAPONAIS JAPONES	DUTCH NEERLANDAIS NEERLANDES	DANISH DANOIS DANES	NORWEGIAN NORVEGIEN NORUEGO	SWEDISH SUEDOIS SUECO	HUNGARIAN HONGROIS HUNGARO	POLISH POLONAIS POLACO	SLOVAK SLOVAQUE ESLOVAKO	TURKISH TURC TURCO	
–	–	–	1	–	1	4	5	–	ESTONIAN
–	–	–	–	3	4	2	1	–	ESTONIEN
–	–	–	1	2	1	4	3	–	ESTONIO
1	–	4	7	30	7	3	2	–	FINNISH
1	1	2	6	72	7	3	2	–	FINNOIS
2	–	4	2	57	3	3	–	–	FINLANDES
240	285	171	43	112	90	69	27	98	FRENCH
213	118	194	54	157	82	77	16	–	FRANCAIS
237	138	69	28	70	28	50	19	–	FRANCES
–	1	–	–	–	–	–	–	1	OLD FRENCH
–	3	–	–	1	–	–	–	–	VIEUX FRANCAIS
–	1	–	–	–	–	–	–	–	FRANCES ANTIGUO
–	–	–	–	–	–	2	–	–	GEORGIAN
–	–	–	–	–	–	–	3	–	GEORGIEN
–	–	–	–	–	–	–	1	–	GEORGIANO
230	596	219	78	95	163	112	57	84	GERMAN
164	189	190	81	177	127	114	32	–	ALLEMAND
235	183	118	51	78	45	74	18	–	ALEMAN
–	–	–	–	–	–	–	–	–	MIDDLE HIGH GERMAN
–	–	–	–	–	–	–	–	–	MOYEN ALLEMAND
–	–	–	–	–	–	–	–	–	ALTO ALEMAN MEDIO
5	19	13	–	2	3	13	2	5	CLASSICAL GREEK
1	13	15	2	10	7	8	2	–	GREC CLASSIQUE
5	1	10	2	3	2	9	4	–	GRIEGO CLASICO
–	1	4	1	2	3	2	1	1	MODERN GREEK
–	1	1	–	5	4	3	–	–	GREC MODERNE
–	2	2	–	–	1	–	–	–	GRIEGO MODERNO
–	4	–	2	–	3	1	1	–	HEBREW
1	1	2	1	4	7	2	–	–	HEBREU
–	–	–	1	1	2	3	1	–	HEBREO
–	–	–	–	–	–	–	–	–	HINDUSTANI
–	–	–	–	–	1	–	–	–	HINDOUSTANI
1	–	–	–	–	2	–	–	–	HINDUSTANI
5	4	1	2	4	–	32	27	6	HUNGARIAN
1	1	–	1	3	–	13	18	–	HONGROIS
3	3	–	2	2	–	12	12	–	HUNGARO
1	–	3	4	6	–	–	–	–	ICELANDIC
–	–	5	3	2	–	–	–	–	ISLANDAIS
–	1	5	5	2	–	–	1	–	ISLANDES
29	77	24	24	27	38	15	10	3	ITALIAN
20	20	17	9	19	20	18	7	–	ITALIEN
28	12	9	5	9	10	9	7	–	ITALIANO
–	3	2	2	3	3	2	–	2	JAPANESE
–	–	9	1	2	6	1	1	–	JAPONAIS
–	1	1	–	1	1	–	–	–	JAPONES
–	–	–	–	–	–	–	–	–	KAZAKH
–	–	–	–	–	–	–	–	–	KAZAKH
–	–	–	–	–	–	–	–	–	KAZAK
–	–	–	–	1	1	1	–	–	KIRGHIZ
1	1	–	–	–	–	–	–	–	KIRGHIZE
–	–	–	–	–	1	–	–	–	KIRIGUIZ
7	13	10	2	4	10	13	5	1	LATIN
7	14	4	1	2	10	8	4	–	LATIN
4	7	8	2	1	2	10	–	–	LATIN
–	–	–	–	1	1	–	2	–	LATVIAN
–	–	1	–	1	1	1	–	–	LETTON
–	–	–	–	–	–	2	1	–	LETON
–	–	–	–	–	2	7	3	–	LITHUANIAN
–	–	–	1	1	2	11	–	–	LITUANIEN
–	–	1	–	–	–	6	2	–	LITUANO
–	–	–	–	–	1	–	1	10	MACEDONIAN
–	1	–	–	–	–	–	–	3	MACEDONIEN
–	–	–	–	–	1	2	–	1	MACEDONIO
–	–	–	–	–	–	–	–	–	MALAYSIAN
–	–	1	–	–	–	–	–	–	MALAIS
–	–	–	–	–	–	–	–	–	MALAYO

7.17 Translations by original language and by new language
Translations d'après la langue originale et la nouvelle langue
Traducciones según la lengua original y la lengua nueva

ORIGINAL LANGUAGE / LANGUE ORIGINALE / LENGUA ORIGINAL	YEAR / ANNEE / AÑO	TRANSLATIONS BY LANGUAGE INTO WHICH TRANSLATED / TRADUCTIONS SELON LA LANGUE DANS LAQUELLE ELLES SONT TRADUITES / TRADUCCIONES SEGUN LA LENGUA EN QUE HAN SIDO TRADUCIDAS						
		ENGLISH ANGLAIS INGLES	FRENCH FRANCAIS FRANCES	SPANISH ESPAGNOL ESPAÑOL	RUSSIAN RUSSE RUSO	ARABIC ARABE ARABE	GERMAN ALLEMAND ALEMAN	ITALIAN ITALIEN ITALIANO
MOLDAVIAN	1979	1	–	–	29	1	–	–
MOLDAVE	1980	1	1	–	33	–	–	–
MODAVO	1981	1	1	–	25	–	–	–
NORWEGIAN	1979	30	5	11	3	–	53	4
NORVEGIEN	1980	26	11	8	6	1	53	3
NORUEGO	1981	17	3	2	4	–	28	2
PERSIAN	1979	16	2	1	2	2	5	–
PERSAN	1980	22	13	1	14	2	11	3
PERSA	1981	10	2	–	11	1	6	3
POLISH	1979	100	38	13	91	–	136	10
POLONAIS	1980	93	68	31	80	–	131	10
POLACO	1981	69	37	19	63	–	110	12
PORTUGUESE	1979	20	11	68	4	–	28	10
PORTUGAIS	1980	19	33	58	8	–	28	4
PORTUGUES	1981	16	9	67	7	–	15	9
ROMANIAN	1979	95	48	14	36	–	69	–
ROMAIN	1980	82	54	19	32	–	73	2
RUMANO	1981	103	47	20	52	–	50	2
RUSSIAN	1979	750	273	411	–	105	687	111
RUSSE	1980	752	405	383	–	114	646	97
RUSO	1981	782	321	345	–	99	548	86
SANSKRIT	1979	52	3	2	1	1	7	1
SANSCRIT	1980	57	26	3	2	–	21	4
SANSCRITO	1981	46	8	3	1	–	12	5
SERBO-CROATIAN	1979	61	31	19	29	1	39	16
SERBO-CROATE	1980	55	35	21	25	11	36	17
SERVIOCROATA	1981	33	24	8	12	–	26	13
SLOVAK	1979	6	–	–	–	–	5	4
SLOVAQUE	1980	–	1	–	1	–	3	2
ESLOVACO	1981	2	1	–	–	–	3	3
SLOVENE	1979	12	4	–	26	4	30	1
SLOVENE	1980	3	4	–	16	–	11	2
ESLOVENO	1981	2	3	1	19	–	13	–
SPANISH	1979	137	58	–	28	3	128	80
ESPAGNOL	1980	114	151	–	27	2	149	45
ESPAÑOL	1981	73	82	–	31	3	87	33
SWEDISH	1979	122	17	16	11	–	172	12
SUEDOIS	1980	116	35	13	6	1	175	11
SUECO	1981	64	18	22	10	1	100	8
TADZHIK	1979	–	–	–	12	–	–	–
TADJIK	1980	–	–	–	15	1	–	–
TADJIK	1981	–	–	–	14	1	–	–
TATAR	1979	–	–	–	22	–	1	–
TATAR	1980	–	–	1	23	–	–	–
TARTARO	1981	1	–	–	26	–	–	–
THAI	1979	2	–	–	–	–	1	–
THAILANDAIS	1980	–	–	–	–	–	–	–
TAILANDES	1981	–	1	–	–	–	1	–
TIBETAN	1979	9	–	–	–	–	2	1
TIBETAIN	1980	5	4	1	–	–	4	2
TIBETANO	1981	6	4	–	1	–	9	–
TURKISH	1979	5	3	2	5	1	14	1
TURC	1980	3	8	–	3	1	11	–
TURCO	1981	5	3	1	3	1	16	2
TURKOMAN	1979	1	–	–	16	1	–	–
TURKMENE	1980	–	–	–	16	–	–	–
TURCOMANO	1981	–	–	–	19	1	–	–
UKRAINIAN	1979	39	5	2	76	–	10	–
UKRAINIEN	1980	24	4	–	67	–	9	–
UCRANIANO	1981	29	5	–	77	–	6	1
URDU	1979	9	–	–	2	1	2	–
OURDU	1980	17	1	–	–	–	2	–
URDU	1981	3	–	–	1	–	–	–
UZBEK	1979	1	1	–	49	4	–	–
OUZBEK	1980	2	–	–	34	–	–	–
UZBECO	1981	–	5	–	37	3	1	–

TRANSLATIONS BY LANGUAGE INTO WHICH TRANSLATED / TRADUCTIONS SELON LA LANGUE DANS LAQUELLE ELLES SONT TRADUITES / TRADUCCIONES SEGUN LA LENGUA EN QUE HAN SIDO TRADUCIDAS									ORIGINAL LANGUAGE / LANGUE ORIGINALE / LENGUA ORIGINAL
JAPANESE JAPONAIS JAPONES	DUTCH NEERLANDAIS NEERLANDES	DANISH DANOIS DANES	NORWEGIAN NORVEGIEN NORUEGO	SWEDISH SUEDOIS SUECO	HUNGARIAN HONGROIS HUNGARO	POLISH POLONAIS POLACO	SLOVAK SLOVAQUE ESLOVAKO	TURKISH TURC TURCO	
–	–	–	–	–	1	–	5	–	MOLDAVIAN
–	–	–	–	–	–	–	–	–	MOLDAVE
–	–	–	–	–	–	–	–	–	MODAVO
3	5	72	–	55	4	4	1	1	NORWEGIAN
–	2	77	–	75	3	6	2	–	NORVEGIEN
1	3	54	–	22	2	3	2	–	NORUEGO
2	1	–	–	–	1	2	–	5	PERSIAN
–	–	–	–	1	2	1	–	–	PERSAN
1	–	–	–	1	–	1	–	–	PERSA
3	4	3	3	7	46	–	23	1	POLISH
6	–	2	1	6	28	–	21	–	POLONAIS
5	4	2	4	4	12	–	18	–	POLACO
2	2	1	3	2	1	4	–	–	PORTUGUESE
4	1	4	3	2	6	7	–	–	PORTUGAIS
4	1	–	–	1	2	3	1	–	PORTUGUES
1	1	–	–	3	75	8	2	–	ROMANIAN
–	1	1	–	1	75	4	6	–	ROMAIN
3	–	–	–	2	61	–	2	–	RUMANO
107	37	29	19	47	293	195	172	85	RUSSIAN
88	19	27	24	57	232	200	130	3	RUSSE
108	22	30	18	19	106	160	124	2	RUSO
1	1	1	–	1	1	–	–	1	SANSKRIT
–	–	2	–	1	–	–	–	–	SANSCRIT
–	–	1	–	–	–	1	–	–	SANSCRITO
1	–	1	1	1	39	9	16	2	SERBO–CROATIAN
3	–	–	–	2	30	8	12	1	SERBO–CROATE
4	1	1	–	1	35	3	20	–	SERVIOCROATA
–	1	–	–	–	7	1	2	–	SLOVAK
–	–	–	–	–	3	1	–	–	SLOVAQUE
–	1	–	–	–	1	1	2	–	ESLOVACO
–	1	3	–	1	60	7	–	–	SLOVENE
–	–	–	–	–	40	13	–	–	SLOVENE
–	–	–	–	1	31	7	–	–	ESLOVENO
23	22	43	12	19	19	17	15	12	SPANISH
12	7	22	12	9	22	22	8	–	ESPAGNOL
28	3	10	8	15	3	14	4	–	ESPAÑOL
20	46	363	210	–	6	6	7	8	SWEDISH
14	26	274	195	–	7	9	3	–	SUEDOIS
14	19	145	142	–	–	6	3	1	SUECO
–	–	–	–	–	1	–	–	–	TADZHIK
–	–	–	–	–	–	–	–	–	TADJIK
–	–	–	–	–	–	–	–	–	TADJIK
–	–	–	–	–	–	–	–	–	TATAR
–	–	–	–	–	–	–	–	–	TATAR
–	–	–	–	–	–	–	–	–	TARTARO
–	–	–	–	–	–	–	–	–	THAI
4	–	–	–	1	–	–	–	–	THAILANDAIS
9	–	–	–	–	–	1	–	–	TAILANDES
1	1	–	–	–	–	–	–	–	TIBETAN
–	–	–	–	–	–	–	–	–	TIBETAIN
–	–	–	–	–	–	–	–	–	TIBETANO
–	–	3	1	2	1	–	2	–	TURKISH
–	–	3	1	2	1	1	1	–	TURC
2	–	1	1	–	–	–	–	–	TURCO
–	–	–	–	–	–	–	–	–	TURKOMAN
–	–	–	–	–	–	–	–	–	TURKMENE
–	–	–	–	–	–	–	–	–	TURCOMANO
–	–	–	–	–	9	10	8	–	UKRAINIAN
–	–	–	–	–	6	8	4	–	UKRAINIEN
2	–	–	–	–	4	14	2	–	UCRANIANO
–	–	–	–	–	1	–	–	1	URDU
–	–	–	–	–	–	–	–	–	OURDU
–	–	–	–	–	–	–	–	–	URDU
–	–	–	–	–	1	–	1	–	UZBEK
–	–	–	–	–	1	–	1	–	OUZBEK
–	–	–	–	–	–	–	–	–	UZBECO

7.17 **Translations by original language and by new language**
Translations d'après la langue originale et la nouvelle langue
Traducciones según la lengua original y la lengua nueva

ORIGINAL LANGUAGE / LANGUE ORIGINALE / LENGUA ORIGINAL	YEAR / ANNEE / AÑO	TRANSLATIONS BY LANGUAGE INTO WHICH TRANSLATED / TRADUCTIONS SELON LA LANGUE DANS LAQUELLE ELLES SONT TRADUITES / TRADUCCIONES SEGUN LA LENGUA EN QUE HAN SIDO TRADUCIDAS						
		ENGLISH ANGLAIS INGLES	FRENCH FRANCAIS FRANCES	SPANISH ESPAGNOL ESPAÑOL	RUSSIAN RUSSE RUSO	ARABIC ARABE ARABE	GERMAN ALLEMAND ALEMAN	ITALIAN ITALIEN ITALIANO
VIETNAMESE	1979	3	–	1	6	–	2	1
VIETNAMIEN	1980	–	–	–	7	–	1	–
VIETNAMITA	1981	–	–	1	7	1	–	–
YIDDISH	1979	26	5	2	12	–	15	–
YIDDISH	1980	13	6	–	11	–	8	4
YIDDISH	1981	9	3	2	14	–	6	7

TRANSLATIONS BY LANGUAGE INTO WHICH TRANSLATED TRADUCTIONS SELON LA LANGUE DANS LAQUELLE ELLES SONT TRADUITES TRADUCCIONES SEGUN LA LENGUA EN QUE HAN SIDO TRADUCIDAS									ORIGINAL LANGUAGE
JAPANESE JAPONAIS JAPONES	DUTCH NEERLANDAIS NEERLANDES	DANISH DANOIS DANES	NORWEGIAN NORVEGIEN NORUEGO	SWEDISH SUEDOIS SUECO	HUNGARIAN HONGROIS HUNGARO	POLISH POLONAIS POLACO	SLOVAK SLOVAQUE ESLOVAKO	TURKISH TURC TURCO	LANGUE ORIGINALE LENGUA ORIGINAL
–	–	–	–	–	–	–	–	6	VIETNAMESE
1	–	–	–	–	1	1	–	–	VIETNAMIEN
–	–	–	–	–	–	1	–	–	VIETNAMITA
–	3	3	1	8	–	1	–	1	YIDDISH
–	–	2	2	6	–	1	–	–	YIDDISH
–	–	–	1	1	–	1	–	–	YIDDISH

7.18 Authors most frequently translated
Auteurs les plus traduits
Autores más traducidos

AUTHORS AUTEURS AUTORES	COUNTRY WITH WHICH THE AUTHOR'S WORKS ARE ASSOCIATED PAYS AUQUEL APPARTIENT L'OEUVRE LITTERAIRE DE L'AUTEUR PAIS AL QUE PERTENECE LA OBRA LITERARIA DEL AUTOR	NUMBER OF TRANSLATIONS NOMBRE DE TRADUCTIONS NUMERO DE TRADUCCIONES					NUMBER OF TRANSLATING COUNTRIES IN 1981 NOMBRE DE PAYS TRADUCTEURS EN 1981 NUMERO DE PAISES TRADUCTORES EN 1981
		1981	1980	1979	1978	1961–1970	
V.I. LENIN‡	U.S.S.R.	384	468	416	413	2354	15
W. DISNEY (PRD'N)‡	U.S.A	226	285	230	279	1102	13
A. CHRISTIE	UNITED KINGDOM	216	189	180	282	920	18
L.I. BREZNEV‡	U.S.S.R.	154	109	181	210	279	11
J. VERNE	FRANCE	152	172	230	279	1102	22
B. CARTLAND	UNITED KINGDOM	111	135	124	137	38	11
K. MARX	GERMANY	111	136	144	186	819	16
H.C. ANDERSEN	DENMARK	110	91	81	153	611	20
J. GRIMM	GERMANY	109	103	109	110	571	14
F. ENGELS	GERMANY	97	132	121	36	616	16
C.PERRAULT	FRANCE	85	33	56	136	169	8
I. ASIMOV	U.S.A.	84	82	60	61	237	15
A. MACLEAN	UNITED KINGDOM	84	57	91	83	387	14
E. BLYTON	UNITED KINGDOM	81	147	126	117	974	10
A.C. DOYLE	UNITED KINGDOM	81	48	25	29	326	18
J. LONDON	U.S.A.	79	93	98	115	539	15
W. SHAKESPEARE	UNITED KINGDOM	78	112	92	93	1227	20
L.N. TOLSTOJ‡	U.S.S.R.	78	79	144	136	1063	15
M. TWAIN	U.S.A.	77	88	85	83	642	15
JOANNES PAULUS II	HOLY SEE	65	70	73	1	–	13
G. SIMENON	BELGIUM	63	82	104	105	1076	15
R.L. STEVENSON	UNITED KINGDOM	63	63	67	86	465	17
C. DICKENS	UNITED KINGDOM	61	59	78	77	604	16
F.M. DOSTOEVSKIJ‡	U.S.S.R.	61	85	73	75	872	16
H.G. KONSALIK	GERMANY	60	72	52	66	139	13
R. GOSCINNY	FRANCE	58	101	89	73	37	8
E.S. GARDNER	U.S.A.	57	54	33	40	752	8
E.L. STRATEMEYER	U.S.A.	56	44	66	52	–	1
E. SALGARY	ITALY	55	16	38	36	78	4
M. GORKIJ‡	U.S.S.R.	54	40	77	72	702	14
C.M. SCHULZ	U.S.A.	54	35	26	16	78	4
H. DE BALZAC	FRANCE	53	48	36	50	620	12
G. GREENE	UNITED KINGDOM	52	63	55	49	497	17
R. SCARRY	U.S.A.	51	27	31	49	50	8
E. HEMINGWAY	U.S.A.	50	64	61	77	626	16
D. DEFOE	UNITED KINGDOM	49	50	42	48	319	16
E. FROMM	U.S.A.	49	39	32	33	179	13
R. STEINER	GERMANY	46	38	36	39	130	12
A. MATHER	...	42	39	–	21	–	6
H. ROBBINS‡	U.S.A.	42	60	68	41	144	14
A.N. KOLMOGOROV‡	U.S.S.R.	41	59	59	63	7	2
A.S. PUSHKIN‡	U.S.S.R.	41	44	40	34	384	12
H. HESSE	GERMANY	40	62	61	67	199	10
E.A. POE	U.S.A.	39	43	44	34	248	8
N.A. TIHONOV‡	U.S.S.R.	39	3	4	1	12	2
J.W. GOETHE	GERMANY	37	35	41	38	368	15
A.P. CEHOV‡	U.S.S.R.	36	51	54	40	520	17
J. DAILEY	U.S.A.	36	24	–	11	–	6

AUTHORS / AUTEURS / AUTORES	COUNTRY WITH WHICH THE AUTHOR'S WORKS ARE ASSOCIATED / PAYS AUQUEL APPARTIENT L'OEUVRE LITTERAIRE DE L'AUTEUR / PAIS AL QUE PERTENECE LA OBRA LITERARIA DEL AUTOR	NUMBER OF TRANSLATIONS / NOMBRE DE TRADUCTIONS / NUMERO DE TRADUCCIONES					NUMBER OF TRANSLATING COUNTRIES IN 1981 / NOMBRE DE PAYS TRADUCTEURS EN 1981 / NUMERO DE PAISES TRADUCTORES EN 1981
		1981	1980	1979	1978	1961–1970	
Z. GREY	U.S.A.	36	11	19	23	342	3
J.N. MAKARYCEV‡	U.S.S.R.	36	44	43	42	–	1
PLATO	GREECE	36	41	32	30	407	14
G. DE VILLIERS	FRANCE	36	43	37	20	22	6
T. CALDWELL	U.S.A.	35	41	30	20	96	8
J.H. CHASE	UNITED KINGDOM	35	23	23	21	320	10
J.F. COOPER	U.S.A.	35	38	30	36	276	9
A. DUMAS (PERE)	FRANCE	35	50	78	60	514	12
W. SCOTT	UNITED KINGDOM	35	38	32	29	247	10
I.B. SINGER	U.S.A.	35	48	65	35	60	14
STENDHAL	FRANCE	35	23	24	37	316	12
O. WILDE	UNITED KINGDOM	34	27	36	34	249	13
HOMER	GREECE	33	42	49	26	327	13
A. HUXLEY	UNITED KINGDOM	33	32	17	29	182	12
R. KIPLING	UNITED KINGDOM	33	31	34	38	268	8
J.P. SARTRE	FRANCE	33	45	50	38	489	13
K.H. SCHEER	GERMANY	32	19	–	20	18	2
P.S. BUCK	U.S.A.	31	70	47	83	659	11
A. CAMUS	FRANCE	31	30	33	23	317	10
L. L'AMOUR	U.S.A.	31	27	1	21	164	5
S. FREUD	AUSTRIA	30	35	56	31	224	7
S. LEM	POLAND	30	30	32	34	76	12
A.E. LINDGREN	SWEDEN	30	49	69	44	368	12
PEYO	BELGIUM	30	45	–	13	–	3
R. CROMPTON	...	29	10	6	3	65	2
C. DARLTON	...	29	10	20	13	11	2
J.V. HODAKOV‡	U.S.S.R.	29	31	33	23	10	1
V. SOTIROVIC	YUGOSLAVIA	29	6	2	2	–	1
L. WERNER	DENMARK	29	31	–	14	21	1
E. ZOLA	FRANCE	29	18	17	34	417	11
N.V. GOGOL‡	U.S.S.R.	28	32	32	27	369	10
F. KAFKA	AUSTRIA	28	28	–	35	236	12
H. MILLER	U.S.A.	28	43	31	35	222	8
A. MORAVIA	ITALY	28	27	23	17	411	12
M. SJOWALL	SWEDEN	28	30	2	31	30	6
C. COLLODI	ITALY	27	26	22	29	133	5
J. CONRAD	UNITED KINGDOM	27	28	31	19	163	10
V. HUGO	FRANCE	27	27	41	27	404	10
A.I. KUPRIN‡	U.S.S.R.	27	10	6	16	87	2
J. LE CARRE	UNITED KINGDOM	27	34	–	18	138	11
J. PIAGET	SWITZERLAND	27	19	37	33	113	10
L. CARROLL	UNITED KINGDOM	26	39	31	42	140	11
C. COOKSON	UNITED KINGDOM	26	24	26	40	44	6
W. DURANT	U.S.A.	26	–	3	–	106	5
D. A. EPSTEJN‡	U.S.S.R.	26	22	–	–	4	1
P. WAHLOO	SWEDEN	26	32	52	5	46	6
V. WINSPEAR	...	26	34	1	8	11	5
S. ZWEIG	AUSTRIA	26	24	1	6	284	10
R. ARTHUR	UNITED KINGDOM	25	31	25	17	22	5
I.A. FEDOSOV‡	U.S.S.R	25	23	28	15	1	1
G. FLAUBERT	FRANCE	25	33	36	19	233	11
F.W. NIETZCHE	GERMANY	25	37	34	28	92	7
E. QUEEN	U.S.A.	25	21	43	30	376	8
J. STEINBECK	U.S.A.	25	29	36	36	601	12
L.M. ALCOTT	U.S.A.	24	19	37	32	228	3
B.B. BUHOVCEV‡	U.S.S.R.	24	29	–	15	–	1
M F. CERNYSOV‡	U.S.S.R.	24	–	–	7	–	1
A.J. CRONIN	UNITED KINGDOM	24	40	32	46	426	9
J. HIGGINS	UNITED KINGDOM	24	20	22	21	6	11
G. DE MAUPASSANT	FRANCE	24	30	32	33	437	13
G.J. MJAKISEV‡	U.S.S.R	24	29	29	13	3	1
D. BAGLEY	UNITED KINGDOM	23	18	40	15	44	8
G. GARCIA MARQUEZ	COLOMBIA	23	35	30	26	21	11
P.A. GLORIOZOV‡	U.S.S.R.	23	22	25	2	2	1
D. H. LAWRENCE	UNITED KINGDOM	23	28	–	27	214	12
S. SHELDON	U.S.A.	23	19	28	23	–	14
I. CALVINO	ITALY	22	17	15	10	86	11
M.L. FISCHER	GERMANY	22	26	31	36	64	5

7.18 Authors most frequently translated
Auteurs les plus traduits
Autores más traducidos

AUTHORS / AUTEURS / AUTORES	COUNTRY WITH WHICH THE AUTHOR'S WORKS ARE ASSOCIATED / PAYS AUQUEL APPARTIENT L'OEUVRE LITTERAIRE DE L'AUTEUR / PAIS AL QUE PERTENECE LA OBRA LITERARIA DEL AUTOR	NUMBER OF TRANSLATIONS / NOMBRE DE TRADUCTIONS / NUMERO DE TRADUCCIONES					NUMBER OF TRANSLATING COUNTRIES IN 1981 / NOMBRE DE PAYS TRADUCTEURS EN 1981 / NUMERO DE PAISES TRADUCTORES EN 1981
		1981	1980	1979	1978	1961–1970	
F. FORSYTH	UNITED KINGDOM	22	22	28	18	2	11
M. GROVER	U.S.A.	22	59	57	23	361	3
R.A. HEINLEIN	U.S.A.	22	28	25	23	78	8
G. HEYER	UNITED KINGDOM	22	38	36	44	125	5
E. KARDELJ	YUGOSLAVIA	22	25	–	14	41	2
U.K. LE GUIN	U.S.A.	22	25	28	19	–	10
D. LESSING	UNITED KINGDOM	22	24	20	15	34	9
T.R. LOBSANG	...	22	40	50	14	44	5
L. MASTERSON	NORWAY	22	55	20	22	2	4
I. WALLACE	U.S.A.	22	21	35	20	77	8
M.L. WEST	AUSTRIA	22	34	36	36	234	10
P.G. WODEHOUSE	UNITED KINGDOM	22	10	16	18	127	8
E.V. AGIBALOVA‡	U.S.S.R.	21	11	10	14	1	1
C. AJTMATOV‡	U.S.S.R.	21	25	26	34	175	6
W. ALLEN	U.S.A	21	9	6	2	–	10
A.C. CLARKE	UNITED KINGDOM	21	21	27	38	115	8
G.M. DONSKOJ‡	U.S.S.R.	21	11	–	–	2	1
N. CARTER	U.S.A.	21	35	62	72	179	3
L. KENT	U.S.A.	21	31	29	19	271	3
J. KRISNAMURTI	INDIA	21	10	20	27	64	10
ED. MCBAIN‡	U.S.A	21	35	42	34	208	8
A. NIN	FRANCE	21	28	32	25	18	11
R. TAGORE	INDIA	21	13	30	19	555	6
I.S. TURGENEV‡	U.S.S.R.	21	24	28	31	391	11
N.S. VILENKIN‡	U.S.S.R.	21	30	26	25	14	2
R. ZELAZNY	U.S.A.	21	13	6	12	2	7
ARISTOTELES	GREECE	20	28	20	33	234	9
H. BOLL	GERMANY	20	22	22	33	191	10
R. BRADBURY	U.S.A.	20	15	14	24	98	12
R.S. CERKASOV‡	U.S.S.R.	20	15	–	–	2	1
R. DAHL	UNITED KINGDOM	20	15	19	34	52	6
L. DEIGHTON	UNITED KINGDOM	20	25	–	10	74	7
H.H. KIRST	GERMANY	20	18	12	12	195	8
C. LAMB	UNITED KINGDOM	20	24	–	–	–	6
J.SWIFT	UNITED KINGDOM	20	28	25	38	216	6
E. WALLACE	U.S.A.	20	26	41	49	269	4

General note/Note général/Note general:

E--> In addition in 1981, the Bible was translated 238 times in 18 countries (in 1980, 232 times in 22 countries; total 1961-1970: 2,126) and *Arabian Nights* 36 times in 7 countries (in 1980, 34 times in 5 countries, total 1961-1970: 288). For Russian authors, the system of transliteration of cyrillic characters adopted by the International Organization for Standardization and followed by *Index Translationum* has been used. The number of translations for these authors also includes works published in the U.S.S.R.. In 1981, these figures were: V.I. Lenin: 305, L. Breznev: 138, L.N. Tolstoj: 38, F.M. Dostoevskij: 6, M. Gorkij: 28, A.N. Kolmogorov: 40, A.S. Pushkin: 12, N.A. Tihonov: 38, A.P. Cehov: 10, J.N. Makarycev: 36, J.V. Hodakov: 29, N.V. Gogol: 6, A.I. Kuprin: 26, D.A. Epstejn: 26, I.A. Fedosov: 25, B.B. Buhocev: 24,, M.F. Cernysov: 24, G.J. Mjakisev: 24, P.A. Gloriosov: 23, E.V. Agibalova: 21, C. Ajmatov: 13, G.M. Donskoj: 21, I.S. Turgenev: 9, N.S. Vilenkin: 20, R.S. Cerkasov: 20.

FR-> En outre, il est paru en 1981, 238 traductions de la Bible dans 18 pays (en 1980, 232 dans 22 pays; total 1961-1970: 2 126) 36 traductions des *Mille et une nuits* dans 7 pays (en 1980, 34 dans 5 pays; total 1961-1970: 288). Pour les auteurs russes, on a utilisé le système de translittération des caractères cyrilliques établi par l'Organisation internationale de normalisation et adopté par l'*Index Translationum*. Le nombre de traductions pour ces auteurs comprend également les traductions parues en U.R.S.S. En 1981, ces chiffres étaient les suivants: V.I. Lenin: 305, L. Breznev: 138, L.N. Tolstoj: 38, F.M. Dostoevskij: 6, M. Gorkij: 28, A.N. Kolmogorov: 40, A.S. Pushkin: 12, N.A. Tihonov: 38, A.P. Cehov: 10, J.N. Makarycev: 36, J.V. Hodakov: 29, N.V. Gogol: 6, A.I. Kuprin: 26, D.A. Epstejn: 26, I.A. Fedosov: 25, B.B. Buhocev: 24,, M.F. Cernysov: 24, G.J. Mjakisev: 24, P.A. Gloriosov: 23, E.V. Agibalova: 21, C. Ajmatov: 13, G.M. Donskoj: 21, I.S. Turgenev: 9, N.S. Vilenkin: 20, R.S. Cerkasov: 20.

ESP> Se publicaron además, en 1981, 238 traducciones de la Biblia, en 18 países (en 1980, 232 en 22 países; de 1961 a 1970 en total 2 126), 36 traducciones de *Las mil y una noches* en 7 países (en 1980, 34 en 5 países; de 1961 a 1970 en total: 288). En el caso de los autores rusos, se ha utilizado el sistema de transcripción de los caracteres cirílicos establecido por la Organización internacional de normalización y adoptado por el *Index Translationum*. El número de traducciones de estos autores comprende también las publicadas en la U.R.S.S. En 1981, las cifras fueron las siguentes: V.I. Lenin: 305, L. Breznev: 138, L.N. Tolstoj: 38, F.M. Dostoevskij: 6, M. Gorkij: 28, A.N. Kolmogorov: 40, A.S. Pushkin: 12, N.A. Tihonov: 38, A.P. Cehov: 10, J.N. Makarycev: 36, J.V. Hodakov: 29, N.V. Gogol: 6, A.I. Kuprin: 26, D.A. Epstejn: 26, I.A. Fedosov: 25, B.B. Buhocev: 24,, M.F. Cernysov: 24, G.J. Mjakisev: 24, P.A. Gloriosov: 23, E.V. Agibalova: 21, C. Ajmatov: 13, G.M. Donskoj: 21, I.S. Turgenev: 9, N.S. Vilenkin: 20, R.S. Cerkasov: 20.

V.I. Lenin:

E--> See general note.

FR-> Voir la note générale.

ESP> Véase la nota general.

Walt Disney:

E--> All works under the name of W. Disney were not necessarily written by him.

FR-> Des oeuvres sont publiées sous le nom de W. Disney dont il n'était pas nécessairement l'auteur.

ESP> Se publican bajo el nombre de W. Disney obras de las que no era necesaramente el autor.

L.I Breznev:

E--> See general note.

FR-> Voir la note générale.

ESP> Véase la nota general.

L.N. Tolstoj:

E--> See general note.

FR-> Voir la note générale.

ESP> Véase la nota general.

F.M. Dostoevskij:

E--> See general note.

FR-> Voir la note générale.

F.M. Dostoevskij: (Cont):
ESP> Véase la nota general.
M. Gorkij:
E--> See general note.
FR-> Voir la note générale.
ESP> Véase la nota general.
H. Robbins:
E--> Including 2 under the pen-name of H. Rubin in 1979.
FR-> Dont 2 sous le pseudonyme de H. Rubin en 1979.
ESP> De las cuales 2 con el seudónimo de H. Rubin en 1979.
A.N. Kolmogorov:
E--> See general note.
FR-> Voir la note générale.
ESP> Véase la nota general.
A.S. Pushkin:
E--> See general note.
FR-> Voir la note générale.
ESP> Véase la nota general.
N.A. Tihonov:
E--> See general note.
FR-> Voir la note générale.
ESP> Véase la nota general.
A.P. Cehov:
E--> See general note.
FR-> Voir la note générale.
ESP> Véase la nota general.
J.N. Makarycev:
E--> See general note.
FR-> Voir la note générale.
ESP> Véase la nota general.
J.V. Hodakov:
E--> See general note.
FR-> Voir la note générale.
ESP> Véase la nota general.
N.V. Gogol:
E--> See general note.
FR-> Voir la note générale.
ESP> Véase la nota general.
A.I. Kuprin:
E--> See general note.
FR-> Voir la note générale.
ESP> Véase la nota general.
D.A. Epstejn:
E--> See general note.
FR-> Voir la note générale.
ESP> Véase la nota general.
I.A. Fedosov:
E--> See general note.

I.A. Fedosov: (Cont):
FR-> Voir la note générale.
ESP> Véase la nota general.
B.B. Buhocev:
E--> See general note.
FR-> Voir la note générale.
ESP> Véase la nota general.
M.F. Cernysov:
E--> See general note.
FR-> Voir la note générale.
ESP> Véase la nota general.
G.J. Mjakisev:
E--> See general note.
FR-> Voir la note générale.
ESP> Véase la nota general.
P.A. Gloriozov:
E--> See general note.
FR-> Voir la note générale.
ESP> Véase la nota general.
E.V. Agibalova:
E--> See general note.
FR-> Voir la note générale.
ESP> Véase la nota general.
C. Ajtmatov:
E--> See general note.
FR-> Voir la note générale.
ESP> Véase la nota general.
G.M. Donskoj:
E--> See general note.
FR-> Voir la note générale.
ESP> Véase la nota general.
E. McBain:
E--> Including 9 under the pen-name of E. Hunter in 1979.
FR-> Dont 9 sous le pseudonyme de E. Hunter en 1979.
ESP> De las cuales 9 con el seudónimo de E. Hunter en 1979.
I.S. Turgenev:
E--> See general note.
FR-> Voir la note générale.
ESP> Véase la nota general.
N.S. Vilenkin:
E--> See general note.
FR-> Voir la note générale.
ESP> Véase la nota general.
R.S. Cerkasov:
E--> See general note.
FR-> Voir la note générale.
ESP> Véase la nota general.

7.19 Daily general-interest newspapers: number and circulation (total and per 1,000 inhabitants)

Journaux quotidiens d'information générale: nombre et tirage (total et pour 1 000 habitants)

Periódicos diarios de información general: número y tirada (total y por 1 000 habitantes)

NUMBER OF COUNTRIES AND TERRITORIES PRESENTED IN THIS TABLE: 169

NOMBRE DE PAYS ET DE TERRITOIRES PRESENTES DANS CE TABLEAU: 169

NUMERO DE PAISES Y DE TERRITORIOS PRESENTADOS EN ESTE CUADRO: 169

COUNTRY / PAYS / PAIS	DAILY NEWSPAPERS / JOURNAUX QUOTIDIENS / PERIODICOS DIARIOS											
	NUMBER / NOMBRE / NUMERO				ESTIMATED CIRCULATION / TIRAGE (ESTIMATION) / TIRAGE (ESTIMACION): TOTAL (IN THOUSANDS) / TOTAL (EN MILLIERS) / TOTAL (EN MILLARES)				PER 1,000 INHABITANTS / POUR 1 000 HABITANTS / POR 1 000 HABITANTES			
	1970	1975	1979	1984	1970	1975	1979	1984	1970	1975	1979	1984
	(1)	(2)	(3)	(4)	(5)	(6)	(7)	(8)	(9)	(10)	(11)	(12)
AFRICA												
ALGERIA	4	4	4	5	275	285	425	570	20	18	24	27
ANGOLA‡	...	4	5	4	...	14	...	112	...	...	...	13
BENIN	2	1	1	1	2	1	1	*1	1	0.3	0.4	*0.3
BOTSWANA	2	1	1	1	13	14	17	18	21	19	19	17
BURKINA FASO	1	1	1	1	2	2	2	2	0.3	0.3	0.2	0.2
BURUNDI	1	1	1	1	0.3	2	...	...	0.1	0.4	...	...
CAMEROON	2	2	...	1	17	25	...	35	3	3	...	4
CHAD	...	4	4	1	...	...	...	1	...	...	...	...
CONGO	3	3	1	1	...	...	...	8	...	...	...	5
COTE D'IVOIRE‡	3	3	1	1	44	35	53	80	8	...	7	9
EGYPT‡	14	12	9	...	745	1 095	2 475	...	23	30	...	...
EQUATORIAL GUINEA	...	...	2	1	...	...	...	...	...	...	...	...
ETHIOPIA‡	8	3	5	3	28	44	52	40	...	1	1	1
GABON	...	1	1	1	...	...	...	15	...	...	...	13
GAMBIA	–	–	–	1	–	–	–	2	–	–	–	3
GHANA‡	...	4	5	4	...	500	345	460	...	51	...	35
GUINEA	1	1	1	1	5	5	20	13	1	1	4	2
GUINEA-BISSAU	1	1	1	1	...	6	6	6	...	10	8	7
KENYA	4	3	3	4	155	134	156	255	14	10	10	13
LESOTHO	...	1	3	3	...	...	32	44	...	...	24	30
LIBERIA‡	2	3	3	3	7	13	11	16	5	8	6	...
LIBYAN ARAB JAMAHIRIYA	8	2	...	4	...	41	...	...	...	17	...	...
MADAGASCAR‡	13	...	5	5	53	...	23	46	8	...	...	5
MALAWI	...	...	2	2	...	...	31	32	...	...	5	5
MALI	...	...	2	1	...	...	...	4	...	...	...	1
MAURITIUS	...	12	8	8	...	82	74	76	...	94	79	74
MOROCCO‡	14	7	9	10	243	245	230	190	...	...	...	...
MOZAMBIQUE‡	6	...	2	2	55	...	42	54	...	...	4	4
NAMIBIA	3	...	...	4	...	...	...	29	...	...	...	19
NIGER	...	2	1	1	...	...	...	5	...	...	...	1
NIGERIA‡	21	12	15	14	319	613	...	516	...	...	...	...
REUNION	...	2	3	2	...	27	52	51	...	56	103	97
RWANDA	...	1	...	1	...	0.2	...	0.3	...	0.0	...	0.1
SENEGAL	1	1	1	1	20	25	25	30	5	5	5	5
SEYCHELLES	2	2	2	1	2	4	4	3	39	62	...	44
SIERRA LEONE	...	2	1	1	...	30	10	10	...	10	3	3
SOMALIA	2	...	1	1	5	...	...	...	2	...	...	...
SOUTH AFRICA‡	22	...	...	23	...	...	...	1 299	...	...	...	...
SUDAN	...	4	...	6	...	...	...	105	...	...	...	5
SWAZILAND‡	–	–	1	2	–	–	9	10	–	–	16	...
TOGO‡	1	1	1	2	...	7	7	10	...	3	3	...
TUNISIA	...	4	5	5	...	190	271	272	...	34	44	39
UGANDA	7	...	1	1	83	...	20	25	9	...	2	2
UNITED REPUBLIC OF TANZANIA‡	...	3	2	2	...	70	189	101	...	...	10	5
ZAIRE‡	13	...	6	7	200	...	45	30	10	...	...	1

COUNTRY / PAYS / PAIS	DAILY NEWSPAPERS / JOURNAUX QUOTIDIENS / PERIODICOS DIARIOS											
	NUMBER / NOMBRE / NUMERO				ESTIMATED CIRCULATION / TIRAGE (ESTIMATION) / TIRAGE (ESTIMACION)							
					TOTAL (IN THOUSANDS) / TOTAL (EN MILLIERS) / TOTAL (EN MILLARES)				PER 1,000 INHABITANTS / POUR 1 000 HABITANTS / POR 1 000 HABITANTES			
	1970	1975	1979	1984	1970	1975	1979	1984	1970	1975	1979	1984
	(1)	(2)	(3)	(4)	(5)	(6)	(7)	(8)	(9)	(10)	(11)	(12)
ZAMBIA	1	2	2	2	57	106	109	109	14	22	20	17
ZIMBABWE	4	3	2	3	83	116	111	190	16	19	16	22
AMERICA, NORTH												
ANTIGUA AND BARBUDA	1	1	1	1	...	4	6	...	...	59	...	...
BAHAMAS	3	2	3	3	28	31	33	38	164	152	157	168
BARBADOS	1	1	1	2	23	24	21	40	96	98	85	158
BELIZE	1	1	2	1	4	4	7	...	33	31	48	...
BERMUDA	1	1	1	1	11	11	13	16	195	181	...	205
CANADA‡	...	121	126	112	...	4 872	5 700	5 544	...	214	239	220
COSTA RICA	8	6	4	5	177	174	155	183	102	89	70	72
CUBA‡	16	15	9	18	...	53	891	1 437	...	...	92	144
DOMINICAN REPUBLIC‡	...	10	7	7	...	197	220	183	...	...	40	30
EL SALVADOR‡	13	12	12	6	365	234	335	296	...	...	...	...
GRENADA‡	2	1	1	–	3	...	...	–	...	...	...	–
GUADELOUPE	2	2	1	1	24	24	18	32	76	73	56	96
GUATEMALA‡	8	10	9	5	...	249	...	187	...	41	...	...
HAITI‡	7	7	4	4	79	93	32	39	17	18	6	...
HONDURAS‡	...	8	7	6	...	99	223	236	...	...	63	...
JAMAICA	...	3	3	3	...	131	128	104	...	64	60	45
MARTINIQUE	2	2	1	1	...	27	26	32	...	81	80	97
MEXICO	200	256	...	312	...	...	...	9 252	...	...	...	120
NETHERLANDS ANTILLES‡	5	5	5	7	33	55	54	53	147	228	214	...
NICARAGUA‡	...	7	8	3	...	91	170	149	...	...	63	47
PANAMA‡	7	6	6	6	130	131	148	119	85	75	78	...
PUERTO RICO	4	...	4	4	495	...	475	539	182	...	150	59
ST. CHRISTOPHER AND NEVIS AND ANGUILLA	2	1	–	–	...	1.5	–	–	...	...	–	–
ST. LUCIA	...	...	–	–	...	...	–	–	...	...	–	–
TRINIDAD AND TOBAGO‡	3	3	...	4	140	100	...	176	147	...	...	151
UNITED STATES	1 763	1 775	1 787	1 687	62 108	60 655	62 223	63 263	303	281	276	268
U.S. VIRGIN ISLANDS	3	3	4	1	14	17	19	6	219	179	...	58
AMERICA, SOUTH												
ARGENTINA‡	179	164	133	...	4 247	2 773	...	...	...	...	...	...
BOLIVIA‡	21	14	14	13	208	199	214	311	...	41	39	50
BRAZIL‡	...	299	328	322	...	4 895	5 094	6 134	...	47	44	46
CHILE	...	47	37	...	...	921	945	...	...	89	86	...
COLOMBIA‡	...	40	38	31	...	1 248	1 273	1 165	...	...	...	...
ECUADOR‡	25	...	38	16	250	...	400	637	41	...	51	...
FRENCH GUIANA	1	1	1	1	1.5	1.5	1.6	1	31	27	...	...
GUYANA	3	...	3	2	44	...	67	78	61	...	79	83
PARAGUAY‡	11	8	5	5	99	73	88	158	...	...	...	...
PERU‡	85	49	59	...	1 660	1 377	...	...	...	91	...	...
SURINAME‡	5	7	5	4	20	33	32	40	54	...	...	...
URUGUAY‡	...	30	28	21	...	637	...	553	...	...	...	...
VENEZUELA‡	...	49	69	...	...	1 067	2 383	...	...	...	164	...
ASIA												
AFGHANISTAN‡	18	...	14	13	101	...	69	65	7	...	...	...
BAHRAIN‡	–	–	–	3	–	–	–	25	–	–	–	...
BANGLADESH‡	...	30	30	47	...	356	404	544	...	...	5	6
BURMA	8	7	7	7	...	319	329	511	...	11	10	14
CHINA	...	...	...	*60	...	...	...	*30 000	...	...	...	*29
CYPRUS‡	10	12	12	10	68	78	67	78	111	...	...	118
DEMOCRATIC KAMPUCHEA	16	16	17	10	...	...	...	...	...	...	...	...
DEMOCRATIC YEMEN‡	...	...	3	3	...	...	12	12	...	...	...	6
HONG KONG	57	82	41	60	...	...	...	...	...	...	...	...
INDIA	...	835	1 087	...	...	9 383	13 033	...	...	15	19	...
INDONESIA	...	*60	...	55	...	*2 200	...	2 878	...	...	...	...
IRAN, ISLAMIC REPUBLIC OF‡	33	...	24	23	222	...	...	970	...	...	...	22
IRAQ‡	4	7	5	5	...	192	325	262	...	17	...	...
ISRAEL‡	24	23	24	26	600	...	...	707	202	...	...	...
JAPAN	178	176	178	125	53 304	60 782	65 881	67 380	511	545	570	562
JORDAN	5	4	5	4	56	58	59	71	24	22	20	21
KOREA, DEMOCRATIC PEOPLE'S REPUB. OF‡	...	...	11	11	...	...	...	1 000	...	...	...	...
KOREA, REPUBLIC OF‡	44	...	29	14	4 396	...	6 496	5 906	138	...	...	...
KUWAIT	5	8	7	8	20	...	...	335	27	...	...	197
LAO PEOPLE'S DEMOCRATIC REPUBLIC‡	...	8	3	3	...	5	...	...	...	...	...	...

7.19 Daily newspapers
Journaux quotidiens
Periódicos diarios

COUNTRY / PAYS / PAIS	DAILY NEWSPAPERS / JOURNAUX QUOTIDIENS / PERIODICOS DIARIOS											
	NUMBER / NOMBRE / NUMERO				ESTIMATED CIRCULATION / TIRAGE (ESTIMATION) / TIRAGE (ESTIMACION)							
					TOTAL (IN THOUSANDS) / TOTAL (EN MILLIERS) / TOTAL (EN MILLARES)				PER 1,000 INHABITANTS / POUR 1 000 HABITANTS / POR 1 000 HABITANTES			
	1970	1975	1979	1984	1970	1975	1979	1984	1970	1975	1979	1984
	(1)	(2)	(3)	(4)	(5)	(6)	(7)	(8)	(9)	(10)	(11)	(12)
LEBANON‡	...	33	25	13	...	283	...	234	...	...	...	...
MACAU‡	6	...	6	10	...	...	59	242	...	...	...	...
MALAYSIA	37	31	44	*40	783	1 038	1 796	*1 670	72	84	...	323
MALDIVES	...	1	...	–	...	...	...	–	...	...	...	–
MONGOLIA	2	1	1	1	133	112	112	156	107	78	69	84
NEPAL‡	16	29	29	13	27	96	...	48	...	...	...	...
PAKISTAN‡	...	102	119	...	...	358	1 095	...	...	...	13	...
PHILIPPINES‡	17	15	19	22	502	686	972	2 022	...	...	...	...
QATAR	–	1	3	...	–	...	...	...	–	...	...	...
SAUDI ARABIA	5	...	12	12	60	...	...	...	10	...	...	...
SINGAPORE	12	10	11	10	...	449	588	700	...	198	246	277
SRI LANKA	24	18	22	21	612	...	...	...	49	...	...	...
SYRIAN ARAB REPUBLIC‡	5	6	6	6	...	...	104	89	...	...	12	...
THAILAND‡	35	...	18	25	749	...	1 943	...	21	...	...	...
TURKEY‡	437	...	1 115	457	...	...	3 880	...	...	...	...	...
UNITED ARAB EMIRATES‡	...	2	3	7	...	2	28	86	...	...	...	...
VIET-NAM‡	...	...	3	3	...	...	500	500	...	...	...	...
YEMEN	6	...	...	3	56	...	...	...	12	...	...	...
EUROPE												
ALBANIA‡	3	2	2	2	105	115	145	145	...	47	54	49
AUSTRIA‡	33	30	...	29	...	2 405	...	2 735	...	320	...	365
BELGIUM	49	30	26	26	...	2 340	2 242	2 209	...	239	228	223
BULGARIA	12	13	12	12	1 642	2 023	2 093	2 298	193	232	237	255
CZECHOSLOVAKIA	28	29	30	27	3 641	4 436	4 641	4 609	254	300	306	298
DENMARK	58	49	49	47	1 790	1 723	1 876	1 837	363	341	367	359
FINLAND	67	60	62	67	...	2 100	2 289	2 599	...	446	480	535
FRANCE‡	106	92	90	101	12 067	10 615	10 619	11 598	238	201	199	212
GERMAN DEMOCRATIC REPUBLIC	...	40	39	39	...	7 946	8 658	9 199	...	472	517	550
GERMANY, FEDERAL REPUBLIC OF‡	1 093	375	380	...	19 701	22 702	25 016	21 362	...	...	...	350
GIBRALTAR	2	1	1	1	6	3	2	*2	242	111	...	*17
GREECE	110	106	116	...	705	921	...	...	80	102	...	...
HOLY SEE‡	1	1	1	1	70	70	70	70	.	.	.	.
HUNGARY	27	27	27	27	2 207	2 455	2 585	2 718	213	233	242	254
ICELAND	5	5	6	4	86	93	127	113	421	427	561	469
IRELAND	7	7	7	7	686	693	771	663	232	216	229	186
ITALY	73	78	75	...	*7 700	*6 469	5 308	...	*144	*116	94	...
LIECHTENSTEIN	1	...	2	2	5	...	12	15	248	...	...	536
LUXEMBOURG	7	7	5	4	130	130	130	...	384	359	358	...
MALTA	6	6	5	4	...	...	...	...	...	...	...	...
MONACO	3	2	2	2	...	...	11	...	...	...	407	...
NETHERLANDS	169	...	80	84	*4 100	...	4 553	4 474	*315	...	323	310
NORWAY	81	80	83	82	1 487	1 657	1 859	2 071	384	414	457	501
POLAND	43	44	44	45	6 832	8 429	8 433	7 887	209	248	239	214
PORTUGAL‡	33	30	22	30	*743	*612	*493	599	*86	*65	*50	...
ROMANIA	55	20	35	36	3 422	*3 015	*3 998	3 609	168	*142	*182	*158
SAN MARINO‡	3	...	3	7	1	...	1	...	...	...	...	...
SPAIN	116	115	105	102	3 450	3 491	...	3 053	102	98	...	80
SWEDEN	114	112	114	99	4 324	4 413	4 378	4 340	538	539	529	521
SWITZERLAND	117	...	88	90	2 318	...	2 501	2 494	370	...	395	392
UNITED KINGDOM‡	...	111	120	108	...	24 127	25 221	23 206	...	431	...	414
YUGOSLAVIA	24	26	27	27	1 738	1 896	2 282	2 609	85	89	103	114
OCEANIA												
AMERICAN SAMOA	1	1	2	2	3	4	10	8	96	120	313	229
AUSTRALIA	58	70	63	...	4 028	5 336	4 851	...	321	392	335	...
COOK ISLANDS	...	1	1	1	...	0.8	2	2	...	44	...	100
FIJI‡	1	1	2	2	16	20	54	21	31	35	87	...
FRENCH POLYNESIA	4	4	2	...	10	11	13	...	93	83	87	...
GUAM	2	1	1	1	17	18	25	18	195	191	235	161
NEW CALEDONIA	1	...	1	1	7	...	15	13	64	...	...	86
NEW ZEALAND	40	40	37	37	1 058	...	1 068	...	375	...	338	...
PAPUA NEW GUINEA	1	1	1	1	...	...	19	27	...	...	6	8
U.S.S.R.												
U.S.S.R.	639	691	...	724	81 633	100 928	...	116 096	338	398	...	422
BYELORUSSIAN S.S.R.	24	25	27	28	1 765	2 214	2 397	2 513	195	237	251	...
UKRAINIAN S.S.R.‡	2 618	2 029	1 755	1 743	...	24 344	23 837	23 000	...	...	...	...

General note/Note generale/Nota general:

E--> It is known or believed that no daily general-interest newspapers are published in the following 39 countries and territories: Africa: Cape Verde, Central African Republic, Comoros, Djibouti, Mauritania, St Helena, Sao Tome and Principe, Western Sahara. America, North: British Virgin Islands, Cayman Islands, Dominica, Greenland, Grenada, Montserrat, Panama-Former Canal Zone, St. Christopher Nevis and Anguilla, St. Lucia, St. Pierre and Miquelon, St. Vincent and the Grenadines, Turks and Caicos Islands. America, South: Falkland Islands (Malvinas). Asia: Bhutan, Brunei Darussalam, East Timor, Maldives, Oman. Europe: Andorra, Faeroe Islands. Oceania: Kiribati, Nauru, Niue, Norfolk Island, Pacific Islands, Samoa, Solomon Islands, Tokelau, Tonga, Tuvalu, Vanuatu.

FR-> Les renseignements disponibles indiquent ou permettent de penser qu'il ne paraît aucun journal quotidien d'information générale dans les 39 pays ou territoires dont la liste suit: Afrique: Cap-Vert, Comores, Djibouti, Mauritanie, Republique Centrafricaine, Sahara occidental, Sainte-Hélène, Sao Tomé et Principe. Amérique du Nord: Dominique, Grenade, Groe$nland, Iles Cai$manes, Iles Vierges britanniques, Iles Turques et Cai$ques, Montserrat, Panama Ancienne Zone du Canal, Saint-Christophe et Nevis et Anguilla, Sainte Lucie, Saint-Pierre et Miquelon, St.-Vincent-et-Grenadines. Amérique du Sud: Iles Falkland (Malvinas). Asie: Bhutan, Brunei Darussalam, Maldives, Oman, Timor Oriental. Europe: Andorre, Iles Féroé. Océanie: Ile Norfolk, Iles du Pacifique, Iles Salomon, Kiribati Nauru, Nioué, Samoa, Tokelaou, Tonga, Tuvalu, Vanuatu.

ESP> La información disponible indica o permite pensar que no se publica ningún periódico diario de información general en los 39 países y territorios siguientes: Africa: Cabo Verde, Comores, Mauritania, República centroafricana, Sahara occidental, Santa Elena, Santo Tome y Principe, Yibuti. América del Norte: Dominica, Granada, Groenlandia, Islas Caimán, Islas Turcas y Caicos, Islas Virgenes Británicas, Montserrat, Panamá Antigua Zona del Canal, Santa Lucía, San Cristobal y Nevis y Anguilla, San Pedro y Miquelón, San Vicente y Granadinas. América del Sur: Islas Falkland (Malvinas). Asia: Brunei Darussalam, Bután, Maldivas, Omán, Timor Oriental. Europa: Andorra, Islas Feroé. Oceanía: Isla Norfolk, Islas del Pacífico, Islas Salomón, Kiribati, Nauru, Niue, Samoa, Tokelau, Tonga, Tuvalu, Vanuatu.

AFRICA:

Angola:

E--> For 1975, the circulation figure refers to 1 daily only.

FR-> Pour 1975, le chiffre relatif au tirage ne se réfère qu'à 1 quotidien.

ESP> En 1975, la cifra relativa a la tirada se refiere a 1 diario solamente.

Côte d'Ivoire:

E--> For 1975, the circulation figure refers to 2 dailies only.

FR-> Pour 1975, le chiffre relatif au tirage ne se réfère qu'à 2 quotidiens.

ESP> En 1975, la cifra relativa a la tirada se refiere a 2 diarios solamente.

Egypt:

E--> For 1979, the circulation figure refers to 8 dailies only.

FR-> Pour 1979, le chiffre relatif au tirage ne se réfère qu'à 8 quotidiens.

ESP> En 1979, la cifra relativa a la tirada se refiere a 8 diarios solamente.

Ethiopia:

E--> For 1970, the circulation figure refers to 6 dailies only.

FR-> Pour 1970, le chiffre relatif au tirage ne se réfère qu'à 6 quotidiens.

ESP> En 1970, la cifra relativa a la tirada se refiere a 6 diarios solamente.

Ghana:

E--> For 1979, the circulation figure refers to 4 dailies only.

FR-> Pour 1979, le chiffre relatif au tirage ne se réfère qu'à 4 quotidiens.

ESP> En 1979, la cifra relativa a la tirada se refiere a 4 diarios solamente.

Liberia:

E--> For 1984, the circulation figure refers to 2 dailies only.

FR-> Pour 1984, le chiffre relatif au tirage ne se réfère qu'à 2 quotidiens.

ESP> En 1984, la cifra relativa a la tirada se refiere a 2 diarios solamente.

Madagascar:

E--> For 1979, the circulation figure refers to 3 dailies only.

FR-> Pour 1979, le chiffre relatif au tirage ne se réfère qu'à 3 quotidiens.

ESP> En 1979, la cifra relativa a la tirada se refiere a 3 diarios solamente.

Morocco:

E--> Data on circulation refer, in 1970 to 10 dailies, in 1975 to 6 dailies, in 1979 and in 1984 to 7 dailies only.

FR-> Les données relatives au tirage concernent 10 quotidiens en 1970, 6 quotidiens en 1975 et 7 quotidiens en 1979 et 1984.

ESP> Los datos relativos a la tirada se refieren a 10 diarios en 1970, a 6 diarios en 1975 y a 7 diarios en 1979 y 1984.

Mozambique:

E--> For 1970, the circulation figure refers to 5 dailies only.

Mozambique: (Cont):

FR-> Pour 1970, le chiffre relatif au tirage ne se réfère qu'à 5 quotidiens.

ESP> En 1970, la cifra relativa a la tirada se refiere a 5 diarios solamente.

Nigeria:

E--> Data on circulation refer, in 1970, to 15 dailies, in 1975 to 10 dailies and in 1984 to 5 dailies only.

FR-> Les données relatives au tirage concernent 15 quotidiens en 1970, 10 quotidiens en 1975 et 5 quotidiens en 1984.

ESP> Los datos relativos a la tirada se refieren a 15 diarios en 1970, a 10 diarios en 1975 y a 5 diarios en 1984.

South Africa:

E--> For 1984, the circulation figure refers to 21 dailies only.

FR-> Pour 1984, le chiffre relatif au tirage ne se réfère qu'à 21 quotidiens.

ESP> En 1984, la cifra relativa a la tirada se refiere a 21 diarios solamente.

Swaziland:

E--> For 1984, the circulation figure refers to 1 daily only.

FR-> Pour 1984, le chiffre relatif au tirage ne se réfère qu'à 1 quotidien.

ESP> En 1984, la cifra relativa a la tirada se refiere a 1 diario solamente.

Togo:

E--> For 1984, the circulation figure refers to 1 daily only.

FR-> Pour 1984, le chiffre relatif au tirage ne se réfère qu'à 1 quotidien.

ESP> En 1984, la cifra relativa a la tirada se refiere a 1 diario solamente.

Tanzania, United Republic of:

E--> For 1975, the circulation figure refers to 2 dailies only.

FR-> Pour 1975, le chiffre relatif au tirage ne se réfère qu'à 2 quotidiens.

ESP> En 1975, la cifra relativa a la tirada se refiere a 2 diarios solamente.

Zaire:

E--> For 1979, the circulation figure refers to 3 dailies only.

FR-> Pour 1979, le chiffre relatif au tirage ne se réfère qu'à 3 quotidiens.

ESP> En 1979, la cifra relativa a la tirada se refiere a 3 diarios solamente.

AMERICA, NORTH:

Canada:

E--> For 1975, the circulation figure refers to 117 dailies only.

FR-> Pour 1975, le chiffre relatif au tirage ne se réfère qu'à 117 quotidiens.

ESP> En 1975, la cifra relativa a la tirada se refiere a 117 diarios solamente.

Cuba:

E--> For 1975, the circulation figure refers to 2 dailies only.

FR-> Pour 1975, le chiffre relatif au tirage ne se réfère qu'à 2 quotidiens.

ESP> En 1975, la cifra relativa a la tirada se refiere a 2 diarios solamente.

Dominican Republic:

E--> For 1975, the circulation figure refers to 7 dailies only.

FR-> Pour 1975, le chiffre relatif au tirage ne se réfère qu'à 7 quotidiens.

ESP> En 1975, la cifra relativa a la tirada se refiere a 7 diarios solamente.

El Salvador:

E--> Data on circulation refer, in 1970 to 10 dailies, in 1975 to 8 dailies, in 1979 to 9 dailies and in 1984 to 5 dailies.

FR-> Les données relatives au tirage concernent 10 quotidiens en 1970, 8 quotidiens en 1975, 9 quotidiens en 1979 et 5 quotidiens en 1984.

ESP> Los datos relativos a la tirada se refieren a 10 diarios en 1970, 8 en 1975, 9 en 1979 y 5 diarios en 1984.

Grenada:

E--> For 1970, the circulation figure refers to 1 daily only.

FR-> Pour 1970, le chiffre relatif au tirage ne se réfère qu'à 1 quotidien.

ESP> En 1970, la cifra relativa a la tirada se refiere a 1 diario solamente.

Guatemala:

E--> For 1984, the circulation figure refers to 3 dailies only.

FR-> Pour 1984, le chiffre relatif au tirage ne se réfère qu'à 3 quotidiens.

ESP> En 1984, la cifra relativa a la tirada se refiere a 3 diarios solamente.

Haiti:

E--> For 1984, the circulation figure refers to 3 dailies only.

FR-> Pour 1984, le chiffre relatif au tirage ne se réfère qu'à 3 quotidiens.

ESP> En 1984, la cifra relativa a la tirada se refiere a 3 diarios solamente.

Honduras:
E--> Data on circulation refer, in 1975 to 4, and in 1984 to 5 dailies only.
FR-> Les données relatives au tirage ne concernent que 4 quotidiens en 1975 et 5 quotidiens en 1984.
ESP> Los datos relativos a la tirada se refieren a 4 diarios en 1975 y a 5 diarios en 1984.
Netherlands Antilles:
E--> For 1984, the circulation figure refers to 5 dailies only.
FR-> Pour 1984, le chiffre relatif au tirage ne se réfère qu'à 5 quotidiens.
ESP> En 1984, la cifra relativa a la tirada se refiere a 5 diarios solamente.
Nicaragua:
E--> For 1975, the circulation figure refers to 6 dailies only.
FR-> Pour 1975, le chiffre relatif au tirage ne se réfère qu'à 6 quotidiens.
ESP> En 1975, la cifra relativa a la tirada se refiere a 6 diarios solamente.
Panama:
E--> For 1984, the circulation figure refers to 5 dailies only.
FR-> Pour 1984, le chiffre relatif au tirage ne se réfère qu'à 5 quotidiens.
ESP> En 1984, la cifra relativa a la tirada se refiere a 5 diarios solamente.
Trinidad and Tobago:
E--> For 1975, the circulation figure refers to 2 dailies only.
FR-> Pour 1975, le chiffre relatif au tirage ne se réfère qu'à 2 quotidiens.
ESP> En 1975, la cifra relativa a la tirada se refiere a 2 diarios solamente.
AMERICA, SOUTH:
Argentina:
E--> Data on circulation refer, in 1970, to 154 dailies, in 1975 to 147.
FR-> Les données relatives au tirage concernent 154 quotidiens en 1970 et 147 en 1975.
ESP> Los datos relativos a la tirada se refieren a 154 diarios en 1970 y a 147 en 1975.
Bolivia:
E--> For 1970, the circulation figure refers to 13 dailies only.
FR-> Pour 1970, le chiffre relatif au tirage ne se réfère qu'à 13 quotidiens.
ESP> En 1970, la cifra relativa a la tirada se refiere a 13 diarios solamente.
Brazil:
E--> Data shown in the 1975 and 1979 columns refer to 1976 and 1978 respectively.
FR-> Les données pour 1975 et 1979 se réfèrent à 1976 et 1978 respectivement.
ESP> Los datos en 1975 y 1979 se refieren a 1976 y 1978 respectivamente.
Colombia:
E--> Data on circulation refer in 1975 to 34 dailies, in 1979 to 33, and in 1984 to 26.
FR-> Les données relatives au tirage concernent 34 quotidiens en 1975, 33 en 1979, et 26 en 1984.
ESP> Los datos relativos a la tirada se refieren a 34 diarios en 1975, a 33 en 1979 y a 26 en 1984.
Ecuador:
E--> For 1984, the circulation figure refers to 15 dailies only.
FR-> Pour 1984, le chiffre relatif au tirage ne se réfère qu'à 15 quotidiens.
ESP> En 1984, la cifra relativa a la tirada se refiere a 15 diarios solamente.
Paraguay:
E--> Data on circulation refer in 1970 to 5 dailies, in 1975, 1979 and 1984 to 4 dailies only.
FR-> Pour 1970, les données relatives au tirage se réfèrent à 5 quotidiens; en 1975, 1979 et 1984 à 4 quotidiens seulement.
ESP> En 1970, las cifras relativas a la tirada se refieren a 5 diarios; en 1975, 1979 y 1984 a 4 diarios solamente.
Peru:
E--> For 1970, the circulation figure refers to 59 dailies only.
FR-> Pour 1970, le chiffre relatif au tirage ne se réfère qu'à 59 quotidiens.
ESP> En 1970, la cifra relativa a la tirada se refiere a 59 diarios solamente.
Suriname:
E--> For 1975, the circulation figure refers to 6 dailies, in 1979 to 3 dailies and in 1984 to 2 dailies only.
FR-> Pour 1979, le chiffre relatif au tirage ne se réfère qu'à 6 quotidiens, 3 quotidiens en 1979 et 2 quotidiens en 1984.
ESP> En 1975, la cifra relativa a la tirada se refiere a 6 diarios y a 3 diarios en 1979 y a 2 diarios en 1984 solamente.
Uruguay:
E--> Data on circulation refer in 1975 to 19 dailies, and in 1984 to 17 dailies only.

Uruguay: (Cont):
FR-> Les données relatives au tirage en 1975 concernent 19 quotidiens et en 1984, 17 quotidiens seulement.
ESP> Los datos relativos a la tirada se refieren a 19 diarios en 1975 y a 17 diarios en 1984.
Venezuela:
E--> For 1975, the circulation figure refers to 30 dailies only.
FR-> Pour 1975, le chiffre relatif au tirage ne se réfère qu'à 30 quotidiens.
ESP> En 1975, la cifra relativa a la tirada se refiere a 30 diarios solamente.
ASIA:
Afghanistan:
E--> Data on circulation refer in 1979 to 9 dailies and in 1984 to 7 dailies only.
FR-> Les chiffres relatifs au tirage ne concernent que 9 quotidiens en 1979 et 7 quotidiens en 1984.
ESP> Las cifras relativas a la tirada se refieren a 9 diarios en 1979 y a 7 diarios en 1984.
Bahrain:
E--> For 1984, the circulation figure refers to 2 dailies only.
FR-> Pour 1984, le chiffre relatif au tirage ne se réfère qu'à 2 quotidiens.
ESP> En 1984, la cifra relativa a la tirada se refiere a 2 diarios solamente.
Bangladesh:
E--> For 1975, the circulation figure refers to 27 dailies only.
FR-> Pour 1975, le chiffre relatif au tirage ne se réfère qu'à 27 quotidiens.
ESP> En 1975, la cifra relativa a la tirada se refiere a 27 diarios solamente.
Cyprus:
E--> For 1975, the circulation figure refers to 10 dailies and in 1979 to 9 dailies only.
FR-> Pour 1975, le chiffre relatif au tirage ne se réfère qu'à 10 quotidiens et en 1979 à 9 quotidiens.
ESP> En 1975, la cifra relativa a la tirada se refiere a 10 diarios y en 1979 a 9 diarios solamente.
Democratic Yemen:
E--> For 1979 and 1984, the circulation figures refer to only 2 dailies.
FR-> Pour 1979 et 1984, les chiffres relatifs au tirage ne se réfèrent qu'à 2 quotidiens.
ESP> En 1979 y 1984, las cifras relativas a la tirada se refieren a 2 diarios solamente.
Iran, Islamic Republic of:
E--> For 1970, the circulation figure refers to 18 dailies only.
FR-> Pour 1970, le chiffre relatif au tirage ne se réfère qu'à 18 quotidiens.
ESP> En 1970, la cifra relativa a la tirada se refiere a 18 diarios solamente.
Iraq:
E--> Data on circulation refer in 1975 to 5 dailies, in 1979 and 1984 to 4 dailies only.
FR-> Les données relatives au tirage en 1975 concernent 5 quotidiens, en 1979 et 1984 4 quotidiens seulememnt.
ESP> Los datos relativos a la tirada se refieren a 5 diarios en 1975, a 4 diarios en 1979 y 1984 solamente.
Israel:
E--> For 1984, the circulation figure refers to 23 dailies only.
FR-> Pour 1984, le chiffre relatif au tirage ne se réfère qu'à 23 quotidiens.
ESP> En 1984, la cifra relativa a la tirada se refiere a 23 diarios solamente.
Korea, Democratic People's Republic of:
E--> For 1984, the circulation figure refers to 1 daily only.
FR-> Pour 1984, le chiffre relatif au tirage ne se réfère qu'à 1 quotidien.
ESP> En 1984, la cifra relativa a la tirada se refiere a 1 diario solamente.
Korea, Republic of:
E--> For 1979, the circulation figure refers to 26 dailies and in 1984 to 13 dailies only.
FR-> Pour 1979, le chiffre relatif au tirage ne se réfère qu'à 26 quotidiens, et en 1984 à 13 quotidiens.
ESP> En 1979, la cifra relativa a la tirada se refiere a 26 diarios y en 1984 a 13 diarios solamente.
Lao, People's Democratic Republic:
E--> For 1975, the circulation figure refers to 1 daily only.
FR-> Pour 1975, le chiffre relatif au tirage ne se réfère qu'à 1 quotidien.
ESP> En 1975, la cifra relativa a la tirada se refiere a 1 diario solamente.
Lebanon:
E--> Data on circulation refer in 1975 to 17 dailies, and in 1984 to 6 dailies only.
FR-> Les données relatives au tirage en 1975 ne se réfèrent qu'à 17 quotidiens et en 1984 à 6 quotidiens.

Lebanon: (Cont):
ESP> Los datos relativos a la tirada se refieren a 17 diarios en 1975 y a 6 diarios en 1984.
Macau:
E--> Data on circulation refer in 1979 and 1984 to 5 dailies only.
FR-> Les données relatives au tirage en 1979 et 1984 ne se réfèrent qu'à 5 quotidiens.
ESP> Los datos relativos a la tirada se refieren a 5 diarios en 1979 y 1984.
Nepal:
E--> Data for circulation refer, in 1970, to 11 dailies, in 1975 to 13 and in 1984 to 7 dailies only.
FR-> Les données relatives au tirage se réfèrent en 1970 à 11 quotidiens, en 1975 à 13 et en 1984 à 7 quotidiens seulement.
ESP> Los datos relativos a la tirada se refieren a 11 diarios en 1970, a 13 en 1975 y a 7 diarios en 1984 solamente.
Pakistan:
E--> For 1975, the circulation figure refers to 18 dailies only.
FR-> Pour 1975, le chiffre relatif au tirage ne se réfère qu'à 18 quotidiens.
ESP> En 1975, la cifra relativa a la tirada se refiere a 18 diarios solamente.
Philippines:
E--> Data on circulation refer, in 1970, to 14 dailies, in 1975 to 12, in 1979 to 18 and in 1984 to 21 dailies only.
FR-> Les données relatives au tirage en 1970 se réfèrent à 14 quotidiens, en 1975 à 12, en 1979 à 18 et en 1984 à 21 quotidiens seulement.
ESP> Los datos relativos a la tirada se refieren a 14 diarios en 1970, a 12 en 1975, a 18 en 1979 y a 21 diarios en 1984 solamente.
Syrian Arab Republic:
E--> For 1984, the circulation figure refers to 5 dailies only.
FR-> Pour 1984, le chiffre relatif au tirage ne se réfère qu'à 5 quotidiens.
ESP> En 1984, la cifra relativa a la tirada se refiere a 5 diarios solamente.
Thailand:
E--> For 1979, the circulation figure refers to 17 dailies only.
FR-> Pour 1979, le chiffre relatif au tirage ne se réfère qu'à 17 quotidiens.
ESP> En 1979, la cifra relativa a la tirada se refiere a 17 diarios solamente.
Turkey:
E--> For 1979, data include non-daily newspapers.
FR-> Pour 1979, les données incluent les journaux non quotidiens.
ESP> En 1979, los datos incluyen los periódicos que no son diarios.
United Arab Emirates:
E--> Data on circulation refer in 1975 to 1 daily, in 1979 to 2 and in 1984 to 4 dailies only.
FR-> Les données relatives au tirage en 1975 se réfèrent à 1 quotidien, en 1979 à 2 et en 1984 à 4 quotidiens seulement.
ESP> Los datos relativos a la tirada se refieren a 1 diario en 1975, a 2 en 1979 y a 4 diarios en 1984.
Viet-Nam:
E--> For 1979, the circulation figure refers to 2 dailies and in 1984 to 1 daily only.
FR-> Pour 1979, le chiffre relatif au tirage ne se réfère qu'à 2 quotidiens et en 1984 à 1 quotidien.
ESP> En 1979, la cifra relativa a la tirada se refiere a 2 diarios y en 1984 a 1 diario solamente.
EUROPE:
Albania:
E--> For 1970, the circulation figure refers to 2 dailies only.
FR-> Pour 1970, le chiffre relatif au tirage ne se réfère qu'à 2 quotidiens.
ESP> En 1970, la cifra relativa a la tirada se refiere a 2 diarios solamente.
Austria:
E--> For 1979, the circulation figure refers to 26 dailies only.
FR-> Pour 1979, le chiffre relatif au tirage ne se réfère qu'à 26 quotidiens.
ESP> En 1979, la cifra relativa a la tirada se refiere a 26 diarios solamente.
France:
E--> Data shown in the 1975, 1979 and 1984 columns refer to 1976, 1978 and 1983 respectively.
FR-> Les données pour 1975, 1979 et 1984 se réfèrent à 1976, 1978 et 1983 respectivement.
ESP> Los datos en 1975, 1979 y 1984 se refieren a 1976, 1978 y 1983 respectivamente.
Germany, Federal Republic of:
E--> For 1970, the number of dailies includes regional editions. For 1975 and 1979 the data include non-daily newspapers. Data for 1984 refers to 1983.
FR-> Pour 1970 le nombre de quotidiens inclut les éditions régionales. Pour 1975 et 1979 les données incluent les journaux non quotidiens. Les données pour 1984 se réfèrent à 1983.
ESP> En 1970 el número de diarios incluye las ediciones regionales. En 1975 y 1979 los datos incluyen los periódicos que no son diarios. Los datos en 1984 se refieren a 1983.
Holy See:
E--> The figures refer to the State of the Vatican City.
FR-> Les chiffres se réfèrent à l'Etat de la Cité du Vatican.
ESP> Las cifras se refieren al Estado de la Ciudad del Vaticano.
Portugal:
E--> For 1984, the circulation figure refers to 17 dailies only.
FR-> Pour 1984, le chiffre relatif au tirage ne se réfère qu'à 17 quotidiens.
ESP> En 1984, la cifra relativa a la tirada se refiere a 17 diarios solamente.
San Marino:
E--> The circulation figures refer to 1 daily only.
FR-> Les chiffres relatifs au tirage ne se réfèrent qu'à 1 quotidien.
ESP> Las cifras relativas a la tirada se refieren a 1 diario solamente.
United Kingdom:
E--> For 1979, the circulation figure refers to 117 dailies only.
FR-> Pour 1979, le chiffre relatif au tirage ne se réfère qu'à 117 quotidiens.
ESP> En 1979, la cifra relativa a la tirada se refiere a 117 diarios solamente.
OCEANIA:
Fiji:
E--> For 1984, the circulation figure refers to 1 daily only.
FR-> Pour 1984, le chiffre relatif au tirage ne se réfère qu'à 1 quotidien.
ESP> En 1984, la cifra relativa a la tirada se refiere a 1 diario solamente.
U.S.S.R.:
Ukrainian S.S.R.:
E--> Data include non-daily newspapers.
FR-> Les données incluent les journaux non quotidiens.
ESP> Los datos incluyen los periódicos que no son diarios.

7.20 Non-daily general-interest newspapers and other periodicals: number and circulation (total and per 1,000 inhabitants)

Journaux non quotidiens d'information générale et autres périodiques: nombre et tirage (total et pour 1 000 habitants)

Periódicos de información general que no son diarios y otras publicaciones periódicas: número y tirada (total y por 1 000 habitantes)

NUMBER OF COUNTRIES AND TERRITORIES PRESENTED IN THIS TABLE: 102

NOMBRE DE PAYS ET DE TERRITOIRES PRESENTES DANS CE TABLEAU: 102

NUMERO DE PAISES Y DE TERRITORIOS PRESENTADOS EN ESTE CUADRO: 102

COUNTRY / PAYS / PAIS	YEAR / ANNEE / AÑO	NON-DAILY NEWSPAPERS / JOURNAUX NON QUOTIDIENS / PERIODICOS NO DIARIOS: NUMBER / NOMBRE / NUMERO			NON-DAILY NEWSPAPERS: ESTIMATED CIRCULATION / TIRAGE (ESTIMATION) / TIRADA (ESTIMACION)		OTHER PERIODICALS / AUTRES PERIODIQUES / OTRAS PUBLICACIONES PERIODICAS	OTHER PERIODICALS: ESTIMATED CIRCULATION / TIRAGE (ESTIMATION) / TIRADA (ESTIMACION)	
		TOTAL / TOTAL / TOTAL	1 – 3 TIMES A WEEK / 1 A 3 FOIS PAR SEMAINE / 1 A 3 VECES POR SEMANA	ISSUED LESS FREQUENTLY / PARAISSANT MOINS FREQUEMMENT / PUBLICADOS CON MENOR FRECUENCIA	TOTAL (000) / TOTAL (000) / TOTAL (000)	PER 1,000 INHABITANTS / POUR 1 000 HABITANTS / POR 1 000 HABITANTES	NUMBER / NOMBRE / NUMERO	TOTAL (000) / TOTAL (000) / TOTAL (000)	PER 1,000 INHABITANTS / POUR 1 000 HABITANTS / POR 1 000 HABITANTES
		(1)	(2)	(3)	(4)	(5)	(6)	(7)	(8)
AFRICA									
ALGERIA	1982	15	3	12	309	16	27	476	24
BOTSWANA	1984	...	...	...	...	...	20	153	144
BURKINA FASO	1984	1	5	...	5.0	1	...	...	...
CAMEROON	1984	3	3	...	35	4	...	...	...
CHAD	1983	1	1	–	1	...	...	...	...
CONGO	1984	2	2	–	15	9	...	...	...
COTE D'IVOIRE	1982	6	6	–	145	17	12	325	37
EGYPT	1982	25	13	12	1 996	46	204	1 841	42
ETHIOPIA	1984	4	4	–	40	1	3	178	4
KENYA	1982	2	2	–	281	15	...	...	...
LESOTHO	1982	1	1	–	10	7	2	11	7
MADAGASCAR	1982	11	11	–	36	4	...	...	...
MAURITIUS	1982	7	7	–	92	93	...	...	...
REUNION	1982	2	1	1	9.0	17	...	...	...
RWANDA‡	1984	4	1	3	33	6	8	...	...
ST. HELENA	1982	1	1	–	1.2	240	...	...	...
SENEGAL	1984	4	4	–	...	...	29	...	...
SEYCHELLES	1984	1	1	–	3.2	44	2	1.6	22
SUDAN	1984	9	6	3	121	6	25	195	9
ZAIRE	1984	9	7	2	115	4	106	225	8
AMERICA, NORTH									
BELIZE	1981	7	6	1	45	285	...	...	...
BERMUDA	1984	1	1	–	14	182	...	...	...
BRITISH VIRGIN ISLANDS	1984	2	2	–	3.6	300	20	*23	*1 950
CANADA‡	1984	1 229	1 085	144	14 200	565	1 382	59 071	2 348
COSTA RICA	1982	4	4	–	818	341	274	163	68
CUBA	1984	5	5	–	62	6	47	2 279	228
GUADELOUPE	1982	26	8	18	69	208	45	142	427
MARTINIQUE	1982	8	7	1	17	52	8	17	52
MEXICO	1984	43	39	4	708	9	232	26 509	344
ST. CHRISTOPHER AND NEVIS AND ANGUILLA	1984	3	3	–	7.0	...	...	...	...
ST. LUCIA	1984	1	1	–	4.5	35	...	...	...
UNITED STATES‡	1984	7 464	7 398	66	...	...	59 609	...	...
U.S. VIRGIN ISLANDS	1982	2	2	–	9.0	89	...	...	...
AMERICA, SOUTH									
BOLIVIA	1982	...	...	...	...	...	106	...	...
BRAZIL	1982	1 049	718	331	6 636	52	3 892	946	7
CHILE	1983	25	25	–	44	4	118	909	78
FALKLAND ISLANDS (MALVINAS)	1984	...	...	...	...	...	3	1.6	800
FRENCH GUIANA	1982	14	4	10	29	392	7	6.3	85

COUNTRY / PAYS / PAIS	YEAR / ANNEE / AÑO	NON-DAILY NEWSPAPERS / JOURNAUX NON QUOTIDIENS / PERIODICOS NO DIARIOS					OTHER PERIODICALS / AUTRES PERIODIQUES / OTRAS PUBLICACIONES PERIODICAS		
		NUMBER / NOMBRE / NUMERO			ESTIMATED CIRCULATION / TIRAGE (ESTIMATION) / TIRADA (ESTIMACION)			ESTIMATED CIRCULATION / TIRAGE (ESTIMATION) / TIRADA (ESTIMACION)	
		TOTAL / TOTAL / TOTAL	1 – 3 TIMES A WEEK / 1 A 3 FOIS PAR SEMAINE / 1 A 3 VECES POR SEMANA	ISSUED LESS FREQUENTLY / PARAISSANT MOINS FREQUEMMENT / PUBLICADOS CON MENOR FRECUENCIA	TOTAL (000) / TOTAL (000) / TOTAL (000)	PER 1,000 INHABITANTS / POUR 1 000 HABITANTS / POR 1 000 HABITANTES	NUMBER / NOMBRE / NUMERO	TOTAL (000) / TOTAL (000) / TOTAL (000)	PER 1,000 INHABITANTS / POUR 1 000 HABITANTS / POR 1 000 HABITANTES
		(1)	(2)	(3)	(4)	(5)	(6)	(7)	(8)
PERU	1982	37	37	——>	...	...	507	...	...
SURINAME	1983	...	...	...	...	...	22	44	119
URUGUAY	1982	...	...	...	...	...	545	...	...
VENEZUELA	1982	45	31	14	468	29	160	4 649	292
ASIA									
BANGLADESH	1984	129	108	21	522	5	...	...	...
BRUNEI DARUSSALAM	1984	1	1	–	46	209	19	128	582
CHINA	1982	224	144	80	46 089	45	3 100	138 852	136
CYPRUS‡	1984	51	12	39	155	235	35	93	141
HONG KONG	1984	5	2	3	...	...	495	...	...
INDIA	1982	...	...	...	...	...	19 937	50 094	70
INDONESIA	1982	206	127	79	4 306	27	...	...	...
IRAN, ISLAMIC REPUBLIC OF	1982	41	25	11	...	...	180	...	...
ISRAEL	1981	52	26	26	...	...	1 100	...	...
JAPAN	1984	...	...	...	...	...	2 138	36 293	303
JORDAN	1984	4	4	–	2.2	1	41	211	62
KUWAIT	1982	3	3	–	475	314	45	982	649
MALAYSIA	1984	20	20	–	4 292	283	1 631	1 689	111
MONGOLIA	1984	35	33	2	718	387	38	663	357
QATAR	1982	1	1	–	3.5	14	...	...	...
SAUDI ARABIA	1984	7	4	3	...	...	58	...	...
SINGAPORE	1984	7	7	–	425	168	1 786	...	...
SRI LANKA‡	1984	81	43	38	...	...	454	42 512	2 106
THAILAND	1984	216	163	53	...	...	1 189	...	...
TURKEY	1984	519	206	313	...	...	1 257	...	...
YEMEN	1984	15	12	3	...	...	40	...	...
EUROPE									
ANDORRA	1984	...	4	...	...	...	15	15	374
AUSTRIA	1984	143	143	–	...	...	2 315	...	...
BELGIUM	1984	2	2	–	22	2	11 256	...	...
BULGARIA	1984	37	34	3	1 092	121	1 758	10 211	1 133
CZECHOSLOVAKIA	1984	118	118	–	1 239	80	926	22 123	1 428
DENMARK	1984	11	11	–	1 249	244	...	...	...
FAEROE ISLANDS	1983	8	...	...	36	878	...	...	...
FINLAND	1984	311	287	24	...	...	4 432	...	...
FRANCE	1981	526	412	114	16 282	303	22 443	195 381	3 630
GERMAN DEMOCRATIC REPUBLIC	1984	30	30	–	9 302	556	1 191	23 116	1 383
GERMANY, FEDERAL REPUBLIC OF	1983	46	46	–	4 550	74	6 702	255 905	4 188
GIBRALTAR	1984	5	5	–	*5.7	*184	15	3.8	123
GREECE	1982	875	213	662	...	...	821	...	...
HOLY SEE	1984	...	...	...	...	...	48	42	42 000
HUNGARY	1984	94	17	77	6 007	562	1 535	13 278	1 243
IRELAND	1984	59	59	–	1 785	500	252	2 959	829
ITALY	1982	414	...	...	...	...	8 265	...	...
LIECHTENSTEIN	1984	1	–	1	3.9	139	...	...	...
LUXEMBOURG‡	1982	4	4	...	...	...	427	...	...
MALTA	1984	9	7	2	...	...	264	...	...
MONACO	1982	...	...	...	...	...	105	792	30 465
NETHERLANDS	1984	*110	*110	–	*800	*55	...	...	...
NORWAY	1984	81	81	–	407	99	3 881	...	...
POLAND‡	1984	51	49	2	2 846	77	2 718	39 057	1 061
PORTUGAL	1982	...	107	...	...	...	915	...	...
ROMANIA	1984	24	24	–	122	5	435	709	31
SAN MARINO	1982	8	–	8	11	524	11	...	...
SWEDEN	1984	75	75	–	467	56	...	...	...
SWITZERLAND	1982	167	151	16	883	139	...	...	...
UNITED KINGDOM	1984	882	882	–	30 196	538	6 408	...	...
YUGOSLAVIA	1984	3 036	212	2 824	23 852	1 040	1 474	4 968	217

COUNTRY / PAYS / PAIS	YEAR / ANNEE / AÑO	NON-DAILY NEWSPAPERS / JOURNAUX NON QUOTIDIENS / PERIODICOS NO DIARIOS — NUMBER / NOMBRE / NUMERO: TOTAL	1 – 3 TIMES A WEEK / 1 A 3 FOIS PAR SEMAINE / 1 A 3 VECES POR SEMANA	ISSUED LESS FREQUENTLY / PARAISSANT MOINS FREQUEMMENT / PUBLICADOS CON MENOR FRECUENCIA	ESTIMATED CIRCULATION / TIRAGE (ESTIMATION) / TIRADA (ESTIMACION): TOTAL (000)	PER 1,000 INHABITANTS / POUR 1 000 HABITANTS / POR 1 000 HABITANTES	OTHER PERIODICALS / AUTRES PERIODIQUES / OTRAS PUBLICACIONES PERIODICAS: NUMBER / NOMBRE / NUMERO	ESTIMATED CIRCULATION / TIRAGE (ESTIMATION) / TIRADA (ESTIMACION): TOTAL (000)	PER 1,000 INHABITANTS / POUR 1 000 HABITANTS / POR 1 000 HABITANTES
		(1)	(2)	(3)	(4)	(5)	(6)	(7)	(8)
OCEANIA									
COOK ISLANDS	1982	2	1	1	2.4	126	3	4.4	232
FIJI	1982	4	4	...	74	114	...	...	...
NEW CALEDONIA	1982	3	1	2	24	166	15	27	186
NEW ZEALAND	1984	*148	*118	*30	...	...	*5 788	...	...
TONGA	1982	2	2	–	8.0	79	...	...	...
VANUATU	1984	1	1	–	2.0	15	...	...	...
U.S.S.R.									
U.S.S.R.	1984	7 603	6 476	1 127	69 179	251	5 357	4 279 930	15 544
BYELORUSSIAN S.S.R.	1984	179	167	12	2 655	...	106	2 555	...

AFRICA:
Rwanda:
E--> The circulation figure in column 4 refers to 1 non daily only.
FR-> Le chiffre relatif au tirage, colonne 4 se réfère à 1 non quotidien seulement.
ESP> La cifra sobre la tirada, columna 4, se refiere a 1 periódico no diario solamente.
AMERICA, NORTH:
Canada:
E--> The figure for other periodicals refers to 1983.
FR-> Le chiffre relatif aux autres périodiques se réfère à 1983.
ESP> La cifra relativa a las otras publicaciones periódicas se refiere a 1983.
United States:
E--> The figure for other periodicals refers to 1980 and does not include parish and school magazines.
FR-> Le chiffre relatif aux autres périodiques se réfère à 1980 et ne comprend ni les bulletins paroissiaux ni ceux des écoles.
ESP> La cifra relativa a las otras publicaciones periódicas se refiere a 1980 y no incluye los boletines parroquiales y los boletines escolares.
ASIA:
Cyprus:
E--> Data on other periodicals do not include children's, comics, parish, school magazines and 'house organs'.
FR-> Les données relatives aux autres périodiques ne comprennent pas les périodiques pour enfants, les périodiques humoristiques, les bulletins paroissiaux et des écoles.
ESP> Los datos relativos a las otras publicaciones peiódicas no incluyen los periódicos para niños, los periódicos humorísticos, los boletines parroquiales y los boletines escolares.
Sri Lanka:
E--> The figure for other periodicals refer to 1983.
FR-> Le chiffre relatif aux autres périodiques se réfère à 1983.
ESP> La cifra relativa a las otras publicaciones periódicas se refiere a 1983.
EUROPE:
Luxembourg:
E--> The figure for other periodicals refers to 1984.
FR-> Le chiffre relatif aux autres périodiques se réfère à 1984.
ESP> La cifra relativa a las otras publicaciones periódicas se refiere a 1984.
Poland:
E--> The figures for other periodicals do not include comics, parish and school magazines.
FR-> Les chiffres relatifs aux autres périodiques excluent les périodiques humoristiques, les bulletins paroissiaux et des écoles.
ESP> Los datos relativos a las otras publicaciones periódicas no incluyen los periódicos humorísticos, los boletines parroquiales y escolares.

7.21 Periodicals, other than general-interest newspapers: number and circulation by subject group

Périodiques autres que les journaux d'information générale classés par sujets: nombre et tirage

Publicaciones periódicas distintas de los diarios de información general: número y tirada clasificados por materias

NUMBER = NUMBER OF PERIODICALS

COPIES = ESTIMATED CIRCULATION (IN THOUSANDS)

FOR THE UNIVERSAL DECIMAL CLASSIFICATION (UDC), SEE SECTION 3 OF THE INTRODUCTORY TEXT TO THIS CHAPTER.

NUMBER OF COUNTRIES AND TERRITORIES PRESENTED IN THIS TABLE: 57

NUMBER = NOMBRE DE PERIODIQUES

COPIES = TIRAGE (ESTIMATION) (EN MILLIERS)

POUR LA CLASSIFICATION DECIMALE UNIVERSELLE (CDU), VOIR LA SECTION 3 DU TEXTE D'INTRODUCTION A CE CHAPITRE.

NOMBRE DE PAYS ET DE TERRITOIRES PRESENTES DANS CE TABLEAU: 57

NUMBER = NUMERO DE PUBLICACIONES PERIODICAS

COPIES = TIRADA (ESTIMACION) (EN MILLARES)

PARA LA CLASIFICACION DECIMAL UNIVERSAL (CDU), VEASE LA SECCION 3 DEL TEXTO DE LA INTRODUCCION A ESTE CAPITULO.

NUMERO DE PAISES Y DE TERRITORIOS PRESENTADOS EN ESTE CUADRO: 57

AFRICA

SUBJECT GROUP GROUPE DE SUJETS	ALGERIA (1982)		EGYPT‡ (1982)		LESOTHO (1982)		RWANDA (1984)	SUDAN (1984)	
GRUPO DE MATERIAS	NUMBER	COPIES	NUMBER	COPIES	NUMBER	COPIES	NUMBER	NUMBER	COPIES
TOTAL A+B	27	476.0	204	1841.0	2	10.5	8	25	195.3
A. TOTAL	25	388.0	197	1593.0	2	10.5	8	23	130.5
1. GENERALITIES	–	–	14	158.0	–	–	3	1	15.0
2. PHILOSOPHY, PSYCHOLOGY	–	–	–	–	–	–	–	–	–
3. RELIGION, THEOLOGY	3	49.0	39	272.0	1	.5	–	–	–
4. SOCIOLOGY, STATISTICS	3	12.0	68	399.0	–	–	–	9	25.9
5. POLITICAL SCIENCE ...	4	27.5	./.	./.	–	–	–	3	1.3
6. LAW ...	–	–	./.	./.	–	–	2	–	–
7. MILITARY ART ...	–	–	./.	./.	–	–	1	–	–
8. EDUCATION	–	–	./.	./.	1	10.0	–	4	37.3
9. TRADE, TRANSPORT ...	–	–	./.	./.	–	–	1	1	5.0
10. ETHNOGRAPHY, FOLKLORE ...	1	.5	./.	./.	–	–	–	1	3.0
11. LINGUISTICS, PHILOLOGY	–	–	–	–	–	–	–	–	–
12. MATHEMATICS	–	–	4	20.0	–	–	–	–	–
13. NATURAL SCIENCES	–	–	./.	./.	–	–	–	–	–
14. MEDICAL SCIENCES ...	2	1.5	54	552.0	–	–	–	–	–
15. INDUSTRIES ...	1	4.5	./.	./.	–	–	–	1	3.0
16. AGRICULTURE	–	–	./.	./.	–	–	1	–	–
17. DOMESTIC SCIENCE	–	–	./.	./.	–	–	–	–	–
18. COMMERCIAL TECHNIQUES ...	–	–	./.	./.	–	–	–	–	–
19. ARTS ...	2	13.0	12	162.0	–	–	–	2	31.0
20. GAMES, SPORTS ...	2	124.0	./.	./.	–	–	–	1	9.0
21. LITERATURE	5	148.0	4	28.0	–	–	–	–	–
22. GEOGRAPHY, TRAVEL	–	–	2	2.0	–	–	–	–	–
23. HISTORY, BIOGRAPHY	2	8.0	./.	./.	–	–	–	–	–
B. TOTAL	2	88.0	7	248.0	–	–	–	2	64.8
1. CHILD. & ADOLESCENTS MAGAZINES	1	38.0	7	248.0	–	–	–	2	64.8
2. COMICS AND HUMOUR MAGAZINES	1	50.0	–	–	–	–	–	–	–
3. PARISH MAGAZINES	–	–	–	–	–	–	–	–	–
4. SCHOOL MAGAZINES & NEWSPAPERS	–	–	–	–	–	–	–	–	–
5. 'HOUSE ORGANS'	–	–	–	–	–	–	–	–	–

AMERICA, NORTH

SUBJECT GROUP / GROUPE DE SUJETS / GRUPO DE MATERIAS	ZAIRE (1984)		BRITISH VIRGIN ISLANDS (1984)		CANADA (1983)		COSTA RICA (1982)	
	NUMBER	COPIES	NUMBER	COPIES	NUMBER	COPIES	NUMBER	COPIES
TOTAL A+B	106	225	20	*23.4	1 382	59 071	274	162.7
A. TOTAL	47	132	20	*23.4	1 382	59 071	274	162.7
1. GENERALITIES	8	24	2	*.3	238	12 337	10	13.0
2. PHILOSOPHY, PSYCHOLOGY	1	1	–	–	1	28	3	4.5
3. RELIGION, THEOLOGY	6	12	–	–	30	1 198	–	–
4. SOCIOLOGY, STATISTICS	1	2	–	–	9	600	7	7.5
5. POLITICAL SCIENCE ...	2	2	–	–	14	515	6	9.0
6. LAW ...	3	28	8	*.3	27	526	–	–
7. MILITARY ART ...	2	2	–	–	6	21	4	13.0
8. EDUCATION	1	11	2	*.3	26	548	121	12.1
9. TRADE, TRANSPORT ...	3	5	–	–	80	1 445	–	–
10. ETHNOGRAPHY, FOLKLORE ...	–	–	–	–	10	2 042	–	–
11. LINGUISTICS, PHILOLOGY	2	2	–	–	1	1 472	1	2.5
12. MATHEMATICS	–	–	–	–	17	380	2	2.0
13. NATURAL SCIENCES	–	–	–	–	70	1 431	10	2.5
14. MEDICAL SCIENCES ...	2	3	2	*.5	145	2 959	7	7.0
15. INDUSTRIES ...	–	–	–	–	149	4 791	–	–
16. AGRICULTURE	3	5	–	–	62	4 131	16	34.5
17. DOMESTIC SCIENCE	–	–	–	–	136	3 023	–	–
18. COMMERCIAL TECHNIQUES ...	2	3	–	–	32	692	–	–
19. ARTS ...	3	4	–	–	62	1 336	–	–
20. GAMES, SPORTS ...	4	23	–	–	224	15 835	–	–
21. LITERATURE	–	–	1	*1.0	6	69	85	52.1
22. GEOGRAPHY, TRAVEL	3	4	1	*20.0	32	3 618	–	–
23. HISTORY, BIOGRAPHY	1	1	4	*1.0	5	74	2	3.0
B. TOTAL	59	93	–	–	...	...	–	–
1. CHILD. & ADOLESCENTS MAGAZINES	3	15	–	–	...	...	–	–
2. COMICS AND HUMOUR MAGAZINES	1	5	–	–	...	...	–	–
3. PARISH MAGAZINES	16	36	–	–	...	...	–	–
4. SCHOOL MAGAZINES & NEWSPAPERS	23	8	–	–	...	...	–	–
5. 'HOUSE ORGANS'	16	29	–	–	...	...	–	–

AMERICA, SOUTH

SUBJECT GROUP / GROUPE DE SUJETS / GRUPO DE MATERIAS	CUBA (1984)		GUADELOUPE (1982)		MARTINIQUE (1982)		UNITED STATES‡ (1980)	BOLIVIA (1982)
	NUMBER	COPIES	NUMBER	COPIES	NUMBER	COPIES	NUMBER	NUMBER
TOTAL A+B	47	2279.1	45	142	8	17.0	59 609	106
A. TOTAL	39	1213.7	21	80	8	17.0	54 398	90
1. GENERALITIES	5	573.3	16	50	–	–	1 735	8
2. PHILOSOPHY, PSYCHOLOGY	–	–	–	–	–	–	821	2
3. RELIGION, THEOLOGY	–	–	–	–	1	2.0	2 370	1
4. SOCIOLOGY, STATISTICS	1	3.6	–	–	1	1.0	290	6
5. POLITICAL SCIENCE ...	3	35.2	–	–	–	–	1 588	2
6. LAW ...	–	–	1	10	–	–	4 997	3
7. MILITARY ART ...	4	102.1	–	–	–	–	372	1
8. EDUCATION	–	–	–	–	1	1.0	6 961	7
9. TRADE, TRANSPORT ...	3	23.5	2	7	1	4.0	2 480	7
10. ETHNOGRAPHY, FOLKLORE ...	–	–	–	–	–	–	3 506	4
11. LINGUISTICS, PHILOLOGY	–	–	–	–	–	–	./.	2
12. MATHEMATICS	–	–	–	–	–	–	128	1
13. NATURAL SCIENCES	–	–	–	–	–	–	1 885	2
14. MEDICAL SCIENCES ...	1	13.9	–	–	–	–	3 985	4
15. INDUSTRIES ...	3	59.7	–	–	–	–	7 322	3
16. AGRICULTURE	2	47.2	–	–	–	–	3 458	6
17. DOMESTIC SCIENCE	–	–	–	–	–	–	1 218	–
18. COMMERCIAL TECHNIQUES ...	–	–	–	–	2	7.0	3 174	8
19. ARTS ...	11	298.8	–	–	1	1.0	1 823	8
20. GAMES, SPORTS ...	2	20.9	2	13	1	1.0	3 086	5
21. LITERATURE	4	35.5	–	–	–	–	1 737	2
22. GEOGRAPHY, TRAVEL	–	–	–	–	–	–	677	3
23. HISTORY, BIOGRAPHY	–	–	–	–	–	–	785	5
B. TOTAL	8	1065.4	24	62	–	–	5 211	16
1. CHILD. & ADOLESCENTS MAGAZINES	4	539.1	–	–	–	–	257	3
2. COMICS AND HUMOUR MAGAZINES	4	526.3	–	–	–	–	252	4
3. PARISH MAGAZINES	–	–	1	2	–	–	...	5
4. SCHOOL MAGAZINES & NEWSPAPERS	–	–	3	4	–	–	...	1
5. 'HOUSE ORGANS'	–	–	20	56	–	–	4 702	3

SUBJECT GROUP GROUPE DE SUJETS GRUPO DE MATERIAS	BRAZIL (1982)		FRENCH GUIANA (1982)		PERU (1982)		SURINAME (1983)		URUGUAY (1982)
	NUMBER	COPIES	NUMBER	COPIES	NUMBER		NUMBER	COPIES	NUMBER
TOTAL A+B	3 892	945.5	7	6.3	507		22	44.0	545
A. TOTAL	3 325	837.5	6	5.6	466		20	43.0	485
1. GENERALITIES	1 209	403.6	–	–	95		1	.4	22
2. PHILOSOPHY, PSYCHOLOGY	35	3.4	–	–	3		–	–	2
3. RELIGION, THEOLOGY	224	135.0	–	–	23		2	2.0	31
4. SOCIOLOGY, STATISTICS	80	1.1	–	–	22		–	–	138
5. POLITICAL SCIENCE ...	134	13.0	–	–	55		2	14.5	16
6. LAW ...	330	47.5	–	–	32		3	3.0	20
7. MILITARY ART ...	5	.2	–	–	9		–	–	3
8. EDUCATION	95	12.1	–	–	24		–	–	22
9. TRADE, TRANSPORT ...	118	21.3	2	.5	23		–	–	9
10. ETHNOGRAPHY, FOLKLORE ...	7	.1	–	–	5		1	.9	–
11. LINGUISTICS, PHILOLOGY	10	.01	–	–	4		–	–	–
12. MATHEMATICS	2	.004	–	–	1		–	–	4
13. NATURAL SCIENCES	29	.2	–	–	8		–	–	12
14. MEDICAL SCIENCES ...	156	9.8	–	–	12		–	–	26
15. INDUSTRIES ...	177	13.8	–	–	31		–	–	24
16. AGRICULTURE	181	13.1	1	.6	17		1	.2	25
17. DOMESTIC SCIENCE	30	25.0	–	–	1		–	–	–
18. COMMERCIAL TECHNIQUES ...	49	1.7	–	–	15		7	18.0	82
19. ARTS ...	113	59.1	1	2.0	16		–	–	5
20. GAMES, SPORTS ...	248	50.5	2	2.5	12		3	4.0	18
21. LITERATURE	56	21.0	–	–	14		–	–	13
22. GEOGRAPHY, TRAVEL	20	2.1	–	–	7		–	–	5
23. HISTORY, BIOGRAPHY	17	3.9	–	–	37		–	–	8
B. TOTAL	567	108.0	1	.7	41		2	1.0	60
1. CHILD. & ADOLESCENTS MAGAZINES	25	17.5	–	–	2		–	–	5
2. COMICS AND HUMOUR MAGAZINES	71	53.1	–	–	5		–	–	7
3. PARISH MAGAZINES	66	11.5	1	.7	6		1	.5	14
4. SCHOOL MAGAZINES & NEWSPAPERS	27	1.0	–	–	10		1	.5	34
5. 'HOUSE ORGANS'	378	24.9	–	–	18		–	–	–

ASIA

SUBJECT GROUP GROUPE DE SUJETS GRUPO DE MATERIAS	VENEZUELA (1982)		BRUNEI DARUSSALAM (1984)		CHINA‡ (1982)		CYPRUS‡ (1984)		HONG KONG (1984)
	NUMBER	COPIES	NUMBER	COPIES	NUMBER	COPIES	NUMBER	COPIES	NUMBER
TOTAL A+B	160	4649.2	19	128	3 100	138 852	35	93	495
A. TOTAL	160	4649.2	9	47	2 984	120 641	35	93	454
1. GENERALITIES	30	1061.8	1	5	136	15 812	12	42	57
2. PHILOSOPHY, PSYCHOLOGY	1	7.9	–	–	346	16 382	1	1	–
3. RELIGION, THEOLOGY	–	–	–	–	–	–	2	2	12
4. SOCIOLOGY, STATISTICS	1	...	–	–	./.	./.	2	2	2
5. POLITICAL SCIENCE ...	–	–	–	–	–	–	2	2	30
6. LAW ...	8	169.0	–	–	–	–	2	4	18
7. MILITARY ART ...	–	–	–	–	–	–	–	–	6
8. EDUCATION	3	8.0	–	–	306	19 363	1	1	2
9. TRADE, TRANSPORT ...	22	235.1	–	–	–	–	1	5	11
10. ETHNOGRAPHY, FOLKLORE ...	–	–	–	–	–	–	–	–	12
11. LINGUISTICS, PHILOLOGY	–	–	–	–	–	–	–	–	–
12. MATHEMATICS	–	–	1	5	–	–	–	–	–
13. NATURAL SCIENCES	–	–	–	–	1 745	30 063	1	1	3
14. MEDICAL SCIENCES ...	7	33.5	–	–	–	–	2	4	6
15. INDUSTRIES ...	2	7.7	–	–	–	–	–	–	47
16. AGRICULTURE	8	7.1	–	–	–	–	3	6	1
17. DOMESTIC SCIENCE	15	1501.7	–	–	–	–	–	–	13
18. COMMERCIAL TECHNIQUES ...	10	62.0	–	–	–	–	1	5	60
19. ARTS ...	14	399.1	–	–	–	–	3	15	30
20. GAMES, SPORTS ...	19	959.8	–	–	–	–	–	–	111
21. LITERATURE	7	61.0	5	16	451	39 021	2	3	13
22. GEOGRAPHY, TRAVEL	5	135.5	1	10	–	–	2	2	20
23. HISTORY, BIOGRAPHY	–	–	1	11	–	–	–	–	–
B. TOTAL	...	...	10	81	116	18 211	–	–	41
1. CHILD. & ADOLESCENTS MAGAZINES	...	...	10	81	51	13 882	–	–	18
2. COMICS AND HUMOUR MAGAZINES	...	...	–	–	65	4 329	–	–	2
3. PARISH MAGAZINES	...	...	–	–	–	–	–	–	11
4. SCHOOL MAGAZINES & NEWSPAPERS	...	...	–	–	–	–	–	–	10
5. 'HOUSE ORGANS'	...	...	–	–	–	–	–	–	–

SUBJECT GROUP GROUPE DE SUJETS GRUPO DE MATERIAS	INDIA‡ (1982)		IRAN, ISLAMIC REPUBLIC OF (1982)	ISRAEL‡ (1981)	JAPAN‡ (1984)	
	NUMBER	COPIES	NUMBER	NUMBER	NUMBER	COPIES
TOTAL A+B	19 937	50094.0	180	1 100	2 138	36 293
A. TOTAL	19 681	47625.0	173	1 061	1 742	18 952
1. GENERALITIES	8 711	26300.0	14	25	100	4 935
2. PHILOSOPHY, PSYCHOLOGY	1 595	2250.0	3	100	13	198
3. RELIGION, THEOLOGY	./.	./.	29	139	11	16
4. SOCIOLOGY, STATISTICS	117	158.0	6	12	36	25
5. POLITICAL SCIENCE ...	–	–	12	144	141	633
6. LAW ...	884	1171.0	1	224	24	46
7. MILITARY ART ...	234	281.0	3	–	–	–
8. EDUCATION	331	240.0	16	74	111	319
9. TRADE, TRANSPORT ...	103	123.0	9	22	51	183
10. ETHNOGRAPHY, FOLKLORE ...	–	–	–	–	–	–
11. LINGUISTICS, PHILOLOGY	–	–	–	–	34	297
12. MATHEMATICS	–	–	2	29	–	–
13. NATURAL SCIENCES	–	–	4	./.	38	141
14. MEDICAL SCIENCES ...	482	638.0	15	34	115	195
15. INDUSTRIES ...	951	854.0	25	57	234	535
16. AGRICULTURE	370	622.0	10	73	25	68
17. DOMESTIC SCIENCE	344	436.0	–	–	112	1 775
18. COMMERCIAL TECHNIQUES ...	–	–	–	./.	–	–
19. ARTS ...	488	2207.0	7	35	119	1 049
20. GAMES, SPORTS ...	111	463.0	6	40	497	8 228
21. LITERATURE	2 872	8958.0	6	53	65	265
22. GEOGRAPHY, TRAVEL	90	913.0	1	–	16	44
23. HISTORY, BIOGRAPHY	1 998	2011.0	4	–	./.	./.
B. TOTAL	256	2469.0	7	39	396	17 341
1. CHILD. & ADOLESCENTS MAGAZINES	256	2469.0	5	39	71	6 081
2. COMICS AND HUMOUR MAGAZINES	–	–	2	–	225	7 313
3. PARISH MAGAZINES	–	–	–	–	–	–
4. SCHOOL MAGAZINES & NEWSPAPERS	–	–	–	–	56	1 411
5. 'HOUSE ORGANS'	–	–	–	–	44	2 536

SUBJECT GROUP GROUPE DE SUJETS GRUPO DE MATERIAS	JORDAN (1984)		KUWAIT (1982)		MALAYSIA (1984)		SAUDI ARABIA (1984)	SINGAPORE (1984)
	NUMBER	COPIES	NUMBER	COPIES	NUMBER	COPIES	NUMBER	NUMBER
TOTAL A+B	41	211	45	981.7	1 631	1688.7	58	1 786
A. TOTAL	33	171	44	925.7	1 292	1187.3	57	1 130
1. GENERALITIES	–	–	16	511.5	64	12.8	–	90
2. PHILOSOPHY, PSYCHOLOGY	–	–	–	–	3	1.2	–	9
3. RELIGION, THEOLOGY	3	10	3	102.0	66	39.6	5	37
4. SOCIOLOGY, STATISTICS	–	–	1	10.0	72	57.6	5	74
5. POLITICAL SCIENCE ...	2	13	4	190.5	411	328.8	–	257
6. LAW ...	1	12	3	7.0	229	110.9	7	104
7. MILITARY ART ...	6	30	–	–	20	60.0	10	20
8. EDUCATION	3	25	1	3.0	64	51.2	1	59
9. TRADE, TRANSPORT ...	4	14	–	–	38	30.4	3	106
10. ETHNOGRAPHY, FOLKLORE ...	1	6	–	–	–	–	–	1
11. LINGUISTICS, PHILOLOGY	–	–	–	–	6	3.0	–	11
12. MATHEMATICS	–	–	–	–	5	3.0	–	1
13. NATURAL SCIENCES	1	4	1	4.0	24	12.0	–	15
14. MEDICAL SCIENCES ...	4	14	3	7.5	34	27.2	2	69
15. INDUSTRIES ...	2	10	2	7.0	49	73.5	15	59
16. AGRICULTURE	2	6	2	5.0	74	148.0	–	6
17. DOMESTIC SCIENCE	–	–	–	–	8	24.0	–	20
18. COMMERCIAL TECHNIQUES ...	1	12	1	14.0	22	17.6	1	37
19. ARTS ...	–	–	1	5.0	19	24.7	5	32
20. GAMES, SPORTS ...	1	3	3	30.0	47	141.0	2	53
21. LITERATURE	2	12	3	29.2	5	4.0	5	18
22. GEOGRAPHY, TRAVEL	–	–	–	–	24	7.2	–	8
23. HISTORY, BIOGRAPHY	–	–	–	–	8	9.6	1	44
B. TOTAL	8	40	1	56.0	339	501.4	1	656
1. CHILD. & ADOLESCENTS MAGAZINES	3	16	1	56.0	29	87.0	1	12
2. COMICS AND HUMOUR MAGAZINES	–	–	–	–	7	21.0	–	1
3. PARISH MAGAZINES	–	–	–	–	12	2.4	–	118
4. SCHOOL MAGAZINES & NEWSPAPERS	4	18	–	–	35	7.0	–	146
5. 'HOUSE ORGANS'	1	6	–	–	256	384.0	–	379

EUROPE

SUBJECT GROUP / GROUPE DE SUJETS / GRUPO DE MATERIAS	SRI LANKA (1983)		THAILAND (1984)	ANDORRA (1984)		AUSTRIA‡ (1984)	BELGIUM (1984)	BULGARIA (1984)	
	NUMBER	COPIES	NUMBER	NUMBER	COPIES	NUMBER	NUMBER	NUMBER	COPIES
TOTAL A+B	454	42511.6	1 189	15	14.6	2 315	11 256	1 758	10 211
A. TOTAL	424	32124.3	1 072	11	10.6	2 058	10 907	1 355	7 596
1. GENERALITIES	8	29.8	104	1	1	141	2 396	277	298
2. PHILOSOPHY, PSYCHOLOGY	5	20.8	23	–	–	./.	70	7	6
3. RELIGION, THEOLOGY	106	422.2	46	–	–	188	476	4	19
4. SOCIOLOGY, STATISTICS	–	–	29	1	.8	./.	233	45	565
5. POLITICAL SCIENCE ...	92	1664.5	29	3	1.5	147	1 298	175	1 132
6. LAW ...	50	297.0	50	–	–	237	935	38	204
7. MILITARY ART ...	–	–	39	–	–	26	120	12	110
8. EDUCATION	16	68.6	65	–	–	105	604	52	372
9. TRADE, TRANSPORT ...	11	86.0	39	2	.5	49	266	34	157
10. ETHNOGRAPHY, FOLKLORE ...	–	–	19	1	.5	58	77	15	875
11. LINGUISTICS, PHILOLOGY	1	48.0	23	–	–	62	54	10	19
12. MATHEMATICS	1	1.6	26	–	–	./.	18	4	3
13. NATURAL SCIENCES	12	44.1	24	–	–	./.	220	66	217
14. MEDICAL SCIENCES ...	16	175.2	74	–	–	61	410	138	557
15. INDUSTRIES ...	8	83.9	58	1	.5	348	1 018	169	876
16. AGRICULTURE	15	380.7	52	–	–	92	344	67	453
17. DOMESTIC SCIENCE	–	–	30	–	–	./.	136	4	777
18. COMMERCIAL TECHNIQUES ...	2	1.3	45	–	–	31	315	76	337
19. ARTS ...	10	193.4	105	1	.5	153	578	49	200
20. GAMES, SPORTS ...	2	1.3	91	–	–	195	663	37	559
21. LITERATURE	65	28577.4	27	–	–	49	315	51	489
22. GEOGRAPHY, TRAVEL	2	27.2	43	–	–	47	76	3	10
23. HISTORY, BIOGRAPHY	2	1.3	31	1	.8	69	285	22	61
B. TOTAL	30	10387.3	117	4	4	257	349	403	2 615
1. CHILD. & ADOLESCENTS MAGAZINES	8	10288.9	25	–	–	59	56	19	1 318
2. COMICS AND HUMOUR MAGAZINES	–	–	18	–	–	19	59	1	374
3. PARISH MAGAZINES	9	24.1	15	2	2	./.	17	121	290
4. SCHOOL MAGAZINES & NEWSPAPERS	8	7.0	22	1	1	./.	106	26	34
5. 'HOUSE ORGANS'	5	67.3	37	1	1	179	111	236	599

SUBJECT GROUP / GROUPE DE SUJETS / GRUPO DE MATERIAS	CZECHOSLOVAKIA (1984)		GERMAN DEMOCRATIC REPUBLIC‡ (1984)		GERMANY, FEDERAL REPUBLIC OF‡ (1983)		GIBRALTAR (1984)	
	NUMBER	COPIES	NUMBER	COPIES	NUMBER	COPIES	NUMBER	COPIES
TOTAL A+B	926	22 123	1 191	23 116	6 702	255 905	15	3.8
A. TOTAL	630	16 022	533	21 116	6 702	255 905	11	1.6
1. GENERALITIES	13	286	12	722	321	17 234	–	–
2. PHILOSOPHY, PSYCHOLOGY	10	108	15	302	./.	./.	–	–
3. RELIGION, THEOLOGY	26	356	34	374	318	9 218	–	–
4. SOCIOLOGY, STATISTICS	7	42	2	3	./.	./.	8	.8
5. POLITICAL SCIENCE ...	33	737	26	1 379	./.	./.	–	–
6. LAW ...	45	988	16	603	1 548	7 696	1	.3
7. MILITARY ART ...	12	490	4	114	./.	./.	–	–
8. EDUCATION	29	411	55	5 724	242	2 983	–	–
9. TRADE, TRANSPORT ...	27	321	13	105	507	7 017	–	–
10. ETHNOGRAPHY, FOLKLORE ...	15	135	5	10	./.	./.	–	–
11. LINGUISTICS, PHILOLOGY	15	29	10	29	123	302	–	–
12. MATHEMATICS	11	26	9	38	179	344	–	–
13. NATURAL SCIENCES	56	118	65	286	./.	./.	1	.3
14. MEDICAL SCIENCES ...	57	382	54	654	544	20 741	–	–
15. INDUSTRIES ...	54	684	74	1 111	1 363	84 354	–	–
16. AGRICULTURE	51	1 028	29	258	209	2 717	–	–
17. DOMESTIC SCIENCE	18	1 731	14	4 442	./.	./.	–	–
18. COMMERCIAL TECHNIQUES ...	6	56	8	94	./.	./.	–	–
19. ARTS ...	36	1 547	30	996	./.	./.	–	–
20. GAMES, SPORTS ...	52	5 923	29	3 002	1 348	103 299	1	.2
21. LITERATURE	25	220	14	144	./.	./.	–	–
22. GEOGRAPHY, TRAVEL	14	374	6	705	./.	./.	–	–
23. HISTORY, BIOGRAPHY	18	30	9	21	./.	./.	–	–
B. TOTAL	296	6 101	658	2 000	./.	./.	4	2.2
1. CHILD. & ADOLESCENTS MAGAZINES	35	3 588	15	3 695	./.	./.	–	–
2. COMICS AND HUMOUR MAGAZINES	4	1 061	1	1 000	./.	./.	–	–
3. PARISH MAGAZINES	33	92	9	14	./.	./.	4	2.2
4. SCHOOL MAGAZINES & NEWSPAPERS	...	...	–	–	./.	./.	–	–
5. 'HOUSE ORGANS'	224	1 360	658	2 000	./.	./.	–	–

7.21 Other periodicals
Autres périodiques
Otras publicaciones periódicas

SUBJECT GROUP / GROUPE DE SUJETS / GRUPO DE MATERIAS	HOLY SEE (1984)		HUNGARY (1984)		IRELAND (1984)		ITALY (1982)	LUXEMBOURG (1982)	MALTA (1984)
	NUMBER	COPIES	NUMBER	COPIES	NUMBER	COPIES	NUMBER	NUMBER	NUMBER
TOTAL A+B	48	41.7	1 535	13278.4	252	2958.6	8 265	427	264
A. TOTAL	47	41.2	789	9051.3	234	2820.3	5 697	388	166
1. GENERALITIES	–	–	38	391.2	21	162.3	997	31	45
2. PHILOSOPHY, PSYCHOLOGY	1	.8	8	15.3	–	–	76	4	–
3. RELIGION, THEOLOGY	37	31.4	16	190.1	48	589.5	568	13	60
4. SOCIOLOGY, STATISTICS	–	–	15	27.8	3	5.0	109	29	–
5. POLITICAL SCIENCE ...	–	–	48	904.1	–	–	413	42	1
6. LAW ...	2	1.6	63	424.4	14	52.7	357	73	3
7. MILITARY ART ...	–	–	–	–	2	4.6	15	2	1
8. EDUCATION	1	1.0	45	301.4	10	34.4	139	17	3
9. TRADE, TRANSPORT ...	–	–	23	223.7	36	521.2	248	10	–
10. ETHNOGRAPHY, FOLKLORE ...	–	–	3	3.6	–	–	97	–	1
11. LINGUISTICS, PHILOLOGY	2	3.5	15	68.0	–	–	57	2	1
12. MATHEMATICS	–	–	11	17.0	–	–	12	–	–
13. NATURAL SCIENCES	–	–	39	113.9	–	–	131	16	5
14. MEDICAL SCIENCES ...	–	–	62	1041.7	15	45.2	431	8	1
15. INDUSTRIES ...	–	–	162	599.7	19	201.5	396	18	5
16. AGRICULTURE	–	–	53	321.0	18	444.1	324	16	3
17. DOMESTIC SCIENCE	–	–	3	405.9	4	140.5	123	1	5
18. COMMERCIAL TECHNIQUES ...	–	–	56	1055.9	13	50.6	88	–	4
19. ARTS ...	1	1.0	36	282.1	4	93.0	311	17	1
20. GAMES, SPORTS ...	–	–	41	2124.2	9	48.2	399	74	22
21. LITERATURE	–	–	36	386.5	2	4.0	146	2	1
22. GEOGRAPHY, TRAVEL	–	–	4	98.0	13	422.8	115	–	3
23. HISTORY, BIOGRAPHY	3	1.9	12	55.8	3	.7	145	13	1
B. TOTAL	1	.5	746	4227.1	18	138.3	2 568	39	98
1. CHILD. & ADOLESCENTS MAGAZINES	–	–	16	1447.7	2	46.7	84	12	5
2. COMICS AND HUMOUR MAGAZINES	–	–	4	1369.6	–	–	9	–	3
3. PARISH MAGAZINES	–	–	–	–	–	–	700	10	37
4. SCHOOL MAGAZINES & NEWSPAPERS	1	.5	110	69.6	8	37.6	64	13	11
5. 'HOUSE ORGANS'	–	–	616	1340.2	8	54.0	1 711	4	42

SUBJECT GROUP / GROUPE DE SUJETS / GRUPO DE MATERIAS	MONACO (1982)		POLAND‡ (1984)		PORTUGAL‡ (1982)	SAN MARINO (1982)	YUGOSLAVIA (1984)	
	NUMBER	COPIES	NUMBER	COPIES	NUMBER	NUMBER	NUMBER	COPIES
TOTAL A+B	105	792.1	2 718	39 057	915	11	1 474	4 968
A. TOTAL	105	792.1	2 614	38 138	618	11	1 385	4 276
1. GENERALITIES	77	485.9	437	12 763	298	–	172	272
2. PHILOSOPHY, PSYCHOLOGY	–	–	36	43	6	–	18	17
3. RELIGION, THEOLOGY	–	–	131	1 461	54	–	60	558
4. SOCIOLOGY, STATISTICS	–	–	86	397	87	5	67	124
5. POLITICAL SCIENCE ...	–	–	200	2 337	./.	–	138	280
6. LAW ...	1	1.0	139	2 002	./.	1	89	170
7. MILITARY ART ...	–	–	32	450	./.	–	28	261
8. EDUCATION	3	17.5	107	1 272	./.	1	76	167
9. TRADE, TRANSPORT ...	–	–	34	305	./.	–	8	48
10. ETHNOGRAPHY, FOLKLORE ...	–	–	6	17	./.	–	11	12
11. LINGUISTICS, PHILOLOGY	–	–	46	1 356	6	–	29	31
12. MATHEMATICS	–	–	23	52	23	2	14	125
13. NATURAL SCIENCES	–	–	187	328	./.	–	88	220
14. MEDICAL SCIENCES ...	–	–	126	1 294	83	–	106	301
15. INDUSTRIES ...	–	–	433	2 461	./.	2	100	337
16. AGRICULTURE	–	–	212	2 389	./.	–	55	186
17. DOMESTIC SCIENCE	–	–	20	2 001	./.	–	4	340
18. COMMERCIAL TECHNIQUES ...	–	–	82	948	./.	–	70	246
19. ARTS ...	3	3.0	76	1 168	43	–	61	239
20. GAMES, SPORTS ...	10	245.0	53	2 999	./.	–	28	112
21. LITERATURE	10	39.2	40	1 771	7	–	93	157
22. GEOGRAPHY, TRAVEL	–	–	35	207	11	–	20	23
23. HISTORY, BIOGRAPHY	1	.5	73	117	./.	–	50	50
B. TOTAL	–	–	104	919	297	–	89	692
1. CHILD. & ADOLESCENTS MAGAZINES	–	–	75	6 436	42	–	22	333
2. COMICS AND HUMOUR MAGAZINES	–	–	...	...	1	–	2	135
3. PARISH MAGAZINES	–	–	...	...	159	–	–	–
4. SCHOOL MAGAZINES & NEWSPAPERS	–	–	...	...	14	–	6	26
5. 'HOUSE ORGANS'	–	–	104	919	81	–	59	198

SUBJECT GROUP / GROUPE DE SUJETS / GRUPO DE MATERIAS	OCEANIA: NEW CALEDONIA (1982)		U.S.S.R.: U.S.S.R. (1984)		U.S.S.R.: BYELORUSSIAN S.S.R. (1984)	
	NUMBER	COPIES	NUMBER	COPIES	NUMBER	COPIES
TOTAL A+B	15	26.8	5 357	4 279 930	106	2 555
A. TOTAL	14	25.3	5 231	3 339 013	97	2 320
1. GENERALITIES	1	2.5	38	9 785	44	1 465
2. PHILOSOPHY, PSYCHOLOGY	–	–	37	42 296	–	–
3. RELIGION, THEOLOGY	1	1.0	16	5 517	–	–
4. SOCIOLOGY, STATISTICS	5	4.5	162	18 591	–	–
5. POLITICAL SCIENCE ...	2	5.0	433	965 214	–	–
6. LAW ...	1	1.0	88	140 771	–	–
7. MILITARY ART ...	–	–	58	33 886	–	–
8. EDUCATION	–	–	224	480 850	10	241
9. TRADE, TRANSPORT ...	1	2.5	347	73 400	–	–
10. ETHNOGRAPHY, FOLKLORE ...	–	–	2	37	–	–
11. LINGUISTICS, PHILOLOGY	–	–	45	2 820	–	–
12. MATHEMATICS	–	–	127	1 697	–	–
13. NATURAL SCIENCES	1	3.5	291	10 888	12	35
14. MEDICAL SCIENCES ...	–	–	199	233 111	1	18
15. INDUSTRIES ...	–	–	1 323	108 238	16	248
16. AGRICULTURE	–	–	295	78 383	6	35
17. DOMESTIC SCIENCE	–	–	81	8 573	–	–
18. COMMERCIAL TECHNIQUES ...	–	–	830	23 754	–	–
19. ARTS ...	1	4.5	138	97 153	4	124
20. GAMES, SPORTS ...	–	–	55	30 024	1	3
21. LITERATURE	–	–	228	937 060	3	151
22. GEOGRAPHY, TRAVEL	–	–	175	36 212	–	–
23. HISTORY, BIOGRAPHY	1	.8	39	753	–	–
B. TOTAL	1	1.5	126	940 917	9	235
1. CHILD. & ADOLESCENTS MAGAZINES	–	–	103	619 571	2	88
2. COMICS AND HUMOUR MAGAZINES	–	–	23	321 346	1	125
3. PARISH MAGAZINES	–	–	–	–	–	–
4. SCHOOL MAGAZINES & NEWSPAPERS	–	–	...	...	–	–
5. 'HOUSE ORGANS'	1	1.5	...	...	6	22

AFRICA:
Egypt:
E--> Periodicals of groups 5, 6, 7, 8, 9, and 10 are included in group 4; 13 in group 12; 15, 16, 17, 18 in group 14; 20 in group 19, 23 in group 22.
FR-> Les périodiques des groupes 5, 6, 7, 8, 9, et 10 sont inclus dans le groupe 4; 13 dans le groupe 12; 15, 16, 17 et 18 dans le groupe 14; 20 dans le groupe 19, 23 dans le groupe 22.
ESP> Las publicaciones periódicas de los grupos 5, 6, 7, 8, 9, y 10 quedan incluídas en el grupo 4; 13 en el grupo 12; 15, 16, 17 y 18 en el grupo 14; 20 en el grupo 19, 23 en el grupo 22.
AMERICA, NORTH:
United States:
E--> Data do not include parish and school magazines.
FR-> Les données ne comprennent ni les bulletins paroissiaux ni ceux des écoles.
ESP> Los datos no incluyen los boletines parroquiales y boletines escolares.
ASIA:
China:
E--> Periodicals of group 4 are included in group 2.
FR-> Les périodiques du groupe 4 sont inclus dans le groupe 2.
ESP> Las publicaciones periódicas del grupo 4 quedan incluidas en el grupo 2.
Cyprus:
E--> Data do not include children's, comics, parish, school magazines and 'house organs'.
FR-> Les données ne comprennent pas les périodiques pour enfants, les périodiques humoristiques, les bulletins paroissiaux et des écoles.
ESP> Los datos relativos a las otras publicaciones periódicas no incluyen los periódicos para niños, los periódicos humorísticos, los boletines parroquiales, y los boletines escolares.
India:
E--> Periodicals of groups 2 and 3 are counted together.
FR-> Les périodiques des groupes 2 et 3 sont comptés ensemble.
ESP> Las publicaciones periódicas de los grupos 2 y 3 figuran en la misma rúbrica.
Israel:
E--> Periodicals of group 13 are included in group 12; 18 in group 9.
FR-> Les périodiques du groupe 13 sont inclus dans le groupe 12; groupe 18 dans le groupe 9.

Israel: (Cont):
ESP> Las publicaciones periódicas del grupo 13 quedan incluídas en el grupo 12; grupo 18 en el grupo 9.
Japan:
E--> Periodicals of groups 22 and 23 are counted together.
FR-> Les périodiques des groupes 22 et 23 sont comptés ensemble.
ESP> Las publicaciones periódicas de los grupos 22 y 23 figuran en la misma rúbrica.
EUROPE:
Austria:
E--> Periodicals of groups 12 and 13 are included in group 23. For other subject groups, the symbol ./. means that the data are included elsewhere. Parish magazines are included in group 3 (religion, theology).
FR-> Les périodiques des groupes 12 et 13 sont compris dans le groupe 23. Pour les autres groupes de sujets, le symbole ./. signifie que les données sont comprises dans un autre groupe. Les bulletins paroissiaux sont compris dans le groupe 3 (religion, théologie).
ESP> Las publicaciones periódicas de los grupos 12 y 13 quedan incluídas en el grupo 23. Para los otros grupos de matérias, el símbolo ./. significa que los datos están incluídos en un otro grupo. Los boletines parroquiales quedan incluídos en el grupo 3 (religión, teología).
German Democratic Republic:
E--> Children's magazines, comics and parish magazines shown under sub-total B are already distributed among the 23 groups.
FR-> Les périodiques pour enfants, les périodiques humoristiques et les bulletins paroissiaux comptés dans le sous-total B sont déjà répartis dans les 23 groupes.
ESP> Los periódicos para niños,los periódicos humorísticos y los boletines parroquiales incluídos en el subtotal B están ya distribuidos en los 23 grupos.
Germany, Federal Republic of:
E--> Periodicals of groups 12 and 13 are counted together. For other subject groups, the symbol ./. means that the data are included elsewhere.
FR-> Les périodiques des groupes 12 et 13 sont comptés ensemble. Pour les autres groupes de sujets, le symbole ./. signifie que les données sont incluses dans un autre groupe.
ESP> Las publicaciones periódicas de los grupos 22 y 23 figuran en la misma rúbrica. Para los otros grupos de matérias, el símbolo ./. significa que los datos están incluidas en un otro grupo.

Poland:
E--> Children's magazines are included in the 23 groups.
FR-> Les périodiques pour enfants sont comptés dans les 23 groupes.
ESP> Los periódicos para niños están incluídos en los 23 grupos.

Portugal:
E--> Periodicals of groups 5, 6, 7, 8, 9 and 10 are included in group 4; group 13 in group 12; groups 15, 16, 17 and 18 in group 14; group 20 in 19 and group 23 in 22.

Portugal: (Cont):
FR-> Les périodiques des groupes 5, 6, 7, 8, 9 et 10 sont inclus dans le groupe 4; le groupe 13 dans le groupe 12; les groupes 15, 16, 17 et 18 dans le groupe 14; le groupe 20 dans le groupe 19; le groupe 23 dans le groupe 22.
ESP> Las publicaciones periódicas de los grupos 5, 6, 7, 8, 9 y 10 quedan incluídas en el grupo 4; las del grupo 13 en el 12; las de los grupos 15, 16, 17 y 18 en el grupo 14; las del grupo 20 en el 19 y las del grupo 23 en el grupo 22.

7.22 Newsprint and other printing and writing paper: production, imports, exports and consumption (total and per 1,000 inhabitants)

Papier journal et autre papier d'impression et d'écriture: production, importations, exportations et consommation (total et pour 1 000 habitants)

Papel de periódico y otro papel de imprenta y de escribir: producción, importaciones, exportaciones y consumo (total y por 1 000 habitantes)

A = PRODUCTION (METRIC TONS)
B = IMPORTS (METRIC TONS)
C = EXPORTS (METRIC TONS)
D = CONSUMPTION (METRIC TONS)
E = CONSUMPTION PER 1,000 INHABITANTS (KILOGRAMS)

NUMBER OF COUNTRIES AND TERRITORIES PRESENTED IN THIS TABLE: 137

A = PRODUCTION (TONNES METRIQUES)
B = IMPORTATIONS (TONNES METRIQUES)
C = EXPORTATIONS (TONNES METRIQUES)
D = CONSOMMATION (TONNES METRIQUES)
E = CONSOMMATION POUR 1 000 HABITANTS (KILOGRAMMES)

NOMBRE DE PAYS ET DE TERRITOIRES PRESENTES DANS CE TABLEAU: 137

A = PRODUCCION (TONELADAS METRICAS)
B = IMPORTACIONES (TONELADAS METRICAS)
C = EXPORTACIONES (TONELADAS METRICAS)
D = CONSUMO (TONELADAS METRICAS)
E = CONSUMO POR 1 000 HABITANTES (KILOGRAMOS)

NUMERO DE PAISES Y DE TERRITORIOS PRESENTADOS EN ESTE CUADRO: 137

COUNTRY PAYS PAIS	DEFINITION OF DATA CODE TIPO DE DATOS	NEWSPRINT / PAPIER JOURNAL / PAPEL DE PERIODICO 1970	1975	1980	1983	OTHER PRINTING AND WRITING PAPER / AUTRE PAPIER D'IMPRESSION ET D'ECRITURE / OTRO PAPEL DE IMPRENTA Y DE ESCRIBIR 1970	1975	1980	1983
AFRICA									
ALGERIA	A					23 000	18 000	30 000	30 000
	B	6 200	8 900	12 000	5 700	19 000	7 200	3 200	3 100
	D	6 200	8 900	12 000	5 700	42 000	25 200	33 200	33 100
	E	451	556	643	279	3 055	1 573	1 779	1 619
ANGOLA	A	600	1 000	1 000		1 500	3 000	3 000	
	B	100	1 100	1 500	1 000	2 000			
	D	700	2 100	2 500	1 000	3 500	5 700	5 700	
	E	89	322	324	120	626	874	738	
BENIN	B		100	100	100		500	500	500
	D		100	100	100		500	500	500
	E		33	29	26		164	143	131
CAMEROON	B	100		500	1 100	1 300	2 000	4 000	2 300
	D	100		500	1 100	1 300	2 000	4 000	2 300
	E	15		58	118	193	264	464	246
CENTRAL AFRICAN REPUBLIC	B					200			
	D					200			
	E					107			
CHAD	B						100	200	200
	D						100	200	200
	E						25	45	42
CONGO	B					200	200	100	100
	D					200	200	100	100
	E					166	148	65	61
COTE D'IVOIRE	B	900	800	800	1 600		4 200	4 200	4 000
	D	900	800	800	1 600		4 200	4 200	4 000
	E	162	118	98	176		621	514	439
EGYPT	A					40 000	24 000	66 000	39 000
	B	32 900	40 200	67 000	99 700	5 000	34 000	53 600	60 900
	D	32 900	40 200	67 000	99 700	45 000	58 000	119 600	99 900
	E	995	1 108	1 614	2 233	1 361	1 598	2 881	2 238
ETHIOPIA	A						3 500	3 500	3 500
	B	900	400	2 000	1 500	900	2 800	200	900
	D	900	400	2 000	1 500	900	6 300	3 700	4 400
	E	29	12	52	36	29	184	96	106

7.22 Newsprint, printing and writing paper
Papier journal, papier d'impression et papier d'écriture
Papel de periódico, papel de imprenta y papel de escribir

COUNTRY / PAYS / PAIS	DEFINITION OF DATA / CODE / TIPO DE DATOS	NEWSPRINT / PAPIER JOURNAL / PAPEL DE PERIODICO				OTHER PRINTING AND WRITING PAPER / AUTRE PAPIER D'IMPRESSION ET D'ECRITURE / OTRO PAPEL DE IMPRENTA Y DE ESCRIBIR			
		1970	1975	1980	1983	1970	1975	1980	1983
GABON	B					100	12 600	1 300	1 300
	D					100	12 600	1 300	1 300
	E					105	12 576	1 222	1 167
GHANA	B	3 600	7 300	1 500	1 000	7 600	6 700	3 300	3 300
	D	3 600	7 300	1 500	1 000	7 600	6 700	3 300	3 300
	E	418	745	130	79	882	684	285	259
GUINEA	B		100	100	100				
	D		100	100	100				
	E		23	21	19				
GUINEA-BISSAU	B		100	100					
	D		100	100					
	E		159	124					
KENYA	A				6 000		8 000	19 000	17 000
	B	5 000	3 900	7 900	3 800	6 900	3 000	1 900	1 400
	C					100	400	8 300	600
	D	5 000	3 900	7 900	9 800	6 800	10 600	12 600	17 800
	E	443	285	471	517	602	774	752	939
LIBERIA	B	100				200	450	500	
	D	100				200	450	500	
	E	73				147	285	267	
LIBYAN ARAB JAMAHIRIYA	B	800	100	800	7 100	1 400	8 700	3 500	4 900
	D	800	100	800	7 100	1 400	8 700	3 500	4 900
	E	403	41	269	2 130	705	3 582	1 177	1 470
MADAGASCAR	A	300	817	3 500	1 000	3 900	8 200		7 000
	B							600	800
	C					1 300	800		
	D	300	817	3 500	1 000	2 600	7 400	600	7 800
	E	45	107	402	106	387	973	69	825
MALAWI	A						1 000	1 000	1 000
	B	200	500	600	700	2 500	2 200	2 500	2 700
	C	200	200	100	100	600	500	100	100
	D	200	300	500	600	1 900	2 700	3 400	3 600
	E	44	58	84	92	420	523	571	552
MALI	B	200	100				200	200	200
	D	200	100				200	200	200
	E	35	16				32	28	26
MAURITIUS	B	600	600	500	1 100	800	1 000	1 600	1 300
	D	600	600	500	1 100	800	1 000	1 600	1 300
	E	708	691	523	1 088	944	1 152	1 675	1 285
MOROCCO	A					10 000	16 500	17 000	17 000
	B	3 100	2 800	5 400	3 800	2 000	1 300	3 200	3 200
	D	3 100	2 800	5 400	3 800	12 000	17 800	20 200	20 200
	E	202	162	279	182	784	1 029	1 042	965
MOZAMBIQUE	B	200	1 700	1 500	2 000			4 000	4 000
	D	200	1 700	1 500	2 000			4 000	4 000
	E	25	175	124	152			330	303
NIGER	B		150	100	100		100	100	100
	D		150	100	100		100	100	100
	E		32	19	17		21	19	17
NIGERIA	A					2 000	2 000	3 500	3 500
	B	17 100	23 700	29 000	20 000	25 200	29 000	41 900	41 900
	D	17 100	23 700	29 000	20 000	27 200	31 000	45 400	45 400
	E	299	350	360	225	475	458	564	510
REUNION	B	400	500	1 000	1 500	300			1 400
	D	400	500	1 000	1 500	300			1 400
	E	906	1 035	1 962	2 868	679			2 677
SENEGAL	B	500	1 800	900	1 000	3 300	1 200	1 800	13 000
	D	500	1 800	900	1 000	3 300	1 200	1 800	13 000
	E	125	377	159	163	823	251	317	2 124
SIERRA LEONE	B	200	100	200	200	200			
	D	200	100	200	200	200			
	E	71	33	61	58	71			
SOMALIA	B	500	300	200	200	100	100	1 300	100
	D	500	300	200	200	100	100	1 300	100
	E	190	92	50	46	38	31	323	23
SOUTH AFRICA	A	160 000	210 000	224 000	564 000	70 000	77 000	178 000	278 000
	B	52 500	300		100	130 500	74 000	92 600	64 700
	C		14 500	70 000	135 000	3 600	6 800	14 400	7 100
	D	212 500	195 800	154 000	429 100	196 900	144 200	256 200	335 600
	E	9 336	7 678	5 382	13 922	8 651	5 655	8 954	10 889

COUNTRY / PAYS / PAIS	DEFINITION OF DATA CODE / TIPO DE DATOS	NEWSPRINT / PAPIER JOURNAL / PAPEL DE PERIODICO				OTHER PRINTING AND WRITING PAPER / AUTRE PAPIER D'IMPRESSION ET D'ECRITURE / OTRO PAPEL DE IMPRENTA Y DE ESCRIBIR			
		1970	1975	1980	1983	1970	1975	1980	1983
SUDAN	B	2 700	3 400	1 500	2 200	3 700	5 000	7 200	6 500
	D	2 700	3 400	1 500	2 200	3 700	5 000	7 200	6 500
	E	195	212	80	108	267	312	385	320
TUNISIA	A						15 000	21 000	23 000
	B		2 900	5 500	9 100			11 100	3 200
	C						3 800	100	
	D		2 900	5 500	9 100		11 200	32 000	26 200
	E		517	860	1 337		1 996	5 006	3 849
UGANDA	B	1 000	500	200	200	2 600	400	500	500
	D	1 000	500	200	200	2 600	400	500	500
	E	102	45	15	14	265	36	38	35
UNITED REPUBLIC OF TANZANIA	B	1 500	4 500	3 500	3 500	5 100	5 000	7 000	7 000
	D	1 500	4 500	3 500	3 500	5 100	5 000	7 000	7 000
	E	111	283	186	167	377	314	371	334
ZAIRE	B	500	1 000	1 000	1 000	2 400	2 000	2 700	2 700
	D	500	1 000	1 000	1 000	2 400	2 000	2 700	2 700
	E	26	45	39	35	123	89	104	96
ZAMBIA	B	2 100	4 300	3 000	3 000	5 300	4 400	6 300	6 300
	D	2 100	4 300	3 000	3 000	5 300	4 400	6 300	6 300
	E	501	888	531	481	1 265	909	1 115	1 010
ZIMBABWE	A	10 000	12 000	16 000	18 000				
	B				1 000			8 500	5 800
	D	10 000	12 000	16 000	19 000			8 500	5 800
	E	1 884	1 930	2 172	2 322			1 154	709
AMERICA, NORTH									
BAHAMAS	B	1 000	600	9 000	1 100	500	200	100	
	D	1 000	600	9 000	1 100	500	200	100	
	E	5 848	2 941	42 857	4 955	2 924	980	476	
BARBADOS	B	900	500	1 500	1 700	500	800	2 800	1 500
	D	900	500	1 500	1 700	500	800	2 800	1 500
	E	3 772	2 045	6 024	6 717	2 096	3 272	11 245	5 927
BELIZE	B	200	200	200	100	100	100	300	300
	D	200	200	200	100	100	100	300	300
	E	1 667	1 527	1 379	649	833	763	2 069	1 948
CANADA	A	7 996 000	7 010 000	8 625 000	8 486 000	821 000	679 000	1 511 000	1 726 000
	B					35 000	146 700	126 800	185 200
	C	7 339 300	6 348 800	7 706 800	7 475 100	300 100	275 600	652 700	713 100
	D	656 700	661 200	918 200	1 010 900	555 900	550 100	985 100	1 198 100
	E	30 676	29 093	38 116	40 632	25 968	24 205	40 893	48 156
COSTA RICA	B	11 100	11 200	12 000	11 400	4 000	2 800	7 600	7 700
	D	11 100	11 200	12 000	11 400	4 000	2 800	7 600	7 700
	E	6 411	5 696	5 267	4 621	2 310	1 424	3 336	3 121
CUBA	A					20 000	30 000	31 300	33 800
	B	22 800	26 700	32 000	38 700	6 500	22 000	15 400	15 600
	D	22 800	26 700	32 000	38 700	26 500	52 000	46 700	49 400
	E	2 660	2 861	3 288	3 889	3 091	5 573	4 799	4 965
DOMINICAN REPUBLIC	B	4 200	6 600	12 400	14 100	3 600	5 900	25 900	28 000
	D	4 200	6 600	12 400	14 100	3 600	5 900	25 900	28 000
	E	979	1 335	2 231	2 359	839	1 193	4 660	4 685
EL SALVADOR	B	13 000	10 300	15 000	12 800	2 100	4 100		2 200
	C		100				400	500	500
	D	13 000	10 200	15 000	12 800	2 100	3 700		1 700
	E	3 628	2 463	3 127	2 442	586	893		324
GUATEMALA	A		600			6 700	9 000	14 700	10 000
	B	8 300	7 500	17 000	10 800	1 100	1 600	5 600	14 600
	C					4 100	4 400	13 500	5 100
	D	8 300	8 100	17 000	10 800	3 700	6 200	6 800	19 500
	E	1 582	1 345	2 458	1 433	705	1 029	983	2 588
HAITI	B	700	800	300	600	300	300	600	600
	D	700	800	300	600	300	300	600	600
	E	152	155	52	96	65	58	103	96
HONDURAS	B	2 700	2 100	6 500	4 200	2 500	2 500	5 400	500
	C						200		
	D	2 700	2 100	6 500	4 200	2 500	2 300	5 400	500
	E	1 023	679	1 761	1 027	947	744	1 463	122
JAMAICA	B	8 600	8 700	3 500	4 600	4 100	6 300	6 900	5 600
	D	8 600	8 700	3 500	4 600	4 100	6 300	6 900	5 600
	E	4 601	4 258	1 611	2 020	2 194	3 084	3 175	2 459

7.22 Newsprint, printing and writing paper
Papier journal, papier d'impression et papier d'écriture
Papel de periódico, papel de imprenta y papel de escribir

COUNTRY / PAYS / PAIS	DEFINITION OF DATA CODE / TIPO DE DATOS	NEWSPRINT / PAPIER JOURNAL / PAPEL DE PERIODICO				OTHER PRINTING AND WRITING PAPER / AUTRE PAPIER D'IMPRESSION ET D'ECRITURE / OTRO PAPEL DE IMPRENTA Y DE ESCRIBIR			
		1970	1975	1980	1983	1970	1975	1980	1983
MARTINIQUE	B			800	1 000				
	D			800	1 000				
	E			2 453	3 032				
MEXICO	A	40 000	29 000	116 000	157 000	122 000	256 000	526 000	404 000
	B	118 800	185 600	110 000	67 000	236 800	64 000	65 300	98 200
	D	158 800	214 600	226 000	224 000	358 800	320 000	591 300	502 200
	E	3 103	3 568	3 257	2 979	7 011	5 320	8 521	6 679
NETHERLANDS ANTILLES	B	600	500	600	1 500	600	600	1 100	1 100
	D	600	500	600	1 500	600	600	1 100	1 100
	E	2 703	2 092	2 381	5 814	2 703	2 510	4 365	4 264
NICARAGUA	B	3 700	4 000	3 000	3 700	2 500	1 800	1 900	4 100
	D	3 700	4 000	3 000	3 700	2 500	1 800	1 900	4 100
	E	1 802	1 661	1 083	1 208	1 217	748	686	1 338
PANAMA	A							3 000	5 000
	B	5 900	3 400	2 600	5 700	5 900	3 200	1 800	7 900
	D	5 900	3 400	2 600	5 700	5 900	3 200	4 800	12 900
	E	3 853	1 946	1 329	2 724	3 853	1 831	2 453	6 165
TRINIDAD AND TOBAGO	B	5 600	6 300	5 100	10 400	2 800	1 900	4 300	4 200
	D	5 600	6 300	5 100	10 400	2 800	1 900	4 300	4 200
	E	5 859	6 252	4 658	9 040	2 929	1 886	3 927	3 651
UNITED STATES	A	3 143 000	3 348 000	4 238 000	4 687 000	9 684 000	9 708 000	13 829 000	15 405 000
	B	6 019 300	5 305 000	6 593 600	6 277 100	278 200	190 000	652 300	1 058 700
	C	130 300	149 800	158 600	267 500	162 100	365 700	212 300	239 600
	D	9 032 000	8 503 200	10 673 000	10 696 600	9 800 100	9 532 300	14 269 000	16 224 100
	E	44 048	39 372	46 872	45 675	47 793	44 137	62 665	69 277
AMERICA, SOUTH									
ARGENTINA	A	3 200		97 000	168 000	122 700	94 000	152 000	174 000
	B	274 300	148 800	174 000	28 000	4 200	6 200	38 000	25 600
	C	100		200	9 200	4 200	1 500	11 000	2 200
	D	277 400	148 800	270 800	186 800	122 700	98 700	179 000	197 400
	E	11 577	5 712	9 590	6 312	5 121	3 789	6 339	6 671
BOLIVIA	B	4 700	4 700	6 000	6 500	3 900	3 900	6 000	6 000
	D	4 700	4 700	6 000	6 500	3 900	3 900	6 000	6 000
	E	1 087	961	1 077	1 077	902	797	1 077	994
BRAZIL	A	103 000	125 000	105 000	106 000	254 000	416 000	870 000	952 000
	B	108 800	116 000	167 100	158 200	58 000	60 000	68 000	36 000
	C	200	300	500	1 200	900	6 000	135 000	255 300
	D	211 600	240 700	271 600	263 000	311 100	470 000	803 000	732 700
	E	2 208	2 228	2 239	2 027	3 246	4 351	6 621	5 647
CHILE	A	124 400	120 000	131 000	155 000		41 000	48 000	53 000
	B					7 900	3 000	13 000	26 800
	C	78 300	78 300	63 000	92 200		14 000	15 000	8 400
	D	46 100	41 700	68 000	62 800	7 900	30 000	46 000	71 400
	E	4 876	4 034	6 111	5 373	836	2 902	4 134	6 109
COLOMBIA	A					43 800	44 000	71 000	67 000
	B	59 200	44 400	71 000	77 900	2 500	9 200	24 300	13 700
	C					3 400	900	2 500	5 000
	D	59 200	44 400	71 000	77 900	42 900	52 300	92 800	75 700
	E	2 846	1 916	2 753	2 829	2 062	2 257	3 598	2 749
ECUADOR	A						3 000	4 200	5 000
	B	13 900	10 800	32 600	32 000	5 900	11 000	19 000	21 200
	D	13 900	10 800	32 600	32 000	5 900	14 000	23 200	26 200
	E	2 297	1 535	4 013	3 611	975	1 990	2 856	2 957
GUYANA	B	1 200	1 400	1 500	500	1 200	1 400	800	800
	D	1 200	1 400	1 500	500	1 200	1 400	800	800
	E	1 691	1 792	1 735	544	1 691	1 792	925	871
PARAGUAY	A							2 000	2 000
	B	4 100	3 100	8 000	3 000	500	1 400	3 800	3 600
	D	4 100	3 100	8 000	3 000	500	1 400	5 800	5 600
	E	1 790	1 153	2 525	865	218	521	1 831	1 615
PERU	A			30 000	10 000	22 000	38 000	42 400	37 000
	B	49 400	51 400	6 500	37 900	2 700	4 200	3 200	2 600
	C		100			2 700		400	500
	D	49 400	51 300	36 500	47 900	22 000	42 200	45 200	39 100
	E	3 744	3 383	2 110	2 560	1 667	2 783	2 613	2 089
SURINAME	B	500	400	600	900		2 000	2 000	2 100
	D	500	400	600	900		2 000	2 000	2 100
	E	1 337	1 100	1 691	2 437		5 502	5 635	5 686

COUNTRY / PAYS / PAIS	DEFINITION OF DATA / CODE / TIPO DE DATOS	NEWSPRINT / PAPIER JOURNAL / PAPEL DE PERIODICO				OTHER PRINTING AND WRITING PAPER / AUTRE PAPIER D'IMPRESSION ET D'ECRITURE / OTRO PAPEL DE IMPRENTA Y DE ESCRIBIR			
		1970	1975	1980	1983	1970	1975	1980	1983
URUGUAY	A					14 500	10 800	25 400	18 000
	B	20 800	10 600	15 200	8 600	100	800	4 100	300
	C						1 000	8 400	7 700
	D	20 800	10 600	15 200	8 600	14 600	10 600	21 100	10 600
	E	7 409	3 747	5 226	2 891	5 200	3 747	7 255	3 564
VENEZUELA	A					26 200	55 700	84 200	82 000
	B	84 300	85 600	141 000	166 700	8 800	5 000	7 200	7 000
	D	84 300	85 600	141 000	166 700	35 000	60 700	91 400	89 000
	E	7 951	6 758	9 385	10 189	3 301	4 793	6 084	5 440
ASIA									
AFGHANISTAN	B		1 200	100	100	400	1 300	500	500
	D		1 200	100	100	400	1 300	500	500
	E		78	6	6	29	85	31	31
BAHRAIN	B					400	1 500	1 700	2 400
	D					400	1 500	1 700	2 400
	E					1 825	5 517	4 899	6 137
BANGLADESH	A	36 000	20 000	37 000	54 000	32 000	24 000	27 000	71 000
	C		5 300	18 000	8 000		400	1 000	1 700
	D	36 000	14 700	19 000	46 000	32 000	23 600	26 000	69 300
	E	540	192	215	480	480	308	295	723
BRUNEI DARUSSALAM	B	100	200	200	300	200	200	500	1 500
	D	100	200	200	300	200	200	500	1 500
	E	769	1 282	1 081	1 422	1 538	1 282	2 703	7 109
BURMA	A					400	7 000	7 000	7 000
	B	15 900	6 500	4 000	6 000	11 700	7 400	8 000	8 000
	D	15 900	6 500	4 000	6 000	12 100	14 400	15 000	15 000
	E	587	214	119	168	446	473	445	419
CHINA	A	392 000	712 000	1 081 000	1 143 000	809 000	1 318 000	1 950 000	2 027 000
	B	13 600	51 300	155 500	172 100	2 100	3 600	6 700	8 900
	C	13 000	1 900	700		13 300	21 300	34 200	25 600
	D	392 600	761 400	1 235 800	1 315 100	797 800	1 300 300	1 922 500	2 010 300
	E	473	821	1 241	1 270	960	1 402	1 930	1 941
CYPRUS	B	1 700	1 300	2 600	3 100	4 100	1 900	3 300	4 300
	D	1 700	1 300	2 600	3 100	4 100	1 900	3 300	4 300
	E	2 764	2 131	4 132	4 758	6 666	3 115	5 244	6 600
DEMOCRATIC KAMPUCHEA	A	500				2 400			
	D	500				2 400			
	E	72				346			
DEMOCRATIC YEMEN	B		100	500	500	400	1 800	1 000	900
	D		100	500	500	400	1 800	1 000	900
	E		60	269	247	267	1 087	537	445
HONG KONG	B	48 200	54 700	90 000	94 900	53 700	51 100	117 400	70 400
	C	3 200	1 400	14 200	5 800	4 300	4 300	5 000	1 100
	D	45 000	53 300	75 800	89 100	49 400	46 800	112 400	69 300
	E	11 417	12 124	15 044	16 654	12 533	10 646	22 308	12 953
INDIA	A	37 300	52 000	155 000	230 000	444 700	504 000	514 000	815 000
	B	144 200	100 800	270 000	171 000	2 800	2 700	12 200	40 000
	C					14 200	100	1 500	500
	D	181 500	152 800	425 000	401 000	433 300	506 600	524 700	854 500
	E	327	246	617	548	781	816	762	1 169
INDONESIA	A	3 000				6 000	45 000	121 000	173 000
	B	40 600	46 700	66 000	110 800	44 000	8 000	34 700	19 200
	D	43 600	46 700	66 000	110 800	50 000	53 000	155 700	192 200
	E	362	344	437	691	416	391	1 031	1 198
IRAN, ISLAMIC REPUBLIC OF	A					12 000	36 000	45 000	45 000
	B	10 900	32 800	14 000	16 000	99 800	33 800	32 000	27 000
	D	10 900	32 800	14 000	16 000	111 800	69 800	77 000	72 000
	E	384	984	362	380	3 937	2 093	1 993	1 709
IRAQ	A						8 000	9 000	9 000
	B	3 100	4 900	14 000	10 000	11 100	5 600	1 500	1 500
	D	3 100	4 900	14 000	10 000	11 100	13 600	10 500	10 500
	E	331	445	1 053	676	1 186	1 234	790	710
ISRAEL	A	9 400	7 000	4 000	2 000	31 800	47 000	41 000	67 000
	B	24 600	30 700	34 100	47 700	5 100	2 400	10 000	28 100
	C					1 500	1 400	2 300	100
	D	34 000	37 700	38 100	49 700	35 400	48 000	48 700	95 000
	E	11 428	10 911	9 824	12 129	11 898	13 892	12 557	23 185

7.22 Newsprint, printing and writing paper
Papier journal, papier d'impression et papier d'écriture
Papel de periódico, papel de imprenta y papel de escribir

COUNTRY / PAYS / PAIS	DEFINITION OF DATA / CODE / TIPO DE DATOS	NEWSPRINT / PAPIER JOURNAL / PAPEL DE PERIODICO 1970	1975	1980	1983	OTHER PRINTING AND WRITING PAPER / AUTRE PAPIER D'IMPRESSION ET D'ECRITURE / OTRO PAPEL DE IMPRENTA Y DE ESCRIBIR 1970	1975	1980	1983
JAPAN	A	1 917 000	2 160 000	2 674 000	2 562 000	2 410 000	2 772 000	4 137 000	4 319 000
	B	88 000	29 500	126 900	260 100	2 000	24 500	26 300	63 000
	C	32 000	107 300	97 500	85 300	191 000	194 400	247 000	317 000
	D	1 973 000	2 082 200	2 703 400	2 736 800	2 221 000	2 602 100	3 916 300	4 065 000
	E	18 911	18 670	23 144	23 005	21 288	23 332	33 528	34 170
JORDAN	B	600	700	2 600	8 500	500	2 000	7 100	5 000
	D	600	700	2 600	8 500	500	2 000	7 100	5 000
	E	261	269	890	2 602	217	769	2 429	1 530
KOREA, DEMOCRATIC PEOPLE'S REPUB. OF	B	1 300	1 300	1 300	1 300	2 100	2 100	2 100	2 100
	D	1 300	1 300	1 300	1 300	2 100	2 100	2 100	2 100
	E	94	82	72	67	151	132	117	108
KOREA, REPUBLIC OF	A	101 700	155 000	249 000	232 000	22 300	132 000	293 000	416 000
	B	6 600				400	100	400	1 400
	C		4 400	22 000	1 000		10 900	50 500	43 900
	D	108 300	150 600	227 000	231 000	22 700	121 200	242 900	373 500
	E	3 392	4 269	5 954	5 759	711	3 435	6 371	9 311
KUWAIT	B		4 800	19 000	14 000	6 700	12 000	26 500	26 500
	C					300	1 200	3 800	3 800
	D		4 800	19 000	14 000	6 400	10 800	22 700	22 700
	E		4 764	13 819	8 725	8 596	10 719	16 510	14 148
LAO PEOPLE'S DEMOCRATIC REPUBLIC	B	300	200	200		400	500	500	
	D	300	200	200		400	500	500	
	E	99	58	54		133	146	136	
LEBANON	B	5 100	6 300	7 000	6 000	23 500	25 400	33 200	34 300
	D	5 100	6 300	7 000	6 000	23 500	25 400	33 200	34 300
	E	2 066	2 277	2 623	2 235	9 518	9 179	12 438	12 778
MACAU	B	3 700	2 800	6 200	6 200	2 500	1 900		
	D	3 700	2 800	6 200	6 200	2 500	1 900		
	E	15 102	10 769	19 195	17 080	10 204	7 308		
MALAYSIA	A						1 000	1 000	
	B	38 400	34 100	66 000	95 000	20 500	31 100	61 700	71 100
	C					600	500	100	
	D	38 400	34 100	66 000	95 000	19 900	31 600	62 600	71 100
	E	3 534	2 771	4 795	6 405	1 832	2 567	4 548	4 793
MONGOLIA	B	2 400	2 600	2 300	3 800		1 700	1 900	3 100
	D	2 400	2 600	2 300	3 800		1 700	1 900	3 100
	E	1 924	1 800	1 383	2 103		1 177	1 142	1 715
OMAN	B				200				3 800
	D				200				3 800
	E				178				3 375
PAKISTAN	A					6 300	17 000	25 000	33 000
	B	500	6 700	33 100	34 400	7 000	45 000	23 200	35 800
	C					400			
	D	500	6 700	33 100	34 400	12 900	62 000	48 200	68 800
	E	8	90	384	364	196	830	560	729
PHILIPPINES	A	30 000	68 000	80 000	70 000	30 000	38 000	70 000	28 000
	B	45 500	800	20 000	1 200	10 700	11 600	12 000	19 400
	C		100				100	200	
	D	75 500	68 700	100 000	71 200	40 700	49 500	81 800	47 400
	E	2 011	1 614	2 070	1 369	1 084	1 163	1 693	912
QATAR	B					600	1 400	3 400	3 400
	D	600	1 400	1 400		600	1 400	3 400	3 400
	E	5 430	8 178	6 236		5 430	8 178	15 145	12 579
SAUDI ARABIA	B	500	2 300	13 000	5 500	6 700	12 200	45 200	55 300
	D	500	2 300	13 000	5 500	6 700	12 200	45 200	55 300
	E	87	317	1 387	520	1 166	1 682	4 823	5 228
SINGAPORE	B	24 500	30 300	60 000	78 300	23 600	28 900	71 100	119 800
	C	900	2 100	4 300	9 800	3 300	9 600	17 900	20 700
	D	23 600	28 200	55 700	68 500	20 300	19 300	53 200	99 100
	E	11 373	12 463	23 069	27 370	9 783	8 530	22 034	39 597
SRI LANKA	A					8 900	9 000	12 500	15 500
	B	18 300	6 500	8 000	13 500	4 300	6 200	15 600	13 800
	D	18 300	6 500	8 000	13 500	13 200	15 200	28 100	29 300
	E	1 462	478	540	862	1 055	1 117	1 896	1 871
SYRIAN ARAB REPUBLIC	B	1 500	900	3 700	7 400	7 200	12 000	30 000	12 000
	D	1 500	900	3 700	7 400	7 200	12 000	30 000	12 000
	E	240	121	420	756	1 151	1 613	3 409	1 225

COUNTRY / PAYS / PAIS	DEFINITION OF DATA / CODE / TIPO DE DATOS	NEWSPRINT / PAPIER JOURNAL / PAPEL DE PERIODICO				OTHER PRINTING AND WRITING PAPER / AUTRE PAPIER D'IMPRESSION ET D'ECRITURE / OTRO PAPEL DE IMPRENTA Y DE ESCRIBIR			
		1970	1975	1980	1983	1970	1975	1980	1983
THAILAND	A					32 000	51 000	73 000	36 000
	B	36 300	63 400	91 600	131 600	12 500	2 100	8 800	9 400
	C					300	1 800	300	200
	D	36 300	63 400	91 600	131 600	44 200	51 300	81 500	45 200
	E	998	1 532	1 969	2 660	1 215	1 240	1 752	913
TURKEY	A	10 700	86 000	86 000	147 000	42 400	72 000	69 000	85 000
	B	15 400	12 200	71 400	4 200	4 300	2 400	2 800	8 700
	D	26 100	98 200	157 400	151 200	46 700	74 400	71 800	93 700
	E	739	2 453	3 540	3 188	1 322	1 859	1 615	1 976
VIET-NAM	A					15 000	18 000	17 000	17 000
	B	21 700	2 000	2 500	2 500	100			
	D	21 700	2 000	2 500	2 500	15 100	18 000	17 000	17 000
	E	508	42	46	43	353	375	314	295
EUROPE									
AUSTRIA	A	170 000	147 000	176 000	176 000	394 000	523 000	618 000	721 000
	B	400	4 600	1 500	12 700	8 100	12 100	56 700	100 600
	C	100	200	1 200	10 100	288 100	409 800	562 100	687 500
	D	170 300	151 400	176 300	178 600	114 000	125 300	112 600	134 100
	E	22 866	20 132	23 490	23 819	15 307	16 661	15 003	17 884
BELGIUM‡	A	95 000	77 000	102 000	99 000	352 000	330 000	436 000	417 000
	B	110 300	105 400	126 000	125 200	208 300	155 500	337 700	326 900
	C	25 600	20 500	31 000	33 600	237 400	201 800	288 400	197 200
	D	179 700	161 900	197 000	190 600	322 900	283 700	485 300	546 700
	E	18 644	16 527	19 996	19 306	33 501	28 961	49 260	55 375
BULGARIA	A					41 000	42 000	36 000	79 000
	B	35 400	49 000	46 200	41 500	9 500	18 400	13 400	12 700
	D	35 400	49 000	46 200	41 500	50 500	60 400	49 400	91 700
	E	4 158	5 618	5 214	4 630	5 931	6 925	5 575	10 230
CZECHOSLOVAKIA	A	81 400	77 000	71 000	68 000	176 500	152 000	168 000	173 000
	B	9 000	8 000	8 000	9 600	26 000	30 000	20 000	6 200
	C	40 700	17 000	7 000	9 400	39 000	48 000	34 000	6 200
	D	49 700	68 000	72 000	68 200	163 500	134 000	154 000	173 000
	E	3 461	4 594	4 702	4 423	11 384	9 053	10 058	11 218
DENMARK	A					71 000	59 000	113 000	155 000
	B	149 200	125 700	153 300	165 800	84 600	91 600	135 800	132 100
	C	200	400	700	700	10 800	14 700	57 600	87 400
	D	149 000	125 300	152 600	165 100	144 800	135 900	191 200	199 700
	E	30 230	24 765	29 787	32 235	29 378	26 860	37 322	38 990
FINLAND	A	1 305 000	992 000	1 569 000	1 613 000	981 000	1 340 000	2 027 000	2 382 000
	B	900				1 600	3 000	4 300	6 000
	C	1 187 000	776 200	1 431 900	1 467 000	779 200	1 176 800	1 750 000	2 092 000
	D	118 900	215 800	137 100	146 000	203 400	166 200	281 300	296 000
	E	25 814	45 796	28 685	30 202	44 160	35 270	58 856	61 232
FRANCE	A	430 200	238 000	261 000	221 000	1 418 000	1 311 000	2 011 000	2 123 000
	B	177 000	165 000	371 400	343 300	228 000	362 000	596 600	746 000
	C	1 700	1 000	3 600	4 500	158 000	262 000	528 200	589 000
	D	605 500	402 000	628 800	559 800	1 488 000	1 411 000	2 079 400	2 280 000
	E	11 950	7 627	11 706	10 342	29 366	26 771	38 713	42 122
GERMAN DEMOCRATIC REPUBLIC	A	96 800	95 900	106 000	105 000	197 000	180 700	182 000	182 000
	B	36 900	50 000	45 300	44 000	1 100	20 000	36 000	76 000
	C	16 400	5 700	10 000	10 000	21 900	18 900	14 000	41 000
	D	117 300	140 200	141 300	139 000	176 200	181 800	204 000	217 000
	E	6 873	8 321	8 442	8 319	10 325	10 790	12 188	12 987
GERMANY, FEDERAL REPUBLIC OF	A	408 000	486 000	606 000	654 000	1 889 000	1 716 000	2 879 000	3 368 000
	B	695 300	654 800	869 100	745 500	520 800	605 000	1 076 700	1 236 400
	C	48 200	64 100	81 100	143 500	287 200	277 600	685 300	1 059 500
	D	1 055 100	1 076 700	1 394 000	1 256 000	2 122 600	2 043 400	3 270 400	3 544 900
	E	17 382	17 413	22 642	20 554	34 969	33 048	53 120	58 012
GREECE	A			9 000	15 000	30 000	35 000	80 000	53 000
	B	31 600	48 000	40 000	61 600	5 700	34 300	42 500	50 100
	C		100	7 900	1 800		300	28 300	2 200
	D	31 600	47 900	41 100	74 800	35 700	69 000	94 200	100 900
	E	3 594	5 295	4 262	7 647	4 060	7 628	9 769	10 316
HUNGARY	A					74 200	101 000	115 000	126 000
	B	53 600	56 300	63 000	66 200	35 400	42 700	44 000	41 700
	C			2 000		1 200	19 200	24 300	22 200
	D	53 600	56 300	61 000	66 200	108 400	124 500	134 700	145 500
	E	5 177	5 341	5 695	6 199	10 470	11 811	12 576	13 626
ICELAND	B	3 100	3 000	4 000	5 000	1 800	1 800	3 200	2 700
	D	3 100	3 000	4 000	5 000	1 800	1 800	3 200	2 700
	E	15 166	13 768	17 528	21 097	8 806	8 261	14 023	11 392

7.22 Newsprint, printing and writing paper
Papier journal, papier d'impression et papier d'écriture
Papel de periódico, papel de imprenta y papel de escribir

COUNTRY PAYS PAIS	DEFINITION OF DATA CODE TIPO DE DATOS	NEWSPRINT PAPIER JOURNAL PAPEL DE PERIODICO				OTHER PRINTING AND WRITING PAPER AUTRE PAPIER D'IMPRESSION ET D'ECRITURE OTRO PAPEL DE IMPRENTA Y DE ESCRIBIR			
		1970	1975	1980	1983	1970	1975	1980	1983
IRELAND	A	6 000	10 000			10 000	19 000	23 000	
	B	48 200	47 000	60 800	54 000	5 300	8 900	22 100	36 000
	C		300	200	100	1 000	2 100	6 700	2 000
	D	54 200	56 700	60 600	53 900	14 300	25 800	38 400	34 000
	E	18 351	17 686	17 818	15 270	4 842	8 047	11 291	9 633
ITALY	A	311 000	243 000	277 000	194 000	1 167 000	1 054 000	1 799 000	1 671 000
	B	13 800	11 500	63 700	178 200	24 100	33 900	147 900	259 300
	C	42 500	9 600	13 000	1 300	133 000	111 000	330 400	377 600
	D	282 300	244 900	327 700	370 900	1 058 100	976 900	1 616 500	1 552 700
	E	5 270	4 387	5 742	6 487	19 754	17 498	28 325	27 158
MALTA	B	300	200	700	700	2 900	2 400	2 300	2 300
	D	300	200	700	700	2 900	2 400	2 300	2 300
	E	919	580	1 897	1 862	8 885	6 957	6 231	6 119
NETHERLANDS	A	167 000	125 000	171 000	179 000	489 000	406 000	571 000	526 000
	B	247 300	257 400	331 900	286 600	213 000	249 400	394 300	389 900
	C	35 600	22 700	45 100	62 400	151 200	193 900	283 600	309 300
	D	378 700	359 700	457 800	403 200	550 800	461 500	681 700	606 600
	E	29 057	26 074	32 354	28 080	42 263	33 454	48 177	42 246
NORWAY	A	554 000	435 000	589 000	711 000	317 000	292 000	337 000	243 000
	B					4 900	16 400	52 800	77 000
	C	475 600	380 500	522 800	584 600	223 600	163 400	231 300	191 300
	D	78 400	54 500	66 200	126 400	98 300	145 000	158 500	128 700
	E	20 218	13 602	16 203	30 687	25 350	36 189	38 795	31 245
POLAND	A	87 900	83 000	91 000	83 000	188 100	210 000	199 000	208 000
	B	15 000	38 000	36 000	45 600	21 000	56 000	28 000	13 900
	C	15 000				100	2 000	2 000	
	D	87 900	121 000	127 000	128 600	209 000	264 000	225 000	221 900
	E	2 692	3 556	3 570	3 528	6 400	7 759	6 325	6 088
PORTUGAL	A	700	1 000			43 200	54 000	87 000	99 000
	B	43 500	28 500	41 000	36 100	1 500	2 300	4 300	12 100
	C	200	2 100			300	14 400	14 000	27 800
	D	44 000	27 400	41 000	36 100	44 400	41 900	77 300	83 300
	E	5 100	2 907	4 148	3 579	5 146	4 446	7 821	8 259
ROMANIA	A	53 000	44 000	103 000	91 000	123 000	121 000	141 000	139 000
	B	9 500	12 500	12 000	11 000	4 000	1 200		
	C	10 800	12 400	59 000	42 000	45 100	38 000	57 000	46 000
	D	51 700	44 100	56 000	60 000	81 900	84 200	84 000	93 000
	E	2 539	2 076	2 522	2 651	4 023	3 963	3 784	4 109
SPAIN	A	115 000	103 000	108 000	115 000	322 800	521 000	717 000	692 000
	B	78 800	101 800	57 600	117 000	11 300	53 000	82 000	85 000
	C		900	3 200		15 900	64 300	42 900	86 000
	D	193 800	203 900	162 400	232 000	318 200	509 700	756 100	691 000
	E	5 737	5 728	4 339	6 088	9 420	14 319	20 200	18 132
SWEDEN	A	1 030 000	1 213 000	1 534 000	1 349 000	537 000	448 000	998 000	1 121 000
	B				5 200	16 100	18 400	32 700	50 500
	C	686 600	920 800	1 238 400	1 087 500	283 800	277 500	510 100	581 400
	D	343 400	292 200	295 600	266 700	269 300	188 900	520 600	590 100
	E	42 700	35 665	35 569	32 035	33 486	23 057	62 644	70 881
SWITZERLAND	A	143 000	143 000	210 000	213 000	249 000	180 000	284 000	275 000
	B	24 600	6 000	24 600	33 000	77 300	82 400	156 600	167 000
	C	100	8 200	27 600	29 000	8 900	28 700	76 000	89 000
	D	167 500	140 800	207 000	217 000	317 400	233 700	364 600	353 000
	E	26 733	21 979	32 718	34 157	50 657	36 481	57 629	55 563
UNITED KINGDOM	A	756 900	319 000	363 000	80 000	1 145 300	952 000	937 000	903 000
	B	789 100	943 000	1 076 500	1 244 000	274 700	531 000	814 500	1 169 000
	C	1 800	4 900	58 400	9 000	69 000	58 400	111 800	135 000
	D	1 544 200	1 257 100	1 381 100	1 315 000	1 351 000	1 424 600	1 639 700	1 937 000
	E	27 833	22 434	24 687	23 461	24 351	25 423	29 309	34 558
YUGOSLAVIA	A	75 000	85 000	45 000	29 000	139 900	157 000	292 000	334 000
	B	23 500	1 600	5 300	7 000	14 800	22 000	12 900	8 100
	C	10 000	1 500	20 300	17 500	33 400	15 900	35 100	43 800
	D	88 500	85 100	30 000	18 500	121 300	163 100	269 800	298 300
	E	4 344	3 986	1 345	813	5 954	7 639	12 099	13 114
OCEANIA									
AUSTRALIA	A	173 300	196 000	221 000	376 000	126 300	160 000	210 000	179 000
	B	275 300	324 500	336 800	134 600	123 000	163 900	181 100	184 100
	C	67 000	30 800	39 100	46 000	17 100	12 900	16 200	11 900
	D	381 600	489 700	518 700	464 600	232 200	311 000	374 900	351 200
	E	30 405	35 932	35 297	30 372	18 501	22 820	25 511	22 959
FIJI	B	800	900	1 700	2 000	500	2 600	2 400	2 200
	D	800	900	1 700	2 000	500	2 600	2 400	2 200
	E	1 538	1 560	2 701	3 001	961	4 508	3 814	3 301

COUNTRY / PAYS / PAIS	DEFINITION OF DATA / CODE / TIPO DE DATOS	NEWSPRINT / PAPIER JOURNAL / PAPEL DE PERIODICO				OTHER PRINTING AND WRITING PAPER / AUTRE PAPIER D'IMPRESSION ET D'ECRITURE / OTRO PAPEL DE IMPRENTA Y DE ESCRIBIR			
		1970	1975	1980	1983	1970	1975	1980	1983
FRENCH POLYNESIA	B	400	300	100	1 000				
	D	400	300	100	1 000				
	E	3 670	2 256	676	6 369				
NEW CALEDONIA	B		1 100	1 300	1 300				
	D		1 100	1 300	1 300				
	E		8 271	9 353	8 784				
NEW ZEALAND	A	213 900	219 000	319 000	269 000	29 700	34 000	33 000	35 000
	B	500	2 300	300	13 000	16 900	12 600	26 400	15 700
	C	118 600	106 400	241 200	143 700	400	300	1 600	1 800
	D	95 800	114 900	78 100	138 300	46 200	46 300	57 800	48 900
	E	33 984	37 206	24 647	42 405	16 389	14 993	18 241	14 994
PAPUA NEW GUINEA	B	600	500			700			
	D	600	500			700			
	E	248	185			289			
SAMOA	B	200				300			1 100
	D	200				300			1 100
	E	1 399				2 098			6 875
U.S.S.R.									
U.S.S.R.	A	1 101 000	1 361 000	1 354 000	1 482 000	883 000	1 136 000	1 141 000	1 249 000
	B	86 800	45 700	30 100	33 200	143 200	171 300	278 700	305 000
	C	259 600	268 000	320 000	341 000	24 800	48 800	48 300	45 200
	D	928 200	1 138 700	1 064 100	1 174 200	1 001 400	1 258 500	1 371 400	1 508 800
	E	3 840	4 494	4 008	4 310	4 143	4 967	5 165	5 538

Belgium:
E--> Including Luxembourg.

Belgium: (Cont):
FR-> Y compris le Luxembourg.
ESP> Incluído Luxemburgo.

8 Cultural heritage

Patrimoine culturel

Patrimonio cultural

The statistics in this chapter refer to cultural heritage in the form of museums, historical monuments and archeological sites, archives, etc. This grouping is new and stems from a concern to bring together in one chapter statistics relating to cultural heritage as delineated in the Unesco Framework for Cultural Statistics (FCS).

Section 1.

Unesco's first attempt to establish international statistics on museums and related institutions was made in the early 1950's. From 1962 onward, the statistical questionnaire was sent out every two years until 1974 when it was decided that the surveys should be conducted at regular intervals of three years in view of the rather infrequent changes in this field.

What renders the international collection of museum statistics relatively difficult is the almost complete absence of generally accepted standards and norms. Some countries, for instance, include in their museum statistics historical monuments and archaeological sites but leave out zoological and botanical gardens, aquaria, nature reserves, etc. For other countries it is just the reverse. Furthermore, not all countries take account of museums which are owned by individuals or private organizations.

The lack of internationally accepted definitions and classifications affects in no small measure the quality, quantity and completeness of the statistics collected. Consequently any kind of international comparison has to be made with great caution.

In order to achieve at least a minimum degree of comparability the categories and terms used in the 1977, 1980 and 1985 surveys have been based on definitions established by the *International Council of Museums (ICOM)*.

For the purpose of these surveys the term *museum* is defined as a *non profit-making, permanent institution in the service of society and its development and open to the public, which acquires, conserves, researches, communicates and exhibits for purposes of study, education and employment, material evidence of man and his environment.* In addition to museums designated as such, the following, recognized by ICOM as being of museum nature, are also included in the surveys:

a: Conservation institutes and exhibition galleries permanently maintained by libraries and archive centers;

b: Natural, archaeological and ethnographic monuments and sites and historical monuments and sites *of a museum nature* for their acquisition, conservation and communication activities;

c: Institutions displaying live specimens, such as botanical and zoological gardens, aquaria, vivaria etc;

d: Nature reserves;

e: Science centres and planetaria.

For statistical purposes, museums and related institutions have been counted by number of administrative units rather than by number of collections.

For the classification of museums and related institutions by *predominant subject of exhibits and collections* the following categories have been used:

a: *Art museums:* museums for the display of works of fine and applied arts. Within this group fall museums such as museums of sculpture, picture galleries, museums of photography and cinema, museums of architecture, etc. Also included in this category are conservation institutes and exhibition galleries permanently maintained by libraries and archive centres;

b: *Archaeology and history museums:* the aim of history museums is to present the historical evolution of a region, country or province over a limited period or over the centuries. Museums of archaeology are distinguished by the fact that they owe all or part of their collections to excavations. Within this group fall museums of collections of historical objects and relics, memorial museums, museums of archives, military museums, museums of historical figures, museums of archaeology, museums of antiquities, etc;

c: *Natural history and natural science museums:* museums for the display of subjects related to either one or several of the disciplines such as biology, geology, botany, zoology, palaeontology and ecology;

d: *Science and technology museums:* museums in this category relate to one or several exact sciences or technologies such as astronomy, mathematics, physics, chemistry, medical science, construction and building industries, manufactured articles, etc. Also included in this category are planeteria and science centres;

e: *Ethnography and anthropology museums:* museums displaying materials on culture, social structures, beliefs, customs, traditional arts, etc;

f: *Specialized museums:* museums which are concerned with reserach and display of all aspects of a *single theme or subject* not covered within one of the categories (a) to (e);

g: *Regional museums:* museums which illustrate a more or less extensive region constituting a historical and cultural entity and sometimes also an ethnical, economic or social one, i.e., the collections refer to a specific territory rather than to a specific theme or subject;

h: *General museums:* museums which have mixed collections and cannot be identified by any one principal field;

i: *Other museums:* museums and related institutions

not included in any of the above categories;

j and k: *Historical monuments and archaeological sites:* architectural or sculptural works and topographical areas of special interest from an archaeological, historical, ethnographical or anthropological point of view;

l and m: *Zoological and botanical gardens, aquaria and nature reserves:* the specific feature of these entities of a museum nature is that they display live specimens.

The classification of museums proper by *ownership or governing authority* covers the following three categories:

a: *National museums:* museums which are owned or administered by central or federal government authorities;

b: *Other public museums:* museums which are owned or governed by other public authorities (federated state, province, county, city, town, etc.) or by public societies, foundations, educational institutions, churches, etc;

c: *Private museums:* museums which are owned by individuals or private organizations.

Figures on *annual attendance* for the different types of museum represent the number of *visitors*. Data on attendance in groups (school and other organized visits) are reported separately but not published in this *Yearbook*.

Data on *receipts* refer to total annual receipts and are given in national currency.

With regard to *personnel employed* by museums and related institutions a distinction is made between *professional* and *other* staff, whereby:

Professional staff are defined as employees doing work that requires specialized education, training or experience. This category includes personnel such as curators, designers, librarians, technicians engaged in restoration work, taxidermists, laboratory technicians, archaeologists, etc;

Other staff (non-professional) include custodial, security and clerical staff, animal attendants, packers, cleaning personnel, etc.

A distinction is also made between paid personnel and volunteers, the latter performing jobs that otherwise would require the hiring of paid personnel. Part-time paid staff is given in full-time equivalent.

Data on current expenditure refer to total annual expenditure and are shown in national currency.

Table 8.1

The figures given in this table show the number of establishments, annual attendance, receipts, personnel and current expenditure by ownership or governing authority. The table gives the most recent data available from either the 1980 or 1985 survey. It should be noted, however, that while data prior to 1983 refer to museums *and* related institutions (monuments, sites, zoological gardens, etc.), those for 1985 and later refer only to museums proper.

Table 8.2

The data shown in this table refer to museums and related institutions by predominant subject of collection, and have been obtained through either the 1980 or 1985 survey. For statistics reported in the 1980 survey, the totals shown in this table are identical to those in the preceding one. In the case of statistics from the 1985 survey, only the total numbers of museums proper can be related to the figures shown in Table 8.1.

Section 2.

The first international collection of statistics on archives and records centres was conducted in early 1984 by means of a questionnaire adapted from a statistical model developed with the assistance of the International Council on Archives (ICA) and pilot-tested in 1981 with a view to streamlining classification categories used in the world and achieving a common archival terminology and classification system. The definitions used in the 1984 survey were based upon a multilingual international glossary of archival terminology published by the International Council on Archives. The definitions relevant to the statistical information published in this *Yearbook* are the following:

1. *Archival institution.* Regardless of its formal title, any agency whose primary functions include:

a) the preservation of archival holdings received by transfer or otherwise;

b) the organization of these holdings for use by persons other than staff members of the institution itself.

Records centre. Irrespective of its title, any institution providing temporary accommodation for the storage and further processing of semi-current records which are no longer frequently used in the conduct of current business, but which cannot yet be disposed of or are not yet ready for transfer to an archival institution.

1.1 *Administrative unit.* An archival institution or a group of archival institutions under a single director or a single administration.

1.2 *General archival institution.* A public archival institution, regardless of its formal title, that is responsible for the preservation of the archives of all or most agencies at a given level of administration, as shown below. General archival institutions are thus categorized as:

a) National, central or general state archives (in unitary countries) or federal archives (in federal countries);

b) Regional archives (in unitary countries) or state archives (of component states in federal countries);

c) Local archives (in both unitary and federal countries).

1.3 *Special archival institution.* An archival institution, either public or private and regardless of its formal title, restricted mainly to:

a) archival holdings transferred by one government agency and its subordinate administrative units (for instance, archives of a parliament or of a defence or foreign ministry), or by a number of similar types of public or private institutions and organizations (i.e. chambers of commerce, trade unions, business firms, ecclesiastic institutions, academies of science, hospitals, universities, political parties, families, etc.);

b) archival holdings acquired on the basis of subject content or common physical form (i.e. archives of literature and art, economic archives, audio-visual archives, motion picture or sound archives, machine-readable archives, etc.).

2. *Holdings.* The totality of archival material in the custody of an archival institution.

2.1 *Conventional archives.* The term is used to refer to manuscript and typescript material, generally on paper. This category includes:

a) printed archives (separately maintained as such);

b) computer print-outs selected for preservation, and

c) conventional archives directly related to cartographic, audio-visual and machine-readable archives, even if physically located separately from the other conventional archives.

With regard to records centres, a distinction should be made between semi-current records and active records.

2.2 *Cartographic archives.* Material, separately maintained in a cartographic section or area, that in graphic or photogrammetric form depicts a portion of a linear surface (such as maps, plans, globes, topographic and hydrographic charts, architectural materials, cartograms, relief models and aerial photographs).

2.3 *Audio-visual archives.* Material in pictorial and/or aural form, regardless of format. Audio-visual archives are categorized as:

a) photographs (still pictures): negatives and prints, slides and transparencies, and film-strips, but excluding aerial photographs separately maintained and included under cartographic archives;

b) motion pictures (moving images) with or without sound: films, film loops, video tapes and other similar material not elsewhere classified;

c) sound recordings (phonograms): discs, tapes, cassettes, etc. and earlier forms thereof.

2.4 *Machine-readable archives.* Material, usually in code, recorded on media such as magnetic discs, drums, tapes, punched cards and tapes, etc. whose contents are accessible only by machine.

2.5 *Microforms.* All material, whether in negative or positive form, carrying transparent photographic images on a reduced scale requiring magnification for their use. Only microforms that have been acquired as part of the archival holdings should be reported. Microforms created or acquired as part of the library holdings should be reported only under that heading. Archival holdings of microforms are categorized as:

a) microfilm in roll form;

b) microfiche and other microforms.

2.6 *Drawings and prints.* Pictorial material other than cartographic archives, audio-visual archives, and microforms, separately maintained in a special section or area.

2.7 *Seals and other three-dimensional objects.* Only unattached and separately-maintained seals should be included.

2.8 *Library material.* A distinction should be made for reporting purposes between material acquired and maintained for reference use by the staff and researchers, and material acquired as a result of legal deposit responsibilities.

3. *Accessions.* Additions to the holdings, acquired mainly by transfer (including transfers from records centres), but also by permanent or revocable deposit, gift, purchase or other method.

4. *Arrangement and description.* All activities involved in bringing holdings under administrative and intellectual control, including the physical organization of the holdings and the preparation of published or unpublished finding aids (guides, inventories, catalogues, calendars, lists, indexes, location indexes/registers, etc.). This does not include any finding aids transferred or acquired with the records and not created by the archival agency.

5. *Reference service.* Providing information about or from the holdings, including making them available for use in search rooms, and loan of holdings.

5.1 *Visitor.* A person actually using search room services, excluding persons in guided group visits.

5.2 *Visit.* Attendance of one visitor during one day or part of a day. If a visitor checks in more than once on the same day, this interrupted attendance should be counted as only one visit.

5.3 *Storage unit.* Any physical unit of archival material, such as a volume, bundle, etc. made available in the search room(s).

5.4 *Recorded inquiries,* other than direct contact in the search room. This includes inquiries answered by telephone or in writing, including the sending of prepared general information, such as leaflets.

6. *Personnel.* All persons employed under the authority of the archival institution in carrying out its functions. In the total number of positions all part-time positions should be included in terms of full-time equivalents.

6.1 *Permanent staff.* Personnel on the budget of the archival institution, such as professional archivists, technical staff, clerical staff, etc.

6.1.1 *Professional archivist.* A person working in an archival institution or records centre who has an education or training considered by the institution as adequate for the performance of professional work with records and/or archives. The education and training may be:

a) university training only, or
b) university plus formal archival training, or
c) formal archival training without any university education.

6.2 *Supernumerary and occasional (non-permanent) personnel.* Personnel not on the budget of the archival institution, such as unpaid apprentices or trainees, volunteers, etc.

Table 8.3

For the 1984 survey, data were requested on general archives (national, regional and local) as well as on special archives (institution-oriented and subject-oriented). The replies received, however, referred in the majority of cases to national archives only and in a few instances to national and regional archives. Hardly any country appeared to be in a position to report on local general archives or on special archives. Table 8.1 shows, therefore, only data on national and regional archives. It is hoped that further surveys will provide more comprehensive statistics; i.e., will include other types of archival institutions as well.

Les statistiques de ce chapitre se réfèrent au patrimoine culturel, représenté par les musées, les monuments et sites historiques, archives etc. Ce regroupement est nouveau et provient du désir de rassembler dans un seul chapitre les statistiques relatives au patrimoine culturel, comme décrit dans le Cadre de l'Unesco pour les statistiques culturelles (CSC).

Section 1.

La première tentative de l'Unesco pour établir des statistiques internationales relatives aux musées et aux institutions assimilées date du début des années cinquante. A partir de 1962, le questionnaire a été envoyé tous les deux ans jusqu'en 1974; il a été décidé alors que les enquêtes devraient être effectuées à des intervalles réguliers de trois ans, compte tenu des changements peu fréquents qui interviennent dans ce domaine.

Ce qui rend relativement difficile la collecte internationale de données statistiques sur les musées est l'absence presque complète de normes et de classifications généralement acceptées. Quelques pays, par exemple, comprennent dans leurs statistiques sur les musées, les monuments historiques et les sites archéologiques mais ne tiennent pas compte des jardins zoologiques et botaniques, des aquariums et réserves naturelles, etc. Pour d'autres pays, c'est juste le contraire qui se produit. De plus, tous les pays ne prennent pas en considération les musées qui appartiennent à des particuliers ou à des organismes privés.

Le manque de définitions et de classifications qui soient acceptées du point de vue international affecte sensiblement la qualité, la quantité et la portée des statistiques recueillies. Par conséquent, toute sorte de comparaison internationale doit être effectuée avec beaucoup de prudence.

Dans le but d'assurer un minimum de comparabilité, les catégories et les termes utilisés dans les enquêtes de 1977, 1980 et 1985 ont été choisis sur la base des définitions établies par le *Conseil International des Musées (ICOM).*

Aux fins de ces enquêtes, on entend par 'musée' une institution permanente, sans but lucratif, au service de la société et de son développement, ouverte au public, et qui fait des recherches concernant les témoins matériels de l'homme et de son environnement, acquiert ceux-là, les conserve, les communique et notamment les expose à des fins d'études, d'éducation et délectation. Outre les musées désignés comme tels, les entités suivantes, reconnues par l'ICOM comme étant assimilées à l'appellation de musées sont également couvertes par cette enquête:

a: Les instituts de conservation et galeries d'exposition dépendant des bibliothèques et des centres d'archives;

b: Les sites et monuments archéologiques, ethnographiques et naturels et les sites et monuments historiques *ayant un caractère de musée* par leurs activités d'acquisition, de conservation et de communication;

c: Les institutions qui présentent des spécimens vivants, tels que les jardins botaniques et zoologiques, aquariums, vivariums, etc.;

d: Les réserves naturelles;

e: Les centres scientifiques et planétariums.

Les unités statistiques correspondent, pour les musées et institutions assimilées, aux unités administratives et non au nombre de collections.

Pour la classification des musées et institutions assimilées *d'après la nature prédominante des sujets exposés et des collections* les catégories suivantes ont été utilisées:

a: *Musées d'art:* musées consacrés aux beaux-arts et aux arts appliqués. Ce groupe comprend les musées de sculpture, les galeries de peinture, les musées de la photographie et du cinéma, les musées d'architecture, etc. Les instituts de conservation et galeries d'exposition dépendant des bibliothèques et des centres d'archives sont également compris dans cette catégorie.

b: *Musées d'archéologie et d'histoire:* les musées d'histoire ont pour but de présenter l'évolution historique d'une région, d'un pays ou d'une province pour des périodes limitées dans le temps ou au cours des siècles. Les musées d'archéologie se distinguent par le fait que leurs collections proviennent en partie ou en totalité de fouilles. Ce groupe englobe les musées de collections d'objets historiques ou de vestiges, musées commémoratifs, musées d'archives, musées militaires, musées de personnalités historiques, musées d'archéologie, musées d'antiquités, etc.;

c: *Musées de science et d'histoire naturelles:* musées consacrés aux sujets se rapportant à une ou à plusieurs disciplines telles que la biologie, la botanique, la zoologie, la paléontologie et l'écologie;

d: *Musées des science et des techniques:* musées consacrés aux sujets se rapportant à une ou plusieurs sciences exactes ou techniques telles que l'astronomie, les mathématiques, la physique, la chimie, les sciences médicales, la construction et les industries du bâtiment, les articles manufacturés, etc. Sont également inclus dans cette catégorie les planétariums et les centres scientifiques.

e: *Musées d'ethnographie et d'anthropologie:* musées qui exposent des matériels se rapportant à la culture, aux structures sociales, aux croyances, aux coutumes, aux arts traditionnels, etc.

f: *Musées spécialisés:* musées concernés par la recherche et l'exposition de tous aspects relatifs à *un thème ou sujet unique* non inclus dans l'une des catégories (a) à (e).

g: *Musées régionaux:* musées dont le thème illustre une région plus ou moins étendue constituant une entité historique et culturelle et parfois même une entité ethnique, économique ou sociale, c'est-à-dire dont les collections se rapportent davantage à un territoire spécifique qu'à un thème ou à un sujet particulier;

h: *Musées généraux:* musées ayant des collections hétérogènes et ne pouvant pas être identifiés par un domaine principal;

i: *Autres musées:* musées et institutions assimilées n'entrant dans aucune des catégories précédentes;

j et k: *Monuments historiques et sites archéologiques protégés:* travaux architecturaux et sculpturaux et zones topographiques présentant un intérêt spécial des points de vue archéologique, historique, ethnologique ou anthropologique;

l et m: *Jardins zoologiques et botaniques, aquariums et réserves naturelles:* Leur caractéristique spécifique est qu'elles présentent des spécimens vivants;

La classification des musées proprement dits selon leur *propriété ou leur statut administratif* couvre les trois catégories suivantes:

a: *Musées nationaux:* musées qui sont la propriété ou qui sont administrés par les autorités de l'Etat (central ou fédéral);

b: *Autres musées publics:* musées qui sont la propriété ou qui sont administrés par d'autres autorités publiques (Etat fédératif, province, municipalité, commune, etc.) ou par des collectivités à caractère public telles que des sociétés, des fondations, des institutions éducatives, des églises, etc.

c: *Musées privés:* musées qui sont la propriété de particuliers ou d'organismes privés.

Les données statistiques concernant la *fréquentation annuelle* des différents types de musées représentent le nombre de *visiteurs*. Les données concernant la fréquentation des groupes (écoles et autres groupes organisés) sont fournies séparément mais ne sont pas publiées dans cet Annuaire.

Les données sur les *recettes* se réfèrent au total des recettes annuelles exprimé en monnaie nationale.

En ce qui concerne le *personnel employé* par les musées et autres institutions assimilées une distinction est établie entre le *personnel professionnel* et *l'autre personnel* comme suit:

Le *personnel professionnel* se rapporte aux employés exécutant un travail nécessitant une formation, une instruction ou une expérience spécialisées. Cette catégorie inclut du personnel tel que les administrateurs, réalisateurs, bibliothécaires, taxidermistes, restaurateurs, techniciens de laboratoire, archéologues, etc.

L'*autre personnel* (non professionnel) comprend les gardiens, commis, responsables de services de sécurité, soigneurs d'animaux, emballeurs, personnel de nettoyage, etc.

Une distinction est aussi établie entre les *salariés* et les *volontaires*, ces derniers faisant des travaux qui, autrement, nécessiteraient l'embauchage de salariés. Le personnel salarié à temps partiel est indiqué en équivalent à plein temps.

Les données sur les *dépenses de fonctionnement* se réfèrent au total annuel de ces dépenses exprimé en monnaie nationale.

Tableau 8.1

Les chiffres présentés dans ce tableau montrent le nombre d'établissements, la fréquentation annuelle, les recettes, les dépenses pour le personnel et les dépenses ordinaires selon la propriété ou le statut administratif. Ce tableau présente les données disponibles les plus récentes, provenant soit de l'enquête de 1980 soit de celle de 1985. Cependant, il est à noter que les données antérieures à 1983 se réfèrent aux musées *et* aux institutions assimilées (monuments, sites, jardins zoologiques, etc.), alors que les données de 1985 se réfèrent seulement aux musées proprement dits.

Tableau 8.2

Les données présentées dans ce tableau se réfèrent aux musées et institutions assimilées d'après la nature prédominante de leurs collections et proviennent soit de l'enquête de 1980 soit de celle de 1985. En ce qui concerne les statistiques de l'enquête de 1980, les totaux figurant dans ce tableau sont identiques à ceux du tableau précédent. Dans le cas des statistiques de l'enquête de 1985, seul le total des musées proprement dits peut se rapporter aux chiffres indiqués dans le tableau 8.1.

Section 2.

Le premier rassemblement au niveau international des statistiques sur les centres d'archives et les dépôts de préarchivage a été effectué au début de 1984 au moyen d'un questionnnaire basé sur un questionnaire modèle élaboré avec l'assistance du Conseil International des Archives (CIA) et testé en 1981 dans le but de concilier les catégories de classification utilisées dans le monde et d'établir une terminologie commune pour les archives et un système de classification commun. Les définitions utilisées dans l'enquête de 1984 étaient basées sur un glossaire international multilingue de terminologie archivistique, publié par le Conseil International des Archives. Les définitions relatives aux informations statistiques publiées dans cet *Annuaire* sont les suivantes:

1. *Institution d'archives.* Quelle que soit son appellation, toute institution dont les fonctions principales sont:

a) la conservation des fonds d'archives, soit versés, soit acquis par d'autres voies;

b) le traitement de ces fonds en vue de leur utilisation par des personnes autres que les membres du personnel de l'institution.

Dépôts de préarchivage. Toute institution, quelle qu'en soit l'appellation, qui prend en charge à titre temporaire la conservation et le traitement des documents semi-courants (second âge), qui ne sont plus fréquemment utilisés pour l'expédition des affaires mais qui ne peuvent encore être ni éliminés ni versés à une institution d'archives.

1.1 *Unité administrative.* Toute institution ou groupe d'institutions d'archives relevant d'un même directeur ou d'une même administration.

1.2 *Institution d'archives générales.* Quelle que soit son appellation, toute institution publique d'archives chargée de la conservation des archives de la plupart ou de toutes les institutions d'un niveau administratif donné, comme indiqué ci-dessous. Les institutions d'archives générales sont donc classées comme suit:

a) *Archives nationales, centrales* ou *générales* (dans les pays unitaires) ou *fédérales* (dans les pays fédéraux);

b) *Archives régionales* (dans les pays unitaires) ou d'Etat (dans les pays fédéraux);

c) *Archives locales* (dans les pays unitaires ainsi que dans les pays fédéraux).

1.3 *Institution d'archives spéciales.* Quelle que soit son appellation, toute institution d'archives publique ou privée, dont le champ de compétence se limite:

a) aux fonds versés par une administration publique donnée et les unités administratives qui lui sont subordonnées (par exemple, archives d'un Parlement, d'un Ministère de la défense ou d'un Ministère des affaires étrangères) ou par des institutions et chambres de commerce, syndicats de travailleurs, firmes économiques, institutions ecclésiastiques, académies des sciences, hôpitaux, universités, partis politiques, familles, etc.);

b) aux fonds et documents collectés d'après leur sujet ou leurs caractéristiques physiques communes) par exemple, archives littéraires et artistiques, archives économiques, archives audiovisuelles, films cinématographiques ou enregistrements sonores, archives lisibles par machine, etc.).

2. *Fonds et collections.* La totalité des documents d'archives conservés dans une institution d'archives.

2.1 *Archives conventionnelles.* Le terme est utilisé pour les documents manuscrits et dactylographiés, en général, sur papier. Sont incluses dans cette catégorie:

a) les archives imprimées (conservées séparément comme telles);

b) les imprimés de sortie d'ordinateurs sélectionnés pour conservation, ainsi que

c) les archives conventionnelles directement rattachées aux archives cartographiques, audiovisuelles et lisibles par machine, même si elles sont physiquement séparées des autres archives conventionnelles.

En ce qui concerne les centres de préarchivage, la distinction devrait être faite entre les documents semi-courants et les documents courants.

2.2 *Archives cartographiques.* Documents conservés séparément dans une section cartographique ou un local particulier qui sous une forme graphique ou photogrammétrique reproduisent une partie d'une surface (cartes, plans, globes, cartes topographiques et hydrographiques, plans et bleus d'architecte, cartogrammes, maquettes du relief, photographies aériennes).

2.3 *Archives audiovisuelles.* Documents consistant en reproductions d'images et enregistrements sonores de tous formats. Les archives audiovisuelles sont classées selon les catégories suivantes:

a) Photographies (images fixes): négatifs et épreuves photographiques, diapositives, images fixes montées sur bande à l'exception des photographies aériennes conservées séparément et incluses dans la catégorie archives cartographiques;

b) Films cinématographiques (images animées) avec ou sans bande sonore (films, films en boucle, bandes-vidéo et autres documents similaires non classés ailleurs);

c) Enregistrements sonores: disques, bandes, cassettes, etc., et matériel de type plus ancien.

2.4 *Archives lisibles par machine.* Documents, habituellement codés, enregistrés sur des supports tels que disques magnétiques, tambours, bandes, cartes perforées, etc., que l'on ne peut consulter que par l'intermédiaire d'une machine.

2.5 *Microcopies.* Toute reproduction photographique réduite de documents, effectuée sur support transparent négatif ou positif et lisible uniquement par agrandissement. Ne doivent être mentionnées que les microcopies acquises en tant que matériel d'archives. Les microcopies produites ou acquises en tant que matériel de bibliothèque doivent être reportées sous cette rubrique. Les microcopies d'archives sont classées sous les catégories suivantes:

a) microfilms en rouleaux
b) microfiches et autres microcopies

2.6 *Dessins et estampes (documents iconographiques).* Tous documents à images autres que les archives cartographiques, audiovisuelles et les microcopies, conservés séparément dans une section spéciale ou un local particulier.

2.7 *Sceaux et autres objets tridimensionnels.* Ne doivent être pris en compte que les sceaux non attachés aux documents et conservés séparément.

2.8 *Matériel de bibliothèque.* Dans ces statistiques une distinction doit être faite entre le matériel acquis et conservé pour l'usage du personnel ou des chercheurs et le matériel acquis par dépôt légal.

3. *Entrées.* Accroissement des collections, principalement par versement (y compris des centres de préarchivage) mais aussi par dépôt permanent ou révocable, don, achat ou par toute autre méthode.

4. *Classement et inventaire.* Toutes opérations nécessaires pour effectuer le contrôle administratif et intellectuel des fonds d'archives, y compris l'organisation matérielle de ces collections et la préparation des instruments de recherche, publiés ou non publiés (guides, catalogues, inventaires sommaires ou analytiques, répertoires, tables, registres des emplacements, etc.). Ceci n'inclut pas les instruments de recherche acquis avec les versements et qui n'ont pas été produits par le service d'archives.

5. *Service des renseignements.* Communication de renseignements sur ou à partir des fonds d'archives y compris la communication des documents dans les salles de lecture et le prêt des documents.

5.1 *Chercheur:* personne utilisant les salles de lecture et de recherche, à l'exception des groupes en visites guidées.

5.2 *Visite:* présence d'un chercheur pendant un jour ou une fraction de jour. Si un chercheur est enregistré plus d'une fois dans la même journée, sa présence intermittente ne doit être comptée que pour une seule visite.

5.3 *Articles communiqués:* toutes unités matérielles telles que cartons, registres, liasses, etc., communiquées dans les salles de lecture et de recherche.

5.4 *Demandes de renseignements enregistrées:* renseignements communiqués par téléphone et par correspondance y compris l'envoi d'imprimés (par exemple brochures d'information).

6 *Personnel.* Toute personne employée par l'institution d'archives et y exerçant ses fonctions. Dans le total des postes pourvus doivent être inclus tous les postes à temps partiel (équivalents en postes à plein temps).

6.1 *Personnel permanent des services d'archives.* Personnel inscrit au budget de l'institution d'archives, tel que: archiviste professionnel, personnel technique, personnel administratif, etc.

6.1.1 *Archiviste professionnel.* Personne travaillant dans une institution d'archives ou un centre de préarchivage qui a suivi un enseignement ou une formation que l'institution d'archives ou le centre de préarchivage considère approprié en vue du traitement des documents d'archives au niveau professionnel. L'enseignement et la formation peuvent être:

a) seulement une éducation universitaire générale, ou
b) une éducation universitaire et une formation archivistique spéciale ou
c) une formation archivistique organisée sans éducation universitaire.

6.2 *Personnel surnuméraire et temporaire.* Personnel non inscrit au budget de l'institution d'archives, tels que: apprentis ou stagiaires non rétribués, volontaires, vacataires, etc.

Tableau 8.3

Pour l'enquête de 1984, les données demandées portaient sur les archives générales (nationales, régionales et locales) ainsi que sur les archives spéciales (selon l'origine administrative et le sujet). Cependant, les réponses reçues concernaient en général les archives nationales seulement et dans quelques cas les archives nationales et régionales. Presque aucun pays n'a semblé être en mesure de fournir des renseignements sur les archives générales locales ni les archives spéciales. Le tableau 8.3 ne présente donc que des données sur les archives nationales et régionales. Il est à souhaiter que les prochaines enquêtes apporteront des statistiques plus complètes, c'est-à-dire qu'elles comprendront également d'autres types d'institutions d'archives.

Las estadísticas de este capítulo se refieren al patrimonio cultural, presentado por los museos, monumentos y sitios históricos, archivos etc. Este es un nuevo agrupamiento, que refleja el deseo de presentar conjuntamente, y en un solo capítulo, las estadísticas del patrimonio cultural, tal como es indicado en el marco de la Unesco de estadísticas culturales (MEC).

Seccion 1.

La primera tentativa de la Unesco para establecer estadísticas internacionales relativas a los museos e instituciones conexas se situa a principios de los años cincuenta. A partir de 1962 y hasta 1974 los cuestionarios estadísticos se enviaron cada dos años, decidiéndose en 1974 que la encuesta se efectuaría a intervalos regulares de tres años, dado que los cambios que se producen en esta materia son poco frecuentes.

Lo que rinde relativamente difícil la recolección internacional de datos estadísticos sobre museos, es la ausencia casi completa de normas y de clasificaciones generalmente aceptadas. Algunos países, por ejemplo, comprenden en las estadísticas relativas a los museos los monumentos históricos y lugares arqueológicos pero no tienen en cuenta los jardines zoológicos y botánicos, los acuarios y reservas naturales, etc. En otros países, es lo contrario que se produce. Además, no todos los países toman en considéracion los museos que pertenecen a particulares o a organismos privados.

La falta de definiciones y de clasificaciones internacionalmente aceptadas, afecta sensiblemente la calidad, la cantidad y el alcance de las estadísticas reunidas. Por consiguiente, toda clase de comparaciones internacionales deben efectuarse con mucha prudencia.

Con vistas a asegurar un mínimo de comparabilidad, las categorías y los términos utilizados en las encuestas de 1977, 1980 y 1985 han sido redactadas sobre la base de las definiciones establecidas por el *Consejo Internacional de Museos (ICOM).*

Para los fines de esta encuesta, el término *museo* significa *una institución permanente, sin fines lucrativos, al servicio de la sociedad y de su desarrollo, abierta al público y que efectua investigaciones sobre los* testimonios materiales del hombre y de su medio ambiente, adquiridos, conservados, comunicados y sobre todo expuestos para fines de estudio, de eduación y de deleite. Además de los museos citados, las entidades siguientes, también reconocidas por el ICOM como museos, se tomarán en consideración en esta encuesta:

a: Los institutos de conservación y las galerías de exposición que dependen de las bibliotecas y de los centros de archivo;
b: Los sitios y monumentos arqueológicos, etnográficos y naturales y los lugares y monumentos históricos que por su actividades de adquisición, de conservación y de comunicación *tienen el carácter de un museo;*
c: Las instituciones que exponen especies vivientes, tales como los jardines botánicos y zoológicos, los acuarios, los viveros, etc.;
d: Las reservas naturales;
e: Los planetariums y los centros científicos.

Con referencia a la unidad estadística empleada, los museos y las instituciones conexas han sido contados según el número de unidades administrativas y no según el número de colecciones.

Para la clasificación de los museos y de las instituciones conexas segun la *naturaleza predominante de sus exposiciones y de sus colecciones,* se han utilizado las categorías siguientes:

a: *Museos de arte:* museos para la exposición de obras de bellas artes y de artes aplicadas. Forman parte de este grupo museos tales como las galerias de pintura, los museos de escultura, museos de fotografía y de cinematografía, museos de arquitectura, etc. De esta categoría forman parte también los institutos de conservación y las galerías de exposición que dependen de las bibliotecas y de los centros de archivo;
b: *Museos de arqueología y de historia:* los museos de historia son aquellos cuya finalidad es la de presentar la evolución histórica de una región, país o provincia durante un período determinado o a través

de los siglos. Los museos de arqueología se distinguen por el hecho de que sus colecciones provienen en todo o en parte de excavaciones. De este grupo forman parte los museos de colecciones de objetos históricos y de vestigios, museos conmemorativos, museos de archivos, museos militares, museos de figuras históricas, museos de arqueología, museos de antiguedades, etc.;

c: *Museos de historia y ciencias naturales:* museos para la exposición de temas relacionados con una o varias disciplinas como biología, geología, botánica, zoología, paleontología, ecología;

d: *Museos de ciencia y de tecnología:* los museos de esta categoría se dedican a una o varias ciencias exactas o tecnológicas tales como astronomía, matemáticas, física, química, ciencias médicas, industrias de la construcción, artículos manufacturados, etc.; incluídos igualmente en esta categoría los planetariums y los centros científicos.

e: *Museos de etnografía y de antropología:* museos que exponen materiales sobre la cultura, las estructuras sociales, las creencias, las costumbres, las artes tradicionales, etc.;

f: *Museos especializados:* museos que ilustran una región mas o menos extensa que constituye una entidad histórica y cultural y, algunas veces, también étnica, económica o social, es decir, que las colecciones se refieren mas a un territorio determinado que a un tema o sujeto particular;

h: *Museos generales:* museos que poseen colecciones mixtas y que no pueden ser identificados por su esfera principal;

i: *Otros museos:* museos e instituciones conexas que no están cubiertos en una de las anteriores categorías.

j y k: *Monumentos históricos y sitios arqueológicos protegidos:* obras arquitectónicas o esculturales y zonas topográficas que presentan especial interés desde un punto de vista arqueológico, histórico, etnológico o antropológico;

l y m: *Jardines zoológicos y botánicos, acuarios y reservas naturáles:* la característica específica de estas entidades es la de exponer especímenes vivientes;

La clasificación de los museos según su *propiedad o su estatuto administrativo* cubre las tres categorías siguientes:

a: *Museos nacionales:* museos que pertenecen o que son administrados por las autoridades del Estado (central o federal);

b: *Otros museos públicos:* museos que pertenecen o que son administrados por otras autoridades públicas (de los estados, de provincias, de distritos, municipalidades, etc.) o por sociedades, fundaciones, instituciones educativas, religiosas, etc., que pueden tener carácter público;

c: *Museos privados:* museos que pertenecen a particulares o a organismos privados.

Los datos sobre la *frecuentación anual* en los diferentes tipos de museos se refieren al número de *visitantes*. Los datos relativos a la frecuentación en grupos (escuelas y otros grupos organizados) se presentan separadamente, pero no son publicados en este Anuario.

Los datos sobre los *ingresos* se refieren al total de los ingresos anuales indicados en moneda nacional.

Con respecto al *personal empleado* en los museos e instituciones conexas, se establece una distinción entre personal *profesional* y *otro* personal, como sigue:

Personal profesional: son los empleados cuyo trabajo requiere una enseñanza, una formación profesional o una experienca especializadas. Esta categoría incluye los conservadores, dibujantes, bibliotecarios, técnios de los servicios de restauración, taxidermistas, técnicos de laboratorio, arqueólogos, etc.

Otro personal (no profesional) incluye los guardianes, el servicio de seguridad y los empleados de despacho, los cuidadores de animales, los embaladores, el personal de limpieza, etc. También se hace una distinción entre los empleados *remunerados* y los *voluntarios*, estos últimos efectuando trabajos que en otro caso requerirían el empleo de personal remunerado. El personal remunerado de jornada parcial será indicado en equivalente a jornada completa.

Los datos sobre los *gastos ordinarios* se refieren al total anual de los gastos ordinarios, que será indicado en moneda nacional.

Cuadro 8.1

Las cifras en este cuadro presentan la cantidad de establecimientos, la frecuentación anual, los ingresos, los gastos de personal y los gastos ordinarios, de acuerdo con la propiedad o estatuto administrativo del establecimiento. Este cuadro presenta los datos más recientes, que provienen de la encuesta de 1980 o de la de 1985. Sin embargo, hay que notar que los datos anteriores a 1983 se refieren a los museos *e* instituciones asimiladas (monumentos, sitios, jardines zoolozgicos, etc.) mientras que los datos de 1985 se refieren únicamente a los museos clasificados como tales.

Cuadro 8.2

Los datos presentados en este cuadro se refieren a los museos e instituticiones asimilados en este categoría, de acuerdo con la naturaleza predominante de las colecciones cuya descripción proviene, sea de la encuesta de 1980 o de la de 1985. En el caso de utilización de datos de la encuesta de 1985, sólo el total de museos, clasificados como tales, pueden ser relacionados con las cifras indicadas en el cuadro 8.1.

Seccion 2.

La primera recolección de estadísticas a nivel internacional sobre centros de archivos y depósitos de prearchivage, se llevó a cabo a principios de 1984 utilizando un cuestionario basado en un cuestionario modelo, que fué desarrollado con la ayuda del Consejo Internacional de Archivos (CIA). Dicho cuestionario fué probado en un estudio piloto en 1981, para conciliar las categorías de clasificación utilizadas en el mundo y establecer una terminología para los archivos y establecer un sistema de clasificación comun. Las definiciones utilizadas en la encuesta de 1984 estaban basados en un glosario internacional multilingue de terminología archivística, publicado por el Consejo Internacional de Archivos. Las definiciones relativas a las informaciones estadísticas publicadas en este *Anuario* son las siguientes:

1. *Institución de archivos.* Sea cual fuere su denominación, toda institución cuya función principal consista en:

a) la conservación de fondos de archivos, ya sean transferidos o bien adquiridos de otro modo;

b) la organización de esos fondos para su utilización por parte de otras personas distintas de los miembros del personal de la institución.

Centros de archivo intermedio. Toda institución, cualquiera que sea su denominación, que se encargue provisionalmente de la conservación y el tratamiento de los documentos semicorrientes que no se utilicen ya frecuentemente para la ejecución de los asuntos en curso, pero que no se puedan todavía ni eliminar ni ceder a una institución de archivos.

1.1 *Unidad administrativa.* Toda institución o conjunto de instituciones de archivo que dependan de un mismo director o de una misma administración.

1.2 Institución de archivos generales. Sea cual fuere su denominación, toda institución pública de archivos encargada de la conservación de los archivos de la mayoría o de todas las instituciones sea cual sea su nivel gubernamental. Las instituciones de archivos generales se clasifican del modo siguiente:

a) Archivos nacionales, centrales o generales (en los países con régimen unitario) o federales (en los países con régimen federal);

b) Archivos regionales (en los países con régimen unitario) o de Estado (en los países con régimen federal);

c) Archivos locales (tanto en los países con régimen unitario como federal).

1.3 *Institución de archivos especiales.* Sea cual sea su denominación, toda institución de archivos pública o privada, cuya competencia se limite:

a) a los fondos cedidos por una administración pública determinada y las unidades administrativas que dependen de ella (por ejemplo, archivos de un Parlamento, de un Ministerio de Defensa o de un Ministerio de Relaciones Exteriores) o por instituciones y organizaciones públicas o privadas de tipo similar (por ejemplo, cámaras de comercio, sindicatos de trabajadores, empresas económicas instituciones eclesiásticas, academias de ciencias, hospitales, universidades, partidos políticos, familias, etc.);

b) a los fondos y documentos recopilados de acuerdo con su tema o sus características físicas comunes (por ejemplo, archivos literarios y artísticos, archivos económicos, archivos audiovisuales, películas o grabaciones sonoras, archivos legibles por máquina, etc.).

2. *Fondos y colecciones.* La totalidad de los documentos de archivos conservados en una institución de archivos.

2.1 *Documentos convencionales.* El término se utiliza para los documentos manuscritos y mecanografiados, por lo general, en papel. Esta categoría abarca:

a) los documentos impresos (conservados como tales por separado);

b) los impresos de salida de computadora, seleccionados para su conservación, y

c) los documentos convencionales que dependen directamente de los documentos cartográficos, audiovisuales y legibles por máquina, incluso si están físicamente separados de los demás documentos (convencionales).

En lo que se refiere a los centros de archivo intermedio se debería distinguir entre los documentos semiactivos y los documentos activos.

2.2 *Documentos cartográficos.* Documentos conservados por separado en una sección cartográfica o un local particular, que, en forma gráfica o fotogramétrica, reproducen una parte de una superficie (mapas, planos, globos, mapas topográficos e hidrográficos, planos y copias azules de arquitectura, cartogramas, maquetas de relieve, fotografías aéreas).

2.3 *Documentos audiovisuales.* Documentos que consisten en reproducciones de imágenes y en grabaciones sonoras de cualquier formato. Los documentos audiovisuales se clasifican dentro de las categorías siguientes:

a) Fotografías (imágenes fijas): Negativos y pruebas fotográficas, diapositivas, películas fijas, exceptuando las fotografías aéreas conservadas por separado e incluídas en la categoría de documentos cartográficos;

b) *Películas cinematográficas (imágenes en movimiento) con o sin banda sonora: películas, bucles de película, cintas video y otros documentos similares no clasificados en otros sitios;*

c) Grabaciones sonoras: discos, cintas, casetes, etc., y material de tipo más antiguo.

2.4 Documentos legibles por máquina. Documentos, por lo común codificados, registrados en soportes informáticos como discos magnéticos, tambores, cintas, tarjetas perforadas, etc., y que sólo pueden leerse con ayuda de una máquina.

2.5 *Microcopias.* Documentos presentados en imágen fotográfica reducida realizada sobre un soporte transparente negativo o positivo y legibile únicamente mediante ampliación. Sólo se deben mencionar las microcopias adquiridas en calidad de material de archivos. Las microcopias producidas o adquiridas como material de biblioteca deben figurar bajo esta rúbrica. Las microcopias de archivos se clasifican en las categorías siguientes:

a) microfilmes en rollos;

b) microfichas y otras microformas.

2.6 *Dibujos y estampas (documentos inconográficos).* Todos los documentos que contengan imágenes que no sean las de los documentos cartográficos, audiovisuales y las microcopias, conservados por separdo en una sección especial o en un local particular.

2.7 *Sellos y otros objectos tridimensionales.* Sólo deben considerarse los sellos sueltos y que se conservan por separado.

2.8 *Material de biblioteca.* A los fines de estas estadísticas, se debe distinguir entre el material adquirido y conservado para uso del personal o de investigadores y el material adquirido por depósito legal.

3. *Ingresos:* Aumento de las colecciones, principalmente por transferencia (comprendidas las de los centros de archivo intermedio), pero también por depósito permanente o revocable, donación, compra o por cualquier otro procedimiento.

4. *Clasificación e inventario.* Todas las operaciones necesarias para llevar a cabo el control administrativo e intelectual de los fondos de los archivos, incluida la organización material de las colecciones y la elaboración de instrumentos de búsqueda, publicados o no publicados (guías, catálogos, inventarios someros o analíticos, repertorios, índices, registros de ubicación etc.). No se incluyen aquí los instrumentos de búsqueda adquiridos con las transferencias y donaciones etc. y que no han sido producidos por el servicio de archivos.

5. *Servicio de informaciones.* Comunicación de informaciones acerca de los fondos de los archivos, incluida la comunicación de documentos en las salas de lectura y el préstamo de documentos.

5.1 *Investigador:* Persona que utiliza las salas de investigación, exceptuando las visitas de grupos.

5.2 *Visita:* Presencia de un investigador durante un día o una parte del día. Si se registra más de una vez a un investigador en el mismo día, su presencia intermitente debe contarse sólo como una visita.

5.3 *Unidad de almacenamiento:* Toda unidad física de documentos de archivo, como volumen, legajo, etc., que se facilita en las salas de investigación.

5.4 *Solicitudes de informaciones registradas:* informaciones comunicadas por teléfono y por correspondencia incluido el envío de impresos (por ejemplo, folletos de información).

6. *Personal.* Toda persona empleada por la institución de archivos y que ejerce en ella sus funciones. En el número total de puestos cubiertos se deben incluir todos los puestos de jornada parcial (equivalentes en puestos a jornada completa).

6.1 *Personal permanente de los servicios de archivos.* Personal inscrito en el presupuesto de la institución de archivos, como, por ejemplo: archivero profesional, personal técnico, personal administrativo, etc.

6.1.1 *Archivero profesional:* Persona que trabaja en una institución de archivos o un centro de archivo intermedio y que ha recibido la educación y formación específica necesaria para el tratamiento de los documentos de archivo a nivel profesional. La educación y la formación pueden ser:

a) solamente una educación universitaria general, o

b) una educación universitaria y una formación específica en archivística y ciencias auxiliares, o

c) una formación organizada en archivística sin educación universitaria.

6.2 *Personal supernumerario y temporero:* personal no inscrito en el presupuesto de la institución de archivos, como, por ejemplo: aprendices o pasantes sin remuneración, voluntarios, etc.

Cuadro 8.3

Para el muestreo de 1984, se solicitaban datos sobre archivos generales (nacionales, regionales y locales) así como los archivos especiales (de acuerdo con el orígen administrativo y con el tópico). Las respuestas recibidas se refieren en general a los archivos nacionales y solamente en algunos casos, a los archivos nacionales y regionales. Casi ningún país pudo proporcionar información sobre archivos generales locales o sobre archivos especiales. El Cuadro 8.3 presenta, solamente, datos sobre archivos nacionales y regionales. Se espera que en el futuro, los muestreos proveerán datos más completos, es decir, que incluirán igualmente, otros tipos de archivos.

8.1 Number of museums by ownership: visitors, personnel and annual current expenditure

Nombre de musées selon leur propriété: visiteurs, personnel et dépenses ordinaires annuelles

Número de museos según su propiedad: visitantes, personal y gastos ordinarios anuales

OWNERSHIP OF MUSEUMS (OR RELATED INSTITUTIONS):

A. NATIONAL MUSEUMS
B. OTHER PUBLIC MUSEUMS
C. PRIVATE MUSEUMS

ANNUAL CURRENT EXPENDITURE AND RECEIPTS ARE SHOWN IN NATIONAL CURRENCY

NUMBER OF COUNTRIES AND TERRITORIES PRESENTED IN THIS TABLE: 110

PROPRIETE DES MUSEES (OU INSTITUTIONS SIMILAIRES):

A. MUSEES NATIONAUX
B. AUTRES MUSEES PUBLICS
C. MUSEES PRIVES

LES DEPENSES ORDINAIRES ET LES RECETTES ANNUELLES SONT EXPRIMEES EN MONNAIE NATIONALE

NOMBRE DE PAYS ET DE TERRITOIRES PRESENTES DANS CE TABLEAU: 110

COUNTRY PAYS PAIS	YEAR ANNEE AÑO	OWNERSHIP OF MUSEUMS (OR RELATED INSTITUTIONS) PROPRIETE DES MUSEES (OU INSTITUTIONS SIMILAIRES) PROPIEDAD DE LOS MUSEOS (O INSTITUCIONES SIMILARES)	TOTAL NUMBER OF MUSEUMS NOMBRE TOTAL DE MUSEES NUMERO TOTAL DE MUSEOS	ATTENDANCE / FREQUENTATION / FRECUENTACION NUMBER OF MUSEUMS REPORTING NOMBRE DE MUSEES AYANT FOURNI CES DONNEES NUMERO DE MUSEOS QUE DIERON ESTE DATO	NUMBER OF VISITORS (000) NOMBRE DE VISITEURS (000) NUMERO DE VISITANTES (000)	ANNUAL RECEIPTS / RECETTES ANNUELLES / INGRESOS ANUALES NUMBER OF MUSEUMS REPORTING NOMBRE DE MUSEES AYANT FOURNI CES DONNEES NUMERO DE MUSEOS QUE DIERON ESTE DATO	TOTAL (000)
AFRICA							
ALGERIA	1979	TOTAL	32	13	260	.	.
		A. NATIONAL MUSEUMS	13	10	235	.	.
		B. OTHER PUBLIC MUSEUMS	19	3	25	.	.
BENIN	1984	TOTAL	5	3	8	2	202
		A. NATIONAL MUSEUMS	4	3	8	2	202
		C. PRIVATE MUSEUMS	1	–	...	–	...
BOTSWANA	1979	TOTAL	2	2	52	.	.
		A. NATIONAL MUSEUMS	1	1	45	.	.
		B. OTHER PUBLIC MUSEUMS	1	1	7	.	.
BURUNDI	1984	TOTAL	2	2	6	1	120
		A. NATIONAL MUSEUMS	1	1	3	1	120
		B. OTHER PUBLIC MUSEUMS	1	1	3	–	...
CAMEROON‡	1979	TOTAL	12	12	4 641	.	.
		A. NATIONAL MUSEUMS	1	1	881	.	.
		B. OTHER PUBLIC MUSEUMS	7	7	2 710	.	.
		C. PRIVATE MUSEUMS	4	4	1 050	.	.
CENTRAL AFRICAN REPUBLIC	1979	TOTAL	65	1	1	.	.
		A. NATIONAL MUSEUMS	14	...	...	.	.
		B. OTHER PUBLIC MUSEUMS	50	...	...	.	.
		C. PRIVATE MUSEUMS	1	...	...	.	.
CHAD	1984	TOTAL	5	1	3	–	...
CONGO	1984	TOTAL	5	4	57	–	...
		A. NATIONAL MUSEUMS	1	–	...	–	...
		B. OTHER PUBLIC MUSEUMS	4	4	57	–	...
ETHIOPIA	1984	A. NATIONAL MUSEUMS	1	1	6	1	6
GHANA	1979	TOTAL	4	4	69	.	.
		A. NATIONAL MUSEUMS	2	2	31	.	.
		B. OTHER PUBLIC MUSEUMS	2	2	38	.	.
GUINEA	1984	TOTAL	5	5	21	–	...
		A. NATIONAL MUSEUMS	1	1	14	–	...
		B. OTHER PUBLIC MUSEUMS	4	4	7	–	...

PROPIEDAD DE LOS MUSEOS (O INSTITUCIONES SIMILARES):

A. MUSEOS NACIONALES
B. OTROS MUSEOS PUBLICOS
C. MUSEOS PRIVADOS

LOS GASTOS ORDINARIOS Y LOS INGRESOS ANUARIOS SE EXPRESAN EN MONEDA NACIONAL

NUMERO DE PAISES Y DE TERRITORIOS PRESENTADOS EN ESTE CUADRO: 110

PERSONNEL / PERSONNEL / PERSONAL						ANNUAL CURRENT EXPENDITURE / DEPENSES ANNUELLES ORDINAIRES / GASTOS ORDINARIOS ANUALES		
		PROFESSIONAL STAFF / PERSONNEL PROFESSIONNEL / PERSONAL PROFESIONAL		OTHER STAFF / AUTRE PERSONNEL / OTRO PERSONAL				
NUMBER OF MUSEUMS REPORTING / NOMBRE DE MUSEES AYANT FOURNI CES DONNEES / NUMERO DE MUSEOS QUE DIERON ESTE DATO	TOTAL STAFF / TOTAL DU PERSONNEL / TOTAL DE PERSONAL	PAID STAFF / SALARIES / REMUNERADOS	VOLUNTEERS / VOLONTAIRES / VOLUNTARIOS	PAID STAFF / SALARIES / REMUNERADOS	VOLUNTEERS / VOLONTAIRES / VOLUNTARIOS	NUMBER OF MUSEUMS REPORTING / NOMBRE DE MUSEES AYANT FOURNI CES DONNEES / NUMERO DE MUSEOS QUE DIERON ESTE DATO	TOTAL (000) / TOTAL (000) / TOTAL (000)	COUNTRY / PAYS / PAIS
								AFRICA
32	389	38	–	351	–	–	...	ALGERIA
13	...	...	...	...	...	–	...	
19	...	...	...	...	...	–	...	
4	66	28	–	38	–	–	...	BENIN
4	66	28	–	38	–	–	...	
–	...	...	...	...	...	–	...	
2	32	5	2	25	–	2	133	BOTSWANA
1	29	4	2	23	–	1	90	
1	3	1	–	2	–	1	43	
2	28	28	–	–	–	1	4 312	BURUNDI
1	21	21	–	–	–	1	4 312	
1	7	7	–	–	–	–	...	
12	31	31	–	–	–	8	8 050	CAMEROON‡
1	10	10	–	–	–	1	5 550	
7	15	15	–	–	–	7	2 500	
4	6	6	–	–	–	–	...	
1	21	15	2	4	–	1	400	CENTRAL AFRICAN REPUBLIC
...	...	...	...	...	...	...	...	
...	...	...	...	...	...	...	...	
1	6	6	–	–	–	1	952	CHAD
5	57	23	–	34	–	5	131 000	CONGO
1	12	11	–	1	–	1	5 000	
4	45	12	–	33	–	4	126 000	
1	45	15	–	30	–	–	...	ETHIOPIA
4	162	25	–	137	–	4	2 210	GHANA
2	113	22	–	91	–	...	...	
2	49	3	–	46	–	...	...	
5	41	19	–	22	–	5	208	GUINEA
1	12	10	–	2	–	1	160	
4	29	9	–	20	–	4	48	

8.1 **Number of museums by ownership**
Nombre de musées selon leur propriété
Número de museos según su propiedad

COUNTRY / PAYS / PAIS	YEAR / ANNEE / AÑO	OWNERSHIP OF MUSEUMS (OR RELATED INSTITUTIONS) / PROPRIETE DES MUSEES (OU INSTITUTIONS SIMILAIRES) / PROPIEDAD DE LOS MUSEOS (O INSTITUCIONES SIMILARES)	TOTAL NUMBER OF MUSEUMS / NOMBRE TOTAL DE MUSEES / NUMERO TOTAL DE MUSEOS	ATTENDANCE / FREQUENTATION / FRECUENTACION: NUMBER OF MUSEUMS REPORTING / NOMBRE DE MUSEES AYANT FOURNI CES DONNEES / NUMERO DE MUSEOS QUE DIERON ESTE DATO	ATTENDANCE / FREQUENTATION / FRECUENTACION: NUMBER OF VISITORS (000) / NOMBRE DE VISITEURS (000) / NUMERO DE VISITANTES (000)	ANNUAL RECEIPTS / RECETTES ANNUELLES / INGRESOS ANUALES: NUMBER OF MUSEUMS REPORTING / NOMBRE DE MUSEES AYANT FOURNI CES DONNEES / NUMERO DE MUSEOS QUE DIERON ESTE DATO	ANNUAL RECEIPTS / RECETTES ANNUELLES / INGRESOS ANUALES: TOTAL (000)
KENYA	1984	TOTAL	6	6	531	6	1 131
		A. NATIONAL MUSEUMS	6	6	531	6	1 131
LIBYAN ARAB JAMAHIRIYA	1979	TOTAL	26	...	50		
MADAGASCAR	1984	A. NATIONAL MUSEUMS	4	3	21	–	...
MALAWI	1984	TOTAL	2	2	80	2	1
		A. NATIONAL MUSEUMS	2	2	80	2	1
MAURITIUS	1983	TOTAL	3	3	237	–	...
		A. NATIONAL MUSEUMS	3	3	237	–	...
MOROCCO‡	1984	TOTAL	11	11	1 580	11	4 741
		A. NATIONAL MUSEUMS	1	1	...	1	...
		B. OTHER PUBLIC MUSEUMS	10	10	...	10	...
NIGER	1979	A. NATIONAL MUSEUMS	1	1	600	.	.
REUNION	1984	TOTAL	2	2	79	–	...
		B. OTHER PUBLIC MUSEUMS	2	2	79	–	...
ST. HELENA	1979	TOTAL	1	–	...	.	.
		A. NATIONAL MUSEUMS	1	–	...	.	.
SENEGAL	1979	TOTAL	4	4	55	.	.
		A. NATIONAL MUSEUMS	1	1	...	.	.
		B. OTHER PUBLIC MUSEUMS	3	3	...	.	.
SEYCHELLES	1979	TOTAL	1	1	8	.	.
		A. NATIONAL MUSEUMS	1	1	8	.	.
SIERRA LEONE	1979	TOTAL	19	1	178	.	.
		A. NATIONAL MUSEUMS	19	1	178	.	.
SUDAN	1984	TOTAL	7	7	*221	–	...
		A. NATIONAL MUSEUMS	1	1	...	–	...
		B. OTHER PUBLIC MUSEUMS	6	6	...	–	...
TUNISIA	1984	TOTAL	35	32	367	32	116
ZAMBIA	1984	TOTAL	3	3	12	3	5
		A. NATIONAL MUSEUMS	3	3	12	3	5
ZIMBABWE	1984	TOTAL	9	6	162	5	36
		A. NATIONAL MUSEUMS	6	6	162	5	36
		C. PRIVATE MUSEUMS	3	–	...	–	...
AMERICA, NORTH							
ANTIGUA AND BARBUDA	1979	TOTAL	3	–	...	.	.
		B. OTHER PUBLIC MUSEUMS	2	–	...	.	.
		C. PRIVATE MUSEUMS	1	–	...	.	.
BAHAMAS	1979	TOTAL	7	–	...	.	.
		A. NATIONAL MUSEUMS	1	–	...	.	.
		C. PRIVATE MUSEUMS	6	–	...	.	.
BARBADOS	1984	TOTAL	1	1	30	1	8 336
BELIZE	1979	TOTAL	5	5	9	.	.
		A. NATIONAL MUSEUMS	5	5	9	.	.
BRITISH VIRGIN ISLANDS	1984	TOTAL	1	1	1	1	6
		A. NATIONAL MUSEUMS	1	1	1	1	6
CANADA‡	1984	TOTAL	661	644	16 165	627	162 625
		A. NATIONAL MUSEUMS	18	15	2 112	18	23 824
		B. OTHER PUBLIC MUSEUMS	583	572	13 215	562	136 287
		C. PRIVATE MUSEUMS	45	44	364	33	2 078
COSTA RICA	1984	TOTAL	16	11	473	5	36 600
		A. NATIONAL MUSEUMS	7	4	73	3	29 400
		B. OTHER PUBLIC MUSEUMS	8	7	400	2	7 200
		C. PRIVATE MUSEUMS	1	–	...	–	...

PERSONNEL / PERSONNEL / PERSONAL						ANNUAL CURRENT EXPENDITURE / DEPENSES ANNUELLES ORDINAIRES / GASTOS ORDINARIOS ANUALES		
NUMBER OF MUSEUMS REPORTING / NOMBRE DE MUSEES AYANT FOURNI CES DONNEES / NUMERO DE MUSEOS QUE DIERON ESTE DATO	TOTAL STAFF / TOTAL DU PERSONNEL / TOTAL DE PERSONAL	PROFESSIONAL STAFF / PERSONNEL PROFESSIONNEL / PERSONAL PROFESIONAL		OTHER STAFF / AUTRE PERSONNEL / OTRO PERSONAL		NUMBER OF MUSEUMS REPORTING / NOMBRE DE MUSEES AYANT FOURNI CES DONNEES / NUMERO DE MUSEOS QUE DIERON ESTE DATO	TOTAL (000) / TOTAL (000) / TOTAL (000)	COUNTRY / PAYS / PAIS
		PAID STAFF / SALARIES / REMUNERADOS	VOLUNTEERS / VOLONTAIRES / VOLUNTARIOS	PAID STAFF / SALARIES / REMUNERADOS	VOLUNTEERS / VOLONTAIRES / VOLUNTARIOS			
6	555	202	–	353	–	6	1 027	KENYA
6	555	202	–	353	–	6	1 027	
...	1 100	40	...	...	...	...	1 500	LIBYAN ARAB JAMAHIRIYA
4	21	21	–	–	–	4	228	MADAGASCAR
1	50	19	1	30	–	2	150	MALAWI
1	50	19	1	30	–	2	150	
3	40	5	–	35	–	3	1 050	MAURITIUS
3	40	5	–	35	–	3	1 050	
...	*500	...	...	...	...	–	...	MOROCCO‡
...	...	...	...	...	...	–	...	
...	...	...	...	...	...	–	...	
1	116	115	1	–	–	1	15 500	NIGER
2	14	12	2	–	–	2	380	REUNION
2	14	12	2	–	–	2	380	
–	...	...	...	...	...	–	...	ST. HELENA
–	...	...	...	...	...	–	...	
4	14	14	–	–	–	–	...	SENEGAL
1	...	...	–	–	–	–	...	
3	...	...	–	–	–	–	...	
1	1	–	–	1	–	1	30	SEYCHELLES
1	1	–	–	1	–	1	30	
1	8	2	–	6	–	19	7	SIERRA LEONE
1	8	2	–	6	–	19	7	
7	134	14	–	119	1	–	...	SUDAN
1	66	7	–	58	1	–	...	
6	68	7	–	61	–	–	...	
13	215	201	–	14	–	33	63	TUNISIA
3	3	–	–	3	–	3	9	ZAMBIA
3	3	–	–	3	–	3	9	
6	187	49	–	138	–	6	1 349	ZIMBABWE
6	187	49	–	138	–	6	1 349	
–	...	...	...	...	...	...	...	
								AMERICA, NORTH
–	...	...	...	...	...	–	...	ANTIGUA AND BARBUDA
–	...	...	...	...	...	–	...	
–	...	...	...	...	...	–	...	
4	12	2	–	7	3	–	...	BAHAMAS
1	8	1	–	7	–	–	...	
3	4	1	–	–	3	–	...	
1	19	4	2	13	–	1	356	BARBADOS
5	23	1	–	22	–	5	88	BELIZE
5	23	1	–	22	–	5	88	
1	3	–	–	1	2	1	5	BRITISH VIRGIN ISLANDS
1	3	–	–	1	2	1	5	
650	16 736	4 708	12 028	./.	./.	611	158 493	CANADA‡
18	887	605	282	./.	./.	18	22 913	
573	15 038	4 013	11 025	./.	./.	545	133 073	
44	574	70	504	./.	./.	34	2 031	
16	179	82	1	93	3	7	35 600	COSTA RICA
7	121	54	–	66	1	3	28 350	
8	56	26	1	27	2	3	6 850	
1	2	2	–	–	–	1	400	

8.1 Number of museums by ownership
Nombre de musées selon leur propriété
Número de museos según su propiedad

COUNTRY / PAYS / PAIS	YEAR / ANNEE / AÑO	OWNERSHIP OF MUSEUMS (OR RELATED INSTITUTIONS) / PROPRIETE DES MUSEES (OU INSTITUTIONS SIMILAIRES) / PROPIEDAD DE LOS MUSEOS (O INSTITUCIONES SIMILARES)	TOTAL NUMBER OF MUSEUMS / NOMBRE TOTAL DE MUSEES / NUMERO TOTAL DE MUSEOS	ATTENDANCE / FREQUENTATION / FRECUENTACION		ANNUAL RECEIPTS / RECETTES ANNUELLES / INGRESOS ANUALES	
				NUMBER OF MUSEUMS REPORTING / NOMBRE DE MUSEES AYANT FOURNI CES DONNEES / NUMERO DE MUSEOS QUE DIERON ESTE DATO	NUMBER OF VISITORS (000) / NOMBRE DE VISITEURS (000) / NUMERO DE VISITANTES (000)	NUMBER OF MUSEUMS REPORTING / NOMBRE DE MUSEES AYANT FOURNI CES DONNEES / NUMERO DE MUSEOS QUE DIERON ESTE DATO	TOTAL (000) / TOTAL (000) / TOTAL (000)
CUBA‡	1984	TOTAL	241	241	8 159	–	–
		A. NATIONAL MUSEUMS	5	5	380	–	–
		B. OTHER PUBLIC MUSEUMS	236	236	7 779	–	–
EL SALVADOR	1979	TOTAL	20	8	1 333	.	.
		A. NATIONAL MUSEUMS	20	8	1 333	.	.
GRENADA	1984	TOTAL	1	1	8	1	19
		A. NATIONAL MUSEUMS	1	1	8	1	19
GUADELOUPE	1979	TOTAL	5	1	31	.	.
		B. OTHER PUBLIC MUSEUMS	4	–	...	.	.
		C. PRIVATE MUSEUMS	1	1	31	.	.
GUATEMALA	1984	TOTAL	18	12	58	5	16
		A. NATIONAL MUSEUMS	13	12	58	5	16
		B. OTHER PUBLIC MUSEUMS	3	–	...	–	...
		C. PRIVATE MUSEUMS	2	–	...	–	...
MEXICO‡	1983	TOTAL	216	216	13 070	–	...
MONTSERRAT	1984	TOTAL	1	1	2	1	4
		B. OTHER PUBLIC MUSEUMS	1	1	2	1	4
ST. LUCIA	1979	TOTAL	1	1	7	.	.
		C. PRIVATE MUSEUMS	1	1	7	.	.
ST. PIERRE AND MIQUELON	1979	TOTAL	1	1	4	.	.
		C. PRIVATE MUSEUMS	1	1	4	.	.
UNITED STATES‡	1978	TOTAL	4 609	...	352 736	.	.
U.S. VIRGIN ISLANDS	1979	TOTAL	10	7	995	.	.
		A. NATIONAL MUSEUMS	3	3	919	.	.
		B. OTHER PUBLIC MUSEUMS	4	3	36	.	.
		C. PRIVATE MUSEUMS	3	1	40	.	.
AMERICA, SOUTH							
BRAZIL	1982	TOTAL	571	571	7 859	–	...
		A. NATIONAL MUSEUMS	243	243	...	–	...
		B. OTHER PUBLIC MUSEUMS	154	154	...	–	...
		C. PRIVATE MUSEUMS	174	174	...	–	...
COLOMBIA	1979	TOTAL	74	58	1 542	.	.
		A. NATIONAL MUSEUMS	24	19	597	.	.
		B. OTHER PUBLIC MUSEUMS	23	18	528	.	.
		C. PRIVATE MUSEUMS	27	21	416	.	.
FALKLAND ISLANDS (MALVINAS)	1979	TOTAL	1	–	...	.	.
		B. OTHER PUBLIC MUSEUMS	1	–	...	.	.
GUYANA	1979	TOTAL	2	1	97	.	.
		A. NATIONAL MUSEUMS	2	1	97	.	.
PERU	1984	TOTAL	12	12	201	12	189 600
		A. NATIONAL MUSEUMS	12	12	201	12	189 600
URUGUAY	1984	TOTAL	19	2	17	–	...
		A. NATIONAL MUSEUMS	18	1	13	–	...
		B. OTHER PUBLIC MUSEUMS	1	1	4	–	...
VENEZUELA	1979	TOTAL	133	–	...	.	.
		A. NATIONAL MUSEUMS	83	–	...	.	.
		B. OTHER PUBLIC MUSEUMS	45	–	...	.	.
		C. PRIVATE MUSEUMS	5	–	...	.	.
ASIA							
AFGHANISTAN	1979	TOTAL	7	7	7	.	.
		B. OTHER PUBLIC MUSEUMS	7	7	7	.	.
BAHRAIN	1984	TOTAL	2	2	99	–	...
		A. NATIONAL MUSEUMS	1	1	24	–	...
		B. OTHER PUBLIC MUSEUMS	1	1	75	–	...

PERSONNEL / PERSONNEL / PERSONAL						ANNUAL CURRENT EXPENDITURE / DEPENSES ANNUELLES ORDINAIRES / GASTOS ORDINARIOS ANUALES		
NUMBER OF MUSEUMS REPORTING / NOMBRE DE MUSEES AYANT FOURNI CES DONNEES / NUMERO DE MUSEOS QUE DIERON ESTE DATO	TOTAL STAFF / TOTAL DU PERSONNEL / TOTAL DE PERSONAL	PROFESSIONAL STAFF / PERSONNEL PROFESSIONNEL / PERSONAL PROFESIONAL: PAID STAFF / SALARIES / REMUNERADOS	PROFESSIONAL STAFF: VOLUNTEERS / VOLONTAIRES / VOLUNTARIOS	OTHER STAFF / AUTRE PERSONNEL / OTRO PERSONAL: PAID STAFF / SALARIES / REMUNERADOS	OTHER STAFF: VOLUNTEERS / VOLONTAIRES / VOLUNTARIOS	NUMBER OF MUSEUMS REPORTING / NOMBRE DE MUSEES AYANT FOURNI CES DONNEES / NUMERO DE MUSEOS QUE DIERON ESTE DATO	TOTAL (000)	COUNTRY / PAYS / PAIS
241	2 364	...	–	...	–	–	...	CUBA‡
5	202	...	–	...	–	–	...	
236	2 162	...	–	...	–	–	...	
8	213	49	–	164	–	8	929	EL SALVADOR
8	213	49	–	164	–	8	929	
1	5	3	2	–	–	1	16	GRENADA
1	5	3	2	–	–	1	16	
5	12	1	–	11	–	1	179	GUADELOUPE
4	8	1	–	7	–	–	...	
1	4	–	–	4	–	1	179	
13	89	24	–	65	–	12	152	GUATEMALA
13	89	24	–	65	–	12	152	
–	...	...	...	...	...	–	...	
–	...	...	...	...	...	–	...	
–	...	...	...	...	...		...	MEXICO‡
1	4	–	2	–	2	1	5	MONTSERRAT
1	4	–	2	–	2	1	5	
1	2	–	1	1	–	1	5	ST. LUCIA
1	2	–	1	1	–	1	5	
1	2	–	–	1	1	1	48	ST. PIERRE AND MIQUELON
1	2	–	–	1	1	1	48	
...	118 556	42 259	76 297	./.	./.	...	784 343	UNITED STATES‡
7	101	36	–	53	12	7	1 720	U.S. VIRGIN ISLANDS
3	67	23	–	44	–	3	1 400	
3	14	5	–	5	4	3	120	
1	20	8	–	4	8	1	200	
								AMERICA, SOUTH
571	6 152	2 745	–	3 407	–	–	...	BRAZIL
243	...	...	–	...	–	–	...	
154	...	...	–	...	–	–	...	
174	...	...	–	...	–	–	...	
69	601	145	22	404	30	35	40 113	COLOMBIA
23	199	57	11	124	7	10	9 554	
21	186	71	9	90	16	9	5 009	
25	216	17	2	190	7	16	25 550	
1	2	–	–	–	2	–	...	FALKLAND ISLANDS (MALVINAS)
1	2	–	–	–	2	–	...	
2	32	7	–	25	–	2	526	GUYANA
2	32	7	–	25	–	2	526	
12	*150	*25	–	*125	–	12	*837 629	PERU
12	*150	*25	–	*125	–	12	*837 629	
11	173	...	...	...	...	–	...	URUGUAY
10	168	...	...	...	...	–	...	
1	5	...	...	...	...	–	...	
81	576	–	–	–	–	81	103 046	VENEZUELA
81	576	–	–	–	–	81	103 046	
–	...	...	...	...	...	–	...	
–	...	...	...	...	...	–	...	
								ASIA
7	103	103	–	–	–	7	3 100	AFGHANISTAN
7	103	103	–	–	–	7	3 100	
2	88	88	–	–	–	1	383	BAHRAIN
1	46	46	–	–	–	–	...	
1	42	42	–	–	–	1	383	

8.1 Number of museums by ownership
Nombre de musées selon leur propriété
Número de museos según su propiedad

COUNTRY / PAYS / PAIS	YEAR / ANNEE / AÑO	OWNERSHIP OF MUSEUMS (OR RELATED INSTITUTIONS) / PROPRIETE DES MUSEES (OU INSTITUTIONS SIMILAIRES) / PROPIEDAD DE LOS MUSEOS (O INSTITUCIONES SIMILARES)	TOTAL NUMBER OF MUSEUMS / NOMBRE TOTAL DE MUSEES / NUMERO TOTAL DE MUSEOS	ATTENDANCE / FREQUENTATION / FRECUENTACION: NUMBER OF MUSEUMS REPORTING / NOMBRE DE MUSEES AYANT FOURNI CES DONNEES / NUMERO DE MUSEOS QUE DIERON ESTE DATO	NUMBER OF VISITORS (000) / NOMBRE DE VISITEURS (000) / NUMERO DE VISITANTES (000)	ANNUAL RECEIPTS / RECETTES ANNUELLES / INGRESOS ANUALES: NUMBER OF MUSEUMS REPORTING / NOMBRE DE MUSEES AYANT FOURNI CES DONNEES / NUMERO DE MUSEOS QUE DIERON ESTE DATO	TOTAL (000)
BHUTAN	1979	TOTAL	1	1	16	.	.
		A. NATIONAL MUSEUMS	1	1	16	.	.
BRUNEI DARUSSALAM	1984	TOTAL	3	3	112	–	...
		A. NATIONAL MUSEUMS	3	3	112	–	...
CYPRUS	1979	TOTAL	26	26	95	.	.
		A. NATIONAL MUSEUMS	23	23	43	.	.
		B. OTHER PUBLIC MUSEUMS	2	2	49	.	.
		C. PRIVATE MUSEUMS	1	1	2	.	.
INDONESIA	1983	TOTAL	100	100	7 171	100	2 096 467
IRAQ	1984	TOTAL	13	13	63	13	60
ISRAEL	1984	TOTAL	95	67	6 780	–	...
JAPAN	1978	TOTAL	493	485	98 487	.	.
		A. NATIONAL MUSEUMS	28	...	...	.	.
		B. OTHER PUBLIC MUSEUMS	222	...	...	.	.
		C. PRIVATE MUSEUMS	243	...	...	.	.
JORDAN	1984	TOTAL	16	10	147	7	150
KOREA, REPUBLIC OF	1984	TOTAL	146	58	665	1	13 040
KUWAIT	1979	TOTAL	3	3	259	.	.
		A. NATIONAL MUSEUMS	3	3	259	.	.
MALAYSIA‡	1979	TOTAL	228	10	3 561	.	.
		A. NATIONAL MUSEUMS	2	2	2 925	.	.
		B. OTHER PUBLIC MUSEUMS	226	8	636	.	.
MALDIVES	1984	TOTAL	1	1	3	1	17
		A. NATIONAL MUSEUMS	1	1	3	1	17
PAKISTAN	1979	TOTAL	10	10	561	.	.
		A. NATIONAL MUSEUMS	1	1	50	.	.
		C. PRIVATE MUSEUMS	9	9	511	.	.
PHILIPPINES	1984	TOTAL	61	–	...	–	...
		A. NATIONAL MUSEUMS	25	–	...	–	...
		B. OTHER PUBLIC MUSEUMS	21	–	...	–	...
		C. PRIVATE MUSEUMS	15	–	...	–	...
QATAR	1978	TOTAL	1	1	60	.	.
		A. NATIONAL MUSEUMS	1	1	60	.	.
SAUDI ARABIA	1984	TOTAL	1	1	40	–	...
		A. NATIONAL MUSEUMS	1	1	40	–	...
SINGAPORE	1979	TOTAL	10	10	4 282	.	.
		A. NATIONAL MUSEUMS	4	4	2 257	.	.
		B. OTHER PUBLIC MUSEUMS	6	6	2 025	.	.
THAILAND‡	1979	TOTAL	119	40	1 103	.	.
		A. NATIONAL MUSEUMS	40	40	1 103	.	.
		B. OTHER PUBLIC MUSEUMS	79	–	...	.	.
TURKEY	1984	TOTAL	127	109	5 476	109	605 546
		A. NATIONAL MUSEUMS	127	109	5 476	109	605 546
UNITED ARAB EMIRATES	1979	TOTAL	3	2	244	.	.
VIET-NAM	1979	TOTAL	9	8	1 918	.	.
		A. NATIONAL MUSEUMS	5	...	1 054	.	.
		B. OTHER PUBLIC MUSEUMS	4	...	864	.	.
EUROPE							
ANDORRA	1979	TOTAL	4	4	51 600	.	.
		A. NATIONAL MUSEUMS	1	1	3 000	.	.
		B. OTHER PUBLIC MUSEUMS	3	3	48 600	.	.
AUSTRIA	1984	TOTAL	209	209	8 943	–	...
		A. NATIONAL MUSEUMS	32	32	2 497	–	...
		B. OTHER PUBLIC MUSEUMS	177	177	6 446	–	...

	PERSONNEL / PERSONNEL / PERSONAL						ANNUAL CURRENT EXPENDITURE / DEPENSES ANNUELLES ORDINAIRES / GASTOS ORDINARIOS ANUALES		
NUMBER OF MUSEUMS REPORTING / NOMBRE DE MUSEES AYANT FOURNI CES DONNEES / NUMERO DE MUSEOS QUE DIERON ESTE DATO	TOTAL STAFF / TOTAL DU PERSONNEL / TOTAL DE PERSONAL	PROFESSIONAL STAFF / PERSONNEL PROFESSIONNEL / PERSONAL PROFESIONAL		OTHER STAFF / AUTRE PERSONNEL / OTRO PERSONAL		NUMBER OF MUSEUMS REPORTING / NOMBRE DE MUSEES AYANT FOURNI CES DONNEES / NUMERO DE MUSEOS QUE DIERON ESTE DATO	TOTAL (000) / TOTAL (000) / TOTAL (000)	COUNTRY / PAYS / PAIS
		PAID STAFF / SALARIES / REMUNERADOS	VOLUNTEERS / VOLONTAIRES / VOLUNTARIOS	PAID STAFF / SALARIES / REMUNERADOS	VOLUNTEERS / VOLONTAIRES / VOLUNTARIOS			
1	11	2	–	9	–	1	150	BHUTAN
1	11	2	–	9	–	1	150	
3	174	49	–	75	–	3	7 024	BRUNEI DARUSSALAM
3	174	49	–	75	–	3	7 024	
26	87	76	–	11	–	26	121	CYPRUS
23	78	67	–	11	–	23	96	
2	7	7	–	–	–	2	23	
1	2	2	–	–	–	1	2	
–	...	...	...	...	...	–	...	INDONESIA
13	80	67	–	13	–	–	...	IRAQ
67	1 265	473	...	792	...	–	...	ISRAEL
493	7 476	1 360	–	6 116	–	–	...	JAPAN
28	617	187	–	430	–	–	...	
222	3 330	535	–	2 795	–	–	...	
243	3 529	638	–	2 891	–	–	...	
16	99	86	13	–	–	9	850	JORDAN
94	920	220	94	606	–	43	5 271 000	KOREA, REPUBLIC OF
3	124	72	–	52	–	3	76	KUWAIT
3	124	72	–	52	–	3	76	
11	379	137	–	242	–	9	3 577	MALAYSIA‡
2	273	89	–	184	–	2	2 759	
9	106	48	–	58	–	7	818	
1	16	1	–	15	–	1	57	MALDIVES
1	16	1	–	15	–	1	57	
10	391	36	105	250	–	10	3 114	PAKISTAN
1	89	16	–	73	–	1	1 059	
9	302	20	105	177	–	9	2 055	
61	699	...	...	...	...	–	...	PHILIPPINES
25	514	...	...	...	...	–	...	
21	109	...	...	...	...	–	...	
15	76	...	...	...	...	–	...	
1	50	50	–	–	–	–	...	QATAR
1	50	50	–	–	–	–	...	
1	17	10	–	7	–	–	...	SAUDI ARABIA
1	17	10	–	7	–	–	...	
10	505	66	–	439	–	10	6 544	SINGAPORE
4	261	59	–	202	–	4	2 723	
6	244	7	–	237	–	6	3 821	
40	548	112	33	403	–	40	28 120	THAILAND‡
40	548	112	33	403	–	40	28 120	
–	...	...	...	...	...	–	...	
127	2 342	461	–	1 881	–	127	254 490	TURKEY
127	2 342	461	–	1 881	–	127	254 490	
3	134	10	–	124	–	2	9 591	UNITED ARAB EMIRATES
8	297	297	–	–	–	8	1 404	VIET-NAM
...	188	188	–	–	–	...	836	
...	109	109	–	–	–	...	568	
								EUROPE
4	9	4	–	5	–	4	7 662	ANDORRA
1	4	2	–	2	–	1	4 142	
3	5	2	–	3	–	3	3 520	
–	...	...	...	...	...	–	...	AUSTRIA
–	...	...	...	...	...	–	...	
–	...	...	...	...	...	–	...	

8.1 Number of museums by ownership
Nombre de musées selon leur propriété
Número de museos según su propiedad

COUNTRY / PAYS / PAIS	YEAR / ANNEE / AÑO	OWNERSHIP OF MUSEUMS (OR RELATED INSTITUTIONS) / PROPRIETE DES MUSEES (OU INSTITUTIONS SIMILAIRES) / PROPIEDAD DE LOS MUSEOS (O INSTITUCIONES SIMILARES)	TOTAL NUMBER OF MUSEUMS / NOMBRE TOTAL DE MUSEES / NUMERO TOTAL DE MUSEOS	ATTENDANCE / FREQUENTATION / FRECUENTACION: NUMBER OF MUSEUMS REPORTING / NOMBRE DE MUSEES AYANT FOURNI CES DONNEES / NUMERO DE MUSEOS QUE DIERON ESTE DATO	NUMBER OF VISITORS (000) / NOMBRE DE VISITEURS (000) / NUMERO DE VISITANTES (000)	ANNUAL RECEIPTS / RECETTES ANNUELLES / INGRESOS ANUALES: NUMBER OF MUSEUMS REPORTING / NOMBRE DE MUSEES AYANT FOURNI CES DONNEES / NUMERO DE MUSEOS QUE DIERON ESTE DATO	TOTAL (000)
BULGARIA	1984	TOTAL	206	206	15 535	206	28 401
		A. NATIONAL MUSEUMS	30	30	1 507	30	4 296
		B. OTHER PUBLIC MUSEUMS	176	176	14 028	176	24 105
CZECHOSLOVAKIA	1984	TOTAL	348	348	17 666	348	41 025
DENMARK	1979	TOTAL	282	268	9 622	.	.
		A. NATIONAL MUSEUMS	40	40	2 285	.	.
		B. OTHER PUBLIC MUSEUMS	216	203	6 521	.	.
		C. PRIVATE MUSEUMS	26	25	816	.	.
FINLAND	1984	TOTAL	572	517	2 897	23	298
		A. NATIONAL MUSEUMS	43	...	...	...	...
		B. OTHER PUBLIC MUSEUMS	512	...	...	...	...
		C. PRIVATE MUSEUMS	17	...	...	...	...
FRANCE	1979	A. NATIONAL MUSEUMS	37	37	12 922	.	.
		B. OTHER PUBLIC MUSEUMS	*1 400	...	...	.	.
GERMAN DEMOCRATIC REPUBLIC	1984	TOTAL	684	684	33 700	684	52
		A. NATIONAL MUSEUMS	66	66	7 900	66	10
		B. OTHER PUBLIC MUSEUMS	618	618	25 800	618	42
GERMANY, FEDERAL REPUBLIC OF‡	1984	TOTAL	2 025	1 586	56 748	–	...
		A. NATIONAL MUSEUMS	14	13	1 025	–	...
		B. OTHER PUBLIC MUSEUMS	1 203	983	33 575	–	...
		C. PRIVATE MUSEUMS	808	590	22 148	–	...
GIBRALTAR	1984	TOTAL	1	1	17	–	...
		B. OTHER PUBLIC MUSEUMS	1	1	17	–	...
HOLY SEE	1984	TOTAL	13	13	1 928	–	...
		A. NATIONAL MUSEUMS	13	13	1 928	–	...
HUNGARY‡	1984	TOTAL	594	541	19 200	–	...
		A. NATIONAL MUSEUMS	30	29	3 574	–	...
		B. OTHER PUBLIC MUSEUMS	564	512	15 626	–	...
IRELAND	1979	TOTAL	49	26	824	.	.
		A. NATIONAL MUSEUMS	...	1	378	.	.
		B. OTHER PUBLIC MUSEUMS	...	16	377	.	.
		C. PRIVATE MUSEUMS	...	9	68	.	.
ITALY‡	1978	TOTAL	1 275	1 112	44 395	.	.
		A. NATIONAL MUSEUMS	181	181	23 524	.	.
		B. OTHER PUBLIC MUSEUMS	1 094	931	20 871	.	.
MALTA	1979	TOTAL	22	16	712	.	.
		A. NATIONAL MUSEUMS	15	15	653	.	.
		B. OTHER PUBLIC MUSEUMS	6	1	59	.	.
		C. PRIVATE MUSEUMS	1	–	...	.	.
MONACO	1979	TOTAL	4	4	1 552	.	.
		A. NATIONAL MUSEUMS	1	1	83	.	.
		B. OTHER PUBLIC MUSEUMS	2	2	1 398	.	.
		C. PRIVATE MUSEUMS	1	1	71	.	.
NETHERLANDS‡	1984	TOTAL	548	539	15 959	537	307 853
NORWAY	1978	TOTAL	195	139	4 573	.	.
		A. NATIONAL MUSEUMS	17	14	1 039	.	.
		B. OTHER PUBLIC MUSEUMS	178	125	3 534	.	.
POLAND	1984	TOTAL	525	475	19 642	416	4 233
		A. NATIONAL MUSEUMS	468	425	18 908	416	4 233
		B. OTHER PUBLIC MUSEUMS	57	50	734	–	...
PORTUGAL‡	1984	TOTAL	139	139	3 800	139	863 784
		A. NATIONAL MUSEUMS	35	35	2 282	35	555 226
		B. OTHER PUBLIC MUSEUMS	96	96	1 346	96	294 018
		C. PRIVATE MUSEUMS	8	8	172	8	14 540
ROMANIA	1979	TOTAL	412	412	16 331	.	.
		A. NATIONAL MUSEUMS	5	5	...	.	.
		B. OTHER PUBLIC MUSEUMS	407	407	...	.	.

PERSONNEL / PERSONNEL / PERSONAL						ANNUAL CURRENT EXPENDITURE / DEPENSES ANNUELLES ORDINAIRES / GASTOS ORDINARIOS ANUALES		
NUMBER OF MUSEUMS REPORTING / NOMBRE DE MUSEES AYANT FOURNI CES DONNEES / NUMERO DE MUSEOS QUE DIERON ESTE DATO	TOTAL STAFF / TOTAL DU PERSONNEL / TOTAL DE PERSONAL	PROFESSIONAL STAFF / PERSONNEL PROFESSIONNEL / PERSONAL PROFESIONAL: PAID STAFF / SALARIES / REMUNERADOS	PROFESSIONAL STAFF: VOLUNTEERS / VOLONTAIRES / VOLUNTARIOS	OTHER STAFF / AUTRE PERSONNEL / OTRO PERSONAL: PAID STAFF / SALARIES / REMUNERADOS	OTHER STAFF: VOLUNTEERS / VOLONTAIRES / VOLUNTARIOS	NUMBER OF MUSEUMS REPORTING / NOMBRE DE MUSEES AYANT FOURNI CES DONNEES / NUMERO DE MUSEOS QUE DIERON ESTE DATO	TOTAL (000) / TOTAL (000) / TOTAL (000)	COUNTRY / PAYS / PAIS
206	3 153	3 153	–	–	–	206	26 869	BULGARIA
30	681	681	–	–	–	30	4 001	
176	2 472	2 472	–	–	–	176	22 868	
348	6 131	4 882	–	1 249	–	80	230 753	CZECHOSLOVAKIA
–	...	...	...	...	...	–	...	DENMARK
–	...	...	...	...	...	–	...	
–	...	...	...	...	...	–	...	
–	...	...	...	...	...	–	...	
519	...	571	–	...	–	504	55 968	FINLAND
...	...	...	–	...	–	...	...	
...	...	...	–	...	–	...	...	
...	...	...	–	...	–	...	...	
34	...	557	...	1 107	...	34	121 730	FRANCE
...	...	...	...	...	...	...	...	
684	6 830	3 000	–	3 830	–	684	171	GERMAN DEMOCRATIC REPUBLIC
66	1 932	1 003	–	929	–	66	40	
618	4 898	1 997	–	2 901	–	618	131	
–	...	...	...	...	...	–	...	GERMANY, FEDERAL REPUBLIC OF‡
–	...	...	...	...	...	–	...	
–	...	...	...	...	...	–	...	
–	...	...	...	...	...	–	...	
1	8	1	–	7	–	1	35	GIBRALTAR
1	8	1	–	7	–	1	35	
13	264	10	–	254	–	–	...	HOLY SEE
13	264	10	–	254	–	–	...	
456	5 613	1 887	–	2 040	–	–	...	HUNGARY‡
23	1 695	669	–	555	–	–	...	
433	3 918	1 218	–	1 485	–	–	...	
30	371	53	52	164	102	20	919	IRELAND
1	96	25	–	71	–	1	400	
18	194	20	19	72	83	14	402	
11	81	8	33	21	19	5	117	
–	...	...	...	...	...	181	59 751	ITALY‡
–	...	...	...	...	...	181	59 751	
–	...	...	...	...	...	–	...	
16	72	8	–	64	–	16	116	MALTA
15	68	7	–	61	–	15	110	
1	4	1	–	3	–	1	6	
–	...	...	...	...	...	–	...	
4	127	122	–	5	–	2	1 319	MONACO
1	10	10	–	–	–	1	1 220	
2	115	110	–	5	–	–	...	
1	2	2	–	–	–	1	99	
548	4 426	1 483	298	2 355	291	537	307 853	NETHERLANDS‡
–	...	...	...	...	...	–	...	NORWAY
–	...	...	...	...	...	–	...	
–	...	...	...	...	...	–	...	
416	9 506	4 768	–	4 738	–	416	4 351	POLAND
416	9 506	4 768	–	4 738	–	416	4 351	
–	...	...	–	...	–	–	...	
139	1 938	815	14	995	114	139	983 601	PORTUGAL‡
35	1 018	444	5	510	59	35	427 212	
96	798	336	9	398	55	96	427 047	
8	122	35	–	87	–	8	129 342	
–	...	...	...	...	...	–	...	ROMANIA
–	...	...	...	...	...	–	...	
–	...	...	...	...	...	–	...	

8.1 **Number of museums by ownership**
Nombre de musées selon leur propriété
Número de museos según su propiedad

COUNTRY / PAYS / PAIS	YEAR / ANNEE / AÑO		OWNERSHIP OF MUSEUMS (OR RELATED INSTITUTIONS) / PROPRIETE DES MUSEES (OU INSTITUTIONS SIMILAIRES) / PROPIEDAD DE LOS MUSEOS (O INSTITUCIONES SIMILARES)	TOTAL NUMBER OF MUSEUMS / NOMBRE TOTAL DE MUSEES / NUMERO TOTAL DE MUSEOS	ATTENDANCE / FREQUENTATION / FRECUENTACION: NUMBER OF MUSEUMS REPORTING / NOMBRE DE MUSEES AYANT FOURNI CES DONNEES / NUMERO DE MUSEOS QUE DIERON ESTE DATO	NUMBER OF VISITORS (000) / NOMBRE DE VISITEURS (000) / NUMERO DE VISITANTES (000)	ANNUAL RECEIPTS / RECETTES ANNUELLES / INGRESOS ANUALES: NUMBER OF MUSEUMS REPORTING / NOMBRE DE MUSEES AYANT FOURNI CES DONNEES / NUMERO DE MUSEOS QUE DIERON ESTE DATO	TOTAL (000)
SAN MARINO	1979		TOTAL	11	11	741	.	.
		A.	NATIONAL MUSEUMS	9	9	...	.	.
		C.	PRIVATE MUSEUMS	2	2	...	.	.
SPAIN‡	1979		TOTAL	610	610	13 897	.	.
		A.	NATIONAL MUSEUMS	86	86	4 750	.	.
		B.	OTHER PUBLIC MUSEUMS	441	441	8 200	.	.
		C.	PRIVATE MUSEUMS	83	83	947	.	.
SWEDEN‡	1983		TOTAL	167	167	12 192	167	643
		A.	NATIONAL MUSEUMS	14	14	2 401	14	81
		B.	OTHER PUBLIC MUSEUMS	153	153	9 791	153	562
YUGOSLAVIA	1982		TOTAL	522	452	11 851	–	...
		B.	OTHER PUBLIC MUSEUMS	522	452	11 851	–	...
OCEANIA								
AMERICAN SAMOA	1979		TOTAL	1	1	52	.	.
AUSTRALIA‡	1979		TOTAL	15	14	5 279	.	.
		A.	NATIONAL MUSEUMS	2	1	734	.	.
		B.	OTHER PUBLIC MUSEUMS	13	13	4 545	.	.
FIJI	1984		TOTAL	1	1	40	1	205
		A.	NATIONAL MUSEUMS	1	1	40	1	205
NEW CALEDONIA‡	1979		TOTAL	1	1	30	.	.
		B.	OTHER PUBLIC MUSEUMS	1	1	30	.	.
NORFOLK ISLAND	1979		TOTAL	1	1	20	.	.
		A.	NATIONAL MUSEUMS	1	1	20	.	.
PACIFIC ISLANDS	1980		TOTAL	5	–	...	.	.
		C.	PRIVATE MUSEUMS	5	–	...	.	.
PAPUA NEW GUINEA	1979		TOTAL	2	2	100	.	.
		A.	NATIONAL MUSEUMS	2	2	100	.	.
U.S.S.R.								
U.S.S.R.‡	1984		TOTAL	1 479	1 370	174 363	–	...
BYELORUSSIAN S.S.R.‡	1984		TOTAL	68	56	4 209	–	...
UKRAINIAN S.S.R.‡	1984		TOTAL	140	140	32 700	–	...

PERSONNEL / PERSONNEL / PERSONAL						ANNUAL CURRENT EXPENDITURE / DEPENSES ANNUELLES ORDINAIRES / GASTOS ORDINARIOS ANUALES		
NUMBER OF MUSEUMS REPORTING		PROFESSIONAL STAFF / PERSONNEL PROFESSIONNEL / PERSONAL PROFESIONAL		OTHER STAFF / AUTRE PERSONNEL / OTRO PERSONAL		NUMBER OF MUSEUMS REPORTING	TOTAL (000)	COUNTRY
NOMBRE DE MUSEES AYANT FOURNI CES DONNEES	TOTAL STAFF	PAID STAFF	VOLUNTEERS	PAID STAFF	VOLUNTEERS	NOMBRE DE MUSEES AYANT FOURNI CES DONNEES	TOTAL (000)	PAYS
NUMERO DE MUSEOS QUE DIERON ESTE DATO	TOTAL DU PERSONNEL	SALARIES	VOLONTAIRES	SALARIES	VOLONTAIRES	NUMERO DE MUSEOS QUE DIERON ESTE DATO	TOTAL (000)	PAIS
	TOTAL DE PERSONAL	REMUNERADOS	VOLUNTARIOS	REMUNERADOS	VOLUNTARIOS			
–	...	...	...	...	...	11	403 500	SAN MARINO
–	...	...	...	...	...	9	...	
–	...	...	...	...	...	2	...	
610	4 684	613	775	2 494	1 196	610	685 443	SPAIN‡
86	1 674	219	245	910	414	86	248 443	
441	2 440	256	400	1 364	700	441	240 000	
83	570	138	130	220	82	83	197 000	
167	3 354		...	...	...	–	...	SWEDEN‡
14	1 054	...	...	...	...	–	...	
153	2 300	...	...	...	...	–	...	
522	3 999	2 165	→	1 834	→	–	...	YUGOSLAVIA
522	3 999	2 165	→	1 834	→	–	...	
								OCEANIA
1	7		–	–		1	260	AMERICAN SAMOA
15	1 747	456	21	928	342	15	31 524	AUSTRALIA‡
2	233	11	–	112	33	2	9 471	
13	1 514	368	21	816	309	13	22 053	
1	9	2	–	5	1	1	198	FIJI
1	9	2		5	1	1	198	
1	9	9		–	–	1	2 500	NEW CALEDONIA‡
1	9	9		–	–	1	2 500	
1	14	14	–	–	–	1	260	NORFOLK ISLAND
1	14	14	–	–	–	1	260	
2	4	–	–	4	–	–	...	PACIFIC ISLANDS
2	4	–	–	4	–	–	...	
2	65	32	2	30	1	2	530	PAPUA NEW GUINEA
2	65	32	2	30	1	2	530	
								U.S.S.R.
–	...	...	...	...	...	–	...	U.S.S.R.‡
–	...	...	...	...	...	–	...	BYELORUSSIAN S.S.R.‡
–	...	...	...	...	...	–	...	UKRAINIAN S.S.R.‡

AFRICA:
Cameroon:
E--> Total does not include 30 historical and archaeological monuments and sites.
FR-> Le total n'inclut pas 30 monuments et sites historiques et archéologiques.
ESP> El total no incluye 30 monumentos y lugares históricos y arqueológicos.
Morocco:
E--> Personnel includes staff working on protected monuments and sites.
FR-> Le personnel inclut les employés qui travaillent dans des monuments et sites protégés.
ESP> El personal incluye los empleados qui trabajan en los monumentos y sitios protegidos.
AMERICA, NORTH:
Canada:
E--> Total includes 15 museums for which ownership has not been communicated.
FR-> Le total inclut 15 musées pour lesquels la répartition selon leur propriété n'a pas été communiquée.
ESP> El total incluye 15 museos cuya distribución según propiedad no ha sido comunicada.
Cuba:
E--> Total includes 103 monuments and sites.
FR-> Le total inclut 103 monuments et sites.

Cuba: (Cont):
ESP> El total incluye 103 monumentos y sitios.
Mexico:
E--> Total includes 125 monuments and sites.
FR-> Le total inclut 125 monuments et sites.
ESP> El total incluye 125 monumentos y sitios.
United States:
E--> Professional and other staff are counted together.
FR-> Le personnel professionnel et l'autre personnel sont comptés ensemble.
ESP> El personal profesional y otro personal están contados conjunamente.
ASIA:
Malaysia:
E--> Expenditure under national museums includes expenditure for 2 public museums.
FR-> Les dépenses relatives aux musées nationaux comprennent les dépenses pour 2 musées publics.
ESP> Los gastos relativos a los museos nacionales incluyen los gastos de 2 museos públicos.
Thailand:
E--> National museums include 8 private museums.
FR-> Les musées nationaux incluent 8 musées privés.
ESP> Los museos nacionales incluyen 8 museos privados.
EUROPE:

Germany, Federal Republic of:

E--> The category 'Other public museums' includes 26 museums owned either by foreign countries or jointly by two or more official bodies.

FR-> La categorie 'Autres musées publics' comprend 26 musées appartenant soit à des pays étrangers soit à deux organismes officiels, ou plus.

ESP> La categoría 'Otros museos públicos' comprende 26 museos que pertencen a otros países, o que pertenecen a dos o más organizaciones oficiales.

Hungary:

E--> Total includes 152 monuments and sites.

FR-> Le total inclut 152 monuments et sites.

ESP> El total incluye 152 monumentos y sitios.

Italy:

E--> Other public museums include private museums.

FR-> Les autres musées publics comprennent les musées privés.

ESP> Otros museos públicos incluye los museos privados.

Netherlands:

E--> Data on receipts and expenditure refer to 1983.

FR-> Les données relatives aux recettes et aux dépenses se réfèrent à 1983.

ESP> Los datos relativos a los ingresos y gastos se refieren a 1983.

Portugal:

E--> Figures shown for total number of museums are incomplete and refer only to those museums which have been able to report statistics on attendance, receipts, personnel and expenditure.

FR-> Les chiffres concernant le nombre total de musées sont incomplets; ils se réfèrent seulement aux musées qui ont pu fournir des statistiques sur la fréquentation, les recettes, le personnel et les dépenses.

ESP> Las cifras sobre el número total de museos son incompletas; ellas se refieren solamente a los museos que han podido proporcionar estadísticas sobre la frecuentación, ingresos, personal y gastos.

Spain:

E--> Total does not include historial and archaeological monuments.

FR-> Le total n'inclut pas les monuments historiques et archéologiques.

ESP> El total no incluye los monumentos históricos y arqueológicos.

Sweden:

E--> Other public museums include private museums.

FR-> Les autres musées publics incluent les musées privés.

ESP> Otros museos públicos incluyen los museos privados.

OCEANIA:

Australia:

E--> Figures shown for total number of museums are incomplete and refer only to those museums which have been able to report statistics on attendance, receipts, personnel and expenditure.

FR-> Les chiffres concernant le nombre total de musées sont incomplets; ils se réfèrent seulement aux musées qui ont pu fournir des statistiques sur la fréquentation, les recettes, le personnel et les dépenses.

ESP> Las cifras sobre el número total de museos son incompletas; ellas se refieren solamente a los museos que han podido proporcionar estadísticas sobre la frecuentación, ingresos, personal y gastos.

New Caledonia:

E--> Expenditure does not include expenditure on personnel.

FR-> Les dépenses n'incluent pas les dépenses relatives au personnel.

ESP> Gastos no incluye los gastos sobre el personal.

U.S.S.R.:

U.S.S.R.:

E--> Total does not include Permanent Exhibition of Economic Achievements of the U.S.S.R. in Moscow which reported 11.6 million visitors.

FR-> Le total ne comprend pas l'Exposition Permanente des Réalisations Economiques de l'U.R.S.S. à Moscou pour laquelle on a compté 11.6 millions de visiteurs.

ESP> El total no incluye la Exposición Permanente de los Materializaciones Económicas Realizados por la U.R.S.S. en Moscú, que fueron de 11.6 millones de visitantes.

Byelorussian S.S.R.:

E--> Total does not include Permanent Exhibition of Economic Achievements of the Byelorussian S.S.R. which reported 259,000 visitors.

FR-> Le total ne comprend pas l'Exposition Permanente des Réalisations Economiques de la R.S.S. de Biélorussie pour laquelle on a compté 259 000 visiteurs.

ESP> El total no incluye la Exposición Permanente de los Materializaciones Económicas Realizados por la R.S.S. de Bielorrusia, que fueron de 259 000 de visitantes.

Ukrainian S.S.R.:

E--> Number of visitors includes visitors to memorials.

FR-> Le nombre de visiteurs inclut les visiteurs des mémorials.

ESP> El número de visitantes incluye los visitantes a los memoriales.

8.2 Number of museums by subject of collection: visitors, personnel and annual current expenditure

Nombre de musées d'après la nature des collections: visiteurs, personnel et dépenses ordinaires annuelles

Número de museos según la naturaleza de sus colecciones: visitantes, personal y gastos ordinarios anuales

SUBJECT OF COLLECTION OR TYPE OF INSTITUTION:

A. ART MUSEUMS
B. ARCHAEOLOGY AND HISTORY MUSEUMS
C. NATURAL HISTORY AND NATURAL SCIENCE MUSEUMS
D. SCIENCE AND TECHNOLOGY MUSEUMS
E. ETHNOGRAPHY AND ANTHROPOLOGY MUSEUMS
F. SPECIALIZED MUSEUMS
G. REGIONAL MUSEUMS
H. GENERAL MUSEUMS
I. OTHER MUSEUMS
J. HISTORICAL AND ARCHAEOLOGICAL MONUMENTS AND SITES
K. ZOOS, BOTANICAL GARDENS, ETC.

NATURE DES COLLECTIONS OU TYPE D'INSTITUTION:

A. MUSEES D'ART
B. MUSEES D'ARCHEOLOGIE ET D'HISTOIRE
C. MUSEES DE SCIENCE ET D'HISTOIRE NATURELLES
D. MUSEES DES SCIENCES ET DES TECHNIQUES
E. MUSEES D'ETHNOGRAPHIE ET D'ANTHROPOLOGIE
F. MUSEES SPECIALISES
G. MUSEES REGIONAUX
H. MUSEES GENERAUX
I. AUTRES MUSEES
J. MONUMENTS ET SITES HISTORIQUES ET ARCHEOLOGIQUES
K. JARDINS ZOOLOGIQUES ET BOTANIQUES, ETC.

THE TOTAL SHOWN FOR YEARS PRIOR TO 1982 REFERS TO MUSEUMS AND RELATED INSTITUTIONS: FROM 1982, TO MUSEUMS ONLY. ANNUAL CURRENT EXPENDITURE AND RECEIPTS ARE EXPRESSED IN NATIONAL CURRENCY.

LE TOTAL INDIQUE POUR LES ANNEES ANTERIEURES A 1982 SE REFERE AUX MUSEES ET INSTITUTIONS ASSIMILEES; A PARTIR DE 1982, AUX MUSEES SEULEMENT. LES DEPENSES ORDINAIRES ET LES RECETTES ANNUELLES SONT EXPRIMEES EN MONNAIE NATIONALE.

NUMBER OF COUNTRIES AND TERRITORIES PRESENTED IN THIS TABLE: 109

NOMBRE DE PAYS ET DE TERRITOIRES PRESENTES DANS CE TABLEAU: 109

COUNTRY / PAYS / PAIS	YEAR / ANNEE / AÑO	SUBJECT OF COLLECTION OR TYPE OF INSTITUTION / NATURE DES COLLECTIONS OU TYPE D'INSTITUTION / NATURALEZA DE LAS COLECCIONES O TIPO DE INSTITUCION	TOTAL NUMBER OF MUSEUMS / NOMBRE TOTAL DE MUSEES / NUMERO TOTAL DE MUSEOS	ATTENDANCE / FREQUENTATION / FRECUENTACION: NUMBER OF MUSEUMS REPORTING / NOMBRE DE MUSEES AYANT FOURNI CES DONNEES / NUMERO DE MUSEOS QUE DIERON ESTE DATO	ATTENDANCE / FREQUENTATION / FRECUENTACION: NUMBER OF VISITORS (000) / NOMBRE DE VISITEURS (000) / NUMERO DE VISITANTES (000)	ANNUAL RECEIPTS / RECETTES ANNUELLES / INGRESOS ANUALES: NUMBER OF MUSEUMS REPORTING / NOMBRE DE MUSEES AYANT FOURNI CES DONNEES / NUMERO DE MUSEOS QUE DIERON ESTE DATO	ANNUAL RECEIPTS / RECETTES ANNUELLES / INGRESOS ANUALES: TOTAL (000)
AFRICA							
ALGERIA	1979	TOTAL	32	13	260	.	.
		A. ART	1	1	7	.	.
		B. ARCHAEOLOGY AND HISTORY	15	11	240	.	.
		E. ETHNOGRAPHY AND ANTHROPOLOGY	4	1	13	.	.
		F. SPECIALIZED MUSEUMS	8	–	...	.	.
		K. ZOOS, BOTANICAL GARDENS, ETC.	4	–	...	.	.
BENIN	1984	TOTAL	5	3	8	2	202
		B. ARCHAEOLOGY AND HISTORY	3	2	5	1	98
		E. ETHNOGRAPHY AND ANTHROPOLOGY	1	1	3	1	104
		I. OTHER MUSEUMS	1	–	...	–	...
		J. MONUMENTS AND SITES	*15	...	...	...	...
		K. ZOOS, BOTANICAL GARDENS, ETC.	*3	...	...	...	...
BOTSWANA	1979	TOTAL	2	2	52	.	.
		H. GENERAL MUSEUMS	1	1	...	.	.
		J. MONUMENTS AND SITES	1	1	...	.	.
BURUNDI	1984	TOTAL	2	2	6	1	120
		E. ETHNOGRAPHY AND ANTHROPOLOGY	1	1	3	...	...
		I. OTHER MUSEUMS	1	1	3	1	120
CAMEROON	1979	TOTAL	42	12	4 641	.	.
		A. ART	1	1	881	.	.
		G. REGIONAL MUSEUMS	7	7	2 710	.	.
		I. OTHER MUSEUMS	4	4	1 050	.	.
		J. MONUMENTS AND SITES	30	–	...	.	.

NUMBER OF MUSEUMS REPORTING NOMBRE DE MUSEES AYANT FOURNI CES DONNEES NUMERO DE MUSEOS QUE DIERON ESTE DATO	PERSONNEL / PERSONNEL / PERSONAL TOTAL STAFF TOTAL DU PERSONNEL TOTAL DE PERSONAL	PROFESSIONAL STAFF / PERSONNEL PROFESSIONNEL / PERSONAL PROFESIONAL PAID STAFF SALARIES REMUNERADOS	 VOLUNTEERS VOLONTAIRES VOLUNTARIOS	OTHER STAFF / AUTRE PERSONNEL / OTRO PERSONAL PAID STAFF SALARIES REMUNERADOS	 VOLUNTEERS VOLONTAIRES VOLUNTARIOS	ANNUAL CURRENT EXPENDITURE / DEPENSES ANNUELLES ORDINAIRES / GASTOS ORDINARIOS ANUALES NUMBER OF MUSEUMS REPORTING NOMBRE DE MUSEES AYANT FOURNI CES DONNEES NUMERO DE MUSEOS QUE DIERON ESTE DATO	 TOTAL (000) TOTAL (000) TOTAL (000)	COUNTRY PAYS PAIS
1	21	15	2	4	–	1	400	CENTRAL AFRICAN REPUBLIC
...	...	...	...	...	–	...	...	
...	...	...	...	...	–	...	...	
...	...	...	...	...	–	...	...	
...	...	...	...	...	–	...	...	
...	...	...	...	...	–	...	...	
1	6	6	–	–	–	1	952	CHAD
...	...	...	–	–	–	...	...	
...	...	...	–	–	–	...	...	
...	...	...	–	–	–	...	...	
...	...	...	–	–	–	...	...	
5	57	23	–	34	–	5	131 000	CONGO
1	38	9	–	29	–	1	120 000	
3	7	3	–	4	–	3	6 000	
1	12	11	–	1	–	1	5 000	
1	45	15	–	30	–	–	...	ETHIOPIA
30	30	22	–	18	–	15	414	
4	162	25	–	137	–	4	2 210	GHANA
1	35	2	–	33	–	1	...	
1	14	1	–	13	–	1	...	
2	113	22	–	91	–	2	...	
5	41	19	–	22	–	5	208	GUINEA
1	12	10	–	2	–	1	160	
4	29	9	–	20	–	4	48	
–	...	...	–	...	–	–	...	
–	...	...	–	...	–	–	...	
6	555	202	–	353	–	6	1 027	KENYA
5	...	...	–	...	–	5	...	
1	...	...	–	...	–	1	...	
–	...	...	–	...	–	–	...	
...	1 100	40	...	...	...	...	1 500	LIBYAN ARAB JAMAHIRIYA
...	...	...	...	...	...	...	...	
...	...	...	...	...	...	...	...	
...	...	...	...	...	...	...	...	
...	...	...	...	...	...	...	...	
3	19	19	–	–	–	3	...	MADAGASCAR
1	2	2	–	–	–	1	...	
1	50	19	1	30	–	2	150	MALAWI
1	50	19	1	30	–	2	150	
1	52	23	–	29	–	1	202	
6	415	138	5	272	–	11	147	
3	40	5	–	35	–	3	1 050	MAURITIUS‡
1	40	5	–	35	–	1	1 050	
1	./.	./.	–	./.	–	1	./.	
1	./.	./.	–	./.	–	1	./.	
–	...	...	...	...	...	–	...	
...	*500	...	...	...	...	–	...	MOROCCO
4	...	...	...	...	...	–	...	
7	...	...	...	...	...	–	...	
15 000	./.	...	...	...	...	–	...	
1	116	115	1	–	–	1	15 500	NIGER
2	14	12	2	–	–	2	380	REUNION
1	...	...	...	–	–	1	...	
1	...	...	...	–	–	1	...	
–	...	...	...	...	...	–	...	ST. HELENA
–	...	...	...	...	...	–	...	

8.2 Number of museums by subject of collection
Nombre de musées d'après la nature des collections
Número de museos según la naturaleza de sus colecciones

COUNTRY / PAYS / PAIS	YEAR / ANNEE / AÑO	SUBJECT OF COLLECTION OR TYPE OF INSTITUTION / NATURE DES COLLECTIONS OU TYPE D'INSTITUTION / NATURALEZA DE LAS COLECCIONES O TIPO DE INSTITUCION	TOTAL NUMBER OF MUSEUMS / NOMBRE TOTAL DE MUSEES / NUMERO TOTAL DE MUSEOS	ATTENDANCE / FREQUENTATION / FRECUENTACION: NUMBER OF MUSEUMS REPORTING / NOMBRE DE MUSEES AYANT FOURNI CES DONNEES / NUMERO DE MUSEOS QUE DIERON ESTE DATO	ATTENDANCE / FREQUENTATION / FRECUENTACION: NUMBER OF VISITORS (000) / NOMBRE DE VISITEURS (000) / NUMERO DE VISITANTES (000)	ANNUAL RECEIPTS / RECETTES ANNUELLES / INGRESOS ANUALES: NUMBER OF MUSEUMS REPORTING / NOMBRE DE MUSEES AYANT FOURNI CES DONNEES / NUMERO DE MUSEOS QUE DIERON ESTE DATO	ANNUAL RECEIPTS / RECETTES ANNUELLES / INGRESOS ANUALES: TOTAL (000)
SENEGAL	1979	TOTAL	4	4	55	.	.
		A. ART	1	1	9	.	.
		B. ARCHAEOLOGY AND HISTORY	1	1	10	.	.
		D. SCIENCE AND TECHNOLOGY	1	1	3	.	.
		J. MONUMENTS AND SITES	1	1	33	.	.
SEYCHELLES	1979	TOTAL	1	1	8	.	.
		H. GENERAL MUSEUMS	1	1	8	.	.
SIERRA LEONE	1979	TOTAL	19	1	178	.	.
		H. GENERAL MUSEUMS	1	1	178	.	.
		J. MONUMENTS AND SITES	18	–	...	.	.
SUDAN	1984	TOTAL	7	7	*221	–	...
		B. ARCHAEOLOGY AND HISTORY	3	3	*127	–	...
		C. NAT. HISTORY AND NAT. SCIENCE.	1	1	*45	–	...
		G. REGIONAL MUSEUMS	3	3	*49	–	...
		J. MONUMENTS AND SITES	13	–	...	–	...
TUNISIA	1984	TOTAL	35	32	367	32	116
		A. ART	1	–	...	–	...
		B. ARCHAEOLOGY AND HISTORY	25	25	343	25	111
		C. NAT. HISTORY AND NAT. SCIENCE.	1	–	...	–	...
		D. SCIENCE AND TECHNOLOGY	1	–	...	–	...
		E. ETHNOGRAPHY AND ANTHROPOLOGY	7	7	24	7	5
		J. MONUMENTS AND SITES	46	6	61	6	22
		K. ZOOS, BOTANICAL GARDENS, ETC.	1	1	876	1	55
ZAMBIA	1984	TOTAL	3	3	12	3	5
		B. ARCHAEOLOGY AND HISTORY	3	3	12	3	5
		J. MONUMENTS AND SITES	1 549	–	...	–	...
		K. ZOOS, BOTANICAL GARDENS, ETC.	12	12	6	–	...
ZIMBABWE	1984	TOTAL	9	6	162	5	36
		B. ARCHAEOLOGY AND HISTORY	2	2	68	2	22
		C. NAT. HISTORY AND NAT. SCIENCE.	1	1	40	1	10
		E. ETHNOGRAPHY AND ANTHROPOLOGY	1	1	44	1	3
		F. SPECIALIZED MUSEUMS	1	1	10	1	1
		G. REGIONAL MUSEUMS	1	1	0	–	...
		I. OTHER MUSEUMS	3	–	...	–	...
		J. MONUMENTS AND SITES	162	...	...	...	...
AMERICA, NORTH							
ANTIGUA AND BARBUDA	1979	TOTAL	3	–	...	.	.
		B. ARCHAEOLOGY AND HISTORY	3	–	...	.	.
BAHAMAS	1979	TOTAL	7	–	...	.	.
		B. ARCHAEOLOGY AND HISTORY	2	–	...	.	.
		E. ETHNOGRAPHY AND ANTHROPOLOGY	3	–	...	.	.
		F. SPECIALIZED MUSEUMS	1	–	...	.	.
		H. GENERAL MUSEUMS	1	–	...	.	.
BARBADOS‡	1984	TOTAL	1	1	30	1	8 336
		B. ARCHAEOLOGY AND HISTORY	1	1	30	1	8 336
BELIZE	1979	TOTAL	5	5	9	.	.
		J. MONUMENTS AND SITES	5	5	9	.	.
BRITISH VIRGIN ISLANDS	1984	TOTAL	1	1	1	1	6
		H. GENERAL MUSEUMS	1	1	1	1	6
		J. MONUMENTS AND SITES	2	2	*30	–	...
		K. ZOOS, BOTANICAL GARDENS, ETC.	1	–	...	–	...
CANADA‡	1984	TOTAL	661	644	16 165	627	162 625
		A. ART	112	108	3 782	111	48 664
		B. ARCHAEOLOGY AND HISTORY	61	56	2 468	56	16 468
		C. NAT. HISTORY AND NAT. SCIENCE.	23	23	699	20	11 101
		D. SCIENCE AND TECHNOLOGY	21	21	1 813	17	16 704
		F. SPECIALIZED MUSEUMS	29	28	624	27	3 973
		G. REGIONAL MUSEUMS	344	340	1 451	326	10 872
		H. GENERAL MUSEUMS	22	21	4 246	22	48 265
		I. OTHER MUSEUMS	49	47	1 082	48	6 578
		J. MONUMENTS AND SITES	244	243	16 052	223	71 562
		K. ZOOS, BOTANICAL GARDENS, ETC.	117	113	31 547	111	129 995

PERSONNEL / PERSONNEL / PERSONAL						ANNUAL CURRENT EXPENDITURE / DEPENSES ANNUELLES ORDINAIRES / GASTOS ORDINARIOS ANUALES		
		PROFESSIONAL STAFF / PERSONNEL PROFESSIONNEL / PERSONAL PROFESIONAL		OTHER STAFF / AUTRE PERSONNEL / OTRO PERSONAL				
NUMBER OF MUSEUMS REPORTING / NOMBRE DE MUSEES AYANT FOURNI CES DONNEES / NUMERO DE MUSEOS QUE DIERON ESTE DATO	TOTAL STAFF / TOTAL DU PERSONNEL / TOTAL DE PERSONAL	PAID STAFF / SALARIES / REMUNERADOS	VOLUNTEERS / VOLONTAIRES / VOLUNTARIOS	PAID STAFF / SALARIES / REMUNERADOS	VOLUNTEERS / VOLONTAIRES / VOLUNTARIOS	NUMBER OF MUSEUMS REPORTING / NOMBRE DE MUSEES AYANT FOURNI CES DONNEES / NUMERO DE MUSEOS QUE DIERON ESTE DATO	TOTAL (000) / TOTAL (000) / TOTAL (000)	COUNTRY / PAYS / PAIS
4	14	14	–	–	–	–	...	SENEGAL
1	9	9	–	–	–	–	...	
1	1	1	–	–	–	–	...	
1	3	3	–	–	–	–	...	
1	1	1	–	–	–	–	...	
1	1	–	–	1	–	1	30	SEYCHELLES
1	1	–	–	1	–	1	30	
1	8	2	–	6	–	19	7	SIERRA LEONE
1	8	2	–	6	–	1	6	
–	...	...	–	...	–	18	1	
7	134	14	–	119	1	–	...	SUDAN
3	...	...	–	...	...	–	...	
1	...	...	–	...	...	–	...	
3	...	...	–	...	...	–	...	
–	...	...	...	...	...	–	...	
13	215	201	–	14	–	33	63	TUNISIA
1	29	15	–	14	–	1	45	
5	161	161	–	–	–	25	14	
–	...	...	–	...	–	–	...	
–	...	...	–	...	–	–	...	
7	25	25	–	–	–	7	4	
46	208	–	–	208	–	46	254	
1	132	102	–	30	–	1	450	
3	3	–	–	3	–	3	9	ZAMBIA
3	3	–	–	3	–	3	9	
18	16	3	–	13	–	3	179	
12	7	–	–	7	–	–	...	
6	187	49	–	138	–	6	1 349	ZIMBABWE
2	77	18	–	59	–	2	475	
1	57	15	–	42	–	1	458	
1	37	10	–	27	–	1	287	
1	13	4	–	9	–	1	118	
1	3	2	–	1	–	1	11	
–	...	...	–	...	–	–	...	
...	...	...	...	...	...	...	...	
								AMERICA, NORTH
–	...	...	...	...	...	–	...	ANTIGUA AND BARBUDA
–	...	...	...	...	...	–	...	
4	12	2	–	7	3	–	...	BAHAMAS
–	...	–	–	–	...	–	...	
3	11	1	–	7	3	–	...	
1	1	1	–	–	–	–	...	
–	...	–	–	–	...	–	...	
1	19	4	2	13	–	1	356	BARBADOS‡
1	19	4	2	13	–	1	356	
5	23	1	–	22	–	5	88	BELIZE
5	23	1	–	22	–	5	88	
1	3	–	–	1	2	1	5	BRITISH VIRGIN ISLANDS
1	3	–	–	1	2	1	5	
–	...	...	...	...	...	–	...	
1	5	–	1	4	–	–	...	
650	16 736	4 708	12 028	./.	./.	611	158 493	CANADA‡
111	4 954	1 203	3 751	./.	./.	108	46 948	
60	1 015	425	590	./.	./.	55	15 456	
22	579	341	238	./.	./.	22	11 257	
20	683	483	200	./.	./.	16	16 113	
29	714	163	551	./.	./.	26	3 402	
340	5 594	564	5 030	./.	./.	314	9 703	
21	2 270	1 297	973	./.	./.	22	49 361	
47	928	233	695	./.	./.	48	6 253	
242	6 049	2 988	3 061	./.	./.	230	66 331	
116	5 219	4 187	1 032	./.	./.	111	114 643	

8.2 Number of museums by subject of collection
Nombre de musées d'après la nature des collections
Número de museos según la naturaleza de sus colecciones

COUNTRY PAYS PAIS	YEAR ANNEE AÑO	SUBJECT OF COLLECTION OR TYPE OF INSTITUTION NATURE DES COLLECTIONS OU TYPE D'INSTITUTION NATURALEZA DE LAS COLECCIONES O TIPO DE INSTITUCION	TOTAL NUMBER OF MUSEUMS NOMBRE TOTAL DE MUSEES NUMERO TOTAL DE MUSEOS	ATTENDANCE / FREQUENTATION / FRECUENTACION NUMBER OF MUSEUMS REPORTING NOMBRE DE MUSEES AYANT FOURNI CES DONNEES NUMERO DE MUSEOS QUE DIERON ESTE DATO	ATTENDANCE / FREQUENTATION / FRECUENTACION NUMBER OF VISITORS (000) NOMBRE DE VISITEURS (000) NUMERO DE VISITANTES (000)	ANNUAL RECEIPTS / RECETTES ANNUELLES / INGRESOS ANUALES NUMBER OF MUSEUMS REPORTING NOMBRE DE MUSEES AYANT FOURNI CES DONNEES NUMERO DE MUSEOS QUE DIERON ESTE DATO	ANNUAL RECEIPTS / RECETTES ANNUELLES / INGRESOS ANUALES TOTAL (000) TOTAL (000) TOTAL (000)
COSTA RICA	1984	TOTAL	16	11	473	5	36 600
		A. ART	1	1	3	1	4 000
		B. ARCHAEOLOGY AND HISTORY	3	2	46	1	400
		C. NAT. HISTORY AND NAT. SCIENCE.	2	1	3	–	...
		D. SCIENCE AND TECHNOLOGY	2	1	1	–	...
		E. ETHNOGRAPHY AND ANTHROPOLOGY	1	1	2	–	...
		F. SPECIALIZED MUSEUMS	3	3	394	2	7 200
		H. GENERAL MUSEUMS	1	1	14	1	25 000
		I. OTHER MUSEUMS	3	1	12	–	...
CUBA‡	1984	TOTAL	241	241	8 159	–	–
		A. ART	20	20	985	–	–
		B. ARCHAEOLOGY AND HISTORY	2	2	58	–	–
		C. NAT. HISTORY AND NAT. SCIENCE.	83	83	2 292	–	–
		G. REGIONAL MUSEUMS	124	124	4 026	–	–
		I. OTHER MUSEUMS	12	12	798	–	–
		K. ZOOS, BOTANICAL GARDENS, ETC.	7	7	5 846	1	63
EL SALVADOR	1979	TOTAL	20	8	1 333	.	.
		A. ART	1	1	18	.	.
		C. NAT. HISTORY AND NAT. SCIENCE.	1	1	241	.	.
		G. REGIONAL MUSEUMS	1	1	97	.	.
		H. GENERAL MUSEUMS	1	1	32	.	.
		J. MONUMENTS AND SITES	15	3	237	.	.
		K. ZOOS, BOTANICAL GARDENS, ETC.	1	1	708	.	.
GRENADA	1984	TOTAL	1	1	8	1	19
		B. ARCHAEOLOGY AND HISTORY	1	1	8	1	19
GUADELOUPE	1979	TOTAL	5	1	31	.	.
		B. ARCHAEOLOGY AND HISTORY	3	–	...	.	.
		E. ETHNOGRAPHY AND ANTHROPOLOGY	1	–	...	.	.
		J. MONUMENTS AND SITES	1	1	31	.	.
GUATEMALA	1984	TOTAL	18	12	58	5	16
		A. ART	2	2	22	1	2
		B. ARCHAEOLOGY AND HISTORY	8	7	25	3	12
		C. NAT. HISTORY AND NAT. SCIENCE.	2	1	3	–	...
		E. ETHNOGRAPHY AND ANTHROPOLOGY	3	1	6	1	2
		F. SPECIALIZED MUSEUMS	1	–	...	–	...
		G. REGIONAL MUSEUMS	1	1	2	–	...
		H. GENERAL MUSEUMS	1	–	...	–	...
		J. MONUMENTS AND SITES	153	3	46	2	25
		K. ZOOS, BOTANICAL GARDENS, ETC.	14	–	...	–	...
MEXICO‡	1983	TOTAL	91	91	13 070	–	...
		A. ART	23	23	...	–	...
		B. ARCHAEOLOGY AND HISTORY	17	17	...	–	...
		C. NAT. HISTORY AND NAT. SCIENCE.	2	2	...	–	...
		D. SCIENCE AND TECHNOLOGY	1	1	...	–	...
		E. ETHNOGRAPHY AND ANTHROPOLOGY	4	4	...	–	...
		F. SPECIALIZED MUSEUMS	22	22	...	–	...
		G. REGIONAL MUSEUMS	22	22	...	–	...
		J. MONUMENTS AND SITES	125	125	...	–	...
MONTSERRAT	1984	TOTAL	1	1	2	1	4
		H. GENERAL MUSEUMS	1	1	2	1	4
		J. MONUMENTS AND SITES	3	–	...	–	...
		K. ZOOS, BOTANICAL GARDENS, ETC.	1	–	...	–	...
ST. LUCIA	1979	TOTAL	1	1	7	.	.
		B. ARCHAEOLOGY AND HISTORY	1	1	7	.	.
ST. PIERRE AND MIQUELON	1979	TOTAL	1	1	4	.	.
		G. REGIONAL MUSEUMS	1	1	4	.	.
UNITED STATES‡	1978	TOTAL	4 609	...	352 736	.	.
		A. ART	624	...	41 451	.	.
		B. ARCHAEOLOGY AND HISTORY	2 323	...	84 488	.	.
		D. SCIENCE AND TECHNOLOGY	832	...	157 931	.	.
		F. SPECIALIZED MUSEUMS	213	...	11 997	.	.
		H. GENERAL MUSEUMS	395	...	22 739	.	.
		I. OTHER MUSEUMS	53	...	2 602	.	.
		K. ZOOS, BOTANICAL GARDENS, ETC.	169	...	31 528	.	.

PERSONNEL / PERSONNEL / PERSONAL						ANNUAL CURRENT EXPENDITURE / DEPENSES ANNUELLES ORDINAIRES / GASTOS ORDINARIOS ANUALES		
NUMBER OF MUSEUMS REPORTING		PROFESSIONAL STAFF / PERSONNEL PROFESSIONNEL / PERSONAL PROFESIONAL		OTHER STAFF / AUTRE PERSONNEL / OTRO PERSONAL		NUMBER OF MUSEUMS REPORTING	TOTAL (000)	COUNTRY
NOMBRE DE MUSEES AYANT FOURNI CES DONNEES	TOTAL STAFF / TOTAL DU PERSONNEL	PAID STAFF / SALARIES	VOLUNTEERS / VOLONTAIRES	PAID STAFF / SALARIES	VOLUNTEERS / VOLONTAIRES	NOMBRE DE MUSEES AYANT FOURNI CES DONNEES	TOTAL (000)	PAYS
NUMERO DE MUSEOS QUE DIERON ESTE DATO	TOTAL DE PERSONAL	REMUNERADOS	VOLUNTARIOS	REMUNERADOS	VOLUNTARIOS	NUMERO DE MUSEOS QUE DIERON ESTE DATO	TOTAL (000)	PAIS
16	179	82	1	93	3	7	35 600	COSTA RICA
1	26	9	–	17	–	1	3 000	
3	12	4	–	8	–	2	600	
2	15	15	–	–	–	1	400	
2	9	6	–	3	–	–	...	
1	1	–	1	–	–	–	...	
3	33	7	–	26	–	2	6 600	
1	79	41	–	38	–	1	25 000	
3	4	–	–	1	3	–	...	
241	2 364	...	–	...	–	–	...	CUBA‡
20	354	...	–	...	–	–	...	
2	15	...	–	...	–	–	...	
83	671	...	–	...	–	–	...	
124	1 126	...	–	...	–	–	...	
12	198	...	–	...	–	–	...	
–	...	...	...	...	...	–	...	
8	213	49	–	164	–	8	929	EL SALVADOR
1	5	3	–	2	–	1	14	
1	15	4	–	11	–	1	52	
1	12	2	–	10	–	1	5	
1	22	17	–	5	–	1	40	
3	86	16	–	70	–	3	301	
1	73	7	–	66	–	1	517	
1	5	3	2	–	–	1	16	GRENADA
1	5	3	2	–	–	1	16	
5	12	1	–	11	–	1	179	GUADELOUPE
3	5	1	–	4	–	–	...	
1	3	–	–	3	–	–	...	
1	4	–	–	4	–	1	179	
13	89	24	–	65	–	12	152	GUATEMALA
2	14	6	–	8	–	2	20	
7	55	13	–	42	–	6	94	
1	5	2	–	3	–	1	13	
1	8	2	–	6	–	1	17	
1	4	1	–	3	–	1	4	
1	3	–	–	3	–	1	4	
–	...	...	–	...	–	–	...	
33	1 025	52	–	973	–	33	2 639	
–	...	...	...	...	...	–	...	
–	...	...	...	...	...	–	...	MEXICO‡
–	...	...	...	...	...	–	...	
–	...	...	...	...	...	–	...	
–	...	...	...	...	...	–	...	
–	...	...	...	...	...	–	...	
–	...	...	...	...	...	–	...	
–	...	...	...	...	...	–	...	
–	...	...	...	...	...	–	...	
–	...	...	...	...	...	–	...	
1	4	–	2	–	2	1	5	MONTSERRAT
1	4	–	2	–	2	1	5	
3	4	–	4	–	–	–	...	
1	1	–	1	–	–	–	...	
1	2	–	1	1	–	1	5	ST. LUCIA
1	2	–	1	1	–	1	5	
1	2	–	–	1	1	1	48	ST. PIERRE AND MIQUELON
1	2	–	–	1	1	1	48	
...	118 556	42 259	76 297	./.	./.	...	784 343	UNITED STATES‡
...	20 266	9 164	11 102	./.	./.	...	202 327	
...	34 540	12 658	21 882	./.	./.	...	169 796	
...	50 972	14 657	36 315	./.	./.	...	309 564	
...	3 539	1 393	2 146	./.	./.	...	15 195	
...	7 349	3 349	4 000	./.	./.	...	66 106	
...	845	335	510	./.	./.	...	7 296	
...	1 045	703	342	./.	./.	...	14 059	

8.2 Number of museums by subject of collection
Nombre de musées d'après la nature des collections
Número de museos según la naturaleza de sus colecciones

COUNTRY / PAYS / PAIS	YEAR / ANNEE / AÑO	SUBJECT OF COLLECTION OR TYPE OF INSTITUTION / NATURE DES COLLECTIONS OU TYPE D'INSTITUTION / NATURALEZA DE LAS COLECCIONES O TIPO DE INSTITUCION	TOTAL NUMBER OF MUSEUMS / NOMBRE TOTAL DE MUSEES / NUMERO TOTAL DE MUSEOS	ATTENDANCE / FREQUENTATION / FRECUENTACION: NUMBER OF MUSEUMS REPORTING / NOMBRE DE MUSEES AYANT FOURNI CES DONNEES / NUMERO DE MUSEOS QUE DIERON ESTE DATO	ATTENDANCE / FREQUENTATION / FRECUENTACION: NUMBER OF VISITORS (000) / NOMBRE DE VISITEURS (000) / NUMERO DE VISITANTES (000)	ANNUAL RECEIPTS / RECETTES ANNUELLES / INGRESOS ANUALES: NUMBER OF MUSEUMS REPORTING / NOMBRE DE MUSEES AYANT FOURNI CES DONNEES / NUMERO DE MUSEOS QUE DIERON ESTE DATO	ANNUAL RECEIPTS / RECETTES ANNUELLES / INGRESOS ANUALES: TOTAL (000)
U.S. VIRGIN ISLANDS	1979	TOTAL	10	7	995	.	.
		B. ARCHAEOLOGY AND HISTORY	4	4	76	.	.
		G. REGIONAL MUSEUMS	1	1	735	.	.
		J. MONUMENTS AND SITES	2	1	91	.	.
		K. ZOOS, BOTANICAL GARDENS, ETC.	3	1	93	.	.
AMERICA, SOUTH							
BRAZIL‡	1982	TOTAL	571	571	7 859	–	...
		A. ART	115	115	...	–	...
		B. ARCHAEOLOGY AND HISTORY	201	201	...	–	...
		C. NAT. HISTORY AND NAT. SCIENCE.	29	29	...	–	...
		D. SCIENCE AND TECHNOLOGY	24	24	...	–	...
		E. ETHNOGRAPHY AND ANTHROPOLOGY	30	30	...	–	...
		I. OTHER MUSEUMS	172	172	...	–	...
COLOMBIA	1979	TOTAL	74	58	1 542	.	.
		A. ART	18	15	618	.	.
		B. ARCHAEOLOGY AND HISTORY	12	9	258	.	.
		D. SCIENCE AND TECHNOLOGY	8	6	91	.	.
		E. ETHNOGRAPHY AND ANTHROPOLOGY	22	17	286	.	.
		F. SPECIALIZED MUSEUMS	2	2	13	.	.
		G. REGIONAL MUSEUMS	1	–	...	.	.
		H. GENERAL MUSEUMS	7	7	161	.	.
		I. OTHER MUSEUMS	1	1	13	.	.
		J. MONUMENTS AND SITES	2	–	...	.	.
		K. ZOOS, BOTANICAL GARDENS, ETC.	1	1	100	.	.
FALKLAND ISLANDS (MALVINAS)	1979	TOTAL	1	–	...	.	.
		H. GENERAL MUSEUMS	1	–	...	.	.
GUYANA	1979	TOTAL	2	1	97	.	.
		B. ARCHAEOLOGY AND HISTORY	1	–	...	.	.
		H. GENERAL MUSEUMS	1	1	97	.	.
PERU	1984	TOTAL	12	12	201	12	189 600
		A. ART	3	3	13	3	26 338
		B. ARCHAEOLOGY AND HISTORY	3	3	143	3	149 886
		G. REGIONAL MUSEUMS	6	6	45	6	13 376
		J. MONUMENTS AND SITES	28	28	392	28	1 741 359
URUGUAY	1984	TOTAL	19	2	17	–	...
		A. ART	2	–	...	–	...
		B. ARCHAEOLOGY AND HISTORY	9	–	...	–	...
		C. NAT. HISTORY AND NAT. SCIENCE.	1	1	13	–	...
		E. ETHNOGRAPHY AND ANTHROPOLOGY	1	–	...	–	...
		G. REGIONAL MUSEUMS	5	–	...	–	...
		I. OTHER MUSEUMS	1	1	4	–	...
VENEZUELA	1979	TOTAL	133	–	...	.	.
		A. ART	14	–	...	.	.
		B. ARCHAEOLOGY AND HISTORY	11	–	...	.	.
		C. NAT. HISTORY AND NAT. SCIENCE.	3	–	...	.	.
		E. ETHNOGRAPHY AND ANTHROPOLOGY	7	–	...	.	.
		F. SPECIALIZED MUSEUMS	8	–	...	.	.
		G. REGIONAL MUSEUMS	3	–	...	.	.
		H. GENERAL MUSEUMS	4	–	...	.	.
		I. OTHER MUSEUMS	4	–	...	.	.
		K. ZOOS, BOTANICAL GARDENS, ETC.	79	–	...	.	.
ASIA							
AFGHANISTAN	1979	TOTAL	7	7	7	.	.
		H. GENERAL MUSEUMS	7	7	7	.	.
BAHRAIN	1984	TOTAL	2	2	99	–	...
		B. ARCHAEOLOGY AND HISTORY	1	1	24	–	...
		E. ETHNOGRAPHY AND ANTHROPOLOGY	1	1	75	–	...
		J. MONUMENTS AND SITES	22	11	3	–	...
BHUTAN	1979	TOTAL	1	1	16	.	.
		H. GENERAL MUSEUMS	1	1	16	.	.
BRUNEI DARUSSALAM	1984	TOTAL	3	3	112	–	...
		H. GENERAL MUSEUMS	1	1	65	–	...
		I. OTHER MUSEUMS	2	2	47	–	...

NUMBER OF MUSEUMS REPORTING / NOMBRE DE MUSEES AYANT FOURNI CES DONNEES / NUMERO DE MUSEOS QUE DIERON ESTE DATO	PERSONNEL / PERSONNEL / PERSONAL: TOTAL STAFF / TOTAL DU PERSONNEL / TOTAL DE PERSONAL	PROFESSIONAL STAFF / PERSONNEL PROFESSIONNEL / PERSONAL PROFESIONAL: PAID STAFF / SALARIES / REMUNERADOS	PROFESSIONAL STAFF: VOLUNTEERS / VOLONTAIRES / VOLUNTARIOS	OTHER STAFF / AUTRE PERSONNEL / OTRO PERSONAL: PAID STAFF / SALARIES / REMUNERADOS	OTHER STAFF: VOLUNTEERS / VOLONTAIRES / VOLUNTARIOS	ANNUAL CURRENT EXPENDITURE / DEPENSES ANNUELLES ORDINAIRES / GASTOS ORDINARIOS ANUALES: NUMBER OF MUSEUMS REPORTING / NOMBRE DE MUSEES AYANT FOURNI CES DONNEES / NUMERO DE MUSEOS QUE DIERON ESTE DATO	ANNUAL CURRENT EXPENDITURE: TOTAL (000)	COUNTRY / PAYS / PAIS
7	101	36	–	53	12	7	1 720	U.S. VIRGIN ISLANDS
4	34	13	–	9	12	4	320	
1	52	20	–	32	–	1	1 100	
1	11	2	–	9	–	1	230	
1	4	1	–	3	–	1	70	
								AMERICA, SOUTH
571	6 152	2 745	–	3 407	–	–	...	BRAZIL‡
115	...	...	–	...	–	–	...	
201	...	...	–	...	–	–	...	
29	...	...	–	...	–	–	...	
24	...	...	–	...	–	–	...	
30	...	...	–	...	–	–	...	
172	...	...	–	...	–	–	...	
69	601	145	22	404	30	35	40 113	COLOMBIA
18	177	34	10	123	10	9	5 537	
9	76	13	1	52	10	8	9 714	
8	97	43	2	51	1	5	12 285	
20	156	34	7	114	1	9	5 660	
2	11	6	–	5	–	–	...	
1	2	1	–	1	–	–	...	
7	42	5	2	27	8	2	70	
1	5	5	–	–	–	1	100	
2	3	–	–	3	–	–	...	
1	32	4	–	28	–	1	6 747	
								FALKLAND ISLANDS (MALVINAS)
1	2	–	–	–	2	–	...	
1	2	–	–	–	2	–	...	
2	32	7	–	25	–	2	526	GUYANA
1	5	2	–	3	–	1	80	
1	27	5	–	22	–	1	446	
12	*150	*25	–	*125	–	12	*837 629	PERU
3	*12	*3	–	*9	–	3	*52 856	
3	*104	*20	–	*84	–	3	*603 510	
6	*34	*2	–	*32	–	6	*181 263	
28	*67	*38	–	*29	–	28	*1 096 327	
11	173	...	...	...	...	–	...	URUGUAY
1	29	...	...	...	...	–	...	
8	107	...	...	...	...	–	...	
1	32	...	...	...	...	–	...	
–	...	...	...	...	...	–	...	
–	...	...	...	...	...	–	...	
1	5	...	...	...	...	–	...	
81	576	–	–	–	–	81	103 046	VENEZUELA
1	90	–	–	–	–	1	10 000	
–	...	...	...	...	...	–	...	
–	...	...	...	...	...	–	...	
–	...	...	...	...	...	–	...	
1	22	–	–	–	–	1	1 209	
–	...	...	...	...	...	–	...	
–	...	...	...	...	...	–	...	
–	...	...	...	...	...	–	...	
79	464	–	–	–	–	79	91 837	
								ASIA
7	103	103	–	–	–	7	3 100	AFGHANISTAN
7	103	103	–	–	–	7	3 100	
2	88	88	–	–	–	1	383	BAHRAIN
1	46	46	–	–	–	–	...	
1	42	42	–	–	–	1	383	
11	43	28	–	15	–	11	547	
1	11	2	–	9	–	1	150	BHUTAN
1	11	2	–	9	–	1	150	
3	174	49	–	75	–	3	7 024	BRUNEI DARUSSALAM
1	116	49	–	67	1	1	5 024	
2	8	–	–	8	–	2	2 000	

8.2 Number of museums by subject of collection
Nombre de musées d'après la nature des collections
Número de museos según la naturaleza de sus colecciones

COUNTRY / PAYS / PAIS	YEAR / ANNEE / AÑO	SUBJECT OF COLLECTION OR TYPE OF INSTITUTION / NATURE DES COLLECTIONS OU TYPE D'INSTITUTION / NATURALEZA DE LAS COLECCIONES O TIPO DE INSTITUCION	TOTAL NUMBER OF MUSEUMS / NOMBRE TOTAL DE MUSEES / NUMERO TOTAL DE MUSEOS	ATTENDANCE / FREQUENTATION / FRECUENTACION: NUMBER OF MUSEUMS REPORTING / NOMBRE DE MUSEES AYANT FOURNI CES DONNEES / NUMERO DE MUSEOS QUE DIERON ESTE DATO	NUMBER OF VISITORS (000) / NOMBRE DE VISITEURS (000) / NUMERO DE VISITANTES (000)	ANNUAL RECEIPTS / RECETTES ANNUELLES / INGRESOS ANUALES: NUMBER OF MUSEUMS REPORTING / NOMBRE DE MUSEES AYANT FOURNI CES DONNEES / NUMERO DE MUSEOS QUE DIERON ESTE DATO	TOTAL (000)
CYPRUS	1979	TOTAL	26	26	95	.	.
		B. ARCHAEOLOGY AND HISTORY	3	3	36	.	.
		E. ETHNOGRAPHY AND ANTHROPOLOGY	2	2	20	.	.
		G. REGIONAL MUSEUMS	6	6	1	.	.
		J. MONUMENTS AND SITES	15	15	38	.	.
INDONESIA	1983	TOTAL	100	100	7 171	100	2 096 467
		A. ART	8	8	133	8	5 732
		B. ARCHAEOLOGY AND HISTORY	40	40	1 286	40	93 158
		C. NAT. HISTORY AND NAT. SCIENCE.	5	5	1 337	5	829 103
		D. SCIENCE AND TECHNOLOGY	7	7	707	7	157 048
		E. ETHNOGRAPHY AND ANTHROPOLOGY	20	20	564	20	46 309
		F. SPECIALIZED MUSEUMS	4	4	45	4	661
		G. REGIONAL MUSEUMS	1	1	20	1	1 527
		H. GENERAL MUSEUMS	8	8	192	8	1 232
		I. OTHER MUSEUMS	7	7	2 887	7	961 697
		K. ZOOS, BOTANICAL GARDENS, ETC.	10	10	3 575	9	950 001
IRAQ	1984	TOTAL	13	13	63	13	60
		B. ARCHAEOLOGY AND HISTORY	13	13	63	13	60
		J. MONUMENTS AND SITES	18	–	...	–	...
ISRAEL	1984	TOTAL	95	67	6 780	–	...
		A. ART	14	12	947	–	...
		B. ARCHAEOLOGY AND HISTORY	34	29	2 997	–	...
		C. NAT. HISTORY AND NAT. SCIENCE.	10	8	721	–	...
		D. SCIENCE AND TECHNOLOGY	5	5	139	–	...
		E. ETHNOGRAPHY AND ANTHROPOLOGY	4	4	164	–	...
		F. SPECIALIZED MUSEUMS	5	3	340	–	...
		H. GENERAL MUSEUMS	3	3	1 407	–	...
		I. OTHER MUSEUMS	4	3	65	–	...
		J. MONUMENTS AND SITES	33	33	6 200	–	...
		K. ZOOS, BOTANICAL GARDENS, ETC.	184	16	2 506	–	...
JAPAN‡	1978	TOTAL	493	485	98 487	.	.
		A. ART	135	133	11 244	.	.
		B. ARCHAEOLOGY AND HISTORY	136	134	13 749	.	.
		C. NAT. HISTORY AND NAT. SCIENCE.	59	58	10 646	.	.
		H. GENERAL MUSEUMS	75	75	5 829	.	.
		K. ZOOS, BOTANICAL GARDENS, ETC.	88	85	57 019	.	.
JORDAN	1984	TOTAL	16	10	147	7	150
		A. ART	1	1	12	–	...
		B. ARCHAEOLOGY AND HISTORY	10	5	62	3	125
		C. NAT. HISTORY AND NAT. SCIENCE.	1	1	3	–	...
		E. ETHNOGRAPHY AND ANTHROPOLOGY	4	3	120	4	25
		J. MONUMENTS AND SITES	3 500	3	638	2	480
		K. ZOOS, BOTANICAL GARDENS, ETC.	2	1	28	1	6
KOREA, REPUBLIC OF	1984	TOTAL	146	58	665	1	13 040
		A. ART	2	1	225	1	13 040
		B. ARCHAEOLOGY AND HISTORY	92	57	410	–	...
		C. NAT. HISTORY AND NAT. SCIENCE.	1	–	...	–	...
		D. SCIENCE AND TECHNOLOGY	2	–	...	–	...
		E. ETHNOGRAPHY AND ANTHROPOLOGY	17	–	...	–	...
		F. SPECIALIZED MUSEUMS	11	–	...	–	...
		G. REGIONAL MUSEUMS	17	–	...	–	...
		I. OTHER MUSEUMS	4	–	...	–	...
		J. MONUMENTS AND SITES	1 200	–	...	–	...
		K. ZOOS, BOTANICAL GARDENS, ETC.	84	–	...	–	...
KUWAIT	1979	TOTAL	3	3	259	.	.
		C. NAT. HISTORY AND NAT. SCIENCE.	1	1	235	.	.
		E. ETHNOGRAPHY AND ANTHROPOLOGY	2	2	24	.	.
MALAYSIA‡	1979	TOTAL	228	10	3 561	.	.
		A. ART	2	1	28	.	.
		B. ARCHAEOLOGY AND HISTORY	1	–	...	.	.
		F. SPECIALIZED MUSEUMS	3	1	1	.	.
		G. REGIONAL MUSEUMS	7	6	607	.	.
		H. GENERAL MUSEUMS	2	2	2 925	.	.
		I. OTHER MUSEUMS	1	–	...	.	.
		J. MONUMENTS AND SITES	208	–	...	.	.
		K. ZOOS, BOTANICAL GARDENS, ETC.	4	–	...	.	.

PERSONNEL / PERSONNEL / PERSONAL						ANNUAL CURRENT EXPENDITURE / DEPENSES ANNUELLES ORDINAIRES / GASTOS ORDINARIOS ANUALES		
NUMBER OF MUSEUMS REPORTING		PROFESSIONAL STAFF / PERSONNEL PROFESSIONNEL / PERSONAL PROFESIONAL		OTHER STAFF / AUTRE PERSONNEL / OTRO PERSONAL		NUMBER OF MUSEUMS REPORTING	TOTAL (000)	COUNTRY
NOMBRE DE MUSEES AYANT FOURNI CES DONNEES	TOTAL STAFF / TOTAL DU PERSONNEL	PAID STAFF / SALARIES	VOLUNTEERS / VOLONTAIRES	PAID STAFF / SALARIES	VOLUNTEERS / VOLONTAIRES	NOMBRE DE MUSEES AYANT FOURNI CES DONNEES	TOTAL (000)	PAYS
NUMERO DE MUSEOS QUE DIERON ESTE DATO	TOTAL DE PERSONAL	REMUNERADOS	VOLUNTARIOS	REMUNERADOS	VOLUNTARIOS	NUMERO DE MUSEOS QUE DIERON ESTE DATO	TOTAL (000)	PAIS
26	87	76	–	11	–	26	121	CYPRUS
3	60	49	–	11	–	3	32	
2	3	3	–	–	–	2	6	
6	7	7	–	–	–	6	20	
15	17	17	–	–	–	15	63	
–	...	...	...	...	...	–	...	INDONESIA
–	...	...	...	...	...	–	...	
–	...	...	...	...	...	–	...	
–	...	...	...	...	...	–	...	
–	...	...	...	...	...	–	...	
–	...	...	...	...	...	–	...	
–	...	...	...	...	...	–	...	
–	...	...	...	...	...	–	...	
–	...	...	...	...	...	–	...	
–	...	...	...	...	...	–	...	
–	...	...	...	...	...	–	...	
13	80	67	–	13	–	–	...	IRAQ
13	80	67	–	13	–	–	...	
18	54	54	–	–	–	–	...	
67	1 265	473	...	792	...	–	...	ISRAEL
12	203	75	...	128	...	–	...	
29	266	122	...	144	...	–	...	
8	116	66	...	50	...	–	...	
5	16	12	...	4	...	–	...	
4	35	13	...	22	...	–	...	
3	139	12	...	127	...	–	...	
3	482	169	...	313	...	–	...	
3	8	4	...	4	...	–	...	
–	...	...	...	...	...	–	...	
–	...	...	...	...	...	–	...	
493	7 476	1 360	–	6 116	–	–	...	JAPAN‡
135	1 538	355	–	1 183	–	–	...	
136	1 271	314	–	957	–	–	...	
59	1 058	305	–	753	–	–	...	
75	819	210	–	609	–	–	...	
88	2 790	176	–	2 614	–	–	...	
16	99	86	13	–	–	9	850	JORDAN
1	5	5	–	–	–	–	...	
7	45	45	–	–	–	7	640	
1	9	4	5	–	–	–	...	
4	40	32	8	–	–	2	210	
8	210	210	–	–	–	3	900	
1	15	15	–	–	–	–	...	
94	920	220	94	606	–	43	5 271 000	KOREA, REPUBLIC OF
2	67	18	–	49	–	1	396 000	
64	617	165	94	358	–	42	4 875 000	
–	...	...	...	...	–	–	...	
–	...	...	...	...	–	–	...	
11	75	16	1	69	–	–	...	
3	19	3	–	16	–	–	...	
10	82	15	–	67	–	–	...	
4	50	3	–	47	–	–	...	
–	...	...	...	...	...	–	...	
24	837	7	...	830	...	–	...	
3	124	72	–	52	–	3	76	KUWAIT
1	90	70	–	20	–	1	53	
2	34	2	–	32	–	2	23	
11	379	137	–	242	–	9	3 577	MALAYSIA‡
1	17	3	–	14	–	1	225	
1	16	4	–	12	–	./.	./.	
3	10	4	–	6	–	–	...	
4	63	37	–	26	–	6	593	
2	273	89	–	184	–	2	2 759	
–	...	...	–	...	–	–	...	
–	...	...	–	...	–	–	...	
–	...	...	–	...	–	–	...	

8.2 Number of museums by subject of collection
Nombre de musées d'après la nature des collections
Número de museos según la naturaleza de sus colecciones

COUNTRY / PAYS / PAIS	YEAR / ANNEE / AÑO	SUBJECT OF COLLECTION OR TYPE OF INSTITUTION / NATURE DES COLLECTIONS OU TYPE D'INSTITUTION / NATURALEZA DE LAS COLECCIONES O TIPO DE INSTITUCION	TOTAL NUMBER OF MUSEUMS / NOMBRE TOTAL DE MUSEES / NUMERO TOTAL DE MUSEOS	ATTENDANCE / FREQUENTATION / FRECUENTACION: NUMBER OF MUSEUMS REPORTING / NOMBRE DE MUSEES AYANT FOURNI CES DONNEES / NUMERO DE MUSEOS QUE DIERON ESTE DATO	ATTENDANCE / FREQUENTATION / FRECUENTACION: NUMBER OF VISITORS (000) / NOMBRE DE VISITEURS (000) / NUMERO DE VISITANTES (000)	ANNUAL RECEIPTS / RECETTES ANNUELLES / INGRESOS ANUALES: NUMBER OF MUSEUMS REPORTING / NOMBRE DE MUSEES AYANT FOURNI CES DONNEES / NUMERO DE MUSEOS QUE DIERON ESTE DATO	ANNUAL RECEIPTS / RECETTES ANNUELLES / INGRESOS ANUALES: TOTAL (000)
MALDIVES	1984	TOTAL	1	1	3	1	17
		H. GENERAL MUSEUMS	1	1	3	1	17
		J. MONUMENTS AND SITES	222	–	...	–	...
PAKISTAN	1979	TOTAL	10	10	561	.	.
		B. ARCHAEOLOGY AND HISTORY	6	6	64	.	.
		I. OTHER MUSEUMS	4	4	497	.	.
PHILIPPINES	1984	TOTAL	61	–	...	–	...
		A. ART	4	–	...	–	...
		B. ARCHAEOLOGY AND HISTORY	19	–	...	–	...
		C. NAT. HISTORY AND NAT. SCIENCE.	2	–	...	–	...
		E. ETHNOGRAPHY AND ANTHROPOLOGY	18	–	...	–	...
		F. SPECIALIZED MUSEUMS	2	–	...	–	...
		H. GENERAL MUSEUMS	16	–	...	–	...
		J. MONUMENTS AND SITES	38	–	...	–	...
QATAR	1978	TOTAL	1	1	60	.	.
		H. GENERAL MUSEUMS	1	1	60	.	.
SAUDI ARABIA	1984	TOTAL	1	1	40	–	...
		B. ARCHAEOLOGY AND HISTORY	1	1	40	–	...
SINGAPORE	1979	TOTAL	10	10	4 282	.	.
		C. NAT. HISTORY AND NAT. SCIENCE.	1	1	313	.	.
		D. SCIENCE AND TECHNOLOGY	1	1	197	.	.
		H. GENERAL MUSEUMS	1	1	430	.	.
		J. MONUMENTS AND SITES	1	1	298	.	.
		K. ZOOS, BOTANICAL GARDENS, ETC.	6	6	3 044	.	.
THAILAND	1979	TOTAL	119	40	1 103	.	.
		A. ART	4	4	30	.	.
		B. ARCHAEOLOGY AND HISTORY	35	35	320	.	.
		C. NAT. HISTORY AND NAT. SCIENCE.	7	–	...	.	.
		D. SCIENCE AND TECHNOLOGY	2	1	753	.	.
		E. ETHNOGRAPHY AND ANTHROPOLOGY	4	–	...	.	.
		F. SPECIALIZED MUSEUMS	12	–	...	.	.
		J. MONUMENTS AND SITES	4	–	...	.	.
		K. ZOOS, BOTANICAL GARDENS, ETC.	51	–	...	.	.
TURKEY	1984	TOTAL	127	109	5 476	109	605 546
		B. ARCHAEOLOGY AND HISTORY	101	86	3 094	86	213 181
		E. ETHNOGRAPHY AND ANTHROPOLOGY	26	23	2 382	23	392 365
		J. MONUMENTS AND SITES	14 352	46	1 729	46	134 911
UNITED ARAB EMIRATES	1979	TOTAL	3	2	244	.	.
		E. ETHNOGRAPHY AND ANTHROPOLOGY	1	1	23	.	.
		H. GENERAL MUSEUMS	1	–	...	.	.
		K. ZOOS, BOTANICAL GARDENS, ETC.	1	1	221	.	.
VIET–NAM	1979	TOTAL	9	8	1 918	.	.
		A. ART	1	1	139	.	.
		B. ARCHAEOLOGY AND HISTORY	7	7	1 779	.	.
		C. NAT. HISTORY AND NAT. SCIENCE.	1	–	...	.	.
EUROPE							
ANDORRA	1979	TOTAL	4	4	51 600	.	.
		B. ARCHAEOLOGY AND HISTORY	1	1	3 000	.	.
		E. ETHNOGRAPHY AND ANTHROPOLOGY	1	1	6 200	.	.
		J. MONUMENTS AND SITES	2	2	42 400	.	.
AUSTRIA	1984	TOTAL	209	209	8 943	–	...
		A. ART	8	8	1 243	–	...
		B. ARCHAEOLOGY AND HISTORY	4	4	123	–	...
		C. NAT. HISTORY AND NAT. SCIENCE.	1	1	294	–	...
		D. SCIENCE AND TECHNOLOGY	1	1	176	–	...
		E. ETHNOGRAPHY AND ANTHROPOLOGY	4	4	30	–	...
		F. SPECIALIZED MUSEUMS	28	28	3 018	–	...
		G. REGIONAL MUSEUMS	163	163	4 059	–	...
		K. ZOOS, BOTANICAL GARDENS, ETC.	2	2	728	–	...

PERSONNEL / PERSONNEL / PERSONAL						ANNUAL CURRENT EXPENDITURE / DEPENSES ANNUELLES ORDINAIRES / GASTOS ORDINARIOS ANUALES		
NUMBER OF MUSEUMS REPORTING		PROFESSIONAL STAFF / PERSONNEL PROFESSIONNEL / PERSONAL PROFESIONAL		OTHER STAFF / AUTRE PERSONNEL / OTRO PERSONAL		NUMBER OF MUSEUMS REPORTING	TOTAL (000)	COUNTRY
NOMBRE DE MUSEES AYANT FOURNI CES DONNEES	TOTAL STAFF / TOTAL DU PERSONNEL	PAID STAFF / SALARIES	VOLUNTEERS / VOLONTAIRES	PAID STAFF / SALARIES	VOLUNTEERS / VOLONTAIRES	NOMBRE DE MUSEES AYANT FOURNI CES DONNEES	TOTAL (000)	PAYS
NUMERO DE MUSEOS QUE DIERON ESTE DATO	TOTAL DE PERSONAL	REMUNERADOS	VOLUNTARIOS	REMUNERADOS	VOLUNTARIOS	NUMERO DE MUSEOS QUE DIERON ESTE DATO	TOTAL (000)	PAIS
1	16	1	–	15	–	1	57	MALDIVES
1	16	1	–	15	–	1	57	
–	...	...	...	...		–	...	
10	391	36	105	250	–	10	3 114	PAKISTAN
6	240	16	63	161	–	6	1 786	
4	151	20	42	89	–	4	1 328	
61	699	...	...	...		–	...	PHILIPPINES
4	24	...	...	...	...	–	...	
19	98	...	...	...	...	–	...	
2	9	...	...	...	...	–	...	
18	108	...	...	...	...	–	...	
2	10	...	...	...	...	–	...	
16	450	...	...	...	...	–	...	
–	...	...	...	...	...	–	...	
1	50	50	–	–	–	–	...	QATAR
1	50	50	–	–	–	–	...	
1	17	10	–	7	–	–	...	SAUDI ARABIA
1	17	10	–	7	–	–	...	
10	505	66	–	439	–	10	6 544	SINGAPORE
1	3	–	–	3	–	1	31	
1	78	25	–	53	–	1	1 549	
1	40	14	–	26	–	1	704	
1	4	–	–	4	–	1	49	
6	380	27	–	353	–	6	4 211	
40	548	112	33	403	–	40	28 120	THAILAND
4	35	8	–	27	–	4	800	
35	285	35	30	220	–	35	17 800	
–	...	...	...	...	–	–	...	
1	228	69	3	156	–	1	9 520	
–	...	...	...	...	–	–	...	
–	...	...	...	...	–	–	...	
–	...	...	...	...	–	–	...	
–	...	...	...	...	–	–	...	
127	2 342	461	–	1 881	–	127	254 490	TURKEY
–	...	...	–	...	–	101	237 506	
–	...	...	–	...	–	26	16 984	
123	175	–	–	175	–	–	...	
3	134	10	–	124	–	2	9 591	UNITED ARAB EMIRATES
1	6	1	–	5	–	–	...	
1	8	2	–	6	–	1	591	
1	120	7	–	113	–	1	9 000	
8	297	297	–	–	–	8	1 404	VIET–NAM
1	57	57	–	–	–	1	228	
7	240	240	–	–	–	7	1 175	
–	...	...	–	–	–	–	...	
								EUROPE
4	9	4	–	5	–	4	7 662	ANDORRA
1	4	2	–	2	–	1	4 142	
1	2	1	–	1	–	1	2 000	
2	3	1	–	2	–	2	1 520	
–	...	...	...	...	...	–	...	AUSTRIA
–	...	...	...	...	...	–	...	
–	...	...	...	...	...	–	...	
–	...	...	...	...	...	–	...	
–	...	...	...	...	...	–	...	
–	...	...	...	...	...	–	...	
–	...	...	...	...	...	–	...	
–	...	...	...	...	...	–	...	
–	...	...	...	...	...	–	...	

8.2 Number of museums by subject of collection
Nombre de musées d'après la nature des collections
Número de museos según la naturaleza de sus colecciones

COUNTRY PAYS PAIS	YEAR ANNEE AÑO	SUBJECT OF COLLECTION OR TYPE OF INSTITUTION NATURE DES COLLECTIONS OU TYPE D'INSTITUTION NATURALEZA DE LAS COLECCIONES O TIPO DE INSTITUCION	TOTAL NUMBER OF MUSEUMS NOMBRE TOTAL DE MUSEES NUMERO TOTAL DE MUSEOS	ATTENDANCE / FREQUENTATION / FRECUENTACION		ANNUAL RECEIPTS / RECETTES ANNUELLES / INGRESOS ANUALES	
				NUMBER OF MUSEUMS REPORTING NOMBRE DE MUSEES AYANT FOURNI CES DONNEES NUMERO DE MUSEOS QUE DIERON ESTE DATO	NUMBER OF VISITORS (000) NOMBRE DE VISITEURS (000) NUMERO DE VISITANTES (000)	NUMBER OF MUSEUMS REPORTING NOMBRE DE MUSEES AYANT FOURNI CES DONNEES NUMERO DE MUSEOS QUE DIERON ESTE DATO	TOTAL (000) TOTAL (000) TOTAL (000)
BULGARIA	1984	TOTAL	206	206	15 535	206	28 401
		A. ART	41	41	2 846	41	4 785
		B. ARCHAEOLOGY AND HISTORY	102	102	6 591	102	6 827
		C. NAT. HISTORY AND NAT. SCIENCE.	4	4	274	4	321
		D. SCIENCE AND TECHNOLOGY	4	4	93	4	570
		E. ETHNOGRAPHY AND ANTHROPOLOGY	8	8	1 040	8	1 455
		F. SPECIALIZED MUSEUMS	23	23	751	23	437
		H. GENERAL MUSEUMS	24	24	3 940	24	14 006
		J. MONUMENTS AND SITES	37 649	–	...	37 649	18 050
		K. ZOOS, BOTANICAL GARDENS, ETC.	105	7	1 286	7	851
CZECHOSLOVAKIA‡	1984	TOTAL	348	348	17 666	348	41 025
		A. ART	22	22	1 849	22	2 334
		B. ARCHAEOLOGY AND HISTORY	28	28	1 445	28	3 019
		D. SCIENCE AND TECHNOLOGY	24	24	2 076	24	2 231
		E. ETHNOGRAPHY AND ANTHROPOLOGY	5	5	475	5	2 825
		F. SPECIALIZED MUSEUMS	28	28	3 399	28	8 375
		G. REGIONAL MUSEUMS	194	194	8 139	194	21 665
		I. OTHER MUSEUMS	47	47	283	47	577
		J. MONUMENTS AND SITES	51 148	106	6 000	106	18 000
		K. ZOOS, BOTANICAL GARDENS, ETC.	1 452	–	...	–	...
DENMARK	1979	TOTAL	282	268	9 622	.	.
		A. ART	48	48	1 638	.	.
		B. ARCHAEOLOGY AND HISTORY	13	13	1 046	.	.
		C. NAT. HISTORY AND NAT. SCIENCE.	11	9	410	.	.
		D. SCIENCE AND TECHNOLOGY	2	2	145	.	.
		F. SPECIALIZED MUSEUMS	65	61	2 454	.	.
		G. REGIONAL MUSEUMS	120	112	1 403	.	.
		I. OTHER MUSEUMS	6	6	197	.	.
		J. MONUMENTS AND SITES	12	12	535	.	.
		K. ZOOS, BOTANICAL GARDENS, ETC.	5	5	1 794	.	.
FINLAND‡	1984	TOTAL	572	517	2 897	23	298
		A. ART	48	46	1 846	–	...
		B. ARCHAEOLOGY AND HISTORY	36	./.	./.	–	...
		C. NAT. HISTORY AND NAT. SCIENCE.	23	21	242	23	298
		D. SCIENCE AND TECHNOLOGY	19	./.	./.	–	...
		E. ETHNOGRAPHY AND ANTHROPOLOGY	2	./.	./.	–	...
		F. SPECIALIZED MUSEUMS	40	./.	./.	–	...
		G. REGIONAL MUSEUMS	403	450	1 169	–	...
		H. GENERAL MUSEUMS	1	./.	./.	–	...
		J. MONUMENTS AND SITES	10 158	3	387	–	...
		K. ZOOS, BOTANICAL GARDENS, ETC.	53	–	...	–	...
GERMAN DEMOCRATIC REPUBLIC‡	1984	TOTAL	684	684	33 700	684	52
		A. ART	77	77	11 100	77	26
		B. ARCHAEOLOGY AND HISTORY	109	109	7 600	109	9
		C. NAT. HISTORY AND NAT. SCIENCE.	50	50	3 800	50	5
		D. SCIENCE AND TECHNOLOGY	36	36	1 900	36	2
		F. SPECIALIZED MUSEUMS	45	45	1 500	45	2
		G. REGIONAL MUSEUMS	367	367	7 800	367	8
		J. MONUMENTS AND SITES	65 445	–	...	–	...
		K. ZOOS, BOTANICAL GARDENS, ETC.	903	137	16 800	–	...
GERMANY, FEDERAL REPUBLIC OF	1984	TOTAL	2 025	1 586	56 748	–	...
		A. ART	251	206	11 289	–	...
		B. ARCHAEOLOGY AND HISTORY	32	24	3 091	–	...
		C. NAT. HISTORY AND NAT. SCIENCE.	130	101	2 932	–	...
		D. SCIENCE AND TECHNOLOGY	138	106	7 517	–	...
		E. ETHNOGRAPHY AND ANTHROPOLOGY	1 057	815	12 219	–	...
		F. SPECIALIZED MUSEUMS	241	181	5 592	–	...
		H. GENERAL MUSEUMS	52	52	5 739	–	...
		I. OTHER MUSEUMS	124	101	8 369	–	...
GIBRALTAR	1984	TOTAL	1	1	17	–	...
		G. REGIONAL MUSEUMS	1	1	17	–	...
HOLY SEE	1984	TOTAL	13	13	1 928	–	...
		A. ART	10	10	...	–	...
		B. ARCHAEOLOGY AND HISTORY	1	1	...	–	...
		E. ETHNOGRAPHY AND ANTHROPOLOGY	1	1	...	–	...
		F. SPECIALIZED MUSEUMS	1	1	...	–	...

PERSONNEL / PERSONNEL / PERSONAL						ANNUAL CURRENT EXPENDITURE / DEPENSES ANNUELLES ORDINAIRES / GASTOS ORDINARIOS ANUALES		
NUMBER OF MUSEUMS REPORTING		PROFESSIONAL STAFF / PERSONNEL PROFESSIONNEL / PERSONAL PROFESIONAL		OTHER STAFF / AUTRE PERSONNEL / OTRO PERSONAL		NUMBER OF MUSEUMS REPORTING	TOTAL (000)	COUNTRY
NOMBRE DE MUSEES AYANT FOURNI CES DONNEES	TOTAL STAFF	PAID STAFF	VOLUNTEERS	PAID STAFF	VOLUNTEERS	NOMBRE DE MUSEES AYANT FOURNI CES DONNEES	TOTAL (000)	PAYS
NUMERO DE MUSEOS QUE DIERON ESTE DATO	TOTAL DU PERSONNEL / TOTAL DE PERSONAL	SALARIES / REMUNERADOS	VOLONTAIRES / VOLUNTARIOS	SALARIES / REMUNERADOS	VOLONTAIRES / VOLUNTARIOS	NUMERO DE MUSEOS QUE DIERON ESTE DATO	TOTAL (000)	PAIS
206	3 153	3 153	–	–	–	206	26 869	BULGARIA
41	477	477	–	–	–	41	4 617	
102	1 040	1 040	–	–	–	102	6 064	
4	63	63	–	–	–	4	303	
4	68	68	–	–	–	4	550	
8	278	278	–	–	–	8	1 343	
23	97	97	–	–	–	23	418	
24	1 130	1 130	–	–	–	24	13 574	
37 649	2 180	1 970	–	210	–	37 649	18 050	
7	165	108	1	57	–	105	802	
348	6 131	4 882	–	1 249	–	80	230 753	CZECHOSLOVAKIA‡
22	549	281	–	268	–	17	52 014	
28	574	391	–	183	–	1	37 357	
24	325	241	–	84	–	2	13 248	
5	97	97	–	–	–	–	...	
28	602	409	–	193	–	17	51 599	
194	3 969	3 453	–	516	–	39	75 754	
47	15	10	–	5	–	4	781	
152	900	500	–	400	–	33 648	650 000	
–	...	...	...	...	...	–	...	
–	...	...	...	...	...	–	...	DENMARK
–	...	...	...	...	...	–	...	
–	...	...	...	...	...	–	...	
–	...	...	...	...	...	–	...	
–	...	...	...	...	...	–	...	
–	...	...	...	...	...	–	...	
–	...	...	...	...	...	–	...	
–	...	...	...	...	...	–	...	
–	...	...	...	...	...	–	...	
519	...	571	–	...	–	504	55 968	FINLAND‡
47	...	177	–	...	–	47	24 993	
./.	...	./.	–	...	–	./.	./.	
22	...	108	–	...	–	7	1 051	
./.	...	./.	–	...	–	./.	./.	
./.	...	./.	–	...	–	./.	./.	
./.	...	./.	–	...	–	./.	./.	
450	...	286	–	...	–	450	29 923	
./.	...	./.	–	...	–	./.	./.	
35	*270	19	–	*251	–	35	2 400	
...	...	...	...	...	...	–	...	
684	6 830	3 000	–	3 830	–	684	171	GERMAN DEMOCRATIC REPUBLIC‡
77	2 103	622	–	1 481	–	77	64	
109	1 821	960	–	860	–	109	47	
50	610	386	–	224	–	50	9	
36	229	105	–	124	–	36	6	
45	223	78	–	145	–	45	3	
367	1 844	849	–	996	–	367	42	
65 445	9 625	352	7 673	1 600	...	48 000	2 000	
137	1 889	...	...	...	...	–	...	
–	...	...	...	...	...	–	...	GERMANY, FEDERAL REPUBLIC OF
–	...	...	...	...	...	–	...	
–	...	...	...	...	...	–	...	
–	...	...	...	...	...	–	...	
–	...	...	...	...	...	–	...	
–	...	...	...	...	...	–	...	
–	...	...	...	...	...	–	...	
–	...	...	...	...	...	–	...	
–	...	...	...	...	...	–	...	
1	8	1	–	7	–	1	35	GIBRALTAR
1	8	1	–	7	–	1	35	
13	264	10	–	254	–	–	...	HOLY SEE
10	...	...	–	...	–	–	...	
1	...	...	–	...	–	–	...	
1	...	...	–	...	–	–	...	
1	...	...	–	...	–	–	...	

8.2 **Number of museums by subject of collection**
Nombre de musées d'après la nature des collections
Número de museos según la naturaleza de sus colecciones

COUNTRY / PAYS / PAIS	YEAR / ANNEE / AÑO	SUBJECT OF COLLECTION OR TYPE OF INSTITUTION / NATURE DES COLLECTIONS OU TYPE D'INSTITUTION / NATURALEZA DE LAS COLECCIONES O TIPO DE INSTITUCION	TOTAL NUMBER OF MUSEUMS / NOMBRE TOTAL DE MUSEES / NUMERO TOTAL DE MUSEOS	ATTENDANCE / FREQUENTATION / FRECUENTACION		ANNUAL RECEIPTS / RECETTES ANNUELLES / INGRESOS ANUALES	
				NUMBER OF MUSEUMS REPORTING / NOMBRE DE MUSEES AYANT FOURNI CES DONNEES / NUMERO DE MUSEOS QUE DIERON ESTE DATO	NUMBER OF VISITORS (000) / NOMBRE DE VISITEURS (000) / NUMERO DE VISITANTES (000)	NUMBER OF MUSEUMS REPORTING / NOMBRE DE MUSEES AYANT FOURNI CES DONNEES / NUMERO DE MUSEOS QUE DIERON ESTE DATO	TOTAL (000) / TOTAL (000) / TOTAL (000)
HUNGARY	1984	TOTAL	442	402	14 658	–	...
		A. ART	89	80	5 348	–	...
		B. ARCHAEOLOGY AND HISTORY	92	84	2 887	–	...
		C. NAT. HISTORY AND NAT. SCIENCE.	18	11	621	–	...
		D. SCIENCE AND TECHNOLOGY	38	36	814	–	...
		E. ETHNOGRAPHY AND ANTHROPOLOGY	39	36	849	–	...
		F. SPECIALIZED MUSEUMS	34	30	783	–	...
		G. REGIONAL MUSEUMS	76	75	2 887	–	...
		H. GENERAL MUSEUMS	1	1	47	–	...
		I. OTHER MUSEUMS	55	49	422	–	...
		J. MONUMENTS AND SITES	152	139	4 540	–	...
IRELAND	1979	TOTAL	49	26	824	.	.
		A. ART	...	1	6	.	.
		B. ARCHAEOLOGY AND HISTORY	...	10	56	.	.
		D. SCIENCE AND TECHNOLOGY	...	1	4	.	.
		F. SPECIALIZED MUSEUMS	...	2	25	.	.
		G. REGIONAL MUSEUMS	...	6	215	.	.
		H. GENERAL MUSEUMS	...	3	394	.	.
		I. OTHER MUSEUMS	...	3	123	.	.
ITALY	1978	TOTAL	1 275	1 112	44 395	.	.
		A. ART	83	83	5 879	.	.
		B. ARCHAEOLOGY AND HISTORY	710	710	15 158	.	.
		C. NAT. HISTORY AND NAT. SCIENCE.	112	77	594	.	.
		D. SCIENCE AND TECHNOLOGY	83	23	59	.	.
		E. ETHNOGRAPHY AND ANTHROPOLOGY	38	36	449	.	.
		F. SPECIALIZED MUSEUMS	66	31	548	.	.
		H. GENERAL MUSEUMS	30	23	225	.	.
		J. MONUMENTS AND SITES	98	98	17 644	.	.
		K. ZOOS, BOTANICAL GARDENS, ETC.	55	31	3 839	.	.
MALTA‡	1979	TOTAL	22	16	526	.	.
		A. ART	8	3	81	.	.
		B. ARCHAEOLOGY AND HISTORY	2	2	43	.	.
		C. NAT. HISTORY AND NAT. SCIENCE.	2	2	66	.	.
		F. SPECIALIZED MUSEUMS	2	2	48	.	.
		J. MONUMENTS AND SITES	7	7	288	.	.
		K. ZOOS, BOTANICAL GARDENS, ETC.	1	–	...	.	.
MONACO	1979	TOTAL	4	4	1 552	.	.
		F. SPECIALIZED MUSEUMS	2	2	154	.	.
		K. ZOOS, BOTANICAL GARDENS, ETC.	2	2	1 398	.	.
NETHERLANDS‡	1984	TOTAL	548	539	15 959	537	307 853
		A. ART	58	57	3 188	...	...
		B. ARCHAEOLOGY AND HISTORY	296	292	5 366	...	...
		C. NAT. HISTORY AND NAT. SCIENCE.	48	48	1 769	...	...
		D. SCIENCE AND TECHNOLOGY	113	110	2 676	...	...
		E. ETHNOGRAPHY AND ANTHROPOLOGY	11	10	340	...	...
		H. GENERAL MUSEUMS	22	22	2 620	...	...
NORWAY	1978	TOTAL	195	139	4 573	.	.
		A. ART	18	14	1 077	.	.
		B. ARCHAEOLOGY AND HISTORY	4	4	457	.	.
		C. NAT. HISTORY AND NAT. SCIENCE.	17	15	564	.	.
		D. SCIENCE AND TECHNOLOGY	2	2	121	.	.
		E. ETHNOGRAPHY AND ANTHROPOLOGY	1	–	...	.	.
		F. SPECIALIZED MUSEUMS	38	28	1 442	.	.
		G. REGIONAL MUSEUMS	115	76	912	.	.
POLAND	1984	TOTAL	525	475	19 642	416	4 233
		A. ART	68	...	...	...	...
		B. ARCHAEOLOGY AND HISTORY	157	...	...	...	...
		C. NAT. HISTORY AND NAT. SCIENCE.	30	...	...	...	...
		D. SCIENCE AND TECHNOLOGY	25	...	...	...	...
		E. ETHNOGRAPHY AND ANTHROPOLOGY	28	...	...	...	...
		G. REGIONAL MUSEUMS	158	...	...	...	...
		I. OTHER MUSEUMS	59	...	...	...	...
		J. MONUMENTS AND SITES	500	–	...	–	...

PERSONNEL / PERSONNEL / PERSONAL						ANNUAL CURRENT EXPENDITURE / DEPENSES ANNUELLES ORDINAIRES / GASTOS ORDINARIOS ANUALES		
NUMBER OF MUSEUMS REPORTING / NOMBRE DE MUSEES AYANT FOURNI CES DONNEES / NUMERO DE MUSEOS QUE DIERON ESTE DATO	TOTAL STAFF / TOTAL DU PERSONNEL / TOTAL DE PERSONAL	PROFESSIONAL STAFF / PERSONNEL PROFESSIONNEL / PERSONAL PROFESIONAL: PAID STAFF / SALARIES / REMUNERADOS	PROFESSIONAL STAFF: VOLUNTEERS / VOLONTAIRES / VOLUNTARIOS	OTHER STAFF / AUTRE PERSONNEL / OTRO PERSONAL: PAID STAFF / SALARIES / REMUNERADOS	OTHER STAFF: VOLUNTEERS / VOLONTAIRES / VOLUNTARIOS	NUMBER OF MUSEUMS REPORTING / NOMBRE DE MUSEES AYANT FOURNI CES DONNEES / NUMERO DE MUSEOS QUE DIERON ESTE DATO	TOTAL (000) / TOTAL (000) / TOTAL (000)	COUNTRY / PAYS / PAIS
343	5 248	1 857	–	1 862	–	–	...	HUNGARY
69	1 107	254	–	437	–	–	...	
71	881	313	–	310	–	–	...	
11	267	150	–	67	–	–	...	
27	387	138	–	122	–	–	...	
26	323	112	–	124	–	–	...	
24	395	159	–	142	–	–	...	
71	1 742	695	–	618	–	–	...	
1	13	2	–	4	–	–	...	
43	133	34	–	38	–	–	...	
113	365	30	–	178	–	–	...	
30	371	53	52	164	102	20	919	IRELAND
1	18	4	–	6	8	1	104	
10	69	7	46	7	9	5	32	
2	5	2	–	3	–	–	...	
3	13	4	2	5	2	1	17	
6	112	5	3	32	72	5	194	
5	109	26	–	77	6	5	424	
3	45	5	1	34	5	3	148	
–	...	...	...	...	...	181	59 751	ITALY
–	...	...	...	...	...	...	...	
–	...	...	...	...	...	...	...	
–	...	...	...	...	...	...	...	
–	...	...	...	...	...	...	...	
–	...	...	...	...	...	...	...	
–	...	...	...	...	...	...	...	
–	...	...	...	...	...	...	...	
–	...	...	...	...	...	...	...	
–	...	...	...	...	...	...	...	
16	72	8	–	64	–	16	116	MALTA‡
–	...	...	...	...	...	–	...	
–	...	...	...	...	...	–	...	
–	...	...	...	...	...	–	...	
–	...	...	...	...	...	–	...	
–	...	...	...	...	...	–	...	
–	...	...	...	...	...	–	...	
4	127	122	–	5	–	2	1 319	MONACO
2	12	12	–	–	–	2	1 319	
2	115	110	–	5	–	–	...	
548	4 426	1 483	298	2 355	291	537	307 853	NETHERLANDS‡
58	682	200	14	450	18	...	...	
296	1 413	491	139	618	165	...	...	
48	320	139	38	125	18	...	...	
113	753	240	78	351	83	...	...	
11	214	109	3	100	1	...	...	
22	1 044	303	25	711	5	...	...	
–	...	...	...	...	...	–	...	NORWAY
–	...	...	...	...	...	–	...	
–	...	...	...	...	...	–	...	
–	...	...	...	...	...	–	...	
–	...	...	...	...	...	–	...	
–	...	...	...	...	...	–	...	
–	...	...	...	...	...	–	...	
–	...	...	...	...	...	–	...	
416	9 506	4 768	–	4 738	–	416	4 351	POLAND
...	...	...	–	...	–	...	...	
...	...	...	–	...	–	...	...	
...	...	...	–	...	–	...	...	
...	...	...	–	...	–	...	...	
...	...	...	–	...	–	...	...	
...	...	...	–	...	–	...	...	
...	...	...	–	...	–	...	...	
–	...	...	...	...	...	–	...	

8.2 Number of museums by subject of collection
Nombre de musées d'après la nature des collections
Número de museos según la naturaleza de sus colecciones

COUNTRY / PAYS / PAIS	YEAR / ANNEE / AÑO	SUBJECT OF COLLECTION OR TYPE OF INSTITUTION / NATURE DES COLLECTIONS OU TYPE D'INSTITUTION / NATURALEZA DE LAS COLECCIONES O TIPO DE INSTITUCION	TOTAL NUMBER OF MUSEUMS / NOMBRE TOTAL DE MUSEES / NUMERO TOTAL DE MUSEOS	ATTENDANCE / FREQUENTATION / FRECUENTACION		ANNUAL RECEIPTS / RECETTES ANNUELLES / INGRESOS ANUALES	
				NUMBER OF MUSEUMS REPORTING / NOMBRE DE MUSEES AYANT FOURNI CES DONNEES / NUMERO DE MUSEOS QUE DIERON ESTE DATO	NUMBER OF VISITORS (000) / NOMBRE DE VISITEURS (000) / NUMERO DE VISITANTES (000)	NUMBER OF MUSEUMS REPORTING / NOMBRE DE MUSEES AYANT FOURNI CES DONNEES / NUMERO DE MUSEOS QUE DIERON ESTE DATO	TOTAL (000) / TOTAL (000) / TOTAL (000)
PORTUGAL‡	1984	TOTAL	134	134	2 886	134	691 798
		A. ART	40	40	1 249	40	464 931
		B. ARCHAEOLOGY AND HISTORY	31	31	633	31	25 883
		C. NAT. HISTORY AND NAT. SCIENCE.	8	8	48	8	60 707
		D. SCIENCE AND TECHNOLOGY	2	2	207	2	58 573
		E. ETHNOGRAPHY AND ANTHROPOLOGY	15	15	95	15	28 335
		F. SPECIALIZED MUSEUMS	10	10	380	10	22 526
		G. REGIONAL MUSEUMS	12	12	173	12	89 660
		H. GENERAL MUSEUMS	11	11	93	11	20 481
		I. OTHER MUSEUMS	5	5	8	5	1 396
		J. MONUMENTS AND SITES	2	2	170	2	8 815
		K. ZOOS, BOTANICAL GARDENS, ETC.	3	3	744	3	163 171
ROMANIA	1979	TOTAL	412	412	16 331	.	.
		A. ART	89	89	4 981	.	.
		B. ARCHAEOLOGY AND HISTORY	59	59	2 189	.	.
		C. NAT. HISTORY AND NAT. SCIENCE.	46	46	4 541	.	.
		D. SCIENCE AND TECHNOLOGY	7	7	242	.	.
		E. ETHNOGRAPHY AND ANTHROPOLOGY	45	45	694	.	.
		F. SPECIALIZED MUSEUMS	76	76	888	.	.
		H. GENERAL MUSEUMS	90	90	2 796	.	.
SAN MARINO	1979	TOTAL	11	11	741	.	.
		A. ART	2	2	...	.	.
		F. SPECIALIZED MUSEUMS	3	3	...	.	.
		I. OTHER MUSEUMS	2	2	...	.	.
		J. MONUMENTS AND SITES	4	4	...	.	.
SPAIN‡	1979	TOTAL	610	610	13 897	.	.
		A. ART	73	73	2 700	.	.
		B. ARCHAEOLOGY AND HISTORY	74	74	1 700	.	.
		C. NAT. HISTORY AND NAT. SCIENCE.	21	21	800	.	.
		D. SCIENCE AND TECHNOLOGY	17	17	600	.	.
		E. ETHNOGRAPHY AND ANTHROPOLOGY	19	19	550	.	.
		F. SPECIALIZED MUSEUMS	132	132	1 200	.	.
		G. REGIONAL MUSEUMS	63	63	750	.	.
		H. GENERAL MUSEUMS	62	62	750	.	.
		I. OTHER MUSEUMS	93	93	2 647	.	.
		K. ZOOS, BOTANICAL GARDENS, ETC.	56	56	2 200	.	.
SWEDEN	1983	TOTAL	167	167	12 192	167	643
		A. ART	28	28	...	28	...
		B. ARCHAEOLOGY AND HISTORY	4	4	...	4	...
		C. NAT. HISTORY AND NAT. SCIENCE.	10	10	...	10	...
		D. SCIENCE AND TECHNOLOGY	7	7	...	7	...
		E. ETHNOGRAPHY AND ANTHROPOLOGY	39	39	...	39	...
		F. SPECIALIZED MUSEUMS	37	37	...	37	...
		G. REGIONAL MUSEUMS	23	23	...	23	...
		H. GENERAL MUSEUMS	15	15	...	15	...
		I. OTHER MUSEUMS	4	4	...	4	...
YUGOSLAVIA	1982	TOTAL	522	452	11 851	–	...
		A. ART	99	83	2 218	–	...
		B. ARCHAEOLOGY AND HISTORY	154	134	5 315	–	...
		C. NAT. HISTORY AND NAT. SCIENCE.	18	17	433	–	...
		E. ETHNOGRAPHY AND ANTHROPOLOGY	47	41	478	–	...
		F. SPECIALIZED MUSEUMS	27	22	199	–	...
		H. GENERAL MUSEUMS	175	154	3 121	–	...
		I. OTHER MUSEUMS	2	1	86	–	...
		K. ZOOS, BOTANICAL GARDENS, ETC.	10	10	2 031	10	221 612
OCEANIA							
AMERICAN SAMOA	1979	TOTAL	1	1	52	.	.
		H. GENERAL MUSEUMS	1	1	52	.	.
AUSTRALIA‡	1979	TOTAL	15	14	5 279	.	.
		A. ART	5	4	1 200	.	.
		B. ARCHAEOLOGY AND HISTORY	1	1	734	.	.
		D. SCIENCE AND TECHNOLOGY	2	2	902	.	.
		H. GENERAL MUSEUMS	7	7	2 443	.	.
FIJI	1984	TOTAL	1	1	40	1	205
		H. GENERAL MUSEUMS	1	1	40	1	205
NEW CALEDONIA‡	1979	TOTAL	1	1	30	.	.
		E. ETHNOGRAPHY AND ANTHROPOLOGY	1	1	30	.	.

NUMBER OF MUSEUMS REPORTING NOMBRE DE MUSEES AYANT FOURNI CES DONNEES NUMERO DE MUSEOS QUE DIERON ESTE DATO	PERSONNEL / PERSONNEL / PERSONAL TOTAL STAFF TOTAL DU PERSONNEL TOTAL DE PERSONAL	PROFESSIONAL STAFF / PERSONNEL PROFESSIONNEL / PERSONAL PROFESIONAL PAID STAFF SALARIES REMUNERADOS	 VOLUNTEERS VOLONTAIRES VOLUNTARIOS	OTHER STAFF / AUTRE PERSONNEL / OTRO PERSONAL PAID STAFF SALARIES REMUNERADOS	 VOLUNTEERS VOLONTAIRES VOLUNTARIOS	ANNUAL CURRENT EXPENDITURE / DEPENSES ANNUELLES ORDINAIRES / GASTOS ORDINARIOS ANUALES NUMBER OF MUSEUMS REPORTING NOMBRE DE MUSEES AYANT FOURNI CES DONNEES NUMERO DE MUSEOS QUE DIERON ESTE DATO	 TOTAL (000) TOTAL (000) TOTAL (000)	COUNTRY PAYS PAIS
134	1 650	706	12	818	114	134	811 285	PORTUGAL‡
40	711	302	4	345	60	40	394 275	
31	251	63	3	182	3	31	94 836	
8	108	93	1	14	–	8	53 498	
2	110	28	1	81	–	2	58 553	
15	108	46	1	55	6	15	45 272	
10	133	90	–	43	–	10	81 065	
12	119	71	2	34	12	12	40 512	
11	61	12	–	48	1	11	41 371	
5	49	1	–	16	32	5	1 903	
2	36	6	–	30	–	2	17 521	
3	252	103	2	147	–	3	154 795	
–	...	...	...	...	...	–	...	ROMANIA
–	...	...	...	...	...	–	...	
–	...	...	...	...	...	–	...	
–	...	...	...	...	...	–	...	
–	...	...	...	...	...	–	...	
–	...	...	...	...	...	–	...	
–	...	...	...	...	...	–	...	
–	...	...	...	...	...	–	...	
–	...	...	...	...	...	11	403 500	SAN MARINO
–	...	...	...	...	...	2	...	
–	...	...	...	...	...	3	...	
–	...	...	...	...	...	2	...	
–	...	...	...	...	...	4	...	
610	4 684	613	775	2 494	1 196	610	685 443	SPAIN‡
73	1 250	185	170	664	296	73	170 000	
74	1 000	149	140	501	190	74	160 000	
21	150	50	20	105	10	21	45 000	
17	100	30	15	135	5	17	24 000	
19	110	35	25	104	5	19	30 000	
132	800	45	130	290	370	132	69 000	
63	150	20	30	105	25	63	19 000	
62	400	25	40	155	210	62	26 000	
93	324	15	125	175	9	93	61 443	
56	400	59	80	260	76	56	81 000	
167	3 354	...	...	...	...	–	...	SWEDEN
28	...	...	...	...	...	–	...	
4	...	...	...	...	...	–	...	
10	...	...	...	...	...	–	...	
7	...	...	...	...	...	–	...	
39	...	...	...	...	...	–	...	
37	...	...	...	...	...	–	...	
23	...	...	...	...	...	–	...	
15	...	...	...	...	...	–	...	
4	...	...	...	...	...	–	...	
522	3 999	2 165	——>	1 834	——>	–	...	YUGOSLAVIA
99	674	365	——>	309	——>	–	...	
154	865	509	——>	356	——>	–	...	
18	145	103	——>	42	——>	–	...	
47	175	109	——>	66	——>	–	...	
27	263	187	——>	76	——>	–	...	
175	1 869	1 191	——>	678	——>	–	...	
2	8	3	——>	5	——>	–	...	
10	205	115	——>	90	——>	10	149 769	
								OCEANIA
1	7	7	–	–	–	1	260	AMERICAN SAMOA
1	7	7	–	–	–	1	260	
15	1 747	456	21	928	342	15	31 524	AUSTRALIA‡
5	714	167	1	327	219	5	16 341	
1	143	30	–	80	33	1	2 016	
2	181	47	2	92	40	2	1 578	
7	709	212	18	429	50	7	11 589	
1	9	2	–	5	1	1	198	FIJI
1	9	2	–	5	1	1	198	
1	9	9	–	–	–	1	2 500	NEW CALEDONIA‡
1	9	9	–	–	–	1	2 500	

8.2 Number of museums by subject of collection
Nombre de musées d'après la nature des collections
Número de museos según la naturaleza de sus colecciones

COUNTRY / PAYS / PAIS	YEAR / ANNEE / AÑO	SUBJECT OF COLLECTION OR TYPE OF INSTITUTION / NATURE DES COLLECTIONS OU TYPE D'INSTITUTION / NATURALEZA DE LAS COLECCIONES O TIPO DE INSTITUCION	TOTAL NUMBER OF MUSEUMS / NOMBRE TOTAL DE MUSEES / NUMERO TOTAL DE MUSEOS	ATTENDANCE / FREQUENTATION / FRECUENTACION: NUMBER OF MUSEUMS REPORTING / NOMBRE DE MUSEES AYANT FOURNI CES DONNEES / NUMERO DE MUSEOS QUE DIERON ESTE DATO	NUMBER OF VISITORS (000) / NOMBRE DE VISITEURS (000) / NUMERO DE VISITANTES (000)	ANNUAL RECEIPTS / RECETTES ANNUELLES / INGRESOS ANUALES: NUMBER OF MUSEUMS REPORTING / NOMBRE DE MUSEES AYANT FOURNI CES DONNEES / NUMERO DE MUSEOS QUE DIERON ESTE DATO	TOTAL (000)
NORFOLK ISLAND	1979	TOTAL	1	1	20	.	.
		J. MONUMENTS AND SITES	1	1	20	.	.
PACIFIC ISLANDS	1980	TOTAL	5	–	...	.	.
		G. REGIONAL MUSEUMS	5	–	...	.	.
PAPUA NEW GUINEA	1979	TOTAL	2	2	100	.	.
		E. ETHNOGRAPHY AND ANTHROPOLOGY	1	1	20	.	.
		H. GENERAL MUSEUMS	1	1	80	.	.
U.S.S.R.							
U.S.S.R.‡	1984	TOTAL	1 479	1 370	174 363	–	...
		A. ART	285	264	36 561	–	...
		B. ARCHAEOLOGY AND HISTORY	355	337	79 683	–	...
		C. NAT. HISTORY AND NAT. SCIENCE.	34	30	3 240	–	...
		F. SPECIALIZED MUSEUMS	51	39	3 405	–	...
		G. REGIONAL MUSEUMS	753	699	39 874	–	...
		J. MONUMENTS AND SITES	393	365	17 229	–	...
BYELORUSSIAN S.S.R.‡	1984	TOTAL	68	56	4 209	–	...
		A. ART	3	2	281	–	...
		B. ARCHAEOLOGY AND HISTORY	22	18	1 907	–	...
		C. NAT. HISTORY AND NAT. SCIENCE.	3	3	165	–	...
		G. REGIONAL MUSEUMS	40	33	1 856	–	...
		J. MONUMENTS AND SITES	8	7	491	–	...
UKRAINIAN S.S.R.‡	1984	TOTAL	140	140	32 700	–	...
		A. ART	34	34	...	–	...
		B. ARCHAEOLOGY AND HISTORY	38	38	...	–	...
		C. NAT. HISTORY AND NAT. SCIENCE.	1	1	...	–	...
		F. SPECIALIZED MUSEUMS	11	11	...	–	...
		G. REGIONAL MUSEUMS	56	56	...	–	...
		J. MONUMENTS AND SITES	34	34	...	–	...

NUMBER OF MUSEUMS REPORTING / NOMBRE DE MUSEES AYANT FOURNI CES DONNEES / NUMERO DE MUSEOS QUE DIERON ESTE DATO	PERSONNEL / PERSONNEL / PERSONAL: TOTAL STAFF / TOTAL DU PERSONNEL / TOTAL DE PERSONAL	PROFESSIONAL STAFF / PERSONNEL PROFESSIONNEL / PERSONAL PROFESIONAL: PAID STAFF / SALARIES / REMUNERADOS	PROFESSIONAL STAFF: VOLUNTEERS / VOLONTAIRES / VOLUNTARIOS	OTHER STAFF / AUTRE PERSONNEL / OTRO PERSONAL: PAID STAFF / SALARIES / REMUNERADOS	OTHER STAFF: VOLUNTEERS / VOLONTAIRES / VOLUNTARIOS	ANNUAL CURRENT EXPENDITURE / DEPENSES ANNUELLES ORDINAIRES / GASTOS ORDINARIOS ANUALES: NUMBER OF MUSEUMS REPORTING / NOMBRE DE MUSEES AYANT FOURNI CES DONNEES / NUMERO DE MUSEOS QUE DIERON ESTE DATO	TOTAL (000)	COUNTRY / PAYS / PAIS
1	14	14	–	–	–	1	260	NORFOLK ISLAND
1	14	14	–	–	–	1	260	
2	4	–	–	4	–		...	PACIFIC ISLANDS
2	4	–	–	4	–		...	
2	65	32	2	30	1	2	530	PAPUA NEW GUINEA
1	4	1	–	3	–	1	16	
1	61	31	2	27	1	1	504	
								U.S.S.R.
–	...	...	...	...	...	–	...	U.S.S.R.‡
–	...	...	...	...	...	–	...	
–	...	...	...	...	...	–	...	
–	...	...	...	...	...	–	...	
–	...	...	...	...	...	–	...	
–	...	...	...	...	...	–	...	
–	...	...	...	...	...	–	...	
–	...	...	...	...	...	–	...	BYELORUSSIAN S.S.R.‡
–	...	...	...	...	...	–	...	
–	...	...	...	...	...	–	...	
–	...	...	...	...	...	–	...	
–	...	...	...	...	...	–	...	
–	...	...	...	...	...	–	...	UKRAINIAN S.S.R.‡
–	...	...	...	...	...	–	...	
–	...	...	...	...	...	–	...	
–	...	...	...	...	...	–	...	
–	...	...	...	...	...	–	...	
–	...	...	...	...	...	–	...	
–	...	...	...	...	...	–	...	

AFRICA:
Mauritius:

E--> Data on personnel and expenditure of natural history and natural science museums and other museums are included under archaeology and history museums.

FR-> Les données relatives au personnel et aux dépenses des musées d'histoire et de science naturelles et d'autres musées sont comptées avec les musées d'archéologie et d'histoire.

ESP> Los datos relativos al personal y gastos de museos de historia y ciencias naturales y otros museos, se cuenta junto con los museos de arqueología e historia.

AMERICA, NORTH:
Barbados:

E--> Includes only history museums.

FR-> Comprend seulement les musées d'histoire.

ESP> Incluye solamente los museos de historia.

Canada:

E--> Archaeology and history museums include ethnography and anthropology museums. Professional and other staff are counted together.

FR-> Les musées d'archéologie et d'histoire incluent les musées d'ethnographie et d'anthropologie. Le personnel professionnel et l'autre personnel sont comptés ensemble.

ESP> Los museos de arqueología e historia incluye museos de etnografía y antropología. El personal profesional y otro personal están contados conjuntamente.

Cuba:

E--> Total includes 103 monuments and sites.

FR-> Le total inclut 103 monuments et sites.

ESP> El total incluye 103 monumentos y sitios.

Mexico:

E--> Number of visitors includes visitors to 125 monuments and sites.

FR-> Le nombre de visiteurs inclut les visiteurs de 125 monuments et sites.

ESP> El número de visitantes incluye las visitantes de 125

Mexico: (Cont):
monumentos y sitios.

United States:

E--> Archaeology and history museums include natural history and natural science museums, ethnography and anthropology museums, and historical and archaeological monuments and sites. Professional and other staff are counted together.

FR-> Les musées d'archéologie et d'histoire comprennent les musées d'histoire et de sciences naturelles, d'ethnographie et d'anthropologie, les monuments et sites historiques et archéologiques. Le personnel professionnel et l'autre personnel sont comptés ensemble.

ESP> Los muiseos de arqueología y de historia incluyen los museos de historia y ciencias naturales, de etnografía y de antropología, los monumentos y lugares históricos y arqueológicos. El personal profesional y el otro personal se cuentan conjuntamente.

AMERICA, SOUTH:
Brazil:

E--> Natural history and natural science museums include 5 museums specialized in botany. Ethnography and anthropology museums include 21 museums specialized in folklore.

FR-> Les musées d'histoire et de sciences naturelles incluent 5 musées spécialisés en botanique. Les musées d'ethnographie et d'antrhopologie incluent 21 musées spécialisés dans le folklore.

ESP> Los museos de historia y ciencias naturales incluyen 5 museos especializados en botánica. Los museos de etnografía y antropología incluyen 21 museos especializados en folklore.

ASIA:
Japan:

E--> Natural history and natural science museums include science and technology museums.

FR-> Les musées d'histoire et des sciences naturelles comprennent ls musées des sciences et des techniques.

ESP> Los museos de historia y de ciencias naturales incluyen los museos de ciencias y de tecnología.

Malaysia:

E--> Expenditure under general museums includes expenditure for

Malaysia: (Cont):
archaeology and history museums.
FR-> Les dépenses des musées généraux incluent les dépenses des musées d'histoire et d'archéologie.
ESP> Los gastos de museos generales incluyen los gastos de museos de historia y de arqueología.
EUROPE:
Czechoslovakia:
E--> Archaeology and history museums include natural history and natural science museums. Regional museums include general museums. Data under zoological and botanical gardens, aquaria, vivaria, etc. refer only to zoological gardens and nature reserves.
FR-> Les musées d'archéologie et d'histoire incluent les musées d'histoire et de sciences naturelles. Les musées régionaux incluent les musées généraux. Les données relatives aux jardins botaniques et zoologiques, aquariums, vivariums, etc. se réfèrent seulement aux jardins zoologiques et aux réserves naturelles.
ESP> Los museos de arqueología e historia incluyen los museos de historia y ciencias naturales. Los museos regionales incluyen los museos generales. Los datos relativos a los jardines zoológicos y botánicos, acuarios, viveros, etc., se refieren a los jardines zoológicos y a reservas naturales solamente.
Finland:
E--> Data on attendance, professional staff and expenditure for archaeology and history museums, science and technology museums, ethnography and anthropology museums, specialized and general museums are included under regional museums.
FR-> Les données relatives à la fréquentation, au personnel professionnel et aux dépenses des musées d'archéologie et d'histoire, des sciences et techniques, d'ethnographie et d'anthropologie, des musées généraux et spécialisés sont comptées avec les musées régionaux.
ESP> Los datos relativos a la frecuentación, al personal profesional y a los gastos de los museos de arqueología e historia, de ciencia y tecnología, de etnografía y antropología, de museos generales y especializados se incluyen en los museos regionales.
German Democratic Republic:
E--> Data on zoological and botanical gardens, aquaria, reserves, etc. do not include data on botanical gardens.
FR-> Les données sur les jardins zoologiques et botaniques, les aquariums, les réserves, etc. n'incluent pas les jardins botaniques.
ESP> Los datos sobre los jarines botánicos y zoológicos, acuarios, viveros, reservas naturales, etc., excluyen los jarines botánicos.
Malta:
E--> Number of visitors does not include 186,000 visitors in organized groups.
FR-> Le nombre de visiteurs n'inclut pas 186 000 visiteurs de groupes organisés.
ESP> El número de los vistantes excluye 186 000 visitantes de los grupos organizados.
Netherlands:
E--> Data on receipts and expenditure refer to 1983.
FR-> Les données relatives aux recettes et aux dépenses se réfèrent à 1983.
ESP> Los datos relativos a los ingresos y gastos se refieren a 1983.
Portugal:
E--> Figures shown for total number of museums are incomplete and refer only to those museums which have been able to report statistics on attendance, receipts, personnel and expenditure.

Portugal: (Cont):
FR-> Les chiffres concernant le nombre total de musées sont incomplets; ils se réfèrent seulement aux musées qui ait pu fournir des statistiques sur la fréquentation, les recettes, le personnel et les dépenses.
ESP> Las cifras sobre el total de museos son incompletos; se refieren solamente a los museos que han podido proporcionar estadísticas sobre frecuentación, ingresos, personal y gastos.
Spain:
E--> Total does not include 6,500 monuments and sites.
FR-> Le total n'inclut pas 6 500 monuments et sites.
ESP> El total excluye 6 500 monumentos y sitios.
OCEANIA:
Australia:
E--> Figures shown for total number of museums are incomplete and refer only to those museums which have been able to report statistics on attendance, receipts, personnel and expenditure.
E--> Figures shown for total number of museums are incomplete and refer only to those museums which have been able to report statistics on attendance, receipts, personnel and expenditure.
FR-> Les chiffres concernant le nombre total de musées sont incomplets; ils se réfèrent seulement aux musées qui ait pu fournir des statistiques sur la fréquentation, les recettes, le personnel et les dépenses.
ESP> Las cifras sobre el total de museos son incompletos; se refieren solamente a los museos que han podido proporcionar estadísticas sobre frecuentación, ingresos, personal y gastos.
New Caledonia:
E--> Expenditure does not include expenditure on personnel.
FR-> Les dépenses ne comprennent pas les dépenses de personnel.
ESP> Los gastos excluyen los gastos de personal.
U.S.S.R.:
U.S.S.R.:
E--> Total does not include Permanent Exhibition of Economic Achievements of the U.S.S.R. in Moscow which reported 11.6 million visitors.
FR-> Le total ne comprend pas l'Exposition Permanente des Réalisations Economiques de l'U.R.S.S. à Moscou pour laquelle on a compté 11.6 millions de visiteurs. Les musées spécialisés incluent les autres musées.
ESP> El total no incluye la Exposición Permanente de los Materializaciones Económicas Realizados por la U.R.S.S. en Moscú, que fueron de 11.6 millones de visitantes. Los museos especializdos incluyen los otros museos.
Byelorussian S.S.R.:
E--> Total does not include Permanent Exhibition of Economic Achievements of the Byelorussian S.S.R. which reported 259,000 visitors.
FR-> Le total ne comprend pas l'Exposition Permanente des Réalisations Economiques de la R.S.S. de Biélorussie pour laquelle on a compté 259 000 visiteurs.
ESP> El total no incluye la Exposición Permanente de los Materializaciones Económicas Realizados por la R.S.S. de Bielorrusia, que fueron de 259 000 de visitantes.
Ukrainian S.S.R.:
E--> Number of visitors includes visitors to memorials.
FR-> Le nombre de visiteurs inclut les visiteurs des mémorials.
ESP> El número de visitantes incluye los visitantes a los memoriales.

8.3 Archival institutions: holdings, accessions, reference service, personnel and current expenditure

Institutions d'archives: fonds et collections, entrées, service des renseignements, personnel et dépenses courantes

Instituciones de archivos: fondos y colecciones, ingresos, servicio de informaciones, personal y gastos corrientes

CATEGORIE DE DONNEES (UNITES DE MESURE)	CATEGORIA DE DATOS (UNIDADES DE MEDIDA)
1. NOMBRE D'INSTITUTIONS	1. NUMERO DE INSTITUCIONES
FONDS ET COLLECTIONS	FONDOS Y COLECCIONES
2. ARCHIVES CONVENTIONNELLES (METRES)	2. DOCUMENTOS CONVENCIONALES (METROS)
3. DONT: DOCUMENTS CONTEMPORAINS	3. DE LOS CUALES: DOCUMENTOS CONTEMPORANEOS
4. ARCHIVES CARTOGRAPHIQUES (ARTICLES)	4. DOCUMENTOS CARTOGRAFICOS (ARTICULOS)
5. ARCHIVES AUDIOVISUELLES (ARTICLES)	5. DOCUMENTOS AUDIOVISUALES (ARTICULOS)
6. MICROCOPIES (ARTICLES)	6. MICROCOPIAS (ARTICULOS)
7. AUTRES ARCHIVES (METRES)	7. OTROS DOCUMENTOS (METROS)
8. AUTRES ARCHIVES (ARTICLES)	8. OTROS DOCUMENTOS (ARTICULOS)
ENTREES	INGRESOS
9. ARCHIVES CONVENTIONNELLES (METRES)	9. DOCUMENTOS CONVENCIONALES (METROS)
10. DONT: DOCUMENTS CONTEMPORAINS	10. DE LOS CUALES: DOCUMENTOS CONTEMPORANEOS
11. ARCHIVES CARTOGRAPHIQUES (ARTICLES)	11. DOCUMENTOS CARTOGRAFICOS (ARTICULOS)
12. ARCHIVES AUDIOVISUELLES (ARTICLES)	12. DOCUMENTOS AUDIOVISUALES (ARTICULOS)
13. MICROCOPIES (ARTICLES)	13. MICROCOPIAS (ARTICULOS)
14. AUTRES ARCHIVES (METRES)	14. OTROS DOCUMENTOS (METROS)
15. AUTRES ARCHIVES (ARTICLES)	15. OTROS DOCUMENTOS (ARTICULOS)
ELABORATION DES INSTRUMENTS DE RECHERCHE	ELABORACION DE LOS INSTRUMENTOS DE BUSQUEDA
16. ARCHIVES CONVENTIONNELLES (METRES)	16. DOCUMENTOS CONVENCIONALES (METROS)
17. AUTRES ARCHIVES (ARTICLES)	17. OTROS DOCUMENTOS (ARTICULOS)
SERVICE DES RENSEIGNEMENTS	SERVICIO DE INFORMACIONES
18. NOMBRE DE CHERCHEURS	18. NUMERO DE INVESTIGADORES
19. NOMBRE DE VISITES DANS LES SALLES DE LECTURE ET DE RECHERCHE	19. NUMERO DE VISITAS EN LAS SALAS DE LECTURA Y DE INVESTIGACION
20. NOMBRE D'ARTICLES CONSULTES	20. NUMERO DE ARTICULOS CONSULTADOS
21. NOMBRE DE DEMANDES	21. NUMERO DE SOLICITUDES
EQUIPEMENT	EQUIPO
22. CAPACITE TOTALE DE RAYONNAGE (METRES)	22. CAPACIDAD TOTAL DE LAS ESTANTERIAS (METROS)
23. DONT: RAYONNAGES OCCUPES	23. DE LA CUALE: ESTANTERIAS OCUPADAS
PERSONNEL	PERSONAL
24. NOMBRE DE PERSONNEL PERMANENT	24. NUMERO DE PERSONAL PERMANENTE
25. DONT: PROFESSIONNEL	25. DEL CUAL: PROFESIONAL
26. TECHNIQUE ET AUTRE	26. TECNICO Y OTRO
27. DEPENSES COURANTES (000)	27. GASTOS CORRIENTES (000)

NUMBER OF COUNTRIES AND TERRITORIES PRESENTED IN THIS TABLE: 62

NOMBRE DE PAYS ET DE TERRITOIRES PRESENTES DANS CE TABLEAU: 62

NUMERO DE PAISES Y DE TERRITORIOS PRESENTADOS EN ESTE CUADRO: 62

AFRICA

TYPE OF DATA (UNITS OF MEASUREMENT) / CATEGORIE DE DONNEES (UNITES DE MESURE) / CATEGORIA DE DATOS (UNIDADES DE MEDIDA)	BURUNDI‡ (1983) NATIONAL	CHAD‡ (1984) NATIONAL	CONGO (1982) NATIONAL	ETHIOPIA (1982) NATIONAL	GABON (1982) NATIONAL	MAURITIUS (1982) NATIONAL	REUNION (1982) NATIONAL	RWANDA‡ (1982) NATIONAL
1. NUMBER OF INSTITUTIONS	1	1	1	1	1	1	1	1
HOLDINGS								
2. CONVENTIONAL ARCHIVES (METRES)	96	226	296	266	1 400	1 265	6 000	300
3. OF WHICH: CONTEMPORARY RECORDS	96	226	294	266	1 400	543	4 000	300
4. CARTOGRAPHIC ARCHIVES (ITEMS)	*20	–	–	370	379	2 360	680	–
5. AUDIOVISUAL ARCHIVES (ITEMS)	–	–	–	1 655	577	...	518	–
6. MICROFORMS (ITEMS)	2 200	–	–	...	265	238	...	–
7. OTHER ARCHIVES (METRES)	30	–	82	...	...	426	580	15
8. OTHER ARCHIVES (ITEMS)	–	–	–	...	...	2 391	–	–
ACCESSIONS								
9. CONVENTIONAL ARCHIVES (METRES)	96	–	12	43	...	12	163	100
10. OF WHICH: CONTEMPORARY RECORDS	96	–	–	43	...	12	163	100
11. CARTOGRAPHIC ARCHIVES (ITEMS)	*20	–	–	–	...	2	...	–
12. AUDIOVISUAL ARCHIVES (ITEMS)	–	–	–	–	...	12	518	–
13. MICROFORMS (ITEMS)	2 200	–	–	...	...	42	...	–
14. OTHER ARCHIVES (ITEMS)	30	–	6	...	...	8	15	5
15. OTHER ARCHIVES (ITEMS)	–	–	–	...	...	7	...	–
ARCHIVES UNDER FINDING-AID CONTROL								
16. CONVENTIONAL ARCHIVES (METRES)	15	50	85	60	35	12	–	100
17. OTHER ARCHIVES (ITEMS)	–	–	–	2 025	...	63	2 354	–
REFERENCE SERVICE								
18. NUMBER OF VISITORS	12	7	69	...	79	396	555	–
19. NUMBER OF VISITS TO SEARCH ROOM(S)	*100	10	...	...	...	1 329	2 125	–
20. NUMBER OF STORAGE UNITS CONSULTED	...	...	180	...	600	2 930	9 159	–
21. NUMBER OF INQUIRIES	4	...	193	...	30	524	333	–
EQUIPMENT								
22. TOTAL SHELVING CAPACITY (METRES)	456	...	...	...	...	2 400	...	500
23. OF WHICH: OCCUPIED SHELVING	...	...	...	...	...	1 755	6 500	400
PERSONNEL								
24. NUMBER OF PERMANENT STAFF	7	5	10	10	7	21	18	9
25. OF WHICH: PROFESSIONAL	–	2	9	7	5	...	2	3
26. TECHNICAL AND OTHER	7	3	1	3	2	...	16	6
27. CURRENT EXPENDITURE (000)	1 154	2 583	...	...	...	1 128	2 443	2 700

AMERICA, NORTH

TYPE OF DATA (UNITS OF MEASUREMENT) / CATEGORIE DE DONNEES (UNITES DE MESURE) / CATEGORIA DE DATOS (UNIDADES DE MEDIDA)	SENEGAL (1982) NATIONAL	SEYCHELLES‡ (1982) NATIONAL	SIERRA LEONE (1984) NATIONAL	ZAIRE (1984) NATIONAL	ZIMBABWE‡ (1982) NATIONAL	BARBADOS‡ (1983) NATIONAL	BERMUDA (1981) NATIONAL	CANADA (1983) NATIONAL
1. NUMBER OF INSTITUTIONS	1	1	1	1	1	1	1	1
HOLDINGS								
2. CONVENTIONAL ARCHIVES (METRES)	10 767	181	1 500	1 000	49 491	...	575	46 143
3. OF WHICH: CONTEMPORARY RECORDS	10 512	...	1 050	1 000	48 545	...	6	*41 528
4. CARTOGRAPHIC ARCHIVES (ITEMS)	...	...	80	670	6 214	...	*30	846 000
5. AUDIOVISUAL ARCHIVES (ITEMS)	...	...	200	3 000	*26 229	...	*4 030	9 628 688
6. MICROFORMS (ITEMS)	...	...	200	–	*3 603	215	335	31 839
7. OTHER ARCHIVES (METRES)	*600	...	6	120	*2 300	196	4	6 413
8. OTHER ARCHIVES (ITEMS)	–	...	...	–	...	...	*62	126 777
ACCESSIONS								
9. CONVENTIONAL ARCHIVES (METRES)	73	181	...	110	2 703	...	1	10 275
10. OF WHICH: CONTEMPORARY RECORDS	70	...	...	110	2 703	...	–	9 246
11. CARTOGRAPHIC ARCHIVES (ITEMS)	–	...	...	–	110	...	–	70 858
12. AUDIOVISUAL ARCHIVES (ITEMS)	–	...	...	–	758	...	–	...
13. MICROFORMS (ITEMS)	...	...	...	–	3	...	*15	4 223
14. OTHER ARCHIVES (ITEMS)	*21	...	...	8	...	...	1	*152
15. OTHER ARCHIVES (ITEMS)	–	...	...	–	117	280	–	2 227
ARCHIVES UNDER FINDING-AID CONTROL								
16. CONVENTIONAL ARCHIVES (METRES)	...	...	300	70	2 694	...	*1	2 231
17. OTHER ARCHIVES (ITEMS)	–	...	...	300	1 182	...	*15	*225 710
REFERENCE SERVICE								
18. NUMBER OF VISITORS	2 226	400	...	946	...	316	...	6 853
19. NUMBER OF VISITS TO SEARCH ROOM(S)	...	...	...	100	2 948	316	362	28 674
20. NUMBER OF STORAGE UNITS CONSULTED	...	...	...	1 273	2 541	386	*730	80 074
21. NUMBER OF INQUIRIES	...	15	36	80	*643	56	157	97 729
EQUIPMENT								
22. TOTAL SHELVING CAPACITY (METRES)	12 200	...	...	3 920	*53 110	...	2 151	...
23. OF WHICH: OCCUPIED SHELVING	...	...	...	2 000	51 660	...	...	...
PERSONNEL								
24. NUMBER OF PERMANENT STAFF	52	10	7	29	68	15	4	743
25. OF WHICH: PROFESSIONAL	42	2	2	17	22	4	1	124
26. TECHNICAL AND OTHER	10	8	5	12	46	11	3	619
27. CURRENT EXPENDITURE (000)	...	718	80	2 303	428	376	88	33 395

AMERICA, SOUTH

TYPE OF DATA (UNITS OF MEASUREMENT) CATEGORIE DE DONNEES (UNITES DE MESURE) CATEGORIA DE DATOS (UNIDADES DE MEDIDA)	COSTA RICA (1982) NATIONAL	JAMAICA (1982) NATIONAL	MARTINIQUE (1982) NATIONAL	MEXICO‡ (1982) NATIONAL	UNITED STATES‡ (1982) NATIONAL	ARGENTINA (1982) NATIONAL	BRAZIL (1984) NATIONAL	CHILE (1983) NATIONAL
1. NUMBER OF INSTITUTIONS	1	1	1	1	1	1	*1	1
HOLDINGS								
2. CONVENTIONAL ARCHIVES (METRES)	6 000	12 147	3 656	22 333	47 763	7 670	1 600	15 000
3. OF WHICH: CONTEMPORARY RECORDS	2 000	...	106	9 170	...	*1 788	...	7 240
4. CARTOGRAPHIC ARCHIVES (ITEMS)	...	7 320	292	...	8 000 000	1 780	11 000	841
5. AUDIOVISUAL ARCHIVES (ITEMS)	15 060	...	690	5 022 740	5 177 050	331 661	357 000	–
6. MICROFORMS (ITEMS)	–	56	6 644	123 066	...	1 525	...	572
7. OTHER ARCHIVES (METRES)	–	9	528	4 449	21 398	884	...	110
8. OTHER ARCHIVES (ITEMS)	–	30	267	10 000	7 500	–	500	46
ACCESSIONS								
9. CONVENTIONAL ARCHIVES (METRES)	–	6	177	436	492	113	...	180
10. OF WHICH: CONTEMPORARY RECORDS	–	–	170	431	...	113	...	152
11. CARTOGRAPHIC ARCHIVES (ITEMS)	–	–	20	10 000	1 000	5	...	–
12. AUDIOVISUAL ARCHIVES (ITEMS)	–	–	662	5 000 000	19 940	68	...	–
13. MICROFORMS (ITEMS)	–	–	139	120 000	...	1 525	...	–
14. OTHER ARCHIVES (ITEMS)	2	2	28	1 332	155	101	...	18
15. OTHER ARCHIVES (ITEMS)	–	–	50	–	...	–	...	–
ARCHIVES UNDER FINDING–AID CONTROL								
16. CONVENTIONAL ARCHIVES (METRES)	...	2	120	8 158	...	141	500	274
17. OTHER ARCHIVES (ITEMS)	–	–	1 150	14 460	38 076	4 269	5	–
REFERENCE SERVICE								
18. NUMBER OF VISITORS	4 075	190	1 238	2 333	...	6 547	1 619	4 832
19. NUMBER OF VISITS TO SEARCH ROOM(S)	20 732	360	3 994	10 000	...	683	1 200	262
20. NUMBER OF STORAGE UNITS CONSULTED	...	1 454	8 148	...	95 520	108	...	910 750
21. NUMBER OF INQUIRIES	9 962	100	105	...	132 121	36	...	13 244
EQUIPMENT								
22. TOTAL SHELVING CAPACITY (METRES)	...	...	6 000	...	382 285	9 392	5 287	...
23. OF WHICH: OCCUPIED SHELVING	6 000	...	3 700	...	225 470	9 392	4 123	...
PERSONNEL								
24. NUMBER OF PERMANENT STAFF	58	19	14	340	2 995	58	253	28
25. OF WHICH: PROFESSIONAL	16	3	1	152	351	30	86	7
26. TECHNICAL AND OTHER	42	16	13	188	2 644	28	167	21
27. CURRENT EXPENDITURE (000)	...	260	359	123 000	84 076	8 040 000	2 001 429	...

ASIA

TYPE OF DATA (UNITS OF MEASUREMENT) CATEGORIE DE DONNEES (UNITES DE MESURE) CATEGORIA DE DATOS (UNIDADES DE MEDIDA)	COLOMBIA (1981) NATIONAL	PERU (1982) NATIONAL	BRUNEI DARUSSALAM (1984) NATIONAL	CYPRUS (1982) NATIONAL	HONG KONG‡ (1982) NATIONAL	INDIA‡ (1982) NATIONAL	INDONESIA (1984) NATIONAL	INDONESIA (1984) REGIONAL
1. NUMBER OF INSTITUTIONS	1	1	1	1	1	1	1	1
HOLDINGS								
2. CONVENTIONAL ARCHIVES (METRES)	3 800	16 276	1 728	1 180	6 155	28 700	20 000	428
3. OF WHICH: CONTEMPORARY RECORDS	250	6 853	–	926	...	11 900	5 500	425
4. CARTOGRAPHIC ARCHIVES (ITEMS)	5 000	151	59	332	1 386	45 000	3 500	–
5. AUDIOVISUAL ARCHIVES (ITEMS)	–	–	3 197	...	2 009	–	1 066 990	–
6. MICROFORMS (ITEMS)	2 600	304	1 987	–	4 424	3 168	8 000	–
7. OTHER ARCHIVES (METRES)	172	24	147	47	295	3 520	100	–
8. OTHER ARCHIVES (ITEMS)	–	–	194	30	1	29	–	–
ACCESSIONS								
9. CONVENTIONAL ARCHIVES (METRES)	–	295	109	191	265	160	169	–
10. OF WHICH: CONTEMPORARY RECORDS	–	295	–	191	265	5	169	–
11. CARTOGRAPHIC ARCHIVES (ITEMS)	–	–	60	–	278	–	–	–
12. AUDIOVISUAL ARCHIVES (ITEMS)	–	–	270	–	200	–	11 278	–
13. MICROFORMS (ITEMS)	597	50	59	–	3 336	395	...	...
14. OTHER ARCHIVES (ITEMS)	–	24	5	...	9	*1 462	...	...
15. OTHER ARCHIVES (ITEMS)	1	–	13	–	–	–	...	...
ARCHIVES UNDER FINDING–AID CONTROL								
16. CONVENTIONAL ARCHIVES (METRES)	30	2 570	109	...	6 155	98	...	...
17. OTHER ARCHIVES (ITEMS)	–	129	4 859	–	7 819	*10 000	...	...
REFERENCE SERVICE								
18. NUMBER OF VISITORS	296	3 761	77	...	...	1 255	230	454
19. NUMBER OF VISITS TO SEARCH ROOM(S)	1 733	...	...	...	...	10 800	200	100
20. NUMBER OF STORAGE UNITS CONSULTED	4 124	...	...	...	...	46 436	...	...
21. NUMBER OF INQUIRIES	182	188	...	...	...	95	50	...
EQUIPMENT								
22. TOTAL SHELVING CAPACITY (METRES)	...	2 177	2 829	2 000	8 625	30 782	...	...
23. OF WHICH: OCCUPIED SHELVING	...	2 045	...	1 227	...	...	20 830	...
PERSONNEL								
24. NUMBER OF PERMANENT STAFF	25	176	7	4	41	*445	253	24
25. OF WHICH: PROFESSIONAL	10	56	1	–	5	*127	20	7
26. TECHNICAL AND OTHER	15	120	6	4	36	*318	233	17
27. CURRENT EXPENDITURE (000)	8 000	506	133	25	2 676	812	...	...

EUROPE

TYPE OF DATA (UNITS OF MEASUREMENT) CATEGORIE DE DONNEES (UNITES DE MESURE)	ISRAEL (1982)	JAPAN (1982)	KOREA, REP. OF (1982)	LEBANON (1982)	MALAYSIA (1982)	SRI LANKA‡ (1982)	THAILAND‡ (1984)	ANDORRA (1982)
CATEGORIA DE DATOS (UNIDADES DE MEDIDA)	NATIONAL	NATIONAL	NATIONAL	NATIONAL	NATIONAL	NATIONAL	NATIONAL	
1. NUMBER OF INSTITUTIONS	1		1	1	1	1	1	1
HOLDINGS								
2. CONVENTIONAL ARCHIVES (METRES)	25 000	*14 372	8 731	4 138	11 826	10 000	4 176	4
3. OF WHICH: CONTEMPORARY RECORDS	24 800	...	8 726	2 000	11 222	6 000	1 525	4
4. CARTOGRAPHIC ARCHIVES (ITEMS)	*5 000	...	1 548 953	–	6 852	1 560	6 500	227
5. AUDIOVISUAL ARCHIVES (ITEMS)	*32 450	*200 256	64 555	4 319	54 143	104	223 078	1 963
6. MICROFORMS (ITEMS)	*2 000	3 281	93 156	28 877	6 439	411	1 118	12 542
7. OTHER ARCHIVES (METRES)	502	*14 232	3 115	1 842	1 048	6 435	105	3
8. OTHER ARCHIVES (ITEMS)	1 830	–	2 531	24 739	1 493	1 988	–	72
ACCESSIONS								
9. CONVENTIONAL ARCHIVES (METRES)	1 500	*547	2 652	2 022	535	307	440	–
10. OF WHICH: CONTEMPORARY RECORDS	1 500	*545	2 652	2 022	431	307	205	–
11. CARTOGRAPHIC ARCHIVES (ITEMS)	–	–	...	–	117	–	2 500	*150
12. AUDIOVISUAL ARCHIVES (ITEMS)	–	–	5 273	4 319	1 569	–	13 009	*300
13. MICROFORMS (ITEMS)	–	–	10 500	11 702	447	28	750	268
14. OTHER ARCHIVES (ITEMS)	8	*66	450	690	357	435	2	1
15. OTHER ARCHIVES (ITEMS)	–	–	110	7 502	276	–	–	*23
ARCHIVES UNDER FINDING-AID CONTROL								
16. CONVENTIONAL ARCHIVES (METRES)	...	35	786	2	1 574	118	125	–
17. OTHER ARCHIVES (ITEMS)	–	–	5 437	13	5 193	28	11 677	*588
REFERENCE SERVICE								
18. NUMBER OF VISITORS	177	5 495	14 215	60	1 020	3 863	750	28
19. NUMBER OF VISITS TO SEARCH ROOM(S)	1 024	...	14 215	450	1 846	3 887	650	57
20. NUMBER OF STORAGE UNITS CONSULTED	6 172	100 864	374 883	800	8 554	9 142	9	1 069
21. NUMBER OF INQUIRIES	950	558	1 732	250	1 400	4 544	52	1 069
EQUIPMENT								
22. TOTAL SHELVING CAPACITY (METRES)	28 000	40 000	...	6 000	37 193	15 931	13 000	...
23. OF WHICH: OCCUPIED SHELVING	25 600	28 604	...	4 358	25 455	15 000	5 800	...
PERSONNEL								
24. NUMBER OF PERMANENT STAFF	25	44	122	21	314	127	50	3
25. OF WHICH: PROFESSIONAL	17	8	11	5	61	12	22	1
26. TECHNICAL AND OTHER	8	36	111	16	253	115	28	2
27. CURRENT EXPENDITURE (000)	13 700	307 040	880 891	...	4 428	10 088	2 344	1 438

TYPE OF DATA (UNITS OF MEASUREMENT) CATEGORIE DE DONNEES (UNITES DE MESURE)	AUSTRIA‡ (1983)	BELGIUM‡ (1982)		DENMARK (1982)		FINLAND‡ (1982)	
CATEGORIA DE DATOS (UNIDADES DE MEDIDA)	NATIONAL	NATIONAL	REGIONAL	NATIONAL	REGIONAL	NATIONAL	REGIONAL
1. NUMBER OF INSTITUTIONS	1	1	14	1	5	1	8
HOLDINGS							
2. CONVENTIONAL ARCHIVES (METRES)	102 000	45 000	115 000	100 000	118 535	34 206	40 973
3. OF WHICH: CONTEMPORARY RECORDS	42 000	20 000	45 000	...	...	23 736	25 962
4. CARTOGRAPHIC ARCHIVES (ITEMS)	365 000	166 850	9 600	...	...	103 235	655 846
5. AUDIOVISUAL ARCHIVES (ITEMS)	280 000	5 608	4 750	...	...	–	–
6. MICROFORMS (ITEMS)	5 000	54 165	1 200	...	...	38 317	28 484
7. OTHER ARCHIVES (METRES)	22 000	...	...	1 140	...	1 448	3 697
8. OTHER ARCHIVES (ITEMS)	36 000	36 385	3 500	1 600	...	./.	./.
ACCESSIONS							
9. CONVENTIONAL ARCHIVES (METRES)	760	...	...	320	2 943	764	853
10. OF WHICH: CONTEMPORARY RECORDS	*650	...	...	...	...	721	798
11. CARTOGRAPHIC ARCHIVES (ITEMS)	1 630	3	52	...	...	1 435	216 353
12. AUDIOVISUAL ARCHIVES (ITEMS)	–	341	–	...	...	–	–
13. MICROFORMS (ITEMS)	1 191	748	–	–	8	3 461	11 746
14. OTHER ARCHIVES (ITEMS)	60	...	...	10	...	24	180
15. OTHER ARCHIVES (ITEMS)	–	...	...	40	...	./.	./.
ARCHIVES UNDER FINDING-AID CONTROL							
16. CONVENTIONAL ARCHIVES (METRES)	194	...	...	...	...	8	94
17. OTHER ARCHIVES (ITEMS)	3 231	1 963	–	...	...	4 724	13 087
REFERENCE SERVICE							
18. NUMBER OF VISITORS	1 879	3 274	8 202	24 140	46 716	...	...
19. NUMBER OF VISITS TO SEARCH ROOM(S)	12 326	19 546	42 424	...	...	31 146	30 728
20. NUMBER OF STORAGE UNITS CONSULTED	24 304	91 791	275 203	93 317	238 603	37 198	48 657
21. NUMBER OF INQUIRIES	7 203	2 205	4 982	13 519	2 083	1 313	8 053
EQUIPMENT							
22. TOTAL SHELVING CAPACITY (METRES)	*105 000	...	...	140 000	156 910	52 000	52 550
23. OF WHICH: OCCUPIED SHELVING	...	...	...	...	...	37 780	43 190
PERSONNEL							
24. NUMBER OF PERMANENT STAFF	134	68	51	81	65	77	78
25. OF WHICH: PROFESSIONAL	43	29	37	28	21	25	20
26. TECHNICAL AND OTHER	91	39	14	53	44	52	58
27. CURRENT EXPENDITURE (000)	36 685	85 915	79 331	32 900	4 200	7 239	6 221

TYPE OF DATA (UNITS OF MEASUREMENT) CATEGORIE DE DONNEES (UNITES DE MESURE) CATEGORIA DE DATOS (UNIDADES DE MEDIDA)	FRANCE‡ (1982)		GIBRALTAR (1983)	HUNGARY‡ (1983)		IRELAND‡ (1982)	
	NATIONAL	REGIONAL	NATIONAL	REGIONAL	NATIONAL	REGIONAL	NATIONAL
1. NUMBER OF INSTITUTIONS	1	100	1	2	20	2	1
HOLDINGS							
2. CONVENTIONAL ARCHIVES (METRES)	150 000	1 283 735	550	45 959	129 994	22 400	100
3. OF WHICH: CONTEMPORARY RECORDS	...	...	*25	...	...	2 400	10
4. CARTOGRAPHIC ARCHIVES (ITEMS)	...	...	–	26 500	108 250	14 500	–
5. AUDIOVISUAL ARCHIVES (ITEMS)	...	...	–	740 965	70 619	60 000	–
6. MICROFORMS (ITEMS)	673 079	...	–	40222 012	550 448	2 400	4
7. OTHER ARCHIVES (METRES)	...	...	1	1 928	7 000	300	–
8. OTHER ARCHIVES (ITEMS)	...	...	–	26 700	7 450	–	–
ACCESSIONS							
9. CONVENTIONAL ARCHIVES (METRES)	13 907	50 316	–	1 419	3 977	412	15
10. OF WHICH: CONTEMPORARY RECORDS	12 750	34 000	–	5	34	247	15
11. CARTOGRAPHIC ARCHIVES (ITEMS)	...	...	–	–	–	100	–
12. AUDIOVISUAL ARCHIVES (ITEMS)	...	...	–	–	–	–	–
13. MICROFORMS (ITEMS)	111 161	80 000	–	512 245	343 498	45	3
14. OTHER ARCHIVES (ITEMS)	170	780	–	30	90	10	–
15. OTHER ARCHIVES (ITEMS)	85	...	–	–	4	–	–
ARCHIVES UNDER FINDING-AID CONTROL							
16. CONVENTIONAL ARCHIVES (METRES)	80	233	–	2 605	5 393	455	*20
17. OTHER ARCHIVES (ITEMS)	3	20	–	5 028	8 739	145	–
REFERENCE SERVICE							
18. NUMBER OF VISITORS	12 755	91 841	*30	1 217	2 668	9 600	15
19. NUMBER OF VISITS TO SEARCH ROOM(S)	...	...	*80	9 596	13 935	6 232	17
20. NUMBER OF STORAGE UNITS CONSULTED	232 830	1 442 906	...	...	...	25 558	...
21. NUMBER OF INQUIRIES	10 000	...	60	4 346	10 661	7 804	...
EQUIPMENT							
22. TOTAL SHELVING CAPACITY (METRES)	...	1 592 734	...	...	137 150	22 430	500
23. OF WHICH: OCCUPIED SHELVING	...	1 283 735	551	...	129 047	...	150
PERSONNEL							
24. NUMBER OF PERMANENT STAFF	368	627	1	191	428	39	1
25. OF WHICH: PROFESSIONAL	110	272	1	140	315	13	1
26. TECHNICAL AND OTHER	258	355	–	51	113	26	–
27. CURRENT EXPENDITURE (000)	83 600	./.	7	29 997	59 000	323	14

TYPE OF DATA (UNITS OF MEASUREMENT) CATEGORIE DE DONNEES (UNITES DE MESURE) CATEGORIA DE DATOS (UNIDADES DE MEDIDA)	ITALY‡ (1982)		NETHERLANDS (1980)		NORWAY‡ (1982)		POLAND‡ (1982)	
	NATIONAL	REGIONAL	NATIONAL	REGIONAL	NATIONAL	REGIONAL	NATIONAL	REGIONAL
1. NUMBER OF INSTITUTIONS	1	94	1	7	1	6	1	1
HOLDINGS								
2. CONVENTIONAL ARCHIVES (METRES)	52 000	992 986	133 200	4 300	37 300	33 000	14 388	155 987
3. OF WHICH: CONTEMPORARY RECORDS	...	...	*66 633	*2 200	...	...	...	...
4. CARTOGRAPHIC ARCHIVES (ITEMS)	...	...	237 400	8 300	*41 000	*500	33 741	279 095
5. AUDIOVISUAL ARCHIVES (ITEMS)	...	...	*60 394	3 500	–	*150 000	...	...
6. MICROFORMS (ITEMS)	...	...	294 402	6 000	*10 500	...	...	...
7. OTHER ARCHIVES (METRES)	72 811	695 634	*5 400	400	1 795	1 859	...	...
8. OTHER ARCHIVES (ITEMS)	...	...	*149 658	*400	*90 820	–	2 000	2 671
ACCESSIONS								
9. CONVENTIONAL ARCHIVES (METRES)	...	...	*8 200	...	1 303	2 225	137	5 333
10. OF WHICH: CONTEMPORARY RECORDS	...	...	...	...	...	...	...	...
11. CARTOGRAPHIC ARCHIVES (ITEMS)	...	...	*12 000	...	9 021	–	...	...
12. AUDIOVISUAL ARCHIVES (ITEMS)	...	...	...	...	–	5 173	...	...
13. MICROFORMS (ITEMS)	...	...	–	...	41	50	...	...
14. OTHER ARCHIVES (ITEMS)	...	...	*4 500	...	37	50	...	...
15. OTHER ARCHIVES (ITEMS)	...	...	*650	...	–	–	...	...
ARCHIVES UNDER FINDING-AID CONTROL								
16. CONVENTIONAL ARCHIVES (METRES)	3 749	349 762	2 905	60	*900	...	332	1 717
17. OTHER ARCHIVES (ITEMS)	...	...	–	...	1 497	...	1 000	9 071
REFERENCE SERVICE								
18. NUMBER OF VISITORS	1 017	24 132	20 652	200	...	...	820	4 921
19. NUMBER OF VISITS TO SEARCH ROOM(S)	4 176	150 407	77 022	300	12 659	19 255	8 434	26 866
20. NUMBER OF STORAGE UNITS CONSULTED	23 193	366 973	546 300	*400	21 885	98 041	27 608	178 398
21. NUMBER OF INQUIRIES	1 023	6 466	*32 100	*400	4 930	21 212	1 452	22 196
EQUIPMENT								
22. TOTAL SHELVING CAPACITY (METRES)	55 000	1 005 033	224 647	8 223	78 000	39 365	...	...
23. OF WHICH: OCCUPIED SHELVING	52 000	992 986	136 436	5 342	...	33 171	...	...
PERSONNEL								
24. NUMBER OF PERMANENT STAFF	151	2 344	304	10	51	80	980	./.
25. OF WHICH: PROFESSIONAL	61	818	128	9	27	30	679	./.
26. TECHNICAL AND OTHER	90	1 526	176	1	24	50	301	./.
27. CURRENT EXPENDITURE (000)	...	13347 000	...	...	10 448	14 147	196 229	./.

TYPE OF DATA (UNITS OF MEASUREMENT) / CATEGORIE DE DONNEES (UNITES DE MESURE) / CATEGORIA DE DATOS (UNIDADES DE MEDIDA)	SPAIN‡ (1982)		SWEDEN‡ (1982)	SWITZERLAND (1982)	UNITED KINGDOM‡ (1983)	YUGOSLAVIA (1981)	OCEANIA: AUSTRALIA (1982)	OCEANIA: FRENCH POLYNESIA‡ (1982)
	NATIONAL	REGIONAL	NATIONAL	NATIONAL	NATIONAL	NATIONAL	NATIONAL	NATIONAL
1. NUMBER OF INSTITUTIONS	1	1	3	1	2	1	1	1
HOLDINGS								
2. CONVENTIONAL ARCHIVES (METRES)	88 216	296 889	*147 000	19 000	183 633	191 610	334 900	1 110
3. OF WHICH: CONTEMPORARY RECORDS	...	...	*25 000	16 000	*93 570	...	334 800	1 006
4. CARTOGRAPHIC ARCHIVES (ITEMS)	...	...	*495 000	10 000	162 400	...	42 750	1 260
5. AUDIOVISUAL ARCHIVES (ITEMS)	639	...	*455 000	20 000	...	...	7 309 304	1 260
6. MICROFORMS (ITEMS)	124	13 603	*242 100	300	*11 200	...	106 900	6 150
7. OTHER ARCHIVES (METRES)	56 034	...	*9 600	1 005	5 100	...	7 090	100
8. OTHER ARCHIVES (ITEMS)	21 451	88 143	*51 270	10 300	...	...	344 426	...
ACCESSIONS								
9. CONVENTIONAL ARCHIVES (METRES)	1 868	77 202	2 449	900	2 228	7 280	11 020	66
10. OF WHICH: CONTEMPORARY RECORDS	...	...	1 100	900	1 922	...	11 020	62
11. CARTOGRAPHIC ARCHIVES (ITEMS)	...	...	69 500	–	4 838	...	–	...
12. AUDIOVISUAL ARCHIVES (ITEMS)	...	...	*20 750	100	...	...	7 678	970
13. MICROFORMS (ITEMS)	...	5 357	437	20	200	...	27 387	...
14. OTHER ARCHIVES (ITEMS)	4 096	4 808	*61	51	120	...	...	25
15. OTHER ARCHIVES (ITEMS)	...	...	*522	120	...	...	...	...
ARCHIVES UNDER FINDING–AID CONTROL								
16. CONVENTIONAL ARCHIVES (METRES)	2 694	31 867	*5 500	1 000	...	8 187	300 227	20
17. OTHER ARCHIVES (ITEMS)	1 542	1 828	*13 684	–	...	...	7 803 130	1 170
REFERENCE SERVICE								
18. NUMBER OF VISITORS	30 746	12 895	*3 200	500	...	13 797	...	500
19. NUMBER OF VISITS TO SEARCH ROOM(S)	...	...	*23 192	3 200	144 555	29 178	5 082	4 000
20. NUMBER OF STORAGE UNITS CONSULTED	...	...	*94 518	10 000	156 030	3 132	30 333	15 000
21. NUMBER OF INQUIRIES	4 641	3 587	*6 302	500	51 350	...	...	3 500
EQUIPMENT								
22. TOTAL SHELVING CAPACITY (METRES)	93 115	359 876	178 000	20 000	188 200	...	392 597	...
23. OF WHICH: OCCUPIED SHELVING		...	147 000	...	164 322	...	339 821	...
PERSONNEL								
24. NUMBER OF PERMANENT STAFF	161	506	179	17	544	...	...	6
25. OF WHICH: PROFESSIONAL	34	103	91	9	88	...	...	1
26. TECHNICAL AND OTHER	127	403	88	8	456	...	...	5
27. CURRENT EXPENDITURE (000)	11 566	29 922	20 238	1 290	10 585	...	...	620

TYPE OF DATA (UNITS OF MEASUREMENT) / CATEGORIE DE DONNEES (UNITES DE MESURE) / CATEGORIA DE DATOS (UNIDADES DE MEDIDA)	GUAM (1982)	KIRIBATI‡ (1983)	NEW ZEALAND‡ (1981)	PAPUA NEW GUINEA (1982)
	NATIONAL	NATIONAL	NATIONAL	NATIONAL
1. NUMBER OF INSTITUTIONS	1	1	1	1
HOLDINGS				
2. CONVENTIONAL ARCHIVES (METRES)	22	540	*17 000	5 790
3. OF WHICH: CONTEMPORARY RECORDS	18	530	*13 500	5 787
4. CARTOGRAPHIC ARCHIVES (ITEMS)	–	100	*400 000	1 062
5. AUDIOVISUAL ARCHIVES (ITEMS)	–	530	*15 000	1 931
6. MICROFORMS (ITEMS)	–	2 800	*4 000	108
7. OTHER ARCHIVES (METRES)	–	30	*250	50
8. OTHER ARCHIVES (ITEMS)	–	...	*500	–
ACCESSIONS				
9. CONVENTIONAL ARCHIVES (METRES)	11	10	1 065	...
10. OF WHICH: CONTEMPORARY RECORDS	11	10	*1 000	...
11. CARTOGRAPHIC ARCHIVES (ITEMS)	–	5	3 064	...
12. AUDIOVISUAL ARCHIVES (ITEMS)	–	76	...	...
13. MICROFORMS (ITEMS)	–	24	17	...
14. OTHER ARCHIVES (ITEMS)	–	2	...	...
15. OTHER ARCHIVES (ITEMS)	–	...	...	...
ARCHIVES UNDER FINDING–AID CONTROL				
16. CONVENTIONAL ARCHIVES (METRES)	9	510	*800	...
17. OTHER ARCHIVES (ITEMS)	–	900	*52 500	...
REFERENCE SERVICE				
18. NUMBER OF VISITORS	–	100	...	92
19. NUMBER OF VISITS TO SEARCH ROOM(S)	–	300	2 490	114
20. NUMBER OF STORAGE UNITS CONSULTED	–	3 000	8 804	...
21. NUMBER OF INQUIRIES	–	200	1 341	152
EQUIPMENT				
22. TOTAL SHELVING CAPACITY (METRES)	160	916	27 200	...
23. OF WHICH: OCCUPIED SHELVING	138	590	23 500	5 787
PERSONNEL				
24. NUMBER OF PERMANENT STAFF	1	2	20	19
25. OF WHICH: PROFESSIONAL	1	1	13	2
26. TECHNICAL AND OTHER	–	1	7	17
27. CURRENT EXPENDITURE (000)	36	17	450	108

AFRICA:

Burundi:

E--> The figure in line 27 refers only to labour costs.

FR-> Le chiffre de la ligne 27 se réfère seulement aux dépenses de personnel.

ESP> La cifra de la línea 27 se refiere solamente a los gastos de personal.

Chad:

E--> The figure in line 27 refers only to labour costs.

FR-> Le chiffre de la ligne 27 se réfère seulement aux dépenses de personnel.

ESP> La cifra de la línea 27 se refiere solamente a los gastos de personal.

Rwanda:

E--> The figure in line 27 refers only to labour costs.

FR-> Le chiffre de la ligne 27 se réfère seulement aux dépenses de personnel.

ESP> La cifra de la línea 27 se refiere solamente a los gastos de personal.

Seychelles:

E--> The figure in line 21 refers only to the number of recorded inquiries answered in writing. The data in line 27 also include current expenditure for the National Museum.

FR-> Le chiffre de la ligne 21 se réfère seulement aux demandes de renseignements fournies par correspondance. Les données de la ligne 27 comprennent aussi les dépenses courantes pour le Musée National.

ESP> La cifra de la línea 21 se refiere solamente a las solicitudes de información suministradas por correspondencia. Los datos de la línea 27 incluyen igualmente los gastos corrientes por el museo nacional.

Zimbabwe:

E--> The figure in line 15 refers only to drawings and prints. The data in line 20 do not include library material.

FR-> Le chiffre de la ligne 15 se réfère seulement aux dessins et estampes. Les données de la ligne 20 ne comprennent pas le matériel de bibliothèque.

ESP> La cifra de la línea 15 se refiere solamente a los dibujos y estampas. Los datos de la línea 20 no incluyen el material dé biblioteca.

AMERICA, NORTH:

Barbados:

E--> The figure in line 21 refers only to the number of recorded inquiries answered in writing.

FR-> Le chiffre de la ligne 21 se réfère seulement aux demandes de renseignements fournies par correspondance.

ESP> La cifra de la línea 21 se refiere solamente a las solicitudes de información suministradas por correspondencia.

Mexico:

E--> The figure in line 15 refers only to drawings and prints.

FR-> Le chiffre de la ligne 15 se réfère seulement aux dessins et estampes.

ESP> La cifra de la línea 15 se refiere solamente a los dibujos y estampas.

United States:

E--> Data refer only to the National Archives in Washington D.C.

FR-> Les données se réfèrent seulement aux archives nationales à Washington D.C.

ESP> Los datos se refieren solamente a los archivos nacionales en Washington D.C.

AMERICA, SOUTH:

Peru:

E--> Lines 2, 16, 24, 25, 26 refer to three institutions and lines 3, 9, 10 and 18 to two institutions.

E--> Les lignes 2, 16, 24, 25, 26 se réfèrent à trois institutions et les lignes 3, 9, 10 et 18 à deux institutions.

E--> Las líneas 2, 16, 24, 25, 26 se refieren a tres instituciones y las líneas 3, 9, 10 y 18 a dos instituciones.

ASIA:

Hong Kong:

E--> The figures in lines 8 and 17 do not include drawings and prints.

FR-> Les chiffres des lignes 8 et 17 ne comprennent pas les dessins et estampes.

ESP> Las cifras de las líneas 8 y 17 no incluyen los dibujos y estampas.

India:

E--> The figure in line 8 does not include drawings and prints.

FR-> Le chiffre de la ligne 8 ne comprend pas les dessins et estampes.

ESP> La cifra de la línea 8 no incluye los dibujos y estampas.

Sri Lanka:

E--> The figure in line 27 refers only to labour costs.

FR-> Le chiffre de la ligne 27 se réfère seulement aux dépenses de personnel.

ESP> La cifra de la línea 27 se refiere solamente a los gastos de personal.

Thailand:

E--> The figure in line 27 refers only to labour costs.

FR-> Le chiffre de la ligne 27 se réfère seulement aux dépenses de personnel.

Thailand: (Cont):

ESP> La cifra de la línea 27 se refiere solamente a los gastos de personal.

EUROPE:

Austria:

E--> The figure in line 8 does not include drawings and prints.

FR-> Le chiffre de la ligne 8 ne comprend pas les dessins et estampes.

ESP> La cifra de la línea 8 no incluye los dibujos y estampas.

Belgium:

E--> The figure in line 8 does not include drawings and prints; that in line 21 refers only to the number of recorded inquiries answered in writing.

FR-> Le chiffre de la ligne 8 ne comprend pas les dessins et estampes; celui de la ligne 21 se réfère seulement aux demandes de renseignements fournies par correspondance.

ESP> La cifra de la línea 8 no incluye los dibujos y estampas; la de la línea 21 se refiere solamente a las solicitudes de información suministradas por correspondencia.

Finland:

E--> Drawings and prints are included with cartographic archives (lines 4 and 11) rather than in lines 8 and 15.

FR-> Les dessins et estampes sont comptés avec les archives cartographiques (lignes 4 et 11) plutôt que dans les lignes 8 et 15.

ESP> Los dibujos y estampas están incluídos con los documentos cartográficos (líneas 4 y 11) y no en las líneas 8 y 15.

France:

E--> The figure in line 27 refers only to labour costs.

FR-> Le chiffre de la ligne 27 se réfère seulement aux dépenses de personnel.

ESP> La cifra de la línea 27 se refiere solamente a los gastos de personal.

Hungary:

E--> The figure in line 8 does not include drawings and prints.

FR-> Le chiffre de la ligne 8 ne comprend pas les dessins et estampes.

ESP> La cifra de la línea 8 no incluye los dibujos y estampas.

Ireland:

E--> Data in lines 3, 4, 11, 17, 18, 19 and 20 refer to one institution only. The figure in line 27 refers only to labour costs.

FR-> Les données des lignes 3, 4, 11, 17, 18, 19 et 20 ne se réfèrent qu'à une institution. Le chiffre de la ligne 27 se réfère seulement aux dépenses de personnel.

ESP> Los datos de las líneas 3, 4, 11, 17, 18, 19 y 20 se refieren a una institución solamente. La cifra de la línea 27 se refiere solamente a los gastos de personal.

Italy:

E--> Line 7 refers to library material counted in volumes, line 16 refers to the number of items, line 21 to the number of recorded inquiries answered in writing only and line 27 does not include labour costs.

FR-> La ligne 7 se réfère au matériel de bibliothèque compté en volumes, la ligne 16 se réfère au nombre d'articles, la ligne 21 seulement aux demandes de renseignements fournies par correspondance et la ligne 27 ne comprend pas les dépenses de personnel.

ESP> La línea 7 se refiere al material de biblioteca calculado en volumenes, la línea 16 se refiere al número de artículos, la línea 21 solamente a las solicitudes de información suministradas por correspondencia y la línea 27 no incluye los gastos de personal.

Norway:

E--> The figure in line 19 also includes the number of visits to the State Archives in Oslo.

FR-> Le chiffre de la ligne 19 comprend aussi le nombre de visites au centre d'archives d'Etat à Oslo.

ESP> La cifra de la línea 19 también incluye el número de visitas al archivo del Estado en Oslo.

Poland:

E--> The figure in line 8 does not include tapes, drawings and prints; the figure in column 1, line 17, refers only to cartographic archives while that in column 2 refers also to audiovisual archives, seals and other three-dimensional objects.

FR-> Le chiffre de la ligne 8 ne comprend pas les cassettes, les dessins et estampes; le chiffre de la ligne 17, colonne 1, se réfère seulement aux archives cartographiques tandis que celui de la colonne 2 se réfère aussi aux archives audiovisuelles et aux sceaux et autres objets tridimensionnels.

ESP> La cifra de la línea 8 no incluye las cintas, los dibujos y estampas; la cifra de la línea 17, columna 1, se refiere solamente a los documentos cartográficos mientras que la de la columna 2 se refiere igualmente a los documentos audiovisuales así como a los sellos y otros objetos tridimensionales.

Spain:

E--> The figure in line 21 refers only to the number of recorded inquiries answered in writing.

FR-> Le chiffre de la ligne 21 se réfère seulement aux demandes de renseignements fournies par correspondance.

ESP> La cifra de la línea 21 se refiere solamente a las solicitudes de información suministradas por correspondencia.

Sweden:
E--> Data on seals and other three-dimensional objects (lines 8 and 15), drawings and prints (line 17) and contemporary records (line 10) refer to one institution only. The figure in line 21 refers only to labour costs.
FR-> Les données relatives aux sceaux et autres objets tridimensionnels (lignes 8 et 15), aux dessins et estampes (ligne 17) et aux documents contemporains (ligne 10) ne se réfèrent qu'à une institution. Le chiffre de la ligne 21 se réfère seulement aux dépenses de personnel.
ESP> Los datos relativos a los sellos y otros objetos tridimensionales (líneas 8 y 15), a los dibujos y estampas (línea 17) y a los documentos contemporáneos (líneas 10) no se refieren que a una institución. La cifra de la línea 21 se refiere solamente a los gastos de personal.
United Kingdom:
E--> Data in lines 7 and 14 refer to library material only.
FR-> Les données des lignes 7 et 14 se réfèrent au matériel de bibliothèque seulement.
ESP> Los datos de las líneas 7 y 14 se refieren solamente al material de biblioteca.
OCEANIA:
French Polynesia:
E--> The figure in line 5 refers only to photographs. Data in lines 7 and
French Polynesia: (Cont):
14 do not include punched cards.
FR-> Le chiffre de la ligne 5 se réfère seulement à des photographies. Les données des lignes 7 et 14 ne comprennent pas les cartes perforées.
ESP> La cifra de la línea 5 se refiere solamente a unas fotografías. Los datos de las líneas 7 y 14 no incluyen las tarjetas perforadas.
Kiribati:
E--> Data in lines 7 and 14 do not include punched cards.
FR-> Les données des lignes 7 et 14 ne comprennent pas les cartes perforées.
ESP> Los datos de las líneas 7 y 14 no incluyen las tarjetas perforadas.
New Zealand:
E--> The figure in line 21 refers only to the number of recorded inquiries answered in writing.
FR-> Le chiffre de la ligne 21 se réfère seulement aux demandes de renseignements fournies par correspondance.
ESP> La cifra de la línea 21 se refiere solamente a las solicitudes de información suministradas por correspondencia.

9 Film and cinema

Films et cinémas

Películas y cines

The statistics in this chapter relate to the production and importation of long films intended for commercial exhibition in cinemas, and to the number, seating capacity and annual attendance of such cinemas. The minimum length for films classified as *long films* varies considerably from country to country, ranging from less than 1,000 metres in some countries to more than 3,000 metres in others; a number of countries, however, have adopted standards close to 2,000 metres. Wherever possible, the minimum length of the films covered by the statistics is given. Where such information is lacking, data refer, without exact definition, to long or *feature* films.

The criteria used to determine that a film has been *produced* or *imported* during the year of reference are shown in the texts of the tables on the production and importation of films.

Table 9.1

This table gives, for 1965, 1970, 1975, 1980 and 1983, the number of long films produced for commercial exhibition in cinemas. Films produced solely for television broadcasting are not included. Figures on international co-productions are usually included in the national figures of each of the countries concerned, but they are also shown separately, where available. The table shows for each country the minimum length for films considered as long films (feature films). The criterion used for characterizing films as *produced* during the year of reference is one of the following:

P: Production completed in the year stated;
C: Approved by censor for public showing in the year stated;
S: Commercially shown for the first time in the year stated;
O: Other criteria.

Table 9.2

The data in this table refer, for the two latest available years of the period 1978 to 1983, to the number of long films imported for commercial exhibition in cinemas. The importation data are classified according to the principal countries of origin. Films imported solely for television broadcasting are not included in this table. The criterion used for characterizing films as *imported* during the year of reference is one of the following:

I: Imported in the year stated;
C: Approved by censor for public showing in the year stated;
S: Commercially shown for the first time in the year stated;
O: Other criteria.

Table 9.3

The statistics shown in this table refer to fixed cinemas and mobile units regularly used for commercial exhibition of long films of 16 mm and over.

The term *fixed cinema* used in this table refers to establishments possessing their own equipment and includes indoor cinemas (those with a permanent fixed roof over most of the seating accommodation), outdoor cinemas and drive-ins (establishments designed to enable the audience to watch a film while seated in their automobile). *Mobile units* are defined as projection units equipped and used to serve more than one site.

The capacity for fixed cinemas refers to the number of seats in the case of cinema halls and to the number of automobiles multiplied by a factor of 4 in the case of drive-ins.

Cinema attendance is calculated from the number of tickets sold during a given year and, wherever possible, shown separately for the three types of cinema establishments (cinema halls, drive-ins and mobile units).

As a rule, figures refer only to commercial establishments but in the case of mobile units, it is possible that the figures for some countries may also include non-commercial units. Gross receipts are given in national currency.

Countries for which data refer to years prior to 1978 have been omitted from this table. For these figures the reader should consult previous editions of the *Yearbook*.

Les statistiques de ce chapitre se rapportent à la production et à l'importation de films de long métrage destinés à la projection cinématographique commerciale, ainsi qu'au nombre de cinémas, au nombre de sièges et à la fréquentation annuelle des cinémas. En ce qui concerne la longueur minimale des films considérés comme des *longs métrages*, les définitions diffèrent considérablement selon les pays: elles peuvent varier entre moins de 1 000 à plus de 3 000 mètres; cependant, beaucoup de pays ont adopté un chiffre voisin de 2 000 mètres. Chaque fois que cela était possible, on a signalé la longueur minimale des films sur lesquels portent les statistiques. En l'absence de telles informations, les chiffres donnés correspondent grosso modo aux films de long métrage ou aux *films vedettes* des programmes.

Les divers critères utilisés pour considérer qu'un film a été *produit* ou *importé* au cours de l'année de référence sont indiqués dans les textes des tableaux relatifs à la production et à l'importation de films.

Tableau 9.1

Ce tableau présente pour 1965, 1970, 1975, 1980 et 1983 le nombre de films de long métrage produits pour la projection cinématographique commerciale. Les films produits uniquement pour les besoins de la télévision sont exclus. Les données sur les coproductions internationales sont généralement comprises dans les données nationales de chaque pays concerné, mais elles sont aussi présentées séparément lorsque les chiffres sont disponibles. Le tableau donne pour chaque pays la longueur minimale des films considérés comme de long métrage (films vedettes). Les critères utilisés pour considérer qu'un film a été *produit* au cours de l'année de référence est un des suivants:

P: Production terminée dans l'année indiquée;

C: Approuvé par la censure pour sa projection en public dans l'année indiquée;
S: Mis en exploitation commerciale pour la première fois dans l'année indiquée;
O: Autres critères.

Tableau 9.2

Les données de ce tableau se réfèrent, pour les deux dernières années disponibles de la période 1978 à 1983, aux films de long métrage importés pour la projection commerciale dans les cinémas. Les données sur l'importation de films ont été classées d'après les principaux pays d'origine. Les films importés uniquement pour les besoins de la télévision sont exclus de ce tableau. Les critères utilisés pour considérer qu'un film a été *importé* au cours de l'année de référence est un des suivants:
I: Importation effective du film au cours de l'année indiquée;
C: Approuvé par la censure pour sa projection en public au cours de l'année indiquée;
S: Mis en exploitation commerciale pour la première fois au cours de l'année indiquée;
O: Autres critères.

Tableau 9.3

Les statistiques présentées dans ce tableau concernent les établissements fixes et les cinémas itinérants d'exploitation commerciale de films de long métrage de 16 mm. et plus.

Dans ce tableau, le terme *établissement fixe* désigne tout établissement doté de son propre équipement; il englobe les salles fermées (c'est-à-dire celles où un toit fixe recouvre la plupart des places), les cinémas de plein air et les cinémas pour automobilistes ou *drive-ins* (conçus pour permettre aux spectateurs d'assister à la projection sans quitter leur voiture). Les *cinémas itinérants* sont définis comme groupes mobiles de projection équipés de manière à pouvoir être utilisés dans des lieux différents.

La capacité des cinémas fixes se réfère au nombre de sièges dans les salles de cinéma et celle des cinémas pour automobilistes (*drive-ins*) au nombre d'automobiles multiplié par le facteur 4.

La fréquentation des cinémas est calculée sur la base du nombre de billets vendus au cours d'une année donnée et, chaque fois que cela était possible, présentée séparément pour chacun des trois types d'établissements cinématographiques (salles de cinéma, cinémas pour automobilistes et cinémas itinérants).

En général, les statistiques présentées ne concernent que les établissements commerciaux; toutefois, dans le cas des cinémas itinérants, il se peut que les données relatives à certains pays tiennent compte aussi des établissements non-commerciaux. Les recettes brutes sont indiquées en monnaie nationale.

Les pays dont les données se réfèrent aux années antérieures à 1978 ont été supprimés de ce tableau. Ces données peuvent être obtenues en consultant les précédentes éditions de l'*Annuaire*.

Las estadísticas de este capítulo se refieren a la producción y a la importación de películas de largo metraje destinadas a la proyección cinematográfica comercial, al igual que al número de cines, al número de asientos y a la frecuentación anual de los cines. En lo que se refiere a la longitud mínima de las películas consideradas como *largo metraje*, las definiciones difieren considerablemente según los países. Pueden variar de menos de 1 000 a más de 3 000 metros, pero son muchos los países que han adoptado una cifra próxima de 2 000 metros. Cada vez que ello es posible, se ha señalado la longitud mínima de las películas a que se refieren las estadísticas. A falta de esas informaciones, las cifras dadas corresponden, grosso modo, a las películas de largo metraje o a las *películas principales* de los programas.

Los diversos criterios utilizados para considerar que una película ha sido *producida* o *importada* durante el año de referencia, se indican en los textos de los cuadros relativos a la producción y a la importación de películas.

Cuadro 9.1

Este cuadro presenta para 1965, 1970, 1975, 1980 y 1983 el número de películas de largo metraje destinadas a la proyección cinematográfica comercial. Las películas producidas exclusivamente para las necesidades de la televisión quedan excluídas. Los datos sobre las coproducciones internacionales se incluyen generalmente en la producción de cada país interesado, pero también son presentados por separado cuando las cifras son disponibles. Este cuadro indica para cada país la longitud mínima de las películas consideradas de largo metraje (películas principales). El criterio utilizado para considerar que una película ha sido *producida* durante el año dé referencia, es uno de los siguientes:
P: Producción terminada en el año indicado;
C: Aprobada por la censura para su presentación al público en el año indicado;
S: Puesta en explotación comercial por primera vez en el año indicado;
O: Otros criterios.

Cuadro 9.2

Los datos de este cuadro se refieren, para los dos últimos años disponibles en el período 1978 a 1983, a las películas de largo metraje importadas y destinadas a la proyección cinematográfica comercial. Los datos sobre las importaciones han sido clasificados según los principales países de origen. Las películas importadas exclusivamente para las necesidades de la televisión quedan excluidas. El criterio utilizado para considerar que una película ha sido importada durante el año de referencia, es uno de los siguientes:
I: Película efectivamente importada en el año indicado;
C: Aprobada por la censura para su presentación al público en el año indicado;
S: Puesta en explotación comercial por primera vez en el año indicado;
O: Otros criterios.

Cuadro 9.3

Las estadísticas presentadas en este cuadro se refieren a los establecimientos fijos y grupos móviles de explotación comercial de películas de largo metraje de 16 mm. o mas.

El término *Establecimiento fijo* utilizado en este cuadro, designa todo establecimiento dotado de su propio equipo y se comprenden en ella las salas cerradas (es decir, aquellas en las que un techo fijo protege la mayor parte de los asientos), los cines al aire libre y los cines para automovilistas o 'drive-ins' (concebidos para que los espectadores puedan asistir a la proyección sin salir de su vehículo). Los *cines ambulantes* se definen como grupos móviles de proyección equipados de modo que puedan utilizarse en lugares diferentes.

La capacidad de los establecimientos fijos se refiere al número de asientos en el caso de los cines y la de los cines para automovilistas (*drive-ins*) al número de automóviles multiplicado por el factor 4.

La frecuentación de los cines se calcula tomando como base el número de billetes vendidos en el curso de un año dado y, cada vez que es posible, muestra por separado las tres tipos de establecimientos cinematográficos (cines, *drive-ins* y grupos móviles).

En general, las estadísticas que se presentan sólo se refieren a los establecimientos comerciales. No obstante, en el caso de los cines ambulantes, es posible que los datos relativos a ciertos países tengan también en cuenta establecimientos no comerciales. La recaudación total se indica en moneda nacional.

Los países cuyos datos se refieren a los años anteriores a 1978 se han omitido de este cuadro. Estas cifras pueden ser obtenidas consultando las precedentes ediciones del *Anuario*.

9.1 Long films: number of films produced

Films de long métrage: nombre de films produits

Películas de largo metraje: número de películas producidas

DEFINITION OF DATA:

P = PRODUCTION COMPLETED IN THE YEAR STATED

C = APPROVED BY CENSOR FOR PUBLIC SHOWING IN THE YEAR STATED

S = COMMERCIALLY SHOWN FOR THE FIRST TIME IN THE YEAR STATED

O = OTHER CRITERIA

LENGTH = MINIMUM LENGTH (IN METRES) WHICH CATEGORIZES THE FILM AS A 'LONG FILM'

NUMBER OF COUNTRIES AND TERRITORIES PRESENTED IN THIS TABLE: 70

CODE:

P = PRODUCTION TERMINEE DANS L'ANNEE INDIQUEE

C = FILMS APPROUVES PAR LA CENSURE POUR LEUR PROJECTION EN PUBLIC DANS L'ANNEE INDIQUEE

S = MISE EN EXPLOITATION COMMERCIALE POUR LA PREMIERE FOIS DANS L'ANNEE INDIQUEE

O = AUTRES CRITERES

LONGUEUR = LONGUEUR MINIMALE (EN METRES) DES FILMS CONSIDERES COMME DE 'LONG METRAGE'

NOMBRE DE PAYS ET DE TERRITOIRES PRESENTES DANS CE TABLEAU: 70

TIPO DE DATOS:

P = PRODUCCION TERMINADA EN EL AÑO INDICADO

C = PELICULAS APROBADAS POR LA CENSURA PARA SU PRESENTACION AL PUBLICO EN EL AÑO INDICADO

S = PUESTA EN EXPLOTACION COMERCIAL POR PRIMERA VEZ EN EL AÑO INDICADO

O = OTROS CRITERIOS

LONGITUD = LONGITUD MINIMA (EN METROS) DE LAS PELICULAS CONSIDERADAS DE 'LARGO METRAJE'

NUMERO DE PAISES Y DE TERRITORIOS PRESENTADOS EN ESTE CUADRO: 70

COUNTRY PAYS PAIS		LENGTH LONGUEUR LONGITUD	DEFINITION OF DATA CODE TIPO DE DATOS	NUMBER OF FILMS PRODUCED NOMBRE DE FILMS PRODUITS NUMERO DE PELICULAS PRODUCIDAS				
				1965	1970	1975	1980	1983
		(1)	(2)	(3)	(4)	(5)	(6)	(7)
AFRICA								
ALGERIA	TOTAL	2 500	S	5	3	3	...	7
	(COPRODUCTIONS/COPRODUCCIONES)			1	2	2	...	3
CAMEROON	TOTAL	3 000	...	...	...	1	...	...
	(COPRODUCTIONS/COPRODUCCIONES)			...	...	–	...	...
EGYPT‡	TOTAL	2 000	P	47	47	90	...	52
	(COPRODUCTIONS/COPRODUCCIONES)			5	1	–	...	–
GHANA	TOTAL	2 400	P	–	3	1	–	...
LIBYAN ARAB JAMAHIRIYA	TOTAL	...	...	...	...	2	...	...
	(COPRODUCTIONS/COPRODUCCIONES)			...	...	1	...	...
MOROCCO	TOTAL	2 150	C	...	...	...	...	12
NIGERIA	TOTAL	1 800	C	...	...	...	20	...
	(COPRODUCTIONS/COPRODUCCIONES)			...	...	...	20	...
SIERRA LEONE	TOTAL	...	...	...	2	...	...	...
	(COPRODUCTIONS/COPRODUCCIONES)			...	–	...	...	...
SUDAN	TOTAL	...	...	...	...	...	1	2
	(COPRODUCTIONS/COPRODUCCIONES)			...	...	...	1	1
TUNISIA	TOTAL	...	...	...	3	...	...	...
AMERICA, NORTH								
CANADA	TOTAL	2 060	...	4	...	41	32	...
CUBA	TOTAL	2 000	P	...	1	8	6	8
	(COPRODUCTIONS/COPRODUCCIONES)			...	–	–	–	1
MEXICO	TOTAL	...	P	52	124	162	109	105
	(COPRODUCTIONS/COPRODUCCIONES)			3	2	...	48	8
UNITED STATES‡	TOTAL	...	...	191	236	176	264	396

9.1 Production of long films
Production de films de long métrage
Producción de películas de largo metraje

COUNTRY PAYS PAIS		LENGTH LONGUEUR LONGITUD	DEFINITION OF DATA CODE TIPO DE DATOS	NUMBER OF FILMS PRODUCED / NOMBRE DE FILMS PRODUITS / NUMERO DE PELICULAS PRODUCIDAS				
				1965	1970	1975	1980	1983
		(1)	(2)	(3)	(4)	(5)	(6)	(7)
AMERICA, SOUTH								
ARGENTINA	TOTAL	1 650	P	32	28	34	27	15
	(COPRODUCTIONS/COPRODUCCIONES)			1	...	1	–	1
BRAZIL	TOTAL	1 650	...	...	72	90	103	...
	(COPRODUCTIONS/COPRODUCCIONES)			...	...	1	...	...
COLOMBIA	TOTAL	2 500	...	...	...	2	...	–
	(COPRODUCTIONS/COPRODUCCIONES)			...	...	–	...	–
GUYANA	TOTAL	3 200	S	...	...	4	...	...
	(COPRODUCTIONS/COPRODUCCIONES)			...	...	–	...	...
PERU	TOTAL	2 000	...	...	...	1	1	...
	(COPRODUCTIONS/COPRODUCCIONES)			...	...	–	1	...
VENEZUELA	TOTAL	2 380	S	...	3	9	12	...
	(COPRODUCTIONS/COPRODUCCIONES)			...	3	1	4	...
ASIA								
AFGHANISTAN	TOTAL	...	...	...	1	...	2	...
	(COPRODUCTIONS/COPRODUCCIONES)			...	–	...	–	...
BRUNEI DARUSSALAM	TOTAL	2 300	...	...	6	...	...	...
BURMA	TOTAL	...	...	81	...	66	...	...
	(COPRODUCTIONS/COPRODUCCIONES)			–	...	–	...	...
HONG KONG	TOTAL	...	C	203	137	112	141	118
	(COPRODUCTIONS/COPRODUCCIONES)			–	–	3	–	2
INDIA	TOTAL	2 000	C	325	396	475	742	741
	(COPRODUCTIONS/COPRODUCCIONES)			–	–	–	–	–
INDONESIA	TOTAL	2 000	P	...	14	41	73	76
	(COPRODUCTIONS/COPRODUCCIONES)			...	...	3	–	1
IRAN, ISLAMIC REPUBLIC OF	TOTAL	2 500	...	...	...	68	...	24
	(COPRODUCTIONS/COPRODUCCIONES)			...	...	–	...	–
IRAQ	TOTAL	...	...	...	...	...	2	2
	(COPRODUCTIONS/COPRODUCCIONES)			...	...	...	–	–
ISRAEL	TOTAL	2 000	C	6	8	8	15	17
	(COPRODUCTIONS/COPRODUCCIONES)			2	8	...	–	–
JAPAN	TOTAL	1 600	S	490	423	333	320	...
	(COPRODUCTIONS/COPRODUCCIONES)			3	...	...	1	...
KOREA, REPUBLIC OF	TOTAL	2 500	C	193	224	99	91	91
	(COPRODUCTIONS/COPRODUCCIONES)			–	6	7	2	5
LEBANON	TOTAL	...	...	15	6	...	...	...
MALAYSIA	TOTAL	2 000	...	...	4	5	14	13
	(COPRODUCTIONS/COPRODUCCIONES)			...	–	2	–	–
PAKISTAN	TOTAL	3 600	O	89	141	120	...	82
	(COPRODUCTIONS/COPRODUCCIONES)			...	1	1	...	2
PHILIPPINES	TOTAL	2 400	...	208	...	143	...	...
QATAR	TOTAL	...	...	...	...	1	...	...
SINGAPORE	TOTAL	2 500	C	11	...	4	...	–
	(COPRODUCTIONS/COPRODUCCIONES)			...	...	1	...	–
SRI LANKA	TOTAL	3 600	C	24	25	31	40	33
	(COPRODUCTIONS/COPRODUCCIONES)			–	–	1	3	–
SYRIAN ARAB REPUBLIC	TOTAL	2 800	...	...	...	...	1	...
	(COPRODUCTIONS/COPRODUCCIONES)			...	...	...	–	...
THAILAND	TOTAL	...	...	...	...	55	...	...
TURKEY	TOTAL	2 500	C	...	...	160	74	72
	(COPRODUCTIONS/COPRODUCCIONES)			...	...	...	1	...
VIET-NAM	TOTAL	1 800	...	...	...	7	16	...
	(COPRODUCTIONS/COPRODUCCIONES)			...	...	–	...	...
EUROPE								
ALBANIA	TOTAL	...	P	...	...	...	...	14

COUNTRY / PAYS / PAIS		LENGTH / LONGUEUR / LONGITUD	DEFINITION OF DATA CODE / TIPO DE DATOS	NUMBER OF FILMS PRODUCED / NOMBRE DE FILMS PRODUITS / NUMERO DE PELICULAS PRODUCIDAS				
				1965	1970	1975	1980	1983
		(1)	(2)	(3)	(4)	(5)	(6)	(7)
AUSTRIA	TOTAL	2 000	S	21	7	6	8	16
	(COPRODUCTIONS/COPRODUCCIONES)			5	4	2	2	7
BELGIUM	TOTAL	1 600	P	1	13	7	5	14
	(COPRODUCTIONS/COPRODUCCIONES)			1	7	...	3	7
BULGARIA	TOTAL	2 000	P	12	16	25	31	32
	(COPRODUCTIONS/COPRODUCCIONES)			1	2	3	...	–
CZECHOSLOVAKIA‡	TOTAL	1 800	C	45	54	62	52	45
	(COPRODUCTIONS/COPRODUCCIONES)			3	2	8	–	8
DENMARK	TOTAL	1 600	S	18	18	17	12	11
	(COPRODUCTIONS/COPRODUCCIONES)			...	...	2	–	–
FINLAND	TOTAL	1 642	S	9	13	5	10	13
	(COPRODUCTIONS/COPRODUCCIONES)			...	8	...	3	...
FRANCE	TOTAL	1 600	O	142	138	222	189	131
	(COPRODUCTIONS/COPRODUCCIONES)			108	72	62	45	30
GERMAN DEMOCRATIC REPUBLIC	TOTAL	2 300	P	15	...	16	17	16
	(COPRODUCTIONS/COPRODUCCIONES)			...	...	1	1	–
GERMANY, FEDERAL REPUBLIC OF	TOTAL	1 600	S	72	129	81	49	83
	(COPRODUCTIONS/COPRODUCCIONES)			47	27	26	12	8
GREECE	TOTAL	2 000	C	112	112	70	27	47
	(COPRODUCTIONS/COPRODUCCIONES)			...	...	...	–	–
HUNGARY	TOTAL	2 000	P	23	23	19	26	25
	(COPRODUCTIONS/COPRODUCCIONES)			–	2	–	5	2
ICELAND	TOTAL	2 000	...	...	...	...	3	4
	(COPRODUCTIONS/COPRODUCCIONES)			...	...	...	–	–
IRELAND	TOTAL	1 500	C	1	5	2	–	...
	(COPRODUCTIONS/COPRODUCCIONES)			...	...	...	–	...
ITALY	TOTAL	1 600	S	188	240	203	160	128
	(COPRODUCTIONS/COPRODUCCIONES)			126	135	43	32	12
NETHERLANDS	TOTAL	1 776	S	1	3	16	7	...
	(COPRODUCTIONS/COPRODUCCIONES)			–	–	–	–	...
NORWAY	TOTAL	2 000	C	11	9	14	10	8
	(COPRODUCTIONS/COPRODUCCIONES)			1	2	1	–	–
POLAND	TOTAL	2 000	P	26	28	36	37	35
	(COPRODUCTIONS/COPRODUCCIONES)			–	–	–	2	1
PORTUGAL	TOTAL	1 600	C	6	4	...	9	3
	(COPRODUCTIONS/COPRODUCCIONES)			...	–	...	1	1
ROMANIA	TOTAL	1 800	P	15	11	23	32	32
	(COPRODUCTIONS/COPRODUCCIONES)			1	2	–	–	1
SPAIN	TOTAL	1 650	C	135	105	105	118	99
	(COPRODUCTIONS/COPRODUCCIONES)			73	63	21	36	18
SWEDEN	TOTAL	2 000	S	21	20	14	20	15
	(COPRODUCTIONS/COPRODUCCIONES)			...	7	–	3	2
SWITZERLAND	TOTAL	1 600	P	10	5	30	13	22
	(COPRODUCTIONS/COPRODUCCIONES)			...	...	2	1	6
UNITED KINGDOM	TOTAL	2 000	O	69	85	70	57	39
	(COPRODUCTIONS/COPRODUCCIONES)			...	2	4	...	...
YUGOSLAVIA	TOTAL	2 000	S	19	29	21	22	29
	(COPRODUCTIONS/COPRODUCCIONES)			6	5	3	3	2
OCEANIA								
AUSTRALIA	TOTAL	1 500	O	...	11	43	...	23
U.S.S.R.								
U.S.S.R.	TOTAL	1 800	P	167	218	184	156	156
	(COPRODUCTIONS/COPRODUCCIONES)			...	3	8	6	6
BYELORUSSIAN S.S.R.	TOTAL	2 100	P	...	...	...	...	6

AFRICA:
Egypt:

E--> Figures prior to 1975 refer to 35 mm films only.

FR-> Les données antérieures à 1975 se réferent aux films de 35 mm seulement.

ESP> Los datos anteriores a 1975 se refieren a las películas de 35 mm solamente.

AMERICA, NORTH:
United States:

E--> While figures 1975 are taken from the 'Film Production Chart' of 'Variety', which, for various reasons, includes only part of the films made by the independents those for 1980 and 1983 have been provided by the Motion Picture Association of America (MPAA).

FR-> Les données de 1975 sont extraites de la 'Film production chart', du magazine 'Variety'; pour diverses raisons elles ne comprennent qu'une partie des films produits par les 'independents', celles de 1980 et 1983 ont été fournies par la 'Motion Picture Association of America'.

ESP> Los datos por 1975 proceden de la 'Film production chart' que figura en 'Variety'; por diversas razones los datos comprenden solamente una parte de las películas producidas por los 'independents', y los correspondientes a 1980 y 1983 han sido proporcionados por la 'Motion Picture Association of America (MPAA).

United States: (Cont):

EUROPE:
Czechoslovakia:

E--> Figures for 1965, 1970 and 1975 include films produced for television broadcasting.

FR-> Les données pour 1965, 1970 et 1975 comprennent les films produits pour la télévision.

ESP> Los datos para 1965, 1970 y 1975 incluyen las películas producidas para la televisión.

9.2 Long films: number of films imported, by country of origin

Films de long métrage: nombre de films importés, par pays d'origine

Películas de largo metraje: número de películas importadas, por país de origen

DEFINITION OF DATA:

I = IMPORTED IN THE YEAR STATED

C = APPROVED BY CENSOR FOR PUBLIC SHOWING IN THE YEAR STATED

S = COMMERCIALLY SHOWN FOR THE FIRST TIME IN THE YEAR STATED

O = OTHER CRITERIA

NUMBER OF COUNTRIES AND TERRITORIES PRESENTED IN THIS TABLE: 89

CODE:

I = IMPORTATION EFFECTIVE DANS L'ANNEE INDIQUEE

C = FILMS APPROUVES PAR LA CENSURE POUR LEUR PROJECTION EN PUBLIC DANS L'ANNEE INDIQUEE

S = MISE EN EXPLOITATION COMMERCIALE POUR LA PREMIERE FOIS DANS L'ANNEE INDIQUEE

O = AUTRES CRITERES

NOMBRE DE PAYS ET DE TERRITOIRES PRESENTES DANS CE TABLEAU: 89

TIPO DE DATOS:

I = EFECTIVAMENTE IMPORTADA EN EL AÑO INDICADO

C = PELICULAS APROBADAS POR LA CENSURA PARA SU PRESENTACION AL PUBLICO EN EL AÑO INDICADO

S = PUESTA EN EXPLOTACION COMERCIAL POR PRIMERA VEZ EN EL AÑO INDICADO

O = OTROS CRITERIOS

NUMERO DE PAISES Y DE TERRITORIOS PRESENTADOS EN ESTE CUADRO: 89

COUNTRY / PAYS / PAIS	YEAR / ANNEE / AÑO	DEFINITION OF DATA / CODE / TIPO DE DATOS	TOTAL	PRINCIPAL COUNTRIES OF ORIGIN / PRINCIPAUX PAYS D'ORIGINE / PRINCIPALES PAISES DE ORIGEN									OTHER COUNTRIES / AUTRES PAYS / OTROS PAISES
				UNITED STATES %	FRANCE %	ITALY %	INDIA %	USSR %	UNITED KINGDOM %	FEDERAL REPUBLIC OF GERMANY %	JAPAN %	HONG-KONG %	%
AFRICA													
ALGERIA	1982	C	107	31.8	12.2	5.6	17.8	7.5	1.9	0.9	0.9	–	21.5
	1983	C	135	46.7	4.4	2.2	22.2	3.0	2.2	0.7	–	–	18.5
ANGOLA	1978	I	182	12.6	22.0	17.0	0.5	12.1	8.2	2.7	0.5	–	24.2
	1979	I	186	15.1	18.3	9.1	1.1	14.0	11.3	1.6	2.2	–	27.4
COTE D'IVOIRE	1978	I	498	38.0	36.3	10.8	7.0	./.	1.0	–	./.	./.	6.8
	1979	I	595	31.3	34.8	11.1	8.2	./.	–	–	./.	./.	14.6
EGYPT	1982	I	182	89.0	0.5	2.7	–	–	5.5	–	–	–	2.2
	1983	I	248	75.4	1.2	10.5	0.8	–	6.5	–	–	0.4	5.2
ETHIOPIA	1980	...	293	47.8	–	3.4	11.3	30.4	–	–	–	1.0	6.1
	1981	...	211	60.7	1.4	6.2	9.0	17.1	–	–	–	0.5	5.2
GHANA	1980	I	24	12.5	–	4.2	–	–	–	–	–	83.3	–
	1981	I	26	23.1	–	57.7	–	–	–	–	–	19.2	–
LIBYAN ARAB JAMAHIRIYA	1978	S	180	38.9	–	9.4	9.4	3.3	10.6	–	0.6	2.8	25.0
	1979	S	169	60.4	2.4	10.1	5.3	–	3.0	–	4.1	5.9	8.9
MAURITANIA	1980	I	208	48.1	13.5	9.6	28.8	–	–	–	–	–	–
	1981	I	190	31.6	21.1	5.3	42.1	–	–	–	–	–	–
MAURITIUS	1982	C	276	–	76.4	–	23.6	–	–	–	–	–	–
	1983	C	321	–	78.5	–	21.5	–	–	–	–	–	–
MOROCCO	1982	C	380	19.2	13.9	5.5	21.8	2.6	5.5	0.3	2.6	23.2	5.3
	1983	C	302	21.2	17.2	9.3	18.9	2.0	7.9	1.0	2.6	15.9	4.0
MOZAMBIQUE	1982	...	66	6.1	10.6	1.5	4.5	48.5	1.5	1.5	–	1.5	24.2
	1983	...	68	7.4	2.9	10.3	–	16.2	4.4	–	27.9	–	30.9
NIGERIA	1978	C	150	72.0	–	–	–	–	28.0	–	–	–	–
	1979	C	105	100.0	–	–	–	–	–	–	–	–	–
RWANDA	1980	C	138	23.9	3.6	0.7	31.2	2.9	–	–	0.7	5.8	31.2
	1981	C	164	22.6	7.9	2.4	32.9	–	–	–	–	6.1	28.0

9.2 Importation of long films
Importation de films de long métrage
Importación de películas de largo metraje

COUNTRY / PAYS / PAIS	YEAR / ANNEE / AÑO	DEFINITION OF DATA / CODE / TIPO DE DATOS	TOTAL	PRINCIPAL COUNTRIES OF ORIGIN / PRINCIPAUX PAYS D'ORIGINE / PRINCIPALES PAISES DE ORIGEN									OTHER COUNTRIES / AUTRES PAYS / OTROS PAISES %
				UNITED STATES %	FRANCE %	ITALY %	INDIA %	USSR %	UNITED KINGDOM %	FEDERAL REPUBLIC OF GERMANY %	JAPAN %	HONG-KONG %	
SOMALIA	1982	...	317	–	–	45.4	51.1	–	–	–	–	–	3.5
	1983	...	449	–	–	74.4	25.6	–	–	–	–	–	–
SUDAN	1981	C	139	...	...	...	13.0	...	...	...	...	...	87.1
	1982	C	137	18.2	7.3	3.7	25.5	7.3	10.9	3.7	–	7.3	16.1
UNITED REPUBLIC OF TANZANIA	1980	C	178	28.1	1.1	6.7	29.2	0.6	7.9	1.1	2.8	21.3	1.1
	1981	C	162	32.7	1.2	11.1	32.1	8.0	4.9	0.6	1.2	8.0	–
ZAMBIA	1978	C	131	63.4	0.8	3.1	–	–	25.2	–	–	7.6	–
	1979	C	154	64.9	–	1.9	–	–	24.0	–	–	9.1	–
AMERICA, NORTH													
BERMUDA	1980	I	135	79.3	0.7	–	–	–	6.7	–	–	13.3	–
	1981	I	122	79.5	1.6	–	–	–	9.0	–	–	8.2	1.6
CANADA	1980	I	777	38.0	13.1	11.7	10.7	./.	1.7	2.3	./.	14.5	8.0
	1982	I	468	45.1	28.6	11.1	1.5	./.	3.2	6.0	./.	–	4.5
CUBA	1982	I	122	9.0	8.2	6.6	–	16.4	4.9	–	7.4	–	47.5
	1983	I	133	10.5	6.0	6.0	–	12.0	4.5	3.0	6.8	–	51.1
GRENADA	1978	...	55	29.1	9.1	–	–	–	47.3	–	–	14.5	–
	1979	...	50	16.0	6.0	–	–	–	24.0	–	20.0	34.0	–
GUATEMALA	1982	...	332	46.7	3.0	14.2	–	–	3.0	1.5	–	–	31.6
	1983	...	296	45.6	2.4	11.1	–	–	4.1	0.7	–	–	36.1
HAITI	1980	...	366	37.4	38.3	2.5	–	–	1.1	–	–	14.5	6.3
	1981	...	422	40.8	41.5	0.7	–	–	1.9	–	–	10.0	5.2
MEXICO	1982	C	407	46.9	4.2	5.7	–	1.5	3.9	4.7	3.2	10.3	19.7
	1983	C	309	53.7	5.5	5.5	–	1.0	6.5	2.6	1.9	3.9	19.4
NICARAGUA	1980	S	222	49.1	6.3	14.9	–	1.8	8.6	0.5	0.5	2.3	16.2
	1981	S	231	68.8	1.7	5.2	–	0.4	3.0	–	–	2.2	18.6
TRINIDAD AND TOBAGO	1978	S	401	50.4	1.5	6.0	16.5	–	4.5	0.2	–	–	20.9
AMERICA, SOUTH													
ARGENTINA	1982	C	230	40.4	10.0	20.0	–	1.3	3.5	2.6	1.3	0.4	20.4
	1983	C	205	51.2	5.9	18.5	0.5	1.5	2.4	3.4	1.5	–	15.1
BOLIVIA	1978	S	452	42.9	4.4	12.6	0.7	0.7	2.7	0.9	0.9	5.3	29.0
	1979	S	394	44.4	3.6	16.2	0.5	3.6	4.6	1.5	1.3	2.8	21.6
BRAZIL	1980	C	497	42.3	3.4	26.6	–	0.2	1.8	4.0	3.8	13.1	4.8
	1981	C	385	46.5	9.4	18.2	–	0.8	1.0	2.6	8.1	6.0	7.5
COLOMBIA	1982	C	355	43.7	3.1	11.8	–	0.3	4.5	2.8	3.7	3.1	27.3
	1983	C	363	46.3	2.8	9.1	–	0.3	2.8	0.3	1.4	1.7	35.5
GUYANA	1980	C	497	72.4	–	–	14.5	–	–	–	–	13.1	–
	1981	C	367	63.2	–	–	17.7	–	–	–	–	19.1	–
PERU	1980	C	682	43.7	4.7	19.2	2.5	1.5	2.1	3.2	0.7	1.8	20.7
	1981	C	707	44.0	3.5	12.2	1.1	1.4	2.0	1.8	1.8	4.0	28.1
VENEZUELA	1980	I	904	38.3	6.6	16.3	–	2.0	–	2.4	1.4	8.7	24.2
	1981	I	606	54.6	4.6	12.9	–	2.5	–	1.7	0.2	5.9	17.7
ASIA													
AFGHANISTAN	1978	I	116	./.	./.	./.	28.4	43.1	./.	./.	–	–	28.4
	1979	I	41	./.	./.	./.	2.4	85.4	./.	./.	–	–	12.2
BRUNEI DARUSSALAM	1980	...	395	32.4	–	–	–	–	0.8	–	–	45.6	21.3
	1981	...	437	33.0	–	–	–	–	1.1	–	–	41.2	24.7
HONG KONG	1982	C	407	28.5	10.3	9.1	0.5	1.7	4.9	6.4	10.1	.	28.5
	1983	C	429	28.4	5.1	6.8	0.7	0.5	4.9	7.7	8.2	.	37.8
INDIA	1980	I	119	21.0	0.8	0.8	.	13.4	8.4	–	0.8	0.8	53.8
	1981	I	190	12.1	3.7	1.6	.	5.8	1.6	1.6	1.1	–	72.6
INDONESIA	1982	...	216	35.6	2.3	4.2	17.1	–	2.3	–	4.2	26.9	7.4
	1983	...	212	34.0	2.4	6.1	10.4	–	5.7	0.5	1.4	30.7	9.0

COUNTRY PAYS PAIS	YEAR ANNEE AÑO	DEFINITION OF DATA CODE TIPO DE DATOS	TOTAL	PRINCIPAL COUNTRIES OF ORIGIN / PRINCIPAUX PAYS D'ORIGINE / PRINCIPALES PAISES DE ORIGEN									OTHER COUNTRIES AUTRES PAYS OTROS PAISES
				UNITED STATES %	FRANCE %	ITALY %	INDIA %	USSR %	UNITED KINGDOM %	FEDERAL REPUBLIC OF GERMANY %	JAPAN %	HONG-KONG %	%
IRAN, ISLAMIC REPUBLIC OF	1982	...	51	23.5	2.0	11.8	–	35.3	5.9	2.0	–	–	19.6
	1983	...	96	13.5	2.1	22.9	–	26.0	10.4	–	2.1	–	22.9
IRAQ	1980	...	186	22.0	10.2	8.6	10.8	3.2	21.5	0.5	–	–	23.1
	1981	...	93	35.5	7.5	6.5	10.8	3.2	3.2	–	–	–	33.3
ISRAEL	1982	...	202	51.5	10.9	9.4	–	1.0	9.4	3.0	2.5	3.0	9.4
	1983	...	267	44.6	8.2	8.6	–	2.2	6.7	2.6	2.2	0.4	24.3
JAPAN	1981	S	223	62.3	8.1	3.6	0.9	4.5	6.3	1.8	.	2.2	10.3
	1982	S	199	58.3	10.6	8.5	–	2.0	3.5	3.5	.	2.0	11.6
JORDAN	1982	...	397	31.5	1.3	18.9	11.3	–	0.5	–	–	6.3	30.2
	1983	...	438	30.8	1.1	19.4	11.4	–	0.7	–	–	6.8	29.7
KOREA, REPUBLIC OF	1982	C	29	72.4	3.4	3.4	–	–	–	6.9	–	13.8	–
	1983	C	26	61.5	3.8	7.7	–	–	3.8	3.8	–	11.5	7.7
KUWAIT	1982	...	145	–	2.1	24.1	62.1	–	–	1.4	4.8	5.5	–
	1983	...	150	–	–	21.3	56.7	–	–	2.0	6.7	13.3	–
LAO PEOPLE'S DEMOCRATIC REPUBLIC	1980	...	113	–	–	–	18.6	80.5	–	–	–	–	0.9
	1981	...	78	–	–	–	23.1	60.3	–	–	–	–	16.7
MALAYSIA	1982	...	983	20.4	5.1	3.5	14.3	0.8	3.2	2.6	1.9	32.0	16.1
	1983	...	1 045	22.3	1.3	3.5	11.9	0.3	6.5	2.0	2.6	36.6	13.0
MALDIVES	1982	C	52	3.8	–	–	92.3	–	–	–	–	–	3.8
	1983	C	49	8.2	2.0	–	85.7	2.0	–	–	–	–	2.0
PAKISTAN	1982	I	77	...	...	...	...	...	...	...	...	...	...
	1983	I	81	...	...	...	...	...	...	...	...	...	...
PHILIPPINES	1980	...	...	45.1	–	0.7	–	–	11.0	0.5	0.4	39.0	3.2
	1981	...	...	42.3	1.3	2.1	–	–	22.0	0.4	1.7	27.6	2.5
QATAR	1982	...	896	29.5	–	–	44.3	–	–	–	–	–	26.2
	1983	...	887	31.9	–	–	39.5	–	–	–	–	–	28.6
SINGAPORE	1982	...	702	31.5	1.6	3.6	11.1	–	2.1	0.6	2.8	25.5	21.2
	1983	...	533	34.7	1.7	5.1	12.8	–	4.1	3.0	1.7	26.1	10.9
SRI LANKA	1982	I	167	29.9	–	0.6	27.5	4.2	33.5	1.8	–	2.4	–
	1983	I	151	48.3	–	0.7	18.5	0.7	27.8	0.7	–	2.6	0.7
SYRIAN ARAB REPUBLIC	1982	...	78	–	–	–	2.6	–	–	–	–	–	97.4
	1983	...	149	–	–	–	8.7	5.4	19.5	–	–	–	66.4
THAILAND	1978	C	401	42.1	./.	5.2	3.5	./.	1.0	./.	3.2	40.2	4.7
	1979	C	260	23.1	./.	2.7	5.4	./.	1.9	./.	1.9	60.0	5.0
TURKEY	1980	S	143	62.9	11.9	10.5	–	1.4	4.9	1.4	1.4	5.6	–
	1981	S	208	55.8	8.7	15.9	0.5	3.8	2.9	5.8	–	5.3	1.4
UNITED ARAB EMIRATES	1978	...	130	68.5	1.5	13.8	16.2	–	–	–	–	–	–
	1979	...	142	63.4	2.1	14.8	19.7	–	–	–	–	–	–
VIET-NAM	1978	I	207	–	–	–	–	43.5	–	–	–	–	56.5
	1979	I	229	–	–	–	–	37.6	–	–	–	–	62.4
YEMEN	1980	...	181	27.6	2.8	5.5	22.1	5.5	4.4	2.8	4.4	2.8	22.1
	1981	...	174	28.7	2.9	5.7	20.1	5.7	4.0	2.9	4.0	2.9	23.0
EUROPE													
ALBANIA	1982	I	8	–	25.0	25.0	–	–	–	–	25.0	–	25.0
	1983	I	7	–	28.6	14.3	–	–	14.3	14.3	28.6	–	–
AUSTRIA	1982	S	331	37.2	13.0	10.3	–	–	3.3	16.9	0.3	6.3	12.7
	1983	S	314	36.0	14.7	13.7	–	0.6	3.5	12.7	–	1.3	17.5
BULGARIA	1982	...	171	3.5	3.5	0.6	1.2	31.6	2.9	2.9	4.7	–	49.1
	1983	...	164	7.9	4.3	3.0	1.8	32.3	–	0.6	3.0	–	47.0
CZECHOSLOVAKIA	1982	S	165	13.3	4.8	3.0	–	26.7	–	4.8	1.8	–	45.5
	1983	S	177	10.2	9.0	3.4	–	22.0	2.8	3.4	–	–	49.2
DENMARK	1982	S	259	55.2	9.3	5.4	–	0.4	4.6	4.2	1.5	0.8	18.5
	1983	S	233	51.1	6.9	7.7	–	0.4	7.3	7.7	0.4	3.0	15.5
FINLAND	1982	S	215	48.4	3.7	1.9	–	6.0	6.5	5.1	1.4	–	27.0
	1983	S	212	48.6	3.8	4.7	–	7.1	3.8	2.4	0.9	–	28.8

COUNTRY / PAYS / PAIS	YEAR / ANNEE / AÑO	DEFINITION OF DATA / CODE / TIPO DE DATOS	TOTAL	PRINCIPAL COUNTRIES OF ORIGIN / PRINCIPAUX PAYS D'ORIGINE / PRINCIPALES PAISES DE ORIGEN: UNITED STATES %	FRANCE %	ITALY %	INDIA %	USSR %	UNITED KINGDOM %	FEDERAL REPUBLIC OF GERMANY %	JAPAN %	HONG-KONG %	OTHER COUNTRIES / AUTRES PAYS / OTROS PAISES %
FRANCE	1982	C	329	40.7	.	11.6	2.7	1.2	4.9	4.3	1.2	17.9	12.5
	1983	C	241	44.0	.	14.1	4.6	1.7	7.9	5.8	2.1	14.9	5.0
GERMAN DEMOCRATIC REPUBLIC	1982	I	130	4.6	4.6	4.6	–	34.6	1.5	1.5	4.6	–	43.8
	1983	I	118	5.9	5.1	2.5	–	30.5	–	6.8	2.5	–	46.6
GERMANY, FEDERAL REPUBLIC OF	1982	S	321	38.3	9.0	10.0	–	0.3	2.2	.	0.9	6.9	32.4
	1983	S	322	34.2	8.1	12.7	–	0.3	4.7	.	0.3	1.6	38.2
GIBRALTAR‡	1980	...	376	88.8	–	–	–	–	./.	1.6	–	–	9.6
	1981	...	369	89.7	–	–	–	–	./.	1.9	–	–	8.4
GREECE	1982	C	376	42.3	14.6	17.8	0.3	1.1	4.0	6.9	1.1	7.2	4.8
	1983	C	261	39.1	14.6	18.4	–	0.8	5.4	8.8	0.4	3.4	9.2
HUNGARY	1982	I	203	18.2	10.3	5.4	–	18.7	1.5	2.5	3.9	–	39.4
	1983	I	198	20.2	9.6	6.6	5.6	19.7	3.0	5.1	0.5	–	29.8
IRELAND	1981	C	214	59.8	1.4	4.2	–	–	23.4	2.8	–	2.3	6.1
	1982	C	192	58.9	2.1	5.7	–	–	21.9	2.6	0.5	1.0	7.3
ITALY	1982	S	259	40.2	25.1	.	–	1.9	3.5	8.9	1.2	1.9	17.4
	1983	S	275	45.1	24.0	.	–	5.5	5.8	8.4	–	1.1	10.2
NETHERLANDS	1981	S	360	42.8	14.7	7.5	–	1.1	6.4	10.8	1.7	8.1	6.9
	1982	S	332	56.3	13.3	2.4	–	–	4.8	10.5	0.9	4.2	7.5
NORWAY	1982	C	273	49.8	9.2	5.9	–	1.8	7.7	2.9	–	0.4	22.3
	1983	C	284	51.4	10.9	7.0	–	1.1	9.5	3.5	1.1	–	15.5
POLAND	1982	S	87	3.4	2.3	–	–	36.8	1.1	1.1	1.1	–	54.0
	1983	S	90	11.1	3.3	2.2	–	40.0	1.1	1.1	–	–	41.1
PORTUGAL	1982	I	338	42.6	16.3	16.3	0.9	0.6	8.6	4.7	0.9	2.7	6.5
	1983	I	282	40.4	9.6	19.5	–	0.7	14.5	3.9	–	3.5	7.8
ROMANIA	1982	I	131	15.3	1.5	5.3	3.1	24.4	4.6	–	3.1	–	42.7
	1983	I	113	5.3	3.5	2.7	–	38.9	1.8	–	–	–	47.8
SAN MARINO	1982	...	358	32.4	7.3	43.9	–	0.6	4.5	2.0	0.3	7.3	2.0
	1983	...	314	31.2	12.4	39.2	–	1.0	7.3	3.5	0.3	1.3	3.8
SPAIN	1980	C	404	36.4	11.6	23.0	–	1.0	9.9	4.7	0.7	0.7	11.9
	1981	C	463	40.6	7.1	16.2	–	1.7	8.4	7.3	0.4	2.2	16.0
SWEDEN	1978	S	276	53.6	8.7	8.3	–	1.8	4.3	7.6	0.4	0.4	14.9
	1979	S	318	52.5	14.2	6.0	–	2.8	7.2	4.7	–	–	12.6
SWITZERLAND	1982	I	441	42.0	21.1	11.8	1.1	0.2	1.8	11.8	0.5	3.9	5.9
	1983	I	466	40.6	21.7	7.9	1.3	0.4	4.3	11.4	5.4	2.8	6.4
UNITED KINGDOM	1982	I	241	50.2	./.	./.	./.	./.	.	./.	./.	./.	49.8
	1983	I	265	54.7	./.	./.	./.	./.	.	./.	./.	./.	45.3
YUGOSLAVIA	1982	I	208	37.5	9.6	3.8	2.4	8.7	3.4	1.9	3.8	10.6	18.3
	1983	I	189	34.9	7.9	10.6	–	7.9	6.9	4.8	1.1	7.4	18.5
OCEANIA													
AUSTRALIA	1982	C	1 095	35.9	4.5	2.6	1.6	3.0	4.7	9.4	0.7	16.9	20.5
	1983	C	900	37.0	5.2	3.9	0.3	2.2	5.8	4.3	1.3	17.9	22.0
NEW ZEALAND	1978	C	504	43.7	11.3	3.8	0.2	1.4	12.9	5.8	2.6	3.4	15.1
	1979	C	564	49.1	9.6	3.7	0.2	1.1	13.3	6.9	1.6	2.5	12.1
NORFOLK ISLAND	1978	I	106	81.1	–	–	–	–	18.9	–	–	–	–
	1979	I	120	60.0	–	–	–	–	40.0	–	–	–	–
TONGA	1978	C	464	*44.8	–	./.	–	./.	./.	–	./.	*44.8	10.3
	1979	C	421	*45.1	–	./.	–	./.	./.	–	./.	*45.1	*9.7
VANUATU	1980	I	175	21.1	38.3	13.7	–	–	6.9	9.1	1.1	9.7	–
	1981	I	207	18.4	39.6	8.2	–	–	8.2	11.1	3.9	10.6	–

General note/ Note générale/ Nota general:

E--> Due to lack of precise information the column 'Other countries' may include data for certain of the principal countries of origin and the symbol ./. has been used in such cases.

FR-> Le symbole ./. indique qu'il n'y a pas des informations précises sur les principaux pays d'origine concernés, qui peuvent se trouver compris dans la colonne 'Autres pays'.

General note/ Note générale/ Nota general: (Cont):

ESP> El símbolo ./. indica que no se dispone de informaciones precisas sobre los principales países de origen en el que figura, que pueden estar comprendidos en la columna 'Otros países'.

EUROPE:

Gibraltar:

E--> Data on films imported from the United Kingdom and the United

Gibraltar: (Cont):
States are counted together.
FR-> Les données relatives aux films importés du Royaume-Uni et des

Gibraltar: (Cont):
Etats-Unis sont comptées ensemble.
ESP> Los datos relativos a las películas importadas del Reino Unido y de los Estados Unidos se cuentan conjuntamente.

9.3 Cinemas: number, seating capacity and annual attendance

Cinémas: nombre d'établissements, nombre de sièges et fréquentation annuelle

Cines: número de establecimientos, número de asientos y frecuentación anual

COUNTRY / PAYS / PAIS	YEAR / ANNEE / AÑO	FIXED CINEMAS / ETABLISSEMENTS FIXES / ESTABLECIMIENTOS FIJOS				MOBILE UNITS / CINEMAS ITINERANTS / UNIDADES MOVILES	
		NUMBER 35 MM AND OVER / NOMBRE 35 MM ET PLUS / NUMERO 35 MM Y MAS	NUMBER 16 MM / NOMBRE 16 MM / NUMERO 16 MM	SEATING CAPACITY / NOMBRE DE SIEGES / NUMERO DE ASIENTOS (000)	ANNUAL ATTENDANCE / FREQUENTATION ANNUELLE / FRECUENTACION ANUAL (000 000)	NUMBER 35 MM + 16 MM / NOMBRE 35 MM + 16 MM / NUMERO 35 MM + 16 MM	ANNUAL ATTENDANCE / FREQUENTATION ANNUELLE / FRECUENTACION ANUAL (000 000)
AFRICA							
ALGERIA	1982	280	–	5 3 0	2 3 8	–	–
ANGOLA	1979	55	–	34.0	6.4	–	–
BURKINA FASO	1981	12	–	14.0	4.0	–	–
BURUNDI	1981	3	4	2.5	0.1	–	–
CAMEROON	1979	52	–	29.0	...	31	...
COTE D'IVOIRE	1979	42	30	42.0	6.6	4	0.4
EGYPT	1983	194	8	185	41.5	–	–
ETHIOPIA	1981	40	–	35.5	...	–	–
GHANA	1981	7	–	9.0	3.9	...	...
LIBERIA	1979	13	–	9.2	1.5	–	–
LIBYAN ARAB JAMAHIRIYA	1979	49	–	22.0	10.1	100	1.2
MAURITANIA	1980	19	–	7.6	...	...	...
MAURITIUS	1983	46	–	42.0	10.5	–	–
MOROCCO	1983	267	–	161.5	39.0	17	...
MOZAMBIQUE	1983	70	–	27.0	9.6	...	...
NIGERIA	1981	*240	–	...	*4.5	20	0.07
RWANDA	1981	2	10	3.6	0.3	–	–
ST. HELENA	1983	...	2	0.9	...	–	–
SUDAN	1983	56	–	97.2	3.0	30	*10.0
UNITED REPUBLIC OF TANZANIA	1981	34	–	14.7	4.0	–	–
AMERICA, NORTH							
BAHAMAS	1979	13	–	5.8	...	–	–
BERMUDA	1981	4	–	1.6	0.2	–	–
CANADA	1982	983	./.	620.0	87.6	–	–
CAYMAN ISLANDS	1979	3	1	1.2	0.2	–	–
CUBA	1983	525	–	276.0	44.7	880	41.6
GUATEMALA	1982	115	./.	72.2	7.9	25	...
HAITI	1981	28	–	13.8	2.1	...	...
MEXICO	1983	2 963	./.	...	211.5	63	...
NICARAGUA	1981	127	–	74.3	5.0	–	–
TRINIDAD AND TOBAGO	1979	72	–	57.0	...	19	0.1
UNITED STATES	1983	16 032	–	5611.0	1053.3	–	–

NUMERO DE PAISES Y DE TERRITORIOS
PRESENTADOS EN ESTE CUADRO: 101

DRIVE-IN CINEMAS CINEMAS POUR AUTOMOBILISTES CINES PARA AUTOMOVILISTAS				ALL CINEMAS TOUS LES CINEMAS TODOS LOS CINES				
NUMBER NOMBRE NUMERO	CAPACITY CAPACITE CAPACIDAD (000)	ANNUAL ATTENDANCE FREQUENTATION ANNUELLE FRECUENTACION ANUAL (000 000)		SEATS PER 1,000 INHABITANTS SIEGES POUR 1 000 HABITANTS ASIENTOS POR 1 000 HABITANTES	ANNUAL ATTENDANCE PER INHABITANT FREQUENTATION ANNUELLE PAR HABITANT FRECUENTACION ANUAL POR HABITANTE	GROSS BOX OFFICE RECEIPTS RECETTES BRUTES RECAUDACION TOTAL DE TAQUILLA (000 000)	CURRENCY MONNAIE MONEDA	COUNTRY PAYS PAIS
								AFRICA
–	–	–		7.5	1.2	101.7	DINAR	ALGERIA
–	–	–		4.9	0.9	167.1	KWANSA	ANGOLA
–	–	–		2.0	0.6	0.5	FRANC C.F.A.	BURKINA FASO
–	–	–		0.6	0.0	17.7	FRANC	BURUNDI
–	–	–		3.5	...	...	FRANC C.F.A.	CAMEROON
–	–	–		5.3	0.9	2500.0	FRANC C.F.A.	COTE D'IVOIRE
–	–	–		4.0	0.9	17.4	POUND	EGYPT
–	–	–		1.1	...	...	BIRR	ETHIOPIA
...	...	...		0.7	...	1.7	CEDI	GHANA
–	–	–		5.1	0.8	...	DOLLAR	LIBERIA
–	–	–		7.7	3.5	...	DINAR	LIBYAN ARAB JAMAHIRIYA
–	–	–		4.7	...	...	OUGUIYA	MAURITANIA
–	–	–		42.3	10.6	...	RUPEE	MAURITIUS
–	–	–		7.3	1.8	114.6	DIRHAM	MOROCCO
...	...	...		2.0	0.7	...	METICAL	MOZAMBIQUE
–	–	–		...	0.1	...	NAIRA	NIGERIA
–	–	–		0.7	0.1	61.5	FRANC	RWANDA
1	0.5	...		...	...	...	POUND STERLING	ST. HELENA
–	–	–		4.8	0.6	...	POUND	SUDAN
–	–	–		0.8	0.2	72	SHILLING	UNITED REPUBLIC OF TANZANIA
								AMERICA, NORTH
3	1.2	...		31.8	...	...	DOLLAR	BAHAMAS
–	–	–		...	...	0.8	DOLLAR	BERMUDA
270	544.0	9.7		30.7	4.0	354.3	DOLLAR	CANADA‡
...	...	...		...	...	...	JAMAICAN DOLLAR	CAYMAN ISLANDS
...	...	...		27.9	8.7	27.9	PESO	CUBA
...	...	...		9.4	1.0	9.2	QUETZAL	GUATEMALA
4	...	0.0		2.7	0.4	8.4	GOURDE	HAITI
5	...	./.		...	2.8	11834.5	PESO	MEXICO
1	1.8	0.2		27.0	1.9	30.2	CORDOBA	NICARAGUA
3	2.0	0.1		52.4	...	3.7	DOLLAR	TRINIDAD AND TOBAGO
2 852	6044.0	143.6		23.9	5.1	3766.0	DOLLAR	UNITED STATES

COUNTRY / PAYS / PAIS	YEAR / ANNEE / AÑO	FIXED CINEMAS / ETABLISSEMENTS FIXES / ESTABLECIMIENTOS FIJOS				MOBILE UNITS / CINEMAS ITINERANTS / UNIDADES MOVILES	
		NUMBER 35 MM AND OVER / NOMBRE 35 MM ET PLUS / NUMERO 35 MM Y MAS	NUMBER 16 MM / NOMBRE 16 MM / NUMERO 16 MM	SEATING CAPACITY / NOMBRE DE SIEGES / NUMERO DE ASIENTOS (000)	ANNUAL ATTENDANCE / FREQUENTATION ANNUELLE / FRECUENTACION ANUAL (000 000)	NUMBER 35 MM + 16 MM / NOMBRE 35 MM + 16 MM / NUMERO 35 MM + 16 MM	ANNUAL ATTENDANCE / FREQUENTATION ANNUELLE / FRECUENTACION ANUAL (000 000)
AMERICA, SOUTH							
ARGENTINA	1983	919	...	622.2	49.9	2	...
BOLIVIA	1979	200	9	160.0	31.0	16	...
BRAZIL	1981	2 189	32	906.1	137.5	20	0.063
CHILE	1983	161	–	100.0	12.2	...	...
COLOMBIA	1983	323	–	183.9	66.0	...	...
FALKLAND ISLANDS (MALVINAS)	1979	–	2	0.5	0.0	2	0.0
GUYANA	1981	50	–	40.0	13.0	...	...
PERU	1980	425	...	...	33.0	–	–
URUGUAY	1981	120	–	80.0	6.2	–	–
VENEZUELA	1981	535	./.	...	67.6	...	...
ASIA							
AFGHANISTAN	1979	34	–	19.4	...	13	...
BHUTAN	1979	12	–	5.0	...	–	–
BRUNEI DARUSSALAM	1981	7	–	6.4	2.3	12	...
DEMOCRATIC YEMEN	1982	24	–	24.2	3.9	...	...
HONG KONG	1983	90	–	103.0	65.0	–	–
INDIA	1983	7 516	4 768	5660	4850	...	...
INDONESIA	1983	1 560	–	978.3	...	...	...
IRAN, ISLAMIC REPUBLIC OF	1983	398	...	180.9	...	116	...
ISRAEL	1978	214	./.	152.3	24.2	–	–
JAPAN	1981	2 298	–	918.0	149.5	–	–
JORDAN	1979	41	–	20.0	15.0	–	–
KOREA, REPUBLIC OF	1983	301	–	232.0	44.0	–	–
KUWAIT	1981	12	...	15.1	3.6	...	...
MALDIVES	1983	5	2	2.8	...	–	–
PAKISTAN	1979	630	–	305.0	172.7	85	2.9
QATAR	1983	4	–	3.8	0.5	...	...
SINGAPORE	1983	57	–	63.0	30.7	–	–
SRI LANKA	1983	329	–	...	41.9	–	–
SYRIAN ARAB REPUBLIC	1983	90	–	50.6	15.0	–	–
THAILAND	1979	682	...	424.0	...	–	–
TURKEY	1980	938	./.	506.3	62.5	3	0.0
VIET-NAM	1980	244	...	...	...	816	...
YEMEN	1980	35	–	28.0	15.0	...	...
EUROPE							
ALBANIA	1983	103	...	28	...	237	3.5
AUSTRIA	1983	532	–	139.0	18.4	4	./.
BELGIUM	1982	472	./.	...	20.5	–	–
BULGARIA	1983	2 988	257	715.2	93.5	41	...
CZECHOSLOVAKIA	1981	2 136	835	861.0	81.0	10	...
DENMARK	1983	453	–	92.0	13.8	5	0.1
FINLAND	1983	368	...	85.0	9.0	8	...
FRANCE	1983	4 894	1 410	1311.5	198.0	...	...
GERMAN DEMOCRATIC REPUBLIC	1983	2 089	–	334.0	61.5	3 553	11.3
GERMANY, FEDERAL REPUBLIC OF	1983	3 664	–	821.0	125.3	25	./.
GIBRALTAR	1981	4	–	2.3	0.2	–	–
HUNGARY	1983	1 095	2 481	547.0	68.9	124	./.
ICELAND	1980	47	...	...	2.6	...	...
IRELAND	1983	177	–	...	...	–	–
ITALY	1983	6 361	./.	...	161.6	...	0.4
MALTA	1983	26	–	19.0	1.4	–	–
MONACO	1981	3	–	1.4	0.1	–	–
NETHERLANDS	1981	551	–	154.3	27.0	11	2.0
NORWAY	1983	467	–	133.0	14.7	26	...
POLAND	1983	1 737	59	483.5	99.7	297	8.4
PORTUGAL	1983	415	./.	215.0	23.7	...	...
ROMANIA	1983	717	4 897	253.0	209.4	114	6.7
SAN MARINO	1983	7	–	3.2	0.1	–	–
SPAIN	1983	4 861	–	...	141.1	...	...
SWEDEN	1983	1 220	–	...	19.0	...	...

DRIVE-IN CINEMAS / CINEMAS POUR AUTOMOBILISTES / CINES PARA AUTOMOVILISTAS			ALL CINEMAS / TOUS LES CINEMAS / TODOS LOS CINES			CURRENCY	COUNTRY
NUMBER / NOMBRE / NUMERO	CAPACITY / CAPACITE / CAPACIDAD (000)	ANNUAL ATTENDANCE / FREQUENTATION ANNUELLE / FRECUENTACION ANUAL (000 000)	SEATS PER 1,000 INHABITANTS / SIEGES POUR 1 000 HABITANTS / ASIENTOS POR 1 000 HABITANTES	ANNUAL ATTENDANCE PER INHABITANT / FREQUENTATION ANNUELLE PAR HABITANT / FRECUENTACION ANUAL POR HABITANTE	GROSS BOX OFFICE RECEIPTS / RECETTES BRUTES / RECAUDACION TOTAL DE TAQUILLA (000 000)	MONNAIE / MONEDA	PAYS / PAIS
							AMERICA, SOUTH
13	27.2	...	21.2	1.7	69.0	PESO	ARGENTINA
1	1.8	0.1	29.8	5.7	120.0	PESO	BOLIVIA
23	12.6	1.3	...	...	11701.0	CRUZEIRO	BRAZIL
...	...	...	8.6	1.0	...	PESO	CHILE
...	...	...	6.7	2.4	2839	PESO	COLOMBIA
–	–	–	250.0	10.5	...	POUND STERLING	FALKLAND ISLANDS (MALVINAS)
1	1.5	0.3	46.0	14.7	29.0	DOLLAR	GUYANA
–	–	–	...	1.9	5500	SOL	PERU
–	–	–	27.3	2.1	86.5	PESO	URUGUAY
20	...	...	...	4.7	376.0	BOLIVAR	VENEZUELA
							ASIA
...	...	...	1.3	...	...	AFGHANI	AFGHANISTAN
–	–	–	3.9	...	...	NGULTRUM	BHUTAN
–	–	–	33.3	13.0	...	DOLLAR	BRUNEI DARUSSALAM
–	–	–	11.2	1.8	...	DINAR	DEMOCRATIC YEMEN
–	–	–	19.4	12.2	...	DOLLAR	HONG KONG
3	4.3	0.9	7.7	6.6	4050.0	RUPEE	INDIA
1	3.4	0.1	6.1	...	...	RUPIAH	INDONESIA
...	...	...	4.3	...	...	RIAL	IRAN, ISLAMIC REPUBLIC OF
...	...	...	41.3	6.6	550.0	SHEKEL	ISRAEL
–	–	–	7.8	1.3	163259	YEN	JAPAN
–	–	–	6.5	4.9	...	DINAR	JORDAN
–	–	–	5.8	1.1	73.0	WON	KOREA, REPUBLIC OF
2	2.1	0.1	11.8	2.5	...	DINAR	KUWAIT
–	–	–	16.7	...	...	RUFIYAA	MALDIVES
3	8.0	0.7	3.9	2.2	...	RUPEE	PAKISTAN
...	...	...	13.5	1.8	4.7	RIYAL	QATAR
1	3.9	0.5	26.7	12.5	27.6	DOLLAR	SINGAPORE
–	–	–	...	2.7	...	RUPEE	SRI LANKA
–	–	–	5.3	1.6	30.0	POUND	SYRIAN ARAB REPUBLIC
–	–	–	9.2	...	...	BAHT	THAILAND
–	–	–	11.3	1.4	...	LIRA	TURKEY
47	...	...	...	5.4	...	DONG	VIET-NAM
...	...	...	4.7	2.5	...	RIAL	YEMEN
							EUROPE
...	...	...	9.9	...	...	LEK	ALBANIA
2	4.0	./.	18.9	2.4	863.8	SCHILLING	AUSTRIA
...	...	...	...	2.1	2289.7	FRANC	BELGIUM
–	–	–	80.0	10.6	42.7	LEV	BULGARIA
–	–	–	56.2	5.3	415.9	KORUNA	CZECHOSLOVAKIA
–	–	–	18.0	2.7	286.8	KRONE	DENMARK
–	–	–	17.5	1.9	172.5	MARKKA	FINLAND
...	...	...	24.0	3.6	3877.1	FRANC	FRANCE‡
–	–	–	20.0	4.4	...	DDR MARK	GERMAN DEMOCRATIC REPUBLIC
23	...	./.	14.1	2.0	872.3	D. MARK	GERMANY, FEDERAL REPUBLIC OF
–	–	–	76.7	5.7	...	POUND STERLING	GIBRALTAR
–	–	–	51.2	6.5	606.8	FORINT	HUNGARY
...	...	...	...	11.4	...	KRONA	ICELAND
–	–	–	...	...	...	POUND	IRELAND
...	...	...	...	2.9	505175.7	LIRA	ITALY
–	–	–	50.4	3.7	0.6	LIRA	MALTA
–	–	–	53.9	3.8	...	FRENCH FRANC	MONACO
2	2.8	./.	11.0	2.0	212.8	GUILDER	NETHERLANDS
–	–	–	32.2	3.6	271.5	KRONE	NORWAY
–	–	–	13.2	3.0	...	ZLOTY	POLAND
–	–	–	21.6	2.4	2643.1	ESCUDO	PORTUGAL
–	–	–	11.2	9.6	...	LEU	ROMANIA‡
–	–	–	145.5	4.6	85.4	LIRA	SAN MARINO
...	...	...	...	3.7	28640.2	PESETA	SPAIN
...	...	...	...	...	456.9	KRONA	SWEDEN

COUNTRY / PAYS / PAIS	YEAR / ANNEE / AÑO	FIXED CINEMAS / ETABLISSEMENTS FIXES / ESTABLECIMIENTOS FIJOS: NUMBER 35 MM AND OVER / NOMBRE 35 MM ET PLUS / NUMERO 35 MM Y MAS	NUMBER 16 MM / NOMBRE 16 MM / NUMERO 16 MM	SEATING CAPACITY / NOMBRE DE SIEGES / NUMERO DE ASIENTOS (000)	ANNUAL ATTENDANCE / FREQUENTATION ANNUELLE / FRECUENTACION ANUAL (000 000)	MOBILE UNITS / CINEMAS ITINERANTS / UNIDADES MOVILES: NUMBER 35 MM + 16 MM / NOMBRE 35 MM + 16 MM / NUMERO 35 MM + 16 MM	ANNUAL ATTENDANCE / FREQUENTATION ANNUELLE / FRECUENTACION ANUAL (000 000)
SWITZERLAND	1983	445	–	140.3	19.7	–	–
UNITED KINGDOM	1983	1 327	–	504.8	64.4	–	–
YUGOSLAVIA	1983	1 221	3	431	85.0	94	1.5
OCEANIA							
AUSTRALIA	1983	703	–	333.4	...	–	–
NEW CALEDONIA	1983	7	–	2.0	0.3	–	–
NEW ZEALAND	1979	172	–	103.0	...	...	...
NORFOLK ISLAND	1981	–	1	0.1	0.0	–	–
SAMOA	1979	2	4	5.6	0.5	–	–
TONGA	1979	3	–	2.0	0.1	5	0.0
U.S.S.R.							
U.S.S.R.	1983	141 641	./.	...	4051.1	9 629	./.
BYELORUSSIAN S.S.R.	1983	6 893	./.	...	138.0	407	./.
UKRAINIAN S.S.R.	1983	27 200	./.	...	788.0	700	...

DRIVE-IN CINEMAS CINEMAS POUR AUTOMOBILISTES CINES PARA AUTOMOVILISTAS			ALL CINEMAS TOUS LES CINEMAS TODOS LOS CINES				
NUMBER / NOMBRE / NUMERO	CAPACITY / CAPACITE / CAPACIDAD (000)	ANNUAL ATTENDANCE / FREQUENTATION ANNUELLE / FRECUENTACION ANUAL (000 000)	SEATS PER 1,000 INHABITANTS / SIEGES POUR 1 000 HABITANTS / ASIENTOS POR 1 000 HABITANTES	ANNUAL ATTENDANCE PER INHABITANT / FREQUENTATION ANNUELLE PAR HABITANT / FRECUENTACION ANUAL POR HABITANTE	GROSS BOX OFFICE RECEIPTS / RECETTES BRUTES / RECAUDACION TOTAL DE TAQUILLA (000 000)	CURRENCY / MONNAIE / MONEDA	COUNTRY / PAYS / PAIS
–	–	–	21.6	3.0	161.6	FRANC	SWITZERLAND
–	–	–	9.0	1.1	122.4	POUND STERLING	UNITED KINGDOM
–	–	–	19.1	3.8	2891.7	DINAR	YUGOSLAVIA
							OCEANIA
*30	./.	...	21.7	...	...	DOLLAR	AUSTRALIA
1	2.4	0.0	29.5	2.0	6.7	FRANC C.F.P.	NEW CALEDONIA
...	...	...	33.2	...	...	DOLLAR	NEW ZEALAND
–	–	–	0.1	5.0	...	AUSTRALIAN DOLLAR	NORFOLK ISLAND
–	–	–	36.1	3.2	0.3	TALA	SAMOA
–	–	–	20.0	1.0	...	PA'ANGA	TONGA
							U.S.S.R.
–	–	–	...	14.9	...	ROUBLE	U.S.S.R.
–	–	–	...	14.1	...	ROUBLE	BYELORUSSIAN S.S.R.
–	–	–	...	15.6	...	ROUBLE	UKRAINIAN S.S.R.

AMERICA, NORTH:
Canada:
E--> Receipts do not include taxes.
FR-> Les recettes ne tiennent pas compte des taxes.
ESP> Las recaudaciones no toman en cuenta los impuestos.
EUROPE:
France
E--> Data on seating capacity refer to 35 mm cinemas only.
FR-> Les données sur le nombre de sièges se réfèrent aux cinémas de 35 mm seulement.
ESP> Los datos sobre el número de asientos se refieren a los cines de 35 mm solamente.
Romania:
E--> Data on seating capacity refer to 35 mm cinemas only.
FR-> Les données sur le nombre de sièges se réfèrent aux cinémas de 35 mm seulement.
ESP> Los datos sobre el número de asientos se refieren a los cines de 35 mm solamente.

10 Broadcasting
Radiodiffusion
Radiodifusión

This chapter presents statistical information on radio and television broadcasting. The figures shown in the 9 tables of this chapter have been obtained from statistical surveys carried out in 1980, 1982 and 1984. The questionnaire used in these surveys was based on definitions and classifications proposed in the Recommendation concerning the International Standardization of Statistics on Radio and Television adopted by the General Conference in 1976.

The response rate of the surveys on radio and television broadcasting has been somewhat disappointing, which explains why Tables 10.5 to 10.9 contain only half the number of countries shown in the tables on receivers/licences issued, for which the statistics have been supplemented from various sources other than the regular Unesco questionnaires. It is hoped that following better application by all countries of the provisions laid down in the 1976 Recommendation, future surveys may result in the publication of more comprehensive and reliable broadcasting statistics.

As concerns television broadcasting, the information available leads to the assumption that in the following 34 countries and territories no television service has yet been introduced:

Africa: Botswana, Burundi, Cameroon, Cape Verde, Chad, Comoros, Gambia, Guinea-Bissau, Lesotho, Malawi, Mali, Rwanda, St. Helena, Sao Tome and Principe.

America, North: Belize, Cayman Islands, Dominica, Turks and Caicos Islands.

America, South: Falkland Islands (Malvinas), Guyana.

Asia: Bhutan, East Timor, Nepal.

Europe: Faeroe Islands.

Oceania: Cook Islands, Fiji, Kiribati, Nauru, Niue, Norfolk Island, Papua New Guinea, Solomon Islands, Tonga, Vanuatu.

Table 10.1

This table gives the latest data available on the number of radio transmitters and their total transmitting power for the period 1978-1983. The figures relate in principle to transmitters used for domestic broadcasting to the general public, excluding transmitters used primarily for external broadcasting. The table also gives data separately according to the type of agency responsible for the transmitters (government, public service, or commercial). Where only the total is given, this indicates that a breakdown by type of organization operating the transmitter has not been communicated. For transmitters operating in the VHF and SHF bands, the transmitting power is given in maximum ERP (Effective radiated power).

Table 10.2

This table gives information on the number of radio receivers and/or licences for the years 1965, 1970, 1975, 1980 and 1983. Generally, data refer to the end of the year stated. The figures on receivers relate to all types of receivers for radio broadcasts to the general public, including those connected to a cable distribution system (wired receivers). The data include such individual private receivers as car radios, portable radio sets and private sets installed in public places as well as communal receivers. Data on receivers are estimates of the number of receivers in use. Such data vary widely in reliability from country to country and should be treated with caution. The number of radio licences as shown in this table is composed of the number of licences for radio receivers plus the number of combined radio/television licences, where applicable.

Table 10.3

This table gives the latest data available on the number of television transmitters and their transmitting power (in maximum ERP) for the period 1978-1983. The figures relate to transmitters operating on a regular basis and used for broadcasting to the general public, regardless of whether the responsibility for them lies with broadcasting institutions or with other bodies such as the national postal or telecommunication services. Unless otherwise stated the data on transmitters relate to both main and relay transmitters. As is the case for radio transmitters, this table also provides information on the agency responsible for the transmitters. Information is also given on the number of television transmitters which broadcast programmes in colour.

Table 10.4

This table gives statistics on the number of television receivers and/or licences for 158 countries and territories out of the 204 represented in this Yearbook.

The number of television receivers/licences per thousand inhabitants for the years 1965, 1970, 1975, 1980 and 1983 has been calculated on the basis of data available.

As is the case for radio, data relating to television *receivers* represent the estimated total number of receivers in use.

Table 10.5

Table 10.5 shows statistics on sound broadcasting programmes for the years 1979, 1981 or 1983. The total annual broadcasting time has been broken down according to programme functions, e.g., information, education, advertisement, entertainment etc. The table also indicates whether the broadcasting institutions are governmental, public service or commercial.

Table 10.6

This table on television programmes has basically the same structure and content as Table 10.5.

Tables 10.7 to 10.9

The three tables on personnel (10.7), revenue (10.8) and current expenditure (10.9) show data on both radio and television grouped together. This has been made necessary by the fact that quite a number of broadcasting institutions which provide both radio and television services have not been able to furnish the corresponding statistics separately.

Ce chapitre donne des renseignements statistiques sur la radio et la télévision. Les chiffres qui apparaissent dans les 9 tableaux de ce chapître ont été obtenus grâce à des enquêtes statistiques effectuées en 1980, 1982 et 1984. Le questionnaire utilisé pour ces enquêtes a été préparé sur la base des définitions et classifications qui figurent dans la Recommandation concernant la normalisation internationale des statistiques relatives à la radio et à la télévision, adoptée par la Conférence générale en 1976.

Le taux de réponse aux enquêtes sur la radio et la télévision a été plutôt décevant, ce qui explique pourquoi les tableaux 10.5 à 10.9 ne présentent que la moitié des pays qui figurent dans les tableaux sur les récepteurs et les licences délivrées, pour lesquels les statistiques ont été obtenues de différentes sources autres que les questionnaires de l'Unesco. Il faut espérer qu'avec une meilleure application par tous les pays des dispositions qui figurent dans la Recommandation de 1976, les prochaines enquêtes permettront la publication de statistiques plus complètes et plus fiables sur la radiodiffusion.

En ce qui concerne la télévision, les renseignements disponibles permettent de conclure que dans les 34 pays et territoires suivants, il n'existe pas encore de service de télévision:

Afrique: Botswana, Burundi, Cameroun, Cap-Vert, Comores, Gambie, Guinée-Bissau, Lesotho, Malawi, Mali, Rwanda, Sainte-Hélène, Sao Tome et Principe, Tchad.

Amérique du Nord: Belize, Iles Caîmanes, Dominique, Iles Turques et Caîques..

Amérique du Sud: Iles Falkland (Malvinas), Guyana.

Asie: Bhoutan, Népal, Timor oriental.

Europe: Iles Féroé.

Océanie: Iles Cook, Fidji, Kiribati, Nauru, Nioué, Ile Norfolk, Papouasie-Nouvelle-Guinée, Iles Salomon, Tonga, Vanuatu.

Tableau 10.1

Ce tableau présente les dernières données disponibles pour la période 1978-1983 sur le nombre de postes émetteurs de radio et leur puissance totale d'émission. Les données se réfèrent en principe aux émetteurs en service qui diffusent des programmes destinés au public qui réside dans le pays et ne comprend pas les émetteurs réservés principalement aux émissions vers l'étranger. Le tableau présente également des données séparées sur le type d'institution responsable des émetteurs (gouvernemental, service public, ou commercial). Lorsque seul le total est présenté, il faut considérer que la répartition par type d'institution responsable des émetteurs n'a pas été communiquée. En ce qui concerne les émetteurs qui diffusent en ondes métriques et centimétriques, la puissance totale d'émission est exprimée en PAR maximale (puissance apparente rayonnée maximale).

Tableau 10.2

Ce tableau présente des renseignements sur le nombre de récepteurs de radio et/ou sur le total de licences délivrées, pour les années 1965, 1970, 1975, 1980 et 1983. En général, les données se réfèrent à la fin de l'année indiquée. Les statistiques portent sur tous les genres de postes récepteurs destinés à capter les programmes radiodiffusés à l'intention du grand public, y compris les postes récepteurs reliés à un réseau de distribution par câble. Les données se réfèrent à tous les postes individuels privés, comme les récepteurs pour automobiles, les postes portatifs et les postes privés installés dans des lieux publics de même qu'aux récepteurs destinés à l'écoute collective. Les données sur les récepteurs sont des estimations du nombre de récepteurs en service. La fiabilité de ces données varie sensiblement d'un pays à l'autre et elles doivent donc être considérées avec prudence. Le nombre de licences de radio présenté dans ce tableau se compose du nombre de licences délivrées pour les récepteurs de radio seulement, ajouté au nombre de licences combinées de radio et de télévision, lorsque c'est applicable.

Tableau 10.3

Ce tableau présente les dernières données disponibles sur le nombre d'émetteurs de télévision et leur puissance d'émission (en PAR maximale) pour la période 1978-1983. Les données se réfèrent aux émetteurs qui fonctionnent régulièrement et qui diffusent des programmes destinés au grand public, sans considérer si leur responsabilité appartient à une institution de radiodiffusion ou à d'autres organismes, comme par exemple les Postes et Télécommunications. Sauf indication contraire, les données sur les émetteurs comprennent les émetteurs principaux et les émetteurs auxiliaires. Comme dans le cas des émetteurs de radio, ce tableau présente également des renseignements sur l'autorité responsable des émetteurs. Des renseignements sont procurés également sur le nombre d'émetteurs de télévision qui diffusent des programmes en couleur.

Tableau 10.4

Le tableau 10.4 présente des statistiques sur le nombre de récepteurs de télévision et/ou les licences délivrées pour 158 pays et territoires, sur les 204 qui figurent dans cet Annuaire.

Sur la base des données disponibles, on a calculé le nombre de récepteurs/licences de télévision pour 1 000 habitants, pour les années 1965, 1970, 1975, 1980 et 1983.

Commme pour la radio, les données relatives aux récepteurs de télévision représentent une estimation du nombre total des récepteurs en service.

Tableau 10.5

Le tableau 10.5 présente des statistiques sur les programmes de radiodiffusion sonore pour les années 1979, 1981 ou 1983. La durée totale annuelle de diffusion a été répartie selon les fonctions des programmes, c'est-à-dire, information, éducation, publicité, divertissement, etc. De plus, le tableau indique si les organismes de radiodiffusion sont gouvernementaux, de service public ou commerciaux.

Tableau 10.6

Ce tableau se réfère aux programmes de télévision et présente exactement la même structure et le même contenu que le tableau 10.5.

Tableaux 10.7 à 10.9

Les trois tableaux contiennent à la fois pour la radiodiffusion sonore et la télévision des données regroupées sur le personnel (10.7), les ressources financières (10.8) et les dépenses courantes (10.9). Ceci a été rendu nécessaire par le fait qu'un grand nombre d'organismes responsables en même temps des services de radio et de télévision n'ont pas été en mesure de fournir séparément les statistiques correspondantes.

Este capítulo proporciona información sobre la radio y la televisión. Los datos que figuran en los 9 cuadros de este capítulo han sido obtenidos por medio de encuestas estadísticas efectuadas en 1980, 1982 y en 1984. El cuestionario utilizado en estas encuestas esta basado en las definiciones y clasificaciones contenidas en la Recomendación sobre la normalización internacional de las estadísticas relativas a la radio y la televisión, adoptada por la Conferencia General en 1976.

La tasa de respuesta de las encuestas sobre la radio y la televisión ha sido desalentador, lo que explica por qué en los cuadros 10.5 a 10.9, aparecen sólo la mitad de los países que forman parte de los cuadros sobre los receptores y licencias existentes, para las cuales las estadísticas han sido obtenidas de varias fuentes, diferentes de los cuestionarios de la Unesco. Es de esperar que con una mejor aplicación por parte de todos los países de las disposiciones que figuran en la Recomendación de 1976, las encuestas futuras permitirán la publicación de estadísticas más completas y más fiables sobre la radiodifusión.

En lo que se refiere a la televisión, de la información disponible se desprende que en los 34 países y territorios siguientes no existe todavía un servicio de televisión:

Africa: Botswana, Burundi, Cabo Verde, Camerún, Chad, Comores, Gambia, Guinea-Bissau, Lesotho, Malawi, Mali, Rwanda, Santa Elena, Santo Tomé y Príncipe.

América del Norte: Belize, Islas Caimán, Dominica, Islas Turcas y Caicos.

América del Sur: Islas Falkland (Malvinas), Guyana.

Asia: Bután, Nepal, Timor oriental.

Europa: Islas Feroé.

Oceanía: Islas Cook, Kiribati, Nauru, Niue, Isla Norfolk, Papua Nueva Guinea, Islas Salomón, Tonga, Vanuatú, Viti.

Cuadro 10.1

Este cuadro presenta los últimos datos disponibles sobre el número de transmisores de radio y su potencia total, para el periodo 1978-1983. En principio, los datos se refieren a los transmisores en funcionamiento que emiten programas destinados al público que reside en el país y no incluyen los transmisores reservados principalmente a las emisiones destinadas al extranjero. El cuadro también presenta datos sobre el tipo de institución responsable de los transmisores (gubernamental, servicio público, o comercial). Cuando sólo se presenta el total, debe considerarse que la distribución por tipo de institución responsable de los transmisores no ha sido comunicada. En lo que se refiere a los transmisores que emiten en muy alta y super alta frecuencia, la potencia total de emisión se expresa en ERP máxima (potencia efectiva radiada máxima).

Cuadro 10.2

Este cuadro procura información sobre el número de receptores de radio y/o los permisos existentes para 1965, 1970, 1975, 1980 y 1983. En general, los datos se refieren al final del año indicado. Las estadísticas se refieren a todos los tipos de receptores destinados a captar los programas emitidos para el público en general, incluídos los que están conectados por cable a una red de distribución. Los datos abarcan todos los receptores individuales privados, como los de los automóviles, los portátiles y los receptores privados instalados en locales públicos así como los receptores destinados a una escucha colectiva. Los datos sobre los receptores son estimaciones del número de receptores en uso. La fiabilidad de estos datos varía sensiblemente de un país a otro y por eso deben ser considerados con prudencia. El número de permisos de radio que figura en este cuadro se refiere al número de permisos concedidos para los receptores de radio solamente, además del número de permisos combinados de radio y de televisión, cuando ello es aplicable.

Cuadro 10.3

Este cuadro presenta los últimos datos disponibles sobre el número de transmisores de televisión y su potencia de emisión (en ERP máxima) para el periodo 1978-1983. Los datos se refieren a los transmisores que funcionan con carácter regular y que emiten programas destinados al público en general, sin considerar si la responsabilidad reside en una institución de radiodifusión o en otros organismos, como por ejemplo correos y telégrafos. Salvo indicación contraria, los datos relativos a los transmisores comprenden los transmisores principales y los auxiliares. Igual que para los transmisores de radio, este cuadro también proporciona información sobre la autoridad responsable de los transmisores. Se presenta igualmente información con respecto al número de transmisores de televisión que emiten programas en color.

Cuadro 10.4

Este cuadro presenta estadísticas sobre el número de receptores de televisión y/o permisos concedidos para 158 países y territorios, sobre los 204 que figuran en este Anuario.

Sobre la base de los datos disponibles, se ha calculado el número de receptores/permisos de televisión por 1 000 habitantes para los años 1965, 1970, 1975, 1980 y 1983.

Como para la radio, los datos relativos a los receptores de televisión representan una estimación del número total de los receptores en uso.

Cuadro 10.5

El cuadro 10.5 presenta, para 1979, 1981 o 1983, las estadíticas sobre los programas de radiodifusión. La duración anual total de radiodifusión ha sido repartida según las funciones de los programas, i.e., información, educación, publicidad, programas recreativos, etc. El cuadro indica también si las instituciones de radiodifusión son gubernamentales, de servicio público o comerciales.

Cuadro 10.6

Este cuadro se refiere a los programas de televisión y presenta exactamente la misma estructura y los mismos criterios que el cuadro 10.5.

Cuadros 10.7 a 10.9

Los tres cuadros sobre personal (10.7), fuentes de ingreso (10.8) y gastos ordinarios (10.9) indican datos sobre radio y televsión en conjunto. Esta agrupación ha sido necesaria por el hecho de que una gran cantidad de organismos responsables a la vez de los servicios de radio y de televisión, no han podido proporcionarnos las estadísticas correspondientes por separado.

10.1 Radio broadcasting: number of transmitters and transmitting power by frequency band

Radiodiffusion sonore: nombre d'émetteurs et puissance d'émission par bande de fréquence

Radiodifusión sonora: número de transmisores y potencia de emisión por banda de frecuencia

T = TOTAL
G = GOVERNMENTAL
P = PUBLIC
C = COMMERCIAL

FIGURES RELATE TO TRANSMITTERS IN SERVICE USED FOR DOMESTIC RADIO BROADCASTS TO THE GENERAL PUBLIC

TRANSMITTING POWER IS EXPRESSED IN KILOWATTS FOR LOW, MEDIUM AND HIGH FREQUENCY TRANSMITTERS, IN EFFECTIVE RADIATED POWER (ERP) FOR VERY AND SUPER HIGH FREQUENCY TRANSMITTERS.

NUMBER OF COUNTRIES AND TERRITORIES PRESENTED IN THIS TABLE: 166

T = TOTAL
G = GOUVERNEMENTAL
P = PUBLIC
C = COMMERCIAL

LES DONNEES SE RAPPORTENT AUX EMETTEURS EN SERVICE QUI DIFFUSENT DES PROGRAMMES DESTINES AU PUBLIC QUI RESIDE DANS LE PAYS

LA PUISSANCE D'EMISSION EST EXPRIMEE EN KILOWATTS POUR LES EMETTEURS D'ONDES KILOMETRIQUES, HECTOMETRIQUES ET DECAMETRIQUES, EN PUISSANCE APPARENTE RAYONNEE (PAR) POUR LES EMETTEURS D'ONDES METRIQUES ET CENTIMETRIQUES

NOMBRE DE PAYS ET DE TERRITOIRES PRESENTES DANS CE TABLEAU: 166

T = TOTAL
G = GUBERNAMENTAL
P = PUBLICA
C = COMERCIAL

LOS DATOS SE REFIEREN A LOS TRANSMISORES EN FUNCIONAMIENTO QUE EMITEN PROGRAMAS DESTINADOS AL PUBLICO QUE RESIDE EN EL PAIS

LA POTENCIA DE EMISION SE EXPRESA EN KILOVATIOS PARA LOS TRANSMISORES DE BAJA, MEDIA Y ALTA FRECUENCIA; EN POTENCIA EFECTIVA RADIADA (ERP) PARA LOS TRANSMISORES EN MUY ALTA FRECUENCIA Y EN SUPER ALTA FRECUENCIA

NUMERO DE PAISES Y DE TERRITORIOS PRESENTADOS EN ESTE CUADRO: 166

COUNTRY / PAYS / PAIS	YEAR / ANNEE / AÑO	OWNERSHIP / PROPRIETE / PROPIEDAD	FREQUENCY / ONDES / FRECUENCIA: LOW / KILOMETRIQUES / BAJA — NUMBER OF TRANSMITTERS / NOMBRE D'EMETTEURS / NUMERO DE TRANSMISORES	LOW — TRANSMITTING POWER / PUISSANCE D'EMISSION / POTENCIA DE EMISION	MEDIUM / HECTOMETRIQUES / MEDIA — NUMBER OF TRANSMITTERS / NOMBRE D'EMETTEURS / NUMERO DE TRANSMISORES	MEDIUM — TRANSMITTING POWER / PUISSANCE D'EMISSION / POTENCIA DE EMISION	HIGH / DECAMETRIQUES / ALTA — NUMBER OF TRANSMITTERS / NOMBRE D'EMETTEURS / NUMERO DE TRANSMISORES	HIGH — TRANSMITTING POWER / PUISSANCE D'EMISSION / POTENCIA DE EMISION	V. HIGH & SUPER HIGH / METRIQUES & CENTIMET. / MUY ALTA Y SUPER ALTA — NUMBER OF TRANSMITTERS / NOMBRE D'EMETTEURS / NUMERO DE TRANSMISORES	V. HIGH & SUPER HIGH — TRANSMITTING POWER / PUISSANCE D'EMISSION / POTENCIA DE EMISION
			(1)	(2)	(3)	(4)	(5)	(6)	(7)	(8)
AFRICA										
ALGERIA	1981	P	2	1 500	39	2 610	14	1 050	–	–
ANGOLA	1979	G	–	–	25	297	25	520	5	7
BENIN	1981	G	–	–	4	90	3	80	–	–
BOTSWANA	1983	G	–	–	3	101	3	70	3	52
BURKINA FASO	1979	G	–	–	3	151	2	24	4	...
BURUNDI	1979	G	–	–	–	–	1	25	4	6
CAMEROON	1980	G	–	–	8	102	9	386	2	...
CAPE VERDE	1979	G	–	–	–	–	2	2	1	...
CENTRAL AFRICAN REPUBLIC	1979	G	–	–	1	1	2	200	1	...
CHAD	1983	G	–	–	3	22	3	106	1	...
COMOROS	1979	G	–	–	2	50	2	18	3	...
CONGO	1983	G	–	–	5	52	5	133	–	–
COTE D'IVOIRE	1979	G	–	–	3	14	3	135	18	360
DJIBOUTI	1979	G	–	–	2	8	1	4	–	–
EGYPT	1983	G	–	–	127	5 831	27	3 522	–	–

COUNTRY / PAYS / PAIS	YEAR / ANNEE / AÑO	OWNERSHIP / PROPRIETE / PROPIEDAD	FREQUENCY / ONDES / FRECUENCIA: LOW / KILOMETRIQUES / BAJA		MEDIUM / HECTOMETRIQUES / MEDIA		HIGH / DECAMETRIQUES / ALTA		V. HIGH & SUPER HIGH / METRIQUES & CENTIMET. / MUY ALTA Y SUPER ALTA	
			NUMBER OF TRANSMITTERS / NOMBRE D'EMETTEURS / NUMERO DE TRANSMISORES	TRANSMITTING POWER / PUISSANCE D'EMISSION / POTENCIA DE EMISION	NUMBER OF TRANSMITTERS / NOMBRE D'EMETTEURS / NUMERO DE TRANSMISORES	TRANSMITTING POWER / PUISSANCE D'EMISSION / POTENCIA DE EMISION	NUMBER OF TRANSMITTERS / NOMBRE D'EMETTEURS / NUMERO DE TRANSMISORES	TRANSMITTING POWER / PUISSANCE D'EMISSION / POTENCIA DE EMISION	NUMBER OF TRANSMITTERS / NOMBRE D'EMETTEURS / NUMERO DE TRANSMISORES	TRANSMITTING POWER / PUISSANCE D'EMISSION / POTENCIA DE EMISION
			(1)	(2)	(3)	(4)	(5)	(6)	(7)	(8)
EQUATORIAL GUINEA	1979	T	–	–	–	–	3	210	–	–
		G	–	–	–	–	1	10	–	–
		C	–	–	–	–	2	200	–	–
ETHIOPIA	1983	G	–	–	4	252	5	500	–	–
GABON	1979	G	–	–	7	83	7	284	2	...
GAMBIA	1979	T	–	–	2	25	–	–	1	...
		G	–	–	1	20	–	–	1	...
		C	–	–	1	5	–	–	–	–
GHANA	1981	G	–	–	–	–	4	5 820	...	...
GUINEA	1979	G	–	–	2	201	5	276	1	3
GUINEA-BISSAU	1983	G	–	–	1	100	1	10	–	–
KENYA	1979	G	–	–	11	660	9	275	2	2
LESOTHO	1979	G	–	–	2	101	1	100	1	1
LIBERIA‡	1978	T	...	...	2	60	5	130	2	...
		G	...	...	1	50	1	10	1	...
		P	...	...	1	10	4	120	–	–
		C	...	...	–	–	–	–	1	...
LIBYAN ARAB JAMAHIRIYA	1979	G	–	–	12	2 141	5	2 100	3	...
MADAGASCAR	1979	G	–	–	11	14	9	260	1	...
MALAWI	1983	P	–	–	14	197	2	120	–	–
MALI	1981	G	–	–	2	130	2	130	10	372
MAURITANIA	1979	G	–	–	1	20	3	300	–	–
MAURITIUS	1983	P	–	–	2	20	2	20	1	5
MOROCCO	1979	G	1	800	27	2 656	4	250	4	12
MOZAMBIQUE	1979	G	–	–	13	196	25	902	1	...
NAMIBIA	1979	G	–	–	–	–	4	200	9	9
NIGER	1979	G	–	–	10	4	6	82	3	3
NIGERIA	1978	T	–	–	60	2 550	36	1 070	15	86
		G	–	–	12	1 050	10	510	–	–
		P	–	–	48	1 500	26	560	15	86
REUNION	1979	P	–	–	2	40	–	–	23	2
RWANDA‡	1983	G	–	–	–	–	2	55	6	11
ST. HELENA	1981	G	–	–	2	1	–	–	–	–
SAO TOME AND PRINCIPE	1979	G	–	–	2	25	1	10	2	1
SENEGAL	1981	G	–	–	7	266	4	138	–	–
SIERRA LEONE	1982	G	–	–	1	10	1	250	1	1
SOMALIA	1979	G	–	–	2	160	2	100	–	–
SUDAN	1983	G	–	–	6	2 400	–	–	–	–
SWAZILAND	1983	G	–	–	2	110	–	–	6	113
TOGO	1979	G	–	–	3	31	4	210	4	...
TUNISIA	1979	G	–	–	6	2 560	3	300	3	...
UGANDA	1979	G	–	–	9	571	4	273	–	–
UNITED REP. OF TANZANIA	1979	G	–	–	9	303	6	220	4	...
ZAMBIA	1979	G	–	–	10	508	5	290	1	1

COUNTRY / PAYS / PAIS	YEAR / ANNEE / AÑO	OWNERSHIP / PROPRIETE / PROPIEDAD	FREQUENCY / ONDES / FRECUENCIA: LOW / KILOMETRIQUES / BAJA — NUMBER OF TRANSMITTERS / NOMBRE D'EMETTEURS / NUMERO DE TRANSMISORES	LOW / KILOMETRIQUES / BAJA — TRANSMITTING POWER / PUISSANCE D'EMISSION / POTENCIA DE EMISION	MEDIUM / HECTOMETRIQUES / MEDIA — NUMBER OF TRANSMITTERS / NOMBRE D'EMETTEURS / NUMERO DE TRANSMISORES	MEDIUM / HECTOMETRIQUES / MEDIA — TRANSMITTING POWER / PUISSANCE D'EMISSION / POTENCIA DE EMISION	HIGH / DECAMETRIQUES / ALTA — NUMBER OF TRANSMITTERS / NOMBRE D'EMETTEURS / NUMERO DE TRANSMISORES	HIGH / DECAMETRIQUES / ALTA — TRANSMITTING POWER / PUISSANCE D'EMISSION / POTENCIA DE EMISION	V. HIGH & SUPER HIGH / METRIQUES & CENTIMET. / MUY ALTA Y SUPER ALTA — NUMBER OF TRANSMITTERS / NOMBRE D'EMETTEURS / NUMERO DE TRANSMISORES	V. HIGH & SUPER HIGH / METRIQUES & CENTIMET. / MUY ALTA Y SUPER ALTA — TRANSMITTING POWER / PUISSANCE D'EMISSION / POTENCIA DE EMISION
			(1)	(2)	(3)	(4)	(5)	(6)	(7)	(8)
AMERICA, NORTH										
ANTIGUA AND BARBUDA‡	1979	T	–	–	3	25	–	–	2	...
		G	–	–	1	5	–	–	–	–
		P	–	–	1	10	–	–	1	...
		C	–	–	1	10	–	–	1	...
BAHAMAS	1979	P	–	–	3	22	–	–	2	...
BELIZE	1983	G	–	–	5	23	1	1	5	21
BERMUDA	1979	C	–	–	3	3	–	–	2	16
BRITISH VIRGIN ISLANDS	1983	C	–	–	1	10	–	–	–	–
CANADA	1983	T	–	–	754	5 517	–	–	786	24 192
		P	–	–	338	953	–	–	359	7 354
		C	–	–	416	4 564	–	–	427	16 838
CAYMAN ISLANDS	1981	T	–	–	2	11	–	–	2	...
		G	–	–	2	11	–	–	1	...
		P	–	–	–	–	–	–	1	...
COSTA RICA	1981	T	–	–	65	532	10	14	48	50
		G	–	–	1	50	1	3	1	1
		P	–	–	10	108	4	6	3	5
		C	–	–	54	374	5	5	44	44
CUBA	1983	G	–	–	150	1 116	–	–	–	–
DOMINICA	1979	T	–	–	3	70	–	–	–	–
		G	–	–	1	10	–	–	–	–
		P	–	–	1	10	–	–	–	–
		C	–	–	1	50	–	–	–	–
DOMINICAN REPUBLIC	1979	C	–	–	123	455	9	168	56	...
EL SALVADOR	1979	T	–	–	74	316	1	10	–	–
		P	–	–	6	42	1	10	–	–
		C	–	–	68	274	–	–	–	–
GREENLAND	1979	G	–	–	7	100	1	1	10	1
GRENADA	1979	G	–	–	1	1	2	10	–	–
GUADELOUPE	1979	P	–	–	2	44	–	–	3	...
GUATEMALA	1979	C	–	–	90	387	14	69	11	...
HAITI	1979	C	–	–	32	116	6	8	10	...
HONDURAS	1979	C	–	–	116	332	12	35	25	...
JAMAICA	1979	C	–	–	8	40	–	–	11	36
MARTINIQUE	1979	P	–	–	2	40	–	–	4	...
MEXICO	1983	T	...	...	651	...	29	...	192	...
		G	...	...	27	...	11	...	13	...
		C	...	...	624	...	18	...	179	...
MONTSERRAT‡	1979	T	–	–	3	221	–	–	–	–
		G	–	–	1	1	–	–	–	–
		C	–	–	2	220	–	–	–	–
NETHERLANDS ANTILLES‡	1979	T	–	–	13	523	–	–	3	...
		P	–	–	2	510	–	–	–	–
		C	–	–	11	13	–	–	3	...
NICARAGUA	1979	T	–	–	70	497	6	152	11	...
		P	–	–	3	116	2	150	–	–
		C	–	–	67	381	4	2	11	...
ST. CHRISTOPHER–NEVIS AND ANGUILLA	1979	T	–	–	2	70	–	–	–	–
		P	–	–	1	50	–	–	–	–
		C	–	–	1	20	–	–	–	–

COUNTRY / PAYS / PAIS	YEAR / ANNEE / AÑO	OWNERSHIP / PROPRIETE / PROPIEDAD	FREQUENCY / ONDES / FRECUENCIA: LOW / KILOMETRIQUES / BAJA — NUMBER OF TRANSMITTERS / NOMBRE D'EMETTEURS / NUMERO DE TRANSMISORES	LOW — TRANSMITTING POWER / PUISSANCE D'EMISSION / POTENCIA DE EMISION	MEDIUM / HECTOMETRIQUES / MEDIA — NUMBER OF TRANSMITTERS / NOMBRE D'EMETTEURS / NUMERO DE TRANSMISORES	MEDIUM — TRANSMITTING POWER / PUISSANCE D'EMISSION / POTENCIA DE EMISION	HIGH / DECAMETRIQUES / ALTA — NUMBER OF TRANSMITTERS / NOMBRE D'EMETTEURS / NUMERO DE TRANSMISORES	HIGH — TRANSMITTING POWER / PUISSANCE D'EMISSION / POTENCIA DE EMISION	V. HIGH & SUPER HIGH / METRIQUES & CENTIMET. / MUY ALTA Y SUPER ALTA — NUMBER OF TRANSMITTERS / NOMBRE D'EMETTEURS / NUMERO DE TRANSMISORES	V. HIGH & SUPER HIGH — TRANSMITTING POWER / PUISSANCE D'EMISSION / POTENCIA DE EMISION
			(1)	(2)	(3)	(4)	(5)	(6)	(7)	(8)
ST. LUCIA	1979	C	–	–	4	71	–	–	–	–
ST. PIERRE AND MIQUELON	1979	P	–	–	1	20	–	–	3	...
ST. VINCENT AND THE GRENADINES	1979	C	–	–	1	10	–	–	–	–
TRINIDAD AND TOBAGO	1979	T	–	–	3	71	–	–	2	40
		G	–	–	1	50	–	–	1	20
		C	–	–	2	21	–	–	1	20
TURKS AND CAICOS ISLANDS	1983	P	–	–	2	3	–	–	–	–
U.S. VIRGIN ISLANDS	1979	C	...	...	5	...	4	...	...	...
AMERICA, SOUTH										
ARGENTINA	1979	T	–	–	152	2 146	14	...	36	...
		G	–	–	30	619	3	151	9	...
		P	–	–	11	198	2	...	3	...
		C	–	–	111	1 329	9	86	24	...
BOLIVIA	1981	T	–	–	114	233	58	149	12	32
		G	–	–	1	10	3	30	1	10
		P	–	–	21	91	3	11	1	10
		C	–	–	92	132	52	108	10	12
BRAZIL	1983	T	–	–	1 202	...	123	...	493	...
		G	–	–	5	...	8	...	14	...
		P	–	–	5	...	–	...	10	...
		C	–	–	1 192	...	115	...	469	...
CHILE	1979	T	21	171	54	382	8	45	26	80
		G	2	101	11	228	2	11	9	25
		P	2	1	6	14	–	–	4	4
		C	17	69	37	140	6	34	13	51
FRENCH GUIANA	1981	P	–	–	2	20	2	14	9	1
GUYANA	1979	G	–	–	6	51	1	10	1	1
PARAGUAY	1979	T	–	–	34	403	6	114	16	...
		G	–	–	1	100	2	105	–	–
		C	–	–	33	303	4	9	16	...
SURINAME	1979	T	–	–	6	79	2	14	8	10
		C	–	–	6	79	2	14	8	10
URUGUAY	1981	T	–	–	89	650	1	10	4	400
		G	–	–	3	150	–	–	1	100
		C	–	–	86	500	1	10	3	300
ASIA										
AFGHANISTAN	1979	G	–	–	10	143	4	168	–	–
BAHRAIN	1979	G	–	–	2	21	–	–	1	3
BANGLADESH	1979	G	–	–	9	1 266	4	218	10	13
BHUTAN	1979	P	–	–	–	–	1	0	–	–
BRUNEI DARUSSALAM	1983	G	–	–	4	421	–	–	4	20
BURMA	1979	G	–	–	1	50	5	250	1	...
CYPRUS	1983	P	–	–	4	43	–	–	2	40
DEMOCRATIC KAMPUCHEA	1979	G	–	–	2	...	4	...	–	–
DEMOCRATIC YEMEN	1979	G	–	–	2	250	4	308	–	–
HONG KONG	1983	T	–	–	6	72	–	–	18	16
		G	–	–	2	40	–	–	9	10
		P	–	–	1	2	–	–	5	5
		C	–	–	3	30	–	–	4	...
INDIA	1983	G	–	–	128	5 240	30	1 565	4	60

COUNTRY / PAYS / PAIS	YEAR / ANNEE / AÑO	OWNERSHIP / PROPRIETE / PROPIEDAD	FREQUENCY / ONDES / FRECUENCIA — LOW / KILOMETRIQUES / BAJA		MEDIUM / HECTOMETRIQUES / MEDIA		HIGH / DECAMETRIQUES / ALTA		V. HIGH & SUPER HIGH / METRIQUES & CENTIMET. / MUY ALTA Y SUPER ALTA	
			NUMBER OF TRANSMITTERS / NOMBRE D'EMETTEURS / NUMERO DE TRANSMISORES	TRANSMITTING POWER / PUISSANCE D'EMISSION / POTENCIA DE EMISION	NUMBER OF TRANSMITTERS / NOMBRE D'EMETTEURS / NUMERO DE TRANSMISORES	TRANSMITTING POWER / PUISSANCE D'EMISSION / POTENCIA DE EMISION	NUMBER OF TRANSMITTERS / NOMBRE D'EMETTEURS / NUMERO DE TRANSMISORES	TRANSMITTING POWER / PUISSANCE D'EMISSION / POTENCIA DE EMISION	NUMBER OF TRANSMITTERS / NOMBRE D'EMETTEURS / NUMERO DE TRANSMISORES	TRANSMITTING POWER / PUISSANCE D'EMISSION / POTENCIA DE EMISION
			(1)	(2)	(3)	(4)	(5)	(6)	(7)	(8)
INDONESIA	1981	G	–	–	50	1 146	146	1 586	105	16
IRAN, ISLAMIC REPUBLIC OF	1983	G	–	–	148	11 517	11	3 800	34	52
IRAQ	1983	G	–	–	11	4 670	24	10 700	11	110
ISRAEL	1983	T	–	–	22	2 059	16	1 550	25	820
JAPAN	1983	T	–	–	526	4 596	7	310	537	173
		P	–	–	322	3 473	–	–	497	123
		C	–	–	204	1 123	7	310	40	50
JORDAN	1983	G	–	–	9	2 232	2	200	6	148
KUWAIT	1983	G	–	–	3	3 200	–	–	3	25
LAO PEOPLE'S DEMOCRATIC REPUBLIC‡	1978	G	...	...	3	30	1	25	...	...
LEBANON	1979	T	–	–	4	165	3	215	3	34
		G	–	–	2	110	2	200	3	34
		P	–	–	2	55	1	15	–	–
MACAU	1979	T	–	–	3	20	–	–	2	1
		G	–	–	2	10	–	–	1	1
		C	–	–	1	10	–	–	1	...
MALAYSIA	1983	G	–	–	60	2 510	21	2 630	2	11
MALDIVES	1983	G	–	–	1	3	2	16	–	–
OMAN	1983	G	–	–	6	320	4	163	2	2
PAKISTAN	1983	G	–	–	23	2 272	16	1 161	36	21
PHILIPPINES	1981	T	97	518	86	375	46	386	66	270
		G	7	70	9	38	6	7	4	15
		P	1	41	8	26	7	270	1	10
		C	89	407	69	311	33	109	61	245
QATAR	1983	G	–	–	8	1 752	1	250	2	20
SAUDI ARABIA	1979	T	...	...	3	600	9	1 200	...	...
SINGAPORE	1983	G	–	–	9	830	7	310	5	100
SRI LANKA	1983	G	–	–	27	563	15	405	19	10
SYRIAN ARAB REPUBLIC	1983	G	–	–	10	2 300	4	2 000	15	150
TURKEY	1983	P	3	1 520	9	3 054	5	1 750	27	960
UNITED ARAB EMIRATES‡	1983	G	–	–	8	3 150	5	2 120	2	3
VIET-NAM	1979	G	–	–	16	...	22	...	1	...
YEMEN	1979	G	–	–	3	130	3	125	–	–
EUROPE										
ALBANIA	1983	G	–	–	11	500	2	30	1	100
ANDORRA	1979	C	–	–	2	1 200	1	10	1	...
AUSTRIA	1983	P	–	–	18	1 486	–	–	549	2 476
BELGIUM	1983	P	–	–	8	1 180	–	–	33	131
BULGARIA	1979	G	–	–	24	3 512	–	–	11	...
CZECHOSLOVAKIA	1983	G	1	1 500	72	5 046	9	1 040	41	1 136
DENMARK	1981	P	1	200	1	250	1	50	46	1 293
FAEROE ISLANDS	1979	P	–	–	1	5	–	–	3	7
FINLAND	1983	P	1	200	6	248	4	380	90	...

COUNTRY / PAYS / PAIS	YEAR / ANNEE / AÑO	OWNERSHIP / PROPRIETE / PROPIEDAD	FREQUENCY / ONDES / FRECUENCIA: LOW / KILOMETRIQUES / BAJA — NUMBER OF TRANSMITTERS / NOMBRE D'EMETTEURS / NUMERO DE TRANSMISORES	LOW / KILOMETRIQUES / BAJA — TRANSMITTING POWER / PUISSANCE D'EMISSION / POTENCIA DE EMISION	MEDIUM / HECTOMETRIQUES / MEDIA — NUMBER OF TRANSMITTERS / NOMBRE D'EMETTEURS / NUMERO DE TRANSMISORES	MEDIUM / HECTOMETRIQUES / MEDIA — TRANSMITTING POWER / PUISSANCE D'EMISSION / POTENCIA DE EMISION	HIGH / DECAMETRIQUES / ALTA — NUMBER OF TRANSMITTERS / NOMBRE D'EMETTEURS / NUMERO DE TRANSMISORES	HIGH / DECAMETRIQUES / ALTA — TRANSMITTING POWER / PUISSANCE D'EMISSION / POTENCIA DE EMISION	V. HIGH & SUPER HIGH / METRIQUES & CENTIMET. / MUY ALTA Y SUPER ALTA — NUMBER OF TRANSMITTERS / NOMBRE D'EMETTEURS / NUMERO DE TRANSMISORES	V. HIGH & SUPER HIGH / METRIQUES & CENTIMET. / MUY ALTA Y SUPER ALTA — TRANSMITTING POWER / PUISSANCE D'EMISSION / POTENCIA DE EMISION
			(1)	(2)	(3)	(4)	(5)	(6)	(7)	(8)
FRANCE	1983	P	1	2 000	39	4 161	19	4 700	781	1 113
GERMAN DEMOCRATIC REPUBLIC	1983	G	1	750	60	3 196	–	–	56	3 371
GERMANY, FEDERAL REPUBLIC OF‡	1983	P	2	750	49	8 755	34	7 750	384	8 475
GIBRALTAR	1983	P	–	–	1	2	–	–	2	...
HUNGARY	1983	G	–	–	13	2 820	7	745	31	191
IRELAND	1980	P	–	–	7	733	–	–	14	618
ITALY	1983	P	1	10	128	2 790	9	585	2 013	5 553
MALTA	1979	G	–	–	2	20	–	–	1	5
MONACO	1981	P	1	2 000	3	1 600	2	200	6	2 000
NETHERLANDS	1983	P	–	–	7	935	5	410	38	886
NORWAY	1981	P	2	210	5	231	4	590	753	2 810
PORTUGAL	1983	P	–	–	35	825	8	750	40	536
ROMANIA	1979	G	1	...	28	3 010	10	...	32	201
SPAIN	1983	P	–	–	75	3 408	16	27 870	173	669
SWEDEN	1980	P	1	300	3	350	4	...	332	6 101
UNITED KINGDOM	1979	P	3	500	132	2 268	–	–	352	4 783
YUGOSLAVIA	1983	P	–	–	362	8 198	5	270	436	4 226
OCEANIA										
AMERICAN SAMOA	1981	C	–	–	1	10	–	–	–	–
AUSTRALIA	1981	T	–	–	234	1 429	7	102	43	878
		G	–	–	4	10	–	–	–	–
		P	–	–	98	997	7	102	36	767
		C	–	–	132	422	–	–	7	111
FIJI	1979	P	–	–	11	56	–	–	1	1
FRENCH POLYNESIA	1979	P	–	–	1	24	5	68	–	–
KIRIBATI	1981	P	–	–	1	10	–	–	–	–
NAURU	1979	G	–	–	1	0	–	–	–	–
NEW CALEDONIA	1979	P	–	–	1	20	1	20	1	20
NEW ZEALAND	1979	T	–	–	65	497	–	–	–	–
		P	–	–	57	470	–	–	–	–
		C	–	–	8	27	–	–	–	–
NIUE	1983	G	–	–	1	1	–	–	–	–
NORFOLK ISLAND	1983	G	–	–	1	0	1	0	–	–
PACIFIC ISLANDS	1979	T	–	–	10	23	–	–	1	...
		G	–	–	8	21	–	–	–	–
		P	–	–	1	1	–	–	–	–
		C	–	–	1	1	–	–	1	...
SAMOA	1981	G	–	–	6	18	–	–	–	–
TONGA	1983	P	–	–	2	10	–	–	–	–
TUVALU	1983	G	–	–	1	5	–	–	–	–
VANUATU	1983	G	–	–	1	10	2	10	1	...

AFRICA:

Liberia:

E--> Data on high frequency transmitters do not include 8 transmitters of the Voice of America.

FR-> Les données relatives aux émetteurs d'ondes décamétriques n'incluent pas 8 émetteurs de la 'Voix de l'Amérique'.

ESP> Los datos relativos a los transmisores de ondas de alta frecuencia no incluyen 8 transmisores de la 'Voz de América'.

Rwanda:

E--> Data exclude transmitters of 'Deutsche Welle'.

FR-> Les données ne comprennent pas les émetteurs de 'Deutsche Welle'.

ESP> Los datos excluyen los transmisores de 'Deutsche Welle'.

AMERICA, NORTH:

Antigua and Barbuda:

E--> Data do not include transmitters of BBC and 'Deutsche Welle'.

FR-> Les données ne tiennent pas compte des émetteurs de la 'BBC' et de la 'Deutsche Welle'.

ESP> Los datos excluyen los transmisores de la 'BBC' y de la Deutsche Welle'.

Montserrat:

E--> Data exclude transmitters of BBC and 'Deutsche Welle'.

FR-> Les données ne tiennent pas compte des émetteurs de la 'BBC' et de la 'Deutsche Welle'.

ESP> Los datos excluyen los transmisores de la 'BBC' y de la

Montserrat: (Cont):

'Deutsche Welle'.

Netherlands Antilles:

E--> Data exclude high frequency transmitters of Transworld Radio and 'Radio Nederland'.

FR-> Les données ne tiennent pas compte des émetteurs d'ondes décamétriques de 'Transworld Radio' et 'Radio Nederland'.

ESP> Los datos excluyen los transmisores de ondas de alta frecuencia de 'Transworld Radio' y 'Radio Nederland'.

ASIA:

Lao People's Democratic Republic:

E--> Not including 7 regional stations

FR-> Non compris 7 stations régionales.

ESP> No incluye 7 estaciones regionales.

United Arab Emirates:

E--> Data refer to Abu Dhabi only.

FR-> Les données se réfèrent à Abu Dhabi seulement.

ESP> Los datos se refieren a Abu Dhabi solamente.

EUROPE:

Germany, Federal Republic of:

E--> Data do not include transmitters of foreign military forces.

FR-> Les données ne tiennent pas compte des émetteurs des forces militaires étrangères.

ESP> Los datos excluyen los transmisores de las fuerzas militares extranjeras.

10.2 Radio broadcasting: number of receivers and receivers per 1,000 inhabitants

Radiodiffusion sonore: nombre de récepteurs et de récepteurs pour 1 000 habitants

Radiodifusión sonora: número de receptores y de receptores por 1 000 habitantes

L = NUMBER OF LICENCES ISSUED OR SETS DECLARED

R = ESTIMATED NUMBER OF RECEIVERS IN USE

NUMBER OF COUNTRIES AND TERRITORIES PRESENTED IN THIS TABLE: 198

L = NOMBRE DE LICENCES DELIVREES OU DE POSTES DECLARES

R = ESTIMATION DU NOMBRE DE RECEPTEURS EN SERVICE

NOMBRE DE PAYS ET DE TERRITOIRES PRESENTES DANS CE TABLEAU: 198

L = NUMERO DE PERMISOS EXISTENTES O DE RECEPTORES DECLARADOS

R = ESTIMACION DEL NUMERO DE RECEPTORES EN FUNCIONAMIENTO

NUMERO DE PAISES Y DE TERRITORIOS PRESENTADOS EN ESTE CUADRO: 198

COUNTRY / PAYS / PAIS	DEFINITION OF DATA / CODE / TIPO DE DATOS	NUMBER OF RECEIVERS IN USE AND/OR LICENCES ISSUED (THOUSANDS) / NOMBRE DE POSTES RECEPTEURS EN SERVICE ET/OU DE LICENCES DELIVREES (MILLIERS) / NUMERO DE RECEPTORES EN FUNCIONAMIENTO Y/O DE PERMISOS EXISTENTES (EN MILES)					NUMBER OF RECEIVERS IN USE AND/OR LICENCES ISSUED PER 1,000 INHABITANTS / NOMBRE DE POSTES RECEPTEURS EN SERVICE ET/OU DE LICENCES DELIVREES POUR 1 000 HABITANTS / NUMERO DE RECEPTORES EN FUNCIONAMIENTO Y/O DE PERMISOS EXISTENTES POR 1 000 HABITANTES				
		1965	1970	1975	1980	1983	1965	1970	1975	1980	1983
		(1)	(2)	(3)	(4)	(5)	(6)	(7)	(8)	(9)	(10)
AFRICA											
ALGERIA	R	...	...	3 000	3 700	4 400	...	...	179	198	215
	L	480	870	–	–	–	40	61	–	–	–
ANGOLA	R	79	95	113	125	163	15	*17	18	18	20
BENIN	R	35	85	150	230	290	15	31	48	67	78
BOTSWANA	R	4	20	57	...	120	8	35	82	...	119
BURKINA FASO	R	50	87	100	110	123	10	16	18	18	19
BURUNDI	R	...	65	100	150	178	...	18	26	35	40
CAMEROON	R	*115	170	232	760	830	*19	25	31	89	91
CAPE VERDE	R	4	5	31	41	47	16	17	104	137	150
CENTRAL AFRICAN REPUBLIC	R	30	46	70	120	140	...	...	34	52	57
CHAD	R	400	450	500	750	1 050	121	124	124	168	219
COMOROS	R	5	24	36	42	56	21	89	120	125	133
CONGO	R	47	65	81	93	750	44	54	60	61	454
COTE D'IVOIRE	R	60	75	300	1 000	1 200	14	14	44	125	129
DJIBOUTI	R	...	...	13	21	23	...	...	62	67	70
EGYPT	R	2 700	4 400	5 120	6 000	8 000	92	132	138	142	174
EQUATORIAL GUINEA	R	...	...	78	100	115	...	...	241	275	303
ETHIOPIA	R	...	160	1 000	3 000	3 000	...	6	36	97	89
GABON	R	36	62	90	96	102	40	65	90	90	90
GAMBIA	R	...	50	61	73	77	...	108	116	121	125
GHANA	R	555	703	1 060	1 700	2 200	71	82	107	148	173
GUINEA	R	75	91	110	135	160	21	23	25	28	31
GUINEA-BISSAU	R	3	4	10	25	28	6	8	16	31	32
KENYA	R	...	...	400	540	640	...	...	30	33	34

COUNTRY / PAYS / PAIS	DEFINITION OF DATA / CODE / TIPO DE DATOS	NUMBER OF RECEIVERS IN USE AND/OR LICENCES ISSUED (THOUSANDS) / NOMBRE DE POSTES RECEPTEURS EN SERVICE ET/OU DE LICENCES DELIVREES (MILLIERS) / NUMERO DE RECEPTORES EN FUNCIONAMIENTO Y/O DE PERMISOS EXISTENTES (EN MILES)					NUMBER OF RECEIVERS IN USE AND/OR LICENCES ISSUED PER 1,000 INHABITANTS / NOMBRE DE POSTES RECEPTEURS EN SERVICE ET/OU DE LICENCES DELIVREES POUR 1 000 HABITANTS / NUMERO DE RECEPTORES EN FUNCIONAMIENTO Y/O DE PERMISOS EXISTENTES POR 1 000 HABITANTES				
		1965	1970	1975	1980	1983	1965	1970	1975	1980	1983
		(1)	(2)	(3)	(4)	(5)	(6)	(7)	(8)	(9)	(10)
LESOTHO	R	5	5	22	30	40	5	5	19	22	28
LIBERIA	L	150	195	264	335	380	126	143	170	179	185
LIBYAN ARAB JAMAHIRIYA	R	50	85	500	646	750	31	43	206	217	223
MADAGASCAR	R	...	541	720	1 700	2 000	...	80	94	194	213
MALAWI	R	80	106	170	275	...	20	24	32	46	...
MALI	R	20	60	81	105	121	4	12	13	15	16
MAURITANIA	R	...	55	82	150	180	...	44	58	92	101
MAURITIUS	L	62	85	124	201	235	80	101	141	209	236
MOROCCO	R	700	935	1 400	3 000	3 600	53	60	81	150	163
MOZAMBIQUE	R	60	90	200	255	275	8	11	21	21	21
NIGER	R	45	145	...	250	280	13	36	...	47	49
NIGERIA	R	...	1 275	5 000	6 100	7 000	...	22	74	76	79
REUNION	R	46	79	91	100	120	117	177	191	204	219
RWANDA	R	...	30	65	150	300	...	8	15	30	53
ST. HELENA	R	...	1	1	2	2	...	140	180	300	400
SAO TOME AND PRINCIPE	R	2	6	17	23	25	33	81	213	271	272
SENEGAL	R	230	268	287	340	440	64	63	58	60	70
SEYCHELLES	R	6	7	16	21	23	128	135	276	323	359
SIERRA LEONE	R	27	40	280	450	700	10	14	92	136	202
SOMALIA	R	35	50	68	112	134	14	18	22	24	25
SOUTH AFRICA	R	1 500	2 000	2 337	8 000	8 800	77	89	92	280	286
SUDAN	R	...	...	1 150	3 500	5 000	...	...	73	187	246
SWAZILAND	R	8	30	55	81	93	21	71	111	148	154
TOGO	R	30	40	350	550	590	18	20	157	209	214
TUNISIA	R	...	388	808	1 000	1 124	...	76	144	156	163
UGANDA	R	...	...	250	295	320	...	...	22	22	22
UNITED REPUBLIC OF TANZANIA	R	115	150	232	500	591	10	11	15	28	29
WESTERN SAHARA	R	...	...	16	25	32	...	...	137	185	218
ZAIRE	R	...	630	1 000	1 500	3 000	...	29	44	57	96
ZAMBIA	R	43	75	100	135	170	12	18	20	23	27
ZIMBABWE	R	...	145	180	240	350	...	27	29	33	45
AMERICA, NORTH											
ANTIGUA AND BARBUDA	R	...	10	15	17	20	...	150	211	227	256
BAHAMAS	R	40	...	95	108	117	282	...	500	514	527
BARBADOS	R	40	89	...	135	191	164	374	...	534	758
BELIZE	R	30	48	59	71	79	278	400	454	473	506
BERMUDA	R	...	38	50	60	67	...	731	926	1 111	1 218
BRITISH VIRGIN ISLANDS	R	...	...	...	...	6	...	...	...	...	462
CANADA	R	...	15 000	...	17 734	20 551	...	703	...	741	825
CAYMAN ISLANDS	R	2	...	4	16	18	222	...	286	889	947
COSTA RICA	R	...	130	151	180	205	...	75	77	80	86

COUNTRY / PAYS / PAIS	DEFINITION OF DATA / CODE / TIPO DE DATOS	NUMBER OF RECEIVERS IN USE AND/OR LICENCES ISSUED (THOUSANDS) / NOMBRE DE POSTES RECEPTEURS EN SERVICE ET/OU DE LICENCES DELIVREES (MILLIERS) / NUMERO DE RECEPTORES EN FUNCIONAMIENTO Y/O DE PERMISOS EXISTENTES (EN MILES)					NUMBER OF RECEIVERS IN USE AND/OR LICENCES ISSUED PER 1,000 INHABITANTS / NOMBRE DE POSTES RECEPTEURS EN SERVICE ET/OU DE LICENCES DELIVREES POUR 1 000 HABITANTS / NUMERO DE RECEPTORES EN FUNCIONAMIENTO Y/O DE PERMISOS EXISTENTES POR 1 000 HABITANTES				
		1965	1970	1975	1980	1983	1965	1970	1975	1980	1983
		(1)	(2)	(3)	(4)	(5)	(6)	(7)	(8)	(9)	(10)
CUBA	R	...	1 330	1 805	2 914	3 121	...	156	194	300	316
DOMINICA	R	...	...	6	35	44	...	...	77	438	550
DOMINICAN REPUBLIC	R	...	...	...	900	1 200	...	...	...	165	201
EL SALVADOR	R	396	583	1 100	1 550	1 900	135	165	275	326	363
GREENLAND	R	6	7	13	15	19	155	154	260	300	365
GRENADA	R	10	15	22	35	38	103	160	210	318	345
GUADELOUPE	L	...	...	32	35	39	...	...	100	109	123
GUATEMALA	R	...	220	262	310	340	...	42	42	43	43
HAITI	R	63	76	93	101	120	16	18	20	20	...
HONDURAS	R	...	108	142	176	200	...	41	46	48	49
JAMAICA	R	350	500	550	800	890	199	268	269	369	394
MARTINIQUE	L	...	42	47	49	55	...	123	141	158	177
MEXICO	R	8 600	...	...	9 000	13 020	208	...	...	130	173
MONTSERRAT	R	...	...	...	6	7	...	...	...	423	523
NETHERLANDS ANTILLES	R	100	115	132	...	180	481	535	548	...	703
NICARAGUA	R	100	137	...	700	850	62	75	...	256	278
PANAMA	R	...	215	260	300	335	...	150	155	158	160
FORMER CANAL ZONE	R	...	...	37	38	46	...	...	902	...	...
PUERTO RICO	R	...	1 525	1 760	2 000	2 450	...	561	601	623	731
ST. CHRISTOPHER–NEVIS AND ANGUILLA	R	6	...	...	20	21	103	...	...	299	...
ST. LUCIA	R	...	...	82	91	96	...	...	745	755	758
ST. PIERRE AND MIQUELON	R	1	2	2	4	4	200	267	350	583	617
TRINIDAD AND TOBAGO	R	165	...	225	300	360	169	...	223	275	313
TURKS AND CAICOS ISLANDS	R	...	1	3	3	5	...	217	500	471	575
UNITED STATES	R	240 000	290 000	401 000	453 000	479 000	1 235	1 415	1 857	1 989	2 043
U.S. VIRGIN ISLANDS	R	25	43	75	85	90	568	652	833	850	891
AMERICA, SOUTH											
ARGENTINA	R	6 600	9 000	9 890	12 000	16 000	298	379	386	433	540
BOLIVIA	R	...	402	1 150	2 800	3 500	...	82	235	500	575
BRAZIL	R	...	11 800	16 980	35 000	50 000	...	128	162	295	386
CHILE	R	...	1 400	1 700	3 250	3 550	...	149	167	293	304
COLOMBIA	R	1 600	2 217	2 808	3 250	3 650	89	108	119	120	133
ECUADOR	R	540	1 700	...	2 650	2 950	107	285	...	317	319
FALKLAND ISLANDS (MALVINAS)	R	1	1	1	1	2	500	550	600	650	750
FRENCH GUIANA	R	3	...	...	30	60	61	...	...	469	857
	L	...	5	6	...	...	...	92	107	...	...
GUYANA	R	80	94	266	303	350	124	133	341	343	381
PARAGUAY	R	...	...	180	224	260	...	...	67	71	75
PERU	R	...	1 748	2 050	2 750	3 100	...	132	135	159	166
SURINAME	R	...	92	110	189	220	...	246	302	540	627
URUGUAY	R	900	1 000	1 500	1 630	1 700	331	347	530	560	573

COUNTRY PAYS PAIS	DEFINITION OF DATA CODE TIPO DE DATOS	NUMBER OF RECEIVERS IN USE AND/OR LICENCES ISSUED (THOUSANDS) NOMBRE DE POSTES RECEPTEURS EN SERVICE ET/OU DE LICENCES DELIVREES (MILLIERS) NUMERO DE RECEPTORES EN FUNCIONAMIENTO Y/O DE PERMISOS EXISTENTES (EN MILES)					NUMBER OF RECEIVERS IN USE AND/OR LICENCES ISSUED PER 1,000 INHABITANTS NOMBRE DE POSTES RECEPTEURS EN SERVICE ET/OU DE LICENCES DELIVREES POUR 1 000 HABITANTS NUMERO DE RECEPTORES EN FUNCIONAMIENTO Y/O DE PERMISOS EXISTENTES POR 1 000 HABITANTES				
		1965	1970	1975	1980	1983	1965	1970	1975	1980	1983
		(1)	(2)	(3)	(4)	(5)	(6)	(7)	(8)	(9)	(10)
VENEZUELA	R	...	...	4 775	5 600	6 800	...	...	398	403	415
ASIA											
AFGHANISTAN	R	...	...	...	1 200	1 350	...	...	...	75	78
BAHRAIN	R	...	56	85	125	175	...	260	332	357	441
BANGLADESH	L	...	...	500	730	770	...	...	6	8	8
BHUTAN	L	2	...	...	7	12	2	...	...	5	9
BRUNEI DARUSSALAM	R	10	15	24	...	49	95	115	150	...	188
BURMA	R	335	400	662	774	864	14	15	22	23	23
CHINA	R	11 500	12 000	...	55 000	70 000	15	15	...	55	67
	L	1 307	1 444	1 486	–	–	2	2	2	–	–
CYPRUS	R	130	167	180	300	410	220	276	292	477	626
	L	...	...	90	123	...	...	...	146	196	...
DEMOCRATIC KAMPUCHEA	R	97	103	110	600	900	16	15	15	94	131
DEMOCRATIC YEMEN	R	...	...	96	118	132	...	...	57	60	61
EAST TIMOR	L	1	3	...	...	...	3	5	...	...	...
HONG KONG	R	529	694	2 200	2 550	2 750	147	175	500	506	518
INDIA	R	...	...	...	...	40 000	...	...	...	...	55
	L	5 401	11 747	17 228	–	–	11	22	29	–	–
INDONESIA	R	1 250	2 550	5 010	15 000	22 000	12	21	37	101	138
IRAN, ISLAMIC REPUBLIC OF	R	...	1 800	2 050	6 400	7 500	...	63	61	169	180
IRAQ	R	793	1 026	1 252	2 000	2 750	99	109	113	153	188
ISRAEL	R	...	477	595	950	1 107	...	160	172	245	270
JAPAN	R	20 425	23 250	58 026	79 200	85 000	207	223	520	678	713
JORDAN	R	269	370	450	536	620	141	161	167	184	191
KOREA, REPUBLIC OF	R	1 961	4 012	13 509	15 000	18 000	68	124	383	393	451
KUWAIT	R	...	105	...	387	480	...	141	...	282	287
LAO PEOPLE'S DEMOCRATIC REPUBLIC	R	...	50	150	350	430	...	17	45	94	102
LEBANON	R	...	600	1 321	2 000	2 100	...	243	477	749	797
MACAU	R	5	9	61	76	100	19	37	226	238	329
MALAYSIA	R	421	430	1 420	5 760	6 100	46	41	119	430	410
	L	...	...	824	1 396	1 673	...	...	69	104	113
MALDIVES	R	...	1	3	7	15	...	11	21	47	90
MONGOLIA	R	...	...	114	166	182	...	...	79	99	101
NEPAL	R	40	55	113	300	390	4	5	9	21	25
OMAN	R	...	...	...	...	700	...	...	...	...	619
PAKISTAN	R	...	...	4 000	5 500	7 000	...	...	56	67	78
	L	972	...	1 390	1 800	1 328	18	...	20	22	15
PHILIPPINES	R	619	1 500	1 800	2 100	2 342	19	41	43	44	45
QATAR	R	...	25	...	110	131	...	225	...	458	466
SAUDI ARABIA	R	...	...	950	2 500	3 300	...	...	131	279	317
SINGAPORE	L	...	274	345	459	681	...	132	153	191	272
SRI LANKA	R	...	...	700	1 454	1 800	...	...	52	99	117
	L	438	500	527	1 200	...	39	40	39	81	...
SYRIAN ARAB REPUBLIC	R	...	1 170	...	1 720	1 970	...	187	...	192	205
THAILAND	R	2 188	2 775	5 200	5 910	7 350	71	76	124	127	149

COUNTRY / PAYS / PAIS	DEFINITION OF DATA / CODE / TIPO DE DATOS	NUMBER OF RECEIVERS IN USE AND/OR LICENCES ISSUED (THOUSANDS) / NOMBRE DE POSTES RECEPTEURS EN SERVICE ET/OU DE LICENCES DELIVREES (MILLIERS) / NUMERO DE RECEPTORES EN FUNCIONAMIENTO Y/O DE PERMISOS EXISTENTES (EN MILES)					NUMBER OF RECEIVERS IN USE AND/OR LICENCES ISSUED PER 1,000 INHABITANTS / NOMBRE DE POSTES RECEPTEURS EN SERVICE ET/OU DE LICENCES DELIVREES POUR 1 000 HABITANTS / NUMERO DE RECEPTORES EN FUNCIONAMIENTO Y/O DE PERMISOS EXISTENTES POR 1 000 HABITANTES				
		1965	1970	1975	1980	1983	1965	1970	1975	1980	1983
		(1)	(2)	(3)	(4)	(5)	(6)	(7)	(8)	(9)	(10)
TURKEY	R	...	...	...	5 000	6 000	...	...	...	113	127
	L	2 443	3 096	4 154	4 046	...	78	89	104	91	...
UNITED ARAB EMIRATES	R	...	...	52	240	310	...	...	102	245	257
YEMEN	R	...	...	87	110	125	...	...	16	19	20
EUROPE											
ALBANIA	R	130	152	175	...	476	69	71	73	...	168
ANDORRA	R	...	...	...	7	7	...	...	...	170	212
AUSTRIA	L	...	2 012	2 255	3 322	4 000	...	271	300	443	530
BELGIUM	L	3 026	3 396	3 891	4 508	4 617	319	352	397	457	468
BULGARIA‡	L	2 055	2 291	1 394	2 149	2 055	251	270	160	242	230
CZECHOSLOVAKIA	L	3 727	3 858	3 914	...	4 165	263	269	264	...	270
DENMARK	R	...	...	3 750	...	...	...	...	741	...	...
	L	1 587	1 634	1 693	1 944	2 005	334	330	335	379	392
FAEROE ISLANDS	L	12	14	...	...	17	324	359	...	...	378
FINLAND	R	...	...	...	4 000	4 800	...	...	...	837	987
	L	1 542	1 783	2 099	–	–	338	387	446	–	–
FRANCE	R	...	...	...	39 900	47 000	...	...	...	743	860
	L	15 336	15 995	17 199	–	–	315	315	326	–	–
GERMAN DEMOCRATIC REPUBLIC	L	5 743	5 985	6 167	6 409	6 415	337	351	366	383	384
GERMANY, FEDERAL REPUBLIC OF	L	17 878	19 622	21 125	22 750	24 604	303	323	342	370	401
GIBRALTAR	R	...	...	30	33	34	...	...	1 000	1 100	1 155
GREECE	R	893	990	2 500	3 310	4 000	104	113	276	343	406
HUNGARY	R	...	...	...	5 340	5 770	...	...	...	499	540
	L	2 484	2 530	2 537	–	–	244	245	241	–	–
ICELAND	L	52	104	115	133	139	268	510	528	583	586
IRELAND	R	610	...	907	1 500	1 600	212	...	285	441	456
	L	524	578	–	–	–	182	196	–	–	–
ITALY	L	10 615	11 636	12 818	13 781	14 213	204	217	230	241	250
LIECHTENSTEIN	L	4	...	7	13	17	221	...	308	500	654
LUXEMBOURG	R	121	157	176	186	235	364	464	492	520	644
MALTA	L	75	99	111	137	153	235	303	338	376	406
MONACO	R	6	7	8	9	10	274	275	320	346	356
NETHERLANDS	R	...	...	...	9 200	11 385	...	...	...	650	793
	L	3 093	3 716	3 909	4 376	4 630	250	285	286	309	322
NORWAY	R	...	...	...	2 900	3 200	...	...	...	710	775
	L	1 089	1 191	1 284	...	...	292	307	320	...	...
POLAND	L	5 646	5 657	8 127	8 666	9 050	179	174	239	244	247
PORTUGAL	R	...	...	...	1 600	1 700	...	...	...	163	171
	L	1 173	1 368	1 511	–	–	128	151	160	–	–
ROMANIA	L	2 790	3 085	3 085	3 205	3 223	147	152	145	144	143
SAN MARINO	L	3	4	6	10	11	176	222	300	476	500
SPAIN	R	4 550	7 700	9 050	9 600	10 900	142	228	254	256	285
SWEDEN	R	...	...	...	7 000	7 150	...	...	...	842	858
	L	2 985	2 847	3 140	–	–	386	354	383	–	–
SWITZERLAND	R	...	...	4 500	...	...	...	...	703	...	...
	L	1 654	1 864	2 105	2 250	2 358	282	297	329	352	364
UNITED KINGDOM	R	...	34 706	39 000	53 000	56 000	...	626	698	947	993
	L	13 516	18 430	–	–	–	248	333	–	–	–

COUNTRY PAYS PAIS	DEFINITION OF DATA CODE TIPO DE DATOS	NUMBER OF RECEIVERS IN USE AND/OR LICENCES ISSUED (THOUSANDS) NOMBRE DE POSTES RECEPTEURS EN SERVICE ET/OU DE LICENCES DELIVREES (MILLIERS) NUMERO DE RECEPTORES EN FUNCIONAMIENTO Y/O DE PERMISOS EXISTENTES (EN MILES)					NUMBER OF RECEIVERS IN USE AND/OR LICENCES ISSUED PER 1,000 INHABITANTS NOMBRE DE POSTES RECEPTEURS EN SERVICE ET/OU DE LICENCES DELIVREES POUR 1 000 HABITANTS NUMERO DE RECEPTORES EN FUNCIONAMIENTO Y/O DE PERMISOS EXISTENTES POR 1 000 HABITANTES				
		1965	1970	1975	1980	1983	1965	1970	1975	1980	1983
		(1)	(2)	(3)	(4)	(5)	(6)	(7)	(8)	(9)	(10)
YUGOSLAVIA	L	2 783	3 380	4 181	4 851	5 419	143	166	196	218	238
OCEANIA											
AMERICAN SAMOA	R	...	...	...	40	43	...	...	...	1 250	1 265
AUSTRALIA	R	...	7 250	13 900	15 000	20 000	...	580	1 001	1 021	1 301
COOK ISLANDS	R	2	2	7	8	10	105	105	368	417	588
FIJI	R	...	...	...	300	330	...	...	...	475	493
FRENCH POLYNESIA	R	30	...	70	80	84	326	...	526	533	535
GUAM	R	28	77	85	100	140	378	895	850	909	1 261
KIRIBATI	R	2	...	8	12	13	38	...	139	195	213
NAURU	R	...	...	4	4	6	...	...	500	500	688
NEW CALEDONIA	R	14	25	60	76	82	156	223	451	543	550
NEW ZEALAND	R	...	...	2 704	2 755	2 850	...	...	878	886	890
NIUE	R	.3	.6	.8	1	1	60	120	160	333	333
NORFOLK ISLAND	R	.4	.5	1.3	2	2	400	500	635	1 000	...
PACIFIC ISLANDS	R	6	53	72	...	...	70	558	595	...	...
PAPUA NEW GUINEA	R	...	...	110	200	215	...	...	41	67	67
SAMOA	R	14	...	...	32	70	110	...	...	205	435
SOLOMON ISLANDS	R	6	8	10	20	24	42	52	53	90	93
TOKELAU	R	...	...	...	...	1	...	...	...	...	500
TONGA	R	4	8	...	70	75	54	90	...	722	721
VANUATU	R	...	10	11	26	30	...	120	116	239	242
U.S.S.R.											
U.S.S.R.	R	73 800	94 600	122 477	130 000	140 000	318	390	481	490	514
BYELORUSSIAN S.S.R.	R	...	1 390	...	2 145	2 300	...	154	...	222	235
UKRAINIAN S.S.R.	R	14 927	18 424	23 539	28 941	33 594	331	389	480	578	665

EUROPE:
Bulgaria:

E--> Data for 1975, 1980 and 1983 do not include licences for receivers connected by wire to a redistribution system.

FR-> Les données pour 1975, 1980 et 1983 ne tiennent pas compte des licences délivrées pour les récepteurs reliés par fil à un réseau de redistribution.

ESP> Los datos para 1975, 1980 y 1983 no incluyen los permisos existentes para los receptores conectados por cable a una red de distribución.

10.3 Television broadcasting: number of transmitters and transmitting power

Télévision: nombre d'émetteurs et puissance d'émission

Televisión: número de transmisores y potencia de emisión

T = TOTAL
G = GOVERNMENTAL
P = PUBLIC
C = COMMERCIAL

FIGURES RELATE TO TRANSMITTERS OPERATING ON A REGULAR BASIS AND USED FOR BROADCASTING TO THE GENERAL PUBLIC

TRANSMITTING POWER IS EXPRESSED IN EFFECTIVE RADIATED POWER (ERP)

NUMBER OF COUNTRIES AND TERRITORIES PRESENTED IN THIS TABLE: 73

T = TOTAL
G = GOUVERNEMENTAL
P = PUBLIC
C = COMMERCIAL

LES DONNEES SE RAPPORTENT AUX EMETTEURS QUI FONCTIONNENT DE FACON REGULIERE ET QUI DIFFUSENT DES EMISSIONS DESTINEES AU GRAND PUBLIC

LA PUISSANCE D'EMISSION EST EXPRIMEE EN PUISSANCE APPARENTE RAYONNEE (PAR)

NOMBRE DE PAYS ET DE TERRITOIRES PRESENTES DANS CE TABLEAU: 73

T = TOTAL
G = GUBERNAMENTAL
P = PUBLICA
C = COMERCIAL

LOS DATOS SE REFIEREN A LOS TRANSMISORES QUE FUNCIONAN CON CARACTER REGULAR Y QUE EMITEN PROGRAMAS DESTINADOS AL PUBLICO EN GENERAL

LA POTENCIA DE EMISION SE EXPRESA EN POTENCIA EFECTIVA RADIADA (ERP)

NUMERO DE PAISES Y DE TERRITORIOS PRESENTADOS EN ESTE CUADRO: 73

COUNTRY / PAYS / PAIS	YEAR / ANNEE / AÑO	OWNERSHIP / PROPRIETE / PROPIEDAD	TOTAL: NUMBER OF TRANSMITTERS / NOMBRE D'EMETTEURS / NUMERO DE TRANSMISORES	TOTAL: TRANSMITTING POWER / PUISSANCE D'EMISSION / POTENCIA DE EMISION	VERY HIGH FREQUENCY / ONDES METRIQUES / MUY ALTA FRECUENCIA: NUMBER OF TRANSMITTERS / NOMBRE D'EMETTEURS / NUMERO DE TRANSMISORES	VHF: TRANSMITTING POWER / PUISSANCE D'EMISSION / POTENCIA DE EMISION	ULTRA HIGH FREQUENCY / ONDES DECIMETRIQUES / ULTRA ALTA FRECUENCIA: NUMBER OF TRANSMITTERS / NOMBRE D'EMETTEURS / NUMERO DE TRANSMISORES	UHF: TRANSMITTING POWER / PUISSANCE D'EMISSION / POTENCIA DE EMISION	NUMBER OF COLOUR TRANSMITTERS / NOMBRE D'EMETTEURS COULEUR / NUMERO DE TRANSMISORES EN COLOR
			(1)	(2)	(3)	(4)	(5)	(6)	(7)
AFRICA									
ALGERIA	1981	P	44	2 665	44	2 665	–	–	...
BENIN	1981	G	2	11	2	11	–	–	...
BURKINA FASO	1983	G	2	...	...	...	...	...	...
EGYPT	1983	G	74	261	–	–	–	–	–
ETHIOPIA	1983	G	2	2	2	2	–	–	–
GHANA	1981	G	7	166	7	166	–	–	2
MADAGASCAR	1979	G	14	0	14	0	–	–	14
MAURITIUS	1983	P	4	5	4	5	–	–	4
MOROCCO	1979	G	20	1 340	20	1 340	–	–	20
NIGERIA	1981	G	41	3 150	41	3 150	–	–	41
SENEGAL	1981	G	1	120	1	120	–	–	...
SIERRA LEONE	1982	G	2	11	2	11	–	–	2
SUDAN	1983	G	20	80	20	80	–	–	...
TOGO	1979	G	4	1 280	4	1 280	–	–	4
TUNISIA	1983	G	20	4 900	16	2 200	4	2 700	20
ZAMBIA	1979	G	5	...	5	...	–	–	5
AMERICA, NORTH									
CANADA	1983	T	2 131	48 844	1 059	24 046	172	24 798	1 231
		P	599	25 132	461	9 530	138	15 602	599
		C	632	23 712	598	14 516	34	9 196	632

COUNTRY PAYS PAIS	YEAR ANNEE AÑO	OWNERSHIP PROPRIETE PROPIEDAD	TOTAL NUMBER OF TRANSMITTERS NOMBRE D'EMETTEURS NUMERO DE TRANSMISORES	TOTAL TRANSMITTING POWER PUISSANCE D'EMISSION POTENCIA DE EMISION	VERY HIGH FREQUENCY / ONDES METRIQUES / MUY ALTA FRECUENCIA NUMBER OF TRANSMITTERS NOMBRE D'EMETTEURS NUMERO DE TRANSMISORES	VERY HIGH FREQUENCY / ONDES METRIQUES / MUY ALTA FRECUENCIA TRANSMITTING POWER PUISSANCE D'EMISSION POTENCIA DE EMISION	ULTRA HIGH FREQUENCY / ONDES DECIMETRIQUES / ULTRA ALTA FRECUENCIA NUMBER OF TRANSMITTERS NOMBRE D'EMETTEURS NUMERO DE TRANSMISORES	ULTRA HIGH FREQUENCY / ONDES DECIMETRIQUES / ULTRA ALTA FRECUENCIA TRANSMITTING POWER PUISSANCE D'EMISSION POTENCIA DE EMISION	NUMBER OF COLOUR TRANSMITTERS NOMBRE D'EMETTEURS COULEUR NUMERO DE TRANSMISORES EN COLOR
			(1)	(2)	(3)	(4)	(5)	(6)	(7)
CUBA	1983	G	58	1 868	58	1 868	–	–	58
GUADELOUPE	1979	P	8	2	7	1	1	0	8
MARTINIQUE	1979	P	8	2	7	1	1	1	7
MEXICO	1983	T	405	...	383	...	22	...	...
		G	230	...	226	...	4	...	...
		C	175	...	157	...	18	...	...
ST. CHRISTOPHER AND NEVIS	1983	G	4	51	4	51	–	–	4
ST. PIERRE AND MIQUELON	1979	G	3	0	3	0	–	–	3
TRINIDAD AND TOBAGO	1981	C	6	86	4	80	2	6	6
U.S. VIRGIN ISLANDS	1979	C	3	85	3	85	–	–	3
AMERICA, SOUTH									
BRAZIL	1983	T	137	...	137	...	...	...	...
		G	2	...	2	...	...	...	...
		P	12	...	12	...	...	...	...
		C	123	...	123	...	...	...	...
COLOMBIA	1983	P	49	271	49	271	–	–	–
FRENCH GUIANA	1979	P	8	14	7	11	1	3	8
URUGUAY	1983	T	33	5 930	33	5 930	–	–	33
		G	12	1 870	12	1 870	–	–	12
		C	21	4 060	21	4 060	–	–	21
ASIA									
AFGHANISTAN	1979	G	1	1	1	1	–	–	1
BAHRAIN	1979	G	1	70	1	70	–	–	1
BANGLADESH	1979	G	8	86	8	86	–	–	8
BRUNEI DARUSSALAM	1983	G	2	30	2	30	–	–	2
CYPRUS	1983	P	29	240	2	40	27	200	29
HONG KONG‡	1983	C	52	64	–	–	52	64	52
INDIA	1981	G	19	127	19	127	–	–	–
INDONESIA	1981	G	231	250	172	250	59	0	...
IRAN, ISLAMIC REPUBLIC OF	1983	G	478	187	453	185	25	2	...
IRAQ	1983	G	35	5 829	29	5 778	6	51	35
ISRAEL	1978	P	48	800	28	500	20	300	48
JAPAN	1983	T	12 756	2 212	1 475	968	11 270	1 243	12 756
		P	6 903	550	985	421	5 916	129	6 903
		C	5 853	1 662	490	547	5 354	1 114	5 853
JORDAN	1983	G	46	2 278	11	2 207	35	71	35
KUWAIT	1983	G	13	56	10	55	3	1	13
MALAYSIA	1983	G	59	324	59	324	–	–	59
MALDIVES	1983	G	2	1	2	1	–	–	2
OMAN	1983	G	8	2 491	8	2 491	–	–	8
PAKISTAN	1983	G	19	1 914	19	1 914	–	–	19
PHILIPPINES	1981	T	43	793	43	793	–	–	–
		G	4	145	4	145	–	–	–
		C	39	648	39	648	–	–	–
QATAR	1983	G	3	1 495	2	800	1	695	3

10.3 Television broadcasting: transmitters
Télévision: émetteurs
Televisión: transmisores

COUNTRY / PAYS / PAIS	YEAR / ANNEE / AÑO	OWNERSHIP / PROPRIETE / PROPIEDAD	TOTAL: NUMBER OF TRANSMITTERS / NOMBRE D'EMETTEURS / NUMERO DE TRANSMISORES	TOTAL: TRANSMITTING POWER / PUISSANCE D'EMISSION / POTENCIA DE EMISION	VERY HIGH FREQUENCY / ONDES METRIQUES / MUY ALTA FRECUENCIA: NUMBER OF TRANSMITTERS / NOMBRE D'EMETTEURS / NUMERO DE TRANSMISORES	VERY HIGH FREQUENCY / ONDES METRIQUES / MUY ALTA FRECUENCIA: TRANSMITTING POWER / PUISSANCE D'EMISSION / POTENCIA DE EMISION	ULTRA HIGH FREQUENCY / ONDES DECIMETRIQUES / ULTRA ALTA FRECUENCIA: NUMBER OF TRANSMITTERS / NOMBRE D'EMETTEURS / NUMERO DE TRANSMISORES	ULTRA HIGH FREQUENCY / ONDES DECIMETRIQUES / ULTRA ALTA FRECUENCIA: TRANSMITTING POWER / PUISSANCE D'EMISSION / POTENCIA DE EMISION	NUMBER OF COLOUR TRANSMITTERS / NOMBRE D'EMETTEURS COULEUR / NUMERO DE TRANSMISORES EN COLOR
			(1)	(2)	(3)	(4)	(5)	(6)	(7)
SINGAPORE	1983	G	8	400	8	400	–	–	8
SRI LANKA	1983	G	4	420	4	420	–	–	4
SYRIAN ARAB REPUBLIC	1981	G	11	180	11	180	–	–	11
TURKEY	1981	G	153	1 988	153	1 988	–	–	...
UNITED ARAB EMIRATES‡	1983	G	15	8 963	7	4 556	8	4 406	15
EUROPE									
ALBANIA	1983	G	176	457	155	420	31	37	186
AUSTRIA	1983	P	864	8 274	264	852	600	7 421	864
BELGIUM	1981	P	31	6 671	15	410	16	6 261	31
BULGARIA	1979	P	339	351	...	...	...	...	...
CZECHOSLOVAKIA‡	1983	G	74	15 260	31	1 550	43	13 710	74
DENMARK	1981	P	32	1 516	31	1 516	1	2	32
FINLAND	1983	P	172	12 736	85	...	87	...	172
FRANCE	1983	T	10 670	129 537	38	1 447	10 632	128 090	10 670
		P	10 613	128 000	–	–	10 613	128 000	10 613
		C	57	1 537	38	1 447	19	90	57
GERMANY, FEDERAL REPUBLIC OF‡	1983	P	5 718	35 500	1 129	2 458	4 589	33 042	5 718
GIBRALTAR	1983	P	4	1	2	0	2	0	2
HUNGARY	1983	T	98	29	63	10	35	19	...
ITALY	1983	P	2 445	25 873	1 081	1 830	1 364	24 043	2 445
MALTA	1979	G	4	...	2	5	2	...	3
MONACO	1981	C	5	2 700	1	1 200	4	1 500	5
NETHERLANDS	1983	P	29	4 188	4	220	25	3 968	29
NORWAY	1981	P	1 389	1 797	1 346	1 792	43	5	1 389
POLAND	1981	G	118	951	...	...	...	...	...
PORTUGAL	1983	P	23	4 305	13	700	10	3 605	23
ROMANIA	1981	G	344	...	...	...	...	...	–
SPAIN‡	1983	P	1 027	13 989	558	2 464	469	11 525	1 027
SWEDEN	1983	P	803	...	...	...	...	...	...
UNITED KINGDOM	1979	P	1 643	52 399	156	4 834	1 487	47 565	1 487
YUGOSLAVIA	1983	P	1 040	22 244	...	...	...	...	...
OCEANIA									
AMERICAN SAMOA	1981	G	3	...	3	...	–	–	3
AUSTRALIA	1981	T	386	9 230	376	8 620	10	610	386
		G	4	650	2	50	2	600	4
		P	230	4 158	230	4 158	–	–	230
		C	152	4 422	144	4 412	8	10	152
FRENCH POLYNESIA	1979	P	10	25	–	–	10	25	10
NEW CALEDONIA	1979	P	20	3	20	3	–	–	20
U.S.S.R.									
U.S.S.R.	1979	G	2 882	...	...	...	...	...	...

ASIA:
Hong Kong:
E--> Not including relay transmitters.
FR-> Non compris les réémetteurs.
ESP> Excluídos los retransmisores.
United Arab Emirates:
E--> Data refer to Abu Dhabi only.
FR-> Les données se réfèrent à Abu Dhabi seulement.
ESP> Los datos se refieren a Abu Dhabi solamente.
EUROPE:
Czechoslovakia:
E--> Not including relay transmitters.
FR-> Non compris les réémetteurs.
ESP> Excluídos los retransmisores.
Germany, Federal Republic of:
E--> Not including transmitting power for 2007 UHF transmitters.
FR-> Non compris la puissance de transmission pour 2007 émetteurs UHF.
ESP> Excluída la potencia de transmisión por 2007 transmisores UHF.
Spain:
E--> Data on transmitters operated by commercial broadcasting organizations have not been communicated.
FR-> Les données relatives aux émetteurs dépendant d'organismes commerciaux n'ont pas été communiquées.
ESP> Los datos relativos a los transmisores que dependen de organismos comerciales no han sido comunicados.

10.4 Television broadcasting: number of receivers and receivers per 1,000 inhabitants

Télévision: nombre de récepteurs et de récepteurs pour 1 000 habitants

Televisión: número de receptores y de receptores por 1 000 habitantes

L = NUMBER OF LICENCES ISSUED OR SETS DECLARED

R = ESTIMATED NUMBER OF RECEIVERS IN USE

NUMBER OF COUNTRIES AND TERRITORIES PRESENTED IN THIS TABLE: 158

L = NOMBRE DE LICENCES DELIVREES OU DE POSTES DECLARES

R = ESTIMATION DU NOMBRE DE RECEPTEURS EN SERVICE

NOMBRE DE PAYS ET DE TERRITOIRES PRESENTES DANS CE TABLEAU: 158

L = NUMERO DE PERMISOS EXISTENTES O DE RECEPTORES DECLARADOS

R = ESTIMACION DEL NUMERO DE RECEPTORES EN FUNCIONAMIENTO

NUMERO DE PAISES Y DE TERRITORIOS PRESENTADOS EN ESTE CUADRO: 158

COUNTRY / PAYS / PAIS	DEFINITION OF DATA / CODE / TIPO DE DATOS	NUMBER OF RECEIVERS IN USE AND/OR LICENCES ISSUED (THOUSANDS) / NOMBRE DE POSTES RECEPTEURS EN SERVICE ET/OU DE LICENCES DELIVREES (MILLIERS) / NUMERO DE RECEPTORES EN FUNCIONAMIENTO Y/O DE PERMISOS EXISTENTES (EN MILES)					NUMBER OF RECEIVERS IN USE AND/OR LICENCES ISSUED PER 1,000 INHABITANTS / NOMBRE DE POSTES RECEPTEURS EN SERVICE ET/OU DE LICENCES DELIVREES POUR 1 000 HABITANTS / NUMERO DE RECEPTORES EN FUNCIONAMIENTO Y/O DE PERMISOS EXISTENTES POR 1 000 HABITANTES				
		1965	1970	1975	1980	1983	1965	1970	1975	1980	1983
		(1)	(2)	(3)	(4)	(5)	(6)	(7)	(8)	(9)	(10)
AFRICA											
ALGERIA	R	...	...	500	975	1 325	...	...	30	52	65
ANGOLA	R	–	–	–	30	33	–	–	–	4.2	4.3
BENIN	R	–	–	–	5	13	–	–	–	1.3	3.4
BURKINA FASO	R	0.3	6	...	...	35	0.1	1.1	...	...	5
CENTRAL AFRICAN REPUBLIC	R	–	–	–	0.7	1.4	–	–	–	0.3	0.6
CONGO	R	0.4	1.8	2.7	3.5	4.5	0.4	1.5	2.0	2.3	2.7
COTE D'IVOIRE	R	6	...	110	300	380	1	...	16	37	41
DJIBOUTI	R	...	1.0	3.1	5	6	...	11	15	16	17
EGYPT	R	323	529	620	1 400	2 000	11	16	17	33	44
EQUATORIAL GUINEA	R	–	–	0.5	1.1	2.0	–	–	1.5	2.8	5
ETHIOPIA	R	2.5	8	20	30	40	0.1	0.5	0.8	1.0	1.2
	L	...	...	...	25	25	...	...	...	0.8	1.0
GABON	R	...	1.2	...	9	20	...	1.3	...	8	18
GHANA	R	0.9	16	33	57	76	0.1	1.9	3.3	5	6
GUINEA	R	–	–	–	6	8	–	–	–	1.2	1.4
KENYA	R	10	16	38	65	75	1.0	1.4	2.8	4.0	4.0
LIBERIA	R	3.0	7	9	21	24	2.4	4.9	6	11	12
LIBYAN ARAB JAMAHIRIYA	R	–	1.0	85	165	220	–	0.5	35	55	66
MADAGASCAR	R	–	3.5	8	45	71	–	0.5	1.0	5	8
MAURITIUS	L	3.6	19	40	79	95	5	23	46	83	96
MOROCCO	L	33	174	448	749	860	2	11	26	37	39
MOZAMBIQUE	R	–	–	1.1	1.5	2.1	–	–	0.1	0.1	0.2
NIGER	R	–	–	...	5	11	–	–	...	0.9	1.9
NIGERIA	R	30	75	100	450	457	0.6	1.3	1.4	6	5
REUNION	R	3	21	41	80	91	7	47	86	163	166
SENEGAL	R	–	1.4	1.8	4.0	6	–	0.3	0.4	0.7	1.0

COUNTRY PAYS PAIS	DEFI-NITION OF DATA CODE TIPO DE DATOS	NUMBER OF RECEIVERS IN USE AND/OR LICENCES ISSUED (THOUSANDS) NOMBRE DE POSTES RECEPTEURS EN SERVICE ET/OU DE LICENCES DELIVREES (MILLIERS) NUMERO DE RECEPTORES EN FUNCIONAMIENTO Y/O DE PERMISOS EXISTENTES (EN MILES)					NUMBER OF RECEIVERS IN USE AND/OR LICENCES ISSUED PER 1,000 INHABITANTS NOMBRE DE POSTES RECEPTEURS EN SERVICE ET/OU DE LICENCES DELIVREES POUR 1 000 HABITANTS NUMERO DE RECEPTORES EN FUNCIONAMIENTO Y/O DE PERMISOS EXISTENTES POR 1 000 HABITANTES				
		1965	1970	1975	1980	1983	1965	1970	1975	1980	1983
		(1)	(2)	(3)	(4)	(5)	(6)	(7)	(8)	(9)	(10)
SEYCHELLES	R	–	–	–	–	0.5	–	–	–	–	8
SIERRA LEONE	R	1.1	3.0	8	20	22	0.5	1.1	2.6	6	6
SOUTH AFRICA	R	...	...	100	2 000	2 300	...	...	3.9	70	75
SUDAN	R	10	45	100	800	1 000	0.7	2.9	6	43	49
SWAZILAND	R	–	–	–	1.0	2.5	–	–	–	1.8	4.1
TOGO	R	–	–	...	10	13	–	–	...	3.7	4.7
TUNISIA	R	...	72	191	300	370	...	14	34	47	54
UGANDA	R	6	...	70	74	81	0.7	...	6	6	6
UNITED REPUBLIC OF TANZANIA	R	...	...	4.3	7	9	...	...	0.3	0.4	0.4
WESTERN SAHARA	R	...	...	2.0	2.4	2.7	...	...	17	18	18
ZAIRE	R	...	7	8	10	12	...	0.3	0.3	0.4	0.4
ZAMBIA	R	9	17	23	60	76	2.3	4.0	5	10	12
ZIMBABWE	R	...	50	57	73	97	...	9	9	10	12
AMERICA, NORTH											
ANTIGUA AND BARBUDA	R	2	...	15	16	19	25	...	211	213	244
BAHAMAS	R	–	–	–	31	36	–	–	–	149	162
BARBADOS	R	6	16	46	50	55	25	67	189	198	218
BERMUDA	R	...	17	20	30	39	...	327	370	556	709
BRITISH VIRGIN ISLANDS	R	...	...	...	2.2	2.5	...	...	...	169	208
CANADA	R	5 310	7 100	9 390	10 617	11 976	270	333	413	443	481
CAYMAN ISLANDS	R	–	–	–	1.8	3.5	–	–	–	100	184
COSTA RICA	R	50	100	128	162	181	34	58	65	72	76
CUBA	R	...	...	595	1 273	1 658	...	...	64	131	168
DOMINICAN REPUBLIC	R	50	100	180	400	550	14	25	38	74	92
EL SALVADOR	R	35	92	135	300	340	12	26	34	63	65
GREENLAND	R	...	...	2.8	3.5	4.4	...	...	56	70	85
GUADELOUPE	L	0.7	7	16	33	38	2.3	22	49	103	119
GUATEMALA	R	55	72	110	175	203	12	14	18	24	26
HAITI	R	...	11	13	16	19	...	2.6	2.8	3.2	...
HONDURAS	R	2.2	22	34	49	52	1.0	8	11	13	13
JAMAICA	R	25	70	110	167	200	14	37	54	77	89
MARTINIQUE	L	1.5	10	22	38	42	5	28	67	122	135
MEXICO	R	1 200	...	...	3 820	8 100	29	...	...	55	108
NETHERLANDS ANTILLES	R	25	32	35	43	57	120	149	145	172	221
NICARAGUA	R	16	55	83	175	205	10	30	39	64	67
PANAMA	R	70	...	185	220	255	57	...	110	116	122
FORMER CANAL ZONE	R	...	...	20	20	20	...	...	488	...	...
PUERTO RICO	R	...	410	630	800	980	...	151	215	249	293
ST. CHRISTOPHER-NEVIS AND ANGUILLA	R	–	–	–	4.2	4.5	–	–	–	63	...
ST. LUCIA	R	...	1.5	1.7	1.8	2.0	...	15	15	15	16
ST. PIERRE AND MIQUELON	R	...	1.3	1.7	3.2	3.4	...	217	283	533	558

10.4 Television broadcasting: receivers
Télévision: récepteurs
Televisión: receptores

COUNTRY / PAYS / PAIS	DEFINITION OF DATA / CODE / TIPO DE DATOS	NUMBER OF RECEIVERS IN USE AND/OR LICENCES ISSUED (THOUSANDS) / NOMBRE DE POSTES RECEPTEURS EN SERVICE ET/OU DE LICENCES DELIVREES (MILLIERS) / NUMERO DE RECEPTORES EN FUNCIONAMIENTO Y/O DE PERMISOS EXISTENTES (EN MILES)					NUMBER OF RECEIVERS IN USE AND/OR LICENCES ISSUED PER 1,000 INHABITANTS / NOMBRE DE POSTES RECEPTEURS EN SERVICE ET/OU DE LICENCES DELIVREES POUR 1 000 HABITANTS / NUMERO DE RECEPTORES EN FUNCIONAMIENTO Y/O DE PERMISOS EXISTENTES POR 1 000 HABITANTES				
		1965	1970	1975	1980	1983	1965	1970	1975	1980	1983
		(1)	(2)	(3)	(4)	(5)	(6)	(7)	(8)	(9)	(10)
TRINIDAD AND TOBAGO	R	20	60	105	210	310	21	58	104	193	270
UNITED STATES	R	70 350	84 600	121 000	155 800	185 300	362	413	560	684	790
U.S. VIRGIN ISLANDS	R	...	9	30	50	56	...	142	333	500	554
AMERICA, SOUTH											
ARGENTINA	R	1 600	3 500	4 000	5 140	5 910	72	147	156	185	199
BOLIVIA	R	...	...	45	300	386	...	...	9	54	64
BRAZIL	R	...	6 100	...	15 000	16 500	...	66	...	126	127
CHILE	R	...	500	700	1 225	1 350	...	53	69	110	116
COLOMBIA	R	350	810	1 600	2 250	2 700	19	39	68	83	98
ECUADOR	R	42	150	252	500	570	8	25	36	60	62
FRENCH GUIANA	L	...	2	5	10	12	...	36	80	164	171
PARAGUAY	R	...	...	54	68	82	...	...	20	21	24
PERU	R	210	395	610	850	950	18	30	40	49	51
SURINAME	R	7	28	34	40	43	21	75	93	114	121
URUGUAY	R	200	...	351	363	370	74	...	124	125	125
VENEZUELA	R	650	...	1 284	1 710	2 100	75	...	107	123	128
ASIA											
AFGHANISTAN	R	–	–	–	45	51	–	–	–	2.8	3.0
BAHRAIN	R	...	13	30	90	130	...	60	117	257	327
BANGLADESH	R	...	...	25	80	84	...	...	0.3	0.9	0.9
BRUNEI DARUSSALAM	R	...	...	14	26	29	...	...	88	137	138
BURMA	R	–	–	–	1.0	6	–	–	–	0.1	0.1
CHINA	R	...	...	...	4 000	7 000	...	...	...	4	7
	L	62	510	913	–	–		1	1	–	–
CYPRUS	R	...	...	...	86	91	...	...	...	137	139
	L	14	49	54	–	–	24	82	87	–	–
DEMOCRATIC KAMPUCHEA	R	7	...	30	35	60	1.1	...	3.7	5	9
DEMOCRATIC YEMEN	R	13	21	31	35	39	10	15	18	18	18
HONG KONG	R	50	444	837	1 114	1 210	14	112	190	221	228
INDIA	L	0.8	25	455	1 548	2 780	0.0	0.0	0.8	1.7	4
INDONESIA	R	45	90	300	3 000	3 600	0.4	0.8	2.2	20	23
IRAN, ISLAMIC REPUBLIC OF	R	110	533	1 700	2 000	2 300	4	19	51	53	55
IRAQ	R	171	350	410	650	800	21	37	37	50	55
ISRAEL	R	...	...	...	900	1 050	...	...	...	232	256
	L	14	356	475	480	500	5	120	137	124	122
JAPAN	R	...	...	...	62 976	67 200	...	...	...	539	563
	L	18 080	22 883	26 427	29 140	30 799	183	219	237	250	258
JORDAN	R	–	46	120	171	220	–	20	44	59	68
KOREA, REPUBLIC OF	L	45	418	1 860	6 280	7 000	1.6	13	53	165	175
KUWAIT	R	...	100	...	353	431	...	134	...	258	258
LEBANON	R	135	260	410	750	780	63	105	148	281	296
MALAYSIA	R	53	130	452		1 425	6	13	38		96
	L	...	...	446	1 119	1 673	...	...	37	84	113
MALDIVES	L	–	–	–	0.8	...	–	–	–	6	...
MONGOLIA	R	...	1.0	3.5	5	11	...	0.8	2.4	3.0	6

COUNTRY / PAYS / PAIS	DEFINITION OF DATA / CODE / TIPO DE DATOS	NUMBER OF RECEIVERS IN USE AND/OR LICENCES ISSUED (THOUSANDS) / NOMBRE DE POSTES RECEPTEURS EN SERVICE ET/OU DE LICENCES DELIVREES (MILLIERS) / NUMERO DE RECEPTORES EN FUNCIONAMIENTO Y/O DE PERMISOS EXISTENTES (EN MILES)					NUMBER OF RECEIVERS IN USE AND/OR LICENCES ISSUED PER 1,000 INHABITANTS / NOMBRE DE POSTES RECEPTEURS EN SERVICE ET/OU DE LICENCES DELIVREES POUR 1 000 HABITANTS / NUMERO DE RECEPTORES EN FUNCIONAMIENTO Y/O DE PERMISOS EXISTENTES POR 1 000 HABITANTES				
		1965	1970	1975	1980	1983	1965	1970	1975	1980	1983
		(1)	(2)	(3)	(4)	(5)	(6)	(7)	(8)	(9)	(10)
OMAN	R	...	...	2.5	35	49	...	...	3.3	39	43
PAKISTAN	R	10	99	380	938	1 116	0.2	1.6	5	11	12
PHILIPPINES	R	120	400	756	1 000	1 350	3.8	11	18	21	26
QATAR	R	...	...	20	80	143	...	...	118	333	509
SAUDI ARABIA	R	...	...	...	2 100	2 750	...	...	...	234	264
SINGAPORE	L	63	157	280	397	472	33	76	124	165	188
SRI LANKA	R	–	–	–	35	50	–	–	–	2.4	3.3
SYRIAN ARAB REPUBLIC	R	65	116	224	385	423	12	19	30	43	44
THAILAND	R	200	...	670	810	840	6	...	16	17	17
TURKEY	R	...	...	...	3 500	6 000	...	...	...	79	127
	L	2	...	1 000	3 410	5 543		...	25	77	117
UNITED ARAB EMIRATES	R	–	–	25	93	112	–	–	49	95	93
YEMEN	R	–	–	–	5	17	–	–	–	0.8	2.7
EUROPE											
ALBANIA	R	1.0	2.1	5	...	196	0.5	1.0	1.9	...	69
ANDORRA	R	1.0	2.1	2.0	4.0	5.0	50	90	74	100	147
AUSTRIA	L	...	1 420	1 905	2 225	2 348	...	191	253	296	311
BELGIUM	L	1 543	2 100	2 549	2 934	2 981	162	217	260	298	303
BULGARIA	L	185	1 028	1 508	1 652	1 691	23	121	173	186	189
CZECHOSLOVAKIA	L	2 113	3 091	3 689	4 292	4 323	149	216	249	280	280
DENMARK	L	1 084	1 359	1 556	1 856	1 889	228	274	308	362	369
FINLAND	R	...	...	1 658	1 980	2 100	...	...	352	414	432
	L	732	1 059	1 336	1 538	1 738	160	230	284	322	357
FRANCE	R	...	...	...	19 000	20 500	...	...	...	354	375
	L	6 489	10 968	14 162	15 978	...	133	216	269	297	...
GERMAN DEMOCRATIC REPUBLIC	L	3 216	4 499	5 224	5 731	5 970	189	264	310	342	358
GERMANY, FEDERAL REPUBLIC OF	L	11 379	16 675	19 226	20 762	22 132	193	275	311	337	360
GIBRALTAR	L	...	...	6	7	7	...	...	200	225	241
GREECE	L	–	170	1 050	1 500	1 750	–	19	116	156	178
HUNGARY	R	...	...	...	...	3 970	...	...	...	...	371
	L	831	1 769	2 295	2 766	2 864	82	171	218	258	268
ICELAND	L	...	41	51	64	70	...	201	234	281	293
IRELAND	R	329	447	...	785	875	114	152	...	231	249
	L	256	438	531	616	...	89	149	167	181	...
ITALY	R	...	...	...	22 000	...	...	...	...	385	...
	L	6 045	9 775	12 103	13 361	13 831	116	182	217	234	243
LIECHTENSTEIN	R	...	...	...	7	8	...	...	...	269	308
LUXEMBOURG	R	31	71	87	90	94	93	208	242	251	256
MALTA	L	27	44	58	76	100	83	134	178	207	265
MONACO	R	...	...	16	17	17	...		648	654	637
NETHERLANDS	R	...	...	...	5 650	6 460	...	...	...	399	450
	L	2 113	3 086	3 646	4 181	4 454	171	237	267	296	310
NORWAY	L	490	854	1 044	1 195	1 316	132	220	260	292	319
POLAND	L	2 078	4 215	6 472	7 954	8 542	66	130	190	224	234
PORTUGAL	L	180	389	722	1 400	1 523	20	43	77	143	153

COUNTRY / PAYS / PAIS	DEFINITION OF DATA CODE / TIPO DE DATOS	NUMBER OF RECEIVERS IN USE AND/OR LICENCES ISSUED (THOUSANDS) / NOMBRE DE POSTES RECEPTEURS EN SERVICE ET/OU DE LICENCES DELIVREES (MILLIERS) / NUMERO DE RECEPTORES EN FUNCIONAMIENTO Y/O DE PERMISOS EXISTENTES (EN MILES)					NUMBER OF RECEIVERS IN USE AND/OR LICENCES ISSUED PER 1,000 INHABITANTS / NOMBRE DE POSTES RECEPTEURS EN SERVICE ET/OU DE LICENCES DELIVREES POUR 1 000 HABITANTS / NUMERO DE RECEPTORES EN FUNCIONAMIENTO Y/O DE PERMISOS EXISTENTES POR 1 000 HABITANTES				
		1965	1970	1975	1980	1983	1965	1970	1975	1980	1983
		(1)	(2)	(3)	(4)	(5)	(6)	(7)	(8)	(9)	(10)
ROMANIA	L	501	1 485	2 692	3 714	3 912	26	73	127	167	173
SAN MARINO	L	1.5	2.4	...	6	7	88	133	...	286	295
SPAIN	R	...	4 115	6 640	9 424	9 850	...	122	187	252	258
SWEDEN	L	2 085	2 513	2 909	3 165	3 245	270	312	355	381	390
SWITZERLAND	R	...	...	2 050	2 300	2 450	...	...	320	360	378
	L	621	1 281	1 781	2 000	...	106	204	278	313	...
UNITED KINGDOM	R	...	...	20 200	22 600	27 000	...	...	361	404	479
	L	13 516	16 309	17 936	18 522	...	248	294	321	331	...
YUGOSLAVIA	L	577	1 798	3 076	4 442	4 818	30	88	144	200	211
OCEANIA											
AMERICAN SAMOA	R	...	2.1	5	6	6	...	72	172	180	182
AUSTRALIA	R	1 954	2 758	4 549	5 600	6 600	172	221	328	381	429
FRENCH POLYNESIA	R	0.5	8	14	16	26	5	73	105	107	162
GUAM	R	28	40	...	75	78	378	465	...	682	703
NEW CALEDONIA	R	0.4	8	15	25	30	4.4	71	113	179	201
NEW ZEALAND	R	413	661	799	862	922	157	235	259	277	288
PACIFIC ISLANDS	R	–	1.2	3.0	7	7	–	13	25	48	49
SAMOA	R	–	–	–	2.5	3.5	–	–	–	16	25
U.S.S.R.											
U.S.S.R.	R	15 700	34 800	55 200	81 000	84 000	68	143	217	305	308
BYELORUSSIAN S.S.R.	R	...	1 111	...	2 100	2 250	...	123	...	218	229
UKRAINIAN S.S.R.	R	2 797	7 167	11 035	12 722	14 761	62	152	225	254	292

General note/Note générale/Nota general:

E--> For the countries listed below, only the estimated number of receivers in use, but not the number of licences has been communicated, although it is known or believed that a licence system is in force:

FR-> Pour les pays ci-dessous, seule une estimation du nombre de récepteurs en service a été communiquée. Bien que certains renseignements indiquent ou permettent de penser qu'un système de redevances est en vigueur, le nombre de licences délivrées n'a pas été fourni:

ESP> Para los países que figuran a continuación, sólo se ha comunicado una estimación de los receptores en servicio. Aunque ciertas informaciones indiquen o permitan pensar que está en vigor un sistema de permisos, el número de permisos concedidos no nos ha sido facilitado:

Africa/Afrique/Africa:
Burkina Faso
Congo
Djibouti/Yibuti
Egypt/Egypte/Egipto
Ethiopia/Ethiopie/Etiopía
Ghana
Kenya/Kenia
Madagascar
Nigeria/Nigéria
Reunion/Réunion/Reunión
Sierra Leone/Sierra Leona
Tunisia/Tunisie/Túnez
Uganda/Ouganda
United Republic of Tanzania/République-Unie de Tanzanie/República Unida de Tanzania
Western Sahara/Sahara occidental
Zimbabwe

General note/Note générale/Nota general: (Cont):

America, North/Amérique du Nord/América del Norte:
Antigua and Barbuda/Antigua et Barbuda/Antigua y Barbuda
Barbados/Barbade
Bermuda/Bermudes/Bermudas
British Virgin Islands/Iles Vierges britanniques/ Islas Vírgenes británicas
Canada/Canadá
Costa Rica
St. Lucia/Sainte-Lucie/Santa Lucía
St. Pierre and Miquelon/Saint-Pierre-et-Miquelon/ San Pedro y Miquelón

Asia/Asie/Asia:
Bahrain/Bahrein
Democratic Kampuchea/Kampuchea démocratique/ Kampuchea democrática
Indonesia/Indonésie
Jordan/Jordanie/Jordania
Kuwait/Koweit/Kuweit
Mongolia/Mongolie
Qatar
Syrian Arab Republic/République arabe syrienne/ República árabe siria

Europe/Europe/Europa:
Albania/Albanie
Andorra/Andorre

Oceania/Océanie/Oceanía:
American Samoa/Samoa américaines/Samoa americanas
French Polynesia/Polynésie française/Polinesia francesa
New Caledonia/Nouvelle-Calédonie/Nueva Caledonia
New Zealand/Nouvelle-Zélande/Nueva Zelandia
Pacific Islands/Iles du Pacifique/Islas del Pacífico

10.5 Radio broadcasting: programmes by function and by type of institution

Radiodiffusion sonore: programmes d'après leur fonction et le type d'organisme

Radiodifusión sonora: programas clasificados según su función y el tipo de institución

TOTAL ANNUAL BROADCASTING HOURS	= TOTAL ANNUEL D'HEURES DE DIFFUSION	= TOTAL ANUAL DE HORAS DE DIFUSION
INFORMATIVE PROGRAMMES	= PROGRAMMES D'INFORMATION	= PROGRAMAS INFORMATIVOS
NEWS BULLETINS	= BULLETINS D'INFORMATION	= BOLETINES DE NOTICIAS
OTHER INFORMATIVE PROGRAMMES	= AUTRES PROGRAMMES D'INFORMATION	= OTROS PROGRAMAS INFORMATIVOS
EDUCATIONAL PROGRAMMES	= PROGRAMMES EDUCATIFS	= PROGRAMAS EDUCATIVOS
RELATED TO A SPECIFIC CURRICULUM	= LIES A UN ENSEIGNEMENT PARTICULIER	= RELACIONADOS CON UN PROGRAMA DE ESTUDIOS ESPECIFICOS
FOR RURAL DEVELOPMENT	= DESTINES AU DEVELOPPEMENT RURAL	= PARA EL DESARROLLO RURAL
OTHER EDUCATIONAL PROGRAMMES	= AUTRES PROGRAMMES EDUCATIFS	= OTROS PROGRAMAS EDUCATIVOS
CULTURAL PROGRAMMES	= PROGRAMMES CULTURELS	= PROGRAMAS CULTURALES
RELIGIOUS PROGRAMMES	= PROGRAMMES RELIGIEUX	= PROGRAMAS RELIGIOSOS
ADVERTISEMENTS	= PUBLICITE	= PUBLICIDAD
ENTERTAINMENT	= DIVERTISSEMENT	= PROGRAMAS RECREATIVOS
PLAYS	= DRAMATIQUES	= DRAMAS
MUSIC	= MUSIQUE	= MUSICA
SPORTS PROGRAMMES	= PROGRAMMES SPORTIFS	= PROGRAMAS DEPORTIVOS
OTHER ENTERTAINMENT PROGRAMMES	= AUTRES PROGRAMMES DE DIVERTISSEMENT	= OTROS PROGRAMAS RECREATIVOS
OTHER NOT ELSEWHERE CLASSIFIED	= PROGRAMMES NON CLASSES	= PROGRAMAS NO CLASIFICADOS

GOVT = GOVERNMENTAL
PUBLIC = PUBLIC
COMM = COMMERCIAL

GOVT = GOUVERNEMENTAL
PUBLIC = PUBLIC
COMM = COMMERCIAL

GOVT = GUBERNAMENTAL
PUBLIC = PUBLICA
COMM = COMERCIAL

NUMBER OF COUNTRIES AND TERRITORIES PRESENTED IN THIS TABLE: 95

NOMBRE DE PAYS ET DE TERRITOIRES PRESENTES DANS CE TABLEAU: 95

NUMERO DE PAISES Y DE TERRITORIOS PRESENTADOS EN ESTE CUADRO: 95

AFRICA

TYPE OF PROGRAMME BY FUNCTION PROGRAMMES D'APRES LEUR FONCTION PROGRAMAS SEGUN SU FUNCION	ALGERIA‡ (1979) PUBLIC	ANGOLA (1979) GOVT	BENIN (1981) PUBLIC	BOTSWANA (1984) GOVT	BURKINA FASO (1983) GOVT	BURUNDI (1979) GOVT	CONGO (1983) GOVT
TOTAL ANNUAL BROADCASTING HOURS	19 981	25 064	5 331	6 833	6 106	11 262	5 757
INFORMATIVE PROGRAMMES	14.7	77.3	47.0	18.9	30.6	14.1	23.9
NEWS BULLETINS, ETC.	9.3	...	41.3	10.9	...	...	15.6
OTHER INFORMATIVE PROGRAMMES	5.4	...	5.7	8.0	...	...	8.3
EDUCATIONAL PROGRAMMES	4.3	4.6	13.2	10.5	14.7	11.6	19.3
RELATED TO A SPECIFIC CURRICULUM	...	0.4	1.1	...	6.2	4.6	–
FOR RURAL DEVELOPMENT	...	0.6	11.2	...	8.6	5.8	5.1
OTHER EDUCATIONAL PROGRAMMES	...	3.7	1.0	...	–	1.2	14.2
CULTURAL PROGRAMMES	9.7	2.7	6.8	2.3	8.5	3.9	13.3
RELIGIOUS PROGRAMMES	7.2	–	–	6.6	3.4	0.5	–
ADVERTISEMENTS	–	–	9.3	2.7	16.0	0.0	0.2
ENTERTAINMENT	57.6	4.1	22.6	59.0	11.0	69.9	30.7
PLAYS	1.1	–	–	1.9	3.2	0.8	0.8
MUSIC	56.5	2.6	19.7	57.1	4.9	66.8	19.3
SPORTS PROGRAMMES	./.	1.2	2.9	–	1.9	2.3	1.7
OTHER ENTERTAINMENT PROGRAMMES	...	0.4	–	–	1.1	–	8.9
OTHER NOT ELSEWHERE CLASSIFIED	6.5	11.3	1.1	–	15.7	–	12.5

TYPE OF PROGRAMME BY FUNCTION PROGRAMMES D'APRES LEUR FONCTION PROGRAMAS SEGUN SU FUNCION	EGYPT (1983) GOVT	EQUATORIAL GUINEA (1983) GOVT	ETHIOPIA (1983) GOVT	GHANA (1983) GOVT	MADAGASCAR (1979) GOVT	MALAWI (1981) PUBLIC	MALI (1981) GOVT
TOTAL ANNUAL BROADCASTING HOURS	56 455	6 205	8 569	8 952	6 565	6 914	5 100
INFORMATIVE PROGRAMMES	9.0	16.2	50.4	35.4	15.0	17.7	45.4
NEWS BULLETINS, ETC.	...	12.5	16.1	28.6	...	14.8	42.4
OTHER INFORMATIVE PROGRAMMES	...	3.7	34.3	6.9	...	3.0	3.1
EDUCATIONAL PROGRAMMES	1.8	15.6	5.6	4.7	24.8	22.5	15.8
RELATED TO A SPECIFIC CURRICULUM	...	8.8	–	2.0	...	17.0	1.2
FOR RURAL DEVELOPMENT	...	6.7	5.6	1.2	10.0	4.0	14.1
OTHER EDUCATIONAL PROGRAMMES	...	–	–	1.5	...	1.5	0.5
CULTURAL PROGRAMMES	14.7	2.9	3.8	1.7	32.2	1.8	7.5
RELIGIOUS PROGRAMMES	18.6	3.1	–	2.9	–	1.8	2.5
ADVERTISEMENTS	0.2	–	–	1.7	4.0	–	4.4
ENTERTAINMENT	44.0	42.9	40.3	17.2	22.0	56.2	24.5
PLAYS	...	0.2	8.6	0.3	...	3.0	2.0
MUSIC	...	42.7	29.1	15.4	...	53.3	2.2
SPORTS PROGRAMMES	...	–	2.6	1.5	...	...	2.8
OTHER ENTERTAINMENT PROGRAMMES	...	–	–	–	...	–	17.5
OTHER NOT ELSEWHERE CLASSIFIED	11.8	19.3	–	36.4	2.0	–	–

TYPE OF PROGRAMME BY FUNCTION PROGRAMMES D'APRES LEUR FONCTION PROGRAMAS SEGUN SU FUNCION	MAURITIUS (1983) PUBLIC	MOROCCO (1979) GOVT	REUNION (1979) PUBLIC	RWANDA (1983) GOVT	ST. HELENA (1981) GOVT	SENEGAL (1981) GOVT	SUDAN (1981) GOVT
TOTAL ANNUAL BROADCASTING HOURS	7 818	31 680	6 207	5 003	1 144	7 616	6 480
INFORMATIVE PROGRAMMES	17.5	18.0	12.0	18.1	20.1	29.0	25.0
NEWS BULLETINS, ETC.	14.0	...	...	18.1	8.9	10.2	11.1
OTHER INFORMATIVE PROGRAMMES	3.5	...	...	–	11.2	18.8	13.9
EDUCATIONAL PROGRAMMES	9.0	5.9	0.1	17.4	17.1	5.8	6.0
RELATED TO A SPECIFIC CURRICULUM	7.0	...	...	2.1	9.2	0.7	1.0
FOR RURAL DEVELOPMENT	2.0	...	...	8.1	–	3.1	5.0
OTHER EDUCATIONAL PROGRAMMES	–	...	...	7.2	8.0	2.0	–
CULTURAL PROGRAMMES	–	17.0	–	–	0.8	3.8	15.0
RELIGIOUS PROGRAMMES	2.0	5.5	–	3.0	9.0	9.2	10.0
ADVERTISEMENTS	–	–	1.9	1.8	2.6	6.8	5.0
ENTERTAINMENT	71.4	53.6	86.0	59.2	49.2	35.2	37.8
PLAYS	3.3	30.0	...	1.0	–	2.4	10.0
MUSIC	52.4	18.7	...	51.9	38.4	30.7	15.0
SPORTS PROGRAMMES	0.7	4.9	...	–	1.7	2.0	2.8
OTHER ENTERTAINMENT PROGRAMMES	15.0	–	...	6.3	9.1	–	10.0
OTHER NOT ELSEWHERE CLASSIFIED	–	–	–	0.5	1.1	10.2	1.2

				AMERICA, NORTH	
TYPE OF PROGRAMME BY FUNCTION PROGRAMMES D'APRES LEUR FONCTION PROGRAMAS SEGUN SU FUNCION	SWAZILAND (1983) GOVT	UNITED REP. OF TANZANIA (1979) GOVT	ZIMBABWE (1981) PUBLIC	BELIZE (1983) GOVT	BRITISH VIRGIN ISL. (1983) COMM
TOTAL ANNUAL BROADCASTING HOURS	5 386	9 191	18 200	11 492	4 716
INFORMATIVE PROGRAMMES	14.4	33.1	33.0	22.2	26.7
NEWS BULLETINS, ETC.	4.6	33.1	6.0	12.9	23.2
OTHER INFORMATIVE PROGRAMMES	9.8	–	26.9	9.3	3.6
EDUCATIONAL PROGRAMMES	21.3	11.5	5.5	3.7	5.0
RELATED TO A SPECIFIC CURRICULUM	–	3.3	2.7	1.7	3.3
FOR RURAL DEVELOPMENT	11.5	8.2	1.4	1.1	1.1
OTHER EDUCATIONAL PROGRAMMES	9.8	–	1.4	0.9	0.6
CULTURAL PROGRAMMES	15.4	2.5	22.0	2.5	–
RELIGIOUS PROGRAMMES	6.7	1.9	0.8	3.6	12.1
ADVERTISEMENTS	15.4	5.0	5.5	4.4	–
ENTERTAINMENT	17.0	46.0	26.9	63.6	56.2
PLAYS	4.8	1.1	7.1	0.9	–
MUSIC	9.8	44.9	13.2	59.8	56.2
SPORTS PROGRAMMES	2.3	–	4.4	0.2	–
OTHER ENTERTAINMENT PROGRAMMES	–	–	2.2	2.7	–
OTHER NOT ELSEWHERE CLASSIFIED	9.8	–	6.3	–	–

TYPE OF PROGRAMME BY FUNCTION / PROGRAMMES D'APRES LEUR FONCTION / PROGRAMAS SEGUN SU FUNCION	CAYMAN ISLANDS (1981)				CUBA‡ (1983)	GUADELOUPE (1979)	MARTINIQUE (1979)
	TOTAL	GOVT	PUBLIC		GOVT	PUBLIC	PUBLIC
TOTAL ANNUAL BROADCASTING HOURS	8 790	6 400	2 390		365 484	6 061	6 283
INFORMATIVE PROGRAMMES	5.6	7.2	1.3		16.5	20.9	14.0
NEWS BULLETINS, ETC.	5.6	7.2	1.3		5.1	...	...
OTHER INFORMATIVE PROGRAMMES	–	–	–		11.5	...	...
EDUCATIONAL PROGRAMMES	11.0	15.0	0.2		2.0	1.1	0.8
RELATED TO A SPECIFIC CURRICULUM	1.5	2.0	–		0.3	...	...
FOR RURAL DEVELOPMENT	–	–	–		1.2	...	...
OTHER EDUCATIONAL PROGRAMMES	9.5	13.0	0.2		0.5	...	...
CULTURAL PROGRAMMES	12.2	12.5	11.3		./.	–	–
RELIGIOUS PROGRAMMES	9.9	12.0	4.2		–	–	–
ADVERTISEMENTS	3.4	4.7	–		11.9	5.0	2.3
ENTERTAINMENT	57.6	48.3	82.4		69.6	73.0	82.9
PLAYS	1.6	1.6	1.7		1.3	...	...
MUSIC	55.2	46.1	79.5		50.3	...	...
SPORTS PROGRAMMES	–	–	–		3.1	...	...
OTHER ENTERTAINMENT PROGRAMMES	0.8	0.7	1.3		15.0	...	...
OTHER NOT ELSEWHERE CLASSIFIED	0.4	0.3	0.6		–	–	–

TYPE OF PROGRAMME BY FUNCTION / PROGRAMMES D'APRES LEUR FONCTION / PROGRAMAS SEGUN SU FUNCION	MEXICO (1983)				ST. PIERRE & MIQUELON (1979)	TURKS AND CAICOS ISL. (1981)	U.S. VIRGIN ISLANDS (1979)
	TOTAL	GOVT	PUBLIC	COMM	PUBLIC	GOVT	COMM
TOTAL ANNUAL BROADCASTING HOURS	4 900 000	350 000	310 000	4 240 000	5 953	5 564	8 778
INFORMATIVE PROGRAMMES	6.5	–	1.8	7.4	15.6	17.2	14.6
NEWS BULLETINS, ETC.	...	...	...	...	...	14.0	14.0
OTHER INFORMATIVE PROGRAMMES	...	...	...	...	...	3.2	0.6
EDUCATIONAL PROGRAMMES	3.8	11.3	45.2	0.2	–	–	–
RELATED TO A SPECIFIC CURRICULUM	–	–	–	–	–	–	–
FOR RURAL DEVELOPMENT	1.7	8.9	16.1	–	–	–	–
OTHER EDUCATIONAL PROGRAMMES	2.2	2.4	29.0	0.2	–	–	–
CULTURAL PROGRAMMES	3.3	1.4	37.1	1.0	–	2.8	–
RELIGIOUS PROGRAMMES	–	–	–	–	–	14.5	–
ADVERTISEMENTS	27.7	36.2	2.3	28.9	–	0.4	11.4
ENTERTAINMENT	52.4	48.6	6.5	56.0	84.4	65.1	74.0
PLAYS	1.2	–	–	1.4	...	–	–
MUSIC	42.9	48.6	6.5	45.0	...	65.1	74.0
SPORTS PROGRAMMES	2.2	–	–	2.5	...	–	–
OTHER ENTERTAINMENT PROGRAMMES	6.1	–	–	7.1	...	–	–
OTHER NOT ELSEWHERE CLASSIFIED	6.3	2.6	7.3	6.5	–	–	–

TYPE OF PROGRAMME BY FUNCTION / PROGRAMMES D'APRES LEUR FONCTION / PROGRAMAS SEGUN SU FUNCION	AMERICA, SOUTH				ASIA		
	BRAZIL (1982)	FALKLAND ISLANDS (1979)	FRENCH GUIANA (1979)	URUGUAY (1983)	AFGHANISTAN (1981)	BAHRAIN (1979)	BANGLADESH (1979)
	TOTAL	GOVT	PUBLIC	TOTAL	GOVT	GOVT	GOVT
TOTAL ANNUAL BROADCASTING HOURS	8 354 788	1 924	5 907	645 000	10 044	5 194	32 120
INFORMATIVE PROGRAMMES	12.7	24.7	11.4	24.2	6.0	19.9	8.3
NEWS BULLETINS, ETC.	10.9	22.6	...	17.1	6.0	16.4	4.5
OTHER INFORMATIVE PROGRAMMES	1.7	2.1	...	7.1	–	3.5	3.7
EDUCATIONAL PROGRAMMES	4.3	3.1	0.4	1.4	9.1	5.5	4.4
RELATED TO A SPECIFIC CURRICULUM	2.6	–	...	0.2	3.3	2.5	...
FOR RURAL DEVELOPMENT	0.9	–	...	0.5	3.2	–	...
OTHER EDUCATIONAL PROGRAMMES	0.7	3.1	...	0.7	2.6	3.0	...
CULTURAL PROGRAMMES	1.1	1.3	–	0.5	10.7	3.5	1.5
RELIGIOUS PROGRAMMES	3.0	2.7	–	0.4	1.3	2.0	0.6
ADVERTISEMENTS	16.6	–	2.6	19.1	2.4	–	4.0
ENTERTAINMENT	60.6	68.2	85.5	54.4	33.0	69.1	81.2
PLAYS	1.3	7.8	...	0.1	1.2	3.5	17.7
MUSIC	55.1	51.6	...	47.2	21.7	63.2	62.0
SPORTS PROGRAMMES	3.1	1.0	...	5.5	0.3	2.3	1.2
OTHER ENTERTAINMENT PROGRAMMES	1.0	7.8	...	1.6	9.8	–	0.3
OTHER NOT ELSEWHERE CLASSIFIED	1.7	–	–	–	37.6	–	0.1

TYPE OF PROGRAMME BY FUNCTION / PROGRAMMES D'APRES LEUR FONCTION / PROGRAMAS SEGUN SU FUNCION	BRUNEI DARUSSALAM (1983)	CYPRUS (1983)	HONG KONG (1981)			INDIA (1983)	INDONESIA‡ (1981)
	GOVT	PUBLIC	TOTAL	GOVT	COMM	GOVT	GOVT
TOTAL ANNUAL BROADCASTING HOURS	10 637	12 836	63 329	42 523	20 806	383 931	266 708
INFORMATIVE PROGRAMMES	30.4	10.6	16.9	17.3	16.2	21.5	32.3
NEWS BULLETINS, ETC.	12.9	7.4	11.7	11.6	11.8	...	...
OTHER INFORMATIVE PROGRAMMES	17.5	3.1	5.2	5.7	4.4	...	...
EDUCATIONAL PROGRAMMES	7.4	3.7	1.7	2.5	–	15.9	19.0
RELATED TO A SPECIFIC CURRICULUM	–	0.4	–	–	–	6.4	...
FOR RURAL DEVELOPMENT	3.2	0.4	–	–	–	6.8	...
OTHER EDUCATIONAL PROGRAMMES	4.2	2.8	1.7	2.5	–	2.7	...
CULTURAL PROGRAMMES	1.5	4.2	0.8	0.8	0.8	11.1	7.6
RELIGIOUS PROGRAMMES	7.7	5.6	1.1	0.5	2.2	0.1	./.
ADVERTISEMENTS	–	2.4	–	–	–	2.3	./.
ENTERTAINMENT	53.0	72.2	72.3	70.2	76.7	46.1	35.3
PLAYS	16.1	1.6	2.5	3.0	1.5	3.2	...
MUSIC	22.9	68.9	66.2	65.5	67.6	38.6	...
SPORTS PROGRAMMES	5.4	0.2	1.8	1.6	2.0	–	...
OTHER ENTERTAINMENT PROGRAMMES	8.6	1.5	1.9	0.1	5.7	4.3	...
OTHER NOT ELSEWHERE CLASSIFIED	–	1.3	7.2	8.8	4.0	3.1	5.7

TYPE OF PROGRAMME BY FUNCTION / PROGRAMMES D'APRES LEUR FONCTION / PROGRAMAS SEGUN SU FUNCION	IRAN, ISL. REP. OF (1983)	ISRAEL‡ (1983)	JAPAN‡ (1983)			JORDAN (1983)	KUWAIT (1983)
	GOVT	PUBLIC	TOTAL	PUBLIC	COMM	GOVT	GOVT
TOTAL ANNUAL BROADCASTING HOURS	8 760	34 281	497 351	20 312	477 039	36 264	22 680
INFORMATIVE PROGRAMMES	20.2	11.5	13.5	22.9	13.1	24.2	10.5
NEWS BULLETINS, ETC.	19.3	5.1	...	...	...	24.2	8.8
OTHER INFORMATIVE PROGRAMMES	0.9	6.4	...	...	...	–	1.7
EDUCATIONAL PROGRAMMES	6.2	2.4	6.1	26.3	5.2	17.7	–
RELATED TO A SPECIFIC CURRICULUM	1.7	2.4	...	...	...	13.5	–
FOR RURAL DEVELOPMENT	1.7	–	...	...	...	4.1	–
OTHER EDUCATIONAL PROGRAMMES	2.7	–	...	...	...	–	–
CULTURAL PROGRAMMES	18.7	8.1	19.9	30.4	19.4	15.1	4.6
RELIGIOUS PROGRAMMES	7.6	0.8	./.	./.	./.	16.7	10.8
ADVERTISEMENTS	–	2.3	0.7	–	0.7	–	–
ENTERTAINMENT	5.9	48.6	59.6	20.4	61.3	26.4	67.1
PLAYS	0.7	0.2	...	...	...	3.3	3.6
MUSIC	4.6	21.8	...	...	...	22.4	53.4
SPORTS PROGRAMMES	1.0	./.	...	...	...	0.7	0.9
OTHER ENTERTAINMENT PROGRAMMES	–	26.6	...	...	...	–	9.1
OTHER NOT ELSEWHERE CLASSIFIED	41.4	26.2	0.2	–	0.3	–	7.1

TYPE OF PROGRAMME BY FUNCTION / PROGRAMMES D'APRES LEUR FONCTION / PROGRAMAS SEGUN SU FUNCION	MALAYSIA (1983)	MALDIVES (1983)	PAKISTAN (1983)	PHILIPPINES (1981)			
	GOVT	GOVT	GOVT	TOTAL	GOVT	PUBLIC	COMM
TOTAL ANNUAL BROADCASTING HOURS	23 270	3 926	78 206	3 949 560	1 282 360	354 240	2 312 960
INFORMATIVE PROGRAMMES	13.8	21.1	25.4	6.4	7.0	0.7	7.0
NEWS BULLETINS, ETC.	13.8	7.7	14.7	...	...	...	...
OTHER INFORMATIVE PROGRAMMES	–	13.3	10.7	...	...	...	...
EDUCATIONAL PROGRAMMES	14.8	7.3	11.9	20.0	20.0	20.0	20.0
RELATED TO A SPECIFIC CURRICULUM	–	0.7	4.3	...	...	...	...
FOR RURAL DEVELOPMENT	7.2	2.0	7.6	...	...	...	...
OTHER EDUCATIONAL PROGRAMMES	7.6	4.6	–	...	...	...	...
CULTURAL PROGRAMMES	–	1.3	5.0	17.0	17.0	17.0	17.0
RELIGIOUS PROGRAMMES	8.3	12.9	9.6	3.0	3.0	3.0	3.0
ADVERTISEMENTS	4.3	14.3	2.3	13.6	13.0	19.3	13.0
ENTERTAINMENT	57.7	43.0	45.8	35.0	35.0	35.0	35.0
PLAYS	3.9	0.7	1.0	...	...	...	...
MUSIC	52.2	0.7	44.3	...	...	...	...
SPORTS PROGRAMMES	1.6	0.3	0.4	...	...	...	...
OTHER ENTERTAINMENT PROGRAMMES	–	41.4	–	...	...	...	...
OTHER NOT ELSEWHERE CLASSIFIED	1.1	–	–	5.0	5.0	5.0	5.0

10.5 **Radio broadcasting: programmes**
Radiodiffusion sonore: programmes
Radiodifusión sonora: programas

TYPE OF PROGRAMME BY FUNCTION / PROGRAMMES D'APRES LEUR FONCTION / PROGRAMAS SEGUN SU FUNCION	QATAR (1983) GOVT	SAUDI ARABIA (1981) GOVT	SINGAPORE (1983) GOVT	SRI LANKA (1983) GOVT	SYRIAN ARAB REPUBLIC (1979) TOTAL	TURKEY (1983) PUBLIC	UNITED ARAB EMIRATES (1983) GOVT
TOTAL ANNUAL BROADCASTING HOURS	15 408	36 865	33 336	34 609	2 363	81 057	18 460
INFORMATIVE PROGRAMMES	10.3	14.0	17.5	11.3	25.5	12.6	15.5
NEWS BULLETINS, ETC.	...	...	8.7	7.7	...	10.6	12.2
OTHER INFORMATIVE PROGRAMMES	...	...	8.8	3.7	...	1.9	3.4
EDUCATIONAL PROGRAMMES	0.6	2.0	12.7	11.0	–	15.5	8.1
RELATED TO A SPECIFIC CURRICULUM	...	...	–	5.4	–	3.7	...
FOR RURAL DEVELOPMENT	...	...	–	5.5	–	4.6	...
OTHER EDUCATIONAL PROGRAMMES	...	...	12.7	0.1	–	7.2	...
CULTURAL PROGRAMMES	9.5	34.0	14.0	4.3	13.4	1.0	10.8
RELIGIOUS PROGRAMMES	6.2	30.0	2.1	8.9	6.5	0.9	11.1
ADVERTISEMENTS	–	–	2.7	3.0	–	3.8	4.1
ENTERTAINMENT	64.6	20.0	51.1	58.0	53.1	65.7	47.5
PLAYS	5.0	...	3.6	4.7	6.6	3.4	4.3
MUSIC	...	...	46.3	47.5	22.1	59.1	41.0
SPORTS PROGRAMMES	...	...	0.2	2.0	0.6	–	0.5
OTHER ENTERTAINMENT PROGRAMMES	...	...	1.0	3.8	23.7	3.2	1.6
OTHER NOT ELSEWHERE CLASSIFIED	3.8	–	–	3.5	1.5	0.6	2.8

EUROPE

TYPE OF PROGRAMME BY FUNCTION / PROGRAMMES D'APRES LEUR FONCTION / PROGRAMAS SEGUN SU FUNCION	ALBANIA (1983) GOVT	BELGIUM‡ (1983) PUBLIC	BULGARIA‡ (1983) PUBLIC	CZECHO-SLOVAKIA (1983) GOVT	DENMARK‡ (1981) TOTAL	DENMARK‡ (1981) GOVT	DENMARK‡ (1981) PUBLIC
TOTAL ANNUAL BROADCASTING HOURS	6 600	49 175	45 332	42 975	14 909	133	14 776
INFORMATIVE PROGRAMMES	21.2	17.5	37.8	15.5	12.2	–	12.3
NEWS BULLETINS, ETC.	18.2	9.9	14.8	11.6	10.5	–	10.6
OTHER INFORMATIVE PROGRAMMES	3.0	7.6	23.0	4.1	1.7	–	1.7
EDUCATIONAL PROGRAMMES	8.2	1.4	2.8	4.2	0.9	100.0	–
RELATED TO A SPECIFIC CURRICULUM	5.5	0.5	–	2.4	...	–	–
FOR RURAL DEVELOPMENT	1.4	–	–	0.1	...	–	–
OTHER EDUCATIONAL PROGRAMMES	1.4	0.9	2.8	1.6	...	–	–
CULTURAL PROGRAMMES	5.5	./.	5.7	18.8	23.2	–	23.4
RELIGIOUS PROGRAMMES	–	0.7	–	–	1.9	–	1.9
ADVERTISEMENTS	–	–	1.9	0.4	–	–	–
ENTERTAINMENT	64.8	64.7	47.3	47.2	59.4	–	60.0
PLAYS	4.1	0.6	2.1	2.3	1.2	–	1.2
MUSIC	56.5	55.8	40.4	41.3	47.2	–	47.6
SPORTS PROGRAMMES	3.5	1.8	0.5	1.0	–	–	–
OTHER ENTERTAINMENT PROGRAMMES	0.8	6.5	4.3	2.6	11.0	–	11.1
OTHER NOT ELSEWHERE CLASSIFIED	0.3	15.7	4.6	13.9	2.4	–	2.5

TYPE OF PROGRAMME BY FUNCTION / PROGRAMMES D'APRES LEUR FONCTION / PROGRAMAS SEGUN SU FUNCION	FINLAND‡ (1983) PUBLIC	FRANCE (1981) PUBLIC	GERMAN DEM. REPUBLIC (1983) GOVT	GIBRALTAR (1983) PUBLIC	HUNGARY (1983) GOVT	IRELAND‡ (1981) PUBLIC	ITALY (1983) PUBLIC
TOTAL ANNUAL BROADCASTING HOURS	17 535	129 953	49 257	6 570	23 603	11 097	48 412
INFORMATIVE PROGRAMMES	18.3	17.6	22.9	14.3	7.4	25.4	23.5
NEWS BULLETINS, ETC.	5.2	...	9.9	14.3	4.9	10.3	21.6
OTHER INFORMATIVE PROGRAMMES	13.1	...	13.0	–	2.6	15.1	1.9
EDUCATIONAL PROGRAMMES	1.7	1.1	3.1	–	5.6	1.5	0.3
RELATED TO A SPECIFIC CURRICULUM	...	...	0.9	–	3.3	1.1	0.1
FOR RURAL DEVELOPMENT	...	...	–	–	0.2	–	–
OTHER EDUCATIONAL PROGRAMMES	...	...	2.2	–	2.2	0.4	0.2
CULTURAL PROGRAMMES	18.6	9.1	3.0	0.8	5.7	./.	35.4
RELIGIOUS PROGRAMMES	1.3	0.6	0.1	1.1	0.1	2.4	0.3
ADVERTISEMENTS	–	0.8	–	0.5	0.9	./.	2.0
ENTERTAINMENT	25.9	70.1	71.0	83.3	60.9	64.3	37.4
PLAYS	0.4	...	–	0.8	2.2	1.9	1.8
MUSIC	22.1	...	65.5	77.9	55.7	53.1	30.7
SPORTS PROGRAMMES	2.5	...	1.5	3.2	1.2	2.8	1.1
OTHER ENTERTAINMENT PROGRAMMES	0.9	...	3.9	1.5	1.7	6.4	3.8
OTHER NOT ELSEWHERE CLASSIFIED	3.4	0.7	–	–	19.3	6.4	1.1

TYPE OF PROGRAMME BY FUNCTION / PROGRAMMES D'APRES LEUR FONCTION / PROGRAMAS SEGUN SU FUNCION	MALTA (1979) GOVT	MONACO (1981) PUBLIC	NORWAY‡ (1981) PUBLIC	POLAND (1983) GOVT	PORTUGAL (1983) PUBLIC	ROMANIA (1983) GOVT	SPAIN‡ (1983) PUBLIC
TOTAL ANNUAL BROADCASTING HOURS	22 002	14 091	11 539	44 253	32 670	32 812	40 460
INFORMATIVE PROGRAMMES	13.7	9.4	46.9	43.3	9.5	18.6	36.2
NEWS BULLETINS, ETC.	10.3	9.2	37.2	18.1	9.5	15.4	31.8
OTHER INFORMATIVE PROGRAMMES	3.4	0.2	9.7	25.2	–	3.2	4.4
EDUCATIONAL PROGRAMMES	2.0	0.2	1.2	1.5	0.6	15.1	2.1
RELATED TO A SPECIFIC CURRICULUM	0.3	0.1	0.9	...	–	2.2	1.6
FOR RURAL DEVELOPMENT	0.5	0.1	–	...	0.4	1.2	–
OTHER EDUCATIONAL PROGRAMMES	1.3	0.1	0.4	...	0.2	11.7	0.5
CULTURAL PROGRAMMES	0.5	0.5	./.	...	18.5	6.7	11.8
RELIGIOUS PROGRAMMES	2.1	14.7	2.0	–	0.9	–	0.3
ADVERTISEMENTS	0.2	8.8	–	1.7	5.8	0.4	0.7
ENTERTAINMENT	78.2	60.7	37.4	52.5	54.8	57.3	48.3
PLAYS	3.4	...	1.3	2.1	0.3	2.1	1.3
MUSIC	73.2	...	24.7	42.0	50.1	53.8	31.0
SPORTS PROGRAMMES	0.6	...	0.4	1.7	3.2	0.7	1.3
OTHER ENTERTAINMENT PROGRAMMES	0.9	...	11.0	6.7	1.2	0.6	14.7
OTHER NOT ELSEWHERE CLASSIFIED	3.3	5.6	12.4	0.9	9.8	1.8	0.6

TYPE OF PROGRAMME BY FUNCTION PROGRAMMES D'APRES LEUR FONCTION PROGRAMAS SEGUN SU FUNCION	SWEDEN (1979) PUBLIC	UNITED KINGDOM (1979) PUBLIC	YUGOSLAVIA (1983) PUBLIC	OCEANIA AMERICAN SAMOA (1981) COMM	FIJI (1979) PUBLIC	FRENCH POLYNESIA (1979) PUBLIC	KIRIBATI‡ (1979) PUBLIC
TOTAL ANNUAL BROADCASTING HOURS	19 112	278 745	385 399	8 760	12 592	5 617	2 975
INFORMATIVE PROGRAMMES	21.7	13.1	18.0	17.9	25.8	11.7	21.8
NEWS BULLETINS, ETC.	8.1	5.8	6.3	16.7	15.5	...	...
OTHER INFORMATIVE PROGRAMMES	13.6	7.2	11.7	1.2	10.3	...	...
EDUCATIONAL PROGRAMMES	3.7	2.1	4.2	1.1	7.1	1.2	16.0
RELATED TO A SPECIFIC CURRICULUM	...	0.6	2.1	–	4.0	...	12.6
FOR RURAL DEVELOPMENT	...	–	2.1	–	1.8	...	./.
OTHER EDUCATIONAL PROGRAMMES	...	1.4	–	1.1	1.3	...	3.4
CULTURAL PROGRAMMES	7.2	40.7	2.5	0.1	0.8	–	28.6
RELIGIOUS PROGRAMMES	2.3	0.7	–	3.0	2.5	...	5.0
ADVERTISEMENTS	–	5.7	4.5	19.4	4.1	3.2	1.7
ENTERTAINMENT	61.2	37.5	68.5	58.5	59.6	83.9	26.9
PLAYS	–	0.4	–	1.4	3.5	...	1.7
MUSIC	47.9	31.9	61.8	56.3	55.5	...	25.2
SPORTS PROGRAMMES	2.8	1.4	1.8	0.8	0.4	...	–
OTHER ENTERTAINMENT PROGRAMMES	10.5	3.9	4.8	–	0.2	...	–
OTHER NOT ELSEWHERE CLASSIFIED	3.8	0.2	2.3	–	–	–	–

TYPE OF PROGRAMME BY FUNCTION PROGRAMMES D'APRES LEUR FONCTION PROGRAMAS SEGUN SU FUNCION	NEW CALEDONIA (1979) PUBLIC	NORFOLK ISLAND (1983) GOVT	PACIFIC ISLANDS (1981) COMM	SAMOA (1981) GOVT	TONGA (1981) PUBLIC	VANUATU (1983) GOVT	U.S.S.R. BYELORUSSIAN S.S.R. (1979) GOVT
TOTAL ANNUAL BROADCASTING HOURS	5 700	5 512	19 710	3 686	3 886	4 500	9 760
INFORMATIVE PROGRAMMES	9.6	13.7	5.1	22.8	27.9	22.2	15.6
NEWS BULLETINS, ETC.	...	4.7	5.1	8.7	21.9	13.3	15.6
OTHER INFORMATIVE PROGRAMMES	...	9.0	–	14.1	6.0	8.9	–
EDUCATIONAL PROGRAMMES	1.4	–	5.1	15.2	19.6	11.1	–
RELATED TO A SPECIFIC CURRICULUM	...	–	3.8	8.1	9.9	–	–
FOR RURAL DEVELOPMENT	...	–	1.3	3.3	6.7	7.8	–
OTHER EDUCATIONAL PROGRAMMES	...	–	–	3.8	3.0	3.3	–
CULTURAL PROGRAMMES	–	–	5.1	2.7	5.8	11.1	9.4
RELIGIOUS PROGRAMMES	–	1.9	10.1	11.3	10.2	11.1	–
ADVERTISEMENTS	3.7	–	10.1	5.6	3.9	1.1	–
ENTERTAINMENT	85.2	54.7	64.5	42.3	32.6	40.0	52.3
PLAYS	...	3.8	–	4.2	–	–	3.1
MUSIC	...	42.5	64.5	23.2	32.6	33.3	48.0
SPORTS PROGRAMMES	...	5.7	–	4.2	–	6.7	1.3
OTHER ENTERTAINMENT PROGRAMMES	...	2.8	–	10.6	–	–	–
OTHER NOT ELSEWHERE CLASSIFIED	–	29.7	–	–	–	3.3	22.6

AFRICA:
Algeria:
E--> Sport programmes are included with news bulletins.
FR-> Les programmes sportifs sont comptés avec les bulletins d'information.
ESP> Los programas deportivos se incluyen con los boletines de noticias.
AMERICA, NORTH:
Cuba:
E--> Cultural programmes are included with entertainment programmes.
FR-> Les programmes culturels sont comptés avec les programmes de divertissement.
ESP> Los programas culturales se incluyen con los programas recreativos.
ASIA:
Indonesia:
E--> Religious programmes are included with educational programmes. Advertisements are included with unclassified programmes.
FR-> Les programmes religieux sont comptés avec les programmes éducatifs. La publicité est comptée avec les programmes non classés.
ESP> Los programas religiosos se incluyen con los programas educativos. La publicidad se incluye con las programas no clasificados.
Israel:
E--> Sport programmes are included with sports news.
FR-> Les programmes sportifs sont comptés avec les nouvelles sportives.
ESP> Los programas deportivas se incluyen con las noticias deportivas.
Japan:
E--> Religious programmes are included with educational programmes.
FR-> Les programmes religieux sont comptés avec les programmes éducatifs.
ESP> Los programas religiosos se incluyen con los programas educativos.
EUROPE:
Belgium:
E--> Cultural programmes are included with other informative programmes. The category 'programmes not elsewhere classified' includes regional programmes and programmes for a specific audience.
FR-> Les programmes culturels sont comptés avec les autres programmes d'information. La rubrique 'Programmes non classés' inclut les programmes régionaux et les programmes destinés à une audience spécifique.
ESP> Los programas culturales se incluyen con los otros programas informativos. La rúbrica 'Programas no clasificados' incluye los programas regionales y los programas orientados a un alcance específico.
Bulgaria:
E--> Sports news are included with sport programmes.
FR-> Les nouvelles sportives sont comptées avec les programmes sportifs.
ESP> Las noticias deportivas se incluyen en los programas deportivos.
Denmark:
E--> Data do not include 3,600 hours of regional programmes.
FR-> Les données excluent 3 600 heures de programmes régionaux.
ESP> Los datos excluyen 3 600 horas de programas regionales.
Finland:
E--> The total annual broadcasting time includes 5,407 hours of programmes in Swedish for which a breakdown by type of programmes is not known.
FR-> Le total annuel d'heures de diffusion inclut 5 407 heures de programmes en suédois pour lesquels la répartition par type de programmes n'est pas connue.
ESP> El total anual de horas de difusión incluye 5 407 horas de programas en sueco por los cuales la repartición por tipo de programas se desconoce.
Ireland:
E--> Cultural programmes and advertisements are included with entertainment.
FR-> Les programmes culturels et la publicité sont comptés avec les programmes de divertissement.
ESP> Los programas culturales y la publicidad figuran incluídos en los programas recreativos.
Norway:
E--> Cultural programmes are included partly with informative programmes and partly with entertainment programmes.
FR-> Les programmes culturels sont comptés en partie avec les programmes d'information et en partie avec les programmes de divertissement.
ESP> Los programas culturales se incluyen en parte con los programas informativos y en parte con los programas recreativos.
Spain:
E--> Data on commercial broadcasting organizations are not available.
FR-> Les données relatives aux organismes commerciaux ne sont pas disponibles.
ESP> Los datos relativos a los organismos comerciales no están disponibles.
OCEANIA:
Kiribati:
E--> Educational programmes for rural development purposes are included with programmes related to a specific curriculum.
FR-> Les programmes éducatifs destinés au développement rural sont inclus avec les programmes liés à un enseignement particulier.
ESP> Los programas educativos para el desarollo rural se incluyen con los programas relacionados con un programa de estudios especificos.

10.6 Television broadcasting: programmes by function and by type of institution

Télévision: programmes d'après leur fonction et le type d'organisme

Televisión: programas clasificados según su función y el tipo de institución

TOTAL ANNUAL BROADCASTING HOURS	= TOTAL ANNUEL D'HEURES DE DIFFUSION	= TOTAL ANUAL DE HORAS DE DIFUSION
INFORMATIVE PROGRAMMES	= PROGRAMMES D'INFORMATION	= PROGRAMAS INFORMATIVOS
NEWS BULLETINS	= BULLETINS D'INFORMATION	= BOLETINES DE NOTICIAS
OTHER INFORMATIVE PROGRAMMES	= AUTRES PROGRAMMES D'INFORMATION	= OTROS PROGRAMAS INFORMATIVOS
EDUCATIONAL PROGRAMMES	= PROGRAMMES EDUCATIFS	= PROGRAMAS EDUCATIVOS
RELATED TO A SPECIFIC CURRICULUM	= LIES A UN ENSEIGNEMENT PARTICULIER	= RELACIONADOS CON UN PROGRAMA DE ESTUDIOS ESPECIFICOS
FOR RURAL DEVELOPMENT	= DESTINES AU DEVELOPPEMENT RURAL	= PARA EL DESARROLLO RURAL
OTHER EDUCATIONAL PROGRAMMES	= AUTRES PROGRAMMES EDUCATIFS	= OTROS PROGRAMAS EDUCATIVOS
CULTURAL PROGRAMMES	= PROGRAMMES CULTURELS	= PROGRAMAS CULTURALES
RELIGIOUS PROGRAMMES	= PROGRAMMES RELIGIEUX	= PROGRAMAS RELIGIOSOS
ADVERTISEMENTS	= PUBLICITE	= PUBLICIDAD
ENTERTAINMENT	= DIVERTISSEMENT	= PROGRAMAS RECREATIVOS
CINEMA FILMS	= FILMS CINEMATOGRAPHIQUES	= PELICULAS CINEMATOGRAFICAS
PLAYS	= DRAMATIQUES	= DRAMAS
MUSIC PROGRAMMES	= MUSIQUE	= MUSICA
SPORTS PROGRAMMES	= PROGRAMMES SPORTIFS	= PROGRAMAS DEPORTIVOS
OTHER ENTERTAINMENT PROGRAMMES	= AUTRES PROGRAMMES DE DIVERTISSEMENT	= OTROS PROGRAMAS RECREATIVOS
OTHER NOT ELSEWHERE CLASSIFIED	= PROGRAMMES NON CLASSES	= PROGRAMAS NO CLASIFICADOS

GOVT = GOVERNMENTAL
PUBLIC = PUBLIC
COMM = COMMERCIAL

GOVT = GOUVERNEMENTAL
PUBLIC = PUBLIC
COMM = COMMERCIAL

GOVT = GUBERNAMENTAL
PUBLIC = PUBLICA
COMM = COMERCIAL

NUMBER OF COUNTRIES AND TERRITORIES PRESENTED IN THIS TABLE: 75

NOMBRE DE PAYS ET DE TERRITOIRES PRESENTES DANS CE TABLEAU: 75

NUMERO DE PAISES Y DE TERRITORIOS PRESENTADOS EN ESTE CUADRO: 75

AFRICA

TYPE OF PROGRAMME BY FUNCTION PROGRAMMES D'APRES LEUR FONCTION PROGRAMAS SEGUN SU FUNCION	ALGERIA (1979)	ANGOLA (1979)	BENIN (1981)			BURKINA FASO (1983)	EGYPT (1983)
	PUBLIC	GOVT	TOTAL	GOVT	PUBLIC	GOVT	GOVT
TOTAL ANNUAL BROADCASTING HOURS	3 163	892	572	362	210	1 300	9 648
INFORMATIVE PROGRAMMES	12.6	21.9	43.2	59.4	15.2	16.8	12.8
NEWS BULLETINS, ETC.	9.0	...	36.4	49.2	14.3	16.8	...
OTHER INFORMATIVE PROGRAMMES	3.6	...	6.8	10.2	1.0	–	...
EDUCATIONAL PROGRAMMES	13.1	3.4	17.5	19.3	14.3	0.5	10.9
RELATED TO A SPECIFIC CURRICULUM	5.7	...	–	–	–	0.5	...
FOR RURAL DEVELOPMENT	–	...	7.0	8.3	4.8	–	...
OTHER EDUCATIONAL PROGRAMMES	7.5	...	10.5	11.0	9.5	–	...
CULTURAL PROGRAMMES	3.9	10.1	16.3	12.4	22.9	12.8	16.5
RELIGIOUS PROGRAMMES	2.1	–	–	–	–	0.5	7.6
ADVERTISEMENTS	–	–	–	–	–	0.8	2.9
ENTERTAINMENT	64.3	38.1	23.1	8.8	47.6	58.8	11.5
CINE FILMS	36.6	16.8	3.5	–	9.5	18.0	...
PLAYS	...	...	5.6	–	15.2	9.2	...
MUSIC PROGRAMMES	11.0	6.2	9.1	–	11.9	25.4	...
SPORTS PROGRAMMES	7.0	9.0	4.5	1.4	10.0	2.3	...
OTHER ENTERTAINMENT PROGRAMMES	9.7	6.2	0.4	–	1.0	3.8	...
OTHER NOT ELSEWHERE CLASSIFIED	4.1	26.6	–	–	–	10.0	37.7

TYPE OF PROGRAMME BY FUNCTION PROGRAMMES D'APRES LEUR FONCTION PROGRAMAS SEGUN SU FUNCION	ETHIOPIA (1983)	GHANA (1983)	MADAGASCAR (1979)		MAURITIUS (1983)		MOROCCO (1979)
	GOVT	GOVT	GOVT		PUBLIC		GOVT
TOTAL ANNUAL BROADCASTING HOURS	1 326	1 114	2 300		2 583		2 576
INFORMATIVE PROGRAMMES	43.3	30.4	24.0		15.4		18.0
NEWS BULLETINS, ETC.	37.4	17.6	9.6		15.4		...
OTHER INFORMATIVE PROGRAMMES	5.9	12.8	14.4		–		...
EDUCATIONAL PROGRAMMES	32.1	21.4	23.0		17.4		4.5
RELATED TO A SPECIFIC CURRICULUM	2.9	–	...		7.4		...
FOR RURAL DEVELOPMENT	–	11.7	...		–		...
OTHER EDUCATIONAL PROGRAMMES	29.1	9.7	...		10.1		...
CULTURAL PROGRAMMES	2.9	7.0	21.0		9.1		17.5
RELIGIOUS PROGRAMMES	–	3.5	–		1.0		5.6
ADVERTISEMENTS	0.9	2.7	–		–		1.5
ENTERTAINMENT	20.9	32.7	32.0		57.1		52.5
CINE FILMS	7.8	–	10.9		40.3		...
PLAYS	–	11.7	10.4		–		18.0
MUSIC PROGRAMMES	5.9	3.5	4.3		–		4.5
SPORTS PROGRAMMES	5.2	11.7	3.0		1.5		...
OTHER ENTERTAINMENT PROGRAMMES	2.0	5.8	3.3		15.3		...
OTHER NOT ELSEWHERE CLASSIFIED	–	2.3	–		–		0.4

TYPE OF PROGRAMME BY FUNCTION PROGRAMMES D'APRES LEUR FONCTION PROGRAMAS SEGUN SU FUNCION	NIGERIA (1981)			REUNION (1979)	SENEGAL (1981)	SUDAN (1981)	ZIMBABWE (1981)
	TOTAL	GOVT	PUBLIC	PUBLIC	GOVT	GOVT	PUBLIC
TOTAL ANNUAL BROADCASTING HOURS	797	104	693	2 590	1 602	2 190	1 800
INFORMATIVE PROGRAMMES	70.6	100.0	66.2	23.2	28.5	23.0	30.6
NEWS BULLETINS, ETC.	34.3	–	39.4	...	22.8	...	21.1
OTHER INFORMATIVE PROGRAMMES	36.4	100.0	26.8	...	5.7	...	9.4
EDUCATIONAL PROGRAMMES	3.3	–	3.8	0.2	24.4	9.0	2.8
RELATED TO A SPECIFIC CURRICULUM	–	–	–	...	–	...	–
FOR RURAL DEVELOPMENT	–	–	–	...	–	...	1.4
OTHER EDUCATIONAL PROGRAMMES	3.3	–	3.8	...	24.4	...	1.4
CULTURAL PROGRAMMES	3.3	–	3.8	–	8.9	8.0	4.4
RELIGIOUS PROGRAMMES	–	–	–	0.7	0.7	9.0	1.7
ADVERTISEMENTS	–	–	–	–	–	7.0	13.9
ENTERTAINMENT	22.8	–	26.7	72.6	28.9	36.0	35.6
CINE FILMS	–	–	–	...	8.1	24.0	5.6
PLAYS	6.5	–	7.5	...	4.9	3.0	13.9
MUSIC PROGRAMMES	–	–	–	...	12.7	9.0	4.4
SPORTS PROGRAMMES	13.0	–	15.0	...	3.2	...	5.6
OTHER ENTERTAINMENT PROGRAMMES	3.3	–	3.8	...	...	...	6.1
OTHER NOT ELSEWHERE CLASSIFIED	–	–	–	3.3	8.6	8.0	11.1

AMERICA, NORTH

TYPE OF PROGRAMME BY FUNCTION PROGRAMMES D'APRES LEUR FONCTION PROGRAMAS SEGUN SU FUNCION	CANADA‡ (1983)			CUBA‡ (1983)	GUADELOUPE (1979)	MARTINIQUE (1979)	MEXICO‡ (1982)
	TOTAL	PUBLIC	COMM	GOVT	PUBLIC	PUBLIC	TOTAL
TOTAL ANNUAL BROADCASTING HOURS	732 810	445 163	287 647	10 096	2 382	2 395	3 900 000
INFORMATIVE PROGRAMMES	25.0	25.5	24.2	38.7	16.7	17.2	0.6
NEWS BULLETINS, ETC.	7.9	7.2	9.1	2.9	...	...	...
OTHER INFORMATIVE PROGRAMMES	17.0	18.3	15.1	35.8	...	...	...
EDUCATIONAL PROGRAMMES	12.9	15.2	9.3	3.8	1.1	1.4	13.3
RELATED TO A SPECIFIC CURRICULUM	5.6	6.8	3.7	0.6	...	...	...
FOR RURAL DEVELOPMENT	–	–	–	–	...	...	...
OTHER EDUCATIONAL PROGRAMMES	7.3	8.4	5.6	3.2	...	...	...
CULTURAL PROGRAMMES	0.7	1.2	0.0	./.	–	–	./.
RELIGIOUS PROGRAMMES	4.5	4.6	4.3	–	0.5	–	...
ADVERTISEMENTS	–	–	–	6.3	–	0.6	33.3
ENTERTAINMENT	56.7	53.3	62.1	51.2	78.4	77.8	42.9
CINE FILMS	8.0	8.1	7.9	12.9	...	...	...
PLAYS	./.	./.	./.	18.1	...	...	...
MUSIC PROGRAMMES	1.4	1.4	1.2	11.0	...	...	...
SPORTS PROGRAMMES	6.7	7.1	5.9	9.2	...	...	...
OTHER ENTERTAINMENT PROGRAMMES	40.7	36.6	47.0	–	...	...	...
OTHER NOT ELSEWHERE CLASSIFIED	0.1	0.2	–	–	3.3	3.0	9.9

TYPE OF PROGRAMME BY FUNCTION / PROGRAMMES D'APRES LEUR FONCTION / PROGRAMAS SEGUN SU FUNCION	ST. PIERRE AND MIQUELON (1979)	TRINIDAD AND TOBAGO (1981)	AMERICA, SOUTH BRAZIL (1982)	COLOMBIA (1983)	FRENCH GUIANA (1979)	URUGUAY (1983)	ASIA AFGHANISTAN (1981)
	PUBLIC	COMM	TOTAL	PUBLIC	PUBLIC	TOTAL	GOVT
TOTAL ANNUAL BROADCASTING HOURS	2 357	4 944	574 972	10 868	2 372	47 020	752
INFORMATIVE PROGRAMMES	17.8	5.0	14.4	13.9	17.0	6.6	36.3
NEWS BULLETINS, ETC.	...	4.5	11.6	7.9	...	6.2	33.5
OTHER INFORMATIVE PROGRAMMES	...	0.5	2.8	6.0	...	0.4	2.8
EDUCATIONAL PROGRAMMES	–	–	6.2	...	0.9	2.6	4.8
RELATED TO A SPECIFIC CURRICULUM	–	–	3.6	...	...	1.6	3.7
FOR RURAL DEVELOPMENT	–	–	1.0	...	...	0.6	–
OTHER EDUCATIONAL PROGRAMMES	–	–	1.6	...	...	0.3	1.1
CULTURAL PROGRAMMES	–	3.0	3.1	3.1	–	0.3	2.0
RELIGIOUS PROGRAMMES	0.6	1.9	2.3	0.2	0.5	0.2	2.9
ADVERTISEMENTS	...	23.3	13.8	13.6	–	20.8	–
ENTERTAINMENT	78.8	64.6	51.6	64.6	78.4	69.5	53.9
CINE FILMS	...	8.4	21.2	...	...	65.6	26.6
PLAYS	...	0.1	9.6	...	...	2.8	–
MUSIC PROGRAMMES	...	4.2	4.6	...	...	0.4	6.6
SPORTS PROGRAMMES	...	10.8	4.9	...	...	0.6	17.8
OTHER ENTERTAINMENT PROGRAMMES	...	41.1	11.3	...	...	0.1	2.8
OTHER NOT ELSEWHERE CLASSIFIED	2.8	2.1	8.7	4.5	3.2	–	0.1

TYPE OF PROGRAMME BY FUNCTION / PROGRAMMES D'APRES LEUR FONCTION / PROGRAMAS SEGUN SU FUNCION	BAHRAIN (1979)	BANGLADESH (1979)	BRUNEI DARUSSALAM (1983)	CYPRUS (1983)	HONG KONG‡ (1981)		
	GOVT	GOVT	GOVT	PUBLIC	TOTAL	GOVT	COMM
TOTAL ANNUAL BROADCASTING HOURS	2 304	2 007	3 285	2 440	24 068	1 489	22 579
INFORMATIVE PROGRAMMES	15.8	19.7	9.9	23.1	10.0	15.6	9.6
NEWS BULLETINS, ETC.	...	...	8.3	11.5	6.1	–	6.5
OTHER INFORMATIVE PROGRAMMES	...	...	1.6	11.6	3.9	15.6	3.1
EDUCATIONAL PROGRAMMES	4.3	11.5	14.2	2.1	6.3	68.4	2.2
RELATED TO A SPECIFIC CURRICULUM	–	6.1	3.2	1.6	4.2	68.0	–
FOR RURAL DEVELOPMENT	0.6	2.7	–	0.5	–	–	–
OTHER EDUCATIONAL PROGRAMMES	3.7	2.7	11.1	–	2.1	0.4	2.2
CULTURAL PROGRAMMES	4.3	...	3.2	12.6	1.1	0.9	1.1
RELIGIOUS PROGRAMMES	4.2	1.7	4.7	0.2	0.1	–	0.1
ADVERTISEMENTS	10.5	9.1	–	11.1	7.8	–	8.3
ENTERTAINMENT	60.9	58.0	67.9	47.3	72.5	10.2	76.6
CINE FILMS	11.9	27.3	15.5	10.2	34.2	–	36.5
PLAYS	31.7	5.4	1.6	1.0	18.3	8.0	19.0
MUSIC PROGRAMMES	4.8	19.9	4.7	6.8	4.4	0.5	4.7
SPORTS PROGRAMMES	5.9	5.4	6.3	0.5	2.7	0.5	2.9
OTHER ENTERTAINMENT PROGRAMMES	6.5	–	39.7	28.8	12.8	1.7	13.6
OTHER NOT ELSEWHERE CLASSIFIED	–	–	–	3.5	2.3	4.9	2.1

10.6 Television broadcasting: programmes
Télévision: programmes
Televisión: programas

TYPE OF PROGRAMME BY FUNCTION / PROGRAMMES D'APRES LEUR FONCTION / PROGRAMAS SEGUN SU FUNCION	INDIA (1981)	INDONESIA (1981)	IRAN, ISL. REPUBLIC OF (1983)	ISRAEL‡ (1983)		
	GOVT	GOVT	GOVT	TOTAL	GOVT	PUBLIC
TOTAL ANNUAL BROADCASTING HOURS	21 960	25 578	5 078	4 368	2 002	2 366
INFORMATIVE PROGRAMMES	11.9	28.0	19.8	8.7	–	16.1
NEWS BULLETINS, ETC.	7.4	25.0	16.7	6.5	–	12.1
OTHER INFORMATIVE PROGRAMMES	4.5	3.0	3.0	2.2	–	4.0
EDUCATIONAL PROGRAMMES	15.8	20.2	11.3	45.8	100.0	–
RELATED TO A SPECIFIC CURRICULUM	6.7	7.3	2.3	28.0	61.1	–
FOR RURAL DEVELOPMENT	6.8	2.8	1.3	17.8	38.9	–
OTHER EDUCATIONAL PROGRAMMES	2.3	10.1	7.7	–	–	–
CULTURAL PROGRAMMES	1.5	8.1	4.2	8.1	–	15.0
RELIGIOUS PROGRAMMES	2.3	2.8	11.8	0.9	–	1.6
ADVERTISEMENTS	0.3	–	–	–	–	–
ENTERTAINMENT	46.1	38.9	25.4	15.6	–	28.8
CINE FILMS	13.8	1.8	4.3	3.6	–	6.6
PLAYS	5.1	18.2	0.7	5.3	–	9.7
MUSIC PROGRAMMES	8.8	18.1	11.2	1.6	–	3.0
SPORTS PROGRAMMES	8.6	0.8	6.3	1.4	–	2.5
OTHER ENTERTAINMENT PROGRAMMES	9.8	–	2.9	3.8	–	7.0
OTHER NOT ELSEWHERE CLASSIFIED	22.0	2.0	27.5	20.8	–	38.5

TYPE OF PROGRAMME BY FUNCTION / PROGRAMMES D'APRES LEUR FONCTION / PROGRAMAS SEGUN SU FUNCION	JAPAN‡ (1983)			JORDAN (1983)	KUWAIT (1983)	MALAYSIA (1983)	MALDIVES (1983)
	TOTAL	PUBLIC	COMM	GOVT	GOVT	GOVT	GOVT
TOTAL ANNUAL BROADCASTING HOURS	667 761	13 099	654 662	5 380	5 315	5 624	1 458
INFORMATIVE PROGRAMMES	14.7	20.6	14.6	10.0	9.9	17.6	33.4
NEWS BULLETINS, ETC.	...	...	...	10.0	8.1	17.6	...
OTHER INFORMATIVE PROGRAMMES	...	...	...	–	1.9	–	...
EDUCATIONAL PROGRAMMES	13.1	46.9	12.4	19.5	–	7.1	7.1
RELATED TO A SPECIFIC CURRICULUM	...	...	...	19.5	–	3.2	...
FOR RURAL DEVELOPMENT	...	...	...	–	–	3.9	...
OTHER EDUCATIONAL PROGRAMMES	...	...	...	–	–	–	...
CULTURAL PROGRAMMES	24.2	21.5	24.2	17.1	11.4	–	2.7
RELIGIOUS PROGRAMMES	./.	./.	./.	3.1	9.3	7.4	5.1
ADVERTISEMENTS	0.6	–	0.6	0.3	2.7	7.6	2.1
ENTERTAINMENT	46.7	11.1	47.4	42.7	52.7	60.3	38.9
CINE FILMS	...	...	...	4.8	8.2	19.4	...
PLAYS	...	...	...	30.6	25.4	25.9	...
MUSIC PROGRAMMES	...	...	...	2.9	5.2	10.1	...
SPORTS PROGRAMMES	...	...	...	1.9	6.2	4.9	...
OTHER ENTERTAINMENT PROGRAMMES	...	...	...	2.4	7.8	–	...
OTHER NOT ELSEWHERE CLASSIFIED	0.8	–	0.8	7.2	13.9	–	10.8

TYPE OF PROGRAMME BY FUNCTION PROGRAMMES D'APRES LEUR FONCTION PROGRAMAS SEGUN SU FUNCION	OMAN (1983)	PAKISTAN (1983)	PHILIPPINES (1981)				QATAR (1983)
	GOVT	GOVT	TOTAL	GOVT	PUBLIC	COMM	GOVT
TOTAL ANNUAL BROADCASTING HOURS	3 299	2 924	376 246	107 566	14 040	254 640	5 887
INFORMATIVE PROGRAMMES	12.6	21.0	7.0	7.0	7.0	7.0	18.5
NEWS BULLETINS, ETC.	...	12.8	...	...	...	...	...
OTHER INFORMATIVE PROGRAMMES	...	8.3	...	...	...	...	...
EDUCATIONAL PROGRAMMES	5.5	5.3	20.0	20.0	20.0	20.0	12.2
RELATED TO A SPECIFIC CURRICULUM	...	–	...	...	...	...	...
FOR RURAL DEVELOPMENT	...	2.2	...	...	...	...	...
OTHER EDUCATIONAL PROGRAMMES	...	3.1	...	...	...	...	...
CULTURAL PROGRAMMES	9.5	5.2	17.0	17.0	17.0	17.0	7.6
RELIGIOUS PROGRAMMES	11.0	10.4	3.0	3.0	3.0	3.0	15.5
ADVERTISEMENTS	–	9.3	13.0	13.0	13.0	13.0	2.1
ENTERTAINMENT	61.5	40.9	35.0	35.0	35.0	35.0	37.0
CINE FILMS	./.	5.2	...	...	...	...	...
PLAYS	./.	7.7	...	...	...	...	...
MUSIC PROGRAMMES	./.	6.8	...	...	...	...	...
SPORTS PROGRAMMES	4.7	19.5	...	...	...	...	...
OTHER ENTERTAINMENT PROGRAMMES	–	1.8	...	...	...	...	...
OTHER NOT ELSEWHERE CLASSIFIED	–	7.8	5.0	5.0	5.0	5.0	7.1

TYPE OF PROGRAMME BY FUNCTION PROGRAMMES D'APRES LEUR FONCTION PROGRAMAS SEGUN SU FUNCION	SAUDI ARABIA (1981)	SINGAPORE‡ (1983)	SRI LANKA (1983)	SYRIAN ARAB REPUBLIC‡ (1979)	TURKEY (1983)	UNITED ARAB EMIRATES‡ (1983)	EUROPE ALBANIA (1983)
	GOVT	GOVT	GOVT	TOTAL	PUBLIC	GOVT	GOVT
TOTAL ANNUAL BROADCASTING HOURS	2 920	6 016	1 604	863	1 811	6 420	2 090
INFORMATIVE PROGRAMMES	14.6	19.4	20.6	12.7	26.0	8.6	19.0
NEWS BULLETINS, ETC.	...	9.6	17.1	...	26.0	8.6	16.5
OTHER INFORMATIVE PROGRAMMES	...	9.8	3.6	...	–	–	2.6
EDUCATIONAL PROGRAMMES	6.2	15.8	3.7	13.2	13.3	8.4	18.5
RELATED TO A SPECIFIC CURRICULUM	3.1	–	0.8	...	6.6	...	6.2
FOR RURAL DEVELOPMENT	2.1	–	2.9	...	1.1	...	3.6
OTHER EDUCATIONAL PROGRAMMES	1.1	15.8	./.	...	5.5	...	8.6
CULTURAL PROGRAMMES	6.2	2.2	21.8	./.	8.4	9.3	10.8
RELIGIOUS PROGRAMMES	12.5	–	3.1	4.6	2.6	15.6	–
ADVERTISEMENTS	...	–	–	–	3.6	3.1	6.1
ENTERTAINMENT	39.6	62.7	37.4	28.9	43.0	45.6	44.6
CINE FILMS	12.5	47.2	16.6	11.4	13.1	14.0	13.4
PLAYS	14.6	./.	2.3	–	13.8	15.6	7.2
MUSIC PROGRAMMES	12.5	11.5	5.9	3.9	6.4	8.3	14.4
SPORTS PROGRAMMES	–	4.0	7.7	2.4	3.1	4.7	7.2
OTHER ENTERTAINMENT PROGRAMMES	–	./.	4.9	11.1	6.5	3.1	2.5
OTHER NOT ELSEWHERE CLASSIFIED	20.9	–	13.3	40.6	3.1	9.3	1.0

TYPE OF PROGRAMME BY FUNCTION / PROGRAMMES D'APRES LEUR FONCTION / PROGRAMAS SEGUN SU FUNCION	BELGIUM‡ (1983) PUBLIC	BULGARIA‡ (1983) PUBLIC	CZECHO-SLOVAKIA (1983) GOVT	DENMARK‡ (1981) GOVT	FINLAND‡ (1983) TOTAL	PUBLIC	COMM
TOTAL ANNUAL BROADCASTING HOURS	8 756	5 024	9 650	2 486	4 507	3 509	998
INFORMATIVE PROGRAMMES	22.2	21.4	27.3	28.2	30.4	33.6	19.1
NEWS BULLETINS, ETC.	8.3	16.7	15.3	9.2	9.7	9.2	11.3
OTHER INFORMATIVE PROGRAMMES	14.0	4.6	12.0	19.0	20.7	24.4	7.8
EDUCATIONAL PROGRAMMES	14.7	17.4	9.6	4.7	5.6	7.2	–
RELATED TO A SPECIFIC CURRICULUM	10.7	7.1	6.1	...	5.2	6.7	–
FOR RURAL DEVELOPMENT	–	1.0	0.1	...	–	–	–
OTHER EDUCATIONAL PROGRAMMES	4.0	9.3	3.5	...	0.4	0.5	–
CULTURAL PROGRAMMES	./.	2.2	3.0	9.8	...	...	–
RELIGIOUS PROGRAMMES	2.1	–	–	1.0	1.1	1.4	–
ADVERTISEMENTS	–	1.1	1.7	–	2.6	–	11.8
ENTERTAINMENT	51.0	34.2	52.8	39.8	46.1	41.2	63.4
CINE FILMS	5.2	15.0	9.2	8.5	9.1	7.4	14.8
PLAYS	20.8	3.5	18.0	13.4	16.1	12.2	29.8
MUSIC PROGRAMMES	4.3	5.1	6.5	8.3	6.6	7.5	3.5
SPORTS PROGRAMMES	12.1	6.1	8.9	7.0	6.4	8.1	0.5
OTHER ENTERTAINMENT PROGRAMMES	8.6	4.5	10.2	2.5	7.9	6.0	14.8
OTHER NOT ELSEWHERE CLASSIFIED	9.9	23.9	5.6	16.5	14.2	16.6	5.6

TYPE OF PROGRAMME BY FUNCTION / PROGRAMMES D'APRES LEUR FONCTION / PROGRAMAS SEGUN SU FUNCION	FRANCE (1983) PUBLIC	GERMAN DEM. REPUBLIC (1983) GOVT	GIBRALTAR (1983) PUBLIC	HUNGARY (1983) GOVT	IRELAND‡ (1981) PUBLIC	ITALY‡ (1983) PUBLIC	MALTA (1979) GOVT
TOTAL ANNUAL BROADCASTING HOURS	12 166	7 962	1 850	4 761	5 445	19 257	1 969
INFORMATIVE PROGRAMMES	41.9	23.1	11.2	16.1	18.9	37.9	18.5
NEWS BULLETINS, ETC.	27.9	11.5	7.0	14.1	6.6	33.7	15.2
OTHER INFORMATIVE PROGRAMMES	13.9	11.6	4.2	2.0	12.3	4.2	3.3
EDUCATIONAL PROGRAMMES	...	9.2	2.8	13.7	5.5	3.3	3.0
RELATED TO A SPECIFIC CURRICULUM	...	...	–	13.4	5.3	3.3	–
FOR RURAL DEVELOPMENT	...	...	–	0.3	–	–	–
OTHER EDUCATIONAL PROGRAMMES	...	...	2.8	–	0.2	–	3.0
CULTURAL PROGRAMMES	...	...	3.2	7.0	./.	21.5	2.6
RELIGIOUS PROGRAMMES	1.3	...	0.5	–	1.9	./.	1.5
ADVERTISEMENTS	1.4	...	–	4.0	./.	1.6	3.0
ENTERTAINMENT	41.8	58.9	82.2	51.9	62.9	32.2	71.2
CINE FILMS	2.8	...	4.2	19.3	12.0	6.6	13.2
PLAYS	12.6	28.8	2.8	1.1	27.6	4.7	3.7
MUSIC PROGRAMMES	15.7	13.8	2.8	2.5	5.2	9.9	20.3
SPORTS PROGRAMMES	4.3	8.4	–	8.7	8.2	7.6	6.0
OTHER ENTERTAINMENT PROGRAMMES	6.4	7.9	72.4	20.4	9.9	3.4	28.0
OTHER NOT ELSEWHERE CLASSIFIED	13.7	8.8	–	7.2	10.7	3.6	–

TYPE OF PROGRAMME BY FUNCTION PROGRAMMES D'APRES LEUR FONCTION PROGRAMAS SEGUN SU FUNCION	MONACO (1981) COMM	NETHERLANDS‡ (1979) PUBLIC	NORWAY (1981) PUBLIC	POLAND (1983) GOVT	PORTUGAL‡ (1983) PUBLIC	ROMANIA (1983) GOVT	SPAIN (1983) PUBLIC
TOTAL ANNUAL BROADCASTING HOURS	1 742	4 514	2 414	8 115	13 650	5 057	6 497
INFORMATIVE PROGRAMMES	8.0	31.3	39.3	44.4	17.3	14.9	15.6
NEWS BULLETINS, ETC.	4.0	13.2	14.0	18.1	17.3	12.0	12.4
OTHER INFORMATIVE PROGRAMMES	4.0	18.1	25.3	26.2	–	2.9	3.2
EDUCATIONAL PROGRAMMES	–	9.1	7.7	12.7	8.9	16.6	1.6
RELATED TO A SPECIFIC CURRICULUM	–	9.1	6.8	...	./.	3.4	–
FOR RURAL DEVELOPMENT	–	–	–	...	./.	2.6	–
OTHER EDUCATIONAL PROGRAMMES	–	–	1.0	...	./.	10.6	1.6
CULTURAL PROGRAMMES	–	3.7	...	...	2.0	5.2	16.3
RELIGIOUS PROGRAMMES	3.8	3.2	1.0	–	2.1	–	1.4
ADVERTISEMENTS	7.5	4.3	–	1.7	1.7	1.0	3.7
ENTERTAINMENT	80.7	38.1	45.2	36.5	57.0	54.7	47.1
CINE FILMS	27.0	20.3	4.5	20.1	8.5	12.8	11.4
PLAYS	...	./.	18.4	2.0	22.9	3.0	13.9
MUSIC PROGRAMMES	...	2.4	7.0	4.7	1.5	22.6	6.4
SPORTS PROGRAMMES	3.4	6.7	7.8	6.1	7.6	4.8	7.0
OTHER ENTERTAINMENT PROGRAMMES	50.2	8.4	7.5	3.7	16.4	11.4	8.6
OTHER NOT ELSEWHERE CLASSIFIED	–	10.3	6.9	4.7	10.9	7.7	14.1

				OCEANIA			U.S.S.R.
TYPE OF PROGRAMME BY FUNCTION PROGRAMMES D'APRES LEUR FONCTION PROGRAMAS SEGUN SU FUNCION	SWEDEN (1981) PUBLIC	UNITED KINGDOM (1979) PUBLIC	YUGOSLAVIA‡ (1983) PUBLIC	AMERICAN SAMOA (1981) GOVT	FRENCH POLYNESIA (1979) PUBLIC	NEW CALEDONIA (1979) PUBLIC	BYELORUSSIAN S.S.R. (1979) GOVT
TOTAL ANNUAL BROADCASTING HOURS	4 691	17 377	22 734	5 212	2 478	2 391	5 130
INFORMATIVE PROGRAMMES	33.6	18.9	30.7	8.8	21.1	15.7	30.8
NEWS BULLETINS, ETC.	10.6	5.4	16.3	6.5	...	...	9.7
OTHER INFORMATIVE PROGRAMMES	23.0	13.5	14.4	2.3	...	...	21.0
EDUCATIONAL PROGRAMMES	–	14.9	7.7	74.8	1.7	1.2	4.7
RELATED TO A SPECIFIC CURRICULUM	–	6.4	5.5	74.8	...	...	4.7
FOR RURAL DEVELOPMENT	–	1.4	–	–	...	...	–
OTHER EDUCATIONAL PROGRAMMES	–	7.1	2.2	–	...	...	–
CULTURAL PROGRAMMES	–	17.6	./.	0.4	–	...	1.9
RELIGIOUS PROGRAMMES	0.9	1.5	–	3.2	1.3	0.8	–
ADVERTISEMENTS	–	3.0	3.3	–	–	–	0.8
ENTERTAINMENT	47.6	36.8	36.2	11.5	73.7	79.0	55.5
CINE FILMS	5.9	9.3	14.9	5.0	...	...	24.6
PLAYS	16.2	8.5	4.8	0.4	...	...	7.9
MUSIC PROGRAMMES	6.7	3.8	6.9	1.5	...	...	7.8
SPORTS PROGRAMMES	8.0	9.8	7.3	4.2	...	...	1.2
OTHER ENTERTAINMENT PROGRAMMES	10.8	5.4	2.4	0.4	...	...	14.0
OTHER NOT ELSEWHERE CLASSIFIED	17.9	7.3	22.1	1.2	2.1	3.3	6.4

AMERICA, NORTH:

Canada:

E--> Plays are included with cinema films.

FR-> Les dramatiques sont comptées avec les films cinématographiques.

ESP> Los dramas se incluyen en las peliculas cinematográficas.

Cuba:

E--> Cultural programmes are included with entertainment programmes.

FR-> Les programmes culturels sont comptés avec les programmes de divertissement.

ESP> Los programas culturales se incluyen con los programas recreativos.

Mexico:

E--> Cultural programmes are included with educational programmes.

FR-> Les programmes culturels sont comptés avec les programmes éducatifs.

ESP> Los programas culturales se incluyen con los programas educativos.

ASIA:

Hong Kong:

E--> The figure shown under column 'Governmental' does not include 389 hours of repeats.

FR-> Le nombre figurant dans la colonne 'Gouvernemental' n'inclut pas 389 heures de rediffusion.

ESP> La cifra que figura en la columna 'gubernamental' no incluye 389 horas de redifusión.

Israel:

E--> The category 'Programmes not elsewhere classified' includes 312 hours of chidren's programmes.

FR-> La rubrique 'Programmes non classés' inclut 312 heures de programmes pour enfants.

ESP> La rúbrica 'programas no clasificados' incluye 312 horas de programas para niños.

Japan:

E--> Religious programmes are included with educational programmes.

FR-> Les programmes religieux sont inclus avec les programmes éducatifs.

ESP> Los programas religiosos se incluyen en los programas educativos.

Singapore:

E--> Cinema films include plays and other entertainment programmes.

FR-> Les films cinématographiques incluent les dramatiques et les autres programmes de divertissement.

ESP> Las películas cinematográficas incluyen las dramas y los otros programas recreativos.

Syrian Arab Republic:

E--> Cultural programmes are included with educational programmes.

FR-> Les programmes culturels sont inclus avec les programmes éducatifs.

ESP> Los programas culturales se incluyen con los programas educativos.

United Arab Emirates:

E--> Data refer to Abu Dhabi only.

FR-> Les données ne concernent qu'Abu Dhabi.

ESP> Los datos se refieren a Abu Dhabi solamente.

EUROPE:

Belgium:

E--> Cultural programmes are included with other informative programmes. The category 'Programmes not elsewhere classified' includes programmes for a specific audience.

Belgium: (Cont):

FR-> Les programmes culturels sont comptés avec les autres programmes d'information. La rubrique 'Programmes non classés' inclut les programmes destinés à une audience spécifique.

ESP> Los programas culturales se incluyen con los otros programas informativos. La rúbrica 'Programas no clasificados' incluye los programas orientados a un alcance específico.

Bulgaria:

E--> Sport news are included with sport programmes.

FR-> Les nouvelles sportives sont comptées avec les programmes sportifs.

ESP> Las noticias deportivas se incluyen en los programas deportivos.

Denmark:

E--> Children's programmes (384 hours) are included with other programmes not elsewhere classified.

FR-> Les programmes pour les enfants (384 heures) sont comptés avec les programmes non classés.

ESP> Los programas para los niños (384 horas) se incluyen en los programas no clasificados.

Finland:

E--> The total annual broadcasting time includes 235 hours of programme intervals for which a breakdown by type of broadcasting institutions has not been reported. The category 'programmes not elsewhere classified' includes 390 hours of children's programmes.

FR-> Le total annuel d'heures de diffusion inclut 235 heures d'intervalles entre programmes pour lesquels une répartition par types d'organismes n'est pas connue. La rubrique 'programmes non classés' inclut 390 heures de programmes pour enfants.

ESP> El total anual de horas de difusión incluye 235 horas de intervalo por dentro de los programas por los cuales la repartición por tipos de instituciones se desconoce. La rúbrica 'programas no clasificados' incluye 390 horas de programas para niños.

Ireland:

E--> Cultural programmes and advertisements are included with entertainment.

FR-> Les programmes culturels et la publicité sont comptés avec les programmes de divertissement.

ESP> Los programas culturales y la publicidad figuran incluídos en los programas recreativos.

Italy:

E--> Religious programmes are included with cultural programmes.

FR-> Les programmes religieux sont comptés avec les programmes culturels.

ESP> Los programas religiosos se incluyen en los programas culturales.

Netherlands:

E--> Plays are included with cinema films.

FR-> Les dramatiques sont comptées avec les films cinématographiques.

ESP> Los dramas se incluyen con las películas cinematográficas.

Portugal:

E--> Children's programmes (228 hours) are included with other programmes not elsewhere classified.

FR-> Les programmes pour les enfants (228 heures) sont comptés avec les programmes non classés.

ESP> Los programas para los niños (228 horas) se incluyen en los programas non clasificados.

Yugoslavia:

E--> Cultural programmes are included with entertainment programmes.

FR-> Les programmes culturels sont compris avec les programmes de divertissement.

ESP> Los programas culturales se incluyen en los programas recreativos.

10.7 Radio and television broadcasting: personnel employed by type of personnel and type of institution

Radiodiffusion sonore et télévision: personnel employé d'après le type de personnel et le type d'organisme

Radiodifusión sonora y televisión: personal que trabaja según el tipo de personal y de la institución

GOVT = GOVERNMENTAL

PUB = PUBLIC

COMM = COMMERCIAL

NUMBER OF COUNTRIES AND TERRITORIES PRESENTED IN THIS TABLE: 103

GOVT = GOUVERNEMENTAL

PUB = PUBLIC

COMM = COMMERCIAL

NOMBRE DE PAYS ET DE TERRITOIRES PRESENTES DANS CE TABLEAU: 103

GOVT = GUBERNAMENTAL

PUB = PUBLICA

COMM = COMERCIAL

NUMERO DE PAISES Y DE TERRITORIOS PRESENTADOS EN ESTE CUADRO: 103

COUNTRY / PAYS / PAIS	YEAR / ANNEE / AÑO	TYPE OF INSTITUTION / TYPE D'ORGANISME / TIPO DE INSTITUCION		TOTAL STAFF / PERSONNEL TOTAL / PERSONAL TOTAL	TYPE OF PERSONNEL / TYPE DE PERSONNEL / TIPO DE PERSONAL: PROGRAMME / DES PROGRAMMES / DE PROGRAMAS	JOURNALISTIC / JOURNALISTIQUE / PERIODISTICO	TECHNICAL PRODUCTION / TECHNIQUE DE PRODUCTION / TECNICO DE PRODUCCION	TECHNICAL TRANSMISSION / TECHNIQUE DE DIFFUSION / TECNICO DE RADIODIFUSION	OTHER TECHNICAL / AUTRE TECHNIQUE / OTRO TECNICO	ADMINISTRATIVE / ADMINISTRATIF / ADMINISTRATIVO	OTHER / DIVERS / OTROS TIPOS
AFRICA											
ALGERIA	1981	RADIO+TV	PUB	2 800	16.1	7.9	39.3	——>	——>	16.1	20.7
ANGOLA	1979	RADIO	GOVT	512	19.5	21.7	13.7	10.2	1.6	20.5	12.9
		TV	GOVT	385	10.9	6.0	30.4	11.7	7.8	17.1	16.1
BENIN	1981	RADIO	PUB	78	66.7	33.3	–	–	–	–	–
		TV	GOVT	76	46.1	7.9	19.7	9.2	–	17.1	–
BOTSWANA	1983	RADIO	GOVT	231	9.5	18.6	8.7	4.3	–	12.6	46.3
BURKINA FASO	1983	RADIO	GOVT	165	32.1	24.2	30.3	——>	——>	7.3	6.1
		TV	GOVT	52	–	19.2	38.5	19.2	3.8	9.6	9.6
BURUNDI	1979	RADIO	GOVT	165	27.9	17.0	11.5	9.7	3.0	21.8	9.1
CAMEROON	1979	RADIO	GOVT	280	–	50.0	26.8	17.9	5.4	–	–
CHAD	1983	RADIO	GOVT	125	43.2	11.2	10.4	17.6	2.4	5.6	9.6
ETHIOPIA	1983	RADIO	GOVT	514	20.8	4.5	7.4	16.7	2.9	41.8	5.8
		TV	GOVT	267	22.1	9.4	18.7	7.5	2.6	15.4	24.3
GHANA	1983	RADIO+TV	GOVT	3 229	6.8	3.3	2.8	20.7	24.0	6.2	36.2
GUINEA–BISSAU	1981	RADIO	GOVT	89	12.4	16.9	39.3	18.0	5.6	–	7.9
MADAGASCAR	1979	RADIO	GOVT	280	21.4	10.7	32.1	——>	——>	3.6	32.1
		TV	GOVT	90	33.3	13.3	36.7	——>	——>	6.7	10.0
MALAWI	1983	RADIO	PUB	433	38.8	——>	49.4	——>	——>	11.8	–
MALI	1981	RADIO	GOVT	178	20.2	9.6	24.7	14.0	–	9.0	22.5
		TV	GOVT	158	22.8	10.8	27.8	15.8	12.7	10.1	–
MAURITIUS	1983	RADIO+TV	PUB	181	21.0	12.2	16.6	4.4	7.7	17.7	20.4
MOROCCO	1979	RADIO	GOVT	1 061	31.1	8.8	10.4	21.2	1.2	15.5	11.9
		TV	GOVT	546	20.0	9.2	18.3	15.6	1.8	15.9	19.2

10.7 Radio and television broadcasting: personnel
Radiodiffusion sonore et télévision: personnel
Radiodifusión sonora y televisión: personal

COUNTRY / PAYS / PAIS	YEAR / ANNEE / AÑO	TYPE OF INSTITUTION / TYPE D'ORGANISME / TIPO DE INSTITUCION		TOTAL STAFF / PERSONNEL TOTAL / PERSONAL TOTAL	PROGRAMME / DES PROGRAMMES / DE PROGRAMAS	JOURNALISTIC / JOURNALISTIQUE / PERIODISTICO	TECHNICAL PRODUCTION / TECHNIQUE DE PRODUCTION / TECNICO DE PRODUCCION	TECHNICAL TRANSMISSION / TECHNIQUE DE DIFFUSION / TECNICO DE RADIODIFUSION	OTHER TECHNICAL / AUTRE TECHNIQUE / OTRO TECNICO	ADMINISTRATIVE / ADMINISTRATIF / ADMINISTRATIVO	OTHER / DIVERS / OTROS TIPOS
					TYPE OF PERSONNEL / TYPE DE PERSONNEL / TIPO DE PERSONAL						
REUNION	1979	RADIO	PUB	38	7.9	13.2	18.4	13.2	5.3	23.7	18.4
		TV	PUB	50	4.0	12.0	40.0	10.0	4.0	16.0	14.0
RWANDA	1983	RADIO	GOVT	84	33.3	16.7	11.9	–	8.3	11.9	17.9
ST. HELENA	1981	RADIO	GOVT	22	9.1	–	–	–	–	–	90.9
SENEGAL	1981	RADIO+TV	GOVT	914	22.5	10.1	38.3	10.5	2.0	8.8	7.9
SIERRA LEONE	1982	RADIO+TV	GOVT	634	26.2	5.0	12.9	3.2	21.1	23.7	7.9
SUDAN	1983	RADIO	GOVT	436	64.0	——>	29.1	——>	——>	6.9	–
		TV	GOVT	473	46.3	——>	48.0	——>	——>	5.7	–
SWAZILAND	1983	RADIO	GOVT	104	16.3	15.4	7.7	16.3	9.6	8.7	26.0
UNITED REPUBLIC OF TANZANIA	1979	RADIO	GOVT	557	24.6	——>	10.8	16.2	3.6	1.4	43.4
ZAMBIA	1979	RADIO	GOVT	327	26.3	4.3	24.8	9.2	10.7	12.5	12.2
		TV	GOVT	134	42.5	–	40.3	——>	–	11.9	5.2
AMERICA, NORTH											
BELIZE	1983	RADIO	GOVT	58	24.1	10.3	13.8	13.8	6.9	10.3	20.7
BRITISH VIRGIN ISLANDS	1983	RADIO	COMM	6	50.0	16.7	–	–	–	33.3	–
CANADA	1983	RADIO+TV	PUB	12 334	60.4	——>	12.6	——>	——>	24.0	3.0
		RADIO	COMM	9 666	59.1	——>	4.4	——>	——>	16.8	19.7
		TV	COMM	6 905	62.7	——>	12.4	——>	——>	14.4	10.5
CAYMAN ISLANDS	1981	RADIO	GOVT	21	9.5	19.0	4.8	4.8	–	19.0	42.9
CUBA	1983	RADIO	GOVT	5 332	–	–	48.0	——>	——>	12.7	39.3
		TV	GOVT	3 090	–	–	49.7	——>	——>	11.9	38.3
GUADELOUPE	1979	RADIO	PUB	40	7.5	10.0	22.5	15.0	5.0	25.0	15.0
		TV	PUB	51	5.9	15.7	37.3	11.8	3.9	13.7	11.8
MARTINIQUE	1979	RADIO	PUB	42	9.5	11.9	23.8	11.9	4.8	21.4	16.7
		TV	PUB	51	3.9	13.7	39.2	9.8	3.9	15.7	13.7
MEXICO	1982	RADIO	GOVT	739	41.4	0.1	18.9	——>	——>	18.8	20.7
			COMM	5 113	22.9	0.5	14.9	——>	——>	16.7	45.0
		TV	GOVT	486	13.8	0.4	81.3	——>	——>	2.1	2.5
			COMM	11 675	29.5	0.2	19.3	——>	——>	22.6	28.5
ST. PIERRE AND MIQUELON	1979	RADIO	PUB	22	18.2	13.6	31.8	4.5	4.5	22.7	4.5
		TV	PUB	25	4.0	12.0	44.0	8.0	8.0	16.0	8.0
TRINIDAD AND TOBAGO	1981	TV	COMM	178	19.7	6.2	43.8	3.9	–	9.6	16.9
TURKS AND CAICOS ISLANDS	1983	RADIO	PUB	5	40.0	——>	20.0	——>	——>	40.0	–
U.S. VIRGIN ISLANDS	1979	RADIO+TV	COMM	13	46.2	——>	7.7	7.7	7.7	7.7	23.1
AMERICA, SOUTH											
BOLIVIA	1981	RADIO	GOVT	27	3.7	33.3	14.8	–	48.1	–	–
			PUB	216	13.0	45.8	3.2	–	38.0	–	–
			COMM	740	0.9	53.8	2.2	–	43.1	–	–
CHILE	1982	RADIO+TV	GOVT	1 004	17.3	12.5	17.7	8.6	1.7	29.1	13.1
			PUB	469	4.7	5.8	3.4	10.7	2.8	7.2	65.5
			COMM	1 787	7.3	8.7	8.3	13.3	4.4	19.6	38.3
COLOMBIA	1983	RADIO	PUB	96	18.8	1.0	13.5	66.7	–	–	
		TV	PUB	1 030	4.2	0.1	29.7	32.1	–	12.4	21.5
FALKLAND ISLANDS (MALVINAS)	1979	RADIO	GOVT	6	16.7	16.7	–	50.0	–	16.7	–
FRENCH GUIANA	1981	RADIO+TV	PUB	94	13.8	16.0	40.4	6.4	–	10.6	12.8
GUYANA	1979	RADIO	GOVT	90	30.0	11.1	12.2	7.8	20.0	7.8	11.1

COUNTRY / PAYS / PAIS	YEAR / ANNEE / AÑO	TYPE OF INSTITUTION / TYPE D'ORGANISME / TIPO DE INSTITUCION		TOTAL STAFF / PERSONNEL TOTAL / PERSONAL TOTAL	TYPE OF PERSONNEL / TYPE DE PERSONNEL / TIPO DE PERSONAL						
					PROGRAMME / DES PROGRAMMES / DE PROGRAMAS	JOURNALISTIC / JOURNALISTIQUE / PERIODISTICO	TECHNICAL PRODUCTION / TECHNIQUE DE PRODUCTION / TECNICO DE PRODUCCION	TECHNICAL TRANSMISSION / TECHNIQUE DE DIFFUSION / TECNICO DE RADIODIFUSION	OTHER TECHNICAL / AUTRE TECHNIQUE / OTRO TECNICO	ADMINISTRATIVE / ADMINISTRATIF / ADMINISTRATIVO	OTHER / DIVERS / OTROS TIPOS
ASIA											
AFGHANISTAN	1981	RADIO	GOVT	965	25.9	2.1	25.5	–	8.0	5.2	33.4
		TV	GOVT	622	30.1	3.2	30.7	–	11.3	8.0	16.7
BAHRAIN	1979	RADIO	GOVT	109	27.5	13.8	22.0	9.2	–	14.7	12.8
		TV	GOVT	205	31.2	4.9	29.3	3.4	7.3	23.9	–
BANGLADESH	1979	RADIO	GOVT	2 088	19.9	——>	24.9	——>	——>	55.2	–
		TV	GOVT	838	25.1	5.4	35.6	10.1	6.4	15.5	1.9
BHUTAN	1979	RADIO	PUB	25	52.0	12.0	16.0	8.0	–	12.0	–
BRUNEI DARUSSALAM	1983	RADIO+TV	GOVT	839	32.8	6.0	42.3	4.8	–	2.9	11.3
CYPRUS	1983	RADIO+TV	PUB	930	22.2	5.2	12.0	18.7	4.1	3.2	34.6
HONG KONG	1981	RADIO+TV	GOVT	595	22.2	18.7	13.1	3.5	13.9	10.3	18.3
		RADIO	COMM	235	41.4	12.2	9.3	——>	——>	5.1	32.1
		TV	COMM	2 755	19.8	4.2	20.9	1.9	9.0	13.9	30.3
INDIA	1981	RADIO	GOVT	15 415	31.0	0.7	23.9	–	2.8	6.8	34.7
		TV	GOVT	4 526	29.8	1.5	10.6	23.9	4.9	16.8	12.5
INDONESIA	1981	RADIO	GOVT	4 633	23.4	15.0	32.8	——>	——>	28.8	–
		TV	GOVT	4 216	19.6	9.3	20.8	20.5	2.0	27.8	–
IRAN, ISLAMIC REPUBLIC OF	1983	RADIO+TV	GOVT	11 541	5.0	——>	29.6	——>	——>	41.3	24.2
IRAQ	1979	RADIO+TV	GOVT	2 981	...	...	...	...	...	...	...
ISRAEL	1983	RADIO	PUB	918	67.1	——>	20.2	——>	——>	12.7	–
		TV	PUB	578	60.7	——>	22.3	——>	——>	17.0	–
JAPAN	1983	RADIO+TV	PUB	16 150	17.8	11.6	17.1	9.2	4.3	10.4	29.7
			COMM	25 928	19.5	13.5	14.4	7.0	1.1	12.7	31.7
JORDAN	1983	RADIO	GOVT	500	40.0	12.0	–	24.0		24.0	–
		TV	GOVT	860	16.9	16.0	20.9	5.1	5.9	17.7	17.4
KUWAIT	1983	RADIO	GOVT	530	7.4	——>	6.8	12.8	48.1	20.9	4.0
		TV	GOVT	1 420	2.8	——>	75.8	——>	——>	21.3	–
MALAYSIA	1983	RADIO+TV	GOVT	5 905	40.4	4.2	37.7	——>	——>	17.6	–
MALDIVES	1983	RADIO	GOVT	62	22.6	——>	6.5	27.4	–	25.8	17.7
		TV	GOVT	49	24.5	——>	26.5	6.1	14.3	28.6	–
OMAN	1983	RADIO	GOVT	102	9.8	29.4	24.5	–	–	36.3	–
		TV	GOVT	161	5.0	9.3	49.7	5.6	3.7	8.7	18.0
PAKISTAN	1983	RADIO	GOVT	5 485	18.0	3.9	26.9	——>	——>	38.5	12.8
PHILIPPINES	1981	RADIO+TV	GOVT	1 664	20.0	——>	30.0	——>	——>	50.0	–
			PUB	650	20.0	——>	30.2	——>	——>	49.8	–
			COMM	16 472	20.0	——>	30.0	——>	——>	50.0	–
QATAR	1983	RADIO	GOVT	354	15.8	6.2	9.0	14.7	5.4	27.1	21.8
		TV	GOVT	540	37.0	7.4	23.1	8.3	13.9	10.2	–
SAUDI ARABIA	1981	RADIO	GOVT	529	31.8	6.0	10.6	8.1	10.2	5.1	28.2
		TV	GOVT	649	17.6	3.2	9.4	7.7	30.7	4.3	27.1
SINGAPORE	1983	RADIO+TV	GOVT	2 503	20.4	4.9	13.5	2.6	1.1	22.5	34.9
SRI LANKA	1983	RADIO	GOVT	2 091	18.7	3.6	31.0	——>	——>	18.7	28.1
		TV	GOVT	472	31.8	7.0	25.8	8.9	0.2	14.2	12.1
SYRIAN ARAB REP.	1983	RADIO+TV	GOVT	2 203	3.1	——>	83.4	——>	——>	12.9	0.6
TURKEY	1983	RADIO	PUB	1 930	32.5	——>	23.1	——>	——>	27.9	16.6
		TV	PUB	1 709	32.9	29.7	18.0	——>	——>	13.0	6.4
UNITED ARAB EMIRATES‡	1983	RADIO	GOVT	223	18.4	12.6	20.2	17.9	–	15.2	15.7
		TV	GOVT	385	19.2	2.6	38.4	7.5	–	9.4	22.9
EUROPE											
AUSTRIA	1983	RADIO+TV	PUB	3 230	34.4	——>	48.3	——>		10.7	6.7

10.7 Radio and television broadcasting: personnel
Radiodiffusion sonore et télévision: personnel
Radiodifusión sonora y televisión: personal

COUNTRY / PAYS / PAIS	YEAR / ANNEE / AÑO	TYPE OF INSTITUTION / TYPE D'ORGANISME / TIPO DE INSTITUCION		TOTAL STAFF / PERSONNEL TOTAL / PERSONAL TOTAL	TYPE OF PERSONNEL / TYPE DE PERSONNEL / TIPO DE PERSONAL						
					PROGRAMME / DES PROGRAMMES / DE PROGRAMAS	JOURNALISTIC / JOURNALISTIQUE / PERIODISTICO	TECHNICAL PRODUCTION / TECHNIQUE DE PRODUCTION / TECNICO DE PRODUCCION	TECHNICAL TRANSMISSION / TECHNIQUE DE DIFFUSION / TECNICO DE RADIODIFUSION	OTHER TECHNICAL / AUTRE TECHNIQUE / OTRO TECNICO	ADMINISTRATIVE / ADMINISTRATIF / ADMINISTRATIVO	OTHER / DIVERS / OTROS TIPOS
BELGIUM	1983	RADIO+TV	PUB	5 308	28.4	——>	42.2	——>	——>	8.1	21.3
DENMARK	1981	RADIO+TV	PUB	3 179	25.7	——>	24.8	–	11.5	32.4	5.6
FINLAND	1983	RADIO+TV	PUB	4 355	28.9	0.4	29.5	9.8	9.8	13.3	8.4
FRANCE	1983	RADIO	PUB	3 256	4.8	16.6	3.4	19.0	2.0	25.2	29.2
		TV	PUB	6 220	19.5	17.3	38.2	–	3.0	19.5	2.6
GIBRALTAR	1983	RADIO+TV	PUB	62	40.3	4.8	19.4	8.1	–	25.8	1.6
HOLY SEE	1983	RADIO	GOVT	343	55.4	——>	10.8	14.6	9.0	10.2	–
HUNGARY	1983	RADIO	GOVT	2 090	19.7	15.8	11.4	3.1	6.7	21.7	21.6
		TV	GOVT	3 217	30.7	1.2	16.4	1.3	2.9	20.1	27.3
IRELAND	1981	RADIO+TV	PUB	2 354	30.1	5.6	25.4	6.8	15.4	14.0	2.7
ITALY	1983	RADIO+TV	PUB	13 582	11.4	11.6	28.6	8.4	7.8	27.9	4.3
MALTA	1979	RADIO	GOVT	450	2.7	1.3	8.7	–	11.1	2.7	73.6
		TV	GOVT	89	24.7	13.5	18.0	2.2	7.9	4.5	29.2
MONACO	1981	RADIO	PUB	601	18.3	14.6	12.8	7.2	10.6	31.3	5.2
		TV	COMM	94	33.0	–	37.2	6.4	4.3	13.8	5.3
NETHERLANDS	1983	RADIO+TV	PUB	6 320	...	...	...	...	...	...	...
NORWAY	1981	RADIO+TV	PUB	2 470	29.8	4.7	27.0	–	13.6	15.6	9.2
POLAND	1979	RADIO+TV	GOVT	12 290	62.9	——>	——>	23.8	——>	4.9	8.4
PORTUGAL	1983	RADIO	PUB	2 042	25.2	9.8	11.6	11.4	1.3	13.1	27.6
		TV	PUB	2 413	14.1	9.0	–	11.9	23.8	26.6	14.6
SPAIN	1983	RADIO	PUB	2 994	12.5	21.3	32.4	2.9	1.2	20.3	9.3
		TV	PUB	4 864	30.8	11.6	38.2	–	1.8	11.7	6.0
SWEDEN	1981	RADIO	PUB	...	...	...	...	...	...	...	...
		TV	PUB	3 463	34.5	——>	44.8	–	7.7	11.9	1.1
UNITED KINGDOM	1979	RADIO+TV	PUB	40 883	...	...	...	...	...	...	...
YUGOSLAVIA	1983	RADIO+TV	PUB	19 175	24.6	20.9	21.3	——>	——>	19.2	14.0
OCEANIA											
AMERICAN SAMOA	1981	RADIO	COMM	11	54.5	9.1	–	9.1	–	18.2	9.1
		TV	GOVT	35	31.4	11.4	31.4	11.4	–	8.6	5.7
FIJI	1981	RADIO	PUB	158	25.3	17.7	14.6	10.8	–	25.3	6.3
FRENCH POLYNESIA	1979	RADIO	PUB	34	11.8	17.6	26.5	14.7	5.9	17.6	5.9
		TV	PUB	40	2.5	17.5	40.0	12.5	5.0	15.0	7.5
KIRIBATI	1979	RADIO	PUB	25	40.0	20.0	12.0	——>	–	20.0	8.0
NEW CALEDONIA	1979	RADIO	PUB	32	9.4	15.6	18.8	25.0	6.3	15.6	9.4
		TV	PUB	40	5.0	15.0	35.0	20.0	5.0	10.0	10.0
NIUE	1983	RADIO	GOVT	6	33.3	33.3	–	–	–	–	33.3
NORFOLK ISLAND	1983	RADIO	GOVT	18	88.9	——>	–	5.6	–	5.6	–
PACIFIC ISLANDS	1981	RADIO	COMM	18	22.2	16.7	27.8	–	–	33.3	–
SAMOA	1979	RADIO	GOVT	62	24.2	9.7	4.8	9.7	9.7	14.5	27.4
TONGA	1983	RADIO	PUB	34	26.5	11.8	17.6	11.8	–	23.5	8.8
TUVALU	1983	RADIO	GOVT	7	28.6	28.6	14.3	–	14.3	–	–
VANUATU	1983	RADIO	GOVT	40	22.5	27.5	7.5	5.0	2.5	20.0	15.0
U.S.S.R.											
BYELORUSSIAN S.S.R.	1979	RADIO	GOVT	1 265	36.8	5.0	7.4	35.7	–	3.7	11.5
		TV	GOVT	2 049	46.8	2.1	46.7	–	–	4.5	–

ASIA:
United Arab Emirates:
E--> Data refer to Abu Dhabi only.

United Arab Emirates: (Cont):
FR-> Les données se réfèrent à Abu Dhabi.
ESP> Los datos se refieren a Abu Dhabi solamente.

10.8 Radio and television broadcasting: annual revenue by source and by type of institution

Radiodiffusion sonore et télévision: ressources financières annuelles d'après l'origine des ressources et le type d'organisme

Radiodifusión sonora y televisión: fuentes de ingreso anuales según el origen de los fondos y el tipo de institución

GOVT = GOVERNMENTAL
PUB = PUBLIC
COMM = COMMERCIAL

TOTAL REVENUE IS SHOWN IN NATIONAL CURRENCY

NUMBER OF COUNTRIES AND TERRITORIES PRESENTED IN THIS TABLE: 83

GOVT = GOUVERNEMENTAL
PUB = PUBLIC
COMM = COMMERCIAL

LE TOTAL DES RESSOURCES EST EXPRIME EN MONNAIE NATIONALE

NOMBRE DE PAYS ET DE TERRITOIRES PRESENTES DANS CE TABLEAU: 83

GOVT = GUBERNAMENTAL
PUB = PUBLICA
COMM = COMERCIAL

LOS FONDOS TOTALES SE EXPRESAN EN MONEDA NACIONAL

NUMERO DE PAISES Y DE TERRITORIOS PRESENTADOS EN ESTE CUADRO: 83

COUNTRY / PAYS / PAIS	YEAR / ANNEE / AÑO	TYPE OF INSTITUTION / TYPE D'ORGANISME / TIPO DE INSTITUCION		REVENUE / RESSOURCES / FONDOS					
					OF WHICH (%) / DONT (EN %) / DE LOS CUALES (EN %)				
				TOTAL (000 000) / TOTAL (000 000) / TOTAL (000 000)	GOVERNMENT FUNDS / FONDS PUBLICS / FONDOS PUBLICOS	LICENCE FEES / REDEVANCES / DERECHOS DE PERMISOS	PRIVATE ENDOWMENTS / DOTATIONS PRIVEES / DONATIVOS PRIVADOS	ADVERTISING / PUBLICITE / PUBLICIDAD	OTHER INCOME / RECETTES DIVERSES / OTROS INGRESOS
AFRICA									
ALGERIA	1981	RADIO+TV	PUB	...	95.0	–	–	–	5.0
ANGOLA	1979	RADIO+TV	GOVT	...	100.0	–	–	–	–
BENIN	1981	RADIO+TV	PUB	203.9	39.0	13.0	–	26.0	22.0
BOTSWANA	1983	RADIO	GOVT	1.8	100.0	–	–	–	–
BURKINA FASO	1983	RADIO+TV	GOVT	...	100.0	–	–	–	–
BURUNDI	1979	RADIO	GOVT	...	98.0	–	–	2.0	–
ETHIOPIA	1983	RADIO	GOVT	5.4	100.0	–	–	–	–
		TV	GOVT	4.1	73.0	16.0	–	11.0	–
GHANA	1983	RADIO+TV	GOVT	72.0	90.3	3.0	–	3.0	3.7
MADAGASCAR	1979	RADIO	GOVT	450.0	99.9	0.0	–	0.1	–
		TV	GOVT	100.0	90.0	10.0	–	–	–
MALAWI	1983	RADIO	PUB	2.9	71.7	–	–	20.7	7.6
MAURITIUS	1983	RADIO+TV	PUB	17.7	14.2	32.6	–	47.3	6.0
MOROCCO	1979	RADIO+TV	GOVT	96.9	49.8	30.9	–	18.3	1.0
REUNION	1979	RADIO	PUB	9.6	–	53.0	–	46.4	0.6
		TV	PUB	10.8	–	99.5	–	–	0.5
RWANDA	1981	RADIO	GOVT	51.2	94.2	3.6	–	2.2	–
ST. HELENA	1981	RADIO	GOVT	0.005	100.0	–	–	–	–

COUNTRY / PAYS / PAIS	YEAR / ANNEE / AÑO	TYPE OF INSTITUTION / TYPE D'ORGANISME / TIPO DE INSTITUCION		REVENUE / RESSOURCES / FONDOS: TOTAL (000 000) / TOTAL (000 000) / TOTAL (000 000)	OF WHICH (%) / DONT (EN %) / DE LOS CUALES (EN %): GOVERNMENT FUNDS / FONDS PUBLICS / FONDOS PUBLICOS	LICENCE FEES / REDEVANCES / DERECHOS DE PERMISOS	PRIVATE ENDOWMENTS / DOTATIONS PRIVEES / DONATIVOS PRIVADOS	ADVERTISING / PUBLICITE / PUBLICIDAD	OTHER INCOME / RECETTES DIVERSES / OTROS INGRESOS
SENEGAL	1981	RADIO+TV	GOVT	1317.0	88.6	–	–	10.8	0.7
UNITED REPUBLIC OF TANZANIA	1979	RADIO	GOVT	...	100.0	–	–	–	–
ZAMBIA	1979	RADIO+TV	GOVT	...	100.0	–	–	–	–
ZIMBABWE	1981	RADIO	PUB	3.6	2.8	24.1	–	69.9	3.2
		TV	PUB	4.2	8.4	33.8	–	52.0	5.8
AMERICA, NORTH									
BELIZE	1983	RADIO	GOVT	0.8	100.0	–	–	–	–
BRITISH VIRGIN ISLANDS	1983	RADIO	COMM	...	–	–	–	100.0	–
CANADA	1983	RADIO+TV	PUB	872.0	–	84.0	–	15.0	1.0
		RADIO	COMM	492.0	–	–	–	97.0	3.0
		TV	COMM	833.0	–	–	–	89.0	11.0
CAYMAN ISLANDS	1981	RADIO	GOVT	0.7	54.2	–	–	45.8	–
			PUB	0.1	–	–	–	–	100.0
CUBA	1983	RADIO+TV	GOVT	...	100.0	–	–	–	–
GUADELOUPE	1979	RADIO	PUB	7.3	–	44.6	–	55.0	0.4
		TV	PUB	9.0	–	99.4	–	–	0.6
MARTINIQUE	1979	RADIO	PUB	7.5	–	49.0	–	51.0	–
		TV	PUB	9.3	–	99.2	–	–	0.8
MEXICO	1982	RADIO	GOVT	152.0	...	...	...	...	...
			COMM	3712.0	...	...	...	...	...
		TV	GOVT	61.0	...	...	...	...	...
			COMM	2104.0	...	...	...	...	...
ST. PIERRE AND MIQUELON	1979	RADIO	PUB	4.2	15.0	85.0	–	–	–
		TV	PUB	5.5	18.0	82.0	–	–	–
TRINIDAD AND TOBAGO	1981	TV	COMM	23.0	–	–	–	99.0	1.0
TURKS AND CAICOS ISLANDS	1983	RADIO	PUB	0.1	100.0	–	–	–	–
AMERICA, SOUTH									
CHILE	1982	RADIO+TV	GOVT	2062.9	1.1	–	0.1	82.5	16.3
			PUB	323.2	1.1	–	2.2	93.3	3.4
			COMM	897.5	0.9	–	0.6	92.9	5.6
FALKLAND ISLANDS (MALVINAS)	1979	RADIO	GOVT	0.018	0.97	19.5	–	17.5	63.0
FRENCH GUIANA	1979	RADIO	PUB	5.0	–	82.0	–	18.0	–
		TV	PUB	6.3	–	99.1	–	–	0.9
GUYANA	1979	RADIO	GOVT	2.3	–	13.0	–	87.0	–
ASIA									
AFGHANISTAN	1981	RADIO	GOVT	31.8	–	1.6	–	40.3	58.1
		TV	GOVT	2.3	–	65.2	–	21.7	13.1
BANGLADESH	1979	RADIO	GOVT	104.6	84.0	9.8	–	5.9	0.4
		TV	GOVT	61.4	64.8	16.5	–	18.8	–
BHUTAN	1979	RADIO	PUB	0.3	100.0	–	–	–	–
BRUNEI DARUSSALAM	1983	RADIO+TV	GOVT	22.0	–	95.0	–	5.0	–
CYPRUS	1983	RADIO+TV	PUB	5.2	3.9	36.8	–	56.1	3.3
HONG KONG	1981	RADIO	GOVT	25.9	100.0	–	–	–	–
		TV	GOVT	38.8	100.0	–	–	–	–
INDIA	1981	RADIO	GOVT	590.0	50.0	25.6	24.4	–	–
		TV	GOVT	148.5	–	33.0	–	67.0	–
INDONESIA	1981	RADIO	GOVT	18494.1	100.0	–	–	–	–
		TV	GOVT	42823.0	–	37.0	63.0	–	–

COUNTRY PAYS PAIS	YEAR ANNEE AÑO	TYPE OF INSTITUTION TYPE D'ORGANISME TIPO DE INSTITUCION		REVENUE / RESSOURCES / FONDOS TOTAL (000 000) TOTAL (000 000) TOTAL (000 000)	OF WHICH (%) / DONT (EN %) / DE LOS CUALES (EN %) GOVERNMENT FUNDS FONDS PUBLICS FONDOS PUBLICOS	LICENCE FEES REDEVANCES DERECHOS DE PERMISOS	PRIVATE ENDOWMENTS DOTATIONS PRIVEES DONATIVOS PRIVADOS	ADVERTISING PUBLICITE PUBLICIDAD	OTHER INCOME RECETTES DIVERSES OTROS INGRESOS
IRAN, ISLAMIC REPUBLIC OF	1983	RADIO	GOVT	6708.0	100.0	–	–	–	–
		TV	GOVT	10734.0	100.0	–	–	–	–
IRAQ	1979	RADIO+TV	GOVT	10.1	...	...	...	...	...
ISRAEL	1983	RADIO+TV	PUB	...	19.0	49.0	–	26.0	6.0
JAPAN	1983	RADIO+TV	PUB	287 746	–	97.1	–	–	2.9
			COMM	1 161 202	–	–	–	94.8	5.2
KUWAIT	1983	RADIO	GOVT	...	100.0	–	–	–	–
		TV	GOVT	...	100.0	–	–	–	–
MALAYSIA	1983	RADIO+TV	GOVT	267.7	49.4	15.5	–	36.1	–
MALDIVES	1983	RADIO	GOVT	1.0	84.0	–	–	10.0	6.0
		TV	GOVT	1.1	–	28.8	–	60.3	10.9
PAKISTAN	1983	RADIO	GOVT	215.4	64.4	17.6	–	17.8	0.3
		TV	GOVT	548.0	35.9	26.0	–	32.0	6.1
PHILIPPINES	1981	RADIO	GOVT	...	...	...	...	...	...
			COMM	169.5	–	–	–	95.0	5.0
		TV	GOVT	38.0	79.0	–	–	21.0	–
			COMM	356.3	–	–	–	68.0	32.0
QATAR	1983	RADIO	GOVT	...	–	100.0	–	–	–
SINGAPORE	1983	RADIO+TV	GOVT	97.0	–	23.0	–	65.0	12.0
SRI LANKA‡	1983	RADIO	GOVT	...	–	38.8	–	42.3	18.9
		TV	GOVT	...	...	...	...	...	...
TURKEY	1983	RADIO	PUB	951.0	–	–	–	100.0	–
		TV	PUB	846.5	2.5	26.9	–	67.9	2.7
UNITED ARAB EMIRATES‡	1983	RADIO	GOVT	26.0	–	74.0	–	26.0	–
		TV	GOVT	75.0	–	76.0	–	24.0	–
EUROPE									
AUSTRIA	1983	RADIO	PUB	1334.0	–	56.1	–	39.9	4.0
		TV	PUB	3514.0	–	56.1	–	36.3	7.6
BELGIUM	1983	RADIO+TV	PUB	10487.0	84.3	–	1.0	–	14.7
DENMARK	1981	RADIO+TV	PUB	1174.0	3.1	90.6	–	–	6.3
FINLAND	1983	RADIO+TV	PUB	958.5	0.3	76.3	–	20.8	2.6
		TV	COMM	395.4	–	–	–	92.8	7.2
FRANCE	1983	RADIO	PUB	1832.0	6.9	85.6	–	1.6	5.9
		TV	PUB	6605.0	0.4	56.3	–	39.9	3.4
GIBRALTAR	1983	RADIO+TV	PUB	1.0	63.0	12.0	–	25.0	–
HUNGARY	1983	RADIO	GOVT	977.0	93.0	–	–	–	7.0
		TV	GOVT	2347.0	100.0	–	–	–	–
IRELAND	1981	RADIO+TV	PUB	...	–	42.0	–	47.0	11.0
ITALY	1983	RADIO+TV	PUB	1223868.0	–	55.2	–	33.7	11.1
MALTA	1979	RADIO	GOVT	0.4	–	–	–	19.0	81.0
		TV	GOVT	0.4	–	–	–	95.0	5.0
MONACO	1981	RADIO	PUB	263.0	–	–	–	100.0	–
		TV	COMM	34.4	–	–	–	56.2	43.8
NETHERLANDS	1983	RADIO+TV	PUB	975.8	–	69.3	–	26.6	4.1
NORWAY	1981	RADIO+TV	PUB	905.8	–	78.2	–	–	21.8
PORTUGAL	1983	RADIO	PUB	...	...	...	–	...	...
		TV	PUB	5396.0	5.7	39.3	–	40.8	14.2
SPAIN	1983	RADIO	PUB	15128.1	–	–	–	11.0	89.0
		TV	PUB	49815.6	–	–	–	95.6	4.4
SWEDEN	1981	RADIO	PUB	...	...	...	...	...	...
		TV	PUB	904.0	–	97.0	–	–	3.0

10.8 Radio and television broadcasting: revenue
Radiodiffusion sonore et télévision: ressources financières
Radiodifusión sonora y televisión: fuentes de ingreso

COUNTRY / PAYS / PAIS	YEAR / ANNEE / AÑO	TYPE OF INSTITUTION / TYPE D'ORGANISME / TIPO DE INSTITUCION		TOTAL (000 000)	REVENUE / RESSOURCES / FONDOS — OF WHICH (%) / DONT (EN %) / DE LOS CUALES (EN %): GOVERNMENT FUNDS / FONDS PUBLICS / FONDOS PUBLICOS	LICENCE FEES / REDEVANCES / DERECHOS DE PERMISOS	PRIVATE ENDOWMENTS / DOTATIONS PRIVEES / DONATIVOS PRIVADOS	ADVERTISING / PUBLICITE / PUBLICIDAD	OTHER INCOME / RECETTES DIVERSES / OTROS INGRESOS
UNITED KINGDOM	1979	RADIO+TV	PUB	732.0	–	42.6	–	55.2	2.2
YUGOSLAVIA	1983	RADIO+TV	PUB	14459.0	5.5	69.3	–	22.6	2.6
OCEANIA									
AMERICAN SAMOA	1981	RADIO	COMM	...	–	–	–	100.0	–
		TV	GOVT	...	75.0	–	–	–	25.0
FIJI	1981	RADIO	PUB	2.0	50.0	–	–	50.0	–
FRENCH POLYNESIA	1979	RADIO	PUB	8.0	8.0	65.5	–	26.0	0.5
		TV	PUB	9.5	9.0	90.0	–	–	1.0
KIRIBATI	1979	RADIO	PUB	0.2	92.0	–	–	5.0	3.0
NEW CALEDONIA	1979	RADIO	PUB	7.9	7.8	66.7	–	24.5	1.0
		TV	PUB	8.9	8.1	76.6	–	14.4	0.9
SAMOA	1979	RADIO	GOVT	0.2	–	–	–	100.0	–
TONGA	1983	RADIO	PUB	0.3	–	–	–	40.0	60.0
TUVALU	1983	RADIO	GOVT	...	100.0	–	–	–	–
VANUATU	1983	RADIO	GOVT	35.0	98.0	–	–	1.0	1.0

ASIA:
Sri Lanka:
E--> Data cover six months only.
FR-> Les données couvrent une période de 6 mois seulement.
ESP> Los datos cubren un período de 6 meses solamente.

United Arab Emirates:
E--> Data refer to Abu Dhabi only.
FR-> Les données se réfèrent à Abu Dhabi seulement.
ESP> Los datos se refieren a Abu Dhabi solamente.

10.9 Radio and television broadcasting: annual current expenditure by purpose and by type of institution

Radiodiffusion sonore et télévision: dépenses courantes annuelles d'après leur destination et le type d'organisme

Radiodifusión sonora y televisión: gastos ordinarios anuales según su destino y el tipo de institución

G = GOVERNMENTAL
P = PUBLIC
C = COMMERCIAL

TOTAL EXPENDITURE IS SHOWN IN NATIONAL CURRENCY

NUMBER OF COUNTRIES AND TERRITORIES PRESENTED IN THIS TABLE: 76

G = GOUVERNEMENTAL
P = PUBLIC
C = COMMERCIAL

LE TOTAL DES DEPENSES EST EXPRIME EN MONNAIE NATIONALE

NOMBRE DE PAYS ET DE TERRITOIRES PRESENTES DANS CE TABLEAU: 76

G = GUBERNAMENTAL
P = PUBLICA
C = COMERCIAL

LOS GASTOS TOTALES SE EXPRESAN EN MONEDA NACIONAL

NUMERO DE PAISES Y DE TERRITORIOS PRESENTADOS EN ESTE CUADRO: 76

COUNTRY / PAYS / PAIS	YEAR / ANNEE / AÑO	TYPE OF INSTITUTION / TYPE D'ORGANISME / TIPO DE INSTITUCION		EXPENDITURE / DEPENSES / GASTOS					
				TOTAL (000 000) / TOTAL (000 000) / TOTAL (000 000)	OF WHICH (%) / DONT (EN %) / DE LOS CUALES (EN %)				
					PROGRAMME PRODUCTION / PRODUCTION DES PROGRAMMES / PRODUCCION DE PROGRAMAS	PROGRAMME PURCHASING / ACHATS DES PROGRAMMES / ADQUISICION DE PROGRAMAS	PRODUCTION FACILITIES / MOYENS DE PRODUCTION / MEDIOS DE PRODUCCION	TRANSMISSION FACILITIES / MOYENS DE DIFFUSION / MEDIOS DE DIFUSION	PERSONNEL, MANAGEMENT AND ADMINISTRATION / PERSONNEL, GESTION ET ADMINISTRATION / PERSONAL, GESTION Y ADMINISTRACION
AFRICA									
ALGERIA	1981	RADIO+TV	PUB	210.0	...	...	...	...	...
BENIN	1981	RADIO+TV	PUB	477.6	15.0	29.0	7.0	12.0	37.0
BOTSWANA	1983	RADIO	GOVT	1.8	18.0	2.0	20.0	30.0	30.0
BURUNDI	1979	RADIO	GOVT	...	10.0	5.0	13.0	5.0	67.0
ETHIOPIA	1983	RADIO	GOVT	4.6	16.0	7.0	2.0	17.0	58.0
		TV	GOVT	3.4	23.0	7.0	5.0	39.0	26.0
GHANA	1983	RADIO+TV	GOVT	75.9	20.0	30.0	20.0	10.0	20.0
LESOTHO	1983	RADIO	GOVT	75.9	20.0	30.0	20.0	10.0	20.0
MADAGASCAR	1979	RADIO+TV	GOVT	400.0	36.2	2.5	20.0	22.5	18.8
MALAWI	1983	RADIO	PUB	3.8	0.8	0.8	23.6	——>	74.9
MAURITIUS	1983	RADIO+TV	PUB	20.9	23.9	——>	76.1	——>	——>
MOROCCO	1979	RADIO+TV	GOVT	75.8	8.7	2.9	5.9	34.4	48.1

10.9 Radio and television broadcasting: expenditure
Radiodiffusion sonore et télévision: dépenses
Radiodifusión sonora y televisión: gastos

COUNTRY / PAYS / PAIS	YEAR / ANNEE / AÑO	TYPE OF INSTITUTION / TYPE D'ORGANISME / TIPO DE INSTITUCION		EXPENDITURE / DEPENSES / GASTOS: TOTAL (000 000) / TOTAL (000 000) / TOTAL (000 000)	OF WHICH (%) / DONT (EN %) / DE LOS CUALES (EN %): PROGRAMME PRODUCTION / PRODUCTION DES PROGRAMMES / PRODUCCION DE PROGRAMAS	PROGRAMME PURCHASING / ACHATS DES PROGRAMMES / ADQUISICION DE PROGRAMAS	PRODUCTION FACILITIES / MOYENS DE PRODUCTION / MEDIOS DE PRODUCCION	TRANSMISSION FACILITIES / MOYENS DE DIFFUSION / MEDIOS DE DIFUSION	PERSONNEL, MANAGEMENT AND ADMINISTRATION / PERSONNEL, GESTION ET ADMINISTRATION / PERSONAL, GESTION Y ADMINISTRACION
REUNION	1979	RADIO	PUB	9.6	11.1	–	49.0	11.6	28.3
		TV	PUB	10.8	7.0	–	55.6	11.3	26.1
RWANDA	1981	RADIO	GOVT	48.8	52.0	48.0	–	–	–
ST. HELENA	1981	RADIO	GOVT	0.0	15.0	20.0	15.0	30.0	20.0
ZAMBIA	1979	RADIO+TV	GOVT	2.3	14.0	22.0	6.0	10.0	48.0
ZIMBABWE	1981	RADIO	PUB	3.6	35.1	0.6	6.6	24.4	33.2
		TV	PUB	4.2	35.9	7.9	14.6	22.1	19.4
AMERICA, NORTH									
BELIZE	1983	RÁDIO	GOVT	...	10.0	10.0	10.0	30.0	40.0
CANADA	1983	RADIO+TV	PUB	834.0	58.0	——>	20.0	——>	22.0
		RADIO	COMM	438.0	36.0	——>	5.0	——>	59.0
		TV	COMM	635.0	62.0	——>	8.0	——>	30.0
CAYMAN ISLANDS	1981	RADIO	GOVT	0.4	3.3	4.8	6.9	33.5	51.4
			PUB	0.0	–	5.9	–	35.3	58.8
GUADELOUPE	1979	RADIO	PUB	7.3	21.2	–	40.0	13.4	25.4
		TV	PUB	9.0	11.4	–	56.6	12.8	19.2
MARTINIQUE	1979	RADIO	PUB	7.5	23.5	–	38.0	13.4	25.1
		TV	PUB	9.3	11.6	–	54.5	10.5	23.4
MEXICO	1982	RADIO	GOVT	159.0	...	...	...	...	...
			COMM	3397.0	...	...	...	...	...
		TV	GOVT	61.0	...	...	...	...	...
			COMM	1874.0	...	...	...	...	...
ST. PIERRE AND MIQUELON	1979	RADIO	PUB	4.7	8.0	–	60.4	7.4	24.2
		TV	PUB	5.0	6.3	–	63.3	10.7	19.7
TURKS AND CAICOS ISLANDS	1983	RADIO	PUB	0.1	–	11.0	8.0	——>	81.0
AMERICA, SOUTH									
CHILE	1982	RADIO+TV	GOVT	2059.8	25.5	9.0	11.3	5.4	48.8
			PUB	517.0	23.6	20.3	8.9	0.7	46.5
			COMM	962.2	3.6	1.1	19.7	2.9	72.7
FALKLAND ISLANDS (MALVINAS)	1979	RADIO	GOVT	0.03	...	...	...	...	...
FRENCH GUIANA	1979	RADIO	PUB	5.0	14.3	–	49.9	12.2	23.6
		TV	PUB	6.3	10.6	–	60.3	11.9	17.2
GUYANA	1979	RADIO	GOVT	2.5	20.0	——>	80.0	——>	——>
ASIA									
AFGHANISTAN	1981	RADIO+TV	GOVT	153.4	...	...	...	...	...
BHUTAN	1979	RADIO	PUB	0.3	65.1	–	32.6	2.3	–
BRUNEI DARUSSALAM	1983	RADIO+TV	GOVT	22.0	15.0	15.0	10.0	10.0	50.0
CYPRUS	1983	RADIO+TV	PUB	4.8	25.0	14.0	18.0	20.0	23.0
HONG KONG	1981	RADIO	GOVT	25.9	50.5	–	1.6	35.7	12.2
		TV	GOVT	38.8	85.3	–	2.9	–	11.8
INDIA	1981	RADIO	GOVT	848.7	...	...	...	...	...
		TV	GOVT	158.0	6.1	5.5	18.3	18.0	52.1
IRAN, ISLAMIC REPUBLIC OF	1983	RADIO	GOVT	6708.0	24.0	–	32.0	——>	44.0
		TV	GOVT	10734.0	35.0	1.0	25.0	——>	39.0
IRAQ	1979	RADIO+TV	GOVT	10.9	...	...	...	...	...
ISRAEL	1983	RADIO	PUB	...	50.0	——>	27.0	13.0	10.0
		TV	PUB	653.0	59.0	8.0	16.0	3.0	14.0

COUNTRY PAYS PAIS	YEAR ANNEE AÑO	TYPE OF INSTITUTION TYPE D'ORGANISME TIPO DE INSTITUCION		EXPENDITURE / DEPENSES / GASTOS					
					OF WHICH (%) / DONT (EN %) / DE LOS CUALES (EN %)				
				TOTAL (000 000) TOTAL (000 000) TOTAL (000 000)	PROGRAMME PRODUCTION PRODUCTION DES PROGRAMMES PRODUCCION DE PROGRAMAS	PROGRAMME PURCHASING ACHATS DES PROGRAMMES ADQUISICION DE PROGRAMAS	PRODUCTION FACILITIES MOYENS DE PRODUCTION MEDIOS DE PRODUCCION	TRANSMISSION FACILITIES MOYENS DE DIFFUSION MEDIOS DE DIFUSION	PERSONNEL, MANAGEMENT AND ADMINISTRATION PERSONNEL, GESTION ET ADMINISTRATION PERSONAL, GESTION Y ADMINISTRACION
JAPAN	1983	RADIO+TV	PUB	277207	35.2	——>	64.8	——>	——>
			COMM	1054888	61.8	——>	38.2	——>	——>
JORDAN	1983	RADIO	GOVT	...	30.0	20.0	50.0	——>	——>
		TV	GOVT	3.9	6.0	17.0	7.0	32.0	38.0
MALAYSIA	1983	RADIO+TV	GOVT	177.3	18.0	0.5	28.3	3.2	50.1
MALDIVES	1983	RADIO	GOVT	...	...	...	...	...	...
		TV	GOVT	0.8	8.8	–	12.3	48.6	30.3
PAKISTAN	1983	RADIO	GOVT	181.0	24.1	——>	16.8	——>	59.1
		TV	GOVT	283.6	18.0	5.7	22.6	17.2	36.5
QATAR	1983	RADIO	GOVT	...	35.0	——>	45.0	——>	20.0
SAUDI ARABIA	1981	RADIO+TV	GOVT	178.3	...	...	...	...	...
SINGAPORE	1983	RADIO	GOVT	17.0	41.0	——>	13.0	23.0	23.0
		TV	GOVT	57.0	40.0	13.0	16.0	1.0	30.0
SRI LANKA	1983	RADIO	GOVT	...	3.0	–	97.0	——>	——>
		TV	GOVT	...	...	...	...	...	...
UNITED ARAB EMIRATES‡	1983	RADIO	GOVT	26.0	15.0	13.0	8.0	4.0	50.0
		TV	GOVT	75.0	7.0	27.0	24.0	9.0	33.0
EUROPE									
ANDORRA	1983	RADIO	PUB	0.3	15.0	–	18.0	23.0	44.0
AUSTRIA	1983	RADIO	PUB	1508.0	...	...	...	...	...
		TV	PUB	3351.0	...	...	...	...	...
BELGIUM	1983	RADIO+TV	PUB	10074.0	...	...	...	...	...
DENMARK‡	1981	RADIO+TV	PUB	295.0	78.3	–	14.2	6.8	0.7
		TV	PUB	391.0	51.4	5.4	34.8	7.1	1.3
FINLAND	1983	RADIO+TV	PUB	786.6	61.3	2.2	8.1	9.0	19.4
		TV	COMM	393.0	86.6	——>	13.4	——>	——>
FRANCE	1983	RADIO	PUB	1759.0	60.8	–	–	21.4	17.8
		TV	PUB	6496.0	34.9	33.2	–	19.4	12.5
GIBRALTAR	1983	RADIO+TV	PUB	1.0	58.0	——>	42.0	——>	——>
HUNGARY	1983	RADIO	GOVT	935.0	8.2	–	26.3	44.2	21.3
		TV	GOVT	2168.0	66.5	1.7	3.5	17.2	11.1
IRELAND	1981	RADIO+TV	PUB	...	68.0	——>	——>	32.0	——>
ITALY	1983	RADIO+TV	PUB	1244525.0	–	–	–	19.0	81.0
MALTA	1979	RADIO	GOVT	0.5	24.0	3.0	1.0	23.0	49.0
		TV	GOVT	0.4	39.0	11.0	3.0	17.0	30.0
MONACO	1981	RADIO	PUB	193.0	45.0	–	17.0	18.0	20.0
		TV	COMM	34.4	48.2	19.9	51.8	——>	——>
NETHERLANDS	1983	RADIO+TV	PUB	1023.2	...	...	...	...	...
NORWAY	1981	RADIO	PUB	353.8	61.4	–	9.2	12.0	17.4
		TV	PUB	491.7	58.4	–	9.9	13.0	18.7
PORTUGAL	1983	RADIO	PUB	...	...	...	...	...	...
		TV	PUB	6080.0	11.4	9.4	21.3	13.2	44.7
SPAIN	1983	RADIO	PUB	15128.1	–	6.4	4.8	1.7	87.1
		TV	PUB	49815.6	–	–	4.8	5.4	42.6
SWEDEN	1981	RADIO	PUB	...	...	...	...	...	...
		TV	COMM	976.0	74.0	7.0	16.0	–	3.0
UNITED KINGDOM	1979	RADIO+TV	PUB	584.0	32.5	——>	67.5	——>	——>
YUGOSLAVIA	1983	RADIO+TV	PUB	14540.0	...	...	...	...	...

COUNTRY / PAYS / PAIS	YEAR / ANNEE / AÑO	TYPE OF INSTITUTION / TYPE D'ORGANISME / TIPO DE INSTITUCION		EXPENDITURE / DEPENSES / GASTOS: TOTAL (000 000)	OF WHICH (%) / DONT (EN %) / DE LOS CUALES (EN %): PROGRAMME PRODUCTION / PRODUCTION DES PROGRAMMES / PRODUCCION DE PROGRAMAS	PROGRAMME PURCHASING / ACHATS DES PROGRAMMES / ADQUISICION DE PROGRAMAS	PRODUCTION FACILITIES / MOYENS DE PRODUCTION / MEDIOS DE PRODUCCION	TRANSMISSION FACILITIES / MOYENS DE DIFFUSION / MEDIOS DE DIFUSION	PERSONNEL, MANAGEMENT AND ADMINISTRATION / PERSONNEL, GESTION ET ADMINISTRATION / PERSONAL, GESTION Y ADMINISTRACION
OCEANIA									
AMERICAN SAMOA	1981	RADIO	COMM	...	5.0	5.0	5.0	25.0	60.0
		TV	GOVT	...	20.0	15.0	15.0	30.0	20.0
FIJI	1981	RADIO	PUB	2.0	25.0	——>	40.0	——>	35.0
FRENCH POLYNESIA	1979	RADIO	PUB	8.0	9.2	——>	54.5	17.7	18.6
		TV	PUB	9.5	5.9	——>	61.1	15.4	17.6
KIRIBATI	1979	RADIO	PUB	0.2	...	...	...	...	...
NEW CALEDONIA	1979	RADIO	PUB	7.9	11.7	——>	46.8	24.1	17.4
		TV	PUB	8.9	9.8	——>	56.7	20.0	13.5
NIUE	1983	RADIO	GOVT	0.6	...	...	...	...	...
SAMOA	1979	RADIO	GOVT	0.2	36.0	4.0	20.0	26.0	14.0
TONGA	1983	RADIO	PUB	0.3	15.0	–	18.0	23.0	44.0
VANUATU	1983	RADIO	GOVT	35.0	20.0	8.7	14.3	28.6	28.6
U.S.S.R.									
BYELORUSSIAN S.S.R.	1979	RADIO	GOVT	7740.0	24.4	0.1	13.9	59.7	1.9
		TV	GOVT	28062.0	19.0	0.2	18.3	56.6	5.9

ASIA:
United Arab Emirates:
E--> Data refer to Abu Dhabi only.
FR-> Les données se réfèrent à Abu Dhabi seulement.
ESP> Los datos se refieren a Abu Dhabi solamente.

EUROPE
Denmark:
E--> Not including expenditure for central management.
FR-> Non compris les dépenses de l'administration centrale.
ESP> Excluídos los gastos de la administración central.

Appendixes
Annexes
Anexos

A Member States and Associate Members of Unesco

Etats membres et Membres associés de l'Unesco

Estados miembros y Miembros asociados de la Unesco

MEMBER STATE ETAT MEMBRE ESTADO MIEMBRO	DATE OF ENTRY DATE D'ADHESION FECHA DE INGRESO	SCALE OF CONTRIBUTIONS BAREME DES CONTRIBUTIONS ESCALA DE CONTRIBUCIONES %	CONTRIBUTIONS TO THE BUDGET 1986-87 CONTRIBUTIONS AU BUDGET 1986-87 CONTRIBUCIONES AL PRESUPUESTO 1986-87 $
TOTAL		100.00	364 980 000
AFGHANISTAN	4.V.1948	0.01	36 498
ALBANIA	16.X.1958	0.01	36 498
ALGERIA	15.X.1962	0.14	510 972
ANGOLA	11.III.1977	0.01	36 498
ANTIGUA AND BARBUDA	15.VII.1982	0.01	36 498
ARGENTINA	15.IX.1948	0.61	2 226 378
AUSTRALIA	4.XI.1946	1.64	5 985 672
AUSTRIA	13.VIII.1948	0.73	2 664 354
BAHAMAS	23.IV.1981	0.01	36 498
BAHRAIN	18.I.1972	0.02	72 996
BANGLADESH	27.X.1972	0.02	72 996
BARBADOS	24.X.1968	0.01	36 498
BELGIUM	29.XI.1946	1.17	4 270 266
BELIZE	10.V.1982	0.01	36 498
BENIN	18.X.1960	0.01	36 498
BHUTAN	13.IV.1982	0.01	36 498
BOLIVIA	13.XI.1946	0.01	36 498
BOTSWANA	16.I.1980	0.01	36 498
BRAZIL	4.XI.1946	1.38	5 036 724
BULGARIA	17.V.1956	0.16	583 968
BURKINA FASO	14.XI.1960	0.01	36 498
BURMA	27.VI.1949	0.01	36 498
BURUNDI	16.XI.1962	0.01	36 498
BYELORUSSIAN S.S.R.	12.V.1954	0.34	1 240 932
CAMEROON	11.XI.1960	0.01	36 498
CANADA	4.XI.1946	3.02	11 022 396
CAPE VERDE	15.II.1978	0.01	36 498
CENTRAL AFRICAN REPUBLIC	11.XI.1960	0.01	36 498
CHAD	19.XII.1960	0.01	36 498
CHILE	7.VII.1953	0.07	255 486
CHINA	4.XI.1946	0.78	2 846 844
COLOMBIA	31.X.1947	0.13	474 474
COMOROS	22.III.1977	0.01	36 498
CONGO	24.X.1960	0.01	36 498
COSTA RICA	19.V.1950	0.02	72 996
COTE D'IVOIRE	27.X.1960	0.02	72 996
CUBA	29.VIII.1947	0.09	328 482
CYPRUS	6.II.1961	0.02	72 996
CZECHOSLOVAKIA	4.XI.1946	0.69	2 518 362
DEMOCRATIC KAMPUCHEA	3.VII.1951	0.01	36 498
DEMOCRATIC YEMEN	16.X.1968	0.01	36 498
DENMARK	4 XI.1946	0.71	2 591 358
DOMINICA	9.I.1979	0.01	36 498
DOMINICAN REPUBLIC	4.XI.1946	0.03	109 494
ECUADOR	22.I.1947	0.03	109 494
EGYPT	4.XI.1946	0.07	255 486
EL SALVADOR	28.IV.1948	0.01	36 498
EQUATORIAL GUINEA	29.XI.1979	0.01	36 498
ETHIOPIA	1.VII.1955	0.01	36 498
FIJI	14.VII.1983	0.01	36 498
FINLAND	10.X.1956	0.49	1 788 402
FRANCE	4.XI.1946	6.29	22 957 242

MEMBER STATE ETAT MEMBRE ESTADO MIEMBRO	DATE OF ENTRY DATE D'ADHESION FECHA DE INGRESO	SCALE OF CONTRIBUTIONS BAREME DES CONTRIBUTIONS ESCALA DE CONTRIBUCIONES %	CONTRIBUTIONS TO THE BUDGET 1986–87 CONTRIBUTIONS AU BUDGET 1986–87 CONTRIBUCIONES AL PRESUPUESTO 1986–87 $
GABON	16.XI.1960	0.03	109 494
GAMBIA	1.VIII.1973	0.01	36 498
GERMAN DEMOCRATIC REPUBLIC	24.XI.1972	1.31	4 781 238
GERMANY, FEDERAL REPUBLIC OF	11.VII.1951	8.16	29 782 368
GHANA	11.IV.1958	0.01	36 498
GREECE	4.XI.1946	0.43	1 569 414
GRENADA	17.II.1975	0.01	36 498
GUATEMALA	2.I.1950	0.02	72 996
GUINEA	2.II.1960	0.01	36 498
GUINEA-BISSAU	1.XI.1974	0.01	36 498
GUYANA	21.III.1967	0.01	36 498
HAITI	18.XI.1946	0.01	36 498
HONDURAS	16.XII.1947	0.01	36 498
HUNGARY	14.IX.1948	0.22	802 956
ICELAND	8.VI.1964	0.03	109 494
INDIA	4.XI.1946	0.34	1 240 932
INDONESIA	27.V.1950	0.14	510 972
IRAN, ISLAMIC REPUBLIC OF	6.IX.1948	0.62	2 262 876
IRAQ	21.X.1948	0.12	437 976
IRELAND	3.X.1961	0.18	656 984
ISRAEL	16.IX.1949	0.22	802 956
ITALY	27.I.1948	3.74	13 650 252
JAMAICA	7.XI.1962	0.02	72 996
JAPAN	2.VII.1951	10.71	39 089 358
JORDAN	14.VI.1950	0.01	36 498
KENYA	7.IV.1964	0.01	36 498
KOREA, DEMOCRATIC PEOPLE'S REPUBLIC	18.X.1974	0.05	182 490
KOREA, REPUBLIC OF	14.VI.1950	0.20	729 960
KUWAIT	18.XI.1960	0.29	1 058 442
LAO PEOPLE'S DEMOCRATIC REPUBLIC	9.VII.1951	0.01	36 498
LEBANON	4.XI.1946	0.01	36 498
LESOTHO	29.IX.1967	0.01	36 498
LIBERIA	6.III.1947	0.01	36 498
LIBYAN ARAB JAMAHIRIYA	27.VI.1953	0.26	948 948
LUXEMBOURG	27.X.1947	0.05	182 490
MADAGASCAR	10.XI.1960	0.01	36 498
MALAWI	27.X.1964	0.01	36 498
MALAYSIA	16.VI.1958	0.10	364 980
MALDIVES	18.VII.1980	0.01	36 498
MALI	7.XI.1960	0.01	36 498
MALTA	10.II.1965	0.01	36 498
MAURITANIA	10.I.1962	0.01	36 498
MAURITIUS	25.X.1968	0.01	36 498
MEXICO	4.XI.1946	0.88	3 211 824
MONACO	6.VII.1949	0.01	36 498
MONGOLIA	1.XI.1962	0.01	36 498
MOROCCO	7.XI.1956	0.05	182 490
MOZAMBIQUE	11.X.1976	0.01	36 498
NAMIBIA	2.XI.1978	...	...
NEPAL	1.V.1953	0.01	36 498
NETHERLANDS	1.I.1947	1.72	6 277 656
NEW ZEALAND	4.XI.1946	0.24	875 952
NICARAGUA	22.II.1952	0.01	36 498
NIGER	10.XI.1960	0.01	36 498
NIGERIA	14.XI.1960	0.19	693 462
NORWAY	4.XI.1946	0.53	1 934 394
OMAN	10.II.1972	0.02	72 996
PAKISTAN	14.IX.1949	0.06	218 988
PANAMA	10.I.1950	0.02	72 996
PAPUA NEW GUINEA	4.X.1976	0.01	36 498
PARAGUAY	20.VI.1955	0.02	72 996
PERU	21.XI.1946	0.07	255 486
PHILIPPINES	21.XI.1946	0.10	364 980
POLAND	6.XI.1946	0.63	2 299 374
PORTUGAL	12.III.1965	0.18	656 964
QATAR	27.I.1972	0.04	145 992
ROMANIA	27.VII.1956	0.19	693 462
RWANDA	7.XI.1962	0.01	36 498

MEMBER STATE ETAT MEMBRE ESTADO MIEMBRO	DATE OF ENTRY DATE D'ADHESION FECHA DE INGRESO	SCALE OF CONTRIBUTIONS BAREME DES CONTRIBUTIONS ESCALA DE CONTRIBUCIONES %	CONTRIBUTIONS TO THE BUDGET 1986-87 CONTRIBUTIONS AU BUDGET 1986-87 CONTRIBUCIONES AL PRESUPUESTO 1986-87 $
SAINT CHRISTOPHER AND NEVIS	26.X.1983	0.01	36 498
SAINT LUCIA	6.III.1980	0.01	36 498
SAINT VINCENT AND THE GRENADINES	15.II.1983	0.01	36 498
SAMOA	3.IV.1981	0.01	36 498
SAN MARINO	12.XI.1974	0.01	36 498
SAO TOME AND PRINCIPE	22.I.1980	0.01	36 498
SAUDI ARABIA	4.XI.1946	0.96	3 503 808
SENEGAL	10.XI.1960	0.01	36 498
SEYCHELLES	18.X.1976	0.01	36 498
SIERRA LEONE	28.III.1962	0.01	36 498
SOMALIA	15.XI.1960	0.01	36 498
SPAIN	30.I.1953	2.00	7 299 600
SRI LANKA	14.XI.1949	0.01	36 498
SUDAN	26.XI.1956	0.01	36 498
SURINAME	16.VII.1976	0.01	36 498
SWAZILAND	25.I.1978	0.01	36 498
SWEDEN	23.I.1950	1.24	4 525 752
SWITZERLAND	28.I.1949	1.11	4 051 278
SYRIAN ARAB REPUBLIC	16.XI.1946	0.04	145 992
THAILAND	1.I.1949	0.09	328 482
TOGO	17.XI.1960	0.01	36 498
TONGA	29.IX.1980	0.01	36 498
TRINIDAD AND TOBAGO	2.XI.1962	0.04	145 992
TUNISIA	8.XI.1956	0.03	109 494
TURKEY	4.XI.1946	0.34	1 240 932
UGANDA	9.XI.1962	0.01	36 498
UKRAINIAN S.S.R.	12.V.1954	1.26	4 598 748
U.S.S.R.	21.IV.1954	10.08	36 789 984
UNITED ARAB EMIRATES	21.IV.1972	0.18	656 964
UNITED REPUBLIC OF TANZANIA	6.III.1962	0.01	36 498
URUGUAY	8.XI.1947	0.04	145 992
VENEZUELA	25.XI.1946	0.59	2 153 382
VIET-NAM	6.VII.1951	0.01	36 498
YEMEN	2.IV.1962	0.01	36 498
YUGOSLAVIA	31.III.1950	0.45	1 642 410
ZAIRE	25.XI.1960	0.01	36 498
ZAMBIA	9.XI.1964	0.01	36 498
ZIMBABWE	22.IX.1980	0.02	72 996

GENERAL NOTE/NOTE GENERALE/NOTA GENERAL:

E—> THE SCALE OF CONTRIBUTIONS IS BASED UPON THE SCALE OF CONTRIBUTIONS OF THE UNITED NATIONS, ADJUSTED TO TAKE INTO ACCOUNT THE DIFFERENCE IN THE MEMBERSHIP OF THE TWO ORGANIZATIONS. THE TOTAL CONTRIBUTIONS 1986-87 DOES NOT INCLUDE ADVANCES TO THE WORKING CAPITAL FUND. THE TOTAL BUDGET SHOWN INCLUDES THE FOLLOWING AMOUNTS, WHICH REPRESENT THE CONTRIBUTIONS OF THREE MEMBER STATES THAT HAVE WITHDRAWN FROM THE ORGANISATION: UNITED STATES (91 245 000, 25%), UNITED KINGDOM (17 519 040, 4.8%) AND SINGAPORE (364 980, 0.1%).

FR—> LE BAREME DES CONTRIBUTIONS EST ETABLI SUR LA BASE DU BAREME DE L'ORGANISATION DES NATIONS UNIES, AJUSTE DE FACON A TENIR COMPTE DE LA COMPOSITION DIFFERENTE DES DEUX ORGANISATIONS. LE MONTANT DES CONTRIBUTIONS 1986/87 NE TIENT PAS COMPTE DES AVANCES AU FONDS DE ROULEMENT. LE BUDGET TOTAL PRESENTE INCLUT LES MONTANTS DES CONTRIBUTIONS DE TROIS ETATS MEMBRES AYANT QUITTE L'ORGANISATION: ETATS UNIS (91 245 000, 25%), ROYAUME-UNI (17 519 040, 4.8%) ET SINGAPOUR (364 980, 0.1%)

ESP> LA ESCALA DE CONTRIBUCIONES SE BASA EN LA ESCALA DE CONTRIBUCIONES DE LAS NACIONES UNIDAS, REAJUSTADA TENIENDO EN CUENTA LA DISTINTA COMPOSICION DE LOS DOS ORGANIZACIONES. EL TOTAL DE 1986-87 NO INCLUYE LOS ANTICIPOS AL FONDO DE OPERACIONES. EL PRESUPUESTO TOTAL PRESENTADO INCLUYE LOS IMPORTES DE LAS CONTRIBUCIONES DE TRES ESTADOS MIEMBROS QUE DEJAN LA ORGANIZACION: ESTADOS UNIDOS (91 245 000, 25%), REINO UNIDO (17 519 040, 4.8%) Y SINGAPUR (364980, 0.1%).

ASSOCIATE MEMBERS AND THEIR DATE OF ENTRY
MEMBRES ASSOCIES ET DATE D'ADHESION
MIEMBROS ASOCIADOS Y FECHA DE INGRES

ASOCIATE MEMBERS MEMBRES ASSOCIES MIEMBROS ASOCIADOS	DATE OF ENTRY DATE D'ADHESION FECHA DE INGRESO	CONTRIBUTION CONTRIBUTION CONTRIBUCION
BRITISH VIRGIN ISLANDS	26.XI.1983	THE CONTRIBUTIONS OF ASSOCIATE MEMBERS ARE ASSESSED AT 60 % OF THE MINIMUM PERCENTAGE ASSESSMENT OF MEMBER STATES. LES CONTRIBUTIONS DES MEMBRES ASSOCIES SONT FIXEES A 60 % DE LA CONTRIBUTION MINIMALE DES ETATS MEMBRES. LA CONTRIBUCION DE LOS MIEMBROS ASOCIADOS SE FIJA EN UN 60 % DE LA CONTRIBUCION MINIMA DE LOS ESTADOS MIEMBROS.
NETHERLANDS ANTILLES	26.X.1983	

B School and financial years

Année scolaire et exercice financier

Año escolar y ejercicio económico

IN THE FOLLOWING TABLE, THE MONTHS ARE REPRESENTED BY ROMAN NUMERALS:

JANUARY = I
FEBRUARY = II
MARCH = III
APRIL = IV
MAY = V
JUNE = VI
JULY = VII
AUGUST = VIII
SEPTEMBER = IX
OCTOBER = X
NOVEMBER = XI
DECEMBER = XII

DANS LE TABLEAU SUIVANT, LES MOIS SONT REPRESENTES PAR DES CHIFFRES ROMAINS:

JANVIER = I
FEVRIER = II
MARS = III
AVRIL = IV
MAI = V
JUIN = VI
JUILLET = VII
AOUT = VIII
SEPTEMBRE = IX
OCTOBRE = X
NOVEMBRE = XI
DECEMBRE = XII

EN EL CUADRO SIGUIENTE, LOS MESES ESTAN REPRESENTADOS POR CIFRAS ROMANAS:

ENERO = I
FEBRERO = II
MARZO = III
ABRIL = IV
MAYO = V
JUNIO = VI
JULIO = VII
AGOSTO = VIII
SEPTIEMBRE = IX
OCTUBRE = X
NOVIEMBRE = XI
DECIEMBRE = XII

COUNTRY / PAYS / PAIS	SCHOOL YEAR / ANNEE SCOLAIRE / AÑO ESCOLAR		START OF FINANCIAL YEAR / DEBUT DE L'EXERCICE FINANCIER / COMIENZO DEL EJERCICIO ECONOMICO
	START / DEBUT / COMIENZO	END / FIN / FIN	
AFRICA			
ALGERIA	IX	VI	I
ANGOLA	IX	VII	I
BENIN	X	VII	I
BOTSWANA	I	XII	IV
BURKINA FASO	X	VII	I
BURUNDI	IX	VI	I
CAMEROON			VII
	IX	VI	
	X	VI	
CAPE VERDE	X	VI	I
CENTRAL AFRICAN REPUBLIC	X	VI	II
CHAD	IX	VI	I
COMOROS	X	VI	I
CONGO	X	VI	I
COTE D'IVOIRE	IX	VI	I
DJIBOUTI	IX	VI	I
EGYPT	X	V	VII
EQUATORIAL GUINEA	IX	VI	I
ETHIOPIA	IX	VI	VII
GABON	X	VI	I
GAMBIA	IX	VII	VII
GHANA	IX	VII	I
GUINEA	X	VII	I
GUINEA-BISSAU	X	VII	I
KENYA	I	XII	VII
LESOTHO	I	XII	IV
LIBERIA	III	XII	VII
LIBYAN ARAB JAMAHIRIYA	X	VI	I
MADAGASCAR	X	VI	I
MALAWI	X	VII	IV
MALI	X	VI	I
MAURITANIA	X	VI	I
MAURITIUS	I	XI	VII
MOROCCO	IX	VI	I
MOZAMBIQUE	II	XII	I
NAMIBIA	II	...	IV
NIGER	X	VI	X
NIGERIA	IX	VI	IV
REUNION	IX	VI	I
RWANDA	IX	VII	I
ST. HELENA	IX	VIII	I
SAO TOME AND PRINCIPE	IV	XII	I
SENEGAL	X	VI	VII
SEYCHELLES	I	XII	I
SIERRA LEONE	IX	VII	VII
SOMALIA	XI	VI	I
SUDAN	VII	III	VII
SWAZILAND	I	XII	IV
TOGO	IX	VI	I
TUNISIA	IX	VI	I
UGANDA	I	XII	VII
UNITED REP. OF TANZANIA	I	XII	VII
WESTERN SAHARA	IX	VIII	I
ZAIRE	IX	VII	I
ZAMBIA	I	XII	III
ZIMBABWE	I	XII	VII
AMERICA, NORTH			
ANTIGUA AND BARBUDA	IX	VII	I
BAHAMAS	IX	VI	I
BARBADOS	IX	VII	IV
BELIZE	VIII	VII	I
BERMUDA	IX	VII	IV

COUNTRY PAYS PAIS	SCHOOL YEAR / ANNEE SCOLAIRE / AÑO ESCOLAR: START DEBUT COMIENZO	END FIN FIN	START OF FINANCIAL YEAR DEBUT DE L'EXERCICE FINANCIER COMIENZO DEL EJERCICIO ECONOMICO
BRITISH VIRGIN ISLANDS	IX	VII	I
CANADA	IX	VI	IV
CAYMAN ISLANDS	IX	VII	I
COSTA RICA	III	XI	I
CUBA	IX	VI	I
DOMINICA	IX	VII	I
DOMINICAN REPUBLIC	IX	VI	I
	I	IX	
EL SALVADOR	I	XI	I
GRENADA	IX	VII	I
GUADELOUPE	IX	VI	I
GUATEMALA	I	X	I
HAITI	X	VI	X
HONDURAS	II	XI	I
JAMAICA	IX	VII	IV
MARTINIQUE	IX	VI	I
MEXICO	IX	VI	I
MONTSERRAT	IX	VII	I
NETHERLANDS ANTILLES	VIII	VII	I
NICARAGUA	II	XI	I
PANAMA	IV	XII	I
FORMER CANAL ZONE	IX	VI	...
PUERTO RICO	IX	VI	VII
ST. CHRISTOPHER AND NEVIS	IX	VIII	I
ST. LUCIA	IX	VII	IV
ST. PIERRE AND MIQUELON	IX	VII	I
ST. VINCENT AND THE GRENADINES	IX	VII	...
TRINIDAD AND TOBAGO	IX	VII	I
TURKS AND CAICOS ISLANDS	IX	VII	III
UNITED STATES	IX	V	X
U.S. VIRGIN ISLANDS	IX	VI	X
AMERICA, SOUTH			
ARGENTINA	III	XI	I
	IX	V	
BOLIVIA	II	X	I
BRAZIL	II	XII	I
CHILE	III	XII	I
COLOMBIA	II	XI	I
	IX	VI	
ECUADOR	X	VII	I
	V	I	
FALKLAND ISLANDS (MALVINAS)	II	XII	IV
FRENCH GUIANA	IX	VI	I
GUYANA	IX	VII	I
PARAGUAY	III	XI	I
PERU	IV	XII	I
SURINAME	X	VIII	I
URUGUAY	III	XII	I
VENEZUELA	X	VII	I
ASIA			
AFGHANISTAN	III	XII	II
	IX	VI	
BAHRAIN	X	VI	I
BANGLADESH	I	XII	VII
BHUTAN	III	XII	IV
BRUNEI DARUSSALAM	I	XII	I
BURMA	IV	III	IV
CHINA	IX	VII	...
CYPRUS	IX	VI	I
DEMOCRATIC KAMPUCHEA	X	VI	...
DEMOCRATIC YEMEN	X	VI	I
EAST TIMOR	X	VII	...
HONG KONG	IX	VII	IV
INDIA	IV	III	IV
INDONESIA	VII	VI	IV
IRAN, ISLAMIC REP. OF	IX	VI	III

COUNTRY PAYS PAIS	SCHOOL YEAR / ANNEE SCOLAIRE / AÑO ESCOLAR: START DEBUT COMIENZO	END FIN FIN	START OF FINANCIAL YEAR DEBUT DE L'EXERCICE FINANCIER COMIENZO DEL EJERCICIO ECONOMICO
IRAQ	IX	VI	I
ISRAEL	IX	VI	IV
JAPAN	IV	III	IV
JORDAN	IX	V	I
KOREA, DEMOCRATIC PEOPLE'S REPUB. OF	IX	VIII	...
KOREA, REPUBLIC OF	III	II	I
KUWAIT	IX	V	VII
LAO PEOPLE'S DEMOCRATIC REPUBLIC	IX	VI	I
LEBANON	X	VI	I
MACAU	X	VII	I
MALAYSIA			
PENINSULAR MALAYSIA	I	XI	I
SABAH	I	XI	I
SARAWAK	I	XI	I
MALDIVES	II	XII	I
MONGOLIA	IX	VI	I
NEPAL	II	I	IX
	XII	XI	
OMAN	IX	VI	I
PAKISTAN	IV	III	VII
	VII	VI	
PHILIPPINES	VI	III	I
QATAR	IX	VI	IV
SAUDI ARABIA	X	VI	IV
SINGAPORE	I	XII	IV
SRI LANKA	I	XII	I
SYRIAN ARAB REPUBLIC	IX	V	I
THAILAND	IV	III	X
TURKEY	IX	V	I
UNITED ARAB EMIRATES	IX	VI	I
VIET–NAM	IX	V	I
YEMEN	IX	VI	VII
EUROPE			
ALBANIA	IX	VI	I
ANDORRA	IX	VI	XII
AUSTRIA	IX	VI	I
BELGIUM	IX	VI	I
BULGARIA	IX	VI	I
CZECHOSLOVAKIA	IX	VI	I
DENMARK	VIII	VI	I
FINLAND	VIII	V	I
FRANCE	IX	VI	I
GERMAN DEMOCRATIC REP.	IX	VII	I
GERMANY, FEDERAL REP. OF	VIII	VII	I
GIBRALTAR	IX	VII	IV
GREECE	IX	VI	I
HUNGARY	IX	VI	I
ICELAND	IX	V	I
IRELAND	VII	VI	I
	IX	VI	
ITALY	IX	VI	I
LIECHTENSTEIN	IV	III	I
LUXEMBOURG	IX	VII	I
MALTA	IX	VII	I
MONACO	IX	VI	I
NETHERLANDS	VIII	VII	I
NORWAY	VIII	VI	I
POLAND	IX	VI	I
PORTUGAL	X	VII	I
ROMANIA	IX	VI	I
SAN MARINO	IX	VI	I
SPAIN	IX	VI	I
SWEDEN	VIII	VI	VII
SWITZERLAND	IV	III	I
	IX	VII	
UNITED KINGDOM	IX	VII	IV
YUGOSLAVIA	IX	VI	I

COUNTRY / PAYS / PAIS	SCHOOL YEAR / ANNEE SCOLAIRE / AÑO ESCOLAR		START OF FINANCIAL YEAR / DEBUT DE L'EXERCICE FINANCIER / COMIENZO DEL EJERCICIO ECONOMICO
	START / DEBUT / COMIENZO	END / FIN / FIN	
OCEANIA			
AMERICAN SAMOA	IX	VI	X
AUSTRALIA	I	XII	VII
COOK ISLANDS	II	XII	IV
FIJI	I	XI	I
FRENCH POLYNESIA	IX	VI	I
GUAM	IX	VI	X
KIRIBATI	II	XII	I
NAURU	I	XI	VII
NEW CALEDONIA	III	XII	I
NEW ZEALAND	II	XII	IV
NIUE	II	XII	IV
NORFOLK ISLAND	I	XII	VII
PACIFIC ISLANDS	IX	VI	X
PAPUA NEW GUINEA	I	XII	I
SAMOA	I	XII	I
SOLOMON ISLANDS	I	XI	I
TOKELAU	II	XII	III
TONGA	II	XII	VII
TUVALU	I	XII	...
VANUATU	II	XII	...
U.S.S.R.			
U.S.S.R.	IX	V/VI	I
BYELORUSSIAN S.S.R.	IX	VI	I
UKRAINIAN S.S.R.	IX	VI	I

GENERAL NOTE

FOR CERTAIN COUNTRIES, 2 LINES ARE SHOWN INSTEAD OF 1 AS CONCERNS THE START AND THE END OF THE SCHOOL YEAR. THE AREAS OR TYPES OF SCHOOLS TO WHICH THESE LINES REFER ARE INDICATED IN THE FOLLOWING TABLE:

NOTE GENERALE

POUR CERTAINS PAYS SUIVANTS, LES DONNEES RELATIVES AU DEBUT ET A LA FIN DE L'ANNEE SCOLAIRE SONT PRESENTEES EN DEUX LIGNES A LA PLACE D'UNE. LES REGIONS OU LES TYPES D'ECOLES CONCERNES PAR CES LIGNES SONT INDIQUES DANS LE TABLEAU SUIVANT:

NOTA GENERAL

PARA LOS PAISES SIGUIENTES, LOS DATOS RELATIVOS AL COMIENZO Y AL FINAL DEL AÑO ESCOLAR SE PRESENTAN EN DOS LINEAS EN VEZ DE UNA. LAS REGIONES O LOS TIPOS DE ESCUELAS A QUE SE REFIEREN DICHAS LINEAS, SE INDICAN EN EL CUADRO SIGUIENTE:

COUNTRY / PAYS / PAIS	LINE / LIGNE / LINEA	REGION OR TYPES OF SCHOOLS / REGION OU TYPES D'ECOLES / REGION O TIPOS DE ESCUELAS
CAMEROON	1	WESTERN / OCCIDENTAL
	2	EASTERN / ORIENTAL
DOMINICAN REPUBLIC	2	COFFEE-GROWING REGION / REGION DES PLANTATIONS DE CAFE / ZONA CAFETALERA
ARGENTINA	2	COLD REGIONS / REGIONS FROIDES / REGIONES FRIAS
COLOMBIA	2	VALLE, CAUCA AND NARINO DEPARTMENTS / DEPARTEMENTS DE VALLE, CAUCA ET NARINO / DEPARTAMENTOS DE VALLE, CAUCA Y NARINO
ECUADOR	1	SIERRA
	2	COASTAL REGION / REGION COTIERE / REGION COSTERA
AFGHANISTAN	2	WARM REGIONS / REGIONS CHAUDES / REGIONES CALIDAS
NEPAL	1	COLD REGIONS / REGIONS FROIDES / REGIONES FRIAS
	2	WARM REGIONS / REGIONS CHAUDES / REGIONES CALIDAS
PAKISTAN	2	KARACHI REGION / REGION DE KARACHI
IRELAND	1	FIRST LEVEL / PREMIER DEGRE / PRIMER GRADO
	2	SECOND LEVEL / SECOND DEGRE / SEGUNDO GRADO
SWITZERLAND	2	CERTAIN CANTONS / CERTAINS CANTONS / ALGUNOS CANTONES

SUMMARY OF THE START OF THE SCHOOL YEAR, 1984 — SOMMAIRE RELATIF A L'ANNEE SCOLAIRE, 1984 — RESUMEN RELATIVO AL AÑO ESCOLAR, 1984

CONTINENTS / CONTINENTS / CONTINENTES	NUMBER OF COUNTRIES IN WHICH SCHOOL YEARS BEGINS IN / NOMBRE DE PAYS DONT L'ANNEE SCOLAIRE COMMENCE EN / NUMERO DE PAISES EN LOS QUE EL AÑO ESCOLAR EMPIEZA EN							
	JANUARY FEBRUARY / JANVIER FEVRIER / ENERO FEBRERO	MARCH APRIL / MARS AVRIL / MARZO ABRIL	MAY JUNE / MAI JUIN / MAYO JUNIO	JULY AUGUST / JUILLET AOUT / JULIO AGOSTO	SEPTEMBER OCTOBER / SEPTEMBRE OCTOBRE / SEPTIEMBRE OCTUBRE	NOVEMBER DECEMBER / NOVEMBRE DECEMBRE / NOVIEMBRE DICIEMBRE	MIXED OR NOT SPECIFIED / MIXTE OU NON SPECIFIE / MIXTO O SIN ESPECIFICAR	TOTAL
AFRICA	12	2	0	1	37	1	1	54
AMERICA, NORTH	4	2	0	2	26	0	1	35
AMERICA, SOUTH	3	4	0	0	4	0	3	14
ASIA	9	6	1	1	25	0	2	44
EUROPE (INCL. U.S.S.R.)	0	1	0	6	26	0	2	35
OCEANIA	15	1	0	0	4	0	0	20
ARAB STATES	(0)	(0)	(0)	(1)	(19)	(1)	(0)	(21)
TOTAL	43	16	1	10	122	1	9	202

SUMMARY OF THE START OF THE FINANCIAL YEAR, 1984 — SOMMAIRE RELATIF A L'EXERCICE FINANCIER, 1984 — RESUMEN RELATIVO AL EJERCICIO ECONOMICO, 1984

CONTINENTS / CONTINENTS / CONTINENTES	NUMBER OF COUNTRIES IN WHICH FINANCIAL YEAR BEGINS IN / NOMBRE DE PAYS DONT L'EXERCICE FINANCIER COMMENCE EN / NUMERO DE PAISES EN LOS QUE EL EJERCICIO ECONOMICO EMPIEZA EN							
	JANUARY FEBRUARY / JANVIER FEVRIER / ENERO FEBRERO	MARCH APRIL / MARS AVRIL / MARZO ABRIL	MAY JUNE / MAI JUIN / MAYO JUNIO	JULY AUGUST / JUILLET AOUT / JULIO AGOSTO	SEPTEMBER OCTOBER / SEPTEMBRE OCTOBRE / SEPTIEMBRE OCTUBRE	NOVEMBER DECEMBER / NOVEMBRE DECEMBRE / NOVIEMBRE DICIEMBRE	MIXED OR NOT SPECIFIED / MIXTE OU NON SPECIFIE / MIXTO O SIN ESPECIFICAR	TOTAL
AFRICA	33	7	0	13	1	0	0	54
AMERICA, NORTH	23	6	0	1	3	0	2	35
AMERICA, SOUTH	13	1	0	0	0	0	0	14
ASIA	23	11	0	4	2	0	4	44
EUROPE (INCL. U.S.S.R.)	31	2	0	1	0	0	1	35
OCEANIA	7	4	0	4	3	0	2	20
ARAB STATES	(15)	(2)	(0)	(4)	(0)	(0)	(0)	(21)
TOTAL	130	31	0	23	9	0	9	202

C Exchange rates

Cours des changes

Tipos de cambio

The following table lists rates of exchange for the figures on expenditure or revenue expressed in national currencies which appear in Tables 4.1 to 4.4, 5.9 to 5.15, 5.17, 5.19, 8.1, 8.2, 9.3, 10.8 and 10.9.

The exchange rates are expressed in terms of the number of units of national currency corresponding to one United States dollar; in previous editions of the *Yearbook* exchange rates were expressed in terms of the value in United States dollars of one unit of national currency.

The reader's attention is drawn to the fact that most countries and territories whose monetary unit is that of another country have been omitted from the table of exchange rates; the relevant information can however easily be found by referring to the data for the country with which the currency is identified.

For most countries, the data were provided by the International Monetary Fund, and refer to average annual exchange rates. For additional information concerning the methodology used to calculate these rates the reader may wish to consult the monthly bulletin *International Financial Statistics* published by the International Monetary Fund. For the remaining countries (indicated by a note) the exchange rates have been extracted from the *Monthly Bulletin of Statistics* of the United Nations.

Le tableau ci-après présente les cours des changes applicables aux données relatives aux dépenses ou aux ressources financières, qui sont exprimées en monnaie nationale dans les tableaux 4.1 à 4.4, 5.9 à 5.15, 5.17, 5.19, 8.1, 8.2, 9.3, 10.8 et 10.9.

Les cours des changes sont exprimés en nombre d'unités de monnaie nationale pour un dollar des Etats-Unis; dans les précédentes éditions de l'*Annuaire*, les cours des changes étaient exprimés en nombre de dollars des Etats-Unis par unité de monnaie nationale.

Le lecteur est prié de noter que les pays ou territoires dont l'unité monétaire est la même que celle d'un autre pays ont été supprimés du tableau des cours des changes. On peut cependant trouver facilement l'information pertinente en se référant aux données du pays dont la monnaie est originaire.

Pour la plupart des pays, les données nous ont été fournies par le Fonds Monétaire International et se réfèrent au cours moyen de l'année. Pour plus de renseignements sur la méthodologie appliquée pour le calcul de ces cours, le lecteur peut consulter le bulletin mensuel *International Financial Statistics* du Fonds Monétaire International. Pour les autres pays (signalés par une note), les cours des changes ont été tirés du *Bulletin Mensuel de Statistiques des Nations Unies.*

En el cuadro que figura a continuación, se indican los tipos de cambio que deben aplicarse a los datos relativos a los gastos o a las fuentes de ingreso expresadas en moneda nacional en los cuadros 4.1 a 4.4, 5.9 a 5.15, 5.17, 5.19, 8.1, 8.2, 9.3, 10.8 y 10.9.

Las tasas de cambio están expresadas en el número de unidades de moneda nacional por dólar de los Estados Unidos; en las ediciones anteriores del *Anuario*, los tipos de cambio estaban expresados en forma inversa, es decir el número de dólares de los Estados Unidos por unidad de moneda nacional.

Nos permitimos indicar al lector que los países o territorios cuya unidad monetaria es la misma que la de otro país, han sido suprimidos del cuadro; la información correspondiente puede ser obtenida refiriéndose a los datos del país de origen.

Para la mayor parte de los países, los datos nos han sido proporcionados por el Fondo Monetario Internacional y se refieren al curso medio del año. Para mayor información sobre la metodología aplicada para el cálculo de los tipos de cambio, el lector puede consultar el boletín mensual *International Financial Statistics* del Fondo Monetario Internacional. Para los demás países (indicados por una nota), los tipos de cambio han sido obtenidos del *Monthly Bulletin of Statistics* (Boletín Mensual de Estadísticas) de las Naciones Unidas.

Ø PRIOR TO 1983, DATA FOR COUNTRIES SHOWN WITH THIS SYMBOL HAVE BEEN TAKEN FROM THE 'MONTHLY BULLETIN OF STATISTICS' PUBLISHED BY THE UNITED NATIONS.

Ø AVANT 1983, LES DONNEES CONCERNANT LES PAYS SIGNALES PAR CE SYMBOLE ONT ETE EXTRAITES DU 'BULLETIN MENSUEL DE STATISTIQUES' PUBLIE PAR LES NATIONS UNIES.

Δ DATA FOR COUNTRIES SHOWN WITH THIS SYMBOL ARE THE NON-COMMERCIAL RATES APPLIED TO TOURISM AND TO REMITTANCES FROM OUTSIDE THE ROUBLE AREA AND HAVE BEEN TAKEN FROM THE 'MONTHLY BULLETIN OF STATISTICS' PUBLISHED BY THE UNITED NATIONS.

Δ LES DONNEES CONCERNANT LES PAYS SIGNALES PAR CE SYMBOLE SONT LES TAUX NON-COMMERCIAUX APPLIQUES AUX TOURISME ET ENVOIS DE FONDS PROVENANT DES PAYS EXTERIEURS A LA ZONE ROUBLE, ET ONT ETE EXTRAITES DU 'BULLETIN MENSUEL DE STATISTIQUES' PUBLIE PAR LES NATIONS UNIES.

COUNTRY PAYS PAIS	NATIONAL CURRENCY MONNAIE NATIONALE MONEDA NACIONAL	NATIONAL CURRENCY PER UNITED STATES DOLLAR VALEUR DU DOLLAR DES ETATS-UNIS EN MONNAIE NATIONALE VALOR DEL DOLAR DE LOS ESTADOS UNIDOS EN MONEDA NACIONAL				
		1960	1965	1970	1975	1976
AFRICA						
ALGERIA	DINAR	4.937	4.937	4.937	3.949	4.163
BENIN	FRANC C.F.A.	246.85	246.85	277.71	214.31	238.95
BOTSWANA	PULA	0.714	0.714	0.714	0.739	0.87
BURKINA FASO	FRANC C.F.A.	246.85	246.85	277.71	214.31	238.95
BURUNDI	FRANC	50.00	84.38	87.50	78.75	86.25
CAMEROON	FRANC C.F.A.	246.85	246.85	277.71	214.31	238.95
CAPE VERDE Ø	ESCUDO	28.75	28.75	28.75	27.47	31.55
CENTRAL AFRICAN REPUBLIC	FRANC C.F.A.	246.85	246.85	277.71	214.31	238.95
CHAD	FRANC C.F.A.	246.85	246.85	277.71	214.31	238.95
COMOROS	FRANC C.F.A	246.85	246.85	277.71	214.31	238.95
CONGO	FRANC C.F.A	246.85	246.85	277.71	214.31	238.95
COTE D'IVOIRE	FRANC C.F.A.	246.85	246.85	277.71	214.31	238.95
DJIBOUTI	FRANC	...	...	...	...	...
EGYPT	POUND	0.348	0.435	0.435	0.391	0.391
EQUATORIAL GUINEA‡	FRANC C.F.A	59.99	59.99	69.98	59.77	68.29
ETHIOPIA	BIRR	2.484	2.50	2.50	2.07	2.07
GABON	FRANC C.F.A	246.85	246.85	277.71	214.31	238.95
GAMBIA	DALASI	1.786	1.786	2.083	1.808	2.226
GHANA	CEDI	0.714	0.714	1.02	1.15	1.15
GUINEA Ø	SYLI	24.69	24.69	24.69	21.09	21.25
GUINEA-BISSAU Ø	PESO	28.75	28.75	28.75	27.47	31.55
KENYA	SHILLING	7.143	7.143	7.143	7.343	8.367
LESOTHO	MALOTI	0.714	0.714	0.714	0.740	0.87
LIBERIA	DOLLAR	1.00	1.00	1.00	1.00	1.00
LIBYAN ARAB JAMAHIRIYA	DINAR	0.357	0.357	0.357	0.296	0.296
MADAGASCAR	FRANC	246.85	246.85	277.71	214.32	238.98
MALAWI	KWACHA	0.714	0.714	0.833	0.864	0.913
MALI‡	FRANC C.F.A.	246.85	246.85	277.71	214.31	238.95
MAURITANIA	OUGUIYA	49.37	49.37	55.542	43.104	45.022
MAURITIUS	RUPEE	4.762	4.762	5.556	6.026	6.682
MOROCCO	DIRHAM	5.06	5.06	5.06	4.052	4.419
MOZAMBIQUE	METICAL	...	...	...	...	...
NAMIBIA	SOUTH AFRICAN RAND	0.714	0.714	0.714	0.739	0.869
NIGER	FRANC C.F.A.	246.85	246.85	277.71	214.31	238.95
NIGERIA	NAIRA	0.714	0.714	0.714	0.616	0.626
RWANDA	FRANC	50.00	50.00	100.00	92.84	92.84
SAO TOME AND PRINCIPE Ø	DOBRA	28.75	28.75	28.75	27.47	31.55
SENEGAL	FRANC C.F.A.	246.85	246.85	277.71	214.31	238.95
SEYCHELLES	RUPEE	4.762	4.762	5.555	6.027	7.419
SIERRA LEONE	LEONE	0.714	0.714	0.833	0.904	1.113
SOMALIA	SHILLING	7.143	7.143	7.143	6.295	6.295
SOUTH AFRICA	RAND	0.714	0.714	0.714	0.739	0.869
SUDAN	POUND	0.348	0.348	0.348	0.348	0.348
SWAZILAND	LILANGENI	0.714	0.714	0.714	0.739	0.87
TOGO	FRANC C.F.A.	246.85	246.85	277.71	214.31	238.95
TUNISIA	DINAR	0.42	0.53	0.525	0.402	0.429
UGANDA	SHILLING	7.143	7.143	7.143	7.422	8.266
UNITED REPUBLIC OF TANZANIA	SHILLING	7.143	7.143	7.143	7.367	8.377
ZAIRE	ZAIRE	0.05	0.165	0.50	0.50	0.792
ZAMBIA	KWACHA	0.714	0.714	0.714	0.643	0.721
ZIMBABWE	DOLLAR	0.714	0.714	0.714	0.57	0.626

Ø LOS DATOS PARA LOS PAISES INDICADOS POR ESTE SIMBOLO HAN SIDO EXTRAIDOS DEL 'MONTHLY BULLETIN OF STATISTICS' (BOLETIN MENSUAL DE ESTADISTICAS) PUBLICADO POR LAS NACIONES UNIDAS.

Δ LOS DATOS PARA LOS PAISES INDICADOS POR ESTE SIMBOLO CORRESPONDEN A LOS TIPOS DE CAMBIO NO-COMERCIABLES UTILIZADOS PARA EL TURISMO Y ENVIOS DE FONDOS QUE PROVIENEN DE LOS PAISES EXTERNOS A LA ZONA DE RUBLES, Y HAN SIDOS EXTRAIDOS DEL 'MONTHLY BULLETIN OF STATISTICS' (BOLETIN MENSUAL DE ESTADISTICAS) PUBLICADO POR LAS NACIONES UNIDAS.

NATIONAL CURRENCY PER UNITED STATES DOLLAR VALEUR DU DOLLAR DES ETATS-UNIS EN MONNAIE NATIONALE VALOR DEL DOLAR DE LOS ESTADOS UNIDOS EN MONEDA NACIONAL								
1977	1978	1979	1980	1981	1982	1983	1984	1985
4.147	3.966	3.853	3.837	4.315	4.592	4.788	4.983	5.028
245.68	225.66	212.72	211.28	271.73	328.61	381.06	436.96	449.26
0.842	0.828	0.815	0.777	0.837	1.030	1.097	1.298	1.903
245.68	225.66	212.72	211.28	271.73	328.61	381.06	436.96	449.26
90.00	90.00	90.00	90.00	90.00	90.00	92.948	119.709	120.691
245.68	225.66	212.72	211.28	271.73	328.61	381.06	436.96	449.26
33.90	35.94	38.31	42.49	50.86	63.04	71.686	84.878	91.632
245.68	225.66	212.72	211.28	271.73	328.61	381.06	436.96	449.26
245.68	225.66	212.72	211.28	271.73	328.61	381.06	436.96	449.26
245.68	225.66	212.72	211.28	271.73	328.61	381.06	436.96	449.261
245.68	225.66	212.72	211.28	271.73	328.61	381.06	436.96	449.26
245.68	225.66	212.72	211.28	271.73	328.61	381.06	436.96	449.26
...	...	...	...	...	...	177.721	177.721	177.721
0.391	0.391	0.70	0.70	0.70	0.70	0.70	0.70	0.70
80.91	70.11	66.15	158.50	194.90	251.20	286.86	321.52	449.26
2.07	2.07	2.07	2.07	2.07	2.07	2.07	2.07	2.07
245.68	225.66	212.72	211.28	271.73	328.61	381.06	436.96	449.26
2.293	2.086	1.888	1.721	1.99	2.290	2.639	3.584	3.894
1.15	1.764	2.75	2.75	2.75	2.75	8.83	35.986	54.365
20.32	18.95	18.739	19.355	21.208	22.378	23.095	24.090	24.333
34.27	33.77	33.401	34.499	37.802	39.887	42.099	105.287	159.620
8.277	7.729	7.475	7.420	9.048	10.922	13.312	14.414	16.432
0.87	0.87	0.842	0.779	0.878	1.084	1.114	1.475	2.229
1.00	1.00	1.00	1.00	1.00	1.00	1.00	1.00	1.00
0.296	0.296	0.296	0.296	0.296	0.296	0.296	0.296	0.296
245.67	225.64	212.72	211.30	271.73	349.71	430.45	576.60	662.48
0.903	0.844	0.817	0.812	0.895	1.055	1.175	1.413	1.719
245.68	225.66	212.72	211.28	271.73	328.61	381.06	436.96	449.26
45.587	46.163	45.893	45.914	48.296	51.769	54.812	63.803	77.085
6.607	6.163	6.308	7.684	8.937	10.873	11.706	13.80	15.443
4.503	4.167	3.899	3.937	5.172	6.023	7.111	8.811	10.063
...	...	...	...	...	...	40.183	42.443	...
0.869	0.869	0.842	0.778	0.877	1.084	1.114	1.475	2.229
245.68	225.66	212.72	211.28	271.73	328.61	381.06	436.96	449.26
0.645	0.635	0.604	0.547	0.618	0.673	0.724	0.765	0.894
92.84	92.84	92.84	92.84	92.84	92.84	94.343	100.172	101.262
37.25	34.73	34.35	35.48	38.88	41.02	42.335	44.159	44.604
245.68	225.66	212.72	211.28	271.73	328.61	381.06	436.96	449.26
7.643	6.952	6.333	6.392	6.315	6.553	6.768	7.059	7.134
1.147	1.047	1.057	1.05	1.159	1.239	1.885	2.51	5.094
6.295	6.295	6.295	6.295	6.295	10.750	15.788	20.019	39.487
0.869	0.869	0.842	0.778	0.877	1.084	1.114	1.475	2.229
0.348	0.377	0.429	0.50	0.559	0.952	1.30	1.30	2.304
0.87	0.87	0.842	0.778	0.877	1.084	1.114	1.475	2.223
245.68	225.66	212.72	211.28	271.73	328.61	381.06	436.96	449.26
0.429	0.416	0.407	0.405	0.494	0.591	0.678	0.777	0.834
8.259	7.736	7.483	7.417	50.052	94.047	153.86	359.70	672.02
8.289	7.712	8.217	8.197	8.284	9.283	11.143	15.292	17.472
0.857	0.836	1.728	2.80	4.384	5.75	12.889	36.129	49.873
0.79	0.801	0.793	0.789	0.87	0.929	1.259	1.813	3.140
0.628	0.677	0.68	0.643	0.69	0.759	1.013	1.257	1.614

COUNTRY PAYS PAIS	NATIONAL CURRENCY MONNAIE NATIONALE MONEDA NACIONAL	NATIONAL CURRENCY PER UNITED STATES DOLLAR VALEUR DU DOLLAR DES ETATS-UNIS EN MONNAIE NATIONALE VALOR DEL DOLAR DE LOS ESTADOS UNIDOS EN MONEDA NACIONAL				
		1960	1965	1970	1975	1976
AMERICA, NORTH						
ANTIGUA AND BARBUDA	E. CARIBBEAN DOLLAR	1.714	1.714	2.00	2.17	2.615
BAHAMAS	DOLLAR	1.02	1.02	1.00	1.00	1.00
BARBADOS	DOLLAR	1.714	1.714	2.00	2.02	2.003
BELIZE	DOLLAR	1.429	1.429	1.667	1.808	2.226
BERMUDA	DOLLAR	0.86	0.86	1.00	1.00	1.00
CANADA	DOLLAR	0.970	1.081	1.048	1.017	0.986
COSTA RICA	COLON	5.615	6.625	6.625	8.57	8.57
CUBA Δ	PESO	1.00	1.00	1.00	0.83	0.83
DOMINICA	E. CARIBBEAN DOLLAR	1.714	1.714	2.00	2.17	2.615
DOMINICAN REPUBLIC	PESO	1.00	1.00	1.00	1.00	1.00
EL SALVADOR	COLON	2.50	2.50	2.50	2.50	2.50
GRENADA	E. CARIBBEAN DOLLAR	1.714	1.714	2.00	2.17	2.615
GUATEMALA	QUETZAL	1.00	1.00	1.00	1.00	1.00
HAITI	GOURDE	5.00	5.00	5.00	5.00	5.00
HONDURAS	LEMPIRA	2.00	2.00	2.00	2.00	2.00
JAMAICA	DOLLAR	0.714	0.714	0.833	0.909	0.909
MEXICO	PESO	12.50	12.50	12.50	12.50	15.426
MONTSERRAT	E. CARIBBEAN DOLLAR	1.714	1.714	2.00	2.17	2.614
NETHERLANDS ANTILLES	GUILDER	1.886	1.886	1.886	1.80	1.80
NICARAGUA	CORDOBA	7.00	7.00	7.00	7.026	7.026
PANAMA	BALBOA	1.00	1.00	1.00	1.00	1.00
FORMER CANAL ZONE	UNITED STATES DOLLAR	1.00	1.00	1.00	1.00	1.00
ST. CHRISTOPHER AND NEVIS	E. CARIBBEAN DOLLAR	1.714	1.714	2.00	2.17	2.61
ST. LUCIA	E. CARIBBEAN DOLLAR	1.714	1.714	2.00	2.17	2.61
ST. VINCENT AND THE GRENADINES	E. CARIBBEAN DOLLAR	1.714	1.714	2.00	2.17	2.61
TRINIDAD AND TOBAGO	DOLLAR	1.714	1.714	2.00	2.17	2.436
UNITED STATES	DOLLAR	1.00	1.00	1.00	1.00	1.00
AMERICA, SOUTH						
ARGENTINA‡	PESO	0.83	1.68	3.76	21.79	0.014
BOLIVIA	PESO	11.88	11.88	11.88	20.00	20.00
BRAZIL	CRUZEIRO	0.19	1.90	4.59	8.13	10.67
CHILE	PESO	0.001	0.003	0.01	4.911	13.054
COLOMBIA	PESO	6.635	10.475	18.443	30.929	34.694
ECUADOR	SUCRE	15.00	18.00	20.917	25.00	25.00
GUYANA	DOLLAR	1.714	1.714	2.00	2.355	2.55
PARAGUAY	GUARANI	123.17	126.00	126.00	126.00	126.00
PERU	SOL	26.87	26.82	38.70	40.54	56.42
SURINAME	GUILDER	1.886	1.886	1.886	1.785	1.785
URUGUAY	PESO	0.011	0.030	0.25	2.254	3.336
VENEZUELA	BOLIVAR	3.22	4.45	4.45	4.290	4.293
ASIA						
AFGHANISTAN	AFGHANI	20.00	45.00	45.00	45.00	45.00
BAHRAIN	DINAR	...	...	0.476	0.396	0.396
BANGLADESH	TAKA	...	...	...	12.019	15.347
BHUTAN	NGULTRUM	4.762	4.762	7.50	8.38	8.96
BRUNEI DARUSSALAM	DOLLAR	3.06	3.06	3.06	2.39	2.54
BURMA	KYAT	4.762	4.762	4.762	6.376	6.767
CHINA	YUAN	2.462	2.462	2.462	1.86	1.941
CYPRUS	POUND	0.357	0.357	0.417	0.368	0.41
DEMOCRATIC YEMEN	DINAR	0.36	0.36	0.417	0.345	0.345
HONG KONG Ø	DOLLAR	5.71	5.71	6.06	4.94	4.88
INDIA	RUPEE	4.762	4.762	7.50	8.38	8.96
INDONESIA	RUPIAH	...	...	362.83	415.00	415.00
IRAN, ISLAMIC REPUBLIC OF	RIAL	75.75	75.75	75.75	67.639	70.222
IRAQ	DINAR	0.357	0.357	0.357	0.295	0.295
ISRAEL	SHEKEL	0.18	0.30	0.35	0.634	0.794
JAPAN	YEN	360.00	360.00	360.00	296.79	296.55
JORDAN	DINAR	0.357	0.357	0.357	0.320	0.332
KOREA, REPUBLIC OF	WON	63.13	266.40	310.56	484.00	484.00
KUWAIT	DINAR	0.357	0.357	0.357	0.296	0.296
LAO PEOPLE'S DEMOCRATIC REP. Ø	KIP	...	...	...	...	...
LEBANON	POUND	3.169	3.072	3.269	2.302	2.872
MACAU	PATACA	...	...	...	...	...
MALAYSIA	RINGGIT	3.061	3.061	3.061	2.394	2.542
MALDIVES Ø	RUFIYAA	4.762	4.762	5.95	6.13	8.63
MONGOLIA Δ	TUGRIK	...	4.00	4.00	3.32	3.32
NEPAL	RUPEE	7.50	7.619	10.125	11.00	12.50
OMAN	RIAL	0.357	0.357	0.417	0.345	0.345
PAKISTAN	RUPEE	4.762	4.762	4.762	9.90	9.90
PHILIPPINES	PESO	2.00	3.90	5.904	7.248	7.44
QATAR	RIYAL	...	...	4.762	3.931	3.963

NATIONAL CURRENCY PER UNITED STATES DOLLAR VALEUR DU DOLLAR DES ETATS-UNIS EN MONNAIE NATIONALE VALOR DEL DOLAR DE LOS ESTADOS UNIDOS EN MONEDA NACIONAL								
1977	1978	1979	1980	1981	1982	1983	1984	1985
2.70	2.70	2.70	2.70	2.70	2.70	2.70	2.70	2.70
1.00	1.00	1.00	1.00	1.00	1.00	1.00	1.00	1.00
2.007	2.011	2.011	2.011	2.011	2.011	2.011	2.011	2.011
2.00	2.00	2.00	2.00	2.00	2.00	2.00	2.00	2.00
1.00	1.00	1.00	1.00	1.00	1.00	1.00	1.00	1.00
1.063	1.141	1.171	1.169	1.199	1.234	1.232	1.295	1.365
8.57	8.57	8.57	8.57	21.763	37.407	41.094	44.533	50.620
0.83	0.74	0.72	0.71	0.83	0.85	0.87	0.90	...
2.70	2.70	2.70	2.70	2.70	2.70	2.70	2.70	2.70
1.00	1.00	1.00	1.00	1.00	1.00	1.00	1.00	3.113
2.50	2.50	2.50	2.50	2.50	2.50	2.50	2.50	2.50
2.70	2.70	2.70	2.70	2.70	2.70	2.70	2.70	2.70
1.00	1.00	1.00	1.00	1.00	1.00	1.00	1.00	1.00
5.00	5.00	5.00	5.00	5.00	5.00	5.00	5.00	5.00
2.00	2.00	2.00	2.00	2.00	2.00	2.00	2.00	2.00
0.909	1.413	1.765	1.781	1.781	1.781	1.932	3.943	5.559
22.573	22.767	22.805	22.951	24.515	56.402	120.094	167.828	256.872
2.70	2.70	2.70	2.70	2.70	2.70	2.70	2.70	2.70
1.80	1.80	1.80	1.80	1.80	1.80	1.80	1.80	1.80
7.026	7.026	9.255	10.05	10.05	10.05	10.05	10.05	26.504
1.00	1.00	1.00	1.00	1.00	1.00	1.00	1.00	1.00
1.00	1.00	1.00	1.00	1.00	1.00	1.00	1.00	1.00
2.70	2.70	2.70	2.70	2.70	2.70	2.70	2.70	2.70
2.70	2.70	2.70	2.70	2.70	2.70	2.70	2.70	2.70
2.70	2.70	2.70	2.70	2.70	2.70	2.70	2.70	2.70
2.40	2.40	2.40	2.40	2.40	2.40	2.40	2.40	2.45
1.00	1.00	1.00	1.00	1.00	1.00	1.00	1.00	1.00
0.041	0.08	0.133	0.184	0.44	2.592	10.53	67.649	601.81
20.00	20.00	20.39	24.51	24.51	63.81	229.78	2314.00	...
14.14	18.07	26.95	52.71	93.12	179.51	577.04	1848.03	6200.00
21.529	31.656	37.246	39.00	39.00	50.909	78.842	98.656	161.081
36.775	39.095	42.55	47.28	54.491	64.085	78.854	100.817	142.311
25.00	25.00	25.00	25.00	25.00	30.026	44.115	62.536	69.556
2.55	2.55	2.55	2.55	2.813	3.00	3.00	3.832	4.252
126.00	126.00	126.00	126.00	126.00	126.00	126.00	201.00	240.00
83.81	156.33	224.55	288.86	422.32	697.57	1628.59	3466.90	10974.20
1.785	1.785	1.785	1.785	1.785	1.785	1.785	1.785	1.785
4.678	6.06	7.861	9.099	10.82	13.909	34.54	56.122	101.422
4.293	4.293	4.293	4.293	4.293	4.293	4.298	7.018	7.500
45.00	45.00	43.733	44.129	49.481	50.60	50.60	50.60	50.60
0.396	0.387	0.382	0.377	0.376	0.376	0.376	0.376	0.376
15.375	15.016	15.552	15.454	17.987	22.118	24.615	25.354	27.994
8.739	8.193	8.126	7.863	8.658	9.455	10.099	11.363	12.369
2.46	2.32	2.19	2.18	2.30	2.34	2.128	2.141	2.226
7.121	6.885	6.654	6.60	7.281	7.791	8.036	8.386	8.475
1.858	1.684	1.555	1.498	1.705	1.889	1.976	2.32	2.937
0.408	0.373	0.354	0.353	0.421	0.475	0.527	0.588	0.612
0.345	0.345	0.345	0.345	0.345	0.345	0.345	0.345	0.345
4.66	...	4.96	5.14	5.69	6.515	7.265	7.818	7.791
8.739	8.193	8.126	7.863	8.658	9.455	10.099	11.363	12.369
415.00	442.05	623.06	626.99	631.76	661.42	909.26	1025.94	1110.58
70.617	70.475	70.475	70.615	78.328	83.603	86.358	90.03	91.051
0.295	0.295	0.295	0.295	0.295	0.298	0.311	0.311	0.311
1.046	1.746	2.544	5.124	0.011	0.022	0.056	0.293	1.178
268.51	210.44	219.14	226.74	220.54	249.08	237.51	237.52	238.54
0.329	0.306	0.30	0.298	0.33	0.352	0.363	0.384	0.394
484.00	484.00	484.00	607.43	681.03	731.08	775.75	805.98	870.02
0.296	0.275	0.276	0.27	0.279	0.287	0.291	0.296	0.301
2.00	4.00	10.00	10.00	30.00	35.00	35.00	35.000	
3.069	2.955	3.243	3.436	4.314	4.744	4.528	6.511	16.417
...	...	...	...	...	...	7.464	8.045	7.941
2.461	2.316	2.188	2.177	2.304	2.335	2.321	2.344	2.483
8.93	8.63	7.55	7.55	7.55	7.05	7.05	7.05	7.098
3.26	3.00	2.90	2.85	3.15	3.27	3.39	3.79	...
12.50	12.11	12.00	12.00	12.336	13.244	14.545	16.459	18.305
0.345	0.345	0.345	0.345	0.345	0.345	0.345	0.345	0.345
9.90	9.90	9.90	9.90	9.90	11.848	13.117	14.046	15.928
7.402	7.366	7.377	7.511	7.90	8.54	11.113	16.699	18.607
3.959	3.877	3.773	3.656	3.64	3.64	3.64	3.64	3.64

COUNTRY / PAYS / PAIS	NATIONAL CURRENCY / MONNAIE NATIONALE / MONEDA NACIONAL	NATIONAL CURRENCY PER UNITED STATES DOLLAR / VALEUR DU DOLLAR DES ETATS-UNIS EN MONNAIE NATIONALE / VALOR DEL DOLAR DE LOS ESTADOS UNIDOS EN MONEDA NACIONAL				
		1960	1965	1970	1975	1976
SAUDI ARABIA	RIYAL	4.50	4.50	4.50	3.517	3.53
SINGAPORE Ø	DOLLAR	3.061	3.061	3.061	2.371	2.471
SRI LANKA	RUPEE	4.762	4.762	5.952	7.007	8.412
SYRIAN ARAB REPUBLIC	POUND	3.58	3.82	3.82	3.70	3.853
THAILAND	BAHT	21.182	20.80	20.80	20.379	20.40
TURKEY	LIRA	4.867	9.00	11.50	14.442	16.053
UNITED ARAB EMIRATES	DIRHAM	...	...	4.762	3.961	3.953
VIET-NAM Ø	DONG	...	...	...	...	...
YEMEN	RIAL	...	...	5.456	4.566	4.563
EUROPE						
ALBANIA Δ	LEK	5.00	5.00	5.00	4.10	4.10
AUSTRIA	SCHILLING	26.00	26.00	26.00	17.417	17.94
BELGIUM	FRANC	50.00	50.00	50.00	36.779	38.605
BULGARIA Δ	LEV	1.17	1.17	1.17	0.97	0.97
CZECHOSLOVAKIA Δ	KORUNA	...	...	...	11.66	11.40
DENMARK	KRONE	69.07	6.907	7.50	5.746	6.045
FINLAND	MARKKA	3.20	3.20	4.20	3.679	3.864
FRANCE	FRANC	4.937	4.937	5.554	4.286	4.779
GERMAN DEMOCRATIC REPUBLIC	DDR MARK	...	...	...	2.55	2.40
GERMANY, FEDERAL REPUBLIC OF	DEUTSCHE MARK	4.20	4.00	3.66	2.46	2.518
GREECE	DRACHMA	30.00	30.00	30.00	32.051	36.518
HUNGARY	FORINT	...	...	60.00	43.971	41.575
ICELAND	KRONA	0.344	0.43	0.88	1.537	1.822
IRELAND	POUND	0.357	0.357	0.417	0.452	0.557
ITALY	LIRA	623.99	625.00	625.00	652.85	832.34
LIECHTENSTEIN	SWISS FRANC	4.373	4.373	4.373	2.581	2.50
LUXEMBOURG	FRANC	50.00	50.00	50.00	36.779	38.605
MALTA	LIRA	0.357	0.357	0.417	0.385	0.425
MONACO	FRENCH FRANC	4.937	4.937	5.554	4.286	4.779
NETHERLANDS	GUILDER	3.80	3.62	3.62	2.529	2.644
NORWAY	KRONE	7.143	7.143	7.143	5.227	5.457
POLAND Δ	ZLOTY	...	...	...	19.92	19.92
PORTUGAL	ESCUDO	28.75	28.75	28.75	25.553	30.229
ROMANIA	LEU	6.00	6.00	6.00	20.00	20.00
SAN MARINO	LIRA	625.00	625.00	625.00	652.85	832.34
SPAIN	PESETA	60.00	60.00	70.00	57.407	66.903
SWEDEN	KRONA	5.173	5.173	5.173	4.152	4.355
SWITZERLAND	FRANC	4.373	4.373	4.373	2.581	2.50
UNITED KINGDOM	POUND STERLING	0.357	0.357	0.417	0.452	0.557
YUGOSLAVIA	DINAR	3.00	6.958	12.50	17.344	18.178
OCEANIA						
AUSTRALIA	DOLLAR	0.893	0.893	0.893	0.764	0.818
FIJI	DOLLAR	0.793	0.793	0.871	0.824	0.897
FRENCH POLYNESIA	FRANC C.F.P.	89.77	89.77	101.01	77.82	86.88
NEW CALEDONIA	FRANC C.F.P.	89.77	89.77	101.01	77.82	86.88
NEW ZEALAND	DOLLAR	0.714	0.719	0.893	0.833	1.005
PAPUA NEW GUINEA	KINA	0.893	0.893	0.893	0.764	0.793
SAMOA	TALA	0.714	0.719	0.721	0.633	0.795
TONGA	PA'ANGA	0.89	0.89	0.89	0.76	0.82
VANUATU	VATU	...	...	...	...	...
U.S.S.R.						
U.S.S.R. Δ	ROUBLE	0.90	0.90	0.90	0.75	0.75
BYELORUSSIAN S.S.R. Δ	ROUBLE	0.90	0.90	0.90	0.75	0.75
UKRAINIAN S.S.R. Δ	ROUBLE	0.90	0.90	0.90	0.75	0.75

NATIONAL CURRENCY PER UNITED STATES DOLLAR
VALEUR DU DOLLAR DES ETATS-UNIS EN MONNAIE NATIONALE
VALOR DEL DOLAR DE LOS ESTADOS UNIDOS EN MONEDA NACIONAL

1977	1978	1979	1980	1981	1982	1983	1984	1985
3.525	3.40	3.361	3.326	3.383	3.427	3.455	3.524	3.622
2.439	2.274	2.175	2.141	2.113	2.14	2.113	2.133	2.200
8.873	15.611	15.572	16.534	19.246	20.812	23.529	25.438	27.163
3.925	3.925	3.925	3.925	3.925	3.925	3.925	3.925	3.925
20.40	20.336	20.419	20.476	21.82	23.00	23.00	23.639	27.159
18.002	24.282	31.078	76.038	111.219	162.553	225.457	366.678	521.983
3.903	3.871	3.815	3.707	3.671	3.671	3.671	3.671	3.671
...	...	2.022	2.088	9.045	9.757	10.018	...	...
4.563	4.563	4.563	4.563	4.563	4.563	4.578	5.353	6.414
4.10	7.60	7.00	7.00	7.00	7.00	7.00	7.00	...
16.527	14.522	13.368	12.938	15.927	17.059	17.963	20.009	20.689
35.843	31.492	29.319	29.242	37.129	45.691	51.132	57.784	59.378
0.97	0.88	0.88	0.85	0.85	0.85	0.98	0.98	...
11.24	10.64	10.44	10.94	11.94	12.44	12.84	12.11	...
6.003	5.515	5.261	5.636	7.123	8.332	9.145	10.357	10.596
4.029	4.117	3.895	3.73	4.315	4.82	5.57	6.01	6.198
4.914	4.513	4.254	4.226	5.435	6.572	7.621	8.739	8.985
2.25	1.90	1.74	1.95	2.20	2.50	2.70	3.05	...
2.322	2.009	1.833	1.818	2.26	2.427	2.553	2.846	2.944
36.838	36.745	37.038	42.617	55.408	66.803	88.064	112.717	138.119
40.961	37.911	35.578	32.532	34.314	36.631	42.671	48.042	50.119
1.989	2.711	3.526	4.798	7.224	12.352	24.843	31.694	41.508
0.573	0.522	0.489	0.487	0.621	0.705	0.805	0.923	0.946
882.39	848.66	830.86	856.45	1136.77	1352.51	1518.85	1756.96	1909.44
2.404	1.788	1.663	1.676	1.964	2.03	2.099	2.35	2.457
35.843	31.492	29.319	29.242	37.129	45.691	51.132	57.784	59.378
0.422	0.385	0.358	0.345	0.387	0.412	0.432	0.461	0.469
4.914	4.513	4.254	4.226	5.435	6.572	7.621	8.739	8.985
2.454	2.164	2.006	1.988	2.495	2.67	2.854	3.209	3.321
5.324	5.242	5.064	4.939	5.74	6.454	7.296	8.161	8.597
19.92	33.20	33.20	33.20	33.20	88.00	95.00	122.00	...
38.278	43.937	48.923	50.062	61.546	79.473	110.78	146.39	170.395
20.00	18.36	18.00	18.00	15.00	15.00	17.129	21.28	17.141
882.39	848.66	830.86	856.45	1136.77	1352.51	1518.85	1756.96	1909.44
75.962	76.667	67.125	71.702	92.32	109.859	143.30	160.761	170.044
4.482	4.518	4.287	4.23	5.063	6.283	7.667	8.272	8.604
2.404	1.788	1.663	1.676	1.964	2.03	2.099	2.35	2.457
0.573	0.522	0.472	0.43	0.498	0.572	0.66	0.752	0.779
18.289	18.637	18.973	24.639	34.966	50.276	92.839	152.822	270.163
0.901	0.874	0.895	0.878	0.87	0.986	1.11	1.139	1.432
0.917	0.847	0.836	0.818	0.855	0.932	1.017	1.083	1.153
89.37	81.90	77.28	76.75	98.23	118.76	138.57	158.89	163.373
89.37	81.90	77.28	76.75	98.23	118.76	138.57	158.89	163.37
1.03	0.964	0.979	1.027	1.153	1.333	1.497	1.764	2.023
0.791	0.709	0.712	0.671	0.673	0.738	0.836	0.899	1.004
0.786	0.736	0.826	0.919	1.034	1.207	1.549	1.862	2.245
0.90	...	...	...	...	...	1.11	1.139	1.432
...	...	...	...	...	...	99.368	99.233	106.032
0.72	0.66	0.65	0.66	0.72	0.73	0.766	0.85	...
0.72	0.66	0.65	0.66	0.72	0.73	0.766	0.850	...
0.72	0.66	0.65	0.66	0.72	0.73	0.766	0.850	...

AFRICA:
Equatorial Guinea:
E--> Prior to 1985, the national currency refers to the Ekuele.
FR-> Avant 1985, la monnaie nationale se réfère à l'Ekuelé.
ESP> Antes de 1985, la moneda nacional se refiere al Ekuelé.
Mali:
E--> The C.F.A. Franc was introduced in August, 1984.
FR-> Le Franc C.F.A. a été introduit en Août 1984.
ESP> El 'Franc C.F.A.' fue introducido en Agosto de 1984.

AMERICA, SOUTH:
Argentina:
E--> Prior to 1975, exchange rates refer to the *old peso*. (1 new peso = 10,000 old pesos).
FR-> Avant 1975, les cours des changes se rapportent à l'*ancien peso*. (1 nouveau peso = 10 000 anciens pesos).
ESP> Antes de 1975, los tipos de cambio se refieren al *antiguo peso*. (1 nuevo peso = 10 000 antiguos pesos).

D Selected list of Unesco statistical publications

Liste sélective d'ouvrages statistiques publiés par l'Unesco

Lista selectiva de obras de estadísticas publicadas por la Unesco

THIS APPENDIX IS IN THREE SECTIONS PRESENTING RESPECTIVELY SELECTIVE LISTS OF STATISTICAL PUBLICATIONS IN ENGLISH, FRENCH AND SPANISH. THUS, THOSE PUBLICATIONS IN THE THREE LANGUAGES ARE SHOWN IN EACH LIST WHILST WORKS AVAILABLE IN ONLY A SPECIFIC LANGUAGE ARE SHOWN IN THE RELEVANT SECTION. THOSE PUBLISHED IN A BILINGUAL, TRILINGUAL OR MULTILINGUAL VERSION ARE INDICATED ACCORDINGLY IN THE APPROPRIATE LISTS. WORKS PUBLISHED IN ARABIC OR RUSSIAN ARE ALSO LISTED, APPROPRIATELY INDICATED. PUBLICATIONS PRIOR TO 1980 ARE NOT SHOWN IN THIS LIST. READERS SHOULD CONTACT THE OFFICE OF STATISTICS FOR FURTHER INFORMATIONS CONCERNING THESE PUBLICATIONS.

- -

CETTE ANNEXE EST PRESENTEE EN TROIS PARTIES (PUBLICATIONS EN ANGLAIS, EN FRANCAIS ET EN ESPAGNOL) OU SONT INDIQUES LES OUVRAGES STATISTIQUES PUBLIES DANS LA LANGUE CORRESPONDANTE. LES PUBLICATIONS PARUES EN ANGLAIS, FRANCAIS ET ESPAGNOL FIGURENT PAR CONSEQUENT DANS LES TROIS PARTIES. CELLES QUI NE SONT PAS PUBLIEES DANS LES TROIS LANGUES, SE TROUVENT SEULEMENT DANS LES PARTIES CONCERNEES. SI UNE PUBLICATION EST EN VERSION BILINGUE, TRILINGUE OU POLYGLOTTE, LE FAIT EST INDIQUE DANS LES LISTES APPROPRIEES. LES OUVRAGES PARUS EN RUSSE ET EN ARABE SONT EGALEMENT MENTIONNES. LES PUBLICATIONS ANTERIEURES A 1980 NE SONT PAS PRESENTEES DANS CETTE LISTE. POUR PLUS D'INFORMATIONS SUR CES DOCUMENTS,LE LECTEUR EST PRIE DE CONTACTER L'OFFICE DES STATISTIQUES DE L'UNESCO

- -

ESTE ANEXO SE PRESENTA EN TRES PARTES (PUBLICACIONES EN INGLES, EN FRANCES Y EN ESPAÑOL) EN LAS QUE SE INDICAN LAS OBRAS ESTADISTICAS PUBLICADAS EN EL IDIOMA CORRESPONDIENTE. LAS PUBLICACIONES APARECIDAS EN INGLES, FRANCES Y ESPAÑOL FIGURAN POR CONSIGUIENTE EN LAS TRES PARTES; LAS QUE NO SE PUBLICAN EN LAS TRES LENGUAS SOLO SE ENCUENTRAN EN LAS PARTES QUE LAS ATANEN. CUANDO UNA PUBLICACION ES BILINGUE, TRILINGUE O PLURILINGUE, SE DA LA DEBIDA INDICACION EN LAS LENGUAS APROPIADAS. TAMBIEN SE SENALAN LAS OBRAS APARECIDAS EN RUSO Y EN ARABE.
LAS PUBLICACIONES ANTERIOR A 1980 NO ESTAN INCLUIDAS EN ESTA LISTA. PARA MAYOR INFORMACION SOBRE DICHOS DOCUMENTOS, SE SUPLICA AL LECTOR EL CONTACTAR LA OFICINA DE ESTADISTICA DE LA UNESCO.

IDENTIFICATION	TITLE	PUBLISHED IN	AVAILABILITY/ PRICE
ISBN 92-3-002351-5	UNESCO STATISTICAL YEARBOOK, 1985 TRILINGUAL: ENGLISH/FRENCH/SPANISH - PUBLISHED ANNUALLY FROM 1963 TO 1985	1985	FF 350
	STATISTICS ON SCIENCE AND TECHNOLOGY PUBLISHED ANNUALLY SINCE 1984. TRILINGUAL: ENGLISH/ FRENCH/ SPANISH	1985	ON REQUEST
	STATISTICAL REPORTS AND STUDIES		
NO. 23	STATISTICS ON RADIO AND TELEVISION, 1960-1976	1979	FF 14
NO. 24	ANALYZING AND PROJECTING SCHOOL ENROLMENT IN DEVELOPING COUNTRIES - A MANUAL OF METHODOLOGY (ALSO PUBLISHED IN FRENCH)	1981	FF 16
NO. 25	STATISTICS ON FILM AND CINEMA, 1955-1977	1981	FF 10
NO. 26	AN INTERNATIONAL SURVEY OF BOOK PRODUCTION DURING THE LAST DECADES	1982	FF 14
NO. 27	STATISTICS OF STUDENTS ABROAD, 1974-1978 BILINGUAL: ENGLISH/FRENCH	1982	FF 32
NO. 28	INTERNATIONAL FLOWS OF SELECTED CULTURAL GOODS	1986	FF 32
	CURRENT SURVEYS AND RESEARCH IN STATISTICS (CSR)		
CSR-S-8	STATISTICS ON SCIENCE AND TECHNOLOGY - LATEST AVAILABLE DATA TRILINGUAL: ENGLISH/FRENCH/SPANISH	1980	ON REQUEST
CSR-S-9	PARTICIPATION OF WOMEN IN R&D - A STATISTICAL STUDY (ALSO PUBLISHED IN FRENCH AND SPANISH)	1980	ON REQUEST
CSR-S-10	STATISTICS ON SCIENCE AND TECHNOLOGY - LATEST AVAILABLE DATA TRILINGUAL: ENGLISH/FRENCH/SPANISH	1980	ON REQUEST
CSR-S-11	STATISTICS ON SCIENCE AND TECHNOLOGY - LATEST AVAILABLE DATA TRILINGUAL: ENGLISH/FRENCH/SPANISH	1981	ON REQUEST
CSR-S-12	HUMAN AND FINANCIAL RESOURCES FOR RESEARCH AND EXPERIMENTAL DEVELOPMENT IN THE PRODUCTIVE SECTOR (ALSO PUBLISHED IN FRENCH AND SPANISH)	1982	ON REQUEST
CSR-S-13	TRENDS IN HUMAN AND FINANCIAL RESOURCES FOR RESEARCH AND EXPERIMENTAL DEVELOPMENT TRILINGUAL: ENGLISH/FRENCH/SPANISH	1982	ON REQUEST
CSR-S-14	STATISTICS ON SCIENCE AND TECHNOLOGY - LATEST AVAILABLE DATA. TRILINGUAL: ENGLISH/FRENCH/SPANISH	1982	ON REQUEST
CSR-S-15	PROPOSALS FOR A METHODOLOGY OF DATA COLLECTION ON SCIENTIFIC AND TECHNOLOGICAL EDUCATION AND TRAINING AT THE THIRD LEVEL. (ALSO PUBLISHED IN FRENCH AND SPANISH)	1983	ON REQUEST
CSR-S-16	HUMAN AND FINANCIAL RESOURCES FOR RESEARCH AND EXPERIMENTAL DEVELOPMENT IN AGRICULTURE (ALSO PUBLISHED IN FRENCH AND SPANISH)	1983	ON REQUEST
CSR-S-17	ESTIMATED WORLD RESOURCES FOR RESEARCH AND EXPERIMENTAL DEVELOPMENT 1970-1980 (ALSO PUBLISHED IN FRENCH AND SPANISH)	1984	ON REQUEST
CSR-S-19	ESTIMATED OF POTENTIAL QUALIFIED GRADUATES FROM HIGHER EDUCATION (ALSO PUBLISHED IN FRENCH AND SPANISH)	1985	ON REQUEST
CSR-S-20	SCIENCE AND TECHNOLOGY FOR DEVELOPMENT: SCANDINAVIAN EFFORTS TO FOSTER DEVELOPMENT RESEARCH AND TRANSFER RESOURCES FOR RESEARCH AND EXPERIMENTAL DEVELOPMENT TO DEVELOPING COUNTRIES (IN ENGLISH ONLY)	1985	ON REQUEST
CSR-S-21	INTEGRATED APPROACH TO INDICATORS FOR SCIENCE AND TECHNOLOGY (ALSO PUBLISHED IN FRENCH AND SPANISH)	1986	ON REQUEST

IDENTIFICATION	TITLE	PUBLISHED IN	AVAILABILITY/ PRICE
CSR-E-34	GUIDELINES FOR THE COLLECTION OF STATISTICS ON LITERACY PROGRAMMES (PRELIMINARY MANUAL) (ALSO PUBLISHED IN FRENCH AND SPANISH)	1979	ON REQUEST
CSR-E-35	THE ALLOCATION OF RESOURCES TO EDUCATION THROUGHOUT THE WORLD (ALSO PUBLISHED IN FRENCH AND SPANISH)	1980	ON REQUEST
CSR-E-36	COMPARATIVE ANALYSIS OF MALE AND FEMALE SCHOOL ENROLMENT AND ILLITERACY (ALSO PUBLISHED IN FRENCH AND SPANISH)	1980	ON REQUEST
CSR-E-37	WASTAGE IN PRIMARY AND GENERAL SECONDARY EDUCATION: A STATISTICAL STUDY OF TRENDS AND PATTERNS IN REPETITION AND DROPOUT (ALSO PUBLISHED IN FRENCH)	1980	ON REQUEST
CSR-E-38	ISCED HANDBOOK: UNION OF SOVIET SOCIALIST REPUBLICS (RUSSIAN ONLY)	1980	ON REQUEST
CSR-E-39	WORLD SCHOOL-AGE POPULATION UNTIL YEAR 2000: SOME IMPLICATIONS FOR THE EDUCATION SECTOR (ALSO PUBLISHED IN FRENCH)	1981	ON REQUEST
CSR-E-40	STATISTICAL METHODS FOR IMPROVING THE ESTIMATION OF REPETITION AND DROP-OUT. TWO METHODOLOGICAL STUDIES (IN ENGLISH ONLY)	1981	ON REQUEST
CSR-E-42	DEVELOPMENT OF EDUCATION IN THE LEAST DEVELOPED COUNTRIES SINCE 1970: A STATISTICAL STUDY (ALSO PUBLISHED IN FRENCH)	1983	ON REQUEST
CSR-E-44	STATISTICS OF EDUCATIONAL ATTAINMENT AND ILLITERACY 1970-1980. TRILINGUAL: ENGLISH/FRENCH/SPANISH	1983	ON REQUEST
CSR-E-46	TRENDS AND PROJECTIONS OF ENROLMENT BY LEVEL OF EDUCATION AND BY AGE, 1960-2000 (AS ASSESSED IN 1982) (IN ENGLISH ONLY)	1983	ON REQUEST
CSR-E-47	TECHNICAL AND VOCATIONAL EDUCATION IN THE WORLD 1970-1980 STATISTICAL REPORT. (ALSO PUBLISHED IN FRENCH)	1983	ON REQUEST
CSR-E-50	FEMALE PARTICIPATION IN HIGHER EDUCATION. ENROLMENT TRENDS, 1975-1982. (ALSO PUBLISHED IN FRENCH)	1985	ON REQUEST
CSR-E-51	ISCED HANDBOOK: KINGDOM OF SAUDI ARABIA. (IN ENGLISH ONLY)	1985	ON REQUEST
CSR-E-52	METHODOLOGICAL AND PRACTICAL GUIDE TO FORMULATING AN ECONOMIC ACCOUNTING SYSTEM FOR EDUCATION SECTOR (ALSO PUBLISHED IN FRENCH)	1986	ON REQUEST
CSR-E-53	EDUCATIONAL STATISTICS- LATEST YEAR AVAILABLE TRILINGUAL: ENGLISH/ FRENCH/ SPANISH	1986	ON REQUEST
CSR-C-1	CULTURAL PAPER: CONSUMPTION, PRODUCTION AND SELF-SUFFICIENCY FOR THE WORLD REGIONS (IN ENGLISH ONLY)	1978	ON REQUEST
CSR-C-2	PRELIMINARY STUDY ON THE SCOPE AND COVERAGE OF A FRAMEWORK FOR CULTURAL STATISTICS (IN ENGLISH ONLY)	1981	ON REQUEST
CSR-C-3	REPORT OF SECOND JOINT UNESCO/ECE MEETING ON CULTURAL STATISTICS (IN ENGLISH ONLY)	1981	ON REQUEST
CSR-C-5	CULTURAL INDICATORS: THEORY AND PRACTICE (IN ENGLISH ONLY)	1981	ON REQUEST
CSR-C-10	INDICATORS OF CULTURAL DEVELOPMENT WITHIN THE EUROPEAN CONTEXT (IN ENGLISH ONLY)	1981	ON REQUEST
CSR-C-11	FROM CULTURAL STATISTICS TO INDICATORS: STRUCTURE AND METHODS (IN ENGLISH ONLY)	1981	ON REQUEST
CSR-C-12	REPORT ON THE INTERNATIONAL PILOT SURVEY ON STATISTICS OF ARCHIVAL INSTITUTIONS AND RECORDS CENTRES (IN ENGLISH ONLY)	1981	ON REQUEST
CSR-C-13	MODEL OF SURVEY ON ACCESS TO CULTURAL RESOURCES AND ON PARTICIPATION IN CULTURAL ACTIVITIES (ALSO PUBLISHED IN FRENCH AND SPANISH)	1982	ON REQUEST

IDENTIFICATION	TITLE	PUBLISHED IN	AVAILABILITY/ PRICE
CSR-C-16	SOURCES OF STATISTICAL DATA ON THE 'LIVE' PERFORMANCE OF MUSIC (IN ENGLISH ONLY)	1981	ON REQUEST
CSR-C-18	REPORT OF THE MEETING OF EXPERTS ON STATISTICS AND INDICATORS OF CULTURE, VIENNA 1979. (IN ENGLISH ONLY)	1981	ON REQUEST
CSR-C-21	STATISTICS IN THE FIELD OF SOUND RECORDINGS (IN ENGLISH ONLY)	1981	ON REQUEST
CSR-C-22	METHODOLOGICAL STUDY ON STATISTICAL NEEDS IN THE FIELD OF THE PRESS (ALSO PUBLISHED IN FRENCH)	1982	ON REQUEST
CSR-C-27	CULTURAL STATISTICS AND CULTURAL DEVELOPMENT - A WORLD STATISTICAL SURVEY OF SOME MEDIA AS CULTURAL DEVELOPMENT SUPPORT - MONDIACULT (ALSO PUBLISHED IN FRENCH, SPANISH AND RUSSIAN)	1982	ON REQUEST
CSR-C-28	FIRST MEETING OF WORKING GROUP (FRAMEWORK GROUP) ON UNESCO FRAMEWORK FOR CULTURAL STATISTICS (FCS) (IN ENGLISH ONLY)	1982	ON REQUEST
CSR-C-29	SOME INTERNATIONAL EXCHANGE PATTERNS IN THE BOOK CULTURAL INDUSTRY (1965-1979) (IN ENGLISH ONLY)	1982	ON REQUEST
CSR-C-30	APPLICATIONS OF INDICATORS TO THE TASK OF CULTURAL PLANNING AT THE NATIONAL LEVEL (IN ENGLISH ONLY)	1982	ON REQUEST
CSR-C-33	MODEL SURVEY ON WOMEN'S ACCESS TO AND PARTICIPATION IN CULTURAL LIFE (ALSO PUBLISHED IN FRENCH)	1982	ON REQUEST
CSR-C-36	SECOND MEETING OF WORKING GROUP (FRAMEWORK GROUP) ON UNESCO FRAMEWORK FOR CULTURAL STATISTICS (FCS) (IN ENGLISH ONLY)	1983	ON REQUEST
CSR-C-47	THE COLLECTION OF DATA ON SOCIO-CULTURAL ACTIVITIES. (ALSO PUBLISHED IN FRENCH)	1984	ON REQUEST
CSR-C-52	THIRD MEETING OF THE FRAMEWORK GROUP ON THE UNESCO FRAMEWORK FOR CULTURAL STATISTICS (FCS) (IN ENGLISH ONLY)	1984	ON REQUEST
CSR-C-55	CULTURAL INDICATORS PROJECT (INDICATORS LINKED TO FCS) (ALSO PUBLISHED IN SPANISH)	1985	ON REQUEST
CSR-C-63	FOURTH MEETING OF THE FRAMEWORK GROUP ON THE UNESCO FRAMEWORK FOR CULTURAL STATISTICS (FCS) (ALSO PUBLISHED IN FRENCH)	1985	ON REQUEST
	ALSO PUBLISHED IN THE CSR-C SERIES AND AVAILABLE UPON REQUEST ARE: A) REPORT OF MEETINGS OF THE JOINT STUDY GROUPS ON THE DIFFERENT CULTURAL CATEGORIES OF THE FRAMEWORK FOR CULTURAL STATISTICS (FCS); AND B) REPERTORIES OF AVAILABLITY OF STATISTICS ON SELECTED FCS CATEGORIES IN INDIVIDUAL COUNTRIES AND REPORTS ON THE RESULTS OF TESTING THEIR APLICABILITY.		
	ANNOTATED ACCESSIONS LISTS OF STUDIES AND REPORTS IN THE FIELD OF SCIENCE STATISTICS		
NO. 15	ST.80/WS/23, OCTOBER 1980 (ALSO PUBLISHED IN FRENCH AND SPANISH)	1980	ON REQUEST
NO. 16	ST.81/WS/12, SEPTEMBER 1981 (ALSO PUBLISHED IN FRENCH AND SPANISH)	1981	ON REQUEST
NO. 17	ST.82/WS/21, SEPTEMBER 1982 (ALSO PUBLISHED IN FRENCH AND SPANISH)	1982	ON REQUEST
NO. 18	ST.84/WS/1, FEBRUARY 1984 (ALSO PUBLISHED IN FRENCH AND SPANISH)	1984	ON REQUEST
NO. 19	ST/84/WS/20, NOVEMBER 1984 (ALSO PUBLISHED IN FRENCH AND SPANISH)	1984	ON REQUEST
NO. 20	ST/85/WS/15, DECEMBER 1985 (ALSO PUBLISHED IN FRENCH AND SPANISH)	1985	ON REQUEST

Selected list of Unesco statistical publications
Liste sélective d'ouvrages statistiques publiés par l'Unesco
Lista selectiva de obras de estadísticas publicadas por la Unesco

IDENTIFICATION	TITLE	PUBLISHED IN	AVAILABILITY/ PRICE
	INTERNATIONAL RECOMMENDATIONS AND CLASSIFICATIONS		
	RECOMMENDATION CONCERNING THE INTERNATIONAL STANDARDIZATION OF STATISTICS RELATING TO BOOK PRODUCTION AND PERIODICALS ADOPTED BY THE GENERAL CONFERENCE AT ITS THIRTEENTH SESSION, PARIS, 19 NOVEMBER 1964 MULTILINGUAL: ENGLISH/FRENCH/SPANISH/RUSSIAN	1964	ON REQUEST
	RECOMMENDATION CONCERNING THE INTERNATIONAL STANDARDIZATION OF LIBRARY STATISTICS ADOPTED BY THE GENERAL CONFERENCE AT ITS SIXTEENTH SESSION, PARIS, 13 NOVEMBER 1970 MULTILINGUAL: ENGLISH/FRENCH/SPANISH/RUSSIAN	1970	ON REQUEST
	RECOMMENDATION CONCERNING THE INTERNATIONAL STANDARDIZATION OF STATISTICS ON RADIO AND TELEVISION ADOPTED BY THE GENERAL CONFERENCE AT ITS NINETEENTH SESSION, NAIROBI, 22 NOVEMBER 1976 MULTILINGUAL: ARABIC/ENGLISH/FRENCH/ SPANISH/RUSSIAN	1976	ON REQUEST
	REVISED RECOMMENDATION CONCERNING THE INTERNATIONAL STANDARDIZATION OF EDUCATIONAL STATISTICS, ADOPTED BY THE GENERAL CONFERENCE AT ITS TWENTIETH SESSION, PARIS, 27 NOVEMBER 1978 MULTILINGUAL: ARABIC/ ENGLISH/FRENCH/SPANISH/RUSSIAN	1978	ON REQUEST
	RECOMMENDATION CONCERNING THE INTERNATIONAL STANDARDIZATION OF STATISTICS ON SCIENCE AND TECHNOLOGY, ADOPTED BY THE GENERAL CONFERENCE OF UNESCO AT ITS TWENTIETH SESSION, PARIS, 27 NOVEMBER 1978 MULTILINGUAL: ARABIC/ ENGLISH/FRENCH/SPANISH/RUSSIAN	1978	ON REQUEST
	RECOMMENDATION CONCERNING THE INTERNATIONAL STANDARDIZATION OF STATISTICS ON THE PUBLIC FINANCING OF CULTURAL ACTIVITIES ADOPTED BY THE GENERAL CONFERENCE AT ITS TWENTY-FIRST SESSION, BELGRADE, 27 OCTOBER 1980 MULTILINGUAL: ARABIC/CHINESE/ENGLISH/FRENCH/ SPANISH/RUSSIAN	1980	ON REQUEST
	REVISED RECOMMENDATION CONCERNING THE INTERNATIONAL STANDARDIZATION OF STATISTICS ON THE PRODUCTION AND DISTRIBUTION OF BOOKS, NEWSPAPERS AND PERIODICALS ADOPTED BY THE GENERAL CONFERENCE AT ITS TWENTY-THIRD SESSION, SOFIA, 1ST NOVEMBER 1985		
ST.80/WS/18	NATIONAL STATISTICAL SYSTEMS FOR COLLECTION OF DATA ON SCIENTIFIC AND TECHNOLOGICAL ACTIVITIES IN THE COUNTRIES OF LATIN AMERICA, PART I - VENEZUELA, COLOMBIA, MEXICO AND CUBA (ALSO PUBLISHED IN FRENCH AND SPANISH)	1980	ON REQUEST
ST.80/WS/29	NATIONAL STATISTICAL SYSTEMS FOR COLLECTION OF DATA ON SCIENTIFIC AND TECHNOLOGICAL ACTIVITIES IN THE COUNTRIES OF LATIN AMERICA, PART II - BRAZIL AND PERU (ALSO PUBLISHED IN FRENCH AND SPANISH)	1980	ON REQUEST
ST.81/WS/14	NATIONAL STATISTICAL SYSTEMS FOR COLLECTION OF DATA ON SCIENTIFIC AND TECHNOLOGICAL ACTIVITIES IN THE COUNTRIES OF LATIN AMERICA. PART III - URUGUAY, ARGENTINA AND CHILE (ALSO PUBLISHED IN FRENCH AND SPANISH)	1981	ON REQUEST
ST-84/WS/12	MANUAL FOR STATISTICS ON SCIENTIFIC AND TECHNOLOGICAL ACTIVITIES (ALSO PUBLISHED IN ARABIC, FRENCH, SPANISH AND RUSSIAN)	1984	ON REQUEST
ST.84/WS/18	GUIDE TO STATISTICS ON SCIENTIFIC AND TECHNOLOGICAL INFORMATION AND DOCUMENTATION (STID), (PROVISIONAL) (ALSO PUBLISHED IN FRENCH AND SPANISH)	1984	ON REQUEST
ST.84/WS/19	GUIDE TO STATISTICS ON SCIENCE AND TECHNOLOGY (ALSO PUBLISHED IN ARABIC, FRENCH, SPANISH AND RUSSIAN)	1984	ON REQUEST
UNESCO:CES/ AC. 23/27	STANDARDIZATION AND INTERNATIONAL COMPARABILITY OF STATISTICS OF EDUCATION (ALSO PUBLISHED IN FRENCH AND RUSSIAN)	1982	ON REQUEST

IDENTIFICATION	TITLE	PUBLISHED IN	AVAILABILITY/ PRICE
UNESCO:CES/ AC. 23/28	SOCIAL INDICATORS IN THE FIELD OF EDUCATION (ALSO PUBLISHED IN FRENCH AND RUSSIAN)	1982	ON REQUEST
COM/ST/ISCED	INTERNATIONAL STANDARD CLASSIFICATION OF EDUCATION (ISCED) (ALSO PUBLISHED IN FRENCH, RUSSIAN AND SPANISH)	1976	ON REQUEST
ED/BIE/CONFIN- TED 35/REF. 8	ABRIDGED VERSION OF ISCED (ALSO PUBLISHED IN ARABIC, FRENCH, RUSSIAN AND SPANISH)	1975	ON REQUEST
	MISCELLANEOUS REPORTS AND DOCUMENTS		
ED/BIE/CONFINTED 39/REF. 1	A SUMMARY STATISTICAL REVIEW OF EDUCATION IN THE WORLD, 1960-1982 INTERNATIONAL CONFERENCE ON EDUCATION 39TH. SESSION, OCTOBER 1984 (ALSO PUBLISHED IN FRENCH AND SPANISH)	1984	ON REQUEST
ED-85/MINEDAP- REF. 2	DEVELOPMENT OF EDUCATION IN ASIA AND THE PACIFIC: A STATISTICAL REVIEW	1985	ON REQUEST
ED-80/MINED- EUROPE/REF. 2	DEVELOPMENT OF EDUCATION IN EUROPE: A STATISTICAL REVIEW (ALSO PUBLISHED IN FRENCH, SPANISH AND RUSSIAN)	1980	ON REQUEST
ED-82/MINEDAF/ REF. 2	DEVELOPMENT OF EDUCATION IN AFRICA: A STATISTICAL REVIEW (ALSO PUBLISHED IN FRENCH)	1982	ON REQUEST
ST/FIN/5	PUBLIC EXPENDITURE ON EDUCATION IN THE WORLD. REGIONAL AND COUNTRY TRENDS, 1970-1982. (ALSO PUBLISHED IN FRENCH)	1985	ON REQUEST
	STUDY ABROAD. INTERNATIONAL SCHOLARSHIPS AND COURSES (PUBLISHED BIENNIALLY) TRILINGUAL: ENGLISH/FRENCH/SPANISH (VOL. XXIV, 1983-84,1984-85,1985-86)	1983	FF 55

IDENTIFICATION	TITRE	PUBLIES EN	DISPONIBILITE/ PRIX
ISBN 92-3- 002351-5	ANNUAIRE STATISTIQUE DE L'UNESCO, 1985 TRILINGUE: ANGLAIS/FRANCAIS/ESPAGNOL - PUBLIE CHAQUE ANNEE DE 1963 A 1985	1985	FF 350
	STATISTIQUES RELATIVES A LA SCIENCE ET A LA TECHNOLOGIE PUBLIEES TOUS LES ANS DEPUIS 1984 TRILINGUE: ANGLAIS/ FRANCAIS/ ESPAGNOL	1985	SUR DEMANDE
	RAPPORTS ET ETUDES STATISTIQUES		
NO. 24	ANALYSE ET PROJECTION DES EFFECTIFS SCOLAIRES DANS LES PAYS EN DEVELOPPEMENT: MANUEL DE METHODOLOGIE (PUBLIE AUSSI EN ANGLAIS)	1982	FF 24
NO. 27	STATISTIQUES DES ETUDIANTS A L'ETRANGER 1974-1978 BILINGUE: ANGLAIS/FRANCAIS	1982	FF 32
	ENQUETES ET RECHERCHES STATISTIQUES		
	TRAVAUX EN COURS (CSR)		
CSR-S-8	STATISTIQUES RELATIVES AUX SCIENCES ET A LA TECHNOLOGIE - DERNIERES DONNEES DISPONIBLES TRILINGUE: ANGLAIS/FRANCAIS/ESPAGNOL	1980	SUR DEMANDE

IDENTIFICATION	TITRE	PUBLIES EN	DISPONIBILITE/ PRIX
CSR-S-9	LA PARTICIPATION DES FEMMES A LA RECHERCHE ET AU DEVELOPPEMENT EXPERIMENTAL (R-D) - ETUDE STATISTIQUE (PUBLIE AUSSI EN ANGLAIS ET EN ESPAGNOL)	1980	SUR DEMANDE
CSR-S-10	STATISTIQUES RELATIVES AUX SCIENCES ET A LA TECHNOLOGIE - DERNIERES DONNEES DISPONIBLES TRILINGUE: ANGLAIS/FRANCAIS/ESPAGNOL	1980	SUR DEMANDE
CSR-S-11	STATISTIQUES RELATIVES AUX SCIENCES ET A LA TECHNOLOGIE - DERNIERES DONNEES DISPONIBLES TRILINGUE: ANGLAIS/FRANCAIS/ESPAGNOL	1981	SUR DEMANDE
CSR-S-12	RESSOURCES HUMAINES ET FINANCIERES CONSACREES A LA RECHERCHE ET AU DEVELOPPEMENT EXPERIMENTAL DANS LE SECTEUR DE LA PRODUCTION (PUBLIE AUSSI EN ANGLAIS ET EN ESPAGNOL)	1982	SUR DEMANDE
CSR-S-13	TENDANCES DES RESSOURCES HUMAINES ET FINANCIERES CONSACREES A LA RECHERCHE ET AU DEVELOPPEMENT EXPERIMENTAL TRILINGUE: ANGLAIS/FRANCAIS/ESPAGNOL	1982	SUR DEMANDE
CSR-S-14	STATISTIQUES RELATIVES AUX SCIENCES ET A LA TECHNOLOGIE - DERNIERES DONNEES DISPONIBLES. TRILINGUE: ANGLAIS/FRANCAIS/ESPAGNOL	1982	SUR DEMANDE
CSR-S-15	PROPOSITIONS POUR UNE METHODE DE RASSEMBLEMENT DES DONNEES RELATIVES A L'ENSEIGNEMENT ET LA FORMATION SCIENTIFIQUE ET TECHNIQUE DU TROISIEME DEGRE (PUBLIE AUSSI EN ANGLAIS ET EN ESPAGNOL)	1983	SUR DEMANDE
CSR-S-16	RESSOURCES HUMAINES ET FINANCIERES CONSACREES A LA RECHERCHE ET AU DEVELOPPEMENT EXPERIMENTAL DANS L'AGRICULTURE (PUBLIE AUSSI EN ANGLAIS ET EN ESPAGNOL)	1983	SUR DEMANDE
CSR-S-17	ESTIMATIONS DES RESSOURCES MONDIALES CONSACREES A LA RECHERCHE ET AU DEVELOPPEMENT EXPERIMENTAL 1970-1980 (PUBLIE AUSSI EN ANGLAIS ET EN ESPAGNOL)	1984	SUR DEMANDE
CSR-S-19	ESTIMATION DES POTENTIELS QUALIFIES DIPLOMES DE L'ENSEIGNEMENT SUPERIEUR (PUBLIE AUSSI EN ANGLAIS ET EN ESPAGNOL)	1985	SUR DEMANDE
CSR-S-21	APPROCHE INTEGREE AUX INDICATEURS POUR LA SCIENCE ET LA TECHNOLOGIE (PUBLIE AUSSI EN ANGLAIS ET EN ESPAGNOL)	1986	SUR DEMANDE
CSR-E-35	L'ALLOCATION DES RESSOURCES A L'EDUCATION DANS LE MONDE (PUBLIE AUSSI EN ANGLAIS ET ESPAGNOL)	1979	SUR DEMANDE
CSR-E-36	ANALYSE COMPARATIVE DE LA SCOLARISATION ET DE L'ANALPHABETISME FEMININS ET MASCULINS (PUBLIE AUSSI EN ANGLAIS ET ESPAGNOL)	1980	EPUISE
CSR-E-37	LES DEPERDITIONS SCOLAIRES DANS L'ENSEIGNEMENT PRIMAIRE ET DANS L'ENSEIGNEMENT GENERAL DU SECOND DEGRE: ETUDE STATISTIQUE DE L'EVOLUTION ET DES PROFILS DU REDOUBLEMENT ET DE L'ABANDON (PUBLIE AUSSI EN ANGLAIS)	1982	SUR DEMANDE
CSR-E-38	GUIDE DE LA CLASSIFICATION INTERNATIONALE TYPE DE L'EDUCATION: UNION DES REPUBLIQUES SOCIALISTES SOVIETIQUES (EN RUSSE SEULEMENT)	1980	SUR DEMANDE
CSR-E-39	POPULATION MONDIALE D'AGE SCOLAIRE JUSQU'A L'AN 2000: INCIDENCES SUR LE SECTEUR DE L'EDUCATION (PUBLIE AUSSI EN ANGLAIS)	1982	SUR DEMANDE
CSR-E-42	DEVELOPPEMENT DE L'EDUCATION DANS LES PAYS LES MOINS AVANCES DEPUIS 1970: ETUDE STATISTIQUE (PUBLIE AUSSI EN ANGLAIS)	1982	SUR DEMANDE
CSR-E-44	STATISTIQUES SUR LE NIVEAU D'INSTRUCTION ET L'ANALPHABETISME, 1970-1980. TRILINGUE: ANGLAIS/FRANCAIS/ESPAGNOL	1983	SUR DEMANDE

IDENTIFICATION	TITRE	PUBLIES EN	DISPONIBILITE/ PRIX
CSR-E-47	L'ENSEIGNEMENT TECHNIQUE ET PROFESSIONNEL DANS LE MONDE 1970-1980. RAPPORT STATIS- TIQUE (PUBLIE AUSSI EN ANGLAIS)	1983	SUR DEMANDE
CSR-E-50	LA PARTICIPATION FEMININE DANS L'ENSEIGNEMENT SUPERIEUR. EVOLUTION DES EFFECTIFS, 1975-1982. (PUBLIE AUSSI EN ANGLAIS)	1985	SUR DEMANDE
CSR-E-52	GUIDE METHODOLOGIQUE ET PRATIQUE POUR L'ELABORATION D'UNE COMPTABILITE ECONOMIQUE DE L'EDUCATION (PUBLIE AUSSI EN ANGLAIS)	1986	SUR DEMANDE
CSR-E-53	STATISTIQUES SCOLAIRES- DERNIERE ANNEE DISPONIBLE. TRILINGUE: ANGLAIS/ FRANCAIS/ ESPAGNOL	1986	SUR DEMANDE
CSR-C-13	MODELE D'ENQUETE SUR L'ACCES AUX RESSOURCES CULTURELLES ET SUR LA PARTICIPATION AUX ACTIVITES CULTURELLES (PUBLIE AUSSI EN ANGLAIS ET EN ESPAGNOL)	1982	SUR DEMANDE
CSR-C-22	ETUDE METHODOLOGIQUE SUR LES BESOINS STATISTIQUES DANS LE DOMAINE DE LA PRESSE (PUBLIE AUSSI EN ANGLAIS)	1981	SUR DEMANDE
CSR-C-27	STATISTIQUES CULTURELLES ET DEVELOPPEMENT CULTUREL - ETUDE STATISTIQUE MONDIALE SUR QUELQUES MEDIAS COMME SUPPORT DU DEVELOPPEMENT CULTUREL - MONDIACULT (PUBLIE AUSSI EN ANGLAIS, ESPAGNOL ET RUSSE)	1982	SUR DEMANDE
CSR-C-33	MODELE D'ENQUETE SUR L'ACCES ET LA PARTICIPATION DES FEMMES A LA VIE CULTURELLE (PUBLIE AUSSI EN ANGLAIS)	1982	SUR DEMANDE
CSR-C-39	STATUT DES LANGUES ET LANGUES D'ENSEIGNEMENT DANS LES ETATS MEMBRES DE L'UNESCO (EN FRAN- CAIS SEULEMENT)	1983	SUR DEMANDE
CSR-C-47	LA COLLECTE DES DONNEES DES ACTIVITES SOCIO- CULTURELLES (PUBLIE AUSSI EN ANGLAIS)	1984	SUR DEMANDE
CSR-C-63	QUATRIEME REUNION DU GROUPE CADRE SUR LE CADRE DE L'UNESCO POUR LES STATISTIQUES CULTURELLES (FSC). (PUBLIE AUSSI EN ANGLAIS)	1985	SUR DEMANDE
	SONT EGALEMENT PUBLIES DANS LA SERIE DES CSR-C ET DISPONIBLES SUR DEMANDE: A) LES RAPPORTS SUR LES REUNIONS DU GROUPE D'ETUDES EN COMMUN SUR LES DIFFERENTES CATEGORIES CULTURELLES DU CADRE POUR LES STATISTIQUES CULTURELLES (FCS); ET B) LES REPERTOIRES SUR LES STATISTIQUES DE CATEGORIES CHOISIES DE LA FCS DISPONIBLES DANS CERTAINS PAYS AINSI QUE DES RAPPORTS SUR LES RESULTATS DES TESTS DE LEUR APPLICATION		
	LISTE ANNOTEE DES ACQUISITIONS NOUVELLES: ETUDES ET RAPPORTS CONCERNANT LES STATISTIQUES RELATIVES AUX SCIENCES		
NO. 15	ST.80/WS/23, OCTOBRE 1980 (PUBLIE AUSSI EN ANGLAIS ET EN ESPAGNOL)	1980	SUR DEMANDE
NO. 16	ST.81/WS/12, SEPTEMBRE 1981 (PUBLIE AUSSI EN ANGLAIS ET EN ESPAGNOL)	1981	SUR DEMANDE
NO. 17	ST.82/WS/21, SEPTEMBRE 1982 (PUBLIE AUSSI EN ANGLAIS ET EN ESPAGNOL)	1982	SUR DEMANDE
NO. 18	ST.84/WS/1, FEVRIER 1984 (PUBLIE AUSSI EN ANGLAIS ET EN ESPAGNOL)	1984	SUR DEMANDE
NO. 19	ST.84/WS/19, NOVEMBRE 1984 (PUBLIE AUSSI EN ANGLAIS ET EN ESPAGNOL)	1984	SUR DEMANDE
NO. 20	ST/85/WS/15, DECEMBER 1985 (PUBLIE AUSSI EN ANGLAIS ET EN ESPAGNOL)	1985	SUR DEMANDE

IDENTIFICATION	TITRE	PUBLIES EN	DISPONIBILITE/ PRIX
	RECOMMANDATIONS ET CLASSIFICATIONS INTERNATIONALES		
	RECOMMANDATION CONCERNANT LA NORMALISATION INTERNATIONALE DES STATISTIQUES DE L'EDITION DE LIVRES ET DE PERIODIQUES ADOPTEE PAR LA CONFERENCE GENERALE A SA TREIZIEME SESSION, PARIS, 19 NOVEMBRE 1964 POLYGLOTTE: ANGLAIS/FRANCAIS/ESPAGNOL/RUSSE	1964	SUR DEMANDE
	RECOMMANDATION CONCERNANT LA NORMALISATION INTERNATIONALE DES STATISTIQUES RELATIVES AUX BIBLIOTHEQUES ADOPTEE PAR LA CONFERENCE GENE-RALE A SA SEIZIEME SESSION, PARIS, LE 13 NOVEMBRE 1970 POLYGLOTTE: ANGLAIS/FRANCAIS/ESPAGNOL/RUSSE	1970	SUR DEMANDE
	RECOMMANDATION CONCERNANT LA NORMALISATION INTERNATIONALE DES STATISTIQUES RELATIVES A LA RADIO ET A LA TELEVISION, ADOPTEE PAR LA CONFERENCE GENERALE A SA DIX-NEUVIEME SESSION, NAIROBI, 22 NOVEMBRE 1976 POLYGLOTTE: ANGLAIS/ARABE/FRANCAIS/ESPAGNOL/ RUSSE	1976	SUR DEMANDE
	RECOMMANDATION REVISEE CONCERNANT LA NORMALISA-TION INTERNATIONALE DES STATISTIQUES DE L'EDU-CATION, ADOPTEE PAR LA CONFERENCE GENERALE A SA VINGTIEME SESSION, PARIS, 27 NOVEMBRE 1978 POLYGLOTTE: ANGLAIS/ARABE/FRANCAIS/ESPAGNOL/ RUSSE	1978	SUR DEMANDE
	RECOMMANDATION CONCERNANT LA NORMALISATION INTERNATIONALE DES STATISTIQUES RELATIVES A LA SCIENCE ET A LA TECHNOLOGIE, ADOPTEE PAR LA CONFERENCE GENERALE A SA VINGTIEME SESSION, PARIS, 27 NOVEMBRE 1978 POLYGLOTTE: ANGLAIS/ARABE/ESPAGNOL/FRANCAIS/ RUSSE	1978	SUR DEMANDE
	RECOMMANDATION CONCERNANT LA NORMALISATION INTERNATIONALE DES STATISTIQUES RELATIVES AU FINANCEMENT PUBLIC DES ACTIVITES CULTURELLES, ADOPTEE PAR LA CONFERENCE GENERALE A SA VINGT ET UNIEME SESSION, BELGRADE, 27 OCTOBRE 1980 POLYGLOTTE: ANGLAIS/ARABE/ESPAGNOL/FRANCAIS RUSSE/CHINOIS	1980	SUR DEMANDE
	RECOMMANDATION REVISEE CONCERNANT LA NORMALISATION INTERNATIONALE DES STATISTIQUES RELATIVES A LA PRODUCTION ET A LA DISTRIBUTION DE LIVRES, DE JOURNAUX ET DE PERIODIQUES, ADOPTEE PAR LA CONFERENCE GENERALE A SA VINGT-TROISIEME SESSION, SOFIA, 1ER NOVEMBRE 1985	1985	SUR DEMANDE
ST.80/WS/18	LES SYSTEMES STATISTIQUES NATIONAUX DE COLLECTE DE DONNEES SUR L'ACTIVITE SCIENTIFIQUE ET TECHNIQUE DANS LES PAYS D'AMERIQUE LATINE PARTIE I - VENEZUELA, COLOMBIE, MEXIQUE ET CUBA (PUBLIE AUSSI EN ANGLAIS ET EN ESPAGNOL)	1980	SUR DEMANDE
ST.80/WS/29	LES SYTEMES STATISTIQUES NATIONAUX DE COLLECTE DE DONNEES SUR L'ACTIVITE SCIENTIFIQUE ET TECHNIQUE DANS LES PAYS D'AMERIQUE LATINE, PARTIE II BRESIL ET PEROU (PUBLIE AUSSI EN ANGLAIS ET EN ESPAGNOL)	1980	SUR DEMANDE
ST.81/WS/14	LES SYSTEMES STATISTIQUES NATIONAUX DE COLLECTE DE DONNEES SUR L'ACTIVITE SCIEN-TIFIQUE ET TECHNIQUE DANS LES PAYS D'AMERIQUE LATINE. PARTIE III - URUGUAY, ARGENTINE ET CHILI (PUBLIE AUSSI EN ANGLAIS ET EN ESPAGNOL)	1981	SUR DEMANDE
ST.84/WS/12	MANUEL POUR LES STATISTIQUES RELATIVES AUX ACTIVITES SCIENTIFIQUES ET TECHNIQUES (PUBLIE AUSSI EN ANGLAIS, ARABE, ESPAGNOL ET RUSSE)	1984	SUR DEMANDE
ST.84/WS/18	GUIDE DES STATISTIQUES RELATIVES A L'INFORMATION ET A LA DOCUMENTATION SCIENTIFIQUES ET TECHNIQUES (IDST) (VERSION PROVISOIRE) (PUBLIE AUSSI EN ANGLAIS ET EN ESPAGNOL)	1984	SUR DEMANDE

IDENTIFICATION	TITRE	PUBLIES EN	DISPONIBILITE/ PRIX
ST.84/WS/19	GUIDE DES STATISTIQUES RELATIVES A LA SCIENCE ET A LA TECHNOLOGIE (PUBLIE AUSSI EN ANGLAIS, ARABE, ESPAGNOL ET RUSSE)	1984	SUR DEMANDE
UNESCO: CES/AC. 23/27	NORMALISATION ET COMPARABILITE INTERNATIONALE DES STATISTIQUES DE L'EDUCATION (PUBLIE AUSSI EN ANGLAIS ET RUSSE)	1982	SUR DEMANDE
UNESCO: CES/AC. 23/28	INDICATEURS SOCIAUX DANS LE DOMAINE DE L'EDUCATION (PUBLIE AUSSI EN ANGLAIS ET RUSSE)	1982	SUR DEMANDE
COM/ST/ISCED	CLASSIFICATION INTERNATIONALE TYPE DE L'EDUCATION (CITE) (PUBLIE AUSSI EN ANGLAIS, ESPAGNOL ET RUSSE)	1976	SUR DEMANDE
ED/BIE/CONFIN-TED 35/ REF.8	VERSION ABREGEE DE LA CITE (PUBLIE AUSSI EN ANGLAIS, ARABE, ESPAGNOL, ET RUSSE)	1975	SUR DEMANDE
	RAPPORTS ET DOCUMENTS DIVERS		
ED/BIE/CONFIN-TED 39/REF. 1	ETUDE STATISTIQUE SOMMAIRE SUR L'EDUCATION DANS LE MONDE, 1960 A 1982 CONFERENCE INTERNATIONALE DE L'EDUCATION, 39EME SESSION, OCTOBRE 1984 (PUBLIE AUSSI EN ANGLAIS ET EN ESPAGNOL)	1984	SUR DEMANDE
ED-80/MINED-EUROPE/REF. 2	DEVELOPPEMENT DE L'EDUCATION EN EUROPE: ANALYSE STATISTIQUE (PUBLIE AUSSI EN ANGLAIS, ESPAGNOL ET RUSSE)	1980	SUR DEMANDE
ED-82 MINEDAF/ REF. 2	DEVELOPPEMENT DE L'EDUCATION EN AFRIQUE: ETUDE STATISTIQUE (PUBLIE AUSSI EN ANGLAIS)	1982	SUR DEMANDE
ST/FIN/5	DEPENSES PUBLIQUES D'EDUCATION DANS LE MONDE - TENDANCES REGIONALES ET PAR PAYS, 1970-1982 (PUBLIE AUSSI EN ANGLAIS)	1985	SUR DEMANDE
	ETUDES A L'ETRANGER. BOURSES ET COURS INTERNATIONAUX. PARAIT TOUS LES DEUX ANS. TRILINGUE: ANGLAIS/FRANCAIS/ESPAGNOL VOL. XXIV, 1983-84, 1984-85, 1985-86	1983	FF 55

IDENTIFICACION	TITULO	PUBLICADO EN	DISPONIBILIDAD/ PRECIO
ISBN 92-3 002351-5	ANUARIO ESTADISTICO DE LA UNESCO 1985 TRILINGUE: INGLES/FRANCES/ESPAÑOL PUBLICADO ANUALMENTE DE 1963 A 1985	1985	FF 350
	ESTADISTICAS RELATIVAS A LA CIENCIA Y A LA TECNOLOGIA PUBLICADAS ANUALMENTE DESDE 1984 TRILINGUE: INGLES/ FRANCES/ ESPAÑOL	1985	SUR DEMANDE
	INFORMES Y ESTUDIOS ESTADISTICOS		
	ENCUESTAS E INVESTIGACIONES ESTADISTICAS:		
	TRABAJOS EN CURSO (CSR):		
CSR-S-8	ESTADISTICAS RELATIVAS A LA CIENCIA Y A LA TECNOLOGIA - ULTIMOS DATOS DISPONIBLES TRILINGUE: INGLES/FRANCES/ESPAÑOL	1980	A PETICION
CSR-S-9	PARTICIPACION DE LA MUJER EN LAS ACTIVIDADES DE I Y D: UN ESTUDIO ESTADISTICO (PUBLICADO IGUALMENTE EN INGLES Y EN FRANCES)	1980	A PETICION
CSR-S-10	ESTADISTICAS RELATIVAS A LA CIENCIA Y A LA TECNOLOGIA - ULTIMOS DATOS DISPONIBLES TRILINGUE: INGLES/FRANCES/ESPAÑOL	1980	A PETICION

IDENTIFICACION	TITULO	PUBLICADO EN	DISPONIBILIDAD/ PRECIO
CSR-S-11	ESTADISTICAS RELATIVAS A LA CIENCIA Y A LA TECNOLOGIA – ULTIMOS DATOS DISPONIBLES TRILINGUE: INGLES/FRANCES/ESPAÑOL	1981	A PETICION
CSR-S-12	RECURSOS HUMANOS Y FINANCIEROS PARA LA INVESTIGACION Y EL DESARROLLO EXPERIMENTAL EN EL SECTOR PRODUCTIVO (PUBLICADO IGUALMENTE EN INGLES Y EN FRANCES)	1982	A PETICION
CSR-S-13	TENDENCIAS DE LOS RECURSOS HUMANOS Y FINANCIEROS PARA LAS ACTIVIDADES DE INVESTIGACION Y DE DESARROLLO EXPERIMENTAL TRILINGUE: INGLES/FRANCES/ESPAÑOL	1982	A PETICION
CSR-S-14	ESTADISTICAS RELATIVAS A LA CIENCIA Y A LA TECNOLOGIA – ULTIMOS DATOS DISPONIBLES. TRILINGUE: INGLES/ FRANCES/ESPAÑOL	1982	A PETICION
CSR-S-15	PROPUESTAS PARA UNA METODOLOGIA DEL ACOPIO DE DATOS SOBRE ENSEÑANZA Y FORMACION CIENTIFICA Y TECNOLOGICA DEL TERCER GRADO (PUBLICADO IGUALMENTE EN INGLES Y EN FRANCES)	1983	A PETICION
CSR-S-16	RECURSOS HUMANOS Y FINANCIEROS PARA LA INVESTIGACION Y EL DESARROLLO EXPERIMENTAL EN LA AGRICULTURA (PUBLICADO IGUALMENTE EN INGLES Y EN FRANCES)	1983	A PETICION
CSR-S-17	ESTIMACION DE LOS RECURSOS MUNDIALES PARA INVESTIGACION Y DESARROLLO EXPERIMENTAL 1970–1980 (PUBLICADO IGUALMENTE EN INGLES Y FRANCES)	1984	A PETICION
CSR-S-19	ESTIMACION DE POTENCIALES CALIFICADOS TITULADOS DE LA ENSEÑANZA SUPERIOR (PUBLICADO IGUALMENTE EN INGLES Y EN FRANCES)	1985	A PETICION
CSR-S-21	CONCEPCION INTEGRADA DE LOS INDICADORES SOBRE CIENCIA Y TECNOLOGIA (PUBLICADO IGUALMENTE EN INGLES Y EN FRANCES)	1986	A PETICION
CSR-E-35	LA ASIGNACION DE RECURSOS PARA LA EDUCACION EN EL MUNDO (PUBLICADO IGUALMENTE EN INGLES Y EN FRANCES)	1980	A PETICION
CSR-E-36	ANALISIS COMPARADO DE LA ESCOLARIZACION Y DEL ANALFABETISMO FEMENINOS Y MASCULINOS (PUBLICADO IGUALMENTE EN INGLES Y EN FRANCES)	1980	A PETICION
CSR-E-38	GUIA DE LA CLASIFICACION INTERNACIONAL NORMALIZADA DE LA EDUCACION: UNION DE REPUBLICAS SOCIALISTAS SOVIETICAS (EN RUSO SOLAMENTE)	1980	A PETICION
CSR-E-44	ESTADISTICAS SOBRE EL NIVEL DE INSTRUCCION Y EL ANALFABETISMO, 1970–1980. TRILINGUE: INGLES/FRANCES/ESPAÑOL	1983	A PETICION
CSR-E-53	ESTADISTICAS DE LA EDUCACION: ULTIMO AÑO DISPONIBLE TRILINGUE:INGLES/FRANCES/ESPAÑOL	1986	A PETICION
CSR-C-13	MODELO DE ENCUESTA SOBRE ACCESO A RECURSOS CULTURALES Y REALIZACION DE ACTIVIDADES CULTURALES	1982	A PETICION
CSR-C-27	ESTADISTICAS CULTURALES Y DESARROLLO CULTURAL – ENCUESTA ESTADISTICA MUNDIAL SOBRE ALGUNOS MEDIOS DE COMUNICACION DE MASAS QUE HAN SERVIDO DE SOPORTE PARA EL DESARROLLO CULTURAL – MONDIACULT (PUBLICADO IGUALMENTE EN INGLES, FRANCES Y RUSO)	1982	A PETICION
CSR-C-55	PROYECTO DE INDICADORES CULTURALES (PUBLICADO IGUALMENTE EN INGLES)	1985	A PETICION
	<u>LISTA ANOTADA DE LAS NUEVAS ADQUISICIONES:</u> <u>ESTUDIOS E INFORMES SOBRE LAS ESTADISTICAS</u> <u>RELATIVAS A LA CIENCIA</u>		
NO. 15	ST.80/WS/23, OCTUBRE 1980 (PUBLICADA IGUALMENTE EN INGLES Y EN FRANCES)	1980	A PETICION

IDENTIFICACION	TITULO	PUBLICADO EN	DISPONIBILIDAD/ PRECIO
NO. 16	ST.81/WS/12, SEPTIEMBRE 1981 (PUBLICADA IGUALMENTE EN INGLES Y EN FRANCES)	1981	A PETICION
NO. 17	ST.82/WS/21, SEPTIEMBRE 1982 (PUBLICADA IGUALMENTE EN INGLES Y EN FRANCES)	1982	A PETICION
NO. 18	ST.84/WS/1, FEBRERO 1984 (PUBLICADA IGUALMENTE EN INGLES Y EN FRANCES)	1984	A PETICION
NO. 19	ST.84/WS/19, NOVIEMBRE 1984 (PUBLICADA IGUALMENTE EN INGLES Y EN FRANCES)	1984	A PETICION
NO. 20	ST/85/WS/15, DICIEMBRE 1985 (PUBLICADA IGUALMENTE EN INGLES Y EN FRANCES)	1985	A PETICION
	RECOMENDACIONES Y CLASIFICACIONES INTERNACIONALES		
	RECOMENDACION SOBRE LA NORMALIZACION INTERNACIONAL DE LAS ESTADISTICAS RELATIVAS A LA EDICION DE LIBROS Y PUBLICACIONES PERIODICAS, APROBADA POR LA CONFERENCIA GENERAL EN SU DECIMOTERCERA REUNION, PARIS, 19 DE NOVIEMBRE DE 1964. PLURILINGUE: INGLES/FRANCES/ESPAÑOL/RUSO	1964	A PETICION
	RECOMENDACION SOBRE LA NORMALIZACION INTERNACIONAL DE LAS ESTADISTICAS RELATIVAS A LAS BIBLIOTECAS, APROBADA POR LA CONFERENCIA GENERAL EN SU DECIMOSEXTA REUNION, PARIS, 13 DE NOVIEMBRE DE 1970. PLURILINGUE: INGLES/FRANCES/ESPAÑOL/RUSO	1970	A PETICION
	RECOMENDACION SOBRE LA NORMALIZACION INTERNACIONAL DE LAS ESTADISTICAS RELATIVAS A LA RADIO Y LA TELEVISION, APROBADA POR LA CONFERENCIA GENERAL EN SU DECIMONOVENA REUNION, NAIROBI, 22 DE NOVIEMBRE DE 1976. PLURILINGUE: INGLES/FRANCES/ESPAÑOL/RUSO/ARABE	1976	A PETICION
	RECOMENDACION REVISADA SOBRE LA NORMALIZACION INTERNACIONAL DE LAS ESTADISTICAS RELATIVAS A LA EDUCACION, APROBADA POR LA CONFERENCIA GENERAL EN SU VIGESIMA REUNION, PARIS, 27 DE NOVIEMBRE DE 1978. PLURILINGUE: ARABE/INGLES/FRANCES/ESPAÑOL/RUSO	1978	A PETICION
	RECOMENDACION SOBRE LA NORMALIZACION INTERNACIONAL DE LAS ESTADISTICAS RELATIVAS A LA CIENCIA Y LA TECNOLOGIA APROBADA POR LA CONFERENCIA GENERAL EN SU VIGESIMA REUNION, PARIS, 27 DE NOVIEMBRE DE 1978. PLURILINGUE: ARABE/INGLES/ESPAÑOL/FRANCES/RUSO	1978	A PETICION
	RECOMENDACION SOBRE LA NORMALIZACION INTERNACIONAL DE LAS ESTADISTICAS RELATIVAS AL FINANCIAMIENTO PUBLICO DE LAS ACTIVIDADES CULTURALES, APROBADA POR LA CONFERENCIA GENERAL EN SU 21A. REUNION, BELGRADO, 27 DE OCTUBRE DE 1980 PLURILINGUE: ARABE/INGLES/ESPAÑOL/FRANCES/RUSO/ CHINO	1980	A PETICION
	RECOMENDACION REVISADA SOBRE LA NORMALIZACION INTERNACIONAL DE LAS ESTADISTICAS RELATIVAS A LA PRODUCCION Y DISTRIBUCION DE LIBROS, DIARIOS Y OTRAS PUBLICACIONES PERIODICAS, APROBADA POR LA CONFERENCIA GENERAL EN SU 23A REUNION, SOFIA, 10 DE NOVIEMBRE DE 1985	1985	A PETICION
ST.80/WS/8	MANUAL DE ESTADISTICAS SOBRE LAS ACTIVIDADES CIENTIFICAS Y TECNOLOGICAS (VERSION PROVISIONAL) (PUBLICADO IGUALMENTE EN ARABE Y RUSO)	1980	A PETICION
ST.80/WS/15	ESTADISTICAS SOBRE LA EDUCACION DE ADULTOS EN COLOMBIA, 1978 (SECTOR OFICIAL) (EN ESPAÑOL SOLAMENTE)	1980	A PETICION
ST.80/WS/18	LOS SISTEMAS ESTADISTICOS NACIONALES DE RECOLECCION DE DATOS SOBRE ACTIVIDADES CIENTIFICAS Y TECNOLOGICAS EN LOS PAISES LATINOAMERICANOS PARTE I – VENEZUELA, COLOMBIA, MEXICO Y CUBA (PUBLICADO IGUALMENTE EN FRANCES Y EN INGLES)	1980	A PETICION

IDENTIFICACION	TITULO	PUBLICADO EN	DISPONIBILIDAD/ PRECIO
ST.80/WS/29	LOS SISTEMAS ESTADISTICOS NACIONALES DE RECOLECCION DE DATOS SOBRE ACTIVIDADES CIENTIFICAS Y TECNOLOGICAS EN LOS PAISES LATINOAMERICANOS PARTE II – BRASIL Y PERU (PUBLICADO IGUALMENTE EN FRANCES Y EN INGLES)	1980	A PETICION
ST.81/WS/14	LOS SISTEMAS ESTADISTICOS NACIONALES DE RECOLECCION DE DATOS SOBRE ACTIVIDADES CIENTIFICAS Y TECNOLOGICAS EN LOS PAISES LATINOAMERICANOS. PARTE III: URUGUAY, ARGENTINA Y CHILE (PUBLICADO IGUALMENTE EN FRANCES Y EN INGLES)	1981	A PETICION
ST.82/WS/18	LA CONVERSION EN LOS CONCEPTOS NORMALIZADOS DE LA UNESCO DE LAS CATEGORIAS ESTADISTICAS RELATIVAS A LA INVESTIGACION CIENTIFICA Y AL DESARROLLO EXPERIMENTAL UTILIZADAS POR OCHO PAISES LAINOAMERICANOS – GUIA PRACTICA PARA LOS SERVICIOS ESTADISTICOS DE ARGENTINA, BRASIL, COLOMBIA, CHILE, MEXICO, PERU, URUGUAY Y VENEZUELA (EN ESPAÑOL SOLAMENTE)	1982	A PETICION
ST.84/WS/12	MANUAL DE ESTADISTICAS SOBRE LAS ACTIVIDADES CIENTIFICAS Y TECNOLOGIAS (PUBLICADO IGUALMENTE EN ARABE, FRANCES, INGLES Y RUSO)	1984	A PETICION
ST.84/WS/18	GUIA PARA LAS ESTADISTICAS SOBRE INFORMACION Y DOCUMENTACION CIENTIFICA Y TECNOLOGIA (IDCT) (PROVISIONAL)(PUBLICADO IGUALMENTE EN FRANCES Y EN INGLES)	1984	A PETICION
ST.84/WS/19	GUIA DE LAS ESTADISTICAS RELATIVAS A LA CIENCIA Y LA TECNOLOGIA (PUBLICADO IGUALMENTE EN ARABE, FRANCES, INGLES Y RUSO)	1984	A PETICION
COM/ST/ISCED	CLASIFICACION INTERNACIONAL NORMALIZADA DE LA EDUCACION (CINE) (PUBLICADA IGUALMENTE EN FRANCES, INGLES Y RUSO)	1976	A PETICION
ED/BIE/CONFIN-TED 35/REF. 8	EDICION ABREVIADA DE LA 'CINE' (PUBLICADA IGUALMENTE EN ARABE, FRANCES, INGLES Y RUSO)	1975	A PETICION
	INFORMES Y DOCUMENTOS DIVERSOS		
ED/BIE/CONFIN-TED 39/REF. 1	RESUMEN ESTADISTICO DE LA EDUCACION EN EL MUNDO, 1960–1982 CONFERENCIA INTERNACIONAL DE EDUCACION 39A. REUNION, OCTUBRE DE 1984 (PUBLICADO IGUALMENTE EN INGLES Y EN FRANCES)	1984	A PETICION
ED-80/MINED-EUROPE/ REF. 2	DESARROLLO DE LA EDUCACION EN EUROPA: UNA REVISION ESTADISTICA (PUBLICADO IGUALMENTE EN INGLES, FRANCES Y RUSO)	1980	A PETICION
	ESTUDIOS EN EL EXTRANJERO, BECAS Y CURSOS INTERNACIONALES SE PUBLICA CADA DOS AÑOS TRILINGUE: INGLES/FRANCES/ESPAÑOL (VOL. XXIV, 1983-84,1984-85,1985-86)	1983	FF 55

E Tables omitted

Tableaux supprimés

Cuadros suprimidos

THE LAST EDITION IN WHICH THE TABLES APPEARED IS SHOWN IN PARENTHESES FOR EACH TABLE

SUMMARY TABLES FOR ALL LEVELS OF EDUCATION

Estimated foreign-student enrolment at the third level of education (1980 edition, table 2.10)

EDUCATIONAL EXPENDITURE

Public current expenditure per pupil (first level) in United States dollars and index numbers of expenditure per pupil, by level of education (1976 edition, table 6.5).

Public capital expenditure on education: distribution by level of education (1978-79 edition, table 6.3

STATISTICS ON SCIENCE AND TECHNOLOGY

General indicators for current resources and future supply of scientific and technical manpower for research and experimental development (1975 edition, table 9.2)

Number of organizations in the productive and general service by size according to number of scientists and engineers engaged in research and experimental development (1978-79 edition, table 9.4)

THEATRE AND OTHER DRAMATIC ARTS

Number of performances, annual attendance, visits to and from abroad (1982 edition, table 9.1)

Number of theatres, professional companies and amateur troupes (1982 edition, table 9.2)

LA DERNIERE EDITION DANS LAQUELLE LES TABLEAUX ONT ETE PUBLIES EST INDIQUEE DANS CHAQUE CAS ENTRE PARENTHESES.

TABLEAUX RECAPITULATIFS POUR TOUS LES DEGRES D'ENSEIGNEMENT

Estimation des effectifs d'étudiants étrangers dans l'enseignement du troisième degré (édition 1980, tableau 2.10)

DEPENSES DE L'ENSEIGNEMENT

Dépenses publiques ordinaires par élève (premier degré) en dollars des Etats-Unis, et indices des dépenses par élève, par degrés d'enseignement (édition 1976, tableau 6.5)

Dépenses publiques en capital afférentes à l'enseignement: répartition par degrés d'enseignement (édition 1978-79, tableau 6.3)

STATISTIQUES RELATIVES A LA SCIENCE ET LA TECHNOLOGIE

Indicateurs des ressources actuelles et des disponibilités futures en personnel scientifique et technique pour la recherche et le développement expérimental (édition 1975, tableau 9.2)

Nombre d'organisations dans les secteurs de la production et de service général, classées d'après le nombre de scientifiques et d'ingénieurs employés à des travaux de recherche et de développement expérimental (édition 1978-79, tableau 9.4)

THEATRE ET SPECTACLE

Nombre de représentations, fréquentation annuelle, visites vers ou venant de l'étranger (édition 1982, tableau 9.1)

Nombre de theâtres, compagnies de professionnels et troupes d'amateurs (édition 1982, tableau 9.2)

LA ULTIMA EDICION EN LA QUE LOS CUADROS FUERON PUBLICADOS SE INDICA EN CADA CASO ENTRE PARENTESIS.

CUADROS RECAPITULATIVOS PARA TODOS LOS GRADOS DE ENSEÑANZA

Estimación del número de estudiantes extranjeros en la enseñanza de tercer grado (edición 1980, cuadro 2.10))

GASTOS DE LA EDUCACION

Gastos públicos ordinarios por alumno (primer grado) en dólares de los Estados Unidos e indices de los gastos por alumno, por grados de enseñanza (edición 1976, cuadro 6.5))

Gastos públicos de capital destinados a la educación : distribución por grados de enseñanza (edición 1978-79, cuadro 6.3)

ESTADISTICAS RELATIVAS A LA CIENCIA Y LA TECNOLOGIA

Indicadores de los efectivos actuales y de las disponibilidades futuras en personal cientifico y técnico para la investigación y el desarrollo experimental (edición 1975, cuadro 9.2)

Número de organizaciones en los sectores productivo y de servicio general, clasificadas de acuerdo con el número de cientificos e ingenieros empleados en trabajos de investigación y de desarrollo experimental (edición 1978-79, cuadro 9.4)

TEATRO Y ESPECTACULO

Número de representaciones, frecuentación anual, visitas del y al extranjero (edición 1982, cuadro 9.1)

Número de teatros, compañias de profesionales y grupos de aficionados (edición 1982, cuadro 9.2)